Collins

LOND[illegible]

CONTENTS

Key to map pages 2-3

Key to map symbols 4-5

Central London maps 6-37

Main London maps 38-207

Theatres and cinemas map 208

Shopping map 209

Index to street names, place names,
and places of interest 210-376

Published by Collins
An imprint of HarperCollins*Publishers*
77-85 Fulham Palace Road, Hammersmith, London W6 8JB

www.collins.co.uk

Mapping generated from Collins Bartholomew digital databases

London Underground Map by permission of Transport Trading Limited
Registered User No. 05/4084

The grid on this map is the National Grid taken from the Ordnance Survey map with the permission of the Controller of Her Majesty's Stationery Office.

Printed in China

Paperback ISBN 0 00 719199 5 SM11948 BDB
Spiral ISBN 0 00 719200 2 SM11949
Imp 001

e-mail: roadcheck@harpercollins.co.uk

Key to map pages

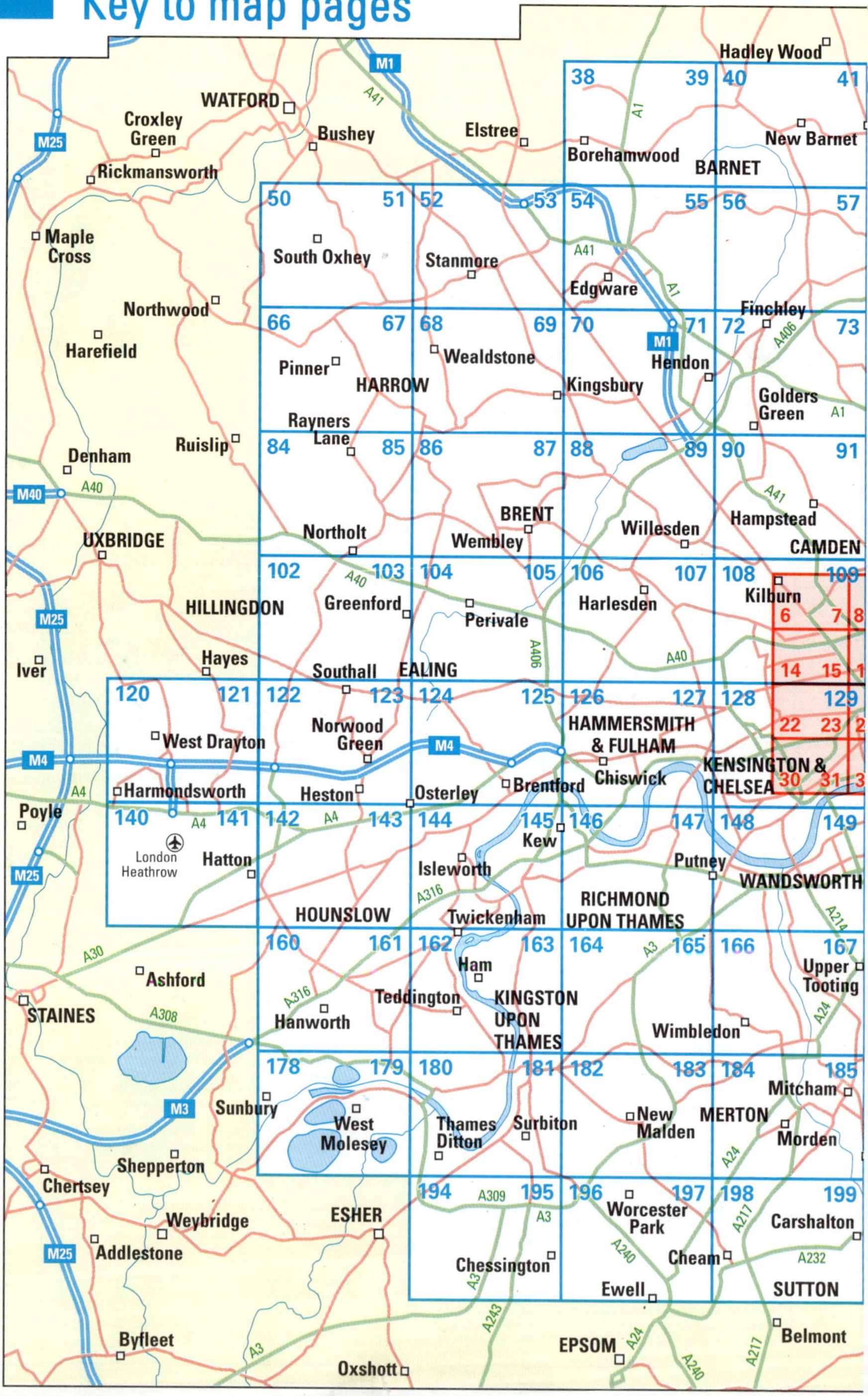

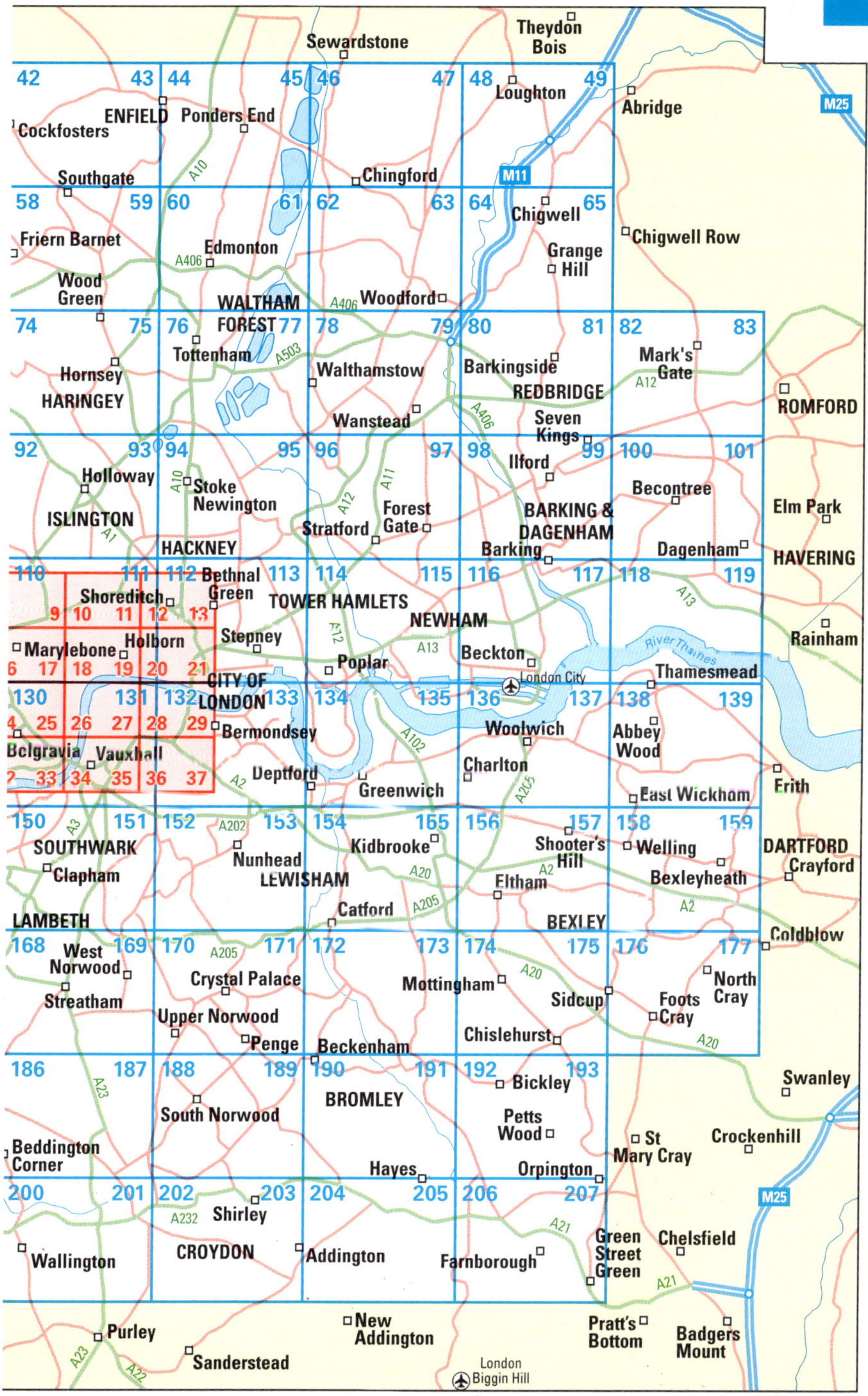
Sewardstone
Theydon Bois
42
43
44
45
46
47
48
49
Loughton
Abridge
M25
ENFIELD
Ponders End
Cockfosters
A10
Southgate
Chingford
M11
58
59
60
61
62
63
64
65
Chigwell
Friern Barnet
Edmonton
Chigwell Row
Grange Hill
A406
Wood Green
WALTHAM FOREST
Woodford
74
75
76
77
78
79
80
81
82
83
Tottenham
A503
Barkingside
Mark's Gate
A12
Hornsey
Walthamstow
REDBRIDGE
ROMFORD
HARINGEY
Wanstead
Seven Kings
92
93
94
95
96
97
98
99
100
101
Holloway
Ilford
Becontree
Stoke Newington
Forest Gate
Elm Park
ISLINGTON
A1
A11
BARKING & DAGENHAM
Stratford
HACKNEY
Barking
Dagenham
HAVERING
110
111
112
113
114
115
116
117
118
119
Bethnal Green
Shoreditch
TOWER HAMLETS
NEWHAM
A13
9
10
11
12
13
Rainham
Marylebone
Holborn
Stepney
Beckton
River Thames
6
17
18
19
20
21
Poplar
CITY OF LONDON
London City
Thamesmead
130
131
132
133
134
135
136
137
138
139
4
25
26
27
28
29
Bermondsey
Woolwich
Abbey Wood
Belgravia
Vauxhall
A102
Charlton
2
33
34
35
36
37
A2
Deptford
Greenwich
A205
East Wickham
Erith
150
151
152
153
154
155
156
157
158
159
A3
A202
Kidbrooke
Shooter's Hill
SOUTHWARK
Welling
DARTFORD
Nunhead
Crayford
Clapham
LEWISHAM
A20
Bexleyheath
Eltham
Catford
LAMBETH
BEXLEY
Coldblow
168
169
170
171
172
173
174
175
176
177
West Norwood
Crystal Palace
Mottingham
North Cray
Streatham
Sidcup
Foots Cray
Upper Norwood
Penge
Chislehurst
Beckenham
186
187
188
189
190
191
192
193
Bickley
Swanley
A23
South Norwood
BROMLEY
Petts Wood
St Mary Cray
Crockenhill
Beddington Corner
Hayes
Orpington
200
201
202
203
204
205
206
207
Shirley
A232
A21
CROYDON
Addington
Farnborough
Green Street Green
Chelsfield
Wallington
Purley
New Addington
Pratt's Bottom
Badgers Mount
Sanderstead
A22
London Biggin Hill

Key to central map symbols

Symbol	Meaning
Dual A4	Primary route
Dual A40	'A' road
B504	'B' road
	Other road
	Street market
	Pedestrian street
	Access restriction
	Track/Footpath
	One way street
	Extent of central London congestion charging zone
CITY	Borough boundary
EC2	Postal district boundary
	Main National Rail station
	Other National Rail station
	London Underground station
	Docklands Light Railway station
	Pedestrian ferry with landing stage
	Bus/Coach station
P	Car park
i	Tourist information centre
	Theatre
	Major hotel

Symbol	Meaning
	Youth hostel
	Historic site
Pol	Police station
PO	Post Office
Lib	Library
	Embassy
Fire Sta	Fire station
	Monument / statue
WC	Public toilet
	Cinema
	Church
	Mosque
	Synagogue
Mormon	Other place of worship
	Leisure & tourism
	Shopping
	Administration & law
	Health & welfare
	Education
	Industry & commerce
	Public open space
	Park/Garden/Sports ground
	Cemetery

A Grid reference

8 Page continuation number

SCALE

1: 10,000 6.3 inches (16cm) to 1 mile/10 cm to 1 km

0 — 1/4 — 1/2 mile

0 — 0.25 — 0.5 — 0.75 kilometre

The reference grid on this atlas coincides with the Ordnance Survey National Grid system. The grid interval is 250 metres.

Key to main map symbols

- M4 Motorway
- Dual A4 Primary route
- Dual A40 'A' road
- B504 'B' road
- Other road/One way street
- Toll
- Street market
- Restricted access road
- Pedestrian street
- Cycle path
- Track/Footpath
- THAMES PATH Long distance footpath
- LC Level crossing
- V P Vehicle/Pedestrian ferry
- County/Borough boundary
- Postal district boundary
- Main National Rail station
- Other National Rail station
- London Underground station
- Docklands Light Railway station
- Tramlink station
- Pedestrian ferry landing stage
- Bus/Coach station

- Leisure & tourism
- Shopping
- Administration & law
- Health & welfare
- Education
- Industry & commerce
- Cemetery
- Golf course
- Public open space/Allotments
- Park/Garden/Sports ground
- Wood/Forest
- USA Embassy
- Pol Police station
- Fire Sta Fire station
- PO/Lib Post Office/Library
- Youth hostel
- Tourist information centre
- Historic Site
- Car park
- Tower block
- Heliport
- Church
- Mosque
- Synagogue

Extent of London congestion charging zone
For more information see website www.cclondon.com

A Grid reference

38 Page continuation number

35 OS National Grid kilometre square

SCALE

1:20,000 3.2 inches (8cm) to 1 mile/5 cm to 1 km

0 — 1/4 — 1/2 mile

0 — 0.25 — 0.5 — 0.75 — 1 kilometre

The reference grid on this atlas coincides with the Ordnance Survey National Grid system. The grid interval is 500 metres.

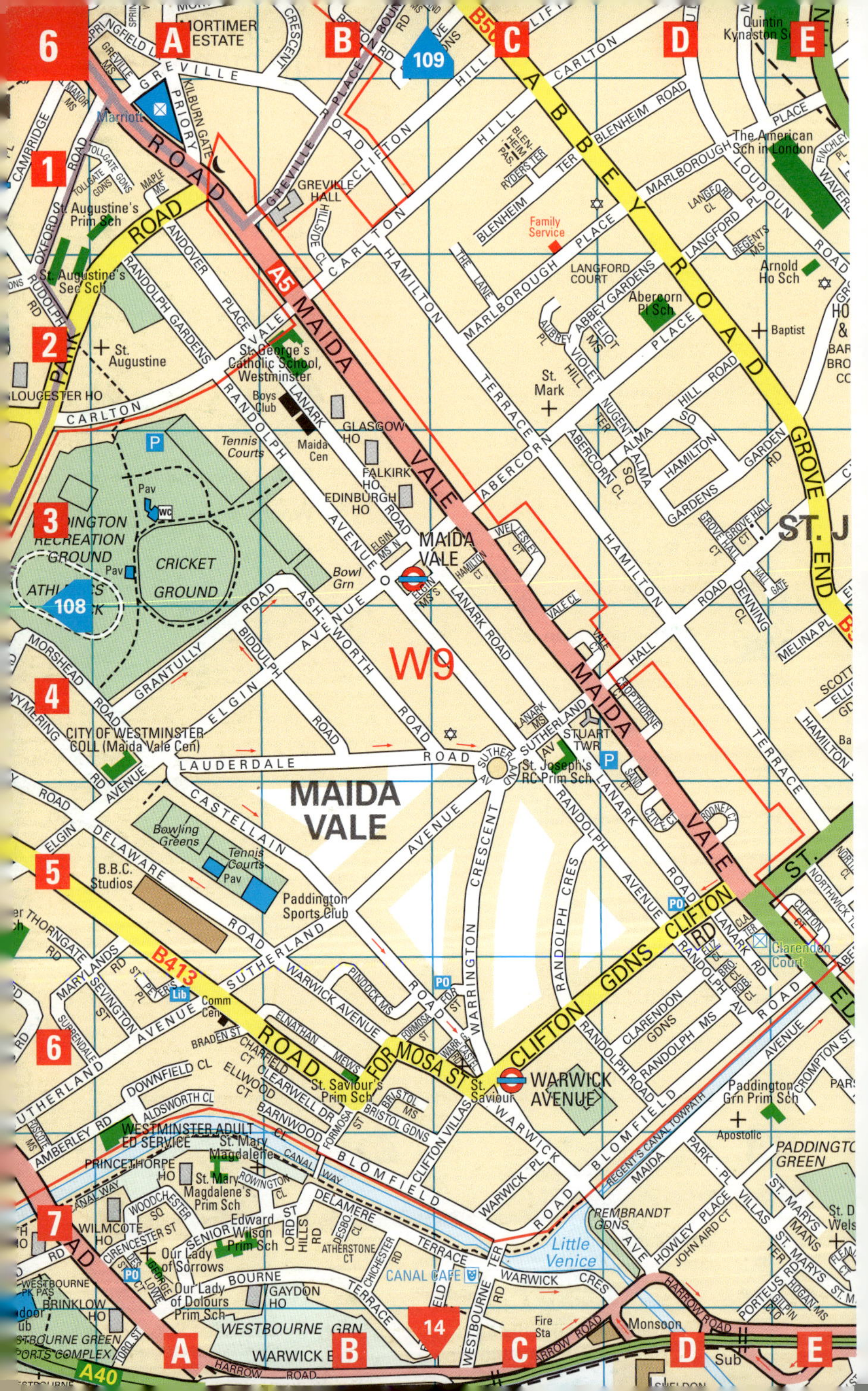

6
A
B
C
D
E
1
2
3
4
5
6
7
MORTIMER ESTATE
109
108
14
B507
A5
B413
A40
Marriott
GREVILLE
KILBURN PRIORY
KILBURN GATE
GREVILLE HALL
GREVILLE PLACE
BOUNDARY RD
CRESCENT
CARLTON HILL
CLIFTON HILL
HILLSIDE CL
HAMILTON TERRACE
ABBEY ROAD
BLENHEIM TER
BLENHEIM ROAD
BLENHEIM PAS
RYDERS TER
THE LANE
MARLBOROUGH PLACE
Family Service
LANGFORD COURT
LANGFORD PL
LANGFORD CL
REGENTS MS
LOUDOUN ROAD
The American Sch in London
Quintin Kynaston Sch
Arnold Ho Sch
Abercorn Pl Sch
ABBEY GARDENS
AUBREY PL
VIOLET HILL
ELIOT MS
Baptist
St. Mark
NUGENT TER
ALMA SQ
ABERCORN PLACE
ABERCORN CL
HILL ROAD
HAMILTON GARDENS
GARDEN RD
GROVE END ROAD
GROVE HALL CT
ST. J
DENNING CL
HALL ROAD
MELINA PL
CAMBRIDGE RD
MANOR MS
TOLLGATE GDNS
MAPLE MS
ROAD
St. Augustine's Prim Sch
St. Augustine's Sec Sch
St. Augustine
OXFORD RD
RUDOLPH RD
PARK ROAD
GLOUCESTER HO
ANDOVER PLACE
RANDOLPH GARDENS
VALE
St. George's Catholic School, Westminster
Boys Club
LANARK ROAD
GLASGOW HO
Maida Cen
FALKIRK HO
EDINBURGH HO
CARLTON
Tennis Courts
Pav
WC
PADDINGTON RECREATION GROUND
CRICKET GROUND
ATHLETICS TRACK
RANDOLPH AVENUE
ELGIN MS N
ELGIN MS S
MAIDA VALE
HAMILTON CT
WELLESLEY CT
VALE CL
Bowl Grn
ASHWORTH ROAD
W9
MORSHEAD ROAD
GRANTULLY ROAD
BIDDULPH ROAD
ELGIN AVENUE
CITY OF WESTMINSTER COLL (Maida Vale Cen)
LAUDERDALE ROAD
MAIDA VALE
SUTHERLAND AVENUE
LANARK MS
STUART TWR
St. Joseph's RC Prim Sch
SAND CT
CLIVE CT
RODNEY CT
COPTHORNE
TERRACE
SCOTT ELLIS GDNS
HAMILTON
CASTELLAIN ROAD
Bowling Greens
Tennis Courts
Pav
B.B.C. Studios
DELAWARE ROAD
ELGIN
Paddington Sports Club
WARRINGTON CRESCENT
RANDOLPH CRES
CLIFTON GDNS
CLIFTON RD
NORTHWICK TER
CLIFTON CT
Clarendon Court
THORNGATE RD
MARYLANDS RD
SEVINGTON ST
ST PETERS
Lib
Comm Cen
SUTHERLAND AVENUE
WARWICK AVENUE
PINDOCK MS
ELNATHAN MS
FORMOSA ST
WARRINGTON
CLARENDON GDNS
RANDOLPH MS
RANDOLPH AV
BRADEN ST
CHARFIELD CT
ELLWOOD CT
CLEARWELL DR
DOWNFIELD CL
St. Saviour's Prim Sch
BRISTOL MS
BRISTOL GDNS
St. Saviour
WARWICK AVENUE
Paddington Grn Prim Sch
Apostolic
CROMPTON ST
PADDINGTON GREEN
SUTHERLAND
ALDSWORTH CL
AMBERLEY RD
WESTMINSTER ADULT ED SERVICE
St. Mary Magdalene
BARNWOOD CL
BLOMFIELD
CLIFTON VILLAS
WARWICK PL
REGENT'S CANAL TOWPATH
MAIDA AVE
PARK PL VILLAS
ST. MARYS MANS
ST. MARYS TER
PRINCETHORPE HO
St. Mary Magdalene's Prim Sch
ROWINGTON CL
CANAL WAY
WOODCHESTER SQ
WILMCOTE HO
CIRENCESTER ST
SENIOR
Edward Wilson Prim Sch
LORD HILLS RD
DELAMERE TERRACE
DESBOROUGH CL
ATHERSTONE CT
CHICHESTER RD
CANAL CAFE
REMBRANDT GDNS
HOWLEY PLACE
JOHN AIRD CT
Little Venice
WARWICK CRES
PORTEUS RD
HOGAN MS
Our Lady of Sorrows
Our Lady of Dolours Prim Sch
BOURNE TERRACE
GAYDON HO
WESTBOURNE PK PAS
BRINKLOW HO
WESTBOURNE GREEN SPORTS COMPLEX
WESTBOURNE GRN
WARWICK
Fire Sta
HARROW ROAD
Monsoon
Sub
WESTBOURNE TER RD

E
F
G
H
J
109
1
2
3
4
5
6
7
8
15
NW8
NW1
ST. JOHN'S WOOD
ST. JOHN'S WOOD BARRACKS
REGEN
LISSON GROVE
MARYLEBONE
LORD'S CRICKET GROUND
M.C.C. MUSEUM
LORD'S TAVERN PH
BOATING LAKE
RUNNING TRACK
Tennis Cts
WINFIELD HOUSE
London Central Mosque
REGENT'S CANAL
WELLINGTON ROAD
PRINCE ALBERT ROAD
ST. JOHN'S WOOD ROAD
PARK ROAD
LISSON GROVE
GLOUCESTER PLACE
MARYLEBONE ROAD
EDGWARE ROAD
OUTER CIRCLE
A41
A5205
A5
A501
B507
TOWNSHEND ESTATE
Robinsfield Inf Sch
Carlton T.V.
St. Christina's Sch
CECILIA COLEMAN GALL
Health Clinic
Barrow Hill Jun Sch
WELLINGTON HOSP N
WELLINGTON HOSP S
HOSP OF ST. JOHN & ST. ELIZABETH
CONVENT OF MERCY
GARDENS
St. John's Wood
Ramada Plaza
BEVERLEY HOUSE
St. Johns Wood Sub Station
Our Lady (RC)
LISSON GREEN ESTATE
ROYAL COLL OF OBSTETRICIANS & GYNAECOLOGISTS
HANOVER GATE MANS
LONDON BUSINESS SCH
Gateway Prim Sch
Health Cen
COCKPIT THEA
Comm Cen
CHURCH STREET ESTATE
LILESTONE ESTATE
Sylvia Young Thea Sch
St. Paul
Evangelical
St. Edward's RC Prim Sch
ST. EDWARD'S CONV
BNP Paribas
LONDON BUS SCH
STEINER
Francis Holland Sch (Marylebone)
St. Cyprian
Ramada Jarvis
Landmark
CHARTER NIGHTINGALE HOSP
Westminster Council Ho
North Westminster Comm Sch Lwr
Christ Church
Christ Ch Bentinck C of E Prim Sch
CITY OF WESTMINSTER COLL
St. Mary
Health Cen
Metropole
HONDURAS
Prim Sch
St. Mary
Swedish
MAG CT
MELCOMBE PL
DORSET SQ
TAUNTON PL
HANOVER GATE
HANOVER TER
KENT TER
SUSSEX PLACE
ALLITSEN ROAD
ACACIA ROAD
ST. JOHN'S WOOD TERRACE
CHARLBERT STREET
NEWCOURT ST
BROADLEY ST
ROSSMORE ROAD
CHURCH STREET
BELL ST
CHAPEL ST
HARCOURT ST
YORK ST
BOSTON PLACE
BALCOMBE ST
IVOR PL
DORSET ST
MELCOMBE ST
MONTAGU STREET
UPPER MONTAGU ST
WYNDHAM ST
ENFORD ST
KNOX ST
CAPLAND STREET
BRAITHWAITE TWR
HALL TWR
PADDINGTON GRN
NEWCASTLE PL
CUNNINGHAM PL
FISHERTON ST
ORCHARDSON ST
PENFOLD ST
CARLISLE MS
SALISBURY ST
ASHBRIDGE ST
SHROTON ST
DAVENTRY ST
COSWAY ST
HAREWOOD AV
BLANDFORD SQ
CHAGFORD ST
GLENTWORTH ST
ELM TREE RD
CAVENDISH AV
GROVE END ROAD
QUEEN'S TER
ALMA SQ
ST. EDMUNDS TER
AVENUE RD
TITCHFIELD RD
MACCLESFIELD BR
EAMONT ST
MACKENNAL ST
VICEROY CT
SHANNON PL
CULWORTH ST
GREENBERRY ST
OSLO CT
BRIDGEMAN ST
COCHRANE ST
ST. ANN'S TER
KINGSMILL TER
AQUILA ST
FB
Amb Sta

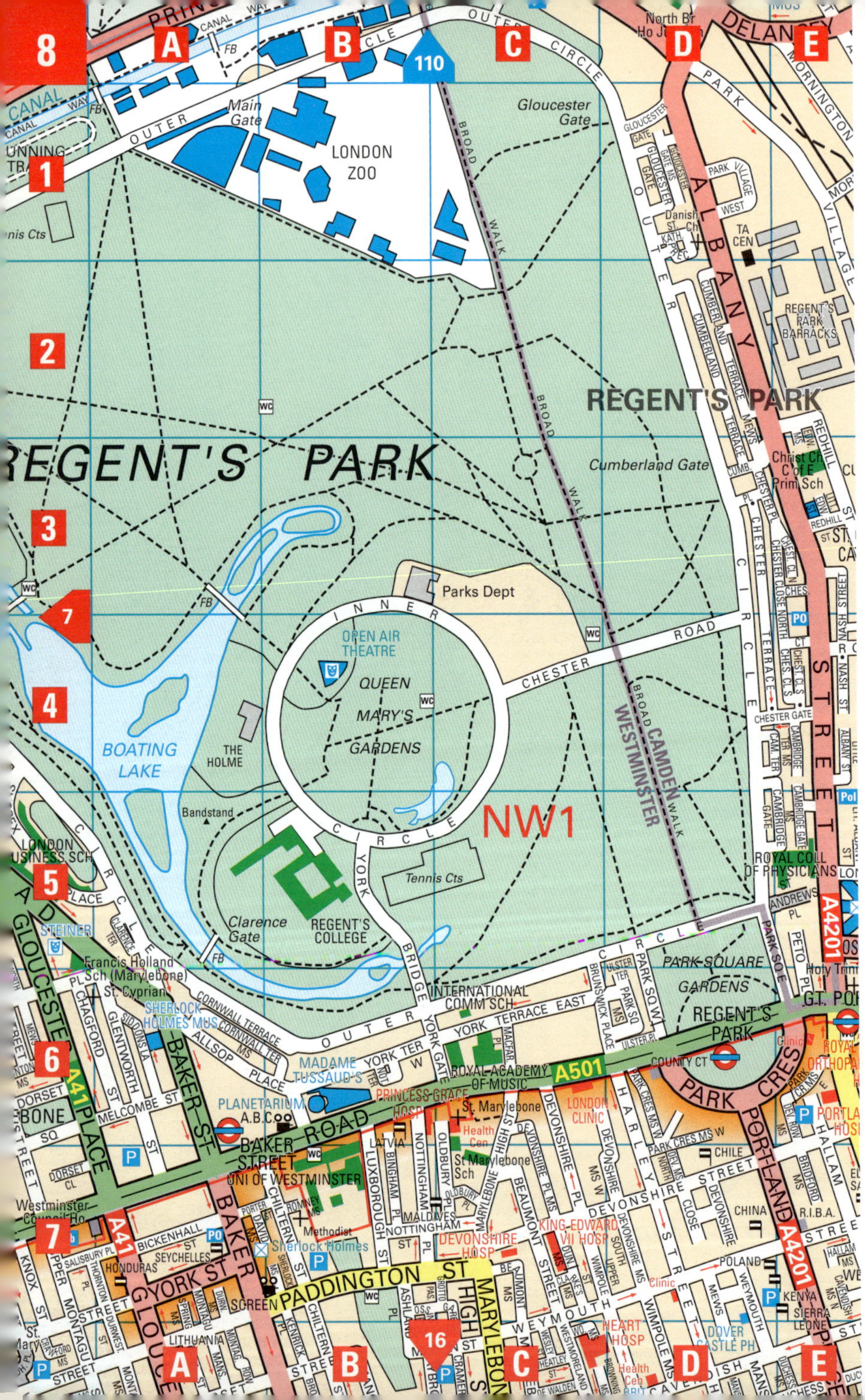
A
B
C
D
E
1
2
3
4
5
6
7
110
16
7
LONDON ZOO
Main Gate
Gloucester Gate
REGENT'S PARK
REGENT'S PARK
BROAD WALK
Cumberland Gate
Parks Dept
INNER CIRCLE
OPEN AIR THEATRE
QUEEN MARY'S GARDENS
CHESTER ROAD
BOATING LAKE
THE HOLME
Bandstand
NW1
Tennis Cts
Clarence Gate
REGENT'S COLLEGE
YORK BRIDGE
OUTER CIRCLE
CAMDEN WALK
WESTMINSTER
REGENT'S PARK BARRACKS
TA CEN
ALBANY STREET
PARK VILLAGE WEST
CUMBERLAND TERRACE
CHESTER TERRACE
CHESTER GATE
CAMBRIDGE GATE
ROYAL COLL OF PHYSICIANS
PARK SQUARE GARDENS
PARK SQUARE EAST
PARK SQ W
ULSTER TER
BRUNSWICK PLACE
INTERNATIONAL COMM SCH
YORK TERRACE EAST
YORK GATE
ROYAL ACADEMY OF MUSIC
A501
MARYLEBONE ROAD
MADAME TUSSAUD'S
PLANETARIUM
PRINCESS GRACE HOSP
BAKER STREET
BAKER ST
SHERLOCK HOLMES MUS
CORNWALL TERRACE
ALLSOP PLACE
LONDON BUSINESS SCH
STEINER
Francis Holland Sch (Marylebone)
St. Cyprian
GLOUCESTER PLACE
A41
DORSET SQ
MELCOMBE ST
UNI OF WESTMINSTER
Westminster Council Ho.
PADDINGTON ST
MARYLEBONE HIGH ST
St. Marylebone Sch
LONDON CLINIC
KING EDWARD VII HOSP
DEVONSHIRE PL
HARLEY ST
WIMPOLE ST
DEVONSHIRE ST
PARK CRESCENT
PORTLAND PL
A4201
GT. PORTLAND ST
ROYAL ORTHOPAEDIC
PORTLAND HOSP
R.I.B.A.
CHINA
CHILE
KENYA
SIERRA LEONE
HONDURAS
LATVIA
LITHUANIA
SEYCHELLES
Sherlock Holmes
DOVER CASTLE PH
HEART HOSP
Health Cen
Clinic
Christ Ch C of E Prim Sch
Holy Trinity
CANAL
FB
REDHILL ST
NASH ST
YORK ST
CHILTERN ST
WEYMOUTH ST
NOTTINGHAM PL
BICKENHALL ST
CHAGFORD ST
GLENTWORTH ST
DELANCEY ST
MORNINGTON

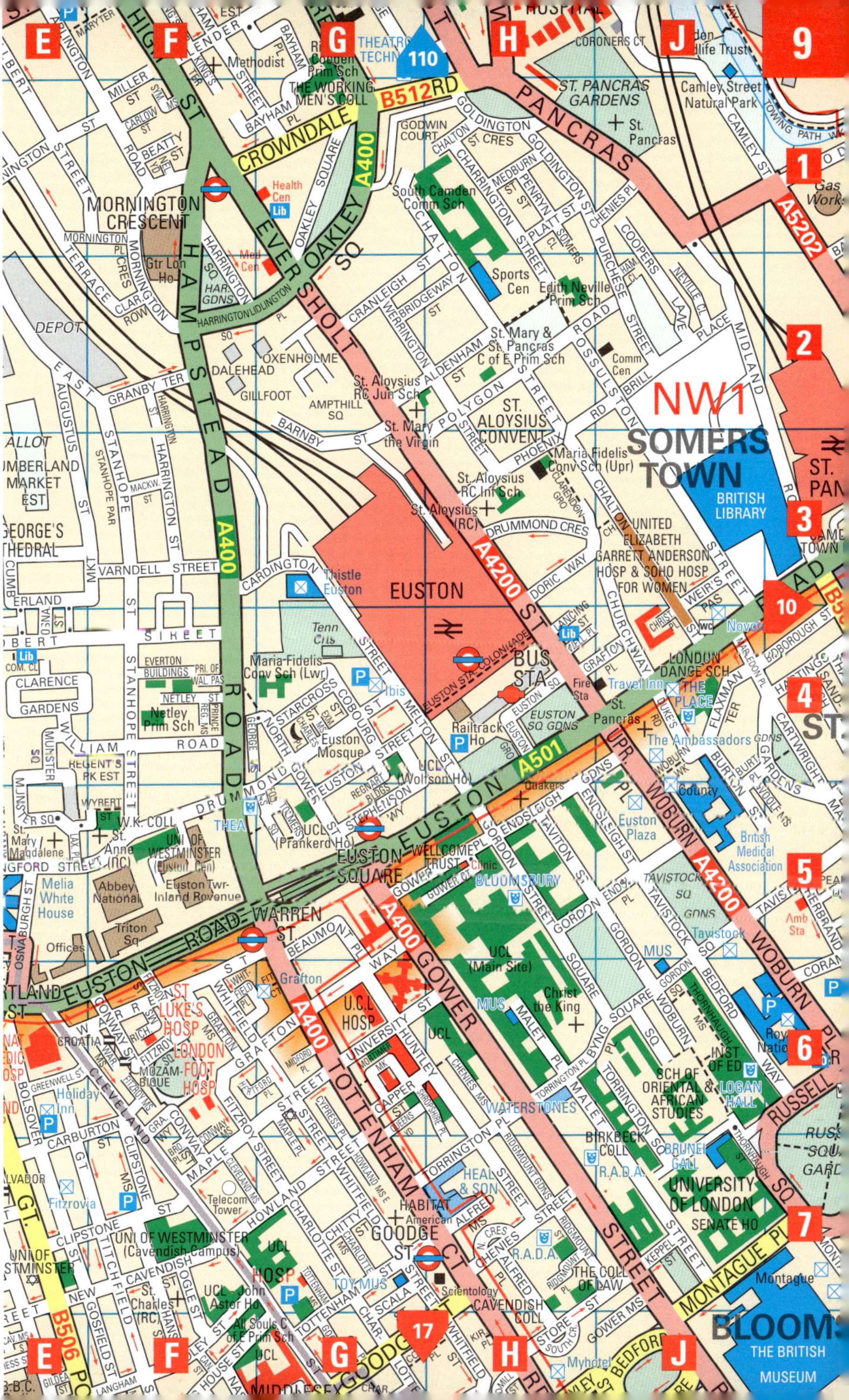
E
F
G
H
J
1
2
3
4
5
6
7
110
10
17
CROWNDALE RD
B512
A400
A4200
A501
A5202
B506
PANCRAS
ST. PANCRAS GARDENS
St. Pancras
Camley Street Natural Park
Camley St
Coroners Ct
Hospital
Theatre Techn
Methodist
The Working Men's Coll
Bayham St
Bayham Pl
Godwin Court
Goldington Cres
Goldington St
Chalton St
Medburn St
Penryn St
Charrington St
Platt St
Somers Cl
Purchese St
Chenies Pl
Coopers Lane
Neville Cl
Midland Rd
Brill Pl
South Camden Comm Sch
Sports Cen
Edith Neville Prim Sch
Health Cen
Lib
Med Cen
MORNINGTON CRESCENT
Mornington Pl
Mornington Terrace
Mornington Cres
Gtr Lon Ho
Clarkson Row
HAMPSTEAD ROAD
EVERSHOLT ST
OAKLEY SQ
Oakley Square
Harrington Sq
Harrington Sq Gdns
Lidlington Pl
Cranleigh St
Werrington St
Bridgeway St
Aldenham St
St. Mary & St. Pancras C of E Prim Sch
Ossulston St
Comm Cen
DEPOT
East St
Augustus St
Granby Ter
Oxenholme
Dalehead
Gillfoot
Ampthill Sq
St. Aloysius RC Jun Sch
Barnby St
Polygon Rd
St. Mary the Virgin
St. Aloysius Convent
Phoenix Rd
Maria Fidelis Conv Sch (Upr)
NW1
SOMERS TOWN
BRITISH LIBRARY
ST. PANCRAS
St. Aloysius RC Inf Sch
St. Aloysius (RC)
Drummond Cres
Doric Way
Chalton St
United Elizabeth Garrett Anderson Hosp & Soho Hosp for Women
Churchway
Weir's Pas
Novotel
ALLOT
Cumberland Market Est
Stanhope Par
Harrington St
Mackw. St
George's Cathedral
Varndell Street
Cardington St
Thistle Euston
EUSTON
Euston Sta Colonnade
Bus Sta
Tenn Ctts
Lib
Lancing St
Grafton Pl
Fire Sta
Travelodge Inn
London Dance Sch
The Place
Flaxman Ter
Cartwright Gardens
Everton Buildings
Clarence Gardens
Netley Prim Sch
Netley St
Stanhope Street
Maria Fidelis Conv Sch (Lwr)
Starcross St
Cobourg St
Melton St
Ibis
Euston Sq Gdns
St. Pancras
Railtrack Ho
Upr. Woburn Pl
The Ambassadors
Burton St
Woburn Wk
County
British Medical Association
William Road
Regent's Pk Est
Munster Sq
Euston Mosque
North Gower St
Drummond St
UCL (Wolfson Ho)
Quakers
Endsleigh Gdns
Endsleigh Pl
Euston Plaza
Wybert St
W.K. Coll
St. Mary Magdalene
St. Anne (RC)
Uni of Westminster (Euston Cen)
UCL (Prankerd Ho)
EUSTON SQUARE
EUSTON ROAD
Wellcome Trust
Clinic
Gower Pl
Gower Ct
Bloomsbury
Gordon Street
Taviton St
Gordon Square
Tavistock Sq
Tavistock Pl
Tavistock
Melia White House
Abbey National
Euston Twr Inland Revenue
Triton Sq
Offices
Warren St
Beaumont Pl
Grafton Way
UCL (Main Site)
Christ the King
MUS
Woburn Pl
Russell Sq
Osnaburgh St
Portland St
St. Luke's Hosp
London Foot Hosp
Whitfield St
U.C.L. Hosp
University St
Huntley St
Malet Pl
Byng Place
Torrington Pl
Sch of Oriental & African Studies
Logan Hall
Inst of Ed
Thornhaugh St
Bedford Way
Holiday Inn
Greenwell St
Bolsover St
Cleveland St
Carburton St
Clipstone St
Conway St
Fitzroy Street
Grafton Way
Maple St
Waterstones
Chenies Ms
Birkbeck Coll
R.A.D.A.
Brunei Gall
University of London
Senate Ho
Fitzrovia
Telecom Tower
Howland St
Charlotte St
Whitfield St
Heal & Son
Habitat
American
Goodge St
Alfred Pl
Ridgmount St
Ridgmount Gdns
Tottenham Court Rd
Gower Street
Montague Pl
Uni of Westminster (Cavendish Campus)
Cavendish Pl
UCL Hosp
UCL John Astor Ho
St. Charles (RC)
All Souls C of E Prim Sch
Toy Mus
Scala St
Scientology
Cavendish Coll
R.A.D.A.
The Coll of Law
Store St
Gower Ms
Keppel St
Montague
BLOOMSBURY
THE BRITISH MUSEUM
Myhotel
Bedford
Goodge St
Middlesex
New Cavendish St
Gosfield St
Langham
UCL
B.B.C.

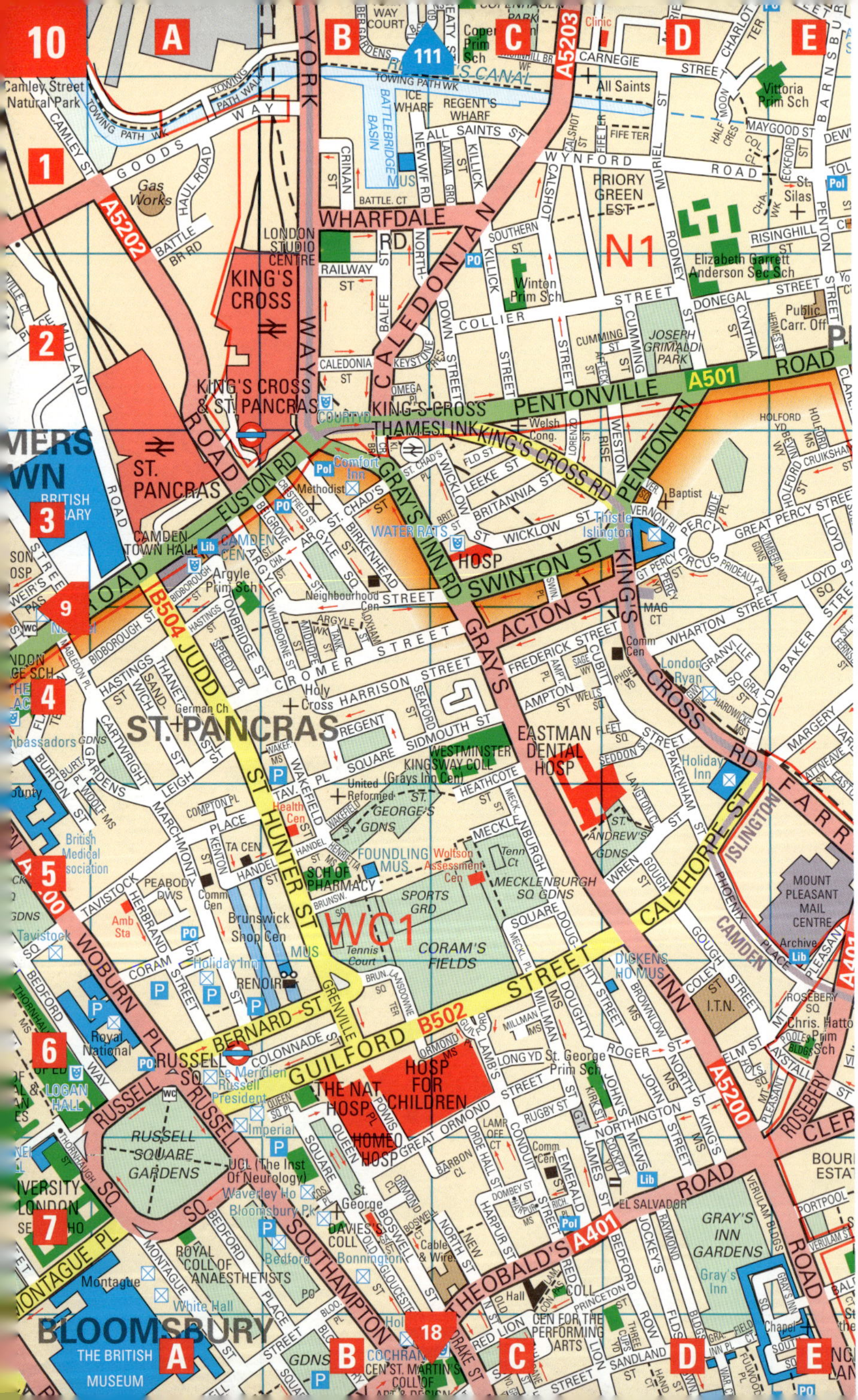
A
B
C
D
E
111
1
2
3
4
5
6
7
Camley Street Natural Park
CAMLEY ST
TOWING PATH WAY
GOODS WAY
Gas Works
HAUL ROAD
BATTLE BR RD
A5202
MIDLAND ROAD
YORK WAY
WAY COURT
REGENT'S CANAL
TOWING PATH WK
ICE WHARF
REGENT'S WHARF
BATTLEBRIDGE BASIN
MUS
CRINAN ST
NEW WHARF RD
LAVINA GRO
KILLICK ST
ALL SAINTS ST
BATTLE CT
Copenhagen Prim Sch
Clinic
A5203
CARNEGIE STREET
All Saints
FIFE TER
CALSHOT ST
WYNFORD ROAD
PRIORY GREEN EST
MURIEL ST
HALF MOON CRES
Vittoria Prim Sch
MAYGOOD ST
ECKFORD ST
St. Silas
Pol
PENTON ST
RISINGHILL ST
Elizabeth Garrett Anderson Sec Sch
N1
RODNEY ST
DONEGAL STREET
Public Carr. Off
CYNTHIA ST
WHARFDALE RD
LONDON STUDIO CENTRE
KING'S CROSS
RAILWAY ST
BALFE ST
NORTH-DOWN ST
CALEDONIAN
SOUTHERN ST
PO
Winton Prim Sch
COLLIER ST
CUMMING ST
JOSEPH GRIMALDI PARK
CALEDONIA ST
KEYSTONE CRES
OMEGA PL
PENTONVILLE ROAD
A501
KING'S CROSS & ST. PANCRAS
COURTYD
KING'S CROSS THAMESLINK
Welsh Cong.
KING'S CROSS RD
LORENZO ST
WESTON RISE
PENTON RI
HOLFORD YD
BEVIN WAY
HOLFORD ST
CRUIKSHANK ST
Baptist
VERNON RI
PERCY CIRCUS
HOLE PL
GREAT PERCY STREET
CUMBERLAND GDNS
PRIDEAUX PL
LLOYD SQ
LLOYD STREET
ST. PANCRAS
BRITISH LIBRARY
EUSTON RD
Pol
Comfort Inn
Methodist
ST. CHAD'S PL
ST. CHAD'S ST
WICKLOW ST
LEEKE ST
BRITANNIA ST
FLD ST
WATER RATS
HOSP
SWINTON ST
Thistle Islington
GT PERCY ST
MAG CT
WHARTON STREET
CAMDEN TOWN HALL
Lib
CAMDEN CEN
ARGYLE ST
ARGYLE SQ
BIRKENHEAD ST
Argyle Prim Sch
Neighbourhood Cen
STREET
ACTON ST
GRAY'S INN RD
KING'S CROSS RD
Comm Cen
GRANVILLE SQ
London Ryan
HARDWICKE ST
LLOYD BAKER ST
9
B504
BIDBOROUGH ST
HASTINGS ST
TONBRIDGE ST
WHIDBORNE ST
MIDHOPE ST
ARGYLE WK
LOXHAM ST
CROMER STREET
FREDERICK STREET
CUBITT ST
JUDD ST
Holy Cross
HARRISON STREET
SEAFORD ST
AMPTON ST
WELLS SQ
MARGERY ST
HASTINGS ST
SANDWICH ST
THANET ST
German Ch
ST. PANCRAS
REGENT SQ
SIDMOUTH ST
EASTMAN DENTAL HOSP
FLEET SQ
SEDDON ST
Holiday Inn
FARRINGDON
Ambassadors
CARTWRIGHT GARDENS
BURTON ST
LEIGH ST
WAKEFIELD MS
TAV. PL
SQUARE
WESTMINSTER KINGSWAY COLL (Grays Inn Cen)
United Reformed
HEATHCOTE ST
MECKLENBURGH PL
LANGTON CL
ISLINGTON
CALTHORPE ST
MOUNT PLEASANT MAIL CENTRE
British Medical Association
COMPTON PL
MARCHMONT ST
Health Cen
WAKEFIELD ST
ST. GEORGE'S GDNS
Tenn Ct
ST. ANDREW'S GDNS
WREN ST
GOUGH ST
PHOENIX PL
TA CEN
HANDEL ST
HENRIETTA MS
FOUNDLING MUS
Wolfson Assessment Cen
MECKLENBURGH SQ GDNS
TAVISTOCK PL
PEABODY DWS
KENTON ST
Comm Cen
SCH OF PHARMACY
BRUNSWICK SQ
SPORTS GRD
WC1
Amb Sta
HERBRAND ST
Brunswick Shop Cen
Tennis Court
CORAM'S FIELDS
DOUGHTY ST
CAMDEN
Archive
Lib
WOBURN PL
CORAM ST
Holiday Inn
MUS
RENOIR
BRUNSWICK SQ
LANSDOWNE TER
DICKENS HO MUS
BROWNLOW MS
GOUGH ST
COLEY ST
I.T.N.
ROSEBERY SQ
Chris. Hatton Prim Sch
Royal National
BERNARD ST
COLONNADE
GRENVILLE ST
B502
GUILFORD STREET
ORMOND MS
MILLMAN ST
MILLMAN MS
LONG YD
St. George Prim Sch
ROGER ST
NORTH MS
ELM ST
AYSTALL BLDGS
POOLES BLDGS
ROSEBERY AVE
A5200
RUSSELL SQ
PO
Le Meridien Russell
President
QUEEN SQ PL
THE NAT HOSP
HOSP FOR CHILDREN
LAMB'S CONDUIT ST
RUGBY ST
NORTHINGTON ST
JOHN'S MEWS
JOHN STREET
KING'S MS
CLERKENWELL
LOGAN HALL
RUSSELL SQUARE GARDENS
Imperial
HOMEO HOSP
GREAT ORMOND ST
LAMB OFF CT
BARBON CL
ORDE HALL ST
Comm Cen
EMERALD ST
COCKPIT YD
Lib
BOURNE ESTATE
UCL (The Inst Of Neurology)
Waverley Ho
Bloomsbury Pk
St. George
DAVIES'S COLL
Bonnington
Cable & Wire
DOMBEY ST
HARPUR ST
RICH. ST
Pol
A401
EL SALVADOR
THEOBALD'S ROAD
GRAY'S INN GARDENS
Gray's Inn
VERULAM BLDGS
PORTPOOL LA
MONTAGUE PL
ROYAL COLL OF ANAESTHETISTS
Bedford
BEDFORD PL
SOUTHAMPTON ROW
BOSWELL ST
GLOUCESTER ST
OLD GLOUCESTER ST
NORTH ST
NEW NORTH ST
Montague
White Hall
BLOOMSBURY
Hol
18
Hall
CEN FOR THE PERFORMING ARTS
PRINCETON ST
JOCKEY'S FIELDS
RAYMOND BLDGS
GRAY'S INN SQ
Chapel
THE BRITISH MUSEUM
GDNS
P
COCHRANE
CEN ST. MARTIN'S COLL OF ART & DESIGN
DRAKE ST
RED LION ST
SANDLAND ST
THREE CUPS YD
Tavistock
THORNHAUGH ST
BEDFORD WAY
RUSSELL SQ

E
F
G
H
J
111
BUSINESS DESIGN CEN
CLOUDESLEY PL
BATCHELOR ST
RITCHIE ST
WARNER
BROMFIELD
PARKFIELD ST
BERNERS RD
N1 Shop Cen
UPPER ST
CHARLTON PL
Our Lady of Czestochowa (RC)
St. John the Evangelist (RC)
RC Prim Sch
ISLINGTON HIGH ST
DUNCAN ST
GERRARD RD
DEVONIA RD
GRANTBRIDGE ST
RHEIDOL TER
ALLINGHAM ST
FROME ST
DAME ST
BURGH ST
HANOVER YD
BALDWIN TER
NOEL ROAD
REGENT'S CANAL
1
MARKET
LION STREET
WHITE LION
CRAFTS COUNCIL
ANGEL
PENTONVILLE
Jurys
The Angel Cen
DUNCAN TER
COLEBROOKE
VINCENT TERRACE
ELIA STREET
QUICK ST
SUDELEY ST
NELSON TER
NELSON PL
GRAHAM ST
CITY GDN ROW
THESEUS WK
Hanover Prim Sch
GRAND JUNC. WF
CITY ROAD BASIN
WENLOCK BASIN
WENLOCK RD
UNION WHARF
PICKFORDS WHARF
WHARF ROAD
2
CITY ROAD
OLD RED LION
CITY & ISLINGTON 6TH FORM COLL
ST. JOHN ST
GOSWELL RD
WAKLEY ST
ANGEL GATE
HALL STREET
PEREGRINE HOUSE
CITY UNI (Walter Sickert Hall)
KESTREL HO
A501
3
MYDDELTON SQUARE
St. Mark
CHADWELL ST
Baptist
ARLINGTON WY
SADLER'S WELLS THEATRE
AMWELL ST
INGLEBERT ST
RIVER ST
MYDDELTON PAS
FINSBURY
Clerkenwell Parochial C of E Prim Sch
NEW RIVER HEAD
SPA GREEN ESTATE
OWEN'S ROW
FRIEND ST
RAWSTORNE ST
HALL ST
NEW CHARLES ST
MORELAND STREET
Moreland Prim Sch
St. Clement
CITY FORUM
12
DINGLEY PL
Hugh Myddelton Jun & Inf Schs
SPENCER ST
Drysdale Bldg
Tait Bldg
CITY UNI
Gonn. Bldg
Coll Bldg
NORTHAMPTON SQUARE
TURNPIKE HO
KINGS SQUARE GDN
Thistle City Barbican
CITY UNI (Health Cen)
HARDWICK ST
St. Peter & Paul (RC)
Town Hall
ROSEBERY AV
CHARLES TOWNSEND HO
FINSBURY EST
Lib
LEVER ST
B502
4
CENTRAL STREET
Swim Pool
ST. LUKE'S GDN
Finsbury Leisure Cen
SKINNER ST
PERCIVAL ST
B501
CITY BUSINESS COLL
THE TRIANGLE
SEWARD STREET
PLEASANT & FIRKIN PH
SPA FIELDS GDNS
Holy Redeemer
Health Cen
Lon. Met. Univ
EXMOUTH MKT
Rosemary Sch
KINGSWAY PL
EC1
Dallington Sch
RC JMI Sch
Sports Cen
CITY UNI
EASTWICK ST
WHITE LION PH
5
COMPTON ST
BREWERY SQ
NORTHBURGH ST
SAPPERTON CT
PARMOOR CT
OLD ST
A5201
Med. Mission
St. James
CLERKENWELL CLOSE
Guardian & Observer
NEWSROOM
FARRINGDON LA
RAY ST
COLL OF PRINTING
CLERKENWELL
St. John
CLERKENWELL RD
QU. MARY (St Bart's Med Coll)
Charterhouse
THE GRN
Italia Conti Acad of Thea Arts
S.O.G.
Leisure Cen
Richard Cloudesley Sch
GOLDEN LANE EST
6
Presbyterian Church of Wales
St. Peter
HATTON GARDEN
B521
A201
CLERKENWELL RD
BRITTON ST
TURNMILL ST
ST. JOHN ST
Chapel
Charterhouse
CHARTERHOUSE SQ
Y.M.C.A.
EXHIB HALLS
FANN ST
COLL OF ART & DESIGN
EAGLE CT
BARBICAN
Charterhouse Sq Sch
BEECH ST
B100
7
St. Alban's C of E Prim Sch
HATTON
LEATHER LANE
ST. CROSS ST
FARRINGDON
FARRINGDON ROAD
COWCROSS ST
Power Sta
GREVILLE ST
LAUDERDALE TWR
THE BARBICAN
ART GALL
City of London Sch for Girls
St. Etheldreda's (RC)
Central Markets (Smithfield)
BARLEY MOW PH
B500
19
LONG LANE
CLOTH FAIR
St. Bartholomew the-great
ALDERSGATE ST
A1
BARBICAN
St.Giles
Barber Surgeons
Ironmongers'
WALLSIDE

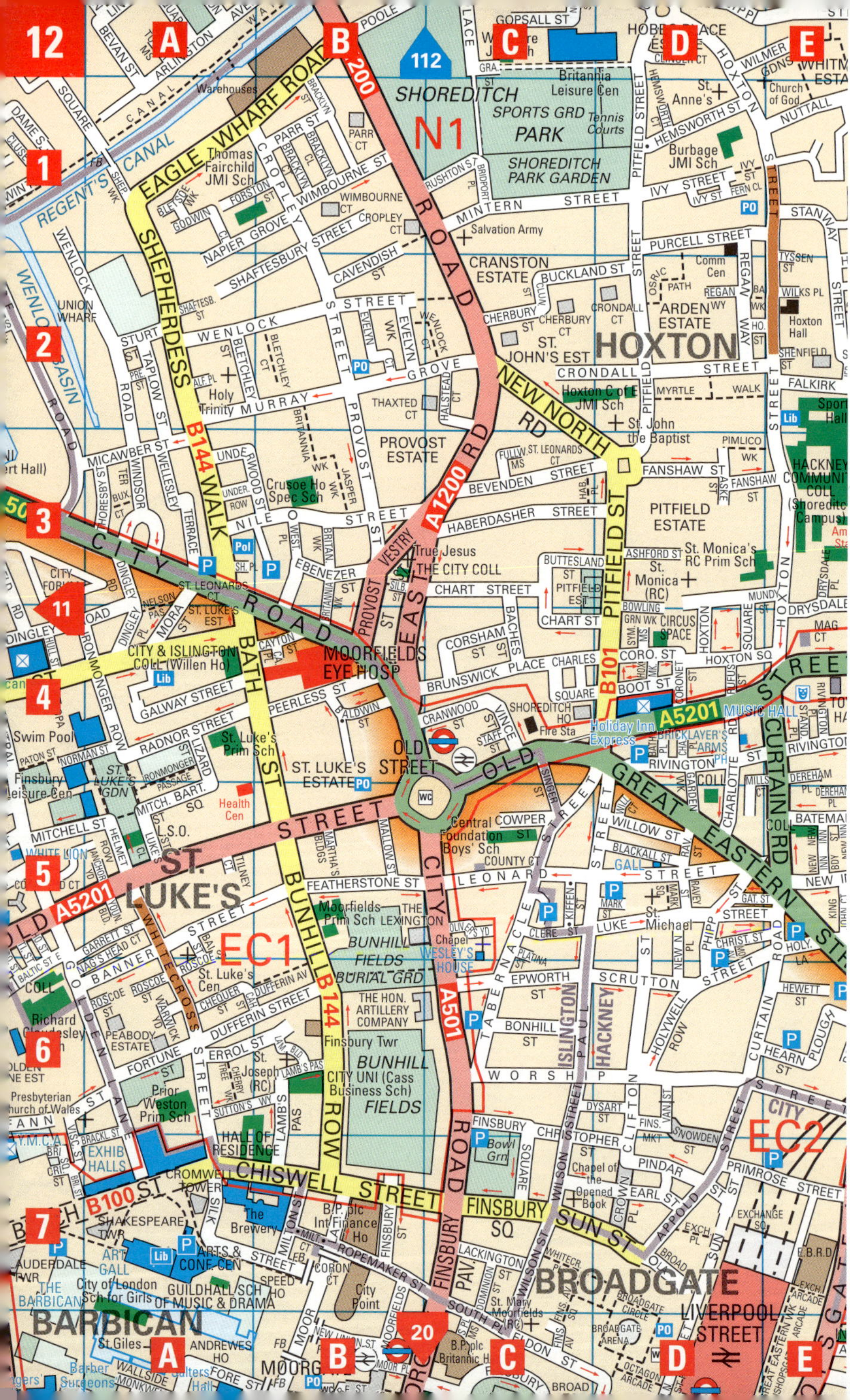
112
SHOREDITCH
N1
SPORTS GRD PARK
SHOREDITCH PARK GARDEN
Britannia Leisure Cen
Tennis Courts
GOPSALL ST
HOBBS PLACE EST
REGENT'S CANAL
EAGLE WHARF ROAD
Warehouses
Thomas Fairchild JMI Sch
WIMBOURNE ST
WIMBOURNE CT
CROPLEY CT
CROPLEY ST
SHEPHERDESS WALK
NAPIER GROVE
SHAFTESBURY STREET
CAVENDISH ST
WENLOCK ROAD
WENLOCK BASIN
UNION WHARF
WENLOCK STREET
MINTERN STREET
Salvation Army
CRANSTON ESTATE
BUCKLAND ST
CHERBURY ST
CHERBURY CT
ST. JOHN'S EST
CRONDALL CT
ARDEN ESTATE
HOXTON
PITFIELD STREET
HEMSWORTH ST
St. Anne's
Burbage JMI Sch
IVY STREET
PO
PURCELL STREET
Comm Cen
Hoxton Hall
CRONDALL STREET
Hoxton C of E JMI Sch
St. John the Baptist
MYRTLE WALK
FALKIRK
Sports Hall
HACKNEY COMMUNITY COLL (Shoreditch Campus)
Lib
HOXTON STREET
Holy Trinity
MURRAY GROVE
THAXTED CT
PROVOST ESTATE
PROVOST STREET
NEW NORTH RD
A1200 RD
B144 WALK
FANSHAW ST
PITFIELD ESTATE
PITFIELD ST
HABERDASHER STREET
BEVENDEN STREET
Crusoe Ho Spec Sch
NILE STREET
CITY ROAD
True Jesus
THE CITY COLL
EAST ROAD
VESTRY ST
CHART STREET
BUTTESLAND ST
ASHFORD ST
St. Monica's RC Prim Sch
St. Monica (RC)
CIRCUS SPACE
CORO. ST
HOXTON SQ
DRYSDALE ST
11
CITY & ISLINGTON COLL (Willen Ho)
MOORFIELDS EYE HOSP
BATH ST
CORSHAM ST
BRUNSWICK PLACE
CHARLES SQUARE
BOOT ST
B101
A5201
MUSIC HALL
Holiday Inn Express
SHOREDITCH HO
Fire Sta
BRICKLAYER'S ARMS PH
RIVINGTON ST
CURTAIN RD
GALWAY STREET
PEERLESS ST
ALDWIN ST
RADNOR STREET
St. Luke's Prim Sch
Swim Pool
Finsbury Leisure Cen
ST. LUKE'S GDN
OLD STREET
ST. LUKE'S ESTATE
Health Cen
MITCH. BART. SQ
L.S.O.
MITCHELL ST
WHITE LION
CENTRAL FOUNDATION Boys' Sch
COWPER ST
OLD STREET
GREAT EASTERN STREET
WILLOW ST
BLACKALL ST
LEONARD STREET
ST. LUKE'S
A5201
OLD STREET
WHITECROSS STREET
EC1
BUNHILL ROW B144
FEATHERSTONE ST
Moorfields Prim Sch
LEXINGTON
BUNHILL FIELDS BURIAL GRD
Chapel
WESLEY'S HOUSE
CITY ROAD A501
TABERNACLE ST
CLERE ST
LUKE ST
St. Michael
PAUL STREET
EPWORTH ST
SCRUTTON STREET
BONHILL ST
HOLYWELL ROW
ISLINGTON
HACKNEY
BANNER ST
St. Luke's Cen
DUFFERIN STREET
ROSCOE ST
PEABODY ESTATE
THE HON. ARTILLERY COMPANY
Finsbury Twr
BUNHILL FIELDS
CITY UNI (Cass Business Sch)
Richard Cloudesley Sch
FORTUNE ST
ERROL ST
St. Joseph (RC)
Prior Weston Prim Sch
WORSHIP ST
CURTAIN RD
HEARN ST
PLOUGH
Presbyterian Church of Wales
Y.M.C.A.
EXHIB HALLS
HALL OF RESIDENCE
CHISWELL STREET
FINSBURY SQUARE
CHRISTOPHER ST
Bowl Grn
Chapel of the Opened Book
EARL ST
PINDAR ST
EC2
PRIMROSE STREET
B100 ST
CROMWELL TOWER
SHAKESPEARE TWR
The Brewery
B.P. plc Int Finance Ho
FINSBURY SQ
SUN ST
EXCHANGE SQ
ART GALL
Lib
ARTS & CONF. CEN
City of London Sch for Girls
GUILDHALL SCH OF MUSIC & DRAMA
THE BARBICAN
BARBICAN
ROPEMAKER ST
City Point
LACKINGTON ST
St. Mary Moorfields (RC)
BROADGATE
BROADGATE ARENA
LIVERPOOL STREET
St Giles
ANDREWES HO
Barber Surgeons
MOORGATE
20
B.P. plc Britannic Ho
A B C D E
1 2 3 4 5 6 7

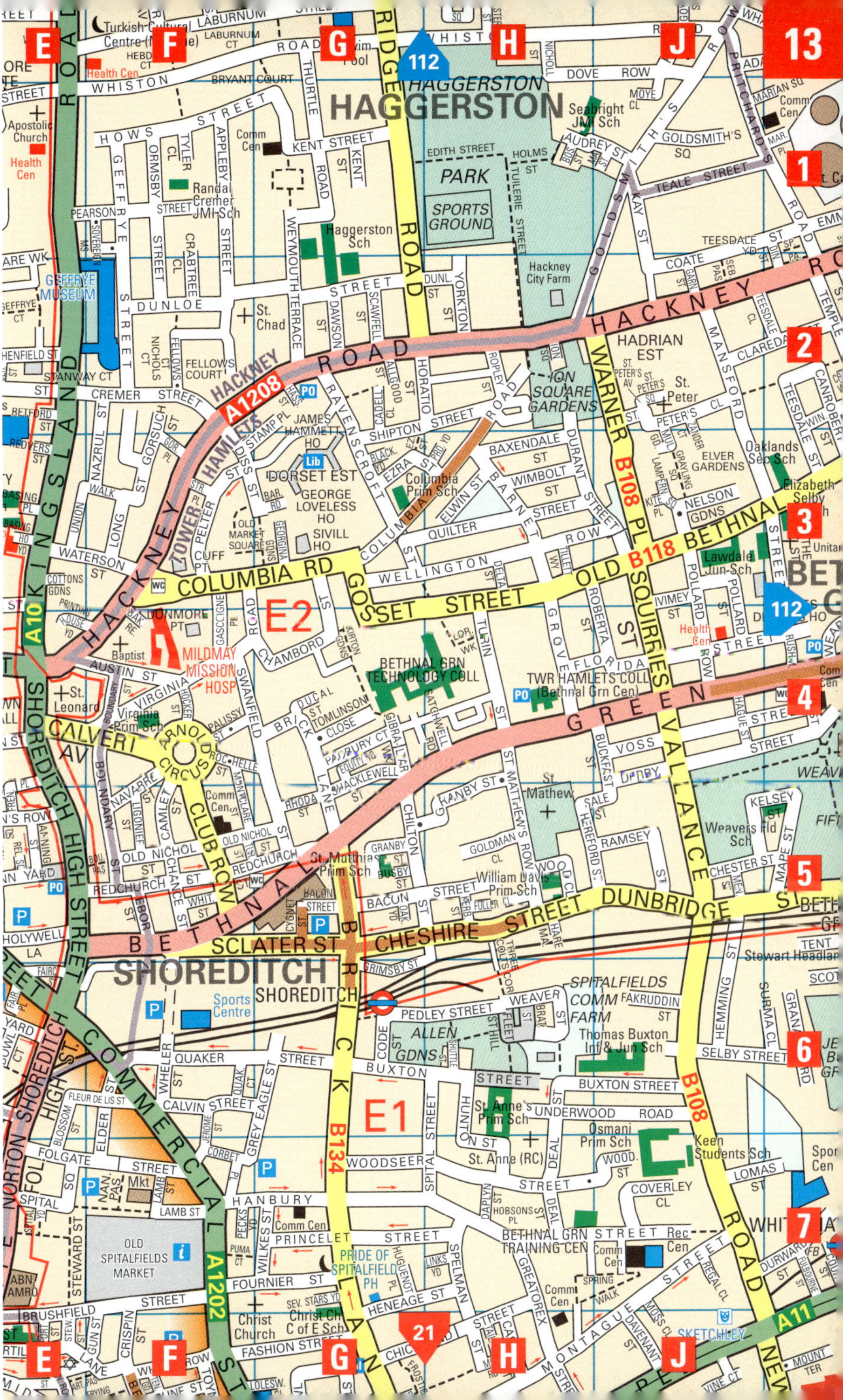
E
F
G
H
J
112
HAGGERSTON
PARK
SPORTS GROUND
Haggerston Sch
Randal Cremer JMI Sch
Seabright JMI Sch
Hackney City Farm
GEFFRYE MUSEUM
St. Chad
KENT STREET
WHISTON ROAD
DOVE ROW
GOLDSMITH'S SQ
TEALE STREET
PRITCHARD'S ROAD
HOWS STREET
DUNLOE STREET
HACKNEY ROAD
A1208
HADRIAN EST
St. Peter
ION SQUARE GARDENS
WARNER PL
B108
B118
OLD BETHNAL GREEN ROAD
Oaklands Sec Sch
Elizabeth Selby
JAMES HAMMETT HO
Lib
DORSET EST
GEORGE LOVELESS HO
SIVILL HO
Columbia Prim Sch
COLUMBIA RD
GOSSET STREET
WELLINGTON ROW
Lawdale Jun Sch
E2
MILDMAY MISSION HOSP
Baptist
St. Leonard
Virginia Prim Sch
CALVERT AV
ARNOLD CIRCUS
CLUB ROW
BETHNAL GREEN TECHNOLOGY COLL
TWR HAMLETS COLL (Bethnal Grn Cen)
BETHNAL GREEN ROAD
St. Mathew
Weavers Fld Sch
VALLANCE ROAD
SQUIRRIES ST
St. Matthias Prim Sch
William Davis Prim Sch
DUNBRIDGE STREET
CHESHIRE STREET
SCLATER ST
SHOREDITCH
Sports Centre
SHOREDITCH HIGH STREET
KINGSLAND ROAD
A10
SPITALFIELDS COMM FARM
Thomas Buxton Inf & Jun Sch
ALLEN GDNS
BRICK LANE
B134
E1
St. Anne's Prim Sch
Osmani Prim Sch
Keen Students Sch
BUXTON STREET
UNDERWOOD ROAD
WOODSEER ST
HANBURY STREET
PRINCELET STREET
FOURNIER ST
PRIDE OF SPITALFIELDS PH
OLD SPITALFIELDS MARKET
Christ Church
Christ Ch C of E Sch
COMMERCIAL ST
A1202
BETHNAL GRN TRAINING CEN
SKETCHLEY
A11
21

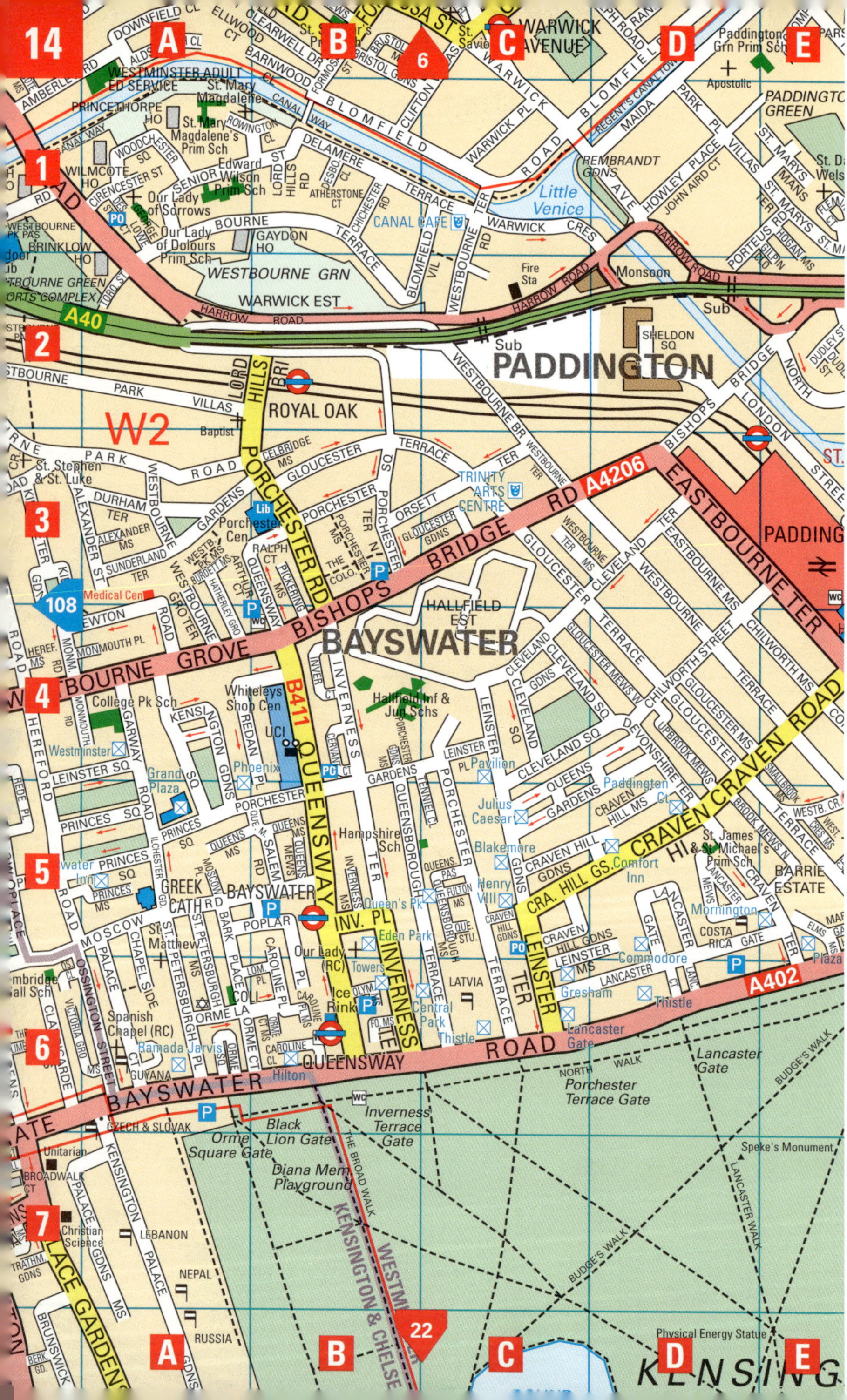
A
B
C
D
E
1
2
3
4
5
6
7
6
22
108
W2
PADDINGTON
BAYSWATER
ROYAL OAK
A40
A4206
A402
B411
WESTBOURNE GRN
WARWICK EST
HARROW ROAD
Little Venice
CANAL CAFE
WESTMINSTER ADULT ED SERVICE
Whiteleys Shop Cen
Hallfield Inf & Jun Schs
HALLFIELD EST
BISHOPS BRIDGE RD
EASTBOURNE TER
WESTBOURNE GROVE
QUEENSWAY
PORCHESTER RD
BAYSWATER ROAD
LEINSTER TER
CRAVEN HILL GS.
CRAVEN ROAD
GLOUCESTER TERRACE
PRINCES SQ
LEINSTER SQ
MOSCOW RD
Greek Cath
Spanish Chapel (RC)
Lancaster Gate
Porchester Terrace Gate
Inverness Terrace Gate
Black Lion Gate
Orme Square Gate
Diana Mem Playground
Speke's Monument
Physical Energy Statue
THE BROAD WALK
LANCASTER WALK
BUDGE'S WALK
KENSINGTON PALACE GARDENS
KENSING

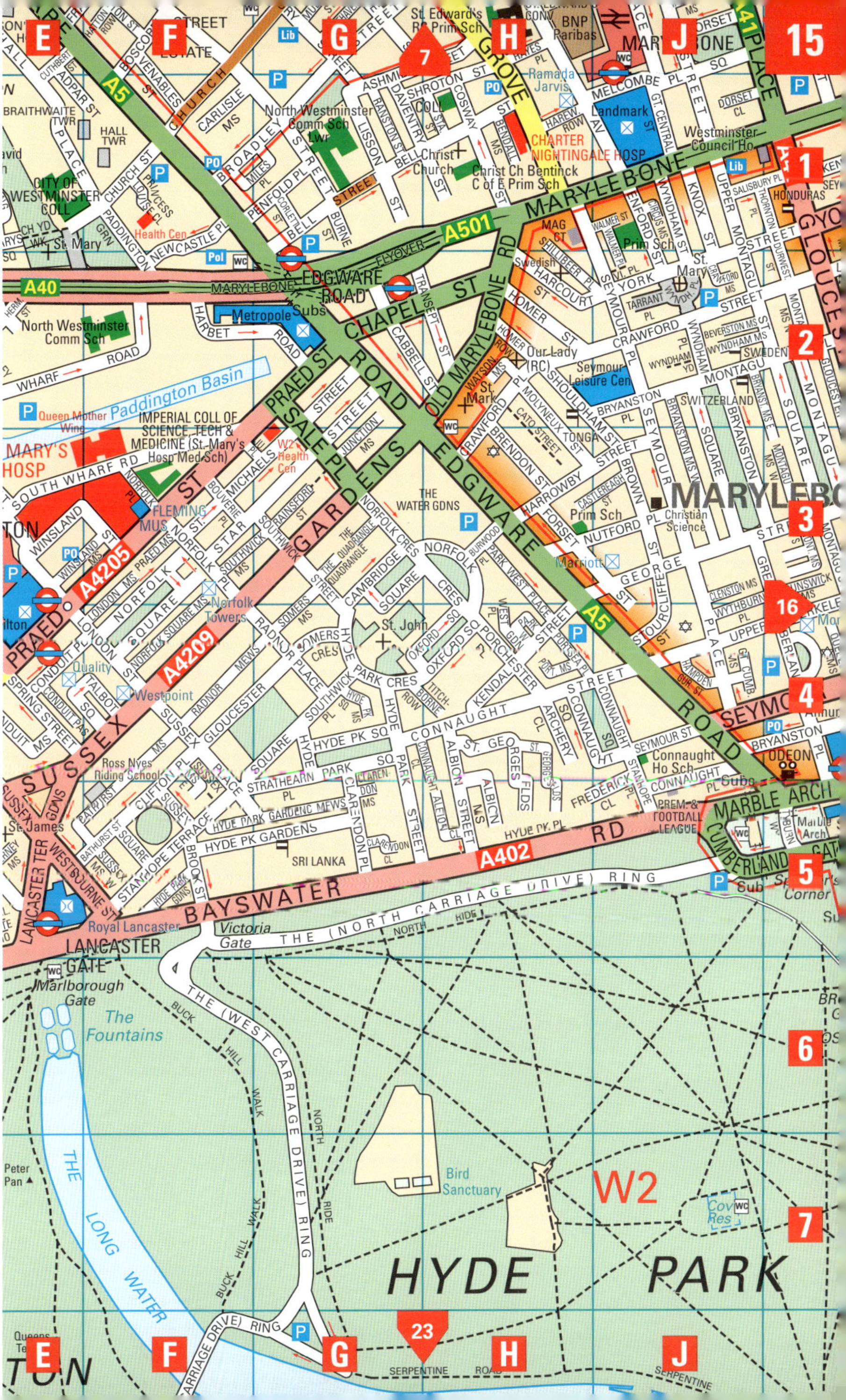
E
F
G
H
J
1
2
3
4
5
6
7
7
16
23
A5
A40
A501
A4205
A4209
A402
Church Street Estate
St Edward's RC Prim Sch
BNP Paribas
Marylebone
Grove
Ramada Jarvis
Landmark
Charter Nightingale Hosp
Westminster Council Ho
Melcombe Pl
Dorset Sq
Harewood Row
Shroton St
Daventry St
Cosway St
Ashmill St
Lisson St
Ranston St
Bell St
Christ Church
Christ Ch Bentinck C of E Prim Sch
North Westminster Comm Sch Lwr
Broadley St
Penfold Pl
Corlett St
Burne St
Church St
Carlisle Ms
Boscobel St
Venables St
Hatton Row
Cuthbert Braithwaite Twr
Hall Twr
Adpar St
City of Westminster Coll
Paddington Grn
Princess Louise Cl
Health Cen
Newcastle Pl
St Mary
Marylebone Rd
Flyover
Edgware Road
Chapel St
Transept St
Old Marylebone Rd
Metropole
Subs
Harbet Road
North Westminster Comm Sch
Wharf Road
Paddington Basin
Queen Mother Wing
Imperial Coll of Science, Tech & Medicine (St Mary's Hosp Med Sch)
St Mary's Hosp
W2 Health Cen
South Wharf Rd
Praed St
Sale Pl
Cabbell St
Junction Ms
Fleming Mus
Norfolk Pl
Winsland St
Winsland Ms
London St
Norfolk Sq
Praed Ms
St Michaels St
Bouverie Pl
Star St
Southwick St
Rainsford St
Sussex Gardens
The Quadrangle
Norfolk Cres
Cambridge Sq
The Water Gdns
Burwood Pl
Park West Place
Harrowby St
Brendon St
Crawford Pl
Molyneux St
Cato St
Shouldham St
Tonga
Watson Ms
St Mark
Our Lady (RC)
Homer Row
Homer St
Harcourt St
Swedish
Shillibeer Pl
Mag Ct
Walmer St
Walmer Pl
Enford St
Prim Sch
Seymour Pl
Crawford St
Tarrant Pl
York St
Wyndham St
Wyndham Yd
St Mary
Seymour Leisure Cen
Bryanston Pl
Montagu St
Beverston Ms
Wyndham Ms
Sweden
Switzerland
Bryanston Ms E
Bryanston Ms W
Bryanston Sq
Montagu Sq
Salisbury Pl
Honduras
Upper Montagu St
Thornton Pl
Knox St
Gloucester Pl
Castlereagh St
Prim Sch
Forset St
Nutford Pl
Brown St
Christian Science
Marylebone
George St
Marriott
Clenston Ms
Wythburn Pl
Upper Berkeley St
Stourcliffe St
Hampden Gurney St
Cumberland
Seymour St
Bryanston Pl
Odeon
Marble Arch
Marble Arch
Cumberland Gate
Subs
Prem. & Football League
Frederick Cl
Connaught Ho Sch
Connaught Pl
Stanhope Pl
Connaught Sq
Connaught St
Archery Cl
Kendal St
Porchester Pl
Oxford Sq
Titchborne Row
Hyde Park Cres
St John
Somers Cres
Somers Ms
Radnor Pl
Radnor Ms
Gloucester Square
Southwick Pl
Hyde Pk Sq
Park St
St George's Flds
Albion St
Albion Cl
Albion Ms
Hyde Pk Pl
Clarendon Pl
Strathearn Pl
Hyde Park Gardens Ms
Hyde Pk Gardens
Sri Lanka
Talbot Sq
Conduit Pl
Spring Street
Quality
Westpoint
Norfolk Towers
Norfolk Square Ms
Sussex Sq
Sussex Pl
Clifton Pl
Ross Nyes Riding School
Bathurst St
Stanhope Terrace
Brook St
Hyde Park Gdns
St James
Lancaster Ter
Westbourne St
Sussex Gdns
Royal Lancaster
Bayswater Rd
Lancaster Gate
Victoria Gate
The (North Carriage Drive) Ring
North Ride
Marlborough Gate
The Fountains
Buck Hill Walk
The (West Carriage Drive) Ring
North Ride
The Long Water
Peter Pan
Bird Sanctuary
W2
Cov Res
Hyde Park
Serpentine Road
Serpentine
Queens Ter

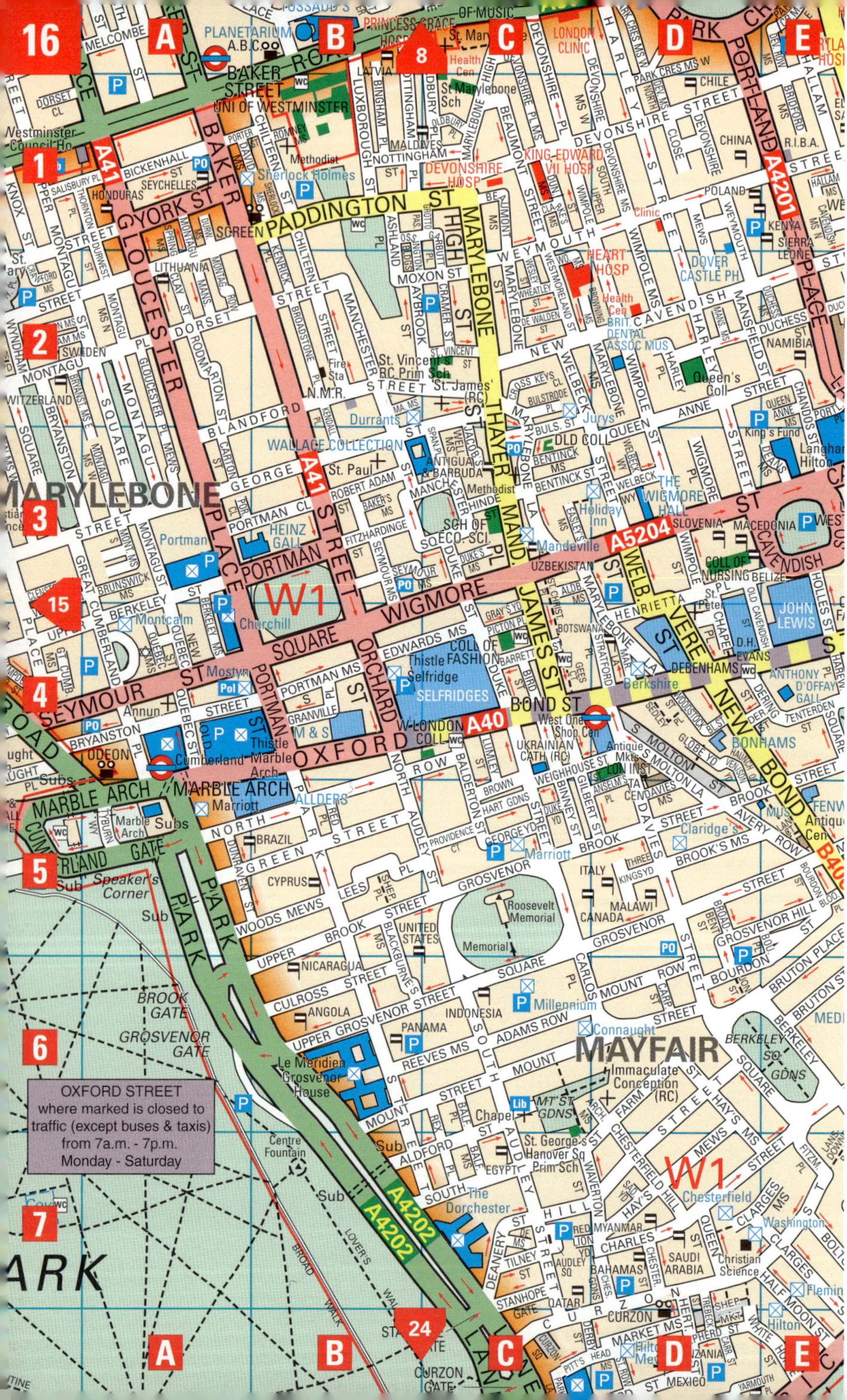
A
B
C
D
E
1
2
3
4
5
6
7
8
15
24
PLANETARIUM
A.B.C.
BAKER STREET
UNI OF WESTMINSTER
PRINCESS GRACE HOSP
LONDON CLINIC
St. Marylebone Sch
Health Cen
LATVIA
MELCOMBE
DORSET CL
Westminster Council Ho
A41
BICKENHALL ST
SEYCHELLES
HONDURAS
YORK ST
GLOUCESTER
BAKER
Sherlock Holmes
Methodist
PADDINGTON ST
MARYLEBONE
HIGH ST
DEVONSHIRE HOSP
KING EDWARD VII HOSP
NOTTINGHAM
LUXBOROUGH
BEAUMONT
DEVONSHIRE
HARLEY
PARK CRES MS W
CHILE
CHINA
R.I.B.A.
PORTLAND PLACE
A4201
POLAND
KENYA
SIERRA LEONE
Clinic
DOVER CASTLE PH
HEART HOSP
Health Cen
BRIT. DENTAL ASSOC MUS
CAVENDISH
NAMIBIA
Queen's Coll
WEYMOUTH
WIMPOLE
MOXON ST
SCREEN
LITHUANIA
DORSET
MONTAGU
SWEDEN
SWITZERLAND
BRYANSTON
SQUARE
MARYLEBONE
Fire Sta
N.M.R.
St. Vincent's RC Prim Sch
St. James' (RC)
Durrants
BLANDFORD
WALLACE COLLECTION
St. Paul
ANTIGUA & BARBUDA
Methodist
THAYER
OLD COLL
BENTINCK
Jurys
QUEEN ANNE
King's Fund
Langham Hilton
THE WIGMORE HALL
Holiday Inn
SLOVENIA
MACEDONIA
COLL OF NURSING
BELIZE
CAVENDISH SQ
JOHN LEWIS
D.H. EVANS
HEINZ GALL
Portman
PORTMAN ST
A41
GEORGE
ROBERT ADAM
SCH OF ECO. SCI.
Mandeville
A5204
UZBEKISTAN
WIGMORE
W1
Churchill
Montcalm
SEYMOUR
Mostyn
Pol
Annun.
BRYANSTON
ODEON
Cumberland
Thistle Marble Arch
OXFORD
ORCHARD
Thistle Selfridge
SELFRIDGES
COLL OF FASHION
M & S
W. LONDON COLL
A40
BOND ST
West One Shop Cen
UKRAINIAN CATH (RC)
BOTSWANA
Berkshire
DEBENHAMS
HENRIETTA
VERE
NEW BOND ST
ANTHONY D'OFFAY GALL
BONHAMS
Antique Mkts
LON INST
SOUTH MOLTON
MARBLE ARCH
Marriott
ALLDERS
Marble Arch
Subs
CUMBERLAND GATE
Speaker's Corner
NORTH ROW
BRAZIL
GREEN ST
CYPRUS
BROOK
Marriott
ITALY
CANADA
MALAWI
GROSVENOR
Claridge's
Roosevelt Memorial
Memorial
UNITED STATES
NICARAGUA
ANGOLA
UPPER GROSVENOR ST
PANAMA
INDONESIA
Millennium
Connaught
MAYFAIR
BERKELEY SQ GDNS
REEVES MS
Le Meridien Grosvenor House
MOUNT ST
Immaculate Conception (RC)
Chapel
MT ST GDNS
St. George's Hanover Sq Prim Sch
EGYPT
The Dorchester
A4202
W1
Chesterfield
Washington
MYANMAR
SAUDI ARABIA
Christian Science
BAHAMAS
QATAR
CURZON
Hilton
Flemings
STANHOPE GATE
CURZON GATE
PARK LANE
PARK
BROOK GATE
GROSVENOR GATE
Centre Fountain
OXFORD STREET where marked is closed to traffic (except buses & taxis) from 7a.m. - 7p.m. Monday - Saturday
ARK
BROAD WALK
LOVER'S WALK
MEXICO
FENWICK
Antiques Cen
B406

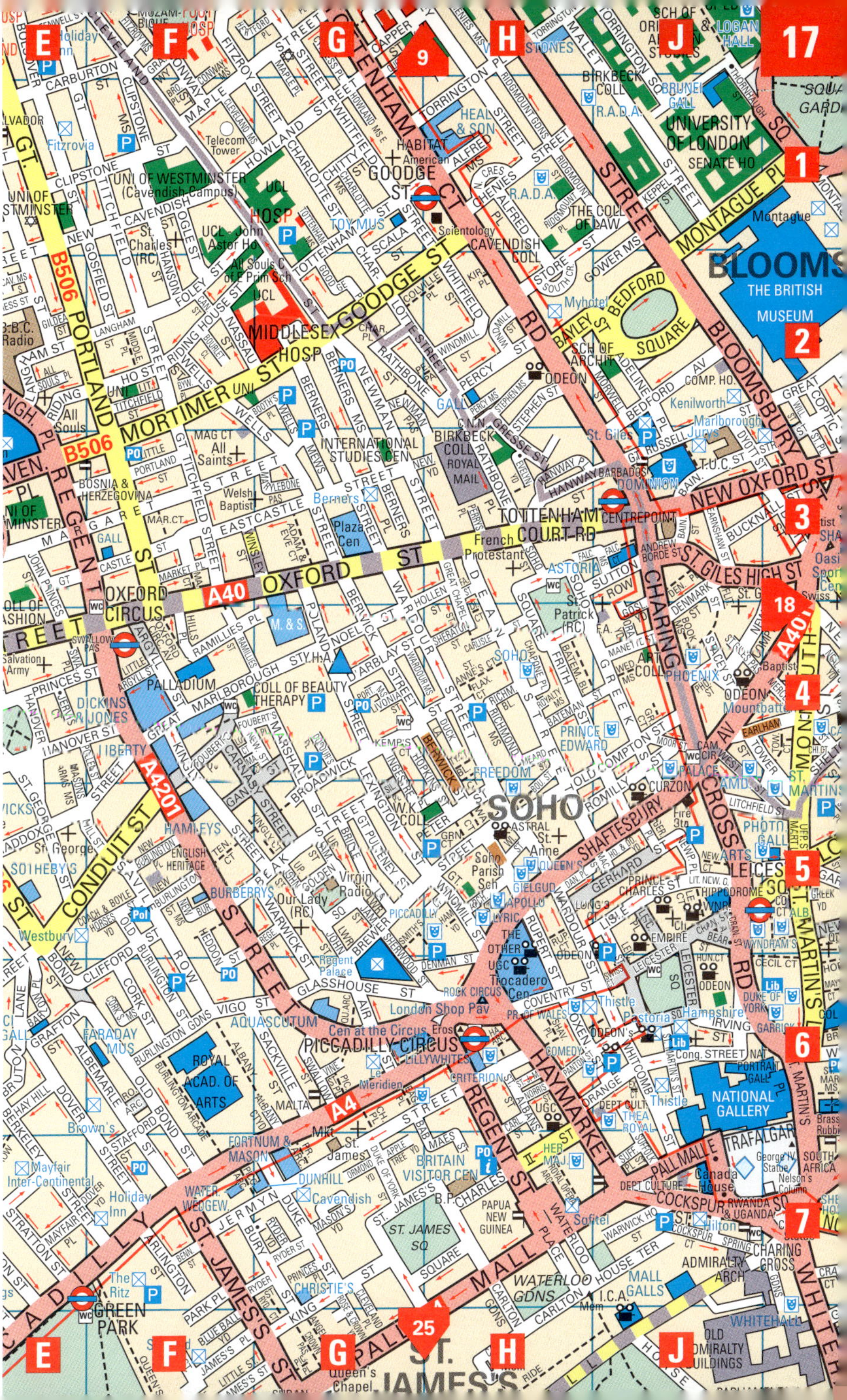
E
F
G
H
J
9
25
1
2
3
4
5
6
7
18
SOHO
BLOOMS
THE BRITISH MUSEUM
UNIVERSITY OF LONDON
SENATE HO
MONTAGUE PL
BEDFORD SQUARE
BLOOMSBURY
NEW OXFORD ST
ST GILES HIGH ST
TOTTENHAM COURT RD
CENTREPOINT
CHARING CROSS RD
OXFORD ST
A40
OXFORD CIRCUS
REGENT ST
GT. PORTLAND ST
B506
MORTIMER ST
GOODGE ST
GOODGE ST
MIDDLESEX HOSP
UCL HOSP
UNI OF WESTMINSTER (Cavendish Campus)
Telecom Tower
Fitzrovia
CARBURTON ST
CLIPSTONE ST
HOWLAND ST
CHARLOTTE ST
CONDUIT ST
A4201
HAMLEYS
LIBERTY
PALLADIUM
CARNABY ST
BROADWICK
SHAFTESBURY AV
CURZON
PICCADILLY CIRCUS
Cen at the Circus
London Shop Pav
Trocadero Cen
LEICESTER SQ
HIPPODROME
EMPIRE
ODEON
NATIONAL GALLERY
TRAFALGAR
Canada House
CHARING CROSS
ADMIRALTY ARCH
COCKSPUR ST
PALL MALL
HAYMARKET
WATERLOO PLACE
ST. JAMES SQ
JERMYN ST
PICCADILLY
GREEN PARK
The Ritz
ROYAL ACAD. OF ARTS
FORTNUM & MASON
BRITAIN VISITOR CEN
SOTHEBY'S
Brown's
Mayfair Inter-Continental
Holiday Inn
ST. JAMES'S
Queen's Chapel
OLD ADMIRALTY BUILDINGS
WHITEHALL
MALL GALLS
ASTORIA
PHOENIX
PRINCE EDWARD
GIELGUD
APOLLO
LYRIC
QUEEN'S
COMEDY
CRITERION
Thistle
Sofitel
Hilton
AQUASCUTUM
BURBERRYS
SAVILE ROW
REGENT ST

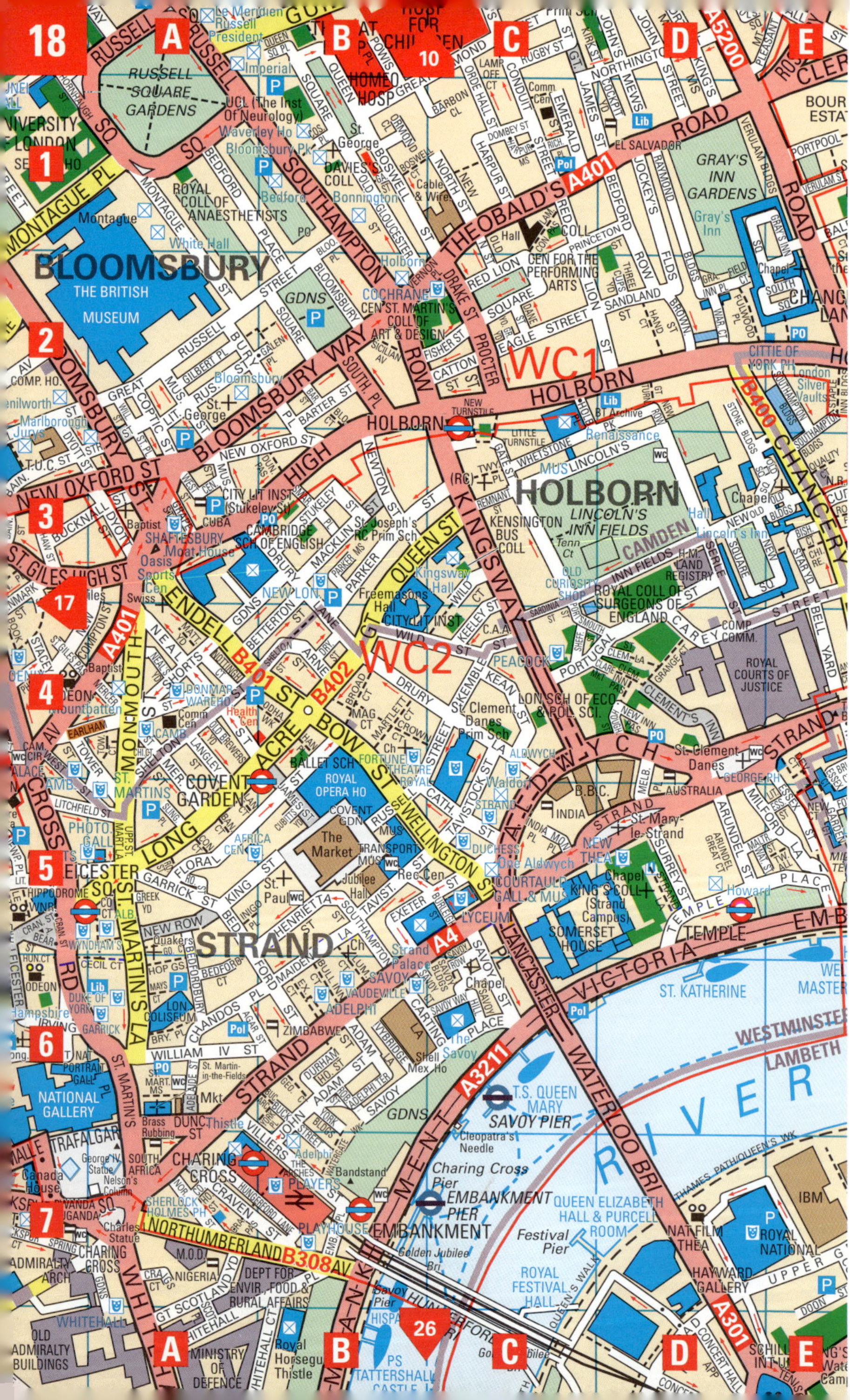
A
B
C
D
E
1
2
3
4
5
6
7
BLOOMSBURY
THE BRITISH MUSEUM
RUSSELL SQUARE GARDENS
ROYAL COLL OF ANAESTHETISTS
SOUTHAMPTON ROW
THEOBALD'S ROAD
A401
GRAY'S INN GARDENS
Gray's Inn
CEN FOR THE PERFORMING ARTS
CEN ST. MARTIN'S COLL OF ART & DESIGN
WC1
HOLBORN
BLOOMSBURY WAY
NEW OXFORD ST
HIGH HOLBORN
KINGSWAY
HOLBORN
LINCOLN'S INN FIELDS
CAMDEN
ROYAL COLL OF SURGEONS OF ENGLAND
ROYAL COURTS OF JUSTICE
CHANCERY LANE
B400
WC2
COVENT GARDEN
ROYAL OPERA HO
The Market
LONG ACRE
SHAFTESBURY
B401
B402
BOW ST
WELLINGTON ST
ALDWYCH
STRAND
St. Clement Danes
B.B.C.
AUSTRALIA
INDIA
COURTAULD GALL & MUS
KING'S COLL (Strand Campus)
SOMERSET HOUSE
TEMPLE
VICTORIA EMBANKMENT
A4
LANCASTER PL
WATERLOO BRI
A3211
A301
T.S. QUEEN MARY
SAVOY PIER
Cleopatra's Needle
Charing Cross Pier
EMBANKMENT PIER
EMBANKMENT
QUEEN ELIZABETH HALL & PURCELL ROOM
Festival Pier
ROYAL FESTIVAL HALL
NAT FILM THEA
HAYWARD GALLERY
ROYAL NATIONAL
IBM
RIVER
WESTMINSTER
LAMBETH
NATIONAL GALLERY
TRAFALGAR
CHARING CROSS
NORTHUMBERLAND AV
B308
DEPT FOR ENVIR, FOOD & RURAL AFFAIRS
MINISTRY OF DEFENCE
WHITEHALL
OLD ADMIRALTY BUILDINGS
ST. MARTIN'S LA
LEICESTER SQ
CHARING CROSS RD
MONMOUTH ST
A401
17
10
26
Thistle
STRAND PALACE
SAVOY
ADELPHI
VAUDEVILLE
LYCEUM
LON COLISEUM
PLAYERS
PLAYHOUSE

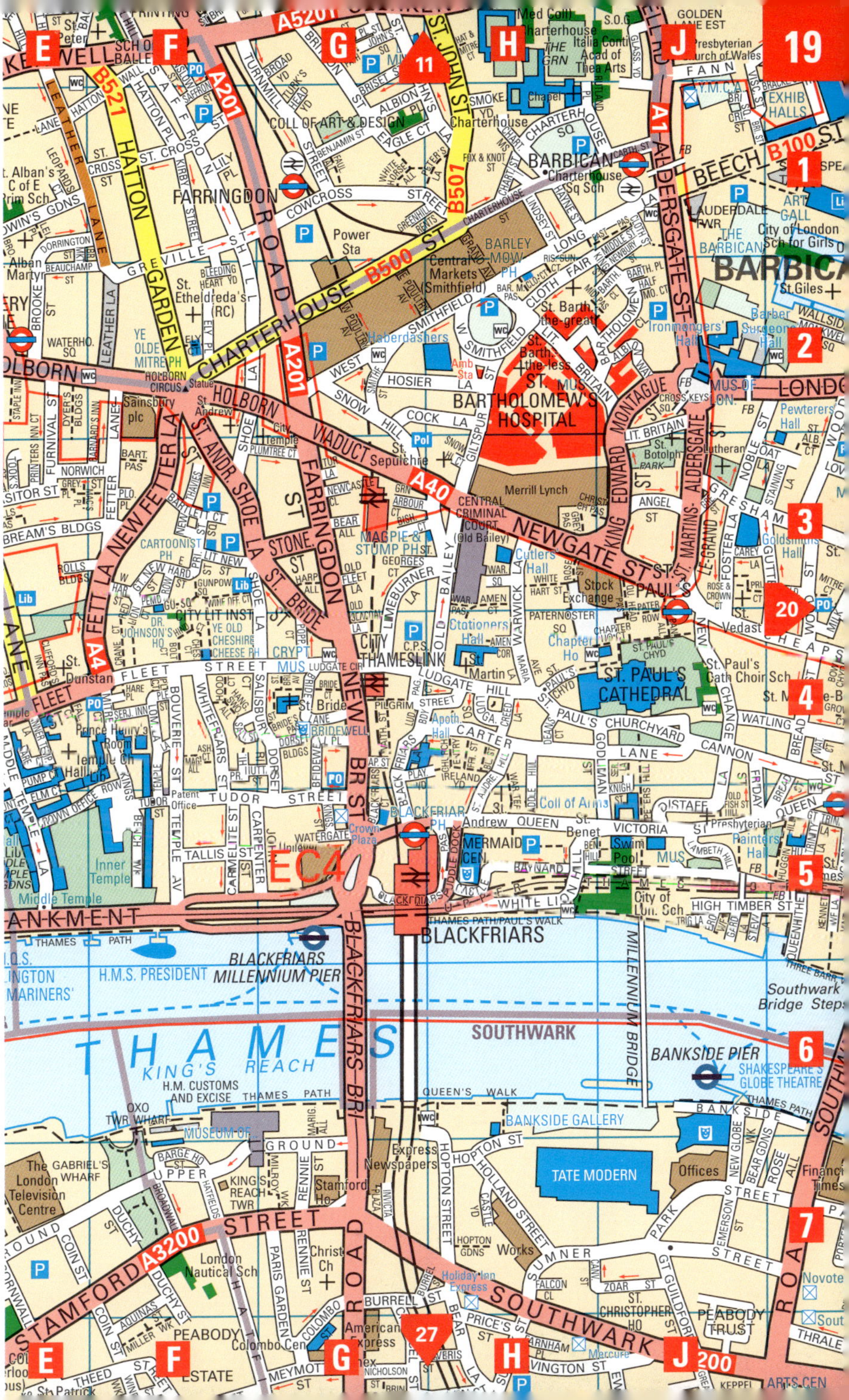
E
F
G
H
J
11
1
2
3
4
5
6
7
20
27
FARRINGDON
BARBICAN
Charterhouse
COLL OF ART & DESIGN
Power Sta
Central Markets (Smithfield)
CHARTERHOUSE
HATTON GARDEN
B521
B501
B500
B100
A5201
A201
A1
A40
A4
A3200
BEECH ST
ALDERSGATE ST
HOLBORN
HOLBORN CIRCUS
HOLBORN VIADUCT
FARRINGDON ST
FARRINGDON ROAD
ST. BARTHOLOMEW'S HOSPITAL
Merrill Lynch
CENTRAL CRIMINAL COURT (Old Bailey)
NEWGATE ST
KING EDWARD ST
ST. PAUL'S
ST. PAUL'S CATHEDRAL
Stock Exchange
Chapter Ho
Stationers Hall
Cutlers Hall
MAGPIE & STUMP PH
St. Sepulchre
CITY THAMESLINK
LUDGATE HILL
FLEET STREET
NEW BR ST
NEW FETTER LA
CHANCERY LANE
St. Bride
BRIDEWELL
TUDOR STREET
QUEEN VICTORIA ST
CANNON ST
BLACKFRIARS
Crown Plaza
MERMAID CEN
City of Lon. Sch
HIGH TIMBER ST
Inner Temple
Middle Temple
EMBANKMENT
THAMES PATH
H.M.S. PRESIDENT
BLACKFRIARS MILLENNIUM PIER
MILLENNIUM BRIDGE
THAMES
KING'S REACH
SOUTHWARK
BANKSIDE PIER
SHAKESPEARE'S GLOBE THEATRE
Southwark Bridge Steps
BANKSIDE
BANKSIDE GALLERY
TATE MODERN
Offices
H.M. CUSTOMS AND EXCISE
OXO TWR WHARF
GABRIEL'S WHARF
London Television Centre
Express Newspapers
HOPTON STREET
HOLLAND STREET
SUMNER STREET
SOUTHWARK STREET
STAMFORD STREET
London Nautical Sch
BLACKFRIARS ROAD
Holiday Inn Express
PEABODY TRUST
PEABODY ESTATE
Colombo Cen
American Express
EC4

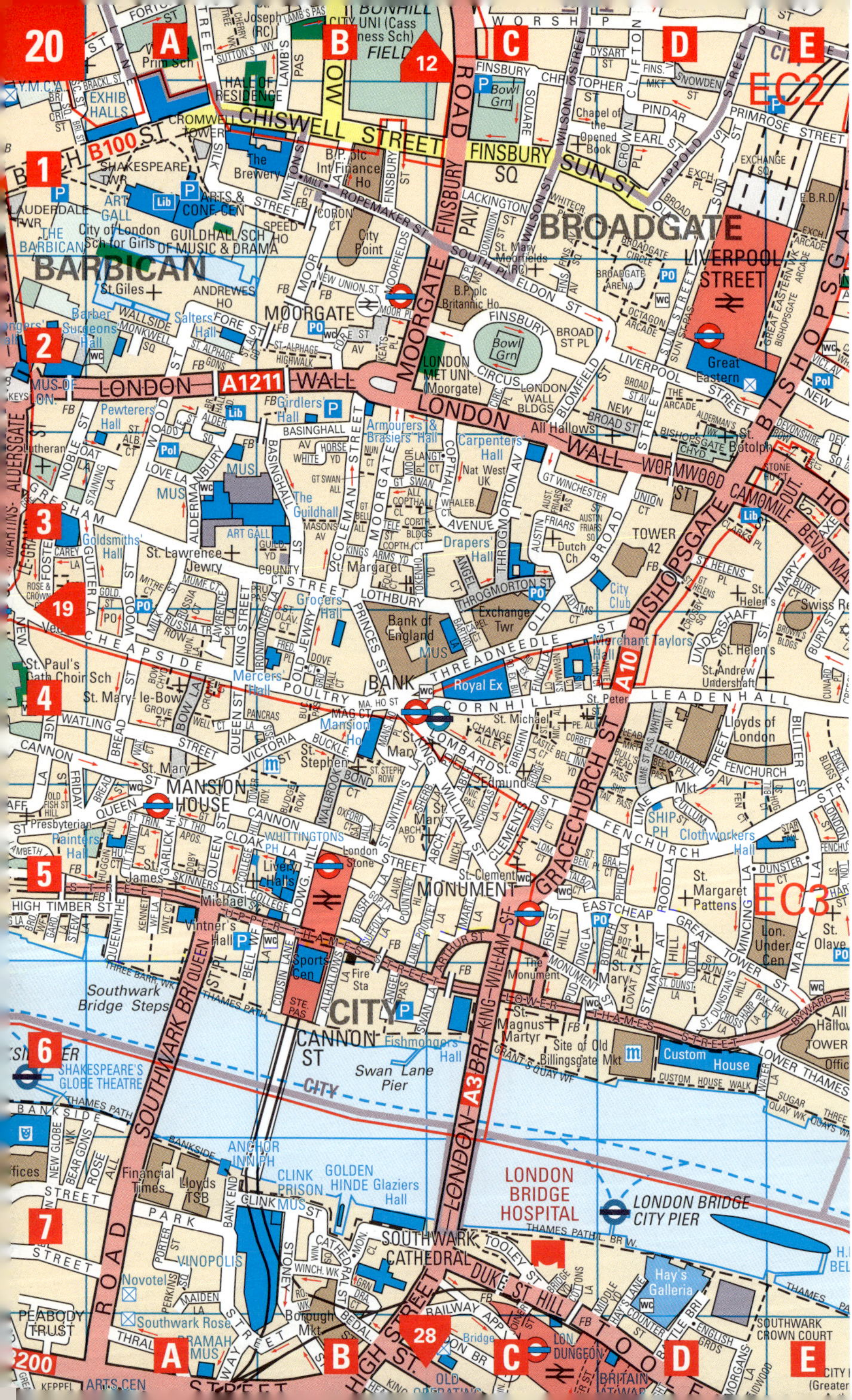
A
B
C
D
E
1
2
3
4
5
6
7
12
19
28
EC2
EC3
BARBICAN
BROADGATE
CITY
MOORGATE
Y.M.C.A.
EXHIB HALLS
HALL OF RESIDENCE
CHISWELL STREET
B100
The Brewery
B.P. plc Int Finance Ho
CITY UNI (Cass Business Sch)
BUNHILL FIELDS
FINSBURY SQ
FINSBURY PAV.
FINSBURY SQUARE
SUN ST
WORSHIP
CHRISTOPHER ST
WILSON STREET
DYSART ST
CLIFTON ST
SNOWDEN ST
PINDAR ST
PRIMROSE STREET
EARL ST
APPOLD ST
EXCHANGE SQ
Chapel of the Opened Book
Bowl Grn
ROPEMAKER ST
CITY Point
SHAKESPEARE TWR
LAUDERDALE TWR
ART GALL
ARTS & CONF CEN
Lib
City of London Sch for Girls
GUILDHALL SCH OF MUSIC & DRAMA
THE BARBICAN
SPEED HO
CORONER CT
NEW UNION ST
MOORFIELDS
MOOR PL
SOUTH PL
St. Mary Moorfields (RC)
B.P. plc Britannic Ho
ELDON ST
BROADGATE CIRCLE
BROADGATE ARENA
LIVERPOOL STREET
OCTAGON ARCADE
SUN ST PAS
St.Giles
ANDREWS HO
Barber Surgeons' Hall
WALLSIDE
MONKWELL SQ
Salters' Hall
FORE ST
FORE ST AV
ST. ALPHAGE HIGHWALK
FINSBURY CIRCUS
LONDON MET UNI (Moorgate)
LONDON WALL BLDGS
BROAD ST PL
BLOMFIELD ST
LIVERPOOL STREET
Great Eastern
Pol
MUS OF LON
LONDON WALL
A1211
Girdlers' Hall
Pewterers' Hall
BASINGHALL AV
Armourers & Brasiers' Hall
Carpenters' Hall
All Hallows
NEW BROAD ST
WORMWOOD ST
BISHOPSGATE
ALDERSGATE
Lutheran
NOBLE ST
WOOD ST
LOVE LA
ALDERMANBURY
GUILDHALL
BASINGHALL ST
COLEMAN ST
MOORGATE
COPTHALL AV
Nat West UK
WHITE HORSE YD
GT SWAN ALL
GT WINCHESTER ST
AUSTIN FRIARS
Dutch Ch
OLD BROAD ST
TOWER 42
ST HELENS PL
St. Helen's
CAMOMILE ST
BEVIS MARKS
HOUNDSDITCH
Swiss Re
MUS
The Guildhall
ART GALL
GRESHAM ST
Goldsmiths' Hall
St. Lawrence Jewry
MASONS AV
St. Margaret
LOTHBURY
COPTHALL AV
THROGMORTON AV
THROGMORTON ST
Drapers' Hall
Exchange Twr
City Club
UNDERSHAFT
St. Helen's
St. Andrew Undershaft
CHEAPSIDE
Grocers' Hall
Bank of England
PRINCES ST
THREADNEEDLE ST
Royal Ex
Merchant Taylors Hall
A10
St. Paul's Cath Choir Sch
St. Mary-le-Bow
POULTRY
BANK
Mercers' Hall
CORNHILL
LEADENHALL ST
St. Peter
Lloyds of London
FENCHURCH AV
BILLITER ST
WATLING ST
BOW LA
QUEEN ST
VICTORIA ST
MANSION HOUSE
Mansion Ho
St. Stephen
St. Mary
St. Michael
LOMBARD ST
CHANGE ALLEY
BIRCHIN LA
St. Edmund
GRACECHURCH ST
LIME ST
FENCHURCH ST
Clothworkers' Hall
St. Margaret Pattens
CANNON ST
QUEEN VICTORIA ST
St. James
Presbyterian
Painters' Hall
WHITTINGTONS
Livery Halls
London Stone
CANNON STREET
MONUMENT
St. Clement
EASTCHEAP
GREAT TOWER ST
MINCING LA
MARK LA
Lon. Under. Cen
St. Olave
HIGH TIMBER ST
UPPER THAMES STREET
Vintner's Hall
Sports Cen
Fire Sta
ARTHUR ST
The Monument
KING WILLIAM ST
Southwark Bridge Steps
QUEENHITHE
SOUTHWARK BR
CITY
CANNON ST
Fishmongers' Hall
LOWER THAMES ST
St. Magnus Martyr
Site of Old Billingsgate Mkt
Custom House
CUSTOM HOUSE WALK
All Hallows
TOWER
BYWARD ST
LOWER THAMES ST
SHAKESPEARE'S GLOBE THEATRE
Swan Lane Pier
CITY
A3
LONDON BRIDGE
BANKSIDE
THAMES PATH
ANCHOR INN PH
CLINK PRISON
GOLDEN HINDE
Glaziers Hall
LONDON BRIDGE HOSPITAL
LONDON BRIDGE CITY PIER
Financial Times
Lloyds TSB
CLINK ST
PARK ST
SOUTHWARK ST
SOUTHWARK CATHEDRAL
TOOLEY ST
VINOPOLIS
Novotel
Southwark Rose
Hay's Galleria
PEABODY TRUST
DRAMAH MUS
Borough Mkt
BOROUGH HIGH ST
LON DUNGEON
BRITAIN AT WAR
SOUTHWARK CROWN COURT
THAMES PATH

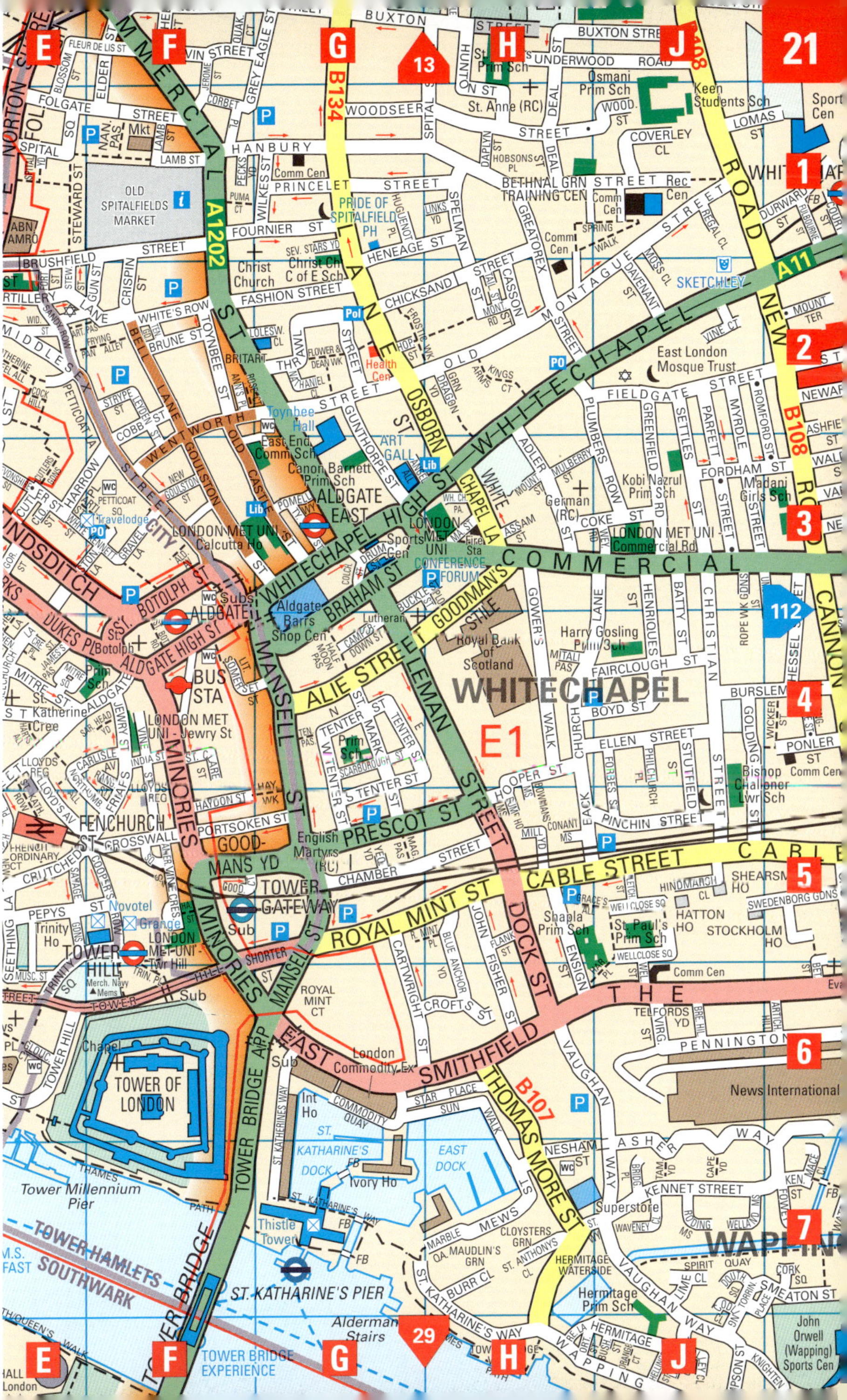
E
F
G
H
J
13
29
112
1
2
3
4
5
6
7
WHITECHAPEL
E1
BUXTON STREET
UNDERWOOD ROAD
WOODSEER
HANBURY
PRINCELET STREET
FOURNIER ST
HENEAGE ST
FASHION STREET
FOLGATE STREET
FLEUR DE LIS ST
ELDER
BLOSSOM ST
SPITAL SQ
LAMB ST
OLD SPITALFIELDS MARKET
BRUSHFIELD STREET
STEWARD ST
CRISPIN ST
GUN ST
ARTILLERY LANE
WHITE'S ROW
BRUNE ST
BELL LANE
TOYNBEE ST
WENTWORTH
GOULSTON
OLD CASTLE ST
MIDDLESEX ST
PETTICOAT LANE
HARROW PL
STRYPE ST
COBB ST
COMMERCIAL ST
A1202
B134
BRICK LANE
WILKES ST
CHRIST CHURCH
Christ Ch C of E Sch
SPELMAN
GREATOREX
HUGUENOT PL
CHICKSAND ST
CASSON ST
OSBORN ST
OLD MONTAGUE ST
WHITECHAPEL HIGH ST
WHITECHAPEL RD
A11
NEW ROAD
B108
CANNON STREET RD
FIELDGATE STREET
PLUMBERS ROW
GREENFIELD RD
SETTLES ST
FORDHAM ST
MYRDLE ST
ROMFORD ST
ADLER ST
MULBERRY ST
COKE ST
COMMERCIAL RD
COMMERCIAL ST
GOWER'S WALK
CHURCH LANE
HENRIQUES ST
BATTY ST
CHRISTIAN ST
FAIRCLOUGH ST
BOYD ST
BURSLEM ST
ELLEN STREET
HOOPER ST
PINCHIN STREET
CABLE STREET
BRAHAM ST
LEMAN STREET
ALIE STREET
GOODMAN'S STILE
PRESCOT ST
CHAMBER STREET
MANSELL ST
TENTER ST
ROYAL MINT ST
JOHN FISHER ST
DOCK ST
CARTWRIGHT ST
THE HIGHWAY
EAST SMITHFIELD
THOMAS MORE ST
B107
VAUGHAN WAY
PENNINGTON ST
News International
ASHER WAY
KENNET STREET
WAPPING
ST. KATHARINE'S WAY
WAPPING HIGH ST
TOWER BRIDGE APP
TOWER BRIDGE
TOWER OF LONDON
TOWER HILL
MINORIES
ALDGATE HIGH ST
ALDGATE
ALDGATE EAST
HOUNDSDITCH
DUKES PL
ST. BOTOLPH ST
FENCHURCH ST
CRUTCHED FRIARS
COOPER'S ROW
PEPYS ST
TRINITY SQ
Trinity Ho
BYWARD ST
THAMES PATH
Tower Millennium Pier
ST. KATHARINE'S PIER
ST. KATHARINE'S DOCK
EAST DOCK
Ivory Ho
Thistle Tower
Int Ho
TOWER HAMLETS
SOUTHWARK
TOWER BRIDGE EXPERIENCE
Alderman Stairs
ROYAL MINT CT
London Commodity Ex
TOWER GATEWAY
GOODMANS YD
SHORTER ST
Novotel
Grange
LONDON MET UNI Twr Hill
LONDON MET UNI Jewry St
LONDON MET UNI Calcutta Ho
LONDON MET UNI Commercial Rd
Royal Bank of Scotland
Harry Gosling Prim Sch
Bishop Challoner Lwr Sch
Kobi Nazrul Prim Sch
Madani Girls Sch
East London Mosque Trust
Toynbee Hall
Canon Barnett Prim Sch
East End Comm Sch
Aldgate Barrs Shop Cen
English Martyrs (RC)
Shapla Prim Sch
St. Paul's Prim Sch
Osmani Prim Sch
Keen Students Sch
St. Anne (RC)
Sports Cen
Hermitage Prim Sch
John Orwell (Wapping) Sports Cen
Superstore
Comm Cen
Health Cen
ART GALL
PRIDE OF SPITALFIELDS PH
SKETCHLEY
Travelodge
BUS STA
FORUM
CONFERENCE
HATTON HO
STOCKHOLM HO
SWEDENBORG GDNS
SHEARSMITH HO
TELFORDS YD
CHAPEL
ST. ANTHONYS CL
MARBLE QUAY
CLOYSTERS GRN
OA. MAUDLIN'S GRN
BURR CL
HERMITAGE WATERSIDE
SPIRIT QUAY
SMEATON ST

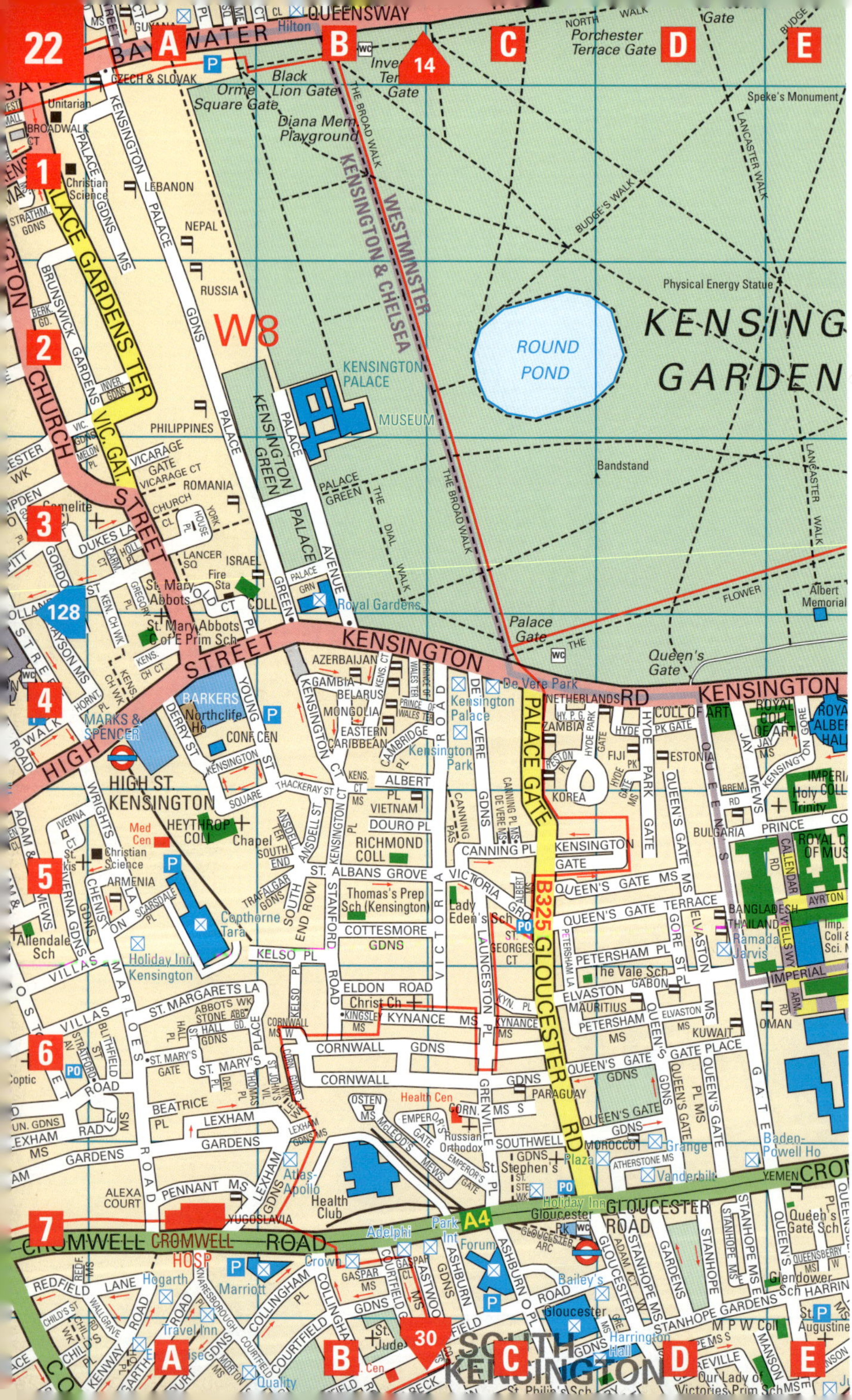
A
B
C
D
E
1
2
3
4
5
6
7
14
30
128
QUEENSWAY
BAYSWATER
Hilton
CZECH & SLOVAK
Unitarian
BROADWALK CT
Christian Science
Orme Square Gate
Black Lion Gate
Inverness Terrace Gate
Porchester Terrace Gate
NORTH WALK
Gate
Speke's Monument
Diana Mem. Playground
THE BROAD WALK
KENSINGTON & CHELSEA
WESTMINSTER
BUDGE'S WALK
LANCASTER WALK
Physical Energy Statue
KENSINGTON GARDENS
ROUND POND
KENSINGTON PALACE
MUSEUM
Bandstand
PALACE GREEN
THE DIAL WALK
Albert Memorial
FLOWER WALK
Palace Gate
Queen's Gate
Royal Gardens
W8
LEBANON
NEPAL
RUSSIA
PHILIPPINES
ROMANIA
ISRAEL
KENSINGTON PALACE GARDENS
PALACE GARDENS TER
BRUNSWICK GARDENS
CHURCH STREET
VIC. GAT.
VICARAGE GATE
VICARAGE CT
KENSINGTON GREEN
PALACE AVENUE
Carmelite
DUKES LA
LANCER SQ
Fire Sta
St. Mary Abbots
St. Mary Abbots C of E Prim Sch
COLL
KENSINGTON HIGH STREET
BARKERS
Northcliffe Ho
CONF CEN
MARKS & SPENCER
HIGH ST. KENSINGTON
YOUNG ST
DERRY ST
KENSINGTON SQUARE
THACKERAY ST
AZERBAIJAN
GAMBIA
BELARUS
MONGOLIA
EASTERN CARIBBEAN
Kensington Palace
Kensington Park
De Vere Park
NETHERLANDS
ZAMBIA
ALBERT PL
VIETNAM
DOURO PL
RICHMOND COLL
CANNING PL
HYDE PARK GATE
FIJI
ESTONIA
KOREA
KENSINGTON GATE
COLL OF ART
ROYAL COLL OF ART
ROYAL ALBERT HALL
IMPERIAL COLL
Holy Trinity
BULGARIA
PRINCE CONSORT RD
ROYAL COLL OF MUSIC
Med Cen
HEYTHROP COLL
Chapel
Christian Science
ARMENIA
ANSDELL ST
ST. ALBANS GROVE
Thomas's Prep Sch (Kensington)
Lady Eden's Sch
VICTORIA GRO
VICTORIA ROAD
QUEEN'S GATE MS
QUEEN'S GATE TERRACE
B325
GLOUCESTER ROAD
PALACE GATE
BANGLADESH
THAILAND
Ramada Jarvis
Imp. Coll & Sci. M
AYRTON
IMPERIAL
Copthorne Tara
Holiday Inn Kensington
Allendale Sch
COTTESMORE GDNS
KELSO PL
ST. GEORGES CT
PETERSHAM PL
The Vale Sch
ELVASTON PL
MAURITIUS
PETERSHAM MS
KUWAIT
OMAN
ST. MARGARETS LA
ABBOTS WK
STONE HALL GDNS
ELDON ROAD
Christ Ch
KYNANCE MS
CORNWALL GDNS
ST. MARY'S GATE
LAUNCESTON PL
GRENVILLE PL
QUEEN'S GATE GDNS
GATE PLACE
PARAGUAY
Health Cen
EMPEROR'S GATE
Russian Orthodox
BEATRICE PL
LEXHAM GARDENS
LEXHAM MS
SOUTHWELL GDNS
St. Stephen's
MOROCCO
Grange
Plaza
ATHERSTONE MS
Vanderbilt
Baden-Powell Ho
YEMEN
Atlas-Apollo
Health Club
ALEXA COURT
PENNANT MS
YUGOSLAVIA
Holiday Inn Gloucester
A4
CROMWELL ROAD
CROMWELL HOSP
Adelphi
Park Int
Forum
GLOUCESTER ARC
GLOUCESTER ROAD
STANHOPE GARDENS
Queen's Gate Sch
Glendower Sch
HARRINGTON
REDFIELD LANE
Hogarth
Marriott
Crown
GASPAR MS
COLLINGHAM PL
COURTFIELD GDNS
ASHBURN GDNS
ASHBURN PL
Bailey's
Gloucester
Harrington Hall
Travel Inn
Quality
St. Jude
SOUTH KENSINGTON
M P W Coll
St. Augustine
Our Lady of Victories Prim Sch
St. Philip's Sch

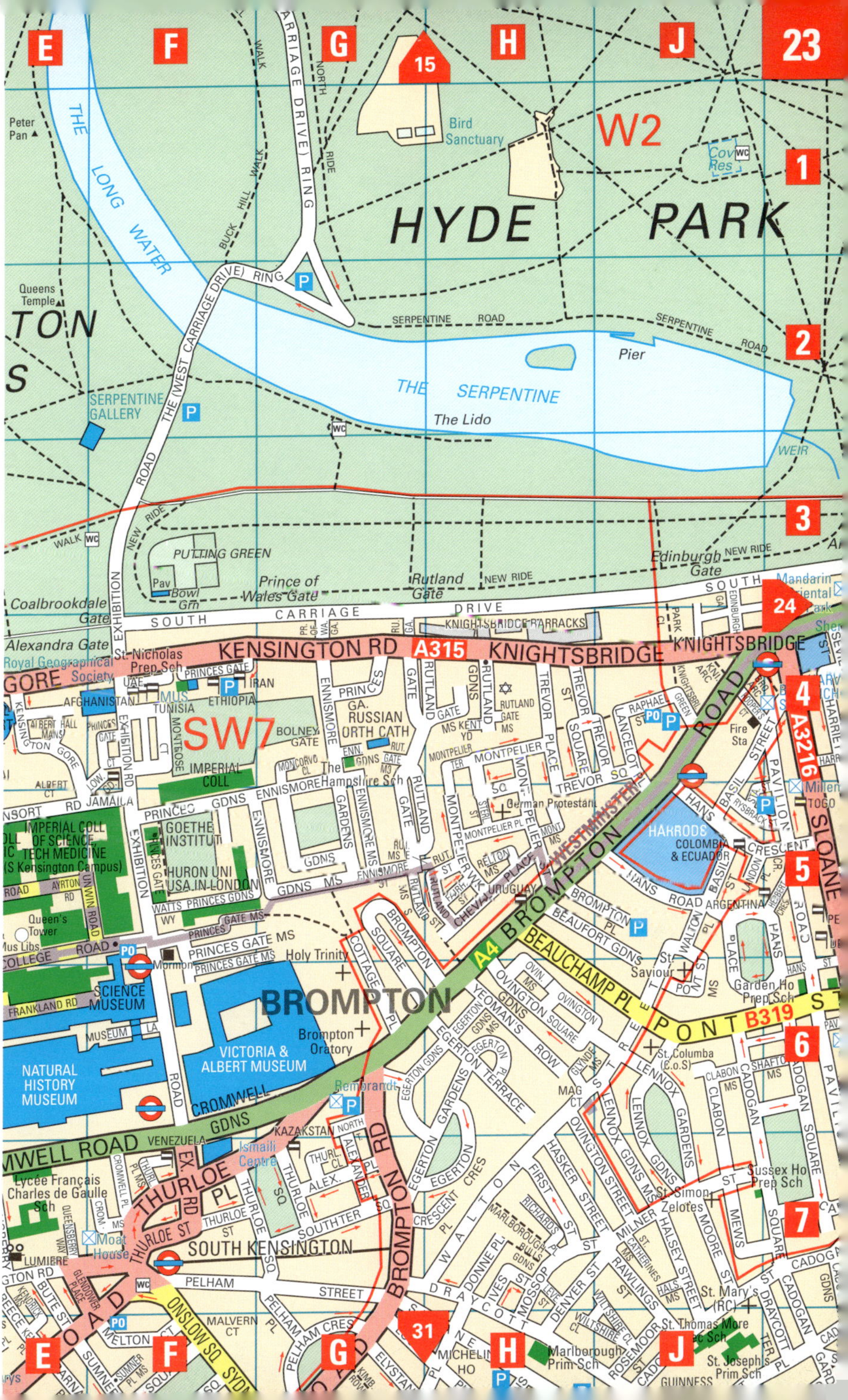
E
F
G
H
J
15
1
2
3
4
5
6
7
24
31
W2
HYDE PARK
SW7
BROMPTON
SOUTH KENSINGTON
Peter Pan
THE LONG WATER
Queens Temple
Bird Sanctuary
Cov Res
BUCK HILL WALK
NORTH RIDE
CARRIAGE DRIVE RING
THE WEST CARRIAGE DRIVE RING
SERPENTINE ROAD
THE SERPENTINE
Pier
The Lido
WEIR
SERPENTINE GALLERY
ROAD
NEW RIDE
WALK
PUTTING GREEN
Pav
Bowl Grn
Prince of Wales Gate
Rutland Gate
Edinburgh Gate
Coalbrookdale Gate
Alexandra Gate
SOUTH CARRIAGE DRIVE
KNIGHTSBRIDGE BARRACKS
Mandarin Oriental Park
Royal Geographical Society
St. Nicholas Prep Sch
KENSINGTON RD
A315
KNIGHTSBRIDGE
EXHIBITION RD
PRINCES GATE
IRAN
AFGHANISTAN
UAE
MUS
TUNISIA
ETHIOPIA
BOLNEY GATE
ENNISMORE GDNS
PRINCES GA.
RUSSIAN ORTH CATH
RUTLAND GATE
MS KENT YD
RUTLAND GATE MS
TREVOR PLACE
TREVOR SQUARE
LANCELOT PL
RAPHAEL ST
KNIGHTSBRIDGE GREEN
Fire Sta
A3216
SLOANE STREET
BASIL STREET
PAVILION ROAD
MONTPELIER ST
MONTPELIER SQ
MONTPELIER PL
MONTPELIER WALK
MONTPELIER TER
German Protestant
TREVOR SQ
IMPERIAL COLL
The Hampshire Sch
MONCORVO CL
ENNISMORE MS
ENNISMORE ST
PRINCES GDNS
JAMAICA
IMPERIAL COLL OF SCIENCE TECH MEDICINE (S Kensington Campus)
GOETHE INSTITUT
HURON UNI USA IN LONDON
WATTS PRINCES GDNS
PRINCES GATE MS
Queen's Tower
Mus Libs
COLLEGE ROAD
FRANKLAND RD
SCIENCE MUSEUM
Mormon
Holy Trinity
VICTORIA & ALBERT MUSEUM
Brompton Oratory
NATURAL HISTORY MUSEUM
MUSEUM LA
CROMWELL GDNS
CROMWELL ROAD
VENEZUELA
Ismaili Centre
KAZAKSTAN
THURLOE PL
THURLOE SQ
THURLOE ST
Lycée Français Charles de Gaulle Sch
Moat House
LUMIERE
SOUTH KENSINGTON
PELHAM STREET
ONSLOW SQ
MELTON CT
MALVERN CT
PELHAM CRES
BROMPTON RD
A4
BROMPTON SQUARE
COTTAGE PL
HARRODS
COLOMBIA & ECUADOR
HANS CRESCENT
HANS ROAD
ARGENTINA
BEAUFORT GDNS
BROMPTON PL
BEAUCHAMP PL
St Saviour
WALTON PL
PONT ST
B319
PONT ST MS
HANS PLACE
Garden Ho Prep Sch
St. Columba (C.o.S)
OVINGTON SQUARE
OVINGTON GDNS
YEOMAN'S ROW
EGERTON TERRACE
EGERTON GARDENS
EGERTON CRES
Rembrandt
LENNOX GARDENS
LENNOX GDNS MS
CLABON MS
SHAFTO MS
CADOGAN SQUARE
Sussex Ho Prep Sch
St. Simon Zelotes
HASKER STREET
OVINGTON STREET
FIRST ST
WALTON ST
MILNER ST
RAWLINGS ST
DRAYCOTT PL
MOORE ST
St. Mary's (RC)
St. Thomas More RC Sch
St. Joseph's Prim Sch
Marlborough Prim Sch
ELYSTAN
DENYER ST
HALSEY STREET
UGANDA
URUGUAY
Knightsbridge
Cadogan

A
B
C
D
E
1
2
3
4
5
6
7
16
23
32
W1
Le Meridien Grosvenor House
Immaculate Conception
Centre Fountain
Sub
A4202
MOUNT ST GDNS
St. George's Hanover Sq Prim Sch
The Dorchester
ALDFORD
SOUTH
DEANERY
TILNEY
STANHOPE GATE
AUDLEY SQ
CHARLES
MYANMAR
BAHAMAS
QATAR
SAUDI ARABIA
Chesterfield
Christian Science
Washington
CLARGES
HALF MOON ST
Fleming
Hilton
CURZON
MARKET MS
SHEPHERD
Hilton Mews
TANZANIA
ST MEXICO
HERTFORD
Christ Church
Sheraton
JAPAN
Athenaeum
Metropolitan
Four Seasons
Inter-Continental
BRICK
HAMILTON PLACE
PARK LANE
A4
GREEN PARK
ARK
BROAD WALK
LOVER'S WALK
STANHOPE GATE
CURZON GATE
Subway
ACHILLES WAY
Achilles Statue
Queen Elizabeth Gate
Bandstand
War Memorial
Holocaust Memorial
WEIR
APSLEY HOUSE WELLINGTON MUS
Gates
ROTTEN ROW
NEW RIDE
Albert Gate
CARRIAGE DRIVE
HYDE PARK CORNER
HYDE PK CORNER
Wellington Arch
Memls.
DUKE OF WELLINGTON PL
CONSTITUTION HILL
Closed to Traffic
BUCKINGHAM PALACE GARDENS
Mandarin Oriental Hyde Park
FRANCE
Lanesborough
KNIGHTSBRIDGE
Berkeley
Sheraton
HARVEY NICHOLS
Basil Street
Fire Sta
A3216
Millennium
TOGO
PAKISTAN
CARLTON TWR PL
Lowndes
PERU
DENMARK
More Ho Sch
Garden Ho Prep Sch
Sheraton
Cadogan
B319
SLOANE STREET
CADOGAN PLACE
Tennis Court
KENSINGTON & CHELSEA
LOWNDES STREET
WILTON PL
WILTON CRES
St. Paul
GROSVENOR CRES
PEMBROKE CL
HALKIN STREET
HEADFORT PL
MONTROSE PL
SINGAPORE
SYRIA
MEXICO
MALAYSIA
TURKEY
TRINIDAD & TOBAGO
COTE D'IVOIRE
GHANA
PORTUGAL
BRUNEI
AUSTRIA
GERMANY
SPAIN
FINLAND
NORWAY
HUNGARY
BELGIUM
BOLIVIA
ALBANIA
LESOTHO
BELGRAVE SQUARE
B310
CHESHAM
BELGRAVIA
ECCLESTON
EATON
A3217
A302
GROSVENOR PLACE
IRELAND
CHESTER
FRANCES SCH OF ENGLISH
St. Peter
HOBART PL
LWR GROSVENOR PL
GROSVENOR GDNS
St. Peter's Eaton Sq C of E Prim Sch
ECCLESTON ST
A3213
Victoria Place
PALACE
INCHBALD SCH OF DESIGN
ICELAND
St. Michael
EBURY
ELIZABETH
Sussex Ho Prep Sch
CADOGAN GDNS
St. Mary's (RC)
Holy Trinity Prim Sch
Moat House
Prim Sch
St. Joseph's Prim Sch
SLOANE SQ
PETER JONES
COACH STA
Lib
PO

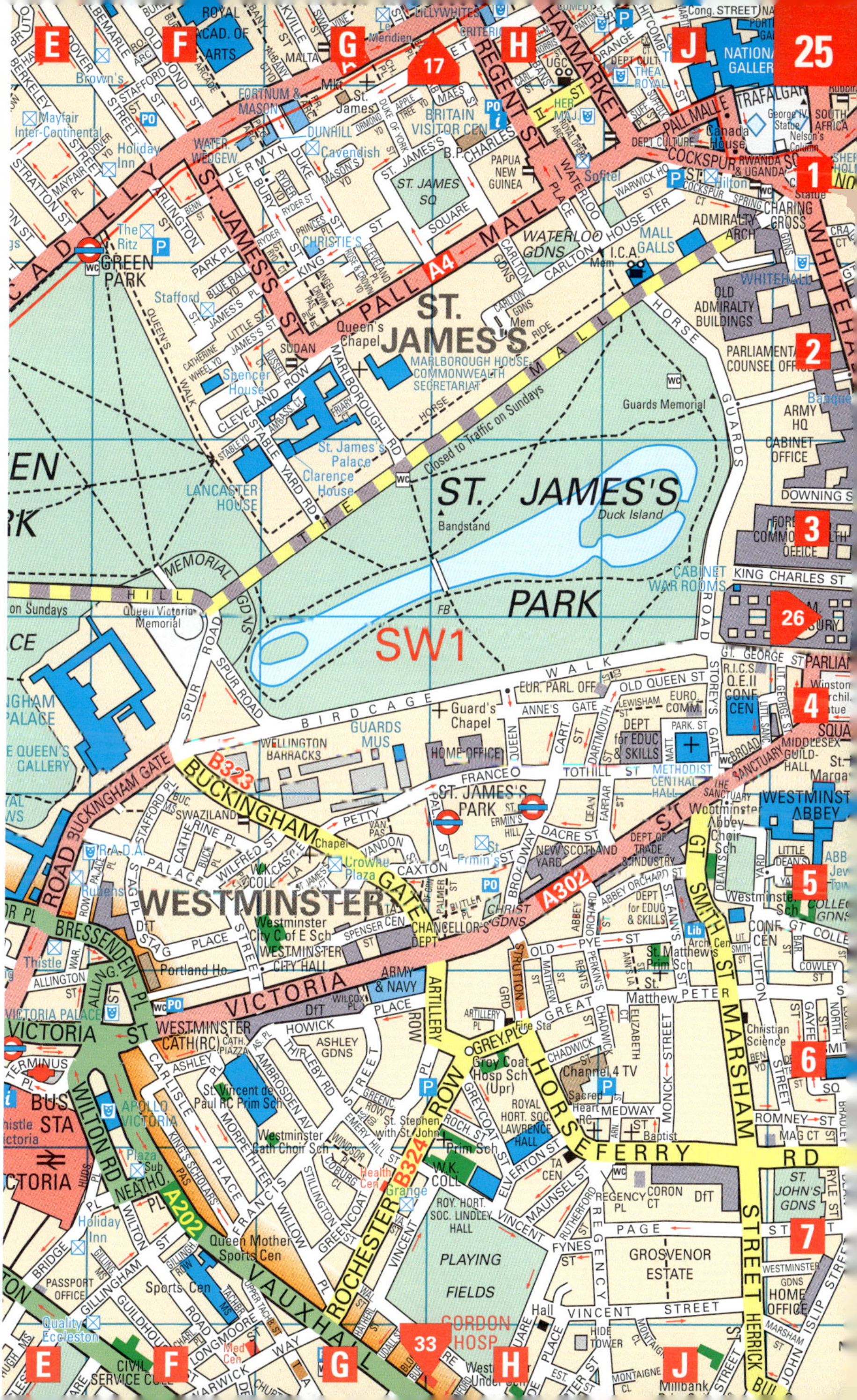
E
F
G
H
J
17
ROYAL ACAD. OF ARTS
Brown's
Mayfair Inter-Continental
Holiday Inn
FORTNUM & MASON
DUNHILL
Cavendish
BRITAIN VISITOR CEN
HAYMARKET
REGENT ST
NATIONAL GALLERY
TRAFALGAR
PALL MALL E
Canada House
COCKSPUR
George IV Statue
Nelson's Column
SOUTH AFRICA
RWANDA & UGANDA
Sofitel
Hilton
CHARING CROSS
ST. JAMES'S SQUARE
PAPUA NEW GUINEA
The Ritz
GREEN PARK
CHRISTIE'S
PALL A4 MALL
WATERLOO GDNS
CARLTON HOUSE TER
I.C.A.
MALL GALLS
ADMIRALTY ARCH
WHITEHALL
OLD ADMIRALTY BUILDINGS
ST. JAMES'S
Queen's Chapel
MARLBOROUGH HOUSE COMMONWEALTH SECRETARIAT
Spencer House
Stafford
St. James's Palace
Clarence House
LANCASTER HOUSE
PARLIAMENTARY COUNSEL OFFICE
Guards Memorial
ARMY HQ
CABINET OFFICE
DOWNING ST
HORSE GUARDS ROAD
Closed to Traffic on Sundays
ST. JAMES'S PARK
Duck Island
Bandstand
CABINET WAR ROOMS
KING CHARLES ST
26
Queen Victoria Memorial
SW1
BIRDCAGE WALK
Guard's Chapel
GUARDS MUS
WELLINGTON BARRACKS
HOME OFFICE
OLD QUEEN ST
DEPT for EDUC & SKILLS
METHODIST CENTRAL HALL
Q.E.II CONF CEN
PARLIAMENT SQUARE
MIDDLESEX GUILD-HALL
WESTMINSTER ABBEY
BUCKINGHAM GATE
B323
ST. JAMES'S PARK
TOTHILL ST
NEW SCOTLAND YARD
DEPT OF TRADE & INDUSTRY
Crowne Plaza
CAXTON
WESTMINSTER
BROADWAY
CHRIST GDNS
A302
VICTORIA ST
Westminster City C of E Sch
WESTMINSTER CITY HALL
ARMY & NAVY
Portland Ho
Thistle
BRESSENDEN PL
VICTORIA
VICTORIA PALACE
WESTMINSTER CATH(RC)
ASHLEY GDNS
ARTILLERY ROW
GREYCOAT PL
Grey Coat Hosp Sch (Upr)
Channel 4 TV
HORSEFERRY RD
MARSHAM ST
Christian Science
St. Vincent de Paul RC Prim Sch
Westminster Cath Choir Sch
St. Stephen with St. John Prim Sch
ROYAL HORT. SOC. LAWRENCE HALL
W.K. COLL
BUS STA
VICTORIA
WILTON RD
NEATHOUSE PL
A202
VAUXHALL BRIDGE RD
Queen Mother Sports Cen
ROCHESTER ROW
B324
ROY. HORT. SOC. LINDLEY HALL
PLAYING FIELDS
GROSVENOR ESTATE
ST. JOHN'S GDNS
WESTMINSTER GDNS
HOME OFFICE
Holiday Inn
PASSPORT OFFICE
Sports Cen
Quality Eccleston
CIVIL SERVICE CLUB
GORDON HOSP
33
VINCENT ST
Millbank
1
2
3
4
5
6
7

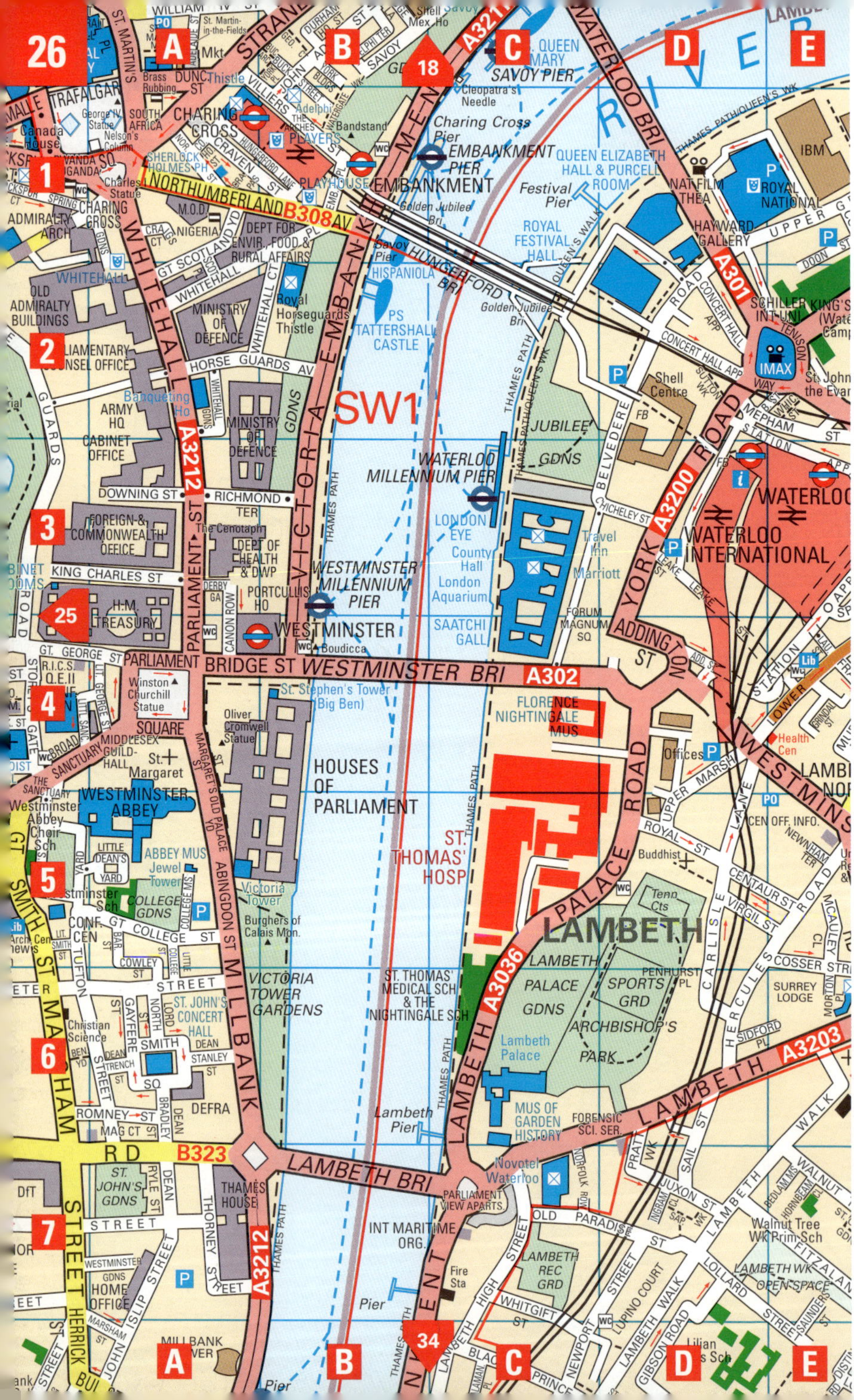
A
B
C
D
E
1
2
3
4
5
6
7
18
25
34
TRAFALGAR
STRAND
CHARING CROSS
Canada House
Nelson's Column
George IV Statue
SOUTH AFRICA
Brass Rubbing
St. Martin-in-the-Fields
Mkt
DUNCANNON ST
Thistle
VILLIERS ST
CRAVEN ST
Adelphi
PLAYERS
Bandstand
SAVOY
Savoy
Shell Mex. Ho
A3211
QUEEN MARY
SAVOY PIER
Cleopatra's Needle
Charing Cross Pier
EMBANKMENT PIER
EMBANKMENT
PLAYHOUSE
SHERLOCK HOLMES PH
Charles I Statue
NORTHUMBERLAND B308 AV
ADMIRALTY ARCH
M.O.D.
NIGERIA
GT SCOTLAND YD
DEPT FOR ENVIR. FOOD & RURAL AFFAIRS
WHITEHALL
WHITEHALL PL
WHITEHALL CT
OLD ADMIRALTY BUILDINGS
MINISTRY OF DEFENCE
Royal Horseguards Thistle
HORSE GUARDS AV
PARLIAMENTARY COUNSEL OFFICE
Banqueting Ho
ARMY HQ
CABINET OFFICE
A3212
MINISTRY OF DEFENCE
GDNS
DOWNING ST
RICHMOND TER
FOREIGN & COMMONWEALTH OFFICE
The Cenotaph
DEPT OF HEALTH & DWP
KING CHARLES ST
H.M. TREASURY
PORTCULLIS HO
CANON ROW
DERBY GA
WESTMINSTER
Boudicca
PARLIAMENT ST
VICTORIA EMBANKMENT
GUARDS
SW1
THAMES PATH
HUNGERFORD BRI
Golden Jubilee Bri
Savoy Pier
HISPANIOLA
PS TATTERSHALL CASTLE
WESTMINSTER MILLENNIUM PIER
WATERLOO MILLENNIUM PIER
RIVER
QUEEN ELIZABETH HALL & PURCELL ROOM
Festival Pier
ROYAL FESTIVAL HALL
QUEEN'S WALK
WATERLOO BRI
NAT FILM THEA
IBM
ROYAL NATIONAL
HAYWARD GALLERY
UPPER GROUND
THAMES PATH/QUEEN'S WK
A301
CONCERT HALL APP
SCHILLER INT UNI
KING'S (Waterloo Camp)
IMAX
TENISON WAY
St. John the Evan
Shell Centre
SUTTON WK
BELVEDERE RD
JUBILEE GDNS
LONDON EYE
County Hall
London Aquarium
SAATCHI GALL
Travel Inn
Marriott
CHICHELEY ST
FORUM MAGNUM SQ
YORK ROAD
A3200
MEPHAM ST
STATION APP
WATERLOO
WATERLOO INTERNATIONAL
LEAKE ST
ADDINGTON ST
LOWER MARSH
Lib
Health Cen
GT. GEORGE ST
PARLIAMENT SQUARE
BRIDGE ST
WESTMINSTER BRI
A302
R.I.C.S.
Q.E.II
Winston Churchill Statue
St. Stephen's Tower (Big Ben)
FLORENCE NIGHTINGALE MUS
Offices
Oliver Cromwell Statue
MIDDLESEX GUILD-HALL
St. Margaret
BROAD SANCTUARY
THE SANCTUARY
WESTMINSTER ABBEY
Westminster Abbey Choir Sch
HOUSES OF PARLIAMENT
ST. THOMAS' HOSP
UPPER MARSH
ROYAL ST
CEN OFF. INFO.
WESTMINSTER BRIDGE ROAD
LAMBETH NORTH
NEWNHAM TER
Buddhist
CENTAUR ST
VIRGIL ST
LITTLE DEAN'S YARD
ABBEY MUS
Jewel Tower
MARGARET ST
OLD PALACE YD
ABINGDON ST
Victoria Tower
Burghers of Calais Mon.
LAMBETH PALACE ROAD
Tenn Cts
LAMBETH
CARLISLE LANE
HERCULES RD
COSSER ST
McAULEY CL
Westminster Sch
COLLEGE GDNS
CONF. CEN
GT COLLEGE ST
GT SMITH ST
TUFTON ST
COWLEY ST
BARTON ST
VICTORIA TOWER GARDENS
ST. THOMAS' MEDICAL SCH & THE NIGHTINGALE SCH
A3036
LAMBETH PALACE GDNS
SPORTS GRD
PENHURST PL
SURREY LODGE
MORTON PL
Christian Science
GAYFERE ST
LORD NORTH ST
ST. JOHN'S CONCERT HALL
SMITH SQ
DEAN STANLEY ST
MARSHAM ST
ROMNEY ST
DEFRA
MILLBANK
Lambeth Palace
ARCHBISHOP'S PARK
SIDFORD PL
A3203
Lambeth Pier
MUS OF GARDEN HISTORY
FORENSIC SCI. SER.
LAMBETH RD
SAIL ST
WALK
HORSEFERRY RD
B323
MAG CT
ST. JOHN'S GDNS
RYLE ST
DEAN RYLE ST
THAMES HOUSE
LAMBETH BRI
Novotel Waterloo
PARLIAMENT VIEW APARTS
NORFOLK ROW
PRATT WK
JUXON ST
INGRAM CL
LAMBETH WALK
BEDLAM MS
HORNBEAM CL
WALNUT TREE WALK
DfT
STREET
THORNEY STREET
INT MARITIME ORG.
OLD PARADISE ST
Walnut Tree Wk Prim Sch
LAMBETH REC GRD
FITZALAN ST
LAMBETH WK OPEN SPACE
WESTMINSTER GDNS
HOME OFFICE
ISLIP STREET
MARSHAM ST
HERRICK STREET
JOHN ISLIP ST
MILLBANK TOWER
Fire Sta
Pier
LAMBETH HIGH STREET
ALBERT EMBANKMENT
WHITGIFT ST
NEWPORT ST
LUPINO COURT
LAMBETH WALK
GIBSON ROAD
LOLLARD STREET
SAUNDERS ST
Lilian Baylis Sch
BLACK PRINCE RD
LAMAN PL
Pier

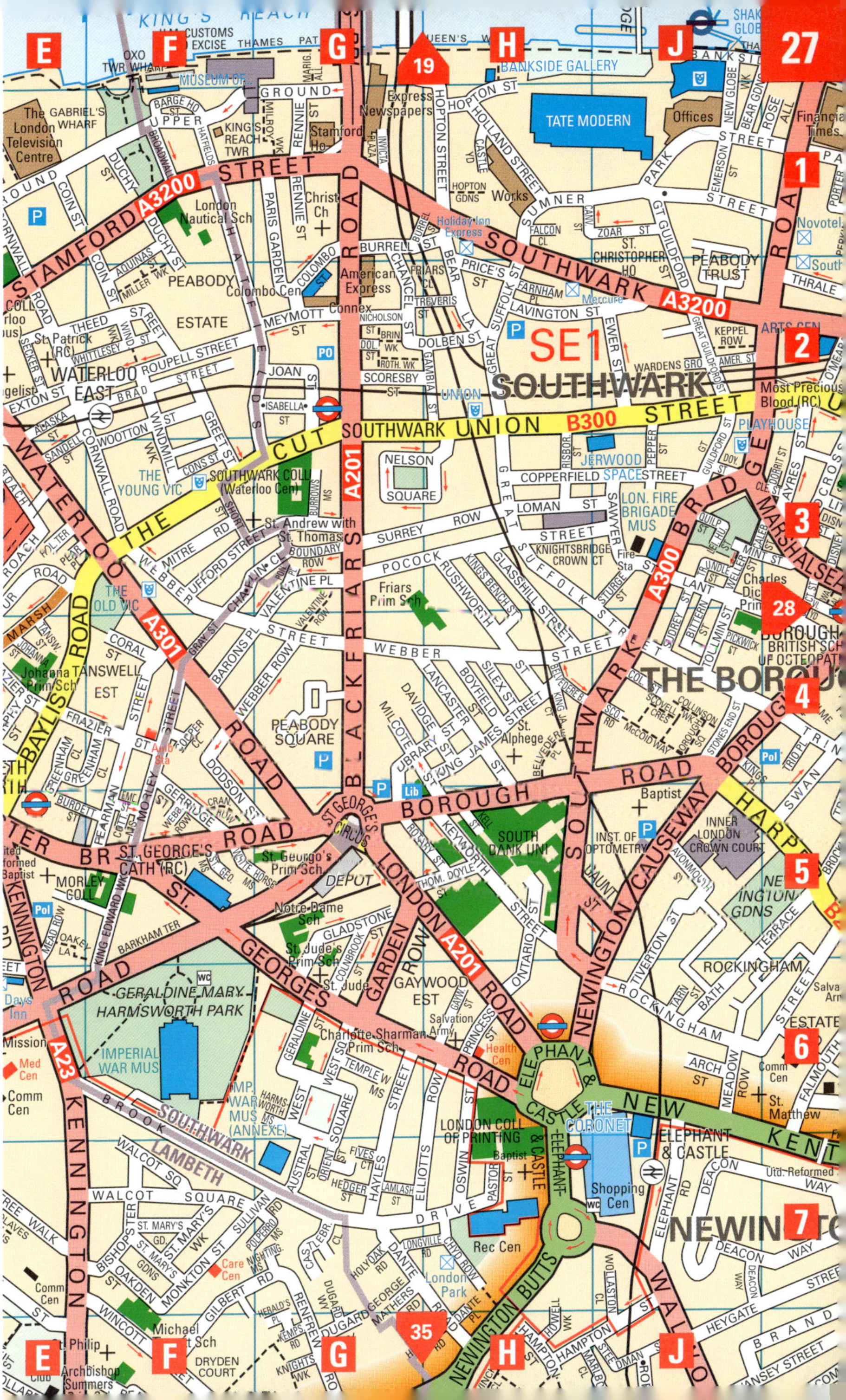
E
F
G
H
J
19
35
28
1
2
3
4
5
6
7
KING'S REACH
THAMES
OXO TWR WHARF
CUSTOMS EXCISE
MUSEUM OF...
BANKSIDE GALLERY
TATE MODERN
Offices
Financial Times
The London Television Centre
GABRIEL'S WHARF
UPPER GROUND
Express Newspapers
Stamford Ho
HOPTON ST
HOLLAND STREET
SUMNER STREET
Works
STAMFORD STREET
A3200
London Nautical Sch
Christ Ch
BLACKFRIARS ROAD
Holiday Inn Express
SOUTHWARK STREET
A3200
PEABODY TRUST
Novotel
Mercure
PEABODY ESTATE
Colombo Cen
American Express
Connex
SE1
SOUTHWARK
WATERLOO EAST
ROUPELL STREET
MEYMOTT ST
PO
UNION
SOUTHWARK UNION STREET
B300
PLAYHOUSE
JERWOOD SPACE
Most Precious Blood (RC)
THE CUT
A201
NELSON SQUARE
COPPERFIELD STREET
THE YOUNG VIC
Southwark Coll (Waterloo Cen)
LON. FIRE BRIGADE MUS
SURREY ROW
LOMAN ST
St. Andrew with St. Thomas
Fire Sta
WATERLOO ROAD
A301
THE OLD VIC
Friars Prim Sch
POCOCK ST
WEBBER STREET
A300
BOROUGH HIGH ST
Charles Dickens Prim Sch
BRITISH SCH OF OSTEOPATHY
THE BOROUGH
BAYLIS ROAD
Johanna Prim Sch
TANSWELL EST
PEABODY SQUARE
St. Alphege
BOROUGH ROAD
Lib
Pol
Baptist
ST GEORGE'S CIRCUS
SOUTH BANK UNI
INST. OF OPTOMETRY
INNER LONDON CROWN COURT
NEWINGTON CAUSEWAY
ST. GEORGE'S CATH (RC)
St. George's Prim Sch
DEPOT
Notre Dame Sch
MORLEY COLL
St. Jude's Prim Sch
LONDON ROAD
A201
GAYWOOD EST
ROCKINGHAM
ROCKINGHAM ST
KENNINGTON ROAD
GERALDINE MARY HARMSWORTH PARK
IMPERIAL WAR MUS
ST. GEORGES ROAD
Charlotte Sharman Prim Sch
Salvation Army
Health Cen
ELEPHANT & CASTLE
THE CORONET
NEW KENT ROAD
St. Matthew
Comm Cen
Med Cen
A23
KENNINGTON
BROOK DRIVE
IMP. WAR MUS (ANNEXE)
SOUTHWARK
LAMBETH
LONDON COLL OF PRINTING
Baptist
Shopping Cen
ELEPHANT & CASTLE
Utd. Reformed
NEWINGTON
DEACON WAY
WALCOT SQUARE
Care Cen
Rec Cen
London Park
NEWINGTON BUTTS
WALWORTH
HEYGATE STREET
BRANDON STREET
St. Philip
Archbishop Summers
Michael Faraday Prim Sch
DRYDEN COURT

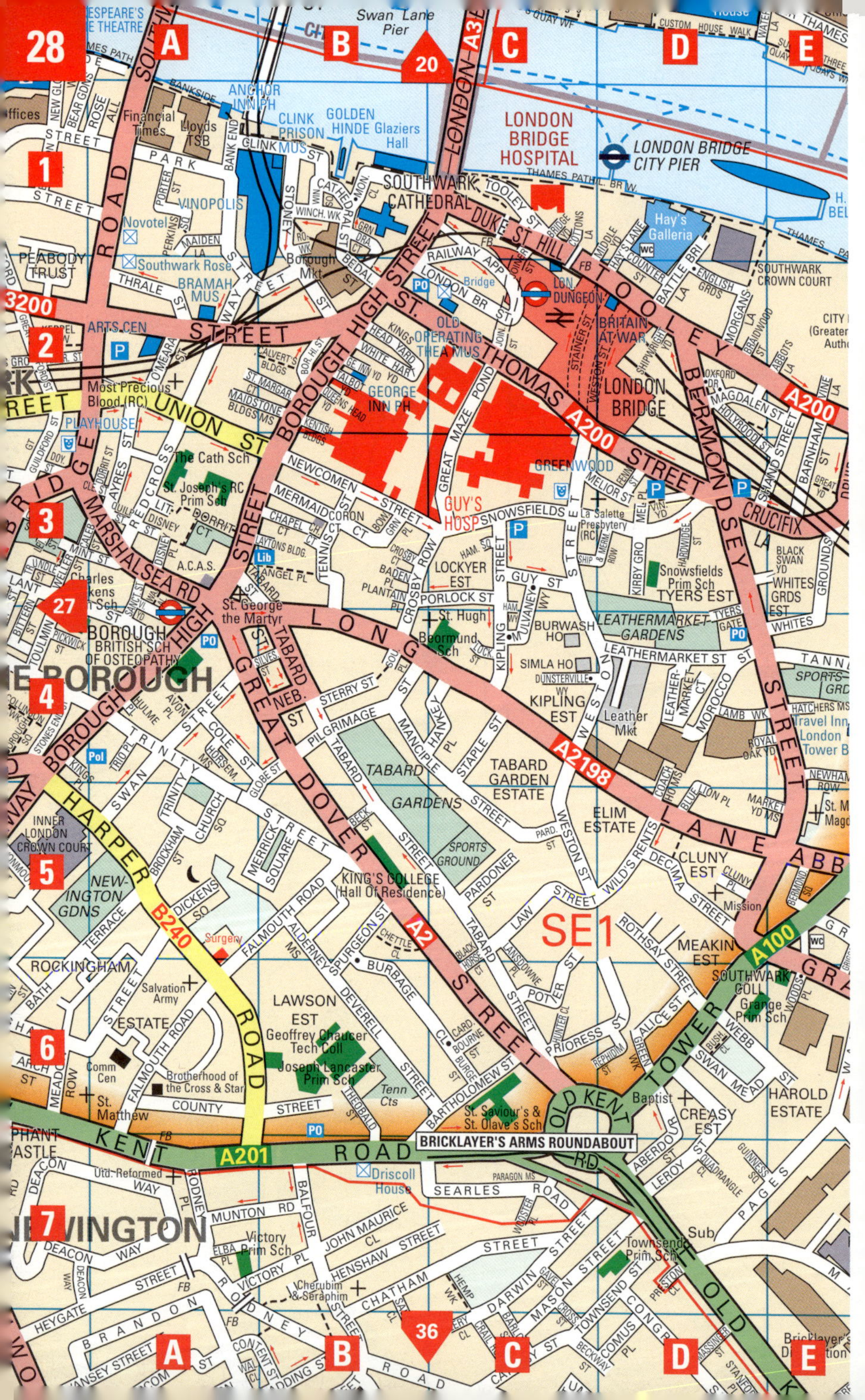
A
B
C
D
E
1
2
3
4
5
6
7
20
27
36
Swan Lane Pier
LONDON BRIDGE HOSPITAL
LONDON BRIDGE CITY PIER
ANCHOR INN PH
CLINK PRISON MUS
GOLDEN HINDE
Glaziers Hall
Financial Times
Lloyds TSB
VINOPOLIS
Novotel
Southwark Rose
BRAMAH MUS
SOUTHWARK CATHEDRAL
Borough Mkt
Hay's Galleria
SOUTHWARK CROWN COURT
LON. DUNGEON
BRITAIN AT WAR
LONDON BRIDGE
OLD OPERATING THEA MUS
GEORGE INN PH
GUY'S HOSP
PEABODY TRUST
ARTS CEN
Most Precious Blood (RC)
PLAYHOUSE
The Cath Sch
St. Joseph's RC Prim Sch
A.C.A.S.
Charles Dickens Sch
BOROUGH
BRITISH SCH OF OSTEOPATHY
St. George the Martyr
THE BOROUGH
GREENWOOD
La Salette Presbytery (RC)
Snowsfields Prim Sch
TYERS EST
LOCKYER EST
St. Hugh
Beormund Sch
BURWASH HO
SIMLA HO
KIPLING EST
LEATHERMARKET GARDENS
Leather Mkt
TABARD GARDENS
TABARD GARDEN ESTATE
SPORTS GROUND
ELIM ESTATE
CLUNY EST
Mission
MEAKIN EST
SOUTHWARK COLL
Grange Prim Sch
HAROLD ESTATE
CREASY EST
Baptist
SE1
KING'S COLLEGE (Hall Of Residence)
INNER LONDON CROWN COURT
NEWINGTON GDNS
Surgery
Salvation Army
ROCKINGHAM ESTATE
LAWSON EST
Geoffrey Chaucer Tech Coll
Joseph Lancaster Prim Sch
Brotherhood of the Cross & Star
St. Matthew
St. Saviour's & St. Olave's Sch
BRICKLAYER'S ARMS ROUNDABOUT
Driscoll House
Utd. Reformed
NEWINGTON
Victory Prim Sch
Cherubim & Seraphim
Townsend Prim Sch
Travel Inn London Tower B
BLACK SWAN YD
WHITES GRDS EST
A3
A200
A2198
A2
A100
A201
B240
A3200
BOROUGH HIGH ST.
TOOLEY STREET
ST. THOMAS STREET
LONG LANE
GREAT DOVER STREET
BERMONDSEY STREET
OLD KENT ROAD
NEW KENT ROAD
HARPER ROAD
SOUTHWARK STREET
UNION ST
MARSHALSEA RD
TOWER BRIDGE ROAD
CRUCIFIX LA
SNOWSFIELDS
NEWCOMEN STREET
TRINITY STREET
SWAN ST
FALMOUTH ROAD
DEVERELL STREET
SEARLES ROAD
CHATHAM ST
BRANDON ST
HEYGATE STREET

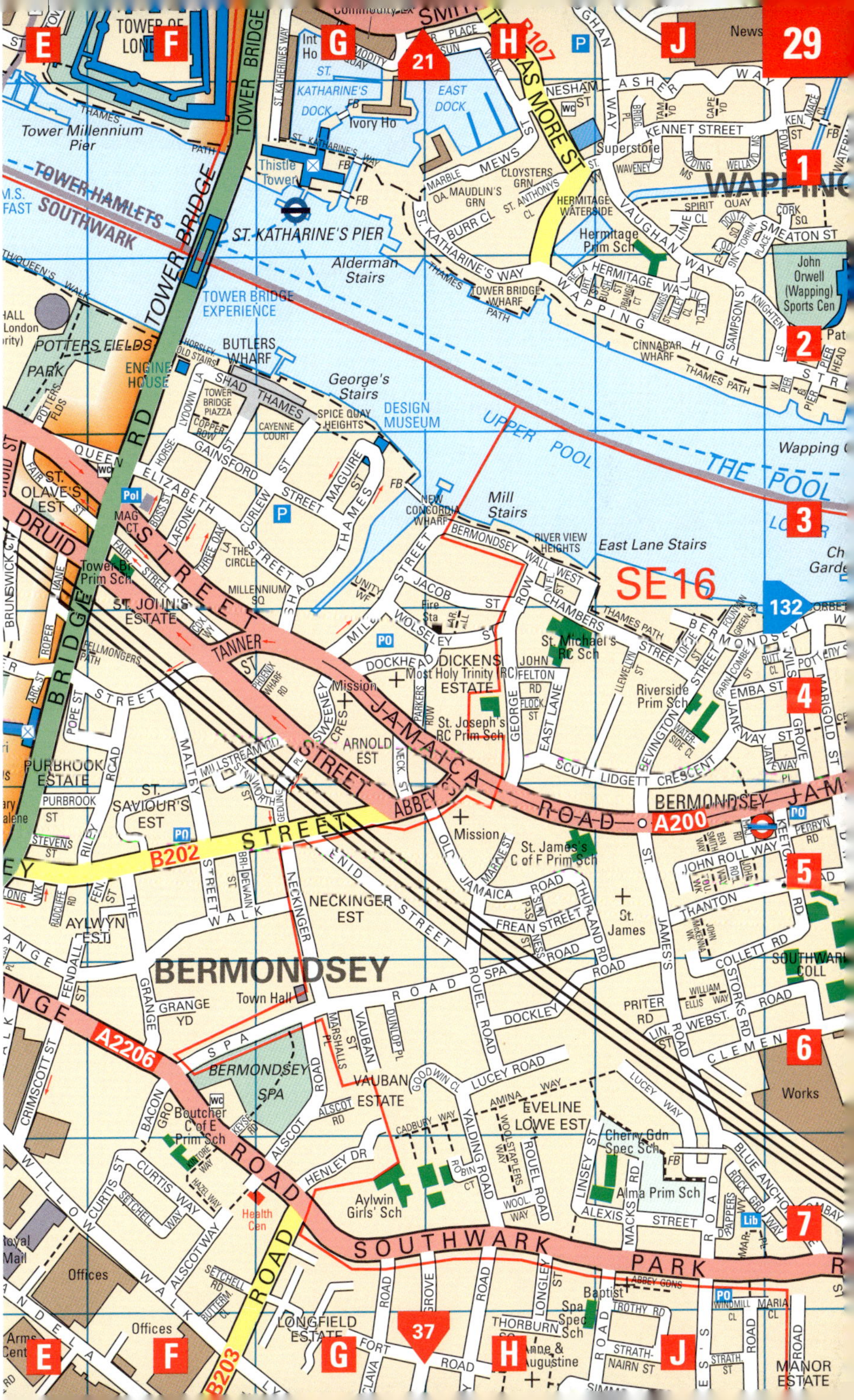
E
F
G
H
J
21
TOWER OF LONDON
Int Ho
ST. KATHARINE'S DOCK
EAST DOCK
Ivory Ho
Tower Millennium Pier
THAMES PATH
TOWER BRIDGE
Thistle Tower
ST. KATHARINE'S WAY
FB
TOWER HAMLETS
SOUTHWARK
ST. KATHARINE'S PIER
Alderman Stairs
TOWER BRIDGE EXPERIENCE
THOMAS MORE ST
B107
MARBLE QUAY
MEWS
CLOYSTERS GRN
QA. MAUDLIN'S GRN
ST. ANTHONYS CL
BURR CL
HERMITAGE WATERSIDE
Superstore
NESHAM ST
ASHER WAY
KENNET STREET
WAVENEY CL
RUDING MS
WELLAND MS
News
WAPPING
SPIRIT QUAY
CORK SQ
SMEATON ST
Hermitage Prim Sch
VAUGHAN WAY
HERMITAGE WALL
John Orwell (Wapping) Sports Cen
WAPPING HIGH STREET
CINNABAR WHARF
THAMES PATH
TOWER BRIDGE WHARF
1
2
3
4
5
6
7
HALL London
POTTERS FIELDS PARK
ENGINE HOUSE
BUTLERS WHARF
SHAD THAMES
TOWER BRIDGE PIAZZA
George's Stairs
SPICE QUAY HEIGHTS
DESIGN MUSEUM
UPPER POOL
THE POOL
Wapping
COPPER ROW
CAYENNE COURT
GAINSFORD ST
QUEEN ELIZABETH ST
TOOLEY ST
ST. OLAVE'S EST
DRUID ST
TOWER BRIDGE RD
MAGUIRE ST
CURLEW STREET
THAMES ST
NEW CONCORDIA WHARF
Mill Stairs
BERMONDSEY WALL WEST
RIVER VIEW HEIGHTS
East Lane Stairs
SE16
132
LAFONE ST
THREE OAK LA
THE CIRCLE
MILLENNIUM SQ
Tower Br Prim Sch
ST. JOHN'S ESTATE
TANNER ST
UNITY WF
JACOB ST
Fire Sta
MILL ST
WOLSELEY ST
CHAMBERS ST
THAMES PATH
St. Michael's RC Sch
BERMONDSEY WALL EAST
DOCKHEAD
DICKENS ESTATE
Most Holy Trinity (RC)
JOHN FELTON RD
Mission
JAMAICA ROAD
St. Joseph's RC Prim Sch
ARNOLD EST
FLOCK ST
EAST LANE
Riverside Prim Sch
EMBA ST
SCOTT LIDGETT CRESCENT
BERMONDSEY
A200
PURBROOK ESTATE
PURBROOK ST
ST. SAVIOUR'S EST
MALTBY ST
MILLSTREAM RD
ABBEY ST
B202
STEVENS ST
RILEY RD
Mission
OLD JAMAICA ROAD
St. James's C of E Prim Sch
JOHN ROLL WAY
THANTON
NECKINGER EST
ENID STREET
FREAN STREET
St. James
SOUTHWARK COLL
COLLETT RD
AYLWYN EST
BERMONDSEY
Town Hall
GRANGE YD
SPA ROAD
DOCKLEY ROAD
PRITER RD
WILLIAM ELLIS WAY
STORKS RD
CLEMENTS RD
A2206
BERMONDSEY SPA
VAUBAN ESTATE
LUCEY ROAD
EVELINE LOWE EST
Works
Boutcher C of E Prim Sch
Cherry Gdn Spec Sch
HENLEY DR
Aylwin Girls' Sch
Alma Prim Sch
ALEXIS STREET
Lib
Health Cen
SOUTHWARK PARK ROAD
Royal Mail
Offices
Offices
Baptist
Spa Spec Sch
THORBURN SQ
ROAD
LONGFIELD ESTATE
37
Arms Cent
B203
St. Anne & Augustine
MANOR ESTATE
STRATHNAIRN ST

A
B
C
D
E
1
2
3
4
5
6
7
CROMWELL ROAD
CROMWELL HOSP
GLOUCESTER ROAD
SOUTH KENSINGTON
EARLS COURT
WEST BROMPTON
BROMPTON CEMETERY
SW10
STAMFORD BRIDGE CHELSEA FC
WESTMINSTER & CHELSEA HOSP
BROMPTON ROAD
FULHAM ROAD
FULHAM BROADWAY
REDCLIFFE GARDENS
FINBOROUGH ROAD
EDITH GROVE
GUNTER GRO
CREMORNE RD
ASHBURNHAM RD
A4
A3220
A3218
A308
A304
22
128
129
St. Stephen's
Holiday Inn
Gloucester
Harrington Hall
Collingham Sch
St. Jude
Y.H.A.
Bousfield Prim Sch
St. Marys
Coleherne Court
St. Lukes
Redcliffe Sch
Servite Prim Sch
Kensington & Chelsea Coll (Hortensia Cen)
Coleridge Square
The London Oratory Sec Sch
Sports Cen.
World's End Est
Paray house Sch
Ashburnham Prim Sch
Salvation Army
St. John with St. Andrew
Park Wk Prim Sch
UGC
Falkner Ho Sch
Our Lady of Victories Prim Sch
St. Augustines
Queen's Gate Sch
Glendower Sch
Baden-Powell Ho
Kensington & Chelsea
Hammersmith & Fulham

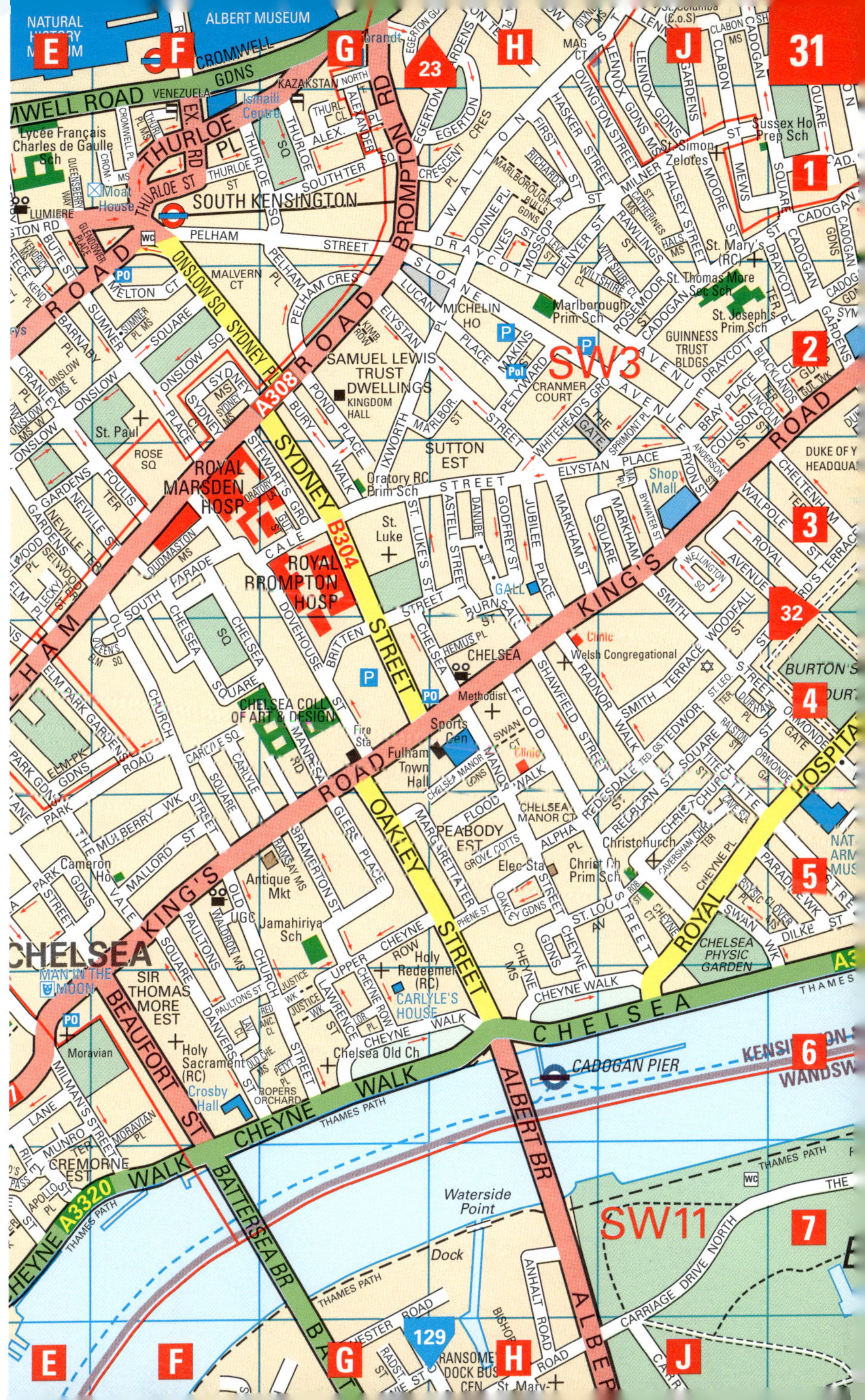
NATURAL HISTORY MUSEUM
ALBERT MUSEUM
CROMWELL GDNS
CROMWELL ROAD
VENEZUELA
Ismaili Centre
KAZAKSTAN
THURLOE PL
THURLOE SQ
THURLOE ST
Lycée Français Charles de Gaulle Sch
Moat House
SOUTH KENSINGTON
LUMIERE
PELHAM STREET
ONSLOW SQ
SYDNEY PL
SYDNEY STREET
MELTON CT
MALVERN CT
PELHAM CRES
FULHAM ROAD
BROMPTON RD
EGERTON CRES
EGERTON GDNS
CRESCENT PL
WALTON ST
DRAYCOTT AVENUE
HASKER ST
FIRST ST
OVINGTON STREET
LENNOX GDNS
CLABON MS
CADOGAN SQUARE
Sussex Ho Prep Sch
St. Simon Zelotes
MILNER ST
HALSEY STREET
MOORE ST
St. Mary's (RC)
St. Thomas More Sec Sch
St. Joseph's Prim Sch
GUINNESS TRUST BLDGS
Marlborough Prim Sch
MICHELIN HO
SLOANE AVENUE
LUCAN PL
ELYSTAN ST
SAMUEL LEWIS TRUST DWELLINGS
KINGDOM HALL
SW3
CRANMER COURT
PETYWARD
WHITEHEAD'S GRO
SUTTON EST
ELYSTAN PLACE
Shop Mall
St. Paul
ROSE SQ
ROYAL MARSDEN HOSP
Oratory RC Prim Sch
St. Luke
ROYAL BROMPTON HOSP
CALE STREET
DOVEHOUSE ST
BRITTEN ST
CHELSEA SQ
CHELSEA COLL OF ART & DESIGN
Fire Sta
Fulham Town Hall
Sports Cen
Methodist
Welsh Congregational
Clinic
KING'S ROAD
SMITH STREET
ROYAL AVENUE
WELLINGTON SQ
DUKE OF YORK HEADQUARTERS
BURTON'S COURT
ST. LEONARD'S TERRACE
ROYAL HOSPITAL ROAD
CHELTENHAM TER
WALPOLE ST
JUBILEE PLACE
MARKHAM ST
MARKHAM SQUARE
FLOOD ST
SHAWFIELD STREET
RADNOR WALK
TEDWORTH SQUARE
PEABODY EST
CHELSEA MANOR CT
Elec Sta
Christchurch
Christ Ch Prim Sch
REDBURN ST
ST. LOO AV
CHELSEA PHYSIC GARDEN
NAT. ARMY MUS
OAKLEY STREET
GLEBE PLACE
BRAMERTON ST
Antique Mkt
Jamahiriya Sch
UGC
OLD CHURCH ST
PAULTONS SQUARE
CHELSEA
MAN IN THE MOON
SIR THOMAS MORE EST
Holy Sacrament (RC)
Crosby Hall
ROPERS ORCHARD
Moravian
BEAUFORT ST
Holy Redeemer (RC)
CARLYLE'S HOUSE
Chelsea Old Ch
CHEYNE WALK
CHELSEA EMBANKMENT
THAMES
CADOGAN PIER
KENSINGTON
WANDSWORTH
THAMES PATH
ALBERT BR
BATTERSEA BR
CREMORNE EST
A3320
A308
B304
Waterside Point
Dock
SW11
CARRIAGE DRIVE NORTH
ANHALT ROAD
RANSOME'S DOCK
23
32
129
E F G H J
1 2 3 4 5 6 7

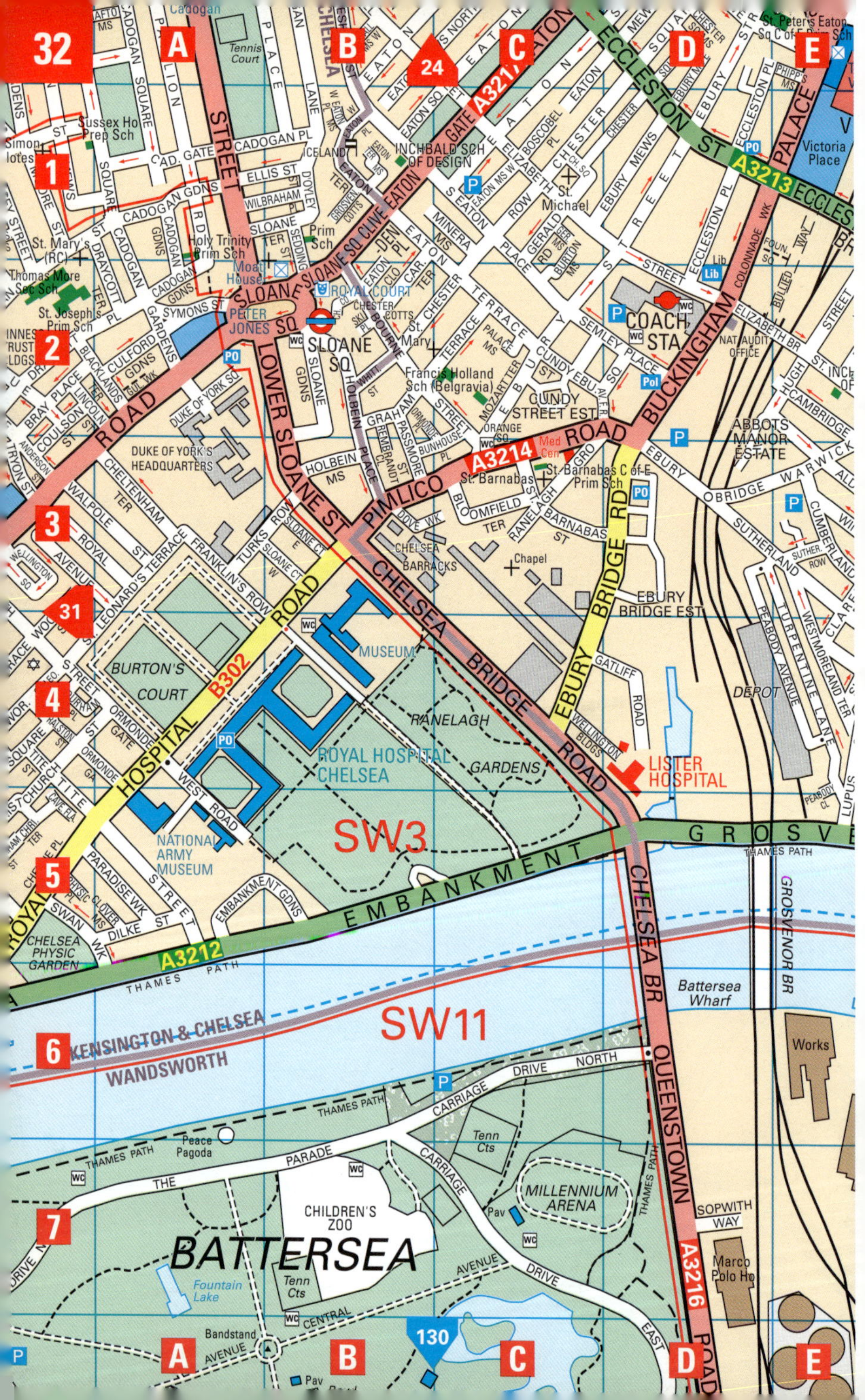
A
B
C
D
E
1
2
3
4
5
6
7
24
31
130
Cadogan
CADOGAN SQUARE
PAVILION
STREET
Tennis Court
PLACE
LANE
CHELSEA
EATON
EATON SQ
EATON GATE
A3214
ECCLESTON ST
A3213
St. Peter's Eaton Sq C of E Prim Sch
Victoria Place
PALACE
Sussex Ho Prep Sch
CAD. GATE
CADOGAN PL
ICELAND
INCHBALD SCH OF DESIGN
ELLIS ST
WILBRAHAM
DOYLEY
CADOGAN GDNS
CADOGAN GDNS
Holy Trinity Prim Sch
SLOANE TER
Prim Sch
SLOANE SQ
CLIVE
St. Mary's (RC)
Thomas More Sec Sch
St. Joseph's Prim Sch
DRAYCOTT
SYMONS ST
Moat House
PETER JONES
ROYAL COURT
SLOANE SQ
SLOANE GDNS
CHESTER
St. Mary
TERRACE
Francis Holland Sch (Belgravia)
CULFORD GDNS
BLACKLANDS TER
LINCOLN ST
COULSON ST
BRAY PLACE
ANDERSON
TRYON ST
ROAD
DUKE OF YORK SQ
DUKE OF YORK'S HEADQUARTERS
CHELTENHAM TER
WALPOLE ST
ROYAL AVENUE
WELLINGTON SQ
ST. LEONARD'S TERRACE
FRANKLIN'S ROW
TURKS ROW
LOWER SLOANE ST
HOLBEIN MS
HOLBEIN PLACE
GRAHAM TER
PIMLICO ROAD
A3214
Med Cen
St. Barnabas
St. Barnabas C of E Prim Sch
BLOOMFIELD TER
RANELAGH GRO
BARNABAS ST
DOVE WK
CHELSEA BARRACKS
Chapel
MINERA MS
ELIZABETH ST
BOSCOBEL PL
CHESTER SQ
St. Michael
GERALD RD
EBURY MEWS
EBURY STREET
ECCLESTON PL
COLONNADE WK
ELIZABETH BR
Lib
COACH STA
SEMLEY PLACE
CUNDY STREET EST
CUNDY ST
BUCKINGHAM PALACE ROAD
NAT. AUDIT OFFICE
HUGH ST
CAMBRIDGE ST
ABBOTS MANOR ESTATE
WARWICK WAY
EBURY SQ
EBURY BRIDGE RD
OBRIDGE
SUTHERLAND ST
SUTHER. ROW
CUMBERLAND ST
ALDERNEY
EBURY BRIDGE EST
PEABODY AVENUE
TURPENTINE LANE
WESTMORELAND TER
CLARE
DEPOT
GATLIFF ROAD
WELLINGTON BLDGS
LISTER HOSPITAL
CHELSEA BRIDGE ROAD
MUSEUM
RANELAGH GARDENS
ROYAL HOSPITAL CHELSEA
BURTON'S COURT
HOSPITAL ROAD
B302
ORMONDE GATE
WEST ROAD
NATIONAL ARMY MUSEUM
SW3
TITE ST
CHRISTCHURCH
PARADISE WK
EMBANKMENT GDNS
SWAN WK
DILKE ST
ROYAL
CHELSEA PHYSIC GARDEN
EMBANKMENT
A3212
GROSVENOR ROAD
THAMES PATH
GROSVENOR BR
CHELSEA BR
Battersea Wharf
Works
SW11
KENSINGTON & CHELSEA
WANDSWORTH
NORTH CARRIAGE DRIVE
QUEENSTOWN ROAD
A3216
Peace Pagoda
THE PARADE
Tenn Cts
MILLENNIUM ARENA
CARRIAGE DRIVE
CHILDREN'S ZOO
SOPWITH WAY
Marco Polo Ho
BATTERSEA
Fountain Lake
Tenn Cts
AVENUE
EAST DRIVE
CENTRAL AVENUE
Bandstand
Pav

E
F
G
H
J
25
VICTORIA STA
WILTON RD
NEATHOUSE PL
A202
St. Vincent de Paul RC Prim Sch
Westminster Cath Choir Sch
Holiday Inn
Queen Mother Sports Cen
Sports Cen
PASSPORT OFFICE
Quality Eccleston
CIVIL SERVICE COLL
VAUXHALL BRIDGE ROAD
ROCHESTER ROW
B323
Grange
Health Cen
W.K. COLL
ROY. HORT. SOC. LINDLEY HALL
PLAYING FIELDS
GORDON HOSP
Westminster Under Sch
HORSEFERRY RD
MEDWAY ST
Sacred Heart RC
St. Baptist
DfT
REGENCY PL
CORON CT
PAGE ST
GROSVENOR ESTATE
VINCENT STREET
HIDE TOWER
MONTAIGNE CL
Millbank Prim Sch
Grey Coat Hosp Sch
Amb Sta
ST. JOHN'S GDNS
WESTMINSTER GDNS
HOME OFFICE
MARSHAM ST
JOHN ISLIP ST
TATE BRITAIN
ATTERBURY ST
MILLBANK BARRACKS
PONSONBY PL
CURETON ST
ERASMUS ST
1
2
3
4
5
6
7
Med Cen
WARWICK WAY
BELGRAVE ROAD
LILLINGTON GARDENS EST
St. James the Less
BALD SCH DESIGN
ECCLESTON SQUARE
ST. GEORGES DRIVE
WARWICK SQUARE
DENBIGH ST
MORETON ST
CHARLWOOD ST
RAMPAYNE ST
Off. Nat Stats.
Lib
PO
PIMLICO
ST GEO. SQ
BESSBOROUGH ST
DRUMMOND GATE
Prim Sch
BESSB. GDNS
A202
34
RIVERSIDE GARDENS
GOVT OFF FOR LOND
St. Gabriel
Holy Apostles (RC)
PIMLICO
GLOUCESTER STREET
LUPUS STREET
St. Saviour
Pimlico Sch
Churchill Gdns Prim Sch
TACHBROOK EST
Offices
GLASGOW TERRACE
CHICHESTER ST
CLAVERTON ST
ST GEORGE'S SQUARE
Dolphin Sq
DOLPHIN SQUARE
CHURCHILL GARDENS
St. Gabriel's C of E Prim Sch
CHURCHILL GARDENS ROAD
PAXTON TER
TELFORD TER
SW1
GROSVENOR ROAD
A3212
THAMES PATH
Westminster Boat Ho
RIVERSIDE COURT
ELM QUAY COURT
RIVER THAMES
Jetty
Nine Elms Pier
Battersea Power Station (Disused)
Waste Auth. Site
Tideway Ind Estate
H.M. Stationery Office Warehouse
Southbank Business Centre
FB Flower Mkt
Depot
Superstore
POST OFFICE WAY
NEW COVENT GARDEN SORTING OFFICE
NINE ELMS LANE
A3205
CRINGLE STREET
KIRTLING ST
PONTON ROAD
NINE ELMS
Depot
SW8
Toll
130
PARK ROAD
John Milton Prim Sch
SLEAFORD ST
PASCAL STREET
HEMANS ST
Squash Cen
A3036
WANDSWORTH ROAD

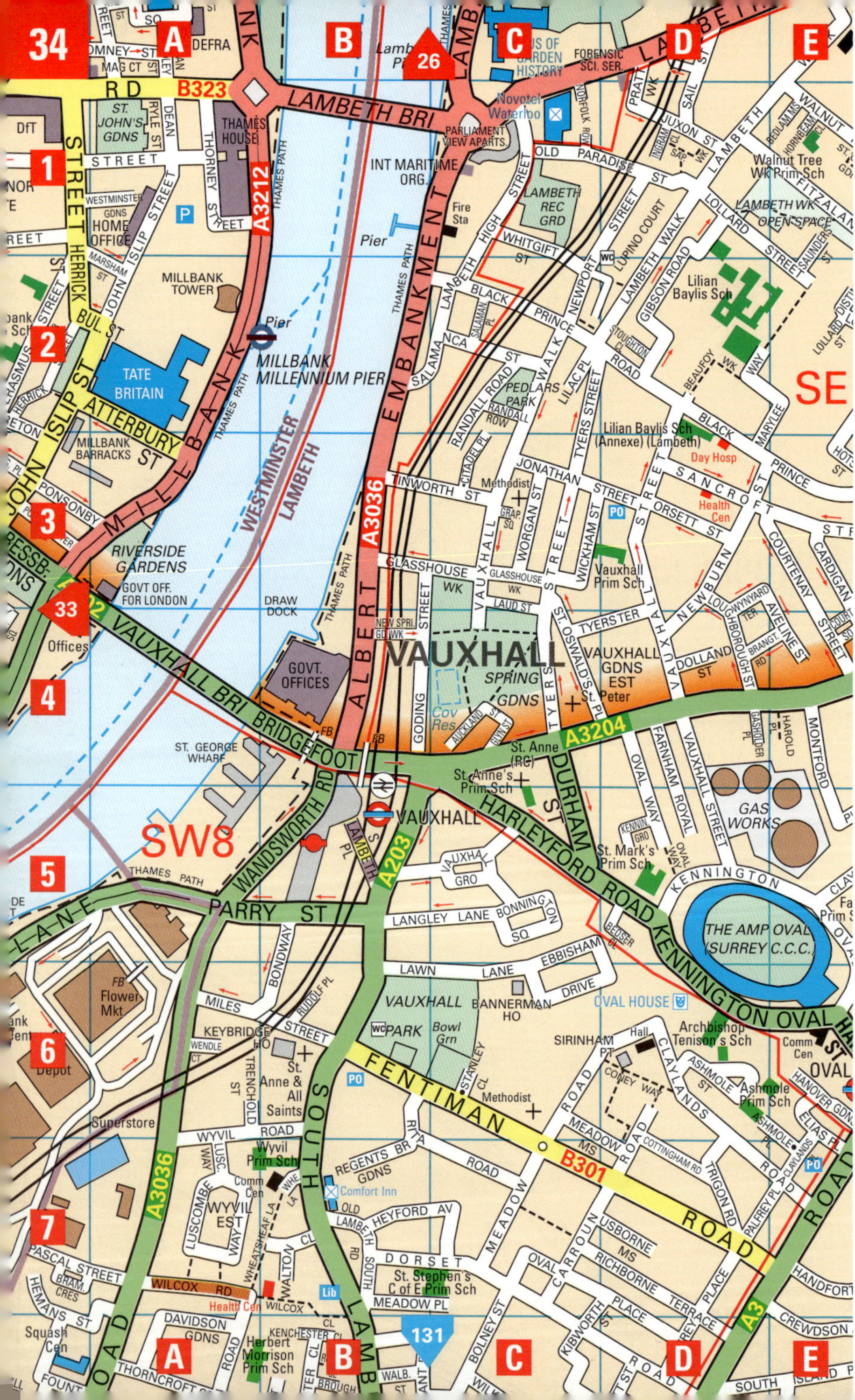

A
B
C
D
E
1
2
3
4
5
6
7
26
33
131
B323
A3212
A3036
A3204
A203
B301
A3
DEFRA
ROMNEY ST
MAG CT
ST. JOHN'S GDNS
RYLE ST
DEAN
THORNEY
THAMES HOUSE
DfT
STREET
WESTMINSTER GDNS
HOME OFFICE
MARSHAM ST
HERRICK
JOHN ISLIP STREET
MILLBANK TOWER
BUL. ST
TATE BRITAIN
ATTERBURY
MILLBANK BARRACKS
ST
PONSONBY
RIVERSIDE GARDENS
GOVT OFF. FOR LONDON
Offices
VAUXHALL BRI
BRIDGEFOOT
MILLBANK
THAMES PATH
Pier
MILLBANK MILLENNIUM PIER
WESTMINSTER
LAMBETH
LAMBETH BRI
INT MARITIME ORG.
PARLIAMENT VIEW APARTS.
DRAW DOCK
GOVT. OFFICES
ST. GEORGE WHARF
SW8
THAMES PATH
WANDSWORTH RD
PARRY ST
LANE
Flower Mkt
Depot
Superstore
MILES
BONDWAY
RUDOLF PL
KEYBRIDGE HO
WENDLE CT
TRENCHOLD ST
St. Anne & All Saints
STREET
WYVIL ROAD
Wyvil Prim Sch
Comm Cen
WYVIL EST
LUSCOMBE WAY
WHEATSHEAF LA
WALTON CL
WILCOX RD
Health Cen
DAVIDSON GDNS
Herbert Morrison Prim Sch
KENCHESTER CL
THORNCROFT ST
PASCAL STREET
BRAM. CRES
HEMANS ST
Squash Cen
SOUTH LAMBETH RD
ALBERT EMBANKMENT
Fire Sta
Pier
Lamb Pi
GARDEN HISTORY
FORENSIC SCI. SER.
Novotel Waterloo
OLD PARADISE ST
LAMBETH HIGH STREET
LAMBETH REC GRD
WHITGIFT ST
BLACK PRINCE RD
SALAMANCA ST
RANDALL ROAD
RANDALL ROW
PEDLARS PARK
CITADEL PL
TINWORTH ST
Methodist
JONATHAN STREET
GRAP. SQ
WORGAN ST
GLASSHOUSE WALK
GLASSHOUSE WK
LAUD ST
NEW SPRI. GD. WK
VAUXHALL
SPRING GDNS
Cov Res
GODING
AUCKLAND ST
TYERS ST
TYERS STREET
LILAC PL
NEWPORT
LUPINO COURT
LAMBETH WALK
GIBSON ROAD
NORFOLK ROW
PRATT WK
JUXON ST
INGRAM CL
SAIL ST
LAMBETH ROAD
WALNUT TREE WK
Walnut Tree Wk Prim Sch
LAMBETH WK OPEN SPACE
LOLLARD STREET
FITZALAN
Lilian Baylis Sch
Lilian Baylis Sch (Annexe) (Lambeth)
Day Hosp
BEAUFOY WK
STOUGHTON CL
SE
MARYLEE WAY
BLACK PRINCE
SANCROFT ST
Health Cen
ORSETT ST
COURTENAY ST
CARDIGAN STREET
WICKHAM ST
PO
Vauxhall Prim Sch
TYERS TER
ST. OSWALD'S PL
VAUXHALL GDNS EST
St. Peter
VAUXHALL WALK
NEWBURN
LOUGHBOROUGH ST
WYNYARD TER
BRANGT. RD
AVELINE ST
DOLLAND ST
GASHOLDER PL
HAROLD PL
MONTFORD
FARNHAM ROYAL
VAUXHALL STREET
OVAL WAY
GAS WORKS
St. Anne (RC)
St. Anne's Prim Sch
DURHAM ST
HARLEYFORD ROAD
St. Mark's Prim Sch
KENNINGTON OVAL
THE AMP OVAL (SURREY C.C.C.)
VAUXHALL
LAMBETH PL
VAUXHALL GRO
BONNINGTON SQ
LANGLEY LANE
LAWN LANE
EBBISHAM DRIVE
BEDSER CL
VAUXHALL PARK
Bowl Grn
BANNERMAN HO
OVAL HOUSE
STANLEY CL
FENTIMAN ROAD
Methodist
SIRINHAM PT
Hall
Archbishop Tenison's Sch
CLAYLANDS ROAD
ASHMOLE ST
Ashmole Prim Sch
CONEY WAY
MEADOW ROAD
MEADOW MS
COTTINGHAM RD
TRIGON RD
Comm Cen
HANOVER GDNS
ELIAS PL
REGENTS BR GDNS
RITA ROAD
Comfort Inn
OLD LAMBETH
HEYFORD AV
DORSET ROAD
St. Stephen's C of E Prim Sch
MEADOW PL
Lib
USBORNE MS
RICHBORNE TERRACE
CARROUN ROAD
OVAL PL
PALFREY PL
KIBWORTH ST
BOLNEY ST
WALB.
HANDFORTH
CREWDSON
SOUTH ISLAND PL

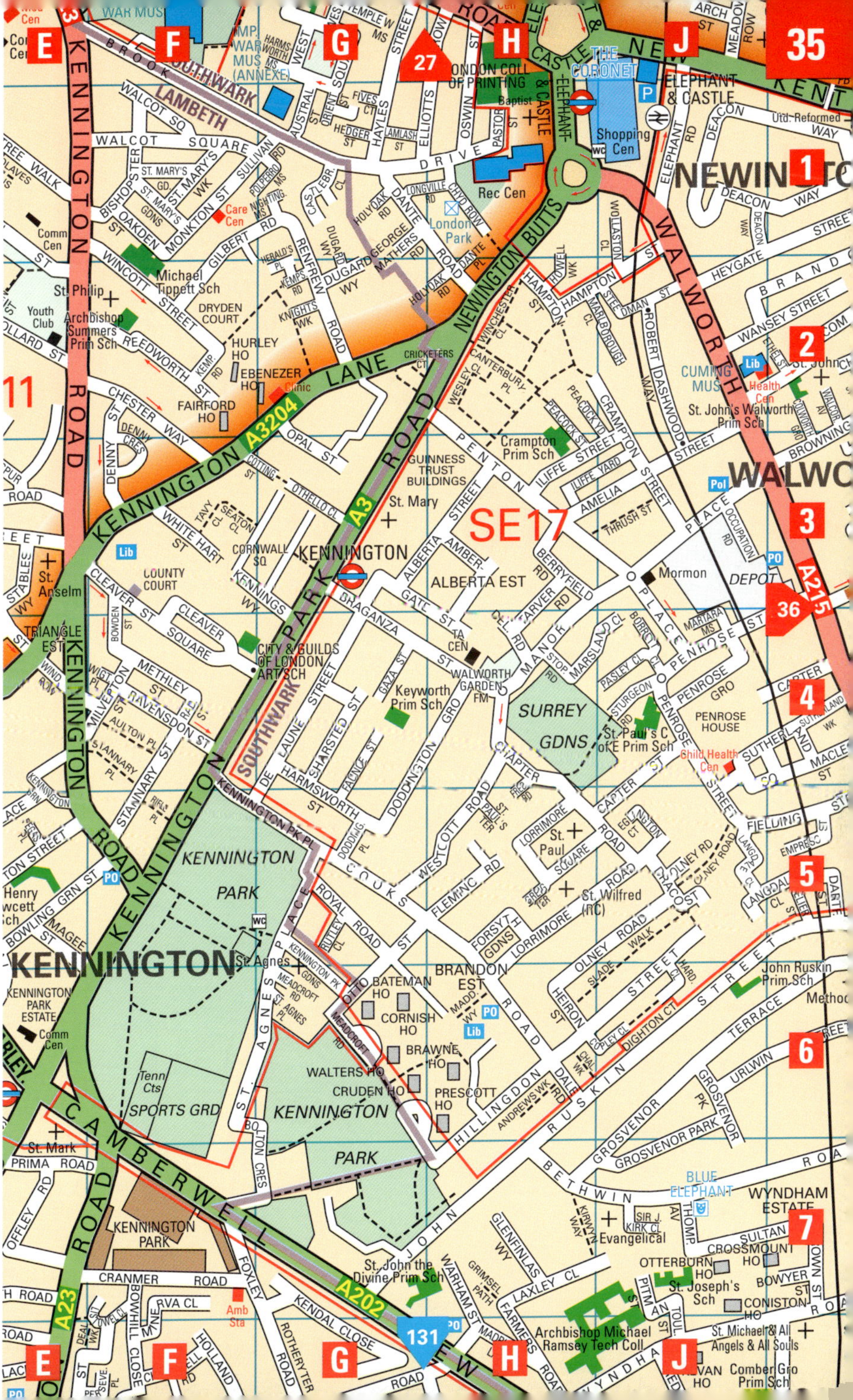
E
F
G
H
J
27
WAR MUS
IMP. WAR MUS (ANNEXE)
LONDON COLL OF PRINTING
THE CORONET
ELEPHANT & CASTLE
Shopping Cen
NEWINGTON
Utd. Reformed
Rec Cen
London Park
Care Cen
Comm Cen
Michael Tippett Sch
St. Philip
Youth Club
Archbishop Summers Prim Sch
DRYDEN COURT
HURLEY HO
EBENEZER HO
Clinic
FAIRFORD HO
CUMING MUS
Lib
Health Cen
St. John's Walworth Prim Sch
Crampton Prim Sch
GUINNESS TRUST BUILDINGS
St. Mary
SE17
KENNINGTON
ALBERTA EST
Mormon
WALWORTH
DEPOT
PO
Pol
COUNTY COURT
CITY & GUILDS OF LONDON ART SCH
TA CEN
WALWORTH GARDEN FM
Keyworth Prim Sch
SURREY GDNS
St. Paul's C of E Prim Sch
PENROSE HOUSE
Child Health Cen
St. Anselm
TRIANGLE EST
St. Paul
St. Wilfred (RC)
KENNINGTON PARK
St Agnes
KENNINGTON PARK ESTATE
Comm Cen
Henry Fawcett Sch
BATEMAN HO
CORNISH HO
BRAWNE HO
WALTERS HO
CRUDEN HO
PRESCOTT HO
BRANDON EST
Tenn Cts
SPORTS GRD
St. Mark
KENNINGTON PARK
Amb Sta
St. John the Divine Prim Sch
John Ruskin Prim Sch
Method
BLUE ELEPHANT
WYNDHAM ESTATE
Evangelical
St. Joseph's Sch
CONISTON HO
OTTERBURN HO
CROSSMOUNT HO
BOWYER
Archbishop Michael Ramsey Tech Coll
St. Michael & All Angels & All Souls
Comber Gro Prim Sch
131
36
11
1
2
3
4
5
6
7
A3
A3204
A23
A202
A215
KENNINGTON ROAD
KENNINGTON LANE
KENNINGTON PARK ROAD
NEWINGTON BUTTS
WALWORTH ROAD
CAMBERWELL NEW ROAD
SOUTHWARK
LAMBETH
BROOK DRIVE
WALCOT SQUARE
RUSKIN WALK
CAMBERWELL
PENTON PLACE
MANOR PLACE
COOKS ROAD
ROYAL ROAD
HILLINGDON STREET
JOHN RUSKIN STREET
GROSVENOR PARK
CRANMER ROAD
KENDAL CLOSE

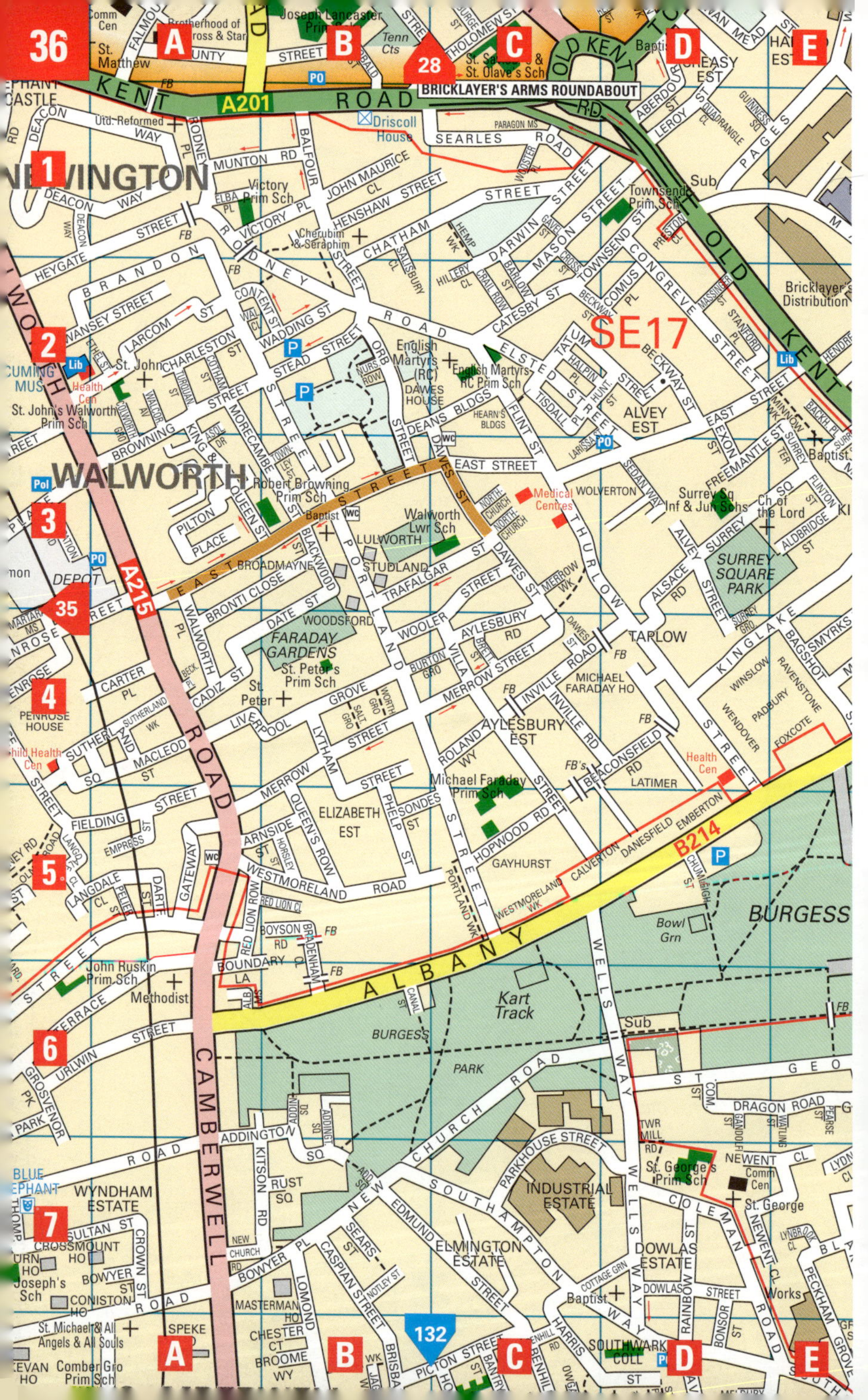
A
B
C
D
E
1
2
3
4
5
6
7
28
35
132
SE17
NEWINGTON
WALWORTH
KENT ROAD
A201
BRICKLAYER'S ARMS ROUNDABOUT
OLD KENT RD
OLD KENT ROAD
A215
WALWORTH ROAD
CAMBERWELL ROAD
B214
ALBANY ROAD
BURGESS PARK
Kart Track
Bowl Grn
DEACON WAY
HEYGATE STREET
BRANDON ST
RODNEY ROAD
MUNTON RD
BALFOUR ST
JOHN MAURICE CL
HENSHAW STREET
CHATHAM ST
DARWIN ST
MASON STREET
TOWNSEND ST
CONGREVE STREET
SEARLES ROAD
PARAGON MS
Driscoll House
Victory Prim Sch
Cherubim & Seraphim
Townsend Prim Sch
English Martyrs (RC)
English Martyrs RC Prim Sch
DAWES HOUSE
EAST STREET
DEANS BLDGS
HEARN'S BLDGS
FLINT ST
ELSTED STREET
CATESBY ST
BECKWAY ST
ALVEY EST
TATUM ST
FREEMANTLE ST
Surrey Sq Inf & Jun Schs
Ch of the Lord
SURREY SQUARE PARK
Baptist
WOLVERTON
Medical Centres
THURLOW STREET
TAPLOW
MICHAEL FARADAY HO
AYLESBURY EST
Michael Faraday Prim Sch
BEACONSFIELD RD
LATIMER
Health Cen
KINGLAKE STREET
WINSLOW
WENDOVER
PADBURY
RAVENSTONE
FOXCOTE
BAGSHOT
GAYHURST
EMBERTON
DANESFIELD
CALVERTON
WESTMORELAND WK
PORTLAND STREET
LULWORTH
STUDLAND
TRAFALGAR STREET
Walworth Lwr Sch
Robert Browning Prim Sch
BROADMAYNE
WOODSFORD
FARADAY GARDENS
St. Peter's Prim Sch
St. Peter
MERROW STREET
LIVERPOOL GROVE
LYTHAM STREET
QUEEN'S ROW
ELIZABETH EST
PHELP ST
SONDES ST
HOPWOOD RD
WESTMORELAND ROAD
ARNSIDE ST
RED LION ROW
BOYSON RD
BRADENHAM
BOUNDARY LA
FIELDING STREET
EMPRESS ST
LANGDALE CL
GATEWAY
MACLEOD ST
SUTHERLAND SQ
CARTER PL
PENROSE HOUSE
DEPOT
St. John's Walworth Prim Sch
St. John
CUMING MUS
Health Cen
John Ruskin Prim Sch
Methodist
URLWIN STREET
GROSVENOR PARK
WYNDHAM ESTATE
SULTAN ST
CROSSMOUNT HO
BOWYER ST
CONISTON HO
CROWN ST
St. Michael & All Angels & All Souls
Comber Gro Prim Sch
Joseph's Sch
ADDINGTON SQ
KITSON RD
RUST SQ
NEW CHURCH RD
MASTERMAN HO
CHESTER CT
BROOME WY
CASPIAN STREET
SEARS ST
EDMUND ST
ELMINGTON ESTATE
SOUTHAMPTON WAY
CHURCH STREET
PARKHOUSE STREET
INDUSTRIAL ESTATE
WELLS WAY
St. George's Prim Sch
St. George
NEWENT CL
COLEMAN ROAD
DOWLAS ESTATE
DOWLAS STREET
SOUTHWARK COLL
PICTON STREET
ST GEORGE'S WAY
DRAGON ROAD
Comm Cen
Works
PECKHAM GROVE
Baptist
BURGESS PARK

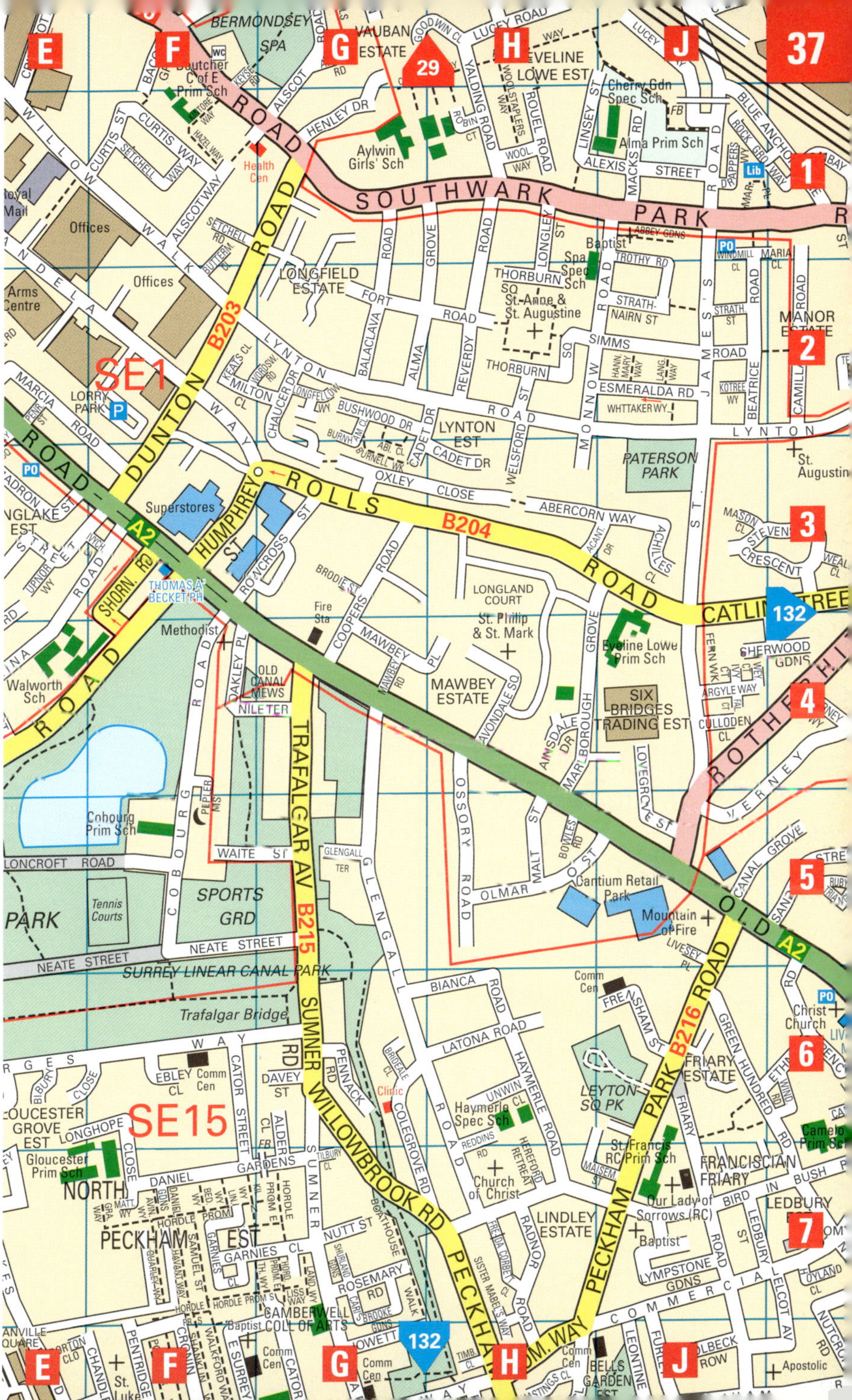

E
F
G
H
J
1
2
3
4
5
6
7
29
132
BERMONDSEY SPA
VAUBAN ESTATE
EVELINE LOWE EST
Boutcher C of E Prim Sch
Health Cen
Aylwin Girls' Sch
Cherry Gdn Spec Sch
Alma Prim Sch
Lib
SOUTHWARK PARK ROAD
Royal Mail
Offices
Arms Centre
LONGFIELD ESTATE
Baptist
Spa Spec Sch
St. Anne & St. Augustine
MANOR ESTATE
PO
SE1
LORRY PARK
P
B203
DUNTON ROAD
LYNTON ROAD
LYNTON EST
PATERSON PARK
St. Augustine
A2
Superstores
ROLLS ROAD
B204
ABERCORN WAY
CATLIN STREET
THOMAS A' BECKET PH
Methodist
Fire Sta
LONGLAND COURT
St. Philip & St. Mark
Eveline Lowe Prim Sch
Walworth Sch
OLD CANAL MEWS
MAWBEY ESTATE
SIX BRIDGES TRADING EST
ROTHERHITHE
VERNEY
Cobourg Prim Sch
LONCROFT ROAD
WAITE ST
GLENGALL TER
Cantium Retail Park
Mountain of Fire
OLD KENT ROAD
SPORTS GRD
Tennis Courts
PARK
NEATE STREET
SURREY LINEAR CANAL PARK
Trafalgar Bridge
TRAFALGAR AV
B215
Comm Cen
Christ Church
B216
PECKHAM PARK ROAD
FRIARY ESTATE
LEYTON SQ PK
SE15
GLOUCESTER GROVE EST
Gloucester Prim Sch
EBLEY CL
Clinic
Haymerle Spec Sch
St Francis RC Prim Sch
Camelot Prim Sch
FRANCISCIAN FRIARY
Church of Christ
Our Lady of Sorrows (RC)
LINDLEY ESTATE
Baptist
NORTH PECKHAM EST
WILLOWBROOK RD
PECKHAM HILL ST
CAMBERWELL COLL OF ARTS
COMMERCIAL WAY
BELLS GARDEN EST
Apostolic
St. Luke

A
B
C
D
E
1
2
3
4
5
6
7
20
21
97
96
95
54
ROAD PITCHES
BELHAVEN CT
LEEMING RD
CLIFTON WY
BLYTH
HORNB CL
BIRCH WK
CROWN
ALBAN
CRES
CAISHOWE ROAD
ODDESEY RD
ROAD
PO
Prim Schs
WINSTRE ROAD
NORTHFIELD RD
EDULF ROAD
SHENLEY
HILL
ROAD
B5378
WARENFORD WAY
RANSKILL RD
NORTON CL
GROVE
ABERFORD LAKE
CATTERICK WAY
LINTON AVENUE
CROXDALE ROAD
ABERFORD PARK
Comm Cen
SPORTS GROUND
Pav
ABERFORD
CANTERBURY HO
CANTERBURY RD
BROOK
ELDON
HARTFORDE RD
BROUGHINGE ROAD
MEADOW PARK
Borehamwood FC & Enfield FC
Pav
Tenn Cts
Prim Sch
Bowl Grn
MEAD RD
CIVIC OFFS
Clinic
Lib
Pol
Amb Sta
Fire Sta
ELSTREE
WAY
A5135
Imperial Studios
Studios
War Memorial
B.B.C. Elstree Studios
GROSVENOR
CLARENDON RD
ESSEX RD
MALDEN RD
WELBECK
STRATFIELD
CHANDOS
LEXINGTON CT
Boulevard 25 Retail Park
Works
Hall
Metropolis Centre
Cinema
PO
BOREHAMWOOD
Superstore
MAXWELL PK
WHITEHOUSE AVENUE
CARDINAL AVENUE
FURZEHILL
MILDRED AV
DRAYTON ROAD
STATION RD
GLENHAVEN AV
Comm Cen
HOLT CL
SHENLEY
LANE
ELSTREE & BOREHAMWOOD
Gas Works
BROWN RD
HILLSIDE
OAKWOOD
ELMWOOD AV
Prim Sch
WD6
Prim Sch
AVENUE
Sec Sch
Sports Cen
POTTERS
WILCOX
DANZIGER WAY
GATE
GREGSON
COOPERS
DENHAM
DENHAM WAY
ROBESON WAY
ALEXANDRA ROAD
KENT CL
NOVELLO WAY
ROWLEY
LANE
Rowley Farm
Mops & Brooms PH
Hertswood School (Annex)
Oaklands College
Swimming Pool
New Horizons
STUDIO
RUTHERFORD CL
BOREHAMWOOD IND PARK
YORK WAY
YORK CRES
Tenn Cts
G.E.C. SPORTS GROUND
Works
Warehouses
Works
MANOR WAY
BULLHEAD ROAD
CHESTER ROAD
WARWICK RD
Works
Moat House Elstree
DURHAM RD
Depot
KING GEORGES PLAYING FLD
Pav
Prim Sch
NEWARK GRN
TON WAY
KENILWORTH DR
KENILWORTH DRIVE
TEMPSFORD GREEN
BARNET BYPASS
WANSFORD PARK
BUCKINGHAM RD
THORNBURY GARDENS
FEATHERSTONE GARDENS
NORFOLK GARDENS
BUCKINGHAM DRIVE
BALMORAL DRIVE
HOWARD
KNEBW. PATH
EASTON GDNS
Prim Sch
Comm Cen
RIPON PARK
RIPON WAY
MONKS MEAD
LEMSFORD CT
ARUNDEL DRIVE
CLEVELAND CRES
GRANTHAM GRN
BURGHLEY AVENUE
DACRE GARDENS
CLYDESDALE
FARRIERS WAY
Works
Depot
Superstore
STIRLING WAY
A1
MELROSE AVENUE
TENNISON AVENUE
MILTON
MASEFIELD AVENUE
LULLINGTON GARTH
CARRINGTON
Furze Hill
ASHLEY
BYRON
VALE AVENUE
ALLOT
DEACONS HILL
HARTFIELD
AVENUE
BERKELEY CL
ASCOT CL
SHEPHERDS
WENTWORTH
SHERATON CL
NICHOLAS
CLARE CL
BELMOR
SUMMIT
ELSTREE
A411
LANE
BARNET LANE
Woodcock Hill Farm
TUNNEL
Airshafts
Deacons Hill
DEACONS HILL OPEN SPACE
Stirling Corner
ELSTREE PARK
BARNET
ARKLEY PARK
HYVER HILL
Hyver Hall
FROGHALL WOOD
SCRATCH WOOD
FB
BOYS HILL WOOD
THISTLE WOOD
NW7
GRAVEL PIT WOOD
CLUMP OF TREES WOOD
Depot
TARGET

E
F
22
G
H
23
J
BRIDGEDOW
GOLF
COURSE
ALLOTMEN
1
BYPASS
A1
WROTHAM
PARK
OPEN
SPACE
Fold Farm
LANE
Homestead
Farm
POOR CLARE
MONASTERY
HERTFORDSHIRE
BYNG R
PLAYING F
2
Barn
R.F.C.
ALLOT
97
HERTSMERE
BARNET
ARKLEY
LANE
OPEN
SPACE
SPORTS
GROUND
GALLEY
A1
DRIVING
RANGE
Clubhouse
Woodlands
Farm
ARKLEY
Sec
Sch
3
OLD FOLD VIEW
CAVENDISH ROAD
GRIMSDYKE CRESCENT
GRIMSDYKE
CRES
JENNINGS
WY
KINGS
ELIZABETH
CL
QUEENS ROAD
Rowley Green
Farm
ARKLEY
OPEN SPACE
40
Nursery
ARGYLE
RD
EN5
WOOD
ROAD
Three
Elms Farm
LANE
WHALEBONE
PARK
ROWLEY
Pav
Rowley
Green
ARKLEY
GOLF
COURSE
ARKLEY
RISE
ESTATE
OPEN
SPACE
OAKLANDS
FIELD END
STONE CROFT
GARDEN CL
KERRY CL
ELMBANK
4
OWLEY
LANE
GOLF
OURSE
OAKLANDS
ARKLEY VW
BARNET
WELLHOUSE
WELLSIDE
96
Arkley
Manor Farm
CARRINGTON CL
ARKLEY DRIVE
HEDGEROW LA
HAZEL ME.
QUINTA
GARTHLAND
MALINS CL
NORTH CL
ENDERSBY RD
ESCOT WAY
AITKEN RD
DENTS
HILL CL
TRINDER
PEPYS CRES
SPRING CL
Clubhouse
COV
RES
ROAD
War
Memorial
Rowley Bank
Nurseries
ROWLEY GREEN
5
Water Tower
PO
COV
RES
KATES CL
MEAD
ROAD
GLEBE LA
Arkley
WEST CL
ST. PETER'S CL
BEECROFT
HACKFORTH CL
CRESCENT
FARM CL
BRETT ROAD
DRIVE
Prim
Sch
WHITINGS
ROAD
PALMER GDNS
DORMER CL
EDWYN CL
STANHOPE
DEXTER RD
WHITINGS
HILL
OPEN
SPACE
GREENLAND RD
NUPTON DRIVE
MAYS
WINDMILL LA
DINGLE CL
ROCKWAYS
WYLO DR
Tennis
Courts
Pavs.
BARNET
GATE
SPORTS
GRD
BRICKFIELD
HAW GRD
ROCKWAYS
SHELF RD
BISH. CL
6
PARTRIDGE CL
SPORTS
GROUND
The
Gate
PH
Barnet
Gate
LANE
Whitings
Hill Farm
Cottage
Farm
Duc
A411
HENDON
FB
95
OLD ELIZABETHANS
(BARNET)
MEMORIAL PLAYING
FIELDS
Pav
Dollis Brook
BARNET
GATE
WOOD
NEW RD
GATE
MAYS
LANE
Brent Lodge Farm
ALTHORP CL
FB
7
MOAT
MOUNT
OPEN SPACE
Dollis Brook
WOOD
B552
55
CHOLMELEIAN
SPORTS
GROUND
E
F
22
G
H
23
J
TOTTERIDGE

A
24
B
C
25
D
E
1
2
3
4
5
6
7
97
96
95
39
56
GOLF
OURSE
OLD FOLD MANOR
GOLF COURSE
ALLOTMENTS
Clubhouse
MOAT
Old Fold Manor
Monken Hadley
Battle of Barnet 1471
Rectory Farm
Prim Sch
Jun Sch
War Memorial
ST. MARTHA'S CONVENT
Bournwell Hill
MONKEN
Priddeon's Hill
Electricity Sta
BYNG ROAD PLAYING FIELDS
High Barnet
Barnet R.F.C.
Prim Sch
ALLOT
Hadley
KING GEORGE'S FIELD
BARNET
SPORTS GROUND
A1081
ST ALBANS ROAD
A1000
HADLEY GREEN
HADLEY HIGHSTONE
HADLEY COMMON
HADLEY GREEN
SUNSET VW
HADLEY GRO
CHRISTCHURCH LA
TA Cen
Mkt
Lib
The Spires Shop Cen
HIGH STREET
Sec Sch
Swim Pool
Works
Tenn Cts
Jun Sch
PO
MUS
THE BULL THEATRE
Barnet Coll
Pol
Sports Cen
BARNET TRADING EST
A411
WOOD STREET
UNION STREET
WHALEBONE PARK
BARNET GENERAL HOSP
CEMETERY
EN5
CHIPPING BARNET
HIGH BARNET
BARNET HILL
GREAT NORTH ROAD
STATION
REC GRD
Bowl Grn
Tenn Cts
BELLS HILL ALLOT
ALLOT
Prim Schs
Comm Cen
Prim Sch
Valley Cen
Underhill
SPORTS GROUND
BARNET FC
Clubhouse
Cinema
Fire Sta
BARNET PLAYING FIELDS
Pavs.
Prim Sch
KING GEORGE V PLAYING FIELDS
Ducks Island
SPORTS GROUND
Pav
Tennis Courts
PLAYING FIELD
GRANGE PLAYING FIELDS
DOLLIS VALLEY GREEN WALK
LONDON LOOP
Sec Sch
OAKLANDS ROAD
N20
SOUTH HERTS GOLF COURSE
WYATTS FARM OPEN SPACE
BROOK FARM OPEN SPACE
TOTTERIDGE COMMON
TOTTERIDGE LANE

E
F
G
H
J
26
27
HADLEY WOOD
Great Beechgates Hill
BEECH HILL
WALMAR CLOSE
CORBAR CL
CAMLET WAY
Clubhouse
FERNYHILL WOOD
1
BEECH HILL PARK
HADLEY WOOD GOLF COURSE
Green Brook
BROADGATE AV
PARKGATE CRES
PARKGATE AV
AVENUE
NEWMANS WAY
GREENBROOK AV
MUSGRAVE CL
COVERT WAY
COVERT WAY OPEN SPACE
Sewit's Hill
FISH PONDS
GREENOAK PL
COCKFOSTERS ROAD
HADLEY COMMON
ENFIELD
BARNET
EN4
2
Water Tower
OAK WOOD
COOMBEHURST CL
COOMBEH CL
Newman's Hill
BEECH HILL LAKE
BAKERS HILL
THE SPIN.
TUDOR GOLF COURSE
TUDOR SPORTS GRD
FAIRGREEN
BOURN CL
COV RES
97
Monument
Sec Sch
Prim Sch
Clubhouse
Tenn Cts
Pavs.
ALLOT
ARUNDEL RD
NORTHFIELD RD
LINTHORPE ROAD
Ludgrove Hall
GAMES ROAD
War Memorial
3
Gas Works
WESTBROOK CRESCENT
LAWTON ROAD
GROVE ROAD
SPORTS GROUND
SPORTS GRDS
Bowl Club
42
TRENT PARK CEM
FORDHAM ROAD
MT PLEASANT
CHALK LA
VICTORIA REC GRD
Tenn Cts
APPLETREE GDNS
KENLEY CL
ST JAMES CL
PARK ROAD
CROMER ROAD
HEXHAM RD
BULWER RD
Amb Sta
GLYN AV
VICTORIA ROAD
Pymme's Brook
PYMMES BROOK DR
PENDALL CL
HAMILTON ROAD
MOUNT PLEASANT
BEVAN ROAD
LANGFORD CRES
BELMONT CL
4
Prim Sch
NEW BARNET
War Memi
PO
Comm Cen
COCKFOSTERS
EAST BARNET ROAD
ROAD
STATION APP
Superstore
VICTORIA CL
ROLFE CL
ECCLESTON CL
EVELYN RD
NORRYS CL
NORRYS RD
96
NEW BARNET
SOMERSET ROAD
MOUNT RD
HIGH ST
PILGRIMS RI
HEDDON RD
ASHURST RD
GARDENS
Sch
GLOUCESTER ROAD
RICHMOND ROAD
Health Cen
KEELY CL
ALLOT
5
Tenn Cts
DENEWOOD
LANCASTER ROAD
BROOKHILL ROAD
CAT HILL
A110
GLOUCESTER RD
EVERSLEIGH ROAD
Lib
CHESTNUT GRO
LAKESIDE CRES
DOGGETTS CT
Prim Sch
Sec Sch
A110
FAIRWAY
HASLUCK GDNS
LONGMORE AVENUE
B193
BARNET RD
DRIVE
BOHUN GROVE
DANELAND
MANSFIELD AV
VERNON CRES
LYONSDOWN
CALTON RD
SOMA GRO
Prim Sch
6
ROAD
DALMENY RD
JACKSON ROAD
CHURCHMEAD CL
WINDSOR AVENUE
RIDGEWAY
DANELAND
WILLENHALL AV
HOLYROOD ROAD
EAST BARNET
COUNTY GATE
NORTHUMBERLAND ROAD
95
WALFIELD AVENUE
HIGH ROAD
OAK HILL PARK
Bandstand
Pav
MOUNT DRIVE
AVENUE
PO
OAKLEIGH PARK
Miniature
7
Bowl Grn
Pav
ALLOT
THATCHAM GDNS
BUCKINGHAM ROAD
A1000
TEMPLE AVENUE
STUART ROAD
Sch
Swim Pool
Youth Cen
Sch
Tenn Cts
Pav
PARKSIDE
ALLOT
Superstore
MARYROSE WY
57
GRANGE AV
AVONDALE
CONNAUGHT RD
Works
CHANDOS
ALICE OWEN'S GRD
26
E
F
G
H
J

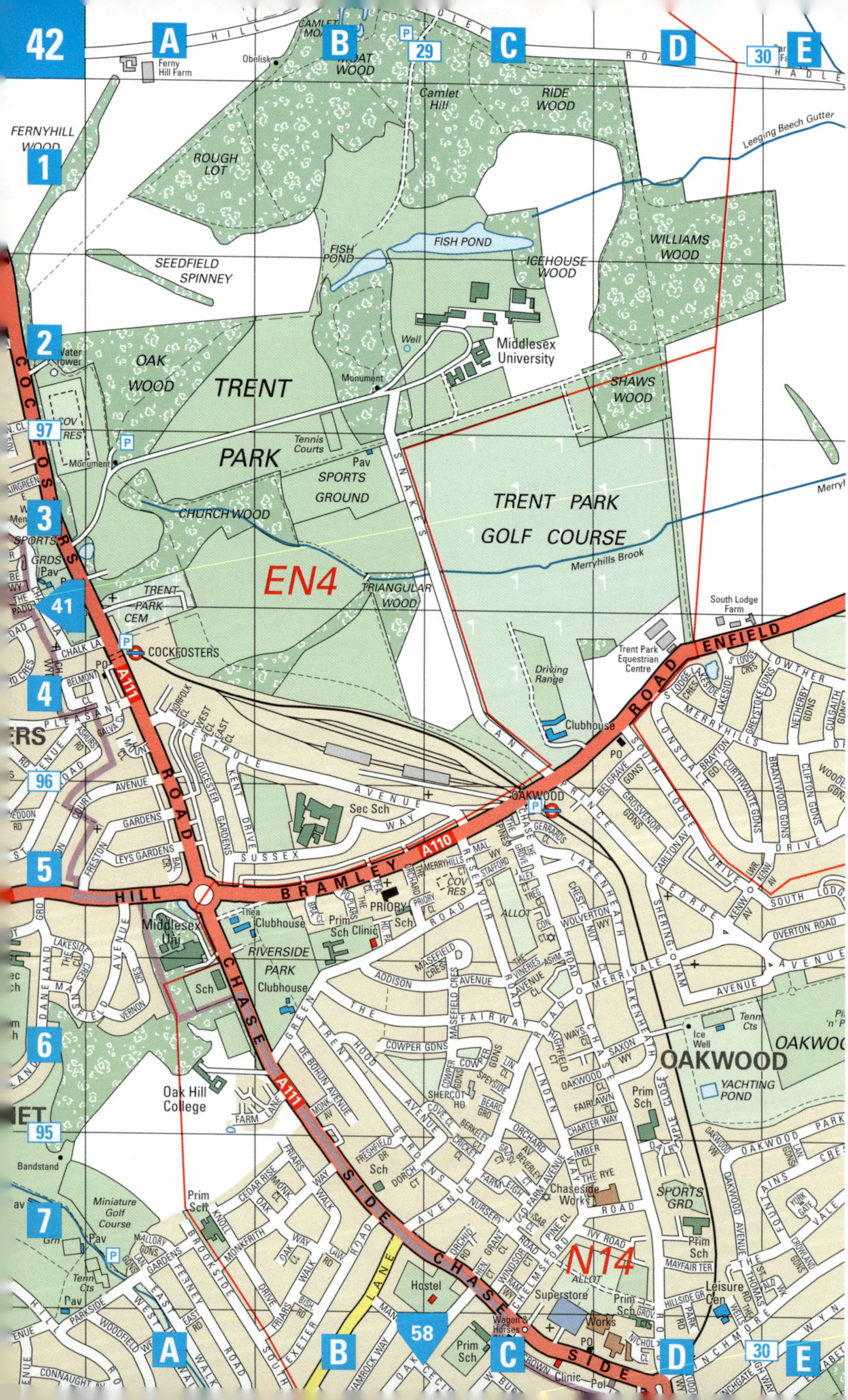
A
B
C
D
E
1
2
3
4
5
6
7
29
30
97
96
95
41
58
Ferny Hill Farm
Obelisk
CAMLET MOAT
MOAT WOOD
Camlet Hill
RIDE WOOD
FERNYHILL WOOD
ROUGH LOT
Leeging Beech Gutter
FISH POND
WILLIAMS WOOD
SEEDFIELD SPINNEY
ICEHOUSE WOOD
Well
Middlesex University
Water Tower
OAK WOOD
TRENT PARK
Monument
SHAWS WOOD
COV RES
Tennis Courts
Pav
SPORTS GROUND
SNAKES LANE
TRENT PARK GOLF COURSE
CHURCH WOOD
Merryhills Brook
EN4
TRIANGULAR WOOD
TRENT PARK CEM
South Lodge Farm
COCKFOSTERS
Trent Park Equestrian Centre
Driving Range
Clubhouse
ENFIELD ROAD
COCKFOSTERS ROAD
A111
CHALK LA
BELMONT CL
PLEASANT
MOUNT
NORFOLK CL
WEST CL
EAST CL
WESTPOLE AVENUE
KENT DRIVE
GLOUCESTER GARDENS
AVENUE
Sec Sch
GARDENS
LEYS GARDENS
SUSSEX WAY
OAKWOOD
BRAMLEY ROAD
A110
MERRYHILLS
RESERVOIR ROAD
PRIORY
Prim Sch
Clinic
COV RES
ALLOT
HILL
Middlesex Uni
Clubhouse
RIVERSIDE PARK
Clubhouse
CHASE SIDE
Sch
Oak Hill College
FARM LANE
LAKENHEATH
BELGRAVE GDNS
GROSVENOR GDNS
CARLTON AV
SOUTH LODGE DRIVE
LONSDALE DR
MERRYHILLS
GEORGE
SHERINGHAM AVENUE
OVERTON ROAD
SOUTH LODGE
MERRIVALE
ADDISON AVENUE
MASEFIELD CRES
THE FAIRWAY
COWPER GDNS
DE BOHUN AVENUE
GREEN
TRENT
HOOD
OAKWOOD
Ice Well
YACHTING POND
Tenn Cts
Prim Sch
SPORTS GRD
Prim Sch
Chaseside Works
THE RYE
N14
IVY ROAD
MAYFAIR TER
Leisure Cen
ALLOT
Superstore
Prim Sch
Works
Wagon & Horses
Hostel
Prim Sch
Clinic
PO
Pol
Bandstand
Miniature Golf Course
Pav
Tenn Cts
Pav
Prim Sch
MONKFRITH
CEDAR RISE
FRIARS WALK
BROOKSIDE
PARKSIDE
WOODFIELD
CONNAUGHT
OAKWOOD PARK
OAKWOOD AVENUE
FOUNTAINS CRES
YORK GATE
THE VALE
CROWN LANE
WINCHMORE HILL
OAKWOOD CRES

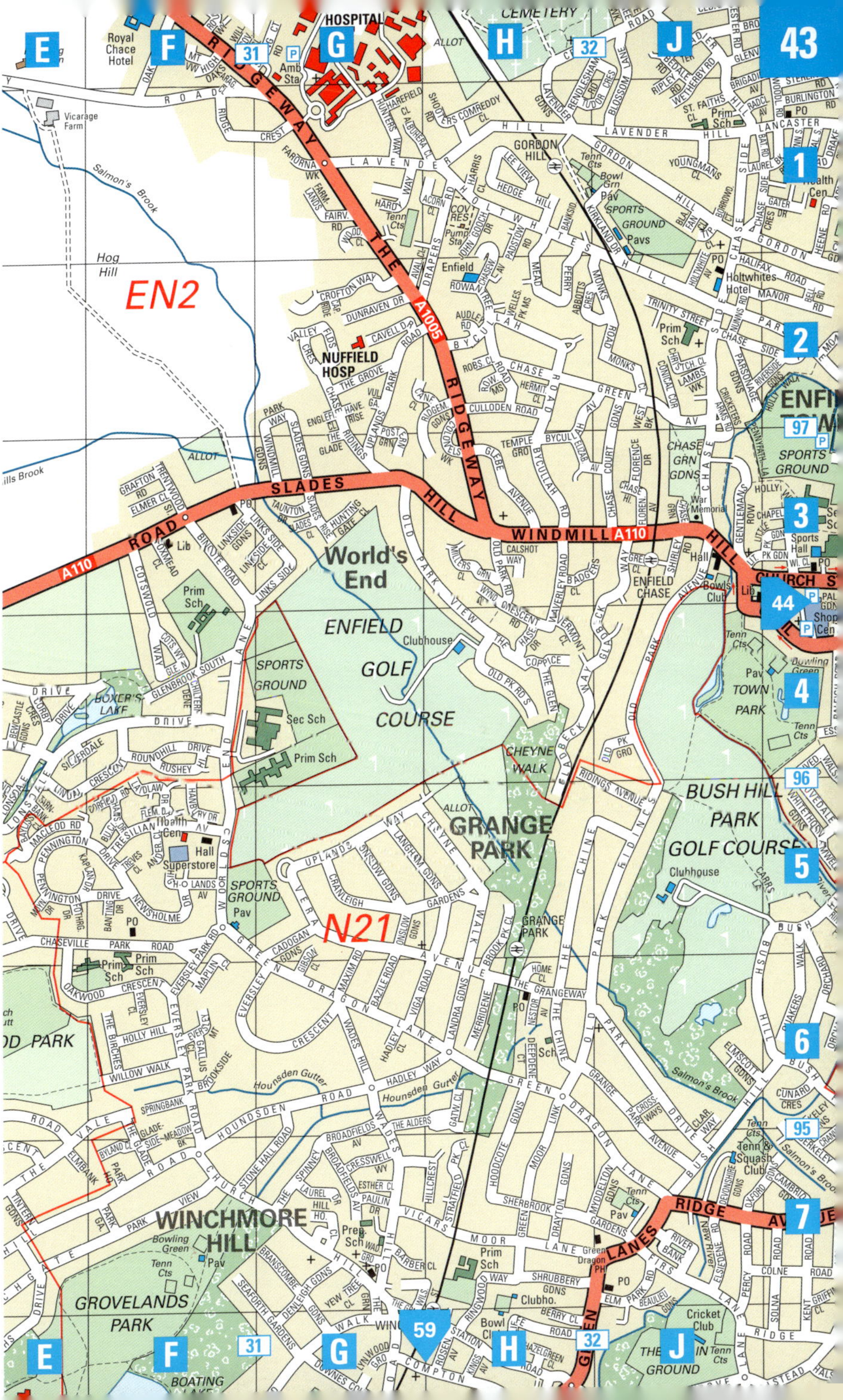
E
F
G
H
J
1
2
3
4
5
6
7
Royal Chace Hotel
HOSPITAL
CEMETERY
Vicarage Farm
Salmon's Brook
Hog Hill
EN2
RIDGEWAY
THE RIDGEWAY
A1005
LAVENDER HILL
GORDON HILL
SPORTS GROUND
Holtwhites Hotel
NUFFIELD HOSP
ENFIELD TOWN
SLADES HILL
WINDMILL HILL
A110
ROAD
World's End
ENFIELD GOLF COURSE
Clubhouse
ENFIELD CHASE
CHURCH ST
TOWN PARK
BOXER'S LAKE
Sec Sch
Prim Sch
CHEYNE WALK
GRANGE PARK
BUSH HILL PARK GOLF COURSE
N21
Superstore
Health Cen
OD PARK
Hounsden Gutter
WINCHMORE HILL
Bowling Green
GROVELANDS PARK
BOATING LAKE
RIDGE AVENUE
GREEN LANES
Cricket Club
THE GROUND
Salmon's Brook
31
32
44
59
95
96
97

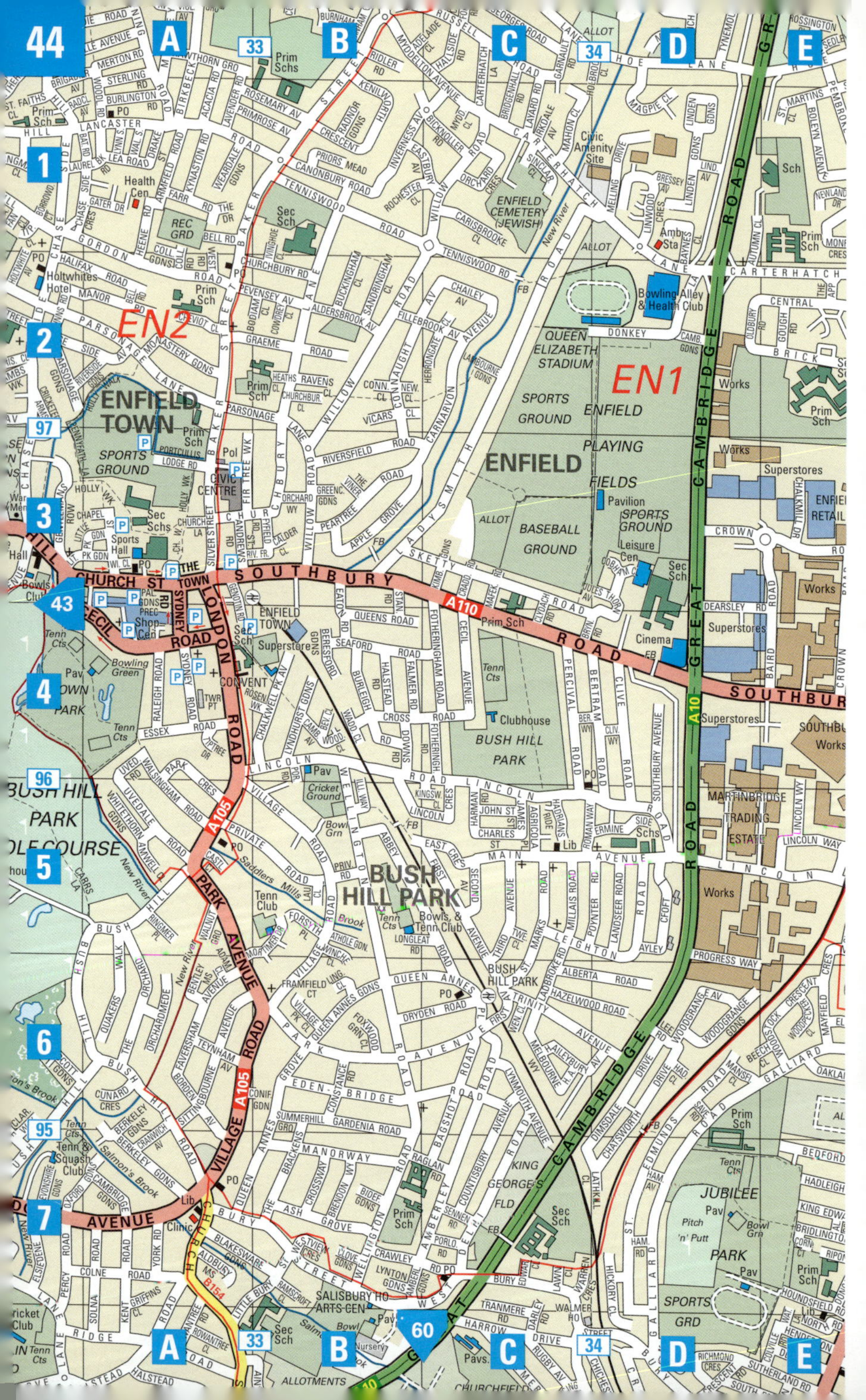

EN2
EN1
ENFIELD TOWN
ENFIELD
BUSH HILL PARK
ENFIELD PLAYING FIELDS
SPORTS GROUND
BASEBALL GROUND
QUEEN ELIZABETH STADIUM
BUSH HILL PARK GOLF COURSE
JUBILEE PARK
KING GEORGE'S FLD
ENFIELD CEMETERY (JEWISH)
CIVIC CENTRE
Civic Amenity Site
Bowling Alley & Health Club
MARTINBRIDGE TRADING ESTATE
ENFIELD RETAIL
SALISBURY HO ARTS CEN
Superstores
Works
Leisure Cen
Cinema
Clubhouse
GREAT CAMBRIDGE ROAD
SOUTHBURY ROAD
A110
A105
A10
B154
LONDON ROAD
PARK AVENUE
VILLAGE ROAD
CHURCH ST
SILVER STREET
BAKER STREET
CHASE SIDE
LANCASTER RD
GORDON ROAD
CARTERHATCH LANE
LADYSMITH ROAD
WILLOW ROAD
CHURCHBURY LANE
LINCOLN ROAD
MAIN AVENUE
QUEEN ANNES PL
BUSH HILL
BURY STREET
BURY STREET WEST
RIDGE AVENUE
CAMBRIDGE GDNS
New River
Salmon's Brook
ALLOTMENTS
33
34
43
60
95
96
97

E
F
G
H
J
35
36
97
96
95
46
61
1
2
3
4
5
6
7
EN3
N9
Enfield Highway
Brimsdown
Ponders End
HERTFORD RD
HERTFORD ROAD
HIGH STREET
A1010
A1055
A110
B137
MERIDIAN WAY
MOLLISON AVENUE
NAGS HEAD ROAD
LEA VALLEY ROAD
SOUTH STREET
CARTERHATCH LANE
GREEN STREET
DURANTS ROAD
ALMA ROAD
BRIMSDOWN AVENUE
NIGHTINGALE ROAD
WHARF ROAD
BRIMSDOWN SPORTS GROUND
DURANTS PARK
ALMA ROAD OPEN SPACE
HERTFORD ROAD CEMETERY
Enfield Coll
Enfield Coll Sports Hall
Middlesex University
REC GRD
ALLOTMENTS
ST. GEORGE'S FIELD
PLAYING FIELD
BRIMSDOWN INDUSTRIAL ESTATE
CENTENARY ESTATE
PONDERS END IND EST
VALLEY LINK IND EST
RIVERSIDE IND EST
ENFIELD ENERGY CEN
Electricity Station
Chimney
Elec Sta
THE ARENA
OPEN SPACE
VALLEY PARK
Gas Works
Ponders End Mills
Superstore
Leisure Cen
Health Cen
Cinema
LEE VALLEY
GOLF
SPORTS PITCH
WILLIAM
GEOF
RESE
KI
River Lee Navigation
Overflow Channel
LEA VALLEY WALK
Boundary Ditch

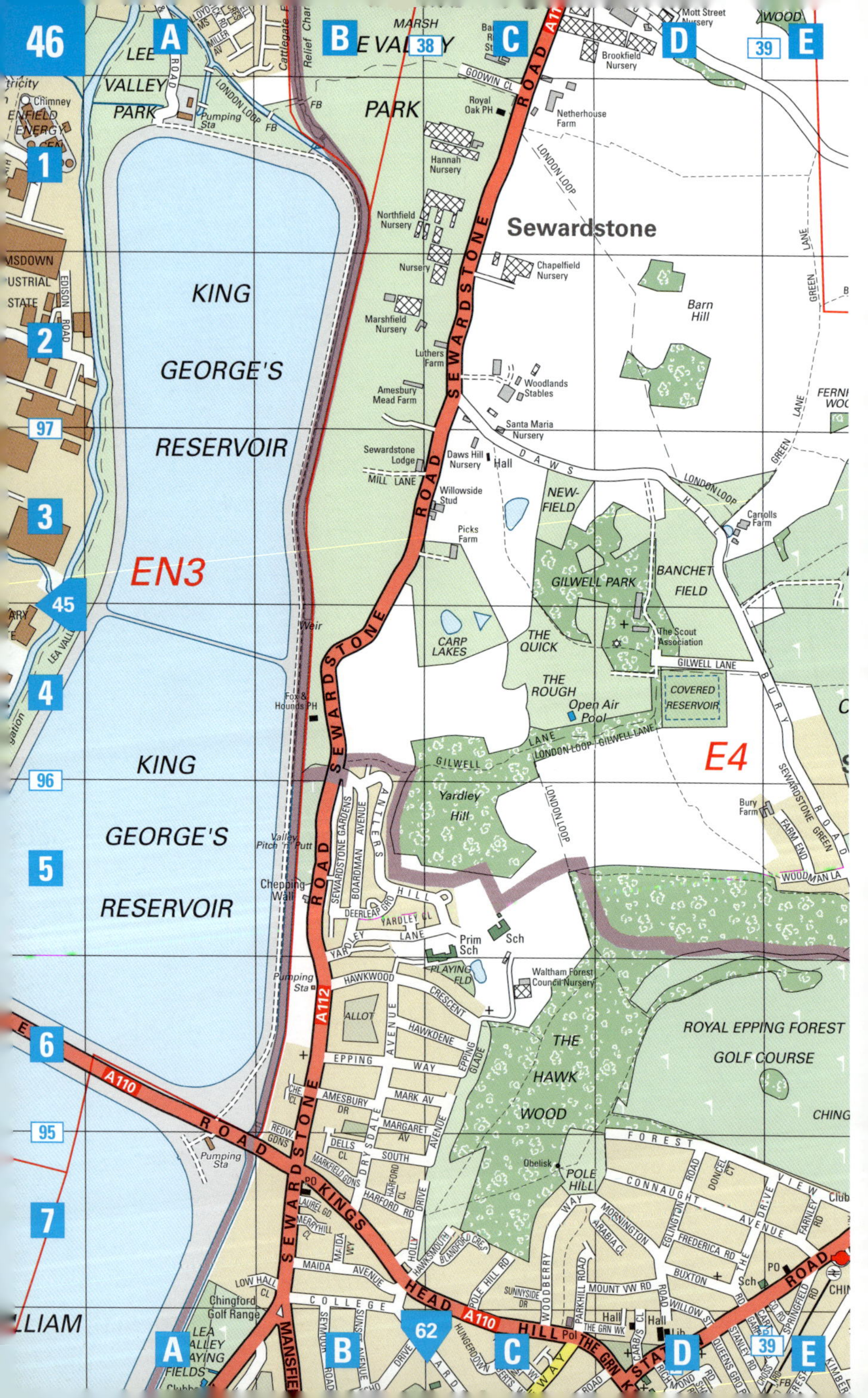
A
B
C
D
E
1
2
3
4
5
6
7
38
39
97
96
95
45
62
LEE VALLEY PARK
MARSH
PARK
Chimney
ENFIELD ENERGY
Pumping Sta
FB
LONDON LOOP
ROAD
Relief Chan
Cattlegate
GODWIN CL
Royal Oak PH
Mott Street Nursery
Brookfield Nursery
Netherhouse Farm
Hannah Nursery
Northfield Nursery
Nursery
Marshfield Nursery
Luthers Farm
Amesbury Mead Farm
Sewardstone Lodge
MILL LANE
Sewardstone
Chapelfield Nursery
Barn Hill
Woodlands Stables
Santa Maria Nursery
Daws Hill Nursery
Hall
DAWS HILL
Willowside Stud
Picks Farm
NEW-FIELD
Carolls Farm
GREEN LANE
BANCHET FIELD
GILWELL PARK
The Scout Association
GILWELL LANE
CARP LAKES
THE QUICK
THE ROUGH
Open Air Pool
COVERED RESERVOIR
E4
EN3
KING GEORGE'S RESERVOIR
KING GEORGE'S RESERVOIR
EDISON ROAD
Weir
LEA VALLEY
Fox & Hounds PH
SEWARDSTONE ROAD
A112
Yardley Hill
LONDON LOOP
Bury Farm
SEWARDSTONE GREEN
FARM END
BURY ROAD
WOODMAN LA
Valley Pitch 'n' Putt
Chepping Wall
SEWARDSTONE GARDENS
BOARDMAN AVENUE
ANTLERS HILL
DEERLEAP GRO
YARDLEY CL
YARDLEY LANE
Prim Sch
Sch
PLAYING FLD
Waltham Forest Council Nursery
Pumping Sta
HAWKWOOD CRESCENT
ALLOT
HAWKDENE
EPPING WAY
EPPING GLADE
THE HAWK WOOD
ROYAL EPPING FOREST GOLF COURSE
CHING
AMESBURY DR
MARK AV
MARGARET AV
DELLS CL
SOUTH
DRYSDALE AVENUE
MARKFIELD GDNS
HARFORD CL
HARFORD RD
HOLLY DRIVE
REDW GDNS
A110
ROAD
KINGS HEAD HILL
Pumping Sta
PO
LAUREL GD
MERRYHILL CL
MAIDA AVENUE
MAIDA WY
HAWKSMOUTH
BLANDFORD CRES
POLE HILL RD
Obelisk
POLE HILL
FOREST VIEW
CONNAUGHT AVENUE
DONCEL CT
EGLINGTON RD
MORNINGTON RD
ARABIA CL
FREDERICA RD
FARNLEY RD
BUXTON RD
THE DRIVE
Club
PO
Sch
SUNNYSIDE DR
WOODBERRY WAY
PARKHILL ROAD
MOUNT VW RD
WILLOW ST
Hall
Lib
THE GRN WK
CARBIS CL
THE GRN
STANLEY RD
SPRINGFIELD RD
LOW HALL CL
Chingford Golf Range
LEA VALLEY PLAYING FIELDS
COLLEGE
SEYMOUR ROAD
SUNSET AVENUE
MANSFIELD
HUNGERDOWN
KINGS HEAD HILL
STATION ROAD
RICHMOND RD
QUEENS GRO
LLIAM

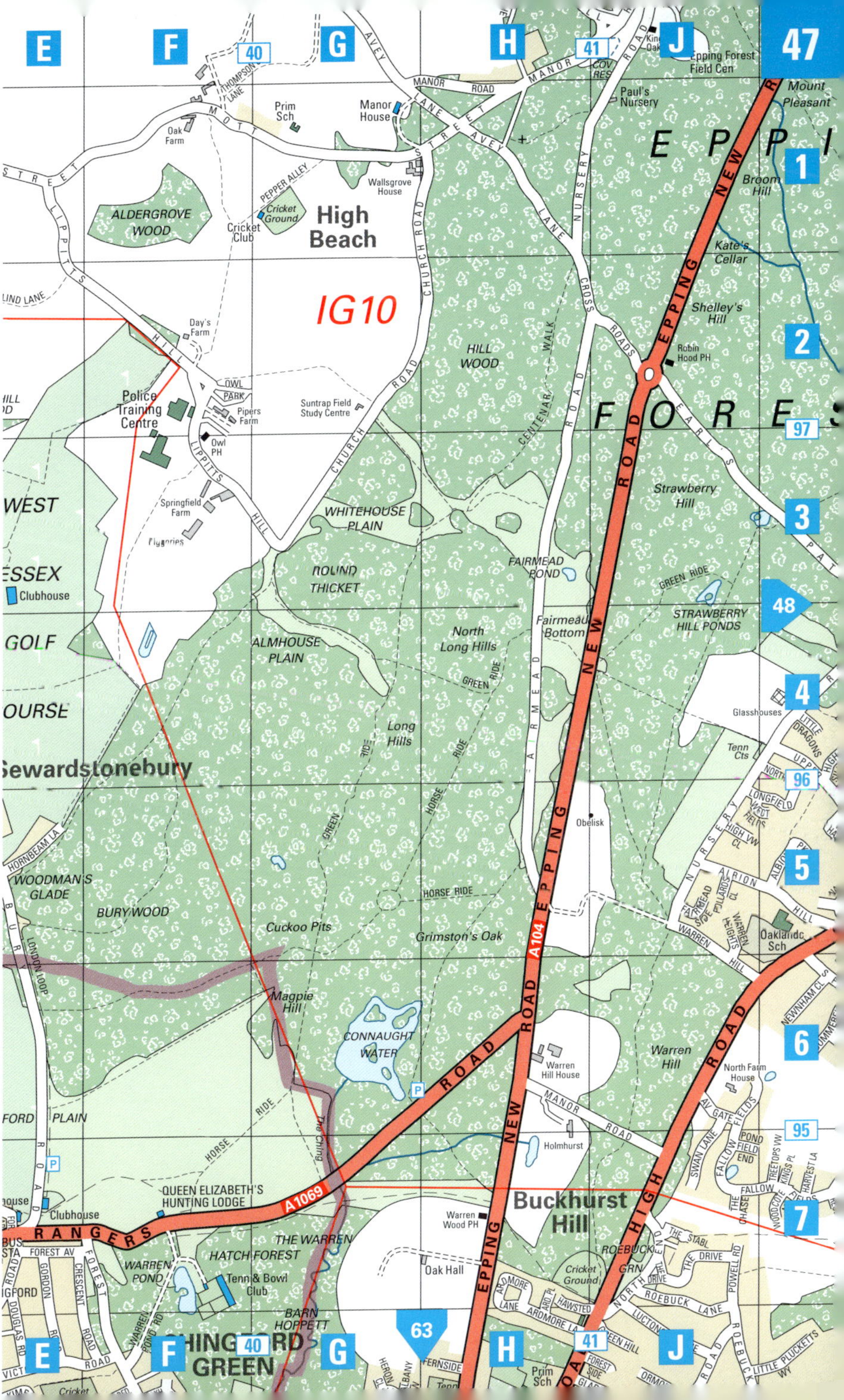
E
F
G
H
J
40
41
Epping Forest Field Cen
Mount Pleasant
1
2
3
4
5
6
7
48
97
96
95
63
THOMPSON LANE
MOTT STREET
Oak Farm
Prim Sch
Manor House
MANOR ROAD
MANOR LANE
AVEY LANE
COV RES
Paul's Nursery
NURSERY LANE
EPPING FOREST
Broom Hill
Kate's Cellar
Shelley's Hill
Robin Hood PH
Wallsgrove House
PEPPER ALLEY
Cricket Ground
Cricket Club
ALDERGROVE WOOD
High Beach
LIPPITTS HILL
CHURCH ROAD
CROSS ROADS
LIND LANE
IG10
Day's Farm
HILL WOOD
CENTENARY WALK
OWL PARK
Pipers Farm
Police Training Centre
Owl PH
Suntrap Field Study Centre
EARL'S PATH
Strawberry Hill
Springfield Farm
WHITEHOUSE PLAIN
FAIRMEAD POND
FAIRMEAD ROAD
WEST ESSEX GOLF COURSE
Clubhouse
ROUND THICKET
GREEN RIDE
STRAWBERRY HILL PONDS
Fairmead Bottom
North Long Hills
ALMHOUSE PLAIN
EPPING NEW ROAD
Glasshouses
LITTLE DRAGONS
Tenn Cts
Long Hills
HORSE RIDE
Sewardstonebury
Obelisk
LONGFIELD
HIGH VW CL
HORNBEAM LA
WOODMAN'S GLADE
ALBION HILL
WARREN HILL
BURY WOOD
Oaklands Sch
Cuckoo Pits
Grimston's Oak
A104
LONDON LOOP
Magpie Hill
NEWNHAM CL
CONNAUGHT WATER
Warren Hill House
Warren Hill
North Farm House
HIGH ROAD
CHINGFORD PLAIN
The Ching
MANOR ROAD
Holmhurst
SWAN LANE
FALLOW FIELDS
POND FIELD END
QUEEN ELIZABETH'S HUNTING LODGE
A1069
Buckhurst Hill
THE CHASE
RANGERS ROAD
THE WARREN
Warren Wood PH
HATCH FOREST
WARREN POND
Tenn & Bowl Club
Oak Hall
ARDMORE LANE
HAWSTED
Cricket Ground
ROEBUCK GRN
THE DRIVE
ROEBUCK LANE
POWELL RD
FOREST AV
GORDON RD
CRESCENT ROAD
DOUGLAS RD
BARN HOPPETT
CHINGFORD GREEN
QUEENS HILL
LITTLE PLUCKETTS WY
FERNSIDE
Prim Sch

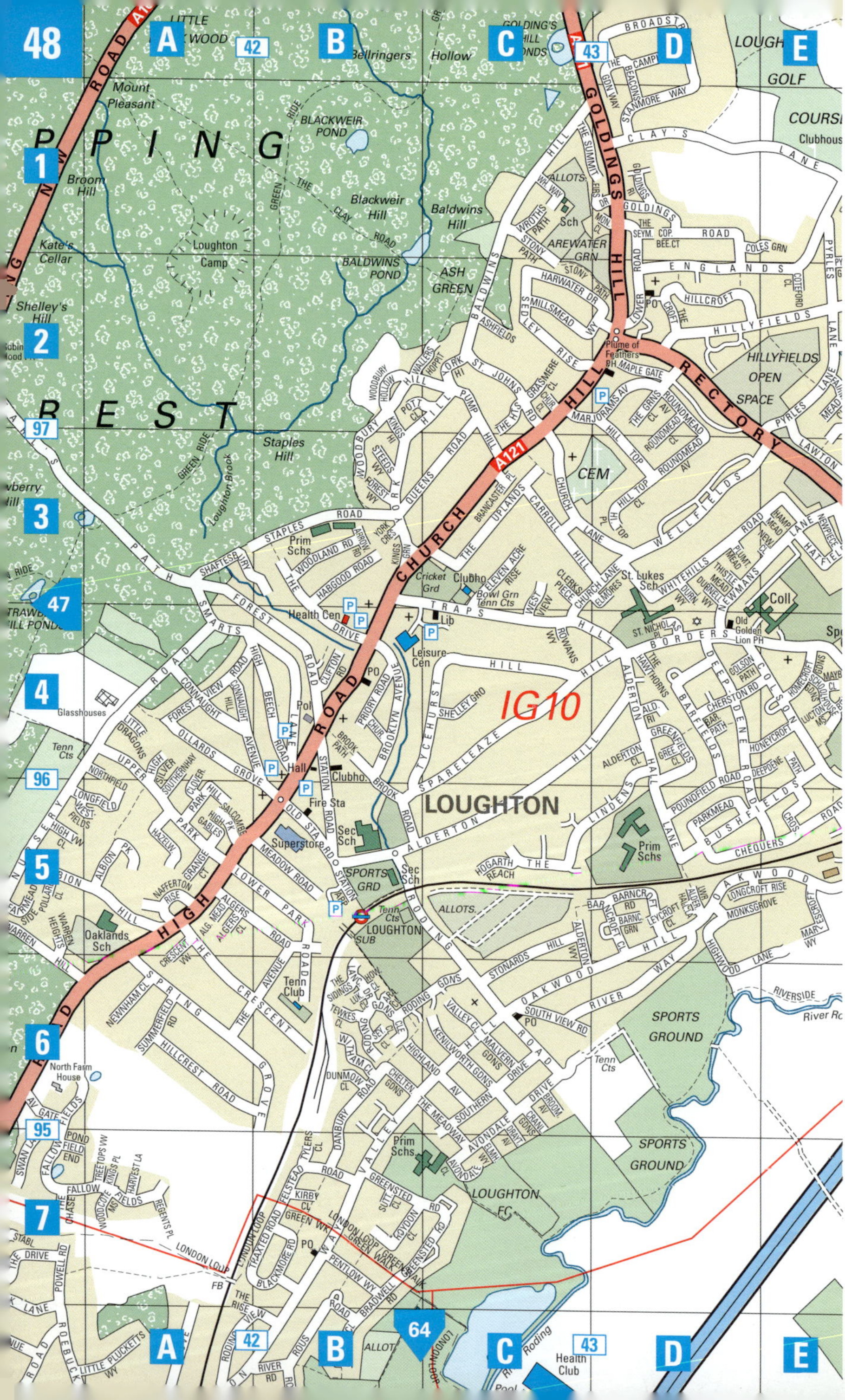
A
B
C
D
E
1
2
3
4
5
6
7
42
43
97
96
95
47
64
Little Wood
Bellringers
Hollow
Golding's Hill Ponds
Loughton Golf Course
Clubhouse
Mount Pleasant
Epping Forest
Broom Hill
Blackweir Pond
Blackweir Hill
Baldwins Hill
Kate's Cellar
Loughton Camp
Baldwins Pond
Ash Green
Shelley's Hill
Staples Hill
Loughton Brook
Green Ride
Goldings Hill
Clay's Lane
Englands Lane
Hillyfields
Hillyfields Open Space
Rectory Lane
Plume of Feathers PH
Church Hill
A121
CEM
Staples Road
Prim Schs
Woodland Rd
Habgood Road
Cricket Grd
Clubho
Bowl Grn
Tenn Cts
Traps Hill
Health Cen
Lib
Leisure Cen
St. Lukes Sch
Coll
Old Golden Lion PH
Borders Lane
IG10
Glasshouses
Tenn Cts
Forest Road
Smarts Road
High Road
Pol
Hall
Clubho
Fire Sta
Superstore
Sec Sch
LOUGHTON
Alderton Hill
Sports Grd
Sec Sch
Loughton
Allots
Oakwood Hill
Oaklands Sch
Tenn Club
Riverside
River Rd
Sports Ground
Tenn Cts
North Farm House
Prim Schs
Loughton FC
Sports Ground
London Loop
FB
Roding
Health Club
Pool

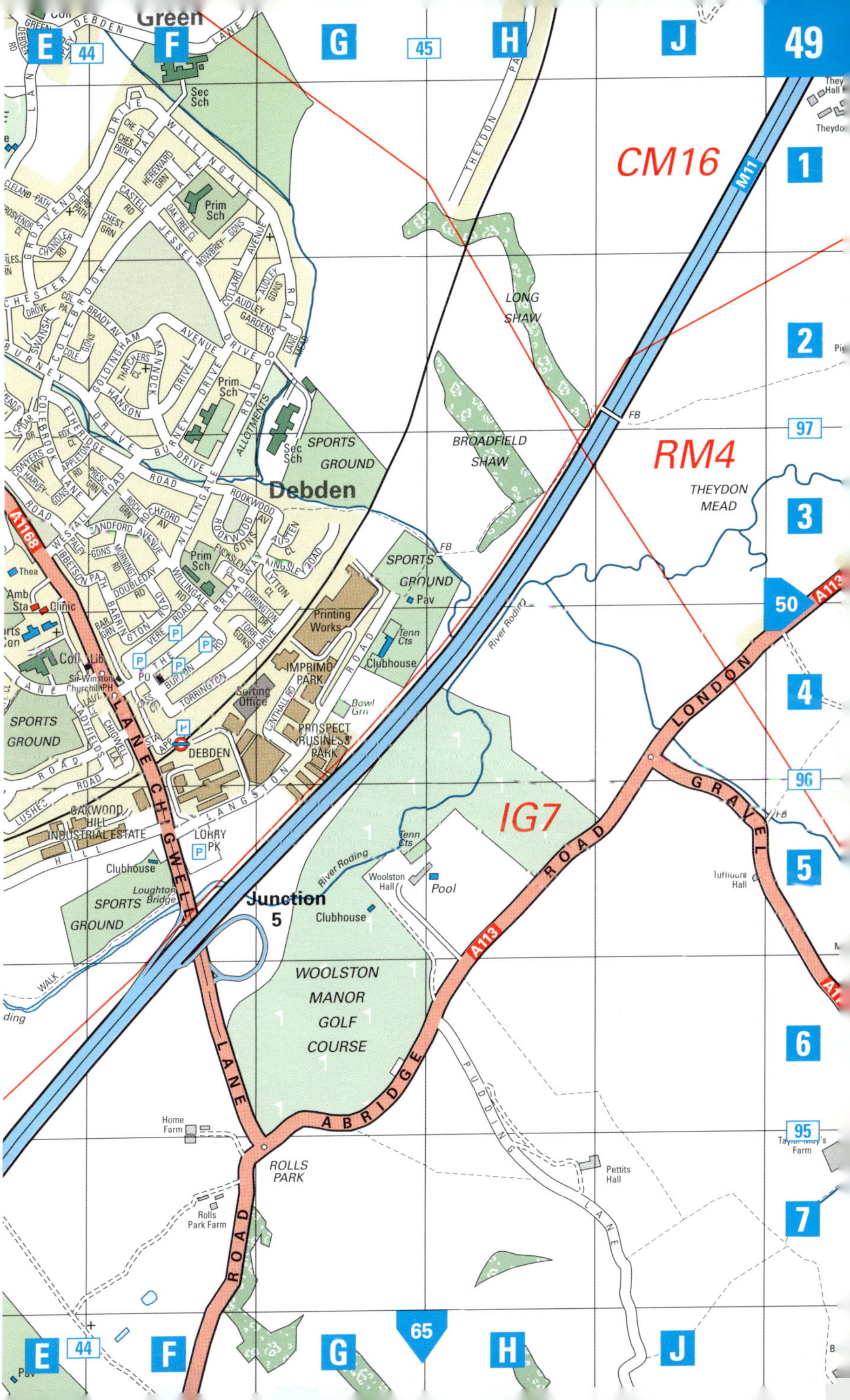

Debden
Green
CM16
RM4
IG7
M11
A1168
A113
50
65
44
45
97
96
95
E
F
G
H
J
1
2
3
4
5
6
7
Sec Sch
Prim Sch
SPORTS GROUND
THEYDON
LONG SHAW
BROADFIELD SHAW
THEYDON MEAD
FB
River Roding
Printing Works
IMPRIMO PARK
Sorting Office
PROSPECT BUSINESS PARK
Tenn Cts
Clubhouse
Pav
Bowl Grn
DEBDEN
OAKWOOD HILL INDUSTRIAL ESTATE
LORRY PK
Loughton Bridge
Junction 5
Woolston Hall
Pool
WOOLSTON MANOR GOLF COURSE
ABRIDGE ROAD
LONDON ROAD
GRAVEL LANE
PUDDING LANE
CHIGWELL LANE
ROLLS PARK
Rolls Park Farm
Home Farm
Pettits Hall
Thea
Amb Sta
Clinic
Coll
Lib
Sir Winston Churchill PH
PO
WILLINGALE ROAD
BURNEY DRIVE
ROCHFORD AV
ROOKWOOD AV
TORRINGTON DR
LANGSTON ROAD
OAKWOOD HILL
HANSON DRIVE
ETHERIDGE ROAD
COLEBROOK LANE
GROSVENOR DRIVE
AUDLEY GARDENS
CHESTER ROAD

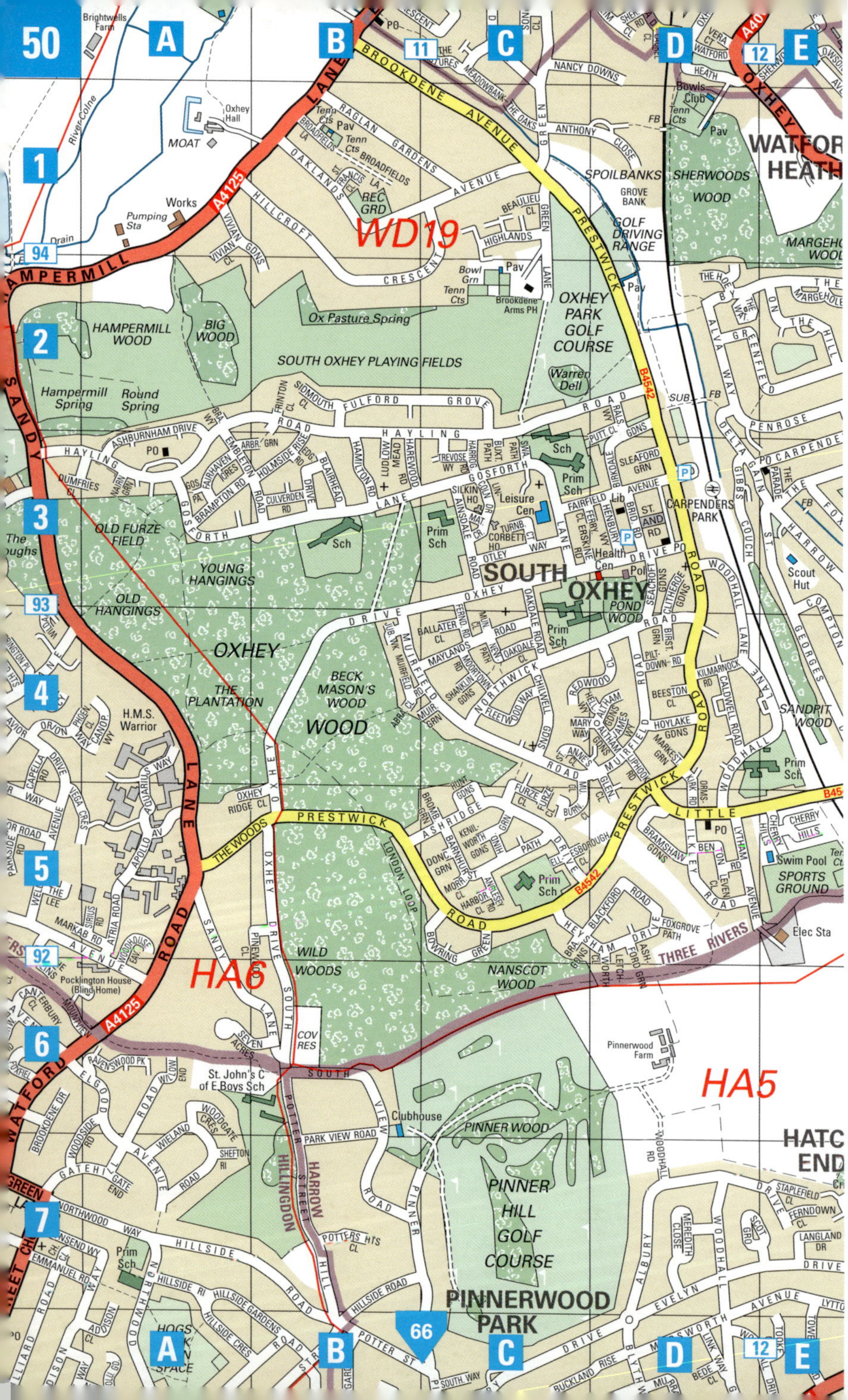
A
B
C
D
E
1
2
3
4
5
6
7
11
12
94
93
92
66
WD19
HA6
HA5
Brightwells Farm
River Colne
Oxhey Hall
MOAT
Works
Pumping Sta
Drain
HAMPERMILL
A4125
LANE
BROOKDENE AVENUE
RAGLAN GARDENS
BROADFIELDS
OAKLANDS
ST. FRANCIS LA
REC GRD
HILLCROFT CRESCENT
VIVIAN GDNS
AVENUE
BEAULIEU CL
HIGHLANDS
Bowl Grn
Tenn Cts
Pav
Brookdene Arms PH
NANCY DOWNS
THE OAKS
MEADOWBANK
ANTHONY CLOSE
SPOILBANKS
GROVE BANK
GOLF DRIVING RANGE
SHERWOODS WOOD
WATFORD HEATH
Bowls Club
Tenn Cts
MARGEHOLE WOOD
PRESTWICK
GREEN LANE
OXHEY PARK GOLF COURSE
Warren Dell
B4542
HAMPERMILL WOOD
BIG WOOD
Ox Pasture Spring
SOUTH OXHEY PLAYING FIELDS
Hampermill Spring
Round Spring
SANDY
SIDMOUTH CL
FULFORD GROVE
ROAD
HAYLING ROAD
ASHBURNHAM DRIVE
FRINTON CL
HAYLING
PO
DUMFRIES CL
NAIRN GRN
FAIRHAVEN CRES
EMBLETON RD
HOLMSIDE RISE
BLAIRHEAD DRIVE
HAMILTON RD
LUDLOW MEAD
HAREWOOD RD
TREVOSE WY
GOSFORTH LANE
Sch
Prim Sch
SLEAFORD GRN
BIRKDALE
CARPENDERS PARK
OLD FURZE FIELD
YOUNG HANGINGS
OLD HANGINGS
GOSFORTH
CULVERDEN RD
Leisure Cen
FAIRFIELD AVENUE
Lib
ST. ANDREW RD
Health Cen
SOUTH OXHEY
POND WOOD
OXHEY DRIVE
BALLATER CL
MAYLANDS RD
OAKDALE RD
SEACROFT GDNS
CLITHEROE GDNS
OXHEY
THE PLANTATION
BECK MASON'S WOOD
WOOD
MUIRFIELD RD
NORTHWICK
REDWOOD
FLEETWOOD WAY
CHILWELL GDNS
BEESTON CL
HOYLAKE GDNS
KILMARNOCK RD
CALDWELL ROAD
WOODHALL LANE
SANDPIT WOOD
Prim Sch
H.M.S. Warrior
ORION WAY
CAPELLA RD
VEGA CRES
AQUARIUS WAY
APOLLO AV
OXHEY RIDGE CL
PRESTWICK
THE WOODS
ASHRIDGE
LONDON LOOP
LITTLE
OXHEY LANE
BRAMSHAW GDNS
ILKLEY RD
LYTHAM AVENUE
CHERRY HILLS
Swim Pool
SPORTS GROUND
Elec Sta
THREE RIVERS
FOXGROVE PATH
HEYSHAM DRIVE
BLACKFORD ROAD
BOWRING GREEN
MARKAB RD
SIRIUS RD
ATRIA ROAD
Pocklington House (Blind Home)
SANDY LANE
PINEWOOD CL
WILD WOODS
NANSCOT WOOD
COV RES
SEVEN ACRES
SOUTH
St. John's C of E Boys Sch
WATFORD ROAD
RAVENSWOOD PK
ELGOOD AV
BROOKDENE DR
WOODGATE CRES
WIELAND ROAD
GATEHILL
GATE END
SHEFTON RI
POTTER STREET
HARROW
HILLINGDON
PARK VIEW ROAD
Clubhouse
PINNER WOOD
PINNER HILL GOLF COURSE
VIEW
Pinnerwood Farm
HATCH END
WOODHALL RD
MEREDITH CLOSE
STAPLEFIELD CL
FERNDOWN CL
LANGLAND DR
DRIVE
NORTHWOOD WAY
HILLSIDE
Prim Sch
EMMANUEL RD
HILLSIDE RI
HILLSIDE GARDENS
HILLSIDE CRES
HILLSIDE ROAD
POTTERS HTS CL
PINNERWOOD PARK
POTTER ST
SOUTH WAY
BUCKLAND RISE
EVELYN AVENUE
ALBURY DRIVE
WOODHALL
HOGS BACK OPEN SPACE
ADDISON

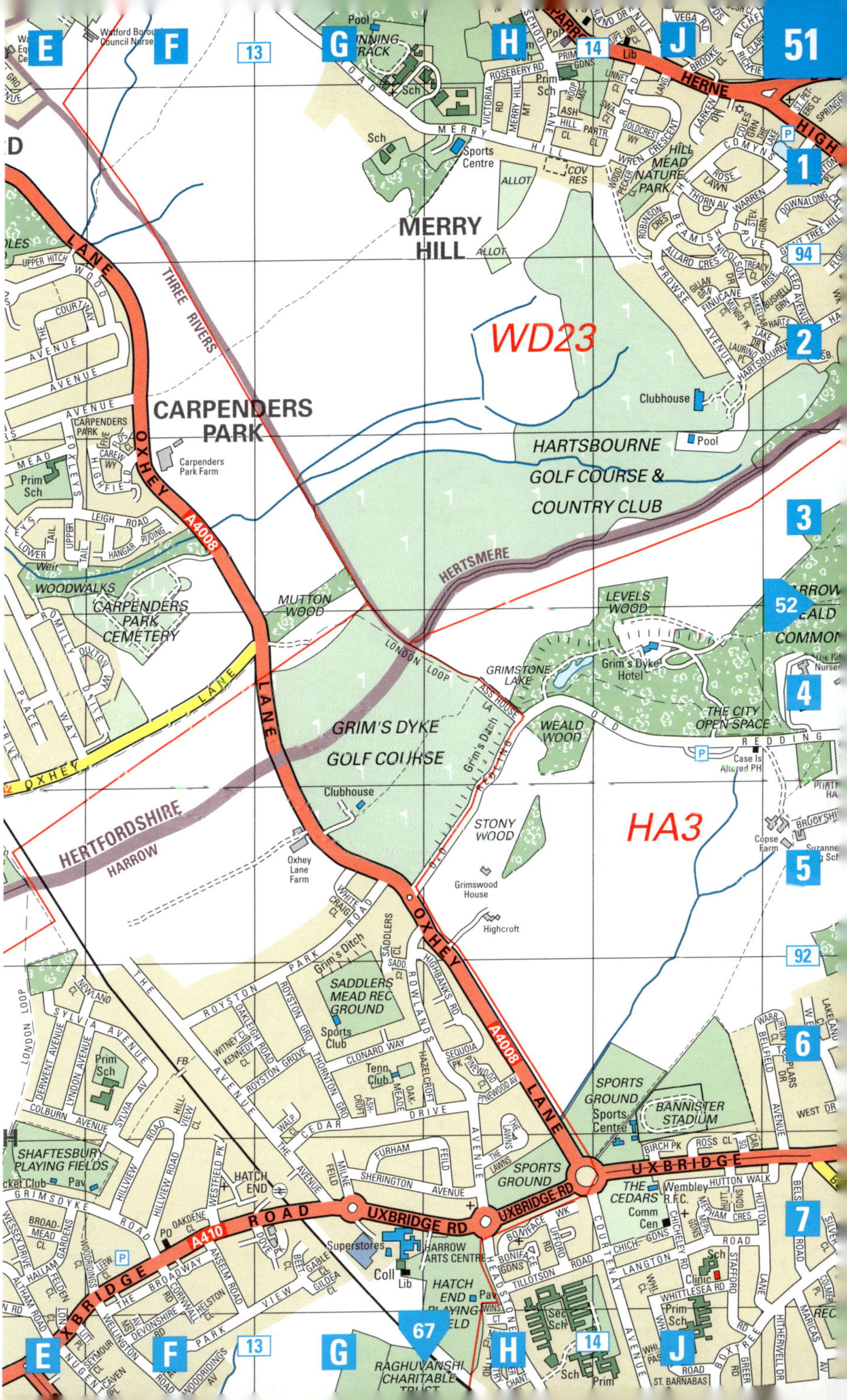
E
F
G
H
J
13
14
1
2
3
4
5
6
7
52
67
94
92
MERRY HILL
WD23
HA3
CARPENDERS PARK
Carpenders Park Farm
HARTSBOURNE GOLF COURSE & COUNTRY CLUB
Clubhouse
Pool
Sports Centre
ALLOT
COV RES
HILL MEAD NATURE PARK
HERTSMERE
THREE RIVERS
HERTFORDSHIRE
HARROW
MUTTON WOOD
LEVELS WOOD
GRIMSTONE LAKE
Grim's Dyke Hotel
THE CITY OPEN SPACE
WEALD WOOD
GRIM'S DYKE GOLF COURSE
Grim's Ditch
STONY WOOD
Grimswood House
Highcroft
Oxhey Lane Farm
Copse Farm
Case Is Altered PH
WOODWALKS
CARPENDERS PARK CEMETERY
Weir
Prim Sch
SADDLERS MEAD REC GROUND
Sports Club
Tenn Club
SPORTS GROUND
BANNISTER STADIUM
SHAFTESBURY PLAYING FIELDS
Pav
HATCH END
Superstores
HARROW ARTS CENTRE
Coll
Lib
HATCH END PLAYING FIELD
THE CEDARS Comm Cen
Wembley R.F.C.
Sec Sch
Clinic
RAGHUVANSHI CHARITABLE TRUST
OXHEY LANE
A4008
UXBRIDGE ROAD
A410
UXBRIDGE RD
MERRY HILL ROAD
HERNE RD
LONDON LOOP
OLD REDDING
Watford Borough Council Nursery

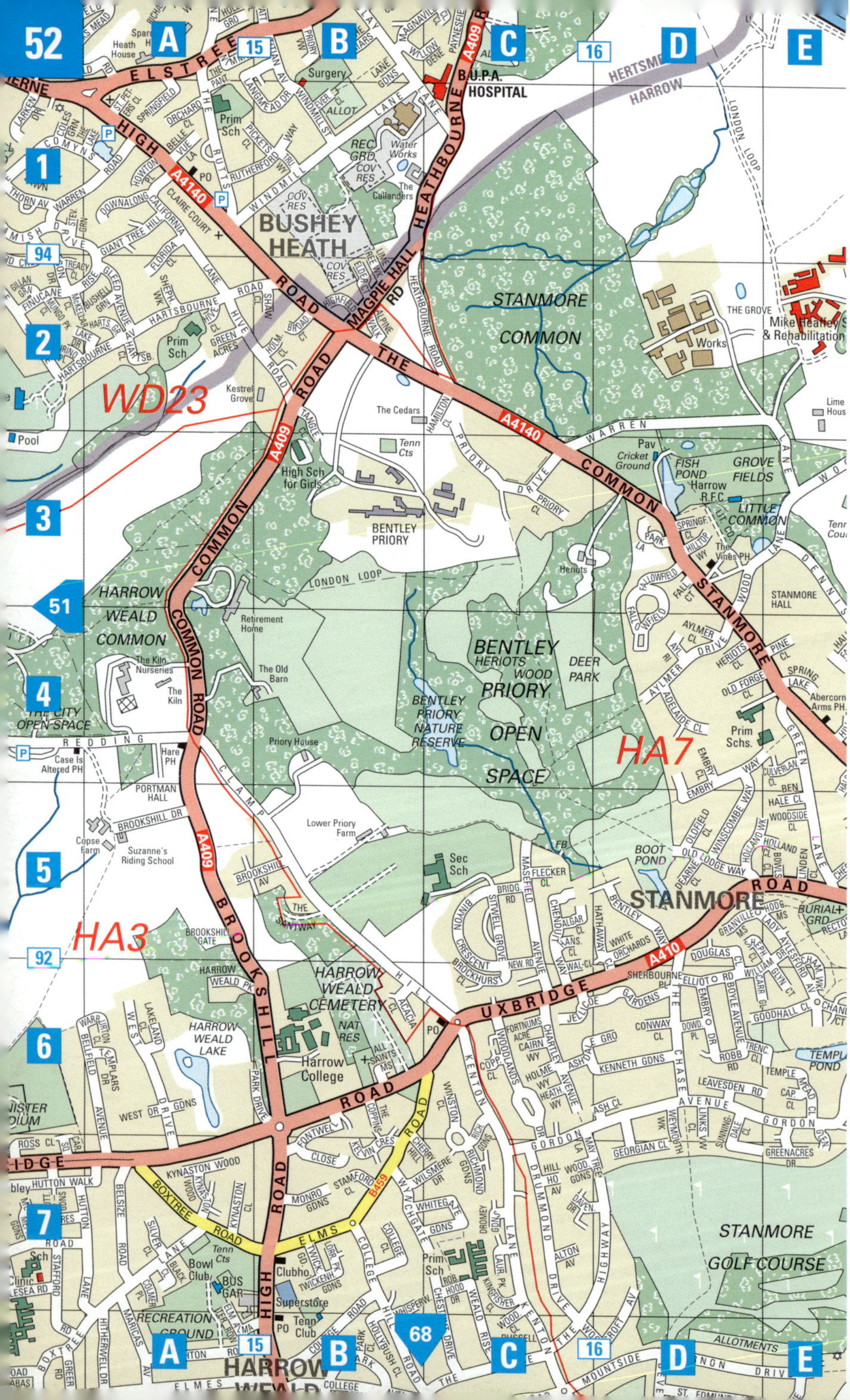
A
B
C
D
E
1
2
3
4
5
6
7
15
16
94
51
92
68
ELSTREE
HIGH ROAD
Heath House
Surgery
B.U.P.A. HOSPITAL
HERTSMERE
HARROW
HEATHBOURNE
A409
A4140
COMYNS ROAD
THORN AV
WARREN DRIVE
DOWNALONG
CALIFORNIA
CLAIRE COURT
GIANT TREE HILL
FLORIDA CL
HARTSBOURNE
Prim Sch
PO
RUTHERFORD WAY
WINDMILL
REC GRD
COV RES
Water Works
The Callanders
BUSHEY HEATH
MAGPIE HALL RD
STANMORE COMMON
THE GROVE
Works
Mike Heaffey S & Rehabilitation
WD23
Kestrel Grove
Pool
The Cedars
Tenn Cts
HAMILTON CL
PRIORY DRIVE
WARREN
LANE
Pav
Cricket Ground
FISH POND
GROVE FIELDS
Harrow R.F.C.
LITTLE COMMON
High Sch for Girls
BENTLEY PRIORY
COMMON ROAD
LONDON LOOP
THE COMMON
STANMORE HILL
Heriots
The Vines PH
STANMORE HALL
HARROW WEALD COMMON
Retirement Home
The Old Barn
The Kiln Nurseries
The Kiln
THE CITY OPEN SPACE
BENTLEY PRIORY OPEN SPACE
HERIOTS WOOD
DEER PARK
BENTLEY PRIORY NATURE RESERVE
HA7
ALYMER DRIVE
OLD FORGE CL
SPRING LAKE
Abercorn Arms PH
Prim Schs.
REDDING
Case Is Altered PH
Hare PH
Priory House
CLAMP HILL
PORTMAN HALL
BROOKSHILL DR
Copse Farm
Suzanne's Riding School
Lower Priory Farm
FB
BOOT POND
EMBRY WAY
WINSCOMBE WAY
OLD LODGE WAY
STANMORE
BURIAL GRD
HA3
BROOKSHILL
BROOKSHILL GATE
THE GATEWAY
Sec Sch
FLECKER CL
NORMAN CRESCENT
SITWELL GROVE
BRIDG. RD
MASEFIELD AVENUE
CHENDUIT WAY
ALGAR CL
HATHAWAY CL
BENTLEY WAY
WHITE ORCHARDS
BROCKHURST CL
NEW RD
HARROW WEALD PK
HARROW WEALD CEMETERY
UXBRIDGE ROAD
A410
SHERBOURNE PL
ELLIOTT RD
DOUGLAS
JELLICOE GARDENS
BOYLE AVENUE
GOODHALL CL
HARROW WEALD LAKE
LAKELAND CL
WEST DRIVE
TEMPLARS DR
BELLFIELD AVENUE
Harrow College
NAT RES
ALL SAINTS
PO
KENTON LANE
WOODLANDS
CAIRN WY
CONWAY CL
ROBB RD
KENNETH GDNS
TEMPLE POND
LEAVESDEN RD
CHASE AVENUE
GORDON AVENUE
ASH CL
GEORGIAN CL
GREENACRES DR
WEST DR GDNS
ROSS CL
FONTWELL CLOSE
KELVIN CRES
WINSTON
CHERRY HILL
COPPINGS
STANMORE GOLF COURSE
KYNASTON WOOD
BOXTREE ROAD
MONRO GDNS
STAMFORD CL
B459
ELMS ROAD
WILSMERE DR
WHITEGATE GDNS
COLLEGE HILL
HUTTON WALK
HILL HO AV
ALTON AV
HIGHWAY
DRUMMOND DRIVE
Tenn Cts
Bowl Club
BUS GAR
Clubho
Superstore
Prim Sch
Clinic
Sch
STAFFORD ROAD
PO
Tenn Club
RECREATION GROUND
WHISPERW
KINGSHER
WOODCROFT AV
MOUNTSIDE
ALLOTMENTS
BELSIZE ROAD
HITHERWELL DR
HARROW WEALD
ELMES
COLLEGE

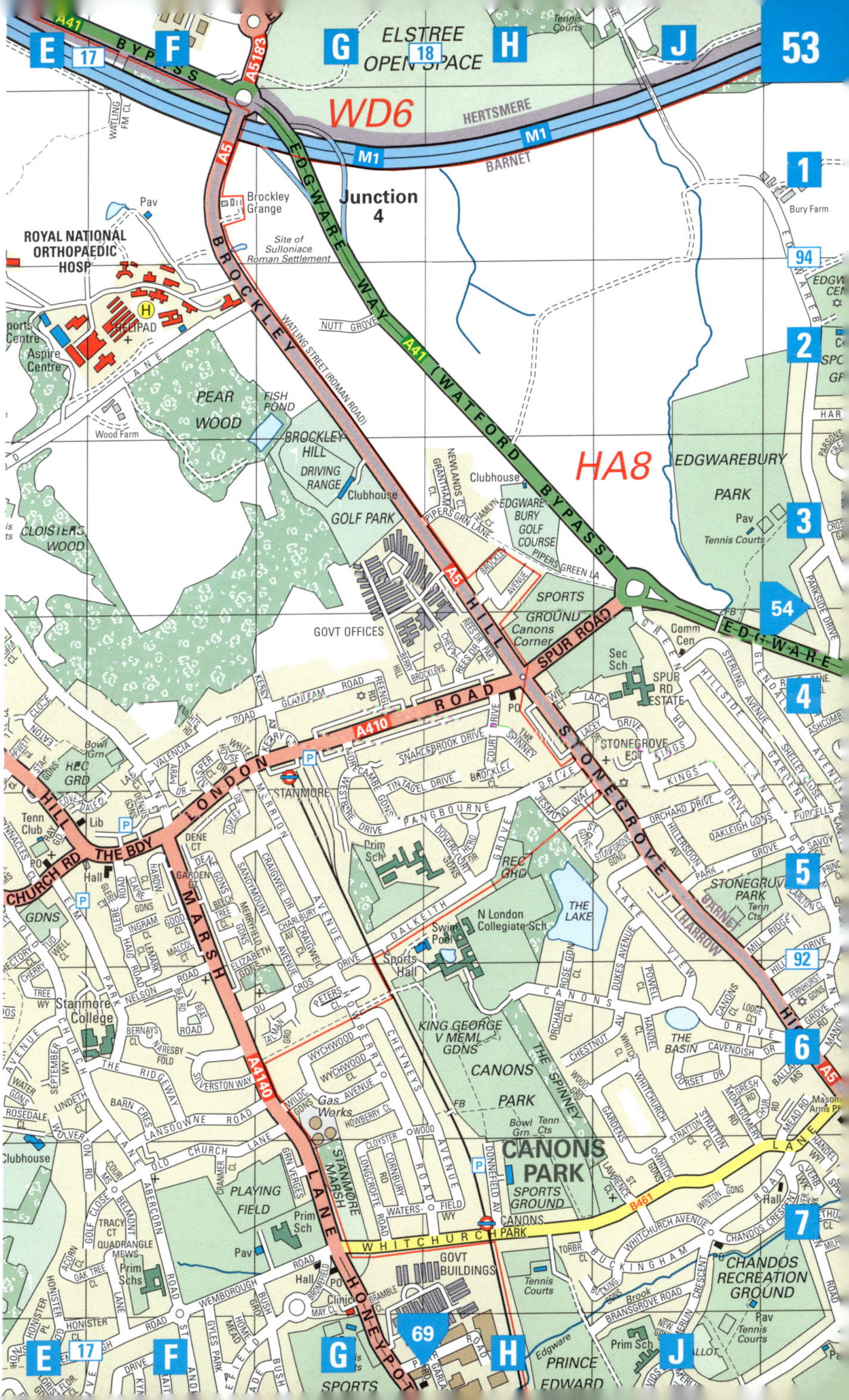
E
F
G
H
J
17
18
ELSTREE OPEN SPACE
WD6
HERTSMERE
BARNET
M1
A41
A5183
A5
BYPASS
Junction 4
Brockley Grange
Site of Sulloniace Roman Settlement
ROYAL NATIONAL ORTHOPAEDIC HOSP
HELIPAD
Aspire Centre
Wood Farm
PEAR WOOD
FISH POND
BROCKLEY HILL
DRIVING RANGE
Clubhouse
GOLF PARK
CLOISTERS WOOD
EDGWARE WAY
WATLING STREET (ROMAN ROAD)
NUTT GROVE
(WATFORD BYPASS)
HA8
EDGWAREBURY PARK
EDGWAREBURY GOLF COURSE
PIPERS GREEN LA
PIPERS GRN LANE
Tennis Courts
Pav
Bury Farm
94
1
2
3
4
5
6
7
54
92
69
SPORTS GROUND Canons Corner
SPUR ROAD
GOVT OFFICES
Comm Cen
Sec Sch
SPUR RD ESTATE
STONEGROVE EST
BROCKLEY HILL
A410
LONDON ROAD
STANMORE
HILL
THE BDY
CHURCH RD
HEC GRD
Tenn Club
Lib
Hall
GDNS
MARSH
A4140
SNARESBROOK DRIVE
TINTAGEL DRIVE
PANGBOURNE DRIVE
Prim Sch
REC GRD
THE LAKE
N London Collegiate Sch
Swim Pool
Sports Hall
DALKEITH
STONEGROVE
STONEGROVE PARK
HARROW
KING GEORGE V MEML GDNS
CANONS PARK
THE SPINNEY
THE BASIN
CANONS DRIVE
CAVENDISH DR
Stanmore College
THE RIDGEWAY
Gas Works
STANMORE MARSH
LANSDOWNE ROAD
CHURCH LANE
PLAYING FIELD
Prim Sch
CANONS PARK SPORTS GROUND
B461
WHITCHURCH LANE
CANONS PARK
GOVT BUILDINGS
Tennis Courts
CHANDOS RECREATION GROUND
BUCKINGHAM
BRANSGROVE ROAD
HONEYPOT LANE
Clinic
Prim Schs
QUADRANGLE MEWS
WEMBOROUGH ROAD
Clubhouse
Edgware Brook
PRINCE EDWARD
SPORTS

A
B
C
D
E
38
THISTLE WOOD
21
1
2
3
4
5
6
7
94
92
53
70
Bury Farm
Depot
London Gateway Services
CLUMP OF TREES WOOD
TARGET WOOD
MILL HILL GOLF COURSE
NUT WOOD
HEMMINGS WOOD
STONEY WOOD LAKE
STONEY WOOD
Days Inn
Clubhouse
EDGWAREBURY CEMETERY
REC GRD
SPORTS GRD
EDGWAREBURY PARK
Tennis Courts
EDGWARE WAY
WATFORD BY-PASS
A41
A1
M1
NORTHWAY CIRCUS
Apex Corner
CONVENT
A5100
HALE LANE
SELVAGE LANE
MARSH LANE
Jolly Badger PH
EDGWARE
HA8
ALLOTMENTS
BUS STA
Broadwalk Shopping Centre
BUS DEPOT
STATION ROAD
HIGH STREET
A5
A5109
DEANS LANE
DEANSBROOK ROAD
Deans Brook
Edgware Brook
Premier Lodge
Wealdstone FC
Masons Arms PH
CHANDOS RECREATION GROUND
EDGWARE COMMUNITY HOSPITAL
TA Cen
SPORTS GROUND
WATLING PARK
LYNDHURST PARK
BURNT OAK
BURNT STREET
Silk Stream
GOLD LANE
WATLING AVENUE

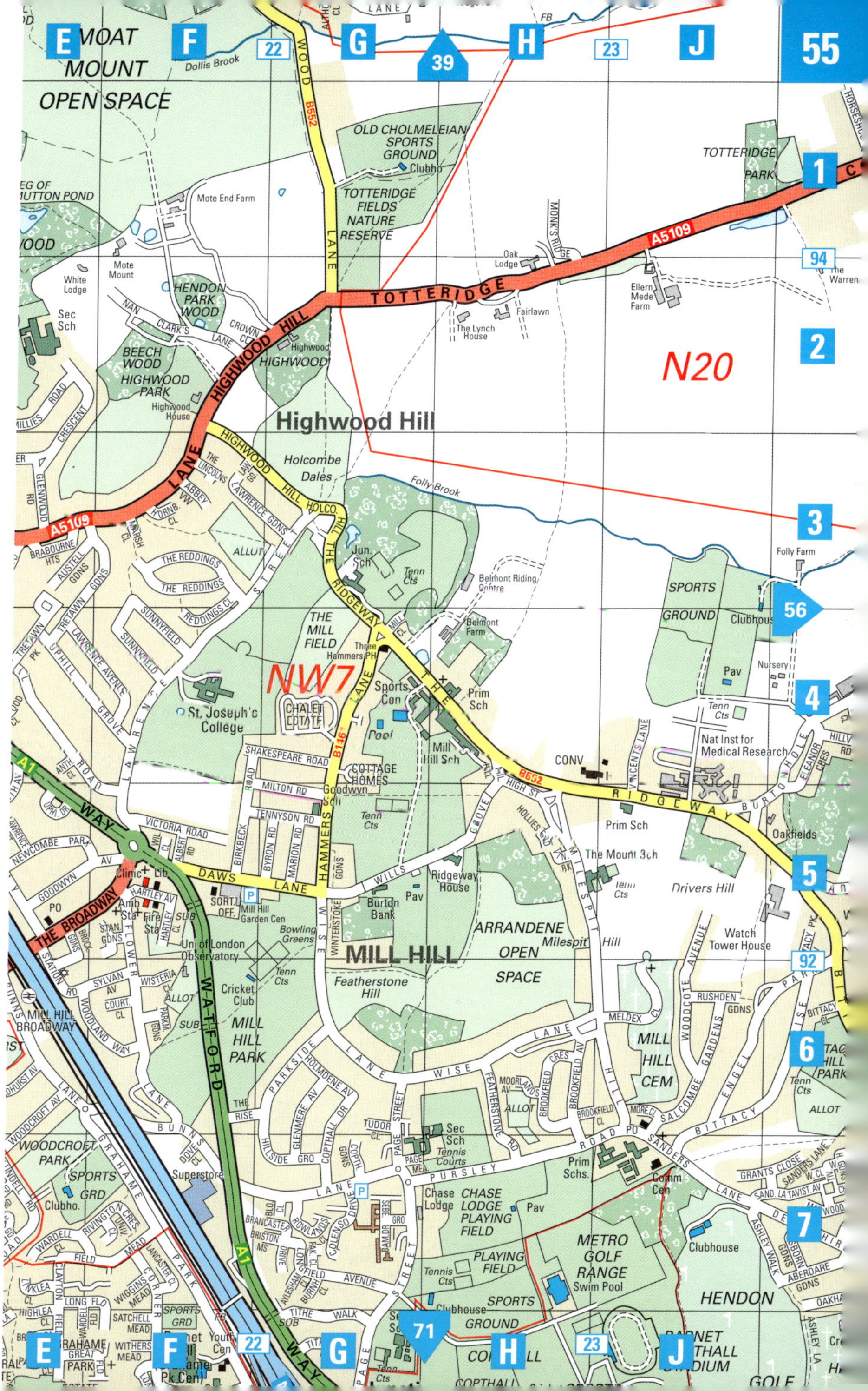
E
F
G
H
J
22
23
39
MOAT MOUNT OPEN SPACE
Dollis Brook
WOOD
B552
LANE
OLD CHOLMELEIAN SPORTS GROUND
Clubho
TOTTERIDGE FIELDS NATURE RESERVE
Mote End Farm
Mote Mount
White Lodge
Sec Sch
HENDON PARK WOOD
CLARK'S
CROWN
HIGHWOOD HILL
Highwood
HIGHWOOD
BEECH WOOD
HIGHWOOD PARK
Highwood House
TOTTERIDGE
A5109
Oak Lodge
MONK'S RIDGE
Fairlawn
The Lynch House
Ellern Mede Farm
TOTTERIDGE PARK
The Warren
94
1
2
N20
Highwood Hill
Holcombe Dales
Folly Brook
3
HOLCO.
THE RIDGEWAY
Jun. Sch
Tenn Cts
Belmont Riding Centre
Belmont Farm
THE MILL FIELD
Three Hammers PH
Folly Farm
SPORTS GROUND
Clubhouse
56
Pav
Nursery
4
NW7
St. Joseph's College
CHALET ESTATE
Sports Cen
Pool
Prim Sch
Mill Hill Sch
B116
SHAKESPEARE ROAD
MILTON RD
COTTAGE HOMES
Goodwyn Sch
TENNYSON RD
HAMMERS LANE
CONV
VINCENTS LANE
Nat Inst for Medical Research
B552
RIDGEWAY
HIGH ST
Prim Sch
The Mount Sch
Oakfields
Drivers Hill
5
A1
VICTORIA ROAD
DAWS LANE
Clinic
Lib
Amb Sta
Fire Sta
THE BROADWAY
PO
SORTG. OFF.
Mill Hill Garden Cen
Uni of London Observatory
Bowling Greens
Burton Bank
Ridgeway House
Pav
ARRANDENE OPEN SPACE
Milespit Hill
MILL HILL
Watch Tower House
92
Featherstone Hill
Cricket Club
MILL HILL PARK
WATFORD
MILL HILL BROADWAY
MILL HILL CEM
6
WISE LANE
MELDEX CL
RUSHDEN GDNS
BITTACY
Sec Sch
Tennis Courts
PURSLEY
Prim Schs.
Comm Cen
SANDERS LANE
WOODCROFT PARK
SPORTS GRD
Clubho.
Superstore
Chase Lodge
CHASE LODGE PLAYING FIELD
Pav
METRO GOLF RANGE
Swim Pool
Clubhouse
7
PLAYING FIELD
Tennis Cts
Clubhouse
SPORTS GROUND
HENDON
BARNET COPTHALL STADIUM
71
SPORTS GRD
Youth Cen
GOLF

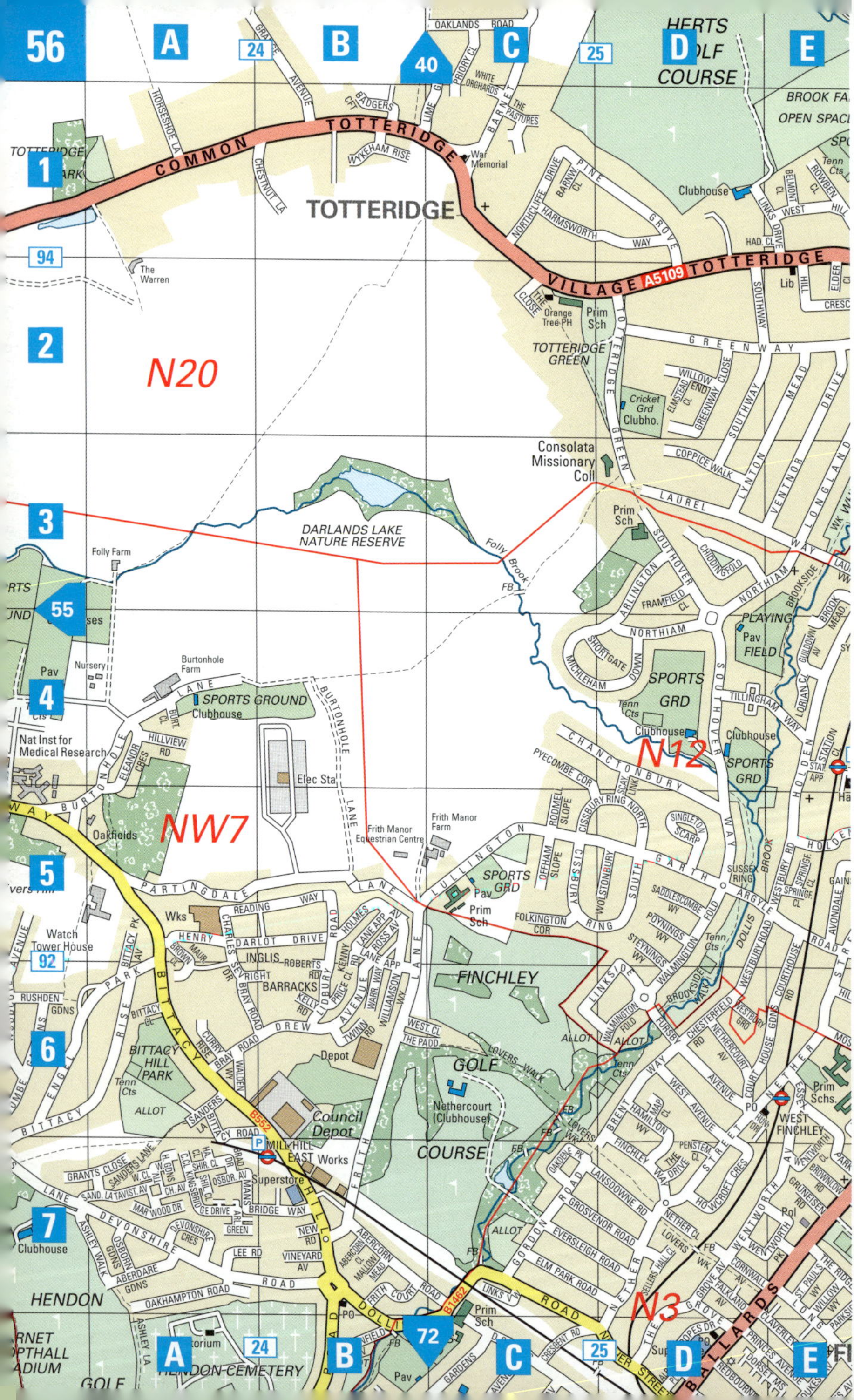
A
B
C
D
E
24
25
40
55
72
92
94
1
2
3
4
5
6
7
HERTS GOLF COURSE
BROOK FARM OPEN SPACE
TOTTERIDGE PARK
TOTTERIDGE COMMON
TOTTERIDGE
TOTTERIDGE VILLAGE
A5109
TOTTERIDGE LANE
OAKLANDS ROAD
GRANGE AVENUE
HORSESHOE LA
BADGERS CFT
LIME GR
PRIORY CL
WHITE ORCHARDS
BARNET LA
THE PASTURES
WYKEHAM RISE
CHESTNUT LA
War Memorial
The Warren
N20
NORTHCLIFFE DRIVE
BARNW CL
PINE GROVE
HARMSWORTH WAY
Clubhouse
LINKS DRIVE
BELMONT CL
ROWBEN CL
WEST HILL
HAD. CL
Tenn Cts
Lib
ELDER CL
CRESC
SOUTHWAY
THE CLOSE
Orange Tree PH
Prim Sch
TOTTERIDGE GREEN
GREENWAY
WILLOW END
ELMSTEAD CL
GREENWAY CLOSE
MEAD
DRIVE
Cricket Grd Clubho.
Consolata Missionary Coll
COPPICE WALK
LYNTON
VENTNOR
LONGLAND
LAUREL WAY
DARLANDS LAKE NATURE RESERVE
Folly Brook
FB
Folly Farm
Nursery
Pav
Burtonhole Farm
BURTONHOLE LANE
BURT. CL
SPORTS GROUND
Clubhouse
Nat Inst for Medical Research
HILLVIEW RD
ELEANOR CRES
Elec Sta
Oakfields
NW7
Frith Manor Farm
Frith Manor Equestrian Centre
SOUTHOVER
CHIDDINGFOLD
NORTHIAM
ARLINGTON
FRAMFIELD CL
SHORTGATE
MICHLEHAM
DOWN
SPORTS GRD
PLAYING FIELD
BROOKSIDE
GUILDOWN AV
BROOK MEAD
TILLINGHAM WAY
LOBIAN CL
Clubhouse
SPORTS GRD
N12
HOLDEN RD
STATION APP
CHANCTONBURY WAY
PYECOMBE COR
RODMELL SLOPE
CISSBURY RING NORTH
SCAYNES LINK
SINGLETON SCARP
LULLINGTON GARTH
OFFHAM SLOPE
CISSBURY RING SOUTH
WOLSTONBURY
SADDLESCOMBE WY
POYNINGS WY
STEYNINGS WY
WALMINGTON FOLD
FOLKINGTON COR
SUSSEX RING
ARGYLE ROAD
DOLLIS BROOK
WESTBURY RD
SPRINGF. CL
AVONDALE
PARTINGDALE LANE
READING WAY
CHARLES SEVRIGHT DR
DARLOT DRIVE
INGLIS BARRACKS
ROBERTS
HOLMES
LANE APP
ROSS AV
Wks
HENRY
MAUR
BROWN CL
BITTACY PK AV
Watch Tower House
RUSHDEN GDNS
BITTACY RISE
BITTACY HILL PARK
BITTACY HILL
DREW AV
CURRY RISE
BRAY RD
WALDEN WY
Depot
KELLY
LIDBURY
PRICE CL
KENNY
AVENUE
WARR
WILLIAMSON WY
TWINN RD
WEST CL
THE PADD
FINCHLEY GOLF COURSE
LOVERS WALK
Nethercourt (Clubhouse)
ALLOT
Tenn Cts
ALLOT
SANDERS LA
BITTACY ROAD
B552
Council Depot
MILL HILL EAST
Works
Superstore
FRITH LANE
LINKSIDE
BROOKSIDE WALK
FURSBY
CHESTERFIELD RD
NETHERCOURT AV
WESTBURY GRD
COURTHOUSE GDNS
NETHER ST
PO
WEST FINCHLEY
Prim Schs
HAMILTON WY
WEST AVENUE
BRENT WAY
FINCHLEY WAY
THE DRIVE
PENSTEMON CL
HOWCROFT CRES
OAKDENE PK
LANSDOWNE RD
GROSVENOR ROAD
EVERSLEIGH ROAD
ELM PARK ROAD
NETHER CL
LOVERS WK
GORDON ROAD
WENTWORTH AV
WENTWORTH PK
CORNWALL AV
FALKLAND AV
GROVE AV
CLAVERLEY GR
PRINCES AVENUE
DORSET MS
BALLARDS LANE
N3
GRUNEISEN RD
BROWNLOW RD
ST. PAUL'S
THE RIDGE
WILLOW WY
PARKSIDE
Pol
GRANTS CLOSE
SANDERS LANE
W. CL
TAVIST. AV
CH. AV
OSBOR. AV
KINGSBRIDGE DRIVE
BRIDGE WAY
MAR WOOD DR
ARL. GREEN
DEVONSHIRE ROAD
DEVONSHIRE CRES
ASHLEY WALK
OSBORN GDNS
ABERDARE GDNS
LEE RD
NEW RD
VINEYARD AV
ABERCORN CL
MALLOW MEAD
FRITH COURT ROAD
OAKHAMPTON ROAD
HENDON
Clubhouse
DOLLIS ROAD
B1462
LINKS VW
Prim Sch
CRESCENT RD
ASHLEY LA
HENDON CEMETERY
FB
Pav
GARDENS

E
F
G
H
J
26
41
73
58
92
94
EN4
N20
1
2
3
4
5
6
7
OAKLEIGH PARK
WHETSTONE
BRUNSWICK PARK
NORTH FINCHLEY
FRIERN BARNET
TOTTERIDGE & WHETSTONE
NORTH MIDDLESEX GOLF COURSE
Clubhouse
BETHUNE PARK GOLF COURSE
SWAN LANE OPEN SPACE
FRIARY PARK
DAME ALICE OWEN'S GRD
SPORTS GRD
COPPETTS WOOD
FINCHLEY MEMORIAL HOSP
GLEBELANDS OPEN SPACE
Great North Leisure Park
MUSWELL HILL SPORTS GRO
Barnet Coll
Crematorium
Woodhouse Coll
Youth Cen
Bowling Club
Recycling Cen
Sports Cen
Tenn Club
Superstore
Hospice
Depot
Works
WINGATE & FINCHLEY F.C.
FINCHLEY R.F.C.
Bowl Clubs
Bowling Alley
Cinema
OAKLEIGH ROAD
FRIERN BARNET LANE
FRIERN BARNET ROAD
RUSSELL LANE
HIGH ROAD
WOODHOUSE ROAD
NORTH CIRCULAR ROAD
BOBBY MOORE WAY
COLNEY HATCH LANE
BALLARDS LANE
A1000
A109
A1003
B550
A598
A406

A
B
C
D
E
1
2
3
4
5
6
7
42
30
94
57
92
74
OSIDGE
SOUTHGATE
N14
BRUNSWICK PARK
NEW SOUTHGATE
N11
NEW SOUTHGATE CEMETERY & CREMATORIUM
SOUTHGATE CEMETERY
ARNOS PARK
MUSWELL HILL GOLF COURSE
FRIERN BRIDGE RETAIL PARK
PRINCESS PARK MANOR
Middlesex Uni
Southgate College
Barnet Coll
NEW SOUTHGATE REC GRD
BRUNSWICK IND PARK
BOUNDS GREEN
ARNOS GROVE
SCOUT PARK
SPORTS GROUND
Pymme's Brook
Bounds Green Brook
CHASE SIDE
THE BOURNE
HIGH STREET
CANNON HILL
OSIDGE LANE
OAKLEIGH ROAD SOUTH
WATERFALL ROAD
BOWES ROAD
BARNET ROAD
STATION ROAD
PINKHAM WAY
TELFORD ROAD
BOUNDS GREEN ROAD
POWYS LANE
WILMER WAY
BROWNLOW ROAD
DURNSFORD ROAD
A1004
A1003
A109
A1110
A406
B1453
B1452
B106
B550

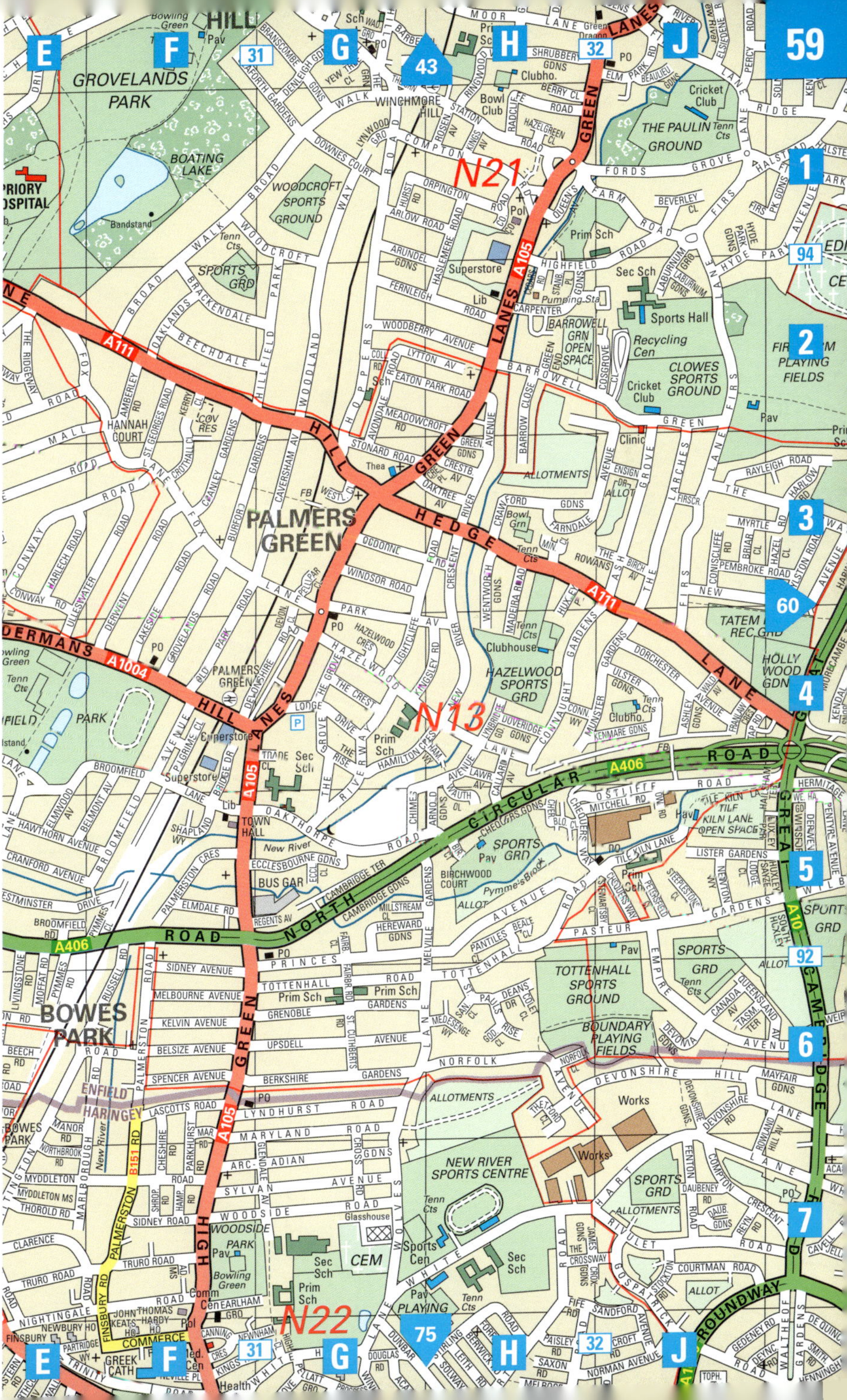

E
F
G
H
J
43
31
32
1
2
3
4
5
6
7
60
94
92
75
GROVELANDS PARK
BOATING LAKE
Bandstand
PRIORY HOSPITAL
WINCHMORE HILL
N21
N13
N22
PALMERS GREEN
BOWES PARK
THE PAULIN GROUND
Cricket Club
WOODCROFT SPORTS GROUND
SPORTS GRD
Superstore
Sports Hall
Recycling Cen
CLOWES SPORTS GROUND
BARROWELL GRN OPEN SPACE
ALLOTMENTS
HAZELWOOD SPORTS GRD
Clubhouse
TATEM PK REC GRD
HOLLY WOOD GDNS
TOWN HALL
New River
BUS GAR
KILN LANE OPEN SPACE
TOTTENHALL SPORTS GROUND
BOUNDARY PLAYING FIELDS
NEW RIVER SPORTS CENTRE
Works
CEM
WOODSIDE PARK
Bowling Green
ENFIELD
HARINGEY
A105
A111
A1004
A406
A10
B151
GREEN LANES
HEDGE LANE
HILL
NORTH CIRCULAR ROAD
GREAT CAMBRIDGE ROAD
HIGH ROAD
PALMERSTON RD
ROUNDWAY

A
B
C
D
E
1
2
3
4
5
6
7
33
44
34
94
59
92
76
LOWER EDMONTON
EDMONTON
UPPER EDMONTON
TOTTENHAM
N18
N17
EDMONTON CEMETERY
TOTTENHAM CEMETERY
FIRS FARM PLAYING FIELDS
CHURCH STREET REC GRD
CHURCHFIELD REC GRD
PYMMES PARK
NORTH MIDDLESEX HOSPITAL
HOLLYWOOD GDNS
TILE KILN LANE OPEN SPACE
THE ROYAL LONDON ESTATE
WINGATE TRADING EST
TOTTENHAM HOTSPUR FC
CRAIG PARK
SALISBURY HO ARTS CEN
Edmonton Green Shopping Cen
GREAT CAMBRIDGE ROAD
CHURCH STREET
STERLING WAY
ANGEL ROAD
FORE STREET
HIGH ROAD
HERTFORD ROAD
SILVER STREET
WHITE HART LANE
THE ROUNDWAY
PARK LANE
A10
A406
A1010
B154
ENFIELD
HARINGEY
SPORTS GROUND
ALLOTMENTS

45
62
77
94
92
35
WILLIAM GIRLING RESERVOIR
LEE VALLEY GOLF COURSE
DRIVING RANGE
DEEPHAMS SEWAGE TREATMENT WORKS
LEE VALLEY PARK
BANBURY RESERVOIR
SOUTH CHINGFORD
E4
N9
MONTAGU RECREATION GROUND
TOTTENHAM PARK CEMETERY
WESTERN SYNAGOGUE CEMETERY
MERIDIAN WAY
NORTH SOUTH ROUTE
LEA VALLEY VIADUCT
SOUTHEND ROAD
ANGEL ROAD
CONDUIT LANE
MONTAGU ROAD
HALL LANE
WALTHAM WAY
Cooks Wharf Roundabout
Hall La
Sunday Market
PICKETTS LOCK LANE
Pickett's Lock
Filter Beds
Storage Tanks
ELEY ESTATE
MOWLEM TRADING ESTATE
HASTINGWOOD TRADING ESTATE
LEA VALLEY TRAD EST
RAVENSIDE RETAIL PK
CHINGFORD IND CEN
CHINGFORD HALL PARK
Gas Works
Electricity Station
Refuge Plant
Pumping Station
Lee Valley Watersports
Fairways Cen
FAIRWAY GOLF RANGE
BRITANNIA SPORTS GROUND
River Lee Navigation
River Lee Diversion
Lee Flood Relief Channel
Overflow Channel
LEA VALLEY WALK
William Morris Sch
BILLET ROAD
A1009
A1037
A406
B137

A
B
C
D
E
46
39
94
61
92
78
1
2
3
4
5
6
7
CHINGFORD
CHINGFORD HATCH
FRIDAY HILL
HIGHAMS PARK
HALE END
E4
Chingford Golf Range
LEA VALLEY PLAYING FIELDS
MANSFIELD PARK
RIDGEWAY PARK
CHINGFORD MOUNT CEMETERY
ALLOTMENTS
LARKSWOOD PLAYING FIELDS
LARKS WOOD
WAR MEML. REC GRD
JUBILEE SPORTS GRD
PIMP HALL PARK
AINSLIE WOOD (Nat-Res)
ROLLS SPORTS GRD
HIGHAMS IND EST
SALISBURY HALL BLADES PLAYING FIELDS
SPORTS GRD
WALTHAMSTOW STADIUM
THE LONDON HOSPITAL SPORTS GRD
BRITANNIA SPORTS GROUND
Sports Centre
Crooked Billet Roundabout
GREENTHORPE HOSP
Holiday Inn Express
WALTHAM FOREST
ENFIELD
A1037
A112
A110
A1009
B169
B160
B146
A406
NORTH CIRCULAR RD
MANSFIELD HILL
OLD CHURCH ROAD
CHINGFORD MOUNT ROAD
CHINGFORD ROAD
NEW ROAD
HATCH LA
LARKSHALL ROAD
WINCHESTER ROAD
STATION ROAD
KINGS ROAD
THE GRN
HILL
THE RIDGEWAY
ENDLEBURY ROAD
CHINGFORD AVENUE
LARKSWOOD ROAD
NORMANSHIRE DRIVE
HIGHAM STATION AVENUE
SOUTHEND RD
COLLEGE GARDENS
SEWARDSTONE ROAD
FRIDAY HILL
SIMMONS LANE
WITHY MEAD
EPPING

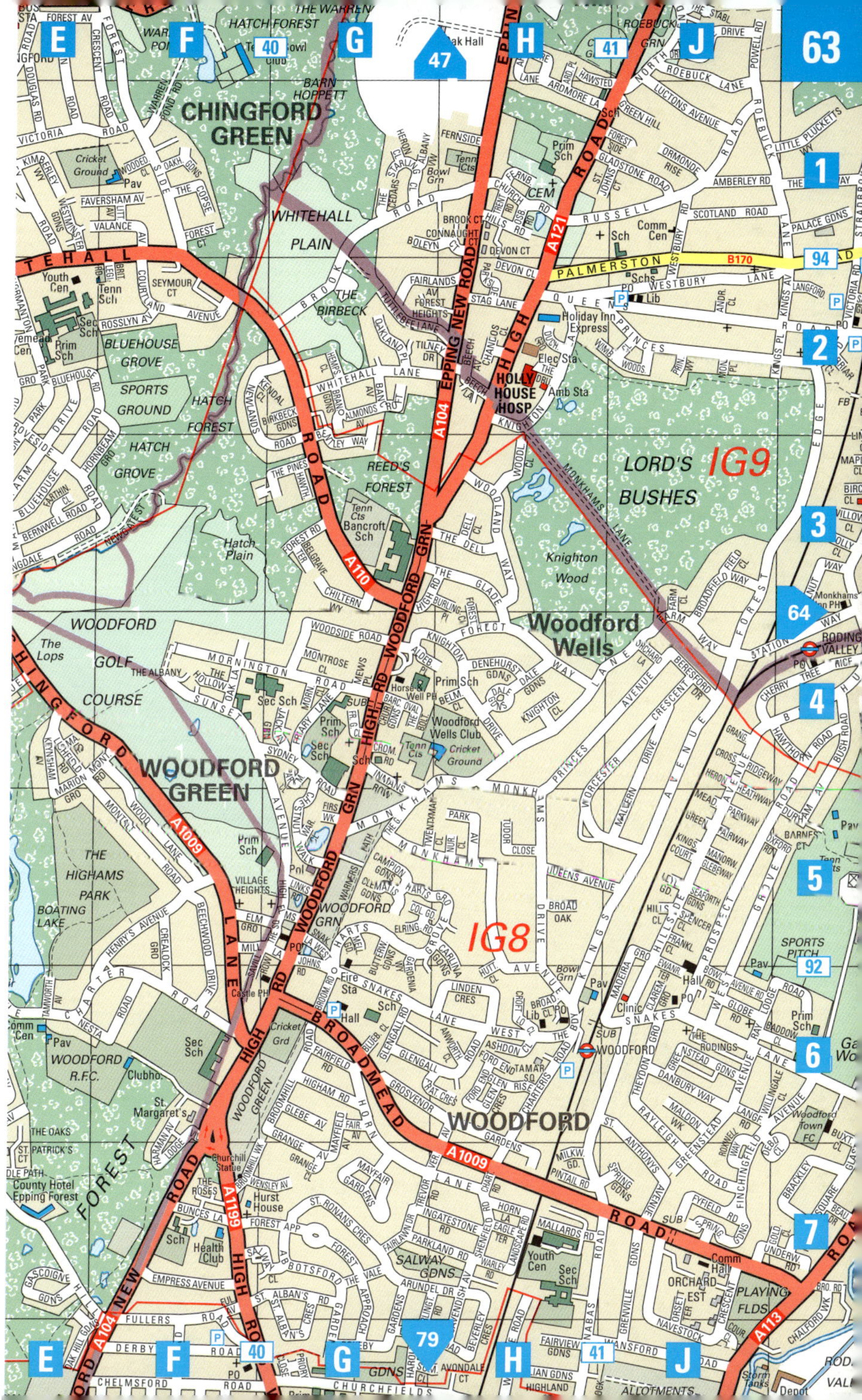
E
F
G
H
J
47
40
41
CHINGFORD GREEN
WHITEHALL PLAIN
THE BIRBECK
BLUEHOUSE GROVE
SPORTS GROUND
HATCH FOREST
HATCH GROVE
REED'S FOREST
Hatch Plain
LORD'S BUSHES
IG9
Knighton Wood
Woodford Wells
WOODFORD GOLF COURSE
The Lops
WOODFORD GREEN
THE HIGHAMS PARK
BOATING LAKE
WOODFORD R.F.C.
IG8
WOODFORD
FOREST
County Hotel Epping Forest
Churchill Statue
Holiday Inn Express
HOLLY HOUSE HOSP
Amb Sta
Elec Sta
Woodford Wells Club
Cricket Ground
Fire Sta
Clinic
WOODFORD
PLAYING FLDS
Woodford Town F.C.
SPORTS PITCH
RODING VALLEY
EPPING NEW ROAD
A104
A121
A110
A1009
A1199
A113
B170
HIGH ROAD
PALMERSTON ROAD
QUEENS ROAD
PRINCES
KNIGHTON LANE
MONKHAMS LANE
MONKHAMS AVENUE
BROADMEAD ROAD
SNAKES LANE
CHINGFORD LANE
WOODFORD NEW ROAD
1
2
3
4
5
6
7
94
64
92
79

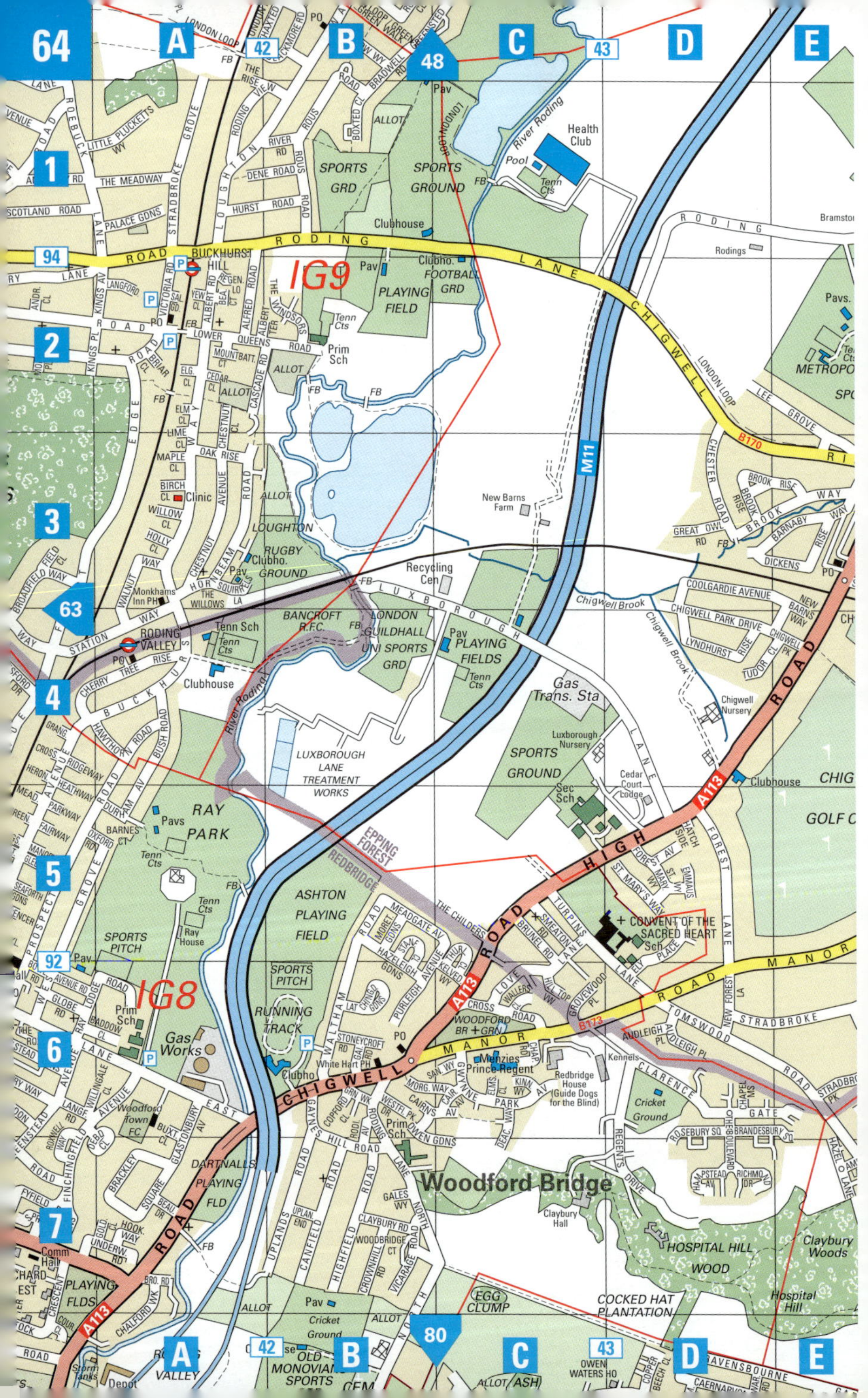
A
B
C
D
E
1
2
3
4
5
6
7
42
43
48
63
80
92
94
IG9
IG8
BUCKHURST HILL
RODING LANE
CHIGWELL LANE
LONDON LOOP
River Roding
Health Club
Pool
Tenn Cts
SPORTS GRD
SPORTS GROUND
Clubhouse
Clubho.
FOOTBALL GRD
PLAYING FIELD
Pav
Prim Sch
ALLOT
LOUGHTON RUGBY GROUND
Recycling Cen
M11
Chigwell Brook
New Barns Farm
Rodings
Bramston
Pavs.
METROPO
B170
Monkhams Inn PH
RODING VALLEY
Tenn Sch
BANCROFT R.F.C.
LONDON GUILDHALL UNI SPORTS GRD
LUXBOROUGH LANE
PLAYING FIELDS
Gas Trans. Sta
Luxborough Nursery
Chigwell Nursery
COOLGARDIE AVENUE
CHIGWELL PARK DRIVE
LYNDHURST RISE
GREAT OWL RD
DICKENS
BROOK RISE
BARNABY WAY
CHESTER ROAD
LUXBOROUGH LANE TREATMENT WORKS
Cedar Court Lodge
Sec Sch
A113
CHIG
GOLF C
EPPING FOREST
REDBRIDGE
RAY PARK
Pavs
Ray House
SPORTS PITCH
ASHTON PLAYING FIELD
RUNNING TRACK
CONVENT OF THE SACRED HEART Sch
HIGH ROAD
MANOR ROAD
B173
TOMSWOOD ROAD
STRADBROKE
Gas Works
Woodford Town FC
White Hart PH
Menzies Prince Regent
Redbridge House (Guide Dogs for the Blind)
Kennels
Cricket Ground
Woodford Bridge
DARTNALLS PLAYING FLD
Claybury Hall
HOSPITAL HILL WOOD
Claybury Woods
Hospital Hill
COCKED HAT PLANTATION
EGG CLUMP
OLD MONOVIANS SPORTS
Cricket Ground
Comm Hall
PLAYING FLDS
Storm Tanks
Depot
VALLEY
OWEN WATERS HO
RAVENSBOURNE

E
F
G
H
J
44
49
81
94
93
92
1
2
3
4
5
6
7
IG7
IG6
Chigwell
Grange Hill
HAINAULT
HIGH ROAD
HAINAULT ROAD
FENCEPIECE ROAD
A113
A123
B173
MANOR ROAD
LAMBOURNE ROAD
VICARAGE LANE
GREEN LANE
FROGHALL LANE
LONDON LOOP
PUDDING LANE
COURTLAND DRIVE
PARKLANDS
MEADOW WAY
Ross Bridge
Chigwell Brook
Oaks Farm
Old Farm
Burnt House
Fulham's Farm
Miller's Farm
Chase Farm Riding Stables
Hillside
White Ridge
COV RES
Forest House
CHIGWELL ROW WATER WORKS
Filter Beds
RESERVOIR
Settling Tanks
RES
SPORTS GROUND
Chigwell Hall
CEM
Sec Sch
Prim Sch
Cricket Grd
Tenn Cts
Pav
Grange Court
ALLOT
Nursery Farm
CHIGWELL CEMETERY
GRANGE HILL
Sch and Training Cen
Chig Well (Site of)
PLAYING FIELD
REC GRD
Woodview
Fairview
L.R.T. DEPOT
Bald Hind PH
Hall
Lib
Health Cen
Comm Cen
Fire Sta
Works
P. & O. Nedlloyd
HAINAULT RECREATION GROUND
FAIRLOP OAK PLAYING FIELD
ILFORD WANDERERS R.F.C.
Clubho.
Bowl Club
Bowl Grn
BRACKEN INDUSTRIAL ESTATE
FOREST INDUSTRIAL PARK
Old Maypole PH
Schs.
Tomswood Hill
BROCKET WAY
BURROW ROAD
ARROWSMITH ROAD
CROSS BOW ROAD
COPPERFIELD
NEW NORTH ROAD
TRELAWNEY ROAD
ARAGON DRIVE
CRESCENT
COVERT ROAD
LIME GROVE
CYPRESS GRO
BEECH GROVE
PENRITH ROAD
ROVER AV
KELSIE WAY
WALDEN WAY
INVERNESS DRIVE
TOMSWOOD

A
B
C
D
E
1
2
3
4
5
6
7
50
84
12
88
89
90
PINNERWOOD PARK
GOLF COURSE
HOGS BACK OPEN SPACE
NORTHWOOD & PINNER COMMUNITY HOSP
Sports Centre
HA6
NORTHWOOD HILLS
RICKMANSWORTH RD
A404
UXBRIDGE ROAD
MONTESOLE PLAYING FIELDS
PINNER GREEN
LITTLE COMMON
REC GRD
PINNER MEMORIAL PARK
HA5
CUCKOO HILL
B466
B472
JOEL STREET
HIGH ROAD
EASTCOTE VILLAGE
Haydon Hall
Eastcote CC
EASTCOTE HO GRD
Squash Club
FIELD END ROAD
GOVERNMENT OFFICES
EASTCOTE
THE CROFT PLAYING FIELD
CANNONBURY AVENUE
Swim Pool & Fitness Cen
WARRENDER PARK
HA4
EASTERN AVENUE
EASTCOTE
HILLINGDON
HARROW
ROXBOURNE
RUISLIP
Superstore
Grangewood Sch
High Sch
Prim Schs
Tennis Club

E
F
G
H
J
13
14
51
85
68
89
90
88
1
2
3
4
5
6
7
PINNER PARK
PINNER
HEADSTONE
NORTH HARROW
WEST HARROW
HARROW
HA1
HA2
UXBRIDGE ROAD
ST. THOMAS' DRIVE
GEORGE V AVENUE
PINNER ROAD
STATION RD
IMPERIAL DRIVE
A404
A4090
RAGHUVANSHI CHARITABLE TRUST SPORTS GROUND
HARROW ARTS CENTRE
Superstores
SPORTS GROUND
RECREATION GROUND
PINNER NEW CEMETERY
Fire Training Cen
Harrow Mus & Heritage Cen
MOAT
PINNER VILLAGE GARDENS
Old Lyonian Sports Club
WEST HARROW REC GRD
Pinner Park Farm
BLOOMSBURY COURT
CHISWICK COURT
HEADSTONE LANE
HEADSTONE DRIVE
RAYNERS LANE
WHITMORE
River Pinn
Yeading Brook
ALLOT
CEM

A
B
C
D
E
1
2
3
4
5
6
7
15
16
52
67
86
88
89
90
HARROW WEALD
BELMONT
WEALDSTONE
HARROW
HA1
HA3
GOLF COURSE
ALLOTMENTS
RECREATION GROUND
WAVERLEY INDUSTRIAL ESTATE
SPORTS GROUND
HARROW & WEALDSTONE
CIVIC CENTRE
CIVIC AMENITY SITE
HAWTHORN CENTRE
KENTON RECREATION GROUND
WEALDSTONE CEM
BYRON REC GRD
Leisure Centre
Sports Centre
DRIVING CENTRE
HARROW REC GROUND
CEM
St. Ann's Centre
HARROW-ON-THE-HILL
COLLEGE BUS STA
Harrow Coll
HARROW HILL GOLF COURSE
THE GROVE OPEN SPACE
MINIATURE RIFLE RANGE
University of Westminster
NORTHWICK PARK & ST. MARK'S HOSPITALS
Superstore
Safari Cinema
HIGH STREET
GEORGE GANGE WAY
RAILWAY APP
STATION ROAD
SHEEPCOTE ROAD
KENTON ROAD
TYBURN LA
LOWLANDS RD
BESSBOROUGH ROAD
WATFORD ROAD
HEADSTONE DRIVE
A409
A404
A312
B458
B457
NORTHWICK PARK
KENTON

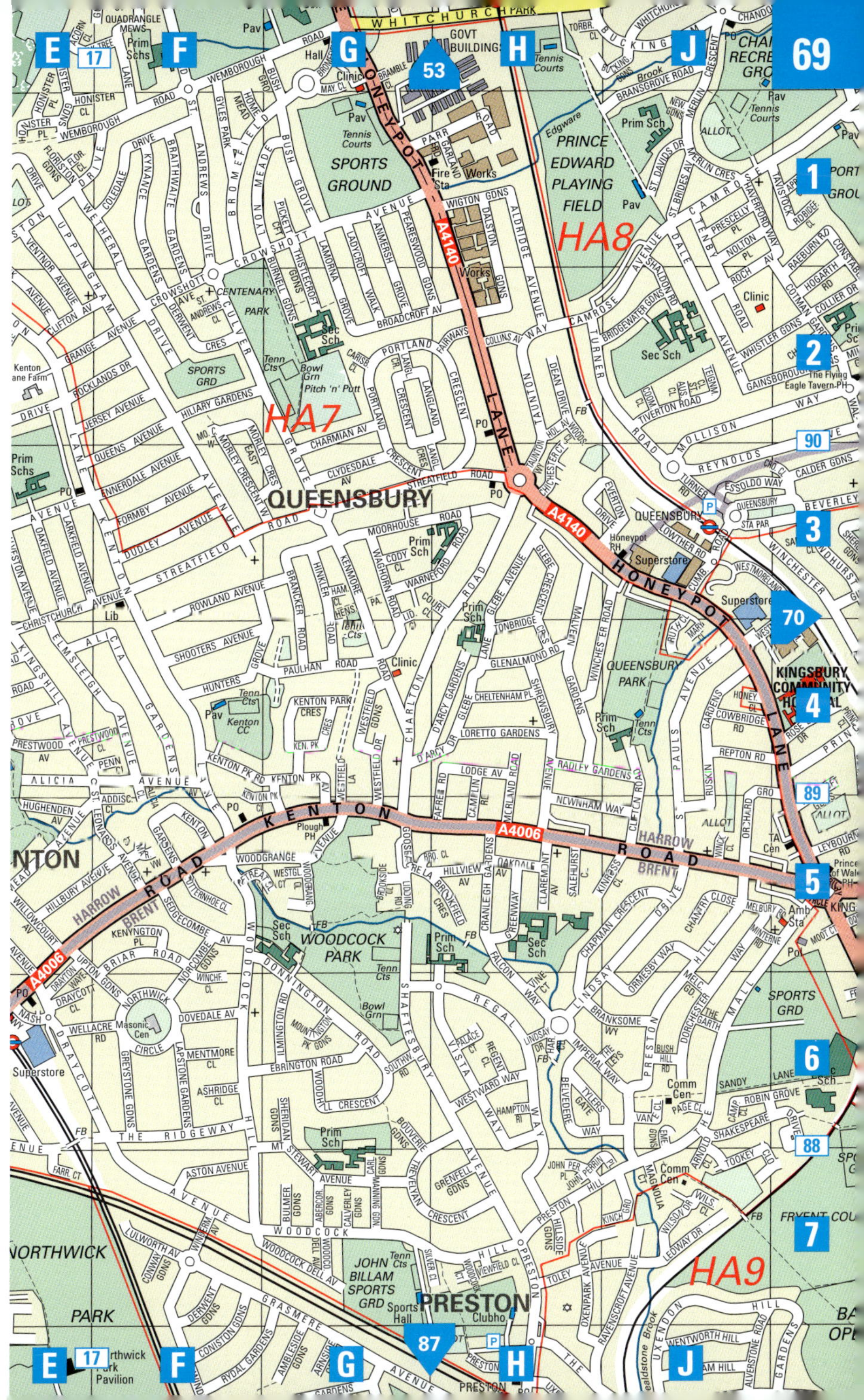

E
F
G
H
J
1
2
3
4
5
6
7
17
53
70
87
88
89
90
QUEENSBURY
HA7
HA8
HA9
A4140
A4006
HONEYPOT LANE
KENTON ROAD
WHITCHURCH PARK
GOVT BUILDINGS
SPORTS GROUND
PRINCE EDWARD PLAYING FIELD
CENTENARY PARK
SPORTS GRD
QUEENSBURY PARK
KINGSBURY COMMUNITY HOSPITAL
WOODCOCK PARK
JOHN BILLAM SPORTS GRD
PRESTON
NORTHWICK PARK
KENTON
HARROW BRENT
The Flying Eagle Tavern PH
Honeypot PH
Plough PH
Superstore
Kenton CC
Masonic Cen
Northwick Park Pavilion
Prince of Wales PH
Sec Sch
Prim Sch
Clinic
Fire Sta
Works
Tennis Courts
Pitch 'n' Putt
Bowl Grn
Comm Cen
Sports Hall
Clubho
Lib
Amb Sta
Pav
Edgware Brook
ALLOT
STREATFIELD ROAD
CROWSHOTT AVENUE
CAMROSE AVENUE
MOLLISON WAY
REYNOLDS DRIVE
PORTLAND CRESCENT
CHARLTON ROAD
SHAFTESBURY AVENUE
WOODCOCK HILL
THE RIDGEWAY
PRESTON HILL
PRESTON ROAD
UXENDON HILL
WENTWORTH HILL
GRASMERE AVENUE
ELMSLEIGH AVENUE
KINGSHILL AVENUE
ALICIA AVENUE
WEMBOROUGH ROAD
BUSH GROVE
ALDRIDGE AVENUE
DEAN DRIVE
TAUNTON WAY
GLEBE AVENUE
MALVERN GARDENS
WINCHESTER ROAD
TURNER ROAD
SANDY LANE
THE MALL
FRYENT COUNTRY PARK

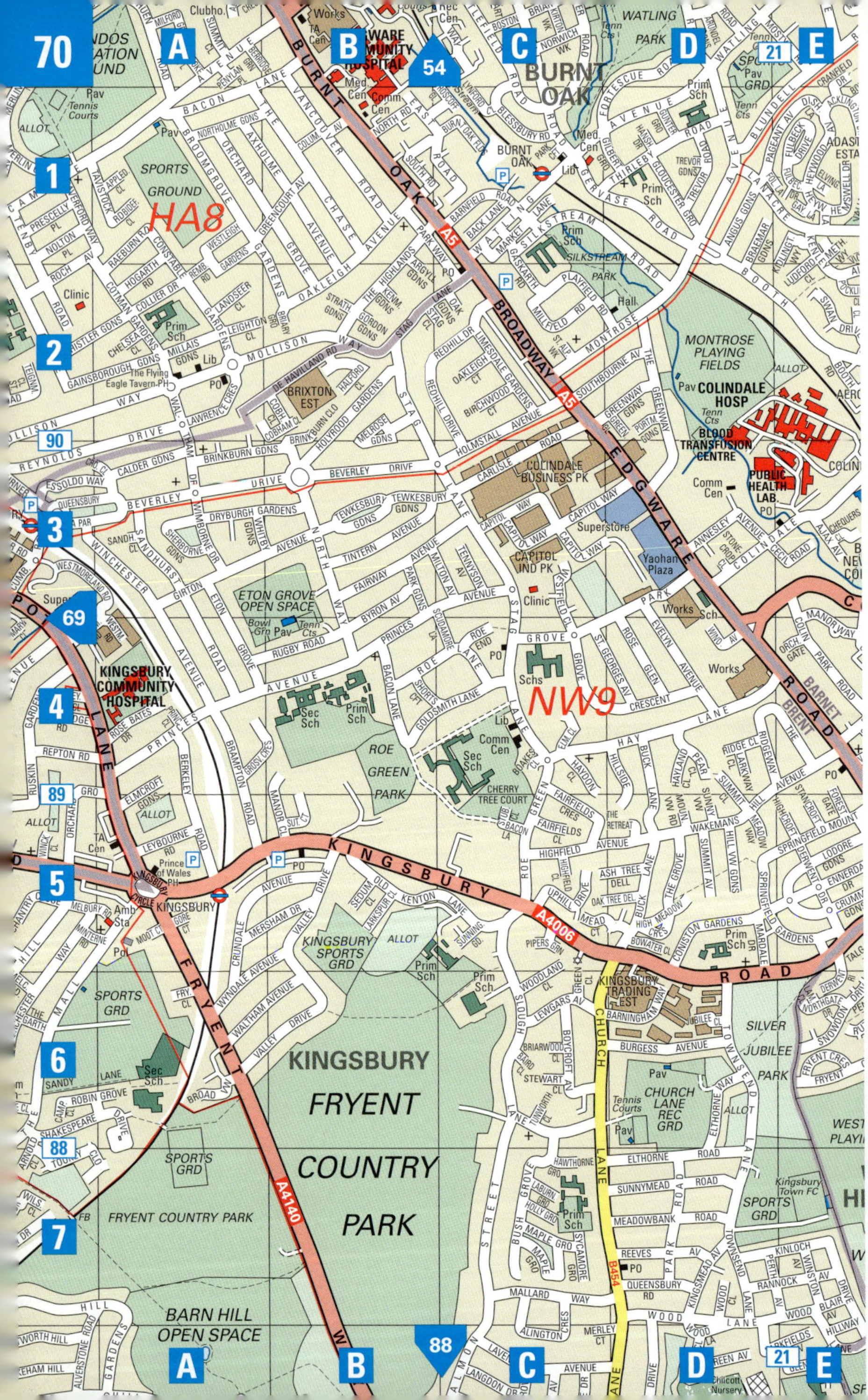

A
B
C
D
E
54
21
1
2
3
4
5
6
7
90
69
89
88
BURNT OAK
WATLING PARK
HA8
NW9
SPORTS GROUND
Clinic
Prim Sch
Lib
PO
Pav
Tennis Courts
ALLOT
TA Cen
Works
EDGWARE COMMUNITY HOSPITAL
Med Cen
Comm Cen
BURNT OAK BROADWAY
A5
EDGWARE ROAD
BURNT OAK
BACON LANE
VANCOUVER ROAD
CHASE
AVENUE
BROOMGROVE
ORCHARD
AXHOLME
THE GREENCOURT AV
WESTLEIGH GARDENS
OAKLEIGH
MOLLISON WAY
MOLLISON
DE HAVILLAND RD
STAG LANE
GAINSBOROUGH GDNS
The Flying Eagle Tavern PH
REYNOLDS DRIVE
BRIXTON EST
HOLYROOD GARDENS
BRINKBURN GDNS
CALDER GDNS
BEVERLEY DRIVE
BEVERLEY
TEWKESBURY
TINTERN AVENUE
DRYBURGH GARDENS
WIMBORNE DR
WINCHESTER
SANDHURST
GIRTON
ETON
ETON GROVE OPEN SPACE
Bowl Grn
Tenn Cts
RUGBY ROAD
BYRON AV
FAIRWAY
PRINCES
AVENUE
COLINDALE BUSINESS PK
CAPITOL WAY
CAPITOL IND PK
Superstore
Yaohan Plaza
COLINDALE AVENUE
MONTROSE PLAYING FIELDS
COLINDALE HOSP
BLOOD TRANSFUSION CENTRE
PUBLIC HEALTH LAB.
SILKSTREAM PARK
SILKSTREAM ROAD
MONTROSE
SOUTHBOURNE AV
HOLMSTALL AVENUE
CARLISLE ROAD
BARNET
BRENT
GROVE
PARK
Schs
Sec Sch
Prim Sch
ROE GREEN PARK
GOLDSMITH LANE
ROE LANE
CHERRY TREE COURT
HAY LANE
BUCK LANE
SUMMIT
WAKEMANS
KINGSBURY COMMUNITY HOSPITAL
ROSE BATES DR
REPTON RD
ELMCROFT GDNS
LEYBOURNE RD
Prince of Wales PH
KINGSBURY
KINGSBURY ROAD
A4006
KENTON LANE
KINGSBURY SPORTS GRD
ALLOT
FRYENT WAY
A4140
KINGSBURY FRYENT COUNTRY PARK
FRYENT COUNTRY PARK
SPORTS GRD
ROBIN GROVE
SHAKESPEARE
BARN HILL OPEN SPACE
KINGSBURY TRADING EST
BARNINGHAM WAY
BURGESS AVENUE
SILVER JUBILEE PARK
CHURCH LANE REC GRD
CHURCH LANE
B454
ELTHORNE ROAD
SUNNYMEAD ROAD
MEADOWBANK ROAD
REEVES AV
QUEENSBURY RD
WOOD LANE
MALLARD WAY
SLOUGH LANE
STREET
BUSH GROVE
MAPLE GRO
SYCAMORE GRO
Kingsbury Town FC
SPORTS GRD
ROAD

E
F
G
H
J
1
2
3
4
5
6
7
22
23
55
72
88
89
90
Clubhouse
METRO GOLF
HENDON
BARNET COPTHALL STADIUM
COPTHALL SPORTS GROUND
COPTHALL PLAYING FIELDS
Cricket Club
Junction 2
Five Ways Corner
Hendon R.F.C.
HOLDERS HILL
GREAT NORTH WAY
NW4
SUNNY HILL PARK
Barnet Coll (Grahame Pk Cen)
GRAHAME PARK
Comm Cen
Health Cen
RAF MUSEUMS
Warehouses
Peel Cen (Metropolitan Pol Training & Driving School)
SPORTS GRD
AERODROME ROAD
WATFORD WAY
M1
A41
A1
A5150
A502
A5
B552
B551
THE HYDE
HENDON
Middlesex Uni
Town Hall
CHURCH ROAD
FINCHLEY
GARDEN HOSP
Thistle Hendon Hall
Church Farm House Mus
Fire Sta
Clinic
Lib
Mkt
HENDON CENTRAL
QUEENS ROAD
HENDON PARK
War Memorial
Hendon Sidings
Superstore
Works
MALCOLM PARK
STATION ROAD
WEST HENDON
Welsh Harp
Sailing Cen
HENDON PLAYING FIELDS
YORK PARK
BROADWAY
Brent Cross Shopping Centre
Holiday Inn
Refuse Disposal Works
Junction 1
River Brent
ALLOTMENTS
Cool Oak Bridge
OODFIELD PARK
BRENT RESERVOIR
Bowl Grn
Bowling Green

A
B
C
D
E
1
2
3
4
5
6
7
24
25
56
71
88
89
90
NW7
NW4
N3
NW11
HOLDERS HILL
GOLF COURSE
HENDON CEMETERY
Crematorium
CHURCH END
FINCHLEY CENTRAL
GOLDERS GREEN
BIG WOOD
LITTLE WOOD
HENDON PARK
BRENT CROSS
CARMELITE MONASTERY
HOOP LANE CEMETERY (JEWISH)
GARDEN OF REMEMBRANCE
GOLDERS GREEN DEPOT
Golders Green Hippodrome
PRINCES PARK
WINDSOR OPEN SPACE
AVENUE HOUSE GRDS
College Farm
Superstores
Holiday Inn
NORTH CIRCULAR ROAD
REGENTS PARK ROAD
FINCHLEY ROAD
HENDON LANE
BALLARDS LANE
EAST END ROAD
FALLODEN WAY
GOLDERS GREEN ROAD
BRENT STREET
HOLDERS HILL ROAD
DOLLIS ROAD
NETHER STREET
BRIDGE LANE
HAMPSTEAD WAY
TEMPLE FORTUNE HILL
A1
A41
A406
A502
A504
A598
B552

E
F
G
H
J
26
57
MEMORIAL HOSP
OPEN SPACE
Great North Leisure Park
Cinema
VICTORIA PARK
FINCHLEY
NORTH CIRCULAR ROAD
A406
A1000
HIGH ROAD
GREAT NORTH ROAD
MUSWELL HILL SPORTS GROUND
COPPETTS WOOD HOSP
Crematorium
ST. PANCRAS & ISLINGTON CEMETERY
N2
COLDFALL WOOD
BARNET
HARINGEY
Fire Sta
Bowl Club
CHANDOS ROAD
CREIGHTON AVENUE
HERTFORD ROAD
BEDFORD ROAD
HUNTINGDON ROAD
LEICESTER ROAD
LINCOLN ROAD
TWYFORD AVENUE
FORTIS GREEN
A504
EAST END ROAD
EAST FINCHLEY CEMETERY
NAZARETH HO CONVENT
EAST FINCHLEY
East Finchley
FORTIS GREEN
CHERRY TREE WOOD
SOUTHERN ROAD
HIGH ROAD
LYTTELTON ROAD
A1
LYTTELTON PLAYING FIELDS
HAMPSTEAD GARDEN SUBURB
AYLMER ROAD
BAKERS LA
ARCHWAY
HIGHGATE GOLF COURSE
Clubhouse
N6
HAMPSTEAD HEATH EXTENSION
HAMPSTEAD GOLF COURSE
Bunkers Hill
TURNERS WOOD
HAMPSTEAD LANE
B519
Highgate Sch
Kenwood House
ATHLONE HOUSE
1
2
3
4
5
6
7
74
88
89
90
91

N10
N6
MUSWELL HILL
ALEXANDRA PARK
ALEXANDRA PALACE
FORTIS GREEN
HIGHGATE WOOD
QUEEN'S WOOD
CROUCH END
HARINGEY
ISLINGTON
PRIORY PARK
THE GROVE
ST.LUKE'S WOODSIDE HOSPITAL
SOUTHWOOD HOSP
HIGHGATE
CROUCH END PLAYING FIELDS
SPORTS GROUND
Ice Rink
Pitch 'n' Putt
TRAIN DEPOT
DEPOT
A B C D E
1 2 3 4 5 6 7
58
73
92
90
89
88
30
ALEXANDRA PARK ROAD
MUSWELL HILL ROAD
MUSWELL HILL BROADWAY
FORTIS GREEN
PRIORY ROAD
PARK ROAD
ARCHWAY ROAD
NORTH HILL
MUSWELL HILL
CROUCH END HILL
HORNSEY LANE
HORNSEY RISE
DURNSFORD ROAD
ALBERT ROAD
SHEPHERDS HILL
HIGHGATE HIGH STREET
B550
B519
B106
B540
A504
A1201
A103
A1

E
F
G
H
J
1
2
3
4
5
6
7
31
32
59
76
88
89
90
93
N22
N8
N15
N4
WOOD GREEN
NOEL PARK
HORNSEY
HARRINGAY
STROUD GREEN
WEST GREEN
FINSBURY
LORDSHIP RECREATION GROUND
DOWNHILLS PARK
CHESTNUTS PARK
BELMONT REC GRD
AMERICAN GDNS
ST. ANN'S HOSPITAL
WD GRN COMMON
RESERVOIR
HORNSEY WATER TREATMENT WORKS
Filter Beds
Gas Works
Shopping City
TRAIN DEPOT
Warehouses
New River
HARRINGAY GREEN LANES
Superstores
RAILWAY FLDS
Cricket Ground
MANOR HOUSE
Seven Sisters Bridge
WOODBERRY DOWN ESTATE
STATIONERS PARK
LORDSHIP LANE
HIGH ROAD
WESTBURY AVENUE
GREEN LANES
TURNPIKE LANE
WIGHTMAN ROAD
TOTTENHAM LANE
HORNSEY PARK ROAD
DOWNHILLS WAY
THE ROUNDWAY
STATION ROAD
SEVEN SISTERS ROAD
CROUCH HILL
ST ANN'S ROAD
WEST GREEN ROAD
A105
A109
A1080
A504
B138
B150
B151
B152
B155

A
B
C
D
E
1
2
3
4
5
6
7
33
34
60
75
88
89
90
94
TOTTENHAM
N17
N15
N16
SOUTH TOTTENHAM
LORDSHIP RECREATION GROUND
The Moselle
DOWNHILLS PARK
BRUCE CASTLE PARK
BRUCE CASTLE MUS
TOWER GDNS
PEABODY EST
BROADWATER FARM EST
THE ROUNDWAY
LORDSHIP LANE
BRUCE GROVE
LANSDOWNE ROAD
HIGH ROAD
WEST GREEN ROAD
PHILIP LANE
MONUMENT WAY
HALE RD
FERRY LANE
BROAD LANE
SEVEN SISTERS ROAD
ST ANN'S ROAD
ST ANN'S HOSPITAL
AMHURST PARK
STAMFORD HILL
CLAPTON COMMON
DOWN LANE REC GRD
LEE VALLEY TECHNOPARK
LOCKWOOD INDUSTRIAL PARK
TOTTENHAM HALE
Tottenham Hale Retail Park
Bowling Alley
HIGH CROSS CENTRE
Coll of N E London
TOWN HALL
Markfield Beam Engine
MARKFIELD REC GRD
WARWICK RESERVOIR WEST
River Lee or Lea
SPRINGHILL SPORTS GRD
SPRINGFIELD PARK
EAST RESERVOIR
New River
SEVEN SISTERS
Superstore
Leisure Cen
Warehouses
HARINGEY
HACKNEY
WATERMEAD WAY
LEA VALLEY WALK
Civic Amenity Site
Cricket Stad
Seven Sisters Bridge
Youth Club

NORTHUMBERLAND PARK
LEE VALLEY PARK
LRT DEPOT
TOTTENHAM MARSHES
LOCKWOOD RESERVOIR
HIGH MAYNARD RESERVOIR
LOW MAYNARD RESERVOIR
Walthamstow Marsh Nature Reserve
Tottenham Lock
Stonebridge Lock
Aqueduct
Lee Flood Relief Channel
UPLANDS BUSINESS PARK
HIGHAMS LODGE BUSINESS CEN
HIGHAM HILL REC GRD
HIGHAM HILL
BILLET ROAD
BLACKHORSE LANE
BLACKHORSE ROAD
FOREST ROAD
A503
A1006
B179
E17
DOUGLAS EYRE PLAYING FIELDS
RESERVOIR NUMBER FOUR
RESERVOIR NUMBER TWO
RESERVOIR NUMBER ONE
RESERVOIR NUMBER THREE
RESERVOIR NUMBER FIVE
COPPERMILLS TREATMENT WORKS
COPPERMILL PLAYING FIELD
ST. JAMES'S PARK
LOW HALL SPORTS GROUND
RECYCLING CENTRE
ALLOTMENTS
LEYTON IND VILLAGE
FOREST BUSINESS PK
ROXWELL TRADING PK
DORMA TRADING PK
WALTHAMSTOW CEM
WALTHAMSTOW QUEENS ROAD
ST JAMES STREET
MARKHOUSE ROAD
HIGH STREET
BRITANNIA SPORTS GROUND
LLOYD PARK
Kimberley Ind Est
Billet Works
Leisure Cen
Selborne Walk Shop
Coppermill Bridge
Horse Shoe Point
Horse Shoe Bridge
Anchor & Hope PH
E F G H J
1 2 3 4 5 6 7
35 61 78 88 89 90 95

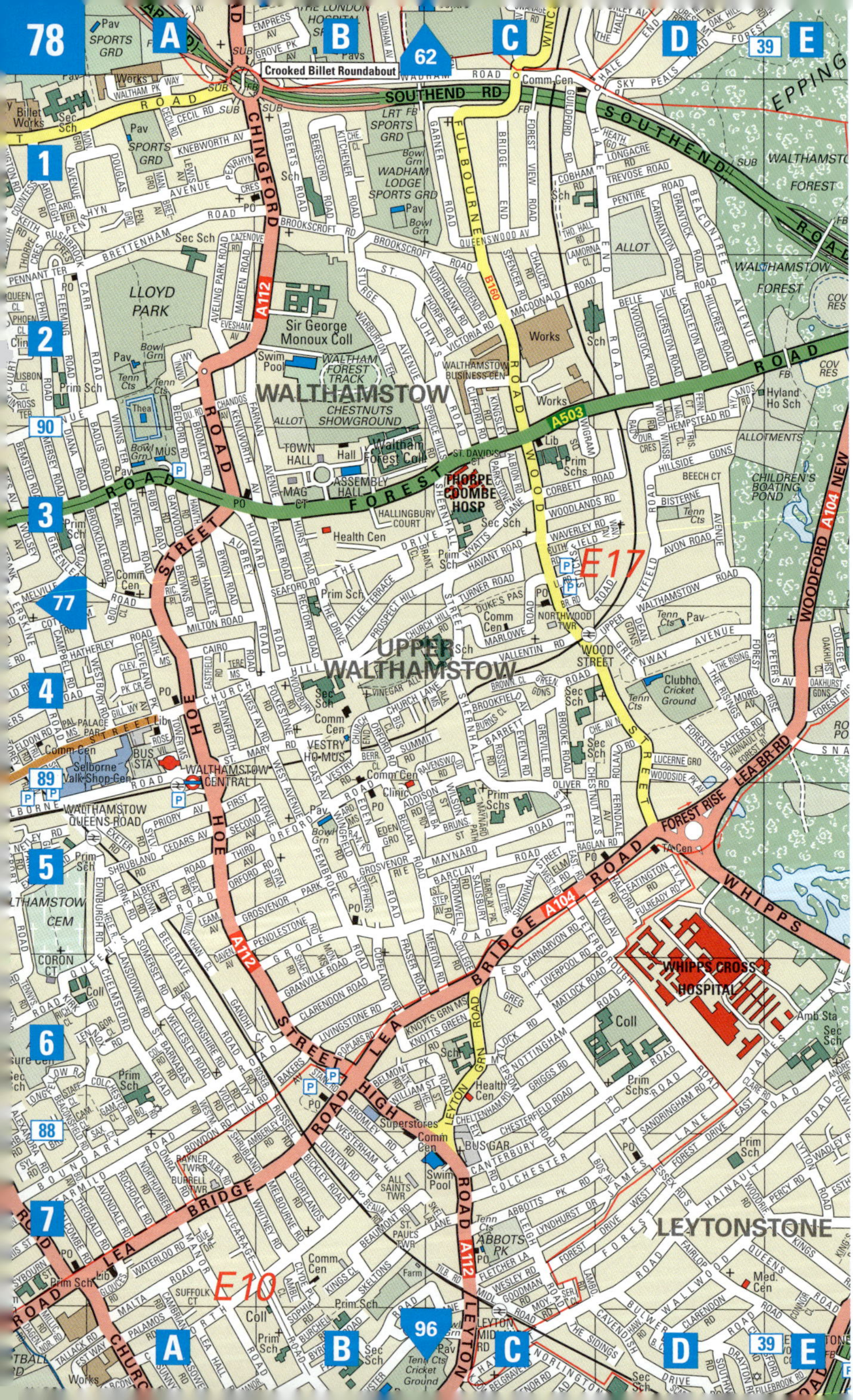
A
B
C
D
E
62
39
Crooked Billet Roundabout
SOUTHEND RD
SOUTHEND ROAD
EPPING
WALTHAMSTOW FOREST
CHINGFORD ROAD
A112
LLOYD PARK
Sir George Monoux Coll
WALTHAM FOREST TRACK
WALTHAMSTOW
CHESTNUTS SHOWGROUND
TOWN HALL
ASSEMBLY HALL
Waltham Forest Coll
FOREST ROAD
A503
THORPE COOMBE HOSP
Health Cen
E17
UPPER WALTHAMSTOW
WOOD STREET
Clubho. Cricket Ground
CHILDREN'S BOATING POND
A104 NEW
WOODFORD
FOREST RISE
LEA BR RD
WHIPPS
WHIPPS CROSS HOSPITAL
HOE STREET
WALTHAMSTOW CENTRAL
Selborne Walk Shop Cen
WALTHAMSTOW QUEENS ROAD
WALTHAMSTOW CEM
LEA BRIDGE ROAD
A104
HIGH ROAD
LEYTON GRN
Superstores
Swim Pool
LEYTONSTONE
E10
LEYTON
Cricket Ground
90
77
89
88
96
1
2
3
4
5
6
7

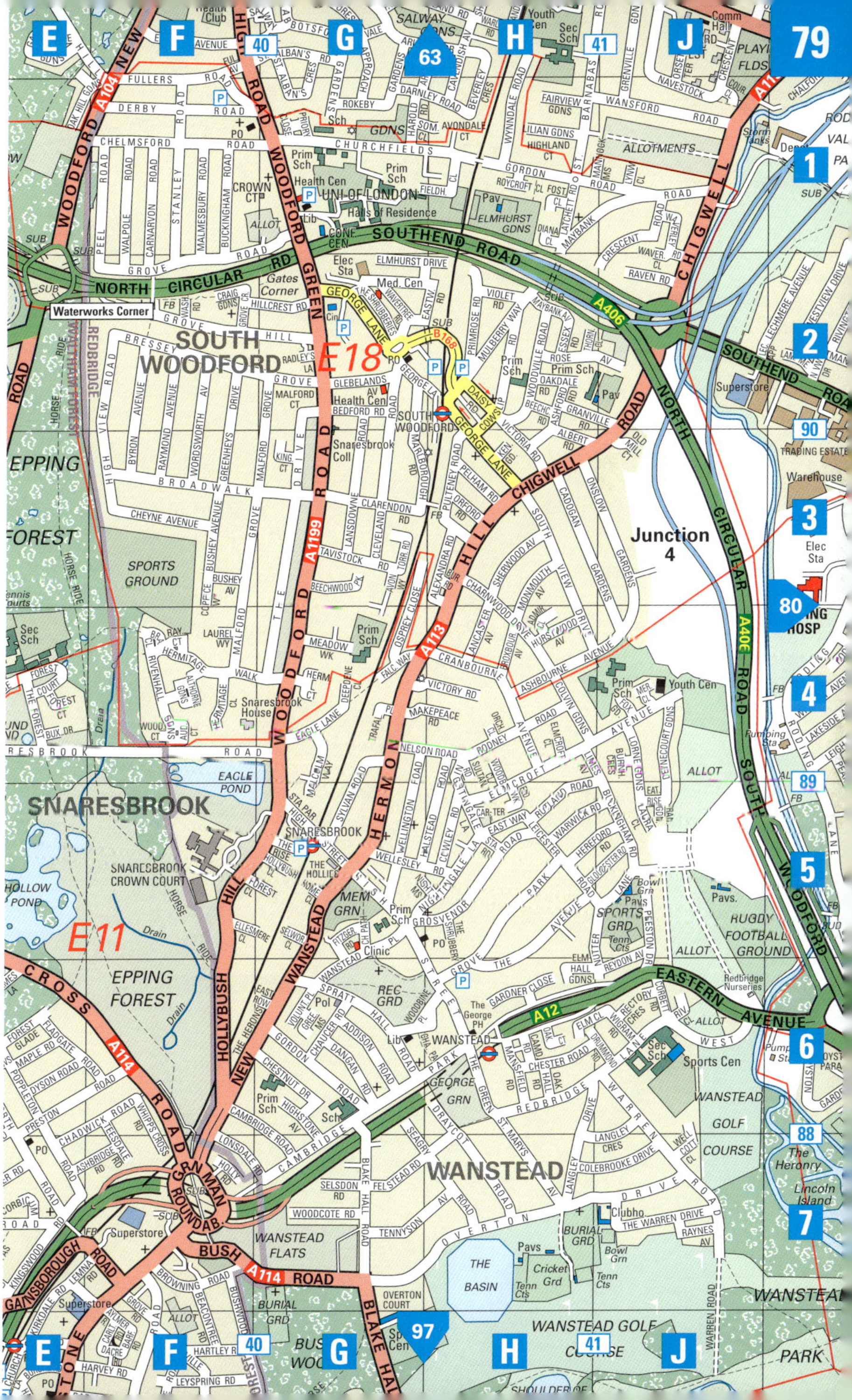

E
F
G
H
J
63
40
41
1
2
3
4
5
6
7
80
90
89
88
97
SOUTH WOODFORD
E18
SNARESBROOK
E11
WANSTEAD
EPPING FOREST
Waterworks Corner
Gates Corner
NORTH CIRCULAR RD
SOUTHEND ROAD
WOODFORD NEW ROAD
WOODFORD GREEN ROAD
HIGH ROAD
HOLLYBUSH HILL
NEW WANSTEAD
HERMON HILL
CHIGWELL ROAD
CHIGWELL HILL
GEORGE LANE
EASTERN AVENUE
CAMBRIDGE PARK
BUSH ROAD
BLAKE HALL ROAD
CROSS ROAD
GREEN MAN ROUNDAB.
HIGH STREET
NORTH CIRCULAR ROAD
WOODFORD ROAD SOUTH
Junction 4
UNI OF LONDON
Halls of Residence
SOUTH WOODFORD
SNARESBROOK
WANSTEAD
Snaresbrook Coll
Snaresbrook House
SNARESBROOK CROWN COURT
EAGLE POND
HOLLOW POND
SPORTS GROUND
RUGBY FOOTBALL GROUND
WANSTEAD GOLF COURSE
WANSTEAD FLATS
THE BASIN
WANSTEAD PARK
Superstore
TRADING ESTATE
Warehouse
Sports Cen
Redbridge Nurseries
The Heronry
Lincoln Island
A104
A1199
A113
A114
A12
A406
B168

A
B
C
D
E
1
2
3
4
5
6
7
64
98
79
42
43
90
89
88
IG8
IG5
IG4
IG1
CLAYHALL
GANTS HILL
REDBRIDGE
RODING VALLEY PARK
OLD MONOVIANS SPORTS GRD
WANSTEAD Clubhouse R.F.C.
SPORTS GROUND
EGG CLUMP
COCKED HAT PLANTATION
ASH PLANTATION
HOSPITAL HILL WOOD
Hospital Hill
UNITY TRADING ESTATE
Superstore
RODING HOSP
RECREATION GROUND
REC GRD
CLAYHILL PARK
TIPTREE ESTATE
GARDEN OF REST
RUGBY FOOTBALL GROUND
PORT OF LONDON AUTH. REC GRD
VALENTINES PARK
Valentines Mansion
DRIVING RANGE
The Heronry
Lincoln Island
Rook Island
ORNAMENTAL WATERS
WANSTEAD PARK
WOODFORD AVENUE
EASTERN AVENUE
WOODFORD ROAD
CLAYHALL AVENUE
CRANBROOK ROAD
BEEHIVE LANE
ROAD SOUTH
A12
A113
A1400
A406
B192

E
F
G
H
J
44
65
82
90
89
88
99
1
2
3
4
5
6
7
Fullwell Cross
IG6
FAIRLOP
FAIRLOP WATER
FAIRLOP WATERS GOLF COURSE
DRIVING RANGE
SPORTS GROUND
FOREST INDUSTRIAL PARK
BRACKEN INDUSTRIAL ESTATE
Sailing Centre
Forest Farm
Sports Cen
ALDBOROUGH HATCH
Aldborough Hall Farm
Aldborough Hatch Farm
Riding School
BARKINGSIDE
BARKINGSIDE CEM
BARKINGSIDE REC GRD
BARNARDOS VILLAGE
Barkingside FC & Ford Utd FC
A123
HIGH ST
ROAD
NEWBURY PARK
EASTERN AVENUE
A12
IG2
IG3
FORD'S SPORTS GROUND
SEVEN KINGS PARK
SEVEN KINGS
MELBOURNE FIELD
Cran Brook
Seven Kings Water
PAINTERS
NORTH ROAD
ALDBOROUGH ROAD
CHASE LANE
OAKS LANE
FOREST ROAD
HORNS ROAD
MEADS LANE
BENTON ROAD
WARDS ROAD
HERTFORD ROAD
PERTH ROAD
SPORTS GRD
REC GRD

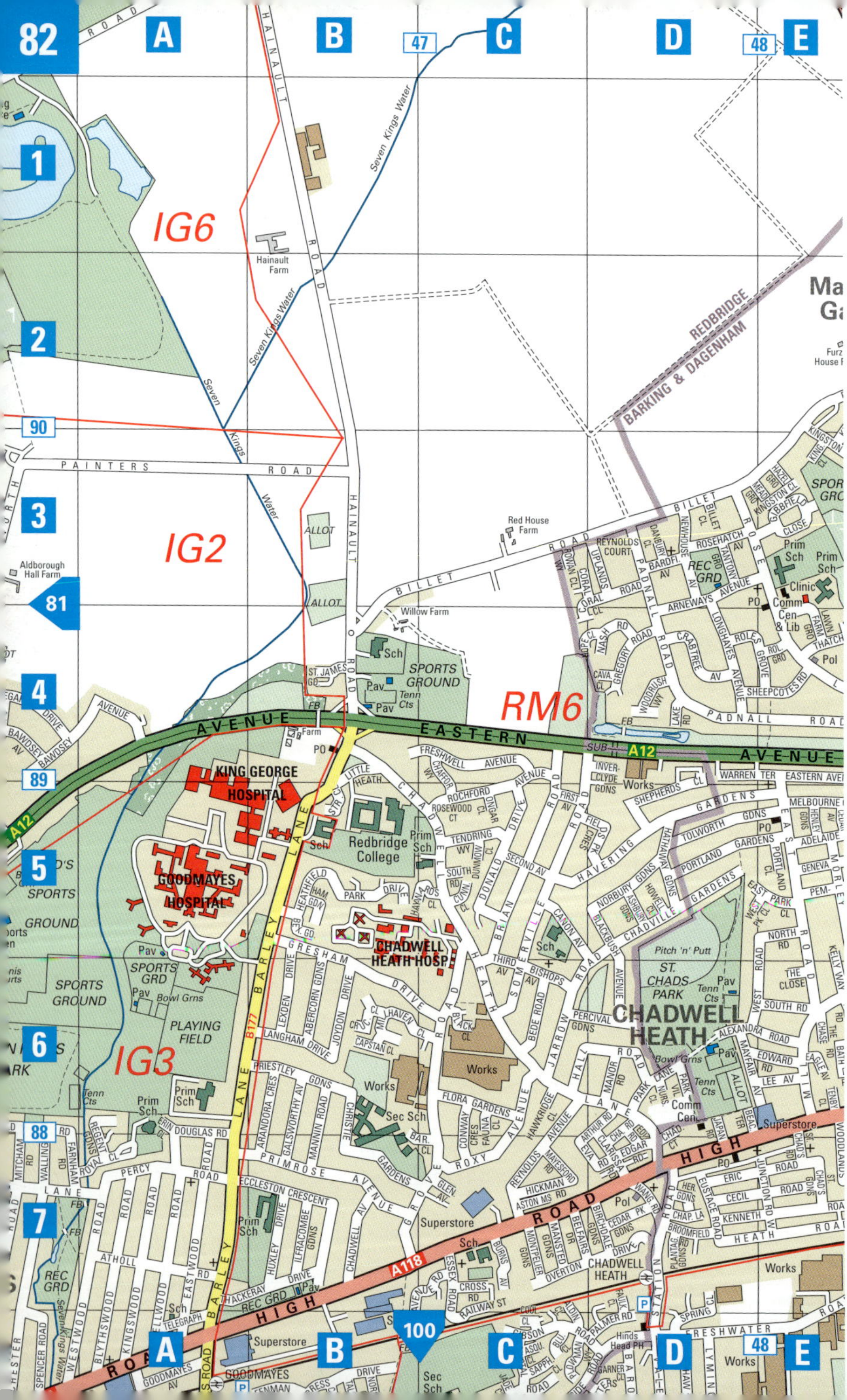
A
B
C
D
E
47
48
1
2
3
4
5
6
7
90
89
88
81
100
IG6
IG2
IG3
RM6
Hainault Farm
Seven Kings Water
Seven Kings Water
HAINAULT ROAD
PAINTERS ROAD
ALLOT
ALLOT
Aldborough Hall Farm
Red House Farm
Willow Farm
BILLET ROAD
REDBRIDGE
BARKING & DAGENHAM
Furze House Farm
REYNOLDS COURT
UPLANDS
CORAL CL
ROWAN CL
DANBURY CL
NEWHOUSE AV
BARDFIELD AV
ROSEHATCH AV
TANTONY GRO
REC GRD
ROSE LANE
Prim Sch
Prim Sch
Clinic
Comm Cen & Lib
PO
ARNEWAYS AVENUE
LONGHAYES AVENUE
CRABTREE AV
ROLFES GROVE
SHEEPCOTES RD
PADNALL ROAD
NASH RD
GREGORY ROAD
WOODRUSH WY
LAKE RD
KINGSTON CL
MEAD GRO
HAZEL GRO
FARM GRO
THATCHES GRO
SPORTS GROUND
Pol
Sch
SPORTS GROUND
Pav
Tenn Cts
Pav
ST. JAMES GDNS
FB
AVENUE
EASTERN
AVENUE
A12
SUB
Farm
PO
KING GEORGE HOSPITAL
GOODMAYES HOSPITAL
Redbridge College
Prim Sch
Sch
CHADWELL HEATH HOSP.
LITTLE HEATH
FRESHWELL AVENUE
CHAFFORD WY
ROCHFORD AVENUE
ROSEWOOD CT
ONGAR CL
TENDRING WY
DUNMOW CL
SOUTH RD
CUNN. CL
DONALD DRIVE
SECOND AV
THIRD AV
BRIAN
SOMERVILLE
HEATH ROAD
FIRST AV
FIELDS PK CRES
INVERCLYDE GDNS
Works
SHEPHERDS CL
WARREN TER
EASTERN AVENUE
GARDENS
TOLWORTH GDNS
HAVERING GARDENS
PORTLAND GARDENS
NORBURY GDNS
ASHBURY GDNS
HOWELL CL
HATHAWAY GDNS
BLACKBUSH AVENUE
CHADVILLE GARDENS
CANON AV
BISHOPS AV
Sch
MELBOURNE GDNS
HENLEY GDNS
ADELAIDE
GENEVA
EAST PARK CL
WEST PK CL
NORTH RD
EAST ROAD
MORLEY
KELLY WAY
THE CLOSE
SOUTH RD
WEST ROAD
Pitch 'n' Putt
ST. CHADS PARK
Tenn Cts
Pav
CHADWELL HEATH
ALEXANDRA ROAD
EDWARD RD
LEE AV
EAGLE AV
Bowl Grns
Pav
Tenn Cts
ALLOT
MAYFAIR AV
PERCIVAL GDNS
JARROW ROAD
HALL LANE
MANOR RD
PARK LANE
BEDE ROAD
Works
Works
FLORA GARDENS
HAWKRIDGE CL
AVENUE
CONWAY CRES
FAUNA CL
ROXY AV
REYNOLDS AVENUE
MAYESFORD RD
HICKMAN
ASTON MS RD
ARTHUR RD
EVA RD
CLARISSA RD
EDGAR RD
Comm Cen
Superstore
HIGH ROAD
A118
Pol
CEDAR PK GDNS
BIRCHDALE GDNS
BELFAIRS DR
MANSTED GDNS
MONTPELIER GDNS
OVERTON DRIVE
CHADWELL HEATH
STATION ROAD
HER. GDNS
CHAP. LA
BROOMFIELD
EUSTACE ROAD
ERIC ROAD
CECIL ROAD
KENNETH ROAD
HEATH ROAD
JUNCTION RD W
CHADS GDNS
WOODLANDS
Works
SPRING CL
FRESHWATER
Works
Hinds Head PH
PALMER RD
GOODMAYES LANE
BARLEY LANE
B177
HEATHFIELD PARK DRIVE
GRESHAM DRIVE
LEXDEN DRIVE
ABERCORN GDNS
JOYDON DRIVE
LANGHAM DRIVE
CAPSTAN CL
HAVEN CL
BLACKSMITH CL
PRIESTLEY GDNS
ARANDORA CRES
GALSWORTHY AV
MANNIN ROAD
CHRISTIE GARDENS
Sec Sch
BAR. CL
PRIMROSE AVENUE
GLEN AV
GROVE
ECCLESTON CRESCENT
Prim Sch
HUXLEY DRIVE
ILFRACOMBE GDNS
CHADWELL AV
Superstore
Sch
ESSEX ROAD
CROSS RD
RAILWAY ST
BURNS AV
THACKERAY DRIVE
REC GRD
Pav
Sch
TELEGRAPH
Superstore
GOODMAYES AV
GOODMAYES
Sec Sch
SPORTS GROUND
SPORTS GRD
Pav
Bowl Grns
PLAYING FIELD
Prim Sch
Prim Sch
ERIN CL
DOUGLAS RD
REGENT GDNS
ROYAL CL
PERCY ROAD
EASTWOOD ROAD
ATHOLL ROAD
KINGSWOOD
ELLWOOD
BLYTHSWOOD
WESTWOOD
SPENCER ROAD
REC GRD
FB
FB
LANE
MITCHAM RD
WALLING RD
FARNHAM RD
BAWDSEY AV
BAWDSEY AVENUE
DRIVE
Tenn Cts
SPORTS GROUND
Ma Ga
A

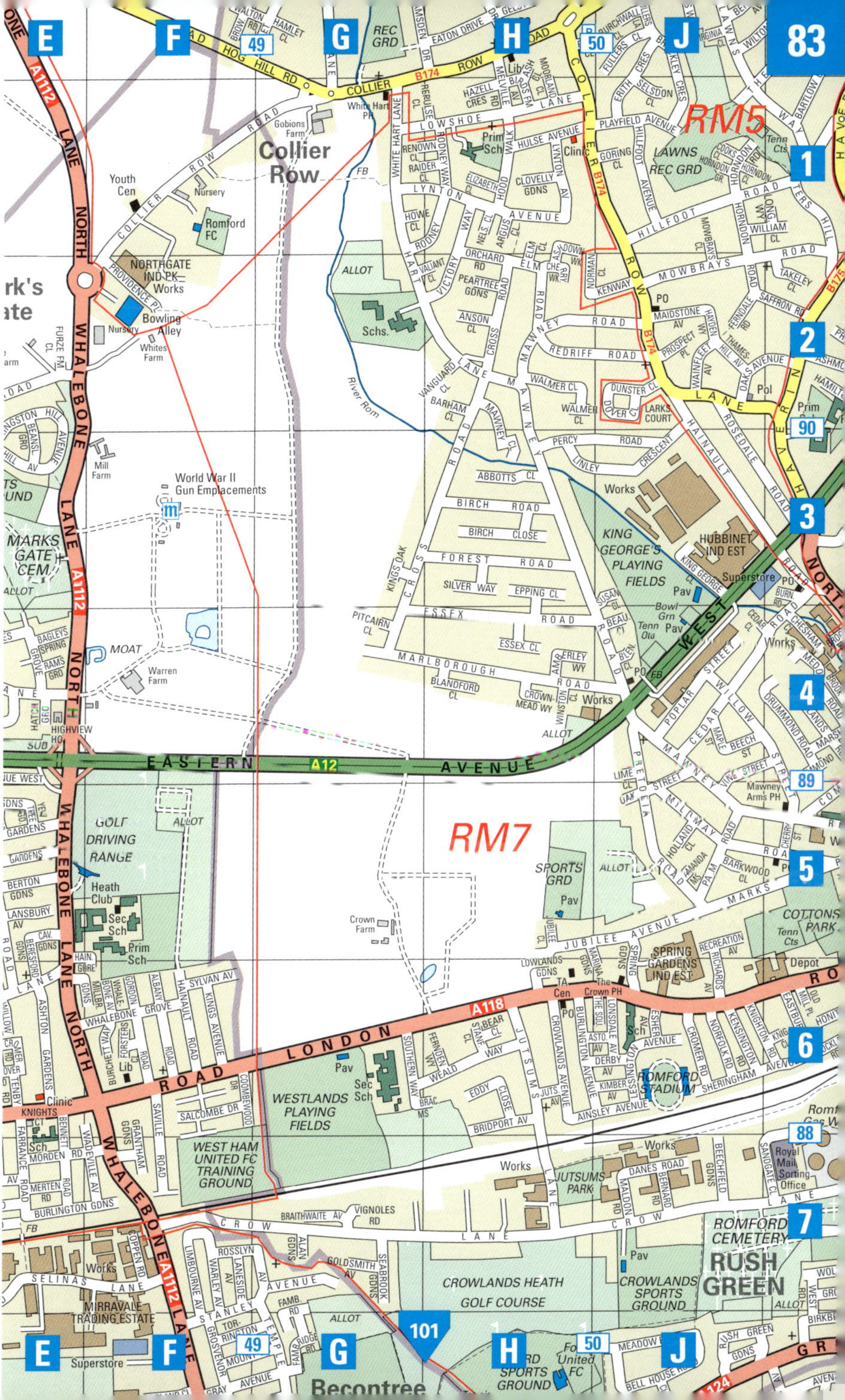

E
F
G
H
J
1
2
3
4
5
6
7
49
50
90
89
88
101
RM5
RM7
Collier Row
COLLIER ROW
HOG HILL RD
B174
White Hart PH
White Hart Lane
Gobions Farm
Youth Cen
Nursery
Romford FC
NORTHGATE IND PK
Works
Bowling Alley
PROVIDENCE PL
Whites Farm
FURZE FM CL
A1112
WHALEBONE LANE NORTH
River Rom
ALLOT
Schs.
Lib
Prim Sch
Clinic
LAWNS REC GRD
REC GRD
EATON DRIVE
LOWSHOE
HULSE AVENUE
PLAYFIELD AVENUE
HILLFOOT AVENUE
MOWBRAYS ROAD
MAIDSTONE AV
PO
REDRIFF ROAD
LARKS COURT
HAINAULT ROAD
MAWNEY ROAD
VANGUARD CL
CROSS ROAD
ABBOTTS CL
BIRCH ROAD
BIRCH CLOSE
FOREST ROAD
SILVER WAY
EPPING CL
ESSEX ROAD
ESSEX CL
PITCAIRN CL
MARLBOROUGH ROAD
BLANDFORD CL
CROWN MEAD WY
KINGS OAK
PERCY ROAD
LINLEY CRESCENT
Works
HUBBINET IND EST
KING GEORGE'S PLAYING FIELDS
Superstore
Pav
Bowl Grn
Tenn Ctn
WEST
POPLAR STREET
Mill Farm
World War II Gun Emplacements
MARKS GATE CEM
MOAT
Warren Farm
HIGHVIEW
EASTERN AVENUE
A12
GOLF DRIVING RANGE
Heath Club
Sec Sch
Prim Sch
ALLOT
Crown Farm
SPORTS GRD
JUBILEE AVENUE
SPRING GARDENS IND EST
RECREATION AV
COTTONS PARK
Depot
The Crown PH
A118
LONDON ROAD
WESTLANDS PLAYING FIELDS
WEST HAM UNITED FC TRAINING GROUND
Sec Sch
Pav
ROMFORD STADIUM
SHERINGHAM AVENUE
AINSLEY AVENUE
JUTSUMS PARK
Works
Royal Mail Sorting Office
CROW LANE
ROMFORD CEMETERY
RUSH GREEN
CROWLANDS HEATH GOLF COURSE
CROWLANDS SPORTS GROUND
MIRRAVALE TRADING ESTATE
SELINAS LANE
Superstore
Becontree
United FC
SPORTS GROUND
Clinic
KNIGHTS
Lib
Sch
BURLINGTON GDNS
WHALEBONE GROVE
SAVILLE ROAD
GOLDSMITH AV

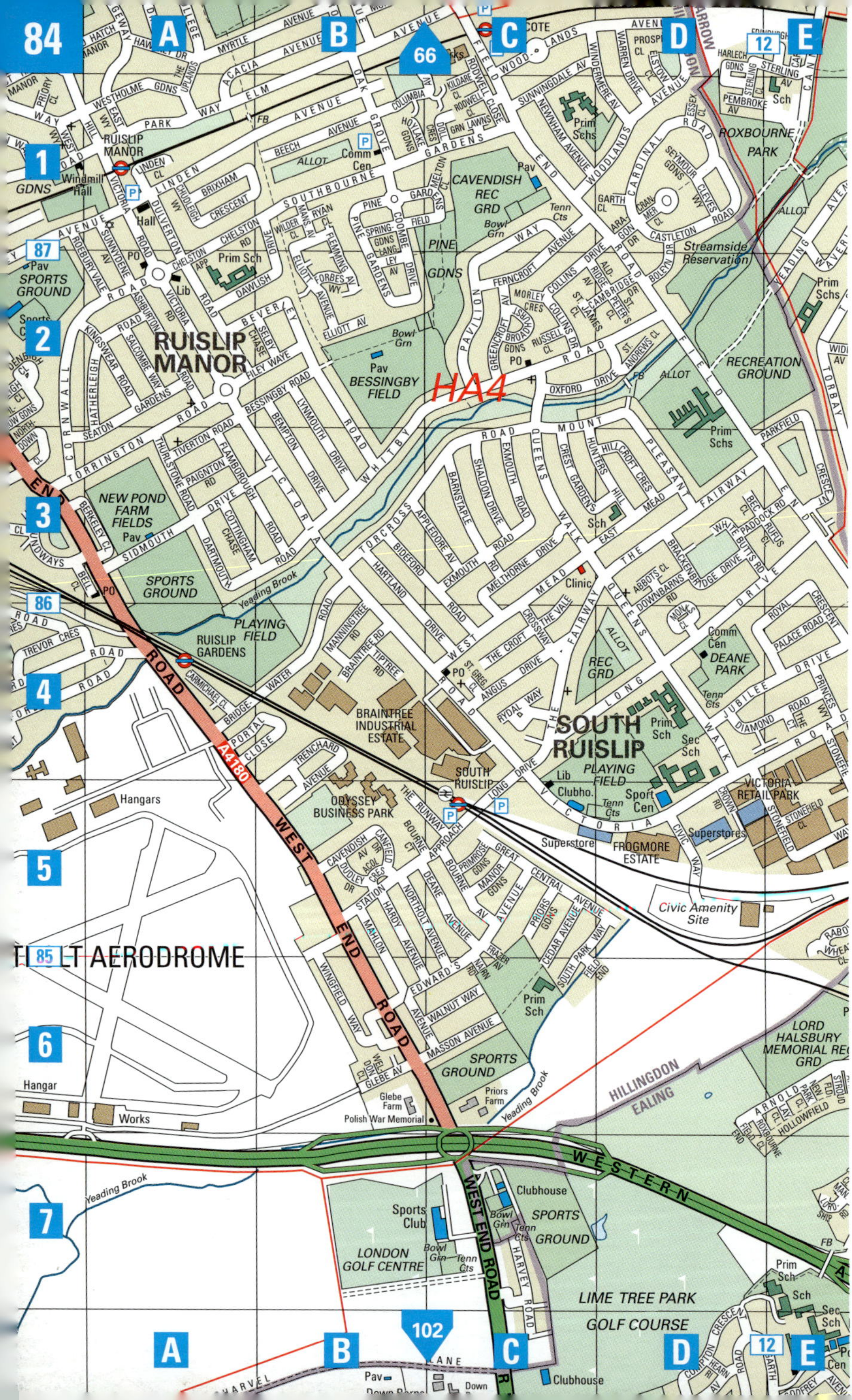

A
B
C
D
E
66
12
87
86
85
102
1
2
3
4
5
6
7
RUISLIP MANOR
RUISLIP MANOR
SOUTH RUISLIP
HA4
CAVENDISH REC GRD
PINE GDNS
BESSINGBY FIELD
ROXBOURNE PARK
Streamside Reservation
RECREATION GROUND
SPORTS GROUND
NEW POND FARM FIELDS
RUISLIP GARDENS
PLAYING FIELD
BRAINTREE INDUSTRIAL ESTATE
ODYSSEY BUSINESS PARK
DEANE PARK
REC GRD
VICTORIA RETAIL PARK
FROGMORE ESTATE
Superstore
Superstores
Civic Amenity Site
AERODROME
Hangars
Hangar
Works
Glebe Farm
Polish War Memorial
Priors Farm
Yeading Brook
HILLINGDON
EALING
LORD HALSBURY MEMORIAL REC GRD
WESTERN
LONDON GOLF CENTRE
Sports Club
Clubhouse
LIME TREE PARK GOLF COURSE
A4180
WEST END ROAD
VICTORIA ROAD
Windmill Hall
Prim Sch
Prim Schs
Sec Sch
Comm Cen
Sport Cen
Clinic
Lib
ALLOT

RAYNERS LANE
WEST HARROW
SOUTH HARROW
NORTHOLT
HA2
UB5
ALEXANDRA AVENUE
A4090
NORTHOLT ROAD
A312
WHITTON AV W
MANDEVILLE ROAD
CHURCH ROAD
EASTCOTE LANE
ALEXANDRA PARK
NEWTON PARK WEST
NEWTON FM ECOLOGY PK
NORTHOLT RECREATION GRD
ROXETH REC GRD
EARLSMEAD STADIUM
ISLIP MANOR PARK
BELVUE PARK
KELVIN INDUSTRIAL ESTATE
SPORTS GRD
PLAYING FIELD
Air Traffic Radio Sta
Harrow Borough FC
Superstore
Cricket Ground
The Roxbourne
NORTHOLT PARK
THE GREENWOODS
EALING GOLF
67
86
87
103
E F G H J
1 2 3 4 5 6 7
13 14

A
B
C
D
E
1
2
3
4
5
6
7
15
16
68
87
85
104
HA2
HA1
UB6
ROXETH
HARROW ON THE HILL
SUDBURY
NORTHWICK PARK & ST. MARK'S HOSPITALS
MINIATURE RIFLE RANGE
HARROW SCHOOL PLAYING FIELDS
HARROW SCHOOL GOLF COURSE
PARK LAKE
Harrow School Farm
ST. ANDREW'S AT HARROW HOSP
HARROW SCHOOL GOLF COURSE
CLEMENTINE CHURCHILL HOSPITAL
CHASEWOOD PARK
SPORTS GROUND
SPORTS GRD
PLAYING FIELDS
EALING NORTHERN SPORTS GRD
REC GRD
Sudbury Tower
SUDBURY HILL HARROW
SUDBURY HILL
SOUTH HARROW
HORSENDEN WOOD
HORSENDEN HILL GOLF COURSE
HORSENDEN HILL
Horsenden Farm
HOME MEAD
SPORTS GROUND
BERKELEY FIELDS
GREAT BRAMSTONES
GLAXCO WELLCOME
Warehouses
Works
Westway Cross Shopping
GREENFORD
LOWER ROAD
BESSBOROUGH ROAD
ROXETH HILL
LONDON ROAD
SUDBURY HILL
HARROW ROAD
GREENFORD ROAD
SUDBURY COURT DRIVE
WATFORD ROAD
WHITTON AVENUE WEST
WHITTON AVENUE
EASTCOTE AVENUE
WOOD END
CAVENDISH AVENUE
HORSENDEN LANE NORTH
OLDFIELD LANE
MOUNT PARK ROAD
A404
A4005
A4090
A4127
B457

E
F
G
H
J
17
69
105
88
85
1
2
3
4
5
6
7
PRESTON
NORTH WEMBLEY
WEMBLEY PARK
WEMBLEY
ALPERTON
SUDBURY
HA9
HA0
Northwick Park Pavilion
PRESTON PARK
SOUTH KENTON
Windermere PH
PRESTON ROAD
Stanmore Junction
FORTY FARM SPORTS GROUND
WEMBLEY COMMERCIAL CENTRE
G.E.C. ESTATE
Dog & Duck PH
Youth Club
NORTH WEMBLEY
EAST LANE
A4088
VALE FARM SPORTS GROUND
Clubhouse
Swim Pool
WEMBLEY FC
KING EDWARD VII PARK
Green Man Hotel PH
CONFERENCE CEN
STADIUM WAY
EXHIB CEN
ROYAL ROUTE
BRENT COUNCIL OFFICES
WEMBLEY STADI
SUDBURY & HARROW ROAD
BARHAM PARK
HARROW ROAD
HIGH ROAD
WEMBLEY CENTRAL
A404
A4089
A4005
PLAYING FIELDS
DEPOTS
SUDBURY TOWN
Health Centre
EALING ROAD
BRIDGEWATER ROAD
SUDBURY GOLF COURSE
GRAND UNION CANAL (PADDINGTON BRANCH)
ALPERTON CEMETERY
ONE TREE HILL REC GRD
Wealdstone Brook
Wembley Brook
BRENT
EALING
EMPIRE WAY
WEMBLEY HILL RD
ENGINEERS WAY
Elvin Ho
Plaza
Ibis
TOWING PATH

A
B
C
D
E
1
2
3
4
5
6
7
70
87
85
21
106
BARN HILL OPEN SPACE
WELSH HARP OPEN SPACE
Welsh Harp Environmental Education Centre
Wembley Sailing Club
Chilcott Nursery
Woodfield Sch
QUEENSBURY RD
WOOD LANE
SALMON STREET
CHURCH LANE
B454
FORTY LANE
FORTY AVENUE
A4088
BRENT TOWN HALL
BLACKBIRD HILL
NEASDEN LANE
NEASDEN LANE NORTH
OLD CHURCH LANE
TUDOR GDNS
HA9
NW10
Superstore
Health Cen
SPORTS GRD
WEMBLEY PARK
BRIDGE RD
PARK DRIVE
EMPIRE WAY
B4565
CHALKHILL RD
BARNHILL ROAD
BRENT GREEN WALK
Comm Cen
River Brent
SPORTS GRD
FULTON ROAD
Palace of Industry
Superstores
WEMBLEY PK BUS-CEN
STADIUM BUS-CEN
CANNON TRADING EST
Sunday Market
WEMBLEY ARENA
CONFERENCE CEN
EXHIB CEN
WEMBLEY STADIUM REDEVELOPMENT open 2006
Works
NEASDEN RAIL DEPOT
HANNAH CLOSE
GREAT CENTRAL WAY
B4557
SOUTH WAY
DRURY WAY
DRURY WAY IND EST
BRENT PARK
WEMBLEY STADIUM
BRENT COUNCIL OFFICES
SHERRINS FARM OPEN SPACE
TOKYNGTON
TOKYNGTON REC GRD
TOKYNGTON RECREATION GROUND
HARROW ROAD
NORTH CIRCULAR ROAD
A406
IKEA TWR
CHURCH END
GIBBONS REC GRD
Swaminarayan Hindi Mission Temple
Power Station
Mitchel Brook
Wembley Brook
DEPOTS
STONEBRIDGE PARK
Leisure Cen
Brent Junction
BRENTFIELD
HILLSIDE
A404
CRAVEN PK
A407
STONEBRIDGE REC GRD
STONEBRIDGE
Princess Royal Distribution Centre
NORTHFIELDS INDUSTRIAL

E
F
G
H
J
22
23
71
1
2
3
4
5
6
7
90
87
85
107
BRENT RESERVOIR
RIFLE RANGE
SPORTS GRD
Nursery
WELSH HARP
AQUARIUS BUSINESS PARK
STAPLES CORNER BUSINESS PK
Staples Corner
Refuse Disposal Works
Superstore
Holiday Inn
TRAIN DEPOT
WELLINGTON PARK EST
NEASDEN RECREATION GRD
NORTH CIRCULAR ROAD
A406
EDGWARE ROAD
BROADWAY
A5
NW2
NEASDEN
EVANS BUSINESS CEN
GLADSTONE PARK
DOLLIS HILL
Tennis Courts
BUS GARAGE
DUDDEN HILL LANE
A4088
NEASDEN LANE
B453
FALCON PK IND EST
DOLLIS HILL
Coll of North West London
CHANCEL IND EST
CYGNUS BUS CEN
CHARMAN PK IND EST
HIGH ROAD
A407
WILLESDEN
WILLESDEN CEMETERY
WILLESDEN CEMETERY (JEWISH)
NW10
ROUNDWOOD PARK
LIBERAL JEWISH CEM
WILLESDEN COMMUNITY HOSP
WILLESDEN GREEN
WALM LANE
A4003
BRONDESBURY PARK
CRICKLEWOOD

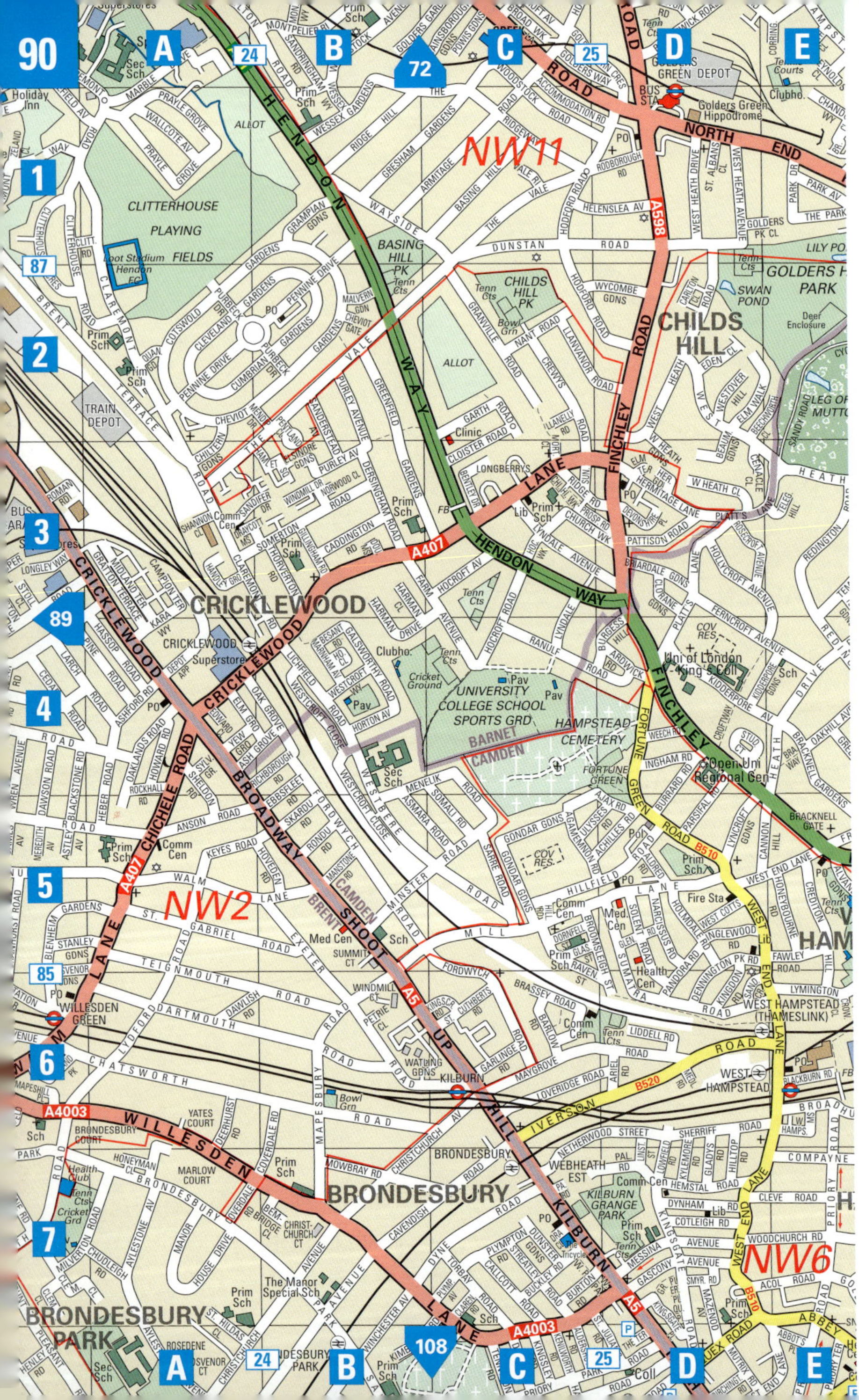

A
B
C
D
E
1
2
3
4
5
6
7
72
89
87
85
108
24
25
NW11
NW2
NW6
CRICKLEWOOD
BRONDESBURY
BRONDESBURY PARK
CHILDS HILL
CLITTERHOUSE PLAYING FIELDS
Hendon FC
GOLDERS GREEN DEPOT
Golders Green Hippodrome
GOLDERS HILL PARK
SWAN POND
Deer Enclosure
BASING HILL PK
CHILDS HILL PK
UNIVERSITY COLLEGE SCHOOL SPORTS GRD
HAMPSTEAD CEMETERY
Cricket Ground
TRAIN DEPOT
Holiday Inn
HENDON WAY
FINCHLEY ROAD
NORTH END ROAD
GOLDERS GREEN ROAD
CRICKLEWOOD LANE
CRICKLEWOOD BROADWAY
SHOOT UP HILL
KILBURN
WILLESDEN LANE
WILLESDEN GREEN
WEST HAMPSTEAD
WEST HAMPSTEAD (THAMESLINK)
BRONDESBURY
CHICHELE ROAD
WALM LANE
MILL LANE
FORTUNE GREEN ROAD
WEST END LANE
IVERSON ROAD
A407
A5
A598
A4003
B510
B520
BARNET
CAMDEN
BRENT
Uni of London King's Coll
Open Uni Regional Cen
KILBURN GRANGE PARK
The Manor Special Sch

HAMPSTEAD HEATH
NW3
N6
PARLIAMENT HILL
HAMPSTEAD
BELSIZE PARK
SOUTH HAMPSTEAD
WEST HAMPSTEAD
PRIMROSE HILL
KENWOOD
Kenwood House
THE IVEAGH BEQUEST KENWOOD HOUSE
ATHLONE HOUSE
SANDY HEATH
WEST HEATH
HEATHLANDS
VALE OF HEALTH
HIGHGATE PONDS
HAMPSTEAD PONDS
VIADUCT POND
LILY POND
STOCK POND
CONCERT POND
KENWOOD LADIES POND
BIRD SANCTUARY POND
BOATING POND
HIGHGATE MEN'S POND
WHITESTONE POND
QUEEN MARY'S HOSP
ROYAL FREE HOSP
FREUD MUSEUM
TAVISTOCK CEN
MAITLAND PARK ESTATE
ST. DOMINIC'S PRIORY
NORTH END WAY
SPANIARDS ROAD
HEATH STREET
HAMPSTEAD HIGH ST
ROSSLYN HILL
HAVERSTOCK HILL
FITZJOHN'S AVENUE
FINCHLEY ROAD
ADELAIDE ROAD
HAMPSTEAD LANE
CYCLE PATH
ATHLETICS TRACK
Cricket Ground
SWISS COTTAGE
CHALK FARM
FINCHLEY ROAD & FROGNAL
FINCHLEY ROAD
A502
A41
B519
B511
B509
E
F
G
H
J
1
2
3
4
5
6
7
26
73
87
92
85
109

A
B
C
D
E
74
30
1
2
3
4
5
6
7
87
91
85
110
N6
N19
NW5
HIGHGATE
HIGHGATE CEMETERY
WATERLOW PARK
WHITTINGTON HOSPITAL
DARTMOUTH PARK
UPPER HOLLOWAY
TUFNELL PARK
GOSPEL OAK
KENTISH TOWN
HILLDROP ESTATE
H.M. PRISON HOLLOWAY
ARCHWAY
ATHLETICS TRACK
LISMORE CIRCUS
CHALK FARM
HIGHGATE HIGH STREET
ARCHWAY ROAD
HOLLOWAY ROAD
JUNCTION ROAD
FORTESS ROAD
KENTISH TOWN ROAD
CAMDEN ROAD
BRECKNOCK ROAD
CHALK FARM ROAD
HORNSEY LANE
HORNSEY RISE
HIGHGATE HILL
DARTMOUTH PARK HILL
GORDON HO ROAD
MANSFIELD ROAD
MALDEN ROAD
PRINCE OF WALES RD
CAMDEN PK RD
YORK WAY
AGAR GROVE
ST. PANCRAS WAY
ROYAL COLLEGE ST
A1
A400
A503
A5200
B518
B519
B517
B540
Youth Cen
Comm Cen
Works
FORUM CLUB
London Met Uni
Royal Mail Delivery Off
Camden Lock Mkt
MTV Studios
Superstore
Roundhouse
Stables Mkt

E
F
G
H
J
31
32
75
87
94
85
111
1
2
3
4
5
6
7
FINSBURY PARK
N4
PARK
FINSBURY
SEVEN SISTERS ROAD
BLACKSTOCK ROAD
HOLLOWAY ROAD
HORNSEY ROAD
TOLLINGTON ROAD
CALEDONIAN ROAD
LIVERPOOL ROAD
HIGHBURY PARK
HIGHBURY GROVE
GREEN LANES
ISLEDON RD
STROUD GREEN ROAD
CROUCH HILL
N7
LOWER HOLLOWAY
HOLLOWAY
N5
HIGHBURY
N1
CANONBURY
BARNSBURY
CLISSOLD
SPORTS GROUND
WEST RESERVOIR
ARSENAL STADIUM
ARSENAL F.C.
PENTONVILLE PRISON
Nags Head Shop.Cen
HIGHBURY & ISLINGTON
ESSEX ROAD
CALEDONIAN ROAD
CALEDONIAN ROAD & BARNSBURY
DRAYTON PARK
HOLLOWAY ROAD
ARSENAL
PARADISE PARK
London Metropolitan Univ
City & Islington Coll
HACKNEY
ISLINGTON
ST. PAUL'S ROAD
CANONBURY ROAD
NEW NORTH ROAD
UPPER STREET
A503
A1
A1201
A105
A103
A5203
A1199
A104
B105
B515

STAMFORD HILL
STOKE NEWINGTON
N16
ABNEY PARK CEMETERY
CLISSOLD PARK
SPORTS GROUND
Clissold House
SHACKLEWELL
HACKNEY DOWNS
BUTTERFIELD GREEN
SHELLGROVE EST
KINGSLAND
DALSTON
E8
N1
DE BEAUVOIR TOWN
LONDON FIELDS
RESERVOIR
Water Works
Kingsland Shop Cen
STOKE NEWINGTON HIGH ST
STOKE NEWINGTON RD
KINGSL HIGH ST
KINGSLAND ROAD
STAMFORD HILL
STOKE NEWINGTON CH ST
NORTHWOLD ROAD
MANOR ROAD
GREEN LANES
NEWINGTON GRN RD
BALLS POND RD
DALSTON LANE
GRAHAM ROAD
QUEENSBRIDGE ROAD
SOUTHGATE ROAD
ALBION ROAD
RECTORY ROAD
EVERING RD
AMHURST RD
PEMBURY ROAD
UPPER CLAPTON
CLAPTON COMMON
SPRINGFIELD PARK
A10
A104
A105
A107
A1199
A1207
B104
B105
B108
B111
B102
A
B
C
D
E
1
2
3
4
5
6
7
33
34
76
85
87
93
112

E
F
G
H
J
35
77
Walthamstow Marsh Nature Reserve
Walthamstow Marsh Nature Reserve
Lee Valley Riding Cen
SPORTS GROUND
LEYTON MARSHES
Lee Valley Ice Centre
NORTH MILLFIELDS RECREATION GROUND
E5
LEA BRIDGE ROAD
A104
Flood Relief Channel
LEE VALLEY PITCH & PUTT GOLF COURSE
River Lee or Lea
NATURE RESERVE
Water Works Bridge
LEA BRIDGE
LEE VALLEY PARK
HACKNEY MARSH
SEYMOUR ROAD PLAYING FIELD
MARSH LANE PLAYING FIELD
Gas Works
FOOTBALL GRD
ALLOT
DORMA TRADING PK
CROMWELL IND EST
ENTERPRISE PARK
LEYTON BUSINESS CEN
WALTHAM FOREST
HACKNEY
LEA VALLEY WALK
River Lee Navigation
CLAPTON PARK
LOWER CLAPTON
LOWER CLAPTON RD
SOUTH MILLFIELDS REC GRD
NYE BEVAN EST
HOMERTON HOSPITAL
HOMERTON HIGH STREET
A102
B112
KINGSMEAD EST
WICK COMMUNITY WOODLAND
Marshgate Bridge
HOMERTON
MABLEY GREEN
E9
EAST CROSS ROUTE
A12
HACKNEY WICK
JOHN HOWARD CEN
MORNING LANE
B113
WICK ROAD
KENWORTHY ROAD
HACKNEY CENTRAL
TOWN HALL
CASSLAND ROAD
A106
WELL STREET COMMON
VICTORIA PARK
OLD FORD
UNION CANAL
SOUTH HACKNEY
MARE ST
A107
WELL ST
CHAPMAN RD
ROTHBURY RD
TOWER HAMLETS
1
2
3
4
5
6
7
85
87
96
113

A
B
C
D
E
78
39
E10
LEYTON
Comm Cen
LEYTON GRANGE EST
CHURCH ROAD
HIGH ROAD
LEYTON
A112
A1006
A106
A12
B161
B161
FRANCIS
ABBOTS PK
LEYTON MIDLAND RD
Tenn Cts
Cricket Ground
Pav
Youth Cen
Med. Cen
Prim Sch
Sec Sch
Pol
Clinic
SIDMOUTH PARK
LEYTON ORIENT FC
COUNCIL OFFS
Lib
ST. PATRICK'S RC CEMETERY
LEYTONSTONE
AVONDALE COURT
LEYTONSTONE HIGH RD
Leisure Cen
Comm Cen
Dep
GREEN
WARREN ROAD
GROVE
CATHALL RD
New Spitalfields Market
ORIENT WAY
MARSH LANE PLAYING FIELD
LEYTON BUSINESS CEN
ORIENT IND PARK
IVE FM SPORTS GRD
Dagenham Brook
ALLOT
Superstore
Works
RECREATION GROUND
River Lee or Lea
ETON MANOR SPORTS GROUND
Lea Valley Sports Centre
RUCKHOLT ROAD
TEMPLE MILL LANE
LEE VALLEY PARK
LEE VALLEY CYCLE CIRCUIT
Lee Valley Campsite
Channelsea River
Cold Stores
WALTHAM FOREST
NEWHAM
DRAPERS FIELD REC GRD
LEYTON ROAD
CHOBHAM ROAD
LEYTONSTONE ROAD
HACKNEY WICK
EASTWAY COMMERCIAL CENTRE
STADIUM (Closed)
EAST CROSS CENTRE
WICK COMMUNITY WOODLAND
95
85
E15
STRATFORD
STRATFORD
Stratford Cen
THE MALL
BUS STA
CONF & LEISURE CEN
Sports Cen
Coll
Mag Ct
Disc Cen
Univ of E Lon
GREAT EASTERN ROAD
A118
BROADWAY
ROMFORD
WEST HAM
THE GROVE
Superstore
Cin
Thea
WHITE POST LA
CARPENTERS ROAD
A115
BOW INDUSTRIAL PARK
Waterworks River
CITY MILL RIVER TOWPATH
BOW BACK RIVERS WALK
Works
Old Ford Locks
Lock
EAST CROSS ROUTE
A12
114
1
2
3
4
5
6
7

E
F
G
H
J
79
41
40
WANSTEAD GOLF COURSE
THE BASIN
PARK
SHOULDER OF MUTTON POND
HERONRY POND
BUSH WOOD
RESERVOIR WOOD
BLAKE HALL ROAD
WOODLANDS AVENUE
NORTHUMBERLAND AVENUE
LEYTONSTONE ROAD
WALTHAM FOREST
REDBRIDGE
E11
E12
ALDERSBROOK ROAD
ALDERSBROOK
CENTRE ROAD
A114
A116
WANSTEAD FLATS
JUBILEE POND
87
98
NEWHAM
MANOR PARK CEMETERY
Crematorium
WEST HAM CEMETERY
JEWISH CEMETERY
HARROW ROAD
DAMES ROAD
CAPEL ROAD
WOODGRANGE ROAD
WANSTEAD PARK
FOREST GATE
ROMFORD ROAD
85
E7
UPTON LANE
GREEN STREET
KATHERINE ROAD
A118
B167
B109
B164
B165
WEST HAM PARK
WEST HAM
UPTON
PLASHET
115
1
2
3
4
5
6
7

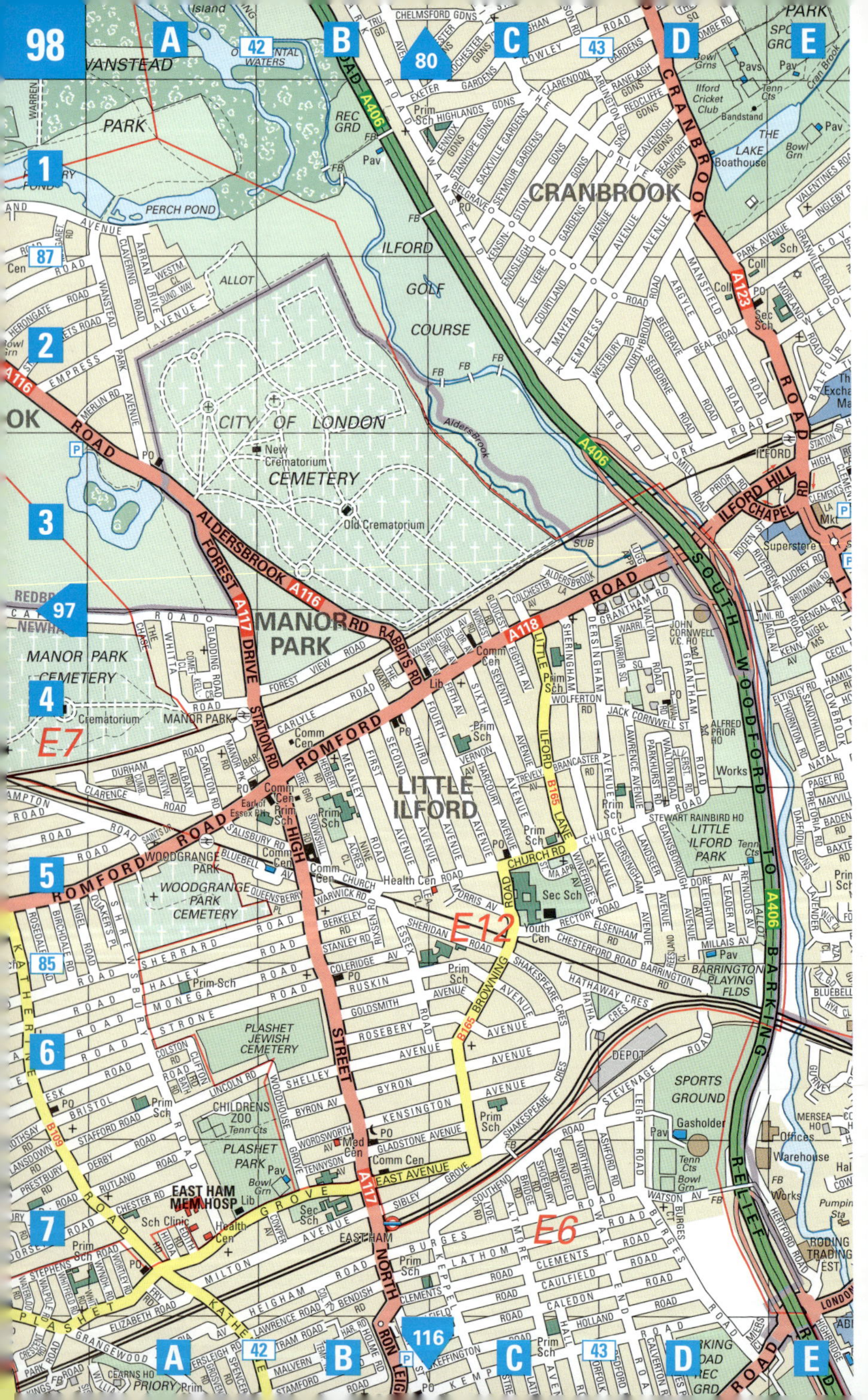
WANSTEAD PARK
PERCH POND
CITY OF LONDON CEMETERY
New Crematorium
Old Crematorium
ILFORD GOLF COURSE
CRANBROOK
Ilford Cricket Club
THE LAKE
Boathouse
MANOR PARK
MANOR PARK CEMETERY
Crematorium
E7
LITTLE ILFORD
LITTLE ILFORD PARK
E12
WOODGRANGE PARK
WOODGRANGE PARK CEMETERY
PLASHET JEWISH CEMETERY
PLASHET PARK
CHILDRENS ZOO
EAST HAM MEM HOSP
SPORTS GROUND
Gasholder
BARRINGTON PLAYING FLDS
E6
RODING TRADING EST
Superstore
ROMFORD ROAD
ALDERSBROOK RD
WOODFORD TO BARKING RELIEF
HIGH STREET NORTH
CRANBROOK ROAD
ILFORD HILL
A406
A116
A117
A118
A123
B165
B109
42
43
80
97
116
87
85

E
F
G
H
J
44
81
SEVEN KINGS
REC GRD
1
2
3
4
5
6
7
87
100
85
117
IG1
IG3
IG11
ILFORD
LOXFORD
BARKING
HIGH ROAD
GREEN LANE
A118
A1083
A124
A123
A12
SOUTH PARK
SOUTH PARK DRIVE
CRICKLEFIELD STADIUM
Ilford FC
ILFORD CEM
KNOX SPORTS FIELD
LOXFORD PARK
BARKING PARK
THE LAKE
BARKING PARK REC GRD
Indoor Bowl Club
Bowling Greens
ALLOTMENTS
LONGBRIDGE ROAD
FANSHAWE AV
NORTHERN RELIEF ROAD
RIPPLE ROAD
WINSTON WAY
GRIGGS AP
LOXFORD LANE
Loxford Water
Mayes Brook
REDBRIDGE
BARKING & DAGENHAM
TRAIN DEPOT
SEVEN KINGS
BARKING HOSPITAL
UPNEY
Health Cen
Health Centre
Sec Sch
Prim Sch
Youth Cen
TA Cen
Swim Pool
Fire Sta
Superstore
TOWN HALL
Clinic
Sixth Form Coll
Comm Cen & Thea
Vicarage Fld Shop Cen
REDBRIDGE ENTERPRISE CEN
The Cauliflower PH
The Royal Oak PH
The Bell PH
PARKWAY
WATER LA
SOUTH PARK TERRACE
MEADWAY
DAWLISH
LEVETT
BREAMORE
EGERTON
WOODBRIDGE
CAVENDISH
SANDRINGHAM
UPNEY LANE
TRIPP BURIAL

A
B
C
D
E
82
48
87
99
85
118
1
2
3
4
5
6
7
IG3
RM8
RM9
GOODMAYES
HIGH ROAD
Superstore
Superstores
GOODMAYES ROAD
BARLEY LANE
KINFAUNS ROAD
CASTLETON ROAD
ASHGROVE ROAD
GREEN LANE
The Lord Napier PH
GOODMAYES PARK
Bowling Club
Prim Sch
Sec Sch
Youth Cen
MAYESBROOK ROAD
ALLOT
Mayes Brook
GOODMAYES PARK REC GRD
GOODMAYES LANE
Sixth Form Coll
Clinic
Comm Cen & Thea
LONGBRIDGE ROAD
Robin Hood PH
Uni of East London
MAYESBROOK PARK
BARKING FC Clubhouse
ARENA
Sports Cen
BOATING LAKE
Pav
WOOD LANE
A124
A1153
B177
B191
BECONTREE AVENUE
BENNETTS CASTLE LANE
VALENCE AVENUE
VALENCE HO MUS
VALENCE MOAT
BECONT
CHADWELL HEATH
Hinds Head PH
Works
SPORTS GROUND
FRESHWATER ROAD
Leisure Centre
PARSLOES PARK
Bowling Green
PORTERS AVENUE
LODGE AVENUE
SPORTS GRD
Roundhouse PH
BECONTREE
Health Cen
Lib
Hall
RIPPLESIDE BURIAL GROUND
MAYBROOK MEADOW EST
GORESBROOK ROAD
Cherry Tree PH
Day Hosp
ALLOT

E
F
G
H
J
83
49
50
CROWLANDS HEATH GOLF COURSE
CROWLANDS SPORTS GROUND
Works
MIRRAVALE TRADING ESTATE
Superstore
ALLOT
Becontree Heath
Sec Sch
FORD SPORTS GROUND
Romford F.C.
Clubhouse
Sports Centre
DRIVING RANGE
Tennis Courts
Pav
Clubhouse
MEADOW ROAD
BELL HOUSE ROAD
RUSH GREEN
A124
RUSH
GREEN
HAVERING
BARKING & DAGENHAM
1
2
3
4
5
6
7
87
86
85
RM7
RM10
Pitch 'n' Putt
SPORTS GROUND
BARKING AND DAGENHAM CIVIC CENTRE
CENTRAL PARK
Fire Sta
Schs
Recycling Centre
Nursery
PARKSIDE HO
FELS FIELD
A1083
WOOD LANE
RAINHAM ROAD NORTH
HEATHWAY
SOUTH LANE
Swim Pool
Comm Cen
Hall
Superstore
Prim Sch
Health Cen
Sec Sch
Lib
Comm Cen
Clinic
Eastbrook PH
STERLING INDUSTRIAL ESTATE
Sports Hall
Dagenham & Redbridge F.C.
Rhone-Poulenc Rorer
DAGENHAM EAST
Railway PH
PONDFIELD PARK
A1240
DAGENHAM
Shopping Centre
DAGENHAM HEATHWAY
A1112
Cross Keys PH
The Bull Inn PH
Schs
Coll
The Gores
GORESBROOK PARK
Clinic
OLD DAGENHAM PARK
ARENA
THE LEYS
SPORTS GRD
Sports Hall
B178
MANOR ROAD SPORTS G
RAINHAM ROAD SOUTH
119
ORCHARD ROAD

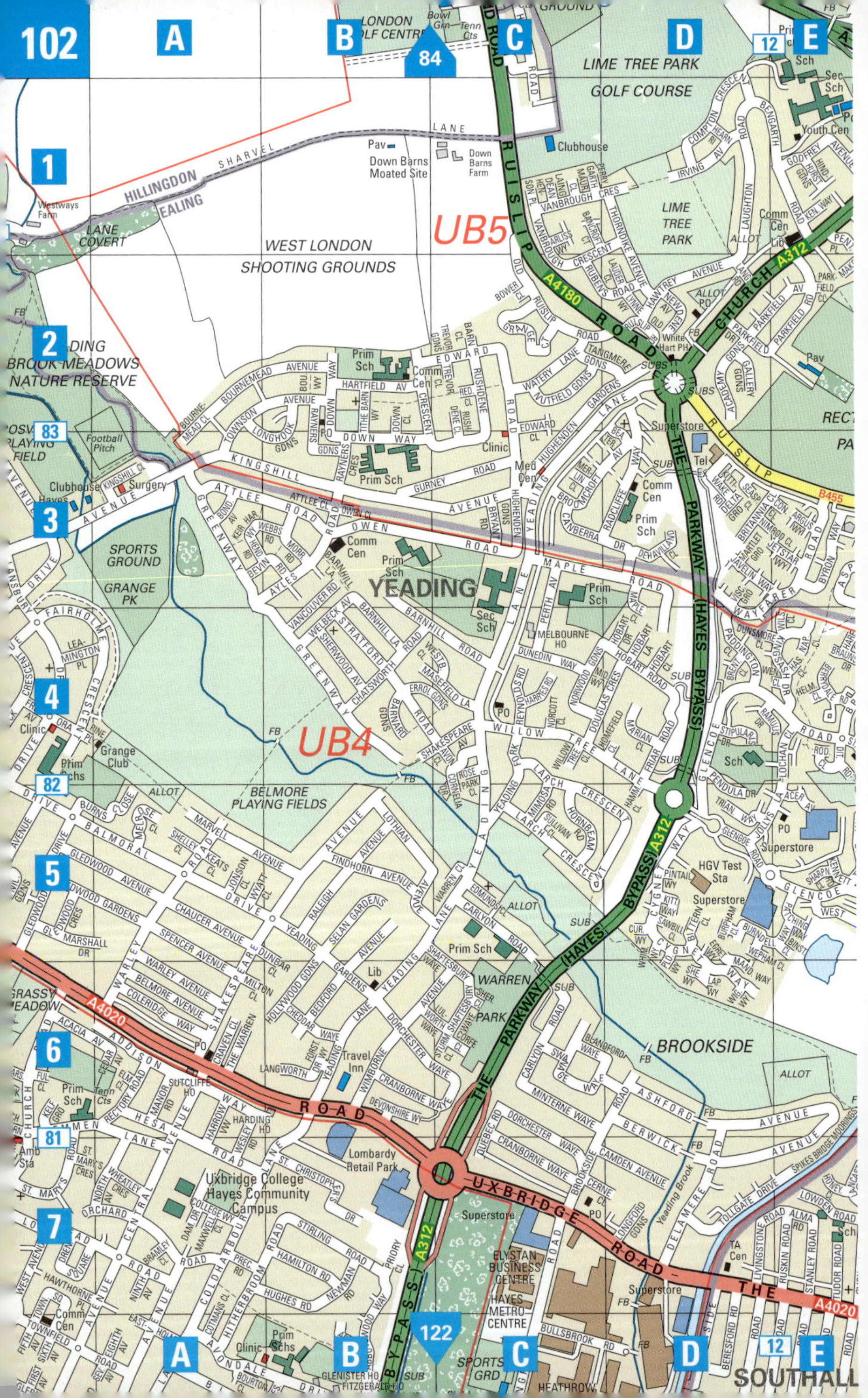

A
B
C
D
E
84
12
122
1
2
3
4
5
6
7
83
82
81
LONDON GOLF CENTRE
LIME TREE PARK GOLF COURSE
Clubhouse
Pav
Down Barns Moated Site
Down Barns Farm
SHARVEL LANE
HILLINGDON
EALING
Westways Farm
LANE COVERT
UB5
WEST LONDON SHOOTING GROUNDS
RUISLIP ROAD
A4180
LIME TREE PARK
ALLOT
Comm Cen
Lib
CHURCH ROAD
A312
COMPTON CRESCENT
BENGARTH ROAD
IRVING AV
GODFREY AVENUE
Youth Cen
Sec Sch
Sch
LAUGHTON ROAD
VANBROUGH CRES
THORNDIKE AVENUE
LAUDER CL
RUBENS ROAD
HANTREY AVENUE
White Hart PH
PARKFIELD AV
PARKFIELD RD
RECT
BROOK MEADOWS NATURE RESERVE
Prim Sch
EDWARD ROAD
HARTFIELD AV
BOURNEMEAD AVENUE
TOWNSON AVENUE
LONGHOOK GDNS
DOWN WAY
RAYNERS CRES
RUSHDENE
WATERY LANE
NUTFIELD GDNS
TANGMERE GDNS
HUGHENDEN GARDENS
Superstore
Tel Ex
RUISLIP ROAD
B455
THE PARKWAY (HAYES BYPASS)
Football Pitch
PLAYING FIELD
Clubhouse Hayes
Surgery
KINGSHILL AVENUE
Clinic
Med Cen
GURNEY ROAD
YEADING LANE
ATTLEE ROAD
OWEN ROAD
Comm Cen
SPORTS GROUND
GRANGE PK
GREENWAY
YEADING
Sec Sch
MAPLE ROAD
MELBOURNE HO
CANBERRA DR
RADCLIFFE
DEHAVILLAND
WAYFARER
DUNSMORE
PADDINGTON
FAIRHOLME
LEAMINGTON PL
CRESCENT
BARNHILL ROAD
VANCOUVER RD
STRATFORD
CHATSWORTH
MASEFIELD LA
ERROL GDNS
DUNEDIN WAY
HOBART ROAD
DOUGLAS CRES
PO
WILLOW TREE LANE
FRIAR ROAD
UB4
FB
Clinic
Grange Club
Prim Schs
BELMORE PLAYING FIELDS
ALLOT
LARCH CRESCENT
HORNBEAM
GLENCOE ROAD
PENDULA DR
Sch
PO
Superstore
HGV Test Sta
Superstore
BALMORAL DRIVE
MARVELL AVENUE
GLEDWOOD AVENUE
GLEDWOOD GARDENS
CHAUCER AVENUE
SPENCER AVENUE
WARLEY AVENUE
BELMORE AVENUE
COLERIDGE WAY
MARSHALL DR
YEADING GARDENS
FINDHORN AVENUE
Prim Sch
WARREN PARK
ALLOT
BROOKSIDE
Lib
GRASSY MEADOW
A4020
ADDISON
PO
Travel Inn
CRANBORNE WAYE
DORCHESTER WAYE
CARLYON ROAD
ASHFORD
BERWICK AVENUE
CAMDEN AVENUE
Prim Sch
Tenn Cts
Amb Sta
CHURCH
ROAD
HARDING HO
Lombardy Retail Park
Uxbridge College Hayes Community Campus
UXBRIDGE ROAD
Superstore
ELYSTAN BUSINESS CENTRE
HAYES METRO CENTRE
BYPASS
A312
PO
Yeading Brook
DELAMERE ROAD
TOLLGATE DRIVE
TA Cen
THE
A4020
Superstore
ST. MARY'S
ORCHARD
STIRLING ROAD
HAMILTON RD
NEWMAN
HUGHES RD
Comm Cen
Prim Schs
Clinic
GLENISTER HO
FITZGERALD HO
SUB
SPORTS GRD
BULLSBROOK RD
HEATHROW
SOUTHALL

E
F
G
H
J
13
14
85
104
83
82
81
123
1
2
3
4
5
6
7
UB5
UB1
GREENFORD
RAVENOR PARK
DORMER'S WELLS
WEST MIDDLESEX GOLF COURSE
NORTHOLT GOLF COURSE
KENSINGTON & CHELSEA PLAYING FIELDS
BELVUE PARK
EALING GOLF RANGE
THE METROPOLITAN CENTRE
KELVIN INDUSTRIAL ESTATE
MARNHAM FIELDS
BIRKBECK COLLEGE SPORTS GROUND
SPORTS GROUND
SMITHS FARM EST
WESTERN AVENUE
A40
CHURCH ROAD
RUISLIP ROAD
THE BROADWAY
GREENFORD ROAD
A4127
GREENFORD PARK REC GRD
GREENFORD PARK CEMETERY
JUBILEE PARK
KING GEORGE'S FIELD
EALING
HILLINGDON
Sports Hall
Water Tower
Taylor Woodrow
Cricket Club
Greenford Recycling Centre
Greenford Depot
MARNHAM FIELD
Greenford Bridge
BRENT LODGE PARK
Cricket Ground
Clubhouse
WILLOWTREE MARINA
IND EST
BROADWAY
HIGH STREET
BRIDGE
UXBRIDGE ROAD
Red Lion
Mkt
White Hart PH
Hare & Hounds PH
Red Lion PH
GLENEAGLES TWR
ST. ANDREWS TWR
SHERINGHAM TWR
MASEFIELD AV
CARLYLE AVENUE
DORMERS WELLS LANE
ALLENBY ROAD
LADY MARGARET ROAD
KINGS AVENUE
QUEENS AVENUE
CORNWALL AVENUE
SOMERSET ROAD
WINDMILL LANE
OLDFIELD LANE
FERRYMEAD GARDENS
RAVENOR PARK ROAD
MARNHAM CRESCENT
WESTBURY AVENUE
GREENFORD GARDENS
STICKLETON CL
HILLSIDE ROAD
EASTMEAD AVENUE
BEECHWOOD AVENUE
BURNS AVENUE
NORTH ROAD
NORTHCOTE AVENUE
SAXON ROAD
DANE ROAD
MOUNT AV
DORMERS AVENUE
EVELYN GROVE
ORCHARD AVENUE

A
B
C
D
E
15
16
86
1
2
3
4
5
6
7
83
103
82
81
124
FIELDS
HILL
BRABSTONES
Horsenden Farm
FIRST AVENUE
STATION APPROACH
Westway Cross Shopping Park
GREEN PARK WAY
ROCKWARE AV
GREENFORD
UNEEDA DR
BIRKBECK AVENUE
BIRKBECK COLLEGE SPORTS GROUND
OLDFIELD REC GRD
INGRAM WAY
DOWNING DRIVE
THORPE WK
SPORTS GROUND
Works
Warehouse
PERIVALE WOOD (Nature Reserve)
UB6
Comm Cen
BILTON
Lib
BUCKINGHAM AV
SUNLEY GDNS
SELBORNE GDNS
PERIVALE INDUSTRIAL
PERIVALE
JUBILEE ROAD
ALLOT
SPORTS GROUND
Clubhouse
Prim Sch
GREENFORD ROAD
CRESCENT
CONWAY
WOODHOUSE CL
WOODHOUSE AV
TEES AVENUE
THAMES
MEDWAY DRIVE
HODDER
RUNNYMEDE
DRIVE
GARDENS
COLWYN AV
SCORTON AV
EALING CENTRAL SPORTS GRD
CHILHAM CL
TAVISTOCK AV
ROCKFORD AV
BIDEFORD
Superstore
DAWLISH AV
Tenn Cts
Comm Cen
WELLAND GDNS
MEDWAY PAR
TEIGNMOUTH GARDENS
WESTERN
A40
SOUTH GREENFORD
LEAVER GARDENS
DAVID AV
AVENUE
ATHLETICS TRACK
PERIVALE PARK SPORTS GROUND
Clubho.
CENTRAL PARADE
Mylett Arms PH
Travel Inn
Clubhouse
Hanwell Town FC
PERIVALE LANE
STOCKDOVE WAY
Med. Cen
SPORTS GRD
Leisure Centre
B452
ARGYLE ROAD
FB
CYCLE PATH
GOLF
FARNDALE CRESCENT
Nature Res
COSTONS AVENUE
BETHAM ROAD
WEDMORE RD
OAKFIELD GDNS
LOCARNO ROAD
CLIFTON RD
PERIVALE PARK GOLF COURSE
EAST
River Brent
RUISLIP ROAD
B455
Greenford Bridge
SPORTS GROUND
Sports Hall
Sch
KESTREL HO
DUNLIN HO
FALCON HO
GURNELL GRO
BRENTS CL
ARGYLE CL
CROSSWAY
Bowl Grn
Clubhouse
Pav
PITSHANGER PARK
BELLEVUE ROAD
BRENTCOT
SCOTCH COMMON
CLIVEDON CT
SPORTS GROUND
Tenn Cts
AVALON CL
VALLIS WAY
BROOKBANK AVENUE
ELMBANK WAY
KENNEDY
WINE RD
CUCKOO DENE
GIFFORD GARDENS
BEECHMOUNT AVENUE
White Hart PH
BERESFORD AVENUE
Med. Cen
MAYFIELD GARDENS
HANWAY ROAD
HIGHLAND AV
HOBBAYNE RD
STUDLAND ROAD
BRENT VALLEY PARK
Greenford Recycling Centre
Greenford Depot
MARNHAM FIELD
ALLOT
Prim Sch
Sec Sch
UPFIELD
GREATDOWN ROAD
COPLEY CLOSE
CASTLE BAR PARK
TEMPLEMAN ROAD
ELLIS CT
Comm Cen
CUCKOO PARK
WESTCOTT
STEPHENSON RD
HOMEFARM ROAD
BROWNING AVENUE
CHEYNE PATH
CAVENDISH AVENUE
HATHAWAY GDNS
FOSSE WAY
BRUTON WAY
ROBINSON CL
CLEVELAND PARK
THE MEAD
CLEVELAND ROAD
KINGSLEY AVENUE
HIGHVIEW
LYNTON AVENUE
ROSEMOUNT RD
BRABANK
ROSEBERY GDNS
ST. STEPHENS AV
COLEBROOKE AV
CHESTER GDNS
SUTHERLAND RD
COURTFIELD GDNS
W13
BRENT VALLEY GOLF COURSE
W7
EAGLES TWR
FRAMFIELD ROAD
DRYDEN AVENUE
ALLOT
DRAYTON GREEN
DRAYTON ROAD
COWPER ROAD
SHAKESPEARE ROAD
MILTON ROAD
ALLINGHAM CL
TENNYSON RD
Works
WEST EALING
Superstore
ALEXANDRIA RD
DRAYTON GREEN ROAD
DRAYTON GDNS
DRAYTON AVENUE
MANOR ROAD
Clubhouse
Cricket Ground
Clubhouse
CHURCH ROAD
GLEBE CL
OAKLEY CL
HIGH TREE CT
CHURCHFIELDS RECREATION GROUND
ZOO
BRENT LODGE PARK
Weir
Bowl Grn
Viaduct
HANWELL
STATION
KENSINGTON & CHELSEA CEMETERY
ECCLESTON ROAD
FELIX ROAD
THE BROADWAY
Lib
PO

E
F
G
H
J
17
87
HA0
ALPERTON CEMETERY
ONE TREE REC GRD
BRAEMAR AVENUE
Comm Cen
Clinic
Sec Sch
ALPERTON
PERIVALE
Prim Schs.
PERIVALE NEW BUSINESS CENTRE
WADSWORTH BUSINESS CENTRE
SHERATON BUSINESS CEN
CAPITAL BUSINESS CEN
METROPOLITAN POLICE TRAFFIC UNIT
ALPERTON SPORTS GROUND
MIDDLESEX HO Superstore
Superstore
ABBEY IND EST
Grand Union Canal
River Brent
Holiday Inn Express
EALING ROAD
HANGER LANE
NORTH CIRCULAR
WESTERN AVENUE
A4005
A406
A4020
B456
B455
ALPERTON LANE
WEST WORLD
HANGER LANE
Holiday Inn
ALLOTMENTS
PITSHANGER PARK
SPORTS GRD
GREYSTOKE PARK TERRACE
FOX WOOD
HANGER HILL PARK
Pitch & Putt
PLAYING FIELD
MOUNT VIEW
THE ORCHARD
MONTPELIER PARK
BARCLAYS BANK SPORTS GROUND
Pool
Cricket Ground
Clubho.
CASTLEBAR HILL
W5
NORTH EALING
WEST ACTON
EALING BROADWAY
EALING
TOWN HALL
Arcadia Shop Cen
Ealing Broadway Shop Cen
THE BROADWAY
THE MALL
UXBRIDGE RD
UXBRIDGE ROAD
NEW BDY
Cinema
PITSHANGER MANOR MUS
WALPOLE
EALING COMMON
GUNNERSBURY LANE
Ramada Jarvis
Tenn Club
Castle Ho
1
2
3
4
5
6
7
82
83
81
106
125

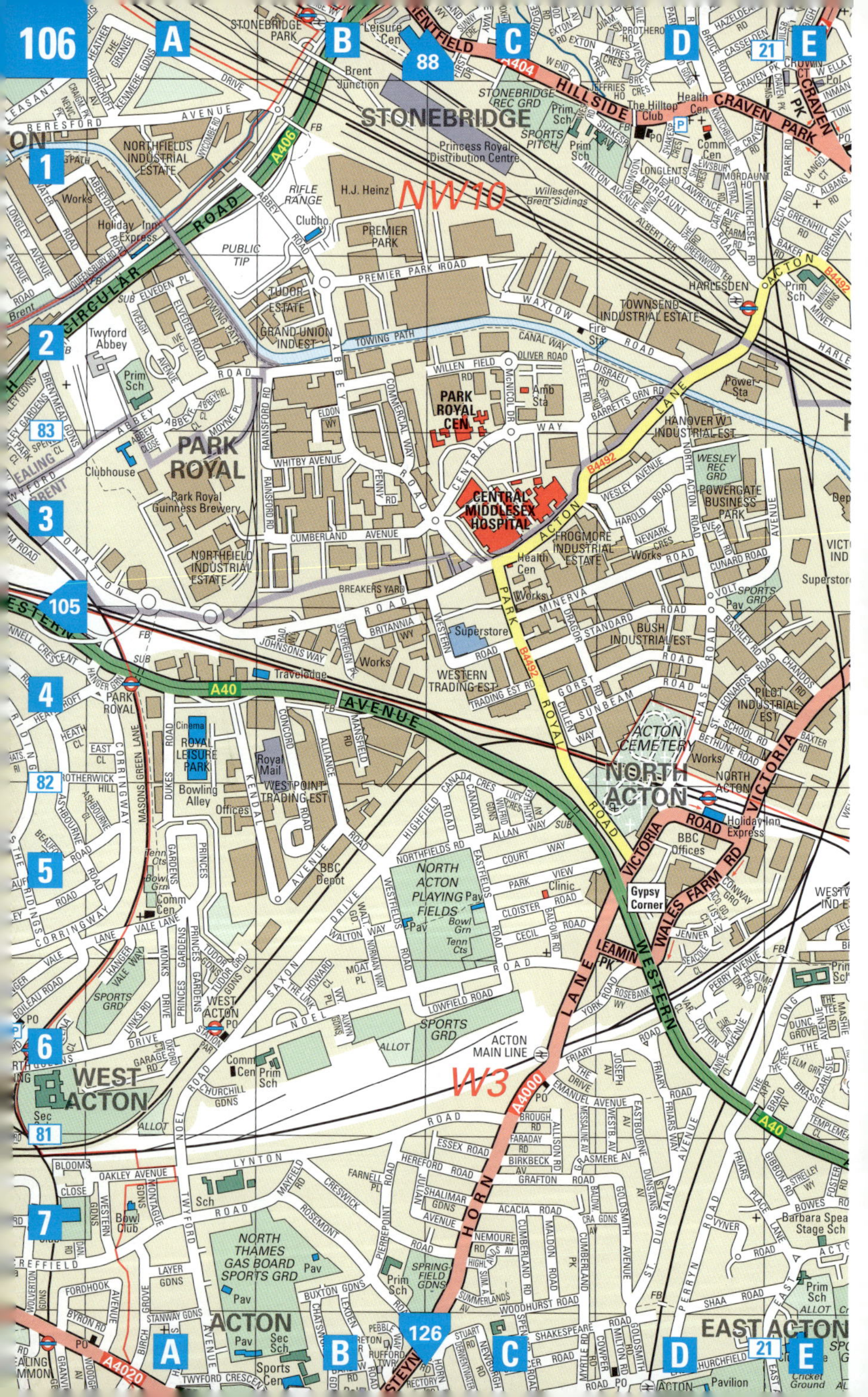
A
B
C
D
E
1
2
3
4
5
6
7
88
21
83
82
81
105
126
STONEBRIDGE
STONEBRIDGE PARK
Brent Junction
Leisure Cen
Princess Royal Distribution Centre
STONEBRIDGE REC GRD
HILLSIDE
CRAVEN PARK
NW10
H.J. Heinz
Willesden Brent Sidings
NORTHFIELDS INDUSTRIAL ESTATE
RIFLE RANGE
Clubho
PREMIER PARK
PREMIER PARK ROAD
PUBLIC TIP
NORTH CIRCULAR ROAD
A406
Holiday Inn Express
Twyford Abbey
TUDOR ESTATE
GRAND UNION IND EST
TOWING PATH
HARLESDEN
TOWNSEND INDUSTRIAL ESTATE
WAXLOW ROAD
PARK ROYAL CEN
ABBEY ROAD
PARK ROYAL
Clubhouse
Park Royal Guinness Brewery
HANOVER W INDUSTRIAL EST
WESLEY REC GRD
POWERGATE BUSINESS PARK
CENTRAL MIDDLESEX HOSPITAL
ACTON LANE
B4492
FROGMORE INDUSTRIAL ESTATE
NORTHFIELD INDUSTRIAL ESTATE
CUMBERLAND AVENUE
BREAKERS YARD
Superstore
BUSH INDUSTRIAL EST
WESTERN TRADING EST
PILOT INDUSTRIAL EST
Travelodge
WESTERN AVENUE
A40
PARK ROYAL
ROYAL LEISURE PARK
Royal Mail
WESTPOINT TRADING EST
ACTON CEMETERY
NORTH ACTON
VICTORIA ROAD
BBC Depot
NORTH ACTON PLAYING FIELDS
Gypsy Corner
WALES FARM RD
WEST ACTON
ACTON MAIN LINE
SPORTS GRD
W3
HORN LANE
A4000
NORTH THAMES GAS BOARD SPORTS GRD
ACTON
EAST ACTON
Barbara Speake Stage Sch
A4020

NW10
W10
W12
HARLESDEN
KENSAL GREEN
KENSAL RISE
NORTH KENSINGTON
WHITE CITY
OLD OAK COMMON
WORMWOOD SCRUBS
BRONDESBURY PARK
KING EDWARD VII SPORTS GRD
WILLESDEN STADIUM
SPORTS GRD
ROUNDWOOD PARK
Willesden Junction
ST. MARY'S RC CEMETERY
KENSAL GREEN CEMETERY
Crematorium
GRAND UNION CANAL (Paddington Branch)
Gas Works
MAINTENANCE DEPOT
LITTLE WORMWOOD SCRUBS REC GRD
NORTH POLE INTERNATIONAL DEPOT
DEPOT
Freightliner Terminal
GATEWAY INDUSTRIAL ESTATE
HYTHE RD IND EST
Superstores
Cumberland Ho
Westmorland Ho
Rutland Bldgs
CUMBERLAND PK
LINFORD CHRISTIE STADIUM
Wormwood Scrubs Pony Centre
QUEEN CHARLOTTE & CHELSEA HOSP
HAMMERSMITH HOSPITAL
H.M. PRISON WORMWOOD SCRUBS
B.B.C. Worldwide
B.B.C. Offices
B.B.C. Television Centre
Westway Sports Cen
WHITE CITY EST
Daytona Raceway
WORMHOLT PARK
HAMMERSMITH PARK
SPORTS GROUND
PEABODY ESTATE
SUTTON EST
PRINCESS LOUISE HOSP
WESTWAY
A40
A404
A4000
A219
A220
HARROW ROAD
SCRUBS LANE
WOOD LANE
DU CANE ROAD
OLD OAK COMMON LANE
ST. QUINTIN AVENUE
TUBBS ROAD
STATION RD
HIGH STREET
MANOR PK RD
CRAVEN PK RD
CHAMBERLAYNE ROAD
DOYLE
BATHURST GARDENS
PALERMO ROAD
LEIGHTON GARDENS
HERBERT GARDENS
WHITMORE GARDENS
CLIFFORD GARDENS
BUCHANAN GARDENS
MITRE WAY
NORTH POLE ROAD
EAST ACTON
SHEPHERD'S
89
127
108
22
23
83
87
81
E F G H J
1 2 3 4 5 6 7

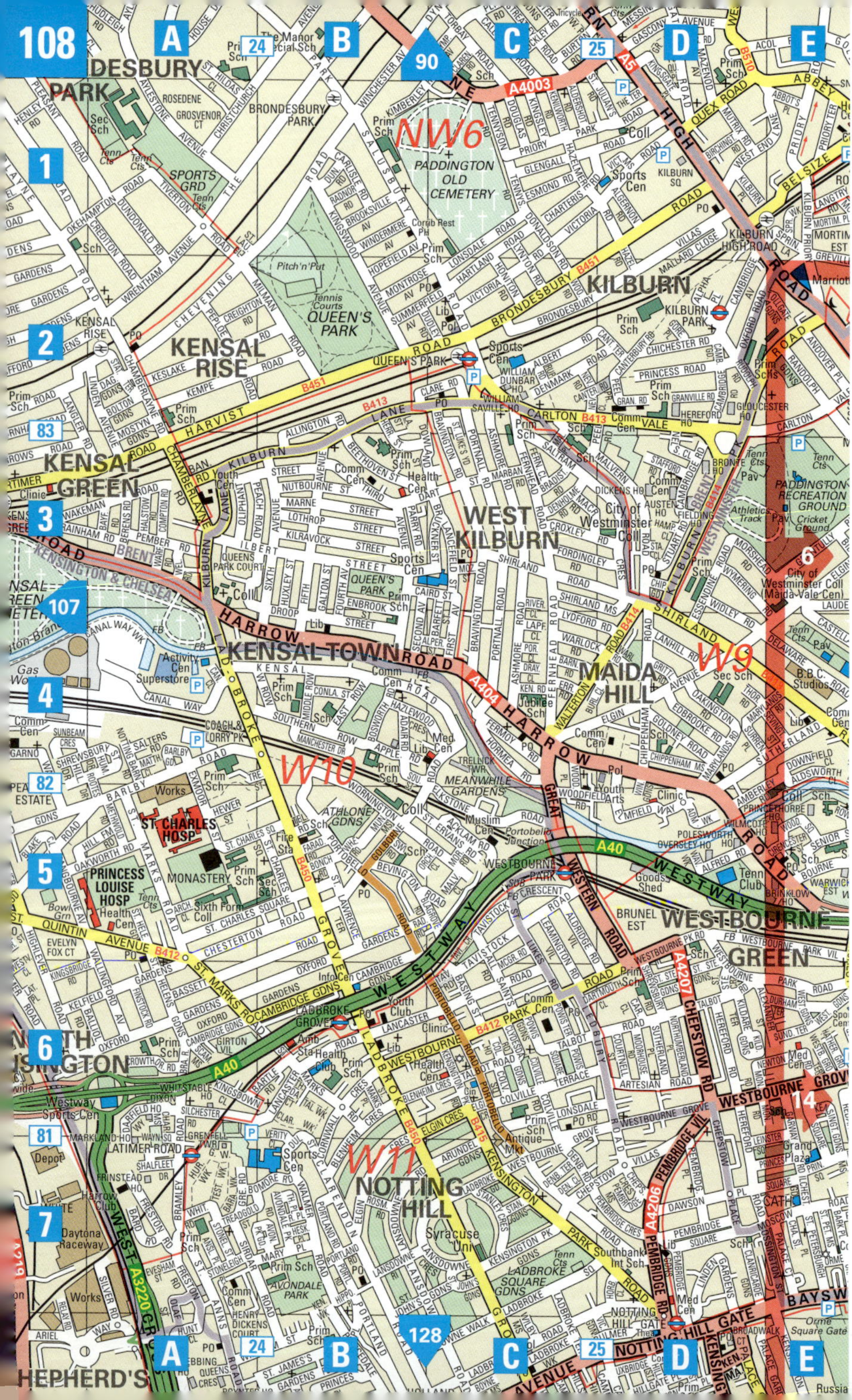

A
B
C
D
E
1
2
3
4
5
6
7
24
25
90
128
83
82
81
107
14
6
NW6
W9
W10
W11
BRONDESBURY PARK
PADDINGTON OLD CEMETERY
QUEEN'S PARK
KENSAL RISE
KILBURN
KILBURN HIGH ROAD
KILBURN PARK
QUEEN'S PARK
KENSAL GREEN
WEST KILBURN
KENSAL TOWN
MAIDA HILL
PADDINGTON RECREATION GROUND
WESTBOURNE GREEN
WESTBOURNE PARK
WESTWAY
NOTTING HILL
NOTTING HILL GATE
LADBROKE GROVE
LATIMER ROAD
ST. CHARLES HOSP
PRINCESS LOUISE HOSP
MEANWHILE GARDENS
HARROW ROAD
KILBURN LANE
LADBROKE GROVE
PORTOBELLO ROAD
CHEPSTOW RD
PEMBROKE VIL
WESTBOURNE GROVE
BRONDESBURY VILLAS
SHIRLAND ROAD
ELGIN AVENUE
CARLTON VALE
QUEX ROAD
ABBEY ROAD
BELSIZE
A4003
A5
B510
B451
B413
B414
A404
A40
B450
B412
B4
A4207
A4206
B415
A3220
WEST CROSS ROUTE

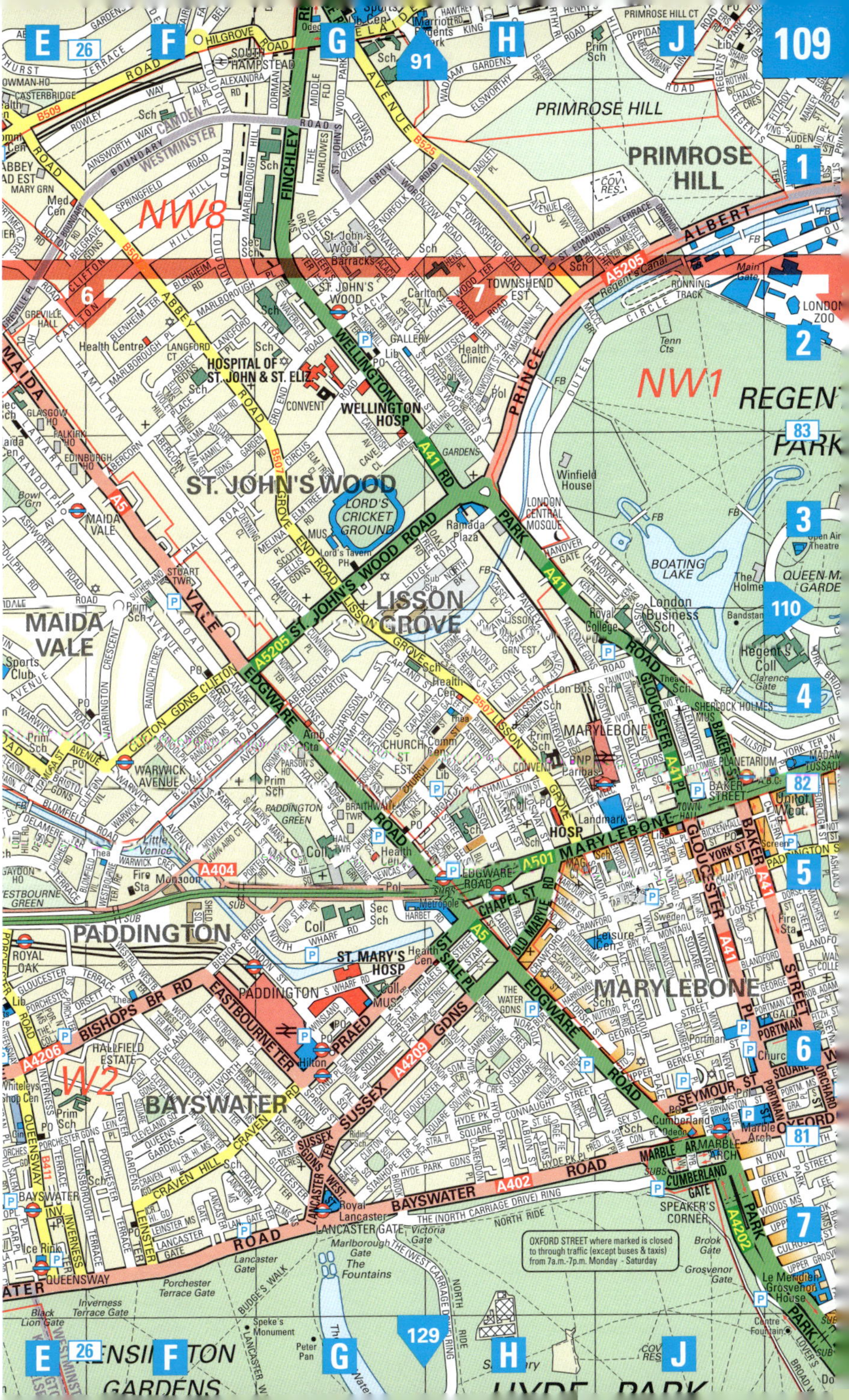
PRIMROSE HILL
PRIMROSE HILL
NW8
NW1
REGENT'S PARK
ST. JOHN'S WOOD
LORD'S CRICKET GROUND
LISSON GROVE
MAIDA VALE
PADDINGTON
BAYSWATER
W2
MARYLEBONE
WELLINGTON HOSP
HOSPITAL OF ST. JOHN & ST. ELIZ.
ST. MARY'S HOSP
LONDON ZOO
BOATING LAKE
Winfield House
LONDON CENTRAL MOSQUE
Regent's Canal
ALBERT
PRINCE ALBERT RD
FINCHLEY ROAD
WELLINGTON RD
PARK RD
ABBEY ROAD
EDGWARE ROAD
MARYLEBONE RD
BAYSWATER ROAD
BAKER STREET
GLOUCESTER PL
PRAED ST
SUSSEX GDNS
EASTBOURNE TER
BISHOPS BR RD
CRAVEN HILL
QUEENSWAY
SEYMOUR ST
OXFORD ST
MARBLE ARCH
SPEAKER'S CORNER
THE (NORTH CARRIAGE DRIVE) RING
KENSINGTON GARDENS
HYDE PARK
OXFORD STREET where marked is closed to through traffic (except buses & taxis) from 7a.m.-7p.m. Monday - Saturday
A5205
A41
A5
A501
A404
A4206
A4209
A402
A4202
B509
B525
B507
B411
E
F
G
H
J
1
2
3
4
5
6
7
26
91
129
110
83
82
81

A
B
C
D
E
1
2
3
4
5
6
7
92
30
83
109
82
81
130
8
9
KING'S CROSS
CAMDEN TOWN
NW1
REGENT'S PARK
LONDON ZOO
QUEEN MARY'S GARDENS
Open Air Theatre
Regent's Coll
ST. GEORGE'S CATHEDRAL
Regent's Park Barracks
SOMERS TOWN
BRITISH LIB
ST PANCRAS HOSP
EUSTON
EUSTON SQUARE
University College London
University of London
BRITISH MUSEUM
MIDDLESEX HOSP
Telecom Tower
LONDON CLINIC
MADAME TUSSAUDS
PLANETARIUM
Royal Acad. of Music
SELFRIDGES
OXFORD CIRCUS
SOHO
W1
MAYFAIR
HAMLEYS
LIBERTY
PICCADILLY CIRCUS
ROYAL ACAD. OF ARTS
Roosevelt Memorial
Royal Veterinary Coll
Sorting Office
Parcelforce
A400
A4201
A5202
A4200
A41
A501
B506
EUSTON ROAD
OXFORD STREET
REGENT STREET
TOTTENHAM COURT ROAD
BAKER STREET
MARYLEBONE HIGH ST
WIGMORE STREET
HAMPSTEAD ROAD
CAMDEN HIGH ST
ALBANY STREET
PARKWAY
SHAFTESBURY AV
CHARING CROSS RD
GOWER ST
ST PANCRAS WAY
PARK LANE

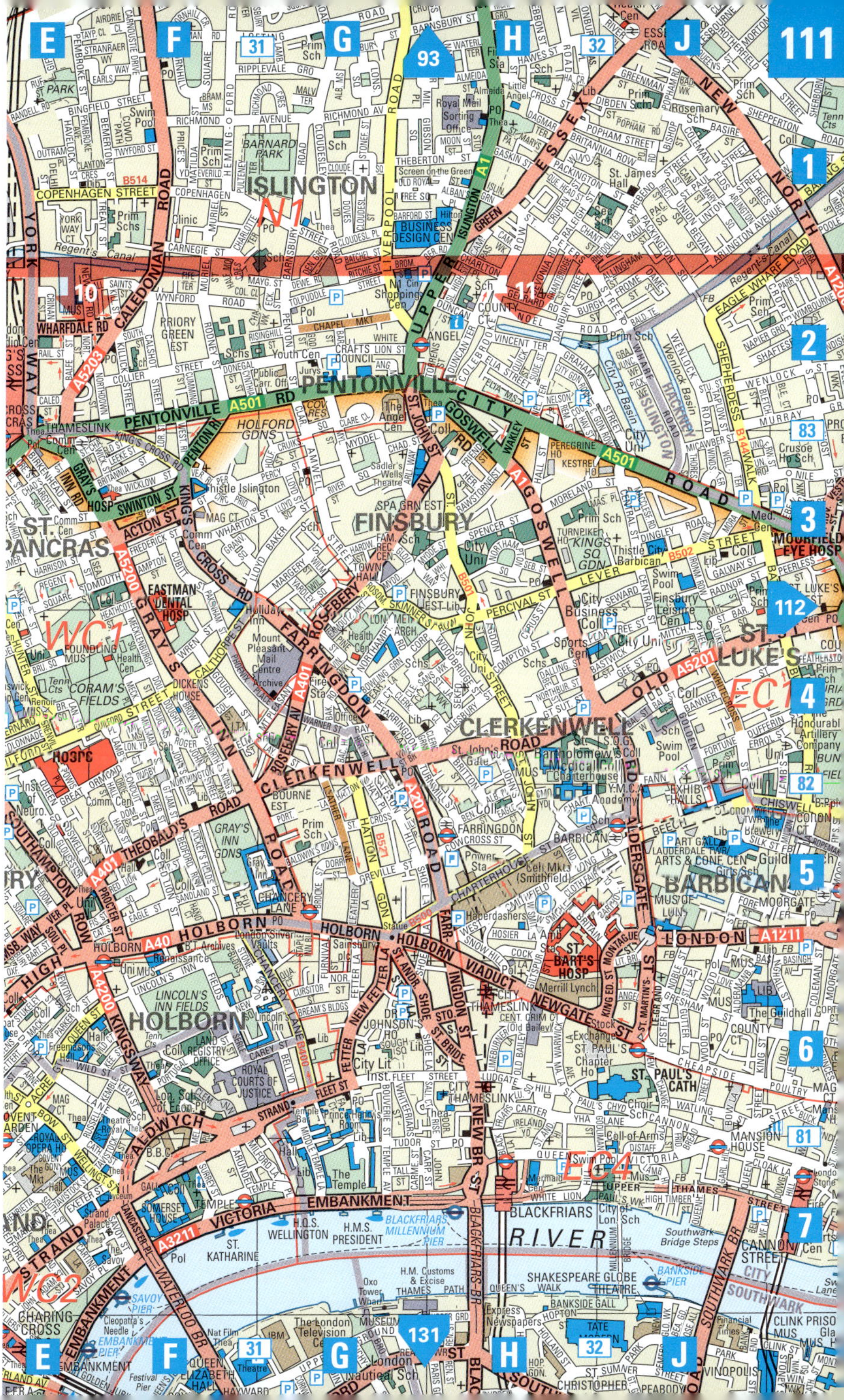
E
F
G
H
J
31
93
32
1
2
3
4
5
6
7
83
112
82
81
131
ISLINGTON
N1
PENTONVILLE
PENTONVILLE RD
A501
FINSBURY
CLERKENWELL
CLERKENWELL ROAD
ST. PANCRAS
WC1
EC1
ST. LUKE'S
BARBICAN
HOLBORN
ALDWYCH
EC4
WC2
STRAND
VICTORIA EMBANKMENT
RIVER
BLACKFRIARS
CALEDONIAN ROAD
COPENHAGEN STREET
YORK WAY
GRAY'S INN ROAD
KING'S CROSS RD
FARRINGDON ROAD
ROSEBERY AV
ST. JOHN ST
GOSWELL ROAD
CITY ROAD
OLD STREET
ALDERSGATE
LONDON WALL
HOLBORN VIADUCT
NEWGATE ST
THEOBALD'S ROAD
KINGSWAY
SOUTHAMPTON ROW
FLEET ST
NEW BR ST
CHEAPSIDE
CANNON ST
QUEEN VICTORIA ST
UPPER STREET
ESSEX ROAD
NEW NORTH ROAD
BARNSBURY ST
LIVERPOOL ROAD
ANGEL
BARNARD PARK
Regent's Canal
CORAM'S FIELDS
EASTMAN DENTAL HOSP
Mount Pleasant Mail Centre
ST. BART'S HOSP
ST. PAUL'S CATH
MANSION HOUSE
CHARING CROSS
SHAKESPEARE GLOBE THEATRE
H.Q.S. WELLINGTON
H.M.S. PRESIDENT
BLACKFRIARS MILLENNIUM PIER
EMBANKMENT PIER
SAVOY PIER
BANKSIDE PIER
CANNON STREET
TATE MODERN
ROYAL COURTS OF JUSTICE
LINCOLN'S INN FIELDS
GRAY'S INN GDNS
SOUTHWARK
WATERLOO BR
BLACKFRIARS BR
SOUTHWARK BR
MOORFIELD EYE HOSP
Honourable Artillery Company
CITY UNI
Sadler's Wells Theatre

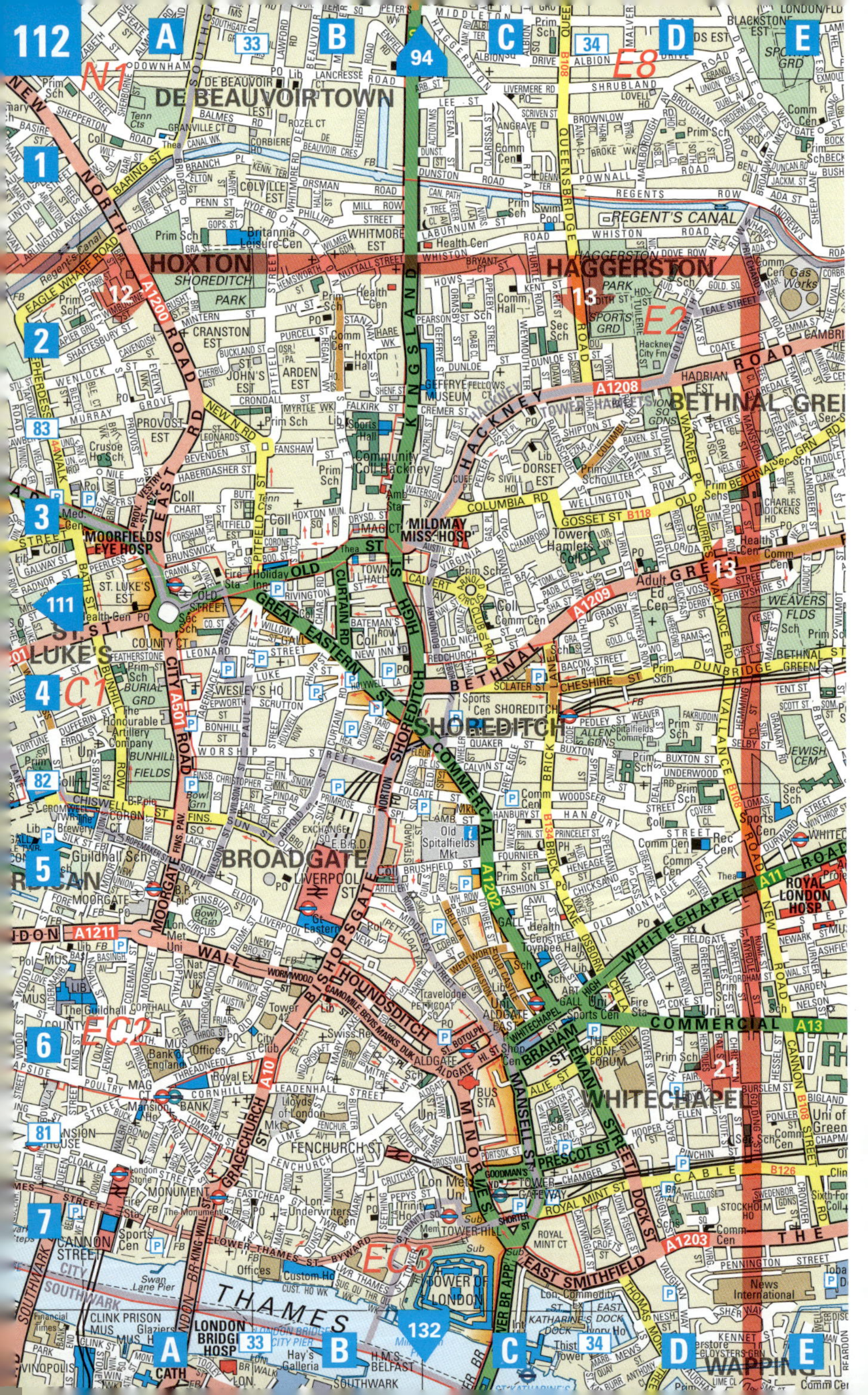
A
B
C
D
E
1
2
3
4
5
6
7
33
34
94
83
111
82
81
132
N1
E8
E2
C1
EC2
EC3
DE BEAUVOIR TOWN
HOXTON
HAGGERSTON
BETHNAL GREEN
SHOREDITCH
BROADGATE
WHITECHAPEL
ST. LUKE'S
WAPPING
THAMES
REGENT'S CANAL
KINGSLAND ROAD
HACKNEY ROAD
NEW NORTH ROAD
EAST RD
CITY ROAD
OLD ST
GREAT EASTERN ST
SHOREDITCH HIGH ST
COMMERCIAL ST
BETHNAL GREEN ROAD
WHITECHAPEL ROAD
COMMERCIAL ROAD
CAMBRIDGE HEATH ROAD
QUEENSBRIDGE ROAD
HOUNDSDITCH
BISHOPSGATE
MINORIES
EAST SMITHFIELD
CABLE STREET
FENCHURCH ST
LONDON WALL
MOORGATE
TOWER OF LONDON
MOORFIELDS EYE HOSP
ROYAL LONDON HOSP
MILDMAY MISS. HOSP
BUNHILL FIELDS
SOUTHWARK
CANNON STREET
LONDON BRIDGE HOSP
A1200
A1208
A1209
A501
A1211
A10
A1202
A11
A13
A1203
B108
B118
B134
B126

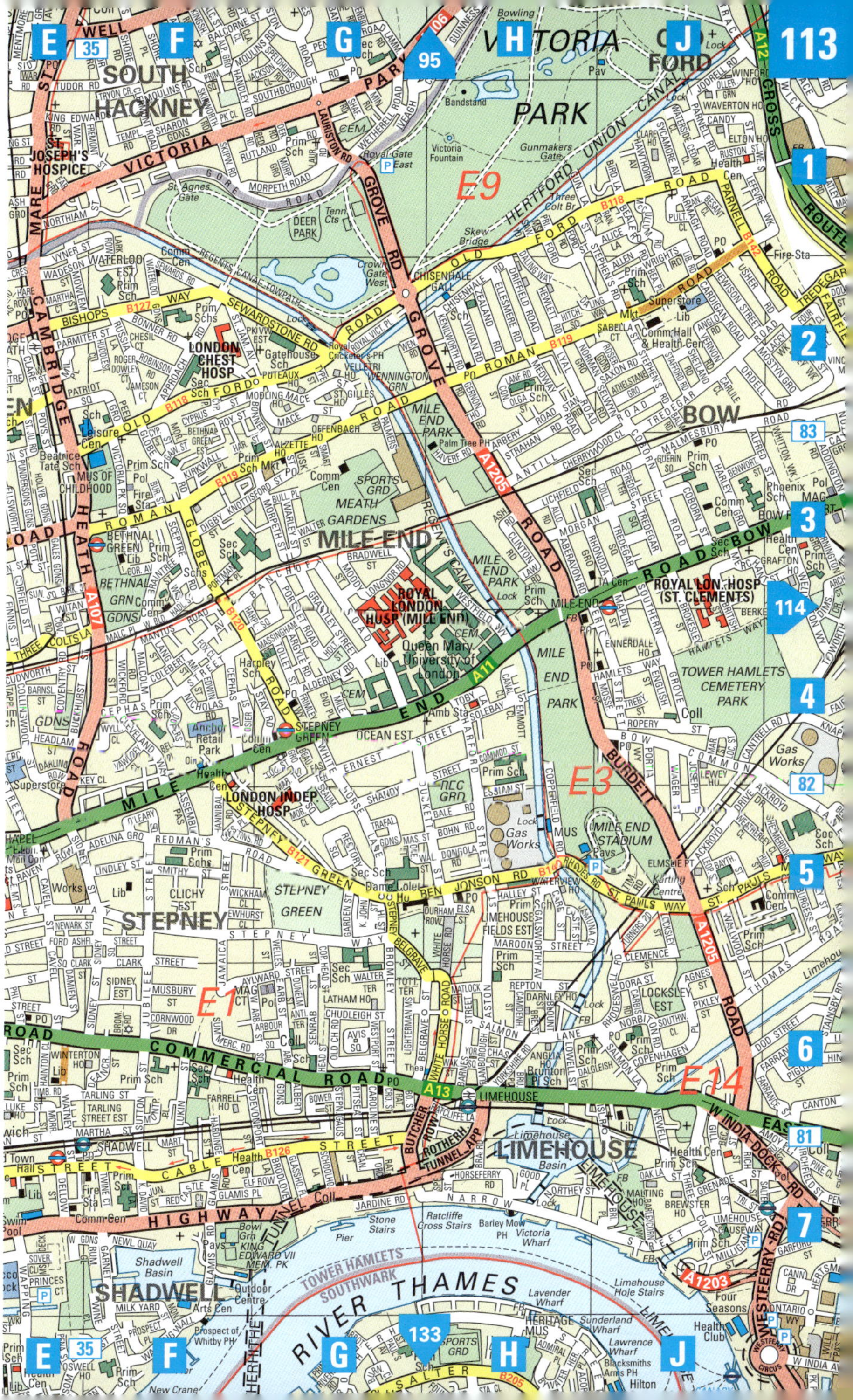
SOUTH HACKNEY
VICTORIA PARK
E9
BOW
MILE END
E3
STEPNEY
E1
LIMEHOUSE
E14
SHADWELL
RIVER THAMES
TOWER HAMLETS
SOUTHWARK
VICTORIA PARK ROAD
GROVE RD
OLD FORD ROAD
ROMAN ROAD
BOW ROAD
MILE END ROAD
COMMERCIAL ROAD
CABLE STREET
HIGHWAY
BURDETT ROAD
CAMBRIDGE HEATH ROAD
BISHOPS WAY
SEWARDSTONE RD
REGENTS CANAL
HERTFORD UNION CANAL
LONDON CHEST HOSP
ROYAL LONDON HOSP (MILE END)
ROYAL LON. HOSP (ST. CLEMENTS)
LONDON INDEP HOSP
ST. JOSEPH'S HOSPICE
Queen Mary University of London
MILE END PARK
MILE END STADIUM
TOWER HAMLETS CEMETERY PARK
MEATH GARDENS
STEPNEY GREEN
Limehouse Basin
Shadwell Basin
Gas Works
E F G H J
1 2 3 4 5 6 7
35 95 106 83 114 82 81 133

A
B
C
D
E
96
39
1
2
3
4
5
6
7
83
82
81
113
134
E15
E3
E14
BOW
BROMLEY
POPLAR
Old Ford Locks
PUDDING MILL LANE
River Lee or Lea
City Mill River
Bow Back River
GREENWAY
BLACKWALL TUNNEL NORTHERN APP
HIGH ST
A118
A11
A12
A1205
A1203
A1261
A1011
B142
B140
B125
B133
B164
Stratford Market Depot
Holiday Inn Ex
Univ of E Lon
Gas Works
Pumping Station
THREE MILLS GREEN
LEE VALLEY PARK
Three Mills Studios
Prescott Channel
Channelsea River
WEST HAM
GROVE HALL PARK
BOW BRIDGE EST
BOW CHURCH
DEVONS EST
BROMLEY BY BOW
ST ANDREW'S HOSP
DEVONS RD
MEMORIAL GDNS
Bow Lock
CODY ROAD BUSINESS CEN
Mail Centre
Elec Sta
NEWHAM
TOWER HAMLETS
Bow Creek
BLACKWALL TRADING EST
LANGDON PARK
BARTLETT PARK
LANSBURY EST
Limehouse Cut
EAST INDIA DOCK RD
LIMMO PENINSULA ECOLOGICAL PARK
EAST INDIA DOCK BASIN NATURE RESERVE
EAST INDIA
ASPEN WAY
POPLAR HIGH STREET
POPLAR BUSINESS PK
COUNCIL OFFICES
WEST INDIA QUAY
BLACKWALL
Reuters
Airshaft
Civic Amenity Site
Blackwall Pier
Jetty
Four Seasons
HSBC
Barclays
WESTFERRY CIRCUS
Travelodge
TOWER HAMLETS CEMETERY PK

E
F
G
H
J
1
2
3
4
5
6
7
40
41
97
116
83
82
81
135
WEST HAM
UPTON PARK
PLAISTOW
CANNING TOWN
E13
E16
EAST LONDON CEMETERY
Crematorium
MEMORIAL RECREATION GROUND
HERMIT RD REC GRD
SPORTS GROUND
NEWHAM GENERAL HOSPITAL
PLAISTOW HOSP
TERENCE McMILLAN STADIUM
CANNING TOWN REC GRD
KING GEORGE PARK
BOLEYN GRD WEST HAM UTD. F.C.
ROYAL VICTORIA DOCK
ExCeL
Sunborn Yacht Hotel
Holiday Inn
ROYAL VICTORIA
CUSTOM HOUSE
PRINCE REGENT
LEA CROSSING
Bow Creek
Trinity Buoy Wharf
Thames Wharf
Millennium Mills
Go Karting
Superstore
PORTWAY
PLASHET ROAD
STOPFORD ROAD
UPTON
NEW PLAISTOW RD
PLAISTOW ROAD
HIGH STREET
THE BDY
GREENGATE ST
BARKING ROAD
BALAAM STREET
PRINCE REGENT LANE
NEWHAM WAY
SILVERTOWN WAY
VICTORIA DOCK ROAD
CONNAUGHT BRIDGE
GREEN STREET
CENTRAL PARK ROAD
A112
A124
A13
B164
B165
B166
B167

A
B
C
D
E
1
2
3
4
5
6
7
42
43
98
115
136
83
82
81
UPTON PARK
EAST HAM
E6
NORTH BECKTON
BECKTON
CUSTOM HOUSE
E16
BARKING ROAD
A124
HIGH STREET NORTH
HIGH STREET SOUTH
A117
NEWHAM WAY
A13
WOOLWICH MANOR WAY
ROYAL ALBERT WAY
A1020
STRAIT ROAD
ROYAL ALBERT DOCK
LONDON CITY AIRPORT
KING GEORGE V DOCK
CENTRAL PARK
EAST HAM JEWISH CEMETERY
BRAMPTON PARK
BOLEYN GRD WEST HAM UTD. F.C.
PRIORY PARK
BARKING ROAD REC GRD
FLANDERS RD PLAYING FLDS
GOOSELEY'S PLAYING FIELDS
BECKTON TRIANGLE RETAIL PARK
PLAYING FIELDS
TERENCE McMILLAN STADIUM
BECKTON DISTRICT PARK NORTH
BECKTON DISTRICT PARK SOUTH
KING GEORGE V PARK
NEW BECKTON PARK
BECKTON RETAIL PARK
ALPINE BUSINESS CEN
Nature Reserve
Sewage Works
Civic Amenity Site
Dry Ski Slope
Newham Riding Centre
Pumping Sta
London Regatta Centre
Uni of East London
ROYAL ALBERT
BECKTON PARK
CYPRUS
Boathouse
Ramada
Sunborn Yacht Hotel
Go Karting
Grain Mills
TERMINAL BUILDINGS
TOWN HALL
Shopping Cen
Travel Inn
Gymnastic Centre
Newham City Farm
Hospice

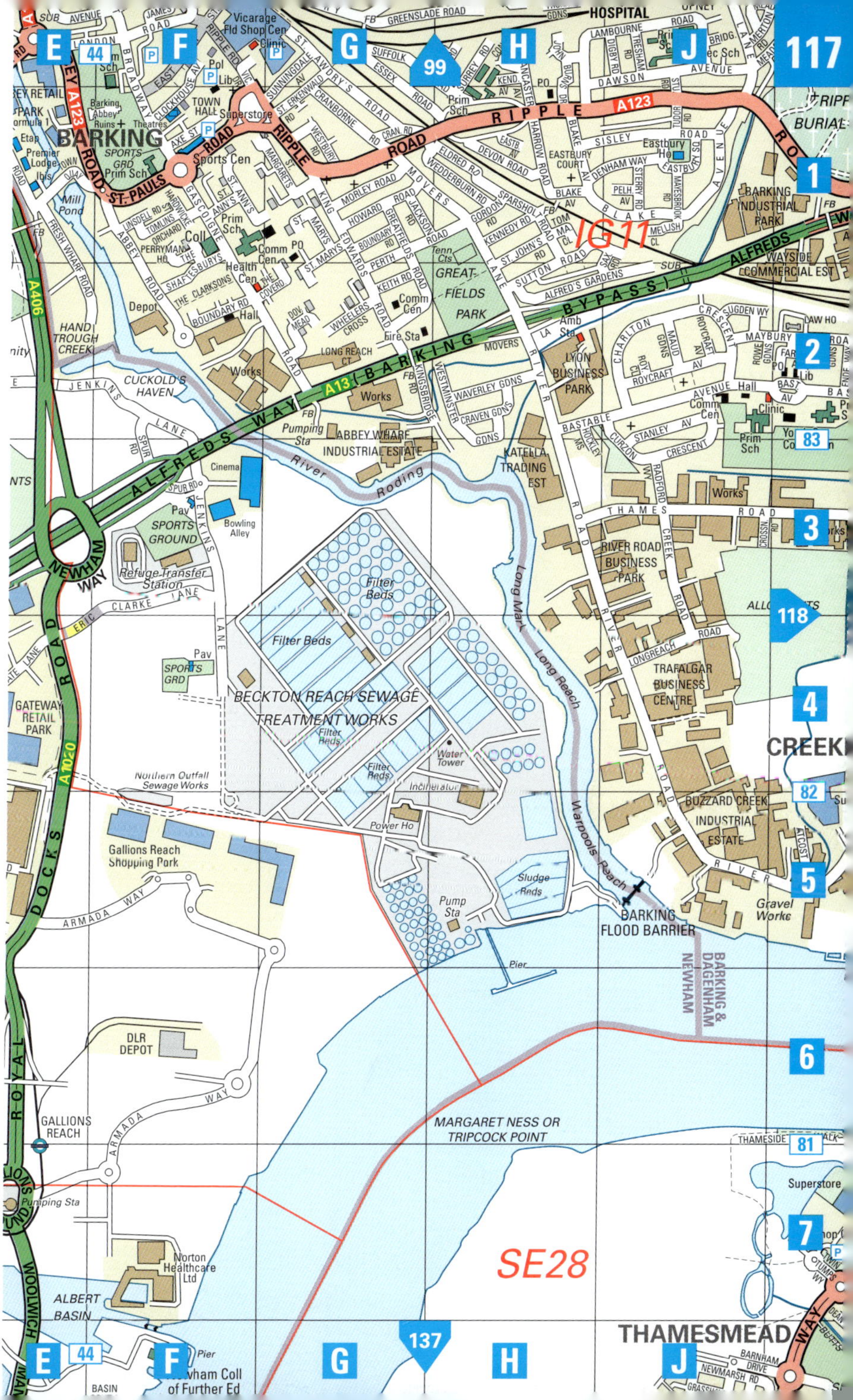
E
F
G
H
J
44
99
1
2
3
4
5
6
7
118
83
82
81
137
BARKING
IG11
SE28
CREEK
THAMESMEAD
HOSPITAL
GREENSLADE ROAD
LAMBOURNE
Vicarage Fld Shop Cen
Clinic
RIPPLE RD
SUFFOLK
ESSEX ROAD
Prim Sch
DAWSON
AVENUE
RIPPLE ROAD
A123
BURIAL
Barking Abbey Ruins
Theatres
TOWN HALL
Superstore
Pol
Lib
SPORTS GRD
Prim Sch
Sports Cen
ST. PAULS
Premier Lodge
Ibis
Mill Pond
FRESH WHARF ROAD
A406
SISLEY
Eastbury Ho
EASTBURY COURT
DENHAM WAY
BLAKE
BARKING INDUSTRIAL PARK
WAYSIDE COMMERCIAL EST
ALFREDS
MORLEY ROAD
HOWARD
MOVERS
GREATFIELDS PARK
Tenn Cts
Comm Cen
Fire Sta
Health Cen
Coll
Depot
Hall
SUTTON ROAD
ALFRED'S GARDENS
BYPASS
BARKING
A13
ALFREDS WAY
Amb Sta
LYON BUSINESS PARK
CHARLTON
ROYCRAFT
MAYBURY
Clinic
Comm Cen
Prim Sch
HAND TROUGH CREEK
CUCKOLD'S HAVEN
JENKINS LANE
Works
Pumping Sta
ABBEY WHARF INDUSTRIAL ESTATE
WAVERLEY GDNS
CRAVEN GDNS
KATELLA TRADING EST
BASTABLE
STANLEY AV
CRESCENT
River Roding
Cinema
Bowling Alley
SPORTS GROUND
Refuge Transfer Station
NEWHAM WAY
CLARKE LANE
ERIC
THAMES ROAD
RIVER ROAD BUSINESS PARK
ALLOTMENTS
Filter Beds
Long Mark
Long Reach
LONGREACH ROAD
TRAFALGAR BUSINESS CENTRE
SPORTS GRD
Pav
BECKTON REACH SEWAGE TREATMENT WORKS
GATEWAY RETAIL PARK
A1020
DOCKS ROAD
Water Tower
Incinerator
Northern Outfall Sewage Works
Power Ho
BUZZARD CREEK INDUSTRIAL ESTATE
Gallions Reach Shopping Park
Sludge Beds
Pump Sta
Warpools Reach
BARKING FLOOD BARRIER
Gravel Works
ARMADA WAY
Pier
NEWHAM
BARKING & DAGENHAM
DLR DEPOT
MARGARET NESS OR TRIPCOCK POINT
GALLIONS REACH
THAMESIDE
Superstore
ROYAL
Pumping Sta
Norton Healthcare Ltd
ALBERT BASIN
WOOLWICH
Pier
Newham Coll of Further Ed
BARNHAM DRIVE
NEWMARSH RD
BASIN

A
B
C
D
E
1
2
3
4
5
6
7
100
48
83
117
82
81
138
RIPPLESIDE
BURIAL GROUND
LODGE
ROAD
A1153
MAYBROOK
MEADOW
STAMFORD
ROAD
GORESBROOK
ROAD
CASTLE GREEN
GORESBROOK
SPORTS
GROUND
BARKING
R.F.C.
Clubhouse
Leisure
Cen
BARKING
INDUSTRIAL
PARK
ALFREDS
WAY
ALFREDS WAY
IND ESTATE
WAYSIDE
COMMERCIAL EST
RIPPLE
ROAD
A13
RENWICK
IND ESTATE
Ship &
Shovel PH
TRAIN
DEPOT
RIPPLESIDE
COMMERCIAL ESTATE
MAYBELLS
COMM EST
SCRATTONS
TERRACE
BOX LANE
Freight Depot
WIVENHOE
ROAD
BASTABLE
AVENUE
Youth &
Comm Cen
ALDERMAN AVENUE
STERN CLOSE
BLESSING
WAY
CHOATS
RIVERSIDE
INDUSTRIAL ESTATE
THAMES
ROAD
City Farm
& Ecology
Park
The Ripple
Nature
Reserve
IG11
The Gores
POWER
STATION
RENWICK
CREEKMOUTH
Superstore
Works
INDUSTRIAL
ESTATE
Gravel
Works
Pier
Jetty
BARKING & DAGENHAM
Barking or
False Point
CROSSNESS
LIGHTHOUSE
THAMESMEAD
NORTH
Ecology
Study Area
BEXLEY
GREENWICH
SE28
Crossway
Lake
RIVERSIDE
GOLF
COURSE
THAMESIDE
WALK
Pumping
Sta
Thamesmere
Lake
Swim
Pool
Superstore
Shop Cen
CENTRAL
WAY
CARLYLE
MANORWAY
GREEN
CROSSWAY
Thamesmead
Town FC
CROSSWAY
PARK
SPORTS
GROUND
MOORINGS
EASTERN
ESMEAD

E
F
G
H
J
49
50
101
1
2
3
4
5
6
7
83
82
81
139
RM10
RM9
SE2
DA17
GORESBROOK PARK
DAGENHAM ROAD
CART ROAD
Tenn Cts
TRESWELL RD
ARNOLD RD
DOWNING RD
DARCY GDNS
DIGBY GDNS
LW. BROAD ST
DOWNS
ROWDOWNS
COOMBES
BROWNE
Hall
SUB
Social Club
WALLERS CL
HORSEBRIDGE CL
BADEN
POWELL CL
STAR CL
BURDETTS
BLOSSOM CL
BUTLER ROAD
Prim Sch
PO
NHAM RE.PK
MORGAN CL
CAUSTON SQ
Admiral Vernon
MOR.PH
DAY HOSP
SCHOOL ROAD
ORCHARD ROAD
WHITEBARN LANE
MARSH GRN RD
BADDOW CL
NORTH CL
SOUTH CL
Prim Sch
OVAL ROAD NORTH
REVIEW ROAD
BALLARDS ROAD
BALL CL
RIDGE CL
Sec Sch
Clubhouse
Pav
DAGENHAM PARK
THE LEYS
B178
CROSBY ROAD
BEAM AVENUE
THIRD AVENUE
SECOND AVENUE
FIRST AVENUE
CENTRE ROAD
NORTH
Comm Cen
FB
WELLINGTON DRIVE
Prim Sch
CHANTRESS CL
CLEMENCE ROAD
LEYS
Cen
CANBERRA
Beam
BARKING & DAGENHAM
HAVERING
RIPPLE ROAD
NEW ROAD
Gores Bridge
Superstore
MERRIELANDS CRES
SUB
Bowling Alley
LINK RD
Fire Sta
OVAL ROAD SOUTH
NEW ROAD
Prim Sch
Beam Bridge
FORD MOTOR WORKS
NORWICH ROAD
KENT AVENUE
POOLES
Works
THAMES AVENUE
DAGENHAM DOCK
CHEQUERS LANE
MANOR WAY
Water Tower
A13
GATEWAY
BREACH LANE
CHOATS MANOR WAY
DAGENHAM BREACH
FB
MARDYKE
LOWER MARDYKE AVENUE
LOWEN
Comm Cen
SOUTH STREET
WALDEN AVENUE
DEARSLEY HO
QUEENS GDNS
CORTINA DRIVE
CAR COMPOUND
ROAD
Dep
A1306
MANOR WAY
CHOATS ROAD
HINDMANS WAY
Power Station
DAGENHAM DIESEL CENTRE
Storage Tanks
FIESTA DR
CONSUL AVENUE
COURIER
FIESTA DRIVE
THAMES AVENUE
HORNCHURCH MARSHES
CAR COMPOUND
Centre for Engineering Manufacturing Excellence
Horse Shoe Corner
UNDERER ROAD
HINDMANS WAY
CHEQUERS LANE
PERRY RD
Oil Storage Depot
Depot
Jetty
Jetty
Dock
Landing Stage
THAMES
FORD MOTOR WORKS
FD
COURIER ROAD
CAR COMPOUND
Jetty
Hornchurch Shoot
Old Man
WALK
Crossness Pumping Station
Jetty
COVERED RESERVOIRS
Crossness Sewage Treatment Works
Sludge Incinerator
SPORTS GROUND
Jetty
Wharf
Warehouses
Depot
ROAD
Jenningtree Point
JENNINGTREE LIGHTHOUSE
2016

YIEWSLEY
WEST DRAYTON
Harmondsworth
Sipson
UB7
Stockley Park Roundabout
Cherry Lane Roundabout
RAINBOW INDUSTRIAL ESTATE
HORTON IND PARK
GlaxoSmith-Kline
SPORTS GROUND
Uxbridge FC
R.A.F. West Drayton
HEATHPARK GOLF COURSE
Crowne Plaza Hotel
Novotel Heathrow
Holiday Inn Heathrow
Heathrow Garden Centre
HEATHROW COACH CEN
Wyevale Garden Centre
Berkeley Nurseries
THE CLOSES RECREATION GROUND
SOUTHLANDS ARTS CEN
United Biscuits
Frays Island Nat Res
West Drayton Cricket Club
Anglers Retreat PH
HARMONDSWORTH MOOR COUNTRY PARK
HARMONDSWORTH CEM
Tithe Barn
Sheraton Heathrow Hotel
Arora International Hotel
Warehouses
SIPSON WAR MEML. REC GRD
Park Inn
Holiday Inn
Thistle Heathrow
British Airways PLC
Bigley Ditch
HILLINGDON
HORTON ROAD
HIGH STREET
STATION APP
CHURCH ROAD
PORTERS WAY
THORNTON ROAD
SIPSON ROAD
CHERRY LANE
HOLLOWAY LANE
HARMONDSWORTH LANE
HATCH LANE
BATH ROAD
STOCKLEY ROAD
A408
A3044
M4
Junction
80
79
78
06
07
140

DAWLEY ROAD
A437
BOLINGBROKE WAY
BOTWELL COMMON ROAD
Clubhouse
The Arena
Offices
STOCKLEY PARK
LONGWALK ROAD
ROUNDWOOD AVENUE
FURZEGROUND WAY
THE SQUARE
Works
Grand Union Canal
Warehouses
RIGBY LANE
Civic Amenity Site
ADLER IND EST
BETAM ROAD
KESTREL WAY
SWALLOWFIELD WAY
ABERGLEN INDUSTRIAL ESTATE
E.M.I. SPORTS GROUND
LONDON LOOP
WARNFORD IND EST
CLAYTON ROAD
BLYTH ROAD
HAYES TOWN
COMPTON ROAD
BOTWELL LANE
Swim Pool
BOTWELL GRN
Prim Sch
CROWN CLOSE
PROVIDENCE INDUSTRIAL ESTATE
SILVERDALE
HAYES & HARLINGTON
KEITH ROAD
NORTH HYDE ROAD
STATION ROAD
Depot
THE SQUARE TRADING ESTATE
Sports & Social Club
GOVERNMENT BUILDINGS
BOURNE AVENUE
BOURNE FARM FIELD
ALLOTMENTS
PINKWELL PARK
PINKWELL LANE
UB3
Clinic
Youth Cen
Lib
CHERRY LANE CEMETERY
Frog's Ditch Farm
Sec Sch
Sports Hall
SAM PHILIP REC GRD
SHEPISTON LANE
Fire Sta
Comfort Inn
HIGH STREET
M4
CRANFORD MEADOW
CRANFORD PARK
IMPERIAL COLLEGE SPORTS GROUND
LITTLE HARLINGTON FIELD
VICTORIA LANE
SIPSON MEADOW
SPORTS GROUND
HARLINGTON
Elder Farm
CRANFORD LANE
Poultry Farm
The White House
WEST END LANE
Radisson Edwardian Hotel
Marriott Hotel
Sheraton Skyline
Holiday Inn Ariel
Ibis
BATH ROAD
A4
Travel Inn
Europa House
141
122

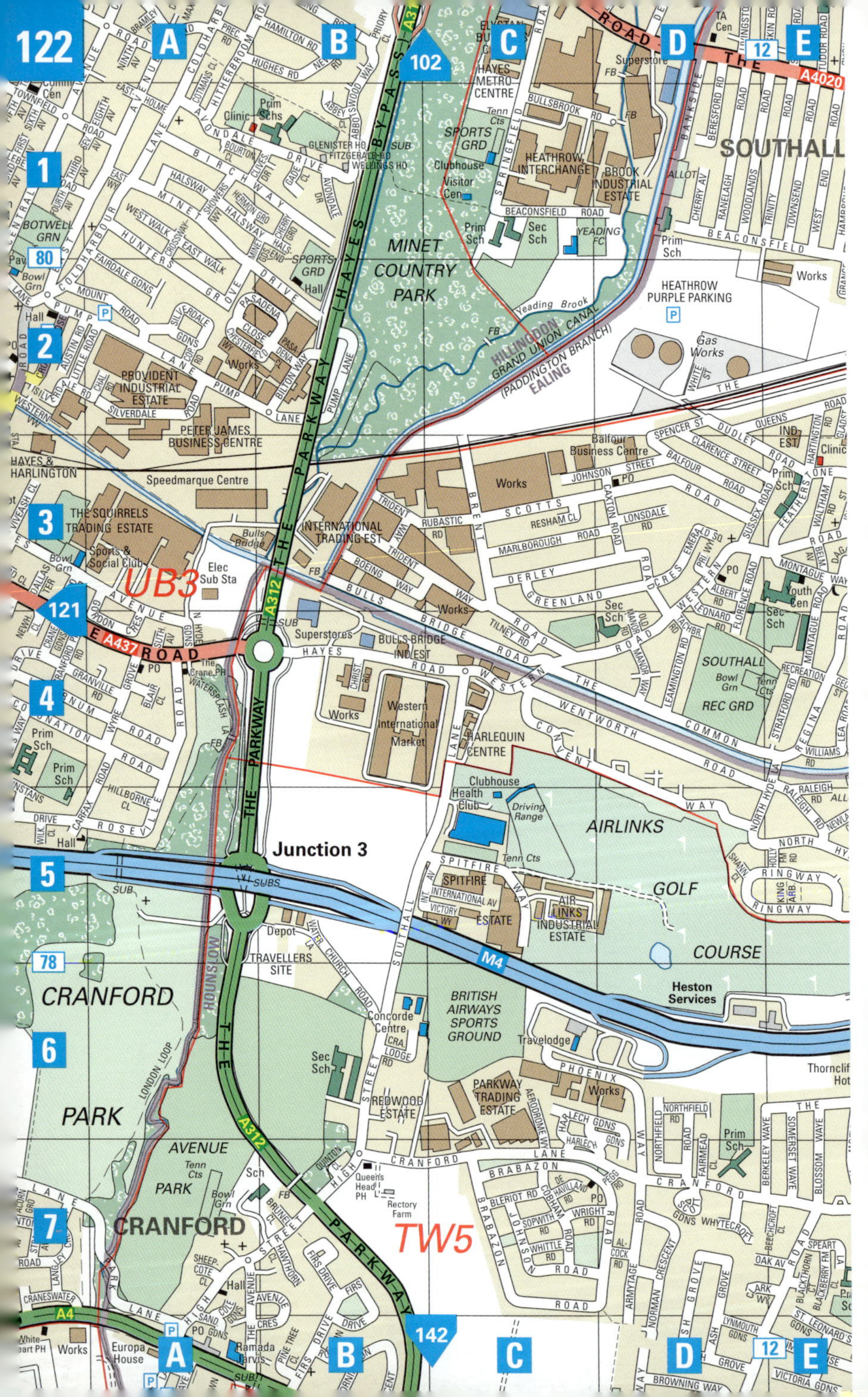
A
B
C
D
E
102
12
1
2
3
4
5
6
7
80
78
121
142
SOUTHALL
MINET COUNTRY PARK
HAYES METRO CENTRE
HEATHROW INTERCHANGE
BROOK INDUSTRIAL ESTATE
SPORTS GRD
Clubhouse
Visitor Cen
YEADING FC
HEATHROW PURPLE PARKING
Gas Works
GRAND UNION CANAL (PADDINGTON BRANCH)
HILLINGDON
EALING
Yeading Brook
BOTWELL GRN
PROVIDENT INDUSTRIAL ESTATE
PETER JAMES BUSINESS CENTRE
HAYES & HARLINGTON
Speedmarque Centre
THE SQUIRRELS TRADING ESTATE
INTERNATIONAL TRADING EST
Balfour Business Centre
Works
UB3
THE PARKWAY
A312
A437
HAYES ROAD
BULLS BRIDGE IND EST
Superstores
Western International Market
HARLEQUIN CENTRE
SOUTHALL
REC GRD
AIRLINKS
GOLF
COURSE
Junction 3
M4
SPITFIRE
INTERNATIONAL AV
AIR LINKS INDUSTRIAL ESTATE
Heston Services
Depot
TRAVELLERS SITE
CRANFORD
PARK
BRITISH AIRWAYS SPORTS GROUND
Concorde Centre
Travelodge
PARKWAY TRADING ESTATE
REDWOOD ESTATE
AVENUE PARK
CRANFORD
TW5
A4
Europa House
Ramada Jarvis
A4020
Thornclif Hot

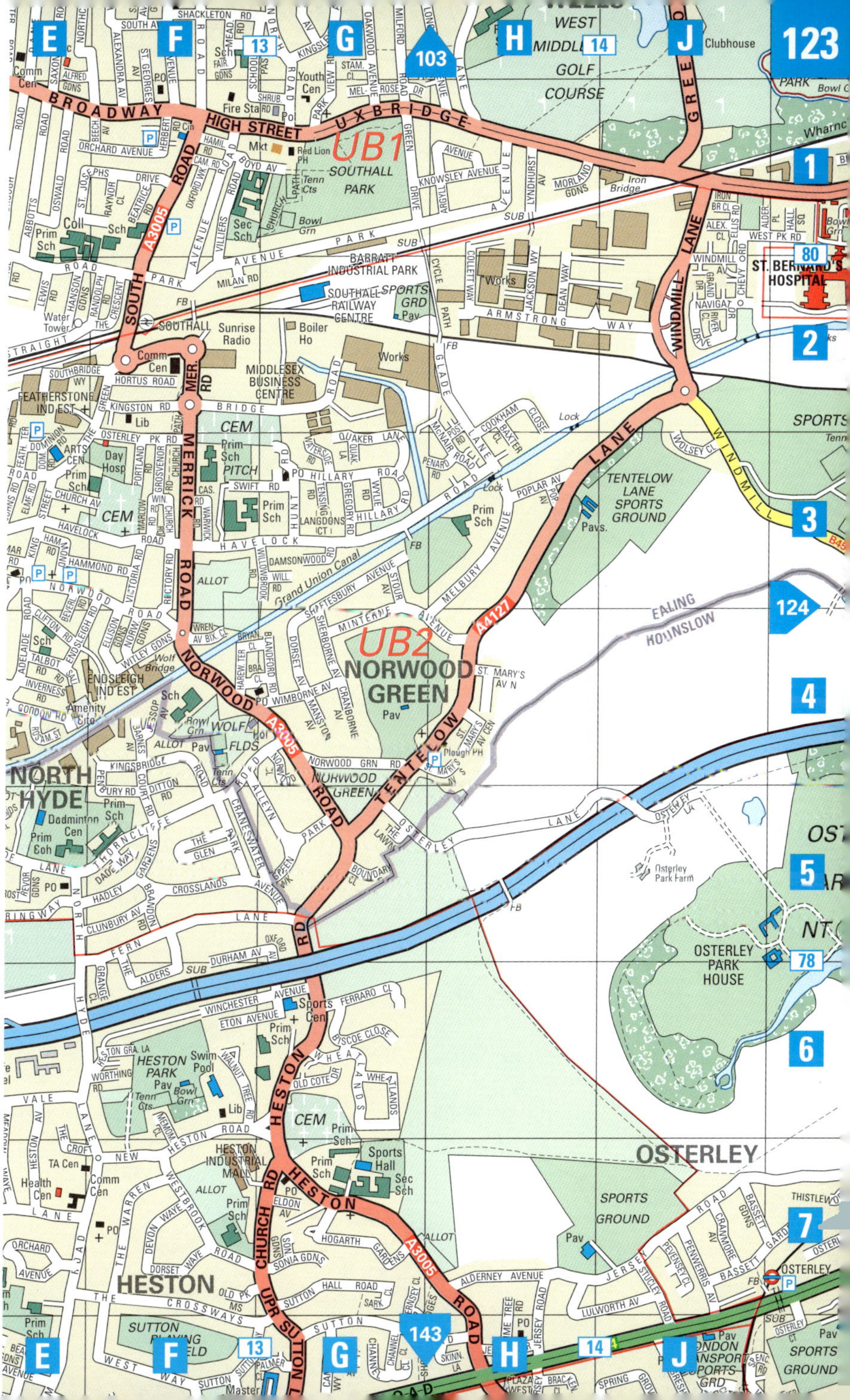

E
F
G
H
J
13
14
103
143
124
78
80
1
2
3
4
5
6
7
WEST MIDDLESEX GOLF COURSE
Clubhouse
BROADWAY
HIGH STREET
UXBRIDGE ROAD
UB1
SOUTHALL PARK
Red Lion PH
Mkt
Fire Sta
Youth Cen
SHACKLETON RD
ORCHARD AVENUE
BOYD AV
KNOWSLEY AVENUE
LYNDHURST AV
MORLAND GDNS
Iron Bridge
WINDMILL LANE
ST. BERNARD'S HOSPITAL
WEST PK RD
PARK AVENUE
BARRATT INDUSTRIAL PARK
SOUTHALL SPORTS RAILWAY CENTRE
SPORTS GRD
ARMSTRONG WAY
Works
SOUTHALL
Sunrise Radio
Boiler Ho
MIDDLESEX BUSINESS CENTRE
FEATHERSTONE IND EST
HORTUS ROAD
KINGSTON RD
BRIDGE ROAD
MERRICK ROAD
CEM
PITCH
Prim Sch
Sec Sch
Day Hosp
QUAKER LANE
HILLARY ROAD
SWIFT RD
HAVELOCK ROAD
NORWOOD ROAD
Grand Union Canal
Lock
TENTELOW LANE SPORTS GROUND
Pavs.
TENTELOW LANE
A4127
A3005
B455
EALING
HOUNSLOW
UB2
NORWOOD GREEN
ST. MARY'S AV N
WIMBORNE AV
SHAFTESBURY AVENUE
MINTERNE AVENUE
ENDSLEIGH IND EST
Amenity Site
WOLF FLDS
Wolf Bridge
NORTH HYDE
Dadminton Cen
NORWOOD GRN RD
NORWOOD GREEN
Plough PH
OSTERLEY LANE
THE GLEN
CROSSLANDS AVENUE
BOUNDARY CL
CLUNBURY AV
RINGWAY
FERN LANE
DURHAM AV
ALDERS
Osterley Park Farm
OSTERLEY PARK HOUSE
HESTON PARK
Swim Pool
Sports Cen
WINCHESTER AVENUE
ETON AVENUE
FERRARO CL
BISCOE CLOSE
WHEATLANDS
HESTON ROAD
HESTON INDUSTRIAL MALL
ALLOT
CEM
Sports Hall
OSTERLEY
SPORTS GROUND
TA Cen
Health Cen
Comm Cen
HESTON
CHURCH RD
SUTTON HALL ROAD
ALDERNEY AVENUE
JERSEY RD
LULWORTH AV
BASSETT GARDENS
CRANMORE AV
THISTLEWORTH
OSTERLEY
SUTTON PLAYING FIELD
WESTBROOK ROAD
DORSET WAYE
THE CROSSWAYS
THE WARREN
ORCHARD AVENUE
HOGARTH GARDENS
SONIA GDNS
ELDON AV
UPR SUTTON LANE
SUTTON LANE
WEST WAY
SKINN. LA
LONDON TRANSPORT SPORTS GRD
SPORTS GROUND
Pav

A
B
C
D
E
1
2
3
4
5
6
7
15
16
104
80
123
78
144
BRENT LODGE PARK
CHURCHFIELDS RECREATION GROUND
Wharncliffe Viaduct
KENSINGTON & CHELSEA CEMETERY
THE BROADWAY
A4020
UXBRIDGE ROAD
ST. BERNARD'S HOSPITAL
EALING HOSPITAL N.H.S. TRUST
HANWELL
HANWELL CEMETERY
LWR BOSTON RD
BOSTON ROAD
A3002
SPORTS GROUND
Sports Centre
WATERSIDE TRADING CENTRE
W7
BRENT RIVER PARK
ELTHORNE PARK
ELTHORNE PARK EXTENSION
RIVER BRENT BUS. PARK
GRAND UNION CANAL WALK
W13
UB2
LONG WOOD (Nature Reserve)
M4
WINDMILL LANE
B454
BOSTON MANOR
LONDON PLAYING FIELDS
Grand Union Canal
WYKE GREEN GOLF COURSE
OSTERLEY PARK NT
OSTERLEY HOUSE
Hare & Hounds PH
Wyevale Garden Centre
B.A.A. SPORTS GRD
MACFARLANE SPORT FIELD
Grasshoppers R.F.C.
CENTAURS BUSINESS CEN
Centaurs R.F.C.
Sky T.V.
WEST CROSS CENTRE
Refuse Transfer Sta
Gallows Bridge
SYON LANE
SPORTS GROUND
Conquest Club
Gillette Ltd.
Gillette Corner
GREAT WEST ROAD
A4
TW7
JERSEY ROAD
OSTERLEY
Brunel University (Osterley Campus)
SYON LANE
SPUR ROAD
DEPOT

E
F
G
H
J
105
17
UXBRIDGE RD
NEW
Ealing Broadway
Lib
PITSHANGER MANOR MUS
Thames Valley Uni
EALING COMMON
WALPOLE PARK
Coll
Ealing Studios
Grange Tavern PH
EALING COMMON
A4020
1
DEPOT
80
GUNNERSBURY AVENUE
NORTH CIRCULAR ROAD
LAMMAS PARK
Thames Valley Uni
W5
ALLOT
POPEFIELD PLAYING FIELDS
2
LAMMAS
PARK
B452
NORTHFIELD AVENUE
SOUTH EALING
SOUTH EALING ROAD
ST MARY'S RD
Superstore
B4491
POPES LANE
SMALL MANSION ARTS CEN
3
GUNNERSBURY PARK MUSEUM
BOATING LAKE
Gunnersbury Nursery
NORTHFIELDS
W3
Miniature Golf
126
LITTLE EALING LANE
B455
SOUTH EALING CEMETERY
LITTLE EALING
CLAYPONDS HOSP
GUNNERSBURY PARK
International Sch of Lond
4
CEMETERY
REC GRD
POTOMAC (FISH POND)
EMC Twr
A3002
WINDMILL RD
SPORTS GRD
Junction 2
M4
PHOENIX PARK
Agfa Gevaert
Leisure
5
BOSTON MANOR
Works
Glaxo SmithKline
CARVILLE HALL PARK
KEW BRIDGE STEAM MUS
KEW BRIDGE
78
BRENTFORD FC
A315
KEW BRIDGE RD
HOLLAND GARDENS
Travelodge
BRENTFORD AIT
6
BRENTFORD
BRENTSIDE EXECUTIVE CENTRE
HIGH STREET
WATERMANS ARTS CEN
Herbarium & Library
KEW GREEN
KEW
TW8
BRENTFORD BUSINESS CENTRE
Sir Joseph Banks Building
KEW PALACE
Orangery
Kew Shop
Filmy Fern House
KEW GARDENS GALLERY
Alpine House
7
LONDON RD
River Brent
Thames Lock
Marina
Glasshouses
The Princess of Wales Conservatory
KEW ROAD
ROYAL
TW9
Waterlily House
THE POND
Temple of Arethusa
Palm House
Battles of Brentford 1016 & 1642
145
BOTANIC GARDENS
Victoria Gate Visitor Cen
Aquatic Experience

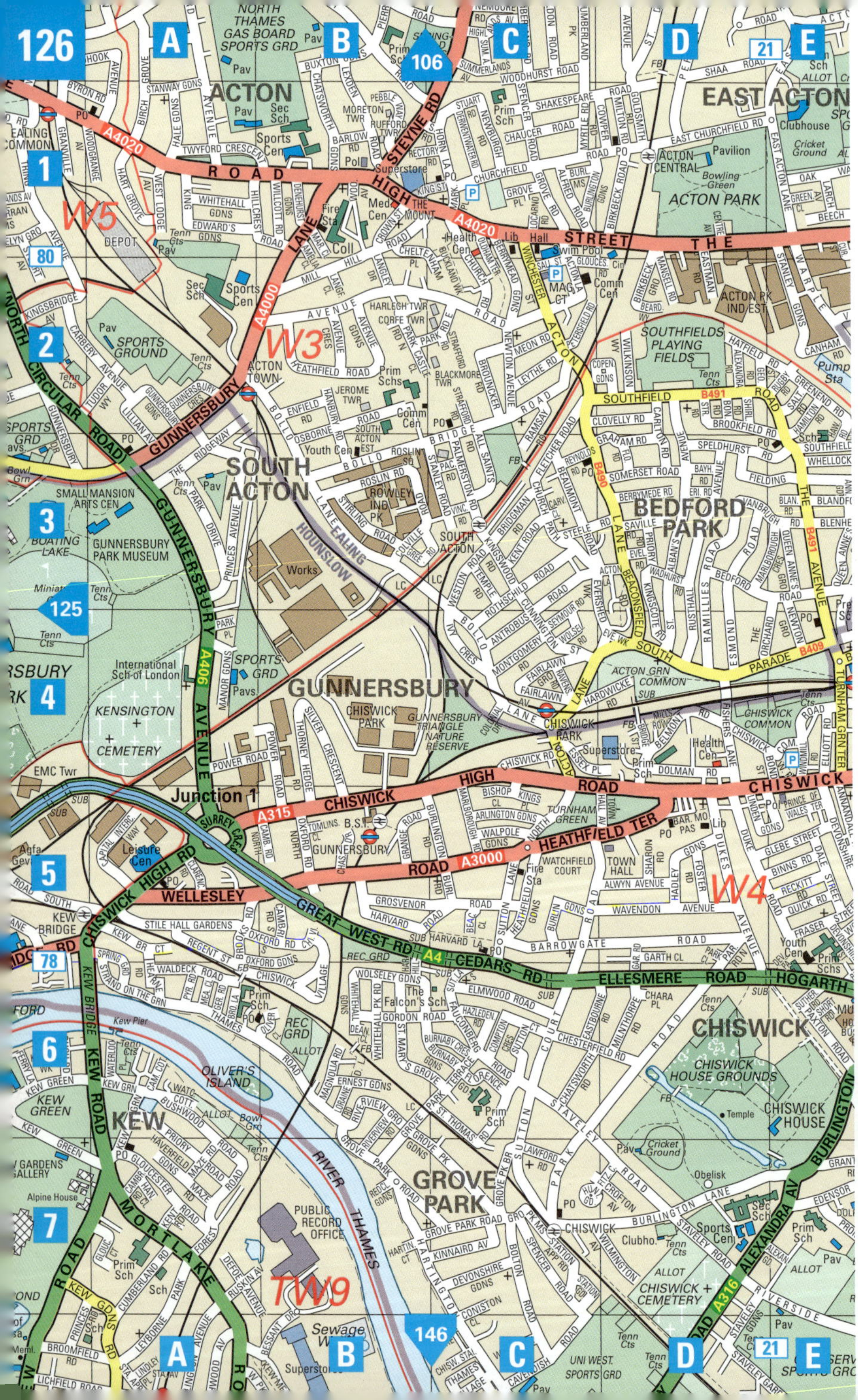
A
B
C
D
E
1
2
3
4
5
6
7
106
125
146
21
80
78
ACTON
EAST ACTON
NORTH THAMES GAS BOARD SPORTS GRD
EALING COMMON
W5
W3
W4
TW9
ACTON CENTRAL
ACTON PARK
ACTON TOWN
SOUTH ACTON
BEDFORD PARK
SOUTHFIELDS PLAYING FIELDS
ACTON PK IND EST
GUNNERSBURY
GUNNERSBURY PARK MUSEUM
SMALL MANSION ARTS CEN
BOATING LAKE
International Sch of London
KENSINGTON CEMETERY
EMC Twr
Junction 1
CHISWICK PARK
GUNNERSBURY TRIANGLE NATURE RESERVE
ACTON GRN COMMON
CHISWICK COMMON
TURNHAM GREEN
CHISWICK
CHISWICK HOUSE GROUNDS
CHISWICK HOUSE
OLIVER'S ISLAND
RIVER THAMES
KEW
KEW GREEN
KEW BRIDGE
GROVE PARK
PUBLIC RECORD OFFICE
CHISWICK CEMETERY
UNI WEST SPORTS GRD
HIGH STREET
THE VALE
GUNNERSBURY AVENUE
NORTH CIRCULAR ROAD
CHISWICK HIGH ROAD
GREAT WEST RD
CEDARS RD
ELLESMERE ROAD
HOGARTH
HEATHFIELD TER
BURLINGTON LANE
MORTLAKE RD
KEW ROAD
A4020
A4000
A406
A315
A3000
A4
A316
B491
B490
B409

E
F
G
H
J
22
107
23
1
2
3
4
5
6
7
80
128
78
147
SHEPHERD'S BUSH
W12
W6
SW13
CASTELNAU
HAMMERSMITH
VALE
A4020 UXBRIDGE ROAD
GOLDHAWK ROAD
A402
A315 KING STREET
HIGH ROAD
A4 GREAT WEST ROAD
HAMMERSMITH FLYOVER
SHEPHERDS BUSH ROAD
SHEPHERDS BUSH GRN
A219
FULHAM PALACE ROAD
GLENTHORNE RD
BEADON RD
A306 CASTELNAU
LONSDALE ROAD
B350
B408
B409
A316
CHISWICK LA
PADDENSWICK ROAD
STAMFORD BROOK RD
LOFTUS ROAD STADIUM QPR FC
Television Centre
Racquet Club
SPORTS GROUND
DEPT OF SOCIAL SECURITY
WORMHOLT PARK
GREEK CATH
Acton & West London Coll
RAVENSCOURT PARK
STARCH GREEN
THE STAMFORD
WENDELL PARK
BUS DEPOT
STAMFORD BROOK
TURNHAM GREEN
Ilogarth Club
HOMEFIELD REC. GRD
Clubhouse
Hogarth Roundabout
Brewery
CHISWICK EYOT
The Swedish Sch
St. Paul's Prep Sch
HAMMERSMITH TER
The Dove Pier
UPPER MALL
LOWER MALL
FURNIVAL GDNS
QUEEN CAROLINE EST
RIVERSIDE STUDIOS
FRANK BANFIELD PARK
CHARING CROSS HOSP
HAMMERSMITH & FULHAM
RICHMOND UPON THAMES
LEG OF MUTTON NATURE RESERVE
HARROD'S SPORTS GRD
The Harrodian
Chiswick Pier
RIVERSIDE RECREATION GROUND
ST. MARY'S CONVENT
THE WETLANDS CENTRE
Visitor Centre
Harrods Wharf
Blakes Wharves
Novotel London West
Lyric Thea
Kings Mall
Superstore
LRT DEPOT
TOWN HALL
The Ark
Apollo
Thames Path

A
B
C
D
E
1
2
3
4
5
6
7
24
25
108
80
127
22
30
78
148
SHEPHERD'S BUSH
W11
NOTTING HILL GATE
HOLLAND PARK
HOLLAND PARK AVENUE
W8
KENSINGTON
HOLLAND PARK
HOLLAND HOUSE
Holland Park Roundabout
West 12 Shopping Centre
KENSINGTON (OLYMPIA)
OLYMPIA
W14
COMMONWEALTH INST
KENSINGTON HIGH ST
HOLLAND ROAD
HAMMERSMITH ROAD
TALGARTH ROAD
WEST CROMWELL RD
CROMWELL RD
WARWICK GDNS
WEST KENSINGTON
EARLS COURT
EARLS COURT EXHIBITION CENTRE
SW5
HAMMERSMITH
HAMMERSMITH FLYOVER
HAMMERSMITH CEMETERY
W6
CHARING CROSS HOSP
QUEENS CLUB
FULHAM PALACE ROAD
LILLIE ROAD
DAWES ROAD
FULHAM CEMETERY
SW6
NORTH END ROAD
WEST BROMPTON
FULHAM BROADWAY
FULHAM BDY
PARSONS GREEN
EEL BROOK COMMON
FULHAM
A3220
A402
A4020
A219
A315
A4
A3218
A3219
A304
A4204
B317

KENSINGTON GARDENS
W2
HYDE PARK
ROUND POND
THE SERPENTINE
The Lido
The Long Water
SERPENTINE ROAD
SERPENTINE GALLERY
KENSINGTON PALACE
Bird Sanctuary
Lancaster Gate
Marlborough Gate
Inverness Terrace Gate
Black Lion Gate
Speke's Monument
Peter Pan
Physical Energy Statue
Queens Temple
Bandstand
War Memorial
Holocaust Memorial
ROTTEN ROW
CYCLE PATH
NEW RIDE
Albert Memorial
Alexandra Gate
Prince of Wales Gate
Rutland Gate
Edinburgh Gate
Albert Gate
Queen's Gate
Palace Gate
Coalbrookdale Gate
OXFORD STREET where marked is closed to through traffic (except buses & taxis) from 7a.m.-7p.m. Monday - Saturday
KENSINGTON ROAD
KENSINGTON GORE
KNIGHTSBRIDGE
A315
A4
SW7
Royal Geo. Soc
ROYAL ALBERT HALL
PRINCE CONSORT RD
Royal Coll of Music
Imperial Coll
Queen's Tower
SCIENCE MUSEUM
NATURAL HISTORY MUSEUM
VICTORIA & ALBERT MUSEUM
HARRODS
SOUTH KENSINGTON
CROMWELL ROAD
GLOUCESTER ROAD
BROMPTON ROAD
BROMPTON
FULHAM ROAD
KING'S ROAD
ROYAL MARSDEN HOSP
ROYAL BROMPTON HOSP
CHELSEA
CHELSEA & WEST HOSP
SW10
SW3
SLOANE SQUARE
SLOANE STREET
A3216
A3217
A308
A3220
A3212
B302
B304
B325
Duke of York's Headquarters
ROYAL HOSPITAL
NAT ARMY MUS
CHELSEA PHYSIC GDNS
Carlyle's House
CHEYNE WALK
CHELSEA EMBANKMENT
ALBERT BR
BATTERSEA BR
CADOGAN PIER
Chelsea Reach
Peace Pagoda
BATTERSEA PARK
CHILDREN'S ZOO
FOUNTAIN LAKE
SW11
REDCLIFFE GARDENS
BROMPTON CEMETERY
EDITH GROVE
GUNTER GROVE
CREMORNE RD
WORLD'S END EST
Chelsea Wharf
Chelsea Creek
Gas Works
Waterside Point
E
F
G
H
J
1
2
3
4
5
6
7
26
80
78
109
130
149
30
31

MAYFAIR
GREEN PARK
ST. JAMES'S
ST. JAMES'S PARK
BUCKINGHAM PALACE GDNS
BUCKINGHAM PALACE
THE QUEEN'S GALLERY
THE ROYAL MEWS
WESTMINSTER
BELGRAVIA
VICTORIA
PIMLICO
RIVER THAMES
SW1
SW8
SW11
NINE ELMS
KENSINGTON & CHELSEA
WANDSWORTH
ROYAL HOSPITAL CHELSEA
Chelsea Barracks
LISTER HOSPITAL
Battersea Power Station (Disused)
New Covent Garden Market
Millennium Arena
BOATING LAKE
TATE BRITAIN
PLAYING FIELDS
GROSVENOR ROAD
CHELSEA BRIDGE RD
QUEENSTOWN ROAD
PICCADILLY
CONSTITUTION HILL
Closed to Traffic on Sundays
Wellington Arch
HYDE PARK CORNER
VAUXHALL BRIDGE ROAD
BUCKINGHAM PALACE ROAD
EMBANKMENT
WESTMINSTER CITY HALL
HORSEFERRY ROAD
MILLBANK
WHITEHALL
Horse Guards Parade
DUCK ISLAND
GOVT OFF. FOR LONDON
Nine Elms Pier
Battersea Dogs Home
Gas Works
Westminster Boat Ho
110
129
150
80
78
30
32
33
A
B
C
D
E
1
2
3
4
5
6
7

RIVER
ST. KATHARINE PIER
CHARING CROSS
EMBANKMENT
SAVOY PIER
EMBANKMENT PIER
Cleopatra's Needle
Festival Pier
ROYAL FESTIVAL HALL
QUEEN ELIZABETH HALL
HAYWARD GALLERY
National Theatre
Nat Film Thea
IBM
The London Television Cen
London Nautical Sch
TATE MODERN
BANKSIDE GALL
SHAKESPEARE GLOBE THEATRE
Southwark Bridge Steps
CLINK PRISON MUS
Financial Times
VINOPOLIS
BRAMAH MUS
PEABODY TRUST
ST. SUMNER STREET
CHRISTOPHER HO
SOUTHWARK
SE1
STAMFORD
BLACKFRIARS RD
WATERLOO EAST
IMAX Cin
TATTERSHALL CASTLE
London Eye
JUBILEE GARDENS
WATERLOO MILLENNIUM PIER
County Hall
London Aquarium
WESTMINSTER MILLENNIUM PIER
WESTMINSTER
WESTMINSTER BR A302
WATERLOO
WATERLOO INTERNATIONAL
YORK ROAD
THE CUT
Southwark Coll
UNION STREET
Arts Cen
COPPERFIELD STREET
THE BOROUGH
BOROUGH
BOROUGH HIGH STREET
MARSHALSEA RD
GREAT DOVER ST
Big Ben
HOUSES OF PARLIAMENT
ST. THOMAS' HOSP
FLORENCE NIGHTINGALE MUS
LAMBETH NORTH
WESTMINSTER BRIDGE RD
ST. GEORGE'S CIRCUS
BOROUGH RD
South Bank University
LONDON ROAD
SOUTHWARK BRIDGE RD
NEWINGTON CAUSEWAY
ST. GEORGE'S CATHEDRAL
ST. GEORGES ROAD
Victoria Tower
Burghers of Calais Mon.
St. Thomas' Medical Sch & The Nightingale Sch
LAMBETH PALACE GDNS
SPORTS GRD.
LAMBETH PALACE ROAD
Lambeth Palace
Lambeth Pier
LAMBETH
LAMBETH BR
LAMBETH RD A3203
GERALD MARY HARMSWORTH PARK
IMPERIAL WAR MUSEUM
ELEPHANT & CASTLE
Elephant & Castle Shopping Cen
NEWINGTON
INN. LON. CROWN COURT
ROCKINGHAM EST
NEW KENT ROAD A201
SE17
SE11
KENNINGTON ROAD
KENNINGTON LANE
NEWINGTON BUTTS
WALWORTH ROAD A215
ALBERTA EST
DEPOT
HEYGATE STREET
BRANDON ST
Walworth Garden Farm
SURREY GDNS
KENNINGTON
KENNINGTON PARK ROAD A3
VAUXHALL
KENNINGTON OVAL
THE OVAL (SURREY C.C.C.)
KENNINGTON PARK
SPORTS GRD
Gas Works
HARLEYFORD RD
KENNINGTON A3204
ALBERT EMBANKMENT A3036
SOUTH LAMBETH ROAD A203
FENTIMAN ROAD
CLAPHAM ROAD
CAMBERWELL NEW ROAD
CAMBERWELL ROAD
CAMBERWELL
SE5
WYNDHAM EST
BRANDON EST
MEDLAR ST
GREEK CATHEDRAL
NEW ROAD A202
SOUTH LAMBETH
MILLBANK MILLENNIUM PIER
DRAW DOCK
GOVT OFF.

A
B
C
D
E
1
2
3
4
5
6
7
33
34
112
131
152
80
78
THAMES
EC3
E1
SE1
SE17
WAPPING
BERMONDSEY
WALWORTH
CAMBERWELL
PECKHAM
BURGESS PARK
TOWER BRIDGE EXPERIENCE
GUY'S HOSPITAL
LONDON BRIDGE HOSP
CLINK PRISON MUS
LONDON BRIDGE CITY PIER
Hay's Galleria
H.M.S. BELFAST
SOUTHWARK CROWN CT
CITY HALL
POTTERS FIELDS PARK
Tower Millennium Pier
ST. KATHARINE'S PIER
ST. KATHARINE'S DOCK
DESIGN MUS
News International
TOOLEY ST
ST. THOMAS ST
BERMONDSEY ST
LONG LANE
GREAT DOVER STREET
TOWER BRIDGE ROAD
JAMAICA ROAD
DRUID STREET
ABBEY STREET
GRANGE ROAD
SOUTHWARK PARK ROAD
OLD KENT ROAD
ROTHERHITHE NEW ROAD
ALBANY ROAD
CAMBERWELL ROAD
EAST STREET
ROLLS ROAD
BRICKLAYER'S ARMS DISTRIBUTION CEN
Royal Mail
Offices
Warehouses
Superstores
Cantium Retail Park
SIX BRIDGES TRADING EST
NORTH PECKHAM ESTATE
INDUSTRIAL EST
Kart Track
Bowl Grn
Trafalgar Bridge
SPORTS GRD
A200
A2198
A2
A2205
A100
A2206
A2207
A1203
A215
B202
B203
B204
B214
B216
29
36
37

E
F
G
H
J
35
113
SHADWELL
RIVER THAMES
TOWER HAMLETS
SOUTHWARK
WAPPING
ROTHERHITHE
SE16
Surrey Water
Canada Water
Greenland Dock
South Dock
Russia Dock Woodland
Southwark Park
Deptford Park
Pepys Park
DEPTFORD
SE8
SE14
SE15
Limehouse Reach
Canary Wharf Pier
Nelson Dock Pier
Greenland Pier
South Bermondsey
The Den Millwall FC
New Cross
New Cross Gate
Fordham Park
Folkestone Gdns
Bridge House Meadows
Gas Works
Lewisham Lions Cen
1
2
3
4
5
6
7
80
78
134
153
A200
A2
A2202
A2208
A1206
B205
B206
B207
B2227
LEWISHAM

A
B
C
D
E
1
2
3
4
5
6
7
114
133
154
80
39
78
POPLAR
ASPEN
WEST INDIA QUAY
A1261
Billingsgate Fish Mkt
BLACKWALL
Blackwall
Jetty
Reach
BLACKWALL TUNNEL
Civic Amenity Site
Airshaft
Airy's Point
MERIDIAN GARDENS
THE DOME
Health Club
WESTFERRY CIRCUS
W INDIA AV
CABOT
HSBC
N COLONNADE
S COLONNADE
CANARY WHARF
Superstore
Barclays
Blackwall Basin
Poplar Dock
Canada Square
Citigroup
HERON QUAYS
MACKENZIE WK
HERON QUAY
BANK STREET
CANARY WHARF
Works
ISLE
OF
DOGS
WEST INDIA DOCKS
The International Hotel
West India Dock Pier
MARSH WALL
S Quay Plaza
Thames Quay (L.D.D.C.)
MERIDIAN GATE
SOUTH QUAY
PRESTONS ROAD
Pier
Pumping Sta
Jetty
Delta Wharf
Works
BUS STA
A102 BLACKWALL TUNNEL
Gas Works
Express Wharf
Health Cen
OCEAN WHARF
KNIGHTHEAD PT
Comm Cen
BOWSPRIT PT
GDNS
WESTFERRY ROAD
Great Eastern Enterprise Cen
HARBOUR EX SQ
SKYLINES VILLAGE
Clinic
Tenn Cts
CUBITT TOWN
London Arena (closed)
CROSSHARBOUR & LONDON ARENA
MILLHARBOUR
INNER DOCK
MANCHESTER ROAD
Lib
Health Cen
Comm Cen
Prim Sch
A1206
Telegraph & Express Print Works
MILLWALL
MILLWALL OUTER DOCK
Docklands Sailing Cen
Comm Cen
Superstore
MUDCHUTE
E14
PARK
MUDCHUTE ALLOT
TOWER HAMLETS
GREENWICH
Pier
Primrose Wharf
Morden Wharf
Works
Pier
Jetty
Enderby's Wharf
Piper's Wharf
GLOBE ROPE WK
MILLWALL PARK
Comm Cen
ISLAND GARDENS
Medical Cen
Works
Prim Sch
Sch
Newcastle Draw Dock
Leisure Cen
Granite Wharf
Lovell's Wharf
Landing Stage
Palmer's Wharf
Payne's Wharf
MASTHOUSE TERRACE PIER
Fire Sta
ST. DAVIDS SQUARE
Ferry House PH
Rowing Club
SAUNDERS NESS RD
Comm Cen
GREENWICH FOOT TUNNEL
REACH
High Bridge Wharf
Trafalgar Rowing Cen
Power Sta
DEPTFORD
SE8
Borthwick Wf
Landing Stage
GREENWICH PIER
Greenwich Pier
GIPSY MOTH IV
CUTTY SARK
Trinity College
Univ of Greenwich
Wood Wharf
ROMNEY RD
A206
TRAFALGAR
QUEEN'S HOUSE
NATIONAL MARITIME MUSEUM
GREENWICH
GREENWICH PARK
One Tree Hill
The Arches Leisure Cen
MAZE HILL
PRINCE STREET
CREEK ROAD
A200
Laban
Clinic
Barnados
DEPTFORD CH ST
Wavelength Sports Complex
FAIRCHARM TRADING ESTATE
LEWISHAM
GREENWICH
DEPTFORD CREEK
Comm Cen
Health Cen
Prim Sch
Lib
GREENWICH
Sch of Management
A206 HIGH RD
Lib
Mkt
Clinic
FAN MUS
FLAMSTEED HOUSE (Old Royal Observatory)
Circus Gate
Charlton Sch
SE10
Croom's Hill Gate
RANGER'S HOUSE
Blackheath
Bandstand
A2209
DEPTFORD BRIDGE
Lewisham Coll
A2
DEPTFORD BRIDGE
BLACKHEATH
Pumping Sta
B208
B209
SOUTH ST
Sec Sch
ROYAL HILL
HYDE VALE
Fire Sta

ROYAL VICTORIA DOCK
115
40
41
E16
SILVERTOWN WAY
NORTH WOOLWICH ROAD
A1020
DLR under construction (opens 2005)
Millennium Mills
Pontoon Dock
Grain Mills
Go Karting
Sunborn Yacht Hotel
THAMES BARRIER PARK
SILVERT
Thames Wharf
Trinity Buoy Wharf
Pier
Millennium Pier
Phoenix Wharf
Manhattan Wharf
GREENSHIELDS IND EST
LYLE PARK
Works
RIVER THAMES
NEWHAM
GREENWICH
WOOLWICH
THAMES FLOOD BARRIER
Barrier Control Building
SE10
Mudlark Pier
Slipway
Pontoon
Jetty
Greenwich Yacht Club
GREENWICH PENINSULA ECOLOGY PARK
THAMES ANCHORAGE POINT IND EST
MERIDIAN TRADING ESTATE
136
NEW CHARLTON
CABLE TRADE PARK
Superstores
GREENWICH INDUSTRIAL ESTATE
Stone Lake Retail Pk
Holiday Inn Express
COUNCIL DEPOT
BLACKWALL LANE
A2203
BLACKWALL TUNNEL APPROACH
WOOLWICH ROAD
A206
EAST GREENWICH PLEASAUNCE
Health Cen
Fire Sta
Warehouses
WESTCOMBE PARK
THE VALLEY CHARLTON ATHLETIC FC
CHARLTON
78
SE7
SE3
A102
HAROLD GIBBONS COURT
RECTORY FIELD Blackheath R.F.C.
CHARLTON ROAD
B210
SHOOTER'S HILL ROAD
A207
OLD DOVER ROAD
B211
VANBRUGH PARK
The Gardens
THE WILDERNESS (DEER PARK)
ART GALL
155
E F G H J
1 2 3 4 5 6 7

A
B
C
D
E
1
2
3
4
5
6
7
42
43
116
135
156
80
78
E16
SE18
SE7
LONDON CITY AIRPORT
KING GEORGE V DOCK
TERMINAL BUILDINGS
ROYAL ALBERT DOCK
London Regatta Centre
Go Karting
Grain Mills
HARTMANN ROAD
CONNAUGHT BRIDGE
CONNAUGHT RD
HART RD
CAMEL ROAD
DREW RD
NORTH WOOLWICH RD
ALBERT ROAD
FACTORY ROAD
A112
Warehouse
SILVERTOWN & LONDON CITY AIRPORT
SILVERTOWN
NORTH WOOLWICH
THAMESIDE INDUSTRIAL EST
STANDARD INDUSTRIAL ESTATE
NORTH WOOLWICH
PIER RD
A117
ROYAL VICTORIA GDNS
North Woolwich Pier
Woolwich Ferry Pier
WOOLWICH FOOT TUNNEL
Tate & Lyle Jetty
REACH
THAMES FLOOD BARRIER
Barrier Gardens Pier
Barrier Control Building
Jetty
VISITORS CEN
HARRINGTON WAY
HARLINGER STREET
BOWATER RD
MELLISH IND EST
WOOLWICH FREE FERRY
South Pontoon
SE. London Aquatic Cen
Leisure Cen
Firepower
NEW FERRY APP
WOOLWICH CHURCH STREET
A206
WOOLWICH ROAD
WOOLWICH DOCKYARD
ST MARY'S GDNS
WOOLWICH HIGH ST
BERESFORD
WELLINGTON ST
Town Hall
Council Offices
Halls of Res
MARYON PARK
MARYON ROAD
Tennis Courts
CHILDRENS ZOO
MARYON WILSON PARK
THE VALLEY CHARLTON ATHLETIC FC
Superstores
HILLREACH
ARTILLERY PLACE
B210
Royal Artillery Barracks
WOOLWICH
BARRACK FIELD
MUS OF ARTILLERY
Dry Ski Slope
GRAND DEPOT RD
WOOLWICH NEW RD
HEATH
LITTLE HEATH
CHARLTON PARK ROAD
THE VILLAGE
CHARLTON
Charlton House
CHARLTON PARK
CHARLTON CEMETERY
WOOLWICH GARRISON
Charlton Pk Sch
REPOSITORY ROAD
CIRCULAR WAY
WOOLWICH COMMON
A205
ACADEMY ROAD
QUEEN ELIZABETH HOSPITAL
Rugby Grd
Royal Military Academy
PRINCE IMPERIAL RD
HORNFAIR PARK
HORNFAIR ROAD
Bowling Green
Lido
A207
SHOOTERS HILL
WOOLWICH COMMON
GREEN CHAIN WALK
ROYAL HERBERT PAVILIONS
Sixth-Form Coll
NIGHTINGALE PL
Youth Club
HERBERT ROAD

E
F
G
H
J
117
THAMESMEAD
SE28
1
2
3
4
5
6
7
80
78
44
138
157
Newham Coll of Further Ed
BASIN SOUTH
ALBERT BASIN
Pier
GALLIONS REACH
North East Wharf
BROADWATER
BROADWATER GRN
WOOLWICH CROWN CT
H.M. PRISON BELMARSH
West Thamesmead Business Park
Southern Outfall Sewer
A2016
WESTERN WAY
THAMESMEAD WEST
PLUMSTEAD ROAD
A206
BUS GAR
POLTHORNE EST
PLUMSTEAD
REC GRD
PLUMSTEAD GARDENS
PLUMSTEAD HIGH STREET
Fire Sta
Leisure Cen
SE18
WINN'S COMMON
PLUMSTEAD COMMON
SHREWSBURY PARK
WOOLWICH CEM
ROCK. GDNS
WOOLWICH CEMETERY
SPORTS GRD
SHOOTER'S HILL GOLF COURSE
EAST WICKHAM OPEN SPACE
WICKHAM LANE
Superstore
Delivery Office
Works
ALLOT

A
B
C
D
E
1
2
3
4
5
6
7
118
137
158
80
78
48
THAMESMEAD
Thamesmead Town FC
SE28
SE2
DA16
EASTERN WAY
CENTRAL WAY
HARROW MANORWAY
BIRCHMERE PARK
Birchmere
SPORTS GRD
SOUTHMERE PARK
SOUTHMERE
LAKESIDE CENTRE
Boating Centre
Southmere
ABBEY WOOD PARK
ABBEY WOOD
Abbey Wood
THISTLEBROOK INDUSTRIAL EST
Delivery Office
Civic Amenity Site
Works
ABBEY WOOD PARK
Health Cen
Lib
Clinic
Prim Sch
Sec Sch
Sports Cen
SPORTS GROUND
CROSSNESS PARK
WOODLANDS WAY
ALLOT
ABBEY ROAD
B213
A2041
A206
A209
MC LEOD ROAD
KNEE HILL
Harrow Inn PH & Hall
Comm Cen
Lesnes Abbey (ruins)
GREEN CHAIN WALK
ABBEY WOOD
ABBEY WOOD CARAVAN CLUBS SITE
BOSTALL HEATH
BOSTALL HILL
HURST ESTATE
WOOLWICH ROAD
WEST HEATH
Coll
CLAM FIELD RECREATION GROUND
BOSTALL WOODS
BOSTALL HEATH
Bowling Green
GOLDIE LEIGH HOSPITAL
GREENWICH
BEXLEY
Bowl Grn
REC GRD
PLUMSTEAD CEMETERY
WOOLWICH CEMETERY
EAST WICKHAM
EAST WICKHAM OPEN SPACE
WICKHAM LANE
UPPER WICKHAM LANE
PLUMSTEAD HIGH STREET
BOSTALL PARK AVENUE
Superstore
Rock. Gdns
Bramley Court

E
F
G
H
J
49
50
117
159
80
79
78
1
2
3
4
5
6
7
Warehouses
Wharf
Depot
Jenningtree Point
JENNINGTREE POINT LIGHTHOUSE
Works
A2016
ERITH MARSHES
Belvedere Sub Sta
DA18
EASTERN WY
WAY
BELVEDERE INDUSTRIAL ESTATE
ANDERSON WAY
MULBERRY
THAMESMEAD SPINE RD
Works
EASTERN IND EST
HAILEY ROAD
Bexley Business Academy
WALDRIST WAY
KENCOT
YARNTON
CHURCH MANORWAY INDUSTRIAL ESTATE
CRABTREE MANORWAY IND EST
BRONZE
Gas Works
SUTHERLAND RD
MAIDA RD
CALDY ROAD
STATION ROAD N
BELVEDERE
PICARDY MANORWAY
POPPY CLOSE
NORMAN ROAD
Superstore
Comm Cen
Sch
KEATS ROAD
VIKING WAY
Prim Sch
ALLOT
DYLAN
LAYMARSH
GILBERT RD
PICARDY ST
LOWER ROAD
B213
Clinic
ELSTREE GARDENS
KINGSWOOD AV
HADLEY RD
RIPLEY ROAD
COLEMAN
SHERIDAN
GERTRUDE RD
LYNDON
UPPER ABBEY ROAD
B250
HALT ROBIN ROAD
DA17
BELVEDERE
FRANK'S PARK
Bexley Coll
LEATHER BOTTLE LANE
Leather Bottle PH
CHUCK WALK
GREEN
KENTISH
PICARDY
FREMANTLE RD
Trinity Sch
Fire Sta
PLAYING FIELD
LESSNESS PARK
NELSON RD
Eardley Arms PH
EARDLEY ROAD
ERITH ROAD
ROAD
A206
REC GRD
Lib
Pol
Prim Sch
ALBERT ROAD ESTATE
VICTORIA STREET
HOLLY
Bexley Coll
LESSNESS HEATH
FRASER
Coll
RIVERDALE
ERITH CEMETERY
BROOK STREET CEMETERY
BELVEDERE SPORTS GRD
Tenn Cts
Clubho
Fox PH
BARNFIELD ROAD
GROSVENOR ROAD
STREAMWAY
DA8
Works
CARLTON
MONASTERY
Prim Sch
ERITH & DISTR HOSP
BEDONWELL ROAD
NORTHUMBERLAND HEATH REC GRD
Pav
THE DRIVE
MANORWAY
PARSONAGE
MATFIELD RD
Prim Schs.
DA7
STAPLETON
HURLINGHAM
PO
Earl Haig PH
BELMONT
Prim Sch
NURSTEAD ROAD
HORSA
Lib
NORTHUMBERLAND PK
BEXLEY
Sec Sch
NORTHUMBERLAND HEATH
COLYERS
WEST HOLME
EAST HOLME
HEATH WAY
CARTMEL
CRESCENT
BIRCHINGTON
BROOK ST
MILL
Prim Sch

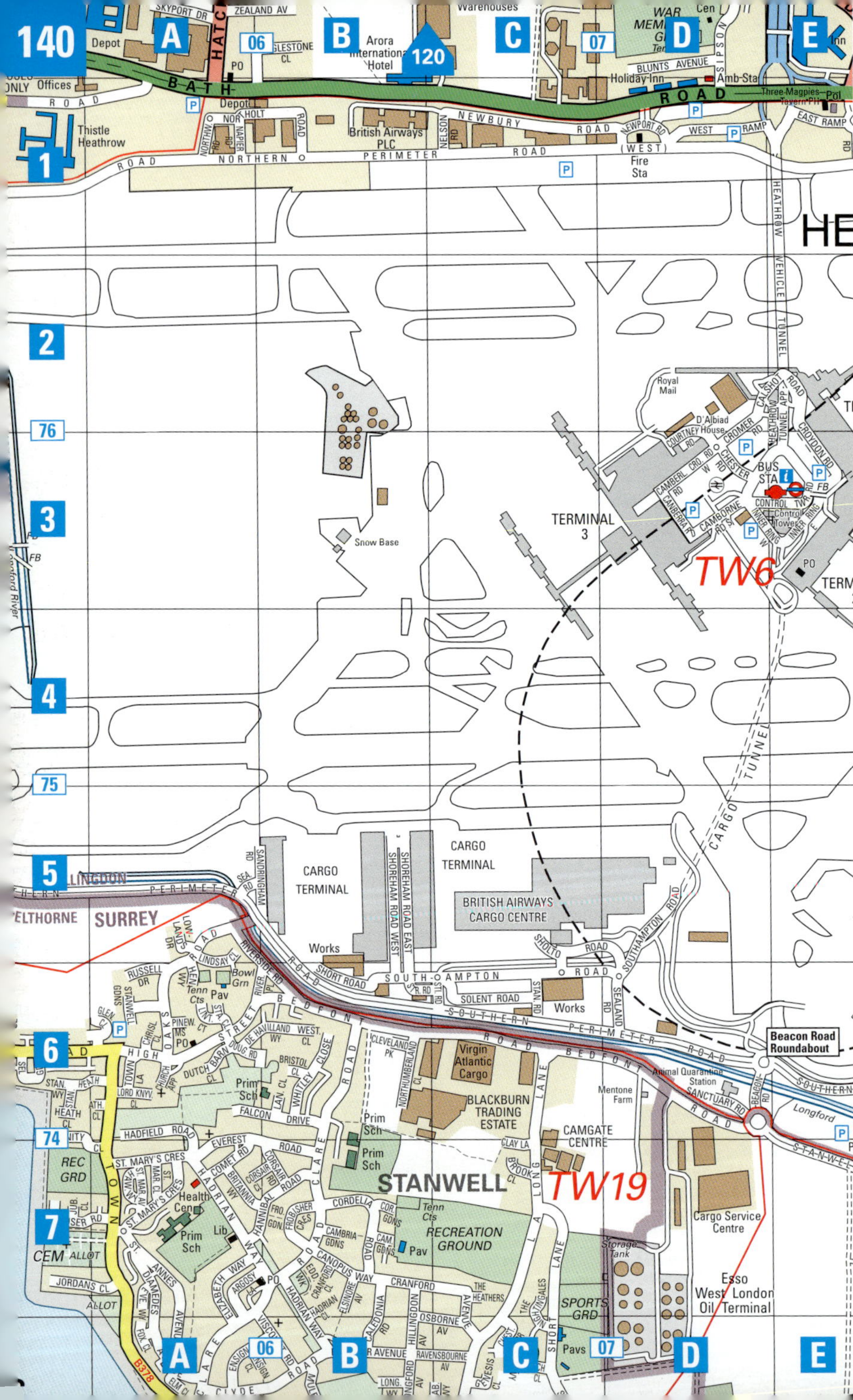
A
B
C
D
E
1
2
3
4
5
6
7
06
07
76
75
74
120
SKYPORT DR
ZEALAND AV
Depot
HATCH
PO
GLESTONE CL
Arora International Hotel
Warehouses
WAR MEM
Cen
BLUNTS AVENUE
Holiday Inn
Amb Sta
SIPSON
Inn
Offices
ROAD
BATH ROAD
Three Magpies Tavern PH
Pol
EAST RAMP
Thistle Heathrow
NORTHWOOD RD
NORMAN RD
NAPIER RD
HOLT ROAD
Depot
British Airways PLC
NELSON RD
NEWBURY ROAD
NEWPORT RD
WEST RAMP
(WEST)
NORTHERN PERIMETER ROAD
Fire Sta
HEATHROW VEHICLE TUNNEL
HE
Royal Mail
D'Albiac House
COURTNEY RD
CROMER RD
CALSHOT RD
HEATHROW TUNNEL APP
CROYDON RD
CHESTER RD
CAMBERLEY RD
CANBERRA RD
CAMBORNE RD S
BUS STA
FB
CONTROL TWR RD
Control Tower
INNER RING W
INNER RING E
Snow Base
TERMINAL 3
TW6
PO
TERM 2
CARGO TUNNEL
CARGO TERMINAL
CARGO TERMINAL
SANDRINGHAM RD
SHOREHAM ROAD WEST
SHOREHAM ROAD EAST
BRITISH AIRWAYS CARGO CENTRE
SOUTHAMPTON ROAD
SHOLTO ROAD
SOUTHAMPTON ROAD
SEALAND RD
SEA RD
HILLINGDON
SOUTHERN PERIMETER ROAD
SPELTHORNE
SURREY
LOWLANDS DR
RIVERSIDE RD
Works
SHORT ROAD
STAN RD
SOLENT ROAD
Works
Beacon Road Roundabout
LINDSAY CL
RUSSELL DR
Bowl Grn
Tenn Cts
Pav
STANWELL GDNS
BEDFONT ROAD
GLEN CL
HIGH STREET
OAKS
PINEWOOD CT
DE HAVILLAND WY
WEST CL
DUTCH BARN CL
BRISTOL CL
CLOSE
CLEVELAND PK
NORTHUMBERLAND CL
Virgin Atlantic Cargo
BEDFONT LANE
Animal Quarantine Station
Mentone Farm
SANCTUARY RD
BEACON RD
Longford
STANWELL
Prim Sch
FALCON DRIVE
WHITLEY CL
BLACKBURN TRADING ESTATE
HADFIELD ROAD
EVEREST ROAD
CLARE ROAD
CLAY LA
CAMGATE CENTRE
BROOK CL
LONG LANE
TW19
STANWELL
REC GRD
ST. MARY'S CRES
COMET RD
HADRIAN WAY
CORSAIR RD
CORDELIA GDNS
Health Cen
Tenn Cts
RECREATION GROUND
Pav
Cargo Service Centre
Prim Sch
Lib
HANNIBAL WAY
FROBISHER CRES
CAMBRIA GDNS
CANOPUS WAY
CRANFORD AV
THE HEATHERS
Storage Tank
Esso West London Oil Terminal
CEM
ALLOT
JORDANS CL
ALLOT
ELIZABETH WAY
ARGOSY LA
CALEDONIA RD
HILLINGDON AV
OSBORNE AV
THE NIGHTINGALES
SPORTS GRD
ST. ANNES AVENUE
DIAMEDES AV
VISCOUNT RD
RAVENSBOURNE AV
Pavs
SHORT LA
CLYDE
B378
ENSIGN CL
LONG.

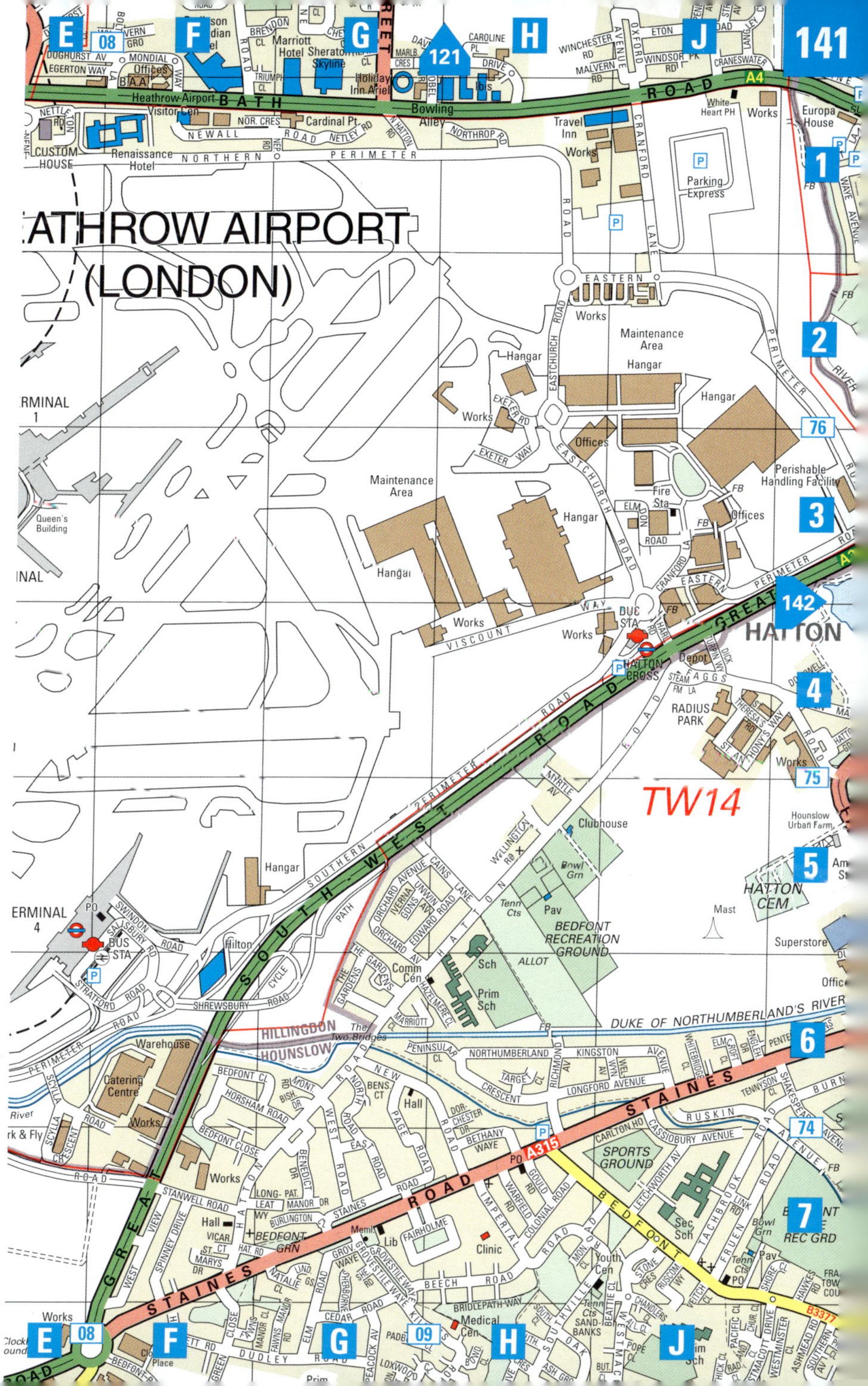

HEATHROW AIRPORT (LONDON)
TW14
HATTON
121
142
08
09
BATH ROAD
A4
Heathrow Airport Visitor Cen
Marriott Hotel
Sheraton Skyline
Holiday Inn Ariel
Ibis
Bowling Alley
Cardinal Pt
Renaissance Hotel
CUSTOM HOUSE
NORTHERN PERIMETER
NEWALL ROAD
NETLEY RD
NORTHROP RD
Travel Inn
Works
Parking Express
CRANFORD LANE
Europa House
EASTERN PERIMETER
EASTCHURCH ROAD
Maintenance Area
Hangar
Offices
Perishable Handling Facility
Fire Sta
EXETER RD
EXETER WAY
ELMDON ROAD
CRANFORD LA
VISCOUNT WAY
DUC STA
HATTON CROSS
Depot
FAGGS
RADIUS PARK
ST. ANTHONY'S WAY
THERESA'S RD
Hounslow Urban Farm
HATTON CEM
Mast
Superstore
GREAT SOUTH WEST ROAD
SOUTHERN PERIMETER ROAD
TERMINAL 1
TERMINAL 4
Queen's Building
BUS STA
SWINDON ROAD
SALISBURY RD
STRATFORD ROAD
Hilton
SHREWSBURY ROAD
CYCLE PATH
MYRTLE AV
WELLINGTON RD
Clubhouse
Bowl Grn
Tenn Cts
Pav
BEDFONT RECREATION GROUND
ALLOT
Sch
Prim Sch
Comm Cen
ORCHARD AVENUE
IVERNA GDNS
UNWIN AV
EDWARD ROAD
CAINS LANE
HAZELMERE CL
MARRIOTT CL
THE GARDENS
DUKE OF NORTHUMBERLAND'S RIVER
HILLINGDON
HOUNSLOW
The Two Bridges
Warehouse
Catering Centre
SCYLLA CRESCENT
PENINSULAR CL
NORTHUMBERLAND
KINGSTON AVENUE
RICHMOND AV
TARGET CL
LONGFORD AVENUE
CRESCENT
BEDFONT CL
HORSHAM ROAD
BEDFONT CLOSE
NEW ROAD
NORTH ROAD
EAST ROAD
WEST ROAD
PAGE ROAD
Hall
DORCHESTER RD
BETHANY WAYE
STAINES ROAD
A315
BEDFONT
SPORTS GROUND
CASSIOBURY AVENUE
LETCHWORTH AV
RUSKIN AVENUE
TENNYSON
SHAKESPEARE AVENUE
Sec Sch
TACHBROOK
FRUEN RD
BEDFONT REC GRD
B3377
STANWELL ROAD
SPINNEY DRIVE
HATTON ROAD
BURLINGTON
FAIRHOLME
Lib
Clinic
IMPERIAL RD
COLONIAL ROAD
GOULD RD
Youth Cen
BEECH ROAD
BRIDLEPATH WAY
Medical Cen
CEDAR ROAD
DUDLEY ROAD
PEACOCK AV
SOUTHVILLE
Works
Place

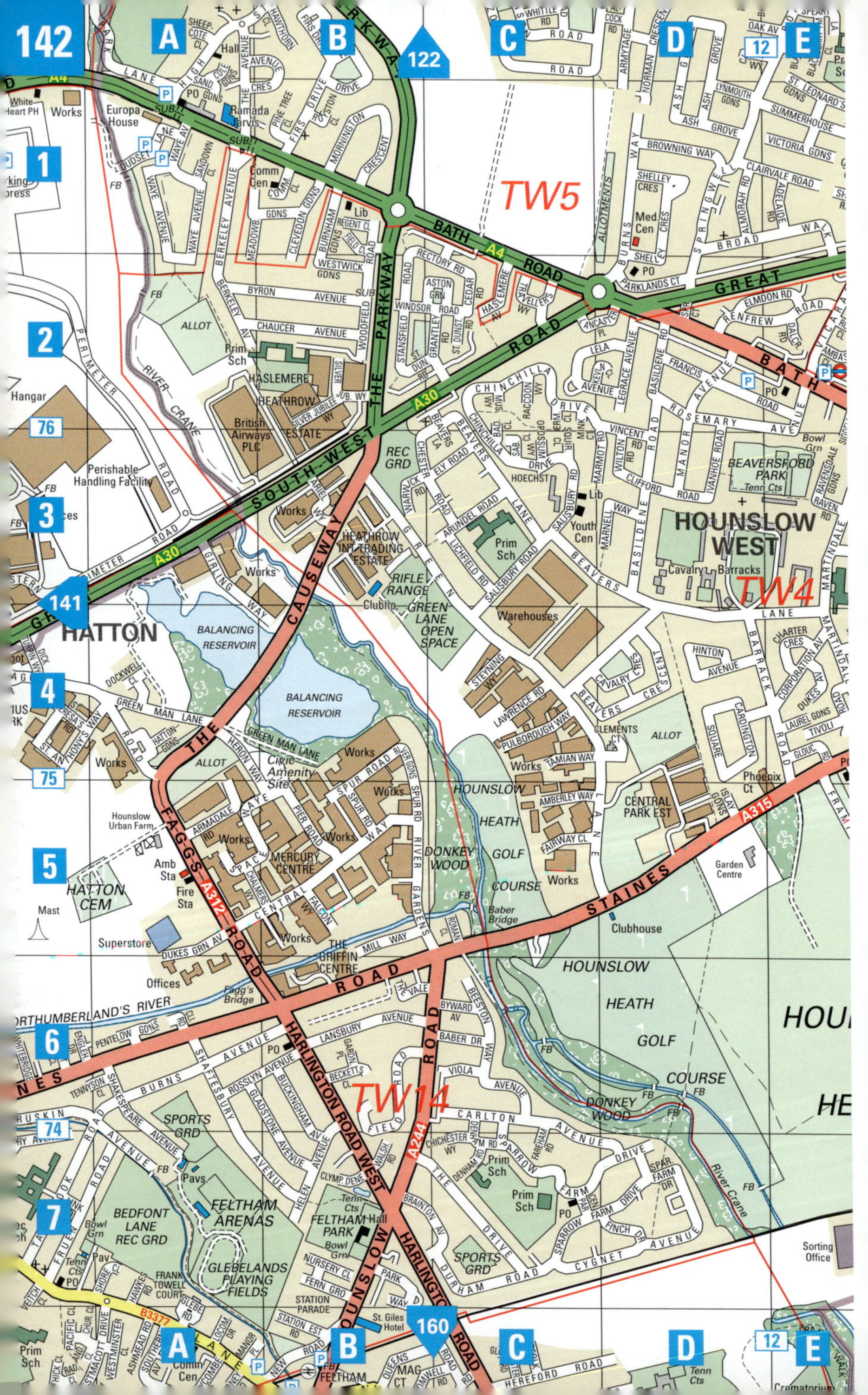

A
B
C
D
E
1
2
3
4
5
6
7
122
141
160
12
76
75
74
TW5
TW4
TW14
HATTON
HOUNSLOW WEST
A4
A30
A312
A315
A244
B3377
BATH ROAD
GREAT SOUTH-WEST ROAD
THE PARKWAY
PERIMETER ROAD
THE CAUSEWAY
STAINES ROAD
FAGG'S ROAD
HARLINGTON ROAD WEST
HOUNSLOW ROAD
HARLINGTON ROAD
GREAT WEST ROAD
BEAVERS LANE
BARRACK ROAD
GREEN LANE
GREEN MAN LANE
CENTRAL WAY
SPUR ROAD
FALCON WAY
CHINCHILLA DRIVE
ROSEMARY AVENUE
CIVIC WAY
SALISBURY ROAD
HIGH STREET
SHELLEY CRES
BROWNING WAY
ADELAIDE RD
SPRINGWELL ROAD
BROAD WALK
CARLTON AVENUE
CYGNET AVENUE
SPARROW FARM DRIVE
BURNS AVENUE
SHAFTESBURY AVENUE
ROSSLYN AVENUE
LANSBURY AVENUE
VIOLA AVENUE
BYRON AVENUE
CHAUCER AVENUE
BERKELEY AVENUE
WAYE AVENUE
CLEVEDON GDNS
WESTWICK GDNS
MORNINGTON CRESCENT
WINDSOR ROAD
RECTORY RD
Europa House
Ramada Jarvis
Works
White Heart PH
Comm Cen
Lib
Med. Cen
PO
Hangar
Perishable Handling Facility
British Airways PLC
HASLEMERE HEATHROW ESTATE
HEATHROW INT. TRADING ESTATE
Prim Sch
ALLOT
REC GRD
RIFLE RANGE
GREEN LANE OPEN SPACE
Clubho.
Warehouses
Youth Cen
BALANCING RESERVOIR
Civic Amenity Site
MERCURY CENTRE
THE GRIFFIN CENTRE
Hounslow Urban Farm
Amb Sta
Fire Sta
HATTON CEM
Mast
Superstore
Offices
Fagg's Bridge
NORTHUMBERLAND'S RIVER
HOUNSLOW HEATH GOLF COURSE
DONKEY WOOD
Baber Bridge
Clubhouse
Garden Centre
CENTRAL PARK EST
Phoenix Ct
BEAVERSFORD PARK
Tenn Cts
Bowl Grn
Cavalry Barracks
River Crane
Sorting Office
SPORTS GRD
FELTHAM ARENAS
BEDFONT LANE REC GRD
GLEBELANDS PLAYING FIELDS
FELTHAM PARK
STATION PARADE
St. Giles Hotel
FELTHAM
Crematorium

E
F
G
H
J
HESTON
13
123
14
SUTTON PLAYING FIELD
WEST ROAD
A4
LAMPTON
LONDON TRANSPORT SPORTS GRD
SPORTS GROUND
SPRING GROVE
B363
LAMPTON PARK
HOUNSLOW CIVIC CENTRE
HOUNSLOW WEST
HOUNSLOW EAST
HOUNSLOW CENTRAL
SUTTON LANE
A3063
A3005
A3006
BULSTRODE AVENUE
BULSTRODE ROAD
HIGH STREET
HANWORTH RD
Treaty Centre
Hounslow Centre
HOUNSLOW
STAINES ROAD
TW3
INWOOD PARK
144
76
75
74
WELLINGTON ROAD N
WELLINGTON ROAD SOUTH
HANWORTH ROAD
A314
B361
B358
Metropolitan Police Training Centre
HOUNSLOW HEATH
LONDON LOOP
HOUNSLOW RICHMOND UPON THAMES
MURRAY PARK
KNELLER
SPORTS GROUND
NELSON ROAD
WHITTON DENE
WHITTON ROAD
TW2
WHITTON
BOROUGH CEMETERY
HOSPITAL BRIDGE
CHERTSEY
161
1
2
3
4
5
6
7

A
B
C
D
E
1
2
3
4
5
6
7
15
16
124
76
143
75
74
162
OSTERLEY
SPORTS GROUND
Campion House Coll
Brunel University (Osterley Campus)
ISLEWORTH CROWN CRT
SPRING GROVE
SPORTS GRD
West Thames Coll
SYON LANE
GROVE ROAD
B363
LONDON ROAD
A315
ISLEWORTH
THE METRO CENTRE
WEST MIDDLESEX UNIVERSITY HOSP
CEM
A310
TWICKENHAM ROAD
WOODLANDS
THORNBURY PLAYING FIELDS
ST. JOHN'S GDNS
ST JOHN'S ROAD
ISLEWORTH
SOUTH ST
RICHMOND RD
VICTORY BUSINESS CENTRE
TW7
TW3
BUS GAR
WORTON HALL INDUSTRIAL ESTATE
MOGDEN WATER TREATMENT WORKS
Filter Beds
REDLEES PARK
Boys Club
CONV
Brunel Univers
ST. MARGARETS ROAD
A3004
ST. MARGARETS
IVYBRIDGE ESTATE
Superstores
Superstore
MOGDEN LANE
Queen's Bridge
GLEN WALK
WHITTON DENE
HOUNSLOW
RICHMOND UPON THAMES
THE RUGBY FOOTBALL UNION TWICKENHAM
TWICKENHAM TRADING EST
Royal Military Sch of Music
B361
WHITTON ROAD
CHERTSEY ROAD
A316
TW2
RICHMOND UPON THAMES COLLEGE
Stoop Memorial Ground Harlequins R.F.C.
PLAYING FIELD
TWICKENHAM
LONDON ROAD
MOOR MEAD GRD
YORK ST
RICHMOND ROAD
CIVIC CEN
Hall
MURRAY PARK
ALLOTMENTS

E
F
G
H
J
17
125
ROYAL
BOTANIC GARDENS
Waterlily House
THE POND
Temple of Arethusa
Palm House
War Meml.
Victoria Gate Visitor Centre
Delivery Office
REC GRD
Aquatic Experience
Great Conservatory
London Butterfly House
Battles of Brentford 1016 & 1642
Wyevale Garden Centre
SYON HOUSE
SYON PARK
THE LAKE
ARBORETUM
Glasshouse
Temperate House
Evolution House
WATER LILY POND
KEW
MARIANNE NORTH GALLERY
QUEEN'S COTTAGE GARDENS
Queen Charlotte's Cottage
Restaurant Pavilion
Pagoda
Lion Gate
HOLLY WALK
Duke of Northumberland Estate
RIVER THAMES
Syon Reach
HOUNSLOW
RICHMOND UPON THAMES
Obelisk
ISLEWORTH
ROYAL MID-SURREY GOLF COURSE
TW9
Kew Observatory
OBSERVATORY GARDENS
SPORTS GRD
London Welsh R.F.C. & Richmond C.C.
RICHMOND ATHLETIC GROUND
Clubhouse
ROYAL HOSP
Bowl Club
Lido
Swim Pool
OLD DEER PARK RECREATION GROUND
Richmond Lock
Richmond Footbridge
Obelisks
TWICKENHAM ROAD
LOWER MORTLAKE ROAD
KEW ROAD
KEW GARDENS
SANDYCOMBE ROAD
MANOR ROAD
A307
A316
A305
B353
B321
B322
Superstore
146
NORTH SHEEN
76
75
74
1
2
3
4
5
6
7
RICHMOND
RICHMOND GREEN
Richmond Palace Remains
THE SQUARE
SHEEN ROAD
GEORGE ST
PARADISE RD
RED LION ST
HILL ST
HILL RISE
White Cross Hotel PH
CORP. ISLAND
Lib & Mus
Comm Cen
PESTHOUSE COMMON
RICHMOND CEMETERY
QUEENS ROAD
KINGS ROAD
FRIARS STILE ROAD
RICHMOND BR
PETERSHAM ROAD
POPPY FACTORY MUS
TERRACE GDNS
TERRACE FIELD
Richmond Hill Hotel
Royal Star & Garter Home
Richmond Coll
BISHOP'S PONDS
CONDUIT WOOD
Richmond Gate
TW10
SAWYER'S HILL
Open During
PETERSHAM COMMON
PETERSHAM MEADOWS
GLOVER'S ISLAND
KIDNEY WOOD
STAR & GARTER HILL
ST MARGARETS ROAD
CROWN ROAD
RICHMOND ROAD
MARBLE HILL PARK
MARBLE HILL HOUSE
MEADOWBANK
Meadowbank Club
Sec Sch
ORLEANS HOUSE GALLERY
ORLEANS ROAD
TW1
RIVER THAMES
163
PETERSHAM ROAD
LONDON THAMES CYCLE ROUTE

A
B
C
D
E
126
21
1
2
3
4
5
6
7
76
145
75
74
164
KEW
KEW GARDENS
BROOMFIELD RD
LICHFIELD ROAD
STA. PAR
STA AV
HIGH PARK RD
WEST PARK RD
CUMBERLAND
LEYBORNE
BURLINGTON AVENUE
BEECHWOOD AV
DEFOE AV
RUSKIN AV
AVENUE
BESSANT DR
KEW MEADOW PATH
Sewage Works
Superstores
MELLISS AV
WHITCOMBE MS
Recycling Cen
HARTINGTON CT
KINNAIRD AV
DEVONSHIRE GDNS
CONISTON CL
CHISWICK STAITHE
CHISW. STAI
THAMES VILLAGE
CHISW. QUAY
WINDRUSH CL
CAVENDISH
Yacht Basin
IBIS LA
SPORTS GRD
Boathouses
UNI WEST. SPORTS GRD
STADIUM
Tenn Cts
CHISWICK CEMETERY
A316
CHERTSEY ROAD
GREAT CHERTSEY ROAD
DUKE'S MEADOW
ALLOT
STAVELEY GARDENS
RIVERSIDE
CIVIL SERV SPORTS GRD
Riverside Club
DUKE'S MEADOW GOLF COURSE
W4
Chiswick R.F.C.
Driving Range
Practice Range
Clubhouse
Pitch
HOUNSLOW
RICHMOND UPON THAMES
A205
SOUTH CIRCULAR ROAD
TW9
NORTH SHEEN CEMETERY
Crematorium
HAMMERSMITH CEMETERY
CHISWICK BR
CLIFFORD AVENUE
CLIFFORD AV
The Ship PH
Courage Brewery
THAMES BK
SHIP LA
A3003
MORTLAKE HIGH ST
ROYAL MAIL
LOWER RICHMOND RD
MORTLAKE
NORTH WORPLE WAY
SOUTH WORPLE WAY
BARNES HOSP
MORTL. CEM
SHALSTONE RD
KINGSWAY
FB
NORTH SHEEN
Bowl Grn
Pav
Sch
Prim Sch
SANDYCOMBE ROAD
B353
VICTORIA COTTS
CLARENCE ROAD
ELIZ. COTT
BRANSTONE
NYLANDS AV
REC GRD
ATWOOD AV
PENSFORD AVENUE
CHELWOOD GDNS
TAYLOR AVENUE
CHAUCER AV
THOMPSON AV
MARKSBURY AVENUE
CHILTON ROAD
DANCER RD
DARELL RD
THE HAVEN
LOWER RICHMOND RD
A316
Fire Sta
THE CLOSE
SOMERTON AV
BICESTER RD
LAMBERT AVENUE
Superstore
MANOR ROAD
MANOR GROVE
GROVE
LEONARD'S RD
ORMONDE RD
HOLMESDALE RD
CARLTON RD
CONNAUGHT AV
LEINSTER AV
ELM RD
Health Cen
Lib
PO
B351
SHEEN LANE
UPPER RICHMOND ROAD WEST
UPPER RICHMOND ROAD WEST
NORTH SHEEN ALLOT
TANGIER RD
CLYDESDALE AV
BURDENSHOTT AV
ROTHESAY AV
WARREN AV
KINGS FARM AV
CARRING. RD
ORCHARD RISE
BERWYN ROAD
STANLEY ROAD
DERBY RD
COVAL LA
COVAL GDNS
COVAL RD
DEANHILL RD
MEDCROFT GDNS
SHEEN GATE GDNS
COLSTON RD
PALMERSTON ROAD
OBSERVATORY RD
EAST SHEEN
SW14
EAST SHEEN AVENUE
GILPIN AVENUE
WALLORTON GDNS
PARKFIELD AV
Sec Sch
Leisure Cen
PARK DRIVE
SUNBURY AV
HERTFORD AV
Twr Ho Sch
TEMPLE SHEEN
WELL LANE
The Plough PH
CHRIST CHURCH RD
Prim Sch
WAYSIDE
VICARAGE ROAD
VICARAGE DR
STONEHILL ROAD
CLARE LAWN AV
PALEWELL COMMON
PALEWELL PLAYING FIELDS
THE MALL
Tennis & Squash Club
FIFE ROAD
YORK AVENUE
HOOD AV
EAST SHEEN COMMON (NT)
PLAYING FIELD
Bowl Grn
Tenn Cts
Bowl Club
ROAD
Black Horse PH
COURTLANDS
PESTHOUSE COMMON
Sec Sch
ALLOT
EAST SHEEN CEMETERY
RICHMOND CEMETERY
QUEENS ROAD
LOWER GROVE RD
GDNS
ROEDEAN CRESCENT
THE BANK OF ENGLAND SPORTS GROUND
Pitch & Putt
East Sheen Gate
TECK PLANTATION
ADAM'S POND
Bog Gate
The Bog
SHEEN WOOD
CYCLE PATH
HORSE RIDE
Roehampton Gate
Cambrian Gate
SHEEN CROSS WOOD
SAWYER'S HILL
POLO FIELD
TW10
CONDUIT WOOD
BARN WOOD POND
Open During Daylight Hours Only
SAW PIT PLANTATION
QUEEN'S RIDE
JUBILEE PLANTATION
DUCHESS WOOD
WHITE LODGE PLANTATIONS

E
F
G
H
J
22
23
127
165
148
1
2
3
4
5
6
7
74
75
76
SW13
SW15
BARNES
ROEHAMPTON
PUTNEY HEATH
PUTNEY
THE WETLANDS CENTRE
BARN ELMS PLAYING FIELDS
BARN ELMS SCHOOL SPORTS CENTRE
BARNES COMMON
PUTNEY LOWER COMMON
PUTNEY HOSP
CRAVEN COTTAGE FULHAM FC
ROEHAMPTON PRIORY HOSPITAL
ROEHAMPTON GOLF COURSE
QUEEN MARY'S UNI HOSP
ROEHAMPTON PLAYING FIELDS
Southlands College
Digby Stuart College
University of Surrey
Froebel College
South Thames Coll
Wandsworth Adult Ed Coll
Bellerbys Coll
MARYFIELD CONVENT
Whitelands College
ST. MARY'S CONVENT
Rosslyn Park R.F.C.
Roehampton Club
Putney Leisure Cen
Putney Park Sch
Tibbet's Corner
The Telegraph PH
SCIO POND
KING'S MERE
Kingsfarm Plantation
Killcat Corner
Beverley Brook
RIVER THAMES
A205
A306
A3003
B306
B350
UPPER RICHMOND ROAD
SOUTH CIRCULAR ROAD
LOWER RICHMOND ROAD
ROEHAMPTON LANE
ROCKS LANE
CASTELNAU
CHURCH ROAD
BARNES HIGH ST
THE TERRACE
LONSDALE ROAD
MILL HILL ROAD
STATION ROAD
QUEENS RIDE
QUEEN ELIZABETH WALK
HOWARDS LANE
PUTNEY HEATH
CLARENCE LANE
DANEBURY AVENUE
HIGHCLIFFE DRIVE
WESTLEIGH AVENUE
CHARTFIELD AVENUE
DOVER HOUSE ROAD
PUTNEY PARK LANE
TELEGRAPH ROAD
WILDCROFT ROAD
TIBBET'S RIDE

A
B
C
D
E
1
2
3
4
5
6
7
24
25
128
147
166
76
75
74
PARSONS GREEN
EEL BROOK COMMON
FULHAM
Fulham Palace
FULHAM PALACE GARDENS
BISHOP'S PARK
RIVER THAMES
PUTNEY BRIDGE
HURLINGHAM PARK
HURLINGHAM CLUB
Hurlingham Ho
SOUTH PARK
SW6
SW15
SW18
PUTNEY
WANDSWORTH
WANDSWORTH PARK
EAST PUTNEY
HAMMERSMITH & FULHAM
Chelsea Coll of Art & Design
Putney Exchange Shop Cen
ROYAL HOSPITAL
Univ of Surrey-Whitelands Coll
KING GEORGE'S PARK
Tibbet's Corner
SOUTHFIELDS
Metropolitan Club
Wandsworth Shopping Cen
FULHAM PALACE ROAD
FULHAM ROAD
NEW KINGS ROAD
KINGS ROAD
WANDSWORTH BRIDGE
PUTNEY HIGH ST
PUTNEY HILL
UPPER RICHMOND ROAD
WEST HILL
MERTON ROAD
PUTNEY BRIDGE ROAD
RICHMOND ROAD
LOWER RICHMOND ROAD
TIBBET'S RIDE
A219
A304
A308
A3209
A205
A3
A217
A218
B306

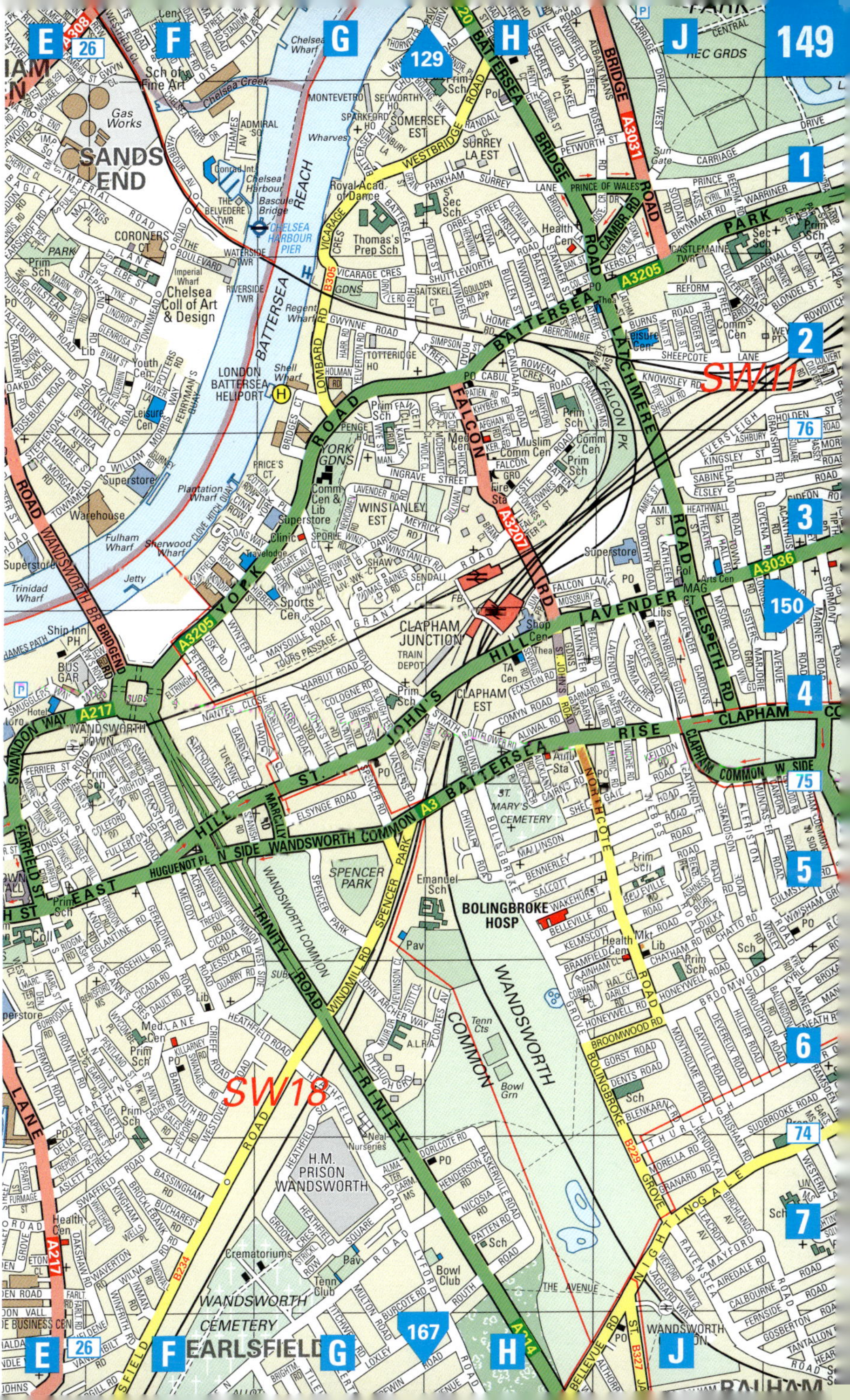
SANDS END
Gas Works
Sch of Fine Art
Chelsea Creek
Chelsea Wharf
Chelsea Harbour
CHELSEA HARBOUR PIER
BATTERSEA REACH
Chelsea Coll of Art & Design
Imperial Wharf
Regent Wharf
Wharves
Royal Acad of Dance
Thomas's Prep Sch
LONDON BATTERSEA HELIPORT
Shell Wharf
Plantation Wharf
Fulham Wharf
Sherwood Wharf
Trinidad Wharf
Jetty
Superstore
Warehouse
Travelodge
Sports Cen
CLAPHAM JUNCTION
TRAIN DEPOT
CLAPHAM EST
WINSTANLEY EST
YORK GDNS
Comm Cen & Lib
BATTERSEA BRIDGE
BATTERSEA BRIDGE ROAD
BRIDGE ROAD
PRINCE OF WALES DR
PARK
BATTERSEA PARK ROAD
FALCON ROAD
LATCHMERE ROAD
FALCON PK
YORK ROAD
LAVENDER HILL
ST JOHN'S HILL
BATTERSEA RISE
NORTHCOTE ROAD
CLAPHAM COMMON W SIDE
WANDSWORTH COMMON
SPENCER PARK
BOLINGBROKE HOSP
ST. MARY'S CEMETERY
Emanuel Sch
TRINITY ROAD
H.M. PRISON WANDSWORTH
WANDSWORTH CEMETERY
Crematorium
EARLSFIELD
WANDSWORTH TOWN
WANDSWORTH BRIDGE RD
SWANDON WAY
FAIRFIELD ST
EAST HILL
NIGHTINGALE LANE
BOLINGBROKE GROVE
BALHAM
SW11
SW18
A3205
A3031
A3207
A3036
A217
A3
A214
B305
B229
B234
B327
129
150
167
26
74
75
76
E
F
G
H
J
1
2
3
4
5
6
7

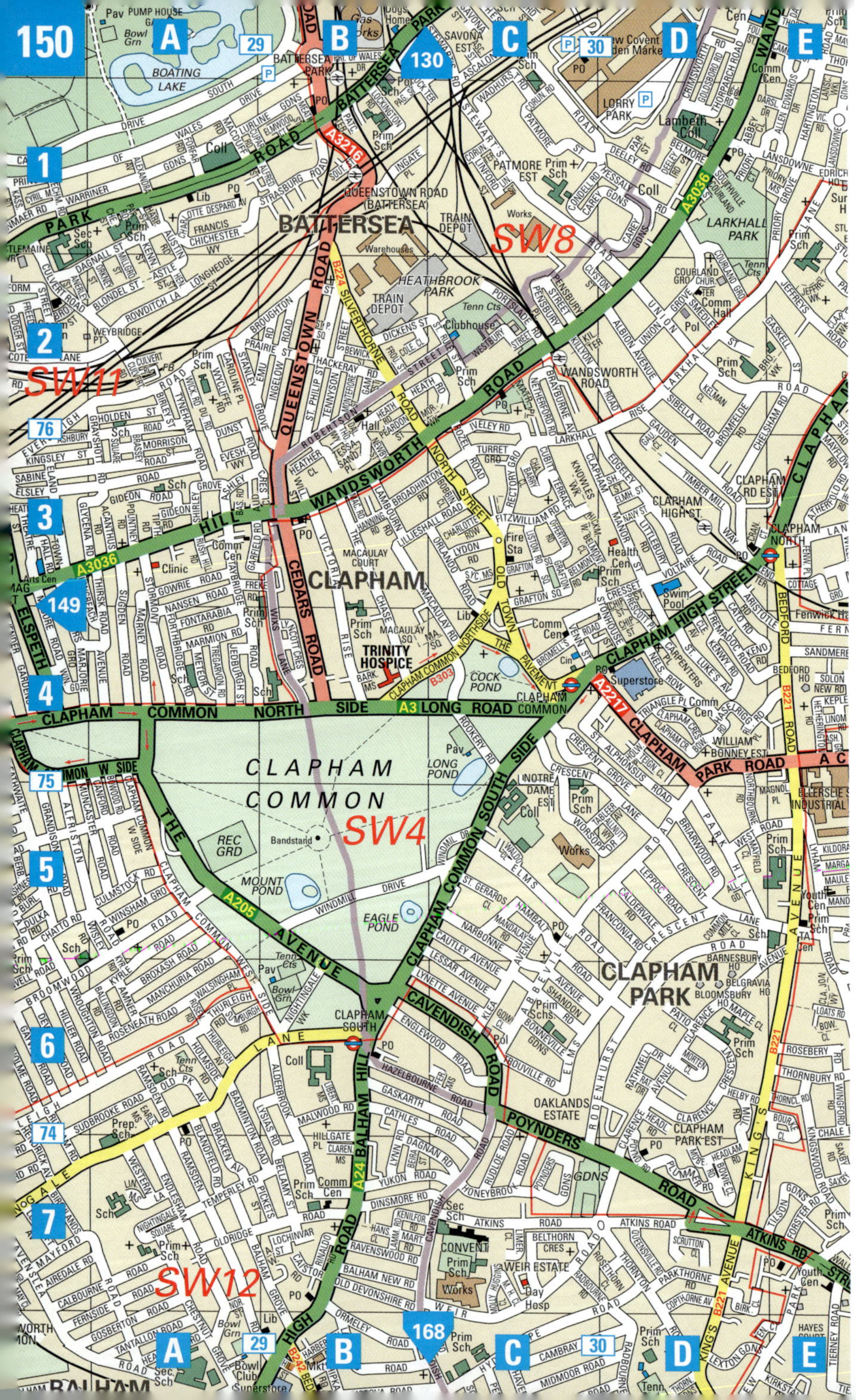
A
B
C
D
E
1
2
3
4
5
6
7
29
30
130
76
149
75
74
168
BATTERSEA
BATTERSEA PARK
BOATING LAKE
SW11
SW8
SW4
SW12
CLAPHAM
CLAPHAM COMMON
CLAPHAM PARK
CLAPHAM NORTH
CLAPHAM COMMON
CLAPHAM SOUTH
CLAPHAM HIGH ST.
CLAPHAM HIGH STREET
CLAPHAM COMMON NORTH SIDE
CLAPHAM COMMON SOUTH SIDE
CLAPHAM PARK ROAD
QUEENSTOWN ROAD
QUEENSTOWN ROAD (BATTERSEA)
CEDARS ROAD
WANDSWORTH ROAD
LAVENDER HILL
LONG ROAD
THE AVENUE
BALHAM HIGH ROAD
CAVENDISH ROAD
POYNDERS ROAD
KING'S AVENUE
BEDFORD ROAD
ATKINS RD
SILVERTHORNE ROAD
NORTH STREET
OLD TOWN
THE PAVEMENT
NIGHTINGALE LANE
HEATHBROOK PARK
LARKHALL PARK
PATMORE EST
OAKLANDS ESTATE
WEIR ESTATE
CONVENT
TRINITY HOSPICE
MOUNT POND
EAGLE POND
LONG POND
COCK POND
REC GRD
Bandstand
TRAIN DEPOT
Warehouses
Superstore
Swim Pool
A3036
A3216
A3
A205
A24
A2217
B224
B303
B221
B242

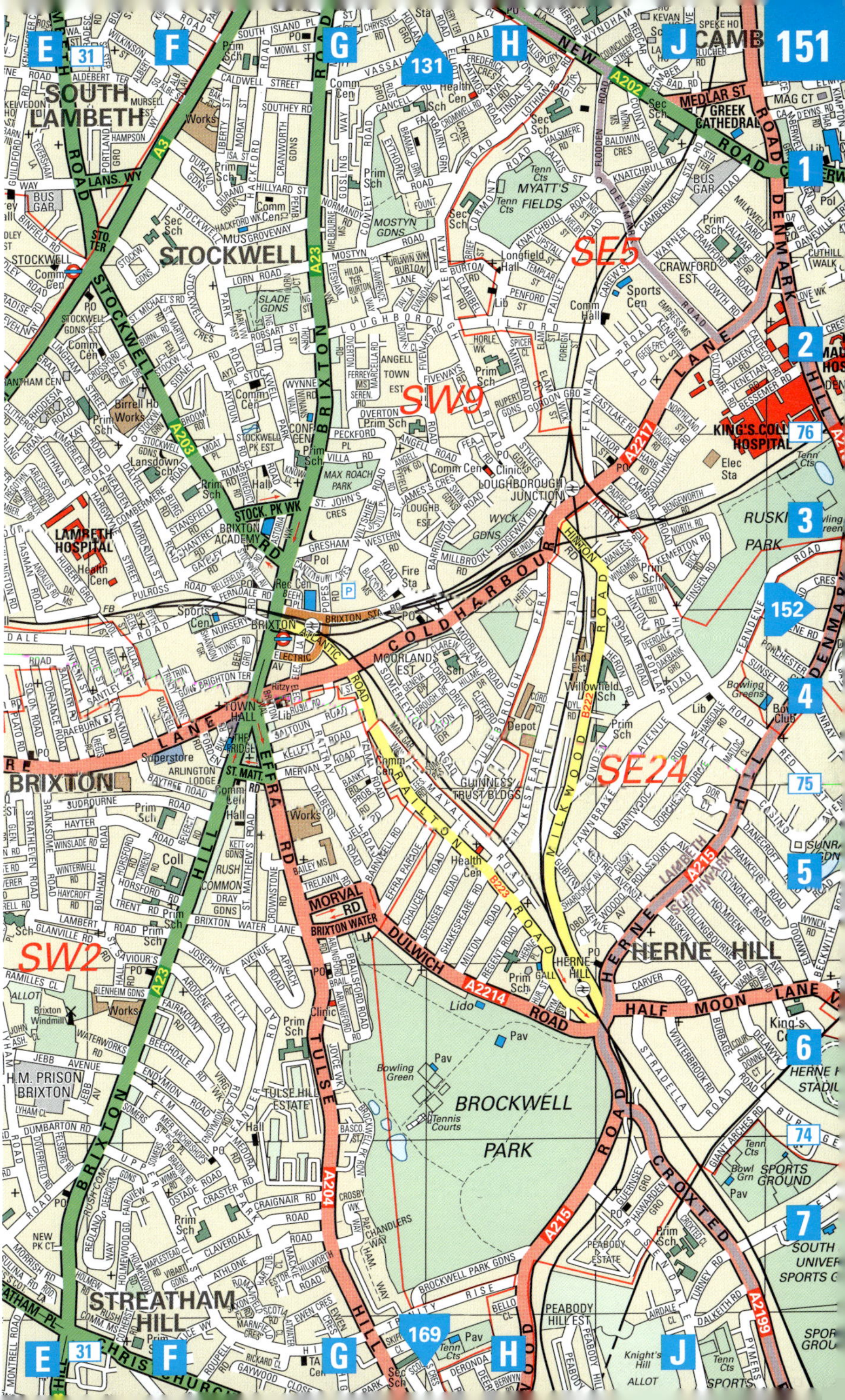
E
F
G
H
J
31
131
152
169
76
75
74
1
2
3
4
5
6
7
SOUTH LAMBETH
STOCKWELL
SE5
SW9
SE24
SW2
BRIXTON
HERNE HILL
STREATHAM HILL
CAMB
MYATT'S FIELDS
LOUGHBOROUGH JUNCTION
KING'S COLL HOSPITAL
LAMBETH HOSPITAL
BROCKWELL PARK
RUSKIN PARK
GREEK CATHEDRAL
H.M. PRISON BRIXTON
TULSE HILL ESTATE
GUINNESS TRUST BLDGS
COLDHARBOUR
HALF MOON LANE
DULWICH ROAD
BRIXTON WATER LANE
DENMARK HILL
EFFRA RD
RAILTON ROAD
MILKWOOD ROAD
CROXTED
NEW ROAD
STOCKWELL ROAD
LANS. WY
STOCKWELL PK WK
MORVAL RD
PECKHAM
Lido
Pav
Bowling Green
Tennis Courts
A3
A23
A202
A203
A204
A215
A2199
A2214
A2217
B222
B223

A
B
C
D
E
33
34
132
PECKHAM
CAMBERWELL CH ST
PECKHAM ROAD
PECKHAM HIGH ST
A202
DENMARK HILL
A215
SE5
THE MAUDSLEY HOSPITAL
KING'S COLLEGE HOSPITAL
CHAMPION PK
William Booth College
GROVE LANE
DOG KENNEL HILL
CHAMPION HILL EST
DENMARK HILL EST
RUSKIN PARK
76
151
75
74
1
2
3
4
5
6
7
LUCAS GDNS
WARWICK GDNS
PECKHAM RYE
A2215
RYE LANE
EAST DULWICH
GROVE VALE
EAST DULWICH RD
KING'S COLLEGE HOSP DULWICH
PECKHAM RYE COMMON
SE22
LORDSHIP LANE
A2216
GREENDALE PLAYING FIELDS
ST. OLAVE'S REC GRD
SUNRAY GDNS
SPORTS GROUND
EAST DULWICH GROVE
A2214
NORTH DULWICH
HERNE HILL STADIUM
VILLAGE WAY
DULWICH
SE21
SOUTH BANK UNIVERSITY SPORTS GROUND
DULWICH PARK
Dulwich Coll
DULWICH PICTURE GALL
DAWSON HEIGHTS ESTATE
170
A2199
LEWISHAM

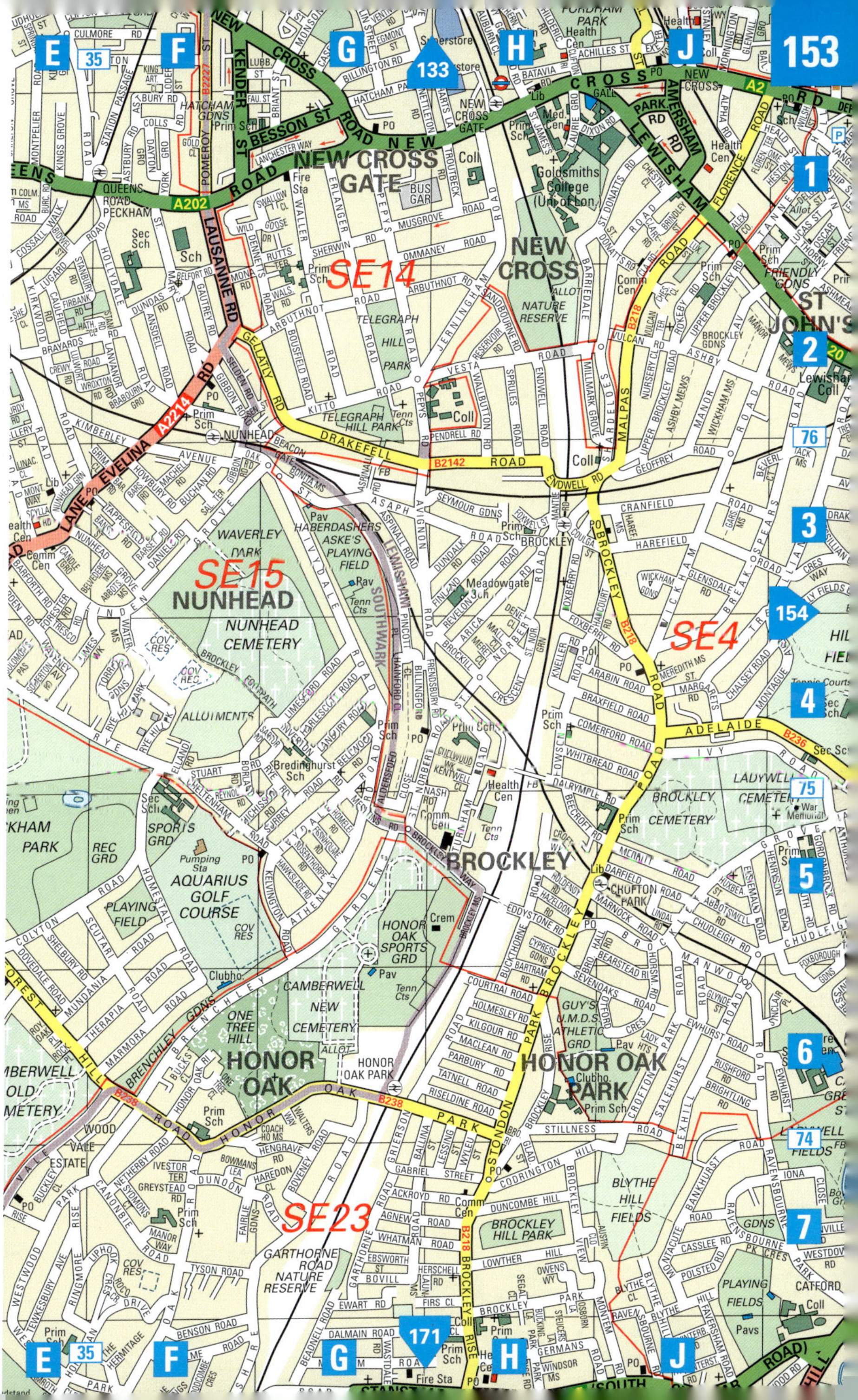
E
F
G
H
J
133
1
2
3
4
5
6
7
154
171
35
76
75
74
NEW CROSS
NEW CROSS GATE
SE14
NEW CROSS
NATURE RESERVE
ST JOHN'S
TELEGRAPH HILL PARK
GOLDSMITHS COLLEGE (Univ of Lon)
LAUSANNE RD
QUEENS ROAD PECKHAM
A202
A2
B2142
DRAKEFELL ROAD
NUNHEAD
SE15
NUNHEAD CEMETERY
WAVERLEY PARK
HABERDASHERS ASKE'S PLAYING FIELD
EVELINA ROAD
A2214
SE4
BROCKLEY
BROCKLEY ROAD
B218
ADELAIDE ROAD
B236
LADYWELL CEMETERY
BROCKLEY CEMETERY
AQUARIUS GOLF COURSE
HONOR OAK SPORTS GRD
CAMBERWELL NEW CEMETERY
ONE TREE HILL
HONOR OAK
HONOR OAK PARK
B238
STONDON PARK
SE23
BLYTHE HILL FIELDS
BROCKLEY HILL PARK
GARTHORNE ROAD NATURE RESERVE
BROCKLEY RISE
PECKHAM RYE PARK
CAMBERWELL OLD CEMETERY
PLAYING FIELDS

A
B
C
D
E
1
2
3
4
5
6
7
134
153
172
39
76
75
74
BLACKHEATH ROAD
BLACKHEATH HILL
SHOOTER'S HILL
BLACKH
ST JOHN'S
SE4
SE13
LEWISHAM
HILLY FIELDS
LADYWELL
LADYWELL CEMETERY
UNIVERSITY HOSPITAL LEWISHAM
LADYWELL CENTRE
LEWISHAM PARK
MOUNTFIELD PARK
PLAYING FIELDS
LADYWELL FIELDS
CATFORD GREYHOUND STADIUM
MANOR PARK
HITHER GREEN
CATFORD
LOAMPIT VALE
LOAMPIT HILL
LEWISHAM HIGH STREET
MOLESWORTH STREET
BROWNHILL ROAD
S CIRCULAR
CATFORD ROAD
LADYWELL ROAD
ADELAIDE AVENUE
BROCKLEY ROAD
LEE HIGH ROAD
BELMONT HILL
GREENWICH SOUTH ST
THURSTON RD
BROOKMILL ROAD
A2
A20
A21
A205
A206
A209
A2209
A2210
A2211
B220
B236
Lewisham Centre
Lewisham Bus Sta
Superstore
Superstores
Comm Hall
Lewisham Coll
Depot
Leisure Cen
Fire Sta
Bowling Green
Tennis Courts
Hospital (Closed)
Town Hall
PRIVATE BANKS SPORTS GRD
Ladywell Arena
Deptford Bridge
Catford Bridge
Ranger's House
Blackheath Gate
Croom's Hill Gate
Water Works
George Inn PH

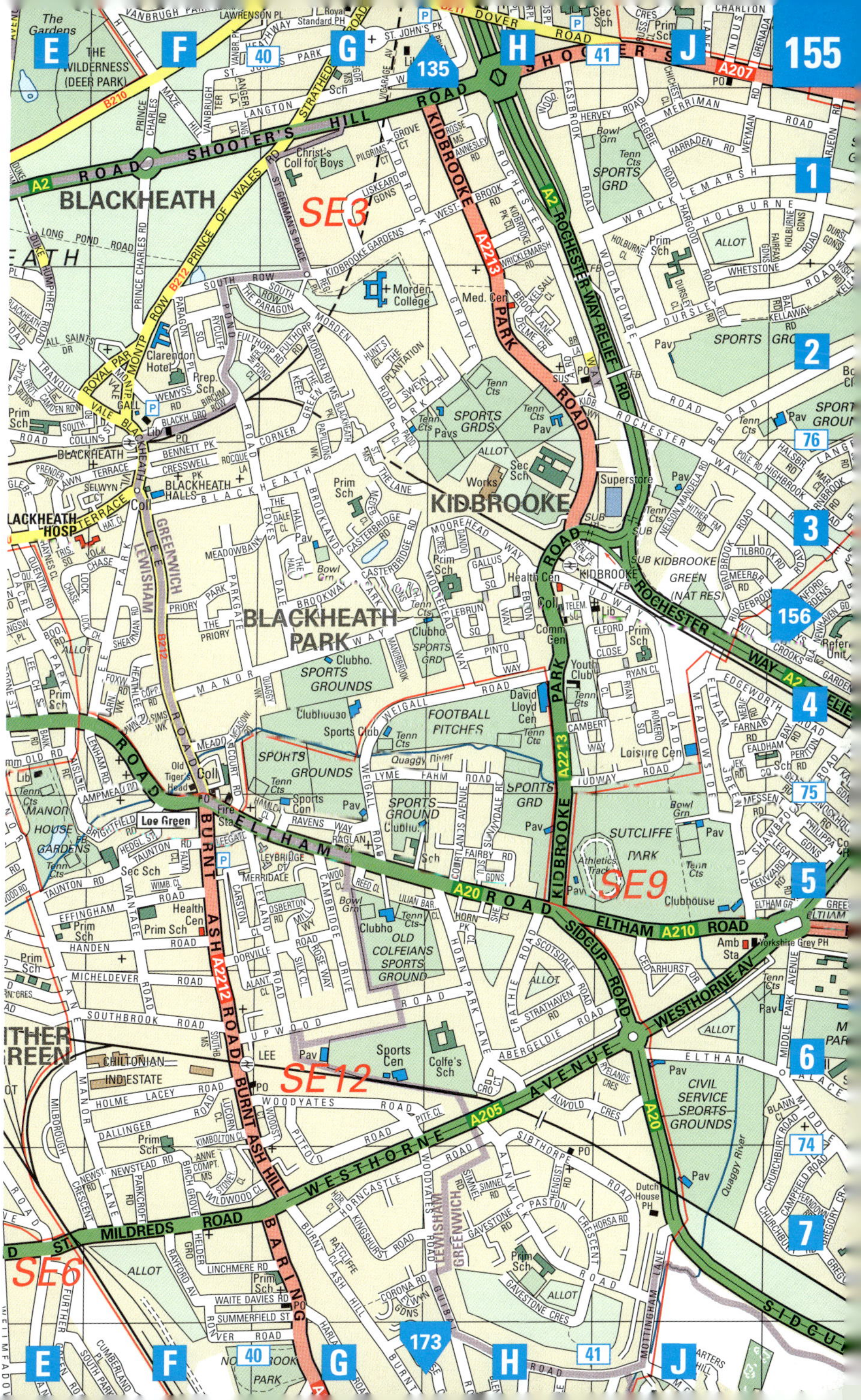

E
F
G
H
J
135
40
41
1
2
3
4
5
6
7
76
156
75
74
173
BLACKHEATH
SE3
KIDBROOKE
BLACKHEATH PARK
SE9
SE12
SE6
The Gardens
THE WILDERNESS (DEER PARK)
SHOOTER'S HILL ROAD
ROCHESTER WAY RELIEF RD
KIDBROOKE PARK ROAD
PRINCE OF WALES RD
Christ's Coll for Boys
Morden College
Clarendon Hotel
SPORTS GRDS
Superstore
KIDBROOKE GREEN (NAT RES)
FOOTBALL PITCHES
SPORTS GROUNDS
Quaggy River
Lee Green
BURNT ASH ROAD
ELTHAM ROAD
SIDCUP ROAD
WESTHORNE AVENUE
SUTCLIFFE PARK
Athletics Track
OLD COLFEIANS SPORTS GROUND
CIVIL SERVICE SPORTS GROUNDS
MANOR HOUSE GARDENS
CHILTONIAN IND ESTATE
MILDREDS ROAD
BARING ROAD
LEWISHAM
GREENWICH
Colfe's Sch
Sports Cen
Loisure Cen
David Lloyd Cen
Dutch House PH
Yorkshire Grey PH
ELTHAM
MANOR
HITHER GREEN

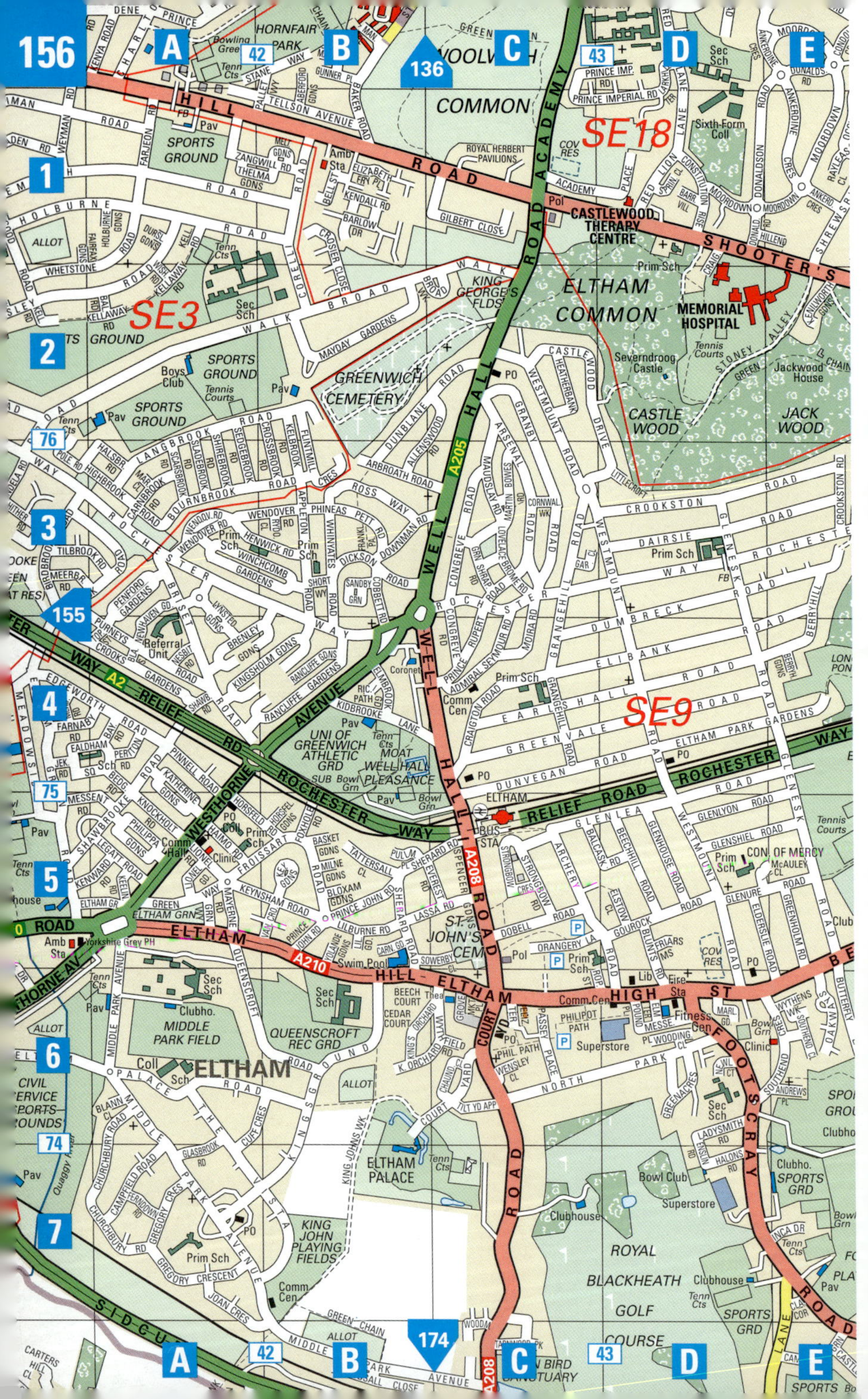
A
B
C
D
E
1
2
3
4
5
6
7
136
155
174
42
43
76
75
74
WOOLWICH COMMON
SE18
SE3
SE9
ELTHAM
HILL ROAD
SHOOTER'S HILL
ACADEMY ROAD
WELL HALL ROAD
A205
A2
A208
A210
ROCHESTER WAY RELIEF ROAD
ROCHESTER WAY
WESTHORNE AVENUE
ELTHAM HILL
ELTHAM HIGH ST
FOOTSCRAY ROAD
COURT ROAD
SIDCUP ROAD
BROAD WALK
KIDBROOKE PARK ROAD
ROYAL HERBERT PAVILIONS
CASTLEWOOD THERAPY CENTRE
MEMORIAL HOSPITAL
ELTHAM COMMON
CASTLE WOOD
JACK WOOD
Severndroog Castle
Jackwood House
KING GEORGE'S FLDS
GREENWICH CEMETERY
SPORTS GROUND
Boys Club
UNI OF GREENWICH ATHLETIC GRD
MOAT
WELL HALL PLEASANCE
Referral Unit
Prim Sch
Sec Sch
Sixth Form Coll
ST. JOHN'S CEM
Swim Pool
Superstore
MIDDLE PARK FIELD
QUEENSCROFT REC GRD
ELTHAM PALACE
KING JOHN PLAYING FIELDS
ROYAL BLACKHEATH GOLF COURSE
Clubhouse
Bowl Club
CIVIL SERVICE SPORTS GROUNDS
Quaggy River
Yorkshire Grey PH
CON. OF MERCY
Fitness Cen
Comm Cen
BUS STA
CROOKSTON ROAD
DAIRSIE ROAD
DUMBRECK ROAD
ELIBANK ROAD
EARLSHALL ROAD
GREENVALE ROAD
DUNVEGAN ROAD
ELTHAM PARK GARDENS
GLENLEA ROAD
GLENLYON ROAD
GLENESK ROAD
WESTMOUNT ROAD
GRANGEHILL ROAD
CONGREVE ROAD
WHETSTONE ROAD
HOLBURNE ROAD
KELLAWAY RD
LANGBROOK ROAD
BOURNBROOK ROAD
DUNBLANE ROAD
ARBROATH ROAD
MAYDAY GARDENS
GILBERT CLOSE
PRINCE IMPERIAL RD
PALACE ROAD
NORTH PARK
GLENURE ROAD
SHERARD ROAD
KEYNSHAM ROAD
PRINCE JOHN RD
LILBURNE RD
ORANGERY LA
SOUTHEND CRES
ANDREWS
MIDDLE PARK AVENUE
QUEENSCROFT ROAD
KINGSGROUND
CHURCHBURY ROAD
GREGORY CRESCENT
JOAN CRES
GREEN CHAIN WK
KING JOHNS WK
CARTERS HILL CL
BIRD SANCTUARY

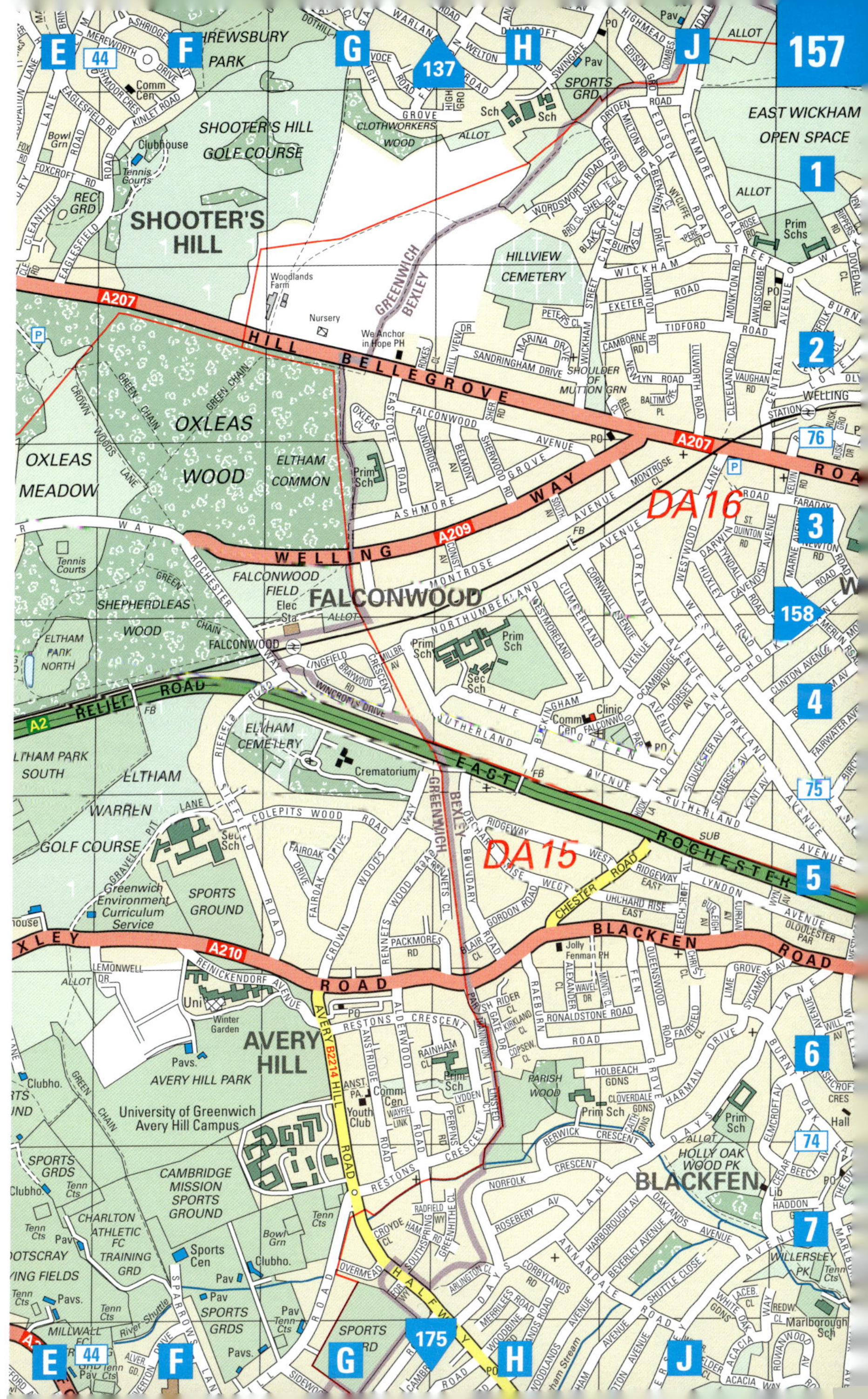
E
F
G
H
J
44
137
1
2
3
4
5
6
7
158
76
75
74
175
SHREWSBURY PARK
SHOOTER'S HILL GOLF COURSE
SHOOTER'S HILL
Clubhouse
Tennis Courts
REC GRD
Bowl Grn
Comm Cen
EAGLESFIELD RD
KINLET ROAD
FOXCROFT RD
CLEANTHUS RD
MEREWORTH DRIVE
CLOTHWORKERS WOOD
ALLOT
GROVE
WARLAND ROAD
WELTON ROAD
DUNCROFT
SWINGATE
SPORTS GRD
Sch
Pav
PO
HIGHMEAD
EDISON GRO
COMBES
EAST WICKHAM OPEN SPACE
Prim Schs
DRYDEN ROAD
MILTON RD
KEATS RD
GLENMORE ROAD
WORDSWORTH ROAD
BLENHEIM DRIVE
WYCLIFFE CL
CHAUCER
HILLVIEW CEMETERY
WICKHAM STREET
HONITON
EXETER RD
WICKHAM
TIDFORD ROAD
CAMBORNE RD
NEWLYN ROAD
LULWORTH ROAD
MONKTON RD
AWLISCOMBE RD
CENTRAL AVENUE
CLEVELAND ROAD
VAUGHAN RD
PETERS CL
MARINA DRIVE
SHOULDER OF MUTTON GRN
SANDRINGHAM DRIVE
HILL VIEW DR
Woodlands Farm
Nursery
We Anchor in Hope PH
GREENWICH
BEXLEY
A207
BELLEGROVE
HILL
ROAD
WELLING
STATION
OXLEAS WOOD
OXLEAS MEADOW
ELTHAM COMMON
GREEN CHAIN
CROWN WOODS LANE
EASTCOTE ROAD
SUNDRIDGE AV
BELMONT AV
SHERWOOD RD
FALCONWOOD AVENUE
ASHMORE GROVE
Prim Sch
MONTROSE AVENUE
A209
WELLING WAY
DA16
FALCONWOOD FIELD
FALCONWOOD
Elec Sta
Tennis Courts
SHEPHERDLEAS WOOD
ELTHAM PARK NORTH
ROCHESTER WAY
NORTHUMBERLAND
WESTMORELAND
CUMBERLAND AV
CORNWALL AVENUE
YORKLAND AVENUE
WESTWOOD LANE
DARWIN
HUXLEY
CAVENDISH
MARNIE AVENUE
NEWTON ROAD
FARADAY
HOOK LANE
CLINTON AVENUE
FAIRWATER AVE
Sec Sch
CAMBRIDGE AV
DORSET AV
Clinic
A2
RELIEF ROAD
LINGFIELD CRESCENT
WINCROFTS DRIVE
ELTHAM CEMETERY
Crematorium
ELTHAM PARK SOUTH
ELTHAM WARREN GOLF COURSE
EAST ROCHESTER WAY
SUTHERLAND AVENUE
GLOUCESTER AV
SOMERSET AV
COLEPITS WOOD ROAD
FAIROAK DRIVE
WOODS
RIDGEWAY
DA15
BOUNDARY
CHESTER ROAD
RIDGEWAY EAST
ORCHARD RISE EAST
LYNDON AVENUE
BLACKFEN ROAD
Jolly Fenman PH
GORDON ROAD
PACKMORES RD
BLAIR CL
Greenwich Environment Curriculum Service
SPORTS GROUND
A210
BEXLEY ROAD
LEMONWELL DR
REINICKENDORF AVENUE
Uni
Winter Garden
AVERY HILL
AVERY HILL PARK
B2214
AVERY HILL ROAD
Pavs.
University of Greenwich Avery Hill Campus
RESTONS CRESCENT
ALDERWOOD ROAD
RAINHAM CL
Comm Cen
Youth Club
QUEENSWOOD ROAD
RONALDSTONE ROAD
HARMAN DRIVE
HOLBEACH GDNS
CLOVERDALE GDNS
PARISH WOOD
Prim Sch
HOLLY OAK WOOD PK
BLACKFEN
DAYS LANE
BERWICK CRESCENT
NORFOLK CRESCENT
ROSEBERY AV
HARBOROUGH AV
OAKLANDS AVENUE
BEVERLEY AVENUE
SHUTTLE CLOSE
WILLERSLEY PK
Marlborough Sch
CAMBRIDGE MISSION SPORTS GROUND
CHARLTON ATHLETIC FC TRAINING GRD
SPORTS GRDS
Sports Cen
Bowl Grn
Clubho.
River Shuttle
MILLWALL FC
SPARROWS LANE
HALFWAY STREET
OVERMEAD
CROYDE CL
CORBYLANDS RD
ARLINGTON CL
Lib
PO

A
B
C
D
E
1
2
3
4
5
6
7
138
157
176
48
76
75
74
EAST WICKHAM
EAST WICKHAM OPEN SPACE
DA16
WELLING
DANSON
PARK
THE LAKE
The Boathouse
Danson Mansion
SPORTS GRD
Bexley Grammer Sch
DA15
STEVENS PARK
PENHILL PARK
MARLBOROUGH PARK
SIDCUP
Welling United FC
Clubhouse
Tennis Courts
Swim Pools
Westbrooke Sch
Sports Centre
Day Hosp
Red House
Three Blackbirds PH
WICKHAM LANE
WELLING HIGH STREET
PARK VIEW ROAD
CROOK LOG
A207
DANSON ROAD
A221
EAST ROCHESTER WAY
A2
BLACKFEN ROAD
A210
BLENDON ROAD
B2210
PENHILL ROAD
OKEHAMPTON CRESCENT
BUDLEIGH CRESCENT
AXMINSTER ROAD
BERWICK ROAD
WROTHAM ROAD
SWANLEY ROAD
FARNHAM ROAD
ELSA ROAD
BALLIOL ROAD
SOMERHILL RD
LYNMERE ROAD
NORTHDOWN ROAD
WESTBROOKE ROAD
GIPSY ROAD
BRAMPTON ROAD
WELLING STATION
BEAN ROAD
DITTON ROAD
SHERWOOD PARK AVENUE
BURNT OAK LANE
ROWLEY AVENUE
BLADINDON DRIVE
RIVERSIDE WALK
THE DRIVE
BEECH WAY
WESTERHAM DRIVE
GWILLIM CLOSE
LODGE LA
WOODSIDE

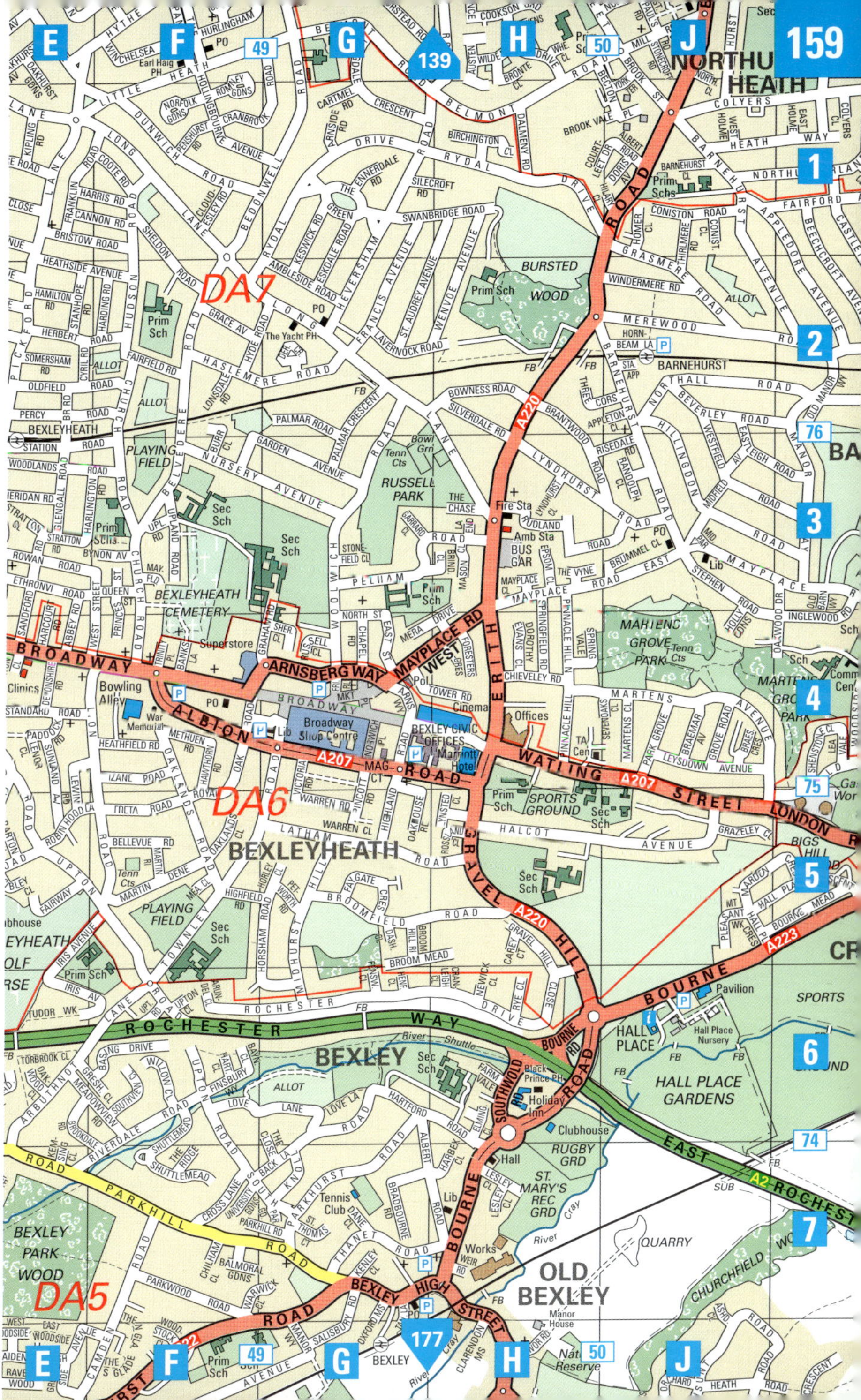
E
F
G
H
J
49
50
139
NORTHUMBERLAND HEATH
1
2
3
4
5
6
7
DA7
DA6
DA5
BEXLEYHEATH
BEXLEY
OLD BEXLEY
BARNEHURST
BEXLEYHEATH STATION
BROADWAY
ARNSBERG WAY
MAYPLACE RD WEST
ALBION ROAD
WATLING STREET
LONDON ROAD
ERITH ROAD
GRAVEL HILL
BOURNE ROAD
BOURNE WAY
ROCHESTER WAY
EAST ROCHESTER WAY
A2
A207
A220
A223
BEXLEY HIGH STREET
PARKHILL ROAD
LONG LANE
BROOK STREET
BELMONT ROAD
RYDAL DRIVE
SWANBRIDGE ROAD
HASLEMERE ROAD
GRACE AV
LAVERNOCK ROAD
BOWNESS ROAD
SILVERDALE RD
LYNDHURST ROAD
NORTHALL ROAD
BEVERLEY ROAD
MAYPLACE ROAD EAST
MARTENS AVENUE
HALCOT AVENUE
LATHAM ROAD
BROOMFIELD ROAD
UPTON ROAD
ROCHESTER DRIVE
HURST ROAD
PALMAR ROAD
NURSERY AVENUE
GARDEN AVENUE
BURSTED WOOD
RUSSELL PARK
MARTENS GROVE PARK
BEXLEYHEATH CEMETERY
PLAYING FIELD
HALL PLACE
HALL PLACE GARDENS
RUGBY GRD
ST. MARY'S REC GRD
BEXLEY PARK WOOD
QUARRY
SPORTS GROUND
Broadway Shop Centre
BEXLEY CIVIC OFFICES
Marriott Hotel
Holiday Inn
Black Prince PH
The Yacht PH
Earl Haig PH
Superstore
Bowling Alley
War Memorial
Clinics
Cinema
Offices
Fire Sta
Amb Sta
BUS GAR
Pavilion
Hall Place Nursery
Clubhouse
Tennis Club
Works
Manor House
Nat Reserve
River Shuttle
River Cray
Prim Sch
Sec Sch
Lib
PO
Pol
MKT
Hall
177
76
75
74
BEXLEY

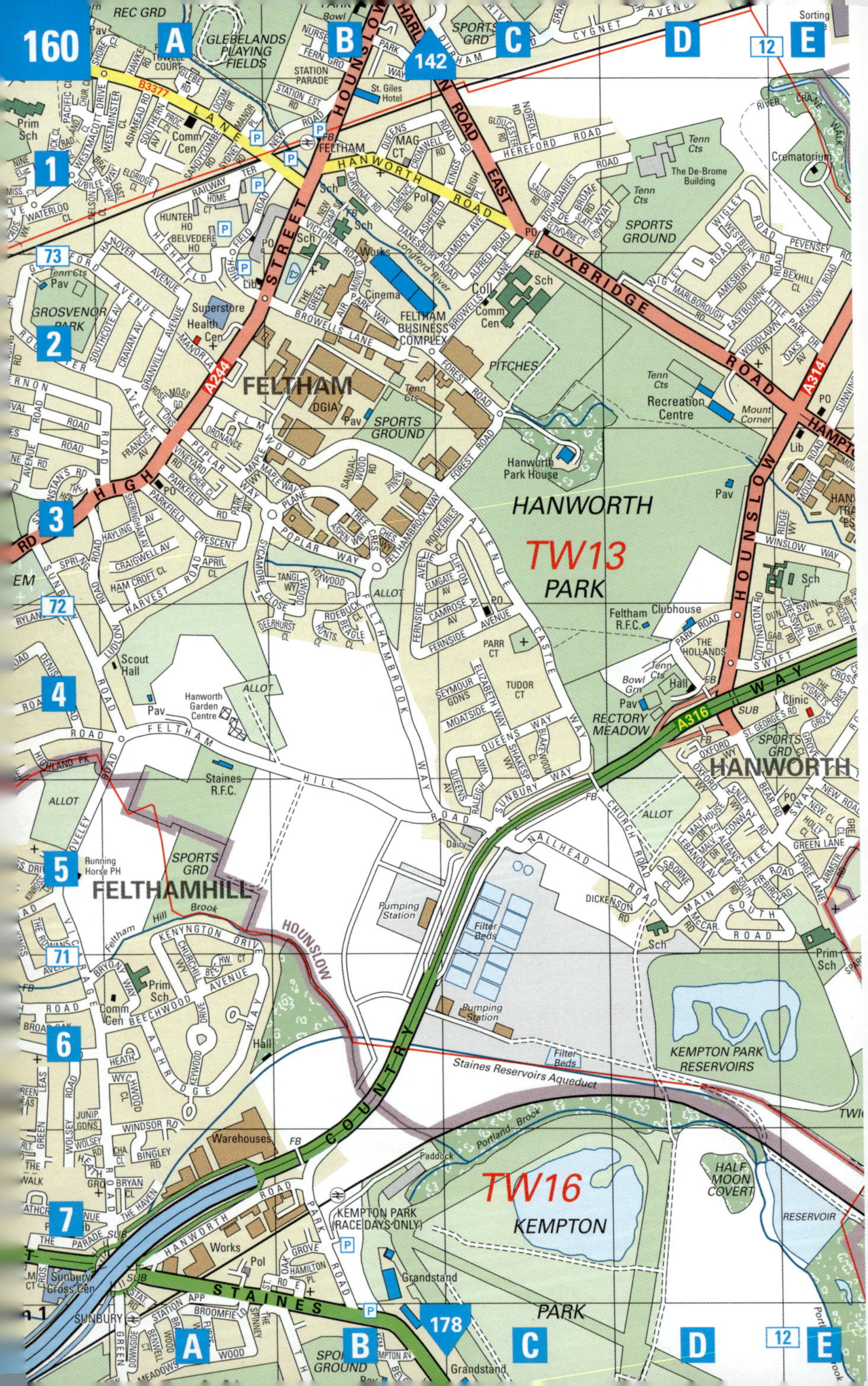

A
B
C
D
E
12
142
REC GRD
GLEBELANDS PLAYING FIELDS
STATION PARADE
St. Giles Hotel
SPORTS GRD
CYGNET AVENUE
Sorting
B3377
LANE
HANWORTH ROAD
FELTHAM
HOUNSLOW ROAD
HARLINGTON ROAD EAST
HEREFORD ROAD
Tenn Cts
The De-Brome Building
Crematorium
RIVER CRANE
SPORTS GROUND
Prim Sch
1
WATERLOO CL
HUNTER HO
BELVEDERE HO
HIGHFIELD
RAILWAY TER
UXBRIDGE ROAD
Longford River
Works
Cinema
FELTHAM BUSINESS COMPLEX
Coll
Comm Cen
Sch
73
GROSVENOR PARK
Superstore
Health Cen
2
AVENUE
HANOVER AVENUE
PITCHES
Recreation Centre
Mount Corner
A314
A244
FELTHAM
DGIA
Pav
SPORTS GROUND
ELMWOOD AVENUE
FOREST ROAD
Hanworth Park House
HAMPTON
HIGH STREET
HANWORTH
TW13
PARK
3
CRESCENT
POPLAR WAY
FELTHAMBROOK WAY
WINSLOW WAY
ALLOT
72
Scout Hall
FELTHAM BROOK
Feltham R.F.C.
Clubhouse
THE HOLLANDS
SWIFT
4
Hanworth Garden Centre
TUDOR CT
Bowl Grn
Hall
Clinic
RECTORY MEADOW
A316
FELTHAM HILL ROAD
Staines R.F.C.
QUEENS WAY
SUNBURY WAY
SPORTS GRD
HANWORTH
5
Running Horse PH
FELTHAMHILL
SPORTS GRD
Brook
HOUNSLOW
NALLHEAD ROAD
Pumping Station
Filter Beds
DICKENSON RD
Sch
SOUTH ROAD
71
KENYNGTON DRIVE
Prim Sch
Comm Cen
BEECHWOOD AVENUE
Prim Sch
Pumping Station
6
Hall
Filter Beds
KEMPTON PARK RESERVOIRS
Staines Reservoirs Aqueduct
COUNTRY WAY
WINDSOR RD
Warehouses
FB
Portland Brook
Paddock
TW16
HALF MOON COVERT
KEMPTON
RESERVOIR
7
HANWORTH ROAD
Works
KEMPTON PARK (RACE DAYS ONLY)
THE PARADE
Sunbury Cross Cen
Pol
Grandstand
STAINES
SUNBURY
178
PARK
SPORTS GROUND
Grandstand

E
F
G
H
J
13
14
143
162
179
71
73
1
2
3
4
5
6
7
WHITTON
BOROUGH CEMETERY
CORONATION WALK
HEATHFIELD REC GRD
TWICKENHAM CEMETERY
TW2
TW12
CRANE PARK
NATURE RESERVE
RICHMOND UPON THAMES
GREAT CHERTSEY ROAD
CHERTSEY RD
A316
PLAYING FIELD
Hospital Bridge
HOSPITAL BRIDGE ROAD
SIXTH CROSS ROAD
B358
A305
STAINES ROAD
TWICKENHAM RD
TWICKENHAM PARK GOLF CENTRE
Clubhouse
FULWELL PARK
FULWELL GOLF COURSE
SPORTS GRD
DRIVING RANGE
HAMPTON FARM IND EST
A312
WEST
Apex Retail Park
Warehouses
Glasshouses
Superstore
UXBRIDGE ROAD
HAMPTON RD
BURTONS ROAD
PARK ROAD
A313
War Meml.
Hampton Community Coll
Junior Sch
Sch
Health Cen
Youth Cen
PLAYING FIELD
HANWORTH ROAD
ACACIA RD
WINDMILL ROAD
REC GRD
ST. CLARE BUSINESS PARK
HAMPTON HILL
Cricket Ground
A311
HIGH STREET
Pantile Bridge
Works
Longford River
CEM
CARLISLE PARK
BROAD LANE
PERCY ROAD
TUDOR RD
Open Air Pool
COBBLERS WALK
HAMPTON
HOUNSLOW
TWICKENHAM R.F.C. Clubhouse
Clubhouse Football
KINGSWAY BUSINESS PARK
HYDES
STATION ROAD
Nursery

A
B
C
D
E
1
2
3
4
5
6
7
15
16
144
161
180
73
71
TW2
TW11
TWICKENHAM
STRAWBERRY HILL
STRAWBERRY HILL GOLF COURSE
HAMPTON HILL
TEDDINGTON
BUSHY
NATIONAL PHYSICAL LABORATORY
BUSHY HOUSE
TEDDINGTON CEM
EEL PIE ISLAND
TWICKENHAM RIFLE CLUB
Thames Young Mariners Base
Teddington Lock
Ham Riverside Lands
THAMES PATH / TOWING PATH
Cross Deep
KNELLER GARDENS
TWICKENHAM GREEN
St. Mary's Uni Coll
PLAYING FIELD
CANAL PLANTATION
ROUND PLANTATION
HAMPTON HILL POND
SPORTS GRD
Cricket Ground
Open Air Pool
Longford River
Bartons Cottage
Open During Daylight Hours Only
HEATH ROAD
THE GREEN
HAMPTON ROAD
CROSS DEEP
KING ST
YORK ST
LONDON RD
STRAWBERRY VALE
TWICKENHAM RD
WALDEGRAVE ROAD
WELLINGTON ROAD
STANLEY ROAD
FULWELL ROAD
SHACKLEGATE LANE
CHURCH ROAD
SOUTH RD
CROSS ROAD
HIGH STREET
BROAD STREET
PARK ROAD
SANDY LANE
QUEEN'S ROAD
STATION ROAD
WALDEGRAVE PARK
CAMBRIDGE PARK
PRINCES ROAD
CONNAUGHT ROAD
TWINING AVENUE
CHERTSEY ROAD
MEADWAY
POPES GROVE
POPES AVENUE
WELLESLEY ROAD
CROMWELL ROAD
FAIRFAX ROAD
HARROWDENE GARDENS
SHAEF WAY
COBBLERS WALK
A305
A311
A310
A309
A313
B360
B358
A316

E
F
G
H
J
17
145
TW1
MARBLE HILL HOUSE PARK
GLOVER'S ISLAND
PETERSHAM MEADOWS
PETERSHAM COMMON
RIVER THAMES
ORLEANS HOUSE GALLERY
Riverside Ho
ORLEANS GDNS
Yacht Club
LONDON THAMES CYCLE ROUTE
WARREN
RIVER LANE
Petersham Nurseries
CHURCH LANE
Hall
Dysarts PH
A307
STAR & GARTER HILL
B353
KIDNEY WOOD
Open During Daylight Hours Only
HORSE RIDE
SIDMOUTH WOOD
DRIFT WAY
1
The German Sch
Stables
Ham Polo Club
HAM HOUSE (NT)
Fox & Duck PH
TREE CL
ASHFIELD CL
CEDAR HTS
KING HENRY VIII MOUND
PETERSHAM
REC GRD
Tenn Cts
HAM STREET
KING GEORGE'S FIELD
HAM HOUSE GARDENS
Prim Sch
Sch
SANDPITS RD
SUDBROOK LA
BUTE AV
PETERSHAM PARK
73
P
THE COPSE
MEADLANDS DRIVE
CLIFFORD RD
PETERSHAM CL
DICKENS CL
HAZEL LANE
MELANCHOLY WALK
ALLOT
BUCKINGHAM ROAD
SANDY LANE EST
PETERSHAM ROAD
2
TW10
SANDY LANE
RIVERSIDE DRIVE
MURRAY RD
STRETTON RD
RUSSELL GDNS
NEVILLE RD
ST MARYS
ARLINGTON RD
ASHLEY GDNS
LAUDERDALE DRIVE
Clubhouse
SPORTS GRD
Sec Sch
RICHMOND GOLF COURSE
SUDBROOK PARK
The Wilderness
HORSE RIDE
WOODVILLE ROAD
Hall
Lib
HAM
MARTINGALES CL
BISHOPS CL
ASHBURNHAM ROAD
ST. MICHAEL'S CONVENT
3
SUDBROOK GDNS
THE COMMON
MOWBRAY RD
SHERIDAN RD
CLEVES RD
MEAD RD
PO
Ormeley Lodge
Ham Bottom
HAM COMMON
HAM GATE AVENUE
HAM
HORNBEAM WALK
164
HAM CROSS PLANTATION
Prim Sch
LOCK RD
NEW RD
CRAIG RD
UPPER HAM RD
A307
HAM FARM ROAD
CHURCH ROAD
COMMON
B352
Ham Gate
4
Ham Dip
LANGHAM HO CL
THE CASSEL HOSPITAL
KINGFISHER DRIVE
DUKES AVENUE
RAND
PARKLEYS
Parkgate House
CHURCH ROAD
TOWING PATH
LAMMAS RD
BURNELL AVENUE
DYSART AVENUE
PO
BARNFIELD AVENUE
BEECH CL
HAM RIDINGS
ALLOT
Teddington Weir
FB
Fire Sta
TUDOR DRIVE
ARAGON RD
Hemand Cen
SOPWITH WAY
Teddington Studios
Lensbury
SHELL SPORTS GRD
TOWING PATH
BIGGIN HILL CL
Tenn Cts
Bowl Grn
Hawker Cen
RICHMOND ROAD
LANCASTER GDNS
CARDINAL AVENUE
GARTH RD
Comm Cen
Riding Sch
5
Pav
Tenn Cts
SPORTS GRD Clubho
BROOM WATER
TROWLOCK ISLAND
KINGSTON UPON THAMES
RICHMOND UPON THAMES
FERNHILL GDNS
WOLSEY DRIVE
ALLOT
PO
HOLLYBUSH RD
Lib
TUDOR DRIVE
WOODCOTE CL
71
ST. WINIFRED'S ROAD
ATBARA ROAD
BUCKLANDS RD
TROWLOCK AVE
Sec Sch
Coll
Prim Sch
REC GRD
Pav
LATCHMERE LANE
ALDERSBROOK DR
CRANLEIGH RD
KING EDWARDS GROVE
KEEPERS MS
MUNSTER ROAD
BLAGDON WK
Tenn Cts
Clubho
Sec Sch
Clubho
Sailing Club
Sailing Cen
GROSVENOR GDNS
DURLSTON RD
ST. ALBAN'S RD
KT2
Prim Sch
PARK ROAD
KELVEDON CL
6
HOLMESDALE ROAD
BROOM ROAD REC GRD
ROWLOCK WAY
Pav
ALBANY PARK ROAD
LOWER HAM ROAD
THAMES PATH
A307
LATCHMERE ROAD
STAUNTON ROAD
UPPER PARK ROAD
BOCKHAMPTON RD
DINTON RD
A310
FAIRWAYS
THAMESIDE
Boathouse
LANGDON PK
BROOM CL
STEVEN'S EYOT
BANK LANE
WYNDHAM ROAD
KINGS ROAD
NEW ROAD
CONIFERS CL
Ave Cen
Bowl Club
RICHMOND ROAD
WOODSIDE RD
PARK FM RD
BURTON RD
SHORTLANDS ROAD
PO
7
NORMANSFIELD AVENUE
Prim Sch
The Boater's Inn PH
CHESTNUT RD
Clinic
Family Cen
ALEXANDRA RD
FB
Superstore
HAMBLE CT
Prim Sch
Tenn Cts
Bowl Grns
EASTBURY RD
CLIFTON RD
YORK ROAD
Prim Sch
TEDDINGTON RD
UPPER
CANBURY GDNS
181
Superstore
RICHMOND RD
GIBBON RD
Prim Sch
DAGMAR RD
GLENVILLE RD
Offices
CEDARS RD
SAMUEL GRAY GDNS
BATE AV
BASIN RD
BERESFORD RD

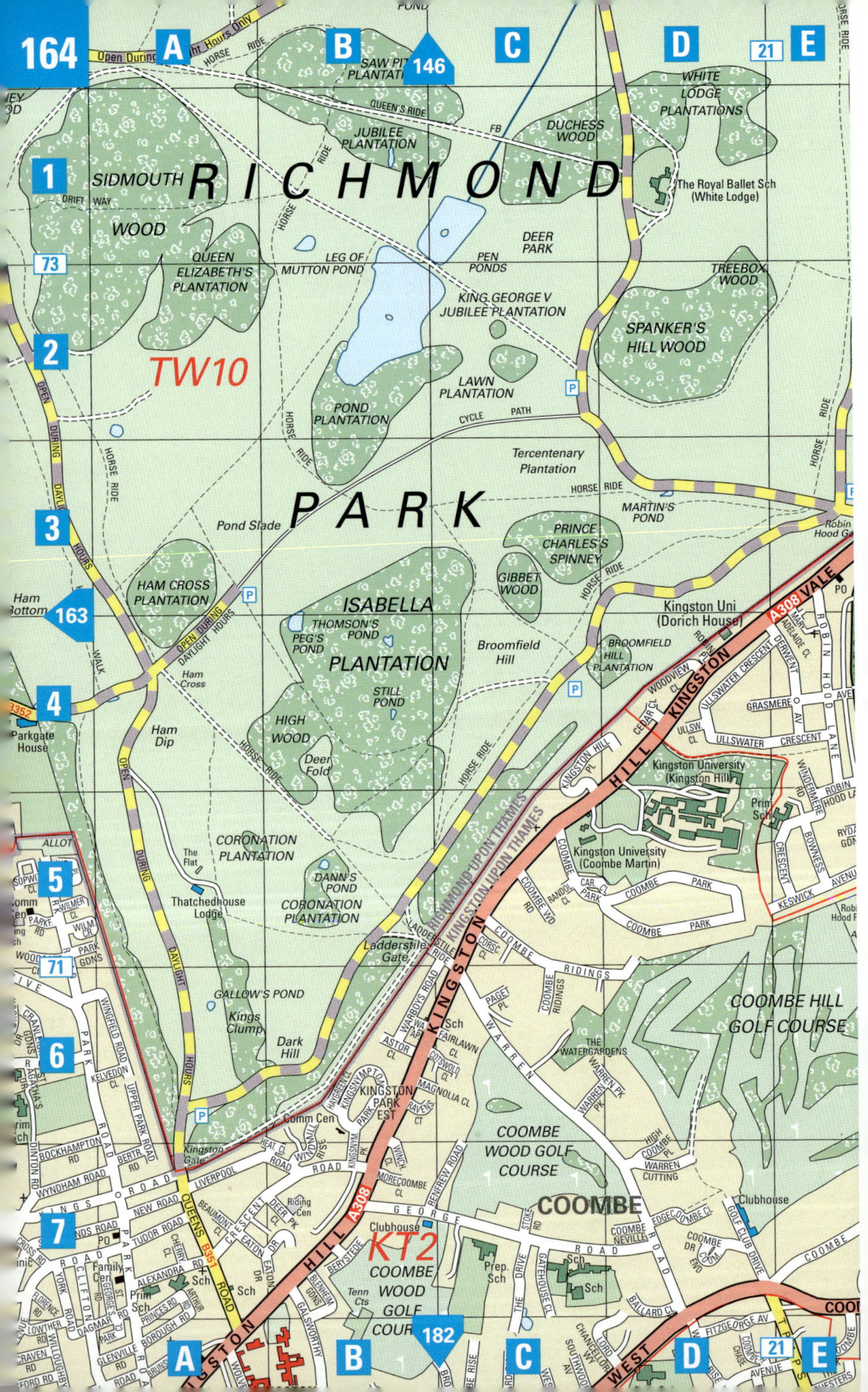

A
B
C
D
E
21
146
Open During Daylight Hours Only
HORSE RIDE
SAW PIT PLANTATION
QUEEN'S RIDE
JUBILEE PLANTATION
FB
DUCHESS WOOD
WHITE LODGE PLANTATIONS
The Royal Ballet Sch (White Lodge)
1
SIDMOUTH
DRIFT WAY
WOOD
RICHMOND
PARK
73
QUEEN ELIZABETH'S PLANTATION
LEG OF MUTTON POND
PEN PONDS
DEER PARK
KING GEORGE V JUBILEE PLANTATION
TREEBOX WOOD
SPANKER'S HILL WOOD
2
TW10
LAWN PLANTATION
POND PLANTATION
CYCLE PATH
OPEN DURING DAYLIGHT HOURS
HORSE RIDE
Tercentenary Plantation
MARTIN'S POND
3
Pond Slade
PRINCE CHARLES'S SPINNEY
GIBBET WOOD
Robin Hood Ga
HAM CROSS PLANTATION
Ham Bottom
163
ISABELLA PLANTATION
THOMSON'S POND
PEG'S POND
STILL POND
Broomfield Hill
BROOMFIELD HILL PLANTATION
Kingston Uni (Dorich House)
A308
VALE
PO
Ham Cross
WALK
4
B352
Parkgate House
HIGH WOOD
Ham Dip
Deer Fold
WOODVIEW CL
KINGSTON
ULLSWATER CRESCENT
GRASMERE AV
ULLSWATER CRESCENT
ROBIN HOOD LANE
Kingston University (Kingston Hill)
Prim Sch
CORONATION PLANTATION
The Flat
Thatchedhouse Lodge
DANN'S POND
CORONATION PLANTATION
RICHMOND UPON THAMES
KINGSTON UPON THAMES
Kingston University (Coombe Martin)
COOMBE PARK
5
ALLOT
WILMER CL
PARKE RD
PARK GDNS
71
LADDERSTILE RIDE
Ladderstile Gate
COOMBE RIDINGS
KESWICK
WINDERMERE RD
BOWNESS CRESCENT
6
WINGFIELD ROAD
KELVEDON CL
UPPER PARK ROAD
GALLOW'S POND
Kings Clump
Dark Hill
WARBOYS ROAD
Sch
FAIRLAWN CL
ASTOR CL
COTSWOLD CL
MAGNOLIA CL
KINGSTON PARK EST
WARREN
THE WATERGARDENS
WARREN PK
COOMBE HILL GOLF COURSE
COOMBE WOOD GOLF COURSE
Comm Cen
Kingston Gate
BOCKHAMPTON RD
BERTRAND
WYNDHAM ROAD
LIVERPOOL ROAD
HIGH COOMBE PL
WARREN CUTTING
COOMBE
Clubhouse
GOLF CLUB DRIVE
7
QUEENS ROAD
B351
NEW ROAD
TUDOR ROAD
MORECOOMBE CL
RENFREW ROAD
GEORGE ROAD
Riding Cen
KT2
Clubhouse
COOMBE NEVILLE
EDGECOOMBE CL
COOMBE END
KINGS ROAD
Family Cen
Prim Sch
ALEXANDRA RD
Sch
BERYSTEDE
COOMBE WOOD GOLF COURSE
Tenn Cts
Prep. Sch
Sch
Sch
BALLARD CL
FITZGEORGE AV
COOMBE ROAD
YORK ROAD
CLIFTON ROAD
DAGMAR RD
GLENVILLE RD
BOROUGH RD
GALSWORTHY
182
WEST
21
KINGSTON HILL
HILL

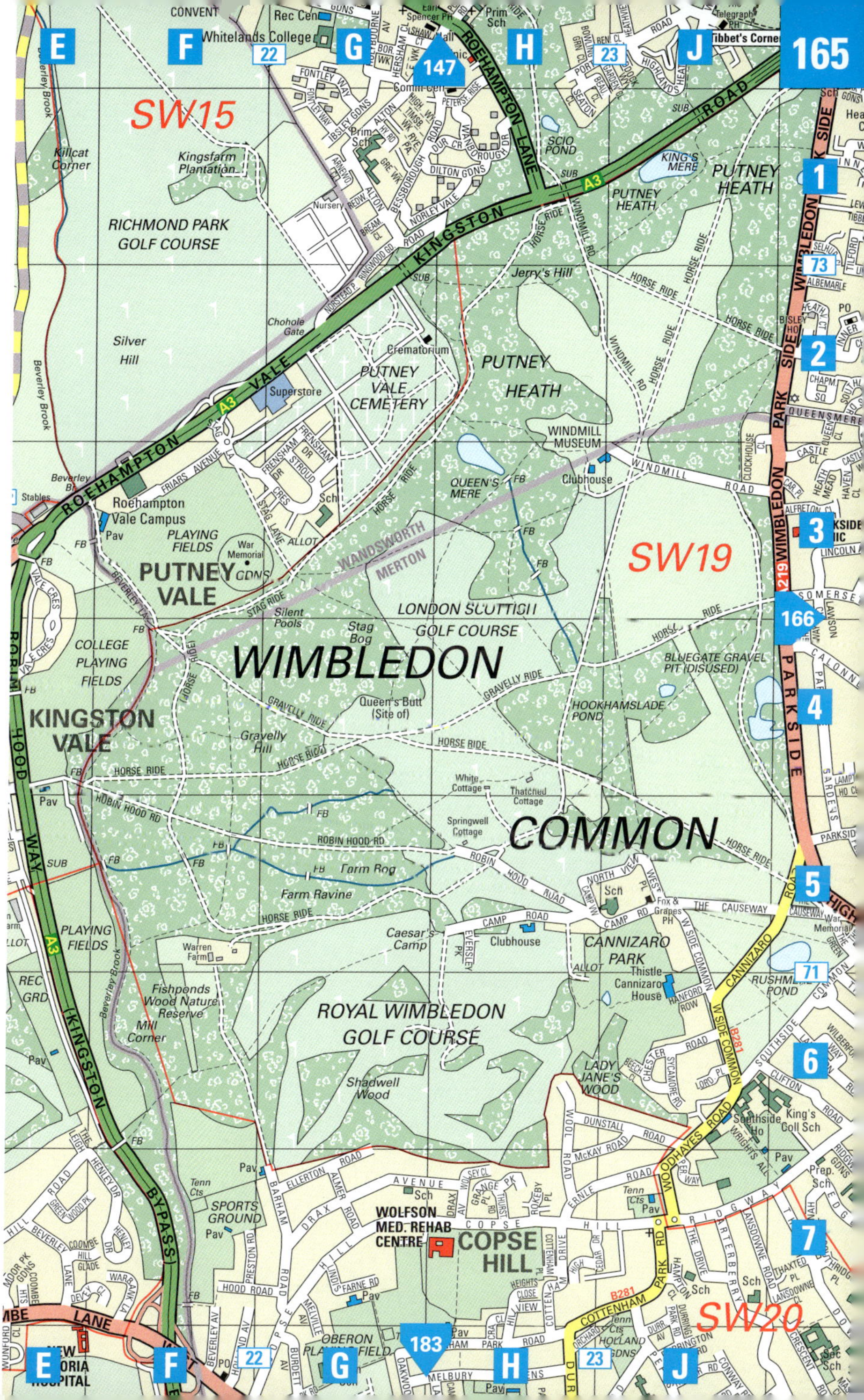

SW15
Killcat Corner
Kingsfarm Plantation
RICHMOND PARK GOLF COURSE
Silver Hill
Beverley Brook
CONVENT
Whitelands College
Rec Cen
147
Prim Sch
ROEHAMPTON LANE
Tibbet's Corner
SCIO POND
KING'S MERE
PUTNEY HEATH
KINGSTON ROAD
A3
Jerry's Hill
HORSE RIDE
WINDMILL RD
Chohole Gate
Crematorium
PUTNEY VALE CEMETERY
Superstore
A3 VALE
ROEHAMPTON
FRIARS AVENUE
WINDMILL MUSEUM
Clubhouse
WINDMILL ROAD
QUEEN'S MERE
Stables
Roehampton Vale Campus
PLAYING FIELDS
War Memorial
PUTNEY VALE
WANDSWORTH
MERTON
SW19
166
LONDON SCOTTISH GOLF COURSE
Stag Bog
Silent Pools
WIMBLEDON
COLLEGE PLAYING FIELDS
BLUEGATE GRAVEL PIT (DISUSED)
GRAVELLY RIDE
Queen's Butt (Site of)
HOOKHAMSLADE POND
KINGSTON VALE
Gravelly Hill
ROBIN HOOD WAY
White Cottage
Thatched Cottage
ROBIN HOOD RD
Springwell Cottage
COMMON
Farm Bog
Farm Ravine
PARKSIDE
CAMP ROAD
Clubhouse
Caesar's Camp
CANNIZARO PARK
THE CAUSEWAY
Fox & Grapes PH
Warren Farm
Thistle Cannizaro House
RUSHMERE POND
Fishponds Wood Nature Reserve
Mill Corner
ROYAL WIMBLEDON GOLF COURSE
LADY JANE'S WOOD
Shadwell Wood
REC GRD
PLAYING FIELDS
(KINGSTON BYPASS)
King's Coll Sch
Southside Ho
WOODHAYES ROAD
SPORTS GROUND
WOLFSON MED. REHAB CENTRE
COPSE HILL
RIDGWAY
BARHAM ROAD
DRAX AVENUE
COTTENHAM PARK RD
SW20
COMBE LANE
OBERON PLAYING FIELD
183
B281
71
73
22
23
E F G H J
1 2 3 4 5 6 7

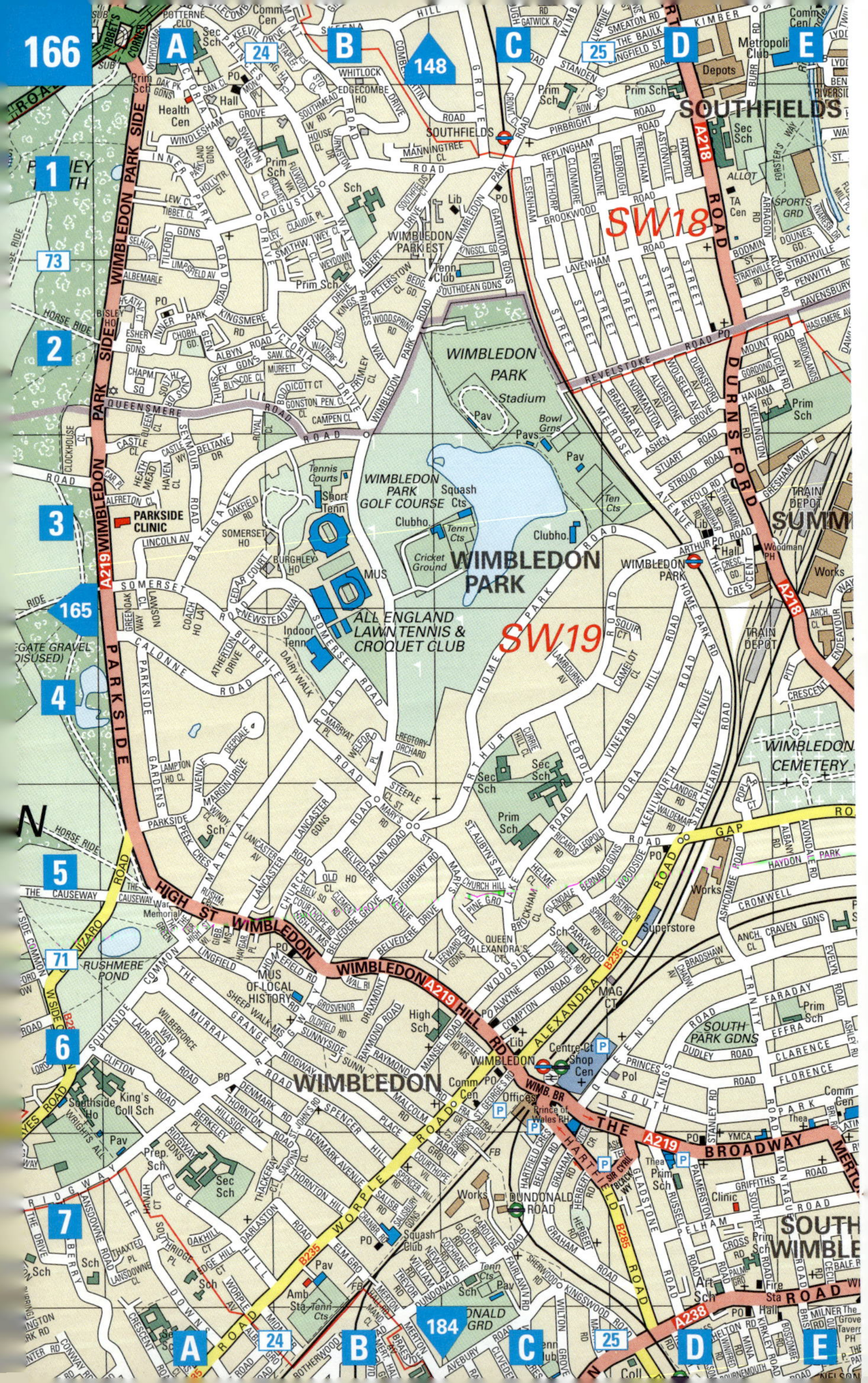

A
B
C
D
E
1
2
3
4
5
6
7
148
165
184
24
25
71
73
SOUTHFIELDS
SW18
SW19
WIMBLEDON PARK
WIMBLEDON PARK Stadium
WIMBLEDON PARK GOLF COURSE
ALL ENGLAND LAWN TENNIS & CROQUET CLUB
WIMBLEDON
WIMBLEDON CEMETERY
PARKSIDE CLINIC
RUSHMERE POND
SOUTH PARK GDNS
TRAIN DEPOT
Metropolitan Club
Centre Ct Shop Cen
MUS OF LOCAL HISTORY
WIMBLEDON PARK SIDE
PARKSIDE
A219
A218
A238
B235
B285
DURNSFORD ROAD
QUEENSMERE ROAD
REVELSTOKE ROAD
HIGH ST WIMBLEDON
WIMBLEDON HILL RD
WORPLE ROAD
THE BROADWAY
ALEXANDRA ROAD
HARTFIELD ROAD
ARTHUR ROAD
HOME PARK ROAD
CHURCH ROAD
SOMERSET ROAD
THE CAUSEWAY
THE RIDGWAY
KINGSWOOD RD
WIMBLEDON

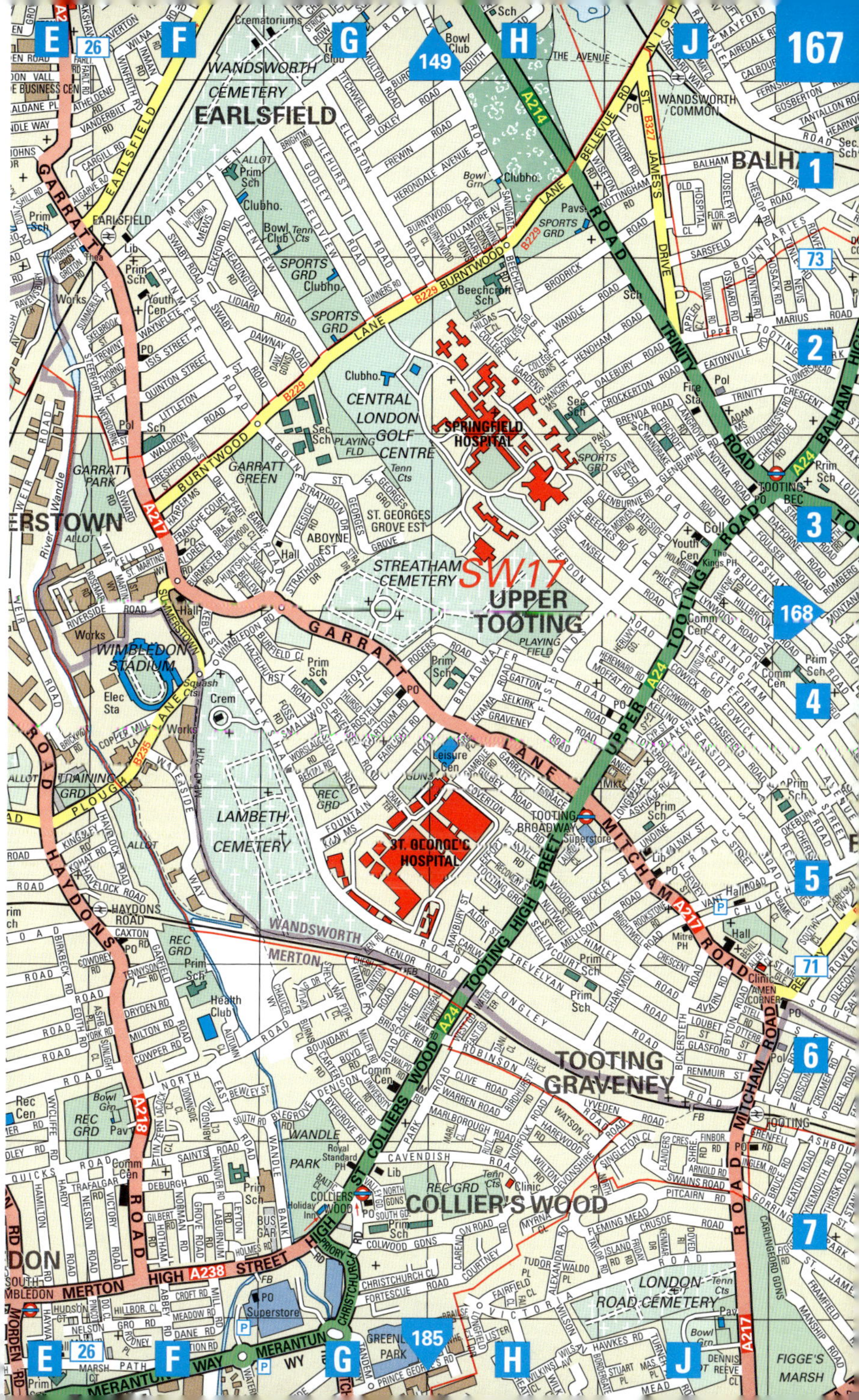
EARLSFIELD
WANDSWORTH CEMETERY
WANDSWORTH COMMON
BALHAM
SPRINGFIELD HOSPITAL
CENTRAL LONDON GOLF CENTRE
GARRATT GREEN
GARRATT PARK
STREATHAM CEMETERY
SW17
UPPER TOOTING
WIMBLEDON STADIUM
LAMBETH CEMETERY
ST. GEORGE'S HOSPITAL
TOOTING BROADWAY
TOOTING BEC
TOOTING GRAVENEY
COLLIER'S WOOD
WANDLE PARK
LONDON ROAD CEMETERY
FIGGE'S MARSH
BURNTWOOD LANE
GARRATT LANE
TRINITY ROAD
UPPER TOOTING ROAD
TOOTING HIGH STREET
MITCHAM ROAD
HAYDONS ROAD
PLOUGH LANE
MERTON HIGH STREET
MERANTUN WAY
HIGH ST. COLLIERS WOOD
A217
A214
A24
A218
A238
B229
B235
B327
149
168
185
26
73
71
E
F
G
H
J
1
2
3
4
5
6
7

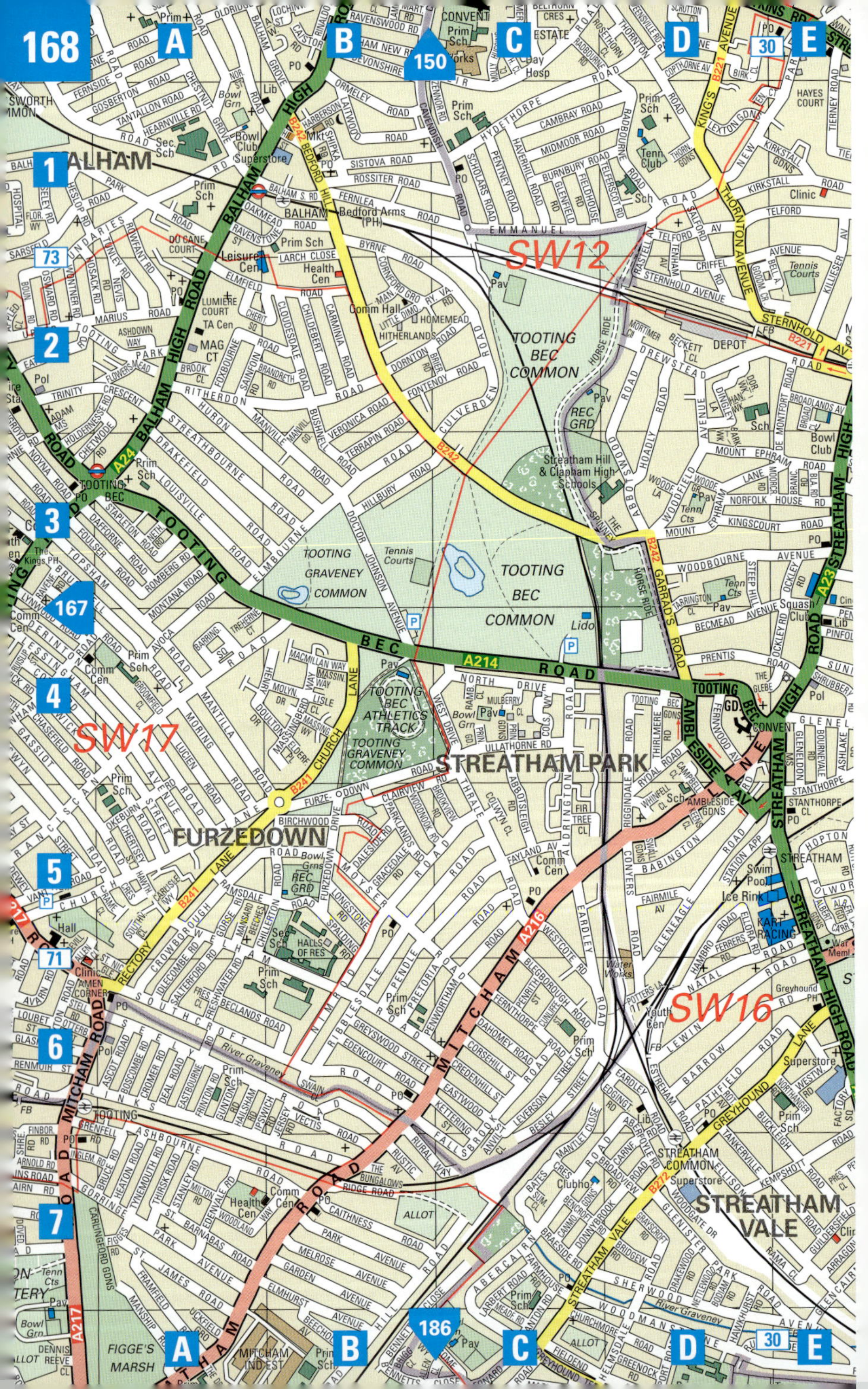
A
B
C
D
E
150
30
1
2
3
4
5
6
7
73
167
71
186
BALHAM
SW12
SW17
SW16
TOOTING BEC COMMON
TOOTING GRAVENEY COMMON
TOOTING BEC ATHLETICS TRACK
STREATHAM PARK
FURZEDOWN
STREATHAM COMMON
STREATHAM VALE
FIGGE'S MARSH
MITCHAM IND EST
BALHAM HIGH ROAD
BEDFORD HILL
BEC ROAD
TOOTING BEC ROAD
CHURCH LANE
MITCHAM ROAD
MITCHAM LANE
STREATHAM HIGH ROAD
GREYHOUND LANE
GARRAD'S ROAD
AMBLESIDE AV
KING'S AVENUE
THORNTON AVENUE
STERNHOLD AV
EMMANUEL ROAD
RECTORY LANE
STREATHAM VALE
A24
A214
A216
A217
A23
B221
B241
B242
B272
River Graveney
Streatham Hill & Clapham High Schools
Bedford Arms (PH)
Superstore
Leisure Cen
Ice Rink
Swim Pool
Kart Racing
Water Works
Hayes Court
Tennis Courts
Lido
Depot
Bowl Club
Greyhound PH
Kings PH

E
F
G
H
J
31
32
151
STREATHAM HILL
SE21
TULSE HILL
CHRISTCHURCH
A205
A23
PALACE ROAD ESTATE
THURLOW PARK
TULSE HILL
SW2
WEST NORWOOD CEMETERY
WEST NORWOOD
170
NORWOOD HIGH ST
KNIGHTS HILL
A215
SE27
STREATHAM
A214
STREATHAM COMMON NORTH
CROWN LANE
CROWN DALE
STREATHAM COMMON
THE ROOKERY
NORWOOD GROVE RECREATION GROUND
BEULAH HILL
CROWN POND
NORWOOD NEW TOWN
SE19
PLAYING FIELD
BIGGIN WOOD
STREATHAM HIGH RD
GREEN LANE
B273
NORBURY
1
2
3
4
5
6
7
73
71
187

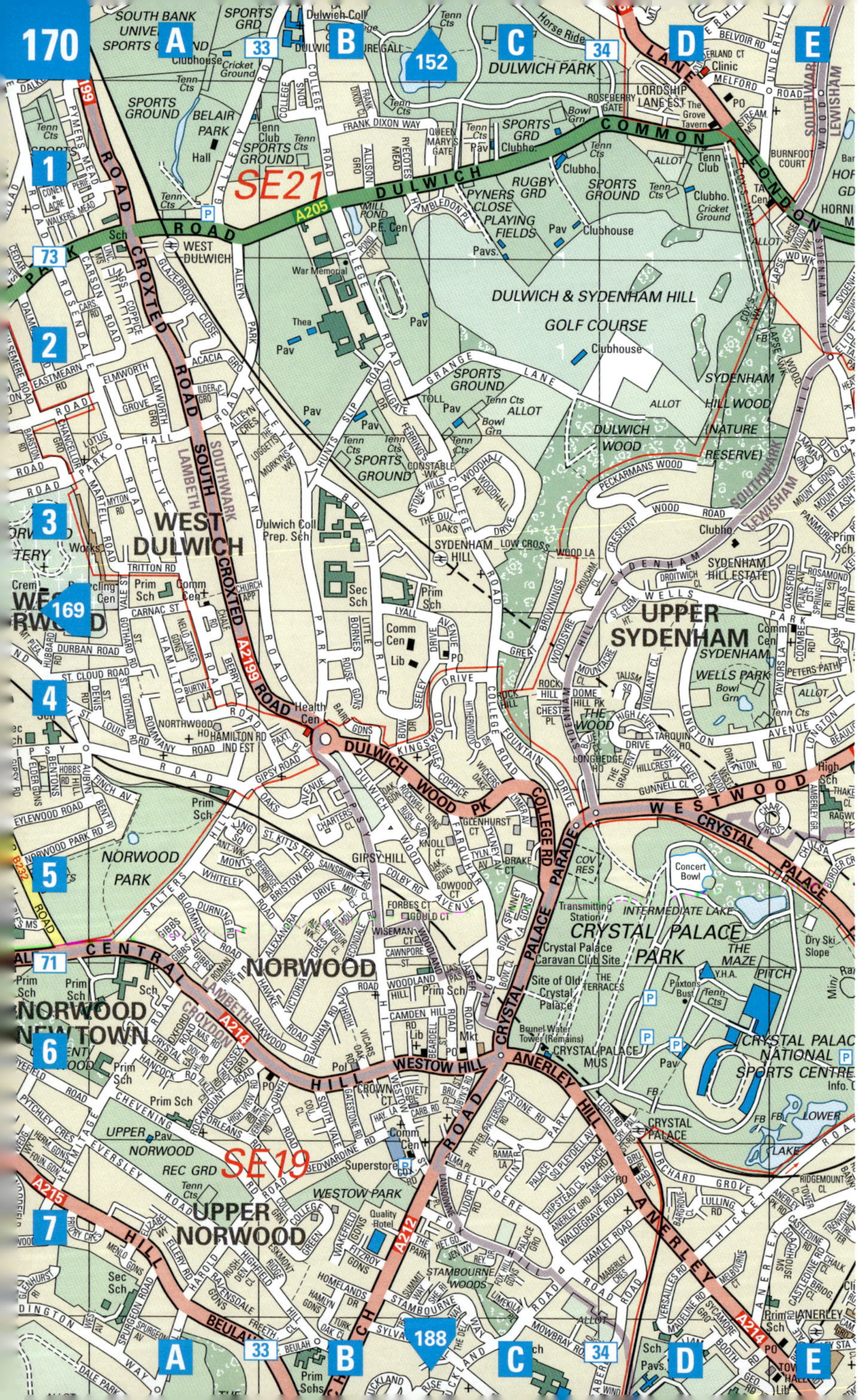
A
B
C
D
E
1
2
3
4
5
6
7
33
34
73
71
152
169
188
SE21
SE19
SOUTH BANK UNIV SPORTS GRD
Clubhouse
Cricket Ground
SPORTS GROUND
BELAIR PARK
Hall
Dulwich Coll
DULWICH PARK
Horse Ride
LORDSHIP LANE EST
The Grove Tavern
Clinic
BELVOIR RD
MELFORD ROAD
PO
FRANK DIXON WAY
SPORTS GRD
Clubho.
ROSEBERRY GATE
Bowl Grn
COMMON
LONDON
BURNFOOT COURT
RUGBY GRD
SPORTS GROUND
Cricket Ground
Clubhouse
PYNERS CLOSE
PLAYING FIELDS
MILL POND
P.E. Cen
DULWICH ROAD
A205
WEST DULWICH
PARK
War Memorial
DULWICH & SYDENHAM HILL
GOLF COURSE
Clubhouse
Thea
Pav
SYDENHAM HILL WOOD (NATURE RESERVE)
DULWICH WOOD
ALLOT
SPORTS GROUND
TOLL
GRANGE LANE
ACACIA GRO
EASTMEARN RD
ELMWORTH GRO
CROXTED ROAD
SOUTH CROXTED ROAD
A2199
WEST DULWICH
LAMBETH
SOUTHWARK
LEWISHAM
Dulwich Coll Prep. Sch
Sec Sch
Prim Sch
Comm Cen
Lib
PO
SYDENHAM HILL
PECKARMANS WOOD
WOOD ROAD
Clubho.
UPPER SYDENHAM
SYDENHAM WELLS PARK
SYDENHAM HILL ESTATE
WELLS PARK
TRITTON RD
CARNAC ST
DURBAN ROAD
ST. CLOUD ROAD
Health Cen
HAMILTON RD IND EST
NORTHWOOD HO
GIPSY ROAD
DULWICH WOOD PK
COLLEGE RD
WESTWOOD HILL
CRYSTAL PALACE
NORWOOD PARK
NORWOOD
GIPSY HILL
Prim Sch
Concert Bowl
INTERMEDIATE LAKE
Transmitting Station
CRYSTAL PALACE PARK
Crystal Palace Caravan Club Site
Site of Old Crystal Palace
THE TERRACES
THE MAZE
Y.H.A.
Dry Ski Slope
Paxtons Bust
Tenn Cts
Brunel Water Tower (Remains)
CRYSTAL PALACE MUS
CRYSTAL PALACE NATIONAL SPORTS CENTRE
Info. C
LOWER LAKE
CENTRAL HILL
A214
CROYDON
NORWOOD NEW TOWN
WESTOW HILL
ANERLEY HILL
ANERLEY ROAD
CRYSTAL PALACE PARADE
Mkt
Pol
Superstore
UPPER NORWOOD REC GRD
UPPER NORWOOD
WESTOW PARK
Quality Hotel
A212
BELVEDERE
STAMBOURNE WOODS
A215
BEULAH HILL
ALLOT
ORCHARD GROVE
THICKET
MELBOURNE
ANERLEY
Prim Sch
Sch
Pavs.
Prim Schs
Sec Sch
PO
Lib

E
F
G
H
J
35
153
172
189
73
71
1
2
3
4
5
6
7
FOREST HILL
SE23
LOWER SYDENHAM
BELL GREEN
SYDENHAM
SE26
NEW BECKENHAM
PENGE
BR3
STANSTEAD ROAD
A205 (SOUTH CIRCULAR ROAD)
WALDRAM PK RD
PERRY VALE
B227
PERRY HILL
CATFORD HILL
A212
DARTMOUTH ROAD
A2216
KIRKDALE
SYDENHAM ROAD
SOUTHEND LANE
NEWLANDS PARK
LENNARD ROAD
PARISH LANE
HIGH STREET
A234
MAYOW PARK
ALEXANDRA REC GRD
CATOR PARK
HOME PARK
LOWER SYDENHAM IND EST
BECKENHAM BUSINESS CEN
H.S.B.C. GROUP SPORTS GRD
NAT WEST BANK SPORTS GRD
SOUTHEND PARK
BELLINGHAM PARK
Blenheim Shopping Cen
Superstore
PENGE EAST
PENGE WEST
NEW BECKENHAM
SYDENHAM
FOREST HILL
LOWER SYDENHAM
GARTHORNE ROAD NATURE RESERVE

CATFORD
SE6
BELLINGHAM
SOUTHEND
BECKENHAM
BR3
BR2
154
171
190
73
71
39
A B C D E
1 2 3 4 5 6 7
S CIRCULAR ROAD
A205
CATFORD ROAD
CATFORD HILL
A212
BROMLEY ROAD
A21
SOUTHEND LANE
A2218
BECKENHAM HILL RD
SOUTHEND ROAD
A2015
CATFORD BRIDGE
BELLINGHAM
BECKENHAM HILL
RAVENSBOURNE
BECKENHAM JUNCTION
FORSTER MEMORIAL PARK
BECKENHAM PLACE PARK
GOLF COURSE
Stumpshill Wood
ASH PLANTATION
SUMMERHOUSE HILL WOOD
PRIVATE BANKS SPORTS GRD
BELLINGHAM PARK
SOUTHEND PARK
NAT WEST BANK SPORTS GRD
KENT C.C.C.
C.G.U. CUACO SPORTS GRD
LEWISHAM BOROUGH SPORTS GROUND
MIDLAND BANK SPORTS GROUND
WARREN AVE PLAYING FIELDS
LEWISHAM
BROMLEY
Ravensbourne River
Pool River
Superstores
Superstore
BUS GAR
Health Cen
Tiger Head PH
WHITEFOOT LANE
DOWNHAM WAY
RANDLESDOWN ROAD
BROADMEAD
ATHELNEY STREET
FOXGROVE ROAD
BRACKLEY ROAD
WORSLEY BRIDGE ROAD
MEADOWVIEW
BRANGBOURNE ROAD
OAKRIDGE
WINLATON
OLDSTEAD ROAD
BROCKMAN RISE
COTTON HILL
HADDINGTON
DOWANHILL ROAD
SANDHURST ROAD
BRAIDWOOD ROAD
KILLEARN ROAD
GLENFARG ROAD
FORDEL ROAD
ARNGASK ROAD
CULVERLEY ROAD
BELLINGHAM ROAD
DANEBY ROAD
CALLANDER ROAD
CRANTOCK ROAD
NEWQUAY ROAD
ARRAN ROAD
INCHMERY ROAD
BARGERY ROAD
PENERLEY ROAD
CONISBOROUGH CRESCENT
HAZELBANK ROAD
BOUNDFIELD ROAD
RAVENSBOURNE AVENUE
SHORTLANDS

E
F
G
H
J
40
41
155
SE12
1
2
3
4
5
6
7
73
174
71
191
GROVE PARK
MOTTINGHAM
DOWNHAM
PLAISTOW
SUNDRIDGE
BR1
NORTHBROOK PARK
HITHER GREEN CEMETERY
Crematorium
UNI OF WESTMINSTER SPORTS GROUND
SPORTS GROUND
CHINBROOK MEADOWS
DOWNHAM FIELDS
SHAFTESBURY PARK REC GRD
KING'S MEADOW PLAYING FIELDS
SUNDRIDGE PARK GOLF COURSE
PLAYING FIELD
TRAIN DEPOT
Bus Sta
GROVE PARK
SUNDRIDGE PARK
Bromley Ct Hotel
Quaggy River
A2212
A21
B226
BARING ROAD
BURNT ASH LANE
CHINBROOK ROAD
COLLEGE RD
LONDON ROAD
MOTTINGHAM LANE
GROVE PARK RD
LINCHMERE RD
WAITE DAVIES RD
SUMMERFIELD ST
WINN ROAD
FARMCOTE ROAD
ASHWATER ROAD
HEATHER ROAD
KINGSAND ROAD
SENLAC ROAD
WESTDEAN
COOPER'S LANE
SANDSTONE RD
BALDER RISE
LE MAY AVENUE
LUFFMAN ROAD
AMBLECOTE ROAD
AMBLECOTE MEADOWS
MARVELS LANE
REIGATE ROAD
VERDANT LANE
CUMBERLAND PLACE
HAFTON ROAD
WHITEFOOT TERRACE
SHROFFOLD ROAD
IVORYDOWN
LAUNCELOT ROAD
DOWNHAM WAY
RIDGEWAY DRIVE
PORTLAND ROAD
LEAMINGTON AVENUE
NEW STREET HILL
KYNASTON ROAD
SANDRINGHAM RD
RANGEFIELD ROAD
AVONDALE ROAD
QUERNMORE RD
KINNAIRD AVENUE
LONDON LANE
PLAISTOW LANE
LANSDOWNE ROAD
EDWARD ROAD
GARDEN ROAD
CRESCENT ROAD
HOLLIGRAVE RD
HAMMELTON RD
GLEBE RD
HIGHLAND RD
ROMNEY RD
PINE WALK

A
B
C
D
E
1
2
3
4
5
6
7
156
173
192
42
43
71
73
SE9
BR1
MOTTINGHAM
NEW ELTHAM
ELMSTEAD
CHISLEHURST WEST
SIDCUP ROAD
A20
A208
B226
B263
MOTTINGHAM ROAD
COURT ROAD
WHITEHORSE HILL
RED HILL
GROVE PARK ROAD
GREEN LANE
ELMSTEAD LANE
WALDEN ROAD
WILLOW GROVE
SOUTH HILL
YESTER PARK ROAD
CAMDEN PARK
CHISLEHURST GOLF COURSE
ROYAL BLACKHEATH GOLF COURSE
TARN BIRD SANCTUARY
THE TARN
FAIRY HILL REC GRD
PLAYING FIELD
SPORTS GROUND
MOTTINGHAM SPORTS GROUND
CHINBROOK ESTATE
LOWER MARVELS WOOD
MARVELS WOOD
GROVE PARK CEMETERY
ELMSTEAD WOOD
Ravensbourne Coll
WHYTES WOODLAND
Bird Sanctuary
Sundridge Park
ROCKPIT WOOD
LOGSHILL WOOD
Botany Bay
ELMSTEAD WOODS
MOTTINGHAM
Eltham Coll
Mottingham Farm
Royal Tavern PH
Leisure Centre

E
F
G
H
J
44
157
1
2
3
4
5
6
7
73
176
71
193
LAMORBEY
DA15
DA14
BR7
LONGLANDS
SIDCUP
TRAINING GRD
Sports Cen
Clubho.
SPORTS GRDS
SPORTS GRD
MILLWALL FC TRAINING GRD
River Shuttle
Works
NEW ELTHAM
SPORTS GRD Clubhouse
Lib
PO
FB
ALLOT
OLD FARM PARK
KING GEORGE'S REC GRD
FOOTSCRAY ROAD
A211
B2214
STREET
WOODLANDS AVENUE
Wyncham Stream
BRAUNDTON AVENUE
WILLERSLEY AVENUE
MAPLE LEAF DRIVE
ACACIA WAY
PINEWOOD AVENUE
LONGMEADOW ROAD
CRADLEY ROAD
SIDEWOOD RD
CROMBIE ROAD
ELLISON ROAD
OAKLEY DR
BROOKLANDS AVENUE
WESTBROOKE RD
YORK AVENUE
GLOUCESTER AVENUE
LITTLE BIRCHES
LONGLANDS PARK CRES
LONGLANDS ROAD
CHARTWELL CL
FRENSHAM RD
HARLAND AV
MARECHAL NIEL AV
SIDCUP BYPASS
A20
MAIN ROAD
JACK NICKLAUS GOLF CENTRE
FLAMINGO PK SPORTS GRD
LONGLANDS REC GRD
CRESCENT
SANDHURST ROAD
Fire Sta
Sports Club SPORTS GROUND
Coll
STATION ROAD
CHISLEHURST ROAD
IMPERIAL WAY
SLADES DRIVE
EDGEHILL ROAD
Stables
Prim Sch
BELMONT LANE OPEN SPACE
Kemnal Manor Stables
Beaver's Wood
Kennels
DOG RACING TRACK
CHISLEHURST CEMETERY
Hoblands Wood
Thompson's Nursery
Frogpool Manor Farm
SPORTS GRD
Frogpool Corner
Sec Sch
OLD ELTHAMIANS SPORTS GRD
UNIVERSITY COLLEGE LONDON SPORTS GRD
Clubho
SPORTS GROUND
A222
PERRY STREET
SCADBURY PARK
NATURE RESERVE
Perry Street Shaw
Bushy Clump
Icehouse Wood
PARK WOOD
Scadbury Moated Manor House Site
Bank's Shaw
HEATHFIELD LANE
HIGH STREET
CENTRE COMMON RD
CHISLEHURST COMMON
War Mem
BROMLEY LANE
ROYAL PAR
Bulls Head Hotel PH
Village Hall
ASHFIELD LANE
PRINCE IMPERIAL ROAD
B263
B264
MANOR PARK RD
WILDERNESS RD
KEMNAL RD
HOLMDALE ROAD
WOODSIDE AVENUE
ACORN CL
DICKENS DR
FOXBURY AVENUE
BEAVERWOOD ROAD
SIDCUP BYPASS
BEXLEY
BROMLEY

A
B
C
D
E
1
2
3
4
5
6
7
158
175
73
71
48
47
DA15
DA14
SIDCUP GOLF COURSE
River Shuttle
Rose Bruford College
LAMORBEY PARK
REC GRD
Comm Cen
Prim Sch
Sec Sch
Marlborough Sch
Ye Old Black Horse Inn PH
Works
Swim Pool
Clubhouse
HURST ROAD
A222
ABBEYHILL PARK
ALLOT
Pav
HURST REC GRD
RUTLAND SHAW
CEM
ALBANY PARK
Clinic
SIDCUP
STA. APP.
Marlowe Ho
Hall
PO
Prim Sch
Sidcup Arts Cen
WARING PARK
Tenn Cts
STATION ROAD
Health Cen
Coll
Pol
SIDCUP HIGH STREET
ELM ROAD
Superstore
THE GREEN
CHURCH RD
War Meml
Sidcup Green
Sports Cen
Bowl Grn
SIDCUP PLACE
Pitch 'n' Putt
CHISLEHURST ROAD
QUEEN MARY'S HOSP
Sch of Nursing & Midwifery
Frognal Corner
GARDEN SHAW
FOOTS CRAY
Spring Shaw
Bank's Shaw
SCADBURY PARK
LITTLE WOOD
BLACK CLUMP
NATURE RESERVE
Irish Plantation
Scadbury Moated Manor House Site
Field Study Centre
Youth Cen
A20
Crittall's Corner
SEVENOAKS ROAD
Sec Sch
Superstore
EDGINGTON WAY
A223
A224
A211
SIDCUP HILL
FOOTS CRAY HIGH ST
MAIDSTONE RD
Works
Glasshouses
RUXLEY CORNER INDUSTRIAL ESTATE
Ruxley Corner
RUXLEY WOOD
Superstore
Ski Centre
Sports Club
Nursery
SIDCUP TECHNOLOGY CENTRE
SPORTS GRD
Seven Stars PH
Prep Sch
Hall
Prim Sch
Comm Cen
Road Safety Cen
SPORTS GROUNDS
Health Club
Merton Ct Sch
Nature Res
Dower House
Foots Cray Place
FOOTS CRAY MEADOWS
River Cray
Five Arch Bridge
NORTH CRAY WOOD
Sec Sch
Prim Sch
BEXLEY LANE
RECTORY LANE
MAYLANDS DRIVE
LONGMEAD DRIVE
BURNT OAK LANE
FOOTS CRAY LANE
Clubhouse
PITCH
Prim Sch
Bowl Grn
Pav

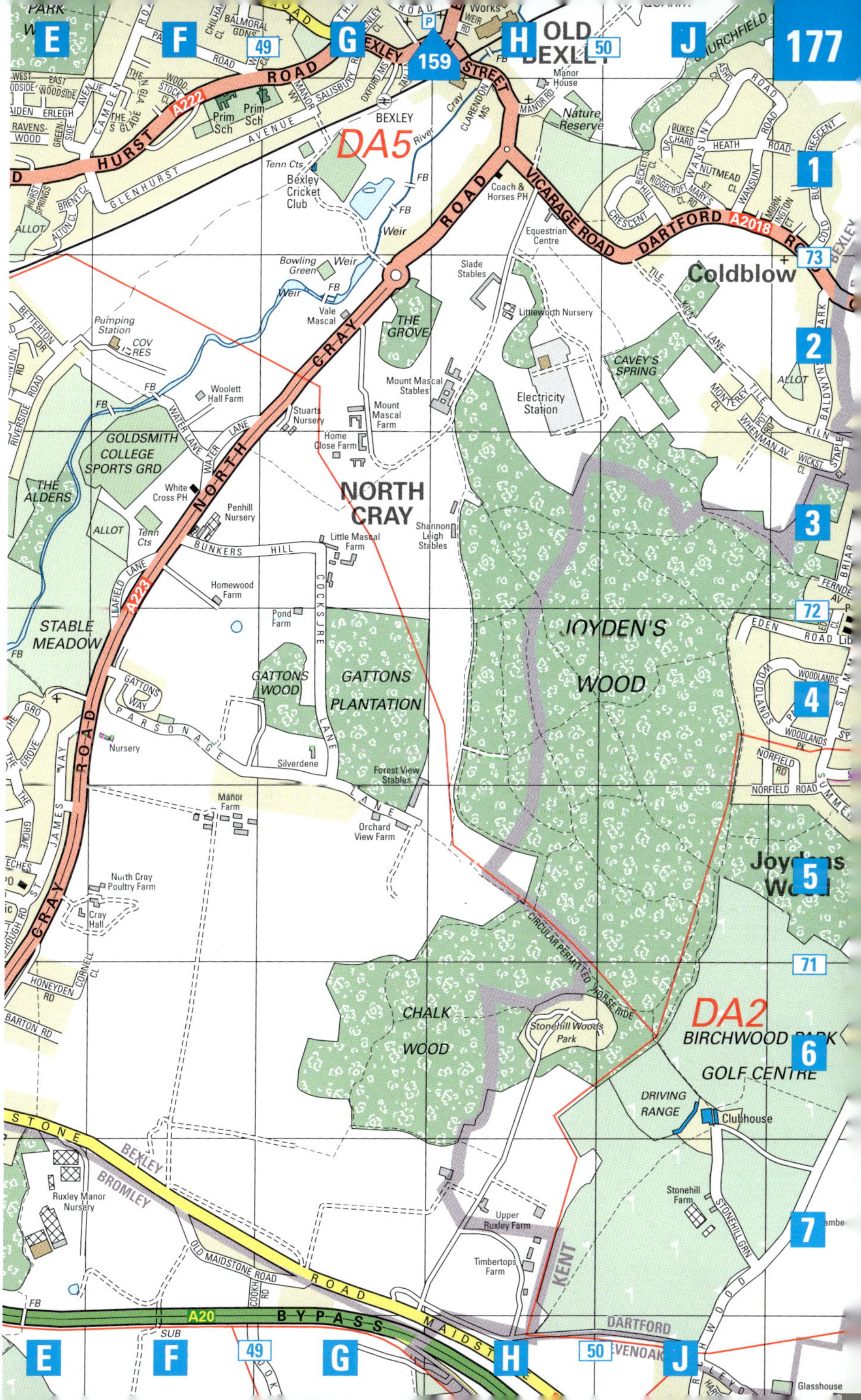
E
F
G
H
J
49
50
159
OLD BEXLEY
DA5
BEXLEY
HURST ROAD
A222
GLENHURST AVENUE
Prim Sch
Prim Sch
Tenn Cts
Bexley Cricket Club
River Cray
FB
Weir
Coach & Horses PH
VICARAGE ROAD
DARTFORD ROAD A2018
Manor House
Nature Reserve
Equestrian Centre
Bowling Green
Vale Mascal
THE GROVE
Slade Stables
Littleworth Nursery
Coldblow
73
Pumping Station
COV RES
Woolett Hall Farm
Stuarts Nursery
Mount Mascal Stables
Mount Mascal Farm
Home Close Farm
Electricity Station
CAVEY'S SPRING
ALLOT
GOLDSMITH COLLEGE SPORTS GRD
THE ALDERS
WATER LANE
White Cross PH
NORTH CRAY ROAD
Penhill Nursery
NORTH CRAY
Shannon Leigh Stables
Little Mascal Farm
BUNKERS HILL
Tenn Cts
Homewood Farm
A223
STABLE MEADOW
Pond Farm
COCKSURE LANE
JOYDEN'S WOOD
72
EDEN ROAD
GATTONS WOOD
GATTONS PLANTATION
GATTONS WAY
PARSONAGE LANE
Nursery
Silverdene
Forest View Stables
Manor Farm
Orchard View Farm
NORFIELD ROAD
Joydens Wood
North Cray Poultry Farm
Cray Hall
CIRCULAR PERMITTED HORSE RIDE
71
HONEYDEN RD
BARTON RD
CHALK WOOD
Stonehill Woods Park
DA2
BIRCHWOOD PARK GOLF CENTRE
DRIVING RANGE
Clubhouse
BEXLEY
BROMLEY
Ruxley Manor Nursery
OLD MAIDSTONE ROAD
MAIDSTONE ROAD
Upper Ruxley Farm
Timbertops Farm
KENT
Stonehill Farm
STONEHILL GRN
A20
BYPASS
SUB
DARTFORD
Glasshouse
1
2
3
4
5
6
7

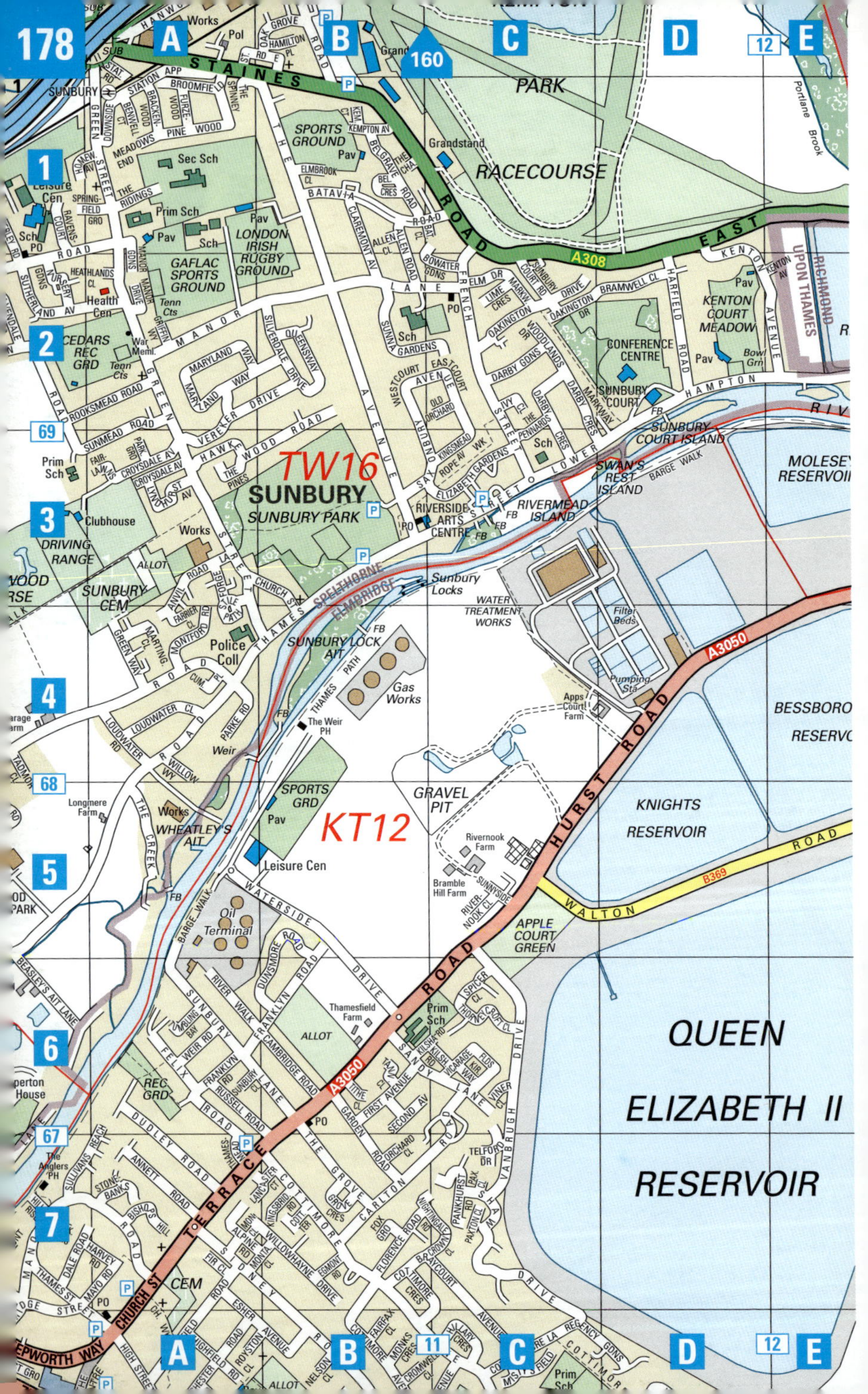
A
B
C
D
E
1
2
3
4
5
6
7
160
12
69
68
67
11
STAINES ROAD
A308
EAST
PARK
RACECOURSE
Grandstand
SPORTS GROUND
Pav
SUNBURY
Sec Sch
Prim Sch
Leisure Cen
Sch
PO
LONDON IRISH RUGBY GROUND
GAFLAC SPORTS GROUND
Tenn Cts
Health Cen
CEDARS REC GRD
War Meml
MANOR LANE
MARYLAND WAY
VERELEY DRIVE
HAWKE WOOD ROAD
SUNMEAD ROAD
ROOKSMEAD ROAD
GREEN STREET
THE AVENUE
FRENCH STREET
KENTON AVENUE
KENTON COURT MEADOW
UPON THAMES
RICHMOND
CONFERENCE CENTRE
SUNBURY COURT
HAMPTON
HARFIELD ROAD
Bowl Grn
TW16
SUNBURY
SUNBURY PARK
RIVERSIDE ARTS CENTRE
RIVERMEAD ISLAND
SWAN'S REST ISLAND
SUNBURY COURT ISLAND
MOLESEY RESERVOIR
BARGE WALK
Sunbury Locks
SUNBURY LOCK AIT
SPELTHORNE
ELMBRIDGE
WATER TREATMENT WORKS
Filter Beds
Pumping Sta
Apps Court Farm
Gas Works
THAMES PATH
Clubhouse
DRIVING RANGE
SUNBURY CEM
Works
Police Coll
CHURCH STREET
THAMES STREET
LOUDWATER ROAD
PARKE RD
Weir
The Weir PH
SPORTS GRD
Pav
Leisure Cen
WHEATLEY'S AIT
Longmere Farm
KT12
GRAVEL PIT
Rivernook Farm
Bramble Hill Farm
HURST ROAD
A3050
BESSBOROUGH RESERVOIR
KNIGHTS RESERVOIR
WALTON ROAD
B369
APPLE COURT GREEN
Oil Terminal
WATERSIDE DRIVE
DUNSMORE ROAD
Thamesfield Farm
ALLOT
Prim Sch
SANDY LANE
QUEEN ELIZABETH II RESERVOIR
REC GRD
TERRACE ROAD
DUDLEY ROAD
ANNETT ROAD
COTTIMORE LANE
CARLTON ROAD
The Anglers PH
CEM
CHURCH ST
EPWORTH WAY
HIGH STREET
VANBRUGH DRIVE
TELFORD DR
REGENCY GDNS

E
F
G
H
J
13
14
161
180
69
68
67
1
2
3
4
5
6
7
HAMPTON
Open Pool
COBBLERS WALK
Clubhouse
Football Grd
HYDES FIELD
Portlane Bridge
KINGSWAY BUSINESS PARK
OLDFIELD PASSAGE
STATION ROAD
ORMOND AVENUE
ORMOND CRESCENT
Hampton FC
BEAVER CL
SHERIDAN PL
HIGH ST
CHURCH ST
UPPER SUNBURY ROAD
A308
THAMES ST
HAMPTON
Bell Inn
Garrick Temple
GARRICK'S AIT
STAIN HILL RESERVOIRS
Filter Beds
GRAND JUNCTION RESERVOIR
SPORTS GRD
Water Works
TW12
SURREY
HURST PARK
BARGE WALK
TERRACE GDNS
LOWER SUNBURY ROAD
SUNNYSIDE RESERVOIR
PLATT'S EYOT
Works
THAMES PATH
RIVER THAMES
EMBRIDGE
BUCKINGHAM AVENUE
THAMES COURT
VICTORIA AV
GARRICK GDNS
HURST ROAD
A3050
PARK WAY
THE FAIRWAY
Cricket Ground
KING'S CHASE
UPPER PALACE RD
Prim Sch
Swim Pool
REC GROUND
Tenn Cts
SPORTS GRD
Vine Hall
ALLOT
CEM
REC GRD
Pav
WALTON ROAD
B369
Clinic
Lib
Med Cen
WOLSEY
REC GRD
Molesey FC
Comm Cen
SOVEREIGN CT
PO
CLINTON AV
WEST MOLESEY
Works
BEAUCHAMP ROAD
SPORTS GROUND
HOSP
KT8
Medical Cen
ISLAND FARM ROAD
FLEETSIDE
FLEET LANE
Dead River
THE WILDERNESS
MOLESEY PARK
River Mole
River Ember
NEILSON PLAYING FIELD
SPORTS GROUND
Sailing Club
Pumping Station
SAND & GRAVEL PIT
ISLAND BARN RESERVOIR
River Mole
IMBER COURT TRADING ESTATE
SPORTS GROUND
FIELDCOMMON LANE
Hall
Fieldcommon Farm
Works
KT10
Filter Beds
Sewage Works
GROVE WAY
Bowl Grn
Sports Club
Tenn Cts
IMBER GROVE
EMBER LANE
IMBER COURT DRIVE
FB

A
B
C
D
E
1
2
3
4
5
6
7
162
179
194
15
16
69
68
67
BUSHY
PARK
TW11
BROOM
CLUMPS
WATERHOUSE
WOODLAND
GARDEN
WATERHOUSE
POND
FISHER'S
POND
Red Brick
Bridge
COBBLERS
COBBLERS WALK
Hawthorn
Lodge
WARREN
PLANTATION
HALF
MOON
PLANTATION
HERON
POND
OVAL
PLANTATION
Boating
Pool
CHESTNUT AV
Diana
Fountain
THE
ROYAL PADDOCKS
HAMPTON COURT ROAD
A308
TERRACE
GDNS
TAGG'S
ISLAND
Pav
Cricket
Ground
Weir
ASH
ISLAND
Hampton Court
House
Hampton
Court
Gate
Lion Gate
Hotel
HAMPTON COURT
HAMPTON
COURT
GREEN
Riding
Sch
Royal
Mews
Molesey
Lock
Mitre
Hotel
Tenn
Cts
MAZE
HAMPTON
COURT
GDNS
THE BROAD WK
NORTH
CANAL
Stud
House
HAMPTON
COURT
PALACE
Hampton
Court
Bri
Pier
Boat
Club
The Long Water
KT8
EAST
MOLESEY
PALACE ROAD
WOLSEY ROAD
RIVER BANK
FELTHAM AV
HAMPTON
COURT
CIGARETTE
ISLAND
PARK
PRIVY
GDN
SOUTH
CANAL
HAMPTON COURT
(HOME
UPPER
PALACE
RD
PARSONS MEAD
Vine
Hall
CHURCH ROAD
ARNISON ROAD
BRIDGE RD
CREEK RD
KENT ROAD
MANOR ROAD
CHALLONERS CL
GROVE RD
SCHOOL RD
HANSLER GROVE
ST JOHNS RD
BRIDGE GDN
B3379
CEDAR RD
OARSMAN PL
QUEENS REACH
Weir
MOLEMBER ROAD
PAVILION TERRACE
DITTON FIELD
Works
Pav
SPORTS
GRD
ALBANY REACH
MOLEM.
COURT
Sch
Pol
ST MARYS RD
SUMMER ROAD
SUMMER AV
SUMMER GDNS
HAMPTON COURT WAY
A309
SPENCER ROAD
MOLE RD
PK RD
BELL ROAD
MATHAM ROAD
Medical Cen
MOLESEY PARK
CL
River Mole
River Ember
RIVERSIDE AV
Pav
SPORTS
GROUND
HAMPTON COURT GOLF COURSE
WOLSEY AV
ARAGON AV
QUEEN'S ROAD
ALEXANDRA RD
RIVER BANK
RIVERSDALE RD
REC
GRD
WARWICK GDNS
WARWICK RD
SPEER ROAD
LEAF CL
THAMES
DITTON
ISLAND
RICHMOND UPON THAMES
GROUND
FARM WAY
EMBER FARM AV
EMBER FARM WAY
HAMPTON CT AV
ESHER
B3379
Tenn
Cts
GARDENS
THISTLEDENE
BROADFIELDS
SOUTHFIELDS
ALLOT
THAMES
DITTON
Works
ORCHARD LANE
LANE
IMBER COURT
TRADING ESTATE
SPORTS
GRD
Met. Police
Training Coll
ENNISMORE
STERRY DR
DENLEIGH GDNS
ELMSWORTHY
Pav
BURIAL
GRD
ST NICHOLAS RD
CHURCH WALK
CHURCH LA
HARVEST LA
BOYLE FARM RD
FITZGERALD RD
BURTENSHAW RD
BOYLE FM
ISLAND
City Wharf
House
KT7
Sch
ASHLEY ROAD
OLD SCHOOL SQ
PO
ST LEONARDS ROAD
QUEENS DRIVE
KINGS DR
FERRY RD
THORKHILL RD
SOUTHBANK
VAUGHAN
Pav
SPORTS
GROUND
EMBERCOURT RD
EMBERCOURT ROAD
EMBER GARDENS
Prim
Sch
COLLEGE DR
Tennis
Club
STATION ROAD
THAMES DITTON
BASINGFIELD RD
BASING WAY
BASING CL
HOME FARM CL
WATTS RD
RIVER AV
PORTSMOUTH AV
Met. Police
Sports Club
SPORTS
GROUND
Pav
Bowl
Grn
Tenn
Cts
RIFLE
RANGE
Tenn Cts
Coll
Prim
Sch
Youth
Club
Health
Cen
MERCER CL
Lib
DEN CL
B364
GIGGS HILL
GIGGS
HILL
GRN
War
Meml.
ANGEL RD
RYTHE CT
The Rythe
HILL GDNS
WESTVILLE RD
SOUTHVILLE RD
THORKHILL
RUSHETT CL
THORKHILL GDNS
ELM TREE AV
WOODSIDE AV
EMBER LANE
IMBER GROVE
SANDON CL
CHESTNUT AVENUE
GROVE WAY
EMBER
Grn
Sports Club
Tenn Cts
DRIVE
WESTON AV
WESTON GREEN
AVENUE
LONGMEAD RD
GREEN
RAPHAEL DRIVE
READ CL
HAYWARD
SAVILL
SPORTS
GROUND
WESTON
OAKLANDS
POUND FARM
GLOUCESTER CL
DITTON LAWN
SCOTT FARM

E
F
G
H
J
17
163
1
2
3
4
5
6
7
182
HAMPTON WICK
THE KINGSFIELD
HAMPTON WICK POND
The Old Ice House
Glasshouse
The Wilderness
Parkfield
OURT PARK
PARK)
THE RICK POND
PALACE
Clubhouse
Watersports Cen
RAVENS AIT
Yacht Club
Sailing Club
Filter Beds
Water Works
Thames Marina
Kingston University
River Thames
THAMES PATH / LONDON LOOP
BARGE WALK
KINGSTON BR
HORSE FAIR
WOOD ST
CLARENCE ST
CROMWELL RD
FAIRFIELD N
LONDON RD
KINGSTON UPON THAMES
Bentalls Cen
Eden Walk Shop Cen
Coronation Stone
GUILDHALL
KINGS HALL RD
HIGH STREET
PENRHYN ROAD
SURBITON ROAD
PORTSMOUTH ROAD
A307
A240
A243
A308
B3363
B3364
B3370
KT1
KT5
KT6
Kingston Uni
Kingston Coll
SURREY COUNTY HALL
KINGSTON CEMET
CEMETE
BERRYLA
SURBITON
SURBITON GENERAL HOSP
Hillcroft Coll
VICTORIA ROAD
UPPER BRIGHTON ROAD
EWELL ROAD
ST. MARK'S HILL
CLAREMONT ROAD
KINGSDOWNE ROAD
VICTORIA REC GRD
FISHPONDS OPEN SPACE
Hogsmill
LONDON LOOP
195
68
69
67
Cockcrow Hill

A
B
C
D
E
1
2
3
4
5
6
7
164
181
196
69
68
67
21
KT1
KT2
KT3
KT5
NORBITON
NEW MALDEN
BERRYLANDS
KINGSTON CEMETERY
SURBITON CEMETERY
COOMBE WOOD GOLF COURSE
KINGSTON HOSPITAL
Kingstonian FC & AFC Wimbledon
Kingston Athletics Cen
Sewage Works
Filter Beds
Sludge Beds
Crematorium
Waste Transfer Station
LONDON LOOP
Hogsmill River
GREEN LANE REC GRD
KINGSTON ROAD REC GRD
HOGSMILL PUBLIC OPEN SPACE
HOGSMILL OPEN SPACE
ALEXANDRA REC
SPORTS GROUND
Bowling Greens
Kingston Uni
Superstore
Superstores
Telephone Ex
Leisure Cen
Comm Cen
Prim Schs
Sec Sch
KINGSTON ROAD
CAMBRIDGE ROAD
COOMBE LANE WEST
COOMBE ROAD
NORBITON ROAD
KINGSTON HILL
LOWER MARSH LANE
SURBITON HILL PARK
MALDEN WAY
KINGSTON BY-PASS
TRAPS LANE
CLARENCE AVENUE
ELM ROAD
BURLINGTON ROAD
A308
A238
A2043
A3
B351
B283

E
F
G
H
J
165
22
23
NEW VICTORIA HOSPITAL
OBERON PLAYING FIELD
SW20
COTTENHAM PARK
COTTENHAM PK REC GRD
HOLLAND GDNS
COOMBE LANE
A238
KINGSTON BY-PASS
BEVERLEY WAY
A3
MALDEN GOLF COURSE
PLAYING FIELDS
SPORTS GROUND
RAYNES PARK SPORTS GRD
RAYNES PARK
WORPLE RD
KINGSTON RD
A298
BUSHEY RD
GRAND DRIVE
B279
B282
B283
PRINCE GEORGE'S PLAYING FIELD
69
184
68
67
MESSINE PLAYING
NEW MALDEN
HIGH STREET
BEVERLEY PARK
KINGSTON UPON THAMES
MERTON
Wyvern Estate
Superstore
BURLINGTON ROAD
MALDEN ROAD
MALDEN WAY
Causeway Cen
Sports Cen
WEST BARNES
WEST BARNES LA
MOTSPUR PARK
UNIVERSITY OF LONDON ATHLETIC GROUND
B.B.C. SPORTS GRD
THE SIR JOSEPH HOOD MEMORIAL PLAYING FIELDS
Gas Works
KT4
SPORTS GROUND
MANOR PARK REC GRD
MORDEN CEMETERY
Crematorium
MERTON & SUTTON JOINT CEMETERY
OLD BLUES R.F.C.
RAYNES PARK PLAYING FIELDS
Recycling Centre
GARTH IND C
197
B284
1
2
3
4
5
6
7

A
B
C
D
E
1
2
3
4
5
6
7
24
25
166
183
198
69
68
67
SW19
SW20
SM4
MERTON
MERTON PARK
MORDEN
MORDEN PARK
BUSHEY MEAD
DUNDONALD REC GRD
NELSON HOSP
WIMBLEDON CHASE
JOHN INNES REC GRD
PRINCE GEORGE'S PLAYING FIELD
JOSEPH HOOD RECREATION GROUND
MESSINES PLAYING FLD
CANNON HILL COMMON
RAYNES PARK PLAYING FIELDS
MORDEN SPORTS GROUND
KING GEORGE'S FIELD
MOSTYN GARDENS
SOUTH MERTON
MORDEN SOUTH
ST. HELIER
MORDEN REC GRD
NURSERY ROAD PLAYING FIELDS
ABBEY REC GRD
GARTH ROAD IND CEN
MERTON SUTTON JOINT CEMETERY
Beverley Brook
Bowling Alley & Health Club
Merton Coll
Travelodge
Swim Pool
Bandstand
Cricket Pitch
Morden Park Pitch 'n' Putt
KINGSTON ROAD
WORPLE ROAD
MARTIN WAY
GRAND DRIVE
TUDOR DRIVE
EPSOM ROAD
LONDON ROAD
CENTRAL ROAD
GREEN LANE
SUTTON COMMON ROAD
LOWER MORDEN LANE
CANNON HILL LANE
HILLCROSS AVENUE
DORSET ROAD
CROWN LA
A238
A298
A24
B235
B286
B279
B285
RAIL DEPOT
CIVIC CEN

E
F
G
H
J
26
167
186
199
69
68
67
1
2
3
4
5
6
7
MERANTUN WAY
STREET
A238
CHRISTCHURCH RD
WESTERN ROAD
A236
LONDON ROAD
A217
MORDEN ROAD
A24
MORDEN HALL ROAD
A297
ST. HELIER AVENUE
MORDEN ROAD
A239
BISHOPSFORD ROAD
CARSHALTON ROAD
A237
CRICKET GRN
MADEIRA RD
CRANMER RD
LONDON ROAD CEMETERY
FIGGE'S MARSH
MERTON INDUSTRIAL PARK
LOMBARD BUSINESS PARK
MORDEN HALL PARK
Snuff Mill Environmental Cen
Morden Hall
Morden Lodge
PHIPPS BRIDGE
BELGRAVE WALK
MORDEN ROAD
ROCK TERRACE REC GRD
BURIAL GROUND
GREENLEA PARK
CR4
SM5
RAVENSBURY PARK
WANDLE IND MUS
MITCHAM
BROOKMEADS
WATERMEADS NT.
Tooting & Mitcham Utd FC
Bishopsford House
POULTER PARK
Pelhamian R.F.C.
SPORTS GROUND
ABBEY IND EST
GRACE BUSINESS CENTRE
EAGLE TRADING EST
MORETON GREEN
ST. HELIER
CARSHALTON SPORTS ARENA
ST. HELIER OPEN SPACE
Wandle Valley Sch
Merton R.F.C.
ROSEHILL
River Wandle
Superstore
Gas Works
Cricket Club
Deen City Farm

168
200
185
A
B
C
D
E
1
2
3
4
5
6
7
30
69
68
67
MITCHAM
CR4
MITCHAM
COMMON
CR0
FIGGE'S MARSH
MITCHAM IND EST
STREATHAM PARK CEMETERY
Crematorium
War Memorial
PLAYING FIELDS
NATIONAL WESTMINSTER BANK SPORTS GROUND
MITCHAM GOLF COURSE
MITCHAM JUNCTION
Clubhouse
GRACE BUSINESS CENTRE
BEDDINGTON CORNER
MILL GREEN
BEDDINGTON LANE
RIFLE RANGE
TRAMSHEDS IND EST
Beddington Farm
Sewage Works
Sorting Office
SHERWOOD PK
PLAYING FIELD
PLAYING FIELD
MERTON
SUTTON
MERTON
Hundred Acre Bridge
Irrigation Bridge
Beehive Bridge
Blue Houses Bridge
Cranmer Bridge
Ravensbury Arms PH
Mill House PH
Jolly Gardeners PH
MITCHAM GARDEN VILLAGE
Eltandia Hall
REC GRD
LONDON ROAD
STREATHAM ROAD
ROWAN ROAD
MANOR ROAD
WINDMILL ROAD
BEDDINGTON LANE
CARSHALTON ROAD
CROYDON ROAD
COMMONSIDE WEST
COMMONSIDE EAST
CRANMER RD
A217
A237
A236
B272

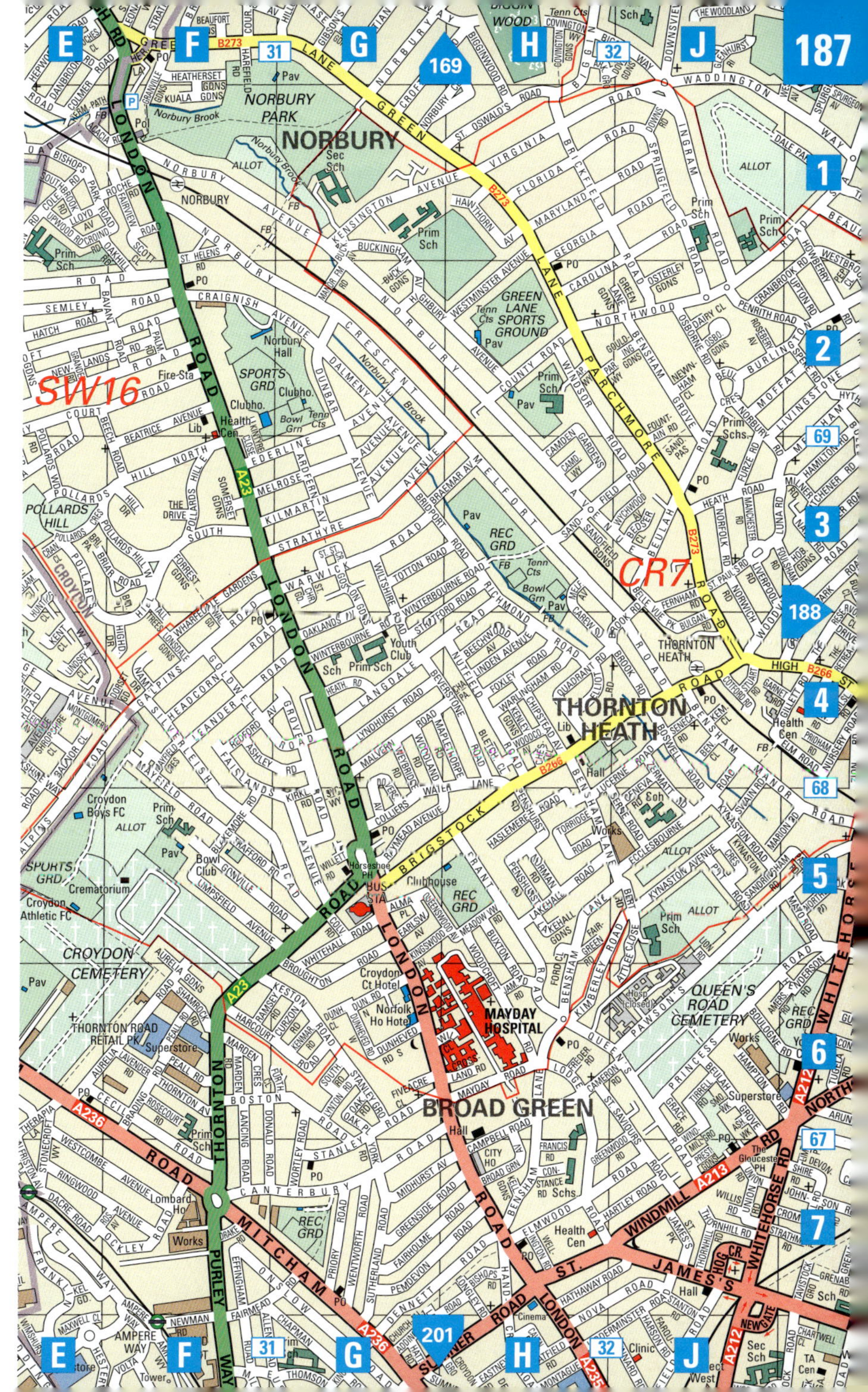
NORBURY
NORBURY PARK
Norbury Brook
Sec Sch
ALLOT
Prim Sch
GREEN LANE SPORTS GROUND
Tenn Cts
Pav
Norbury Hall
SPORTS GRD
Clubho.
Bowl Grn
Fire Sta
Health Cen
Lib
SW16
POLLARDS HILL
CROYDON
REC GRD
CR7
THORNTON HEATH
Youth Club
Prim Sch
Croydon Boys FC
Crematorium
Croydon Athletic FC
CROYDON CEMETERY
THORNTON ROAD RETAIL PK
Superstore
Croydon Ct Hotel
Norfolk Ho Hotel
MAYDAY HOSPITAL
Hosp (closed)
QUEEN'S ROAD CEMETERY
BROAD GREEN
CITY HO
Health Cen
Works
Lombard Ho
Cinema
Clinic
LONDON ROAD
A23
B273
B266
A236
A213
A212
A235
BRIGSTOCK ROAD
PARCHMORE ROAD
GREEN LANE
NORBURY AVENUE
NORBURY CRESCENT
MITCHAM ROAD
THORNTON ROAD
PURLEY WAY
WINDMILL RD
ST. JAMES'S RD
WHITEHORSE RD
HIGH ST
169
201
188
E
F
G
H
J
1
2
3
4
5
6
7
31
32
67
68
69

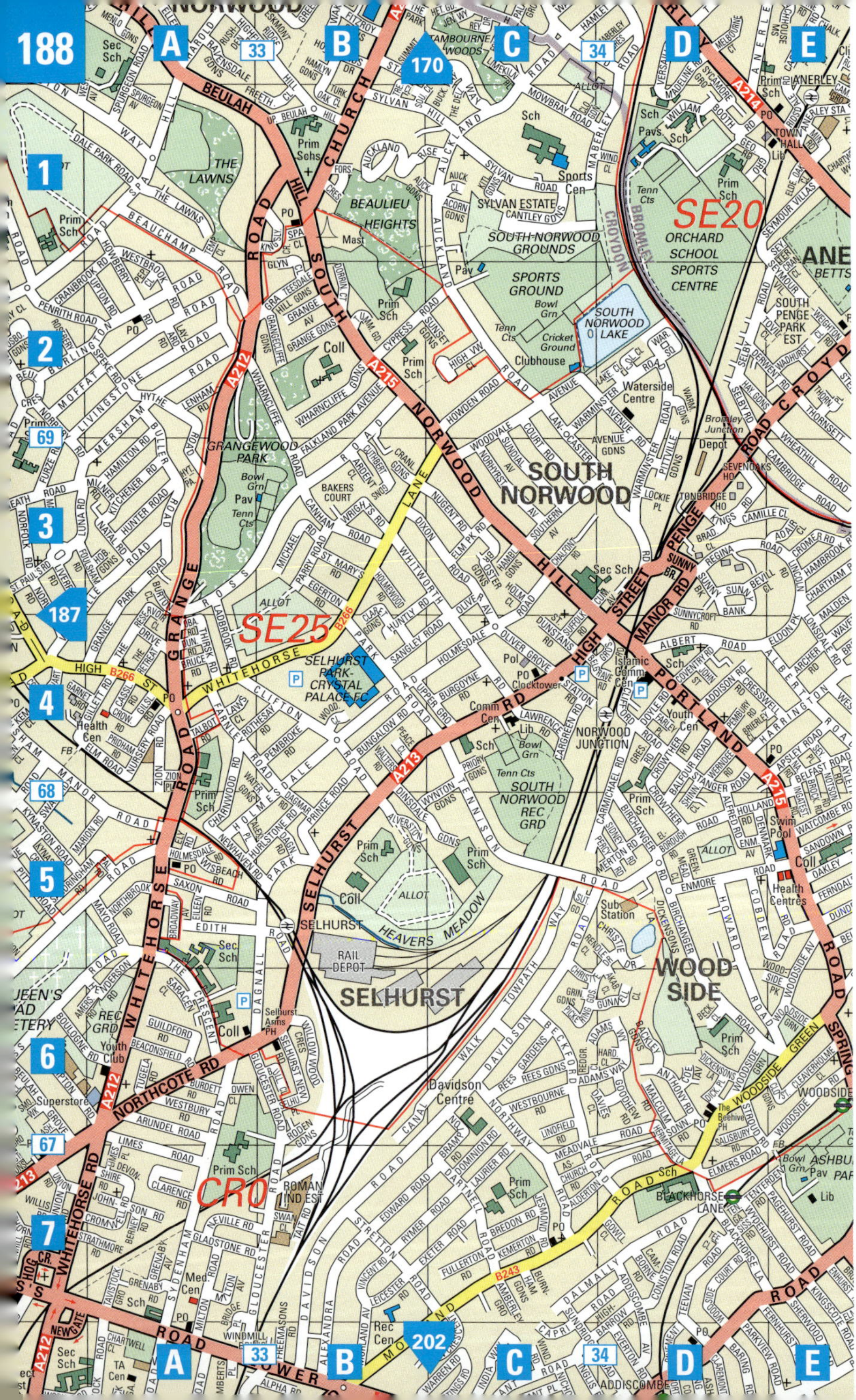

A
B
C
D
E
33
34
170
187
202
69
68
67
1
2
3
4
5
6
7
NORWOOD
BEULAH HILL
THE LAWNS
BEAUCHAMP ROAD
DALE PARK ROAD
SPURGEON AV
CHURCH ROAD
SOUTH NORWOOD HILL
TAMBOURNE WOODS
SYLVAN HILL
MOWBRAY ROAD
BEAULIEU HEIGHTS
SYLVAN ESTATE
SOUTH NORWOOD GROUNDS
SPORTS GROUND
SOUTH NORWOOD LAKE
Clubhouse
Waterside Centre
CROYDON
BROMLEY
SE20
ORCHARD SCHOOL SPORTS CENTRE
ANERLEY
SOUTH PENGE PARK EST
Bromley Junction
Depot
CROYDON ROAD
SOUTH NORWOOD
NORWOOD JUNCTION
PORTLAND ROAD
MANOR RD
HIGH STREET
PENGE
GRANGEWOOD PARK
GRANGE ROAD
SE25
WHITEHORSE LANE
SELHURST PARK CRYSTAL PALACE FC
HIGH ST
Clocktower
SOUTH NORWOOD REC GRD
SELHURST ROAD
HEAVERS MEADOW
RAIL DEPOT
SELHURST
WOODSIDE
WOODSIDE GREEN
Davidson Centre
BLACKHORSE LANE
CR0
ROMAN IND EST
WHITEHORSE ROAD
NORTHCOTE RD
LOWER ADDISCOMBE ROAD
ADDISCOMBE
ASHBURTON PARK
Superstore

171
190
203
35
69
68
67
BR3
CR0
ELMERS END
UPPER ELMERS END
MONKS ORCHARD
SOUTH NORWOOD COUNTRY PARK
BECKENHAM CEMETERY
Crematorium
BECKENHAM HOSPITAL
CROYDON RD REC GROUND
Bandstand
CREASE PARK
CROYDON AND RYLANDS FIELDS
CROYDON SPORTS ARENA
Croydon FC
CROYDON DRIVING RANGE
LONG LANE WOOD
Bird Sanctuary
ASHBURTON PLAYING FIELDS
SHIRLEY OAKS HOSPITAL
BETHLEM ROYAL HOSPITAL
GLADE WOOD
COLD SHAW
Beckenham R.F.C. SPORTS GROUND
PLAYING FIELDS
SPORTS GROUND
Cricket Club
Recycling Cen
Superstore
Depot
Works
KENT HOUSE
BECKENHAM ROAD
AVENUE ROAD
BIRKBECK
HARRINGTON ROAD
ARENA
CLOCK HOUSE
Leisure Cen
Youth Club
Indoor Bowl Club
Blenheim Shopping Cen
BECKENHAM ROAD
CROYDON ROAD
ELMERS END ROAD
UPPER ELMERS END ROAD
LONG LANE
SHIRLEY ROAD
CROYDON ROAD
A234
A214
A213
A222
Pitch 'n' Putt
SPORTS GRD
REC GRD
King William IV PH
Elmer Lodge PH
Sec Sch
Prim Sch

A
B
C
D
E
1
2
3
4
5
6
7
172
189
204
39
69
68
67
BECKENHAM
LEWISHAM
BROMLEY
SHORTLANDS
GOLF
COURSE
Ravensbourne River
THE SLOANE HOSPITAL
BECKENHAM JUNCTION
A2015
A222
A214
B230
B251
BR3
RECTORY ROAD
HIGH STREET
MANOR ROAD
BROMLEY ROAD
ALBEMARLE ROAD
FOXGROVE
THE AVENUE
WICKHAM ROAD
KELSEY PARK
HAYES LANE
HAYES WAY
CROYDON RD REC GROUND
CREASE PARK
HARVINGTON PLAYING FIELD
Beckenham Town FC
EDEN PARK
Langley Court (Research Laboratories)
SOUTH EDEN PARK ROAD
UPPER ELMERS END
CROUCH OAK WOOD
COLD SHAW
HIGH BROOM WOOD
BETHLEM ROYAL HOSPITAL
PARK LANGLEY
SPORTS GROUND
LANGLEY PARK SPORTS GRD
PLAYING FIELD
LANGLEY PARK GOLF COURSE
THE ROOKERY
WEST WICKHAM
BECKENHAM ROAD
LINKS WAY
WELLHOUSE RD
STONE PARK AVENUE
HAWKSBROOK LANE
WICKHAM WAY
BRABOURNE RISE
OAKWOOD AVENUE
The Beck
War Memorial
Clubhouse
Swimming

E
F
G
H
J
40
41
173
192
205
69
68
67
1
2
3
4
5
6
7
BR1
BR2
BROMLEY
Widmore Green
WIDMORE
SHORTLANDS
BROMLEY PARK
A21
A21 WAY
B228
B2212
B265
B251
TWEEDY ROAD
COLLEGE RD
HIGH ST
WIDMORE ROAD
KENTISH WAY
BECKENHAM LANE
MASONS HILL
BROMLEY COMMON
WESTMORELAND ROAD
HAYES ROAD
HAYES LANE
HOMESDALE ROAD
PICKHURST LANE
MEAD WAY
BARNHILL AVENUE
LETCHWORTH DRIVE
CHERITON AVENUE
THE CHASE
PALACE VIEW
ROCHESTER AVENUE
NIGHTINGALE LANE
PLAISTOW LANE
ORCHARD ROAD
SIWARD ROAD
GODWIN ROAD
GLANVILLE ROAD
GUNDULPH RD
WALDO RD
HARWOOD AV
QUEEN ANNE AVENUE
DURHAM AVENUE
RAVENSBOURNE RD
ETHELBERT RD
ELMFIELD RD
RINGERS RD
MARTINS ROAD
STATION RD
QUEENS MEAD ROAD
SOUTH HILL ROAD
The Glades Shop Cen
Leisure Cen
BROMLEY CIVIC CENTRE
CHURCH HOUSE GDNS
QUEEN'S MEAD REC GRD
SPORTS GROUND
MARTIN'S HILL
War Mem
Bandstand
Superstore
Bus Sta
Mkt
BROMLEY NORTH
BROMLEY SOUTH
Westmoreland Place
MAG COURT
COUNTY CT
Clinic
Coll
Lib
Thea
Fire Sta
Pol
Works
Gas Works
Recycling Cen
HAVELOCK REC GRD
Sec Sch
Prim Sch
Sch
Schs
Bromley CC
Tenn Cts
ALLOT
Pav
SOUTH HILL WOOD
CUPOLA WOOD
REC GRD
SPORTS GRD
The Pinnacle Club
Cricket Club
Bromley FC
Bowl Grn
FISHER'S WOOD
NORMAN PARK RECREATION GROUND
ATHLETICS TRACK
SCROGGINHALL WOOD
BROOK WOOD
MAZZARDS WOOD
WOODCOCK GROVE
LORDS WOOD
Ravens Bourne
RES
Hayes Street Farm
The Pickhurst PH
FAIR ACRES
Bromley College of Further & Higher Education
Clubhouse
Bowl Grn Pumping Sta
Tenn Club

A
B
C
D
E
42
43
174
206
191
1
2
3
4
5
6
7
69
68
67
Widmore Green
BR1
BR2
BICKLEY
SOUTHBOROUGH
Bromley Common
CHISLEHURST GOLF COURSE
Clubhouse
LOGS HILL
Sec Sch
ARTS CEN
Prep Sch
Prim Sch
SPORTS GRD
CHALKPIT WOOD
CHISLEHURST
STATION APPROACH
SUMMER HILL
BROMLEY
RAVENSHILL
Coll
GOSHILL WOOD
BIRCH WOOD
CHISLEHURST ROAD
BICKLEY ROAD
A222
B264
B265
A21
PAGE HEATH LANE
BICKLEY PARK ROAD
WOODLANDS ROAD
PRIORY
Bickley Park CC
PLAYING FIELD
REC GRD
Works
Gas Works
Bickley Junction
HAWTHORNE ROAD
OLDFIELD ROAD
Recycling Cen
HAVELOCK REC GRD
Swim Pool
Clinic
WHITEHALL REC GRD
Bowl Grn
Bickley Manor Hotel
Bromley High Sch
BLACKBROOK LANE
THORNET WOOD
JUBILEE COUNTRY PARK
Southborough Lane Stables
SOUTHBOROUGH LANE
SOUTHBOROUGH ROAD
Crooked Billet PH
SOUTHBOROUGH OPEN SPACE
OXHAWTH CRESCENT
SPORTS GROUND
ALLOT
ST. LUKE'S CEM
Youth Cen
PARKFIELD
RECREATION GROUND
BROMLEY GOLF COURSE
Bromley College of Further & Higher Education
LORDS WOOD
Ravens Bourne
MAGPIE LANE REC GRD
Adult Ed Cen
Oakley House
MAZZARDS WOOD
WOODCOCK GROVE
COMMON
Prince's Plain
PLAYING FIELD
SPARROW WOOD
CROFTON HEATH
LONDON LOOP
BLACKBROOK WOOD
Hall
Lib
Amb Sta

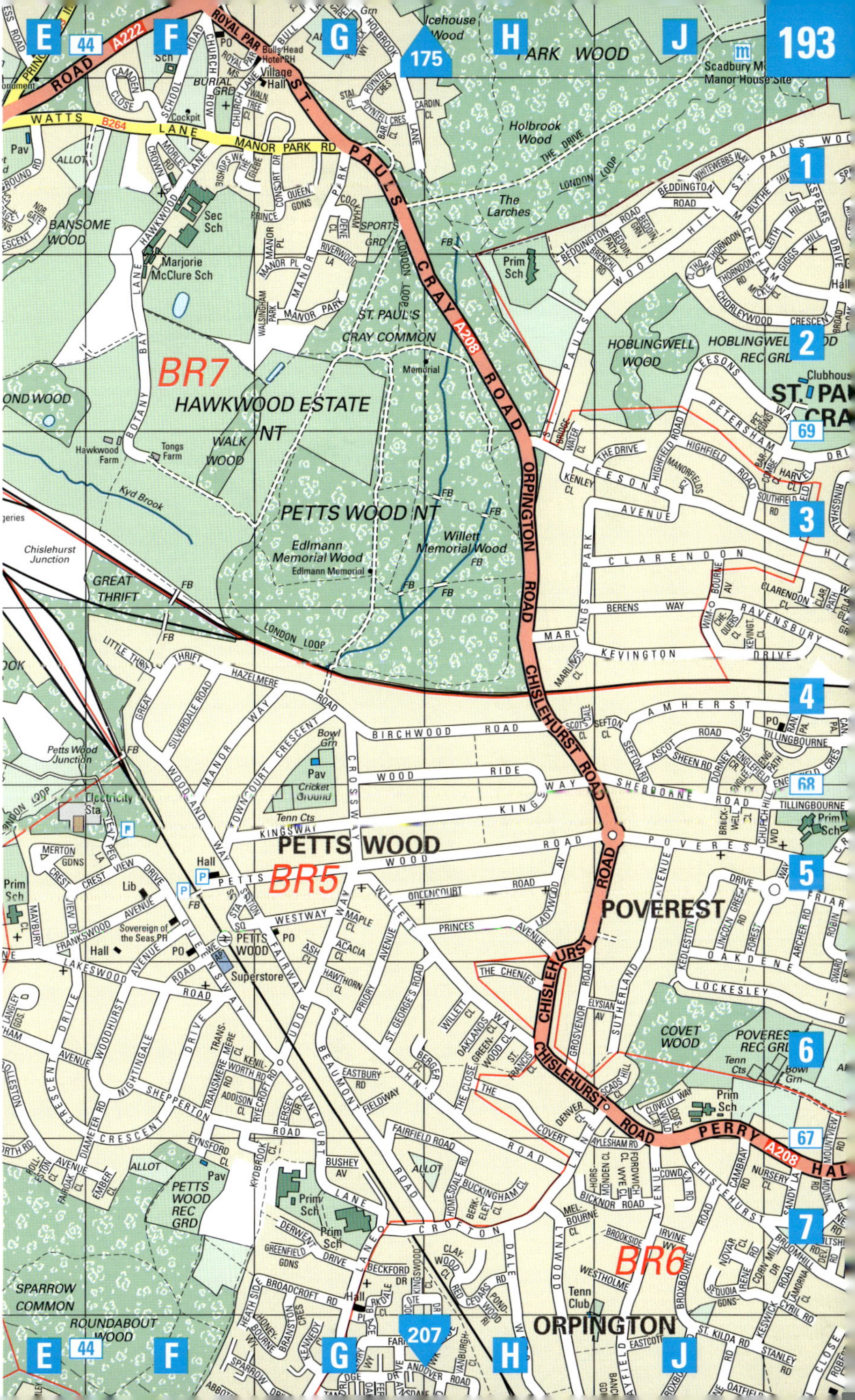
E
F
G
H
J
44
175
207
69
68
67
1
2
3
4
5
6
7
A222
B264
A208
WATTS LANE
ROYAL PAR
ST. PAULS CRAY ROAD
ORPINGTON ROAD
CHISLEHURST ROAD
MANOR PARK RD
Bulls Head Hotel PH
Village Hall
Cockpit
Icehouse Wood
PARK WOOD
Scadbury Manor House Site
Holbrook Wood
THE DRIVE
LONDON LOOP
The Larches
BANSOME WOOD
Sec Sch
Marjorie McClure Sch
Prim Sch
ST. PAUL'S CRAY COMMON
Memorial
HOBLINGWELL WOOD
HOBLINGWELL REC GRD
Clubhouse
BR7
HAWKWOOD ESTATE NT
WALK WOOD
Hawkwood Farm
Tongs Farm
Kyd Brook
PETTS WOOD NT
Edlmann Memorial Wood
Edlmann Memorial
Willett Memorial Wood
Chislehurst Junction
GREAT THRIFT
Petts Wood Junction
Electricity Sta
Bowl Grn
Pav
Cricket Ground
Tenn Cts
PETTS WOOD
BR5
POVEREST
Sovereign of the Seas PH
Superstore
Lib
Hall
PO
COVET WOOD
POVEREST REC GRD
PETTS WOOD REC GRD
SPARROW COMMON
ROUNDABOUT WOOD
Tenn Club
ORPINGTON
BR6
BIRCHWOOD ROAD
WOOD RIDE
KINGSWAY
HAZELMERE
SILVERDALE ROAD
TOWNCOURT CRESCENT
CROSSWAY
WOODLAND WAY
QUEENSWAY
WESTWAY
FAIRWAY
PRINCES AVENUE
LADYWOOD AV
POVEREST ROAD
AMHERST
SHERBORNE ROAD
TILLINGBOURNE
CLARENDON
BERENS WAY
KEVINGTON DRIVE
RAVENSBURY
MARLINGS PARK AVENUE
LEESONS
HIGHFIELD ROAD
BEDDINGTON ROAD
MICKLEHAM
CHORLEYWOOD CRESCENT
OAKDENE
LOCKESLEY
SUTHERLAND
GROSVENOR ROAD
LAKESWOOD ROAD
FRANKSWOOD AVENUE
NIGHTINGALE
SHEPPERTON
CRESCENT
TOWNCOURT LANE
CROFTON LANE
CROFTON
BUCKINGHAM CL
FAIRFIELD ROAD
THE COVERT
PERRY HALL
LYNWOOD
BROXBOURNE
ST. KILDA RD
STANLEY
EASTCOTT
BROADCROFT RD
BECKFORD DR
BUSHEY AV
ALLOT

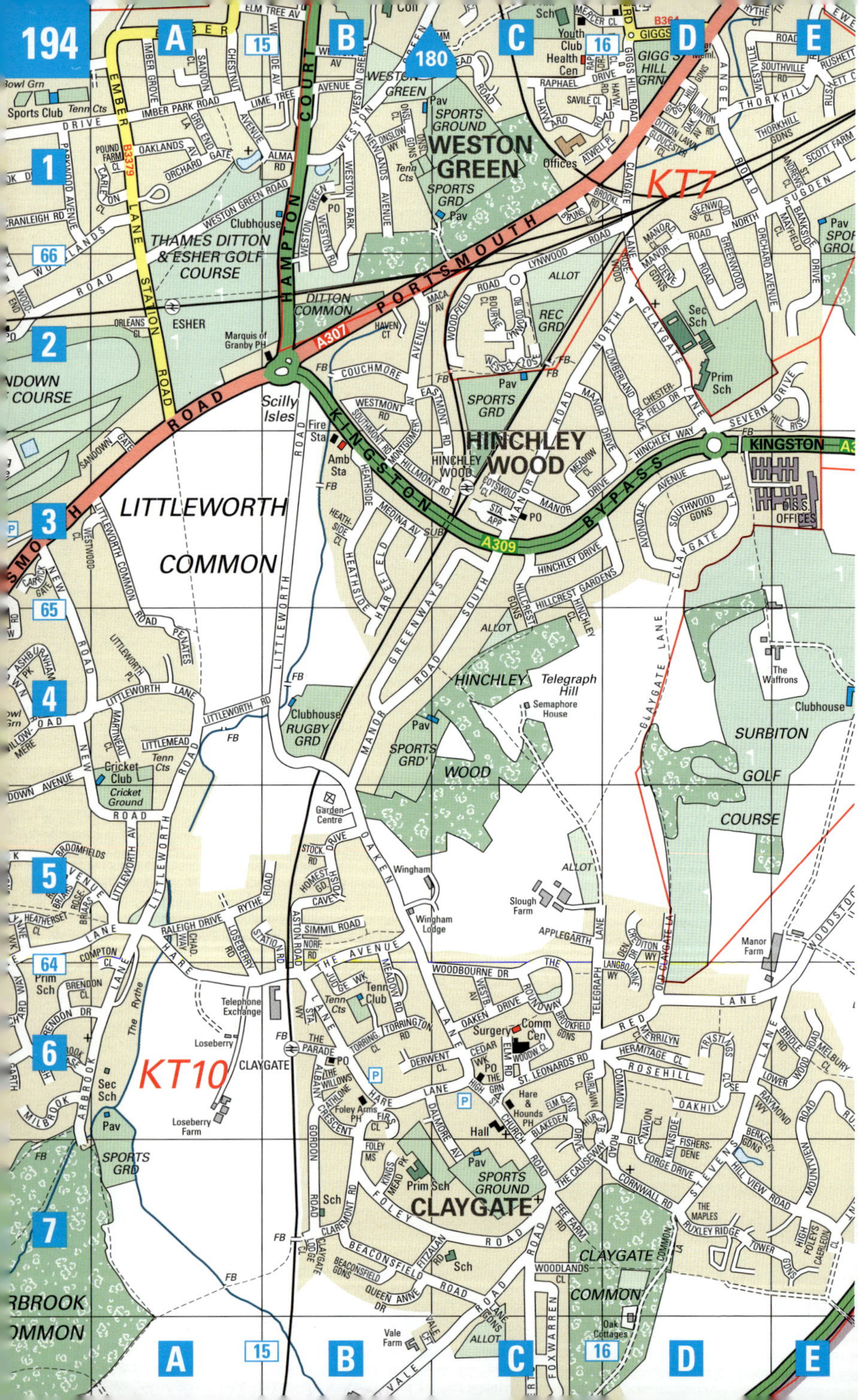
A
B
C
D
E
1
2
3
4
5
6
7
15
16
66
65
64
180
KT7
KT10
WESTON GREEN
SPORTS GROUND
SPORTS GRD
THAMES DITTON & ESHER GOLF COURSE
DITTON COMMON
ESHER
Marquis of Granby PH
Scilly Isles
LITTLEWORTH COMMON
HINCHLEY WOOD
HINCHLEY WOOD
Telegraph Hill
Semaphore House
SURBITON GOLF COURSE
The Waffrons
Clubhouse
D.S.S. OFFICES
KINGSTON BYPASS
A309
A307
PORTSMOUTH ROAD
HAMPTON COURT
B3379
B364
EMBER LANE
STATION ROAD
IMBER PARK ROAD
WESTON GREEN ROAD
LITTLEWORTH ROAD
LITTLEWORTH LANE
LITTLEWORTH COMMON ROAD
NEW ROAD
MANOR ROAD
CLAYGATE LANE
OAKEN LANE
HARE LANE
RED LANE
GREENWAYS
COUCHMORE AV
WESTMONT RD
HINCHLEY DRIVE
HILLCREST GARDENS
RALEIGH DRIVE
RYTHE ROAD
THE AVENUE
CLAYGATE COMMON
FOLEY ROAD
BEACONSFIELD RD
QUEEN ANNE DR
FOXWARREN
CLAYGATE
RUGBY GRD
Cricket Club
Cricket Ground
Garden Centre
Wingham
Wingham Lodge
Slough Farm
Manor Farm
Telephone Exchange
Loseberry
Loseberry Farm
Prim Sch
Sec Sch
Sch
Surgery
Comm Cen
Hare & Hounds PH
Foley Arms PH
Hall
Vale Farm
Oak Cottages
REC GRD
ALLOT
Pav
PO
FB
Fire Sta
Amb Sta
Offices
Youth Club
Health Cen
GIGGS HILL GRN
Sports Club
Tenn Cts

E
F
G
H
J
17
181
18
196
64
66
1
2
3
4
5
6
7
KT6
KT9
LONG DITTON
HOOK
CHESSINGTON
TOLWORTH
Cockcrow Hill
SURREY
ELMBRIDGE
KINGSTON UPON THAMES
KINGSTON BYPASS
A3
A243
A240
B3364
HOOK ROAD
EWELL ROAD
KINGSDOWNE ROAD
DITTON ROAD
ESHER BYPASS
Manor House
Management Training Cen
Woodstock Garden Centre
Hill Park Nursery
Ditton Nurseries
CEM
ALLOT
SPORTS GROUND
KING EDWARD REC GRD
MEML. GRD
LOVELACE PLAYING FIELD
Stables
Youth Cen
Elm Farm
LOWER WOOD
THE GRAPSOME
Barwell Court
Winey Hill
REC GRD
Cricket Club
CHURCH FIELDS
Bowl Club
Comm Cen
Clinic
Lib
Comm Coll
Sports Cen
Prim Sch
Sec Sch
Works
KING GEORGE'S TRADING
HOOK RISE SOUTH IND PK
Blackamoors Head PH
CHESSINGTON NORTH
CHESSINGTON SOUTH
CHESSINGTON GOLF CENTRE
Driving Range
Clubhouse
BARWELL BUSINESS PARK
Bonesgate Stream
Earthworks
Castle Hill
Dysart Sch
TOLWORTH HOSPITAL

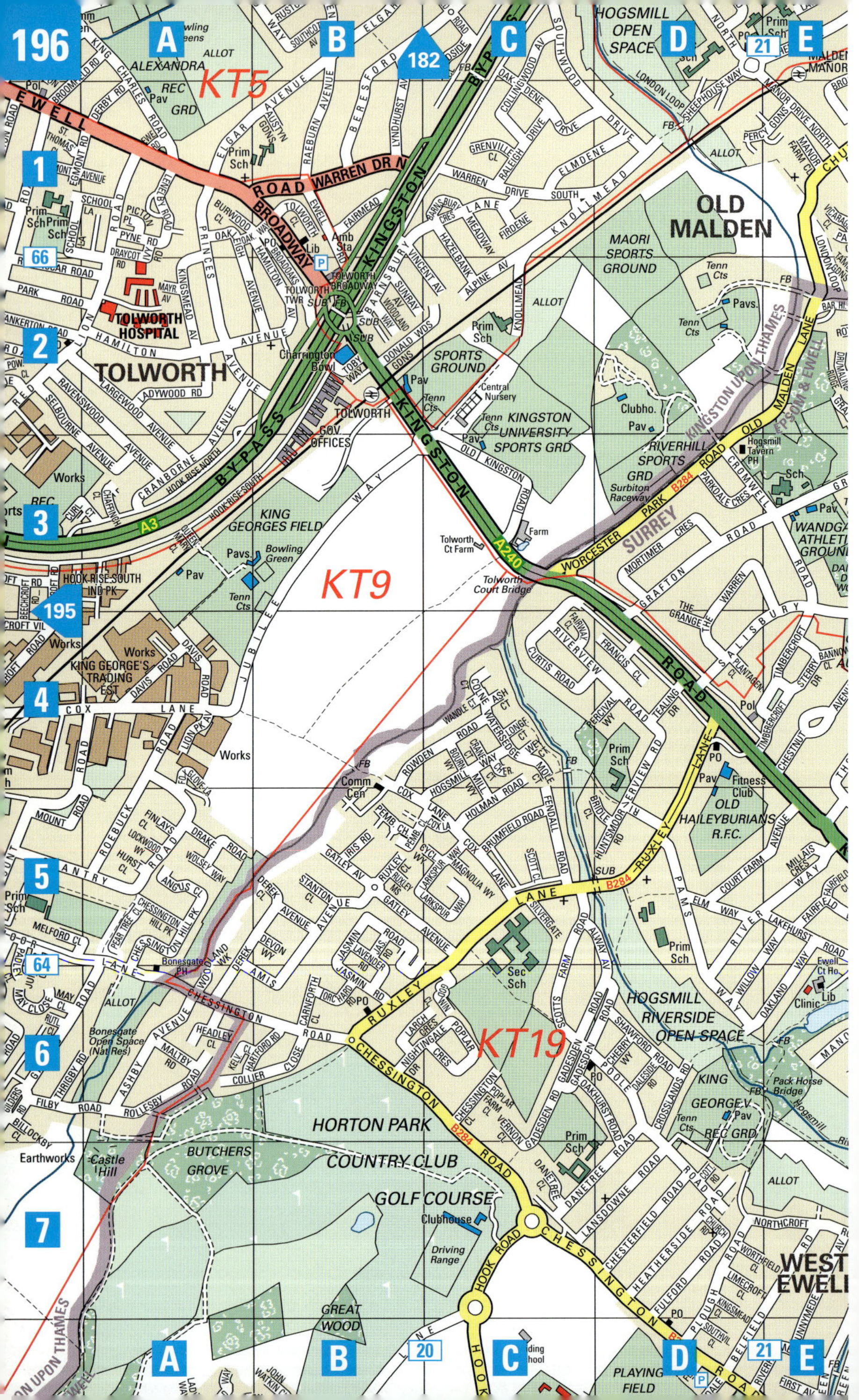
A
B
182
C
D
E
HOGSMILL OPEN SPACE
ALEXANDRA REC GRD
KT5
EWELL ROAD
BROADWAY
WARREN DR N
KINGSTON BY PASS
1
2
3
4
5
6
7
66
64
21
195
20
OLD MALDEN
MAORI SPORTS GROUND
TOLWORTH HOSPITAL
TOLWORTH
SPORTS GROUND
KINGSTON UNIVERSITY SPORTS GRD
RIVERHILL SPORTS GRD
KINGSTON UPON THAMES
EPSOM & EWELL
KING GEORGES FIELD
HOOK RISE SOUTH IND PK
KING GEORGE'S TRADING EST
KT9
SURREY
WORCESTER PARK ROAD
KINGSTON ROAD
A3
A240
B284
JUBILEE WAY
Tolworth Ct Farm
Tolworth Court Bridge
COX LANE
OLD HALEYBURIANS R.F.C.
HOGSMILL RIVERSIDE OPEN SPACE
KT19
RUXLEY LANE
CHESSINGTON ROAD
HORTON PARK COUNTRY CLUB GOLF COURSE
BUTCHERS GROVE
Castle Hill
Earthworks
GREAT WOOD
HOOK ROAD
KING GEORGE V REC GRD
WEST EWELL
PLAYING FIELD
Bonesgate Open Space (Nat Res)
Driving Range
Clubhouse

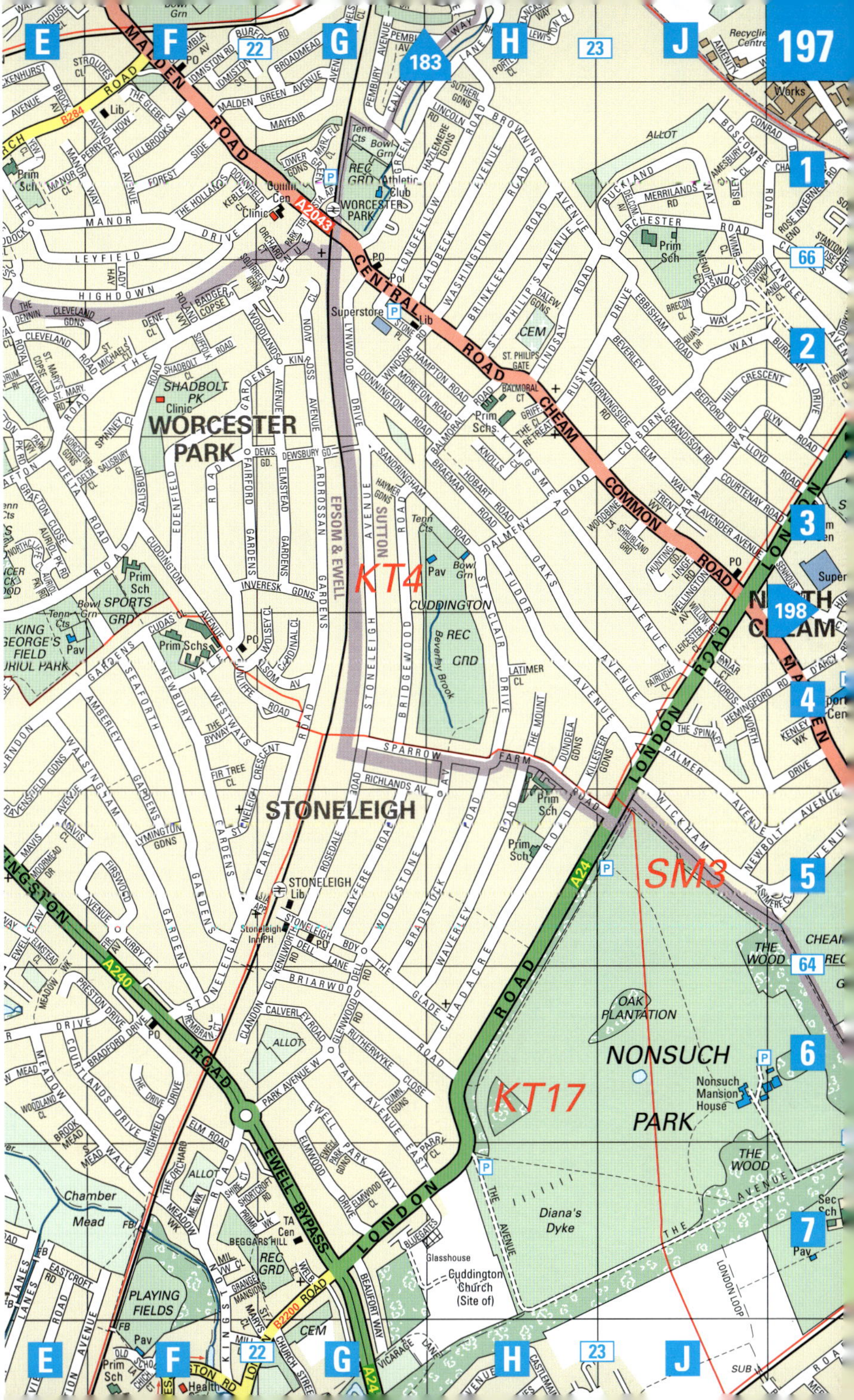
E
F
G
H
J
22
23
183
198
1
2
3
4
5
6
7
66
64
WORCESTER PARK
STONELEIGH
NORTH CHEAM
NONSUCH PARK
KT4
KT17
SM3
EPSOM & EWELL
SUTTON
MALDEN ROAD
A2043
CENTRAL ROAD
CHEAM COMMON ROAD
LONDON ROAD
A24
A240
KINGSTON ROAD
EWELL BYPASS
B284
B2200
SPARROW FARM ROAD
WICKHAM AVENUE
MANOR DRIVE
LEYFIELD
HIGHDOWN
THE AVENUE
DORCHESTER ROAD
CUDDINGTON REC GRD
Beverley Brook
SHADBOLT PK
KING GEORGE'S FIELD
SPORTS GRD
Superstore
Recycling Centre
Works
ALLOT
CEM
OAK PLANTATION
THE WOOD
Nonsuch Mansion House
Diana's Dyke
Glasshouse
Cuddington Church (Site of)
Chamber Mead
PLAYING FIELDS
LONDON LOOP
STONELEIGH Lib
Stoneleigh Inn PH
BEGGARS HILL
REC GRD
Prim Sch
Prim Schs
PO
Lib
Clinic

A
B
C
D
E
1
2
3
4
5
6
7
24
25
184
66
197
64
GARTH ROAD IND CEN
Works
CONRAD DR
BOSCOMBE RD
CHARMINSTER RD
TRAFALGAR AV
ST. ANTHONY'S HOSP
St. Raphael's Hospice
CLARKES AV
LANGLEY AVENUE
ROSE INVERNESS RD
STANTON CL
DORKING CL
BURNHAM DR
HILL CRESCENT
BEDFORD RD
GLYN ROAD
LLOYD ROAD
COURTENAY ROAD
LONDON ROAD
STONECOT HILL
STONECOT CL
ASH ROAD
OAKDENE MS
TONFIELD ROAD
POPLAR RD
FIR RD
BEECHES AV
RIDGE ROAD
MORLEY RD
ALLOT
Prim Sch
Lib
PO
Comm Cen
TA Cen
Pyl Brook
SM3
SUTTON CEMETERY
KIMPTON TRADE BUSINESS CENTRE
MINDEN ROAD
SANDIFORD RD
KIMPTON ROAD
WEALDSTONE RD
Recycling Cen
Superstore
KIMPTON LINK
WILLOW WALK
WHITTAKER RD
GARTH ROAD
SALCOMBE DR
DUNSTER AVENUE
DUDLEY DR
ARAGON AV
CHATHAM CL
GILLIAN PK RD
ELSWOOD RD
COMMON ROAD
SUTTON COMMON ROAD
B279
MORDEN WAY
ACACIA DR
TAUNTON CL
BARRINGTON RD
SHERBORNE CL
ALCORN CL
GLENTHORNE GDNS
ANGLE CL
REIGATE AVENUE REC GRD
Sec Sch
Tenn Cts
Pav
REC GRD
HARTLAND ROAD
GLASTONBURY RD
HEXHAM RD
KENSHAM RD
KIRKSTED RD
HUNSTON RD
REIGATE AVENUE
ROSE
Tennis Centre
SUTTON COMMON
FAIRLANDS AV
HURSTCOURT RD
CLENSHAM LANE
BURFORD RD
LYMESCOTE GDNS
MARLBOROUGH RD
DIBDIN RD
STAYTON ROAD
BLENHEIM ROAD
COOMBE WK
VERMONT RD
HALLMEAD RD
SUNNYHURST CL
Oldfields Trading Est
NORTHSPUR RD
ANTON CRES
COLLINGWOOD ROAD
SOUTHY CL
ALEXANDRA AV
CHAUCER AV
CHAUCER HO
SORRENTO RD
RECTORY CL
VICARAGE RD
BUSHEY RD
VALE ROAD
BUS GAR
Gas Works
Mkt
B2230
SM1
COLLINGWOOD PARK
Sutton Utd. FC
Tenn Cts
OLDFIELDS ROAD
A217
ST. DUNSTAN'S HILL
Clubho.
Bowl Grn
SPORTS GRD
Comm Cen
Superstore
CAMBERLEY CLOSE
MARLOW DRIVE
EGHAM CL
STAINES AV
CAVERSHAM AV
GANDER GREEN LANE
WATSON AV
HAMILTON AV
WESTBOURNE AV
WARNER AV
CHERTSEY DRIVE
MOLESEY DR
GREEN DRIVE
KEW CRESCENT
WALTON AVENUE
SUNBURY RD
THE MEADS
HENLEY AVENUE
BROCKS DRIVE
ST. MARGARET'S AV
KINGSTON AVENUE
CRESCENT
ESHER AV
FROGMORE CL
WINDSOR AVENUE
NORTH CHEAM
HILBERT ROAD
HAYES CRES
WRAYFIELD ROAD
MATLOCK CRES
CHARTWELL GDNS
BUXTON CRES
CARLTON CRES
ABBOTTS ROAD
NORTHFIELD CRES
MATLOCK PL
FRIENDS HILL
Fire Sta
WESTFIELD ROAD
SALTASH CL
ST. ALBAN'S ROAD
HILLDALE ROAD
ELMBROOK RD
JEFFS RD
FREDERICK RD
ALBERTA AVENUE
ALMA CRES
Clinic
Sports Cen
D'ARCY RD
CHURCH HILL ROAD
PRIORY CRESCENT
PRIORY AVENUE
PRIORY ROAD
KENLEY WK
HEMINGFORD RD
MALDEN ROAD
A2043
SPINNEY
NEWBOLT AVENUE
ASHMERE CL
NETLEY CL
CHATSWORTH RD
STOUGHTON AVENUE
TILEHURST ROAD
SOWDON ROAD
FROMONDES ROAD
FIELDSEND RD
Sec Sch
Schs
Tenn Club
ALLOT
Sutton Water Services
SHEARWATER RD
BOUR WAY
PERRETS FIELD
LOVE LA
GANDER GRN LA
WEST SUTTON
ST. JAMES AVENUE
NORMAN AVENUE
SYDNEY ROAD
BEULAH ROAD
BEAUCHAMP ROAD
ORCHARD RD
BURGESS RD
CROWN RD
CLYDE RD
Coll Youth Cen
HOOD RD
ROBIN HOOD
Prim Sch
Health Cen
CAMDEN RD
GIBSON
Sch
WESTERN ROAD
Thea
Holiday Inn
SPORTS GRD
Squash Club
A232
SUTTON
Sutton High Sch
GROVE AVENUE
THE WOOD
CHEAM REC GRD
Pav
Tenn Cts
Bowl Grn
CHEAM PARK
CHEAM
Nonsuch Mansion House
TUDOR CL
LUMLEY RD
MICKLEHAM GDNS
CHEAM PK WAY
PARK LA
PARKSIDE
BROADWAY
THE BROADWAY
Lib
Hall
HIGH ST
CHEAM ROAD
QUARRY PARK RD
REVELL RD
FAIRHOLME RD
ROSEBERY RD
DERBY ROAD
YORK ROAD
BRIDGEFIELD RD
LANDSEER RD
BERGAMS GROVE
A232 EWELL RD
EWELL ROAD
JUBILEE CL
QUEENS ACRE
ANNE BOLEYN'S WALK
KINGSWAY
STATION WAY
CHEAM MANS
SCOTSDALE CL
CHEAM
BELMONT RISE
SALISBURY AVENUE
MULGRAVE ROAD
HILLSIDE RD
ARUNDEL RD
BERESFORD ROAD
CORNWALL ROAD
HEATHER GDNS
VILLAGE ROW
WORCESTER ROAD
BRAMBLEACRES CL
GRANGE ROAD
OVERTON ROAD
LESLIE GDNS
CONWAY DR
WEYMOUTH CT
BANBURY CL
CAMBORNE RD
AUDLEY
SACKVILLE RD
PENSHURST
Nursery
OVERTON PARK REC GRD
SM2
SANDY LANE
BURDON LA
BURDON PK
UPPER MULGRAVE RD
CHAMPNEYS CL
MANOR
ARUNDEL GDNS
Sch
B283
BELMONT
GLEBE ROAD
PEACHES CLOSE
SPORTS GRD
Harefield Bridge
HOLMWOOD CL
Cricket Ground
LONDON LOOP
THE GLADE
Prim Sch
Sec Sch
Pav
SUB

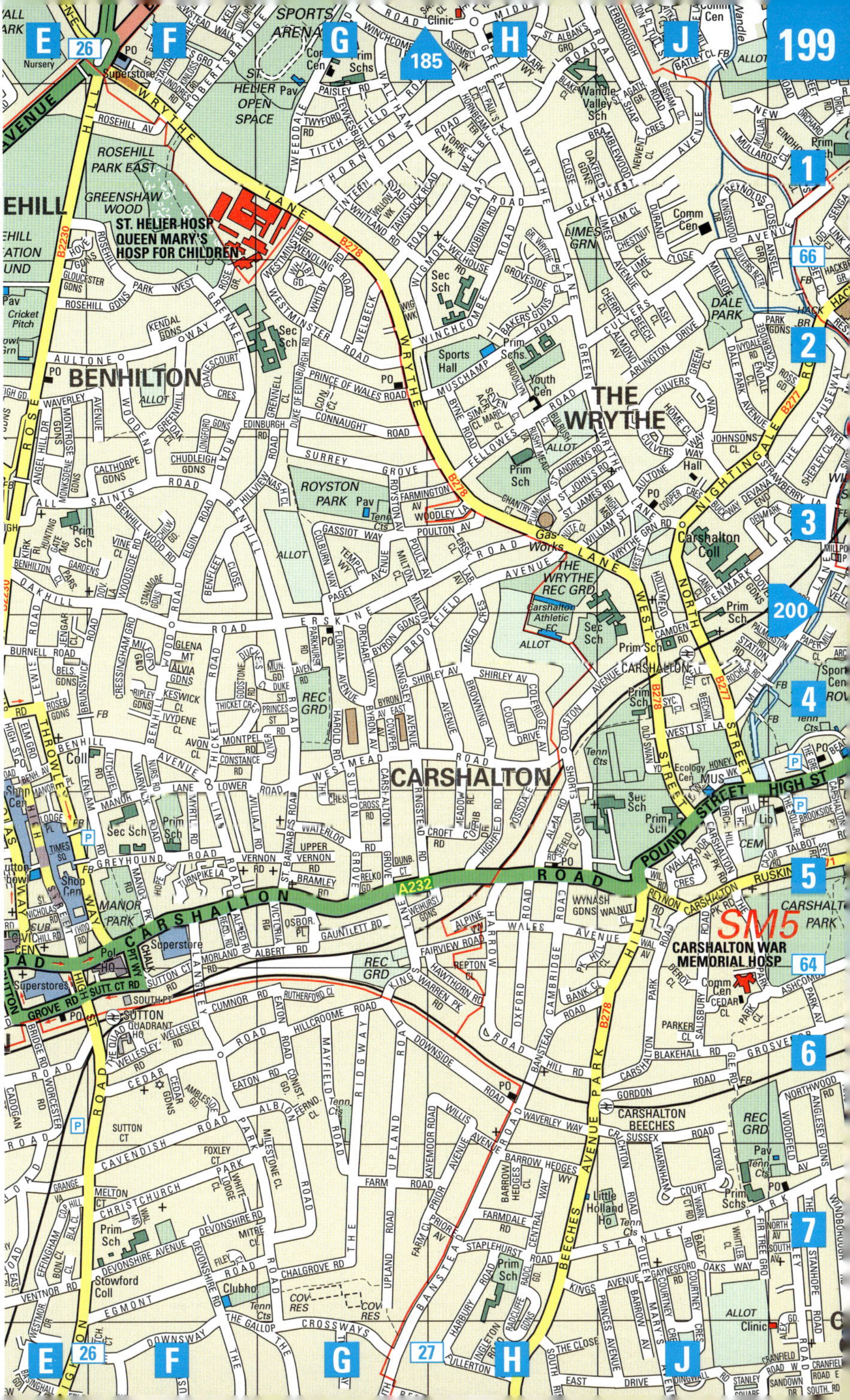
E
F
G
H
J
26
185
200
27
64
66
1
2
3
4
5
6
7
SPORTS ARENA
ST. HELIER OPEN SPACE
ROSEHILL PARK EAST
GREENSHAW WOOD
ST. HELIER HOSP
QUEEN MARY'S HOSP FOR CHILDREN
BENHILTON
THE WRYTHE
ROYSTON PARK
THE WRYTHE REC GRD
Carshalton Athletic FC
CARSHALTON
Carshalton Coll
MANOR PARK
CARSHALTON PARK
SM5
CARSHALTON WAR MEMORIAL HOSP
CARSHALTON BEECHES
Little Holland Ho
Stowford Coll
LIMES GRN
DALE PARK
Wandle Valley Sch
Sports Hall
Youth Cen
Gas Works
Ecology Cen
Superstore
Superstores
Sutton
WRYTHE LANE
ROSEHILL AV
ROSEHILL GDNS
WINCHCOMBE
ERSKINE ROAD
CARSHALTON ROAD
POUND STREET
HIGH ST
WEST STREET
NORTH STREET
NIGHTINGALE RD
CULVERS AV
BEECHES AVENUE
BANSTEAD ROAD
CHALGROVE RD
DEVONSHIRE AVENUE
CROSSWAYS
DOWNSWAY
THE GALLOP
EGMONT
A232
B278
B277
B2230

A
B
C
D
E
186
30
1
2
3
4
5
6
7
66
199
64
29
HACKBRIDGE
BEDDINGTON
BEDDINGTON PARK
WALLINGTON
SOUTH BEDDINGTON
CARSHALTON ON THE HILL
SM5
SM6
LONDON ROAD
MANOR ROAD
WOODCOTE ROAD
CROYDON ROAD
ACRE LANE
HIGH ST
STREET
NIGHTINGALE ROAD
HACKBRIDGE ROAD
BEDDINGTON LANE
PLOUGH LANE
HILLIERS LANE
SANDY LANE S
FORESTERS
STAFFORD ROAD
STANLEY PARK RD
RUSKIN ROAD
PARK LANE
BOUNDARY RD
MILE ROAD
A232
A237
B271
B272
B277
RESERVOIR
Sewage Works
Filter Beds
Sludge Beds
Irrigation Bridge
Mile Road Bridge
Beddington Farm
Sorting Office
PIONEERS INDUSTRIAL PARK
BEDDINGTON TRADING PARK WEST
FELNEX TRADING ESTATE
THE GRANGE GARDENS
WILDERNESS ISLAND
DALE PARK
THE GROVE
CARSHALTON PARK
BANDON HILL CEMETERY
MELLOWS PARK
ROUNDSHAW PARK
River Wandle
SPORTS GRD
Sports Cen
Superstore
Health Cen
Clinic
Fire Sta
ALLOT

E
F
G
H
J
31
32
187
202
66
64
1
2
3
4
5
6
7
WADDON
CROYDON
SOUTH CROYDON
CR0
CR2
PURLEY WAY
A23
A232
A236
A235
A212
B275
B271
DUPPAS HILL RD
DUPPAS HILL
WANDLE PARK
ROMAN WAY
OLD TOWN
SUMNER ROAD
LONDON RD
WELLESLEY ROAD
HIGH ST
PARK LANE
BRIGHTON ROAD
STAFFORD ROAD
DENNING AVENUE
WARHAM ROAD
WADDON WAY
PURLEY WAY PLAYING FIELDS
ROUNDSHAW PLAYING FIELD
ROUNDSHAW OPEN SPACE
HALING PARK
HALING GROVE
Whitgift Centre
Drummond Cen
Croydon Flyover
CROYDON SUB STATION
MILL LANE TRADING ESTATE
PROGRESS BUSINESS PK
STAFFORD CROSS IND EST
AMPERE WAY IND EST
WADDON MARSH
WEST CROYDON
REEVES CORNER
CHURCH STREET
GEORGE STREET
WELLESLEY ROAD
Croydon Airport Vis Cen
Aerodrome Hotel
Leisure Cen
SPORTS GRD
SPORTS GROUND
Civic Amenity Site
Superstore
Works

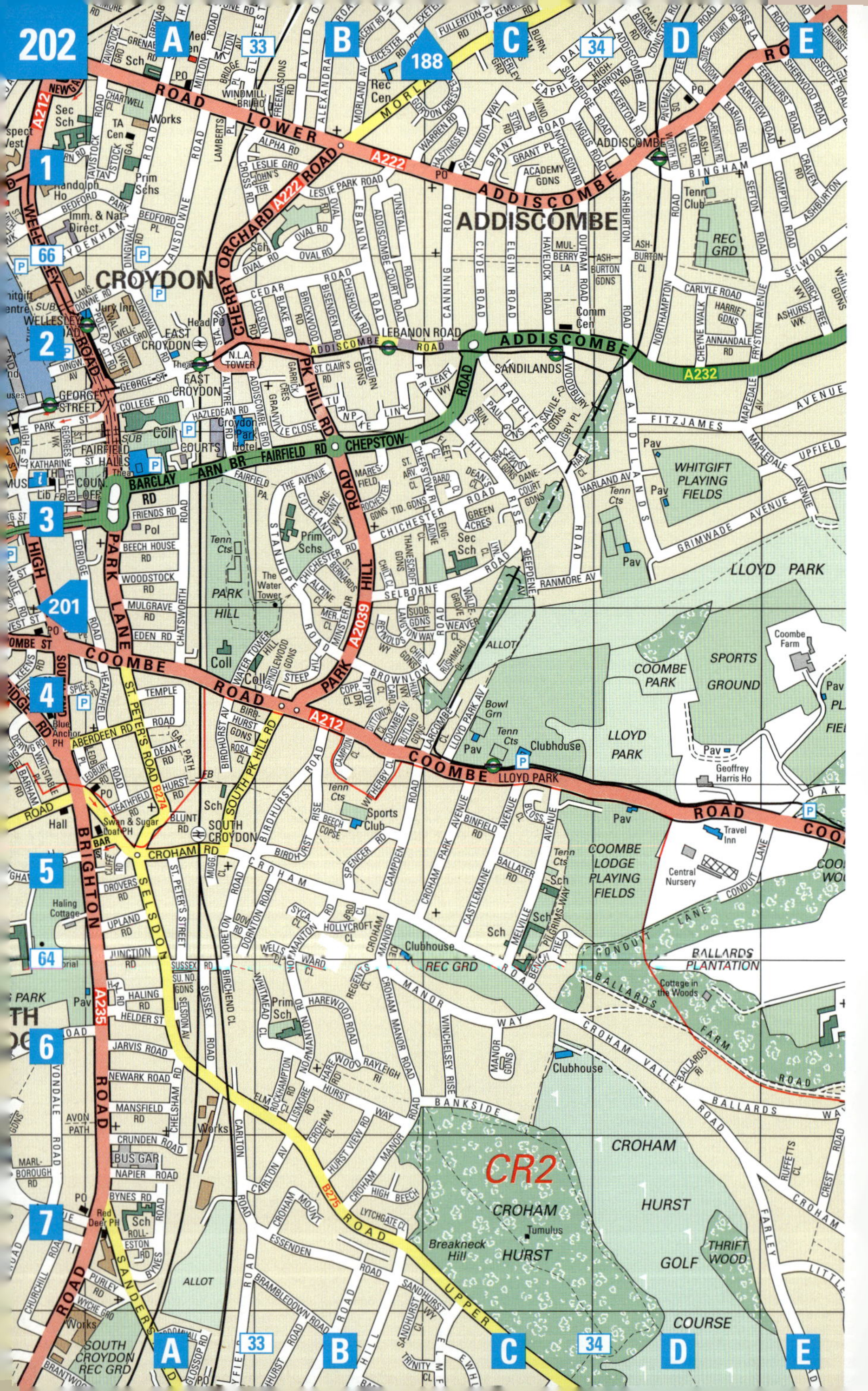
A
B
C
D
E
1
2
3
4
5
6
7
33
34
188
201
66
64
CROYDON
ADDISCOMBE
LOWER ADDISCOMBE ROAD
ADDISCOMBE ROAD
A222
A232
A212
A235
A2039
B274
B275
CHERRY ORCHARD ROAD
LEBANON ROAD
SANDILANDS
EAST CROYDON
GEORGE STREET
WELLESLEY ROAD
CHEPSTOW RD
BARCLAY RD
PARK LANE
PARK HILL RD
PARK HILL
COOMBE ROAD
LLOYD PARK
COOMBE PARK
SPORTS GROUND
WHITGIFT PLAYING FIELDS
COOMBE LODGE PLAYING FIELDS
BALLARDS PLANTATION
CROHAM HURST
CROHAM HURST GOLF COURSE
THRIFT WOOD
Breakneck Hill
Tumulus
CR2
SOUTH CROYDON
BRIGHTON ROAD
SELSDON ROAD
UPPER SELSDON ROAD
CROHAM ROAD
CROHAM MANOR ROAD
CROHAM VALLEY ROAD
BALLARDS WAY
BALLARDS FARM ROAD
CONDUIT LANE
SOUTH CROYDON REC GRD
REC GRD
Travel Inn
Central Nursery
Geoffrey Harris Ho
Coombe Farm
Clubhouse
Sports Club
Fairfield Halls
Croydon Park Hotel
The Water Tower
ALLOT
FITZJAMES AVENUE
GRIMWADE AVENUE
UPFIELD
SELWOOD RD
ASHBURTON RD
RANMORE AV
HARLAND AV
BIRDHURST RD
ST PETER'S ROAD
SOUTH PK HILL RD
CARLTON RD
ESSENDEN RD
BRAMBLEDOWN ROAD
FARLEY ROAD
BANKSIDE
HOLLYCROFT CL
WINCHELSEA RISE
MANOR WAY
CASTLEMAINE AV
COOMBE

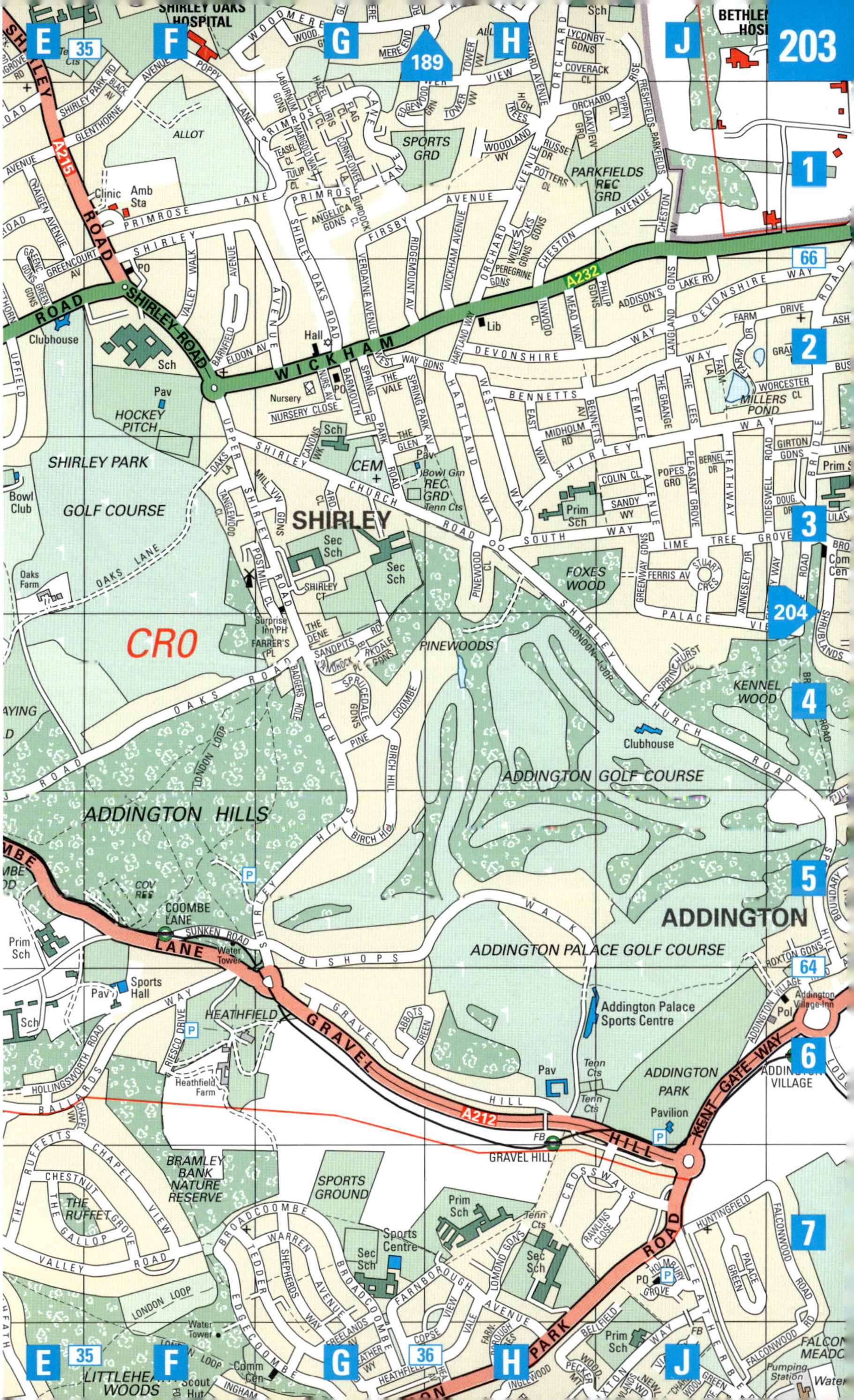

E
F
G
H
J
35
36
189
204
66
64
1
2
3
4
5
6
7
SHIRLEY OAKS HOSPITAL
SHIRLEY ROAD
A215
A232
A212
WICKHAM ROAD
SPORTS GRD
PARKFIELDS REC GRD
Clinic
Amb Sta
PRIMROSE LANE
Clubhouse
Sch
HOCKEY PITCH
SHIRLEY PARK GOLF COURSE
Bowl Club
Oaks Farm
OAKS LANE
CR0
SHIRLEY
Sec Sch
CEM
REC GRD
Bowl Grn
Tenn Cts
Prim Sch
FOXES WOOD
MILLERS POND
PINEWOODS
KENNEL WOOD
ADDINGTON GOLF COURSE
ADDINGTON HILLS
OAKS ROAD
LONDON LOOP
COOMBE LANE
SUNKEN ROAD
Water Tower
BISHOPS WALK
ADDINGTON
ADDINGTON PALACE GOLF COURSE
Addington Palace Sports Centre
Addington Village Inn
ADDINGTON VILLAGE
ADDINGTON PARK
Pavilion
KENT GATE WAY
GRAVEL HILL
HEATHFIELD
Heathfield Farm
Sports Hall
BALLARDS WAY
BRAMLEY BANK NATURE RESERVE
SPORTS GROUND
THE RUFFET
VALLEY ROAD
Sports Centre
Prim Sch
Sec Sch
FARNBOROUGH AVENUE
PARK ROAD
LITTLEHEATH WOODS
Scout Hut
Comm Cen
Pumping Station

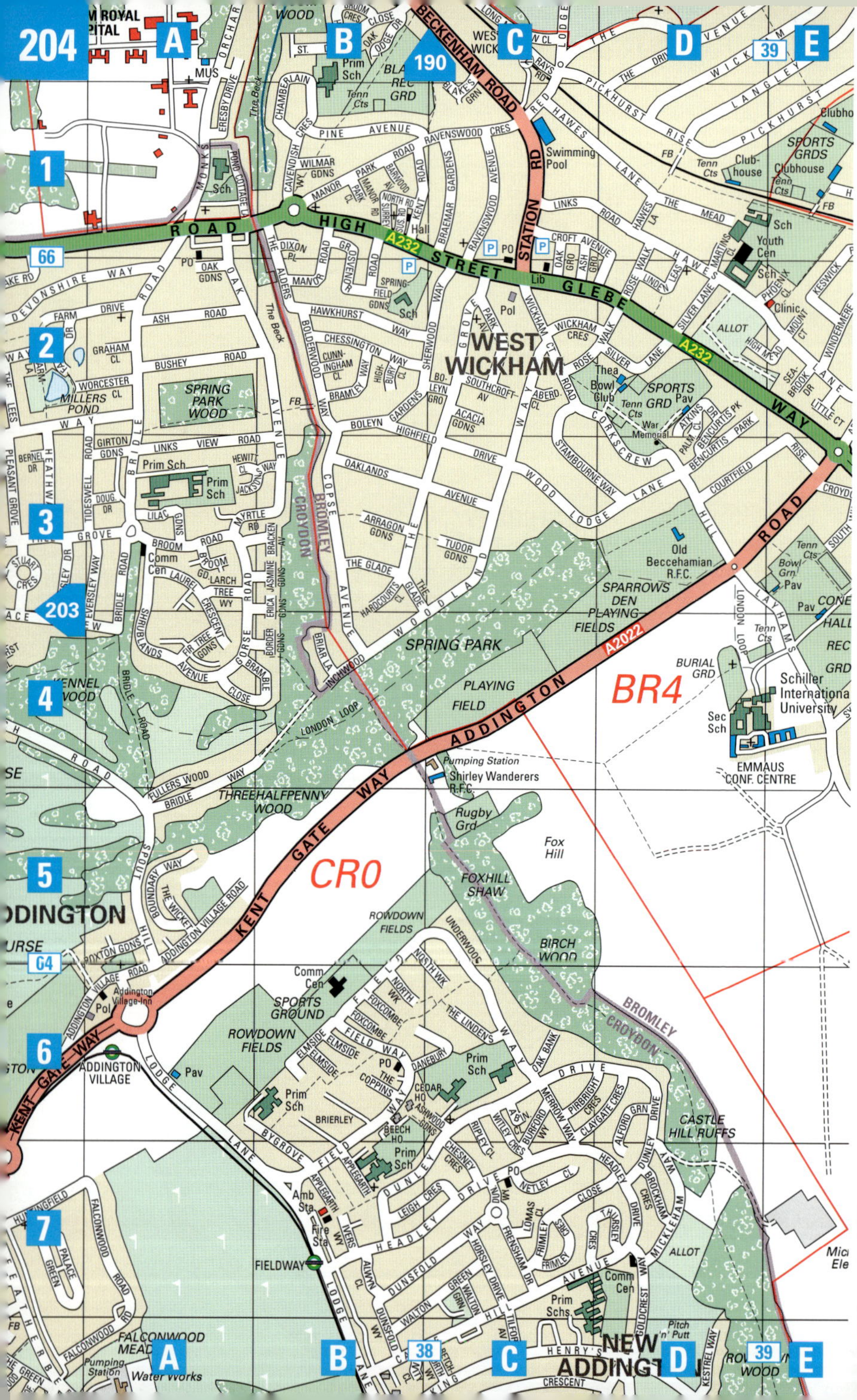
A
B
C
D
E
1
2
3
4
5
6
7
190
203
39
66
64
38
WEST WICKHAM
NEW ADDINGTON
ADDINGTON VILLAGE
BR4
CR0
HIGH STREET
GLEBE WAY
A232
A2022
ADDINGTON ROAD
KENT GATE WAY
BECKENHAM ROAD
STATION RD
CORKSCREW HILL
WOOD LODGE LANE
LAYHAMS ROAD
SPRING PARK
PLAYING FIELD
SPRING PARK WOOD
THREEHALFPENNY WOOD
KENNEL WOOD
SPARROWS DEN PLAYING FIELDS
FOXHILL SHAW
Fox Hill
BIRCH WOOD
CASTLE HILL RUFFS
ROWDOWN FIELDS
SPORTS GROUND
MILLERS POND
Old Beccehamian R.F.C.
Shirley Wanderers R.F.C.
Pumping Station
Rugby Grd
Schiller International University
EMMAUS CONF. CENTRE
BURIAL GRD
Swimming Pool
Youth Cen
SPORTS GRDS
Thea
Bowl Club
War Memorial
Comm Cen
Prim Sch
Sec Sch
Pol
PO
Lib
Clinic
Hall
ALLOT
Addington Village Inn
FIELDWAY
Amb Sta
Fire Sta
Water Works
Pitch 'n' Putt
BROMLEY
CROYDON
The Beck
SOUTHCROFT AV
ACACIA GDNS
HIGHFIELD DRIVE
OAKLANDS AVENUE
BOLEYN GARDENS
ARRAGON GDNS
TUDOR GDNS
THE GLADE
HARDCOURTS CL
INCHWOOD
BRIAR LA
LONDON LOOP
FULLERS WOOD
BRIDLE WAY
SPOUT HILL
BOUNDARY WAY
THE WICKET
ADDINGTON VILLAGE ROAD
POXTON GDNS
LODGE LANE
BYGROVE
FIELD WAY
ELMSIDE
FOXCOMBE
NORTH WK
UNDERWOOD
THE LINDENS
DANEBURY
THE COPPINS
CEDAR HO
ASHWOOD GDNS
BEECH HO
BRIERLEY
APPLEGARTH
DUNLEY DRIVE
HEADLEY DRIVE
LEIGH CRES
CHESNEY CRES
RIPLEY CL
WITLEY CRES
BURFORD WY
MERROW WAY
PIRBRIGHT CRES
CLAYGATE CRES
ALFORD GRN
NETLEY CL
LOMAS CL
FRIMLEY CRES
FRENSHAM DR
TAUNSLEY
BROCKHAM CRES
MICKLEHAM WAY
GOLDCREST WAY
CASTLE HILL AVENUE
HORSLEY DRIVE
DUNSFOLD WY
WALTON GRN
ALWYN CL
KESTREL WAY
HENRY'S
CRESCENT
FALCONWOOD ROAD
FALCONWOOD MEAD
HUNTINGFIELD
PALACE GREEN
HEATHFIELD
DEVONSHIRE WAY
FARM DRIVE
GRAHAM CL
BUSHEY ROAD
WORCESTER CL
ASH ROAD
OAK GDNS
OAK AVENUE
LINKS VIEW ROAD
GIRTON GDNS
BERNEL DR
TIDESWELL ROAD
DOUG. DR
LILAC GDNS
BROOM ROAD
BROOM GD.
LAUREL CRESCENT
LARCH TREE WY
FIR TREE GDNS
JASMINE GDNS
BRACKEN AV
ERICA GDNS
BORDER GDNS
GORSE ROAD
BRAMBLE CLOSE
SHRUBLANDS AVENUE
HEWITT CL
JACKSONS WAY
MYRTLE RD
EVERSLEY WAY
BRIDLE ROAD
STUART CRES
PLEASANT GROVE
MONKS ORCHARD
ERESBY DRIVE
POND COTTAGE LA
CHAMBERLAIN CRES
CAVENDISH WAY
WILMAR GDNS
PINE AVENUE
RAVENSWOOD CRES
RAVENSWOOD AVENUE
BRAEMAR GARDENS
KENT ROAD
NORTH RD
MANOR PARK CL
MANOR ROAD
DIXON PL
GROSVENOR ROAD
SPRINGFIELD GDNS
HAWKHURST WAY
CHESSINGTON WAY
CUNNINGHAM CL
BRAMLEY WAY
HIGHBURY CL
BOLDERWOOD WAY
SHERWOOD WAY
GROVE PARK AV
BOLEYN GRO
COPSE AVENUE
WOODLAND WAY
WICKHAM CT ROAD
WICKHAM CRES
ROSE WALK
SILVER LANE
ABERDEEN CL
STAMBOURNE WAY
ATKINS CL
PALM CL
BENCURTIS PK
BENCURTIS PARK
COURTFIELD RISE
CROFT AVENUE
OAK GRO
ASH GRO
LINKS ROAD
HAWES LANE
HAWES LA
THE MEAD
MARTINS CL
PHOENIX CL
MOUNT CT
HIGH MEAD
SEABROOK DR
WINDERMERE
KESWICK
LITTLE CT
PICKHURST RISE
PICKHURST LANE
LANGLEY WAY
WICKHAM WAY
THE DRIVE
RAYS RD
RED LODGE
BLAKES GRN
BLAKE REC GRD
Tenn Cts
Club-house
Clubhouse
Pav
FB
MUS
Sch

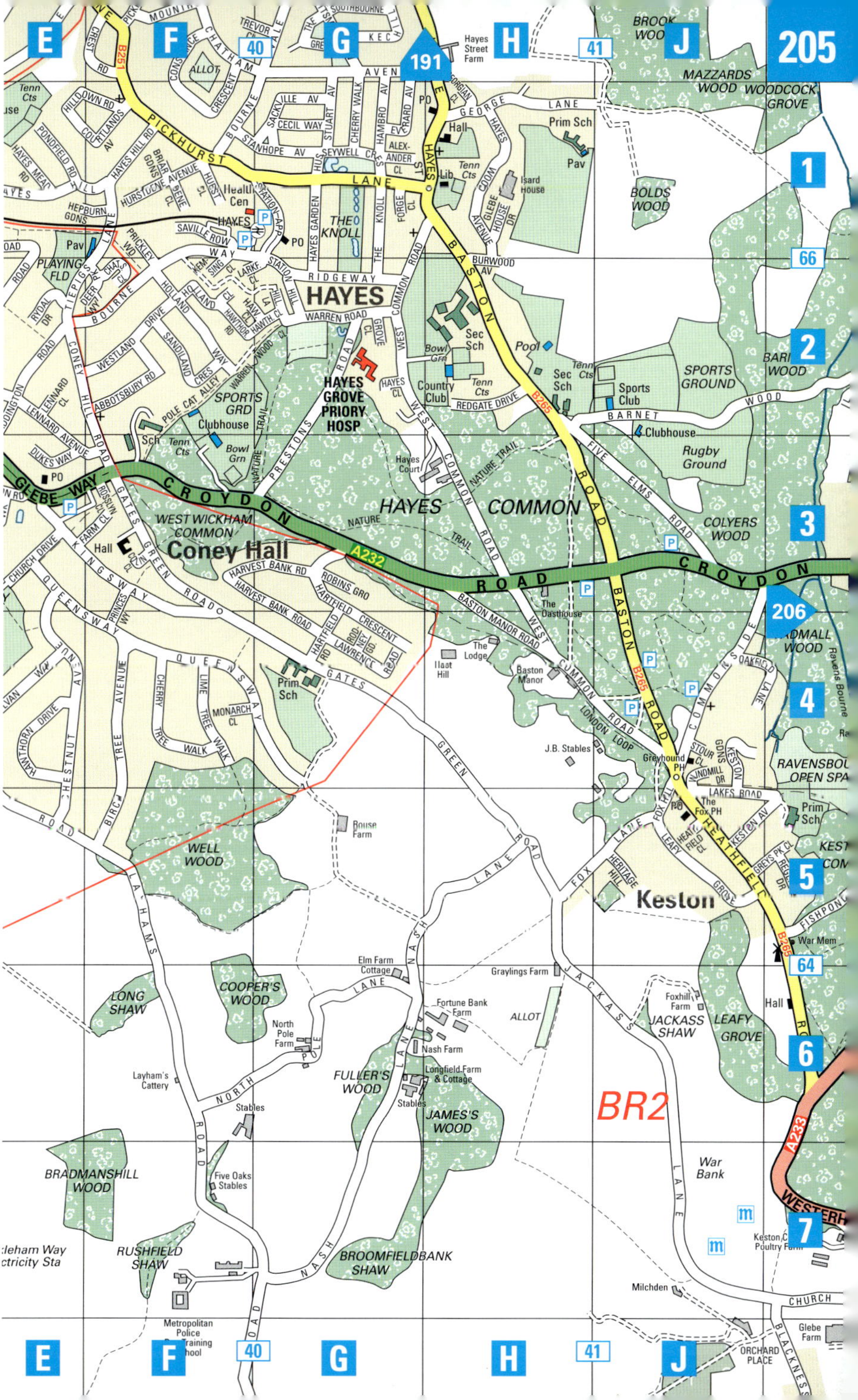
E
F
G
H
J
40
41
191
206
1
2
3
4
5
6
7
66
64
HAYES
Coney Hall
Keston
HAYES COMMON
WEST WICKHAM COMMON
HAYES GROVE PRIORY HOSP
PICKHURST LANE
CROYDON ROAD
BASTON ROAD
HEATHFIELD ROAD
A232
B265
B251
A233
BR2
MAZZARDS WOOD
WOODCOCK GROVE
BOLDS WOOD
SPORTS GROUND
Rugby Ground
COLYERS WOOD
RAVENSBOURNE OPEN SPACE
WELL WOOD
COOPER'S WOOD
LONG SHAW
FULLER'S WOOD
JAMES'S WOOD
BRADMANSHILL WOOD
RUSHFIELD SHAW
BROOMFIELDBANK SHAW
JACKASS SHAW
LEAFY GROVE
JACKASS LANE
NASH LANE
LAYHAMS ROAD
NORTH POLE LANE
GATES GREEN ROAD
FIVE ELMS ROAD
WEST COMMON ROAD
BARNET WOOD
COMMONSIDE
FOX LANE
CHURCH ROAD
BLACKNESS
ORCHARD PLACE
Metropolitan Police Training School
War Bank
Keston Court Poultry Farm
Milchden
Glebe Farm
Rouse Farm
Elm Farm Cottage
Graylings Farm
Fortune Bank Farm
Nash Farm
Longfield Farm & Cottage
North Pole Farm
Layham's Cattery
Stables
Five Oaks Stables
Foxhill Farm
J.B. Stables
Baston Manor
The Oasthouse
The Lodge
Hayes Court
Hayes Street Farm
Isard House
War Mem
Prim Sch
Sec Sch
Country Club
Sports Club
Clubhouse
Health Cen
PO
Lib
Hall
Pav
Tenn Cts
Bowl Grn
THE KNOLL
RIDGEWAY
WARREN ROAD
QUEENSWAY
KINGSWAY
CHURCH DRIVE
HAWTHORN DRIVE
GLEBE WAY
CONEY HILL ROAD
HARVEST BANK RD
HARTFIELD CRESCENT
STATION HILL
HOLLAND WAY
WESTLAND DRIVE
SANDILANDS CRES
POLE CAT ALLEY
PRESTONS ROAD
REDGATE DRIVE
BURWOOD AV
GEORGE LANE
BOURNE WAY
LAKES ROAD
KESTON AV
FISHPONDS RD
Greyhound PH
The Fox PH
ALLOT
Ilaat Hill

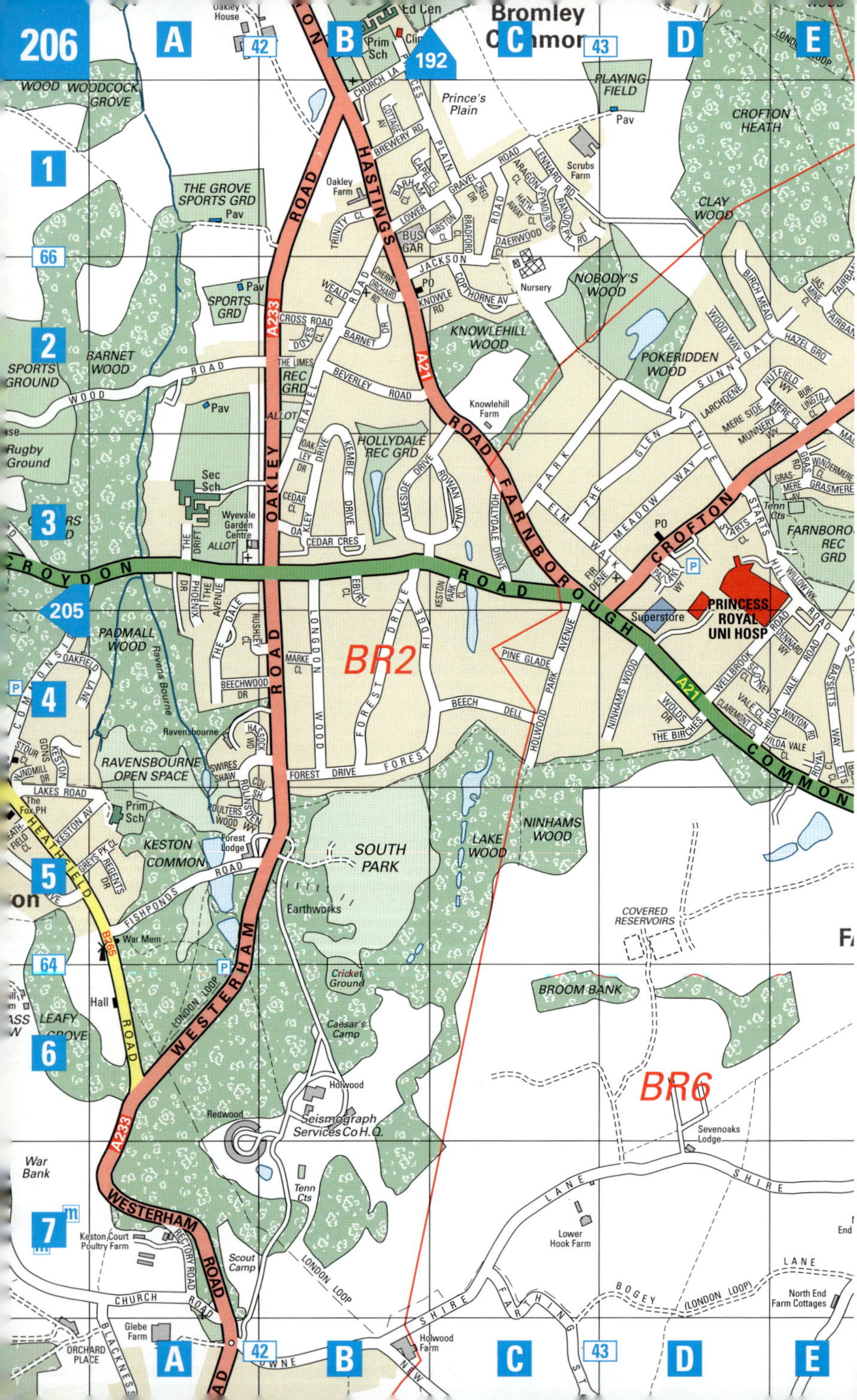
A
B
C
D
E
1
2
3
4
5
6
7
42
43
192
205
66
64
Bromley Common
Prince's Plain
PLAYING FIELD
CROFTON HEATH
WOOD
WOODCOCK GROVE
THE GROVE SPORTS GRD
Pav
SPORTS GRD
SPORTS GROUND
BARNET WOOD
Rugby Ground
Oakley Farm
HASTINGS ROAD
OAKLEY ROAD
A233
A21
CHURCH LA
BREWERY RD
COTTAGE AV
PLAIN
BARHAM CL
CAPEL CL
GRAVEL RD
LOWER GRAVEL RD
TRINITY CL
RIBSTON CL
BRADFORD DR
DAERWOOD CL
ARAGON CL
SEYMOUR DR
HATHAWAY CL
LENNARD RD
RANDOLPH RD
Scrubs Farm
CLAY WOOD
NOBODY'S WOOD
Nursery
JACKSON RD
CHERRY ORCHARD RD
PO
KNOWLE RD
COPTHORNE AV
WEALD CL
BUS GAR
CROSS ROAD
DOVES CL
BARNET DR
KNOWLEHILL WOOD
POKERIDDEN WOOD
THE LIMES REC GRD
BEVERLEY ROAD
Knowlehill Farm
WOOD ROAD
ALLOT
HOLLYDALE REC GRD
HOLLYDALE DRIVE
KEMBLE DRIVE
LAKESIDE DRIVE
ROWAN WALK
FARNBOROUGH ROAD
CROFTON ROAD
Sec Sch
Wyevale Garden Centre
THE DRIFT
CEDAR CL
CEDAR CRES
OAKLEY DR
PARK AVENUE
ELM WALK
THE GLEN
MEADOW WAY
SUNNYDALE
LARCHDENE
WOOD WAY
BIRCH MEAD
HAZEL GRO
NUTFIELD WY
MERE SIDE
MERE CL
MUNNERY WY
WINDERMERE RD
GRASMERE RD
Tenn Cts
FARNBOROUGH REC GRD
PRINCESS ROYAL UNI HOSP
Superstore
FIR DENE
PALLANT WY
STARTS CL
STARTS HILL
WILLOW WK
DENNARD WY
CROYDON ROAD
EBURY CL
KESTON PARK CL
RIDGE
PADMALL WOOD
Ravens Bourne
THE AVENUE
PHOENIX DR
RUSHEY CL
THE DALE
LONGDON WOOD
MARKE CL
BEECHWOOD DR
FOREST DRIVE
BEECH DELL
PINE GLADE
HOLWOOD PARK AVENUE
NINHAMS WOOD
WOLDS DR
THE BIRCHES
WELLBROOK RD
SCONEY
CLAREMONT CL
VALE CL
HILDA VALE RD
WINTON RD
BASSETTS WAY
COMMON
BR2
OAKFIELD LANE
KESTON GDNS
STOUR CL
WINDMILL DR
Ravensbourne
RAVENSBOURNE OPEN SPACE
HASSOCK WD
SWIRES SHAW
COLE SH
ROUNDEN WY
POULTERS WOOD
Forest Lodge
LAKES ROAD
The Fox PH
HEATHFIELD
KESTON AV
GREYS PK CL
REGENTS DR
Prim Sch
KESTON COMMON
FISHPONDS ROAD
SOUTH PARK
LAKE WOOD
NINHAMS WOOD
Earthworks
COVERED RESERVOIRS
War Mem
B265
Cricket Ground
Caesar's Camp
BROOM BANK
Hall
LEAFY GROVE
LONDON LOOP
WESTERHAM ROAD
Holwood
Seismograph Services Co H.Q.
Redwood
BR6
Sevenoaks Lodge
SHIRE LANE
War Bank
Tenn Cts
Lower Hook Farm
Keston Court Poultry Farm
RECTORY ROAD
Scout Camp
CHURCH ROAD
FARTHING ST
BOGEY LANE
North End Farm Cottages
Glebe Farm
ORCHARD PLACE
BLACKNESS
Holwood Farm
NEW

E
F
G
H
J
44
193
45
66
65
64
1
2
3
4
5
6
7
ORPINGTON
BR5
BR6
ROUNDABOUT WOOD
GUMPING COMMON
CROFTON ROAD
STATION ROAD
SEVENOAKS ROAD
HIGH STREET
FARNBOROUGH WAY
FARNBOROUGH HILL
FARNBOROUGH HIGH STREET
A232
A223
B2158
ORPINGTON HOSPITAL
NEWSTEAD WOOD
DARRICK COMMON
DARRICK WOOD
PLAYING FIELD
THE GREEN
FARNBOROUGH
Sports Club
SPORTS GRD
ALLOT
The Manse
Mill Hill
CHURCH END PLANTATION
RAMUS WOOD
Green Street Green
COCKSETT PLANTATION
Cocksett Hill
HIGH ELMS COUNTRY PARK
Nature Centre
Woodpiece
WHITELANDS WOOD
Clubhouse
Clockhouse
THE ROOKERY
HIGH ELMS
BLACKLANDS
LONDON LOOP
Denbarn Farm
Chelsfield Hall Farm
ROUNDS WOOD
Rose & Crown PH
Social Club
GLENTRAMMON REC GRD
Pav
BUS STA
Tenn Club
Swim Pool
Clinic
Pumping Sta
War Mem

West End theatres & cinemas

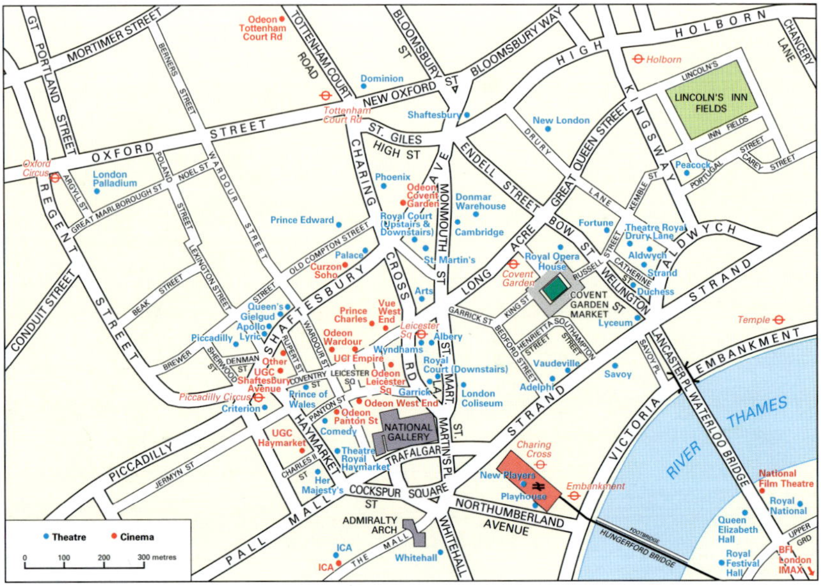

Theatres

Adelphi *0870 403 0303*
Albery *0870 060 6621*
Aldwych *020 7379 3367*
Apollo *020 7494 5070*
Arts *020 7836 2132*
Cambridge *020 7494 5080*
Comedy *0870 060 6637*
Criterion *020 7839 8811*
Dominion *08706 077400*
Donmar Warehouse *0870 060 6624*
Duchess *020 7494 5075*
Fortune *0870 060 6626*
Garrick *020 7494 5085*
Gielgud *020 7494 5065*
Her Majesty's *020 7494 5400*
ICA *020 7930 3647*
London Coliseum *020 7632 8300*
London Palladium *020 7494 5020*
Lyceum *08706 063441*
Lyric *020 7494 5045*
New London *0870 890 0141*
New Players *0870 033 2626*
Palace *0870 895 5579*
Peacock *020 7863 8222*
Phoenix *0870 060 6629*
Piccadilly *0870 060 6630*
Playhouse *020 7839 4401*
Prince Edward *020 7447 5400*
Prince of Wales *0870 850 0393*
Queen Elizabeth Hall *020 7921 0600*
Queen's *020 7494 5040*
Royal Court Jerwood Theatre Downstairs *020 7565 5050*
Royal Court Jerwood Theatre Upstairs *020 7565 5050*
Royal Festival Hall *020 7921 0600*
Royal National *020 7452 3400*
Royal Opera House *020 7304 4000*
St. Martin's *020 7836 1443*
Savoy *020 7836 8888*
Shaftesbury *020 7379 5399*
Strand *0870 850 9170*
Theatre Royal, Drury Lane *020 7494 5060*
Theatre Royal, Haymarket *020 7930 8890*
Vaudeville *08708 900511*
Whitehall *0870 060 6632*
Wyndhams *0870 060 6633*

Cinemas

BFI London IMAX *0870 787 2525*
Curzon Soho *020 7734 2255*
ICA *020 7930 3647*
National Film Theatre *020 7928 3232*
Odeon Leicester Sq *0871 224 4007*
Odeon Panton St *0871 224 4007*
Odeon Covent Garden *0871 224 4007*
Odeon Tottenham Court Rd *0871 224 4007*
Odeon Wardour Street *0871 224 4007*
Odeon West End *0871 224 4007*
Other *020 7437 0757*
Prince Charles *020 7437 7003*
UCI Empire Leicester Sq *08700 102030*
UGC Haymarket *08709 070712*
UGC Shaftesbury Avenue *0871 200 2000*
Vue West End *0871 224 0240*

West End shopping

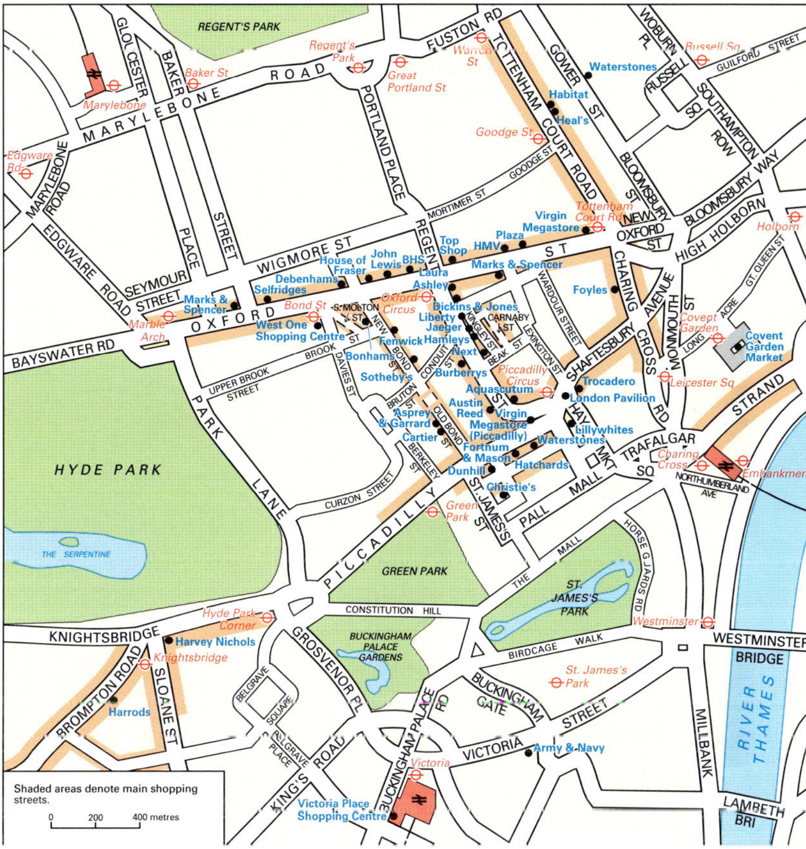

Shops

Aquascutum *020 7675 8200*
Army & Navy *020 7834 1234*
Asprey & Garrard
020 7493 6767
Austin Reed *020 7534 7777*
BHS (Oxford St)
020 7629 2011
Bonhams *020 7393 3900*
Burberrys *020 7968 0000*
Cartier *020 7408 5700*
Christie's *020 7839 9060*
Covent Garden Market
020 7836 9136
Debenhams *020 7580 3000*
Dickins & Jones *020 7734 7070*
Dunhill *020 7355 9500*
Fenwick *020 7629 9161*
Fortnum & Mason
020 7734 8040
Foyles *020 7437 5660*
Habitat (Tottenham Court Rd)
020 7631 3880
Hamleys *08703 332455*
Harrods *020 7730 1234*
Harvey Nichols *020 7235 5000*
Hatchards *020 7439 9921*
Heal's *020 7636 1666*
HMV *020 7631 3423*
House of Fraser *0870 160 7258*
Jaeger *020 7200 4015*
John Lewis *020 7629 7711*
Laura Ashley (Regent St)
020 7355 1363
Liberty *020 7734 1234*
Lillywhites *0870 333 9602*
London Pavilion *020 7439 1791*
Marks & Spencer
(Marble Arch) *020 7935 4422*
Marks & Spencer Pantheon
(Oxford St) *020 7437 7722*
Next (Regent St)
020 7434 2515
Plaza Shopping Centre, Oxford St
020 7637 8811
Selfridges *0870 837 7377*
Sotheby's *020 7293 5000*
Top Shop & Top Man
020 7636 7700
Trocadero *09068 881100*
Victoria Place Shopping Centre
020 7931 8811
Virgin Megastore
020 7631 1234
Virgin Megastore (Piccadilly)
020 7439 2500
Waterstones (Gower St)
020 7636 1577
Waterstones (Piccadilly)
020 7851 2400

Index

How to use this index

This index combines entries for street names, place names and places of interest.

Place names are shown in capital letters,

e.g. **ACTON**, W3 . . . .**126** A1

These include towns, villages and localities within the area covered by this atlas.

Places of interest are shown with a star symbol,

e.g. ★ **British Mus**, WC1 . . . . .**18** A2

These include parks, museums, galleries, and other important buildings or locations of tourist interest.

All other entries are for street names. When there is more than one street with exactly the same name then that name is shown only once in the index. It is then followed by a list of entries for each postal district that contains a street with that same name. For example, there are three streets called Appleby Close in this atlas and the index entry shows that one of these is in London postal district E4, one is in London postal district N15 and one is in Twickenham, TW2.

Appleby Cl, E4 . . . .**62** C6
N15 . . . .**76** A5
Twickenham TW2 . . . . .**162** A2

All entries are followed by the page number and grid reference on which the name will be found. So, in the example above, **Appleby Close,** E4 will be found on page **62** in square C6. All entries are indexed to the largest scale map on which they are shown.

The index also contains some street names which are not actually shown on the maps because there is not enough space to name them. In these cases the adjoining or nearest named thoroughfare to such streets is shown in the index in *italics,* and the reference indicates where the unnamed street is located *off* the named thoroughfare.

e.g. **Bacton St**, E2
off Roman Rd **113** F3

This means that Bacton Street is not named on the map, but it is located *off* Roman Road on page **113** in square F3.

A strict letter-by-letter alphabetical order is followed in this index. All non-alphabetic characters such as spaces, hyphens or apostrophes are not included in the index order. For example Belle Vue Road and Bellevue Road will be found listed together.

Standard terms such as Avenue, Close, Rise and Road are abbreviated in the index but are ordered alphabetically as if given in full. So, for example, **Abbots Ri** comes before **Abbots Rd**.

Names beginning with a definite article (i.e. The) are indexed from their second word onwards with the article being placed at the end of the name,

e.g. **Avenue, The**, E4 . . . .**62** D6

The alphabetical order extends to include postal information so that where two or more streets have exactly the same name, London postal district references are given first in alpha-numeric order and are followed by non-London post town references in alphabetical order, e.g. Appleby Close, E4 is followed by Appleby Close, N15 and then Appleby Close, Twickenham TW2.

In cases where there are two or more streets of the same name in the same postal area, extra information is given in brackets to aid location. For example, High St, Orpington BR6 (Farnborough), and High St, Orpington BR6 (Green St Grn), distinguishes between two streets called High Street which are both in the post town of Orpington, within the same postal district of BR6.

Extra locational information is also given for some localities within large post towns. This is also to aid location.

e.g. **Alford Grn**, Croy. (New Adgtn.) CR0

This street is within the locality of New Addington which is part of the post town of Croydon, and it is within postal district CR0.

A full list of locality and post town abbreviations used in this atlas is given below.

General abbreviations

Acad	Academy	Br	Bridge	Circ	Circus	Cov	Covered
All	Alley	BUPA	British United Provident Association	Cl	Close	Crem	Crematorium
Allot	Allotments			Co	County	Cres	Crescent
Amb	Ambulance			Coll	College	Ct	Court
App	Approach	C of E	Church of England	Comb	Combined	Cts	Courts
Arc	Arcade			Comm	Community	Ctyd	Courtyard
Assoc	Association	Cath	Cathedral	Comp	Comprehensive	Dep	Depot
Av	Avenue	Cem	Cemetery	Conf	Conference	Dept	Department
Bdy	Broadway	Cen	Central, Centre	Cont	Continuing	Dev	Development
Bk	Bank	Cft	Croft	Conv	Convent	Dr	Drive
Bldg	Building	Cfts	Crofts	Cor	Corner	Dws	Dwellings
Bldgs	Buildings	Ch	Church	Coron	Coroners	E	East
Boul	Boulevard	Chyd	Churchyard	Cors	Corners	Ed	Education, Educational
Bowl	Bowling	Cin	Cinema	Cotts	Cottages		

Elec	Electricity
Embk	Embankment
Est	Estate
Ex	Exchange
Exhib	Exhibition
FB	Footbridge
FC	Football Club
Fld	Field
Flds	Fields
Fm	Farm
GM	Grant Maintained
Gall	Gallery
Gar	Garage
Gdn	Garden
Gdns	Gardens
Gen	General
Govt	Government
Gra	Grange
Grad	Graduate
Gram	Grammar
Grd	Ground
Grds	Grounds
Grn	Green
Grns	Greens
Gro	Grove
Gros	Groves
Gt	Great
HQ	Headquarters
Ho	House
Hos	Houses
Hosp	Hospital
Hts	Heights
Ind	Industrial
Indep	Independent
Inf	Infant(s)
Inst	Institute
Int	International
JM	Junior Mixed
JMI	Junior Mixed & Infant(s)
Jun	Junior
Junct	Junction
La	Lane
Las	Lanes
Lib	Library
Lit	Literary
Lo	Lodge
Lwr	Lower
Mag	Magistrates
Mans	Mansions
Med	Medical, Medicine
Mem	Memorial
Met	Metropolitan
Mid	Middle
Mkt	Market
Mkts	Markets
Ms	Mews
Mt	Mount
Mus	Museum
N	North
NHS	National Health Service
NT	National Trust
Nat	National
Nurs	Nursery
PH	Public House
PO	Post Office
PRU	Pupil Referral Unit
Par	Parade
Pas	Passage
Pav	Pavilion
Pk	Park
Pl	Place
Pol	Police
Poly	Polytechnic
Prec	Precinct
Prep	Preparatory
Prim	Primary
Prom	Promenade
Pt	Point
Quad	Quadrant
RC	Roman Catholic
Rd	Road
Rds	Roads
Rec	Recreation
Rehab	Rehabilitation
Res	Reservoir, Residence
Ri	Rise
S	South
SM	Secondary Mixed
Sch	School
Schs	Schools
Sec	Secondary
Sen	Senior
Shop	Shopping
Spec	Special
Sq	Square
St	Street
St.	Saint
Sta	Station
Sts	Streets
Sub	Subway
Swim	Swimming
TA	Territorial Army
TH	Town Hall
Tech	Technical, Technology
Tenn	Tennis
Ter	Terrace
Thea	Theatre
Trd	Trading
Twr	Tower
Twrs	Towers
Uni	University
Upr	Upper
VA	Voluntary Aided
VC	Voluntary Controlled
Vet	Veterinary
Vil	Villa
Vil	Villas
Vw	View
W	West
Wd	Wood
Wds	Woods
Wf	Wharf
Wk	Walk
Wks	Works
Yd	Yard

Locality and post town abbreviations

In the list of abbreviations shown below, post towns are in **bold** type

Bark.	**Barking**
Barn.	**Barnet**
Barne.	Barnehurst
Beck.	**Beckenham**
Bedd.	Beddington
Bedd.Cor.	Beddington Corner
Belv.	**Belvedere**
Bex.	**Bexley**
Bexh.	**Bexleyheath**
Borwd.	**Borehamwood**
Brent.	**Brentford**
Brom.	**Bromley**
Buck.H.	**Buckhurst Hill**
Bushey Hth	Bushey Heath
Carp.Pk	Carpenders Park
Cars.	**Carshalton**
Chad.Hth	Chadwell Heath
Chess.	**Chessington**
Chig.	**Chigwell**
Chis.	**Chislehurst**
Clay.	Claygate
Cockfos.	Cockfosters
Coll.Row	Collier Row
Cran.	Cranford
Croy.	**Croydon**
Dag.	**Dagenham**
Dart.	**Dartford**
E.Bed.	East Bedfont
E.Croy.	East Croydon
E.Mol.	**East Molesey**
Ealing Com.	Ealing Common
Eastcote Vill.	Eastcote Village
Edg.	**Edgware**
Elm.Wds	Elmstead Woods
Enf.	**Enfield**
Epp.	**Epping**
Farnboro.	Farnborough
Felt.	**Feltham**
Grn St Grn	Green Street Green
Grnf.	**Greenford**
Hackbr.	Hackbridge
Han.	Hanworth
Har.	**Harrow**
Har.Hill	Harrow on the Hill
Har.Wld	Harrow Weald
Harm.	Harmondsworth
Hat.	**Hatfield**
Hatt.Cr.	Hatton Cross
High Barn.	High Barnet
Highams Pk	Highams Park
Hinch.Wd	Hinchley Wood
Hmptn H.	Hampton Hill
Hmptn W.	Hampton Wick
Hmptn.	Hampton
Houns.	**Hounslow**
Houns.W.	Hounslow West
Hthrw Air.	Heathrow Airport
Hthrw Air.N.	Heathrow Airport North
Ilf.	**Ilford**
Islw.	**Isleworth**
Kes.	**Keston**
Kings.T.	**Kingston upon Thames**
Long Dit.	Long Ditton
Loug.	**Loughton**
Lt.Hth	Little Heath
Lwr Sydenham	**Lower Sydenham**
Mitch.	**Mitcham**
Mitch.Com.	Mitcham Common
Mord.	**Morden**
Mots.Pk	Motspur Park
N.Finchley	North Finchley
N.Har.	North Harrow
N.Mal.	**New Malden**
New Adgtn	New Addington
New Barn.	New Barnet
Northumb.Hth	Northumberland Heath
Norwood Junct.	Norwood Junction
Nthlt.	Northolt
Nthwd.	**Northwood**
Orp.	**Orpington**
Petts Wd	Petts Wood
Pnr.	**Pinner**
Pot.B.	**Potters Bar**
Pur.	**Purley**
Rain.	Rainham
Rich.	**Richmond**
Rod.Val.	Roding Valley
Rom.	**Romford**
Ruis.	**Ruislip**
S.Croy.	**South Croydon**
S.Har.	South Harrow
S.Norwood	South Norwood
S.Oxhey	South Oxhey
S.Ruis.	South Ruislip
Scad.Pk	Scadbury Park
Short.	Shortlands
Sid.	**Sidcup**
St.P.Cray	St. Paul's Cray
Stai.	**Staines**
Stan.	**Stanmore**
Stanw.	Stanwell
Sthl Grn	Southall Green
Sthl.	**Southall**
Sun.	**Sunbury-on-Thames**
Surb.	**Surbiton**
Sutt.	**Sutton**
T.Ditt.	**Thames Ditton**
Tedd.	**Teddington**
Th.Hth.	**Thornton Heath**
They.B.	Theydon Bois
Tkgtn	Tokyngton
Twick.	**Twickenham**
Uxb.	**Uxbridge**
W.Croy.	West Croydon
W.Ealing	West Ealing
W.Ewell	West Ewell
W.Mol.	**West Molesey**
W.Wick.	**West Wickham**
Wall.	**Wallington**
Walt.	**Walton-on-Thames**
Wat.	**Watford**
Wdf.Grn.	**Woodford Green**
Well.	**Welling**
Wem.	**Wembley**
West Dr.	**West Drayton**
Wldste	Wealdstone
Woodside Pk	Woodside Park
Wor.Pk.	**Worcester Park**
Yiew.	Yiewsley

1 Canada Sq, E14 . . . **134** B1
30 St. Mary Axe, EC3
off St. Mary Axe . . . **112** B6
99 Bishopsgate, EC2
off Bishopsgate . . . **112** B6

A

Aaron Hill Rd, E6 . . . **116** D5
Abberley Ms, SW4
off Cedars Rd . . . **150** B3
Abbess Cl, E6
off Oliver Gdns . . . **116** B5
SW2 . . . **169** H1
Abbeville Ms, SW4
off Clapham Pk Rd . . . **150** D4
Abbeville Rd, N8
off Barrington Rd . . . **74** D4
SW4 . . . **150** C6
Abbey Av, Wem. HA0 . . . **105** H2
Abbey Business Cen, SW8
off Ingate Pl . . . **150** B1
Abbey Cl, E5 . . . **94** D4
SW8 . . . **150** D1
Hayes UB3 . . . **122** B1
Northolt UB5
off Invicta Gro . . . **103** F3
Pinner HA5 . . . **66** B3
Abbey Cres, Belv. DA17 . . **139** G4
Abbeydale Rd, Wem.
HA0 . . . **106** A1
Abbey Dr, SW17
off Church La . . . **168** A5
Abbeyfield Rd, SE16 . . . **133** F4
Abbeyfields Cl, NW10 . . . **106** A2
Abbey Gdns, NW8 . . . **6** C2
SE16 . . . **37** J1
W6 . . . **128** B6
Chislehurst BR7 . . . **192** D1
Abbey Gro, SE2 . . . **138** B4
Abbeyhill Rd, Sid.
DA15 . . . **176** C2
Abbey Ind Est, Mitch.
CR4 . . . **185** J5
Wembley HA0 . . . **105** J1
Abbey La, E15 . . . **114** C2
Beckenham BR3 . . . **172** A7
Abbey Ms, E17
off Leamington Av . . . **78** A5
Abbey Orchard St, SW1 . . . **25** J5
Abbey Par, SW19
off Merton High St . . . **167** F7
W5 *off Hanger La* . . . **105** J3
Abbey Pk, Beck. BR3 . . . **172** A7
Abbey Retail Pk, Bark.
IG11 . . . **117** E1
Abbey Rd, E15 . . . **114** E2
NW6 . . . **90** E7
NW8 . . . **109** F2
NW10 . . . **106** B2
SE2 . . . **138** D4
SW19 . . . **167** F7
Barking IG11 . . . **99** E7
Belvedere DA17 . . . **138** D4
Bexleyheath DA7 . . . **159** E4
Croydon CR0 . . . **201** H3
Enfield EN1 . . . **44** B5
Ilford IG2 . . . **81** G5
Abbey Rd Est, NW8 . . . **109** E1
Abbey St, E13 . . . **115** G4
SE1 . . . **28** E5
Abbey Ter, SE2 . . . **138** C4
Abbey Vw, NW7 . . . **55** F3
Abbey Wk, W.Mol. KT8 . . . **179** H3
Abbey Way, SE2 . . . **138** D3
Abbey Wf Ind Est, Bark.
IG11 . . . **117** G2
ABBEY WOOD, SE2 . . . **138** B3
**Abbey Wd Caravan Club
Site**, SE2 . . . **138** C5
Abbey Wd Rd, SE2 . . . **138** B4
Abbotsbury Cl, E15 . . . **114** C2
W14
off Abbotsbury Rd . . . **128** C2
Abbotsbury Gdns, Pnr.
HA5 . . . **66** C6
Abbotsbury Ms, SE15 . . . **153** F3
Abbotsbury Rd, W14 . . . **128** B2
Bromley BR2 . . . **205** F2
Morden SM4 . . . **184** E5
Abbots Cl, N1
off Alwyne Rd . . . **93** J6
Orpington BR5 . . . **207** F1
Ruislip HA4 . . . **84** D3
Abbots Dr, Har. HA2 . . . **85** G2
Abbotsford Av, N15 . . . **75** J4
Abbotsford Gdns, Wdf.Grn.
IG8 . . . **63** G7
Abbotsford Rd, Ilf. IG3 . . . **100** A2
Abbots Gdns, N2 . . . **73** G4
W8 . . . **22** A6
Abbots Grn, Croy. CR0 . . . **203** G6
Abbotshade Rd, SE16 . . . **133** G1
Abbotshall Av, N14 . . . **58** C3
Abbotshall Rd, SE6 . . . **172** D1
Abbots La, SE1 . . . **28** E2
Abbotsleigh Cl, Sutt.
SM2 . . . **198** E7
Abbotsleigh Rd, SW16 . . . **168** C4
Abbots Manor Est, SW1 . . **32** D2
Abbotsmede Cl, Twick.
TW1 . . . **162** C2
Abbots Pk, SW2 . . . **169** G1
Abbot's Pl, NW6 . . . **108** E1
Abbot's Rd, E6 . . . **116** A1
Abbots Rd, Edg. HA8 . . . **54** C7
Abbots Ter, N8 . . . **74** E6
Abbotstone Rd, SW15 . . . **147** J3
Abbot St, E8 . . . **94** C6
Abbots Wk, W8 . . . **22** A6
Abbots Way, Beck. BR3 . . **189** H5
Abbotswell Rd, SE4 . . . **153** J5
Abbotswood Cl, Belv. DA17
off Coptefield Dr . **138/139** E3
Abbotswood Gdns, Ilf.
IG5 . . . **80** C3
Abbotswood Rd, SE22 . . . **152** B4
SW16 . . . **168** D3
Abbotswood Way, Hayes
UB3 . . . **122** B1
Abbott Av, SW20 . . . **184** A2
Abbott Cl, Hmptn. TW12 . **161** E6
Northolt UB5 . . . **85** F6
Abbott Rd, E14 . . . **114** C5
Abbotts Cl, SE28 . . . **118** C7
Romford RM7 . . . **83** H3
Abbotts Cres, E4 . . . **62** D4
Enfield EN2 . . . **43** H2
Abbotts Dr, Wem. HA0 . . . **86** E2
Abbotts Pk Rd, E10 . . . **78** C7
Abbotts Rd, Barn. EN5 . . . **40** E4
Mitcham CR4 . . . **186** C4
Southall UB1 . . . **123** E1
Sutton SM3 . . . **198** C3
Abbotts Wk, Bexh. DA7 . . **138** D7
Abchurch La, EC4 . . . **20** C5
Abchurch Yd, EC4 . . . **20** B5
Abdale Rd, W12 . . . **127** H1
Aberavon Rd, E3 . . . **113** H3
Abercairn Rd, SW16 . . . **168** C7
Aberconway Rd, Mord.
SM4 . . . **184** E3
Abercorn Cl, NW7 . . . **56** B7
NW8 . . . **6** C2
Abercorn Cres, Har. HA2 . . **85** H1
Abercorn Gdns, Har. HA3 . **69** G7
Romford RM6 . . . **82** B6
Abercorn Pl, NW8 . . . **6** C3
Abercorn Rd, NW7 . . . **56** B7
Stanmore HA7 . . . **53** F7
Abercorn Way, SE1 . . . **37** H3
Abercrombie Dr, Enf. EN1
off Linwood Cres . . . **44** D1
Abercrombie St, SW11 . . . **149** H2
Aberdale Ct, SE16
off Poolmans St . . . **133** G2
Aberdare Cl, W.Wick.
BR4 . . . **204** C2
Aberdare Gdns, NW6 . . . **91** E7
NW7 . . . **56** A7
Aberdare Rd, Enf. EN3 . . . **45** F4
Aberdeen La, N5 . . . **93** H5
Aberdeen Par, N18
off Angel Rd . . . **60/61** E5
Aberdeen Pk, N5 . . . **93** H5
Aberdeen Pk Ms, N5 . . . **93** J4
Aberdeen Pl, NW8 . . . **6** E6
Aberdeen Rd, N5 . . . **93** J4
N18 . . . **60** E5
NW10 . . . **89** F5
Croydon CR0 . . . **201** J4
Harrow HA3 . . . **68** C2
Aberdeen Sq, E14
off Westferry Circ . . . **133** J1
Aberdeen Ter, SE3 . . . **154** D2
Aberdour Rd, Ilf. IG3 . . . **100** B3
Aberdour St, SE1 . . . **36** D1
Aberfeldy St, E14 . . . **114** C6
Aberford Gdns, SE18 . . . **156** B1
Aberford Rd, Borwd. WD6 . **38** A2
Aberfoyle Rd, SW16 . . . **168** D6
Abergeldie Rd, SE12 . . . **155** H6
Aberglen Ind Est, Hayes
UB3 . . . **121** G2
Abernethy Rd, SE13 . . . **154** E4
Abersham Rd, E8 . . . **94** C5
Abery St, SE18 . . . **137** H4
Abingdon Cl, NW1
off Camden Sq . . . **92** D6
SE1 . . . **37** G3
SW19 . . . **167** F6
Abingdon Rd, N3 . . . **73** F2
SW16 . . . **186** E2
W8 . . . **128** D3
Abingdon St, SW1 . . . **26** A5
Abingdon Vil, W8 . . . **128** D3
Abinger Cl, Bark. IG11 . . . **100** A4
Bromley BR1 . . . **192** B3
Croydon CR0 . . . **204** C6
Wallington SM6 . . . **201** E5
Abinger Gdns, Islw. TW7 . **144** B3
Abinger Gro, SE8 . . . **133** J6
Abinger Ms, W9
off Warlock Rd . . . **108** D4
Abinger Rd, W4 . . . **127** E3
Ablett St, SE16 . . . **133** F5
Abney Gdns, N16
*off Stoke Newington
High St* . . . **94** C2
Aboyne Dr, SW20 . . . **183** G2
Aboyne Est, SW17 . . . **167** G3
Aboyne Rd, NW10 . . . **88** E3
SW17 . . . **167** G3
Abraham Cl, Wat. WD19 . . . **50** B4
Abridge Rd, Chig. IG7 . . . **49** G6
Abridge Way, Bark. IG11 . . **118** B2
Abyssinia Cl, SW11
off Cairns Rd . . . **149** H4
Abyssinia Rd, SW11
off Auckland Rd . . . **149** H4
Acacia Av, N17 . . . **60** A7
Brentford TW8 . . . **124** E7
Mitcham CR4
off Acacia Rd . . . **186** B2
Ruislip HA4 . . . **84** A1
Wembley HA9 . . . **87** H5
Acacia Cl, SE8 . . . **133** H4
SE20 *off Selby Rd* . . . **188** D2
Orpington BR5 . . . **193** G5
Stanmore HA7 . . . **52** B6
Acacia Dr, Sutt. SM3 . . . **198** C1
Acacia Gdns, NW8 . . . **7** F1
West Wickham BR4 . . . **204** C2
Acacia Gro, SE21 . . . **170** A2
New Malden KT3 . . . **182** D3
Acacia Ms, West Dr. UB7 . **120** A6
Acacia Pl, NW8 . . . **7** F1
Acacia Rd, E11 . . . **97** E2
E17 . . . **77** H6
N22 . . . **75** G1
NW8 . . . **7** F1
SW16 . . . **187** E1
W3 . . . **106** C7
Beckenham BR3 . . . **189** J3
Enfield EN2 . . . **44** A1
Hampton TW12 . . . **161** G6
Mitcham CR4 . . . **186** B2
Acacia Way, Sid. DA15 . . . **175** J1
Academy Gdns, W8
*off Duchess of
Bedford's Wk* . . . **128** D2
Croydon CR0 . . . **202** C1
Northolt UB5 . . . **102** D2
Academy Pl, SE18 . . . **156** C1
Academy Rd, SE18 . . . **156** C1
Acanthus Dr, SE1 . . . **37** H3
Acanthus Rd, SW11 . . . **150** A3
Accommodation Rd,
NW11 . . . **72** C7
A.C. Ct, T.Ditt. KT7
off Harvest La . . . **180** D6
Acer Av, Hayes UB4 . . . **102** E5
Acfold Rd, SW6 . . . **148** E1
Achilles Cl, SE1 . . . **37** J3
Achilles Rd, NW6 . . . **90** D5
Achilles St, SE14 . . . **133** H7
Achilles Way, W1 . . . **24** C2
Acklam Rd, W10 . . . **108** C5
Acklington Dr, NW9 . . . **70** E1
Ackmar Rd, SW6 . . . **148** D1
Ackroyd Dr, E3 . . . **113** J5
Ackroyd Rd, SE23 . . . **153** G7
Acland Cl, SE18
off Clothworkers Rd . . **137** G7
Acland Cres, SE5 . . . **152** A4
Acland Rd, NW2 . . . **89** H6
Acle Cl, Ilf. IG6 . . . **64** E7
Acock Gro, Nthlt. UB5 . . . **85** H4
Acol Cres, Ruis. HA4 . . . **84** B5
Acol Rd, NW6 . . . **90** D7
Aconbury Rd, Dag. RM9 . . **118** B1
Acorn Cl, E4 . . . **62** A5
Chislehurst BR7 . . . **175** F5
Enfield EN2 . . . **43** H1
Hampton TW12 . . . **161** H6
Stanmore HA7 . . . **53** E7
Acorn Ct, Ilf. IG2 . . . **81** H6
Acorn Gdns, SE19 . . . **188** C1
W3 . . . **106** D5
Acorn Gro, Hayes UB3 . . . **121** J7
Acorn Par, SE15
off Carlton Gro . . . **132/133** E7
Acorns, The, Chig. IG7 . . . **65** H4
Acorn Wk, SE16 . . . **133** H1
Acorn Way, SE23 . . . **171** G3
Beckenham BR3 . . . **190** C5
Orpington BR6 . . . **207** E4
Acre Dr, SE22 . . . **152** D4
Acre La, SW2 . . . **150** E4
Carshalton SM5 . . . **200** A4
Wallington SM6 . . . **200** A4
Acre Path, Nthlt. UB5
off Arnold Rd . . . **84/85** E6
Acre Rd, SW19 . . . **167** G6
Dagenham RM10 . . . **101** H7
Kingston upon Thames
KT2 . . . **181** H1
Acris St, SW18 . . . **149** F5
ACTON, W3 . . . **126** A1
Acton Cl, N9 . . . **60** D2
Acton Hill Ms, W3
off Uxbridge Rd . . . **126** B1
Acton La, NW10 . . . **106** E2
W3 . . . **126** C2
W4 . . . **126** D3
Acton Ms, E8 . . . **112** C1
Acton Pk Ind Est, W3 . . . **126** D2
Acton St, WC1 . . . **10** C4
Acuba Rd, SW18 . . . **166** E2
Acworth Cl, N9
off Turin Rd . . . **45** F7
Ada Gdns, E14 . . . **114** D6
E15 . . . **115** F1
Adair Cl, SE25 . . . **188** E3
Adair Rd, W10 . . . **108** B4
Adair Twr, W10
off Appleford Rd . . . **108** B4
Adam & Eve Ct, W1 . . . **17** G3
Adam & Eve Ms, W8 . . . **128** D3
Adam Cl, SE6 . . . **171** J4
Adam Ct, SW7 . . . **30** D1
Adam Pl, N16
*off Stoke Newington
High St* . . . **94** C2
Adam Rd, E4 . . . **61** J6
Adams Cl, N3
off Falkland Av . . . **56** D7
NW9 . . . **88** B2
Surbiton KT5 . . . **181** J6
Adams Ct, EC2 . . . **20** C3
Adams Gdns Est, SE16
off St. Marychurch St . **133** F2
Adams Ms, N22 . . . **58** E7
SW17 . . . **167** J2
Adamson Rd, E16 . . . **115** G6
NW3 . . . **91** G7
Adamson Way, Beck. BR3
off Creswell Dr . . . **190** B5
Adams Pl, N7
off George's Rd . . . **93** F5
Adamsrill Cl, Enf. EN1 . . . **44** A6
Adamsrill Rd, SE26 . . . **171** H4
Adams Rd, N17 . . . **76** A2
Beckenham BR3 . . . **189** H5
Adams Row, W1 . . . **16** C6
Adams Sq, Bexh. DA6
off Regency Way . **158/159** E3
Adam St, WC2 . . . **18** B6
Adams Wk, Kings.T. KT1 . **181** H2
Adams Way, Croy. CR0 . . . **188** C6
Adam Wk, SW6 . . . **127** J7
Ada Pl, E2 . . . **112** D1
Adare Wk, SW16 . . . **169** F3
Ada Rd, SE5 . . . **132** B7
Wembley HA0 . . . **87** G3
Adastral Est, NW9 . . . **70** E1
Ada St, E8 . . . **112** E1
Adcock Wk, Orp. BR6
off Borkwood Pk . . . **207** J4
Adderley Gdns, SE9 . . . **174** D4
Adderley Gro, SW11
off Culmstock Rd . . . **150** A5
Adderley Rd, Har. HA3 . . . **68** C1
Adderley St, E14 . . . **114** C6
ADDINGTON, Croy. CR0 . **203** J5
Addington Ct, SW14 . . . **146** D3
Addington Dr, N12 . . . **57** F6
Addington Gro, SE26 . . . **171** H4
Addington Rd, E3 . . . **114** A3
E16 . . . **115** E4
N4 . . . **75** G6
Croydon CR0 . . . **201** G1
West Wickham BR4 . . . **204** E2
Addington Sq, SE5 . . . **36** A7
Addington St, SE1 . . . **26** D4

Addington Village Rd, Croy. CR0 . . . 204 A5
Addis Cl, Enf. EN3 . . . 45 G1
ADDISCOMBE, Croy. CR0 . . . 202 C1
Addiscombe Av, Croy. CR0 . . . 188 D7
Addiscombe Cl, Har. HA3 . . . 69 F5
Addiscombe Ct Rd, Croy. CR0 . . . 202 B1
Addiscombe Gro, Croy. CR0 . . . 202 A2
Addiscombe Rd, Croy. CR0 . . . 202 B2
Addison Av, N14 . . . 42 B6
W11 . . . 128 B1
Hounslow TW3 . . . 143 J1
Addison Br Pl, W14 . . . 128 C4
Addison Cl, Nthwd. HA6 . . 66 A1
Orpington BR5 . . . 193 F6
Addison Cres, W14 . . . 128 B3
Addison Dr, SE12 *off Eltham Rd* . . . 155 H5
Addison Gdns, W14 . . . 128 A3
Surbiton KT5 . . . 181 J4
Addison Gro, W4 . . . 127 E3
Addison Pl, W11 . . . 128 B1
Southall UB1 *off Longford Av* . . . 103 G7
Addison Rd, E11 . . . 79 G6
E17 . . . 78 B5
SE25 . . . 188 D4
W14 . . . 128 C3
Bromley BR2 . . . 191 J5
Enfield EN3 . . . 45 F1
Ilford IG6 . . . 81 F1
Teddington TW11 . . . 162 E6
Addison's Cl, Croy. CR0 . . 203 J2
Addison Way, NW11 . . . 72 C4
Hayes UB3 . . . 102 A6
Addle Hill, EC4 . . . 19 H5
Addle St, EC2 . . . 20 A2
Addy Ho, SE16 *off Rotherhithe New Rd* . . . 133 F4
Adecroft Way, W.Mol. KT8 . . . 179 J3
Adela Av, N.Mal. KT3 . . . 183 H5
Adelaide Av, SE4 . . . 153 J4
Adelaide Cl, SW9 *off Broughton Dr* . . . 151 G4
Stanmore HA7 . . . 52 D4
Adelaide Cotts, W7 . . . 124 C2
Adelaide Gdns, Rom. RM6 . . . 82 E5
Adelaide Gro, W12 . . . 127 G1
Adelaide Rd, E10 . . . 96 B3
NW3 . . . 91 G7
SW18 *off Putney Br Rd* . . . 148 D5
W13 . . . 124 D1
Chislehurst BR7 . . . 175 E5
Hounslow TW5 . . . 142 E1
Ilford IG1 . . . 99 E2
Richmond TW9 . . . 145 J4
Southall UB2 . . . 123 E4
Surbiton KT6 . . . 181 H5
Teddington TW11 . . . 162 C6
Adelaide St, WC2 . . . 18 A6
Adelaide Ter, Brent. TW8 . 125 G5
Adela St, W10 *off Kensal Rd* . . . 108 B4
Adelina Gro, E1 . . . 113 F5
Adelina Ms, SW12 *off King's Av* . . . 168 D1
Adeline Pl, WC1 . . . 17 J2
Adeliza Cl, Bark. IG11 *off North St* . . . 98/99 E7
Adelphi Ct, SE16 *off Poolmans St* . . . 133 G2
Adelphi Ter, WC2 . . . 18 B6
Adeney Cl, W6 . . . 128 A6
Aden Gro, N16 . . . 94 A4
Adenmore Rd, SE6 . . . 154 A7
Aden Rd, Enf. EN3 . . . 45 H4
Ilford IG1 . . . 81 E7
Aden Ter, N16 . . . 94 A4
Adie Rd, W6 . . . 127 J3
Adine Rd, E13 . . . 115 H4
Adler Ind Est, Hayes UB3 . . . 121 G2
Adler St, E1 . . . 21 H3
Adley St, E5 . . . 95 H5
Adlington Cl, N18 . . . 60 A5
Admaston Rd, SE18 . . . 137 F7
Admiral Ct, NW4 *off Barton Cl* . . . 71 G5
Admiral Ho, Tedd. TW11 *off Twickenham Rd* . . . 162 D4
Admiral Pl, N8 *off Effingham Rd* . . . 75 H4
SE16 . . . 133 H1
Admirals Cl, E18 . . . 79 H4
Admiral Seymour Rd, SE9 . . . 156 C4
Admirals Gate, SE10 . . . 154 B1
Admiral Sq, SW10 . . . 149 G1
Admiral St, SE8 . . . 154 A2
Admirals Wk, NW3 . . . 91 F3
Admirals Way, E14 . . . 134 A2
★Admiralty Arch, SW1 . . . 25 J1
Admiralty Cl, SE8 *off Reginald Sq* . . . 134 A7
Admiralty Way, Tedd. TW11 . . . 162 C6
Admiral Wk, W9 . . . 108 D5
Adolf St, SE6 . . . 172 B4
Adolphus Rd, N4 . . . 93 H2
Adolphus St, SE8 . . . 133 J7
Adomar Rd, Dag. RM8 . . . 100 D3
Adpar St, W2 . . . 7 E6
Adrian Av, NW2 *off North Circular Rd* . . 89 H1
Adrian Cl, Barn. EN5 . . . 40 A6
Adrian Ms, SW10 . . . 30 B5
Adriatic Bldg, E14 *off Narrow St* . . . 113 H7
Adrienne Av, Sthl. UB1 . . . 103 F4
Advance Rd, SE27 . . . 169 J4
Advent Ct, Wdf.Grn. IG8 *off Wood La* . . . 63 F5
Adventurers Ct, E14 *off Newport Av* . . . 114 D7
Advent Way, N18 . . . 61 G5
Adys Rd, SE15 . . . 152 C3
Aerodrome Rd, NW4 . . . 71 F2
NW9 . . . 71 F2
Aerodrome Way, Houns. TW5 . . . 122 C6
Aeroville, NW9 . . . 71 E2
Affleck St, N1 . . . 10 D2
Afghan Rd, SW11 . . . 149 H2
★Africa Cen, WC2 . . . 18 A5
Africa Ho, SE16 . . . 133 E3
Agamemnon Rd, NW6 . . . 90 C5
Agar Cl, Surb. KT6 . . . 195 J2
Agar Gro, NW1 . . . 92 C7
Agar Gro Est, NW1 . . . 92 D7
Agar Pl, NW1 . . . 92 C7
Agar St, WC2 . . . 18 A6
Agate Cl, E16 . . . 116 A6
Agate Rd, W6 . . . 127 J3
Agatha Cl, E1 *off Prusom St* . . . 132/133 E1
Agaton Rd, SE9 . . . 175 F2
Agave Rd, NW2 . . . 89 J4
Agdon St, EC1 . . . 11 G5
Agincourt Rd, NW3 . . . 91 J4
Agnes Av, Ilf. IG1 . . . 98 E4
Agnes Cl, E6 . . . 116 D7
Agnesfield Cl, N12 . . . 57 H6
Agnes Gdns, Dag. RM8 . . 100 D4
Agnes Rd, W3 . . . 127 F1
Agnes St, E14 . . . 113 J6
Agnew Rd, SE23 . . . 153 G7
Agricola Ct, E3 *off Parnell Rd* . . . 113 J1
Agricola Pl, Enf. EN1 . . . 44 C5
Aidan Cl, Dag. RM8 . . . 100 E4
Aileen Wk, E15 . . . 97 F7
Ailsa Av, Twick. TW1 . . . 144 D5
Ailsa Rd, Twick. TW1 . . . 145 E5
Ailsa St, E14 . . . 114 C5
Ainger Ms, NW3 *off Ainger Rd* . . . 91 J7
Ainger Rd, NW3 . . . 91 J7
Ainsdale Cl, Orp. BR6 . . . 207 G1
Ainsdale Cres, Pnr. HA5 . . . 67 G3
Ainsdale Dr, SE1 . . . 37 H4
Ainsdale Rd, W5 . . . 105 G4
Watford WD19 . . . 50 C3
Ainsley Av, Rom. RM7 . . . 83 H6
Ainsley Cl, N9 . . . 60 B1
Ainsley St, E2 . . . 112 E3
Ainslie Wk, SW12 . . . 150 B7
Ainslie Wd Cres, E4 . . . 62 B5
Ainslie Wd Gdns, E4 . . . 62 B4
Ainslie Wd Rd, E4 . . . 62 A5
Ainsty Est, SE16 . . . 133 G2
Ainsworth Cl, NW2 . . . 89 G3
SE15 *off Lyndhurst Gro* . . 152 B2
Ainsworth Rd, E9 . . . 95 F7
Croydon CR0 . . . 201 H2
Ainsworth Way, NW8 . . . 109 F1
Aintree Av, E6 . . . 116 B1
Aintree Cres, Ilf. IG6 . . . 81 F2
Aintree Est, SW6 *off Dawes Rd* . . . 128 B7
Aintree Rd, Grnf. UB6 . . . 105 E2
Aintree St, SW6 . . . 128 B7
Aird Ct, Hmptn. TW12 *off Oldfield Rd* . . . 179 F1
Airdrie Cl, N1 . . . 93 F7
Hayes UB4 *off Glencoe Rd* . . . 102/103 E5
Airedale Av, W4 . . . 127 F4
Airedale Av S, W4 *off Netheravon Rd S* . . . 127 F5
Airedale Rd, SW12 . . . 149 J7
W5 . . . 125 F3
Airlie Gdns, W8 . . . 128 D2
Ilford IG1 . . . 99 E1
Air Links Ind Est, Houns. TW5 . . . 122 C5
Air Pk Way, Felt. TW13 . . . 160 B2
Airport Roundabout, E16 *off Connaught Br* . . . 136 A1
Air St, W1 . . . 17 G6
Airthrie Rd, Ilf. IG3 . . . 100 B2
Aisgill Av, W14 . . . 128 C5
Aisher Rd, SE28 . . . 118 C7
Aislibie Rd, SE12 . . . 155 E4
Aiten Pl, W6 *off Standish Rd* . . . 127 G4
Aitken Cl, E8 *off Pownall Rd* . . . 112 D1
Mitcham CR4 . . . 185 J7
Aitken Rd, SE6 . . . 172 B2
Barnet EN5 . . . 39 J5
Ajax Av, NW9 . . . 70 E3
Ajax Rd, NW6 . . . 90 D5
Akabusi Cl, Croy. CR0 . . . 188 D6
Akehurst St, SW15 . . . 147 G6
Akenside Rd, NW3 . . . 91 G5
Akerman Rd, SW9 . . . 151 H2
Surbiton KT6 . . . 181 F6
Alabama St, SE18 . . . 137 G7
Alacross Rd, W5 . . . 125 F2
Alandale Dr, Pnr. HA5 . . . 66 B2
Aland Ct, SE16 *off Finland St* . . . 133 H3
Alander Ms, E17 . . . 78 C4
Alan Dr, Barn. EN5 . . . 40 B6
Alan Gdns, Rom. RM7 . . . 83 G7
Alan Hocken Way, E15 . . . 114 E2
Alan Rd, SW19 . . . 166 B5
Alanthus Cl, SE12 . . . 155 F6
Alaska St, SE1 . . . 27 E2
Alba Cl, Hayes UB4 *off Ramulis Dr* . . . 102 D4
Albacore Cres, SE13 . . . 154 B6
Alba Gdns, NW11 . . . 72 B6
Alban Cres, Borwd. WD6 . . 38 B1
Alban Highwalk, EC2 *off London Wall* . . . 111 J5
Albany, W1 . . . 17 F6
Albany, The, Wdf.Grn. IG8 . 63 F4
Albany Cl, N15 . . . 75 H4
SW14 . . . 146 B4
Bexley DA5 . . . 158 C7
Albany Ct, E4 *off Chelwood Cl* . . . 46 B6
Albany Ctyd, W1 . . . 17 G6
Albany Cres, Edg. HA8 . . . 54 A7
Esher (Clay.) KT10 . . . 194 B6
Albany Mans, SW11 . . . 129 H7
Albany Ms, N1 *off Barnsbury Pk* . . . 93 G7
SE5 . . . 36 A6
Bromley BR1 . . . 173 G6
Kingston upon Thames KT2 *off Albany Pk Rd* . . . 163 G6
Sutton SM1 *off Camden Rd* . . . 198/199 E5
Albany Pk Av, Enf. EN3 . . . 45 F1
Albany Pk Rd, Kings.T. KT2 . . . 163 H6
Albany Pas, Rich. TW10 . . 145 J5
Albany Pl, Brent. TW8 *off Albany Rd* . . . 125 H6
Albany Rd, E10 . . . 78 A7
E12 . . . 98 A4
E17 . . . 77 H6
N4 . . . 75 F6
N18 . . . 61 E5
SE5 . . . 36 B6
SW19 . . . 166 E5
W13 . . . 104 E7
Belvedere DA17 . . . 139 F6
Bexley DA5 . . . 158 C7
Brentford TW8 . . . 125 G6
Chislehurst BR7 . . . 174 E5
New Malden KT3 . . . 182 D4
Richmond TW10 *off Albert Rd* . . . 145 J5
Romford RM6 . . . 83 F6
Albany St, NW1 . . . 8 D1
Albany Ter, NW1 *off Marylebone Rd* . . . 110 B4
Albany Vw, Buck.H. IG9 . . . 63 G1
Alba Pl, W11 *off Portobello Rd* . . . 108 C6
Albatross Cl, E6 *off Woolwich Manor Way* . . . 116 C4
Albatross St, SE18 . . . 137 H7
Albatross Way, SE16 . . . 133 G2
Albemarle, SW19 . . . 166 A2
Albemarle App, Ilf. IG2 . . . 81 E6
Albemarle Av, Twick. TW2 . 161 F1
Albemarle Gdns, Ilf. IG2 . . . 81 E6
New Malden KT3 . . . 182 D4
Albemarle Pk, Stan. HA7 *off Marsh La* . . . 53 F5
Albemarle Rd, Barn. EN4 . . 41 H7
Beckenham BR3 . . . 190 B1
Albemarle St, W1 . . . 17 E6
Albemarle Way, EC1 . . . 11 G6
Alberon Gdns, NW11 . . . 72 C4
Alberta Av, Sutt. SM1 . . . 198 B4
Alberta Est, SE17 . . . 35 H3
Alberta Rd, Enf. EN1 . . . 44 C6
Erith DA8 . . . 159 J1
Alberta St, SE17 . . . 35 G3
Albert Av, E4 . . . 62 A4
SW8 . . . 131 F7
Albert Br, SW3 . . . 31 H6
SW11 . . . 31 H6
Albert Br Rd, SW11 . . . 31 H7
Albert Carr Gdns, SW16 . 168 E5
Albert Cl, E9 *off Northiam St* . . 112/113 E1
N22 . . . 74 D1
Albert Ct, SW7 . . . 23 E4
Albert Cres, E4 . . . 62 A4
Albert Dr, SW19 . . . 166 B2
Albert Embk, SE1 . . . 34 B4
Albert Gdns, E1 . . . 113 G6
Albert Gate, SW1 . . . 24 A3
Albert Gro, SW20 . . . 184 A1
Albert Hall Mans, SW7 . . . 23 E4
Albert Mans, SW11 *off Albert Br Rd* . . . 149 J1
★Albert Mem, SW7 . . . 22 E3
Albert Ms, E14 *off Narrow St* . . . 113 H7
N4 *off Albert Rd* . . . 93 F1
SE4 *off Arabin Rd* . . . 153 H4
W8 . . . 22 C5
Albert Pl, N3 . . . 72 D1
N17 *off High Rd* . . . 76 C3
W8 . . . 22 B4
Albert Rd, E10 . . . 96 C2
E16 . . . 136 B1
E17 . . . 78 A5
E18 . . . 79 H3
N4 . . . 93 F1
N15 . . . 76 B6
N22 . . . 74 C1
NW4 . . . 72 A4
NW6 . . . 108 C2
NW7 . . . 55 F5
SE9 . . . 174 B3
SE20 . . . 171 G7
SE25 . . . 188 D4
W5 . . . 105 E4
Barnet EN4 . . . 41 F4
Belvedere DA17 . . . 139 F5
Bexley DA5 . . . 159 G6
Bromley BR2 . . . 192 A5
Buckhurst Hill IG9 . . . 64 A2
Dagenham RM8 . . . 101 G1
Hampton (Hmptn H.) TW12 . . . 161 J5
Harrow HA2 . . . 67 J3
Hayes UB3 . . . 121 H3
Hounslow TW3 . . . 143 G4
Ilford IG1 . . . 99 E3
Kingston upon Thames KT1 . . . 181 J2
Mitcham CR4 . . . 185 J3
New Malden KT3 . . . 183 F4
Richmond TW10 . . . 145 H5
Southall UB2 . . . 122 D3
Sutton SM1 . . . 199 G5
Teddington TW11 . . . 162 C6
Twickenham TW1 . . . 162 C1
West Drayton UB7 . . . 120 B1
Albert Rd Est, Belv. DA17 . . . 139 F5
Albert Sq, E15 . . . 97 E5
SW8 . . . 131 F7
Albert St, N12 . . . 57 F5
NW1 . . . 110 B1
Albert Ter, NW1 . . . 110 A1
NW10 . . . 106 D1
Buckhurst Hill IG9 . . . 64 A2

Albert Ter Ms, NW1
off Regents Pk Rd 110 A1
Albert Way, SE15 132 E7
Albion Av, N10 74 A1
SW8 150 D2
Albion Bldgs, EC1
off Bartholomew Cl 111 J5
Albion Cl, W2 15 H5
Albion Dr, E8 94 C7
Albion Est, SE16 133 G2
Albion Gro, N16 94 B4
Albion Hill, Loug. IG10 47 J5
Albion Ms, N1 111 G1
NW6
off Kilburn High Rd 90 C7
W2 15 H4
W6 *off Galena Rd* 127 H4
Albion Par, N16
off Albion Rd 94 A4
Albion Pk, Loug. IG10 48 A5
Albion Pl, EC1 19 G1
SE25 *off High St* 188 D3
W6 127 H4
Albion Riverside Bldg, SW11
off Hester Rd 129 H7
Albion Rd, E17 78 C3
N16 94 A4
N17 76 C2
Bexleyheath DA6 159 F4
Hounslow TW3 143 G4
Kingston upon Thames
KT2 182 C1
Sutton SM2 199 G6
Twickenham TW2 162 B1
Albion Sq, E8 94 C7
Albion St, SE16 133 F2
W2 15 H4
Croydon CR0 201 H1
Albion Ter, E8 94 C7
Albion Vil Rd, SE26 171 F3
Albion Wk, N1
off York Way 110 E2
Albion Way, EC1 19 J2
SE13 154 C4
Wembley HA9
off North End Rd 88 B3
Albion Yd, N1
off Balfe St 110 E2
Albon Ho, SW18
off Neville Gill Cl 148 E6
Albrighton Rd, SE22 152 B3
Albuhera Cl, Enf. EN2 43 G1
Albury Av, Bexh. DA7 158 E2
Isleworth TW7 124 C7
Albury Cl, Hmptn. TW12 161 G6
Albury Ct, Sutt. SM1
off Ripley Gdns 199 F4
Albury Dr, Pnr. HA5 50 D7
Albury Ms, E12 97 J1
Albury Rd, Chess. KT9 195 H5
Albury St, SE8 134 A6
Albyfield, Brom. BR1 192 C3
Albyn Rd, SE8 154 A1
Alcester Cres, E5 95 E2
Alcester Rd, Wall. SM6 200 B4
Alcock Cl, Wall. SM6 200 D7
Alcock Rd, Houns. TW5 122 D7
Alconbury Rd, E5 94 D2
Alcorn Cl, Sutt. SM3 198 D3
Alcott Cl, W7
off Westcott Cres 104 C5
Alcuin Ct, Stan. HA7
off Old Ch La 53 F7
ALDBOROUGH HATCH,
Ilf. IG2 81 H3
Aldborough Rd, Dag.
RM10 101 J6
Aldborough Rd N, Ilf.
IG2 81 J5
Aldborough Rd S, Ilf. IG3 99 H1
Aldbourne Rd, W12 127 F1
Aldbridge St, SE17 36 E3
Aldburgh Ms, W1 16 C3
Aldbury Av, Wem. HA9 88 B7
Aldbury Ms, N9 44 A7
Aldebert Ter, SW8 131 E7
Aldeburgh Cl, E5
off Southwold Rd 94/95 E2
Aldeburgh Pl, SE10
off Aldeburgh St 135 G4
Woodford Green IG8 63 G4
Aldeburgh St, SE10 135 G5
Alden Av, E15 115 F3
Aldenham St, NW1 9 G2
Aldensley Rd, W6 127 H3
Alderbrook Rd, SW12 150 B6
Alderbury Rd, SW13 127 G6
Alder Cl, SE15 37 G6
Alder Gro, NW2 89 H2
Aldergrove Gdns, Houns. TW3
off Bath Rd 142/143 E2
Alderholt Way, SE15
off Blakes Rd 132 B7
Alderman Av, Bark. IG11 118 A3
Aldermanbury, EC2 20 A3
Aldermanbury Sq, EC2 20 A2
Alderman Judge Mall, Kings.T.
KT1 *off Eden St* 181 H2
Aldermans Hill, N13 58 E4
Alderman's Wk, EC2 20 D2
Aldermary Rd, Brom.
BR1 191 G1
Alder Ms, N19
off Bredgar Rd 92 C2
Aldermoor Rd, SE6 171 J3
Alderney Av, Houns.
TW5 123 H7
Alderney Gdns, Nthlt.
UB5 85 F7
Alderney Ms, SE1 28 B5
Alderney Rd, E1 113 G4
Alderney St, SW1 32 E3
Alder Rd, SW14 146 D3
Sidcup DA14 175 J3
Alders, The, N21 43 G6
Feltham TW13 160 E4
Hounslow TW5 123 F6
West Wickham BR4 204 B1
Alders Av, Wdf.Grn. IG8 62 E6
ALDERSBROOK, E12 97 H2
Aldersbrook Av, Enf. EN1 44 B2
Aldersbrook Dr, Kings.T.
KT2 163 J6
Aldersbrook La, E12 98 C3
Aldersbrook Rd, E11 97 H2
E12 98 A3
Alders Cl, E11
off Aldersbrook Rd 97 H2
W5 125 G3
Edgware HA8 54 C5
Aldersey Gdns, Bark. IG11 99 G6
Aldersford Cl, SE4 153 G5
Aldersgate St, EC1 19 J3
Alders Gro, E.Mol. KT8
off Esher Rd 180 A5
Aldersgrove Av, SE9 173 J3
Aldershot Rd, NW6 108 C1
Aldersmead Av, Croy.
CR0 189 G6
Aldersmead Rd, Beck.
BR3 171 H7
Alderson Pl, Sthl. UB2 123 J1
Alderson St, W10
off Kensal Rd 108 B4
Alders Rd, Edg. HA8 54 C5
Alderton Cl, NW10 88 D3
Loughton IG10 48 D4
Alderton Cres, NW4 71 H5
Alderton Hall La, Loug.
IG10 48 D4
Alderton Hill, Loug. IG10 48 B5
Alderton Ms, Loug. IG10
off Alderton Hall La 48 D4
Alderton Ri, Loug. IG10 48 D4
Alderton Rd, SE24 151 J3
Croydon CR0 188 C7
Alderton Way, NW4 71 H5
Loughton IG10 40 C5
Alderville Rd, SW6 148 C2
Alder Wk, Ilf. IG1 99 F5
Alderwick Dr, Houns.
TW3 144 A3
Alderwood Rd, SE9 157 G6
Aldford St, W1 24 B1
Aldgate, EC3 21 F4
Aldgate Av, E1 21 F3
Aldgate Barrs Shop Cen,
E1 21 G3
Aldgate High St, EC3 21 F4
Aldine Ct, W12
off Aldine St 127 J1
Aldine Pl, W12
off Uxbridge Rd 127 J1
Aldine St, W12 127 J2
Aldington Cl, Dag. RM8 82 C7
Aldington Rd, SE18 136 A3
Aldis Ms, SW17
off Aldis St 167 H5
Aldis St, SW17 167 H5
Aldred Rd, NW6 90 D5
Aldren Rd, SW17 167 F3
Aldriche Way, E4 62 C6
Aldrich Gdns, Sutt. SM3 198 C3
Aldrich Ter, SW18
off Lidiard Rd 167 F2
Aldridge Av, Edg. HA8 54 B3
Ruislip HA4 84 D2
Stanmore HA7 69 H1
Aldridge Ri, N.Mal. KT3 182 E7
Aldridge Rd Vil, W11 108 C5
Aldridge Wk, N14 42 E7
Aldrington Rd, SW16 168 C5
Aldsworth Cl, W9 6 A6
Aldwick Cl, SE9 175 G3
Aldwick Rd, Croy. CR0 201 F3
Aldworth Gro, SE13 154 C6
Aldworth Rd, E15 96 E7
Aldwych, WC2 18 C5
Aldwych Av, Ilf. IG6 81 F4
Aldwych Underpass, WC2
off Kingsway 111 F6
Alers Rd, Bexh. DA6 158 D5
Alesia Cl, N22
off Nightingale Rd 58/59 E7
Alestan Beck Rd, E16 116 A5
Alexa Ct, W8 30 A1
Sutton SM2
off Mulgrave Rd 198 D6
Alexander Av, NW10 89 H7
Alexander Cl, Barn. EN4 41 G4
Bromley BR2 205 G1
Sidcup DA15 157 H5
Southall UB2 123 J1
Twickenham TW2 162 C2
Alexander Evans Ms, SE23
off Sunderland Rd 171 G1
★**Alexander Fleming**
Laboratory Mus, W2 15 F3
Alexander Ho, Kings.T. KT2
off Kingsgate Rd 181 H1
Alexander Ms, W2 14 A3
Alexander Pl, SW7 31 G1
Alexander Rd, N19 92 E3
Bexleyheath DA7 158 D2
Chislehurst BR7 175 E5
Alexander Sq, SW3 31 G1
Alexander St, W2 108 D6
Alexandra Av, N22 74 D1
SW11 150 A1
W4 126 D7
Harrow HA2 85 F1
Southall UB1 103 F7
Sutton SM1 198 D3
Alexandra Cl, SE8 133 J6
Harrow HA2
off Alexandra Av 85 G3
Alexandra Cotts, SE14 153 J1
Alexandra Ct, N14 42 C5
N16 *off Belgrade Rd* 94 C4
Wembley HA9 87 J4
Alexandra Cres, Brom.
BR1 173 F6
Alexandra Dr, SE19 170 B5
Surbiton KT5 182 A7
Alexandra Gdns, N10 74 B4
W4 126 D7
Hounslow TW3 143 H2
Alexandra Gro, N4 93 H1
N12 57 E5
Alexandra Ms, N2
off Fortis Grn 73 J3
SW19
off Alexandra Rd 166 D6
★**Alexandra Palace**, N22 74 D2
Alexandra Palace Way,
N22 74 C3
Alexandra Pk Rd, N10 74 B2
N22 74 D2
Alexandra Pl, NW8 109 F1
SE25 188 A5
Croydon CR0
off Alexandra Rd 202 B1
Alexandra Rd, E6 116 D3
E10 96 C3
E17 77 J6
E18 79 H3
N8 75 G3
N9 44 E7
N10 58 B6
N15 76 A5
NW4 72 A4
NW8 91 F7
SE26 171 G6
SW14 146 D3
SW19 166 C6
W4 126 D2
Brentford TW8 125 G6
Croydon CR0 202 B1
Enfield EN3 45 G4
Hounslow TW3 143 H2
Kingston upon Thames
KT2 164 A7
Mitcham CR4 167 H7
Richmond TW9 145 J2
Romford (Chad.Hth) RM6 82 D6
Thames Ditton KT7 180 C5
Twickenham TW1 145 F6
Alexandra Sq, Mord.
SM4 184 D5
Alexandra St, E16 115 G5
SE14 133 H7
Alexandra Wk, SE19 170 B5
Alexandria Rd, W13 104 D7
Alexis St, SE16 37 H1
Alfearn Rd, E5 95 F4
Alford Grn, Croy. (New Adgtn)
CR0 204 D6
Alford Pl, N1 12 A2
Alfoxton Av, N15 75 H4
Alfreda St, SW11 150 B1
Alfred Cl, W4
off Belmont Rd 126 D4
Alfred Gdns, Sthl. UB1 103 E7
Alfred Ms, W1 17 H1
Alfred Pl, WC1 17 H1
Alfred Prior Ho, E12 98 D4
Alfred Rd, E15 97 F5
SE25 188 D5
W2 108 D5
W3 126 C1
Belvedere DA17 139 F5
Buckhurst Hill IG9 64 A2
Feltham TW13 160 C2
Kingston upon Thames
KT1 181 H3
Sutton SM1 199 F5
Alfred's Gdns, Bark. IG11 117 H2
Alfred St, E3 113 J3
Alfreds Way, Bark. IG11 117 F3
Alfreds Way Ind Est,
Bark. IG11 118 A1
Alfreton Cl, SW19 166 A3
Alfriston Av, Croy. CR0 186 E7
Harrow HA2 67 G6
Alfriston Cl, Surb. KT5 181 J5
Alfriston Rd, SW11 149 J5
Algar Cl, Islw. TW7
off Algar Rd 144 D3
Stanmore HA7 52 C5
Algar Rd, Islw. TW7 144 D3
Algarve Rd, SW18 167 E1
Algernon Rd, NW4 71 G6
NW6 108 D1
SE13 154 B4
Algers Cl, Loug. IG10 48 A5
Algers Mead, Loug. IG10 48 A5
Algers Rd, Loug. IG10 48 A5
Algiers Rd, SE13 154 A4
Alibon Gdns, Dag.
RM10 101 G5
Alibon Rd, Dag.
RM9, RM10 101 F5
Alice Cl, Barn. EN5 41 F4
Alice Ct, SW15
off Deodar Rd 148 C4
Alice Gilliatt Ct, W14 128 C6
Alice La, E3 113 J1
Alice Ms, Tedd. TW11
off Luther Rd 162 C5
Alice St, SE1 28 D6
Alice Thompson Cl, SE12 173 J2
Alice Walker Cl, SE24
off Shakespeare Rd 151 H4
Alice Way, Houns. TW3 143 H4
Alicia Av, Har. HA3 69 E4
Alicia Cl, Har. HA3 69 F4
Alicia Gdns, Har. HA3 69 E4
Alie St, E1 21 G4
Alington Cres, NW9 88 C1
Alison Cl, E6 116 D6
Croydon CR0
off Shirley Oaks Rd 203 G1
Aliwal Rd, SW11 149 H4
Alkerden Rd, W4 127 E5
Alkham Rd, N16 94 C2
Allan Barclay Cl, N15
off High Rd 76 C6
Allan Cl, N.Mal. KT3 182 D5
Allandale Av, N3 72 B3
Allan Way, W3 106 C5
Allard Cres, Bushey
(Bushey Hth) WD23 51 J1
Allard Gdns, SW4 150 D5
Allardyce St, SW4 151 F4
Allbrook Cl, Tedd. TW11 162 B5
Allcroft Rd, NW5 92 A5
Allder Way, S.Croy. CR2 201 H7
Allenby Cl, Grnf. UB6 103 G3
Allenby Rd, SE23 171 H3
SE28
off Broadwater Rd 137 F3
Southall UB1 103 G6
Allen Cl, Mitch. CR4 186 B1
Sunbury-on-Thames
TW16 178 B1
Allen Ct, Grnf. UB6 86 C5

Allendale Av, Sthl. UB1 **103** G6
Allendale Cl, SE5
off Daneville Rd **152** A1
SE26 **171** G5
Allendale Rd, Grnf. UB6 **86** E6
Allen Edwards Dr, SW8 **150** E1
Allenford Ho, SW15
off Tunworth Cres **147** F6
Allen Pl, Twick. TW1
off Church St **162** D1
Allen Rd, E3 **113** J2
N16 **94** B4
Beckenham BR3 **189** G2
Croydon CR0 **187** F7
Sunbury-on-Thames TW16 **178** B1
Allensbury Pl, NW1 **92** D7
Allens Rd, Enf. EN3 **45** F5
Allen St, W8 **128** D3
Allenswood Rd, SE9 **156** B3
Allerford Ct, Har. HA2 **67** H5
Allerford Rd, SE6 **172** B4
Allerton Ct, NW4
off Holders Hill Rd **72** A2
Allerton Rd, N16 **93** J2
Allerton Wk, N7
off Durham Rd **93** F2
Allestree Rd, SW6 **128** B7
Alleyn Cres, SE21 **170** A2
Alleyndale Rd, Dag. RM8 **100** C2
Alleyn Pk, SE21 **170** A2
Southall UB2 **123** F4
Alleyn Rd, SE21 **170** A3
Allfarthing La, SW18 **149** E6
Allgood Cl, Mord. SM4 **184** A6
Allgood St, E2 **13** G2
Allhallows La, EC4 **20** B6
★**All Hallows-on-the-Wall C of E Ch**, EC2 **20** C2
Allhallows Rd, E6 **116** B5
All Hallows Rd, N17 **76** B1
Alliance Cl, Wem. HA0 **87** G4
Alliance Ct, W3
off Alliance Rd **106** B4
Alliance Rd, E13 **115** J4
SE18 **138** A6
W3 **106** B4
Allied Way, W3
off Larden Rd **126/127** E2
Allingham Cl, W7 **104** C7
Allingham Ms, N1 **11** J1
Allingham St, N1 **11** J1
Allington Av, N17 **60** B6
Allington Cl, SW19 *off High St Wimbledon* **166** A5
Greenford UB6 **85** J7
Allington Ct, Enf. EN3 **45** G5
Allington Rd, NW4 **71** H5
W10 **108** B2
Harrow HA2 **67** J5
Orpington BR6 **207** G2
Allington St, SW1 **25** F6
Allison Cl, SE10
off Dartmouth Hill **154** C1
Allison Gro, SE21 **170** B1
Allison Rd, N8 **75** G5
W3 **106** C6
Allitsen Rd, NW8 **7** G2
Allnutt Way, SW4 **150** D5
Alloa Rd, SE8 **133** G5
Ilford IG3 **100** A2
Allonby Gdns, Wem. HA9 **87** F1
Allotment Way, NW2
off Midland Ter **90** A3
Alloway Rd, E3 **113** H3
Allports Ms, E1
off Stepney Grn **113** F4
All Saints Cl, N9 **60** C2
SW8 *off Lansdowne Way* **150/151** E1
All Saints Dr, SE3 **155** E2
All Saints Ms, Har. HA3 **52** B6
All Saints Pas, SW18
off Wandsworth High St **148/149** E5
All Saints Rd, SW19 **167** F7
W3 **126** C3
W11 **108** C5
Sutton SM1 **199** E3
All Saints St, N1 **10** C1
All Saints Twr, E10 **78** B7
Allsop Pl, NW1 **8** A6
All Souls Av, NW10 **107** H2
All Souls Pl, W1 **17** E2
Allum Way, N20 **57** F1
Allwood Cl, SE26 **171** G4
Alma Av, E4 **62** C7
Almack Rd, E5 **95** F4
Alma Cres, Sutt. SM1 **198** B5
Alma Gro, SE1 **37** G2
Alma Pl, NW10
off Harrow Rd **107** H3
SE19 **170** C7
Thornton Heath CR7 **187** G5
Alma Rd, N10 **58** A7
SW18 **149** F5
Carshalton SM5 **199** H5
Enfield EN3 **45** H5
Esher KT10 **194** B1
Sidcup DA14 **176** A3
Southall UB1 **102** E7
Alma Row, Har. HA3 **68** A1
Alma Sq, NW8 **6** D3
Alma St, E15 **96** D6
NW5 **92** B6
Alma Ter, SW18 **149** G7
W8 *off Allen St* **128** D3
Almeida St, N1 **93** H7
Almeric Rd, SW11 **149** J4
Almer Rd, SW20 **165** G7
Almington St, N4 **93** F1
Almond Av, W5 **125** H3
Carshalton SM5 **199** J2
West Drayton UB7 **120** D3
Almond Cl, SE15 **152** D2
Bromley BR2 **192** D7
Feltham TW13
off Highfield Rd **160** A1
Almond Gro, Brent. TW8 **124** E7
Almond Rd, N17 **60** D7
SE16 **133** E4
Almonds Av, Buck.H. IG9 **63** G2
Almond Way, Borwd. WD6 **38** B4
Bromley BR2 **192** D7
Harrow HA2 **67** H2
Mitcham CR4 **186** D5
Almorah Rd, N1 **94** A7
Hounslow TW5 **142** D1
Alnwick Gro, Mord. SM4
off Bordesley Rd **184/185** E4
Alnwick Rd, E16 **115** J6
SE12 **155** H7
ALPERTON, Wem. HA0 **105** J1
Alperton La, Grnf. UB6 **105** G3
Wembley HA0 **105** G3
Alperton St, W10 **108** B4
Alphabet Gdns, Cars. SM5 **185** G6
Alphabet Sq, E3
off Hawgood St **114** A5
Alpha Cl, NW1 **7** H4
Alpha Gro, E14 **134** A2
Alpha Pl, NW6 **108** D2
SW3 **31** H5
Alpha Rd, E4 **62** B3
N18 **60** D6
SE14 **153** J1
Croydon CR0 **202** B1
Enfield EN3 **45** H4
Surbiton KT5 **181** J6
Teddington TW11 **162** A5
Alpha St, SE15 **152** D2
Alphea Cl, SW19
off Courtney Rd **167** H7
Alpine Av, Surb. KT5 **196** C2
Alpine Business Cen, E6 **116** D5
Alpine Cl, Croy. CR0 **202** B3
Alpine Copse, Brom. BR1 **192** D2
Alpine Gro, E9 **95** F7
Alpine Rd, E10 **96** B2
SE16 **133** F4
Walton-on-Thames KT12 **178** A7
Alpine Vw, Cars. SM5 **199** H5
Alpine Wk, Stan. HA7 **52** B2
Alpine Way, E6 **116** D5
Alric Av, NW10 **88** D7
New Malden KT3 **183** E3
Alroy Rd, N4 **75** G7
Alsace Rd, SE17 **36** D3
Alscot Rd, SE1 **37** G1
Alscot Way, SE1 **37** F1
Alsike Rd, SE2 **138** D3
Erith DA18 **138** E3
Alsom Av, Wor.Pk. KT4 **197** G4
Alston Cl, Surb. KT6 **181** E7
Alston Rd, N18 **60** E5
SW17 **167** G4
Barnet EN5 **40** B3
Altair Cl, N17 **60** C6
Altash Way, SE9 **174** C2
Altenburg Av, W13 **125** E3
Altenburg Gdns, SW11 **149** J4
Alt Gro, SW19
off St. George's Rd **166** C7
Altham Gdns, Wat. WD19 **50** D4
Altham Rd, Pnr. HA5 **51** E7
Althea St, SW6 **149** E3
Althorne Gdns, E18 **79** F4
Althorne Way, Dag. RM10 **101** G2
Althorp Cl, Barn. EN5 **39** G7
Althorpe Gro, SW11
off Westbridge Rd **149** G1
Althorpe Ms, SW11
off Battersea High St **149** G1
Althorpe Rd, Har. HA1 **67** J5
Althorp Rd, SW17 **167** J1
Altmore Av, E6 **98** C7
Alton Av, Stan. HA7 **52** C7
Alton Cl, Bex. DA5 **177** E1
Isleworth TW7 **144** C2
Alton Gdns, Beck. BR3 **172** A7
Twickenham TW2 **144** A7
Alton Rd, N17 **76** A3
SW15 **165** G1
Croydon CR0 **201** G3
Richmond TW9 **145** H4
Alton St, E14 **114** B5
Altyre Cl, Beck. BR3 **189** J5
Altyre Rd, Croy. CR0 **202** A2
Altyre Way, Beck. BR3 **189** J5
Alvanley Gdns, NW6 **90** E5
Alva Way, Wat. WD19 **50** D2
Alverstone Av, SW19 **166** D2
Barnet EN4 **41** H7
Alverstone Gdns, SE9 **175** F1
Alverstone Rd, E12 **98** D4
NW2 **89** J7
New Malden KT3 **183** F4
Wembley HA9 **87** J1
Alverston Gdns, SE25 **188** B5
Alverton St, SE8 **133** J5
Alveston Av, Har. HA3 **68** E3
Alvey Est, SE17 **36** D2
Alvey St, SE17 **36** D3
Alvia Gdns, Sutt. SM1 **199** F4
Alvington Cres, E8 **94** C5
Alway Av, Epsom KT19 **196** C5
Alwold Cres, SE12 **155** H6
Alwyn Av, W4 **126** D5
Alwyn Cl, Croy. (New Adgtn) CR0 **204** B7
Alwyne La, N1
off Alwyne Vil **93** H7
Alwyne Pl, N1 **93** J6
Alwyne Rd, N1 **93** J7
SW19 **166** C6
W7 **104** B7
Alwyne Sq, N1 **93** J6
Alwyne Vil, N1 **93** H7
Alwyn Gdns, NW4 **71** G4
W3 **106** B6
Alyth Gdns, NW11 **72** D6
Alzette Ho, E2 **113** G3
Amalgamated Dr, Brent. TW8 **124** D6
Amanda Cl, Chig. IG7 **65** G6
Amanda Ms, Rom. RM7 **83** J5
Amazon Apartments, N8
off High St **75** F4
Amazon St, E1
off Hessel St **112/113** E6
Ambassador Cl, Houns. TW3 **142** E2
Ambassador Gdns, E6 **116** C5
Ambassador's Ct, SW1 **25** G2
Ambassador Sq, E14
off Cahir St **134** B4
Amber Av, E17 **77** H1
Amber Ct, SW17
off Brudenell Rd **168** A4
Amberden Av, N3 **72** D3
Ambergate St, SE17 **35** H3
Amber Gro, NW2
off Prayle Gro **90** A1
Amber La, Ilf. IG6 **64** E7
Amberley Cl, Orp. BR6
off Warnford Rd **207** J5
Pinner HA5 **67** F3
Amberley Ct, Sid. DA14 **176** C5
Amberley Gdns, Enf. EN1 **44** B7
Epsom KT19 **197** F4
Amberley Gro, SE26 **170** E4
Croydon CR0 **188** C7
Amberley Rd, E10 **78** B7
N13 **59** F2
SE2 **138** D6
W9 **108** D5
Buckhurst Hill IG9 **63** J1
Amberley Rd, Enf. EN1 **44** C7
Amberley Way, Houns. TW4 **142** C5
Morden SM4 **184** C7
Amberley Way, Rom. RM7 **83** H4
Amber Ms, N22
off Brampton Pk Rd **75** G3
Amberside Cl, Islw. TW7 **144** A6
Amber St, E15
off Great Eastern Rd **96** D6
Amber Wf, E2
off Nursery La **112** C1
Amberwood Cl, Wall. SM6
off The Chase **200/201** E5
Amberwood Ri, N.Mal. KT3 **182** E6
Amblecote Cl, SE12 **173** H3
Amblecote Meadows, SE12 **173** H3
Amblecote Rd, SE12 **173** H3
Ambler Rd, N4 **93** H3
Ambleside, Brom. BR1 **172** D6
Ambleside Av, SW16 **168** D4
Beckenham BR3 **189** H5
Ambleside Cl, E9
off Churchill Wk **95** F5
E10 **78** B7
Ambleside Cres, Enf. EN3 **45** G3
Ambleside Gdns, SW16 **168** D5
Ilford IG4 **80** B4
Sutton SM2 **199** F6
Wembley HA9 **87** G1
Ambleside Pt, SE15
off Ilderton Rd **133** F7
Ambleside Rd, NW10 **89** F7
Bexleyheath DA7 **159** G2
Ambrooke Rd, Belv. DA17 **139** G3
Ambrosden Av, SW1 **25** G6
Ambrose Av, NW11 **72** B7
Ambrose Cl, E6
off Lovage App **116** B5
Orpington BR6
off Stapleton Rd **207** J3
Ambrose Ms, SW11 **149** H2
Ambrose St, SE16 **132** E4
Ambrose Wk, E3
off Malmesbury Rd **114** A2
Amelia Cl, W3 **126** B1
Amelia St, SE17 **35** H3
Amen Cor, EC4 **19** H4
SW17 **167** J6
Amen Ct, EC4 **19** H3
Amenity Way, Mord. SM4 **183** J7
America Sq, EC3 **21** F5
America St, SE1 **27** J2
Amerland Rd, SW18 **148** C6
Amersham Av, N18 **60** A6
Amersham Gro, SE14 **133** J7
Amersham Rd, SE14 **133** J7
Croydon CR0 **187** J6
Amersham Vale, SE14 **133** J7
Amery Gdns, NW10 **107** H1
Amery Rd, Har. HA1 **86** D2
Amesbury Av, SW2 **169** E2
Amesbury Cl, Wor.Pk. KT4 **197** J1
Amesbury Dr, E4 **46** B6
Amesbury Rd, Brom. BR1 **192** A3
Dagenham RM9 **100** D7
Feltham TW13 **160** D2
Amesbury Twr, SW8
off Westbury St **150** C2
Amethyst Cl, N11 **58** D7
Amethyst Rd, E15 **96** D4
Amherst Av, W13 **105** F6
Amherst Dr, Orp. BR5 **193** J4
Amherst Rd, W13 **105** F6
Amhurst Gdns, Islw. TW7 **144** C1
Amhurst Par, N16
off Amhurst Pk **76** C7
Amhurst Pk, N16 **76** A7
Amhurst Pas, E8 **94** D4
Amhurst Rd, E8 **94** E5
N16 **94** C4
Amhurst Ter, E8 **94** D4
Amhurst Wk, SE28
off Pitfield Cres **138** A1
Amidas Gdns, Dag. RM8 **100** B4
Amiel St, E1 **113** F4
Amies St, SW11 **149** J3
Amina Way, SE16 **29** H6
Amis Av, Epsom KT19 **196** B6
Amity Gro, SW20 **183** J1
Amity Rd, E15 **115** F1
Ammanford Grn, NW9
off Ruthin Cl **70/71** E6
Amner Rd, SW11 **150** A6
Amor Rd, W6 **127** J3

Amott Rd, SE15 . . . **152** D3
Amoy Pl, E14 . . . **114** A6
Ampere Way, Croy. CR0 . . **187** E7
Ampleforth Rd, SE2 . . . **138** B2
Ampthill Sq, NW1 . . . **9** G2
Ampton Pl, WC1 . . . **10** C4
Ampton St, WC1 . . . **10** C4
Amroth Cl, SE23 . . . **171** E1
Amroth Grn, NW9
off Fryent Gro . . . **70/71** E6
Amsterdam Rd, E14 . . . **134** C3
Amundsen Ct, E14
off Napier Av . . . **134** A5
Amwell Cl, Enf. EN2 . . . **44** A5
Amwell Ct Est, N4 . . . **93** J1
Amwell St, EC1 . . . **11** E3
Amyand Cotts, Twick. TW1
off Amyand Pk Rd . **144/145** E6
Amyand La, Twick. TW1
off Marble Hill Gdns . . . **144/145** E7
Amyand Pk Gdns, Twick. TW1
off Amyand Pk Rd . **144/145** E7
Amyand Pk Rd, Twick. TW1 . . . **144** D7
Amy Cl, Wall. SM6
off Mollison Dr . . . **200/201** E7
Amyruth Rd, SE4 . . . **154** A5
Amy Warne Cl, E6
off Evelyn Denington Rd . . . **116** B4
Anatola Rd, N19
off Dartmouth Pk Hill . . **92** B2
Ancaster Cres, N.Mal. KT3 . . . **183** G6
Ancaster Ms, Beck. BR3 . . **189** G3
Ancaster Rd, Beck. BR3 . . **189** G3
Ancaster St, SE18 . . . **137** H7
Anchorage Cl, SW19 . . . **166** D5
Anchorage Pt, E14
off Cuba St . . . **134** A2
Anchorage Pt Ind Est, SE7 . . . **135** J3
Anchor & Hope La, SE7 . . **135** H3
Anchor Cl, Bark. IG11 . . . **118** B3
Anchor Ms, N1
off Balls Pond Rd . . . **94** B6
SW12
off Hazelbourne Rd . . . **150** B6
Anchor Retail Pk, E1 . . . **113** F4
Anchor St, SE16 . . . **132** E4
Anchor Ter, E1
off Cephas Av . . . **113** F4
Anchor Wf, E3
off Watts Gro . . . **114** B5
Anchor Yd, EC1 . . . **12** A5
Ancill Cl, W6 . . . **128** B6
Ancona Rd, NW10 . . . **107** G2
SE18 . . . **137** G5
Andace Pk Gdns, Brom. BR1 . . . **191** J1
Andalus Rd, SW9 . . . **151** E3
Ander Cl, Wem. HA0 . . . **87** G4
Anderson Cl, N21 . . . **43** F5
W3 . . . **106** D6
Sutton SM3 . . . **198** D1
Anderson Ho, Bark. IG11
off The Coverdales . . . **117** G2
Anderson Pl, Houns. TW3 . . . **143** H4
Anderson Rd, E9 . . . **95** G6
Woodford Green IG8 . . . **80** A3
Andersons Sq, N1
off Gaskin St . . . **111** H1
Anderson St, SW3 . . . **31** J3
Anderson Way, Belv. DA17 . . . **139** H2
Anderton Cl, SE5 . . . **152** A3
Andmark Ct, Sthl. UB1
off Herbert Rd . . . **123** F1
Andover Av, E16
off King George Av . . . **116** A6
Andover Cl, Grnf. UB6
off Ruislip Rd . . . **103** H4
Andover Pl, NW6 . . . **6** A1
Andover Rd, N7 . . . **93** F2
Orpington BR6 . . . **207** G1
Twickenham TW2 . . . **162** A1
Andre St, E8 . . . **94** D5
Andrew Borde St, WC2 . . . **17** J3
Andrew Cl, Ilf. IG6 . . . **65** G6
Andrewes Gdns, E6 . . . **116** B6
Andrewes Ho, EC2 . . . **20** A2
Andrew Pl, SW8
off Cowthorpe Rd . . . **150** D1
Andrew Reed Ho, SW18
off Linstead Way . . . **148** B7
Andrews Cl, E6
off Linton Gdns . . . **116** B6
Andrews Cl, Buck.H. IG9 . . **63** J2
Harrow HA1
off Bessborough Rd . . . **68** A7
Worcester Park KT4 . . . **198** A2
Andrews Crosse, WC2 . . . **18** E4
Andrews Pl, SE9 . . . **156** E6
Andrew's Rd, E8 . . . **112** E1
Andrew St, E14 . . . **114** C6
Andrews Wk, SE17 . . . **35** H6
Andwell Cl, SE2 . . . **138** B2
ANERLEY, SE20 . . . **188** E1
Anerley Gro, SE19 . . . **170** C7
Anerley Hill, SE19 . . . **170** C6
Anerley Pk, SE20 . . . **170** D7
Anerley Pk Rd, SE20 . . . **170** E7
Anerley Rd, SE19 . . . **170** D7
SE20 . . . **170** D7
Anerley Sta Rd, SE20 . . . **188** E1
Anerley St, SW11 . . . **149** J2
Anerley Vale, SE19 . . . **170** C7
Anfield Cl, SW12
off Belthorn Cres . . . **150** C7
Angel All, E1 . . . **21** G3
Angel Cl, N18 . . . **60** C4
Angel Cor Par, N18
off Fore St . . . **60** D5
Angel Ct, EC2 . . . **20** C3
SW1 . . . **25** G2
SW17 . . . **167** J4
Angel Edmonton, N18
off Angel Rd . . . **60** D5
Angelfield, Houns. TW3 . . **143** H4
Angel Gate, EC1 . . . **11** H3
Angel Hill, Sutt. SM1
off Sutton Common Rd . . . **198/199** E3
Angel Hill Dr, Sutt. SM1 . . **199** E3
Angelica Dr, E6 . . . **116** D5
Angelica Gdns, Croy. CR0 . . . **203** G1
Angelis Apartments, N1
off Graham St . . . **111** H2
Angel La, E15 . . . **96** D6
Angell Pk Gdns, SW9 . . . **151** G3
Angell Rd, SW9 . . . **151** G3
Angell Town Est, SW9 . . . **151** G2
Angel Ms, E1
off Cable St . . . **112** D7
N1 . . . **11** F2
SW15
off Roehampton High St . . . **147** G7
Angel Pas, EC4 . . . **20** B6
Angel Pl, N18 . . . **60** D5
SE1 . . . **28** B3
Angel Rd, N18 . . . **60** E5
Harrow HA1 . . . **68** B6
Thames Ditton KT7 . . . **180** D7
Angel Rd Wks, N18 . . . **61** F5
Angel Sq, EC1 . . . **11** F2
Angel St, EC1 . . . **19** J3
Angel Wk, W6 . . . **127** J4
Angerstein La, SE3 . . . **135** F7
Angle Grn, Dag. RM8 . . . **100** C1
Anglers Cl, Rich. TW10
off Locksmeade Rd . . . **163** F4
Angler's La, NW5 . . . **92** B6
Anglers Reach, Surb. KT6 . . . **181** G5
Anglesea Av, SE18 . . . **136** E4
Anglesea Ms, SE18
off Anglesea Av . . **136/137** E4
Anglesea Rd, SE18 . . . **136** E4
Kingston upon Thames KT1 . . . **181** G4
Anglesea Ter, W6
off Wellesley Av . . . **127** H3
Anglesey Ct Rd, Cars. SM5 . . . **200** A6
Anglesey Gdns, Cars. SM5 . . . **200** A6
Anglesey Rd, Enf. EN3 . . . **45** E4
Watford WD19 . . . **50** C5
Anglesmede Cres, Pnr. HA5 . . . **67** G3
Anglesmede Way, Pnr. HA5 . . . **67** F3
Angles Rd, SW16 . . . **169** E4
Anglia Cl, N17
off Park La . . . **60/61** E7
Anglia Ct, Dag. RM8
off Spring Cl . . . **100** D1
Anglia Ho, E14 . . . **113** H6
Anglian Rd, E11 . . . **96** D3
Anglia Wk, E6 . . . **116** C1
Anglo Rd, E3 . . . **113** J2
Angrave Ct, E8 . . . **112** C1
Angrave Pas, E8
off Haggerston Rd . . . **112** C1
Angus Cl, Chess. KT9 . . . **196** A5
Angus Dr, Ruis. HA4 . . . **84** C4
Angus Gdns, NW9 . . . **70** D1
Angus Rd, E13 . . . **115** J3
Angus St, SE14 . . . **133** H7
Anhalt Rd, SW11 . . . **31** H7
Ankerdine Cres, SE18 . . . **136** D7
Anlaby Rd, Tedd. TW11 . . . **162** B5
Anley Rd, W14 . . . **128** A2
Anmersh Gro, Stan. HA7 . . **69** G1
Annabel Cl, E14 . . . **114** B6
Anna Cl, E8 . . . **112** C1
Annandale Rd, SE10 . . . **135** F6
W4 . . . **126** E4
Croydon CR0 . . . **202** D2
Sidcup DA15 . . . **157** H7
Anna Neagle Cl, E7
off Dames Rd . . . **97** G4
Anne Boleyn's Wk, Kings.T. KT2 . . . **163** H5
Sutton SM3 . . . **198** A7
Anne Case Ms, N.Mal. KT3
off Sycamore Gro . . . **182** D3
Anne Compton Ms, SE12 . . . **155** F7
Annesley Av, NW9 . . . **70** D3
Annesley Cl, NW10 . . . **88** E3
Annesley Dr, Croy. CR0 . . **203** J3
Annesley Rd, SE3 . . . **155** H1
Annesley Wk, N19 . . . **92** C2
Anne St, E13 . . . **115** G4
Annette Cl, Har. HA3
off Spencer Rd . . . **68** B2
Annette Cres, N1
off Essex Rd . . . **93** J7
Annette Rd, N7 . . . **93** F4
Annett Rd, Walt. KT12 . . . **178** A7
Anne Way, Ilf. IG6 . . . **65** F6
West Molesey KT8 . . . **179** H4
Annie Besant Cl, E3 . . . **113** J1
Annie Taylor Ho, E12
off Walton Rd . . . **98** D4
Anning St, EC2 . . . **13** E5
Annington Rd, N2 . . . **73** J3
Annis Rd, E9 . . . **95** H6
Ann La, SW10 . . . **30** E7
Ann Moss Way, SE16 . . . **133** F3
Ann's Cl, SW1 . . . **24** A4
Ann's Pl, E1 . . . **21** F2
Ann St, SE18 . . . **137** G4
Annsworthy Av, Th.Hth. CR7
off Grange Pk Rd . . . **188** A3
Annsworthy Cres, SE25
off Grange Rd . . . **188** A2
Ansdell Rd, SE15 . . . **153** F2
Ansdell St, W8 . . . **22** B5
Ansdell Ter, W8 . . . **22** B5
Ansell Gro, Cars. SM5 . . . **200** A1
Ansell Rd, SW17 . . . **167** H3
Anselm Cl, Croy. CR0
off Park Hill Ri . . . **202** C3
Anselm Rd, SW6 . . . **128** D6
Pinner HA5 . . . **51** F7
Ansford Rd, Brom. BR1 . . . **172** C5
Ansleigh Pl, W11 . . . **108** A7
Anson Cl, Rom. RM7 . . . **83** H2
Anson Ho, E1
off Shandy St . . . **113** H4
Anson Pl, SE28 . . . **137** G2
Anson Rd, N7 . . . **92** C4
NW2 . . . **90** A5
Anson Ter, Nthlt. UB5 . . . **85** H6
Anstey Rd, SE15 . . . **152** D3
Anstey Wk, N15 . . . **75** H4
Anstice Cl, W4 . . . **127** E7
Anstridge Path, SE9 . . . **157** G6
Anstridge Rd, SE9 . . . **157** G6
Antelope Rd, SE18 . . . **136** C3
Anthony Cl, NW7 . . . **55** E4
Watford WD19 . . . **50** C1
★**Anthony d'Offay Gall**, W1 . . . **16** E4
Anthony Rd, SE25 . . . **188** D6
Greenford UB6 . . . **104** B2
Welling DA16 . . . **158** A1
Anthony St, E1 *off Commercial Rd* . . . **112/113** E6
Anthony Way, N18 . . . **61** G6
Antigua Cl, SE19
off Salters Hill . . . **170** A5
Antigua Wk, SE19 . . . **170** A5
Antill Rd, E3 . . . **113** H3
N15 . . . **76** C4
Antill Ter, E1 . . . **113** G6
Antlers Hill, E4 . . . **46** B5
Anton Cres, Sutt. SM1 . . . **198** D3
Antoneys Cl, Pnr. HA5 . . . **66** D2
Anton Pl, Wem. HA9 . . . **88** B3
Anton St, E8 . . . **94** D5
Antrim Gro, NW3 . . . **91** J6
Antrim Mans, NW3 . . . **91** H6
Antrim Rd, NW3 . . . **91** J6
Antrobus Cl, Sutt. SM1 . . **198** C5
Antrobus Rd, W4 . . . **126** C4
Anvil Cl, SW16 . . . **168** C7
Anvil Rd, Sun. TW16 . . . **178** A3
Anworth Cl, Wdf.Grn. IG8 . . . **63** H6
Apex Cl, Beck. BR3 . . . **190** B1
Apex Cor, NW7 . . . **54** D4
Apex Ind Est, NW10
off Hythe Rd . . . **107** G3
Apex Retail Pk, Felt. TW13 . . . **161** F3
Apex Twr, N.Mal. KT3 . . . **182** E3
Aplin Way, Islw. TW7 . . . **144** B1
Apollo, E14
off Newton Pl . . . **134** A4
Apollo Av, Brom. BR1
off Rodway Rd . . . **191** H1
Northwood HA6 . . . **50** A5
★**Apollo Hammersmith**, W6 . . . **127** J5
Apollo Pl, E11 . . . **96** E3
SW10 . . . **31** E7
★**Apollo Thea**, W1 . . . **17** H5
★**Apollo Victoria Thea**, SW1 . . . **25** F6
Apollo Way, SE28
off Broadwater Rd . . . **137** G3
Apostle Way, Th.Hth. CR7 . . . **187** H2
Apothecary St, EC4 . . . **19** G4
Appach Rd, SW2 . . . **151** G6
Apple Blossom Ct, SW8
off Pascal St . . . **130** D7
Appleby Cl, E4 . . . **62** C6
N15 . . . **76** A5
Twickenham TW2 . . . **162** A2
Appleby Rd, E8 . . . **94** D7
E16 . . . **115** F6
Appleby St, E2 . . . **13** F1
Appledore Av, Bexh. DA7 . **159** J1
Ruislip HA4 . . . **84** B3
Appledore Cl, SW17 . . . **167** J2
Bromley BR2 . . . **191** F5
Edgware HA8 . . . **70** A1
Appledore Cres, Sid. DA14 . . . **175** H3
Appledore Way, NW7
off Tavistock Av . . . **56** A7
Appleford Rd, W10 . . . **108** B4
Apple Garth, Brent. TW8 . **125** G4
Applegarth, Croy.
(New Adgtn) CR0 . . . **204** B7
Esher (Clay.) KT10 . . . **194** C5
Applegarth Dr, Ilf. IG2 . . . **81** J4
Applegarth Rd, SE28 . . . **138** B1
W14 . . . **128** A3
Apple Gro, Chess. KT9 . . . **195** H4
Enfield EN1 . . . **44** B3
Apple Mkt, Kings.T. KT1
off Eden St . . . **181** G2
Apple Rd, E11 . . . **96** E3
Appleton Cl, Bexh. DA7 . . **159** J2
Appleton Gdns, N.Mal. KT3 . . . **183** G6
Appleton Rd, SE9 . . . **156** B3
Loughton IG10 . . . **49** E3
Appleton Sq, Mitch. CR4
off Silbury Av . . . **185** H1
Appletree Cl, SE20
off Jasmine Gro . . **188/189** E1
Appletree Gdns, Barn. EN4 . . . **41** H4
Apple Tree Yd, SW1 . . . **25** G1
Applewood Cl, N20 . . . **57** H1
NW2 . . . **89** H3
Applewood Dr, E13 . . . **115** H4
Appold St, EC2 . . . **20** D1
Apprentice Way, E5
off Clarence Rd . . . **94/95** E4
Approach, The, NW4 . . . **72** A5
W3 . . . **106** D6
Enfield EN1 . . . **44** E2
Orpington BR6 . . . **207** J2
Approach Cl, N16
off Cowper Rd . . . **94** B4
Approach Rd, E2 . . . **113** F2
SW20 . . . **183** J2
Barnet EN4 . . . **41** G4
West Molesey KT8 . . . **179** G5
Aprey Gdns, NW4 . . . **71** J4
April Cl, W7 . . . **104** B7
Feltham TW13 . . . **160** A3
Orpington BR6
off Briarswood Way . . **207** J5
April Glen, SE23 . . . **171** G3

April St, E8 . . . . **94** C4
Apsley Cl, Har. HA2 . . . . . . **67** J5
★**Apsley Ho, Wellington Mus**, W1 . . . . **24** B3
Apsley Rd, SE25 . . . . **188** E4
New Malden KT3 . . . . . **182** C3
Apsley Way, NW2 . . . . **89** G2
W1 . . . . **24** C3
Aquarius Business Pk, NW2 . . . . **89** G1
Aquarius Way, Nthwd. HA6 . . . . **50** A5
★**Aquatic Experience**, Brent. TW8 . . . . **145** E1
Aquila St, NW8 . . . . **7** F1
Aquinas St, SE1 . . . . **27** F2
Arabella Dr, SW15 . . . . . . **147** E4
Arabia Cl, E4 . . . . **46** D7
Arabin Rd, SE4 . . . . **153** H4
Aragon Av, T.Ditt. KT7 . . . . **180** C5
Aragon Cl, Brom. BR2 . . . **206** C1
Loughton IG10 . . . . **48** B6
Aragon Dr, Ilf. IG6 . . . . **65** F7
Ruislip HA4 . . . . **84** D1
Aragon Rd, Kings.T. KT2 . . . . **163** H5
Morden SM4 . . . . **184** A6
Aragon Twr, SE8 . . . . **133** J4
Arandora Cres, Rom. RM6 . . . . **82** B7
Aran Dr, Stan. HA7 . . . . . . **53** F4
Arbery Rd, E3 . . . . **113** H3
Arbor Cl, Beck. BR3 . . . . . **190** B2
Arbor Ct, N16
off Lordship Rd **94** A2
Arborfield Cl, SW2 . . . . . . **169** F1
Arbor Rd, E4 . . . . **62** D3
Arbour Rd, Enf. EN3 . . . . . **45** G4
Arbour Sq, E1 . . . . **113** G6
Arbroath Grn, Wat. WD19 . . **50** A3
Arbroath Rd, SE9 . . . . **156** B3
Arbury Ter, SE26
off Oaksford Av . . **170/171** E3
Arbuthnot La, Bex. DA5 . . **159** E6
Arbuthnot Rd, SE14 . . . . . **153** G2
Arbutus St, E8 . . . . **112** B1
Arcade, The, EC2 . . . . **20** D2
Croydon CR0
off High St **201** J3
Arcadia Av, N3 . . . . **72** D1
Arcadia Cl, Cars. SM5 . . . **200** A4
Arcadian Av, Bex. DA5 . . . **158** E6
Arcadian Cl, Bex. DA5 . . . **158** E6
Arcadian Gdns, N22 . . . . . . **59** F7
Arcadian Pl, SW18
off Sutherland Gro . . . **148** D7
Arcadian Rd, Bex. DA5 . . . **158** E6
Arcadia Shop Cen, W5 . . . **105** G7
Arcadia St, E14 . . . . **114** A6
Archangel St, SE16 . . . . . **133** G2
Archbishops Pl, SW2 . . . . **151** F6
Archdale Pl, N.Mal. KT3 . . **182** B3
Archdale Rd, SE22 . . . . . . **152** C5
Archel Rd, W14 . . . . **128** C6
Archer Cl, Kings.T. KT2 . . **163** H7
Archer Ho, SW11
off Vicarage Cres **149** G1
Archer Ms, Hmptn. (Hmptn H.) TW12
off Windmill Rd **161** J6
Archer Rd, SE25 . . . . **188** E4
Archers Dr, Enf. EN3 . . . . . **45** F2
Archer Sq, SE14
off Knoyle St **133** H6
Archer St, W1 . . . . **17** H5
Archery Cl, W2 . . . . **15** H4
Harrow HA3 . . . . **68** C3
Archery Rd, SE9 . . . . **156** C5
Arches, The, SW6
off Munster Rd **148** C2
WC2 . . . . **26** B1
Harrow HA2 . . . . **85** H2
Archibald Ms, W1 . . . . **16** C6
Archibald Rd, N7 . . . . **92** D4
Archibald St, E3 . . . . **114** A3
Archie Cl, West Dr. UB7 . . **120** D2
Archie St, SE1 . . . . **29** E4
Arch St, SE1 . . . . **27** J6
Archway Cl, N19
off St. Johns Way **92** C2
SW19 . . . . **166** E4
W10 . . . . **108** A5
Wallington SM6 . . . . . . **200** D3
Archway Mall, N19
off Magdala Av **92** C2
Archway Ms, SW15
off Putney Br Rd **148** B4
Archway Rd, N6 . . . . **73** J6
N19 . . . . **92** C1
Archway St, SW13 . . . . . . **147** E3
Arcola St, E8 . . . . **94** C5
Arctic St, NW5
off Gillies St **92** A5
Arcus Rd, Brom. BR1 . . . . **173** E6
Ardbeg Rd, SE24 . . . . **152** A6
Arden Cl, SE28
off Redbourne Dr. **118** D6
Harrow HA1 . . . . **86** A3
Arden Ct Gdns, N2 . . . . **73** G6
Arden Cres, E14 . . . . **134** A4
Dagenham RM9 . . . . . . **100** C7
Arden Est, N1 . . . . **12** D2
Arden Gro, Orp. BR6 . . . . **207** E4
Arden Ho, SW9
off Grantham Rd . **150/151** E2
Arden Ms, E17 . . . . **78** B5
Arden Mhor, Pnr. HA5 . . . . **66** B4
Arden Rd, N3 . . . . **72** B3
W13 . . . . **105** F7
Ardent Cl, SE25 . . . . **188** B3
Ardfern Av, SW16 . . . . **187** G3
Ardfillan Rd, SE6 . . . . **172** D1
Ardgowan Rd, SE6 . . . . . . **154** E7
Ardilaun Rd, N5 . . . . **93** J4
Ardingly Cl, Croy. CR0 . . . **203** G3
Ardleigh Gdns, Sutt. SM3 . . . . **184** D7
Ardleigh Ho, Bark. IG11
off St. Ann's **117** F1
Ardleigh Ms, Ilf. IG1
off Bengal Rd **98/99** E3
Ardleigh Rd, E17 . . . . **77** J1
N1 . . . . **94** A6
Ardleigh Ter, E17 . . . . **77** J1
Ardley Cl, NW10 . . . . **88** E3
SE6 . . . . **171** H3
Ardlui Rd, SE27 . . . . **169** J2
Ardmay Gdns, Surb. KT6 . . . . **181** H5
Ardmere Rd, SE13 . . . . . . **154** D6
Ardmore La, Buck.H. IG9 . . **47** H7
Ardmore Pl, Buck.H. IG9 . . **47** H7
Ardoch Rd, SE6 . . . . **172** D2
Ardra Rd, N9 . . . . **61** G3
Ardrossan Gdns, Wor.Pk. KT4 . . . . **197** G3
Ardshiel Cl, SW15
off Bemish Rd **148** A3
Ardwell Av, Ilf. IG6 . . . . **81** F5
Ardwell Rd, SW2 . . . . **168** E2
Ardwick Rd, NW2 . . . . **90** D4
Arewater Grn, Loug. IG10 . . . . **48** C1
Argali Ho, Erith DA18
off Kale Rd **138/139** F3
Argall Av, E10 . . . . **77** G7
Argall Way, E10 . . . . **95** G1
Argenta Way, NW10 . . . . . . **88** B7
Argon Ms, SW6 . . . . **128** D7
Argon Rd, N18 . . . . **61** F5
Argosy La, Stai. (Stanw.) TW19 . . . . **140** A7
Argus Cl, Rom. RM7 . . . . . . **83** H1
Argus Way, Nthlt. UB5 . . . **102** E3
Argyle Av, Houns. TW3 . . . **143** G6
Argyle Cl, W13 . . . . **104** D4
Argyle Pas, N17 . . . . **76** C1
Argyle Pl, W6 . . . . **127** H4
Argyle Rd, E1 . . . . **113** G4
E15 . . . . **96** E4
E16 . . . . **115** J6
N12 . . . . **56** D5
N17 . . . . **76** D1
N18 . . . . **60** D4
W13 . . . . **104** D5
Barnet EN5 . . . . **39** J4
Greenford UB6 . . . . **104** C3
Harrow HA2 . . . . **67** H6
Hounslow TW3 . . . . **143** H5
Ilford IG1 . . . . **98** D2
Teddington TW11 . . . . . **162** B5
Argyle Sq, WC1 . . . . **10** B3
Argyle St, WC1 . . . . **10** A3
Argyle Wk, WC1 . . . . **10** B4
Argyle Way, SE16 . . . . **37** J4
Argyll Av, Sthl. UB1 . . . . . **123** H1
Argyll Cl, SW9
off Dalyell Rd **151** F3
Argyll Gdns, Edg. HA8 . . . . **70** B2
Argyll Rd, SE18 . . . . **137** F3
W8 . . . . **128** D2
Argyll St, W1 . . . . **17** F4
Arica Rd, SE4 . . . . **153** H4
Ariel Rd, NW6 . . . . **90** D6
Ariel Way, W12 . . . . **127** J1
Hounslow TW4 . . . . **142** B3
Aristotle Rd, SW4 . . . . **150** D3
Arkell Gro, SE19 . . . . **169** H7
Arkindale Rd, SE6 . . . . . . **172** C3
ARKLEY, Barn. EN5 . . . . . . **39** G5
Arkley Cres, E17 . . . . **77** J5
Arkley Dr, Barn. EN5 . . . . . **39** G4
Arkley La, Barn. EN5 . . . . . **39** G3
Arkley Pk, Barn. EN5 . . . . . **38** D6
Arkley Rd, E17 . . . . **77** J5
Arkley Vw, Barn. EN5 . . . . . **39** H4
Arklow Ms, Surb. KT6
off Vale Rd S **195** H2
Arklow Rd, SE14 . . . . **133** J6
Arkwright Rd, NW3 . . . . . . **91** F5
Arlesey Cl, SW15
off Lytton Gro **148** B6
Arlesford Rd, SW9 . . . . . . **151** E3
Arlingford Rd, SW2 . . . . . **151** G5
Arlington, N12 . . . . **56** D3
Arlington Av, N1 . . . . **111** J2
Arlington Cl, SE13 . . . . . . **154** D6
Sidcup DA15 . . . . **157** H7
Sutton SM1 . . . . **198** D2
Twickenham TW1 . . . . . . **145** F6
Arlington Ct, Hayes UB3
off Shepiston La **121** G5
Arlington Dr, Cars. SM5 . . **199** J2
Arlington Gdns, W4 . . . . . **126** C5
Ilford IG1 . . . . **98** D1
Arlington Grn, NW7 . . . . . . **56** A7
Arlington Lo, SW2 . . . . **151** F4
Arlington Ms, Twick. TW1
off Arlington Rd **145** F6
Arlington Pl, SE10
off Greenwich S St . . . **134** C7
Arlington Rd, N14 . . . . **58** B2
NW1 . . . . **110** B1
W13 . . . . **104** E6
Richmond TW10 . . . . . . **163** G2
Surbiton KT6 . . . . **181** G6
Teddington TW11 . . . . . **162** C4
Twickenham TW1 . . . . . **145** F6
Woodford Green IG8 . . . **79** G1
Arlington Sq, N1 . . . . **111** J1
Arlington St, SW1 . . . . **25** F1
Arlington Way, EC1 . . . . . . **11** F3
Arliss Way, Nthlt. UB5 . . . **102** C1
Arlow Rd, N21 . . . . **59** G1
Armada Ct, SE8
off Watergate St **134** A6
Armadale Cl, N17 . . . . **76** E4
Armadale Rd, SW6 . . . . . . **128** D7
Feltham TW14 . . . . **142** A5
Armada Way, E6 . . . . **117** E5
Armagh Rd, E3 . . . . **113** J1
Armfield Cl, W.Mol. KT8 . . **179** F5
Armfield Cres, Mitch. CR4 . . . . **185** J2
Armfield Rd, Enf. EN2 . . . . **44** A1
Arminger Rd, W12 . . . . . . **127** H1
Armistice Gdns, SE25
off Penge Rd **188** D3
Armitage Rd, NW11 . . . . . . **90** C1
SE10 . . . . **135** F5
Armour Cl, N7
off Roman Way **93** F6
Armoury Rd, SE8 . . . . **154** B2
Armoury Way, SW18 . . . . **148** D5
Armstead Wk, Dag. RM10 . . . . **101** G7
Armstrong Av, Wdf.Grn. IG8 . . . . **62** E6
Armstrong Cl, E6
off Porter Rd **116** C6
Borehamwood WD6 . . . . **38** C3
Dagenham RM8
off Palmer Rd **100** D1
Pinner HA5 . . . . **66** A6
Walton-on-Thames KT12
off Sunbury La **178** A6
Armstrong Cres, Barn. EN4 . . . . **41** G3
Armstrong Rd, SE18 . . . . **137** F3
SW7 . . . . **22** E6
W3 . . . . **127** F1
Feltham TW13 . . . . **160** E5
Armstrong Way, Sthl. UB2 . . . . **123** H2
Armytage Rd, Houns. TW5 . . . . **122** D7
Arnal Cres, SW18 . . . . **148** B7
Arncliffe Cl, N11
off Kettlewell Cl. **58** A6
Arncroft Ct, Bark. IG11
off Renwick Rd. **118** B3
Arndale Wk, SW18
off Garratt La **148/149** E5
Arne Gro, Orp. BR6 . . . . . **207** J3
Arne St, WC2 . . . . **18** B4
Arnett Sq, E4 . . . . **61** J6
Arne Wk, SE3 . . . . **155** F4
Arneways Av, Rom. RM6 . . **82** D3
Arneway St, SW1 . . . . **25** J6
Arnewood Cl, SW15 . . . . . **165** G1
Arney's La, Mitch. CR4 . . . **186** A6
Arngask Rd, SE6 . . . . **154** D7
Arnhem Pl, E14 . . . . **134** A3
Arnhem Way, SE22
off East Dulwich Gro . . **152** B5
Arnhem Wf, E14
off Arnhem Pl **134** A3
Arnison Rd, E.Mol. KT8 . . **180** A4
Arnold Bennett Way, N8
off Burghley Rd. **75** G3
Arnold Circ, E2 . . . . **13** F4
Arnold Cl, Har. HA3 . . . . . . **69** J7
Arnold Cres, Islw. TW7 . . . **144** A5
Arnold Dr, Chess. KT9 . . . **195** G6
Arnold Est, SE1 . . . . **29** G4
Arnold Gdns, N13 . . . . **59** H5
Arnold Rd, E3 . . . . **114** A3
N15 . . . . **76** C3
SW17 . . . . **167** J7
Dagenham RM9, RM10 . **101** F7
Northolt UB5 . . . . **84** D6
Arnos Gro, N14 . . . . **58** D4
Arnos Rd, N11 . . . . **58** C5
Arnott Cl, SE28
off Applegarth Rd **118** C7
W4 *off Fishers La* **126** D4
Arnould Av, SE5 . . . . **152** A4
Arnsberg Way, Bexh. DA7 . . . . **159** G4
Arnside Gdns, Wem. HA9 . **87** G1
Arnside Rd, Bexh. DA7 . . . **159** G1
Arnside St, SE17 . . . . **36** A5
Arnulf St, SE6 . . . . **172** B4
Arnulls Rd, SW16 . . . . **169** G6
Arodene Rd, SW2 . . . . **151** F6
Arosa Rd, Twick. TW1 . . . . **145** G6
Arpley Sq, SE20
off High St. **171** F7
Arragon Gdns, SW16 . . . . **168** E7
West Wickham BR4 . . . . **204** B3
Arragon Rd, E6 . . . . **116** A1
SW18 . . . . **166** E1
Twickenham TW1 . . . . . **144** D7
Arran Cl, Wall. SM6 . . . . . **200** B4
Arran Dr, E12 . . . . **98** A1
Arran Grn, Wat. WD19
off Prestwick Rd **50** C1
Arran Ms, W5 . . . . **125** J1
Arran Rd, SE6 . . . . **172** B2
Arran Wk, N1 . . . . **93** J7
Arras Av, Mord. SM4 . . . . **185** F5
Arrol Rd, Beck. BR3 . . . . . **189** F3
Arrow Rd, E3 . . . . **114** B3
Arrowscout Wk, Nthlt. UB5
off Argus Way **102/103** E3
Arrowsmith Cl, Chig. IG7 . . **65** J6
Arrowsmith Path, Chig. IG7 . . . . **65** J5
Arrowsmith Rd, Chig. IG7 . . . . **65** H5
Loughton IG10 . . . . **48** B3
★**Arsenal FC**, N5 . . . . **93** H3
Arsenal Rd, SE9 . . . . **156** C2
Arsenal Way, SE18 . . . . . . **137** F3
Arterberry Rd, SW20 . . . . **165** J7
Artesian Cl, NW10 . . . . **88** D7
Artesian Gro, Barn. EN5 . . **41** F4
Artesian Rd, W2 . . . . **108** D6
Artesian Wk, E11 . . . . **96** E3
Arthingworth St, E15 . . . . **114** E1
Arthur Ct, W2 . . . . **14** A3
Arthurdon Rd, SE4 . . . . . . **154** A5
Arthur Gro, SE18 . . . . **137** F4
Arthur Henderson Ho, SW6 . . . . **148** C2
Arthur Horsley Wk, E7
off Magpie Cl **97** F5
Arthur Rd, E6 . . . . **116** C2
N7 . . . . **93** F4
N9 . . . . **60** C2
SW19 . . . . **166** D3
Kingston upon Thames KT2 . . . . **164** A7
New Malden KT3 . . . . . **183** H5
Romford RM6 . . . . **82** C7
Arthur St, EC4 . . . . **20** C6
Arthur Walls Ho, E12
off Grantham Rd. **98** D3
Artichoke Hill, E1
off Pennington St. **112/113** E7
Artichoke Pl, SE5
off Camberwell Ch St . **152** A1
Artillery Cl, Ilf. IG2
off Horns Rd **81** F6
Artillery La, E1 . . . . **20** E2
W12 . . . . **107** G6

Artillery Pas, E1 **21** E2
Artillery Pl, SE18 **136** C5
SW1 **25** H6
Harrow HA3 *off Chicheley Rd* **51** J7
Artillery Row, SW1 **25** H6
Artington Cl, Orp. BR6 **207** F4
Artisan Cl, E6 *off Ferndale St* **116/117** E6
Artizan St, E1 **21** E3
Arundel Av, Mord. SM4 **184** C4
Arundel Cl, E15 **97** E4
SW11 *off Chivalry Rd* **149** H5
Bexley DA5 **159** F6
Croydon CR0 **201** H3
Hampton (Hmptn H.) TW12 **161** H5
Arundel Ct, N12 **57** H6
Harrow HA2 **85** G4
Arundel Dr, Borwd. WD6 **38** C5
Harrow HA2 **85** F4
Woodford Green IG8 **63** G7
Arundel Gdns, N21 **59** G1
W11 **108** C7
Edgware HA8 **54** D7
Ilford IG3 **100** A2
Arundel Gt Ct, WC2 **18** D5
Arundel Gro, N16 **94** B5
Arundel Pl, N1 **93** G6
Arundel Rd, Barn. EN4 **41** H3
Croydon CR0 **188** A6
Hounslow TW4 **142** C3
Kingston upon Thames KT1 **182** B2
Sutton SM2 **198** C7
Arundel Sq, N7 **93** G6
Arundel St, WC2 **18** D5
Arundel Ter, SW13 **127** H6
Arvon Rd, N5 **93** G5
Asbaston Ter, Ilf. IG1 *off Buttsbury Rd* **99** F5
Ascalon St, SW8 **130** C7
Ascham Dr, E4 *off Rushcroft Rd* **62** B7
Ascham End, E17 **77** H1
Ascham St, NW5 **92** C5
Aschurch Rd, Croy. CR0 **188** C7
Ascot Cl, Borwd. (Elstree) WD6 **38** A5
Ilford IG6 **65** H6
Northolt UB5 **85** G5
Ascot Gdns, Sthl. UB1 **103** F5
Ascot Rd, E6 **116** C3
N15 **76** A5
N18 **60** D4
SW17 **168** A6
Orpington BR5 **193** J4
Ascott Av, W5 **125** H2
Ashanti Ms, E8 *off Lower Clapton Rd* **94/95** E5
Ashbourne Av, E18 **79** H4
N20 **57** J2
NW11 **72** C5
Bexleyheath DA7 **139** E7
Harrow HA2 **86** A2
Ashbourne Cl, N12 **57** E4
W5 **106** A5
Ashbourne Ct, E5 *off Daubeney Rd* **95** H4
Ashbourne Gro, NW7 **54** D5
SE22 **152** C5
W4 **127** E5
Ashbourne Par, W5 *off Ashbourne Rd* **105** J4
Ashbourne Ri, Orp. BR6 **207** G4
Ashbourne Rd, W5 **105** J5
Mitcham CR4 **168** A6
Ashbourne Ter, SW19 **166** D7
Ashbourne Way, NW11 *off Ashbourne Av* **72** C5
Ashbridge Rd, E11 **79** F7
Ashbridge St, NW8 **7** G6
Ashbrook Rd, N19 **92** D1
Dagenham RM10 **101** H3
Ashburn Gdns, SW7 **30** C1
Ashburnham Av, Har. HA1 **68** C6
Ashburnham Cl, N2 **73** G3
Watford WD19 *off Ashburnham Dr* **50** A3
Ashburnham Dr, Wat. WD19 **50** A3
Ashburnham Gdns, Har. HA1 **68** C6
Ashburnham Gro, SE10 **134** B7
Ashburnham Pl, SE10 **134** B7
Ashburnham Retreat, SE10 **134** B7
Ashburnham Rd, NW10 **107** J3
SW10 **129** F7
Ashburnham Rd, Belv. DA17 **139** J4
Richmond TW10 **163** E3
Ashburn Pl, SW7 **30** C1
Ashburton Av, Croy. CR0 **202** E1
Ilford IG3 **99** H4
Ashburton Cl, Croy. CR0 **202** D1
Ashburton Ct, Pnr. HA5 **66** D3
Ashburton Gdns, Croy. CR0 **202** D2
Ashburton Rd, E16 **115** G6
Croydon CR0 **202** D1
Ruislip HA4 **84** A2
Ashburton Ter, E13 *off Grasmere Rd* **115** G2
Ashbury Gdns, Rom. RM6 **82** D5
Ashbury Pl, SW19 **167** F6
Ashbury Rd, SW11 **149** J3
Ashby Av, Chess. KT9 **196** A6
Ashby Gro, N1 **93** J7
Ashby Ms, SE4 **153** J2
SW2 *off Prague Pl* **150/151** E5
Ashby Rd, N15 **76** D5
SE4 **153** J2
Ashby St, EC1 **11** H4
Ashby Wk, Croy. CR0 **187** J6
Ashby Way, West Dr. UB7 **120** D7
Ashchurch Gro, W12 **127** G2
Ashchurch Pk Vil, W12 **127** G3
Ashchurch Ter, W12 **127** G3
Ash Cl, SE20 **189** F2
Carshalton SM5 **199** J2
Edgware HA8 **54** C4
New Malden KT3 **182** D2
Orpington BR5 **193** G5
Sidcup DA14 **176** B3
Stanmore HA7 **52** D6
Ashcombe Av, Surb. KT6 **181** G7
Ashcombe Gdns, Edg. HA8 **54** A4
Ashcombe Ho, Enf. EN3 **45** G3
Ashcombe Pk, NW2 **89** E3
Ashcombe Rd, SW19 **166** D5
Carshalton SM5 **200** A6
Ashcombe Sq, N.Mal. KT3 **182** C3
Ashcombe St, SW6 **148** E2
Ash Ct, Epsom KT19 **196** C4
Ashcroft, Pnr. HA5 **51** G6
Ashcroft Av, Sid. DA15 **158** A6
Ashcroft Ct, N20 *off Oakleigh Rd N* **57** G2
Ashcroft Cres, Sid. DA15 **158** A6
Ashcroft Rd, E3 **113** H3
Chessington KT9 **195** J3
Ashcroft Sq, W6 *off King St* **127** J4
Ashdale Cl, Twick. TW2 **143** J7
Ashdale Gro, Stan. HA7 **52** C6
Ashdale Rd, SE12 **173** H1
Ashdale Way, Twick. TW2 *off Ashdale Cl* **143** J7
Ashdene, SE15 **152** E1
Pinner HA5 **66** C3
Ashdon Cl, Wdf.Grn. IG8 **63** H6
Ashdon Rd, NW10 **107** E1
Ashdown Cl, Beck. BR3 **190** B2
Bexley DA5 **159** J7
Ashdown Cres, NW5 *off Queen's Cres* **92** A5
Ashdown Est, E11 *off High Rd Leytonstone* **96/97** E4
Ashdown Pl, T.Ditt. KT7 **180** D7
Ashdown Rd, Enf. EN3 **45** F3
Kingston upon Thames KT1 **181** H2
Ashdown Wk, E14 **134** A4
Romford RM7 **83** H2
Ashdown Way, SW17 **168** A2
Ashen, E6 *off Downings* **116** D6
Ashenden Rd, E5 **95** G5
Ashen Gro, SW19 **166** D3
Ashentree Ct, EC4 **19** F4
Asher Loftus Way, N11 **57** J6
Asher Way, E1 **29** J1
Ashfield Av, Felt. TW13 **160** B1
Ashfield Cl, Beck. BR3 **172** A7
Richmond TW10 **163** H1
Ashfield La, Chis. BR7 **175** F6
Ashfield Par, N14 **58** D1
Ashfield Rd, N4 **75** J6
N14 **58** C3
W3 **127** F1
Ashfields, Loug. IG10 **48** C2
Ashfield St, E1 **112** E5
Ashfield Yd, E1 *off Ashfield St* **112/113** E5
Ashford Av, N8 **74** E4
Hayes UB4 **102** D6
Ashford Cl, E17 **77** J6
Ashford Cres, Enf. EN3 **45** F2
Ashford Grn, Wat. WD19 **50** D5
Ashford Ms, N17 *off Vicarage Rd* **76** D1
Ashford Rd, E6 **98** D6
E18 **79** H2
NW2 **90** A4
Ashford St, N1 **12** D3
Ash Gro, E8 **113** E1
N13 **59** J3
NW2 **90** A4
SE20 **189** F2
W5 **125** H2
Enfield EN1 **44** B7
Hounslow TW5 **142** D1
Southall UB1 **103** G5
Wembley HA0 **86** D4
West Wickham BR4 **204** C2
Ashgrove Rd, Brom. BR1 **172** D6
Ilford IG3 **99** J1
Ash Hill Cl, Bushey WD23 **51** H1
Ash Hill Dr, Pnr. HA5 **66** C3
Ashingdon Cl, E4 **62** C3
Ashington Rd, SW6 **148** C2
Ash Island, E.Mol. KT8 **180** A3
Ashlake Rd, SW16 **168** E4
Ashland Pl, W1 **16** B1
Ashlar Pl, SE18 *off Masons Hill* **136/137** E4
Ashleigh Gdns, Sutt. SM1 **198** E2
Ashleigh Pt, SE23 *off Dacres Rd* **171** G3
Ashleigh Rd, SE20 **189** E3
SW14 **146** E3
Ashley Av, Ilf. IG6 **81** E2
Morden SM4 **184** D5
Ashley Cl, NW4 **71** J2
Pinner HA5 **66** B2
Ashley Cres, N22 **75** G2
SW11 **150** A3
Ashley Dr, Borwd. WD6 **38** C5
Isleworth TW7 **124** B6
Twickenham TW2 **143** H7
Ashley Gdns, N13 **59** J4
SW1 **25** G6
Orpington BR6 **207** H5
Richmond TW10 **163** G3
Wembley HA9 **87** H2
Ashley Gro, Loug. IG10 *off Staples Rd* **48** B3
Ashley La, NW4 **71** J2
Croydon CR0 **201** H4
Ashley Pl, SW1 **25** F6
Ashley Rd, E4 **62** A5
E7 **97** J7
N17 **76** D3
N19 **92** E1
SW19 **166** E6
Enfield EN3 **45** F2
Hampton TW12 **179** G1
Richmond TW9 *off Jocelyn Rd* **145** H3
Thames Ditton KT7 **180** C6
Thornton Heath CR7 **187** F4
Ashley Wk, NW7 **55** J7
Ashling Rd, Croy. CR0 **202** D1
Ashlin Rd, E15 **96** D4
Ashlone Rd, SW15 **147** J3
Ashlyns Way, Chess. KT9 **195** G6
Ashmead, N14 **42** C5
Ashmead Gate, Brom. BR1 **191** J1
Ashmead Ho, E9 *off Kingsmead Way* **95** H5
Ashmead Rd, SE8 **154** A2
Feltham TW14 **160** A1
Ashmere Av, Beck. BR3 **190** D2
Ashmere Cl, Sutt. SM3 **197** J5
Ashmere Gro, SW2 **150** E4
Ashmill St, NW1 **15** G1
Ashmole Pl, SW8 **34** E6
Ashmole St, SW8 **34** D6
Ashmore Cl, SE15 *off Lisford St* **152** C1
Ashmore Ct, Houns. TW5 *off Wheatlands* **123** G6
Ashmore Gro, Well. DA16 **157** G3
Ashmore Rd, W9 **108** C4
Ashmount Est, N19 *off Ashmount Rd* **74** D7
Ashmount Rd, N15 **76** C5
N19 **74** C7
Ashmount Ter, W5 *off Murray Rd* **125** G4
Ashneal Gdns, Har. HA1 **86** A3
Ashness Gdns, Grnf. UB6 **86** E6
Ashness Rd, SW11 **149** J5
Ashridge Cl, Har. HA3 **69** F6
Ashridge Cres, SE18 **137** F7
Ashridge Dr, Wat. WD19 **50** C5
Ashridge Gdns, N13 **58** D5
Pinner HA5 **66** E4
Ashridge Way, Mord. SM4 **184** C3
Sunbury-on-Thames TW16 **160** A6
Ash Rd, E15 **97** E5
Croydon CR0 **204** A2
Orpington BR6 **207** J7
Sutton SM3 **184** B7
Ash Row, Brom. BR2 **192** D7
Ashtead Rd, E5 **76** D7
Ashton Cl, Sutt. SM1 **198** D4
Ashton Ct, E4 *off Connington Cres* **62** E3
Ashton Gdns, Houns. TW4 **143** F4
Romford RM6 **83** E6
Ashton Rd, E15 **96** D5
Ashton St, E14 **114** C7
Ashtree Av, Mitch. CR4 **185** H2
Ash Tree Cl, Croy. CR0 **189** H6
Ashtree Cl, Orp. BR6 *off Broadwater Gdns.* **206/207** E4
Ash Tree Cl, Surb. KT6 **195** H1
Ash Tree Dell, NW9 **70** C5
Ash Tree Way, Croy. CR0 **189** H5
Ashurst Cl, SE20 **189** E1
Ashurst Dr, Ilf. IG2, IG6 **81** E6
Ashurst Rd, N12 **57** H5
Barnet EN4 **41** J5
Ashurst Wk, Croy. CR0 **202** E2
Ashvale Rd, SW17 **167** J5
Ashville Rd, E11 **96** D2
Ash Wk, SW2 **169** F1
Wembley HA0 **87** F4
Ashwater Rd, SE12 **173** G1
Ashwell Cl, E6 *off Northumberland Rd* **116** B6
Ashwin St, E8 **94** C6
Ashwood Gdns, Croy. (New Adgtn) CR0 **204** B6
Hayes UB3 *off Cranford Dr* **121** J4
Ashwood Rd, E4 **62** D3
Ashworth Cl, SE5 *off Love Wk* **152** A2
Ashworth Rd, W9 **6** B3
Askern Cl, Bexh. DA6 **158** D4
Aske St, N1 **12** D3
Askew Cres, W12 **127** F2
Askew Rd, W12 **127** F1
Askham Ct, W12 **127** G1
Askham Rd, W12 **127** G1
Askill Dr, SW15 *off Keswick Rd* **148** B5
Asland Rd, E15 **114** E1
Aslett St, SW18 **149** E7
Asmara Rd, NW2 **90** B5
Asmuns Hill, NW11 **72** D5
Asmuns Pl, NW11 **72** C5
Asolando Dr, SE17 **36** A2
Aspen Cl, N19 *off Hargrave Pk* **92** C2
W5 **125** J2
West Drayton UB7 **120** C1
Aspen Copse, Brom. BR1 **192** C2
Aspen Ct, Hayes UB3 **121** H4
Aspen Dr, Wem. HA0 **86** D4
Aspen Gdns, W6 **127** H5
Mitcham CR4 **186** A5
Aspen Grn, Erith DA18 **139** F3
Aspen La, Nthlt. UB5 **102** E3
Aspenlea Rd, W6 **128** A6
Aspen Way, E14 **114** A7
Feltham TW13 **160** B3
Aspern Gro, NW3 **91** H5
Aspinall Rd, SE4 **153** G3
Aspinden Rd, SE16 **133** E4
Aspley Rd, SW18 **149** E5
Asplins Rd, N17 **76** D1
Asprey Ms, Beck. BR3 **189** J5
Asprey Pl, Brom. BR1 *off Chislehurst Rd* **192** A2
Asquith Cl, Dag. RM8 **100** C1
Assam St, E1 **21** H3
Assata Ms, N1 *off St. Paul's Rd* **93** H6
Assembly Pas, E1 **113** F5
Assembly Wk, Cars. SM5 **185** H7
Ass Ho La, Har. HA3 **51** H4

Assurance Cotts, Belv.
DA17 *off Heron Hill* . . . **139** F5
Astall Cl, Har. HA3 . . . . **68** B1
Astbury Business Pk, SE15
off Station Pas. **153** F1
Astbury Rd, SE15. . . . . . . **153** F1
Astell St, SW3 . . . . **31** H3
Aste St, E14 . . . . **134** C2
Asteys Row, N1
off River Pl **93** H7
Asthall Gdns, Ilf. IG6 . . . . . **81** F4
Astle St, SW11. . . . . **150** A2
Astley Av, NW2 . . . . **89** J5
Aston Av, Har. HA3 . . . . . . **69** F7
Aston Cl, Sid. DA14 . . . . . **176** A3
Aston Grn, Houns. TW4 . . **142** C2
Aston Ms, Rom. RM6. . . . . **82** C7
Aston Pl, SW16
off Averil Gro **169** H6
Aston Rd, SW20. . . . . **183** J2
W5. . . . . **105** G6
Esher (Clay.) KT10. . . . . **194** B5
Aston St, E14 . . . . **113** H6
Aston Ter, SW12
off Cathles Rd **150** B6
Astonville St, SW18. . . . . **166** D1
Astor Av, Rom. RM7 . . . . . **83** J6
Astor Cl, Kings.T. KT2 . . . **164** B6
Astoria Wk, SW9 . . . . **151** G3
Astrop Ms, W6 . . . . **127** J3
Astrop Ter, W6 . . . . **127** J3
Astwood Ms, SW7. . . . . . . **30** C1
Asylum Rd, SE15 . . . . **133** E7
Atalanta St, SW6. . . . . . . **148** A1
Atbara Ct, Tedd. TW11 . . . **163** E6
Atbara Rd, Tedd. TW11 . . . **163** E6
Atcham Rd, Houns. TW3 . **143** J4
Atcost Rd, Bark. IG11 . . . . **118** A5
Atheldene Rd, SW18 . . . . **167** E1
Athelney St, SE6 . . . . **172** A3
Athelstane Gro, E3. . . . . . **113** J2
Athelstane Ms, N4
off Stroud Grn Rd **93** G1
Athelstan Ho, E9
off Kingsmead Way. . . . **95** J5
Athelstan Rd, Kings. I.
KT1 . . . . **181** J4
Athelstone Rd, Har. HA3 . . **68** A2
Athena Cl, Har. HA2
off Byron Hill Rd **86** B2
Kingston upon Thames
KT1 . . . . **181** J3
Athenaeum Pl, N10
off Fortis Grn Rd **74** B3
Athenaeum Rd, N20 . . . . . **57** F1
Athenlay Rd, SE15 . . . . . . **153** G5
Athens Gdns, W9
off Harrow Rd **108** D4
Atherden Rd, E5. . . . . **95** F4
Atherfold Rd, SW9. . . . . . **150** E3
Atherley Way, Houns.
TW4. . . . . **143** F7
Atherstone Ct, W2 . . . . **14** B1
Atherstone Ms, SW7 . . . . . **30** D1
Atherton Cl, Stai. (Stanw.)
TW19. . . . . **140** A6
Atherton Dr, SW19. . . . . . **166** A4
Atherton Hts, Wem. HA0 . . **87** F6
Atherton Ms, E7. . . . . **97** F6
Atherton Pl, Har. HA2 . . . . **68** A3
Southall UB1 . . . . **103** H7
Atherton Rd, E7 . . . . **97** F5
SW13. . . . . **127** G7
Ilford IG5. . . . . **80** B2
Atherton St, SW11 . . . . . . **149** H2
Athlone, Esher (Clay.)
KT10 . . . . **194** B6
Athlone Cl, E5
off Goulton Rd. **94/95** E4
Athlone Rd, SW2 . . . . **151** F7
Athlone St, NW5 . . . . **92** A6
Athlon Rd, Wem. HA0 . . . **105** G2
Athol Cl, Pnr. HA5 . . . . **66** B1
Athole Gdns, Enf. EN1. . . . **44** B5
Athol Gdns, Pnr. HA5. . . . . **66** B1
Atholl Rd, Ilf. IG3 . . . . **82** A7
Athol Rd, Erith DA8 . . . . . **139** J5
Athol Sq, E14 . . . . **114** C6
Atkins Dr, W.Wick. BR4 . . **204** D2
Atkinson Rd, E16 . . . . **115** J5
Atkins Rd, E10 . . . . **78** B6
SW12. . . . . **150** D7
Atlantic Rd, SW9 . . . . **151** G4
Atlantis Cl, Bark. IG11. . . . **118** B3
Atlas Gdns, SE7. . . . . **135** J4
Atlas Ms, E8 *off Tyssen St* . **94** C6
N7 . . . . **93** F6
Atlas Rd, E13 . . . . **115** G2
N11 . . . . **58** B6
Atlas Rd, NW10 . . . . **107** E3
Wembley HA9. . . . . **88** C4
Atley Rd, E3 . . . . **114** A1
Atlip Rd, Wem. HA0 . . . . . **105** H1
Atney Rd, SW15. . . . . **148** B4
Atria Rd, Nthwd. HA6 . . . . **50** A5
Attenborough Cl, Wat. WD19
off Harrow Way **50/51** E3
Atterbury Rd, N4 . . . . **75** G6
Atterbury St, SW1 . . . . **33** J2
Attewood Av, NW10 . . . . . **88** E3
Attewood Rd, Nthlt. UB5. . **85** E6
Attfield Cl, N20 . . . . **57** G2
Attlee Cl, Hayes UB4 . . . . **102** B3
Thornton Heath CR7 . . . **187** J6
Attlee Rd, SE28 . . . . **118** B7
Hayes UB4. . . . . **102** A3
Attlee Ter, E17 . . . . **78** B4
Attneave St, WC1. . . . . **10** E4
Atwater Cl, SW2 . . . . **169** G1
Atwell Cl, E10
off Belmont Pk Rd. **78** B6
Atwell Pl, T.Ditt. KT7. . . . . **194** C1
Atwell Rd, SE15
off Rye La **152** D2
Atwood Av, Rich. TW9 . . . **146** A2
Atwood Rd, W6 . . . . **127** H4
Atwoods All, Rich. TW9
off Leyborne Pk. **146** A1
Aubert Pk, N5. . . . . **93** H4
Aubert Rd, N5 . . . . **93** H4
Aubrey Pl, NW8 . . . . **6** C2
Aubrey Rd, E17. . . . . **78** A3
N8 . . . . **75** E5
W8. . . . . **128** C1
Aubrey Wk, W8. . . . . **128** C1
Auburn Cl, SE14. . . . . **133** H7
Aubyn Hill, SE27 . . . . **169** J4
Aubyn Sq, SW15 . . . . **147** G4
Auckland Cl, SE19 . . . . . . **188** C1
Auckland Gdns, SE19. . . . **188** B1
Auckland Hill, SE27 . . . . . **169** J4
Auckland Ri, SE19 . . . . . . **188** B1
Auckland Rd, E10. . . . . **96** B3
SE19 . . . . **188** C1
SW11 . . . . **149** H4
Ilford IG1. . . . . **99** E1
Kingston upon Thames
KT1 . . . . **181** J4
Auckland St, SE11 . . . . **34** C4
Auden Pl, NW1 . . . . **110** A1
Sutton SM3
off Wordsworth Dr. . . . **197** J4
Audleigh Pl, Chig. IG7 . . . . **64** D6
Audley Cl, N10 . . . . **58** B7
SW11 . . . . **150** A3
Borehamwood WD6 . . . . **38** A3
Audley Ct, E18 . . . . **79** F4
Pinner HA5
off Rickmansworth Rd . **66** C2
Audley Dr, E16
off Wesley Av **135** H1
Audley Gdns, Ilf. IG3 . . . . . **99** J2
Loughton IG10 . . . . **49** F2
Audley Pl, Sutt. SM2 . . . . **198** D7
Audley Rd, NW4. . . . . **71** H6
W5. . . . . **105** J5
Enfield EN2. . . . . **43** H2
Richmond TW10 . . . . . . **145** J5
Audley Sq, W1 . . . . **24** C1
Audrey Cl, Beck. BR3 . . . . **190** B6
Audrey Gdns, Wem. HA0 . . **87** E2
Audrey Rd, Ilf. IG1 . . . . **98** E3
Audrey St, E2. . . . . **13** H1
Audric Cl, Kings.T. KT2. . . **182** A1
Augurs La, E13 . . . . **115** H3
Augusta Cl, W.Mol. KT8
off Freeman Dr **179** F3
Augusta Rd, Twick. TW2 . . **161** J2
Augusta St, E14 . . . . **114** B6
Augustine Rd, W14. . . . . . **128** A3
Harrow HA3 . . . . **67** H1
Augustus Cl, W12
off Goldhawk Rd. **127** H2
Brentford TW8. . . . . **125** F7
Augustus Rd, SW19 . . . . . **166** B1
Augustus St, NW1 . . . . **9** E2
Aultone Way, Cars. SM5 . **199** J3
Sutton SM1 . . . . **199** E2
Aulton Pl, SE11. . . . . **35** F4
Aurelia Gdns, Croy. CR0. . **187** F5
Aurelia Rd, Croy. CR0. . . . **187** E6
Auriga Ms, N16 . . . . **94** A5
Auriol Cl, Wor.Pk. KT4
off Auriol Pk Rd . . **196/197** E3
Auriol Dr, Grnf. UB6. . . . . . **86** A7
Auriol Pk Rd, Wor.Pk. KT4 . **197** E3
Auriol Rd, W14 . . . . **128** B4
Austell Gdns, NW7 . . . . . . **55** E3
Austen Cl, SE28 . . . . **138** B1
Loughton IG10 . . . . **49** G3
Austen Ho, NW6. . . . . **108** D3
Austen Rd, Erith DA8 . . . . **139** H7
Harrow HA2 . . . . **85** H2
Austin Av, Brom. BR2. . . . **192** B5
Austin Cl, SE23 . . . . **153** J7
Twickenham TW1 . . . . . **145** F5
Austin Ct, E6
off Kings Rd. **115** J1
Austin Friars, EC2. . . . . **20** C3
Austin Friars Pas, EC2 . . . . **20** C3
Austin Friars Sq, EC2 . . . . **20** C3
Austin Rd, SW11 . . . . **150** A1
Hayes UB3 . . . . **121** J2
Austin St, E2 . . . . **13** F4
Austral Cl, Sid. DA15 . . . . **175** J3
Australia Rd, W12. . . . . . . **107** H7
Austral St, SE11 . . . . **35** G1
Austyn Gdns, Surb. KT5 . **196** B1
Autumn Cl, SW19. . . . . . . **167** F6
Enfield EN1 . . . . **44** D1
Autumn St, E3 . . . . **114** A1
Avalon Cl, SW20. . . . . **184** B2
W13 . . . . **104** D5
Enfield EN2. . . . . **43** G2
Avalon Rd, SW6. . . . . **148** E1
W13 . . . . **104** D4
Avard Gdns, Orp. BR6 . . . **207** F4
Avarn Rd, SW17 . . . . **167** J6
Avebury Ct, N1
off Poole St **112** A1
Avebury Pk, Surb. KT6. . . **181** G7
Avebury Rd, E11
off Southwest Rd **96** D1
SW19. . . . . **184** C1
Orpington BR6 . . . . **207** G3
Avebury St, N1
off Poole St **112** A1
Aveline St, SE11. . . . . **34** E3
Aveling Pk Rd, E17. . . . . . . **78** A2
Ave Maria La, EC4 . . . . **19** H4
Avenell Rd, N5 . . . . **93** H3
Avening Rd, SW18
off Brathway Rd **148** D7
Avening Ter, SW18 . . . . . . **148** D6
Avenons Rd, E13 . . . . **115** G4
Avenue, The, E4 . . . . **62** D6
E11 (Leytonstone) **97** F2
E11 (Wanstead) **79** H6
N3 . . . . **72** D2
N8 . . . . **75** G3
N10 . . . . **74** C2
N11 . . . . **58** B4
N17 . . . . **76** B2
NW6 . . . . **108** A1
SE10 . . . . **134** D7
SW4. . . . . **150** A5
SW11 . . . . **149** H7
SW18. . . . . **149** H7
W4. . . . . **126** E3
W13 . . . . **104** E7
Barnet EN5 . . . . **40** B3
Beckenham BR3 . . . . . . **190** B1
Bexley DA5 . . . . **158** D7
Bromley BR1. . . . . **192** A3
Carshalton SM5 . . . . . . **200** A7
Croydon CR0. . . . . **202** B3
Epsom KT17 . . . . **197** H7
Esher (Clay.) KT10. . . . . **194** B6
Hampton TW12 . . . . **161** F6
Harrow HA3 . . . . **68** C1
Hounslow TW3 . . . . **143** H5
Hounslow (Cran.) TW5 . **142** A1
Isleworth TW7 . . . . **124** A6
Keston BR2 . . . . **206** A3
Loughton IG10 . . . . **48** A6
Orpington BR6 . . . . **207** J2
Orpington (St.P.Cray)
BR5 . . . . **176** B7
Pinner HA5 . . . . **67** F6
Pinner (Hatch End) HA5 . **51** G7
Richmond TW9 . . . . **145** J2
Sunbury-on-Thames
TW16. . . . . **178** B1
Surbiton KT5. . . . . **181** J6
Sutton (Cheam) SM3 . . **197** J7
Twickenham TW1 . . . . . **145** F5
Wembley HA9. . . . . **87** J2
West Drayton UB7 . . . . **120** B3
West Wickham BR4. . . . **190** C7
Worcester Park KT4. . . . **197** F2
Avenue Cl, N14. . . . . **42** C6
NW8 . . . . **109** H1
Hounslow TW5
off The Avenue **142** A1
West Drayton UB7 . . . . **120** A3
Avenue Cres, W3 . . . . **126** B2
Hounslow TW5. . . . . . . **122** B7
Avenue Elmers, Surb.
KT6 . . . . **181** H5
Avenue Gdns, SE25 . . . . . **188** D3
SW14. . . . . **146** E3
W3. . . . . **126** B2
Hounslow TW5
off The Avenue **122** A7
Teddington TW11. . . . . . **162** C7
Avenue Gate, Loug. IG10. . **47** J6
Avenue Ind Est, E4. . . . . . . **61** J6
Avenue Ms, N10 . . . . **74** B3
Avenue Pk Rd, SE27. . . . . **169** H2
Avenue Rd, E7 . . . . **97** H5
N6 . . . . **74** C7
N12 . . . . **57** F4
N14 . . . . **42** B7
N15 . . . . **76** A5
NW3 . . . . **91** G7
NW8 . . . . **91** G7
NW10. . . . . **107** F2
SE20 . . . . **189** F1
SE25 . . . . **188** D2
SW16. . . . . **186** D2
SW20. . . . . **183** H2
W3. . . . . **126** B2
Beckenham BR3 . . . . . . **189** F1
Belvedere DA17 . . . . . . **139** J4
Bexleyheath DA7 . . . . . **158** E3
Brentford TW8. . . . . **125** F5
Erith DA8. . . . . **139** J7
Hampton TW12 . . . . **179** H1
Isleworth TW7 . . . . **144** C1
Kingston upon Thames
KT1 . . . . **181** H3
New Malden KT3 . . . . . **182** E4
Pinner HA5 . . . . **66** E3
Romford (Chad.Hth)
RM6. . . . . **82** B7
Southall UB1. . . . . **123** F2
Teddington TW11. . . . . . **162** D7
Wallington SM6 . . . . . . **200** C7
Woodford Green IG8 . . . **63** J6
Avenue S, Surb. KT5 . . . . **181** J7
Avenue Ter, N.Mal. KT3
off Kingston Rd. **182** C3
Averil Gro, SW16 . . . . **169** H6
Averill St, W6 . . . . **128** A6
Avern Gdns, W.Mol. KT8 . **179** H4
Avern Rd, W.Mol. KT8 . . . **179** H5
Avery Fm Row, SW1 . . . . . **32** C2
Avery Gdns, Ilf. IG2 . . . . . . **80** C5
AVERY HILL, SE9 . . . . **157** F6
★**Avery Hill Pk**, SE9 . . . . . **157** F6
Avery Hill Rd, SE9 . . . . . . **157** G6
Avery Row, W1. . . . . **16** D5
Avey La, Loug. IG10 . . . . . . **47** H1
Aviary Cl, E16 . . . . **115** F5
Aviemore Cl, Beck. BR3 . . **189** J5
Aviemore Way, Beck.
BR3 . . . . **189** H5
Avignon Rd, SE4 . . . . **153** G3
Avington Ct, SE1
off Old Kent Rd. **132** B4
Avington Gro, SE20 . . . . . **171** F7
Avington Way, SE15. . . . . . **37** F7
Avion Cres, NW9 . . . . **71** G1
Avis Sq, E1 . . . . **113** G6
Avoca Rd, SW17. . . . . **168** A4
Avocet Ms, SE28 . . . . **137** G3
Avon Cl, Hayes UB4. . . . . **102** C4
Sutton SM1. . . . . **199** F4
Worcester Park KT4. . . . **197** G2
Avon Ct, Grnf. UB6
off Braund Av **103** H4
Avondale Av, N12. . . . . **56** E5
NW2 . . . . **89** E3
Barnet EN4 . . . . **57** J1
Esher KT10 . . . . **194** D3
Worcester Park KT4. . . . **197** F1
Avondale Cl, Loug. IG10 . . **48** C7
Avondale Ct, E11 . . . . **96** E1
E16 *off Avondale
Rd*. **114/115** E5
E18 . . . . **79** H1
Avondale Cres, Enf. EN3 . . **45** H3
Ilford IG4. . . . . **80** A5
Avondale Dr, Hayes UB3 . **122** A1
Loughton IG10 . . . . **48** C7
Avondale Gdns, Houns.
TW4 . . . . **143** F5
Avondale Ms, Brom. BR1
off Avondale Rd **173** G6
Avondale Pk Gdns, W11 . . **108** B7
Avondale Pk Rd, W11 . . . . **108** B7
Avondale Pavement, SE1
off Avondale Sq **132** D5
Avondale Ri, SE15 . . . . . . **152** C3
Avondale Rd, E16. . . . . . . **115** E5
E17 . . . . **78** A7

Avondale Rd, N3 73 F1
N13 59 G2
N15 75 H5
SE9 174 B2
SW14 146 D3
SW19 166 E5
Bromley BR1 173 E6
Harrow HA3 68 C3
South Croydon CR2 201 J6
Welling DA16 158 C2
Avondale Sq, SE1 37 H4
Avonley Rd, SE14 133 F7
Avon Ms, Pnr. HA5 67 F1
Avonmore Gdns, W14 *off Avonmore Rd* 128 C4
Avonmore Pl, W14 *off Avonmore Rd* 128 B4
Avonmore Rd, W14 128 C4
Avonmouth St, SE1 27 J5
Avon Path, S.Croy. CR2 201 J6
Avon Pl, SE1 28 A4
Avon Rd, E17 78 D3
SE4 154 A3
Greenford UB6 103 G4
Avonstowe Cl, Orp. BR6 207 F3
Avon Way, E18 79 G3
Avonwick Rd, Houns. TW3 143 H2
Avril Way, E4 62 C5
Avro Way, Wall. SM6 201 E7
Awlfield Av, N17 76 A1
Awliscombe Rd, Well. DA16 157 J2
Axe St, Bark. IG11 117 F1
Axholme Av, Edg. HA8 70 A1
Axminster Cres, Well. DA16 158 C1
Axminster Rd, N7 93 E3
Aybrook St, W1 16 B2
Aycliffe Cl, Brom. BR1 192 C4
Aycliffe Rd, W12 127 F1
Aylands Cl, Wem. HA9 *off Preston Rd* 87 H2
Aylesbury Cl, E7 *off Atherton Rd* 97 F6
Aylesbury Ct, Sutt. SM1 *off Benhill Wd Rd* 199 F3
Aylesbury Est, SE17 36 C4
Aylesbury Rd, SE17 36 C4
Bromley BR2 191 G3
Aylesbury St, EC1 11 G6
NW10 88 D3
Aylesford Av, Beck. BR3 189 H5
Aylesford St, SW1 33 H3
Aylesham Cen, The, SE15 152 D1
Aylesham Cl, NW7 55 G7
Aylesham Rd, Orp. BR6 193 J7
Ayles Rd, Hayes UB4 102 B3
Aylestone Av, NW6 108 A1
Aylett Rd, SE25 188 E4
Isleworth TW7 144 B2
Ayley Cft, Enf. EN1 44 D5
Ayliffe Cl, Kings.T. KT1 *off Cambridge Gdns* 182 A2
Aylmer Cl, Stan. HA7 52 D4
Aylmer Dr, Stan. HA7 52 D4
Aylmer Par, N2 73 J5
Aylmer Rd, E11 97 F1
N2 73 H5
W12 127 E2
Dagenham RM8 100 E3
Ayloffe Rd, Dag. RM9 101 F6
Aylton Est, SE16 *off Renforth St* 133 F2
Aylward Rd, SE23 171 G2
SW20 184 C2
Aylwards Ri, Stan. HA7 52 D4
Aylward St, E1 113 F6
Aylwyn Est, SE1 29 F5
Aynhoe Rd, W14 128 A4
Aynscombe La, SW14 146 C3
Aynscombe Path, SW14 *off Thames Bk* 146 C2
Ayr Ct, W3 *off Monks Dr* 106 A5
Ayres Cl, E13 115 G3
Ayres Cres, NW10 88 D7
Ayres St, SE1 28 A3
Ayrsome Rd, N16 94 B3
Ayrton Rd, SW7 23 E5
Aysgarth Ct, Sutt. SM1 *off Sutton Common Rd* 198/199 E3
Aysgarth Rd, SE21 152 B6
Aytoun Pl, SW9 151 F2
Aytoun Rd, SW9 151 F2
Azalea Cl, W7 124 C1
Azalea Cl, Ilf. IG1 98 E5
Azalea Ct, Wdf.Grn. IG8 *off The Bridle Path* 62/63 E7
Azalea Wk, Pnr. HA5 66 B5
Southall UB2 *off Navigator Dr* 123 J2
Azania Ms, NW5 92 B5
Azenby Rd, SE15 152 C2
Azile Everitt Ho, SE18 *off Blendon Ter* 137 F5
Azof St, SE10 135 E4

B

Baalbec Rd, N5 93 H5
Babbacombe Cl, Chess. KT9 195 G5
Babbacombe Gdns, Ilf. IG4 80 B4
Babbacombe Rd, Brom. BR1 191 G1
Baber Dr, Felt. TW14 142 C6
Babington Ri, Wem. HA9 88 A6
Babington Rd, NW4 71 H4
SW16 168 D5
Dagenham RM8 100 C5
Babmaes St, SW1 17 G6
Bacchus Wk, N1 12 D2
Baches St, N1 12 C4
Back Ch La, E1 21 H5
Back Hill, EC1 11 E6
Backhouse Pl, SE17 36 E2
Back La, N8 74 E5
NW3 *off Heath St* 91 F4
Bexley DA5 159 G7
Brentford TW8 125 G6
Edgware HA8 70 C1
Richmond TW10 163 F3
Romford RM6 *off St. Chad's Rd* 82/83 E7
Backley Gdns, SE25 188 D6
Back Rd, Sid. DA14 176 A4
Bacon Gro, SE1 29 F6
Bacon La, NW9 70 B4
Edgware HA8 70 A1
Bacons La, N6 92 A1
Bacon St, E1 13 G5
E2 13 G5
Bacon Ter, Dag. RM8 *off Fitzstephen Rd* 100 B5
Bacton, NW5 92 A5
Bacton St, E2 *off Roman Rd* 113 F3
Baddow Cl, Dag. RM10 119 G1
Woodford Green IG8 64 A6
Baddow Wk, N1 111 J1
Baden Pl, SE1 28 B3
Baden Powell Cl, Dag. RM9 119 E1
Surbiton KT6 195 J2
Baden Rd, N8 74 D4
Ilford IG1 98 E5
Badger Cl, Felt. TW13 *off Sycamore Cl* 160 A3
Hounslow TW4 142 C3
Ilford IG2 81 F7
Badgers Cl, Enf. EN2 43 H3
Harrow HA1 68 A6
Badgers Copse, Orp. BR6 207 J2
Worcester Park KT4 197 F2
Badgers Cft, N20 56 B1
SE9 174 D3
Badgers Hole, Croy. CR0 203 G4
Badgers Wk, N.Mal. KT3 182 E2
Badlis Rd, E17 78 A2
Badma Cl, N9 *off Hudson Way* 61 F3
Badminton Cl, Borwd. WD6 38 A2
Harrow HA1 68 B4
Northolt UB5 85 G6
Badminton Ms, E16 *off Hanameel St* 135 G1
Badminton Rd, SW12 150 A6
Badric Ct, SW11 *off Yelverton Rd* 149 G2
Badsworth Rd, SE5 131 J7
Baffin Way, E14 *off Prestons Rd* 114 C7
Bagley Cl, West Dr. UB7 120 B2
Bagley's La, SW6 149 E1
Bagleys Spring, Rom. RM6 83 E4
Bagshot Ct, SE18 *off Prince Imperial Rd* 156 D1
Bagshot Rd, Enf. EN1 44 C7
Bagshot St, SE17 36 E4
Baildon St, SE8 133 J7
Bailey Cl, E4 62 C4
N11 58 D7
Bailey Cres, Chess. KT9 *off Nigel Fisher Way* 195 G6
Bailey Ms, SW2 151 G5
Bailey Pl, SE26 171 G6
Baillies Wk, W5 *off Liverpool Rd* 125 G2
Bainbridge Cl, Rich. (Ham) TW10 *off Latchmere Cl* 163 H5
Bainbridge Rd, Dag. RM9 101 F4
Bainbridge St, WC1 17 J3
Baines Cl, S.Croy. CR2 *off Brighton Rd* 201 J5
Baird Av, Sthl. UB1 103 H7
Baird Cl, E10 *off Marconi Rd* 96 A1
NW9 70 C6
Baird Gdns, SE19 170 B4
Baird Rd, Enf. EN1 44 E4
Baird St, EC1 12 A5
Bairny Wd App, Wdf.Grn. IG8 *off Broadway Cl* 63 H6
Baizdon Rd, SE3 154 E2
Baker La, Mitch. CR4 186 A2
Baker Pas, NW10 *off Acton La* 106/107 E1
Baker Rd, NW10 106 E1
SE18 136 B7
Bakers Av, E17 78 B6
Bakers Ct, SE25 188 B3
Bakers End, SW20 184 B2
Bakers Fld, N7 *off Crayford Rd* 92 D4
Bakers Gdns, Cars. SM5 199 H2
Bakers Hall Ct, EC3 20 E6
Bakers Hill, E5 95 F1
Barnet EN5 41 E2
Bakers La, N6 73 J5
Baker's Ms, W1 16 B3
Bakers Ms, Orp. BR6 207 J6
Bakers Pas, NW3 *off Heath St* 91 F4
Baker's Rents, E2 13 F4
Bakers Row, E15 114 E2
Baker's Row, EC1 11 E6
Baker St, NW1 8 A6
W1 16 A1
Enfield EN1 44 A3
Baker's Yd, EC1 *off Baker's Row* 111 G4
Bakery Cl, SW9 151 F1
Bakery Path, Edg. HA8 *off Station Rd* 54 B6
Bakery Pl, SW11 *off Altenburg Gdns* 149 J4
Bakewell Way, N.Mal. KT3 182 E2
Balaams La, N14 58 D2
Balaam St, E13 115 G3
Balaclava Rd, SE1 37 G2
Surbiton KT6 181 F7
Bala Grn, NW9 *off Snowdon Dr* 70/71 E6
Balcaskie Rd, SE9 156 C5
Balchen Rd, SE3 156 A2
Balchier Rd, SE22 152 E6
Balcombe Cl, Bexh. DA6 158 D4
Balcombe St, NW1 7 J6
Balcon Ct, W5 *off Boileau Rd* 105 J6
Balcon Way, Borwd. WD6 38 C1
Balcorne St, E9 95 F7
Balder Ri, SE12 173 H2
Balderton St, W1 16 C4
Baldock St, E3 114 B2
Baldry Gdns, SW16 169 E6
Baldwin Cres, SE5 151 J1
Baldwin Gdns, Houns. TW3 *off Chamberlain Gdns* 143 J1
Baldwin's Gdns, EC1 18 E1
Baldwins Hill, Loug. IG10 48 C2
Baldwin St, EC1 12 B4
Baldwin Ter, N1 11 J1
Baldwyn Gdns, W3 106 C7
Bale Rd, E1 113 H5
Balfern Gro, W4 127 E5
Balfern St, SW11 149 H1
Balfe St, N1 10 B2
Balfour Av, W7 124 C1
Balfour Business Cen, Sthl. UB2 122 D3
Balfour Gro, N20 57 J3
Balfour Ho, W10 *off St. Charles Sq* 108 A5
Balfour Ms, N9 *off The Broadway* 60 D3
W1 24 C1
Balfour Pl, SW15 147 H4
W1 16 C6
Balfour Rd, N5 93 J4
SE25 188 D4
SW19 166 E7
W3 106 C5
W13 124 D2
Bromley BR2 192 A5
Carshalton SM5 199 J7
Harrow HA1 68 A5
Hounslow TW3 143 H3
Ilford IG1 98 E2
Southall UB2 122 D3
Balfour St, SE17 36 B1
Balfron Twr, E14 *off St. Leonards Rd* 114 C6
Balgonie Rd, E4 62 D1
Balgowan Cl, N.Mal. KT3 183 E5
Balgowan Rd, Beck. BR3 189 H3
Balgowan St, SE18 137 J4
BALHAM, SW12 167 J1
Balham Continental Mkt, SW12 *off Shipka Rd* 168 B1
Balham Gro, SW12 150 A7
Balham High Rd, SW12 168 A1
SW17 168 A2
Balham Hill, SW12 150 B7
Balham New Rd, SW12 150 B7
Balham Pk Rd, SW12 167 J1
Balham Rd, N9 60 D2
Balham Sta Rd, SW12 168 B1
Balkan Wk, E1 *off Pennington St* 112/113 E7
Balladier Wk, E14 114 B5
Ballamore Rd, Brom. BR1 173 G3
Ballance Rd, E9 95 G6
Ballantine St, SW18 149 F4
Ballard Cl, Kings.T. KT2 164 D7
Ballards Cl, Dag. RM10 119 H1
Ballards Fm Rd, Croy. CR0 202 D6
South Croydon CR2 202 D6
Ballards La, N3 72 D1
N12 72 D1
Ballards Ms, Edg. HA8 54 A6
Ballards Ri, S.Croy. CR2 202 D6
Ballards Rd, NW2 89 G2
Dagenham RM10 119 H1
Ballards Way, Croy. CR0 203 E6
South Croydon CR2 202 D6
Ballast Quay, SE10 134 D5
Ballater Cl, Wat. WD19 50 C4
Ballater Rd, SW2 151 E4
South Croydon CR2 202 C5
Ball Ct, EC3 *off Cornhill* 112 A6
Ballina St, SE23 153 G6
Ballingdon Rd, SW11 150 A6
Ballinger Pt, E3 *off Bromley High St* 114 B3
Balliol Av, E4 62 D4
Balliol Rd, N17 76 B1
W10 107 J6
Welling DA16 158 B2
Balloch Rd, SE6 172 D1
Ballogie Av, NW10 89 E4
Ballow Cl, SE5 *off Harris St* 132 B7
Balls Pond Pl, N1 *off Balls Pond Rd* 94 A6
Balls Pond Rd, N1 94 A6
Balmain Cl, W5 125 G1
Balmer Rd, E3 113 J2
Balmes Rd, N1 112 A1
Balmoral Apartments, W2 *off Praed St* 109 H5
Balmoral Av, N11 58 A5
Beckenham BR3 189 H4
Balmoral Cl, SW15 *off Westleigh Av* 148 A6
Balmoral Ct, Wor.Pk. KT4 197 H2
Balmoral Cres, W.Mol. KT8 179 G3
Balmoral Dr, Borwd. WD6 38 D5
Southall UB1 103 F4
Balmoral Gdns, W13 124 D3
Bexley DA5 159 F7
Ilford IG3 99 J1
Balmoral Gro, N7 93 F6
Balmoral Ms, W12 127 F2
Balmoral Rd, E7 97 J4
E10 96 B2
NW2 89 H6
Harrow HA2 85 G4
Balmoral Rd, Kings.T. KT1 181 J4
Worcester Park KT4 197 H3
Balmore Cl, E14 114 C6

Balmore Cres, Barn. EN4 . . **42** A5
Balmore St, N19. . . . . **92** B2
Balmuir Gdns, SW15 . . . . **147** J4
Balnacraig Av, NW10 . . . . . **89** E4
Balniel Gate, SW1 . . . . **33** J3
Baltic Cl, SW19. . . . . **167** G7
Baltic Ct, SE16
off Timber Pond Rd . . . **133** G2
Baltic Pl, N1
off Kingsland Rd **112** D1
Baltic St E, EC1 . . . . **11** J6
Baltic St W, EC1 . . . . **11** J6
Baltimore Pl, Well. DA16 . **157** J2
Balvaird Pl, SW1 . . . . **33** J4
Balvernie Gro, SW18 . . . . **148** C7
Bamber Ho, Bark. IG11
off St. Margarets **117** F1
Bamber Rd, SE15
off Moody Rd **152** C1
Bamborough Gdns, W12 . **127** J2
Bamford Av, Wem. HA0 . . **105** J1
Bamford Ct, E15
off Clays La **96** B5
Bamford Rd, Bark. IG11 . . . **99** F6
Bromley BR1 . . . . **172** C5
Bampfylde Cl, Wall. SM6 . **200** C3
Bampton Dr, NW7 . . . . **55** G7
Bampton Rd, SE23. . . . . . **171** G3
Banavie Gdns, Beck. BR3 . **190** C1
Banbury Cl, Enf. EN2
off Holtwhites Hill **43** H1
Banbury Ct, WC2 . . . . **18** A5
Sutton SM2. . . . . **198** D7
Banbury Enterprise Cen, Croy.
CR0 *off Factory La*. . . . **201** H2
Banbury Rd, E9 . . . . **95** G7
E17 . . . . **61** G7
Banbury St, SW11 . . . . . . **149** H2
Banbury Wk, Nthlt. UB5
off Brabazon Rd **103** G2
Banchory Rd, SE3 . . . . . . **135** H7
Bancroft Av, N2 . . . . **73** H5
Buckhurst Hill IG9. . . . . . **63** G2
Bancroft Ct, Nthlt. UB5 . . **102** C1
Bancroft Gdns, Har. HA3 . . **67** J1
Orpington BR6 . . . . **207** J1
Bancroft Rd, E1. . . . . **113** F3
Harrow HA3 . . . . **67** J2
Bandon Ri, Wall. SM6 . . . **200** D5
Banfield Rd, SE15 . . . . . . **152** E4
Bangalore St, SW15. . . . . **147** J3
Bangor Cl, Nthlt. UB5 . . . . **85** H5
Banim St, W6 . . . . **127** H3
Banister Rd, W10 . . . . **108** A3
Bank, The, N6
off Cholmeley Pk **92** B1
Bank Av, Mitch. CR4. . . . . **185** G2
Bank End, SE1 . . . . **28** A1
Bankfoot Rd, Brom. BR1 . **173** E4
Bankhurst Rd, SE6. . . . . . **153** J7
Bank La, SW15. . . . . **146** E5
Kingston upon Thames
KT2 . . . . **163** H7
Bank Ms, Sutt. SM1
off Sutton Ct Rd **199** F6
★**Bank of England**, EC2 . . . **20** B4
★**Bank of England Mus**,
EC2 . . . . **20** C4
Banksian Wk, Islw. TW7 . . **144** B1
Banksia Rd, N18. . . . . **61** F5
Bankside, SE1 . . . . **19** J6
Enfield EN2. . . . . **43** H1
South Croydon CR2 . . . **202** C6
Southall UB1. . . . . **122** D1
Bankside Av, Nthlt. UB5
off Townson Av **102** A2
Bankside Cl, Cars. SM5 . . **199** H6
Isleworth TW7 . . . . **144** C4
Bankside Dr, T.Ditt. KT7 . . **194** E1
★**Bankside Gall**, SE1 . . . . . **19** H6
Bankside Rd, Ilf. IG1 . . . . . **99** F5
Bankside Way, SE19
off Lunham Rd **170** B6
Banks La, Bexh. DA6 . . . . **159** F4
Banks Rd, Borwd. WD6 . . . **38** C2
Bank St, E14. . . . . **134** A1
Banks Way, E12
off Grantham Rd. **98** D4
Bankton Rd, SW2. . . . . . . **151** G4
Bankwell Rd, SE13. . . . . . **155** E4
Bannerman Ho, SW8 . . . . . **34** C6
Banner St, EC1. . . . . **12** A6
Banning St, SE10. . . . . . . **134** E5
Bannister Cl, SW2
off Ewen Cres **169** G1
Greenford UB6 . . . . **86** A5
Bannister Ho, E9
off Homerton High St . . **95** G5
Bannockburn Rd, SE18 . . **137** H4
Bannow Cl, Epsom KT19 . **196** E4
★**Banqueting Ho**, SW1 . . . **26** A2
Banstead Gdns, N9 . . . . . . **60** B3
Banstead Rd, Cars. SM5 . **199** H6
Banstead St, SE15 . . . . . . **153** F3
Banstead Way, Wall. SM6. **201** E5
Banstock Rd, Edg. HA8 . . . **54** B6
Banting Dr, N21 . . . . **43** F5
Banton Cl, Enf. EN1
off Central Av. **11/16** E2
Bantry St, SE5 . . . . **132** A7
Banwell Rd, Bex. DA5
off Woodside La **158** D6
Banyard Rd, SE16
off Southwark
Pk Rd **132/133** E3
Baptist Gdns, NW5
off Queen's Cres **92** A6
Barandon Wk, W11 . . . . . . **108** A7
Barbara Brosnan Ct, NW8 . . **7** E2
Barbara Hucklesby Cl, N22
off The Sandlings. **75** H2
Barbauld Rd, N16. . . . . **94** B3
Barber Cl, N21 . . . . **43** G7
Barber's All, E13. . . . . **115** H3
Barbers Rd, E15 . . . . **114** B2
BARBICAN, EC2 . . . . **19** J2
★**Barbican Arts & Conf Cen**,
EC2 . . . . **20** A1
Barbican Rd, Grnf. UB6 . . **103** H6
Barb Ms, W6. . . . . **127** J3
Barbon Cl, WC1 . . . . **18** C1
Barbot Cl, N9 . . . . **60** D3
Barchard St, SW18. . . . . . **148** E5
Barchester Cl, W7. . . . . . . **124** C1
Barchester Rd, Har. HA3 . . **68** A2
Barchester St, E14 . . . . . . **114** B5
Barclay Cl, SW6 . . . . **128** D7
Barclay Oval, Wdf.Grn.
IG8. . . . . **63** G4
Barclay Path, E17 . . . . **78** C5
Barclay Rd, E11. . . . . **97** E1
E13. . . . . **115** J4
E17 . . . . **78** C5
N18 . . . . **60** A6
SW6 . . . . **128** D7
Croydon CR0. . . . . **202** A3
Barclay Way, SE22
off Lordship La **152** D7
Barcombe Av, SW2 . . . . . **169** E2
Barcombe Cl, Orp. BR5 . . **193** J3
Barden St, SE18. . . . . **137** H7
Bardfield Av, Rom. RM6. . . **82** D3
Bardney Rd, Mord. SM4 . **185** E4
Bardolph Rd, N7 . . . . **92** E4
Richmond TW9
off St. Georges Rd . . . **145** J3
Bard Rd, W10 . . . . **108** A7
Bardsey Pl, E1
off Mile End Rd **113** F5
Bardsey Wk, N1
off Clephane Rd **93** J6
Bardsley Cl, Croy. CR0 . . . **202** C3
Bardsley La, SE10. . . . . . . **134** C6
Barfett St, W10. . . . . **108** C4
Barfield Av, N20 . . . . **57** H2
Barfield Rd, E11 . . . . **97** F1
Bromley BR1 . . . . **192** D3
Barfields, Loug. IG10 . . . . . **48** D4
Barfields Gdns, Loug. IG10
off Barfields **48** D4
Barfields Path, Loug.
IG10. . . . . **48** D4
Barford Cl, NW4. . . . . **71** G1
Barford St, N1. . . . . **111** G1
Barforth Rd, SE15 . . . . . . **153** E3
Barfreston Way, SE20. . . . **189** E1
Bargate Cl, SE18 . . . . **137** J5
New Malden KT3 . . . . . **183** G6
Barge Ho Rd, E16. . . . . . . **136** E1
Barge Ho St, SE1 . . . . **27** F1
Bargery Rd, SE6. . . . . **172** B1
Barge Wk, E.Mol. KT8 . . . **181** G2
Kingston upon Thames
KT1 . . . . **181** G1
Walton-on-Thames
KT12 . . . . **178** D3
Bargrove Cl, SE20 . . . . . . **170** D7
Bargrove Cres, SE6
off Elm La **171** J2
Barham Cl, Brom. BR2 . . . **206** B1
Chislehurst BR7. . . . . . . **174** E5
Romford RM7 . . . . **83** H2
Wembley HA0. . . . . **87** E6
Barham Rd, SW20 . . . . **165** G7
Chislehurst BR7. . . . . . . **174** E5
South Croydon CR2 . . . **201** J5
Baring Cl, SE12. . . . . **173** G2
Baring Rd, SE12 . . . . **155** G7
Baring Rd, Barn. EN4. . . . . **41** G3
Croydon CR0. . . . . **202** D1
Baring St, N1 . . . . **112** A1
Barkantine Shop Par, The,
E14 *off The Quarterdeck*. **134** A2
Barker Cl, N.Mal. KT3. . . . **182** B4
Barker Dr, NW1 . . . . **92** C7
Barker Ms, SW4 . . . . **150** B4
Barker St, SW10. . . . . **30** C5
Barker Wk, SW16 . . . . **168** D3
Barker Way, SE22
off Dulwich Common . **170** D1
Barkham Rd, N17. . . . . **60** A7
Barkham Ter, SE1. . . . . **27** F5
BARKING, IG11 . . . . **117** E1
Barking Ind Pk, Bark.
IG11 . . . . **117** J1
Barking Rd, E6 . . . . **116** A2
E13. . . . . **115** H4
E16. . . . . **115** F5
BARKINGSIDE, Ilf. IG6 . . . . **81** E3
Bark Pl, W2 . . . . **14** A5
Barkston Gdns, SW5 . . . . . **30** A3
Barkwood Cl, Rom. RM7 . . **83** J5
Barkworth Rd, SE16. . . . . **133** E5
Barlborough St, SE14 . . . **133** F7
Barlby Gdns, W10. . . . . . . **108** A4
Barlby Rd, W10. . . . . **108** A5
Barleycorn Way, E14 . . . . **113** J7
Barleyfields Cl, Rom. RM6 . **82** B7
Barley La, Ilf. IG3 . . . . **100** A1
Romford RM6 . . . . **82** B6
Barley Mow Pas, EC1. . . . . **19** H2
W4. . . . . **126** D5
Barley Shotts Business Pk,
W10 *off St. Ervans Rd*. . **108** C5
Barlow Cl, Wall. SM6 . . . . **200** E7
Barlow Dr, SE18. . . . . **156** B1
Barlow Pl, W1. . . . . **17** E6
Barlow Rd, NW6 . . . . **90** C6
W3. . . . . **126** B1
Hampton TW12 . . . . **161** G7
Barlow St, SE17. . . . . **36** C2
Barmeston Rd, SE6 . . . . . **172** B2
Barmor Cl, Har. HA2. . . . . . **67** H2
Barmouth Av, Grnf. UB6 . . **104** C2
Barmouth Rd, SW18 . . . . **149** F6
Croydon CR0. . . . . **203** G2
Barnabas Ct, N21
off Cheyne Wk. **43** G5
Barnabas Rd, E9. . . . . **95** G5
Barnaby Cl, Har. HA2 . . . . . **85** J2
Barnaby Pl, SW7 . . . . **31** E2
Barnaby Way, Chig. IG7 . . . **64** E3
Barnard Cl, SE18 . . . . **136** D4
Chislehurst BR7 . . . . **193** G1
Sunbury-on-Thames
TW16 *off Oak Gro*. . . . **160** B7
Wallington SM6 . . . . . . **200** D7
Barnard Gdns, Hayes
UB4 . . . . **102** B4
New Malden KT3 . . . . . **183** G4
Barnard Gro, E15
off Vicarage La **97** F7
Barnard Hill, N10 . . . . **74** A2
Barnard Ms, SW11 . . . . . . **149** H4
Barnardo Dr, Ilf. IG6. . . . . . **81** F4
Barnardo Gdns, E1
off Devonport St **113** G7
Barnardo St, E1
off Devonport St **113** G6
Barnardos Village, Ilf. IG6. . **81** F3
Barnard Rd, SW11 . . . . . . **149** H4
Enfield EN1 . . . . **45** E2
Mitcham CR4. . . . . **186** A3
Barnard's Inn, EC1 . . . . **19** F3
Barnby Sq, E15
off Barnby St **114/115** E1
Barnby St, E15 . . . . **114** E1
NW1 . . . . **9** G2
Barn Cl, Nthlt. UB5. . . . . . **102** C2
Barn Cres, Stan. HA7 . . . . . **53** F6
Barncroft Cl, Loug. IG10. . . **48** D5
Barncroft Grn, Loug. IG10 . **48** D5
Barncroft Rd, Loug. IG10 . . **48** D5
Barneby Cl, Twick. TW2
off Rowntree Rd **162** B1
Barnehurst Av, Bexh.
DA7 . . . . **159** J1
Erith DA8. . . . . **159** J1
Barnehurst Cl, Erith DA8 . **159** J1
Barnehurst Rd, Bexh.DA7 . **159** J2
Barn Elms Pk, SW15 . . . . **147** J2
BARNES, SW13 . . . . **147** G2
Barnes All, Hmptn. TW12
off Hampton Ct Rd . . . **179** J2
Barnes Av, SW13 . . . . **127** G7
Southall UB2. . . . . **123** F4
Barnes Br, SW13 . . . . **147** E2
Barnes Br, W4. . . . . **147** E2
Barnesbury Ho, SW4 . . . . **150** D5
Barnes Cl, E12 . . . . **98** A4
★**Barnes Common**,
SW13. . . . . **147** G3
Barnes Ct, E16
off Ridgwell Rd **115** J5
Woodford Green IG8 . . . **64** A5
Barnes End, N.Mal. KT3. . **183** G5
Barnes High St, SW13 . . . **147** F2
Barnes Ho, Bark. IG11
off St. Marys **117** G1
Barnes Pikle, W5. . . . . **105** G7
Barnes Rd, N18 . . . . **61** F4
Ilford IG1. . . . . **99** F5
Barnes St, E14 . . . . **113** H6
Barnes Ter, SE8. . . . . **133** J5
BARNET, EN4 & EN5 . . . . . **40** C3
Barnet Bypass, Barn. EN5 . **38** E3
Barnet Dr, Brom. BR2 . . . **206** B2
BARNET GATE, Barn. EN5. **39** F6
Barnet Gate La, Barn.
EN5 . . . . **39** F6
Barnet Gro, E2 . . . . **13** H3
Barnet Hill, Barn. EN5 . . . . **40** D4
Barnet Ho, N20 . . . . **57** F2
Barnet La, N20. . . . . **56** C1
Barnet EN5 . . . . **40** C6
★**Barnet Mus**, Barn. EN5
off Wood St. **40** B4
Barnet Rd, Barn. EN5. . . . . **39** H5
Barnet Trd Est, Barn. EN5. . **40** C3
Barnett St, E1
off Cannon St Rd . **112/113** E6
Barnet Way, NW7. . . . . **38** D7
Barnet Wd Rd, Brom. BR2. **205** J2
Barney Cl, SE7 . . . . **135** J5
Barnfield, N.Mal. KT3. . . . **182** E6
Barnfield Av, Croy. CR0 . . **203** F2
Kingston upon Thames
KT2 . . . . **163** H5
Mitcham CR4. . . . . **186** B4
Barnfield Cl, N4
off Crouch Hill **74/75** E7
SW17. . . . . **167** F3
Barnfield Gdns, SE18
off Plumstead
Common Rd **136/137** E6
Kingston upon Thames
KT2 . . . . **163** H4
Barnfield Pl, E14. . . . . **134** A4
Barnfield Rd, SE18 . . . . . . **137** E6
W5. . . . . **105** F4
Belvedere DA17 . . . . . . **139** F6
Edgware HA8 . . . . **70** C1
Barnfield Wd Cl, Beck.
BR3 . . . . **190** D6
Barnfield Wd Rd, Beck.
BR3 . . . . **190** D6
Barnham Dr, SE28 . . . . . . **137** J1
Barnham Rd, Grnf. UB6 . . **103** J3
Barnham St, SE1 . . . . **28** E3
Barnhill, Pnr. HA5. . . . . **66** C5
Barn Hill, Wem. HA9. . . . . . **88** D2
Barnhill Av, Brom. BR2. . . **191** F5
Barnhill La, Hayes UB4 . . **102** B3
Barnhill Rd, Hayes UB4 . . **102** B4
Wembley HA9. . . . . **88** C3
Barnhurst Path, Wat.
WD19. . . . . **50** C5
Barningham Way, NW9 . . . **70** D6
Barnlea Cl, Felt. TW13 . . . **161** E2
Barnmead Gdns, Dag.
RM9 . . . . **101** F5
Barnmead Rd, Beck. BR3 . **189** H1
Dagenham RM9 . . . . . . **101** F5
Barn Ri, Wem. HA9. . . . . . . **88** A1
BARNSBURY, N1 . . . . **93** F7
Barnsbury Cl, N.Mal. KT3. **182** C4
Barnsbury Cres, Surb.
KT5 . . . . **196** C1
Barnsbury Est, N1
off Barnsbury Rd. **111** G1
Barnsbury Gro, N7. . . . . . . **93** F7
Barnsbury La, Surb. KT5 . **196** B2
Barnsbury Pk, N1 . . . . **93** G7
Barnsbury Rd, N1. . . . . **10** E1
Barnsbury Sq, N1. . . . . **93** G7
Barnsbury St, N1 . . . . **93** G7
Barnsbury Ter, N1. . . . . **93** F7
Barnscroft, SW20 . . . . **183** H3
Barnsdale Av, E14. . . . . . . **134** A4
Barnsdale Rd, W9. . . . . . . **108** C4
Barnsley St, E1 . . . . **113** E4
Barnstaple Rd, Ruis. HA4. . **84** C3
Barnston Wk, N1
off Popham St **111** J1
Barn St, N16 *off Stoke*
Newington Ch St **94** B3

Barn Way, Wem. HA9 . . . . . **88** A1
Barnwell Rd, SW2 . . . . . . **151** G5
Barnwood Cl, N20 . . . . **56** C1
W9 . . . . **6** A6
Baron Cl, N11
off Balmoral Av **58** A5
Baroness Rd, E2 . . . . **13** G3
Baronet Gro, N17
off St. Paul's Rd **76** D1
Baronet Rd, N17 . . . . **76** D1
Baron Gdns, Ilf. IG6 . . . . . . **81** F3
Baron Gro, Mitch. CR4 . . . **185** H4
Baron Rd, Dag. RM8 . . . . . **100** D1
Barons, The, Twick. TW1 . . **145** E6
Barons Ct, Wall. SM6
off Whelan Way **200** D3
Barons Ct Rd, W14 . . . . . . **128** B5
Baronsfield Rd, Twick.
TW1 . . . . **145** E6
Barons Gate, Barn. EN4 . . . **41** H6
Barons Keep, W14 . . . . . . **128** B5
Barons Mead, Har. HA1 . . . **68** B4
Baronsmead Rd, SW13 . . **147** G1
Baronsmede, W5 . . . . **125** J2
Baronsmere Rd, N2 . . . . . . **73** H4
Barons Pl, SE1 . . . . **27** F4
Baron St, N1 . . . . **11** E1
Barons Wk, Croy. CR0 . . . **189** H6
Baron Wk, E16 . . . . **115** F5
Mitcham CR4 . . . . **185** H4
Barque Ms, SE8
off Watergate St **134** A6
Barrack Rd, Houns. TW4 . . **142** D4
Barracks La, Barn. EN5
off High St **40** B3
Barratt Av, N22 . . . . **75** F2
Barratt Ind Pk, Sthl. UB1 . **123** G2
Barratt Way, Har. HA3
off Tudor Rd **68** A3
Barrenger Rd, N10 . . . . **73** J1
Barrett Rd, E17 . . . . **78** C4
Barretts Grn Rd, NW10 . . . **106** C2
Barretts Gro, N16 . . . . **94** B5
Barrett St, W1 . . . . **16** C4
Barrhill Rd, SW2 . . . . **169** E2
Barriedale, SE14 . . . . **153** H1
Barrie Est, W2 . . . . **14** E5
Barrier App, SE7 . . . . **136** A3
Barrier Pt Rd, E16 . . . . . . **135** J1
Barrier Pt Twr, E16
off Barrier Pt Rd **135** J2
Barringer Sq, SW17 . . . . . **168** A4
Barrington Cl, NW5 . . . . . . **92** A5
Ilford IG5 . . . . **80** C1
Loughton IG10
off Barrington Rd **49** F4
Barrington Grn, Loug.
IG10 . . . . **49** F4
Barrington Rd, E12 . . . . **98** D6
N8 . . . . **74** D5
SW9 . . . . **151** H3
Bexleyheath DA7 . . . . . **158** D2
Loughton IG10 . . . . **49** F3
Sutton SM3 . . . . **198** D1
Barrington Vil, SE18 . . . . . **156** D1
Barrow Av, Cars. SM5 . . . . **199** J7
Barrow Cl, N21 . . . . **59** H3
Barrowdene Cl, Pnr. HA5
off Paines La **66/67** E2
Barrowell Grn, N21 . . . . . . **59** H2
Barrowfield Cl, N9 . . . . **61** E3
Barrowgate Rd, W4 . . . . . **126** C5
Barrow Hedges Cl, Cars.
SM5 . . . . **199** H7
Barrow Hedges Way, Cars.
SM5 . . . . **199** H7
Barrow Hill, Wor.Pk. KT4 . **196** E2
Barrow Hill Cl, Wor.Pk. KT4
off Barrow Hill . . . **196/197** E2
Barrow Hill Est, NW8
off Barrow Hill Rd **109** H2
Barrow Hill Rd, NW8 . . . . . . **7** G2
Barrow Pt Av, Pnr. HA5 . . . **66** E2
Barrow Pt La, Pnr. HA5 . . . **66** E2
Barrow Rd, SW16 . . . . **168** D6
Croydon CR0 . . . . **201** G5
Barrow Wk, Brent. TW8
off Glenhurst Rd **125** F5
Barrs Rd, NW10 . . . . **88** D7
Barry Av, N15
off Craven Pk Rd **76** C6
Bexleyheath DA7 . . . . . **138** E7
Barry Cl, Orp. BR6 . . . . . . **207** H3
Barry Rd, E6 . . . . **116** B6
NW10 . . . . **88** C7
SE22 . . . . **152** D6
Barset Rd, SE15 . . . . **153** F3
Barson Cl, SE20 . . . . **171** F7
Barston Rd, SE27 . . . . **169** J3
Barstow Cres, SW2 . . . . . **169** F1
Barter St, WC1 . . . . **18** B2
Barters Wk, Pnr. HA5
off High St **66/67** E3
Barth Ms, SE18
off Barth Rd **137** H4
Bartholomew Cl, EC1 . . . . . **19** J2
SW18 . . . . **149** F4
Bartholomew Ct, E14
off Newport Av **114** D7
Bartholomew La, EC2 . . . . **20** C4
Bartholomew Pl, EC1 . . . . . **19** J2
Bartholomew Rd, NW5 . . . **92** C6
Bartholomew Sq, E1
off Coventry Rd . . **112/113** E4
EC1 . . . . **12** A5
Bartholomew St, SE1 . . . . **28** B6
Bartholomew Vil, NW5 . . . **92** C6
Barth Rd, SE18 . . . . **137** H4
Bartle Av, E6 . . . . **116** B2
Bartle Rd, W11 . . . . **108** B6
Bartlett Cl, E14 . . . . **114** A6
Bartlett Ct, EC4 . . . . **19** F3
Bartletts Pas, EC4 . . . . **19** F3
Bartlett St, S.Croy. CR2 . . **202** A5
Barton Av, Rom. RM7 . . . . **101** H1
Barton Cl, E6 . . . . **116** C6
E9 *off Churchill Wk* **95** F5
NW4 . . . . **71** G5
SE15 *off Kirkwood*
Rd **152/153** E3
Bexleyheath DA6 . . . . . **158** E5
Chigwell IG7 . . . . **65** F2
Barton Grn, N.Mal. KT3 . . **182** D2
Barton Ho, SW6 *off*
Wandsworth Br Rd . **148/149** E3
Barton Meadows, Ilf. IG6 . . **81** F4
Barton Rd, W14 . . . . **128** B5
Sidcup DA14 . . . . **177** E6
Barton St, SW1 . . . . **26** A5
Bartonway, NW8
off Queen's Ter **109** G2
Barton Way, Borwd. WD6 . . **38** A2
Bartram Rd, SE4 . . . . **153** H5
Barts Cl, Beck. BR3 . . . . . . **190** A5
Barville Cl, SE4
off St. Norbert Rd **153** H4
Barwick Rd, E7 . . . . **97** H4
Barwood Av, W.Wick.
BR4 . . . . **204** B1
Bascombe St, SW2 . . . . . **151** G6
Basden Gro, Felt. TW13 . . **161** G2
Basedale Rd, Dag. RM9 . . **100** B7
Baseing Cl, E6 . . . . **116** D7
Basevi Way, SE8 . . . . **134** B6
Bashley Rd, NW10 . . . . . . **106** D4
Basil Av, E6 . . . . **116** B2
Basildene Rd, Houns.
TW4 . . . . **142** D2
Basildon Av, Ilf. IG5 . . . . . . **80** D1
Basildon Rd, SE2 . . . . **138** A5
Basil Gdns, SE27 . . . . **169** J5
Croydon CR0
off Primrose La **203** G1
Basilon Rd, Bexh. DA7 . . . **158** E2
Basil St, SW3 . . . . **23** J5
Basin App, E14
off Commercial Rd . . . **113** H6
Basing Cl, T.Ditt. KT7 . . . . **180** C7
Basing Ct, SE15 . . . . **152** C1
Basingdon Way, SE5 . . . . **152** A4
Basing Dr, Bex. DA5 . . . . . **159** F6
Basingfield Rd, T.Ditt.
KT7 . . . . **180** C7
Basinghall Av, EC2 . . . . **20** B2
Basinghall St, EC2 . . . . **20** B3
Basing Hill, NW11 . . . . **90** C1
Wembley HA9 . . . . **87** J2
Basing Ho, Bark. IG11
off St. Margarets **117** G1
Basing Ho Yd, E2 . . . . **13** E3
Basing Pl, E2 . . . . **13** E3
Basing St, W11 . . . . **108** C6
Basing Way, N3 . . . . **72** D3
Thames Ditton KT7 . . . . **180** C7
Basire St, N1 . . . . **111** J1
Baskerville Rd, SW18 . . . . **149** H7
Basket Gdns, SE9 . . . . **156** B5
Baslow Cl, Har. HA3 . . . . . . **68** A1
Baslow Wk, E5
off Overbury St **95** G4
Basnett Rd, SW11 . . . . . . **150** A3
Basque Ct, SE16
off Poolmans St **133** G2
Bassano St, SE22 . . . . **152** C5
Bassant Rd, SE18 . . . . **137** J6
Bassein Pk Rd, W12 . . . . . **127** F2
Bassett Gdns, Islw. TW7 . . **123** J7
Bassett Ho, Dag. RM9 . . . **118** B1
Bassett Rd, W10 . . . . **108** A6
Bassetts Cl, Orp. BR6 . . . . **206** E4
Bassett St, NW5 . . . . **92** A6
Bassetts Way, Orp. BR6 . . **206** E4
Bassett Way, Grnf. UB6 . . **103** H6
Bassingham Rd, SW18 . . **149** F7
Wembley HA0 . . . . **87** G6
Bassishaw Highwalk, EC2
off London Wall **111** J5
Bastable Av, Bark. IG11 . . . **117** H2
Bastion Highwalk, EC2
off London Wall **111** J5
Bastion Ho, EC2
off London Wall **111** J5
Bastion Rd, SE2 . . . . **138** A5
Baston Manor Rd, Brom.
BR2 . . . . **205** H3
Baston Rd, Brom. BR2 . . . **205** H1
Bastwick St, EC1 . . . . **11** J5
Basuto Rd, SW6 . . . . **148** D1
Batavia Cl, Sun. TW16 . . . **178** C1
Batavia Ms, SE14
off Goodwood Rd **133** H7
Batavia Rd, SE14 . . . . **133** H7
Sunbury-on-Thames
TW16 . . . . **178** B1
Batchelor St, N1 . . . . **11** E1
Bateman Cl, Bark. IG11
off Glenny Rd **99** F6
Bateman Ho, SE17 . . . . **35** G6
Bateman Rd, E4 . . . . **62** A6
Bateman's Bldgs, W1 . . . . . **17** H4
Bateman's Row, EC2 . . . . . **12** E5
Bateman St, W1 . . . . **17** H4
Bates Cres, SW16 . . . . **168** C7
Croydon CR0 . . . . **201** G5
Bateson St, SE18 . . . . **137** H4
Bates Pt, E13
off Pelly Rd **115** G1
Bate St, E14
off Three Colt St **113** J7
Bath Cl, SE15
off Asylum Rd . . . **132/133** E7
Bath Ct, EC1 . . . . **11** E6
Bathgate Rd, SW19 . . . . . **166** A3
Bath Ho Rd, Croy. CR0 . . . **200** E1
Bath Pas, Kings.T. KT1
off St. James Rd **181** G2
Bath Pl, EC2 . . . . **12** D4
Barnet EN5 . . . . **40** C3
Bath Rd, E7 . . . . **98** A6
N9 . . . . **61** E2
W4 . . . . **126** E4
Hayes UB3 . . . . **141** F1
Hounslow TW3, TW4,
TW5, TW6 . . . . **142** D2
Mitcham CR4 . . . . **185** G3
Romford RM6 . . . . **82** E6
West Drayton UB7 . . . . **140** A1
Baths Rd, Brom. BR2 . . . . **192** A4
Bath St, EC1 . . . . **12** A4
Bath Ter, SE1 . . . . **27** J6
Bathurst Av, SW19
off Brisbane Av . . **184/185** E1
Bathurst Gdns, NW10 . . . . **107** H2
Bathurst Ms, W2 . . . . **15** E5
Bathurst Rd, Ilf. IG1 . . . . . . **98** E1
Bathurst St, W2 . . . . **15** E5
Bathway, SE18 . . . . **136** D4
Batley Cl, Mitch. CR4 . . . . **185** J7
Batley Pl, N16 . . . . **94** C3
Batley Rd, N16 *off Stoke*
Newington High St **94** C3
Enfield EN2 . . . . **43** J1
Batman Cl, W12 . . . . **127** H1
Batoum Gdns, W6 . . . . . . **127** J3
Batson St, W12 . . . . **127** G2
Batsworth Rd, Mitch.
CR4 . . . . **185** G3
Battenburg Wk, SE19
off Brabourne Cl **170** B5
Batten Cl, E6
off Savage Gdns **116** C6
Batten St, SW11 . . . . **149** H3
Battersby Rd, SE6 . . . . . . **172** D2
BATTERSEA, SW11 . . . . . . **150** B1
Battersea Br, SW3 . . . . **31** F7
SW11 . . . . **31** F7
Battersea Br Rd, SW11 . . . **129** H7
Battersea Ch Rd, SW11 . . **149** G1
★**Battersea Dogs Home**,
SW8 . . . . **130** B7
Battersea High St, SW11 . **149** G1
★**Battersea Park**, SW11 . . . **32** A7
Battersea Pk Rd, SW8 . . . **150** B1
SW11 . . . . **149** H2
Battersea Ri, SW11 . . . . . . **149** H5
Battersea Sq, SW11
off Battersea High St . **149** G1
Battery Rd, SE28 . . . . **137** H2
Battishill Gdns, N1
off Waterloo Ter **93** H7
Battishill St, N1
off Waterloo Ter **93** H7
Battlebridge Ct, N1 . . . . . . **10** B1
Battle Br La, SE1 . . . . **28** D2
Battle Br Rd, NW1 . . . . **10** A2
Battle Cl, SW19
off North Rd **167** F6
Battledean Rd, N5 . . . . **93** H5
Battle Rd, Belv. DA17 . . . . **139** J4
Erith DA8 . . . . **139** J4
Batty St, E1 . . . . **21** J3
Baudwin Rd, SE6 . . . . **172** E2
Baugh Rd, Sid. DA14 . . . . **176** C5
Baulk, The, SW18 . . . . **148** D7
Bavant Rd, SW16 . . . . **187** E2
Bavaria Rd, N19 . . . . **92** E2
Bavdene Ms, NW4
off The Burroughs **71** H4
Bavent Rd, SE5 . . . . **151** J2
Bawdale Rd, SE22 . . . . . . **152** C5
Bawdsey Av, Ilf. IG2 . . . . . . **81** J4
Bawtree Rd, SE14 . . . . . . **133** H7
Bawtry Rd, N20 . . . . **57** J3
Baxendale, N20 . . . . **57** F2
Baxendale St, E2 . . . . **13** H3
Baxter Cl, Sthl. UB2 . . . . . **123** H2
Baxter Rd, E16 . . . . **115** J6
N1 . . . . **94** A6
N18 . . . . **60** E4
NW10 . . . . **106** E4
Ilford IG1 . . . . **98** E5
Bay Ct, W5
off Popes La **125** H3
Baycroft Cl, Pnr. HA5 . . . . . **66** C3
Baydon Ct, Brom. BR2 . . . **191** F3
Bayes Cl, SE26 . . . . **171** F5
Bayfield Rd, SE9 . . . . **156** A4
Bayford Ms, E8
off Bayford St **94/95** E7
Bayford Rd, NW10 . . . . . . **108** A3
Bayford St, E8 . . . . **95** E7
Bayham Pl, NW1 . . . . **9** F1
Bayham Rd, W4 . . . . **126** D3
W13 . . . . **104** E7
Morden SM4 . . . . **185** E4
Bayham St, NW1 . . . . **110** C1
Bayley St, WC1 . . . . **17** H2
Bayley Wk, SE2
off Woolwich Rd . . **138/139** E5
Baylin Rd, SW18
off Garratt La **148/149** E6
Baylis Ms, Twick. TW1
off Amyand Pk Rd **144** D7
Baylis Rd, SE1 . . . . **27** E4
Bayliss Av, SE28 . . . . **118** D7
Bayliss Cl, N21 . . . . **43** E5
Southall UB1 . . . . **103** H6
Bayne Cl, E6
off Savage Gdns **116** C6
Baynes Cl, Enf. EN1 . . . . . . **44** D2
Baynes Ms, NW3
off Belsize La **91** G6
Baynes St, NW1 . . . . **92** C7
Baynham Cl, Bex. DA5 . . . **159** F6
Bayonne Rd, W6 . . . . **128** B6
Bayshill Ri, Nthlt. UB5 . . . . **85** H6
Bayston Rd, N16 . . . . **94** C3
BAYSWATER, W2 . . . . **14** B4
Bayswater Rd, W2 . . . . **15** F5
Baythorne St, E3 . . . . **113** J5
Bay Tree Cl, Brom. BR1 . . . **191** J1
Ilford IG6
off Hazel La **64/65** E7
Baytree Cl, Sid. DA15 . . . . **175** J1
Baytree Ho, E4
off Dells Cl **46** B7
Baytree Rd, SW2 . . . . **151** F4
Bazalgette Cl, N.Mal.
KT3 . . . . **182** D5
Bazalgette Gdns, N.Mal.
KT3 . . . . **182** D5
Bazely St, E14 . . . . **114** C7
Bazile Rd, N21 . . . . **43** G6
Beacham Cl, SE7 . . . . **136** A5
Beachborough Rd, Brom.
BR1 . . . . **172** C4
Beachcroft Rd, E11 . . . . **97** E3
Beachcroft Way, N19 . . . . . **92** D1
Beach Gro, Felt. TW13 . . . **161** G2
Beachy Rd, E3 . . . . **96** A7
Beacon Gate, SE14 . . . . . . **153** G3
Beacon Gro, Cars. SM5 . . **200** A4
Beacon Hill, N7 . . . . **92** E5
Beacon Rd, SE13 . . . . **154** D6
Hounslow (Hthrw Air.)
TW6 . . . . **140** D6

Beacon Rd Roundabout, Houns.
(Hthrw Air.) TW6 . . . . . **140** E6
Beacons Cl, E6
off Oliver Gdns **116** B5
Beaconsfield Cl, N11 . . . . . **58** A4
SE3 . . . . **135** G6
W4 . . . . **126** C5
Beaconsfield Gdns, Esher
(Clay.) KT10 . . . . **194** B7
Beaconsfield Par, SE9
off Beaconsfield Rd . . . **174** B4
Beaconsfield Rd, E10 . . . . . **96** C2
E16 . . . . **115** F4
E17 . . . . **77** J6
N9 . . . . **60** D4
N11 . . . . **58** A3
N15 . . . . **76** B4
NW10 . . . . **89** F6
SE3 . . . . **135** F7
SE9 . . . . **174** B2
SE17 . . . . **36** C4
W4 . . . . **126** D3
W5 . . . . **125** F2
Bromley BR1 . . . . **192** A3
Croydon CR0 . . . . **188** A6
Esher (Clay.) KT10 . . . . . **194** B7
Hayes UB4 . . . . **122** C1
New Malden KT3 . . . . . **182** D2
Southall UB1 . . . . **122** D1
Surbiton KT5 . . . . **181** J7
Twickenham TW1 . . . . . **144** E6
Beaconsfield Ter, Rom.
RM6 . . . . **82** D6
Beaconsfield Ter Rd, W14 . **128** B3
Beaconsfield Wk, E6 *off East
Ham Manor Way* **116** D6
SW6 . . . . **148** C1
Beacontree Av, E17 . . . . . . **78** D1
Beacontree Rd, E11 . . . . . . **79** F7
Beadlow Cl, Cars. SM5
off Olveston Wk **185** G6
Beadman Pl, SE27
off Norwood High St . **169** H4
Beadman St, SE27 . . . . . . **169** H4
Beadnell Rd, SE23 . . . . . . **171** G1
Beadon Rd, W6 . . . . **127** J4
Bromley BR2 . . . . **191** G4
Beaford Gro, SW20 . . . . . **184** B3
Beagle Cl, Felt. TW13 . . . . **160** B4
Beak St, W1 . . . . **17** G5
Beal Cl, Well. DA16 . . . . . . **158** A1
Beale Cl, N13 . . . . **59** H5
Beale Pl, E3 . . . . **113** J2
Beale Rd, E3 . . . . **113** J1
Beal Rd, Ilf. IG1 . . . . **98** D2
Beam Av, Dag. RM10 . . . . **119** H1
Beaminster Gdns, Ilf. IG6 . . **80** E2
Beamish Dr, Bushey
(Bushey Hth) WD23 . . . . **51** J1
Beamish Rd, N9 . . . . **60** D1
Beanacre Cl, E9 . . . . **95** J6
Bean Rd, Bexh. DA6 . . . . . **158** D4
Beanshaw, SE9 . . . . **174** D4
Beansland Gro, Rom.
RM6 . . . . **83** E2
Bear All, EC4 . . . . **19** G3
Bear Cl, Rom. RM7 . . . . **83** H6
Beardell St, SE19 . . . . **170** C6
Beardow Gro, N14 . . . . **42** C6
Beard Rd, Kings.T. KT2 . . . **163** J5
Beardsfield, E13
off Valetta Gro **115** G1
Beard's Hill, Hmptn.
TW12 . . . . **179** G1
Beard's Hill Cl, Hmptn. TW12
off Beard's Hill **179** G1
Beardsley Ter, Dag. RM8
off Fitzstephen Rd **100** B5
Beardsley Way, W3 . . . . . . **126** D2
Bearfield Rd, Kings.T.
KT2 . . . . **163** H7
Bear Gdns, SE1 . . . . **27** J1
Bear La, SE1 . . . . **27** H1
Bear Rd, Felt. TW13 . . . . . **160** D5
Bearstead Ri, SE4 . . . . . . **153** J5
Bearsted Ter, Beck. BR3 . . **190** A1
Bear St, WC2 . . . . **17** J5
Beaton Cl, SE15 . . . . **152** C1
Beatrice Av, SW16 . . . . . . **187** F3
Wembley HA9 . . . . **87** H5
Beatrice Cl, E13
off Chargeable La **115** G4
Pinner HA5
off Reid Cl **66** A4
Beatrice Ct, Buck.H. IG9 . . . **64** A2
Beatrice Pl, W8 . . . . **22** A6
Beatrice Rd, E17 . . . . **78** A5
N4 . . . . **75** G7
N9 . . . . **45** F7
Beatrice Rd, SE1 . . . . **37** J2
Richmond TW10
off Albert Rd **145** J5
Southall UB1 . . . . **123** F1
Beatson Wk, SE16 . . . . . . **133** G1
Beattock Ri, N10 . . . . **74** B4
Beatty Rd, N16 . . . . **94** B4
Stanmore HA7 . . . . **53** F6
Beatty St, NW1 . . . . **9** F1
Beattyville Gdns, Ilf.
IG6 . . . . **80** D3
Beauchamp Cl, W4
off Church Path **126** C3
Beauchamp Ct, Stan. HA7
off Hardwick Cl **53** F5
Beauchamp Pl, SW3 . . . . . . **23** H5
Beauchamp Rd, E7 . . . . **97** H7
SE19 . . . . **188** A1
SW11 . . . . **149** H4
East Molesey KT8 . . . . . **179** H5
Sutton SM1 . . . . **198** D5
Twickenham TW1 . . . . . **144** D7
West Molesey KT8 . . . . **179** H5
Beauchamp St, EC1 . . . . . . **19** E2
Beauchamp Ter, SW15
off Dryburgh Rd **147** H3
Beauclerc Rd, W6 . . . . **127** H3
Beauclerk Cl, Felt. TW13
off Florence Rd **160** B1
Beaudesert Ms, West Dr.
UB7 . . . . **120** B2
Beaufort, E6
off Newark Knok **116** D5
Beaufort Av, Har. HA3 . . . . **68** D4
Beaufort Cl, E4
off Higham Sta Av **62** B6
SW15 . . . . **147** H7
W5 . . . . **105** J5
Romford RM7 . . . . **83** J4
Beaufort Ct, Rich. TW10
off Beaufort Rd **163** F4
Beaufort Dr, NW11 . . . . **72** D4
Beaufort Gdns, NW4 . . . . . . **71** J6
SW3 . . . . **23** H5
SW16 . . . . **169** F7
Hounslow TW5 . . . . **143** E1
Ilford IG1 . . . . **98** D1
Beaufort Ms, SW6
off Lillie Rd **128** C6
Beaufort Pk, NW11 . . . . **72** D4
Beaufort Rd, W5 . . . . **105** J5
Kingston upon Thames
KT1 . . . . **181** H4
Richmond TW10 . . . . . . **163** F4
Twickenham TW1 . . . . . **145** F7
Beaufort St, SW3 . . . . **31** F6
Beaufort Way, Epsom
KT17 . . . . **197** G7
Beaufoy Rd, N17 . . . . **60** B7
Beaufoy Wk, SE11 . . . . **34** D2
Beaulieu Av, E16 . . . . **135** H1
SE26 . . . . **170** E4
Beaulieu Cl, NW9 . . . . **71** E4
SE5 . . . . **152** A3
Hounslow TW4 . . . . **143** F5
Mitcham CR4 . . . . **186** A1
Twickenham TW1 . . . . . **145** G7
Watford WD19 . . . . **50** C1
Beaulieu Dr, Pnr. HA5 . . . . **66** D6
Beaulieu Gdns, N21 . . . . . . **43** J7
Beaulieu Pl, W4
off Rothschild Rd **126** C3
Beaumanor Gdns, SE9 . . . **174** D4
Beaumaris Dr, Wdf.Grn.
IG8 . . . . **64** A7
Beaumaris Grn, NW9
off Goldsmith Av . . . **70/71** E6
Beaumont Av, W14 . . . . . . **128** C5
Harrow HA2 . . . . **67** H6
Richmond TW9 . . . . **145** J3
Wembley HA0 . . . . **87** F5
Beaumont Cl, Kings.T.
KT2 . . . . **164** A7
Beaumont Cres, W14 . . . . **128** C5
Beaumont Gdns, NW3 . . . . **90** D3
Beaumont Gro, E1 . . . . . . **113** G4
Beaumont Ms, W1 . . . . **16** C1
Pinner HA5 . . . . **66** E3
Beaumont Pl, W1 . . . . **9** G5
Barnet EN5 . . . . **40** C1
Isleworth TW7 . . . . **144** C5
Beaumont Ri, N19 . . . . **92** D1
Beaumont Rd, E10 . . . . **78** B7
E13 . . . . **115** H3
SE19 . . . . **169** J6
SW19 . . . . **148** B7
W4 . . . . **126** C3
Orpington BR5 . . . . **193** G6
Beaumont Sq, E1 . . . . **113** G4
Beaumont St, W1 . . . . **16** C1
Beaumont Wk, NW3 . . . . . . **91** J7
Beauvais Ter, Nthlt. UB5 . . **102** D3
Beauval Rd, SE22 . . . . **152** C6
Beaverbank Rd, SE9 . . . . . **175** G1
Beaver Cl, SE20
off Lullington Rd **170** D7
Hampton TW12 . . . . **179** H1
Beaver Gro, Nthlt. UB5
off Jetstar Way . . . **102/103** E3
Beavers Cres, Houns.
TW4 . . . . **142** C4
Beavers La, Houns. TW4 . **142** C3
Beavers La Camp, Houns.
TW4 *off Beavers La* . . **142** C3
Beaverwood Rd, Chis.
BR7 . . . . **175** H6
Beavor Gro, W6
off Beavor La **127** G4
Beavor La, W6 . . . . **127** G4
Bebbington Rd, SE18 . . . . **137** H4
Bebletts Cl, Orp. BR6 . . . . **207** J5
Beccles Dr, Bark. IG11 . . . . **99** H6
Beccles St, E14 . . . . **113** J7
Bec Cl, Ruis. HA4 . . . . **84** D3
Beck Cl, SE13 . . . . **154** B1
Beck Ct, Beck. BR3 . . . . . . **189** G3
BECKENHAM, BR3 . . . . . . **190** A1
Beckenham Business Cen,
Beck. BR3 . . . . **171** H6
Beckenham Gdns, N9 . . . . **60** B3
Beckenham Gro, Brom.
BR2 . . . . **190** D2
Beckenham Hill Rd, SE6 . . **172** B5
Beckenham BR3 . . . . . . **172** B5
Beckenham La, Brom.
BR2 . . . . **191** E2
Beckenham Pl Pk, Beck.
BR3 . . . . **172** B7
Beckenham Rd, Beck.
BR3 . . . . **189** G1
West Wickham BR4 . . . . **190** B7
Beckers, The, N16
off Rectory Rd **94** D3
Becket Av, E6 . . . . **116** D3
Becket Cl, SE25 . . . . **188** D6
Becket Fold, Har. HA1
off Courtfield Cres **68** C5
Becket Rd, N18 . . . . **61** F4
Becket St, SE1 . . . . **28** B5
Beckett Cl, NW10 . . . . **88** D6
SW16 . . . . **168** D2
Belvedere DA17
off Tunstock Way . **138/139** E3
Becketts Cl, Bex. DA5 . . . **177** J1
Feltham TW14 . . . . **142** B6
Orpington BR6 . . . . **207** J3
Becketts Pl, Kings.T.
(Hmptn W.) KT1 . . . . . . **181** G1
Beckett Wk, Beck. BR3 . . . **171** H6
Beckford Dr, Orp. BR5 . . . **193** G7
Beckford Pl, SE17 . . . . **36** A4
Beckford Rd, Croy. CR0 . . **188** C6
Beck La, Beck. BR3 . . . . . . **189** G3
Becklow Gdns, W12
off Becklow Rd **127** G2
Becklow Ms, W12
off Becklow Rd **127** F2
Becklow Rd, W12 . . . . **127** G2
Beck River Pk, Beck. BR3 . **189** J1
Beck Rd, E8 . . . . **112** E1
Becks Rd, Sid. DA14 . . . . . **176** A3
BECKTON, E6 . . . . **116** D5
Beckton Pk Roundabout, E16
off Royal Albert Way . . **116** C7
Beckton Retail Pk, E6 . . . . **116** D5
Beckton Rd, E16 . . . . **115** F5
Beckton Triangle Retail Pk,
E6 . . . . **116** D4
Beck Way, Beck. BR3 . . . . **189** J3
Beckway Rd, SW16 . . . . . **186** D2
Beckway St, SE17 . . . . **36** C2
Beckwith Rd, SE24 . . . . . . **152** A6
Beclands Rd, SW17 . . . . . **168** A6
Becmead Av, SW16 . . . . . **168** D4
Harrow HA3 . . . . **68** E5
Becondale Rd, SE19 . . . . . **170** B5
BECONTREE, Dag. RM8 . . **100** E3
Becontree Av, Dag. RM8 . **100** B4
BECONTREE HEATH, Dag.
RM8 . . . . **101** G1
Bective Pl, SW15
off Bective Rd **148** C4
Bective Rd, E7 . . . . **97** G4
SW15 . . . . **148** C4
Becton Pl, Erith DA8 . . . . **139** H7
Bedale St, SE1 . . . . **28** B2
BEDDINGTON, Croy.
CR0 . . . . **200** D2
BEDDINGTON CORNER,
Mitch. CR4 . . . . **186** A7
Beddington Cross, Croy.
CR0 . . . . **200** D1
Beddington Fm Rd, Croy.
CR0 . . . . **200** E1
Beddington Gdns, Cars.
SM5 . . . . **200** A6
Wallington SM6 . . . . . . **200** B6
Beddington Grn, Orp.
BR5 . . . . **193** J1
Beddington Gro, Wall.
SM6 . . . . **200** D5
Beddington La, Croy.
CR0 . . . . **186** C5
Beddington Path, Orp.
BR5 . . . . **193** J1
Beddington Rd, Ilf. IG3 . . . **81** J7
Orpington BR5 . . . . **193** H2
Beddington Trd Pk W,
Croy. CR0 . . . . **200** E1
Bede Cl, Pnr. HA5 . . . . **66** D1
Bedenham Way, SE15 . . . . **37** F7
Bedens Rd, Sid. DA14 . . . **176** E6
Bede Rd, Rom. RM6 . . . . . . **82** C6
Bedevere Rd, N9
off Salisbury Rd **60** D3
Bedfont Cl, Felt. TW14 . . . **141** F6
Mitcham CR4 . . . . **186** A2
Bedfont La, Felt. TW13,
TW14 . . . . **141** J7
Bedfont Rd, Stai. (Stanw.)
TW19 . . . . **140** B6
Bedford Av, WC1 . . . . **17** J2
Barnet EN5 . . . . **40** C5
Hayes UB4 . . . . **102** B6
Bedfordbury, WC2 . . . . **18** A5
Bedford Cl, N10 . . . . **58** A7
W4 . . . . **127** E6
Bedford Cor, W4
off The Avenue . . **126/127** E4
Bedford Ct, WC2 . . . . **18** A6
Bedford Gdns, W8 . . . . . . **128** D1
Bedford Hill, SW12 . . . . . . **168** B1
SW16 . . . . **168** B1
Bedford Ho, SW4 . . . . **150** E4
Bedford Ms, N2
off Bedford Rd **73** H3
SE6 *off Aitken Rd* **172** B2
BEDFORD PARK, W4 . . . . **126** D3
Bedford Pk, Croy. CR0 . . . **201** J1
Bedford Pk Cor, W4
off Bath Rd **126/127** E4
Bedford Pas, SW6
off Dawes Rd **128** B7
Bedford Pl, WC1 . . . . **18** A1
Croydon CR0 . . . . **202** A1
Bedford Rd, E6 . . . . **116** D1
E17 . . . . **78** A2
E18 . . . . **79** G2
N2 . . . . **73** H3
N8 . . . . **74** D6
N9 . . . . **44** E7
N15 . . . . **76** B4
N22 . . . . **74** E1
NW7 . . . . **54** E3
SW4 . . . . **150** E3
W4 . . . . **126** D3
W13 . . . . **104** E7
Harrow HA1 . . . . **67** J6
Ilford IG1 . . . . **99** E3
Sidcup DA15 . . . . **175** H3
Twickenham TW2 . . . . . **162** A3
Worcester Park KT4 . . . . **197** J2
Bedford Row, WC1 . . . . **18** D1
Bedford Sq, WC1 . . . . **17** J2
Bedford St, WC2 . . . . **18** A5
Bedford Ter, SW2
off Lyham Rd **150/151** E5
Bedford Way, WC1 . . . . **9** J6
Bedgebury Gdns,
SW19 . . . . **166** B2
Bedgebury Rd, SE9 . . . . . **156** A4
Bedivere Rd, Brom. BR1 . **173** G3
Bedlam Ms, SE11 . . . . **34** D1
Bedlow Way, Croy. CR0 . . **201** F4
Bedonwell Rd, SE2 . . . . . **138** E6
Belvedere DA17 . . . . . . **139** G6
Bexleyheath DA7 . . . . . **139** G6
Bedser Cl, SE11 . . . . **34** D5
Thornton Heath CR7 . . . **187** J3
Bedser Dr, Grnf. UB6 . . . . . **86** A5
Bedster Gdns, W.Mol.
KT8 . . . . **179** H2
Bedwardine Rd, SE19 . . . . **170** B7
Bedwell Gdns, Hayes
UB3 . . . . **121** H5
Bedwell Rd, N17 . . . . **76** B1
Belvedere DA17 . . . . . . **139** G5

Beeby Rd, E16 **115** H5
Beech Av, N20 **57** H1
W3 **126** E1
Brentford TW8 **125** E7
Buckhurst Hill IG9 **63** H2
Ruislip HA4 **84** B1
Sidcup DA15 **158** A7
Beech Cl, N9 **44** D6
SE8 *off Clyde St* **133** J6
SW15 **147** G7
SW19 **165** J6
Carshalton SM5 **199** J2
Loughton IG10 *off Cedar Dr* **48/49** E2
Staines (Stanw.) TW19 *off St. Mary's Cres* **140** A7
Sunbury-on-Thames TW16 *off Harfield Rd* **178** D2
West Drayton UB7 **120** D3
Beech Copse, Brom. BR1 **192** C2
South Croydon CR2 **202** B5
Beech Ct, E17 **78** D3
SE9 **156** B6
Ilford IG1 *off Riverdene Rd* **98** D3
Beechcroft, Chis. BR7 **174** D7
Beechcroft Av, NW11 **72** C7
Harrow HA2 **67** G7
New Malden KT3 **182** C1
Southall UB1 **123** F1
Beechcroft Cl, Houns. TW5 **122** E7
Orpington BR6 **207** G4
Beechcroft Gdns, Wem. HA9 **87** J3
Beechcroft Lo, Sutt. SM2 *off Devonshire Rd* **199** F7
Beechcroft Rd, E18 **79** H2
SW14 *off Elm Rd* **146** C3
SW17 **167** H2
Chessington KT9 **195** J3
Orpington BR6 **207** G4
Beechdale, N21 **59** F2
Beechdale Rd, SW2 **151** F6
Beech Dell, Kes. BR2 **206** C4
Beech Dr, N2 **73** J3
Beechen Cliff Way, Islw. TW7 *off Henley Cl* **144** C1
Beechen Gro, Pnr. HA5 **67** F3
Beeches, The, Houns. TW3 **143** H1
Beeches Av, Cars. SM5 **199** H7
Beeches Cl, SE20 *off Genoa Rd* **189** F1
Beeches Rd, SW17 **167** H3
Sutton SM3 **198** B1
Beechfield Cotts, Brom. BR1 *off Widmore Rd* **191** J2
Beechfield Gdns, Rom. RM7 **83** J7
Beechfield Rd, N4 **75** J6
SE6 **171** J1
Bromley BR1 **191** J2
Beech Gdns, EC2 *off Aldersgate St* **111** J5
W5 **125** H2
Dagenham RM10 **101** H7
Beech Gro, Ilf. IG6 **65** H6
Mitcham CR4 **186** D4
New Malden KT3 **182** D3
Beech Hall Cres, E4 **62** D7
Beech Hall Rd, E4 **62** C7
Beech Hill Av, Barn. EN4 **41** F1
Beechhill Rd, SE9 **156** D5
Beech Ho, Croy. CR0 **204** B6
Beech Ho Rd, Croy. CR0 **202** A3
Beech La, Buck.H. IG9 **63** H2
Beech Lawns, N12 **57** G5
Beechmont Cl, Brom. BR1 **172** E5
Beechmore Gdns, Sutt. SM3 **198** A2
Beechmore Rd, SW11 **149** J1
Beechmount Av, W7 **104** A5
Beecholme Av, Mitch. CR4 **186** B1
Beecholme Est, E5 *off Prout Rd* **94/95** E3
Beech Rd, N11 **59** E6
SW16 **187** E2
Feltham TW14 **141** H7
Beech Row, Rich. TW10 **163** H4
Beech St, EC2 **19** J1
Romford RM7 **83** J4
Beech Tree Cl, Stan. HA7 **53** F5
Beech Tree Glade, E4 *off Forest Side* **63** F1
Beech Tree Pl, Sutt. SM1 *off St. Nicholas Way* **198/199** E5
Beechvale Cl, N12 **57** H5
Beech Wk, NW7 **54** E6
Beech Way, NW10 **88** D7
Beechway, Bex. DA5 **158** D6
Beech Way, Twick. TW2 **161** G3
Beechwood Av, N3 **72** C3
Greenford UB6 **103** H3
Harrow HA2 **85** H3
Orpington BR6 **207** H5
Richmond TW9 **146** A1
Sunbury-on-Thames TW16 **160** A6
Thornton Heath CR7 **187** H4
Beechwood Circle, Har. HA2 *off Beechwood Gdns* **85** H3
Beechwood Cl, NW7 **54** D5
Surbiton KT6 **181** F7
Beechwood Ct, Cars. SM5 **199** J4
Sunbury-on-Thames TW16 **160** A6
Beechwood Cres, Bexh. DA7 **158** D3
Beechwood Dr, Kes. BR2 **206** A4
Woodford Green IG8 **63** F5
Beechwood Gdns, NW10 *off St. Annes Gdns* **105** J3
Harrow HA2 **85** H3
Ilford IG5 **80** C5
Beechwood Gro, W3 *off East Acton La* **106/107** E7
Surbiton KT6 **181** F7
Beechwood Ms, N9 **60** D2
Beechwood Pk, E18 **79** G3
Beechwood Ri, Chis. BR7 **175** E4
Beechwood Rd, E8 **94** C6
N8 **74** D4
Beechwoods Ct, SE19 *off Crystal Palace Par* **170** C5
Beechworth Cl, NW3 **90** D2
Beecroft La, SE4 *off Beecroft Rd* **153** H5
Beecroft Ms, SE4 *off Beecroft Rd* **153** H5
Beecroft Rd, SE4 **153** H5
Beehive Cl, E8 **94** C7
Beehive La, Ilf. IG1, IG4 **80** C6
Beehive Pas, EC3 **20** D4
Beehive Pl, SW9 **151** G3
Beeken Dene, Orp. BR6 *off Isabella Dr* **207** F4
Beeleigh Rd, Mord. SM4 **185** E4
Beeston Cl, E8 *off Ferncliff Rd* **94** D5
Watford WD19 **50** D4
Beeston Pl, SW1 **24** E6
Beeston Rd, Barn. EN4 **41** G6
Beeston Way, Felt. TW14 **142** C6
Beethoven St, W10 **108** B3
Beeton Cl, Pnr. HA5 **51** G7
Begbie Rd, SE3 **155** J1
Beggars Hill, Epsom KT17 **197** F7
Beggars Roost La, Sutt. SM1 **198** D6
Begonia Cl, E6 **116** B5
Begonia Pl, Hmptn. TW12 *off Gresham Rd* **161** G6
Begonia Wk, W12 *off Du Cane Rd* **107** F6
Beira St, SW12 **150** B7
Bekesbourne St, E14 *off Ratcliffe La* **113** H6
Belcroft Cl, Brom. BR1 *off Hope Pk* **173** F7
Beldham Gdns, W.Mol. KT8 **179** H3
Belfairs Dr, Rom. RM6 **82** C7
Belfairs Grn, Wat. WD19 *off Heysham Dr* **50** D5
Belfast Rd, N16 **94** C2
SE25 **188** E4
Belfont Wk, N7 **93** E4
Belford Gro, SE18 **136** D4
Belfort Rd, SE15 **153** F2
Belfour Ter, N3 **72** E2
Belfry Cl, SE16 *off Masters Dr* **132/133** E5
Belgrade Rd, N16 **94** B4
Hampton TW12 **179** H1
Belgrave Cl, N14 *off Prince George Av* **42** C5
NW7 **54** D5
W3 *off Avenue Rd* **126** C2
Belgrave Ct, E14 *off Westferry Circ* **134** A1
Belgrave Cres, Sun. TW16 **178** B1
Belgrave Gdns, N14 **42** D5
NW8 **109** E1
Stanmore HA7 *off Copley Rd* **53** F5
Belgrave Hts, E11 **97** G1
Belgrave Ms N, SW1 **24** B4
Belgrave Ms S, SW1 **24** C5
Belgrave Ms W, SW1 **24** B5
Belgrave Pl, SW1 **24** C5
Belgrave Rd, E10 **96** C1
E11 **97** G2
E13 **115** J4
E17 **78** A5
SE25 **188** C4
SW1 **33** F2
SW13 **127** F7
Hounslow TW4 **143** F3
Ilford IG1 **98** C1
Mitcham CR4 **185** G3
Sunbury-on-Thames TW16 **178** B1
Belgrave Sq, SW1 **24** B5
Belgrave St, E1 **113** G6
Belgrave Ter, Wdf.Grn. IG8 **63** G3
Belgrave Wk, Mitch. CR4 **185** G3
Belgrave Yd, SW1 **24** D6
BELGRAVIA, SW1 **24** B6
Belgravia Cl, Barn. EN5 **40** C3
Belgravia Gdns, Brom. BR1 **172** E6
Belgravia Ho, SW4 **150** D6
Belgravia Ms, Kings.T. KT1 **181** G4
Belgrove St, WC1 **10** A3
Belham Wk, SE5 *off D'Eynsford Rd* **152** A1
Belinda Rd, SW9 **151** H3
Belitha Vil, N1 **93** F7
Bellamy Cl, E14 *off Byng St* **134** A2
W14 *off Aisgill Av* **128** C5
Edgware HA8 **54** C3
Bellamy Dr, Stan. HA7 **68** E1
Bellamy Rd, E4 **62** B6
Enfield EN2 **44** A2
Bellamy St, SW12 **150** B7
Bellarmine Cl, SE28 **137** J2
Bellasis Av, SW2 **168** E2
Bell Av, West Dr. UB7 **120** C4
Bell Cl, Pnr. HA5 **66** C3
Bellclose Rd, West Dr. UB7 **120** B2
Bell Ct, Surb. KT5 *off Barnsbury La* **196** B2
Bell Dr, SW18 **148** B7
Bellefields Rd, SW9 **151** F3
Bellegrove Cl, Well. DA16 **157** J2
Bellegrove Par, Well. DA16 *off Bellegrove Rd* **157** J3
Bellegrove Rd, Well. DA16 **157** G2
Bellenden Rd, SE15 **152** C2
Bellestaines Pleasaunce, E4 **62** A2
Belleville Rd, SW11 **149** J5
Belle Vue, Grnf. UB6 **104** A1
Belle Vue Est, NW4 *off Bell La* **71** J4
Belle Vue La, Bushey (Bushey Hth) WD23 **52** A1
Bellevue Ms, N11 *off Bellevue Rd* **58** A5
Bellevue Par, SW17 *off Bellevue Rd* **167** H1
Belle Vue Pk, Th.Hth. CR7 **187** J3
Bellevue Pl, E1 **113** F4
Belle Vue Rd, E17 **78** D2
Bellevue Rd, N11 **58** A4
Belle Vue Rd, NW4 *off Bell La* **71** J4
Bellevue Rd, SW13 **147** G2
SW17 **167** H1
W13 **104** E4
Bellevue Rd, Bexleyheath DA6 **159** F5
Kingston upon Thames KT1 **181** H3
Bellew St, SW17 **167** F3
Bell Fm Av, Dag. RM10 **101** J3
Bellfield Av, Har. HA3 **51** J6
Bellfield Cl, SE3 *off Charlton Rd* **135** G7
Bellflower Cl, E6 *off Sorrel Gdns* **116** B5
Bell Gdns, E10 *off Church Rd* **96** A1
E17 *off Markhouse Rd* **77** J5
Bellgate Ms, NW5 *off York Ri* **92** B3
BELL GREEN, SE6 **171** J3
Bell Grn, SE26 **171** J3
Bell Grn La, SE26 **171** H5
Bell Hill, Croy. CR0 *off Surrey St* **201** J3
Bell Ho Rd, Rom. RM7 **101** J1
BELLINGHAM, SE6 **172** B3
Bellingham Ct, Bark. IG11 *off Renwick Rd* **118** B3
Bellingham Grn, SE6 **172** A3
Bellingham Rd, SE6 **172** B3
Bell Inn Yd, EC3 **20** C4
Bell La, E1 **21** F2
E16 **135** G1
NW4 **72** A4
Twickenham TW1 *off The Embankment* **162** D1
Wembley HA9 *off Magnet Rd* **87** G2
Bellmaker Ct, E3 *off St. Pauls Way* **114** A5
Bell Meadow, SE19 *off Dulwich Wd Av* **170** B4
Bello Cl, SE24 **151** H7
Bellot Gdns, SE10 *off Bellot St* **134/135** E5
Bellot St, SE10 **135** E5
Bellring Cl, Belv. DA17 **139** G6
Bell Rd, E.Mol. KT8 **180** A5
Enfield EN1 **44** A1
Hounslow TW3 **143** H4
Bells All, SW6 **148** D2
Bells Gdn Est, SE15 *off Buller Cl* **132** D7
Bells Hill, Barn. EN5 **40** A5
Bell St, NW1 **15** G1
SE18 **156** B1
Belltrees Gro, SW16 **169** F5
Bell Water Gate, SE18 **136** D3
Bell Wf La, EC4 **20** A5
Bellwood Rd, SE15 **153** G4
Bell Yd, WC2 **18** E3
Bell Yd Ms, SE1 *off Bermondsey St* **132** B2
Belmarsh Rd, SE28 *off Western Way* **137** H2
BELMONT, Har. HA3 **68** D2
Belmont Av, N9 **60** D1
N13 **59** E5
N17 **75** J3
Barnet EN4 **41** J5
New Malden KT3 **183** G5
Southall UB2 **122** E3
Welling DA16 **157** H3
Wembley HA0 **105** J1
Belmont Circle, Har. HA3 **68** E1
Belmont Cl, E4 **62** D5
N20 **56** E1
SW4 **150** C3
Barnet EN4 **41** J4
Woodford Green IG8 **63** H4
Belmont Ct, NW11 **72** C5
Belmont Gro, SE13 **154** D3
W4 *off Belmont Rd* **126** D4
Belmont Hall Ct, SE13 *off Belmont Gro* **154** D3
Belmont Hill, SE13 **154** D3
Belmont La, Chis. BR7 **175** F5
Stanmore HA7 **63** F7
Belmont Ms, SW19 *off Chapman Sq* **166** A2
Belmont Pk, SE13 **154** D4
Belmont Pk Cl, SE13 *off Belmont Pk* **154** D4
Belmont Pk Rd, E10 **78** B6
Belmont Ri, Sutt. SM2 **198** C6
Belmont Rd, N15 **75** J4
N17 **75** J4
SE25 **188** E5
SW4 **150** C3
W4 **126** D4
Beckenham BR3 **189** J2
Chislehurst BR7 **175** E5
Belmont Rd, Erith DA8 **139** G7
Harrow HA3 **68** C3
Ilford IG1 **99** F3
Twickenham TW2 **162** A2
Wallington SM6 **200** B5
Belmont St, NW1 **92** A7
Belmont Ter, W4 *off Belmont Rd* **126** D4
Belmor, Borwd. (Elstree) WD6 **38** A5
Belmore Av, Hayes UB4 **102** A6
Belmore La, N7 **92** D5
Belmore St, SW8 **150** D1
Beloe Cl, SW15 **147** G3
Belper Ct, E5 *off Pedro St* **95** G4

Belsham St, E9 . . . . **95** F6
Belsize Av, N13 . . . . **59** F6
NW3 . . . . **91** G6
W13 . . . . **125** E3
Belsize Ct, NW3
off Belsize La **91** H5
Belsize Cres, NW3 . . . . **91** G5
Belsize Gdns, Sutt. SM1 . **199** E4
Belsize Gro, NW3 . . . . **91** H6
Belsize La, NW3 . . . . **91** G6
Belsize Ms, NW3
off Belsize La **91** G6
BELSIZE PARK, NW3 . . . . . **91** H6
Belsize Pk, NW3 . . . . **91** G6
Belsize Pk Gdns, NW3 . . . . **91** H6
Belsize Pk Ms, NW3
off Belsize La **91** G6
Belsize Pl, NW3
off Belsize La **91** G6
Belsize Rd, NW6 . . . . **108** E1
Harrow HA3 . . . . **52** A7
Belsize Sq, NW3 . . . . **91** G6
Belsize Ter, NW3 . . . . **91** G6
Belson Rd, SE18 . . . . **136** C4
Beltane Dr, SW19 . . . . **166** A3
Belthorn Cres, SW12 . . . . **150** C7
Belton Rd, E7 . . . . **97** H7
E11 . . . . **96** E4
N17 . . . . **76** B3
NW2 . . . . **89** G6
Sidcup DA14 . . . . **176** A4
Belton Way, E3 . . . . **114** A5
Beltran Rd, SW6 . . . . **148** E2
Beltwood Rd, Belv. DA17 . **139** J4
BELVEDERE, DA17 . . . . . . **139** H4
Belvedere Av, SW19 . . . . . **166** B5
Ilford IG5 . . . . **80** E2
Belvedere Bldgs, SE1 . . . . . **27** H4
Belvedere Cl, Tedd. TW11 . **162** B5
Belvedere Ct, N2 . . . . **73** G5
Belvedere Dr, SW19 . . . . . **166** B5
Belvedere Gdns, W.Mol.
KT8 . . . . **179** F5
Belvedere Gro, SW19 . . . . **166** B5
Belvedere Ho, Felt. TW13 . **160** A1
Belvedere Ind Est, Belv.
DA17 . . . . **139** J3
Belvedere Ms, SE3
off Langton Way **155** F1
SE15 . . . . **153** E3
Belvedere Pl, SE1 . . . . **27** H4
SW2 *off Acre La* **151** F4
Belvedere Rd, E10 . . . . **95** H1
SE1 . . . . **26** D3
SE2 . . . . **138** D1
SE19 . . . . **170** C7
W7 . . . . **124** C3
Bexleyheath DA7 . . . . . **159** F3
Belvedere Sq, SW19 . . . . . **166** D5
Belvedere Strand, NW9 . . . **71** F2
Belvedere Twr, The,
SW10 . . . . **149** F1
Belvedere Way, Har. HA3 . . **69** H6
Belvoir Cl, SE9 . . . . **174** B3
Belvoir Rd, SE22 . . . . **152** D7
Belvue Cl, Nthlt. UB5 . . . . . **85** G7
Belvue Rd, Nthlt. UB5 . . . . **85** G7
Bembridge Cl, NW6 . . . . . . **90** B7
Bemerton Est, N1 . . . . **93** F7
Bemerton St, N1 . . . . **111** F1
Bemish Rd, SW15 . . . . . . **148** A3
Bempton Dr, Ruis. HA4 . . . **84** B2
Bemsted Rd, E17 . . . . **77** J3
Benares Rd, SE18 . . . . **137** J4
Benbow Rd, W6 . . . . **127** H3
Benbow St, SE8 . . . . **134** A6
Benbury Cl, Brom. BR1 . . **172** C5
Bench Fld, S.Croy. CR2 . . **202** C6
Bencroft Rd, SW16 . . . . . . **168** C7
Bencurtis Pk, W.Wick.
BR4 . . . . **204** D3
Bendall Ms, NW1 . . . . **15** H1
Bendemeer Rd, SW15 . . . **148** A3
Bendish Rd, E6 . . . . **98** B7
Bendmore Av, SE2 . . . . . . **138** A5
Bendon Valley, SW18 . . . . **148** E7
Benedict Cl, Belv. DA17
off Tunstock Way . **138/139** E3
Orpington BR6 . . . . **207** H3
Benedict Dr, Felt. TW14 . . **141** G7
Benedict Rd, SW9 . . . . . . **151** F3
Mitcham CR4 . . . . **185** G3
Benedict Way, N2 . . . . **73** F3
Benenden Grn, Brom. BR2 . **191** G5
Benett Gdns, SW16 . . . . . **186** E2
Benfleet Cl, Sutt. SM1 . . . **199** F3
Benfleet Way, N11 . . . . **58** A2
Bengal Ct, EC3
off Birchin La **112** A6
Bengal Rd, Ilf. IG1 . . . . **98** E4
Bengarth Dr, Har. HA3 . . . . **68** A2
Bengarth Rd, Nthlt. UB5 . **102** D1
Bengeworth Rd, SE5 . . . . **151** J3
Harrow HA1 . . . . **86** D2
Ben Hale Cl, Stan. HA7 . . . **52** E4
Benham Cl, SW11 . . . . . . **149** G3
Chessington KT9
off Merritt Gdns **195** F6
Benham Gdns, Houns.
TW4 . . . . **143** F5
Benham Rd, W7 . . . . **104** B5
Benhams Pl, NW3
off Holly Wk **91** F4
Benhill Av, Sutt. SM1 . . . . **199** E4
Benhill Rd, SE5 . . . . **132** A7
Sutton SM1 . . . . **199** F3
Benhill Wd Rd, Sutt. SM1 . **199** F3
BENHILTON, Sutt. SM1 . . **199** E2
Benhilton Gdns, Sutt.
SM1 . . . . **199** E3
Benhurst Ct, SW16 . . . . . **169** G5
Benhurst La, SW16 . . . . . **169** G5
Benin St, SE13 . . . . **154** D7
Benjafield Cl, N18
off Brettenham Rd . . **60/61** E4
Benjamin Cl, E8 . . . . **112** D1
Benjamin St, EC1 . . . . **19** G1
Ben Jonson Rd, E1 . . . . . . **113** H5
Benledi St, E14 . . . . **114** D6
Bennelong Cl, W12 . . . . . . **107** H7
Bennerley Rd, SW11 . . . . . **149** H5
Bennetsfield Rd, Uxb.
UB11 . . . . **120** E1
Bennet's Hill, EC4 . . . . **19** H5
Bennett Cl, Kings.T.
(Hmptn W.) KT1 . . . . . . **181** F1
Welling DA16 . . . . **158** A2
Bennett Gro, SE13 . . . . . . **154** B1
Bennett Pk, SE3 . . . . **155** F3
Bennett Rd, E13 . . . . **115** J4
N16 . . . . **94** B4
Romford RM6 . . . . **83** E6
Bennetts Av, Croy. CR0 . . **203** H2
Greenford UB6 . . . . **104** B1
Bennetts Castle La, Dag.
RM8 . . . . **100** C4
Bennetts Cl, N17 . . . . **60** C6
Mitcham CR4 . . . . **186** B1
Bennetts Copse, Chis.
BR7 . . . . **174** B6
Bennett St, SW1 . . . . **25** F1
W4 . . . . **126** E6
Bennetts Way, Croy. CR0 . **203** H2
Bennetts Yd, SW1 . . . . **25** J6
Benningholme Rd, Edg.
HA8 . . . . **54** E6
Bennington Rd, N17 . . . . . . **76** B1
Woodford Green IG8 . . . **63** E7
Benn St, E9 . . . . **95** H6
Benn's Wk, Rich. TW9
off Rosedale Rd **145** H4
Benrek Cl, Ilf. IG6 . . . . **81** F1
Bensbury Cl, SW15 . . . . . **147** H7
Bensham Cl, Th.Hth.
CR7 . . . . **187** J4
Bensham Gro, Th.Hth.
CR7 . . . . **187** J2
Bensham La, Croy. CR0 . . **187** H7
Thornton Heath CR7 . . . **187** H4
Bensham Manor Rd,
Th.Hth. CR7 . . . . **187** J4
Bensington Ct, Felt.
TW14 . . . . **141** G6
Bensley Cl, N11 . . . . **57** J5
Ben Smith Way, SE16 . . . . **29** J5
Benson Av, E6 . . . . **115** J2
Benson Cl, Houns. TW3 . . **143** G4
Benson Quay, E1
off Garnet St **113** F7
Benson Rd, SE23 . . . . **171** F1
Croydon CR0 . . . . **201** G3
Bentalls Cen, Kings.T.
KT1 . . . . **181** G2
Bentfield Gdns, SE9
off Aldersgrove Av . . . **173** J3
Benthal Rd, N16 . . . . **94** D2
Bentham Ct, N1
off Rotherfield St **93** J7
Bentham Rd, E9 . . . . **95** G6
SE28 . . . . **118** B7
Bentham Wk, NW10 . . . . . . **88** C5
Ben Tillet Cl, Bark. IG11 . . **100** A7
Ben Tillett Cl, E16
off Newland St **136** C1
Bentinck Ms, W1 . . . . **16** C3
Bentinck Rd, West Dr.
UB7 . . . . **120** A1
Bentinck St, W1 . . . . **16** C3
Bentley Dr, NW2 . . . . **90** C3
Ilford IG2 . . . . **81** F6
Bentley Ms, Enf. EN1 . . . . . **44** A6
★**Bentley Priory**, Stan.
HA7 . . . . **52** B3
Bentley Rd, N1
off Tottenham Rd **94** B6
Bentley Way, Stan. HA7 . . . **52** D5
Woodford Green IG8 . . . **63** G3
Benton Rd, Ilf. IG1 . . . . **99** G1
Watford WD19 . . . . **50** D5
Bentons La, SE27 . . . . **169** J4
Bentons Ri, SE27 . . . . **170** A5
Bentry Cl, Dag. RM8 . . . . . **101** E2
Bentry Rd, Dag. RM8 . . . . **101** E2
Bentworth Rd, W12 . . . . . **107** H6
Benwell Ct, Sun. TW16 . . . **178** A1
Benwell Rd, N7 . . . . **93** G4
Benwick Cl, SE16
off Aspinden Rd . . **132/133** E3
Benworth St, E3 . . . . **113** J3
Benyon Rd, N1
off Southgate Rd **112** A1
Berberis Wk, West Dr.
UB7 . . . . **120** B4
Berber Pl, E14
off Birchfield St **114** A7
Berber Rd, SW11 . . . . **149** J5
Berberry Cl, Edg. HA8
off Larkspur Gro **54** C4
Bercta Rd, SE9 . . . . **175** F2
Berenger Wk, SW10 . . . . . . **30** E7
Berens Rd, NW10 . . . . **108** A3
Berens Way, Chis. BR7 . . . **193** J4
Beresford Av, N20 . . . . **57** J2
W7 . . . . **104** A5
Surbiton KT5 . . . . **196** B1
Twickenham TW1 . . . . . **145** F6
Wembley HA0 . . . . **105** J1
Beresford Dr, Brom. BR1 . **192** A3
Woodford Green IG8 . . . **63** J4
Beresford Gdns, Enf.
EN1 . . . . **44** B4
Hounslow TW4 . . . . **143** F5
Romford RM6 . . . . **83** E5
Beresford Rd, E4 . . . . **62** E1
E17 . . . . **78** B1
N2 . . . . **73** H3
N5 . . . . **93** J5
N8 . . . . **75** G5
Harrow HA1 . . . . **68** A5
Kingston upon Thames
KT2 . . . . **181** J1
New Malden KT3 . . . . . **182** C4
Southall UB1 . . . . **122** D1
Sutton SM2 . . . . **198** C7
Beresford Sq, SE18 . . . . . **136** E4
Beresford St, SE18 . . . . . . **136** E3
Beresford Ter, N5 . . . . **93** J5
Berestede Rd, W6 . . . . **127** F5
Bere St, E1
off Cranford St **113** G7
Bergen Sq, SE16
off Norway Gate **133** H3
Berger Cl, Orp. BR5 . . . . . **193** G6
Berger Rd, E9 . . . . **95** G6
Berghem Ms, W14
off Blythe Rd **128** A3
Bergholt Av, Ilf. IG4 . . . . . . **80** B5
Bergholt Cres, N16 . . . . **76** B7
Bergholt Ms, NW1
off Rossendale Way . . . **92** C7
Berglen Ct, E14
off Branch Rd **113** H6
Bering Sq, E14
off Napier Av **134** A5
Bering Wk, E16 . . . . **116** A6
Berisford Ms, SW18 . . . . . **149** F6
Berkeley Av, Bexh. DA7 . . . **158** D1
Greenford UB6 . . . . **86** B6
Hounslow TW4 . . . . **142** A2
Ilford IG5 . . . . **80** D2
Berkeley Cl, Borwd. (Elstree)
WD6 . . . . **38** A5
Kingston upon Thames
KT2 . . . . **163** H7
Orpington BR5 . . . . **193** H7
Ruislip HA4 . . . . **84** A3
Berkeley Ct, N14 . . . . **42** C6
Wallington SM6 . . . . . . **200** C3
Berkeley Cres, Barn. EN4 . . **41** G5
Berkeley Dr, W.Mol. KT8 . . **179** F3
Berkeley Gdns, N21 . . . . . . **44** A7
W8
off Brunswick Gdns . . . **128** D1
Esher (Clay.) KT10 . . . . **194** D6
Berkeley Ho, E3 . . . . **114** A4
Berkeley Ms, W1 . . . . **16** A3
Berkeley Pl, SW19 . . . . . . **166** A6
Berkeley Rd, E12 . . . . **98** B5
N8 . . . . **74** D5
N15 . . . . **76** A6
NW9 . . . . **70** A4
SW13 . . . . **147** G1
Berkeley Sq, W1 . . . . **16** E6
Berkeley St, W1 . . . . **17** E6
Berkeley Twr, E14
off Westferry Circ **133** J1
Berkeley Wk, N7
off Durham Rd **93** F2
Berkeley Waye, Houns.
TW5 . . . . **122** D7
Berkhampstead Rd, Belv.
DA17 . . . . **139** G5
Berkhamsted Av, Wem.
HA9 . . . . **87** J6
Berkley Gro, NW1
off Berkley Rd **91** J7
Berkley Rd, NW1 . . . . **91** J7
Berkshire Gdns, N13 . . . . . **59** G6
N18 . . . . **60** E5
Berkshire Rd, E9 . . . . **95** J6
Berkshire Sq, Mitch. CR4
off Berkshire Way . **186/187** E4
Berkshire Way, Mitch.
CR4 . . . . **186** E4
Bermans Way, NW10 . . . . . **89** E4
BERMONDSEY, SE1 . . . . . . **29** F6
Bermondsey Sq, SE1 . . . . . **28** E5
Bermondsey St, SE1 . . . . . **28** D2
Bermondsey Wall E, SE16 . **29** J4
Bermondsey Wall W, SE16 . **29** H3
Bernal Cl, SE28
off Haldane Rd **118** D7
Bernard Ashley Dr, SE7 . . **135** H5
Bernard Av, W13 . . . . **125** E3
Bernard Cassidy St, E16 . . **115** F5
Bernard Gdns, SW19 . . . . **166** C5
Bernard Rd, N15 . . . . **76** C5
Romford RM7 . . . . **83** J7
Wallington SM6 . . . . . . **200** B4
Bernards Cl, Ilf. IG6 . . . . . . **65** F6
Bernard St, WC1 . . . . **10** A6
Bernays Cl, Stan. HA7 . . . . **53** F6
Bernays Gro, SW9 . . . . . . **151** F4
Bernel Dr, Croy. CR0 . . . . **203** J3
Berne Rd, Th.Hth. CR7 . . . **187** J5
Berners Dr, W13 . . . . **104** D6
Bernersmede, SE3
off Blackheath Pk **155** G3
Berners Ms, W1 . . . . **17** G2
Berners Pl, W1 . . . . **17** G3
Berners Rd, N1 . . . . **11** F1
N22 . . . . **75** G1
Berners St, W1 . . . . **17** G2
Berney Rd, Croy. CR0 . . . . **188** A7
Bernhardt Cres, NW8 . . . . . . **7** G5
Bernhart Cl, Edg. HA8 . . . . . **54** C7
Bernville Way, Har. HA3
off Kenton Rd **69** J5
Bernwell Rd, E4 . . . . **63** E3
Berridge Grn, Edg. HA8 . . . **54** A7
Berridge Ms, NW6
off Hillfield Rd **90** D5
Berridge Rd, SE19 . . . . . . **170** A5
Berriman Rd, N7 . . . . **93** F3
Berriton Rd, Har. HA2 . . . . **85** F1
Berrybank Cl, E4
off Greenbank Cl **62** C2
Berry Cl, N21 . . . . **59** H1
NW10 . . . . **88** E7
Dagenham RM10 . . . . . . **101** G5
Berry Ct, Houns. TW4 . . . . **143** F5
Berrydale Rd, Hayes UB4 . **102** E4
Berryfield Cl, E17 . . . . **78** B4
Bromley BR1 . . . . **192** B1
Berryfield Rd, SE17 . . . . . . **35** H3
Berryhill, SE9 . . . . **156** E4
Berry Hill, Stan. HA7 . . . . . **53** G4
Berryhill Gdns, SE9 . . . . . **156** E4
BERRYLANDS, Surb. KT5 . **181** J5
Berrylands, SW20 . . . . **183** J3
Surbiton KT5 . . . . **182** A5
Berrylands Rd, Surb.
KT5 . . . . **181** J6
Berry La, SE21 . . . . **170** A4
Berryman Cl, Dag. RM8
off Bennetts Castle La . **100** C3
Berrymans La, SE26 . . . . . **171** G4
Berrymead Gdns, W3 . . . . **126** C1
Berrymede Rd, W4 . . . . . . **126** D3
Berry Pl, EC1 . . . . **11** H4
Berry St, EC1 . . . . **11** H5
Berry Way, W5 . . . . **125** H3
Bertal Rd, SW17 . . . . **167** G4
Berthon St, SE8 . . . . **134** A7
Bertie Rd, NW10 . . . . **89** G6
SE26 . . . . **171** G6

Bertram Cotts, SW19
off Hartfield Rd **166** D7
Bertram Rd, NW4 **71** G6
Enfield EN1 **44** D4
Kingston upon Thames KT2 **164** A7
Bertram St, N19 **92** B2
Bertram Way, Enf. EN1 **44** C4
Bertrand St, SE13 **154** B3
Bertrand Way, SE28 **118** B7
Bert Rd, Th.Hth. CR7 **187** J5
Berwick Av, Hayes UB4 **102** D6
Berwick Cl, Stan. HA7
off Gordon Av **52** C7
Twickenham TW2 **161** G1
Berwick Cres, Sid. DA15 **157** H6
Berwick Gdns, Sutt. SM1
off Woodside Rd **199** F3
Berwick Rd, E16 **115** H6
N22 **75** H1
Welling DA16 **158** B1
Berwick St, W1 **17** H4
Berwyn Av, Houns. TW3 **143** H1
Berwyn Rd, SE24 **169** H1
Richmond TW10 **146** B4
Beryl Av, E6 **116** B5
Beryl Ho, SE18
off Spinel Cl **137** J5
Beryl Rd, W6 **128** A5
Berystede, Kings.T. KT2 **164** B7
Besant Ct, N1
off Newington Grn Rd **94** A5
Besant Rd, NW2 **90** B4
Besant Wk, N7
off Newington Barrow Way **93** F2
Besant Way, NW10 **88** C5
Besley St, SW16 **168** C6
Bessant Dr, Rich. TW9 **146** B1
Bessborough Gdns, SW1 **33** J3
Bessborough Pl, SW1 **33** H3
Bessborough Rd, SW15 **165** G1
Harrow HA1 **86** A1
Bessborough St, SW1 **33** H3
Bessemer Rd, SE5 **151** J2
Bessie Lansbury Cl, E6 **116** D6
Bessingby Rd, Ruis. HA4 **84** A2
Bessingham Wk, SE4
off Frendsbury Rd **153** G4
Besson St, SE14 **153** F1
Bessy St, E2
off Roman Rd **113** F3
Bestwood St, SE8 **133** G4
Beswick Ms, NW6
off Lymington Rd **90/91** E6
Betam Rd, Hayes UB3 **121** G2
Beta Pl, SW4
off Santley St **150/151** E4
Betchworth Cl, Sutt. SM1
off Turnpike La **199** G5
Betchworth Rd, Ilf. IG3 **99** H2
Betham Rd, Grnf. UB6 **104** A3
Bethany Waye, Felt. TW14 **141** H7
Bethecar Rd, Har. HA1 **68** B5
Bethell Av, E16 **115** F4
Ilford IG1 **80** D7
Bethel Rd, Well. DA16 **158** C3
Bethersden Cl, Beck. BR3 **171** J7
BETHNAL GREEN, E2 **112** D2
Bethnal Grn Est, E2 **113** F3
★**Bethnal Green Mus of Childhood**, E2 **113** E3
Bethnal Grn Rd, E1 **13** F5
E2 **13** F5
Bethune Av, N11 **57** J4
Bethune Rd, N16 **76** A7
NW10 **106** D4
Bethwin Rd, SE5 **35** H7
Betjeman Cl, Pnr. HA5 **67** G4
Betony Cl, Croy. CR0
off Primrose La **203** G1
Betoyne Av, E4 **62** E4
Betstyle Circ, N11 **58** B4
Betstyle Rd, N11 **58** B4
Betterton Dr, Sid. DA14 **177** E2
Betterton St, WC2 **18** A4
Bettons Pk, E15 **115** E1
Bettridge Rd, SW6 **148** C2
Betts Cl, Beck. BR3
off Kendall Rd **189** H2
Betts Ms, E17
off Queen's Rd **77** J6
Betts Rd, E16
off Victoria Dock Rd **115** H7
Betts St, E1
off The Highway **112/113** E7
Betts Way, SE20 **189** E1
Betts Way, Surb. KT6 **195** E1
Beulah Av, Th.Hth. CR7
off Beulah Rd **187** J2
Beulah Cl, Edg. HA8 **54** B3
Beulah Cres, Th.Hth. CR7 **187** J2
Beulah Gro, Croy. CR0 **187** J6
Beulah Hill, SE19 **169** H6
Beulah Path, E17
off Addison Rd **78** B5
Beulah Rd, E17 **78** B5
SW19 **166** C7
Sutton SM1 **198** D4
Thornton Heath CR7 **187** J3
Bevan Av, Bark. IG11 **100** A7
Bevan Ct, Croy. CR0 **201** G5
Bevan Rd, SE2 **138** B5
Barnet EN4 **41** J4
Bevan St, N1 **111** J1
Bev Callender Cl, SW8
off Daley Thompson Way **150** B3
Bevenden St, N1 **12** C3
Bevercote Wk, Belv. DA17
off Osborne Rd **139** F6
Beveridge Rd, NW10
off Curzon Cres **88/89** E7
Beverley Av, SW20 **183** F1
Hounslow TW4 **143** F4
Sidcup DA15 **157** J7
Beverley Cl, N21 **59** J1
SW11 *off Maysoule Rd* **149** G4
SW13 **147** F2
Chessington KT9 **195** F4
Enfield EN1 **44** B4
Beverley Cotts, SW15
off Kingston Vale **164** D4
Beverley Ct, N14 **42** C7
N20 *off Farnham Cl* **41** F7
SE4 **153** J3
Beverley Cres, Wdf.Grn. IG8 **79** H1
Beverley Dr, Edg. HA8 **70** B3
Beverley Gdns, NW11 **72** B7
SW13 **147** F3
Stanmore HA7 **68** D1
Wembley HA9 **87** J1
Worcester Park KT4
off Green La **197** G1
Beverley Ho, NW8 **7** G4
Beverley La, SW15 **165** F3
Kingston upon Thames KT2 **165** E7
Beverley Ms, E4
off Beverley Rd **62** D6
Beverley Path, SW13 **147** F2
Beverley Rd, E4 **62** D6
E6 **116** A3
SE20
off Wadhurst Cl **188/189** E2
SW13 **147** F3
W4 **127** F5
Bexleyheath DA7 **159** J2
Bromley BR2 **206** B2
Dagenham RM9 **101** E4
Kingston upon Thames KT1 **181** F1
Mitcham CR4 **186** D4
New Malden KT3 **183** G4
Ruislip HA4 **84** A2
Southall UB2 **123** E3
Worcester Park KT4 **197** J2
Beverley Trd Est, Mord. SM4
off Garth Rd **184** A7
Beverley Way, SW20 **183** F1
New Malden KT3 **183** F1
Beversbrook Rd, N19 **92** D3
Beverstone Rd, SW2 **151** F5
Thornton Heath CR7 **187** G4
Beverston Ms, W1 **15** J2
Bevill Allen Cl, SW17 **167** J5
Bevill Cl, SE25 **188** D3
Bevin Cl, SE16
off Stave Yd Rd **133** H1
Bevin Ct, WC1
off Holford St **111** G3
Bevington Path, SE1
off Tanner St **132** C2
Bevington Rd, W10 **108** B5
Beckenham BR3 **190** B2
Bevington St, SE16 **29** J4
Bevin Rd, Hayes UB4 **102** A3
Bevin Sq, SW17 **167** J3
Bevin Way, WC1 **10** E3
Bevis Marks, EC3 **20** E3
Bewcastle Gdns, Enf. EN2 **43** E4
Bew Ct, SE22
off Lordship La **152** D7
Bewdley St, N1 **93** G7
Bewick Ms, SE15 **132** E7
Bewick St, SW8 **150** B2
Bewley St, E1
off Dellow St **112/113** E7
SW19 **167** F6
Bewlys Rd, SE27 **169** H5
Bexhill Cl, Felt. TW13 **160** E2
Bexhill Rd, N11 **58** D5
SE4 **153** J7
SW14 **146** C3
Bexhill Wk, E15
off Mitre Rd **114/115** E2
BEXLEY, DA5 **159** G6
Bexley Gdns, N9 **60** A3
Romford (Chad.Hth) RM6 **82** B5
BEXLEYHEATH, DA6 & DA7 **159** F5
Bexley High St, Bex. DA5 **159** G7
Bexley La, Sid. DA14 **176** C3
Bexley Rd, SE9 **156** E5
Erith DA8 **139** J7
Beynon Rd, Cars. SM5 **199** J5
Bianca Ho, N1
off Crondall St **112** B2
Bianca Rd, SE15 **37** H6
Bibsworth Rd, N3 **72** C2
Bibury Cl, SE15 **37** E6
Bicester Rd, Rich. TW9 **146** A3
Bickenhall St, W1 **16** A1
Bickersteth Rd, SW17 **167** J6
Bickerton Rd, N19 **92** C2
BICKLEY, Brom. BR1 **192** C3
Bickley Cres, Brom. BR1 **192** B4
Bickley Pk Rd, Brom. BR1 **192** B3
Bickley Rd, E10 **78** B7
Bromley BR1 **192** A2
Bickley St, SW17 **167** H5
Bicknell Rd, SE5 **151** J3
Bicknoller Rd, Enf. EN1 **44** C1
Bicknor Rd, Orp. BR6 **193** H7
Bidborough Cl, Brom. BR2 **191** F5
Bidborough St, WC1 **10** A4
Biddenden Way, SE9 **174** D4
Bidder St, E16 **114** E5
Biddestone Rd, N7 **93** F4
Biddulph Rd, W9 **6** A4
Bideford Av, Grnf. UB6 **104** E2
Bideford Cl, Edg. HA8 **70** A1
Feltham TW13 **161** F3
Bideford Gdns, Enf. EN1 **44** B7
Bideford Rd, Brom. BR1 **173** F3
Ruislip HA4 **84** B3
Welling DA16 **138** B7
Bidwell Gdns, N11 **58** C7
Bidwell St, SE15 **153** E1
★**Big Ben (St. Stephens Tower)**, SW1 **26** B4
Bigbury Cl, N17 **60** B7
Biggerstaff Rd, E15 **114** C1
Biggerstaff St, N4 **93** G2
Biggin Av, Mitch. CR4 **185** J1
Biggin Hill, SE19 **169** H7
Biggin Hill Cl, Kings.T. KT2 **163** F5
Biggin Way, SE19 **169** H7
Bigginwood Rd, SW16 **169** H7
Biggs Row, SW15
off Felsham Rd **148** A3
Big Hill, E5 **95** E1
Bigland St, E1 **112** E6
Bignell Rd, SE18 **136** E5
Bignold Rd, E7 **97** G4
Bigwood Rd, NW11 **72** E5
Billet Cl, Rom. RM6 **82** D3
Billet Rd, E17 **77** G2
Romford RM6 **82** B3
Billets Hart Cl, W7 **124** B2
Billet Wks, E17 **77** J1
Bill Hamling Cl, SE9 **174** C2
Billingford Cl, SE4 **153** G4
Billing Pl, SW10 **30** B7
Billing Rd, SW10 **30** B7
Billings Cl, Dag. RM9
off Ellerton Rd **100** C7
★**Billingsgate Mkt**, E14 **134** B1
Billing St, SW10 **30** B7
Billington Ms, W3
off High St **126** B1
Billington Rd, SE14 **133** G7
Billiter Sq, EC3 **20** E5
Billiter St, EC3 **20** E4
Bill Nicholson Way, N17
off High Rd **60** C7
Billockby Cl, Chess. KT9 **195** J6
Billson St, E14 **134** C4
Bilsby Gro, SE9 **174** A4
Bilton Rd, Grnf. UB6 **105** E1
Bilton Way, Enf. EN3 **45** H1
Hayes UB3 **122** B2
Bina Gdns, SW5 **30** C2
Bincote Rd, Enf. EN2 **43** F3
Binden Rd, W12 **127** F3
Bindon Grn, Mord. SM4 **185** E4
Binfield Rd, SW4 **151** E1
South Croydon CR2 **202** C5
Bingfield St, N1 **111** E1
Bingham Ct, N1
off Halton Rd **93** H7
Bingham Pl, W1 **16** B1
Bingham Pt, SE18
off Whitworth Pl **136/137** E4
Bingham Rd, Croy. CR0 **202** D1
Bingham St, N1 **94** A6
Bingley Rd, E16 **115** J6
Greenford UB6 **103** J5
Sunbury-on-Thames TW16 **160** A7
Binley Ho, SW15
off Highcliffe Dr **147** G6
Binney St, W1 **16** C5
Binns Rd, W4 **126** E5
Binns Ter, W4
off Binns Rd **126/127** E5
Binsey Wk, SE2 **138** C1
Binstead Cl, Hayes UB4 **102** E5
Binyon Cres, Stan. HA7 **52** C5
Birbetts Rd, SE9 **174** C2
Bircham Path, SE4
off St. Norbert Rd **153** G4
Birchanger Rd, SE25 **188** D5
Birch Av, N13 **59** J3
Birch Cl, E16 **115** E5
N19 *off Hargrave Pk* **92** C2
SE15
off Bournemouth Rd **152** D2
Brentford TW8 **124** E7
Buckhurst Hill IG9 **64** A3
Hounslow TW3 **144** A3
Romford RM7 **83** H3
Teddington TW11 **162** D5
Birchdale Gdns, Rom. RM6 **82** D7
Birchdale Rd, E7 **97** J5
Birchdene Dr, SE28 **138** A2
Birchen Cl, NW9 **88** D2
Birchend Cl, S.Croy. CR2 **202** A6
Birchen Gro, NW9 **88** D2
Birches, The, N21 **43** F6
SE7 **135** H6
Orpington BR6 **206** D4
Birches Cl, Mitch. CR4 **185** J3
Pinner HA5 **66** E5
Birchfield St, E14 **114** A7
Birch Gdns, Dag. RM10 **101** J3
Birch Grn, NW9
off Clayton Fld **54/55** E7
Birch Gro, E11 **96** E3
SE12 **155** F7
W3 **126** A1
Welling DA16 **158** A4
Birch Hill, Croy. CR0 **203** G5
Birchington Cl, Bexh. DA7 **159** H1
Birchington Rd, N8 **74** D6
NW6 **108** D1
Surbiton KT5 **181** J7
Birchin La, EC3 **20** C4
Birchlands Av, SW12 **149** J7
Birch Mead, Orp. BR6 **206** D2
Birchmead Av, Pnr. HA5 **66** C4
Birchmere Business Pk, SE28
off Eastern Way **138** A2
Birchmere Row, SE3 **155** F2
Birchmore Wk, N5 **93** J3
Birch Pk, Har. HA3 **51** J7
Birch Rd, Felt. TW13 **160** D5
Romford RM7 **83** H3
Birch Row, Brom. BR2 **192** D7
Birch Tree Av, W.Wick. BR4 **205** F5
Birch Tree Way, Croy. CR0 **202** E2
Birchville Ct, Bushey (Bushey Hth) WD23
off Heathbourne Rd **52** B1
Birch Wk, Borwd. WD6 **38** A1
Erith DA8 **139** J6
Mitcham CR4 **186** B1
Birchway, Hayes UB3 **122** A1
Birchwood Av, N10 **74** A3
Beckenham BR3 **189** J4
Sidcup DA14 **176** B2
Wallington SM6 **200** A3
Birchwood Cl, Mord. SM4 **184** E4

Birchwood Ct, N13 . . . . 59 H5
Edgware HA8 . . . . 70 C2
Birchwood Dr, NW3 . . . . 91 E3
Birchwood Gro, Hmptn. TW12 . . . . 161 G6
Birchwood Rd, SW17 . . . . 168 B5
Orpington BR5 . . . . 193 G4
Birdbrook Cl, Dag. RM10 . 101 J7
Birdbrook Rd, SE3 . . . . . . 155 J3
Birdcage Wk, SW1 . . . . 25 G4
Birdham Cl, Brom. BR1 . . 192 B5
Birdhurst Av, S.Croy. CR2 . . . . 202 A4
Birdhurst Gdns, S.Croy. CR2 . . . . 202 A4
Birdhurst Ri, S.Croy. CR2 . . . . 202 B5
Birdhurst Rd, SW18 . . . . . 149 F4
SW19 . . . . 167 H6
South Croydon CR2 . . . 202 B5
Bird in Bush Rd, SE15 . . . . 37 J7
Bird-in-Hand La, Brom. BR1 . . . . 192 A2
Bird-in-Hand Pas, SE23 *off Dartmouth Rd* 171 F2
Birds Fm Av, Rom. RM5 . . . 83 H1
Birdsfield La, E3 . . . . 113 J1
Bird St, W1 . . . . 16 C4
Bird Wk, Twick. TW2 . . . . . 161 F1
Birdwood Cl, Tedd. TW11 . 162 B4
Birkbeck Av, W3 . . . . 106 C7
Greenford UB6 . . . . 103 J1
Birkbeck Gdns, Wdf.Grn. IG8 . . . . 63 F2
Birkbeck Gro, W3 . . . . 126 D2
Birkbeck Hill, SE21 . . . . . . 169 H2
Birkbeck Ms, E8 *off Sandringham Rd* . . . 94 C5
W3 *off Birkbeck Rd* 126 D1
Birkbeck Pl, SE21 . . . . 169 J1
Birkbeck Rd, E8 . . . . 94 C5
N8 . . . . 75 E4
N12 . . . . 57 F5
N17 . . . . 76 C1
NW7 . . . . 55 F5
SW19 . . . . 167 E5
W3 . . . . 126 D1
W5 . . . . 125 F4
Beckenham BR3 . . . . . . 189 F2
Enfield EN2 . . . . 44 A1
Ilford IG2 . . . . 81 G5
Sidcup DA14 . . . . 176 A3
Birkbeck St, E2 . . . . 113 E3
Birkbeck Way, Grnf. UB6 . 103 J1
Birkdale Av, Pnr. HA5 . . . . . 67 G3
Birkdale Cl, SE16 *off Masters Dr* . . . 132/133 E5
SE28 *off Redbourne Dr* 118 D6
Orpington BR6 . . . . 193 G7
Birkdale Gdns, Croy. CR0 . . . . 203 G4
Watford WD19 . . . . 50 D3
Birkdale Rd, SE2 . . . . 138 A4
W5 . . . . 105 H4
Birkenhead Av, Kings.T. KT2 . . . . 181 J2
Birkenhead St, WC1 . . . . . . 10 B3
Birkhall Rd, SE6 . . . . 172 D1
Birkwood Cl, SW12 . . . . . . 150 D7
Birley Rd, N20 . . . . 57 F2
Birley St, SW11 . . . . 150 A2
Birnam Rd, N4 . . . . 93 F2
Birrell Ho, SW9 *off Stockwell Rd* 151 F2
Birse Cres, NW10 . . . . 89 E4
Birstall Grn, Wat. WD19 . . . 50 D4
Birstall Rd, N15 . . . . 76 B5
Biscay Rd, W6 . . . . 128 A5
Biscoe Cl, Houns. TW5 . . . 123 G6
Biscoe Way, SE13 . . . . 154 D3
Bisenden Rd, Croy. CR0 . . 202 B2
Bisham Cl, Cars. SM5 . . . 199 J1
Bisham Gdns, N6 . . . . 92 A1
Bishop Butt Cl, Orp. BR6 *off Stapleton Rd* 207 J3
Bishop Cl, W4 . . . . 126 C5
Bishop Fox Way, W.Mol. KT8 . . . . 179 F4
Bishop Ken Rd, Har. HA3 . . 68 C2
Bishop Kings Rd, W14 . . . 128 B4
Bishop Rd, N14 . . . . 42 B7
Bishop's Av, E13 . . . . 115 H1
SW6 . . . . 148 A2
Bishops Av, Brom. BR1 . . 191 J2
Romford RM6 . . . . 82 C6
Bishops Av, The, N2 . . . . . . 73 G7
Bishops Br, W2 . . . . 14 D3
Bishops Br Rd, W2 . . . . 14 B4
Bishops Cl, E17 . . . . 78 B4
N19 *off Wyndham Cres* . . 92 C3
SE9 . . . . 175 F2
Barnet EN5 . . . . 40 A6
Enfield EN1 *off Central Av* 44/45 E2
Richmond TW10 . . . . . . 163 G3
Bishop's Cl, Sutt. SM1 . . . 198 D3
Bishop's Ct, EC4 . . . . 19 G3
WC2 . . . . 18 E3
Bishops Dr, Felt. TW14 . . . 141 G6
Northolt UB5 . . . . 103 E1
Bishopsford Rd, Mord. SM4 . . . . 185 F7
Bishopsgate, EC2 . . . . 20 D4
Bishopsgate Arc, EC2 . . . . . 20 E2
Bishopsgate Chyd, EC2 . . . 20 D2
Bishops Gro, N2 . . . . 73 G6
Hampton TW12 . . . . 161 F4
Bishop's Hall, Kings.T. KT1 . . . . 181 G2
Bishops Hill, Walt. KT12 . . 178 A7
Bishop's Pk, SW6 . . . . 148 A2
Bishop's Pk Rd, SW6 . . . . . 148 A2
Bishops Pk Rd, SW16 . . . . 187 E1
Bishops Pl, Sutt. SM1 *off Lind Rd* 199 F5
Bishops Rd, N6 . . . . 74 A6
SW6 . . . . 148 C1
Bishop's Rd, SW11 . . . . . . 129 H7
Bishops Rd, W7 . . . . 124 B2
Croydon CR0 . . . . 187 H7
Bishops Ter, SE11 . . . . 35 F1
Bishopsthorpe Rd, SE26 . 171 G4
Bishop St, N1 . . . . 111 J1
Bishops Wk, Chis. BR7 . . . 193 F1
Croydon CR0 . . . . 203 G5
Bishop's Wk, Pnr. HA5 *off High St* 66/67 E3
Bishops Way, E2 . . . . 113 E2
Bishopswood Rd, N6 . . . . . 73 J7
Bishop Way, NW10 . . . . 88 E7
Bishop Wilfred Wd Cl, SE15 *off Moncrieff St* 152 D2
Bisley Cl, Wor.Pk. KT4 . . . 197 J1
Bisley Ho, SW19 . . . . 166 A2
Bispham Rd, NW10 . . . . . 105 J3
Bisson Rd, E15 . . . . 114 C2
Bisterne Av, E17 . . . . 78 D3
Bittacy Cl, NW7 . . . . 56 A6
Bittacy Hill, NW7 . . . . 56 A6
Bittacy Pk Av, NW7 . . . . . . 56 A6
Bittacy Ri, NW7 . . . . 55 J6
Bittacy Rd, NW7 . . . . 56 A6
Bittern Cl, Hayes UB4 . . . . 102 D5
Bittern Pl, N22 *off Coburg Rd* 75 F2
Bittern St, SE1 . . . . 27 J4
Bittoms, The, Kings.T. KT1 . . . . 181 G3
Bixley Cl, Sthl. UB2 . . . . . 123 F4
Blackall St, EC2 . . . . 12 D5
Blackberry Fm Cl, Houns. TW5 . . . . 122 E7
Blackbird Hill, NW9 . . . . . . 88 C2
Blackbird Yd, E2 . . . . 13 G3
Blackborne Rd, Dag. RM10 . . . . 101 G6
Black Boy La, N15 . . . . 75 J5
Blackbrook La, Brom. BR1, BR2 . . . . 192 D3
Blackburne's Ms, W1 . . . . . 16 B5
Blackburn Rd, NW6 . . . . . . 90 E6
Blackburn Trd Est, Stai. (Stanw.) TW19 . . . . . . 140 C6
Blackbush Av, Rom. RM6 . . 82 D5
Blackbush Cl, Sutt. SM2 . 199 E7
Blackdown Cl, N2 . . . . 73 F2
Blackdown Ter, SE18 *off Prince Imperial Rd* . 136 D7
Blackett St, SW15 . . . . . . 148 A3
Black Fan Cl, Enf. EN2 . . . . 43 J1
BLACKFEN, Sid. DA15 . . . 157 J7
Blackfen Rd, Sid. DA15 . . . 157 H5
Blackford Rd, Wat. WD19 . . 50 D5
Blackford's Path, SW15 *off Roehampton High St* 147 G7
Blackfriars Br, EC4 . . . . 19 G5
SE1 . . . . 19 G5
Blackfriars Ct, EC4 . . . . 19 G5
Black Friars La, EC4 . . . . . . 19 G5
Blackfriars Pas, EC4 . . . . . . 19 G5
Blackfriars Rd, SE1 . . . . 27 G4
Black Gates, Pnr. HA5 *off Church La* 67 F3
BLACKHEATH, SE3 . . . . 155 E1
★**Blackheath**, SE3 . . . . . . 154 D1
Blackheath Av, SE10 . . . . 134 D7
Blackheath Gro, SE3 . . . . 155 F2
Blackheath Hill, SE10 . . . . 154 C1
BLACKHEATH PARK, SE3 . . . . 155 F4
Blackheath Pk, SE3 . . . . . 155 F3
Blackheath Ri, SE13 . . . . . 154 C2
Blackheath Rd, SE10 . . . . 154 B1
Blackheath Vale, SE3 . . . . 155 E2
Blackheath Village, SE3 . . 155 F2
Black Horse Ct, SE1 . . . . . . 28 C5
Blackhorse La, E17 . . . . 77 G4
Croydon CR0 . . . . 188 D7
Blackhorse Ms, E17 *off Blackhorse La* 77 G3
Blackhorse Rd, E17 . . . . . . 77 G4
SE8 . . . . 133 H5
Sidcup DA14 . . . . 176 A4
Blacklands Rd, SE6 . . . . . 172 C4
Blacklands Ter, SW3 . . . . . . 31 J2
Black Lion La, W6 . . . . 127 G4
Black Lion Ms, W6 *off Black Lion La* 127 G4
Blackmore Av, Sthl. UB1 . . . . 124 A1
Blackmore Rd, Buck.H. IG9 . . . . 48 B7
Blackmores Gro, Tedd. TW11 . . . . 162 D6
Blackmore Twr, W3 . . . . . . 126 C2
Black Path, E10 . . . . 77 G7
Blackpool Rd, SE15 . . . . . . 152 E2
Black Prince Rd, SE1 . . . . . 34 C2
SE11 . . . . 34 D2
Black Rod Cl, Hayes UB3 . 121 J3
Blackshaw Pl, N1 *off Hertford Rd* 94 B7
Blackshaw Rd, SW17 . . . . . 167 F4
Blacksmiths Cl, Rom. RM6 . . . . 82 C6
Blacks Rd, W6 *off Queen Caroline St* . 127 J4
Blackstock Ms, N4 *off Blackstock Rd* 93 H2
Blackstock Rd, N4 . . . . 93 H2
N5 . . . . 93 H2
Blackstone Est, E8 . . . . 94 E7
Blackstone Rd, NW2 . . . . . 89 J5
Black Swan Yd, SE1 . . . . . . 28 E3
Blackthorn Av, West Dr. UB7 . . . . 120 D4
Blackthorn Ct, Houns. TW5 . . . . 122 E7
Blackthorne Av, Croy. CR0 . . . . 189 F7
Blackthorne Dr, E4 . . . . 62 D4
Blackthorn Gro, Bexh. DA7 . . . . 158 D3
Blackthorn St, E3 . . . . 114 A4
Blacktree Ms, SW9 . . . . . . 151 G3
Blackwall La, SE10 . . . . . . 135 E5
Blackwall Pier, E14 . . . . . . 114 E7
Blackwall Trd Est, E14 . . . . 114 D5
Blackwall Tunnel, E14 . . . . 134 D1
Blackwall Tunnel App, SE10 . . . . 134 E2
Blackwall Tunnel Northern App, E3 . . . . 114 A2
E14 . . . . 114 A2
Blackwall Way, E14 . . . . . . 114 C7
Blackwater Cl, E7 . . . . 97 F4
Blackwater Rd, Sutt. SM1 *off High St* 198/199 E4
Blackwater St, SE22 . . . . . 152 C5
Blackwell Cl, E5 . . . . 95 G4
Harrow HA3 . . . . 52 A7
Blackwell Gdns, Edg. HA8 . . . . 54 A3
Blackwood Av, N18 *off Harbet Rd* 61 G5
Blackwood St, SE17 . . . . . . 36 B3
Blade Ms, SW15 *off Deodar Rd* 148 C4
Blades Ct, SW15 *off Deodar Rd* 148 C4
Bladindon Dr, Bex. DA5 . . 158 C7
Bladon Gdns, Har. HA2 . . . 67 H6
Blagdens Cl, N14 . . . . 58 C2
Blagdens La, N14 . . . . 58 D2
Blagdon Rd, SE13 . . . . . . 154 B6
New Malden KT3 . . . . . 183 F4
Blagdon Wk, Tedd. TW11 . 163 F6
Blagrove Rd, W10 . . . . 108 B5
Blair Av, NW9 . . . . 70 E7
Blair Cl, N1 . . . . 93 J6
Hayes UB3 . . . . 122 A4
Sidcup DA15 . . . . 157 H5
Blairderry Rd, SW2 . . . . . . 169 E2
Blairhead Dr, Wat. WD19 . . 50 B3
Blair St, E14 . . . . 114 C6
Blake Apartments, N8 *off High St* 75 F4
Blake Av, Bark. IG11 . . . . . 117 H1
Blake Cl, W10 . . . . 107 J5
Carshalton SM5 . . . . . . 185 H7
Welling DA16 . . . . 157 H1
Blakeden Dr, Esher (Clay.) KT10 . . . . 194 C6
Blake Gdns, SW6 . . . . 148 E1
Blake Hall Cres, E11 . . . . . . 97 G1
Blake Hall Rd, E11 . . . . 79 G7
Blakehall Rd, Cars. SM5 . . 199 J6
Blake Ho, Beck. BR3 . . . . . 172 A6
Blake Ms, Rich. TW9 *off High Pk Rd* 146 A1
Blakemore Rd, SW16 . . . . 168 E3
Thornton Heath CR7 . . . 187 F5
Blakemore Way, Belv. DA17 . . . . 139 E3
Blakeney Av, Beck. BR3 . . 189 J1
Blakeney Cl, E8 *off Ferncliff Rd* 94 D5
N20 . . . . 57 F1
NW1 *off Rossendale Way* . . . 92 D7
Blakeney Rd, Beck. BR3 . . 171 J7
Blakenham Rd, SW17 . . . 167 J4
Blaker Ct, SE7 *off Fairlawn* 135 J7
Blake Rd, E16 . . . . 115 F4
N11 . . . . 58 C7
Croydon CR0 . . . . 202 B2
Mitcham CR4 . . . . 185 H3
Blaker Rd, E15 . . . . 114 C1
Blakes Av, N.Mal. KT3 . . . 183 F5
Blake's Grn, W.Wick. BR4 . . . . 204 C1
Blakes La, N.Mal. KT3 . . . 183 F5
Blakesley Av, W5 . . . . 105 F6
Blakesley Ho, E12 *off Grantham Rd* 98 D3
Blakesley Wk, SW20 *off Kingston Rd* 184 C2
Blakes Rd, SE15 . . . . 36 E7
Blakes Ter, N.Mal. KT3 . . . 183 G5
Blake St, SE8 *off Watergate St* 134 A6
Blakesware Gdns, N9 . . . . . 44 A7
Blakewood Cl, Felt. TW13 . . . . 160 C4
Blanchard Cl, SE9 . . . . 174 B3
Blanchard Way, E8 . . . . 94 D6
Blanch Cl, SE15 *off Culmore Rd* 133 F7
Blanchedowne, SE5 . . . . . 152 A4
Blanche St, E16 . . . . 115 F4
Blanchland Rd, Mord. SM4 . . . . 184 E5
Blandfield Rd, SW12 . . . . 150 A6
Blandford Av, Beck. BR3 . . 189 H2
Twickenham TW2 . . . . . 161 H1
Blandford Cl, N2 . . . . 73 F4
Croydon CR0 . . . . 201 E3
Romford RM7 . . . . 83 H4
Blandford Cres, E4 . . . . 40 C7
Blandford Rd, W4 . . . . 126 E3
W5 . . . . 125 G2
Beckenham BR3 . . . . . . 189 F2
Southall UB2 . . . . 123 G4
Teddington TW11 . . . . . 162 A5
Blandford Sq, NW1 . . . . 7 H6
Blandford St, W1 . . . . 16 A3
Blandford Waye, Hayes UB4 . . . . 102 C6
Bland St, SE9 . . . . 156 A4
Blaney Cres, E6 . . . . 116 E3
Blanmerle Rd, SE9 . . . . . . 174 E1
Blann Cl, SE9 . . . . 156 A6
Blantyre St, SW10 . . . . 30 E7
Blantyre Wk, SW10 . . . . . . 30 E7
Blashford, NW3 . . . . 91 J7
Blashford St, SE13 . . . . . . 154 D7
Blasker Wk, E14 . . . . 134 A5
Blawith Rd, Har. HA1 . . . . . 68 B4
Blaydon Cl, N17 . . . . 60 E7
Blaydon Wk, N17 . . . . 60 E7
Bleak Hill La, SE18 . . . . . . 137 J6
Blean Gro, SE20 . . . . 171 F7
Bleasdale Av, Grnf. UB6 . . 104 D2
Blechynden St, W10 *off Bramley Rd* 108 A7
Bleddyn Cl, Sid. DA15 . . . 158 C6
Bledlow Cl, SE28 . . . . 118 C7
Bledlow Ri, Grnf. UB6 . . . 103 J2
Bleeding Heart Yd, EC1 . . . 19 F2
Blegborough Rd, SW16 . . 168 C6
Blendon Dr, Bex. DA5 . . . 158 D6
Blendon Path, Brom. BR1 . . . . 173 F7

Blendon Rd, Bex. DA5 . . . 158 D6
Blendon Ter, SE18 . . . . 137 F5
Blendworth Pt, SW15
off Wanborough Dr . . . 165 H1
Blendworth Way, SE15
off Blakes Rd. 132 B7
Blenheim Av, Ilf. IG2 . . . . . 80 D6
Blenheim Cl, N21
off Elm Pk Rd 59 J1
SE12 . . . . 173 H1
SW20. . . . . 183 J3
Greenford UB6
off Leaver Gdns. 104 A2
Romford RM7 . . . . 83 J4
Wallington SM6 . . . . . . 200 C7
Blenheim Ct, N19
off Marlborough Rd 92/93 E2
Sidcup DA14 . . . . 175 G3
Sutton SM2
off Wellesley Rd 199 F6
Woodford Green IG8
off Navestock Cres 63 J7
Blenheim Cres, W11 . . . . . 108 B6
South Croydon CR2 . . . 201 J7
Blenheim Dr, Well. DA16 . 157 J1
Blenheim Gdns, NW2 . . . . 89 J5
SW2. . . . . 151 F6
Kingston upon Thames KT2 . . . . 164 B7
Wallington SM6 . . . . . . 200 C6
Wembley HA9. . . . . 87 H3
Blenheim Gro, SE15. . . . . 152 D2
Blenheim Pas, NW8 . . . . 6 C1
Blenheim Pl, Tedd. TW11 . 162 C5
Blenheim Ri, N15
off Talbot Rd 76 C4
Blenheim Rd, E6. . . . . 116 A3
E15 . . . . 97 E4
E17 . . . . 77 G3
NW8 . . . . 6 C1
SE20 *off Maple Rd* 171 F7
SW20. . . . . 183 J3
W4. . . . . 126 E3
Barnet EN5 . . . . 40 A3
Bromley BR1 . . . . 192 B4
Harrow HA2 . . . . 67 H6
Northolt UB5. . . . . 85 H6
Sidcup DA15 . . . . 176 C1
Sutton SM1. . . . . 198 D3
Blenheim Shop Cen, SE20 . . . . 171 F7
Blenheim St, W1 . . . . 16 D4
Blenheim Ter, NW8 . . . . 6 C1
Blenheim Way, Islw. TW7 . 144 D1
Blenkarne Rd, SW11. . . . . . 149 J6
Bleriot Rd, Houns. TW5 . . 122 C7
Blessbury Rd, Edg. HA8. . . 70 C1
Blessington Cl, SE13 . . . . 154 D3
Blessington Rd, SE13. . . . 154 D3
Blessing Way, Bark. IG11 . 118 C3
Bletchingley Cl, Th.Hth. CR7 . . . . 187 H4
Bletchley Ct, N1 . . . . 12 B2
Bletchley St, N1 . . . . 12 A2
Bletchmore Cl, Hayes UB3 . . . . 121 G5
Bletsoe Wk, N1. . . . . 12 A1
Blewbury Ho, SE2
off Yarnton Way. 138 D2
Blincoe Cl, SW19 . . . . 166 A2
Blind La, Loug. (High Beach) IG10. . . . . 46 E2
Bliss Cres, SE13 . . . . 154 B2
Blissett St, SE10. . . . . 154 C1
Bliss Ms, W10
off Third Av 108 B3
Blisworth Cl, Hayes UB4
off Braunston Dr . 102/103 E4
Blithbury Rd, Dag. RM9 . . 100 B6
Blithdale Rd, SE2 . . . . 138 A4
Blithfield St, W8. . . . . 22 A6
Blockley Rd, Wem. HA0 . . . 86 E2
Bloemfontein Av, W12 . . . 127 H1
Bloemfontein Rd, W12 . . . 107 H7
Blomfield Rd, W9. . . . . 14 C1
Blomfield St, EC2. . . . . 20 C2
Blomfield Vil, W2 . . . . 14 B2
Blomville Rd, Dag. RM8 . . 101 E3
Blondell Cl, West Dr. UB7. 120 A6
Blondel St, SW11 . . . . 150 A2
Blondin Av, W5. . . . . 125 F4
Blondin St, E3 . . . . 114 A2
Bloomburg St, SW1. . . . . . 33 G2
Bloomfield Cres, Ilf. IG2. . . 81 E6
Bloomfield Pl, W1 . . . . 16 E5
Bloomfield Rd, N6 . . . . 74 A6
SE18 . . . . 137 E5
Bromley BR2. . . . . 192 A5
Bloomfield Rd, Kings.T. KT1 . . . . 181 H4
Bloomfield Ter, SW1. . . . . . 32 C3
Bloom Gro, SE27 . . . . 169 H3
Bloomhall Rd, SE19 . . . . . 170 A5
Bloom Pk Rd, SW6. . . . . . 128 C7
BLOOMSBURY, WC1 . . . . . 17 J2
Bloomsbury Cl, NW7 . . . . . 55 G7
W5. . . . . 105 J7
Bloomsbury Ct, WC1 . . . . . 18 B2
Pinner HA5 . . . . 67 F3
Bloomsbury Ho, SW4 . . . 150 D6
Bloomsbury Pl, SW18
off Fullerton Rd. 149 F5
WC1. . . . . 18 B1
Bloomsbury Sq, WC1. . . . . 18 B2
Bloomsbury St, WC1 . . . . . 17 J2
Bloomsbury Way, WC1. . . . 18 A3
Blore Cl, SW8
off Thessaly Rd 150 D1
Blore Ct, W1 . . . . 17 H4
Blossom Cl, W5
off Almond Av. 125 H2
Dagenham RM9 . . . . . . 119 F1
South Croydon CR2 . . . 202 C5
Blossom La, Enf. EN2 . . . . 43 J1
Blossom St, E1. . . . . 21 E1
Blossom Way, West Dr. UB7. . . . . 120 D4
Blossom Waye, Houns. TW5. . . . . 122 E7
Blount St, E14 . . . . 113 H6
Bloxam Gdns, SE9. . . . . . 156 B5
Bloxhall Rd, E10. . . . . 95 J1
Bloxham Cres, Hmptn. TW12 . . . . 161 F7
Bloxworth Cl, Wall. SM6 . 200 C3
Blucher Rd, SE5 . . . . 131 J7
Blue Anchor All, Rich. TW9
off Kew Rd 145 H4
Blue Anchor La, SE16. . . . . 37 J1
Blue Anchor Yd, E1. . . . . . . 21 H5
Blue Ball Yd, SW1 . . . . 25 F2
Bluebell Av, E12. . . . . 98 A5
Bluebell Cl, E9
off Moulins Rd. 113 F1
SE26 . . . . 170 C4
Northolt UB5. . . . . 85 F6
Orpington BR6 . . . . 207 F2
Wallington SM6 . . . . . . 200 B1
Bluebell Way, Ilf. IG1 . . . . . 98 E6
Blueberry Cl, Wdf.Grn. IG8. . . . . 63 G6
Bluebird La, Dag. RM10 . . 101 G7
Bluebird Way, SE28 . . . . . 137 G2
Bluefield Cl, Hmptn. TW12. . . . . 161 G5
Bluegates, Epsom (Ewell) KT17 . . . . 197 G7
Bluehouse Rd, E4. . . . . 63 E3
Bluelion Pl, SE1 . . . . 28 D5
Blueprint Apartments, SW12 *off Balham Gro*. 150 B7
Bluewater Ho, SW18 *off Smugglers Way* . 148/149 E4
Blundell Cl, E8
off Amhurst Rd. 94 D5
Blundell Rd, Edg. HA8 . . . . 70 D1
Blundell St, N7. . . . . 92 E7
Blunden Cl, Dag. RM8 . . . 100 C1
Blunt Rd, S.Croy. CR2 . . . 202 A5
Blunts Av, West Dr. UB7. . 120 D7
Blunts Rd, SE9. . . . . 156 D5
Blurton Rd, E5 . . . . 95 F4
Blyth Cl, E14
off Manchester Rd. . . . 134 D4
Twickenham TW1
off Grimwood Rd 144 C6
Blythe Cl, SE6 . . . . 153 J7
Blythe Hill, SE6 . . . . 153 J7
Orpington BR5 . . . . 193 J1
Blythe Hill La, SE6 . . . . . . 153 J7
Blythe Hill Pl, SE23
off Brockley Pk 153 H7
Blythe Ms, W14
off Blythe Rd. 128 A3
Blythe Rd, W14. . . . . 128 A3
Blythe St, E2. . . . . 112 E3
Blythe Vale, SE6 . . . . 171 J1
Blyth Rd, E17 . . . . 77 J7
SE28 . . . . 118 C7
Bromley BR1 . . . . 191 F1
Hayes UB3 . . . . 121 H2
Blyth's Wf, E14
off Narrow St. 113 H7
Blythswood Rd, Ilf. IG3 . . 100 A1
Blyth Wd Pk, Brom. BR1
off Blyth Rd. 191 F1
Blythwood Rd, N4 . . . . 75 E7
Blythwood Rd, Pnr. HA5 . . 66 D1
Boades Ms, NW3
off New End 91 G4
Boadicea St, N1
off Copenhagen St . . . 111 F1
Boakes Cl, NW9 . . . . 70 C4
Boardman Av, E4 . . . . 46 B5
Boardman Cl, Barn. EN5 . . 40 B5
Boardwalk Pl, E14 . . . . . . 134 C1
Boar's Head Yd, Brent. TW8
off Brent Way 125 G7
Boathouse Wk, SE15 . . . . . 37 G7
Richmond TW9 . . . . 145 H1
Boat Lifter Way, SE16
off Sweden Gate. 133 H4
Boat Quay, E16
off Royal Albert Way . . 115 J7
Bob Anker Cl, E13
off Chesterton Rd 115 G3
Bobbin Cl, SW4 . . . . 150 C3
Bobby Moore Way, N10 . . . 57 J7
Bob Marley Way, SE24
off Mayall Rd. 151 G4
Bockhampton Rd, Kings.T. KT2 . . . . 163 J7
Bocking St, E8 . . . . 112 E1
Boddicott Cl, SW19 . . . . . 166 B2
Bodiam Cl, Enf. EN1. . . . . . 44 A2
Bodiam Rd, SW16 . . . . 168 D7
Bodicea Ms, Houns. TW4. 143 F7
Bodley Cl, N.Mal. KT3 . . . 182 E5
Bodley Manor Way, SW2
off Papworth Way 151 G7
Bodley Rd, N.Mal. KT3. . . 182 D6
Bodmin Cl, Har. HA2 . . . . . 85 F3
Bodmin Gro, Mord. SM4 . 185 E5
Bodmin St, SW18 . . . . . . 166 D1
Bodnant Gdns, SW20 . . . 183 G3
Bodney Rd, E8 . . . . 94 E5
Boeing Way, Sthl. UB2. . . 122 B3
Boevey Path, Belv. DA17 . 139 F6
Bogey La, Orp. BR6 . . . . . 206 D7
Bognor Gdns, Wat. WD19
off Bowring Grn 50 C5
Bognor Rd, Well. DA16. . . 158 D1
Bohemia Pl, E8. . . . . 95 E6
Bohn Rd, E1 . . . . 113 H5
Bohun Gro, Barn. EN4 . . . . 41 H6
Boileau Par, W5
off Boileau Rd. 105 J6
Boileau Rd, SW13 . . . . . . 127 G7
W5. . . . . 105 J6
Bolden St, SE8. . . . . 154 B2
Bolderwood Way, W.Wick. BR4 . . . . 204 B2
Boldmere Rd, Pnr. HA5 . . . 66 C7
Boleyn Av, Enf. EN1 . . . . . . 44 E1
Boleyn Cl, E17 . . . . 78 A4
Loughton IG10
off Roding Gdns 48 B6
Boleyn Ct, Buck.H. IG9. . . . 63 G1
Boleyn Dr, Ruis. HA4 . . . . . 84 D2
West Molesey KT8 . . . . 179 F3
Boleyn Gdns, Dag. RM10 . 101 J7
West Wickham BR4. . . . 204 B2
Boleyn Gro, W.Wick. BR4 . . . . 204 C2
Boleyn Rd, E6. . . . . 116 A2
E7 . . . . 97 G7
N16 . . . . 94 B5
Boleyn Way, Barn. EN5 . . . 41 F3
Ilford IG6. . . . . 65 F6
Bolina Rd, SE16 . . . . 133 F5
Bolingbroke Gro, SW11 . . 149 H4
Bolingbroke Rd, W14 . . . . 128 A3
Bolingbroke Wk, SW11. . . 129 G7
Bolingbroke Way, Hayes UB3. . . . . 121 G1
Bolliger Ct, NW10
off Park Royal Rd. . . . 106 C4
Bollo Br Rd, W3 . . . . 126 B3
Bollo La, W3. . . . . 126 B2
W4. . . . . 126 C4
Bolney Gate, SW7 . . . . 23 G4
Bolney St, SW8 . . . . 131 F7
Bolney Way, Felt. TW13 . . 161 E3
Bolsover St, W1 . . . . 9 E6
Bolstead Rd, Mitch. CR4 . . 186 B1
Bolt Ct, EC4 . . . . 19 F4
Boltmore Cl, NW4 . . . . 72 A3
Bolton Cl, SE20
off Selby Rd 188 D2
Chessington KT9. . . . . . 195 G6
Bolton Cres, SE5 . . . . 35 F6
Bolton Gdns, NW10 . . . . . 108 A2
SW5. . . . . 30 A3
Bromley BR1. . . . . 173 F6
Teddington TW11. . . . . . 162 D6
Bolton Gdns Ms, SW10 . . . 30 C3
Bolton Rd, E15. . . . . 97 F6
N18 . . . . 60 C5
NW8 . . . . 109 E1
NW10. . . . . 107 E1
W4. . . . . 126 C7
Chessington KT9. . . . . . 195 G6
Harrow HA1 . . . . 67 J4
Boltons, The, SW10 . . . . . . 30 C3
Wembley HA0. . . . . 86 C4
Woodford Green IG8 . . . 63 G4
Boltons La, Hayes UB3 . . 121 F7
Boltons Pl, SW5. . . . . 30 C3
Bolton St, W1. . . . . 24 E1
Bolton Wk, N7
off Durham Rd 93 F2
Bombay St, SE16. . . . . . . 132 E4
Bomer Cl, West Dr. UB7. . 120 D7
Bomore Rd, W11. . . . . 108 A7
Bonar Pl, Chis. BR7 . . . . . 174 B7
Bonar Rd, SE15 . . . . 132 D7
Bonchester Cl, Chis. BR7 . 174 D7
Bonchurch Cl, Sutt. SM2 . 199 E7
Bonchurch Rd, W10 . . . . . 108 B5
W13. . . . . 124 E1
Bond Ct, EC4 . . . . 20 B4
Bondfield Av, Hayes UB4. 102 A3
Bondfield Rd, E6
off Lovage App 116 B5
Bond Gdns, Wall. SM6. . . 200 C4
Bonding Yd Wk, SE16
off Finland St 133 H3
Bond Rd, Mitch. CR4 . . . . 185 H2
Surbiton KT6. . . . . 195 J2
Bond St, E15 . . . . 96 E5
W4. . . . . 126 E4
W5. . . . . 105 G7
Bondway, SW8 . . . . 34 B6
Boneta Rd, SE18 . . . . 136 C3
Bonfield Rd, SE13 . . . . . . 154 C4
Bonham Gdns, Dag. RM8. . . . . 100 D2
Bonham Rd, SW2. . . . . . . 151 F5
Dagenham RM8 . . . . . . 100 D2
Bonheur Rd, W4. . . . . 126 D2
Bonhill St, EC2. . . . . 12 C6
Boniface Gdns, Har. HA3 . . 51 H7
Boniface Wk, Har. HA3. . . 51 H7
Bonington Ho, Enf. EN1
off Ayley Cft 44 D5
Bonita Ms, SE4 . . . . 153 G3
Bon Marche Ter Ms, SE27
off Gipsy Rd 170 B4
Bonner Hill Rd, Kings.T. KT1 . . . . 181 J3
Bonner Rd, E2 . . . . 113 F2
Bonnersfield Cl, Har. HA1. . . . . 68 C6
Bonnersfield La, Har. HA1. . . . . 68 D6
Bonner St, E2. . . . . 113 F2
Bonneville Gdns, SW4. . . 150 C6
Bonnington Sq, SW8. . . . . 34 C5
Bonnington Twr, Brom. BR2 . . . . 192 B6
Bonny St, NW1 . . . . 92 C7
Bonser Rd, Twick. TW1 . . . 162 C2
Bonsor St, SE5. . . . . 132 B7
Bonville Gdns, NW4
off Handowe Cl. 71 G4
Bonville Rd, Brom. BR1 . . 173 F5
Bookbinders' Cotts, N20
off Manor Dr. 57 J3
Booker Cl, E14
off Wallwood St. 113 J5
Booker Rd, N18 . . . . 60 D5
Book Ms, WC2 . . . . 17 J4
Boone Ct, N9 . . . . 61 F3
Boones Rd, SE13 . . . . 155 E4
Boone St, SE13 . . . . 155 E4
Boord St, SE10. . . . . 135 E3
Boothby Rd, N19 . . . . 92 D2
Booth Cl, E9
off Victoria Pk Rd . 112/113 E1
SE28 . . . . 118 B7
Booth Rd, NW9 . . . . 70 E2
Croydon CR0
off Waddon New Rd . . 201 H2
Booth's Pl, W1 . . . . 17 G2
Boot St, N1 . . . . 12 D4
Bordars Rd, W7 . . . . 104 B5
Bordars Wk, W7 . . . . 104 B5
Borden Av, Enf. EN1. . . . . . 44 A6
Border Cres, SE26 . . . . . . 170 E5
Border Gdns, Croy. CR0. . 204 B4
Bordergate, Mitch. CR4 . . 185 H1
Border Rd, SE26. . . . . 171 E5
Borders La, Loug. IG10 . . . 48 D4
Bordesley Rd, Mord. SM4. 185 E4
Bordon Wk, SW15 . . . . . . 147 G7

Boreas Wk, N1 **11** H2
Boreham Av, E16 **115** G6
Boreham Cl, E11
off Hainault Rd **96** C1
Boreham Rd, N22 **75** J2
BOREHAMWOOD, WD6 **38** B3
Borehamwood Ind Pk,
Borwd. WD6 **38** D2
Borgard Rd, SE18 **136** C4
Borkwood Pk, Orp. BR6 **207** J4
Borkwood Way, Orp. BR6 **207** H4
Borland Rd, SE15 **153** F4
Teddington TW11 **162** E6
Borneo St, SW15 **147** J3
BOROUGH, THE, SE1 **27** J4
Borough High St, SE1 **27** J4
Borough Hill, Croy. CR0 **201** H3
★**Borough Mkt**, SE1 **28** B2
Borough Rd, SE1 **27** G5
Isleworth TW7 **144** B1
Kingston upon Thames
KT2 **182** A1
Mitcham CR4 **185** H2
Borough Sq, SE1 **27** J4
Borrett Cl, SE17 **35** J4
Borrodaile Rd, SW18 **149** E6
Borrowdale Av, Har. HA3 **68** D2
Borrowdale Cl, Ilf. IG4 **80** B4
Borrowdale Ct, Enf. EN2 **43** J1
Borthwick Ms, E15
off Borthwick Rd **96/97** E4
Borthwick Rd, E15 **96** E4
NW9
off West Hendon Bdy **71** F6
Borthwick St, SE8 **134** A5
Borwick Av, E17 **77** J3
Bosbury Rd, SE6 **172** C3
Boscastle Rd, NW5 **92** B3
Boscobel Cl, Brom. BR1 **192** C2
Boscobel Pl, SW1 **32** C1
Boscobel St, NW8 **7** F6
Bosco Cl, Orp. BR6
off Strickland Way **207** J4
Boscombe Av, E10 **78** D7
Boscombe Cl, E5 **95** H5
Boscombe Gdns, SW16 **169** E6
Boscombe Rd, SW17 **100** A6
SW19 **184** E1
W12 **127** G1
Worcester Park KT4 **197** J1
Bose Cl, N3
off Claremont Pk **72** B1
Bosgrove, E4 **62** C1
Boss Ho, SE1 **29** F3
Boss St, SE1 **29** F3
Bostall Heath, SE2 **138** C5
Bostall Hill, SE2 **138** A5
Bostall La, SE2 **138** B5
Bostall Manorway, SE2 **138** B4
Bostall Pk Av, Bexh.
DA7 **138** E7
Bostall Rd, Orp. BR5 **176** B7
Bostal Row, Bexh. DA7
off Harlington Rd **159** F3
Boston Gdns, W4 **127** E6
W7 **124** D4
Brentford TW8 **124** D4
★**Boston Manor**, Brent.
TW8 **125** E5
Boston Manor Rd, Brent.
TW8 **124** E4
Boston Pk Rd, Brent.
TW8 **125** F5
Boston Pl, NW1 **7** J6
Boston Rd, E6 **116** B3
E17 **78** A6
W7 **124** B1
Croydon CR0 **187** F6
Edgware HA8 **54** C7
Boston St, E2 **13** H1
Bostonthorpe Rd, W7 **124** B2
Boston Vale, W7 **124** D4
Bosun Cl, E14 *off Byng St* **134** A2
Boswell Ct, WC1 **18** B1
Boswell Path, Hayes UB3
off Croyde Av **121** J4
Boswell Rd, Th.Hth. CR7 **187** J4
Boswell St, WC1 **18** B1
Bosworth Cl, E17 **77** J1
Bosworth Rd, N11 **58** D6
W10 **108** B4
Barnet EN5 **40** D3
Dagenham RM10 **101** G4
Botany Bay La, Chis.
BR7 **193** F3
Botany Cl, Barn. EN4 **41** H4
Boteley Cl, E4 **62** D2
Botham Cl, Edg. HA8
off Pavilion Way **54** C7
Botha Rd, E13 **115** H5
Bothwell Cl, E16 **115** F5
Bothwell St, W6
off Delorme St **128** A6
Botolph All, EC3 **20** D5
Botolph La, EC3 **20** D5
Botsford Rd, SW20 **184** B2
Botts Ms, W2
off Chepstow Rd **108** D6
Botts Pas, W2
off Chepstow Rd **108** D6
Botwell La, Hayes UB3 **121** H1
Boucher Cl, Tedd. TW11 **162** C5
Boughton Av, Brom. BR2 **191** F7
Boughton Rd, SE28 **137** H3
Boulcott St, E1 **113** G6
Boulevard, The, SW6 **149** F1
SW17
off Balham High Rd **168** A2
SW18
off Smugglers
Way **148/149** E4
Pinner HA5
off Pinner Rd **67** G4
Woodford Green IG8 **64** D7
Boulevard 25 Retail Pk,
Borwd. WD6 **38** A3
Boulogne Rd, Croy. CR0 **187** J6
Boulton Ho, Brent. TW8
off Green Dragon La **125** H5
Boulton Rd, Dag. RM8 **101** E3
Boultwood Rd, E6 **116** B6
Bounces La, N9 **60** E2
Bounces Rd, N9 **60** E1
Boundaries Rd, SW12 **167** J2
Feltham TW13 **160** C1
Boundary Av, E17 **77** J7
Boundary Cl, SE20
off Haysleigh Gdns **188** D2
Barnet EN5 **40** C1
Ilford IG3
off Loxford La **99** H4
Kingston upon Thames
KT1 **182** B3
Southall UB2 **123** G5
Boundary La, E13 **116** A3
SE17 **36** A6
Boundary Pas, E2 **13** F5
Boundary Rd, E13 **115** J2
E17 **77** J7
N9 **45** F6
N22 **75** H3
NW8 **109** E1
SW19 **167** G6
Barking IG11 **117** F2
Carshalton SM5 **200** B6
Pinner HA5 **66** D6
Sidcup DA15 **157** H5
Wallington SM6 **200** B6
Wembley HA9 **87** H3
Boundary Row, SE1 **27** G3
Boundary St, E2 **13** F4
Boundary Way, Croy.
CR0 **204** A5
Boundfield Rd, SE6 **172** F3
Bounds Grn Rd, N11 **58** C6
N22 **58** C6
Bourchier St, W1 **17** H5
Bourdon Pl, W1 **16** E5
Bourdon Rd, SE20 **189** F2
Bourdon St, W1 **16** E5
Bourke Cl, NW10
off Mayo Rd **88/89** E6
SW4 **150** E6
Bourlet Cl, W1 **17** F2
Bourn Av, N15 **76** A4
Barnet EN4 **41** G5
Bournbrook Rd, SE3 **156** A3
Bourne, The, N14 **58** D1
Bourne Av, N14 **58** E2
Hayes UB3 **121** F3
Ruislip HA4 **84** C5
Bourne Cl, T.Ditt. KT7 **194** C2
Bourne Ct, Ruis. HA4 **84** B5
Bourne Dr, Mitch. CR4 **185** G2
Bourne Est, EC1 **18** E1
Bourne Gdns, E4 **62** B4
Bourne Hill, N13 **58** E1
Bourne Hill Cl, N13
off Bourne Hill **59** F2
Bournemead Av, Nthlt.
UB5 **102** A2
Bournemead Cl, Nthlt.
UB5 **102** A2
Bournemead Way, Nthlt.
UB5 **102** B2
Bournemouth Cl, SE15 **152** D2
Bournemouth Rd, SE15 **152** D2
SW19 **184** D1
Bourne Pl, W4
off Dukes Av **126** D5
Bourne Rd, E7 **97** F3
N8 **75** E6
Bexley DA5 **159** H6
Bromley BR2 **192** A4
Dartford DA1 **159** J6
Bourneside Cres, N14 **58** D1
Bourneside Gdns, SE6 **172** C5
Bourne St, SW1 **32** B2
Croydon CR0
off Waddon New Rd **201** H2
Bourne Ter, W2 **14** A1
Bourne Vale, Brom. BR2 **191** G7
Bournevale Rd, SW16 **168** E4
Bourne Vw, Grnf. UB6 **86** C6
Bourne Way, Brom. BR2 **205** F2
Epsom KT19 **196** C4
Sutton SM1 **198** C5
Bournewood Rd, SE18 **138** A7
Bournville Rd, SE6 **154** A7
Bournwell Cl, Barn. EN4 **41** J3
Bourton Cl, Hayes UB3 **122** A1
Bousfield Rd, SE14 **153** G2
Boutflower Rd, SW11 **149** H4
Bouverie Gdns, Har. HA3 **69** G6
Bouverie Ms, N16
off Bouverie Rd **94** B2
Bouverie Pl, W2 **15** F3
Bouverie Rd, N16 **94** B2
Harrow HA1 **67** J7
Bouverie St, EC4 **19** F4
Boveney Rd, SE23 **153** G7
Bovill Rd, SE23 **153** G7
Bovingdon Av, Wem.
HA9 **88** A6
Bovingdon Cl, N19
off Brookside Rd **92** C2
Bovingdon La, NW9 **71** E1
Bovingdon Rd, SW6 **148** E1
Bovingdon Sq, Mitch. CR4
off Leicester Av **186/187** E4
BOW, E3 **113** J2
Bowater Cl, NW9 **70** D5
SW2 **150** E6
Bowater Gdns, Sun.
TW16 **178** B2
Bowater Pl, SE3 **135** H7
Bowater Rd, SE18 **136** A3
Wembley HA9
off Chalkhill Rd **88** B3
Bow Back Rivers Wk,
E15 **96** B7
Bow Br Est, E3 **114** B3
Bow Chyd, EC4 **20** A4
Bow Common La, E3 **113** J4
Bowden St, SE11 **35** F4
Bowditch, SE8 **133** J5
Bowdon Rd, E17 **78** A7
Bowen Dr, SE21 **170** B3
Bowen Rd, Har. HA1 **67** J7
Bowen St, E14 **114** B6
Bower Av, SE10 **154** E1
Bower Cl, Nthlt. UB5 **102** C2
Bowerdean St, SW6 **148** F1
Bowerman Av, SE14 **133** H6
Bower St, E1 **113** G6
Bowers Wk, E6 **116** B6
Bowes Cl, Sid. DA15 **158** B6
BOWES PARK, N22 **59** E6
Bowes Rd, N11 **58** B5
N13 **58** E5
W3 **106** E7
Dagenham RM8 **100** C4
Bowfell Rd, W6 **127** J6
Bowford Av, Bexh. DA7 **158** E1
Bowhill Cl, SW9 **35** F7
Bowie Cl, SW4 **150** D7
Bow Ind Pk, E15 **96** A7
Bowland Rd, SW4 **150** D4
Woodford Green IG8 **63** J6
Bowland Yd, SW1 **24** A4
Bow La, EC4 **20** A4
N12 **73** F1
Morden SM4 **184** B6
Bowl Ct, EC2 **12** E6
Bowles Rd, SE1 **37** H5
Bowley Cl, SE19 **170** C6
Bowley La, SE19 **170** C5
Bowling Grn Cl, SW15 **147** H7
Bowling Grn La, EC1 **11** F5
Bowling Grn Pl, SE1 **28** B3
Bowling Grn Row, SE18
off Samuel St **136** C3
Bowling Grn St, SE11 **35** E5
Bowling Grn Wk, N1 **12** D3
Bowls, The, Chig. IG7 **65** H4
Bowls Cl, Stan. HA7 **52** E5
Bowman Av, E16 **115** F7
Bowman Ms, SW18 **166** C1
Bowmans Cl, W13 **124** E1
Bowmans Lea, SE23 **153** F7
Bowmans Meadow, Wall.
SM6 **200** B3
Bowmans Ms, E1 **21** H5
N7 *off Seven*
Sisters Rd **92/93** E3
Bowmans Pl, N7
off Holloway Rd **92/93** E3
Bowman's Trd Est, NW9
off Westmoreland Rd **69** J3
Bowmead, SE9 **174** C2
Bowmore Wk, NW1
off St. Paul's Cres **92** D7
Bowness Cl, E8
off Beechwood Rd **94** C6
Bowness Cres, SW15 **164** E5
Bowness Dr, Houns. TW4 **143** E4
Bowness Rd, SE6 **154** B7
Bexleyheath DA7 **159** H2
Bowood Rd, SW11 **150** A4
Enfield EN3 **45** G2
Bowring Grn, Wat. WD19 **50** C5
Bow Rd, E3 **113** J3
Bowrons Av, Wem. HA0 **87** G7
Bowsley Ct, Felt. TW13
off Highfield Rd **160** A1
Bowsprit Pt, E14 **134** A3
Bow St, E15 **96** E5
WC2 **18** B4
Bowyer Cl, E6 **116** C5
Bowyer Pl, SE5 **36** A7
Bowyer St, SE5 **35** J7
Boxall Rd, SE21 **152** B6
Boxgrove Rd, SE2 **138** C3
Box La, Bark. IG11 **118** B2
Boxley Rd, Mord. SM4 **185** F4
Boxley St, E16 **135** H1
Boxmoor Rd, Har. HA3 **68** E4
Boxoll Rd, Dag. RM9 **101** F4
Boxted Cl, Buck.H. IG9 **64** B1
Boxtree La, Har. HA3 **67** J1
Boxtree Rd, Har. HA3 **52** A7
Boxwood Cl, West Dr. UB7
off Hawthorne Cres **120** C2
Boxworth Cl, N12 **57** G5
Boxworth Gro, N1
off Richmond Av **111** F1
Boyard Rd, SE18 **136** E5
Boyce St, SE1 **26** D2
Boyce Way, E13 **115** G4
Boycroft Av, NW9 **70** C6
Boyd Av, Sthl. UB1 **123** F1
Boyd Cl, Kings.T. KT2
off Crescent Rd **164** A7
Boydell Ct, NW8
off St. John's Wd Pk **91** G7
Boyd Rd, SW19 **167** G6
Boyd St, E1 **21** H4
Boyfield St, SE1 **27** H4
Boyland Rd, Brom. BR1 **173** F5
Boyle Av, Stan. HA7 **52** D6
Boyle Fm Island, T.Ditt.
KT7 **100** D6
Boyle Fm Rd, T.Ditt. KT7 **180** D6
Boyle St, W1 **17** F5
Boyne Av, NW4 **72** A4
Boyne Rd, SE13 **154** C3
Dagenham RM10 **101** G3
Boyne Ter Ms, W11 **128** C1
Boyseland Ct, Edg. HA8 **54** C2
Boyson Rd, SE17 **36** B5
Boyton Cl, E1
off Stayner's Rd **113** G4
N8 **75** E3
Boyton Rd, N8 **75** E3
Brabant Ct, EC3 **20** D5
Brabant Rd, N22 **75** F2
Brabazon Av, Wall. SM6 **200** E7
Brabazon Rd, Houns.
TW5 **122** C7
Northolt UB5 **103** G2
Brabazon St, E14 **114** B6
Brabourne Cl, SE19 **170** B5
Brabourne Cres, Bexh.
DA7 **139** F6
Brabourne Hts, NW7 **55** E3
Brabourne Ri, Beck. BR3 **190** C5
Brabourn Gro, SE15 **153** F2
Bracewell Av, Grnf. UB6 **86** C5
Bracewell Rd, W10 **107** J5
Bracewood Gdns, Croy.
CR0 **202** C3
Bracey Ms, N4
off Bracey St **92/93** E2
Bracey St, N4 **93** E2
Bracken, The, E4
off Hortus Rd **62** C2

Bracken Av, SW12 150 A6
Croydon CR0 204 B3
Brackenbridge Dr, Ruis. HA4 84 D3
Brackenbury Gdns, W6 127 H3
Brackenbury Rd, N2 73 F3
W6 127 H3
Bracken Cl, E6 116 C5
Borehamwood WD6 38 B1
Twickenham TW2 *off Hedley Rd* 143 G7
Brackendale, N21 59 F2
Brackendale Cl, Houns. TW3 143 H1
Bracken Dr, Chig. IG7 65 E6
Bracken End, Islw. TW7 144 A5
Brackenfield Cl, E5 *off Tiger Way* 94/95 E4
Bracken Gdns, SW13 147 G2
Bracken Hill Cl, Brom. BR1 *off Bracken Hill La* 191 F1
Bracken Hill La, Brom. BR1 191 F1
Bracken Ind Est, Ilf. IG6 65 J7
Bracken Ms, E4 *off Hortus Rd* 62 C2
Romford RM7 83 G6
Brackens, The, Enf. EN1 44 B7
Brackenwood, Sun. TW16 178 A1
Brackley Av, SE15 *off Linden Gro* 152 D3
Brackley Cl, Wall. SM6 201 E7
Brackley Rd, W4 127 E5
Beckenham BR3 171 J7
Brackley Sq, Wdf.Grn. IG8 64 A7
Brackley St, EC1 19 J1
Brackley Ter, W4 127 E5
Bracklyn Cl, N1 12 B1
Bracklyn Ct, N1 12 B1
Bracklyn St, N1 12 B1
Bracknell Cl, N22 75 G1
Bracknell Gdns, NW3 90 E4
Bracknell Gate, NW3 90 E5
Bracknell Way, NW3 90 E4
Bracondale Rd, SE2 138 A4
Bradbourne Rd, Bex. DA5 159 G7
Bradbourne St, SW6 148 D2
Bradbury Cl, Borwd. WD6 38 B1
Southall UB2 123 F4
Bradbury Ms, N16 *off Bradbury St* 94 B5
Bradbury St, N16 94 B5
Braddock Cl, Islw. TW7 144 C3
Braddon Rd, Rich. TW9 145 J3
Braddyll St, SE10 134 E5
Bradenham Av, Well. DA16 158 A4
Bradenham Cl, SE17 36 B5
Bradenham Rd, Har. HA3 68 E4
Braden St, W9 6 A6
Bradfield Dr, Bark. IG11 100 A5
Bradfield Rd, E16 135 G2
Ruislip HA4 85 E5
Bradford Cl, N17 *off Commercial Rd* 60 B6
SE26 *off Coombe Rd* 170/171 E4
Bromley BR2 206 C1
Bradford Dr, Epsom KT19 197 F6
Bradford Rd, W3 *off Warple Way* 126/127 E2
Ilford IG1 99 G1
Bradgate Rd, SE6 154 A6
Brading Cres, E11 97 H2
Brading Rd, SW2 151 F7
Croydon CR0 187 F6
Brading Ter, W12 127 H3
Bradiston Rd, W9 108 C3
Bradley Cl, N1 11 F1
N7 *off Sutterton St* 93 F6
Bradley Gdns, W13 104 E6
Bradley Ms, SW17 *off Bellevue Rd* 167 J1
Bradley Rd, N22 75 F2
SE19 169 J6
Bradley Stone Rd, E6 116 C5
Bradman Row, Edg. HA8 *off Pavilion Way* 54 C7
Bradmead, SW8 130 B7
Bradmore Pk Rd, W6 127 H3
Bradshaw Cl, SW19 166 D6
Bradshaw Dr, NW7 56 A7
Bradshaws Cl, SE25 188 D3
Bradstock Rd, E9 95 G6
Epsom KT17 197 G5
Brad St, SE1 27 F2
Bradwell Av, Dag. RM10 101 G2
Bradwell Cl, E18 79 F4
Bradwell Ms, N18 *off Lyndhurst Rd* 60 D4
Bradwell Rd, Buck.H. IG9 64 B1
Bradwell St, E1 113 G3
Brady Av, Loug. IG10 49 F2
Bradymead, E6 116 D6
Brady St, E1 112 E4
Braemar Av, N22 75 E1
NW10 88 D3
SW19 166 D2
Bexleyheath DA7 159 J4
Thornton Heath CR7 187 G3
Wembley HA0 87 G7
Braemar Cl, SE16 *off Masters Dr* 132/133 E5
Braemar Gdns, NW9 70 D1
Sidcup DA15 175 G3
West Wickham BR4 204 C1
Braemar Rd, E13 115 F4
N15 76 B5
Brentford TW8 125 H6
Worcester Park KT4 197 H3
Braeside, Beck. BR3 172 A5
Braeside Av, SW19 184 B1
Braeside Cl, Pnr. HA5 *off The Avenue* 51 G7
Braeside Cres, Bexh. DA7 159 J4
Braeside Rd, SW16 168 C7
Braes St, N1 93 H7
Braesyde Cl, Belv. DA17 139 F4
Brafferton Rd, Croy. CR0 201 J4
Braganza St, SE17 35 G3
Bragg Cl, Dag. RM8 *off Porters Av* 100 B6
Braham St, E1 21 G4
Braid Av, W3 106 E6
Braid Cl, Felt. TW13 161 F2
Braid Ct, W4 *off Lawford Rd* 126 C7
Braidwood Pas, EC1 *off Aldersgate St* 111 J5
Braidwood Rd, SE6 172 D1
Braidwood St, SE1 28 D2
Brailsford Cl, Mitch. CR4 167 H7
Brailsford Rd, SW2 151 G5
Brainton Av, Felt. TW14 142 B7
Braintree Av, Ilf. IG4 80 B4
Braintree Ind Est, Ruis. HA4 84 B4
Braintree Rd, Dag. RM10 101 G3
Ruislip HA4 84 B4
Braintree St, E2 113 F3
Braithwaite Av, Rom. RM7 83 G7
Braithwaite Gdns, Stan. HA7 69 F1
Braithwaite Ho, EC1 *off Bunhill Row* 112 A4
Braithwaite Rd, Enf. EN3 45 J3
Braithwaite Twr, W2 15 E1
Bramah Grn, SW9 151 G1
★**Bramah Mus**, SE1 28 A2
Bramalea Cl, N6 74 A6
Bramall Cl, E15 *off Idmiston Rd* 97 F5
Bramber Ct, Brent. TW8 *off Sterling Pl* 125 H4
Bramber Ho, Kings.T. KT2 *off Kingsgate Rd* 181 H1
Bramber Rd, N12 57 H5
W14 128 C6
Brambleacres Cl, Sutt. SM2 198 D7
Bramblebury Rd, SE18 137 F5
Bramble Cl, N15 *off Broad La* 76 D4
Beckenham BR3 190 C5
Chigwell IG7 *off High Rd* 65 F1
Croydon CR0 204 A4
Stanmore HA7 53 G7
Bramble Cft, Erith DA8 139 J4
Brambledown Cl, W.Wick. BR4 191 E5
Brambledown Rd, Cars. SM5 200 A7
South Croydon CR2 202 B7
Wallington SM6 200 B7
Bramble Gdns, W12 *off Wallflower St* 107 F7
Bramble La, Hmptn. TW12 161 F6
Brambles, The, Chig. IG7 *off Clayside* 65 F5
West Drayton UB7 120 B4
Brambles Cl, Islw. TW7 124 E7
Bramblewood Cl, Cars. SM5 199 H1
Bramblings, The, E4 62 D4
Bramcote Av, Mitch. CR4 185 J4
Bramcote Ct, Mitch. CR4 *off Bramcote Av* 185 J4
Bramcote Gro, SE16 133 F5
Bramcote Rd, SW15 147 H4
Bramdean Cres, SE12 173 G1
Bramdean Gdns, SE12 173 G1
Bramerton Rd, Beck. BR3 189 J3
Bramerton St, SW3 31 G5
Bramfield Ct, N4 *off Queens Dr* 93 J2
Bramfield Rd, SW11 149 H6
Bramford Ct, N14 58 D2
Bramford Rd, SW18 149 F4
Bramham Gdns, SW5 30 A3
Chessington KT9 195 G4
Bramhope La, SE7 135 H6
Bramlands Cl, SW11 149 H3
Bramley Cl, E17 77 H2
N14 42 B5
Hayes UB3 102 A7
Orpington BR6 207 E1
South Croydon CR2 201 H5
Twickenham TW2 143 J6
Woodford Green IG8 *off Orsett Ter* 63 J7
Bramley Ct, Well. DA16 158 B1
Bramley Cres, SW8 33 J7
Ilford IG2 80 D6
Bramley Gdns, Wat. WD19 50 C5
Bramley Hill, S.Croy. CR2 201 H5
Bramley Ho, SW15 *off Tunworth Cres* 147 F6
Bramley Rd, N14 42 B5
W5 125 F3
W10 108 A7
Sutton SM1 199 G5
Bramley Way, Houns. TW4 143 F5
West Wickham BR4 204 B2
Brampton Cl, E5 95 E2
Brampton Gdns, N15 *off Brampton Rd* 75 J5
Brampton Gro, NW4 71 H4
Harrow HA3 68 D4
Wembley HA9 88 A1
Brampton La, NW4 71 J4
Brampton Pk Rd, N22 75 G3
Brampton Rd, E6 116 A3
N15 75 J5
NW9 70 A4
SE2 138 C6
Bexleyheath DA7 138 D7
Croydon CR0 188 C7
Watford WD19 50 A3
Bramshaw Gdns, Wat. WD19 50 D5
Bramshaw Ri, N.Mal. KT3 183 E6
Bramshaw Rd, E9 95 G6
Bramshill Cl, Chig. IG7 *off Tine Rd* 65 H5
Bramshill Gdns, NW5 92 B3
Bramshill Rd, NW10 107 F2
Bramshot Av, SE7 135 G6
Bramshot Way, Wat. WD19 50 A2
Bramston Cl, Ilf. IG6 65 J6
Bramston Rd, NW10 107 G2
SW17 167 F3
Bramwell Cl, Sun. TW16 178 D2
Bramwell Ms, N1 111 F1
Brancaster Dr, NW7 55 F7
Brancaster Pl, Loug. IG10 48 C3
Brancaster Rd, E12 98 C4
SW16 168 E3
Ilford IG2 81 G6
Brancepeth Gdns, Buck.H. IG9 63 G2
Branch Hill, NW3 91 F3
Branch Pl, N1 112 A1
Branch Rd, E14 113 H7
Branch St, SE15 132 B7
Brancker Cl, Wall. SM6 *off Brown Cl* 200/201 E7
Brancker Rd, Har. HA3 69 G3
Brancroft Way, Enf. EN3 45 H1
Brand Cl, N4 93 H1
Brandesbury Sq, Wdf.Grn. IG8 64 D7
Brandlehow Rd, SW15 148 C4
Brandon Est, SE17 35 H6
Brandon Ms, EC2 *off The Barbican* 111 J5
Brandon Rd, E17 78 C3
N7 92 E7
Southall UB2 123 F5
Sutton SM1 198 E4
Brandon St, SE17 35 J2
Brandram Ms, SE13 *off Brandram Rd* 154/155 E3
Brandram Rd, SE13 154 E3
Brandreth Rd, E6 116 C6
SW17 168 B2
Brandries, The, Wall. SM6 200 D3
Brand St, SE10 134 C7
Brandville Gdns, Ilf. IG6 81 E4
Brandville Rd, West Dr. UB7 120 B2
Brandy Way, Sutt. SM2 198 D7
Brangbourne Rd, Brom. BR1 172 C5
Brangton Rd, SE11 34 D4
Brangwyn Cres, SW19 185 G1
Branksea St, SW6 128 B7
Branksome Av, N18 60 C5
Branksome Cl, Tedd. TW11 162 A4
Branksome Rd, SW2 151 E5
SW19 184 D1
Branksome Way, Har. HA3 69 H6
New Malden KT3 182 C1
Bransby Rd, Chess. KT9 195 H6
Branscombe Gdns, N21 43 G7
Branscombe St, SE13 154 B3
Bransdale Cl, NW6 *off West End La* 108/109 E1
Bransgrove Rd, Edg. HA8 69 J1
Branston Cres, Orp. BR5 207 G1
Branstone Rd, Rich. TW9 145 J1
Brants Wk, W7 104 B4
Brantwood Av, Erith DA8 139 J7
Isleworth TW7 144 D4
Brantwood Cl, E17 78 B3
Brantwood Gdns, Enf. EN2 42 E4
Ilford IG4 80 B4
Brantwood Rd, N17 60 C6
SE24 151 J5
Bexleyheath DA7 159 H2
Brasenose Dr, SW13 127 J6
Brasher Cl, Grnf. UB6 86 A5
Brassett Pt, E15 114 E1
Brassey Cl, Felt. TW14 160 A1
Brassey Rd, NW6 90 C6
Brassey Sq, SW11 150 A3
Brassie Av, W3 106 E6
Brass Tally All, SE16 *off Middleton Dr* 133 G2
Brasted Cl, SE26 171 F4
Bexleyheath DA6 158 D5
Brathway Rd, SW18 148 D7
Bratley St, E1 13 H6
Braund Av, Grnf. UB6 103 H4
Braundton Av, Sid. DA15 175 J1
Braunston Dr, Hayes UB4 102 E4
Bravington Pl, W9 *off Bravington Rd* 108 C4
Bravington Rd, W9 108 C2
Bravingtons Wk, N1 *off Pentonville Rd* 110 E2
Brawne Ho, SE17 35 G6
Braxfield Rd, SE4 153 H4
Braxted Pk, SW16 169 F6
Bray, NW3 91 H7
Brayards Rd, SE15 152 E2
Braybourne Dr, Islw. TW7 124 C7
Braybrooke Gdns, SE19 *off Fox Hill* 170 C7
Braybrook St, W12 107 F5
Brayburne Av, SW4 150 C2
Bray Cl, Borwd. WD6 38 C1
Braycourt Av, Walt. KT12 178 B7
Bray Cres, SE16 *off Marlow Way* 133 G2
Braydon Rd, N16 94 C1
Bray Dr, E16 115 F7
Brayfield Ter, N1 *off Lofting Rd* 93 G7
Brayford Sq, E1 *off Summercourt Rd* 113 F6
Bray Pas, E16 115 G7
Bray Pl, SW3 31 J2
Bray Rd, NW7 56 A6
Brayton Gdns, Enf. EN2 42 D4
Braywood Rd, SE9 157 G4

Brazil Cl, Croy. (Bedd.) CR0 **186** E7
Breach La, Dag. RM9 **119** G3
Bread St, EC4 **20** A4
Breakspears Ms, SE4
off Breakspears Rd **154** A2
Breakspears Rd, SE4 **153** J3
Bream Cl, N17 **77** E4
Bream Gdns, E6 **116** D3
Breamore Cl, SW15 **165** G1
Breamore Rd, Ilf. IG3 **99** J2
Bream's Bldgs, EC4 **18** E3
Bream St, E3 **96** A7
Breamwater Gdns, Rich. TW10 **163** E3
Brearley Cl, Edg. HA8
off Pavilion Way **54** C7
Breasley Cl, SW15 **147** H4
Brechin Pl, SW7 **30** D2
Brecknock Rd, N7 **92** C4
N19 **92** C4
Brecknock Rd Est, N7 **92** C4
Breckonmead, Brom. BR1
off Wanstead Rd **191** J2
Brecon Cl, Mitch. CR4 **186** E3
Worcester Park KT4 **197** J2
Brecon Grn, NW9
off Goldsmith Av **70/71** E6
Brecon Rd, W6 **128** B6
Enfield EN3 **45** F4
Brede Cl, E6 **116** D3
Bredgar, SE13 **154** C5
Bredgar Rd, N19 **92** C2
Bredhurst Cl, SE20 **171** F6
Bredon Rd, Croy. CR0 **188** C7
Breer St, SW6 **148** E3
Breezers Hill, E1 **21** J6
Brember Rd, Har. HA2 **85** J2
Bremer Ms, E17
off Church La **78** B4
Bremner Rd, SW7 **22** D4
Brenchley Cl, Brom. BR2 **191** F6
Chislehurst BR7 **192** D1
Brenchley Gdns, SE23 **153** F6
Brenchley Rd, Orp. BR5 **193** J1
Brenda Rd, SW17 **167** J2
Brende Gdns, W.Mol. KT8 **179** H4
Brendon Av, NW10 **89** E4
Brendon Cl, Hayes UB3 **121** F7
Brendon Gdns, Har. HA2 **85** H4
Ilford IG2 **81** H5
Brendon Gro, N2 **73** F2
Brendon Rd, SE9 **175** G2
Dagenham RM8 **101** F1
Brendon St, W1 **15** H3
Brendon Way, Enf. EN1 **44** B7
Brenley Cl, Mitch. CR4 **186** A3
Brenley Gdns, SE9 **156** A4
Brent Cl, Bex. DA5 **177** E1
Brentcot Cl, W13 **104** E4
Brent Cres, NW10 **105** J2
Brent Cross Gdns, NW4
off Haley Rd **72** A6
Brent Cross Shop Cen, NW4 **71** J7
Brentfield, NW10 **88** B7
Brentfield Cl, NW10
off Normans Mead **88** D6
Brentfield Gdns, NW2
off Hendon Way **72** A7
Brentfield Rd, NW10 **88** D6
BRENTFORD, TW8 **125** G6
Brentford Business Cen, Brent. TW8 **125** F7
Brentford Cl, Hayes UB4 **102** D4
★**Brentford FC**, Brent. TW8 **125** G6
Brent Grn, NW4 **71** J5
Brent Grn Wk, Wem. HA9 **88** C3
Brentham Way, W5 **105** G4
Brenthouse Rd, E9 **95** E7
Brenthurst Rd, NW10 **89** F5
Brent Lea, Brent. TW8 **125** F7
Brentmead Cl, W7 **104** B7
Brentmead Gdns, NW10 **105** J2
Brentmead Pl, NW11
off North Circular Rd **72** A6
Brenton St, E14 **113** H6
Brent Pk, NW10 **88** D5
Brent Pk Rd, NW4 **71** H7
NW9 **89** G1
Brent Pl, Barn. EN5 **40** D5
Brent Rd, E16 **115** G5
SE18 **136** E7
Brentford TW8 **125** F6
Southall UB2 **122** C3
Brent Side, Brent. TW8 **125** F6
Brentside Cl, W13 **104** D4
Brentside Executive Cen, Brent. TW8 **125** E6
Brent St, NW4 **71** J4
Brent Ter, NW2 **89** J2
Brentvale Av, Sthl. UB1 **124** A1
Wembley HA0 **105** J1
Brent Vw Rd, NW9 **71** G7
Brent Way, N3 **56** D6
Brentford TW8 **125** G7
Wembley HA9 **88** B6
Brentwick Gdns, Brent. TW8 **125** H4
Brentwood Cl, SE9 **175** F1
Brentwood Ho, SE18
off Shooter's Hill Rd **136** A7
Brereton Rd, N17 **60** C7
Bressenden Pl, SW1 **25** E5
Bressey Av, Enf. EN1 **44** D1
Bressey Gro, E18 **79** F2
Brett Cl, N16
off Yoakley Rd **94** B2
Northolt UB5
off Broomcroft Av **102** D3
Brett Ct, N9 **61** F2
Brett Cres, NW10 **88** D7
Brettell St, SE17 **36** C4
Brettenham Av, E17 **78** A1
Brettenham Rd, E17 **78** A2
N18 **60** E4
Brett Gdns, Dag. RM9 **100** E7
Brett Ho Cl, SW15
off Putney Heath La **148** A6
Brett Pas, E8
off Kenmure Rd **94/95** E5
Brett Rd, E8 **95** E5
Barnet EN5 **39** J5
Brewer's Grn, SW1 **25** H5
Brewers Hall Gdns, EC2 **20** A2
Brewers La, Rich. TW9 **145** G5
Brewer St, W1 **17** G5
★**Brewery, The**, EC1 **20** A1
Brewery Cl, Wem. HA0 **86** D5
Brewery La, Twick. TW1 **144** C7
Brewery Rd, N7 **92** E7
SE18 **137** G5
Bromley BR2 **206** B1
Brewery Sq, EC1 **11** H5
SE1
off Horselydown La **132** C1
Brewhouse La, E1 **133** E1
SW15 **148** B3
Brewhouse Rd, SE18 **136** C4
Brewhouse Wk, SE16 **133** H1
Brewhouse Yd, EC1 **11** H5
Brewood Rd, Dag. RM8 **100** B6
Brewster Gdns, W10 **107** J5
Brewster Ho, E14 **113** J7
Brewster Rd, E10 **96** B1
Brian Rd, Rom. RM6 **82** C5
Briants Cl, Pnr. HA5 **67** F2
Briant St, SE14 **153** G1
Briar Av, SW16 **169** F7
Briarbank Rd, W13 **104** D6
Briar Cl, N2 **73** E3
N13 **59** J3
Buckhurst Hill IG9 **64** A2
Hampton TW12 **101** F5
Isleworth TW7 **144** C5
Briar Ct, Sutt. SM3 **197** J4
Briar Cres, Nthlt. UB5 **85** H6
Briardale Gdns, NW3 **90** D3
Briarfield Av, N3 **72** E2
Briarfield Cl, Bexh. DA7
off Palmar Rd **159** G2
Briar Gdns, Brom. BR2 **205** F1
Briaris Cl, N17 **60** E7
Briar La, Croy. CR0 **204** B4
Briar Pas, SW16 **187** E3
Briar Pl, SW16 **187** F3
Briar Rd, NW2 **89** J4
SW16 **187** E3
Harrow HA3 **69** F5
Twickenham TW2 **162** B1
Briarswood Way, Orp. BR6 **207** J5
Briar Wk, SW15 **147** H4
W10 *off Droop St* **108** B4
Edgware HA8 **54** C7
Briar Way, West Dr. UB7 **120** D2
Briarwood Cl, NW9 **70** C6
Briarwood Dr, Nthwd. HA6 **66** A2
Briarwood Rd, SW4 **150** D5
Epsom KT17 **197** G6
Briary Cl, NW3
off Fellows Rd **91** H7
Briary Ct, E16
off Turner St **115** F6
Sidcup DA14 **176** B5
Briary Gdns, Brom. BR1 **173** H5
Briary Gro, Edg. HA8 **70** B2
Briary La, N9 **60** C3
Brick Ct, EC4 **18** E4
Brick Fm Cl, Rich. TW9 **146** B1
Brickfield Cl, Brent. TW8 **125** F7
Brickfield Cotts, SE18 **137** J6
Brickfield Fm Gdns, Orp. BR6 **207** F4
Brickfield La, Barn. EN5 **39** F6
Hayes UB3 **121** G6
Brickfield Rd, SW19 **167** E4
Thornton Heath CR7 **187** H1
Brickfields, Har. HA2 **86** A2
Brickfields Way, West Dr. UB7 **120** C3
Brick La, E1 **13** G5
E2 **13** G4
Enfield EN1, EN3 **44** E2
Stanmore HA7
off Honeypot La **53** G7
Bricklayer's Arms Distribution Cen, SE1 **36** E2
Bricklayer's Arms Roundabout, SE1 **36** B1
Brick St, W1 **24** D2
Brickwood Cl, SE26 **171** E3
Brickwood Rd, Croy. CR0 **202** B2
Brideale Cl, SE15 **37** G6
Bride Ct, EC4 **19** G4
Bride La, EC4 **19** G4
Bridel Ms, N1
off Colebrooke Row **111** H1
Brides Pl, N1
off De Beauvoir Rd **94** B7
Bride St, N7 **93** F6
Bridewain St, SE1 **29** F5
Bridewell Pl, E1
off Brewhouse La **132/133** E1
EC4 **19** G4
Bridford Ms, W1 **16** E1
Bridge, The, Har. HA3 **68** B3
Bridge App, NW1 **92** A7
Bridge Av, W6 **127** J5
W7 **104** A5
Bridge Cl, W10
off Kingsdown Cl **108** A6
Enfield EN1 **45** E2
Teddington TW11
off Shacklegate La. **162** C4
Bridge Ct, E14
off Newport Av **114** D7
Bridge Dr, N13 **59** F4
Bridge End, E17 **78** C1
Bridgefield Rd, Sutt. SM1 **198** D6
Bridgefoot, SE1 **34** A4
Bridge Gdns, N16
off Green Las **94** A4
East Molesey KT8 **180** A4
Bridge Gate, N21
off Ridge Av **43** J7
Bridge Ho Quay, E14
off Prestons Rd **134** C1
Bridgeland Rd, E16 **115** G7
Bridge La, NW11 **72** B5
SW11 **149** H1
Bridgeman Rd, N1 **93** F7
Teddington TW11 **162** D6
Bridgeman St, NW8 **7** G2
Bridge Meadows, SE14 **133** G6
Bridgend Rd, SW18 **149** F4
Bridgenhall Rd, Enf. EN1 **44** C1
Bridgen Rd, Bex. DA5 **158** E6
Bridge Pk, SW18 **148** D5
Bridge Pl, SW1 **33** E1
Croydon CR0 **188** A7
Bridgeport Pl, E1 **29** J1
Bridge Rd, E6 **98** C7
E15 **96** D7
E17 **77** J7
N9 *off The Broadway* **60** D3
N22 **74** E1
NW10 **88** E6
Beckenham BR3 **171** J7
Bexleyheath DA7 **159** E2
Chessington KT9 **195** H5
East Molesey KT8 **180** B4
Hounslow TW3 **144** A2
Isleworth TW7 **144** A3
Southall UB2 **123** F2
Sutton SM2 **199** E6
Twickenham TW1 **144** E6
Wallington SM6 **200** C5
Wembley HA9 **88** A3
Bridge Row, Croy. CR0
off Cross Rd **202** A1
Bridges Ct, SW11 **149** G3
Bridges La, Croy. CR0 **200** E4
Bridges Pl, SW6 **148** C1
Bridges Rd, SW19 **166** E6
Stanmore HA7 **52** C5
Bridges Rd Ms, SW19
off Bridges Rd **166/167** E6
Bridge St, SW1 **26** A4
W4 **126** D4
Pinner HA5 **66** D3
Richmond TW9 **145** G5
Bridge Ter, E15
off Bridge Rd. **96** D7
SE13 *off Mercator Rd* **154** D4
Bridgetown Cl, SE19
off St. Kitts Ter. **170** B5
Bridge Vw, W6 **127** J5
Bridgeview Ct, Ilf. IG6 **65** G6
Bridgewater Cl, Chis. BR7 **193** H3
Bridgewater Gdns, Edg. HA8 **69** J2
Bridgewater Rd, Ruis. HA4 **84** A4
Wembley HA0 **87** F7
Bridgewater Sq, EC2 **19** J1
Bridgewater St, EC2 **19** J1
Bridge Way, N11
off Pymmes Grn Rd **58** C3
NW11 **72** C5
Bridgeway, Bark. IG11 **99** J7
Bridge Way, Twick. TW2 **143** J7
Bridgeway, Wem. HA0 **87** H7
Bridgeway St, NW1 **9** H2
Bridge Wf Rd, Islw. TW7
off Church St **144/145** E3
Bridgewood Cl, SE20 **170** E7
Bridgewood Rd, SW16 **168** D7
Worcester Park KT4 **197** G4
Bridge Yd, SE1 **28** C1
Bridgford St, SW18 **167** F3
Bridgman Rd, W4 **126** C3
Bridgwater Rd, E15 **114** C1
Bridle Cl, Epsom KT19 **196** D5
Kingston upon Thames KT1 **181** G4
Sunbury-on-Thames TW16 *off Forge La.* **178** A3
Bridle La, W1 **17** G6
Twickenham TW1
off Crown Rd **144/145** E6
Bridle Path, Croy. CR0 **201** F3
Bridle Path, The, Wdf.Grn. IG8 **62** E7
Bridle Rd, Croy. CR0 **204** A3
Esher (Clay.) KT10 **194** E6
Pinner HA5 **66** C6
Bridle Way, Croy. CR0 **204** A5
Orpington BR6 **207** F1
Bridleway, The, Wall. SM6 **200** C4
Bridlington Rd, N9 **44** E7
Watford WD19 **50** D3
Bridport Av, Rom. RM7 **83** H6
Bridport Pl, N1 **12** C1
Bridport Rd, N18 **60** B5
Greenford UB6 **103** H1
Thornton Heath CR7 **187** G3
Bridport Ter, SW8
off Wandsworth Rd **150** D1
Bridstow Pl, W2
off Talbot Rd **108** D6
Brief St, SE5 **151** H1
Brierley, Croy. (New Adgtn) CR0 **204** B6
Brierley Av, N9 **61** F1
Brierley Cl, SE25 **188** D4
Brierley Rd, E11 **96** D4
SW12 **168** C2
Brierly Gdns, E2
off Royston St **113** F2
Brigade Cl, Har. HA2 **86** A2
Brigade St, SE3
off Royal Par **155** F2
Brigadier Av, Enf. EN2 **43** J1
Briggeford Cl, E5
off Geldeston Rd. **94** D2
Briggs Cl, Mitch. CR4 **186** B1
Bright Cl, Belv. DA17 **138** D4
Brightfield Rd, SE12 **155** F5
Brightling Rd, SE4 **153** J6
Brightlingsea Pl, E14 **113** J7
Brightman Rd, SW18 **167** G1
Brighton Av, E17 **77** J5
Brighton Dr, Nthlt. UB5 **85** G6
Brighton Gro, SE14
off Harts La **153** H1
Brighton Rd, E6 **116** D3
N2 **73** F2
N16 **94** B4
South Croydon CR2 **201** J5

Brighton Rd, Surb. KT6 . . 181 F6
Brighton Ter, SW9 . . . . . . 151 F4
Brightside, The, Enf. EN3 . . 45 G1
Brightside Rd, SE13 . . . . . 154 D6
Bright St, E14 . . . . 114 B6
Brightwell Cl, Croy. CR0
off Sumner Rd 201 G1
Brightwell Cres, SW17 . . . 167 J5
Brig Ms, SE8
off Watergate St 134 A6
Brigstock Rd, Belv. DA17 . 139 H4
Thornton Heath CR7 . . . 187 G5
Brill Pl, NW1 . . . . 9 J2
Brim Hill, N2 . . . . 73 F4
Brimpsfield Cl, SE2 . . . . . 138 B3
BRIMSDOWN, Enf. EN3 . . . 45 H3
Brimsdown Av, Enf. EN3 . . 45 H2
Brimsdown Ind Est, Enf.
EN3 . . . . 45 J2
Brindle Gate, Sid. DA15 . . 175 H1
Brindley Cl, Bexh. DA7 . . . 159 H3
Wembley HA0 . . . . 105 F1
Brindley Ho, SW2
off New Pk Rd . . . 150/151 E7
Brindley St, SE14 . . . . 153 J1
Brindley Way, Brom.
BR1 . . . . 173 G5
Southall UB1 . . . . 103 H7
Brindwood Rd, E4 . . . . 61 J3
Brinkburn Cl, SE2 . . . . 138 A4
Edgware HA8 . . . . 70 B2
Brinkburn Gdns, Edg.
HA8 . . . . 70 A3
Brinkley, Kings.T. KT1
off Burritt Rd 182 A2
Brinkley Rd, Wor.Pk.
KT4 . . . . 197 H2
Brinklow Cres, SE18 . . . . . 137 E7
Brinklow Ho, W2 . . . . 14 A1
Brinkworth Rd, Ilf. IG5 . . . . 80 B3
Brinkworth Way, E9 . . . . . . 95 J6
Brinsdale Rd, NW4 . . . . 72 A4
Brinsley Rd, Har. HA3 . . . . . 68 A2
Brinsley St, E1
off Watney St 112/113 E6
Brinsworth Cl, Twick.
TW2 . . . . 162 A2
Brinton Wk, SE1 . . . . 27 G2
Brion Pl, E14 . . . . 114 C5
Brisbane Av, SW19 . . . . . . 184 E1
Brisbane Ct, N10
off Sydney Rd 58 B7
Brisbane Rd, E10 . . . . 96 B2
W13 . . . . 124 D2
Ilford IG1 . . . . 81 E7
Brisbane St, SE5 . . . . 132 A7
Briscoe Cl, E11 . . . . 97 F2
Briscoe Rd, SW19 . . . . 167 G6
Briset Rd, SE9 . . . . 156 A3
Briset St, EC1 . . . . 19 G1
Briset Way, N7 . . . . 93 F2
Bristol Cl, Stai. (Stanw.)
TW19 . . . . 140 B6
Wallington SM6 . . . . . . 200 E7
Bristol Gdns, SW15
off Portsmouth Rd 147 J7
W9 . . . . 6 B6
Bristol Ms, W9 . . . . 6 B6
Bristol Pk Rd, E17 . . . . 77 H4
Bristol Rd, E7 . . . . 97 J6
Greenford UB6 . . . . 103 H1
Morden SM4 . . . . 185 F5
Briston Gro, N8 . . . . 75 E6
Briston Ms, NW7 . . . . 55 G7
Bristowe Cl, SW2
off Tulse Hill 151 G6
Bristow Rd, SE19 . . . . 170 B5
Bexleyheath DA7 . . . . . 159 E1
Croydon CR0 . . . . 200 E4
Hounslow TW3 . . . . 143 J3
★**Britain at War Experience**,
SE1 . . . . 28 D2
Britannia Cl, SW4
off Bowland Rd 150 D4
Northolt UB5 . . . . 102 D3
Britannia Gate, E16 . . . . . 135 G1
Britannia La, Twick. TW2 . . 143 J7
Britannia Rd, E14 . . . . 134 A4
N12 . . . . 57 F3
SW6 . . . . 128 E7
Ilford IG1 . . . . 98 E3
Surbiton KT5 . . . . 181 J7
Britannia Row, N1 . . . . . . 111 H1
Britannia St, WC1 . . . . 10 C3
Britannia Wk, N1 . . . . 12 B3
Britannia Way, NW10 . . . . 106 B4
SW6 *off Britannia*
Rd 148/149 E1
Staines (Stanw.) TW19 . 140 A7
★**British Dental Assoc Mus**,
W1 . . . . 16 D2
British Gro, W4 . . . . 127 F5
British Gro Pas, W4 . . . . . 127 F5
British Gro S, W4
off British Gro Pas 127 F5
British Legion Rd, E4 . . . . . 63 F2
★**British Lib**, NW1 . . . . 9 J3
★**British Lib Newspaper** . . . .
Collection, NW9 . . . . 70 E3
★**British Med Assoc**, WC1 . . 9 J5
★**British Mus**, WC1 . . . . . . 18 A2
★**British Red Cross Mus &** . .
Archives, SW1 . . . . 24 B4
British St, E3 . . . . 113 J3
Brittain Rd, Dag. RM8 . . . 101 E3
Britten Cl, NW11 . . . . 90 E1
Brittenden Cl, Orp. BR6 . . 207 H6
Brittenden Par, Orp. BR6
off Glentrammon Rd . . 207 J6
Britten Dr, Sthl. UB1 . . . . 103 G6
Britten St, SW3 . . . . 31 G4
Britton Cl, SE6
off Brownhill Rd 154 D7
Britton St, EC1 . . . . 11 G6
Brixham Cres, Ruis. HA4 . . 84 A1
Brixham Gdns, Ilf. IG3 . . . . 99 H5
Brixham Rd, Well. DA16 . . 158 D1
Brixham St, E16 . . . . 136 C1
BRIXTON, SW2 . . . . 151 E4
★**Brixton Acad, The**,
SW9 . . . . 151 F3
Brixton Est, Edg. HA8 . . . . 70 B2
Brixton Hill, SW2 . . . . 151 E7
Brixton Hill Pl, SW2
off Brixton Hill . . . 150/151 E7
Brixton Oval, SW2 . . . . . . 151 G4
Brixton Rd, SW9 . . . . 151 G2
Brixton Sta Rd, SW9 . . . . 151 G4
Brixton Water La, SW2 . . . 151 F5
Broadbent Cl, N6 . . . . 92 B1
Broadbent St, W1 . . . . 16 D5
Broadberry Ct, N18 . . . . . . 60 E5
Broadbridge Cl, SE3 . . . . . 135 G7
Broadcoombe, S.Croy.
CR2 . . . . 203 F7
Broad Ct, WC2 . . . . 18 B4
Broadcroft Av, Stan. HA7 . . 69 G2
Broadcroft Rd, Orp. BR5 . 193 G7
Broadeaves Cl, S.Croy.
CR2 . . . . 202 B5
Broadfield Cl, NW2 . . . . . . 89 J3
Croydon CR0
off Progress Way 201 F2
Broadfield Ct, Bushey
(Bushey Hth) WD23 . . . 52 B2
Broadfield La, NW1 . . . . . . 92 E7
Broadfield Rd, SE6 . . . . . . 154 E7
Broadfields, E.Mol. KT8 . . 180 A6
Harrow HA2 . . . . 67 H2
Broadfields Av, N21 . . . . . . 43 G7
Edgware HA8 . . . . 54 B4
Broadfields Hts, Edg. HA8 . 54 B4
Broadfields La, Wat.
WD19 . . . . 50 B1
Broadfield Sq, Enf. EN1 . . . 45 E2
Broadfields Way, NW10 . . . 89 F5
Broadfield Way, Buck.H.
IG9 . . . . 63 J3
BROADGATE, EC2 . . . . 20 C1
Broadgate, E13 . . . . 115 J2
EC2 *off Liverpool St* . . . 112 B5
Broadgate Circle, EC2 . . . . 20 D1
Broadgate Rd, E16 . . . . . . 116 A6
Broadgates Av, Barn.
EN4 . . . . 41 E1
Broadgates Rd, SW18
off Ellerton Rd 167 G1
BROAD GREEN, Croy.
CR0 . . . . 187 G6
Broad Grn Av, Croy. CR0 . 187 H7
Broadhead Strand, NW9 . . 71 F1
Broadheath Dr, Chis.
BR7 . . . . 174 C5
Broadhinton Rd, SW4 . . . 150 B3
Broadhurst Av, Edg. HA8 . . 54 B4
Ilford IG3 . . . . 99 J4
Broadhurst Cl, NW6
off Broadhurst Gdns . . . 91 F6
Richmond TW10
off Lower Gro Rd 145 J5
Broadhurst Gdns, NW6 . . . 90 E6
Chigwell IG7 . . . . 65 F4
Ruislip HA4 . . . . 84 C2
Broadlands, Felt. TW13 . . 161 F3
Broadlands Av, SW16 . . . . 168 E2
Enfield EN3 . . . . 45 E3
Broadlands Cl, N6 . . . . 74 A7
SW16 . . . . 168 E2
Broadlands Cl, Enf. EN3 . . . 45 E3
Broadlands Rd, N6 . . . . 73 J7
Bromley BR1 . . . . 173 H4
Broadlands Way, N.Mal.
KT3 . . . . 183 F6
Broad La, EC2 . . . . 20 D1
N8 *off Tottenham La* 75 F5
N15 . . . . 76 C4
Hampton TW12 . . . . 161 G6
Broad Lawn, SE9 . . . . 174 D2
Broadlawns Ct, Har. HA3 . . 68 C1
Broadley St, NW8 . . . . 15 F1
Broadley Ter, NW1 . . . . 7 H6
Broadmayne, SE17 . . . . 36 B3
Broadmead, SE6 . . . . 172 A3
Broadmead Av, Wor.Pk.
KT4 . . . . 183 G7
Broadmead Cl, Hmptn.
TW12 . . . . 161 G6
Pinner HA5 . . . . 51 E7
Broadmead Rd, Hayes
UB4 . . . . 102 E4
Northolt UB5 . . . . 102 E4
Woodford Green IG8 . . . 63 G6
Broad Oak, Wdf.Grn. IG8 . . 63 H5
Broad Oak Cl, E4 . . . . 62 A5
Broadoaks, Surb. KT6 . . . 196 B1
Broadoaks Way, Brom.
BR2 . . . . 191 F5
Broad Sanctuary, SW1 . . . 25 J4
Broadstone Pl, W1 . . . . 16 B2
Broad St, Dag. RM10 . . . . 101 G7
Teddington TW11 . . . . . . 162 C6
Broad St Av, EC2 . . . . 20 D2
Broad St Pl, EC2 . . . . 20 C2
Broad Vw, NW9 . . . . 70 A6
Broadview Rd, SW16 . . . . 168 D7
Broadwalk, E18 . . . . 79 F3
Broad Wk, N21 . . . . 59 F2
NW1 . . . . 8 D4
SE3 . . . . 155 J3
W1 . . . . 24 B1
Broadwalk, Har. HA2 . . . . . 67 G5
Broad Wk, Houns. TW5 . . 142 D1
Richmond TW9 . . . . 125 J7
Broad Wk, The, W8 . . . . . . 14 B6
East Molesey KT8 . . . . . 180 C3
Broadwalk Ct, W8 . . . . . . 128 D1
Broad Wk La, NW11 . . . . . . 72 C7
Broadwalk Shop Cen,
Edg. HA8 . . . . 54 B6
Broadwall, SE1 . . . . 27 F1
Broadwater Fm Est, N17 . . 76 A2
Broadwater Gdns, Orp.
BR6 . . . . 207 E4
Broadwater Rd, N17 . . . . . 76 B1
SE28 . . . . 137 G3
SW17 . . . . 167 H4
Broadway, E15 . . . . 96 D7
SW1 . . . . 25 H5
Barking IG11 . . . . 99 F7
Bexleyheath DA6 . . . . . 159 E4
Broadway, The, E4 . . . . 62 C6
E13 . . . . 115 H2
N8 . . . . 74 E6
N9 . . . . 60 D3
N14
off Winchmore Hill Rd . . 58 D1
N22 . . . . 75 G2
NW7 . . . . 55 F5
SW13 *off The*
Terrace 146/147 E2
SW19 . . . . 166 C6
W5 . . . . 105 G7
W7 *off Cherington Rd* . . 124 B1
W7 (W.Ealing) 124 D1
W13 . . . . 124 D1
Broadway, The,
Croydon CR0
off Croydon Rd . . 200/201 E4
Dagenham RM8 . . . . . . 101 F2
Greenford UB6 . . . . 103 J4
Harrow HA2 . . . . 68 B2
Loughton IG10 . . . . 49 F4
Pinner HA5 . . . . 51 F7
Southall UB1 . . . . 102 D7
Stanmore HA7 . . . . 53 F5
Sutton SM1
off Manor La 199 F5
Sutton (Cheam) SM3 . . 198 B6
Thames Ditton KT7
off Hampton Ct Way . . 194 B1
Wembley HA9
off East La 87 H3
Woodford Green IG8 . . . 63 H6
Broadway Av, Croy. CR0 . 188 A5
Twickenham TW1 . . . . . 144 E6
Broadway Cl, Wdf.Grn.
IG8 . . . . 63 H6
Broadway Ct, SW19
off The Broadway 166 D6
Broadway Gdns, Mitch.
CR4 . . . . 185 H4
Broadway Ho, Brom. BR1
off Elmfield Pk 191 G3
Broadway Mkt, E8 . . . . . . 112 E1
Broadway Mkt Ms, E8
off Regents Row 112 D1
Broadway Ms, E5 . . . . 76 C7
N13 *off Elmdale Rd* 59 F5
N21 *off Compton Rd* 59 H1
Broadway Par, N8 . . . . 74 E6
Hayes UB3
off Coldharbour La . . . 122 A1
Broadway Pl, SW19
off Hartfield Rd 166 C6
Broadway Shop Cen, W6 *off*
Hammersmith Bdy . . . 127 J4
Bexleyheath DA6 . . . . . 159 G4
Broadwick St, W1 . . . . 17 G5
Broadwood Ter, W8
off Pembroke Rd 128 C4
Broad Yd, EC1 . . . . 11 G6
Brocas Cl, NW3
off Fellows Rd 91 H7
Brockbridge Ho, SW15
off Tangley Gro 147 F6
Brockdish Av, Bark. IG11 . . 99 J5
Brockenhurst, W.Mol.
KT8 . . . . 179 F6
Brockenhurst Av, Wor.Pk.
KT4 . . . . 197 E1
Brockenhurst Gdns,
NW7 . . . . 55 E5
Ilford IG1 . . . . 99 F5
Brockenhurst Ms, N18
off Lyndhurst Rd 60 D4
Brockenhurst Rd, Croy.
CR0 . . . . 188 E7
Brockenhurst Way,
SW16 . . . . 186 D2
Brocket Cl, Chig. IG7
off Burrow Rd 65 J5
Brocket Way, Chig. IG7 . . . 65 H5
Brockham Cl, SW19 . . . . . 166 C5
Brockham Cres, Croy.
(New Adgtn) CR0 . . . . 204 D7
Brockham Dr, SW2
off Fairview Pl 151 F7
Ilford IG2 . . . . 81 E6
Brockham St, SE1 . . . . 28 A5
Brockhurst Cl, Stan. HA7 . . 52 C6
Brockill Cres, SE4 . . . . 153 H4
Brocklebank Rd, SE7 . . . . 135 H4
SW18 . . . . 149 F7
Brocklehurst St, SE14 . . . 133 G7
Brocklesby Rd, SE25 . . . . 188 E4
BROCKLEY, SE4 . . . . 153 H5
Brockley Av, Stan. HA7 . . . 53 H3
Brockley Cl, Stan. HA7 . . . . 53 H4
Brockley Cross, SE4
off Endwell Rd 153 H3
Brockley Footpath, SE15 . 153 F4
Brockley Gdns, SE4 . . . . . 153 J2
Brockley Gro, SE4 . . . . . . 153 J5
Brockley Hall Rd, SE4 . . . 153 H6
Brockley Hill, Stan. HA7 . . . 53 F1
Brockley Ms, SE4 . . . . 153 H5
Brockley Pk, SE23 . . . . . . 153 H7
Brockley Ri, SE23 . . . . 153 H6
Brockley Rd, SE4 . . . . 153 J3
Brockleyside, Stan. HA7 . . 53 G4
Brockley Vw, SE23 . . . . . . 153 H7
Brockley Way, SE4 . . . . . . 153 G5
Brockman Ri, Brom. BR1 . 172 D4
Brock Pl, E3 . . . . 114 B4
Brock Rd, E13 . . . . 115 H5
Brocks Dr, Sutt. SM3 . . . . 198 B3
Brockshot Cl, Brent. TW8 . 125 G6
Brock St, SE15
off Evelina Rd 153 F3
Brockway Cl, E11 . . . . 97 E1
Brockwell Av, Beck. BR3 . 190 B5
Brockwell Cl, Orp. BR5 . . 193 J5
★**Brockwell Park**, SE24 . . 151 H6
Brockwell Pk Gdns, SE24 . 151 G7
Brockwell Pk Row, SW2 . 151 G6
Brodewater Rd, Borwd.
WD6 . . . . 38 B2
Brodia Rd, N16 . . . . 94 B3
Brodie Rd, E4 . . . . 62 C1
Brodie St, SE1 . . . . 37 G3
Brodlove La, E1 . . . . 113 G7
Brodrick Gro, SE2 . . . . . . 138 B4
Brodrick Rd, SW17 . . . . . . 167 H2
Brograve Gdns, Beck.
BR3 . . . . 190 B2
Broken Wf, EC4 . . . . 19 J5

Brokesley St, E3 113 J4
Broke Wk, E8 112 D1
Bromar Rd, SE5 152 B3
Bromborough Grn, Wat. WD19 50 C5
Bromefield, Stan. HA7 69 F1
Bromehead Rd, E1 113 F6
Bromehead St, E1 *off Commercial Rd* 113 F6
Bromell's Rd, SW4 150 C4
Brome Rd, SE9 156 C3
Bromfelde Rd, SW4 150 D2
Bromfelde Wk, SW4 150 D2
Bromfield St, N1 11 F1
Bromhall Rd, Dag. RM8, RM9 100 B6
Bromhedge, SE9 174 C3
Bromholm Rd, SE2 138 B3
Bromleigh Ct, SE23 *off Lapse Wd Wk* 170/171 E2
BROMLEY, E3 114 B4
BROMLEY, BR1 & BR2 191 F2
Bromley Av, Brom. BR1 173 E7
BROMLEY COMMON, Brom. BR2 192 C7
Bromley Common, Brom. BR2 191 J4
Bromley Cres, Brom. BR2 191 F3
Bromley Gdns, Brom. BR2 191 F3
Bromley Gro, Brom. BR2 190 D2
Bromley Hall Rd, E14 114 C5
Bromley High St, E3 114 B3
Bromley Hill, Brom. BR1 172 E5
Bromley La, Chis. BR7 175 F7
Bromley Mall, The, Brom. BR1 191 G3
BROMLEY PARK, Brom. BR1 190 E1
Bromley Pk, Brom. BR1 *off London Rd* 191 F1
Bromley Pl, W1 17 F1
Bromley Rd, E10 78 B6
E17 78 A2
N17 76 C1
N18 60 A3
SE6 172 B1
Beckenham BR3 190 B1
Bromley (Downham) BR1 172 C4
Bromley (Short.) BR2 190 C2
Chislehurst BR7 192 E1
Bromley St, E1 113 G5
BROMPTON, SW3 23 G6
Brompton Arc, SW3 23 J4
Brompton Cl, SE20 *off Selby Rd* 188 D2
Hounslow TW4 143 F6
Brompton Gro, N2 73 H4
★**Brompton Oratory**, SW7 23 G6
Brompton Pk Cres, SW6 30 A6
Brompton Pl, SW3 23 H5
Brompton Rd, SW1 23 H5
SW3 31 G1
SW7 23 H5
Brompton Sq, SW3 23 G5
Brompton Ter, SE18 *off Prince Imperial Rd* 156 D1
Bromwich Av, N6 92 A2
Bromyard Av, W3 127 E1
Bromyard Ho, SE15 132 E7
BRONDESBURY, NW2 90 B7
Brondesbury Ct, NW2 89 J6
Brondesbury Ms, NW6 *off Willesden La* 90 D7
BRONDESBURY PARK, NW6 89 J7
Brondesbury Pk, NW2 89 H6
NW6 90 A7
Brondesbury Rd, NW6 108 C2
Brondesbury Vil, NW6 108 C2
Bronsart Rd, SW6 128 B7
Bronson Rd, SW20 184 A2
Bronte Cl, E7 *off Bective Rd* 97 G4
Erith DA8 139 H7
Ilford IG2 80 D5
Bronte Ho, NW6 108 D3
Bronti Cl, SE17 36 A4
Bronze Age Way, Belv. DA17 139 J3
Erith DA8 139 J3
Bronze St, SE8 134 A7
Brook Av, Dag. RM10 101 H7
Edgware HA8 54 B6
Wembley HA9 88 A3
Brookbank Av, W7 104 A5
Brookbank Rd, SE13 154 A3
Brook Cl, NW7 *off Frith Ct* 56 B7
SW17 168 A2
SW20 183 H3
W3 *off West Lo Av* 126 A1
Borehamwood WD6 38 B3
Staines (Stanw.) TW19 140 C7
Brook Ct, Buck.H. IG9 63 H1
Brook Cres, E4 62 A4
N9 60 E4
Brookdale, N11 58 C4
Brookdale Rd, E17 78 A3
SE6 154 B6
Bexley DA5 159 E6
Brookdene Rd, SE18 137 J4
Brook Dr, SE11 27 F6
Harrow HA1 67 J4
Brooke Av, Har. HA2 85 J3
Brookehowse Rd, SE6 172 B3
Brookend Rd, Sid. DA15 175 H1
Brooke Rd, E5 94 D3
E17 78 C4
N16 94 C3
Brooke's Ct, EC1 19 E1
Brookes Mkt, EC1 19 F1
Brooke St, EC1 19 E2
Brookfield, N6 92 A3
Brookfield Av, E17 78 C4
NW7 55 H6
W5 105 G4
Sutton SM1 199 G4
Brookfield Cl, NW7 55 H6
Brookfield Ct, Grnf. UB6 103 J3
Harrow HA3 69 G5
Brookfield Cres, NW7 55 H6
Harrow HA3 69 H5
Brookfield Gdns, Esher (Clay.) KT10 194 C6
Brookfield Pk, NW5 92 B3
Brookfield Path, Wdf.Grn. IG8 62 E6
Brookfield Rd, E9 95 H6
N9 60 D3
W4 126 D2
Brookfields, Enf. EN3 45 G4
Brookfields Av, Mitch. CR4 185 H5
Brook Gdns, E4 62 B4
SW13 147 F3
Kingston upon Thames KT2 182 C1
Brook Gate, W1 16 A6
Brook Grn, W6 128 A4
Brookhill Cl, SE18 136 E5
Barnet EN4 41 H5
Brookhill Rd, SE18 136 E5
Barnet EN4 41 H5
Brookhouse Gdns, E4 62 E4
Brook Ind Est, Hayes UB4 122 D1
Brooking Cl, Dag. RM8 100 C3
Brooking Rd, E7 97 G5
Brookland Cl, NW11 72 D4
Brookland Garth, NW11 72 E4
Brookland Hill, NW11 72 D4
Brookland Ri, NW11 72 D4
Brooklands Av, SW19 166 E2
Sidcup DA15 175 G2
Brooklands Dr, Grnf. UB6 105 G1
Brooklands Pk, SE3 155 G3
Brooklands Pas, SW8 *off Belmore St* 150 D1
Brooklands Rd, T.Ditt. KT7 194 C1
Brook La, SE3 155 H2
Bexley DA5 158 D6
Bromley BR1 173 G6
Brook La N, Brent. TW8 125 G5
Brooklea Cl, NW9 71 E1
Brooklyn Av, SE25 189 E4
Loughton IG10 48 B4
Brooklyn Cl, Cars. SM5 199 H2
Brooklyn Gro, SE25 189 E4
Brooklyn Rd, SE25 188 E4
Bromley BR2 192 A5
Brooklyn Way, West Dr. UB7 120 A3
Brookmarsh Ind Est, SE10 *off Norman Rd* 134 B7
Brook Mead, Epsom KT19 197 E6
Brookmead Av, Brom. BR1 192 C5
Brook Meadow, N12 56 E4
Brook Meadow Cl, Wdf.Grn. IG8 62 E6
Brookmead Rd, Croy. CR0 186 C6
Brookmeads Est, Mitch. CR4 185 H5
Brook Ms N, W2 14 D5
Brookmill Rd, SE8 154 A1
Brook Par, Chig. IG7 *off High Rd* 64/65 E3
Brook Pk Cl, N21 43 H6
Brook Path, Loug. IG10 48 B4
Brook Pl, Barn. EN5 40 D5
Brook Ri, Chig. IG7 64 D3
Brook Rd, N8 74 E4
N22 75 F3
NW2 89 G2
Borehamwood WD6 38 A2
Buckhurst Hill IG9 63 G2
Ilford IG2 81 H6
Loughton IG10 48 B5
Surbiton KT6 195 H2
Thornton Heath CR7 187 J4
Twickenham TW1 144 D6
Brook Rd S, Brent. TW8 125 G6
Brooks Av, E6 116 C4
Brooksbank St, E9 95 F6
Brooksby Ms, N1 *off Brooksby St* 93 G7
Brooksby St, N1 93 G7
Brooksby's Wk, E9 95 G5
Brooks Cl, SE9 174 D2
Brooks Ct, E15 *off Clays La* 96 B5
Brookscroft Rd, E17 78 B1
Brookshill, Har. HA3 52 A5
Brookshill Av, Har. HA3 52 A5
Brookshill Dr, Har. HA3 52 A5
Brookshill Gate, Har. (Har.Wld) HA3 52 A5
Brookside, N21 43 F6
Barnet EN4 41 H6
Carshalton SM5 200 A5
Ilford IG6 65 F6
Orpington BR6 193 J7
Brookside Cl, Barn. EN5 40 B6
Feltham TW13 *off Sycamore Cl* 160 A3
Harrow (Kenton) HA2 60 C6
Harrow (S.Har.) HA3 85 E4
Brookside Cres, Wor.Pk. KT4 *off Green La* 197 G1
Brookside Rd, N9 60 E4
N19 92 C2
NW11 72 B6
Hayes UB4 102 C7
Brookside S, Barn. EN4 42 A7
Brookside Wk, N3 72 B2
N12 56 D6
NW4 72 B4
NW11 72 B4
Brookside Way, Croy. CR0 189 G6
Brooks La, W4 126 A6
Brook's Ms, W1 16 D5
Brook Sq, SE18 *off Shooter's Hill Rd* 156 B1
Brooks Rd, E13 115 G1
W4 126 A6
Brook St, N17 *off High Rd* 76 C2
W1 16 C5
W2 15 F5
Belvedere DA17 139 H5
Erith DA8 139 H6
Kingston upon Thames KT1 181 H2
Brooksville Av, NW6 108 B1
Brook Vale, Erith DA8 159 H1
Brookview Rd, SW16 168 C5
Brookville Rd, SW6 128 C7
Brook Wk, N2 73 G1
Edgware HA8 54 D6
Brookway, SE3 155 G3
Brook Way, Chig. IG7 64 D3
Brookwood Av, SW13 147 F3
Brookwood Cl, Brom. BR2 191 F4
Brookwood Rd, SW18 166 C1
Hounslow TW3 143 H1
Broom Cl, Brom. BR2 192 B6
Teddington TW11 163 G7
Broomcroft Av, Nthlt. UB5 102 C3
Broome Rd, Hmptn. TW12 161 F7
Broome Way, SE5 131 J7
Broomfield, E17 77 J7
Sunbury-on-Thames TW16 178 A1
Broomfield Av, N13 59 F5
Loughton IG10 48 C6
Broomfield La, N13 59 F4
Broomfield Pl, W13 *off Broomfield Rd* 124/125 E1
Broomfield Rd, N13 59 E5
W13 125 E1
Beckenham BR3 189 H3
Bexleyheath DA6 159 G5
Richmond TW9 145 J1
Romford RM6 82 D7
Surbiton KT5 195 J1
Teddington TW11 *off Melbourne Rd* 163 F6
Broomfield St, E14 114 A5
Broom Gdns, Croy. CR0 204 A3
Broomgrove Gdns, Edg. HA8 70 A1
Broomgrove Rd, SW9 151 F2
Broomhill Ct, Wdf.Grn. IG8 *off Broomhill Rd* 63 G6
Broomhill Ri, Bexh. DA6 159 G5
Broomhill Rd, SW18 148 D5
Ilford IG3 100 A2
Woodford Green IG8 63 G6
Broomhill Wk, Wdf.Grn. IG8 63 F7
Broomhouse La, SW6 148 D2
Broomhouse Rd, SW6 148 D2
Broomloan La, Sutt. SM1 198 D2
Broom Lock, Tedd. TW11 163 F6
Broom Mead, Bexh. DA6 159 G5
Broom Pk, Tedd. TW11 163 G7
Broom Rd, Croy. CR0 204 A3
Teddington TW11 163 F6
Broomsleigh St, NW6 90 C5
Broom Water, Tedd. TW11 163 F6
Broom Water W, Tedd. TW11 163 F5
Broomwood Cl, Croy. CR0 189 G5
Broomwood Rd, SW11 149 J6
Broseley Gro, SE26 171 H5
Broster Gdns, SE25 188 C3
Brougham Rd, E8 112 D1
W3 106 C6
Brougham St, SW11 149 J2
Brough Cl, SW8 *off Kenchester Cl* 130/131 E7
Kingston upon Thames KT2 163 G5
Broughinge Rd, Borwd. WD6 38 B2
Broughton Av, N3 72 B3
Richmond TW10 163 E3
Broughton Dr, SW9 151 G4
Broughton Gdns, N6 74 C6
Broughton Rd, SW6 148 E2
W13 105 E7
Orpington BR6 207 G2
Thornton Heath CR7 187 G6
Broughton Rd App, SW6 *off Wandsworth Br Rd* 148/149 E2
Broughton St, SW8 150 A2
Brouncker Rd, W3 126 C2
Browells La, Felt. TW13 160 B2
Brown Cl, Wall. SM6 200 E7
Brownfield St, E14 114 B6
Browngraves Rd, Hayes UB3 121 F7
Brown Hart Gdns, W1 16 C5
Brownhill Rd, SE6 154 B7
Browning Av, W7 104 C6
Sutton SM1 199 H4
Worcester Park KT4 197 H1
Browning Cl, E17 78 C4
W9 6 D6
Hampton TW12 161 F4
Welling DA16 157 H1
Browning Ho, W12 *off Wood La* 107 J6
Browning Ms, W1 16 D2
Browning Rd, E11 79 F7
E12 98 C6
Browning St, SE17 36 A3
Browning Way, Houns. TW5 142 D1
Brownlea Gdns, Ilf. IG3 100 A2
Brownlow Cl, Barn. EN4 41 G5
Brownlow Ms, WC1 10 D6
Brownlow Rd, E7 *off Woodford Rd* 97 H4
E8 112 C1
N3 56 E7
N11 58 E6
NW10 89 E7
W13 124 D1
Borehamwood WD6 38 A4

Brownlow Rd, Croy. CR0 **202** B4
Brownlow St, WC1 **18** D2
Brown's Bldgs, EC3 **20** E4
Brownsea Wk, NW7 *off Sanders La.* **56** A6
Browns La, NW5 **92** B5
Brownspring Dr, SE9 **175** E4
Browns Rd, E17 **78** A3
Surbiton KT5 **181** J7
Brown St, W1 **15** J3
Brownswell Rd, N2 **73** G2
Brownswood Rd, N4 **93** H3
Broxash Rd, SW11 **150** A6
Broxbourne Av, E18 **79** H4
Broxbourne Rd, E7 **97** G3
Orpington BR6 **193** J7
Broxholm Rd, SE27 **169** G3
Broxted Rd, SE6 **171** J2
Broxwood Way, NW8 **109** H1
★**Bruce Castle Mus**, N17 **76** B1
Bruce Castle Rd, N17 **76** C1
Bruce Cl, W10 *off Ladbroke Gro.* **108** B5
Welling DA16 **158** B1
Bruce Gdns, N20 *off Balfour Gro* **57** J3
Bruce Gro, N17 **76** B1
Bruce Hall Ms, SW17 *off Brudenell Rd* **168** A4
Bruce Rd, E3 **114** B3
NW10 **88** D7
SE25 **188** A4
Barnet EN5 *off St. Albans Rd.* **40** B3
Harrow HA3 **68** B2
Mitcham CR4 **168** A7
Bruckner St, W10 **108** C3
Brudenell Rd, SW17 **167** J3
Bruffs Meadow, Nthlt. UB5 **85** E6
Bruford Ct, SE8 *off Creekside* **134** B6
Bruges Pl, NW1 *off Randolph St.* **92** C7
Brumfield Rd, Epsom KT19 **196** C5
Brummel Cl, Bexh. DA7 **159** J3
★**Brunei Gall**, WC1 **17** J1
Brunel Cl, SE19 **170** C6
Hounslow TW5 **122** B7
Northolt UB5 **103** F3
★**Brunel Engine Ho**, SE16 **133** F2
Brunel Est, W2 **108** D5
Brunel Pl, Sthl. UB1 **103** H6
Brunel Rd, E17 **77** H6
SE16 **133** F2
W3 **106** E5
Woodford Green IG8 **64** C5
Brunel St, E16 *off Victoria Dock Rd.* **115** F6
Brunel Wk, N15 **76** B4
Twickenham TW2 *off Stephenson Rd* **143** G7
Brune St, E1 **21** F2
Brunner Cl, NW11 **73** F5
Brunner Rd, E17 **77** J5
W5 **105** G4
Bruno Pl, NW9 **88** C2
Brunswick Av, N11 **58** A3
Brunswick Cl, Bexh. DA6 **158** D4
Pinner HA5 **67** E6
Brunswick Cl, Thames Ditton KT7 **194** C1
Twickenham TW2 **162** A3
Brunswick Ct, EC1 *off Northampton Sq* **111** H3
SE1 **29** E4
Barnet EN4 **41** G5
Brunswick Cres, N11 **58** A3
Brunswick Gdns, W5 **105** H3
W8 **128** D1
Ilford IG6 **65** F7
Brunswick Gro, N11 **58** A3
Brunswick Ind Pk, N11 **58** B4
Brunswick Ms, SW16 *off Potters La.* **168** D6
W1 **16** A3
BRUNSWICK PARK, N11 **57** J2
Brunswick Pk, SE5 **152** A1
Brunswick Pk Gdns, N11 **58** A2
Brunswick Pk Rd, N11 **58** A2
Brunswick Pl, N1 **12** C4
NW1 **8** C5
SE19 **170** D7
Brunswick Quay, SE16 **133** G3
Brunswick Rd, E10 **96** C1
Brunswick Rd, E14 *off Blackwall Tunnel Northern App* **114** C6
N15 **76** B5
W5 **105** G4
Bexleyheath DA6 **158** D4
Kingston upon Thames KT2 **182** A1
Sutton SM1 **199** E4
Brunswick Shop Cen, WC1 **10** A5
Brunswick Sq, N17 **60** C6
WC1 **10** B6
Brunswick St, E17 **78** C5
Brunswick Vil, SE5 **152** B1
Brunswick Way, N11 **58** B4
Brunton Pl, E14 **113** H6
Brushfield St, E1 **21** E2
Brussels Rd, SW11 **149** G4
Bruton Cl, Chis. BR7 **174** C7
Bruton La, W1 **16** E6
Bruton Pl, W1 **16** E6
Bruton Rd, Mord. SM4 **185** F5
Bruton St, W1 **16** E6
Bruton Way, W13 **104** D5
Bryan Av, NW10 **89** H7
Bryan Cl, Sun. TW16 **160** A7
Bryan Rd, SE16 **133** J2
Bryan's All, SW6 *off Wandsworth Br Rd.* **148/149** E2
Bryanston Av, Twick. TW2 **161** H1
Bryanston Cl, Sthl. UB2 **123** F4
Bryanstone Ct, Sutt. SM1 *off Oakhill Rd* **199** F4
Bryanstone Rd, N8 **74** D5
Bryanston Ms E, W1 **15** J2
Bryanston Ms W, W1 **15** J2
Bryanston Pl, W1 **15** J2
Bryanston Sq, W1 **15** J2
Bryanston St, W1 **15** J4
Bryant Cl, Barn. EN5 **40** C5
Bryant Ct, E2 **13** F1
Bryant Rd, Nthlt. UB5 **102** C3
Bryant St, E15 **96** D7
Bryantwood Rd, N7 **93** G5
Brycedale Cres, N14 **58** D4
Bryce Rd, Dag. RM8 **100** C4
Brydale Ho, SE16 *off Rotherhithe New Rd* **133** G4
Bryden Cl, SE26 **171** H5
Brydges Pl, WC2 **18** A6
Brydges Rd, E15 **96** D5
Brydon Wk, N1 *off Outram Pl* **110/111** E1
Bryer Ct, EC2 *off Aldersgate St* **111** J5
Bryett Rd, N7 **93** E3
Brymay Cl, E3 **114** A2
Brynmaer Rd, SW11 **149** J1
Bryn-y-Mawr Rd, Enf. EN1 **44** C4
Bryony Cl, Loug. IG10 **48** E4
Bryony Rd, W12 **107** G7
Buchanan Cl, N21 **43** F5
Buchanan Ct, Borwd. WD6 **38** C2
Buchanan Gdns, NW10 **107** H2
Buchan Rd, SE15 **153** F3
Bucharest Rd, SW18 **149** F7
Buckden Cl, N2 *off Southern Rd* **73** J4
SE12 *off Upwood Rd* **155** F6
Buckfast Ct, W13 *off Romsey Rd.* **104** D7
Buckfast Rd, Mord. SM4 **185** E4
Buckfast St, E2 **13** J4
Buck Hill Wk, W2 **15** F6
Buckhold Rd, SW18 **148** D6
Buckhurst Av, Cars. SM5 **199** H1
BUCKHURST HILL, IG9 **47** H7
Buckhurst St, E1 **113** E4
Buckhurst Way, Buck.H. IG9 **64** A4
Buckingham Arc, WC2 **18** B6
Buckingham Av, N20 **41** F7
Feltham TW14 **142** B6
Greenford UB6 **104** D1
Thornton Heath CR7 **187** G1
Welling DA16 **157** H4
West Molesey KT8 **179** H3
Buckingham Cl, W5 **105** F5
Enfield EN1 **44** B2
Hampton TW12 **161** F5
Orpington BR5 **193** H7
Buckingham Ct, NW4 **71** G3
Loughton IG10 *off Rectory La* **48** D2
Buckingham Dr, Chis. BR7 **175** E5
Buckingham Gdns, Edg. HA8 **53** J7
Thornton Heath CR7 **187** G2
West Molesey KT8 *off Buckingham Av* **179** H2
Buckingham Gate, SW1 **25** F4
Buckingham La, SE23 **153** H7
Buckingham Ms, N1 *off Buckingham Rd* **94** B6
NW10 *off Buckingham Rd* **107** F2
SW1 **25** F5
★**Buckingham Palace**, SW1 **24** E4
Buckingham Palace Rd, SW1 **32** D2
Buckingham Pl, SW1 **25** F5
Buckingham Rd, E10 **96** B3
E11 **79** J5
E15 **97** F5
E18 **79** F1
N1 **94** B6
N22 **74** E1
NW10 **107** F2
Borehamwood WD6 **38** D4
Edgware HA8 **53** J7
Hampton TW12 **161** F4
Harrow HA1 **68** A5
Ilford IG1 **99** G2
Kingston upon Thames KT1 **181** J4
Mitcham CR4 **186** E5
Richmond TW10 **163** G2
Buckingham St, WC2 **18** B6
Buckland Cres, NW3 **91** G7
Buckland Ri, Pnr. HA5 **66** C1
Buckland Rd, E10 **96** C2
Chessington KT9 **195** J5
Orpington BR6 **207** H4
Bucklands Rd, Tedd. TW11 **163** F6
Buckland St, N1 **12** C2
Buckland Wk, W3 **126** C2
Morden SM4 **185** F4
Buckland Way, Wor.Pk. KT4 **197** J1
Buck La, NW9 **70** D5
Buckleigh Av, SW20 **184** B3
Buckleigh Rd, SW16 **168** D6
Buckleigh Way, SE19 **188** C1
Buckler Gdns, SE9 *off Southold Ri* **174** C3
Bucklers All, SW6 **128** C6
Bucklersbury, EC4 **20** B4
Bucklersbury Pas, EC4 **20** B4
Bucklers Way, Cars. SM5 **199** J3
Buckles Ct, Belv. DA17 *off Fendyke Rd* **138** D3
Buckle St, E1 **21** G3
Buckley Cl, SE23 **153** E7
Buckley Rd, NW6 **90** C7
Buckley St, SE1 *off Mepham St* **131** G1
Buckmaster Cl, SW9 *off Stockwell Pk Rd* **151** F3
Buckmaster Rd, SW11 **149** H4
Bucknall St, WC2 **17** J3
Bucknall Way, Beck. BR3 **190** B4
Bucknell Cl, SW2 **151** F4
Buckner Rd, SW2 **151** F4
Buckrell Rd, E4 **62** D2
Buckstone Cl, SE23 **153** F6
Buckstone Rd, N18 **60** D6
Buck St, NW1 **92** B7
Buckters Rents, SE16 **133** H1
Buckthorne Rd, SE4 **153** H6
Buck Wk, E17 *off Wood St* **78** D4
Budd Cl, N12 **57** E4
Buddings Circle, Wem. HA9 **88** C3
Budd's All, Twick. TW1 *off Arlington Cl* **145** F5
Bude Cl, E17 **77** J5
Budge La, Mitch. CR4 **185** J7
Budge Row, EC4 **20** B5
Budge's Wk, W2 **22** C1
Budleigh Cres, Well. DA16 **158** C1
Budoch Ct, Ilf. IG3 **100** A2
Budoch Dr, Ilf. IG3 **100** A2
Buer Rd, SW6 **148** B2
Bugsby's Way, SE7 **135** G4
SE10 **135** F4
Bulganak Rd, Th.Hth. CR7 **187** J4
Bulinga St, SW1 **33** J2
Bullace Row, SE5 **132** A7
Bull All, Well. DA16 *off Welling High St* **158** B3
Bullards Pl, E2 **113** G3
Bullbanks Rd, Belv. DA17 **139** J4
Bullen St, SW11 **149** H2
Buller Cl, SE15 **132** D7
Buller Rd, N17 **76** D2
N22 **75** G2
NW10 *off Chamberlayne Rd* **108** A3
Barking IG11 **99** H7
Thornton Heath CR7 **188** A2
Bullers Cl, Sid. DA14 **176** E5
Bullers Wd Dr, Chis. BR7 **174** B7
Bullescroft Rd, Edg. HA8 **54** A3
Bullhead Rd, Borwd. WD6 **38** C3
Bullied Way, SW1 **32** E2
Bull Inn Ct, WC2 **18** B6
Bullivant St, E14 **114** C7
Bull La, N18 **60** B5
Chislehurst BR7 **175** G7
Dagenham RM10 **101** H3
Bull Rd, E15 **115** F2
Bullrush Cl, Croy. CR0 **188** B6
Bull's All, SW14 **146** D2
Bulls Br Ind Est, Sthl. UB2 **122** B4
Bulls Br Rd, Sthl. UB2 **122** B3
Bullsbrook Rd, Hayes UB4 **122** C1
Bulls Gdns, SW3 **31** H1
Bull's Head Pas, EC3 **20** D4
Bull Yd, SE15 *off Peckham High St* **152** D1
Bulmer Gdns, Har. HA3 **69** G7
Bulmer Ms, W11 *off Ladbroke Rd.* **108** D7
Bulmer Pl, W11 **128** D1
Bulow Est, SW6 *off Broughton Rd.* **148/149** E2
Bulrush Cl, Cars. SM5 **199** H2
Bulstrode Av, Houns. TW3 **143** F2
Bulstrode Gdns, Houns. TW3 **143** F3
Bulstrode Pl, W1 **16** C2
Bulstrode Rd, Houns. TW3 **143** G3
Bulstrode St, W1 **16** C3
Bulwer Ct Rd, E11 **96** D1
Bulwer Gdns, Barn. EN5 *off Bulwer Rd* **41** F4
Bulwer Rd, E11 **78** D7
N18 **60** B4
Barnet EN5 **41** E4
Bulwer St, W12 **127** J1
Bunces La, Wdf.Grn. IG8 **63** F7
Bungalow Rd, SE25 **188** B4
Bungalows, The, SW16 **168** B7
Wallington SM6 **200** B5
Bunhill Row, EC1 **12** B5
Bunhouse Pl, SW1 **32** B3
Bunkers Hill, NW11 **73** F7
Belvedere DA17 **139** G4
Sidcup DA14 **177** F3
Bunning Way, N7 **93** E7
Bunns La, NW7 **55** F6
Bunsen St, E3 *off Kenilworth Rd* **113** H2
Buntingbridge Rd, Ilf. IG2 **81** G5
Bunting Cl, N9 *off Dunnock Cl* **61** G1
Mitcham CR4 **185** J5
Bunton St, SE18 **136** D3
Bunyan Ct, EC2 *off Beech St* **111** J5
Bunyan Rd, E17 **77** H3
Buonaparte Ms, SW1 **33** H3
Burbage Cl, SE1 **28** B6
Burbage Rd, SE21 **152** A6
SE24 **151** J6
Burberry Cl, N.Mal. KT3 **182** E2
Burbridge Way, N17 **76** C2
Burcham St, E14 **114** B6
Burcharbro Rd, SE2 **138** D6
Burchell Rd, E10 **96** B1
SE15 **153** E1
Burchett Way, Rom. RM6 **83** F6
Burcote Rd, SW18 **167** G1
Burden Cl, Brent. TW8 **125** F5
Burdenshott Av, Rich. TW10 **146** B4
Burden Way, E11 *off Brading Cres* **97** H2
Burder Cl, N1 **94** B6
Burder Rd, N1 *off Balls Pond Rd* **94** B6
Burdett Av, SW20 **183** G1

Burdett Cl, W7
off Cherington Rd 124 C2
Sidcup DA14 176 E5
Burdett Ms, NW3
off Belsize Cres 91 G6
W2 14 A3
Burdett Rd, E3 113 J4
E14 113 J4
Croydon CR0 188 A6
Richmond TW9 145 J3
Burdetts Rd, Dag. RM9 119 F1
Burdett St, SE1 27 E5
Burdock Cl, Croy. CR0 203 G1
Burdock Rd, N17 76 D3
Burdon La, Sutt. SM2 198 B7
Burfield Cl, SW17 167 G4
Burford Cl, Dag. RM8 100 C3
Ilford IG6 81 F4
Burford Gdns, N13 59 F3
Burford Rd, E6 116 B3
E15 96 D7
SE6 171 J2
Brentford TW8 125 H5
Bromley BR1 192 B4
Sutton SM1 198 D2
Worcester Park KT4 183 F7
Burford Wk, SW6
off Cambria St 128/129 E7
Burford Way, Croy.
(New Adgtn) CR0 204 C6
Burges Ct, E6 98 D7
Burges Gro, SW13 127 H7
Burges Rd, E6 98 B7
Burgess Av, NW9 70 D6
Burgess Cl, Felt. TW13 160 E4
Burgess Hill, NW2 90 D4
Burgess Rd, E15 96 E4
Sutton SM1 198 E4
Burgess St, E14 114 A5
Burge St, SE1 28 C6
★**Burgh Ho (Hampstead Mus)**,
NW3 *off New End Sq* 91 G4
Burghill Rd, SE26 171 H4
Burghley Av, Borwd.
WD6 38 C5
New Malden KT3 182 D1
Burghley Hall Cl, SW19 148 B7
Burghley Ho, SW19 166 B3
Burghley Pl, Mitch. CR4 186 A5
Burghley Rd, E11 97 E1
N8 75 G3
NW5 92 B5
SW19 166 A4
Burghley Twr, W3 107 F7
Burgh St, N1 11 H1
Burgon St, EC4 19 H4
Burgos Cl, Croy. CR0 201 G6
Burgos Gro, SE10 154 B1
Burgoyne Rd, N4 75 H6
SE25 188 C4
SW9 151 F3
Burham Cl, SE20
off Maple Rd 171 F7
Burhill Gro, Pnr. HA5 66 E2
Burke Cl, SW15 147 E4
Burke St, E16 115 F6
Burket Cl, Sthl. UB2
off Kingsbridge Rd 123 F4
Burland Rd, SW11 149 J5
Burleigh Av, Sid. DA15 157 J5
Wallington SM6 200 A3
Burleigh Gdns, N14 58 C1
Burleigh Ho, W10
off St. Charles Sq 108 A5
Burleigh Pl, SW15 148 A5
Burleigh Rd, Enf. EN1 44 B4
Sutton SM3 198 B1
Burleigh St, WC2 18 C5
Burleigh Wk, SE6
off Muirkirk Rd 172 C1
Burleigh Way, Enf. EN2
off Church St 44 A3
Burley Cl, E4 62 A5
SW16 186 D2
Burley Rd, E16 115 J6
Burlington Arc, W1 17 F6
Burlington Av, Rich.
TW9 146 A1
Romford RM7 83 H6
Burlington Cl, E6 *off*
Northumberland Rd 116 B6
W9 108 C4
Feltham TW14 141 G7
Orpington BR6 206 E2
Pinner HA5 66 B3
Burlington Gdns, W1 17 F6
W3 126 C1
W4 126 C5
Romford RM6 83 E7
Burlington La, W4 126 E7
Burlington Ms, SW15 148 C5
W3 126 C1
Burlington Pl, SW6
off Burlington Rd 148 B2
Woodford Green IG8 63 G3
Burlington Ri, Barn. EN4 57 H1
Burlington Rd, N10
off Tetherdown 74 A2
N17 76 D1
SW6 148 B2
W4 126 C5
Enfield EN2 44 A1
Isleworth TW7 144 A1
New Malden KT3 183 G4
Thornton Heath CR7 187 J2
Burma Rd, N16 94 A4
Burmester Rd, SW17 167 F3
Burnaby Cres, W4 126 B6
Burnaby Gdns, W4 126 C6
Burnaby St, SW10 129 F7
Burnbrae Cl, N12 57 E6
Burnbury Rd, SW12 168 C1
Burncroft Av, Enf. EN3 45 F2
Burndell Way, Hayes
UB4 102 E5
Burne Jones Ho, W14 128 C4
Burnell Av, Rich. TW10 163 F5
Welling DA16 158 A2
Burnell Gdns, Stan. HA7 69 G1
Burnell Rd, Sutt. SM1 199 E4
Burnell Wk, SE1 37 G3
Burnels Av, E6 116 D3
Burness Cl, N7
off Roman Way 93 F6
Burne St, NW1 15 G1
Burnett Cl, E9 95 F5
Burney Av, Surb. KT5 181 J5
Burney Dr, Loug. IG10 49 E2
Burney St, SE10 134 C7
Burnfoot Av, SW6 148 B1
Burnfoot Ct, SE22 170 E1
Burnham, NW3 91 H7
Burnham Cl, NW7 55 G7
SE1 37 G2
Harrow (Wldste) HA3 68 D4
Burnham Ct, NW4 71 J4
Burnham Cres, E11 79 J4
Burnham Dr, Wor.Pk.
KT4 198 A2
Burnham Gdns, Croy.
CR0 188 C7
Hayes UB3 121 G3
Hounslow TW4 142 B1
Burnham Rd, E4 61 J5
Dagenham RM9 100 B7
Morden SM4 185 F5
Sidcup DA14 176 E2
Burnham St, E2 113 F3
Kingston upon Thames
KT2 182 A1
Burnham Way, SE26 171 J5
W13 124 E4
Burnhill Cl, SE15
off Gervase St 132/133 E7
Burnhill Rd, Beck. BR3 190 A2
Burnley Cl, Wat. WD19 50 C5
Burnley Rd, NW10 89 G5
SW9 151 F2
Burnsall St, SW3 31 H3
Burns Av, Felt. TW14 142 A6
Romford (Chad.Hth)
RM6 82 C7
Sidcup DA15 158 B6
Southall UB1 103 G7
Burns Cl, E17 78 C4
SW19 167 G6
Welling DA16 157 J1
Burnside Av, E4 61 J6
Burnside Cl, SE16 133 G1
Barnet EN5 40 D3
Twickenham TW1 144 D6
Burnside Cres, Wem.
HA0 105 G1
Burnside Rd, Dag. RM8 100 C2
Burns Rd, NW10 107 F1
SW11 149 J2
W13 124 E2
Wembley HA0 105 G2
Burns Way, Houns. TW5 142 D2
Burnt Ash Hill, SE12 155 F6
Burnt Ash La, Brom. BR1 173 G6
Burnt Ash Rd, SE12 155 F5
Burnthwaite Rd, SW6 128 D7
BURNT OAK, Edg. HA8 54 C7
Burnt Oak Bdy, Edg. HA8 54 B7
Burnt Oak Flds, Edg.
HA8 70 C1
Burnt Oak La, Sid. DA15 158 A6
Burntwood Cl, SW18 167 G1
Burntwood Gra Rd,
SW18 167 G1
Burntwood La, SW17 167 H2
Burntwood Vw, SE19
off Bowley La 170 C5
Buross St, E1
off Commercial Rd 112/113 E6
Burpham Cl, Hayes UB4 102 D5
Burrage Gro, SE18 137 F4
Burrage Pl, SE18 137 F5
Burrage Rd, SE18 137 F6
Burrard Rd, E16 115 H6
NW6 90 D5
Burr Cl, E1 29 H1
Bexleyheath DA7 159 F3
Burrell Cl, Croy. CR0 189 H6
Edgware HA8 54 B2
Burrell Row, Beck. BR3
off High St 190 A2
Burrell St, SE1 27 G1
Burrells Wf Sq, E14 134 B5
Burrell Twr, E10 78 A7
Burritt Rd, Kings.T. KT1 182 A2
Burroughs, The, NW4 71 H5
Burroughs Gdns, NW4 71 H4
Burroughs Par, NW4
off The Burroughs 71 H4
Burrow Cl, Chig. IG7
off Burrow Rd 65 J5
Burrow Grn, Chig. IG7 65 J5
Burrow Rd, SE22 152 B4
Chigwell IG7 65 J5
Burrows Ms, SE1 27 G3
Burrows Rd, NW10 107 J3
Burrow Wk, SE21
off Rosendale Rd 151 J7
Burr Rd, SW18 148 D7
Bursdon Cl, Sid. DA15 175 J2
Bursland Rd, Enf. EN3 45 G4
Burslem St, E1 21 J4
Burstock Rd, SW15 148 B4
Burston Rd, SW15 148 A5
Burston Vil, SW15
off St. John's Av 148 A5
Burstow Rd, SW20 184 B1
Burtenshaw Rd, T.Ditt.
KT7 180 D7
Burtley Cl, N4 93 J1
Burton Cl, Chess. KT9 195 G7
Thornton Heath CR7 188 A3
Burton Ct, SW3
off Franklin's Row 129 J5
Burton Gdns, Houns.
TW5 143 F1
Burton Gro, SE17 36 B4
Burtonhole Cl, NW7 56 A4
Burtonhole La, NW7 56 B4
Burton La, SW9 151 G2
Burton Ms, SW1 32 C2
Burton Pl, WC1 9 J4
Burton Rd, E18 79 H3
NW6 90 C7
SW9 151 H2
Kingston upon Thames
KT2 163 H7
Loughton IG10 49 F4
Burtons Rd, Hmptn.
(Hmptn H.) TW12 161 H4
Burton St, WC1 9 J4
Burt Rd, E16 135 J1
Burtwell La, SE27 170 A4
Burwash Ho, SE1 28 C4
Burwash Rd, SE18 137 G5
Burwell Av, Grnf. UB6 86 B6
Burwell Cl, E1
off Bigland St 112/113 E6
Burwell Rd, E10 95 H1
Burwell Wk, E3 114 A4
Burwood Av, Brom. BR2 205 H2
Pinner HA5 66 C5
Burwood Cl, Surb. KT6 196 A1
Burwood Pl, W2 15 H3
Bury Cl, SE16
off Rotherhithe St 133 G1
Bury Ct, EC3 20 E3
Bury Gro, Mord. SM4 184 E5
Bury Pl, WC1 18 A2
Bury Rd, E4 47 E5
N22 75 G3
Dagenham RM10 101 H5
Buryside Cl, Ilf. IG2 81 J4
Bury St, EC3 20 E4
N9 60 D1
SW1 25 F1
Bury St W, N9 44 A7
Bury Wk, SW3 31 G2
Busbridge Ho, E14
off Brabazon St 114 A5
Busby Pl, NW5 92 D6
Busby St, E2 13 G5
Bushbaby Cl, SE1 28 D6
Bushberry Rd, E9 95 H6
Bush Cl, Ilf. IG2 81 G5
Bush Cotts, SW18
off Putney Br Rd 148 D5
Bush Ct, W12 *off*
Shepherds Bush Grn 128 A2
Bushell Cl, SW2 169 F2
Bushell Grn, Bushey
(Bushey Hth) WD23 52 A2
Bushell St, E1 29 J2
Bushell Way, Chis. BR7 174 D5
Bushey Av, E18 79 F3
Orpington BR5 193 G7
Bushey Cl, E4 62 C3
Bushey Ct, SW20 183 H2
Bushey Down, SW12
off Bedford Hill 168 B2
BUSHEY HEATH, Bushey
WD23 52 B1
Bushey Hill Rd, SE5 152 B1
Bushey La, Sutt. SM1 198 D4
Bushey Lees, Sid. DA15
off Fen Gro 157 J6
BUSHEY MEAD, SW20 184 A3
Bushey Rd, E13 115 J2
N15 76 B6
SW20 183 H3
Croydon CR0 204 A2
Hayes UB3 121 H4
Sutton SM1 198 E4
Bushey Way, Beck. BR3 190 D6
Bushfield Cl, Edg. HA8 54 B2
Bushfield Cres, Edg. HA8 54 B2
Bushfields, Loug. IG10 48 D5
Bush Gro, NW9 70 C7
Stanmore HA7 69 G1
Bushgrove Rd, Dag.
RM8 100 D4
Bush Hill, N21 43 J7
BUSH HILL PARK, Enf.
EN1 44 B5
Bush Hill Rd, N21 44 A6
Harrow HA3 69 J6
Bush Ind Est, NW10 106 D4
Bush La, EC4 20 B5
Bushmead Cl, N15
off Copperfield Dr 76 C4
Bushmoor Cres, SE18 137 F7
Bushnell Rd, SW17 168 B2
Bush Rd, E8 112 E1
E11 79 F7
SE8 133 G4
Buckhurst Hill IG9 64 A4
Richmond TW9 125 J6
Bushway, Dag. RM8 100 D4
Bushwood, E11 97 F1
Bushwood Dr, SE1 37 G2
Bushwood Rd, Rich.
TW9 126 A6
★**Bushy Park**, Tedd. TW11 180 C1
Bushy Pk, Hmptn.
(Hmptn H.) TW12 180 C1
Teddington TW11 180 C1
Bushy Pk Gdns, Tedd.
TW11 162 A5
Bushy Pk Rd, Tedd.
TW11 163 E7
Bushy Rd, Tedd. TW11 162 C6
★**Business Design Cen**,
N1 111 G1
Butcher Row, E1 113 G7
E14 113 G7
Butchers Rd, E16 115 G6
Bute Av, Rich. TW10 163 H2
Bute Ct, Wall. SM6
off Bute Rd 200 C5
Bute Gdns, W6 128 A4
Wallington SM6 200 C5
Bute Gdns W, Wall.
SM6 200 C5
Bute Ms, NW11
off Northway 72/73 E5
Bute Rd, Croy. CR0 201 G1
Ilford IG6 81 E5
Wallington SM6 200 C4
Bute St, SW7 31 E1
Bute Wk, N1
off Marquess Rd 94 A6
Butler Av, Har. HA1 68 A7
Butler Ct, Wem. HA0
off Harrow Rd 86 D4
Butler Pl, SW1 25 H5
Butler Rd, NW10
off Curzon Cres 89 F7
Dagenham RM8 100 B4
Harrow HA1 67 J7

Butler St, E2
off Knottisford St 113 F3
Butlers Wf, SE1 29 G2
Buttercup Cl, Nthlt. UB5 85 F6
Butterfield Cl, N17
off Devonshire Rd 59 J6
SE16
off Wilson Gro 132/133 E2
Twickenham TW1
off Rugby Rd 144 C6
Butterfields, E17 78 C5
Butterfield Sq, E6
off Harper Rd 116 C6
Butterfly La, SE9 156 E6
Butterfly Wk, SE5
off Denmark Hill 152 A1
Butter Hill, Cars. SM5 200 A3
Wallington SM6 200 A3
Butteridges Cl, Dag. RM9 119 F1
Buttermere Cl, E15 96 D4
SE1 37 F1
Morden SM4 184 A6
Buttermere Dr, SW15 148 B5
Buttermere Wk, E8 94 C6
Butterwick, W6 127 J4
Butterworth Gdns, Wdf.Grn. IG8 63 G6
Buttesland St, N1 12 C3
Buttfield Cl, Dag. RM10 101 H6
Buttmarsh Cl, SE18 137 E5
Butts, The, Brent. TW8 125 G6
Sunbury-on-Thames TW16
off Elizabeth Gdns 178 C3
Buttsbury Rd, Ilf. IG1 99 F5
Butts Cotts, Felt. TW13 161 F3
Butts Cres, Felt. TW13 161 G3
Butts Piece, Nthlt. UB5
off Longhook Gdns 102 B2
Butts Rd, Brom. BR1 173 E5
Buxhall Cres, E9 95 J6
Buxted Rd, E8 94 C7
N12 57 H5
SE22 152 B4
Buxton Cl, N9 61 F2
Woodford Green IG8 64 A6
Buxton Ct, N1 12 A3
Buxton Cres, Sutt. SM3 198 B4
Buxton Dr, E11 79 E4
New Malden KT3 182 D2
Buxton Gdns, W3 106 B7
Buxton Ms, SW4
off Larkhall La 150 D2
Buxton Path, Wat. WD19 50 C3
Buxton Rd, E4 46 D7
E6 116 B3
E15 96 E5
E17 77 H4
N19 92 D1
NW2 89 H6
SW14 147 E3
Ilford IG2 81 H6
Thornton Heath CR7 187 H5
Buxton St, E1 13 G6
Buzzard Creek Ind Est, Bark. IG11 117 J5
Byam St, SW6 149 F2
Byards Cft, SW16 186 D1
Byatt Wk, Hmptn. TW12
off Victors Dr 160/161 E6
Bychurch End, Tedd. TW11
off Church Rd 162 C5
Bycroft Rd, Sthl. UB1 103 G4
Bycroft St, SE20
off Parish La 171 G7
Bycullah Av, Enf. EN2 43 H3
Bycullah Rd, Enf. EN2 43 H3
Bye, The, W3 107 E6
Byegrove Rd, SW19 167 G6
Byeway, The, SW14 146 C3
Bye Way, The, Har. HA3 68 B1
Byeways, Twick. TW2 161 H3
Byeways, The, Surb. KT5 182 A5
Byfeld Gdns, SW13 147 G1
Byfield Cl, SE16 133 H2
Byfield Pas, Islw. TW7 144 D3
Byfield Rd, Islw. TW7 144 D3
Byford Cl, E15 97 E7
Bygrove, Croy. (New Adgtn) CR0 204 B6
Bygrove St, E14 114 B6
Byland Cl, N21 43 F7
Bylands Cl, SE2
off Finchale Rd 138 B3
SE16
off Rotherhithe St 133 G1
Byne Rd, SE26 171 F6
Carshalton SM5 199 H2
Bynes Rd, S.Croy. CR2 202 A7
Byng Pl, WC1 9 H6
Byng Rd, Barn. EN5 40 A3
Byng St, E14 134 A2
Bynon Av, Bexh. DA7 159 E3
Byre, The, N14 *off Farm La* 42 B6
Byre Rd, N14 *off Farm La* 42 A6
Byrne Rd, SW12 168 B1
Byron Av, E12 98 B6
E18 79 F3
NW9 70 B4
Borehamwood WD6 38 A5
Hounslow TW4 142 A2
New Malden KT3 183 G5
Sutton SM1 199 G4
Byron Av E, Sutt. SM1 199 G4
Byron Cl, E8 112 D1
SE26 *off Porthcawe Rd* 171 H4
SE28 138 C1
Hampton TW12 161 F4
Byron Ct, W9
off Lanhill Rd 108 D4
Enfield EN2
off Bycullah Rd 43 H2
Harrow HA1 68 B6
Byron Dr, N2 73 G6
Erith DA8 139 H7
Byron Gdns, Sutt. SM1 199 G4
Byron Hill Rd, Har. HA2 86 A1
Byron Ho, Beck. BR3 172 A6
Byron Ms, NW3 91 H5
W9 *off Shirland Rd* 108 D4
Byron Rd, E10 96 B1
E17 78 A3
NW2 89 H2
NW7 55 G5
W5 125 J1
Harrow HA1 68 B6
Harrow (Wldste) HA3 68 C2
Wembley HA0 87 F3
Byron St, E14
off St. Leonards Rd 114 C6
Byron Ter, N9 45 F7
Byron Way, Nthlt. UB5 102 E3
West Drayton UB7 120 C4
Bysouth Cl, N15 76 A4
Ilford IG5 80 E1
By the Wd, Wat. WD19 50 D2
Bythorn St, SW9 151 F3
Byton Rd, SW17 167 J6
Byward Av, Felt. TW14 142 C6
Byward St, EC3 20 E6
Bywater Pl, SE16 133 H1
Bywater St, SW3 31 J3
Byway, The, Epsom KT19 197 F4
Bywell Pl, W1 17 F2
Bywood Av, Croy. CR0 189 F6
Byworth Wk, N19
off Courtauld Rd 92 D1

C

Cabbell St, NW1 15 G2
★**Cabinet War Rooms**, SW1 25 J3
Cabinet Way, E4 61 J6
Cable Pl, SE10
off Diamond Ter 154 C1
Cable St, E1 21 H5
Cable Trade Pk, SE7 135 J4
Cabot Pl, E14 134 A1
Cabot Sq, E14 134 A1
Cabot Way, E6
off Parr Rd 116 A1
Cabul Rd, SW11 149 H2
Cactus Cl, SE15
off Lyndhurst Gro 152 B2
Cactus Wk, W12
off Du Cane Rd 107 F6
Cadbury Cl, Islw. TW7 144 D1
Cadbury Way, SE16 29 G6
Caddington Cl, Barn. EN4 41 H5
Caddington Rd, NW2 90 B3
Caddis Cl, Stan. HA7
off Daventer Dr 52 C7
Cadell Cl, E2 13 G2
Cade Rd, SE10 154 D1
Cader Rd, SW18 149 F6
Cadet Dr, SE1 37 G3
Cadet Pl, SE10 134 E5
Cadiz Rd, Dag. RM10 101 J7
Cadiz St, SE17 36 A4
Cadley Ter, SE23 171 F2
Cadman Cl, SW9
off Langton Rd 131 H7
Cadmer Cl, N.Mal. KT3 182 E4
Cadmus Cl, SW4
off Aristotle Rd 150 D3
Cadnam Pt, SW15
off Dilton Gdns 165 H1
Cadogan Cl, E9
off Cadogan Ter 95 J7
Beckenham BR3
off Albemarle Rd 190 D1
Harrow HA2 85 H4
Teddington TW11 162 B5
Cadogan Ct, Sutt. SM2 199 E6
Cadogan Gdns, E18 79 H3
N3 72 E1
N21 43 G5
SW3 32 A1
Cadogan Gate, SW1 32 A1
Cadogan La, SW1 24 B6
Cadogan Pl, SW1 24 A5
Cadogan Rd, SE18 137 F3
Surbiton KT6 181 G5
Cadogan Sq, SW1 24 A6
Cadogan St, SW3 31 J2
Cadogan Ter, E9 95 J6
Cadoxton Av, N15 76 C6
Cadwallon Rd, SE9 175 E2
Caedmon Rd, N7 93 F4
Caerleon Cl, Esher (Clay.) KT10 194 E7
Sidcup DA14 176 C5
Caerleon Ter, SE2
off Blithdale Rd 138 B4
Caernarvon Cl, Mitch. CR4 186 E3
Caernarvon Dr, Ilf. IG5 80 D1
Caesars Wk, Mitch. CR4 185 J5
Cahill St, EC1 12 A6
Cahir St, E14 134 B4
Cains La, Felt. TW14 141 H5
Caird St, W10 108 B3
Cairn Av, W5 125 G1
Cairndale Cl, Brom. BR1 173 F7
Cairnes Ms, SE18
off Shooter's Hill Rd 156 B1
Cairnfield Av, NW2 89 E3
Cairngorm Cl, Tedd. TW11
off Vicarage Rd 162 D5
Cairns Av, Wdf.Grn. IG8 64 B6
Cairns Rd, SW11 149 H5
Cairn Way, Stan. HA7 52 C6
Cairo New Rd, Croy. CR0 201 H2
Cairo Rd, E17 78 A4
Caishowe Rd, Borwd. WD6 38 B1
Caistor Ms, SW12
off Caistor Rd 150 B7
Caistor Pk Rd, E15 115 F1
Caistor Rd, SW12 150 B7
Caithness Gdns, Sid. DA15 157 J6
Caithness Rd, W14 128 A4
Mitcham CR4 168 B7
Calabria Rd, N5 93 H6
Calais Gate, SE5
off Calais St 151 H1
Calais St, SE5 151 H1
Calbourne Rd, SW12 149 J7
Calcott Wk, SE9 174 A4
Caldbeck Av, Wor.Pk. KT4 197 G2
Caldecot Rd, SE5 151 J2
Caldecott Way, E5 95 G3
Calder Av, Grnf. UB6 104 C2
Calder Cl, Enf. EN1 44 B3
Calder Gdns, Edg. HA8 70 A3
Calderon Pl, W10
off St. Quintin Gdns 107 J5
Calderon Rd, E11 96 C4
Calder Rd, Mord. SM4 185 F5
Caldervale Rd, SW4 150 D5
Calderwood St, SE18 136 D4
Caldicot Grn, NW9
off Snowdon Dr 70/71 E6
Caldwell Rd, Wat. WD19 50 D4
Caldwell St, SW9 131 F7
Caldwell Yd, EC4
off Upper Thames St 111 J7
Caldy Rd, Belv. DA17 139 H3
Caldy Wk, N1
off Clephane Rd 93 J6
Caleb St, SE1 27 J3
Caledonian Cl, Ilf. IG3 100 B1
Caledonian Rd, N1 10 B2
N7 93 F5
Caledonian Wf, E14 134 D4
Caledonia St, N1 10 B2
Caledon Rd, E6 116 B1
Wallington SM6 200 A4
Cale St, SW3 31 G3
Caletock Way, SE10 135 F5
Calico Row, SW11
off York Pl 149 F3
Calidore Cl, SW2
off Endymion Rd 151 F6
California La, Bushey (Bushey Hth) WD23 52 A1
California Rd, N.Mal. KT3 182 C4
Callaby Ter, N1
off Wakeham St 94 A6
Callaghan Cl, SE13
off Glenton Rd 154/155 E4
Callander Rd, SE6 172 B2
Callard Av, N13 59 H5
Callcott Rd, NW6 90 C7
Callcott St, W8
off Hillgate Pl 128 D1
Callendar Rd, SW7 22 E5
Callingham Cl, E14
off Wallwood St 113 J5
Callis Fm Cl, Stai. (Stanw.) TW19
off Bedfont Rd 140 B6
Callis Rd, E17 77 J6
Callow St, SW3 30 D5
Calmont Rd, Brom. BR1 172 D6
Calne Av, Ilf. IG5 80 E1
Calonne Rd, SW19 166 A4
Calshot Rd, Houns. (Hthrw Air.) TW6 140 D2
Calshot St, N1 10 C1
Calshot Way, Enf. EN2 43 H3
Hounslow (Hthrw Air.) TW6
off Calshot Rd 140/141 E2
Calthorpe Gdns, Edg. HA8
off Jesmond Way 53 H5
Sutton SM1 199 F3
Calthorpe St, WC1 10 D5
Calton Av, SE21 152 B5
Calton Rd, Barn. EN5 41 F6
Calverley Cl, Beck. BR3 172 B6
Calverley Cres, Dag. RM10 101 G2
Calverley Gdns, Har. HA3 69 G7
Calverley Gro, N19 92 D1
Calverley Rd, Epsom KT17 197 G6
Calvert Av, E2 13 E4
Calvert Cl, Belv. DA17 139 G4
Sidcup DA14 176 E6
Calverton, SE5 36 C5
Calverton Rd, E6 116 D1
Calvert Rd, SE10 135 F5
Barnet EN5 40 A2
Calvert's Bldgs, SE1 28 B2
Calvert St, NW1
off Chalcot Rd 110 A1
Calvin St, E1 13 F6
Calydon Rd, SE7 135 H5
Calypso Cres, SE15
off Samuel St 132 C7
Calypso Way, SE16 133 J3
Camac Rd, Twick. TW2 162 A1
Cambalt Rd, SW15 148 A5
Camberley Av, SW20 183 H2
Enfield EN1 44 B4
Camberley Cl, Sutt. SM3 198 A3
Camberley Rd, Houns. (Hthrw Air.) TW6 140 D3
Cambert Way, SE3 155 H4
CAMBERWELL, SE5 131 J7
Camberwell Ch St, SE5 152 A1
Camberwell Glebe, SE5 152 A1
Camberwell Grn, SE5 152 A1
Camberwell Gro, SE5 152 A1
Camberwell New Rd, SE5 35 E6
Camberwell Pas, SE5
off Camberwell Grn 151 J1
Camberwell Rd, SE5 36 A6
Camberwell Sta Rd, SE5 151 J1
Cambeys Rd, Dag. RM10 101 H5
Camborne Av, W13 125 E2
Camborne Cl, Houns. (Hthrw Air.) TW6
off Camborne Rd S 140 D3
Camborne Ms, W11
off St. Marks Rd 108 B6
Camborne Rd, SW18 148 D7
Croydon CR0 188 D7
Morden SM4 184 A5
Sidcup DA14 176 C3
Sutton SM2 198 D7
Welling DA16 157 J2
Camborne Rd N, Houns. (Hthrw Air.) TW6
off Camborne Rd S 140 D3
Camborne Rd S, Houns. (Hthrw Air.) TW6 140 D3

Camborne Way, Houns. TW5 143 G1
Hounslow (Hthrw Air.) TW6 *off Camborne Rd S* 140 D3
Cambourne Av, N9 45 G7
Cambray Rd, SW12 168 C1
Orpington BR6 193 J7
Cambria Cl, Houns. TW3 143 G4
Sidcup DA15 175 G1
Cambria Ct, Felt. TW14 *off Hounslow Rd* 142 B7
Cambria Gdns, Stai. TW19 140 B7
Cambria Ho, SE26 *off High Level Dr* 170 D4
Cambrian Av, Ilf. IG2 81 H5
Cambrian Cl, SE27 169 H3
Cambrian Grn, NW9 *off Snowdon Dr* 70/71 E5
Cambrian Rd, E10 78 A7
Richmond TW10 145 J6
Cambria Rd, SE5 151 J3
Cambria St, SW6 129 E7
Cambridge Av, NW6 108 D2
Greenford UB6 86 C5
New Malden KT3 183 F2
Welling DA16 157 J4
Cambridge Barracks Rd, SE18 136 C4
Cambridge Circ, WC2 17 J4
Cambridge Cl, E17 77 J6
N22 *off Pellatt Gro* 75 G1
NW10 *off Lawrence Way* 88 C3
SW20 183 H1
Hounslow TW4 143 E4
West Drayton UB7 120 A6
Cambridge Cotts, Rich. TW9 126 A6
Cambridge Cres, E2 112 E2
Teddington TW11 162 D5
Cambridge Dr, SE12 155 G5
Ruislip HA4 84 C2
Cambridge Gdns, N10 74 B1
N13 59 G5
N17 *off Great Cambridge Rd* 60 A7
N21 44 A7
NW6 108 D2
W10 108 B6
Enfield EN1 44 D2
Kingston upon Thames KT1 182 A2
Cambridge Gate, NW1 8 E4
Cambridge Gate Ms, NW1 8 E4
Cambridge Grn, SE9 174 E1
Cambridge Gro, SE20 188 E1
W6 127 H4
Cambridge Gro Rd, Kings.T. KT1 182 A2
Cambridge Heath Rd, E1 113 E2
E2 113 E2
Cambridge Mans, SW11 *off Cambridge Rd* 149 J1
Cambridge Par, Enf. EN1 *off Great Cambridge Rd* 44 D1
Cambridge Pk, E11 79 G7
Twickenham TW1 145 G7
Cambridge Pk Rd, E11 *off Cambridge Pk* 79 F7
Cambridge Pl, W8 22 B4
Cambridge Rd, E4 62 D1
E11 79 F6
NW6 108 D3
SE20 188 E3
SW11 149 J1
SW13 147 F2
SW20 183 G1
W7 124 C2
Barking IG11 99 F7
Bromley BR1 173 G7
Carshalton SM5 199 H6
Hampton TW12 161 F7
Harrow HA2 67 G5
Hounslow TW4 143 E4
Ilford IG3 99 H1
Kingston upon Thames KT1 181 J2
Mitcham CR4 186 C3
New Malden KT3 182 E4
Richmond TW9 126 A7
Sidcup DA14 175 H4
Southall UB1 123 F1
Teddington TW11 162 C4
Twickenham TW1 145 G6
Walton-on-Thames KT12 178 B6
West Molesey KT8 179 F4
Cambridge Rd N, W4 126 B5
Cambridge Rd S, W4 126 B5
Cambridge Row, SE18 137 E5
Cambridge Sq, W2 15 G3
Cambridge St, SW1 32 E2
Cambridge Ter, N13 59 G5
NW1 8 E4
Cambridge Ter Ms, NW1 8 E4
Cambstone Cl, N11 58 A2
Cambus Cl, Hayes UB4 103 E5
Cambus Rd, E16 115 G5
Camdale Rd, SE18 137 J7
★**Camden Arts Cen**, NW3 91 F5
Camden Av, Felt. TW13 160 C2
Hayes UB4 102 C7
Camden Cl, Chis. BR7 175 F7
Camden Gdns, NW1 *off Kentish Town Rd* 92 B7
Sutton SM1 198 E5
Thornton Heath CR7 187 H3
Camden Gro, Chis. BR7 175 E6
Camden High St, NW1 110 B1
Camden Hill Rd, SE19 170 B6
Camdenhurst St, E14 113 H6
Camden La, N7 *off Rowstock Gdns* 92 D6
★**Camden Lock Mkt & Waterbuses**, NW1 92 B7
Camden Lock Pl, NW1 *off Chalk Fm Rd* 92 B7
Camden Ms, NW1 92 D6
Camden Pk Rd, NW1 92 D6
Chislehurst BR7 174 C7
Camden Pas, N1 111 H1
Camden Rd, E11 79 H6
E17 77 J6
N7 92 D5
NW1 110 C1
Bexley DA5 177 F1
Carshalton SM5 199 J4
Sutton SM1 198 D5
Camden Row, SE3 155 E2
Camden Sq, NW1 92 D6
SE15 *off Watts St* 152 C1
Camden St, NW1 92 B7
Camden Ter, NW1 *off North Vil* 92 D6
CAMDEN TOWN, NW1 110 C1
Camden Wk, N1 111 H1
Camden Way, Chis. BR7 174 C7
Thornton Heath CR7 187 H3
Camelford Wk, W11 *off Lancaster Rd* 108 B6
Camel Gro, Kings.T. KT2 163 G5
Camellia Ct, Wdf.Grn. IG8 *off The Bridle Path* 62/63 E7
Camellia Pl, Twick. TW2 143 H7
Camellia St, SW8 130 E7
Camelot Cl, SE28 137 G2
SW19 166 D4
Camelot St, SE15 *off Bird in Bush Rd* 132/133 E7
Camel Rd, E16 136 A1
Camera Pl, SW10 30 E6
Cameron Cl, N18 61 E4
N20 *off Myddelton Pk* 57 H2
Cameron Pl, E1 *off Varden St* 112/113 E6
Cameron Rd, SE6 171 J2
Bromley BR2 191 G4
Croydon CR0 187 H6
Ilford IG3 99 H1
Cameron Sq, Mitch. CR4 185 H1
Camerton Cl, E8 *off Buttermere Wk* 94 C6
Camgate Cen, Stai. (Stanw.) TW19 140 C6
Camilla Rd, SE16 132 E4
Camille Cl, SE25 188 D3
Camlan Rd, Brom. BR1 173 F4
Camlet St, E2 13 F5
Camlet Way, Barn. EN4 40 D2
Camley St, NW1 9 J1
★**Camley St Natural Pk**, NW1 9 J1
Camm Gdns, Kings.T. KT1 *off Church Rd* 181 J2
Thames Ditton KT7 180 B7
Camms Ter, Dag. RM10 101 J5
Camomile Av, Mitch. CR4 185 J1
Camomile St, EC3 20 D3
Campana Rd, SW6 148 D1
Campbell Av, Ilf. IG6 81 F4
Campbell Cl, SE18 *off Moordown* 156 D1
SW16 168 D4
Campbell Cl, Ruis. HA4 66 A6
Twickenham TW2 162 A2
Campbell Ct, N17 76 C1
SE22 *off Lordship La* 152 D7
Campbell Cft, Edg. HA8 54 A5
Campbell Gordon Way, NW2 89 H4
Campbell Rd, E3 114 A3
E6 116 B1
E15 *off Trevelyan Rd* 97 F4
E17 77 J4
N17 76 D1
W7 104 B7
Croydon CR0 187 H7
East Molesey KT8 *off Hampton Ct Rd* 180 C3
Twickenham TW2 162 A2
Campbell Wk, N1 *off Outram Pl* 110/111 E1
Campdale Rd, N7 92 D3
Campden Cres, Dag. RM8 100 B4
Wembley HA0 87 E2
Campden Gro, W8 128 D2
Campden Hill Ct, W8 *off Campden Hill Rd* 128 D2
Campden Hill Gdns, W8 128 D1
Campden Hill Gate, W8 *off Duchess of Bedford's Wk* 128 D2
Campden Hill Pl, W11 *off Holland Pk Av* 128 C1
Campden Hill Rd, W8 128 D1
Campden Hill Sq, W8 128 C1
Campden Hill Twrs, W11 *off Notting Hill Gate* 128 D1
Campden Ho Cl, W8 *off Hornton St* 128 D2
Campden Rd, S.Croy. CR2 202 B5
Campden St, W8 128 D1
Campen Cl, SW19 166 B2
Camperdown St, E1 21 G4
Campfield Rd, SE9 156 A7
Campion Cl, E6 116 C7
Croydon CR0 202 B4
Harrow HA3 69 J6
Campion Gdns, Wdf.Grn. IG8 63 G5
Campion Pl, SE28 138 B1
Campion Rd, SW15 147 J4
Isleworth TW7 144 C1
Campion Ter, NW2 90 A3
Campion Way, Edg. HA8 54 C4
Camplin Rd, Har. HA3 69 H5
Camplin St, SE14 133 G7
Camp Rd, SW19 165 J5
Campsbourne, The, N8 *off High St* 74/75 E4
Campsbourne Rd, N8 75 E3
Campsey Gdns, Dag. RM9 100 B7
Campsey Rd, Dag. RM9 100 B7
Campsfield Rd, N8 *off Campsbourne Rd* 74/75 E3
Campshill Pl, SE13 *off Campshill Rd* 154 C5
Campshill Rd, SE13 154 C5
Campus Rd, E17 77 J6
Campus Way, NW4 *off Greyhound Hill* 71 H3
Camp Vw, SW19 165 H5
Cam Rd, E15 114 D1
Camrose Av, Edg. HA8 69 J1
Erith DA8 139 H6
Feltham TW13 160 B4
Camrose Cl, Croy. CR0 189 H7
Morden SM4 184 D4
Camrose St, SE2 138 A5
Canada Av, N18 59 J6
Canada Cres, W3 106 C5
Canada Est, SE16 133 F3
Canada Gdns, SE13 154 C5
Canada Rd, W3 106 C4
Canada Sq, E14 134 B1
Canada St, SE16 133 G2
Canada Way, W12 107 H7
Canadian Av, SE6 172 B1
Canal App, SE8 133 H6
Canal Cl, E1 113 H4
W10 108 A4
Canal Gro, SE15 37 J5
Canal Path, E2 112 C1
Canal St, SE5 36 B6
Canal Wk, N1 112 A1
SE26 171 F5
Croydon CR0 188 B6
Canal Way, N1 12 A1
Canal Way, NW1 7 H3
NW8 7 G4
NW10 107 F4
W10 108 A4
Canal Way Wk, W10 108 A4
Canberra Cl, NW4 71 G3
Canberra Dr, Hayes UB4 102 C3
Northolt UB5 102 C3
Canberra Rd, E6 *off Barking Rd* 116 C1
SE7 135 J6
W13 124 D1
Bexleyheath DA7 138 D6
Hounslow (Hthrw Air.) TW6 140 D3
Canbury Av, Kings.T. KT2 181 J1
Canbury Ms, SE26 *off Wells Pk Rd* 170 D3
Canbury Pk Rd, Kings.T. KT2 181 H1
Canbury Pas, Kings.T. KT2 181 G1
Cancell Rd, SW9 151 G1
Candahar Rd, SW11 149 H2
Candle Gro, SE15 153 E3
Candlemakers Apartments, SW18 *off York Rd* 149 G3
Candler St, N15 76 A6
Candover Cl, West Dr. UB7 120 A7
Candover St, W1 17 F2
Candy St, E3 113 J1
Caney Ms, NW2 *off Claremont Rd* 90 A2
Canfield Dr, Ruis. HA4 84 B5
Canfield Gdns, NW6 91 F7
Canfield Pl, NW6 *off Canfield Gdns* 91 F6
Canfield Rd, Wdf.Grn. IG8 64 B7
Canford Av, Nthlt. UB5 103 E1
Canford Cl, Enf. EN2 43 G2
Canford Gdns, N.Mal. KT3 182 D6
Canford Pl, Tedd. TW11 163 E6
Canford Rd, SW11 150 A5
Canham Rd, SE25 188 B3
W3 126 E2
Canmore Gdns, SW16 168 C7
Cann Hall Rd, E11 96 E4
Canning Cres, N22 75 F1
Canning Cross, SE5 152 B2
Canning Pas, W8 22 C5
Canning Pl, W8 22 C5
Canning Pl Ms, W8 22 C4
Canning Rd, E15 114 E2
E17 77 H4
N5 93 H3
Croydon CR0 202 C2
Harrow HA3 68 C3
Cannington Rd, Dag. RM9 100 C6
CANNING TOWN, E16 115 G6
Cannizaro Rd, SW19 165 J6
Cannonbury Av, Pnr. HA5 66 D6
Cannon Cl, SW20 183 J3
Hampton TW12 *off Hanworth Rd* 161 H6
Cannon Ct, EC1 *off St. John St* 111 H4
Cannon Dr, E14 114 A7
Cannon Hill, N14 58 D3
NW6 90 D5
Cannon Hill La, SW20 184 B3
Cannon La, NW3 91 G3
Pinner HA5 84 E1
Cannon Pl, NW3 91 G3
SE7 136 B5
Cannon Rd, N14 58 E3
Bexleyheath DA7 159 E1
Cannon St, EC4 19 J4
Cannon St Rd, E1 112 E6
Cannon Trd Est, Wem. HA9 88 B4
Cannon Way, W.Mol. KT8 179 G4
Cannon Wf Business Cen, SE8 133 H4
Cannon Workshops, E14 *off Cannon Dr* 114 A7
Canon Av, Rom. RM6 82 C5
Canon Beck Rd, SE16 133 F2
Canonbie Rd, SE23 153 F7
CANONBURY, N1 93 J6
Canonbury Cres, N1 93 J7
Canonbury Gro, N1 93 J7
Canonbury La, N1 93 H7
Canonbury Pk N, N1 93 J6

Canonbury Pk S, N1 93 J6
Canonbury Pl, N1 93 H6
Canonbury Rd, N1 93 H6
Enfield EN1 44 B1
Canonbury Sq, N1 93 H7
Canonbury St, N1 93 J7
Canonbury Vil, N1 93 H7
Canonbury Yd, N1
off New N Rd 111 J1
Canonbury Yd W, N1
off Compton Rd 93 H6
Canon Mohan Cl, N14
off Farm La 42 B6
Canon Rd, Brom. BR1 191 J3
Canon Row, SW1 26 A4
Canons Cl, N2 73 G7
Edgware HA8 53 J6
Canons Cor, Edg. HA8 53 H4
Canons Dr, Edg. HA8 53 H6
Canonsleigh Rd, Dag.
RM9 100 B7
CANONS PARK, Edg.
HA8 53 H7
Canons Pk Cl, Edg. HA8
off Donnefield Av 53 H7
Canon St, N1 111 J1
Canons Wk, Croy. CR0 203 G3
Canopus Way, Nthwd. HA6 50 A4
Staines TW19 140 B7
Canrobert St, E2 112 E3
Cantelowes Rd, NW1 92 D6
Canterbury Av, Ilf. IG1 80 B7
Sidcup DA15 176 C2
Canterbury Cl, E6
off Harper Rd 116 C6
Beckenham BR3 190 B1
Chigwell IG7 65 J3
Greenford UB6 103 H6
Canterbury Cres, SW9 151 G3
Canterbury Gro, SE27 169 H3
Canterbury Ho, Borwd.
WD6 38 A2
Canterbury Pl, SE17 35 H2
Canterbury Rd, E10 78 C7
NW6 108 D2
Borehamwood WD6 38 A2
Croydon CR0 187 F7
Feltham TW13 161 E3
Harrow HA1, HA2 67 H5
Morden SM4 185 F5
Canterbury Ter, NW6 108 D2
Cantium Retail Pk, SE1 37 J5
Cantley Gdns, SE19 188 C1
Ilford IG2 81 F6
Cantley Rd, W7 124 D3
Canton St, E14 114 A6
Cantrell Rd, E3 113 J4
Cantwell Rd, SE18 136 E7
Canute Gdns, SE16 133 G4
Canvey St, SE1 27 H1
Cape Cl, Bark. IG11
off North St 99 F6
Capel Av, Wall. SM6 201 F5
Capel Cl, N20 57 F3
Bromley BR2 206 B1
Capel Ct, EC2 20 C4
SE20 off Melvin Rd 189 F1
Capel Gdns, Ilf. IG3 99 J4
Pinner HA5 67 F4
Capel Pt, E7 97 H4
Capel Rd, E7 97 H4
E12 97 J4
Barnet EN4 41 H6
Capener's Cl, SW1 24 B4
Capern Rd, SW18
off Cargill Rd 167 F1
Cape Rd, N17
off High Cross Rd 76 D3
Cape Yd, E1 29 J1
Capital Business Cen, Wem.
HA0 105 G2
Capital Ind Est, Mitch. CR4
off Willow La 185 J5
Capital Interchange Way,
Brent. TW8 126 A5
Capitol Ind Pk, NW9 70 C3
Capitol Way, NW9 70 C3
Capland St, NW8 7 F5
Caple Par, NW10
off Harley Rd 106/107 E2
Caple Rd, NW10 107 F2
Capper St, WC1 9 G6
Caprea Cl, Hayes UB4
off Triandra Way 102 D5
Capri Rd, Croy. CR0 202 C1
Capstan Cl, Rom. RM6 82 B6
Capstan Ride, Enf. EN2 43 G2
Capstan Rd, SE8 133 J4
Capstan Sq, E14 134 C2
Capstan Way, SE16 133 H1
Capstone Rd, Brom. BR1 173 F4
Capthorne Av, Har. HA2 85 E1
Capuchin Cl, Stan. HA7 52 E6
Capulet Ms, E16
off Hanover Av 135 G1
Capworth St, E10 96 A1
Caradoc Cl, W2 108 D6
Caradoc St, SE10 134 E5
Caradon Cl, E11
off Brockway Cl 96/97 E2
Caradon Way, N15 76 A4
Caravel Cl, E14
off Tiller Rd 134 A3
Caravelle Gdns, Nthlt. UB5
off Javelin Way 102 D3
Caravel Ms, SE8
off Watergate St 134 A6
Caraway Cl, E13 115 H5
Caraway Pl, Wall. SM6 200 B3
Carberry Rd, SE19 170 B6
Carbery Av, W3 125 J2
Carbis Cl, E4 62 D1
Carbis Rd, E14 113 J6
Carbuncle Pas Way, N17 76 D2
Carburton St, W1 17 E1
Cardale St, E14
off Plevna St 134 C3
Carden Rd, SE15 152 E3
Cardiff Rd, W7 124 D3
Enfield EN3 45 E4
Cardiff St, SE18 137 H7
Cardigan Gdns, Ilf. IG3 100 A2
Cardigan Rd, E3 113 J2
SW13 147 G2
SW19 off Haydons Rd 167 F6
Richmond TW10 145 H6
Cardigan St, SE11 34 E3
Cardigan Wk, N1
off Ashby Gro 93 J7
Cardinal Av, Borwd. WD6 38 B3
Kingston upon Thames
KT2 163 H5
Morden SM4 184 B6
Cardinal Bourne St, SE1 28 C6
Cardinal Cl, Chis. BR7 193 G1
Edgware HA8
off Abbots Rd 54 D7
Morden SM4 184 B7
Worcester Park KT4 197 G4
Cardinal Ct, Borwd. WD6
off Cardinal Av 38 B3
Cardinal Cres, N.Mal.
KT3 182 C2
Cardinal Dr, Ilf. IG6 65 F6
Cardinal Hinsley Cl,
NW10 107 G2
Cardinal Pl, SW15 148 A4
Cardinal Rd, Felt. TW13 160 B1
Ruislip HA4 84 D1
Cardinals Wk, Hmptn.
TW12 161 J7
Cardinals Way, N19 92 D1
Cardinal Way, Har. HA3
off Wolseley Rd 68 B3
Cardine Ms, SE15 132 E7
Cardington Sq, Houns.
TW4 142 D4
Cardington St, NW1 9 F3
Cardinham Rd, Orp.
BR6 207 J4
Cardozo Rd, N7 93 E5
Cardrew Av, N12 57 G5
Cardrew Cl, N12 57 H5
Cardross St, W6 127 H3
Cardwell Rd, N7 92 E4
Carew Cl, N7 93 F2
Carew Rd, N17 76 D2
W13 125 F2
Mitcham CR4 186 A2
Thornton Heath CR7 187 H3
Wallington SM6 200 C6
Carew St, SE5 151 J2
Carew Way, Wat. WD19 51 F3
Carey Ct, Bexh. DA6 159 H5
Carey Gdns, SW8 150 C1
Carey La, EC2 19 J3
Carey Pl, SW1 33 H2
Carey Rd, Dag. RM9 101 E4
Carey St, WC2 18 D4
Carey Way, Wem. HA9 88 B4
Carfax Pl, SW4
off Holwood Pl 150 D4
Carfax Rd, Hayes UB3 121 J5
Carfree Cl, N1
off Bewdley St 93 G7
Cargill Rd, SW18 167 E1
Cargreen Pl, SE25
off Cargreen Rd 188 C4
Cargreen Rd, SE25 188 C4
Carholme Rd, SE23 171 J1
Carisbrooke Av, Bex.
DA5 176 D1
Carisbrooke Cl, Enf. EN1 44 C1
Stanmore HA7 69 G2
Carisbrooke Gdns, SE15 37 G7
Carisbrooke Ho, Kings.T. KT2
off Kingsgate Rd 181 H1
Carisbrooke Rd, E17 77 H4
Bromley BR2 191 J4
Mitcham CR4 186 D4
Carker's La, NW5 92 B5
Carleton Cl, Esher KT10 194 A1
Carleton Rd, N7 92 D5
Carleton Vil, NW5
off Leighton Gro 92 C5
Carlile Cl, E3 113 J2
Carlina Gdns, Wdf.Grn.
IG8 63 H5
Carlingford Gdns, Mitch.
CR4 167 J7
Carlingford Rd, N15 75 H3
NW3 91 G4
Morden SM4 184 A6
Carlisle Av, EC3 21 E4
W3 106 E6
Carlisle Cl, Kings.T. KT2 182 A1
Pinner HA5 66 E7
Carlisle Gdns, Har. HA3 69 G7
Ilford IG1 80 B6
Carlisle La, SE1 26 D6
Carlisle Ms, NW8 15 F1
Carlisle Pl, N11 58 B4
SW1 25 F6
Carlisle Rd, E10 96 A2
N4 75 G7
NW6 108 B1
NW9 70 C3
Hampton TW12 161 H7
Sutton SM1 198 C5
Carlisle St, W1 17 H4
Carlisle Wk, E8
off Laurel St 94 C6
Carlisle Way, SW17 168 A5
Carlos Pl, W1 16 C6
Carlow St, NW1 9 F1
Carlton Av, N14 42 D5
Feltham TW14 142 C6
Harrow HA3 68 E5
Hayes UB3 121 H4
South Croydon CR2 202 B7
Carlton Av E, Wem. HA9 87 H1
Carlton Av W, Wem. HA0 86 E2
Carlton Cl, NW3 90 D2
Borehamwood WD6 38 D4
Chessington KT9 195 G6
Edgware HA8 54 A5
Northolt UB5
off Whitton Av W 85 J5
Carlton Ct, SW9 151 H1
Ilford IG6 81 G3
Carlton Cres, Sutt. SM3 198 B4
Carlton Dr, SW15 148 B5
Ilford IG6 81 G3
Carlton Gdns, SW1 25 H2
W5 105 F6
Carlton Gro, SE15 152 E1
Carlton Hill, NW8 109 F2
Carlton Ho, Felt. TW14 141 J7
Carlton Ho Ter, SW1 25 H2
Carlton Pk Av, SW20 183 J2
Carlton Rd, E11 97 F1
E12 98 A4
E17 77 H1
N4 75 G7
N11 58 A5
SW14 146 C3
W4 126 D2
W5 105 F7
Erith DA8 139 H6
New Malden KT3 182 E2
Sidcup DA14 175 J5
South Croydon CR2 202 A6
Walton-on-Thames
KT12 178 B7
Welling DA16 158 B3
Carlton Sq, E1
off Argyle Rd 113 G4
Carlton St, SW1 17 H6
Carlton Ter, E11 79 H5
N18 60 A3
SE26 171 F3
Carlton Twr Pl, SW1 24 A5
Carlton Vale, NW6 108 E2
Carlton Vil, SW15
off St. John's Av 147 J5
Carlwell St, SW17 167 H5
Carlyle Av, Brom. BR1 192 A3
Carlyle Av, Sthl. UB1 103 F7
Carlyle Cl, N2 73 F6
West Molesey KT8 179 H2
Carlyle Gdns, Sthl. UB1 103 F7
Carlyle Lo, Barn.
(New Barn.) EN5
off Richmond Rd 41 F5
Carlyle Ms, E1
off Alderney Rd 113 G4
Carlyle Pl, SW15 148 A4
Carlyle Rd, E12 98 B4
NW10 106 D1
SE28 118 B7
W5 125 F5
Croydon CR0 202 D2
★Carlyle's Ho, SW3 31 G6
Carlyle Sq, SW3 31 F4
Carlyon Av, Har. HA2 85 F4
Carlyon Cl, Wem. HA0 105 H1
Carlyon Rd, Hayes UB4 102 C6
Wembley HA0 105 H2
Carmalt Gdns, SW15 147 J4
Carmarthen Grn, NW9
off Snowdon Dr 70/71 E6
Carmarthen Pl, SE1
off Bermondsey St 132 B2
Carmel Ct, W8 22 A3
Wembley HA9 88 B2
Carmelite Cl, Har. HA3 67 J1
Carmelite Rd, Har. HA3 67 J1
Carmelite St, EC4 19 F5
Carmelite Wk, Har. HA3 67 J1
Carmelite Way, Har. HA3 67 J2
Carmen St, E14 114 B6
Carmichael Cl, SW11
off Darien Rd 149 G3
Ruislip HA4 84 A4
Carmichael Ms, SW18 149 G7
Carmichael Rd, SE25 188 D5
Carminia Rd, SW17 168 B2
Carnaby St, W1 17 F4
Carnac St, SE27 170 A4
Carnanton Rd, E17 78 D1
Carnarvon Av, Enf. EN1 44 C3
Carnarvon Dr, Hayes
UB3 121 F3
Carnarvon Rd, E10 78 C6
E15 97 F6
E18 79 F1
Barnet EN5 40 B3
Carnation St, SE2 138 B5
Carnbrook Rd, SE3 156 A3
Carnecke Gdns, SE9 156 B5
Carnegie Cl, Surb. KT6
off Fullers Av 195 J2
Carnegie Pl, SW19 166 A3
Carnegie St, N1 111 F1
Carnforth Cl, Epsom
KT19 196 B6
Carnforth Rd, SW16 168 D7
Carnie Lo, SW17
off Manville Rd 168 B3
Carnoustie Cl, SE28
off Redbourne Dr 118 D6
Carnoustie Dr, N1 93 F7
Carnwath Rd, SW6 148 D3
Carol Cl, NW4 72 A4
Carolina Cl, E15 96 E5
Carolina Rd, Th.Hth. CR7 187 H2
Caroline Cl, N10
off Alexandra Pk Rd 74 B2
SW16 169 F4
W2 14 B6
Croydon CR0 202 B4
Isleworth TW7 124 A7
West Drayton UB7 120 A2
Caroline Ct, Stan. HA7
off The Chase 52 D6
Caroline Gdns, SE15 132 E7
Caroline Pl, SW11 150 A2
W2 14 B5
Hayes UB3 121 H7
Caroline Pl Ms, W2 14 B6
Caroline Rd, SW19 166 C7
Caroline St, E1 113 G6
Caroline Ter, SW1 32 B2
Caroline Wk, W6 128 B6
Carol St, NW1 110 C1
Carpenders Av, Wat.
WD19 50 E3
CARPENDERS PARK,
Wat. WD19 51 F2
Carpenders Pk, Wat.
WD19 51 E2
Carpenter Gdns, N21 59 H2
Carpenters Arms Path, SE9
off Eltham High St 156 C6
Carpenters Ct, Twick.
TW2 162 B2

Carpenters Ms, N7
off North Rd 92 E5
Carpenters Pl, SW4 150 D4
Carpenters Rd, E15 96 B6
Carpenter St, W1 16 D6
Carrara Cl, SW9
off Eaton Dr. 151 H4
Carrara Ms, E8 94 D5
Carrara Wf, SW6 148 B3
Carr Cl, Stan. HA7 52 F6
Carr Gro, SE18 136 B4
Carriage Dr E, SW11 32 B7
Carriage Dr N, SW11 32 C6
Carriage Dr S, SW11 149 J1
Carriage Dr W, SW11 129 J7
Carriage Ms, Ilf. IG1 99 F2
Carriage Pl, N16 94 A3
SW16 *off Eardley Rd.* 168 C5
Carriage St, SE18 137 E3
Carrick Cl, Islw. TW7 144 D3
Carrick Dr, Ilf. IG6 81 F1
Carrick Gdns, N17
off Flexmere Rd 60 B7
Carrick Ms, SE8
off Watergate St 134 A6
Carrill Way, Belv. DA17 138 D4
Carrington Av, Borwd.
WD6 38 B5
Hounslow TW3 143 H5
Carrington Cl, Barn.
EN5 39 G5
Borehamwood WD6 38 C5
Croydon CR0 189 H7
Kingston upon Thames
KT2 164 C5
Carrington Gdns, E7
off Woodford Rd 97 H4
Carrington Rd, Rich.
TW10 146 A4
Carrington Sq, Har. HA3 51 J7
Carrington St, W1 24 D2
Carrol Cl, NW5 92 B4
Carroll Cl, E15 97 F5
Carroll Hill, Loug. IG10 48 C3
Carronade Pl, SE28 137 F3
Carron Cl, E14 114 B6
Carroun Rd, SW8 34 C7
Carroway La, Grnf. UB6
off Cowgate Rd 104 A3
Carrow Rd, Dag. RM9 100 B7
Carr Rd, E17 77 J2
Northolt UB5 85 G6
Carrs La, N21 43 J5
Carr St, E14 113 H5
CARSHALTON, SM5 199 G4
Carshalton Gro, Sutt.
SM1 199 G4
Carshalton Pk Rd, Cars.
SM5 199 J5
Carshalton Pl, Cars.
SM5 200 A4
Carshalton Rd, Cars.
SM5 199 F5
Mitcham CR4 186 A4
Sutton SM1 199 F5
Carslake Rd, SW15 147 J6
Carson Rd, E16 115 G4
SE21 170 A2
Barnet EN4 41 J4
Carstairs Rd, SE6 172 C3
Carston Cl, SE12 155 F5
Carswell Cl, Ilf. IG4
off Roding La S 80 A4
Carswell Rd, SE6 154 C7
Carter Cl, Wall. SM6 200 D7
Carter Ct, EC4
off Carter La 111 H6
Carteret St, SW1 25 H4
Carteret Way, SE8 133 H4
Carterhatch La, Enf. EN1 44 D2
Carterhatch Rd, Enf. EN3 45 F2
Carter La, EC4 19 H4
Carter Pl, SE17 36 A4
Carter Rd, E13 115 H1
SW19 167 G6
Carters Cl, Wor.Pk. KT4 198 A2
Carters Hill Cl, SE9 173 J1
Carters La, SE23 171 H2
Carter St, SE17 35 J5
Carters Yd, SW18 *off*
Wandsworth High St. 148 D5
Carthew Rd, W6 127 H3
Carthew Vil, W6 127 H3
Carthusian St, EC1 19 J1
Cartier Circle, E14 134 B1
Carting La, WC2 18 B6
Cart La, E4 46 D7
Cartmel Cl, N17
off Heybourne Rd 60/61 E7
Cartmel Gdns, Mord.
SM4 185 F5
Cartmel Rd, Bexh. DA7 159 G1
Carton St, W1 16 A3
Cartridge Pl, SE18 137 E3
Cartwright Gdns, WC1 10 A4
Cartwright Rd, Dag.
RM9 101 F7
Cartwright St, E1 21 G5
Cartwright Way, SW13 127 H7
Carver Cl, W4 126 C3
Carver Rd, SE24 151 J6
Carville Cres, Brent. TW8 125 H4
Cary Rd, E11 97 E4
Carysfort Rd, N8 74 D5
N16 94 A3
Cascade Av, N10 74 C4
Cascade Cl, Buck.H. IG9
off Cascade Rd 64 A2
Cascade Rd, Buck.H. IG9 64 A2
Casella Rd, SE14 133 G7
Casewick Rd, SE27 169 H4
Casey Cl, NW8 7 G4
Casimir Rd, E5 95 E3
Casino Av, SE24 151 J5
Caspian St, SE5 36 B7
Caspian Wk, E16 116 A6
Caspian Wf, E3
off Violet Rd 114 B5
Cassandra Cl, Nthlt. UB5 86 A4
Casselden Rd, NW10 88 D7
Cassidy Rd, SW6 128 D7
Cassilda Rd, SE2 138 A4
Cassilis Rd, Twick. TW1 145 E5
Cassiobury Av, Felt.
TW14 141 J6
Cassiobury Rd, E17 77 G5
Cassis Ct, Loug. IG10 49 F4
Cassland Rd, E9 95 F7
Thornton Heath CR7 188 A4
Casslee Rd, SE6 153 J7
Casson St, E1 21 H2
Castalia Sq, E14
off Roserton St 134 C2
Castalia St, E14
off Plevna St 134 C2
Castellain Rd, W9 6 C6
Castellane Cl, Stan. HA7
off Daventer Dr 52 C7
Castello Av, SW15 147 J5
Castell Rd, Loug. IG10 49 F1
CASTELNAU, SW13 127 G6
Castelnau, SW13 127 H6
Castelnau Gdns, SW13
off Arundel Ter 127 H6
Castelnau Pl, SW13
off Castelnau 127 H6
Castelnau Row, SW13
off Lonsdale Rd 127 H6
Casterbridge, NW6 109 E1
Casterbridge Rd, SE3 155 G3
Casterton St, E8
off Wilton Way 94/95 E6
Castile Rd, SE18 136 D4
Castillon Rd, SE6 172 E2
Castlands Rd, SE6 171 J2
Castle Av, E4 62 D5
Castlebar Hill, W5 105 E5
Castlebar Ms, W5 105 F5
Castlebar Pk, W5 105 E4
Castlebar Rd, W5 105 F5
Castle Baynard St, EC4 19 H5
Castlebrook Cl, SE11 35 G1
Castle Cl, E9
off Swinnerton St 95 H5
SW19 166 A3
W3 126 B2
Bromley BR2 190 E3
Castlecombe Dr, SW19 148 A7
Castlecombe Rd, SE9 174 B4
Castle Ct, EC3 20 C4
SE26 *off Champion Rd* 171 H4
SW15 *off Brewhouse La* 148 B3
Castledine Rd, SE20 170 E7
Castle Dr, Ilf. IG4 80 B6
Castleford Av, SE9 174 E1
Castleford Cl, N17 60 C6
Castlegate, Rich. TW9 145 J3
Castlehaven Rd, NW1 92 B7
Castle La, SW1 25 G5
Castleleigh Ct, Enf. EN2 44 A5
Castlemaine Av, S.Croy.
CR2 202 C5
Castlemaine Twr, SW11 149 J1
Castle Ms, N12
off Castle Rd 57 F5
NW1 *off Castle Rd* 92 B6
Hampton TW12
off Station Rd 179 H1
Castle Par, Epsom KT17
off Ewell Bypass 197 G7
Castle Pl, NW1 92 B6
W4
off Windmill Rd 126/127 E4
Castle Pt, E13 115 J2
Castlereagh St, W1 15 J3
Castle Rd, N12 57 F5
NW1 92 B6
Dagenham RM9 118 B1
Enfield EN3 45 H1
Isleworth TW7 144 C2
Northolt UB5 85 H6
Southall UB2 123 F3
Castle St, E6 115 J2
Kingston upon Thames
KT1 181 H2
Castleton Av, Wem. HA9 87 H4
Castleton Cl, Croy. CR0 189 H6
Castleton Gdns, Wem.
HA9 87 H3
Castleton Rd, E17 78 D2
SE9 174 A4
Ilford IG3 100 A1
Mitcham CR4 186 D4
Ruislip HA4 84 D1
Castletown Rd, W14 128 B5
Castleview Cl, N4 93 J1
Castleview Gdns, Ilf. IG1 80 B6
Castle Wk, Sun. TW16
off Elizabeth Gdns 178 C3
Castle Way, SW19 166 A3
Feltham TW13 160 C4
Castlewood Dr, SE9 156 C2
Castlewood Rd, N15 76 D6
N16 76 D7
Barnet EN4 41 G3
Castle Yd, N6
off North Rd 74 A7
SE1 27 H1
Richmond TW10
off Hill St 145 G5
Castor La, E14 114 B7
Caterham Av, Ilf. IG5 80 C2
Caterham Rd, SE13 154 C3
Catesby St, SE17 36 C2
CATFORD, SE6 172 B1
Catford Bdy, SE6 154 B7
Catford Hill, SE6 171 J2
Catford Ms, SE6
off Holbeach Rd 154 B7
Catford Rd, SE6 172 A1
Cathall Rd, E11 96 D3
Cathay St, SE16 133 E2
Cathay Wk, Nthlt. UB5
off Brabazon Rd 103 G2
Cathcart Dr, Orp. BR6 207 H2
Cathcart Hill, N19 92 C3
Cathcart Rd, SW10 30 D5
Cathcart St, NW5 92 B6
Cathedral Piazza, SW1 25 F6
Cathedral St, SE1 28 B1
Catherall Rd, N5 93 J3
Catherine Cl, Loug. IG10
off Roding Gdns 48 C6
Catherine Ct, N14
off Conisbee Ct 42 C5
Catherine Dr, Rich. TW9 145 H4
Catherine Gdns, Houns.
TW3 144 A4
Catherine Griffiths Ct,
EC1 11 F5
Catherine Gro, SE10 154 B1
Catherine Pl, SW1 25 F5
Harrow HA1 68 C5
Catherine Rd, Surb. KT6 181 G5
Catherine's Cl, West Dr.
UB7 *off Money La* 120 A3
Catherine St, WC2 18 C5
Catherine Wheel All, E1 20 E2
Catherine Wheel Rd,
Brent. TW8 125 G7
Catherine Wheel Yd, SW1 25 F2
Cat Hill, Barn. EN4 41 H6
Cathles Rd, SW12 150 B6
Cathnor Rd, W12 127 H2
Catling Cl, SE23 171 F3
Catlins La, Pnr. HA5 66 B3
Catlin St, SE16 37 J4
Cator La, Beck. BR3 189 J2
Cato Rd, SW4 150 D3
Cator Rd, SE26 171 G6
Carshalton SM5 199 J5
Cator St, SE15 37 F6
Cato St, W1 15 H2
Catterick Cl, N11 58 A6
Cattistock Rd, SE9 174 B5
Cattley Cl, Barn. EN5
off Wood St 40 B4
Catton St, WC1 18 C2
Caulfield Rd, E6 98 C7
SE15 153 E2
Causeway, The, N2 73 H4
SW18 148 E4
SW19 166 A5
Carshalton SM5 200 A3
Chessington KT9 195 H4
Esher (Clay.) KT10 194 C7
Feltham TW14 142 A4
Hounslow TW4 142 A4
Teddington TW11
off Broad St 162 C6
Causeyware Rd, N9 45 E7
Causton Rd, N6 74 B7
Causton Sq, Dag. RM10 101 G7
Causton St, SW1 33 J2
Cautley Av, SW4 150 C5
Cavalier Cl, Rom. RM6 82 D4
Cavalry Barracks, Houns.
TW4 142 D3
Cavalry Cres, Houns.
TW4 142 D4
Cavalry Gdns, SW15 148 B5
Cavan Pl, Pnr. HA5 67 F1
Cavaye Pl, SW10 30 D4
Cavell Dr, Enf. EN2 43 G2
Cavell Rd, N17 60 A7
Cavell St, E1 113 E5
Cavendish Av, N3 72 D2
NW8 7 F2
W13 104 D5
Erith DA8 139 J6
Harrow HA1 86 A4
New Malden KT3 183 H5
Ruislip HA4 84 B5
Sidcup DA15 158 A7
Welling DA16 157 J3
Woodford Green IG8 79 H1
Cavendish Cl, N18 61 E5
NW6 *off Cavendish Rd* 90 C7
NW8 7 F3
Cavendish Ct, EC3 20 E3
Cavendish Cres, Borwd.
(Elstree) WD6 38 A4
Cavendish Dr, E11 96 D1
Edgware HA8 53 J6
Esher (Clay.) KT10 194 B5
Cavendish Gdns, Bark.
IG11 99 H5
Ilford IG1 98 D1
Romford RM6 83 E5
Cavendish Ms N, W1 16 E1
Cavendish Ms S, W1 16 E2
Cavendish Par, Houns. TW4
off Bath Rd 142/143 E2
Cavendish Pl, W1 16 E3
Cavendish Rd, E4 62 C6
N4 75 G6
Cavendish Rd, N18 60 E5
NW6 90 B7
SW12 150 B6
SW19 167 G7
W4 146 C1
Barnet EN5 39 J3
Croydon CR0 201 H1
New Malden KT3 183 F5
Sutton SM2 199 F7
Cavendish Sq, W1 16 E3
Cavendish St, N1 12 B2
Cavendish Ter, Felt. TW13
off High St 160 A2
Cavendish Way, W.Wick.
BR4 204 B1
Cavenham Gdns, Ilf. IG1 99 G3
Caverleigh Way, Wor.Pk.
KT4 197 G1
Cave Rd, E13 115 H2
Richmond TW10 163 F4
Caversham Av, N13 59 G3
Sutton SM3 198 B2
Caversham Ct, N11 58 A3
Caversham Flats, SW3 31 J5
Caversham Rd, N15 75 J4
NW5 92 C6
Kingston upon Thames
KT1 181 J2
Caversham St, SW3 31 J5
Caverswall St, W12 107 J6
Caveside Cl, Chis. BR7 192 D1
Cawdor Cres, W7 124 D4
Cawnpore St, SE19 170 B5
Caxton Gro, E3 114 A3
Caxton Ms, Brent. TW8
off The Butts 125 G6
Caxton Rd, N22 75 F2
SW19 167 F5
W12 128 A2
Southall UB2 122 D3

Caxton St, SW1 ..... **25** G5
Caxton St N, E16
off Victoria Dock Rd **115** F7
Cayenne Ct, SE1 ..... **29** G2
Caygill Cl, Brom. BR2 ..... **191** F4
Cayley Cl, Wall. SM6 ..... **200** E7
Cayley Rd, Sthl. UB2
off McNair Rd **123** H3
Cayton Pl, EC1 ..... **12** B4
Cayton Rd, Grnf. UB6 ..... **104** B2
Cayton St, EC1 ..... **12** B4
Cazenove Rd, E17 ..... **78** A1
N16 ..... **94** C2
Cearns Ho, E6 ..... **116** A1
Cecil Av, Bark. IG11 ..... **99** G7
Enfield EN1 ..... **44** C4
Wembley HA9 ..... **87** J5
Cecil Cl, W5
off Helena Rd **105** G5
Chessington KT9 ..... **195** G4
Cecil Ct, WC2 ..... **17** J6
Barnet EN5 ..... **40** A3
Cecile Pk, N8 ..... **75** E6
Cecilia Cl, N2 ..... **73** F3
★**Cecilia Coleman Gall**, NW8 ..... **7** F1
Cecilia Rd, E8 ..... **94** D5
Cecil Pk, Pnr. HA5 ..... **67** E4
Cecil Pl, Mitch. CR4 ..... **185** J5
Cecil Rd, E11 ..... **97** E3
E13 ..... **115** G1
E17 ..... **78** A1
N10 ..... **74** B2
N14 ..... **58** C1
NW9 ..... **70** E3
NW10 ..... **106** E1
SW19 ..... **166** E7
W3 ..... **106** C5
Croydon CR0 ..... **187** F6
Enfield EN2 ..... **44** A4
Harrow HA3 ..... **68** B3
Hounslow TW3 ..... **143** J2
Ilford IG1 ..... **98** E4
Romford RM6 ..... **82** D7
Sutton SM1 ..... **198** C6
★**Cecil Sharp Ho**, NW1 ..... **110** A1
Cecil Way, Brom. BR2 ..... **205** G1
Cedar Av, Barn. EN4 ..... **41** H7
Enfield EN3 ..... **45** F2
Hayes UB3 ..... **102** A6
Romford RM6 ..... **82** E5
Ruislip HA4 ..... **84** C6
Sidcup DA15 ..... **158** A7
Twickenham TW2 ..... **143** H6
West Drayton UB7 ..... **120** C1
Cedar Cl, E3 ..... **113** J1
SE21 ..... **169** J1
SW15 ..... **164** D4
Borehamwood WD6 ..... **38** B4
Bromley BR2 ..... **206** B3
Buckhurst Hill IG9 ..... **64** A2
Carshalton SM5 ..... **199** J6
East Molesey KT8
off Cedar Rd **180** B4
Romford RM7 ..... **83** J4
Cedar Copse, Brom. BR1 ..... **192** C2
Cedar Ct, E11
off Grosvenor Rd **79** H5
N1 *off Essex Rd* **93** J7
SE9 ..... **156** B6
SW19 ..... **166** A3
Cedar Cres, Brom. BR2 ..... **206** B3
Cedarcroft Rd, Chess. KT9 ..... **195** J4
Cedar Dr, N2 ..... **73** H4
Loughton IG10 ..... **49** E2
Pinner HA5 ..... **51** G6
Cedar Gdns, Sutt. SM2 ..... **199** F6
Cedar Gro, W5 ..... **125** H3
Bexley DA5 ..... **158** C6
Southall UB1 ..... **103** G5
Cedar Hts, Rich. TW10 ..... **163** H1
Cedar Ho, Croy. CR0 ..... **204** B6
Cedarhurst, Brom. BR1
off Elstree Hill **172/173** E7
Cedarhurst Dr, SE9 ..... **155** J5
Cedar Lawn Av, Barn. EN5 ..... **40** B5
Cedar Mt, SE9 ..... **174** A1
Cedarne Rd, SW6 ..... **128** E7
Cedar Pk, Chig. IG7
off High Rd **64/65** E4
Cedar Pk Gdns, Rom. RM6 ..... **82** D7
Cedar Pl, SE7
off Floyd Rd **135** J5
Cedar Ri, N14 ..... **42** A7
Cedar Rd, N17 ..... **76** C1
Cedar Rd, NW2 ..... **89** J4
Bromley BR1 ..... **191** J2
Croydon CR0 ..... **202** B2
East Molesey KT8 ..... **180** B4
Hounslow TW4 ..... **142** C2
Romford RM7 ..... **83** J4
Sutton SM2 ..... **199** F6
Teddington TW11 ..... **162** D5
Cedars, The, E15
off Portway **115** F1
W13 *off Heronsforde* **105** F6
Buckhurst Hill IG9 ..... **63** G1
Teddington TW11
off Adelaide Rd **162** C6
Cedars Av, E17 ..... **78** A5
Mitcham CR4 ..... **186** A4
Cedars Cl, NW4 ..... **72** A3
SE13 ..... **154** D3
Cedars Ct, N9
off Church St **60** B2
Cedars Ms, SW4
off Cedars Rd **150** B4
Cedars Rd, E15 ..... **97** E6
N9 *off Church St* **60** D2
N21 ..... **59** H2
SW4 ..... **150** B3
SW13 ..... **147** F2
W4 ..... **126** C5
Beckenham BR3 ..... **189** H2
Croydon CR0 ..... **201** E3
Kingston upon Thames (Hmptn W.) KT1 ..... **181** F1
Morden SM4 ..... **184** D4
Cedar Ter, Rich. TW9 ..... **145** H4
Cedar Tree Gro, SE27 ..... **169** H5
Cedarville Gdns, SW16 ..... **169** F6
Cedar Vista, Rich. TW9
off Kew Rd **145** H1
Cedar Wk, Esher (Clay.) KT10 ..... **194** C6
Cedar Way, NW1 ..... **92** D7
Cedra Ct, N16 ..... **94** D1
Cedric Rd, SE9 ..... **175** F3
Celadon Cl, Enf. EN3 ..... **45** H3
Celandine Cl, E14 ..... **114** A5
Celandine Dr, E8 ..... **94** C7
SE28 ..... **138** B1
Celandine Way, E15 ..... **115** E3
Celbridge Ms, W2 ..... **14** B3
Celestial Gdns, SE13 ..... **154** D4
Celia Rd, N19 ..... **92** C4
Celtic Av, Brom. BR2 ..... **190** E3
Celtic St, E14 ..... **114** B5
Cemetery La, SE7 ..... **136** B6
Cemetery Rd, E7 ..... **97** F4
N17 ..... **60** B7
SE2 ..... **138** B7
Cenacle Cl, NW3 ..... **90** D3
★**Cenotaph, The**, SW1 ..... **26** A3
Centaurs Business Cen, Islw. TW7 ..... **124** D6
Centaur St, SE1 ..... **26** D5
Centenary Est, Enf. EN3 ..... **45** J4
Centenary Rd, Enf. EN3 ..... **45** J4
Centenary Wk, Loug. IG10 ..... **47** H3
Central Av, E11 ..... **96** D2
N2 ..... **73** G2
N9 ..... **60** B3
SW11 ..... **129** J7
Enfield EN1 ..... **44** E2
Hayes UB3 ..... **102** A7
Hounslow TW3 ..... **143** J4
Pinner HA5 ..... **67** F6
Wallington SM6 ..... **201** E5
Welling DA16 ..... **157** J2
West Molesey KT8 ..... **179** F4
Central Circ, NW4
off Hendon Way **71** H5
★**Central Criminal Ct (Old Bailey)**, EC4 ..... **19** H3
Central Gdns, Mord. SM4
off Central Rd **184/185** E5
Central Hill, SE19 ..... **170** A5
Central Ho, E15
off High St **114** C2
Barking IG11
off Cambridge Rd **99** F7
Central Par, Felt. TW14 ..... **142** C7
Greenford UB6 ..... **104** D3
Hounslow TW5
off Heston Rd **123** G7
Surbiton KT6
off St. Mark's Hill **181** H6
Central Pk Av, Dag. RM10 ..... **101** H3
Central Pk Est, Houns. TW4 ..... **142** D5
Central Pk Rd, E6 ..... **116** A2
Central Pl, SE25
off Portland Rd **188/189** E4
Central Rd, Mord. SM4 ..... **184** D5
Wembley HA0 ..... **86** E5
Worcester Park KT4 ..... **197** G2
Central Sch Footpath, SW14 ..... **146** C3
Central Sq, NW11 ..... **72** E6
Wembley HA9
off Station Gro **87** H5
West Molesey KT8 ..... **179** F4
Central St, EC1 ..... **11** J4
Central Way, NW10 ..... **106** C3
SE28 ..... **138** A1
Carshalton SM5 ..... **199** H7
Feltham TW14 ..... **142** B5
Centre, The, Felt. TW13 ..... **160** A2
Centre at the Circ, W1 ..... **17** G6
Centre Av, W3 ..... **126** D1
W10 *off Harrow Rd* **107** J3
Centre Common Rd, Chis. BR7 ..... **175** F6
Centre Ct Shop Cen, SW19 ..... **166** C6
Centrepoint, WC1 ..... **17** J3
Centre Rd, E7 ..... **97** G2
E11 ..... **97** G2
Dagenham RM10 ..... **119** H2
Centre St, E2 ..... **113** E2
Centre Way, E17 ..... **62** C7
N9 ..... **61** F2
Centreway, Ilf. IG1 ..... **99** F2
Centric Cl, NW1
off Oval Rd **110** B1
Centurion Cl, N7 ..... **93** F7
Centurion Ct, Wall. SM6
off Wandle Rd **200** B2
Centurion La, E3
off Libra Rd **113** J2
Centurion Way, Erith DA18 ..... **139** G3
Century Cl, NW4 ..... **72** A5
Century Ms, E5
off Lower Clapton Rd **95** F4
Century Rd, E17 ..... **77** H3
Century Yd, SE23 ..... **171** F2
Cephas Av, E1 ..... **113** F4
Cephas St, E1 ..... **113** F4
Ceres Rd, SE18 ..... **137** J4
Cerise Rd, SE15 ..... **152** D1
Cerne Cl, Hayes UB4 ..... **102** D7
Cerne Rd, Mord. SM4 ..... **185** F6
Cerney Ms, W2 ..... **15** E5
Cervantes Ct, W2 ..... **14** B4
Cester St, E2
off Whiston Rd **112** D1
Ceylon Rd, W14 ..... **128** A3
Chabot Dr, SE15
off Linden Gro **152** D3
Chadacre Av, Ilf. IG5 ..... **80** C3
Chadacre Rd, Epsom KT17 ..... **197** H6
Chadbourn St, E14 ..... **114** B5
Chad Cres, N9 ..... **61** F3
Chadd Dr, Brom. BR1 ..... **192** B3
Chadd Grn, E13 ..... **115** G1
Chadview Ct, Rom. (Chad.Hth) RM6 ..... **82** D7
Chadville Gdns, Rom. RM6 ..... **82** D5
Chadway, Dag. RM8 ..... **100** C1
Chadwell Av, Rom. RM6 ..... **82** B7
CHADWELL HEATH, Rom. RM6 ..... **82** D6
Chadwell Heath La, Rom. RM6 ..... **82** B5
Chadwell St, EC1 ..... **11** F3
Chadwick Av, E4 ..... **62** D4
N21 *off Laidlaw Dr* **43** F5
SW19 ..... **166** D6
Chadwick Cl, SW15 ..... **147** F7
W7 *off Westcott Cres* **104** C5
Teddington TW11 ..... **162** D6
Chadwick Ms, W4
off Thames Rd **126** B6
Chadwick Pl, Surb. KT6 ..... **181** F7
Chadwick Rd, E11 ..... **79** E7
NW10 ..... **107** F1
SE15 ..... **152** C2
Ilford IG1 ..... **99** E3
Chadwick St, SW1 ..... **25** J6
Chadwick Way, SE28 ..... **118** D7
Chadwin Rd, E13 ..... **115** H5
Chadworth Way, Esher (Clay.) KT10 ..... **194** A5
Chaffinch Av, Croy. CR0 ..... **189** G6
Chaffinch Cl, N9 ..... **61** G1
Croydon CR0 ..... **189** G6
Surbiton KT6 ..... **196** A3
Chaffinch Rd, Beck. BR3 ..... **189** H1
Chafford Way, Rom. RM6 ..... **82** C4
Chagford St, NW1 ..... **7** J6
Chailey Av, Enf. EN1 ..... **44** C2
Chailey Cl, Houns. TW5
off Springwell Rd **142** D1
Chailey St, E5 ..... **95** F3
Chalbury Wk, N1 ..... **10** D1
Chalcombe Rd, SE2 ..... **138** B3
Chalcot Cl, Sutt. SM2 ..... **198** D7
Chalcot Cres, NW1 ..... **109** J1
Chalcot Gdns, NW3 ..... **91** J6
Chalcot Ms, SW16 ..... **168** E3
Chalcot Rd, NW1 ..... **92** A7
Chalcot Sq, NW1 ..... **92** A7
Chalcott Gdns, Surb. KT6 ..... **195** F1
Chalcroft Rd, SE13 ..... **154** E5
Chaldon Path, Th.Hth. CR7 ..... **187** H4
Chaldon Rd, SW6 ..... **128** B7
Chale Rd, SW2 ..... **150** E6
Chalet Est, NW7 ..... **55** G4
Chalfont Av, Wem. HA9 ..... **88** B6
Chalfont Ct, NW9 ..... **71** F3
Chalfont Grn, N9 ..... **60** B3
Chalfont Ms, SW19
off Augustus Rd **166** C1
Chalfont Rd, N9 ..... **60** B3
SE25 ..... **188** C3
Hayes UB3 ..... **122** A2
Chalfont Wk, Pnr. HA5
off Willows Cl **66** C2
Chalfont Way, W13 ..... **124** E3
Chalford Cl, W.Mol. KT8 ..... **179** G4
Chalford Rd, SE21 ..... **170** A4
Chalford Wk, Wdf.Grn. IG8 ..... **80** A1
Chalgrove Av, Mord. SM4 ..... **184** D5
Chalgrove Cres, Ilf. IG5 ..... **80** B2
Chalgrove Gdns, N3 ..... **72** B3
Chalgrove Rd, N17 ..... **76** E1
Sutton SM2 ..... **199** G7
Chalice Cl, Wall. SM6
off Lavender Vale **200** D6
Chalkenden Cl, SE20 ..... **170** E7
Chalk Fm Rd, NW1 ..... **92** A7
Chalk Hill Rd, W6
off Shortlands **128** A4
Chalkhill Rd, Wem. HA9 ..... **88** B3
Chalklands, Wem. HA9 ..... **88** C3
Chalk La, Barn. EN4 ..... **41** J4
Chalkley Cl, Mitch. CR4 ..... **185** J2
Chalkmill Dr, Enf. EN1 ..... **44** E3
Chalk Pit Way, Sutt. SM1 ..... **199** F5
Chalk Rd, E13 ..... **115** H5
Chalkstone Cl, Well. DA16 ..... **158** A1
Chalkwell Pk Av, Enf. EN1 ..... **44** B4
Challice Way, SW2 ..... **169** F1
Challin St, SE20 ..... **189** F1
Challis Rd, Brent. TW8 ..... **125** G5
Challoner Cl, N2 ..... **73** G2
Challoner Cres, W14
off Challoner St **128** C5
Challoners Cl, E.Mol. KT8 ..... **180** A4
Challoner St, W14 ..... **128** C5
Chalmers Ho, SW11
off York Rd **149** F3
Chalmers Wk, SE17 ..... **35** H6
Chalmers Way, Felt. TW14 ..... **142** A5
Chaloner Ct, SE1 ..... **28** B3
Chalsey Rd, SE4 ..... **153** J4
Chalton Dr, N2 ..... **73** F6
Chalton St, NW1 ..... **9** J3
Chamberlain Cl, SE28
off Broadwater Rd **137** G3
Chamberlain Cotts, SE5
off Camberwell Gro **152** A1
Chamberlain Cres, W.Wick. BR4 ..... **204** B1
Chamberlain Gdns, Houns. TW3 ..... **143** J1
Chamberlain La, Pnr. HA5 ..... **66** A4
Chamberlain Pl, E17 ..... **77** H3
Chamberlain Rd, N2 ..... **73** F2
N9 ..... **60** D3
W13 *off Midhurst Rd* **124** D2
Chamberlain St, NW1
off Regents Pk Rd **91** J7
Chamberlain Wk, Felt. TW13
off Burgess Cl **160/161** E4
Chamberlain Way, Pnr. HA5 ..... **66** B3

Chamberlain Way, Surb. KT6 . . . 181 H7
Chamberlayne Av, Wem. HA9 . . . 87 H2
Chamberlayne Rd, NW10 . . . 108 A3
Chambers Gdns, N2 . . . 73 G1
Chambers La, NW10 . . . 89 H7
Chambers Pl, S.Croy. CR2 *off Rolleston Rd* . . . 202 A7
Chambers Rd, N7 . . . 92 E4
Chambers St, SE16 . . . 29 H3
Chamber St, E1 . . . 21 G5
Chambers Wk, Stan. HA7 . . . 52 E6
Chambon Pl, W6 *off Beavor La* . . . 127 G4
Chambord St, E2 . . . 13 G4
Champion Cres, SE26 . . . 171 H4
Champion Gro, SE5 . . . 152 A3
Champion Hill, SE5 . . . 152 A3
Champion Hill Est, SE5 . . . 152 B3
Champion Pk, SE5 . . . 152 A2
Champion Pk Est, SE5 *off Denmark Hill* . . . 152 A3
Champion Rd, SE26 . . . 171 H4
Champness Cl, SE27 *off Rommany Rd* . . . 170 A4
Champness Rd, Bark. IG11 . . . 99 J6
Champneys Cl, Sutt. SM2 . . . 198 C7
Chancellor Gro, SE21 . . . 169 J2
Chancellor Pas, E14 *off South Colonnade* . . . 134 A1
Chancellor Pl, NW9 . . . 71 F2
Chancellors Rd, W6 . . . 127 J5
Chancellors St, W6 . . . 127 J5
Chancelot Rd, SE2 . . . 138 B4
Chancel St, SE1 . . . 27 G1
Chancery La, WC2 . . . 18 E3
Beckenham BR3 . . . 190 B2
Chancery Ms, SW17 . . . 167 H2
Chance St, E1 . . . 13 F5
E2 . . . 13 F5
Chanctonbury Cl, SE9 . . . 175 E3
Chanctonbury Gdns, Sutt. SM2 . . . 198 E7
Chanctonbury Way, N12 . . . 56 C4
Chandler Av, E16 . . . 115 G5
Chandler Cl, Hmptn. TW12 . . . 179 G1
Chandler Ms, Twick. TW1 . . . 144 D7
Chandler Rd, Loug. IG10 . . . 49 E1
Chandlers Cl, Felt. TW14 . . . 141 J7
Chandlers Ms, E14 . . . 134 A2
Chandler St, E1 *off Wapping La* . . . 132/133 E1
Chandlers Way, SW2 . . . 151 G7
Chandler Way, SE15 . . . 132 C7
Chandon Lo, Sutt. SM2 *off Devonshire Rd* . . . 199 F7
Chandos Av, E17 . . . 78 A2
N14 . . . 58 C3
N20 . . . 57 F1
W5 . . . 125 F4
Chandos Cl, Buck.H. IG9 . . . 63 H2
Chandos Ct, Stan. HA7 . . . 52 E6
Chandos Cres, Edg. HA8 . . . 53 J7
Chandos Par, Edg. HA8 *off Chandos Cres* . . . 53 J7
Chandos Pl, WC2 . . . 18 A6
Chandos Rd, E15 . . . 96 D5
N2 . . . 73 G2
N17 . . . 76 B2
NW2 . . . 89 J5
NW10 . . . 106 E4
Harrow HA1 . . . 67 J5
Pinner HA5 . . . 66 C7
Chandos St, W1 . . . 16 E2
Chandos Way, NW11 . . . 90 E1
Change All, EC3 . . . 20 C4
Channel Cl, Houns. TW5 . . . 143 G1
Channel Gate Rd, NW10 *off Old Oak La* . . . 107 F3
Channelsea Rd, E15 . . . 114 D1
Chantress Cl, Dag. RM10 . . . 119 J1
Chantrey Rd, SW9 . . . 151 F3
Chantry Cl, NW7 *off Hendon Wd La* . . . 39 F6
SE2 *off Felixstowe Rd* . . . 138 C3
W9 *off Elgin Av* . . . 108 C4
Harrow HA3 . . . 69 J5
Sidcup DA14 *off Ellenborough Rd* . . . 176/177 E5
Sunbury-on-Thames TW16 . . . 160 A7
Chantry Ct, Cars. SM5 . . . 199 H3
Chantry La, Brom. BR2 *off Bromley Common* . . . 192 A5
Chantry Pl, Har. HA3 . . . 67 H1
Chantry Rd, Chess. KT9 . . . 195 J5
Harrow HA3 . . . 67 H1
Chantry Sq, W8 *off St. Mary's Pl* . . . 128/129 E3
Chantry St, N1 . . . 111 H1
Chantry Way, Mitch. CR4 . . . 185 G3
Chant Sq, E15 . . . 96 D7
Chant St, E15 . . . 96 D7
Chapel Ct, N2 . . . 73 H3
SE1 . . . 28 B3
Chapel Fm Rd, SE9 . . . 174 C3
Chapel Gate Ms, SW4 *off Bedford Rd* . . . 150 E3
Chapel Ho St, E14 . . . 134 B5
Chapelier Ho, SW18 *off Point Pleasant* . . . 148 D4
Chapel La, Chig. IG7 . . . 65 J3
Pinner HA5 . . . 66 D3
Romford RM6 . . . 82 D7
Chapel Mkt, N1 . . . 10 E1
Chapel Ms, Wdf.Grn. IG8 . . . 64 D6
Chapelmount Rd, Wdf.Grn. IG8 . . . 64 C6
Chapel Path, E11 . . . 79 G6
Chapel Pl, EC2 . . . 12 D4
N1 . . . 11 F1
N17 *off White Hart La* . . . 60 C7
W1 . . . 16 D4
Chapel Rd, SE27 . . . 169 H4
W13 . . . 125 E1
Bexleyheath DA7 . . . 159 G4
Hounslow TW3 . . . 143 H3
Ilford IG1 . . . 98 D3
Twickenham TW1 . . . 145 E7
Chapel Side, W2 . . . 14 A5
Chapel Stones, N17 . . . 76 C1
Chapel St, NW1 . . . 15 G2
SW1 . . . 24 C5
Enfield EN2 . . . 43 J3
Chapel Ter, Loug. IG10 *off Forest Rd* . . . 48 B4
Chapel Vw, S.Croy. CR2 . . . 203 E6
Chapel Wk, NW4 . . . 71 H4
Croydon CR0 *off Wellesley Rd* . . . 201 J2
Chapel Way, N7 *off Sussex Way* . . . 93 F3
Chapel Yd, SW18 *off Wandsworth High St* . . . 148 D5
Chaplin Cl, SE1 . . . 27 F3
Chaplin Rd, E15 . . . 115 E2
N17 . . . 76 C3
NW2 . . . 89 G6
Dagenham RM9 . . . 101 E7
Wembley HA0 . . . 87 F6
Chaplin Sq, N12 . . . 57 G7
Chapman Cl, West Dr. UB7 . . . 120 C3
Chapman Cres, Har. HA3 . . . 69 H5
Chapman Pk Ind Est, NW10 . . . 89 F6
Chapman Pl, N4 . . . 93 H2
Chapman Rd, E9 . . . 95 J6
Belvedere DA17 . . . 139 G5
Croydon CR0 . . . 201 G1
Chapman's La, SE2 . . . 138 C4
Belvedere DA17 . . . 138 D4
Chapman Sq, SW19 . . . 166 A2
Chapman St, E1 . . . 112 E7
Chapone Pl, W1 . . . 17 H4
Chapter Cl, W4 *off Beaumont Rd* . . . 126 C3
Chapter Ho Ct, EC4 . . . 19 J4
Chapter Rd, NW2 . . . 89 G5
SE17 . . . 35 H4
Chapter St, SW1 . . . 33 H2
Chapter Way, Hmptn. TW12 . . . 161 G4
Chara Pl, W4 . . . 126 D6
Charcot Ho, SW15 *off Highcliffe Dr* . . . 147 F6
Charcroft Gdns, Enf. EN3 . . . 45 G4
Chardin Rd, W4 *off Elliott Rd* . . . 126/127 E4
Chardmore Rd, N16 . . . 94 D1
Chard Rd, Houns. (Hthrw Air.) TW6 *off Heathrow Tunnel App* . . . 140 D3
Chardwell Cl, E6 *off Northumberland Rd* . . . 116 B6
Charecroft Way, W12 . . . 128 A2
Charfield Ct, W9 . . . 6 A6
Charford Rd, E16 . . . 115 G5
Chargeable La, E13 . . . 115 F4
Chargeable St, E16 . . . 115 F4
Chargrove Cl, SE16 *off Marlow Way* . . . 133 G2
Charing Cl, Orp. BR6 . . . 207 J4
Charing Cross, SW1 . . . 26 A1
Charing Cross Rd, WC2 . . . 17 J3
Charlbert St, NW8 . . . 7 G1
Charlbury Av, Stan. HA7 . . . 53 G5
Charlbury Gdns, Ilf. IG3 . . . 99 J2
Charlbury Gro, W5 . . . 105 F6
Charlbury Ho, E12 *off Grantham Rd* . . . 98 D3
Charldane Rd, SE9 . . . 174 E3
Charlecote Gro, SE26 . . . 171 E3
Charlecote Rd, Dag. RM8 . . . 100 E3
Charlemont Rd, E6 . . . 116 C3
Charles Babbage Cl, Chess. KT9 . . . 195 F7
Charles Barry Cl, SW4 . . . 150 C3
Charles Burton Ct, E5 *off Ashenden Rd* . . . 95 H5
Charles Cl, Sid. DA14 . . . 176 B4
Charles Cobb Gdns, Croy. CR0 . . . 201 G5
Charles Coveney Rd, SE15 . . . 152 C1
Charles Cres, Har. HA1 . . . 68 A7
Charles Dickens Ho, E2 . . . 112 E3
Charles Dickens Ter, SE20 *off Maple Rd* . . . 171 F7
Charlesfield, SE9 . . . 173 J3
Charles Flemwell Ms, E16 *off Hanameel St* . . . 135 G1
Charles Grinling Wk, SE18 . . . 136 D4
Charles Haller St, SW2 *off Tulse Hill* . . . 151 G7
Charles Ho, N17 *off Love La* . . . 60 C7
Charles La, NW8 . . . 7 F2
Charlesmere Gdns, SE28 *off Battery Rd* . . . 137 H2
Charles Pl, NW1 . . . 9 G4
Charles Rd, E7 *off Lens Rd* . . . 97 J7
SW19 . . . 184 D1
W13 . . . 104 D6
Romford RM6 . . . 82 D7
Charles II Pl, SW3 *off King's Rd* . . . 129 J5
Charles II St, SW1 . . . 25 H1
Charles Sevright Dr, NW7 . . . 56 A5
Charles Sq, N1 . . . 12 C4
Charles Sq Est, N1 *off Pitfield St* . . . 112 A3
Charles St, E16 . . . 136 A1
SW13 . . . 147 E2
W1 . . . 24 D1
Croydon CR0 . . . 201 J3
Enfield EN1 . . . 44 C5
Hounslow TW3 . . . 140 F2
Charleston Cl, Felt. TW13 *off Vineyard Rd* . . . 160 A3
Charleston St, SE17 . . . 36 A2
Charles Townsend Ho, EC1 . . . 11 F4
Charles Whincup Rd, E16 . . . 135 H1
Charleville Circ, SE26 . . . 170 D5
Charleville Ms, Islw. TW7 *off Railshead Rd* . . . 144/145 E4
Charleville Rd, W14 . . . 128 B5
Charlie Chaplin Wk, SE1 *off Waterloo Rd* . . . 131 G1
Charlieville Rd, Erith DA8 *off Northumberland Pk* . . . 139 J7
Charlmont Rd, SW17 . . . 167 J6
Charlotte Cl, Bexh. DA6 . . . 158 E5
Ilford IG6 *off Connor Cl* . . . 81 F1
Charlotte Ct, W6 *off Goldhawk Rd* . . . 127 G3
Charlotte Despard Av, SW11 . . . 150 A1
Charlotte Ms, W1 . . . 17 G1
W10 . . . 108 A6
W14 *off Munden St* . . . 128 B4
Charlotte Pl, NW9 *off Uphill Dr* . . . 70 C5
SW1 . . . 33 F2
W1 . . . 17 G2
Charlotte Rd, EC2 . . . 12 D5
SW13 . . . 147 F1
Dagenham RM10 . . . 101 H6
Wallington SM6 . . . 200 C6
Charlotte Row, SW4 . . . 150 C3
Charlotte Sq, Rich. TW10 *off Greville Rd* . . . 145 J6
Charlotte St, W1 . . . 17 G1
Charlotte Ter, N1 . . . 111 F1
Charlow Cl, SW6 *off Townmead Rd* . . . 149 F2
CHARLTON, SE7 . . . 135 J6
★**Charlton Athletic FC**, SE7 . . . 135 J5
Charlton Ch La, SE7 . . . 135 J5
Charlton Cres, Bark. IG11 . . . 117 J2
Charlton Dene, SE7 . . . 135 J7
Charlton Kings Rd, NW5 . . . 92 D5
Charlton La, SE7 . . . 136 A5
Charlton Pk La, SE7 . . . 136 A7
Charlton Pk Rd, SE7 . . . 136 A6
Charlton Pl, N1 . . . 11 G1
Charlton Rd, N9 . . . 61 G1
NW10 . . . 107 E1
SE3 . . . 135 G7
SE7 . . . 135 H7
Harrow HA3 . . . 69 G4
Wembley HA9 . . . 87 J1
Charlton Way, SE3 . . . 154 E1
Charlwood Cl, Har. HA3 *off Kelvin Cres* . . . 52 B7
Charlwood Pl, SW1 . . . 33 G2
Charlwood Rd, SW15 . . . 148 A3
Charlwood Sq, Mitch. CR4 . . . 185 G3
Charlwood St, SW1 . . . 33 G2
Charlwood Ter, SW15 *off Cardinal Pl* . . . 148 A4
Charmian Av, Stan. HA7 . . . 69 G3
Charminster Av, SW19 . . . 184 E2
Charminster Ct, Surb. KT6 . . . 181 G7
Charminster Rd, SE9 . . . 174 A4
Worcester Park KT4 . . . 198 A1
Charmouth Rd, Well. DA16 . . . 158 C1
Charnock Rd, E5 . . . 94 E3
Charnwood Av, SW19 . . . 184 D2
Charnwood Cl, N.Mal. KT3 . . . 183 E4
Charnwood Dr, E18 . . . 79 H3
Charnwood Gdns, E14 . . . 134 A4
Charnwood Pl, N20 . . . 57 F3
Charnwood Rd, SE25 . . . 188 A5
Charnwood St, E5 . . . 94 D2
Charrington Rd, Croy. CR0 *off Drayton Rd* . . . 201 H2
Charrington St, NW1 . . . 9 H1
Charsley Rd, SE6 . . . 172 B2
Chart Cl, Brom. BR2 . . . 191 E1
Croydon CR0 *off Stockbury Rd* . . . 189 F6
Charter Av, Ilf. IG2 . . . 99 G1
Charter Ct, N.Mal. KT3 . . . 182 E3
Charter Cres, Houns. TW4 . . . 142 E4
Charter Dr, Bex. DA5 . . . 158 E7
★**Chartered Insurance Institutes Mus**, EC2 *off Aldermanbury* . . . 20 A3
★**Charterhouse**, EC1 . . . 19 H1
Charterhouse Av, Wem. HA0 . . . 87 F4
Charterhouse Bldgs, EC1 . . . 11 H6
Charterhouse Ms, EC1 . . . 19 H1
Charterhouse Rd, E8 . . . 94 D4
Charterhouse Sq, EC1 . . . 19 H1
Charterhouse St, EC1 . . . 19 F2
Charteris Rd, N4 . . . 93 G1
NW6 . . . 108 C1
Woodford Green IG8 . . . 63 H7
Charter Rd, Kings.T. KT1 . . . 182 B3
Charter Rd, The, Wdf.Grn. IG8 . . . 62 E6
Charters Cl, SE19 . . . 170 B5
Charter Sq, Kings.T. KT1 . . . 182 B2
Charter Way, N3 . . . 72 C4
N14 . . . 42 C6
Chartfield Av, SW15 . . . 147 H5
Chartfield Sq, SW15 . . . 148 A5
Chartham Gro, SE27 *off Royal Circ* . . . 169 G3
Chartham Rd, SE25 . . . 188 E3
Chart Hills Cl, SE28 *off Fairway Dr* . . . 118/119 E6
Chartley Av, NW2 . . . 88 E3
Stanmore HA7 . . . 52 C6
Charton Cl, Belv. DA17 *off Nuxley Rd* . . . 139 F6
Chartridge Cl, Barn. EN5 . . . 39 G5
Chart St, N1 . . . 12 C3
Chartwell Cl, SE9 . . . 175 F2
Croydon CR0 . . . 202 A1
Greenford UB6 . . . 103 H1
Chartwell Dr, Orp. BR6 . . . 207 G5

Chartwell Gdns, Sutt. SM3 . . . . 198 B4
Chartwell Pl, Har. HA2 . . . . 86 A2
Sutton SM3 . . . . 198 C4
Chartwell Way, SE20 . . . . 188 E1
Charwood, SW16 . . . . 169 G4
Chase, The, E12 . . . . 98 A4
SW4 . . . . 150 B3
SW16 . . . . 169 F7
SW20 . . . . 184 B1
Bexleyheath DA7 . . . . 159 H3
Bromley BR1 . . . . 191 H3
Chigwell IG7 . . . . 65 F4
Edgware HA8 . . . . 70 B1
Loughton IG10 . . . . 47 J7
Pinner HA5 . . . . 67 F4
Pinner (Eastcote) HA5 . . . . 66 C6
Romford (Chad.Hth) RM6 . . . . 82 E6
Stanmore HA7 . . . . 52 D5
Sunbury-on-Thames TW16 . . . . 178 B1
Wallington SM6 . . . . 200 E5
Chase Ct Gdns, Enf. EN2 . . 43 J3
Chasefield Rd, SW17 . . . . 167 J4
Chase Gdns, E4 . . . . 62 A4
Twickenham TW2 . . . . 144 A6
Chase Grn, Enf. EN2 . . . . 43 J3
Chase Grn Av, Enf. EN2 . . . . 43 H2
Chase Hill, Enf. EN2 . . . . 43 J3
Chase La, Ilf. IG6 . . . . 81 G5
Chaseley Dr, W4 . . . . 126 B5
Chaseley St, E14 . . . . 113 H6
Chasemore Cl, Mitch. CR4 . . . . 185 J7
Chasemore Gdns, Croy. CR0 *off Thorneloe Gdns* . . 201 H5
Chase Ridings, Enf. EN2 . . 43 G2
Chase Rd, N14 . . . . 42 C6
NW10 . . . . 106 D4
W3 . . . . 106 D4
Chase Side, N14 . . . . 42 A6
Enfield EN2 . . . . 43 J3
Chase Side Av, SW20 . . . . 184 B1
Enfield EN2 . . . . 43 J2
Chase Side Cres, Enf. EN2 . 43 J1
Chase Side Pl, Enf. EN2 *off Chase Side* 43 J2
Chaseville Pk Rd, N21 . . . . 43 E5
Chase Way, N14 . . . . 58 B2
Chasewood Av, Enf. EN2 . . 43 H2
Chasewood Pk, Har. HA1 . . 86 C3
Chatfield Rd, SW11 . . . . 149 F3
Croydon CR0 . . . . 201 H1
Chatham Av, Brom. BR2 . . . . 191 F7
Chatham Cl, NW11 . . . . 72 D5
SE18 *off Cadogan Rd* . . 136 E3
Sutton SM3 . . . . 184 C7
Chatham Pl, E9 . . . . 95 F6
Chatham Rd, E17 . . . . 77 H3
E18 *off Grove Hill* 79 F2
SW11 . . . . 149 J6
Kingston upon Thames KT1 . . . . 182 A2
Orpington BR6 . . . . 207 F5
Chatham St, SE17 . . . . 36 B1
Chatsfield Pl, W5 . . . . 105 H6
Chatsworth Av, NW4 . . . . 71 J2
SW20 . . . . 184 B1
Bromley BR1 . . . . 173 H4
Sidcup DA15 . . . . 176 A1
Wembley HA9 . . . . 87 J5
Chatsworth Cl, NW4 . . . . 71 J2
Borehamwood WD6 . . . . 38 A3
West Wickham BR4 . . . . 205 F2
Chatsworth Ct, W8 . . . . 128 D4
Stanmore HA7 *off Marsh La* 53 F5
Chatsworth Cres, Houns. TW3 . . . . 144 A4
Chatsworth Dr, Enf. EN1 . . 44 D7
Chatsworth Est, E5 *off Elderfield Rd* 95 G4
Chatsworth Gdns, W3 . . . 106 B7
Harrow HA2 . . . . 85 H1
New Malden KT3 . . . . 183 F5
Chatsworth Par, Orp. BR5 *off Queensway* 193 F5
Chatsworth Pl, Mitch. CR4 . . . . 185 J3
Teddington TW11 . . . . 162 D4
Chatsworth Ri, W5 . . . . 105 J4
Chatsworth Rd, E5 . . . . 95 F3
E15 . . . . 97 F5
NW2 . . . . 90 A6
W4 . . . . 126 C6
W5 . . . . 105 J4
Croydon CR0 . . . . 202 A4
Chatsworth Rd, Hayes UB4 . . . . 102 B4
Sutton SM3 . . . . 198 A5
Chatsworth Way, SE27 . . 169 H3
Chatterton Ms, N4 *off Chatterton Rd* 93 H3
Chatterton Rd, N4 . . . . 93 H3
Bromley BR2 . . . . 192 A4
Chatto Rd, SW11 . . . . 149 J5
Chaucer Av, Hayes UB4 . . 102 A5
Hounslow TW4 . . . . 142 B2
Richmond TW9 . . . . 146 A2
Chaucer Cl, N11 . . . . 58 C5
Chaucer Ct, N16 . . . . 94 B4
Chaucer Dr, SE1 . . . . 37 G2
Chaucer Gdns, Sutt. SM1 . . . . 198 D3
Chaucer Grn, Croy. CR0 . . 189 E7
Chaucer Ho, Sutt. SM1 . . 198 D3
Chaucer Rd, E7 . . . . 97 G6
E11 . . . . 79 G6
E17 . . . . 78 C2
SE24 . . . . 151 G5
W3 . . . . 126 C1
Sidcup DA15 . . . . 176 C1
Sutton SM1 . . . . 198 D4
Welling DA16 . . . . 157 H1
Chaucer Way, SW19 . . . . 167 G6
Chauncey Cl, N9 . . . . 60 D3
Chaundrye Cl, SE9 . . . . 156 C6
Chauntler Cl, E16 . . . . 115 H7
CHEAM, Sutt. SM3 . . . . 198 A6
Cheam Common Rd, Wor.Pk. KT4 . . . . 197 H2
Cheam Mans, Sutt. SM3 . 198 B7
Cheam Pk Way, Sutt. SM3 . . . . 198 B6
Cheam Rd, Sutt. SM1 . . . . 198 C6
Cheam St, SE15 *off Evelina Rd* . . . 152/153 E3
Cheapside, EC2 . . . . 20 A4
N13 *off Taplow Rd* 59 J4
Cheddar Cl, N11 *off Martock Gdns* 58 A6
Cheddar Rd, Houns. (Hthrw Air.) TW6 *off Cromer Rd* 140 D2
Cheddar Waye, Hayes UB4 . . . . 102 B6
Cheddington Rd, N18 . . . . 60 B3
Chedworth Cl, E16 *off Hallsville Rd* 115 F6
Cheeseman Cl, Hmptn. TW12 . . . . 161 E6
Cheesemans Ter, W14 . . . 128 C5
Cheldon Av, NW7 . . . . 56 A7
Chelford Rd, Brom. BR1 . . 172 D5
Chelmer Cres, Bark. IG11 . 118 B2
Chelmer Rd, E9 . . . . 95 G5
Chelmsford Cl, E6 *off Guildford Rd* 116 C6
W6 . . . . 128 A6
Chelmsford Gdns, Ilf. IG1 . 80 B7
Chelmsford Rd, E11 . . . . 96 D1
E17 . . . . 78 A6
E18 . . . . 79 F1
N14 . . . . 42 C7
Chelmsford Sq, NW10 . . . 107 J1
CHELSEA, SW3 . . . . 31 E5
★**Chelsea Antique Mkt**, SW3 . . . . 31 F5
Chelsea Br, SW1 . . . . 32 D5
SW8 . . . . 32 D5
Chelsea Br Rd, SW1 . . . . 32 B3
Chelsea Cloisters, SW3 *off Lucan Pl* 129 H4
Chelsea Cl, NW10 *off Winchelsea Rd* 106 D1
Edgware HA8 . . . . 70 A2
Hampton (Hmptn H.) TW12 . . . . 161 J5
Worcester Park KT4 . . . . 183 G7
Chelsea Cres, SW10 *off Harbour Av* 149 F1
Chelsea Embk, SW3 . . . . 31 H6
★**Chelsea FC**, SW6 . . . . 30 A7
Chelsea Gdns, W13 *off Hathaway Gdns* . . . 104 C5
Sutton SM3 . . . . 198 B4
Chelsea Harbour, SW10 . . 149 F1
Chelsea Harbour Dr, SW10 . . . . 149 F1
Chelsea Manor Ct, SW3 . . 31 H5
Chelsea Manor Gdns, SW3 . . . . 31 G5
Chelsea Manor St, SW3 . . 31 G4
Chelsea Pk Gdns, SW3 . . . 30 E5
★**Chelsea Physic Gdn**, SW3 . . . . 31 J5
Chelsea Sq, SW3 . . . . 31 F3
Chelsea Vista, SW6 *off The Boulevard* 149 F1
Chelsea Wf, SW10 . . . . 129 G7
Chelsfield Av, N9 . . . . 45 G7
Chelsfield Gdns, SE26 . . . 171 F3
Chelsfield Grn, N9 *off Chelsfield Av* 45 G7
Chelsham Rd, SW4 . . . . 150 D3
South Croydon CR2 . . . 202 A6
Chelston App, Ruis. HA4 . . 84 A2
Chelston Rd, Ruis. HA4 . . 84 A1
Chelsworth Dr, SE18 . . . . 137 G6
Cheltenham Av, Twick. TW1 . . . . 144 D7
Cheltenham Cl, N.Mal. KT3 *off Northcote Rd* 182 C3
Northolt UB5 . . . . 85 H6
Cheltenham Gdns, E6 . . . 116 B2
Loughton IG10 . . . . 48 B6
Cheltenham Pl, W3 . . . . 126 B1
Harrow HA3 . . . . 69 H4
Cheltenham Rd, E10 . . . . 78 C6
SE15 . . . . 153 F4
Cheltenham Ter, SW3 . . . . 32 A3
Chelverton Rd, SW15 . . . . 148 A4
Chelwood, N20 *off Oakleigh Rd N* 57 G2
Chelwood Cl, E4 . . . . 46 B6
Chelwood Gdns, Rich. TW9 . . . . 146 A2
Chelwood Gdns Pas, Rich. TW9 *off Chelwood Gdns* 146 A2
Chelwood Wk, SE4 . . . . 153 H4
Chenappa Cl, E13 . . . . 115 G3
Chenduit Way, Stan. HA7 . . . . 52 C5
Cheney Row, E17 . . . . 77 J1
Cheneys Rd, E11 . . . . 97 E3
Cheney St, Pnr. HA5 . . . . 66 C5
Chenies, The, Orp. BR6 . . 193 H6
Chenies Ms, WC1 . . . . 9 H6
Chenies Pl, NW1 . . . . 9 H1
Chenies St, WC1 . . . . 17 H1
Cheniston Gdns, W8 . . . . 22 A5
Chepstow Cl, SW15 *off Lytton Gro* 148 B6
Chepstow Cres, W11 . . . . 108 D7
Ilford IG3 . . . . 81 H6
Chepstow Gdns, Sthl. UB1 . . . . 103 F6
Chepstow Pl, W2 . . . . 108 D6
Chepstow Ri, Croy. CR0 . . 202 B3
Chepstow Rd, W2 . . . . 108 D6
W7 . . . . 124 D3
Croydon CR0 . . . . 202 B3
Chepstow Vil, W11 . . . . 108 C7
Chepstow Way, SE15 . . . . 132 C7
Chequers, Buck.H. IG9 *off Hills Rd* 63 H1
Chequers Cl, NW9 . . . . 70 E3
Orpington BR5 . . . . 193 J4
Chequers Gdns, N13 . . . . 59 H5
Chequers La, Dag. RM9 . . 119 F4
Chequers Par, SE9 *off Eltham High St* . . . 156 C6
Chequers Rd, Loug. IG10 . . 48 D5
Chequer St, EC1 . . . . 12 A6
Chequers Way, N13 . . . . 59 J5
Cherbury Cl, SE28 . . . . 118 D6
Cherbury Ct, N1 . . . . 12 C2
Cherbury St, N1 . . . . 12 C2
Cherchefelle Ms, Stan. HA7 . . . . 52 E5
Cherimoya Gdns, W.Mol. KT8 *off Kelvinbrook* . . 179 H3
Cherington Rd, W7 . . . . 124 C1
Cheriton Av, Brom. BR2 . . 191 F5
Ilford IG5 . . . . 80 C2
Cheriton Cl, W5 . . . . 105 F5
Barnet EN4 . . . . 41 J3
Cheriton Dr, SE18 . . . . 137 G7
Cheriton Sq, SW17 . . . . 168 A2
Cherry Av, Sthl. UB1 . . . . 122 D1
Cherry Blossom Cl, N13 . . . 59 H5
Cherry Cl, E17 *off Eden Rd* . 78 B4
NW9 . . . . 71 E2
SW2 *off Tulse Hill* 151 G7
W5 . . . . 125 G3
Carshalton SM5 . . . . 199 J2
Morden SM4 . . . . 184 B4
Cherrycot Hill, Orp. BR6 . . 207 G4
Cherrycot Ri, Orp. BR6 . . . 207 F4
Cherry Cres, Brent. TW8 . . 124 E7
Cherrycroft Gdns, Pnr. HA5 *off Westfield Pk* 51 F7
Cherrydown Av, E4 . . . . 61 J3
Cherrydown Cl, E4 . . . . 61 J3
Cherrydown Rd, Sid. DA14 . . . . 176 D2
Cherrydown Wk, Rom. RM7 . . . . 83 H2
Cherry Gdns, Dag. RM9 . . 101 F5
Northolt UB5 . . . . 85 H7
Cherry Gdn St, SE16 . . . . 132 E2
Cherry Garth, Brent. TW8 . . . . 125 G4
Cherry Gro, Hayes UB3 . . 122 B1
Cherry Hill, Barn. EN5 . . . . 41 E6
Harrow HA3 . . . . 52 B6
Cherry Hill Gdns, Croy. CR0 . . . . 201 F4
Cherry Hills, Wat. WD19 . . . 50 E5
Cherrylands Cl, NW9 . . . . 88 C2
Cherry La, West Dr. UB7 . . 120 C4
Cherry La Roundabout, West Dr. UB7 . . . . 120 E4
Cherry Laurel Wk, SW2 *off Beechdale Rd* 151 F6
Cherry Orchard, West Dr. UB7 . . . . 120 B2
Cherry Orchard Gdns, Croy. CR0 *off Oval Rd* 202 A2
West Molesey KT8 . . . . 179 F3
Cherry Orchard Rd, Brom. BR2 . . . . 206 B2
Croydon CR0 . . . . 202 A2
West Molesey KT8 . . . . 179 G3
Cherry Tree Cl, E9 *off Moulins Rd* 113 F1
Wembley HA0 . . . . 86 C4
Cherry Tree Ct, NW9 . . . . 70 C4
Cherry Tree Dr, SW16 . . . . 169 E3
Cherry Tree Ri, Buck.H. IG9 . 63 J4
Cherry Tree Rd, E15 *off Wingfield Rd* 96/97 E4
N2 . . . . 73 J4
Cherry Tree Wk, EC1 . . . . 12 A6
Beckenham BR3 . . . . 189 J4
West Wickham BR4 . . . . 205 F4
Cherry Tree Way, Stan. HA7 . . . . 53 E6
Cherry Wk, Brom. BR2 . . . 205 G1
Cherry Way, Epsom KT19 . 196 D6
Cherrywood Cl, E3 . . . . 113 H3
Kingston upon Thames KT2 . . . . 164 A7
Cherrywood Dr, SW15 . . . 148 A5
Cherrywood La, Mord. SM4 . . . . 184 B4
Cherry Wd Way, W5 *off Hanger Vale La* 106 A5
Cherston Gdns, Loug. IG10 *off Cherston Rd* 48 D4
Cherston Rd, Loug. IG10 . . 48 D4
Chertsey Dr, Sutt. SM3 . . 198 B2
Chertsey Rd, E11 . . . . 96 D2
Ilford IG1 . . . . 99 G4
Twickenham TW1, TW2 . 144 C6
Chertsey St, SW17 . . . . 168 A5
Chervil Cl, Felt. TW13 . . . . 160 A3
Chervil Ms, SE28 . . . . 138 B1
Cherwell Ct, Epsom KT19 . . . . 196 C4
Cheryls Cl, SW6 . . . . 149 E1
Cheseman St, SE26 . . . . 171 E3
Chesfield Rd, Kings.T. KT2 . . . . 163 H7
Chesham Av, Orp. BR5 . . . 192 E6
Chesham Cl, SW1 . . . . 24 B6
Chesham Cres, SE20 . . . . 189 F2
Chesham Ms, SW1 . . . . 24 B5
Chesham Pl, SW1 . . . . 24 B6
Chesham Rd, SE20 . . . . 189 F2
SW19 . . . . 167 G5
Kingston upon Thames KT1 . . . . 182 A1
Chesham St, NW10 . . . . 88 D3
SW1 . . . . 24 B6
Chesham Ter, W13 . . . . 124 E2
Cheshire Cl, E17 . . . . 78 B1
SE4 . . . . 153 J2
Mitcham CR4 . . . . 186 E3
Cheshire Ct, EC4 . . . . 19 F4
Cheshire Gdns, Chess. KT9 . . . . 195 G6
Cheshire Ho, N18 . . . . 61 E4
Cheshire Rd, N22 . . . . 59 F7
Cheshire St, E2 . . . . 13 G5
Chesholm Rd, N16 . . . . 94 B3
Cheshunt Rd, E7 . . . . 97 H6
Belvedere DA17 . . . . 139 G5
Chesil Ct, E2 . . . . 113 F2
Chesilton Rd, SW6 . . . . 148 C1
Chesley Gdns, E6 . . . . 116 A2
Chesney Cres, Croy. (New Adgtn) CR0 . . . . 204 C7

Chesney St, SW11 . . . . . . **150** A1
Chesnut Est, N17 . . . . **76** C3
Chesnut Gro, N17
off Chesnut Rd **76** C3
Chesnut Rd, N17 . . . . **76** C3
Chessell Cl, Th.Hth. CR7 . . **187** H4
CHESSINGTON, KT9 . . . . **195** H6
Chessington Av, N3 . . . . . . **72** B3
Bexleyheath DA7 . . . . . **139** E7
Chessington Cl, Epsom
KT19 . . . . **196** C6
Chessington Ct, Pnr. HA5 . **67** F4
Chessington Hall Gdns,
Chess. KT9 . . . . **195** G7
Chessington Hill Pk, Chess.
KT9 . . . . **196** A5
Chessington Lo, N3 . . . . . . **72** C3
Chessington Way, W.Wick.
BR4 . . . . **204** B2
Chesson Rd, W14 . . . . **128** C6
Chesswood Way, Pnr.
HA5 . . . . **66** D2
Chester Av, Rich. TW10 . . **145** J5
Twickenham TW2 . . . . . **161** F1
Chester Cl, SW1 . . . . **24** C4
SW13 . . . . **147** H3
Loughton IG10 . . . . **49** F1
Sutton SM1 . . . . **198** D2
Chester Cl N, NW1 . . . . **8** E3
Chester Cl S, NW1 . . . . **8** E4
Chester Cotts, SW1 . . . . . . **32** B2
Chester Ct, NW1 . . . . **8** E3
SE5 . . . . **132** A7
Chester Cres, E8
off Ridley Rd **94** C6
Chester Dr, Har. HA2 . . . . . **67** F6
Chesterfield Dr, Esher
KT10 . . . . **194** D2
Chesterfield Gdns, N4 . . . . **75** H5
SE10 *off Crooms Hill* . . . **134** D7
W1 . . . . **24** D1
Chesterfield Gro, SE22 . . . **152** C5
Chesterfield Hill, W1 . . . . . **16** D6
Chesterfield Ms, N4
off Chesterfield Gdns . . **75** H5
Chesterfield Rd, E10 . . . . . . **70** C6
N3 . . . . **56** D6
W4 . . . . **126** C6
Barnet EN5 . . . . **40** A5
Epsom KT19 . . . . **196** D7
Chesterfield St, W1 . . . . . . **24** D1
Chesterfield Wk, SE10 . . . **154** D1
Chesterfield Way, SE15 . . **133** F7
Hayes UB3 . . . . **122** A2
Chesterford Gdns, NW3 . . . **91** E4
Chesterford Ho, SE10
off Shooter's Hill Rd . . **136** A7
Chesterford Rd, E12 . . . . . . **98** C5
Chester Gdns, W13 . . . . . . **104** D6
Enfield EN3 . . . . **45** E6
Morden SM4 . . . . **185** F6
Chester Gate, NW1 . . . . **8** D4
Chester Grn, Loug. IG10 . . **49** F1
Chester Ms, E17
off Chingford Rd **78** A2
SW1 . . . . **24** D6
Chester Path, Loug. IG10 . . **49** F1
Chester Pl, NW1 . . . . **8** D3
Chester Rd, E7 . . . . **98** A7
E11 . . . . **79** H6
E16 . . . . **115** E4
E17 . . . . **77** G5
N9 . . . . **61** E1
N17 . . . . **76** A3
N19 . . . . **92** B2
NW1 . . . . **8** C4
SW19 . . . . **165** J6
Borehamwood WD6 . . . . **38** C3
Chigwell IG7 . . . . **64** D3
Hounslow TW4 . . . . **142** B3
Hounslow (Hthrw Air.)
TW6 . . . . **140** D3
Ilford IG3 . . . . **99** J1
Loughton IG10 . . . . **48** E2
Sidcup DA15 . . . . **157** H5
Chester Row, SW1 . . . . **32** B2
Chesters, The, N.Mal.
KT3 . . . . **182** E1
Chester Sq, SW1 . . . . **32** D1
Chester Sq Ms, SW1 . . . . . **24** D6
Chester St, E2 . . . . **13** J5
SW1 . . . . **24** C5
Chester Ter, NW1 . . . . **8** D3
Chesterton Cl, SW18
off Ericcson Cl **148** D5
Greenford UB6 . . . . **103** H2
Chesterton Ho, SW11
off Ingrave St **149** G3
Chesterton Rd, E13 . . . . . . **115** G3
Chesterton Rd, W10 . . . . . **108** A5
Chesterton Sq, W8
off Pembroke Rd **128** C4
Chesterton Ter, E13 . . . . . . **115** G3
Kingston upon Thames
KT1 . . . . **182** A2
Chester Way, SE11 . . . . **35** F2
Chesthunte Rd, N17 . . . . . . **75** J1
Chestnut All, SW6
off Lillie Rd **128** C6
Chestnut Av, E7 . . . . **97** H4
N8 . . . . **74** E5
SW14 *off Thornton Rd* . . **146** D3
Brentford TW8 . . . . **125** G4
Buckhurst Hill IG9 . . . . . . **64** A3
East Molesey KT8 . . . . . **180** C3
Edgware HA8 . . . . **53** H6
Epsom KT19 . . . . **196** E4
Esher KT10 . . . . **180** A7
Hampton TW12 . . . . **161** G7
Teddington TW11 . . . . . . **180** C2
Wembley HA0 . . . . **86** E5
West Wickham BR4 . . . . **205** E5
Chestnut Av N, E17 . . . . . . **78** C4
Chestnut Av S, E17 . . . . . . **78** C4
Chestnut Cl, N14 . . . . **42** C5
N16 *off Lordship Gro* . . . **94** A2
SE6 . . . . **172** C5
SE14 . . . . **153** J1
SW16 . . . . **169** G4
Buckhurst Hill IG9 . . . . . . **64** A2
Carshalton SM5 . . . . . . **199** J1
Sidcup DA15 . . . . **176** A1
West Drayton UB7 . . . . **121** E7
Chestnut Ct, SW6
off North End Rd **128** C6
Surbiton KT6
off Penners Gdns **181** H7
Chestnut Dr, E11 . . . . **79** G6
Bexleyheath DA7 . . . . . **158** D3
Harrow HA3 . . . . **52** C7
Pinner HA5 . . . . **66** D6
Chestnut Gro, SE20 . . . . . **171** E7
SW12 . . . . **150** A7
W5 . . . . **125** G3
Barnet EN4 . . . . **41** J5
Ilford IG6 . . . . **65** H6
Isleworth TW7 . . . . **144** D4
Mitcham CR4 . . . . **186** D4
New Malden KT3 . . . . . . **182** D3
South Croydon CR2 . . . **203** E7
Wembley HA0 . . . . **86** E5
Chestnut La, N20 . . . . **56** B1
Chestnut Pl, SE26 . . . . . . **170** C4
Chestnut Ri, SE18 . . . . . . **137** G6
Chestnut Rd, SE27 . . . . . . **169** H3
SW20 . . . . **184** A2
Kingston upon Thames
KT2 . . . . **163** H7
Twickenham TW2 . . . . . **162** B2
Chestnut Row, N3
off Nether St **56** D7
Chestnut Wk, Wdf.Grn.
IG8 . . . . **63** G5
Chestnut Way, Felt.
TW13 . . . . **160** B3
Cheston Av, Croy. CR0 . . . **203** H2
Chettle Cl, SE1 . . . . **28** B5
Chettle Ct, N8 . . . . **75** G6
Chetwode Rd, SW17 . . . . . **167** J3
Chetwood Wk, E6 . . . . **116** B6
Chetwynd Av, Barn. EN4 . . **57** J1
Chetwynd Rd, NW5 . . . . **92** B4
Chevalier Cl, Stan. HA7 . . . **53** H4
Cheval Pl, SW7 . . . . **23** H5
Cheval St, E14 . . . . **134** A3
Cheveney Wk, Brom. BR2
off Marina Cl **191** G3
Chevening Rd, NW6 . . . . . **108** A2
SE10 . . . . **135** F5
SE19 . . . . **170** A6
Chevenings, The, Sid.
DA14 . . . . **176** C3
Cheverton Rd, N19 . . . . **92** D1
Chevet St, E9
off Kenworthy Rd **95** H5
Cheviot Cl, Enf. EN1 . . . . . **44** A2
Hayes UB3 . . . . **121** G7
Cheviot Gdns, NW2 . . . . . . **90** A2
SE27 . . . . **169** H4
Cheviot Gate, NW2 . . . . . . **90** B2
Cheviot Rd, SE27 . . . . **169** G5
Cheviot Way, Ilf. IG2 . . . . . . **81** H4
Chevron Cl, E16 . . . . **115** G6
Chevy Rd, Sthl. UB2 . . . . . **123** J2
Chewton Rd, E17 . . . . **77** H4
Cheyne Av, E18 . . . . **79** F3
Twickenham TW2 . . . . . **161** F1
Cheyne Cl, NW4 . . . . **71** J5
Cheyne Cl, Brom. BR2
off Cedar Cres **206** B3
Cheyne Ct, SW3 . . . . **31** J5
Cheyne Gdns, SW3 . . . . . . **31** H5
Cheyne Hill, Surb. KT5 . . . **181** J4
Cheyne Ms, SW3 . . . . **31** H5
Cheyne Path, W7 . . . . **104** C5
Cheyne Pl, SW3 . . . . **31** J5
Cheyne Row, SW3 . . . . **31** G6
Cheyne Wk, N21 . . . . **43** H5
NW4 . . . . **71** J6
SW3 . . . . **31** H6
SW10 . . . . **30** E7
Croydon CR0 . . . . **202** D2
Cheyneys Av, Edg. HA8 . . . **53** G6
Chichele Gdns, Croy.
CR0 . . . . **202** B4
Chichele Rd, NW2 . . . . **90** A5
Chicheley Gdns, Har.
HA3 . . . . **51** J7
Chicheley Rd, Har. HA3 . . . **51** J7
Chicheley St, SE1 . . . . **26** D3
Chichester Cl, E6 . . . . **116** B6
SE3 . . . . **155** J1
Hampton TW12
off Maple Cl **161** F6
Chichester Ct, Stan. HA7 . . **69** H3
Chichester Gdns, Ilf. IG1 . . **80** B7
Chichester Ms, SE27 . . . . **169** G4
Chichester Rents, WC2 . . . **18** E3
Chichester Rd, E11 . . . . **97** E3
N9 . . . . **60** D1
NW6 . . . . **108** D2
W2 . . . . **14** B1
Croydon CR0 . . . . **202** B3
Chichester St, SW1 . . . . . . **33** G4
Chichester Way, E14 . . . . . **134** D4
Feltham TW14 . . . . **142** B7
Chicksand St, E1 . . . . **21** G2
Chiddingfold, N12 . . . . **56** D3
Chiddingstone Av, Bexh.
DA7 . . . . **139** F7
Chiddingstone St, SW6 . . **148** D2
Chieveley Rd, Bexh.
DA7 . . . . **159** H4
Chignell Pl, W13
off The Broadway **124** D1
CHIGWELL, IG7 . . . . **65** E3
Chigwell Hill, E1
off Pennington St . **112/113** E7
Chigwell Hurst Ct, Pnr.
HA5 . . . . **66** D3
Chigwell La, Loug. IG10 . . . **49** F5
Chigwell Pk, Chig. IG7 . . . . **64** E4
Chigwell Pk Dr, Chig. IG7 . **64** D3
Chigwell Ri, Chig. IG7 . . . . **64** D2
Chigwell Rd, E18 . . . . **79** H3
Woodford Green IG8 . . . **79** J2
Chilcombe Ho, SW15
off Fontley Way **147** G7
Chilcot Cl, E14
off Grundy St **114** B6
Chilcott Cl, Wem. HA0 . . . . **87** F4
Childebert Rd, SW17 . . . . **168** B2
Childeric Rd, SE14 . . . . . . **133** H7
Childerley, Kings.T. KT1
off Burritt Rd **182** A3
Childerley St, SW6
off Fulham Palace Rd . **148** A1
Childers, The, Wdf.Grn.
IG8 . . . . **64** C5
Childers St, SE8 . . . . **133** H6
Child La, SE10 . . . . **135** F3
CHILDS HILL, NW2 . . . . **90** D2
Childs Hill Wk, NW2 . . . . . . **90** C3
Childs La, SE19
off Westow St **170** B6
Child's Ms, SW5
off Child's Pl **128** D4
Child's Pl, SW5 . . . . **128** D4
Child's St, SW5 . . . . **128** D4
Child's Wk, SW5
off Child's St **128** D4
Childs Way, NW11 . . . . **72** C5
Chilham Cl, Bex. DA5 . . . . **159** F7
Greenford UB6 . . . . **104** D2
Chilham Rd, SE9 . . . . **174** B4
Chilham Way, Brom. BR2 . **191** G7
Chillerton Rd, SW17 . . . . . **168** A5
Chillington Dr, SW11
off Wynter St **149** F4
Chillingworth Gdns, Twick.
TW1 *off Tower Rd* **162** C3
Chillingworth Rd, N7 . . . . . **93** F5
Chilmark Gdns, N.Mal.
KT3 . . . . **183** F7
Chilmark Rd, SW16 . . . . . **186** D2
Chiltern Av, Twick. TW2 . . . **161** G1
Chiltern Cl, Croy. CR0 . . . **202** B3
Chiltern Cl, Wor. Pk. KT4
off Cotswold Way **197** J2
Chiltern Dene, Enf. EN2 . . . **43** F4
Chiltern Dr, Surb. KT5 . . . **182** B5
Chiltern Gdns, NW2 . . . . . . **90** A3
Bromley BR2 . . . . **191** F4
Chiltern Rd, E3 . . . . **114** A4
Ilford IG2 . . . . **81** H4
Pinner HA5 . . . . **66** C5
Chiltern St, W1 . . . . **16** B1
Chiltern Way, Wdf.Grn.
IG8 . . . . **63** G3
Chilthorne Cl, SE6 *off*
Ravensbourne Pk Cres . **153** J7
Chilton Av, W5 . . . . **125** G4
Chilton Gro, SE8 . . . . **133** G4
Chiltonian Ind Est, SE12 . **155** F6
Chilton Rd, Edg. HA8
off Manor Pk Cres **54** A6
Richmond TW9 . . . . **146** A3
Chiltons, The, E18
off Grove Hill **79** G2
Chilton St, E2 . . . . **13** G5
Chilver St, SE10 . . . . **135** F5
Chilwell Gdns, Wat. WD19 . **50** C4
Chilworth Ct, SW19
off Windlesham Gro . . **166** A1
Chilworth Gdns, Sutt.
SM1 . . . . **199** F3
Chilworth Ms, W2 . . . . **14** D4
Chilworth St, W2 . . . . **14** D4
Chimes Av, N13 . . . . **59** G5
China Hall Ms, SE16
off Lower Rd **133** G3
China Ms, SW2
off Craster Rd **151** F7
★**Chinatown**, W1
off Gerrard St **17** H5
Chinbrook Cres, SE12 . . . **173** H3
Chinbrook Est, SE9 . . . . . **174** A3
Chinbrook Rd, SE12 . . . . . **173** H3
Chinchilla Dr, Houns.
TW4 . . . . **142** C2
Chine, The, N10 . . . . **74** C4
N21 . . . . **43** H6
Wembley HA0 . . . . **87** E5
Ching Ct, WC2 . . . . **18** A4
Chingdale Rd, E4 . . . . **62** E3
CHINGFORD, E4 . . . . **62** B1
Chingford Av, E4 . . . . **62** B3
CHINGFORD GREEN, E4 . . **63** F1
CHINGFORD HATCH, E4 . . **62** C4
Chingford Ind Cen, E4 . . . . **61** H5
Chingford La, Wdf.Grn.
IG8 . . . . **62** E4
Chingford Mt Rd, E4 . . . . . **62** A4
Chingford Rd, E4 . . . . **62** A6
E17 . . . . **78** B1
Chingley Cl, Brom. BR1 . . **172** E6
Ching Way, E4 . . . . **61** J6
Chinnor Cres, Grnf. UB6 . **103** H2
Chipka St, E14 . . . . **134** C2
Chipley St, SE14 . . . . **133** H6
Chipmunk Gro, Nthlt. UB5
off Argus Way **102/103** E3
Chippendale St, E5 . . . . . . **95** G3
Chippenham Av, Wem.
HA9 . . . . **88** B5
Chippenham Gdns, NW6 . **108** D3
Chippenham Ms, W9 . . . . **108** D4
Chippenham Rd, W9 . . . . **108** D4
CHIPPING BARNET, Barn.
EN5 . . . . **40** B4
Chipping Cl, Barn. EN5
off St. Albans Rd **40** B3
Chipstead Av, Th.Hth. CR7 . **187** H4
Chipstead Cl, SE19 . . . . . **170** C7
Chipstead Gdns, NW2 . . . . **89** H2
Chipstead St, SW6 . . . . . . **148** D1
Chip St, SW4 . . . . **150** D3
Chirk Cl, Hayes UB4
off Braunston Dr . **102/103** E4
Chisenhale Rd, E3 . . . . . . **113** H2
Chisholm Rd, Croy. CR0 . . **202** B2
Richmond TW10 . . . . . . **145** J6
Chisledon Wk, E9
off Southmoor Way **95** J6
CHISLEHURST, BR7 . . . . . **174** D7
Chislehurst Av, N12 . . . . . . **57** F7
★**Chislehurst Caves**, Chis.
BR7 *off Caveside Cl* . . **192** D1
Chislehurst Rd, Brom.
BR1 . . . . **192** A2
Chislehurst BR7 . . . . . . **192** A2
Orpington BR5, BR6 . . . **193** H4
Richmond TW10 . . . . . . **145** H6
Sidcup DA14 . . . . **176** A5
CHISLEHURST WEST, Chis.
BR7 . . . . **174** C5

Chislet Cl, Beck. BR3
off Abbey La **172** A7
Chisley Rd, N15 **76** B6
Chiswell Sq, SE3
off Brook La **155** H2
Chiswell St, EC1 **20** A1
CHISWICK, W4 **126** D6
Chiswick Br, SW14 **146** C2
W4 **146** C2
Chiswick Cl, Croy. CR0 **201** F3
Chiswick Common Rd,
W4 **126** D4
Chiswick Ct, Pnr. HA5 **67** F3
Chiswick Grn Studios, W4
off Evershed Wk **126** C4
Chiswick High Rd, W4 **126** D4
Brentford TW8 **125** J5
★**Chiswick Ho**, W4 **126** E6
Chiswick Ho Grds, W4 **126** D6
Chiswick La, W4 **127** E5
Chiswick La S, W4 **127** F5
Chiswick Mall, W4 **127** F6
W6 **127** F6
Chiswick Pk, W4 **126** B4
Chiswick Quay, W4 **146** C1
Chiswick Rd, N9 **60** D2
W4 **126** C4
Chiswick Roundabout, W4
off Chiswick High Rd **126** A5
Chiswick Sq, W4 *off Hogarth Roundabout* **126/127** E6
Chiswick Staithe, W4 **146** C1
Chiswick Ter, W4
off Acton La **126** C4
Chiswick Village, W4 **126** B5
Chiswick Wf, W4 **127** F6
Chitterfield Gate, West Dr.
UB7 **120** D7
Chitty's La, Dag. RM8 **100** D2
Chitty St, W1 **17** G1
Chivalry Rd, SW11 **149** H5
Chivenor Gro, Kings.T.
KT2 **163** G5
Chivers Rd, E4 **62** B3
Choats Manor Way, Dag.
RM9 **118** E2
Choats Rd, Bark. IG11 **118** C2
Dagenham RM9 **118** C2
Chobham Gdns, SW19 **166** A2
Chobham Rd, E15 **96** D5
Cholmeley Cres, N6 **74** B7
Cholmeley Pk, N6 **92** B1
Cholmley Gdns, NW6
off Fortune Grn Rd **90** D5
Cholmley Rd, T.Ditt. KT7 **180** E6
Cholmondeley Av,
NW10 **107** G2
Cholmondeley Wk, Rich.
TW9 **145** F5
Choppins Ct, E1
off Wapping La **132/133** E1
Chopwell Cl, E15
off Bryant St **96** D7
Chorleywood Cres, Orp.
BR5 **193** J2
Choumert Gro, SE15 **152** D2
Choumert Ms, SE15 **152** D2
Choumert Rd, SE15 **152** C3
Choumert Sq, SE15 **152** D2
Chow Sq, E8 *off Arcola St* **94** C5
Chrislaine Cl, Stai. (Stanw.)
TW19 **140** A6
Chrisp St, E14 **114** B5
Christabel Cl, Islw. TW7 **144** B3
Christchurch Av, N12 **57** F6
NW6 **90** B7
Harrow HA3 **69** E4
Teddington TW11 **162** D5
Wembley HA0 **87** H6
Christchurch Cl, N12
off Summers La **57** G7
SW19 **167** G7
Enfield EN2 **43** J2
Christchurch Ct, NW6 **90** B7
Christchurch Gdns, Har.
HA3 **68** D4
Christchurch Grn, Wem.
HA0 **87** H6
Christchurch Hill, NW3 **91** G3
Christchurch La, Barn.
EN5 **40** B2
Christchurch Pk, Sutt.
SM2 **199** F7
Christ Ch Pas, EC1 **19** H3
Christchurch Pas, NW3 **91** F3
Barnet EN5 **40** B3
Christ Ch Path, Hayes
UB3 **121** F3
Christchurch Rd, N8 **74** E6
Christchurch Rd, SW2 **169** F1
SW14 **146** B5
SW19 **185** G1
Christ Ch Rd, Beck. BR3
off Fairfield Rd **190** A2
Christchurch Rd, Houns.
(Hthrw Air.) TW6
off Courtney Rd **140** D3
Ilford IG1 **99** E1
Sidcup DA15 **175** J4
Christ Ch Rd, Surb. KT5 **181** J6
Christchurch Sq, E9
off Victoria Pk Rd **113** F1
Christchurch St, SW3 **31** J5
Christchurch Ter, SW3 **31** J5
Christchurch Way, SE10 **135** E4
Christian Ct, SE16 **133** J1
Christian Flds, SW16 **169** G7
Christian St, E1 **21** J3
Christie Dr, Croy. CR0 **188** D5
Christie Gdns, Rom.
RM6 **82** B6
Christie Rd, E9 **95** H6
Christina Sq, N4
off Adolphus Rd **93** H1
Christina St, EC2 **12** D5
Christine Worsley Cl, N21
off Highfield Rd **59** H2
Christopher Av, W7 **124** D3
Christopher Cl, SE16 **133** G2
Sidcup DA15 **157** J5
Christopher Gdns, Dag.
RM9 *off Wren Rd* **100** D5
Christopher Pl, NW1 **9** J4
Christopher Rd, Sthl.
UB2 **122** B4
Christopher's Ms, W11
off Penzance St **128** B1
Christopher St, EC2 **12** C6
Chryssell Rd, SW9 **131** G7
Chubworthy St, SE14 **133** H6
Chudleigh Cres, Ilf. IG3 **99** H4
Chudleigh Gdns, Sutt.
SM1 **199** F3
Chudleigh Rd, NW6 **90** A7
SE4 **153** J5
Twickenham TW2 **144** C7
Chudleigh St, E1 **113** G6
Chudleigh Way, Ruis.
HA4 **84** A1
Chulsa Rd, SE26 **170** E5
Chumleigh St, SE5 **36** D5
Chumleigh Wk, Surb.
KT5 **181** J4
Church All, Croy. CR0 **201** G1
Church App, SE21 **170** A3
Staines (Stanw.) TW19 **140** A6
Church Av, E4 **62** D6
NW1 *off Kentish Town Rd* **92** B6
SW14 **146** D3
Beckenham BR3 **190** A1
Northolt UB5 **85** F7
Pinner HA5 **67** E6
Sidcup DA14 **176** A5
Southall UB2 **123** E3
Churchbury Cl, Enf. EN1 **44** B2
Churchbury La, Enf. EN1 **44** A3
Churchbury Rd, SE9 **156** A7
Enfield EN1 **44** A2
Church Cl, N20 **57** H3
W8 **22** A3
Edgware HA8 **54** C5
Hounslow TW3
off Bath Rd **143** F3
Loughton IG10 **48** C2
West Drayton UB7 **120** B3
Church Ct, Rich. TW9
off George St **145** G5
Church Cres, E9 **95** G7
N3 **72** C1
N10 **74** B4
N20 **57** H3
Churchcroft Cl, SW12
off Endlesham Rd **150** A7
Churchdown, Brom. BR1 **173** E4
Church Dr, NW9 **88** D1
Harrow HA2 **67** F6
West Wickham BR4 **205** E3
Church Elm La, Dag.
RM10 **101** G6
CHURCH END, N3 **72** C1
CHURCH END, NW10 **88** E6
Church End, E17 **78** B4
NW4 **71** H3
Church Entry, EC4 **19** H4
★**Church Farm Ho Mus**,
NW4 **71** H3
Church Fm La, Sutt.
SM3 **198** B6
Churchfield Av, N12 **57** F6
Churchfield Cl, Har. HA2 **67** J4
Churchfield Rd, W3 **126** C1
W7 **124** B2
W13 **125** E1
Welling DA16 **158** A3
Churchfields, E18 **79** G1
SE10 *off Roan St* **134** C6
Loughton IG10 **48** B4
West Molesey KT8 **179** G3
Churchfields Av, Felt.
TW13 **161** F3
Churchfields Rd, Beck.
BR3 **189** G2
Church Gdns, W5 **125** G2
Wembley HA0 **86** D4
Church Gate, SW6 **148** B3
Church Gro, SE13 **154** B4
Kingston upon Thames
KT1 **181** F1
Church Hill, E17 **78** A4
N21 **43** F7
SE18 **136** C3
SW19 **166** C5
Carshalton SM5 **199** J5
Harrow HA1 **86** B1
Loughton IG10 **48** B3
Church Hill Rd, E17 **78** B4
Barnet EN4 **41** J7
Surbiton KT6 **181** H5
Sutton SM3 **198** A4
Church Hill Wd, Orp.
BR5 **193** J5
Church Hyde, SE18
off Old Mill Rd **137** H6
Churchill Av, Har. HA3 **68** E6
Churchill Ct, W5 **105** J4
Northolt UB5 **85** G5
Churchill Gdns, SW1 **33** F4
W3 **106** A6
Churchill Gdns Rd, SW1 **33** E4
Churchill Ms, Wdf.Grn. IG8
off High Rd
Woodford Grn **63** F6
Churchill Pl, E14 **134** B1
Harrow HA1
off Sandridge Cl **68** B4
Churchill Rd, E16 **115** J6
NW2 **89** H6
NW5 **92** B4
Edgware HA8 **53** J6
South Croydon CR2 **201** J7
Churchill Ter, E4 **62** A4
Churchill Wk, E9 **95** F5
Churchill Way, Brom. BR1
off Ethelbert Rd **191** G3
Sunbury-on-Thames
TW16 **160** A5
Church La, E11 **97** E1
E17 **78** B4
N2 **73** G3
N8 **75** F4
N9 **60** D2
N17 **76** B1
NW9 **88** C2
SW17 **168** B4
SW19 **184** C1
W5 **125** F2
Bromley BR2 **206** B1
Chessington KT9 **195** J6
Chislehurst BR7 **193** F1
Dagenham RM10 **101** H6
Enfield EN1 **44** A3
Harrow HA3 **68** C1
Loughton IG10 **48** C3
Pinner HA5 **67** E3
Richmond TW10 **163** H1
Teddington TW11 **162** C5
Thames Ditton KT7 **180** C6
Twickenham TW1 **162** D1
Wallington SM6 **200** D3
Churchley Rd, SE26 **171** E4
Church Manor Est, SW9
off Vassall Rd **131** G7
Church Manorway, SE2 **137** J4
Church Manorway Ind Est,
Erith DA8 **139** J3
Churchmead Cl, Barn.
EN4 **41** H6
Church Meadow, Surb.
KT6 **195** F2
Churchmead Rd, NW10 **89** G6
Churchmore Rd, SW16 **186** C1
Church Mt, N2 **73** G5
Church Paddock Ct, Wall.
SM6 **200** D3
Church Pas, EC2
off Gresham St **111** J6
Barnet EN5 *off Wood St* **40** C4
Church Pas, Surb. KT6 **181** H5
Church Path, E11 **79** G5
E17 *off St. Mary Rd* **78** B4
N5 **93** H5
N12 **57** F5
N17 *off White Hart La* **60** B7
N20 **57** F4
NW10 **89** E7
SW14 **146** D3
SW19 **184** D2
W4 **126** C3
W7 **124** B1
Mitcham CR4 **185** H3
Southall UB1 **123** G1
Southall (Sthl Grn)
UB2 **123** F3
Church Pl, SW1 **17** G6
W5 *off Church Gdns* **125** G2
Mitcham CR4 **185** H3
Twickenham TW1
off Church St **162/163** E1
Church Ri, SE23 **171** G1
Chessington KT9 **195** J6
Church Rd, E10 **96** B2
E12 **98** B5
E17 **77** H2
N1 **93** J6
N6 **74** A6
N17 **76** B1
NW4 **71** H4
NW10 **89** E6
SE19 **188** B1
SW13 **147** F2
SW19 (Wimbledon) **166** B4
W3 **126** C2
W7 **124** C1
Barking IG11 **99** F6
Bexleyheath DA7 **159** F2
Bromley BR2 **191** G2
Bromley (Short.) BR2 **190** E3
Buckhurst Hill IG9 **63** H1
Croydon CR0 **201** H3
East Molesey KT8 **180** A4
Enfield EN3 **45** F6
Epsom (W.Ewell) KT19 **196** D7
Esher (Clay.)
KT10 **194** C6
Feltham TW13 **160** D5
Hayes UB3 **121** J1
Hounslow (Cran.) TW5 **122** B5
Hounslow (Heston)
TW5 **123** G7
Ilford IG2 **81** G6
Isleworth TW7 **144** A1
Keston BR2 **206** A7
Kingston upon Thames
KT1 **181** J2
Loughton (High Beach)
IG10 **47** H2
Mitcham CR4 **185** G2
Northolt UB5 **85** F7
Orpington (Farnboro.)
BR6 **207** F5
Richmond TW9, TW10 **145** H5
Richmond (Ham) TW10 **163** J5
Sidcup DA14 **176** A4
Southall UB2 **123** F3
Stanmore HA7 **53** E5
Surbiton KT6 **195** F2
Sutton SM3 **198** B6
Teddington TW11 **162** B4
Wallington SM6 **200** C3
Welling DA16 **158** B2
West Drayton UB7 **120** A3
Worcester Park KT4 **196** E1
Church Rd Merton,
SW19 **185** G1
Church Rd Twr Block, Stan.
HA7 *off Church Rd* **53** F5
Church Row, NW3 **91** F4
Chislehurst BR7 **175** F7
Church St, E15 **115** E1
E16 **136** E1
N9 **60** B2
NW8 **15** F1
W2 **15** F1
W4 **127** E6
Croydon CR0 **201** J2
Dagenham RM10 **101** H6
Enfield EN2 **44** A3
Hampton TW12 **179** J1
Isleworth TW7 **144** E3
Kingston upon Thames
KT1 **181** G2
Sunbury-on-Thames
TW16 **178** B3
Sutton SM1
off High St **198/199** E5
Twickenham TW1 **162** D1

Church St Est, NW8 ... 7 F6
Church St N, E15 ... 115 E1
Church St Pas, E15
off Church St ... 114/115 E1
Church Stretton Rd, Houns. TW3 ... 143 J5
Church Ter, NW4 ... 71 H3
SE13 ... 154 E3
SW8 ... 150 D2
Richmond TW10 ... 145 G5
Church Vale, N2 ... 73 J3
SE23 ... 171 F2
Churchview Rd, Twick. TW2 ... 162 A1
Church Wk, N6
off Swains La ... 92 A3
N16 ... 94 A4
NW2 ... 90 C3
NW4 ... 71 J3
NW9 ... 88 D2
SW13 ... 147 G1
SW15 ... 147 H5
SW16 ... 186 C2
SW20 ... 183 J3
Brentford TW8 ... 125 F6
Enfield EN2
off Church La ... 44 A3
Richmond TW9
off Red Lion St ... 145 G5
Thames Ditton KT7 ... 180 C6
Church Way, N20 ... 57 G3
Churchway, NW1 ... 9 J3
Church Way, Barn. EN4 ... 41 J4
Edgware HA8 ... 54 A6
Churchwell Path, E9 ... 95 F5
Churchwood Gdns, Wdf.Grn. IG8 ... 63 G4
Churchyard Row, SE11 ... 35 H1
Church Yd Wk, W2 ... 15 E1
Churston Av, E13 ... 115 H1
Churston Cl, SW2
off Tulse Hill ... 169 H1
Churston Dr, Mord. SM4 ... 184 A5
Churston Gdns, N11 ... 58 C6
Churton Pl, SW1 ... 33 G2
Churton St, SW1 ... 33 G2
Chusan Pl, E14
off Commercial Rd ... 113 J6
Chyngton Cl, Sid. DA15 ... 175 J3
Cibber Rd, SE23 ... 171 G2
Cicada Rd, SW18 ... 149 F5
Cicely Rd, SE15 ... 152 D1
Cinderella Path, NW11
off North End Rd ... 90/91 E1
Cinderford Way, Brom. BR1 ... 173 E4
Cinema Par, W5
off Ashbourne Rd ... 105 J4
Cinnabar Wf, E1 ... 29 J2
Cinnamon Cl, SE15
off Pentridge St. ... 132 C7
Croydon CR0 ... 186 E7
Cinnamon Row, SW11 ... 149 F3
Cinnamon St, E1 ... 133 E1
Cintra Pk, SE19 ... 170 C7
Circle, The, NW2 ... 89 E3
NW7 ... 54 D5
SE1 ... 29 F3
Circle Gdns, SW19 ... 184 D2
Circuits, The, Pnr. HA5 ... 66 C4
Circular Rd, N17 ... 76 C3
Circular Way, SE18 ... 136 C6
Circus Ms, W1 ... 15 J1
Circus Pl, EC2 ... 20 C2
Circus Rd, NW8 ... 6 E3
Circus St, SE10 ... 134 C7
Cirencester St, W2 ... 14 A1
Cirrus Cl, Wall. SM6 ... 200 E7
Cissbury Ring N, N12 ... 56 C5
Cissbury Ring S, N12 ... 56 C5
Cissbury Rd, N15 ... 76 A5
Citadel Pl, SE11 ... 34 C3
Citizen Ho, N7
off Harvist Est ... 93 G4
Citizen Rd, N7 ... 93 G4
C.I.Twr, N.Mal. KT3 ... 183 E3
Citron Ter, SE15
off Nunhead La ... 152/153 E3
City Cross Business Pk, SE10
off Salutation Rd. 134/135 E4
City Forum, EC1 ... 11 J3
City Gdn Row, N1 ... 11 H2
City Gate Ho, Ilf. IG2 ... 80 E6
City Ho, Croy. CR0 ... 187 H7
City Mill River Towpath, E15 ... 96 B7
★**City of Westminster Archives Cen**, SW1 *off St. Ann's St* . 25 J5
City Pt, EC2 ... 20 B1
City Rd, EC1 ... 11 G2
★**City Uni**, EC1 ... 11 G4
Civic Way, Ilf. IG6 ... 81 F4
Ruislip HA4 ... 84 D5
Clabon Ms, SW1 ... 23 J6
Clack St, SE16 ... 133 F2
Clacton Rd, E6 ... 116 A3
E17 ... 77 H6
N17 *off Sperling Rd* ... 76 C2
Claigmar Gdns, N3 ... 72 E1
Claire Ct, N12 ... 57 F3
Bushey (Bushey Hth) WD23 ... 52 A1
Pinner HA5
off Westfield Pk ... 51 F7
Claire Gdns, Stan. HA7 ... 53 F5
Claire Pl, E14 ... 134 A3
Clairvale Rd, Houns. TW5 ... 142 D1
Clairview Rd, SW16 ... 168 B5
Clairville Gdns, W7 ... 124 C1
Clairville Pt, SE23 ... 171 G3
Clamp Hill, Stan. HA7 ... 52 A4
Clancarty Rd, SW6 ... 148 D2
Clandon Cl, W3
off Avenue Rd ... 126 B2
Epsom KT17 ... 197 F6
Clandon Gdns, N3 ... 72 D3
Clandon Rd, Ilf. IG3 ... 99 H2
Clandon St, SE8 ... 154 A2
Clanfield Way, SE15
off Blakes Rd ... 132 B7
Clanricarde Gdns, W2 ... 108 D7
CLAPHAM, SW4 ... 150 B3
★**Clapham Common**, SW4 ... 150 A4
Clapham Common N Side, SW4 ... 150 B4
Clapham Common S Side, SW4 ... 150 B6
Clapham Common W Side, SW4 ... 150 A4
Clapham Cres, SW4 ... 150 D4
Clapham Est, SW11 ... 149 H4
Clapham High St, SW4 ... 150 D4
Clapham Manor St, SW4 ... 150 C3
CLAPHAM PARK, SW4 ... 150 D6
Clapham Pk Est, SW4 ... 150 D6
Clapham Pk Rd, SW4 ... 150 D4
Clapham Rd, SW9 ... 150 E3
Clapham Rd Est, SW4 ... 150 D3
Clap La, Dag. RM10 ... 101 H3
Claps Gate La, E6 ... 116 E4
Clapton Common, E5 ... 76 C7
CLAPTON PARK, E5 ... 95 H4
Clapton Pk Est, E5
off Blackwell Cl ... 95 H4
Clapton Pas, E5 ... 95 F5
Clapton Sq, E5 ... 95 F5
Clapton Ter, N16
off Oldhill St ... 94 D1
Clapton Way, E5 ... 94 D4
Clara Pl, SE18 ... 136 D4
Clare Cl, N2
off Thomas More Way .. 73 F3
Clare Cor, SE9 ... 156 E7
Claredale St, E2 ... 13 J2
Clare Gdns, E7 ... 97 G4
W11 *off Westbourne Pk Rd* ... 108 B6
Barking IG11 ... 99 J6
Clare Ho, E3 ... 113 J1
Clare La, N1 ... 93 J7
Clare Lawn Av, SW14 ... 146 D5
Clare Mkt, WC2 ... 18 C4
Clare Ms, SW6
off Waterford Rd . 128/129 E7
Claremont Av, Har. HA3 ... 69 H5
New Malden KT3 ... 183 G5
Sunbury-on-Thames TW16 ... 178 B1
Claremont Cl, E16 ... 136 D1
N1 ... 11 F2
SW2 *off Streatham Hill* ... 168/169 E1
Orpington BR6 ... 206 D4
Claremont Ct, Surb. KT6
off St. James Rd ... 181 G6
Claremont Gdns, Ilf. IG3 ... 99 H2
Surbiton KT6 ... 181 H5
Claremont Gro, W4
off Edensor Gdns. 126/127 E7
Woodford Green IG8 ... 63 J6
Claremont Pk, N3 ... 72 B1
Claremont Rd, E7 ... 97 H5
E17 ... 77 H2
N6 ... 74 C7
Claremont Rd, NW2 ... 90 A3
W9 ... 108 B2
W13 ... 104 D5
Bromley BR1 ... 192 B4
Croydon CR0 ... 202 D1
Esher (Clay.) KT10 ... 194 B7
Harrow HA3 ... 68 B2
Surbiton KT6 ... 181 H6
Teddington TW11 ... 162 C5
Twickenham TW1 ... 145 F6
Claremont Sq, N1 ... 10 E2
Claremont St, E16 ... 136 D1
N18 ... 60 D6
SE10 ... 134 B6
Claremont Way, NW2 ... 89 J1
Clarence Av, SW4 ... 150 D6
Bromley BR1 ... 192 B4
Ilford IG2 ... 80 D6
New Malden KT3 ... 182 C2
Clarence Cl, Barn. EN4 ... 41 G5
Clarence Cres, SW4 ... 150 D6
Sidcup DA14 ... 176 B3
Clarence Gdns, NW1 ... 9 E4
Clarence Gate, Wdf.Grn. IG8 ... 64 D6
Clarence Gate Gdns, NW1
off Glentworth St ... 109 J4
★**Clarence Ho**, SW1 ... 25 G3
Clarence La, SW15 ... 147 E6
Clarence Ms, E5 ... 95 E5
SE16 ... 133 G1
SW12 ... 150 B7
Clarence Pl, E5 ... 95 E5
Clarence Rd, E5 ... 95 E4
E12 ... 98 A5
E16 ... 115 E4
E17 ... 77 G2
N15 ... 75 J5
N22 ... 59 E7
NW6 ... 90 C7
SE8 ... 134 B6
SE9 ... 174 B2
SW19 ... 166 E6
W4 ... 126 A5
Bexleyheath DA6 ... 158 E4
Bromley BR1 ... 192 A3
Croydon CR0 ... 188 A7
Enfield EN3 ... 45 E5
Richmond TW9 ... 145 J1
Sidcup DA14 ... 176 B3
Sutton SM1 ... 198 E4
Teddington TW11 ... 162 C6
Wallington SM6 ... 200 B5
Clarence St, Kings.T. KT1 ... 181 H2
Richmond TW9 ... 145 H4
Southall UB2 ... 122 D3
Clarence Ter, NW1 ... 8 A5
Hounslow TW3 ... 143 H4
Clarence Wk, SW4 ... 150 E2
Clarence Way, NW1 ... 92 B7
Clarence Way Est, NW1 ... 92 B7
Clarendon Cl, E9 ... 95 F7
W2 ... 15 G5
Clarendon Cres, Twick. TW2 ... 162 A3
Clarendon Cross, W11
off Portland Rd ... 108 B7
Clarendon Dr, SW15 ... 147 J4
Clarendon Gdns, NW4 ... 71 H3
W9 ... 6 D6
Ilford IG1 ... 98 C1
Wembley HA9 ... 87 H4
Clarendon Gro, NW1 ... 9 H3
Mitcham CR4 ... 185 J3
Clarendon Ms, W2 ... 15 G4
Bexley DA5 ... 177 H1
Borehamwood WD6
off Clarendon Rd. ... 38 A3
Clarendon Pl, W2 ... 15 G5
Clarendon Ri, SE13 ... 154 C3
Clarendon Rd, E11 ... 96 D1
E17 ... 78 B6
E18 ... 79 G3
N8 ... 75 F3
N15 ... 75 H4
N18 ... 60 D6
N22 ... 75 F2
SW19 ... 167 H7
W5 ... 105 H4
W11 ... 108 B7
Borehamwood WD6 ... 38 A3
Croydon CR0 ... 201 H2
Harrow HA1 ... 68 B6
Hayes UB3 ... 121 J2
Wallington SM6 ... 200 C6
Clarendon St, SW1 ... 32 E4
Clarendon Ter, W9 ... 6 D5
Clarendon Wk, W11 ... 108 B6
Clarendon Way, N21 ... 43 J6
Chislehurst BR7 ... 193 J3
Orpington BR5 ... 193 J3
Clarens St, SE6 ... 171 J2
Clare Pl, SW15
off Minstead Gdns ... 147 F7
Clare Pt, NW2
off Claremont Rd ... 90 A1
Clare Rd, E11 ... 78 D6
NW10 ... 89 G7
SE14 ... 153 J1
Greenford UB6 ... 86 A6
Hounslow TW4 ... 143 F3
Staines (Stanw.) TW19 . 140 B7
Clare St, E2 ... 113 E2
Claret Gdns, SE25 ... 188 B4
Clareville Gro, SW7 ... 30 D2
Clareville Rd, Orp. BR5 .. 207 F2
Clareville St, SW7 ... 30 D2
Clare Way, Bexh. DA7 ... 158 E1
Clarewood Wk, SW9 ... 151 H4
Clarges Ms, W1 ... 24 D1
Clarges St, W1 ... 24 E1
Claribel Rd, SW9 ... 151 H2
Claridge Rd, Dag. RM8 ... 100 D1
Clarina Rd, SE20
off Evelina Rd ... 171 G7
Clarissa Rd, Rom. RM6 ... 82 D7
Clarissa St, E8 ... 112 C1
Clarke Ms, N9
off Plevna Rd ... 60/61 E3
Clarke Path, N16 ... 94 D1
Clarkes Av, Wor.Pk. KT4 .. 198 A1
Clarke's Ms, W1 ... 16 C1
Clark Lawrence Ct, SW11
off Winstanley Rd ... 149 G3
Clarkson Rd, E16 ... 115 F6
Clarkson Row, NW1 ... 9 F2
Clarksons, The, Bark. IG11 ... 117 F2
Clarkson St, E2 ... 112 E3
Clarks Pl, EC2 ... 20 D3
Clarks Rd, Ilf. IG1 ... 99 G2
Clark St, E1 ... 113 E5
Clark Way, Houns. TW5 .. 122 D7
Classon Cl, West Dr. UB7 ... 120 B2
Claude Rd, E10 ... 96 C2
E13 ... 115 H1
SE15 ... 152 E2
Claude St, E14 ... 134 A4
Claudia Jones Way, SW2 . 150 E6
Claudia Pl, SW19 ... 166 B1
Claughton Rd, E13 ... 115 J2
Clauson Av, Nthlt. UB5 ... 85 H5
Clavell St, SE10 ... 134 C6
Claverdale Rd, SW2 ... 151 F7
Clavering Av, SW13 ... 127 H6
Clavering Cl, Twick. TW1 .. 162 D4
Clavering Rd, E12 ... 98 A1
Claverings Ind Est, N9 ... 61 G2
Claverley Gro, N3 ... 56 D7
Claverley Vil, N3
off Claverley Gro ... 56/57 E7
Claverton St, SW1 ... 33 G4
Clave St, E1
off Cinnamon St . 132/133 E1
Claxton Gro, W6 ... 128 A5
Clay Av, Mitch. CR4 ... 186 B2
Claybank Gro, SE13
off Algernon Rd. ... 154 B3
Claybourne Ms, SE19
off Church Rd ... 170 B7
Claybridge Rd, SE12 ... 173 J4
Claybrook Cl, N2 ... 73 G3
Claybrook Rd, W6 ... 128 A6
Claybury Bdy, Ilf. IG5 ... 80 B3
Claybury Hall, Wdf.Grn. IG8
off Regents Dr. ... 64 C7
Claybury Rd, Wdf.Grn. IG8 ... 64 B7
Claydon Dr, Croy. CR0 ... 201 E4
Claydown Ms, SE18
off Woolwich New Rd . 136 D5
Clayfarm Rd, SE9 ... 175 F2
CLAYGATE, Esher KT10 .. 194 B7
Claygate Cres, Croy. (New Adgtn) CR0 ... 204 C6
Claygate La, Esher KT10 . 194 D2
Thames Ditton KT7 ... 194 D1
Claygate Lo Cl, Esher (Clay.) KT10 ... 194 B7
Claygate Rd, W13 ... 124 E3
CLAYHALL, Ilf. IG5 ... 80 C2
Clayhall Av, Ilf. IG5 ... 80 B3
Clayhill, Surb. KT5 ... 182 A5
Clayhill Cres, SE9 ... 174 A4
Claylands Pl, SW8 ... 34 E7
Claylands Rd, SW8 ... 34 D6

Clay La, Edg. HA8 54 A1
Staines (Stanw.) TW19 140 C7
Claymill Ho, SE18 137 F5
Claymore Cl, Mord. SM4 184 D7
Claymore Ct, E17
off Billet Rd 77 H1
Claypole Dr, Houns.
TW5 143 E1
Claypole Rd, E15 114 C2
Clayponds Av, Brent.
TW8 125 H4
Clayponds Gdns, W5 125 G4
Clayponds La, Brent.
TW8 125 H5
Clay Rd, The, Loug. IG10 48 B1
Clayside, Chig. IG7 65 F6
Clays La, E15 96 B5
Clay's La, Loug. IG10 48 D1
Clays La Cl, E15 96 B5
Clay St, W1 16 A2
Clayton Av, Wem. HA0 87 H7
Clayton Cl, E6
off Brandreth Rd 116 C6
Clayton Cres, N1 111 E1
Brentford TW8 125 G5
Clayton Dr, SE8
off Sapphire Rd 133 H5
Clayton Fld, NW9 55 E7
Clayton Ms, SE10 154 D1
Clayton Rd, SE15 152 D1
Chessington KT9 195 F4
Hayes UB3 121 H2
Isleworth TW7 144 B3
Romford RM7 101 J1
Clayton St, SE11 34 E5
Clayton Ter, Hayes UB4
off Jollys La 102 D5
Claywood Cl, Orp. BR6 193 H7
Clayworth Cl, Sid. DA15 158 B6
Cleanthus Cl, SE18
off Cleanthus Rd 156/157 E1
Cleanthus Rd, SE18 157 E1
Clearbrook Way, E1
off West Arbour St 113 G6
Clearwater Ter, W11
off Lorne Gdns 128 A2
Clearwell Dr, W9 6 A6
Cleave Av, Hayes UB3 121 H4
Orpington BR6 207 H6
Cleaveland Rd, Surb. KT6 181 G5
Cleaverholme Cl, SE25 188 E6
Cleaver Sq, SE11 35 F3
Cleaver St, SE11 35 F3
Cleeve Hill, SE23 171 E1
Cleeve Pk Gdns, Sid.
DA14 176 B2
Cleeve Way, SW15
off Danebury Av 147 F7
Clegg Ho, SE3
off Pinto Way 155 H4
Clegg St, E1
off Prusom St 132/133 E1
E13 115 G2
Cleland Path, Loug. IG10 49 E1
Clematis Gdns, Wdf.Grn.
IG8 63 G5
Clematis St, W12 107 F7
Clem Attlee Ct, SW6 128 C6
Clem Attlee Est, SW6
off Lillie Rd 128 C6
Clem Attlee Par, SW6
off North End Rd 128 C6
Clemence Rd, Dag.
RM10 119 J1
Clemence St, E14 113 J5
Clement Av, SW4 150 D4
Clement Cl, NW6 89 J7
W4 *off Acton La* 126 D4
Clement Gdns, Hayes
UB3 121 H4
Clementhorpe Rd, Dag.
RM9 100 C6
Clementina Rd, E10 95 J1
Clementine Cl, W13
off Balfour Rd 124/125 E2
Clementine Wk, Wdf.Grn. IG8
off Salway Cl 63 G7
Clement Rd, SW19 166 B5
Beckenham BR3 189 G2
Clements Av, E16 115 G7
Clements Ct, Houns.
TW4 142 D4
Ilford IG1
off Clements La 98/99 E3
Clement's Inn, WC2 18 D4
Clement's Inn Pas, WC2 18 D4
Clements La, EC4 20 C5
Ilford IG1 98 E3
Clements Pl, Brent. TW8 125 G5
Clements Rd, E6 98 C7
SE16 29 J6
Ilford IG1 98 E3
Clendon Way, SE18
off Polthorne Gro 137 G4
Clennam St, SE1 28 A3
Clensham Ct, Sutt. SM1 *off Sutton Common Rd* 198 D2
Clensham La, Sutt. SM1 198 D2
Clenston Ms, W1 15 J3
★**Cleopatra's Needle**,
WC2 26 C1
Clephane Rd, N1 93 J6
Clere St, EC2 12 C5
CLERKENWELL, EC1 11 G6
Clerkenwell Cl, EC1 11 F5
Clerkenwell Grn, EC1 11 F6
Clerkenwell Rd, EC1 10 E6
Clerks Piece, Loug. IG10 48 C3
Clermont Rd, E9 113 F1
Clevedon Cl, N16
off Smalley Cl 94 C3
Clevedon Gdns, Hayes
UB3 121 G3
Hounslow TW5 142 B1
Clevedon Rd, SE20 189 G1
Kingston upon Thames
KT1 182 A2
Twickenham TW1 145 G6
Cleveland Av, SW20 184 C2
W4 127 F4
Hampton TW12 161 F7
Cleveland Cres, Borwd.
WD6 38 C5
Cleveland Gdns, N4 75 J5
NW2 90 A2
SW13 147 F2
W2 14 C4
Worcester Park KT4 197 E2
Cleveland Gro, E1
off Cleveland Way 113 F4
Cleveland Ms, W1 17 F1
Cleveland Pk, Stai. TW19 140 B6
Cleveland Pk Av, E17 78 A4
Cleveland Pk Cres, E17 78 A4
Cleveland Pl, SW1 25 G1
Cleveland Ri, Mord.
SM4 184 A7
Cleveland Rd, E18 79 G3
N1 94 A7
N9 45 E7
SW13 147 F2
W4 *off Antrobus Rd* 126 C3
W13 104 E5
Ilford IG1 99 E3
Isleworth TW7 144 D4
New Malden KT3 182 E4
Welling DA16 157 J2
Worcester Park KT4 197 E2
Cleveland Row, SW1 25 F2
Cleveland Sq, W2 14 C4
Cleveland St, W1 9 F6
Cleveland Ter, W2 14 D3
Cleveland Way, E1 113 F4
Cleveley Cl, SE7 136 A4
Cleveley Cres, W5 105 H2
Cleveleys Rd, E5 95 E3
Cleverly Est, W12 127 G1
Cleve Rd, NW6 90 D7
Sidcup DA14 176 D3
Cleves Cl, Loug. IG10 48 B6
Cleves Rd, E6 116 A1
Richmond TW10 163 F3
Cleves Wk, Ilf. IG6 65 F7
Cleves Way, Hmptn.
TW12 161 F7
Ruislip HA4 84 D1
Clewer Cres, Har. HA3 68 A1
Clewer Ho, SE2
off Wolvercote Rd 138 D2
Clichy Est, E1 113 F5
Clifden Rd, E5 95 F5
Brentford TW8 125 G6
Twickenham TW1 162 C1
Cliffe Rd, S.Croy. CR2 202 A5
Cliffe Wk, Sutt. SM1
off Turnpike La 199 F5
Clifford Av, SW14 146 B3
Chislehurst BR7 174 C6
Ilford IG5 80 E1
Wallington SM6 200 C4
Clifford Cl, Nthlt. UB5 103 E1
Clifford Dr, SW9 151 H4
Clifford Gdns, NW10 107 J2
Hayes UB3 121 G4
Clifford Rd, E16 115 F4
E17 78 C2
N9 45 F6
SE25 188 D4
Clifford Rd, Barn. EN5 41 E3
Hounslow TW4 142 D3
Richmond TW10 163 G2
Wembley HA0 105 G1
Clifford's Inn Pas, EC4 19 E4
Clifford St, W1 17 F6
Clifford Way, NW10 89 F4
Cliff Rd, NW1 92 D6
Cliff Ter, SE8 154 A2
Cliffview Rd, SE13 154 A3
Cliff Vil, NW1 92 D6
Cliff Wk, E16 115 F5
Clifton Av, E17 77 G3
N3 72 C1
W12 127 F1
Feltham TW13 160 C3
Stanmore HA7 69 E2
Wembley HA9 87 J6
Clifton Cl, Orp. BR6 207 F5
Clifton Ct, N4
off Biggerstaff St 93 G2
NW8 6 E5
Woodford Green IG8
off Snakes La W 63 G6
Clifton Cres, SE15 133 E7
Clifton Est, SE15
off Consort Rd 152/153 E1
Clifton Gdns, N15 76 C6
NW11 72 C6
W4 *off Dolman Rd* 126 D4
W9 6 C6
Enfield EN2 42 E4
Clifton Gro, E8 94 D6
Clifton Hill, NW8 109 E2
Clifton Pk Av, SW20 183 J2
Clifton Pl, SE16
off Canon Beck Rd 133 F2
W2 15 F5
Clifton Ri, SE14 133 H7
Clifton Rd, E7 98 A6
E16 115 E5
N1 93 J6
N3 73 F1
N8 74 D6
N22 74 C1
NW10 107 G2
SE25 188 B4
SW19 166 A6
W9 6 D5
Greenford UB6 103 J4
Harrow HA3 69 J5
Hounslow (Hthrw Air.) TW6
off Inner Ring E 140/141 E3
Ilford IG2 81 G6
Isleworth TW7 144 A2
Kingston upon Thames
KT2 163 J7
Loughton IG10 48 B4
Sidcup DA14 175 H4
Southall UB2 123 E4
Teddington TW11 162 B4
Wallington SM6 200 B5
Welling DA16 158 C3
Clifton St, EC2 20 D1
Clifton Ter, N4 93 G2
Clifton Vil, W9 14 B1
Clifton Wk, E6 116 B6
W6 *off Galena Rd* 127 H4
Clifton Way, SE15 133 E7
Borehamwood WD6 38 A1
Wembley HA0 105 H1
Clinch Ct, E16 115 G5
Cline Rd, N11 58 C6
Clinger Ct, N1
off Pitfield St 112 B1
★**Clink Prison Mus**, SE1 28 B1
Clink St, SE1 28 A1
Clinton Av, E.Mol. KT8 179 J4
Welling DA16 157 J4
Clinton Cres, Ilf. IG6 65 H6
Clinton Rd, E3 113 H3
E7 97 G4
N15 76 A4
Clinton Ter, Sutt. SM1
off Manor La 199 F4
Clipper Cl, SE16
off Kinburn St 133 G2
Clipper Way, SE13 154 C4
Clippesby Cl, Chess.
KT9 195 J7
Clipstone Ms, W1 9 F6
Clipstone Rd, Houns.
TW3 143 G3
Clipstone St, W1 17 E1
Clissold Cl, N2 73 J3
Clissold Ct, N4 93 J2
Clissold Cres, N16 94 A3
Clissold Rd, N16 94 A3
Clitheroe Av, Har. HA2 85 G1
Clitheroe Gdns, Wat.
WD19 50 D3
Clitheroe Rd, SW9 151 E2
Clitherow Av, W7 124 D3
Clitherow Pas, Brent.
TW8 125 F5
Clitherow Rd, Brent.
TW8 125 F5
Clitterhouse Cres, NW2 89 J1
Clitterhouse Rd, NW2 89 J1
Clive Av, N18
off Claremont St 60 D6
Clive Ct, W9 6 D5
Cliveden Cl, N12
off Woodside Av 57 F4
Cliveden Pl, SW1 32 B1
Cliveden Rd, SW19 184 C1
Clivedon Ct, W13 104 E5
Clivedon Rd, E4 62 E5
Clive Pas, SE21
off Clive Rd 170 A3
Clive Rd, SE21 170 A3
SW19 167 H6
Belvedere DA17 139 G4
Enfield EN1 44 D4
Feltham TW14 142 A6
Twickenham TW1 162 C4
Clivesdale Dr, Hayes
UB3 122 B1
Clive Way, Enf. EN1 44 D4
Cloak La, EC4 20 A5
Clockhouse Av, Bark.
IG11 117 F1
Clockhouse Cl, SW19 165 J3
Clockhouse Pl, SW15 148 B5
Clock Ho Rd, Beck. BR3 189 H3
★**Clockmakers Company Collection, The, Guildhall Lib**, EC2 20 A3
Clock Twr Ms, N1
off Arlington Av 111 J1
SE28 118 B7
Clock Twr Pl, N7 92 E6
Clock Twr Rd, Islw. TW7 144 C3
Cloister Cl, Tedd. TW11 162 E5
Cloister Gdns, SE25 188 E6
Edgware HA8 54 C5
Cloister Rd, NW2 90 C3
W3 106 C5
Cloisters Av, Brom. BR2 192 C5
Cloisters Business Cen, SW8
off Battersea Pk Rd 130 B7
Cloisters Mall, Kings.T. KT1
off Union St 181 G2
Clonard Way, Pnr. HA5 51 G6
Clonbrock Rd, N16 94 B4
Cloncurry St, SW6 148 A2
Clonmel Cl, Har. HA2 86 A1
Clonmell Rd, N17 76 A3
Clonmel Rd, SW6 128 C7
Teddington TW11 162 A4
Clonmore St, SW18 166 C1
Cloonmore Av, Orp. BR6 207 J4
Clorane Gdns, NW3 90 D3
Close, The, E4
off Beech Hall Rd 62 C7
N14 58 D2
N20 56 C2
SE3 *off Heath La* 154 D2
Barnet EN4 41 J6
Beckenham BR3 189 H4
Bexley DA5 159 G6
Harrow HA2 67 J2
Isleworth TW7 144 A2
Mitcham CR4 185 J4
New Malden KT3 182 C2
Orpington BR5 193 H6
Pinner (Eastcote) HA5 66 C7
Pinner (Rayners La)
HA5 67 F7
Richmond TW9 146 B3
Romford RM6 82 E6
Sidcup DA14 176 B5
Sutton SM3 184 C7
Wembley (Barnhill Rd)
HA9 88 C3
Wembley (Lyon Pk Av)
HA0 87 H6
Cloth Ct, EC1 19 H2
Cloth Fair, EC1 19 H2
Clothier St, E1 21 E3
Cloth St, EC1 19 J1
Clothworkers Rd, SE18 137 G7
Cloudesdale Rd, SW17 168 B2
Cloudesley Pl, N1 111 G1
Cloudesley Rd, N1 111 G1
Bexleyheath DA7 159 F1
Cloudesley Sq, N1 111 G1
Cloudesley St, N1 111 G1

Clouston Cl, Wall. SM6 . . **200** E5
Clova Rd, E7. . . . . **97** F6
Clove Cres, E14. . . . . **114** D7
Clove Hitch Quay, SW11 . **149** F3
Clovelly Av, NW9 . . . . **71** F4
Clovelly Cl, Pnr. HA5 . . . . **66** B3
Clovelly Gdns, SE19. . . . . **188** C1
Enfield EN1 . . . . **44** B7
Romford RM7 . . . . **83** H1
Clovelly Rd, N8. . . . . **74** D4
W4. . . . . **126** C2
W5. . . . . **125** F2
Bexleyheath DA7 . . . . . **138** E6
Hounslow TW3 . . . . **143** G2
Clovelly Way, E1
off Jamaica St. **113** F6
Harrow HA2 . . . . **85** F2
Orpington BR6 . . . . **193** J6
Clover Cl, E11
off Norman Rd **96** D2
Cloverdale Gdns, Sid.
DA15 . . . . **157** J6
Cloverleys, Loug. IG10 . . . . **48** A5
Clover Ms, SW3 . . . . **31** J5
Clover Way, Wall. SM6 . . . **200** A1
Clove St, E13
off Barking Rd **115** G4
Clowders Rd, SE6 . . . . . . **171** J3
Clowser Cl, Sutt. SM1
off Turnpike La. **199** F5
Cloysters Grn, E1 . . . . **29** H1
Cloyster Wd, Edg. HA8. . . . **53** G7
Club Gdns Rd, Brom.
BR2 . . . . **191** G7
Club Row, E1 . . . . **13** F5
E2 . . . . **13** F5
Clunbury Av, Sthl. UB2 . . **123** F5
Clunbury St, N1 . . . . **12** C2
Cluny Est, SE1 . . . . **28** D5
Cluny Ms, SW5. . . . . **128** D4
Cluny Pl, SE1 . . . . **28** D5
Cluse Ct, N1 . . . . **11** J1
Clutton St, E14. . . . . **114** B5
Clydach Rd, Enf. EN1 . . . . . **44** C4
Clyde Circ, N15. . . . . **76** B4
Clyde Pl, E10 . . . . **78** B7
Clyde Rd, N15 . . . . **76** B4
N22 . . . . **74** D1
Croydon CR0. . . . . **202** C1
Sutton SM1. . . . . **198** D5
Wallington SM6 . . . . . . **200** C5
Clydesdale, Enf. EN3 . . . . . **45** G4
Clydesdale Av, Stan. HA7 . **69** G3
Clydesdale Cl, Borwd.
WD6 . . . . **38** D5
Isleworth TW7 . . . . **144** C3
Clydesdale Gdns, Rich.
TW10 . . . . **146** B4
Clydesdale Ho, Erith DA18
off Kale Rd **138/139** E2
Clydesdale Rd, W11 . . . . . **108** C6
Clyde St, SE8 . . . . **133** J6
Clyde Ter, SE23. . . . . **171** F2
Clyde Vale, SE23. . . . . **171** F2
Clymping Dene, Felt.
TW14. . . . . **142** B7
Clyston St, SW8. . . . . **150** C2
Coach & Horses Yd, W1 . . . **17** E5
Coach Ho La, N5
off Highbury Hill **93** H4
SW19. . . . . **166** A4
Coach Ho Ms, SE1 . . . . **28** D5
SE14 *off Waller Rd* **153** G2
Coachhouse Ms, SE20 . . . **170** E7
Coach Ho Ms, SE23 . . . . . **153** G6
Coach Ho Yd, SW18
off Ebner St **148/149** E4
Coachmaker Ms, SW4
off Fenwick Pl. . . . **150/151** E3
Coach Yd Ms, N19
off Trinder Rd. **92/93** E1
Coaldale Wk, SE21
off Lairdale Cl **151** J7
Coalecroft Rd, SW15 . . . . . **147** J4
Coal Wf Rd, W12
off Sterne St **128** A2
Coates Av, SW18 . . . . **149** H6
Coates Hill Rd, Brom.
BR1 . . . . **192** D2
Coate St, E2. . . . . **13** J2
Coates Wk, Brent. TW8. . . **125** H5
Cobb Cl, Borwd. WD6 . . . . **38** C5
Cobbett Rd, SE9. . . . . **156** B3
Twickenham TW2 . . . . . **161** G1
Cobbetts Av, Ilf. IG4. . . . . . **80** A5
Cobbett St, SW8 . . . . **131** F7
Cobble La, N1
off Edwards Ms. **93** H7
Cobble Ms, N5. . . . . **93** J3
Cobblers Wk, E.Mol. KT8 . **180** D1
Hampton TW12 . . . . **161** J7
Kingston upon Thames
KT2 . . . . **180** D1
Teddington TW11. . . . . . **180** D1
Cobblestone Pl, Croy. CR0
off Oakfield Rd **201** J1
Cobbold Est, NW10 . . . . . . **89** F6
Cobbold Ms, W12
off Cobbold Rd **127** F2
Cobbold Rd, E11. . . . . **97** F3
NW10 . . . . **89** F6
W12. . . . . **127** E2
Cobb's Ct, EC4
off Ludgate Hill **111** H6
Cobb's Rd, Houns. TW4 . . **143** F4
Cobb St, E1 . . . . **21** F2
Cobden Rd, E11 . . . . **97** E3
SE25 . . . . **188** D5
Orpington BR6 . . . . **207** G4
Cobham Av, N.Mal. KT3. . **183** G5
Cobham Cl, SW11 . . . . . . **149** H6
Bromley BR2. . . . . **192** B7
Edgware HA8 . . . . **70** B2
Enfield EN1 . . . . **44** D3
Sidcup DA15
off Park Mead **158** B6
Wallington SM6 . . . . . . **200** E6
Cobham Ho, Bark. IG11
off St. Margarets **117** F1
Cobham Ms, NW1
off Agar Gro **92** D7
Cobham Pl, Bexh. DA6. . . **158** D5
Cobham Rd, E17 . . . . **78** C1
N22 . . . . **75** H3
Hounslow TW5 . . . . **122** C7
Ilford IG3. . . . . **99** H2
Kingston upon Thames
KT1 . . . . **182** A1
Cobland Rd, SE12 . . . . . . **173** J4
Coborn Rd, E3 . . . . **113** J3
Coborn St, E3. . . . . **113** J3
Cobourg Rd, SE5 . . . . **37** F5
Cobourg St, NW1. . . . . **9** G4
Coburg Cl, SW1 . . . . **33** G1
Coburg Cres, SW2 . . . . . . **169** F1
Coburg Gdns, Ilf. IG5 . . . . . **80** A2
Coburg Rd, N22 . . . . **75** F3
Cochrane Ms, NW8 . . . . **7** F2
Cochrane Rd, SW19. . . . . . **166** C7
Cochrane St, NW8. . . . . **7** F2
Cockayne Way, SE8 . . . . . **133** H5
Cockerell Rd, E17. . . . . **77** H7
COCKFOSTERS, Barn.
EN4 . . . . **41** H4
Cockfosters Par, Barn. EN4
off Cockfosters Rd. **42** A4
Cockfosters Rd, Barn.
EN4 . . . . **41** J2
Cock Hill, E1. . . . . **21** E2
Cock La, EC1 . . . . **19** G2
Cockpit Steps, SW1 . . . . . . **25** J4
Cockpit Yd, WC1. . . . . **18** D1
Cocks Cres, N.Mal. KT3 . . **183** F4
Cocksett Av, Orp. BR6 . . . **207** H6
Cockspur Ct, SW1 . . . . **25** J1
Cockspur St, SW1 . . . . **25** J1
Cocksure La, Sid. DA14 . . **177** G3
Coda Cen, The, SW6. . . . . **148** B1
Code St, E1 . . . . **13** G6
Codicote Ter, N4
off Green Las **93** J2
Codling Cl, E1 . . . . **29** J1
Codling Way, Wem. HA0 . . **87** G4
Codrington Hill, SE23. . . . **153** H7
Codrington Ms, W11
off Blenheim Cres **108** B6
Cody Cl, Har. HA3 . . . . **69** G3
Wallington SM6
off Alcock Cl **200** D7
Cody Rd, E16 . . . . **114** D4
Cody Rd Business Cen,
E16. . . . . **114** D4
Coe Av, SE25 . . . . **188** D6
Coe's All, Barn. EN5
off Wood St. **40** B4
Cogan Av, E17 . . . . **77** H1
Coin St, SE1. . . . . **27** E1
Coity Rd, NW5 . . . . **92** A6
Cokers La, SE21
off Perifield **170** A1
Coke St, E1. . . . . **21** H3
Colas Ms, NW6
off Birchington Rd. . . . **108** D1
Colbeck Ms, SW7. . . . . **30** B2
Colbeck Rd, Har. HA1. . . . . **67** J7
Colberg Pl, N16 . . . . **76** B7
Colborne Way, Wor.Pk.
KT4 . . . . **197** J3
Colbrook Av, Hayes UB3 . **121** G3
Colbrook Cl, Hayes UB3 . **121** G3
Colburn Av, Pnr. HA5 . . . . . **51** E6
Colburn Way, Sutt. SM1 . . **199** G3
Colby Ms, SE19
off Gipsy Hill **170** B5
Colby Rd, SE19. . . . . **170** B5
Colchester Av, E12 . . . . **98** C3
Colchester Dr, Pnr. HA5 . . . **66** D5
Colchester Rd, E10. . . . . . . **78** C7
E17 . . . . **78** A6
Edgware HA8 . . . . **54** C7
Northwood HA6 . . . . **66** A2
Colchester St, E1 . . . . **21** G3
Coldbath Sq, EC1. . . . . **11** E5
Coldbath St, SE13 . . . . . . **154** B1
COLDBLOW, Bex. DA5 . . . **177** J2
Cold Blow La, SE14 . . . . . **133** G7
Cold Blows, Mitch. CR4 . . **186** A3
Coldershaw Rd, W13 . . . . **124** D1
Coldfall Av, N10 . . . . **73** J2
Cold Harbour, E14 . . . . . . **134** C2
Coldharbour Crest, SE9
off Great Harry Dr **174** D3
Coldharbour La, SE5 . . . . **151** G4
SW9. . . . . **151** G4
Hayes UB3. . . . . **102** A7
Coldharbour Pl, SE5
off Denmark Hill **151** J2
Coldharbour Rd, Croy.
CR0 . . . . **201** G5
Coldharbour Way, Croy.
CR0 . . . . **201** G5
Coldstream Gdns, SW18 . **148** C6
Colebeck Ms, N1 . . . . **93** H6
Colebert Av, E1. . . . . **113** F4
Colebrook Cl, NW7 . . . . . . **56** A7
SW15 *off West Hill* **148** A7
Colebrooke Av, W13. . . . . **104** E6
Colebrooke Dr, E11. . . . . . . **79** H7
Colebrooke Pl, N1
off St. Peters St **111** H1
Colebrooke Ri, Brom.
BR2 . . . . **191** E2
Colebrooke Row, N1 . . . . . **11** G2
Colebrook Gdns, Loug.
IG10. . . . . **49** E2
Colebrook Ho, E14
off Brabazon St **114** B6
Colebrook La, Loug. IG10 . **49** E2
Colebrook Path, Loug.
IG10. . . . . **49** E2
Colebrook Rd, SW16 . . . . **187** E1
Colebrook Way, N11 . . . . . . **58** B5
Coleby Path, SE5
off Harris St. **132** A7
Cole Cl, SE28 . . . . **138** B1
Coledale Dr, Stan. HA7 . . . **69** F1
Coleford Rd, SW18. . . . . . **149** F5
Cole Gdns, Houns. TW5 . . **122** A7
Colegrave Rd, E15 . . . . **96** D5
Colegrove Rd, SE15 . . . . . . **37** G6
Coleherne Ct, SW5. . . . . . . **30** B4
Coleherne Ms, SW10 . . . . . **30** A4
Coleherne Rd, SW10 . . . . . **30** A4
Colehill Gdns, SW6
off Fulham Palace Rd . **148** B2
Colehill La, SW6. . . . . **148** B1
Coleman Cl, SE25 . . . . . . **188** D2
Coleman Flds, N1 . . . . **111** J1
Coleman Rd, SE5. . . . . **36** D7
Belvedere DA17 . . . . . . **139** G4
Dagenham RM9 . . . . . . **101** E6
Colemans Heath, SE9 . . . **174** E3
Coleman St, EC2 . . . . **20** B3
Colenso Dr, NW7 . . . . **55** G7
Colenso Rd, E5. . . . . **95** F4
Ilford IG2. . . . . **99** H1
Cole Pk Gdns, Twick. TW1 **144** D6
Cole Pk Rd, Twick. TW1. . . **144** D6
Cole Pk Vw, Twick. TW1
off Hill Vw Rd **144** D6
Colepits Wd Rd, SE9 . . . . **157** F5
Coleraine Rd, N8 . . . . **75** G3
SE3 . . . . **135** F6
Coleridge Av, E12. . . . . **98** B6
Sutton SM1. . . . . **199** H4
Coleridge Cl, SW8 . . . . . . **150** B2
Coleridge Gdns, NW6
off Fairhazel Gdns. **91** F7
SW10. . . . . **30** B7
Coleridge La, N8
off Coleridge Rd. . . . **74/75** E6
Coleridge Rd, E17. . . . . **77** J4
N4 . . . . **93** G2
N8 . . . . **74** D6
N12 . . . . **57** F5
Croydon CR0. . . . . **189** F7
Coleridge Sq, SW10. . . . . . **30** C7
Coleridge Sq, W13
off Berners Dr **104** D6
Coleridge Wk, NW11 . . . . . **72** D4
Coleridge Way, Hayes
UB4 . . . . **102** A6
West Drayton UB7 . . . . **120** C4
Cole Rd, Twick. TW1 . . . . . **144** D6
Colesburg Rd, Beck. BR3 . **189** J3
Coles Cres, Har. HA2 . . . . . **85** H2
Coles Grn, Bushey
(Bushey Hth) WD23 . . . **51** J1
Loughton IG10 . . . . **48** D1
Coles Grn Ct, NW2. . . . . . . **89** G2
Coles Grn Rd, NW2 . . . . . . **89** G1
Coleshill Rd, Tedd. TW11. . **162** B6
Colestown St, SW11 . . . . **149** H2
Cole St, SE1. . . . . **28** A4
Colet Cl, N13 . . . . **59** H6
Colet Gdns, W14 . . . . **128** A4
Coley St, WC1 . . . . **10** D6
Colfe Rd, SE23 . . . . **171** H1
Colham Av, West Dr.
UB7 . . . . **120** B1
Colham Mill Rd, West Dr.
UB7 . . . . **120** A2
Colina Ms, N15
off Harringay Rd **75** H5
Colina Rd, N15. . . . . **75** H5
Colin Cl, NW9. . . . . **71** E4
Croydon CR0. . . . . **203** J3
West Wickham BR4. . . . **205** F3
Colin Cres, NW9. . . . . **71** F4
Colindale Av, NW9. . . . . . . **70** D3
Colindale Business Pk,
NW9 . . . . **70** C3
Colindeep Gdns, NW4 . . . . **71** G5
Colindeep La, NW4 . . . . . . **70** E3
NW9 . . . . **70** E3
Colin Dr, NW9 . . . . **71** F5
Colinette Rd, SW15 . . . . . **147** J4
Colin Gdns, NW9. . . . . **71** F5
Colin Par, NW9
off Edgware Rd **70/71** E4
Colin Pk Rd, NW9 . . . . **70** E4
Colin Rd, NW10 . . . . **89** G6
Colinton Rd, Ilf. IG3 . . . . . **100** B2
★**Coliseum, The**, WC2 . . . . **18** A6
Coliston Pas, SW18
off Coliston Rd **148** D7
Coliston Rd, SW18. . . . . . **148** D7
Collamore Av, SW18 . . . . **167** H1
Collapit Cl, Har. HA1 . . . . . **67** H5
Collard Av, Loug. IG10 . . . . **49** F2
Collard Grn, Loug. IG10
off Collard Av **49** F2
Collard Pl, NW1
off Harmood St. **92** B7
College App, SE10 . . . . . . **134** C6
College Av, Har. HA3 . . . . . **68** B1
College Cl, E9
off Median Rd. **95** F5
N18 . . . . **60** C5
Harrow HA3 . . . . **52** B7
Twickenham TW2
off Meadway. **162** A1
College Cres, NW3. . . . . . . **91** G6
College Cross, N1 . . . . **93** G7
College Dr, Ruis. HA4 . . . . **66** A7
Thames Ditton KT7 . . . . **180** B7
College Gdns, E4 . . . . **46** B7
N18 . . . . **60** C5
SE21 . . . . **170** B1
SW17. . . . . **167** H2
Enfield EN2. . . . . **44** A1
Ilford IG4. . . . . **80** B5
New Malden KT3 . . . . . **183** F5
College Grn, SE19 . . . . . . **170** B7
College Gro, NW1
off St. Pancras Way . . . **110** D1
College Hill, EC4 . . . . **20** A5
College Hill Rd, Har. HA3. . **68** C1
College La, NW5 . . . . **92** B4
College Ms, SW1 . . . . **26** A5
SW18
off St. Ann's Hill. . **148/149** E5
★**College of Arms**, EC4 . . . **19** H5
College Pk Cl, SE13 . . . . . **154** D4
College Pk Rd, N17
off College Rd. **60** C6
College Pl, E17 . . . . **78** E4
NW1. . . . . **110** C1
SW10. . . . . **30** C7
College Pt, E15. . . . . **97** F6
College Rd, E17 . . . . **78** C5
N17 . . . . **60** C6
N21 . . . . **59** G2
NW10. . . . . **107** J2
SE19 . . . . **170** C5
SE21 . . . . **152** B7

College Rd, SW19 . . . . . . **167** G6
W13. . . . . **104** E6
Bromley BR1 . . . . **173** G7
Croydon CR0. . . . . **202** A2
Enfield EN2. . . . . **44** A2
Harrow (Har.Hill) HA1 . . . **68** B6
Harrow (Har.Wld) HA3 . . **68** B1
Isleworth TW7 . . . . **144** C1
Wembley HA9. . . . . **87** G1
College Row, E9. . . . . **95** G5
College Slip, Brom. BR1. . **191** G1
College St, EC4 . . . . **20** A5
College Ter, E3 . . . . **113** J3
N3 *off Hendon La* **72** C2
College Vw, SE9. . . . . **174** A1
College Wk, Kings.T. KT1
off Grange Rd **181** H2
College Way, Hayes UB3 . **102** A7
College Yd, NW5
off College La **92** B4
Collent St, E9. . . . . **95** F6
Colless Rd, N15 . . . . **76** C5
Collett Rd, SE16. . . . . **29** J6
Collett Way, Sthl. UB2 . . . **123** H1
Collier Cl, E6
off Trader Rd **116/117** E6
Epsom KT19 . . . . **196** A6
Collier Dr, Edg. HA8. . . . . . **70** A2
COLLIER ROW, Rom.
RM5. . . . . **83** G1
Collier Row Rd, Rom.
RM5. . . . . **83** F1
Colliers Shaw, Kes. BR2. . **206** A4
Collier St, N1 . . . . **10** C2
Colliers Water La, Th.Hth.
CR7 . . . . **187** G5
COLLIER'S WOOD,
SW19. . . . . **167** G7
Collindale Av, Erith DA8. . **139** H6
Sidcup DA15 . . . . **176** A1
Collingbourne Rd, W12 . . **127** H1
Collingham Gdns, SW5 . . . **30** B2
Collingham Pl, SW5. . . . . . **30** A2
Collingham Rd, SW5 . . . . . **30** B1
Collings Cl, N22
off Whittington Rd. **59** F6
Collington St, SE10
off Hoskins St **134** D5
Collingtree Rd, SE26 . . . . **171** F4
Collingwood Av, N10 . . . . . **74** A3
Surbiton KT5. . . . . **196** C1
Collingwood Cl, SE20 . . . **189** E1
Twickenham TW2 . . . . . **143** G6
Collingwood Rd, E17 . . . . . **78** A6
N15 . . . . **76** B4
Mitcham CR4. . . . . **185** H2
Sutton SM1. . . . . **198** D3
Collingwood St, E1 . . . . . **113** E4
Collins Av, Stan. HA7 . . . . . **69** H2
Collins Dr, Ruis. HA4 . . . . . **84** C2
Collinson St, SE1. . . . . **27** J4
Collinson Wk, SE1 . . . . **27** J4
Collins Rd, N5 . . . . **93** J4
Collins Sq, SE3
off Tranquil Vale. **155** F2
Collins St, SE3. . . . . **155** E2
Collin's Yd, N1
off Islington Grn **111** H1
Collinwood Av, Enf. EN3 . . **45** F3
Collinwood Gdns, Ilf. IG5. . **80** C5
Collis All, Twick. TW2
off The Green **162** B1
Collison Pl, N16 . . . . **94** B2
Colls Rd, SE15 . . . . **153** F1
Collyer Av, Croy. CR0. . . . **200** E4
Collyer Pl, SE15
off Peckham High St . . **152** D1
Collyer Rd, Croy. CR0. . . . **201** E4
Colman Rd, E16 . . . . **115** J5
Colmar Cl, E1
off Alderney Rd. **113** G4
Colmer Pl, Har. HA3. . . . . . **52** A7
Colmer Rd, SW16. . . . . . . **187** E1
Colmore Ms, SE15 . . . . . . **153** E1
Colmore Rd, Enf. EN3 . . . . **45** F4
Colnbrook St, SE1 . . . . **27** G6
Colne Ct, Epsom KT19. . . **196** C4
Colne Ho, Bark. IG11 . . . . . **99** E6
Colne Rd, E5. . . . . **95** H4
N21 . . . . **44** A7
Twickenham TW1, TW2 . **162** B1
Colne St, E13
off Grange Rd **115** G3
Colney Hatch La, N10 . . . . **58** A7
N11 . . . . **57** J6
Cologne Rd, SW11 . . . . . . **149** G4
Colombo Rd, Ilf. IG1. . . . . . **99** F1
Colombo St, SE1 . . . . **27** G2
Colomb St, SE10 . . . . **135** E5
Colonels Wk, Enf. EN2 . . . . **43** H3
Colonial Av, Twick. TW2 . . **143** J5
Colonial Dr, W4 . . . . **126** C4
Colonial Rd, Felt. TW14 . . **141** H7
Colonnade, WC1. . . . . **10** A6
Colonnades, The, W2 . . . . . **14** B3
Colonnade Wk, SW1 . . . . . **32** D2
Colosseum Ter, NW1
off Albany St **110** B4
Colson Gdns, Loug. IG10
off Colson Rd. **48/49** E4
Colson Path, Loug. IG10 . . **48** D4
Colson Rd, Croy. CR0. . . . **202** B2
Loughton IG10 . . . . **48** E4
Colson Way, SW16. . . . . . **168** C4
Colsterworth Rd, N15 . . . . **76** C4
Colston Av, Cars. SM5 . . . **199** H4
Colston Cl, Cars. SM5
off West St. **199** J4
Colston Rd, E7. . . . . **98** A6
SW14. . . . . **146** C4
Colthurst Cres, N4 . . . . **93** J2
Colthurst Dr, N9. . . . . **60** E3
Coltness Cres, SE2. . . . . . **138** B5
Colton Gdns, N17 . . . . **75** J3
Colton Rd, Har. HA1. . . . . . **68** B5
Columbia Av, Edg. HA8 . . . **70** B1
Ruislip HA4 . . . . **84** B1
Worcester Park KT4. . . . **183** F7
Columbia Pt, SE16
off Moodkee St. **133** F3
Columbia Rd, E2 . . . . **13** F3
E13. . . . . **115** F4
Columbia Sq, SW14 *off*
Upper Richmond Rd W. **146** C4
Columbine Av, E6. . . . . . . **116** B5
South Croydon CR2 . . . **201** H7
Columbine Way, SE13 . . . **154** C2
Columbus Ct, SE16
off Rotherhithe St. . . . **133** F1
Columbus Ctyd, E14
off West India Av. **134** A1
Columbus Gdns, Nthwd.
HA6 . . . . **66** A1
Colva Wk, N19
off Chester Rd. **92** B2
Colvestone Cres, E8. . . . . . **94** C5
Colview Ct, SE9
off Mottingham La . . . **174** A1
Colville Est, N1. . . . . **112** B1
Colville Gdns, W11 . . . . . . **108** C6
Colville Hos, W11 . . . . **108** C6
Colville Ms, W11
off Lonsdale Rd. **108** C6
Colville Pl, W1 . . . . **17** G2
Colville Rd, E11 . . . . **96** C3
E17 . . . . **77** H2
N9 . . . . **60** E1
W3. . . . . **126** B3
W11 . . . . **108** C6
Colville Sq, W11 . . . . **108** C6
Colville Ter, W11 . . . . **108** C6
Colvin Cl, SE26. . . . . **171** F5
Colvin Gdns, E4 . . . . **62** C3
E11. . . . . **79** H4
Ilford IG6. . . . . **81** F1
Colvin Rd, E6 . . . . **98** B7
Thornton Heath CR7 . . . **187** G5
Colwall Gdns, Wdf.Grn.
IG8. . . . . **63** G5
Colwell Rd, SE22 . . . . **152** C5
Colwick Cl, N6 . . . . **74** D7
Colwith Rd, W6 . . . . **127** J6
Colwood Gdns, SW19 . . . **167** G7
Colworth Gro, SE17. . . . . . **36** A2
Colworth Rd, E11 . . . . **78** E6
Croydon CR0. . . . . **202** D1
Colwyn Av, Grnf. UB6 . . . **104** C2
Colwyn Cl, SW16. . . . . . . **168** C5
Colwyn Cres, Houns.
TW3. . . . . **143** J1
Colwyn Grn, NW9
off Snowdon Dr. . . . **70/71** E6
Colwyn Rd, NW2 . . . . **89** H3
Colyer Cl, N1 . . . . **10** D1
SE9 . . . . **175** E2
Colyers La, Erith DA8. . . . **159** J1
Colyton Cl, Well. DA16. . . **158** D1
Wembley HA0
off Bridgewater Rd **87** F6
Colyton La, SW16 . . . . . . **169** G5
Colyton Rd, SE22. . . . . . . **153** E5
Colyton Way, N18. . . . . **60** D5
Combe Av, SE3 . . . . **135** F7
Combedale Rd, SE10 . . . **135** G5
Combe Lo, SE7
off Elliscombe Rd **135** J6
Combemartin Rd, SW18 . **148** B7
Combe Ms, SE3 . . . . **135** F7
Comber Cl, NW2 . . . . **89** H3
Comber Gro, SE5. . . . . . . **151** J1
Combermere Rd, SW9. . . **151** F3
Morden SM4. . . . . **185** E6
Comberton Rd, E5 . . . . **95** E2
Combeside, SE18. . . . . . . **137** J7
Combwell Cres, SE2 . . . . **138** A3
Comely Bk Rd, E17 . . . . . . **78** C5
Comeragh Ms, W14 . . . . . **128** B5
Comeragh Rd, W14 . . . . . **128** B5
Comer Cres, Sthl. UB2
off Windmill Av **123** J2
Comerford Rd, SE4 . . . . . **153** H4
Comet Cl, E12 . . . . **98** A4
Comet Pl, SE8 . . . . **134** A7
Comet Rd, Stai. (Stanw.)
TW19. . . . . **140** A7
Comet St, SE8 . . . . **134** A7
Comfort St, SE15 . . . . **36** D6
Commerce Rd, N22 . . . . . . **75** F1
Brentford TW8. . . . . **125** F7
Commerce Way, Croy.
CR0 . . . . **201** F2
Commercial Rd, E1 . . . . . . **21** H3
E14. . . . . **113** F6
N17 . . . . **60** B6
N18 . . . . **60** B5
Commercial St, E1. . . . . **13** F6
Commercial Way, NW10. . **106** B2
SE15 . . . . **132** C7
Commerell St, SE10. . . . . **135** E5
Commodity Quay, E1 . . . . **21** G6
Commodore St, E1. . . . . . **113** H4
Common, The, E15. . . . . . . **97** E6
W5. . . . . **105** H7
Richmond TW10 . . . . . . **163** G3
Southall UB2. . . . . **122** C4
Stanmore HA7 . . . . **52** B2
Commondale, SW15 . . . . **147** J3
Common La, Esher (Clay.)
KT10 . . . . **194** D7
Common Mile Cl, SW4 . . **150** D5
Common Rd, SW13 . . . . . **147** G3
Esher (Clay.) KT10. . . . . **194** D6
Stanmore HA7 . . . . **52** A4
Commonside, Kes. BR2 . . **205** J4
Commonside E, Mitch.
CR4 . . . . **185** J3
Commonside W, Mitch.
CR4 . . . . **185** J3
Commonwealth Av, W12 . **107** H7
★**Commonwealth Inst**,
W8. . . . . **128** C3
Commonwealth Rd, N17 . . **60** D7
Commonwealth Way,
SE2 . . . . **138** B5
Community Cl, Houns.
TW5 . . . . **142** B1
Community La, N7. . . . . . . **92** D5
Community Rd, E15. . . . . . **96** D5
Greenford UB6 . . . . **103** J1
Como Rd, SE23 . . . . **171** H2
Compass Hill, Rich.
TW10. . . . . **145** G6
Compass Ho, SW18
off Smugglers
Way **148/149** E4
Compayne Gdns, NW6 . . . **90** E7
Compton Av, E6 . . . . **116** A2
N1 . . . . **93** H6
N6 . . . . **73** H7
Wembley HA0. . . . . **87** F4
Compton Cl, E3 . . . . **114** A5
NW1 . . . . **9** E4
NW11 *off The Vale* **90** A3
W13. . . . . **104** D6
Edgware HA8
off Pavilion Way **54** C7
Compton Ct, SE19
off Victoria Cres. **170** B5
Compton Cres, N17 . . . . . . **59** J7
W4. . . . . **126** C6
Chessington KT9. . . . . . **195** H6
Northolt UB5. . . . . **102** D1
Compton Ho, SW11
off Parkham St **149** H1
Compton Pas, EC1 . . . . **11** H5
Compton Pl, WC1. . . . . **10** A5
Watford WD19. . . . . **50** E3
Compton Ri, Pnr. HA5 . . . . **67** E5
Compton Rd, N1 . . . . **93** H6
N21 . . . . **59** G1
NW10. . . . . **108** A3
SW19. . . . . **166** C6
Croydon CR0. . . . . **202** E1
Compton St, EC1 . . . . **11** G5
Compton Ter, N1 . . . . **93** H6
Computer Ho, Brent.
TW8 . . . . **125** F6
Comreddy Cl, Enf. EN2 . . . **43** H1
Comus Pl, SE17 . . . . **36** D2
Comyn Rd, SW11 . . . . **149** H4
Comyns, The, Bushey
(Bushey Hth) WD23. . . . **51** J1
Comyns Cl, E16 . . . . **115** F5
Comyns Rd, Dag. RM9 . . . **101** G7
Conant Ms, E1 . . . . **21** H5
Concanon Rd, SW2 . . . . . **151** F4
Concert Hall App, SE1 . . . . **26** D2
Concord Cl, Nthlt. UB5. . . **102** E3
Concorde Cl, Houns.
TW3 . . . . **143** H2
Concorde Dr, E6. . . . . **116** C5
Concord Rd, W3 . . . . **106** B4
Enfield EN3. . . . . **45** F5
Concord Ter, Har. HA2
off Coles Cres **85** H2
Concourse, The, N9
off New Rd **60** D2
NW9 . . . . **71** F1
Condell Rd, SW8 . . . . **150** C1
Conder St, E14
off Salmon La **113** H6
Condor Path, Nthlt. UB5
off Brabazon Rd **103** G2
Condover Cres, SE18 . . . . **136** E7
Condray Pl, SW11. . . . . . . **129** H7
Conduit Av, SE10
off Crooms Hill **154** D1
Conduit Ct, WC2 . . . . **18** A5
Conduit La, N18. . . . . **61** F5
Croydon CR0. . . . . **202** D5
Enfield EN3
off Morson Rd. **45** H6
South Croydon CR2 . . . **202** D5
Conduit Ms, SE18 . . . . . . **137** E5
W2. . . . . **14** E4
Conduit Pas, W2. . . . . **15** E4
Conduit Pl, W2 . . . . **15** E4
Conduit Rd, SE18. . . . . . . **137** E5
Conduit St, W1. . . . . **17** E5
Conduit Way, NW10. . . . . . **88** C7
Conewood St, N5 . . . . **93** H3
Coney Acre, SE21 . . . . **169** J1
Coney Burrows, E4
off Wyemead Cres . . **62/63** E2
Coneygrove Path, Nthlt. UB5
off Arnold Rd. **84/85** E6
CONEY HALL, W.Wick.
BR4 . . . . **205** F3
Coney Hill Rd, W.Wick.
BR4 . . . . **205** E2
Coney Way, SW8 . . . . **34** D6
Conference Cl, E4
off Greenbank Cl. **62** C2
★**Conference Forum, The**,
E1 . . . . **21** H3
Conference Rd, SE2 . . . . . **138** C4
Congleton Gro, SE18 . . . . **137** F5
Congo Dr, N9 . . . . **61** F3
Congo Rd, SE18 . . . . **137** G5
Congress Rd, SE2. . . . . . . **138** C4
Congreve Rd, SE9 . . . . . . **156** C3
Congreve St, SE17 . . . . **36** D1
Congreve Wk, E16 . . . . . . **116** A5
Conical Cor, Enf. EN2. . . . . **43** J2
Conifer Cl, Orp. BR6. . . . . **207** G4
Conifer Gdns, SW16 . . . . . **169** F3
Enfield EN1 . . . . **44** B6
Sutton SM1 . . . . **198** E2
Conifers Cl, Tedd. TW11 . . **163** E7
Conifer Way, Wem. HA0 . . . **87** F3
Coniger Rd, SW6 . . . . **148** D2
Coningham Ms, W12
off Percy Rd. **127** G1
Coningham Rd, W12 . . . . **127** H2
Coningsby Cotts, W5
off Coningsby Rd **125** G2
Coningsby Gdns, E4 . . . . . **62** B6
Coningsby Rd, N4 . . . . **75** H7
W5. . . . . **125** F2
Conington Rd, SE13. . . . . **154** B2
Conisbee Ct, N14. . . . . **42** C5
Conisborough Cres,
SE6 . . . . **172** C3
Coniscliffe Cl, Chis. BR7. . **192** D1
Coniscliffe Rd, N13. . . . . . . **59** J3
Coniston Av, Bark. IG11 . . . **99** H7
Greenford UB6 . . . . **105** E3
Welling DA16 . . . . **157** H3
Coniston Cl, N20 . . . . **57** F3
SW13 *off Lonsdale Rd* . **127** F7
SW20. . . . . **184** A6
W4. . . . . **146** C1
Barking IG11
off Coniston Av. **99** H7
Bexleyheath DA7 . . . . . **159** J1
Conistone Way, N7. . . . . . . **93** E7

Coniston Gdns, N9 . . . . . . 61 F1
NW9 . . . . 70 D5
Ilford IG4. . . . . 80 B4
Pinner HA5 . . . . 66 A4
Sutton SM2. . . . . 199 G6
Wembley HA9. . . . . 87 F1
Coniston Ho, SE5. . . . . 35 J7
Coniston Rd, N10 . . . . 74 B2
N17 . . . . 60 D6
Bexleyheath DA7 . . . . . 159 J1
Bromley BR1. . . . . 172 E6
Croydon CR0. . . . . 188 D7
Twickenham TW2 . . . . . 143 H6
Coniston Wk, E9
off Clifden Rd 95 F5
Coniston Way, Chess. KT9 . . . . 195 H3
Conlan St, W10. . . . . 108 B4
Conley Rd, NW10. . . . . 89 E6
Conley St, SE10
off Pelton Rd 134/135 E5
Connaught Av, E4 . . . . 46 D7
SW14. . . . . 146 C3
Barnet EN4 . . . . 57 J1
Enfield EN1 . . . . 44 B2
Hounslow TW4 . . . . 143 E5
Loughton IG10 . . . . 48 A4
Connaught Br, E16. . . . . . 136 A1
Connaught Business Cen, Mitch. CR4
off Wandle Way 185 J5
Connaught Cl, E10. . . . . . . 95 H2
W2. . . . . 15 G4
Enfield EN1 . . . . 44 B2
Sutton SM1. . . . . 199 G2
Connaught Ct, E17
off Orford Rd. 78 B4
Buckhurst Hill IG9. . . . . . 63 H1
Connaught Dr, NW11 . . . . . 72 D4
Connaught Gdns, N10 . . . . 74 B5
N13 . . . . 59 H4
Morden SM4. . . . . 185 F4
Connaught Hill, Loug. IG10. . . . . 48 A4
Connaught La, Ilf. IG1
off Connaught Rd 99 G2
Connaught Ms, SE18. . . . 136 D5
Ilford IG1
off Connaught Rd 99 G2
Connaught Pl, W2 . . . . 15 J5
Connaught Rd, E4 . . . . 46 E7
E11. . . . . 96 D1
E16 . . . . 136 A1
E17 . . . . 78 A5
N4 . . . . 75 G7
NW10. . . . . 107 E1
SE18 . . . . 136 D5
W13 . . . . 104 E7
Barnet EN5 . . . . 40 A6
Harrow HA3 . . . . 68 C1
Ilford IG1. . . . . 99 G2
New Malden KT3 . . . . . 183 E4
Richmond TW10
off Albert Rd 145 J5
Sutton SM1. . . . . 199 G2
Teddington TW11. . . . . . 162 A5
Connaught Roundabout, E16
off Connaught Br. 116 A7
Connaught Sq, W2. . . . . . . 15 J4
Connaught St, W2 . . . . 15 G4
Connaught Way, N13. . . . . 59 H4
Connell Cres, W5 . . . . 105 J4
Connemara Cl, Borwd. WD6
off Percheron Rd. 38 D6
Connington Cres, E4 . . . . . 62 D3
Connor Cl, E11 . . . . 78 E7
Ilford IG6. . . . . 81 E1
Connor Rd, Dag. RM9 . . . 101 F4
Connor St, E9
off Lauriston Rd. 113 G1
Conolly Rd, W7. . . . . 124 B1
Conrad Dr, Wor.Pk. KT4 . . 197 J1
Conrad Ho, N16 . . . . 94 B5
Consfield Av, N.Mal. KT3 . 183 G4
Consort Ms, Islw. TW7 . . . 144 A5
Consort Rd, SE15. . . . . . . 152 E1
Cons St, SE1 . . . . 27 F3
Constable Av, E16
off Wesley Av 135 H1
Constable Cl, NW11 . . . . . . 73 E6
Constable Cres, N15 . . . . . 76 D5
Constable Gdns, Edg. HA8. . . . . 70 A1
Isleworth TW7 . . . . 144 A5
Constable Ms, Dag. RM8
off Stonard Rd. 100 B4
Constable Wk, SE21. . . . . . 170 C3
Constance Cres, Brom. BR2 . . . . 191 F7
Constance Rd, Croy. CR0 . . . . 187 H7
Enfield EN1 . . . . 44 B6
Sutton SM1. . . . . 199 F4
Twickenham TW2 . . . . . 143 H7
Constance St, E16
off Albert Rd 136 B1
Constantine Rd, NW3 . . . . 91 H4
Constitution Hill, SW1. . . . 24 D3
Constitution Ri, SE18 . . . 156 D1
Consul Av, Dag. RM9 . . . . 119 J3
Content St, SE17 . . . . 36 A2
Contessa Cl, Orp. BR6 . . . 207 H5
Control Twr Rd, Houns. (Hthrw Air.) TW6 . . . . . 140 D3
Convair Wk, Nthlt. UB5
off Kittiwake Rd. 102 D3
Convent Cl, Beck. BR3 . . . 172 C7
Convent Gdns, W5 . . . . . . 125 F4
W11
off Kensington Pk Rd . 108 C6
Convent Hill, SE19 . . . . . . 169 J6
Convent Way, Sthl. UB2. . 122 C4
Conway Cl, Stan. HA7 . . . . 52 D6
Conway Cres, Grnf. UB6 . 104 B2
Romford RM6 . . . . 82 C7
Conway Dr, Hayes UB3 . . 121 F3
Sutton SM2. . . . . 198 E6
Conway Gdns, Mitch. CR4 . . . . 186 D4
Wembley HA9. . . . . 69 F7
Conway Gro, W3 . . . . 106 D5
Conway Ms, W1. . . . . 9 F6
Conway Rd, N14 . . . . 59 E3
N15 . . . . 75 H5
NW2 . . . . 89 J2
SE18 . . . . 137 G4
SW20. . . . . 183 J1
Feltham TW13 . . . . 160 D5
Hounslow TW4 . . . . 143 F7
Hounslow (Hthrw Air.) TW6
off Inner Ring E . . 140/141 E3
Conway St, E13 . . . . 115 G4
W1. . . . . 9 F6
Conway Wk, Hmptn. TW12
off Fearnley Cres. 161 F6
Conybeare, NW3
off King Henry's Rd. . . . 91 H7
Conyers Cl, Wdf.Grn. IG8. . 62 E6
Conyers Rd, SW16 . . . . . . 168 D5
Conyer St, E3 . . . . 113 H2
Conyers Way, Loug. IG10 . . 49 E3
Cooden Cl, Brom. BR1
off Plaistow La 173 H7
Cook Ct, SE16
off Rotherhithe St. . . . 133 F1
Cooke Cl, E14
off Cabot Sq 134 A1
Cookes Cl, E11 . . . . 97 F2
Cookes La, Sutt. SM3. . . . 198 B6
Cookham Cl, Sthl. UB2 . . 123 H2
Cookham Cres, SE16
off Marlow Way. 133 G2
Cookham Dene Cl, Chis. BR7 . . . . 193 G1
Cookham Rd, Sid. DA14. . 177 G7
Cookhill Rd, SE2 . . . . 138 B2
Cook Rd, Dag. RM9 . . . . . 118 E1
Cooks Cl, Rom. RM5 . . . . . 83 J1
Cookson Gro, Erith DA8. . 139 H7
Cook's Rd, E15 . . . . 114 B2
Cooks Rd, SE17 . . . . 35 G5
Cooks Wf Roundabout, N18 . . . . 61 G5
Coolfin Rd, E16. . . . . 115 G6
Coolgardie Av, E4. . . . . 62 C5
Chigwell IG7 . . . . 64 D3
Coolhurst Rd, N8 . . . . 74 D6
Cool Oak La, NW9 . . . . 71 E7
Coomassie Rd, W9
off Bravington Rd 108 C4
COOMBE, Kings.T. KT2 . . 164 C7
Coombe Av, Croy. CR0. . . 202 B4
Coombe Bk, Kings.T. KT2. 182 E1
Coombe Cl, Edg. HA8 . . . . 69 J2
Hounslow TW3 . . . . 143 G4
Coombe Cor, N21 . . . . 59 H1
Coombe Cres, Hmptn. TW12 . . . . 161 E7
Coombe Dr, Kings.T. KT2. 164 D7
Ruislip HA4 . . . . 84 B1
Coombe End, Kings.T. KT2 . . . . 164 D7
Coombefield Cl, N.Mal. KT3 . . . . 183 E5
Coombe Gdns, SW20. . . . 183 G2
New Malden KT3 . . . . . 183 F4
Coombe Hts, Kings.T. KT2 . . . . 165 E7
Coombe Hill Glade, Kings.T. KT2 . . . . 165 E7
Coombe Hill Rd, Kings.T. KT2 . . . . 164 E7
Coombe Ho Chase, N.Mal. KT3 . . . . 182 D1
Coombehurst Cl, Barn. EN4. . . . . 41 J2
Coombe La, SW20 . . . . . . 183 G1
Croydon CR0. . . . . 202 E5
Coombe La W, Kings.T. KT2 . . . . 164 E7
Coombe Lea, Brom. BR1 . 192 B3
Coombe Neville, Kings.T. KT2 . . . . 164 D7
Coombe Pk, Kings.T. KT2 . . . . 164 D5
Coombe Ridings, Kings.T. KT2 . . . . 164 C5
Coombe Ri, Kings.T. KT2 . . . . 182 C1
Coombe Rd, N22 . . . . 75 G1
NW10 . . . . 88 D3
SE26 . . . . 170 E4
W4. . . . . 127 E5
W13
off Northcroft Rd . 124/125 E3
Croydon CR0. . . . . 202 A4
Hampton TW12 . . . . 161 F6
Kingston upon Thames KT2 . . . . 182 A1
New Malden KT3 . . . . . 182 E2
Coomber Way, Croy. CR0. 186 D7
Coombes Rd, Dag. RM9. . 119 F1
Coombe Wk, Sutt. SM1 . . 198 E3
Coombewood Dr, Rom. RM6. . . . . 83 F6
Coombe Wd Rd, Kings.T. KT2 . . . . 164 C5
Coombs St, N1. . . . . 11 H2
Coomer Ms, SW6
off Coomer Pl 128 C6
Coomer Pl, SW6. . . . . 128 C6
Coomer Rd, SW6
off Coomer Pl 128 C6
Cooms Wk, Edg. HA8
off East Rd 70 C1
Cooperage Cl, N17
off Brantwood Rd 60 C6
Cooper Av, E17. . . . . 77 G1
Cooper Cl, SE1. . . . . 27 F4
Cooper Ct, E15
off Clays La. 96 B5
Cooper Cres, Cars. SM5. . 199 J3
Cooper Rd, NW4 . . . . 72 A6
NW10 . . . . 89 F5
Croydon CR0. . . . . 201 G4
Coopersale Cl, Wdf.Grn. IG8
off Navestock Cres 63 J7
Coopersale Rd, E9 . . . . 95 G5
Coopers Cl, E1 . . . . 113 F4
Dagenham RM10. . . . . . 101 H6
Coopers Cres, Borwd. WD6 . . . . 38 C1
Coopers La, E10. . . . . 96 B1
NW1 . . . . 9 J1
Cooper's La, SE12 . . . . . . 173 H2
Coopers Rd, SE1 . . . . 37 G4
Cooper's Row, EC3 . . . . . . 21 F5
Cooper St, E16
off Lawrence St. 115 F5
Coopers Wk, E15
off Maryland St. 96 D5
Coopers Yd, N1
off Upper St 93 H7
Cooper's Yd, SE19
off Westow Hill 170 B6
Coote Gdns, Dag. RM8. . . 101 F3
Coote Rd, Bexh. DA7 . . . . 159 F1
Dagenham RM8 . . . . . . 101 F3
Copeland Dr, E14. . . . . . . 134 A4
Copeland Rd, E17. . . . . 78 B5
SE15 . . . . 152 D2
Copeman Cl, SE26 . . . . . . 171 F5
Copenhagen Gdns, W4 . . . 126 C2
Copenhagen Pl, E14. . . . . . 113 J6
Copenhagen St, N1 . . . . . 111 E1
Cope Pl, W8 . . . . 128 D3
Copers Cope Rd, Beck. BR3 . . . . 171 J6
Cope St, SE16 . . . . 133 G4
Copford Cl, Wdf.Grn. IG8. . 64 B6
Copford Wk, N1
off Popham St 111 J1
Copgate Path, SW16 . . . . 169 F6
Copinger Wk, Edg. HA8
off North Rd 70 B1
Copland Av, Wem. HA0 . . . 87 G5
Copland Cl, Wem. HA0. . . . 87 F5
Copland Ms, Wem. HA0
off Copland Rd 87 H6
Copland Rd, Wem. HA0 . . . 87 H6
Copleston Ms, SE15
off Copleston Rd. 152 C2
Copleston Pas, SE15 . . . . 152 C3
Copleston Rd, SE15 . . . . . 152 C3
Copley Cl, SE17 . . . . 35 H6
W7. . . . . 104 C5
Copley Dene, Brom. BR1 . . . . 192 A1
Copley Pk, SW16 . . . . 169 F6
Copley Rd, Stan. HA7 . . . . 53 F5
Copley St, E1 . . . . 113 G5
Copnor Way, SE15
off Blakes Rd. 132 B7
Coppard Gdns, Chess. KT9 . . . . 195 F6
Copped Hall, SE21
off Glazebrook Cl 170 A2
Coppelia Rd, SE3 . . . . 155 F4
Coppen Rd, Dag. RM8 . . . . 83 F7
Copperas St, SE8. . . . . . . 134 B6
Copper Beech Cl, Ilf. IG5 . . 80 D1
Copper Beech Ct, Loug. IG10. . . . . 48 D1
Copper Beeches, Islw. TW7
off Eversley Cres. 144 A1
Copper Cl, SE19
off Auckland Rd. 170 C7
Copperdale Rd, Hayes UB3. . . . . 122 A2
Copperfield, Chig. IG7 . . . . 65 G6
Copperfield App, Chig. IG7. . . . . 65 G6
Copperfield Ct, Pnr. HA5
off Copperfield Way . . . 67 F4
Copperfield Dr, N15. . . . . . 76 C4
Copperfield Ms, N18 . . . . . 60 B5
Copperfield Rd, E3 . . . . . . 113 H4
SE28 . . . . 118 C6
Copperfield St, SE1 . . . . . . 27 H3
Copperfield Way, Chis. BR7 . . . . 175 F6
Pinner HA5 . . . . 67 F4
Coppergate Cl, Brom. BR1 . . . . 191 H1
Copper Mead Cl, NW2. . . . 89 J3
Copper Mill Dr, Islw. TW7. . . . . 144 C2
Coppermill La, E17. . . . . . . 77 F6
Copper Mill La, SW17 . . . 167 F4
Copper Row, SE1. . . . . 29 F2
Coppetts Cl, N12 . . . . 57 H7
Coppetts Rd, N10. . . . . 74 A2
Coppice, The, Enf. EN2. . . . 43 H4
Coppice Cl, SW20 . . . . . . 183 J3
Beckenham BR3 . . . . . . 190 B4
Stanmore HA7 . . . . 52 C6
Coppice Dr, SW15 . . . . . . 147 H6
Coppice Wk, N20 . . . . 56 D3
Coppice Way, E18. . . . . 79 F4
Coppies Gro, N11 . . . . 58 A4
Copping Cl, Croy. CR0 . . . 202 B4
Coppins, The, Croy. (New Adgtn) CR0 . . . . 204 B6
Harrow HA3 . . . . 52 B6
Coppock Cl, SW11 . . . . . . 149 H2
Coppsfield, W.Mol. KT8
off Hurst Rd. 179 G3
Copse, The, E4 . . . . 63 F1
Copse Av, W.Wick. BR4 . . 204 B3
Copse Cl, SE7. . . . . 135 H6
West Drayton UB7 . . . . 120 A3
Copse Glade, Surb. KT6. . 195 G1
COPSE HILL, SW20 . . . . . . 165 G7
Copse Hill, SW20 . . . . 165 H7
Sutton SM2. . . . . 199 E7
Copsewood Cl, Sid. DA15 . . . . 157 H6
Coptefield Dr, Belv. DA17 . . . . 138 D3
Copthall Av, EC2 . . . . 20 C3
Copthall Bldgs, EC2. . . . . . 20 B3
Copthall Cl, EC2. . . . . 20 B3
Copthall Ct, EC2. . . . . 20 B3
Copthall Dr, NW7. . . . . 55 G7
Copthall Gdns, NW7 . . . . . 55 G7
Twickenham TW1 . . . . . 162 C1
Copthorne Av, SW12 . . . . 150 D7
Bromley BR2. . . . . 206 C2
Ilford IG6. . . . . 65 E6
Copthorne Ms, Hayes UB3 . . . . 121 H4
Coptic St, WC1. . . . . 18 A2
Copwood Cl, N12. . . . . 57 G4
Coral Cl, Rom. RM6 . . . . . . 82 C4
Coraline Cl, Sthl. UB1 . . . 103 F3
Coralline Wk, SE2. . . . . . . 138 C2

Coral Row, SW11 off Gartons Way . . . 149 F3
Coral St, SE1 . . . 27 F4
Coram St, WC1 . . . 10 A6
Coran Cl, N9 . . . 45 G7
Corban Rd, Houns. TW3 . . . 143 G3
Corbden Cl, SE15 . . . 152 C1
Corbet Cl, Wall. SM6 . . . 200 A1
Corbet Ct, EC3 . . . 20 C4
Corbet Pl, E1 . . . 21 F1
Corbett Gro, N22 . . . 58 E7
Corbett Ho, Wat. WD19 . . . 50 C3
Corbett Rd, E11 . . . 79 J6
E17 . . . 78 C3
Corbetts La, SE16 off Rotherhithe New Rd . . . 133 F4
Corbetts Pas, SE16 off Rotherhithe New Rd . . . 133 F4
Corbicum, E11 . . . 79 E7
Corbidge Ct, SE8 off Glaisher St . . . 134 B6
Corbiere Ct, SW19 off Thornton Rd . . . 166 A6
Corbiere Ho, N1 . . . 112 B1
Corbins La, Har. HA2 . . . 85 H3
Corbridge Cres, E2 . . . 112 E2
Corby Cres, Enf. EN2 . . . 43 E4
Corbylands Rd, Sid. DA15 . . . 157 H7
Corbyn St, N4 . . . 93 E1
Corby Rd, NW10 . . . 106 D2
Corby Way, E3 off Knapp Rd . . . 114 A4
Cordelia Cl, SE24 . . . 151 H4
Cordelia Gdns, Stai. TW19 . . . 140 B7
Cordelia Rd, Stai. TW19 . . . 140 B7
Cordelia St, E14 . . . 114 B6
Cordell Ho, N15 off Newton Rd . . . 76 C5
Cording St, E14 off Chrisp St . . . 114 B5
Cordwainers Wk, E13 off Richmond St . . . 115 G2
Cord Way, E14 off Mellish St . . . 134 A3
Cordwell Rd, SE13 . . . 154 E5
Corefield Cl, N11 off Benfleet Way . . . 58 A2
Corelli Rd, SE3 . . . 156 B2
Corfe Av, Har. HA2 . . . 85 G4
Corfe Cl, Borwd. WD6 off Chester Rd . . . 38 D3
Hayes UB4 . . . 102 C6
Corfe Twr, W3 . . . 126 B2
Corfield Rd, N21 . . . 43 F5
Corfield St, E2 . . . 113 E3
Corfton Rd, W5 . . . 105 H6
Coriander Av, E14 . . . 114 D6
Cories Cl, Dag. RM8 . . . 100 D2
Corinium Cl, Wem. HA9 . . . 87 J4
Corinne Rd, N19 . . . 92 C4
Corinthian Way, Stai.(Stanw.) TW19 off Clare Rd . . . 140 A7
Corker Wk, N7 . . . 93 F2
Corkran Rd, Surb. KT6 . . . 181 G7
Corkscrew Hill, W.Wick. BR4 . . . 204 D2
Cork Sq, E1 off Smeaton St . . . 132/133 E1
Cork St, W1 . . . 17 F6
Cork St Ms, W1 . . . 17 F6
Cork Tree Way, E4 . . . 61 H5
Corlett St, NW1 . . . 15 G1
Cormont Rd, SE5 . . . 151 H1
Cormorant Cl, E17 off Banbury Rd . . . 77 G1
Cormorant Ho, Enf. EN3 off Alma Rd . . . 45 G5
Cormorant Pl, Sutt. SM1 off Sandpiper Rd . . . 198 C5
Cormorant Rd, E7 . . . 97 F4
Cornbury Rd, Edg. HA8 . . . 53 G7
Cornelia Dr, Hayes UB4 . . . 102 C4
Cornelia St, N7 . . . 93 F6
Cornell Cl, Sid. DA14 . . . 177 E6
Corner Grn, SE3 . . . 155 G3
Corner Ho St, WC2 . . . 26 A1
Corner Mead, NW9 . . . 55 F7
Corney Reach Way, W4 . . . 127 E7
Corney Rd, W4 . . . 127 E6
Cornflower La, Croy. CR0 . . . 203 G1
Cornflower Ter, SE22 . . . 152 E6
Cornford Cl, Brom. BR2 . . . 191 G5
Cornford Gro, SW12 . . . 168 B2
Cornhill, EC3 . . . 20 C4
Cornish Ct, N9 . . . 44 E7
Cornish Gro, SE20 . . . 171 E7
Cornish Ho, SE17 . . . 35 G6
Brentford TW8 off Green Dragon La . . . 125 J5
Corn Mill Dr, Orp. BR6 . . . 193 J7
Cornmill La, SE13 . . . 154 B3
Cornmow Dr, NW10 . . . 89 F5
Cornshaw Rd, Dag. RM8 . . . 100 D1
Cornthwaite Rd, E5 . . . 95 F3
Cornwall Av, E2 . . . 113 F3
N3 . . . 56 D7
N22 . . . 75 E1
Esher (Clay.) KT10 off The Causeway . . . 194 C7
Southall UB1 . . . 103 F5
Welling DA16 . . . 157 H3
Cornwall Cl, Bark. IG11 . . . 99 J6
Cornwall Cres, W11 . . . 108 B7
Cornwall Dr, Orp. BR5 . . . 176 C7
Cornwall Gdns, NW10 . . . 89 H6
SW7 . . . 22 B6
Cornwall Gdns Wk, SW7 . . . 22 B6
Cornwall Gro, W4 . . . 127 E5
Cornwallis Av, N9 . . . 61 E2
SE9 . . . 175 G2
Cornwallis Gro, N9 . . . 61 E2
Cornwallis Rd, E17 . . . 77 G4
N9 . . . 61 E2
N19 . . . 92 E2
SE18 off Duke of Wellington Av . . . 137 F3
Dagenham RM9 . . . 100 D4
Cornwallis Sq, N19 . . . 92 E2
Cornwallis Wk, SE9 . . . 156 C3
Cornwall Ms S, SW7 . . . 22 C6
Cornwall Ms W, SW7 . . . 22 B6
Cornwall Rd, N4 . . . 75 G7
N15 . . . 76 A5
N18 off Fairfield Rd . . . 60 D5
SE1 . . . 26 E1
Croydon CR0 . . . 201 H2
Esher (Clay.) KT10 . . . 194 D7
Harrow HA1 . . . 67 J6
Pinner HA5 . . . 51 F7
Sutton SM2 . . . 198 C7
Twickenham TW1 . . . 162 D1
Cornwall Sq, SE11 . . . 35 G3
Cornwall St, E1 off Watney St . . . 112/113 E7
Cornwall Ter, NW1 . . . 8 A6
Cornwall Ter Ms, NW1 . . . 8 A6
Corn Way, E11 . . . 96 D3
Cornwood Cl, N2 . . . 73 G5
Cornwood Dr, E1 . . . 113 F6
Cornworthy Rd, Dag. RM8 . . . 100 C5
Corona Rd, SE12 . . . 155 G7
Coronation Av, N16 off Victorian Rd . . . 94 C3
Coronation Cl, Bex. DA5 . . . 158 D6
Ilford IG6 . . . 81 F4
Coronation Rd, E13 . . . 115 J3
NW10 . . . 105 J3
Hayes UB3 . . . 121 J4
Coronation Wk, Twick. TW2 . . . 161 F1
Coronet St, N1 . . . 12 D4
Corporation Av, Houns. TW4 . . . 142 E4
Corporation Row, EC1 . . . 11 F5
Corporation St, E15 . . . 115 F2
N7 . . . 92 E5
Corrance Rd, SW2 . . . 151 E4
Corri Av, N14 . . . 58 D4
Corrib Dr, Sutt. SM1 . . . 199 H5
Corrigan Cl, NW4 . . . 71 J3
Corringham Ct, NW11 off Corringham Rd . . . 72/73 E7
Corringham Rd, NW11 . . . 72 D7
Wembley HA9 . . . 88 A2
Corringway, NW11 . . . 72 E7
W5 . . . 106 A4
Corris Grn, NW9 off Snowdon Dr . . . 70/71 E6
Corry Dr, SW9 . . . 151 H4
Corsair Cl, Stai. TW19 . . . 140 A7
Corsair Rd, Stai. TW19 . . . 140 B7
Corscombe Cl, Kings.T. KT2 . . . 164 C5
Corsehill St, SW16 . . . 168 C6
Corsham St, N1 . . . 12 C4
Corsica St, N5 . . . 93 H6
Cortayne Rd, SW6 . . . 148 C2
Cortina Dr, Dag. RM9 . . . 119 J3
Cortis Rd, SW15 . . . 147 H6
Cortis Ter, SW15 . . . 147 H6
Corunna Rd, SW8 . . . 150 C1
Corunna Ter, SW8 . . . 150 C1
Corvette Sq, SE10 off Feathers Pl . . . 134 D6
Coryton Path, W9 off Ashmore Rd . . . 108 C4
Cosbycote Av, SE24 . . . 151 J5
Cosdach Av, Wall. SM6 . . . 200 D7
Cosedge Cres, Croy. CR0 . . . 201 G5
Cosgrove Cl, N21 . . . 59 J2
Hayes UB4 off Kingsash Dr . . . 102/103 E4
Cosmo Pl, WC1 . . . 18 B1
Cosmur Cl, W12 . . . 127 F3
Cossall Wk, SE15 . . . 153 E1
Cossar Ms, SW2 off Tulse Hill . . . 151 G6
Cosser St, SE1 . . . 26 E5
Costa St, SE15 . . . 152 D2
Costons Av, Grnf. UB6 . . . 104 A3
Costons La, Grnf. UB6 . . . 104 A3
Coston Wk, SE4 off Hainford Cl . . . 153 G4
Cosway St, NW1 . . . 15 H1
Cotall St, E14 . . . 114 A6
Coteford Cl, Loug. IG10 . . . 48 E2
Pinner HA5 . . . 66 A5
Coteford St, SW17 . . . 167 J4
Cotelands, Croy. CR0 . . . 202 B3
Cotesbach Rd, E5 . . . 95 F3
Cotesmore Gdns, Dag. RM8 . . . 100 C4
Cotford Rd, Th.Hth. CR7 . . . 187 J4
Cotham St, SE17 . . . 36 A2
Cotherstone Rd, SW2 . . . 169 F1
Cotleigh Av, Bex. DA5 . . . 176 D2
Cotleigh Rd, NW6 . . . 90 D7
Cotman Cl, NW11 . . . 73 F6
SW15 off Westleigh Av . . . 148 A6
Cotman Gdns, Edg. HA8 . . . 70 A2
Cotman Ms, Dag. RM8 off Highgrove Rd . . . 100 C5
Cotmans Cl, Hayes UB3 . . . 122 A1
Coton Rd, Well. DA16 . . . 158 A3
Cotsford Av, N.Mal. KT3 . . . 182 C5
Cotswold Cl, Esher KT10 . . . 194 C3
Kingston upon Thames KT2 . . . 164 B6
Cotswold Ct, EC1 . . . 11 J5
N11 . . . 58 A4
Cotswold Gdns, E6 . . . 116 A3
NW2 . . . 90 A2
Ilford IG2 . . . 81 G7
Cotswold Gate, NW2 off Cotswold Gdns . . . 90 B1
Cotswold Grn, Enf. EN2 off Cotswold Way . . . 43 F4
Cotswold Ms, SW11 off Battersea High St . . . 149 G1
Cotswold Ri, Orp. BR6 . . . 193 J6
Cotswold Rd, Hmptn. TW12 . . . 161 G6
Cotswold St, SE27 off Norwood High St . . . 169 H4
Cotswold Way, Enf. EN2 . . . 43 F4
Worcester Park KT4 . . . 197 J2
Cottage Av, Brom. BR2 . . . 206 B1
Cottage Fld Cl, Sid. DA14 . . . 176 C1
Cottage Grn, SE5 . . . 36 C7
Cottage Gro, SW9 . . . 150 E3
Surbiton KT6 . . . 181 G6
Cottage Homes, NW7 . . . 55 G4
Cottage Pl, SW3 . . . 23 G5
Cottage Rd, Epsom KT19 . . . 196 D7
Cottage St, E14 . . . 114 B7
Cottage Wk, N16 off Smalley Cl . . . 94 C3
Cottenham Dr, NW9 . . . 71 F3
SW20 . . . 165 H7
Cottenham Par, SW20 off Durham Rd . . . 183 H2
COTTENHAM PARK, SW20 . . . 183 H1
Cottenham Pk Rd, SW20 . . . 165 H7
Cottenham Pl, SW20 . . . 165 H7
Cottenham Rd, E17 . . . 77 J4
Cotterill Rd, Surb. KT6 . . . 195 H2
Cottesbrook St, SE14 off Nynehead St . . . 133 H7
Cottesloe Ms, SE1 . . . 27 F5
Cottesmore Av, Ilf. IG5 . . . 80 D2
Cottesmore Gdns, W8 . . . 22 B5
Cottimore Cres, Walt. KT12 . . . 178 B7
Cottimore Ter, Walt. KT12 . . . 178 B7
Cottingham Chase, Ruis. HA4 . . . 84 A3
Cottingham Rd, SE20 . . . 171 G7
SW8 . . . 34 D6
Cottington Rd, Felt. TW13 . . . 160 D4
Cottington St, SE11 . . . 35 F3
Cottle Way, SE16 off St. Marychurch St . . . 133 F2
Cotton Av, W3 . . . 106 D6
Cotton Cl, Dag. RM9 off Flamstead Rd . . . 100 C7
Cottongrass Cl, Croy. CR0 off Cornflower La . . . 203 G1
Cotton Hill, Brom. BR1 . . . 172 D4
Cotton Row, SW11 . . . 149 F3
Cottons Gdns, E2 . . . 13 E3
Cottons La, SE1 . . . 28 C1
Cotton St, E14 . . . 114 C7
Cottrell Ct, SE10 off Greenroof Way . . . 135 F3
Cotts Cl, W7 off Westcott Cres . . . 104 C5
Couchmore Av, Esher KT10 . . . 194 B2
Ilford IG5 . . . 80 C2
Coulgate St, SE4 . . . 153 H3
Coulson Cl, Dag. RM8 . . . 82 C7
Coulson St, SW3 . . . 31 J3
Coulter Cl, Hayes UB4 off Berrydale Rd . . . 102/103 E4
Coulter Rd, W6 . . . 127 H3
Councillor St, SE5 . . . 131 J7
Counter Ct, SE1 off Southwark St . . . 132 A1
Counter St, SE1 . . . 28 D2
Countess Rd, NW5 . . . 92 C5
Countisbury Av, Enf. EN1 . . . 44 C7
Country Way, Felt. TW13 . . . 160 B7
Sunbury-on-Thames TW16 . . . 160 B7
County Gate, SE9 . . . 175 F3
Barnet EN5 . . . 41 E6
County Gro, SE5 . . . 151 J1
★County Hall, SE1 . . . 26 C3
County Rd, E6 . . . 116 E5
Thornton Heath CR7 . . . 187 H2
County St, SE1 . . . 28 A6
Coupland Pl, SE18 . . . 137 F5
Courcy Rd, N8 . . . 75 G3
Courier Rd, Dag. RM9 . . . 119 J4
Courland Gro, SW8 . . . 150 D1
Courland Gro Hall, SW8 . . . 150 D2
Courland St, SW8 . . . 150 D1
Course, The, SE9 . . . 174 D3
Court, The, Ruis. HA4 . . . 84 E4
Courtauld Cl, SE28 off Pitfield Cres . . . 138 A1
★Courtauld Inst of Art, WC2 . . . 18 C5
Courtauld Rd, N19 . . . 92 D1
Court Av, Belv. DA17 . . . 139 F5
Court Cl, Har. HA3 . . . 69 H3
Twickenham TW2 . . . 161 H3
Wallington SM6 . . . 200 D7
Court Cl Av, Twick. TW2 . . . 161 H3
Court Cres, Chess. KT9 . . . 195 G5
Court Downs Rd, Beck. BR3 . . . 190 B2
★Court Dress Collection, Kensington Palace, W8 . . . 22 B2
Court Dr, Croy. CR0 . . . 201 F4
Stanmore HA7 . . . 53 H4
Sutton SM1 . . . 199 H4
Courtenay Av, N6 . . . 73 H6
Harrow HA3 . . . 67 J1
Courtenay Dr, Beck. BR3 . . . 190 D2
Courtenay Gdns, Har. HA3 . . . 67 J2
Courtenay Ms, E17 off Cranbrook Ms . . . 77 H5
Courtenay Pl, E17 . . . 77 H5
Courtenay Rd, E11 . . . 97 F3
E17 . . . 77 G4
SE20 . . . 171 G7
Wembley HA9 . . . 87 G3
Worcester Park KT4 . . . 197 J3
Courtenay Sq, SE11 . . . 34 E4
Courtenay St, SE11 . . . 34 E3
Courtens Ms, Stan. HA7 . . . 53 F7
Court Fm Av, Epsom KT19 . . . 196 D5
Court Fm Rd, SE9 . . . 174 A2
Northolt UB5 . . . 85 G7
Courtfield, W5 off Castlebar Hill . . . 105 F5
Courtfield Av, Har. HA1 . . . 68 C5
Courtfield Cres, Har. HA1 . . . 68 C5
Courtfield Gdns, SW5 . . . 30 B1
W13 . . . 104 D6
Courtfield Ms, SW5 . . . 30 C2
Courtfield Ri, W.Wick. BR4 . . . 204 D3
Courtfield Rd, SW7 . . . 30 B2
Court Gdns, N7 . . . 93 G6

Courtgate Cl, NW7 . . . . **55** F6
Courthill Rd, SE13 . . . . . . **154** C4
Courthope Rd, NW3. . . . . . **91** J4
SW19. . . . . **166** B5
Greenford UB6 . . . . **104** A2
Courthope Vil, SW19 . . . . **166** B7
Court Ho Gdns, N3 . . . . . . **56** D6
Courthouse Rd, N12 . . . . . **56** E6
Courtland Av, E4 . . . . **63** F2
NW7 . . . . **54** D3
SW16. . . . . **169** F7
Ilford IG1. . . . . **98** C2
Courtland Cl, Wdf.Grn. IG8. . . . . **79** J1
Courtland Dr, Chig. IG7 . . . **65** E3
Courtland Gro, SE28 . . . . **118** D7
Courtland Rd, E6 *off Harrow Rd* **116** B1
Courtlands, Rich. TW10 . . **146** A4
Courtlands Av, SE12 . . . . **155** H5
Bromley BR2. . . . . **205** F1
Hampton TW12 . . . . **161** F6
Richmond TW9 . . . . **146** B2
Courtlands Dr, Epsom KT19 . . . . **197** E6
Courtlands Rd, Surb. KT5 . **182** A7
Court La, SE21 . . . . **152** B6
Court La Gdns, SE21 . . . . **152** B7
Courtleet Dr, Erith DA8 . . **159** H1
Courtleigh Gdns, NW11 . . . **72** B4
Courtman Rd, N17 . . . . **59** J7
Court Mead, Nthlt. UB5 . . **103** F3
Courtmead Cl, SE24. . . . . **151** J6
Courtnell St, W2. . . . . **108** D6
Courtney Cl, SE19 . . . . . . **170** B6
Courtney Cres, Cars. SM5. . . . . **199** J7
Courtney Pl, Croy. CR0. . . **201** G3
Courtney Rd, N7 *off Bryantwood Rd* **93** G5
SW19. . . . . **167** H7
Croydon CR0 . . . . **201** G3
Hounslow (Hthrw Air.) TW6 . . . . **140** D3
Courtney Way, Houns. (Hthrw Air.) TW6 *off Courtney Rd*. **140** D2
Court Par, Wem. HA0 . . . . . **86** E3
Courtrai Rd, SE23. . . . . . . **153** H6
Court Rd, SE9. . . . . **174** B2
SE25 . . . . **188** C2
Southall UB2. . . . . **123** F4
Courtside, N8 . . . . **74** D6
Court St, E1 *off Durward St* . . . **112/113** E5
Bromley BR1 . . . . **191** G2
Court Way, NW9. . . . . **71** E4
W3. . . . . **106** C6
Ilford IG6. . . . . **81** F3
Twickenham TW2 . . . . . **144** C7
Courtway, Wdf.Grn. IG8. . . **63** J5
Courtway, The, Wat. WD19 . . . . **51** E2
Court Yd, SE9. . . . . **156** B6
Courtyard, The, N1 . . . . **93** F7
Cousin La, EC4. . . . . **20** B6
Couthurst Rd, SE3 . . . . . . **135** H6
Coutts Av, Chess. KT9 . . . **195** H5
Coutts Cres, NW5 . . . . **92** A3
Coval Gdns, SW14 . . . . . . **146** B4
Coval La, SW14 . . . . **146** B4
Coval Rd, SW14 . . . . **146** B4
Covelees Wall, E6 . . . . **116** D6
Covell Ct, SE8 *off Reginald Sq* **134** A7
★**Covent Garden**, WC2 . . . **18** B5
Coventry Cl, E6 *off Harper Rd*. **116** C6
NW6 *off Kilburn High Rd* . . . **108** D1
Coventry Cross, E3 *off Gillender St* **114** C4
Coventry Rd, E1 . . . . **113** E4
E2. . . . . **113** E4
SE25 . . . . **188** D4
Ilford IG1. . . . . **98** E1
Coventry St, W1 . . . . **17** H6
Coverack Cl, N14 . . . . **42** C6
Croydon CR0. . . . . **189** H7
Coverdale Cl, Stan. HA7. . . **53** E5
Coverdale Gdns, Croy. CR0 *off Park Hill Ri* **202** C3
Coverdale Rd, N11 . . . . **58** A6
NW2 . . . . **90** A7
W12. . . . . **127** H1
Coverdales, The, Bark. IG11 . . . . **117** F2
Coverley Cl, E1. . . . . **21** J1
Covert, The, Orp. BR6. . . . **193** H6
Coverton Rd, SW17 . . . . . **167** H5
Covert Rd, Ilf. IG6. . . . . **65** J6
Covert Way, Barn. EN4. . . . **41** F2
Covet Wd Cl, Orp. BR5 *off Lockesley Dr* **193** J6
Covey Cl, SW19 . . . . **184** E2
Covington Gdns, SW16 . . **169** H7
Covington Way, SW16 . . . **169** F6
Cowan Cl, E6 *off Oliver Gdns* **110** D5
Cowbridge La, Bark. IG11 . . **98** E7
Cowbridge Rd, Har. HA3 . . **69** J4
Cowcross St, EC1. . . . . **19** G1
Cowdenbeath Path, N1 . . **111** F1
Cowden Rd, Orp. BR6 . . . **193** J7
Cowden St, SE6 . . . . **172** A4
Cowdrey Cl, Enf. EN1. . . . . **44** B2
Cowdrey Rd, SW19 . . . . . **167** E5
Cowdry Rd, E9 *off Wick Rd* . **95** H6
Cowen Av, Har. HA2. . . . . . **85** J2
Cowgate Rd, Grnf. UB6 . . **104** A2
Cowick Rd, SW17. . . . . . . **167** J4
Cowings Mead, Nthlt. UB5. . . . . **85** E7
Cowland Av, Enf. EN3 . . . . **45** F4
Cow La, Grnf. UB6 . . . . . . **104** A2
Cow Leaze, E6 . . . . **116** D6
Cowleaze Rd, Kings.T. KT2 . . . . **181** H1
Cowley La, E11 *off Cathall Rd*. **96/97** E3
Cowley Pl, NW4. . . . . **71** J5
Cowley Rd, E11 . . . . **79** H5
SW9. . . . . **151** G1
SW14. . . . . **146** E3
W3. . . . . **127** F1
Ilford IG1 . . . . **80** C7
Cowley St, SW1. . . . . **26** A5
Cowling Cl, W11 *off Wilsham St* **128** B1
Cowper Av, E6 . . . . **98** B7
Sutton SM1. . . . . **199** G4
Cowper Cl, Brom. BR2. . . **192** A4
Welling DA16 . . . . **158** A5
Cowper Gdns, N14. . . . . . . **42** C6
Wallington SM6 . . . . . . **200** C6
Cowper Rd, N14. . . . . **58** B1
N16 . . . . **94** B5
N18 . . . . **60** D5
SW19. . . . . **167** F6
W3. . . . . **126** D1
W7. . . . . **104** C7
Belvedere DA17 . . . . . . **139** G4
Bromley BR2. . . . . **192** A4
Kingston upon Thames KT2 . . . . **163** J5
Cowpers Ct, EC3 *off Birchin La* **112** A6
Cowper St, EC2 . . . . **12** C5
Cowper Ter, W10 *off St. Marks Rd* **108** A5
Cowslip Rd, E18. . . . . **79** H2
Cowthorpe Rd, SW8 . . . . . **150** D1
Coxe Pl, Har. (Wldste) HA3. . . . . **68** D4
Cox La, Chess. KT9 . . . . . **195** J4
Epsom KT19 . . . . **196** B5
Coxmount Rd, SE7. . . . . . **136** A5
Coxson Way, SE1 . . . . **29** F4
Cox's Wk, SE21. . . . . **170** D1
Coxwell Rd, SE18. . . . . . . **137** G5
SE19 . . . . **170** B7
Coxwold Path, Chess. KT9 *off Garrison La* **195** H7
Crabbs Cft Cl, Orp. BR6 *off Ladycroft Way* **207** F5
Crab Hill, Beck. BR3 . . . . . **172** D7
Crabtree Av, Rom. RM6 . . . **82** D4
Wembley HA0 . . . . **105** H2
Crabtree Cl, E2. . . . . **13** F2
Crabtree Ct, E15 *off Clays La*. **96** B5
Crabtree La, SW6. . . . . . . **128** A7
Crabtree Manorway Ind Est, Belv. DA17. . . . . **139** H3
Crabtree Manorway N, Belv. DA17. . . . . **139** J2
Crabtree Manorway S, Belv. DA17. . . . . **139** J3
Craddock Rd, Enf. EN1. . . . **44** C3
Craddock St, NW5 *off Prince of Wales Rd*. . **92** A6
Cradley Rd, SE9 . . . . **175** G1
★**Crafts Council**, N1 . . . . . . **11** F2
Craigen Av, Croy. CR0 . . . **203** E1
Craigerne Rd, SE3 . . . . . . **135** H7
Craig Gdns, E18 . . . . **79** F2
Craigholm, SE18 . . . . **156** D2
Craigmuir Pk, Wem. HA0 . **105** J1
Craignair Rd, SW2 . . . . . . **151** G7
Craignish Av, SW16 . . . . . **187** F2
Craig Pk Rd, N18 . . . . **60** E5
Craig Rd, Rich. TW10 . . . . **163** F4
Craigs Ct, SW1. . . . . **26** A1
Craigton Rd, SE9 . . . . **156** C4
Craigweil Cl, Stan. HA7 . . . **53** G5
Craigweil Dr, Stan. HA7 . . . **53** G5
Craigwell Av, Felt. TW13. . **160** A3
Craik Ct, NW6 *off Carlton Vale* **108** C2
Crail Row, SE17. . . . . **36** C2
Cramer Ct, N.Mal. KT3 *off Warwick Rd* **182** C3
Cramer St, W1 . . . . **16** C2
Cramond Cl, W6. . . . . **128** B6
Crampton Rd, SE20 . . . . . **171** F6
Crampton St, SE17 . . . . . . **35** J2
Cranberry Cl, Nthlt. UB5 *off Parkfield Av* **102** D2
Cranberry La, E16. . . . . . . **114** E4
Cranborne Av, Sthl. UB2 . **123** G4
Surbiton KT6. . . . . **196** A3
Cranborne Rd, Bark. IG11 . **117** G1
Cranborne Waye, Hayes UB4 . . . . **102** C7
Cranbourn All, WC2 . . . . . . **17** J5
Cranbourne Av, E11 . . . . . . **79** H4
Cranbourne Cl, SW16. . . . **187** E3
Cranbourne Dr, Pnr. HA5 . . **66** D5
Cranbourne Gdns, NW11 . . **72** B5
Ilford IG6. . . . . **81** F3
Cranbourne Pas, SE16 *off Marigold St* . . **132/133** E2
Cranbourne Rd, E12 *off High St N*. **98** B5
E15 . . . . **96** C4
N10 . . . . **74** B2
Cranbourn St, WC2 . . . . . . **17** J5
CRANBROOK, Ilf. IG1. . . . . . **98** C1
Cranbrook Cl, Brom. BR2. **191** G6
Cranbrook Dr, Twick. TW2 **161** H1
Cranbrook Ms, E17 . . . . . . **77** H5
Cranbrook Pk, N22. . . . . . . **75** F1
Cranbrook Ri, Ilf. IG1 . . . . . **80** C7
Cranbrook Rd, SE8 . . . . . . **154** A1
SW19. . . . . **166** B7
W4. . . . . **127** E5
Barnet EN4 . . . . **41** G6
Bexleyheath DA7 . . . . . **159** F1
Hounslow TW4 . . . . **143** F4
Ilford IG1, IG2, IG6 . . . . . **80** D7
Thornton Heath CR7 . . . **187** J2
Cranbrook St, E2 *off Mace St* **113** G2
Cranbury Rd, SW6 . . . . . . **149** E2
Crane Av, W3 . . . . **106** C7
Isleworth TW7 . . . . **144** D5
Cranebank Ms, Twick. TW1 . . . . **144** D4
Cranebrook, Twick. TW2 *off Manor Rd*. **161** J2
Crane Cl, Dag. RM10 . . . . **101** G6
Harrow HA2 . . . . **85** J3
Crane Ct, EC4. . . . . **19** F4
Epsom KT19 . . . . **196** C4
Craneford Cl, Twick. TW2 . **144** C7
Craneford Way, Twick. TW2. . . . . **144** B7
Crane Gdns, Hayes UB3 . **121** J4
Crane Gro, N7 . . . . **93** G6
Crane Lo Rd, Houns. TW5. . . . . **122** B6
Crane Mead, SE16 . . . . . . **133** G4
Crane Pk Rd, Twick. TW2 . **161** H2
Crane Rd, Twick. TW2 . . . . **162** B1
Cranesbill Cl, NW9 *off Colindale Av* **70** D3
Cranes Dr, Surb. KT5 . . . . **181** H4
Cranes Pk, Surb. KT5 . . . . **181** H4
Cranes Pk Av, Surb. KT5 . **181** H4
Cranes Pk Cres, Surb. KT5 **181** J4
Crane St, SE10 . . . . **134** D5
SE15 . . . . **152** C1
Craneswater, Hayes UB3. . . . . **121** J7
Craneswater Pk, Sthl. UB2. . . . . **123** F5
Cranes Way, Borwd. WD6 . **38** C5
Crane Way, Twick. TW2. . . **143** J7
Cranfield Cl, SE27 *off Dunelm Gro*. **169** J3
Cranfield Dr, NW9 . . . . **54** E7
Cranfield Rd, SE4. . . . . . . **153** J3
Cranfield Row, SE1 . . . . . . **27** F5
CRANFORD, Houns. TW5. . . . . **122** A7
Cranford Av, N13 . . . . **59** E5
Staines TW19. . . . . **140** B7
Cranford Cl, SW20 . . . . . . **183** H1
Staines TW19. . . . . **140** B7
Cranford Cotts, E1 *off Cranford St* **113** G7
Cranford Dr, Hayes UB3. . **121** J4
Cranford La, Hayes UB3. . **121** G6
Hounslow (Hthrw Air.) TW6. . . . . **141** J3
Hounslow (Hthrw Air.N.) TW6. . . . . **141** J1
Hounslow (Heston) TW5 . . . . **122** D7
Cranford Pk Rd, Hayes UB3 . . . . **121** J4
Cranford St, E1. . . . . **113** G7
Cranford Way, N8. . . . . **75** F5
Cranhurst Rd, NW2 . . . . . . **89** J5
Cranleigh Cl, SE20 . . . . . . **188** E2
Bexley DA5 . . . . **159** H6
Cranleigh Gdns, N21 . . . . . **43** G5
SE25 . . . . **188** B3
Barking IG11 . . . . **99** G7
Harrow HA3 . . . . **69** H5
Kingston upon Thames KT2 . . . . **163** J6
Loughton IG10 . . . . **48** C6
Southall UB1. . . . . **103** F6
Sutton SM1. . . . . **198** E2
Cranleigh Gdns Ind Est, Sthl. UB1 *off Cranleigh Gdns* . . . **103** F6
Cranleigh Ms, SW11. . . . . **149** H2
Cranleigh Rd, N15 . . . . **75** J5
SW19. . . . . **184** D3
Cranleigh St, NW1 . . . . **9** G2
Cranley Dene Ct, N10. . . . . **74** B4
Cranley Dr, Ilf. IG2 . . . . **81** F7
Cranley Gdns, N10 . . . . **74** C4
N13 . . . . **59** F3
SW7. . . . . **30** D3
Wallington SM6 . . . . . . **200** C7
Cranley Ms, SW7 . . . . **30** D3
Cranley Par, SE9 *off Beaconsfield Rd*. . . **174** B4
Cranley Pl, SW7 . . . . **31** E2
Cranley Rd, E13 . . . . **115** H5
Ilford IG2. . . . . **81** F6
Cranmer Av, W13 . . . . **124** E3
Cranmer Cl, Mord. SM4. . **184** A6
Ruislip HA4 . . . . **84** D1
Stanmore HA7 . . . . **53** F7
Cranmer Ct, SW3. . . . . **31** H2
SW4. . . . . **150** D3
Hampton (Hmptn H.) TW12 *off Cranmer Rd* **161** H5
Cranmer Fm Cl, Mitch. CR4 . . . . **185** J4
Cranmer Gdns, Dag. RM10 . . . . **101** J4
Cranmer Ho, SW11 *off Surrey La* **149** H1
Cranmer Rd, E7 . . . . **97** H4
SW9. . . . . **35** F7
Croydon CR0 . . . . **201** H3
Edgware HA8 . . . . **54** B3
Hampton (Hmptn H.) TW12. . . . . **161** H5
Kingston upon Thames KT2 . . . . **163** H5
Mitcham CR4. . . . . **185** J4
Cranmer Ter, SW17. . . . . . **167** G5
Cranmore Av, Islw. TW7 . . **123** J7
Cranmore Rd, Brom. BR1 . . . . **173** E3
Chislehurst BR7. . . . . . . **174** C5
Cranmore Way, N10 . . . . . . **74** C4
Cranston Cl, Houns. TW3. **143** E2
Cranston Est, N1 . . . . **12** C2
Cranston Gdns, E4. . . . . . . **62** B5
Cranston Rd, SE23. . . . . . **171** H1
Cranswick Rd, SE16. . . . . **133** E5
Crantock Rd, SE6 . . . . **172** B2
Cranwell Cl, E3. . . . . **114** B4
Cranwich Av, N21. . . . . **44** A7
Cranwich Rd, N16 . . . . **76** A7
Cranwood St, EC1 . . . . **12** B4
Cranworth Cres, E4 . . . . . . **62** D1
Cranworth Gdns, SW9. . . **151** G1
Craster Rd, SW2. . . . . **151** F7
Crathie Rd, SE12 . . . . **155** H6
Cravan Av, Felt. TW13. . . . **160** A2
Craven Av, W5 . . . . **105** F7
Southall UB1. . . . . **103** F5
Craven Cl, Hayes UB4 . . . **102** A6
Craven Gdns, SW19. . . . . **166** D5
Barking IG11 . . . . **117** H2
Ilford IG6. . . . . **81** G2
Craven Hill, W2. . . . . **14** D5
Craven Hill Gdns, W2 . . . . . **14** C5

Craven Hill Ms, W2 14 D5
Craven Ms, SW11
off Taybridge Rd 150 A3
Craven Pk, NW10 106 E1
Craven Pk Ms, NW10 106 E1
Craven Pk Rd, N15 76 C6
NW10 106 E1
Craven Pas, WC2 26 A1
Craven Rd, NW10 106 D1
W2 14 D5
W5 105 F7
Croydon CR0 202 E1
Kingston upon Thames KT2 181 J1
Craven St, WC2 26 A1
Craven Ter, W2 14 D5
Craven Wk, N16 76 D7
Crawford Av, Wem. HA0 87 G5
Crawford Cl, Islw. TW7 144 B2
Crawford Est, SE5 151 J2
Crawford Gdns, N13 59 H3
Northolt UB5 103 F3
Crawford Ms, W1 15 J2
Crawford Pas, EC1 11 E6
Crawford Pl, W1 15 H3
Crawford Rd, SE5 151 J1
Crawford St, NW10
off Fawood Av 88 D7
W1 15 J2
Crawley Rd, E10 96 B1
N22 75 J2
Enfield EN1 44 B7
Crawshay Ct, SW9
off Eythorne Rd 151 G1
Crawthew Gro, SE22 152 C4
Craybrooke Rd, Sid. DA14 176 B4
Craybury End, SE9 175 F2
Crayford Cl, E6
off Neatscourt Rd 116 B5
Crayford Rd, N7 92 D4
Crayke Hill, Chess. KT9 195 H7
Cray Rd, Belv. DA17 139 G6
Sidcup DA14 176 C7
Crealock Gro, Wdf.Grn. IG8 63 F5
Crealock St, SW18 149 E6
Creasy Est, SE1 28 D6
Crebor St, SE22 152 D6
Credenhall Dr, Brom. BR2 206 C1
Credenhill St, SW16 168 C6
Crediton Hill, NW6 90 E5
Crediton Rd, E16
off Pacific Rd 115 G6
NW10 108 A1
Crediton Way, Esher (Clay.) KT10 194 D5
Credon Rd, E13 115 J2
SE16 133 E5
Creechurch La, EC3 20 E4
Creechurch Pl, EC3 21 E4
Creed Ct, EC4
off Ludgate Hill 111 H6
Creed La, EC4 19 H4
Creek, The, Sun. TW16 178 A5
CREEKMOUTH, Bark. IG11 118 A4
Creek Rd, SE8 134 A6
SE10 134 A6
Barking IG11 117 J3
East Molesey KT8 180 B4
Creekside, SE8 134 B7
Creeland Gro, SE6
off Catford Hill 171 J1
Crefeld Cl, W6 128 A6
Creffield Rd, W3 105 J7
W5 105 J7
Creighton Av, E6 116 A2
N2 73 H3
N10 74 A2
Creighton Cl, W12 107 H7
Creighton Rd, N17 60 B7
NW6 108 A2
W5 125 G3
Cremer St, E2 13 F2
Cremorne Est, SW10 31 E7
Cremorne Rd, SW10 129 F7
Crescent, EC3 21 F5
Crescent, The, E17 77 H5
N11 57 J4
NW2 89 H3
SW13 147 F2
SW19 166 D3
W3 106 E6
Barnet EN5 40 E3
Beckenham BR3 190 A1
Bexley DA5 158 C7
Croydon CR0 188 A5
Harrow HA2 86 A1
Crescent, The, Hayes UB3 121 F7
Ilford IG2 80 D6
Loughton IG10 48 A5
New Malden KT3 182 C2
Sidcup DA14 175 J4
Southall UB1 123 F2
Surbiton KT6 181 H5
Sutton SM1 199 G4
Wembley HA0 86 E2
West Molesey KT8 179 G4
West Wickham BR4 190 E6
Crescent Arc, SE10
off Creek Rd 134 C6
Crescent Ct, Surb. KT6 181 G5
Crescent Dr, Orp. BR5 193 E6
Crescent Gdns, SW19 166 D3
Ruislip HA4 66 B6
Crescent Gro, SW4 150 C4
Mitcham CR4 185 H4
Crescent Ho, SE13
off Ravensbourne Pl 154 B2
Crescent La, SW4 150 D5
Crescent Ms, N22
off Palace Gates Rd 74/75 E1
Crescent Pl, SW3 31 G1
Crescent Ri, N22 74 D1
Barnet EN4 41 H5
Crescent Rd, E4 47 E7
E6 115 J1
E10 96 B2
E13 115 G1
E18 79 J2
N3 72 C1
N8 74 D7
N9 60 D1
N11 57 J4
N15 *off Carlingford Rd* 75 H3
N22 74 D1
SE18 136 E5
SW20 184 A1
Barnet EN4 41 H5
Beckenham BR3 190 B2
Bromley BR1 173 G7
Dagenham RM10 101 H4
Enfield EN2 43 H3
Kingston upon Thames KT2 164 A7
Sidcup DA15 175 J3
Crescent Row, EC1 11 J6
Crescent Stables, SW15
off Upper Richmond Rd 148 B4
Crescent St, N1 93 F7
Crescent Vw, Loug. IG10 48 A6
Crescent Way, N12 57 H6
SE4 154 A3
SW16 169 F7
Orpington BR6 207 H5
Crescent Wd Rd, SE26 170 D3
Cresford Rd, SW6 148 E1
Crespigny Rd, NW4 71 H6
Cressage Cl, Sthl. UB1 103 G4
Cresset Rd, E9 95 F6
Cresset St, SW4 150 D3
Cressfield Cl, NW5 92 A5
Cressida Rd, N19 92 C1
Cressingham Gro, Sutt. SM1 199 F4
Cressingham Rd, SE13 154 C3
Edgware HA8 54 D6
Cressington Cl, N16
off Wordsworth Rd 94 B5
Cress Ms, Brom. BR1 172 D5
Cresswell Gdns, SW5 30 C3
Cresswell Pk, SE3 155 F3
Cresswell Pl, SW10 30 C3
Cresswell Rd, SE25 188 D4
Feltham TW13 160 E4
Twickenham TW1 145 G6
Cresswell Way, N21 43 G7
Cressy Ct, E1
off Cressy Pl 113 F5
W6 127 H3
Cressy Pl, E1 113 F5
Cressy Rd, NW3 91 J5
Crest, The, N13 59 G4
NW4 71 J5
Surbiton KT5 182 A5
Crestbrook Av, N13 59 H3
Crestbrook Pl, N13 59 H3
Crestfield St, WC1 10 B3
Crest Gdns, Ruis. HA4 84 C3
Creston Way, Wor.Pk. KT4 198 A1
Crest Rd, NW2 89 F3
Bromley BR2 191 F7
South Croydon CR2 202 E7
Crest Vw, Pnr. HA5 66 D4
Crest Vw Dr, Orp. BR5 193 E5
Crestway, SW15 147 H6
Crestwood Way, Houns. TW4 143 F5
Creswell Dr, Beck. BR3 190 B5
Creswick Rd, W3 106 B7
Creswick Wk, E3
off Malmesbury Rd 114 A3
NW11 72 C4
Creton St, SE18 136 D3
Crewdson Rd, SW9 131 G7
Crewe Pl, NW10 107 F3
Crews St, E14 134 A4
Crewys Rd, NW2 90 C2
SE15 153 E2
Crichton Av, Wall. SM6 200 D5
Crichton Rd, Cars. SM5 199 J6
Crichton St, SW8
off Westbury St 150 C2
Cricketers Arms Rd, Enf. EN2 43 J2
Cricketers Cl, N14 42 C7
Chessington KT9 195 G4
Cricketers Ct, SE11 35 G2
Cricketers Ms, SW18
off East Hill 148/149 E5
Cricketers Ter, Cars. SM5
off Wrythe La 199 H3
Cricketfield Rd, E5 94 E4
Cricket Grn, Mitch. CR4 185 J3
Cricket Grd Rd, Chis. BR7 192 E1
Cricket La, Beck. BR3 171 H6
Cricklade Av, SW2 169 E2
CRICKLEWOOD, NW2 90 A3
Cricklewood Bdy, NW2 89 J3
Cricklewood La, NW2 90 A4
Cridland St, E15
off Church St 115 F1
Crieff Ct, Tedd. TW11 163 F7
Crieff Rd, SW18 149 F6
Criffel Av, SW2 168 D2
Crimscott St, SE1 29 E6
Crimsworth Rd, SW8 150 D1
Crinan St, N1 10 B1
Cringle St, SW8 33 F7
Cripplegate St, EC2 19 J1
Cripps Grn, Hayes UB4
off Stratford Rd 102 B4
Crispe Ho, Bark. IG11
off Dovehouse Mead 117 G2
Crispen Rd, Felt. TW13 160 E4
Crispian Cl, NW10 89 E4
Crispin Cl, Croy. CR0
off Harrington Cl 200/201 E2
Crispin Cres, Croy. CR0 200 D3
Crispin Rd, Edg. HA8 54 C6
Crispin St, E1 21 F2
Crisp Rd, W6 127 J5
Cristowe Rd, SW6 148 C2
Criterion Ms, N19 92 D2
Crittall's Cor, Sid. DA14 176 C7
Crockerton Rd, SW17 167 J2
Crockham Way, SE9 174 D4
Crocus Cl, Croy. CR0
off Cornflower La 203 G1
Crocus Fld, Barn. EN5 40 C6
Croft, The, E4 62 E2
NW10 107 F2
W5 105 H5
Barnet EN5 40 A4
Hounslow TW5 123 E6
Loughton IG10 48 D2
Pinner HA5
off Rayners La 67 F7
Ruislip HA4 84 C4
Wembley HA0 87 F5
Croft Av, W.Wick. BR4 204 C1
Croft Cl, NW7 54 E3
Belvedere DA17 139 F5
Chislehurst BR7 174 C4
Hayes UB3 121 F7
Croft Ct, Borwd. WD6
off Kensington Way 38 D3
Croftdown Rd, NW5 92 A3
Croft End Cl, Chess. KT9
off Ashcroft Rd 195 J3
Crofters Cl, Islw. TW7
off Ploughmans End 144 A5
Crofters Ct, SE8
off Croft St 133 H4
Crofters Way, NW1 110 D1
Croft Gdns, W7 124 D2
Croft Lo Cl, Wdf.Grn. IG8 63 H6
Croft Ms, N12 57 F3
Crofton Av, W4 126 D7
Bexley DA5 158 D7
Orpington BR6 207 F2
Croftongate Way, SE4 153 H5
Crofton Gro, E4 62 D4
Crofton La, Orp. BR5, BR6 193 G7
Crofton Pk Rd, SE4 153 J6
Crofton Rd, E13 115 H4
SE5 152 B1
Orpington BR6 206 D3
Crofton Ter, E5
off Studley Cl 95 H5
Richmond TW9 145 J4
Crofton Way, Barn. EN5
off Wycherley Cres. 40/41 E6
Enfield EN2 43 G2
Croft Rd, SW16 187 G1
SW19 167 F7
Bromley BR1 173 G6
Enfield EN3 45 H1
Sutton SM1 199 H5
Croftside, SE25
off Sunny Bk 188 D3
Crofts La, N22
off Glendale Av 59 G7
Crofts Rd, Har. HA1 68 D6
Crofts St, E1 21 H6
Croft St, SE8 133 H4
Croftway, NW3 90 D4
Richmond TW10 163 E3
Croft Way, Sid. DA15 175 H3
Crogsland Rd, NW1 92 A7
Croham Cl, S.Croy. CR2 202 B6
Croham Manor Rd, S.Croy. CR2 202 B5
Croham Mt, S.Croy. CR2 202 B7
Croham Pk Av, S.Croy. CR2 202 C5
Croham Rd, S.Croy. CR2 202 A5
Croham Valley Rd, S.Croy. CR2 202 C6
Croindene Rd, SW16 187 E1
Cromartie Rd, N19 74 D7
Cromarty Rd, Edg. HA8 54 B2
Crombie Cl, Ilf. IG4 80 C5
Crombie Rd, Sid. DA15 175 G1
Crome Rd, NW10 88 E6
Cromer Pl, Orp. BR6
off Andover Rd 207 G1
Cromer Rd, E10
off James La 78 D6
N17 76 D2
SE25 188 E3
SW17 168 A6
Barnet EN5 41 F4
Hounslow (Hthrw Air.) TW6 140 D3
Romford RM7 83 J6
Romford (Chad.Hth) RM6 83 E6
Woodford Green IG8 63 G4
Cromer Rd W, Houns. (Hthrw Air.) TW6 140 D3
Cromer St, WC1 10 B4
Cromer Ter, E8
off Ferncliff Rd 94 D5
Cromer Vil Rd, SW18 148 C6
Cromford Cl, Orp. BR6 207 H3
Cromford Path, E5
off Overbury St 95 G4
Cromford Rd, SW18 148 D5
Cromford Way, N.Mal. KT3 182 D1
Cromlix Cl, Chis. BR7 192 E2
Crompton St, W2 6 E6
Cromwell Av, N6 92 B1
W6 127 H5
Bromley BR2 191 H4
New Malden KT3 183 F5
Cromwell Cl, E1
off Vaughan Way 132 D1
N2 73 G4
W3 *off High St* 126 C1
Bromley BR2 191 H4
Cromwell Cres, SW5 128 D4
Cromwell Gdns, SW7 23 F6
Cromwell Gro, W6 127 J3
Cromwell Highwalk, EC2
off Beech St 111 J5
Cromwell Ind Est, E10 95 H1
Cromwell Ms, SW7 31 F1
Cromwell Pl, N6 92 B1
SW7 31 F1
SW14 146 C3
W3 *off Grove Pl* 126 C1
Cromwell Rd, E7 97 J7
E17 78 C5
N3 73 F1
N10 58 A7
SW5 128 E4
SW7 30 E1
SW9 151 H1
SW19 166 D5

Cromwell Rd, Beck. BR3 . 189 H2
Croydon CR0 . . . . 188 A7
Feltham TW13 . . . . 160 B1
Hounslow TW3 . . . . 143 G4
Kingston upon Thames
KT2 . . . . 181 H1
Teddington TW11 . . . . . . 162 D6
Wembley HA0 . . . . 105 H2
Worcester Park KT4 . . . . 196 D3
Cromwell St, Houns.
TW3 . . . . 143 G4
Cromwell Twr, EC2 . . . . 20 A1
Crondace Rd, SW6 . . . . . . 148 D1
Crondall Ct, N1 . . . . 12 D2
Crondall Ho, SW15
off Fontley Way 165 G1
Crondall St, N1 . . . . 12 C2
Cronin St, SE15 . . . . 132 C7
Crooked Billet, SW19
off Woodhayes Rd 165 J6
Crooked Billet Roundabout,
E17 . . . . 62 A7
Crooked Billet Yd, E2
off Kingsland Rd 112 B3
Crooked Usage, N3 . . . . . . 72 B3
Crooke Rd, SE8 . . . . 133 H5
Crookham Rd, SW6 . . . . . 148 C1
Crook Log, Bexh. DA6 . . . 158 D3
Crookston Rd, SE9 . . . . . . 156 D3
Croombs Rd, E16 . . . . 115 J5
Crooms Hill, SE10 . . . . . . 134 D7
Crooms Hill Gro, SE10 . . . 134 C7
Cropley Ct, N1 . . . . 12 B1
Cropley St, N1 . . . . 12 B1
Croppath Rd, Dag. RM10 . 101 G4
Cropthorne Ct, W9 . . . . 6 D4
Crosby Cl, Felt. TW13 . . . . 160 E4
Crosby Ct, SE1 . . . . 28 B3
Crosby Rd, E7 . . . . 97 G6
Dagenham RM10 . . . . . . 119 H2
Crosby Row, SE1 . . . . 28 B4
Crosby Sq, EC3 . . . . 20 D4
Crosby Wk, E8
off Laurel St 94 C6
SW2 . . . . 151 G7
Crosier Cl, SE3 . . . . 156 B1
Crosland Pl, SW11
off Taybridge Rd 150 A3
Cross Av, SE10 . . . . 134 D6
Crossbow Rd, Chig. IG7 . . . 65 J5
Crossbrook Rd, SE3 . . . . . 156 B2
Cross Cl, SE15
off Gordon Rd . . . 152/153 E1
Cross Deep, Twick. TW1 . . 162 C2
Cross Deep Gdns, Twick.
TW1 . . . . 162 C2
Crossfield Rd, N17 . . . . 75 J3
NW3 . . . . 91 G7
Crossfields, Loug. IG10 . . . 48 E5
Crossfield St, SE8 . . . . . . 134 A7
Crossford St, SW9 . . . . . . 151 F2
Crossgate, Edg. HA8 . . . . . 54 A3
Greenford UB6 . . . . 87 F6
Cross Keys Cl, N9
off Balham Rd 60 D2
W1 . . . . 16 C2
Cross Keys Sq, EC1 . . . . . . 19 J2
Cross Lances Rd, Houns.
TW3 . . . . 143 H4
Crossland Rd, Th.Hth.
CR7 . . . . 187 H6
Crosslands Av, W5 . . . . . . 125 J1
Southall UB2 . . . . 123 F5
Crosslands Rd, Epsom
KT19 . . . . 196 D6
Cross La, EC3 . . . . 20 D6
N8 . . . . 75 F3
Bexley DA5 . . . . 159 F7
Crosslet St, SE17 . . . . 36 C1
Crosslet Vale, SE10 . . . . . . 154 B1
Crossley St, N7 . . . . 93 G6
Crossmead, SE9 . . . . 174 C1
Crossmead Av, Grnf.
UB6 . . . . 103 G3
Crossmount Ho, SE5 . . . . . 35 J7
Crossness La, SE28 . . . . . 118 D7
★**Crossness Pumping Sta**,
SE2 . . . . 119 E6
Crossness Rd, Bark. IG11 . 117 J3
Cross Rd, E4 . . . . 62 E1
N11 . . . . 58 B5
N22 . . . . 59 G7
SE5 . . . . 152 B2
SW19 . . . . 166 D7
Bromley BR2 . . . . 206 B2
Croydon CR0 . . . . 202 A1
Enfield EN1 . . . . 44 B4
Feltham TW13 . . . . 160 E4
Harrow HA1 . . . . 68 A4
Cross Rd, Har. (S.Har.) HA2 . 85 H3
Harrow (Wldste) HA3 . . . 68 D2
Kingston upon Thames
KT2 . . . . 163 J7
Romford RM7 . . . . 83 G3
Romford (Chad.Hth) RM6 . 82 C7
Sidcup DA14
off Sidcup Hill 176 B4
Sutton SM2 . . . . 199 G5
Woodford Green IG8 . . . 64 C6
Cross Rds, Loug.
(High Beach) IG10 . . . . . 47 H2
Cross St, N1 . . . . 111 H1
SW13 . . . . 147 E2
Hampton (Hmptn H.)
TW12 . . . . 161 J5
Crossthwaite Av, SE5 . . . . 152 A4
Crosswall, EC3 . . . . 21 F5
Crossway, N12 . . . . 57 G6
N16 . . . . 94 B5
NW9 . . . . 71 F4
SE28 . . . . 118 C6
SW20 . . . . 183 J4
W13 . . . . 104 D4
Dagenham RM8 . . . . . . 100 C3
Enfield EN1 . . . . 44 B7
Hayes UB3 . . . . 122 A1
Orpington BR5 . . . . 193 G4
Pinner HA5 . . . . 66 B2
Ruislip HA4 . . . . 84 C4
Woodford Green IG8 . . . 63 J4
Crossway, The, N22 . . . . . . 59 H7
SE9 . . . . 174 A2
Cross Way, The, Har. HA3 . . 68 B2
Crossways, N21 . . . . 43 J6
South Croydon CR2 . . . 203 H7
Crossways, The, Houns.
TW5 . . . . 123 F7
Wembley HA9 . . . . 88 A2
Crossways Rd, Beck.
BR3 . . . . 190 A4
Mitcham CR4 . . . . 186 B3
Croston St, E8 . . . . 112 D1
Crothall Cl, N13 . . . . 59 F3
Crouch Av, Bark. IG11 . . . . 118 B2
Crouch Cl, Beck. BR3
off Abbey La 172 A6
Crouch Cft, SE9 . . . . 174 D3
CROUCH END, N8 . . . . 74 C6
Crouch End Hill, N8 . . . . . . 74 D7
Crouch Hall Rd, N8 . . . . 74 D6
Crouch Hill, N4 . . . . 74 E6
N8 . . . . 74 E6
Crouchman's Cl, SE26 . . . 170 C3
Crouch Rd, NW10 . . . . 88 D7
Crowborough Path, Wat.
WD19
off Prestwick Rd 50 D4
Crowborough Rd, SW17 . 168 A6
Crowden Way, SE28 . . . . . 118 C7
Crowder St, E1 . . . . 112 E7
Crowfoot Cl, E9 *off*
Lee Conservancy Rd . . . 95 J5
SE28 *off Hill Vw Dr* 137 H1
Crowhurst Cl, SW9 . . . . . 151 G2
Crowland Av, Hayes UB3 . 121 H4
Crowland Gdns, N14 . . . . . 42 E7
Crowland Rd, N15 . . . . 76 C5
Thornton Heath CR7 . . . 188 A4
Crowlands Av, Rom. RM7 . 83 H6
Crowland Ter, N1 . . . . 94 A7
Crowland Wk, Mord.
SM4 . . . . 185 E6
Crow La, Rom. RM7 . . . . . . 83 F7
Crowley Cres, Croy. CR0 . 201 G5
Crowline Wk, N1
off St. Paul's Rd 94 A6
Crowmarsh Gdns, SE23
off Tyson Rd 153 F7
Crown Arc, Kings.T. KT1
off Union St 181 G2
Crown Cl, E3 . . . . 114 A1
N22 *off Winkfield Rd* . . . 75 G1
NW6 . . . . 90 E6
NW7 . . . . 55 F2
Hayes UB3 . . . . 121 J2
Walton-on-Thames
KT12 . . . . 178 C7
Crown Ct, EC2 . . . . 20 A4
SE12 . . . . 155 H6
WC2 . . . . 18 B4
Bromley BR2
off Victoria Rd 192 A5
Crown Dale, SE19 . . . . 169 H6
Crowndale Rd, NW1 . . . . 9 F1
Crownfield Av, Ilf. IG2 . . . . 81 H5
Crownfield Rd, E15 . . . . 96 D5
Crown Hill, Croy. CR0
off Church St 201 J2
Crownhill Rd, NW10 . . . . . 107 F1
Woodford Green IG8 . . . 64 B7
Crown Ho, Bark. IG11
off Linton Rd 99 F7
Crown La, N14 . . . . 58 C1
SW16 . . . . 169 G5
Bromley BR2 . . . . 192 A5
Chislehurst BR7 . . . . . . 193 F1
Morden SM4 . . . . 184 E3
Crown La Gdns, SW16
off Crown La 169 G5
Crown La Spur, Brom.
BR2 . . . . 192 A6
Crownmead Way, Rom.
RM7 . . . . 83 H4
Crown Ms, E13
off Waghorn Rd 115 J1
W6 . . . . 127 G4
Crown Office Row, EC4 . . . 19 E5
Crown Pas, SW1 . . . . 25 G2
Kingston upon Thames
KT1 *off Church St* 181 G2
Crown Pl, EC2 . . . . 20 D1
NW5
off Kentish Town Rd . . . 92 B6
SE16 *off Varcoe Rd* 132 E5
Crown Pt Par, SE19
off Beulah Hill 169 H6
Crown Reach, SW1
off Grosvenor Rd 130 D5
Crown Rd, N10 . . . . 58 A7
Borehamwood WD6 . . . . 38 A1
Enfield EN1 . . . . 44 E4
Ilford IG6 . . . . 81 G4
Morden SM4 . . . . 184 E4
New Malden KT3 . . . . . 182 C1
Ruislip HA4 . . . . 84 D5
Sutton SM1 . . . . 198 E4
Twickenham TW1 . . . . . 145 E6
Crownstone Rd, SW2 . . . . 151 G5
Crown St, SE5 . . . . 36 A7
W3 . . . . 126 B1
Dagenham RM10 . . . . . . 101 J6
Harrow HA2 . . . . 86 A1
Crown Ter, Rich. TW9 . . . . 145 J4
Crowntree Cl, Islw. TW7 . . 124 C6
Crown Wk, Wem. HA9 . . . . . 87 J3
Crown Way, West Dr. UB7 . 120 C1
Crown Wds La, SE9 . . . . . 157 E2
SE18 . . . . 157 E2
Crown Wds Way, SE9 . . . . 157 G5
Crown Wks, E2
off Temple St 112/113 E2
Crown Yd, Houns. TW3
off High St 143 J3
Crowshott Av, Stan. HA7 . . 69 F1
Crows Rd, E15 . . . . 114 D3
Barking IG11 . . . . 99 E6
Crowther Av, Brent. TW8 . 125 H4
Crowther Rd, SE25 . . . . . . 188 D4
Crowthorne Cl, SW18 . . . . 166 C1
Crowthorne Rd, W10 . . . . 108 A6
Croxden Cl, Edg. HA8 . . . . 69 J3
Croxden Wk, Mord. SM4 . 185 F6
Croxford Gdns, N22 . . . . . . 59 H7
Croxley Rd, W9 . . . . 108 C3
Croxted Cl, SE21 . . . . 151 J7
Croxted Ms, SE24
off Croxted Rd 151 J6
Croxted Rd, SE21 . . . . 151 J7
SE24 . . . . 151 J7
Croyde Av, Grnf. UB6 . . . . 103 J3
Hayes UB3 . . . . 121 H4
Croyde Cl, Sid. DA15 . . . . 157 G7
CROYDON, CR0 . . . . 202 A2
Croydon Flyover, Croy.
CR0 . . . . 201 H4
Croydon Gro, Croy. CR0 . . 201 H1
★**Croydon Mus**, Croy.
CR0 . . . . 201 J3
Croydon Rd, E13 . . . . 115 F4
SE20 . . . . 188 E2
Beckenham BR3 . . . . . . 189 H4
Bromley BR2 . . . . 205 F3
Croydon (Bedd.) CR0 . . 201 E4
Croydon (Mitch.Com.)
CR0 . . . . 186 A4
Hounslow (Hthrw Air.)
TW6 . . . . 140 E2
Keston BR2 . . . . 205 J3
Mitcham CR4 . . . . 186 A4
Wallington SM6 . . . . . . 200 B4
West Wickham BR4 . . . . 204 E3
Croyland Rd, N9 . . . . 60 D1
Croylands Dr, Surb. KT6 . 181 H7
Croysdale Av, Sun. TW16 . 178 A3
Crozier Ho, SE3
off Ebdon Way 155 H3
Crozier Ter, E9 . . . . 95 G5
Crucible Cl, Rom. RM6 . . . . 82 B6
Crucifix La, SE1 . . . . 28 D3
Cruden Ho, SE17 . . . . 35 G6
Cruden St, N1 . . . . 111 H1
Cruikshank Rd, E15 . . . . . . 97 E4
Cruikshank St, WC1 . . . . . . 10 E3
Crummock Gdns, NW9 . . . 70 E5
Crumpsall St, SE2 . . . . . . 138 C4
Crundale Av, NW9 . . . . 70 A5
Crunden Rd, S.Croy. CR2 . 202 A7
Crusader Gdns, Croy. CR0
off Cotelands 202 B3
Crusoe Ms, N16 . . . . 94 A2
Crusoe Rd, Mitch. CR4 . . . 167 J7
Crutched Friars, EC3 . . . . . 21 E5
Crutchley Rd, SE6 . . . . . . 173 E2
Crystal Ct, SE19
off College Rd 170 C5
Crystal Ho, SE18
off Spinel Cl 137 J5
Crystal Palace Caravan Club,
SE19 . . . . 170 C5
★**Crystal Palace FC**,
SE25 . . . . 188 B4
★**Crystal Palace Nat Sport**
Cen, SE19 . . . . 170 D6
Crystal Palace Par, SE19 . 170 C6
★**Crystal Palace Pk**, SE19 . 170 C5
Crystal Palace Pk Rd,
SE26 . . . . 170 D5
Crystal Palace Rd, SE22 . . 152 D4
Crystal Palace Sta Rd,
SE19 . . . . 170 D6
Crystal Ter, SE19 . . . . 170 A6
Crystal Vw Ct, Brom. BR1
off Winlaton Rd 172 D4
Crystal Way, Dag. RM8 . . . 100 C1
Harrow HA1 . . . . 68 C5
Crystal Wf, N1
off Graham St 111 H2
Cuba Dr, Enf. EN3 . . . . 45 F2
Cuba St, E14 . . . . 134 A2
Cubitt Sq, Sthl. UB2
off Windmill Av 123 J1
Cubitt Steps, E14
off Cabot Sq 134 A1
Cubitt St, WC1 . . . . 10 C4
Croydon CR0 . . . . 201 F5
Cubitts Yd, WC2 . . . . 18 B5
Cubitt Ter, SW4 . . . . 150 C3
CUBITT TOWN, E14 . . . . . . 134 C3
Cuckoo Av, W7 . . . . 104 B4
Cuckoo Dene, W7 . . . . 104 A5
Cuckoo Hall La, N9 . . . . 45 F7
Cuckoo Hill, Pnr. HA5 . . . . . 66 C3
Cuckoo Hill Dr, Pnr. HA5 . . 66 C3
Cuckoo Hill Rd, Pnr. HA5 . . 66 C4
Cuckoo La, W7 . . . . 104 B7
Cudas Cl, Epsom KT19 . . . 197 F4
Cuddington Av, Wor.Pk.
KT4 . . . . 197 F3
Cudham St, SE6 . . . . 154 C7
Cudworth St, E1 . . . . 113 E4
Cuff Cres, SE9 . . . . 156 A6
Cuff Pt, E2 . . . . 13 F3
Culford Gdns, SW3 . . . . 32 A2
Culford Gro, N1 . . . . 94 B6
Culford Ms, N1
off Culford Rd 94 B6
Culford Rd, N1 . . . . 94 B7
Culgaith Gdns, Enf. EN2 . . 42 E4
Cullen Way, NW10 . . . . . . 106 C4
Culling Rd, SE16
off Lower Rd 133 F3
Cullington Cl, Har. HA3 . . . 68 D4
Cullingworth Rd, NW10 . . . 89 G5
Culloden Cl, SE16 . . . . 37 J4
Culloden Rd, Enf. EN2 . . . . 43 H2
Culloden St, E14 . . . . 114 C6
Cullum St, EC3 . . . . 20 D5
Culmington Rd, W13 . . . . 125 F2
Culmore Rd, SE15 . . . . . . 133 E7
Culmstock Rd, SW11 . . . . 150 A5
Culpeper Cl, Ilf. IG6 . . . . . . 65 E6
Culpepper Cl, N18
off Dysons Rd 60 E5
Culross Cl, N15 . . . . 75 J4
Culross St, W1 . . . . 16 B6
Culsac Rd, Surb. KT6 . . . . 195 H2
Culverden Rd, SW12 . . . . 168 C2
Watford WD19 . . . . 50 B3
Culver Gro, Stan. HA7 . . . . 69 F2
Culverhouse Gdns,
SW16 . . . . 169 F3
Culverlands Cl, Stan. HA7 . 52 E4
Culverley Rd, SE6 . . . . 172 B1
Culvers Av, Cars. SM5 . . . 199 J2
Culvers Retreat, Cars.
SM5 . . . . 199 J1

Culverstone Cl, Brom. BR2 **191** F6
Culvers Way, Cars. SM5 **199** J2
Culvert Pl, SW11 **150** A2
Culvert Rd, N15 **76** B5
SW11 **149** J2
Culworth St, NW8 **7** G2
Cumberland Av, NW10 **106** B3
Welling DA16 **157** H3
Cumberland Cl, E8 **94** C6
SW20 *off Lansdowne Rd* **166** A7
Ilford IG6 **81** F1
Twickenham TW1 *off Westmorland Cl* **144/145** E6
Cumberland Ct, Well. DA16 *off Bellegrove Rd* **157** H2
Cumberland Cres, W14 **128** B4
Cumberland Dr, Bexh. DA7 **138** E7
Chessington KT9 **195** J3
Esher KT10 **194** D2
Cumberland Gdns, NW4 **72** B2
WC1 **10** D3
Cumberland Gate, W1 **15** J5
Cumberland Mkt, NW1 **9** E3
Cumberland Mkt Est, NW1 **9** E3
Cumberland Mills Sq, E14 *off Saunders Ness Rd* **134** D5
Cumberland Pk, NW10 **107** G3
W3 **106** C7
Cumberland Pl, NW1 **8** D3
SE6 **173** F1
Sunbury-on-Thames TW16 **178** A4
Cumberland Rd, E12 **98** A4
E13 **115** H5
E17 **77** H2
N9 **61** F1
N22 **75** F2
SE25 **189** E6
SW13 **147** F1
W3 **106** C7
W7 **124** C2
Bromley BR2 **190** E4
Harrow HA1 **67** H5
Richmond TW9 **126** A7
Stanmore HA7 **69** J3
Cumberland St, SW1 **32** E3
Cumberland Ter, NW1 **8** D2
Cumberland Ter Ms, NW1 **8** D2
Cumberland Vil, W3 *off Cumberland Rd* **106** C7
Cumberlow Av, SE25 **188** C3
Cumberton Rd, N17 **76** A1
Cumbrae Gdns, Surb. KT6 **195** G2
Cumbrian Gdns, NW2 **90** A2
★**Cuming Mus**, SE17 **35** J2
Cumming St, N1 **10** C2
Cumnor Gdns, Epsom KT17 **197** G6
Cumnor Rd, Sutt. SM2 **199** F6
Cunard Cres, N21 **44** A6
Cunard Pl, EC3 **20** E4
Cunard Rd, NW10 **106** D3
Cunard St, SE5 *off Albany Rd* **132** B6
Cunard Wk, SE16 **133** H4
Cundy Rd, E16 **115** J6
Cundy St, SW1 **32** C2
Cundy St Est, SW1 **32** C2
Cunliffe Rd, Epsom KT19 **197** F4
Cunliffe St, SW16 **168** C6
Cunningham Cl, Rom. RM6 **82** C5
West Wickham BR4 **204** B2
Cunningham Pk, Har. HA1 **67** J5
Cunningham Pl, NW8 **7** E5
Cunningham Rd, N15 **76** D4
Cunnington St, W4 **126** C3
Cupar Rd, SW11 **150** A1
Cupola Cl, Brom. BR1 **173** H5
Cureton St, SW1 **33** J2
Curfew Ho, Bark. IG11 *off St. Ann's* **117** F1
Curie Gdns, NW9 *off Pasteur Cl* **70/71** E2
Curlew Cl, SE28 **118** D7
Curlew Ct, Surb. KT6 **195** J3
Curlew Ho, Enf. EN3 *off Allington Ct* **45** G5
Curlew St, SE1 **29** F3
Curlew Ter, Ilf. IG5 *off Tiptree Cres* **80** D3
Curlew Way, Hayes UB4 **102** D5
Curness St, SE13 *off Lewisham High St* **154** C4
Curnick's La, SE27 *off Chapel Rd* **169** J4
Curnock Est, NW1 *off Plender St* **110** C1
Curran Av, Sid. DA15 **157** J5
Wallington SM6 **200** A3
Currey Rd, Grnf. UB6 **86** A6
Curricle St, W3 **126** E1
Currie Hill Cl, SW19 **166** C4
Curry Ri, NW7 **56** A6
Cursitor St, EC4 **18** E3
Curtain Pl, EC2 *off Curtain Rd* **112** B3
Curtain Rd, EC2 **12** D6
Curthwaite Gdns, Enf. EN2 **42** D4
Curtis Dr, W3 **106** D6
Curtis Fld Rd, SW16 **169** F4
Curtis La, Wem. HA0 *off Montrose Cres* **87** H6
Curtis Rd, Epsom KT19 **196** C4
Hounslow TW4 **143** F7
Curtis St, SE1 **37** F1
Curtis Way, SE1 **37** F1
SE28 *off Tawney Rd* **118** B7
Curve, The, W12 **107** G7
Curwen Av, E7 *off Woodford Rd* **97** H4
Curwen Rd, W12 **127** G2
Curzon Av, Enf. EN3 **45** G5
Stanmore HA7 **68** D1
Curzon Cl, Orp. BR6 **207** G4
Curzon Cres, NW10 **89** F7
Barking IG11 **117** J2
Curzon Gate, W1 **24** C2
Curzon Pl, Pnr. HA5 **66** C5
Curzon Rd, N10 **74** B2
W5 **105** E4
Thornton Heath CR7 **187** G6
Curzon Sq, W1 **24** C2
Curzon St, W1 **24** C2
Cusack Cl, Twick. TW1 *off Waldegrave Rd* **162** C4
CUSTOM HOUSE, E16 **116** A6
Custom Ho Reach, SE16 **133** J2
Custom Ho Wk, EC3 **20** D6
Cut, The, SE1 **27** F3
Cutcombe Rd, SE5 **151** J2
Cuthberga Cl, Bark. IG11 *off George St* **99** F7
Cuthbert Gdns, SE25 **188** B3
Cuthbert Rd, E17 **78** C3
N18 *off Fairfield Rd* **60** D5
Croydon CR0 **201** H2
Cuthbert St, W2 **15** E1
Cuthill Wk, SE5 **152** A1
Cutlers Gdns, E1 **21** E3
Cutlers Gdns Arc, EC2 *off Cutler St* **112** B6
Cutlers Sq, E14 *off Britannia Rd* **134** A4
Cutlers Ter, N1 *off Balls Pond Rd* **94** A6
Cutler St, E1 **21** E3
Cutthroat All, Rich. TW10 *off Ham St* **163** F2
★**Cutty Sark**, SE10 **134** C6
Cutty Sark Gdns, SE10 *off King William Wk* **134** C6
Cuxton Cl, Bexh. DA6 **158** E5
Cyclamen Cl, Hmptn. TW12 *off Gresham Rd* **161** G6
Cyclamen Way, Epsom KT19 **196** B5
Cyclops Ms, E14 **134** A4
Cygnet Av, Felt. TW14 **142** C7
Cygnet Cl, NW10 **88** D5
Borehamwood WD6 **38** C1
Cygnets, The, Felt. TW13 **160** E4
Cygnet St, E1 **13** G5
Cygnet Way, Hayes UB4 **102** D5
Cygnus Business Cen, NW10 **89** F6
Cymbeline Ct, Har. HA1 **68** C6
Cynthia St, N1 **10** D2
Cyntra Pl, E8 **95** E7
Cypress Av, Twick. TW2 **143** J7
Cypress Gdns, SE4 **153** H5
Cypress Gro, Ilf. IG6 **65** H6
Cypress Pl, W1 **9** G6
Cypress Rd, SE25 **188** B2
Harrow HA3 **68** A2
Cypress Tree Cl, Sid. DA15 *off White Oak Gdns* **157** J7
Cyprus Av, N3 **72** B2
Cyprus Cl, N4 *off Atterbury Rd* **75** H6
Cyprus Gdns, N3 **72** B2
Cyprus Pl, E2 **113** F2
E6 **116** D7
Cyprus Rd, N3 **72** C2
N9 **60** C2
Cyprus Roundabout, E16 *off Royal Albert Way* **116** D7
Cyprus St, E2 **113** F2
Cyrena Rd, SE22 **152** C6
Cyril Mans, SW11 **149** J1
Cyril Rd, Bexh. DA7 **159** E2
Cyrus St, EC1 **11** H5
Czar St, SE8 **134** A6

D

Dabbs Hill La, Nthlt. UB5 **85** H5
Dabin Cres, SE10 **154** C1
Dacca St, SE8 **133** J6
Dace Rd, E3 **96** A7
Dacre Av, Ilf. IG5 **80** D2
Dacre Cl, Chig. IG7 **65** F4
Greenford UB6 **103** H2
Dacre Gdns, SE13 **154** E4
Borehamwood WD6 **38** D5
Chigwell IG7 **65** F4
Dacre Pk, SE13 **155** E3
Dacre Pl, SE13 **154** E3
Dacre Rd, E11 **97** F1
E13 **115** H1
Croydon CR0 **187** E7
Dacres Rd, SE23 **171** G3
Dacre St, SW1 **25** H5
Dade Way, Sthl. UB2 **123** F5
Daerwood Cl, Brom. BR2 **206** C1
Daffodil Cl, Croy. CR0 *off Primrose La* **203** G1
Daffodil Gdns, Ilf. IG1 **98** E5
Daffodil Pl, Hmptn. TW12 *off Gresham Rd* **161** G6
Daffodil St, W12 **107** F7
Dafforne Rd, SW17 **168** A3
DAGENHAM, RM8 - RM10 **101** G6
Dagenham Av, Dag. RM9 **118** E1
Dagenham Rd, E10 **95** J1
Dagenham RM10 **101** J4
Dagmar Av, Wem. HA9 **87** J4
Dagmar Gdns, NW10 **108** A2
Dagmar Ms, Sthl. UB2 *off Dagmar Rd* **122/123** E3
Dagmar Pas, N1 *off Cross St* **111** H1
Dagmar Rd, N4 **75** G7
N15 *off Cornwall Rd* **76** A4
N22 **74** D1
SE5 **152** B1
SE25 **188** B5
Dagenham RM10 **101** J7
Kingston upon Thames KT2 **181** J1
Southall UB2 **122** E3
Dagmar Ter, N1 **111** H1
Dagnall Pk, SE25 **188** B6
Dagnall Rd, SE25 **188** B5
Dagnall St, SW11 **149** J2
Dagnan Rd, SW12 **150** B7
Dagonet Gdns, Brom. BR1 **173** G3
Dagonet Rd, Brom. BR1 **173** G3
Dahlia Gdns, Ilf. IG1 **99** E6
Mitcham CR4 **186** D4
Dahlia Rd, SE2 **138** B4
Dahomey Rd, SW16 **168** C6
Daimler Way, Wall. SM6 **200** E7
Daines Cl, E12 *off Colchester Av* **98** C3
Dainford Cl, Brom. BR1 **172** D5
Dainton Cl, Brom. BR1 **191** H1
Daintry Cl, Har. HA3 **68** D4
Daintry Way, E9 *off Osborne Rd* **95** J6
Dairsie Rd, SE9 **156** D3
Dairy Cl, NW10 **107** G1
Thornton Heath CR7 **187** J2
Dairy Fm Pl, SE15 *off Queens Rd* **153** F1
Dairy La, SE18 **136** C4
Dairyman Cl, NW2 *off Claremont Rd* **90** B3
Dairy Ms, SW9 **151** E3
Dairy Wk, SW19 **166** B4
Daisy Cl, Croy. CR0 *off Primrose La* **203** G1
Daisy Dobbins Wk, N19 *off Hillrise Rd* **74/75** E7
Daisy La, SW6 **148** D3
Daisy Rd, E16 *off Cranberry La* **114/115** E4
Daisy Rd, E18 **79** H2
Dakota Cl, Wall. SM6 **201** F7
Dakota Gdns, E6 **116** B4
Northolt UB5 *off Argus Way* **102/103** E3
Dalberg Rd, SW2 **151** G4
Dalberg Way, SE2 *off Lanridge Rd* **138** D3
Dalby Rd, SW18 **149** F4
Dalby St, NW5 **92** B6
Dalcross Rd, Houns. TW4 **142** E2
Dale, The, Kes. BR2 **206** A4
Dale Av, Edg. HA8 **69** J1
Hounslow TW4 **143** E3
Dalebury Rd, SW17 **167** H2
Dale Cl, SE3 **155** G3
Barnet EN5 **41** E6
Pinner HA5 **66** B1
Dale Gdns, Wdf.Grn. IG8 **63** H4
Dale Grn Rd, N11 **58** B3
Dale Gro, N12 **57** F5
Daleham Gdns, NW3 **91** G5
Daleham Ms, NW3 **91** G6
Dalehead, NW1 **9** F2
Dalemain Ms, E16 *off Hanover Av* **135** G1
Dale Pk Av, Cars. SM5 **199** J2
Dale Pk Rd, SE19 **187** J1
Dale Rd, NW5 *off Grafton Rd* **92** A5
SE17 **35** H6
Greenford UB6 **103** H5
Sutton SM1 **198** C4
Dale Row, W11 *off St. Marks Rd* **108** B6
Daleside Gdns, Chig. IG7 **65** F3
Daleside Rd, SW16 **168** B5
Epsom KT19 **196** D6
Dales Path, Borwd. WD6 *off Farriers Way* **38** D5
Dales Rd, Borwd. WD6 **38** D5
Dale St, W4 **126** E5
Dale Vw Av, E4 **62** C2
Dale Vw Cres, E4 **62** C2
Dale Vw Gdns, E4 **62** D3
Daleview Rd, N15 **76** B6
Dalewood Gdns, Wor.Pk. KT4 **197** H2
Dale Wd Rd, Orp. BR6 **193** H7
Daley St, E9 **95** G6
Daley Thompson Way, SW8 **150** B2
Dalgarno Gdns, W10 **107** J5
Dalgarno Way, W10 **107** J4
Dalgleish St, E14 **113** H6
Daling Way, E3 **113** H1
Dalkeith Gro, Stan. HA7 **53** G5
Dalkeith Rd, SE21 **169** J1
Ilford IG1 **99** F3
Dallas Rd, NW4 **71** G7
SE26 **170** E4
W5 **105** J5
Sutton SM3 **198** B6
Dallas Ter, Hayes UB3 **121** J3
Dallinger Rd, SE12 **155** F6
Dalling Rd, W6 **127** H3
Dallington Sq, EC1 *off Dallington St* **111** H4
Dallington St, EC1 **11** H5
Dallin Rd, SE18 **137** E7
Bexleyheath DA6 **158** D4
Dalmain Rd, SE23 **171** G1
Dalmally Rd, Croy. CR0 **188** C7
Dalmeny Av, N7 **92** D4
SW16 **187** G2
Dalmeny Cl, Wem. HA0 **87** F6
Dalmeny Cres, Houns. TW3 **144** A4
Dalmeny Rd, N7 **92** D3
Barnet EN5 **41** F6
Carshalton SM5 **200** A7
Erith DA8 **159** H1
Worcester Park KT4 **197** H3
Dalmeyer Rd, NW10 **89** F6
Dalmore Av, Esher (Clay.) KT10 **194** C6
Dalmore Rd, SE21 **169** J2
Dalrymple Cl, N14 **42** D7
Dalrymple Rd, SE4 **153** H4
DALSTON, E8 **94** D7
Dalston Gdns, Stan. HA7 **69** H1
Dalston La, E8 **94** C6
Dalton Av, Mitch. CR4 **185** H2
Dalton Cl, Orp. BR6 **207** H3
Dalton Rd, Har. (Har.Wld) HA3 **68** A2
Dalton St, SE27 **169** H2
Dalwood St, SE5 **152** B1

Daly Ct, E15
off Clays La **96** C5
Dalyell Rd, SW9 **151** F3
Damascene Wk, SE21
off Lovelace Rd **169** J1
Damask Cres, E16
off Cranberry La **114/115** E4
Damer Ter, SW10
off Tadema Rd **129** F7
Dames Rd, E7 **97** G3
Dame St, N1 **11** J1
Damien St, E1 **113** E6
Damon Cl, Sid. DA14 **176** B3
Damson Dr, Hayes UB3 **102** A7
Damsonwood Rd, Sthl.
UB2 **123** G3
Danbrook Rd, SW16 **187** E1
Danbury Cl, Rom. RM6 **82** D3
Danbury Ms, Wall. SM6 **200** B4
Danbury Rd, Loug. IG10 **48** B7
Danbury St, N1 **11** H1
Danbury Way, Wdf.Grn.
IG8 **63** J6
Danby St, SE15 **152** C3
Dancer Rd, SW6 **148** C1
Richmond TW9 **146** A3
Dando Cres, SE3 **155** H3
Dandridge Cl, SE10 **135** F5
Danebury, Croy. (New Adgtn)
CR0 **204** B6
Danebury Av, SW15 **147** E6
Daneby Rd, SE6 **172** B3
Dane Cl, Bex. DA5 **159** G7
Orpington BR6 **207** G5
Danecourt Gdns, Croy.
CR0 **202** C3
Danecroft Rd, SE24 **151** J5
Danehill Wk, Sid. DA14
off Hatherley Rd **176** A3
Danehurst Gdns, Ilf. IG4 **80** B5
Danehurst St, SW6 **148** B1
Daneland, Barn. EN4 **41** J6
Danemead Gro, Nthlt.
UB5 **85** H5
Danemere St, SW15 **147** J3
Dane Pl, E3
off Roman Rd **113** H2
Dane Rd, N18 **61** F3
SW19 **185** F1
W13 **125** F1
Ilford IG1 **99** F5
Southall UB1 **103** E7
Danesbury Rd, Felt. TW13 **160** B1
Danescombe, SE12
off Winn Rd **173** G1
Danes Ct, Wem. HA9 **88** B3
Danescourt Cres, Sutt.
SM1 **199** F2
Danescroft, NW4 **72** A5
Danescroft Av, NW4 **72** A5
Danescroft Gdns, NW4 **72** A5
Danesdale Rd, E9 **95** H6
Danesfield, SE5 **36** D5
Danes Gate, Har. HA1 **68** B3
Danes Rd, Rom. RM7 **83** J7
Dane St, WC1 **18** C2
Daneswood Av, SE6 **172** C3
Danethorpe Rd, Wem.
HA0 **87** G6
Danetree Cl, Epsom
KT19 **196** C7
Danetree Rd, Epsom
KT19 **196** C7
Danette Gdns, Dag.
RM10 **101** F2
Daneville Rd, SE5 **152** A1
Dangan Rd, E11 **79** G6
Daniel Bolt Cl, E14
off Uamvar St **114** B5
Daniel Cl, N18 **61** F4
SW17 **167** H6
Hounslow TW4
off Harvey Rd **143** F7
Daniel Gdns, SE15 **37** F7
Daniell Way, Croy. CR0 **201** E1
Daniel Pl, NW4 **71** H6
Daniel Rd, W5 **105** J7
Daniels Rd, SE15 **153** F3
Dan Leno Wk, SW6
off Britannia Rd **128/129** E7
Dan Mason Dr, W4
off Great Chertsey Rd **146** C2
Dansey Pl, W1 **17** H5
Dansington Rd, Well.
DA16 **158** A4
Danson Cres, Well. DA16 **158** B3
Danson La, Well. DA16 **158** A4
Danson Mead, Well.
DA16 **158** C3
★**Danson Park**, Well.
DA16 **158** C4
Danson Pk, Bexh. DA6 **158** C4
Danson Rd, Bex. DA5 **158** D5
Bexleyheath DA6 **158** D5
Danson Underpass, Sid. DA15
off Danson Rd **158** C6
Dante Pl, SE11 **35** H1
Dante Rd, SE11 **35** G1
Danube St, SW3 **31** H3
Danvers Rd, N8 **74** D4
Danvers St, SW3 **31** F6
Danziger Way, Borwd.
WD6 **38** C1
Daphne Gdns, E4
off Gunners Gro **62** C3
Daphne St, SW18 **149** F6
Daplyn St, E1 **21** H1
D'Arblay St, W1 **17** G4
Darby Cres, Sun. TW16 **178** C2
Darby Gdns, Sun. TW16 **178** C2
Darcy Av, Wall. SM6 **200** C4
Darcy Cl, N20 **57** G2
D'Arcy Dr, Har. HA3 **69** G4
Darcy Gdns, Dag. RM9 **119** F1
D'Arcy Gdns, Har. HA3 **69** H4
D'Arcy Pl, Brom. BR2 **191** G4
Darcy Rd, SW16 **186** E2
Isleworth TW7
off London Rd **144** D1
D'Arcy Rd, Sutt. SM3 **198** A4
Dare Gdns, Dag. RM8
off Grafton Rd **100/101** E3
Darell Rd, Rich. TW9 **146** A3
Darenth Rd, N16 **76** C7
Welling DA16 **158** A1
Darfield Rd, SE4 **153** J5
Darfield Way, W10 **108** A6
Darfur St, SW15 **148** A3
Dargate Cl, SE19
off Chipstead Cl **170** C7
Darien Rd, SW11 **149** G3
Dark Ho Wk, EC3
off King William St **112** B7
Darlands Dr, Barn. EN5 **40** A5
Darlan Rd, SW6 **128** C7
Darlaston Rd, SW19 **166** A7
Darley Cl, Croy. CR0 **189** H6
Darley Dr, N.Mal. KT3 **182** D2
Darley Gdns, Mord. SM4 **185** E6
Darley Rd, N9 **60** C1
SW11 **149** J6
Darling Rd, SE4 **154** A3
Darling Row, E1 **113** E4
Darlington Rd, SE27 **169** H5
Darmaine Cl, S.Croy. CR2
off Churchill Rd **201** J7
Darnaway Pl, E14
off Abbott Rd **114** C6
Darndale Cl, E17 **77** J2
Darnley Ho, E14 **113** H6
Darnley Rd, E9 **95** E6
Woodford Green IG8 **79** G1
Darnley Ter, W11
off St. James's Gdns **128** B1
Darrell Rd, SE22 **152** D5
Darren Cl, N4 **75** F7
Darrick Wd Rd, Orp. BR6 **207** G2
Darris Cl, Hayes UB4 **103** E4
Darsley Dr, SW8 **150** E1
Dartford Av, N9 **45** F6
Dartford Gdns, Rom. (Chad.Hth)
RM6
off Heathfield Pk Dr **82** B6
Dartford Rd, Bex. DA5 **177** J1
Dartford St, SE17 **36** A5
Dartmoor Wk, E14
off Charnwood Gdns **134** A4
Dartmouth Cl, W11 **108** C6
Dartmouth Gro, SE10 **154** C1
Dartmouth Hill, SE10 **154** C1
Dartmouth Ho, Kings.T. KT2
off Kingsgate Rd **181** H1
DARTMOUTH PARK, NW5 **92** B3
Dartmouth Pk Av, NW5 **92** B3
Dartmouth Pk Hill, N19 **92** B1
NW5 **92** B1
Dartmouth Pk Rd, NW5 **92** B4
Dartmouth Pl, SE23
off Dartmouth Rd **171** F2
W4 **127** E6
Dartmouth Rd, E16
off Fords Pk Rd **115** G6
NW2 **90** A6
NW4 **71** G6
SE23 **171** F3
SE26 **171** F3
Bromley BR2 **191** G7
Ruislip HA4 **84** A3
Dartmouth Row, SE10 **154** C2
Dartmouth St, SW1 **25** H4
Dartmouth Ter, SE10 **154** D1
Dartnell Rd, Croy. CR0 **188** C7
Dartrey Wk, SW10 **30** D7
Dart St, W10 **108** B3
Darville Rd, N16 **94** C3
Darwell Cl, E6 **116** D2
Darwin Cl, N11 **58** B3
Orpington BR6 **207** G5
Darwin Dr, Sthl. UB1 **103** H6
Darwin Gdns, Wat. WD19
off Barnhurst Path **50** C5
Darwin Rd, N22 **75** H1
W5 **125** F5
Welling DA16 **157** J3
Darwin St, SE17 **36** C1
Daryngton Dr, Grnf. UB6 **104** A2
Dashwood Cl, Bexh. DA6 **159** G5
Dashwood Rd, N8 **75** F6
Dassett Rd, SE27 **169** H5
Datchelor Pl, SE5 **152** A1
Datchet Rd, SE6 **171** J3
Datchworth Ct, N4
off Queens Dr **93** J3
Date St, SE17 **36** B4
Daubeney Gdns, N17 **59** J7
Daubeney Rd, E5 **95** H4
N17 **59** J7
Daubeney Twr, SE8 **133** J4
Dault Rd, SW18 **149** F6
Davema Cl, Chis. BR7
off Brenchley Cl **192** D1
Davenant Rd, N19 **92** D2
Croydon CR0
off Duppas Hill Rd **201** H4
Davenant St, E1 **21** J2
Davenport Cl, Tedd. TW11 **162** D6
Davenport Rd, SE6 **154** B6
Sidcup DA14 **176** D2
Daventer Dr, Stan. HA7 **52** C7
Daventry Av, E17 **78** A5
Daventry St, NW1 **15** G1
Davern Cl, SE10 **135** F4
Davey Cl, N7 **93** F6
Davey Rd, E9 **96** A7
Davey St, SE15 **37** G6
David Av, Grnf. UB6 **104** B3
David Cl, Hayes UB3 **121** G7
Davidge St, SE1 **27** G4
David Lee Pt, E15 **115** E1
David Ms, W1 **16** A1
David Rd, Dag. RM8 **100** E2
Davidson Gdns, SW8 **130** E7
Davidson La, Har. HA1
off Grove Hill **68** C7
Davidson Rd, Croy. CR0 **188** C6
Davids Rd, SE23 **171** F1
David St, E15 **96** D6
David's Way, Ilf. IG6 **65** H7
David Twigg Cl, Kings.T.
KT2 **181** H1
Davies Cl, Croy. CR0 **188** D6
Davies La, E11 **97** E2
Davies Ms, W1 **16** D5
Davies St, W1 **16** D5
Davington Gdns, Dag.
RM8 **100** B5
Davington Rd, Dag. RM8 **100** B6
Davinia Cl, Wdf.Grn. IG8
off Deacon Way **64** C6
Davis Rd, W3 **127** F1
Chessington KT9 **196** A4
Davis St, E13 **115** H2
Davisville Rd, W12 **127** G2
Dawes Av, Islw. TW7 **144** D5
Dawes Ho, SE17 **36** C2
Dawes Rd, SW6 **128** B7
Dawes St, SE17 **36** C3
Dawley Rd, Hayes UB3 **121** H3
Dawlish Av, N13 **58** E4
SW18 **166** E2
Greenford UB6 **104** D2
Dawlish Dr, Ilf. IG3 **99** H4
Pinner HA5 **67** E5
Ruislip HA4 **84** A2
Dawlish Rd, E10 **96** C2
N17 **76** D3
NW2 **90** A6
Dawnay Gdns, SW18 **167** G2
Dawnay Rd, SW18 **167** F2
Dawn Cl, Houns. TW4 **143** E3
Dawn Cres, E15
off Bridge Rd **114** D1
Dawpool Rd, NW2 **89** F2
Daws Hill, E4 **46** C3
Daws La, NW7 **55** F5
Dawson Av, Bark. IG11 **99** H7
Dawson Cl, SE18 **137** F4
Dawson Gdns, Bark. IG11
off Dawson Av **99** J7
Dawson Hts Est, SE22 **152** D7
Dawson Pl, W2 **108** D7
Dawson Rd, NW2 **89** J5
Kingston upon Thames
KT1 **181** J3
Dawson St, E2 **13** G2
Dax Ct, Sun. TW16
off Thames St **178** C3
Daybrook Rd, SW19 **184** E2
Daylesford Av, SW15 **147** G4
Daymer Gdns, Pnr. HA5 **66** B4
Daysbrook Rd, SW2 **169** F2
Days La, Sid. DA15 **157** H7
Dayton Gro, SE15 **153** F1
Deacon Ms, N1 **94** A7
Deacon Rd, NW2 **89** G5
Kingston upon Thames
KT2 **181** J1
Deacons Cl, Borwd. (Elstree)
WD6 **38** A4
Pinner HA5 **66** B2
Deacons Leas, Orp. BR6 **207** G4
Deacons Ri, N2 **73** G5
Deacons Wk, Hmptn. TW12
off Bishops Gro **161** F4
Deacon Way, SE17 **35** J1
Woodford Green IG8 **64** C7
Deal Ms, W5
off Darwin Rd **125** G4
Deal Porters Way, SE16 **133** F3
Deal Rd, SW17 **168** A6
Deal's Gateway, SE10
off Blackheath Rd **154** B1
Deal St, E1 **21** H1
Dealtry Rd, SW15 **147** J4
Deal Wk, SW9
off Mandela St **131** G7
Dean Bradley St, SW1 **26** A6
Dean Cl, E9
off Churchill Wk **95** F5
SE16
off Surrey Water Rd **133** G1
Dean Ct, Wem. HA0 **87** E3
Deancross St, E1 **113** F6
Dean Dr, Stan. HA7 **69** H2
Deane Av, Ruis. HA4 **84** C5
Deane Cft Rd, Pnr. HA5 **66** B6
Deanery Cl, N2 **73** H4
Deanery Ms, W1 **24** C1
Deanery Rd, E15 **97** E6
Deanery St, W1 **24** C1
Deane Way, Ruis. HA4 **66** B6
Dean Farrar St, SW1 **25** H5
Dean Gdns, E17 **78** D4
W13
off Northfield Av **124/125** E1
Deanhill Rd, SW14 **146** B4
Dean Rd, NW2 **89** J6
SE28 **118** A7
Croydon CR0 **202** A4
Hampton TW12 **161** G5
Hounslow TW3 **143** H5
Dean Ryle St, SW1 **26** A1
Deansbrook Cl, Edg. HA8 **54** C7
Deansbrook Rd, Edg. HA8 **54** C6
Deans Bldgs, SE17 **36** B2
Deans Cl, W4 **126** B6
Dean's Cl, Croy. CR0 **202** C3
Deans Cl, Edg. HA8 **54** C6
Deans Ct, EC4 **19** H4
Deanscroft Av, NW9 **88** C2
Deans Dr, N13 **59** H6
Edgware HA8 **54** D5
Dean's Gate Cl, SE23 **171** G3
Deans La, W4 **126** B6
Edgware HA8 **54** C6
Deans Ms, W1 **16** E3
Deans Rd, W7 **124** C1
Sutton SM1 **198** E3
Dean Stanley St, SW1 **26** A6
Dean St, E7 **97** G5
W1 **17** H3
Deansway, N2 **73** G4
N9 **60** B3
Deans Way, Edg. HA8 **54** C5
Dean's Yd, SW1 **25** J5
Dean Trench St, SW1 **26** A6
Dean Wk, Edg. HA8
off Deansbrook Rd **54** C6
Dean Way, Sthl. UB2 **123** H2
Dearne Cl, Stan. HA7 **52** D5
De'Arn Gdns, Mitch. CR4 **185** H3
Dearsley Rd, Enf. EN1 **44** D3
Deason St, E15
off High St **114** C1
De Barowe Ms, N5
off Leigh Rd **93** H4

DEBDEN, Loug. IG10 **49** G3
Debden Cl, Kings.T. KT2 **163** G5
Woodford Green IG8 **63** J7
De Beauvoir Cres, N1 **112** B1
De Beauvoir Est, N1 **112** A1
De Beauvoir Rd, N1 **112** B1
De Beauvoir Sq, N1 **94** B7
DE BEAUVOIR TOWN, N1 **112** A1
Debnams Rd, SE16 *off Rotherhithe New Rd* **133** F4
De Bohun Av, N14 **42** B6
Deborah Cl, Islw. TW7 **144** B1
De Brome Rd, Felt. TW13 **160** C1
Deburgh Rd, SW19 **167** F7
Decima St, SE1 **28** D5
Deck Cl, SE16 *off Thame Rd* **133** G2
Decoy Av, NW11 **72** B5
De Crespigny Pk, SE5 **152** A2
Deeley Rd, SW8 **150** D1
Deena Cl, W3 **105** J6
Deepdale, SW19 **166** A4
Deepdale Av, Brom. BR2 **191** F4
Deepdale Cl, N11 *off Ribblesdale Av* **58** A6
Deepdene, W5 **105** J4
Deepdene Av, Croy. CR0 **202** C3
Deepdene Cl, E11 **79** G4
Deepdene Ct, N21 **43** H6
Deepdene Gdns, SW2 **151** F7
Deepdene Path, Loug. IG10 **48** D4
Deepdene Pt, SE23 *off Dacres Rd* **171** G3
Deepdene Rd, SE5 **152** A4
Loughton IG10 **48** D4
Welling DA16 **158** A3
Deepwell Cl, Islw. TW7 **144** D1
Deepwood La, Grnf. UB6 *off Cowgate Rd* **104** A3
Deerbrook Rd, SE24 **169** H1
Deerdale Rd, SE24 **151** J4
Deerfield Cl, NW9 *off Rookery Cl* **71** F5
Deerhurst Cl, Felt. TW13 **160** A4
Deerhurst Cres, Hmptn. (Hmptn H.) TW12 **161** J5
Deerhurst Rd, NW2 **90** A6
SW16 **169** F5
Deerings Dr, Pnr. HA5 **66** A5
Deerleap Gro, E4 **46** B5
Dee Rd, Rich. TW9 **145** J4
Deer Pk Cl, Kings.T. KT2 **164** B7
Deer Pk Gdns, Mitch. CR4 **185** G3
Deer Pk Rd, SW19 **185** E2
Deer Pk Way, W.Wick. BR4 **205** F2
Deeside Rd, SW17 **167** G3
Dee St, E14 **114** C6
Defiance Wk, SE18 **136** C3
Defiant Way, Wall. SM6 **200** E7
Defoe Av, Rich. TW9 **126** A7
Defoe Cl, SE16 *off Vaughan St* **133** J2
SW17 **167** H6
Defoe Ho, EC2 **20** A1
Defoe Pl, EC2 *off Beech St* **111** J5
SW17 *off Lessingham Av* **167** J4
Defoe Rd, N16 **94** B2
De Frene Rd, SE26 **171** G4
De Gama Pl, E14 *off Maritime Quay* **134** A5
Degema Rd, Chis. BR7 **174** E5
Dehar Cres, NW9 **71** F7
Dehavilland Cl, Nthlt. UB5 **102** D3
De Havilland Dr, SE18 *off Cambridge Row* **136** E5
De Havilland Rd, Edg. HA8 **70** B2
Hounslow TW5 **122** C7
De Havilland Way, Stai. (Stanw.) TW19 **140** A6
Dekker Rd, SE21 **152** B6
Delacourt Rd, SE3 *off Old Dover Rd* **135** H7
Delafield Rd, SE7 **135** H5
Delaford Rd, SE16 **133** E5
Delaford St, SW6 **128** B7
Delamare Cres, Croy. CR0 **189** F6
Delamere Gdns, NW7 **54** D6
Delamere Rd, SW20 **184** A1
W5 **125** H1
Borehamwood WD6 **38** B1
Hayes UB4 **102** D7
Delamere Ter, W2 **14** B1
Delancey Pas, NW1 *off Delancey St* **110** B1
Delancey St, NW1 **110** B1
De Laune St, SE17 **35** G4
Delaware Rd, W9 **6** A5
Delawyk Cres, SE24 **151** J6
Delcombe Av, Wor.Pk. KT4 **197** J1
Delft Way, SE22 *off East Dulwich Gro* **152** B5
Delhi Rd, Enf. EN1 **44** C7
Delhi St, N1 **111** E1
Delia St, SW18 **149** E7
Delisle Rd, SE28 **137** H1
Delius Gro, E15 **114** D2
Dell, The, SE2 **138** A5
SE19 **188** C1
Brentford TW8 **125** F6
Feltham TW14 *off Harlington Rd W* **142** B7
Pinner HA5 **66** D2
Wembley HA0 **87** E5
Woodford Green IG8 **63** H3
Della Path, E5 *off Napoleon Rd* **94/95** E3
Dellbow Rd, Felt. TW14 *off Central Way* **142** B5
Dell Cl, E15 **114** D1
Wallington SM6 **200** D4
Woodford Green IG8 **63** H3
Dellfield Cl, Beck. BR3 *off Foxgrove Rd* **172** C7
Dell La, Epsom KT17 **197** G5
Dellors Cl, Barn. EN5 **40** A5
Dellow Cl, Ilf. IG2 **81** G7
Dellow St, E1 **113** E7
Dell Rd, Epsom KT17 **197** G6
West Drayton UB7 **120** C3
Dells Cl, E4 **46** B7
Teddington TW11 *off Middle La* **162** C6
Dell's Ms, SW1 **33** G2
Dell Wk, N.Mal. KT3 **183** E2
Dell Way, W13 **105** F6
Dellwood Gdns, Ilf. IG5 **80** D3
Delmare Cl, SW9 *off Brighton Ter* **151** F4
Delme Cres, SE3 **155** H2
Delmey Cl, Croy. CR0 *off Radcliffe Rd* **202** C3
Deloraine St, SE8 **154** A1
Delorme St, W6 **128** A6
Delta Cl, Wor.Pk. KT4 **197** F3
Delta Ct, NW2 **89** G2
Delta Gain, Wat. WD19 **50** D2
Delta Gro, Nthlt. UB5 **102** D3
Delta Rd, Wor.Pk. KT4 **197** E3
Delta St, E2 **13** H3
De Luci Rd, Erith DA8 **139** J5
De Lucy St, SE2 **138** B4
Delvan Cl, SE18 *off Ordnance Rd* **136** D7
Delvers Mead, Dag. RM10 **101** J4
Delverton Rd, SE17 **35** H4
Delvino Rd, SW6 **148** D1
De Mandeville Gate, Enf. EN1 *off Southbury Rd* **44** D4
Demesne Rd, Wall. SM6 **200** D5
Demeta Cl, Wem. HA9 **88** C3
De Montfort Par, SW16 *off Streatham High Rd* **168/169** E3
De Montfort Rd, SW16 **168** E3
De Morgan Rd, SW6 **149** E3
Dempster Cl, Surb. KT6 **195** F1
Dempster Rd, SW18 **149** F5
Denbar Par, Rom. RM7 *off Mawney Rd* **83** J4
Denberry Dr, Sid. DA14 **176** B3
Denbigh Cl, NW10 **88** E7
W11 **108** C7
Chislehurst BR7 **174** C6
Southall UB1 **103** F6
Sutton SM1 **198** C5
Denbigh Dr, Hayes UB3 **121** F2
Denbigh Gdns, Rich. TW10 **145** J5
Denbigh Ms, SW1 **33** F2
Denbigh Pl, SW1 **33** F3
Denbigh Rd, E6 **116** A3
W11 **108** C7
W13 **105** E7
Hounslow TW3 **143** H2
Southall UB1 **103** F6
Denbigh St, SW1 **33** F2
Denbigh Ter, W11 **108** C7
Denbridge Rd, Brom. BR1 **192** C2
Den Cl, Beck. BR3 **190** D3
Dene, The, W13 **104** E5
Croydon CR0 **203** G4
Wembley HA9 **87** H4
West Molesey KT8 **179** F5
Dene Av, Houns. TW3 **143** F3
Sidcup DA15 **158** B7
Dene Cl, SE4 **153** H3
Bromley BR2 **205** F1
Worcester Park KT4 **197** F2
Dene Ct, Stan. HA7 *off Marsh La* **53** F5
Dene Gdns, Stan. HA7 **53** F5
Thames Ditton KT7 **194** D2
Denehurst Gdns, NW4 **71** J6
W3 **126** B1
Richmond TW10 **146** A4
Twickenham TW2 **144** A7
Woodford Green IG8 **63** H4
Dene Rd, N11 **57** J1
Buckhurst Hill IG9 **64** A1
Denewood, Barn. EN5 **41** F5
Denewood Rd, N6 **73** J6
Denford St, SE10 *off Woolwich Rd* **135** F5
Dengie Wk, N1 *off Basire St* **111** J1
Denham Cl, Well. DA16 *off Park Vw Rd* **158** C3
Denham Cres, Mitch. CR4 **185** J4
Denham Dr, Ilf. IG2 **81** F6
Denham Rd, N20 **57** J3
Feltham TW14 **142** C6
Denham St, SE10 **135** G5
Denham Way, Bark. IG11 **117** H1
Borehamwood WD6 **38** D1
Denholme Rd, W9 **108** C3
Denison Cl, N2 **73** F3
Denison Rd, SW19 **167** G6
W5 **105** F4
Deniston Av, Bex. DA5 **176** E1
Denis Way, SW4 *off Gauden Rd* **150** D3
Denleigh Gdns, N21 **59** G1
Thames Ditton KT7 **180** B6
Denman Dr, NW11 **72** D5
Esher (Clay.) KT10 **194** D5
Denman Dr N, NW11 **72** D5
Denman Dr S, NW11 **72** D5
Denman Pl, W1 *off Great Windmill St* **110** D7
Denman Rd, SE15 **152** C1
Denman St, W1 **17** H6
Denmark Av, SW19 **166** B7
Denmark Ct, Mord. SM4 **184** D5
Denmark Gdns, Cars. SM5 **199** J3
Denmark Gro, N1 **11** E1
Denmark Hill, SE5 **152** A1
Denmark Hill Dr, NW9 **71** F4
Denmark Hill Est, SE5 **152** A4
Denmark Pl, WC2 **17** J3
Denmark Rd, N8 **75** G4
NW6 **108** C2
SE5 **151** J1
SE25 **188** D5
SW19 **166** A6
W13 **105** E7
Bromley BR1 **191** H1
Carshalton SM5 **199** J3
Kingston upon Thames KT1 **181** H3
Twickenham TW2 **162** A3
Denmark St, E11 *off High Rd Leytonstone* **96/97** E3
E13 **115** H5
N17 **76** E1
WC2 **17** J4
Denmark Wk, SE27 **169** J4
Denmead Ho, SW15 *off Highcliffe Dr* **147** F6
Denmead Rd, Croy. CR0 **201** H1
Denmead Way, SE15 *off Pentridge St* **132** C7
Dennan Rd, Surb. KT6 **195** J1
Dennard Way, Orp. BR6 **206** E4
Denner Rd, E4 **62** A2
Denne Ter, E8 **112** C1
Dennett Rd, Croy. CR0 **201** G1
Dennetts Gro, SE14 *off Dennetts Rd* **153** G2
Dennetts Rd, SE14 **153** F1
Denning Av, Croy. CR0 **201** G4
Denning Cl, NW8 **6** D3
Hampton TW12 **161** F6
Denning Rd, NW3 **91** G4
Dennington Cl, E5 *off Detmold Rd* **94/95** E2
Dennington Pk Rd, NW6 **90** D6
Denningtons, The, Wor.Pk. KT4 **197** E2
Dennis Av, Wem. HA9 **87** J5
Dennis Gdns, Stan. HA7 **53** F5
Dennis La, Stan. HA7 **52** E3
Dennison Pt, E15 **96** C7
Dennis Pk Cres, SW20 **184** B1
Dennis Reeve Cl, Mitch. CR4 **185** J1
Dennis Rd, E.Mol. KT8 **179** J4
Denny Cl, E6 *off Linton Gdns* **116** B5
Denny Cres, SE11 **35** F2
Denny Gdns, Dag. RM9 *off Canonsleigh Rd* **100** B7
Denny Rd, N9 **60** E1
Denny St, SE11 **35** F3
Den Rd, Brom. BR2 **190** D3
Densham Rd, E15 **115** E1
Densole Cl, Beck. BR3 *off Kings Hall Rd* **189** H1
Densworth Gro, N9 **61** F2
Denton Cl, Barn. EN5 **39** J5
Denton Rd, N8 **75** F5
N18 **60** B4
Twickenham TW1 **145** G6
Welling DA16 **138** C7
Denton St, SW18 **149** E6
Denton Way, E5 **95** G3
Dents Rd, SW11 **149** J6
Denver Cl, Orp. BR6 **193** H6
Denver Rd, N16 **76** B7
Denyer St, SW3 **31** H2
Denzil Rd, NW10 **89** F5
Deodara Cl, N20 **57** H3
Deodar Rd, SW15 **148** B4
★**Department for Environment, Food & Rural Affairs (D.E.F.R.A.)**, SW1 **26** A1
★**Department for Transport (D.f.T.)**, SW1 **33** J1
★**Department of Health & Dept for Work & Pensions (D.W.P.)**, SW1 **26** A3
Depot App, NW2 **90** A4
Depot Rd, W12 *off Wood La* **107** J7
Hounslow TW3 **144** A3
DEPTFORD, SE8 **133** J5
Deptford Br, SE8 **154** A1
Deptford Bdy, SE8 **154** A1
Deptford Ch St, SE8 **134** A6
Deptford Ferry Rd, E14 **134** A4
Deptford Grn, SE8 **134** A6
Deptford High St, SE8 **134** A6
Deptford Strand, SE8 **133** J4
Deptford Wf, SE8 **133** J4
De Quincey Ms, E16 *off Wesley Av* **135** G1
De Quincey Rd, N17 **76** A1
Derby Av, N12 **57** F5
Harrow HA3 **68** A1
Romford RM7 **83** J6
Derby Ct, E5 *off Overbury St* **95** G4
Derby Gate, SW1 **26** A3
Derby Hill, SE23 **171** F2
Derby Hill Cres, SE23 **171** F2
Derby Rd, E7 **97** J7
E9 **113** G1
E18 **79** F1
N18 **61** F5
SW14 **146** B4
SW19 *off Russell Rd* **166** D7
Croydon CR0 **201** H2
Enfield EN3 **45** E5
Greenford UB6 **103** H1
Hounslow TW3 **143** H4
Surbiton KT5 **196** A1
Sutton SM1 **198** C6
Derby Rd Ind Est, Houns. TW3 *off Derby Rd* **143** H4
Derbyshire St, E2 **13** J4
Derby St, W1 **24** C2
Dereham Pl, EC2 **12** E4
Dereham Rd, Bark. IG11 **99** J6
Derek Av, Epsom KT19 **196** A5
Wallington SM6 **200** B4
Wembley HA9 **88** B7
Derek Cl, Epsom (Ewell) KT19 **196** B5
Derek Walcott Cl, SE24 *off Shakespeare Rd* **151** H5
Dericote St, E8 **112** D1
Deridene Cl, Stai. (Stanw.) TW19 *off Bedfont Rd* **140** B6
Derifall Cl, E6 **116** C5
Dering Pl, Croy. CR0 **201** J4

Dering Rd, Croy. CR0 . . . . 201 J4
Dering St, W1 . . . . 16 D4
Derinton Rd, SW17 . . . . . 167 J4
Derley Rd, Sthl. UB2 . . . . 122 C3
Dermody Gdns, SE13 . . . . 154 D5
Dermody Rd, SE13 . . . . . . 154 D5
Deronda Rd, SE24 . . . . . . 169 H1
Deroy Cl, Cars. SM5 . . . . . 199 J6
Derrick Gdns, SE7
off Anchor & Hope La . 135 J4
Derrick Rd, Beck. BR3 . . . . 189 J3
Derry Rd, Croy. CR0 . . . . . 200 E3
Derry St, W8 . . . . 22 A4
Dersingham Av, E12 . . . . . . 98 D5
Dersingham Rd, NW2 . . . . 90 B3
Derwent Av, N18 . . . . 60 A5
NW7 . . . . 54 D5
SW15 . . . . 164 E4
Barnet EN4 . . . . 57 J1
Pinner HA5 . . . . 51 E6
Derwent Cl, Esher (Clay.)
KT10 . . . . 194 B6
Derwent Cres, N20 . . . . 57 F3
Bexleyheath DA7 . . . . . 159 G2
Derwent Cres,
Stanmore HA7 . . . . 69 F2
Derwent Dr, NW9 . . . . 70 E5
Orpington BR5 . . . . 193 G7
Derwent Gdns, Ilf. IG4 . . . . 80 B4
Wembley HA9 . . . . 69 F7
Derwent Gro, SE22 . . . . . 152 C4
Derwent Ri, NW9 . . . . 70 E6
Derwent Rd, N13 . . . . 59 F4
SE20 . . . . 188 D2
SW20 . . . . 184 A6
W5 . . . . 125 F3
Southall UB1 . . . . 103 G6
Twickenham TW2 . . . . . 143 H6
Derwent St, SE10 . . . . 134 E5
Derwent Wk, Wall. SM6 . . 200 B7
Derwentwater Rd, W3 . . . 126 C1
Derwent Yd, W5
off Northfield Av 125 F3
Desborough Cl, W2 . . . . . . 14 B1
Desborough St, W2 . . . . . . 14 A1
Desenfans Rd, SE21 . . . . . 152 B6
Desford Ms, E16
off Desford Rd . . . 114/115 E4
Desford Rd, E16 . . . . 115 E4
★**Design Mus**, SE1 . . . . 29 G2
Desmond St, SE14 . . . . . . 133 H6
Desmond Tutu Dr, SE23
off St. Germans Rd . . . 171 H1
Despard Rd, N19 . . . . 92 C1
Detling Rd, Brom. BR1 . . . 173 G5
Detmold Rd, E5 . . . . 95 F2
Devalls Cl, E6 . . . . 116 D7
Devana End, Cars. SM5 . . 199 J3
Devas Rd, SW20 . . . . 183 J1
Devas St, E3 . . . . 114 B4
Devenay Rd, E15 . . . . 97 F7
Devenish Rd, SE2 . . . . 138 A2
Deventer Cres, SE22 . . . . 152 B5
Deveraux Cl, Beck. BR3
off Creswell Dr 190 B5
De Vere Cotts, W8
off Canning Pl 129 F3
De Vere Gdns, W8 . . . . 22 C4
Ilford IG1 . . . . 98 C2
Deverell St, SE1 . . . . 28 B6
De Vere Ms, W8 . . . . 22 C5
Devereux Ct, WC2 . . . . 18 E4
Devereux La, SW13 . . . . . 127 H7
Devereux Rd, SW11 . . . . . 149 J6
Deverill Ct, SE20 . . . . 189 F1
Devey Cl, Kings.T. KT2 . . . 165 E7
Devizes St, N1 off Poole St . 112 A1
Devon Av, Twick. TW2 . . . . 161 J1
Devon Cl, N17 . . . . 76 C3
Buckhurst Hill IG9 . . . . . . 63 H2
Greenford UB6 . . . . 105 F1
Devon Ct, Buck.H. IG9 . . . . 63 H1
Devoncroft Gdns, Twick.
TW1 . . . . 144 D7
Devon Gdns, N4 . . . . 75 H6
Devonhurst Pl, W4
off Heathfield Ter 126 D5
Devonia Gdns, N18 . . . . . . 59 J6
Devonia Rd, N1 . . . . 11 H1
Devonport Gdns, Ilf. IG1 . . 80 C6
Devonport Ms, W12
off Devonport Rd 127 H1
Devonport Rd, W12 . . . . . 127 H2
Devonport St, E1 . . . . 113 F6
Devon Ri, N2 . . . . 73 G4
Devon Rd, Bark. IG11 . . . . 117 H1
Devons Est, E3 . . . . 114 B3
Devonshire Av, Sutt.
SM2 . . . . 199 F7
Devonshire Cl, E15 . . . . 97 E4
N13 . . . . 59 G4
W1 . . . . 16 D1
Devonshire Cres, NW7 . . . . 56 A7
Devonshire Dr, SE10 . . . . 134 B7
Surbiton KT6 . . . . 195 G1
Devonshire Gdns, N17 . . . . 59 J6
N21 . . . . 43 J7
W4 . . . . 126 C7
Devonshire Gro, SE15 . . . . 133 F6
Devonshire Hill La, N17 . . . 59 J6
Devonshire Ho, Sutt. SM2
off Devonshire Av 199 F7
Devonshire Ms, SW10
off Park Wk 129 G6
W4 off Glebe St . . . 126/127 E5
Devonshire Ms N, W1 . . . . 16 D1
Devonshire Ms S, W1 . . . . . 16 D1
Devonshire Ms W, W1 . . . . . 8 D6
Devonshire Pas, W4 . . . . . 126 E5
Devonshire Pl, NW2 . . . . . . 90 D3
W1 . . . . 8 C6
W8 . . . . 22 A6
Devonshire Pl Ms, W1 . . . . . 8 C6
Devonshire Rd, E16 . . . . . 115 H6
E17 . . . . 78 A6
N9 . . . . 61 F1
N13 . . . . 59 F4
N17 . . . . 59 J6
NW7 . . . . 56 A7
SE9 . . . . 174 B2
SE23 . . . . 171 F1
SW19 . . . . 167 H7
W4 . . . . 126 E5
W5 . . . . 125 F3
Bexleyheath DA6 . . . . . 159 E4
Carshalton SM5 . . . . . . 200 A4
Croydon CR0 . . . . 188 A7
Feltham TW13 . . . . 160 E3
Harrow HA1 . . . . 68 A6
Ilford IG2 . . . . 81 G7
Pinner (Eastcote) HA5 . . . 66 C6
Pinner (Hatch End) HA5 . 67 F1
Southall UB1 . . . . 103 G5
Sutton SM2 . . . . 199 F7
Devonshire Row, EC2 . . . . 20 E2
Devonshire Row Ms, W1 . . . 8 E6
Devonshire Sq, EC2 . . . . . . 20 E3
Bromley BR2 . . . . 191 H4
Devonshire St, W1 . . . . 16 C1
W4 . . . . 126 E5
Devonshire Ter, W2 . . . . 14 D4
Devonshire Way, Croy.
CR0 . . . . 203 H2
Hayes UB4 . . . . 102 B6
Devons Rd, E3 . . . . 114 A5
Devon St, SE15 . . . . 132 E6
Devon Way, Chess. KT9 . . 195 F5
Epsom KT19 . . . . 196 B5
Devon Waye, Houns.
TW5 . . . . 123 F7
De Walden St, W1 . . . . 16 C2
Dewar St, SE15 . . . . 152 D3
Dewberry Gdns, E6 . . . . . 116 B6
Dewberry St, E14 . . . . 114 C5
Dewey Rd, N1 . . . . 10 E1
Dagenham RM10 . . . . . . 101 H6
Dewey St, SW17 . . . . 167 J5
Dewhurst Rd, W14 . . . . . . 128 A3
Dewlands Ct, NW4
off Holders Hill Rd 72 A2
Dewsbury Cl, Pnr. HA5 . . . 67 F6
Dewsbury Ct, W4
off Chiswick Rd 126 C4
Dewsbury Gdns, Wor.Pk.
KT4 . . . . 197 G3
Dewsbury Rd, NW10 . . . . . 89 G5
Dewsbury Ter, NW1
off Camden High St . . . 110 B1
Dexter Ho, Erith DA18
off Kale Rd 138/139 E3
Dexter Rd, Barn. EN5 . . . . . 40 A6
Deyncourt Rd, N17 . . . . 75 J1
Deynecourt Gdns, E11 . . . . 79 J4
D'Eynsford Rd, SE5 . . . . . 152 A1
Diadem Ct, W1 . . . . 17 H4
Dial Wk, The, W8 . . . . 22 B3
Diamedes Av, Stai. (Stanw.)
TW19 . . . . 140 A7
Diameter Rd, Orp. BR5 . . 193 E7
Diamond Cl, Dag. RM8 . . 100 C1
Diamond Rd, Ruis. HA4 . . . 84 D4
Diamond St, NW10 . . . . . . 88 D7
SE15 . . . . 132 B7
Diamond Ter, SE10 . . . . . . 154 C1
Diamond Way, SE8
off Deptford High St . . 134 A7
Diana Cl, E18 . . . . 79 H1
SE8 off Staunton St . . . 133 J6
Diana Gdns, Surb. KT6 . . 195 J2
Diana Ho, SW13 . . . . 147 F1
★**Diana Princess of Wales Mem**, W2 . . . . 23 F2
Diana Rd, E17 . . . . 77 J3
Dianne Way, Barn. EN4 . . . 41 H5
Dianthus Cl, SE2
off Carnation St 138 B5
Dibden Row, SE1
off Gerridge St 131 G3
Dibden St, N1 . . . . 111 H1
Dibdin Cl, Sutt. SM1 . . . . 198 D3
Dibdin Rd, Sutt. SM1 . . . . 198 D3
Dicey Av, NW2 . . . . 89 J5
Dickens Av, N3 . . . . 73 F1
Dickens Cl, Erith DA8 . . . . 139 H7
Hayes UB3
off Croyde Av 121 H4
Richmond TW10 . . . . . . 163 H2
Dickens Dr, Chis. BR7 . . . . 175 F6
Dickens Est, SE1 . . . . 29 H4
SE16 . . . . 29 H4
Dickens Ho, NW6 . . . . 108 D3
★**Dickens Ho Mus**, WC1 . . . 10 D6
Dickens La, N18 . . . . 60 B5
Dickenson Cl, N9
off Croyland Rd 60 D1
Dickenson Rd, N8 . . . . 75 E7
Feltham TW13 . . . . 160 C5
Dickensons La, SE25 . . . . 188 D5
Dickensons Pl, SE25 . . . . . 188 D6
Dickenson St, NW5
off Dalby St 92 B6
Dickens Ri, Chig. IG7 . . . . . 64 D3
Dickens Rd, E6 . . . . 116 A2
Dickens Sq, SE1 . . . . 28 A5
Dickens St, SW8 . . . . 150 B2
Dickenswood Cl, SE19 . . . 169 H7
Dickerage La, N.Mal.
KT3 . . . . 182 C3
Dickerage Rd, Kings.T.
KT1 . . . . 182 C1
New Malden KT3 . . . . . 182 C1
Dickinson Ct, EC1
off St. John St 111 H4
Dickson Fold, Pnr. HA5 . . . 66 D4
Dickson Rd, SE9 . . . . 156 B3
Dick Turpin Way, Felt.
TW14 . . . . 141 J4
Didsbury Cl, E6
off Barking Rd 116 C1
Dieppe Cl, W14
off Gibbs Grn 128 C5
Digby Cres, N4 . . . . 93 J2
Digby Gdns, Dag. RM10 . . 119 G1
Digby Pl, Croy. CR0 . . . . . 202 C3
Digby Rd, E9 . . . . 95 G6
Barking IG11 . . . . 99 J7
Digby St, E2 . . . . 113 F3
Diggon St, E1
off Stepney Way 113 G5
Dighton Ct, SE5 . . . . 35 J6
Dighton Rd, SW18 . . . . . . 149 F5
Dignum St, N1 . . . . 11 E1
Digswell St, N7
off Holloway Rd 93 G6
Dilhorne Cl, SE12 . . . . 173 H3
Dilke St, SW3 . . . . 32 A5
Dilloway Yd, Sthl. UB2
off The Green 122/123 E2
Dillwyn Cl, SE26 . . . . 171 H4
Dilston Cl, Nthlt. UB5
off Yeading La 102 C3
Dilston Gro, SE16
off Abbeyfield Rd 133 F4
Dilton Gdns, SW15 . . . . . . 165 G1
Dilwyn Ct, E17
off Hillyfield 77 H3
Dimes Pl, W6
off King St 127 H4
Dimmock Dr, Grnf. UB6 . . . 86 A5
Dimond Cl, E7 . . . . 97 G4
Dimsdale Dr, NW9 . . . . 88 C1
Enfield EN1 . . . . 44 D6
Dimsdale Wk, E13
off Stratford Rd 115 G1
Dimson Cres, E3 . . . . 114 A4
Dingle Cl, Barn. EN5 . . . . . . 39 F6
Dingle Gdns, E14 . . . . 114 A7
Dingley La, SW16 . . . . 168 D2
Dingley Pl, EC1 . . . . 12 A4
Dingley Rd, EC1 . . . . 11 J4
Dingwall Av, Croy. CR0 . . . 201 J2
Dingwall Gdns, NW11 . . . . 72 D6
Dingwall Rd, SW18 . . . . . . 149 F7
Croydon CR0 . . . . 202 A2
Dinmont St, E2
off Coate St 112/113 E2
Dinsdale Gdns, SE25 . . . . 188 B5
Dinsdale Gdns, Barn. EN5 . 41 E5
Dinsdale Rd, SE3 . . . . 135 F6
Dinsmore Rd, SW12 . . . . . 150 B7
Dinton Rd, SW19 . . . . 167 G6
Kingston upon Thames
KT2 . . . . 163 J7
Diploma Av, N2 . . . . 73 H4
Diploma Ct, N2
off Diploma Av 73 H4
Dirleton Rd, E15 . . . . 115 F1
Disbrowe Rd, W6 . . . . 128 D6
Discovery Business Pk, SE16
off St. James's Rd 132 D3
Discovery Wk, E1 . . . . 132 E1
Dishforth La, NW9 . . . . 70 E1
Disney Ms, N4
off Chesterfield Gdns . . 75 H5
Disney Pl, SE1 . . . . 28 A3
Disney St, SE1 . . . . 28 A3
Dison Cl, Enf. EN3 . . . . 45 G1
Disraeli Cl, SE28 . . . . 138 C1
W4 off Acton La 126 D4
Disraeli Gdns, SW15
off Fawe Pk Rd 148 C4
Disraeli Rd, E7 . . . . 97 G6
NW10 . . . . 106 C2
SW15 . . . . 148 B4
W5 . . . . 125 G1
Diss St, E2 . . . . 13 F3
Distaff La, EC4 . . . . 19 J5
Distillery La, W6
off Fulham Palace Rd . 127 J5
Distillery Rd, W6 . . . . 127 J5
Distillery Wk, Brent. TW8 . 125 H6
Distin St, SE11 . . . . 34 E2
District Rd, Wem. HA0 . . . . 86 E5
Ditch All, SE10 . . . . 154 B1
Ditchburn St, E14 . . . . 114 C7
Ditchfield Rd, Hayes UB4 . 102 E4
Dittisham Rd, SE9 . . . . . . 174 B4
Ditton Cl, T.Ditt. KT7 . . . . . 180 D7
Dittoncroft Cl, Croy. CR0 . 202 B4
Ditton Gra Cl, Surb. KT6 . 195 G1
Ditton Gra Dr, Surb. KT6 . 195 G1
Ditton Hill, Surb. KT6 . . . . 195 F1
Ditton Hill Rd, Surb. KT6 . 195 F1
Ditton Lawn, T.Ditt. KT7 . . 194 D1
Ditton Pl, SE20 . . . . 189 E1
Ditton Reach, T.Ditt. KT7 . . 180 E6
Ditton Rd, Bexh. DA6 . . . . 158 D5
Southall UB2 . . . . 123 F4
Surbiton KT6 . . . . 195 H1
Divis Way, SW15 . . . . 147 H6
Dixon Clark Ct, N1
off Canonbury Rd 93 H6
Dixon Cl, E6
off Brandreth Rd 116 C6
Dixon Ho, W10 . . . . 108 A6
Dixon Pl, W.Wick. BR4 . . . 204 B1
Dixon Rd, SE14 . . . . 153 H1
SE25 . . . . 188 B3
Dixon's All, SE16 . . . . 132 E2
Dobbin Cl, Har. HA3 . . . . . . 68 D2
Dobell Path, SE9
off Dobell Rd 156 C5
Dobell Rd, SE9 . . . . 156 C5
Dobree Av, NW10 . . . . 89 H7
Dobson Cl, NW6 . . . . 91 G7
Doby Ct, EC4 . . . . 20 A5
Dockers Tanner Rd, E14 . . 134 A3
Dockhead, SE1 . . . . 29 G4
Dock Hill Av, SE16 . . . . . . 133 G2
Dockland St, E16 . . . . 136 D1
Dockley Rd, SE16 . . . . 29 H6
Dock Rd, E16 . . . . 115 F7
Brentford TW8 . . . . 125 G7
Dockside Rd, E16 . . . . 116 A7
Dock St, E1 . . . . 21 H5
Dockwell Cl, Felt. TW14 . . 142 A4
Dockyard Ind Est, SE18
off Woolwich Ch St . . . 136 B3
Doctor Johnson Av,
SW17 . . . . 168 B3
★**Doctor Johnson's Ho**,
EC4 . . . . 19 F4
Doctors Cl, SE26 . . . . 171 F5
Docwra's Bldgs, N1 . . . . . . 94 B6
Dodbrooke Rd, SE27 . . . . 169 G3
Doddington Gro, SE17 . . . . 35 G5
Doddington Pl, SE17 . . . . . 35 G5
Dodsley Pl, N9 . . . . 61 E3
Dodson St, SE1 . . . . 27 F4
Dod St, E14 . . . . 113 J6
Doebury Wk, SE18
off Prestwood Cl 138 A6
Doel Cl, SW19 . . . . 167 F7
Doggets Ct, Barn. EN4 . . . . 41 H5
Doggett Rd, SE6 . . . . 154 A7
Doghurst Av, Hayes UB3 . 121 E7

Doghurst Dr, West Dr. UB7 **121** E7
Dog Kennel Hill, SE22 **152** B3
Dog Kennel Hill Est, SE22 **152** B3
Dog La, NW10 **89** E4
Doherty Rd, E13 **115** G4
Dokal Ind Est, Sthl. UB2 *off Hartington Rd* **122/123** E3
Dolben St, SE1 **27** G2
Dolby Rd, SW6 **148** C2
Dolland St, SE11 **34** D4
Dollis Av, N3 **72** C1
Dollis Brook Wk, Barn. EN5 **40** B6
Dollis Cres, Ruis. HA4 **84** C1
DOLLIS HILL, NW2 **89** H3
Dollis Hill Av, NW2 **89** H3
Dollis Hill La, NW2 **89** H3
Dollis Ms, N3 *off Dollis Pk* **72** C1
Dollis Pk, N3 **72** C1
Dollis Rd, N3 **56** B7
NW7 **56** B7
Dollis Valley Dr, Barn. EN5 **40** C6
Dollis Valley Grn Wk, N20 *off Totteridge La* **57** F2
Barnet EN5 **40** B6
Dollis Valley Way, Barn. EN5 **40** C6
Dolman Cl, N3 *off Avondale Rd* **73** F2
Dolman Rd, W4 **126** D4
Dolman St, SW4 **151** F4
Dolphin Cl, SE16 *off Kinburn St* **133** G2
SE28 **118** D6
Surbiton KT6 **181** G6
Dolphin Ct, NW11 **72** B6
Dolphin Ho, SW18 *off Smugglers Way* **148/149** E4
Dolphin La, E14 **114** B7
Dolphin Rd, Nthlt. UB5 **103** F2
Dolphin Sq, SW1 **33** G4
W4 **126** E7
Dolphin St, Kings.T. KT1 **181** H1
Dolphin Twr, SE8 *off Abinger Gro* **133** J6
Dombey St, WC1 **18** C1
★**Dome, The**, SE10 **134** E1
Dome Hill Pk, SE26 **170** C4
Domett Cl, SE5 **152** A4
Domfe Pl, E5 *off Rushmore Rd* **95** F4
Domingo St, EC1 **11** J5
Dominica Cl, E13 **115** J2
Dominion Rd, Croy. CR0 **188** C7
Southall UB2 **123** E3
Dominion St, EC2 **20** C1
★**Dominion Thea**, W1 **17** J3
Domonic Dr, SE9 **174** E4
Domville Cl, N20 **57** G2
Donald Dr, Rom. RM6 **82** C5
Donald Rd, E13 **115** H1
Croydon CR0 **187** F6
Donaldson Rd, NW6 **108** C1
SE18 **156** D1
Donald Wds Gdns, Surb. KT5 **196** B2
Donato Dr, SE15 *off Wells Way* **132** B7
Doncaster Dr, Nthlt. UB5 **85** F5
Doncaster Gdns, N4 *off Stanhope Gdns* **75** J6
Northolt UB5 **85** F5
Doncaster Grn, Wat. WD19 **50** C5
Doncaster Rd, N9 **44** E7
Doncel Ct, E4 **46** D7
Donegal St, N1 **10** D2
Doneraile St, SW6 **148** A2
Dongola Rd, E1 **113** H5
E13 **115** H3
N17 **76** B3
Dongola Rd W, E13 *off Balaam St* **115** H3
Donington Av, Ilf. IG6 **81** F5
Donkey All, SE22 **152** D7
Donkey La, Enf. EN1 **44** D2
Donne Ct, SE24 **151** J6
Donnefield Av, Edg. HA8 **53** H7
Donne Pl, SW3 **31** H1
Mitcham CR4 **186** B4
Donne Rd, Dag. RM8 **100** C2
Donnington Rd, NW10 **89** H7
Harrow HA3 **69** G5
Worcester Park KT4 **197** G2
Donnybrook Rd, SW16 **168** C7
Donovan Av, N10 **74** B2
Don Phelan Cl, SE5 **152** A1
Doone Cl, Tedd. TW11 **162** D6
Doon St, SE1 **26** E2
Doral Way, Cars. SM5 **199** J5
Dorando Cl, W12 **107** H7
Doran Gro, SE18 **137** H7
Doran Wk, E15 **96** C7
Dora Rd, SW19 **166** D5
Dora St, E14 **113** J6
Dorchester Av, N13 **59** J4
Bexley DA5 **176** D1
Harrow HA2 **67** J6
Dorchester Cl, Nthlt. UB5 **85** H5
Orpington BR5 *off Grovelands Rd* **176** A7
Dorchester Ct, N14 **42** B7
SE24 **151** J5
Dorchester Dr, SE24 **151** J5
Feltham TW14 **141** H6
Dorchester Gdns, E4 **62** A4
NW11 **72** D4
Dorchester Gro, W4 **127** E5
Dorchester Ms, N.Mal. KT3 *off Elm Rd* **182** D4
Twickenham TW1 **145** F7
Dorchester Rd, Mord. SM4 **185** E7
Northolt UB5 **85** H5
Worcester Park KT4 **197** J1
Dorchester Way, Har. HA3 **69** J6
Dorchester Waye, Hayes UB4 **102** C6
Dorcis Av, Bexh. DA7 **158** E2
Dordrecht Rd, W3 **127** E1
Dore Av, E12 **98** D5
Doreen Av, NW9 **88** D1
Dore Gdns, Mord. SM4 **185** E7
Dorell Cl, Sthl. UB1 **103** F5
Doria Rd, SW6 **148** C2
Doric Way, NW1 **9** H3
Dorien Rd, SW20 **184** A2
Doris Av, Erith DA8 **159** J1
Doris Rd, E7 **97** G7
Dorking Cl, SE8 **133** J6
Worcester Park KT4 **198** A2
Dorlcote Rd, SW18 **149** G7
Dorman Pl, N9 *off Balham Rd* **60** D2
Dorman Wk, NW10 *off Garden Way* **88** D5
Dorman Way, NW8 **109** G1
Dorma Trd Pk, E10 **95** G1
Dormay St, SW18 **148** E5
Dormer Cl, E15 **97** F6
Barnet EN5 **40** A5
Dormers Av, Sthl. UB1 **103** G6
Dormers Ri, Sthl. UB1 **103** H6
DORMER'S WELLS, Sthl. UB1 **103** H7
Dormers Wells La, Sthl. UB1 **103** G6
Dornberg Cl, SE3 **135** G7
Dornberg Rd, SE3 *off Banchory Rd* **135** H7
Dorncliffe Rd, SW6 **148** B2
Dorney, NW3 **91** H7
Dorney Ri, Orp. BR5 **193** J4
Dorney Way, Houns. TW4 **143** E5
Dornfell St, NW6 **90** C5
Dornton Rd, SW12 **168** B2
South Croydon CR2 **202** A5
Dorothy Av, Wem. HA0 **87** H7
Dorothy Evans Cl, Bexh. DA7 **159** H4
Dorothy Gdns, Dag. RM8 **100** B4
Dorothy Rd, SW11 **149** J3
Dorrell Pl, SW9 *off Brixton Rd* **151** G4
Dorrien Wk, SW16 **168** D2
Dorrington Ct, SE25 **188** B2
Dorrington Pt, E3 *off Bromley High St* **114** B3
Dorrington St, EC1 **19** E1
Dorrington Way, Beck. BR3 *off Creswell Dr* **190** B5
Dorrit Ms, N18 **60** B4
Dorrit St, SE1 **28** A3
Dorrit Way, Chis. BR7 **175** F6
Dors Cl, NW9 **88** D1
Dorset Av, Sthl. UB2 **123** G4
Welling DA16 **157** J4
Dorset Bldgs, EC4 **19** G4
Dorset Cl, NW1 **15** J1
Dorset Dr, Edg. HA8 **53** J6
Dorset Est, E2 **13** G3
Dorset Gdns, Mitch. CR4 **187** F4
Dorset Ms, N3 **72** D1
Dorset Ms, SW1 **24** D5
Dorset Pl, E15 **96** D6
Dorset Ri, EC4 **19** G4
Dorset Rd, E7 **97** J7
N15 **76** A4
N22 **75** E1
SE9 **174** B2
SW8 **34** B7
SW19 **184** D1
W5 **125** F3
Beckenham BR3 **189** G3
Harrow HA1 **67** J6
Mitcham CR4 **185** H2
Dorset Sq, NW1 **7** J6
Dorset St, W1 **16** A2
Dorset Way, Twick. TW2 **162** A1
Dorset Waye, Houns. TW5 **123** F7
Dorton Cl, SE15 *off Chandler Way* **132** C7
Dorville Cres, W6 **127** H3
Dorville Rd, SE12 **155** F5
Dothill Rd, SE18 **137** G7
Douai Gro, Hmptn. TW12 **179** J1
Doubleday Rd, Loug. IG10 **49** F3
Doughty Ms, WC1 **10** C6
Doughty St, WC1 **10** C5
Douglas Av, E17 **78** A1
New Malden KT3 **183** H4
Wembley HA0 **87** H7
Douglas Cl, Stan. HA7 **52** D5
Wallington SM6 **201** E7
Douglas Cres, Hayes UB4 **102** C4
Douglas Dr, Croy. CR0 **204** A3
Douglas Ms, NW2 **90** B3
Douglas Path, E14 *off Manchester Rd* **134** C5
Douglas Rd, E4 **47** E7
E16 **115** G5
N1 **93** J7
N22 **75** G1
NW6 **108** C1
Hounslow TW3 **143** H3
Ilford IG3 **82** A6
Kingston upon Thames KT1 **182** B2
Staines (Stanw.) TW19 **140** A6
Surbiton KT6 **195** J2
Welling DA16 **158** B1
Douglas Sq, Mord. SM4 **184** D6
Douglas St, SW1 **33** H2
Douglas Ter, E17 *off Douglas Av* **78** A1
Douglas Way, SE8 **133** J7
Doulton Ms, NW6 *off Lymington Rd* **90/91** E6
Dounesforth Gdns, SW18 **166** E1
Douro Pl, W8 **22** B5
Douro St, E3 **114** A2
Douthwaite Sq, E1 **29** J1
Dove App, E6 **116** B5
Dove Cl, NW7 *off Bunns La* **55** F7
Northolt UB5 *off Wayfarer Rd* **102** D4
Wallington SM6 **201** F7
Dovecot Cl, Pnr. HA5 **66** B5
Dovecote Av, N22 **75** G3
Dovecote Gdns, SW14 *off Avondale Rd* **146** D3
Dove Ct, EC2 **20** B4
Dovedale Av, Har. HA3 **69** F6
Ilford IG5 **80** D2
Dovedale Cl, Well. DA16 **158** A2
Dovedale Ri, Mitch. CR4 **167** J7
Dovedale Rd, SE22 **153** E5
Dovedon Cl, N14 **58** E2
Dove Ho Gdns, E4 **62** A2
Dovehouse Mead, Bark. IG11 **117** G2
Dovehouse St, SW3 **31** G3
Dove Ms, SW5 **30** C2
Dove Pk, Pnr. HA5 **51** G7
Dover Cl, NW2 *off Brent Ter* **90** A2
Romford RM5 **83** J2
Dovercourt Av, Th.Hth. CR7 **187** G4
Dovercourt Est, N1 **94** A6
Dovercourt Gdns, Stan. HA7 **53** H5
Dovercourt La, Sutt. SM1 **199** F3
Dovercourt Rd, SE22 **152** B6
Doverfield Rd, SW2 **151** E6
Dover Flats, SE1 *off Old Kent Rd* **132** B4
Dover Gdns, Cars. SM5 **199** J3
Dover Ho Rd, SW15 **147** G4
Doveridge Gdns, N13 **59** H4
Dove Rd, N1 **94** A6
Dove Row, E2 **112** D1
Dover Pk Dr, SW15 **147** H6
Dover Patrol, SE3 *off Kidbrooke Way* **155** H2
Dover Rd, E12 **97** J2
N9 **61** F2
SE19 **170** A6
Romford RM6 **82** E6
Dover St, W1 **17** E6
Dover Yd, W1 **25** F1
Doves Cl, Brom. BR2 **206** B2
Doves Yd, N1 **111** G1
Doveton Rd, S.Croy. CR2 **202** A5
Doveton St, E1 *off Malcolm Rd* **113** F4
Dove Wk, SW1 **32** B3
Dowanhill Rd, SE6 **172** D1
Dowdeswell Cl, SW15 **147** E4
Dowding Pl, Stan. HA7 **52** D6
Dowdney Cl, NW5 **92** C5
Dowgate Hill, EC4 **20** B5
Dowland St, W10 **108** B2
Dowlas Est, SE5 **36** D7
Dowlas St, SE5 **36** D7
Dowlerville Rd, Orp. BR6 **207** J6
Dowman Cl, SW19 *off Nelson Gro Rd* **184/185** E1
Downage, NW4 **71** J3
Downalong, Bushey (Bushey Hth) WD23 **52** A1
Downbarns Rd, Ruis. HA4 **84** D3
Downbury Ms, SW18 *off Merton Rd* **148** D6
Down Cl, Nthlt. UB5 **102** B2
Downderry Rd, Brom. BR1 **172** D3
Downe Cl, Well. DA16 **138** C7
Downend, SE18 *off Moordown* **136/137** E7
Downe Rd, Mitch. CR4 **185** J2
Downers Cotts, SW4 *off The Pavement* **150** C4
Downes Cl, Twick. TW1 *off St. Margarets Rd* **144/145** E6
Downes Ct, N21 **59** G1
Downfield, Wor.Pk. KT4 **197** F1
Downfield Cl, W9 **6** A6
Down Hall Rd, Kings.T. KT2 **181** G1
DOWNHAM, Brom. BR1 **173** F5
Downham La, Brom. BR1 *off Downham Way* **172** D5
Downham Rd, N1 **94** A7
Downham Way, Brom. BR1 **172** D5
Downhills Av, N17 **76** A3
Downhills Pk Rd, N17 **75** J3
Downhills Way, N17 **75** J3
Downhurst Av, NW7 **54** D5
Downing Cl, Har. HA2 **67** J3
Downing Dr, Grnf. UB6 **104** A1
Downing Rd, Dag. RM9 **119** F1
Downings, E6 **116** D6
Downing St, SW1 **26** A3
Downland Cl, N20 **57** F1
Downleys Cl, SE9 **174** B2
Downman Rd, SE9 **156** B3
Down Pl, W6 **127** H4
Down Rd, Tedd. TW11 **163** E6
Downs, The, SW20 **166** A7
Downs Av, Chis. BR7 **174** C5
Pinner HA5 **67** F6
Downs Br Rd, Beck. BR3 **190** D1
Downsbury Ms, SW18 *off Merton Rd* **148** D5
Downsell Rd, E15 **96** C4
Downsfield Rd, E17 **77** H6
Downshall Av, Ilf. IG3 **81** H6
Downs Hill, Beck. BR3 **172** D7
Downshire Hill, NW3 **91** G4
Downside, Sun. TW16 **178** A1
Twickenham TW1 **162** C3
Downside Cl, SW19 **167** F6
Downside Cres, NW3 **91** H5
W13 **104** D4
Downside Rd, Sutt. SM2 **199** G6
Downside Wk, Nthlt. UB5 **103** F3
Downs La, E5 *off Downs Rd* **94/95** E4
Downs Pk Rd, E5 **94** D5
E8 **94** C5
Downs Rd, E5 **94** D4
Beckenham BR3 **190** B2
Enfield EN1 **44** B4
Thornton Heath CR7 **187** J1

Down St, W1 . . . . **24** D2
West Molesey KT8 . . . . **179** G5
Down St Ms, W1 . . . . **24** D2
Downs Vw, Islw. TW7. . . . **124** C7
Downsview Gdns, SE19. . **169** H7
Downsview Rd, SE19. . . . **169** J7
Downsway, Orp. BR6. . . . **207** H5
Downton Av, SW2 . . . . . . **169** E2
Downtown Rd, SE16 . . . . **133** H2
Down Way, Nthlt. UB5 . . . **102** B3
Dowrey St, N1
off Richmond Av **111** G1
Dowsett Rd, N17 . . . . **76** C2
Dowson Cl, SE5 . . . . **152** A4
Doyce St, SE1 . . . . **27** J3
Doyle Gdns, NW10 . . . . . . **107** G1
Doyle Rd, SE25. . . . . **188** D4
D'Oyley St, SW1 . . . . **32** B1
Doynton St, N19 . . . . **92** B2
Draco St, SE17 . . . . **35** J5
Dragonfly Cl, E13
off Hollybush St **115** H3
Dragon Rd, SE15 . . . . **36** D6
Dragoon Rd, SE8 . . . . **133** J5
Dragor Rd, NW10 . . . . **106** C4
Drake Cl, SE16
off Middleton Dr **133** G2
Drake Ct, SE19 . . . . **170** C5
W12. . . . . **127** J2
Harrow HA2 . . . . **85** F1
Drake Cres, SE28 . . . . **118** C6
Drakefell Rd, SE4 . . . . **153** G2
SE14 . . . . **153** G2
Drakefield Rd, SW17 . . . . **168** A3
Drakeley Ct, N5
off Highbury Hill **93** H4
Drake Rd, SE4 . . . . **154** A3
Chessington KT9. . . . . . **196** A5
Croydon CR0. . . . . **187** F7
Harrow HA2 . . . . **85** F2
Mitcham CR4. . . . . **186** A6
Drakes Ctyd, NW6 . . . . **90** C7
Drake St, WC1 . . . . **18** C2
Enfield EN2 . . . . **44** A1
Drakes Wk, E6. . . . . **116** C1
Drakewood Rd, SW16 . . . **168** D7
Draper Cl, Belv. DA17. . . . **139** F4
Isleworth TW7 . . . . **144** A2
Draper Ho, SE1
off Newington Butts . . **131** H4
Draper Pl, N1
off Dagmar Ter. **111** H1
Drapers Gdns, EC2
off Copthall Av. **112** A6
Drapers Rd, E15 . . . . **96** D4
N17 . . . . **76** C3
Enfield EN2 . . . . **43** H2
Drappers Way, SE16. . . . . . **37** J1
Draven Cl, Brom. BR2 . . . **191** F7
Drawdock Rd, SE10 . . . . . **134** D1
Drawell Cl, SE18. . . . . **137** H5
Drax Av, SW20 . . . . **165** H7
Draxmont, SW19 . . . . **166** B6
Draycot Rd, E11 . . . . **79** H6
Surbiton KT6. . . . . **196** A1
Draycott Av, SW3. . . . . **31** H1
Harrow HA3 . . . . **69** E6
Draycott Cl, NW2. . . . . **90** A3
SE5 *off Edmund St*. . . . **132** A7
Harrow HA3 . . . . **69** E6
Draycott Ms, SW6
off New Kings Rd **148** C2
Draycott Pl, SW3 . . . . **31** J2
Draycott Ter, SW3 . . . . **32** A1
Drayford Cl, W9 . . . . **108** C4
Dray Gdns, SW2. . . . . **151** F5
Draymans Ms, SE15
off Chadwick Rd **152** C2
Draymans Way, Islw. TW7 . **144** C3
Drayside Ms, Sthl. UB2
off Kingston Rd. **123** F2
Drayson Ms, W8. . . . . **128** D2
Drayton Av, W13. . . . . **104** D7
Loughton IG10 . . . . **48** C6
Orpington BR6 . . . . **207** E1
Drayton Br Rd, W7 . . . . . . **104** C7
W13 . . . . **104** C7
Drayton Cl, Houns. TW4. . **143** F5
Ilford IG1 . . . . **99** G1
Drayton Gdns, N21 . . . . . . **43** H7
SW10. . . . . **30** D3
W13 . . . . **104** D7
West Drayton UB7 . . . . **120** B2
Drayton Grn, W13. . . . . . . **104** D7
Drayton Grn Rd, W13 . . . . **104** E7
Drayton Gro, W13. . . . . . . **104** D7
Drayton Pk, N5. . . . . **93** G5
Drayton Pk Ms, N5
off Drayton Pk. **93** G5
Drayton Rd, E11 . . . . **96** D1
N17 . . . . **76** B2
NW10. . . . . **107** F1
W13 . . . . **104** D7
Borehamwood WD6 . . . . **38** A4
Croydon CR0. . . . . **201** H2
Drayton Waye, Har. HA3. . . **69** E6
Dresden Cl, NW6 . . . . **91** E6
Dresden Rd, N19 . . . . **92** D1
Dressington Av, SE4 . . . . **154** A6
Drew Av, NW7 . . . . **56** B6
Drew Gdns, Grnf. UB6. . . . **86** C6
Drew Rd, E16 . . . . **136** B1
Drewstead Rd, SW16. . . . . **168** D2
Driffield Rd, E3 . . . . **113** H2
Drift, The, Brom. BR2 . . . . **206** A3
Drift Way, Rich. TW10 . . . . **163** J1
Driftway, The, Mitch. CR4. **186** A1
Drinkwater Rd, Har. HA2 . . **85** H2
Drive, The, E4 . . . . **46** D7
E17 . . . . **78** B4
E18 . . . . **79** G4
N3 . . . . **56** D7
N6 . . . . **73** J5
N11 . . . . **58** C6
NW10 *off Longstone Av*. . **107** F1
NW11. . . . . **72** B7
SW6 *off Fulham Rd*. . . . **148** B2
SW16. . . . . **187** F3
SW20. . . . . **165** J7
W3. . . . . **106** C6
Barking IG11 . . . . **99** J7
Barnet (High Barn.) EN5 . **40** B3
Barnet (New Barn.) EN5 . **41** F6
Beckenham BR3 . . . . . . **190** A2
Bexley DA5 . . . . **158** C6
Buckhurst Hill IG9 . . . . . . **47** J7
Chislehurst BR7 . . . . . . **193** J3
Chislehurst (Scad.Pk)
BR7 . . . . **193** H1
Edgware HA8 . . . . **54** A5
Enfield EN2 . . . . **44** A1
Epsom KT19 . . . . **197** F6
Erith DA8. . . . . **139** H7
Feltham TW14 . . . . **142** C7
Harrow HA2 . . . . **67** G7
Hounslow TW3 . . . . **144** A3
Ilford IG1 . . . . **98** C1
Isleworth TW7 . . . . **144** A2
Kingston upon Thames
KT2 . . . . **161** G7
Loughton IG10 . . . . **48** B3
Morden SM4. . . . . **185** G5
Orpington BR6 . . . . **207** J2
Romford (Coll.Row)
RM5. . . . . **83** J1
Sidcup DA14 . . . . **176** B3
Surbiton KT6. . . . . **181** H7
Thornton Heath CR7 . . . **188** A4
Wembley HA9. . . . . **88** C2
West Wickham BR4. . . . . **190** D7
Driveway, The, E17
off Hoe St **78** B6
Droitwich Cl, SE26 . . . . . . **170** D3
Dromey Gdns, Har. HA3 . . **68** C7
Dromore Rd, SW15 . . . . . . **148** B6
Dronfield Gdns, Dag.
RM8. . . . . **100** C5
Droop St, W10 . . . . **108** B4
Drovers Pl, SE15. . . . . **133** E7
Drovers Rd, S.Croy. CR2 . **202** A5
Droveway, Loug. IG10 . . . . **49** E2
Druce Rd, SE21 . . . . **152** B6
Druid St, SE1 . . . . **28** E3
Druids Way, Brom. BR2 . . **190** D4
Drumaline Ridge, Wor.Pk.
KT4 . . . . **197** E2
Drummond Cen, Croy.
CR0 . . . . **201** J2
Drummond Cres, NW1 . . . . **9** H3
Drummond Dr, Stan. HA7 . **52** C7
Drummond Gate, SW1 . . . **33** J3
Drummond Pl, Twick.
TW1. . . . . **144** E6
Drummond Rd, E11 . . . . . . **79** H6
SE16 . . . . **132** E3
Croydon CR0. . . . . **201** J2
Drummonds, The, Buck.H.
IG9. . . . . **63** H2
Drummonds Pl, Rich.
TW9. . . . . **145** H4
Drummond St, NW1 . . . . . . **9** F5
Drum St, E1 . . . . **21** G3
Drury Cres, Croy. CR0 . . . **201** G2
Drury La, WC2 . . . . **18** B4
Drury Rd, Har. HA1 . . . . **67** J7
Drury Way, NW10. . . . . **88** D5
Drury Way Ind Est, NW10. . **88** C5
Dryad St, SW15 . . . . **148** A3
Dryburgh Gdns, NW9 . . . . **70** A3
Dryburgh Rd, SW15. . . . . **147** H3
Dryden Av, W7 . . . . **104** C6
Dryden Cl, Ilf. IG6. . . . . **65** J6
Dryden Ct, SE11 . . . . **35** F2
Dryden Rd, SW19. . . . . . . **167** F6
Enfield EN1 . . . . **44** B6
Harrow HA3 . . . . **68** C1
Welling DA16 . . . . **157** H1
Dryden St, WC2 . . . . **18** B4
Dryfield Cl, NW10 . . . . **88** C6
Dryfield Rd, Edg. HA8 . . . . **54** C6
Dryfield Wk, SE8
off New King St **134** A6
Dryhill Rd, Belv. DA17 . . . **139** F6
Dryland Av, Orp. BR6. . . . **207** J4
Drylands Rd, N8. . . . . **75** E6
Drysdale Av, E4 . . . . **46** B7
Drysdale Pl, N1 . . . . **12** E3
Drysdale St, N1 . . . . **12** E4
Dublin Av, E8 . . . . **112** D1
Du Burstow Ter, W7 . . . . . **124** B2
Ducal St, E2 . . . . **13** G4
Du Cane Cl, W12. . . . . **107** J6
Du Cane Ct, SW17 . . . . . . **168** A1
Du Cane Rd, W12 . . . . **107** F6
Duchess Cl, N11 . . . . **58** B5
Sutton SM1 . . . . **199** F4
Duchess Gro, Buck.H. IG9 . **63** H2
Duchess Ms, W1. . . . . **16** E2
Duchess of Bedford's Wk,
W8. . . . . **128** D2
Duchess St, W1 . . . . **16** E2
Duchy St, SE1 . . . . **27** F1
Ducie St, SW4 . . . . **151** F4
Duckett Ms, N4
off Duckett Rd **75** H6
Duckett Rd, N4. . . . . **75** H6
Duckett St, E1. . . . . **113** G4
Duck La, W1 . . . . **17** H4
Duck Lees La, Enf. EN3 . . . **45** H4
DUCKS ISLAND, Barn.
EN5 . . . . **40** A6
Ducks Wk, Twick. TW1. . . . **145** F5
Du Cros Dr, Stan. HA7 . . . . **53** G6
Du Cros Rd, W3
off The Vale. **126/127** E1
Dudden Hill La, NW10 . . . . **89** F4
Duddington Cl, SE9 . . . . . **174** A4
Dudley Av, Har. HA3. . . . . . **69** F3
Dudley Ct, NW11 . . . . **72** C4
Dudley Dr, Mord. SM4. . . **184** B7
Ruislip HA4 . . . . **84** B5
Dudley Gdns, W13 . . . . . . **125** E2
Harrow HA2 . . . . **86** A1
Dudley Ms, SW2
off Bascombe St **151** G6
Dudley Pl, Hayes UB3 . . . **121** G4
Dudley Rd, E17. . . . . **78** A2
N3 . . . . **72** E2
NW6 . . . . **108** B2
SW19. . . . . **166** D6
Harrow HA2 . . . . **85** J2
Ilford IG1 . . . . **99** E4
Kingston upon Thames
KT1 . . . . **181** J3
Richmond TW9 . . . . **145** J2
Southall UB2. . . . . **122** D2
Walton-on-Thames
KT12 . . . . **178** A6
Dudley St, W2 . . . . **14** E2
Dudlington Rd, E5 . . . . **95** F2
Dudmaston Ms, SW3. . . . . . **31** F3
Dudrich Ms, SE22
off Melbourne Gro . . . **152** C5
Dudsbury Rd, Sid. DA14 . **176** B6
Dudset La, Houns. TW5 . . **142** A1
Dufferin Av, EC1 . . . . **12** B6
Dufferin St, EC1 . . . . **12** A6
Duffield Cl, Har. HA1 . . . . . **68** C5
Duffield Dr, N15
off Copperfield Dr **76** C4
Duff St, E14 . . . . **114** B6
Dufour's Pl, W1. . . . . **17** G4
Dugard Way, SE11 . . . . **35** G1
Duggan Dr, Chis. BR7
off Wood Dr. **174** B6
Dugolly Av, Wem. HA9
off Chalkhill Rd **88** B3
Duke Gdns, Ilf. IG6
off Duke Rd **81** G4
Duke Humphrey Rd,
SE3 . . . . **155** E1
Duke of Cambridge Cl,
Twick. TW2 . . . . **144** A6
Duke of Edinburgh Rd,
Sutt. SM1 . . . . **199** G2
Duke of Wellington Av,
SE18 . . . . **137** E3
Duke of Wellington Pl,
SW1 . . . . **24** C3
Duke of York Sq, SW3 . . . . **32** A2
Duke of York St, SW1 . . . . . **25** G1
Duke Rd, W4. . . . . **126** D5
Ilford IG6. . . . . **81** G4
Dukes Av, N3 . . . . **72** E1
N10 . . . . **74** C3
W4. . . . . **126** D5
Edgware HA8 . . . . **53** J6
Harrow HA1 . . . . **68** B4
Harrow (N.Har.) HA2 . . . . **67** F6
Hounslow TW4 . . . . **142** E4
Kingston upon Thames
KT2 . . . . **163** F4
New Malden KT3 . . . . . **183** F3
Northolt UB5. . . . . **85** E7
Richmond TW10 . . . . . . **163** F4
Dukes Cl, Hmptn. TW12 . . **161** F5
Dukes Ct, E6. . . . . **116** D1
Dukes Gate, W4
off Acton La. **126** C4
Dukes Grn Av, Felt.
TW14. . . . . **142** A5
Dukes Head Yd, N6
off Highgate High St. . . **92** B1
Duke Shore Pl, E14
off Narrow St. **113** J7
Duke Shore Wf, E14
off Narrow St. **113** J7
Dukes La, W8 . . . . **128** D2
Duke's Meadows, W4
off Great Chertsey Rd. **146** C2
Dukes Ms, N10
off Dukes Av **74** B3
Duke's Ms, W1 . . . . **16** C3
Dukes Orchard, Bex. DA5. **177** J1
Duke's Pas, E17 . . . . **78** C4
Dukes Pl, EC3. . . . . **21** E4
Dukes Rd, E6 . . . . **116** D1
W3. . . . . **106** A5
Duke's Rd, WC1 . . . . **9** J4
Dukesthorpe Rd, SE26 . . . **171** G4
Duke St, SW1. . . . . **25** G1
W1. . . . . **16** C3
Richmond TW9 . . . . **145** G4
Sutton SM1. . . . . **199** G4
Duke St Hill, SE1 . . . . **28** C1
Dukes Way, W.Wick. BR4 . **205** E3
Duke's Yd, W1. . . . . **16** C5
Dulas St, N4
off Everleigh St. **93** F1
Dulford St, W11 . . . . **108** B7
Dulka Rd, SW11 . . . . **149** J5
Dulverton Rd, SE9 . . . . . . **175** F2
Ruislip HA4 . . . . **84** A1
DULWICH, SE21 . . . . **152** B7
★**Dulwich Coll Picture Gall**,
SE21 . . . . **152** B7
Dulwich Common, SE21 . **170** B1
SE22 . . . . **170** B1
Dulwich Lawn Cl, SE22
off Colwell Rd **152** C5
Dulwich Oaks, The, SE21 . **170** B3
Dulwich Rd, SE24 . . . . . . **151** G5
Dulwich Village, SE21 . . . **152** B6
Dulwich Wd Av, SE19. . . . **170** B4
Dulwich Wd Pk, SE19. . . . **170** B4
Dumbarton Rd, SW2 . . . . **151** E6
Dumbleton Cl, Kings.T. KT1
off Gloucester Rd **182** B1
Dumbreck Rd, SE9. . . . . . **156** C4
Dumont Rd, N16 . . . . **94** B3
Dumpton Pl, NW1
off Gloucester Av **92** A7
Dunbar Av, SW16. . . . . . . **187** G2
Beckenham BR3 . . . . . . **189** H4
Dagenham RM10. . . . . . **101** G3
Dunbar Cl, Hayes UB4 . . . **102** A5
Dunbar Ct, Sutt. SM1. . . . **199** G5
Dunbar Gdns, Dag. RM10. **101** G5
Dunbar Rd, E7 . . . . **97** G6
N22 . . . . **75** G1
New Malden KT3 . . . . . **182** C4
Dunbar St, SE27. . . . . **169** J3
Dunblane Cl, Edg. HA8
off Tayside Dr **54** B2
Dunblane Rd, SE9 . . . . . . **156** B3
Dunboyne Rd, NW3. . . . . . . **91** J5
Dunbridge Ho, SW15
off Highcliffe Dr. **147** F6
Dunbridge St, E2 . . . . **13** J5
Duncan Cl, Barn. EN5 . . . . **41** F4
Duncan Gro, W3 . . . . **106** E6
Duncannon St, WC2. . . . . . **18** A6
Duncan Rd, E8 . . . . **112** E1
Richmond TW9 . . . . **145** H4
Duncan St, N1 . . . . **11** G1
Duncan Ter, N1 . . . . **11** G2

Dunch St, E1
off Watney St **112/113** E6
Duncombe Hill, SE23. . . . **153** H7
Duncombe Rd, N19 . . . . . . **92** D1
Duncrievie Rd, SE13. . . . . **154** D6
Duncroft, SE18. . . . . **137** H7
Dundalk Rd, SE4 . . . . **153** H3
Dundas Gdns, W.Mol.
KT8 . . . . **179** H3
Dundas Rd, SE15 . . . . **153** F2
Dundee Rd, E13 . . . . **115** H2
SE25 . . . . **188** E5
Dundee St, E1 . . . . **132** E1
Dundee Way, Enf. EN3 . . . . **45** H3
Dundela Gdns, Wor.Pk.
KT4 . . . . **197** H4
Dundonald Cl, E6 *off*
Northumberland Rd . . **116** B6
Dundonald Rd, NW10. . . . **108** A1
SW19. . . . . **166** B7
Dunedin Ho, E16
off Manwood St **136** C1
Dunedin Rd, E10 . . . . **96** B3
Ilford IG1 . . . . **99** F1
Dunedin Way, Hayes UB4 **102** C4
Dunelm Gro, SE27 . . . . . . **169** J4
Dunelm St, E1 . . . . **113** G6
Dunfield Gdns, SE6 . . . . . **172** B4
Dunfield Rd, SE6 . . . . **172** B5
Dunford Rd, N7 . . . . **93** F4
Dungarvan Av, SW15 . . . . **147** G4
Dunheved Cl, Th.Hth.
CR7 . . . . **187** G6
Dunheved Rd N, Th.Hth.
CR7 . . . . **187** G6
Dunheved Rd S, Th.Hth.
CR7 . . . . **187** G6
Dunheved Rd W, Th.Hth.
CR7 . . . . **187** G6
Dunhill Pt, SW15
off Dilton Gdns **165** H1
Dunholme Grn, N9. . . . . . . **60** C3
Dunholme La, N9
off Dunholme Rd **60** C3
Dunholme Rd, N9 . . . . **60** C3
Dunkeld Rd, SE25 . . . . . . **188** A4
Dagenham RM8 . . . . . . **100** B2
Dunkery Rd, SE9 . . . . **174** A4
Dunkirk St, SE27
off Waring St. **169** J4
Dunlace Rd, E5. . . . . **95** F4
Dunleary Cl, Houns. TW4. **143** F7
Dunley Dr, Croy.
(New Adgtn) CR0 . . . . **204** B7
Dunlin Ho, W13 . . . . **104** C4
Dunloe Av, N17 . . . . **76** A3
Dunloe St, E2. . . . . **13** F2
Dunlop Pl, SE16. . . . . **29** G6
Dunmore Pt, E2 . . . . **13** F4
Dunmore Rd, NW6. . . . . . **108** B1
SW20. . . . . **183** J1
Dunmow Cl, Felt. TW13 . . **160** E4
Loughton IG10 . . . . **48** B6
Romford RM6 . . . . **82** C5
Dunmow Ho, Dag. RM9 . . **118** B1
Dunmow Rd, E15. . . . . **96** D4
Dunmow Wk, N1
off Popham St **111** J1
Dunnage Cres, SE16
off Plough Way **133** H4
Dunn Mead, NW9
off Field Mead. **55** F7
Dunnock Cl, N9 . . . . **61** G1
Borehamwood WD6 . . . . **38** A4
Dunnock Rd, E6 . . . . **116** B6
Dunns Pas, WC1. . . . . **18** B3
Dunn St, E8 . . . . **94** C5
Dunollie Pl, NW5
off Dunollie Rd **92** C5
Dunollie Rd, NW5 . . . . **92** C5
Dunoon Rd, SE23. . . . . . . **153** F7
Dunraven Dr, Enf. EN2. . . . **43** G2
Dunraven Rd, W12 . . . . . . **127** G1
Dunraven St, W1 . . . . **16** A5
Dunsany Rd, W14. . . . . . . **128** A3
Dunsfold Way, Croy.
(New Adgtn) CR0 . . . . **204** B7
Dunsford Way, SW15
off Dover Pk Dr **147** H6
Dunsmore Cl, Hayes
UB4 . . . . **102** D4
Dunsmore Rd, Walt.
KT12. . . . . **178** B6
Dunsmure Rd, N16. . . . . . . **94** B1
Dunspring La, Ilf. IG5 . . . . . **80** E2
Dunstable Ms, W1 . . . . **16** C1
Dunstable Rd, Rich. TW9 . **145** H4
West Molesey KT8 . . . . **179** F4
Dunstall Rd, SW20. . . . . . **165** H6
Dunstall Way, W.Mol.
KT8 . . . . **179** H3
Dunstan Cl, N2
off Thomas More Way. . **73** F3
Dunstan Rd, NW11. . . . . . . **90** C1
Dunstans Gro, SE22. . . . . **152** E6
Dunstans Rd, SE22 . . . . . **152** D7
Dunster Av, Mord. SM4 . . **198** A1
Dunster Cl, Barn. EN5 . . . . **40** A4
Romford RM5 . . . . **83** J2
Dunster Ct, EC3 . . . . **20** D5
Borehamwood WD6
off Kensington Way. . . . **38** D3
Dunster Dr, NW9 . . . . **88** C1
Dunster Gdns, NW6. . . . . . **90** C7
Dunsterville Way, SE1 . . . . **28** C4
Dunster Way, Har. HA2 . . . **85** E3
Wallington SM6
off Helios Rd. **200** A1
Dunston Rd, E8 . . . . **112** C1
SW11 . . . . **150** A2
Dunston St, E8. . . . . **112** C1
Dunton Cl, Surb. KT6. . . . **195** H1
Dunton Rd, E10 . . . . **78** B7
SE1 . . . . **37** F3
Duntshill Rd, SW18 . . . . . **167** E1
Dunvegan Cl, W.Mol.
KT8 . . . . **179** H4
Dunvegan Rd, SE9 . . . . . . **156** C4
Dunwich Rd, Bexh. DA7. . **159** F1
Dunworth Ms, W11
off Portobello Rd. **108** C6
Duplex Ride, SW1 . . . . **24** A4
Dupont Rd, SW20 . . . . . . **184** A2
Duppas Av, Croy. CR0
off Violet La **201** H4
Duppas Hill La, Croy. CR0
off Duppas Hill Rd. . . . **201** H4
Duppas Hill Rd, Croy.
CR0 . . . . **201** H4
Duppas Hill Ter, Croy.
CR0 . . . . **201** H3
Duppas Rd, Croy. CR0 . . . **201** G3
Dupree Rd, SE7 . . . . **135** H5
Dura Den Cl, Beck. BR3 . . **172** B7
Durand Cl, Cars. SM5 . . . **199** J1
Durand Gdns, SW9 . . . . . **151** F1
Durands Wk, SE16 . . . . . . **133** J2
Durand Way, NW10 . . . . . . **88** C7
Durants Pk Av, Enf. EN3 . . **45** G4
Durants Rd, Enf. EN3. . . . . **45** F4
Durant St, E2. . . . . **13** H3
Durban Gdns, Dag. RM10. **101** J7
Durban Rd, E15 . . . . **114** E3
E17 . . . . **77** J1
N17 . . . . **60** B6
SE27 . . . . **169** J4
Beckenham BR3 . . . . . . **189** J2
Ilford IG2. . . . . **99** H1
Durbin Rd, Chess. KT9. . . **195** H4
Durdans Rd, Sthl. UB1 . . . **103** F6
Durell Gdns, Dag. RM9 . . **100** D5
Durell Rd, Dag. RM9. . . . . **100** D5
Durford Cres, SW15 . . . . . **165** G1
Durham Av, Brom. BR2 . . **191** F4
Hounslow TW5 . . . . **123** F5
Woodford Green IG8 . . . **64** A5
Durham Cl, SW20
off Durham Rd **183** H2
Durham Hill, Brom. BR1. . **173** F4
Durham Ho St, WC2. . . . . . **18** B6
Durham Pl, SW3. . . . . **31** J4
Ilford IG1 *off Eton Rd* . . . **99** F4
Durham Ri, SE18 . . . . **137** F5
Durham Rd, E12. . . . . **98** A4
E16. . . . . **115** E4
N2 . . . . **73** H3
N7 . . . . **93** F2
N9 . . . . **60** D2
SW20. . . . . **183** H1
W5. . . . . **125** G3
Borehamwood WD6 . . . . **38** C3
Bromley BR2. . . . . **191** F3
Dagenham RM10. . . . . . **101** J5
Feltham TW14 . . . . **142** C7
Harrow HA1 . . . . **67** H5
Sidcup DA14 . . . . **176** B5
Durham Row, E1 . . . . **113** H5
Durham St, SE11 . . . . **34** C4
Durham Ter, W2 . . . . **14** A3
Durham Wf, Brent. TW8
off London Rd. **125** F7
Durham Yd, E2
off Teesdale St . . . **112/113** E3
Durley Av, Pnr. HA5 . . . . . . **67** E7
Durley Rd, N16. . . . . **76** B7
Durlston Rd, E5 . . . . **94** D2
Kingston upon Thames
KT2 . . . . **163** H6
Durnell Way, Loug. IG10. . . **48** D3
Durnford St, N15 . . . . **76** B5
SE10
off Greenwich Ch St . . **134** C6
Durning Rd, SE19. . . . . . . **170** A5
Durnsford Av, SW19. . . . . **166** D2
Durnsford Rd, N11 . . . . **74** D1
SW19. . . . . **166** D2
Durrant Way, Orp. BR6. . . **207** G5
Durrell Rd, SW6 . . . . **148** C1
Durrington Av, SW20 . . . . **183** J1
Durrington Pk Rd, SW20 . **165** J7
Durrington Rd, E5 . . . . **95** H4
Durrington Twr, SW8
off Westbury St. **150** C2
Dursley Cl, SE3 . . . . **155** J2
Dursley Gdns, SE3. . . . . . **156** A1
Dursley Rd, SE3. . . . . **155** J2
Durward St, E1. . . . . **112** E5
Durweston Ms, W1 . . . . **16** A1
Durweston St, W1 . . . . **16** A1
Dury Rd, Barn. EN5 . . . . . . **40** C1
Dutch Barn Cl, Stai.
(Stanw.) TW19. . . . . . . **140** A6
Dutch Gdns, Kings.T. KT2
off Windmill Ri **164** B6
Dutch Yd, SW18
off Wandsworth
High St **148** D5
Dutton St, SE10 . . . . **154** C1
Duxberry Cl, Brom. BR2
off Southborough La. . **192** B5
Duxford Ho, SE2
off Wolvercote Rd **138** D2
Dwight Ct, SW6
off Burlington Rd **148** B2
Dye Ho La, E3. . . . . **114** A1
Dyer's Bldgs, EC1. . . . . **19** E2
Dyers Hall Rd, E11 . . . . **96** E1
Dyers La, SW15 . . . . **147** H4
Dykes Way, Brom. BR2. . . **191** F3
Dylan Rd, SE24 . . . . **151** H4
Belvedere DA17 . . . . . . **139** G3
Dylways, SE5. . . . . **152** A4
Dymchurch Cl, Ilf. IG5 . . . . **80** D2
Orpington BR6 . . . . **207** H4
Dymes Path, SW19
off Queensmere Rd. . . **166** A2
Dymock St, SW6 . . . . **148** E3
Dymond Est, SW17
off Glenburnie Rd **167** H3
Dyneley Rd, SE12. . . . . . . **173** J4
Dyne Rd, NW6. . . . . **90** C7
Dynevor Rd, N16 . . . . **94** B3
Richmond TW10 . . . . . . **145** H5
Dynham Rd, NW6 . . . . **90** D7
Dyott St, WC1 . . . . **18** A3
Dysart Av, Kings.T. KT2 . . **163** F5
Dysart St, EC2 . . . . **12** D6
Dyson Rd, E11 . . . . **79** E6
E15 . . . . **97** F6
Dysons Rd, N18 . . . . **61** E5

E

Eade Rd, N4. . . . . **75** J7
Eagans Cl, N2
off Market Pl. **73** H3
Eagle Av, Rom. RM6 . . . . . **82** E6
Eagle Cl, SE16
off Varcoe Rd. **133** F5
Enfield EN3. . . . . **45** F4
Wallington SM6 . . . . . . **201** E6
Eagle Ct, EC1 . . . . **19** G1
Eagle Dr, NW9 . . . . **71** E2
Eagle Hts, SW11
off Bramlands Cl. **149** H3
Eagle Hill, SE19 . . . . **170** A6
Eagle La, E11 . . . . **79** G4
Eagle Ms, N1
off Tottenham Rd. **94** B6
Eagle Pl, SW1. . . . . **17** G6
SW7. . . . . **30** D3
Eagle Rd, Wem. HA0 . . . . . **87** G7
Eaglesfield Rd, SE18 . . . . **137** E7
Eagle St, WC1 . . . . **18** C2
Eagle Ter, Wdf.Grn. IG8 . . . **63** H7
Eagle Trd Est, Mitch. CR4
off Willow La. **185** J6
Eagle Wf, E14
off Broomfield St. **114** B5
Eagle Wf Rd, N1. . . . . **12** A1
Ealdham Sq, SE9. . . . . . . **155** J4
EALING, W5 . . . . **105** F7
Ealing Bdy Shop Cen,
W5. . . . . **105** G7
Ealing Cl, Borwd. WD6. . . . **38** D1
★**Ealing Common**, W5. . . **125** H1
Ealing Downs Ct, Grnf. UB6
off Perivale La. **104** D3
Ealing Grn, W5. . . . . **125** G1
Ealing Pk Gdns, W5 . . . . . **125** F4
Ealing Rd, Brent. TW8 . . . **125** G5
Northolt UB5. . . . . **85** G7
Wembley HA0 . . . . **105** G1
Ealing Village, W5. . . . . . **105** H6
Eamont St, NW8 . . . . **7** G1
Eardley Cres, SW5 . . . . . . **128** D5
Eardley Pt, SE18
off Wilmount St . . **136/137** E4
Eardley Rd, SW16 . . . . . . **168** C5
Belvedere DA17 . . . . . . **139** G5
Earl Cl, N11. . . . . **58** B5
Earldom Rd, SW15. . . . . . **147** J4
Earle Gdns, Kings.T.
KT2 . . . . **163** H6
Earlham Gro, E7. . . . . **97** F5
N22 . . . . **59** F7
Earlham St, WC2 . . . . **17** J4
Earl Ri, SE18. . . . . **137** G4
Earl Rd, SW14 *off Elm Rd* . **146** C4
EARLS COURT, SW5 . . . . **128** C5
★**Earls Court Exhib Cen**,
SW5. . . . . **128** D5
Earls Ct Gdns, SW5 . . . . . . **30** A2
Earls Ct Rd, SW5 . . . . **128** D4
W8. . . . . **128** D4
Earls Ct Sq, SW5 . . . . **30** A3
Earls Cres, Har. HA1. . . . . . **68** B4
Earlsdown Ho, Bark. IG11
off Wheelers Cross . . . **117** G2
Earlsferry Way, N1 . . . . **93** F7
EARLSFIELD, SW18 . . . . . **167** F1
Earlsfield Ho, Kings.T. KT2
off Kingsgate Rd **181** H1
Earlsfield Rd, SW18 . . . . . **167** F1
Earlshall Rd, SE9 . . . . **156** C4
Earlsmead, Har. HA2 . . . . . **85** F4
Earlsmead Rd, N15 . . . . . . **76** C5
NW10. . . . . **107** J2
Earl's Path, Loug. IG10. . . . **47** J2
Earls Ter, W8. . . . . **128** C3
Earlsthorpe Ms, SW12 . . . **150** A6
Earlsthorpe Rd, SE26 . . . . **171** G4
Earlstoke St, EC1 . . . . **11** G3
Earlston Gro, E9. . . . . **113** E1
Earl St, EC2 . . . . **20** D1
Earls Wk, W8. . . . . **128** D3
Dagenham RM8 . . . . . . **100** B4
Earls Way, Orp. BR6
off Station Rd **207** J2
Earlswood Av, Th.Hth.
CR7 . . . . **187** G5
Earlswood Gdns, Ilf. IG5 . . **80** D3
Earlswood St, SE10 . . . . . **135** E5
Early Ms, NW1
off Arlington Rd. **110** B1
Earnshaw St, WC2 . . . . **17** J3
Earsby St, W14. . . . . **128** B4
Easby Cres, Mord. SM4 . . **185** E6
Easebourne Rd, Dag.
RM8. . . . . **100** C5
Easedale Ho, Islw. TW7
off Summerwood Rd . **144** C5
Eashing Pt, SW15
off Wanborough Dr. . . **165** H1
Easley's Ms, W1 . . . . **16** C3
EAST ACTON, W3. . . . . . . **126** D1
East Acton La, W3 . . . . . . **106** E7
East Arbour St, E1 . . . . . . **113** G6
East Av, E12. . . . . **98** B7
E17 . . . . **78** B4
Hayes UB3 . . . . **121** J2
Southall UB1 . . . . **103** F7
Wallington SM6 . . . . . . **201** F5
East Bk, N16. . . . . **76** B7
Eastbank Rd, Hmptn.
(Hmptn H.) TW12 . . . . **161** J5
EAST BARNET, Barn. EN4. **41** H6
East Barnet Rd, Barn. EN4. **41** H6
Eastbourne Av, W3. . . . . . **106** D6
Eastbourne Gdns, SW14 . **146** C3
Eastbourne Ms, W2 . . . . . . **14** D3
Eastbourne Rd, E6 . . . . . . **116** D3
E15. . . . . **115** E1
N15 . . . . **76** B6
SW17. . . . . **168** A6
W4. . . . . **126** C6
Brentford TW8. . . . . **125** F5
Feltham TW13 . . . . **160** D2
Eastbourne Ter, W2 . . . . . . **14** D3
Eastbournia Av, N9 . . . . . . **61** E3
Eastbrook Av, N9. . . . . **45** F7
Dagenham RM10. . . . . . **101** J4
Eastbrook Rd, SE3. . . . . . **135** H7
Eastbury Av, Bark. IG11 . . **117** H1
Enfield EN1. . . . . **44** B1

Eastbury Ct, Bark. IG11 117 H1
Eastbury Gro, W4 127 E5
★**Eastbury Ho**, Bark. IG11 117 J1
Eastbury Rd, E6 116 D4
Kingston upon Thames KT2 163 H7
Orpington BR5 193 G6
Eastbury Sq, Bark. IG11 117 J1
Eastbury Ter, E1 113 G4
Eastcastle St, W1 17 F3
Eastcheap, EC3 20 C5
East Churchfield Rd, W3 126 D1
Eastchurch Rd, Houns. (Hthrw Air.) TW6 141 H2
East Cl, W5 106 A4
Barnet EN4 42 A4
Greenford UB6 103 J2
Eastcombe Av, SE7 135 H6
EASTCOTE, Pnr. HA5 66 C6
Eastcote, Orp. BR6 207 J1
Eastcote Av, Grnf. UB6 86 D5
Harrow HA2 85 H2
West Molesey KT8 179 F5
Eastcote La, Har. HA2 85 G3
Northolt UB5 85 G7
Eastcote La N, Nthlt. UB5 85 F6
Eastcote Pl, Pnr. HA5 66 B6
Eastcote Rd, Har. HA2 85 J3
Pinner HA5 66 D5
Pinner (Eastcote Vill.) HA5 66 A6
Welling DA16 157 G2
Eastcote St, SW9 151 F2
Eastcote Vw, Pnr. HA5 66 C4
EASTCOTE VILLAGE, Pnr. HA5 66 B5
Eastcourt, Sun. TW16 178 C2
East Ct, Wem. HA0 87 F2
East Cres, N11 57 J4
Enfield EN1 44 C5
Eastcroft Rd, Epsom KT19 197 E7
East Cross Cen, E15 96 A6
East Cross Route, E3 95 J7
E9 95 J7
Eastdown Pk, SE13 154 D4
East Duck Lees La, Enf. EN3 45 H4
EAST DULWICH, SE22 152 D6
East Dulwich Gro, SE22 152 B6
East Dulwich Rd, SE15 152 C4
SE22 152 C4
East End Rd, N2 73 F3
N3 72 D2
East End Way, Pnr. HA5 67 E3
East Entrance, Dag. RM10 119 H2
Eastern Av, E11 79 J6
Ilford IG2, IG4 80 B6
Pinner HA5 66 D7
Romford RM6 82 C4
Eastern Av W, Rom. RM1, RM5, RM6, RM7 83 E4
Eastern Gateway, E16 115 J7
Eastern Ind Est, Erith DA18 139 G2
Eastern Perimeter Rd, Houns. (Hthrw Air.) TW6 141 J3
Eastern Quay Apartments, E16 *off Rayleigh Rd* 135 H1
Eastern Rd, E13 115 H2
E17 78 C5
N2 73 J3
N22 75 E1
SE4 154 A4
Easternville Gdns, Ilf. IG2 81 F6
Eastern Way, SE2 138 D1
SE28 138 A2
Belvedere DA17 139 H2
Erith DA18 138 D1
East Ferry Rd, E14 134 B3
Eastfield Cotts, Hayes UB3 121 H5
Eastfield Gdns, Dag. RM10 101 G4
Eastfield Rd, E17 78 A4
N8 74 E3
Dagenham RM9, RM10 101 G4
Eastfields, Pnr. HA5 66 C5
Eastfields Av, SW18 *off Point Pleasant* 148 D4
Eastfields Rd, W3 106 C5
Mitcham CR4 186 A2
Eastfield St, E14 113 H5
EAST FINCHLEY, N2 73 G4
East Gdns, SW17 167 H6
Eastgate Cl, SE28 118 D6
Eastglade, Pnr. HA5 67 E3
EAST HAM, E6 116 B2
Eastham Cl, Barn. EN5 40 B5
East Ham Ind Est, E6 116 B4
East Ham Manor Way, E6 116 D6
East Ham Shop Hall, E6 *off Myrtle Rd* 116 B1
East Harding St, EC4 19 F3
East Heath Rd, NW3 91 G3
East Hill, SW18 149 E5
Wembley HA9 88 A2
Eastholm, NW11 73 E4
Eastholme, Hayes UB3 122 A1
East India Dock Rd, E14 114 A6
East India Way, Croy. CR0 202 C1
Eastlake Rd, SE5 151 H2
Eastlands Cres, SE21 152 C6
East La, SE16 29 H4
Kingston upon Thames KT1 *off High St* 181 G3
Wembley HA0, HA9 87 G3
Eastlea Ms, E16 *off Desford Rd* 114/115 E4
Eastleigh Av, Har. HA2 85 H2
Eastleigh Cl, NW2 89 E3
Sutton SM2 199 E7
Eastleigh Rd, E17 77 J2
Bexleyheath DA7 159 J2
Hounslow (Hthrw Air.) TW6 *off Cranford La* 141 J3
Eastleigh Wk, SW15 147 G7
Eastleigh Way, Felt. TW14 160 A1
Eastman Rd, W3 126 D1
East Mascalls, SE7 *off Mascalls Rd* 135 J6
East Mead, Ruis. HA4 84 D3
Eastmead Av, Grnf. UB6 103 H3
Eastmead Cl, Brom. BR1 192 B2
Eastmearn Rd, SE21 169 J2
EAST MOLESEY, KT8 180 A4
Eastmont Rd, Esher KT10 194 B2
Eastmoor Pl, SE7 *off Eastmoor St* 136 A3
Eastmoor St, SE7 136 A3
East Mt St, E1 113 E5
Eastney Rd, Croy. CR0 201 H1
Eastney St, SE10 134 D5
Eastnor Rd, SE9 175 F1
Easton Gdns, Borwd. WD6 38 D4
Easton St, WC1 10 E4
East Pk Cl, Rom. RM6 82 D5
East Parkside, SE10 135 E2
East Pas, EC1 19 H1
East Pier, E1 *off Wapping High St* 132/133 E1
East Pl, SE27 *off Pilgrim Hill* 169 J4
East Poultry Av, EC1 19 G2
East Ramp, Houns. (Hthrw Air.) TW6 140 E1
East Rd, E15 115 G1
N1 12 B4
SW19 167 F6
Barnet EN4 58 A1
Edgware HA8 70 B1
Feltham TW14 141 G7
Kingston upon Thames KT2 181 H1
Romford (Chad.Hth) RM6 82 E5
Welling DA16 158 B2
West Drayton UB7 120 C4
East Rochester Way, SE9 157 H4
Bexley DA5 158 D6
Sidcup DA15 157 H4
East Row, E11 79 G6
W10 108 B4
Eastry Av, Brom. BR2 191 F6
Eastry Rd, Erith DA8 139 G7
EAST SHEEN, SW14 146 D4
East Sheen Av, SW14 146 D4
Eastside Rd, NW11 72 C4
East Smithfield, E1 21 G6
East St, SE17 36 A3
Barking IG11 99 F7
Bexleyheath DA7 159 G4
Brentford TW8 125 F7
Bromley BR1 191 G2
East Surrey Gro, SE15 132 C7
East Tenter St, E1 21 G4
East Twrs, Pnr. HA5 66 D5
East Vw, E4 62 C5
Barnet EN5 40 C3
Eastview Av, SE18 137 H7
Eastville Av, NW11 72 C6
East Wk, Barn. EN4 42 A7
Hayes UB3 122 A1
Eastway, E9 95 J6
East Way, E11 79 H5
Bromley BR2 191 G7
Croydon CR0 203 H2
Hayes UB3 122 A1
Eastway, Mord. SM4 184 A5
East Way, Ruis. HA4 84 A1
Eastway, Wall. SM6 200 C4
Eastway Commercial Cen, E9 96 A5
Eastway Cres, Har. HA2 *off Eliot Dr* 85 H2
Eastwell Cl, Beck. BR3 189 H1
Eastwick Ct, SW19 *off Victoria Dr* 166 A1
EAST WICKHAM, Well. DA16 138 A7
Eastwood Cl, E18 *off George La* 79 G2
N7 *off Eden Gro* 93 G5
N17 *off Northumberland Gro* 60/61 E7
Eastwood Rd, E18 79 G2
N10 74 A2
Ilford IG3 82 A7
West Drayton UB7 120 D2
East Woodside, Bex. DA5 177 E1
Eastwood St, SW16 168 C6
Eatington Rd, E10 78 D5
Eaton Cl, SW1 32 B2
Stanmore HA7 53 E4
Eaton Dr, SW9 151 H4
Kingston upon Thames KT2 164 A7
Eaton Gdns, Dag. RM9 100 E7
Eaton Gate, SW1 32 B1
Eaton Ho, E14 *off Westferry Circ* 134 A1
Eaton La, SW1 24 E6
Eaton Ms N, SW1 32 B1
Eaton Ms S, SW1 32 C1
Eaton Ms W, SW1 32 C1
Eaton Pk Rd, N13 59 G2
Eaton Pl, SW1 24 B6
Eaton Ri, E11 79 J5
W5 105 G6
Eaton Rd, NW4 71 J5
Enfield EN1 44 B3
Hounslow TW3 144 A4
Sidcup DA14 176 D2
Sutton SM2 199 G6
Eaton Row, SW1 24 D6
Eatons Mead, E4 62 A2
Eaton Sq, SW1 24 D5
Eaton Ter, SW1 32 B1
Eaton Ter Ms, SW1 32 B1
Eatonville Rd, SW17 167 J2
Eatonville Vil, SW17 *off Eatonville Rd* 167 J2
Ebbisham Dr, SW8 34 C5
Ebbisham Rd, Wor.Pk. KT4 197 J2
Ebbsfleet Rd, NW2 90 B4
Ebdon Way, SE3 155 H3
Ebenezer Ho, SE11 35 F2
Ebenezer St, N1 12 B3
Ebenezer Wk, SW16 186 C1
Ebley Cl, SE15 37 F6
Ebner St, SW18 149 E5
Ebor St, E1 13 F5
Ebrington Rd, Har. HA3 69 G6
Ebsworth St, SE23 153 G7
Eburne Rd, N7 93 E3
Ebury Br, SW1 32 D3
Ebury Br Est, SW1 32 D3
Ebury Br Rd, SW1 32 C4
Ebury Cl, Kes. BR2 206 B3
Ebury Ms, SE27 169 H3
SW1 32 C1
Ebury Ms E, SW1 32 D1
Ebury Sq, SW1 32 C2
Ebury St, SW1 32 D1
Ecclesbourne Cl, N13 59 G5
Ecclesbourne Gdns, N13 59 G5
Ecclesbourne Rd, N1 93 J7
Thornton Heath CR7 187 J5
Eccles Rd, SW11 149 J4
Eccleston Br, SW1 32 E1
Eccleston Cl, Barn. EN4 41 J4
Orpington BR6 207 G1
Eccleston Cres, Rom. RM6 82 A7
Ecclestone Ct, Wem. HA9 *off St. John's Rd* 87 H5
Ecclestone Pl, Wem. HA9 87 J5
Eccleston Ms, SW1 24 C6
Eccleston Pl, SW1 32 D1
Eccleston Rd, W13 104 D7
Eccleston Sq, SW1 32 E2
Eccleston Sq Ms, SW1 33 F2
Eccleston St, SW1 24 D6
Echo Hts, E4 *off Mount Echo Dr* 62 B1
Eckersley St, E1 *off Buxton St* 112 D4
Eckford St, N1 10 E1
Eckington Ho, N15 *off Fladbury Rd* 76 A6
Eckstein Rd, SW11 149 H4
Eclipse Rd, E13 115 H5
Ector Rd, SE6 172 E2
Edbrooke Rd, W9 108 D4
Eddiscombe Rd, SW6 148 C2
Eddy Cl, Rom. RM7 83 H6
Eddystone Rd, SE4 153 H5
Eddystone Twr, SE8 133 H4
Eddystone Wk, Stai. TW19 140 B7
Ede Cl, Houns. TW3 143 F3
Edenbridge Cl, SE16 *off Masters Dr* 132/133 E5
Edenbridge Rd, E9 95 G7
Enfield EN1 44 B6
Eden Cl, NW3 90 D2
W8 *off Adam & Eve Ms* 128 D3
Wembley HA0 105 G1
Edencourt Rd, SW16 168 B6
Edenfield Gdns, Wor.Pk. KT4 197 F3
Eden Gro, E17 78 B5
N7 93 F5
Edenham Way, W10 *off Elkstone Rd* 108 C5
Edenhurst Av, SW6 148 C3
Eden Ms, SW17 *off Huntspill St* 167 F3
EDEN PARK, Beck. BR3 190 A5
Eden Pk Av, Beck. BR3 189 H4
Eden Rd, E17 78 B5
SE27 169 H5
Beckenham BR3 189 H4
Bexley DA5 177 J4
Croydon CR0 202 A4
Edensor Gdns, W4 127 E7
Edensor Rd, W4 126 E7
Eden St, Kings.T. KT1 181 G2
Edenvale Cl, Mitch. CR4 *off Edenvale Rd* 168 A7
Edenvale Rd, Mitch. CR4 168 A7
Edenvale St, SW6 149 E2
Eden Wk, Kings.T. KT1 *off Eden St* 181 H2
Eden Wk Shop Cen, Kings.T. KT1 181 H2
Eden Way, Beck. BR3 189 J5
Ederline Av, SW16 187 F3
Edgar Kail Way, SE22 152 B4
Edgarley Ter, SW6 148 B1
Edgar Rd, E3 114 B3
Hounslow TW4 143 F7
Romford RM6 82 D7
Edgbaston Rd, Wat. WD19 50 A3
Edgeborough Way, Brom. BR1 174 A7
Edgebury, Chis. BR7 175 E4
Edgebury Wk, Chis. BR7 175 F4
Edgecombe Ho, SW19 166 B1
Edgecoombe, S.Croy. CR2 203 F7
Edgecoombe Cl, Kings.T. KT2 164 D7
Edgecote Cl, W3 *off Cheltenham Pl* 126 C1
Edgecot Gro, N15 *off Oulton Rd* 76 A5
Edgefield Av, Bark. IG11 99 J7
Edge Hill, SE18 136 E6
SW19 166 A7
Edge Hill Av, N3 72 D3
Edge Hill Ct, SW19 166 A7
Edgehill Gdns, Dag. RM10 101 G4
Edgehill Rd, W13 105 F5
Chislehurst BR7 175 F3
Mitcham CR4 186 B1
Edgeley La, SW4 *off Edgeley Rd* 150 D3
Edgeley Rd, SW4 150 D3
Edgel St, SW18 *off Ferrier St* 148/149 E4
Edgepoint Cl, SE27 *off Knights Hill* 169 H5
Edge St, W8 *off Kensington Ch St* 128 D1
Edgewood Dr, Orp. BR6 207 J5

Edgewood Grn, Croy. CR0 . . . . 203 G1
Edgeworth Av, NW4 . . . . . 71 G5
Edgeworth Cl, NW4 . . . . . . 71 G5
Edgeworth Cres, NW4 . . . . 71 G5
Edgeworth Rd, SE9 . . . . . 155 J4
Barnet EN4 . . . . 41 H4
Edgington Rd, SW16 . . . . 168 D6
Edgington Way, Sid. DA14 . . . . 176 C7
EDGWARE, HA8 . . . . 54 B5
Edgwarebury Gdns, Edg. HA8 . . . . 54 A5
Edgwarebury La, Edg. HA8 . . . . 54 A4
Edgware Ct, Edg. HA8 *off Cavendish Dr* 54 A6
Edgware Rd, NW2 . . . . 89 H1
NW9 . . . . 70 D3
W2 . . . . 15 H3
Edgware Rd Sub, W2 *off Edgware Rd* 109 H5
Edgware Way, Edg. HA8 . . 53 J4
Edinburgh Cl, E2 *off Russia La* 113 F2
Pinner HA5 . . . . 66 D7
Edinburgh Ct, SW20 . . . . 184 A5
Edinburgh Dr, Rom. RM7 *off Eastern Av W* 83 J4
Edinburgh Gate, SW1 . . . . 23 J3
Edinburgh Ho, W9 . . . . 6 B3
Edinburgh Rd, E13 . . . . . . 115 H2
E17 . . . . 78 A5
N18 . . . . 60 D5
W7 . . . . 124 C2
Sutton SM1 . . . . 199 F2
Edington Rd, SE2 . . . . 138 B3
Enfield EN3 . . . . 45 F2
Edison Cl, E17 *off Exeter Rd* 78 A5
Edison Ct, SE10 *off Greenroof Way* 135 F3
Edison Dr, Sthl. UB1 . . . . 103 H6
Wembley HA9 . . . . 87 H2
Edison Gro, SE18 . . . . 137 J7
Edison Rd, N8 . . . . 74 D6
Bromley BR2 . . . . 191 G2
Enfield EN3 . . . . 45 J2
Welling DA16 . . . . 157 J1
Edis St, NW1 . . . . 110 A1
Edith Cavell Cl, N19 *off Hornsey Ri Gdns* . . . 74 D7
Edith Cavell Way, SE18 *off Shooter's Hill Rd* . . . 156 B1
Edith Gdns, Surb. KT5 . . . 182 B7
Edith Gro, SW10 . . . . 30 C6
Edithna St, SW9 . . . . 151 E3
Edith Nesbit Wk, SE9 *off Westhorne Av* 156 B4
Edith Rd, E6 . . . . 98 A7
E15 *off Chandos Rd* 96 D5
N11 . . . . 58 D7
SE25 . . . . 188 A5
SW19 . . . . 167 E6
W14 . . . . 128 B4
Romford RM6 . . . . 82 D6
Edith Row, SW6 . . . . 149 E1
Edith St, E2 . . . . 13 H1
Edith Summerskill Ho, SW6 *off Clem Attlee Ct* 128 C7
Edith Ter, SW10 . . . . 30 C7
Edith Vil, SW15 *off Bective Rd* 148 B4
W14 . . . . 128 C4
Edith Yd, SW10 . . . . 30 D7
Edmansons Cl, N17 *off Bruce Gro* 76 B1
Edmeston Cl, E9 . . . . 95 H6
Edmond Halley Way, SE10 . . . . 134 E2
Edmonds Ct, W.Mol. KT8 *off Avern Rd* 179 H4
EDMONTON, N9 . . . . 60 D4
Edmonton Grn, N9 *off Hertford Rd* 60/61 E2
Edmonton Grn Shop Cen, N9 . . . . 60 E2
Edmund Gro, Felt. TW13 . 161 F2
Edmund Hurst Dr, E6 . . . . 116 E5
Edmund Rd, Mitch. CR4 . . 185 H3
Welling DA16 . . . . 158 A3
Edmunds Cl, Hayes UB4 . 102 C5
Edmund St, SE5 . . . . 36 B7
Edmunds Wk, N2 . . . . 73 H4
Edna Rd, SW20 . . . . 184 A2
Edna St, SW11 . . . . 149 H1
Edrich Ho, SW4 . . . . 150 E1
Edrick Rd, Edg. HA8 . . . . . . 54 C6
Edrick Wk, Edg. HA8 . . . . . 54 C6
Edric Rd, SE14 . . . . 133 G7
Edridge Rd, Croy. CR0 . . . 201 J3
Edulf Rd, Borwd. WD6 . . . . 38 B1
Edward Av, E4 . . . . 62 B6
Morden SM4 . . . . 185 G5
Edward Cl, N9 . . . . 44 C7
NW2 . . . . 90 A4
Hampton (Hmptn H.) TW12 *off Edward Rd* 161 J5
Northolt UB5 . . . . 102 C2
Edward Ct, E16 *off Alexandra St* 115 G5
Edwardes Pl, W8 *off Edwardes Sq* 128 C3
Edwardes Sq, W8 . . . . 128 D3
Edward Gro, Barn. EN4 . . . 41 G5
Edward Ms, NW1 . . . . 8 E2
Edward Pl, SE8 . . . . 133 J6
Edward Rd, E17 . . . . 77 G4
SE20 . . . . 171 G7
Barnet EN4 . . . . 41 G5
Bromley BR1 . . . . 173 H7
Chislehurst BR7 . . . . . . 175 E5
Croydon CR0 . . . . 188 B7
Feltham TW14 . . . . 141 G5
Hampton (Hmptn H.) TW12 . . . . 161 J5
Harrow HA2 . . . . 67 J3
Northolt UB5 . . . . 102 C2
Romford RM6 . . . . 82 E6
Edward's Av, Ruis. HA4 . . . 84 B6
Edwards Cl, Wor.Pk. KT4 . 198 A2
Edwards Cotts, N1 *off Compton Av* 93 H6
Edwards Dr, N11 *off Gordon Rd* 58 D7
Edwards La, N16 . . . . 94 A2
Edwards Ms, N1 . . . . 93 G7
W1 . . . . 16 B4
Edward Sq, N1 *off Caledonian Rd* 111 F1
SE16 *off Rotherhithe St* 133 H1
Edwards Rd, Belv. DA17 . 139 G4
Edward St, E16 . . . . 115 G4
SE8 . . . . 133 J6
SE14 . . . . 133 H7
Edward's Way, SE4 *off Adelaide Av* 154 A5
Edwards Yd, Wem. HA0 *off Mount Pleasant* . . . 105 H1
Edward Temme Av, E15 . . . 97 F7
Edward Tyler Rd, SE12 . . . 173 H2
Edwina Gdns, Ilf. IG4 . . . . 80 B5
Edwin Av, E6 . . . . 116 D2
Edwin Cl, Bexh. DA7 . . . . 139 F6
Edwin Pl, Croy. CR0 *off Cross Rd* 202 A1
Edwin Rd, Edg. HA8 . . . . . 54 D6
Twickenham TW1, TW2 . 162 C1
Edwin's Mead, E9 *off Lindisfarne Way* 95 H4
Edwin St, E1 . . . . 113 F4
E16 . . . . 115 G5
Edwyn Cl, Barn. EN5 . . . . . 39 J6
Edwyn Ho, SW18 *off Neville Gill Cl* 148 E6
Eel Brook Cl, SW6 *off King's Rd* 148 E1
Eel Brook Studios, SW6 *off Moore Pk Rd* 128 D7
Eel Pie Island, Twick. TW1 . 162 E1
Effie Pl, SW6 . . . . 128 D7
Effie Rd, SW6 . . . . 128 D7
Effingham Cl, Sutt. SM2 . 199 E7
Effingham Rd, N8 . . . . 75 G5
SE12 . . . . 155 E5
Croydon CR0 . . . . 187 F7
Surbiton KT6 . . . . 181 E7
Effort St, SW17 . . . . 167 H5
Effra Par, SW2 . . . . 151 G5
Effra Rd, SW2 . . . . 151 G4
SW19 . . . . 166 E6
Egbert St, NW1 . . . . 110 A1
Egbury Ho, SW15 *off Tangley Gro* 147 F6
Egerton Cl, Pnr. HA5 . . . . . 66 A4
Egerton Cres, SW3 . . . . 31 H1
Egerton Dr, SE10 . . . . 154 B1
Egerton Gdns, NW4 . . . . . . 71 H4
NW10 . . . . 107 J1
SW3 . . . . 23 G6
W13 . . . . 105 E6
Ilford IG3 . . . . 99 J3
Egerton Gdns Ms, SW3 . . . 23 H6
Egerton Pl, SW3 . . . . 23 H6
Egerton Rd, N16 . . . . 76 C7
SE25 . . . . 188 B3
New Malden KT3 . . . . . 183 F4
Egerton Rd, Twick. TW2 . . 144 B7
Wembley HA0 . . . . 87 J7
Egerton Ter, SW3 . . . . 23 H6
Egerton Way, Hayes UB3 . 121 E7
Eggardon Ct, Nthlt. UB5 *off Lancaster Rd* 85 J6
Egham Cl, SW19 *off Winterfold Cl* 166 B2
Sutton SM3 . . . . 198 B2
Egham Cres, Sutt. SM3 . . 198 A3
Egham Rd, E13 . . . . 115 H5
Eglantine Rd, SW18 . . . . . 149 F5
Egleston Rd, Mord. SM4 . 184 E6
Eglington Ct, SE17 . . . . 35 J5
Eglington Rd, E4 . . . . 46 D7
Eglinton Hill, SE18 . . . . . . 137 E6
Eglinton Rd, SE18 . . . . . . 136 D6
Egliston Ms, SW15 . . . . . . 147 J3
Egliston Rd, SW15 . . . . . . 147 J3
Eglon Ms, NW1 *off Berkley Rd* 91 J7
Egmont Av, Surb. KT6 . . . 195 J1
Egmont Rd, N.Mal. KT3 . . 183 F4
Surbiton KT6 . . . . 195 J1
Sutton SM2 . . . . 199 F7
Walton-on-Thames KT12 . . . . 178 B7
Egmont St, SE14 . . . . 133 G7
Egremont Ho, SE13 *off Conington Rd* 154 B2
Egremont Rd, SE27 . . . . . 169 G3
Egret Way, Hayes UB4 . . . 102 D5
Eider Cl, E7 . . . . 97 F5
Hayes UB4 *off Cygnet Way* 102 D5
Eighteenth Rd, Mitch. CR4 . . . . 186 E4
Eighth Av, E12 . . . . 98 C4
Hayes UB3 . . . . 122 A1
Eileen Rd, SE25 . . . . 188 A5
Eindhoven Cl, Cars. SM5 . 200 A1
Eisenhower Dr, E6 . . . . . . 116 B5
Elaine Gro, NW5 . . . . 92 A5
Elam Cl, SE5 . . . . 151 H2
Elam St, SE5 . . . . 151 H2
Eland Pl, Croy. CR0 *off Eland Rd* 201 H3
Eland Rd, SW11 . . . . 149 J3
Croydon CR0 . . . . 201 H3
Elba Pl, SE17 . . . . 36 A1
Elberon Av, Croy. CR0 . . . 186 C6
Elbe St, SW6 . . . . 149 F2
Elborough Rd, SE25 . . . . . 188 D5
Elborough St, SW18 . . . . 166 D1
Elbury Dr, E16 . . . . 115 G6
Elcho St, SW11 . . . . 129 H7
Elcot Av, SE15 . . . . 132 E7
Elder Av, N8 . . . . 74 E5
Elderberry Cl, Ilf. IG6 *off Hazel La* 64/65 E7
Elderberry Gro, SE27 *off Linton Gro* 169 J5
Elderberry Rd, W5 . . . . . . 125 H2
Elderberry Way, E6 *off Vicarage La* 116 C3
Elder Cl, N20 . . . . 56 E2
Sidcup DA15 . . . . 175 J1
Elder Ct, Bushey (Bushey Hth) WD23 . . . . 52 B2
Elderfield Pl, SW17 . . . . . 168 B4
Elderfield Rd, E5 . . . . 95 F4
Elderfield Wk, E11 . . . . 79 H5
Elderflower Way, E15 . . . . . 96 E7
Elder Gdns, SE27 . . . . 169 J4
Elder Oak Cl, SE20 . . . . . . 188 E1
Elder Rd, SE27 . . . . 169 J5
Elderslie Cl, Beck. BR3 . . . 190 B5
Elderslie Rd, SE9 . . . . 156 D5
Elder St, E1 . . . . 21 F1
Elderton Rd, SE26 . . . . . . 171 H4
Eldertree Pl, Mitch. CR4 *off Eldertree Way* 186 C1
Eldertree Way, Mitch. CR4 . . . . 186 B1
Elder Wk, N1 *off Essex Rd* 111 H1
Elderwood Pl, SE27 *off Elder Rd* 169 J5
Eldon Av, Borwd. WD6 . . . . 38 A2
Croydon CR0 . . . . 203 F2
Hounslow TW5 . . . . 123 G7
Eldon Gro, NW3 . . . . 91 G5
Eldon Pk, SE25 . . . . 188 E4
Eldon Rd, E17 . . . . 77 J4
N9 . . . . 61 F2
N22 . . . . 75 H1
W8 . . . . 22 B6
Eldon St, EC2 . . . . 20 C2
Eldon Way, NW10 . . . . 106 B2
Eldred Rd, Bark. IG11 . . . . 117 H1
Eldridge Cl, Felt. TW14 . . . 160 A1
Eleanor Cl, N15 *off Arnold Rd* 76 C3
SE16 . . . . 133 G2
Eleanor Cres, NW7 . . . . 56 A4
Eleanor Gdns, Barn. EN5 . . 40 A5
Dagenham RM8 . . . . . . 101 F3
Eleanor Gro, SW13 . . . . . . 147 E3
Eleanor Rd, E8 . . . . 94 E7
E15 . . . . 97 F6
N11 . . . . 58 E6
Eleanor St, E3 . . . . 114 A3
Eleanor Wk, SE18 *off Samuel St* 136 C4
Electra Business Pk, E16 *off Bidder St* 114 D5
Electric Av, SW9 . . . . 151 G4
Electric La, SW9 . . . . 151 G4
Electric Par, E18 *off George La* 79 G2
Surbiton KT6 . . . . 181 G6
Elektron Ho, E14 *off Blackwall Way* 114 D7
Elephant & Castle, SE1 . . . 27 H6
Elephant & Castle Shop Cen, SE1 *off Elephant & Castle* 131 J4
Elephant La, SE16 . . . . . . 133 F2
Elephant Rd, SE17 . . . . 35 J1
Elers Rd, W13 . . . . 125 F2
Hayes UB3 . . . . 121 G4
Eleven Acre Ri, Loug. IG10 . . . . 48 C3
Eley Est, N18 . . . . 61 F5
Eley Rd, N18 . . . . 61 G5
Elfindale Rd, SE24 . . . . . . 151 J5
Elfin Gro, Tedd. TW11 *off Broad St* 162 C5
Elford Cl, SE3 . . . . 155 H4
Elfort Rd, N5 . . . . 93 G4
Elfrida Cres, SE6 . . . . 172 A4
Elf Row, E1 . . . . 113 F7
Elfwine Rd, W7 . . . . 104 B5
Elgal Cl, Orp. BR6 *off Orchard Rd* . . . 206/207 E5
Elgar Av, NW10 *off Mitchellbrook Way* . . 88 D6
SW16 . . . . 186 E3
W5 . . . . 125 H2
Surbiton KT5 . . . . 182 B7
Elgar Cl, E13 *off Bushey Rd* 115 J2
SE8 *off Comet St* 134 A7
Buckhurst Hill IG9 . . . . . . 64 A2
Elgar St, SE16 . . . . 133 H3
Elgin Av, W9 . . . . 6 A4
W12 . . . . 127 G2
Harrow HA3 . . . . 68 E2
Elgin Cl, W12 . . . . 127 H2
Elgin Cres, W11 . . . . 108 C6
Hounslow (Hthrw Air.) TW6 *off Eastern Perimeter Rd* 141 H2
Elgin Ms, W11 *off Ladbroke Gro* 108 B6
Elgin Ms N, W9 . . . . 6 B3
Elgin Ms S, W9 . . . . 6 B3
Elgin Rd, N22 . . . . 74 C2
Croydon CR0 . . . . 202 C1
Ilford IG3 . . . . 99 H1
Sutton SM1 . . . . 199 F3
Wallington SM6 . . . . . . 200 C6
Elgood Av, Nthwd. HA6 . . . 50 A6
Elgood Cl, W11 *off Avondale Pk Rd* . . . 108 B7
Elham Cl, Brom. BR1 . . . . 174 A7
Elia Ms, N1 . . . . 11 G2
Elias Pl, SW8 . . . . 34 E6
Elia St, N1 . . . . 11 G2
Elibank Rd, SE9 . . . . 156 D4
Elim Est, SE1 . . . . 28 D5
Elim Way, E13 . . . . 115 F3
Eliot Bk, SE23 . . . . 170 E2
Eliot Cotts, SE3 *off Eliot Pl* 154/155 E2
Eliot Ct, N15 *off Tynemouth Rd* 76 C4
Eliot Dr, Har. HA2 . . . . 85 H2
Eliot Gdns, SW15 . . . . 147 G4
Eliot Hill, SE13 . . . . 154 C2
Eliot Ms, NW8 . . . . 6 D2
Eliot Pk, SE13 . . . . 154 C3
Eliot Pl, SE3 . . . . 154 E2
Eliot Rd, Dag. RM9 . . . . . . 100 D4
Eliot Vale, SE3 . . . . 154 D2
Elizabethan Cl, Stai. (Stanw.) TW19 *off Elizabethan Way* 140 A7

Elizabethan Way, Stai. (Stanw.) TW19 **140** A7
Elizabeth Av, N1 **93** J7
Enfield EN2 **43** H3
Ilford IG1 **99** G2
Elizabeth Blackwell Ho, N22 *off Progress Way* **75** G1
Elizabeth Br, SW1 **32** D2
Elizabeth Cl, E14 *off Grundy St* **114** B6
W9 **6** D5
Barnet EN5 **40** A3
Romford RM7 **83** H1
Sutton SM1 **198** C4
Elizabeth Clyde Cl, N15 **76** B4
Elizabeth Cotts, Rich. TW9 **145** J1
Elizabeth Ct, SW1 **25** J6
Woodford Green IG8 *off Navestock Cres* **63** J7
Elizabeth Est, SE17 **36** B5
Elizabeth Fry Pl, SE18 **156** B1
Elizabeth Fry Rd, E8 *off Lamb La* **94/95** E7
Elizabeth Gdns, W3 **127** F1
Isleworth TW7 **144** D4
Stanmore HA7 **53** F6
Sunbury-on-Thames TW16 **178** C3
Elizabeth Ms, NW3 **91** H6
Elizabeth Pl, N15 **76** A4
Elizabeth Ride, N9 **45** E7
Elizabeth Rd, E6 **116** A1
N15 **76** B5
Elizabeth Sq, SE16 *off Rotherhithe St* **113** H7
Elizabeth St, SW1 **32** C1
Elizabeth Ter, SE9 **156** C6
Elizabeth Way, SE19 **170** A7
Feltham TW13 **160** C4
Elkanette Ms, N20 *off Ridgeview Rd* **57** F2
Elkington Rd, E13 **115** H4
Elkstone Rd, W10 **108** C5
Ellaline Rd, W6 **128** A6
Ellanby Cres, N18 **60** F5
Elland Rd, SE15 **153** F4
Ella Rd, N8 **75** E7
Ellement Cl, Pnr. HA5 **66** D5
Ellenborough Pl, SW15 **147** G4
Ellenborough Rd, N22 **75** J1
Sidcup DA14 **176** D5
Ellen Cl, Brom. BR1 **192** A3
Ellen Ct, N9 *off Densworth Gro* **61** F2
Ellen St, E1 **21** J4
Ellen Webb Dr, Har. (Wldste) HA3 **68** B3
Elleray Rd, Tedd. TW11 **162** C6
Ellerby St, SW6 **148** A1
Ellerdale Cl, NW3 *off Ellerdale Rd* **91** F4
Ellerdale Rd, NW3 **91** F5
Ellerdale St, SE13 **154** D4
Ellerdine Rd, Houns. TW3 **143** J4
Ellerker Gdns, Rich. TW10 **145** H6
Ellerman Av, Twick. TW2 **161** F1
Ellerslie Gdns, NW10 **107** G1
Ellerslie Rd, W12 **127** H1
Ellerslie Sq Ind Est, SW2 **150** E5
Ellerton Gdns, Dag. RM9 **100** C7
Ellerton Rd, SW13 **147** G1
SW18 **167** G1
SW20 **165** G7
Dagenham RM9 **100** C7
Surbiton KT6 **195** J2
Ellery Rd, SE19 **170** A7
Ellery St, SE15 **152** E2
Ellesborough Cl, Wat. WD19 **50** C5
Ellesmere Av, NW7 **54** D3
Beckenham BR3 **190** B2
Ellesmere Cl, E11 **79** F5
Ellesmere Gdns, Ilf. IG4 **80** B5
Ellesmere Gro, Barn. EN5 **40** C5
Ellesmere Rd, E3 **113** H2
NW10 **89** G5
W4 **126** D6
Greenford UB6 **103** J4
Twickenham TW1 **145** F6
Ellesmere St, E14 **114** B6
Ellingfort Rd, E8 **95** E7
Ellingham Rd, E15 **96** D4
W12 **127** G2
Chessington KT9 **195** G6
Ellington Rd, N10 **74** B4
Ellington Rd, Houns. TW3 **143** H2
Ellington St, N7 **93** G6
Elliot Cl, E15 **96** E7
Elliot Rd, NW4 **71** H6
Stanmore HA7 **52** D6
Elliott Av, Ruis. HA4 **84** B2
Elliott Cl, Wem. HA9 **87** J3
Elliott Rd, SW9 **131** H7
W4 **126** E4
Bromley BR2 **192** A4
Thornton Heath CR7 **187** H4
Elliott's Pl, N1 *off St. Peters St* **111** H1
Elliott Sq, NW3 **91** H7
Elliotts Row, SE11 **35** G1
Ellis Cl, NW10 *off High Rd* **89** H6
SE9 **175** F2
Elliscombe Rd, SE7 **135** J5
Ellis Ct, W7 **104** C5
Ellisfield Dr, SW15 **147** F7
Ellison Gdns, Sthl. UB2 **123** F4
Ellison Ho, SE13 *off Lewisham Rd* **154** C2
Ellison Rd, SW13 **147** F2
SW16 **168** D7
Sidcup DA15 **175** G1
Ellis Rd, Mitch. CR4 **185** J6
Southall UB2 **123** J1
Ellis St, SW1 **32** A1
Elliston Ho, SE18 **136** D4
Ellora Rd, SW16 **168** D5
Ellsworth St, E2 **113** E3
Ellwood Ct, W9 **6** A6
Elmar Rd, N15 **76** A4
Elm Av, W5 **125** H1
Ruislip HA4 **84** A1
Elmbank, N14 **43** E7
Elmbank Av, Barn. EN5 **39** J4
Elm Bk Dr, Brom. BR1 **192** A2
Elm Bk Gdns, SW13 **147** E2
Elmbank Way, W7 **104** A5
Elmbourne Dr, Belv. DA17 **139** H4
Elmbourne Rd, SW17 **168** A3
Elmbridge Av, Surb. KT5 **182** B5
Elmbridge Cl, Ruis. HA4 **66** A6
Elmbridge Wk, E8 *off Wilman Gro* **94** D7
Elmbrook Cl, Sun. TW16 **178** B1
Elmbrook Gdns, SE9 **156** B4
Elmbrook Rd, Sutt. SM1 **198** C4
Elm Cl, E11 **79** H6
N19 *off Hargrave Pk* **92** C2
NW4 **72** A5
SW20 *off Grand Dr* **183** J4
Buckhurst Hill IG9 **64** A2
Carshalton SM5 **199** J1
Harrow HA2 **67** H6
Hayes UB3 **102** A6
Romford RM7 **83** H2
South Croydon CR2 **202** B6
Surbiton KT5 **182** C7
Twickenham TW2 **161** H2
Elm Ct, EC4 **19** E5
Mitcham CR4 *off Armfield Cres* **185** J2
Elmcourt Rd, SE27 **169** H2
Elm Cres, W5 **125** H1
Kingston upon Thames KT2 **181** H1
Elmcroft, N8 **75** F5
Elmcroft Av, E11 **79** H5
N9 **44** E6
NW11 **72** C7
Sidcup DA15 **157** J6
Elmcroft Cl, E11 **79** H4
W5 **105** G6
Chessington KT9 **195** H3
Feltham TW14 **141** J6
Elmcroft Cres, NW11 **72** B7
Harrow HA2 **67** G3
Elmcroft Dr, Chess. KT9 **195** H3
Elmcroft Gdns, NW9 **70** A5
Elmcroft St, E5 **95** F4
Elmdale Rd, N13 **59** F5
Elmdene, Surb. KT5 **196** C1
Elmdene Cl, Beck. BR3 **189** J5
Elmdene Rd, SE18 **136** E5
Elmdon Rd, Houns. TW4 **142** D2
Hounslow (Hatt.Cr.) TW6 **141** J3
Elm Dr, Har. HA2 **67** H6
Sunbury-on-Thames TW16 **178** C2
Elmer Cl, Enf. EN2 **43** F3
Elmer Gdns, Edg. HA8 **54** B7
Isleworth TW7 **144** A3
Elmer Rd, SE6 **154** C7
Elmers Dr, Tedd. TW11 *off Kingston Rd* **162/163** E6
ELMERS END, Beck. BR3 **189** H3
Elmers End Rd, SE20 **189** F2
Beckenham BR3 **189** F2
Elmerside Rd, Beck. BR3 **189** H4
Elmers Rd, SE25 **188** D7
Elmfield Av, N8 **74** E5
Mitcham CR4 **186** A1
Teddington TW11 **162** C5
Elmfield Cl, Har. HA1 **86** B2
Elmfield Pk, Brom. BR1 **191** G3
Elmfield Rd, E4 **62** C2
E17 **77** G6
N2 **73** G3
Elmfield Rd, SW17 **168** A2
Bromley BR1 **191** G3
Southall UB2 **123** E3
Elmfield Way, W9 **108** D5
Elm Friars Wk, NW1 **92** D7
Elm Gdns, N2 **73** F3
Esher (Clay.) KT10 **194** C6
Mitcham CR4 **186** D4
Elmgate Av, Felt. TW13 **160** B3
Elmgate Gdns, Edg. HA8 **54** D5
Elm Grn, W3 **106** E6
Elmgreen Cl, E15 *off Church St N* **114/115** E1
Elm Gro, N8 **75** E6
NW2 **90** A4
SE15 **152** C2
SW19 **166** B7
Harrow HA2 **67** G7
Kingston upon Thames KT2 **181** H1
Orpington BR6 **207** J1
Sutton SM1 **199** E4
Woodford Green IG8 **63** F5
Elmgrove Cres, Har. HA1 **68** C5
Elmgrove Gdns, Har. HA1 **68** D5
Elm Gro Par, Wall. SM6 *off Butter Hill* **200** A3
Elm Gro Rd, SW13 **147** G2
W5 **125** H2
Elmgrove Rd, Croy. CR0 **188** E7
Harrow HA1 **68** C5
Elm Hall Gdns, E11 **79** H5
Elmhurst, Belv. DA17 **139** E6
Elmhurst Av, N2 **73** G3
Mitcham CR4 **168** B7
Elmhurst Dr, E18 **79** G2
Elmhurst Gdns, E18 *off Elmhurst Dr* **79** H1
Elmhurst Mans, SW4 *off Edgeley Rd* **150** D3
Elmhurst Rd, E7 **97** H7
N17 **76** C2
SE9 **174** B2
Elmhurst St, SW4 **150** D3
Elmhurst Vil, SE15 *off Cheltenham Rd* **153** F4
Elmhurst Way, Loug. IG10 **48** C7
Elmington Cl, Bex. DA5 **159** H6
Elmington Est, SE5 **36** C7
Elmington Rd, SE5 **152** A1
Elmira St, SE13 **154** B3
Elm La, SE6 **171** J2
Elmlee Cl, Chis. BR7 **174** C6
Elmley Cl, E6 *off Northumberland Rd* **116** B5
Elmley St, SE18 **137** G4
Elm Ms, Rich. TW10 *off Grove Rd* **145** J6
Elmore Cl, Wem. HA0 **105** H2
Elmore Rd, E11 **96** C3
Enfield EN3 **45** G1
Elmores, Loug. IG10 **48** D3
Elmore St, N1 **93** J7
Elm Pk, SW2 **151** F6
Stanmore HA7 **53** E5
Elm Pk Av, N15 **76** C5
Elm Pk Ct, Pnr. HA5 **66** C3
Elm Pk Gdns, NW4 **72** A5
SW10 **31** E4
Elm Pk La, SW3 **30** E4
Elm Pk Mans, SW10 **30** D5
Elm Pk Rd, E10 **95** H1
N3 **56** C7
N21 **43** J7
SE25 **188** C3
SW3 **30** E5
Pinner HA5 **66** C2
Elm Pl, SW7 **31** E3
Elm Quay Ct, SW8 **33** H5
Elm Rd, E7 **97** F6
E11 **96** D2
E17 **78** C5
N22 *off Granville Rd* **75** H1
SW14 **146** C3
Elm Rd, Barn. EN5 **40** C4
Beckenham BR3 **189** J2
Chessington KT9 **195** H4
Epsom KT17 **197** F6
Esher (Clay.) KT10 **194** C6
Kingston upon Thames KT2 **181** J1
New Malden KT3 **182** D4
Romford RM7 **83** H2
Sidcup DA14 **176** A4
Thornton Heath CR7 **188** A4
Wallington SM6 **200** A1
Wembley HA9 **87** H5
Elm Rd W, Sutt. SM3 **184** C7
Elm Row, NW3 **91** F3
Elms, The, SW13 **147** F3
Elms Av, N10 **74** B3
NW4 **72** A5
Elmscott Gdns, N21 **43** J6
Elmscott Rd, Brom. BR1 **173** F5
Elms Ct, Wem. HA0 **86** C4
Elms Cres, SW4 **150** C6
Elmsdale Rd, E17 **77** J4
Elms Gdns, Dag. RM9 **101** F4
Wembley HA0 **86** D4
Elmshaw Rd, SW15 **147** G5
Elmshurst Cres, N2 **73** G4
Elmside, Croy. (New Adgtn) CR0 **204** B6
Elmside Rd, Wem. HA9 **88** A3
Elms La, Wem. HA0 **86** D4
Elmsleigh Av, Har. HA3 **69** E4
Elmsleigh Ct, Sutt. SM1 **198** E3
Elmsleigh Rd, Twick. TW2 **162** A2
Elmslie Cl, Wdf.Grn. IG8 **64** C6
Elmslie Pt, E3 **113** J5
Elms Ms, W2 **14** E5
Elms Pk Av, Wem. HA0 **86** D4
Elms Rd, SW4 **150** C5
Harrow HA3 **52** B7
ELMSTEAD, Chis. BR7 **174** A5
Elmstead Av, Chis. BR7 **174** C5
Wembley HA9 **87** H1
Elmstead Cl, N20 **56** D2
Epsom KT19 **197** E5
Elmstead Cres, Well. DA10 **138** C6
Elmstead Gdns, Wor.Pk. KT4 **197** G3
Elmstead Glade, Chis. BR7 **174** C6
Elmstead La, Chis. BR7 **174** C5
Elmstead Rd, Ilf. IG3 **99** H2
Elmstone Rd, SW6 **148** D1
Elm St, WC1 **10** D6
Elmsworth Av, Houns. TW3 **143** H2
Elm Ter, NW2 **90** D3
SE9 **156** D6
Harrow HA3 **52** A7
Elmton Way, E5 *off Rendlesham Rd* **94** D3
Elm Tree Av, Esher KT10 **180** A7
Elm Tree Cl, NW8 **7** E3
Northolt UB5 **103** F7
Elm Tree Rd, NW8 **7** E3
Elmtree Rd, Tedd. TW11 **162** B4
Elm Wk, NW3 **90** D2
SW20 **183** J4
Orpington BR6 **206** C3
Elm Way, N11 **58** A6
NW10 **88** E4
Epsom KT19 **196** D5
Worcester Park KT4 **197** J3
Elmwood Av, N13 **59** E5
Borehamwood WD6 **38** B4
Feltham TW13 **160** A2
Harrow HA3 **68** D5
Elmwood Cl, Epsom KT17 **197** G7
Wallington SM6 **200** A2
Elmwood Ct, SW11 **150** B1
Wembley HA0 **86** D3
Elmwood Cres, NW9 **70** C4
Elmwood Dr, Bex. DA5 **158** E7
Epsom KT17 **197** G6
Elmwood Gdns, W7 **104** B6
Elmwood Rd, SE24 **152** A5
W4 **126** C6
Croydon CR0 **187** H7
Mitcham CR4 **185** J3
Elmworth Gro, SE21 **170** A2
Elnathan Ms, W9 **6** B6
Elphinstone Rd, E17 **77** J2
Elphinstone St, N5 *off Avenell Rd* **93** H4
Elrington Rd, E8 **94** D6
Woodford Green IG8 **63** G5
Elruge Cl, West Dr. UB7 **120** A3

Elsa Rd, Well. DA16 . . . . . 158 B2
Elsa St, E1 . . . . 113 H5
Elsdale St, E9. . . . . 95 F6
Elsden Ms, E2 *off Old Ford Rd* 113 F2
Elsden Rd, N17. . . . . 76 C1
Elsenham Rd, E12 . . . . 98 D5
Elsenham St, SW18 . . . . . 166 C1
Elsham Rd, E11 . . . . 96 E3
W14. . . . . 128 B2
Elsham Ter, W14. . . . . 128 B2
Elsiedene Rd, N21 . . . . 43 J7
Elsiemaud Rd, SE4. . . . . . 153 J5
Elsie Rd, SE22 . . . . 152 C4
Elsinore Av, Stai. TW19. . . 140 B7
Elsinore Gdns, NW2. . . . . . 90 B3
Elsinore Rd, SE23. . . . . . . 171 H1
Elsinore Way, Rich. TW9 *off Lower Richmond Rd* . . 146 B3
Elsley Rd, SW11 . . . . 149 J3
Elspeth Rd, SW11. . . . . . . 149 J4
Wembley HA0 . . . . 87 H5
Elsrick Av, Mord. SM4 . . . 184 D5
Elstan Way, Croy. CR0 . . . 189 H7
Elstead Ct, Sutt. SM3 *off Stonecot Hill* 198 B1
Elsted St, SE17 . . . . 36 C2
Elstow Cl, SE9 . . . . 156 D5
Ruislip HA4 . . . . 66 D7
Elstow Gdns, Dag. RM9 . . 118 E1
Elstow Rd, Dag. RM9. . . . 100 E7
Elstree Gdns, N9 . . . . 61 E1
Belvedere DA17 . . . . . . 139 E4
Ilford IG1 . . . . 99 F5
Elstree Hill, Brom. BR1. . . 172 E7
Elstree Pk, Borwd. WD6. . . 38 D6
Elstree Way, Borwd. WD6 . . . . 38 B3
Elswick Rd, SE13 . . . . 154 B2
Elswick St, SW6. . . . . 149 F2
Elsworthy, T.Ditt. KT7 . . . . 180 B6
Elsworthy Ri, NW3. . . . . . . 91 H7
Elsworthy Rd, NW3 . . . . . . 109 H1
Elsworthy Ter, NW3 . . . . . . 91 H7
Elsynge Rd, SW18 . . . . . . 149 G5
ELTHAM, SE9. . . . . 156 A6
Eltham Grn, SE9 . . . . 155 J5
Eltham Grn Rd, SE9. . . . . . 155 J4
Eltham High St, SE9 . . . . 156 C6
Eltham Hill, SE9. . . . . 156 A5
★Eltham Palace, SE9. . . . 156 B7
Eltham Palace Rd, SE9. . . 155 J6
Eltham Pk Gdns, SE9. . . . 156 D4
Eltham Rd, SE9 . . . . 155 J5
SE12 . . . . 155 F5
Elthiron Rd, SW6 . . . . 148 D1
Elthorne Av, W7 . . . . 124 C2
Elthorne Ct, Felt. TW13 . . 160 C1
Elthorne Pk Rd, W7 . . . . . . 124 C2
Elthorne Rd, N19 . . . . 92 D2
NW9 . . . . 70 D7
Elthorne Way, NW9 . . . . . . 70 D6
Elthruda Rd, SE13 . . . . . . 154 D6
Eltisley Rd, Ilf. IG1 . . . . . . 98 E4
Elton Av, Barn. EN5 . . . . . . 40 C5
Greenford UB6 . . . . 86 C6
Wembley HA0. . . . . 87 E5
Elton Cl, Kings.T. KT1. . . . 163 F7
Elton Ho, E3 . . . . 113 J1
Elton Pl, N16 . . . . 94 B5
Elton Rd, Kings.T. KT2 . . . 181 J1
Eltringham St, SW18 . . . . 149 F4
Elvaston Ms, SW7 . . . . 22 D5
Elvaston Pl, SW7 . . . . 22 C6
Elveden Pl, NW10. . . . . 106 A2
Elveden Rd, NW10 . . . . . . 106 A2
Elvendon Rd, N13 . . . . 58 E6
Elver Gdns, E2 . . . . 13 J3
Elverson Ms, SE8. . . . . 154 B2
Elverson Rd, SE8 . . . . 154 B2
Elverton St, SW1 . . . . 33 H1
Elvington Grn, Brom. BR2 . . . . 191 F5
Elvington La, NW9. . . . . . . 70 E1
Elvino Rd, SE26 . . . . 171 H5
Elvis Rd, NW2 . . . . 89 J6
Elwill Way, Beck. BR3. . . . 190 C4
Elwin St, E2 . . . . 13 H3
Elwood St, N5 . . . . 93 H3
Elwyn Gdns, SE12 . . . . . . 155 G7
Ely Cl, N.Mal. KT3 . . . . . . 183 F2
Ely Ct, EC1 . . . . 19 F2
Ely Gdns, Borwd. WD6. . . . 38 D5
Dagenham RM10. . . . . . 101 J3
Ilford IG1 *off Canterbury Av* 80 B7
Elyne Rd, N4 . . . . 75 G6
Ely Pl, EC1 . . . . 19 F2
Woodford Green IG8 . . . 64 D6
Ely Rd, E10. . . . . 78 C6
Croydon CR0. . . . . 188 A5
Hounslow (Hthrw Air.) TW6 *off Eastern Perimeter Rd* 141 J2
Hounslow (Houns.W.) TW4 . . . . 142 C3
Elysian Av, Orp. BR5 . . . . 193 J6
Elysium Pl, SW6 *off Fulham Pk Gdns* . . 148 C2
Elysium St, SW6 *off Fulham Pk Gdns* . . 148 C2
Elystan Business Cen, Hayes UB4. . . . . 102 C7
Elystan Pl, SW3 . . . . 31 H3
Elystan St, SW3. . . . . 31 G2
Elystan Wk, N1 *off Cloudesley Rd* 111 G1
Emanuel Av, W3 . . . . 106 C6
Emanuel Dr, Hmptn. TW12. . . . . 161 F5
Embankment, SW15 . . . . 148 A2
Embankment, The, Twick. TW1. . . . . 162 D1
Embankment Gdns, SW3 . 32 A5
Embankment Pl, WC2 . . . . 26 B1
Embassy Ct, Sid. DA14 . . 176 B3
Welling DA16 *off Welling High St* . . . 158 B3
Embassy Gdns, Beck. BR3 *off Blakeney Rd*. 189 J1
Emba St, SE16. . . . . 29 J4
Ember Cl, Orp. BR5 . . . . . 193 F7
Embercourt Rd, T.Ditt. KT7 . . . . 180 B6
Ember Fm Av, E.Mol. KT8 . . . . 180 A6
Ember Fm Way, E.Mol. KT8 . . . . 180 A6
Ember Gdns, T.Ditt. KT7 . . 180 B7
Ember La, E.Mol. KT8 . . . . 180 A7
Esher KT10 . . . . 180 A7
Emberton, SE5. . . . . 36 D5
Embleton Rd, SE13 . . . . . 154 B3
Watford WD19. . . . . 50 A3
Embleton Wk, Hmptn. TW12 *off Fearnley Cres*. 161 F6
Embry Cl, Stan. HA7 . . . . . 52 D4
Embry Dr, Stan. HA7 . . . . . 52 D6
Embry Way, Stan. HA7. . . . 52 D5
Emden Cl, West Dr. UB7 . 120 D2
Emden St, SW6 . . . . 149 E1
Emerald Cl, E16 . . . . 116 B6
Emerald Gdns, Dag. RM8. 101 G1
Emerald Sq, Sthl. UB2 . . . 122 D3
Emerald St, WC1 . . . . 18 C1
Emerson Gdns, Har. HA3. . 69 J6
Emerson Rd, Ilf. IG1. . . . . . 80 D7
Emerson St, SE1 . . . . 27 J1
Emerton Cl, Bexh. DA6 . . 159 E4
Emery Hill St, SW1 . . . . . . 25 G6
Emery St, SE1 . . . . 27 F5
Emes Rd, Erith DA8 . . . . . 139 J7
Emilia Cl, Enf. EN3. . . . . . . 45 E5
Emlyn Gdns, W12. . . . . . . 127 E2
Emlyn Rd, W12. . . . . 127 E2
Emmanuel Rd, SW12. . . . 168 C1
Emma Rd, E13 . . . . 115 F2
Emma St, E2. . . . . 112 E2
Emmaus Way, Chig. IG7 . . 64 D5
Emmott Av, Ilf. IG6. . . . . . . 81 F5
Emmott Cl, E1 . . . . 113 H4
NW11. . . . . 73 F6
Emms Pas, Kings.T. KT1 *off High St*. 181 G2
Emperor's Gate, SW7 . . . . 22 B6
Empire Av, N18 . . . . 59 J5
Empire Ct, Wem. HA9 . . . . 88 B3
Empire Rd, Grnf. UB6. . . . 105 F1
Empire Sq, N7 . . . . 93 E3
SE20 *off High St* 171 G7
Empire Way, Wem. HA9 . . . 87 J4
Empire Wf Rd, E14 . . . . . . 134 D4
Empress Av, E4 . . . . 62 A7
E12 . . . . 97 J2
Ilford IG1. . . . . 98 C2
Woodford Green IG8 . . . 63 F7
Empress Dr, Chis. BR7 . . . 174 E6
Empress Ms, SE5. . . . . . . 151 J2
Empress Pl, SW6 . . . . 128 D5
Empress St, SE17 . . . . 36 A5
Empson St, E3 . . . . 114 B4
Emsworth Cl, N9 . . . . 61 F1
Emsworth Rd, Ilf. IG6. . . . . 81 E2
Emsworth St, SW2 . . . . . 169 F2
Emu Rd, SW8. . . . . 150 B2
Ena Rd, SW16 . . . . 186 E3
Enbrook St, W10. . . . . 108 B3
Endale Cl, Cars. SM5 . . . . 199 J2
Endeavour Ho, Barn. EN5 . . . . 41 F4
Endeavour Way, SW19. . . 166 E4
Barking IG11 . . . . 118 A2
Croydon CR0. . . . . 186 D7
Endell St, WC2 . . . . 18 A3
Enderby St, SE10. . . . . . . 134 E5
Enderley Cl, Har. HA3 *off Enderley Rd*. 68 B1
Enderley Rd, Har. HA3 . . . . 68 B1
Endersby Rd, Barn. EN5 . . 39 J5
Endersleigh Gdns, NW4 . . 71 G4
Endlebury Rd, E4. . . . . 62 B2
Endlesham Rd, SW12 . . . 150 A7
Endsleigh Gdns, WC1 . . . . . 9 H5
Ilford IG1. . . . . 98 C2
Surbiton KT6. . . . . 181 F6
Endsleigh Ind Est, Sthl. UB2. . . . . 123 F4
Endsleigh Pl, WC1 . . . . 9 J5
Endsleigh Rd, W13 . . . . . . 104 D7
Southall UB2. . . . . 123 E4
Endsleigh St, WC1 . . . . 9 H5
Endway, Surb. KT5 . . . . . 182 A7
Endwell Rd, SE4. . . . . 153 H2
Endymion Rd, N4. . . . . 75 G7
SW2. . . . . 151 F6
Energen Cl, NW10 . . . . 88 E6
ENFIELD, EN1 - EN3. . . . . . 44 C3
ENFIELD HIGHWAY, Enf. EN3 . . . . 45 F3
Enfield Retail Pk, Enf. EN1 . . . . 44 E3
Enfield Rd, N1 . . . . 94 B7
W3. . . . . 126 B2
Brentford TW8. . . . . 125 G5
Enfield EN2 . . . . 42 D4
Hounslow (Hthrw Air.) TW6 *off Eastern Perimeter Rd*. 141 H2
ENFIELD TOWN, Enf. EN2 . 44 A2
Enfield Wk, Brent. TW8. . . 125 G5
Enford St, W1. . . . . 15 J1
Engadine Cl, Croy. CR0 . . 202 C3
Engadine St, SW18 . . . . . 166 C1
Engate St, SE13 . . . . 154 C4
Engel Pk, NW7. . . . . 55 J6
Engineer Cl, SE18 . . . . . . 136 D6
Engineers Way, Wem. HA9. 88 A4
Englands La, NW3 . . . . 91 J6
Loughton IG10 . . . . 48 D2
England Way, N.Mal. KT3 182 B4
Englefield Cl, Croy. CR0 *off Queen's Rd*. 187 J6
Enfield EN2. . . . . 43 G2
Orpington BR5 . . . . 193 J4
Englefield Cres, Orp. BR5 . . . . 193 J4
Englefield Path, Orp. BR5 . . . . 193 J4
Englefield Rd, N1. . . . . 94 A6
Engleheart Dr, Felt. TW14 141 J6
Engleheart Rd, SE6 . . . . . 154 B7
Englewood Rd, SW12 . . . 150 B6
English Grds, SE1 . . . . 28 D2
English St, E3. . . . . 113 J4
Enid St, SE16. . . . . 29 G5
Enmore Av, SE25 . . . . 188 D5
Enmore Gdns, SW14 . . . . . 146 D6
Enmore Rd, SE25. . . . . . . 188 D5
SW15. . . . . 147 J4
Southall UB1. . . . . 103 G4
Ennerdale Av, Stan. HA7 . . 69 F3
Ennerdale Cl, Sutt. SM1. . 198 C4
Ennerdale Dr, NW9 . . . . . . 70 E5
Ennerdale Gdns, Wem. HA9. . . . . 87 G1
Ennerdale Ho, E3 . . . . 113 J4
Ennerdale Rd, Bexh. DA7. 159 G1
Richmond TW9 . . . . 145 J2
Ennersdale Rd, SE13 . . . . 154 D5
Ennismore Av, W4 . . . . . . 127 F4
Greenford UB6 . . . . 86 B6
Ennismore Gdns, SW7. . . . 23 G4
Thames Ditton KT7. . . . 180 B6
Ennismore Gdns Ms, SW7 . . . . 23 G5
Ennismore Ms, SW7 . . . . . 23 G5
Ennismore St, SW7 . . . . . . 23 G5
Ennis Rd, N4 . . . . 93 G1
SE18 . . . . 137 F6
Ensign Dr, N13. . . . . 59 J3
Ensign St, E1 . . . . 21 H5
Ensign Way, Wall. SM6. . . 200 E7
Enslin Rd, SE9 . . . . 156 D6
Ensor Ms, SW7 . . . . 30 E3
Enstone Rd, Enf. EN3. . . . . 45 H3
Enterprise Cl, Croy. CR0. . 201 G1
Enterprise Pk, E10 . . . . 95 H1
Enterprise Way, NW10 . . . 107 G3
SW18. . . . . 148 D4
Teddington TW11. . . . . 162 C5
Enterprize Way, SE8 . . . . . 133 J4
Epirus Ms, SW6 . . . . 128 D7
Epirus Rd, SW6 . . . . 128 C7
Epping Cl, E14 . . . . 134 A4
Romford RM7 . . . . 83 H3
★Epping Forest, Epp. & Loug. 47 J1
Epping Glade, E4 . . . . 46 C6
Epping New Rd, Buck.H. IG9. . . . . 63 H2
Loughton IG10 . . . . 47 H5
Epping Pl, N1 *off Liverpool Rd* 93 G6
Epping Way, E4 . . . . 46 B6
Epple Rd, SW6. . . . . 148 C1
Epsom Cl, Bexh. DA7. . . . 159 H3
Northolt UB5. . . . . 85 F5
Epsom Rd, E10. . . . . 78 C6
Croydon CR0. . . . . 201 G4
Ilford IG3. . . . . 81 J6
Morden SM4. . . . . 184 C7
Sutton SM3. . . . . 184 C7
Epsom Sq, Houns. (Hthrw Air.) TW6 *off Eastern Perimeter Rd*. 141 J2
Epstein Rd, SE28 . . . . 138 A1
Epworth Rd, Islw. TW7. . . 124 E7
Epworth St, EC2 . . . . 12 C6
Equity Sq, E2 . . . . 13 G4
Erasmus St, SW1. . . . . 33 J2
Erconwald St, W12. . . . . . 107 F6
Erebus Dr, SE28 . . . . 137 F3
Eresby Dr, Beck. BR3 . . . . 204 A1
Eresby Pl, NW6 . . . . 90 D7
Erica Gdns, Croy. CR0 . . . 204 B4
Erica St, W12 . . . . 107 G7
Eric Clarke La, Bark. IG11 . 117 E4
Eric Cl, E7. . . . . 97 G4
Ericcson Cl, SW18 . . . . . . 148 D5
Eric Rd, E7 . . . . 97 G4
NW10 *off Church Rd*. . . . 89 F6
Romford RM6 . . . . 82 D7
Eric St, E3. . . . . 113 J4
Eridge Rd, W4. . . . . 126 D3
Erin Cl, Brom. BR1 . . . . . . 172 E7
Ilford IG3. . . . . 82 A6
Erindale, SE18 . . . . 137 G6
Erindale Ter, SE18. . . . . . . 137 G6
Erith Cres, Rom. RM5 . . . . 83 J1
Erith Rd, Belv. DA17. . . . . 139 G5
Bexleyheath DA7 . . . . . 159 H4
Erith DA8. . . . . 159 H4
Erlanger Rd, SE14 . . . . . . 153 G1
Erlesmere Gdns, W13. . . . 124 D3
Ermine Cl, Houns. TW4 . . 142 C2
Ermine Ho, N17 *off Moselle St* 60 C7
Ermine Rd, N15 . . . . 76 C6
SE13 . . . . 154 B3
Ermine Side, Enf. EN1 . . . . 44 D5
Ermington Rd, SE9. . . . . . 175 F2
Ernald Av, E6 . . . . 116 B2
Erncroft Way, Twick. TW1 . 144 C6
Ernest Av, SE27 . . . . 169 H4
Ernest Cl, Beck. BR3. . . . . 190 A5
Ernest Gdns, W4 . . . . 126 B6
Ernest Gro, Beck. BR3 . . . 189 J5
Ernest Rd, Kings.T. KT1 . . 182 B2
Ernest Sq, Kings.T. KT1 . . 182 B2
Ernest St, E1. . . . . 113 G4
Ernle Rd, SW20 . . . . 165 H7
Ernshaw Pl, SW15 *off Carlton Dr* 148 B5
★Eros, W1 . . . . 17 H6
Erpingham Rd, SW15. . . . 147 J3
Erridge Rd, SW19 . . . . . . 184 D2
Errington Rd, W9 . . . . 108 C4
Errol Gdns, Hayes UB4. . . 102 B4
New Malden KT3 . . . . . 183 G4
Errol St, EC1. . . . . 12 A6
Erskine Cl, Sutt. SM1 . . . . 199 H3
Erskine Cres, N17. . . . . 76 E4
Erskine Hill, NW11 . . . . 72 D5
Erskine Ms, NW3 *off Erskine Rd*. 91 J7
Erskine Rd, E17 . . . . 77 J4
NW3 . . . . 91 J7
Sutton SM1. . . . . 199 G4
Watford WD19. . . . . 50 C3
Erwood Rd, SE7. . . . . 136 B5
Esam Way, SW16 . . . . 169 G5
Escott Gdns, SE9 . . . . 174 B4
Escot Way, Barn. EN5 . . . . 39 J5
Escreet Gro, SE18 . . . . . . 136 D4
Esher Av, Rom. RM7 . . . . . 83 J6
Sutton SM3. . . . . 198 A3

Esher Av, Walt. KT12 . . . . 178 A7
Esher Bypass, Chess. KT9 . 195 E7
Esher KT10 . . . . 195 E7
Esher Cl, Bex. DA5 . . . . . . 176 E1
Esher Cres, Houns. (Hthrw Air.) TW6 *off Eastern Perimeter Rd* 141 H2
Esher Gdns, SW19 . . . . . . 166 A2
Esher Ms, Mitch. CR4 . . . . 185 J3
Esher Rd, E.Mol. KT8 . . . . 180 A6
Ilford IG3 . . . . 99 H3
Eskdale Av, Nthlt. UB5 . . . 103 F1
Eskdale Cl, Wem. HA9 . . . . 87 G2
Eskdale Rd, Bexh. DA7 . . 159 G2
Eskmont Ridge, SE19 . . . . 170 B7
Esk Rd, E13 . . . . 115 G4
Esmar Cres, NW9 . . . . 71 G7
Esme Ho, SW15 . . . . 147 F4
Esmeralda Rd, SE1 . . . . . . 37 J2
Esmond Rd, NW6 . . . . 108 C1
W4 . . . . 126 D4
Esmond St, SW15 . . . . . . 148 B4
Esparto St, SW18 . . . . 149 E7
Essenden Rd, Belv. DA17 . 139 G5
South Croydon CR2 . . . 202 B7
Essendine Rd, W9 . . . . . . 108 D4
Essex Av, Islw. TW7 . . . . . 144 B3
Essex Cl, E17 . . . . 77 H4
Morden SM4 . . . . 184 A7
Romford RM7 . . . . 83 H4
Ruislip HA4 . . . . 84 D1
Essex Ct, EC4 . . . . 18 E4
SW13 . . . . 147 F2
Essex Gdns, N4 . . . . 75 H6
Essex Gro, SE19 . . . . 170 A6
Essex Ho, E14 *off Giraud St* 114 B6
Essex Pk, N3 . . . . 56 E6
Essex Pk Ms, W3 . . . . 126 E1
Essex Pl, W4 . . . . 126 C4
Essex Pl Sq, W4 *off Chiswick High Rd* . . 126 D4
Essex Rd, E4 . . . . 62 E1
E10 . . . . 78 C6
E12 . . . . 98 B5
E17 . . . . 77 H6
E18 . . . . 79 H2
N1 . . . . 111 H1
NW10 . . . . 89 E7
W3 . . . . 106 C7
W4 *off Belmont Rd* 126 D4
Barking IG11 . . . . 99 G7
Borehamwood WD6 . . . . 38 A3
Dagenham RM10 . . . . . . 101 J5
Enfield EN2 . . . . 44 A4
Romford RM7 . . . . 83 H4
Romford (Chad.Hth) RM6 . 82 C7
Essex Rd S, E11 . . . . 78 D7
Essex St, E7 . . . . 97 G5
WC2 . . . . 18 E5
Essex Twr, SE20 . . . . 189 E1
Essex Vil, W8 . . . . 128 D2
Essex Wf, E5 . . . . 95 F2
Essian St, E1 . . . . 113 H5
Essoldo Way, Edg. HA8 . . . 69 J3
Estate Way, E10 . . . . 95 J1
Estcourt Rd, SE25 . . . . . . 189 E6
SW6 . . . . 128 C7
Estella Av, N.Mal. KT3 . . . 183 H4
Estelle Rd, NW3 . . . . 91 J4
Esterbrooke St, SW1 . . . . . 33 H2
Este Rd, SW11 . . . . 149 H3
Esther Cl, N21 . . . . 43 G7
Esther Rd, E11 . . . . 78 E7
Estoria Cl, SW2 . . . . 151 G7
★**Estorick Collection of Modern Italian Art**, N1 . . 93 H6
Estreham Rd, SW16 . . . . . 168 D6
Estridge Cl, Houns. TW3 . 143 G4
Estuary Cl, Bark. IG11 . . . . 118 B3
Eswyn Rd, SW17 . . . . 167 J4
Etchingham Pk Rd, N3 . . . . 57 E7
Etchingham Rd, E15 . . . . . 96 C4
Eternit Wk, SW6 . . . . 147 J1
Etfield Gro, Sid. DA14 . . . 176 B5
Ethelbert Cl, Brom. BR1 . . 191 G3
Ethelbert Gdns, Ilf. IG2 . . . 80 C5
Ethelbert Rd, SW20 . . . . . 184 A1
Bromley BR1 . . . . 191 G3
Erith DA8 . . . . 139 J7
Ethelbert St, SW12 *off Fernlea Rd* 168 B1
Ethelburga St, SW11 . . . . 149 H1
Etheldene Av, N10 . . . . 74 C4
Ethelden Rd, W12 . . . . 127 H1
Ethel Rd, E16 . . . . 115 H6
Ethel St, SE17 . . . . 35 J2
Etheridge Grn, Loug. IG10 *off Etheridge Rd* 49 F3
Etheridge Rd, NW2 . . . . 71 J7
Loughton IG10 . . . . 49 E2
Etherley Rd, N15 . . . . 75 J5
Etherow St, SE22 . . . . 152 D6
Etherstone Grn, SW16 . . . 169 G4
Etherstone Rd, SW16 . . . . 169 G4
Ethnard Rd, SE15 . . . . 132 E6
Ethronvi Rd, Bexh. DA7 . . 159 E3
Etloe Rd, E10 . . . . 96 A2
Eton Av, N12 . . . . 57 F7
NW3 . . . . 91 G7
Eton Av, Barnet EN4 . . . . . 41 H6
Hounslow TW5 . . . . 123 F6
New Malden KT3 . . . . . 182 D5
Wembley HA0 . . . . 87 E4
Eton Cl, SW18 . . . . 149 E7
Eton Coll Rd, NW3 . . . . 91 J6
Eton Ct, NW3 *off Eton Av* . 91 G7
Wembley HA0 *off Eton Av* 87 F4
Eton Garages, NW3 *off Lambolle Pl* 91 H6
Eton Gro, NW9 . . . . 70 A3
SE13 . . . . 154 E3
Eton Hall, NW3 *off Eton Coll Rd* 91 J6
Eton Pl, NW3 *off Haverstock Hill* 92 A7
Eton Ri, NW3 *off Eton Coll Rd* 91 J6
Eton Rd, NW3 . . . . 91 J7
Hayes UB3 . . . . 121 J7
Ilford IG1 . . . . 99 F5
Eton St, Rich. TW9 . . . . . . 145 H5
Eton Vil, NW3 . . . . 91 J6
Etta St, SE8 . . . . 133 H6
Ettrick St, E14 . . . . 114 C6
Etwell Pl, Surb. KT5 . . . . . 181 J6
Euesden Cl, N9 . . . . 60 E3
Eugenia Rd, SE16 . . . . 133 F4
Eureka Rd, Kings.T. KT1 *off Washington Rd* . . . 182 A2
Europa Pl, EC1 . . . . 11 J4
Europe Rd, SE18 . . . . 136 C3
Eustace Pl, SE18 *off Borgard Rd* 136 C4
Eustace Rd, E6 . . . . 116 B3
SW6 . . . . 128 D7
Romford RM6 . . . . 82 D7
Euston Cen, NW1 *off Triton Sq* 110 C4
Euston Gro, NW1 . . . . 9 H4
Euston Rd, N1 . . . . 10 A3
NW1 . . . . 9 E6
Croydon CR0 . . . . 201 G1
Euston Sq, NW1 . . . . 9 H4
Euston Sta Colonnade, NW1 . . . . 9 H4
Euston St, NW1 . . . . 9 G5
Euston Twr, NW1 . . . . 9 F5
Evandale Rd, SW9 . . . . . . 151 G2
Evangelist Rd, NW5 . . . . . . 92 B4
Evans Business Cen, NW2 . 89 G3
Evans Cl, E8 *off Buttermere Wk* 94 C6
Evans Gro, Felt. TW13 . . . 161 G2
Evans Rd, SE6 . . . . 173 E2
Evanston Av, E4 . . . . 62 C7
Evanston Gdns, Ilf. IG4 . . . 80 B6
Eva Rd, Rom. RM6 . . . . 82 C7
Evelina Rd, SE15 . . . . 153 F3
SE20 . . . . 171 G7
Eveline Lowe Est, SE16 . . . 29 H6
Eveline Rd, Mitch. CR4 . . . 185 J1
Evelyn Av, NW9 . . . . 70 D4
Evelyn Cl, Twick. TW2 . . . . 143 H7
Evelyn Ct, N1 . . . . 12 B2
Evelyn Denington Rd, E6 . 116 B4
Evelyn Dr, Pnr. HA5 . . . . . . 50 D7
Evelyn Fox Ct, W10 . . . . . . 107 J5
Evelyn Gdns, SW7 . . . . 30 E4
Richmond TW9 *off Kew Rd* 145 H4
Evelyn Gro, W5 . . . . 125 J1
Southall UB1 . . . . 103 F6
Evelyn Rd, E16 . . . . 135 H1
E17 . . . . 78 C4
SW19 . . . . 166 E5
W4 . . . . 126 D3
Barnet EN4 . . . . 41 J4
Richmond TW9 . . . . 145 H3
Richmond (Ham) TW10 . 163 F3
Evelyn St, SE8 . . . . 133 H5
Evelyn Ter, Rich. TW9 . . . . 145 H3
Evelyn Wk, N1 . . . . 12 B2
Evelyn Way, Wall. SM6 . . . 200 D4
Evelyn Yd, W1 . . . . 17 H3
Evening Hill, Beck. BR3 . . 172 C7
Evenwood Cl, SW15 . . . . . 148 B5
Everard Av, Brom. BR2 . . . 205 G1
Everard Way, Wem. HA9 . . 87 H3
Everatt Cl, SW18 *off Amerland Rd* 148 C6
Everdon Rd, SW13 . . . . . . 127 G6
Everest Pl, E14 . . . . 114 C5
Everest Rd, SE9 . . . . 156 C5
Staines (Stanw.) TW19 . 140 A7
Everett Cl, Bushey (Bushey Hth) WD23 . . . . 52 B1
Everett Wk, Belv. DA17 *off Osborne Rd* 139 F5
Everglade Strand, NW9 . . . 71 F1
Evergreen Ct, Stai. (Stanw.) TW19 *off Evergreen Way* 140 A7
Evergreen Sq, E8 . . . . 94 C7
Evergreen Way, Stai. (Stanw.) TW19 . . . . 140 A7
Everilda St, N1 . . . . 111 F1
Evering Rd, E5 . . . . 94 C3
N16 . . . . 94 C3
Everington Rd, N10 . . . . . . 73 J2
Everington St, W6 . . . . . . 128 A6
Everitt Rd, NW10 . . . . 106 D3
Everleigh St, N4 . . . . 93 F1
Eve Rd, E11 . . . . 96 E4
E15 . . . . 115 E2
N17 . . . . 76 B3
Isleworth TW7 . . . . 144 D4
Eversfield Gdns, NW7 . . . . 54 E7
Eversfield Rd, Rich. TW9 . 145 J2
Evershed Wk, W4 . . . . 126 D4
Eversholt St, NW1 . . . . 9 G1
Evershot Rd, N4 . . . . 93 F1
Eversleigh Rd, E6 . . . . 116 A1
N3 . . . . 56 C7
SW11 . . . . 149 J3
Barnet EN5 . . . . 41 F5
Eversley Av, Wem. HA9 . . . 88 A2
Eversley Cl, N21 . . . . 43 F6
Loughton IG10 . . . . 49 F3
Eversley Cres, N21 . . . . . . 43 F6
Isleworth TW7 . . . . 144 A1
Eversley Mt, N21 . . . . 43 F6
Eversley Pk, SW19 . . . . . . 165 H5
Eversley Pk Rd, N21 . . . . . . 43 F6
Eversley Rd, SE7 . . . . 135 H6
SE19 . . . . 170 A7
Surbiton KT5 . . . . 181 J4
Eversley Way, Croy. CR0 . 204 A4
Everthorpe Rd, SE15 . . . . 152 C3
Everton Bldgs, NW1 . . . . . . 9 F4
Everton Dr, Stan. HA7 . . . . 69 J3
Everton Rd, Croy. CR0 . . . 202 D1
Evesham Av, E17 . . . . 78 A2
Evesham Cl, Grnf. UB6 . . 103 H2
Sutton SM2 . . . . 198 D7
Evesham Ct, W13 *off Tewkesbury Rd* 124 D1
Evesham Grn, Mord. SM4 . . . . 184 E6
Evesham Rd, E15 . . . . 115 F1
N11 . . . . 58 C5
Morden SM4 . . . . 185 E6
Evesham St, W11 . . . . 108 A7
Evesham Wk, SE5 *off Love Wk* 152 A2
SW9 . . . . 151 G2
Evesham Way, SW11 . . . . 150 A3
Ilford IG5 . . . . 80 D3
Evry Rd, Sid. DA14 . . . . . . 176 C6
Ewald Rd, SW6 . . . . 148 C2
Ewanrigg Ter, Wdf.Grn. IG8 . . . . 63 J5
Ewart Gro, N22 . . . . 75 G1
Ewart Pl, E3 *off Roman Rd* 113 J2
Ewart Rd, SE23 . . . . 153 G7
Ewe Cl, N7 . . . . 93 E6
Ewell Bypass, Epsom KT17 . . . . 197 G7
Ewell Ct Av, Epsom KT19 . 197 E5
Ewellhurst Rd, Ilf. IG5 . . . . 80 B2
Ewell Pk Gdns, Epsom KT17 . . . . 197 G7
Ewell Pk Way, Epsom (Ewell) KT17 . . . . 197 G6
Ewell Rd, Surb. KT6 . . . . . 181 H6
Surbiton (Long Dit.) KT6 . . . . 180 E7
Sutton SM3 . . . . 198 B6
Ewelme Rd, SE23 . . . . 171 F1
Ewen Cres, SW2 . . . . 151 G7
Ewer St, SE1 . . . . 27 J2
Ewhurst Cl, E1 . . . . 113 F5
Ewhurst Rd, SE4 . . . . 153 J6
Exbury Rd, SE6 . . . . 172 A2
★**ExCeL**, E16 . . . . 115 H7
Excel Ct, WC2 . . . . 17 J6
ExCeL Marina, E16 *off Western Gateway* . . 115 H7
Excelsior Cl, Kings.T. KT1 *off Washington Rd* . . . 182 A2
Excelsior Gdns, SE13 . . . . 154 C2
ExCeL Waterfront, E16 *off Western Gateway* . . 115 H7
Exchange Arc, EC2 . . . . 20 E1
Exchange Bldgs, E1 *off Cutler St* 112 B6
Exchange Cl, N11 *off Benfleet Way* 58 A2
Exchange Ct, WC2 . . . . 18 B6
Exchange Ho, N8 *off Crouch End Hill* 74 E6
Exchange Mall, The, Ilf. IG1 . . . . 98 E2
Exchange Pl, EC2 . . . . 20 D1
Exchange Sq, EC2 . . . . 20 D1
Exchange Wk, Pnr. HA5 . . . 66 E7
Exeter Cl, E6 *off Harper Rd* 116 C6
Exeter Gdns, Ilf. IG1 . . . . . . 98 B1
Exeter Ho, SW15 *off Putney Heath* 147 J6
Exeter Ms, NW6 *off West Hampstead Ms* . 90/91 E6
SW6 *off Farm La* 128 D7
Exeter Rd, E16 . . . . 115 G5
E17 . . . . 78 A5
N9 . . . . 61 F2
N14 . . . . 58 B1
NW2 . . . . 90 B5
Croydon CR0 . . . . 188 B7
Dagenham RM10 . . . . . . 101 H6
Enfield EN3 . . . . 45 G3
Feltham TW13 . . . . 161 F3
Harrow HA2 . . . . 85 E2
Hounslow (Hthrw Air.) TW6 . . . . 141 H2
Welling DA16 . . . . 157 J2
Exeter St, WC2 . . . . 18 B5
Exeter Way, SE14 . . . . 133 J7
Hounslow (Hthrw Air.) TW6 . . . . 141 H3
Exford Gdns, SE12 . . . . . . 173 H1
Exford Rd, SE12 . . . . 173 H2
Exhibition Cl, W12 . . . . . . 107 J7
Exhibition Rd, SW7 . . . . 23 F4
Exmoor Cl, Ilf. IG6 . . . . 81 F1
Exmoor St, W10 . . . . 108 A4
Exmouth Mkt, EC1 . . . . 11 E5
Exmouth Ms, NW1 . . . . 9 G4
Exmouth Pl, E8 . . . . 94 E7
Exmouth Rd, E17 . . . . 77 J5
Bromley BR2 . . . . 101 H3
Ruislip HA4 . . . . 84 C3
Welling DA16 . . . . 158 C1
Exmouth St, E1 *off Commercial Rd* . . . 113 F6
Exning Rd, E16 . . . . 115 F4
Exon St, SE17 . . . . 36 D3
Express Dr, Ilf. IG3 . . . . . . 100 B1
Exton Cres, NW10 . . . . 88 C7
Exton Gdns, Dag. RM8 . . . 100 C5
Exton Rd, NW10 . . . . 88 C7
Exton St, SE1 . . . . 27 E2
Eyebright Cl, Croy. CR0 *off Primrose La* 203 G1
Eyhurst Cl, NW2 . . . . 89 G2
Eylewood Rd, SE27 . . . . . . 169 J5
Eynella Rd, SE22 . . . . 152 C7
Eynham Rd, W12 . . . . 107 J6
Eynsford Cl, Orp. BR5 . . . 193 F7
Eynsford Cres, Bex. DA5 . 176 C1
Eynsford Rd, Ilf. IG3 . . . . . . 99 H2
Eynsham Dr, SE2 . . . . 138 A4
Eynswood Dr, Sid. DA14 . 176 B5
Eyot Gdns, W6 . . . . 127 F5
Eyot Grn, W4 *off Chiswick Mall* 127 F6
Eyre Ct, NW8 . . . . 6 E1
Eyre St Hill, EC1 . . . . 11 E6
Eythorne Rd, SW9 . . . . . . 151 G1
Ezra St, E2 . . . . 13 G3

F

Faber Gdns, NW4 . . . . 71 G5
Fabian Rd, SW6 . . . . 128 C7
Fabian St, E6 . . . . 116 C4
Factory La, N17 . . . . 76 C2
Croydon CR0 . . . . 201 G1
Factory Rd, E16 . . . . 136 B1
Factory Sq, SW16 . . . . . . 168 E6
Factory Yd, W7 *off Uxbridge Rd* 124 B1

Faggs Rd, Felt. TW14 142 A5
Fairacre, N.Mal. KT3 182 E3
Fairacres, SW15 147 G4
Fair Acres, Brom. BR2 191 G5
Fairbairn Grn, SW9 151 G1
Fairbank Av, Orp. BR6 206 E2
Fairbank Est, N1 *off East Rd* 112 A2
Fairbanks Rd, N17 76 C3
Fairbourne Rd, N17 76 B3
Fairbridge Rd, N19 92 D2
Fairbrook Cl, N13 59 G5
Fairbrook Rd, N13 59 G6
Fairburn Cl, Borwd. WD6 38 A1
Fairburn Ct, SW15 *off Mercier Rd* 148 B5
Fairby Rd, SE12 155 H5
Faircharm Trd Est, SE8 134 B7
Fairchild Cl, SW11 *off Wye St* 149 G2
Fairchild Pl, EC2 13 E6
Fairchild St, EC2 13 E6
Fairclough St, E1 21 J4
Faircross Av, Bark. IG11 99 F6
Fairdale Gdns, SW15 147 H4
Hayes UB3 122 A1
Fairey Av, Hayes UB3 121 J4
Fairfax Gdns, SE3 156 A1
Fairfax Ms, E16 *off Wesley Av* 135 H1
SW15 147 J4
Fairfax Pl, NW6 91 F7
W14 128 B3
Fairfax Rd, N8 75 G4
NW6 91 F7
W4 127 E3
Teddington TW11 162 D6
Fairfax Way, N10 *off Cromwell Rd* 58 A7
Fairfield Av, NW4 71 H6
Edgware HA8 54 B6
Twickenham TW2 161 H1
Watford WD19 50 C3
Fairfield Cl, N12 57 F4
Enfield EN3 *off Scotland Grn Rd N* 45 H4
Epsom (Ewell) KT19 196 E5
Mitcham CR4 167 H7
Sidcup DA15 157 J6
Fairfield Ct, NW10 107 G1
Northwood HA6 *off Windsor Cl* 66 A2
Fairfield Cres, Edg. HA8 54 B6
Fairfield Dr, SW18 149 E5
Greenford UB6 105 F1
Harrow HA2 67 J3
Fairfield E, Kings.T. KT1 181 H2
Fairfield Gdns, N8 *off Elder Av* 74/75 E5
Fairfield Gro, SE7 136 A5
★**Fairfield Halls**, Croy. CR0 202 A3
Fairfield N, Kings.T. KT1 181 H2
Fairfield Path, Croy. CR0 202 A3
Fairfield Pl, Kings.T. KT1 181 H3
Fairfield Rd, E3 114 A2
E17 77 H2
N8 75 E5
N18 60 D4
W7 124 D3
Beckenham BR3 190 A2
Bexleyheath DA7 159 F2
Bromley BR1 173 G7
Croydon CR0 202 B3
Ilford IG1 99 E6
Kingston upon Thames KT1 181 H2
Orpington BR5 193 G6
Southall UB1 103 F6
West Drayton UB7 120 B1
Woodford Green IG8 63 G6
Fairfields Cl, NW9 70 C5
Fairfields Cres, NW9 70 C4
Fairfield S, Kings.T. KT1 181 H2
Fairfields Rd, Houns. TW3 143 J3
Fairfield St, SW18 149 E5
Fairfield Trade Pk, Kings.T. KT1 181 J3
Fairfield Way, Barn. EN5 40 D5
Epsom KT19 196 E5
Fairfield W, Kings.T. KT1 181 H2
Fairfoot Rd, E3 114 A4
Fairford Av, Croy. CR0 189 G5
Fairford Cl, Croy. CR0 189 H5
Fairford Ct, Sutt. SM2 *off Grange Rd* 198/199 E7
Fairford Gdns, Wor.Pk. KT4 197 F3
Fairford Ho, SE11 35 F2
Fairgreen, Barn. EN4 41 J3
Fairgreen E, Barn. EN4 41 J3
Fairgreen Par, Mitch. CR4 *off London Rd* 185 J3
Fairgreen Rd, Th.Hth. CR7 187 H5
Fairhaven Av, Croy. CR0 189 G6
Fairhaven Cres, Wat. WD19 50 A3
Fairhazel Gdns, NW6 91 E6
Fairholme, Felt. TW14 141 G7
Fairholme Cl, N3 72 B4
Fairholme Gdns, N3 72 B3
Fairholme Rd, W14 128 B5
Croydon CR0 187 G7
Harrow HA1 68 C5
Ilford IG1 80 C7
Sutton SM1 198 C6
Fairholt Cl, N16 94 B1
Fairholt Rd, N16 94 A1
Fairholt St, SW7 23 H5
Fairland Rd, E15 97 F6
Fairlands Av, Buck.H. IG9 63 G2
Sutton SM1 198 D2
Thornton Heath CR7 187 F4
Fairlands Ct, SE9 *off North Pk* 156 D6
Fairlawn, SE7 135 J6
Fairlawn Av, N2 73 H4
W4 126 C4
Bexleyheath DA7 158 D2
Fairlawn Cl, N14 42 C6
Esher (Clay.) KT10 194 C6
Feltham TW13 161 F4
Kingston upon Thames KT2 164 C6
Fairlawn Dr, Wdf.Grn. IG8 63 G7
Fairlawnes, Wall. SM6 *off Maldon Rd* 200 B5
Fairlawn Gdns, Sthl. UB1 103 F7
Fairlawn Gro, W4 126 C4
Fairlawn Pk, SE26 171 H5
Fairlawn Rd, SW19 166 C7
Fairlawns, Pnr. HA5 66 C2
Sunbury-on-Thames TW16 178 A3
Twickenham TW1 145 F6
Fairlea Pl, W5 105 G4
Fairlie Gdns, SE23 153 F7
Fairlight Av, E4 62 D2
NW10 107 E2
Woodford Green IG8 63 G6
Fairlight Cl, E4 62 D2
Worcester Park KT4 197 J4
Fairlight Rd, SW17 167 G4
Fairlop Gdns, Ilf. IG6 65 F7
Fairlop Rd, E11 78 D7
Ilford IG6 81 F2
Fairmead, Brom. BR1 192 C4
Surbiton KT5 196 B1
Fairmead Cl, Brom. BR1 192 C4
Hounslow TW5 122 D7
New Malden KT3 182 D3
Fairmead Cres, Edg. HA8 54 C3
Fairmead Gdns, Ilf. IG4 80 B5
Fairmead Ho, E9 *off Kingsmead Way* 95 H4
Fairmead Rd, N19 92 D3
Croydon CR0 201 F1
Loughton IG10 47 H4
Fairmeads, Loug. IG10 48 E2
Fairmead Side, Loug. IG10 47 J5
Fairmile Av, SW16 168 D5
Fairmile Ho, Tedd. TW11 *off Twickenham Rd* 162 D4
Fairmont Av, E14 *off Blackwall Way* 134 D1
Fairmont Cl, Belv. DA17 139 F5
Fairmount Rd, SW2 151 F6
Fairoak Cl, Orp. BR5 193 E7
Fairoak Dr, SE9 157 G5
Fairseat Cl, Bushey (Bushey Hth) WD23 *off Hive Rd* 52 B2
Fairstead Wk, N1 *off Popham Rd* 111 J1
Fair St, SE1 29 E3
Hounslow TW3 *off High St* 143 J3
Fairthorn Rd, SE7 135 G5
Fairview Av, Wem. HA0 87 G6
Fairview Cl, E17 77 H1
Chigwell IG7 65 H4
Fairview Cres, Har. HA2 85 G1
Fairview Dr, Chig. IG7 65 H4
Orpington BR6 207 G4
Fairview Gdns, Wdf.Grn. IG8 79 H1
Fairview Pl, SW2 151 F7
Fairview Rd, N15 76 C5
SW16 187 F1
Chigwell IG7 65 H4
Enfield EN2 43 G1
Sutton SM1 199 G5
Fairview Way, Edg. HA8 54 A4
Fairwater Av, Well. DA16 158 A4
Fairway, SW20 183 J3
Bexleyheath DA6 159 E5
Orpington BR5 193 G5
Woodford Green IG8 63 J5
Fairway, The, N13 59 J3
N14 42 B6
NW7 54 D3
W3 106 E6
Barnet EN5 41 E6
Bromley BR1 192 C5
New Malden KT3 182 D1
Northolt UB5 85 J6
Ruislip HA4 84 D3
Wembley HA0 87 E3
West Molesey KT8 179 H3
Fairway Av, NW9 70 B3
Borehamwood WD6 38 B2
Fairway Cl, NW11 73 F7
Croydon CR0 189 H5
Epsom KT19 196 C4
Hounslow TW4 142 C5
Fairway Ct, NW7 *off The Fairway* 54 D3
Fairway Dr, SE28 118 D6
Greenford UB6 85 H7
Fairway Gdns, Beck. BR3 190 D6
Ilford IG1 99 F5
Fairways, Stan. HA7 69 H2
Teddington TW11 163 G7
Fairweather Cl, N15 76 B4
Fairweather Rd, N16 76 D6
Fairwyn Rd, SE26 171 H4
Fakenham Cl, NW7 55 G7
Northolt UB5 *off Goodwood Dr* 85 G6
Fakruddin St, E1 13 J6
Falcon Av, Brom. BR1 192 B4
Falconberg Ct, W1 17 J3
Falconberg Ms, W1 17 H3
Falcon Cl, SE1 27 H1
W4 *off Sutton La S* 126 C6
Falcon Ct, EC4 19 E4
Falcon Cres, Enf. EN3 45 G5
Falcon Dr, Stai. (Stanw.) TW19 140 A6
Falconer Wk, N7 *off Newington Barrow Way* 93 F2
Falcon Gro, SW11 149 H3
Falcon Ho, W13 104 C4
Falcon La, SW11 149 H3
Falcon Pk Ind Est, NW10 89 F5
Falcon Rd, SW11 149 H2
Enfield EN3 45 G5
Hampton TW12 161 F7
Falcon St, E13 115 G4
Falcon Ter, SW11 149 H3
Falcon Way, E11 79 G4
E14 134 B4
NW9 71 E2
Feltham TW14 142 B5
Harrow HA3 69 H5
FALCONWOOD, Well. DA16 157 G3
Falconwood Av, Well. DA16 157 G2
Falconwood Par, Well. DA16 157 H4
Falconwood Rd, Croy. CR0 204 A7
Falcourt Cl, Sutt. SM1 198 E5
Falkirk Gdns, Wat. WD19 *off Blackford Rd* 50 D5
Falkirk Ho, W9 6 B3
Falkirk St, N1 12 E2
Falkland Av, N3 56 D7
N11 58 A4
Falkland Pk Av, SE25 188 B3
Falkland Pl, NW5 *off Falkland Rd* 92 C5
Falkland Rd, N8 75 G4
NW5 92 C5
Barnet EN5 40 B2
Fallaize Av, Ilf. IG1 *off Riverdene Rd* 98/99 E4
Falloden Way, NW11 72 D4
Fallow Cl, Chig. IG7 65 J5
Fallow Ct, SE16 37 J4
Fallow Ct Av, N12 57 F7
Fallowfield, Stan. HA7 52 D3
Fallowfield Ct, Stan. HA7 52 D3
Fallow Flds, Loug. IG10 47 J7
Fallowfields Dr, N12 57 H6
Fallows Cl, N2 73 F2
Fallsbrook Rd, SW16 168 C7
Falman Cl, N9 *off Croyland Rd* 60 D1
Falmer Rd, E17 78 B3
N15 75 J5
Enfield EN1 44 B4
Falmouth Av, E4 62 D5
Falmouth Cl, N22 *off Truro Rd* 59 F7
SE12 155 F5
Falmouth Gdns, Ilf. IG4 80 B5
Falmouth Ho, Kings.T. KT2 *off Kingsgate Rd* 181 H1
Falmouth Rd, SE1 28 A5
Falmouth St, E15 96 D5
Falmouth Way, E17 *off Gosport Rd* 77 J5
Falstaff Ms, Hmptn. (Hmptn H.) TW12 *off Hampton Rd* 162 A5
Fambridge Cl, SE26 171 J4
Fambridge Rd, Dag. RM8 101 G1
★**Family Records Cen, Public Record Office**, EC1 11 F4
Fane St, W14 *off North End Rd* 128 C6
★**Fan Mus**, SE10 134 C7
Fann St, EC1 11 J6
EC2 11 J6
Fanshawe Av, Bark. IG11 99 F6
Fanshawe Cres, Dag. RM9 101 E5
Fanshawe Rd, Rich. TW10 163 F4
Fanshaw St, N1 12 D3
Fanthorpe St, SW15 147 J3
Faraday Av, Sid. DA14 176 A2
Faraday Cl, N7 *off Bride St* 93 F6
★**Faraday Mus**, W1 17 F6
Faraday Rd, E15 97 F6
SW19 166 D6
W3 106 C7
W10 108 B5
Southall UB1 103 H7
Welling DA16 158 A3
West Molesey KT8 179 G4
Faraday Way, SE18 136 A3
Croydon CR0 *off Ampere Way* 201 F1
Fareham Rd, Felt. TW14 142 C7
Fareham St, W1 17 H3
Farewell Pl, Mitch. CR4 185 H1
Faringdon Av, Brom. BR2 192 E6
Faringford Rd, E15 96 E7
Farjeon Rd, SE3 156 A1
Farleigh Av, Brom. BR2 191 F6
Farleigh Pl, N16 *off Farleigh Rd* 94 C4
Farleigh Rd, N16 94 C4
Farley Dr, Ilf. IG3 99 H1
Farley Ms, SE6 154 C7
Farley Pl, SE25 188 D4
Farley Rd, SE6 154 B7
South Croydon CR2 202 E7
Farlington Pl, SW15 *off Roehampton La* 147 H7
Farlow Rd, SW15 148 A3
Farlton Rd, SW18 149 E7
Farman Gro, Nthlt. UB5 *off Wayfarer Rd* 102 D3
Farm Av, NW2 90 B3
SW16 169 E4
Harrow HA2 67 F7
Wembley HA0 87 F6
Farmborough Cl, Har. HA1 *off Pool Rd* 68 A7
Farm Cl, SW6 *off Farm La* 128 D7
Barnet EN5 39 J5
Buckhurst Hill IG9 63 J3
Dagenham RM10 101 J7
Southall UB1 103 H7
Sutton SM2 199 G7
West Wickham BR4 205 E3
Farmcote Rd, SE12 173 G1
Farm Ct, NW4 71 G3
Farmdale Rd, SE10 135 G5
Carshalton SM5 199 H7
Farm Dr, Croy. CR0 203 J2
Farm End, E4 46 E5
Farmer Rd, E10 96 B1
Farmers Rd, SE5 35 H7
Farmer St, W8 *off Uxbridge St* 128 D1
Farmfield Rd, Brom. BR1 172 E5
Farmhouse Rd, SW16 168 C7
Farmilo Rd, E17 77 J7

Farmington Av, Sutt. SM1 ... **199** G3
Farmlands, Enf. EN2 ... **43** G1
Pinner HA5 ... **66** A4
Farmlands, The, Nthlt. UB5 ... **85** F6
Farmland Wk, Chis. BR7 ... **174** E5
Farm La, N14 ... **42** A6
SW6 ... **128** D6
Croydon CR0 ... **203** J2
Farm La Trd Cen, SW6
off Farm La ... **128** D6
Farmleigh, N14 ... **42** C7
Farm Pl, W8
off Uxbridge St ... **128** D1
Farm Rd, N21 ... **59** H1
NW10 ... **106** D1
Edgware HA8 ... **54** B6
Hounslow TW4 ... **161** E1
Morden SM4 ... **185** E5
Sutton SM2 ... **199** G7
Farmstead Rd, SE6 ... **172** B4
Harrow HA3 ... **68** A1
Farm St, W1 ... **16** D6
Farm Vale, Bex. DA5 ... **159** H6
Farm Wk, NW11 ... **72** C5
Farm Way, Buck.H. IG9 ... **63** J4
Farmway, Dag. RM8 ... **100** C4
Farm Way, Wor.Pk. KT4 ... **197** J3
Farnaby Rd, SE9 ... **155** J4
Bromley BR1, BR2 ... **172** D7
Farnan Av, E17 ... **78** A2
Farnan Rd, SW16 ... **169** E5
FARNBOROUGH, Orp. BR6 ... **206** E5
Farnborough Av, E17 ... **77** H3
South Croydon CR2 ... **203** G7
Farnborough Cl, Wem. HA9
off Chalkhill Rd ... **88** B2
Farnborough Common, Orp. BR6 ... **206** C3
Farnborough Cres, Brom. BR2
off Saville Row ... **205** F1
Farnborough Hill, Orp. BR6 ... **207** G5
Farnborough Ho, SW15
off Fontley Way ... **165** G1
Farnborough Way, SE15
off Blakes Rd ... **132** B7
Orpington BR6 ... **207** F4
Farncombe St, SE16 ... **29** J4
Farndale Av, N13 ... **59** H3
Farndale Cres, Grnf. UB6 . **103** J3
Farnell Ms, SW5 ... **30** A3
Farnell Pl, W3 ... **106** B7
Farnell Rd, Islw. TW7 ... **144** A3
Farnham Cl, N20 ... **41** F7
Farnham Gdns, SW20 ... **183** H2
Farnham Pl, SE1 ... **27** H2
Farnham Rd, Ilf. IG3 ... **81** J7
Welling DA16 ... **158** C2
Farnham Royal, SE11 ... **34** D4
Farningham Rd, N17 ... **60** D7
Farnley Rd, E4 ... **46** E7
SE25 ... **188** A4
Faro Cl, Brom. BR1 ... **192** D2
Faroe Rd, W14 ... **128** A3
Farorna Wk, Enf. EN2 ... **43** G1
Farquhar Rd, SE19 ... **170** C5
SW19 ... **166** D3
Farquharson Rd, Croy. CR0 ... **201** J1
Farrance Rd, Rom. RM6 ... **83** E6
Farrance St, E14 ... **113** J6
Farrans Ct, Har. HA3 ... **69** E7
Farrant Av, N22 ... **75** G2
Farr Av, Bark. IG11 ... **118** A2
Farrell Ho, E1 ... **113** F6
Farren Rd, SE23 ... **171** H2
Farrer Ms, N8
off Farrer Rd ... **74** C4
Farrer Rd, N8 ... **74** C4
Harrow HA3 ... **69** H5
Farrer's Pl, Croy. CR0 ... **203** G4
Farrier Cl, Sun. TW16 ... **178** A4
Farrier Rd, Nthlt. UB5 ... **103** G2
Farriers Ct, Sutt. SM3
off Forge La ... **198** B7
Farriers Ms, SE15
off Machell Rd ... **153** F3
Farrier St, NW1 ... **92** B7
Farriers Way, Borwd. WD6 . **38** C6
Farrier Wk, SW10 ... **30** C5
Farringdon La, EC1 ... **11** F6
Farringdon Rd, EC1 ... **10** E5
Farringdon St, EC4 ... **19** G3
Farrington Pl, Chis. BR7 ... **175** G7
Farrins Rents, SE16 ... **133** H1
Farrow La, SE14 ... **133** F7
Farrow Pl, SE16
off Ropemaker Rd ... **133** H3
Farr Rd, Enf. EN2 ... **44** A1
Farthingale Wk, E15 ... **96** D7
Farthing All, SE1 ... **29** H4
Farthing Flds, E1
off Raine St ... **132/133** E1
Farthings, The, Kings.T. KT2
off Brunswick Rd ... **182** A1
Farthings Cl, E4 ... **63** E3
Pinner HA5 ... **66** B6
Farthing St, Orp. BR6 ... **206** C7
Farwell Rd, Sid. DA14 ... **176** B3
Farwig La, Brom. BR1 ... **191** F1
Fashion St, E1 ... **21** F2
Fashoda Rd, Brom. BR2 ... **192** A4
Fassett Rd, E8 ... **94** D6
Kingston upon Thames KT1 ... **181** H4
Fassett Sq, E8 ... **94** D6
Fauconberg Rd, W4 ... **126** C6
Faulkner Cl, Dag. RM8 ... **82** D7
Faulkner's All, EC1 ... **19** G1
Faulkner St, SE14 ... **153** F1
Fauna Cl, Rom. RM6 ... **82** C7
Faunce St, SE17 ... **35** G5
Favart Rd, SW6 ... **148** D1
Faversham Av, E4 ... **63** E1
Enfield EN1 ... **44** A6
Faversham Rd, SE6 ... **153** J7
Beckenham BR3 ... **189** J2
Morden SM4 ... **185** E6
Fawcett Cl, SW11 ... **149** G2
SW16 ... **169** G4
Fawcett Est, E5 ... **94** D1
Fawcett Rd, NW10 ... **107** F1
Croydon CR0 ... **201** J3
Fawcett St, SW10 ... **30** C5
Fawcus Cl, Esher (Clay.) KT10 *off Dalmore Av* .. **194** C6
Fawe Pk Rd, SW15 ... **148** C4
Fawe St, E14 ... **114** B5
Fawley Rd, NW6 ... **90** E5
Fawnbrake Av, SE24 ... **151** H5
Fawn Rd, E13 ... **115** J2
Chigwell IG7 ... **65** J5
Fawood Av, NW10 ... **88** D7
Faygate Cres, Bexh. DA6 . **159** G5
Faygate Rd, SW2 ... **169** F2
Fayland Av, SW16 ... **168** C5
Fearnley Cres, Hmptn. TW12 ... **161** E5
Fearon St, SE10 ... **135** G5
Featherbed La, Croy. CR0 **203** J7
Feathers Pl, SE10 ... **134** D6
Featherstone Av, SE23 ... **171** E2
Featherstone Gdns, Borwd. WD6 ... **38** C4
Featherstone Ind Est, Sthl UB2 ... **123** E2
Featherstone Rd, NW7 ... **55** H6
Southall UB2 ... **122** E3
Featherstone St, EC1 ... **12** B5
Featherstone Ter, Sthl. UB2 ... **123** E3
Featley Rd, SW9 ... **151** H3
Federal Rd, Grnf. UB6 ... **105** F2
Federation Rd, SE2 ... **138** B4
Fee Fm Rd, Esher (Clay.) KT10 ... **194** C7
Felbridge Av, Stan. HA7 ... **68** D1
Felbridge Cl, SW16 ... **169** G4
Felbrigge Rd, Ilf. IG3 ... **99** J2
Felday Rd, SE13 ... **154** B6
Felden Cl, Pnr. HA5 ... **51** E7
Felden St, SW6 ... **148** C1
Feldman Cl, N16 ... **94** D1
Felgate Ms, W6 ... **127** H4
Felhampton Rd, SE9 ... **174** E2
Felhurst Cres, Dag. RM10 . **101** H4
Felix Av, N8 ... **74** E6
Felix Rd, W13 ... **104** D7
Walton-on-Thames KT12 ... **178** A6
Felixstowe Ct, E16
off Fishguard Way . **136/137** E2
Felixstowe Rd, N9 ... **60** D4
N17 ... **76** C3
NW10 ... **107** H3
SE2 ... **138** B3
Fellbrigg Rd, SE22 ... **152** C5
Fellbrigg St, E1
off Headlam St ... **112/113** E4
Fellbrook, Rich. TW10 ... **163** E3
Fellmongers Path, SE1 ... **29** E4
Fellmongers Yd, Croy. CR0
off Surrey St ... **201** J2
Fellowes Cl, Hayes UB4
off Paddington Cl ... **102** D4
Fellowes Rd, Cars. SM5 ... **199** H3
Fellows Ct, E2 ... **13** F2
Fellows Rd, NW3 ... **91** G7
Fell Rd, Croy. CR0 ... **201** J3
Felltram Way, SE7
off Woolwich Rd ... **135** G5
Fell Wk, Edg. HA8
off East Rd ... **70** B1
Felmersham Cl, SW4
off Haselrigge Rd ... **150** D4
Felmingham Rd, SE20 ... **189** F2
Felnex Trd Est, Wall. SM6 . **200** A2
Felsberg Rd, SW2 ... **151** E6
Fels Cl, Dag. RM10 ... **101** H3
Fels Fm Av, Dag. RM10 ... **101** J3
Felsham Rd, SW15 ... **148** A3
Felspar Cl, SE18 ... **137** J5
Felstead Av, Ilf. IG5 ... **80** D1
Felstead Gdns, E14
off Ferry St ... **134** C5
Felstead Rd, E11 ... **79** G7
Loughton IG10 ... **48** B7
Felstead St, E9 ... **95** J6
Felsted Rd, E16 ... **116** A6
FELTHAM, TW13 & TW14 . **160** A2
Feltham Av, E.Mol. KT8 ... **180** B4
Felthambrook Way, Felt. TW13 ... **160** B3
Feltham Business Complex, Felt. TW13 ... **160** B2
Feltham Hill Rd, Felt. TW13 ... **160** A4
Feltham Rd, Mitch. CR4 ... **185** J2
Felton Cl, Orp. BR5 ... **192** E6
Felton Gdns, Bark. IG11
off Sutton Rd ... **117** H1
Felton Ho, SE3
off Ryan Cl ... **155** H4
Felton Lea, Sid. DA14 ... **175** J5
Felton Rd, W13
off Camborne Av ... **125** F2
Barking IG11
off Sutton Rd ... **117** H2
Felton St, N1 ... **112** A1
Fencepiece Rd, Chig. IG7 ... **65** F5
Ilford IG6 ... **65** F5
Fenchurch Av, EC3 ... **20** D4
Fenchurch Bldgs, EC3 ... **20** E4
Fenchurch Pl, EC3 ... **20** E5
Fenchurch St, EC3 ... **20** D5
Fen Ct, EC3 ... **20** D5
Fendall Rd, Epsom KT19 . **196** C5
Fendall St, SE1 ... **29** E6
Fendt Cl, E16
off Bowman Av ... **115** F7
Fendyke Rd, Belv. DA17 ... **138** D3
Fenelon Pl, W14 ... **128** C4
Fen Gro, Sid. DA15 ... **157** J6
Fenham Rd, SE15 ... **132** D7
Fenman Ct, N17
off Shelbourne Rd .. **76/77** E1
Fenman Gdns, Ilf. IG3 ... **100** B1
Fenn Cl, Brom. BR1 ... **173** G6
Fennel Cl, E16
off Cranberry La .. **114/115** E4
Croydon CR0
off Primrose La ... **203** G1
Fennel St, SE18 ... **136** D6
Fenner Cl, SE16
off Layard Rd ... **132/133** E4
Fenner Sq, SW11 *off Thomas Baines Rd* ... **149** G3
Fenning St, SE1 ... **28** D3
Fenn St, E9 ... **95** F5
Fenstanton Av, N12 ... **57** G5
Fen St, E16
off Victoria Dock Rd ... **115** F7
Fenswood Cl, Bex. DA5 ... **159** G5
Fentiman Rd, SW8 ... **34** B6
Fenton Cl, E8
off Laurel St ... **94** C6
SW9 ... **151** F2
Chislehurst BR7 ... **174** C5
★**Fenton Ho**, NW3 ... **91** F3
Fenton Rd, N17 ... **59** J7
Fentons Av, E13 ... **115** H2
Fenwick Cl, SE18
off Ritter St ... **136** D6
Fenwick Gro, SE15 ... **152** D3
Fenwick Pl, SW9 ... **150** E3
South Croydon CR2
off Columbine Av ... **201** H7
Fenwick Rd, SE15 ... **152** D3
Ferdinand Pl, NW1
off Ferdinand St ... **92** A7
Ferdinand St, NW1 ... **92** A6
Ferguson Av, Surb. KT5 ... **181** J5
Ferguson Cl, E14 ... **134** A4
Bromley BR2 ... **190** C3
Ferguson Dr, W3 ... **106** D6
Fergus Rd, N5
off Calabria Rd ... **93** H5
Ferme Pk Rd, N4 ... **75** E5
N8 ... **75** E5
Fermor Rd, SE23 ... **171** H1
Fermoy Rd, W9 ... **108** C4
Greenford UB6 ... **103** H4
Fern Av, Mitch. CR4 ... **186** D4
Fernbank, Buck.H. IG9 ... **63** H1
Fernbank Av, Walt. KT12 . **179** E7
Wembley HA0 ... **86** C4
Fernbank Ms, SW12 ... **150** C6
Fernbrook Av, Sid. DA15
off Blackfen Rd ... **157** H5
Fernbrook Cres, SE13 ... **154** E6
Fernbrook Dr, Har. HA2 ... **67** H7
Fernbrook Rd, SE13 ... **154** E6
Ferncliff Rd, E8 ... **94** D5
Fern Cl, N1 ... **12** D1
Ferncroft Av, N12 ... **57** H6
NW3 ... **90** D3
Ruislip HA4 ... **84** C2
Ferndale, Brom. BR1 ... **191** J2
Ferndale Av, E17 ... **78** D5
Hounslow TW4 ... **143** E3
Ferndale Cl, Bexh. DA7 ... **158** E1
Ferndale Ct, SE3 ... **135** F7
Ferndale Rd, E7 ... **97** H7
E11 ... **97** E2
N15 ... **76** C6
SE25 ... **188** E5
SW4 ... **150** E4
SW9 ... **151** F3
Romford RM5 ... **83** J2
Ferndale St, E6 ... **116** E7
Ferndale Ter, Har. HA1 ... **68** C4
Ferndale Way, Orp. BR6 ... **207** G5
Fern Dene, W13
off Templewood .. **104/105** E5
Ferndene Rd, SE24 ... **151** J4
Fernden Way, Rom. RM7 ... **83** H6
Ferndown, Nthwd. HA6 ... **66** A2
Ferndown Av, Orp. BR6 ... **207** G1
Ferndown Cl, Pnr. HA5 ... **50** E7
Sutton SM2 ... **199** G6
Ferndown Rd, SE9 ... **156** A7
Watford WD19 ... **50** C3
Ferney Meade Way, Islw. TW7 ... **144** D2
Ferney Rd, Barn. EN4 ... **42** A7
Fern Gro, Felt. TW14 ... **142** B7
Fernhall Dr, Ilf. IG4 ... **80** A5
Fernham Rd, Th.Hth. CR7 . **187** J3
Fernhead Rd, W9 ... **108** C4
Fernhill Ct, E17 ... **78** D2
Fernhill Gdns, Kings.T. KT2 ... **163** G5
Fernhill St, E16 ... **136** C1
Fernholme Rd, SE15 ... **153** G5
Fernhurst Gdns, Edg. HA8 ... **54** A6
Fernhurst Rd, SW6 ... **148** B1
Croydon CR0 ... **188** D7
Fern La, Houns. TW5 ... **123** F5
Fernlea Rd, SW12 ... **168** B1
Mitcham CR4 ... **186** A2
Fernleigh Cl, W9 ... **108** C3
Croydon CR0
off Stafford Rd ... **201** G4
Fernleigh Ct, Har. HA2 ... **67** H2
Wembley HA9 ... **87** H2
Fernleigh Rd, N21 ... **59** G2
Fernsbury St, WC1 ... **10** E4
Fernshaw Rd, SW10 ... **30** C6
Fernside, NW11
off Finchley Rd ... **90** D2
Buckhurst Hill IG9 ... **63** H1
Fernside Av, NW7 ... **54** D3
Feltham TW13 ... **160** B4
Fernside Rd, SW12 ... **167** J1
Ferns Rd, E15 ... **97** F6
Fern St, E3 ... **114** A4
Fernthorpe Rd, SW16 ... **168** C6
Ferntower Rd, N5 ... **94** A5
Fern Wk, SE16 ... **37** J4
Fernways, Ilf. IG1
off Cecil Rd ... **98/99** E4
Fernwood Av, SW16 ... **168** D4
Wembley HA0
off Bridgewater Rd ... **87** F5
Fernwood Cl, Brom. BR1 . **191** J2
Fernwood Cres, N20 ... **57** J3
Ferranti Cl, SE18 ... **136** A3
Ferraro Cl, Houns. TW5 ... **123** G6
Ferrers Av, Wall. SM6 ... **200** D4
West Drayton UB7 ... **120** A2
Ferrers Rd, SW16 ... **168** D5
Ferrestone Rd, N8 ... **75** F4

Ferrey Ms, SW9 151 G2
Ferriby Cl, N1 *off Bewdley St* 93 G7
Ferrier Pt, E16 *off Forty Acre La* 115 H5
Ferrier St, SW18 149 E4
Ferring Cl, Har. HA2 85 J1
Ferrings, SE21 170 B2
Ferris Av, Croy. CR0 203 J3
Ferris Rd, SE22 152 D4
Ferron Rd, E5 94 E3
Ferrour Ct, N2 73 G3
Ferryhills Cl, Wat. WD19 50 C3
Ferry La, N17 76 D4
SW13 127 F6
Brentford TW8 125 H6
Richmond TW9 125 J6
Ferryman's Quay, SW6 149 F2
Ferrymead Av, Grnf. UB6 103 G3
Ferrymead Dr, Grnf. UB6 103 G2
Ferrymead Gdns, Grnf. UB6 103 J2
Ferrymoor, Rich. TW10 163 E3
Ferry Pl, SE18 *off Woolwich High St* 136 D3
Ferry Rd, SW13 127 G7
Teddington TW11 162 E5
Thames Ditton KT7 180 E6
Twickenham TW1 162 E1
West Molesey KT8 179 G3
Ferry Sq, Brent. TW8 125 H6
Ferry St, E14 134 C5
Festing Rd, SW15 148 A3
Festival Cl, Bex. DA5 176 D1
Festival Wk, Cars. SM5 199 J5
Festoon Way, E16 116 A7
Fetter La, EC4 19 F4
Ffinch St, SE8 134 A7
Field Cl, E4 62 B6
NW2 89 G2
Bromley BR1 191 J2
Buckhurst Hill IG9 63 J3
Chessington KT9 195 F5
Hayes UB3 121 F7
Hounslow TW4 142 B1
West Molesey KT8 179 H5
Fieldcommon La, Walt. KT12 179 F7
Field Ct, WC1 18 D2
Field End, Barn. EN5 39 H4
Northolt UB5 84 D6
Ruislip HA4 84 C6
Fieldend, Twick. TW1 162 C4
Fieldend Rd, SW16 186 C1
Field End Rd, Pnr. HA5 66 B6
Ruislip HA4 85 E4
Fielders Cl, Enf. EN1 *off Woodfield Cl* 44 B4
Harrow HA2 85 J1
Fieldfare Rd, SE28 118 C7
Fieldgate La, Mitch. CR4 185 H3
Fieldgate St, E1 21 J2
Fieldhouse Cl, E18 79 G1
Fieldhouse Rd, SW12 168 C1
Fielding Av, Twick. TW2 161 J3
Fielding Ho, NW6 108 D3
Fielding Ms, SW13 *off Castelnau* 127 H6
Fielding Rd, W4 126 D3
W14 128 A3
Fieldings, The, SE23 171 F1
Fielding St, SE17 35 J5
Fielding Wk, W13 124 E3
Field La, Brent. TW8 125 F7
Teddington TW11 162 D5
Field Mead, NW7 55 E7
NW9 55 E7
Field Pl, N.Mal. KT3 183 F6
Field Rd, E7 97 F4
N17 76 A3
W6 128 B5
Feltham TW14 142 B6
Fieldsend Rd, Sutt. SM3 198 B5
Fields Est, E8 94 D7
Fieldside Cl, Orp. BR6 *off State Fm Av* 207 F4
Fieldside Rd, Brom. BR1 172 D5
Fields Pk Cres, Rom. RM6 82 D5
Field St, WC1 10 C3
Fieldview, SW18 167 G1
Field Way, NW10 *off Twybridge Way* 88 C7
Croydon CR0 204 B6
Fieldway, Dag. RM8 100 B4
Field Way, Grnf. UB6 103 H1
Fieldway, Orp. BR5 193 G6
Fieldway Cres, N5 93 G5
Fiennes Cl, Dag. RM8 100 C1
Fiesta Dr, Dag. RM9 119 J4
Fife Rd, E16 115 G5
N22 59 H7
Fife Rd, SW14 146 C5
Kingston upon Thames KT1 181 H2
Fife Ter, N1 10 D1
Fifield Path, SE23 *off Bampton Rd* 171 G3
Fifth Av, E12 98 C4
W10 108 B3
Hayes UB3 121 J1
Fifth Cross Rd, Twick. TW2 162 A2
Fifth Way, Wem. HA9 88 B4
Figges Rd, Mitch. CR4 168 A7
Fig Tree Cl, NW10 *off Craven Pk* 106/107 E1
Filby Rd, Chess. KT9 195 J6
Filey Av, N16 94 D1
Filey Cl, Sutt. SM2 199 F7
Filey Waye, Ruis. HA4 84 A2
Filigree Ct, SE16 *off Silver Wk* 133 J1
Fillebrook Av, Enf. EN1 44 B2
Fillebrook Rd, E11 96 D1
Filmer Rd, SW6 148 B1
Filston Rd, Erith DA8 *off Riverdale Rd* 139 H5
Finborough Rd, SW10 30 A5
SW17 167 J6
Finchale Rd, SE2 138 A3
Finch Av, SE27 170 A4
Finch Cl, NW10 88 D5
Barnet EN5 40 D5
Finchdean Ho, SW15 *off Tangley Gro* 147 F7
Finch Dr, Felt. TW14 142 D7
Finch Gdns, E4 62 A5
Finchingfield Av, Wdf.Grn. IG8 63 J7
Finch La, EC3 20 C4
FINCHLEY, N3 72 E1
Finchley Ct, N3 57 E6
Finchley La, NW4 71 J4
Finchley Pk, N12 57 F4
Finchley Pl, NW8 6 E1
Finchley Rd, NW2 90 D3
NW3 91 F6
NW8 109 G1
NW11 72 C6
Finchley Way, N3 56 D7
Finch Ms, SE15 132 C7
Finden Rd, E7 97 H5
Findhorn Av, Hayes UB4 102 B5
Findhorn St, E14 114 C6
Findon Cl, SW18 *off Wimbledon Pk Rd* 148 D6
Harrow HA2 85 H3
Findon Rd, N9 60 E1
W12 127 G2
Fingal St, SE10 135 F5
Finland Quay, SE16 *off Finland St* 133 H3
Finland Rd, SE4 153 H3
Finland St, SE16 133 H3
Finlays Cl, Chess. KT9 196 A5
Finlay St, SW6 148 A1
Finney La, Islw. TW7 144 D1
Finnis St, E2 113 E3
Finnymore Rd, Dag. RM9 101 E7
FINSBURY, EC1 11 F3
Finsbury Av, EC2 20 C2
Finsbury Av Sq, EC2 20 C2
Finsbury Circ, EC2 20 C2
Finsbury Cotts, N22 *off Clarence Rd* 58/59 E7
Finsbury Est, EC1 11 G4
Finsbury Ho, N22 75 E1
Finsbury Mkt, EC2 12 D6
FINSBURY PARK, N4 93 G1
★Finsbury Park, N4 75 H7
Finsbury Pk Av, N4 75 J6
Finsbury Pk Rd, N4 93 H2
Finsbury Pavement, EC2 20 C1
Finsbury Rd, N22 75 F1
Finsbury Sq, EC2 20 C1
Finsbury St, EC2 20 B1
Finsbury Twr, EC1 12 B6
Finsbury Way, Bex. DA5 159 F6
Finsen Rd, SE5 151 J3
Finstock Rd, W10 108 A6
Finucane Ri, Bushey (Bushey Hth) WD23 51 J2
Firbank Cl, E16 116 A5
Enfield EN2 *off Gladbeck Way* 43 J4
Firbank Rd, SE15 153 E2
Fir Cl, Walt. KT12 178 A7
Fircroft Gdns, Har. HA1 86 B3
Fircroft Rd, SW17 167 J2
Chessington KT9 195 J4
Fir Dene, Orp. BR6 206 C3
Firdene, Surb. KT5 196 C1
Fire Bell All, Surb. KT6 181 H6
Firecrest Dr, NW3 91 E3
Firefly Cl, Wall. SM6 200 E7
Firefly Gdns, E6 *off Jack Dash Way* 116 B4
★Firepower, SE18 136 E3
Fire Sta All, Barn. EN5 *off Christchurch La* 40 C2
Firethorn Cl, Edg. HA8 *off Larkspur Gro* 54 C4
Fir Gro, N.Mal. KT3 183 F6
Fir Gro Rd, SW9 *off Marcella Rd* 151 G2
Firhill Rd, SE6 172 A4
Fir Rd, Felt. TW13 160 D5
Sutton SM3 198 C1
Firs, The, E17 *off Leucha Rd* 77 H5
N20 57 G1
W5 105 G5
Firs Av, N10 74 A3
N11 58 A6
SW14 146 C4
Firsby Av, Croy. CR0 203 G1
Firsby Rd, N16 94 C1
Firs Cl, N10 *off Firs Av* 74 A3
SE23 153 G7
Esher (Clay.) KT10 194 B6
Mitcham CR4 186 B2
Firscroft, N13 59 J3
Firs Dr, Houns. TW5 122 B7
Loughton IG10 48 D1
Firside Gro, Sid. DA15 175 J1
Firs La, N13 59 J3
N21 59 J2
Firs Pk Av, N21 60 A1
Firs Pk Gdns, N21 59 J1
First Av, E12 98 B4
E13 115 G3
E17 78 A5
N18 61 F4
NW4 71 J4
SW14 146 E3
W3 127 F1
W10 108 C4
Bexleyheath DA7 138 C7
Dagenham RM10 119 H2
Enfield EN1 44 C6
Greenford UB6 86 A7
Hayes UB3 121 J1
Romford RM6 82 C5
Walton-on-Thames KT12 178 B6
Wembley HA9 87 G2
West Molesey KT8 179 F4
First Cl, W.Mol. KT8 179 J3
First Cross Rd, Twick. TW2 162 B2
First Dr, NW10 88 C7
First St, SW3 31 H1
Firstway, SW20 183 J2
First Way, Wem. HA9 88 B4
Firs Wk, Wdf.Grn. IG8 63 G5
Firswood Av, Epsom KT19 197 F5
Firth Gdns, SW6 148 B1
Fir Tree Av, Mitch. CR4 186 A2
West Drayton UB7 120 D3
Fir Tree Cl, SW16 168 C5
W5 105 H6
Epsom (Ewell) KT19 197 F4
Orpington BR6 *off Highfield Av* 207 J5
Fir Tree Gdns, Croy. CR0 204 A4
Fir Tree Gro, Cars. SM5 199 J7
Fir Tree Rd, Houns. TW4 143 E4
Fir Trees Cl, SE16 133 H1
Fir Tree Wk, Dag. RM10 *off Wheel Fm Dr* 101 J3
Enfield EN1 44 A3
Fisher Cl, Croy. CR0 *off Grant Rd* 202 C1
Greenford UB6 103 G3
Fisherman Cl, Rich. TW10 *off Locksmeade Rd* 163 F4
Fishermans Dr, SE16 133 G2
Fisherman's Wk, E14 134 A1
Fishermans Wk, SE28 *off Tugboat St* 137 H2
Fisher Rd, Har. HA3 68 C2
Fishers Cl, SW16 *off Garrad's Rd* 168 D3
Fishers Ct, SE14 *off Besson St* 153 G1
Fishersdene, Esher (Clay.) KT10 194 D7
Fishers La, W4 126 D4
Fisher St, E16 115 G5
WC1 18 B2
Fishers Way, Belv. DA17 139 J1
Fisherton St, NW8 7 E6
Fishguard Way, E16 137 E2
Fishponds Rd, SW17 167 H4
Keston BR2 206 A5
Fish St Hill, EC3 20 C5
Fitzalan Rd, N3 72 B3
Esher (Clay.) KT10 194 B7
Fitzalan St, SE11 34 E1
Fitzgeorge Av, W14 128 B4
New Malden KT3 182 D1
Fitzgerald Av, SW14 147 E3
Fitzgerald Cl, E11 *off Fitzgerald Rd* 79 G5
Fitzgerald Ho, E14 114 B6
Hayes UB3 122 B1
Fitzgerald Rd, E11 79 G5
SW14 146 D3
Thames Ditton KT7 180 D6
Fitzhardinge St, W1 16 B3
Fitzherbert Ho, Rich. TW10 *off Kingsmead* 145 J6
Fitzhugh Gro, SW18 149 G6
Fitzjames Av, W14 128 B4
Croydon CR0 202 D2
Fitzjohn Av, Barn. EN5 40 B5
Fitzjohn's Av, NW3 91 F5
Fitzmaurice Pl, W1 24 E1
Fitzneal St, W12 107 F6
Fitzroy Cl, N6 91 J1
Fitzroy Ct, W1 9 G6
Fitzroy Cres, W4 126 D7
Fitzroy Gdns, SE19 170 B7
Fitzroy Ms, W1 9 F6
Fitzroy Pk, N6 91 J1
Fitzroy Rd, NW1 110 A1
Fitzroy Sq, W1 9 F6
Fitzroy St, W1 9 F6
Fitzroy Yd, NW1 *off Fitzroy Rd* 110 A1
Fitzstephen Rd, Dag. RM8 100 B5
Fitzwarren Gdns, N19 92 C1
Fitzwilliam Av, Rich. TW9 145 J2
Fitzwilliam Ms, E16 *off Hanover Av* 135 G1
Fitzwilliam Rd, SW4 150 C3
Fitzwygram Cl, Hmptn. (Hmptn H.) TW12 161 J5
Five Acre, NW9 71 F1
Fiveacre Cl, Th.Hth. CR7 187 G6
Five Bell All, E14 *off Three Colt St* 113 J7
Five Elms Rd, Brom. BR2 205 H3
Dagenham RM9 101 F3
Five Flds Cl, Wat. WD19 51 F3
Fives Ct, SE11 35 G1
Five Ways Cor, NW4 71 H1
Fiveways Rd, SW9 151 G2
Fladbury Rd, N15 76 A6
Fladgate Rd, E11 79 E6
Flag Cl, Croy. CR0 203 G1
Flag Wk, Pnr. HA5 *off Eastcote Rd* 66 A6
Flambard Rd, Har. HA1 68 D6
Flamborough Rd, Ruis. HA4 84 A3
Flamborough St, E14 113 H6
Flamborough Wk, E14 *off Flamborough St* 113 H6
Flamingo Gdns, Nthlt. UB5 *off Jetstar Way* 102/103 E3
Flamstead Gdns, Dag. RM9 *off Flamstead Rd* 100 C7
Flamstead Rd, Dag. RM9 100 C7
Flamsted Av, Wem. HA9 88 A6
★Flamsteed Ho Mus, SE10 134 D7
Flamsteed Rd, SE7 136 B5
Flanchford Rd, W12 127 F3
Flanders Cres, SW17 167 J7
Flanders Rd, E6 116 C2
W4 127 E4
Flanders Way, E9 95 G6
Flank St, E1 21 H5
Flask Cotts, NW3 *off New End Sq* 91 G4
Flask Wk, NW3 91 G4
Flat Iron Sq, SE1 *off Union St* 131 J1
Flavell Ms, SE10 135 E5
Flaxen Cl, E4 *off Flaxen Rd* 62 B3

Flaxen Rd, E4 62 B3
Flaxley Rd, Mord. SM4 184 E6
Flaxman Ct, W1 17 H4
Flaxman Rd, SE5 151 H2
Flaxman Ter, WC1 9 J4
Flaxton Rd, SE18 157 G1
Flecker Cl, Stan. HA7 52 C5
Fleece Dr, N9 60 D4
Fleece Rd, Surb. KT6 195 F1
Fleece Wk, N7 off Manger Rd 92/93 E6
Fleeming Cl, E17 off Pennant Ter 77 J2
Fleeming Rd, E17 77 J2
Fleet Cl, W.Mol. KT8 179 F5
Fleet La, W.Mol. KT8 179 F6
Fleet Pl, EC4 off Farringdon St 111 G6
Fleet Rd, NW3 91 H5
Fleetside, W.Mol. KT8 179 F6
Fleet Sq, WC1 10 C4
Fleet St, EC4 19 E4
Fleet St Hill, E1 13 H6
Fleetway Business Pk, Grnf. UB6 105 E2
Fleetwood Cl, E16 116 A5
Chessington KT9 195 G7
Croydon CR0 202 C3
Fleetwood Ct, E6 off Evelyn Denington Rd 116 C5
Fleetwood Gro, W3 off East Acton La 106/107 E7
Fleetwood Rd, NW10 89 G5
Kingston upon Thames KT1 182 B3
Fleetwood Sq, Kings.T. KT1 182 B3
Fleetwood St, N16 off Stoke Newington Ch St 94 B2
Fleetwood Way, Wat. WD19 50 C4
Fleming Cl, W9 off Chippenham Rd 108 D4
Fleming Ct, W2 14 E1
Croydon CR0 201 G5
Fleming Dr, N21 43 F5
Fleming Mead, Mitch. CR4 167 H7
Fleming Rd, SE17 35 H5
Southall UB1 103 H6
Fleming Wk, NW9 off Pasteur Cl 70/71 E2
Fleming Way, SE28 118 D7
Isleworth TW7 144 C3
Flemming Av, Ruis. HA4 84 B1
Flempton Rd, E10 77 H7
Fletcher Cl, E6 off Trader Rd 116/117 E6
Fletcher La, E10 78 C7
Fletcher Path, SE8 off New Butt La 134 A7
Fletcher Rd, W4 126 C3
Chigwell IG7 65 J5
Fletchers Cl, Brom. BR2 191 H4
Fletcher St, E1 21 J5
Fletching Rd, E5 95 F3
SE7 135 J6
Fletton Rd, N11 58 E7
Fleur de Lis St, E1 13 E6
Fleur Gates, SW19 off Princes Way 148 A7
Flexmere Gdns, N17 off Flexmere Rd 76 A1
Flexmere Rd, N17 76 A1
Flight App, NW9 71 F2
Flimwell Cl, Brom. BR1 172 E5
Flint Cl, E15 off Vicarage La 96 E7
Flintmill Cres, SE3 156 B2
Flinton St, SE17 36 E3
Flint St, SE17 36 C2
Flitcroft St, WC2 17 J3
Floathaven Cl, SE28 138 A1
Flock Mill Pl, SW18 166 E1
Flockton St, SE16 29 H4
Flodden Rd, SE5 151 J1
Flood La, Twick. TW1 off Church La 162 D1
Flood Pas, SE18 off Samuel St 136 C4
Flood St, SW3 31 H4
Flood Wk, SW3 31 H5
Flora Cl, E14 114 B6
Flora Gdns, W6 127 H4
Romford RM6 82 C6
Floral St, WC2 18 A5
Flora St, Belv. DA17 off Victoria St 139 F5
Florence Av, Enf. EN2 43 J3
Florence Av, Mord. SM4 185 F5
Florence Cantwell Wk, N19 off Hillrise Rd 74/75 E7
Florence Cl, Walt. KT12 off Florence Rd 178 B7
Florence Dr, Enf. EN2 43 J3
Florence Elson Cl, E12 off Grantham Rd 98 D4
Florence Gdns, W4 126 C6
Romford RM6 off Roxy Av 82 C7
★Florence Nightingale Mus, SE1 26 C4
Florence Rd, E6 115 J1
E13 115 F2
N4 93 G1
SE2 138 C3
SE14 153 J1
SW19 166 E6
W4 126 D3
W5 105 H7
Beckenham BR3 189 G2
Bromley BR1 191 G1
Feltham TW13 160 B1
Kingston upon Thames KT2 163 J7
Southall UB2 122 D4
Walton-on-Thames KT12 178 B7
Florence St, E16 115 F4
N1 93 H7
NW4 71 J4
Florence Ter, SE14 153 J1
Florence Way, SW12 167 J1
Florey Sq, N21 off Highlands Av 43 F5
Florfield Pas, E8 off Reading La 94/95 E6
Florfield Rd, E8 off Reading La 94/95 E6
Florian Av, Sutt. SM1 199 G4
Florian Rd, SW15 148 B4
Florida Cl, Bushey (Bushey Hth) WD23 52 A2
Florida Rd, Th.Hth. CR7 187 H1
Florida St, E2 13 H4
Florin Ct, SE1 off Tanner St 132 C2
Floris Pl, SW4 off Fitzwilliam Rd 150 C3
Floriston Cl, Stan. HA7 69 E1
Floriston Ct, Nthlt. UB5 85 H5
Floriston Gdns, Stan. HA7 69 E1
Floss St, SW15 147 J2
Flower & Dean Wk, E1 21 G2
Flower La, NW7 55 F5
Flower Ms, NW11 72 B6
Flower Pot Cl, N15 off St. Ann's Rd 76 C6
Flowers Cl, NW2 89 G3
Flowersmead, SW17 168 A2
Flowers Ms, N19 off Archway Rd 92 C2
Flower Wk, The, SW7 22 C4
Floyd Rd, SE7 135 J5
Floyer Cl, Rich. TW10 off Queens Rd 145 J5
Fludyer St, SE13 154 E4
Foley Ms, Esher (Clay.) KT10 194 B7
Foley Rd, Esher (Clay.) KT10 194 B7
Foley St, W1 17 F2
Folgate St, E1 21 E1
Foliot St, W12 107 F6
Folkestone Rd, E6 116 D2
E17 78 B4
N18 60 D4
Folkingham La, NW9 70 D1
Folkington Cor, N12 56 C5
Follett St, E14 114 C6
Folly La, E4 61 J7
E17 77 H1
Folly Ms, W11 off Portobello Rd 108 C6
Folly Wall, E14 134 C2
Fontaine Rd, SW16 169 F7
Fontarabia Rd, SW11 150 A4
Fontayne Av, Chig. IG7 65 F4
Fontenoy Rd, SW12 168 B2
Fonteyne Gdns, Wdf.Grn. IG8 off Lechmere Av 80 A2
Fonthill Cl, SE20 off Selby Rd 188 D2
Fonthill Ms, N4 off Lennox Rd 93 G2
Fonthill Rd, N4 93 F1
Font Hills, N2 73 F2
Fontley Way, SW15 147 G7
Fontwell Cl, Har. HA3 52 B7
Northolt UB5 85 G6
Fontwell Dr, Brom. BR2 192 D5
Football La, Har. HA1 86 B1
Footpath, The, SW15 147 G5
FOOTS CRAY, Sid. DA14 176 B6
Foots Cray High St, Sid. DA14 176 C6
Foots Cray La, Sid. DA14 176 C1
Footscray Rd, SE9 156 D6
Forbes Cl, NW2 89 G3
Forbes Ct, SE19 170 B5
Forbes St, E1 21 J4
Forbes Way, Ruis. HA4 84 B2
Forburg Rd, N16 94 D1
Ford Cl, E3 off Roman Rd 113 H2
Harrow HA1 68 A7
Thornton Heath CR7 187 H6
Forde Av, Brom. BR1 191 J3
Fordel Rd, SE6 172 D1
Ford End, Wdf.Grn. IG8 63 H6
Fordham Cl, Barn. EN4 41 H3
Fordham Rd, Barn. EN4 41 G3
Fordham St, E1 21 J3
Fordhook Av, W5 105 J7
Fordingley Rd, W9 108 C3
Fordington Ho, SE26 off Sydenham Hill 170 D3
Fordington Rd, N6 73 J5
Fordmill Rd, SE6 172 A2
Ford Rd, E3 113 H1
Dagenham RM9, RM10 101 F7
Fords Gro, N21 59 J1
Fords Pk Rd, E16 115 G6
Ford Sq, E1 113 E5
Ford St, E3 113 H1
E16 115 F6
Fordwich Cl, Orp. BR6 193 J7
Fordwych Rd, NW2 90 B4
Fordyce Ho, SW16 off Colson Way 168 C4
Fordyce Rd, SE13 154 C6
Fordyke Rd, Dag. RM8 101 F2
★Foreign & Commonwealth Office, SW1 26 A3
Foreign St, SE5 151 H2
Foreland Ct, NW4 72 B1
Foreland St, SE18 off Plumstead Rd 137 G4
Foreman Ct, W6 off Hammersmith Bdy 127 J4
Foremark Cl, Ilf. IG6 65 J5
Foreshore, SE8 133 J4
Forest, The, E11 79 E4
Forest App, E4 47 E7
Woodford Green IG8 63 F7
Forest Av, E4 47 E7
Chigwell IG7 64 D5
Forest Business Pk, E17 77 G7
Forest Cl, E11 79 F5
Chislehurst BR7 192 D1
Woodford Green IG8 63 H3
Forest Ct, E4 63 F1
E11 79 E4
Forest Cft, SE23 171 E2
Forestdale, N14 58 D4
Forest Dr, E12 98 A3
Keston BR2 206 B4
Woodford Green IG8 62 D7
Forest Dr E, E11 78 D7
Forest Dr W, E11 78 C7
Forest Edge, Buck.H. IG9 63 J4
Forester Rd, SE15 153 E4
Foresters Cl, Wall. SM6 200 D7
Foresters Cres, Bexh. DA7 159 H4
Foresters Dr, E17 78 D4
Wallington SM6 200 D7
Forest Gdns, N17 76 C2
FOREST GATE, E7 97 G5
Forest Gate, NW9 70 E5
Forest Glade, E4 62 E4
E11 79 E6
Forest Gro, E8 94 C7
Forest Hts, Buck.H. IG9 63 G2
FOREST HILL, SE23 171 G1
Forest Hill Business Cen, SE23 171 F2
Forest Hill Ind Est, SE23 off Perry Vale 171 F2
Forest Hill Rd, SE22 152 E5
SE23 152 E5
Forestholme Cl, SE23 171 F2
Forest Ind Pk, Ilf. IG6 81 H1
Forest La, E7 97 E5
E15 97 E5
Chigwell IG7 64 D5
Forest Mt Rd, Wdf.Grn. IG8 62 D7
Fore St, EC2 20 A2
N9 60 D5
N18 60 C6
Pinner HA5 66 A5
Fore St Av, EC2 20 B2
Forest Ridge, Beck. BR3 190 A3
Keston BR2 206 B4
Forest Ri, E17 78 D5
Forest Rd, E7 97 G4
E8 94 C6
E11 78 D7
E17 77 F4
N9 61 E1
N17 77 F4
Feltham TW13 160 C2
Ilford IG6 81 H1
Loughton IG10 48 A3
Richmond TW9 126 A7
Romford RM7 83 H3
Sutton SM3 198 D1
Woodford Green IG8 63 G3
Forest Side, E4 47 F7
E7 off Capel Rd 97 H4
Buckhurst Hill IG9 63 J1
Worcester Park KT4 197 F1
Forest St, E7 97 G5
Forest Vw, E4 46 D7
E11 off High Rd Leytonstone 79 F7
Forest Vw Av, E10 78 D5
Forest Vw Rd, E12 98 B4
E17 78 C1
Loughton IG10 48 A4
Forest Wk, N10 74 B1
Forest Way, N19 off Hargrave Pk 92 C2
Loughton IG10 48 B3
Orpington BR5 193 J5
Sidcup DA15 157 G7
Woodford Green IG8 63 H4
Forfar Rd, N22 75 H1
SW11 150 A1
Forge Cl, Brom. BR2 205 G1
Hayes UB3 off High St 121 G6
Forge Cotts, W5 off Ealing Grn 125 G1
Forge Dr, Esher (Clay.) KT10 194 D7
Forge La, Felt. TW13 160 E5
Sunbury-on-Thames TW16 178 A3
Sutton SM3 198 B7
Forge Ms, Croy. CR0 off Addington Village Rd 204 A5
Sunbury-on-Thames TW16 off Forge La 178 A3
Forge Pl, NW1 off Malden Cres 92 A6
Forlong Path, Nthlt. UB5 off Arnold Rd 84/85 E6
Forman Pl, N16 off Farleigh Rd 94 C4
Formation, The, E16 off Woolwich Manor Way 136/137 E2
Formby Av, Stan. HA7 69 F3
Formosa St, W9 6 C6
Formunt Cl, E16 off Vincent St 115 F5
Forres Gdns, NW11 72 D6
Forrester Path, SE26 171 G4
Forrest Gdns, SW16 187 F3
Forris Av, Hayes UB3 121 J1
Forset St, W1 15 H3
Forstal Cl, Brom. BR2 off Ridley Rd 191 G3
Forster Cl, E17 62 D7
Forster Rd, E17 77 H6
N17 76 C3
SW2 150 E7
Beckenham BR3 189 H3
Croydon CR0 off Windmill Rd 187 J7
Forsters Cl, Rom. RM6 83 F6
Forster's Way, SW18 166 E1
Forsters Way, Hayes UB4 102 B6
Forston St, N1 12 B1
Forsyte Cres, SE19 188 B1
Forsyth Gdns, SE17 35 H5
Forsythia Cl, Ilf. IG1 98 E5
Forsyth Pl, Enf. EN1 44 B5
Forterie Gdns, Ilf. IG3 100 A3
Fortescue Av, E8 off Mentmore Ter 94/95 E7
Twickenham TW2 161 J3
Fortescue Rd, SW19 167 G7
Edgware HA8 70 D1

Fortess Gro, NW5
off Fortess Rd ... **92** B5
Fortess Rd, NW5 ... **92** B5
Fortess Wk, NW5
off Fortess Rd ... **92** B5
Forthbridge Rd, SW11 ... **150** A4
Fortis Cl, E16 ... **115** J6
FORTIS GREEN, N2 ... **73** J4
Fortis Grn, N2 ... **73** H4
N10 ... **73** H4
Fortis Grn Av, N2 ... **73** J3
Fortis Grn Rd, N10 ... **74** A3
Fortismere Av, N10 ... **74** A3
Fortnam Rd, N19 ... **92** D2
★**Fortnum & Mason**, W1 ... **25** F1
Fortnums Acre, Stan. HA7 ... **52** C6
Fort Rd, SE1 ... **37** G2
Northolt UB5 ... **85** G7
Fortrose Gdns, SW2
off New Pk Rd ... **168** D1
Fort St, E1 ... **21** E2
E16 ... **135** H1
Fortuna Cl, N7
off Vulcan Way ... **93** F6
Fortune Gate Rd, NW10 ... **107** E1
Fortune Grn Rd, NW6 ... **90** D4
Fortunes Mead, Nthlt.
UB5 ... **85** E6
Fortune St, EC1 ... **12** A6
Fortune Wk, SE28
off Broadwater Rd ... **137** G3
Fortune Way, NW10 ... **107** G3
Forty Acre La, E16 ... **115** G5
Forty Av, Wem. HA9 ... **87** J3
Forty Cl, Wem. HA9 ... **87** J2
Forty Footpath, SW14 ... **146** C3
Forty La, Wem. HA9 ... **88** B2
Forum, The, W.Mol. KT8 ... **179** H4
★**Forum Club**, NW5 ... **92** B5
Forum Magnum Sq, SE1 ... **26** C3
Forumside, Edg. HA8
off High St ... **54** A6
Forum Way, Edg. HA8
off High St ... **54** A6
Forval Cl, Mitch. CR4 ... **185** J5
Forward Dr, Har. HA3 ... **68** C4
Fosbury Ms, W2 ... **14** B6
Foscote Ms, W9
off Amberley Rd ... **108** D5
Foscote Rd, NW4 ... **71** H6
Foskett Rd, SW6 ... **148** C2
Foss Av, Croy. CR0 ... **201** G5
Fossdene Rd, SE7 ... **135** H5
Fossdyke Cl, Hayes UB4 ... **103** E5
Fosse Way, W13 ... **104** D5
Fossil Rd, SE13 ... **154** A3
Fossington Rd, Belv.
DA17 ... **138** D4
Foss Rd, SW17 ... **167** G4
Fossway, Dag. RM8 ... **100** C2
Foster La, EC2 ... **19** J3
Foster Rd, E13 ... **115** G4
W3 ... **106** E7
W4 ... **126** D5
Fosters Cl, E18 ... **79** H1
Chislehurst BR7 ... **174** C5
Foster St, NW4 ... **71** J4
Foster Wk, NW4
off New Brent St ... **71** J4
Fothergill Cl, E13 ... **115** G2
Fothergill Dr, N21 ... **43** E5
Fotheringham Rd, Enf.
EN1 ... **44** C4
Foubert's Pl, W1 ... **17** F4
Foulden Rd, N16 ... **94** C4
Foulden Ter, N16
off Foulden Rd ... **94** C4
Foulis Ter, SW7 ... **31** F3
Foulser Rd, SW17 ... **167** J3
Foulsham Rd, Th.Hth.
CR7 ... **187** J3
Founder Cl, E6
off Trader Rd ... **116/117** E6
Founders Ct, EC2 ... **20** B3
Founders Gdns, SE19 ... **169** J7
★**Foundling Mus**, WC1 ... **10** B5
Foundry Cl, SE16 ... **133** H1
Foundry Ms, NW1 ... **9** G5
Fountain Ct, EC4 ... **19** E5
Fountain Dr, SE19 ... **170** C4
Fountain Grn Sq, SE16 ... **29** J3
Fountain Ms, N5
off Highbury Gra ... **93** J4
NW3 ... **91** J6
Fountain Pl, SW9 ... **151** G1
Fountain Rd, SW17 ... **167** G5
Thornton Heath CR7 ... **187** J2
Fountains, The, Loug. IG10
off Fallow Flds ... **48** A7
Fountains Av, Felt. TW13 ... **161** F3
Fountains Cl, Felt. TW13 ... **161** F2
Fountains Cres, N14 ... **42** E7
Fountain Sq, SW1 ... **32** D1
Fountain St, E2
off Columbia Rd ... **112** C3
Fountayne Rd, N15 ... **76** D4
N16 ... **94** D2
Fount St, SW8 ... **130** D7
Fouracres, SW12
off Little Dimocks ... **168** B2
Enfield EN3 ... **45** H1
Fourland Wk, Edg. HA8 ... **54** C6
Fournier St, E1 ... **21** F1
Four Seasons Cl, E3 ... **114** A2
Four Seasons Cres, Sutt.
SM3 ... **198** C2
Fourth Av, E12 ... **98** C4
W10 ... **108** B4
Hayes UB3 ... **121** J1
Fourth Cross Rd, Twick.
TW2 ... **162** A2
Fourth Way, Wem. HA9 ... **88** C4
Four Wents, The, E4
off Kings Rd ... **62** D2
Fowey Av, Ilf. IG4 ... **80** A5
Fowey Cl, E1
off Kennet St ... **132/133** E1
Fowler Cl, SW11 ... **149** G3
Fowler Rd, E7 ... **97** G4
N1 *off Halton Rd* ... **93** H7
Mitcham CR4 ... **186** A2
Fowlers Cl, Sid. DA14
off Thursland Rd ... **176/177** E5
Fowlers Wk, W5 ... **105** G4
Fownes St, SW11 ... **149** H3
Fox & Knot St, EC1 ... **19** H1
Foxberry Rd, SE4 ... **153** H3
Foxborough Gdns, SE4 ... **154** A6
Foxbourne Rd, SW17 ... **168** A2
Foxbury Av, Chis. BR7 ... **175** G6
Foxbury Cl, Brom. BR1 ... **173** H6
Foxbury Rd, Brom. BR1 ... **173** G6
Fox Cl, E1 ... **113** F4
E16 ... **115** G5
Foxcombe, Croy.
(New Adgtn) CR0 ... **204** B6
Foxcombe Cl, E6
off Boleyn Rd ... **116** A2
Foxcombe Rd, SW15
off Alton Rd ... **165** G1
Foxcote, SE5 ... **36** E4
Foxcroft Rd, SE18 ... **157** E1
Foxes Dale, SE3 ... **155** G3
Bromley BR2 ... **190** D3
Foxfield Rd, Orp. BR6 ... **207** G2
Foxglove Cl, Sid. DA15
off Wellington Av ... **158** A6
Southall UB1 ... **103** E7
Foxglove Gdns, E11 ... **79** J4
Foxglove La, Chess. KT9 ... **196** A4
Foxglove Path, SE28
off Hill Vw Dr ... **137** H1
Foxglove St, W12 ... **107** F7
Foxglove Way, Wall. SM6 ... **200** B1
Foxgrove, N14 ... **58** E3
Fox Gro, Walt. KT12 ... **178** B7
Foxgrove Av, Beck. BR3 ... **172** B7
Foxgrove Path, Wat.
WD19 ... **50** D5
Foxgrove Rd, Beck. BR3 ... **172** B7
Foxham Rd, N19 ... **92** D3
Fox Hill, SE19 ... **170** C7
Keston BR2 ... **205** J5
Fox Hill Gdns, SE19 ... **170** C7
Foxhole Rd, SE9 ... **156** B5
Fox Hollow Cl, SE18 ... **137** H5
Fox Hollow Dr, Bexh.
DA7 ... **158** D3
Foxholt Gdns, NW10 ... **88** C7
Foxhome Cl, Chis. BR7 ... **174** D6
Fox Ho Rd, Belv. DA17 ... **139** H4
Foxlands Cres, Dag.
RM10 ... **101** J5
Foxlands La, Dag. RM10 ... **101** J5
Foxlands Rd, Dag. RM10 ... **101** J5
Fox La, N13 ... **59** F3
W5 ... **105** H4
Keston BR2 ... **205** H5
Foxlees, Wem. HA0 ... **86** D4
Foxley Cl, E8
off Ferncliff Rd ... **94** D5
Loughton IG10 ... **49** E2
Foxley Ct, Sutt. SM2 ... **199** F7
Foxley Rd, SW9 ... **35** F7
Thornton Heath CR7 ... **187** H4
Foxleys, Wat. WD19 ... **51** E3
Foxley Sq, SW9
off Cancell Rd ... **131** H7
Foxmead Cl, Enf. EN2 ... **43** F3
Foxmore St, SW11 ... **149** J1
Fox Rd, E16 ... **115** F5
Fox's Path, Mitch. CR4 ... **185** H2
Foxton Gro, Mitch. CR4 ... **185** G2
Foxwell Ms, SE4
off Foxwell St ... **153** H3
Foxwell St, SE4 ... **153** H3
Foxwood Cl, NW7 ... **54** E4
Feltham TW13 ... **160** B3
Foxwood Grn Cl, Enf. EN1 ... **44** B6
Foxwood Rd, SE3 ... **155** F4
Foyle Rd, N17 ... **76** D1
SE3 ... **135** F6
Framfield Cl, N12 ... **56** D3
Framfield Ct, Enf. EN1 ... **44** B6
Framfield Rd, N5 ... **93** H5
W7 ... **104** B6
Mitcham CR4 ... **168** A7
Framlingham Cl, E5
off Detmold Rd ... **95** F2
Framlingham Cres, SE9 ... **174** B4
Frampton Cl, Sutt. SM2 ... **198** D7
Frampton Pk Rd, E9 ... **95** F6
Frampton Rd, Houns.
TW4 ... **142** E5
Frampton St, NW8 ... **7** E6
Francemary Rd, SE4 ... **154** A5
Frances Rd, E4 ... **62** A6
Frances St, SE18 ... **136** C4
Franche Ct Rd, SW17 ... **167** F3
Francis Av, Bexh. DA7 ... **159** G2
Feltham TW13 ... **160** A3
Ilford IG1 ... **99** G2
Francis Barber Cl, SW16
off Well Cl ... **169** F4
Franciscan Rd, SW17 ... **167** J5
Francis Chichester Way,
SW11 ... **150** A1
Francis Cl, E14 *off
Saunders Ness Rd* ... **134** D4
Epsom KT19 ... **196** D4
Francis Gro, SW19 ... **166** C6
Francis Rd, E10 ... **96** C1
N2 *off Lynmouth Rd* ... **73** J4
Croydon CR0 ... **187** H7
Greenford UB6 ... **105** F1
Harrow HA1 ... **68** D5
Hounslow TW4 ... **142** D2
Ilford IG1 ... **99** G2
Pinner HA5 ... **66** C5
Wallington SM6 ... **200** C6
Francis St, E15 ... **96** E5
SW1 ... **33** F1
Ilford IG1 ... **99** G2
Francis Ter, N19
off Junction Rd ... **92** C3
Francis Wk, N1
off Bingfield St ... **111** F1
Francklyn Gdns, Edg.
HA8 ... **54** A3
Franconia Rd, SW4 ... **150** C5
Frank Bailey Wk, E12
off Gainsborough Av ... **98** D5
Frank Burton Cl, SE7
off Victoria Way ... **135** H5
Frank Dixon Cl, SE21 ... **170** B1
Frank Dixon Way, SE21 ... **170** B1
Frankfurt Rd, SE24 ... **151** J5
Frankham St, SE8 ... **134** A7
Frankland Cl, SE16 ... **133** E3
Woodford Green IG8 ... **63** J5
Frankland Rd, E4 ... **62** A5
SW7 ... **23** E6
Franklin Cl, N20 ... **41** F7
SE13 ... **154** B1
SE27 ... **169** H3
Kingston upon Thames
KT1 ... **182** A3
Franklin Cres, Mitch.
CR4 ... **186** C4
Franklin Ho, NW9 ... **71** F7
Franklin Pas, SE9 ... **156** B3
Franklin Pl, SE13 ... **154** B1
Franklin Rd, SE20 ... **171** F7
Bexleyheath DA7 ... **159** E1
Franklins Ms, Har. HA2 ... **85** J2
Franklin Sq, W14
off Marchbank Rd ... **128** C5
Franklin's Row, SW3 ... **32** A3
Franklin St, E3
off St. Leonards St ... **114** B3
N15 ... **76** B6
Franklin Way, Croy. CR0 ... **187** E7
Franklyn Gdns, Ilf. IG6 ... **65** G6
Franklyn Rd, NW10 ... **89** F7
Walton-on-Thames
KT12 ... **178** A6
Franks Av, N.Mal. KT3 ... **182** C4
Frank St, E13 ... **115** G4
Frankswood Av, Orp.
BR5 ... **193** E5
Frank Towell Ct, Felt. TW14
off Glebelands Rd ... **160** A1
Franlaw Cres, N13 ... **59** J4
Fransfield Gro, SE26 ... **171** E3
Frant Cl, SE20 ... **171** F7
Franthorne Way, SE6 ... **172** B2
Frant Rd, Th.Hth. CR7 ... **187** H5
Fraser Cl, E6
off Linton Gdns ... **116** B6
Bexley DA5
off Dartford Rd ... **177** J1
Fraser Ho, Brent. TW8
off Green Dragon La ... **125** J5
Fraser Rd, E17 ... **78** B5
N9 ... **60** E3
Erith DA8 ... **139** J5
Greenford UB6 ... **105** E1
Fraser St, W4 ... **126** E5
Frating Cres, Wdf.Grn.
IG8 ... **63** G6
Frays Av, West Dr. UB7 ... **120** A2
Frays Cl, West Dr. UB7 ... **120** A3
Frazer Av, Ruis. HA4 ... **84** C5
Frazier St, SE1 ... **26** E4
Frean St, SE16 ... **29** H5
Freda Corbett Cl, SE15 ... **37** H7
Frederica Rd, E4 ... **46** D7
Frederica St, N7
off Caledonian Rd ... **93** F7
Frederick Cl, W2 ... **15** J5
Sutton SM1 ... **198** C4
Frederick Ct, NW2
off Douglas Ms ... **90** B3
Frederick Cres, SW9 ... **131** H7
Enfield EN3 ... **45** F2
Frederick Gdns, Croy.
CR0 ... **187** H6
Sutton SM1 ... **198** C5
Frederick Pl, SE18 ... **137** E5
Frederick Rd, SE17 ... **35** H5
Sutton SM1 ... **198** C5
Frederick's Pl, EC2 ... **20** B4
Fredericks Pl, N12 ... **57** F4
Frederick Sq, SE16
off Rotherhithe St ... **113** H7
Frederick's Row, EC1 ... **11** G3
Frederick St, WC1 ... **10** C4
Frederick Ter, E8
off Haggerston Rd ... **112** C1
Frederick Vil, W7
off Lower Boston Rd ... **124** B1
Frederic Ms, SW1 ... **24** A4
Frederic St, E17 ... **77** H5
Fred White Wk, N7
off Market Rd ... **92/93** E6
Fred Wigg Twr, E11 ... **97** F2
Freedom Cl, E17 ... **77** H4
Freedom Rd, N17 ... **76** A2
Freedom St, SW11 ... **149** J2
Freegrove Rd, N7 ... **93** E5
Freeland Pk, NW4 ... **72** B2
Freeland Rd, W5 ... **105** J7
Freelands Gro, Brom.
BR1 ... **191** H1
Freelands Rd, Brom. BR1 ... **191** H1
Freeling St, N1
off Caledonian Rd ... **93** F7
Freeman Cl, Nthlt. UB5 ... **85** E7
Freeman Ct, N7
off Tollington Way ... **92/93** E3
Freeman Dr, W.Mol. KT8 ... **179** F3
Freeman Rd, Mord. SM4 ... **185** G5
Freemantle Av, Enf. EN3 ... **45** G5
Freemantle St, SE17 ... **36** D3
★**Freemason's Hall (United
Grand Lo of England)**,
WC2 ... **18** B3
Freemasons Rd, E16 ... **115** H5
Croydon CR0 ... **202** B1
Freesia Cl, Orp. BR6
off Briarswood Way ... **207** J5
Freethorpe Cl, SE19 ... **188** A1
Free Trade Wf, E1
off The Highway ... **113** G7
★**Freightliners City Fm**,
N7 ... **93** F6
Freke Rd, SW11 ... **150** A3
Fremantle Rd, Belv.
DA17 ... **139** G4
Ilford IG6 ... **81** F2
Fremont St, E9 ... **113** F1
French Ordinary Ct, EC3 ... **21** E5
French Pl, E1 ... **13** E5
French St, Sun. TW16 ... **178** C2
Frendsbury Rd, SE4 ... **153** H4
Frensham Cl, Sthl. UB1 ... **103** F4

Frensham Ct, Mitch. CR4
off Phipps Br Rd 185 G3
Frensham Dr, SW15. . . . . 165 G2
Croydon (New Adgtn)
CR0 . . . . 204 C7
Frensham Rd, SE9 . . . . . . 175 G2
Frensham St, SE15 . . . . . . 37 J6
Frere St, SW11 . . . . 149 H2
Freshfield Av, E8 . . . . 94 C7
Freshfield Cl, SE13
off Marischal Rd 154 D4
Freshfield Dr, N14 . . . . 42 B7
Freshfields, Croy. CR0 . . . 189 J7
Freshford St, SW18 . . . . . 167 F3
Freshwater Cl, SW17 . . . . 168 A6
Freshwater Rd, SW17 . . . 168 A6
Dagenham RM8 . . . . . . 100 D1
Freshwell Av, Rom. RM6 . . 82 C4
Fresh Wf Rd, Bark. IG11 . . 117 E1
Freshwood Cl, Beck. BR3 . 190 B1
Freston Gdns, Barn. EN4 . . 42 A5
Freston Pk, N3 . . . . 72 C2
Freston Rd, W10 . . . . 108 A7
W11 . . . . 108 A7
Freta Rd, Bexh. DA6. . . . . 159 F5
★**Freud Mus**, NW3. . . . . . . 91 F6
Frewin Rd, SW18 . . . . 167 G1
Friar Ms, SE27
off Prioress Rd 169 H3
Friar Rd, Hayes UB4. . . . . 102 D4
Friars, The, Chig. IG7 . . . . . 65 H4
Friars Av, N20. . . . . 57 H3
SW15. . . . . 165 F3
Friars Cl, E4 . . . . 62 C3
N2 . . . . 73 G4
SE1 . . . . 27 H2
Ilford IG1. . . . . 99 G1
Northolt UB5
off Broomcroft Av 102 D3
Friars Gdns, W3
off St. Dunstans Av . . . 106 D6
Friars Gate Cl, Wdf.Grn.
IG8. . . . . 63 G4
Friars La, Rich. TW9 . . . . . 145 G5
Friars Mead, E14 . . . . 134 C3
Friars Ms, SE9 . . . . 156 D5
Friars Pl La, W3. . . . . 106 D7
Friars Rd, E6. . . . . 116 A1
Friars Stile Pl, Rich. TW10
off Friars Stile Rd 145 H6
Friars Stile Rd, Rich.
TW10. . . . . 145 H6
Friar St, EC4. . . . . 19 H4
Friars Wk, N14 . . . . 58 B1
SE2 . . . . 138 D5
Friars Way, W3 . . . . 106 D6
Friary Cl, N12 . . . . 57 H5
Friary Ct, SW1 . . . . 25 C2
Friary Est, SE15 . . . . 37 J6
Friary La, Wdf.Grn. IG8 . . . 63 G4
Friary Rd, N12 . . . . 57 G4
SE15 . . . . 37 J6
W3 . . . . 106 D6
Friary Way, N12 . . . . 57 H4
FRIDAY HILL, E4 . . . . 62 D2
Friday Hill, E4. . . . . 62 E2
Friday Hill E, E4 . . . . 62 E3
Friday Hill W, E4. . . . . 62 E2
Friday Rd, Mitch. CR4. . . . 167 J7
Friday St, EC4. . . . . 19 J4
Frideswide Pl, NW5
off Islip St 92 C5
Friendly Pl, SE13
off Lewisham Rd. 154 B1
Friendly St, SE8 . . . . 154 A1
Friendly St Ms, SE8
off Friendly St 154 A2
Friendship Wk, Nthlt. UB5
off Wayfarer Rd 102 D3
Friendship Way, E15
off Carpenters Rd 114 C1
Friends Rd, Croy. CR0 . . . 202 A3
Friend St, EC1. . . . . 11 G3
FRIERN BARNET, N11 . . . . . 57 H4
Friern Barnet La, N11 . . . . . 57 H4
N20 . . . . 57 H4
Friern Barnet Rd, N11. . . . . 57 J5
Friern Br Retail Pk, N11 . . . 58 B6
Friern Ct, N20. . . . . 57 G3
Friern Mt Dr, N20. . . . . 41 F7
Friern Pk, N12. . . . . 57 F5
Friern Rd, SE22. . . . . 152 D6
Friern Watch Av, N12 . . . . . 57 F4
Frigate Ms, SE8
off Watergate St 134 A6
Frimley Av, Wall. SM6. . . . 201 E5
Frimley Cl, SW19 . . . . 166 B2
Croydon (New Adgtn)
CR0 . . . . 204 C7
Frimley Ct, Sid. DA14. . . . 176 B5
Frimley Cres, Croy.
(New Adgtn) CR0 . . . . 204 C7
Frimley Gdns, Mitch. CR4 . 185 H3
Frimley Rd, Chess. KT9 . . 195 H5
Ilford IG3. . . . . 99 H3
Frimley Way, E1 . . . . 113 G4
Frinstead Ho, W10 . . . . . . 108 A7
Frinton Cl, Wat. WD19 . . . . 50 B2
Frinton Dr, Wdf.Grn. IG8 . . 62 D7
Frinton Ms, Ilf. IG2
off Bramley Cres. 80 D6
Frinton Rd, E6. . . . . 116 A3
N15 . . . . 76 B6
SW17. . . . . 168 A6
Sidcup DA14 . . . . 176 E2
Friston Path, Chig. IG7. . . . 65 H5
Friston St, SW6 . . . . 148 E2
Friswell Pl, Bexh. DA6 . . . 159 G4
Fritham Cl, N.Mal. KT3. . . 182 E6
Frith Ct, NW7 . . . . 56 B7
Frith La, NW7. . . . . 56 B7
Frith Rd, E11. . . . . 96 C4
Croydon CR0. . . . . 201 J2
Frith St, W1 . . . . 17 H4
Frithville Gdns, W12. . . . . 127 J1
Frizlands La, Dag. RM10. . 101 H4
Frobisher Cl, Pnr. HA5 . . . . 66 D7
Frobisher Cres, EC2
off Beech St 111 J5
Staines TW19. . . . . 140 B7
Frobisher Gdns, Stai.
TW19. . . . . 140 B7
Frobisher Pas, E14
off North Colonnade . . 134 A1
Frobisher Rd, E6. . . . . 116 C6
N8 . . . . 75 G4
Frobisher St, SE10 . . . . . . 135 E6
Froghall La, Chig. IG7 . . . . 65 G4
Frogley Rd, SE22 . . . . 152 C4
Frogmore, SW18 . . . . 148 D5
Frogmore Cl, Sutt. SM3 . . 198 A3
Frogmore Est, Ruis. HA4 . . 84 D5
Frogmore Gdns, Sutt.
SM3. . . . . 198 B4
Frogmore Ind Est, NW10 . 106 C3
Frognal, NW3. . . . . 91 F5
Frognal Av, Har. HA1 . . . . . 68 C4
Sidcup DA14 . . . . 176 A5
Frognal Cl, NW3. . . . . 91 F5
Frognal Ct, NW3 . . . . 91 F6
Frognal Gdns, NW3 . . . . 91 F4
Frognal La, NW3 . . . . 90 E5
Frognal Par, NW3
off Frognal Ct 91 F6
Frognal Pl, Sid. DA14. . . . 176 A6
Frognal Ri, NW3. . . . . 91 F4
Frognal Way, NW3 . . . . 91 F4
Froissart Rd, SE9 . . . . 156 A5
Frome Rd, N22
off Westbury Av. 75 H3
Frome St, N1 . . . . 11 J1
Fromondes Rd, Sutt.
SM3. . . . . 198 B5
Frostic Wk, E1 . . . . 21 G2
Froude St, SW8 . . . . 150 B2
Fruen Rd, Felt. TW14 . . . . 141 J7
Fruiterers Pas, EC4
off Southwark Br 111 J7
Fryatt Rd, N17 . . . . 60 A7
Fryday Gro Ms, SW12
off Weir Rd 150 C7
Fryent Cl, NW9. . . . . 70 A6
Fryent Cres, NW9. . . . . 70 E6
Fryent Flds, NW9 . . . . 71 E6
Fryent Gro, NW9 . . . . 70 E6
Fryent Way, NW9 . . . . 70 A5
Frying Pan All, E1. . . . . 21 F2
Fry Rd, E6. . . . . 98 A7
NW10. . . . . 107 F1
Fryston Av, Croy. CR0 . . . 202 D2
Fuchsia St, SE2 . . . . 138 B5
Fulbeck Dr, NW9 . . . . 70 E1
Fulbeck Wk, Edg. HA8
off Knightswood Cl. . . . 54 B2
Fulbeck Way, Har. HA2. . . . 67 J2
Fulbourne Rd, E17 . . . . 78 C1
Fulbourne St, E1
off Durward St . . . 112/113 E5
Fulbrook Rd, N19
off Junction Rd 92 C4
Fulford Gro, Wat. WD19 . . . 50 B2
Fulford Rd, Epsom KT19 . 196 D7
Fulford St, SE16. . . . . 133 E2
FULHAM, SW6. . . . . 148 B2
Fulham Bdy, SW6 . . . . 128 D7
Fulham Ct, SW6
off Shottendane Rd. . . 128 D7
★**Fulham FC**, SW6 . . . . . . 148 A1
Fulham High St, SW6 . . . 148 B2
★**Fulham Palace Mus**,
SW6. . . . . 148 A2
Fulham Palace Rd, SW6. . 128 A7
W6. . . . . 127 J5
Fulham Pk Gdns, SW6. . . 148 C2
Fulham Pk Rd, SW6 . . . . . 148 C2
Fulham Rd, SW3 . . . . 30 E4
SW6. . . . . 30 B7
SW10. . . . . 30 E4
Fullbrooks Av, Wor.Pk.
KT4 . . . . 197 F1
Fuller Cl, E2 . . . . 13 H5
Orpington BR6 . . . . 207 J5
Fuller Rd, Dag. RM8 . . . . . 100 B3
Fullers Av, Surb. KT6 . . . . 195 J2
Woodford Green IG8 . . . 63 F7
★**Fuller's Griffin Brewery**,
W4. . . . . 127 F6
Fullers Rd, E18 . . . . 79 F1
Fuller St, NW4 . . . . 71 J4
Fullers Way N, Surb.
KT6 . . . . 195 J3
Fullers Way S, Chess.
KT9 . . . . 195 H4
Fullers Wd, Croy. CR0. . . . 204 A5
Fuller Ter, Ilf. IG1
off Oaktree Gro. 99 F5
Fullerton Rd, SW18 . . . . . 149 F5
Croydon CR0. . . . . 188 C7
Fuller Way, Hayes UB3. . . 121 J5
Fullwell Av, Ilf. IG5, IG6 . . . 80 C1
FULLWELL CROSS, Ilf.
IG6. . . . . 81 G1
Fullwell Cross Roundabout, Ilf.
IG6 *off High St* 81 G2
Fullwoods Ms, N1 . . . . 12 C3
Fulmar Cl, Surb. KT5 . . . . 181 J6
Fulmead St, SW6. . . . . . . 149 E1
Fulmer Cl, Hmptn. TW12 . 161 E5
Fulmer Rd, E16. . . . . 116 A5
Fulmer Way, W13 . . . . 124 E3
Fulready Rd, E10 . . . . 78 D5
Fulstone Cl, Houns. TW4 . 143 F4
Fulthorp Rd, SE3 . . . . 155 F2
Fulton Ms, W2 . . . . 14 C5
Fulton Rd, Wem. HA9. . . . . 88 A3
Fulwell Pk Av, Twick.
TW2. . . . . 161 H2
Fulwell Rd, Tedd. TW11. . . 162 A4
Fulwood Av, Wem. HA0 . . 105 J1
Fulwood Gdns, Twick.
TW1. . . . . 144 C6
Fulwood Pl, WC1 . . . . 18 D2
Fulwood Wk, SW19 . . . . . 166 B1
Furber St, W6. . . . . 127 H3
Furham Feild, Pnr. HA5 . . . 51 G7
Furley Rd, SE15 . . . . 132 D7
Furlong Cl, Wall. SM6. . . . 200 A1
Furlong Rd, N7. . . . . 93 G6
Furmage St, SW18. . . . . . 149 E7
Furneaux Av, SE27 . . . . . . 169 H5
Furness Rd, NW10 . . . . . . 107 G2
SW6. . . . . 149 E2
Harrow HA2 . . . . 67 H7
Morden SM4 . . . . 185 E7
Furnival St, EC4 . . . . 19 E3
Furrow La, E9. . . . . 95 F5
Fursby Av, N3. . . . . 56 D6
Further Acre, NW9 . . . . 71 F2
Furtherfield Cl, Croy.
CR0 . . . . 187 G6
Further Grn Rd, SE6. . . . . 155 E7
Furze Cl, Wat. WD19. . . . . . 50 C5
FURZEDOWN, SW17 . . . . 168 A5
Furzedown Dr, SW17. . . . 168 B5
Furzedown Hall, SW17
off Spalding Rd. 168 B5
Furzedown Rd, SW17 . . . 168 B5
Furze Fm Cl, Rom. RM6 . . . 83 E2
Furzefield Cl, Chis. BR7 . . 174 E6
Furzefield Rd, SE3 . . . . . . 135 H6
Furzeground Way, Uxb.
UB11 . . . . 121 F1
Furzeham Rd, West Dr.
UB7 . . . . 120 B2
Furzehill Rd, Borwd. WD6 . 38 A4
Furze Rd, Th.Hth. CR7 . . . 187 J3
Furze St, E3 . . . . 114 A5
Furzewood, Sun. TW16 . . 178 A1
Fuschia Ct, Wdf.Grn. IG8
off The Bridle Path . . 62/63 E7
Fyfe Way, Brom. BR1
off Widmore Rd. 191 G2
Fyfield Cl, Brom. BR2. . . . 190 D4
Fyfield Ct, E7 . . . . 97 G6
Fyfield Rd, E17. . . . . 78 D3
SW9. . . . . 151 G3
Enfield EN1 . . . . 44 B3
Fyfield Rd, Wdf. Grn IG8 . . 63 J7
Fynes St, SW1 . . . . 33 H1

G

Gable Cl, Pnr. HA5 . . . . 51 G7
Gable Ct, SE26
off Lawrie Pk Av. . 170/171 E5
Gables, The, Wem. HA9 . . . 87 J3
Gables Cl, SE5 . . . . 152 B1
SE12 . . . . 173 G1
Gabriel Cl, Felt. TW13. . . . 160 D4
Gabrielle Cl, Wem. HA9 . . . 87 J3
Gabrielle Ct, NW3 . . . . 91 G6
Gabriel St, SE23. . . . . 153 G7
Gabriel's Wf, SE1 . . . . 27 E1
Gad Cl, E13. . . . . 115 H3
Gaddesden Av, Wem.
HA9. . . . . 87 J6
Gade Cl, Hayes UB3. . . . . 122 B1
Gadesden Rd, Epsom
KT19 . . . . 196 C6
Gadsbury Cl, NW9. . . . . 71 F6
Gadwall Cl, E16
off Freemasons Rd . . . 115 H6
Gadwall Way, SE28 . . . . . 137 G2
Gage Rd, E16 *off*
Malmesbury Rd . . 114/115 E5
Gage St, WC1. . . . . 18 B1
Gainford St, N1
off Richmond Av 111 G1
Gainsboro Gdns, Grnf.
UB6. . . . . 86 B5
Gainsborough Av, E12 . . . . 98 D5
Gainsborough Cl, Beck.
BR3 . . . . 172 A7
Esher KT10
off Lime Tree Av 194 B1
Gainsborough Ct, N12. . . . 57 E5
W12 *off Lime Gro* 127 J2
Bromley BR2. . . . . 191 J4
Gainsborough Gdns, NW3. 91 G3
NW11. . . . . 72 C7
Edgware HA8 . . . . 69 J2
Isleworth TW7 . . . . 144 A6
Gainsborough Ho, Enf. EN1
off Ayley Cft 44 D5
Gainsborough Ms, SE26
off Panmure Rd . . 170/171 E3
Gainsborough Pl, Chig. IG7. 65 J3
Gainsborough Rd, E11 . . . . 79 E7
E15. . . . . 114 E3
N12 . . . . 57 E5
W4. . . . . 127 F4
Dagenham RM8 . . . . . . 100 B4
New Malden KT3 . . . . . 182 D7
Richmond TW9 . . . . 145 J3
Woodford Green IG8 . . . 64 B6
Gainsborough Sq, Bexh. DA6
off Regency Way 158 D3
Gainsborough St, E9
off Trowbridge Rd 95 J6
Gainsborough Studios, N1
off Poole St 112 A1
Gainsford Rd, E17 . . . . 77 J4
Gainsford St, SE1 . . . . 29 F3
Gairloch Rd, SE5 . . . . 152 B2
Gaisford St, NW5. . . . . 92 C6
Gaitskell Ct, SW11 . . . . . . 149 H2
Gaitskell Rd, SE9 . . . . 175 F1
Galahad Rd, N9
off Salisbury Rd 60 D3
Bromley BR1. . . . . 173 G3
Galata Rd, SW13 . . . . 127 G7
Galatea Sq, SE15
off Scylla Rd. 152/153 E3
Galaxy, E14 *off Crews St* . 134 A4
Galba Ct, Brent. TW8
off Augustus Cl 125 G7
Galbraith St, E14 . . . . 134 C3
Galdana Av, Barn. EN5 . . . 41 F3
Galeborough Av, Wdf.Grn.
IG8. . . . . 62 D7
Gale Cl, Hmptn. TW12
off Stewart Cl. . . . 160/161 E6
Mitcham CR4. . . . . 185 G3
Galena Ho, SE18
off Grosmont Rd. 137 J5
Galena Rd, W6 . . . . 127 H4
Galen Pl, WC1 . . . . 18 B2
Galesbury Rd, SW18 . . . . 149 F6
Gales Gdns, E2. . . . . 113 E3
Gale St, E3 . . . . 114 A5
Dagenham RM9 . . . . . . 118 D1
Gales Way, Wdf.Grn. IG8 . . 64 B7
Galgate Cl, SW19. . . . . . . 166 B1
Gallants Fm Rd, Barn.
EN4. . . . . 41 H7

Galleon Cl, SE16
off Kinburn St 133 G2
Galleons Dr, Bark. IG11 118 A3
Gallery Gdns, Nthlt. UB5 102 D2
Gallery Rd, SE21 170 A1
Galley La, Barn. EN5 39 H3
Galleywall Rd, SE16 132 E4
Galliard Cl, N9 45 F6
Galliard Rd, N9 60 D1
Gallia Rd, N5 93 H5
Gallions Cl, Bark. IG11 118 A3
Gallions Reach Shop Pk, E6 117 F5
Gallions Rd, SE7 135 H4
Gallions Roundabout, E16 116 E7
Gallions Vw Rd, SE28
off Goldfinch Rd 137 H2
Gallon Cl, SE7 135 J4
Gallop, The, S.Croy. CR2 203 E7
Sutton SM2 199 F7
Gallosson Rd, SE18 137 H4
Galloway Path, Croy. CR0 202 A4
Galloway Rd, W12 127 G1
Gallus Cl, N21 43 F6
Gallus Sq, SE3 155 H3
Galpins Rd, Th.Hth. CR7 187 F4
Galsworthy Av, E14 113 H5
Romford RM6 82 B7
Galsworthy Cl, SE28 138 B1
Galsworthy Cres, SE3
off Merriman Rd 155 J1
Galsworthy Rd, NW2 90 B4
Kingston upon Thames KT2 164 B7
Galsworthy Ter, N16
off Hawksley Rd 94 B3
Galton St, W10 108 B4
Galva Cl, Barn. EN4 42 A4
Galvani Way, Croy. CR0
off Ampere Way 201 F1
Galveston Rd, SW15 148 C5
Galway Cl, SE16
off Masters Dr 132/133 E5
Galway St, EC1 12 A4
Gambetta St, SW8 150 B2
Gambia St, SE1 27 H2
Gambier Ho, EC1
off Mora St 111 J3
Gambole Rd, SW17 167 H4
Games Rd, Barn. EN4 41 J3
Gamlen Rd, SW15 148 A4
Gamuel Cl, E17 78 A6
Gander Grn Cres, Hmptn. TW12 179 G1
Gander Grn La, Sutt. SM1, SM3 198 B2
Gandhi Cl, E17 78 A6
Gandolfi St, SE15 36 D6
Ganton St, W1 17 F5
Ganton Wk, Wat. WD19
off Woodhall La 50/51 E4
GANTS HILL, Ilf. IG2 80 D5
Gants Hill, Ilf. IG2
off Eastern Av 80 D6
Gantshill Cres, Ilf. IG2 80 D5
Gap Rd, SW19 166 D5
Garage Rd, W3 106 A6
Garbutt Pl, W1 16 C1
Garden Av, Bexh. DA7 159 G3
Mitcham CR4 168 B7
Garden City, Edg. HA8 54 A6
Garden Cl, E4 62 A5
SE12 173 H3
SW15 147 H7
Barnet EN5 39 J4
Hampton TW12 161 F5
Northolt UB5 103 E1
Wallington SM6 200 E5
Garden Ct, EC4 18 E5
N12 *off Holden Rd* 56/57 E5
Richmond TW9
off Lichfield Rd 145 J1
Stanmore HA7
off Marsh La 53 F5
West Molesey KT8
off Avern Rd 179 H4
Gardeners Cl, N11 58 A2
SE9 174 B3
Gardeners Rd, Croy. CR0 201 H1
Gardenia Rd, Enf. EN1 44 B6
Gardenia Way, Wdf.Grn. IG8 63 G5
Garden La, SW2
off Christchurch Rd 169 F1
Bromley BR1 173 H6
Garden Ms, W2
off Linden Gdns 108 D7
Garden Pl, E8
off Haggerston Rd 112 C1
Garden Rd, NW8 6 D3
SE20 189 F1
Bromley BR1 173 H7
Richmond TW9 146 A3
Walton-on-Thames KT12 178 B6
Garden Row, SE1 27 G6
Gardens, The, SE22 152 D4
Beckenham BR3 190 C2
Feltham TW14 141 G5
Harrow HA1 67 J6
Pinner HA5 67 F6
Garden St, E1 113 G5
Garden Ter, SW1 33 H3
Garden Wk, EC2 12 D4
Beckenham BR3
off Hayne Rd 189 J1
Garden Way, NW10 88 C6
Gardiner Av, NW2 89 J5
Gardiner Cl, Dag. RM8 100 D4
Enfield EN3 45 G6
Gardner Cl, E11 79 H6
Gardner Ct, EC1
off St. John St 111 H4
Gardner Gro, Felt. TW13 161 F2
Gardner Pl, Felt. TW14 142 B6
Gardner Rd, E13 115 H4
Gardners La, EC4 19 J5
Gardnor Rd, NW3
off Flask Wk 91 G4
Gard St, EC1 11 H3
Garendon Gdns, Mord. SM4 184 E7
Garendon Rd, Mord. SM4 184 E7
Gareth Cl, Wor.Pk. KT4
off Burnham Dr 198 A2
Gareth Gro, Brom. BR1 173 G4
Garfield Ms, SW11
off Garfield Rd 150 A3
Garfield Rd, E4 62 D1
E13 115 F4
SW11 150 A3
SW19 167 F5
Enfield EN3 45 F4
Twickenham TW1 162 D1
Garford St, E14 114 A7
Garganey Wk, SE28 118 D7
Garibaldi St, SE18 137 H4
Garland Dr, Houns. TW3 143 J2
Garland Ho, Kings.T. KT2
off Kingsgate Rd 181 H1
Garland Rd, SE18 137 G7
Stanmore HA7 69 H1
Garlands Ct, Croy. CR0
off Chatsworth Rd 202 A4
Garlick Hill, EC4 20 A5
Garlies Rd, SE23 171 H3
Garlinge Rd, NW2 90 C6
Garman Cl, N18 60 A5
Garman Rd, N17 61 F7
Garnault Ms, EC1 11 F4
Garnault Pl, EC1 11 F4
Garner Cl, Dag. RM8 100 D1
Garner Rd, E17 78 C1
Garner St, E2 13 J2
Garnet Rd, NW10 89 E6
Thornton Heath CR7 188 A4
Garnet St, E1 113 F7
Garnett Cl, SE9 156 C3
Garnett Rd, NW3 91 J5
Garnett Way, E17
off McEntee Av 77 H1
Garnet Wk, E6
off Kingfisher St 116 B5
Garnham Cl, N16
off Garnham St 94 C2
Garnham St, N16 94 C2
Garnies Cl, SE15 37 F7
Garrad's Rd, SW16 168 D3
Garrard Cl, Bexh. DA7 159 G3
Chislehurst BR7 175 E5
Garrard Wk, NW10
off Garnet Rd 88/89 E6
Garratt Cl, Croy. CR0 200 E4
Garratt La, SW17 167 G4
SW18 148 E5
Garratt Rd, Edg. HA8 54 A7
Garratt Ter, SW17 167 H4
Garrett Cl, W3
off Jenner Av 106 D5
Garrett St, EC1 12 A5
Garrick Av, NW11 72 B6
Garrick Cl, SW18 149 F4
W5 105 H4
Richmond TW9
off The Green 145 G5
Garrick Cres, Croy. CR0 202 B2
Garrick Dr, NW4 71 J2
SE28
off Broadwater Rd 137 G3
Garrick Gdns, W.Mol. KT8 179 G3
Garrick Pk, NW4 72 A2
Garrick Rd, NW9 71 F6
Greenford UB6 103 H4
Richmond TW9 146 A2
Garricks Ho, Kings.T. KT1
off Wadbrook St 181 G2
Garrick St, WC2 18 A5
Garrick Way, NW4 72 A4
Garrison Cl, SE18
off Red Lion La 136 D7
Hounslow TW4 143 F5
Garrison La, Chess. KT9 195 G7
Garsdale Cl, N11 58 A6
Garside Cl, SE28
off Goosander Way 137 G3
Hampton TW12 161 H6
Garsington Ms, SE4 153 J3
Garter Way, SE16
off Poolmans St 133 G2
Garth, The, N12
off Holden Rd 56/57 E5
Hampton (Hmptn H.) TW12
off Uxbridge Rd 161 H6
Harrow HA3 69 J6
Garth Cl, W4 126 D5
Kingston upon Thames KT2 163 J5
Morden SM4 184 A7
Ruislip HA4 84 D1
Garth Ct, W4 *off Garth Rd* 126 D5
Garthland Dr, Barn. EN5 39 H5
Garth Ms, W5
off Greystoke Gdns 105 H4
Garthorne Rd, SE23 153 G7
Garth Rd, NW2 90 C2
W4 126 D6
Kingston upon Thames KT2 163 J5
Morden SM4 183 J6
Garth Rd Ind Cen, Mord. SM4 184 A7
Garthside, Rich. TW10 163 H5
Garthway, N12 57 H6
Gartmoor Gdns, SW19 166 C1
Gartmore Rd, Ilf. IG3 99 J1
Garton Pl, SW18 149 F6
Gartons Cl, Enf. EN3 45 F5
Gartons Way, SW11 149 F3
Garvary Rd, E16 115 H6
Garway Rd, W2 14 A4
Garwood Cl, N17 76 E1
Gascoigne Gdns, Wdf.Grn. IG8 63 E7
Gascoigne Pl, E2 13 F4
Gascoigne Rd, Bark. IG11 117 F1
Gascony Av, NW6 90 D7
Gascoyne Rd, E9 95 G7
Gaselee St, E14 114 C7
Gasholder Pl, SE11 34 D4
Gaskarth Rd, SW12 150 B6
Edgware HA8 70 C1
Gaskell Rd, N6 73 J6
Gaskell St, SW4 150 E2
Gaskin St, N1 111 H1
Gaspar Cl, SW5 30 B1
Gaspar Ms, SW5 30 B1
Gassiot Rd, SW17 167 J4
Gassiot Way, Sutt. SM1 199 G3
Gastein Rd, W6 128 A6
Gaston Bell Cl, Rich. TW9 145 J3
Gaston Rd, Mitch. CR4 186 A3
Gataker St, SE16 133 E3
Gatcombe Ms, W5 105 J7
Gatcombe Rd, E16 135 G1
N19 92 D3
Gatcombe Way, Barn. EN4 41 J3
Gate Cl, Borwd. WD6 38 C1
Gate End, Nthwd. HA6 50 A7
Gateforth St, NW8 7 G6
Gatehouse Cl, Kings.T. KT2 164 C7
Gatehouse Sq, SE1
off Southwark Br Rd 131 J1
Gateley Rd, SW9 151 F3
Gate Ms, SW7 23 H4
Gater Dr, Enf. EN2 44 A1
Gatesborough St, EC2 12 D5
Gates Grn Rd, Kes. BR2 205 G4
West Wickham BR4 205 F3
Gateside Rd, SW17 167 J3
Gatestone Rd, SE19 170 B6
Gate St, WC2 18 C3
Gateway, SE17 36 A5
Gateway Arc, N1
off Islington High St 111 H2
Gateway Ho, Bark. IG11
off St. Ann's 117 F1
Gateway Ind Est, NW10 107 F3
Gateway Ms, E8
off Shacklewell La 94 C5
Gateway Retail Pk, E6 117 E4
Gateway Rd, E10 96 B3
Gateways, The, SW3 31 H2
Gatfield Gro, Felt. TW13 161 G2
Gathorne Rd, N22 75 G2
Gathorne St, E2
off Mace St 113 G2
Gatley Av, Epsom KT19 196 B5
Gatliff Rd, SW1 32 C4
Gatling Rd, SE2 138 A5
Gatonby St, SE15 152 C1
Gatting Cl, Edg. HA8
off Pavilion Way 54 C7
Gatton Rd, SW17 167 H4
Gattons Way, Sid. DA14 177 F4
Gatward Cl, N21 43 H6
Gatward Grn, N9 60 B2
Gatwick Rd, SW18 148 C7
Gauden Cl, SW4 150 D3
Gauden Rd, SW4 150 D2
Gaumont Ter, W12
off Lime Gro 127 J2
Gauntlet Cl, Nthlt. UB5 84 E7
Gauntlett Ct, Wem. HA0 86 E5
Gauntlett Rd, Sutt. SM1 199 G5
Gaunt St, SE1 27 H5
Gautrey Rd, SE15 153 F2
Gautrey Sq, E6 116 C6
Gavel St, SE17 36 C1
Gaverick Ms, E14
off Westferry Rd 134 A4
Gavestone Cres, SE12 155 H7
Gavestone Rd, SE12 155 H7
Gaviller Pl, E5
off Clarence Rd 94/95 E4
Gavina Cl, Mord. SM4 185 H5
Gavin St, SE18 137 H4
Gawain Wk, N9
off Salisbury Rd 60 D3
Gawber St, E2 113 F3
Gawsworth Cl, E15
off Ash Rd 96/97 E5
Gawthorne Av, NW7
off Lane App 56 B5
Gawthorne Ct, E3
off Mostyn Gro 114 A2
Gay Cl, NW2 89 H5
Gaydon Ho, W2 14 B1
Gaydon La, NW9 70 E1
Gayfere Rd, Epsom KT17 197 G5
Ilford IG5 80 C3
Gayfere St, SW1 26 A6
Gayford Rd, W12 127 F2
Gay Gdns, Dag. RM10 101 J4
Gayhurst, SE17 36 C5
Gayhurst Rd, E8 94 D7
Gaylor Rd, Nthlt. UB5 85 F5
Gaynesford Rd, SE23 171 G2
Carshalton SM5 199 J7
Gaynes Hill Rd, Wdf.Grn. IG8 64 B6
Gay Rd, E15 114 D2
Gaysham Av, Ilf. IG2 80 D5
Gaysham Hall, Ilf. IG5 80 E3
Gay St, SW15 148 A3
Gayton Ct, Har. HA1 68 C6
Gayton Cres, NW3 91 G4
Gayton Ho, E3
off Blackthorn St 114 A4
Gayton Rd, NW3 91 G4
SE2 *off Florence Rd* 138 C3
Harrow HA1 68 C6
Gayville Rd, SW11 149 J6
Gaywood Cl, SW2 169 F1
Gaywood Est, SE1 27 H6
Gaywood Rd, E17 78 A3
Gaywood St, SE1 27 H6
Gaza St, SE17 35 G4
Geariesville Gdns, Ilf. IG6 81 E4
Geary Rd, NW10 89 G5
Geary St, N7 93 F5
G.E.C. Est, Wem. HA9 87 G3
Geddes Pl, Bexh. DA6
off Market Pl 159 G4
Gedeney Rd, N17 75 J1
Gedling Pl, SE1 29 G5
Geere Rd, E15 115 F1
Gees Ct, W1 16 C4
Gee St, EC1 11 J5
Geffrye Ct, N1 12 E2
Geffrye Est, N1
off Stanway St 112 B2

★**Geffrye Mus**, E2 . . . . 13 E2
Geffrye St, E2. . . . . 13 F1
Geldart Rd, SE15 . . . . 132 E7
Geldeston Rd, E5. . . . . 94 D2
Gellatly Rd, SE14. . . . . . . 153 F2
Gemini Gro, Nthlt. UB5
off Javelin Way. . . 102/103 E3
General Gordon Pl, SE18. 136 E4
General Wolfe Rd, SE10 . . 154 D1
Genesta Rd, SE18 . . . . . . 137 E6
Geneva Dr, SW9. . . . . 151 G4
Geneva Gdns, Rom. RM6 . 82 E5
Geneva Rd, Kings.T. KT1 . 181 H4
Thornton Heath CR7 . . . 187 J5
Genever Cl, E4. . . . . 62 A5
Genista Rd, N18. . . . . 61 E5
Genoa Av, SW15 . . . . 147 J5
Genoa Rd, SE20. . . . . 189 F1
Genotin Rd, Enf. EN1. . . . . 44 A3
Genotin Ter, Enf. EN1
off Genotin Rd 44 A3
Gentian Row, SE13
off Sparta St 154 C1
Gentlemans Row, Enf.
EN2 . . . . 43 J3
Gentry Gdns, E13
off Whitwell Rd 115 G4
Geoffrey Cl, SE5. . . . . 151 J2
Geoffrey Gdns, E6 . . . . . . 116 B2
Geoffrey Rd, SE4 . . . . 153 J3
George Beard Rd, SE8 . . . 133 J4
George Comberton Wk, E12
off Gainsborough Av . . 98 D5
George Ct, WC2 . . . . 18 B6
George Cres, N10. . . . . 58 A7
George Downing Est, N16
off Cazenove Rd 94 C2
George V Av, Pnr. HA5. . . . 67 G3
George V Cl, Pnr. HA5
off George V Av. 67 G3
George V Way, Grnf. UB6. 105 E1
George Gange Way, Har.
(Wldste) HA3. . . . . 68 B3
George Gro Rd, SE20. . . . 188 D1
★**George Inn**, SE1 . . . . 28 B2
George Inn Yd, SE1 . . . . . . 28 B2
George La, E18. . . . . 79 G2
SE13 . . . . 154 C6
Bromley BR2. . . . . 205 H1
George Lansbury Ho, N22
off Progress Way. 75 G1
George Loveless Ho, E2. . . 13 G3
George Lowe Ct, W2 . . . . . 14 A1
George Mathers Rd, SE11 . 35 G1
George Ms, NW1 . . . . 9 F4
Enfield EN2
off Sydney Rd. 44 A3
George Pl, N17
off Dongola Rd 76 B3
George Rd, E4 . . . . 62 A6
Kingston upon Thames
KT2 . . . . 164 B7
New Malden KT3 . . . . . 183 F4
George Row, SE16. . . . . 29 H4
George Sq, SW19
off Mostyn Rd. 184 C3
George's Rd, N7. . . . . 93 F5
Georges Sq, SW6
off North End Rd. 128 C6
George St, E16 . . . . 115 F6
W1. . . . . 16 A3
W7 *off The Broadway* . . 124 B1
Barking IG11 . . . . 99 F7
Croydon CR0. . . . . 202 A2
Hounslow TW3 . . . . 143 F2
Richmond TW9 . . . . 145 G5
Southall UB2. . . . . 122 E4
Georgetown Cl, SE19
off St. Kitts Ter. 170 A5
Georgette Pl, SE10
off King George St . . . 134 C7
Georgeville Gdns, Ilf. IG6. . 81 E4
George Wyver Cl, SW19
off Beaumont Rd. 148 B7
George Yd, EC3 . . . . 20 C4
W1. . . . . 16 C5
Georgiana St, NW1 . . . . . 110 C1
Georgian Cl, Brom. BR2. . 191 H7
Stanmore HA7 . . . . 52 D7
Georgian Ct, SW16
off Gleneldon Rd . 168/169 E4
Wembley HA9. . . . . 88 A6
Georgian Way, Har. HA1 . . 86 A2
Georgia Rd, N.Mal. KT3 . . 182 C4
Thornton Heath CR7 . . . 187 H1
Georgina Gdns, E2. . . . . . . 13 G3
Geraint Rd, Brom. BR1 . . 173 G4
Geraldine Rd, SW18. . . . . 149 F5
W4. . . . . 126 A6
Geraldine St, SE11 . . . . 27 G6
Gerald Ms, SW1. . . . . 32 C1
Gerald Rd, E16 . . . . 115 F4
SW1. . . . . 32 C1
Dagenham RM8 . . . . . . 101 F2
Gerard Av, Houns. TW4 . . 143 G7
Gerard Pl, E9
off Groombridge Rd . . . 95 G7
Gerard Rd, SW13 . . . . 147 F1
Harrow HA1 . . . . 68 D6
Gerards Cl, SE16 . . . . 133 F5
Gerda Rd, SE9 . . . . 175 F2
Germander Way, E15 . . . . 115 E3
Gernigan Ho, SW18
off Fitzhugh Gro 149 G6
Gernon Rd, E3 . . . . 113 H2
Geron Way, NW2 . . . . 89 H1
Gerrard Gdns, Pnr. HA5. . . 66 A5
Gerrard Pl, W1 . . . . 17 J5
Gerrard Rd, N1 . . . . 11 H1
Gerrards Cl, N14. . . . . 42 C5
Gerrard St, W1 . . . . 17 H5
Gerridge St, SE1 . . . . 27 F4
Gerry Raffles Sq, E15
off Great Eastern Rd . . . 96 D6
Gertrude Rd, Belv. DA17 . 139 G4
Gertrude St, SW10. . . . . . . 30 D6
Gervase Cl, Wem. HA9. . . . 88 C3
Gervase Rd, Edg. HA8 . . . . 70 C1
Gervase St, SE15 . . . . 133 E7
Ghent St, SE6 . . . . 172 A2
Ghent Way, E8
off Tyssen St 94 C6
Giant Arches Rd, SE24. . . 151 J7
Giant Tree Hill, Bushey
(Bushey Hth) WD23. . . . 52 A1
Gibbard Ms, SW19. . . . . . 166 A5
Gibbfield Cl, Rom. RM6. . . 82 E3
Gibbins Rd, E15 . . . . 96 C7
Gibbon Rd, SE15 . . . . 153 F2
W3. . . . . 106 E7
Kingston upon Thames
KT2 . . . . 181 H1
Gibbons Ms, NW11
off Hayes Cres. 72 C5
Gibbons Rents, SE1
off Magdalen St 132 B1
Gibbons Rd, NW10 . . . . . . 88 D6
Gibbon Wk, SW15
off Swinburne Rd 147 G4
Gibbs Av, SE19. . . . . 170 A5
Gibbs Cl, SE19 . . . . 170 A5
Gibbs Couch, Wat. WD19 . . 50 D3
Gibbs Grn, W14 . . . . 128 C5
Edgware HA8 . . . . 54 C5
Gibbs Rd, N18 . . . . 61 F4
Gibbs Sq, SE19. . . . . 170 A5
Gibraltar Wk, E2. . . . . 13 G4
Gibson Cl, E1
off Colebert Av 113 F4
N21 . . . . 43 G6
Chessington KT9. . . . . . 195 F6
Isleworth TW7 . . . . 144 A3
Gibson Gdns, N16
off Northwold Rd 94 C2
Gibson Ms, Twick. TW1
off Richmond Rd. 145 F7
Gibson Rd, SE11 . . . . 34 D2
Dagenham RM8 . . . . . . 100 C1
Sutton SM1. . . . . 198 E5
Gibson's Hill, SW16 . . . . . 169 G6
Gibson Sq, N1 . . . . 111 G1
Gibson St, SE10. . . . . 134 E5
Gideon Cl, Belv. DA17 . . . 139 H4
Gideon Ms, W5. . . . . 125 G2
Gideon Rd, SW11 . . . . 150 A3
Giesbach Rd, N19. . . . . 92 C2
Giffard Rd, N18 . . . . 60 B5
Giffin St, SE8 . . . . 134 A7
Gifford Gdns, W7 . . . . 104 A5
Gifford St, N1. . . . . 93 E7
Gift La, E15. . . . . 115 E1
Giggs Hill Gdns, T.Ditt.
KT7 . . . . 194 D1
Giggs Hill Rd, T.Ditt.
KT7 . . . . 180 D7
Gilbert Cl, SE18 . . . . 156 C1
Gilbert Gro, Edg. HA8 . . . . 70 D1
Gilbert Ho, EC2
off The Barbican. 111 J5
SE8 *off McMillan St* . . . 134 A6
Gilbert Pl, WC1. . . . . 18 A2
Gilbert Rd, SE11. . . . . 35 F2
SW19. . . . . 167 F7
Belvedere DA17 . . . . . . 139 G3
Bromley BR1 . . . . 173 G7
Pinner HA5 . . . . 66 D4
Gilbert St, E15 . . . . 96 E4
W1. . . . . 16 C4
Gilbert St, Houns. TW3
off High St. 143 J3
Gilbert Way, Croy. CR0
off Beddington
Fm Rd. 200/201 E1
Gilbey Rd, SW17 . . . . 167 H4
Gilbeys Yd, NW1 . . . . 92 A7
Gilbourne Rd, SE18 . . . . . 137 J6
Gilda Av, Enf. EN3 . . . . 45 H5
Gilda Cres, N16 . . . . 94 D1
Gildea Cl, Pnr. HA5 . . . . . . 51 G7
Gildea St, W1 . . . . 17 E2
Gilden Cres, NW5 . . . . 92 A5
Gildersome St, SE18
off Nightingale Vale. . . 136 D6
Gilders Rd, Chess. KT9 . . 195 J6
Giles Coppice, SE19. . . . . 170 C4
Gilkes Cres, SE21. . . . . . . 152 B6
Gilkes Pl, SE21 . . . . 152 B6
Gillan Grn, Bushey
(Bushey Hth) WD23. . . . 51 J2
Gillards Ms, E17
off Gillards Way 78 A4
Gillards Way, E17 . . . . 78 A4
Gill Av, E16 . . . . 115 G6
Gillender St, E3 . . . . 114 C4
E14. . . . . 114 C4
Gillespie Rd, N5 . . . . 93 G3
Gillett Av, E6. . . . . 116 B2
Gillette Cor, Islw. TW7 . . . 124 D7
Gillett Pl, N16
off Gillett St. 94 B5
Gillett Rd, Th.Hth. CR7 . . . 188 A4
Gillett St, N16 . . . . 94 B5
Gillfoot, NW1 . . . . 9 F2
Gillham Ter, N17. . . . . 60 D6
Gillian Pk Rd, Sutt. SM3 . 198 C1
Gillian St, SE13 . . . . 154 B5
Gillies St, NW5. . . . . 92 A5
Gilling Ct, NW3 . . . . 91 H6
Gillingham Ms, SW1 . . . . . 33 F1
Gillingham Rd, NW2 . . . . . 90 B3
Gillingham Row, SW1 . . . . 33 F1
Gillingham St, SW1. . . . . . 33 E1
Gillison Wk, SE16. . . . . 29 J5
Gillman Dr, E15 . . . . 115 F1
Gill St, E14 . . . . 113 J6
Gillum Cl, Barn. EN4 . . . . . 57 J1
Gilmore Rd, SE13. . . . . . . 154 D4
Gilpin Av, SW14. . . . . 146 D4
Gilpin Cl, W2 . . . . 14 E1
Mitcham CR4. . . . . 185 H2
Gilpin Cres, N18. . . . . 60 C5
Twickenham TW2 . . . . . 143 H7
Gilpin Rd, E5 . . . . 95 H4
Gilpin Way, Hayes UB3 . . 121 G7
Gilsland Rd, Th.Hth. CR7 . 188 A4
Gilstead Ho, Bark. IG11 . . 118 B2
Gilstead Rd, SW6. . . . . . . 149 E2
Gilston Rd, SW10. . . . . 30 D4
Gilton Rd, SE6 . . . . 173 E3
Giltspur St, EC1 . . . . 19 H3
Gilwell Cl, E4
off Antlers Hill. 46 D4
Gilwell La, E4. . . . . 46 C4
Gilwell Pk, E4. . . . . 46 C3
Gippeswyck Cl, Pnr. HA5
off Uxbridge Rd 66 D1
Gipsy Hill, SE19 . . . . 170 B4
Gipsy La, SW15 . . . . 147 G3
★**Gipsy Moth IV**, SE10. . . 134 C6
Gipsy Rd, SE27 . . . . 169 J4
Welling DA16 . . . . 158 D1
Gipsy Rd Gdns, SE27. . . . 169 J4
Giralda Cl, E16
off Fulmer Rd 116 A5
Giraud St, E14 . . . . 114 B6
Girdlers Rd, W14 . . . . 128 A4
Girdlestone Wk, N19 . . . . . 92 C2
Girdwood Rd, SW18 . . . . 148 B7
Girling Way, Felt. TW14 . . 142 A3
Gironde Rd, SW6. . . . . . . 128 C7
Girton Av, NW9 . . . . 70 A3
Girton Cl, Nthlt. UB5 . . . . . 85 J6
Girton Gdns, Croy. CR0 . . 204 A3
Girton Rd, SE26 . . . . 171 G5
Northolt UB5. . . . . 85 J6
Girton Vil, W10 . . . . 108 A6
Gisbourne Cl, Wall. SM6 . 200 D3
Gisburn Rd, N8 . . . . 75 F4
Gissing Wk, N1
off Lofting Rd 93 G7
Gittens Cl, Brom. BR1 . . . 173 F4
Given Wilson Wk, E13. . . . 115 F2
Glacier Way, Wem. HA0 . . 105 G2
Gladbeck Way, Enf. EN2. . . 43 H4
Gladding Rd, E12. . . . . 98 A4
Glade, The, N21 . . . . 43 F6
SE7 . . . . 135 J7
Glade, The, Brom. BR1 . . . 192 A2
Croydon CR0. . . . . 189 G5
Enfield EN2. . . . . 43 G3
Epsom KT17 . . . . 197 G5
Ilford IG5. . . . . 80 C1
West Wickham BR4. . . . 204 B3
Woodford Green IG8 . . . 63 H3
Glade Cl, Surb. KT6 . . . . . 195 G2
Glade Ct, Ilf. IG5
off The Glade. 80 C1
Glade Gdns, Croy. CR0 . . 189 H7
Glade La, Sthl. UB2 . . . . . 123 H2
Gladeside, N21. . . . . 43 F6
Croydon CR0. . . . . 189 G6
Gladesmore Rd, N15 . . . . . 76 C6
Glades Shop Cen, The,
Brom. BR1. . . . . 191 G2
Gladeswood Rd, Belv.
DA17 . . . . 139 H4
Gladiator St, SE23 . . . . . . 153 H6
Glading Ter, N16. . . . . 94 C3
Gladioli Cl, Hmptn. TW12
off Gresham Rd. 161 G6
Gladsdale Dr, Pnr. HA5 . . . 66 A4
Gladsmuir Rd, N19. . . . . . . 92 C1
Barnet EN5 . . . . 40 B2
Gladstone Av, E12 . . . . 98 B7
N22 . . . . 75 G2
Feltham TW14 . . . . 142 A6
Twickenham TW2 . . . . . 144 A7
Gladstone Ct, SW19
off Gladstone Rd. 166 D7
Gladstone Gdns, Houns. TW3
off Palmerston Rd. . . . 143 J1
Gladstone Ms, N22
off Pelham Rd 75 G2
NW6 *off Cavendish Rd* . . 90 C7
SE20 . . . . 171 F7
Gladstone Par, NW2
off Edgware Rd. 89 H1
Gladstone Pk Gdns, NW2 . 89 H3
Gladstone Pl, E3
off Roman Rd 113 J2
Barnet EN5 . . . . 40 A4
Gladstone Rd, SW19 . . . . 166 D7
W4 *off Acton La* 126 D3
Buckhurst Hill IG9. . . . . . 63 H1
Croydon CR0. . . . . 188 A7
Kingston upon Thames
KT1 . . . . 182 A3
Orpington BR6 . . . . 207 F5
Southall UB2. . . . . 122 E3
Surbiton KT6. . . . . 195 G2
Gladstone St, SE1 . . . . 27 G5
Gladstone Ter, SE27
off Bentons La. 169 J4
Gladstone Way, Har.
(Wldste) HA3. . . . . 68 B3
Gladwell Rd, N8. . . . . 75 F6
Bromley BR1 . . . . 173 G6
Gladwyn Rd, SW15 . . . . . 148 A3
Gladys Rd, NW6. . . . . 90 D7
Glaisher St, SE8. . . . . 134 A6
Glamis Cres, Hayes UB3 . . 121 F3
Glamis Pl, E1 . . . . 113 F7
Glamis Rd, E1. . . . . 113 F7
Glamis Way, Nthlt. UB5 . . . 85 J6
Glamorgan Cl, Mitch. CR4. 186 E3
Glamorgan Rd, Kings.T.
KT1 . . . . 163 F7
Glanfield Rd, Beck. BR3 . . 189 J4
Glanleam Rd, Stan. HA7 . . 53 G4
Glanville Ms, Stan. HA7. . . 52 D5
Glanville Rd, SW2 . . . . . . 151 E5
Bromley BR2. . . . . 191 H3
Glasbrook Av, Twick. TW2. 161 F1
Glasbrook Rd, SE9. . . . . . 156 A7
Glaserton Rd, N16 . . . . 76 B7
Glasford St, SW17 . . . . . . 167 J6
Glasgow Ho, W9 . . . . 6 B3
Glasgow Rd, E13 . . . . 115 H2
N18 *off Aberdeen Rd*. 60/61 E5
Glasgow Ter, SW1 . . . . 33 F4
Glasse Cl, W13 . . . . 104 D7
Glasshill St, SE1 . . . . 27 H3
Glasshouse Flds, E1 . . . . . 113 G7
Glasshouse St, W1. . . . . . . 17 G6
Glasshouse Wk, SE11. . . . . 34 B3
Glasshouse Yd, EC1 . . . . . . 11 J6
Glasslyn Rd, N8 . . . . 74 D5
Glassmill La, Brom. BR2 . 191 F2
Glass St, E2
off Coventry Rd . . 112/113 E4
Glass Yd, SE18
off Woolwich High St . 136 D3
Glastonbury Av, Wdf.Grn.
IG8. . . . . 64 A7
Glastonbury Pl, E1
off Sutton St 113 F6

Glastonbury Rd, N9 ... **60** D1
Morden SM4 ... **184** D7
Glastonbury St, NW6 ... **90** C5
Glaucus St, E3 ... **114** B5
Glazbury Rd, W14 ... **128** B4
Glazebrook Cl, SE21 ... **170** A2
Glazebrook Rd, Tedd. TW11 ... **162** C7
Glebe, The, SE3 ... **154** E3
SW16 ... **168** D4
Chislehurst BR7 ... **193** F1
West Drayton UB7 ... **120** C4
Worcester Park KT4 ... **197** F1
Glebe Av, Enf. EN2 ... **43** H3
Harrow HA3 ... **69** H3
Mitcham CR4 ... **185** H2
Ruislip HA4 ... **84** B6
Woodford Green IG8 ... **63** G6
Glebe Cl, W4
off Glebe St ... **126/127** E5
Glebe Cotts, Sutt. SM1
off Vale Rd ... **198/199** E4
Glebe Ct, W7 ... **104** A7
Mitcham CR4 ... **185** J3
Stanmore HA7 ... **53** F5
Glebe Cres, NW4 ... **71** J4
Harrow HA3 ... **69** H3
Glebe Gdns, N.Mal. KT3 ... **183** E7
Glebe Ho Dr, Brom. BR2 ... **205** H1
Glebe Hyrst, SE19
off Giles Coppice ... **170** C4
Glebelands, W.Mol. KT8 ... **179** H5
Glebelands Av, E18 ... **79** G2
Ilford IG2 ... **81** G7
Glebelands Cl, SE5
off Grove Hill Rd ... **152** B3
Glebelands Rd, Felt. TW14 ... **142** A7
Glebe La, Barn. EN5 ... **39** G5
Harrow HA3 ... **69** H4
Glebe Path, Mitch. CR4 ... **185** H3
Glebe Pl, SW3 ... **31** G5
Glebe Rd, E8
off Middleton Rd ... **94** C7
N3 ... **73** F1
N8 ... **75** F4
NW10 ... **89** F6
SW13 ... **147** G2
Bromley BR1 ... **191** G1
Carshalton SM5 ... **199** J6
Dagenham RM10 ... **101** H6
Hayes UB3 ... **121** J1
Stanmore HA7 ... **53** F5
Glebe Side, Twick. TW1 ... **144** C6
Glebe St, W4 ... **126** E5
Glebe Ter, E3 *off Bow Rd* ... **114** A3
Glebe Way, Felt. TW13 ... **161** G3
West Wickham BR4 ... **204** C2
Glebeway, Wdf.Grn. IG8 ... **63** J5
Gledhow Gdns, SW5 ... **30** C2
Gledstanes Rd, W14 ... **128** B5
Gleed Av, Bushey (Bushey Hth) WD23 ... **52** A2
Gleeson Dr, Orp. BR6 ... **207** J5
Glegg Pl, SW15 ... **148** A4
Glen, The, Brom. BR2 ... **190** E2
Croydon CR0 ... **203** G2
Enfield EN2 ... **43** H4
Orpington BR6 ... **206** C3
Pinner HA5 ... **67** E7
Pinner (Eastcote) HA5 ... **66** B5
Southall UB2 ... **123** F5
Wembley HA9 ... **87** G4
Glenaffric Av, E14 ... **134** D4
Glen Albyn Rd, SW19 ... **166** A2
Glenalmond Rd, Har. HA3 ... **69** H4
Glenalvon Way, SE18 ... **136** B4
Glena Mt, Sutt. SM1 ... **199** F4
Glenarm Rd, E5 ... **95** F5
Glenavon Cl, Esher (Clay.) KT10 ... **194** D7
Glenavon Rd, E15 ... **97** E7
Glenbarr Cl, SE9
off Dumbreck Rd ... **156/157** E3
Glenbow Rd, Brom. BR1 ... **172** E6
Glenbrook N, Enf. EN2 ... **43** F4
Glenbrook Rd, NW6 ... **90** D5
Glenbrook S, Enf. EN2 ... **43** F4
Glenbuck Ct, Surb. KT6
off Glenbuck Rd ... **181** G6
Glenbuck Rd, Surb. KT6 ... **181** G6
Glenburnie Rd, SW17 ... **167** J3
Glencairn Dr, W5 ... **105** E4
Glencairne Cl, E16 ... **116** A5
Glencairn Rd, SW16 ... **186** E1
Glencoe Av, Ilf. IG2 ... **81** G7
Glencoe Dr, Dag. RM10 ... **101** G4
Glencoe Rd, Hayes UB4 ... **102** D5
Glencorse Grn, Wat. WD19
off Caldwell Rd ... **50** D4
Glen Cres, Wdf.Grn. IG8 ... **63** H6
Glendale Av, N22 ... **59** G7
Edgware HA8 ... **53** J4
Romford RM6 ... **82** C7
Glendale Cl, SE9
off Dumbreck Rd ... **156** D3
Glendale Dr, SW19 ... **166** C5
Glendale Gdns, Wem. HA9 ... **87** G1
Glendale Ms, Beck. BR3 ... **190** B1
Glendale Rd, Erith DA8 ... **139** J4
Glendale Way, SE28 ... **118** C7
Glendall St, SW9 ... **151** F4
Glendarvon St, SW15 ... **148** A3
Glendevon Cl, Edg. HA8
off Tayside Dr ... **54** B3
Glendish Rd, N17 ... **76** D1
Glendor Gdns, NW7 ... **54** D4
Glendower Gdns, SW14
off Glendower Rd ... **146** D3
Glendower Pl, SW7 ... **31** E1
Glendower Rd, E4 ... **62** D1
SW14 ... **146** D3
Glendown Rd, SE2 ... **138** A5
Glendun Rd, W3 ... **107** E7
Gleneagle Ms, SW16
off Ambleside Av ... **168** D5
Gleneagle Rd, SW16 ... **168** D5
Gleneagles, Stan. HA7 ... **52** E6
Gleneagles Cl, SE16
off Ryder Dr ... **132/133** E5
Orpington BR6 ... **207** G1
Staines (Stanw.) TW19 ... **140** A6
Watford WD19 ... **50** D4
Gleneagles Grn, Orp. BR6
off Tandridge Dr ... **207** G1
Gleneagles Twr, Sthl. UB1 ... **103** J6
Gleneldon Ms, SW16 ... **168** E4
Gleneldon Rd, SW16 ... **168** E4
Glenelg Rd, SW2 ... **151** E5
Glenesk Rd, SE9 ... **156** D3
Glenfarg Rd, SE6 ... **172** D1
Glenfield Rd, SW12 ... **168** C1
W13 ... **125** E2
Glenfield Ter, W13 ... **124** E2
Glenfinlas Way, SE5 ... **35** H7
Glenforth St, SE10 ... **135** F5
Glengall Causeway, E14 ... **134** A3
Glengall Gro, E14 ... **134** B3
Glengall Rd, NW6 ... **108** C1
SE15 ... **37** G5
Bexleyheath DA7 ... **159** E3
Edgware HA8 ... **54** B3
Woodford Green IG8 ... **63** G6
Glengall Ter, SE15 ... **37** G5
Glen Gdns, Croy. CR0 ... **201** G3
Glengarnock Av, E14 ... **134** C4
Glengarry Rd, SE22 ... **152** B5
Glenham Dr, Ilf. IG2 ... **80** E5
Glenhaven Av, Borwd. WD6 ... **38** A3
Glenhead Cl, SE9
off Dumbreck Rd ... **156/157** E3
Glenhill Cl, N3 ... **72** D2
Glenhouse Rd, SE9 ... **156** D5
Glenhurst Av, NW5 ... **92** A4
Bexley DA5 ... **177** F1
Glenhurst Ct, SE19 ... **170** C5
Glenhurst Ri, SE19 ... **169** J7
Glenhurst Rd, N12 ... **57** G5
Brentford TW8 ... **125** F6
Glenilla Rd, NW3 ... **91** H6
Glenister Ho, Hayes UB3 ... **122** B1
Glenister Pk Rd, SW16 ... **168** D7
Glenister Rd, SE10 ... **135** F5
Glenister St, E16 ... **136** D1
Glenkerry Ho, E14
off Burcham St ... **114** C6
Glenlea Path, SE9
off Well Hall Rd ... **156** C5
Glenlea Rd, SE9 ... **156** C5
Glenloch Rd, NW3 ... **91** H6
Enfield EN3 ... **45** F2
Glenluce Rd, SE3 ... **135** G7
Glenlyon Rd, SE9 ... **156** D5
Glenmere Av, NW7 ... **55** G7
Glen Ms, E17 *off Glen Rd* ... **77** J5
Glenmill, Hmptn. TW12 ... **161** F5
Glenmore Rd, NW3 ... **91** H6
Welling DA16 ... **157** J1
Glenmore Way, Bark. IG11 ... **118** A3
Glenmount Path, SE18
off Raglan Rd ... **137** F5
Glennie Rd, SE27 ... **169** G3
Glenny Rd, Bark. IG11 ... **99** F6
Glenorchy Cl, Hayes UB4 ... **103** E5
Glenparke Rd, E7 ... **97** H6
Glen Ri, Wdf.Grn. IG8 ... **63** H6
Glen Rd, E13 ... **115** J4
E17 ... **77** J5
Chessington KT9 ... **195** H3
Glenrosa St, SW6 ... **149** F2
Glenrose Ct, Sid. DA14 ... **176** B5
Glenroy St, W12 ... **107** J6
Glensdale Rd, SE4 ... **153** J3
Glenshiel Rd, SE9 ... **156** D5
Glenside, Chig. IG7 ... **65** E6
Glentanner Way, SW17
off Aboyne Rd ... **167** G3
Glen Ter, E14
off Manchester Rd ... **134** C2
Glentham Gdns, SW13
off Glentham Rd ... **127** H6
Glentham Rd, SW13 ... **127** G6
Glenthorne Av, Croy. CR0 ... **203** E1
Glenthorne Cl, Sutt. SM3 ... **198** D1
Glenthorne Gdns, Ilf. IG6 ... **80** D3
Sutton SM3 ... **198** D1
Glenthorne Ms, W6
off Glenthorne Rd ... **127** H4
Glenthorne Rd, E17 ... **77** H5
N11 ... **57** J5
W6 ... **127** J4
Kingston upon Thames KT1 ... **181** J4
Glenthorpe Rd, Mord. SM4 ... **184** A5
Glenton Rd, SE13 ... **154** E4
Glentrammon Av, Orp. BR6 ... **207** J6
Glentrammon Cl, Orp. BR6 ... **207** J6
Glentrammon Gdns, Orp. BR6 ... **207** J6
Glentrammon Rd, Orp. BR6 ... **207** J6
Glentworth St, NW1 ... **8** A6
Glenure Rd, SE9 ... **156** D5
Glenview, SE2 ... **138** D6
Glenview Rd, Brom. BR1 ... **192** A2
Glenville Gro, SE8 ... **133** J7
Glenville Ms, SW18 ... **148** E7
Glenville Rd, Kings.T. KT2 ... **182** A1
Glen Wk, Islw. TW7 ... **144** A5
Glenwood Av, NW9 ... **88** E1
Glenwood Cl, Har. HA1 ... **68** C5
Glenwood Ct, E18
off Clarendon Rd ... **79** G3
Glenwood Gdns, Ilf. IG2 ... **80** D5
Glenwood Gro, NW9 ... **88** C1
Glenwood Rd, N15 ... **75** H5
NW7 ... **55** E3
SE6 ... **171** J1
Epsom KT17 ... **197** G6
Hounslow TW3 ... **144** A3
Glenwood Way, Croy. CR0 ... **189** G6
Glenworth Av, E14 ... **134** D4
Gliddon Dr, E5 ... **94** E4
Gliddon Rd, W14 ... **128** B4
Glimpsing Grn, Erith DA18 ... **139** E3
Global App, E3
off Hancock Rd ... **114** B2
Globe Pond Rd, SE16 ... **133** H1
Globe Rd, E1 ... **113** F3
E2 ... **113** F3
E15 ... **97** F5
Woodford Green IG8 ... **63** J6
Globe Rope Wk, E14 ... **134** C4
Globe St, SE1 ... **28** A5
Globe Ter, E2
off Globe Rd ... **113** F3
Globe Wf, SE16
off Rotherhithe St ... **133** G1
Globe Yd, W1 ... **16** D4
Gloster Rd, N.Mal. KT3 ... **182** E4
Gloucester Arc, SW7 ... **30** C1
Gloucester Av, NW1 ... **92** A7
Sidcup DA15 ... **175** H2
Gloucester Av, Welling DA16 ... **157** J4
Gloucester Circ, SE10 ... **134** C7
Gloucester Cl, NW10 ... **88** D7
Thames Ditton KT7 ... **194** D1
Gloucester Ct, EC3 ... **21** E6
Richmond TW9 ... **126** A7
Gloucester Cres, NW1 ... **110** B1
Gloucester Dr, N4 ... **93** H2
NW11 ... **72** D4
Gloucester Gdns, NW11 ... **72** C7
W2 ... **14** B3
Barnet EN4 ... **42** A4
Gloucester Gdns, Ilf. IG1 ... **80** B7
Sutton SM1 ... **199** E2
Gloucester Gate, NW1 ... **8** D1
Gloucester Gate Ms, NW1 ... **8** D1
Gloucester Gro, Edg. HA8 ... **70** D1
Gloucester Gro Est, SE15 ... **37** E6
Gloucester Ho, NW6 ... **108** D2
Gloucester Ms, E10
off Gloucester Rd ... **78** A7
W2 ... **14** D4
Gloucester Ms W, W2 ... **14** C4
Gloucester Par, Sid. DA15 ... **158** A5
Gloucester Pk, SW7 ... **30** C1
Gloucester Pl, NW1 ... **7** J5
W1 ... **16** A1
Gloucester Pl Ms, W1 ... **16** A2
Gloucester Rd, E10 ... **78** A7
E11 ... **79** H5
E12 ... **98** C3
E17 ... **77** G2
N17 ... **76** A2
N18 ... **60** C5
SW7 ... **22** C5
W3 ... **126** C2
W5 ... **125** F2
Barnet EN5 ... **41** F5
Belvedere DA17 ... **139** F5
Croydon CR0 ... **188** A6
Feltham TW13 ... **160** C1
Hampton TW12 ... **161** H7
Harrow HA1 ... **67** H5
Hounslow TW4 ... **142** E4
Kingston upon Thames KT1 ... **182** B2
Richmond TW9 ... **126** A7
Teddington TW11 ... **162** B5
Twickenham TW2 ... **161** J1
Gloucester Sq, E2
off Whiston Rd ... **112** D1
W2 ... **15** F4
Gloucester St, SW1 ... **33** F4
Gloucester Ter, W2 ... **14** C3
Gloucester Wk, W8 ... **128** D2
Gloucester Way, EC1 ... **11** F4
Glover Cl, SE2 ... **138** C4
Glover Dr, N18 ... **61** F6
Glover Rd, Pnr. HA5 ... **66** D6
Gloxinia Wk, Hmptn. TW12 ... **161** G6
Glycena Rd, SW11 ... **149** J3
Glyn Av, Barn. EN4 ... **41** G4
Glyn Cl, SE25 ... **188** B2
Glyn Ct, SW16 ... **169** G3
Stanmore HA7 ... **52** E6
Glyndebourne Pk, Orp. BR6 ... **207** E2
Glynde Ms, SW3 ... **23** H6
Glynde Rd, Bexh. DA7 ... **158** D3
Glynde St, SE4 ... **153** J6
Glyndon Rd, SE18 ... **137** F4
Glyn Dr, Sid. DA14 ... **176** B4
Glynfield Rd, NW10 ... **89** E7
Glynne Rd, N22 ... **75** G2
Glyn Rd, E5 ... **95** G3
Enfield EN3 ... **45** F4
Worcester Park KT4 ... **198** A2
Glyn St, SE11 ... **34** C4
Glynwood Ct, SE23 ... **171** F2
Goaters All, SW6 ... **128** C7
Goat La, Surb. KT6 ... **195** F2
Goat Rd, Mitch. CR4 ... **186** A7
Goat Wf, Brent. TW8 ... **125** H6
Godalming Av, Wall. SM6 ... **201** E5
Godalming Rd, E14 ... **114** B5
Godbold Rd, E15 ... **114** E3
Goddard Pl, N19 ... **92** C3
Goddard Rd, Beck. BR3 ... **189** G4
Goddards Way, Ilf. IG1 ... **99** G1
Godfrey Av, Nthlt. UB5 ... **102** E1
Twickenham TW2 ... **144** A7
Godfrey Hill, SE18 ... **136** B4
Godfrey Rd, SE18 ... **136** C4
Godfrey St, E15 ... **114** C2
SW3 ... **31** H3
Godfrey Way, Houns. TW4 ... **143** E7
Goding St, SE11 ... **34** B4
Godley Cl, SE14
off Kender St ... **153** F1
Godley Rd, SW18 ... **167** G1
Godliman St, EC4 ... **19** J4
Godman Rd, SE15 ... **152** E2
Godolphin Cl, N13 ... **59** H6
Godolphin Pl, W3
off Vyner Rd ... **106** D7
Godolphin Rd, W12 ... **127** H2
Godson Rd, Croy. CR0 ... **201** G3

Godson St, N1 ... **11** E1
Godstone Rd, Sutt. SM1 . **199** F4
Twickenham TW1 ... **144** D6
Godstow Rd, SE2 ... **138** C2
Godwin Cl, N1 ... **12** A1
Epsom KT19 ... **196** C6
Godwin Ct, NW1 ... **9** G1
Godwin Rd, E7 ... **97** H4
Bromley BR2 ... **191** J3
Goffers Rd, SE3 ... **154** D1
Goidel Cl, Wall. SM6 ... **200** D4
Golborne Gdns, W10
off Golborne Rd ... **108** C4
Golborne Ms, W10
off Portobello Rd ... **108** B5
Golborne Rd, W10 ... **108** B5
Golda Cl, Barn. EN5 ... **40** A6
Goldbeaters Gro, Edg. HA8 ... **54** E6
Goldcliff Cl, Mord. SM4 . . **184** D6
Goldcrest Cl, E16
off Sheerwater Rd ... **116** A5
SE28 ... **118** C7
Goldcrest Ms, W5
off Montpelier Av ... **105** G5
Goldcrest Way, Bushey WD23 ... **51** J1
Golden Ct, Rich. TW9
off George St ... **145** G5
Golden Cres, Hayes UB3 . **121** J1
Golden Cross Ms, W11
off Basing St ... **108** C6
★**Golden Hinde**, SE1 ... **28** B1
Golden Jubilee Br, SE1 ... **26** C2
WC2 ... **26** C1
Golden La, EC1 ... **11** J6
Golden La Est, EC1 ... **11** J6
Golden Manor, W7 ... **104** B7
Golden Plover Cl, E16
off Maplin Rd ... **115** H6
Golden Sq, W1 ... **17** G5
Golden Yd, NW3
off Heath St ... **91** F4
Golders Cl, Edg. HA8 ... **54** B5
Golders Gdns, NW11 ... **72** B7
GOLDERS GREEN, NW11 . . **72** D7
Golders Grn Cres, NW11 . . **72** C7
Golders Grn Rd, NW11 ... **72** B6
Golders Manor Dr, NW11 . . **72** A6
Golders Pk Cl, NW11 ... **90** E1
Golders Ri, NW4 ... **72** A5
Golders Way, NW11 ... **72** C7
Goldfinch Rd, SE28 ... **137** G3
Goldfinch Way, Borwd. WD6 ... **38** A4
Goldhawk Ms, W12
off Devonport Rd ... **127** H2
Goldhawk Rd, W6 ... **127** F4
W12 ... **127** G3
Goldhaze Cl, Wdf.Grn. IG8 . **64** A7
Gold Hill, Edg. HA8 ... **54** D6
Goldhurst Ter, NW6 ... **90** E7
Golding Cl, Chess. KT9
off Coppard Gdns ... **195** F6
Goldingham Av, Loug. IG10 ... **49** F2
Goldings Hill, Loug. IG10 . . **48** D1
Goldings Ri, Loug. IG10 . . **48** D1
Goldings Rd, Loug. IG10 ... **48** D1
Golding St, E1 ... **21** J4
Golding Ter, SW11
off Longhedge St ... **150** A2
Goldington Cres, NW1 ... **9** H1
Goldington St, NW1 ... **9** H1
Gold La, Edg. HA8 ... **54** D6
Goldman Cl, E2 ... **13** H5
Goldmark Ho, SE3
off Lebrun Sq ... **155** H3
Goldney Rd, W9 ... **108** D4
Goldrill Dr, N11 ... **58** A2
Goldsboro Rd, SW8 ... **150** D1
Goldsborough Cres, E4 ... **62** C2
Goldsdown Cl, Enf. EN3 ... **45** H2
Goldsdown Rd, Enf. EN3 ... **45** G2
Goldsmid St, SE18
off Sladedale Rd ... **137** H5
Goldsmith Av, E12 ... **98** B6
NW9 ... **71** F6
W3 ... **106** D7
Romford RM7 ... **83** G7
Goldsmith Cl, W3
off East Acton La . **126/127** E1
Harrow HA2 ... **85** H1
Goldsmith La, NW9 ... **70** B4
Goldsmith Rd, E10 ... **96** A1
E17 ... **77** G2
N11 ... **57** J5
SE15 ... **152** D1
W3 ... **126** D1
★**Goldsmiths' Hall**, EC2 ... **20** A3
Goldsmith's Row, E2 ... **13** H2
Goldsmith's Sq, E2 ... **13** J1
Goldsmith St, EC2 ... **20** A3
Goldsworthy Gdns, SE16 . **133** F4
Goldwell Rd, Th.Hth. CR7 . **187** F4
Goldwin Cl, SE14 ... **153** F1
Goldwing Cl, E16 ... **115** G6
Golf Cl, Stan. HA7 ... **53** F7
Thornton Heath CR7
off Kensington Av ... **187** G1
Golf Club Dr, Kings.T. KT2 ... **164** D7
Golfe Rd, Ilf. IG1 ... **99** G3
Golf Rd, W5
off Boileau Rd ... **105** J6
Bromley BR1 ... **192** D3
Golf Side, Twick. TW2 ... **162** A3
Golfside Cl, N20 ... **57** H3
New Malden KT3 ... **183** E2
Goliath Cl, Wall. SM6 ... **200** E7
Gollogly Ter, SE7 ... **135** J5
Gomer Gdns, Tedd. TW11 . **162** D6
Gomer Pl, Tedd. TW11 ... **162** D6
Gomm Rd, SE16 ... **133** F3
Gomshall Av, Wall. SM6 . . **200** E5
Gondar Gdns, NW6 ... **90** C5
Gonson St, SE8 ... **134** B6
Gonston Cl, SW19 ... **166** B2
Gonville Cres, Nthlt. UB5 . . **85** H6
Gonville Rd, Th.Hth. CR7 . **187** F5
Gonville St, SW6
off Putney Br App ... **148** B3
Gooch Ho, E5 ... **95** E3
Goodall Rd, E11 ... **96** C3
Gooden Ct, Har. HA1 ... **86** B3
Goodenough Rd, SW19 . . **166** C7
Goodey Rd, Bark. IG11 ... **99** J7
Goodge Pl, W1 ... **17** G2
Goodge St, W1 ... **17** G2
Goodhall Cl, Stan. HA7 ... **52** E6
Goodhall St, NW10 ... **107** E3
Goodhart Pl, E14 ... **113** H7
Goodhart Way, W.Wick. BR4 ... **190** F7
Goodhew Rd, Croy. CR0 . **188** D6
Gooding Cl, N.Mal. KT3 . **182** C4
Goodinge Cl, N7 ... **92** E6
Goodman Cres, SW2 ... **168** D2
Goodman Rd, E10 ... **78** C7
Goodmans Ct, E1 ... **21** F5
Wembley HA0 ... **87** G4
Goodman's Stile, E1 ... **21** H4
Goodmans Yd, E1 ... **21** F5
GOODMAYES, Ilf. IG3 ... **100** B2
Goodmayes Av, Ilf. IG3 ... **100** A1
Goodmayes La, Ilf. IG3 ... **100** A4
Goodmayes Rd, Ilf. IG3 ... **100** A1
Goodrich Rd, SE22 ... **152** C6
Goodson Rd, NW10 ... **89** E7
Goods Way, NW1 ... **10** A1
Goodway Gdns, E14 ... **114** D6
Goodwin Cl, SE16 ... **29** G6
Mitcham CR4 ... **185** G3
Goodwin Ct, Barn. EN4 ... **41** H6
Goodwin Dr, Sid. DA14 . . **176** D3
Goodwin Gdns, Croy. CR0 ... **201** H6
Goodwin Rd, N9 ... **61** F1
W12 ... **127** G2
Croydon CR0 ... **201** H5
Goodwins Ct, WC2 ... **18** A5
Goodwin St, N4
off Fonthill Rd ... **93** G2
Goodwood Cl, Mord. SM4 ... **184** D4
Stanmore HA7 ... **53** F5
Goodwood Dr, Nthlt. UB5 . **85** G6
Goodwood Path, Borwd. WD6 *off Stratfield Rd* . . **38** A3
Goodwood Rd, SE14 ... **133** H7
Goodwyn Av, NW7 ... **55** E5
Goodwyns Vale, N10 ... **74** A1
Goodyers Gdns, NW4 ... **72** A5
Goosander Way, SE28 ... **137** G3
Gooseacre La, Har. HA3 ... **69** G5
Gooseley La, E6 ... **116** D3
Goosens Cl, Sutt. SM1
off Turnpike La ... **199** F5
Goose Sq, E6
off Harper Rd ... **116** C6
Gophir La, EC4 ... **20** B5
Gopsall St, N1 ... **112** A1
Gordon Av, E4 ... **62** E6
SW14 ... **146** E4
Stanmore HA7 ... **52** E6
Twickenham TW1 ... **144** D5
Gordonbrock Rd, SE4 ... **154** A5
Gordon Cl, E17 ... **78** A6
Gordon Cl, N19
off Highgate Hill ... **92** C1
Gordon Ct, W12 ... **107** J6
Gordon Cres, Croy. CR0 . . **202** B1
Hayes UB3 ... **122** A3
Gordondale Rd, SW19 ... **166** D2
Gordon Gdns, Edg. HA8 ... **70** B2
Gordon Gro, SE5 ... **151** H2
Gordon Hill, Enf. EN2 ... **43** J1
Gordon Ho, E1
off Glamis Rd ... **113** F7
Gordon Ho Rd, NW5 ... **92** A4
Gordon Pl, W8 ... **128** D2
Gordon Rd, E4 ... **47** E7
E11 ... **79** G6
E15 ... **96** C4
E18 ... **79** H1
N3 ... **56** C7
N9 ... **61** E2
N11 ... **58** D7
SE15 ... **152** E2
W4 ... **126** B6
W5 ... **105** F7
W13 ... **104** E7
Barking IG11 ... **117** H1
Beckenham BR3 ... **189** J3
Belvedere DA17 ... **139** J4
Carshalton SM5 ... **199** J6
Enfield EN2 ... **43** J1
Esher (Clay.) KT10 ... **194** B6
Harrow HA3 ... **68** B3
Hounslow TW3 ... **143** J4
Ilford IG1 ... **99** G3
Kingston upon Thames KT2 ... **181** J1
Richmond TW9 ... **145** J2
Romford RM6 ... **83** F6
Sidcup DA15 ... **157** H5
Southall UB2 ... **123** E4
Surbiton KT5 ... **181** J7
Gordon Sq, WC1 ... **9** J6
Gordon St, E13
off Grange Rd ... **115** G3
WC1 ... **9** H5
Gordon Way, Barn. EN5 ... **40** C4
Bromley BR1 ... **191** G1
Gore Ct, NW9 ... **70** A5
Gorefield Pl, NW6 ... **108** D2
Gore Rd, E9 ... **113** F1
SW20 ... **183** J2
Goresbrook Rd, Dag. RM9 ... **118** B1
Goresbrook Village, Dag. RM9
off Goresbrook Rd ... **118** B1
Gore St, SW7 ... **22** D5
Gorham Pl, W11
off Mary Pl ... **108** B7
Goring Cl, Rom. RM5 ... **83** J1
Goring Gdns, Dag. RM8 . . **100** C4
Goring Rd, N11 ... **58** E6
Goring St, EC3 ... **21** E3
Goring Way, Grnf. UB6 ... **103** J2
Gorleston Rd, N15 ... **76** A5
Gorleston St, W14 ... **128** B4
Gorman Rd, SE18 ... **136** C4
Gorringe Pk Av, Mitch. CR4 ... **167** J7
Gorse Cl, E16 ... **115** G6
Gorse Ri, SW17 ... **168** A5
Gorse Rd, Croy. CR0 ... **204** A4
Gorst Rd, NW10 ... **106** C4
SW11 ... **149** J6
Gorsuch Pl, E2 ... **13** F3
Gorsuch St, E2 ... **13** F3
Gosberton Rd, SW12 ... **168** A1
Gosbury Hill, Chess. KT9 . **195** H4
Gosfield Rd, Dag. RM8 ... **101** G2
Gosfield St, W1 ... **17** F1
Gosford Gdns, Ilf. IG4 ... **80** C5
Gosforth La, Wat. WD19 . . **50** C3
Gosforth Path, Wat. WD19 . **50** A3
Goslett Yd, WC2 ... **17** J4
Gosling Cl, Grnf. UB6 ... **103** G3
Gosling Way, SW9 ... **151** G1
Gospatrick Rd, N17 ... **59** J7
GOSPEL OAK, NW5 ... **92** A4
Gospel Oak Est, NW5 ... **91** J5
Gosport Rd, E17 ... **77** J5
Gosport Wk, N17
off Yarmouth Cres . . **76/77** E5
Gosport Way, SE15
off Blakes Rd ... **132** C7
Gossage Rd, SE18
off Ancona Rd ... **137** G5
Gosset St, E2 ... **13** G3
Gosshill Rd, Chis. BR7 ... **192** D2
Gossington Cl, Chis. BR7
off Beechwood Ri . . **174/175** E4
Gosterwood St, SE8 ... **133** H6
Gostling Rd, Twick. TW2 . . **161** G1
Goston Gdns, Th.Hth. CR7 ... **187** G3
Goswell Rd, EC1 ... **11** J6
Gothic Ct, Hayes UB3
off Sipson La ... **121** G6
Gothic Rd, Twick. TW2 ... **162** A2
Gottfried Ms, NW5
off Fortess Rd ... **92** C4
Goudhurst Rd, Brom. BR1 ... **173** E5
Gough Rd, E15 ... **97** F4
Enfield EN1 ... **44** E2
Gough Sq, EC4 ... **19** F3
Gough St, WC1 ... **10** D5
Gough Wk, E14
off Saracen St ... **114** A6
Gould Ct, SE19 ... **170** C5
Goulden Ho App, SW11 . . **149** H2
Goulding Gdns, Th.Hth. CR7 ... **187** H2
Gould Rd, Felt. TW14 ... **141** H7
Twickenham TW2 ... **162** B1
Gould Ter, E8
off Kenmure Rd ... **94/95** E5
Goulston St, E1 ... **21** F3
Goulton Rd, E5 ... **95** E4
Gourley Pl, N15
off Gourley St ... **76** B5
Gourley St, N15 ... **76** B5
Gourock Rd, SE9 ... **156** D5
Govan St, E2
off Whiston Rd ... **112** D1
Govier Cl, E15 ... **97** E7
Gowan Av, SW6 ... **148** B1
Gowan Rd, NW10 ... **89** H6
Gower Cl, SW4 ... **150** C6
Gower Ct, WC1 ... **9** H5
Gower Ms, WC1 ... **17** H2
Gower Pl, WC1 ... **9** G5
Gower Rd, E7 ... **97** G6
Isleworth TW7 ... **124** C6
Gower St, WC1 ... **9** G5
Gower's Wk, E1 ... **21** H3
Gowland Pl, Beck. BR3 ... **189** J2
Gowlett Rd, SE15 ... **152** D3
Gowlland Cl, Croy. CR0 . . **188** D7
Gowrie Rd, SW11 ... **150** A3
Graburn Way, E.Mol. KT8 ... **180** A3
Grace Av, Bexh. DA7 ... **159** F2
Grace Business Cen, Mitch. CR4 ... **185** J5
Gracechurch St, EC3 ... **20** C5
Grace Cl, SE9 ... **174** A3
Borehamwood WD6 ... **38** D1
Edgware HA8
off Pavilion Way ... **54** C7
Ilford IG6 ... **65** J6
Gracedale Rd, SW16 ... **168** B5
Gracefield Gdns, SW16 . . **169** E3
Grace Jones Cl, E8
off Parkholme Rd ... **94** D6
Grace Path, SE26 ... **171** F4
Grace Pl, E3
off St. Leonards St ... **114** B3
Grace Rd, Croy. CR0 ... **187** J6
Grace's All, E1 ... **21** H5
Graces Ms, SE5 ... **152** B2
Graces Rd, SE5 ... **152** B2
Grace St, E3 ... **114** B3
Gradient, The, SE26 ... **170** D4
Graduate Pl, SE1
off Long La ... **132** B3
Graeme Rd, Enf. EN1 ... **44** A2
Graemesdyke Av, SW14 . . **146** B3
Grafton Cl, W13 ... **104** D6
Hounslow TW4 ... **161** E1
Worcester Park KT4 ... **197** E3
Grafton Cres, NW1 ... **92** B6
Grafton Gdns, N4 ... **75** J6
Dagenham RM8 ... **101** E2
Grafton Ho, E3 ... **114** A3
Grafton Ms, W1 ... **9** F6
Grafton Pk Rd, Wor.Pk. KT4 ... **196** E2
Grafton Pl, NW1 ... **9** H4
Grafton Rd, NW5 ... **92** A5
W3 ... **106** C7
Croydon CR0 ... **201** G1
Dagenham RM8 ... **101** E2
Enfield EN2 ... **43** F3
Harrow HA1 ... **67** J5
New Malden KT3 ... **182** E3
Worcester Park KT4 ... **196** D3
Graftons, The, NW2
off Hermitage La ... **90** D3
Grafton Sq, SW4 ... **150** C3
Grafton St, W1 ... **17** E6

Grafton Ter, NW5 . . . . **91** J5
Grafton Way, W1 . . . . **9** F6
WC1 . . . . **9** F6
West Molesey KT8 . . . . **179** F4
Grafton Yd, NW5
off Prince of Wales Rd. . **92** B6
Graham Av, W13 . . . . **124** E2
Mitcham CR4. . . . . **186** A1
Graham Cl, Croy. CR0 . . . **204** A2
Grahame Pk Est, NW9. . . . **71** E1
Grahame Pk Way, NW7 . . . **55** F7
NW9 . . . . **71** F2
Graham Gdns, Surb. KT6. **195** H1
Graham Rd, E8. . . . . **94** C6
E13. . . . . **115** G4
N15 . . . . **75** H3
NW4 . . . . **71** H6
SW19. . . . . **166** C7
W4. . . . . **126** D3
Bexleyheath DA6 . . . . . **159** G4
Hampton TW12 . . . . **161** G4
Harrow HA3 . . . . **68** B3
Mitcham CR4. . . . . **186** A1
Graham St, N1 . . . . **11** H2
Graham Ter, SW1 . . . . **32** B2
Grainger Cl, Nthlt. UB5
off Lancaster Rd **85** J5
Grainger Rd, N22. . . . . **75** J1
Isleworth TW7 . . . . **144** C2
Gramer Cl, E11
off Norman Rd **96** D2
Grampian Cl, Hayes UB3. **121** G7
Orpington BR6
off Cotswold Ri **193** J6
Sutton SM2
off Devonshire Rd. . . . **199** F7
Grampian Gdns, NW2 . . . . **90** B1
Grampian Ho, N9
off Plevna Rd. **60/61** E2
Granard Av, SW15 . . . . . . **147** H5
Granard Rd, SW12. . . . . . **149** J7
Granary Cl, N9
off Turin Rd **45** F7
Granary Rd, E1. . . . . **112** E4
Granary Sq, N1
off Liverpool Rd **93** G6
Granary St, NW1 . . . . **110** D1
Granby Pl, SE1. . . . . **26** E4
Granby Rd, SE9 . . . . **156** C2
Granby St, E2. . . . . **13** G5
Granby Ter, NW1 . . . . **9** F2
Grand Arc, N12
off Ballards La. **57** F5
Grand Av, EC1 . . . . **19** H1
N10 . . . . **74** A4
Surbiton KT5. . . . . **182** B5
Wembley HA9. . . . . **88** A5
Grand Av E, Wem. HA9 . . . **88** B5
Grand Dep Rd, SE18 . . . . **136** D5
Grand Dr, SW20. . . . . **183** J2
Southall UB2. . . . . **123** J2
Granden Rd, SW16. . . . . . **187** E2
Grandison Rd, SW11 . . . . **149** J5
Worcester Park KT4. . . . **197** J2
Grand Junct Wf, N1 . . . . . . **11** J2
Grand Par Ms, SW15 *off*
Upper Richmond Rd. . **148** B5
Grand Union Canal Wk,
W7. . . . . **124** B3
Grand Union Cl, W9
off Woodfield Rd. **108** C5
Grand Union Cres, E8 . . . . **94** D7
Grand Union Ind Est,
NW10. . . . . **106** B2
Grand Union Wk, NW1 . . . **92** B7
Grand Wk, E1
off Solebay St **113** H4
Granfield St, SW11. . . . . . **149** G1
Grange, The, N2
off Central Av **73** G2
N20 . . . . **57** F1
SE1 . . . . **29** F5
Grange, The, SW19. . . . . . **166** A6
Croydon CR0. . . . . **203** J2
Wembley HA0. . . . . **88** A7
Worcester Park KT4. . . . **196** D3
Grange Av, N12 . . . . **57** F5
N20 . . . . **40** B7
SE25 . . . . **188** B2
Barnet EN4 . . . . **57** H1
Stanmore HA7 . . . . **69** E2
Twickenham TW2 . . . . . **162** B2
Woodford Green IG8 . . . **63** G6
Grangecliffe Gdns, SE25 . **188** B2
Grange Cl, Edg. HA8 . . . . . **54** C5
Hounslow TW5 . . . . **123** F6
Sidcup DA15 . . . . **176** A3
West Molesey KT8 . . . . **179** H4
Woodford Green IG8 . . . **63** G7
Grange Ct, WC2 . . . . **18** D4
Chigwell IG7 . . . . **65** F2
Loughton IG10 . . . . **48** A5
Northolt UB5. . . . . **102** C2
Grangecourt Rd, N16. . . . . **94** B1
Grange Cres, SE28 . . . . . . **118** C6
Chigwell IG7 . . . . **65** G5
Grange Dr, Chis. BR7 . . . . **174** B6
Grange Fm Cl, Har. HA2. . . **85** J2
Grange Gdns, N14 . . . . **58** D1
NW3 . . . . **91** E3
SE25 . . . . **188** B2
Pinner HA5 . . . . **67** F4
Grange Gro, N1 . . . . **93** H6
GRANGE HILL, Chig. IG7 . . **65** G6
Grange Hill, SE25. . . . . . . **188** B2
Edgware HA8 . . . . **54** C5
Grangehill Pl, SE9
off Westmount Rd. . . . **156** C3
Grangehill Rd, SE9. . . . . . **156** C3
Grange Ho, Bark. IG11
off St. Margarets **117** G1
Grange La, SE21. . . . . **170** C2
Grange Mans, Epsom
KT17 . . . . **197** F7
Grangemill Rd, SE6 . . . . . **172** A3
Grangemill Way, SE6 . . . . **172** A2
★**Grange Mus of Comm**
History, NW10
off Neasden La **89** E4
GRANGE PARK, N21 . . . . . **43** H5
Grange Pk, W5 . . . . **125** H1
Grange Pk Av, N21. . . . . . . **43** H6
Grange Pk Pl, SW20. . . . . . **165** H7
Grange Pk Rd, E10. . . . . . . **96** B1
Thornton Heath CR7 . . . **188** A4
Grange Pl, NW6 . . . . **90** D7
Grange Rd, E10 . . . . **96** A1
E13. . . . . **115** F3
E17 . . . . **77** H5
N6 . . . . **74** A6
N17 . . . . **60** D6
N18 . . . . **60** D6
NW10 . . . . **89** H6
SE1 . . . . **28** E5
SE19 . . . . **188** A4
SE25 . . . . **188** A4
SW13. . . . . **147** G1
W4. . . . . **126** B5
W5. . . . . **125** G1
Chessington KT9. . . . . . **195** H4
Edgware HA8 . . . . **54** D6
Harrow HA1 . . . . **68** D6
Harrow (S.Har.) HA2 . . . . **86** A2
Ilford IG1. . . . . **99** E4
Kingston upon Thames
KT1 . . . . **181** H3
Orpington BR6 . . . . **207** F2
Southall UB1. . . . . **122** E2
Sutton SM2. . . . . **198** D7
Thornton Heath CR7 . . . **188** A4
West Molesey KT8 . . . . **179** H4
Grange St, N1. . . . . **112** A1
Grange Vale, Sutt. SM2 . . **199** E7
Grange Vw Rd, N20 . . . . . . **57** F1
Grange Wk, SE1 . . . . **28** E5
Grangeway, N12 . . . . **57** E4
NW6 *off Messina Av*. . . . **90** D7
Woodford Green IG8 . . . **63** J4
Grangeway, The, N21. . . . . **43** H6
Grangeway Gdns, Ilf. IG4. . **80** B5
Grangewood, Bex. DA5
off Hurst Rd. **177** F1
Grangewood Cl, Pnr.
HA5 . . . . **66** A5
Grangewood La, Beck.
BR3 . . . . **171** J6
Grangewood St, E6 . . . . . **115** J1
Grangewood Ter, SE25
off Grange Rd **188** A3
Grange Yd, SE1 . . . . **29** F6
Granham Gdns, N9 . . . . . . **60** C2
Granite St, SE18. . . . . **137** J5
Granleigh Rd, E11 . . . . **96** E2
Gransden Av, E8. . . . . **95** E7
Gransden Rd, W12
off Wendell Rd. **127** F2
Grantbridge St, N1. . . . . . . **11** H1
Grantchester Cl, Har. HA1 . **86** C3
Grant Cl, N14. . . . . **42** C7
Grantham Cen, The, SW9 **151** E2
Grantham Cl, Edg. HA8 . . . **53** H3
Grantham Gdns, Rom.
RM6. . . . . **83** F6
Grantham Grn, Borwd.
WD6 . . . . **38** C5
Grantham Pl, W1 . . . . **24** D2
Grantham Rd, E12 . . . . **98** D4
SW9. . . . . **151** E2
Grantham Rd, W4 . . . . . . **126** E7
Grantley Rd, Houns. TW4. **142** C2
Grantley St, E1 . . . . **113** G3
Grantock Rd, E17. . . . . **78** D1
Granton Rd, SW16. . . . . . **186** C1
Ilford IG3. . . . . **100** A1
Sidcup DA14 . . . . **176** C6
Grant Pl, Croy. CR0 . . . . . **202** C1
Grant Rd, SW11 . . . . **149** G4
Croydon CR0. . . . . **202** C1
Harrow HA3 . . . . **68** B3
Grants Cl, N17 . . . . **76** B2
NW7 . . . . **55** J7
Grant's Quay Wf, EC3. . . . . **20** C6
Grant St, E13 . . . . **115** G3
N1 . . . . **11** E1
Grantully Rd, W9 . . . . **6** A4
Grant Way, Islw. TW7 . . . . **124** D6
Granville Av, N9. . . . . **61** F3
Feltham TW13 . . . . **160** A2
Hounslow TW3 . . . . **143** G5
Granville Cl, Croy. CR0. . . **202** B2
Granville Ct, N1 . . . . **112** A1
Granville Gdns, SW16 . . . **187** F1
W5. . . . . **125** J1
Granville Gro, SE13 . . . . . **154** C3
Granville Ms, Sid. DA14 . . **176** A4
Granville Pk, SE13 . . . . . . **154** C3
Granville Pl, N12 (N.Finchley)
off High Rd **57** F7
SW6 *off Maxwell*
Rd. **128/129** E7
W1. . . . . **16** B4
Pinner HA5 . . . . **66** D3
Granville Rd, E17 . . . . **78** B6
E18 . . . . **79** H2
N4 . . . . **75** F6
N12 . . . . **57** E7
N13 *off Russell Rd* **59** F6
N22 . . . . **75** H1
NW2 . . . . **90** C2
NW6 . . . . **108** D2
SW18. . . . . **148** D7
SW19 *off Russell Rd* . . . **166** D7
Barnet EN5 . . . . **39** J4
Hayes UB3 . . . . **121** J4
Ilford IG1. . . . . **98** E1
Sidcup DA14 . . . . **176** A4
Welling DA16 . . . . **158** C3
Granville Sq, SE15 . . . . . . **132** B7
WC1. . . . . **10** D4
Granville St, WC1. . . . . **10** D4
Grape St, WC2 . . . . **18** A3
Graphite Sq, SE11 . . . . **34** C3
Grapsome Cl, Chess. KT9
off Nigel Fisher Way . . **195** F7
Grasdene Rd, SE18 . . . . . **138** A7
Grasgarth Cl, W3
off Creswick Rd **106** C7
Grasmere Av, SW15. . . . . **164** D4
SW19. . . . . **184** D3
W3. . . . . **106** C7
Hounslow TW3 . . . . **143** H6
Orpington BR6 . . . . **206** E3
Wembley HA9. . . . . **69** G7
Grasmere Cl, Loug. IG10 . . **48** C2
Grasmere Ct, N22
off Palmerston Rd. **59** F6
Grasmere Gdns, Har. HA3 . **68** D2
Ilford IG4. . . . . **80** C5
Orpington BR6 . . . . **206** E3
Grasmere Pt, SE15
off Ilderton Rd. **133** F7
Grasmere Rd, E13. . . . . . . **115** G2
N10 . . . . **74** B1
N17 . . . . **60** D6
SE25 . . . . **189** E6
SW16. . . . . **169** F5
Bexleyheath DA7 . . . . . **159** J1
Bromley BR1. . . . . **191** F1
Orpington BR6 . . . . **206** E3
Grasshaven Way, SE28. . . **137** J1
Grassington Cl, N11
off Ribblesdale Av. **58** A6
Grassington Rd, Sid.
DA14 . . . . **176** A4
Grassmount, SE23. . . . . . **171** E2
Grass Pk, N3 . . . . **72** C1
Grassway, Wall. SM6. . . . **200** C4
Grasvenor Av, Barn. EN5 . . **40** D6
Grately Way, SE15 . . . . **37** F7
Gratton Rd, W14. . . . . **128** B3
Gratton Ter, NW2 . . . . **90** A3
Graveley, Kings.T. KT1
off Willingham Way. . . **182** A2
Graveley Av, Borwd. WD6 . **38** C4
Gravel Hill, N3 . . . . **72** C2
Bexleyheath DA6 . . . . . **159** H5
Croydon CR0. . . . . **203** G6
Gravel Hill Cl, Bexh. DA6 . **159** H5
Gravel La, E1 . . . . **21** F3
Gravelly Ride, SW19 . . . . **165** H4
Gravel Pit La, SE9 . . . . . . **157** F5
Gravel Rd, Brom. BR2 . . . **206** B2
Twickenham TW2 . . . . . **162** B1
Gravelwood Cl, Chis.
BR7 . . . . **175** F3
Graveney Gro, SE20. . . . . **171** F7
Graveney Rd, SW17. . . . . **167** H4
Gravesend Rd, W12 . . . . . **107** G7
Gray Av, Dag. RM8 . . . . . . **101** F1
Grayham Cres, N.Mal.
KT3 . . . . **182** D4
Grayham Rd, N.Mal. KT3. **182** D4
Grayland Cl, Brom. BR1. . **192** A1
Grayling Cl, E16
off Cranberry La. . **114/115** E4
Grayling Rd, N16 . . . . **94** A2
Grayling Sq, E2 . . . . **13** J3
Grayscroft Rd, SW16 . . . . **168** D7
Grayshott Rd, SW11. . . . . **150** A2
★**Gray's Inn**, WC1. . . . . **18** D1
Gray's Inn Pl, WC1 . . . . **18** D2
Gray's Inn Rd, WC1 . . . . . . **10** C4
Gray's Inn Sq, WC1 . . . . . . **18** E1
Gray St, SE1. . . . . **27** F4
Grayswood Gdns, SW20
off Farnham Gdns. . . . **183** H2
Grayswood Pt, SW15
off Norley Vale **165** G1
Gray's Yd, W1 . . . . **16** C4
Graywood Ct, N12. . . . . **57** F7
Grazebrook Rd, N16. . . . . . **94** A2
Grazeley Cl, Bexh. DA6 . . **159** J5
Grazeley Ct, SE19
off Gipsy Hill. **170** B4
Great Acre Ct, SW4
off St. Alphonsus Rd. . **150** D4
Great Arthur Ho, EC1
off Fann St. **111** J4
Great Bell All, EC2 . . . . **20** B3
Great Benty, West Dr.
UB7. . . . . **120** B4
Great Brownings, SE21 . . **170** C4
Great Bushey Dr, N20 . . . . **57** E1
Great Cambridge Junct, N18
off North Circular Rd . . **60** A4
Great Cambridge Rd, N9 . . **60** B1
N17 . . . . **60** A5
N18 . . . . **60** A5
Enfield EN1 . . . . **44** D4
Great Castle St, W1 . . . . . . **17** E3
Great Cen Av, Ruis. HA4 . . **84** C5
Great Cen St, NW1 . . . . **15** J1
Great Cen Way, NW10 . . . . **88** E5
Wembley HA9. . . . . **88** C4
Great Chapel St, W1 . . . . . **17** H3
Great Chart St, SW11
off Wynter St. **149** F4
Great Chertsey Rd, W4. . . **146** C2
Feltham TW13 . . . . **161** G3
Great Ch La, W6. . . . . **128** A5
Great Coll St, SW1. . . . . . . **26** A5
Great Cross Av, SE10 . . . . **134** E7
Great Cumberland Ms,
W1. . . . . **15** J4
Great Cumberland Pl, W1 . . **15** J3
Great Dover St, SE1. . . . . . **28** A4
Greatdown Rd, W7. . . . . . **104** C4
Great Eastern Enterprise Cen,
E14 *off Millharbour*. . . **134** B2
Great Eastern Rd, E15 . . . . **96** D7
Great Eastern St, EC2 . . . . **12** D4
Great Eastern Wk, EC2. . . . **20** E2
Great Elms Rd, Brom.
BR2 . . . . **191** J4
Great Fld, NW9 . . . . **71** E1
Greatfield Av, E6. . . . . **116** C4
Greatfield Cl, N19
off Warrender Rd. **92** C4
SE4 . . . . **154** A4
Greatfields Rd, Bark. IG11 . **117** G1
Great Fleete Way, Bark. IG11
off Choats Rd. **118** C2
Great Galley Cl, Bark.
IG11 . . . . **118** B3
Great Gatton Cl, Croy.
CR0 . . . . **189** H7
Great George St, SW1. . . . **25** J4
Great Guildford St, SE1 . . . **27** J1
Greatham Wk, SW15 . . . . **165** G1
Great Harry Dr, SE9 . . . . . **174** D3
Great James St, WC1. . . . . . **10** C6
Great Marlborough St, W1. **17** F4
Great Maze Pond, SE1. . . . **28** C3
Great Newport St, WC2
off Cranbourn St **110** D7
Great New St, EC4. . . . . . . **19** F3

Great N Leisure Pk, N12 . . 57 G7
Great N Rd, N2. . . . . 73 H4
N6 . . . . 73 H4
Barnet (New Barn.) EN5 . 40 D5
Great N Way, NW4. . . . . . . 71 J2
Great Oaks, Chig. IG7 . . . . 65 F4
Greatorex St, E1 . . . . 21 H1
Great Ormond St, WC1 . . . 18 B1
Great Owl Rd, Chig. IG7 . . 61 D3
Great Percy St, WC1. . . . . 10 D3
Great Peter St, SW1. . . . . 25 H6
Great Portland St, W1 . . . . 17 E1
Great Pulteney St, W1 . . . . 17 G5
Great Queen St, WC2. . . . 18 B4
Great Russell St, WC1 . . . . 17 J3
Great St. Helens, EC3 . . . . 20 D3
Great St. Thomas Apostle,
EC4 . . . . 20 A5
Great Scotland Yd, SW1 . . 26 A2
Great Smith St, SW1. . . . . 25 J5
Great South-West Rd, Felt.
TW14. . . . . 141 F7
Hounslow TW4 . . . . 141 J4
Great Spilmans, SE22 . . . 152 B5
Great Strand, NW9 . . . . . . 71 F1
Great Suffolk St, SE1. . . . . 27 H2
Great Sutton St, EC1 . . . . . 11 H6
Great Swan All, EC2. . . . . . 20 B3
Great Thrift, Orp. BR5. . . . 193 F4
Great Titchfield St, W1 . . . . 17 F3
Great Twr St, EC3. . . . . 20 D5
Great Trinity La, EC4. . . . . . 20 A5
Great Turnstile, WC1. . . . . . 18 D2
Great Western Rd, W2 . . . 108 C5
W9. . . . . 108 C5
W11 . . . . 108 C5
Great W Rd, W4 . . . . 126 B5
W6. . . . . 127 F5
Brentford TW8. . . . . 126 B5
Hounslow TW5 . . . . 142 D2
Isleworth TW7 . . . . 124 B7
Great Wf Rd, E14
off Churchill Pl 134 B1
Great Winchester St, EC2 . 20 C3
Great Windmill St, W1 . . . 17 H5
Greatwood, Chis. BR7 . . . 174 D7
Great Yd, SE1. . . . . 28 E3
Greaves Cl, Bark. IG11
off Norfolk Rd. 99 H7
Greaves Pl, SW17. . . . . . . 167 H4
Grebe Av, Hayes UB4
off Cygnet Way 102 D6
Grebe Cl, E7
off Cormorant Rd 97 F5
E17 . . . . 61 H7
Barking IG11 . . . . 118 A4
Grebe Ct, Sutt. SM1. . . . . 198 C5
Grecian Cres, SE19. . . . . . 169 H6
Gredo Ho, Bark. IG11 . . . . 118 B3
Greek Ct, W1 . . . . 17 J4
★**Greek Orthodox Cath of the Divine Wisdom (St. Sophia)**, W2 . . . 14 A5
Greek St, W1 . . . . 17 J4
Greek Yd, WC2 . . . . 18 A5
Green, The, E4 . . . . 62 C1
E11. . . . . 79 H6
E15 . . . . 97 E6
N9 . . . . 60 D2
N14 . . . . 58 D3
N21 . . . . 43 G7
SW14. . . . . 146 C3
SW19. . . . . 166 A5
W3. . . . . 107 E6
W5 *off High St* 125 G1
Bexleyheath DA7 . . . . . 159 G1
Bromley BR1
off Downham Way . . . 173 G3
Bromley (Hayes) BR2 . . 191 G7
Carshalton SM5 . . . . . . 200 A4
Esher (Clay.) KT10. . . . . 194 C6
Green, The, Feltham
TW13. . . . . 160 B2
Hounslow TW5
off Heston Rd 123 G6
Morden SM4. . . . . 184 B4
New Malden KT3 . . . . . 182 C3
Orpington (St.P.Cray) BR5
off The Avenue 176 B7
Richmond TW9 . . . . 145 G5
Sidcup DA14 . . . . 176 A4
Southall UB2. . . . . 123 E3
Sutton SM1 . . . . 198 E3
Twickenham TW2 . . . . . 162 B1
Welling DA16 . . . . 157 H4
Wembley HA0. . . . . 86 D2
West Drayton UB7 . . . . 120 A3
Woodford Green IG8 . . . 63 G5
Greenacre Cl, Nthlt. UB5 . . 85 F5
Greenacre Gdns, E17 . . . . . 78 C4
Greenacre Pl, Wall. (Hackbr.)
SM6 *off Park Rd* 200 B2
Greenacres, N3 . . . . 72 B2
SE9 . . . . 156 D6
Bushey (Bushey Hth)
WD23 . . . . 52 A2
Green Acres, Croy. CR0 . . 202 C3
Greenacres Cl, Orp. BR6 . 207 F4
Greenacres Dr, Stan. HA7 . 52 E7
Greenacre Sq, SE16
off Fishermans Dr. . . . 133 G2
Greenacre Wk, N14 . . . . . . 58 E3
Green Arbour Ct, EC1 . . . . 19 G3
Green Av, NW7. . . . . 54 D4
W13. . . . . 125 E3
Greenaway Av, N18 . . . . . . 61 G6
Greenaway Gdns, NW3 . . . 90 E4
Green Bk, E1 . . . . 132 E1
N12 . . . . 57 E4
Greenbank Av, Wem. HA0 . 86 D5
Greenbank Cl, E4. . . . . 62 C2
Greenbank Cres, NW4 . . . . 72 B4
Greenbay Rd, SE7 . . . . . . 136 A7
Greenberry St, NW8 . . . . . . 7 G2
Greenbrook Av, Barn. EN4. 41 F1
Green Cl, NW9. . . . . 70 C6
NW11. . . . . 73 F7
Bromley BR2. . . . . 190 E3
Carshalton SM5 . . . . . . 199 J2
Feltham TW13 . . . . 160 E5
Greencoat Pl, SW1. . . . . . . 33 G1
Greencoat Row, SW1 . . . . 25 G6
Greencourt Av, Croy. CR0 . 203 E2
Edgware HA8 . . . . 70 B1
Greencourt Gdns, Croy.
CR0 . . . . 203 E1
Greencourt Rd, Orp. BR5 . 193 G5
Greencrest Pl, NW2
off Dollis Hill La 89 G3
Green Cft, Edg. HA8
off Deans La 54 C5
Greencroft Av, Ruis. HA4 . . 84 C2
Greencroft Cl, E6
off Neatscourt Rd 116 B5
Greencroft Gdns, NW6 . . . 91 E7
Enfield EN1 . . . . 44 B3
Greencroft Rd, Houns.
TW5. . . . . 143 F1
Green Dale, SE5. . . . . 152 A4
SE22 . . . . 152 B5
Green Dale Cl, SE22
off Green Dale. 152 B5
Green Dragon Ct, SE1 . . . . 28 B1
Green Dragon La, N21 . . . . 43 H6
Brentford TW8. . . . . 125 H5
Green Dragon Yd, E1 . . . . . 21 H2
Green Dr, Sthl. UB1 . . . . . 123 G1
Green End, N21 . . . . 59 H2
Chessington KT9. . . . . . 195 H4
Greenend Rd, W4. . . . . . . 126 E2
Greenfarm Cl, Orp. BR6 . . 207 J5
Greenfell Mans, SE8
off Glaisher St. 134 B6
Greenfield Av, Surb. KT5 . 182 B7
Watford WD19. . . . . 50 D2
Greenfield Dr, N2. . . . . 73 J4
Greenfield Gdns, NW2. . . . 90 B2
Dagenham RM9 . . . . . . 118 D1
Orpington BR5 . . . . 193 G7
Greenfield Rd, E1. . . . . 21 J2
N15 . . . . 76 B5
Dagenham RM9 . . . . . . 118 C1
Greenfields, Loug. IG10 . . . 48 D4
Greenfields Cl, Loug.
IG10. . . . . 48 D4
Greenfield Way, Har. HA2 . 67 H3
GREENFORD, UB6 . . . . . . 103 H3
Greenford Av, W7. . . . . . . 104 B4
Southall UB1. . . . . 103 F7
Greenford Gdns, Grnf.
UB6 . . . . 103 H3
Greenford Rd, Grnf. UB6 . 103 J5
Harrow HA1 . . . . 86 B5
Southall UB1. . . . . 123 J1
Sutton SM1. . . . . 198 E4
Green Gdns, Orp. BR6 . . . 207 F5
Greengate, Grnf. UB6 . . . . 86 E6
Greengate St, E13 . . . . . . 115 H2
Greenhalgh Wk, N2 . . . . . . 73 F4
Greenham Cl, SE1 . . . . 27 E4
Greenham Cres, E4 . . . . . . 61 J6
Greenham Rd, N10. . . . . . . 74 A2
Greenhaven Dr, SE28. . . . 118 B6
Greenheys Dr, E18. . . . . . . 79 F3
Greenhill, NW3
off Hampstead High St. 91 G4
SE18 . . . . 136 C5
Green Hill, Buck.H. IG9 . . . 63 J1
Greenhill, Sutt. SM1. . . . . 199 F2
Wembley HA9. . . . . 88 B2
Greenhill Gdns, Nthlt.
UB5 . . . . 103 F2
Greenhill Gro, E12 . . . . 98 B4
Greenhill Pk, NW10 . . . . . 106 E1
Barnet EN5 . . . . 40 E5
Greenhill Rd, NW10 . . . . . 106 E1
Harrow HA1 . . . . 68 B6
Greenhill's Rents, EC1 . . . . 19 H1
Greenhills Ter, N1
off Baxter Rd. 94 A6
Greenhill Ter, SE18. . . . . . 136 C5
Northolt UB5. . . . . 103 F2
Greenhill Way, Har. HA1. . . 68 B6
Wembley HA9. . . . . 88 B2
Greenhithe Cl, Sid. DA15. 157 H7
Greenholm Rd, SE9 . . . . . 156 E5
Green Hundred Rd, SE15. . 37 J6
Greenhurst Rd, SE27 . . . . 169 G5
Greening St, SE2 . . . . 138 C4
Greenland Cres, Sthl.
UB2. . . . . 122 C3
Greenland Ms, SE8
off Trundleys Rd 133 G5
Greenland Pl, NW1
off Greenland Rd. 110 B1
Greenland Quay, SE16. . . 133 G4
Greenland Rd, NW1 . . . . . 110 C1
Barnet EN5 . . . . 39 J6
Greenland St, NW1
off Camden High St. . . 110 B1
Green La, E4. . . . . 46 E3
NW4 . . . . 72 A5
SE9 . . . . 174 D2
SE20 . . . . 171 G7
SW16. . . . . 169 F7
W7. . . . . 124 B2
Chigwell IG7 . . . . 65 G2
Chislehurst BR7. . . . . . . 174 E4
Dagenham RM8 . . . . . . 100 A1
Edgware HA8 . . . . 54 A5
Feltham TW13 . . . . 160 E5
Harrow HA1 . . . . 86 B3
Hounslow TW4 . . . . 142 B3
Ilford IG1, IG3 . . . . 99 F2
Morden SM4. . . . . 184 E6
New Malden KT3 . . . . . 182 C5
Stanmore HA7 . . . . 52 E4
Thornton Heath CR7 . . . 187 G1
Watford WD19. . . . . 50 C1
West Molesey KT8 . . . . 179 H5
Worcester Park KT4. . . . 197 G1
Green La Gdns, Th.Hth.
CR7 . . . . 187 J2
Green Las, N4 . . . . 93 J1
N8 . . . . 75 H3
N13 . . . . 60 F6
N15 . . . . 75 H3
N16 . . . . 93 J3
N21 . . . . 59 H1
Greenlaw Gdns, N.Mal.
KT3 . . . . 183 F7
Greenlawn La, Brent. TW8
off Ealing Rd. 125 G4
Green Lawns, Ruis. HA4 . . 84 C1
Greenlaw St, SE18. . . . . . 136 D3
Green Leaf Av, Wall.
SM6. . . . . 200 D4
Greenleaf Cl, SW2
off Tulse Hill. 151 G7
Greenleafe Dr, Ilf. IG6 . . . . 81 E4
Greenleaf Rd, E6
off Redclyffe Rd. 115 J1
E17 . . . . 77 J3
Greenlea Pk, SW19 . . . . . 185 G1
Green Man Gdns, W13. . . 104 D7
Green Man La, W13 . . . . . 124 D1
Feltham TW14 . . . . 142 A4
Green Man Pas, W13 . . . . 104 D7
Green Man Roundabout,
E11. . . . . 79 F7
Greenman St, N1. . . . . 93 J7
Greenmead Cl, SE25 . . . . 188 D5
Green Moor Link, N21 . . . . 43 H7
Greenmoor Rd, Enf. EN3 . . 45 F2
Greenoak Pl, Barn. EN4 . . . 41 J2
Greenoak Way, SW19. . . . 166 A4
Greenock Rd, SW16. . . . . 186 D1
W3. . . . . 126 B3
★**Green Park**, SW1. . . . . . . 24 E3
Greenpark Ct, Wem. HA0. . 87 F7
Green Pk Way, Grnf. UB6. 104 B1
Green Pt, E15. . . . . 97 E6
Green Pond Cl, E17 . . . . . . 77 J3
Green Pond Rd, E17. . . . . . 77 H3
Green Ride, Loug. IG10 . . . 47 G5
Green Rd, N14 . . . . 42 B6
N20. . . . . 57 F3
Greenroof Way, SE10 . . . . 135 F3
Greens Cl, The, Loug.
IG10. . . . . 48 D2
Green's Ct, W1 . . . . 17 H5
Green's End, SE18 . . . . . . 136 E4
Greenshank Cl, E17
off Banbury Rd 61 H7
Greenshields Ind Est, E16. 135 H1
Greenside, Bex. DA5 . . . . 177 E1
Dagenham RM8 . . . . . . 100 C1
Greenside Cl, N20 . . . . 57 G2
SE6 . . . . 172 D2
Greenside Rd, W12. . . . . . 127 G3
Croydon CR0. . . . . 187 G7
Greenslade Rd, Bark. IG11 . 99 G7
Green Slip Rd, Barn. EN5 . . 40 C2
Greenstead Av, Wdf.Grn.
IG8. . . . . 63 J7
Greenstead Cl, Wdf.Grn. IG8
off Greenstead Gdns . . 63 J6
Greenstead Gdns, SW15 . 147 G5
Woodford Green IG8 . . . 63 J6
Greensted Rd, Loug. IG10 . 48 B7
Greenstone Ms, E11 . . . . . . 79 G6
Green St, E7. . . . . 97 H6
E13. . . . . 115 J1
W1. . . . . 16 A5
Enfield EN3 . . . . 45 F2
Sunbury-on-Thames
TW16. . . . . 178 A1
GREEN STREET GREEN,
Orp. BR6 . . . . 207 H6
Green Ter, EC1 . . . . 11 F4
Green Vale, W5. . . . . 105 J6
Bexleyheath DA6 . . . . . 158 D5
Greenvale Rd, SE9. . . . . . 156 C4
Green Verges, Stan. HA7 . . 53 G7
Green Vw, Chess. KT9 . . . 195 J7
Greenview Av, Beck. BR3. 189 H6
Croydon CR0. . . . . 189 H6
Greenview Cl, W3. . . . . . . 126 E1
Green Wk, NW4 . . . . 72 A5
SE1 . . . . 28 D6
Buckhurst Hill IG9. . . . . . 48 B7
Hampton TW12
off Orpwood Cl 101 F6
Southall UB2. . . . . 123 G5
Woodford Green IG8 . . . 64 B6
Green Wk, The, E4 . . . . 62 C1
Greenway, N14 . . . . 58 E2
N20 . . . . 56 D2
Green Way, SE9 . . . . 156 A5
Greenway, SW20 . . . . 183 J4
Green Way, Brom. BR2. . . 192 B6
Greenway, Chis. BR7 . . . . 174 D5
Dagenham RM8 . . . . . . 100 C2
Harrow HA3 . . . . 69 H5
Hayes UB4 . . . . 102 B4
Pinner HA5 . . . . 66 B2
Green Way, Sun. TW16. . . 178 A4
Greenway, Wall. SM6. . . . 200 C4
Woodford Green IG8 . . . 63 J5
Greenway, The, NW9 . . . . . 70 D2
Harrow HA3 . . . . 68 B1
Hounslow TW4 . . . . 143 F4
Pinner HA5 . . . . 67 F6
Greenway Av, E17 . . . . 78 D4
Greenway Cl, N4 . . . . 93 J2
N11 . . . . 58 A6
N15 *off Copperfield Dr* . . 76 C4
N20 . . . . 56 D2
NW9 . . . . 70 D2
Greenway Gdns, NW9 . . . . 70 D2
Croydon CR0. . . . . 203 J3
Greenford UB6 . . . . 103 G3
Harrow HA3 . . . . 68 B2
Greenways, Beck. BR3 . . . 190 A2
Esher KT10 . . . . 194 B4
Greenways, The, Twick. TW1
off South Western Rd . 144 D6
Greenwell St, W1. . . . . 9 E6
GREENWICH, SE10 . . . . . 134 D6
Greenwich Ch St, SE10 . . 134 C6
Greenwich Cres, E6
off Swan App. 116 B5
Greenwich Foot Tunnel,
E14 . . . . 134 C5
SE10 . . . . 134 C5
Greenwich High Rd,
SE10 . . . . 154 B1
Greenwich Ind Est, SE7. . 135 H4
Greenwich Mkt, SE10
off King William Wk . . 134 C6
★**Greenwich Park**, SE10. . 134 D7
Greenwich Pk St, SE10 . . 134 D5
★**Greenwich Pier**, SE10 . . 134 C6
Greenwich Quay, SE8 . . . 134 B6
Greenwich Shop Pk, SE7
off Bugsby's Way. 135 H4

Greenwich S St, SE10 ... **154** B1
Greenwich Vw Pl, E14 ... **134** B3
Greenwood Av, Dag. RM10 ... **101** H4
Enfield EN3 ... **45** H2
Greenwood Cl, Mord. SM4 ... **184** B4
Orpington BR5 ... **193** H6
Sidcup DA15 *off Hurst Rd* ... **176** A2
Thames Ditton KT7 ... **194** D1
Greenwood Ct, SW1 ... **33** F3
Greenwood Dr, E4 *off Avril Way* ... **62** C5
Greenwood Gdns, N13 ... **59** H3
Ilford IG6 ... **65** F7
Greenwood La, Hmptn. (Hmptn H.) TW12 ... **161** H5
Greenwood Pk, Kings.T. KT2 ... **165** E7
Greenwood Pl, NW5 *off Highgate Rd* ... **92** B5
Greenwood Rd, E8 ... **94** D6
E13 *off Valetta Gro* ... **115** F2
Croydon CR0 ... **187** H7
Isleworth TW7 ... **144** B3
Mitcham CR4 ... **186** D3
Thames Ditton KT7 ... **194** D1
Greenwoods, The, Har. (S.Har.) HA2 ... **85** J2
Greenwood Ter, NW10 ... **106** D1
Green Wrythe Cres, Cars. SM5 ... **199** H1
Green Wrythe La, Cars. SM5 ... **185** G6
Greer Rd, Har. HA3 ... **67** J1
Greet St, SE1 ... **27** F2
Greg Cl, E10 ... **78** C6
Gregor Ms, SE3 ... **135** G7
Gregory Cres, SE9 ... **156** A7
Gregory Pl, W8 ... **22** A3
Gregory Rd, Rom. RM6 ... **82** D4
Southall UB2 ... **123** G3
Gregson Cl, Borwd. WD6 ... **38** C1
Greig Cl, N8 ... **74** E5
Greig Ter, SE17 ... **35** H5
Grenaby Av, Croy. CR0 ... **188** A7
Grenaby Rd, Croy. CR0 ... **188** A7
Grenada Rd, SE7 ... **135** J7
Grenade St, E14 ... **113** J7
Grenadier St, E16 ... **136** D1
Grena Gdns, Rich. TW9 ... **145** J4
Grenard Cl, SE15 *off Lisford St* ... **152** C1
Grena Rd, Rich. TW9 ... **145** J4
Grendon Gdns, Wem. HA9 ... **88** A2
Grendon St, NW8 ... **7** G5
Grenfell Cl, Borwd. WD6 ... **38** C1
Grenfell Gdns, Har. HA3 ... **69** H7
Grenfell Rd, W11 ... **108** A7
Mitcham CR4 ... **167** J6
Grenfell Twr, W11 ... **108** A7
Grenfell Wk, W11 ... **108** A7
Grennell Cl, Sutt. SM1 ... **199** G2
Grennell Rd, Sutt. SM1 ... **199** F2
Grenoble Gdns, N13 ... **59** G6
Grenville Cl, N3 ... **72** C1
Surbiton KT5 ... **196** C1
Grenville Ct, SE19 *off Lymer Av* ... **170** C5
Grenville Gdns, Wdf.Grn. IG8 ... **79** J1
Grenville Ms, N19 *off Grenville Rd* ... **92** E1
SW7 ... **30** D1
Hampton TW12 ... **161** H5
Grenville Pl, NW7 ... **54** D5
SW7 ... **22** C6
Grenville Rd, N19 ... **92** E1
Grenville St, WC1 ... **10** B6
Gresham Av, N20 ... **57** J4
Gresham Cl, Bex. DA5 ... **159** E6
Enfield EN2 ... **43** J3
Gresham Dr, Rom. RM6 ... **82** B5
Gresham Gdns, NW11 ... **90** B1
Gresham Pl, N19 ... **92** D2
Gresham Rd, E6 ... **116** C2
E16 ... **115** H6
NW10 ... **88** D5
SE25 ... **188** D4
SW9 ... **151** G3
Beckenham BR3 ... **189** H2
Edgware HA8 ... **53** J6
Hampton TW12 ... **161** G6
Hounslow TW3 ... **143** J1
Gresham St, EC2 ... **19** J3
Gresham Way, SW19 ... **166** D3
Gresley Cl, E17 ... **77** H6
N15 *off Clinton Rd* ... **76** A4
Gresley Rd, N19 ... **92** C1
Gressenhall Rd, SW18 ... **148** C6
Gresse St, W1 ... **17** H2
Gresswell Cl, Sid. DA14 ... **176** A3
Greswell St, SW6 ... **148** A1
Gretton Rd, N17 ... **60** B7
Greville Cl, Twick. TW1 ... **144** E7
Greville Hall, NW6 ... **6** B1
Greville Ms, NW6 *off Greville Rd* ... **108/109** E2
Greville Pl, NW6 ... **6** B1
Greville Rd, E17 ... **78** C4
NW6 ... **6** A1
Richmond TW10 ... **145** J6
Greville St, EC1 ... **19** F2
Grey Cl, NW11 ... **73** F6
Greycoat Pl, SW1 ... **25** H6
Greycoat St, SW1 ... **25** H6
Greycot Rd, Beck. BR3 ... **172** A5
Grey Eagle St, E1 ... **21** F1
Greyfell Cl, Stan. HA7 *off Coverdale Cl* ... **52/53** E5
Greyfriars Pas, EC1 ... **19** H3
Greyhound Hill, NW4 ... **71** G3
Greyhound La, SW16 ... **168** D6
Greyhound Rd, N17 ... **76** B3
NW10 ... **107** H3
W6 ... **128** A6
W14 ... **128** B6
Sutton SM1 ... **199** F5
Greyhound Ter, SW16 ... **186** C1
Greys Pk Cl, Kes. BR2 ... **205** J5
Greystead Rd, SE23 ... **153** F7
Greystoke Av, Pnr. HA5 ... **67** G3
Greystoke Gdns, W5 ... **105** H4
Enfield EN2 ... **42** D4
Greystoke Pk Ter, W5 ... **105** G3
Greystoke Pl, EC4 ... **19** E3
Greystone Gdns, Har. HA3 ... **69** F6
Ilford IG6 ... **81** F2
Greystone Path, E11 *off Grove Rd* ... **79** F7
Greyswood Av, N18 ... **61** G6
Greyswood St, SW16 ... **168** B6
Grierson Rd, SE23 ... **153** G7
Griffin Cen, The, Felt. TW14 ... **142** B5
Griffin Cl, NW10 ... **89** H5
Griffin Manor Way, SE28 ... **137** G3
Griffin Rd, N17 ... **76** B2
SE18 ... **137** G5
Griffins Cl, N21 ... **44** A7
Griffin Way, Sun. TW16 ... **178** A2
Griffith Cl, Dag. RM8 *off Gibson Rd* ... **100** C1
Griffiths Cl, Wor.Pk. KT4 ... **197** H2
Griffiths Rd, SW19 ... **166** D7
Griggs App, Ilf. IG1 ... **99** F2
Griggs Pl, SE1 ... **28** E6
Griggs Rd, E10 ... **78** C6
Grilse Cl, N9 ... **61** E4
Grimsby Gro, E16 ... **137** E1
Grimsby St, E2 ... **13** G6
Grimsdyke Cres, Barn. EN5 ... **39** J3
Grimsdyke Rd, Pnr. HA5 ... **51** E7
Grimsel Path, SE5 ... **35** H7
Grimshaw Cl, N6 ... **74** A7
Grimston Rd, SW6 ... **148** C2
Grimwade Av, Croy. CR0 ... **202** D3
Grimwade Cl, SE15 ... **153** F3
Grimwood Rd, Twick. TW1 ... **144** C7
Grindall Cl, Croy. CR0 *off Hillside Rd* ... **201** H4
Grindal St, SE1 ... **26** E4
Grindleford Av, N11 ... **58** A2
Grindley Gdns, Croy. CR0 ... **188** C6
Grinling Pl, SE8 ... **134** A6
Grinstead Rd, SE8 ... **133** H5
Grittleton Av, Wem. HA9 ... **88** B6
Grittleton Rd, W9 ... **108** D4
Grizedale Ter, SE23 ... **171** E2
Grocer's Hall Ct, EC2 ... **20** B4
Grogan Cl, Hmptn. TW12 ... **161** F6
Groombridge Cl, Well. DA16 ... **158** A5
Groombridge Rd, E9 ... **95** G7
Groom Cl, Brom. BR2 ... **191** H4
Groom Cres, SW18 ... **149** G7
Groomfield Cl, SW17 ... **168** A4
Groom Pl, SW1 ... **24** C5
Grooms Dr, Pnr. HA5 ... **66** A5
Grosmont Rd, SE18 ... **137** J5
Grosse Way, SW15 ... **147** H6
Grosvenor Av, N5 ... **93** J5
SW14 ... **146** E3
Grosvenor Av, Cars. SM5 ... **199** J6
Harrow HA2 ... **67** H6
Richmond TW10 *off Grosvenor Rd* ... **145** H5
Grosvenor Cl, Loug. IG10 ... **48** E1
Grosvenor Cotts, SW1 ... **32** B1
Grosvenor Ct, N14 ... **42** C7
NW6 ... **108** A1
Grosvenor Cres, NW9 ... **70** A4
SW1 ... **24** C4
Grosvenor Cres Ms, SW1 ... **24** B4
Grosvenor Dr, Loug. IG10 ... **49** E1
Grosvenor Est, SW1 ... **33** J1
Grosvenor Gdns, E6 ... **116** A3
N10 ... **74** C3
N14 ... **42** D5
NW2 ... **89** J5
NW11 ... **72** C6
SW1 ... **24** D5
SW14 ... **146** E3
Kingston upon Thames KT2 ... **163** G6
Wallington SM6 ... **200** C7
Woodford Green IG8 ... **63** G6
Grosvenor Gdns Ms E, SW1 ... **24** E5
Grosvenor Gdns Ms N, SW1 ... **24** D6
Grosvenor Gdns Ms S, SW1 ... **24** E6
Grosvenor Gate, W1 ... **16** A6
Grosvenor Hill, SW19 ... **166** B6
W1 ... **16** D5
Grosvenor Pk, SE5 ... **35** J6
Grosvenor Pk Rd, E17 ... **78** A5
Grosvenor Path, Loug. IG10 ... **49** E1
Grosvenor Pl, SW1 ... **24** C4
Grosvenor Ri E, E17 ... **78** B5
Grosvenor Rd, E6 ... **116** A1
E7 ... **97** H6
E10 ... **96** C1
E11 ... **79** G5
N3 ... **56** C7
N9 ... **60** E1
N10 ... **74** B1
SE25 ... **188** D4
SW1 ... **32** D5
W4 ... **126** B5
W7 ... **124** D1
Belvedere DA17 ... **139** G6
Bexleyheath DA6 ... **158** D5
Borehamwood WD6 ... **38** A3
Brentford TW8 ... **125** G6
Dagenham RM8 ... **101** F1
Hounslow TW3 ... **143** F3
Ilford IG1 ... **99** F3
Orpington BR5 ... **193** H6
Richmond TW10 ... **145** H5
Southall UB2 ... **123** F3
Twickenham TW1 ... **144** D7
Wallington SM6 ... **200** B6
West Wickham BR4 ... **204** B1
Grosvenor Sq, W1 ... **16** C5
Grosvenor St, W1 ... **16** D5
Grosvenor Ter, SE5 ... **35** H7
Grosvenor Way, E5 ... **95** F2
Grosvenor Wf Rd, E14 ... **134** D4
Grote's Bldgs, SE3 ... **155** E2
Grote's Pl, SE3 ... **154** E2
Groton Rd, SW18 ... **167** E2
Grotto Pas, W1 ... **16** C1
Grotto Rd, Twick. TW1 ... **162** C2
Grove, The, E15 ... **96** E6
N3 ... **72** D1
N4 ... **75** F7
N6 ... **92** A1
N8 ... **74** D5
N13 ... **59** G5
N14 ... **42** C5
NW9 ... **70** D5
NW11 ... **72** B7
W5 ... **125** G1
Bexleyheath DA6 ... **158** D4
Edgware HA8 ... **54** B4
Enfield EN2 ... **43** G2
Greenford UB6 ... **103** J6
Isleworth TW7 ... **144** B1
Sidcup DA14 ... **177** E4
Stanmore HA7 ... **52** D2
Teddington TW11 ... **162** D4
Twickenham TW1 *off Bridge Rd* ... **144/145** E6
Walton-on-Thames KT12 ... **178** B7
West Wickham BR4 ... **204** B3
Grove Av, N3 ... **56** D7
N10 ... **74** C2
W7 ... **104** B6
Grove Av, Pnr. HA5 ... **67** E4
Sutton SM1 ... **198** D6
Twickenham TW1 ... **162** C1
Grove Bk, Wat. WD19 ... **50** D1
Grovebury Rd, SE2 ... **138** B2
Grove Cl, N14 *off Avenue Rd* ... **42** B7
SE23 ... **171** G1
Bromley BR2 ... **205** G2
Feltham TW13 ... **160** E4
Kingston upon Thames KT1 ... **181** J4
Grove Cotts, SW3 ... **31** H5
Grove Ct, SE3 ... **155** G1
Barnet EN5 *off High St* ... **40** C3
East Molesey KT8 *off Walton Rd* ... **180** A5
Grove Cres, E18 ... **79** F2
NW9 ... **70** C4
Feltham TW13 ... **160** E4
Kingston upon Thames KT1 ... **181** H3
Walton-on-Thames KT12 ... **178** B7
Grove Cres Rd, E15 ... **96** D6
Grovedale Rd, N19 ... **92** D2
Grove End, E18 *off Grove Hill* ... **79** F2
NW5 *off Chetwynd Rd* ... **92** B4
Grove End Gdns, NW8 *off Grove End Rd* ... **109** G2
Grove End La, Esher KT10 ... **194** A1
Grove End Rd, NW8 ... **6** E2
Grove Fm Ct, Mitch. CR4 *off Brookfields Av* ... **185** J4
Grove Footpath, Surb. KT5 ... **181** H4
Grove Gdns, NW4 ... **71** G4
NW8 ... **7** H4
Dagenham RM10 ... **101** J3
Enfield EN3 ... **45** G1
Teddington TW11 ... **162** D4
Grove Grn Rd, E11 ... **96** C3
Grove Hall Ct, NW8 ... **6** D3
Grove Hill, E18 ... **79** F2
Harrow HA1 ... **68** B7
Grove Hill Rd, SE5 ... **152** B3
Harrow HA1 ... **68** B7
Grove Ho Rd, N8 ... **74** E4
Groveland Av, SW16 ... **169** F7
Groveland Ct, EC4 ... **20** A4
Groveland Rd, Beck. BR3 ... **189** J3
Grovelands, W.Mol. KT8 ... **179** G4
Grovelands Cl, SE5 ... **152** B2
Harrow HA2 ... **85** H3
Grovelands Ct, N14 ... **42** D7
Grovelands Rd, N13 ... **59** F4
N15 ... **76** D6
Orpington BR5 ... **176** A7
Groveland Way, N.Mal. KT3 ... **182** C5
Grove La, SE5 ... **152** A1
Chigwell IG7 ... **65** J3
Kingston upon Thames KT1 ... **181** H4
Grove La Ter, SE5 *off Grove La* ... **152** B3
Grove Mkt Pl, SE9 ... **156** C6
Grove Ms, W6 ... **127** J3
W11 *off Portobello Rd* ... **108** C6
Grove Mill Pl, Cars. SM5 ... **200** A3
GROVE PARK, SE12 ... **173** G2
GROVE PARK, W4 ... **126** B7
Grove Pk, E11 ... **79** H6
NW9 ... **70** C4
Grove Pk, SE5 ... **152** B2
Grove Pk Av, E4 ... **62** B7
Grove Pk Br, W4 ... **126** C7
Grove Pk Gdns, W4 ... **126** B6
Grove Pk Ms, W4 ... **126** C7
Grove Pk Rd, N15 ... **76** B4
SE9 ... **173** J3
W4 ... **126** B7
Grove Pk Ter, W4 ... **126** B6
Grove Pas, E2 ... **113** E2
Teddington TW11 ... **162** D5
Grove Pl, NW3 *off Christchurch Hill* ... **91** G4
SW12 *off Cathles Rd* ... **150** B6
W3 ... **126** C1
W5 *off The Grove* ... **125** G1
Barking IG11 *off Clockhouse Av* ... **117** F1
Grove Rd, E3 ... **113** G1
E4 ... **62** B4
E11 ... **79** F7
E17 ... **78** B6
E18 ... **79** F2

Grove Rd, N11 . . . . 58 B5
N12 . . . . 57 G5
N15 . . . . 76 B5
NW2 . . . . 89 J6
SW13 . . . . 147 F2
SW19 . . . . 167 F7
W3 . . . . 126 C1
W5 . . . . 105 G7
Barnet EN4 . . . . 41 H3
Belvedere DA17 . . . . . . 139 F6
Bexleyheath DA7 . . . . . 159 J4
Borehamwood WD6 . . . . 38 A1
Brentford TW8 . . . . 125 F5
East Molesey KT8 . . . . . 180 A4
Edgware HA8 . . . . 54 A6
Hounslow TW3 . . . . 143 H4
Isleworth TW7 . . . . 144 B1
Mitcham CR4 . . . . 186 B2
Pinner HA5 . . . . 67 F5
Richmond TW10 . . . . . . 145 J6
Romford RM6 . . . . 82 B7
Surbiton KT6 . . . . 181 G5
Sutton SM1 . . . . 199 E6
Thornton Heath CR7 . . . 187 G4
Twickenham TW2 . . . . . 162 A3
Groveside Cl, W3 . . . . 106 A6
Carshalton SM5 . . . . . . 199 H2
Groveside Rd, E4 . . . . 62 E2
Grovestile Waye, Felt. TW14 . . . . 141 G7
Grove St, N18 . . . . 60 C6
SE8 . . . . 133 J4
Grove Ter, NW5 . . . . 92 B3
Teddington TW11 . . . . . . 162 D4
Grove Ter Ms, NW5
off Grove Ter 92 B3
Grove Vale, SE22 . . . . 152 B4
Chislehurst BR7 . . . . 174 D6
Grove Vil, E14 . . . . 114 B7
Groveway, SW9 . . . . 151 F1
Dagenham RM8 . . . . . . 100 D4
Grove Way, Esher KT10 . . 179 J7
Wembley HA9 . . . . 88 B5
Grovewood, Rich. TW9
off Sandycombe Rd . . 146 A1
Grovewood Pl, Wdf.Grn. IG8 . . . . 64 C6
Grummant Rd, SE15 . . . . 152 C1
Grundy St, E14 . . . . 114 B6
Gruneisen Rd, N3 . . . . 56 E7
★**Guards Mus**, SW1 . . . . . . 25 G4
Gubyon Av, SE24 . . . . 151 H5
Guerin Sq, E3 . . . . 113 J3
Guernsey Cl, Houns. TW5 . . . . 143 G1
Guernsey Gro, SE24 . . . . . 151 J7
Guernsey Rd, E11 . . . . 96 D1
Guibal Rd, SE12 . . . . 155 H7
Guildersfield Rd, SW16 . . 168 E7
Guildford Gro, SE10 . . . . . 154 B1
Guildford Rd, E6 . . . . 116 B6
E17 . . . . 78 C1
SW8 . . . . 151 E1
Croydon CR0 . . . . 188 A6
Ilford IG3 . . . . 99 H2
Guildford Way, Wall. SM6 . . . . 201 E5
★**Guildhall, The**, EC2 . . . . . 20 B3
★**Guildhall Art Gall**, Guildhall Lib, EC2 . . . . . 20 A3
Guildhall Bldgs, EC2
off Basinghall St 112 A6
Guildhall Yd, EC2 . . . . 20 B3
Guildhouse St, SW1 . . . . . 33 F1
Guildown Av, N12 . . . . 56 E4
Guild Rd, SE7 . . . . 136 A5
Guildsway, E17 . . . . 77 J1
Guilford Av, Surb. KT5 . . . 181 J5
Guilford Pl, WC1 . . . . 10 C6
Guilford St, WC1 . . . . 10 B6
Guilford Vil, Surb. KT5
off Alpha Rd 181 J6
Guilsborough Cl, NW10 . . . 88 E7
Guinness Cl, E9 . . . . 95 H7
Hayes UB3 . . . . 121 G3
Guinness Sq, SE1 . . . . 36 D1
Guinness Trust Bldgs, SE1
off Snowsfields 132 B2
SE11 . . . . 35 H3
SW3 . . . . 31 J2
SW9 . . . . 151 H4
Guinness Trust Est, N16
off Holmleigh Rd 94 B1
Guion Rd, SW6 . . . . 148 C2
Gulland Wk, N1
off Clephane Rd 93 J6
Gull Cl, Wall. SM6 . . . . . . 200 E7
Gulliver Cl, Nthlt. UB5 . . . 103 F1
Gulliver Rd, Sid. DA15 . . . 175 H2
Gulliver St, SE16 . . . . 133 J3
Gulston Wk, SW3 . . . . 32 A2
Gumleigh Rd, W5 . . . . 125 F4
Gumley Gdns, Islw. TW7 . 144 D3
Gumping Rd, Orp. BR5 . . 207 F2
Gundulph Rd, Brom. BR2 . 191 J3
Gunmakers La, E3 . . . . . . 113 H1
Gunnell Cl, SE26 . . . . 170 D5
Croydon CR0 . . . . 188 D6
Gunner La, SE18 . . . . 136 D5
GUNNERSBURY, W4 . . . . 126 B4
Gunnersbury Av, W3 . . . . 126 A3
W4 . . . . 126 A3
W5 . . . . 125 J1
Gunnersbury Cl, W4
off Grange Rd 126 B5
Gunnersbury Ct, W3
off Bollo La 126 B2
Gunnersbury Cres, W3 . . . 126 A2
Gunnersbury Dr, W5 . . . . 125 J2
Gunnersbury Gdns, W3 . . 126 A2
Gunnersbury La, W3 . . . . 126 A3
Gunnersbury Ms, W4
off Chiswick High Rd . . 126 B5
★**Gunnersbury Park**, W3 . 125 J4
Gunnersbury Pk, W3 . . . . 125 J4
W5 . . . . 125 J4
★**Gunnersbury Park Mus & Art Cen**, W3 . . . . 126 A3
Gunners Gro, E4 . . . . 62 C3
Gunners Rd, SW18 . . . . . . 167 G2
Gunnery Ter, SE18 . . . . . . 137 F4
Gunning St, SE18 . . . . . . 137 H4
Gunpowder Sq, EC4 . . . . . 19 F3
Gunstor Rd, N16 . . . . 94 B4
Gun St, E1 . . . . 21 F2
Gunter Gro, SW10 . . . . 30 C6
Edgware HA8 . . . . 70 D1
Gunterstone Rd, W14 . . . . 128 B4
Gunthorpe St, E1 . . . . 21 G2
Gunton Rd, E5 . . . . 95 E3
SW17 . . . . 168 A6
Gunwhale Cl, SE16 . . . . . 133 G1
Gurdon Rd, SE7 . . . . 135 G5
Gurnell Gro, W13 . . . . 104 C4
Gurney Cl, E15
off Gurney Rd 96/97 E5
E17 . . . . 77 G1
Barking IG11 . . . . 98 E6
Gurney Cres, Croy. CR0 . . 201 F1
Gurney Dr, N2 . . . . 73 F5
Gurney Rd, E15 . . . . 96 E5
SW6 . . . . 149 F3
Carshalton SM5 . . . . . . 200 A4
Northolt UB5 . . . . 102 B3
Guthrie St, SW3 . . . . 31 G3
Gutter La, EC2 . . . . 20 A3
Guyatt Gdns, Mitch. CR4
off Ormerod Gdns 186 A2
Guy Barnett Gro, SE3
off Casterbridge Rd . . . 155 G3
Guy Rd, Wall. SM6 . . . . . . 200 D3
Guyscliff Rd, SE13 . . . . . . 154 C5
Guy St, SE1 . . . . 28 C3
Gwalior Rd, SW15
off Felsham Rd 148 A3
Gwendolen Av, SW15 . . . 148 A5
Gwendolen Cl, SW15 . . . . 148 A5
Gwendoline Av, E13 . . . . . 115 H1
Gwendwr Rd, W14 . . . . . . 128 B5
Gwillim Cl, Sid. DA15 . . . . 158 A5
Gwydor Rd, Beck. BR3 . . . 189 G4
Gwydyr Rd, Brom. BR2 . . 191 F3
Gwyn Cl, SW6 . . . . 129 F7
Gwynne Av, Croy. CR0 . . . 189 G7
Gwynne Cl, W4
off Pumping Sta Rd . . 127 F6
Gwynne Pk Av, Wdf.Grn. IG8 . . . . 64 C6
Gwynne Pl, WC1 . . . . 10 D4
Gwynne Rd, SW11 . . . . . . 149 G2
Gylcote Cl, SE5 . . . . 152 A4
Gyles Pk, Stan. HA7 . . . . . . 69 F1
Gyllyngdune Gdns, Ilf. IG3 . . . . 99 J2
Gypsy Cor, W3 . . . . 106 D5

H

Haarlem Rd, W14 . . . . 128 A3
Haberdasher Est, N1
off Haberdasher St . . . 112 A3
Haberdasher Pl, N1 . . . . . . 12 C3
Haberdasher St, N1 . . . . . . 12 C3
Habgood Rd, Loug. IG10 . . 48 B3
Haccombe Rd, SW19
off Haydons Rd 167 F6
HACKBRIDGE, Wall. SM6 . 200 B2
Hackbridge Grn, Wall. SM6 . . . . 200 A2
Hackbridge Pk Gdns, Cars. SM5 . . . . 200 A2
Hackbridge Rd, Wall. SM6 . . . . 200 A2
Hackford Rd, SW9 . . . . . . 151 F1
Hackford Wk, SW9 . . . . . . 151 F1
Hackforth Cl, Barn. EN5 . . . 39 H5
Hackington Cres, Beck. BR3 . . . . 172 A6
HACKNEY, E8 . . . . 94 E6
★**Hackney City Fm**, E2 . . . . 13 H2
Hackney Cl, Borwd. WD6 . . 38 D5
Hackney Gro, E8
off Reading La 94/95 E6
★**Hackney Marsh**, E9 . . . . . 95 H3
★**Hackney Mus**, E8 . . . . . . 95 E6
Hackney Rd, E2 . . . . 13 F4
HACKNEY WICK, E9 . . . . . . 96 A5
Hackworth Pt, E3
off Rainhill Way 114 B3
Hadar Cl, N20 . . . . 56 E1
Hadden Rd, SE28 . . . . 137 H3
Hadden Way, Grnf. UB6 . . . 86 A6
Haddington Rd, Brom. BR1 . . . . 172 D3
Haddon Cl, Borwd. WD6 . . 38 A3
Enfield EN1 . . . . 44 D6
New Malden KT3 . . . . . 183 F5
Haddonfield, SE8 . . . . 133 G4
Haddon Gro, Sid. DA15 . . 158 A7
Haddon Rd, Sutt. SM1 . . . 198 E4
Haddo St, SE10 . . . . 134 B6
Hadfield Cl, Sthl. UB1
off Adrienne Av 103 F3
Hadfield Rd, Stai. (Stanw.) TW19 . . . . 140 A6
Hadleigh Cl, E1
off Mantus Rd 113 F4
SW20 . . . . 184 C2
Hadleigh Rd, N9 . . . . 44 E7
Hadleigh St, E2 . . . . 113 F4
Hadleigh Wk, E6 . . . . 116 B6
HADLEY, Barn. EN5 . . . . . . 40 C2
Hadley Cl, N21 . . . . 43 G6
Hadley Common, Barn. EN5 . . . . 40 D2
Hadley Gdns, W4 . . . . 126 D5
Southall UB2 . . . . 123 F5
Hadley Grn, Barn. EN5 . . . . 40 C2
Hadley Grn Rd, Barn. EN5 . 40 C2
Hadley Grn W, Barn. EN5 . . 40 C2
Hadley Gro, Barn. EN5 . . . . 40 B2
Hadley Highstone, Barn. EN5 . . . . 40 C1
Hadley Ridge, Barn. EN5 . . 40 C3
Hadley Rd, Barn. (New Barn.) EN5 . . . . 41 E4
Belvedere DA17 . . . . . . 139 F4
Mitcham CR4 . . . . 186 D4
Hadley St, NW1 . . . . 92 B6
Hadley Way, N21 . . . . 43 G6
Hadlow Pl, SE19 . . . . 170 D7
Hadlow Rd, Sid. DA14 . . . 176 A4
Welling DA16 . . . . 138 C7
Hadrian Ct, Sutt. SM2
off Stanley Rd . . . 198/199 E7
Hadrian Est, E2 . . . . 13 J2
Hadrian Ms, N7
off Roman Way 93 F7
Hadrians Ride, Enf. EN1 . . . 44 C5
Hadrian St, SE10 . . . . 134 E5
Hadrian Way, Stai. (Stanw.) TW19 . . . . 140 B7
Hadyn Pk Rd, W12 . . . . . . 127 G2
Hafer Rd, SW11 . . . . 149 J4
Hafton Rd, SE6 . . . . 173 E1
Haggard Rd, Twick. TW1 . . 144 E7
HAGGERSTON, E2 . . . . 13 G1
Haggerston Rd, E8 . . . . 94 C7
Hague St, E2 . . . . 13 J4
Ha-Ha Rd, SE18 . . . . 136 C6
Haig Pl, Mord. SM4
off Green La 184 D6
Haig Rd, Stan. HA7 . . . . . . 53 F5
Haig Rd E, E13 . . . . 115 J3
Haig Rd W, E13 . . . . 115 J3
Haigville Gdns, Ilf. IG6 . . . . 81 E4
Hailes Cl, SW19
off North Rd 167 F6
Haileybury Av, Enf. EN1 . . . 44 C6
Hailey Rd, Erith DA18 . . . . 139 G2
Hailsham Av, SW2 . . . . . . 169 F2
Hailsham Cl, Surb. KT6 . . 181 G7
Hailsham Dr, Har. HA1 . . . . 68 A3
Hailsham Rd, SW17 . . . . . 168 A6
Hailsham Ter, N18 . . . . 59 J5
Haimo Rd, SE9 . . . . 156 A5
HAINAULT, Ilf. IG6 . . . . 65 H7
Hainault Ct, E17 . . . . 78 D4
Hainault Gore, Rom. RM6 . 83 E5
Hainault Gro, Chig. IG7 . . . 65 F4
Hainault Rd, E11 . . . . 96 C1
Chigwell IG7 . . . . 65 E3
Romford RM5 . . . . 83 J2
Romford (Chad.Hth) RM6 . . . . 83 F6
Romford (Lt.Hth) RM6 . . 82 B3
Hainault St, SE9 . . . . 175 E1
Ilford IG1 . . . . 99 E2
Haines Wk, Mord. SM4
off Dorchester Rd . 184/185 E7
Hainford Cl, SE4 . . . . 153 G4
Haining Cl, W4
off Wellesley Rd 126 A5
Hainthorpe Rd, SE27 . . . . 169 H3
Hainton Cl, E1 . . . . 113 E6
Halberd Ms, E5
off Knightland Rd . . 94/95 E2
Halbutt Gdns, Dag. RM9 . 101 F3
Halbutt St, Dag. RM9 . . . . 101 F4
Halcomb St, N1 . . . . 112 B1
Halcot Av, Bexh. DA6 . . . . 159 H5
Halcrow St, E1
off Newark St 112/113 E5
Haldane Cl, N10 . . . . 58 B7
Haldane Pl, SW18 . . . . . . 166 E1
Haldane Rd, E6 . . . . 116 A3
SE28 . . . . 118 D7
SW6 . . . . 128 C7
Southall UB1 . . . . 103 J6
Haldan Rd, E4 . . . . 62 C6
Haldon Cl, Chig. IG7
off Arrowsmith Rd 65 H5
Haldon Rd, SW18 . . . . 148 C5
Hale, The, E4 . . . . 62 D7
N17 . . . . 76 D3
Hale Cl, E4 . . . . 62 C3
Edgware HA8 . . . . 54 C5
Orpington BR6 . . . . 207 F4
Hale Dr, NW7 . . . . 54 C6
HALE END, E4 . . . . 62 D6
Hale End Cl, Ruis. HA4 . . . . 66 A6
Hale End Rd, E4 . . . . 62 D6
E17 . . . . 78 D1
Woodford Green IG8 . . . 62 D7
Halefield Rd, N17 . . . . 76 D1
Hale Gdns, N17 . . . . 76 D3
W3 . . . . 126 A1
Hale Gro Gdns, NW7 . . . . . 54 D5
Hale La, NW7 . . . . 54 D5
Edgware HA8 . . . . 54 B5
Hale Path, SE27 . . . . 169 H4
Hale Rd, E6 . . . . 116 B4
N17 . . . . 76 D3
Halesowen Rd, Mord. SM4 . . . . 184 E7
Hales St, SE8
off Deptford High St . . 134 A7
Hale St, E14 . . . . 114 B7
Halesworth Cl, E5
off Theydon Rd 95 F2
Halesworth Rd, SE13 . . . . 154 B3
Hale Wk, W7 . . . . 104 B5
Haley Rd, NW4 . . . . 71 J6
Half Acre, Brent. TW8 . . . . 125 G6
Half Acre Rd, W7 . . . . 124 B1
Half Moon Ct, EC1 . . . . 19 J2
Half Moon Cres, N1 . . . . . . 10 D1
Half Moon La, SE24 . . . . . 151 J6
Half Moon Pas, E1 . . . . 21 G4
Half Moon St, W1 . . . . 24 E1
Halford Cl, Edg. HA8 . . . . . 70 B2
Halford Rd, E10 . . . . 78 D5
SW6 . . . . 128 D6
Richmond TW10 . . . . . . 145 H5
Halfway St, Sid. DA15 . . . 157 G7
Haliburton Rd, Twick. TW1 . . . . 144 D5
Haliday Wk, N1
off Balls Pond Rd 94 A6
Halidon Cl, E9
off Urswick Rd 95 F5
Halifax Rd, Enf. EN2 . . . . . . 43 J2
Greenford UB6 . . . . 103 H1
Halifax St, SE26 . . . . 171 E4
Halifield Dr, Belv. DA17 . . 138 E3
Haling Gro, S.Croy. CR2 . . 201 J7
Haling Pk, S.Croy. CR2 . . . 201 J6
Haling Pk Gdns, S.Croy. CR2 . . . . 201 H6
Haling Pk Rd, S.Croy. CR2 . . . . 201 H5
Haling Rd, S.Croy. CR2 . . 202 A6
Halkin Arc, SW1 . . . . 24 B5
Halkin Ms, SW1 . . . . 24 B5
Halkin Pl, SW1 . . . . 24 B5

Halkin St, SW1 24 C4
Hall, The, SE3 155 G3
Hallam Cl, Chis. BR7 174 C5
Hallam Gdns, Pnr. HA5 51 E7
Hallam Ms, W1 16 E1
Hallam Rd, N15 75 H4
SW13 147 H3
Hallam St, W1 8 E6
Hall Av, N18
off Weir Hall Av 60 A6
Hall Cl, W5 105 H5
Hall Ct, Tedd. TW11 162 C5
Hall Dr, SE26 171 F5
W7 104 B6
Halley Gdns, SE13 154 D4
Halley Rd, E7 97 J6
E12 98 A6
Halley St, E14 113 H5
Hall Fm Cl, Stan. HA7 52 E4
Hall Fm Dr, Twick. TW2 144 A7
Hallfield Est, W2 14 C4
Hall Gdns, E4 61 J4
Hall Gate, NW8 6 D3
Halliards, The, Walt. KT12
off Felix Rd 178 A6
Halliday Sq, Sthl. UB2 124 A1
Halliford St, N1 93 J7
Hallingbury Ct, E17 78 B3
Halliwell Rd, SW2 151 F6
Halliwick Rd, N10 74 A1
Hall La, E4 61 H5
E4 (Junct) 61 H5
NW4 71 G1
Hayes UB3 121 G7
Hallmark Trd Est, NW10
off Great Cen Way 88 C4
Hallmead Rd, Sutt. SM1 198 E3
Hall Oak Wk, NW6
off Barlow Rd 90 C6
Hallowell Av, Croy. CR0 200 E4
Hallowell Cl, Mitch. CR4 186 A3
Hallowes Cres, Wat. WD19
off Hayling Rd 50 A3
Hallowfield Way, Mitch.
CR4 185 G4
★**Hall Pl**, Bex. DA5 159 J6
Hall Pl, W2 6 E6
Hall Pl Cres, Bex. DA5 159 J5
Hall Rd, E6 116 C1
E15 96 D4
NW8 6 D4
Isleworth TW7 144 A5
Romford (Chad.Hth)
RM6 82 C6
Hall St, EC1 11 H3
N12 57 F5
Hallsville Rd, E16 115 F6
Hallswelle Rd, NW11 72 C5
Hall Twr, W2 15 F1
Hall Vw, SE9 174 A2
Hallywell Cres, E6 116 C5
Halons Rd, SE9 156 D7
Halpin Pl, SE17 36 C2
Halsbrook Rd, SE3 156 A3
Halsbury Cl, Stan. HA7 52 E4
Halsbury Rd, W12 127 H1
Halsbury Rd E, Nthlt. UB5 85 J4
Halsbury Rd W, Nthlt.
UB5 85 H5
Halsend, Hayes UB3 122 B1
Halsey Ms, SW3 31 J1
Halsey St, SW3 31 J1
Halsham Cres, Bark. IG11 99 J6
Halsmere Rd, SE5 151 H1
Halstead Cl, Croy. CR0
off Charles St 201 J3
Halstead Ct, N1 12 C2
Halstead Gdns, N21 60 A1
Halstead Rd, E11 79 G5
N21 59 J1
Enfield EN1 44 B4
Halston Cl, SW11 149 J6
Halstow Rd, NW10 108 A3
SE10 135 G5
Halsway, Hayes UB3 122 A1
Halter Cl, Borwd. WD6
off Clydesdale Cl 38 D5
Halton Cl, N11
off Colney Hatch La 57 J6
Halton Cross St, N1 111 H1
Halton Pl, N1
off Dibden St 111 J1
Halton Rd, N1 93 H7
Halt Robin La, Belv. DA17
off Halt Robin Rd 139 H4
Halt Robin Rd, Belv.
DA17 139 G4
HAM, Rich. TW10 163 G3
Ham, The, Brent. TW8 125 F7
Hambalt Rd, SW4 150 C5
Hamble Ct, Tedd. TW11 163 G7
Hambledon Gdns, SE25 188 C3
Hambledon Pl, SE21 170 B1
Hambledon Rd, SW18 148 C7
Hambledown Rd, Sid.
DA15 157 G7
Hamble St, SW6 149 E3
Hambleton Cl, Wor.Pk. KT4
off Cotswold Way 197 J2
Hamble Wk, Nthlt. UB5
off Brabazon Rd 103 G2
Hambridge Way, SW2 151 G7
Hambro Av, Brom. BR2 205 G1
Hambrook Rd, SE25 188 E3
Hambro Rd, SW16 168 D6
Hambrough Rd, Sthl.
UB1 122 E1
Ham Cl, Rich. TW10 163 F3
Ham Common, Rich.
TW10 163 J4
Ham Cft Cl, Felt. TW13 160 A3
Hamden Cres, Dag.
RM10 101 H3
Hamel Cl, Har. HA3 69 G3
Hamelin St, E14
off St. Leonards Rd 114 C6
Hameway, E6 116 D4
Ham Fm Rd, Rich. TW10 163 G4
Hamfrith Rd, E15 97 F6
Ham Gate Av, Rich. TW10 163 G3
★**Ham Ho**, Rich. TW10 163 F1
Hamilton Av, N9 44 D7
Ilford IG6 81 E4
Surbiton KT6 196 B1
Sutton SM3 198 B2
Hamilton Cl, N17 76 C3
NW8 6 E4
SE16 *off Somerford Way* 133 H2
Barnet EN4 41 H4
Stanmore HA7 52 C2
Hamilton Ct, W5 105 J7
W9 6 C3
Hamilton Cres, N13 59 G4
Harrow HA2 85 F3
Hounslow TW3 143 H5
Hamilton Gdns, NW8 6 D3
Hamilton La, N5
off Hamilton Pk 93 H4
Hamilton Ms, SW18
off Merton Rd 166 D1
W1 24 D3
Hamilton Pk, N5 93 H4
Hamilton Pk W, N5 93 H4
Hamilton Pl, N19
off Wedmore St 92 D3
W1 24 C2
Sunbury-on-Thames
TW16 160 B7
Hamilton Rd, E15 115 E3
E17 77 H2
N2 73 F3
N9 44 D7
NW10 89 G5
NW11 72 A7
SE27 170 A4
SW19 167 E7
W4 126 E2
W5 105 H7
Barnet EN4 41 H4
Bexleyheath DA7 159 E2
Brentford TW8 125 G6
Harrow HA1 68 B5
Hayes UB3 102 B7
Ilford IG1 98 E4
Sidcup DA15 176 A4
Southall UB1 123 F1
Thornton Heath CR7 188 A3
Twickenham TW2 162 B1
Watford WD19 50 B3
Hamilton Rd Ind Est,
SE27 170 A4
Hamilton Sq, N12
off Sandringham Gdns 57 G6
SE1 28 C3
Hamilton St, SE8
off Deptford High St 134 A6
Hamilton Ter, NW8 6 D3
Hamilton Way, N3 56 D6
N13 59 H4
Hamlea Cl, SE12 155 F5
Hamlet, The, SE5 152 A3
Hamlet Cl, SE13
off Old Rd 154/155 E4
Hamlet Gdns, W6 127 G4
Hamleton Ter, Dag. RM9
off Flamstead Rd 100 C7
Hamlet Rd, SE19 170 C7
Hamlet Sq, NW2 90 B3
Hamlets Way, E3 113 J4
Hamlet Way, SE1 28 C3
★**Hamleys**, W1 17 F5
Hamlin Cres, Pnr. HA5 66 C5
Hamlyn Cl, Edg. HA8 53 H3
Hamlyn Gdns, SE19 170 B7
Hammelton Grn, SW9
off Cromwell Rd 151 H1
Hammelton Rd, Brom.
BR1 191 F1
Hammers La, NW7 55 G5
HAMMERSMITH, W6 127 J5
Hammersmith Br, SW13 127 H6
W6 127 H6
Hammersmith Br Rd,
W6 127 J5
Hammersmith Bdy, W6 127 J4
Hammersmith Flyover,
W6 127 J5
Hammersmith Gro, W6 127 J3
Hammersmith Rd, W6 128 A4
W14 128 A4
Hammersmith Ter, W6 127 G5
Hammet Cl, Hayes UB4 102 D5
Hammett St, EC3 21 F5
Hammond Av, Mitch.
CR4 186 B2
Hammond Cl, Barn. EN5 40 B5
Greenford UB6
off Lilian Board Way 86 A5
Hampton TW12 179 G1
Hammond Rd, Enf. EN1 45 E2
Southall UB2 123 E3
Hammonds Cl, Dag. RM8 100 C3
Hammond St, NW5 92 C6
Hammond Way, SE28
off Oriole Way 118 B7
Hamonde Cl, Edg. HA8 54 B2
Hamond Sq, N1
off Hoxton St 112 B2
Ham Pk Rd, E7 97 F7
E15 97 F7
Hampden Av, Beck. BR3 189 H2
Hampden Cl, NW1 9 J2
Hampden Gurney St, W1 15 J4
Hampden La, N17 76 C1
Hampden Rd, N8 75 G4
N10 58 A7
N17 76 D1
N19 *off Holloway Rd* 92 D2
Beckenham BR3 189 H2
Harrow HA3 67 J1
Kingston upon Thames
KT1 182 A3
Hampden Sq, N14
off Osidge La 58 B1
Hampden Way, N14 58 B2
Hampshire Cl, N18
off Berkshire Gdns 60/61 E5
Hampshire Hog La, W6
off King St 127 H4
Hampshire Rd, N22 59 F7
Hampshire St, NW5
off Torriano Av 92 D6
Hampson Way, SW8 151 F1
HAMPSTEAD, NW3 91 G4
Hampstead Av, Wdf.Grn.
IG8 64 D7
Hampstead Cl, SE28 138 B1
Hampstead Gdns, NW11 72 D6
Romford (Chad.Hth)
RM6 82 B5
HAMPSTEAD GARDEN SUBURB, N2 73 F5
Hampstead Grn, NW3 91 H5
Hampstead Gro, NW3 91 F3
★**Hampstead Heath**, NW3 91 G2
Hampstead Hts, N2 73 F4
Hampstead High St, NW3 91 F4
Hampstead Hill Gdns,
NW3 91 G4
Hampstead La, N6 73 G7
NW3 73 G7
Hampstead Rd, NW1 9 F1
Hampstead Sq, NW3 91 F3
Hampstead Wk, E3
off Waterside Cl 113 J1
Hampstead Way, NW11 91 F1
HAMPTON, TW12 179 H1
Hampton Cl, N11
off Balmoral Av 58 B5
NW6 108 D3
SW20 165 J7
Hampton Ct, N1
off Upper St 93 H6
Hampton Ct Av, E.Mol.
KT8 180 A5
Hampton Ct Cres, E.Mol.
KT8 180 A3
★**Hampton Court Palace & Pk**, E.Mol. KT8 180 B3
Hampton Ct Par, E.Mol. KT8
off Creek Rd 180 B4
Hampton Ct Rd, E.Mol.
KT8 180 C3
Hampton TW12 179 J2
Kingston upon Thames
KT1 180 C3
Hampton Ct Way, E.Mol.
KT8 180 B6
Thames Ditton KT7 194 B2
Hampton Fm Ind Est, Felt.
TW13 161 F3
HAMPTON HILL, Hmptn.
TW12 161 J6
Hampton Hill Business Pk,
Hmptn. TW12
off Wellington Rd 161 J5
Hampton La, Felt. TW13 161 E4
Hampton Mead, Loug.
IG10 48 E3
Hampton Ms, NW10
off Minerva Rd 106 D3
Hampton Ri, Har. HA3 69 H6
Hampton Rd, E4 61 J5
E7 97 H5
E11 96 D1
Croydon CR0 187 J6
Hampton (Hmptn H.)
TW12 162 A5
Ilford IG1 99 E4
Teddington TW11 162 A5
Twickenham TW2 162 A3
Worcester Park KT4 197 G2
Hampton Rd E, Felt.
TW13 161 F3
Hampton Rd W, Felt.
TW13 160 E2
Hampton St, SE1 35 H2
SE17 35 H2
HAMPTON WICK, Kings.T.
KT1 181 E1
Ham Ridings, Rich. TW10 163 J5
Hamshades Cl, Sid.
DA15 175 J3
Ham St, Rich. TW10 163 F2
Ham Vw, Croy. CR0 189 H6
Ham Yd, W1 17 H5
Hanah Ct, SW19 166 A7
Hanameel St, E16 135 G1
Hana Ms, E5
off Goulton Rd 95 F4
Hanbury Cl, NW4 71 J3
Hanbury Dr, E11 *off High Rd*
Leytonstone 79 F7
N21 43 F5
Hanbury Ms, N1
off Mary St 111 J1
Hanbury Rd, N17 76 E2
W3 126 B2
Hanbury St, E1 21 F1
Hancock Ct, Borwd. WD6 38 C1
Hancock Rd, E3 114 C3
SE19 170 A6
Handa Wk, N1
off Clephane Rd 94 A6
Hand Ct, WC1 18 D2
Handcroft Rd, Croy. CR0 187 H7
Handel Cl, Edg. HA8 53 J6
Handel Pl, NW10
off Mitchellbrook Way 88 D6
Handel St, WC1 10 A5
Handel Way, Edg. HA8 54 A7
Handen Rd, SE12 155 E5
Handforth Rd, SW9 34 E7
Ilford IG1
off Winston Way 98/99 E3
Handley Gro, NW2 90 A3
Handley Page Rd, Wall.
SM6 201 F7
Handley Rd, E9 95 F7
Handowe Cl, NW4 71 G4
Handside Cl, Wor.Pk. KT4
off Carters Cl 198 A1
Hands Wk, E16 115 G6
Handsworth Av, E4 62 D6
Handsworth Rd, N17 76 A3
Handsworth Way, Wat. WD19
off Hayling Rd 50 A3
Handtrough Way, Bark. IG11
off Fresh Wf Rd 116/117 E2
Hanford Cl, SW18 166 D1
Hanford Row, SW19 165 J6
Hangar Ruding, Wat.
WD19 51 F3
Hanger Grn, W5 106 A4
Hanger La, W5 105 J4
Hanger Vale La, W5 105 J6

Hanger Vw Way, W3 . . . . . 106 A6
Hanging Sword All, EC4 . . 19 F4
Hankey Pl, SE1 . . . . 28 C4
Hankins La, NW7 . . . . 54 E3
Hanley Gdns, N4 . . . . 93 F1
Hanley Pl, Beck. BR3 . . . . 172 A7
Hanley Rd, N4 . . . . 93 E1
Hanmer Wk, N7 off Newington Barrow Way . 93 F3
Hannah Cl, NW10 . . . . 88 C4
Beckenham BR3 . . . . . . 190 C3
Hannah Ct, N13 . . . . 59 F2
Hannah Mary Way, SE1 . . . 37 J2
Hannah Ms, Wall. SM6 . . . 200 C7
Hannay La, N8 . . . . 74 D7
Hannay Wk, SW16 . . . . . . 168 D2
Hannell Rd, SW6 . . . . 128 B7
Hannen Rd, SE27 off Norwood High St . 169 H3
Hannibal Rd, E1 . . . . 113 F5
Staines (Stanw.) TW19 . 140 A7
Hannibal Way, Croy. CR0 . 201 F5
Hannington Rd, SW4 . . . . 150 B3
Hanover Av, E16 . . . . 135 G1
Feltham TW13 . . . . 160 A1
Hanover Cl, Rich. TW9 . . . 126 A7
Sutton SM3 . . . . 198 C4
Hanover Ct, SE19 off Anerley Rd 170 D7
W12 off Uxbridge Rd . . 127 G1
Hanover Dr, Chis. BR7 . . . 175 F4
Hanover Gdns, SE11 . . . . . 34 E6
Ilford IG6 . . . . 65 F7
Hanover Gate, NW1 . . . . 7 H4
Hanover Gate Mans, NW1 . . 7 H5
Hanover Ho, Surb. KT6 off Lenelby Rd 196 A1
Hanover Pk, SE15 . . . . 152 D1
Hanover Pl, E3 off Brokesley St 113 J3
WC2 . . . . 18 B4
Hanover Rd, N15 . . . . 76 C4
NW10 . . . . 89 J7
SW19 . . . . 167 F7
Hanover Sq, W1 . . . . 17 E4
Hanover St, W1 . . . . 17 E4
Croydon CR0 off Abbey Rd 201 H3
Hanover Ter, NW1 . . . . 7 H4
Hanover Ter Ms, NW1 . . . . . 7 H4
Hanover Way, Bexh. DA6 . . . . 158 D3
Hanover W Ind Est, NW10 . . . . 106 D2
Hanover Yd, N1 . . . . 11 H1
Hansard Ms, W14 off Holland Rd 128 A2
Hansart Way, Enf. EN2 off The Ridgeway 43 G1
Hanscomb Ms, SW4 off Bromell's Rd 150 C4
Hans Cres, SW1 . . . . 23 J5
Hanselin Cl, Stan. HA7 . . . . 52 C5
Hansen Dr, N21 . . . . 43 F5
Hanshaw Dr, Edg. HA8 . . . 70 D1
Hansler Gro, E.Mol. KT8 . 180 A4
Hansler Rd, SE22 . . . . . . 152 C5
Hansol Rd, Bexh. DA6 . . . 158 E5
Hanson Cl, SW12 . . . . 150 B7
SW14 . . . . 146 C3
Beckenham BR3 . . . . . . 172 B6
Loughton IG10 off Hanson Dr 49 F2
West Drayton UB7 . . . . 120 C3
Hanson Dr, Loug. IG10 . . . . 49 F2
Hanson Gdns, Sthl. UB1 . 123 E2
Hanson Grn, Loug. IG10 off Hanson Dr 49 F2
Hanson St, W1 . . . . 17 F1
Hans Pl, SW1 . . . . 24 A5
Hans Rd, SW3 . . . . 23 J5
Hans St, SW1 . . . . 24 A6
Hanway Pl, W1 . . . . 17 H3
Hanway Rd, W7 . . . . 104 A6
Hanway St, W1 . . . . 17 H3
HANWELL, W7 . . . . 124 C1
HANWORTH, Felt. TW13 . 160 D4
Hanworth Rd, Felt. TW13 . 160 B1
Hampton TW12 . . . . 161 H6
Hounslow TW3, TW4 . . . 143 H3
Sunbury-on-Thames TW16 . . . . 160 A7
Hanworth Ter, Houns. TW3 . . . . 143 H4
Hanworth Trd Est, Felt. TW13 . . . . 161 E3
Hapgood Cl, Grnf. UB6 . . . 86 A5
Harads Pl, E1 . . . . 21 J6
Harben Rd, NW6 . . . . 91 F7
Harberson Rd, E15 . . . . . . 115 F1
SW12 . . . . 168 B1
Harberton Rd, N19 . . . . 92 C1
Harbet Rd, E4 . . . . 61 G5
N18 . . . . 61 G5
W2 . . . . 15 F2
Harbex Cl, Bex. DA5 . . . . . 159 H7
Harbinger Rd, E14 . . . . . . 134 B4
Harbledown Rd, SW6 . . . 148 D1
Harbord Cl, SE5 off De Crespigny Pk . . 152 A2
Harbord St, SW6 . . . . 148 A1
Harborne Cl, Wat. WD19 . . . 50 C5
Harborough Av, Sid. DA15 . . . . 157 H7
Harborough Rd, SW16 . . . 169 F4
Harbour Av, SW10 . . . . . . 149 F1
Harbour Ex Sq, E14 . . . . . 134 B2
Harbour Reach, SW6 off The Boulevard 149 F1
Harbour Rd, SE5 . . . . 151 J3
Harbour Yd, SW10 off Harbour Av 149 F1
Harbridge Av, SW15 . . . . . 147 F7
Harbut Rd, SW11 . . . . 149 G4
Harcombe Rd, N16 . . . . 94 B3
Harcourt Av, E12 . . . . 98 C4
Edgware HA8 . . . . 54 C3
Sidcup DA15 . . . . 158 C6
Wallington SM6 . . . . . . 200 B4
Harcourt Cl, Islw. TW7 . . . 144 D3
Harcourt Fld, Wall. SM6 . . 200 B4
Harcourt Lo, Wall. SM6 off Croydon Rd 200 B4
Harcourt Rd, E15 . . . . 115 F2
N22 . . . . 74 D1
SE4 . . . . 153 H4
SW19 off Russell Rd . . . 166 D7
Bexleyheath DA6 . . . . . 159 E4
Thornton Heath CR7 . . . 187 F6
Wallington SM6 . . . . . . 200 B4
Harcourt St, W1 . . . . 15 H2
Harcourt Ter, SW10 . . . . . . 30 B4
Hardcastle Cl, Croy. CR0 . . . . 188 D6
Hardcourts Cl, W.Wick. BR4 . . . . 204 B3
Hardel Ri, SW2 . . . . 169 H2
Hardel Wk, SW2 off Papworth Way 151 G7
Hardens Manorway, SE7 . 136 A3
Harders Rd, SE15 . . . . 152 E2
Hardess St, SE24 off Herne Hill Rd 151 J3
Hardie Cl, NW10 . . . . 88 D5
Hardie Rd, Dag. RM10 . . . 101 J2
Harding Cl, SE17 . . . . 35 J5
Croydon CR0 . . . . 202 C3
Hardinge Cres, SE18 off Armstrong Rd 137 F3
Hardinge Rd, N18 . . . . 60 B5
NW10 . . . . 107 H1
Hardinge St, E1 . . . . 113 F6
Harding Ho, Hayes UB3 . . 102 B6
Harding Rd, Bexh. DA7 . . 159 F2
Harding's Cl, Kings.T. KT2 . . . . 181 J1
Hardings La, SE20 . . . . . . 171 G6
Hardman Rd, SE7 . . . . 135 H5
Kingston upon Thames KT2 . . . . 181 H2
Hardwick Cl, Stan. HA7 . . . 53 F5
Hardwicke Av, Houns. TW5 . . . . 143 G1
Hardwicke Ms, WC1 . . . . . . 10 D4
Hardwicke Rd, N13 . . . . . . 58 E6
W4 . . . . 126 D4
Richmond TW10 . . . . . . 163 F4
Hardwicke St, Bark. IG11 . 117 F1
Hardwick Grn, W13 . . . . . 105 E5
Hardwick St, EC1 . . . . 11 F4
Hardwicks Way, SW18 off Buckhold Rd 148 D5
Hardwidge St, SE1 . . . . 28 D3
Hardy Av, E16 off Wesley Av 135 G1
Ruislip HA4 . . . . 84 B5
Hardy Cl, SE16 off Middleton Dr 133 G2
Barnet EN5 . . . . 40 B6
Pinner HA5 . . . . 66 D7
Hardy Rd, E4 . . . . 61 J6
SE3 . . . . 135 F7
SW19 . . . . 167 E7
Hardys Cl, E.Mol. KT8 off Feltham Av 180 B4
Hardy Way, Enf. EN2 . . . . . 43 G1
Hare & Billet Rd, SE3 . . . . 154 D1
Harebell Dr, E6 . . . . 116 D5
Harecastle Cl, Hayes UB4 . . . . 102 E4
Hare Ct, EC4 . . . . 19 E4
Harecourt Rd, N1 . . . . 93 J6
Haredale Rd, SE24 . . . . . . 151 J4
Haredon Cl, SE23 . . . . 153 F7
Harefield, Esher KT10 . . . . 194 B4
Harefield Cl, Enf. EN2 . . . . . 43 G1
Harefield Ms, SE4 . . . . 153 J3
Harefield Rd, N8 . . . . 74 D5
SE4 . . . . 153 J3
SW16 . . . . 169 F7
Sidcup DA14 . . . . 176 D2
Hare La, Esher (Clay.) KT10 . . . . 194 B6
Hare Marsh, E2 . . . . 13 H5
Hare Pl, EC4 . . . . 19 F4
Hare Row, E2 . . . . 113 E2
Haresfield Rd, Dag. RM10 . . . . 101 G6
Hare St, SE18 . . . . 136 D3
Hare Wk, N1 . . . . 12 E2
Harewood Av, NW1 . . . . 7 H6
Northolt UB5 . . . . 85 E7
Harewood Cl, Nthlt. UB5 . . 85 F7
Harewood Dr, Ilf. IG5 . . . . . 80 C2
Harewood Pl, W1 . . . . 16 E4
Harewood Rd, SW19 . . . . 167 H6
Isleworth TW7 . . . . 124 C7
South Croydon CR2 . . . 202 B6
Watford WD19 . . . . 50 B3
Harewood Row, NW1 . . . . . 15 H1
Harewood Ter, Sthl. UB2 . 123 F4
Harfield Gdns, SE5 . . . . . . 152 B3
Harfield Rd, Sun. TW16 . . 178 D2
Harford Cl, E4 . . . . 46 B7
Harford Ms, N19 off Wedmore St 92 D3
Harford Rd, E4 . . . . 46 B7
Harford St, E1 . . . . 113 H4
Harford Wk, N2 . . . . 73 G5
Hargood Cl, Har. HA3 . . . . . 69 H6
Hargood Rd, SE3 . . . . 155 J1
Hargrave Pk, N19 . . . . 92 C2
Hargrave Pl, N7 off Brecknock Rd 92 D5
Hargrave Rd, N19 . . . . 92 C2
Hargwyne St, SW9 . . . . . . 151 F3
Haringey Pk, N8 . . . . 74 E6
Haringey Pas, N4 . . . . 75 H6
N8 . . . . 75 G4
Haringey Rd, N8 . . . . 74 F4
Harington Ter, N9 . . . . 60 A3
N18 . . . . 60 A3
Harkett Cl, Har. HA3 off Byron Rd 68 C2
Harkett Ct, Har. HA3 . . . . . 68 C2
Harland Av, Croy. CR0 . . . 202 C3
Sidcup DA15 . . . . 175 G3
Harland Cl, SW19 . . . . 184 E3
Harland Rd, SE12 . . . . 173 G1
Harlands Gro, Orp. BR6 off Pinecrest Gdns . 206/207 E4
Harlech Gdns, Houns. TW5 . . . . 122 C6
Pinner HA5 . . . . 66 D7
Harlech Rd, N14 . . . . 59 E3
Harlech Twr, W3 . . . . 126 B2
Harlequin Av, Brent. TW8 . 124 D6
Harlequin Cl, Hayes UB4 off Cygnet Way 102 D5
Isleworth TW7 . . . . 144 B5
Harlequin Ho, Erith DA18 off Kale Rd 138/139 E3
Harlequin Rd, Tedd. TW11 . 162 E7
★Harlequins F.C. (Rugby), Twick. TW2 . . . . 144 B7
Harlescott Rd, SE15 . . . . . 153 G4
HARLESDEN, NW10 . . . . . 107 E2
Harlesden Gdns, NW10 . . 107 F1
Harlesden La, NW10 . . . . . 107 G1
Harlesden Rd, NW10 . . . . 107 G1
Harleston Cl, E5 off Theydon Rd 95 F2
Harley Cl, Wem. HA0 . . . . . 87 G6
Harley Ct, E11 off Blake Hall Rd 79 G7
Harley Cres, Har. HA1 . . . . 68 A4
Harleyford, Brom. BR1 . . . 191 H1
Harleyford Rd, SE11 . . . . . . 34 C5
Harleyford St, SE11 . . . . . . 34 E6
Harley Gdns, SW10 . . . . . . 30 D4
Orpington BR6 . . . . 207 H4
Harley Gro, E3 . . . . 113 J3
Harley Pl, W1 . . . . 16 D2
Harley Rd, NW3 . . . . 91 G7
NW10 . . . . 106 E2
Harrow HA1 . . . . 68 A4
Harley St, W1 . . . . 16 D2
Harling Ct, SW11 off Latchmere Rd 149 J2
Harlinger St, SE18 . . . . . . 136 B3
HARLINGTON, Hayes UB3 . . . . 121 F6
Harlington Cl, Hayes UB3 off New Rd 121 F7
Harlington Rd, Bexh. DA7 . 159 E3
Hounslow (Hthrw Air.) TW6 . . . . 141 J4
Harlington Rd E, Felt. TW13, TW14 . . . . 142 B7
Harlington Rd W, Felt. TW14 . . . . 142 B6
Harlow Rd, N13 . . . . 60 A3
Harlyn Dr, Pnr. HA5 . . . . . . 66 B3
Harman Av, Wdf.Grn. IG8 . . 63 F7
Harman Cl, E4 . . . . 62 D4
NW2 . . . . 90 B3
Harman Dr, NW2 . . . . 90 B3
Sidcup DA15 . . . . 157 J6
Harman Rd, Enf. EN1 . . . . . 44 C5
HARMONDSWORTH, West Dr. UB7 . . . . 120 A6
Harmondsworth La, West Dr. UB7 . . . . 120 B6
Harmondsworth Rd, West Dr. UB7 . . . . 120 B5
Harmony Cl, NW11 . . . . 72 B5
Harmony Ter, Har. HA2 off Goldsmith Cl 85 H1
Harmony Way, NW4 off Victoria Rd 71 J4
Harmood Gro, NW1 off Clarence Way 92 B7
Harmood Pl, NW1 off Harmood St 92 B7
Harmood St, NW1 . . . . 92 B7
Harmsworth Ms, SE11 . . . . 27 G6
Harmsworth St, SE17 . . . . 35 G4
Harmsworth Way, N20 . . . . 56 C1
Harness Rd, SE28 . . . . . . 138 A2
Harold Av, Belv. DA17 . . . 139 F5
Hayes UB3 . . . . 121 J3
Harold Est, SE1 . . . . 28 E6
Harold Gibbons Ct, SE7 . . 135 J6
Harold Laski Ho, EC1 . . . . . 11 G4
Harold Pl, SE11 . . . . 34 E4
Harold Rd, E4 . . . . 62 C4
E11 . . . . 96 E1
E13 . . . . 115 H1
N8 . . . . 75 F5
N15 . . . . 76 C5
NW10 . . . . 106 D3
SE19 . . . . 170 B6
Sutton SM1 . . . . 199 G4
Woodford Green IG8 . . . 79 G1
Haroldstone Rd, E17 . . . . . 77 G5
Harp All, EC4 . . . . 10 C3
Harpenden Rd, E12 . . . . . . 97 J2
SE27 . . . . 169 H3
Harpenmead Pt, NW2 off Granville Rd 90 C2
Harper Cl, N14 off Alexandra Ct 42 C5
Harper Ms, SW17 . . . . 167 F3
Harper Rd, E6 . . . . 116 C6
SE1 . . . . 27 J5
Harpers Yd, N17 off Ruskin Rd 76 C1
Harp Island Cl, NW10 . . . . . 88 D2
Harp La, EC3 . . . . 20 D6
Harpley Sq, E1 . . . . 113 F3
Harpour Rd, Bark. IG11 . . . 99 F6
Harp Rd, W7 . . . . 104 C4
Harpsden St, SW11 . . . . . 150 A1
Harpur Ms, WC1 . . . . 18 C1
Harpur St, WC1 . . . . 18 C1
Harraden Rd, SE3 . . . . 155 J1
Harrap St, E14 . . . . 114 C7
Harrier Av, E11 off Eastern Av 79 H6
Harrier Ms, SE28 . . . . 137 G3
Harrier Rd, NW9 . . . . 71 E2
Harriers Cl, W5 . . . . 105 H7
Harrier Way, E6 . . . . 116 C4
Harries Rd, Hayes UB4 . . . 102 C4
Harriet Cl, E8 . . . . 112 D1
Harriet Gdns, Croy. CR0 . . 202 D2
Harriet St, SW1 . . . . 24 A4
Harriet Tubman Cl, SW2 . . 151 G7
Harriet Wk, SW1 . . . . 24 A4
HARRINGAY, N8 . . . . 75 G5
Harringay Gdns, N8 . . . . . . 75 H4
Harringay Rd, N15 . . . . 75 H5
Harrington Cl, NW10 . . . . . 88 D3
Croydon CR0 . . . . 200 E2
Harrington Ct, W10 off Dart St 108 C3

Harrington Gdns, SW7 . . . . 30 B2
Harrington Hill, E5 . . . . 95 E1
Harrington Rd, E11 . . . . 97 E1
SE25 . . . . 188 D4
SW7 . . . . 30 E1
Harrington Sq, NW1 . . . . . . 9 F2
Harrington St, NW1 . . . . 9 F3
Harrington Way, SE18 . . . 136 A3
Harriott Cl, SE10 . . . . 135 F4
Harris Cl, Enf. EN2 . . . . 43 H1
Hounslow TW3 . . . . 143 G1
Harrison Cl, N20 . . . . 57 H1
Harrison Rd, Dag. RM10 . . 101 H6
Harrisons Ri, Croy. CR0 . . 201 H3
Harrison St, WC1 . . . . 10 B4
Harris Rd, Bexh. DA7 . . . . 159 E1
Dagenham RM9 . . . . . . 101 F5
Harris St, E17 . . . . 77 J7
SE5 . . . . 132 A7
★**Harrods**, SW1 . . . . 23 J5
Harrogate Ct, N11
off Coverdale Rd 58 A6
Harrogate Rd, Wat.
WD19 . . . . 50 C3
Harrold Rd, Dag. RM8 . . . 100 B5
HARROW, HA1 - HA3 . . . . . 68 A7
★**Harrow Arts Cen**, Pnr.
HA5 . . . . 51 H7
Harrow Av, Enf. EN1 . . . . . 44 C6
Harroway Rd, SW11 . . . . . 149 G2
Harrowby St, W1 . . . . 15 H3
Harrow Cl, Chess. KT9 . . . 195 G7
Harrowdene Cl, Wem.
HA0 . . . . 87 G4
Harrowdene Gdns, Tedd.
TW11 . . . . 162 D6
Harrowdene Rd, Wem.
HA0 . . . . 87 G3
Harrow Dr, N9 . . . . 60 C1
Harrowes Meade, Edg.
HA8 . . . . 54 A3
Harrow Flds Gdns, Har.
HA1 . . . . 86 B3
Harrowgate Rd, E9 . . . . 95 H6
Harrow Grn, E11
off Harrow Rd 96/97 E3
Harrow La, E14 . . . . 114 C7
Harrow Manorway, SE2 . . 138 C1
★**Harrow Mus & Heritage Cen**, Har. HA2 . . . . 67 J3
HARROW ON THE HILL,
Har. HA1 . . . . 86 B2
Harrow Pk, Har. HA1 . . . . . 86 B2
Harrow Pas, Kings.T. KT1
off Market Pl 181 G2
Harrow Pl, E1 . . . . 21 E3
Harrow Rd, E6 . . . . 116 B1
E11 . . . . 97 E3
NW10 . . . . 107 H3
W2 . . . . 14 A2
W9 . . . . 108 C4
W10 . . . . 108 A4
Barking IG11 . . . . 117 H1
Carshalton SM5 . . . . . . 199 H5
Ilford IG1 . . . . 99 F4
Wembley HA0 . . . . 87 F5
Wembley (Tkgtn) HA9 . . 87 J5
★**Harrow Sch**, Har. HA1 . . . 86 B1
Harrow Vw, Har.
HA1, HA2 . . . . 68 A1
Hayes UB3 . . . . 102 A6
Harrow Vw Rd, W5 . . . . . . 105 E4
Harrow Way, Wat. WD19 . . . 50 E3
HARROW WEALD, Har.
HA3 . . . . 68 A1
Harrow Weald Pk, Har.
HA3 . . . . 52 A6
Hart Cres, Chig. IG7 . . . . . . 65 J5
Harte Rd, Houns. TW3 . . . 143 F2
Hartfield Av, Borwd. (Elstree)
WD6 . . . . 38 A5
Northolt UB5 . . . . 102 B2
Hartfield Cl, Borwd. (Elstree)
WD6 . . . . 38 A5
Hartfield Cres, SW19 . . . . 166 C7
West Wickham BR4 . . . . 205 G3
Hartfield Gro, SE20 . . . . . 189 E1
Hartfield Rd, SW19 . . . . . . 166 C7
Chessington KT9 . . . . . . 195 G5
West Wickham BR4 . . . . 205 G4
Hartfield Ter, E3 . . . . 114 A2
Hartford Av, Har. HA3 . . . . 68 D3
Hartforde Rd, Borwd.
WD6 . . . . 38 A2
Hartford Rd, Bex. DA5 . . . 159 G6
Epsom KT19 . . . . 196 A6
Hart Gro, W5 . . . . 126 A1
Southall UB1 . . . . 103 G5
Hartham Cl, N7 . . . . 93 E5
Hartham Cl, Islw. TW7 . . . 144 D1
Hartham Rd, N7 . . . . 92 E5
N17 . . . . 76 C2
Isleworth TW7 . . . . 144 C1
Harting Rd, SE9 . . . . 174 B4
Hartington Cl, Har. HA1 . . . 86 B4
Hartington Ct, W4 . . . . . . 126 B7
Hartington Rd, E16 . . . . . . 115 H6
E17 . . . . 77 H6
SW8 . . . . 150 E1
W4 . . . . 126 B7
W13 . . . . 105 E7
Southall UB2 . . . . 122 E2
Twickenham TW1 . . . . . 144 E7
Hartismere Rd, SW6 . . . . 128 C7
Hartlake Rd, E9 . . . . 95 G6
Hartland Cl, N21
off Elmscott Gdns 43 J6
Edgware HA8 . . . . 54 A2
Hartland Dr, Edg. HA8 . . . . 54 A2
Ruislip HA4 . . . . 84 B3
Hartland Rd, E15 . . . . 97 F7
N11 . . . . 57 J5
NW1 . . . . 92 B7
NW6 . . . . 108 C2
Hampton (Hmptn H.)
TW12 . . . . 161 H4
Isleworth TW7 . . . . 144 D3
Morden SM4 . . . . 184 D7
Hartlands Cl, Bex. DA5 . . 159 F6
Hartland Way, Croy. CR0 . 203 H2
Morden SM4 . . . . 184 C7
Hartlepool Ct, E16 *off Fishguard Way* . . . 136/137 E2
Hartley Av, E6 . . . . 116 B1
NW7 . . . . 55 F5
Hartley Cl, NW7 . . . . 55 F5
Bromley BR1 . . . . 192 C2
Hartley Rd, E11 . . . . 97 F1
Croydon CR0 . . . . 187 H7
Welling DA16 . . . . 138 C7
Hartley St, E2 . . . . 113 F3
Hartmann Rd, E16 . . . . . . 136 A1
Hartnoll St, N7
off Eden Gro 93 F5
Harton Cl, Brom. BR1 . . . . 192 A1
Harton Rd, N9 . . . . 61 E2
Harton St, SE8 . . . . 154 A1
Hartsbourne Av, Bushey
(Bushey Hth) WD23 . . . . . 51 J2
Hartsbourne Cl, Bushey
(Bushey Hth) WD23 . . . . 52 A2
Hartsbourne Rd, Bushey
(Bushey Hth) WD23 . . . . 52 A2
Harts Gro, Wdf.Grn. IG8 . . . 63 G5
Hartshorn All, EC3 . . . . 21 E4
Hartshorn Gdns, E6 . . . . . 116 D4
Harts La, SE14 . . . . 133 H7
Barking IG11 . . . . 98 E6
Hartslock Dr, SE2 . . . . 138 D2
Hartsmead Rd, SE9 . . . . . 174 C2
Hart St, EC3 . . . . 20 E5
Hartsway, Enf. EN3 . . . . . . 45 F4
Hartswood Gdns, W12 . . . 127 F3
Hartswood Grn, Bushey
(Bushey Hth) WD23 . . . . 52 A2
Hartswood Rd, W12 . . . . . 127 F2
Hartsworth Cl, E13 . . . . . . 115 F2
Hartville Rd, SE10 . . . . . . 137 H4
Hartwell Dr, E4 . . . . 62 C6
Hartwell St, E8
off Dalston La 94 C6
Harvard Hill, W4 . . . . 126 B6
Harvard La, W4 . . . . 126 B5
Harvard Rd, SE13 . . . . 154 C5
W4 . . . . 126 B5
Isleworth TW7 . . . . 144 B1
Harvel Cres, SE2 . . . . 138 D5
Harvest Bk Rd, W.Wick.
BR4 . . . . 205 F3
Harvesters Cl, Islw. TW7 . 144 A5
Harvest La, Loug. IG10 . . . . 48 A7
Thames Ditton KT7 . . . . 180 D6
Harvest Rd, Felt. TW13 . . . 160 A4
Harvey Dr, Hmptn.
TW12 . . . . 179 H1
Harvey Gdns, E11
off Harvey Rd 97 F1
SE7 . . . . 135 J5
Loughton IG10 . . . . 49 E3
Harvey Ho, Brent. TW8
off Green Dragon La . . 125 H5
Harvey Pt, E16 *off Fife Rd* . 115 H5
Harvey Rd, E11 . . . . 97 E1
N8 . . . . 75 F5
SE5 . . . . 152 A1
Hounslow TW4 . . . . 143 F7
Ilford IG1 . . . . 99 E5
Northolt UB5 . . . . 84 C7
Harvey Rd, Walt. KT12 . . . 178 A7
Harvey St, N1 . . . . 112 A1
Harvill Rd, Sid. DA14 . . . . 176 D5
Harvington Wk, E8
off Wilman Gro 94 D7
Harvist Est, N7 . . . . 93 G4
Harvist Rd, NW6 . . . . 108 A3
Harwater Dr, Loug. IG10 . . 48 C2
Harwell Pas, N2 . . . . 73 J4
Harwood Av, Brom. BR1 . 191 H2
Mitcham CR4 . . . . 185 H3
Harwood Cl, N12
off Summerfields Av . . . 57 H6
Wembley HA0
off Harrowdene Rd 87 G4
Harwood Rd, SW6 . . . . . . 128 D7
Harwoods Yd, N21
off Wades Hill 43 G7
Harwood Ter, SW6 . . . . . . 148 E1
Hascombe Ter, SE5
off Love Wk 152 A2
Haselbury Rd, N9 . . . . 60 B4
N18 . . . . 60 B4
Haseley End, SE23
off Tyson Rd 153 F7
Haselrigge Rd, SW4 . . . . . 150 D4
Haseltine Rd, SE26 . . . . . . 171 J4
Haselwood Dr, Enf. EN2 . . 43 H4
Haskard Rd, Dag. RM9 . . . 100 D4
Hasker St, SW3 . . . . 31 H1
Haslam Av, Sutt. SM3 . . . 198 B1
Haslam Cl, N1 . . . . 93 G7
Haslam St, SE15 . . . . 132 C7
Haslemere Av, NW4 . . . . . . 72 A6
SW18 . . . . 166 E2
W7 . . . . 124 D3
W13 . . . . 124 D3
Barnet EN4 . . . . 57 J1
Hounslow TW5 . . . . 142 C2
Mitcham CR4 . . . . 185 G2
Haslemere Cl, Hmptn.
TW12 . . . . 161 F5
Wallington SM6
off Stafford Rd . . . 200/201 E5
Haslemere Gdns, N3 . . . . . 72 C3
Haslemere Heathrow Est,
Houns. TW4 . . . . 142 B2
Haslemere Rd, N8 . . . . 74 D7
N21 . . . . 59 H2
Bexleyheath DA7 . . . . . 159 F2
Ilford IG3 . . . . 99 J2
Thornton Heath CR7 . . . 187 H5
Hasler Cl, SE28 . . . . 118 B7
Hasluck Gdns, Barn. EN5 . . 41 F6
Hassard St, E2 . . . . 13 G2
Hassendean Rd, SE3 . . . . 135 H6
Hassett Rd, E9 . . . . 95 G6
Hassocks Cl, SE26 . . . . . . 171 E3
Hassocks Rd, SW16 . . . . . 186 D1
Hassock Wd, Kes. BR2 . . . 206 A4
Hassop Rd, NW2 . . . . 90 A4
Hassop Wk, SE9 . . . . 174 B4
Hasted Rd, SE7 . . . . 136 A5
Hastings Av, Ilf. IG6 . . . . . . 81 F4
Hastings Cl, SE15 . . . . 132 D7
Hastings Cl, Barnet EN5
off Leicester Rd 41 F4
Wembley HA0 . . . . 87 F4
Hastings Dr, Surb. KT6 . . 181 F6
Hastings Ho, SE18 . . . . . . 136 C4
Hastings Rd, N11 . . . . 58 C5
N17 . . . . 76 A3
W13 . . . . 104 E7
Bromley BR2 . . . . 206 B1
Croydon CR0 . . . . 202 C1
Hastings St, SE18 . . . . . . 137 F3
WC1 . . . . 10 A4
Hastingwood Trd Est,
N18 . . . . 61 G6
Hastoe Cl, Hayes UB4 . . . 102 E4
Hat & Mitre Ct, EC1 . . . . . . 11 H6
Hatch, The, Enf. EN3 . . . . . 45 G1
Hatcham Ms Business Cen,
SE14 *off Hatcham Pk Rd* 153 G1
Hatcham Pk Ms, SE14
off Hatcham Pk Rd . . . 153 G1
Hatcham Pk Rd, SE14 . . . 153 G1
Hatcham Rd, SE15 . . . . . . 133 F6
Hatchard Rd, N19 . . . . 92 D2
Hatchcroft, NW4 . . . . 71 H3
HATCH END, Pnr. HA5 . . . . 50 E6
Hatchers Ms, SE1 . . . . 28 E4
Hatch Gro, Rom. RM6 . . . . 83 E4
Hatch La, E4 . . . . 62 D4
West Drayton UB7 . . . . 120 A7
Hatch Pl, Kings.T. KT2 . . . 163 J5
Hatch Rd, SW16 . . . . 187 E2
Hatch Side, Chig. IG7 . . . . . 64 D5
Hatchwood Cl, Wdf.Grn. IG8
off Sunset Av 63 F4
Hatcliffe Cl, SE3 . . . . 155 F3
Hatcliffe St, SE10
off Woolwich Rd 135 F5
Hatfield Cl, SE14
off Reaston St 133 G7
Ilford IG6 . . . . 81 E3
Mitcham CR4 . . . . 185 G4
Hatfield Mead, Mord. SM4
off Central Rd 184 D5
Hatfield Rd, E15 . . . . 97 E5
W4 . . . . 126 D2
W13 . . . . 124 D1
Dagenham RM9 . . . . . . 101 E6
Hatfields, SE1 . . . . 27 F1
Loughton IG10 . . . . 48 E3
Hathaway Cl, Brom. BR2 . 206 C1
Stanmore HA7 . . . . 52 D5
Hathaway Cres, E12 . . . . . . 98 C6
Hathaway Gdns, W13 . . . . 104 C5
Romford RM6 . . . . 82 D5
Hathaway Rd, Croy. CR0 . 187 H7
Hatherleigh Cl, NW7 . . . . . 56 A7
Chessington KT9 . . . . . . 195 G5
Morden SM4 . . . . 184 D4
Hatherleigh Rd, Ruis. HA4 . 84 A2
Hatherley Cres, Sid.
DA14 . . . . 176 A2
Hatherley Gdns, E6 . . . . . 116 A2
N8 . . . . 74 E6
Hatherley Gro, W2 . . . . 14 A3
Hatherley Ms, E17 . . . . 78 A4
Hatherley Rd, E17 . . . . 77 J4
Richmond TW9 . . . . 145 J2
Sidcup DA14 . . . . 176 A4
Hatherley St, SW1 . . . . 33 G1
Hathern Gdns, SE9 . . . . . . 174 D4
Hatherop Rd, Hmptn.
TW12 . . . . 161 F7
Hathorne Cl, SE15 . . . . . . 153 E2
Hathway St, SE15
off Gibbon Rd 153 F2
Hathway Ter, SE14
off Kitto Rd 153 F2
Hatley Av, Ilf. IG6 . . . . 81 F4
Hatley Cl, N11 . . . . 57 J5
Hatley Rd, N4 . . . . 93 F2
Hatteraick St, SE16
off Brunel Rd 133 F2
Hattersfield Cl, Belv.
DA17 . . . . 139 F4
HATTON, Felt. TW14 . . . . . 141 J4
Hatton Cl, SE18 . . . . 137 G7
Hatton Ct, E5 *off Gilpin Rd* . 95 H4
Hatton Gdn, EC1 . . . . 19 F1
Hatton Gdns, Mitch. CR4 . 185 J5
Hatton Grn, Felt. TW14 . . . 142 A4
Hatton Gro, West Dr.
UB7 . . . . 120 A2
Hatton Ho, E1 . . . . 21 J5
Hatton Pl, EC1 . . . . 11 F6
Hatton Rd, Croy. CR0 . . . . 201 G1
Feltham TW14 . . . . 141 H5
Hatton Row, NW8 . . . . 7 F6
Hatton St, NW8 . . . . 7 F6
Hatton Wall, EC1 . . . . 19 E1
Haul Rd, NW1 . . . . 10 A1
Haunch of Venison Yd, W1 . 16 D4
Havana Rd, SW19 . . . . 166 D2
Havannah St, E14 . . . . 134 A2
Havant Rd, E17 . . . . 78 C3
Havant Way, SE15 . . . . 37 F7
Havelock Pl, Har. HA1 . . . . 68 B6
Havelock Rd, N17 . . . . 76 D2
SW19 . . . . 167 F5
Belvedere DA17 . . . . . . 139 F4
Bromley BR2 . . . . 191 J4
Croydon CR0 . . . . 202 C1
Harrow HA3 . . . . 68 B3
Southall UB2 . . . . 123 F3
Havelock St, N1 . . . . 111 E1
Ilford IG1 . . . . 98 E2
Havelock Ter, SW8 . . . . . . 130 B7
Havelock Wk, SE23 . . . . . . 171 F1
Haven, The, SE26
off Springfield Rd . . 170/171 E5
Richmond TW9 . . . . 146 A3
Sunbury-on-Thames
TW16 . . . . 160 A7
Haven Cl, SE9 . . . . 174 C3
SW19 . . . . 166 A3
Sidcup DA14 . . . . 176 C6
Haven Ct, Esher KT10 . . . 194 B2
Haven Grn, W5 . . . . 105 G6
Haven Grn Ct, W5
off Haven Grn 105 G6
Havenhurst Ri, Enf. EN2 . . 43 G2
Haven La, W5 . . . . 105 H6

Haven Ms, E3
off St. Pauls Way 113 J5
N1 off Liverpool Rd 93 G7
Haven Pl, W5
off The Broadway 105 G7
Haven St, NW1
off Castlehaven Rd 92 B7
Haven Ter, W5
off The Broadway 105 G7
Havenwood, Wem. HA9 88 B3
Haverfield Gdns, Rich.
TW9 126 A7
Haverfield Rd, E3 113 H3
Haverford Way, Edg. HA8 69 J1
Haverhill Rd, E4 62 C1
SW12 168 C1
Havering Gdns, Rom. RM6 82 C5
Havering St, E1
off Devonport St 113 G6
Havering Way, Bark. IG11 118 B3
Haversfield Est, Brent.
TW8 125 H5
Haversham Cl, Twick.
TW1 145 G6
Haversham Pl, N6 91 J2
Haverstock Hill, NW3 91 H5
Haverstock Pl, N1
off Haverstock St 111 H2
Haverstock Rd, NW5 92 A5
Haverstock St, N1 11 H2
Haverthwaite Rd, Orp.
BR6 207 G2
Havil St, SE5 132 B7
Havisham Pl, SE19 169 H6
Hawarden Gro, SE24 151 J7
Hawarden Hill, NW2 89 G3
Hawarden Rd, E17 77 G4
Hawbridge Rd, E11 96 D1
Hawes La, W.Wick. BR4 204 D1
Hawes Rd, N18 60 E6
Bromley BR1 191 H1
Hawes St, N1 93 H7
Haweswater Ho, Islw. TW7
off Summerwood Rd 144 C5
Hawgood St, E3 114 A5
Hawkdene, E4 46 B6
Hawke Pk Rd, N22 75 H3
Hawke Pl, SE16
off Middleton Dr 133 G2
Hawke Rd, SE19 170 B6
Hawkesbury Rd, SW15 147 H5
Hawkesfield Rd, SE23 171 H2
Hawkesley Cl, Twick. TW1 162 D4
Hawkes Rd, Felt. TW14 142 A7
Mitcham CR4 185 H1
Hawke Twr, SE14
off Nynehead St 133 H6
Hawkewood Rd, Sun.
TW16 178 A3
Hawkhurst Gdns, Chess.
KT9 195 H4
Hawkhurst Rd, SW16 186 D1
Hawkhurst Way, N.Mal.
KT3 182 D5
West Wickham BR4 204 B2
Hawkins Cl, NW7
off Hale La 54 D5
Borehamwood WD6
off Banks Rd 38 C2
Harrow HA1 68 A7
Hawkins Rd, Tedd. TW11 163 E6
Hawkins Way, SE6 172 A5
Hawkley Gdns, SE27 169 H2
Hawkridge Cl, Rom. RM6 82 C7
Hawksbrook La, Beck.
BR3 190 B6
Hawkshaw Cl, SW2
off Tierney Rd 150/151 E7
Hawkshead Cl, Brom.
BR1 173 E7
Hawkshead Rd, NW10 89 F7
W4 126 E2
Hawkslade Rd, SE15 153 G5
Hawksley Rd, N16 94 B3
Hawks Ms, SE10
off Luton Pl 134 C7
Hawksmoor Cl, E6
off Allhallows Rd 116 B6
SE18 137 H5
Hawksmoor Ms, E1
off Cable St 112/113 E7
Hawksmoor St, W6 128 A6
Hawksmouth, E4 46 B7
Hawks Rd, Kings.T. KT1 181 J2
Hawkstone Rd, SE16 133 F4
Hawk Ter, Ilf. IG5
off Tiptree Cres 80 D3
Hawkwell Ct, E4
off Colvin Gdns 62 C3
Hawkwell Ho, Dag. RM8 101 G1
Hawkwell Wk, N1
off Basire St 111 J1
Hawkwood Cres, E4 46 B6
Hawkwood La, Chis. BR7 193 F1
Hawkwood Mt, E5 95 E1
Hawlands Dr, Pnr. HA5 66 E7
Hawley Cl, Hmptn. TW12 161 F6
Hawley Cres, NW1 92 B7
Hawley Ms, NW1
off Hawley St 92 B7
Hawley Rd, N18 61 G5
NW1 92 B7
Hawley St, NW1 92 B7
Hawstead Rd, SE6 154 B6
Hawsted, Buck.H. IG9 47 H7
Hawthorn Av, E3 113 J1
N13 59 E5
Carshalton SM5 200 A7
Richmond TW9
off Kew Rd 145 H2
Thornton Heath CR7 187 H1
Hawthorn Cen, Har. HA1 68 C4
Hawthorn Cl, Hmptn.
TW12 161 G5
Hounslow TW5 122 B7
Orpington BR5 193 G6
Hawthorn Cotts, Well. DA16
off Hook La 158 A3
Hawthorn Ct, Rich. TW9
off West Hall Rd 146 B1
Hawthorn Cres, SW17 168 A5
Hawthornden Cl, N12
off Fallowfields Dr 57 H6
Hawthorndene Cl, Brom.
BR2 205 F2
Hawthorndene Rd, Brom.
BR2 205 F2
Hawthorn Dr, Har. HA2 67 F6
West Wickham BR4 205 E4
Hawthorne Av, Har. HA3 68 D6
Mitcham CR4 185 G2
Ruislip HA4 66 B6
Hawthorne Cl, N1 94 B6
Bromley BR1 192 C3
Sutton SM1
off Aultone Way 198/199 E2
Hawthorne Ct, Nthwd. HA6
off Ryefield Cres 66 A2
Hawthorne Cres, West Dr.
UB7 120 C2
Hawthorne Fm Av, Nthlt.
UB5 103 E1
Hawthorne Gro, NW9 70 C7
Hawthorne Ms, Grnf. UB6
off Greenford Rd 103 J6
Hawthorne Rd, E17 78 A3
Bromley BR1 192 D3
Hawthorne Way, N9 60 B2
Staines (Stanw.) TW19 140 A7
Hawthorn Gdns, W5 125 G3
Hawthorn Gro, SE20 171 E7
Barnet EN5 39 F6
Hawthorn Hatch, Brent.
TW8 125 E7
Hawthorn Ms, NW7
off Holders Hill Rd 72 B1
Hawthorn Pl, Erith DA8 139 J5
Hawthorn Rd, N8 74 D3
N18 60 C5
NW10 89 G7
Bexleyheath DA6 159 F4
Brentford TW8 125 E7
Buckhurst Hill IG9 64 A4
Sutton SM1 199 H6
Wallington SM6 200 B7
Hawthorns, Wdf.Grn. IG8 63 G3
Hawthorns, The, Epsom KT17
off Ewell Bypass 197 F6
Loughton IG10 48 D4
Hawthorn Wk, W10
off Droop St 108 B4
Hawtrey Av, Nthlt. UB5 102 D2
Hawtrey Dr, Ruis. HA4 66 A7
Hawtrey Rd, NW3 91 H7
Haxted Rd, Brom. BR1
off North Rd 191 H1
Hay Cl, E15 97 E7
Borehamwood WD6 38 C2
Haycroft Gdns, NW10 107 G1
Haycroft Rd, SW2 151 E5
Surbiton KT6 195 H3
Hay Currie St, E14 114 B6
Hayday Rd, E16 115 G5
Haydens Pl, W11
off Portobello Rd 108 C6
Hayden Way, Rom. RM5 83 J2
Haydns Ms, W3
off Emanuel Av 106 C6
Haydock Av, Nthlt. UB5 85 G6
Haydock Grn, Nthlt. UB5
off Haydock Av 85 G6
Haydon Cl, NW9 70 C4
Enfield EN1
off Mortimer Dr 44 B6
Haydon Dr, Pnr. HA5 66 A4
Haydon Pk Rd, SW19 166 E5
Haydon Rd, Dag. RM8 100 C2
Haydons Rd, SW19 167 E5
Haydon St, EC3 21 F5
Haydon Wk, E1 21 G5
Haydon Way, SW11 149 G4
HAYES, Brom. BR2 205 G2
Hayes Bypass, Hayes UB3,
UB4 102 D4
Hayes Chase, W.Wick.
BR4 190 E5
Hayes Cl, Brom. BR2 205 G2
Hayes Ct, SW2 168 E1
Hayes Cres, NW11 72 C5
Sutton SM3 198 A4
Hayesford Pk Dr, Brom.
BR2 191 F5
Hayes Gdn, Brom. BR2 205 G2
Hayes Gro, SE15 152 C4
Hayes Hill, Brom. BR2 204 E1
Hayes Hill Rd, Brom.
BR2 205 F1
Hayes La, Beck. BR3 190 C3
Bromley BR2 191 G5
Hayes Mead Rd, Brom.
BR2 205 E1
Hayes Metro Cen, Hayes
UB4 102 C7
Hayes Pl, NW1 7 H6
Hayes Rd, Brom. BR2 191 G4
Southall UB2 122 B4
Hayes St, Brom. BR2 205 H1
HAYES TOWN, Hayes
UB3 121 H2
Hayes Way, Beck. BR3 190 C4
Hayes Wd Av, Brom.
BR2 205 H1
Hayfield Pas, E1
off Stepney Grn 113 F4
Hayfield Yd, E1
off Mile End Rd 113 F4
Haygarth Pl, SW19 166 A5
Haygreen Cl, Kings.T. KT2 164 B6
Hay Hill, W1 17 E6
Hayland Cl, NW9 70 D4
Hay La, NW9 70 D4
Hayles St, SE11 35 G1
Haylett Gdns, Kings.T. KT1
off Anglesea Rd 181 G4
Hayling Av, Felt. TW13 160 A3
Hayling Cl, N16
off Boleyn Rd 94 B5
Hayling Rd, Wat. WD19 50 B2
Hayman St, N1
off Cross St 93 H7
Haymarket, SW1 17 H6
Haymarket Arc, SW1 17 H6
Haymer Gdns, Wor.Pk.
KT4 197 G3
Haymerle Rd, SE15 37 H6
Haymill Cl, Grnf. UB6 104 C3
Hayne Rd, Beck. BR3 189 J2
Haynes Cl, N11 58 A3
N17 60 E7
SE3 155 E3
Haynes Dr, N9 60 E3
Haynes La, SE19 170 B6
Haynes Rd, Wem. HA0 87 H7
Hayne St, EC1 19 H1
Haynt Wk, SW20 184 B3
★**Hay's Galleria**, SE1 28 D1
Hay's La, SE1 28 D2
Haysleigh Gdns, SE20 188 D2
Hay's Ms, W1 16 D6
Hay St, E2 112 D1
Hayter Ct, E11 97 H2
Hayter Rd, SW2 151 E5
Hayton Cl, E8
off Buttermere Wk 94 C6
Hayward Cl, SW19 185 E1
★**Hayward Gall**, SE1 26 D1
Hayward Gdns, SW15 147 J6
Hayward Rd, N20 57 F2
Thames Ditton KT7 194 D1
Haywards Cl, Rom.
(Chad.Hth) RM6 82 B5
Hayward's Pl, EC1 11 G6
Haywood Cl, Pnr. HA5 66 D2
Haywood Ri, Orp. BR6 207 H4
Haywood Rd, Brom. BR2 192 A4
Hayworth Cl, Enf. EN3
off Green St 45 H2
Hazel Av, West Dr. UB7 120 D3
Hazelbank, Surb. KT5 196 C1
Hazelbank Rd, SE6 172 D2
Hazelbourne Rd, SW12 150 B6
Hazelbrouck Gdns, Ilf.
IG6 65 G7
Hazelbury Cl, SW19 184 D2
Hazelbury Grn, N9 60 B3
Hazelbury La, N9 60 B3
Hazel Cl, N13 60 A3
N19 off Hargrave Pk 92 C2
NW9 71 E2
SE15 152 D2
Brentford TW8 125 E7
Croydon CR0 189 G7
Mitcham CR4 186 D4
Twickenham TW2 143 J7
Hazelcroft, Pnr. HA5 51 G6
Hazeldean Rd, NW10 88 D7
Hazeldene Dr, Pnr. HA5 66 C3
Hazeldene Rd, Ilf. IG3 100 B2
Welling DA16 158 C2
Hazeldon Rd, SE4 153 H5
Hazeleigh Gdns, Wdf.Grn.
IG8 64 B5
Hazel Gdns, Edg. HA8 54 B4
Hazelgreen Cl, N21 59 H1
Hazel Gro, SE26 171 G4
Enfield EN1
off Dimsdale Dr 44 D6
Orpington BR6 206 E2
Romford RM6 82 E3
Wembley HA0
off Carlyon Rd 105 H1
Hazel Gro Est, SE26 171 G4
Hazelhurst, Beck. BR3 190 D1
Hazelhurst Rd, SW17 167 F4
Hazel La, Ilf. IG6 64 E7
Richmond TW10 163 H2
Hazell Cres, Rom. RM5 83 H1
Hazellville Rd, N19 74 D7
Hazel Mead, Barn. EN5 39 H5
Hazelmere Cl, Felt. TW14 141 G6
Northolt UB5 103 F2
Hazelmere Dr, Nthlt.
UB5 103 F2
Hazelmere Rd, NW6 108 D1
Northolt UB5 103 F2
Orpington BR5 193 F4
Hazelmere Wk, Nthlt.
UB5 103 F2
Hazelmere Way, Brom.
BR2 191 G6
Hazel Ms, N22
off Alexandra Rd 75 G3
Hazel Rd, E15
off Wingfield Rd 96/97 E5
NW10 107 J3
Hazeltree La, Nthlt. UB5 103 E3
Hazel Wk, Brom. BR2 192 D6
Hazel Way, E4 61 J6
SE1 37 F1
Hazelwood, Loug. IG10 48 A5
Hazelwood Av, Mord.
SM4 185 E4
Hazelwood Cl, W5 125 H2
Harrow HA2 67 H4
Hazelwood Ct, NW10
off Neasden La N. 88/89 E3
Hazelwood Cres, N13 59 G4
Hazelwood Cft, Surb.
KT6 181 H6
Hazelwood Dr, Pnr. HA5 66 B2
Hazelwood La, N13 59 G4
Hazelwood Pk Cl, Chig.
IG7 65 H5
Hazelwood Rd, E17 77 H5
Enfield EN1 44 C6
Hazlebury Rd, SW6 148 E2
Hazledean Rd, Croy. CR0 202 A2
Hazledene Rd, W4 126 C6
Hazlemere Gdns, Wor.Pk.
KT4 197 H1
Hazlewell Rd, SW15 147 H5
Hazlewood Cl, E5
off Mandeville St 95 H3
Hazlewood Cres, W10 108 B4
Hazlitt Cl, Felt. TW13 161 E4
Hazlitt Ms, W14
off Hazlitt Rd 128 B3
Hazlitt Rd, W14 128 B3
Headcorn Pl, Th.Hth. CR7
off Headcorn Rd 187 F4
Headcorn Rd, N17 60 C7
Bromley BR1 173 F5
Thornton Heath CR7 187 F4
Headfort Pl, SW1 24 C4
Headingley Cl, Ilf. IG6 65 J6
Headington Rd, SW18 167 F2

Headlam Rd, SW4 **150** D6
Headlam St, E1 **113** E4
Headley App, Ilf. IG2 **80** D5
Headley Av, Wall. SM6 **201** F5
Headley Cl, Epsom KT19 **196** A6
Headley Ct, SE26 **171** E5
Headley Dr, Croy.
(New Adgtn) CR0 **204** B7
Ilford IG2 **80** E6
Head's Ms, W11
off Artesian Rd **108** D6
HEADSTONE, Har. HA2 **67** J4
Headstone Dr, Har.
HA1, HA3 **68** B3
Headstone Gdns,
Har. HA2 **67** J4
Headstone La, Har.
HA2, HA3 **67** H4
Headstone Rd, Har. HA1 **68** B5
Head St, E1 **113** G6
Headway Cl, Rich. TW10
off Locksmeade Rd **163** F4
Heald St, SE14 **153** J1
Healey Dr, Orp. BR6 **207** J4
Healey St, NW1 **92** B6
Heanor Ct, E5
off Pedro St **95** G3
Hearne Rd, W4 **126** A6
Hearn Ri, Nthlt. UB5 **102** D1
Hearn's Bldgs, SE17 **36** C2
Hearn St, EC2 **12** E6
Hearnville Rd, SW12 **168** A1
Heath, The, W7
off Lower Boston Rd **124** B1
Heatham Pk, Twick. TW2 **144** C7
Heath Av, Bexh. DA7 **138** D6
Heathbourne Rd, Bushey
(Bushey Hth) WD23 **52** B2
Stanmore HA7 **52** B2
Heath Brow, NW3
off North End Way **91** F3
Heath Cl, NW11 **72** E7
W5 **105** J4
Hayes UB3 **121** G7
Heathcock Ct, WC2
off Strand **110/111** E7
Heathcote Av, Ilf. IG5 **80** C2
Heathcote Ct, Ilf. IG5
off Heathcote Av **80** C2
Heathcote Gro, E4 **62** C3
Heathcote Pt, E9
off Wick Rd **95** G6
Heathcote Rd, Twick.
TW1 **145** E6
Heathcote St, WC1 **10** C5
Heathcote Way, West Dr. UB7
off Tavistock Rd **120** A1
Heath Ct, Houns. TW4 **143** F4
Heathcroft, NW11 **91** E1
W5 **105** J4
Heathcroft Gdns, E17 **78** D1
Heathdale Av, Houns.
TW4 **143** E3
Heathdene Dr, Belv. DA17 **139** H4
Heathdene Rd, SW16 **169** F7
Wallington SM6 **200** B7
Heath Dr, NW3 **90** E4
SW20 **183** J4
Heathedge, SE26 **170** E2
Heatherbank, SE9 **156** C2
Chislehurst BR7 **192** D2
Heather Cl, E6 **116** E6
N7 *off Newington*
Barrow Way **93** F3
SE13 **154** D6
SW8 **150** B3
Hampton TW12 **179** F1
Isleworth TW7
off Harvesters Cl **144** A5
Heatherdale Cl, Kings.T.
KT2 **164** A6
Heatherdene Cl, N12
off Bow La **73** F1
Mitcham CR4 **185** H4
Heather Dr, Enf. EN2
off Chasewood Av **43** H2
Heather Gdns, NW11 **72** B6
Sutton SM2 **198** D6
Heatherlands, Sun. TW16 **160** A6
Heatherley Dr, Ilf. IG5 **80** B3
Heather Pk Dr, Wem. HA0 **88** A7
Heather Rd, E4 **61** J6
NW2 **89** F2
SE12 **173** G2
Heathers, The, Stai.
TW19 **140** C7
Heatherset Gdns, SW16 **169** F7
Heatherside Rd, Epsom
KT19 **196** D7
Heatherside Rd, Sid. DA14
off Wren Rd **176** D3
Heatherton Ter, N3 **73** E2
Heather Wk, W10
off Droop St **108** B4
Edgware HA8 **54** B5
Twickenham TW2
off Stephenson Rd **143** G7
Heather Way, Stan. HA7 **52** C6
Heatherwood Cl, E12 **97** J2
Heathfield, E4 **62** C3
Chislehurst BR7 **175** F6
Heathfield Av, SW18
off Heathfield Rd **149** G7
Heathfield Cl, E16 **116** A5
Keston BR2 **205** J5
Heathfield Dr, Mitch.
CR4 **185** H1
Heathfield Gdns, NW11 **72** A6
SE3 **154** E2
SW18 *off Heathfield Rd* **149** G6
W4 **126** C5
Croydon CR0
off Coombe Rd **202** A4
Heathfield La, Chis. BR7 **175** E6
Heathfield N, Twick. TW2 **144** C7
Heathfield Pk, NW2 **89** J6
Heathfield Pk Dr, Rom.
(Chad.Hth) RM6 **82** B5
Heathfield Rd, SW18 **149** F6
W3 **126** B2
Bexleyheath DA6 **159** F4
Bromley BR1 **173** F7
Croydon CR0 **202** A4
Keston BR2 **205** J5
Heathfields Ct, Houns. TW4
off Frampton Rd **142/143** E5
Heathfield S, Twick. TW2 **144** C7
Heathfield Sq, SW18 **149** G7
Heathfield St, W11
off Portland Rd **108** B7
Heathfield Ter, SE18 **137** J6
W4 **126** C5
Heath Gdns, Twick. TW1 **162** C1
Heathgate, NW11 **72** E6
Heathgate Pl, NW3
off Agincourt Rd **91** J5
Heath Gro, SE20
off Maple Rd **171** F7
Heath Hurst Rd, NW3 **91** H4
Heathland Rd, N16 **94** B1
Heathlands Cl, Sun.
TW16 **178** A2
Twickenham TW1 **162** C2
Heathlands Way, Houns.
TW4 **143** E5
Heath La, SE3 **154** D2
Heathlee Rd, SE3 **155** F4
Heathley End, Chis. BR7 **175** F6
Heathmans Rd, SW6 **148** C1
Heath Mead, SW19 **166** A3
Heath Pk Dr, Brom. BR1 **192** B3
Heath Pas, NW3 **91** E2
Heath Ri, SW15 **148** A6
Bromley BR2 **191** F6
Heath Rd, SW8 **150** B2
Bexley DA5 **177** J1
Harrow HA1 **67** J7
Hounslow TW3 **143** H4
Romford RM6 **82** D7
Thornton Heath CR7 **187** J3
Twickenham TW1, TW2 **162** C1
★**Heathrow Airport**, Houns.
TW6 **140** E1
Heathrow Ho, Houns. TW5
off Bath Rd **142** A1
Heathrow Interchange,
Hayes UB4 **122** C1
Heathrow Int Trd Est,
Houns. TW4 **142** B3
Heathrow Tunnel App, Houns.
(Hthrw Air.) TW6 **140** E3
Heathrow Vehicle Tunnel,
Houns. (Hthrw Air.) TW6 **140** E1
Heaths Cl, Enf. EN1 **44** B2
Heath Side, NW3 **91** G4
Heathside, Esher KT10 **194** B3
Hounslow TW4 **143** F7
Heath Side, Orp. BR5 **207** F1
Heathside Av, Bexh. DA7 **159** E1
Heathside Cl, Esher KT10 **194** B3
Ilford IG2 **81** G5
Heathstan Rd, W12 **107** G6
Heath St, NW3 **91** F4
Heath Vw, N2 **73** F4
Heath Vw Cl, N2 **73** F4
Heathview Ct, SW19 **166** A2
Heathview Dr, SE2 **138** D6
Heathview Gdns, SW15 **147** J7
Heathview Rd, Th.Hth.
CR7 **187** G4
Heath Vil, SE18 **137** J5
SW18 *off Cargill Rd* **167** F1
Heathville Rd, N19 **74** E7
Heathwall St, SW11 **149** J3
Heathway, SE3 **135** F7
Croydon CR0 **203** J3
Dagenham RM9, RM10 **101** G7
Heath Way, Erith DA8 **159** J1
Heathway, Wdf.Grn. IG8 **63** J4
Heathway Ind Est, Dag. RM10
off Manchester Way **101** H4
Heathwood Gdns, SE7 **136** B4
Heathwood Pt, SE23
off Dacres Rd **171** G3
Heaton Cl, E4 **62** C3
Heaton Rd, SE15 **152** D3
Mitcham CR4 **168** A7
Heaven Tree Cl, N1 **93** J5
Heaver Rd, SW11
off Wye St **149** G3
Heavitree Cl, SE18 **137** G5
Heavitree Rd, SE18 **137** G5
Hebden Ct, E2
off Laburnum St **112** C1
Hebden Ter, N17
off Commercial Rd **60** B6
Hebdon Rd, SW17 **167** H3
Heber Rd, NW2 **90** A5
SE22 **152** C6
Hebron Rd, W6 **127** H3
Hecham Cl, E17 **77** H2
Heckfield Pl, SW6
off Fulham Rd **128** D7
Heckford St, E1
off The Highway **113** G7
Hector St, SE18 **137** H4
Heddington Gro, N7 **93** F5
Heddon Cl, Islw. TW7 **144** D4
Heddon Ct Av, Barn. EN4 **41** J5
Heddon Ct Par, Barn. EN4
off Cockfosters Rd **42** A5
Heddon Rd, Barn. EN4 **41** J5
Heddon St, W1 **17** F5
Hedge Hill, Enf. EN2 **43** H1
Hedge La, N13 **59** H3
Hedgeley, Ilf. IG4 **80** C4
Hedgemans Rd, Dag.
RM9 **100** D7
Hedgemans Way, Dag.
RM9 **100** E6
Hedgerley Gdns, Grnf.
UB6 **103** J2
Hedgerow La, Barn. EN5 **39** H5
Hedgers Cl, Loug. IG10
off Newmans La **48** D4
Hedgers Gro, E9 **95** H6
Hedger St, SE11 **35** G1
Hedge Wk, SE6 **172** B4
Hedgewood Gdns, Ilf. IG5 **80** D5
Hedgley Ms, SE12
off Hedgley St **155** F5
Hedgley St, SE12 **155** F5
Hedingham Cl, N1
off Popham Rd **93** J7
Hedingham Ho, Kings.T. KT2
off Kingsgate Rd **181** H1
Hedingham Rd, Dag.
RM8 **100** B5
Hedley Rd, Twick. TW2 **143** G7
Hedley Row, N5
off Poets Rd **94** A5
Heenan Cl, Bark. IG11
off Glenny Rd **99** F6
Heene Rd, Enf. EN2 **44** A1
Heidegger Cres, SW13
off Trinity Ch Rd **127** H6
Heigham Rd, E6 **98** A7
Heighton Gdns, Croy.
CR0 **201** H5
Heights, The, SE7 **135** J5
Beckenham BR3 **172** C7
Loughton IG10 **48** C2
Northolt UB5 **85** F5
Heights Cl, SW20 **165** H7
★**Heinz Gall, R.I.B.A.**, W1 **16** B3
Heiron St, SE17 **35** H6
Helby Rd, SW4 **150** D6
Helder Gro, SE12 **155** F7
Helder St, S.Croy. CR2 **202** A6
Heldmann Cl, Houns.
TW3 **144** A4
Helegan Cl, Orp. BR6 **207** J4
Helena Pl, E9
off Fremont St **113** F1
Helena Rd, E13 **115** F2
E17 **78** A5
NW10 **89** H5
Helena Rd, W5 **105** G5
Helena Sq, SE16
off Rotherhithe St **113** H7
Helen Av, Felt. TW14 **142** B7
Helen Cl, N2
off Thomas More Way **73** F3
West Molesey KT8 **179** H4
Helenslea Av, NW11 **90** C1
Helen's Pl, E2
off Roman Rd **113** F3
Helen St, SE18
off Wilmount St **136/137** E4
Helios Rd, Wall. SM6 **200** A1
Helix Gdns, SW2
off Helix Rd **151** F6
Helix Rd, SW2 **151** F6
Hellen Way, Wat. WD19 **50** D4
Hellings St, E1 **29** J2
Helme Cl, SW19 **166** C5
Helmet Row, EC1 **12** A5
Helmore Rd, Bark. IG11 **99** J7
Helmsdale Cl, Hayes
UB4 **102** E4
Helmsdale Rd, SW16 **186** C1
Helmsley Pl, E8 **94** E7
Helperby Rd, NW10
off Mayo Rd **88/89** E6
Helsinki Sq, SE16 **133** H3
Helston Cl, Pnr. HA5 **51** F7
Helvetia St, SE6 **171** J2
Hemans St, SW8 **33** J7
Hemberton Rd, SW9 **150** E3
Hemery Rd, Grnf. UB6 **86** A5
Hemingford Cl, N12 **57** G5
Hemingford Rd, N1 **111** F1
Sutton SM3 **197** J4
Heming Rd, Edg. HA8 **54** B7
Hemington Av, N11 **57** J5
Hemlock Rd, W12 **107** F7
Hemming Cl, Hmptn. TW12
off Chandler Cl **179** G1
Hemmings Cl, Sid. DA14 **176** B2
Hemming St, E1 **13** J6
Hempstead Cl, Buck.H.
IG9 **63** G2
Hempstead Rd, E17 **78** D2
Hemp Wk, SE17 **36** C1
Hemsby Rd, Chess. KT9 **195** J6
Hemstal Rd, NW6 **90** D7
Hemswell Dr, NW9 **70** E1
Hemsworth Ct, N1
off Hemsworth St **112** B2
Hemsworth St, N1 **12** D1
Hemus Pl, SW3 **31** H4
Hen & Chicken Ct, EC4
off Fleet St **111** G6
Henbury Way, Wat. WD19 **50** D3
Henchman St, W12 **107** F6
Hendale Av, NW4 **71** G3
Henderson Cl, NW10 **88** C6
Henderson Dr, NW8 **7** E5
Henderson Rd, E7 **97** J6
N9 **60** E1
SW18 **149** H7
Croydon CR0 **188** A6
Hayes UB4 **102** A3
Hendham Rd, SW17 **167** H2
HENDON, NW4 **71** H4
Hendon Av, N3 **72** B1
Hendon Hall Ct, NW4
off Parson St **72** A3
Hendon La, N3 **72** B3
Hendon Pk Row, NW11 **72** C6
Hendon Rd, N9 **60** D2
Hendon Way, NW2 **90** C3
NW4 **71** H6
Staines (Stanw.) TW19 **140** A6
Hendon Wd La, NW7 **39** F6
Hendren Cl, Grnf. UB6
off Dimmock Dr **86** A5
Hendre Rd, SE1 **36** E2
Hendrick Av, SW12 **149** J6
Heneage La, EC3 **20** E4
Heneage St, E1 **21** G1
Henfield Cl, N19 **92** C1
Bexley DA5 **159** G6
Henfield Rd, SW19 **184** C1
Hengelo Gdns, Mitch.
CR4 **185** G4
Hengist Rd, SE12 **155** H7
Erith DA8 **139** H7
Hengist Way, Brom. BR2 **190** E4
Hengrave Rd, SE23 **153** G7
Hengrove Ct, Bex. DA5
off Hurst Rd **176/177** E1
Henley Av, Sutt. SM3 **198** B3
Henley Cl, SE16
off St. Marychurch St **133** F2
Greenford UB6 **103** J2

Henley Cl, Islw. TW7 . . . . . **144** C1
Henley Ct, N14 . . . . **42** C7
Henley Cross, SE3 . . . . . . **155** H3
Henley Dr, SE1 . . . . **37** G1
Kingston upon Thames KT2 . . . . **165** F7
Henley Gdns, Pnr. HA5 . . . **66** B3
Romford RM6 . . . . **82** E5
Henley Rd, E16 . . . . **136** C2
N18 . . . . **60** B4
NW10 . . . . **107** J1
Ilford IG1 . . . . **99** F4
Henley St, SW11 . . . . . . **150** A2
Henley Way, Felt. TW13 . . **160** D5
Henlow Pl, Rich. TW10
off Sandpits Rd **163** G2
Hennel Cl, SE23 . . . . **171** F3
Hennessy Rd, N9 . . . . **61** F2
Henniker Gdns, E6 . . . . . . **116** A3
Henniker Ms, SW3 . . . . **30** E5
Henniker Pt, E15 . . . . **96** E5
Henniker Rd, E15 . . . . **96** D5
Henningham Rd, N17 . . . . . **76** A1
Henning St, SW11 . . . . . . **149** H1
Henrietta Cl, SE8 . . . . . . **134** A6
Henrietta Ms, WC1 . . . . **10** B5
Henrietta Pl, W1 . . . . **16** D4
Henrietta St, E15 . . . . **96** C5
WC2 . . . . **18** B5
Henriques St, E1 . . . . **21** J3
Henry Addlington Cl, E6 . . **116** E5
Henry Cooper Way, SE9 . . **174** A3
Henry Darlot Dr, NW7 . . . . **56** A5
Henry Dent Cl, SE5 . . . . . **152** A3
Henry Dickens Ct, W11 . . . **128** A1
Henry Doulton Dr, SW17 . **168** B4
Henry Jackson Rd, SW15 . . . . **148** A3
Henry Macaulay Av, Kings.T. KT2 . . . . **181** G1
Henry Rd, E6 . . . . **116** B2
N4 . . . . **93** J1
Barnet EN4 . . . . **41** G5
Henry's Av, Wdf.Grn. IG8 . . **63** F5
Henryson Rd, SE4 . . . . . . **154** A5
Henry St, Brom. BR1 . . . . **191** H1
Henry's Wk, Ilf. IG6 . . . . . . **65** G7
Henry Tate Ms, SW16 . . . . **169** G5
Hensford Gdns, SE26
off Wells Pk Rd . . . **170/171** E4
Henshall Pt, E3
off Bromley High St . . **114** B3
Henshall St, N1 . . . . **94** A6
Henshawe Rd, Dag. RM8 . **100** D3
Henshaw St, SE17 . . . . **36** B1
Hensley Pt, E9 *off Wick Rd*. **95** G6
Henslowe Rd, SE22 . . . . . **152** D5
Henson Av, NW2 . . . . **89** J5
Henson Cl, Orp. BR6 . . . . **207** E2
Henson Path, Har. HA3 . . . **69** G3
Henson Pl, Nthlt. UB5 . . . **102** C1
Henstridge Pl, NW8 . . . . **7** G1
Henty Cl, SW11 . . . . **129** H7
Henty Wk, SW15 . . . . **147** H5
Henville Rd, Brom. BR1 . . **191** H1
Henwick Rd, SE9 . . . . **156** A3
Henwood Side, Wdf.Grn. IG8
off Love La **64** C6
Hepburn Gdns, Brom. BR2 . . . . **205** E1
Hepburn Ms, SW11
off Webbs Rd **149** J5
Hepple Cl, Islw. TW7 . . . . **144** E2
Hepplestone Cl, SW15
off Dover Pk Dr **147** H6
Hepscott Rd, E9 . . . . **96** A7
Hepworth Ct, Bark. IG11 . **100** A5
Hepworth Gdns, Bark. IG11 . . . . **100** A5
Hepworth Rd, SW16 . . . . **169** E7
Hepworth Wk, NW3
off Haverstock Hill **91** H5
Heracles Cl, Wall. SM6 . . **200** E7
Herald Gdns, Wall. SM6 . . **200** B3
Herald's Pl, SE11 . . . . **35** G1
Herald St, E2
off Three Colts La . **112/113** E4
Herbal Hill, EC1 . . . . **11** F6
Herbert Cres, SW1 . . . . **24** A5
Herbert Gdns, NW10 . . . . **107** H2
W4 *off Magnolia Rd* . . . **126** B6
Romford RM6 . . . . **82** D7
Herbert Ms, SW2
off Bascombe St **151** G6
Herbert Morrison Ho, SW6
off Clem Attlee Ct **128** C6
Herbert Pl, SE18 *off Plumstead Common Rd* **136/137** E6
Herbert Rd, E12 . . . . **98** B4
Herbert Rd, E17 . . . . **77** J7
N11 . . . . **58** E7
N15 . . . . **76** C5
NW9 . . . . **71** G6
SE18 . . . . **136** D7
SW19 . . . . **166** C7
Bexleyheath DA7 . . . . . **159** E2
Bromley BR2 . . . . **192** A5
Ilford IG3 . . . . **99** H2
Kingston upon Thames KT1 . . . . **181** J3
Southall UB1 . . . . **123** F1
Herbert St, E13 . . . . **115** G2
NW5 . . . . **92** A6
Herbert Ter, SE18
off Herbert Rd . . . **136/137** E6
Herbrand St, WC1 . . . . **10** A5
Hercules Pl, N7
off Hercules St **92/93** E3
Hercules Rd, SE1 . . . . **26** D6
Hercules St, N7 . . . . **93** E3
Hereford Av, Barn. EN4 . . . **57** J1
Hereford Ct, Sutt. SM2
off Worcester Rd **198** D7
Hereford Gdns, SE13
off Longhurst Rd . **154/155** E5
Ilford IG1 . . . . **80** B7
Pinner HA5 . . . . **66** E5
Twickenham TW2 . . . . . **161** J1
Hereford Ho, NW6 . . . . . . **108** D2
Hereford Ms, W2
off Hereford Rd **108** D6
Hereford Pl, SE14
off Royal Naval Pl **133** J7
Hereford Retreat, SE15 . . . **37** H6
Hereford Rd, E11 . . . . **79** H5
W2 . . . . **108** D6
W3 . . . . **106** B7
W5 . . . . **125** F3
Feltham TW13 . . . . **160** C1
Hereford Sq, SW7 . . . . **30** D2
Hereford St, E2 . . . . **13** H5
Hereford Way, Chess. KT9 . . . . **195** F5
Herent Dr, Ilf. IG5 . . . . **80** B4
Hereward Gdns, N13 . . . . . **59** G5
Hereward Grn, Loug. IG10 . . . . **49** F1
Hereward Rd, SW17 . . . . . **167** J4
Herga Ct, Har. HA1 . . . . . . **86** B3
Herga Rd, Har. HA3 . . . . . . **68** C4
Heriot Av, E4 . . . . **62** A2
Heriot Rd, NW4 . . . . **71** J5
Heriots Cl, Stan. HA7 . . . . . **52** D4
Heritage Cl, SW9 . . . . **151** H3
Heritage Hill, Kes. BR2 . . . **205** J5
Heritage Pl, SW18
off Earlsfield Rd **167** F1
Heritage Vw, Har. HA1 . . . . **86** C3
Herlwyn Gdns, SW17 . . . . **167** J4
Hermes Cl, W9
off Chippenham Rd . . . **108** D4
Hermes St, N1 . . . . **10** E2
Hermes Wk, Nthlt. UB5
off Hotspur Rd **103** G2
Hermes Way, Wall. SM6 . . **200** D7
Hermiston Av, N8 . . . . **75** E5
Hermitage, The, SE23 . . . . **171** F1
SW13 . . . . **147** F1
Richmond TW10 . . . . . . **145** G5
Hermitage Cl, E18 . . . . **79** F4
SE2 *off Felixstowe Rd* . . **138** C3
Enfield EN2 . . . . **43** H2
Esher (Clay.) KT10 . . . . . **194** D6
Hermitage Ct, E18 . . . . **79** G4
NW2 *off Hermitage La* . . **90** D3
Hermitage Gdns, NW2 . . . . **90** D3
SE19 . . . . **169** J6
Hermitage La, N18 . . . . **60** A5
NW2 . . . . **90** D3
SE25 . . . . **188** D6
SW16 . . . . **169** F7
Croydon CR0 . . . . **188** D6
Hermitage Path, SW16 . . . **187** E1
Hermitage Rd, N4 . . . . **75** H7
N15 . . . . **75** H7
SE19 . . . . **169** J7
Hermitage Row, E8 . . . . . . **94** D5
Hermitage St, W2 . . . . **15** E2
Hermitage Wk, E18 . . . . **79** F4
Hermitage Wall, E1 . . . . **29** J2
Hermitage Waterside, E1 . . **29** H1
Hermitage Way, Stan. HA7 . . . . **68** D1
Hermit Pl, NW6
off Belsize Rd **108/109** E1
Hermit Rd, E16 . . . . **115** F5
Hermit St, EC1 . . . . **11** G3
Hermon Gro, Hayes UB3 . **122** A1
Hermon Hill, E11 . . . . **79** G5
E18 . . . . **79** G5
Herndon Rd, SW18 . . . . . . **149** F5
Herne Cl, NW10
off North Circular Rd . . **88** D5
HERNE HILL, SE24 . . . . . . **151** J5
Herne Hill, SE24 . . . . **151** J6
Herne Hill Ho, SE24
off Railton Rd **151** H6
Herne Hill Rd, SE24 . . . . . **151** J3
Herne Ms, N18
off Lyndhurst Rd **60** D4
Herne Pl, SE24 . . . . **151** H5
Herne Rd, Surb. KT6 . . . . **195** G2
Heron Cl, E17 . . . . **77** J2
NW10 . . . . **89** E6
Buckhurst Hill IG9 . . . . . . **63** G1
Sutton SM1
off Sandpiper Rd **198** C5
Heron Ct, Brom. BR2 . . . . **191** J4
Heron Cres, Sid. DA14 . . . **175** H3
Herondale Av, SW18 . . . . **167** G1
Heron Dr, N4 . . . . **93** J2
Herongate Rd, E12 . . . . **97** J2
Heron Hill, Belv. DA17 . . . **139** F4
Heron Ms, Ilf. IG1
off Balfour Rd **98/99** E2
Heron Pl, SE16 . . . . **133** H1
Heron Quay, E14 . . . . **134** A1
Heron Rd, SE24 . . . . **151** J4
Croydon CR0
off Tunstall Rd **202** B2
Twickenham TW1 . . . . . **144** D4
Herons, The, E11 . . . . **79** F6
Heronsforde, W13 . . . . **105** F6
Heronsgate, Edg. HA8 . . . . **54** A5
Heronslea Dr, Stan. HA7 . . **53** H5
Heron's Pl, Islw. TW7 . . . . **144** E3
Heron Sq, Rich. TW9
off Bridge St **145** G5
Herons Ri, Barn. EN4 . . . . . **41** H4
Heron Trd Est, W3
off Alliance Rd **106** B4
Heron Way, Felt. TW14 . . . **142** A4
Heronway, Wdf.Grn. IG8 . . . **63** J4
Herrick Rd, N5 . . . . **93** J3
Herrick St, SW1 . . . . **33** J1
Herries St, W10 . . . . **108** B2
Herringham Rd, SE7 . . . . . **135** J3
Herrongate Cl, Enf. EN1 . . . **44** C2
Hersant Cl, NW10 . . . . **107** G1
Herschell Ms, SE5
off Bicknell Rd **151** J3
Herschell Rd, SE23 . . . . . . **153** H7
Hersham Cl, SW15 . . . . . . **147** G7
Hertford Av, SW14 . . . . . . **146** D5
Hertford Cl, Barn. EN4 . . . . **41** G3
Hertford Pl, W1 . . . . **9** F6
Hertford Rd, N1 . . . . **112** B1
N2 . . . . **73** H3
N9 . . . . **60** E2
Barking IG11 . . . . **98** E7
Barnet EN4 . . . . **41** F3
Enfield EN3 . . . . **45** F3
Ilford IG2 . . . . **81** H6
Hertford Sq, Mitch. CR4
off Hertford Way . . **186/187** E4
Hertford St, W1 . . . . **24** D1
Hertford Wk, Belv. DA17
off Hoddesdon Rd **139** G5
Hertford Way, Mitch. CR4 . **186** E4
Hertslet Rd, N7 . . . . **93** F3
Hertsmere Rd, E14 . . . . . . **114** A7
Hervey Cl, N3 . . . . **72** D1
Hervey Pk Rd, E17 . . . . **77** H4
Hervey Rd, SE3 . . . . **155** H1
Hesa Rd, Hayes UB3 . . . . **102** A6
Hesewall Cl, SW4
off Brayburne Av **150** C2
Hesketh Pl, W11 . . . . **108** B7
Hesketh Rd, E7 . . . . **97** G3
Heslop Rd, SW12 . . . . **167** J1
Hesper Ms, SW5 . . . . **30** A3
Hesperus Cres, E14 . . . . . **134** B4
Hessel Rd, W13 . . . . **124** D2
Hessel St, E1 . . . . **112** E6
Hestercombe Av, SW6 . . . **148** B2
Hesterman Way, Croy. CR0 . . . . **201** E1
Hester Rd, N18 . . . . **60** D5
SW11 . . . . **129** H7
Hester Ter, Rich. TW9
off Chilton Rd **146** A3
HESTON, Houns. TW5 . . . . **123** F7
Heston Av, Houns. TW5 . . . **123** E7
Heston Gra La, Houns. TW5 . . . . **123** F6
Heston Ind Mall, Houns. TW5 . . . . **123** F7
Heston Rd, Houns. TW5 . . **123** G7
Heston St, SE14 . . . . **153** J1
Heswell Grn, Wat. WD19
off Fairhaven Cres **50** A3
Hetherington Rd, SW4 . . . **150** E4
Hetley Gdns, SE19 . . . . . . **170** C7
Hetley Rd, W12 . . . . **127** H1
Heton Gdns, NW4 . . . . **71** G4
Hevelius Cl, SE10 . . . . **135** F5
Hever Cft, SE9 . . . . **174** D4
Hever Gdns, Brom. BR1 . . **192** D3
Heverham Rd, SE18 . . . . . **137** H4
Heversham Rd, Bexh. DA7 . . . . **159** G2
Hewer St, W10 . . . . **108** A5
Hewett Cl, Stan. HA7 . . . . . **53** E4
Hewett Rd, Dag. RM8 . . . **100** D5
Hewett St, EC2 . . . . **12** E6
Hewish Rd, N18 . . . . **60** B4
Hewison St, E3 . . . . **113** J2
Hewitt Av, N22 . . . . **75** H2
Hewitt Cl, Croy. CR0 . . . . **204** A3
Hewitt Rd, N8 . . . . **75** G5
Hewlett Rd, E3 . . . . **113** H2
Hexagon, The, N6 . . . . **91** J1
Hexal Rd, SE6 . . . . **172** E3
Hexham Gdns, Islw. TW7 . **124** D7
Hexham Rd, SE27 . . . . . . **169** J2
Barnet EN5 . . . . **41** E4
Morden SM4 . . . . **198** E1
Heybourne Rd, N17 . . . . . . **61** E7
Heybridge Av, SW16 . . . . **169** E7
Heybridge Dr, Ilf. IG6 . . . . . **81** G2
Heybridge Way, E10 . . . . . . **77** H7
Heyford Av, SW8 . . . . **34** B7
SW20 . . . . **184** C3
Heyford Rd, Mitch. CR4 . . **185** H2
Heyford Ter, SW8
off Heyford Av . . . **130/131** E7
Heygate St, SE17 . . . . **35** J2
Heylyn Sq, E3
off Malmesbury Rd . . . **113** J3
Heynes Rd, Dag. RM8 . . . **100** C4
Heysham Dr, Wat. WD19 . . **50** C5
Heysham La, NW3 . . . . **91** E3
Heysham Rd, N15 . . . . **76** A6
Heythorp St, SW18 . . . . . **166** C1
Heywood Av, NW9 . . . . **70** E1
Heyworth Rd, E5 . . . . **94** E4
E15 . . . . **97** F5
Hibbert Rd, E17 . . . . **77** J7
Harrow HA3 . . . . **68** C2
Hibbert St, SW11 . . . . **149** F3
Hibernia Gdns, Houns. TW3 . . . . **143** G4
Hibernia Pt, SE2
off Wolvercote Rd **138** D2
Hibernia Rd, Houns. TW3 . **143** G4
Hibiscus Cl, Edg. HA8
off Campion Way **54** C4
Hichisson Rd, SE15 . . . . . **153** F5
Hickin Cl, SE7 . . . . **136** A4
Hickin St, E14
off Plevna St **134** C3
Hickling Rd, Ilf. IG1 . . . . . . **99** E5
Hickman Av, E4 . . . . **62** C6
Hickman Cl, E16 . . . . **116** A5
Hickman Rd, Rom. RM6 . . . **82** C7
Hickmore Wk, SW4 . . . . . **150** C3
Hickory Cl, N9 . . . . **44** D7
Hicks Av, Grnf. UB6 . . . . . **104** A2
Hicks Cl, SW11 . . . . **149** H3
Hicks St, SE8 . . . . **133** H5
Hidcote Gdns, SW20 . . . . **183** H3
Hide, E6 *off Downings* . . . **116** D6
Hide Pl, SW1 . . . . **33** H2
Hide Rd, Har. HA1 . . . . **68** A4
Hides St, N7
off Sheringham Rd **93** F6
Hide Twr, SW1 . . . . **33** H2
Higgins Wk, Hmptn. TW12
off Abbott Cl **160/161** E6
High Acres, Enf. EN2
off Old Pk Vw **43** H3
HIGHAM HILL, E17 . . . . **77** H2
Higham Hill Rd, E17 . . . . . . **77** H2
Higham Pl, E17 . . . . **77** H3
Higham Rd, N17 . . . . **76** A3
Woodford Green IG8 . . . **63** G6
Highams Ct, E4
off Friars Cl **62** D3
Highams Lo Business Cen, E17 . . . . **77** H3
HIGHAMS PARK, E4 . . . . . . **62** D5
Highams Pk Ind Est, E4 . . . **62** C6
Higham Sta Av, E4 . . . . **62** B6
Higham St, E17 . . . . **77** H3
Highbanks Cl, Well. DA16 . . . . **138** B7

Highbanks Rd, Pnr. HA5 51 H5
Highbank Way, N8 75 G6
HIGH BARNET, Barn. EN5 40 A2
Highbarrow Rd, Croy. CR0 188 D7
HIGH BEACH, Loug. IG10 47 G1
High Beech, S.Croy. CR2 202 B7
High Beeches, Sid. DA14 176 E5
High Beech Rd, Loug. IG10 48 A4
High Br, SE10 134 D5
Highbridge Rd, Bark. IG11 116 E1
High Br Wf, SE10 134 D5
Highbrook Rd, SE3 156 A3
High Broom Cres, W.Wick. BR4 190 B7
HIGHBURY, N5 93 H5
Highbury Av, Th.Hth. CR7 187 G2
Highbury Cl, N.Mal. KT3 182 C4
West Wickham BR4 204 B2
Highbury Cor, N5 93 G6
Highbury Cres, N5 93 G5
Highbury Est, N5 93 J5
Highbury Gdns, Ilf. IG3 99 H2
Highbury Gra, N5 93 H4
Highbury Gro, N5 93 H6
Highbury Hill, N5 93 G3
Highbury Ms, N7 *off Holloway Rd* 93 G6
Highbury New Pk, N5 93 J5
Highbury Pk, N5 93 H3
Highbury Pk Ms, N5 *off Highbury Gra* 93 J4
Highbury Pl, N5 93 H6
Highbury Quad, N5 93 J3
Highbury Rd, SW19 166 B5
Highbury Sta Rd, N1 93 G6
Highbury Ter, N5 93 H5
Highbury Ter Ms, N5 93 H5
High Cedar Dr, SW20 165 H7
Highclere Rd, N.Mal. KT3 182 D3
Highclere St, SE26 171 H4
Highcliffe Dr, SW15 147 F6
Highcliffe Gdns, Ilf. IG4 80 B5
Highcombe, SE7 135 H6
Highcombe Cl, SE9 174 A1
High Coombe Pl, Kings.T. KT2 164 D7
Highcroft, NW9 70 D5
Highcroft Av, Wem. HA0 106 A1
Highcroft Gdns, NW11 72 C6
Highcroft Rd, N19 74 E7
High Cross Cen, N15 76 D4
High Cross Rd, N17 76 D3
Highcross Way, SW15 165 G1
Highdaun Dr, SW16 187 F4
Highdown, Wor.Pk. KT4 197 E2
Highdown Rd, SW15 147 H6
High Dr, N.Mal. KT3 182 C1
High Elms, Chig. IG7 65 H4
Woodford Green IG8 63 G5
Highfield, Bushey (Bushey Hth) WD23 52 B2
Feltham TW13 160 A1
Watford WD19 51 F3
Highfield Av, NW9 70 C5
NW11 72 A7
Erith DA8 139 H6
Greenford UB6 86 B5
Orpington BR6 207 J5
Pinner HA5 67 F5
Wembley HA9 87 J3
Highfield Cl, N22 75 G1
NW9 70 C5
SE13 154 D6
Surbiton KT6 195 F1
Highfield Ct, N14 42 C6
Highfield Dr, Brom. BR2 191 E4
Epsom KT19 197 F7
West Wickham BR4 204 B2
Highfield Gdns, NW11 72 B6
Highfield Hill, SE19 170 A7
Highfield Ms, NW6 *off Compayne Gdns* 90/91 E7
Highfield Rd, N21 59 H2
NW11 72 B6
W3 106 B5
Bexleyheath DA6 159 F5
Bromley BR1 192 C4
Chislehurst BR7 193 J3
Feltham TW13 160 A2
Isleworth TW7 144 C1
Surbiton KT5 182 C7
Sutton SM1 199 H5
Woodford Green IG8 64 B7
Highfields Gro, N6 91 J1
High Foleys, Esher (Clay.) KT10 194 E7
High Gables, Loug. IG10 48 A5
HIGHGATE, N6 92 A2
Highgate Av, N6 74 B6
★**Highgate Cem**, N6 92 A1
Highgate Cl, N6 74 A7
Highgate High St, N6 92 A1
Highgate Hill, N6 92 B1
N19 92 B1
Highgate Ho, SE26 *off Sydenham Hill* 170 D3
Highgate Rd, NW5 92 B4
Highgate Wk, SE23 171 F2
Highgate W Hill, N6 92 A2
High Gro, SE18 137 G7
Bromley BR1 191 J1
Highgrove Cl, N11 *off Balmoral Av* 58 A5
Chislehurst BR7 192 B1
Highgrove Ms, Cars. SM5 199 J3
Highgrove Rd, Dag. RM8 100 C5
Highgrove Way, Ruis. HA4 66 A6
High Hill Est, E5 *off Mount Pleasant La* 94/95 E1
High Hill Ferry, E5 95 E1
High Holborn, WC1 18 B3
Highland Av, W7 104 B6
Dagenham RM10 101 J3
Loughton IG10 48 B6
Highland Cotts, Wall. SM6 200 B4
Highland Ct, E18 79 H1
Highland Cft, Beck. BR3 172 B5
Highland Rd, SE19 170 B6
Bexleyheath DA6 159 G5
Bromley BR1, BR2 191 F1
Highlands, Wat. WD19 50 C1
Highlands, The, Edg. HA8 70 B2
Potters Bar EN6 40 E5
Highlands Av, N21 43 F5
W3 106 C7
Highlands Cl, N4 *off Mount Vw Rd* 74/75 E7
Hounslow TW3 143 H1
Highlands Gdns, Ilf. IG1 98 C1
Highlands Heath, SW15 147 J7
Highlands Rd, Barn. EN5 40 D5
High La, W7 104 A6
High Lawns, Har. HA1 86 B3
Highlea Cl, NW9 71 E1
High Level Dr, SE26 170 D4
Highlever Rd, W10 107 J5
Highmead, SE18 137 J7
High Mead, Chig. IG7 65 F2
Harrow HA1 68 B5
West Wickham BR4 204 D2
Highmead Cres, Wem. HA0 87 J7
High Meadow Cl, Pnr. HA5 *off Daymer Gdns* 66 B4
High Meadow Cres, NW9 70 D5
High Meadows, Chig. IG7 65 G5
High Meads Rd, E16 116 A6
Highmore Rd, SE3 135 E7
High Mt, NW4 71 G6
High Pk Av, Rich. TW9 146 A1
High Pk Rd, Rich. TW9 146 A1
High Path, SW19 185 E1
High Pt, N6 74 A7
SE9 175 E3
High Rd, N2 73 G1
N11 58 B5
N12 57 F6
N15 76 C6
N17 76 C1
N20 41 F7
N22 75 G3
NW10 (Willesden) 89 H6
Buckhurst Hill IG9 63 H2
Bushey (Bushey Hth) WD23 52 A1
Chigwell IG7 64 C5
Harrow (Har.Wld) HA3 52 B7
Ilford IG1 98 E3
Ilford (Seven Kings) IG3 99 J1
Loughton IG10 47 J7
Pinner HA5 66 B4
Romford (Chad.Hth) RM6 100 B1
Wembley HA0, HA9 87 G5
High Rd Leyton, E10 96 B1
E15 96 C3
High Rd Leytonstone, E11 96 E4
E15 96 E4
High Rd Woodford Grn, E18 63 F7
Woodford Green IG8 63 F7
Highshore Rd, SE15 152 C2
High Silver, Loug. IG10 48 A4
Highstone Av, E11 79 G6
High St, E11 79 G5
E13 115 G2
E15 114 C2
E17 77 J5
N8 74 E4
N14 58 D1
NW7 55 H4
NW10 (Harlesden) 107 F2
SE20 171 E6
SE25 (S.Norwood) 188 C4
W3 126 B1
W5 105 G7
Barnet EN5 40 B3
Beckenham BR3 190 A2
Brentford TW8 125 G6
Bromley BR1 191 G2
Carshalton SM5 200 A4
Chislehurst BR7 174 E6
Croydon CR0 201 J2
Edgware HA8 54 A6
Esher (Clay.) KT10 194 C6
Feltham TW13 160 A3
Hampton TW12 161 J6
Harrow HA1, HA2 86 B1
Harrow (Wldste) HA3 68 B3
Hayes UB3 121 H5
Hounslow TW3 143 J3
Hounslow (Cran.) TW5 122 B7
Ilford (Barkingside) IG6 81 F2
Kingston upon Thames KT1 181 G2
Kingston upon Thames (Hmptn W.) KT1 181 F1
New Malden KT3 183 E3
Orpington (Farnboro.) BR6 207 E5
Orpington (Grn St Grn) BR6 207 J7
Pinner HA5 66 E3
Southall UB1 123 F1
Staines (Stanw.) TW19 140 A6
Sutton SM1 198 E4
Sutton (Cheam) SM3 198 B6
Teddington TW11 162 D5
Thames Ditton KT7 180 D7
Thornton Heath CR7 187 J4
Twickenham (Whitton) TW2 143 J7
Wembley HA9 87 J4
West Drayton (Harm.) UB7 120 A6
West Drayton (Yiew.) UB7 120 A1
West Molesey KT8 179 G4
West Wickham BR4 204 B1
High St Colliers Wd, SW19 167 G7
High St Ms, SW19 166 B5
High St N, E6 116 B1
E12 98 B5
High St Ponders End, Enf. EN3 45 F4
High St S, E6 116 C2
High St Wimbledon, SW19 166 A5
High Timber St, EC4 19 J5
High Tor Cl, Brom. BR1 *off Babbacombe Rd* 173 H7
High Tor Vw, SE28 *off Hill Vw Dr* 137 H1
High Tree Ct, W7 104 B7
High Trees, SW2 169 G1
Barnet EN4 41 H5
Croydon CR0 203 H1
Highview, Nthlt. UB5 103 E3
High Vw, Pnr. HA5 66 C4
Highview Av, Edg. HA8 54 C4
Wallington SM6 201 F5
High Vw Cl, SE19 188 C2
Loughton IG10 47 J5
Highview Gdns, N3 72 B3
N11 58 C5
Edgware HA8 54 C4
Highview Ho, Rom. RM6 83 E4
High Vw Rd, E18 79 F3
SE19 170 A6
Highview Rd, W13 104 D5
Sidcup DA14 176 B4
Highway, The, E1 21 J6
E14 21 J6
Stanmore HA7 68 C1
Highwood, Brom. BR2 190 E3
Highwood Av, N12 57 F4
Highwood Cl, Orp. BR6 207 F2
Highwood Dr, Orp. BR6 207 F2
Highwood Gdns, Ilf. IG5 80 C5
Highwood Gro, NW7 54 D5
HIGHWOOD HILL, NW7 55 G2
Highwood Hill, NW7 55 F2
Highwood La, Loug. IG10 48 D5
Highwood Rd, N19 92 E3
High Worple, Har. HA2 67 F7
Highworth Rd, N11 58 D6
Hilary Av, Mitch. CR4 186 A3
Hilary Cl, SW6 30 A7
Erith DA8 159 J1
Hilary Rd, W12 107 F6
Hilbert Rd, Sutt. SM3 198 A3
Hilborough Way, Orp. BR6 207 G5
Hilda Lockert Wk, SW9 *off Fiveways Rd* 151 H2
Hilda Rd, E6 98 A7
E16 115 E4
Hilda Ter, SW9 151 G2
Hilda Vale Cl, Orp. BR6 206 E4
Hilda Vale Rd, Orp. BR6 206 D4
Hildenborough Gdns, Brom. BR1 173 E6
Hildenlea Pl, Brom. BR2 190 E2
Hildreth St, SW12 168 B1
Hildyard Rd, SW6 128 D6
Hiley Rd, NW10 107 J3
Hilgrove Rd, NW6 91 F7
Hiliary Gdns, Stan. HA7 69 F2
Hillary Dr, Islw. TW7 144 C4
Hillary Ri, Barn. EN5 40 D4
Hillary Rd, Sthl. UB2 123 G3
Hillbeck Cl, SE15 133 F7
Hillbeck Way, Grnf. UB6 104 A1
Hillborne Cl, Hayes UB3 122 A5
Hillborough Cl, SW19 167 F7
Hillbrook Rd, SW17 167 J3
Hill Brow, Brom. BR1 192 A1
Hillbrow, N.Mal. KT3 183 F3
Hillbrow Rd, Brom. BR1 172 E7
Hillbury Av, Har. HA3 69 E5
Hillbury Rd, SW17 168 B3
Hill Cl, NW2 89 H3
NW11 72 D6
Barnet EN5 39 J5
Chislehurst BR7 174 E5
Harrow HA1 86 B3
Stanmore HA7 52 E4
Hillcote Av, SW16 169 G7
Hill Ct, Nthlt. UB5 85 G5
Hillcourt Av, N12 56 E6
Hillcourt Est, N16 94 A1
Hillcourt Rd, SE22 152 E6
Hill Cres, N20 56 E2
Bexley DA5 177 J1
Harrow HA1 68 D5
Surbiton KT5 181 J5
Worcester Park KT4 197 J2
Hillcrest, N6 74 A7
N21 43 H7
Hill Crest, Sid. DA15 158 A7
Hillcrest Av, NW11 72 B5
Edgware HA8 54 B4
Pinner HA5 66 D4
Hillcrest Cl, SE26 170 D4
Beckenham BR3 189 J5
Hillcrest Ct, Sutt. SM2 *off Eaton Rd* 199 G6
Hillcrest Gdns, N3 72 B4
NW2 89 G3
Esher KT10 194 C3
Hillcrest Rd, E17 78 D2
E18 79 F2
W3 126 A1
W5 105 H5
Bromley BR1 173 G5
Loughton IG10 48 A6
Hillcrest Vw, Beck. BR3 189 J6
Hillcroft, Loug. IG10 48 D2
Hillcroft Av, Pnr. HA5 67 F6
Hillcroft Cres, W5 105 H6
Ruislip HA4 84 D3
Watford WD19 50 B1
Wembley HA9 87 J4
Hillcroft Rd, E6 116 E5
Hillcroome Rd, Sutt. SM2 199 G6
Hillcross Av, Mord. SM4 184 C5
Hilldale Rd, Sutt. SM1 198 C4
Hilldown Rd, SW16 169 E7
Bromley BR2 205 E1
Hill Dr, NW9 88 C1
SW16 187 F3
Hilldrop Cres, N7 92 D5
Hilldrop Est, N7 92 D5
Hilldrop La, N7 92 D5
Hilldrop Rd, N7 92 D5
Bromley BR1 173 G6
Hillend, SE18 156 D1
Hill End, Orp. BR6 *off The Approach* 207 J2

Hillersdon Av, SW13 . . . . 147 G2
Edgware HA8 . . . . 53 J5
Hillery Cl, SE17 . . . . 36 C2
Hill Fm Rd, W10 . . . . 107 J5
Hillfield Av, N8 . . . . 75 E5
NW9 . . . . 71 E5
Wembley HA0 . . . . 87 H7
Hillfield Cl, Har. HA2 . . . . 67 J4
Hillfield Ct, NW3 . . . . 91 H5
Hillfield Ms, N8
off Hillfield Av 75 F4
Hillfield Par, Mord. SM4 . . 185 H6
Hillfield Pk, N10 . . . . 74 B4
N21 . . . . 59 G2
Hillfield Pk Ms, N10 . . . . 74 B4
Hillfield Rd, NW6 . . . . 90 C5
Hampton TW12 . . . . 161 F7
Hillfoot Av, Rom. RM5 . . . . 83 J1
Hillfoot Rd, Rom. RM5 . . . . 83 J1
Hillgate Pl, SW12 . . . . 150 B7
W8 . . . . 128 D1
Hillgate St, W8 . . . . 128 D1
Hill Gate Wk, N6 . . . . 74 C6
Hill Gro, Felt. TW13
off Watermill Way 161 F2
Hill Ho Av, Stan. HA7 . . . . 52 C7
Hill Ho Cl, N21 . . . . 43 G7
Hill Ho Dr, Hmptn. TW12 . 179 G1
Hill Ho Rd, SW16 . . . . 169 F5
Hilliards Ct, E1
off Wapping High St 132/133 E1
Hillier Cl, Barn. EN5 . . . . 40 E6
Hillier Gdns, Croy. CR0
off Crowley Cres 201 G5
Hillier Pl, Chess. KT9 . . . . 195 F6
Hillier Rd, SW11 . . . . 149 J6
Hilliers La, Croy. CR0 . . . . 200 E3
Hillingdon Rd, Bexh. DA7 . 159 J2
Hillingdon St, SE5 . . . . 35 H6
SE17 . . . . 35 H6
Hillington Gdns, Wdf.Grn. IG8 . . . . 80 A2
Hillman Dr, W10 . . . . 107 J4
Hillman St, E8 . . . . 95 E6
Hillmarton Rd, N7 . . . . 93 E5
Hillmead Dr, SW9 . . . . 151 H4
Hillmont Rd, Esher KT10 . 194 B3
Hillmore Gro, SE26 . . . . 171 G5
Hill Path, SW16
off Valley Rd 169 F5
Hillreach, SE18 . . . . 136 C5
Hill Ri, N9 . . . . 45 E6
NW11 . . . . 73 E4
SE23 *off London Rd*. 170/171 E1
Esher KT10 . . . . 194 E2
Greenford UB6 . . . . 85 J7
Richmond TW10 . . . . 145 G5
Hillrise Rd, N19 . . . . 74 E7
Hill Rd, N10 . . . . 73 J1
NW8 . . . . 6 D2
Carshalton SM5 . . . . 199 H6
Harrow HA1 . . . . 68 D5
Mitcham CR4 . . . . 186 B1
Pinner HA5 . . . . 66 E5
Sutton SM1 . . . . 199 E5
Wembley HA0 . . . . 86 E3
Hillsborough Grn, Wat. WD19
off Ashburnham Dr 50 A3
Hillsborough Rd, SE22 . . . 152 B5
Hillsgrove, Well. DA16 . . . 138 C7
Hillside, NW9 . . . . 70 D4
NW10 . . . . 106 C1
SW19 . . . . 166 A6
Barnet EN5 . . . . 41 F5
Hillside Av, N11 . . . . 57 J6
Borehamwood WD6 . . . . 38 B4
Wembley HA9 . . . . 87 J4
Woodford Green IG8 . . . 63 J5
Hillside Cl, NW8 . . . . 6 B1
Morden SM4 . . . . 184 B4
Woodford Green IG8 . . . 63 J5
Hillside Cres, Har. HA2 . . . 85 J1
Northwood HA6 . . . . 66 A1
Hillside Dr, Edg. HA8 . . . . 54 A6
Hillside Est, N15 . . . . 76 C6
Hillside Gdns, E17 . . . . 78 D3
N6 . . . . 74 A6
SW2 . . . . 169 G2
Barnet EN5 . . . . 40 B4
Edgware HA8 . . . . 53 J4
Harrow HA3 . . . . 69 H7
Northwood HA6 . . . . 50 A7
Wallington SM6 . . . . 200 C7
Hillside Gro, N14 . . . . 42 D7
NW7 . . . . 55 G7
Hillside La, Brom. BR2 . . . 205 G2
Hillside Pas, SW2 . . . . 169 F2
Hillside Ri, Nthwd. HA6 . . . 50 A7
Hillside Rd, N15 . . . . 76 B7
SW2 . . . . 169 G2
W5 . . . . 105 H5
Bromley BR2 . . . . 191 F3
Croydon CR0 . . . . 201 H5
Northwood HA6 . . . . 50 A7
Pinner HA5 . . . . 50 B7
Southall UB1 . . . . 103 G4
Surbiton KT5 . . . . 181 J5
Sutton SM2 . . . . 198 C7
Hillsleigh Rd, W8 . . . . 128 C1
Hills Ms, W5 . . . . 105 H7
Hills Pl, W1 . . . . 17 F4
Hills Rd, Buck.H. IG9 . . . . 63 H1
Hillstowe St, E5 . . . . 95 F2
Hill St, W1 . . . . 24 C1
Richmond TW9 . . . . 145 G5
Hill Top, NW11 . . . . 73 E4
Loughton IG10 . . . . 48 D2
Morden SM4 . . . . 184 D6
Sutton SM3 . . . . 184 C7
Hilltop Av, NW10 . . . . 88 C7
Hill Top Cl, Loug. IG10 . . . . 48 D3
Hilltop Gdns, NW4 . . . . 71 H2
Orpington BR6 . . . . 207 H2
Hill Top Pl, Loug. IG10 . . . . 48 D3
Hilltop Rd, NW6 . . . . 90 D7
Hill Top Vw, Wdf.Grn. IG8 . . 64 C6
Hilltop Way, Stan. HA7 . . . . 52 D3
Hillview, SW20 . . . . 165 H7
Mitcham CR4 . . . . 186 E4
Hillview Av, Har. HA3 . . . . 69 H5
Hillview Cl, Pnr. HA5 . . . . 51 F6
Wembley HA9 . . . . 87 J2
Hillview Cres, Ilf. IG1 . . . . 80 C6
Hill Vw Cres, Orp. BR6 . . . 207 J1
Hill Vw Dr, SE28 . . . . 137 H1
Welling DA16 . . . . 157 H2
Hillview Gdns, NW4 . . . . 72 A4
Hill Vw Gdns, NW9 . . . . 70 D5
Hillview Gdns, Har. HA2 . . 67 G3
Hillview Rd, NW7 . . . . 56 A4
Chislehurst BR7 . . . . 174 D5
Hill Vw Rd, Esher (Clay.) KT10 . . . . 194 D7
Orpington BR6 . . . . 207 J1
Hillview Rd, Pnr. HA5 . . . . 51 F7
Sutton SM1 . . . . 199 F3
Hill Vw Rd, Twick. TW1 . . . 144 D6
Hillway, N6 . . . . 92 A2
NW9 . . . . 88 E1
Hillworth Rd, SW2 . . . . 151 G7
Hillyard Rd, W7 . . . . 104 B5
Hillyard St, SW9 . . . . 151 G1
Hillyfield, E17 . . . . 77 H2
Hillyfield Cl, E9
off Mabley St 95 H5
Hillyfields, Loug. IG10 . . . . 48 D2
Hilly Flds Cres, SE4 . . . . 154 A3
Hilsea Pt, SW15
off Wanborough Dr . . . 165 H1
Hilsea St, E5 . . . . 95 F4
Hilton Av, N12 . . . . 57 G5
Hilversum Cres, SE22
off East Dulwich Gro . . 152 B5
Himley Rd, SW17 . . . . 167 H5
Hinchley Cl, Esher KT10 . . 194 C3
Hinchley Dr, Esher KT10 . 194 C3
Hinchley Way, Esher KT10 . . . . 194 D3
HINCHLEY WOOD, Esher KT10 . . . . 194 C3
Hinckley Rd, SE15 . . . . 152 D4
Hind Cl, Chig. IG7 . . . . 65 J5
Hind Ct, EC4 . . . . 19 F4
Hinde Ms, W1
off Marylebone La 110 A6
Hindes Rd, Har. HA1 . . . . 68 A5
Hinde St, W1 . . . . 16 C3
Hind Gro, E14 . . . . 114 A6
Hindhead Cl, N16 . . . . 94 B1
Hindhead Gdns, Nthlt. UB5 . . . . 102 E1
Hindhead Grn, Wat. WD19 . 50 C5
Hindhead Pt, SW15
off Wanborough Dr . . . 165 H1
Hindhead Way, Wall. SM6 . . . . 200 E5
Hind Ho, N7
off Harvist Est 93 G4
Hindmans Rd, SE22 . . . . 152 D5
Hindmans Way, Dag. RM9 . 119 F4
Hindmarsh Cl, E1 . . . . 21 J5
Hindon Ct, SW1
off Wilton Rd 130 C4
Hindrey Rd, E5 . . . . 94 E5
Hindsley's Pl, SE23 . . . . 171 F2
Hinkler Rd, Har. HA3 . . . . 69 G3
Hinksey Path, SE2 . . . . 138 D3
Hinstock Rd, SE18 . . . . 137 F6
Hinton Av, Houns. TW4 . . 142 D4
Hinton Cl, SE9 . . . . 174 B1
Hinton Rd, N18 . . . . 60 B4
SE24 . . . . 151 H3
Wallington SM6 . . . . 200 C6
Hippodrome Ms, W11
off Portland Rd 108 B7
Hippodrome Pl, W11 . . . . 108 B7
Hirst Cres, Wem. HA9
off East La 87 H3
Hiscocks Ho, NW10 . . . . 88 C7
Hitcham Rd, E17 . . . . 77 J7
Hitchin Sq, E3 . . . . 113 H2
Hithe Gro, SE16
off Lower Rd 133 G3
Hitherbroom Rd, Hayes UB3 . . . . 122 A1
Hither Fm Rd, SE3 . . . . 155 J3
Hitherfield Rd, SW16 . . . . 169 F2
Dagenham RM8 . . . . 101 E2
HITHER GREEN, SE13 . . . 154 E6
Hither Grn La, SE13 . . . . 154 C5
Hitherlands, SW12 . . . . 168 B2
Hitherwell Dr, Har. HA3 . . . 68 A1
Hitherwood Dr, SE19 . . . . 170 C4
Hive Cl, Bushey (Bushey Hth) WD23 . . . . 52 A2
Hive Rd, Bushey (Bushey Hth) WD23 . . . . 52 A2
★**H.M.S. Belfast**, SE1 . . . . 28 E1
★**H.M.S. President**, EC4 . . . 19 F6
★**H.M. Treasury**, SW1 . . . . 26 A3
Hoadly Rd, SW16 . . . . 168 D3
Hobart Cl, N20
off Oakleigh Rd N 57 H2
Hayes UB4 . . . . 102 D4
Hobart Dr, Hayes UB4 . . . 102 D4
Hobart Gdns, Th.Hth. CR7 . . . . 188 A3
Hobart La, Hayes UB4 . . . 102 D4
Hobart Pl, SW1 . . . . 24 D5
Richmond TW10
off Chisholm Rd 145 J6
Hobart Rd, Dag. RM9 . . . . 100 D4
Hayes UB4 . . . . 102 D4
Ilford IG6 . . . . 81 F2
Hobart Rd, Worcester Park KT4 . . . . 197 H3
Hobbayne Rd, W7 . . . . 104 A6
Hobbes Wk, SW15 . . . . 147 H5
Hobbs Grn, N2 . . . . 73 F3
Hobbs Ms, Ilf. IG3
off Ripley Rd 99 J2
Hobbs Pl Est, N1
off Pitfield St 112 B1
Hobbs Rd, SE27 . . . . 169 J4
Hobday St, E14 . . . . 114 B5
Hobill Wk, Surb. KT5 . . . . 181 J6
Hoblands End, Chis. BR7 . 175 H6
Hobsons Pl, E1 . . . . 21 H1
Hobury St, SW10 . . . . 30 D6
Hocker St, E2 . . . . 13 F4
Hockett Cl, SE8
off Grove St 133 J4
Hockley Av, E6 . . . . 116 B2
Hockley Ct, E18
off Churchfields 79 G1
Hockley Ms, Bark. IG11 . . . 117 H2
Hocroft Av, NW2 . . . . 90 C3
Hocroft Rd, NW2 . . . . 90 C4
Hocroft Wk, NW2 . . . . 90 C3
Hodder Dr, Grnf. UB6 . . . . 104 C2
Hoddesdon Rd, Belv. DA17 . . . . 139 G5
Hodford Rd, NW11 . . . . 90 C2
Hodgkin Cl, SE28
off Fleming Way 118 D7
Hodgkins Ms, Stan. HA7 . . 52 E5
Hodister Cl, SE5
off Badsworth Rd 131 J7
Hodnet Gro, SE16 . . . . 133 G4
Hodson Cl, Har. HA2 . . . . 85 F3
Hoe, The, Wat. WD19 . . . . 50 D2
Hoechst, Houns. TW4 . . . . 142 C3
Hoe St, E17 . . . . 78 A4
Hofland Rd, W14 . . . . 128 A3
Hogan Ms, W2 . . . . 14 E1
Hogan Way, E5
off Geldeston Rd 94 D2
Hogarth Business Pk, W4 . 127 E6
Hogarth Cl, E16 . . . . 116 A5
W5 . . . . 105 H5
Hogarth Ct, EC3 . . . . 20 E5
SE19 *off Fountain Dr* . . . 170 C4
Hogarth Cres, SW19 . . . . 185 G1
Croydon CR0 . . . . 187 J7
Hogarth Gdns, Houns. TW5 . . . . 123 G7
Hogarth Hill, NW11 . . . . 72 C4
Hogarth La, W4 . . . . 126 E6
Hogarth Pl, SW5 . . . . 30 A2
Hogarth Reach, Loug. IG10 . . . . 48 C5
Hogarth Rd, SW5 . . . . 30 A2
Dagenham RM8 . . . . 100 B5
Edgware HA8 . . . . 70 A2
Hogarth Roundabout, W4 . 127 F6
Hogarth Roundabout Flyover, W4 *off Burlington La* 126/127 E6
★**Hogarth's Ho**, W4
off Hogarth La 126 E6
Hogarth Way, Hmptn. TW12 . . . . 179 J1
Hogshead Pas, E1
off Pennington St. 112/113 E7
Hogsmill Way, Epsom KT19 . . . . 196 C5
Holbeach Gdns, Sid. DA15 . . . . 157 H6
Holbeach Ms, SW12
off Harberson Rd 168 B1
Holbeach Rd, SE6 . . . . 154 A7
Holbeck Row, SE15 . . . . 132 D7
Holbein Ms, SW1 . . . . 32 B3
Holbein Pl, SW1 . . . . 32 B2
Holbein Ter, Dag. RM8
off Marlborough Rd . . 100 B4
Holberton Gdns, NW10 . . 107 H3
HOLBORN, WC2 . . . . 18 C3
Holborn, EC1 . . . . 18 E2
Holborn Circ, EC1 . . . . 19 F2
Holborn Pl, WC1 . . . . 18 C2
Holborn Rd, E13 . . . . 115 H4
Holborn Viaduct, EC1 . . . . 19 F2
Holborn Way, Mitch. CR4 . 185 J2
Holbrook Cl, N19
off Dartmouth Pk Hill . . 92 B1
Enfield EN1 . . . . 44 C1
Holbrooke Ct, N7 . . . . 93 E4
Holbrooke Pl, Rich. TW10
off Hill Ri 145 G5
Holbrook La, Chis. BR7 . . 175 G7
Holbrook Rd, E15 . . . . 115 F2
Holbrook Way, Brom. BR2 . . . . 192 C6
Holburne Cl, SE3 . . . . 155 J1
Holburne Gdns, SE3 . . . . 156 A1
Holburne Rd, SE3 . . . . 155 J1
Holcombe Hill, NW7 . . . . 55 G3
Holcombe Rd, N17 . . . . 76 C3
Ilford IG1 . . . . 80 D7
Holcombe St, W6 . . . . 127 H5
Holcote Cl, Belv. DA17 *off Blakemore Way* . . 138/139 E3
Holcroft Rd, E9 . . . . 95 F7
Holden Av, N12 . . . . 57 E5
NW9 . . . . 88 C1
Holdenby Rd, SE4 . . . . 153 H5
Holden Cl, Dag. RM8 . . . . 100 B3
Holdenhurst Av, N12 . . . . 57 E7
Holden Pt, E15
off Waddington Rd 96 D6
Holden Rd, N12 . . . . 56 E5
Holden St, SW11 . . . . 150 A2
Holder Cl, N3 . . . . 57 E7
Holdernesse Cl, Islw. TW7 . . . . 144 D1
Holdernesse Rd, SW17 . . 167 J3
Holderness Way, SE27 . . . 169 H5
HOLDERS HILL, NW4 . . . . 72 A2
Holders Hill Av, NW4 . . . . 72 A2
Holders Hill Circ, NW7
off Dollis Rd 56 B7
Holders Hill Cres, NW4 . . . 72 A2
Holders Hill Dr, NW4 . . . . 72 A3
Holders Hill Gdns, NW4 . . . 72 B2
Holders Hill Rd, NW4 . . . . 72 A2
NW7 . . . . 72 A2
Holegate St, SE7
off Westmoor St 136 A3
Holford Ms, WC1 . . . . 10 E2
Holford Pl, WC1 . . . . 10 D3
Holford Rd, NW3 . . . . 91 F3
Holford St, WC1 . . . . 10 E3
Holford Yd, WC1 . . . . 10 E2
Holgate Av, SW11 . . . . 149 G3
Holgate Gdns, Dag. RM10 . . . . 101 G5
Holgate Rd, Dag. RM10 . . 101 G5
Holland Av, SW20 . . . . 183 F1
Holland Cl, Barn. EN5 . . . . 41 G7
Bromley BR2 . . . . 205 F2
Romford RM7 . . . . 83 J5
Stanmore HA7 . . . . 52 E5
Holland Ct, E17
off Evelyn Rd 78 C4

Holland Ct, NW7
off Page St **55** G6
Holland Dr, SE23 . . . . **171** H3
Holland Gdns, W14 . . . . **128** B3
Brentford TW8 . . . . **125** H6
Holland Gro, SW9 . . . . **131** G7
★**Holland Ho & Pk**, W8 . . **128** C2
Holland Pk, W8 . . . . **128** C2
W11 . . . . **128** B2
Holland Pk Av, W11 . . . . **128** B2
Ilford IG3 . . . . **81** H6
Holland Pk Gdns, W14 . . . **128** B1
Holland Pk Ms, W11 . . . . **128** B1
Holland Pk Rd, W14 . . . . **128** C3
Holland Pk Roundabout,
W11 . . . . **128** A2
Holland Pas, N1
off Basire St **111** J1
Holland Pl, W8 . . . . **22** A3
Holland Rd, E6 . . . . **116** C1
E15 . . . . **115** E3
NW10 . . . . **107** G1
SE25 . . . . **188** D5
W14 . . . . **128** A2
Wembley HA0 . . . . **87** G6
Hollands, The, Felt. TW13 . **160** D4
Worcester Park KT4 . . . . **197** F1
Holland St, SE1 . . . . **27** H1
W8 . . . . **128** D2
Holland Vil Rd, W14 . . . . **128** B2
Holland Wk, N19
off Duncombe Rd **92** D1
W8 . . . . **128** C2
Stanmore HA7 . . . . **52** D5
Holland Way, Brom. BR2 . **205** F2
Hollar Rd, N16
off Stoke Newington
High St **94** C3
Hollen St, W1 . . . . **17** H3
Holles Cl, Hmptn. TW12 . . **161** G6
Holles St, W1 . . . . **16** E3
Holley Rd, W3 . . . . **127** E2
Hollickwood Av, N12 . . . . **57** J6
Holliday Sq, SW11
off Fowler Cl **149** G3
Hollidge Way, Dag. RM10 . **101** H6
Hollies, The, E11 . . . . **79** G5
N20 *off Oakleigh Pk N* . . . **57** G1
Harrow HA3 . . . . **68** D4
Hollies Av, Sid. DA15 . . . . **175** J2
Hollies Cl, SW16 . . . . **169** G6
Twickenham TW1 . . . . **162** C2
Hollies End, NW7 . . . . **55** H5
Hollies Rd, W5 . . . . **125** F4
Hollies Way, SW12
off Bracken Av **150** A7
Holligrave Rd, Brom. BR1 . **191** G1
Hollingbourne Av, Bexh.
DA7 . . . . **139** F7
Hollingbourne Gdns,
W13 . . . . **104** E5
Hollingbourne Rd, SE24 . . **151** J5
Hollingsworth Rd, Croy.
CR0 . . . . **203** E6
Hollington Cres, N.Mal.
KT3 . . . . **183** F6
Hollington Rd, E6 . . . . **116** C3
N17 . . . . **76** D2
Hollingworth Cl, W.Mol.
KT8 . . . . **179** F4
Hollingworth Rd, Orp.
BR5 . . . . **192** E6
Hollman Gdns, SW16 . . . . **169** H6
Hollow, The, Wdf.Grn. IG8 . **63** F4
HOLLOWAY, N7 . . . . **92** E4
Holloway Cl, West Dr.
UB7 . . . . **120** B5
Holloway La, West Dr.
UB7 . . . . **120** B6
Holloway Rd, E6 . . . . **116** C3
E11 . . . . **96** E3
N7 . . . . **93** F4
N19 . . . . **92** D2
Holloway St, Houns. TW3 . **143** H3
Hollowfield Wk, Nthlt.
UB5 . . . . **84** E6
Hollows, The, Brent. TW8
off Kew Br Rd **125** J6
Hollow Wk, Rich. TW9
off Kew Rd **125** H7
Holly Av, Stan. HA7 . . . . **69** H2
Hollybank Cl, Hmptn.
TW12 . . . . **161** G5
Hollyberry La, NW3
off Holly Wk **91** F4
Hollybrake Cl, Chis. BR7 . **175** G7
Hollybush Cl, E11 . . . . **79** G5
Harrow HA3 . . . . **68** B1
Hollybush Gdns, E2 . . . . **113** E3
Hollybush Hill, E11 . . . . **79** F6
Holly Bush Hill, NW3 . . . . **91** F4
Holly Bush La, Hmptn.
TW12 . . . . **161** F7
Hollybush Pl, E2
off Bethnal Grn Rd . **112/113** E3
Hollybush Rd, Kings.T.
KT2 . . . . **163** H5
Holly Bush Steps, NW3
off Heath St **91** F4
Hollybush St, E13 . . . . **115** H3
Holly Bush Vale, NW3
off Heath St **91** F4
Holly Cl, NW10 . . . . **88** E7
Beckenham BR3 . . . . **190** C4
Buckhurst Hill IG9 . . . . **64** A3
Feltham TW13 . . . . **160** E5
Wallington SM6 . . . . **200** B7
Holly Ct, Sutt. SM2
off Worcester Rd **198** D7
Holly Cres, Beck. BR3 . . . . **189** J5
Woodford Green IG8 . . . **62** D7
Hollycroft Av, NW3 . . . . **90** D3
Wembley HA9 . . . . **87** J2
Hollycroft Cl, S.Croy.
CR2 . . . . **202** B5
West Drayton UB7 . . . . **120** D6
Hollycroft Gdns, West Dr.
UB7 . . . . **120** D6
Hollydale Cl, Nthlt. UB5
off Dorchester Rd **85** H4
Hollydale Dr, Brom.
BR2 . . . . **206** C3
Hollydale Rd, SE15 . . . . **153** F1
Hollydene, SE15 . . . . **152** E1
Hollydown Way, E11 . . . . **96** D3
Holly Dr, E4 . . . . **46** B7
Brentford TW8 . . . . **124** D6
Holly Fm Rd, Sthl. UB2 . . **122** E5
Hollyfield Av, N11 . . . . **57** J5
Hollyfield Rd, Surb. KT5 . **181** J7
Holly Gdns, Bexh. DA7 . . **159** J4
West Drayton UB7 . . . . **120** C2
Holly Gro, NW9 . . . . **70** C7
SE15 . . . . **152** C2
Pinner HA5 . . . . **67** E1
Holly Hedge Ter, SE13 . . . **154** D5
Holly Hill, N21 . . . . **43** F6
NW3 . . . . **91** F4
Holly Hill Rd, Belv. DA17 . **139** H5
Erith DA8 . . . . **139** H5
Holly Lo Gdns, N6 . . . . **92** A2
Hollymead, Cars. SM5 . . . **199** J3
Holly Ms, SW10 . . . . **30** D4
Holly Mt, NW3
off Holly Bush Hill **91** F4
Hollymount Cl, SE10 . . . . **154** C1
Holly Pk, N3 . . . . **72** C3
N4 . . . . **75** F7
Holly Pk Est, N4
off Blythwood Rd **75** F7
Holly Pk Gdns, N3 . . . . **72** D3
Holly Pk Rd, N11 . . . . **58** A5
W7 . . . . **124** C1
Holly Pl, NW3
off Holly Wk **91** F4
Holly Rd, E11 . . . . **79** F7
W4 *off Dolman Rd* **126** D4
Hampton (Hmptn H.)
TW12 . . . . **161** J6
Hounslow TW3 . . . . **143** H4
Twickenham TW1 . . . . **162** D1
Holly St, E8 . . . . **94** C6
Holly Ter, N6
off Highgate W Hill **92** A1
N20 *off Swan La* **57** F2
Hollytree Cl, SW19 . . . . **166** A1
Holly Vw Cl, NW4 . . . . **71** G6
Holly Village, N6
off Swains La **92** B2
Holly Wk, NW3 . . . . **91** F4
Enfield EN2 . . . . **43** J3
Richmond TW9 . . . . **145** H2
Holly Way, Mitch. CR4 . . . **186** D4
Hollywood Gdns, Hayes
UB4 . . . . **102** B6
Hollywood Ms, SW10 . . . . **30** C5
Hollywood Rd, E4 . . . . **61** H5
SW10 . . . . **30** C4
Hollywood Way, Wdf.Grn.
IG8 . . . . **62** D7
Holman Rd, SW11 . . . . **149** G2
Epsom KT19 . . . . **196** C5
Holmbridge Gdns, Enf.
EN3 . . . . **45** G4
Holmbrook Dr, NW4 . . . . **72** A5
Holmbury Ct, SW17 . . . . **167** J3
SW19
off Cavendish Rd **167** H7
Holmbury Gdns, Hayes
UB3 *off Church Rd* . . . **121** J1
Holmbury Gro, Croy.
CR0 . . . . **203** J7
Holmbury Pk, Brom. BR1 . **174** B7
Holmbury Vw, E5 . . . . **95** E1
Holmbush Rd, SW15 . . . . **148** B6
Holmcote Gdns, N5 . . . . **93** J5
Holmcroft Way, Brom.
BR2 . . . . **192** C5
Holmdale Gdns, NW4 . . . . **72** A5
Holmdale Rd, NW6 . . . . **90** D5
Chislehurst BR7 . . . . **175** F5
Holmdale Ter, N15 . . . . **76** B7
Holmdene Av, NW7 . . . . **55** G6
SE24 . . . . **151** J5
Harrow HA2 . . . . **67** H3
Holmdene Cl, Beck. BR3 . **190** C2
Holmead Rd, SW6 . . . . **129** E7
Holmebury Cl, Bushey
(Bushey Hth) WD23 . . . . **52** B2
Holme Ct, Islw. TW7
off Twickenham Rd . . . **144** D3
Holmefield Ct, NW3 . . . . **91** H6
Holme Lacey Rd, SE12 . . . **155** F6
Holme Rd, E6 . . . . **116** B1
Holmes Av, E17 . . . . **77** J3
NW7 . . . . **56** B5
Holmesdale Av, SW14 . . . **146** B3
Holmesdale Cl, SE25 . . . . **188** C3
Holmesdale Rd, N6 . . . . **74** B7
SE25 . . . . **188** A5
Bexleyheath DA7 . . . . **158** D2
Croydon CR0 . . . . **188** A5
Richmond TW9 . . . . **145** J1
Teddington TW11 . . . . **163** F6
Holmesley Rd, SE23 . . . . **153** H6
Holmes Pl, SW10 . . . . **30** D5
Holmes Rd, NW5 . . . . **92** B5
SW19 . . . . **167** F7
Twickenham TW1 . . . . **162** C2
Holmes Ter, SE1 . . . . **27** E3
Holme Way, Stan. HA7 . . . **52** C6
Holmewood Gdns, SW2 . **151** F7
Holmewood Rd, SE25 . . . **188** B3
SW2 . . . . **151** E7
Holmfield Av, NW4 . . . . **72** A5
Holmhurst Rd, Belv.
DA17 . . . . **139** H5
Holmleigh Rd, N16 . . . . **94** B1
Holmleigh Rd Est, N16
off Holmleigh Rd **94** C1
Holm Oak Cl, SW15
off West Hill **148** C6
Holm Oak Ms, SW4
off King's Av **150/151** E5
Holmshaw Cl, SE26 . . . . **171** H4
Holmside Ri, Wat. WD19 . . **50** B3
Holmside Rd, SW12 . . . . **150** A6
Holmsley Cl, N.Mal. KT3 . **183** F6
Holmsley Ho, SW15
off Tangley Gro **147** F7
Holms St, E2 . . . . **13** H1
Holmstall Av, Edg. HA8 . . . **70** C3
Holm Wk, SE3
off Blackheath Pk **155** G2
Holmwood Cl, Har. HA2 . . . **67** J3
Northolt UB5 . . . . **85** H6
Sutton SM2 . . . . **198** A7
Holmwood Gdns, N3 . . . . **72** D2
Wallington SM6 . . . . **200** B6
Holmwood Gro, NW7 . . . . **54** D5
Holmwood Rd, Chess.
KT9 . . . . **195** G5
Ilford IG3 . . . . **99** H2
Holmwood Vil, SE7
off Woolwich Rd **135** G5
Holne Chase, N2 . . . . **73** F6
Morden SM4 . . . . **184** C6
Holness Rd, E15 . . . . **97** F6
Holroyd Rd, SW15 . . . . **147** J4
Holstein Way, Erith DA18 . **138** E3
Holstock Rd, Ilf. IG1 . . . . **99** F3
Holsworth Cl, Har. HA2 . . . **67** J5
Holsworthy Sq, WC1 . . . . **10** D6
Holsworthy Way, Chess.
KT9 . . . . **195** F5
Holt, The, Ilf. IG6 . . . . **65** F6
Wallington SM6 . . . . **200** C4
Holt Cl, N10 . . . . **74** A4
SE28 . . . . **118** B7
Chigwell IG7 . . . . **65** J5
Holt Ct, E15 *off Clays La* . . **96** C5
Holton St, E1 . . . . **113** G4
Holt Rd, E16 . . . . **136** B1
Wembley HA0 . . . . **87** E3
Holt Way, Chig. IG7 . . . . **65** J5
Holtwhite Av, Enf. EN2 . . . **43** J2
Holtwhites Hill, Enf. EN2 . . **43** H1
Holwell Pl, Pnr. HA5 . . . . **66** E4
Holwood Pk Av, Orp.
BR6 . . . . **206** C4
Holwood Pl, SW4 . . . . **150** D4
Holybourne Av, SW15 . . . **147** G7
Holyhead Cl, E3 . . . . **114** A3
E6 *off Valiant Way* **116** C5
Holyoake Ct, SE16
off Bryan Rd **133** J2
Holyoake Wk, N2 . . . . **73** F3
W5 . . . . **105** F4
Holyoak Rd, SE11 . . . . **35** G1
Holyport Rd, SW6 . . . . **127** J7
Holyrood Av, Har. HA2 . . . **85** E4
Holyrood Gdns, Edg.
HA8 . . . . **70** B3
Holyrood Ms, E16
off Wesley Av **135** G1
Holyrood Rd, Barn. EN5 . . . **41** F6
Holyrood St, SE1 . . . . **28** D2
Holywell Cl, SE3 . . . . **135** G6
SE16 *off Masters Dr* . **132/133** E5
Holywell La, EC2 . . . . **12** E5
Holywell Row, EC2 . . . . **12** D6
Home Cl, Cars. SM5 . . . . **199** J2
Northolt UB5 . . . . **103** F3
Home Ct, Felt. TW13 . . . . **160** A1
Homecroft Gdns, Loug.
IG10 . . . . **48** E4
Homecroft Rd, N22 . . . . **75** J1
SE26 . . . . **171** F5
Home Fm Cl, T.Ditt. KT7 . . **180** C7
Homefarm Rd, W7 . . . . **104** B6
Homefield Av, Ilf. IG2 . . . . **81** H5
Homefield Cl, NW10 . . . . **88** C6
Hayes UB4 . . . . **102** C4
Homefield Gdns, N2 . . . . **73** G3
Mitcham CR4 . . . . **185** F2
Homefield Ms, Beck.
BR3 . . . . **190** A1
Homefield Pk, Sutt. SM1 . **198** E6
Homefield Rd, SW19 . . . . **166** A6
W4 . . . . **127** F4
Bromley BR1 . . . . **191** J1
Edgware HA8 . . . . **54** D6
Walton-on-Thames
KT12 . . . . **179** E7
Wembley HA0 . . . . **86** D4
Homefield St, N1 . . . . **12** D2
Home Gdns, Dag. RM10 . . **101** J3
Homelands Dr, SE19 . . . . **170** B7
Home Lea, Orp. BR6 . . . . **207** J5
Homeleigh Rd, SE15 . . . . **153** G5
Homemead, SW12 . . . . **168** C2
Home Mead, Stan. HA7 . . . **69** F1
Homemead Rd, Brom.
BR2 . . . . **192** C5
Croydon CR0 . . . . **186** C6
★**Home Office**, SW1 . . . . **25** H4
Home Pk Rd, SW19 . . . . **166** D3
Home Pk Wk, Kings.T.
KT1 . . . . **181** G4
Homer Cl, Bexh. DA7 . . . . **159** J1
Homer Dr, E14 . . . . **134** A4
Home Rd, SW11 . . . . **149** H2
Homer Rd, E9 . . . . **95** H6
Croydon CR0 . . . . **189** G6
Homer Row, W1 . . . . **15** H2
Homersham Rd, Kings.T.
KT1 . . . . **182** A2
Homer St, W1 . . . . **15** H2
HOMERTON, E9 . . . . **95** H5
Homerton Gro, E9 . . . . **95** G5
Homerton High St, E9 . . . . **95** F5
Homerton Rd, E9 . . . . **95** H5
Homerton Row, E9 . . . . **95** F5
Homerton Ter, E9
off Morning La **95** F6
Homesdale Cl, E11 . . . . **79** G5
Homesdale Rd, Brom.
BR1, BR2 . . . . **191** J4
Orpington BR5 . . . . **193** H7
Homesfield, NW11 . . . . **72** D5
Homestall Rd, SE22 . . . . **153** F5
Homestead, The, N11 . . . . **58** B4
Homestead Gdns, Esher
(Clay.) KT10 . . . . **194** B5
Homestead Paddock, N14 . **42** B5
Homestead Pk, NW2 . . . . **89** F3
Homestead Rd, SW6 . . . . **128** C7
Dagenham RM8 . . . . **101** F2
Homewillow Cl, N21 . . . . **43** H6
Homewood Cl, Hmptn. TW12
off Fearnley Cres **161** F6
Homewood Cres, Chis.
BR7 . . . . **175** H6
Homildon Ho, SE26
off Sydenham Hill **170** D3
Honduras St, EC1 . . . . **11** J5

Honeybourne Rd, NW6 . . . **90** E5
Honeybourne Way, Orp.
BR5 . . . . **207** G1
Honeybrook Rd, SW12. . . **150** C7
Honey Cl, Dag. RM10 . . . . **101** H6
Honeycroft, Loug. IG10 . . . **48** D4
Honeyden Rd, Sid. DA14 . **177** E6
Honey La, EC2 . . . . **20** A4
Honeyman Cl, NW6 . . . . . . **90** A7
Honeypot Cl, NW9 . . . . . . **69** J4
Honeypot La, NW9 . . . . . . **69** J3
Stanmore HA7 . . . . **69** J3
Honeysett Rd, N17
off Reform Row. **76** C2
Honeysuckle Cl, Sthl.
UB1 . . . . **102** E7
Honeysuckle Gdns, Croy. CR0
off Primrose La **203** G1
Honeywell Rd, SW11 . . . . **149** J6
Honeywood Rd, NW10. . . **107** F2
Isleworth TW7 . . . . **144** D4
Honeywood Wk, Cars.
SM5. . . . . **199** J4
Honister Cl, Stan. HA7. . . . **69** E1
Honister Gdns, Stan. HA7 . **53** E7
Honister Pl, Stan. HA7 . . . . **69** E1
Honiton Gdns, NW7. . . . . . **56** A7
Honiton Ho, Enf. EN3
off Exeter Rd. **45** G3
Honiton Rd, NW6 . . . . **108** C2
Welling DA16 . . . . **157** J2
Honley Rd, SE6 . . . . **154** B7
Honnor Gdns, Islw. TW7 . **144** A2
HONOR OAK, SE23 . . . . . **153** F6
HONOR OAK PARK, SE4 . **153** H6
Honor Oak Pk, SE23. . . . . **153** F6
Honor Oak Ri, SE23 . . . . . **153** F6
Honor Oak Rd, SE23 . . . . **171** F1
Hood Av, N14. . . . . **42** B6
SW14. . . . . **146** C5
Hood Cl, Croy. CR0
off Parson's Mead **201** H1
Hoodcote Gdns, N21 . . . . . **43** H7
Hood Ct, EC4 . . . . **19** F4
Hood Rd, SW20 . . . . **165** F7
Hood Wk, Rom. RM7 . . . . . **83** H1
HOOK, Chess. KT9 . . . . . . **195** H4
Hook, The, Barn. EN5. . . . . **41** G6
Hookers Rd, E17. . . . . **77** G3
Hook Fm Rd, Brom. BR2 . **192** A5
Hooking Grn, Har. HA2 . . . **67** H5
Hook La, Well. DA16. . . . . **157** J5
Hook Ri N, Surb. KT6. . . . **196** A3
Hook Ri S, Surb. KT6. . . . **196** A3
Hook Ri S Ind Pk, Surb.
KT6 . . . . **196** A3
Hook Rd, Chess. KT9 . . . . **195** G5
Surbiton KT6. . . . . **195** H3
Hooks Cl, SE15
off Woods Rd **152/153** E1
Hooks Hall Dr, Dag.
RM10 . . . . **101** J3
Hookstone Way, Wdf.Grn.
IG8. . . . . **64** A7
Hooks Way, SE22
off Dulwich Common . **170** D1
Hook Wk, Edg. HA8 . . . . . . **54** C6
Hooper Rd, E16 . . . . **115** G6
Hooper's Ct, SW3 . . . . **23** J4
Hooper's Ms, Bushey
WD23 . . . . **51** H1
Hooper St, E1. . . . . **21** H5
Hoop La, NW11 . . . . **72** C7
Hope Cl, N1
off Wallace Rd. **93** J6
SE12 . . . . **173** H3
Brentford TW8
off Burford Rd. **125** H5
Romford (Chad.Hth)
RM6. . . . . **82** C4
Sutton SM1 . . . . **199** F5
Woodford Green IG8
off West Gro **63** J6
Hopedale Rd, SE7 . . . . . . **135** H6
Hopefield Av, NW6. . . . . . **108** B2
Hope Pk, Brom. BR1 . . . . **173** F7
Hopes Cl, Houns. TW5
off Old Cote Dr **123** G6
Hope St, SW11. . . . . **149** G3
Hopetown St, E1 . . . . **21** G2
Hopewell St, SE5. . . . . . . **132** A7
Hopewell Yd, SE5
off Hopewell St. **132** A7
Hope Wf, SE16
off St. Marychurch St . **133** F2
Hop Gdns, WC2 . . . . **18** A6
Hopgood St, W12
off Macfarlane Rd **127** J1
Hopkins Cl, N10 . . . . **58** A7
Hopkins Ms, E15
off West Rd **115** F1
Hopkinsons Pl, NW1
off Fitzroy Rd. **110** A1
Hopkins St, W1 . . . . **17** G4
Hoppers Rd, N13 . . . . **59** G2
N21 . . . . **59** G2
Hoppett Rd, E4. . . . . **62** E3
Hopping La, N1
off St. Mary's Gro **93** H6
Hoppingwood Av, N.Mal.
KT3 . . . . **183** E3
Hop St, SE10 . . . . **135** F4
Hopton Gdns, SE1 . . . . **27** H1
New Malden KT3 . . . . . **183** G6
Hopton Rd, SE18
off Cadogan Rd. **136** E3
SW16. . . . . **168** E5
Hopton St, SE1 . . . . **27** H1
Hoptree Cl, N12
off Woodside Pk Rd . **56/57** E4
Hopwood Cl, SW17 . . . . . **167** F3
Hopwood Rd, SE17 . . . . . . **36** C5
Hopwood Wk, E8
off Wilman Gro **94** D7
Horace Av, Rom. RM7 . . . **101** J1
Horace Rd, E7 . . . . **97** H4
Ilford IG6. . . . . **81** F3
Kingston upon Thames
KT1 . . . . **181** J3
Horatio Ct, SE16
off Rotherhithe St **133** F1
Horatio Pl, E14
off Cold Harbour. **134** C2
SW19 *off Kingston Rd*. . **166** D7
Horatio St, E2 . . . . **13** H2
Horatius Way, Croy. CR0 . **201** F5
Horbury Cres, W11 . . . . . . **108** D7
Horbury Ms, W11
off Ladbroke Rd. **108** C7
Horder Rd, SW6. . . . . **148** B1
Hordle Prom E, SE15 . . . . . **37** G7
Hordle Prom N, SE15. . . . . **37** E7
Hordle Prom S, SE15. . . . . **37** E7
Hordle Prom W, SE15
off Blakes Rd. **132** B7
Horizon Way, SE7 . . . . **135** H4
Horle Wk, SE5. . . . . **151** H2
Horley Cl, Bexh. DA6 . . . . **159** G5
Horley Rd, SE9 . . . . **174** B4
Hormead Rd, W9 . . . . **108** C4
Hornbeam Cl, NW7 . . . . . . **55** F3
SE11 . . . . **34** E1
Borehamwood WD6 . . . . **38** A1
Buckhurst Hill IG9
off Hornbeam Rd **64** A3
Ilford IG1. . . . . **99** G5
Northolt UB5. . . . . **85** F5
Hornbeam Cres, Brent.
TW8. . . . . **125** E7
Hornbeam Gro, E4 . . . . **63** E3
Hornbeam La, E4 . . . . **47** E5
Bexleyheath DA7 . . . . . **159** J2
Hornbeam Rd, Buck.H.
IG9. . . . . **64** A3
Hayes UB4. . . . . **102** C5
Hornbeam Sq, E3
off Hawthorn Av **113** J1
Hornbeams Ri, N11 . . . . . . **58** A6
Hornbeam Ter, Cars.
SM5. . . . . **199** H1
Hornbeam Wk, Rich.
TW10. . . . . **163** J3
Hornbeam Way, Brom.
BR2 . . . . **192** D6
Hornblower Cl, SE16
off Greenland Quay . . **133** H4
Hornbuckle Cl, Har. HA2 . . **86** A2
Hornby Cl, NW3. . . . . **91** G7
Horncastle Cl, SE12 . . . . . **155** G7
Horncastle Rd, SE12 . . . . **155** G7
Hornchurch Cl, Kings.T.
KT2 . . . . **163** G4
Horndean Cl, SW15
off Bessborough Rd . . **165** G1
Horndon Cl, Rom. RM5 . . . **83** J1
Horndon Grn, Rom. RM5 . . **83** J1
Horndon Rd, Rom. RM5. . . **83** J1
Horner La, Mitch. CR4 . . . **185** G2
Horne Way, SW15. . . . . . . **147** J2
Hornfair Rd, SE7. . . . . **135** J6
Horniman Dr, SE23 . . . . . . **171** E1
★**Horniman Mus**, SE23 . . **170** E1
Horning Cl, SE9 . . . . **174** B4
Horn La, SE10. . . . . **135** G4
W3. . . . . **106** C7
Woodford Green IG8 . . . **63** G6
Horn Link Way, SE10 . . . . **135** G4
Horn Pk Cl, SE12 . . . . **155** H5
Horn Pk La, SE12 . . . . **155** H5
Horns Cft Cl, Bark. IG11
off Thornhill Gdns. **99** H7
Horns End Pl, Pnr. HA5 . . . **66** C4
HORNSEY, N8 . . . . **75** F3
Hornsey La, N6. . . . . **92** B1
N19 . . . . **92** C1
Hornsey La Est, N19
off Hornsey La. **74** D7
Hornsey La Gdns, N6. . . . . **74** C7
Hornsey Pk Rd, N8. . . . . . . **75** F3
Hornsey Ri, N19 . . . . **74** D7
Hornsey Ri Gdns, N19 . . . . **74** D7
Hornsey Rd, N7 . . . . **93** F2
N19 . . . . **92** E1
Hornsey St, N7. . . . . **93** F5
Hornshay St, SE15. . . . . . **133** F6
Horns Rd, Ilf. IG2, IG6 . . . . **81** F5
Hornton Pl, W8. . . . . **22** A4
Hornton St, W8 . . . . **128** D1
Horsa Rd, SE12 . . . . **155** J7
Erith DA8. . . . . **139** J7
Horse & Dolphin Yd, W1 . . **17** J5
Horsebridge Cl, Dag. RM9. **119** E1
Horsecroft Rd, Edg. HA8 . . **54** D7
Horse Fair, Kings.T. KT1 . . **181** G2
Horseferry Pl, SE10 . . . . . **134** C6
Horseferry Rd, E14 . . . . . . **113** H7
SW1. . . . . **25** H6
Horse Guards Av, SW1 . . . . **26** A2
★**Horse Guards Par**, SW1 . **25** J2
Horse Guards Rd, SW1 . . . **25** J2
Horse Leaze, E6 . . . . **116** D6
Horsell Rd, N5 . . . . **93** G5
Horselydown La, SE1. . . . . **29** F3
Horsemongers Ms, SE1 . . . **28** A4
Horsenden Av, Grnf. UB6. . **86** B5
Horsenden Cres, Grnf.
UB6. . . . . **86** C5
Horsenden La N, Grnf.
UB6. . . . . **86** C6
Horsenden La S, Grnf.
UB6 . . . . **104** D1
Horse Ride, SW1 . . . . **25** G2
Horse Rd, E7 *off Centre Rd* . **97** H3
Horseshoe Cl, E14 . . . . . . **134** C5
NW2 . . . . **00** H2
Horse Shoe Ct, EC1
off St. John St **111** H4
Horse Shoe Cres, Nthlt.
UB5 . . . . **103** G2
Horse Shoe Grn, Sutt. SM1
off Aultone Way . . **198/199** E2
Horseshoe La, N20. . . . . . . **56** A1
Enfield EN2
off Chase Side. **43** J3
Horse Yd, N1
off Essex Rd. **111** H1
Horsfeld Gdns, SE9 . . . . . **156** B5
Horsfeld Rd, SE9 . . . . **156** A5
Horsford Rd, SW2 . . . . . . **151** F5
Horsham Av, N12. . . . . **57** H5
Horsham Rd, Bexh. DA6 . **159** G5
Feltham TW14 . . . . **141** F6
Horsleydown Old Stairs,
SE1 . . . . **29** F2
Horsley Dr, Croy.
(New Adgtn) CR0 . . . . **204** C7
Kingston upon Thames
KT2 . . . . **163** G5
Horsley Rd, E4 . . . . **62** C2
Bromley BR1
off Palace Rd. **191** H1
Horsley St, SE17 . . . . **36** B5
Horsmonden Cl, Orp.
BR6 . . . . **193** H7
Horsmonden Rd, SE4. . . . **153** J5
Hortensia Rd, SW10. . . . . . **30** C6
Horticultural Pl, W4
off Heathfield Ter. **126** D5
Horton Av, NW2. . . . . **90** B4
Horton Br Rd, West Dr.
UB7 . . . . **120** C1
Horton Cl, West Dr. UB7. . **120** C1
Horton Ind Pk, West Dr.
UB7 . . . . **120** C1
Horton Rd, E8. . . . . **94** E6
West Drayton UB7 . . . . **120** D1
Horton St, SE13 . . . . **154** B3
Horton Way, Croy. CR0. . . **189** G5
Hortus Rd, E4. . . . . **62** C2
Southall UB2. . . . . **123** F2
Hosack Rd, SW17. . . . . . . **167** J2
Hoser Av, SE12. . . . . **173** G2
Hosier La, EC1 . . . . **19** G2
Hoskins Cl, E16. . . . . **115** J6
Hayes UB3
off Cranford Dr **121** J5
Hoskins St, SE10 . . . . **134** D5
Hospital Br Rd, Twick.
TW2. . . . . **143** H7
Hospital Rd, E9
off Homerton Row **95** G5
Hounslow TW3 . . . . **143** G3
Hospital Way, SE13
off Lullingstone La . . . **154** D6
Hotham Cl, W.Mol. KT8
off Garrick Gdns **179** G3
Hotham Rd, SW15 . . . . . . **147** J3
SW19. . . . . **167** F7
Hotham Rd Ms, SW19
off Haydons Rd. **167** F7
Hotham St, E15 . . . . **114** E1
Hothfield Pl, SE16
off Lower Rd. **133** F3
Hotspur Rd, Nthlt. UB5 . . **103** G2
Hotspur St, SE11 . . . . **34** E3
Houblon Rd, Rich. TW10. . **145** H5
Houghton Cl, E8
off Buttermere Wk. **94** C6
Hampton TW12 . . . . **161** E6
Houghton Rd, N15
off West Grn Rd. **76** C5
Houghton St, WC2. . . . . . . **18** D4
Houlder Cres, Croy. CR0. . **201** H6
Houndsden Rd, N21. . . . . . **43** F6
Houndsditch, EC3 . . . . **20** E3
Houndsfield Rd, N9 . . . . . . **44** E7
HOUNSLOW,
TW3 - TW6. . . . . **143** F4
Hounslow Av, Houns.
TW3. . . . . **143** H5
Hounslow Business Pk,
Houns. TW3
off Alice Way **143** G4
Hounslow Gdns, Houns.
TW3. . . . . **143** H5
★**Hounslow Heath**, Houns.
TW4. . . . . **142** E6
Hounslow Rd, Felt. (Feltham)
TW14. . . . . **160** B1
Feltham (Han.) TW13. . . **160** D4
Twickenham TW2 . . . . . **143** J6
HOUNSLOW WEST, Houns.
TW4. . . . . **142** D3
Housman Way, SE5
off Hopewell St. **132** A7
★**Houses of Parliament**,
SW1 . . . . **26** B4
Houston Pl, Esher KT10
off Lime Tree Av **194** B1
Houston Rd, SE23 . . . . . . **171** H2
Surbiton KT6. . . . . **181** E6
Hove Av, E17 . . . . **77** J5
Hoveden Rd, NW2 . . . . **90** B5
Hove Gdns, Sutt. SM1 . . . **199** E1
Hoveton Rd, SE28 . . . . . . **118** C6
Hoveton Way, Ilf. IG6 . . . . . **64** E7
Howard Av, Bex. DA5. . . . **176** C1
Howard Bldg, SW8
off Queenstown Rd. . . **130** B6
Howard Cl, N11 . . . . **58** A2
NW2 . . . . **90** B4
W3. . . . . **106** B6
Hampton TW12 . . . . **161** J6
Loughton IG10 . . . . **48** B6
Howard Dr, Borwd. WD6 . . **38** D4
Howard Ms, N5
off Hamilton Pk. **93** H4
Howard Rd, E6 . . . . **116** C2
E11. . . . . **97** E3
E17 . . . . **78** A3
N15 . . . . **76** B6
N16 . . . . **94** A4
NW2 . . . . **90** A4
SE20 . . . . **189** F1
SE25 . . . . **188** D5
Barking IG11 . . . . **117** G1
Bromley BR1. . . . . **173** G7
Ilford IG1. . . . . **99** E4
Isleworth TW7 . . . . **144** C3
New Malden KT3 . . . . . **183** E3
Southall UB1 . . . . **103** H6
Surbiton KT5. . . . . **181** J6
Howards Cl, Pnr. HA5 . . . . **66** B2
Howards Crest Cl, Beck.
BR3 . . . . **190** C2
Howards La, SW15. . . . . . **147** H5
Howards Rd, E13 . . . . **115** G3
Howard St, T.Ditt. KT7 . . . **181** E7
Howard Wk, N2 . . . . **73** F4
Howard Way, Barn. EN5. . . **40** A5
Howarth Ct, E15
off Clays La. **96** C5
Howarth Rd, SE2 . . . . **138** A5
Howberry Cl, Edg. HA8 . . . **53** G6
Howberry Rd, Edg. HA8. . . **53** G6
Stanmore HA7 . . . . **53** G6

Howberry Rd, Th.Hth. CR7 **188** A1
Howbury Rd, SE15 **153** F3
Howcroft Cres, N3 **56** D7
Howcroft La, Grnf. UB6 *off Cowgate Rd* **104** A3
Howden Cl, SE28 **118** D7
Howden Rd, SE25 **188** C2
Howden St, SE15 **152** D3
Howe Cl, Rom. RM7 **83** G1
Howell Cl, Rom. RM6 **82** D5
Howell Wk, SE1 **35** H2
Howes Cl, N3 **72** D3
Howfield Pl, N17 **76** C3
Howgate Rd, SW14 **146** D3
Howick Pl, SW1 **25** G6
Howie St, SW11 **129** H7
Howitt Cl, N16 *off Allen Rd* **94** B4
NW3 *off Howitt Rd* **91** H6
Howitt Rd, NW3 **91** H6
Howland Est, SE16 **133** F3
Howland Ms E, W1 **17** G1
Howland St, W1 **17** F1
Howland Way, SE16 **133** H2
Howletts Rd, SE24 **151** J6
Howley Pl, W2 **14** D1
Howley Rd, Croy. CR0 **201** H3
Howsman Rd, SW13 **127** G6
Howson Rd, SE4 **153** H4
Howson Ter, Rich. TW10 **145** H6
Hows St, E2 **13** F1
Howton Pl, Bushey (Bushey Hth) WD23 **52** A1
HOXTON, N1 **12** D2
Hoxton Mkt, N1 **12** D4
Hoxton Sq, N1 **12** D4
Hoxton St, N1 **12** E4
Hoylake Gdns, Mitch. CR4 **186** C3
Ruislip HA4 **84** B1
Watford WD19 **50** D4
Hoylake Rd, W3 **107** E6
Hoyland Cl, SE15 *off Commercial Way* **132/133** E7
Hoyle Rd, SW17 **167** H5
Hoy St, E16 **115** F6
★**H.Q.S. Wellington, Master Mariners' Hall**, WC2 **19** E5
Hubbard Dr, Chess. KT9 **195** F6
Hubbard Rd, SE27 **169** J4
Hubbard St, E15 **114** E1
Hubbinet Ind Est, Rom. RM7 **83** J3
Hubert Gro, SW9 **151** E3
Hubert Rd, E6 **116** A3
Huddart St, E3 **113** J5
Huddleston Cl, E2 **113** F2
Huddlestone Rd, E7 **97** F4
NW2 **89** H6
Huddleston Rd, N7 **92** D4
Hudson Ct, E14 *off Maritime Quay* **134** A5
SW19 **167** E7
Hudson Gdns, Orp. BR6 *off Superior Dr* **207** J6
Hudson Pl, SE18 **137** F5
Hudson Rd, Bexh. DA7 **159** F2
Hayes UB3 **121** G6
Hudson's Pl, SW1 **33** E1
Hudson Way, N9 **61** F3
NW2 *off Gratton Ter* **90** A3
Huggin Ct, EC4 **20** A5
Huggin Hill, EC4 **20** A5
Huggins Pl, SW2 *off Roupell Rd* **169** F1
Hughan Rd, E15 **96** D5
Hugh Dalton Av, SW6 **128** C6
Hughenden Av, Har. HA3 **69** E5
Hughenden Gdns, Nthlt. UB5 **102** C3
Hughenden Rd, Wor.Pk. KT4 **183** G7
Hughendon Ter, E15 *off Westdown Rd* **96** C4
Hughes Cl, N12 *off Coleridge Rd* **57** F5
Hughes Rd, Hayes UB3 **102** B7
Hughes Ter, SW9 *off Styles Gdns* **151** H3
Hughes Wk, Croy. CR0 *off St. Saviours Rd* **187** J7
Hugh Gaitskell Cl, SW6 **128** C6
Hugh Ms, SW1 **32** E2
Hugh St, SW1 **32** E2
Hugon Rd, SW6 **148** E3
Hugo Rd, N19 **92** C4
Huguenot Pl, E1 **21** G1
SW18 **149** F5
Huguenot Sq, SE15 *off Scylla Rd* **152/153** E3
Hullbridge Ms, N1 *off Sherborne St* **112** A1
Hull Cl, SE16 **133** G2
Hull Pl, E16 *off Fishguard Way* **136/137** E2
Hull St, EC1 **11** J4
Hulme Pl, SE1 **28** A4
Hulse Av, Bark. IG11 **99** G6
Romford RM7 **83** H1
Hulse Ter, Ilf. IG1 *off Buttsbury Rd* **99** F5
Humber Cl, West Dr. UB7 **120** A1
Humber Dr, W10 **108** A4
Humber Rd, NW2 **89** H2
SE3 **135** F6
Humberstone Rd, E13 **115** J3
Humberton Cl, E9 *off Marsh Hill* **95** H5
Humbolt Rd, W6 **128** B6
Humes Av, W7 **124** B3
Hume Ter, E16 *off Prince Regent La* **115** J6
Hume Way, Ruis. HA4 **66** A6
Humphrey Cl, Ilf. IG5 **80** C1
Humphrey St, SE1 **37** F3
Humphries Cl, Dag. RM9 **101** F4
Hundred Acre, NW9 **71** F2
Hungerdown, E4 **62** C1
Hungerford Br, SE1 **26** B1
WC2 **26** B1
Hungerford La, WC2 **26** A1
Hungerford Rd, N7 **92** D5
Hungerford St, E1 *off Commercial Rd* **112/113** E6
Hunsdon Cl, Dag. RM9 **101** E6
Hunsdon Rd, SE14 **133** G6
Hunslett St, E2 *off Royston St* **113** F2
Hunston Rd, Mord. SM4 **198** E1
Hunt Cl, W11 **128** A1
Hunter Cl, SE1 **28** C6
SW12 *off Balham Pk Rd* **168** A1
Borehamwood WD6 **38** C5
Wallington SM6 **200** E7
Huntercrombe Gdns, Wat. WD19 **50** C5
Hunter Ho, Felt. TW13 **160** A1
Hunter Rd, SW20 **183** J1
Ilford IG1 **99** E5
Thornton Heath CR7 **188** A3
Hunters, The, Beck. BR3 **190** C1
Hunters Ct, Rich. TW9 *off Friars La* **145** G5
Hunters Gro, Har. HA3 **69** F4
Hayes UB3 **122** A1
Orpington BR6 **207** E4
Hunters Hall Rd, Dag. RM10 **101** G4
Hunters Hill, Ruis. HA4 **84** C3
Hunters Meadow, SE19 *off Dulwich Wd Av* **170** B4
Hunters Rd, Chess. KT9 **195** H3
Hunters Sq, Dag. RM10 **101** G4
Hunter St, WC1 **10** B5
Hunters Way, Croy. CR0 **202** B4
Enfield EN2 **43** G1
Hunter Wk, E13 **115** G2
Borehamwood WD6 *off Hunter Cl* **38** C5
Huntingdon Cl, Mitch. CR4 **187** E3
Huntingdon Gdns, W4 **126** C7
Worcester Park KT4 **197** J3
Huntingdon Rd, N2 **73** H3
N9 **61** F1
Huntingdon St, E16 **115** F6
N1 **93** F7
Huntingfield, Croy. CR0 **203** J7
Huntingfield Rd, SW15 **147** G4
Hunting Gate Cl, Enf. EN2 **43** G3
Hunting Gate Dr, Chess. KT9 **195** H7
Hunting Gate Ms, Sutt. SM1 **199** E3
Twickenham TW2 *off Colne Rd* **162** B1
Huntings Rd, Dag. RM10 **101** G6
Huntley Cl, Stai. (Stanw.) TW19 *off Cambria Gdns* **140** B7
Huntley Dr, N3 **56** D6
Huntley St, WC1 **9** G6
Huntley Way, SW20 **183** G2
Huntly Rd, SE25 **188** B4
Hunton St, E1 **13** H6
Hunt Rd, Sthl. UB2 **123** G3
Hunt's Cl, SE3 **155** G2
Hunt's Ct, WC2 **17** J6
Hunts La, E15 **114** C2
Huntsmans Cl, Felt. TW13 **160** B4
Huntsman St, SE17 **36** C2
Hunts Mead, Enf. EN3 **45** G3
Hunts Mead Cl, Chis. BR7 **174** C7
Huntsmoor Rd, Epsom KT19 **196** D5
Huntspill St, SW17 **167** F3
Hunts Slip Rd, SE21 **170** B3
Huntsworth Ms, NW1 **7** J6
Hunt Way, SE22 *off Dulwich Common* **170** D1
Hurdwick Pl, NW1 *off Harrington Sq* **110** C2
Hurley Cres, SE16 *off Marlow Way* **133** G2
Hurley Ho, SE11 **35** F2
Hurley Rd, Grnf. UB6 **103** H6
Hurlingham Business Pk, SW6 **148** D3
Hurlingham Ct, SW6 **148** C3
Hurlingham Gdns, SW6 **148** C3
★**Hurlingham Ho**, SW6 **148** D3
★**Hurlingham Park**, SW6 **148** C2
Hurlingham Retail Pk, SW6 *off Carnwath Rd* **148/149** E3
Hurlingham Rd, SW6 **148** C2
Bexleyheath DA7 **139** F7
Hurlingham Sq, SW6 **148** E3
Hurlock St, N5 **93** H3
Hurlstone Rd, SE25 **188** A5
Hurn Ct Rd, Houns. TW4 *off Renfrew Rd* **142** D2
Huron Cl, Orp. BR6 *off Winnipeg Dr* **207** J6
Huron Rd, SW17 **168** A2
Hurren Cl, SE3 **154** E3
Hurricane Rd, Wall. SM6 **201** E7
Hurry Cl, E15 **97** E7
Hursley Rd, Chig. IG7 *off Tufter Rd* **65** J5
Hurst Av, E4 **62** A4
N6 **74** C6
Hurstbourne, Esher (Clay.) KT10 **194** C6
Hurstbourne Gdns, Bark. IG11 **99** H6
Hurstbourne Ho, SW15 *off Tangley Gro* **147** F6
Hurstbourne Rd, SE23 **171** H1
Hurst Cl, E4 **62** A3
NW11 **72** E6
Bromley BR2 **205** F1
Chessington KT9 **196** A5
Northolt UB5 **85** F6
Hurstcourt Rd, Sutt. SM1 **198** E2
Hurstdene Av, Brom. BR2 **205** F1
Hurstdene Gdns, N15 **76** B7
Hurst Est, SE2 **138** D5
Hurstfield, Brom. BR2 **191** G5
Hurstfield Rd, W.Mol. KT8 **179** G3
Hurst La, SE2 **138** D5
East Molesey KT8 **179** J4
Hurstleigh Gdns, Ilf. IG5 **80** C1
Hurstmead Ct, Edg. HA8 **54** B4
Hurst Ri, Barn. EN5 **40** D3
Hurst Rd, E17 **78** B3
N21 **59** G1
Bexley DA5 **176** D1
Buckhurst Hill IG9 **64** A1
Croydon CR0 **202** A5
East Molesey KT8 **179** G3
Erith DA8 **139** J7
Sidcup DA15 **176** A2
Walton-on-Thames KT12 **178** C5
West Molesey KT8 **179** E3
Hurst Springs, Bex. DA5 **177** E1
Hurst St, SE24 **151** H6
Hurst Vw Rd, S.Croy. CR2 **202** B7
Hurst Way, S.Croy. CR2 **202** B6
Hurstway Wk, W11 **108** A7
Hurstwood Av, E18 **79** H4
Bexley DA5 **176** E1
Hurstwood Dr, Brom. BR1 **192** C3
Hurstwood Rd, NW11 **72** B4
Hurtwood Rd, Walt. KT12 **179** F7
Huson Cl, NW3 **91** H7
Hussain Cl, Har. HA1 **86** C4
Hussars Cl, Houns. TW4 **142** E3
Husseywell Cres, Brom. BR2 **205** G1
Hutchings St, E14 **134** A2
Hutchings Wk, NW11 **73** E4
Hutchins Cl, E15 *off Gibbins Rd* **96** C7
Hutchinson Ter, Wem. HA9 **87** G3
Hutchins Rd, SE28 **118** A7
Hutton Cl, Grnf. UB6 *off Mary Peters Dr* **86** A5
Woodford Green IG8 **63** H6
Hutton Gdns, Har. HA3 **51** J7
Hutton Gro, N12 **57** E5
Hutton La, Har. HA3 **51** J7
Hutton Row, Edg. HA8 *off Pavilion Way* **54** C7
Hutton St, EC4 **19** F4
Hutton Wk, Har. HA3 **51** J7
Huxbear St, SE4 **153** J5
Huxley Cl, Nthlt. UB5 **103** E1
Huxley Dr, Rom. RM6 **82** B7
Huxley Gdns, NW10 **105** J3
Huxley Par, N18 **60** A5
Huxley Pl, N13 **59** H4
Huxley Rd, E10 **96** C2
N18 **60** A4
Welling DA16 **157** J3
Huxley Sayze, N18 **60** A5
Huxley St, W10 **108** B3
Hyacinth Cl, Hmptn. TW12 *off Gresham Rd* **161** G6
Ilford IG1 **98** E6
Hyacinth Ct, Pnr. HA5 *off Tulip Ct* **66** C3
Hyacinth Rd, SW15 **165** G1
Hycliffe Gdns, Chig. IG7 **65** F4
HYDE, THE, NW9 **71** F4
Hyde, The, NW9 **71** E5
Hyde Cl, E13 **115** G2
Barnet EN5 **40** C3
Hyde Ct, N20 **57** G3
Hyde Cres, NW9 **71** E5
Hyde Est Rd, NW9 **71** F5
Hyde Fm Ms, SW12 *off Telferscot Rd* **168** D1
Hydefield Cl, N21 **60** A1
Hydefield Ct, N9 **60** B2
Hyde Ho, NW9 **71** E5
Hyde La, SW11 *off Battersea Br Rd* **149** H1
★**Hyde Park**, W2 **23** G1
Hyde Pk, SW7 **23** G1
W1 **23** G1
Hyde Pk Av, N21 **59** J2
Hyde Pk Cor, W1 **24** C3
Hyde Pk Cres, W2 **15** G4
Hyde Pk Gdns, N21 **59** J1
W2 **15** F5
Hyde Pk Gdns Ms, W2 **15** F5
Hyde Pk Gate, SW7 **22** D4
Hyde Pk Gate Ms, SW7 **22** D4
Hyde Pk Pl, W2 **15** H5
Hyde Pk Sq, W2 **15** G4
Hyde Pk Sq Ms, W2 **15** G4
Hyde Pk St, W2 **15** G4
Hyderabad Way, E15 **96** E7
Hyde Rd, N1 **112** A1
Bexleyheath DA7 **159** F2
Richmond TW10 *off Albert Rd* **145** J5
Hydeside Gdns, N9 **60** C2
Hydes Pl, N1 *off Compton Av* **93** H7
Hyde St, SE8 *off Deptford High St* **134** A6
Hydethorpe Av, N9 **60** C2
Hydethorpe Rd, SW12 **168** C1
Hyde Vale, SE10 **134** C7
Hyde Wk, Mord. SM4 **184** D7
Hyde Way, N9 **60** C2
Hayes UB3 **121** J4
Hylands Rd, E17 **78** D2
Hylton St, SE18 **137** J4
Hyndewood, SE23 **171** G3
Hyndman St, SE15 **132** E6
Hynton Rd, Dag. RM8 **100** C2
Hyrstdene, S.Croy. CR2 **201** H4
Hyson Rd, SE16 *off Galleywall Rd* **132/133** E4
Hythe Av, Bexh. DA7 **139** F7
Hythe Cl, N18 **60** D4
Hythe Path, Th.Hth. CR7 **188** A3
Hythe Rd, NW10 **107** G4
Thornton Heath CR7 **188** A2
Hythe Rd Ind Est, NW10 **107** G3
Hyver Hill, NW7 **38** D6

I

Ian Sq, Enf. EN3 *off Lansbury Rd* **45** G1

Ibbetson Path, Loug. IG10 . 49 E3
Ibbotson Av, E16 . . . . 115 F6
Ibbott St, E1
off Mantus Rd 113 F4
Iberian Av, Wall. SM6 . . . . 200 D4
Ibex Ho, E15 *off Forest La* . 96 E6
Ibis La, W4 . . . . 146 C1
Ibis Way, Hayes UB4
off Cygnet Way 102 D6
Ibscott Cl, Dag. RM10 . . . . 101 J6
Ibsley Gdns, SW15 . . . . . . 165 G1
Ibsley Way, Barn. EN4 . . . . 41 H5
★**Ice Ho, Holland Pk**, W8 . 128 C2
Iceland Rd, E3 . . . . 114 A1
Iceni Ct, E3 *off Roman Rd* . 113 J1
Ice Wf, N1 . . . . 10 B1
Ice Wf Marina, N1
off New Wf Rd 110/111 E2
Ickburgh Est, E5
off Ickburgh Rd 94/95 E3
Ickburgh Rd, E5 . . . . 94 E3
Ickleton Rd, SE9 . . . . 174 B4
Icknield Dr, Ilf. IG2 . . . . 81 E5
Ickworth Pk Rd, E17 . . . . . 77 H4
Ida Rd, N15 . . . . 76 A5
Ida St, E14 . . . . 114 C6
Iden Cl, Brom. BR2 . . . . . . 191 E3
Idlecombe Rd, SW17 . . . . 168 A6
Idmiston Rd, E15 . . . . 97 F5
SE27 . . . . 169 J3
Worcester Park KT4 . . . . 183 F7
Idmiston Sq, Wor.Pk. KT4 . 183 F7
Idol La, EC3 . . . . 20 D6
Idonia St, SE8 . . . . 133 J7
Iffley Rd, W6 . . . . 127 H3
Ifield Rd, SW10 . . . . 30 B5
Ifor Evans Pl, E1
off Mile End Rd 113 G4
Ightham Rd, Erith DA8 . . . 139 G7
Ikea Twr, NW10 . . . . 88 D5
Ilbert St, W10 . . . . 108 A3
Ilchester Gdns, W2 . . . . 14 A5
Ilchester Pl, W14 . . . . 128 C3
Ilchester Rd, Dag. RM8 . . 100 B5
Ildersly Gro, SE21 . . . . . . 170 A2
Ilderton Rd, SE16 . . . . 133 F7
SE16 . . . . 133 E5
Ilex Cl, Sun. TW16
off Oakington Dr 178 C2
Ilex Ho, N4 . . . . 75 F7
Ilex Rd, NW10 . . . . 89 F6
Ilex Way, SW16 . . . . 169 G5
ILFORD, IG1 - IG6 . . . . 99 F3
Ilford Hill, Ilf. IG1 . . . . 98 D3
Ilford La, Ilf. IG1 . . . . 98 E3
Ilfracombe Gdns, Rom.
RM6 . . . . 82 B7
Ilfracombe Rd, Brom. BR1 . 173 F3
Iliffe St, SE17 . . . . 35 H3
Iliffe Yd, SE17 . . . . 35 H3
Ilkeston Ct, E5
off Overbury St 95 G4
Ilkley Cl, SE19 . . . . 170 A6
Ilkley Rd, E16 . . . . 115 J5
Watford WD19 . . . . 50 D5
Illingworth Cl, Mitch. CR4 . 185 G3
Illingworth Way, Enf. EN1 . 44 B4
Ilmington Rd, Har. HA3 . . . . 69 G6
Ilminster Gdns, SW11 . . . 149 H4
Imber Cl, N14 . . . . 42 C7
Esher KT10
off Ember La 194 A1
Imber Ct Trd Est, E.Mol.
KT8 . . . . 180 A6
Imber Gro, Esher KT10 . . . 180 A7
Imber Pk Rd, Esher KT10 . 194 A1
Imber St, N1 . . . . 112 A1
Imer Pl, T.Ditt. KT7 . . . . . . 180 C7
Imperial Av, N16
off Victorian Rd 94 C3
Imperial Cl, Har. HA2 . . . . . 67 G6
★**Imperial Coll, Uni of**
London, SW7 . . . . 23 E5
Imperial Coll Rd, SW7 . . . . 22 E6
Imperial Cres, SW6
off William Morris Way . 149 F2
Imperial Dr, Har. HA2 . . . . . 67 G7
Imperial Gdns, Mitch. CR4 . 186 B3
Imperial Ms, E6
off Central Pk Rd 115 J2
Imperial Rd, N22 . . . . 74 E1
SW6 . . . . 149 E1
Feltham TW14 . . . . 141 H7
Imperial Sq, SW6 . . . . 149 E1
Imperial St, E3 . . . . 114 C3
★**Imperial War Mus**, SE1 . . 27 F6
Imperial Way, Chis. BR7 . . 175 F3
Croydon CR0 . . . . 201 F6
Harrow HA3 . . . . 69 H6
Imperial Wf, SW6 . . . . 149 F2
Imprimo Pk, Loug. IG10 . . . 49 G4
Imre Cl, W12
off Ellerslie Rd 127 H1
Inca Dr, SE9 . . . . 156 E7
Inca Ter, N15 *off Milton Rd* . 75 H3
Inchmery Rd, SE6 . . . . 172 B2
Inchwood, Croy. CR0 . . . . 204 B4
Independent Pl, E8
off Downs Pk Rd 94 C5
Independents Rd, SE3
off Blackheath Village . 155 F3
Inderwick Rd, N8 . . . . 75 F5
Indescon Ct, E14 . . . . 134 B2
India Pl, WC2 . . . . 18 C5
India St, EC3 . . . . 21 F4
India Way, W12 . . . . 107 H7
Indigo Ms, E14
off Ashton St 114 C7
N16 . . . . 94 A3
Indus Rd, SE7 . . . . 135 J7
Industry Ter, SW9
off Canterbury Cres . . 151 G3
Ingal Rd, E13 . . . . 115 G4
Ingate Pl, SW8 . . . . 150 B1
Ingatestone Rd, E12 . . . . . . 97 J1
SE25 . . . . 188 E4
Woodford Green IG8 . . . 63 G7
Ingelow Rd, SW8 . . . . 150 B2
Ingersoll Rd, W12 . . . . 127 H1
Ingestre Pl, W1 . . . . 17 G4
Ingestre Rd, E7 . . . . 97 G4
NW5 . . . . 92 B4
Ingham Rd, NW6 . . . . 90 D4
Inglebert St, EC1 . . . . 11 E3
Ingleborough St, SW9 . . . . 151 G2
Ingleby Dr, Har. HA1 . . . . . 86 A3
Ingleby Rd, N7
off Bryett Rd 92/93 E3
Dagenham RM10 . . . . . . 101 H6
Ilford IG1 . . . . 98 E1
Ingleby Way, Chis. BR7 . . . 174 D5
Ingle Cl, Pnr. HA5 . . . . 67 E3
Ingledew Rd, SE18 . . . . . . 137 G5
Inglehurst Gdns, Ilf. IG4 . . . 80 C5
Inglemere Rd, SE23 . . . . . 171 G3
Mitcham CR4 . . . . 167 J7
Inglesham Wk, E9 . . . . 95 J6
Ingleside Cl, Beck. BR3 . . . 172 A7
Ingleside Gro, SE3 . . . . . . 135 F6
Inglethorpe St, SW6 . . . . 148 A1
Ingleton Av, Well. DA16 . . 158 A5
Ingleton Rd, N18 . . . . 60 D6
Ingleton St, SW9 . . . . 151 G2
Ingleway, N12 . . . . 57 G6
Inglewood Cl, E14 . . . . . . 134 A4
Ilford IG6 . . . . 65 J6
Inglewood Copse, Brom.
BR1 . . . . 192 B2
Inglewood Rd, NW6 . . . . . . 90 D5
Inglis Barracks, NW7 . . . . . 56 A5
Inglis Rd, W5 . . . . 105 J7
Croydon CR0 . . . . 202 C1
Inglis St, SE5 . . . . 151 H1
Ingram Av, NW11 . . . . 73 F7
Ingram Cl, SE11 . . . . 34 D1
Stanmore HA7 . . . . 53 F5
Ingram Rd, N2 . . . . 73 H4
Thornton Heath CR7 . . . 187 J1
Ingram Way, Grnf. UB6 . . 104 A1
Ingrave Ho, Dag. RM9 . . . 118 B1
Ingrave St, SW11 . . . . 149 G3
Ingress St, W4
off Devonshire Rd . 126/127 E5
Inigo Jones Rd, SE7 . . . . . 136 B7
Inigo Pl, WC2 . . . . 18 A5
Inkerman Rd, NW5 . . . . 92 B6
Inkerman Ter, W8
off Allen St 128 D3
Inks Grn, E4 . . . . 62 C5
Inkster Ho, SW11
off Ingrave St 149 H3
Inman Rd, NW10 . . . . 106 E1
SW18 . . . . 149 F7
Inmans Row, Wdf.Grn. IG8 . 63 G4
Inner Circle, NW1 . . . . 8 B4
Inner Pk Rd, SW19 . . . . . . 166 A1
Inner Ring E, Houns.
(Hthrw Air.) TW6 . . . . . 140 E3
Inner Ring W, Houns.
(Hthrw Air.) TW6 . . . . . 140 D3
Inner Temple La, EC4 . . . . . 19 E4
Innes Cl, SW20 . . . . 184 B2
Innes Gdns, SW15 . . . . . . 147 H6
Innes St, SE15
off Blakes Rd 132 B7
Innes Yd, Croy. CR0
off Whitgift St 201 J3
Inniskilling Rd, E13 . . . . . . 115 J2
Innovation Cl, Wem. HA0 . 105 H1
Inskip Cl, E10 . . . . 96 B2
Inskip Rd, Dag. RM8 . . . . 100 D1
★**Institute of Contemporary**
Arts (I.C.A.), SW1 . . . . . 25 J1
Institute Pl, E8 . . . . 94 E5
Integer Gdns, E11 . . . . 78 D7
Interchange E Ind Est, E5
off Grosvenor Way 95 F2
International Av, Houns.
TW5 . . . . 122 C5
International Trd Est, Sthl.
UB2 . . . . 122 B3
Inveraray Pl, SE18
off Old Mill Rd 137 G6
Inver Cl, E5
off Theydon Rd 95 F2
Inverclyde Gdns, Rom.
RM6 . . . . 82 D4
Inver Ct, W2 . . . . 14 B4
W6 *off Goldhawk Rd* . . . 127 G3
Inveresk Gdns, Wor.Pk.
KT4 . . . . 197 F3
Inverforth Cl, NW3
off North End Way 91 F2
Inverforth Rd, N11 . . . . 58 B5
Inverine Rd, SE7 . . . . 135 H5
Invermead Cl, W6
off Goldhawk Rd 127 G3
Invermore Pl, SE18 . . . . . . 137 F4
Inverness Av, Enf. EN1 . . . . 44 B1
Inverness Dr, Ilf. IG6 . . . . . . 65 H6
Inverness Gdns, W8 . . . . . . 22 A2
Inverness Ms, E16 . . . . . . 137 F1
W2 . . . . 14 B5
Inverness Pl, W2 . . . . 14 B5
Inverness Rd, N18
off Aberdeen Rd . . . 60/61 E5
Hounslow TW3 . . . . 143 F4
Southall UB2 . . . . 123 E4
Worcester Park KT4 . . . . 198 A1
Inverness St, NW1 . . . . . . 110 B1
Inverness Ter, W2 . . . . 14 B5
Inverton Rd, SE15 . . . . . . 153 G4
Invicta Cl, Chis. BR7 . . . . . 174 D5
Invicta Gro, Nthlt. UB5 . . . 103 F3
Invicta Plaza, SE1 . . . . 27 G1
Invicta Rd, SE3 . . . . 135 G7
Inville Rd, SE17 . . . . 36 C4
Inwen Ct, SE8 . . . . 133 H5
Inwood Av, Houns. TW3 . . 143 J3
Inwood Cl, Croy. CR0 . . . . 203 H2
Inwood Rd, Houns. TW3 . . 143 H4
Inworth St, SW11 . . . . 149 H2
Inworth Wk, N1
off Popham St 111 J1
Iona Cl, SE6 . . . . 154 A7
Morden SM4 . . . . 184 E7
Ionian Bldg, E14
off Narrow St 113 H7
Ion Sq, E2 . . . . 13 H2
Ipswich Rd, SW17 . . . . . . 168 A6
Ireland Cl, E6
off Bradley Stone Rd . . 116 C5
Ireland Pl, N22
off Whittington Rd . . 58/59 E7
Ireland Yd, EC4 . . . . 19 H4
Irene Rd, SW6 . . . . 148 D1
Orpington BR6 . . . . 193 J7
Ireton Cl, N10 . . . . 58 A7
Ireton St, E3
off Tidworth Rd 114 A4
Iris Av, Bex. DA5 . . . . 159 E5
Iris Cl, E6 . . . . 116 B4
Croydon CR0 . . . . 203 G1
Surbiton KT6 . . . . 181 J7
Iris Ct, Pnr. HA5 . . . . 66 C3
Iris Cres, Bexh. DA7 . . . . . 139 F6
Iris Rd, Epsom (W.Ewell)
KT19 . . . . 196 B5
Iris Wk, Edg. HA8
off Ash Cl 54 C4
Iris Way, E4 . . . . 61 J6
Irkdale Av, Enf. EN1 . . . . . . 44 C1
Iron Br Cl, NW10 . . . . 88 E5
Southall UB2 . . . . 123 J1
Iron Br Rd, Uxb. UB11 . . . 120 D2
West Drayton UB7 . . . . 120 D2
Iron Mill Pl, SW18
off Garratt La 148/149 E6
Iron Mill Rd, SW18 . . . . . . 149 E6
Ironmonger La, EC2 . . . . . . 20 B4
Ironmonger Pas, EC1 . . . . . 12 A5
Ironmonger Row, EC1 . . . . 12 A4
Ironmongers Pl, E14
off Spindrift Av 134 A4
Ironside Cl, SE16
off Kinburn St 133 G2
Irvine Av, Har. HA3 . . . . 68 D3
Irvine Cl, N20 . . . . 57 H2
Irvine Way, Orp. BR6 . . . . 193 J7
Irving Av, Nthlt. UB5 . . . . 102 D1
Irving Gro, SW9 . . . . 151 F2
Irving Ms, N1
off Alwyne Rd 93 J6
Irving Rd, W14 . . . . 128 A3
Irving St, WC2 . . . . 17 J6
Irving Way, NW9 . . . . 71 F5
Irwin Av, SE18 . . . . 137 H7
Irwin Gdns, NW10 . . . . . . 107 H1
Isabel Hill Cl, Hmptn. TW12
off Upper Sunbury Rd . . 179 H1
Isabella Cl, N14 . . . . 42 C7
Isabella Ct, Rich. TW10
off Grove Rd 145 J6
Isabella Dr, Orp. BR6 . . . . 207 F4
Isabella Rd, E9 . . . . 95 F5
Isabella St, SE1 . . . . 27 G2
Isabel St, SW9 . . . . 151 F1
Isambard Ms, E14 . . . . . . 134 C3
Isambard Pl, SE16
off Rotherhithe St 133 F1
Isel Way, SE22
off East Dulwich Gro . . 152 B5
Isham Rd, SW16 . . . . 186 E2
Isis Cl, SW15 . . . . 147 J4
Isis St, SW18 . . . . 167 F2
Island Fm Av, W.Mol. KT8 . 179 F5
Island Fm Rd, W.Mol. KT8 . 179 F5
Island Rd, Mitch. CR4 . . . . 167 J7
Island Row, E14 . . . . 113 J6
Isla Rd, SE18 . . . . 137 F6
Islay Gdns, Houns. TW4 . . 142 D5
Islay Wk, N1
off Douglas Rd 93 J7
Isledon Rd, N7 . . . . 93 G3
Islehurst Cl, Chis. BR7 . . . 192 D1
ISLEWORTH, TW7 . . . . 144 C3
Isleworth Business
Complex, Islw. TW7
off St. John's Rd 144 C2
Isleworth Prom, Twick.
TW1 . . . . 144 E4
ISLINGTON, N1 . . . . 111 F1
Islington Grn, N1 . . . . 111 H1
Islington High St, N1 . . . . . 11 F2
Islington Pk Ms, N1
off Islington Pk St 93 G7
Islington Pk St, N1 . . . . 93 G7
Islip Gdns, Edg. HA8 . . . . . 54 D7
Northolt UB5 . . . . 85 E7
Islip Manor Rd, Nthlt. UB5 . 85 E7
Islip St, NW5 . . . . 92 C5
Ismailia Rd, E7 . . . . 97 H7
★**Ismaili Cen & Zamana**
Gall, SW7 . . . . 31 F1
Isom Cl, E13
off Belgrave Rd 115 J4
Ivanhoe Dr, Har. HA3 . . . . . 68 D3
Ivanhoe Rd, SE5 . . . . 152 C3
Hounslow TW4 . . . . 142 D3
Ivatt Pl, W14 . . . . 128 C5
Ivatt Way, N17 . . . . 75 H3
Iveagh Av, NW10 . . . . 106 A2
Iveagh Cl, E9 . . . . 113 G1
NW10 . . . . 106 A2
Iveagh Ter, NW10
off Iveagh Av 106 A2
Ivedon Rd, Well. DA16 . . . 158 C2
Ive Fm Cl, E10 . . . . 96 A2
Ive Fm La, E10 . . . . 96 A2
Iveley Rd, SW4 . . . . 150 C2
Ivere Dr, Barn. EN5 . . . . 40 E6
Iverhurst Cl, Bexh. DA6 . . 158 D5
Iverna Ct, W8 . . . . 128 D3
Iverna Gdns, W8 . . . . 128 D3
Feltham TW14 . . . . 141 G5
Iverson Rd, NW6 . . . . 90 C6
Ivers Way, Croy.
(New Adgtn) CR0 . . . . 204 B7
Ives Rd, E16 . . . . 114 E5
Ives St, SW3 . . . . 31 H1
Ivestor Ter, SE23 . . . . 153 F7
Ivimey St, E2 . . . . 13 J3
Ivinghoe Cl, Enf. EN1 . . . . . 44 B2
Ivinghoe Rd, Dag. RM8 . . 100 B5
Ivor Gro, SE9 . . . . 175 E1
Ivor Pl, NW1 . . . . 7 J6
Ivor St, NW1 . . . . 92 C7
Ivorydown, Brom. BR1 . . . 173 G4
Ivory Sq, SW11
off Gartons Way 149 F3
Ivybridge Cl, Twick. TW1 . . 144 D6
Ivybridge Est, Islw. TW7 . . 144 C5
Ivybridge La, WC2 . . . . 18 B6
Ivychurch Cl, SE20 . . . . . . 171 F7
Ivychurch La, SE17 . . . . 37 F3
Ivy Cl, Har. HA2 . . . . 85 F4

Ivy Cl, Pnr. HA5 66 C7
Sunbury-on-Thames TW16 178 C2
Ivy Cotts, E14 *off Grove Vil.* 114 B7
Ivy Ct, SE16 37 J4
Ivy Cres, W4 126 C4
Ivydale Rd, SE15 153 G3
Carshalton SM5 199 J2
Ivyday Gro, SW16 169 F3
Ivydene, W.Mol. KT8 179 F5
Ivydene Cl, Sutt. SM1 199 F4
Ivy Gdns, N8 74 E6
Mitcham CR4 186 D3
Ivyhouse Rd, Dag. RM9 100 D6
Ivy La, Houns. TW4 143 F4
Ivymount Rd, SE27 169 G3
Ivy Pl, Surb. KT5 *off Alpha Rd* 181 J6
Ivy Rd, E16 *off Pacific Rd* 115 G6
E17 78 A6
N14 42 C7
NW2 89 J4
SE4 153 J4
SW17 *off Tooting High St* 167 H5
Hounslow TW3 143 H4
Surbiton KT6 196 A1
Ivy St, N1 12 D1
Ivy Wk, Dag. RM9 100 E6
Ixworth Pl, SW3 31 G3
Izane Rd, Bexh. DA6 159 F4

J

Jacaranda Cl, N.Mal. KT3 182 E3
Jacaranda Gro, E8 94 C7
Jackass La, Kes. BR2 205 H6
Jack Barnett Way, N22 75 F2
Jack Clow Rd, E15 115 E2
Jack Cornwell St, E12 98 D4
Jack Dash Way, E6 116 B4
Jack Goodchild Way, Kings.T. KT1 *off Kingston Rd* 182 B3
Jacklin Grn, Wdf.Grn. IG8 63 G4
Jackman Ms, NW10 88 E3
Jackman St, E8 112 E1
Jackson Cl, E9 95 F7
Jackson Ct, E11 *off Brading Cres* 97 H1
Jackson Rd, N7 93 F4
Barking IG11 117 G1
Barnet EN4 41 H6
Bromley BR2 206 B2
Jacksons La, N6 74 A7
Jacksons Pl, Croy. CR0 *off Cross Rd* 202 A1
Jackson St, SE18 136 D6
Jacksons Way, Croy. CR0 204 A3
Jackson Way, Sthl. UB2 123 H2
Jack Walker Ct, N5 93 H4
Jacob Ho, Erith DA18 *off Kale Rd* 138 D2
Jacobs Cl, Dag. RM10 101 H4
Jacobs Ho, E13 115 J3
Jacob St, SE1 29 G3
Jacob's Well Ms, W1 16 C3
Jacqueline Cl, Nthlt. UB5 *off Canford Av* 103 F1
Jade Cl, E16 116 A6
NW2 *off Marble Dr* 72 A7
Dagenham RM8 100 C1
Jaffe Rd, Ilf. IG1 99 F1
Jaffray Pl, SE27 *off Chapel Rd* 169 H4
Jaffray Rd, Brom. BR2 192 A4
Jaggard Way, SW12 149 J7
Jago Cl, SE18 137 F6
Jago Wk, SE5 132 A7
Jamaica Rd, SE1 29 G4
SE16 132 C2
Thornton Heath CR7 187 H6
Jamaica St, E1 113 F6
James Av, NW2 89 J5
Dagenham RM8 101 F1
James Bedford Cl, Pnr. HA5 66 C2
James Boswell Cl, SW16 *off Curtis Fld Rd* 169 G4
James Clavell Sq, SE18 *off Cadogan Rd* 136 E3
James Cl, E13 *off Richmond St* 115 G2
NW11 *off Woodlands* 72 B6
James Collins Cl, W9 *off Fermoy Rd* 108 C4
James Ct, N1 *off Morton Rd* 93 J7
James Dudson Ct, NW10 88 C7
James Gdns, N22 59 H7
James Hammett Ho, E2 13 G2
James Joyce Wk, SE24 *off Shakespeare Rd* 151 H4
James La, E10 78 D7
E11 78 D6
James Newman Ct, SE9 *off Great Harry Dr* 174 D3
Jameson Cl, W3 *off Acton La* 126 C2
Jameson Ct, E2 113 F2
Jameson St, W8 128 D1
James Pl, N17 76 C1
James's Cotts, Rich. TW9 *off Kew Rd* 126 A7
James Sinclair Pt, E13 115 J1
James St, W1 16 C3
WC2 18 B5
Barking IG11 99 F7
Enfield EN1 44 C5
Hounslow TW3 144 A3
James Ter, SW14 *off Mullins Path* 146 D3
Jamestown Rd, NW1 110 B1
Jamestown Way, E14 114 D7
James Way, Wat. WD19 50 D4
James Yd, E4 62 D6
Jamieson Ho, Houns. TW4 143 F7
Jamuna Cl, E14 113 H5
Jane St, E1 *off Commercial Rd* 112/113 E6
Janet St, E14 134 A3
Janeway Pl, SE16 *off Janeway St* 132/133 E2
Janeway St, SE16 29 J4
Janice Ms, Ilf. IG1 *off Oakfield Rd* 98/99 E3
Jansen Wk, SW11 *off Hope St* 149 G4
Janson Cl, E15 *off Janson Rd* 96/97 E5
NW10 88 D3
Janson Rd, E15 96 E5
Jansons Rd, N15 76 B3
Japan Cres, N4 93 F1
Japan Rd, Rom. RM6 82 D6
Jardine Rd, E1 113 G7
Jarrett Cl, SW2 169 H1
Jarrow Cl, Mord. SM4 184 E5
Jarrow Rd, N17 76 E4
SE16 133 F4
Romford RM6 82 C6
Jarrow Way, E9 95 H4
Jarvis Cl, Bark. IG11 *off Westbury Rd* 117 G1
Barnet EN5 40 A5
Jarvis Rd, SE22 *off Melbourne Gro* 152 B4
South Croydon CR2 202 A6
Jasmine Cl, Ilf. IG1 99 E5
Orpington BR6 206 E2
Southall UB1 103 E7
Jasmine Gdns, Croy. CR0 204 B3
Harrow HA2 85 G2
Jasmine Gro, SE20 189 E1
Jasmine Ter, West Dr. UB7 120 D2
Jasmine Way, E.Mol. KT8 *off Hampton Ct Way* 180 B4
Jasmin Rd, Epsom KT19 196 B5
Jason Ct, W1 *off Marylebone La* 110 A6
Jason Wk, SE9 174 D4
Jasper Pas, SE19 170 C6
Jasper Rd, E16 116 A6
SE19 170 C5
Jasper Wk, N1 12 B3
Javelin Way, Nthlt. UB5 102 D3
Jaycroft, Enf. EN2 *off The Ridgeway* 43 G1
Jay Gdns, Chis. BR7 174 C4
Jay Ms, SW7 22 D4
Jazzfern Ter, Wem. HA0 *off Maybank Av* 86 D5
Jean Batten Cl, Wall. SM6 201 F7
Jebb Av, SW2 151 E6
Jebb St, E3 114 A2
Jedburgh Rd, E13 115 J3
Jedburgh St, SW11 150 A4
Jeddo Rd, W12 127 F2
Jefferson Cl, W13 125 E3
Ilford IG2 81 E5
Jefferson Wk, SE18 *off Kempt St* 136 D6
Jeffreys Pl, NW1 *off Jeffreys St* 92 C7
Jeffreys Rd, SW4 150 E2
Enfield EN3 45 J3
Jeffreys St, NW1 92 B7
Jeffreys Wk, SW4 150 E2
Jeffries Ho, NW10 106 D1
Jeffs Cl, Hmptn. TW12 *off Uxbridge Rd* 161 H6
Jeffs Rd, Sutt. SM1 198 C4
Jeger Av, E2 112 C1
Jeken Rd, SE9 155 J4
Jelf Rd, SW2 151 G5
Jellicoe Gdns, Stan. HA7 52 C6
Jellicoe Rd, E13 *off Jutland Rd* 115 G4
N17 60 A7
Jemma Knowles Cl, SW2 *off Neil Wates Cres* 169 G1
Jemmett Cl, Kings.T. KT2 182 B1
Jengar Cl, Sutt. SM1 199 E4
Jenkins La, E6 116 D2
Barking IG11 117 E2
Jenkins Rd, E13 115 H4
Jenner Av, W3 106 D5
Jenner Cl, Sid. DA14 176 A4
Jenner Ho, SE3 135 E6
Jenner Pl, SW13 127 H6
Jenner Rd, N16 94 C2
Jennett Rd, Croy. CR0 201 G3
Jennifer Rd, Brom. BR1 173 F3
Jennings Cl, Surb. KT6 181 F7
Jennings Rd, SE22 152 C6
Jennings Way, Barn. EN5 39 J3
Jenningtree Way, Belv. DA17 139 J2
Jenny Hammond Cl, E11 *off Newcomen Rd* 97 F3
Jenson Way, SE19 170 C7
Jenton Av, Bexh. DA7 158 E1
Jephson Rd, E7 97 J7
Jephson St, SE5 *off Grove La* 152 A1
Jephtha Rd, SW18 148 D6
Jeppos La, Mitch. CR4 185 J4
Jepson Ho, SW6 *off Pearscroft Rd* 148/149 E1
Jerdan Pl, SW6 128 D7
Jeremiah St, E14 114 B6
Jeremys Grn, N18 61 E4
Jermyn St, SW1 25 F1
Jerningham Av, Ilf. IG5 80 E2
Jerningham Rd, SE14 153 H2
Jerome Cres, NW8 7 G5
Jerome Pl, Kings.T. KT1 *off Wadbrook St* 181 G2
Jerome St, E1 21 F1
Jerome Twr, W3 126 B2
Jerrard St, N1 12 E2
SE13 154 B3
Jersey Av, Stan. HA7 69 E2
Jersey Dr, Orp. BR5 193 G6
Jersey Par, Houns. TW5 143 H1
Jersey Rd, E11 96 D1
E16 *off Prince Regent La* 115 J6
SW17 168 B6
W7 124 D2
Hounslow TW3, TW5 143 H1
Ilford IG1 99 E4
Isleworth TW7 124 B6
Jersey St, E2 *off Bethnal Grn Rd* 112/113 E3
Jerusalem Pas, EC1 11 G6
Jervis Ct, W1 17 E4
Jerviston Gdns, SW16 169 G6
Jesmond Av, Wem. HA9 87 J6
Jesmond Cl, Mitch. CR4 186 B3
Jesmond Rd, Croy. CR0 188 C7
Jesmond Way, Stan. HA7 53 H5
Jessam Av, E5 94 E1
Jessamine Rd, W7 124 B1
Jessel Dr, Loug. IG10 49 F1
Jesse Rd, E10 96 C1
Jessica Rd, SW18 149 F6
Jessie Blythe La, N19 74 E7
Jessop Av, Sthl. UB2 123 F4
Jessop Rd, SE24 *off Milkwood Rd* 151 H4
Jessop Sq, E14 *off Heron Quay* 134 A1
Jessops Way, Croy. CR0 186 C6
Jessup Cl, SE18 137 F4
Jetstar Way, Nthlt. UB5 102 E3
Jevington Way, SE12 173 H2
Jewel Rd, E17 78 A3
★**Jewel Twr, Hos of Parliament**, SW1 26 A5
★**Jewish Mus**, NW1 *off Albert St* 110 B1
Jewry St, EC3 21 F4
Jew's Row, SW18 149 E4
Jews Wk, SE26 171 E4
Jeymer Av, NW2 89 H5
Jeymer Dr, Grnf. UB6 103 J1
Jeypore Pas, SW18 *off Jeypore Rd* 149 F6
Jeypore Rd, SW18 149 F7
Jillian Cl, Hmptn. TW12 161 G7
Jim Bradley Cl, SE18 *off John Wilson St* 136 D4
Jim Griffiths Ho, SW6 *off Clem Attlee Ct* 128 C6
Joan Cres, SE9 156 A7
Joan Gdns, Dag. RM8 100 E2
Joan Rd, Dag. RM8 100 E2
Joan St, SE1 27 G2
Jocelyn Rd, Rich. TW9 145 H3
Jocelyn St, SE15 152 D1
Jockey's Flds, WC1 18 D1
Jodane St, SE8 133 J4
Jodrell Cl, Islw. TW7 144 D1
Jodrell Rd, E3 113 J1
Joel St, Nthwd. HA6 66 A3
Pinner HA5 66 A3
Johanna St, SE1 27 E4
John Adam St, WC2 18 B6
John Aird Ct, W2 14 D1
John Archer Way, SW18 149 G6
John Ashby Cl, SW2 151 E6
John Austin Cl, Kings.T. KT2 *off Queen Elizabeth Rd* 181 J1
John Barnes Wk, E15 97 F6
John Bradshaw Rd, N14 *off High St* 58 D1
John Burns Dr, Bark. IG11 99 H7
John Campbell Rd, N16 94 B5
John Carpenter St, EC4 19 G5
John Cornwell VC Ho, E12 98 D4
John Drinkwater Cl, E11 *off Browning Rd* 79 F7
John Felton Rd, SE16 29 H4
John Fisher St, E1 21 H5
John Gooch Dr, Enf. EN2 43 H1
John Harrison Way, SE10 135 F3
John Horner Ms, N1 11 J1
John Islip St, SW1 34 A2
John Keats Ho, N22 59 F7
John Kennedy Ho, SE16 *off Rotherhithe Old Rd* 133 G4
John Maurice Cl, SE17 36 B1
John McKenna Wk, SE16 29 J5
John Newton Ct, Well. DA16 158 B3
John Parker Cl, Dag. RM10 101 H7
John Parker Sq, SW11 *off Thomas Baines Rd* 149 G3
John Penn St, SE13 154 B1
John Perrin Pl, Har. HA3 69 H7
John Princes St, W1 17 E3
John Rennie Wk, E1 *off Wine Cl* 132/133 E1
John Roll Way, SE16 29 J5
John Ruskin St, SE5 35 G7
Johns Av, NW4 71 J4
Johns Ct, Sutt. SM2 *off Mulgrave Rd* 198/199 E6
John Silkin La, SE8 133 G5
Johns La, Mord. SM4 185 F5
John's Ms, WC1 10 D6
John Smith Av, SW6 128 C7
John Smith Ms, E14 *off Newport Av* 114 D7
Johnson Cl, E8 112 D1
Johnson Rd, NW10 106 D1
Bromley BR2 192 A5
Croydon CR0 188 A7
Hounslow TW5 122 C7
Johnsons Cl, Cars. SM5 199 J3
Johnson's Ct, EC4 *off Fleet St* 111 G6
Johnsons Dr, Hmptn. TW12 179 J1
Johnson's Pl, SW1 33 F4
Johnson St, E1 *off Cable St* 113 F7
Southall UB2 122 C3
Johnsons Way, NW10 106 B4
John Spencer Sq, N1 93 H6
John's Pl, E1 *off Damien St* 112/113 E6
John's Ter, Croy. CR0 202 A1
Johnston Cl, SW9 *off Hackford Rd* 151 F1
Johnstone Rd, E6 116 C3
Johnston Rd, Wdf.Grn. IG8 63 G5
Johnston Ter, NW2 *off Kara Way* 90 A3
John St, E15 115 F1

John St, SE25 **188** D4
WC1 **10** D6
Enfield EN1 **44** C5
Hounslow TW3 **143** E2
John Trundle Ct, EC2
off The Barbican **111** J5
John Walsh Twr, E11 **97** F2
John Williams Cl, SE14 **133** G6
Kingston upon Thames KT2
off Henry Macaulay Av **181** G1
John Wilson St, SE18 **136** D3
John Woolley Cl, SE13 **154** E4
Joiner's Arms Yd, SE5
off Denmark Hill **152** A1
Joiners Pl, N5
off Leconfield Rd **94** A4
Joiner St, SE1 **28** C2
Joiners Yd, N1
off Caledonia St **110** E2
Jollys La, Har. HA2 **86** A1
Hayes UB4 **102** D5
Jonathan Ct, W4
off Windmill Rd **126/127** E4
Jonathan St, SE11 **34** C3
Jones Rd, E13
off Holborn Rd **115** H4
Jones St, W1 **16** D6
Jones Wk, Rich. TW10
off Pyrland Rd **145** J6
Jonquil Gdns, Hmptn. TW12
off Partridge Rd **161** F6
Jonson Cl, Hayes UB4 **102** A5
Mitcham CR4 **186** B4
Jordan Cl, Dag. RM10
off Muggeridge Rd **101** H4
Harrow HA2
off Hamilton Cres **85** F3
Jordan Ct, SW15
off Charlwood Rd **148** A4
Jordan Rd, Grnf. UB6 **105** E1
Jordans Cl, Islw. TW7 **144** B1
Joseph Av, W3 **106** D6
Joseph Hardcastle Cl, SE14 **133** G7
Josephine Av, SW2 **151** F5
Joseph Powell Cl, SW12
off Hazelbourne Rd **150** B6
Joseph Ray Rd, E11 **97** E2
Joseph St, E3 **113** J4
Joseph Trotter Cl, EC1
off Myddelton St **111** G3
Joshua Cl, N10 **58** B7
South Croydon CR2 **201** H7
Joshua St, E14
off St. Leonards Rd **114** C6
Joubert St, SW11 **149** J2
Jowett St, SE15 **132** C7
Joyce Av, N18 **60** C5
Joyce Dawson Way, SE28
off Thamesmere Dr **118** A7
Joyce Dawson Way Shop Arc, SE28
off Thamesmere Dr **118** A7
Joyce Page Cl, SE7
off Lansdowne La **136** A6
Joyce Wk, SW2 **151** G6
JOYDENS WOOD, Bex. DA5 **177** J5
Joydon Dr, Rom. RM6 **82** B6
Joyners Cl, Dag. RM9 **101** F4
Jubb Powell Ho, N15 **76** B6
Jubilee Av, E4 **62** C6
Romford RM7 **83** H5
Twickenham TW2 **161** J1
Jubilee Cl, NW9 **70** D6
Pinner HA5 **66** C2
Romford RM7 **83** H5
Jubilee Cres, E14 **134** C3
N9 **60** D1
Jubilee Dr, Ruis. HA4 **84** D4
★**Jubilee Gdns**, SE1 **26** C2
Jubilee Gdns, Sthl. UB1 **103** G6
Jubilee La, W5
off Mountfield Rd **105** H6
Jubilee Pl, SW3 **31** H3
Jubilee Rd, Grnf. UB6 **104** E1
Sutton SM3 **198** A7
Jubilee St, E1 **113** F6
Jubilee Wk, Wat. WD19 **50** B4
Jubilee Way, SW19 **185** E1
Chessington KT9 **196** A4
Sidcup DA14 **176** A2
Judd St, WC1 **10** A4
Jude St, E16 **115** F6
Judge Wk, Esher (Clay.) KT10 **194** B6
Juer St, SW11 **129** H7
Jules Thorn Av, Enf. EN1 **44** C3

Julia Gdns, Bark. IG11 **118** D2
Julia Garfield Ms, E16
off Wesley Av **135** H1
Juliana Cl, N2 **73** F3
Julian Av, W3 **106** B7
Julian Cl, Barn. EN5 **40** E3
Julian Hill, Har. HA1 **86** B2
Julian Pl, E14 **134** B5
Julian Tayler Path, SE23 **170** E2
Julia St, NW5
off Oak Village **92** A4
Julien Rd, W5 **125** F3
Juliette Rd, E13 **115** F2
Julius Nyerere Cl, N1
off Copenhagen St **111** G4
Junction App, SE13 **154** C3
SW11 **149** H3
Junction Av, W10
off Harrow Rd **107** J3
Junction Ms, W2 **15** G3
Junction Pl, W2 **15** G3
Junction Rd, E13 **115** H2
N9 **60** D1
N17 **76** D3
N19 **92** C4
W5 **125** G4
Brentford TW8 **125** G4
Harrow HA1 **68** B6
South Croydon CR2 **202** A5
Junction Rd E, Rom. RM6
off Kenneth Rd **82/83** E7
Junction Rd W, Rom. RM6 **82** E7
Junction Shop Cen, The, SW11
off St. John's Hill **149** H4
Juniper Cl, Barn. EN5 **40** A5
Chessington KT9 **195** J6
Wembley HA9 **87** J5
Juniper Cres, NW1 **92** A7
Juniper Gdns, SW16
off Leonard Rd **186** C1
Juniper La, E6 **116** B5
Juniper Rd, Ilf. IG1 **98** D4
Juniper St, E1 **113** F7
Juno Way, SE14 **133** G6
Jupiter Way, N7 **93** F6
Jupp Rd, E15 **96** D7
Jupp Rd W, E15 **114** C1
Justice Wk, SW3 **31** G6
Justin Cl, Brent. TW8 **125** G7
Justin Rd, E4 **61** J6
Jute La, Enf. EN3 **45** H2
Jutland Cl, N19
off Sussex Way **92/93** E1
Jutland Rd, E13 **115** G4
SE6 **154** C7
Jutsums Av, Rom. RM7 **83** H6
Jutsums La, Rom. RM7 **83** H6
Juxon Cl, Har. HA3
off Augustine Rd **67** H1
Juxon St, SE11 **34** D1

K

Kaduna Cl, Pnr. HA5 **66** A5
Kale Rd, Erith DA18 **138** E2
Kambala Rd, SW11 **149** G2
Kangley Br Rd, SE26 **171** J5
Kaplan Dr, N21 **43** E5
Karanjia Ct, NW2
off Walm La **89** J6
Kara Way, NW2 **90** A4
Karen Ct, SE4
off Wickham Rd **153** J2
Bromley BR1
off Blyth Rd **191** F1
Karen Ter, E11
off Montague Rd **97** F2
Karenza Ct, Wem. HA9
off Lulworth Av **69** F7
Kariba Cl, N9 **61** F3
Karina Cl, Chig. IG7 **65** H5
Karoline Gdns, Grnf. UB6
off Oldfield La N **104** A2
Kashgar Rd, SE18 **137** J5
Kashmir Rd, SE7 **136** A7
Kassala Rd, SW11 **149** J1
Katella Trd Est, Bark. IG11 **117** H3
Kates Cl, Barn. EN5 **39** G5
Katharine St, Croy. CR0 **201** J3
Katherine Cl, SE16
off Rotherhithe St **133** G1
Katherine Gdns, SE9 **156** A4
Ilford IG6 **65** F7
Katherine Rd, E6 **98** A7
E7 **97** J5
Twickenham TW1
off London Rd **162** D1

Katherine Sq, W11
off Wilsham St **128** B1
Kathleen Av, W3 **106** C5
Wembley HA0 **87** H7
Kathleen Rd, SW11 **149** J3
Kayemoor Rd, Sutt. SM2 **199** H7
Kay Rd, SW9 **151** E2
Kays Ter, E18
off Walpole Rd **79** F1
Kay St, E2 **13** J1
Welling DA16 **158** B1
Kay Way, SE10
off Greenwich High Rd **134** B7
Kean St, WC2 **18** C4
Keatley Grn, E4 **61** J6
Keats Av, E16
off Wesley Av **135** H1
Keats Cl, E11
off Nightingale La **79** H5
NW3 *off Keats Gro* **91** H4
SE1 **37** F2
SW19 *off North Rd* **167** G6
Chigwell IG7 **65** F6
Enfield EN3 **45** G5
Hayes UB4 **102** A5
Keats Gro, NW3 **91** G4
★**Keats Ho**, NW3 **91** H4
Keats Ho, Beck. BR3 **172** A6
Keats Pl, EC2 **20** B2
Keats Rd, Belv. DA17 **139** J3
Welling DA16 **157** H1
Keats Way, Croy. CR0 **189** F6
Greenford UB6 **103** H5
West Drayton UB7 **120** C4
Keble Cl, Nthlt. UB5 **85** J5
Worcester Park KT4 **197** F1
Keble Pl, SW13
off Somerville Av **127** H6
Keble St, SW17 **167** F4
Kechill Gdns, Brom. BR2 **191** G7
Kedelston Ct, E5
off Redwald Rd **95** G4
Kedeston Ct, Sutt. SM1
off Hurstcourt Rd **198/199** E1
Kedleston Dr, Orp. BR5 **193** J6
Kedleston Wk, E2
off Middleton St **112/113** E3
Keedonwood Rd, Brom. BR1 **172** E5
Keel Cl, SE16 **133** G1
Barking IG11 **118** C2
Keel Ct, E14
off Newport Av **114** D7
Keeley Rd, Croy. CR0 **201** J2
Keeley St, WC2 **18** C4
Keeling Rd, SE9 **156** A5
Keely Cl, Barn. EN4 **41** H5
Keemor Cl, SE18
off Llanover Rd **136** D7
Keens Cl, SW16 **168** D5
Keens Rd, Croy. CR0 **201** J4
Keens Yd, N1
off St. Paul's Rd **93** H6
Keep, The, SE3 **155** G2
Kingston upon Thames KT2 **163** J6
Keepers Ms, Tedd. TW11 **163** F6
Keep La, N11
off Gardeners Cl **58** A2
Keetons Rd, SE16 **132** E3
Keevil Dr, SW19 **148** A7
Keighley Cl, N7
off Penn Rd **92/93** E5
Keightley Dr, SE9 **175** F1
Keildon Rd, SW11 **149** J4
Keir, The, SW19
off West Side Common **165** J5
Keir Hardie Est, E5
off Springfield **94/95** E1
Keir Hardie Ho, W6
off Lochaline St **127** J6
Keir Hardie Way, Bark. IG11 **100** A7
Hayes UB4 **102** A3
Keith Connor Cl, SW8
off Daley Thompson Way **150** B3
Keith Gro, W12 **127** G2
Keith Rd, E17 **77** J1
Barking IG11 **117** G2
Hayes UB3 **121** H3
Kelbrook Rd, SE3 **156** B3
Kelby Path, SE9 **175** E3
Kelceda Cl, NW2 **89** G2
Kelfield Gdns, W10 **107** J6
Kelfield Ms, W10
off Kelfield Gdns **108** A6
Kelland Cl, N8
off Palace Rd **74** D5
Kelland Rd, E13 **115** G4

Kellaway Rd, SE3 **155** J2
Keller Cres, E12 **98** A4
Kellerton Rd, SE13 **154** E5
Kellett Rd, SW2 **151** G4
Kelling Gdns, Croy. CR0 **187** H7
Kellino St, SW17 **167** J4
Kellner Rd, SE28 **137** J3
Kell St, SE1 **27** H5
Kelly Av, SE15 **132** C7
Kelly Cl, NW10 **88** D3
Kelly Ct, Borwd. WD6 **38** C2
Kelly Ms, W9
off Woodfield Rd **108** C5
Kelly Rd, NW7 **56** B6
Kelly St, NW1 **92** B6
Kelly Way, Rom. RM6 **82** E5
Kelman Cl, SW4 **150** D2
Kelmore Gro, SE22 **152** D4
Kelmscott Cl, E17 **77** J2
Kelmscott Gdns, W12 **127** G3
Kelmscott Rd, SW11 **149** H5
Kelross Pas, N5
off Kelross Rd **93** J4
Kelross Rd, N5 **93** H4
Kelsall Cl, SE3 **155** H2
Kelsall Ms, Rich. TW9
off Melliss Av **146** B1
Kelsey Gate, Beck. BR3 **190** B2
Kelsey La, Beck. BR3 **190** A2
Kelsey Pk Av, Beck. BR3 **190** B2
Kelsey Pk Rd, Beck. BR3 **190** A2
Kelsey Sq, Beck. BR3 **190** A2
Kelsey St, E2 **13** J5
Kelsey Way, Beck. BR3 **190** A3
Kelshall Ct, N4
off Brownswood Rd **93** J2
Kelsie Way, Ilf. IG6 **65** H7
Kelson Ho, E14 **134** C3
Kelso Pl, W8 **22** B6
Kelso Rd, Cars. SM5 **185** F7
Kelston Rd, Ilf. IG6 **81** E2
Kelvedon Cl, Kings.T. KT2 **163** J6
Kelvedon Ho, SW8 **150** E1
Kelvedon Rd, SW6 **128** C7
Kelvedon Way, Wdf.Grn. IG8 **64** C6
Kelvin Av, N13 **59** F6
Teddington TW11 **162** D6
Kelvinbrook, W.Mol. KT8 **179** H3
Kelvin Cl, Epsom KT19 **196** A6
Kelvin Cres, Har. HA3 **52** B7
Kelvin Dr, Twick. TW1 **145** E6
Kelvin Gdns, Croy. CR0 **187** E7
Southall UB1 **103** G6
Kelvin Gro, SE26 **170** E3
Chessington KT9 **195** H3
Kelvington Cl, Croy. CR0 **189** H7
Kelvington Rd, SE15 **153** G5
Kelvin Ind Est, Grnf. UB6 **85** H7
Kelvin Par, Orp. BR6 **207** H1
Kelvin Rd, N5 **93** H4
Welling DA16 **158** A3
Kember St, N1
off Carnoustie Dr **93** F7
Kemble Dr, Brom. BR2 **206** B3
Kemble Rd, N17 **76** D1
SE23 **171** G1
Croydon CR0 **201** G3
Kemble St, WC2 **18** C4
Kemerton Rd, SE5 **151** J3
Beckenham BR3 **190** B2
Croydon CR0 **188** C7
Kemeys St, E9 **95** H5
Kemnal Rd, Chis. BR7 **175** G4
Kempe Rd, NW6 **108** A2
Kemp Gdns, Croy. CR0
off St. Saviours Rd **187** J6
Kempis Way, SE22
off East Dulwich Gro **152** B5
Kemplay Rd, NW3 **91** G4
Kemp Rd, Dag. RM8 **100** D1
Kemp's Ct, W1 **17** G4
Kemps Dr, E14
off Morant St **114** A7
Kempsford Gdns, SW5 **128** D5
Kempsford Rd, SE11 **35** F2
Kemps Gdns, SE13
off Thornford Rd **154** C5
Kempshott Rd, SW16 **168** D7
Kempson Rd, SW6 **148** D1
Kempthorne Rd, SE8 **133** H4
Kempton Av, Nthlt. UB5 **85** G6
Sunbury-on-Thames TW16 **178** B1
Kempton Cl, Erith DA8 **139** J6
Kempton Ct, E1
off Durward St **112/113** E5
Sunbury-on-Thames TW16 **178** B1

★**Kempton Park Racecourse**, Sun. TW16 160 C7
Kempton Rd, E6 116 C1
Hampton TW12 179 F2
Kempton Wk, Croy. CR0 189 H6
Kempt St, SE18 136 D6
Kemsing Cl, Bex. DA5 159 E7
Bromley BR2 205 F2
Thornton Heath CR7 187 J4
Kemsing Rd, SE10 135 G5
Kemsley, SE13 154 C5
Kenbury Gdns, SE5 *off Kenbury St* 151 J2
Kenbury St, SE5 151 J2
Kenchester Cl, SW8 131 E7
Kencot Cl, Erith DA18 139 F2
Kendal Av, N18 60 A4
W3 106 A4
Barking IG11 99 H7
Kendal Cl, SW9 35 G7
Woodford Green IG8 63 F2
Kendale Rd, Brom. BR1 172 E5
Kendal Gdns, N18 60 A4
Sutton SM1 199 F2
Kendall Av, Beck. BR3 189 H2
Kendall Ct, SW19 *off Byegrove Rd* 167 G6
Borehamwood WD6 *off Gregson Cl* 38 C1
Kendall Pl, W1 16 B2
Kendall Rd, SE18 156 B1
Beckenham BR3 189 H2
Isleworth TW7 144 D2
Kendalmere Cl, N10 74 B1
Kendal Par, N18 *off Great Cambridge Rd* 60 A4
Kendal Pl, SW15 148 C5
Kendal Rd, NW10 89 G4
Kendal St, W2 15 H4
Kender St, SE14 133 F7
Kendoa Rd, SW4 150 D4
Kendon Cl, E11 *off The Avenue* 79 H5
Kendra Hall Rd, S.Croy. CR2 201 H7
Kendrey Gdns, Twick. TW2 144 B6
Kendrick Ms, SW7 31 E1
Kendrick Pl, SW7 31 E2
Kenelm Cl, Har. HA1 86 D3
Kenerne Dr, Barn. EN5 40 B5
Kenilford Rd, SW12 150 B7
Kenilworth Av, E17 78 A2
SW19 166 D5
Harrow HA2 85 F4
Kenilworth Cl, Borwd. WD6 38 C3
Kenilworth Ct, SW15 *off Lower Richmond Rd* 148 A3
Kenilworth Cres, Enf. EN1 44 B1
Kenilworth Dr, Borwd. WD6 38 C3
Kenilworth Gdns, SE18 156 E2
Ilford IG3 99 J2
Loughton IG10 48 C6
Southall UB1 103 F3
Watford WD19 50 C5
Kenilworth Rd, E3 113 H2
NW6 108 C1
SE20 189 G1
W5 125 H1
Edgware HA8 54 C3
Epsom KT17 197 G6
Orpington BR5 193 F6
Kenley Av, NW9 70 E1
Kenley Cl, Barn. EN4 41 H4
Bexley DA5 159 G7
Chislehurst BR7 193 H3
Kenley Gdns, Th.Hth. CR7 187 H4
Kenley Rd, SW19 184 C2
Kingston upon Thames KT1 182 B2
Twickenham TW1 144 D6
Kenley Wk, W11 108 B7
Sutton SM3 198 A4
Kenlor Rd, SW17 167 G5
Kenmare Dr, N17 76 C2
Mitcham CR4 167 J7
Kenmare Gdns, N13 59 H4
Kenmare Rd, Th.Hth. CR7 187 G6
Kenmere Gdns, Wem. HA0 106 A1
Kenmere Rd, Well. DA16 158 C2
Kenmont Gdns, NW10 107 H3
Kenmore Av, Har. HA3 68 D4
Kenmore Cl, Rich. TW9 *off Kent Rd* 126 A7
Kenmore Gdns, Edg. HA8 70 B2
Kenmore Rd, Har. HA3 69 G3
Kenmure Rd, E8 95 E5
Kenmure Yd, E8 *off Kenmure Rd* 94/95 E5
Kennacraig Cl, E16 *off Hanameel St* 135 G1
Kennard Rd, E15 96 D7
N11 57 J5
Kennard St, E16 136 C1
SW11 150 A2
Kennedy Av, Enf. EN3 45 F6
Kennedy Cl, E13 115 G2
Mitcham CR4 186 A2
Orpington BR5 207 G1
Pinner HA5 51 F6
Kennedy Path, W7 *off Harp Rd* 104 C4
Kennedy Rd, W7 104 B5
Barking IG11 117 H1
Kennedy Wk, SE17 *off Flint St* 132 A4
Kennet Cl, SW11 *off Maysoule Rd* 149 G4
Kenneth Av, Ilf. IG1 98 E4
Kenneth Cres, NW2 89 H5
Kenneth Gdns, Stan. HA7 52 D6
Kenneth More Rd, Ilf. IG1 *off Oakfield Rd* 98/99 E3
Kenneth Rd, Rom. RM6 82 D7
Kenneth Robbins Ho, N17 60 E7
Kennet Rd, W9 108 C4
Isleworth TW7 144 C3
Kennet Sq, Mitch. CR4 185 H1
Kennet St, E1 29 J1
Kennett Dr, Hayes UB4 102 E5
Kennet Wf La, EC4 20 A5
Kenninghall, N18 60 E5
Kenninghall Rd, E5 94 D3
N18 61 F5
Kenning St, SE16 *off Railway Av* 133 F2
Kennings Way, SE11 35 G3
Kenning Ter, N1 112 B1
KENNINGTON, SE11 35 E6
Kennington Grn, SE11 35 E4
Kennington Gro, SE11 34 D5
Kennington La, SE11 35 F3
Kennington Oval, SE11 34 D5
Kennington Pk, SW9 35 F7
Kennington Pk Est, SE11 35 E6
Kennington Pk Gdns, SE11 35 G5
Kennington Pk Pl, SE11 35 F4
Kennington Pk Rd, SE11 35 F5
Kennington Rd, SE1 27 E5
SE11 27 E6
Kenny Rd, NW7 56 B5
Kenrick Pl, W1 16 B1
KENSAL GREEN, NW10 107 J3
★**Kensal Green Cem**, W10 107 J3
KENSAL RISE, NW6 108 A2
Kensal Rd, W10 108 B4
KENSAL TOWN, W10 108 A4
Kensal Wf, W10 *off Ladbroke Gro* 108 A4
KENSINGTON, W8 128 C2
Kensington Av, E12 98 B6
Thornton Heath CR7 187 G1
Kensington Ch Ct, W8 22 A4
Kensington Ch St, W8 128 D1
Kensington Ch Wk, W8 22 A4
Kensington Cl, N11 58 A6
Kensington Ct, NW7 *off Grenville Pl* 54 D5
W8 22 B4
Kensington Ct Gdns, W8 *off Kensington Ct Pl* 128/129 E3
Kensington Ct Ms, W8 22 B4
Kensington Ct Pl, W8 22 B5
Kensington Dr, Wdf.Grn. IG8 80 A1
★**Kensington Gdns**, W2 22 D2
Kensington Gdns, Ilf. IG1 98 C2
Kingston upon Thames KT1 *off Portsmouth Rd* 181 G3
Kensington Gdns Sq, W2 14 A4
Kensington Gate, W8 22 C5
Kensington Gore, SW7 23 E4
Kensington Hall Gdns, W14 *off Beaumont Av* 128 C5
Kensington High St, W8 128 D3
W14 128 B4
Kensington Mall, W8 128 D1
★**Kensington Palace**, W8 22 B2
Kensington Palace Gdns, W8 22 A1
Kensington Pk Gdns, W11 108 C7
Kensington Pk Ms, W11 *off Kensington Pk Rd* 108 C6
Kensington Pk Rd, W11 108 C7
Kensington Pl, W8 128 D1
Kensington Rd, SW7 23 F4
W8 22 B4
Northolt UB5 103 G3
Romford RM7 83 J6
Kensington Sq, W8 22 A4
Kensington Ter, S.Croy. CR2 *off Sanderstead Rd* 202 A7
Kensington Village, W14 *off Avonmore Rd* 128 C4
Kensington Way, Borwd. WD6 38 D3
Kent Av, W13 104 E5
Dagenham RM9 119 G4
Welling DA16 157 J5
Kent Cl, Mitch. CR4 187 E4
Orpington BR6 207 H6
Kent Dr, Barn. EN4 42 A4
Teddington TW11 162 B5
Kentford Way, Nthlt. UB5 102 E1
Kent Gdns, W13 105 E5
Ruislip HA4 66 B6
Kent Gate Way, Croy. CR0 204 A5
Kent Ho La, Beck. BR3 171 H5
Kent Ho Rd, SE26 189 G1
Beckenham BR3 171 H5
Kentish Bldgs, SE1 28 B2
Kentish Rd, Belv. DA17 139 G4
KENTISH TOWN, NW5 92 C6
Kentish Town Rd, NW1 92 B7
NW5 92 B7
Kentish Way, Brom. BR1 191 G2
Kentlea Rd, SE28 137 H2
Kentmere Rd, SE18 137 H4
KENTON, Har. HA3 68 E5
Kenton Av, Har. HA1 68 C7
Southall UB1 103 G7
Sunbury-on-Thames TW16 178 E2
Kenton Ct, W14 *off Kensington High St* 128 C3
Kenton Gdns, Har. HA3 69 F5
Kenton La, Har. HA3 69 F3
Kenton Pk Av, Har. HA3 69 G4
Kenton Pk Cl, Har. HA3 69 F4
Kenton Pk Cres, Har. HA3 69 G4
Kenton Pk Rd, Har. HA3 69 F4
Kenton Rd, E9 95 G6
Harrow HA1, HA3 69 G5
Kenton St, WC1 10 A5
Kent Pas, NW1 7 J5
Kent Rd, N21 60 A1
W4 126 C3
Dagenham RM10 101 H5
East Molesey KT8 179 J4
Kingston upon Thames KT1 *off The Bittoms* 181 G3
Richmond TW9 126 A7
West Wickham BR4 204 B1
Kents Pas, Hmptn. TW12 179 F1
Kent St, E2 13 G1
E13 115 J3
Kent Ter, NW1 7 H4
Kent Vw Gdns, Ilf. IG3 99 H2
Kent Way, Surb. KT6 195 H3
Kentwell Cl, SE4 153 H4
Kentwode Grn, SW13 127 G7
Kent Yd, SW7 23 H4
Kenver Av, N12 57 G6
Kenward Rd, SE9 155 J5
Kenway, Rom. RM5 83 J2
Ken Way, Wem. HA9 88 C2
Kenway Rd, SW5 30 A2
Kenwood Av, N14 42 D5
SE14 *off Besson St* 153 G1
Kenwood Cl, NW3 91 G1
West Drayton UB7 120 D6
Kenwood Dr, Beck. BR3 190 C3
Kenwood Gdns, E18 79 H3
Ilford IG2 80 D4
★**Kenwood Ho (The Iveagh Bequest)**, NW3 91 H1
Kenwood Rd, N6 73 J6
N9 60 D1
Kenworthy Rd, E9 95 H5
Kenwyn Dr, NW2 89 E3
Kenwyn Rd, SW4 150 D4
SW20 183 J1
Kenya Rd, SE7 136 A7
Kenyngton Dr, Sun. TW16 160 A5
Kenyngton Pl, Har. HA3 69 F5
Kenyon St, SW6 148 A1
Keogh Rd, E15 97 E6
Kepler Rd, SW4 150 E4
Keppel Rd, E6 98 C7
Dagenham RM9 100 E4
Keppel Row, SE1 27 J2
Keppel St, WC1 17 J1
Kerbela St, E2 13 H5
Kerbey St, E14 114 B6
Kerfield Cres, SE5 152 A1
Kerfield Pl, SE5 152 A1
Kerri Cl, Barn. EN5 39 J4
Kerridge Ct, N1 94 B6
Kerrison Pl, W5 125 G1
Kerrison Rd, E15 114 D1
SW11 149 H3
W5 125 G1
Kerrison Vil, W5 *off Kerrison Pl* 125 G1
Kerry Av, Stan. HA7 53 G4
Kerry Cl, E16 115 H6
N13 59 F2
Kerry Ct, Stan. HA7 53 G4
Kerry Path, SE14 133 J6
Kerry Rd, SE14 133 J6
Kersey Gdns, SE9 174 B4
Kersfield Rd, SW15 148 A6
Kershaw Cl, SW18 *off Westover Rd* 149 G6
Kershaw Rd, Dag. RM10 101 G3
Kersley Ms, SW11 149 J2
Kersley Rd, N16 94 B3
Kersley St, SW11 149 J2
Kerswell Cl, N15 76 B5
Kerwick Cl, N7 *off Sutterton St* 93 F7
Keslake Rd, NW6 108 A2
Kessock Cl, N17 76 E5
Kesteven Cl, Ilf. IG6 65 J6
Kestlake Rd, Bex. DA5 *off East Rochester Way* 158 C6
KESTON, BR2 205 J5
Keston Av, Kes. BR2 205 J5
Keston Cl, N18 60 A3
Welling DA16 138 C7
Keston Gdns, Kes. BR2 205 J4
Keston Pk Cl, Kes. BR2 206 C3
Keston Rd, N17 76 A3
SE15 152 D3
Thornton Heath CR7 187 G6
Kestral Ct, Wall. SM6 *off Carew Rd* 200 C5
Kestrel Av, E6 *off Swan App* 116 B5
SE24 151 H5
Kestrel Cl, NW9 71 E2
NW10 88 D5
Kingston upon Thames KT2 163 G4
Kestrel Ho, EC1 11 J3
W13 104 C4
Enfield EN3 *off Alma Rd* 45 G5
Kestrel Pl, SE14 *off Milton Ct Rd* 133 H6
Kestrel Way, Hayes UB3 121 G2
Keswick Av, SW15 164 E5
SW19 184 D2
Keswick Bdy, SW15 *off Upper Richmond Rd* 148 B5
Keswick Cl, Sutt. SM1 199 F4
Keswick Gdns, Ilf. IG4 80 B5
Wembley HA9 87 H4
Keswick Ms, W5 125 H1
Keswick Rd, SW15 148 B5
Bexleyheath DA7 159 G2
Orpington BR6 207 J1
Twickenham TW2 143 J6
West Wickham BR4 204 E2
Kettering St, SW16 168 C6
Kett Gdns, SW2 151 F5
Kettlebaston Rd, E10 95 J1
Kettlewell Cl, N11 58 A6
Kevan Ho, SE5 131 J7
Kevelioc Rd, N17 75 J1
Kevin Cl, Houns. TW4 142 D2
Kevington Cl, Orp. BR5 193 J4
Kevington Dr, Chis. BR7 193 J4
Orpington BR5 193 J4
KEW, Rich. TW9 126 A6
Kew Br, Brent. TW8 125 J6
Richmond TW9 125 J6
Kew Br Arches, Rich. TW9 *off Kew Br* 125 J6
Kew Br Ct, W4 126 A5
Kew Br Rd, Brent. TW8 125 J6
★**Kew Bridge Steam Mus**, Brent. TW8 125 J5
Kew Cres, Sutt. SM3 198 B3
Kew Foot Rd, Rich. TW9 145 H4
Kew Gdns Rd, Rich. TW9 125 J7
Kew Grn, Rich. TW9 126 A7
Kew Meadow Path, Rich. TW9 146 A1
★**Kew Observatory**, Rich. TW9 145 E3
★**Kew Palace, Royal Botanic Gdns**, Rich. TW9 125 H7

Kew Retail Pk, Rich. TW9
off Bessant Dr **146** B1
Kew Rd, Rich. TW9 . . . . . . **126** A6
Keybridge Ho, SW8 . . . . . . **34** B6
Key Cl, E1 . . . . **113** E4
Keyes Rd, NW2 . . . . **90** A5
Keymer Rd, SW2 . . . . **169** F2
Keynes Cl, N2 . . . . **73** J3
Keynsham Av, Wdf.Grn.
IG8 . . . . **63** E4
Keynsham Gdns, SE9 . . . **156** B5
Keynsham Rd, SE9 . . . . . . **156** A5
Morden SM4 . . . . **198** E1
Keynsham Wk, Mord.
SM4 . . . . **198** E1
Keyse Rd, SE1 . . . . **29** F6
Keysham Av, Houns. TW5
off The Avenue **142** A1
Keystone Cres, N1 . . . . **10** B2
Keywood Dr, Sun. TW16 . **160** A6
Keyworth Cl, E5 . . . . **95** H4
Keyworth St, SE1 . . . . **27** H5
Kezia St, SE8
off Trundleys Rd **133** H5
Khalsa Ct, N22
off Acacia Rd **75** H1
Khama Rd, SW17 . . . . **167** H4
Khartoum Rd, E13 . . . . . . **115** H3
SW17 . . . . **167** G4
Ilford IG1 . . . . **99** E5
Khyber Rd, SW11 . . . . **149** H2
Kibworth St, SW8 . . . . . . **131** F7
KIDBROOKE, SE3 . . . . **155** H3
Kidbrooke Gdns, SE3 . . . . **155** G2
Kidbrooke Gro, SE3 . . . . . **155** G1
Kidbrooke La, SE9 . . . . . . **156** B4
Kidbrooke Pk Cl, SE3 . . . . . **155** H1
Kidbrooke Pk Rd, SE3 . . . **155** H1
Kidbrooke Way, SE3 . . . . . **155** H2
Kidderminster Pl, Croy. CR0
off Kidderminster Rd. . **201** H1
Kidderminster Rd, Croy.
CR0 . . . . **201** H1
Kidderpore Av, NW3 . . . . . **90** D4
Kidderpore Gdns, NW3 . . . **90** D4
Kidd Pl, SE7 . . . . **136** B5
Kidlington Way, NW9 . . . . . **70** E2
Kielder Cl, Ilf. IG6 . . . . **65** J6
Kiffen St, EC2 . . . . **12** C5
Kilberry Cl, Islw. TW7 . . . . **144** A1
KILBURN, NW6 . . . . **108** D2
Kilburn Br, NW6
off Kilburn High Rd . . . **108** D1
Kilburn Gate, NW6 . . . . **6** A1
Kilburn High Rd, NW6 . . . . **90** C7
Kilburn La, W9 . . . . **108** A3
W10 . . . . **108** A3
Kilburn Pk Rd, NW6 . . . . . **108** D3
Kilburn Pl, NW6 . . . . **108** D1
Kilburn Priory, NW6 . . . . . **108** E1
Kilburn Sq, NW6 . . . . **108** D1
Kilburn Vale, NW6
off Belsize Rd **108/109** E1
Kildare Cl, Ruis. HA4 . . . . . **84** C1
Kildare Gdns, W2 . . . . **108** D6
Kildare Rd, E16 . . . . **115** G5
Kildare Ter, W2 . . . . **108** D6
Kildare Wk, E14
off Farrance St **114** A6
Kildoran Rd, SW2 . . . . **150** E5
Kildowan Rd, Ilf. IG3 . . . . **100** A1
Kilgour Rd, SE23 . . . . **153** H6
Kilkie St, SW6 . . . . **149** F2
Killarney Rd, SW18 . . . . . . **149** F6
Killburns Mill Cl, Wall. SM6
off London Rd **200** B4
Killearn Rd, SE6 . . . . **172** D1
Killester Gdns, Wor.Pk.
KT4 . . . . **197** H4
Killick St, N1 . . . . **10** C1
Killieser Av, SW2 . . . . **168** E2
Killip Cl, E16 . . . . **115** F6
Killowen Av, Nthlt. UB5 . . . **85** J5
Killowen Rd, E9 . . . . **95** G6
Killyon Rd, SW8 . . . . **150** C2
Killyon Ter, SW8 . . . . **150** C2
Kilmaine Rd, SW6 . . . . . . **128** B7
Kilmarnock Gdns, Dag. RM8
off Lindsey Rd **100** C3
Kilmarnock Rd, Wat. WD19 . **50** D4
Kilmarsh Rd, W6 . . . . **127** J4
Kilmartin Av, SW16 . . . . . **187** F3
Kilmartin Rd, Ilf. IG3 . . . . . **100** A2
Kilmeston Way, SE15 . . . . . **37** F7
Kilmington Rd, SW13 . . . **127** G6
Kilmorey Gdns, Twick.
TW1 . . . . **144** E5
Kilmorey Rd, Twick. TW1 . **144** E4
Kilmorie Rd, SE23 . . . . . . **171** H1
Kiln Cl, Hayes UB3
off Brickfield La **121** G6
Kilner St, E14 . . . . **114** A5
Kiln Ms, SW17 . . . . **167** G5
Kiln Pl, NW5 . . . . **92** A5
Kilnside, Esher (Clay.)
KT10 . . . . **194** D7
Kilpatrick Way, Hayes
UB4 . . . . **103** E5
Kilravock St, W10 . . . . **108** B3
Kilsby Wk, Dag. RM9
off Rugby Rd **100** B6
Kilsha Rd, Walt. KT12 . . . . **178** B6
Kimbell Gdns, SW6 . . . . . **148** B1
Kimbell Pl, SE3
off Tudway Rd **155** J4
Kimberley Av, E6 . . . . **116** B2
SE15 . . . . **153** E2
Ilford IG2 . . . . **81** G7
Romford RM7 . . . . **83** J6
Kimberley Dr, Sid.
DA14 . . . . **176** D2
Kimberley Gdns, N4 . . . . . . **75** H5
Enfield EN1 . . . . **44** C3
Kimberley Gate, Brom. BR1
off Oaklands Rd **173** F7
Kimberley Ind Est, E17 . . . . **77** J1
Kimberley Rd, E4 . . . . **62** E1
E11 . . . . **96** D2
E16 . . . . **115** F4
E17 . . . . **77** J1
N17 . . . . **76** D2
N18 . . . . **61** E6
NW6 . . . . **108** B1
SW9 . . . . **151** E2
Beckenham BR3 . . . . . . **189** G2
Croydon CR0 . . . . **187** H6
Kimberley Way, E4 . . . . **63** E1
Kimber Rd, SW18 . . . . **148** D7
Kimble Rd, SW19 . . . . **167** G6
Kimbolton Cl, SE12 . . . . . **155** F6
Kimbolton Grn, Borwd.
WD6 . . . . **38** C4
Kimbolton Row, SW3 . . . . **31** G2
Kimmeridge Gdns, SE9 . . **174** B4
Kimmeridge Rd, SE9 . . . . **174** B4
Kimpton Ho, SW15
off Fontley Way **147** G7
**Kimpton Link Business
Cen**, Sutt. SM3
off Kimpton Rd **198** C2
Kimpton Rd, SE5 . . . . **152** A1
Sutton SM3 . . . . **198** C2
**Kimpton Trade & Business
Cen**, Sutt. SM3 . . . . . . **198** C2
Kinburn St, SE16 . . . . **133** G2
Kincaid Rd, SE15 . . . . **132** E7
Kincardine Gdns, W9
off Harrow Rd **100** C4
Kinch Gro, Wem. HA9 . . . . **69** J7
Kinder Cl, SE28 . . . . **118** D7
Kinder St, E1
off Cannon St Rd . **112/113** E6
Kinfauns Rd, SW2 . . . . . . **169** G2
Ilford IG3 . . . . **100** A1
King Alfred Av, SE6 . . . . . **172** A3
King & Queen Cl, SE9
off St. Keverne Rd **174** B4
King & Queen St, SE17 . . . **36** A2
King & Queen Wf, SE16
off Rotherhithe St **133** G1
King Arthur Cl, SE15 . . . . **133** F7
King Charles Cres, Surb.
KT5 . . . . **181** J7
King Charles Rd, Surb.
KT5 . . . . **181** J5
King Charles St, SW1 . . . . **25** J3
King Charles Ter, E1
off Sovereign Cl . . **112/113** E7
King Charles Wk, SW19
off Princes Way **166** B1
Kingcup Cl, Croy. CR0
off Primrose La **203** G1
King David La, E1 . . . . **113** F7
Kingdon Rd, NW6 . . . . **90** D6
King Edward Dr, Chess. KT9
off Kelvin Gro **195** H3
King Edward Ms, SW13 . . **147** G1
King Edward Rd, E10 . . . . . **96** C1
E17 . . . . **77** H3
Barnet EN5 . . . . **40** D4
King Edward's Gdns, W3 . **126** A1
King Edwards Gro, Tedd.
TW11 . . . . **163** E6
King Edward's Pl, W3
off King Edward's Gdns . . **126** A1
King Edwards Rd, E9 . . . . **113** E1
N9 . . . . **44** E7
Barking IG11 . . . . **117** G1
King Edward's Rd, Enf.
EN3 . . . . **45** G4
King Edward St, EC1 . . . . . **19** J3
King Edward III Ms, SE16
off Paradise St . . . **132/133** E2
King Edward Wk, SE1 . . . . **27** F5
Kingfield Rd, W5 . . . . **105** G4
Kingfield St, E14 . . . . **134** C4
Kingfisher Av, E11
off Eastern Av **79** H6
Kingfisher Cl, SE28 . . . . . . **118** C7
Harrow (Har.Wld) HA3 . . **52** C7
Kingfisher Ct, SW19
off Queensmere Rd . . . **166** B2
Surbiton KT6
off Ewell Rd **181** J7
Sutton SM1
off Sandpiper Rd **198** C5
Kingfisher Dr, Rich. TW10 . **163** E4
Kingfisher Ms, SE13 . . . . . **154** B4
Kingfisher Pl, N22
off Clarendon Rd **75** F2
Kingfisher Sq, SE8 . . . . . . **133** J6
Kingfisher St, E6 . . . . **116** B5
Kingfisher Wk, NW9
off Eagle Dr **70/71** E2
Kingfisher Way, NW10 . . . . **88** D5
Beckenham BR3 . . . . . . **189** G5
King Frederik IX Twr,
SE16 . . . . **133** J3
King Gdns, Croy. CR0 . . . . **201** H5
King George Av, E16 . . . . . **116** A6
Ilford IG2 . . . . **81** G5
King George Cl, Rom.
RM7 . . . . **83** J3
King Georges Dr, Sthl.
UB1 . . . . **103** F5
King George VI Av, Mitch.
CR4 . . . . **185** J4
King George Sq, Rich.
TW10 . . . . **145** J6
King George's Trd Est,
Chess. KT9 . . . . **196** A4
King George St, SE10 . . . **134** C7
Kingham Cl, SW18 . . . . . . **149** F7
W11 . . . . **128** B2
King Harolds Way, Bexh.
DA7 . . . . **138** D7
King Henry Ms, Orp. BR6
off Osgood Av **207** J5
King Henry's Reach, W6 . . **127** J6
King Henry's Rd, NW3 . . . . **91** H7
Kingston upon Thames
KT1 . . . . **182** B3
King Henry St, N16 . . . . . . **94** B5
King Henry's Wk, N1 . . . . . **94** B6
King Henry Ter, E1
off Sovereign Cl . . **112/113** E7
Kinghorn St, EC1 . . . . **19** J2
King James Ct, SE1 . . . . . . **27** H4
King James St, SE1 . . . . . . **27** H4
King John Ct, EC2 . . . . **12** E5
King John St, E1 . . . . **113** G5
King Johns Wk, SE9 . . . . . **174** A1
Kinglake Est, SE17 . . . . **37** E3
Kinglake St, SE17 . . . . **36** D4
Kinglet Cl, E7
off Romford Rd **97** G6
Kingly Ct, W1 . . . . **17** F5
Kingly St, W1 . . . . **17** F4
Kingsand Rd, SE12 . . . . . . **173** G2
Kings Arbour, Sthl. UB2 . . **122** E5
Kings Arms Ct, E1 . . . . **21** H2
Kings Arms Yd, EC2 . . . . . . **20** B3
Kingsash Dr, Hayes UB4 . **102** E4
Kings Av, N10 . . . . **74** A3
N21 . . . . **59** H1
King's Av, SW4 . . . . **150** D7
SW12 . . . . **168** D1
Kings Av, W5 . . . . **105** G6
Bromley BR1 . . . . **173** F6
Buckhurst Hill IG9 . . . . . . **64** A2
Carshalton SM5 . . . . . . **199** H7
Greenford UB6 . . . . **103** H6
Hounslow TW3 . . . . **143** H1
New Malden KT3 . . . . . **183** E4
Romford RM6 . . . . **83** F6
Woodford Green IG8 . . . **63** H6
Kings Bench St, SE1 . . . . . **27** H3
Kings Bench Wk, EC4 . . . . . **19** F4
Kingsbridge Av, W3 . . . . . **125** J2
Kingsbridge Ct, E14
off Dockers Tanner Rd . **134** A4
Kingsbridge Cres, Sthl.
UB1 . . . . **103** F5
Kingsbridge Dr, NW7 . . . . . **56** A7
Kingsbridge Rd, W10 . . . . **107** J6
Barking IG11 . . . . **117** G2
Morden SM4 . . . . **184** A7
Kingsbridge Rd, Sthl.
UB2 . . . . **123** F4
Walton-on-Thames
KT12 . . . . **178** B7
KINGSBURY, NW9 . . . . **70** B6
Kingsbury Circle, NW9 . . . . **70** A5
Kingsbury Rd, N1 . . . . **94** B6
NW9 . . . . **70** B5
Kingsbury Ter, N1 . . . . **94** B6
Kingsbury Trd Est, NW9 . . . **70** D6
Kings Butts, SE9
off Strongbow Cres . . **156** C5
Kings Chace Vw, Enf. EN2
off Crofton Way **43** G2
Kings Chase, E.Mol. KT8 . **179** J3
Kingsclere Cl, SW15 . . . . . **147** G7
Kingsclere Ct, Barn. EN5
off Gloucester Rd **41** F5
Kingsclere Pl, Enf. EN2
off Chase Side **43** J2
Kingscliffe Gdns, SW19 . . **166** C1
Kings Cl, E10 . . . . **78** B7
NW4 . . . . **72** A4
Thames Ditton KT7 . . . . **180** D6
Kings Coll Rd, NW3 . . . . . . **91** H7
Kingscote Rd, W4 . . . . **126** D3
Croydon CR0 . . . . **188** E7
New Malden KT3 . . . . . **182** D3
Kingscote St, EC4 . . . . **19** G5
Kings Ct, E13 . . . . **115** H1
W6 *off King St* **127** G4
Wembley HA9 . . . . **88** B2
Kingscourt Rd, SW16 . . . . **168** D3
Kings Ct S, SW3
off Chelsea Manor Gdns . **129** H5
Kings Cres, N4 . . . . **93** J3
Kings Cres Est, N4 . . . . **93** J2
Kingscroft Rd, NW2 . . . . . . **90** C6
KING'S CROSS, N1 . . . . . . **110** D1
King's Cross Br, N1 . . . . . . **10** B3
King's Cross Rd, WC1 . . . . . **10** D3
Kingsdale Gdns, W11 . . . . **128** A1
Kingsdale Rd, SE18 . . . . . **137** J7
SE20 . . . . **171** G7
Kingsdown Av, W3 . . . . . . **107** E7
W13 . . . . **125** E2
Kingsdown Cl, SE16
off Masters Dr . . . **132/133** E5
W10 . . . . **108** A6
Kingsdowne Rd, Surb.
KT6 . . . . **181** H7
Kingsdown Rd, E11 . . . . . . **97** E3
N19 . . . . **92** E2
Sutton SM3 . . . . **198** B5
Kingsdown Way, Brom.
BR2 . . . . **191** G7
Kings Dr, Edg. HA8 . . . . . . **53** J4
Surbiton KT5 . . . . **182** A7
Teddington TW11 . . . . . . **162** A5
Thames Ditton KT7 . . . . **180** E6
Wembley HA9 . . . . **88** B2
Kings Fm Av, Rich. TW10 . **146** A4
Kingsfield Av, Har. HA2 . . . **67** H4
Kingsfield Ho, SE9 . . . . . . **174** A3
Kingsfield Rd, Har. HA1 . . . **68** A7
Kingsford St, NW5 . . . . **91** J5
Kingsford Way, E6 . . . . . . **116** C5
Kings Gdns, NW6
off West End La **90** D7
Ilford IG1 . . . . **99** G1
King's Garth Ms, SE23
off London Rd **171** F2
Kingsgate, Wem. HA9 . . . . **88** C3
Kingsgate Av, N3 . . . . **72** D3
Kingsgate Cl, Bexh. DA7 . **158** E1
Kingsgate Pl, NW6 . . . . **90** D7
Kingsgate Rd, NW6 . . . . . . **90** D7
Kingston upon Thames
KT2 . . . . **181** H1
Kings Grn, Loug. IG10 . . . . **48** B3
Kingsground, SE9 . . . . . . **156** B7
Kings Gro, SE15 . . . . **133** E7
Kingshall Ms, SE13
off Lewisham Rd **154** C3
Kings Hall Rd, Beck. BR3 . **171** H7
Kings Head Hill, E4 . . . . . . **46** B7
Kings Head Yd, SE1 . . . . . . **28** B2
Kings Highway, SE18 . . . . **137** H6
Kings Hill, Loug. IG10 . . . . **48** B2
Kingshill Av, Har. HA3 . . . . **69** E4
Northolt UB5 . . . . **102** A3
Worcester Park KT4 . . . . **183** G7
Kingshill Cl, Hayes UB4 . . **102** A3
Kingshill Dr, Har. HA3 . . . . **68** E3
Kingshold Est, E9
off Victoria Pk Rd **113** F1
Kingshold Rd, E9 . . . . **95** F7
Kingsholm Gdns, SE9 . . . **156** A4
Kingshurst Rd, SE12 . . . . **155** G7

Kingside Business Pk, SE18
off Woolwich Ch St ... **136** B3
Kings Keep, Kings.T. KT1
off Beaufort Rd **181** H4
KINGSLAND, N1 .... **94** B6
Kingsland, NW8
off Broxwood Way.... **109** H1
Kingsland Grn, E8 .... **94** B6
Kingsland High St, E8 .... **94** C5
Kingsland Pas, E8
off Kingsland Grn **94** B6
Kingsland Rd, E2 .... **13** E3
E8.................. **112** B2
E13................. **115** J3
Kingsland Shop Cen, E8 .. **94** C6
Kings La, Sutt. SM1 ..... **199** G6
Kingslawn Cl, SW15
off Howards La **147** H5
Kingsleigh Cl, Brent. TW8
off Brook Rd S. **125** G6
Kingsleigh Pl, Mitch. CR4
off Chatsworth Pl **185** J3
Kingsleigh Wk, Brom. BR2
off Stamford Dr...... **191** F4
Kingsley Av, W13 .... **104** D6
Hounslow TW3 .... **143** J2
Southall UB1......... **103** G7
Sutton SM1.......... **199** G4
Kingsley Cl, N2.......... **73** F5
Dagenham RM10....... **101** H4
Kingsley Ct, Edg. HA8 .... **54** B2
Kingsley Dr, Wor.Pk. KT4
off Badgers Copse ... **197** F2
Kingsley Flats, SE1
off Old Kent Rd...... **132** B4
Kingsley Gdns, E4 .... **62** A5
Kingsley Ms, E1
off Wapping La ... **112/113** E7
W8.................. **22** B6
Chislehurst BR7 ...... **175** E6
Kingsley Pl, N6.......... **74** A7
Kingsley Rd, E7 .... **97** G7
E17 .... **78** C2
N13 .... **59** G4
NW6 .... **108** C1
SW19............... **167** E5
Croydon CR0......... **201** G1
Harrow HA2 .... **85** J4
Hounslow TW3 .... **143** J2
Ilford IG6............. **81** F1
Loughton IG10 .... **49** G3
Orpington BR6 .... **207** J7
Pinner HA5 .... **67** F4
Kingsley St, SW11 ...... **149** J3
Kingsley Way, N2........ **73** F6
Kingsley Wd Dr, SE9..... **174** C3
Kingslyn Cres, SE19..... **188** B1
Kings Mall, W6......... **127** J4
Kingsman Par, SE18
off Woolwich Ch St ... **136** C3
Kingsman St, SE18 ..... **136** C3
Kingsmead, Barn. EN5.... **40** D4
Richmond TW10 ...... **145** J6
Kingsmead Av, N9 .... **60** E1
NW9 .... **70** D7
Mitcham CR4......... **186** C3
Sunbury-on-Thames
TW16.............. **178** C3
Surbiton KT6......... **196** A2
Worcester Park KT4.... **197** H3
Kingsmead Cl, Epsom
KT19 .... **196** D7
Sidcup DA15 .... **176** A2
Teddington TW11...... **162** D6
Kingsmead Dr, Nthlt. UB5 . **85** F7
Kingsmead Est, E9....... **95** H5
Kingsmead Ho, E9
off Kingsmead Way.... **95** H4
Kings Mead Pk, Esher
(Clay.) KT10 .... **194** B7
Kingsmead Rd, SW2 .... **169** G2
Kingsmead Way, E9 ...... **95** H4
Kingsmere Cl, SW15
off Felsham Rd **148** B3
Kingsmere Pk, NW9...... **88** B1
Kingsmere Pl, N16 .... **94** A1
Kingsmere Rd, SW19.... **166** A2
Kings Ms, SW4
off King's Av..... **150/151** E5
King's Ms, WC1 .... **10** D6
Kings Ms, Chig. IG7...... **65** F2
Kingsmill Gdns, Dag.
RM9................ **101** F5
Kingsmill Rd, Dag. RM9.. **101** F5
Kingsmill Ter, NW8......... **7** F1
Kingsnympton Pk, Kings.T.
KT2............... **164** B6
Kings Oak, Rom. RM7 .... **83** G3
King's Orchard, SE9..... **156** B6
Kings Paddock, Hmptn.
TW12.............. **179** J1
Kings Par, Cars. SM5
off Wrythe La........ **199** H3
Kingspark Ct, E18........ **79** G3
King's Pas, E11 .... **78** E7
Kings Pas, Kings.T. KT1 .. **181** G2
Kings Pl, SE1 .... **27** J4
W4................. **126** C5
Buckhurst Hill IG9...... **63** J2
Loughton IG10 .... **48** A7
King Sq, EC1 .... **11** J4
King's Reach Twr, SE1 .... **27** F1
Kings Ride Gate, Rich.
TW10.............. **146** A4
Kingsridge, SW19....... **166** B2
Kings Rd, E4............ **62** D1
E6................. **115** J1
E11.................. **78** E7
King's Rd, N17 .... **76** C1
Kings Rd, N18 .... **60** D5
N22 .... **75** F1
NW10 .... **89** H7
SE25 .... **188** D3
King's Rd, SW1 .... **31** H3
SW3................. **31** H3
SW6................ **148** E1
SW10............... **148** E1
Kings Rd, SW14 .... **146** D3
SW19............... **166** D6
W5................. **105** G5
Barking IG11
off North St.......... **99** F7
Barnet EN5 .... **39** J3
Feltham TW13 .... **160** C1
Harrow HA2 .... **85** F2
Kingston upon Thames
KT2 .... **163** H7
Mitcham CR4......... **186** A3
Orpington BR6 .... **207** J4
Richmond TW10 ...... **145** J5
Surbiton KT6......... **195** F1
Teddington TW11...... **162** A5
Twickenham TW1 ..... **145** E6
West Drayton UB7 .... **120** C2
Kings Rd Bungalows, Har.
HA2 *off Kings Rd* **85** F3
King's Scholars' Pas, SW1 . **33** F1
King Stairs Cl, SE16
off Elephant La .. **132/133** E2
King's Ter, NW1
off Plender St........ **110** C1
Kings Ter, Islw. TW7
off Worple Rd **144** D3
Kingsthorpe Rd, SE26 ... **171** G4
Kingston Av, Felt. TW14 .. **141** H6
Sutton SM3.......... **198** B3
Kingston Br, Kings.T. KT1 . **181** G2
Kingston Bypass, SW15.. **165** E4
SW20............... **165** E4
Esher KT10 .... **194** D3
New Malden KT3 ..... **183** F1
Surbiton KT5, KT6..... **195** H3
Kingston Cl, Nthlt. UB5 .. **103** F1
Romford RM6 .... **82** E3
Teddington TW11...... **162** E6
Kingston Ct, N4
off Wiltshire Gdns..... **75** J6
Kingston Cres, Beck. BR3. **189** J1
Kingston Gdns, Croy. CR0
off Wandle Rd ... **200/201** E3
Kingston Hall Rd, Kings.T.
KT1 .... **181** G3
Kingston Hill, Kings.T.
KT2 .... **164** C6
Kingston Hill Av, Rom.
RM6................. **83** E3
Kingston Hill Pl, Kings.T.
KT2............... **164** C4
Kingston La, Tedd. TW11 . **162** D5
West Drayton UB7 .... **120** C2
★**Kingston Mus & Heritage Cen**, Kings.T. KT1 .... **181** H2
Kingston Pk Est, Kings.T.
KT2 .... **164** B6
Kingston Pl, Har. HA3
off Richmond Gdns.... **52** C7
Kingston Rd, N9......... **60** D2
SW15............... **165** G1
SW19............... **184** C1
SW20............... **183** J2
Barnet EN4 .... **41** G5
Epsom KT17, KT19..... **196** E5
Ilford IG1............. **99** E4
Kingston upon Thames
KT1 .... **182** B3
New Malden KT3 ..... **182** D4
Southall UB2......... **123** F2
Surbiton KT5......... **196** B2
Kingston Rd, Tedd. TW11 . **162** E5
Worcester Park KT4.... **196** B2
Kingston Sq, SE19 ...... **170** A5
KINGSTON UPON THAMES,
KT1 & KT2.......... **181** H2
KINGSTON VALE, SW15.. **165** E4
Kingston Vale, SW15 .... **164** D4
Kingstown St, NW1 ..... **110** A1
King St, E13 .... **115** G4
EC2 .... **20** A4
N2 .... **73** G3
N17 .... **76** C1
SW1................. **25** G2
W3................. **126** B1
W6................. **127** G4
WC2................. **18** A5
Richmond TW9 .... **145** G5
Southall UB2......... **123** E3
Twickenham TW1 ..... **162** D1
King's Wk, Kings.T. KT2 .. **181** G1
Kings Wk Shop Mall, SW3
off King's Rd **129** J5
Kingswater Pl, SW11
off Battersea Ch Rd... **129** H7
Kingsway, N12.......... **57** F6
SW14............... **146** B3
WC2................. **18** C3
Croydon CR0......... **201** F5
Enfield EN3 .... **45** E5
Kings Way, Har. HA1 ..... **68** B4
Kingsway, N.Mal. KT3 ... **183** J4
Orpington BR5 .... **193** H5
Wembley HA9......... **87** H4
West Wickham BR4.... **205** E3
Woodford Green IG8 ... **63** J5
Kingsway Business Pk,
Hmptn. TW12........ **179** F1
Kingsway Cres, Har. HA2.. **67** J4
Kingsway Pl, EC1 .... **11** F5
Kingsway Rd, Sutt. SM3 . **198** B7
Kingsway Shop Cen, NW3
off Hampstead High St. **91** F4
Kingswear Rd, NW5...... **92** B3
Ruislip HA4........... **84** A2
Kings Wf, E8
off Kingsland Rd **112** B1
Kingswood Av, NW6 .... **108** B1
Belvedere DA17 ...... **139** F4
Bromley BR2......... **190** E3
Hampton TW12 .... **161** H6
Hounslow TW3 .... **143** F1
Thornton Heath CR7 ... **187** G5
Kingswood Cl, N20 ...... **41** F6
SW8................ **131** E7
Enfield EN1 .... **44** B5
New Malden KT3 ..... **183** F6
Orpington BR6 .... **193** G7
Surbiton KT6......... **181** H7
Kingswood Dr, SE19 .... **170** B4
Carshalton SM5 ...... **199** J1
Kingswood Est, SE21
off Bowen Dr........ **170** B4
Kingswood Ms, N15
off Harringay Rd **75** H5
Kingswood Pk, N3....... **72** C2
Kingswood Pl, SE13..... **155** E4
Kingswood Rd, E11 ...... **79** E7
SE20 .... **171** F6
SW2................ **150** E6
SW19............... **166** C7
W4................. **126** C3
Bromley BR2......... **190** D4
Ilford IG3............ **100** A1
Wembley HA9......... **88** A3
Kingswood Ter, W4
off Kingswood Rd.... **126** C3
Kingswood Way, Wall.
SM6............... **201** E5
Kingsworth Cl, Beck.
BR3................ **189** H5
Kingsworthy Cl, Kings.T.
KT1............... **181** J3
King's Yd, SW15
off Stanbridge Rd **147** J3
Kingthorpe Rd, NW10 .... **88** D7
Kingthorpe Ter, NW10 .... **88** D6
Kingweston Cl, NW2
off Windmill Dr **90** B3
King William IV Gdns, SE20
off St. John's Rd **171** F6
King William La, SE10
off Orlop St **134/135** E5
King William St, EC4 ..... **20** C6
King William Wk, SE10... **134** C6
Kingwood Rd, SW6 ..... **148** A1
Kinlet Rd, SE18 .... **157** F1
Kinloch Dr, NW9 .... **70** E7
Kinloch St, N7
off Hornsey Rd **93** F3
Kinloss Ct, N3
off Haslemere Gdns ... **72** C4
Kinloss Gdns, N3........ **72** C4
Kinloss Rd, Cars. SM5 ... **185** F7
Kinnaird Av, W4 .... **126** C7
Bromley BR1......... **173** F6
Kinnaird Cl, Brom. BR1 .. **173** F6
Kinnaird Way, Wdf.Grn.
IG8................. **64** C6
Kinnear Rd, W12........ **127** F2
Kinnerton Pl N, SW1 ..... **24** A4
Kinnerton Pl S, SW1 ..... **24** A4
Kinnerton St, SW1....... **24** B4
Kinnerton Yd, SW1....... **24** A4
Kinnoul Rd, W6 .... **128** B6
Kinross Av, Wor.Pk. KT4 .. **197** G2
Kinross Cl, Edg. HA8
off Tayside Dr **54** B2
Harrow HA3 .... **69** J5
Kinross Ter, E17 .... **77** J2
Kinsale Rd, SE15 .... **152** D3
Kintore Way, SE1 .... **37** F1
Kintyre Cl, SW16 .... **187** F3
Kinveachy Gdns, SE7.... **136** B5
Kinver Rd, SE26 .... **171** F4
Kipling Dr, SW19 .... **167** G6
Kipling Est, SE1 .... **28** C4
Kipling Pl, Stan. HA7
off Uxbridge Rd **52** C6
Kipling Rd, Bexh. DA7 ... **159** E1
Kipling St, SE1.......... **28** C4
Kipling Ter, N9 .... **60** A3
Kippington Dr, SE9 ..... **174** A1
Kirby Cl, Epsom KT19 ... **197** F5
Ilford IG6............. **65** H6
Loughton IG10 .... **48** B7
Kirby Est, SE16......... **132** E3
Kirby Gro, SE1 .... **28** D3
Kirby St, EC1 .... **19** F1
Kirby Way, Walt. KT12 ... **178** C6
Kirchen Rd, W13........ **104** E7
Kirkby Cl, N11
off Coverdale Rd...... **58** A6
Kirkcaldy Grn, Wat. WD19
off Trevose Way....... **50** C3
Kirkdale, SE26 .... **170** E2
Kirkdale Rd, E11 .... **97** E1
Kirkfield Cl, W13
off Broomfield Rd . **124/125** E1
Kirkham Rd, E6......... **116** B6
Kirkham St, SE18....... **137** H6
Kirkland Av, Ilf. IG5 ...... **80** D2
Kirkland Cl, Sid. DA15 ... **157** H6
Kirkland Dr, Enf. EN2..... **43** H1
Kirkland Wk, E8 .... **94** C6
Kirk La, SE18 .... **137** F6
Kirkleas Rd, Surb. KT6... **195** H1
Kirklees Rd, Dag. RM8 ... **100** C5
Thornton Heath CR7 ... **187** G5
Kirkley Rd, SW19 .... **184** D1
Kirkman Pl, W1.......... **17** H2
Kirkmichael Rd, E14
off Dee St **114** C6
Kirk Ri, Sutt. SM1....... **199** E3
Kirk Rd, E17 .... **77** J6
Kirkside Rd, SE3........ **135** G6
Kirkstall Av, N17......... **76** A4
Kirkstall Gdns, SW2..... **168** D1
Kirkstall Rd, SW2....... **168** D1
Kirkstead Ct, E5
off Mandeville St **95** H3
Kirksted Rd, Mord. SM4 . **198** E1
Kirkstone Way, Brom.
BR1 .... **173** E7
Kirk St, WC1 .... **10** C6
Kirkton Rd, N15 .... **76** B4
Kirkwall Pl, E2 .... **113** F3
Kirkwood Rd, SE15 ..... **153** E2
Kirn Rd, W13
off Kirchen Rd ... **104/105** E7
Kirrane Cl, N.Mal. KT3 ... **183** F5
Kirtley Rd, SE26 .... **171** H4
Kirtling St, SW8.......... **33** F7
Kirton Cl, W4
off Dolman Rd....... **126** D4
Kirton Gdns, E2 .... **13** G4
Kirton Rd, E13 .... **115** J2
Kirton Wk, Edg. HA8 ..... **54** C7
Kirwyn Way, SE5 .... **35** H7
Kitcat Ter, E3........... **114** A3
Kitchener Rd, E7 .... **97** H6
E17 .... **78** B1
N2 .... **73** H3
N17 .... **76** A3
Dagenham RM10...... **101** H6
Thornton Heath CR7 ... **188** A3
Kite Pl, E2.............. **13** J3
Kite Yd, SW11
off Cambridge Rd **149** J1

Kitley Gdns, SE19. . . . . . . **188** C1
Kitson Rd, SE5. . . . . **36** A7
SW13. . . . . **147** G1
Kittiwake Pl, Sutt. SM1
off Sandpiper Rd. **198** C5
Kittiwake Rd, Nthlt. UB5 . **102** D3
Kittiwake Way, Hayes
UB4 . . . . **102** D5
Kitto Rd, SE14 . . . . **153** G2
Kiver Rd, N19 . . . . **92** D2
Kiwi Cl, Twick. TW1
off Crown Rd **144/145** E6
Klea Av, SW4 . . . . **150** C6
Knapdale Cl, SE23 . . . . . . **171** E2
Knapmill Rd, SE6 . . . . **172** A2
Knapmill Way, SE6 . . . . . . **172** B2
Knapp Cl, NW10. . . . . **89** E6
Knapp Rd, E3 . . . . **114** A4
Knapton Ms, SW17
off Seely Rd. **168** A6
Knaresborough Dr, SW18 . **166** E1
Knaresborough Pl, SW5. . . **30** A1
Knatchbull Rd, NW10. . . . **106** D1
SE5 . . . . **151** J1
Knebworth Av, E17 . . . . . . **78** A1
Knebworth Path, Borwd.
WD6 . . . . **38** D4
Knebworth Rd, N16
off Nevill Rd **94** B4
Knee Hill, SE2. . . . . **138** C4
Knee Hill Cres, SE2 . . . . . **138** C4
Kneller Gdns, Islw. TW7 . . **144** A5
Kneller Rd, SE4 . . . . **153** H4
New Malden KT3 . . . . . **182** E7
Twickenham TW2 . . . . . **143** J6
Knight Cl, Dag. RM8 . . . . **100** C2
Knighten St, E1 . . . . **29** J2
Knighthead Pt, E14 . . . . . **134** A3
Knightland Rd, E5 . . . . **94** E2
Knighton Cl, S.Croy. CR2 . **201** H7
Woodford Green IG8 . . . **63** H4
Knighton Dr, Wdf.Grn. IG8. **63** G4
Knighton Grn, Buck.H. IG9
off High Rd **63** H2
Knighton La, Buck.H. IG9. . **63** H2
Knighton Pk Rd, SE26 . . . **171** G5
Knighton Rd, E7 . . . . **97** G3
Romford RM7 . . . . **83** J6
Knightrider Ct, EC4
off Godliman St. **111** J7
Knightrider St, EC4 . . . . . . **19** J5
Knights Arc, SW1. . . . . **23** J4
Knights Av, W5. . . . . **125** H2
Knightsbridge, SW1. . . . . . **24** A4
SW7. . . . . **23** H4
Knightsbridge Grn, SW1 . . **23** J4
Knights Cl, E9
off Churchill Wk. **95** F5
Knights Ct, Kings.T. KT1 . **181** H2
Romford RM6 . . . . **83** E6
Knights Hill, SE27 . . . . . . **169** H5
Knights Hill Sq, SE27
off Knights Hill **169** H4
Knights La, N9 . . . . **60** D3
Knights Ms, Sutt. SM2
off York Rd. **198** D7
Knights Pk, Kings.T. KT1 . **181** H3
Knight's Pl, Twick. TW2
off May Rd **162** B1
Knights Rd, E16 . . . . **135** G2
Stanmore HA7 . . . . **53** F4
Knights Wk, SE11. . . . . **35** G2
Knights Way, Ilf. IG6. . . . . **65** F6
Knightswood Cl, Edg.
HA8 . . . . **54** C2
Knightwood Cres, N.Mal.
KT3 . . . . **182** E6
Knivet Rd, SW6 . . . . **128** D6
Knobs Hill Rd, E15 . . . . . . **114** B1
Knockholt Rd, SE9. . . . . . . **156** A5
Knole, The, SE9. . . . . **174** D4
Knole Cl, Croy. CR0
off Stockbury Rd **189** F6
Knole Gate, Sid. DA15
off Woodside Cres. . . . **175** H3
Knoll, The, W13. . . . . **105** F5
Beckenham BR3 . . . . . . **190** B1
Bromley BR2. . . . . **205** G2
Knoll Ct, SE19 . . . . **170** C5
Knoll Dr, N14 . . . . **42** A7
Knollmead, Surb. KT5 . . . . **196** C1
Knoll Ri, Orp. BR6 . . . . . . **207** J1
Knoll Rd, SW18 . . . . **149** F5
Bexley DA5 . . . . **159** G7
Sidcup DA14 . . . . **176** B5
Knolls Cl, Wor.Pk. KT4 . . . **197** H3
Knollys Cl, SW16 . . . . **169** G3
Knollys Rd, SW16 . . . . . . **169** G3
Knottisford St, E2. . . . . . . **113** F3
Knotts Grn Ms, E10 . . . . . . **78** B6
Knotts Grn Rd, E10 . . . . . . **78** B6
Knowle Av, Bexh. DA7 . . . **139** E7
Knowle Cl, SW9. . . . . **151** G3
Knowle Rd, Brom. BR2 . . **206** B2
Twickenham TW2 . . . . . **162** B1
Knowles Cl, West Dr. UB7 . **120** B1
Knowles Hill Cres, SE13. . **154** D5
Knowles Ho, SW18
off Neville Gill Cl. **148** E6
Knowles Wk, SW4 . . . . . . **150** C3
Knowlton Grn, Brom.
BR2 . . . . **191** F5
Knowsley Av, Sthl. UB1 . . **123** G1
Knowsley Rd, SW11 . . . . . **149** J2
Knox Rd, E7 . . . . **97** F6
Knox St, W1 . . . . **15** J1
Knoyle St, SE14 . . . . **133** H6
Kohat Rd, SW19. . . . . **167** E5
Kossuth St, SE10 . . . . **134** E5
Kotree Way, SE1. . . . . **37** J2
Kramer Ms, SW5
off Kempsford Gdns . . **128** D5
Kreedman Wk, E8. . . . . **94** D5
Kreisel Wk, Rich. TW9. . . . **125** J6
Kuala Gdns, SW16 . . . . . . **187** F1
Kuhn Way, E7
off Forest La **97** G5
Kydbrook Cl, Orp. BR5 . . . **193** G7
Kylemore Cl, E6
off Parr Rd **116** A2
Kylemore Rd, NW6 . . . . . . **90** D7
Kymberley Rd, Har. HA1 . . **68** B6
Kynance Gdns, Stan. HA7 . **69** F1
Kynance Ms, SW7 . . . . **22** C6
Kynance Pl, SW7 . . . . **22** C6
Kynaston Av, N16
off Dynevor Rd **94** C3
Thornton Heath CR7 . . . **187** J5
Kynaston Cl, Har. HA3 . . . . **52** A7
Kynaston Cres, Th.Hth.
CR7 . . . . **187** J5
Kynaston Rd, N16 . . . . **94** B3
Bromley BR1 . . . . **173** G5
Enfield EN2 . . . . **44** A1
Thornton Heath CR7 . . . **187** J5
Kynaston Wd, Har. HA3 . . . **52** A7
Kynersley Cl, Cars. SM5
off William St **199** J3
Kynock Rd, N18 . . . . **61** F4
Kyrle Rd, SW11. . . . . **150** A5
Kyverdale Rd, N16 . . . . **94** C2

L

Laburnham Cl, Wem. HA0
off Highcroft Av. **106** A1
Laburnum Av, N9. . . . . **60** B2
N17 . . . . **60** A7
Sutton SM1. . . . . **199** H3
Laburnum Cl, E4 . . . . **61** J6
N11 . . . . **58** A6
SE15 *off Clifton Way* . . . **133** F7
Laburnum Ct, E2
off Laburnum St **112** C1
Stanmore HA7 . . . . **53** F4
Laburnum Cres, Sun. TW16
off Batavia Rd **178** B1
Laburnum Gdns, N21. . . . . **59** J2
Croydon CR0. . . . . **189** G7
Laburnum Gro, N21 . . . . . . **59** J2
NW9 . . . . **70** C7
Hounslow TW3 . . . . **143** F4
New Malden KT3 . . . . . **182** D2
Southall UB1 . . . . **103** F4
Laburnum Ho, Dag. RM10
off Bradwell Av **101** G2
Laburnum Rd, SW19 . . . . **167** F7
Hayes UB3 . . . . **121** J4
Mitcham CR4. . . . . **186** A2
Laburnum St, E2 . . . . **112** C1
Laburnum Way, Brom.
BR2 . . . . **192** D7
Lacebark Cl, Sid. DA15. . . **157** J7
Lacewing Cl, E13
off Sewell St **115** G3
Lacey Cl, N9. . . . . **60** D2
Lacey Dr, Dag. RM8 . . . . . **100** B4
Edgware HA8 . . . . **53** H4
Hampton TW12 . . . . **179** F1
Lacey Wk, E3 . . . . **114** A2
Lackington St, EC2 . . . . **20** C1
Lacock Cl, SW19. . . . . **167** F6
Lacock Ct, W13
off Singapore Rd. **124** D1
Lacon Rd, SE22 . . . . **152** D4
Lacy Rd, SW15. . . . . **148** A4
Ladas Rd, SE27 . . . . **169** J4
Ladbroke Cres, W11
off Ladbroke Gro. **108** B6
Ladbroke Gdns, W11 . . . . **108** C7
Ladbroke Gro, W10. . . . . . **108** A4
W11 . . . . **108** B6
Ladbroke Ms, W11
off Ladbroke Rd **128** B1
Ladbroke Rd, W11 . . . . . . **128** C1
Enfield EN1 . . . . **44** C6
Ladbroke Sq, W11. . . . . . . **108** C7
Ladbroke Ter, W11. . . . . . . **108** C7
Ladbroke Wk, W11 . . . . . . **128** C1
Ladbrook Cl, Pnr. HA5 . . . . **67** F5
Ladbrooke Cres, Sid.
DA14 . . . . **176** D3
Ladbrook Rd, SE25 . . . . . **188** A3
Ladderstile Ride, Kings.T.
KT2 . . . . **164** B5
Ladderswood Way, N11 . . . **58** C5
Lady Aylesford Av, Stan.
HA7 . . . . **52** E5
Lady Booth Rd, Kings.T.
KT1 . . . . **181** H2
Ladybower Ct, E5
off Gilpin Rd **95** H4
Ladycroft Gdns, Orp. BR6 . **207** F5
Ladycroft Rd, SE13. . . . . . **154** B3
Ladycroft Wk, Stan. HA7 . . **69** G1
Ladycroft Way, Orp. BR6 . **207** F5
Lady Dock Path, SE16
off Salter Rd **133** H2
Ladyfield Cl, Loug. IG10. . . **49** E4
Ladyfields, Loug. IG10 . . . . **49** E4
Lady Hay, Wor.Pk. KT4. . . . **197** F2
Lady Margaret Rd, N19 . . . **92** C4
NW5 . . . . **92** C5
Southall UB1. . . . . **103** F5
Ladysmith Av, E6 . . . . **116** B2
Ilford IG2. . . . . **81** G7
Ladysmith Cl, NW7
off Colenso Dr. **55** G7
Ladysmith Rd, E16. . . . . . . **115** F3
N17 . . . . **76** D2
N18 . . . . **61** E5
SE9 . . . . **156** D6
Enfield EN1 . . . . **44** B3
Harrow HA3 . . . . **68** B2
Lady Somerset Rd, NW5 . . **92** B4
LADYWELL, SE13. . . . . . . **154** A5
Ladywell Cl, SE4
off Adelaide Av **153** J4
Ladywell Hts, SE4 . . . . . . **153** J6
Ladywell Rd, SE13 . . . . . . **154** A5
Ladywell St, E15
off Plaistow Gro **115** F1
Ladywood Av, Orp. BR5. . **193** H5
Ladywood Rd, Surb. KT6. **196** A2
Lafone Av, Felt. TW13
off Alfred Rd **160** C1
Lafone St, SE1 . . . . **29** F3
Lagado Ms, SE16 . . . . **133** G1
Lagonda Av, Ilf. IG6 . . . . . . **65** J6
Laidlaw Dr, N21 . . . . **43** F4
Laing Cl, Ilf. IG6 . . . . **65** G6
Laing Dean, Nthlt. UB5 . . **102** C1
Laings Av, Mitch. CR4 . . . **185** J2
Lainlock Pl, Houns. TW3
off Spring Gro Rd **143** H1
Lainson St, SW18 . . . . . . **148** D7
Lairdale Cl, SE21 . . . . **169** J1
Laird Ho, SE5 . . . . **131** J7
Lairs Cl, N7
off Manger Rd **92/93** E6
Laitwood Rd, SW12. . . . . **168** B1
Lake, The, Bushey
(Bushey Hth) WD23. . . . **51** J1
Lake Av, Brom. BR1 . . . . . **173** G6
Lake Cl, SW19
off Lake Rd **166** C5
Dagenham RM8 . . . . **100** D3
Lakedale Rd, SE18 . . . . . . **137** H6
Lake Dr, Bushey
(Bushey Hth) WD23. . . . **51** J2
Lakefield Cl, SE20
off Limes Av. **170/171** E7
Lakefield Rd, N22. . . . . **75** H2
Lake Gdns, Dag. RM10 . . . **101** G5
Richmond TW10 . . . . . . **163** E2
Wallington SM6 . . . . . . **200** B3
Lakehall Gdns, Th.Hth.
CR7 . . . . **187** H5
Lakehall Rd, Th.Hth. CR7 . **187** H5
Lake Ho Rd, E11 . . . . **97** G3
Lakehurst Rd, Epsom
KT19 . . . . **196** E5
Lakeland Cl, Har. HA3 . . . . **52** A6
Lakenheath, N14 . . . . **42** D6
Lake Rd, SW19. . . . . **166** C5
Croydon CR0. . . . . **203** J2
Lake Rd, Rom. RM6 . . . . . . **82** D4
Laker Pl, SW15. . . . . **148** C6
Lakeside, N3. . . . . **73** E2
W13 *off Edgehill Rd* . . . **105** F6
Beckenham BR3 . . . . . . **190** B3
Enfield EN2 . . . . **42** D4
Wallington SM6
off Derek Av **200** B3
Lakeside Av, SE28 . . . . . . **138** A1
Ilford IG4. . . . . **80** A4
Lakeside Cl, SE25. . . . . . . **188** D2
Chigwell IG7 . . . . **65** J4
Sidcup DA15 . . . . **158** C5
Lakeside Ct, N4 . . . . **93** H2
Borehamwood (Elstree)
WD6 *off Cavendish Cres* . **38** A5
Lakeside Cres, Barn. EN4. . **41** J5
Lakeside Dr, Brom. BR2. . **206** B3
Lakeside Rd, N13 . . . . **59** F4
W14. . . . . **128** A3
Lakeside Way, Wem. HA9. . **88** A4
Lakes Rd, Kes. BR2 . . . . . **205** J5
Lakeswood Rd, Orp. BR5. **193** E6
Lake Vw, Edg. HA8 . . . . . . **53** J5
Lakeview Ct, SW19
off Victoria Dr **166** B2
Lakeview Rd, SE27 . . . . . **169** G5
Welling DA16 . . . . **158** B4
Lakis Cl, NW3
off Flask Wk. **91** F4
Laleham Av, NW7 . . . . **54** D3
Laleham Rd, SE6 . . . . **154** C6
Lalor St, SW6. . . . . **148** B2
Lambarde Av, SE9 . . . . . . **174** D4
Lamb Cl, Nthlt. UB5 . . . . . **102** E3
Lamberhurst Rd, SE27. . . **169** G4
Dagenham RM8 . . . . . . **101** F1
Lambert Av, Rich. TW9. . . **146** B3
Lambert Jones Ms, EC2
off The Barbican. **111** J5
Lambert Rd, E16. . . . . **115** H6
N12 . . . . **57** G5
SW2. . . . . **151** E5
Lamberts Pl, Croy. CR0 . . **202** A1
Lamberts Rd, Surb. KT5. . **181** H5
Lambert St, N1 . . . . **93** G7
Lambert Wk, Wem. HA9. . . **87** G3
Lambert Way, N12
off Woodhouse Rd **57** F5
LAMBETH, SE1 . . . . **26** C5
Lambeth Br, SE1 . . . . **34** B1
SW1. . . . . **34** B1
Lambeth High St, SE1 . . . . **34** C2
Lambeth Hill, EC4 . . . . **19** J5
★**Lambeth Palace**, SE1 . . . **26** C6
Lambeth Palace Rd, SE1 . . **26** C6
Lambeth Rd, SE1. . . . . **26** D6
SE11 . . . . **26** D6
Croydon CR0. . . . . **187** G7
Lambeth Wk, SE11 . . . . **34** D1
Lamb La, E8 . . . . **94** E7
Lamble St, NW5. . . . . **92** A5
Lambley Rd, Dag. RM9 . . **100** B6
Lambolle Pl, NW3 . . . . **91** H6
Lambolle Rd, NW3 . . . . **91** H6
Lambourn Cl, W7 . . . . **124** C2
Lambourne Av, SW19. . . . **166** C4
Lambourne Ct, Wdf.Grn. IG8
off Navestock Cres **63** J7
Lambourne Gdns, E4. . . . . **62** A2
Barking IG11
off Lambourne Rd. **99** J7
Enfield EN1 . . . . **44** C2
Lambourne Gro, SE16
off Reculver Rd **133** G5
Kingston upon Thames
KT1 *off Kenley Rd*. . . . **182** B2
Lambourne Pl, SE3
off Shooter's Hill Rd . . **155** H1
Lambourne Rd, E11 . . . . . . **78** C7
Barking IG11 . . . . **99** H7
Chigwell IG7 . . . . **65** H4
Ilford IG3. . . . . **99** H2
Lambourn Rd, SW4 . . . . . **150** B3
Lambrook Ter, SW6 . . . . . **148** B1
Lamb's Bldgs, EC1 . . . . **12** B6
Lambs Conduit Pas, WC1. . **18** C1
Lamb's Conduit St, WC1 . . **10** C6
Lambscroft Av, SE9 . . . . . **173** J3
Lambs Meadow, Wdf.Grn.
IG8 . . . . **80** A2
Lambs Ms, N1
off Colebrooke Row. . . **111** H1
Lamb's Pas, EC1. . . . . **20** B1
Lambs Ter, N9 . . . . **60** A2
Lamb St, E1 . . . . **21** F1
Lambs Wk, Enf. EN2. . . . . . **43** J2
Lambton Ms, N19
off Lambton Rd **92/93** E1

Lambton Pl, W11
off Westbourne Gro. 108 C6
Lambton Rd, N19 92 E1
SW20 183 J1
Lamb Wk, SE1 28 D4
Lamerock Rd, Brom. BR1 173 F4
Lamerton Rd, Ilf. IG6 81 E2
Lamerton St, SE8 134 A6
Lamford Cl, N17 60 A7
Lamington St, W6 127 H4
Lamlash St, SE11 35 G1
Lammas Av, Mitch. CR4 186 A2
Lammas Grn, SE26 170 E3
Lammas Pk, W5 125 F2
Lammas Pk Gdns, W5 125 F2
Lammas Pk Rd, W5 125 F1
Lammas Rd, E9 95 G7
E10 95 H2
Richmond TW10 163 F4
Lammermoor Rd, SW12 150 B7
Lamont Rd, SW10 30 D6
Lamont Rd Pas, SW10
off Lamont Rd 129 G6
LAMORBEY, Sid. DA15 175 J1
Lamorbey Cl, Sid. DA15 175 J1
Lamorna Cl, E17 78 C1
Lamorna Gro, Stan. HA7 69 G1
Lampard Gro, N16 94 C1
Lampern Sq, E2 13 J3
Lampeter Cl, NW9 70 E6
Lampeter Sq, W6
off Humbolt Rd 128 B6
Lamplighter Cl, E1
off Cleveland Way 113 F4
Lampmead Rd, SE12 155 E5
Lamp Office Ct, WC1 10 C6
Lamport Cl, SE18 136 C4
LAMPTON, Houns. TW3 143 H1
Lampton Av, Houns. TW3 143 H1
Lampton Ho Cl, SW19 166 A4
Lampton Pk Rd, Houns. TW3 143 H2
Lampton Rd, Houns. TW3 143 H2
Lanacre Av, NW9 71 F1
Lanark Cl, W5 105 F5
Lanark Ms, W9 6 C4
Lanark Pl, W9 6 D5
Lanark Rd, W9 6 C4
Lanark Sq, E14 134 B3
Lanata Wk, Hayes UB4
off Ramulis Dr 102 D4
Lanbury Rd, SE15 153 G4
Lancashire Ct, W1 16 E5
Lancaster Av, E18 79 H4
SE27 169 H2
SW19 166 A5
Barking IG11 99 H7
Mitcham CR4 186 E5
Lancaster Cl, N1
off Hertford Rd 94 B7
N17 *off Park La* 60 D7
NW9 55 F7
Bromley BR2 191 F4
Kingston upon Thames KT2 163 G5
Staines (Stanw.) TW19 140 B6
Lancaster Cotts, Rich. TW10
off Lancaster Pk 145 H6
Lancaster Ct, SE27 169 H2
SW6 128 C7
W2 14 D6
Walton-on-Thames KT12 178 A7
Lancaster Dr, E14
off Prestons Rd 134 C1
NW3 91 H6
Loughton IG10 48 B6
Lancaster Gdns, SW19 166 B5
W13 125 E2
Bromley BR1 192 B5
Kingston upon Thames KT2 163 G5
Lancaster Gate, W2 14 D6
Lancaster Gro, NW3 91 G6
★**Lancaster Ho**, SW1 25 F3
Lancaster Ms, SW18
off East Hill 148/149 E5
W2 14 D5
Richmond TW10
off Richmond Hill 145 H6
Lancaster Pk, Rich. TW10 145 H5
Lancaster Pl, SW19
off Lancaster Rd 166 A5
WC2 18 C5
Hounslow TW4 142 C2
Ilford IG1
off Staines Rd 99 F5
Twickenham TW1 144 D6
Lancaster Rd, E7 97 G7
Lancaster Rd, E11 97 E2
E17 77 G2
N4 75 G7
N11 58 D6
N18 60 C5
NW10 89 F5
SE25 188 C2
SW19 166 A5
W11 108 B6
Barnet EN4 41 G5
Enfield EN2 44 A1
Harrow HA2 67 G5
Northolt UB5 85 J6
Southall UB1 103 E7
Lancaster St, SE1 27 H4
Lancaster Ter, W2 15 E5
Lancaster Wk, W2 22 E3
Lancaster Way, Wor.Pk. KT4 183 H7
Lancaster W, W11
off Grenfell Rd. 108 A7
Lancastrian Rd, Wall. SM6 201 E7
Lancefield St, W10 108 C3
Lancell St, N16
off Stoke Newington Ch St 94 B2
Lancelot Av, Wem. HA0 87 G4
Lancelot Cres, Wem. HA0 87 G4
Lancelot Gdns, Barn. EN4 42 A7
Lancelot Pl, SW7 23 J4
Lancelot Rd, Ilf. IG6 65 H6
Welling DA16 158 A4
Wembley HA0 87 G5
Lance Rd, Har. HA1 67 J7
Lancer Sq, W8 22 A3
Lancey Cl, SE7
off Cleveley Cl 136 A4
Lanchester Rd, N6 73 J5
Lanchester Way, SE14 153 F1
Lancing Gdns, N9 60 C1
Lancing Rd, W13
off Drayton Grn Rd. 104/105 E7
Croydon CR0 187 F6
Ilford IG2 81 G6
Lancing St, NW1 9 H4
Lancresse Ct, N1 112 B1
Landcroft Rd, SE22 152 C6
Landells Rd, SE22 152 C6
Landford Rd, SW15 147 J3
Landgrove Rd, SW19 166 D5
Landmann Way, SE14 133 G6
Landmark Hts, E5 95 H4
Landon Pl, SW1 23 J5
Landons Cl, E14 134 C1
Landon Wk, E14
off Cottage St 114 B7
Landor Rd, SW9 150 E3
Landor Wk, W12 127 G2
Landport Way, SE15 37 G7
Landra Gdns, N21 43 H6
Landridge Rd, SW6 148 C2
Landrock Rd, N8 75 E6
Landscape Rd, Wdf.Grn. IG8 63 H7
Landseer Av, E12 98 D5
Landseer Cl, SW19
off Brangwyn Cres 185 F1
Edgware HA8 70 A2
Landseer Rd, N19 92 E3
Enfield EN1 44 D5
New Malden KT3 182 D7
Sutton SM1 198 D6
Landstead Rd, SE18 137 G7
Lane, The, NW8 6 C1
SE3 155 G3
Lane App, NW7 56 B5
Lane Cl, NW2 89 H3
Lane End, Bexh. DA7 159 H3
Lane Gdns, Esher (Clay.) KT10 194 C7
Lane Ms, E12
off Colchester Av. 98 C3
Lanercost Cl, SW2 169 G2
Lanercost Gdns, N14 42 E7
Lanercost Rd, SW2 169 G2
Lanesborough Pl, SW1 24 C3
Laneside, Chis. BR7 175 E5
Edgware HA8 54 C5
Laneside Av, Dag. RM8 83 F7
Laneway, SW15 147 H5
Lanfranc Rd, E3 113 H2
Lanfrey Pl, W14
off North End Rd. 128 C5
Langbourne Av, N6 92 A2
Langbourne Pl, E14 134 B5
Langbourne Way, Esher (Clay.) KT10 194 D6
Langbrook Rd, SE3 156 A3
Langcroft Cl, Cars. SM5 199 J3
Langdale Av, Mitch. CR4 185 J3
Langdale Cl, SE17 35 J5
SW14 146 B4
Dagenham RM8 100 C1
Orpington BR6
off Grasmere Rd 206/207 E3
Langdale Cres, Bexh. DA7 139 G7
Langdale Gdns, Grnf. UB6 105 E3
Langdale Rd, SE10 134 C7
Thornton Heath CR7 187 G4
Langdale St, E1
off Burslem St 112/113 E6
Langdon Ct, NW10 106 E1
Langdon Cres, E6 116 D2
Langdon Dr, NW9 88 C1
Langdon Pk, Tedd. TW11 163 F7
Langdon Pk Rd, N6 74 C7
Langdon Pl, SW14
off Rosemary La 146 C3
Langdon Rd, E6 116 D1
Bromley BR2 191 H3
Morden SM4 185 F5
Langdons Ct, Sthl. UB2 123 G3
Langdon Shaw, Sid. DA14 175 J5
Langdon Wk, Mord. SM4 185 F5
Langdon Way, SE1 37 J2
Langford Cl, E8 94 D5
N15 76 B6
NW8 6 D1
W3 126 B2
Langford Ct, NW8 6 C2
Langford Cres, Barn. EN4 41 J4
Langford Grn, SE5 152 B3
Langford Pl, NW8 6 D2
Sidcup DA14 176 A3
Langford Rd, SW6 149 E2
Barnet EN4 41 H4
Woodford Green IG8 63 J6
Langfords, Buck.H. IG9 64 A2
Langham Cl, N15
off Langham Rd 75 H3
Langham Dr, Rom. RM6 82 B6
Langham Gdns, N21 43 G5
W13 105 E7
Edgware HA8 54 C7
Richmond TW10 163 F4
Wembley HA0 87 F2
Langham Ho Cl, Rich. TW10 163 G4
Langham Pk Pl, Brom. BR2 191 F4
Langham Pl, N15 75 H3
W1 16 E2
W4 *off Hogarth Roundabout* 126/127 E6
Langham Rd, N15 75 H3
SW20 183 J1
Edgware HA8 54 C6
Teddington TW11 162 E5
Langham St, W1 17 E2
Langhedge Cl, N18
off Langhedge La 60 C6
Langhedge La, N18 60 C5
Langhedge La Ind Est, N18 60 C6
Langholm Cl, SW12
off King's Av 150 D7
Langholme, Bushey WD23 51 J1
Langhorn Dr, Twick. TW2 144 B7
Langhorne Rd, Dag. RM10 101 G7
Langland Cres, Stan. HA7 69 H3
Langland Dr, Pnr. HA5 50 E7
Langland Gdns, NW3 91 E5
Croydon CR0 203 J2
Langler Rd, NW10 107 J2
Langley Av, Ruis. HA4 84 B1
Surbiton KT6 195 G1
Worcester Park KT4 198 A2
Langley Ct, WC2 18 A5
Beckenham BR3 190 B5
Langley Cres, E11 79 J7
Dagenham RM9 100 C7
Edgware HA8 54 C3
Hayes UB3 121 J7
Langley Dr, E11 79 H7
W3 126 B1
Langley Gdns, Brom. BR2 191 J4
Dagenham RM9 100 C7
Orpington BR5 193 E6
Langley Gro, N.Mal. KT3 182 E2
Langley La, SW8 34 B5
Langley Meadow, Loug. IG10 49 G2
Langley Pk, NW7 54 E6
Langley Pk Rd, Sutt. SM1, SM2 199 F5
Langley Rd, SW19 184 C1
Beckenham BR3 189 H4
Isleworth TW7 144 C2
Surbiton KT6 181 H7
Welling DA16 138 C6
Langley Row, Barn. EN5 40 C1
Langley St, WC2 18 A4
Langley Way, W.Wick. BR4 204 D1
Langmead Dr, Bushey (Bushey Hth) WD23 52 A1
Langmead St, SE27
off Beadman St 169 H4
Langmore Ct, Bexh. DA6
off Regency Way 158 D3
Langridge Ms, Hmptn. TW12 *off Oak Av* 161 F6
Langroyd Rd, SW17 167 J2
Langside Av, SW15 147 G4
Langside Cres, N14 58 D3
Langston Hughes Cl, SE24
off Shakespeare Rd. 151 H4
Langston Rd, Loug. IG10 49 F5
Lang St, E1 113 F4
Langthorn Ct, EC2 20 B3
Langthorne Rd, E11 96 D3
Langthorne St, SW6 128 A7
Langton Av, E6 116 D3
N20 41 F7
Langton Cl, WC1 10 D4
Langton Ho, SW16
off Colson Way 168 C4
Langton Pl, SW18
off Merton Rd 166 D1
Langton Ri, SE23 152 E7
Langton Rd, NW2 89 J3
SW9 131 H7
Harrow HA3 51 J7
West Molesey KT8 179 J4
Langton St, SW10 30 D6
Langton Way, SE3 155 F1
Croydon CR0 202 B4
Langtry Pl, SW6
off Seagrave Rd 128 D6
Langtry Rd, NW8 108 E1
Northolt UB5 102 D2
Langtry Wk, NW8
off Alexandra Pl 91 F7
Langwood Chase, Tedd. TW11 163 F6
Langworth Dr, Hayes UB4 102 A6
Lanhill Rd, W9 108 D4
Lanier Rd, SE13 154 C6
Lanigan Dr, Houns. TW3 143 H5
Lankaster Gdns, N2 73 G1
Lankers Dr, Har. HA2 67 F6
Lankton Cl, Beck. BR3 190 C1
Lannock Rd, Hayes UB3 121 H1
Lannoy Rd, SE9 175 F1
Lanrick Rd, E14 114 D6
Lanridge Rd, SE2 138 D3
Lansbury Av, N18 60 A5
Barking IG11 100 A7
Feltham TW14 142 B6
Romford RM6 83 E5
Lansbury Cl, NW10 88 C5
Lansbury Est, E14 114 B6
Lansbury Gdns, E14 114 D6
Lansbury Rd, Enf. EN3 45 G1
Lansbury Way, N18 60 B5
Lanscombe Wk, SW8 150 E1
Lansdell Rd, Mitch. CR4 186 A2
Lansdowne Av, Bexh. DA7 138 D7
Orpington BR6 207 E1
Lansdowne Cl, SW20 166 A7
Surbiton KT5
off Kingston Rd. 196 B2
Twickenham TW1
off Lion Rd 162 C1
Lansdowne Copse, Wor.Pk. KT4 *off The Avenue* 197 G2
Lansdowne Ct, Wor.Pk. KT *off The Avenue* 197 G2
Lansdowne Cres, W11 108 B7
Lansdowne Dr, E8 94 D6
Lansdowne Gdns, SW8 150 E1
Lansdowne Grn, SW8
off Hartington Rd. 150/151 E1
Lansdowne Gro, NW10 89 E4
Lansdowne Hill, SE27 169 H3
Lansdowne La, SE7 136 A6
Lansdowne Ms, SE7 136 A5
W11 *off Lansdowne Rd.* 128 C1
Lansdowne Pl, SE1 28 C6
SE19 170 C7
Lansdowne Ri, W11 108 B7
Lansdowne Rd, E4 62 A2

Lansdowne Rd, E11 . . . . . . **97** F2
E17 . . . . **78** A5
E18 . . . . **79** G3
N3 . . . . **56** C7
N10 . . . . **74** C2
N17 . . . . **76** C1
SW20 . . . . **165** J7
W11 . . . . **108** B7
Bromley BR1 . . . . **173** G7
Croydon CR0 . . . . **202** A2
Epsom KT19 . . . . **196** C7
Harrow HA1 . . . . **68** B7
Hounslow TW3 . . . . **143** H3
Ilford IG3 . . . . **99** J1
Stanmore HA7 . . . . **53** F6
Lansdowne Row, W1 . . . . . **24** E1
Lansdowne Ter, WC1 . . . . . **10** B6
Lansdowne Wk, W11 . . . . **128** B1
Lansdowne Way, SW8 . . . **150** D1
Lansdowne Wd Cl, SE27 . **169** H3
Lansdown Rd, E7 . . . . **97** J7
Sidcup DA14 . . . . **176** B3
Lansfield Av, N18 . . . . **60** D4
Lantern Cl, SW15 . . . . **147** G4
Wembley HA0 . . . . **87** G5
Lanterns Ct, E14 . . . . **134** A2
Lantern Way, West Dr. UB7 . . . . **120** B2
Lant St, SE1 . . . . **27** J3
Lanvanor Rd, SE15 . . . . . . **153** F2
Lapford Cl, W9 . . . . **108** C4
Lapponum Wk, Hayes UB4 *off Lochan Cl* **102** D5
Lapse Wd Wk, SE23 . . . . . **170** E1
Lapstone Gdns, Har. HA3 . **69** F6
Lapwing Ct, Surb. KT6 *off Chaffinch Cl* **196** A3
Lapwing Twr, SE8 *off Abinger Gro* **133** J6
Lapwing Way, Hayes UB4 . **102** D6
Lara Cl, SE13 . . . . **154** C6
Chessington KT9 . . . . . . **195** H7
Larbert Rd, SW16 . . . . **186** C1
Larch Av, W3 . . . . **126** E1
Larch Cl, E13 . . . . **115** H4
N11 . . . . **58** A7
N19 *off Bredgar Rd* **92** C2
SE8 *off Clyde St* **133** J6
SW12 . . . . **168** B2
Larch Cres, Epsom KT19 . **196** B6
Hayes UB4 . . . . **102** C4
Larchdene, Orp. BR6 . . . . **206** D2
Larch Dr, W4 *off Gunnersbury Av* . . **126** A5
Larches, The, N13 . . . . **59** J3
Larches Av, SW14 . . . . **146** D4
Larch Grn, NW9 *off Clayton Fld* **70/71** E1
Larch Gro, Sid. DA15 . . . . **175** J1
Larch Rd, E10 *off Walnut Rd* **96** A2
NW2 . . . . **89** J4
Larch Tree Way, Croy. CR0 . **204** A3
Larch Way, Brom. BR2 . . . **192** D7
Larchwood Rd, SE9 . . . . . **175** E2
Larcombe Cl, Croy. CR0 . . **202** C4
Larcom St, SE17 . . . . **36** A2
Larden Rd, W3 . . . . **127** E1
Largewood Av, Surb. KT6 . **196** A2
Larissa St, SE17 . . . . **36** C3
Larkbere Rd, SE26 . . . . . . **171** H4
Larken Cl, Bushey WD23 *off Larken Dr* **51** J1
Larken Dr, Bushey WD23 . . **51** J1
Larkfield Av, Har. HA3 . . . . **69** E3
Larkfield Cl, Brom. BR2 . . **205** F2
Larkfield Rd, Rich. TW9 . . **145** H4
Sidcup DA14 . . . . **175** J3
Larkhall La, SW4 . . . . **150** D2
Larkhall Ri, SW4 . . . . **150** C3
Larkhill Ter, SE18 . . . . **156** D1
Lark Row, E2 . . . . **113** F1
Larksfield Gro, Enf. EN1 . . **45** E1
Larks Gro, Bark. IG11 *off Thornhill Gdns* **99** H7
Larkshall Ct, Rom. RM7 . . . **83** J2
Larkshall Cres, E4 . . . . **62** C4
Larkshall Rd, E4 . . . . **62** C5
Larkspur Cl, E6 . . . . **116** B5
N17 *off Fryatt Rd* **60** A7
NW9 . . . . **70** B5
Larkspur Gro, Edg. HA8 . . . **54** C4
Larkspur Way, Epsom KT19 . . . . **196** C5
Larkswood Ct, E4 . . . . **62** D5
Larkswood Leisure Pk, E4 . **62** C4
Larkswood Ri, Pnr. HA5 . . . **66** C4
Larkswood Rd, E4 . . . . **62** A4
Lark Way, Cars. SM5 . . . . **185** H7
Larkway Cl, NW9 . . . . **70** D4
Larnach Rd, W6 . . . . **128** A6
Larpent Av, SW15 . . . . . . **147** J5
Larwood Cl, Grnf. UB6 . . . . **86** A5
Lascelles Av, Har. HA1 . . . . **68** A7
Lascelles Cl, E11 . . . . **96** D2
Lascotts Rd, N22 . . . . **59** F6
Lassa Rd, SE9 . . . . **156** B5
Lassell St, SE10 . . . . **134** D5
Lasseter Pl, SE3 *off Vanbrugh Hill* **135** F6
Latchett Rd, E18 . . . . **79** H1
Latchingdon Ct, E17 . . . . . **77** G4
Latchingdon Gdns, Wdf.Grn. IG8 . . . . **64** B6
Latchmere Cl, Rich. TW10 . **163** H5
Latchmere La, Kings.T. KT2 . . . . **163** J6
Latchmere Pas, SW11 *off Cabul Rd* **149** H2
Latchmere Rd, SW11 . . . . **149** J2
Kingston upon Thames KT2 . . . . **163** H7
Latchmere St, SW11 . . . . **149** J2
Lateward Rd, Brent. TW8 . **125** G6
Latham Cl, E6 *off Oliver Gdns* **116** B6
Twickenham TW1 . . . . . **144** D7
Latham Ho, E1 . . . . **113** G6
Latham Rd, Bexh. DA6 . . . **159** G5
Twickenham TW1 . . . . . **144** C7
Lathams Way, Croy. CR0 . **201** F1
Lathkill Cl, Enf. EN1 . . . . . . **44** D7
Lathom Rd, E6 . . . . **98** C7
Latimer, SE17 . . . . **36** D4
Latimer Av, E6 . . . . **116** C1
Latimer Cl, Pnr. HA5 . . . . . **66** C1
Worcester Park KT4 . . . . **197** H4
Latimer Gdns, Pnr. HA5 . . . **66** C1
Latimer Pl, W10 . . . . **107** J6
Latimer Rd, E7 . . . . **97** H4
N15 . . . . **76** B6
SW19 . . . . **166** E6
W10 . . . . **107** J6
Barnet EN5 . . . . **40** E3
Croydon CR0 *off Abbey Rd* **201** H3
Teddington TW11 . . . . . . **162** C5
Latona Rd, SE15 . . . . **37** H6
La Tourne Gdns, Orp. BR6 . **207** F3
Lattimer Pl, W4 . . . . **127** E6
Latton Cl, Walt. KT12 . . . . **179** E7
Latymer Ct, W6 . . . . **128** A4
Latymer Rd, N9 . . . . **60** C1
Latymer Way, N9 . . . . **60** A2
Lauder Cl, Nthlt. UB5 . . . . **102** D2
Lauderdale Dr, Rich. TW10 . . . . **163** G3
Lauderdale Pl, EC2 *off Beech St* **111** J5
Lauderdale Rd, W9 . . . . **6** A4
Lauderdale Twr, EC2 . . . . . . **19** J1
Laud St, SE11 . . . . **34** C3
Croydon CR0 . . . . **201** J3
Laughton Ct, Borwd. WD6 *off Banks Rd* **38** D2
Laughton Rd, Nthlt. UB5 . **102** D1
Launcelot Rd, Brom. BR1 . **173** G4
Launcelot St, SE1 . . . . **26** E4
Launceston Gdns, Grnf. UB6 . . . . **105** F1
Launceston Pl, W8 . . . . **22** C5
Launceston Rd, Grnf. UB6 . . . . **105** F1
Launch St, E14 . . . . **134** C3
Laundress La, N16 . . . . **94** D3
Laundry La, N1 *off Greenman St* **111** J1
Laundry Ms, SE23 . . . . . . **153** H7
Laundry Rd, W6 . . . . **128** B6
Launton Dr, Bexh. DA6 . . **158** D4
Laura Cl, E11 . . . . **79** J5
Enfield EN1 . . . . **44** B5
Lauradale Rd, N2 . . . . **73** J4
Laura Pl, E5 . . . . **95** F4
Laurel Av, Twick. TW1 . . . . **162** C1
Laurel Bk Gdns, SW6 *off New Kings Rd* **148** C2
Laurel Bk Rd, Enf. EN2 . . . . **43** J1
Laurel Bk Vil, W7 *off Lower Boston Rd* . . **124** B1
Laurel Cl, N19 *off Hargrave Pk* **92** C2
SW17 . . . . **167** H5
Ilford IG6 . . . . **65** F6
Sidcup DA14 . . . . **176** A3
Laurel Cres, Croy. CR0 . . . **204** A3
Laurel Dr, N21 . . . . **43** G7
Laurel Gdns, E4 . . . . **46** B7
Laurel Gdns, NW7 . . . . **54** D3
W7 . . . . **124** B1
Bromley BR1 . . . . **192** B4
Hounslow TW4 . . . . **142** E4
Laurel Gro, SE20 . . . . **171** E7
SE26 . . . . **171** G4
Laurel La, West Dr. UB7 . . **120** B4
Laurel Manor, Sutt. SM2 *off Devonshire Rd* **199** F7
Laurel Pk, Har. HA3 . . . . . . **52** C7
Laurel Rd, SW13 . . . . **147** G2
SW20 . . . . **183** H1
Hampton (Hmptn H.) TW12 . . . . **162** A5
Laurel St, E8 . . . . **94** C6
Laurel Vw, N12 . . . . **56** E3
Laurel Way, E18 . . . . **79** F4
N20 . . . . **56** D3
Laurence Ms, W12 *off Askew Rd* **127** G2
Laurence Pountney Hill, EC4 . . . . **20** B5
Laurence Pountney La, EC4 . . . . **20** B5
Laurie Gro, SE14 . . . . **153** H1
Laurie Rd, W7 . . . . **104** B5
Laurier Rd, NW5 . . . . **92** B3
Croydon CR0 . . . . **188** C7
Laurimel Cl, Stan. HA7 *off September Way* . **52/53** E6
Laurino Pl, Bushey (Bushey Hth) WD23 . . . . **51** J2
Lauriston Rd, E9 . . . . **113** G1
SW19 . . . . **166** A6
Lausanne Rd, N8 . . . . **75** G4
SE15 . . . . **153** F1
Lavell St, N16 . . . . **94** A4
Lavender Av, NW9 . . . . **88** C1
Mitcham CR4 . . . . **185** H1
Worcester Park KT4 . . . . **197** J3
Lavender Cl, SW3 . . . . **31** F6
Bromley BR2 . . . . **192** B6
Carshalton SM5 . . . . **200** A4
Lavender Ct, W.Mol. KT8 *off Molesham Way* . . **179** H3
Lavender Gdns, SW11 . . . **149** J4
Enfield EN2 . . . . **43** H1
Harrow HA3 *off Uxbridge Rd* **52** B6
Lavender Gro, E8 . . . . **94** C7
Mitcham CR4 . . . . **185** H1
Lavender Hill, SW11 . . . . . **149** H4
Enfield EN2 . . . . **43** G1
Lavender Pl, Ilf. IG1 . . . . . . **98** E5
Lavender Ri, West Dr. UB7 . . . . **120** D2
Lavender Rd, SE16 . . . . . . **133** H1
SW11 . . . . **149** G3
Carshalton SM5 . . . . **200** A4
Croydon CR0 . . . . **187** F6
Enfield EN2 . . . . **44** A1
Epsom KT19 . . . . **196** B5
Sutton SM1 . . . . **199** G4
Lavender St, E15 *off Manbey Gro* **96/97** E6
Lavender Sweep, SW11 . . **149** J4
Lavender Ter, SW11 *off Falcon Rd* **149** H3
Lavender Vale, Wall. SM6 . **200** D6
Lavender Wk, SW11 . . . . . **149** J4
Mitcham CR4 . . . . **186** A3
Lavender Way, Croy. CR0 . **189** G6
Lavengro Rd, SE27 . . . . . . **169** J2
Lavenham Rd, SW18 . . . . **166** C2
Lavernock Rd, Bexh. DA7 . **159** G2
Lavers Rd, N16 . . . . **94** B3
Laverstoke Gdns, SW15 . . **147** G7
Laverton Ms, SW5 . . . . **30** B2
Laverton Pl, SW5 . . . . **30** B2
Lavidge Rd, SE9 . . . . **174** B2
Lavina Gro, N1 . . . . **10** C1
Lavington Cl, E9 *off Beanacre Cl* **95** J6
Lavington Rd, W13 . . . . . . **125** E1
Croydon CR0 . . . . **201** F3
Lavington St, SE1 . . . . **27** H2
Lawdons Gdns, Croy. CR0 . . . . **201** H4
Lawford Rd, N1 . . . . **94** B7
NW5 . . . . **92** C6
W4 . . . . **126** C7
Law Ho, Bark. IG11 . . . . . . **118** A2
Lawless St, E14 . . . . **114** B7
Lawley Rd, N14 . . . . **42** B7
Lawley St, E5 . . . . **95** F4
Lawn, The, Sthl. UB2 . . . . **123** G5
Lawn Cl, N9 . . . . **44** C7
Bromley BR1 . . . . **173** H6
New Malden KT3 . . . . . **182** E2
Lawn Cres, Rich. TW9 . . . . **146** A2
Lawn Fm Gro, Rom. RM6 . **82** E4
Lawnfield, NW2 *off Coverdale Rd* **90** A7
Lawn Gdns, W7 . . . . **124** B1
Lawn Ho Cl, E14 . . . . **134** C2
Lawn La, SW8 . . . . **34** B6
Lawn Rd, NW3 . . . . **91** J5
Beckenham BR3 . . . . . . **171** J7
Lawns, The, E4 . . . . **62** A5
SE3 *off Lee Ter* **154/155** E3
SE19 . . . . **188** A1
Pinner HA5 . . . . **51** H7
Sidcup DA14 . . . . **176** B4
Sutton SM2 . . . . **198** B7
Lawns Ct, Wem. HA9 *off The Avenue* **87** J2
Lawnside, SE3 . . . . **155** F4
Lawn Ter, SE3 . . . . **155** E3
Lawn Vale, Pnr. HA5 . . . . . . **66** D2
Lawrence Av, E12 . . . . **98** D4
E17 . . . . **77** G1
N13 . . . . **59** H4
NW7 . . . . **55** E4
NW10 . . . . **106** D1
New Malden KT3 . . . . . **182** D6
Lawrence Bldgs, N16 . . . . . **94** C3
Lawrence Campe Cl, N20 *off Friern Barnet La* **57** G3
Lawrence Cl, E3 . . . . **114** A2
N15 *off Lawrence Rd* . . . **76** B3
Lawrence Ct, NW7 . . . . **55** E5
Lawrence Cres, Dag. RM10 . . . . **101** H3
Edgware HA8 . . . . **70** A2
Lawrence Gdns, NW7 . . . . **55** F3
Lawrence Hill, E4 . . . . **62** A2
Lawrence La, EC2 . . . . **20** A4
Lawrence Pl, N1 *off Outram Pl* **110/111** E1
Lawrence Rd, E6 . . . . **116** A1
E13 . . . . **115** H1
N15 . . . . **76** B4
N18 . . . . **60** E4
SE25 . . . . **188** C4
W5 . . . . **125** G4
Erith DA8 . . . . **139** H7
Hampton TW12 . . . . **161** F7
Hounslow TW4 . . . . **142** C4
Pinner HA5 . . . . **66** D5
Richmond TW10 . . . . . . **163** F4
West Wickham BR4 . . . . **205** G4
Lawrence St, E16 . . . . **115** F5
NW7 . . . . **55** F4
SW3 . . . . **31** G6
Lawrence Way, NW10 . . . . **88** C3
Lawrence Weaver Cl, Mord. SM4 *off Green La* **184** D6
Lawrie Pk Av, SE26 . . . . . **171** E5
Lawrie Pk Cres, SE26 . . . . **171** E5
Lawrie Pk Gdns, SE26 . . . **171** E4
Lawrie Pk Rd, SE26 . . . . . **171** E6
Laws Cl, SE25 . . . . **188** A4
Lawson Cl, E16 . . . . **115** J5
SW19 . . . . **166** A3
Lawson Est, SE1 . . . . **28** B6
Lawson Gdns, Pnr. HA5 . . . . **66** B3
Lawson Rd, Enf. EN3 . . . . . **45** F1
Southall UB1 . . . . **103** F4
Law St, SE1 . . . . **28** C5
Lawton Rd, E3 . . . . **113** H3
E10 . . . . **96** C1
Barnet EN4 . . . . **41** G3
Loughton IG10 . . . . **48** E3
Laxcon Cl, NW10 . . . . **88** C5
Laxey Rd, Orp. BR6 . . . . . **207** J6
Laxley Cl, SE5 . . . . **35** H7
Laxton Pl, NW1 . . . . **9** E5
Layard Rd, SE16 . . . . **133** E4
Enfield EN1 . . . . **44** C1
Thornton Heath CR7 . . . **188** A2
Layard Sq, SE16 . . . . **133** E4
Laycock St, N1 . . . . **93** G6
Layer Gdns, W3 . . . . **106** A7
Layfield Cl, NW4 . . . . **71** H7
Layfield Cres, NW4 . . . . . . **71** H7
Layfield Rd, NW4 . . . . **71** H7
Layhams Rd, Kes. BR2 . . **205** F5
West Wickham BR4 . . . . **204** D3
Laymarsh Cl, Belv. DA17 . . . . **139** F3
Laymead Cl, Nthlt. UB5 . . . **84** E6
Laystall St, EC1 . . . . **10** E6
Layton Cres, Croy. CR0 . . **201** G5
Layton Pl, Rich. TW9 *off Station Av* **146** A1
Layton Rd, Brent. TW8 . . . **125** G5
Hounslow TW3 . . . . **143** H4
Laytons Bldgs, SE1 . . . . . . **28** A3

Layzell Wk, SE9
off Mottingham La . . . 174 A1
Lazar Wk, N7
off Briset Way . . . 93 F2
Leabank Cl, Har. HA1 . . . 86 B3
Leabank Sq, E9 . . . 96 A6
Leabank Vw, N15 . . . 76 D6
Leabourne Rd, N16 . . . 76 D6
LEA BRIDGE, E5 . . . 95 G3
Lea Br Business Cen, E10
off Burwell Rd . . . 95 H1
Lea Br Rd, E5 . . . 95 F3
E10 . . . 95 H1
E17 . . . 78 D4
Lea Cl, Twick. TW2 . . . 143 F7
Leacroft Av, SW12 . . . 149 J7
Leadale Av, E4 . . . 62 A2
Leadale Rd, N15 . . . 76 D6
N16 . . . 76 D6
Leadbeaters Cl, N11
off Goldsmith Rd . . . 57 J5
★**Leadenhall Mkt**, EC3 . . . 20 D4
Leadenhall Pl, EC3 . . . 20 D4
Leadenhall St, EC3 . . . 20 D4
Leadenham Ct, E3
off Spanby Rd . . . 114 A4
Leader Av, E12 . . . 98 D5
Leadings, The, Wem. HA9 . 88 C3
Leaf Cl, T.Ditt. KT7 . . . 180 B5
Leaf Gro, SE27 . . . 169 G5
Leafield Cl, SW16 . . . 169 H6
Leafield La, Sid. DA14 . . . 177 F4
Leafield Rd, SW20 . . . 184 C3
Sutton SM1 . . . 198 D2
Leafy Gro, Kes. BR2 . . . 205 J5
Leafy Oak Rd, SE12 . . . 173 J3
Leafy Way, Croy. CR0 . . . 202 C2
Lea Gdns, Wem. HA9 . . . 87 H4
Leagrave St, E5 . . . 95 F3
Lea Hall Rd, E10 . . . 96 A1
Leahurst Rd, SE13 . . . 154 D5
Leake St, SE1 . . . 26 D3
Lealand Rd, N15 . . . 76 C6
Leamington Av, E17 . . . 78 A5
Bromley BR1 . . . 173 J5
Morden SM4 . . . 184 C4
Orpington BR6 . . . 207 H4
Leamington Cl, E12 . . . 98 B5
Bromley BR1 . . . 173 J5
Hounslow TW3 . . . 143 J5
Leamington Cres, Har.
HA2 . . . 85 E3
Leamington Gdns, Ilf. IG3 . 99 J2
Leamington Pk, W3 . . . 106 D5
Leamington Rd, Sthl.
UB2 . . . 122 D4
Leamington Rd Vil, W11 . . 108 C5
Leamore St, W6 . . . 127 H4
Leamouth Rd, E6
off Remington Rd . . . 116 B6
E14 . . . 114 D6
Leander Ct, SE8 . . . 154 A1
Leander Rd, SW2 . . . 151 F6
Northolt UB5 . . . 103 G2
Thornton Heath CR7 . . . 187 F4
Learner Dr, Har. HA2 . . . 85 G2
Lea Rd, Beck. BR3
off Fairfield Rd . . . 190 A2
Enfield EN2 . . . 44 A1
Southall UB2 . . . 122 E4
Learoyd Gdns, E6 . . . 116 D7
Leas Cl, Chess. KT9 . . . 195 J7
Leas Dale, SE9 . . . 174 D3
Leas Grn, Chis. BR7 . . . 175 J6
Leaside Av, N10 . . . 74 A3
Leaside Rd, E5 . . . 95 F1
Leasowes Rd, E10 . . . 96 A1
Lea Sq, E3
off Lefevre Wk . . . 113 J1
Leatherbottle Grn, Erith
DA18 . . . 139 F3
Leather Bottle La, Belv.
DA17 . . . 139 E4
Leather Cl, Mitch. CR4 . . . 186 A2
Leatherdale St, E1
off Portelet Rd . . . 113 G4
Leather Gdns, E15
off Abbey Rd . . . 114/115 E1
Leatherhead Cl, N16 . . . 94 C1
Leather La, EC1 . . . 19 F2
★**Leather Mkt Bermondsey**,
SE1 . . . 28 D4
Leathermarket Ct, SE1 . . . 28 D4
Leathermarket St, SE1 . . . 28 D4
Leathersellers Cl, Barn. EN5
off The Avenue . . . 40 B4
Leathsail Rd, Har. HA2 . . . 85 H3
Leathwaite Rd, SW11 . . . 149 J4
Leathwell Rd, SE8 . . . 154 B2
Lea Valley Rd, E4 . . . 45 G5
Enfield EN3 . . . 45 G5
Lea Valley Trd Est, N18 . . . 61 G5
Lea Valley Viaduct, E4 . . . 61 G5
N18 . . . 61 G5
Lea Valley Wk, E3 . . . 114 C4
E5 . . . 95 H3
E9 . . . 95 H3
E10 . . . 95 H3
E14 . . . 114 B5
E15 . . . 114 C3
E17 . . . 77 F1
N9 . . . 61 H1
N15 . . . 76 D6
N16 . . . 76 D6
N17 . . . 77 F1
N18 . . . 77 F1
Enfield EN3 . . . 45 J3
Leaveland Cl, Beck. BR3 . . 190 A4
Leaver Gdns, Grnf. UB6 . . 104 A2
Leavesden Rd, Stan. HA7 . 52 D6
Lea Vw Hos, E5
off Springfield . . . 94/95 E1
Leaway, E10 . . . 95 G1
Lebanon Av, Felt. TW13 . . 160 D5
Lebanon Ct, Twick. TW1 . . 144 E7
Lebanon Gdns, SW18 . . . 148 D6
Lebanon Pk, Twick. TW1 . . 144 E7
Lebanon Rd, SW18 . . . 148 D5
Croydon CR0 . . . 202 B1
Lebrun Sq, SE3 . . . 155 H3
Lechmere App, Wdf.Grn.
IG8 . . . 79 J2
Lechmere Av, Chig. IG7 . . . 65 F4
Woodford Green IG8 . . . 80 A2
Lechmere Rd, NW2 . . . 89 H6
Leckford Rd, SW18 . . . 167 F2
Leckwith Av, Bexh. DA7 . . 138 E6
Lecky St, SW7 . . . 31 E3
Leclair Ho, SE3
off Gallus Sq . . . 155 H3
Leconfield Av, SW13 . . . 147 F3
Leconfield Rd, N5 . . . 94 A4
Leda Av, Enf. EN3 . . . 45 G1
Leda Rd, SE18 . . . 136 C3
Ledbury Est, SE15 . . . 132 E7
Ledbury Ms N, W11
off Ledbury Rd . . . 108 D7
Ledbury Ms W, W11
off Ledbury Rd . . . 108 D7
Ledbury Pl, Croy. CR0 . . . 201 J4
Ledbury Rd, W11 . . . 108 C6
Croydon CR0 . . . 201 J4
Ledbury St, SE15 . . . 37 J7
Ledrington Rd, SE19 . . . 170 D6
Ledway Dr, Wem. HA9 . . . 69 J7
LEE, SE12 . . . 154 E4
Lee Av, Rom. RM6 . . . 82 E6
Lee Br, SE13 . . . 154 C3
Leechcroft Av, Sid. DA15 . 157 J5
Leechcroft Rd, Wall. SM6 . 200 A3
Lee Ch St, SE13 . . . 155 E4
Lee Cl, E17 . . . 77 G1
Barnet EN5 . . . 41 F4
Lee Conservancy Rd, E9 . . 95 J5
Leecroft Rd, Barn. EN5 . . . 40 B5
Leeds Pl, N4
off Tollington Pk . . . 93 F2
Leeds Rd, Ilf. IG1 . . . 99 G1
Leeds St, N18 . . . 60 D5
Leefern Rd, W12 . . . 127 G2
Leegate, SE12 . . . 155 F5
Lee Grn, SE12
off Lee High Rd . . . 155 F5
Lee Gro, Chig. IG7 . . . 64 D2
Lee High Rd, SE12 . . . 154 D3
SE13 . . . 154 D3
Leeke St, WC1 . . . 10 C3
Leeland Rd, W13 . . . 124 D1
Leeland Ter, W13 . . . 124 D1
Leeland Way, NW10 . . . 89 F4
Lee Pk, SE3 . . . 155 F4
Lee Pk Way, N9 . . . 61 G4
N18 . . . 61 G4
Leerdam Dr, E14 . . . 134 C3
Lee Rd, NW7 . . . 56 A7
SE3 . . . 155 F3
SW19 . . . 185 E1
Enfield EN1 . . . 44 D6
Greenford UB6 . . . 105 F1
Lees, The, Croy. CR0 . . . 203 J2
Leeside, Barn. EN5 . . . 40 B5
Leeside Ct, SE16
off Rotherhithe St . . . 133 G1
Leeside Cres, NW11 . . . 72 C6
Leeside Rd, N17 . . . 61 E6
Leeson Rd, SE24 . . . 151 G4
Leesons Hill, Chis. BR7 . . 193 H3
Leesons Way, Orp. BR5 . . 193 J2
Lees Pl, W1 . . . 16 B5
Lee St, E8 . . . 112 C1
Lee Ter, SE3 . . . 154 E3
SE13 . . . 154 E3
Lee Valley Pathway, E9 . . 95 J3
E10 . . . 77 F7
E17 . . . 77 F7
Lee Valley Technopark, N17 . 76 D3
Lee Vw, Enf. EN2 . . . 43 H1
Leeward Gdns, SW19 . . . 166 C6
Leeway, SE8 . . . 133 J5
Leeway Cl, Pnr. HA5 . . . 51 F7
Leewood Cl, SE12
off Upwood Rd . . . 155 F6
Lefevre Wk, E3 . . . 113 J1
Lefroy Rd, W12 . . . 127 F2
Legard Rd, N5 . . . 93 H3
Legatt Rd, SE9 . . . 156 A5
Leggatt Rd, E15 . . . 114 C2
Legge St, SE13 . . . 154 C5
Leghorn Rd, NW10 . . . 107 F2
SE18 . . . 137 G5
Legion Cl, N1 . . . 93 G6
Legion Ct, Mord. SM4 . . . 184 D6
Legion Rd, Grnf. UB6 . . . 103 J1
Legion Ter, E3
off Lefevre Wk . . . 113 J1
Legion Way, N12 . . . 57 H7
Legon Av, Rom. RM7 . . . 101 J1
Legrace Av, Houns. TW4 . 142 D2
Leicester Av, Mitch. CR4 . 187 E4
Leicester Cl, Wor.Pk. KT4 . 197 J4
Leicester Ct, WC2 . . . 17 J5
Leicester Gdns, Ilf. IG3 . . . 81 H7
Leicester Ms, N2
off Leicester Rd . . . 73 H3
Leicester Pl, WC2 . . . 17 J5
Leicester Rd, E11 . . . 79 H5
N2 . . . 73 H3
Barnet EN5 . . . 40 E5
Croydon CR0 . . . 188 B7
Leicester Sq, WC2 . . . 17 J6
Leicester St, WC2 . . . 17 J5
Leigh, The, Kings.T. KT2 . . 164 E6
Leigham Av, SW16 . . . 169 E3
Leigham Ct, Wall. SM6
off Stafford Rd . . . 200 C6
Leigham Ct Rd, SW16 . . . 169 E2
Leigham Dr, Islw. TW7 . . . 124 B7
Leigham Vale, SW2 . . . 169 F3
SW16 . . . 169 F3
Leigh Av, Ilf. IG4 . . . 80 A4
Leigh Cl, N.Mal. KT3 . . . 182 D4
Leigh Ct, SE4
off Lewisham Way . . . 154 A2
Borehamwood WD6
off Banks Rd . . . 38 D2
Harrow HA2 . . . 86 B1
Leigh Cres, Croy.
(New Adgtn) CR0 . . . 204 B7
Leigh Gdns, NW10 . . . 107 J2
Leigh Hunt Dr, N14 . . . 58 D1
Leigh Hunt St, SE1 . . . 27 J3
Leigh Orchard Cl, SW16 . . 169 F3
Leigh Pl, EC1 . . . 19 E1
Feltham TW13 . . . 160 C1
Welling DA16 . . . 158 A2
Leigh Rd, E6 . . . 98 D6
E10 . . . 78 C7
N5 . . . 93 H4
Hounslow TW3 . . . 144 A4
Leigh Rodd, Wat. WD19 . . . 51 F3
Leigh St, WC1 . . . 10 A5
Leighton Av, E12 . . . 98 D5
Pinner HA5 . . . 66 E3
Leighton Cl, Edg. HA8 . . . 70 A2
Leighton Cres, NW5
off Leighton Gro . . . 92 C5
Leighton Gdns, NW10 . . . 107 H2
Leighton Gro, NW5 . . . 92 C5
★**Leighton Ho Mus**, W14 . 128 C3
Leighton Pl, NW5 . . . 92 C5
Leighton Rd, NW5 . . . 92 D5
W13 . . . 124 D2
Enfield EN1 . . . 44 C5
Harrow (Har.Wld) HA3 . . 68 A2
Leighton St, Croy. CR0 . . . 201 H1
Leila Parnell Pl, SE7 . . . 135 J6
Leinster Av, SW14 . . . 146 C3
Leinster Gdns, W2 . . . 14 C4
Leinster Ms, W2 . . . 14 C5
Leinster Pl, W2 . . . 14 C4
Leinster Rd, N10 . . . 74 B4
Leinster Sq, W2 . . . 108 D6
Leinster Ter, W2 . . . 14 C5
Leisure Way, N12 . . . 57 G7
Leith Cl, NW9 . . . 88 D1
Leithcote Gdns, SW16 . . . 169 F4
Leithcote Path, SW16 . . . 169 F3
Leith Rd, N22 . . . 75 H1
Leith Yd, NW6
off Quex Rd . . . 108 D1
Lela Av, Houns. TW4 . . . 142 C2
Lelitia Cl, E8
off Pownall Rd . . . 112 D1
Leman St, E1 . . . 21 G4
Lemark Cl, Stan. HA7 . . . 53 F5
Le May Av, SE12 . . . 173 H3
Lemmon Rd, SE10 . . . 134 E6
Lemna Rd, E11 . . . 79 E7
Lemonwell Ct, SE9
off Lemonwell Dr . . . 157 F5
Lemonwell Dr, SE9 . . . 157 F5
Lemsford Cl, N15 . . . 76 D5
Lemsford Ct, N4
off Brownswood Rd . . . 93 J2
Borehamwood WD6 . . . 38 C4
Lemuel St, SW18 . . . 149 E6
Lena Cres, N9 . . . 61 F2
Lena Gdns, W6 . . . 127 J3
Lena Kennedy Cl, E4 . . . 62 B6
Lenanton Steps, E14
off Manilla St . . . 134 A2
Lendal Ter, SW4 . . . 150 D3
Lenelby Rd, Surb. KT6 . . . 196 A1
Len Freeman Pl, SW6
off John Smith Av . . . 128 C7
Lenham Rd, SE12 . . . 155 F4
Bexleyheath DA7 . . . 139 F6
Sutton SM1 . . . 199 E4
Thornton Heath CR7 . . . 188 A2
Lennard Av, W.Wick. BR4 . 205 E2
Lennard Cl, W.Wick. BR4 . 205 E2
Lennard Rd, SE20 . . . 171 F6
Beckenham BR3 . . . 171 G6
Bromley BR2 . . . 206 C1
Croydon CR0 . . . 201 J1
Lennon Rd, NW2 . . . 89 J5
Lennox Gdns, NW10 . . . 89 F4
SW1 . . . 23 J6
Croydon CR0 . . . 201 H4
Ilford IG1 . . . 98 C1
Lennox Gdns Ms, SW1 . . . 23 J6
Lennox Rd, E17 . . . 77 J6
N4 . . . 93 F2
Lenor Cl, Bexh. DA6 . . . 159 E4
Lensbury Way, SE2 . . . 138 C3
Lens Rd, E7 . . . 97 J7
Lenthall Rd, E8 . . . 94 D7
Loughton IG10 . . . 49 G4
Lenthorp Rd, SE10 . . . 135 F4
Lentmead Rd, Brom. BR1 . 173 F3
Lenton Path, SE18 . . . 137 G6
Lenton Ri, Rich. TW9
off Evelyn Ter . . . 145 H3
Lenton St, SE18 . . . 137 G4
Leof Cres, SE6 . . . 172 B5
Leominster Rd, Mord.
SM4 . . . 185 F6
Leominster Wk, Mord.
SM4 . . . 185 F6
Leonard Av, Mord. SM4 . . 185 F5
Leonard Pl, N16
off Allen Rd . . . 94 B4
Leonard Rd, E4 . . . 62 A6
E7 . . . 97 G4
N9 . . . 60 C3
SW16 . . . 186 C1
Southall UB2 . . . 122 D3
Leonard Robbins Path,
SE28 *off Tawney Rd* . . . 118 B7
Leonard St, E16 . . . 136 B1
EC2 . . . 12 C5
Leontine Cl, SE15 . . . 132 D7
Leopards Ct, EC1 . . . 19 E1
Leopold Av, SW19 . . . 166 C5
Leopold Ms, E9
off Fremont St . . . 113 F1
Leopold Rd, E17 . . . 78 A5
N2 . . . 73 G3
N18 . . . 61 E5
NW10 . . . 89 E7
SW19 . . . 166 C4
W5 . . . 125 J1
Leopold St, E3 . . . 113 J5
Leopold Ter, SW19
off Dora Rd . . . 166 D5
Leo St, SE15 . . . 133 E7
Leo Yd, EC1 . . . 11 H6
Leppoc Rd, SW4 . . . 150 D5
Leroy St, SE1 . . . 36 D1
Lerry Cl, W14
off Thaxton Rd . . . 128 C6
Lescombe Cl, SE23 . . . 171 H3
Lescombe Rd, SE23 . . . 171 H3
Lesley Cl, Bex. DA5 . . . 159 H7
Leslie Gdns, Sutt. SM2 . . . 198 D7
Leslie Gro, Croy. CR0 . . . 202 B1

Leslie Gro Pl, Croy. CR0
off Leslie Gro 202 A1
Leslie Pk Rd, Croy. CR0 . . 202 B1
Leslie Rd, E11 . . . . 96 C4
E16 . . . . 115 H6
N2 . . . . 73 G3
Leslie Smith Sq, SE18
off Nightingale Vale . . . 136 D6
★Lesnes Abbey (ruins),
Erith DA18 . . . . 138 D4
Lessar Av, SW4 . . . . 150 C5
Lessingham Av, SW17 . . . 167 J4
Ilford IG5 . . . . 80 D3
Lessing St, SE23 . . . . 153 H7
Lessington Av, Rom. RM7 . 83 J6
Lessness Av, Bexh. DA7 . . 138 D7
LESSNESS HEATH, Belv.
DA17 . . . . 139 H5
Lessness Pk, Belv. DA17 . 139 F5
Lessness Rd, Belv. DA17
off Stapley Rd 139 G5
Morden SM4 . . . . 185 F6
Lester Av, E15 . . . . 115 E3
Leswin Pl, N16
off Leswin Rd 94 C3
Leswin Rd, N16 . . . . 94 C3
Letchford Gdns, NW10 . . . 107 G3
Letchford Ms, NW10
off Letchford Gdns . . . 107 G3
Letchford Ter, Har. HA3 . . . 67 H1
Letchworth Av, Felt. TW14 . 141 J7
Letchworth Cl, Brom.
BR2 . . . . 191 G5
Watford WD19 . . . . 50 D5
Letchworth Dr, Brom.
BR2 . . . . 191 G5
Letchworth St, SW17 . . . . 167 J4
Lethbridge Cl, SE13 . . . . . 154 C1
Letterstone Rd, SW6
off Varna Rd 128 C7
Lettice St, SW6 . . . . 148 C1
Lett Rd, E15 . . . . 96 D7
Lettsom St, SE5 . . . . 152 B2
Lettsom Wk, E13 . . . . 115 G2
Leucha Rd, E17 . . . . 77 H5
Levana Cl, SW19 . . . . 166 B1
Levehurst Way, SW4 . . . . 150 E2
Leven Cl, Wat. WD19 . . . . . 50 D5
Levendale Rd, SE23 . . . . . 171 H2
Leven Rd, E14 . . . . 114 C5
Leverett St, SW3 . . . . 31 H1
Leverholme Gdns, SE9 . . . 174 D3
Leverson St, SW16 . . . . . 168 C6
Lever St, EC1 . . . . 11 H4
Leverton Pl, NW5
off Leverton St 92 C5
Leverton St, NW5 . . . . 92 C5
Levett Gdns, Ilf. IG3 . . . . . 99 J4
Levett Rd, Bark. IG11 . . . . 99 H6
Levine Gdns, Bark. IG11 . . 118 D2
Levison Way, N19
off Grovedale Rd 92 D2
Lewes Cl, Nthlt. UB5 . . . . . 85 G6
Lewesdon Cl, SW19 . . . . . 166 A1
Lewes Rd, N12 . . . . 57 H5
Bromley BR1 . . . . 192 A2
Leweston Pl, N16 . . . . 76 C7
Lewey Ho, E3 . . . . 113 J4
Lewgars Av, NW9 . . . . 70 C6
Lewin Rd, SW14 . . . . 146 D3
SW16 . . . . 168 D6
Bexleyheath DA6 . . . . . 159 E4
Lewis Av, E17 . . . . 78 A1
Lewis Cl, N14
off Orchid Rd 42 C7
Lewis Cres, NW10 . . . . 88 C5
Lewis Gdns, N2 . . . . 73 G2
Lewis Gro, SE13 . . . . 154 C3
LEWISHAM, SE13 . . . . . . 154 B4
Lewisham Cen, SE13 . . . . 154 C3
Lewisham High St, SE13 . 154 C3
Lewisham Hill, SE13 . . . . 154 C2
Lewisham Pk, SE13 . . . . . 154 B6
Lewisham Rd, SE13 . . . . . 154 B1
Lewisham St, SW1 . . . . 25 J4
Lewisham Way, SE4 . . . . . 153 J1
SE14 . . . . 153 J1
Lewis Pl, E8 . . . . 94 D5
Lewis Rd, Mitch. CR4 . . . . 185 G2
Richmond TW10
off Red Lion St 145 G5
Sidcup DA14 . . . . 176 C3
Southall UB1 . . . . 123 E2
Sutton SM1 . . . . 199 E4
Welling DA16 . . . . 158 C3
Lewis St, NW1 . . . . 92 B6
Lewiston Cl, Wor.Pk. KT4 . 183 H7
Lewis Way, Dag. RM10 . . . 101 H6
Lexden Dr, Rom. RM6 . . . . 82 B6
Lexden Rd, W3 . . . . 106 B7
Mitcham CR4 . . . . 186 D4
Lexham Ct, Grnf. UB6 . . . 104 A1
Lexham Gdns, W8 . . . . 30 A1
Lexham Gdns Ms, W8 . . . . 22 B6
Lexham Ho, Bark. IG11
off St. Margarets 117 G1
Lexham Ms, W8 . . . . 128 D4
Lexham Wk, W8 . . . . 22 B6
Lexington, The, EC1 . . . . . . 12 B5
Lexington St, W1 . . . . 17 G4
Lexington Way, Barn. EN5 . 40 A4
Lexton Gdns, SW12 . . . . . 168 D1
Leyborne Av, W13 . . . . 125 E2
Leyborne Pk, Rich. TW9 . . 146 A1
Leybourne Cl, Brom. BR2 . 191 G6
Leybourne Rd, E11 . . . . 97 F1
NW1 . . . . 92 B7
NW9 . . . . 70 A5
Leybourne St, NW1
off Hawley St 92 B7
Leybridge Ct, SE12 . . . . . 155 G5
Leyburn Cl, E17
off Church La 78 B4
Leyburn Gdns, Croy. CR0 . 202 B2
Leyburn Gro, N18 . . . . 60 D6
Leyburn Rd, N18 . . . . 60 D6
Leycroft Cl, Loug. IG10 . . . 48 D5
Leyden St, E1 . . . . 21 F2
Leydon Cl, SE16
off Lagado Ms 133 G1
Leyfield, Wor.Pk. KT4 . . . 197 E1
Leyland Av, Enf. EN3 . . . . . 45 H2
Leyland Gdns, Wdf.Grn.
IG8 . . . . 63 J5
Leyland Rd, SE12 . . . . . . 155 G5
Leylang Rd, SE14 . . . . . . 133 G7
Leys, The, N2 . . . . 73 F4
Harrow HA3 . . . . 69 J6
Leys Av, Dag. RM10 . . . . . 101 J7
Leys Cl, Dag. RM10 . . . . . 101 J7
Harrow HA1 . . . . 68 A5
Leysdown Av, Bexh. DA7 . 159 J4
Leysdown Rd, SE9 . . . . . . 174 B2
Leysfield Rd, W12 . . . . . . 127 G2
Leys Gdns, Barn. EN4 . . . . 42 A5
Leyspring Rd, E11 . . . . 97 F1
Leys Rd E, Enf. EN3 . . . . . . 45 H1
Leys Rd W, Enf. EN3 . . . . . 45 H1
Ley St, Ilf. IG1, IG2 . . . . . . 99 E2
Leyswood Dr, Ilf. IG2 . . . . . 81 H5
Leythe Rd, W3 . . . . 126 C2
LEYTON, E11 . . . . 96 B1
Leyton Business Cen, E10 . 96 A2
Leyton Gra, E10
off Goldsmith Rd 96 B1
Leyton Gra Est, E10 . . . . . . 96 B1
Leyton Grn Rd, E10 . . . . . . 78 C6
Leyton Ind Village, E10 . . . . 77 G7
★Leyton Orient FC, E10 . . . 96 B3
Leyton Pk Rd, E10 . . . . 96 C3
Leyton Rd, E15 . . . . 96 D5
SW19 . . . . 167 F7
LEYTONSTONE, E11 . . . . . . 78 D7
Leytonstone Rd, E15 . . . . . 96 E5
Leywick St, E15 . . . . 114 E2
Lezayre Rd, Orp. BR6 . . . . 207 J6
Liardet St, SE14 . . . . 133 H6
Liberia Rd, N5 . . . . 93 H6
★Liberty, W1 . . . . 17 F4
Liberty Av, SW19 . . . . 185 G1
Liberty Ms, SW12 . . . . 150 B6
Liberty St, SW9 . . . . 151 F1
Libra Rd, E3 . . . . 113 J1
E13 . . . . 115 G2
Library Pl, E1
off Cable St 112/113 E7
Library St, SE1 . . . . 27 G4
Library Way, Twick. TW2
off Nelson Rd 143 J7
Lichfield Cl, Barn. EN4 . . . . 41 J3
Lichfield Ct, Rich. TW9
off Sheen Rd 145 H4
Lichfield Gdns, Rich. TW9 . 145 H4
Lichfield Gro, N3 . . . . 72 D1
Lichfield Rd, E3 . . . . 113 H3
E6 . . . . 116 A3
N9 off Winchester Rd . . . 60 D2
NW2 . . . . 90 B4
Dagenham RM8 . . . . 100 B4
Hounslow TW4 . . . . 142 C3
Northwood HA6 . . . . 66 A3
Richmond TW9 . . . . 145 J1
Woodford Green IG8 . . . 63 E4
Lichlade Cl, Orp. BR6 . . . . 207 J4
Lidbury Rd, NW7 . . . . 56 B6
Lidcote Gdns, SW9 . . . . . 151 G2
Liddall Way, West Dr. UB7 . 120 C1
Liddell Cl, Har. HA3 . . . . . . 69 G3
Liddell Gdns, NW10 . . . . . 107 J2
Liddell Rd, NW6 . . . . 90 D6
Lidding Rd, Har. HA3 . . . . . 69 G5
Liddington Rd, E15 . . . . . 115 F1
Liddon Rd, E13 . . . . 115 H3
Bromley BR1 . . . . 191 J3
Liden Cl, E17
off Hitcham Rd 95 J1
Lidfield Rd, N16 . . . . 94 A4
Lidgate Rd, SE15
off Chandler Way 132 C7
Lidiard Rd, SW18 . . . . 167 F2
Lidlington Pl, NW1 . . . . 9 F2
Lido Sq, N17 . . . . 76 A2
Lidyard Rd, N19 . . . . 92 C1
★Lifetimes Mus, Croy.
CR0 . . . . 201 J3
Liffler Rd, SE18 . . . . 137 H5
Liffords Pl, SW13 . . . . 147 F2
Lifford St, SW15 . . . . 148 A4
Lightcliffe Rd, N13 . . . . 59 G4
Lighter Cl, SE16 . . . . 133 H4
Lighterman Ms, E1 . . . . . . 113 G6
Lightermans Rd, E14 . . . . 134 A2
Lightfoot Rd, N8 . . . . 74 E5
Lightley Cl, Wem. HA0
off Stanley Av 87 J7
Ligonier St, E2 . . . . 13 F5
Lilac Cl, E4 . . . . 61 J6
Lilac Gdns, W5 . . . . 125 G3
Croydon CR0 . . . . 204 A3
Lilac Ms, N8
off Courcy Rd 75 G3
Lilac Pl, SE11 . . . . 34 C2
Lilac St, W12 . . . . 107 G7
Lilburne Gdns, SE9 . . . . . 156 B5
Lilburne Rd, SE9 . . . . 156 B5
Lilburne Wk, NW10 . . . . . . 88 C6
Lile Cres, W7 . . . . 104 B5
Lilestone Est, NW8 . . . . 7 E6
Lilestone St, NW8 . . . . 7 G5
Lilford Rd, SE5 . . . . 151 H2
Lilian Barker Cl, SE12 . . . . 155 G5
Lilian Board Way, Grnf.
UB6 . . . . 86 A5
Lilian Cl, N16
off Barbauld Rd 94 B3
Lilian Gdns, Wdf.Grn. IG8 . 79 H1
Lilian Rd, SW16 . . . . 186 C1
Lillechurch Rd, Dag. RM8 . 100 B6
Lilleshall Rd, Mord. SM4 . 185 G6
Lilley Cl, E1 . . . . 29 J2
Lilley La, NW7 . . . . 54 D5
Lillian Av, W3 . . . . 126 A2
Lillian Rd, SW13 . . . . 127 G6
Lillie Rd, SW6 . . . . 128 B7
Lillieshall Rd, SW4 . . . . . . 150 B3
Lillie Yd, SW6 . . . . 128 D6
Lillingston Ho, N7
off Harvist Est 93 G4
Lillington Gdns Est, SW1 . 33 G2
Lilliput Av, Nthlt. UB5 . . . . 103 F1
Lily Cl, W14 . . . . 128 B4
Lily Dr, West Dr. UB7 . . . . 120 A4
Lily Gdns, Wem. HA0 . . . . 105 F2
Lily Pl, EC1 . . . . 19 F1
Lily Rd, E17 . . . . 78 A6
Lilyville Rd, SW6 . . . . 148 C1
Limbourne Av, Dag. RM8 . . 83 F7
Limburg Rd, SW11 . . . . . . 149 J4
Limeburner La, EC4 . . . . . . 19 G4
Lime Cl, E1 . . . . 29 J1
Bromley BR1 . . . . 192 B4
Buckhurst Hill IG9 . . . . . . 64 A3
Carshalton SM5 . . . . . . 199 J2
Harrow HA3 . . . . 68 C2
Romford RM7 . . . . 83 J4
Lime Ct, Mitch. CR4
off Lewis Rd 185 G2
Lime Cres, Sun. TW16 . . . 178 C2
Limecroft Cl, Epsom KT19 . 196 D7
Limedene Cl, Pnr. HA5 . . . . 66 D1
Lime Gro, E4 . . . . 61 J6
N20 . . . . 56 C1
W12 . . . . 127 J2
Ilford IG6 . . . . 65 J6
New Malden KT3 . . . . . 182 D3
Orpington BR6 . . . . 207 E2
Ruislip HA4 . . . . 66 B7
Sidcup DA15 . . . . 157 J6
Twickenham TW1 . . . . . 144 C6
Limeharbour, E14 . . . . 134 B3
LIMEHOUSE, E14 . . . . 113 H7
Limehouse Causeway,
E14 . . . . 113 J7
Limehouse Flds Est, E14 . 113 H5
Limehouse Link, E14 . . . . 113 H7
Limekiln Dr, SE7 . . . . 135 H6
Limekiln Pl, SE19 . . . . 170 C7
Limerick Cl, SW12 . . . . . . 150 C7
Limerick Ms, N2
off Bedford Rd 73 H3
Lime Rd, Rich. TW9
off St. Mary's Gro 145 J4
Lime Row, Erith DA18
off Northwood Pl 139 F3
Limerston St, SW10 . . . . . . 30 D5
Limes, The, W2
off Linden Gdns 108 D7
Bromley BR2 . . . . 206 B2
Limes Av, E11 . . . . 79 H4
N12 . . . . 57 F4
NW7 . . . . 54 E6
NW11 . . . . 72 B7
SE20 . . . . 171 E7
SW13 . . . . 147 F2
Carshalton SM5 . . . . . . 199 J1
Chigwell IG7 . . . . 65 G6
Croydon CR0 . . . . 201 G3
Limes Av, The, N11 . . . . 58 B5
Limesdale Gdns, Edg.
HA8 . . . . 70 C2
Limes Fld Rd, SW14
off White Hart La . 146/147 E3
Limesford Rd, SE15 . . . . . 153 G4
Limes Gdns, SW18 . . . . . . 148 D6
Limes Gro, SE13 . . . . 154 C4
Limes Pl, Croy. CR0 . . . . . 188 A7
Limes Rd, Beck. BR3 . . . . 190 B2
Croydon CR0 . . . . 188 A6
Limes Row, Orp. BR6
off Orchard Rd . . . 206/207 E5
Limestone Wk, Erith
DA18 . . . . 138 D3
Lime St, E17 . . . . 77 H4
EC3 . . . . 20 D5
Lime St Pas, EC3 . . . . 20 D4
Limes Wk, SE15 . . . . 153 E4
W5 off Chestnut Gro . . . 125 G2
Lime Ter, W7
off Manor Ct Rd 104 B7
Lime Tree Av, Esher KT10 . 194 A1
Thames Ditton KT7 . . . . 194 A1
Limetree Cl, SW2 . . . . 169 F1
Lime Tree Gro, Croy. CR0 . 203 J3
Lime Tree Pl, Mitch. CR4 . . 186 B1
Lime Tree Rd, Houns. TW5 . 143 H1
Limetree Ter, Well. DA16
off Hook La 158 A3
Limetree Wk, SW17
off Church La 168 A5
Lime Tree Wk, Bushey
(Bushey Hth) WD23 . . . . 52 B1
West Wickham BR4 . . . . 205 F4
Lime Wk, E15
off Church St N . . . 114/115 E1
Limewood Cl, E17 . . . . 77 J4
W13
off St. Stephens Rd . 104/105 E6
Beckenham BR3 . . . . . . 190 C5
Limewood Ct, Ilf. IG4 . . . . . 80 C5
Limewood Rd, Erith DA8 . 139 J7
Limpsfield Av, SW19 . . . . 166 A2
Thornton Heath CR7 . . . 187 F5
Linacre Cl, SE15 . . . . 153 E3
Linacre Ct, W6 . . . . 128 A5
Linacre Rd, NW2 . . . . 89 H6
Linberry Wk, SE8 . . . . 133 J4
Linchmere Rd, SE12 . . . . . 155 F7
Lincoln Av, N14 . . . . 58 C3
SW19 . . . . 166 A3
Twickenham TW2 . . . . . 161 H2
Lincoln Cl, SE25
off Woodside Grn 188 D6
Greenford UB6 . . . . 103 J1
Harrow HA2 . . . . 67 F5
Lincoln Ct, N16 . . . . 76 A7
Borehamwood WD6 . . . . 38 D5
Lincoln Cres, Enf. EN1 . . . . 44 B5
Lincoln Dr, Wat. WD19 . . . . 50 C3
Lincoln Gdns, Ilf. IG1 . . . . . 80 B7
Lincoln Grn Rd, Orp. BR5 . 193 J5
Lincoln Ms, NW6
off Willesden La 108 C1
SE21 . . . . 170 A1
Lincoln Rd, E7 . . . . 98 A6
E13 . . . . 115 H4
E18 off Grove Rd 79 G1
N2 . . . . 73 H3
SE25 . . . . 188 E3
Enfield EN1, EN3 . . . . . . 44 D5
Feltham TW13 . . . . 161 F3
Harrow HA2 . . . . 67 F5
Mitcham CR4 . . . . 186 E5
New Malden KT3 . . . . . 182 C3
Sidcup DA14 . . . . 176 B5
Wembley HA0 . . . . 87 G6
Worcester Park KT4 . . . . 197 H1

Lincolns, The, NW7 ...... **55** F3
★**Lincoln's Inn**, WC2...... **18** D3
Lincoln's Inn Flds, WC2 ... **18** C3
Lincoln St, E11 .... **96** E2
SW3................ **31** J2
Lincoln Way, Enf. EN1 .... **44** E5
Lincombe Rd, Brom. BR1. **173** F3
Lindal Cres, Enf. EN2 ..... **43** E4
Lindales, The, N17
off Brantwood Rd **60** C6
Lindal Rd, SE4 .... **153** J5
Linden Av, NW10 .... **108** A2
Enfield EN1 .... **44** D1
Hounslow TW3 .... **143** H5
Ruislip HA4 .... **84** A1
Thornton Heath CR7 ... **187** H4
Wembley HA9......... **87** J5
Linden Cl, N14 .... **42** C6
Ruislip HA4 .... **84** A1
Stanmore HA7 .... **52** E5
Thames Ditton KT7 .... **180** C7
Linden Ct, W12.......... **127** J1
Linden Cres, Grnf. UB6 ... **86** C6
Kingston upon Thames
KT1 .... **181** J2
Woodford Green IG8 ... **63** H6
Lindenfield, Chis. BR7 ... **192** E2
Linden Gdns, W2 .... **108** D7
W4................. **126** D5
Enfield EN1 .... **44** D1
Linden Gro, SE15 .... **153** E3
SE26 .... **171** F6
New Malden KT3 ..... **182** E3
Teddington TW11
off Waldegrave Rd. ... **162** C5
Linden Lawns, Wem. HA9 . **87** J4
Linden Lea, N2.......... **73** F5
Linden Leas, W.Wick. BR4. **204** D2
Linden Ms, N1 .... **94** A5
W2 *off Linden Gdns* ... **108** D7
Linden Pas, W4
off Linden Gdns **126** D5
Linden Pl, Mitch. CR4.... **185** H4
Linden Rd, E17
off High St........... **77** J5
N10 .... **74** B4
N11 .... **57** J2
N15 .... **75** J4
Hampton TW12 .... **161** G7
Lindens, The, N12........ **57** G5
W4 *off Hartington Rd* .. **146** C1
Croydon (New Adgtn)
CR0 .... **204** C6
Loughton IG10 .... **48** C5
Linden Wk, N19
off Hargrave Pk....... **92** C2
Linden Way, N14 .... **42** C6
Lindeth Cl, Stan. HA7 .... **52** E6
Lindfield Gdns, NW3 ..... **91** E5
Lindfield Rd, W5........ **105** F4
Croydon CR0......... **188** C6
Lindfield St, E14........ **114** A6
Lindhill Cl, Enf. EN3...... **45** G1
Lindisfarne Rd, SW20.... **165** G7
Dagenham RM8 ...... **100** C3
Lindisfarne Way, E9 ...... **95** H4
Lindley Est, SE15......... **37** H7
Lindley Pl, Rich. TW9 .... **146** A1
Lindley Rd, E10 .... **96** B2
Lindley St, E1 .... **113** F5
Lindore Rd, SW11....... **149** J4
Lindores Rd, Cars. SM5 .. **185** F7
Lindo St, SE15
off Selden Rd **153** F2
Lind Rd, Sutt. SM1 ...... **199** F5
Lindrop St, SW6........ **149** F2
Lindsay Cl, Chess. KT9... **195** H7
Staines (Stanw.) TW19 . **140** A5
Lindsay Dr, Har. HA3 ..... **69** H6
Lindsay Rd, Hmptn.
(Hmptn H.) TW12..... **161** H4
Worcester Park KT4.... **197** H2
Lindsay Sq, SW1 .... **33** J3
Lindsell St, SE10 .... **154** C1
Lindsey Cl, Brom. BR1 ... **192** A3
Mitcham CR4......... **187** E4
Lindsey Gdns, Felt. TW14. **141** G7
Lindsey Ms, N1 .... **93** J7
Lindsey Rd, Dag. RM8 ... **100** C4
Lindsey St, EC1 .... **19** H1
Lind St, SE8............ **154** B2
Lindum Rd, Tedd. TW11 .. **163** F7
Lindway, SE27 .... **169** H5
Lindwood Cl, E6
off Northumberland Rd. **116** B5
Linfield Cl, NW4......... **71** J3
Linford Rd, E17.......... **78** C3
Linford St, SW8 .... **150** C1
Lingards Rd, SE13 ...... **154** C4
Lingey Cl, Sid. DA15 .... **175** J2
Lingfield Av, Kings.T. KT1 . **181** H4
Lingfield Cl, Enf. EN1..... **44** B6
Lingfield Cres, SE9...... **157** G4
Lingfield Gdns, N9........ **45** E7
Lingfield Rd, SW19...... **166** A5
Worcester Park KT4.... **197** J3
Lingham St, SW9....... **151** E2
Lingholm Way, Barn. EN5 . **40** A5
Lingmere Cl, Chig. IG7.... **65** F2
Ling Rd, E16............ **115** G5
Erith DA8............ **139** J6
Lingrove Gdns, Buck.H. IG9
off Beech La **63** H2
Lings Coppice, SE21 .... **170** A2
Lingwell Rd, SW17....... **167** H3
Lingwood Gdns, Islw.
TW7............... **124** B7
Lingwood Rd, E5 .... **76** D7
Linhope St, NW1 .... **7** J5
Link, The, SE9.......... **174** D3
W3................. **106** B6
Enfield EN3........... **45** H1
Northolt UB5
off Eastcote La **85** F5
Pinner HA5 .... **66** C7
Wembley HA0
off Nathans Rd **87** F1
Linkfield, Brom. BR2 .... **191** G6
West Molesey KT8 .... **179** G3
Linkfield Rd, Islw. TW7.... **144** C2
Link La, Wall. SM6 ...... **200** D6
Linklea Cl, NW9......... **55** E7
Link Rd, N11............ **58** A4
Dagenham RM9 ...... **119** H2
Feltham TW14........ **141** J7
Wallington SM6 ...... **200** A1
Links, The, E17.......... **77** H4
Links Av, Mord. SM4 .... **184** D4
Links Dr, N20........... **56** D1
Links Gdns, SW16 ...... **169** G7
Linkside, N12........... **56** C6
Chigwell IG7.......... **65** F5
New Malden KT3 ..... **183** E2
Linkside Cl, Enf. EN2 ..... **43** F3
Linkside Gdns, Enf. EN2 .. **43** F3
Links Rd, NW2.......... **89** F2
SW17............... **167** J6
W3................. **106** A6
West Wickham BR4.... **204** C1
Woodford Green IG8 ... **63** G5
Links Side, Enf. EN2 ..... **43** G3
Link St, E9 .... **95** F6
Links Vw, N3 .... **56** C7
Links Vw Cl, Stan. HA7 ... **52** D6
Links Vw Rd, Croy. CR0 .. **204** A3
Hampton (Hmptn H.)
TW12 .... **161** J5
Linksway, NW4 .... **72** A2
Links Way, Beck. BR3.... **190** A6
Links Yd, E1 .... **21** H1
Linkway, N4............ **75** J7
SW20............... **183** H3
Link Way, Brom. BR2 .... **192** B7
Linkway, Dag. RM8 ..... **100** C4
Link Way, Pnr. HA5....... **66** D1
Linkway, Rich. TW10 .... **163** E2
Linkway, The, Barn. EN5 .. **40** E6
Linkwood Wk, NW1
off Maiden La **93** D7
Linley Cres, Rom. RM7 ... **83** H3
Linley Rd, N17 .... **76** B2
★**Linley Sambourne Ho**,
W8................. **128** D2
Linnell Cl, NW11......... **72** E6
Linnell Dr, NW11 .... **72** E6
Linnell Rd, N18
off Fairfield Rd **60** D5
SE5 .... **152** B2
Linnet Cl, N9 .... **61** G1
SE28 .... **118** C7
Linnet Ms, SW12 .... **150** A7
Linnett Cl, E4........... **62** C4
Linnet Ter, Ilf. IG5
off Tiptree Cres **80** D3
Linom Rd, SW4 .... **150** E4
Linscott Rd, E5.......... **95** F4
Linsdell Rd, Bark. IG11 ... **117** F1
Linsey St, SE16 .... **37** H1
Linslade Cl, Houns. TW4
off Frampton Rd . **142/143** E5
Pinner HA5 .... **66** B3
Linstead St, NW6........ **90** D7
Linstead Way, SW18 .... **148** B7
Linsted Ct, SE9 .... **157** H6
Linster Gro, Borwd. WD6.. **38** C5
Lintaine Cl, W6
off Moylan Rd....... **128** B6
Linthorpe Av, Wem. HA0 .. **87** F6
Linthorpe Rd, N16 .... **76** B7
Barnet EN4 .... **41** H3
Linton Cl, Mitch. CR4.... **185** J7
Welling DA16
off Anthony Rd **158** B1
Linton Gdns, E6 .... **116** B6
Linton Gro, SE27 .... **169** H5
Linton Rd, Bark. IG11 ..... **99** F7
Lintons, The, Bark. IG11 ... **99** F7
Linton St, N1 .... **111** J1
Lintott Ct, Stai. (Stanw.)
TW19............... **140** A6
Linver Rd, SW6 .... **148** D2
Linwood Cl, SE5........ **152** C2
Linwood Cres, Enf. EN1... **44** D1
Linwood Way, SE15 ...... **37** F7
Linzee Rd, N8........... **74** E4
Lion Av, Twick. TW1
off Lion Rd **162** C1
Lion Cl, SE4 .... **154** A6
Lion Ct, Borwd. WD6 ..... **38** C1
Lionel Gdns, SE9 .... **156** A5
Lionel Ms, W10
off Telford Rd........ **108** B5
Lionel Rd, SE9 .... **156** A5
Lionel Rd N, Brent. TW8.. **125** H4
Lionel Rd S, Brent. TW8.. **125** J5
Lion Gate Gdns, Rich.
TW9 .... **145** J3
Lion Gate Ms, SW18
off Merton Rd **148** D7
Lion Pk Av, Chess. KT9 .. **196** A4
Lion Plaza, EC2
off Threadneedle St... **112** A6
Lion Rd, E6............ **116** C5
N9.................. **60** D2
Bexleyheath DA6 ..... **159** F4
Croydon CR0......... **187** J5
Twickenham TW1 ..... **162** C1
Lions Cl, SE9 .... **173** J3
Lion Way, Brent. TW8.... **125** G7
Lion Wf Rd, Islw. TW7 ... **144** E3
Lion Yd, SW4
off Tremadoc Rd **150** D4
Liphook Cres, SE23 ..... **153** F7
Liphook Rd, Wat. WD19 ... **50** D4
Lippitts Hill, Loug.
(High Beach) IG10..... **47** E1
Lipton Cl, SE28
off Aisher Rd **118** C7
Lipton Rd, E1
off Bower St **113** G6
Lisbon Av, Twick. TW2.... **161** J2
Lisbon Cl, E17 .... **77** J2
Lisburne Rd, NW3 .... **91** J4
Lisford St, SE15 .... **152** C1
Lisgar Ter, W14 .... **128** C4
Liskeard Cl, Chis. BR7 ... **175** F6
Liskeard Gdns, SE3 ..... **155** G1
Lisle Cl, SW17 .... **168** B4
Lisle St, WC2 .... **17** J5
Lismore Circ, NW5....... **92** A5
Lismore Cl, Islw. TW7.... **144** D2
Lismore Rd, N17 .... **76** A3
South Croydon CR2 ... **202** B6
Lismore Wk, N1
off Clephane Rd **93** J6
Lissant Cl, Surb. KT6
off Lovelace Rd...... **181** G7
Lissenden Gdns, NW5 .... **92** A4
Lisson Grn Est, NW8 ...... **7** G4
LISSON GROVE, NW8 ..... **7** F6
Lisson Gro, NW1 .... **7** G5
NW8 .... **7** F4
Lisson St, NW1 .... **15** G1
Liss Way, SE15.......... **37** G7
Lister Cl, W3 .... **106** D5
Mitcham CR4......... **185** H1
Lister Ct, NW9
off Pasteur Cl...... **70/71** E2
Lister Gdns, N18 .... **59** J5
Lister Ho, SE3 .... **135** E6
Lister Rd, E11 .... **97** E1
Lister Wk, SE28
off Haldane Rd **118** D7
Liston Rd, N17 .... **76** D1
SW4................ **150** C3
Liston Way, Wdf.Grn. IG8
off Navestock Cres **63** J7
Listowel Cl, SW9 .... **35** F7
Listowel Rd, Dag. RM10.. **101** G3
Listria Pk, N16 .... **94** B2
Litchfield Av, E15 .... **96** E6
Morden SM4.......... **184** C7
Litchfield Gdns, NW10.... **89** G6
Litchfield Rd, Sutt. SM1.. **199** F4
Litchfield St, WC2 .... **17** J5
Litchfield Way, NW11 ..... **73** E5
Lithos Rd, NW3 .... **91** E6
Little Acre, Beck. BR3.... **190** A3
Little Albany St, NW1 ..... **8** E5
Little Argyll St, W1........ **17** F4
Little Benty, West Dr. UB7. **120** A5
Little Birches, Sid. DA15 . **175** H2
Little Boltons, The, SW5 .. **30** B3
SW10................ **30** B3
Little Bornes, SE21...... **170** B4
Little Britain, EC1 .... **19** J3
Littlebrook Cl, Croy. CR0 . **189** G6
Little Brownings, SE23 .. **170** E2
Littlebury Rd, SW4...... **150** D3
Little Bury St, N9........ **60** A1
Little Cedars, N12
off Woodside Av **57** F4
Little Chester St, SW1 .... **24** C5
Little Cloisters, SW1
off Tufton St......... **130** D3
Little Coll La, EC4
off Upper Thames St.. **112** A7
Little Coll St, SW1 .... **26** A5
Littlecombe, SE7 .... **135** H6
Littlecombe Cl, SW15 ... **148** A6
Little Common, Stan. HA7. **52** D3
Littlecote Cl, SW19 ..... **148** A7
Littlecote Pl, Pnr. HA5 .... **67** E1
Little Ct, W.Wick. BR4 ... **204** E2
Littlecroft, SE9......... **156** D3
Littledale, SE2 .... **138** A6
Little Dean's Yd, SW1..... **26** A5
Little Dimocks, SW12.... **168** B2
Little Dorrit Ct, SE1 ...... **28** A3
Little Dragons, Loug. IG10. **48** A4
LITTLE EALING, W5 ..... **125** F4
Little Ealing La, W5 ..... **125** F4
Little Edward St, NW1..... **8** E3
Little Elms, Hayes UB3 ... **121** G7
Little Essex St, WC2...... **18** E5
Little Ferry Rd, Twick. TW1
off Ferry Rd **162/163** E1
Littlefield Cl, N19
off Tufnell Pk Rd **92** C4
Kingston upon Thames
KT1 *off Fairfield W* ... **181** H2
Littlefield Rd, Edg. HA8 ... **54** C7
Little Friday Rd, E4....... **62** E2
Little Gearies, Ilf. IG6..... **80** E4
Little George St, SW1 ..... **26** A4
Little Gra, Grnf. UB6
off Perivale La....... **104** D3
Little Grn, Rich. TW9 .... **145** G4
Little Grn St, NW5
off College La **92** B4
Littlegrove, Barn. EN4 .... **41** H6
Little Halliards, Walt. KT12
off Felix Rd **178** A6
Little Heath, SE7 .... **136** B6
Romford (Chad.Hth)
RM6................ **82** B4
Little Heath Rd, Bexh.
DA7 .... **159** F1
Littleheath Rd, S.Croy.
CR2 .... **202** E7
★**Little Holland Ho**, Cars.
SM5............... **199** H7
LITTLE ILFORD, E12...... **98** B5
Little Ilford La, E12....... **98** C4
Littlejohn Rd, W7 .... **104** C6
Little Marlborough Ct, W1 . **17** F4
Littlemead, Esher KT10 .. **194** A4
Littlemede, SE9 .... **174** C3
Littlemoor Rd, Ilf. IG1 .... **99** G3
Littlemore Rd, SE2....... **138** A2
Little Moss La, Pnr. HA5 .. **67** E2
Little Newport St, WC2 ... **17** J5
Little New St, EC4 .... **19** F3
Little Orchard Cl, Pnr. HA5
off Barrow Pt La.... **66/67** E2
Little Oxhey La, Wat.
WD19................ **50** D5
Little Pk Dr, Felt. TW13... **160** D2
Little Pk Gdns, Enf. EN2 .. **43** J3
Little Plucketts Way, Buck.H.
IG9 .... **63** J1
Little Portland St, W1..... **17** F3
Little Queens Rd, Tedd.
TW11.............. **162** C6
Little Redlands, Brom.
BR1 .... **192** B2
Little Rd, Croy. CR0
off Lower Addiscombe
Rd **202** B1
Hayes UB3 .... **121** J2
Littlers Cl, SW19
off Runnymede **185** G1
Little Russell St, WC1 .... **18** A2
Little St. James's St, SW1 . **25** F2
Little St. Leonards, SW14 . **146** C3
Little Sanctuary, SW1 .... **25** J4

Little Smith St, SW1 . . . . . **25** J5
Little Somerset St, E1 . . . . **21** F4
Littlestone Cl, Beck. BR3 *off Abbey La* **172** A6
Little Strand, NW9 . . . . . . **71** F2
Little Thrift, Orp. BR5 . . . . **193** F4
Little Titchfield St, W1 . . . . **17** F2
Littleton Av, E4 . . . . **63** F1
Littleton Cres, Har. HA1 . . . **86** C2
Littleton Rd, Har. HA1 . . . . **86** C2
Littleton St, SW18 . . . . . . **167** F2
Little Trinity La, EC4 . . . . . . **20** A5
Little Turnstile, WC1 . . . . . . **18** C3
★**Little Venice (Waterbuses)**, W2 . . . . **14** C1
Littlewood, SE13 . . . . **154** C5
Littlewood Cl, W13 . . . . . . **125** E3
Littleworth Av, Esher KT10 . . . . **194** A5
Littleworth Common Rd, Esher KT10 . . . . **194** A3
Littleworth La, Esher KT10 . . . . **194** A4
Littleworth Pl, Esher KT10 . **194** A4
Littleworth Rd, Esher KT10 . . . . **194** B4
Livermere Rd, E8 . . . . **112** C1
Liverpool Gro, SE17 . . . . . . **36** A4
Liverpool Rd, E10 . . . . **78** C6
E16 . . . . **115** E5
N1 . . . . **111** G2
N7 . . . . **93** G5
W5 . . . . **125** G2
Kingston upon Thames KT2 . . . . **164** A7
Thornton Heath CR7 . . . **187** J3
Liverpool St, EC2 . . . . **20** D2
Livesey Cl, Kings.T. KT1 . . **181** J3
★**Livesey Mus**, SE15 . . . . **132** E6
Livesey Pl, SE15 . . . . **37** J5
Livingstone Ct, E10 *off Matlock Rd* **78** C6
Barnet EN5 *off Christchurch La* **40** B2
Livingstone Pl, E14 *off Ferry St* **134** C5
Livingstone Rd, E15 . . . . . **114** C1
E17 . . . . **78** B6
N13 . . . . **59** E6
SW11 *off Winstanley Rd* **149** G3
Hounslow TW3 . . . . **143** J4
Southall UB1 . . . . **102** D7
Thornton Heath CR7 . . . **187** J2
Livingstone Wk, SW11 . . . **149** G3
Livonia St, W1 . . . . **17** G4
Livsey Cl, SE28 . . . . **137** F3
Lizard St, EC1 . . . . **12** A4
Lizban St, SE3 . . . . **135** H7
Llanelly Rd, NW2 . . . . **90** C2
Llanover Rd, SE18 . . . . **136** D6
Wembley HA9 . . . . **87** G3
Llanthony Rd, Mord. SM4 . **185** G6
Llanvanor Rd, NW2 . . . . . . **90** C2
Llewellyn St, SE16 . . . . **29** J4
Lloyd Av, SW16 . . . . **187** E1
Lloyd Baker St, WC1 . . . . . **10** D4
Lloyd Ct, Pnr. HA5 . . . . **66** D5
Lloyd Pk Av, Croy. CR0 . . . **202** C4
Lloyd Rd, E6 . . . . **116** C1
E17 . . . . **77** G4
Dagenham RM9 . . . . . . **101** F6
Worcester Park KT4 . . . . **197** J3
Lloyd's Av, EC3 . . . . **21** E4
★**Lloyds of London**, EC3 . . **20** D4
Lloyds Pl, SE3 . . . . **155** E2
Lloyd Sq, WC1 . . . . **10** E3
Lloyd's Row, EC1 . . . . **11** F4
Lloyd St, WC1 . . . . **10** E3
Lloyds Way, Beck. BR3 . . . **189** H5
Loampit Hill, SE13 . . . . . . **154** A2
Loampit Vale, SE13 . . . . . **154** B3
Loanda Cl, E8 *off Clarissa St* **112** C1
Loats Rd, SW2 . . . . **150** E6
Lobelia Cl, E6 *off Sorrel Gdns* **116** B5
Locarno Rd, W3 . . . . **126** C1
Greenford UB6 . . . . **103** J4
Lochaber Rd, SE13 . . . . . . **154** E4
Lochaline St, W6 . . . . **127** J6
Lochan Cl, Hayes UB4 . . . **102** E4
Lochinvar St, SW12 . . . . . **150** B7
Lochmere Cl, Erith DA8 . . **139** H6
Lochnagar St, E14 . . . . . . **114** C5
Lock Chase, SE3 . . . . **155** E3
Lock Cl, Sthl. UB2 *off Navigator Dr* **123** J2
Lockesfield Pl, E14 . . . . . . **134** B5
Lockesley Dr, Orp. BR5 . . **193** J6
Lockesley Sq, Surb. KT6 . **181** G6
Locket Rd, Har. HA3 . . . . . . **68** B3
Lockfield Av, Enf. EN3 . . . . **45** H2
Lockgate Cl, E9 *off Lee Conservancy Rd* . . **95** J5
Lockhart Cl, N7 . . . . **93** F6
Enfield EN3 *off Derby Rd* **44/45** E5
Lockhart St, E3 . . . . **113** J4
Lockhurst St, E5 . . . . **95** G4
Lockie Pl, SE25 . . . . **188** D3
Lockier Wk, Wem. HA9 . . . . **87** G3
Lockington Rd, SW8 . . . . **150** B1
Lockmead Rd, N15 . . . . **76** D6
SE13 . . . . **154** C3
Lock Rd, Rich. TW10 . . . . . **163** F4
Locks La, Mitch. CR4 . . . . **185** J1
Locksley Est, E14 . . . . **113** J6
Locksley St, E14 . . . . **113** J5
Locksmeade Rd, Rich. TW10 . . . . **163** F4
Lockswood Cl, Barn. EN4 . . . . **41** J4
Lockton St, W10 *off Bramley Rd* **108** A7
Lockwood Cl, SE26 . . . . . . **171** G4
Lockwood Ind Pk, N17 . . . . **76** E3
Lockwood Sq, SE16 . . . . . **132** E3
Lockwood Way, E17 . . . . . . **77** G2
Chessington KT9 . . . . . . **196** A5
Lockyer Est, SE1 . . . . **28** C3
Lockyer St, SE1 . . . . **28** C4
Locomotive Dr, Felt. TW14 . . . . **160** A1
Loddiges Rd, E9 . . . . **95** F7
Loder St, SE15 . . . . **153** F1
Lodge Av, SW14 . . . . **146** E3
Croydon CR0 . . . . **201** G3
Dagenham RM8, RM9 . . **118** A1
Harrow HA3 . . . . **69** H4
Lodge Cl, N18 . . . . **59** J5
Edgware HA8 . . . . **53** J6
Isleworth TW7 . . . . **144** E1
Wallington SM6 . . . . . . **200** A1
Lodge Ct, Wem. HA0 . . . . . . **87** H5
Lodge Dr, N13 . . . . **59** G4
Lodge Gdns, Beck. BR3 . . **189** J5
Lodge Hill, SE2 . . . . **138** B7
Ilford IG4 . . . . **80** B4
Welling DA16 . . . . **138** B7
Lodgehill Pk Cl, Har. HA2 . . **85** H2
Lodge La, N12 . . . . **57** F5
Bexley DA5 . . . . **158** D6
Croydon (New Adgtn) CR0 . . . . **204** A6
Lodge Pl, Sutt. SM1 . . . . . **199** E5
Lodge Rd, NW4 . . . . **71** J4
NW8 . . . . **7** F4
Bromley BR1 . . . . **173** H7
Croydon CR0 . . . . **187** H6
Sutton SM1 *off Throwley Way* . **198/199** E5
Wallington SM6 . . . . . . **200** B5
Lodge Vil, Wdf.Grn. IG8 . . . **63** F7
Lodore Gdns, NW9 . . . . **70** E5
Lodore St, E14 . . . . **114** C6
Lofthouse Pl, Chess. KT9 . **195** F6
Loftie St, SE16 . . . . **29** J4
Lofting Rd, N1 . . . . **93** F7
Loftus Rd, W12 . . . . **127** H1
Logan Cl, Enf. EN3 . . . . **45** G1
Hounslow TW4 . . . . **143** F3
Logan Ms, W8 . . . . **128** D4
Logan Pl, W8 . . . . **128** D4
Logan Rd, N9 . . . . **61** E2
Wembley HA9 . . . . **87** H2
Loggetts, The, SE21 . . . . . **170** B2
Logs Hill, Brom. BR1 . . . . **174** B7
Chislehurst BR7 . . . . **174** B7
Logs Hill Cl, Chis. BR7 . . . **192** B1
Lolesworth Cl, E1 . . . . **21** G2
Lollard St, SE11 . . . . **34** D1
Loman St, SE1 . . . . **27** H3
Lomas Cl, Croy. CR0 . . . . **204** C7
Lomas Dr, E8 . . . . **94** C7
Lomas St, E1 . . . . **21** J1
Lombard Av, Enf. EN3 . . . . **45** F1
Ilford IG3 . . . . **99** H1
Lombard Business Pk, SW19 . . . . **185** F2
Lombard Ct, EC3 . . . . **20** C5
W3 *off Crown St* **126** B1
Lombard La, EC4 . . . . **19** F4
Lombard Rd, N11 . . . . **58** B5
SW11 . . . . **149** G2
SW19 . . . . **185** E2
Lombard St, EC3 . . . . **20** C4
Lombard Wall, SE7 . . . . . . **135** H3
Lombardy Cl, Ilf. IG6 *off Hazel La* **64/65** E7
Lombardy Pl, W2 . . . . **14** A6
Lombardy Retail Pk, Hayes UB3 . . . . **102** B7
Lomond Cl, N15 . . . . **76** B4
Wembley HA0 . . . . **87** J7
Lomond Gdns, S.Croy. CR2 . . . . **203** H7
Lomond Gro, SE5 . . . . **36** B7
Loncroft Rd, SE5 . . . . **37** E5
Londesborough Rd, N16 . . **94** B4
★**London Aquarium**, SE1 . . **26** C3
★**London Brass Rubbing Cen, St. Martin-in-the-Fields Ch**, WC2 . . . . **18** A6
London Br, EC4 . . . . **28** C1
SE1 . . . . **28** C1
London Br St, SE1 . . . . **28** B2
London Br Wk, SE1 . . . . . . **28** C1
★**London Broncos R.L.C. (share Griffin Pk with Brentford F.C.)**, Brent. TW8 . . . . **125** G6
★**London Butterfly Ho, Syon Pk**, Brent. TW8 . . **145** E1
★**London Canal Mus, The**, N1 *off New Wf Rd* **10** B1
★**London Cen Mosque**, NW8 . . . . **7** H4
★**London City Airport**, E16 . . . . **136** B1
★**London Commodity Exchange**, E1 . . . . **21** G6
★**London Dungeon**, SE1 . . **28** C2
★**London Eye**, SE1 . . . . **26** C3
London Flds, E8 . . . . **94** E7
London Flds E Side, E8 . . . **94** E7
London Flds W Side, E8 . . . **94** D7
★**London Fire Brigade Mus**, SE1 . . . . **27** J3
★**London Heathrow Airport**, Houns. TW6 . . . . **140** E1
London La, E8 . . . . **95** E7
Bromley BR1 . . . . **173** F7
★**London Met Archives**, EC1 . . . . **11** F5
London Ms, W2 . . . . **15** F4
★**London Palladium**, W1 . . **17** F4
★**London Peace Pagoda**, SW11 . . . . **32** A7
★**London Regatta Cen**, E16 . . . . **116** A7
London Rd, E13 . . . . **115** G2
SE1 . . . . **27** G5
SE23 . . . . **170** D1
SW16 . . . . **187** F1
SW17 . . . . **185** J2
Barking IG11 . . . . **99** E7
Brentford TW8 . . . . **125** F7
Bromley BR1 . . . . **173** F7
Croydon CR0 . . . . **187** H7
Enfield EN2 . . . . **44** A3
Harrow HA1 . . . . **86** B2
Hounslow TW3 . . . . **143** J3
Isleworth TW7 . . . . **144** C2
Kingston upon Thames KT2 . . . . **181** J2
Mitcham CR4 . . . . **185** J2
Mitcham (Bedd.Cor.) CR4 . . . . **186** A7
Morden SM4 . . . . **184** D5
Romford (Abridge) RM4 . . . . **49** J4
Romford (Chad.Hth) RM6, RM7 . . . . **83** G6
Stanmore HA7 . . . . **53** F5
Sutton SM3 . . . . **198** A3
Thornton Heath CR7 . . . **187** G5
Twickenham TW1 . . . . . **144** D5
Wallington SM6 . . . . . . **200** B4
Wembley HA9 . . . . **87** H6
London Shop Pav, W1 . . . . **17** H6
★**London Silver Vaults**, WC2 . . . . **18** E2
London Stile, W4 *off Wellesley Rd* **126** A5
★**London Stone**, EC4 . . . . . **20** B5
London St, EC3 . . . . **20** E5
W2 . . . . **15** E4
★**London Transport Mus**, WC2 . . . . **18** B5
London Wall, EC2 . . . . **20** A2
London Wall Bldgs, EC2 . . . **20** C2
★**London Wildlife Trust**, NW1 . . . . **110** D1
★**London Zoo**, NW1 . . . . . . **8** B1
Lonesome Way, SW16 . . . **186** B1
Long Acre, WC2 . . . . **18** A5
Longacre Pl, Cars. SM5 *off Beddington Gdns* . **200** A6
Longacre Rd, E17 . . . . **78** D1
Longbeach Rd, SW11 . . . . **149** J3
Longberrys, NW2 . . . . **90** C3
Longboat Row, Sthl. UB1 . **103** F6
Longbridge Rd, Bark. IG11 . **99** F7
Dagenham RM8 . . . . . . **100** A4
Longbridge Way, SE13 . . . **154** C5
Longcliffe Path, Wat. WD19 *off Gosforth La* **50** A3
Longcroft, SE9 . . . . **174** C3
Longcrofte Rd, Edg. HA8 . . **53** G7
Longcroft Ri, Loug. IG10 . . **48** D5
Long Deacon Rd, E4 . . . . . **62** E1
LONG DITTON, Surb. KT10 . . . . **195** F1
Longdon Wd, Kes. BR2 . . **206** B4
Longdown Rd, SE6 . . . . . **172** A4
Long Dr, W3 . . . . **106** E6
Greenford UB6 . . . . **103** H1
Ruislip HA4 . . . . **84** D4
Long Elmes, Har. HA3 . . . . **67** H1
Longfellow Rd, E17 . . . . . . **77** J6
Worcester Park KT4 . . . . **197** G2
Longfellow Way, SE1 . . . . . **37** G2
Long Fld, NW9 . . . . **55** E7
Longfield, Brom. BR1 . . . . **191** F1
Loughton IG10 . . . . **47** J5
Longfield Av, E17 . . . . **77** H4
NW7 . . . . **55** G7
W5 . . . . **105** F7
Wallington SM6 . . . . . . **200** A1
Wembley HA9 . . . . **87** H1
Longfield Cres, SE26 . . . . **171** F3
Longfield Dr, SW14 . . . . . **146** B5
Mitcham CR4 . . . . **167** H7
Longfield Est, SE1 . . . . **37** G2
Longfield Rd, W5 . . . . **105** F7
Longfield St, SW18 . . . . . . **148** D7
Longfield Wk, W5 . . . . **105** F6
Longford Av, Felt. TW14 . . **141** H6
Southall UB1 . . . . **103** G7
Longford Cl, Hmptn. (Hmptn H.) TW12 . . . . . **161** G4
Hayes UB4 *off Longford Gdns* **102** D7
Longford Ct, E5 *off Pedro St* **95** G4
NW4 . . . . **72** A4
Epsom KT19 . . . . **196** C4
Longford Gdns, Hayes UB4 . . . . **102** D7
Sutton SM1 . . . . **199** F3
Longford Rd, Twick. TW2 . **161** G1
Longford St, NW1 . . . . **8** E5
Longford Wk, SW2 *off Papworth Way* **151** G7
Long Grn, Chig. IG7 . . . . . . **65** H4
Longhayes Av, Rom. RM6 . **82** D4
Longhayes Ct, Rom. RM6 *off Longhayes Av* **82** D4
Longheath Gdns, Croy. CR0 . . . . **189** F5
Longhedge Ho, SE26 . . . . **170** C4
Long Hedges, Houns. TW3 . . . . **143** G1
Longhedge St, SW11 . . . . **150** A2
Longhill Rd, SE6 . . . . **172** D2
Longhook Gdns, Nthlt. UB5 . . . . **102** A2
Longhope Cl, SE15 . . . . . . **37** E6
Longhurst Rd, SE13 . . . . . **154** D5
Croydon CR0 . . . . **189** E6
Longland Ct, SE1 . . . . **37** H3
Longland Dr, N20 . . . . **56** E3
LONGLANDS, Chis. BR7 . **175** F3
Longlands Ct, W11 *off Portobello Rd* **108** C7
Mitcham CR4 *off Summerhill Way* . . **186** A1
Longlands Pk Cres, Sid. DA15 . . . . **175** H3
Longlands Rd, Sid. DA15 . **175** H3
Long La, EC1 . . . . **19** H1
N2 . . . . **73** F2
N3 . . . . **56** E7
SE1 . . . . **28** B4
Bexleyheath DA7 . . . . . **138** D7
Croydon CR0 . . . . **189** F5
Staines (Stanw.) TW19 . **140** C7
Longleat Rd, Enf. EN1 . . . . **44** B5
Longleat Way, Felt. TW14 . **141** G7
Longleigh La, SE2 . . . . . . **138** C6
Bexleyheath DA7 . . . . . **138** C6
Longlents Ho, NW10 . . . . **106** D1
Longley Av, Wem. HA0 . . . **105** J1
Longley Rd, SW17 . . . . . . **167** H6
Croydon CR0 . . . . **187** H7

Longley Rd, Har. HA1 67 J5
Long Leys, E4 62 B6
Longley St, SE1 37 H2
Longley Way, NW2 89 J3
Long Mark Rd, E16 off Fulmer Rd 116 A5
Longmarsh La, SE28 off Hill Vw Dr 137 H1
Long Mead, NW9 71 F1
Longmead, Chis. BR7 192 D2
Longmead Dr, Sid. DA14 176 D2
Long Meadow, NW5 off Torriano Av 92 D5
Long Meadow Cl, W.Wick. BR4 190 C7
Longmeadow Rd, Sid. DA15 175 H1
Longmead Rd, SW17 167 J5
Thames Ditton KT7 180 B7
Longmoore St, SW1 33 F2
Longmoor Pt, SW15 off Norley Vale 165 H1
Longmore Av, Barn. EN4, EN5 41 F6
Longnor Rd, E1 113 G3
Long Pond Rd, SE3 155 E1
Long Reach Ct, Bark. IG11 117 G2
Longreach Rd, Bark. IG11 117 J4
Longridge La, Sthl. UB1 103 H7
Longridge Rd, SW5 128 D4
Long Rd, SW4 150 B4
Long's Ct, WC2 17 H5
Longs Ct, Rich. TW9 off Crown Ter 145 J4
Longshaw Rd, E4 62 D3
Longshore, SE8 133 J4
Longstaff Cres, SW18 148 D6
Longstaff Rd, SW18 148 D6
Longstone Av, NW10 89 F7
Longstone Rd, SW17 168 B5
Long St, E2 13 F3
Longthornton Rd, SW16 186 C2
Longthorpe Ct, W6 off Goldhawk Rd 127 G3
Longton Av, SE26 170 D4
Longton Gro, SE26 170 E4
Longville Rd, SE11 35 G1
Long Wk, SE1 28 E5
SE18 136 E6
SW13 147 E2
New Malden KT3 182 C3
Longwalk Rd, Uxb. UB11 121 E1
Longwood Dr, SW15 147 G6
Longwood Gdns, Ilf. IG5, IG6 80 C4
Longworth Cl, SE28 118 D6
Long Yd, WC1 10 C6
Loning, The, NW9 71 E4
Lonsdale Av, E6 116 A3
Romford RM7 83 J6
Wembley HA9 87 H5
Lonsdale Cl, E6 off Lonsdale Av 116 B4
SE9 174 A3
Edgware HA8 off Orchard Dr 53 J5
Pinner HA5 51 E7
Lonsdale Cres, Ilf. IG2 80 E6
Lonsdale Dr, Enf. EN2 43 E5
Lonsdale Gdns, Th.Hth. CR7 187 F4
Lonsdale Ms, Rich. TW9 off Elizabeth Cotts 146 A1
Lonsdale Pl, N1 off Barnsbury St 93 G7
Lonsdale Rd, E11 79 F7
NW6 108 C2
SE25 188 E4
SW13 127 G6
W4 127 F4
W11 108 C6
Bexleyheath DA7 159 F2
Southall UB2 122 D3
Lonsdale Sq, N1 93 G7
Loobert Rd, N15 76 B3
Looe Gdns, Ilf. IG6 81 E3
Loop Rd, Chis. BR7 175 F6
Lopen Rd, N18 60 B4
Loraine Cl, Enf. EN3 45 F5
Loraine Rd, N7 93 F4
W4 126 B6
Lord Amory Way, E14 134 C2
Lord Av, Ilf. IG5 80 C4
Lord Chancellor Wk, Kings.T. KT2 182 C1
Lordell Pl, SW19 165 J6
Lorden Wk, E2 13 H4
Lord Gdns, Ilf. IG5 80 B4
Lord Hills Br, W2 14 B2
Lord Hills Rd, W2 14 B1
Lord Holland La, SW9 off St. Lawrence Way 151 G1
Lord Knyvett Cl, Stai. (Stanw.) TW19 140 A6
Lord Knyvetts Ct, Stai. (Stanw.) TW19 off De Havilland Way 140 B6
Lord Napier Pl, W6 off Upper Mall 127 G5
Lord N St, SW1 26 A6
Lord Roberts Ms, SW6 off Moore Pk Rd 128/129 E7
Lord Roberts Ter, SE18 136 D5
★Lord's, Middlesex County Cricket Club & Mus, NW8 7 F3
Lord's Cl, SE21 169 J2
Lords Cl, Felt. TW13 161 E2
Lordship Gro, N16 94 A2
Lordship La, N17 75 J1
N22 75 G2
SE22 152 C6
Lordship La Est, SE22 170 D1
Lordship Pk, N16 93 J2
Lordship Pk Ms, N16 off Allerton Rd 93 J2
Lordship Pl, SW3 31 G6
Lordship Rd, N16 94 A2
Northolt UB5 84 E7
Lordship Ter, N16 94 A2
Lordsmead Rd, N17 76 B1
Lord St, E16 136 B1
Lord's Vw, NW8 7 F4
Lord Warwick St, SE18 136 C3
Lorenzo St, WC1 10 C3
Loretto Gdns, Har. HA3 69 H4
Lorian Cl, N12 56 E4
Loring Rd, N20 57 H2
SE14 off St. James's 153 H1
Isleworth TW7 144 C2
Loris Rd, W6 127 J3
Lorn Ct, SW9 151 G2
Lorne Av, Croy. CR0 189 G7
Lorne Cl, NW8 7 H4
Lorne Gdns, E11 79 J4
W11 128 A2
Croydon CR0 189 G7
Lorne Rd, E7 97 H4
E17 78 A5
N4 93 F1
Harrow HA3 68 C2
Richmond TW10 off Albert Rd 145 J5
Lorn Rd, SW9 151 F2
Lorraine Pk, Har. HA3 52 B7
Lorrimore Rd, SE17 35 H5
Lorrimore Sq, SE17 35 H5
Loseberry Rd, Esher (Clay.) KT10 194 A5
Lothair Rd, W5 125 G2
Lothair Rd N, N4 75 H6
Lothair Rd S, N4 75 G7
Lothbury, EC2 20 B3
Lothian Av, Hayes UB4 102 B5
Lothian Cl, Wem. HA0 86 D4
Lothian Rd, SW9 151 H1
Lothrop St, W10 108 B3
Lots Rd, SW10 129 F7
Lotus Cl, SE21 169 J3
Loubet St, SW17 167 J6
Loudoun Av, Ilf. IG6 81 E5
Loudoun Rd, NW8 6 D1
Loudoun Rd Ms, NW8 off Loudoun Rd 109 F1
Loudwater Cl, Sun. TW16 178 A4
Loudwater Rd, Sun. TW16 178 A4
Loughborough Est, SW9 off Loughborough Rd 151 H2
Loughborough Pk, SW9 151 H4
Loughborough Rd, SW9 151 G2
Loughborough St, SE11 34 D3
Lough Rd, N7 93 F6
LOUGHTON, IG10 48 C5
Loughton Way, Buck.H. IG9 64 A1
Louisa Cl, E9 off Wetherell Rd 113 G1
Louisa Gdns, E1 off Louisa St 113 G4
Louisa Ho, SW15 147 E4
Louisa St, E1 113 G4
Louise Aumonier Wk, N19 off Hillrise Rd 74/75 E7
Louise Bennett Cl, SE24 off Shakespeare Rd 151 H4
Louise Ct, E11 off Grosvenor Rd 79 H5
Louise Rd, E15 97 E6
Louis Gdns, Chis. BR7 174 C4
Louis Ms, N10 74 B1
Louisville Rd, SW17 168 A3
Louvaine Rd, SW11 149 G4
Lovage App, E6 116 B5
Lovat Cl, NW2 89 F3
Lovat La, EC3 20 D6
Lovatt Cl, Edg. HA8 54 B6
Lovatt Dr, Ruis. HA4 66 A5
Lovat Wk, Houns. TW5 off Cranford La 122/123 E7
Loveday Rd, W13 125 E1
Lovegrove St, SE1 37 J4
Lovegrove Wk, E14 134 C1
Lovekyn Cl, Kings.T. KT2 off Queen Elizabeth Rd 181 J2
Lovelace Av, Brom. BR2 192 D6
Lovelace Gdns, Bark. IG11 100 A4
Surbiton KT6 181 G7
Lovelace Grn, SE9 156 C3
Lovelace Rd, SE21 169 J2
Barnet EN4 41 H7
Surbiton KT6 181 F7
Love La, EC2 20 A3
N17 60 C7
SE18 136 E4
SE25 189 E3
Bexley DA5 159 F6
Mitcham CR4 185 H3
Morden SM4 184 D7
Pinner HA5 66 E3
Surbiton KT6 195 G2
Sutton SM3 198 B5
Woodford Green IG8 64 C6
Lovel Av, Well. DA16 158 A2
Lovelinch Cl, SE15 133 F6
Lovell Ho, E8 112 D1
Lovell Pl, SE16 off Ropemaker Rd 133 H3
Lovell Rd, Rich. TW10 163 F3
Southall UB1 103 H6
Loveridge Ms, NW6 off Loveridge Rd 90 C6
Loveridge Rd, NW6 90 C6
Lovers Wk, N3 56 D7
NW7 56 C6
SE10 134 E6
Lover's Wk, W1 24 B1
Lovett Dr, Cars. SM5 185 F7
Lovett's Pl, SW18 off Old York Rd 148/149 E4
Lovett Way, NW10 88 C5
Love Wk, SE5 152 A2
Lovibonds Av, Orp. BR6 207 E4
Lowbrook Rd, Ilf. IG1 99 E5
Low Cross Wd La, SE21 170 C3
Lowden Rd, N9 61 E1
SE24 151 H4
Southall UB1 102 E7
Lowe Av, E16 115 G5
Lowell St, E14 113 H6
Lower Addiscombe Rd, Croy. CR0 202 B1
Lower Addison Gdns, W14 128 B2
Lower Alderton Hall La, Loug. IG10 48 D5
Lower Belgrave St, SW1 24 D6
Lower Boston Rd, W7 124 B1
Lower Broad St, Dag. RM10 119 G1
Lower Camden, Chis. BR7 174 C7
Lower Ch St, Croy. CR0 off Waddon New Rd 201 H2
LOWER CLAPTON, E5 95 G4
Lower Clapton Rd, E5 95 E5
Lower Clarendon Wk, W11 off Lancaster Rd 108 B6
Lower Common S, SW15 147 H3
Lower Coombe St, Croy. CR0 201 J4
Lower Downs Rd, SW20 184 A1
Lower Drayton Pl, Croy. CR0 off Drayton Rd 201 H2
LOWER EDMONTON, N9 60 C1
Lower George St, Rich. TW9 off George St 145 G5
Lower Gravel Rd, Brom. BR2 206 B1
Lower Grn Gdns, Wor.Pk. KT4 197 G1
Lower Grn W, Mitch. CR4 185 H3
Lower Grosvenor Pl, SW1 24 D5
Lower Gro Rd, Rich. TW10 145 J6
Lower Hall La, E4 61 H5
Lower Hampton Rd, Sun. TW16 178 C3
Lower Ham Rd, Kings.T. KT2 163 G6
LOWER HOLLOWAY, N7 93 F5
Lower James St, W1 17 G5
Lower John St, W1 17 G5
Lower Kenwood Av, Enf. EN2 42 D5
Lower Kings Rd, Kings.T. KT2 163 H7
Lower Lea Crossing, E14 114 E7
E16 114 E7
Lower Maidstone Rd, N11 off Telford Rd 58 C6
Lower Mall, W6 127 H5
Lower Mardyke Av, Rain. RM13 119 J2
Lower Marsh, SE1 26 E4
Lower Marsh La, Kings.T. KT1 181 J4
Lower Merton Ri, NW3 91 H7
Lower Morden La, Mord. SM4 183 J6
Lower Mortlake Rd, Rich. TW9 145 H4
Lower Pk Rd, N11 58 C5
Belvedere DA17 139 G3
Loughton IG10 48 A5
Lower Queens Rd, Buck.H. IG9 64 A2
Lower Richmond Rd, SW14 146 B3
SW15 147 J3
Richmond TW9 146 A3
Lower Rd, SE8 133 F3
SE16 133 F3
Belvedere DA17 139 G3
Harrow HA2 86 A2
Loughton IG10 48 D2
Sutton SM1 199 F4
Lower Robert St, WC2 off John Adam St 110/111 E7
Lower Sand Hills, T.Ditt. KT7 181 F7
Lower Sloane St, SW1 32 B2
Lower Sq, Islw. TW7 144 E3
Lower Strand, NW9 71 F2
Lower Sunbury Rd, Hmptn. TW12 179 F2
LOWER SYDENHAM, SE26 171 G4
Lower Sydenham Ind Est, SE26 171 J5
Lower Tail, Wat. WD19 51 E3
Lower Talbot Wk, W11 off Lancaster Rd 108 B6
Lower Teddington Rd, Kings.T. KT1 181 G1
Lower Ter, NW3 91 F3
Lower Thames St, EC3 20 C6
Lower Wd Rd, Esher (Clay.) KT10 194 D6
Lowestoft Cl, E5 off Theydon Rd 95 F2
Lowestoft Ms, E16 137 E2
Loweswater Cl, Wem. HA9 87 G2
Lowfield Rd, NW6 90 D7
W3 106 C6
Low Hall Cl, E4 46 A7
Low Hall La, E17 77 H6
Lowick Rd, Har. HA1 68 B4
Lowlands Dr, Stai. (Stanw.) TW19 140 A5
Lowlands Gdns, Rom. RM7 83 H6
Lowlands Rd, Har. HA1 68 B7
Pinner HA5 66 C7
Lowman Rd, N7 93 F4
Lowndes Cl, SW1 24 C6
Lowndes Ct, W1 17 F4
Bromley BR1 off Queens Rd 191 G2
Lowndes Pl, SW1 24 B6
Lowndes Sq, SW1 24 A4
Lowndes St, SW1 24 A5
Lowood Ct, SE19 170 C5
Lowood St, E1 off Dellow St 112/113 E7
Lowry Cres, Mitch. CR4 185 H2
Lowry Rd, Dag. RM8 100 B4
Lowshoe La, Rom. RM5 83 H1
Lowther Dr, Enf. EN2 42 E4
Lowther Gdns, SW7 23 F4
Lowther Hill, SE23 153 H7
Lowther Rd, E17 77 H2
N7 off Mackenzie Rd 93 G5
SW13 147 F1
Kingston upon Thames KT2 181 J1
Stanmore HA7 69 J3
Lowth Rd, SE5 151 J2
LOXFORD, Ilf. IG1 99 F5

Loxford Av, E6 . . . . 116 A2
Loxford La, Ilf. IG1, IG3 . . . 99 F5
Loxford Rd, Bark. IG11 . . . . 99 E6
Loxford Ter, Bark. IG11
off Fanshawe Av 99 F6
Loxham Rd, E4. . . . . 62 A7
Loxham St, WC1 . . . . 10 B4
Loxley Cl, SE26 . . . . 171 G5
Loxley Rd, SW18 . . . . 167 G1
Hampton TW12 . . . . 161 F4
Loxton Rd, SE23. . . . . 171 G1
Loxwood Rd, N17 . . . . 76 B3
Lubbock Rd, Chis. BR7 . . . 174 C7
Lubbock St, SE14. . . . . . . 133 F7
Lucan Pl, SW3 . . . . 31 G2
Lucan Rd, Barn. EN5 . . . . . 40 B3
Lucas Av, E13 . . . . 115 H1
Harrow HA2 . . . . 85 G2
Lucas Cl, NW10
off Pound La 89 G7
Lucas Ct, Har. HA2. . . . . . . 85 G1
Lucas Gdns, N2 . . . . 73 F2
Lucas Rd, SE20. . . . . 171 F6
Lucas Sq, NW11
off Hampstead Way. . . . 72 D6
Lucas St, SE8. . . . . 154 A1
Lucerne Cl, N13 . . . . 58 E4
Lucerne Ct, Erith DA18
off Middle Way. . . 138/139 E3
Lucerne Gro, E17 . . . . 78 D4
Lucerne Ms, W8
off Kensington Mall . . 128 D1
Lucerne Rd, N5 . . . . 93 H4
Orpington BR6 . . . . 207 J1
Thornton Heath CR7 . . . 187 H5
Lucey Rd, SE16 . . . . 29 H6
Lucey Way, SE16 . . . . 29 J6
Lucien Rd, SW17 . . . . 168 A4
SW19. . . . . 166 E2
Lucknow St, SE18 . . . . . . 137 H7
Lucorn Cl, SE12 . . . . 155 F6
Lucton Ms, Loug. IG10. . . . 48 E4
Luctons Av, Buck.H. IG9. . . 63 J1
Lucy Cres, W3. . . . . 106 C5
Lucy Gdns, Dag. RM8
off Grafton Rd . . . 100/101 E5
Luddesdon Rd, Erith DA8 . 139 G7
Ludford Cl, NW9 . . . . 70 E2
Croydon CR0
off Warrington Rd 201 H4
Ludgate Bdy, EC4. . . . . 19 G4
Ludgate Circ, EC4. . . . . 19 G4
Ludgate Hill, EC4 . . . . 19 G4
Ludgate Sq, EC4 . . . . 19 H4
Ludham Cl, SE28
off Rollesby Way 118 C6
Ilford IG6. . . . . 80 E1
Ludlow Cl, Brom. BR2
off Aylesbury Rd 191 G3
Harrow HA2 . . . . 85 F4
Ludlow Mead, Wat. WD19 . 50 B3
Ludlow Rd, W5. . . . . 105 F4
Feltham TW13 . . . . 160 A4
Ludlow St, EC1. . . . . 11 J5
Ludlow Way, N2. . . . . 73 F4
Ludovick Wk, SW15 . . . . . 147 E4
Ludwick Ms, SE14 . . . . . . 133 H7
Luffield Rd, SE2 . . . . 138 B3
Luffman Rd, SE12 . . . . . . 173 H3
Lugard Rd, SE15. . . . . 153 E2
Lugg App, E12 . . . . 98 D3
Luke Ho, E1 . . . . 113 E6
Luke St, EC2. . . . . 12 D5
Lukin Cres, E4 . . . . 62 D3
Lukin St, E1 . . . . 113 F6
Lukintone Cl, Loug. IG10 . . 48 B6
Lullingstone Cl, Orp. BR5
off Lullingstone Cres. . 176 B7
Lullingstone Cres, Orp.
BR5 . . . . 176 A7
Lullingstone La, SE13 . . . 154 D7
Lullingstone Rd, Belv.
DA17 . . . . 139 F6
Lullington Garth, N12 . . . . 56 C5
Borehamwood WD6 . . . . 38 B5
Bromley BR1. . . . . 173 E7
Lullington Rd, SE20 . . . . . 170 D7
Dagenham RM9 . . . . . . 100 E7
Lulot Gdns, N19. . . . . 92 B2
Lulworth, SE17 . . . . 36 B3
Lulworth Av, Houns. TW5 123 H7
Wembley HA9. . . . . 69 F7
Lulworth Cl, Har. HA2 . . . . 85 F3
Lulworth Cres, Mitch.
CR4 . . . . 185 H2
Lulworth Dr, Pnr. HA5 . . . . 66 D7
Lulworth Gdns, Har. HA2. . 85 E2
Lulworth Rd, SE9. . . . . . . 174 B2
SE15 . . . . 153 E2
Lulworth Rd, Well. DA16 . 157 J2
Lulworth Waye, Hayes
UB4 . . . . 102 C6
Lumen Rd, Wem. HA9 . . . . 87 G2
Lumiere Ct, SW17 . . . . . . 168 A2
Lumley Cl, Belv. DA17 . . . 139 G6
Lumley Ct, WC2 . . . . 18 B6
Lumley Gdns, Sutt. SM3 . 198 B5
Lumley Rd, Sutt. SM3 . . . 198 B6
Lumley St, W1 . . . . 10 C4
Luna Rd, Th.Hth. CR7 . . . . 187 J3
Lundin Wk, Wat. WD19
off Woodhall La. 50 D4
Lundy Dr, Hayes UB3. . . . 121 H4
Lundy Wk, N1
off Clephane Rd 93 J6
Lunham Rd, SE19. . . . . . . 170 B6
Lupin Cl, SW2
off Palace Rd. 169 H2
Croydon CR0
off Primrose La 203 G1
West Drayton UB7
off Magnolia St. 120 A5
Lupin Cres, Ilf. IG1
off Bluebell Way. . . . 98/99 E5
Lupino Ct, SE11 . . . . 34 D2
Lupton Cl, SE12 . . . . 173 H3
Lupton St, NW5. . . . . 92 C4
Lupus St, SW1 . . . . 33 G4
Luralda Gdns, E14
off Saunders Ness Rd. 134 C5
Lurgan Av, W6 . . . . 128 A6
Lurline Gdns, SW11 . . . . . 150 A1
Luscombe Ct, Brom. BR2. 190 E2
Luscombe Way, SW8 . . . . . 34 A7
Lushes Ct, Loug. IG10
off Lushes Rd. 48/49 E5
Lushes Rd, Loug. IG10. . . . 49 E5
Lushington Rd, NW10 . . . 107 H2
SE6 . . . . 172 B5
Lushington Ter, E8
off Wayland Av 94 D5
Luther Cl, Edg. HA8 . . . . . . 54 C2
Luther King Cl, E17 . . . . . . 77 H6
Luther Ms, Tedd. TW11
off Luther Rd. 162 C5
Luther Rd, Tedd. TW11 . . . 162 C5
Luton Pl, SE10 . . . . 134 C7
Luton Rd, E17. . . . . 77 J3
Sidcup DA14 . . . . 176 C3
Luton St, NW8. . . . . 7 F6
Lutton Ter, NW3
off Flask Wk. 91 G4
Luttrell Av, SW15 . . . . 147 H5
Lutwyche Rd, SE6 . . . . . . 171 J2
Luxborough La, Chig. IG7 . 64 B3
Luxborough St, W1 . . . . . . 16 B1
Luxembourg Ms, E15
off Leytonstone Rd 96 E5
Luxemburg Gdns, W6 . . . 128 A4
Luxfield Rd, SE9. . . . . 174 B1
Luxford St, SE16 . . . . 133 G4
Luxmore St, SE4 . . . . 153 J1
Luxor St, SE5 . . . . 151 J3
Lyall Av, SE21 . . . . 170 B3
Lyall Ms, SW1 . . . . 24 B6
Lyall Ms W, SW1 . . . . 24 B6
Lyall St, SW1 . . . . 24 B6
Lyal Rd, E3 . . . . 113 H2
Lycée, The, SE11
off Stannary St 131 G6
Lycett Pl, W12
off Becklow Rd 127 G2
Lyconby Gdns, Croy. CR0 . 189 H7
Lydd Cl, Sid. DA14 . . . . . . 175 H3
Lydden Ct, SE9. . . . . 157 H6
Lydden Gro, SW18. . . . . . 148 E7
Lydden Rd, SW18. . . . . . . 148 E7
Lydd Rd, Bexh. DA7 . . . . . 139 F7
Lydeard Rd, E6. . . . . 98 C7
Lydford Cl, N16
off Pellerin Rd. 94 B5
Lydford Rd, N15. . . . . 76 A5
NW2 . . . . 90 A6
W9. . . . . 108 C4
Lydhurst Av, SW2. . . . . . . 169 F2
Lydney Cl, SE15 . . . . 36 E7
SW19 *off Princes Way*. . 166 B2
Lydon Rd, SW4 . . . . 150 C3
Lydstep Rd, Chis. BR7 . . . 174 D4
Lyford Rd, SW18 . . . . 149 G7
Lygon Pl, SW1 . . . . 24 D6
Lyham Cl, SW2. . . . . 151 E6
Lyham Rd, SW2 . . . . 150 E5
Lyle Cl, Mitch. CR4 . . . . . . 186 A7
Lyme Fm Rd, SE12. . . . . . 155 G4
Lyme Gro, E9
off St. Thomas's Sq. . . . 95 F7
Lymer Av, SE19 . . . . 170 C5
Lyme Rd, Well. DA16 . . . . 158 B1
Lymescote Gdns, Sutt.
SM1. . . . . 198 D2
Lyme St, NW1 . . . . 92 C7
Lyme Ter, NW1
off Royal Coll St 92 C7
Lyminge Cl, Sid. DA14 . . . 175 J4
Lyminge Gdns, SW18 . . . 167 H1
Lymington Av, N22 . . . . . . 75 G2
Lymington Cl, E6
off Valiant Way. 116 C5
SW16. . . . . 186 D2
Lymington Gdns, Epsom
KT19 . . . . 197 F5
Lymington Rd, NW6 . . . . . 90 E6
Dagenham RM8 . . . . . . 100 D1
Lyminster Cl, Hayes UB4
off West Quay Dr . 102/103 E5
Lympstone Gdns, SE15 . . . 37 J7
Lynbridge Gdns, N13 . . . . . 59 H4
Lynbrook Cl, SE15 . . . . 36 E7
Lynbrook Gro, SE15
off Newent Cl 132 B7
Lynchen Cl, Houns. TW5
off The Avenue 142 A1
Lynch Wk, SE8
off Prince St 133 J6
Lyncott Cres, SW4 . . . . . . 150 B4
Lyncroft Av, Pnr. HA5. . . . . 66 E5
Lyncroft Gdns, NW6 . . . . . 90 D5
W13. . . . . 125 F2
Hounslow TW3 . . . . 143 J4
Lyndale, NW2. . . . . 90 C4
Lyndale Av, NW2 . . . . 90 C3
Lyndale Cl, SE3 . . . . 135 F6
Lyndhurst Av, N12 . . . . 57 J6
NW7 . . . . 54 E6
SW16. . . . . 186 D2
Pinner HA5 . . . . 66 B1
Southall UB1. . . . . 123 H1
Sunbury-on-Thames
TW16. . . . . 178 A3
Surbiton KT5. . . . . 196 B1
Twickenham TW2 . . . . . 161 F1
Lyndhurst Cl, NW10. . . . . . 88 D3
Bexleyheath DA7 . . . . . 159 H3
Croydon CR0. . . . . 202 C3
Orpington BR6 . . . . 207 E4
Lyndhurst Ct, E18
off Churchfields. 79 G1
Sutton SM2
off Overton Rd 198 D7
Lyndhurst Dr, E10 . . . . 78 C7
New Malden KT3 . . . . . 183 E6
Lyndhurst Gdns, N3. . . . . . 72 B1
NW3 . . . . 91 G5
Barking IG11 . . . . 99 H6
Enfield EN1 . . . . 44 B4
Ilford IG2 . . . . 81 G6
Pinner HA5 . . . . 66 B1
Lyndhurst Gro, SE15 . . . . 152 B2
Lyndhurst Ho, SW15
off Ellisfield Dr 147 G7
Lyndhurst Ri, Chig. IG7 . . . 64 D4
Lyndhurst Rd, E4 . . . . 62 C7
N18 . . . . 60 D4
N22 . . . . 59 F6
NW3 . . . . 91 G5
Bexleyheath DA7 . . . . . 159 H3
Greenford UB6 . . . . 103 H4
Thornton Heath CR7 . . . 187 G4
Lyndhurst Sq, SE15 . . . . . 152 C1
Lyndhurst Ter, NW3 . . . . . . 91 G5
Lyndhurst Way, SE15 . . . . . 152 C1
Sutton SM2. . . . . 198 D7
Lyndon Av, Pnr. HA5 . . . . . 51 E6
Sidcup DA15 . . . . 157 J5
Wallington SM6 . . . . . . 200 A3
Lyndon Rd, Belv. DA17 . . 139 G4
Lyndon Yd, SW17
off Riverside Rd 167 F4
Lyne Cres, E17 . . . . 77 J1
Lyneham Wk, E5 . . . . 95 H5
Lynette Av, SW4. . . . . 150 B6
Lynett Rd, Dag. RM8 . . . . 100 D2
Lynford Cl, Barn. EN5
off Rowley La 39 F5
Edgware HA8 . . . . 54 C7
Lynford Gdns, Edg. HA8 . . 54 B3
Ilford IG3. . . . . 99 J2
Lynmere Rd, Well. DA16. . 158 B2
Lyn Ms, E3
off Tredegar Sq 113 J3
N16 . . . . 94 B4
Lynmouth Av, Enf. EN1 . . . 44 C6
Morden SM4. . . . . 184 A7
Lynmouth Dr, Ruis. HA4 . . 84 B2
Lynmouth Gdns, Grnf.
UB6 . . . . 105 E1
Lynmouth Gdns, Houns.
TW5 . . . . 142 D1
Lynmouth Rd, E17 . . . . 77 H6
N2 . . . . 73 J3
N16 . . . . 94 C1
Greenford UB6 . . . . 105 E1
Lynn Cl, Har. HA3. . . . . 68 A2
Lynne Cl, Orp. BR6. . . . . . 207 J6
Lynne Way, NW10 . . . . 88 E6
Northolt UB5 . . . . 102 D2
Lynn Ms, E11
off Lynn Rd 96/97 E2
Lynn Rd, E11. . . . . 96 E2
SW12. . . . . 150 B7
Ilford IG2. . . . . 81 G7
Lynn St, Enf. EN2. . . . . 44 A1
Lynsted Cl, Bexh. DA6 . . . 159 H5
Bromley BR1 . . . . 191 J2
Lynsted Ct, Beck. BR3
off Churchfields Rd . . . 189 H2
Lynsted Gdns, SE9. . . . . . 156 A3
Lynton Av, N12. . . . . 57 G4
NW9 . . . . 71 F4
W13. . . . . 104 D6
Romford RM7 . . . . 83 G1
Lynton Cl, NW10 . . . . 88 E5
Chessington KT9. . . . . . 195 H4
Isleworth TW7 . . . . 144 C4
Lynton Cres, Ilf. IG2 . . . . . 80 E6
Lynton Est, SE1 . . . . 37 H2
Lynton Gdns, N11 . . . . 58 D6
Enfield EN1 . . . . 44 B7
Lynton Mead, N20 . . . . 56 D3
Lynton Rd, E4. . . . . 62 B5
N8 . . . . 74 D5
NW6 . . . . 108 C1
SE1 . . . . 37 G2
W3. . . . . 106 A7
Croydon CR0. . . . . 187 G6
Harrow HA2 . . . . 85 E2
New Malden KT3 . . . . . 182 D5
Lynton Ter, W3
off Lynton Rd. 106 C6
Lynwood Cl, E18 . . . . 79 J1
Harrow HA2 . . . . 85 E3
Lynwood Dr, Wor.Pk. KT4 . 197 G2
Lynwood Gdns, Croy.
CR0 . . . . 201 F4
Southall UB1. . . . . 103 F6
Lynwood Gro, N21. . . . . . . 59 G1
Orpington BR6 . . . . 193 H7
Lynwood Rd, SW17 . . . . . 167 J3
W5. . . . . 105 H4
Thames Ditton KT7 . . . . 194 C2
Lynx Way, E16
off Festoon Way. 116 A7
Lyon Business Pk, Bark.
IG11 . . . . 117 H2
Lyon Meade, Stan. HA7 . . . 69 F1
Lyon Pk Av, Wem. HA0. . . . 87 H6
Lyon Rd, SW19. . . . . 185 F1
Harrow HA1 . . . . 68 C6
Lyonsdown Av, Barn. EN5 . 41 F6
Lyonsdown Rd, Barn. EN5 . 41 F6
Lyons Pl, NW8 . . . . 7 E5
Lyon St, N1
off Caledonian Rd. 93 F7
Lyons Wk, W14. . . . . 128 B4
Lyon Way, Grnf. UB6 . . . . 104 B1
Lyoth Rd, Orp. BR5 . . . . . 207 F2
Lyric Dr, Grnf. UB6. . . . . . 103 H4
Lyric Ms, SE26 . . . . 171 F4
Lyric Rd, SW13. . . . . 147 F1
★**Lyric Thea**, W6. . . . . 127 J4
Lysander Gdns, Surb. KT6
off Ewell Rd. 181 J6
Lysander Gro, N19. . . . . . . 92 D1
Lysander Ms, N19
off Lysander Gro 92 C1
Lysander Rd, Croy. CR0 . . 201 F6
Lysander Way, Orp. BR6 . 207 F3
Lysias Rd, SW12. . . . . 150 A6
Lysia St, SW6. . . . . 128 A7
Lysons Wk, SW15
off Swinburne Rd 147 G5
Lytchet Rd, Brom. BR1. . . 173 H7
Lytchet Way, Enf. EN3 . . . . 45 F1
Lytchgate Cl, S.Croy. CR2 . 202 B7
Lytcott Dr, W.Mol. KT8
off Freeman Dr 179 F3
Lytcott Gro, SE22. . . . . . . 152 C5
Lyte St, E2
off Bishops Way 113 F2
Lytham Av, Wat. WD19. . . . 50 D5
Lytham Cl, SE28. . . . . 118 E6
Lytham Gro, W5 . . . . 105 J3
Lytham St, SE17 . . . . 36 B4
Lyttelton Cl, NW3 . . . . 91 H7
Lyttelton Rd, E10 . . . . 96 B3

Lyttelton Rd, N2. . . . . 73 F5
N8 . . . . 75 G3
Lytton Av, N13 . . . . 59 G2
Lytton Cl, N2 . . . . 73 G5
Loughton IG10 . . . . 49 G3
Northolt UB5. . . . . 85 F7
Lytton Gdns, Wall. SM6 . . 200 D4
Lytton Gro, SW15 . . . . . . 148 A5
Lytton Rd, E11 . . . . 78 E7
Barnet EN5 . . . . 41 F4
Pinner HA5 . . . . 50 E7
Lytton Strachey Path, SE28
off Titmuss Av 118 B7
Lyveden Rd, SE3 . . . . 135 H7
SW17. . . . . 167 H6

M

Maberley Cres, SE19 . . . . 170 D7
Maberley Rd, SE19. . . . . . 188 C1
Beckenham BR3 . . . . . . 189 G3
Mabledon Pl, WC1 . . . . 9 J4
Mablethorpe Rd, SW6 . . . 128 B7
Mabley St, E9. . . . . 95 H6
McAdam Dr, Enf. EN2
off Rowantree Rd 43 H2
Macaret Cl, N20. . . . . 41 E7
MacArthur Cl, E7 . . . . 97 G6
MacArthur Ter, SE7 . . . . . 136 B6
Macaulay Av, Esher
KT10 . . . . 194 B2
Macaulay Ct, SW4 . . . . . . 150 B3
Macaulay Rd, E6. . . . . 116 A2
SW4. . . . . 150 B3
Macaulay Sq, SW4. . . . . . 150 B4
Macaulay Way, SE28
off Booth Cl. 118 B7
McAuley Cl, SE1. . . . . 26 E5
SE9 . . . . 156 E5
Macauley Ms, SE13 . . . . . 154 C2
Macbean St, SE18 . . . . . . 136 D3
Macbeth St, W6 . . . . 127 H5
McCall Cl, SW4
off Jeffreys Rd . . . 150/151 E2
McCall Cres, SE7 . . . . 136 B5
McCarthy Rd, Felt. TW13 . 160 D5
Macclesfield Br, NW1 . . . . . 7 H1
Macclesfield Rd, EC1 . . . . . 11 J3
SE25 . . . . 189 E5
Macclesfield St, W1 . . . . . . 17 J5
McCoid Way, SE1. . . . . 27 J4
McCrone Ms, NW3
off Belsize La. 91 G6
McCullum Rd, E3 . . . . 113 J1
McDermott Cl, SW11 . . . . 149 H3
McDermott Rd, SE15 . . . . 152 D3
Macdonald Av, Dag.
RM10 . . . . 101 H3
Macdonald Rd, E7 . . . . 97 G4
E17 . . . . 78 C2
N11 . . . . 57 J5
N19 . . . . 92 C2
McDonough Cl, Chess.
KT9 . . . . 195 H4
McDowall Cl, E16 . . . . 115 F5
McDowall Rd, SE5 . . . . . . 151 J1
Macduff Rd, SW11 . . . . . . 150 A1
Mace Cl, E1
off Kennet St 132/133 E1
McEntee Av, E17 . . . . 77 H1
Mace St, E2 . . . . 113 G2
McEwen Way, E15 . . . . . . 114 D1
Macey Ho, SW11
off Surrey La. 149 H1
Macfarland Gro, SE15
off Blakes Rd. 132 B7
MacFarlane La, Islw. TW7. 124 C6
Macfarlane Rd, W12 . . . . . 127 J1
Macfarren Pl, NW1. . . . . 8 C6
McGrath Rd, E15 . . . . 97 F5
Macgregor Rd, E16. . . . . . 115 J5
McGregor Rd, W11 . . . . . . 108 C6
Machell Rd, SE15. . . . . . . 153 F3
McIntosh Cl, Wall. SM6 . . 200 E7
Mackay Rd, SW4 . . . . 150 B3
McKay Rd, SW20 . . . . 165 H7
McKellar Cl, Bushey
(Bushey Hth) WD23. . . . 51 J2
Mackennal St, NW8. . . . . . . 7 H2
Mackenzie Rd, N7 . . . . 93 F6
Beckenham BR3 . . . . . . 189 F2
Mackenzie Wk, E14 . . . . . 134 A1
McKerrell Rd, SE15 . . . . . 152 D1
Mackeson Rd, NW3 . . . . . . 91 J4
Mackie Rd, SW2. . . . . 151 G7
Mackintosh La, E9
off Homerton High St . . 95 G5
Macklin St, WC2. . . . . 18 B3
Mackrow Wk, E14
off Robin Hood La 114 C7
Macks Rd, SE16 . . . . 37 J1
Mackworth St, NW1 . . . . . . 9 F3
Maclaren Ms, SW15
off Clarendon Dr 147 J4
Maclean Rd, SE23 . . . . . . 153 H6
Macleod Rd, N21 . . . . 43 E5
McLeod Rd, SE2. . . . . 138 B4
McLeod's Ms, SW7 . . . . . . 22 B6
Macleod St, SE17. . . . . 36 A4
Maclise Rd, W14. . . . . 128 B3
McMillan St, SE8 . . . . 134 A6
McMillan Student Village,
SE8 *off Creek Rd*. 134 A6
Macmillan Way, SW17 . . . 168 B4
McNair Rd, Sthl. UB2. . . . 123 H2
McNeil Rd, SE5 . . . . 152 B2
McNicol Dr, NW10 . . . . . . 106 C2
Macoma Rd, SE18 . . . . . . 137 G6
Macoma Ter, SE18 . . . . . . 137 G6
Maconochies Rd, E14. . . . 134 B5
Macquarie Way, E14. . . . . 134 B4
McRae La, Mitch. CR4 . . . 185 J7
Macroom Rd, W9 . . . . 108 C3
Mac's Pl, EC4 . . . . 19 E3
★**Madame Tussaud's**, NW1 . 8 B6
Mada Rd, Orp. BR6 . . . . . . 206 E3
Maddams St, E3. . . . . 114 B4
Maddison Cl, Tedd. TW11 . 162 C6
Maddocks Cl, Sid. DA14. . 176 E5
Maddock Way, SE17. . . . . . 35 H6
Maddox St, W1 . . . . 16 E5
Madeira Av, Brom. BR1 . . 172 E7
Madeira Gro, Wdf.Grn.
IG8. . . . . 63 J6
Madeira Rd, E11 . . . . 96 D1
N13 . . . . 59 H4
SW16. . . . . 169 E5
Mitcham CR4. . . . . 185 J4
Madeley Rd, W5 . . . . 105 H6
Madeline Gro, Ilf. IG1. . . . . 99 G5
Madeline Rd, SE20. . . . . . 188 D1
Madge Gill Way, E6
off Ron Leighton Way . 116 B1
Madinah Rd, E8 . . . . 94 D6
Madingley, Kings.T. KT1
off St. Peters Rd 182 A2
Madison Cres, Bexh.
DA7 . . . . 138 C7
Madison Gdns, Bexh.
DA7 . . . . 138 C7
Bromley BR2. . . . . 191 F3
Madras Pl, N7 . . . . 93 G6
Madras Rd, Ilf. IG1 . . . . 99 E4
Madrid Rd, SW13. . . . . . . 147 G1
Madrigal La, SE5 . . . . 131 H7
Madron St, SE17 . . . . 36 E3
Mafeking Av, E6 . . . . 116 A2
Brentford TW8. . . . . 125 H6
Ilford IG2. . . . . 81 G7
Mafeking Rd, E16. . . . . . . 115 F4
N17 . . . . 76 D2
Enfield EN1 . . . . 44 C3
Magdala Av, N19 . . . . 92 B2
Magdala Rd, Islw. TW7. . . 144 D3
South Croydon CR2
off Napier Rd. 202 A7
Magdalene Cl, SE15
off Pilkington Rd . 152/153 E2
Magdalene Gdns, E6 . . . . 116 D4
Magdalen Pas, E1 . . . . 21 G5
Magdalen Rd, SW18 . . . . 167 F1
Magdalen St, SE1 . . . . 28 D2
Magee St, SE11 . . . . 35 E5
Magellan Pl, E14
off Maritime Quay. . . . 134 A5
Maggie Blakes Causeway,
SE1 *off Shad Thames* . 132 C1
Magnet Rd, Wem. HA9 . . . 87 G2
Magnin Cl, E8
off Wilde Cl 112 D1
Magnolia Cl, E10 . . . . 96 A2
Kingston upon Thames
KT2 . . . . 164 C6
Magnolia Ct, Har. HA3. . . . 69 J7
Richmond TW9
off West Hall Rd 146 B1
Wallington SM6
off Parkgate Rd. 200 B5
Magnolia Gdns, Edg. HA8 . 54 C4
Magnolia Pl, SW4 . . . . . . 150 E5
W5 *off Montpelier Rd* . . 105 H5
Magnolia Rd, W4 . . . . 126 B6
Magnolia St, West Dr.
UB7. . . . . 120 A4
Magnolia Way, Epsom
KT19 . . . . 196 C5
Magpie All, EC4 . . . . 19 F4
Magpie Cl, E7. . . . . 97 F5
NW9 *off Eagle Dr*. . . . 70/71 E2
Enfield EN1 . . . . 44 D1
Magpie Hall Cl, Brom.
BR2 . . . . 192 B6
Magpie Hall La, Brom.
BR2 . . . . 192 C5
Magpie Hall Rd, Bushey
(Bushey Hth) WD23. . . . 52 B2
Magpie Pl, SE14
off Milton Ct Rd 133 H6
Magri Wk, E1
off Ashfield St 113 F5
Maguire Dr, Rich. TW10 . . 163 F4
Maguire St, SE1. . . . . 29 G3
Mahlon Av, Ruis. HA4 . . . . 84 B5
Mahogany Cl, SE16 . . . . . 133 H1
Mahon Cl, Enf. EN1 . . . . . . 44 C1
Maida Av, E4 . . . . 46 B7
W2. . . . . 14 D1
MAIDA HILL, W9. . . . . 108 C4
Maida Rd, Belv. DA17 . . . 139 G3
MAIDA VALE, W9 . . . . 6 B5
Maida Vale, W9. . . . . 6 C4
Maida Way, E4 . . . . 46 B7
Maiden Erlegh Av, Bex.
DA5 . . . . 176 E1
Maiden La, NW1 . . . . 92 D7
SE1 . . . . 28 A1
WC2. . . . . 18 B6
Maiden Rd, E15 . . . . 97 E7
Maidenstone Hill, SE10 . . 154 C1
Maids of Honour Row,
Rich. TW9
off The Green 145 G5
Maidstone Av, Rom. RM5 . 83 J2
Maidstone Bldgs Ms, SE1 . 28 A2
Maidstone Ho, E14
off Carmen St 114 B6
Maidstone Rd, N11. . . . . . . 58 C6
Sidcup DA14 . . . . 176 D6
Maidstone St, E2 . . . . 13 J1
Main Av, Enf. EN1 . . . . 44 C5
Main Dr, Wem. HA9 . . . . . . 87 G3
Mainridge Rd, Chis. BR7 . 174 D4
Main Rd, Sid. DA14 . . . . . 175 H3
Main St, Felt. TW13 . . . . . 160 D5
Maisemore St, SE15 . . . . . . 37 J7
Maitland Cl, Houns. TW4 . 143 F3
Maitland Cl Est, SE10
off Greenwich High Rd . 134 B7
Maitland Pk Est, NW3 . . . . 91 J6
Maitland Pk Rd, NW3 . . . . 91 J6
Maitland Pk Vil, NW3. . . . . 91 J6
Maitland Pl, E5
off Clarence Rd 94/95 E4
Maitland Rd, E15 . . . . 97 F6
SE26 . . . . 171 G6
Majendie Rd, SE18. . . . . . 137 G5
Majestic Way, Mitch. CR4. 185 J2
Major Cl, SW9
off Styles Gdns 151 H3
Major Rd, E15 . . . . 96 C5
SE16 . . . . 29 J5
Makepeace Av, N6 . . . . 92 A2
Makepeace Rd, E11 . . . . . . 79 G4
Northolt UB5. . . . . 102 E2
Makins St, SW3. . . . . 31 H2
Malabar St, E14 . . . . 134 A2
Malam Gdns, E14
off Wades Pl. 114 B7
Malbrook Rd, SW15. . . . . 147 H4
Malcolm Ct, Stan. HA7 . . . 53 F5
Malcolm Cres, NW4. . . . . . 71 G6
Malcolm Dr, Surb. KT6 . . . 195 H1
Malcolm Pl, E2 . . . . 113 F4
Malcolm Rd, E1 . . . . 113 F4
SE20 . . . . 171 F7
SE25 . . . . 188 D6
SW19. . . . . 166 B6
Malcolms Way, N14 . . . . . . 42 C5
Malcolm Way, E11 . . . . 79 G5
Malden Av, SE25 . . . . 188 E4
Greenford UB6 . . . . 86 B5
Malden Ct, N.Mal. KT3
off West Barnes La . . . 183 H3
Malden Cres, NW1. . . . . . . 92 A6
Malden Grn Av, Wor.Pk.
KT4 . . . . 197 F1
Malden Hill, N.Mal. KT3. . 183 F3
Malden Hill Gdns, N.Mal.
KT3 . . . . 183 F3
Malden Pk, N.Mal. KT3 . . 183 F6
Malden Pl, NW5
off Grafton Ter. 92 A5
Malden Rd, NW5 . . . . 92 A5
Borehamwood WD6 . . . . 38 A3
New Malden KT3 . . . . . 183 E5
Sutton SM3. . . . . 198 A4
Malden Rd, Wor. Pk KT4. . 183 F7
Malden Way, N.Mal. KT3 . 183 F5
Maldon Cl, E15
off David St. 96 D5
N1 *off Popham Rd*. 111 J1
SE5 . . . . 152 B3
Maldon Ct, Wall. SM6
off Maldon Rd. 200 C5
Maldon Rd, N9. . . . . 60 C3
W3. . . . . 106 C7
Romford RM7 . . . . 83 J7
Wallington SM6 . . . . . . 200 B5
Maldon Wk, Wdf.Grn. IG8 . 63 J6
Malet Pl, WC1 . . . . 9 H6
Malet St, WC1 . . . . 9 H6
Maley Av, SE27 . . . . 169 H2
Malford Ct, E18 . . . . 79 G2
Malford Gro, E18 . . . . 79 F4
Malfort Rd, SE5 . . . . 152 B3
Malham Cl, N11
off Catterick Cl. 58 A6
Malham Rd, SE23. . . . . . . 171 G1
Malins Cl, Barn. EN5 . . . . . 39 H5
Mall, The, E15. . . . . 96 D7
N14 . . . . 58 E3
SW1. . . . . 25 G3
SW14. . . . . 146 C5
W5. . . . . 105 H7
Croydon CR0. . . . . 201 J2
Harrow HA3 . . . . 69 J6
Surbiton KT6. . . . . 181 G5
Mallams Ms, SW9
off St. James's Cres . . 151 H3
Mallard Cl, E9
off Berkshire Rd 95 J6
NW6 . . . . 108 D2
W7. . . . . 124 B2
Barnet EN5
off The Hook 41 G6
Twickenham TW2
off Stephenson Rd . . . 143 G7
Mallard Path, SE28. . . . . . 137 G3
Mallard Pl, Twick. TW1 . . . 162 D3
Mallard Pt, E3
off Rainhill Way 114 B3
Mallards Rd, Bark. IG11 . . 118 A4
Woodford Green IG8 . . . 63 H7
Mallard Wk, Beck. BR3. . . 189 G5
Sidcup DA14 . . . . 176 C5
Mallard Way, NW9 . . . . 70 C7
Mallet Dr, Nthlt. UB5 . . . . . 85 F5
Mallet Rd, SE13 . . . . 154 D6
★**Mall Galleries**, SW1 . . . . 25 J1
Malling, SE13. . . . . 154 C5
Malling Cl, Croy. CR0. . . . 189 F6
Malling Gdns, 185 . . . . F6
Malling Way, Brom. BR2 . 191 F7
Mallinson Rd, SW11. . . . . 149 H5
Croydon CR0. . . . . 200 D3
Mallord St, SW3 . . . . 31 F5
Mallory Cl, SE4 . . . . 153 H4
Mallory Gdns, Barn. EN4 . . 42 A7
Mallory St, NW8 . . . . 7 H5
Mallow Cl, Croy. CR0
off Marigold Way 203 G1
Mallow Mead, NW7. . . . . . . 56 B7
Mallow St, EC1 . . . . 12 B5
Mall Rd, W6 . . . . 127 H5
Malmains Cl, Beck. BR3 . . 190 D5
Malmains Way, Beck. BR3. 190 C4
Malmesbury Rd, E3 . . . . . 113 J3
E16. . . . . 115 E5
E18 . . . . 79 F1
Morden SM4. . . . . 185 F7
Malmesbury Ter, E16 . . . . 115 F5
Malmsmead Ho, E9
off Kingsmead Way. . . . 95 H5
Malpas Dr, Pnr. HA5 . . . . . 66 D5
Malpas Rd, E8 . . . . 94 E6
SE4 . . . . 153 J2
Dagenham RM9 . . . . . . 100 D6
Malta Rd, E10. . . . . 96 A1
Malta St, EC1 . . . . 11 H5
Maltby Rd, Chess. KT9. . . 196 A6
Maltby St, SE1. . . . . 29 F4
Malthouse Dr, W4 . . . . . . 127 E6
Feltham TW13 . . . . 160 D5
Malthouse Pas, SW13
off The Terrace . . . 146/147 E2
Malthus Path, SE28
off Owen Cl. 138 C1
Malting Ho, E14 . . . . 113 J7
Maltings, The, Orp. BR6. . 207 J1
Maltings Cl, SW13
off Cleveland Gdns . 146/147 E2
Maltings Ms, Sid. DA15
off Station Rd 176 A3
Maltings Pl, SW6 . . . . 149 E1
Malting Way, Islw. TW7 . . 144 C3

Malton Ms, SE18
off Malton St **137** H6
W10
off Cambridge Gdns . . **108** B6
Malton Rd, W10
off St. Marks Rd **108** B6
Malton St, SE18 . . . . **137** H6
Maltravers St, WC2 . . . . . . **18** D5
Malt St, SE1 . . . . **37** H5
Malva Cl, SW18
off St. Ann's Hill . . **148/149** E5
Malvern Av, E4 . . . . **62** D7
Bexleyheath DA7 . . . . . **138** E7
Harrow HA2 . . . . **85** E3
Malvern Cl, SE20
off Derwent Rd **188** D2
W10 . . . . **108** C5
Mitcham CR4 . . . . **186** C3
Surbiton KT6 . . . . **195** H1
Malvern Ct, SE14
off Avonley Rd **133** F7
SW7 . . . . **31** F2
Sutton SM2
off Overton Rd **198** D7
Malvern Dr, Felt. TW13 . . . **160** D5
Ilford IG3 . . . . **99** J4
Woodford Green IG8 . . . **63** J5
Malvern Gdns, NW2 . . . . . . **90** B2
NW6 *off Carlton Vale* . . . **108** C2
Harrow HA3 . . . . **69** H3
Loughton IG10 . . . . **48** C6
Malvern Ms, NW6
off Malvern Rd **108** D3
Malvern Pl, NW6 . . . . **108** C3
Malvern Rd, E6 . . . . **116** B1
E8 . . . . **94** D7
E11 . . . . **97** E2
N8 . . . . **75** F3
N17 . . . . **76** D3
NW6 . . . . **108** D3
Hampton TW12 . . . . **161** G7
Hayes UB3 . . . . **121** H7
Surbiton KT6 . . . . **195** H2
Thornton Heath CR7 . . . **187** G4
Malvern Ter, N1 . . . . **111** G1
N9 *off Latymer Rd* **60** C1
Malvern Way, W13
off Templewood . . **104/105** E5
Malwood Rd, SW12 . . . . . **150** B6
Malyons Rd, SE13 . . . . . . **154** B5
Malyons Ter, SE13 . . . . . . **154** B5
Managers St, E14
off Prestons Rd **134** C1
Manatee Pl, Wall. SM6
off Croydon Rd **200** D3
Manaton Cl, SE15 . . . . **152** E3
Manaton Cres, Sthl. UB1 . **103** G6
Manbey Gro, E15 . . . . **96** E6
Manbey Pk Rd, E15 . . . . . . **96** E6
Manbey Rd, E15 . . . . **96** E6
Manbey St, E15 . . . . **96** E6
Manbre Rd, W6 . . . . **127** J6
Manbrough Av, E6 . . . . . . **116** C3
Manchester Ct, E16 . . . . . **115** H6
Manchester Dr, W10 . . . . . **108** B4
Manchester Gro, E14 . . . . **134** C5
Manchester Ms, W1 . . . . . . **16** B2
Manchester Rd, E14 . . . . . **134** C5
N15 . . . . **76** A6
Thornton Heath CR7 . . . **187** J3
Manchester Sq, W1 . . . . . . **16** B3
Manchester St, W1 . . . . **16** B2
Manchester Way, Dag.
RM10 . . . . **101** H4
Manchuria Rd, SW11 . . . . **150** A6
Manciple St, SE1 . . . . **28** B4
Mandalay Rd, SW4 . . . . . **150** C5
Mandarin St, E14
off Salter St **114** A7
Mandarin Way, Hayes
UB4 . . . . **102** D5
Mandela Cl, NW10 . . . . **88** C7
Mandela Rd, E16 . . . . **115** G6
Mandela St, NW1 . . . . **110** C1
SW9 . . . . **131** G7
Mandela Way, SE1 . . . . **36** E1
Mandeville Cl, SE3
off Vanbrugh Pk **135** F7
SW20 . . . . **184** B1
Mandeville Ct, E4 . . . . **61** H4
Mandeville Dr, Surb. KT6. **195** G1
Mandeville Ms, SW4
off Clapham Pk Rd. **150/151** E4
Mandeville Pl, W1 . . . . **16** C3
Mandeville Rd, N14 . . . . . . **58** B2
Isleworth TW7 . . . . **144** D2
Northolt UB5 . . . . **85** G7
Mandeville St, E5 . . . . **95** H3
Mandrake Rd, SW17 . . . . **167** J3
Mandrake Way, E15 . . . . . . **96** E7
Mandrell Rd, SW2 . . . . . . **150** E5
Manette St, W1 . . . . **17** J4
Manford Way, Chig. IG7 . . . **65** H4
Manfred Rd, SW15 . . . . . . **148** C5
Manger Rd, N7 . . . . **93** E6
Mangold Way, Erith DA18 . **138** E3
Manhattan Wf, E16 . . . . . . **135** G2
Manilla St, E14 . . . . **134** A2
Manister Rd, SE2 . . . . **138** A3
Manitoba Ct, SE16
off Renforth St **133** F2
Manitoba Gdns, Orp. BR6
off Superior Dr **207** J6
Manley Ct, N16
*off Stoke Newington
High St* **94** C3
Manley St, NW1 . . . . **110** A1
Mann Cl, Croy. CR0
off Salem Pl **201** J3
Manningford Cl, EC1 . . . . . **11** G3
Manning Gdns, Har. HA3 . . **69** G7
Manning Pl, Rich. TW10
off Grove Rd **145** J6
Manning Rd, E17
off Southcote Rd **77** H5
Dagenham RM10 . . . . . . **101** G6
Manningtree Cl, SW19 . . . **166** B1
Manningtree Rd, Ruis.
HA4 . . . . **84** B4
Manningtree St, E1 . . . . . . **21** H3
Mannin Rd, Rom. RM6 . . . **82** B7
Mannock Dr, Loug. IG10 . . **49** F2
Mannock Ms, E18 . . . . **79** H1
Mannock Rd, N22 . . . . **75** H3
Manns Cl, Islw. TW7 . . . . . **144** C5
Manns Rd, Edg. HA8 . . . . . **54** A6
Manoel Rd, Twick. TW2 . . . **161** J2
Manor Av, SE4 . . . . **153** J2
Hounslow TW4 . . . . **142** D3
Northolt UB5 . . . . **85** F7
Manorbrook, SE3 . . . . **155** G4
Manor Cl, E17
off Manor Rd **77** H2
NW7 *off Manor Dr* **54** D5
NW9 . . . . **70** B5
SE28 . . . . **118** C6
Barnet EN5 . . . . **40** B4
Worcester Park KT4 . . . . **197** E1
Manor Cotts App, N2 . . . . . **73** F2
Manor Ct, E10
off Grange Pk Rd **96** B1
N2 . . . . **73** J5
SW6
off Bagley's La . . . **148/149** E1
Twickenham TW2 . . . . . **161** J2
Wembley HA9 . . . . **87** H5
Manor Ct Rd, W7 . . . . **104** B7
Manor Cres, Surb. KT5 . . **182** A6
Manordene Cl, T.Ditt. KT7 . **194** D1
Manordene Rd, SE28 . . . . **118** C6
Manor Dr, N14 . . . . **42** B7
N20 . . . . **57** H3
NW7 . . . . **54** D6
Epsom KT19 . . . . **196** E6
Esher KT10 . . . . **194** C2
Feltham TW13
off Lebanon Av **160** D5
Sunbury-on-Thames
TW16 . . . . **178** A2
Surbiton KT5 . . . . **181** J6
Wembley HA9 . . . . **87** J4
Manor Dr, The, Wor.Pk.
KT4 . . . . **197** E1
Manor Dr N, N.Mal. KT3 . **182** D7
Worcester Park KT4 . . . . **196** E1
Manor Est, SE16 . . . . **132** E4
Manor Fm Cl, Wor.Pk.
KT4 . . . . **196** E1
Manor Fm Dr, E4 . . . . **63** E3
Manor Fm Rd, Th.Hth.
CR7 . . . . **187** G2
Wembley HA0 . . . . **105** G2
Manorfield Cl, N19
off Junction Rd **92** C4
Manor Flds, SW15 . . . . . . **148** A6
Manorfields Cl, Chis. BR7 . **193** J3
Manor Gdns, N7 . . . . **92** E3
SW20 . . . . **184** C2
W3 . . . . **126** A4
W4
off Devonshire Rd . **126/127** E5
Hampton TW12 . . . . **161** H7
Richmond TW9 . . . . **145** J4
Ruislip HA4 . . . . **84** C5
South Croydon CR2 . . . **202** C6
Sunbury-on-Thames
TW16 . . . . **178** A2
Manor Gate, Nthlt. UB5 . . . **84** E7
Manorgate Rd, Kings.T.
KT2 . . . . **182** A1
Manor Gro, SE15 . . . . **133** F6
Beckenham BR3 . . . . . . **190** B2
Richmond TW9 . . . . **146** A4
Manor Hall Av, NW4 . . . . . **71** J2
Manor Hall Dr, NW4 . . . . . **72** A2
Manorhall Gdns, E10 . . . . . **96** A1
Manor Ho Dr, NW6 . . . . . . **90** A7
Manor Ho Est, Stan. HA7
off Old Ch La **52/53** E6
Manor Ho Way, Islw. TW7 . **144** E3
Manor La, SE12 . . . . **155** E6
SE13 . . . . **154** E4
Feltham TW13 . . . . **160** A2
Hayes UB3 . . . . **121** G6
Sunbury-on-Thames
TW16 . . . . **178** A2
Sutton SM1 . . . . **199** F5
Manor La Ter, SE13 . . . . . **154** E4
Manor Ms, NW6
off Cambridge Av **108** D2
SE4 . . . . **153** J2
Manor Mt, SE23 . . . . **171** F1
Manor Par, NW10
off Station Rd **107** F2
MANOR PARK, E12 . . . . . . **98** B4
Manor Pk, SE13 . . . . **154** D4
Chislehurst BR7 . . . . . . **193** G2
Richmond TW9 . . . . **145** J4
Manor Pk Cl, W.Wick. BR4. **204** B1
Manor Pk Cres, Edg. HA8 . **54** A6
Manor Pk Dr, Har. HA2 . . . **67** H3
Manor Pk Gdns, Edg. HA8. **54** A5
Manor Pk Par, SE13
off Lee High Rd **154** D4
Manor Pk Rd, E12 . . . . **98** A4
N2 . . . . **73** G3
NW10 . . . . **107** F1
Chislehurst BR7 . . . . . . **193** F1
Sutton SM1 . . . . **199** F5
West Wickham BR4 . . . . **204** B1
Manor Pl, SE17 . . . . **35** H4
Chislehurst BR7 . . . . . . **193** G1
Feltham TW14 . . . . **160** A1
Mitcham CR4 . . . . **186** C3
Sutton SM1 . . . . **199** E4
Manor Rd, E10 . . . . **78** A7
E15 . . . . **114** E3
E16 . . . . **114** E3
E17 . . . . **77** H2
N16 . . . . **94** A2
N17 . . . . **76** D1
N22 . . . . **59** E6
SE25 . . . . **188** D4
SW20 . . . . **184** C2
W13 . . . . **104** D7
Barking IG11 . . . . **99** J6
Barnet EN5 . . . . **40** B5
Beckenham BR3 . . . . . . **190** B2
Bexley DA5 . . . . **177** H1
Chigwell IG7 . . . . **64** E5
Dagenham RM10 . . . . . . **101** J6
East Molesey KT8 . . . . . **180** A4
Enfield EN2 . . . . **44** A2
Harrow HA1 . . . . **68** D6
Hayes UB3 . . . . **102** A6
Loughton IG10 . . . . **47** H6
Loughton (High Beach)
IG10 . . . . **47** H1
Mitcham CR4 . . . . **186** C4
Richmond TW9 . . . . **145** J3
Romford (Chad.Hth)
RM6 . . . . **82** D6
Sidcup DA15 . . . . **175** J3
Sutton SM2 . . . . **198** C7
Teddington TW11 . . . . . . **162** E5
Twickenham TW2 . . . . . **161** J2
Wallington SM6 . . . . **200** B4
West Wickham BR4 . . . . **204** B2
Woodford Green IG8 . . . **64** C6
Manor Rd N, Esher KT10 . **194** C3
Thames Ditton KT7 . . . . **194** D2
Wallington SM6 . . . . **200** B4
Manor Rd S, Esher KT10 . **194** B4
Manorside, Barn. EN5 . . . . **40** B4
Manorside Cl, SE2 . . . . . . **138** C4
Manor Sq, Dag. RM8 . . . . **100** D2
Manor Vale, Brent. TW8 . . **125** F5
Manor Vw, N3 . . . . **72** E2
Manor Way, E4 . . . . **62** D4
NW9 . . . . **70** E3
SE3 . . . . **155** F4
SE23 . . . . **153** F7
SE28 . . . . **138** C1
Beckenham BR3 . . . . . . **190** A2
Bexley DA5 . . . . **177** G1
Borehamwood WD6 . . . . **38** C4
Bromley BR2 . . . . **192** B6
Manorway, Enf. EN1 . . . . . **44** B7
Manor Way, Har. HA2 . . . . . **67** H4
Mitcham CR4 . . . . **186** C3
Orpington BR5 . . . . **193** F4
South Croydon CR2 . . . **202** B6
Southall UB2 . . . . **122** D4
Manorway, Wdf.Grn. IG8 . . **63** J5
Manor Way, Wor.Pk. KT4 . **197** E1
Manor Way, The, Wall.
SM6 . . . . **200** B4
Manpreet Ct, E12
off Morris Av **98** C5
Manresa Rd, SW3 . . . . **31** G4
Mansard Beeches, SW17 . **168** A5
Mansard Cl, Pnr. HA5 . . . . . **66** D3
Mansbridge Way, NW7 . . . **56** B7
Manse Cl, Hayes UB3 . . . **121** G6
Mansel Gro, E17 . . . . **78** A1
Mansell Rd, W3 . . . . **126** D2
Greenford UB6 . . . . **103** H5
Mansell St, E1 . . . . **21** G6
Mansel Rd, SW19 . . . . **166** B6
Mansergh Cl, SE18 . . . . . . **136** B7
Manse Rd, N16 . . . . **94** C3
Mansfield Av, N15 . . . . **76** A4
Barnet EN4 . . . . **41** J6
Ruislip HA4 . . . . **84** B1
Mansfield Cl, N9 . . . . **44** D6
Mansfield Hill, E4 . . . . **62** B1
Mansfield Ms, W1 . . . . **16** D2
Mansfield Pl, NW3
off New End **91** F4
Mansfield Rd, E11 . . . . **79** H6
E17 . . . . **77** J4
NW3 . . . . **91** J5
W3 . . . . **106** B4
Chessington KT9 . . . . . . **195** F5
Ilford IG1 . . . . **98** D2
South Croydon CR2 . . . **202** A6
Mansfield St, W1 . . . . **16** D2
Mansford St, E2 . . . . **13** J2
Manship Rd, Mitch. CR4 . **168** A7
Mansion Cl, SW9
off Cowley Rd **151** G1
Mansion Gdns, NW3 . . . . . **91** E3
★**Mansion Ho**, EC4 . . . . . . **20** B4
Mansion Ho Pl, EC4 . . . . . . **20** B4
Mansion Ho St, EC4 . . . . . . **20** B4
Manson Ms, SW7 . . . . **30** D2
Manson Pl, SW7 . . . . **30** E2
Mansted Gdns, Rom. RM6 **82** C7
Manston Av, Sthl. UB2 . . . **123** G4
Manston Cl, SE20
off Garden Rd **189** F1
Manstone Rd, NW2 . . . . . . **90** B5
Manston Gro, Kings.T.
KT2 . . . . **163** G5
Manthorp Rd, SE18 . . . . . **137** F5
Mantilla Rd, SW17 . . . . . . **168** A4
Mantle Rd, SE4 . . . . **153** H3
Mantlet Cl, SW16 . . . . **168** C7
Mantle Way, E15
off Romford Rd **96/97** E7
Manton Av, W7 . . . . **124** C2
Manton Rd, SE2 . . . . **138** A4
Mantua St, SW11 . . . . **149** G3
Mantus Cl, E1
off Mantus Rd **113** F4
Mantus Rd, E1 . . . . **113** F4
Manus Way, N20
off Blakeney Cl **57** F2
Manville Gdns, SW17 . . . . **168** B2
Manville Rd, SW17 . . . . . . **168** A2
Manwood Rd, SE4 . . . . **153** J5
Manwood St, E16 . . . . **136** C1
Manygates, SW12 . . . . . . **168** B2
Mapesbury Ms, NW4
off Station Rd **71** G6
Mapesbury Rd, NW2 . . . . . **90** B6
Mapeshill Pl, NW2 . . . . **89** J6
Mape St, E2 . . . . **112** E4
Maple Av, E4 . . . . **61** J5
W3 . . . . **127** E1
Harrow HA2 . . . . **85** H2
Maple Cl, N3 . . . . **56** D6
N16 . . . . **76** D6
SW4 . . . . **150** D6
Buckhurst Hill IG9 . . . . . . **64** A3
Hampton TW12 . . . . **161** F6
Hayes UB4 . . . . **102** D3
Ilford IG6 . . . . **65** H5
Mitcham CR4 . . . . **186** B1
Orpington BR5 . . . . **193** G5
Ruislip HA4 . . . . **66** B6
Maple Ct, N.Mal. KT3 . . . . **182** E3
Maple Cres, Sid. DA15 . . . **158** A6
Maplecroft Cl, E6
off Allhallows Rd **116** B6
Mapledale Av, Croy. CR0 . **202** D2

Mapledene, Chis. BR7
off Kemnal Rd ... **175** F5
Mapledene Rd, E8 ... **94** C7
Maple Gdns, Edg. HA8 ... **54** E7
Maple Gate, Loug. IG10 ... **48** D2
Maple Gro, NW9 ... **70** C7
W5 ... **125** G3
Brentford TW8 ... **124** E7
Southall UB1 ... **103** F5
Maplehurst Cl, Kings.T.
KT1 ... **181** H4
Maple Ind Est, Felt. TW13
off Maple Way ... **160** A3
Maple Leaf Dr, Sid. DA15 . **175** J1
Mapleleafe Gdns, Ilf. IG6 ... **80** E3
Maple Leaf Sq, SE16
off St. Elmos Rd ... **133** G2
Maple Ms, NW6 ... **6** A1
SW16 ... **169** F5
Maple Pl, W1 ... **9** G6
Maple Rd, E11 ... **79** E6
SE20 ... **189** E1
Hayes UB4 ... **102** C3
Surbiton KT6 ... **181** H5
Maples, The, Esher (Clay.)
KT10 ... **194** D7
Maples Pl, E1
off Raven Row ... **112/113** E5
Maplestead Rd, SW2 ... **151** F7
Dagenham RM9 ... **118** B1
Maple St, W1 ... **17** F1
Romford RM7 ... **83** J4
Maplethorpe Rd, Th.Hth.
CR7 ... **187** H4
Mapleton Cl, Brom. BR2 . **191** G6
Mapleton Cres, SW18 ... **148** E6
Mapleton Rd, E4 ... **62** C3
SW18 ... **148** E6
Enfield EN1 ... **45** E2
Maple Wk, W10
off Droop St ... **108** A4
Maple Way, Felt. TW13 ... **160** A3
Maplin Cl, N21 ... **43** F6
Maplin Ho, SE2
off Wolvercote Rd ... **138** D2
Maplin Rd, E16 ... **115** G6
Maplin St, E3 ... **113** J3
Mapperley Dr, Wdf.Grn.
IG8 *off Forest Dr* ... **62/63** E7
Maran Way, Erith DA18 ... **138** D2
Marathon Way, SE28 ... **137** J2
Marban Rd, W9 ... **108** C3
★**Marble Arch**, W1 ... **16** A5
Marble Cl, W3 ... **126** B1
Marble Dr, NW2 ... **90** A1
Marble Hill Cl, Twick. TW1 . **144** E7
Marble Hill Gdns, Twick.
TW1 ... **144** E7
★**Marble Hill Ho**, Twick.
TW1 ... **145** F7
Marble Ho, SE18
off Felspar Cl ... **137** J5
Marble Quay, E1 ... **29** H1
Marbrook Ct, SE12 ... **173** J3
Marcella Rd, SW9 ... **151** G2
Marcellina Way, Orp. BR6 . **207** H3
Marchant Rd, E11 ... **96** D2
Marchant St, SE14 ... **133** H6
Marchbank Rd, W14 ... **128** C6
Marchmont Gdns, Rich. TW10
off Marchmont Rd ... **145** J5
Marchmont Rd, Rich.
TW10 ... **145** J5
Wallington SM6 ... **200** C7
Marchmont St, WC1 ... **10** A5
March Rd, Twick. TW1 ... **144** D7
Marchside Cl, Houns. TW5
off Springwell Rd ... **142** D1
Marchwood Cl, SE5 ... **132** B7
Marchwood Cres, W5 ... **105** F6
Marcia Rd, SE1 ... **37** E2
Marcilly Rd, SW18 ... **149** G5
Marconi Rd, E10 ... **96** A1
Marconi Way, Sthl. UB1 ... **103** H6
Marcon Pl, E8 ... **94** E6
Marco Rd, W6 ... **127** J3
Marcourt Lawns, W5 ... **105** H4
Marcus Ct, E15 ... **115** E1
Marcus Garvey Ms, SE22
off St. Aidan's Rd . **152/153** E5
Marcus Garvey Way,
SE24 ... **151** G4
Marcus St, E15 ... **115** F1
SW18 ... **149** E6
Marcus Ter, SW18 ... **149** E6
Mardale Dr, NW9 ... **70** D5
Mardell Rd, Croy. CR0 ... **189** G5
Marden Av, Brom. BR2 ... **191** G6
Marden Cres, Bex. DA5 ... **159** J5
Marden Cres, Croy. CR0 ... **187** F6
Marden Rd, N17 ... **76** B3
Croydon CR0 ... **187** F6
Marden Sq, SE16 ... **132** E3
Marder Rd, W13 ... **124** D2
Mardyke Cl, Rain. RM13 ... **119** J2
Marechal Niel Av, Sid.
DA15 ... **175** G3
Maresfield, Croy. CR0 ... **202** B3
Maresfield Gdns, NW3 ... **91** F5
Mare St, E8 ... **113** E1
Marfleet Cl, Cars. SM5 ... **199** H2
Margaret Av, E4 ... **46** B6
Margaret Bondfield Av,
Bark. IG11 ... **100** A7
Margaret Bldgs, N16
off Margaret Rd ... **94** C1
Margaret Ct, W1 ... **17** F3
Margaret Gardner Dr, SE9 . **174** C2
Margaret Ingram Cl, SW6
off John Smith Av ... **128** C7
Margaret Lockwood Cl,
Kings.T. KT1 ... **181** J4
Margaret Rd, N16 ... **94** C1
Barnet EN4 ... **41** G4
Bexley DA5 ... **158** D6
Margaret St, W1 ... **17** E3
Margaretta Ter, SW3 ... **31** G5
Margaretting Rd, E12 ... **97** J2
Margaret Way, Ilf. IG4 ... **80** B6
Margate Rd, SW2 ... **150** E5
Margeholes, Wat. WD19 ... **50** E2
Margery Pk Rd, E7 ... **97** G6
Margery Rd, Dag. RM8 ... **100** D3
Margery St, WC1 ... **10** E4
Margin Dr, SW19 ... **166** A5
Margravine Gdns, W6 ... **128** A5
Margravine Rd, W6 ... **128** A5
Marham Gdns, SW18 ... **167** H1
Morden SM4 ... **185** F6
Maria Cl, SE1
off Beatrice Rd ... **132** D4
Marian Cl, Hayes UB4 ... **102** D4
Marian Ct, Sutt. SM1 ... **198** E5
Marian Pl, E2 ... **112** E2
Marian Rd, SW16 ... **186** C1
Marian Sq, E2 ... **13** J1
Marian St, E2
off Hackney Rd ... **112/113** E2
Marian Way, NW10 ... **89** F7
Maria Ter, E1 ... **113** G5
Maria Theresa Cl, N.Mal.
KT3 ... **182** D5
Maricas Av, Har. HA3 ... **68** A1
Marie Lloyd Gdns, N19
off Hornsey Ri Gdns . **74/75** E7
Marie Lloyd Wk, E8
off Forest Rd ... **94** D6
Marigold All, SE1 ... **19** G6
Marigold Cl, Sthl. UB1
off Lancaster Rd ... **102/103** E7
Marigold Rd, N17 ... **61** F7
Marigold St, SE16 ... **132** E2
Marigold Way, E4
off Silver Birch Av ... **61** J6
Croydon CR0 ... **203** G1
Marina App, Hayes UB4 ... **103** E5
Marina Av, N.Mal. KT3 ... **183** H5
Marina Cl, Brom. BR2 ... **191** G3
Marina Dr, Well. DA16 ... **157** H2
Marina Gdns, Rom. RM7 ... **83** J6
Marina Way, Tedd. TW11
off Fairways ... **163** G7
Marine Dr, SE18 ... **136** C4
Barking IG11 ... **118** B4
Marinefield Rd, SW6 ... **149** E2
Mariner Gdns, Rich. TW10 . **163** F3
Mariner Rd, E12
off Dersingham Av ... **98** C4
Mariners Ms, E14 ... **134** D4
Marine St, SE16 ... **29** H5
Marine Twr, SE8
off Abinger Gro ... **133** J6
Marion Cl, Ilf. IG6 ... **65** G7
Marion Gro, Wdf.Grn. IG8 . **63** E5
Marion Rd, NW7 ... **55** G5
Thornton Heath CR7 ... **187** J5
Marischal Rd, SE13 ... **154** D3
Maritime Ho, SE18
off Green's End ... **136** E4
Barking IG11
off Linton Rd ... **99** F7
Maritime Quay, E14 ... **134** A5
Maritime St, E3 ... **113** J4
Marius Pas, SW17
off Marius Rd ... **168** A2
Marius Rd, SW17 ... **168** A2
Marjorams Av, Loug. IG10 . **48** C2
Marjorie Gro, SW11 ... **149** J4
Marjorie Ms, E1
off Arbour Sq ... **113** G6
Mark Av, E4 ... **46** B6
Mark Cl, Bexh. DA7 ... **158** E1
Southall UB1
off Longford Av ... **123** H1
Marke Cl, Kes. BR2 ... **206** B4
Markeston Grn, Wat.
WD19 ... **50** D4
Market, The, Cars. SM5
off Wrythe La ... **199** F1
Sutton SM1
off Rose Hill ... **199** F1
Market Ct, W1 ... **17** F3
Market Est, N7 ... **92** E6
Market Hill, SE18 ... **136** D3
Market La, Edg. HA8 ... **70** C1
Market Ms, W1 ... **24** D2
Market Pl, N2 ... **73** H3
NW11 ... **73** F4
SE16 ... **37** J1
W1 ... **17** F3
W3 ... **126** C1
Bexleyheath DA6 ... **159** G4
Brentford TW8 ... **125** F7
Enfield EN2
off The Town ... **44** A3
Kingston upon Thames
KT1 ... **181** G2
Market Rd, N7 ... **92** E6
Richmond TW9 ... **146** A3
Market Row, SW9
off Atlantic Rd ... **151** G4
Market Service Rd, The, Sutt.
SM1 *off Rosehill Av* ... **199** F1
Market Sq, E14
off Chrisp St ... **114** B6
N9 *off New Rd* ... **60** D2
Bromley BR1 ... **191** G2
Market St, E6 ... **116** C2
SE18 ... **136** D4
Market Way, E14
off Kerbey St ... **114** B6
Wembley HA0
off Turton Rd ... **87** H5
Market Yd Ms, SE1 ... **28** E5
Markfield Gdns, E4 ... **46** B7
Markfield Rd, N15 ... **76** D4
Markham Pl, SW3 ... **31** J3
Markham Sq, SW3 ... **31** J3
Markham St, SW3 ... **31** H3
Markhole Cl, Hmptn. TW12
off Priory Rd ... **161** F7
Markhouse Av, E17 ... **77** H6
Markhouse Rd, E17 ... **77** J5
Markland Ho, W10 ... **108** A7
Mark La, EC3 ... **20** E6
Markmanor Av, E17 ... **77** H7
Mark Rd, N22 ... **75** H2
Marksbury Av, Rich. TW9 . **146** A3
MARK'S GATE, Rom. RM6 . **82** E2
Mark Sq, EC2 ... **12** D5
Marks Rd, Rom. RM7 ... **83** J5
Mark St, E15 ... **96** E7
EC2 ... **12** D5
Markway, Sun. TW16 ... **178** C2
Markwell Cl, SE26
off Longton Gro ... **170/171** E4
Markyate Rd, Dag. RM8 ... **100** B5
Marlands Rd, Ilf. IG5 ... **80** B3
Marlborough, SW3 ... **31** H1
Marlborough Av, E8 ... **112** D1
N14 ... **58** C3
Edgware HA8 ... **54** B3
Marlborough Cl, N20
off Marlborough Gdns . **57** J3
SE17 ... **35** H2
SW19 ... **167** H6
Orpington BR6
off Aylesham Rd ... **193** J7
Marlborough Ct, W1 ... **17** F4
W8 ... **128** D4
Wallington SM6
off Cranley Gdns ... **200** C7
Marlborough Cres, W4 ... **126** D3
Hayes UB3 ... **121** G7
Marlborough Dr, Ilf. IG5 ... **80** B3
Marlborough Gdns, N20 ... **57** J3
Marlborough Gate Ho, W2 . **14** E5
Marlborough Gro, SE1 ... **37** H4
Marlborough Hill, NW8 ... **109** F1
Harrow HA1 ... **68** C4
★**Marlborough Ho**, SW1 ... **25** G2
Marlborough La, SE7 ... **135** J6
Marlborough Pk Av, Sid.
DA15 ... **158** A7
Marlborough Pl, NW8 ... **6** C2
Marlborough Rd, E4 ... **62** A6
E7 ... **97** J7
Marlborough Rd, E15
off Borthwick Rd ... **96/97** E4
E18 ... **79** G3
N9 ... **60** C1
N19 ... **92** D2
N22 ... **59** E7
SE18 *off Cadogan Rd* ... **136** E3
SW1 ... **25** G2
SW19 ... **167** G6
W4 ... **126** C5
W5 ... **125** G2
Bexleyheath DA7 ... **158** D3
Bromley BR2 ... **191** J4
Dagenham RM8 ... **100** B4
Feltham TW13 ... **160** D2
Hampton TW12 ... **161** G6
Isleworth TW7 ... **144** E1
Richmond TW10 ... **145** H6
Romford RM7 ... **83** G4
South Croydon CR2 ... **201** J7
Southall UB2 ... **122** C3
Sutton SM1 ... **198** D3
Marlborough St, SW3 ... **31** G2
Marlborough Yd, N19 ... **92** D2
Marler Rd, SE23 ... **171** H1
Marlescroft Way, Loug.
IG10 ... **48** E5
Marley Av, Bexh. DA7 ... **138** D6
Marley Cl, N15
off Stanmore Rd ... **75** H4
Greenford UB6 ... **103** G3
Marley Wk, NW2
off Lennon Rd ... **89** J5
Marl Fld Cl, Wor.Pk. KT4 ... **197** G1
Marlingdene Cl, Hmptn.
TW12 ... **161** G6
Marlings Cl, Chis. BR7 ... **193** H4
Marlings Pk Av, Chis. BR7 . **193** H4
Marlins Cl, Sutt. SM1
off Turnpike La ... **199** F5
Marloes Cl, Wem. HA0 ... **87** G4
Marloes Rd, W8 ... **22** A6
Marlow Cl, SE20 ... **189** E3
Marlow Ct, NW6 ... **90** A7
NW9 ... **71** F3
Marlow Cres, Twick. TW1 . **144** C6
Marlow Dr, Sutt. SM3 ... **198** A2
Marlowe Cl, Chis. BR7 ... **175** G6
Ilford IG6 ... **81** F1
Marlowe Ct, SE19
off Lymer Av ... **170** C5
Marlowe Gdns, SE9 ... **156** D6
Marlowe Path, SE8
off Glaisher St ... **134** B6
Marlowe Rd, E17 ... **78** C4
Marlowes, The, NW8 ... **109** G1
Marlowe Sq, Mitch. CR4 ... **186** C4
Marlowe Way, Croy. CR0 ... **201** E2
Marlow Gdns, Hayes UB3 . **121** G3
Marlow Rd, E6 ... **116** C3
SE20 ... **189** E3
Southall UB2 ... **123** F3
Marlow Way, SE16 ... **133** G2
Marl Rd, SW18 ... **149** E4
Marl St, SW18
off Marl Rd ... **149** F4
Marlton St, SE10
off Woolwich Rd ... **136** F6
Marlwood Cl, Sid. DA15 ... **175** H2
Marmadon Rd, SE18 ... **137** J4
Marmion App, E4 ... **62** A4
Marmion Av, E4 ... **61** J4
Marmion Cl, E4 ... **61** J4
Marmion Ms, SW11
off Taybridge Rd ... **150** A3
Marmion Rd, SW11 ... **150** A4
Marmont Rd, SE15 ... **152** D1
Marmora Rd, SE22 ... **153** F6
Marmot Rd, Houns. TW4 . **142** D3
Marne Av, N11 ... **58** B4
Welling DA16 ... **158** A3
Marnell Way, Houns. TW4 . **142** D3
Marne St, W10 ... **108** B3
Marney Rd, SW11 ... **150** A4
Marnfield Cres, SW2 ... **169** F1
Marnham Av, NW2 ... **90** B4
Marnham Cres, Grnf. UB6 . **103** H3
Marnock Rd, SE4 ... **153** H5
Maroon St, E14 ... **113** H5
Maroons Way, SE6 ... **172** A5
Marquess Rd, N1 ... **94** A6
Marquis Cl, Wem. HA0 ... **87** J7
Marquis Rd, N4 ... **93** F1
N22 ... **59** F6
NW1 ... **92** D6
Marrabon Cl, Sid. DA15 ... **176** A1
Marrick Cl, SW15 ... **147** G4
Marriott Cl, Felt. TW14 ... **141** G6
Marriott Rd, E15 ... **114** E1

Marriott Rd, N4 . . . . 93 F1
N10 . . . . 73 J1
Barnet EN5 . . . . 40 A3
Marriotts Cl, NW9 . . . . 71 F6
Marryat Cl, Houns. TW4 . . 143 F4
Marryat Pl, SW19 . . . . 166 B4
Marryat Rd, SW19 . . . . . . 166 A5
Marryat Sq, SW6 . . . . 148 B1
Marsala Rd, SE13 . . . . 154 B4
Marsden Rd, N9 . . . . 60 E2
SE15 . . . . 152 C3
Marsden St, NW5 . . . . 92 A6
Marsden Way, Orp. BR6 . . 207 J4
Marshall Cl, SW18
off Allfarthing La 149 F6
Harrow HA1
off Bowen Rd 68 A7
Hounslow TW4 . . . . 143 F5
Marshall Path, SE28
off Attlee Rd 118 B7
Marshall Rd, E10 . . . . 96 B3
N17 . . . . 76 A1
Marshalls Cl, N11 . . . . 58 B4
Marshall's Gro, SE18 . . . . 136 B4
Marshalls Pl, SE16 . . . . 29 G6
Marshall's Rd, Sutt. SM1 . 198 E4
Marshall St, W1 . . . . 17 G4
Marshalsea Rd, SE1 . . . . . . 28 A3
Marsham Cl, Chis. BR7 . . 174 E5
Marsham St, SW1 . . . . 25 J6
Marsh Av, Mitch. CR4 . . . . 186 A2
Marshbrook Cl, SE3 . . . . . 156 A3
Marsh Cl, NW7 . . . . 55 F3
Marsh Ct, SW19 . . . . 185 F1
Marsh Dr, NW9 . . . . 71 F6
Marsh Fm Rd, Twick. TW2 . 162 C1
Marshfield St, E14 . . . . . . 134 C3
Marshgate La, E15 . . . . . . 114 B1
Marshgate Path, SE28
off Tom Cribb Rd 137 F4
Marshgate Sidings, E15 . . 114 B1
Marsh Grn Rd, Dag. RM10. 119 G1
Marsh Hill, E9. . . . . 95 H5
Marsh La, E10 . . . . 96 A2
N17 . . . . 61 E7
NW7 . . . . 54 E4
Stanmore HA7 . . . . 53 F5
Marsh Rd, Pnr. HA5 . . . . . . 66 E4
Wembley HA0 . . . . 105 G2
Marshside Cl, N9 . . . . 61 F1
Marsh St, E14
off Harbinger Rd 134 B4
Marsh Wall, E14 . . . . 134 A1
Marsland Cl, SE17 . . . . 35 H4
Marston Av, Chess. KT9 . . 195 H6
Dagenham RM10 . . . . . . 101 G2
Marston Cl, NW6 . . . . 91 F7
Dagenham RM10 . . . . . . 101 G3
Marston Rd, Ilf. IG5 . . . . . . 80 B1
Teddington TW11 . . . . . . 162 E5
Marston Way, SE19 . . . . . 169 H7
Marsworth Av, Pnr. HA5 . . 66 D1
Marsworth Cl, Hayes UB4. 103 E5
Martaban Rd, N16 . . . . 94 B2
Martara Ms, SE17 . . . . 35 J4
Martello St, E8 . . . . 94 E7
Martello Ter, E8 . . . . 94 E7
Martell Rd, SE21 . . . . 170 A3
Martel Pl, E8
off Dalston La 94 C6
Marten Rd, E17 . . . . 78 A2
Martens Av, Bexh. DA7 . . 159 J4
Martens Cl, Bexh. DA7 . . . 159 J4
Martha Ct, E2 . . . . 113 E2
Martham Cl, SE28 . . . . . . 118 D7
Ilford IG6 . . . . 80 E1
Martha Rd, E15 . . . . 97 E6
Martha's Bldgs, EC1 . . . . . . 12 B5
Martha St, E1 . . . . 113 E6
Marthorne Cres, Har. HA3 . 68 A2
Martina Ter, Chig. IG7
off Manford Way 65 J5
Martin Bowes Rd, SE9 . . . 156 C3
Martinbridge Trd Est, Enf.
EN1 . . . . 44 D5
Martin Cl, N9 . . . . 61 G1
Martin Cres, Croy. CR0 . . . 201 G1
Martindale, SW14 . . . . . . 146 C5
Martindale Av, E16 . . . . . . 115 G7
Martindale Rd, SW12 . . . . 150 B7
Hounslow TW4 . . . . 142 E3
Martin Dene, Bexh. DA6 . 159 F5
Martin Dr, Nthlt. UB5 . . . . . 85 F5
Martineau Cl, Esher KT10 . 194 A4
Martineau Ms, N5
off Martineau Rd 93 H4
Martineau Rd, N5 . . . . 93 H4
Martineau St, E1 . . . . 113 F7
Martingale Cl, Sun. TW16 178 A4
Martingales Cl, Rich.
TW10 . . . . 163 G3
Martin Gdns, Dag. RM8 . . 100 C4
Martin Gro, Mord. SM4 . . 184 D3
Martin La, EC4 . . . . 20 C5
Martin Ri, Bexh. DA6 . . . . 159 F5
Martin Rd, Dag. RM8 . . . . 100 C4
Martins Cl, W.Wick. BR4 . . 204 D1
Martinsfield Cl, Chig. IG7 . 65 H4
Martins Mt, Barn. EN5 . . . . 40 D4
Martins Pl, SE28
off Martin St 137 H1
Martins Rd, Brom. BR2 . . 191 E2
Martin St, SE28 . . . . 137 H1
Martins Wk, N8
off Alexandra Rd 75 G3
N10 . . . . 74 A1
SE28 . . . . 137 H1
Borehamwood WD6
off Siskin Cl 38 A4
Martin Way, SW20 . . . . . . 184 B3
Morden SM4 . . . . 184 B3
Martlet Gro, Nthlt. UB5 . . 102 D3
Martlett Ct, WC2 . . . . 18 B4
Martley Dr, Ilf. IG2 . . . . 80 E5
Martock Cl, Har. HA3 . . . . . 68 D4
Martock Gdns, N11 . . . . . . 57 J5
Marton Cl, SE6 . . . . 172 A3
Marton Rd, N16 . . . . 94 B2
Martys Yd, NW3
off Hampstead High St . . 91 G4
Marvell Av, Hayes UB4 . . . 102 A5
Marvels Cl, SE12 . . . . 173 H2
Marvels La, SE12 . . . . 173 H2
Marville Rd, SW6 . . . . 128 C7
Marvin St, E8
off Sylvester Rd 94/95 E6
Marwell Cl, W.Wick. BR4
off Deer Pk Way 205 F2
Marwood Cl, Well. DA16 . 158 B3
Marwood Dr, NW7 . . . . 56 A7
Mary Adelaide Cl, SW15 . 164 E4
Mary Ann Gdns, SE8 . . . . 134 A6
Maryatt Av, Har. HA2 . . . . . 85 H2
Marybank, SE18 . . . . 136 C4
Mary Cl, Stan. HA7 . . . . . . 69 J4
Mary Datchelor Cl, SE5 . . 152 A1
Mary Grn, NW8 . . . . 109 E1
Maryland Ind Est, E15
off Maryland Rd 96 D5
Maryland Pk, E15 . . . . 96 E5
Maryland Pt, E15
off Leytonstone Rd . 96/97 E6
Maryland Rd, E15 . . . . 96 D5
N22 . . . . 59 F6
Thornton Heath CR7 . . . 187 H1
Maryland Sq, E15 . . . . 97 E5
Marylands Rd, W9 . . . . . . 108 D4
Maryland St, E15 . . . . 96 D5
Maryland Wk, N1
off Popham St 111 J1
Maryland Way, Sun. TW16. 178 A2
Mary Lawrenson Pl, SE3 . 135 F7
MARYLEBONE, NW1 . . . . . . 15 J3
Marylebone Flyover, NW1 15 F2
W2 . . . . 15 F2
Marylebone High St, W1 . . 16 C1
Marylebone La, W1 . . . . . . 16 D4
Marylebone Ms, W1 . . . . . . 16 D2
Marylebone Pas, W1 . . . . . 17 G3
Marylebone Rd, NW1 . . . . . 15 H1
Marylebone St, W1 . . . . . . 16 C2
Marylee Way, SE11 . . . . 34 D3
Mary Macarthur Ho, W6
off Field Rd 128 B6
Maryon Gro, SE7 . . . . 136 B4
Maryon Ms, NW3
off South End Rd 91 H4
Maryon Rd, SE7 . . . . 136 B4
SE18 . . . . 136 B4
Mary Peters Dr, Grnf. UB6 . 86 A5
Mary Pl, W11 . . . . 108 B7
Mary Rose Cl, Hmptn. TW12
off Ashley Rd 179 G1
Mary Rose Mall, E6
off Frobisher Rd 116 D5
Maryrose Way, N20 . . . . . . 57 G1
Mary Seacole Cl, E8
off Clarissa St 112 C1
Mary's Ter, Twick. TW1 . . . 144 D7
Mary St, E16
off Barking Rd 115 F5
N1 . . . . 111 J1
Mary Ter, NW1 . . . . 110 B1
Mary Way, Wat. WD19 . . . . 50 D4
Masbro Rd, W14 . . . . 128 A3
Mascalls Ct, SE7
off Victoria Way 135 J6
Mascalls Rd, SE7 . . . . 135 J6
Mascotte Rd, SW15 . . . . . 148 A4
Mascotts Cl, NW2 . . . . 89 H3
Masefield Av, Borwd. WD6 . 38 B5
Southall UB1 . . . . 103 G7
Stanmore HA7 . . . . 52 C5
Masefield Cres, N14 . . . . . . 42 C6
Masefield Gdns, E6 . . . . . 116 D4
Masefield La, Hayes UB4 . 102 B4
Masefield Rd, Hmptn. TW12
off Wordsworth Rd . . . 161 F4
Masefield Vw, Orp. BR6 . . 207 F3
Masham Ho, Erith DA18
off Kale Rd 138 D2
Mashie Rd, W3 . . . . 106 E6
Maskall Cl, SW2 . . . . 169 G1
Maskani Wk, SW16
off Bates Cres 168 C7
Maskell Rd, SW17 . . . . . . 167 F3
Maskelyne Cl, SW11 . . . . . 149 H1
Mason Bradbear Ct, N1
off St. Paul's Rd 94 A6
Mason Cl, E16 . . . . 115 G7
SE16 . . . . 37 J3
SW20 . . . . 184 A1
Bexleyheath DA7 . . . . . 159 H3
Borehamwood WD6 . . . . 38 C2
Hampton TW12 . . . . 179 F1
Mason Rd, Sutt. SM1
off Manor Pl 198/199 E5
Woodford Green IG8 . . . 63 E4
Masons Arms Ms, W1 . . . . 17 E4
Masons Av, EC2 . . . . 20 B3
Croydon CR0 . . . . 201 J3
Harrow HA3 . . . . 68 C4
Masons Ct, Wem. HA9
off Mayfields 88 A2
Masons Grn La, W3 . . . . . 106 A5
Masons Hill, SE18 . . . . . . 137 E4
Bromley BR1, BR2 . . . . . 191 G3
Mason's Pl, EC1 . . . . 11 H3
Masons Pl, Mitch. CR4 . . . 185 J1
Mason St, SE17 . . . . 36 C2
Mason's Yd, SW1 . . . . 25 G1
SW19
off High St Wimbledon . 166 A5
Massey Cl, N11
off Grove Rd 58 B5
Massey Ct, E6 . . . . 115 J1
Massie Rd, E8
off Graham Rd 94 D6
Massingberd Way, SW17 . 168 B4
Massinger St, SE17 . . . . . . 36 D2
Massingham St, E1 . . . . . 113 G4
Masson Av, Ruis. HA4 . . . . 84 C6
Master Gunner Pl, SE18 . . 136 B7
Masterman Ho, SE5 . . . . . . 36 B7
Masterman Rd, E6 . . . . . . 116 B3
Masters Cl, SW16
off Blegborough Rd . . 168 C6
Masters Dr, SE16 . . . . 132 E5
Masters St, E1 . . . . 113 G5
Masthouse Ter, E14 . . . . . 134 A4
Mast Leisure Pk, SE16 . . . 133 G3
Mastmaker Rd, E14 . . . . . 134 A2
Maswell Pk Cres, Houns.
TW3 . . . . 143 J5
Maswell Pk Rd, Houns.
TW3 . . . . 143 H5
Matcham Rd, E11 . . . . 97 E3
Matchless Dr, SE18 . . . . . 136 D7
Matfield Cl, Brom. BR2 . . 191 G5
Matfield Rd, Belv. DA17 . . 139 G6
Matham Gro, SE22 . . . . . . 152 C4
Matham Rd, E.Mol. KT8 . . 180 A5
Matheson Rd, W14 . . . . . . 128 C4
Mathews Av, E6 . . . . 116 D2
Mathews Pk Av, E15 . . . . . 97 F6
Matilda Cl, SE19
off Elizabeth Way 170 A7
Matilda St, N1 . . . . 111 F1
Matlock Cl, SE24 . . . . 151 J4
Barnet EN5 . . . . 40 A5
Matlock Ct, SE5
off Denmark Hill Est . . 152 A4
Matlock Cres, Sutt. SM3 . 198 B4
Watford WD19 . . . . 50 C3
Matlock Gdns, Sutt. SM3 . 198 B4
Matlock Pl, Sutt. SM3 . . . 198 B4
Matlock Rd, E10 . . . . 78 C6
Matlock St, E14 . . . . 113 H6
Matlock Way, N.Mal. KT3 . 182 D1
Matrimony Pl, SW8 . . . . . 150 C2
Matson Ct, Wdf.Grn. IG8
off The Bridle Path . . 62/63 E7
Matthew Cl, W10 . . . . 108 A4
Matthew Ct, Mitch. CR4 . . 186 D5
Matthew Parker St, SW1 . . 25 J4
Matthews Rd, Grnf. UB6 . . 86 A5
Matthews St, SW11 . . . . . 149 J2
Matthews Yd, WC2 . . . . 18 A4
Matthias Rd, N16 . . . . 94 A5
Mattingley Way, SE15 . . . . 37 F7
Mattison Rd, N4 . . . . 75 G6
Mattock La, W5 . . . . 125 E1
W13 . . . . 125 E1
Maud Cashmore Way,
SE18 . . . . 136 C3
Maude Rd, E17 . . . . 77 H5
SE5 . . . . 152 B1
Maudesville Cotts, W7
off The Broadway 124 B1
Maude Ter, E17 . . . . 77 H4
Maud Gdns, E13 . . . . 115 F1
Barking IG11 . . . . 117 J2
Maudlin's Grn, E1 . . . . 29 H1
Maud Rd, E10 . . . . 96 C3
E13 . . . . 115 F2
Maudslay Rd, SE9 . . . . . . 156 C3
Maudsley Ho, Brent. TW8
off Green Dragon La . . 125 H5
Maud St, E16 . . . . 115 F5
Maud Wilkes Cl, NW5 . . . . 92 C5
Mauleverer Rd, SW2 . . . . 150 E5
Maundeby Wk, NW10
off Neasden La 88/89 E6
Maunder Rd, W7 . . . . 124 C1
Maunsel St, SW1 . . . . 33 H1
Maurice Av, N22 . . . . 75 H2
Maurice Brown Cl, NW7 . . 56 A5
Maurice St, W12 . . . . 107 H6
Maurice Wk, NW11 . . . . 73 F4
Maurier Cl, Nthlt. UB5 . . . 102 C1
Mauritius Rd, SE10 . . . . . 135 E4
Maury Rd, N16 . . . . 94 D2
Mauveine Gdns, Houns.
TW3 . . . . 143 G4
Mavelstone Cl, Brom.
BR1 . . . . 192 B1
Mavelstone Rd, Brom.
BR1 . . . . 192 B1
Maverton Rd, E3 . . . . 114 A1
Mavis Av, Epsom KT19 . . . 197 E5
Mavis Cl, Epsom KT19 . . . 197 E5
Mavis Wk, E6 . . . . 116 B5
Mawbey Est, SE1 . . . . 37 H4
Mawbey Pl, SE1 . . . . 37 G4
Mawbey Rd, SE1 . . . . 37 G4
Mawbey St, SW8 . . . . 130 E7
Mawney Cl, Rom. RM7 . . . 83 H2
Mawney Rd, Rom. RM7 . . . 83 J4
Mawson Cl, SW20 . . . . 184 B2
Mawson La, W4
off Great W Rd 127 F6
Maxey Gdns, Dag. RM9 . . 101 E4
Maxey Rd, SE18 . . . . 137 F4
Dagenham RM9 . . . . . . 100 E4
Maxfield Cl, N20 . . . . 41 F7
Maxilla Gdns, W10
off Cambridge Gdns . . 108 A6
Maxilla Wk, W10
off Kingsdown Cl 108 A6
Maxim Rd, N21 . . . . 43 G6
Maxted Pk, Har. HA1 . . . . . 68 B7
Maxted Rd, SE15 . . . . 152 C3
Maxwell Cl, Croy. CR0 . . . 201 E1
Hayes UB3 . . . . 102 A7
Maxwell Gdns, Orp. BR6 . 207 J3
Maxwell Rd, SW6 . . . . 128 E7
Borehamwood WD6 . . . . 38 B3
Welling DA16 . . . . 158 A4
West Drayton UB7 . . . . 120 C4
Maxwelton Av, NW7 . . . . . 54 D5
Maxwelton Cl, NW7 . . . . . . 54 D5
Maya Angelou Ct, E4
off Bailey Cl 62 C4
Maya Cl, SE15 . . . . 152 E2
Mayall Rd, SE24 . . . . 151 H5
Maya Pl, N11 . . . . 58 D7
Maya Rd, N2 . . . . 73 F4
Maybank Av, E18 . . . . 79 H2
Wembley HA0 . . . . 86 C5
Maybank Gdns, Pnr. HA5 . 66 A5
Maybank Rd, E18 . . . . 79 H1
May Bate Av, Kings.T. KT2 . 181 G1
Maybells Commercial Est,
Bark. IG11 . . . . 118 D2
Mayberry Pl, Surb. KT5 . . 181 J7
Maybourne Cl, SE26 . . . . . 171 E5
Maybrook Meadow Est,
Bark. IG11 . . . . 100 A7
Maybury Cl, Loug. IG10 . . . 48 E4
Orpington BR5 . . . . 193 E5
Maybury Gdns, NW10 . . . . 89 H6
Maybury Ms, N6 . . . . 74 C7
Maybury Rd, E13 . . . . 115 J4
Barking IG11 . . . . 117 J2
Maybury St, SW17 . . . . . . 167 H5
Maychurch Cl, Stan. HA7 . . 53 G7

May Cl, Chess. KT9 . . . . . 195 J6
May Ct, SW19 . . . . 185 F1
Maycroft, Pnr. HA5. . . . . . . 66 B2
Maycross Av, Mord. SM4. 184 C3
Mayday Gdns, SE3. . . . . . 156 B2
Mayday Rd, Th.Hth. CR7. . 187 H6
Maydew Ho, SE16
off Abbeyfield Rd 133 F4
Mayerne Rd, SE9 . . . . 156 A5
Mayesbrook Rd, Bark.
IG11. . . . . 117 J1
Dagenham RM8 . . . . . . 100 A3
Ilford IG3 . . . . 100 A3
Mayesford Rd, Rom. RM6 . 82 C7
Mayes Rd, N22. . . . . 75 G2
Mayeswood Rd, SE12 . . . 173 J3
MAYFAIR, W1 . . . . 16 D6
Mayfair Av, Bexh. DA7 . . . 158 D1
Ilford IG1 . . . . 98 C2
Romford RM6 . . . . 82 D6
Twickenham TW2 . . . . . 143 J7
Worcester Park KT4. . . . 197 G1
Mayfair Cl, Beck. BR3. . . . 190 B1
Surbiton KT6. . . . . 195 H1
Mayfair Gdns, N17. . . . . . . 60 A6
Woodford Green IG8 . . . 63 G7
Mayfair Ms, NW1
off Regents Pk Rd 91 J7
Mayfair Pl, W1 . . . . 25 E1
Mayfair Ter, N14 . . . . 42 D7
Mayfield, Bexh. DA7 . . . . 159 F3
Mayfield Av, N12 . . . . 57 F4
N14 . . . . 58 D2
W4. . . . . 127 E4
W13. . . . . 124 E3
Harrow HA3 . . . . 68 E5
Orpington BR6 . . . . 207 J1
Woodford Green IG8 . . . 63 G7
Mayfield Cl, E8
off Forest Rd 94 C6
SW4. . . . . 150 D5
Thames Ditton KT7 . . . . 194 E1
Mayfield Cres, N9 . . . . 44 E6
Thornton Heath CR7 . . . 187 F4
Mayfield Dr, Pnr. HA5 . . . . 67 F4
Mayfield Gdns, NW4 . . . . . 72 A6
W7. . . . . 104 A6
Mayfield Mans, SW15
off West Hill. 148 A7
Mayfield Rd, E4 . . . . 62 C2
E8 . . . . 94 C7
E13. . . . . 115 F4
E17 . . . . 77 H2
N8 . . . . 75 F6
SW19. . . . . 184 C1
W3. . . . . 106 B7
W12. . . . . 127 E2
Belvedere DA17 . . . . . . 139 J4
Bromley BR1. . . . . 192 B5
Dagenham RM8 . . . . . . 100 C1
Enfield EN3. . . . . 45 G2
Sutton SM2. . . . . 199 G6
Thornton Heath CR7 . . . 187 F4
Mayfields, Wem. HA9. . . . . 88 A2
Mayfields Cl, Wem. HA9 . . 88 A2
Mayflower Cl, SE16
off Greenland Quay . . 133 G4
Mayflower Ct, SE16
off St. Marychurch St . 133 F2
Mayflower Rd, SW9. . . . . 150 E3
Mayflower St, SE16 . . . . . 133 F2
Mayfly Cl, Pnr. HA5 . . . . . . 66 C7
Mayfly Gdns, Nthlt. UB5
off Ruislip Rd. 102 D3
Mayford Cl, SW12 . . . . . . 149 J7
Beckenham BR3 . . . . . . 189 G3
Mayford Rd, SW12. . . . . . 149 J7
May Gdns, Wem. HA0 . . . 105 F2
Maygood St, N1. . . . . 10 D1
Maygrove Rd, NW6 . . . . . . 90 C6
Mayhew Cl, E4. . . . . 62 A3
Mayhill Rd, SE7 . . . . 135 H6
Barnet EN5 . . . . 40 B6
Maylands Dr, Sid. DA14 . . 176 D3
Maylands Rd, Wat. WD19. . 50 C4
Maynard Cl, N15
off Brunswick Rd. 76 B4
SW6
off Cambria St . . . 128/129 E7
Maynard Path, E17. . . . . . . 78 C5
Maynard Rd, E17 . . . . 78 C5
Maynards Quay, E1
off Garnet St 113 F7
Maynooth Gdns, Cars.
SM5. . . . . 185 J7
Mayola Rd, E5 . . . . 95 F4
Mayo Rd, NW10. . . . . 88 E6
Croydon CR0. . . . . 188 A5
Mayow Rd, SE23 . . . . 171 G3
Mayow Rd, SE26 . . . . 171 G4
Mayplace Cl, Bexh. DA7. . 159 H3
Mayplace La, SE18. . . . . . 137 E7
Mayplace Rd E, Bexh.
DA7 . . . . 159 H3
Dartford DA1 . . . . 159 J3
Mayplace Rd W, Bexh.
DA7 . . . . 159 G4
Maypole Cres, Ilf. IG6. . . . . 65 G7
May Rd, E4. . . . . 62 A6
E13. . . . . 115 G2
Twickenham TW2 . . . . . 162 B1
Mayroyd Av, Surb. KT6 . . 196 A2
May's Bldgs Ms, SE10
off Crooms Hill 134 D7
Mays Ct, WC2. . . . . 18 A6
Mays Hill Rd, Brom. BR2 . 191 E2
Mays La, E4 . . . . 62 D2
Barnet EN5 . . . . 40 B5
Maysoule Rd, SW11 . . . . . 149 G4
Mays Rd, Tedd. TW11 . . . . 162 A5
Mayston Ms, SE10
off Westcombe Hill . . . 135 G5
May St, W14
off North End Rd. 128 C5
Mayswood Gdns, Dag.
RM10 . . . . 101 J6
Mayton St, N7 . . . . 93 F3
Maytree Cl, Edg. HA8 . . . . 54 C3
Maytree Gdns, W5
off South Ealing Rd. . . 125 G2
May Tree La, Stan. HA7 . . . 52 C7
Maytree Wk, SW2 . . . . . . 169 G2
Mayville Est, N16
off King Henry St 94 B5
Mayville Rd, E11. . . . . 96 E2
Ilford IG1 . . . . 98 E5
May Wk, E13. . . . . 115 H2
Maywood Cl, Beck. BR3. . 172 B7
Maze Hill, SE3 . . . . 134 E6
SE10 . . . . 134 E6
Mazenod Av, NW6 . . . . 90 D7
Maze Rd, Rich. TW9 . . . . . 126 A7
Mead, The, N2 . . . . 73 F2
W13. . . . . 104 E5
Beckenham BR3 . . . . . . 190 C1
Wallington SM6 . . . . . . 200 D6
Watford WD19. . . . . 50 E3
West Wickham BR4. . . . 204 D1
Mead Cl, Har. HA3 . . . . 68 A1
Loughton IG10 . . . . 48 E2
Mead Ct, NW9 . . . . 70 C5
Mead Cres, E4 . . . . 62 C4
Sutton SM1. . . . . 199 H4
Meadcroft Rd, SE11 . . . . . . 35 G6
Meade Cl, W4. . . . . 126 A6
Meadfield, Edg. HA8 . . . . . 54 B2
Mead Fld, Har. HA2
off Kings Rd 85 F3
Meadfield Grn, Edg. HA8. . 54 B2
Meadfoot Rd, SW16. . . . . 168 C7
Meadgate Av, Wdf.Grn.
IG8. . . . . 64 B5
Mead Gro, Rom. RM6 . . . . 82 E3
Meadlands Dr, Rich. TW10 163 G2
Meadow, The, Chis. BR7 . 175 F6
Meadow Av, Croy. CR0 . . 189 G6
Meadow Bk, N21 . . . . 43 F6
Meadowbank, NW3. . . . . . 91 J7
SE3 . . . . 155 F3
Surbiton KT5. . . . . 181 J6
Meadowbank Cl, SW6 . . . 127 J7
Meadowbank Gdns,
Houns. TW5. . . . . 142 A2
Meadowbank Rd, NW9 . . . 70 D7
Meadowbanks, Barn. EN5. 39 F5
Meadow Cl, E4
off Mount Echo Av 62 B1
E9 . . . . 95 J5
SE6 . . . . 172 A5
SW20. . . . . 183 J4
Barking IG11
off Meadow Rd. 99 J7
Barnet EN5 . . . . 40 C6
Bexleyheath DA6 . . . . . 159 F5
Chislehurst BR7. . . . . . . 174 E5
Esher KT10 . . . . 194 C3
Hounslow TW4 . . . . 143 G6
Northolt UB5. . . . . 103 G2
Richmond TW10 . . . . . . 163 H1
Sutton SM1
off Aultone Way . . 198/199 E2
Meadowcourt Rd, SE3. . . 155 F4
Meadowcroft, Brom. BR1 . 192 C3
Meadowcroft Rd, N13 . . . . 59 G2
Meadow Dr, N10 . . . . 74 B3
NW4 . . . . 71 J2
Meadow Gdns, Edg. HA8 . 54 B6
Meadow Garth, NW10. . . . 88 C6
Meadowgate Cl, NW7
off Stanhope Gdns 55 F5
Meadow Hill, N.Mal. KT3. 182 E6
Meadow La, SE12 . . . . . . 173 H3
Meadowlea Cl, West Dr.
UB7 . . . . 120 A6
Meadow Ms, SW8 . . . . 34 C6
Meadow Pl, SW8 . . . . 34 B7
W4 *off Edensor Rd*. 126/127 E7
Meadow Rd, SW8 . . . . 34 C7
SW19. . . . . 167 F7
Barking IG11 . . . . 99 J7
Borehamwood WD6 . . . . 38 B2
Bromley BR2. . . . . 191 E1
Dagenham RM9 . . . . . . 101 F6
Esher (Clay.) KT10. . . . . 194 B6
Feltham TW13 . . . . 160 E2
Loughton IG10 . . . . 48 B5
Pinner HA5 . . . . 66 D5
Romford RM7 . . . . 101 J1
Southall UB1 . . . . 103 F7
Sutton SM1. . . . . 199 H5
Meadow Row, SE1 . . . . . . 27 J6
Meadows Cl, E10 . . . . 96 A2
Meadows End, Sun.
TW16. . . . . 178 A1
Meadowside, SE9 . . . . . . 155 J4
Meadow Stile, Croy. CR0
off High St. 201 J3
Meadowsweet Cl, E16
off Monarch Dr 116 A5
SW20. . . . . 183 J5
Meadow Vw, Har. HA1. . . . 86 B1
Sidcup DA15 . . . . 158 B7
Meadowview Rd, SE6 . . . 171 J5
Bexley DA5 . . . . 159 E6
Meadow Vw Rd, Th.Hth.
CR7 . . . . 187 H5
Meadow Wk, E18. . . . . 79 G4
Dagenham RM9 . . . . . . 101 F6
Epsom KT17, KT19. . . . . 197 E6
Wallington SM6 . . . . . . 200 B3
Meadow Way, NW9 . . . . . . 70 D5
Chessington KT9. . . . . . 195 H5
Chigwell IG7 . . . . 65 F3
Orpington BR6 . . . . 206 D3
Ruislip HA4. . . . . 66 B6
Wembley HA9. . . . . 87 G4
Meadow Way, The, Har.
HA3. . . . . 68 B1
Meadow Waye, Houns.
TW5. . . . . 123 E6
Mead Path, SW17 . . . . . . 167 F5
Mead Pl, E9 . . . . 95 F6
Croydon CR0. . . . . 201 H1
Mead Plat, NW10. . . . . 88 C6
Mead Rd, Chis. BR7 . . . . . 175 F6
Edgware HA8 . . . . 54 A6
Richmond TW10 . . . . . . 163 F3
Mead Row, SE1 . . . . 27 E5
Meads, The, Edg. HA8 . . . . 54 D6
Sutton SM3. . . . . 198 B3
Meads La, Ilf. IG3. . . . . 81 H7
Meads Rd, N22. . . . . 75 H2
Enfield EN3. . . . . 45 H1
Mead Ter, Wem. HA9
off Meadow Way. 87 G4
Meadvale Rd, W5 . . . . 105 E4
Croydon CR0. . . . . 188 C7
Meadway, N14. . . . . 58 D2
NW11. . . . . 72 E6
SW20. . . . . 183 J4
Barnet EN5 . . . . 40 D4
Beckenham BR3 . . . . . . 190 C1
Mead Way, Brom. BR2 . . . 191 F6
Croydon CR0. . . . . 203 H2
Meadway, Ilf. IG3. . . . . 99 H4
Surbiton KT5. . . . . 196 C1
Twickenham TW2 . . . . . 162 A1
Woodford Green IG8 . . . 63 J5
Meadway, The, SE3
off Heath La 154 D2
Buckhurst Hill IG9. . . . . . 64 A1
Loughton IG10 . . . . 48 C6
Meadway Cl, NW11 . . . . . . 73 E6
Barnet EN5 . . . . 40 D4
Pinner HA5
off Highbanks Rd 51 H6
Meadway Ct, NW11 . . . . . . 73 E6
Meadway Gate, NW11. . . . 72 D6
Meaford Way, SE20 . . . . . 171 E7
Meakin Est, SE1. . . . . 28 D5
Meanley Rd, E12 . . . . 98 B4
Meard St, W1 . . . . 17 H4
Meath Rd, E15 . . . . 115 F2
Ilford IG1. . . . . 99 F3
Meath St, SW11 . . . . 150 B1
Mecklenburgh Pl, WC1. . . . 10 C5
Mecklenburgh Sq, WC1 . . . 10 C5
Mecklenburgh St, WC1 . . . 10 C5
Medburn St, NW1 . . . . 9 H1
Medcroft Gdns, SW14 . . . 146 C4
Medebourne Cl, SE3 . . . . 155 G3
Medesenge Way, N13 . . . . 59 H6
Medfield St, SW15. . . . . . 147 H7
Medhurst Cl, E3
off Arbery Rd. 113 H2
Medhurst Rd, E3
off Arbery Rd. 113 H2
Median Rd, E5 . . . . 95 F5
★**Medici Galleries**, W1 . . . . 16 E6
Medina Av, Esher KT10 . . 194 B3
Medina Gro, N7
off Medina Rd. 93 G3
Medina Rd, N7. . . . . 93 G3
Medland Cl, Wall. SM6. . . 200 A1
Medland Ho, E14
off Branch Rd 113 H7
Medlar Cl, Nthlt. UB5
off Parkfield Av. . . 102/103 E2
Medlar St, SE5. . . . . 151 J1
Medley Rd, NW6 . . . . 90 D6
Medora Rd, SW2 . . . . 151 F7
Medusa Rd, SE6. . . . . 154 B6
Medway Bldgs, E3
off Medway Rd 113 H2
Medway Cl, Croy. CR0 . . . 189 F6
Ilford IG1 . . . . 99 F5
Medway Dr, Grnf. UB6. . . 104 C2
Medway Gdns, Wem. HA0 . 86 D4
Medway Ms, E3
off Medway Rd 113 H2
Medway Par, Grnf. UB6 . . 104 C2
Medway Rd, E3 . . . . 113 H2
Medway St, SW1 . . . . 25 J6
Medwin St, SW4 . . . . 151 F4
Meerbrook Rd, SE3 . . . . . 155 J3
Meeson Rd, E15 . . . . 115 F1
Meeson St, E5 . . . . 95 H4
Meeting Fld Path, E9
off Chatham Pl 95 F6
Meeting Ho All, E1
off Wapping La. . . 132/133 E1
Meeting Ho La, SE15 . . . . 152 E1
Mehetabel Rd, E9. . . . . 95 F6
Meister Cl, Ilf. IG1 . . . . 99 G1
Melancholy Wk, Rich.
TW10. . . . . 163 F2
Melanda Cl, Chis. BR7 . . . 174 C5
Melanie Cl, Bexh. DA7 . . . 158 E1
Melba Way, SE13 . . . . 154 B1
Melbourne Av, N13 . . . . . . 59 F6
W13. . . . . 124 D1
Pinner HA5 . . . . 67 H3
Melbourne Cl, Orp. BR6. . 193 H7
Wallington SM6
off Melbourne Rd 200 C5
Melbourne Ct, E5
off Daubeney Rd. 95 H4
N10 *off Sydney Rd* 58 B7
SE20 . . . . 170 D7
Melbourne Gdns, Rom.
RM6. . . . . 82 E5
Melbourne Gro, SE22. . . . 152 B4
Melbourne Ho, Hayes
UB4 . . . . 102 C4
Melbourne Ms, SE6 . . . . . 154 C7
SW9. . . . . 151 G1
Melbourne Pl, WC2 . . . . . . 18 D5
Melbourne Rd, E6. . . . . . . 116 C1
E10 . . . . 78 B7
E17 . . . . 77 H4
SW19. . . . . 184 D1
Ilford IG1. . . . . 99 E1
Teddington TW11. . . . . . 163 F6
Wallington SM6 . . . . . . 200 B5
Melbourne Sq, SW9
off Melbourne Ms. . . . 151 G1
Melbourne Ter, SW6
off Waterford Rd . 128/129 E7
Melbourne Way, Enf. EN1 . 44 C6
Melbury Av, Sthl. UB2 . . . 123 H3
Melbury Cl, Chis. BR7 . . . 174 C6
Esher (Clay.) KT10. . . . . 194 E6
Melbury Ct, W8 . . . . 128 C3
Melbury Dr, SE5
off Sedgmoor Pl 132 B7
Melbury Gdns, SW20. . . . 183 H1
Melbury Rd, W14 . . . . 128 C3
Harrow HA3 . . . . 69 J5
Melcombe Gdns, Har.
HA3. . . . . 69 J6
Melcombe Pl, NW1 . . . . . . 15 J1
Melcombe St, NW1 . . . . 8 A6
Meldex Cl, NW7. . . . . 55 J6
Meldon Cl, SW6
off Bagley's La . . . 148/149 E1
Meldone Cl, Surb. KT5. . . 182 B6

Meldrum Rd, Ilf. IG3 . . . . . **100** A2
Melfield Gdns, SE6 . . . . . **172** B4
Melford Av, Bark. IG11 . . . . **99** H6
Melford Cl, Chess. KT9 . . . **195** J5
Melford Rd, E6 . . . . **116** C4
E11 . . . . **96** E2
E17 . . . . **77** H4
SE22 . . . . **152** D7
Ilford IG1 . . . . **99** G2
Melfort Av, Th.Hth. CR7 . . **187** H3
Melfort Rd, Th.Hth. CR7 . . **187** H3
Melgund Rd, N5 . . . . **93** G5
Melina Pl, NW8 . . . . **6** E4
Melina Rd, W12 . . . . **127** H2
Melior Pl, SE1 . . . . **28** D3
Melior St, SE1 . . . . **28** C3
Meliot Rd, SE6 . . . . **172** D2
Meller Cl, Croy. CR0 . . . . . **200** E3
Melling Dr, Enf. EN1 . . . . . **44** D1
Melling St, SE18 . . . . **137** H6
Mellish Cl, Bark. IG11 . . . . **117** J1
Mellish Gdns, Wdf.Grn. IG8 . . . . **63** G5
Mellish Ind Est, SE18 . . . . **136** B3
Mellish St, E14 . . . . **134** A3
Mellison Rd, SW17 . . . . . . **167** H5
Melliss Av, Rich. TW9 . . . . **146** B1
Mellitus St, W12 . . . . **107** F6
Mellor Cl, Walt. KT12 . . . . **179** F7
Mellows Rd, Ilf. IG5 . . . . . . **80** C3
Wallington SM6 . . . . . . **200** D5
Mells Cres, SE9 . . . . **174** C4
Mell St, SE10
off Trafalgar Rd . . . **134/135** E5
Melody La, N5 . . . . **93** H5
Melody Rd, SW18 . . . . . . **149** F5
Melon Pl, W8 . . . . **22** A3
Melon Rd, E11 . . . . **96** E3
SE15 . . . . **152** D1
Melrose Av, N22 . . . . **75** H1
NW2 . . . . **89** H5
SW16 . . . . **187** F3
SW19 . . . . **166** D2
Borehamwood WD6 . . . . **38** B5
Greenford UB6 . . . . **103** H2
Mitcham CR4 . . . . **168** B7
Twickenham TW2 . . . . . **143** H7
Melrose Cl, SE12 . . . . **173** G1
Greenford UB6 . . . . **103** H2
Hayes UB4 . . . . **102** A5
Melrose Ct, W13
off Williams Rd **124** D1
Melrose Cres, Orp. BR6 . . **207** G4
Melrose Dr, Sthl. UB1 . . . **123** G1
Melrose Gdns, W6 . . . . . . **127** J3
Edgware HA8 . . . . **70** B2
New Malden KT3 . . . . . . **182** D3
Melrose Rd, SW13 . . . . . . **147** F2
SW18 . . . . **148** C6
SW19 . . . . **184** D2
W3 *off Stanley Rd* **126** C3
Pinner HA5 . . . . **67** F4
Melrose Ter, W6 . . . . **127** J2
Melsa Rd, Mord. SM4 . . . **185** F6
Melthorne Dr, Ruis. HA4 . . **84** C3
Melthorpe Gdns, SE3 . . . . **156** B1
Melton Cl, Ruis. HA4 . . . . . **84** C1
Melton Ct, SW7 . . . . **31** F2
Sutton SM2 . . . . **199** F7
Melton St, NW1 . . . . **9** G4
Melville Av, SW20 . . . . . . **165** G7
Greenford UB6 . . . . **86** C5
South Croydon CR2 . . . **202** C5
Melville Gdns, N13 . . . . . . **59** H5
Melville Pl, N1
off Essex Rd **111** H1
Melville Rd, E17 . . . . **77** J3
NW10 . . . . **88** D7
SW13 . . . . **147** G1
Sidcup DA14 . . . . **176** C2
Melville Vil Rd, W3
off High St **126** D1
Melvin Rd, SE20 . . . . **189** F1
Melyn Cl, N7
off Anson Rd **92** C4
Memel Ct, EC1 . . . . **11** J6
Memel St, EC1 . . . . **11** J6
Memess Path, SE18 . . . . . **136** D6
Memorial Av, E15 . . . . **114** E3
Memorial Cl, Houns. TW5 . **123** F6
Mendip Cl, SE26 . . . . **171** F4
Hayes UB3 . . . . **121** G7
Worcester Park KT4 . . . . **197** J1
Mendip Dr, NW2 . . . . **90** A2
Mendip Ho, N9
off New Rd **60** D3
Mendip Rd, SW11 . . . . . . **149** F3
Ilford IG2 . . . . **81** H5
Mendora Rd, SW6 . . . . . . **128** B7
Menelik Rd, NW2 . . . . **90** B4
Menlo Gdns, SE19 . . . . . . **170** A7
Menon Dr, N9 . . . . **60** E3
Menotti St, E2 . . . . **13** J5
Mentmore Cl, Har. HA3 . . . **69** F6
Mentmore Ter, E8 . . . . **95** E7
Meon Ct, Islw. TW7 . . . . . **144** B2
Meon Rd, W3 . . . . **126** C2
Meopham Rd, Mitch. CR4 . **186** C1
Mepham Cres, Har. HA3 . . **51** J7
Mepham Gdns, Har. HA3 . . **51** J7
Mepham St, SE1 . . . . **26** D2
Mera Dr, Bexh. DA7 . . . . . **159** G4
Merantun Way, SW19 . . . . **185** F1
Merbury Cl, SE13 . . . . **154** C5
SE28 *off Merbury Rd* . . **137** G1
Merbury Rd, SE28 . . . . . . **137** H2
Mercator Pl, E14
off Napier Av **134** A5
Mercator Rd, SE13 . . . . . . **154** D4
Mercer Cl, T.Ditt. KT7 . . . . **180** C7
Merceron St, E1 . . . . **112** E4
Mercer Pl, Pnr. HA5
off Crossway **66** C2
Mercers Cl, SE10 . . . . **135** F4
Mercers Ms, N19
off Mercers Rd **92** D3
Mercers Pl, W6 . . . . **127** J4
Mercers Rd, N19 . . . . **92** D3
Mercer St, WC2 . . . . **18** A4
Merchants Cl, SE25
off Clifford Rd **188** D4
Merchants Ho, SE10
off Hoskins St **134** D5
Merchant St, E3 . . . . **113** J3
Merchiston Rd, SE6 . . . . . **172** D2
Merchland Rd, SE9 . . . . . . **175** F1
Mercia Gro, SE13 . . . . **154** C4
Mercier Rd, SW15 . . . . . . **148** B5
Mercury Cen, Felt. TW14 . **142** B5
Mercury Way, SE14 . . . . . **133** G6
Mercy Ter, SE13 . . . . **154** B4
Merebank La, Croy. CR0 . . **201** F5
Mere Cl, SW15 . . . . **148** A7
Orpington BR6 . . . . **206** E2
Meredith Av, NW2 . . . . **89** J5
Meredith Cl, Pnr. HA5 . . . . **50** D7
Meredith Ms, SE4 . . . . . . **153** J4
Meredith St, E13 . . . . **115** G3
EC1 . . . . **11** G4
Meredyth Rd, SW13 . . . . . **147** G2
Mere End, Croy. CR0 . . . . **189** G7
Mere Side, Orp. BR6 . . . . **206** D2
Meretone Cl, SE4 . . . . **153** H4
Merevale Cres, Mord.
SM4 . . . . **185** F6
Mereway Rd, Twick. TW2 . **162** A1
Merewood Cl, Brom. BR1 . **192** D2
Merewood Rd, Bexh. DA7 . **159** J2
Mereworth Cl, Brom. BR2 . **191** F5
Mereworth Dr, SE18 . . . . . **137** E7
Merganser Gdns, SE28
off Avocet Ms **137** G3
Meriden Cl, Brom. BR1 . . . **174** A7
Ilford IG6 . . . . **81** F1
Meridian Gate, E14 . . . . . **134** C2
Meridian Pl, E14 . . . . **134** B2
Meridian Rd, SE7 . . . . **136** A7
Meridian Sq, E15 . . . . **96** D7
Meridian Trd Est, SE7 . . . . **135** H4
Meridian Wk, N17
off Commercial Rd **60** B6
Meridian Way, N9 . . . . **61** F5
N18 . . . . **61** F6
Enfield EN3 . . . . **45** G6
Merifield Rd, SE9 . . . . **155** J4
Merino Cl, E11 . . . . **79** J4
Merino Pl, Sid. DA15
off Blackfen Rd **158** A6
Merivale Rd, SW15 . . . . . . **148** B4
Harrow HA1 . . . . **67** J7
Merlewood Dr, Chis. BR7 . **192** C1
Merley Ct, NW9 . . . . **88** C1
Merlin Cl, Croy. CR0 . . . . . **202** B4
Mitcham CR4 . . . . **185** H3
Northolt UB5 . . . . **102** C3
Wallington SM6 . . . . **201** F6
Merlin Cres, Edg. HA8 . . . . **69** J1
Merlin Gdns, Brom. BR1 . . **173** G3
Merling Cl, Chess. KT9
off Coppard Gdns **195** G5
Merlin Gro, Beck. BR3 . . . **189** J4
Ilford IG6 . . . . **65** E7
Merlin Ho, Enf. EN3
off Allington Ct **45** G5
Merlin Rd, E12 . . . . **97** J2
Welling DA16 . . . . **158** A4
Merlin Rd N, Well. DA16 . . **158** A4
Merlins Av, Har. HA2 . . . . . **85** F3
Merlin St, WC1 . . . . **11** E4
Mermaid Ct, SE1 . . . . **28** B3
SE16 . . . . **133** J1
Mermaid Twr, SE8
off Abinger Gro **133** J6
Merredene St, SW2 . . . . . **151** F6
Merriam Av, E9 . . . . **95** J6
Merriam Cl, E4 . . . . **62** C5
Merrick Rd, Sthl. UB2 . . . . **123** F2
Merrick Sq, SE1 . . . . **28** A5
Merridale, SE12 . . . . **155** G5
Merridene, N21 . . . . **43** H6
Merrielands Cres, Dag.
RM9 . . . . **119** F1
Merrilands Rd, Wor.Pk.
KT4 . . . . **197** J1
Merrilees Rd, Sid. DA15 . . **175** H1
Merrilyn Cl, Esher (Clay.)
KT10 . . . . **194** D6
Merriman Rd, SE3 . . . . . . **155** J1
Merrington Rd, SW6 . . . . **128** D6
Merrion Av, Stan. HA7 . . . . **53** G5
Merrion Wk, SE17
off Dawes St **132** A5
Merritt Gdns, Chess. KT9 . **195** F6
Merritt Rd, SE4 . . . . **153** J5
Merrivale, N14 . . . . **42** D6
Merrivale Av, Ilf. IG4 . . . . . **80** A4
Merrow St, SE17 . . . . **36** B5
Merrow Wk, SE17 . . . . **36** C3
Merrow Way, Croy.
(New Adgtn) CR0 . . . . **204** C6
Merrydown Way, Chis.
BR7 . . . . **192** B1
Merryfield, SE3 . . . . **155** F2
Merryfield Gdns, Stan.
HA7 . . . . **53** F5
Merryfield Ho, SE9
off Grove Pk Rd **173** J3
Merryfields Way, SE6 . . . . **154** B7
MERRY HILL, Bushey
WD23 . . . . **51** G1
Merryhill Cl, E4 . . . . **46** B7
Merry Hill Mt, Bushey
WD23 . . . . **51** H1
Merry Hill Rd, Bushey
WD23 . . . . **51** H1
Merryhills Ct, N14 . . . . **42** C5
Merryhills Dr, Enf. EN2 . . . **42** D4
Mersea Ho, Bark. IG11 . . . . **98** E6
Mersey Rd, E17 . . . . **77** J3
Mersey Wk, Nthlt. UB5
off Brabazon Rd **103** G2
Mersham Dr, NW9 . . . . **70** A5
Mersham Pl, SE20 . . . . . . **189** E1
Mersham Rd, Th.Hth. CR7 . **188** A3
Merten Rd, Rom. RM6 . . . . **83** E7
Merthyr Ter, SW13 . . . . . . **127** H6
MERTON, SW19 . . . . **184** D1
Merton Av, W4 . . . . **127** F4
Northolt UB5 . . . . **85** J5
Merton Gdns, Orp. BR5 . . **193** E5
Merton Hall Gdns, SW20 . **184** B1
Merton Hall Rd, SW19 . . . **184** B1
Merton High St, SW19 . . . **167** E7
Merton Ind Pk, SW19 . . . . **185** F1
Merton La, N6 . . . . **91** J2
Merton Mans, SW20 . . . . . **184** A2
MERTON PARK, SW19 . . . **184** D2
Merton Pk Par, SW19
off Kingston Rd **184** C1
Merton Ri, NW3 . . . . **91** H7
Merton Rd, E17 . . . . **78** C5
SE25 . . . . **188** D5
SW18 . . . . **148** D5
SW19 . . . . **166** E7
Barking IG11 . . . . **99** J7
Harrow HA2 . . . . **85** J1
Ilford IG3 . . . . **81** J7
Merton Way, W.Mol. KT8 . **179** H4
Merttins Rd, SE15 . . . . . . **153** G5
Meru Cl, NW5 . . . . **92** A4
Mervan Rd, SW2 . . . . **151** G4
Mervyn Av, SE9 . . . . **175** F3
Mervyn Rd, W13 . . . . **124** D3
Messaline Av, W3 . . . . **106** C6
Messent Rd, SE9 . . . . **155** J5
Messeter Pl, SE9 . . . . **156** D6
Messina Av, NW6 . . . . **90** D7
Metcalf Wk, Felt. TW13
off Gabriel Cl **160/161** E4
Meteor St, SW11 . . . . **150** A4
Meteor Way, Wall. SM6 . . **200** E7
Metheringham Way, NW9 . **70** E1
Methley St, SE11 . . . . **35** F4
★**Methodist Cen Hall**,
SW1 . . . . **25** J4
Methuen Cl, Edg. HA8 . . . . **54** A7
Methuen Pk, N10 . . . . **74** B2
Methuen Rd, Belv. DA17 . **139** H4
Bexleyheath DA6 . . . . . **159** F4
Edgware HA8 . . . . **54** A7
Methwold Rd, W10 . . . . . . **108** A5
Metro Cen, The, Islw. TW7 . **144** B2
Metropolis Cen, Borwd.
WD6 . . . . **38** A3
Metropolitan Cen, The,
Grnf. UB6 . . . . **103** H1
Metropolitan Cl, E14
off Broomfield St **114** A5
Mews, The, N1
off St. Paul St **111** J1
N8 *off Turnpike La* **75** G3
Ilford IG4 . . . . **80** A5
Twickenham TW1
off Bridge Rd **144/145** E6
Mews Deck, E1 . . . . **113** E7
Mews Pl, Wdf.Grn. IG8 . . . . **63** G4
Mews St, E1 . . . . **29** H1
Mexfield Rd, SW15 . . . . . . **148** C5
Meyer Rd, Erith DA8 . . . . **139** J6
Meymott St, SE1 . . . . **27** G2
Meynell Cres, E9 . . . . **95** G7
Meynell Gdns, E9 . . . . **95** G7
Meynell Rd, E9 . . . . **95** G7
Meyrick Rd, NW10 . . . . **89** G6
SW11 . . . . **149** G3
Miah Ter, E1
off Wapping High St . . **132** D1
Miall Wk, SE26 . . . . **171** H4
Micawber St, N1 . . . . **12** A3
Michael Cliffe Ho, EC1
off Skinner St **111** H3
Michael Faraday Ho, SE17 . **36** C4
Michael Gaynor Cl, W7 . . **124** C1
Michaelmas Cl, SW20 . . . **183** J3
Michael Rd, E11 . . . . **97** E1
SE25 . . . . **188** B3
SW6 . . . . **149** E1
Michaels Cl, SE13 . . . . . . **154** E4
Micheldever Rd, SE12 . . . **155** E6
Michelham Gdns, Twick.
TW1 . . . . **162** C3
Michels Row, Rich. TW9
off Kew Foot Rd **145** H4
Michel Wk, SE18
off Cambridge Row . . . **136** E5
Michigan Av, E12 . . . . **98** B4
Michleham Down, N12 . . . **56** C4
Mickleham Cl, Orp. BR5 . **193** J2
Mickleham Gdns, Sutt.
SM3 . . . . **198** B6
Mickleham Rd, Orp. BR5 . **193** J1
Mickleham Way, Croy.
(New Adgtn) CR0 . . . . **204** D7
Micklethwaite Rd, SW6 . . **128** D6
Midas Met Ind Est, The,
Mord. SM4
off Garth Rd **198** A1
Middle Dene, NW7 . . . . **54** D3
Middle Fld, NW8 . . . . **109** G1
Middlefielde, W13 . . . . . . **104** E5
Middlefield Gdns, Ilf. IG2 . . **81** E6
Middle Grn Cl, Surb. KT5
off Alpha Rd **181** J6
Middleham Gdns, N18 . . . . **60** D6
Middleham Rd, N18 . . . . . . **60** D6
Middle La, N8 . . . . **74** E5
Teddington TW11 . . . . . . **162** C6
Middle La Ms, N8
off Middle La **74/75** E5
Middle Pk Av, SE9 . . . . . . **156** A6
Middle Path, Har. HA2
off Middle Rd **86** A1
Middle Rd, E13
off London Rd **115** G2
SW16 . . . . **186** D2
Barnet EN4 . . . . **41** H6
Harrow HA2 . . . . **86** A2
Middle Row, W10 . . . . **108** B4
Middlesborough Rd, N18 . . **60** D6
Middlesex Business Cen,
Sthl. UB2 . . . . **123** G2
Middlesex Cl, Sthl. UB1 . . **103** H4
Middlesex Ct, W4
off British Gro **127** F4
★**Middlesex Guildhall**,
SW1 . . . . **26** A4
Middlesex Ho, Wem. HA0 . **105** G1
Middlesex Pas, EC1 . . . . . . **19** H2
Middlesex Rd, Mitch. CR4 . **186** E5
Middlesex St, E1 . . . . **20** E2
Middlesex Wf, E5 . . . . **95** F2
Middle St, EC1 . . . . **19** J1
Croydon CR0
off Surrey St **201** J3
Middle Temple, EC4 . . . . . . **19** E5
Middle Temple La, EC4 . . . . **18** E4

Middleton Av, E4 . . . **61** J4
Greenford UB6 . . . **104** A2
Sidcup DA14 . . . **176** C6
Middleton Cl, E4 . . . **61** J3
Middleton Dr, SE16 . . . **133** G2
Pinner HA5 . . . **66** A3
Middleton Gdns, Ilf. IG2 . . **80** E6
Middleton Gro, N7 . . . **92** E5
Middleton Ms, N7
off Middleton Gro . . **92/93** E5
Middleton Pl, W1 . . . **17** F2
Middleton Rd, E8 . . . **94** C7
NW11 . . . **72** D7
Carshalton SM5 . . . **185** H7
Morden SM4 . . . **185** F6
Middleton St, E2 . . . **112** E3
Middleton Way, SE13 . . . **154** D4
Middleway, NW11 . . . **73** E5
Middle Way, SW16 . . . **186** D2
Erith DA18 . . . **138** E3
Hayes UB4 . . . **102** C4
Middle Way, The, Har. HA3 . **68** C2
Middle Yd, SE1 . . . **28** C1
Midfield Av, Bexh. DA7 . . **159** J3
Midfield Par, Bexh. DA7 . . **159** J3
Midford Pl, W1 . . . **9** G6
Midholm, NW11 . . . **72** E4
Wembley HA9 . . . **88** A1
Midholm Cl, NW11 . . . **72** E4
Midholm Rd, Croy. CR0 . . **203** H2
Midhope St, WC1 . . . **10** B4
Midhurst Av, N10 . . . **74** A3
Croydon CR0 . . . **187** G7
Midhurst Hill, Bexh. DA6 . **159** G6
Midhurst Rd, W13 . . . **124** D2
Midhurst Way, E5 . . . **94** D4
Midland Cres, NW3
off Finchley Rd . . . **91** F6
Midland Pl, E14
off Ferry St . . . **134** C5
Midland Rd, E10 . . . **78** C7
NW1 . . . **9** J2
Midland Ter, NW2 . . . **90** A3
NW10 . . . **107** E4
Midleton Rd, N.Mal. KT3 . **182** C3
Midlothian Rd, E3
off Burdett Rd . . . **113** J5
Midmoor Rd, SW12 . . . **168** C1
SW19 . . . **184** A1
Midship Cl, SE16
off Surrey Water Rd . . **133** G1
Midship Pt, E14 . . . **134** A2
Midstrath Rd, NW10 . . . **89** E4
Midsummer Av, Houns.
TW4 . . . **143** F4
Midway, Sutt. SM3 . . . **184** C7
Midwinter Cl, Well. DA16
off Hook La . . . **158** A3
Midwood Cl, NW2 . . . **89** H3
Miers Cl, E6 . . . **116** D1
Mighell Av, Ilf. IG4 . . . **80** A5
Milan Rd, Sthl. UB1 . . . **123** F2
Milborne Gro, SW10 . . . **30** D4
Milborne St, E9 . . . **95** F6
Milborough Cres, SE12 . . **155** E6
Milcote St, SE1 . . . **27** G4
Mildenhall Rd, E5 . . . **95** F4
Mildmay Av, N1 . . . **94** A6
Mildmay Gro N, N1 . . . **94** A5
Mildmay Gro S, N1 . . . **94** A5
Mildmay Pk, N1 . . . **94** A5
Mildmay Pl, N16
off Boleyn Rd . . . **94** B5
Mildmay Rd, N1 . . . **94** B5
Ilford IG1
off Winston Way . . . **98/99** E3
Romford RM7 . . . **83** J5
Mildmay St, N1 . . . **94** A6
Mildred Av, Borwd. WD6 . . **38** A4
Hayes UB3 . . . **121** G4
Northolt UB5 . . . **85** H5
MILE END, E1 . . . **113** G3
Mile End, The, E17 . . . **77** G1
Mile End Pl, E1 . . . **113** G4
Mile End Rd, E1 . . . **113** F5
E3 . . . **113** F5
Mile Rd, Wall. SM6 . . . **200** C1
Miles Dr, SE28 . . . **137** G1
Milespit Hill, NW7 . . . **55** H5
Miles Pl, NW1 . . . **15** F1
Surbiton KT5
off Villiers Av . . . **181** J4
Miles Rd, N8 . . . **75** E3
Mitcham CR4 . . . **185** H3
Miles St, SW8 . . . **34** A6
Milestone Cl, N9
off Chichester Rd . . . **60** D2
Sutton SM2 . . . **199** G6
Milestone Rd, SE19 . . . **170** C6
Miles Way, N20 . . . **57** H2
Milfoil St, W12 . . . **107** G7
Milford Cl, SE2 . . . **139** E6
Milford Gdns, Croy. CR0
off Tannery Cl . . . **189** G5
Edgware HA8 . . . **54** A7
Wembley HA0 . . . **87** G5
Milford Gro, Sutt. SM1 . . . **199** F4
Milford La, WC2 . . . **18** D5
Milford Ms, SW16 . . . **169** F3
Milford Rd, W13 . . . **124** E1
Southall UB1 . . . **103** G7
Milford Twrs, SE6
off Thomas La . . . **154** B7
Milk St, E16 . . . **136** E1
EC2 . . . **20** A4
Bromley BR1 . . . **173** H6
Milkwell Gdns, Wdf.Grn.
IG8 . . . **63** H7
Milkwell Yd, SE5 . . . **151** J1
Milkwood Rd, SE24 . . . **151** H5
Milk Yd, E1 . . . **113** F7
Millais Av, E12 . . . **98** D5
Millais Cres, Epsom KT19 . **196** E5
Millais Gdns, Edg. HA8 . . . **70** A2
Millais Rd, E11 . . . **96** C4
Enfield EN1 . . . **44** C5
New Malden KT3 . . . **182** E6
Millais Way, Epsom KT19 . **196** C4
Milland Ct, Borwd. WD6 . . **38** D1
Millard Cl, N16
off Boleyn Rd . . . **94** B5
Millard Ter, Dag. RM10
off Church Elm La . . . **101** G6
Millbank, SW1 . . . **26** A6
Millbank Twr, SW1 . . . **34** A2
Millbank Way, SE12 . . . **155** G5
Millbourne Rd, Felt.
TW13 . . . **161** E4
Millbrook Av, Well. DA16 . **157** G4
Millbrook Gdns, Rom.
(Chad.Hth) RM6 . . . **83** F6
Millbrook Pl, NW1
off Hampstead Rd . . . **110** C2
Millbrook Rd, N9 . . . **60** E1
SW9 . . . **151** H3
Mill Cl, Cars. SM5 . . . **200** A2
West Drayton UB7 . . . **120** A3
Mill Cor, Barn. EN5 . . . **40** C1
Mill Ct, E10 . . . **96** C3
Millcroft Ho, SE6 . . . **172** C4
Millender Wk, SE16 . . . **133** F4
Millennium Br, EC4 . . . **19** J5
SE1 . . . **19** J5
Millennium Cl, E16
off Russell Rd . . . **115** G6
Millennium Dr, E14 . . . **134** D4
Millennium Harbour, E14 . **133** J2
Millennium Pl, E2 . . . **113** E2
Millennium Sq, SE1 . . . **29** G3
Millennium Way, SE10 . . . **134** E2
Miller Cl, Mitch. CR4 . . . **185** J7
Pinner HA5 . . . **66** C2
Miller Rd, SW19 . . . **167** G6
Croydon CR0 . . . **201** F1
Miller's Av, E8 . . . **94** C5
Millers Cl, NW7 . . . **55** G4
Millers Ct, W4
off Chiswick Mall . . . **127** F5
Millers Grn Cl, Enf. EN2 . . . **43** H3
Millers Meadow Cl, SE3
off Meadowcourt Rd . . **155** F5
Miller's Ter, E8 . . . **94** C5
Miller St, NW1 . . . **9** F1
Millers Way, W6 . . . **127** J2
Miller Wk, SE1 . . . **27** F2
Millet Rd, Grnf. UB6 . . . **103** H3
Mill Fm Cl, Pnr. HA5 . . . **66** C2
Mill Fm Cres, Houns. TW4 . **161** E1
Millfield Av, E17 . . . **77** H1
Millfield La, N6 . . . **91** J2
Millfield Pl, N6 . . . **92** A2
Millfield Rd, Edg. HA8 . . . **70** C2
Hounslow TW4 . . . **161** E1
Millfields Est, E5
off Denton Way . . . **95** G3
Millfields Rd, E5 . . . **95** F4
Mill Gdns, SE26 . . . **171** E4
Mill Grn, Mitch. CR4
off London Rd . . . **186** A7
Mill Grn Business Pk, Mitch.
CR4 *off Mill Grn Rd* . . . **186** A7
Mill Grn Rd, Mitch. CR4 . . **185** J7
Millgrove St, SW11 . . . **150** A2
Millharbour, E14 . . . **134** B3
Millhaven Cl, Rom. RM6 . . **82** B6
MILL HILL, NW7 . . . **55** G5
Mill Hill, SW13
off Mill Hill Rd . . . **147** G2
Mill Hill Circ, NW7
off Watford Way . . . **55** F5
Mill Hill Gro, W3
off Mill Hill Rd . . . **126** B1
Mill Hill Rd, SW13 . . . **147** G2
W3 . . . **126** B2
Millhouse Pl, SE27 . . . **169** H4
Millicent Rd, E10 . . . **95** J1
Milligan St, E14 . . . **113** J7
Milliners Ct, Loug. IG10
off The Croft . . . **48** D2
Milliners Ho, SW18
off Point Pleasant . . . **148** D4
Milling Rd, Edg. HA8 . . . **54** D7
Millington Rd, Hayes UB3 . **121** H3
Mill La, E4 . . . **46** B3
NW6 . . . **90** C5
SE18 . . . **136** D5
Carshalton SM5 . . . **199** J4
Croydon CR0 . . . **201** F3
Romford (Chad.Hth)
RM6 . . . **82** E6
Woodford Green IG8 . . . **63** F5
Mill La Trd Est, Croy. CR0 . **201** F3
Millman Ms, WC1 . . . **10** C6
Millman Pl, WC1
off Millman St . . . **111** F4
Millman St, WC1 . . . **10** C6
Millmark Gro, SE14 . . . **153** H2
Millmarsh La, Enf. EN3 . . . **45** H2
Mill Mead Rd, N17 . . . **76** E4
Mill Pl, E14
off Commercial Rd . . . **113** H6
Chislehurst BR7 . . . **192** E1
Kingston upon Thames
KT1 . . . **181** J3
Mill Plat, Islw. TW7 . . . **144** D2
Mill Plat Av, Islw. TW7 . . . **144** D2
Mill Pond Cl, SW8
off Crimsworth Rd . . . **130** D7
Millpond Est, SE16
off West La . . . **132/133** E2
Millpond Pl, Cars. SM5 . . **200** A3
Mill Ridge, Edg. HA8 . . . **53** J5
Mill Rd, E16 . . . **135** H1
SW19 . . . **167** F7
Erith DA8 . . . **139** J7
Ilford IG1 . . . **98** D3
Twickenham TW2 . . . **161** J2
Mill Row, N1 . . . **112** B1
Mills Ct, EC2 . . . **12** E4
Mills Gro, E14
off Dewberry St . . . **114** C5
NW4 . . . **72** A3
Mill Shot Cl, SW6 . . . **127** J7
Millside, Cars. SM5 . . . **199** J2
Millside Pl, Islw. TW7 . . . **144** E2
Millsmead Way, Loug.
IG10 . . . **48** C2
Millson Cl, N20 . . . **57** G2
Mills Row, W4 . . . **126** D4
Millstream Cl, N13 . . . **59** G5
Millstream Rd, SE1 . . . **29** F4
Mill St, SE1 . . . **29** G4
W1 . . . **17** E5
Kingston upon Thames
KT1 . . . **181** H3
Mill Vale, Brom. BR2 . . . **191** F2
Mill Vw Cl, Epsom (Ewell)
KT17 . . . **197** F7
Mill Vw Gdns, Croy. CR0 . **203** G3
MILLWALL, E14 . . . **134** B3
Millwall Dock Rd, E14 . . . **134** A3
★**Millwall FC**, SE16 . . . **133** F5
Millway, NW7 . . . **54** E5
Mill Way, Felt. TW14 . . . **142** B5
Millway Gdns, Nthlt. UB5 . **85** F6
Millwell Cres, Chig. IG7 . . **65** G5
Millwood Rd, Houns. TW3 . **143** J5
Millwood St, W10
off St. Charles Sq . . . **108** B5
Mill Yd, E1 . . . **21** H5
Milman Cl, Pnr. HA5 . . . **66** D3
Milman Rd, NW6 . . . **108** B2
Milman's St, SW10 . . . **31** E6
Milmead Ind Cen, N17 . . . **76** E2
Milne Ct, E18
off Churchfields . . . **79** G1
Milne Feild, Pnr. HA5 . . . **51** G7
Milne Gdns, SE9 . . . **156** B5
Milner Dr, Twick. TW2 . . . **144** A7
Milner Pl, N1 . . . **111** G1
Carshalton SM5
off High St . . . **200** A4
Milner Rd, E15 . . . **114** E3
SW19 . . . **184** E1
Dagenham RM8 . . . **100** C2
Kingston upon Thames
KT1 . . . **181** G3
Milner Rd, Mord. SM4 . . . **185** G5
Thornton Heath CR7 . . . **188** A3
Milner Sq, N1 . . . **93** H7
Milner St, SW3 . . . **31** J1
Milner Wk, SE9 . . . **175** G2
Milnthorpe Rd, W4 . . . **126** D6
Milo Rd, SE22 . . . **152** C6
Milroy Wk, SE1 . . . **27** G1
Milson Rd, W14 . . . **128** B3
Milton Av, E6 . . . **98** A7
N6 . . . **74** C7
NW9 . . . **70** C3
NW10 . . . **106** C1
Barnet EN5 . . . **40** C5
Croydon CR0 . . . **188** A7
Sutton SM1 . . . **199** G3
Milton Cl, N2 . . . **73** F5
SE1 . . . **37** F2
Hayes UB4 . . . **102** A6
Sutton SM1 . . . **199** G3
Milton Ct, EC2 . . . **20** B1
Romford (Chad.Hth) RM6
off Cross Rd . . . **82** C7
Milton Ct Rd, SE14 . . . **133** H6
Milton Cres, Ilf. IG2 . . . **81** F7
Milton Dr, Borwd. WD6 . . . **38** B5
Milton Gdn Est, N16
off Milton Gro . . . **94** B4
Milton Gro, N11 . . . **58** C5
N16 . . . **94** A4
Milton Pk, N6 . . . **74** C7
Milton Pl, N7
off George's Rd . . . **93** G5
Milton Rd, E17 . . . **78** A4
N6 . . . **74** C7
N15 . . . **75** H4
NW7 . . . **55** G5
NW9
off West Hendon Bdy . . **71** G7
SE24 . . . **151** H6
SW14 . . . **146** D3
SW19 . . . **167** F6
W3 . . . **126** D1
W7 . . . **104** C7
Belvedere DA17 . . . **139** G4
Croydon CR0 . . . **202** A1
Hampton TW12 . . . **161** G7
Harrow HA1 . . . **68** B4
Mitcham CR4 . . . **168** A7
Sutton SM1 . . . **198** D3
Wallington SM6 . . . **200** C6
Welling DA16 . . . **157** J1
Milton St, EC2 . . . **20** B1
Milton Way, West Dr. UB7 . **120** C4
Milverton Gdns, Ilf. IG3 . . . **99** J2
Milverton Ho, SE23 . . . **171** H3
Milverton Rd, NW6 . . . **89** J7
Milverton St, SE11 . . . **35** F4
Milverton Way, SE9 . . . **174** D4
Milward St, E1
off Stepney Way . . **112/113** E5
Milward Wk, SE18
off Spearman St . . . **136** D6
Mimosa Rd, Hayes UB4 . . **102** C5
Mimosa St, SW6 . . . **148** C1
Minard Rd, SE6 . . . **154** E7
Mina Rd, SE17 . . . **36** E4
SW19 . . . **184** D1
Minchenden Cres, N14 . . . **58** C3
Mincing La, EC3 . . . **20** D5
Minden Rd, SE20 . . . **188** E1
Sutton SM3 . . . **198** C2
Minehead Rd, SW16 . . . **169** F5
Harrow HA2 . . . **85** G3
Mineral St, SE18 . . . **137** H4
Minera Ms, SW1 . . . **32** C1
Minerva Cl, SW9 . . . **131** G7
Sidcup DA14 . . . **175** H3
Minerva Rd, E4 . . . **62** B7
NW10 . . . **106** C4
Kingston upon Thames
KT1 . . . **181** J2
Minerva St, E2 . . . **112** E2
Minet Av, NW10 . . . **106** E2
Minet Dr, Hayes UB3 . . . **122** A1
Minet Gdns, NW10 . . . **106** E2
Hayes UB3 . . . **122** A1
Minet Rd, SW9 . . . **151** H2
Minford Gdns, W14 . . . **128** A2
Mingard Wk, N7
off Hornsey Rd . . . **93** F2
Ming St, E14 . . . **114** A7
★**Ministry of Defence**,
SW1 . . . **26** A2
Ministry Way, SE9 . . . **174** C2
Miniver Pl, EC4
off Garlick Hill . . . **111** J7
Mink Ct, Houns. TW4 . . . **142** C3
Minniedale, Surb. KT5 . . . **181** J5

Minnow St, SE17 *off East St* **132** B4
Minnow Wk, SE17 . . . . **36** E2
Minories, EC3. . . . . **21** F5
Minshull Pl, Beck. BR3 . . . **172** A7
Minshull St, SW8 *off Wandsworth Rd* . . . **150** D1
Minson Rd, E9 . . . . **113** G1
Minstead Gdns, SW15 . . . **147** F7
Minstead Way, N.Mal. KT3 . . . . **182** E6
Minster Av, Sutt. SM1 *off Leafield Rd*. **198** D2
Minster Ct, EC3 *off Mincing La* **112** A7
Minster Dr, Croy. CR0 . . . **202** B4
Minster Gdns, W.Mol. KT8 . . . . **179** F4
Minster Pavement, EC3 *off Mincing La* **112** A7
Minster Rd, NW2. . . . . **90** B5
Bromley BR1. . . . . **173** H7
Minster Wk, N8 *off Lightfoot Rd* **74/75** E4
Minstrel Gdns, Surb. KT5 . **181** J4
Mint Business Pk, E16 . . . **115** G5
Mintern Cl, N13 . . . . **59** H3
Minterne Av, Sthl. UB2 . . **123** G4
Minterne Rd, Har. HA3. . . . **69** J5
Minterne Waye, Hayes UB4 . . . . **102** C6
Mintern St, N1 . . . . **12** C1
Minton Ms, NW6 *off Lymington Rd*. . . **90/91** E6
Mint Rd, Wall. SM6 . . . . . **200** B4
Mint St, SE1. . . . . **27** J3
Mint Wk, Croy. CR0 *off High St*. **201** J3
Mirabel Rd, SW6 . . . . **128** C7
Miranda Cl, E1 *off Sidney St* **113** F5
Miranda Ct, W3 *off Queens Dr* **105** J6
Miranda Rd, N19 . . . . **92** C1
Mirfield St, SE7 . . . . **136** A4
Miriam Rd, SE18 . . . . **137** H5
Mirravale Trd Est, Dag. RM8. . . . . **83** F7
Mirren Cl, Har. HA2 . . . . . . **85** F4
Mirror Path, SE9 *off Lambscroft Av* **173** J3
Missenden Gdns, Mord. SM4. . . . . **185** F6
Mission Gro, E17 . . . . **77** H5
Mission Pl, SE15 . . . . **152** D1
Mission Sq, Brent. TW8 . . **125** H6
Mistletoe Cl, Croy. CR0 *off Marigold Way* **203** G1
Mitali Pas, E1 . . . . **21** H4
MITCHAM, CR4 . . . . **186** A3
Mitcham Gdn Village, Mitch. CR4. . . . . **186** A5
Mitcham Ind Est, Mitch. CR4 . . . . **186** A1
Mitcham La, SW16. . . . . . **168** C6
Mitcham Pk, Mitch. CR4. . **185** J4
Mitcham Rd, E6 . . . . **116** B3
SW17. . . . . **167** J5
Croydon CR0. . . . . **186** E6
Ilford IG3. . . . . **81** J7
Mitchellbrook Way, NW10 . **88** D6
Mitchell Cl, SE2 . . . . **138** C4
Belvedere DA17 . . . . . . **139** J3
Mitchell Rd, N13 . . . . **59** H5
Orpington BR6 . . . . **207** J4
Mitchell's Pl, SE21 *off Dulwich Village* . . . **152** B7
Mitchell St, EC1 . . . . **11** J5
Mitchell Wk, E6. . . . . **116** B5
Mitchell Way, NW10. . . . . . **88** C6
Bromley BR1. . . . . **191** G1
Mitchison Rd, N1. . . . . **94** A6
Mitchley Rd, N17 . . . . **76** D3
Mitford Cl, Chess. KT9 *off Merritt Gdns* **195** F6
Mitford Rd, N19. . . . . **93** E2
Mitre, The, E14 *off Three Colt St* **113** J7
Mitre Av, E17 *off Greenleaf Rd* **77** J3
Mitre Cl, Brom. BR2 *off Beckenham La* **191** F2
Sutton SM2. . . . . **199** F7
Mitre Ct, EC2 . . . . **20** A3
EC4 . . . . **19** F4
Mitre Rd, E15 . . . . **114** E2
SE1 . . . . **27** F3
Mitre Sq, EC3. . . . . **21** E4
Mitre St, EC3 . . . . **21** E4
Mitre Way, W10. . . . . **107** H4
Moat, The, N.Mal. KT3 . . . **182** E1
Moat Cl, Orp. BR6 . . . . . . **207** J6
Moat Cres, N3 . . . . **72** E3
Moat Cft, Well. DA16 . . . . **158** C3
Moat Dr, E13 *off Boundary Rd* **115** J2
Harrow HA1 . . . . **67** J4
Moat Fm Rd, Nthlt. UB5 . . **85** F6
Moat Pl, SW9 . . . . **151** F3
W3. . . . . **106** B6
Moatside, Enf. EN3 . . . . . . **45** G4
Feltham TW13 . . . . **160** C4
Moberley Rd, SW4. . . . . . **150** D7
Modbury Gdns, NW5 *off Queen's Cres* **92** A6
Modder Pl, SW15. . . . . . . **148** A4
Model Cotts, SW14 *off Upper Richmond Rd W* **146** C4
Model Fm Cl, SE9. . . . . . . **174** B3
Modling Ho, E2. . . . . **113** G2
Moelwyn Hughes Ct, N7 *off Hilldrop Cres* **92** D5
Moelyn Ms, Har. HA1. . . . . **68** D5
Moffat Rd, N13. . . . . **59** E6
SW17. . . . . **167** H4
Thornton Heath CR7 . . . **187** J2
Mogden La, Islw. TW7 . . . **144** B5
Mohmmad Khan Rd, E11 *off Harvey Rd* **97** F1
Moira Cl, N17. . . . . **76** B2
Moira Rd, SE9 . . . . **156** C4
Moland Mead, SE16 *off Crane Mead* **133** G5
Molasses Row, SW11 *off Cinnamon Row* . . . **149** F3
Mole Abbey Gdns, W.Mol. KT8 *off New Rd*. **179** G3
Mole Ct, Epsom KT19 . . . **196** C4
Molember Ct, E.Mol. KT8 . **180** B5
Molember Rd, E.Mol. KT8. **180** B5
Molescroft, SE9 . . . . **175** F3
Molesey Av, W.Mol. KT8 . **179** F4
Molesey Dr, Sutt. SM3. . . **198** B2
Molesey Pk Av, W.Mol. KT8 . . . . **179** H5
Molesey Pk Cl, E.Mol. KT8 . . . . **179** J5
Molesey Pk Rd, E.Mol. KT8. . . . . **180** A5
West Molesey KT8 . . . . **179** H5
Molesey Rd, W.Mol. KT8 . **179** E5
Molesford Rd, SW6 . . . . . **148** D1
Molesham Cl, W.Mol. KT8. **179** H3
Molesham Way, W.Mol. KT8 . . . . **179** H3
Molesworth St, SE13. . . . **154** C3
Mollison Av, Enf. EN3 . . . . **45** H5
Mollison Dr, Wall. SM6 . . **201** E6
Mollison Sq, Wall. SM6 *off Mollison Dr*. . . **200/201** E7
Mollison Way, Edg. HA8 . . **70** A2
Molly Huggins Cl, SW12 . . **150** C7
Molyneux Dr, SW17. . . . . **168** B4
Molyneux St, W1 . . . . **15** H2
Monarch Cl, Felt. TW14 . . **141** H7
West Wickham BR4. . . . **205** F4
Monarch Dr, E16. . . . . **116** A5
Monarch Ms, E17 . . . . **78** B5
SW16. . . . . **169** G5
Monarch Par, Mitch. CR4 *off London Rd*. **185** J2
Monarch Pl, Buck.H. IG9 . . **63** J2
Monarch Rd, Belv. DA17 . **139** G3
Monarchs Ct, NW7 *off Grenville Pl* **54** D5
Mona Rd, SE15 . . . . **153** F2
Monastery Gdns, Enf. EN2 . **44** A2
Mona St, E16 . . . . **115** F5
Monaveen Gdns, W.Mol. KT8 . . . . **179** G3
Monck St, SW1 . . . . **25** J6
Monclar Rd, SE5 . . . . **152** A4
Moncorvo Cl, SW7. . . . . . . **23** G4
Moncrieff Cl, E6 *off Linton Gdns*. **116** B6
Moncrieff Pl, SE15 *off Rye La* **152** D2
Moncrieff St, SE15. . . . . . **152** D2
Mondial Way, Hayes UB3. **121** F7
Monega Rd, E7. . . . . **97** J6
E12 . . . . **98** A6
Money La, West Dr. UB7 . **120** A3
Monier Rd, E3 . . . . **96** A7
Monivea Rd, Beck. BR3 . . **171** J7
Monkchester Cl, Loug. IG10 . . . . **48** D1
Monk Dr, E16 . . . . **115** G6
MONKEN HADLEY, Barn. EN5. . . . . **40** C1
Monkfrith Av, N14 . . . . **42** B6
Monkfrith Cl, N14. . . . . **42** B7
Monkfrith Way, N14 . . . . . **42** A7
Monkhams Av, Wdf.Grn. IG8 . . . . **63** G5
Monkhams Dr, Wdf.Grn. IG8. . . . . **63** H4
Monkhams La, Buck.H. IG9. **63** H3
Woodford Green IG8 . . . **63** G5
Monkleigh Rd, Mord. SM4. . . . . **184** B3
Monk Pas, E16 *off Monk Dr*. **115** G7
Monks Av, Barn. EN5. . . . . **41** F6
West Molesey KT8 . . . . **179** F5
Monks Cl, SE2 . . . . **138** D4
Enfield EN2. . . . . **43** J2
Harrow HA2 . . . . **85** H2
Ruislip HA4. . . . . **84** D4
Monksdene Gdns, Sutt. SM1. . . . . **199** E3
Monks Dr, W3. . . . . **106** A5
Monksgrove, Loug. IG10 . . **48** D5
Monksmead, Borwd. WD6. **38** C4
MONKS ORCHARD, Croy. CR0 . . . . **189** J7
Monks Orchard Rd, Beck. BR3 . . . . **204** A1
Monks Pk, Wem. HA9 . . . . **88** C6
Monks Pk Gdns, Wem. HA9. . . . . **88** B6
Monk's Ridge, N20. . . . . . . **55** H1
Monks Rd, Enf. EN2. . . . . . **43** J2
Monk St, SE18 . . . . **136** D4
Monks Way, NW11 *off Hurstwood Rd* **72** C4
Beckenham BR3 . . . . . . **190** A5
Orpington BR5 . . . . **207** F1
West Drayton UB7 . . . . **120** B6
Monkswell Ct, N10 *off Pembroke Rd*. **74** A1
Monkswood Gdns, Borwd. WD6 . . . . **38** D4
Ilford IG5. . . . . **80** D3
Monkton Rd, Well. DA16 . **157** J2
Monkton St, SE11 . . . . **35** F1
Monkville Av, NW11. . . . . . **72** C4
Monkwell Sq, EC2 . . . . **20** A2
Monmouth Av, E18 . . . . . . **79** H4
Kingston upon Thames KT1 . . . . **163** F7
Monmouth Cl, W4 *off Beaumont Rd*. **126** D3
Mitcham CR4 *off Recreation Way*. **186/187** E4
Welling DA16 . . . . **158** A4
Monmouth Gro, Brent. TW8 *off Sterling Pl* **125** H4
Monmouth Pl, W2 *off Monmouth Rd* **108** D6
Monmouth Rd, E6 . . . . . . **116** C3
N9 . . . . **60** E2
W2. . . . . **108** E6
Dagenham RM9 . . . . **101** F5
Hayes UB3 . . . . **121** H4
Monmouth St, WC2 . . . . . . **18** A4
Monnery Rd, N19. . . . . **92** C3
Monnow Rd, SE1. . . . . **37** H3
Mono La, Felt. TW13 . . . . **160** B2
Monoux Gro, E17. . . . . **78** A1
Monroe Cres, Enf. EN1. . . . **44** E1
Monroe Dr, SW14 . . . . . . **146** B5
Monro Gdns, Har. HA3. . . . **52** B7
Monro Way, E5. . . . . **94** E4
Monsal Ct, E5 *off Redwald Rd*. **95** G4
Monsell Ct, N4 *off Monsell Rd* **93** H3
Monsell Rd, N4 . . . . **93** H3
Monson Rd, NW10. . . . . . **107** G2
SE14 . . . . **133** G7
Mons Way, Brom. BR2 . . **192** B6
Montacute Rd, SE6 . . . . . **153** J7
Morden SM4. . . . . **185** G6
Montagu Cres, N18 . . . . . . **61** E4
Montague Av, SE4 . . . . . . **153** J4
W7. . . . . **124** C1
Montague Cl, SE1 . . . . **28** B1
Walton-on-Thames KT12 . . . . **178** A7
Montague Gdns, W3 . . . . **106** A7
Montague Pl, WC1. . . . . . . **17** J1
Montague Rd, E8. . . . . **94** D5
E11. . . . . **97** F2
N8 . . . . **75** F5
N15 . . . . **76** D4
SW19. . . . . **166** E7
Montague Rd, W7 . . . . . . **124** C1
W13. . . . . **105** E6
Croydon CR0. . . . . **201** H1
Hounslow TW3 . . . . **143** H3
Richmond TW10 . . . . . . **145** H6
Southall UB2. . . . . **122** E4
Montague Sq, SE15 *off Clifton Way*. **133** F7
Montague St, EC1 . . . . **19** J2
WC1. . . . . **18** A1
Montague Waye, Sthl. UB2 . . . . **122** E3
Montagu Gdns, N18 . . . . . **60** E4
Wallington SM6 . . . . . . **200** C4
Montagu Mans, W1 . . . . . . **16** A1
Montagu Ms N, W1 . . . . . . **16** A2
Montagu Ms S, W1 . . . . . . **16** A3
Montagu Ms W, W1 . . . . . . **16** A3
Montagu Pl, W1 . . . . **15** J2
Montagu Rd, N9 . . . . **61** F4
N18 . . . . **61** E5
NW4 . . . . **71** G6
Montagu Rd Ind Est, N18 . **61** F4
Montagu Row, W1 . . . . **16** A2
Montagu Sq, W1 . . . . **16** A2
Montagu St, W1. . . . . **16** A3
Montaigne Cl, SW1 . . . . . . **33** J1
Montalt Rd, Wdf.Grn. IG8 . **63** F5
Montana Gdns, SE26. . . . **171** J5
Sutton SM1 *off Lind Rd* **199** F5
Montana Rd, SW17 . . . . . **168** A4
SW20. . . . . **183** J1
Montbelle Rd, SE9 . . . . . . **174** E3
Montcalm Cl, Brom. BR2 . **191** G6
Hayes UB4 *off Ayles Rd*. **102** B3
Montcalm Rd, SE7 . . . . . . **136** A7
Montclare St, E2 . . . . **13** F4
Monteagle Av, Bark. IG11. . **99** F6
Monteagle Way, E5 *off Rendlesham Rd*. . . . **94** D3
SE15 . . . . **153** E3
Montefiore St, SW8. . . . . **150** B2
Montego Cl, SE24 *off Railton Rd* **151** G4
Montem Rd, SE23 . . . . . . **153** J7
New Malden KT3 . . . . . **182** E4
Montem St, N4 *off Thorpedale Rd* **93** F1
Montenotte Rd, N8 . . . . . . **74** C5
Monterey Cl, Bex. DA5. . . **177** J2
Montesole Ct, Pnr. HA5 . . . **66** C2
Montevetro, SW11 . . . . . . **149** G1
Montford Pl, SE11 . . . . **34** E4
Montford Rd, Sun. TW16 . **178** A4
Montfort Gdns, Ilf. IG6. . . . **65** F6
Montfort Pl, SW19 . . . . . . **166** A1
Montgolfier Wk, Nthlt. UB5 *off Jetstar Way* . . . **102/103** E3
Montgomery Av, Esher KT10 . . . . **194** B3
Montgomery Cl, Mitch. CR4 . . . . **187** F4
Sidcup DA15 . . . . **157** J6
Montgomery Ct, W4 *off St. Thomas' Rd* . . . **126** C6
Montgomery Rd, W4 . . . . **126** C4
Edgware HA8 . . . . **53** J6
Montgomery St, E14 . . . . **134** B1
Montholme Rd, SW11 . . . **149** J6
Monthope Rd, E1. . . . . **21** H2
Montolieu Gdns, SW15 . . **147** H5
Montpelier Av, W5 . . . . . . **105** F5
Bexley DA5 . . . . **158** D7
Montpelier Gdns, E6 . . . . **116** A3
Romford RM6 . . . . **82** C7
Montpelier Gro, NW5 . . . . **92** C5
Montpelier Ms, SW7 . . . . . **23** H5
Montpelier Pl, E1 . . . . **113** F6
SW7. . . . . **23** H5
Montpelier Ri, NW11 . . . . . **72** B7
Wembley HA9. . . . . **87** G1
Montpelier Rd, N3 . . . . **73** F1
SE15 . . . . **153** E1
W5. . . . . **105** G5
Sutton SM1. . . . . **199** F4
Montpelier Row, SE3. . . . **155** F2
Twickenham TW1 . . . . . **145** E7
Montpelier Sq, SW7 . . . . . **23** H4
Montpelier St, SW7. . . . . . **23** H4
Montpelier Ter, SW7 . . . . . **23** H4
Montpelier Vale, SE3 . . . . **155** F2
Montpelier Wk, SW7 . . . . . **23** H5
Montpelier Way, NW11 . . . **72** B7
Montrave Rd, SE20 . . . . . **171** F6
Montreal Pl, WC2 . . . . **18** C5
Montreal Rd, Ilf. IG1. . . . . . **81** F7
Montrell Rd, SW2. . . . . . . **169** E1

Montrose Av, NW6 ... **108** B2
Edgware HA8 ... **70** C2
Sidcup DA15 ... **158** A7
Twickenham TW2 ... **143** H7
Welling DA16 ... **157** G3
Montrose Cl, Well. DA16 . **157** J3
Woodford Green IG8 ... **63** G4
Montrose Ct, SW7 ... **23** F4
Montrose Cres, N12 ... **57** F6
Wembley HA0 ... **87** H6
Montrose Gdns, Mitch.
CR4 ... **185** J3
Sutton SM1 ... **199** E2
Montrose Pl, SW1 ... **24** C4
Montrose Rd, Felt. TW14 . **141** G6
Harrow HA3 ... **68** B2
Montrose Way, SE23 ... **171** G1
Montserrat Av, Wdf.Grn.
IG8 ... **62** D7
Montserrat Cl, SE19 ... **170** A5
Montserrat Rd, SW15 ... **148** B4
★**Monument, The**, EC3 ... **20** C6
Monument Gdns, SE13 .. **154** C5
Monument St, EC3 ... **20** C5
Monument Way, N17 ... **76** C3
Monza St, E1 ... **113** F7
Moodkee St, SE16 ... **133** F3
Moody Rd, SE15 ... **132** C7
Moody St, E1 ... **113** G3
Moon La, Barn. EN5 ... **40** C3
Moon St, N1 ... **111** H1
Moorcroft Gdns, Brom. BR2
off Southborough Rd . **192** B5
Moorcroft Rd, SW16 ... **168** E3
Moorcroft Way, Pnr. HA5 .. **66** E5
Moordown, SE18 ... **156** D1
Moore Cl, SW14
off Little St. Leonards . **146** C3
Mitcham CR4 ... **186** B2
Moore Cres, Dag. RM9 ... **118** B1
Moorefield Rd, N17 ... **76** C2
Moorehead Way, SE3 ... **155** H3
Mooreland Rd, Brom.
BR1 ... **173** F7
Moore Pk Rd, SW6 ... **128** E7
Moore Rd, SE19 ... **169** J6
Moore St, SW3 ... **31** J1
Moore Wk, E7
off Stracey Rd ... **97** G4
Moore Way, SE22
off Lordship La ... **170** D1
Moorey Cl, E15
off Stephen's Rd ... **115** F1
Moorfield Av, W5 ... **105** G4
Moorfield Rd, Chess. KT9 . **195** H5
Enfield EN3 ... **45** F1
Moorfields, EC2 ... **20** B2
Moorfields Highwalk, EC2
off Fore St ... **112** A5
Moorgate, EC2 ... **20** B3
Moorgate Pl, EC2 ... **20** B3
Moorhouse Rd, W2 ... **108** D6
Harrow HA3 ... **69** G3
Moorings, SE28 ... **118** B7
Moorland Cl, Twick. TW2
off Telford Rd ... **143** G7
Moorland Rd, SW9 ... **151** H4
Moorlands Av, NW7 ... **55** H6
Moorlands Est, SW9 ... **151** G1
Moor La, EC2 ... **20** D2
Chessington KT9 ... **195** H4
Moormead Dr, Epsom
KT19 ... **197** E5
Moor Mead Rd, Twick.
TW1 ... **144** D6
Moor Pk Gdns, Kings.T.
KT2 ... **165** E7
Moor Pl, EC2 ... **20** B2
Moorside Rd, Brom. BR1 . **173** E3
Moor St, W1 ... **17** J4
Moortown Rd, Wat. WD19 . **50** C4
Moot Ct, NW9 ... **70** A5
Morant Pl, N22
off Commerce Rd ... **75** F1
Morant St, E14 ... **114** A7
Mora Rd, NW2 ... **89** J4
Mora St, EC1 ... **12** A4
Morat St, SW9 ... **151** F1
Moravian Pl, SW10 ... **31** F6
Moravian St, E2 ... **113** F3
Moray Av, Hayes UB3 ... **121** J1
Moray Cl, Edg. HA8
off Pentland Av ... **54** B2
Moray Ms, N7
off Durham Rd ... **93** F2
Moray Rd, N4 ... **93** F2
Mordaunt Gdns, Dag.
RM9 ... **100** E7
Mordaunt Ho, NW10 ... **106** D1
Mordaunt Rd, NW10 ... **106** D1
Mordaunt St, SW9 ... **151** F3
MORDEN, SM4 ... **184** D3
Morden Ct, Mord. SM4 .. **184** E4
Morden Gdns, Grnf. UB6 .. **86** C5
Mitcham CR4 ... **185** G4
★**Morden Hall Pk N.T.**,
Mord. SM4 ... **185** E3
Morden Hall Rd, Mord.
SM4 ... **185** E3
Morden Hill, SE13 ... **154** C2
Morden La, SE13 ... **154** C1
MORDEN PARK, Mord.
SM4 ... **184** B5
Morden Rd, SE3 ... **155** G2
SW19 ... **185** E1
Mitcham CR4 ... **185** F4
Romford RM6 ... **83** E7
Morden Rd Ms, SE3 ... **155** G2
Morden St, SE13 ... **154** B1
Morden Way, Sutt. SM3 .. **184** D7
Morden Wf Rd, SE10 ... **134** E3
Mordon Rd, Ilf. IG3 ... **81** J7
Mordred Rd, SE6 ... **172** E2
Morecambe Cl, E1 ... **113** G5
Morecambe Gdns, Stan.
HA7 ... **53** G4
Morecambe St, SE17 ... **36** A2
Morecambe Ter, N18 ... **60** A4
More Cl, E16 ... **115** F6
W14 ... **128** B4
Morecoombe Cl, Kings.T.
KT2 ... **164** B7
Moree Way, N18 ... **60** D4
Moreland St, EC1 ... **11** H3
Moreland Way, E4 ... **62** B3
Morella Rd, SW12 ... **149** J7
Morell Cl, Barn. EN5
off Galdana Av ... **41** F3
More London Pl, SE1
off Tooley St ... **132** B1
More London Riverside,
SE1 *off Tooley St* ... **132** B1
Moremead Rd, SE6 ... **171** J4
Morena St, SE6 ... **154** B7
Moresby Av, Surb. KT5 .. **182** B7
Moresby Rd, E5 ... **94** E1
Moresby Wk, SW8 ... **150** B2
Moreton Av, Islw. TW7 ... **144** B1
Moreton Cl, E5 ... **95** F2
N15 ... **76** A6
NW7 ... **55** J6
SW1 ... **33** G3
Moreton Gdns, Wdf.Grn.
IG8 ... **64** B5
Moreton Pl, SW1 ... **33** G3
Moreton Rd, N15 ... **76** A6
South Croydon CR2 ... **202** A5
Worcester Park KT4 ... **197** G2
Moreton St, SW1 ... **33** G3
Moreton Ter, SW1 ... **33** G3
Moreton Ter Ms N, SW1 ... **33** G3
Moreton Ter Ms S, SW1 ... **33** G3
Moreton Twr, W3 ... **126** B1
Morford Cl, Ruis. HA4 ... **66** B7
Morford Way, Ruis. HA4 ... **66** B7
Morgan Av, E17 ... **78** D4
Morgan Cl, Dag. RM10 ... **101** G7
Morgan Rd, N7 ... **93** G5
W10 ... **108** C5
Bromley BR1 ... **173** G7
Morgans La, SE1 ... **28** D2
Morgan St, E3 ... **113** H3
E16 ... **115** F5
Morgan Way, Wdf.Grn. IG8 . **64** B6
Moriatry Cl, N7 ... **92** E4
Morie St, SW18 ... **149** E5
Morieux Rd, E10 ... **95** J1
Moring Rd, SW17 ... **168** A4
Morkyns Wk, SE21 ... **170** B3
Morland Av, Croy. CR0 ... **202** B1
Morland Cl, NW11 ... **91** E1
Hampton TW12 ... **161** F5
Mitcham CR4 ... **185** H3
Morland Gdns, NW10 ... **88** D7
Southall UB1 ... **123** H1
Morland Ms, N1
off Lofting Rd ... **93** G7
Morland Rd, E17 ... **77** G5
SE20 ... **171** G6
Croydon CR0 ... **202** B1
Dagenham RM10 ... **101** G7
Harrow HA3 ... **69** H5
Ilford IG1 ... **98** E2
Sutton SM1 ... **199** F5
Morley Av, E4 ... **62** D7
N18 ... **60** D4
N22 ... **75** G2
Morley Cl, Orp. BR6 ... **207** E2
Morley Cres, Edg. HA8 ... **54** C2
Ruislip HA4 ... **84** C2
Morley Cres E, Stan. HA7 . **69** F2
Morley Cres W, Stan. HA7 . **69** F2
Morley Rd, E10 ... **96** C1
E15 ... **115** F2
SE13 ... **154** C4
Barking IG11 ... **117** G1
Chislehurst BR7 ... **193** F1
Romford RM6 ... **82** E5
Sutton SM3 ... **198** C1
Twickenham TW1 ... **145** G6
Morley St, SE1 ... **27** F5
Morna Rd, SE5 ... **151** J2
Morning La, E9 ... **95** F6
Morningside Rd, Wor.Pk.
KT4 ... **197** H2
Mornington Av, W14 ... **128** C4
Bromley BR1 ... **191** J3
Ilford IG1 ... **80** D7
Mornington Cl, Wdf.Grn.
IG8 ... **63** G4
Mornington Ct, Bex. DA5 . **177** J1
Mornington Cres, NW1 ... **9** F1
Hounslow TW5 ... **142** B1
Mornington Gro, E3 ... **114** A3
Mornington Ms, SE5 ... **151** J1
Mornington Pl, NW1 ... **9** E1
Mornington Rd, E4 ... **46** D7
E11 ... **97** F1
SE8 ... **133** J7
Greenford UB6 ... **103** H5
Loughton IG10 ... **49** F3
Woodford Green IG8 ... **63** F4
Mornington St, NW1 ... **8** E1
Mornington Ter, NW1 ... **110** B1
Mornington Wk, Rich.
TW10 ... **163** G4
Morocco St, SE1 ... **28** D4
Morpeth Gro, E9 ... **113** G1
Morpeth Rd, E9 ... **113** F1
Morpeth St, E2 ... **113** G3
Morpeth Ter, SW1 ... **25** F6
Morpeth Wk, N17
off West Rd ... **60/61** E7
Morrab Gdns, Ilf. IG3 ... **99** J3
Morris Av, E12 ... **98** C5
Morris Cl, Croy. CR0 ... **189** H6
Orpington BR6 ... **207** H3
Morris Ct, E4 ... **62** B3
Morris Gdns, SW18 ... **148** D7
Morrish Rd, SW2 ... **151** E7
Morrison Av, E4 ... **62** A6
N17 ... **76** B3
Morrison Rd, SW9
off Marcella Rd ... **151** G2
Barking IG11 ... **118** E2
Hayes UB4 ... **102** B3
Morrison St, SW11 ... **150** A3
Morris Pl, N4 ... **93** G2
Morris Rd, E14 ... **114** B5
E15 ... **96** E4
Dagenham RM8 ... **101** F2
Isleworth TW7 ... **144** C3
Morris St, E1 ... **113** E6
Morriston Cl, Wat. WD19 .. **50** C5
Morse Cl, E13 ... **115** G3
Morshead Rd, W9 ... **108** D3
Morson Rd, Enf. EN3 ... **45** H6
Morston Gdns, SE9 ... **174** C4
Morten Cl, SW4 ... **150** D6
Morteyne Rd, N17 ... **76** A1
Mortgramit Sq, SE18
off Powis St ... **136** D3
Mortham St, E15 ... **114** D1
Mortimer Cl, NW2 ... **90** C3
SW16 ... **168** D2
Mortimer Cres, NW6 ... **108** E1
Worcester Park KT4 ... **196** D3
Mortimer Dr, Enf. EN1 ... **44** A5
Mortimer Est, NW6 ... **108** E1
Mortimer Ho, W11
off St. Anns Rd ... **128** A1
Mortimer Mkt, WC1 ... **9** G6
Mortimer Pl, NW6 ... **108** E1
Mortimer Rd, E6 ... **116** C3
N1 ... **94** B7
NW10 ... **107** J3
W13 ... **105** F6
Mitcham CR4 ... **185** J1
Mortimer Sq, W11
off St. Anns Rd ... **108** A7
Mortimer St, W1 ... **17** F3
Mortimer Ter, NW5
off Gordon Ho Rd ... **92** B4
MORTLAKE, SW14 ... **146** C3
Mortlake Cl, Croy. CR0
off Richmond Rd . **200/201** E3
Mortlake Dr, Mitch. CR4 .. **185** H1
Mortlake High St, SW14 . **146** D3
Mortlake Rd, E16 ... **115** H6
Ilford IG1 ... **99** F4
Richmond TW9 ... **126** A7
Mortlake Ter, Rich. TW9
off Kew Rd ... **126** A7
Mortlock Cl, SE15
off Cossall Wk ... **152/153** E1
Morton Cl, Wall. SM6 ... **201** F7
Morton Ct, Nthlt. UB5 ... **85** J5
Morton Cres, N14 ... **58** D4
Morton Gdns, Wall. SM6 . **200** C5
Morton Ms, SW5 ... **30** A2
Morton Pl, SE1 ... **26** E6
Morton Rd, E15 ... **97** F7
N1 ... **93** J7
Morden SM4 ... **185** G5
Morton Way, N14 ... **58** C3
Morvale Cl, Belv. DA17 .. **139** F4
Morval Rd, SW2 ... **151** G5
Morven Rd, SW17 ... **167** J3
Morville Ho, SW18
off Fitzhugh Gro ... **149** G6
Morville St, E3 ... **114** A2
Morwell St, WC1 ... **17** J2
Moscow Pl, W2 ... **14** A5
Moscow Rd, W2 ... **14** A5
Moseley Row, SE10 ... **135** F4
Moselle Av, N22 ... **75** G2
Moselle Cl, N8
off Miles Rd ... **75** F3
Moselle Ho, N17
off William St ... **60** C7
Moselle Pl, N17
off High Rd ... **60** C7
Moselle St, N17 ... **60** C7
Mossborough Cl, N12 ... **57** E6
Mossbury Rd, SW11 ... **149** H3
Moss Cl, E1 ... **21** J1
Pinner HA5 ... **67** F2
Mossdown Cl, Belv. DA17 . **139** G4
Mossford Ct, Ilf. IG6 ... **81** E3
Mossford Grn, Ilf. IG6 ... **81** E3
Mossford La, Ilf. IG6 ... **81** E2
Mossford St, E3 ... **113** J4
Moss Gdns, Felt. TW13 .. **160** A2
South Croydon CR2
off Warren Av ... **203** G7
Moss Hall Ct, N12 ... **57** E6
Moss Hall Cres, N12 ... **57** E6
Moss Hall Gro, N12 ... **56** E6
Mossington Gdns, SE16
off Abbeyfield Rd ... **133** F4
Moss La, Pnr. HA5 ... **67** F3
Mosslea Rd, SE20 ... **171** F6
Bromley BR2 ... **192** A5
Orpington BR6 ... **207** F3
Mossop St, SW3 ... **31** H1
Moss Rd, Dag. RM10 ... **101** G7
Mossville Gdns, Mord.
SM4 ... **184** C3
Moston Cl, Hayes UB3
off Fuller Way ... **121** J5
Mostyn Av, Wem. HA9 ... **87** J5
Mostyn Gdns, NW10 ... **108** A2
Mostyn Gro, E3 ... **113** J2
Mostyn Rd, SW9 ... **151** G1
SW19 ... **184** C1
Edgware HA8 ... **54** D7
Mosul Way, Brom. BR2 .. **192** B6
Motcomb St, SW1 ... **24** A5
Moth Cl, Wall. SM6 ... **200** E7
Mothers' Sq, E5 ... **95** E4
Motley Av, EC2 ... **12** D5
Motley St, SW8
off St. Rule St ... **150** C2
MOTSPUR PARK, N.Mal.
KT3 ... **183** G6
Motspur Pk, N.Mal. KT3 . **183** F6
MOTTINGHAM, SE9 ... **173** J2
Mottingham Gdns, SE9 .. **174** A1
Mottingham La, SE9 ... **173** J1
SE12 ... **173** J1
Mottingham Rd, N9 ... **45** G6
SE9 ... **174** B2
Mottisfont Rd, SE2 ... **138** A3
Mott St, Loug. (High Beach)
IG10 ... **47** F1
Moulins Rd, E9 ... **113** F1
Moulsford Ho, N7 ... **92** D5
Moulton Av, Houns. TW3 . **143** E2
Mound, The, SE9 ... **174** D3
Moundfield Rd, N16 ... **76** D6
Mount, The, N20 ... **57** F2
NW3 *off Heath St* ... **91** F4
W3 ... **126** B1
New Malden KT3 ... **183** F3
Wembley HA9 ... **88** B2
Worcester Park KT4 ... **197** H4

Mountacre Cl, SE26 170 C4
Mount Adon Pk, SE22 152 D7
Mountague Pl, E14 114 C7
Mount Angelus Rd, SW15 147 F7
Mount Ararat Rd, Rich. TW10 145 H5
Mount Ash Rd, SE26 170 E3
Mount Av, E4 62 A3
W5 105 G5
Southall UB1 103 G6
Mountbatten Cl, SE18 137 H6
SE19 170 B5
Mountbatten Ct, SE16 *off Rotherhithe St* 133 F1
Buckhurst Hill IG9 64 A2
Mountbatten Gdns, Beck. BR3 *off Balmoral Av* 189 H4
Mountbatten Ms, SW18 *off Inman Rd* 167 F1
Mountbel Rd, Stan. HA7 68 D1
Mount Cl, W5 105 F5
Barnet EN4 42 A4
Bromley BR1 192 B1
Mountcombe Cl, Surb. KT6 181 H7
Mount Cor, Felt. TW13 160 D2
Mount Ct, SW15 *off Weimar St* 148 B3
West Wickham BR4 204 E2
Mount Culver Av, Sid. DA14 176 D6
Mount Dr, Bexh. DA6 158 E5
Harrow HA2 67 F5
Wembley HA9 88 C2
Mountearl Gdns, SW16 169 F3
Mount Echo Av, E4 62 B2
Mount Echo Dr, E4 62 B1
Mount Ephraim La, SW16 168 D3
Mount Ephraim Rd, SW16 168 D3
Mount Est, The, E5 *off Mount Pleasant La* 94/95 E2
Mountfield Cl, SE6 154 D7
Mountfield Rd, E6 116 D2
N3 72 D3
W5 105 G6
Mountfield Ter, SE6 *off Mountfield Cl* 154 D7
Mountford St, E1 21 H3
Mountfort Cres, N1 *off Barnsbury Sq* 93 G7
Mountfort Ter, N1 *off Barnsbury Sq* 93 G7
Mount Gdns, SE26 170 E3
Mount Gro, Edg. HA8 54 C3
Mountgrove Rd, N5 93 H3
Mounthurst Rd, Brom. BR2 191 F7
Mountington Pk Cl, Har. HA3 69 G6
Mountjoy Cl, SE2 138 B2
Mountjoy Ho, EC2 *off The Barbican* 111 J5
Mount Ms, Hmptn. TW12 179 H1
Mount Mills, EC1 11 H4
Mount Nod Rd, SW16 169 F3
Mount Pk Av, Har. HA1 86 A2
Mount Pk Cres, W5 105 G6
Mount Pk Rd, W5 105 G5
Harrow HA1 86 A3
Pinner HA5 66 A5
Mount Pl, W3 *off High St* 126 B1
Mount Pleasant, SE27 169 J4
WC1 10 D6
Barnet EN4 41 H4
Ruislip HA4 84 C2
Wembley HA0 105 H1
Mount Pleasant Cres, N4 75 F7
Mount Pleasant Hill, E5 95 E2
Mount Pleasant La, E5 94 E2
Mount Pleasant Pl, SE18 *off Orchard Rd* 137 G4
Mount Pleasant Rd, E17 77 H2
N17 76 B2
NW10 89 J7
SE13 154 B6
W5 105 F4
Chigwell IG7 65 G4
New Malden KT3 182 C3
Mount Pleasant Vil, N4 75 F7
Mount Pleasant Wk, Bex. DA5 159 J5
Mount Rd, NW2 89 H3
NW4 71 G6
SE19 170 A6
SW19 166 D2
Barnet EN4 41 H5
Bexleyheath DA6 158 D5
gton KT9 195 J5
am RM8 101 F1
Mount Rd, Felt. TW13 160 E3
Hayes UB3 121 J2
Ilford IG1 98 E5
Mitcham CR4 185 H2
New Malden KT3 182 D3
Mount Row, W1 16 D6
Mountsfield Ct, SE13 154 D6
Mountside, Felt. TW13 161 E3
Stanmore HA7 68 C1
Mounts Pond Rd, SE3 154 D2
Mount Sq, The, NW3 *off Heath St* 91 F3
Mount Stewart Av, Har. HA3 69 G6
Mount St, W1 16 C6
Mount Ter, E1 *off New Rd* 112/113 E5
Mount Vernon, NW3 91 F4
Mount Vw, NW7 54 D3
W5 105 G4
Mountview Cl, NW11 91 E1
Mountview Ct, N8 *off Green Las* 75 H4
Mount Vw Rd, E4 46 C7
N4 75 E7
NW9 70 D4
Mountview Rd, Esher (Clay.) KT10 194 E7
Mount Vil, SE27 169 H3
Mountwood, W.Mol. KT8 179 G3
Movers La, Bark. IG11 117 G1
Mowatt Cl, N19 92 D1
Mowbray Rd, NW6 90 B7
SE19 188 C1
Barnet EN5 41 F4
Edgware HA8 54 A4
Richmond TW10 163 F3
Mowbrays Cl, Rom. RM5 83 J1
Mowbrays Rd, Rom. RM5 83 J2
Mowbrey Gdns, Loug. IG10 49 F2
Mowlem St, E2 113 E2
Mowlem Trd Est, N17 61 F7
Mowll St, SW9 131 G7
Moxon Cl, E13 *off Whitelegg Rd* 115 F2
Moxon St, W1 16 B2
Barnet EN5 40 C3
Moye Cl, E2 13 J1
Moyers Rd, E10 78 C7
Moylan Rd, W6 128 B6
Moyne Pl, NW10 106 A2
Moynihan Dr, N21 43 E5
Moys Cl, Croy. CR0 186 E6
Moyser Rd, SW16 168 B5
Mozart St, W10 108 C3
Mozart Ter, SW1 32 C2
Muchelney Rd, Mord. SM4 185 F6
Mud La, W5 105 G5
Muggeridge Cl, S.Croy. CR2 202 A5
Muggeridge Rd, Dag. RM10 101 H4
Muirdown Av, SW14 146 C4
Muir Dr, SW18 149 G6
Muirfield, W3 107 E6
Muirfield Cl, SE16 *off Ryder Dr* 132/133 E5
Watford WD19 50 C4
Muirfield Cres, E14 *off Millharbour* 134 B3
Muirfield Grn, Wat. WD19 50 C4
Muirfield Rd, Wat. WD19 50 D4
Muirkirk Rd, SE6 172 C1
Muir Rd, E5 94 D4
Muir St, E16 *off Newland St* 136 C1
Mulberry Business Cen, SE16 *off Quebec Way* 133 G2
Mulberry Cl, E4 62 A2
N8 74 E5
NW3 *off Hampstead High St* 91 G4
NW4 71 J3
SE7 *off Charlton Pk Rd* 136 A6
SE22 152 D5
SW3 *off Beaufort St* 129 G6
SW16 168 C4
Barnet EN4 41 G4
Northolt UB5 *off Parkfield Av* 102/103 E2
Mulberry Ct, Bark. IG11 *off Westrow Dr* 99 J7
Mulberry Cres, Brent. TW8 125 E7
West Drayton UB7 120 D2
Mulberry La, Croy. CR0 202 C1
Mulberry Ms, SE14 *off Lewisham Way* 153 J1
Wallington SM6 *off Ross Rd* 200 C6
Mulberry Par, West Dr. UB7 120 D3
Mulberry Pl, W6 *off Chiswick Mall* 127 G5
Mulberry Rd, E8 94 C7
Mulberry St, E1 21 H3
Mulberry Wk, SW3 31 F5
Mulberry Way, E18 79 H2
Belvedere DA17 139 J2
Ilford IG6 81 F4
Mulgrave Rd, NW10 89 F4
SE18 136 C4
SW6 128 C6
W5 105 G3
Croydon CR0 202 A3
Harrow HA1 86 D2
Sutton SM2 198 D6
Mulholland Cl, Mitch. CR4 186 B2
Mulkern Rd, N19 92 D1
Mullards Cl, Mitch. CR4 199 J1
Muller Rd, SW4 150 D6
Mullet Gdns, E2 13 J3
Mullins Path, SW14 146 D3
Mullion Cl, Har. HA3 67 H1
Mullion Wk, Wat. WD19 *off Ormskirk Rd* 50 D4
Mull Wk, N1 *off Clephane Rd* 93 J6
Mulready St, NW8 7 G6
Multi-way, W3 *off Valetta Rd* 126/127 E2
Multon Rd, SW18 149 G7
Mulvaney Way, SE1 28 C4
Mumford Ct, EC2 20 A3
Mumford Rd, SE24 *off Railton Rd* 151 H5
Muncaster Rd, SW11 149 J5
Muncies Ms, SE6 172 C2
Mundania Rd, SE22 153 E6
Munday Rd, E16 115 G6
Munden St, W14 128 B4
Mundesley Cl, Wat. WD19 50 C4
Mundford Rd, E5 95 F2
Mundon Gdns, Ilf. IG1 99 G1
Mund St, W14 128 C5
Mundy St, N1 12 D3
Mungo Pk Cl, Bushey (Bushey Hth) WD23 51 J2
Munnery Way, Orp. BR6 206 D3
Munnings Gdns, Islw. TW7 144 A5
Munro Dr, N11 58 C6
Munro Ms, W10 108 B5
Munro Ter, SW10 31 E7
Munslow Gdns, Sutt. SM1 199 G4
Munster Av, Houns. TW4 143 F4
Munster Ct, Tedd. TW11 163 F6
Munster Gdns, N13 59 H4
Munster Ms, SW6 *off Lillie Rd* 128 B7
Munster Rd, SW6 148 C1
Teddington TW11 163 E6
Munster Sq, NW1 9 E4
Munton Rd, SE17 36 A1
Murchison Av, Bex. DA5 176 D1
Murchison Rd, E10 96 C2
Murdock Cl, E16 *off Rogers Rd* 115 F6
Murdock St, SE15 132 E6
Murfett Cl, SW19 166 B2
Muriel St, N1 10 D1
Murillo Rd, SE13 154 D4
Murphy St, SE1 27 E4
Murray Av, Brom. BR1 191 H2
Hounslow TW3 143 H5
Murray Cres, Pnr. HA5 66 D1
Murray Gro, N1 12 A2
Murray Ms, NW1 92 D7
Murray Rd, SW19 166 A6
W5 125 F4
Richmond TW10 163 E2
Murray Sq, E16 115 G6
Murray St, NW1 92 D7
Murrays Yd, SE18 136 E4
Murray Ter, NW3 *off Flask Wk* 91 G4
W5 *off Murray Rd* 125 G4
Mursell Est, SW8 151 F1
Murtwell Dr, Chig. IG7 65 F6
Musard Rd, W6 128 B6
W14 128 B6
Musbury St, E1 113 F6
Muscal, W6 128 B6
Muscatel Pl, SE5 *off Dalwood St* 152 B1
Muschamp Rd, SE15 152 C3
Carshalton SM5 199 H2
Muscovy Ho, Erith DA18 *off Kale Rd* 138/139 E2
Muscovy St, EC3 21 E6
★**Museum in Docklands**, E14 *off Hertsmere Rd* 114 A7
★**Museum Interpretative Cen**, E6 *off Norman Rd* 116 C4
Museum La, SW7 23 E6
★**Museum of Artillery, The Rotunda**, SE18 136 C5
★**Museum of Gdn History**, SE1 26 C6
★**Museum of Instruments, Royal Coll of Music**, SW7 22 E5
★**Museum of London**, EC2 19 J2
★**Museum of Richmond**, Rich. TW9 145 G5
Museum Pas, E2 *off Victoria Pk Sq* 112/113 E3
Museum St, WC1 18 A2
Musgrave Cl, Barn. EN4 41 F1
Musgrave Cres, SW6 148 D1
Musgrave Rd, Islw. TW7 144 C1
Musgrove Rd, SE14 153 G1
Musjid Rd, SW11 *off Kambala Rd* 149 G2
Musket Cl, Barn. EN4 *off East Barnet Rd* 41 G5
Musquash Way, Houns. TW4 142 C2
Muston Rd, E5 94 E2
Mustow Pl, SW6 *off Munster Rd* 148 C2
Muswell Av, N10 74 B2
MUSWELL HILL, N10 74 B3
Muswell Hill, N10 74 B3
Muswell Hill Bdy, N10 74 B3
Muswell Hill Pl, N10 74 B4
Muswell Hill Rd, N6 74 A6
N10 74 A4
Muswell Ms, N10 *off Muswell Rd* 74 B3
Muswell Rd, N10 74 B3
Mutrix Rd, NW6 108 D1
Mutton Pl, NW1 *off Harmood St* 92 B6
Muybridge Rd, N.Mal. KT3 182 C2
Myatt Rd, SW9 151 H1
Myatt's Flds N, SW9 *off Eythorne Rd* 151 G1
Mycenae Rd, SE3 135 G7
Myddelton Cl, Enf. EN1 44 C1
Myddelton Gdns, N21 43 H7
Myddelton Pk, N20 57 G3
Myddelton Pas, EC1 11 F3
Myddelton Rd, N8 75 E4
Myddelton Sq, EC1 11 F3
Myddelton St, EC1 11 F4
Myddleton Av, N4 93 J2
Myddleton Ms, N22 59 E7
Myddleton Rd, N22 59 E7
Myers La, SE14 133 G6
Mylis Cl, SE26 171 E4
Mylius Cl, SE14 *off Kender St* 153 F1
Mylne St, EC1 11 E2
Mynterne Ct, SW19 *off Swanton Gdns* 166 A1
Myra St, SE2 138 A5
Myrdle St, E1 21 J2
Myrna Cl, SW19 167 H7
Myron Pl, SE13 154 C3
Myrtle Av, Felt. TW14 141 H4
Ruislip HA4 66 A7
Myrtleberry Cl, E8 *off Beechwood Rd* 94 C6
Myrtle Cl, Barn. EN4 57 J1
West Drayton UB7 120 C3
Myrtledene Rd, SE2 138 A5
Myrtle Gdns, W7 124 B1
Myrtle Gro, N.Mal. KT3 182 C2
Myrtle Rd, E6 116 B1
E17 77 H6
N13 59 J3
W3 126 C1
Croydon CR0 204 A3
Hampton (Hmptn H.) TW12 161 J6
Hounslow TW3 143 J2
Ilford IG1 99 E2
Sutton SM1 199 F5

Myrtle Wk, N1 . . . . **12** D2
Mysore Rd, SW11. . . . . . . **149** J3
Myton Rd, SE21 . . . . **170** A3

N

N1 Shop Cen, N1 . . . . **11** F1
Nadine St, SE7. . . . . **135** J5
Nafferton Ri, Loug. IG10 . . **48** A5
Nagle Cl, E17 . . . . **78** D2
Nag's Head Ct, EC1 . . . . . . **11** J6
Nags Head La, Well.
DA16 . . . . **158** B3
Nags Head Rd, Enf. EN3 . . **45** F4
Nags Head Shop Cen, N7 . **93** F4
Nairne Gro, SE24 . . . . **152** A5
Nairn Grn, Wat. WD19 . . . . **50** A3
Nairn Rd, Ruis. HA4 . . . . . . **84** C6
Nairn St, E14 . . . . **114** C5
Nallhead Rd, Felt. TW13 . . **160** C5
Namba Roy Cl, SW16. . . . **169** F4
Namton Dr, Th.Hth. CR7 . . **187** F4
Nan Clark's La, NW7 . . . . . **55** F2
Nankin St, E14 . . . . **114** A6
Nansen Rd, SW11 . . . . . . **150** A4
Nansen Village, N12. . . . . . **57** E4
Nantes Cl, SW18 . . . . **149** F4
Nantes Pas, E1. . . . . **21** F1
Nant Rd, NW2 . . . . **90** C2
Nant St, E2
off Cambridge
Heath Rd. **112/113** E3
Naoroji St, WC1 . . . . **11** E4
Napier Av, E14 . . . . **134** A5
SW6. . . . . **148** C3
Napier Cl, SE8
off Amersham Vale . . . **133** J7
W14 *off Napier Rd* **128** C3
West Drayton UB7 . . . . **120** C3
Napier Ct, SW6
off Ranelagh Gdns . . . **148** C3
Napier Gro, N1. . . . . **12** A2
Napier Pl, W14 . . . . **128** C3
Napier Rd, E6 . . . . **116** D1
E11. . . . . **96** E4
E15. . . . . **115** E2
N17 . . . . **76** B3
NW10. . . . . **107** H3
SE25 . . . . **188** E4
W14. . . . . **128** C3
Belvedere DA17 . . . . . . **139** F4
Bromley BR2. . . . . **191** H4
Enfield EN3. . . . . **45** G5
Hounslow (Hthrw Air.)
TW6 . . . . **140** A1
Isleworth TW7 . . . . **144** D4
South Croydon CR2 . . . **202** A7
Wembley HA0. . . . . **87** G5
Napier Ter, N1 . . . . **93** H7
Napoleon Rd, E5 . . . . **94** E3
Twickenham TW1 . . . . . **145** E7
Napton Cl, Hayes UB4 . . . **102** E4
Narbonne Av, SW4. . . . . . **150** C5
Narborough St, SW6 . . . . **148** E2
Narcissus Rd, NW6 . . . . . . **90** D5
Naresby Fold, Stan. HA7 . . **53** F6
Narford Rd, E5 . . . . **94** D3
Narrow Boat Cl, SE28
off Ridge Cl **137** G2
Narrow St, E14. . . . . **113** H7
Narrow Way, Brom. BR2 . **192** B6
Nascot St, W12. . . . . **107** J6
Naseberry Ct, E4
off Merriam Cl. **62** C5
Naseby Cl, NW6. . . . . **91** F7
Isleworth TW7 . . . . **144** B1
Naseby Rd, SE19 . . . . **170** A6
Dagenham RM10. . . . . . **101** G3
Ilford IG5. . . . . **80** C1
Nash Cl, Sutt. SM1. . . . . . **199** G3
Nash Ct, E14
off South Colonnade. . **134** B1
Nash Grn, Brom. BR1. . . . **173** G6
Nash La, Kes. BR2 . . . . . . **205** G5
Nash Rd, N9. . . . . **61** F2
SE4 . . . . **153** G4
Romford RM6 . . . . **82** D4
Nash St, NW1 . . . . **8** E4
Nash Way, Har. HA3. . . . . . **69** E6
Nasmyth St, W6. . . . . **127** H3
Nassau Path, SE28
off Disraeli Cl **138** C1
Nassau Rd, SW13 . . . . . . **147** F1
Nassau St, W1 . . . . **17** F2
Nassington Rd, NW3. . . . . **91** H4
Natalie Cl, Felt. TW14. . . . **141** G7
Natalie Ms, Twick. TW2
off Sixth Cross Rd. . . . **162** A3
Natal Rd, N11 . . . . **58** E6
SW16. . . . . **168** D6
Ilford IG1 . . . . **98** E4
Thornton Heath CR7 . . . **188** A3
Nathaniel Cl, E1 . . . . **21** G2
Nathans Rd, Wem. HA0 . . . **87** F1
Nathan Way, SE28 . . . . . . **137** H4
★**National Army Mus**,
SW3 . . . . **32** A5
★**National Gall**, WC2 . . . . . **17** J6
★**National Maritime Mus**,
SE10 . . . . **134** D6
★**National Portrait Gall**,
WC2 . . . . **17** J6
National Ter, SE16
off Bermondsey
Wall E. **132/133** E2
Nation Way, E4. . . . . **62** C1
★**Natural History Mus**,
SW7 . . . . **23** E6
Naval Row, E14 . . . . **114** C7
Naval Wk, Brom. BR1
off High St. **191** G3
Navarino Gro, E8 . . . . **94** D6
Navarino Rd, E8 . . . . **94** D6
Navarre Rd, E6 . . . . **116** B2
Navarre St, E2 . . . . **13** F5
Navenby Wk, E3
off Rounton Rd **114** A4
Navestock Cl, E4
off Mapleton Rd **62** C3
Navestock Cres, Wdf.Grn.
IG8 . . . . **79** J1
Navestock Ho, Bark. IG11 . **118** B2
Navigator Dr, Sthl. UB2 . . **123** J2
Navigator Pk, Sthl. UB2
off Southall La. **122** C4
Navy St, SW4. . . . . **150** D3
Naxos Bldg, E14
off Hutchings St **134** A2
Nayim Pl, E8
off Amhurst Rd **94/95** E5
Naylor Gro, Enf. EN3
off South St. **45** G5
Naylor Rd, N20. . . . . **57** F2
SE15 . . . . **132** E7
Nazareth Gdns, SE15. . . . **152** E2
Nazrul St, E2 . . . . **13** F3
Neagle Cl, Borwd. WD6
off Balcon Way **38** C1
Neal Av, Sthl. UB1 . . . . . . **103** F4
Neal Cl, Nthwd. HA6 . . . . . **66** A1
Nealden St, SW9 . . . . **151** F3
Neale Cl, N2. . . . . **73** F3
Neal St, WC2 . . . . **18** A4
Neal's Yd, WC2. . . . . **18** A4
Near Acre, NW9 . . . . **71** F1
NEASDEN, NW2. . . . . **89** E3
Neasden Cl, NW10. . . . . . . **89** E5
Neasden La, NW10 . . . . . . **89** E4
Neasden La N, NW10. . . . . **88** D3
Neasham Rd, Dag. RM8. . **100** B5
Neate St, SE5. . . . . **37** E5
Neath Gdns, Mord. SM4 . **185** F6
Neathouse Pl, SW1 . . . . . . **33** F1
Neatscourt Rd, E6 . . . . . . **116** A5
Nebraska St, SE1. . . . . **28** B4
Neckinger, SE16. . . . . **29** G5
Neckinger Est, SE16. . . . . . **29** G5
Neckinger St, SE1 . . . . **29** G4
Nectarine Way, SE13 . . . . **154** B2
Needham Rd, W11
off Westbourne Gro. . . **108** D6
Needham Ter, NW2
off Kara Way **90** A3
Needleman St, SE16 . . . . **133** G2
Neeld Cres, NW4 . . . . **71** H5
Wembley HA9. . . . . **88** A5
Neeld Par, Wem. HA9
off Harrow Rd **88** A5
Neil Wates Cres, SW2 . . . **169** G1
Nelgarde Rd, SE6. . . . . . . **154** A7
Nella Rd, W6. . . . . **128** A6
Nelldale Rd, SE16 . . . . . . **133** F4
Nello James Gdns, SE27 . **170** A4
Nelson Cl, NW6 . . . . **108** D2
Croydon CR0. . . . . **201** H1
Romford RM7 . . . . **83** H1
Nelson Ct, SE16
off Brunel Rd. **133** F1
Nelson Gdns, E2 . . . . **13** J3
Hounslow TW3 . . . . **143** G6
Nelson Gro Rd, SW19 . . . **185** E1
Nelson Mandela Cl, N10 . . **74** A2
Nelson Mandela Rd, SE3. **155** J3
Nelson Pas, EC1. . . . . **12** A4
Nelson Pl, N1 . . . . **11** H2
Sidcup DA14
off Sidcup High St. . . . **176** A4
Nelson Rd, E4 . . . . **62** B6
E11. . . . . **79** G4
N8 . . . . **75** F5
N9 . . . . **61** E2
N15 . . . . **76** B4
SE10 . . . . **134** C6
SW19. . . . . **167** E7
Belvedere DA17 . . . . . . **139** F5
Bromley BR2. . . . . **191** J4
Enfield EN3. . . . . **45** G6
Harrow HA1 . . . . **86** A1
Hounslow TW3, TW4 . . . **143** G6
Hounslow (Hthrw Air.)
TW6 . . . . **140** C1
New Malden KT3 . . . . . **182** D5
Sidcup DA14
off Sidcup High St. . . . **176** A4
Stanmore HA7 . . . . **53** F6
Twickenham TW2 . . . . . **143** J6
★**Nelson's Column**, WC2 . . **26** A1
Nelson Sq, SE1 . . . . **27** G3
Nelson's Row, SW4 . . . . . **150** D4
Nelson St, E1 . . . . **112** E6
E6. . . . . **116** C2
E16
off Huntingdon St **115** F7
Nelsons Yd, NW1 . . . . **9** F1
Nelson Ter, N1 . . . . **11** H2
Nelson Trd Est, SW19. . . . **184** E1
Nelson Wk, SE16
off Rotherhithe St **133** H1
Nemoure Rd, W3 . . . . **106** C7
Nene Gdns, Felt. TW13. . . **161** F2
Nene Rd, Houns.
(Hthrw Air.) TW6 . . . . . **141** E1
Nepaul Rd, SW11 . . . . **149** H2
Nepean St, SW15. . . . . . . **147** G6
Neptune Ct, Borwd. WD6
off Clarendon Rd. **38** A3
Neptune Rd, Har. HA1 . . . . **68** A6
Hounslow (Hthrw Air.)
TW6 . . . . **141** G1
Neptune St, SE16. . . . . . . **133** F3
Nero Ct, Brent. TW8
off Justin Cl. **125** G7
Nesbit Rd, SE9. . . . . **156** A4
Nesbitt Cl, SE3
off Hurren Cl **154/155** E3
Nesbitts All, Barn. EN5
off Bath Pl. **40** C3
Nesbitt Sq, SE19
off Coxwell Rd. **170** B7
Nesham St, E1. . . . . **29** H1
Ness St, SE16 . . . . **29** H5
Nesta Rd, Wdf.Grn. IG8 . . . **63** E6
Nestles Av, Hayes UB3 . . **121** J3
Nestor Av, N21. . . . . **43** H6
Netheravon Rd, W4 . . . . . **127** F4
W7. . . . . **124** C1
Netheravon Rd S, W4. . . . **127** F5
Netherbury Rd, W5 . . . . . **125** G3
Netherby Gdns, Enf. EN2. . **42** E4
Netherby Rd, SE23. . . . . . **153** F7
Nether Cl, N3. . . . . **56** D7
Nethercourt Av, N3 . . . . . . **56** D6
Netherfield Gdns, Bark.
IG11 . . . . **99** G6
Netherfield Rd, N12. . . . . . **57** E5
SW17. . . . . **168** A3
Netherford Rd, SW4. . . . . **150** C2
Netherhall Gdns, NW3. . . . **91** F6
Netherhall Way, NW3
off Netherhall Gdns . . . **91** F5
Netherlands Rd, Barn.
EN5 . . . . **41** G6
Netherleigh Cl, N6 . . . . **92** B1
Nether St, N3. . . . . **72** D1
N12 . . . . **56** D7
Netherton Gro, SW10 . . . . **30** D6
Netherton Rd, N15. . . . . . . **76** A6
Twickenham TW1 . . . . . **144** E5
Netherwood, N2 . . . . **73** G2
Netherwood Pl, W14
off Netherwood Rd. . . **128** A3
Netherwood Rd, W14. . . . **128** A3
Netherwood St, NW6 . . . . **90** C7
Netley Cl, Croy.
(New Adgtn) CR0 . . . . **204** C7
Sutton SM3. . . . . **198** A5
Netley Dr, Walt. KT12. . . . **179** F7
Netley Gdns, Mord. SM4. **185** F7
Netley Rd, E17 . . . . **77** J5
Brentford TW8. . . . . **125** H6
Hounslow (Hthrw Air.)
TW6 . . . . **141** G1
Ilford IG2. . . . . **81** G5
Morden SM4. . . . . **185** F7
Netley St, NW1 . . . . **9** F4
Nettleden Av, Wem. HA9 . . **88** A6
Nettlefold Pl, SE27. . . . . . **169** H3
Nettlestead Cl, Beck. BR3
off Copers Cope Rd. . . **171** J7
Nettleton Rd, SE14 . . . . . **153** G1
Hounslow (Hthrw Air.)
TW6 . . . . **141** E1
Nettlewood Rd, SW16 . . . **168** D7
Neuchatel Rd, SE6 . . . . . . **171** J2
Nevada Cl, N.Mal. KT3
off Georgia Rd. **182** C4
Nevada St, SE10 . . . . **134** C6
Nevern Pl, SW5 . . . . **128** D4
Nevern Rd, SW5. . . . . **128** D4
Nevern Sq, SW5. . . . . **128** D4
Neville Av, N.Mal. KT3 . . . **182** D1
Neville Cl, E11 . . . . **97** F3
NW1 . . . . **9** J2
NW6 . . . . **108** C2
SE15 . . . . **132** D7
W3 *off Acton La* **126** C2
Hounslow TW3 . . . . **143** H2
Sidcup DA15 . . . . **175** J4
Neville Dr, N2. . . . . **73** F6
Neville Gdns, Dag. RM8. . **100** D3
Neville Gill Cl, SW18 . . . . **148** D6
Neville Pl, N22 . . . . **75** F1
Neville Rd, E7. . . . . **97** G7
NW6 . . . . **108** C2
W5. . . . . **105** G4
Croydon CR0. . . . . **188** A7
Dagenham RM8 . . . . . . **100** D2
Ilford IG6. . . . . **81** F1
Kingston upon Thames
KT1 . . . . **182** A2
Richmond TW10 . . . . . . **163** F3
Nevilles Ct, NW2 . . . . **89** G3
Neville St, SW7 . . . . **31** E3
Neville Ter, SW7. . . . . **31** E3
Neville Wk, Cars. SM5
off Green Wrythe La . . **185** H7
Nevill Rd, N16 . . . . **94** B4
Nevill Way, Loug. IG10
off Valley Hill. **48** B7
Nevin Dr, E4. . . . . **62** B1
Nevinson Cl, SW18 . . . . . **149** G6
Nevis Rd, SW17 . . . . **168** A2
New Acres Rd, SE28 . . . . **137** H2
Newall Rd, Houns.
(Hthrw Air.) TW6 . . . . . **141** F1
Newark Cres, NW10. . . . . **106** D3
Newark Grn, Borwd. WD6 . **38** D3
Newark Knok, E6 . . . . **116** D6
Newark Par, NW4
off Greyhound Hill **71** G3
Newark Rd, S.Croy. CR2 . **202** A6
Newark St, E1 . . . . **112** E5
Newark Way, NW4. . . . . **71** G4
New Ash Cl, N2
off Oakridge Dr. **73** G3
New Atlas Wf, E14
off Arnhem Pl **133** J3
New Barn Cl, Wall. SM6. . **201** F6
NEW BARNET, Barn. EN5 . **41** E4
New Barns Av, Mitch.
CR4. . . . . **186** D4
New Barn St, E13. . . . . . . **115** G4
New Barns Way, Chig. IG7. **64** E3
NEW BECKENHAM, Beck.
BR3 . . . . **171** J6
Newbiggin Path, Wat.
WD19 . . . . **50** C4
Newbolt Av, Sutt. SM3 . . **197** J5
Newbolt Rd, Stan. HA7 . . . **52** C6
New Bond St, W1 . . . . **16** D4
Newborough Grn, N.Mal.
KT3 . . . . **182** D4
New Brent St, NW4. . . . . . . **71** J5
Newbridge Pt, SE23
off Windrush La. **171** G3
New Br St, EC4 . . . . **19** G4
New Broad St, EC2 . . . . . . **20** D2
New Bdy, W5 . . . . **105** F7
Hampton (Hmptn H.) TW12
off Hampton Rd **162** A5
New Bdy Bldgs, W5
off New Bdy **105** G7
Newburgh Rd, W3 . . . . . . **126** C1
Newburgh St, W1 . . . . **17** F4
New Burlington Ms, W1. . . **17** F5
New Burlington Pl, W1 . . . **17** F5
New Burlington St, W1 . . . **17** F5
Newburn St, SE11 . . . . **34** D4
Newbury Cl, Nthlt. UB5. . . **85** F6
Newbury Gdns, Epsom
KT19 . . . .
Newbury Ho, N22 . . . . . .
Newbury Ms, NW5
off Malden Rd. . . . .
NEWBURY PARK, Ilf. IG

Newbury Rd, E4 **62** C6
Bromley BR2 **191** G3
Hounslow (Hthrw Air.) TW6 **140** C1
Ilford IG2 **81** G6
Newbury St, EC1 **19** J2
Newbury Way, Nthlt. UB5 **85** E6
New Butt La, SE8 **134** A7
New Butt La N, SE8
off Reginald Rd **134** A7
Newby Cl, Enf. EN1 **44** B2
Newby Pl, E14 **114** C7
Newby St, SW8 **150** B3
New Caledonian Wf, SE16 **133** J3
Newcastle Cl, EC4 **19** G3
Newcastle Pl, W2 **15** F2
Newcastle Row, EC1 **11** F5
New Cavendish St, W1 **17** E1
New Change, EC4 **19** J4
New Chapel Sq, Felt. TW13 **160** B1
New Charles St, EC1 **11** H3
NEW CHARLTON, SE7 **135** J4
New Ch Ct, SE19
off Waldegrave Rd **170** D7
New Ch Rd, SE5 **36** A7
New City Rd, E13 **115** J3
New Cl, SW19 **185** F3
Feltham TW13 **160** E5
New Coll Ct, NW3
off Finchley Rd **91** F6
New Coll Ms, N1
off Islington Pk St **93** G7
New Coll Par, NW3
off Finchley Rd **91** G6
Newcombe Gdns, SW16 **169** E4
Hounslow TW4 **143** F4
Newcombe Pk, NW7 **55** E5
Wembley HA0 **105** J1
Newcombe St, W8
off Kensington Pl **128** D1
Newcomen Rd, E11 **97** F3
SW11 **149** G3
Newcomen St, SE1 **28** B3
New Compton St, WC2 **17** J4
New Concordia Wf, SE1 **29** H3
New Ct, EC4 **18** E5
Newcourt St, NW8 **7** G2
★**New Covent Garden Flower Mkt**, SW8 **34** A6
★**New Covent Garden Mkt**, SW8 **130** D7
New Crane Pl, E1
off Garnet St **133** F1
NEW CROSS, SE14 **153** H1
NEW CROSS GATE, SE14 **153** G1
New Cross Rd, SE14 **133** F7
Newdales Cl, N9
off Balham Rd **60** D2
Newdene Av, Nthlt. UB5 **102** D2
Newell St, E14 **113** J6
NEW ELTHAM, SE9 **174** D2
New End, NW3 **91** F4
New End Sq, NW3 **91** G4
Newent Cl, SE15 **36** D7
Carshalton SM5 **199** J1
New Fm Av, Brom. BR2 **191** G4
New Ferry App, SE18 **136** D3
New Fetter La, EC4 **19** F3
Newfield Cl, Hmptn. TW12
off Percy Rd **179** G1
Newfield Ri, NW2 **89** H3
New Forest La, Chig. IG7 **64** D6
Newgale Gdns, Edg. HA8 **69** J1
New Gdn Dr, West Dr. UB7
off Drayton Gdns **120** B2
Newgate, Croy. CR0 **201** J1
Newgate Cl, Felt. TW13 **161** E2
Newgate St, E4 **63** F3
EC1 **19** H3
New Globe Wk, SE1 **27** J1
New Goulston St, E1 **21** F3
New Grn Pl, SE19
off Hawke Rd **170** B6
Newhams Row, SE1 **28** E4
Newham Way, E6 **115** J5
E16 **115** F5
Newhaven Cl, Hayes UB3 **121** J4
Newhaven Gdns, SE9 **156** A4
Newhaven La, E16 **115** F4
Newhaven Rd, SE25 **188** A5
New Heston Rd, Houns. TW5 **123** F7
New Horizons Ct, Brent. TW8 *off Shield Dr* **124** D6
Newhouse Av, Rom. RM6 **82** D3
Newhouse Cl, N.Mal. KT3 **183** E7
Newhouse Wk, Mord. SM4 **185** F7
Newick Cl, Bex. DA5 **159** H6
Newick Rd, E5 **95** E3
Newing Grn, Brom. BR1 **174** A7
NEWINGTON, SE1 **35** J1
Newington Barrow Way, N7 **93** F3
Newington Butts, SE1 **35** H2
SE11 **35** H2
Newington Causeway, SE1 **27** H3
Newington Grn, N1 **94** A5
N16 **94** A5
Newington Grn Rd, N1 **94** A6
New Inn Bdy, EC2 **12** E5
New Inn Pas, WC2 **18** D4
New Inn Sq, EC2 **12** E5
New Inn St, EC2 **12** E5
New Inn Yd, EC2 **12** E5
New James Ct, SE15
off Nunhead La **152/153** E3
New Jersey Ter, SE15
off Nunhead La **152/153** E3
New Jubilee Ct, Wdf.Grn. IG8 *off Grange Av* **63** G7
New Kent Rd, SE1 **27** J6
New Kings Rd, SW6 **148** C2
New King St, SE8 **134** A6
Newland Cl, Pnr. HA5 **51** E6
Newland Ct, Wem. HA9
off Forty Av **88** A2
Newland Dr, Enf. EN1 **44** E1
Newland Gdns, W13 **124** D2
Newland Rd, N8 **74** E3
Newlands, The, Wall. SM6 **200** C7
Newlands Av, T.Ditt. KT7 **194** B1
Newlands Cl, Edg. HA8 **53** H3
Southall UB2 **122** E5
Wembley HA0 **87** F6
Newlands Ct, SE9 **156** D6
Newlands Pk, SE26 **171** G5
Newlands Pl, Barn. EN5 **40** A5
Newlands Quay, E1 **113** F7
Newlands Rd, SW16 **187** E2
Woodford Green IG8 **63** F2
Newland St, E16 **136** B1
Newlands Way, Chess. KT9 **195** F5
Newling Cl, E6
off Porter Rd **116** C6
New London St, EC3 **21** E5
New Lydenburg St, SE7 **135** J3
Newlyn Cl, Orp. BR6 **207** J4
Newlyn Gdns, Har. HA2 **67** F7
Newlyn Rd, N17 **76** C1
NW2 *off Tilling Rd* **89** J1
Barnet EN5 **40** C4
Welling DA16 **157** J2
NEW MALDEN, KT3 **182** D3
Newman Pas, W1 **17** G2
Newman Rd, E13 **115** H3
E17 *off Southcote Rd* **77** G5
Bromley BR1 **191** G1
Croydon CR0 **201** F1
Hayes UB3 **102** B7
Newmans Cl, Loug. IG10 **48** E3
Newman's Ct, EC3 **20** C4
Newmans La, Loug. IG10 **48** D3
Surbiton KT6 **181** G6
Newman's Row, WC2 **18** D2
Newman St, W1 **17** G2
Newmans Way, Barn. EN4 **41** F1
Newman Yd, W1 **17** H3
Newmarket Av, Nthlt. UB5 **85** G5
Newmarket Grn, SE9
off Middle Pk Av **156** A7
Newmarsh Rd, SE28 **137** J1
Newminster Rd, Mord. SM4 **185** F6
New Mt St, E15 **96** D7
Newnes Path, SW15
off Putney Pk La **147** H4
Newnham Av, Ruis. HA4 **84** C1
Newnham Cl, Loug. IG10 **48** A6
Northolt UB5 **85** J5
Thornton Heath CR7 **187** J2
Newnham Gdns, Nthlt. UB5 **85** J5
Newnham Ms, N22
off Newnham Rd **75** F1
Newnham Rd, N22 **75** F1
Newnhams Cl, Brom. BR1 **192** C3
Newnham Ter, SE1 **26** E5
Newnham Way, Har. HA3 **69** H5
New N Pl, EC2 **12** D6
New N Rd, N1 **12** C2
Ilford IG6 **65** G7
New N St, WC1 **18** C1
Newnton Cl, N4 **76** A7
New Oak Rd, N2 **73** F2
New Orleans Wk, N19 **74** D7
New Oxford St, WC1 **17** J3
New Pk Av, N13 **59** J3
New Pk Cl, Nthlt. UB5 **84** E6
New Pk Ct, SW2 **151** E7
New Pk Par, SW2
off Doverfield Rd **150/151** E6
New Pk Rd, SW2 **168** D1
Newpiece, Loug. IG10 **48** F3
New Pl Sq, SE16 **132** E3
New Plaistow Rd, E15 **115** E1
Newport Av, E13 **115** H4
E14 **114** D7
Newport Ct, WC2 **17** J5
Newport Mead, Wat. WD19
off Kilmarnock Rd **50** D4
Newport Pl, WC2 **17** J5
Newport Rd, E10 **96** C2
E17 **77** H4
SW13 **147** G1
Hounslow (Hthrw Air.) TW6 **140** D1
Newport St, SE11 **34** C2
New Printing Ho Sq, WC1
off Gray's Inn Rd **111** F4
New Priory Ct, NW6
off Mazenod Av **90** D7
New Providence Wf, E14
off Blackwall Way **134** D1
Newquay Cres, Har. HA2 **85** E2
Newquay Gdns, Wat. WD19
off Fulford Gro **50** B2
Newquay Rd, SE6 **172** B2
New Quebec St, W1 **16** A4
New Ride, SW7 **23** J3
New River Av, N8
off High St **75** F4
New River Ct, N5 **94** A4
New River Cres, N13 **59** H4
New River Head, EC1 **11** F3
New River Wk, N1 **93** J6
New River Way, N4 **76** A7
New Rd, E1 **112** E5
E4 **62** B4
N8 **74** E5
N9 **60** D3
N17 **76** C1
N22 **75** J1
NW7 **56** B7
NW7 (Barnet Gate) **39** F7
SE2 **138** D4
Brentford TW8 **125** G6
Dagenham RM9, RM10 **119** G1
Feltham TW14 **160** B1
Feltham (E.Bed.) TW14 **141** G6
Feltham (Han.) TW13 **160** E5
Harrow HA1 **86** C4
Hayes UB3 **121** F7
Hounslow TW3
off Station Rd **143** H4
Ilford IG3 **99** H2
Kingston upon Thames KT2 **104** A7
Mitcham CR4 **199** J1
Richmond TW10 **163** F4
Welling DA16 **158** B2
West Molesey KT8 **179** G3
New Row, WC2 **18** A5
Newry Rd, Twick. TW1 **144** D4
Newsam Av, N15 **76** A5
★**New Scotland Yd**, SW1 **25** H5
Newsholme Dr, N21 **43** F5
NEW SOUTHGATE, N11 **58** D4
New Spring Gdns Wk, SE11 **34** B4
New Sq, WC2 **18** D3
New Sq Pas, WC2
off New Sq **111** F6
Newstead Av, Orp. BR6 **207** G3
Newstead Rd, SE12 **155** E7
Newstead Wk, Cars. SM5 **185** F7
Newstead Way, SW19 **166** A4
New St, EC2 **20** E2
New St Hill, Brom. BR1 **173** H5
New St Sq, EC4 **19** F3
Newton Av, N10 **74** A1
W3 **126** C2
Newton Cl, E17 **77** H6
Harrow HA2 **85** G2
Newton Cres, Borwd. WD6 **38** C4
Newton Gro, W4 **126** E4
Newton Ho, Enf. EN3
off Exeter Rd **45** G3
Newton Pl, E14 **134** A4
Newton Rd, E15 **96** D5
N15 **76** C5
NW2 **89** J3
SW19 **166** B7
Newton Rd, W2 **108** D6
Harrow HA3 **68** B2
Isleworth TW7 **144** C2
Welling DA16 **158** A3
Wembley HA0 **87** J7
Newton St, WC2 **18** B3
Newtons Yd, SW18
off Wandsworth High St **148/149** E5
Newton Wk, Edg. HA8
off North Rd **70** B1
Newton Way, N18 **59** J5
Newtown St, SW11
off Strasburg Rd **150** B1
New Trinity Rd, N2 **73** G3
New Turnstile, WC1 **18** C2
New Union Cl, E14 **134** C3
New Union St, EC2 **20** B2
New Wanstead, E11 **79** F6
New Way Rd, NW9 **71** E4
New Wf Rd, N1 **10** B1
New Zealand Way, W12 **107** H7
Niagara Av, W5 **125** F4
Niagara Cl, N1
off Cropley St **112** A2
Nibthwaite Rd, Har. HA1 **68** B5
Nicholas Cl, Grnf. UB6 **103** H2
Nicholas Ct, E13
off Tunmarsh La **115** H3
Nicholas Gdns, W5 **125** G2
Nicholas La, EC4 **20** C5
Nicholas Ms, W4
off Short Rd **126/127** E6
Nicholas Pas, EC4 **20** C5
Nicholas Rd, E1 **113** F4
Croydon CR0 **201** E4
Dagenham RM8 **101** F2
Nicholay Rd, N19 **92** D1
Nichol Cl, N14 **58** D1
Nicholes Rd, Houns. TW3 **143** G4
Nichol La, Brom. BR1 **173** G7
Nichollsfield Wk, N7
off Hillmarton Rd **93** F5
Nicholls Pt, E15
off Park Gro **115** G1
Nicholl St, E2 **112** D1
Nichols Cl, N4
off Osborne Rd **93** G1
Chessington KT9
off Merritt Gdns **195** F6
Nichols Ct, E2 **13** F2
Nichols Grn, W5
off Montpelier Rd **105** H5
Nicholson Rd, Croy. CR0 **202** C1
Nicholson St, SE1 **27** G2
Nickelby Cl, SE28 **118** C6
Nickols Wk, SW18
off Jew's Row **148/149** E4
Nicola Cl, Har. HA3 **68** A2
South Croydon CR2 **201** J6
Nicola Ms, Ilf. IG6 **65** E7
Nicol Cl, Twick. TW1
off Cassilis Rd **144/145** E6
Nicoll Pl, NW4 **71** H6
Nicoll Rd, NW10 **107** E1
Nicoll Way, Borwd. WD6 **38** D5
Nicolson Dr, Bushey (Bushey Hth) WD23 **51** J1
Nicosia Rd, SW18 **149** H7
Niederwald Rd, SE26 **171** H4
Nield Rd, Hayes UB3 **121** J2
Nigel Cl, Nthlt. UB5
off Church Rd **102/103** E1
Nigel Fisher Way, Chess. KT9 **195** F7
Nigel Ms, Ilf. IG1 **98** E4
Nigel Playfair Av, W6
off King St **127** H4
Nigel Rd, E7 **97** J5
SE15 **152** D3
Nigeria Rd, SE7 **135** J7
Nightingale Av, E4 **62** E5
Harrow HA1 **68** E7
Nightingale Cl, E4 **62** E4
W4 *off Grove Pk Ter* **126** C6
Carshalton SM5 **200** A2
Pinner HA5 **66** C5
Nightingale Ct, E11
off Nightingale La **79** H5
Nightingale Dr, Epsom KT19 **196** B6
Nightingale Est, E5 **94** D3
Nightingale Gro, SE13 **154** D5
Nightingale Hts, SE18
off Nightingale Vale **136** E6
Nightingale La, E11 **79** G5
N6 **91** H1
N8 **74** E4
SW4 **149** J7

Nightingale La, SW12 . . . **149** J7
Bromley BR1 . . . . **191** J2
Richmond TW10 . . . . . . **145** H7
Nightingale Ms, E3
off Chisenhale Rd **113** H2
E11 . . . . **79** G5
SE11 . . . . **35** F1
Kingston upon Thames
KT1 *off South La* **181** G3
Nightingale Pl, SE18 . . . . **136** D6
SW10 . . . . **30** D5
Nightingale Rd, E5 . . . . **94** E3
N1 . . . . **93** J6
N9 . . . . **45** F6
N22 . . . . **75** E1
NW10 . . . . **107** F2
W7 . . . . **124** C1
Carshalton SM5 . . . . . . **199** J3
Hampton TW12 . . . . **161** G5
Orpington BR5 . . . . **193** F6
Walton-on-Thames
KT12 . . . . **178** B7
West Molesey KT8 . . . . **179** H5
Nightingales, The, Stai.
TW19 . . . . **140** C7
Nightingale Sq, SW12 . . . **150** A7
Nightingale Vale, SE18 . . . **136** D6
Nightingale Wk, SW4 . . . . **150** B6
Nightingale Way, E6 . . . . . **116** B5
Nile Cl, N16
off Evering Rd **94** C3
Nile Dr, N9 . . . . **61** F2
Nile Path, SE18
off Jackson St **136** D6
Nile Rd, E13 . . . . **115** J2
Nile St, N1 . . . . **12** A3
Nile Ter, SE15 . . . . **37** F4
Nimegen Way, SE22 . . . . . **152** B5
Nimrod Cl, Nthlt. UB5 . . . **102** D3
Nimrod Pas, N1
off Tottenham Rd **94** B6
Nimrod Rd, SW16 . . . . . . **168** B6
Nina Mackay Cl, E15
off Arthingworth St . **114/115** E1
Nine Acres Cl, E12 . . . . **98** B5
NINE ELMS, SW8 . . . . **33** G7
Nine Elms La, SW8 . . . . . . **33** G6
Nineteenth Rd, Mitch.
CR4 . . . . **186** E4
Ninhams Wd, Orp. BR6 . . **206** D4
Ninth Av, Hayes UB3 . . . . **102** A7
Nisbet Ho, E9
off Homerton High St . . **95** G5
Nithdale Rd, SE18 . . . . . . **137** E7
Niton Cl, Barn. EN5 . . . . . . **40** A6
Niton Rd, Rich. TW9 . . . . . **146** A3
Niton St, SW6 . . . . **128** A7
Niven Cl, Borwd. WD6 . . . . **38** C1
N.L.A. Twr, Croy. CR0 . . . . **202** A2
Nobel Dr, Hayes UB3 . . . . **121** G7
Nobel Rd, N18 . . . . **61** F5
Noble St, EC2 . . . . **19** J3
NOEL PARK, N22 . . . . **75** G2
Noel Pk Rd, N22 . . . . **75** G2
Noel Rd, E6 . . . . **116** B4
N1 . . . . **11** G1
W3 . . . . **106** B6
Noel Sq, Dag. RM8 . . . . . . **100** C4
Noel St, W1 . . . . **17** G4
Noel Ter, SE23
off Dartmouth Rd **171** F2
Nolan Way, E5 . . . . **94** D4
Nolton Pl, Edg. HA8 . . . . . . **69** J1
Nonsuch Cl, Ilf. IG6 . . . . . . **65** E6
★**Nonsuch Mansion Ho**,
Sutt. SM3 . . . . **197** J6
Nora Gdns, NW4 . . . . **72** A4
NORBITON, Kings.T. KT2 . **182** B2
Norbiton Av, Kings.T. KT1 . **182** A2
Norbiton Common Rd,
Kings.T. KT1 . . . . **182** B3
Norbiton Rd, E14 . . . . **113** J6
Norbreck Gdns, NW10
off Lytham Gro **105** J3
Norbreck Par, NW10
off Lytham Gro **105** J3
Norbroke St, W12 . . . . **107** F7
Norburn St, W10
off Chesterton Rd **108** B5
NORBURY, SW16 . . . . **187** G1
Norbury Av, SW16 . . . . . . **187** F1
Hounslow TW3 . . . . **144** A5
Thornton Heath CR7 . . . **187** G2
Norbury Cl, SW16 . . . . . . **187** G1
Norbury Ct Rd, SW16 . . . **186** E3
Norbury Cres, SW16 . . . . **187** F1
Norbury Cross, SW16 . . . **186** E3
Norbury Gdns, Rom. RM6 . **82** D5
Norbury Gro, NW7 . . . . **54** E3
Norbury Hill, SW16 . . . . . **169** G7
Norbury Ri, SW16 . . . . . . **186** E3
Norbury Rd, E4 . . . . **62** A5
Thornton Heath CR7 . . . **187** J2
Norcombe Gdns, Har.
HA3 . . . . **69** F6
Norcott Cl, Hayes UB4 . . . **102** C4
Norcott Rd, N16 . . . . **94** D2
Norcroft Gdns, SE22 . . . . **152** D7
Norcutt Rd, Twick. TW2 . . **162** B1
Norfield Rd, Dart. DA2 . . . **177** J4
Norfolk Av, N13 . . . . **59** H6
N15 . . . . **76** C6
Norfolk Cl, N2
off Park Rd **73** H3
N13 . . . . **59** H6
Barnet EN4 . . . . **42** A4
Twickenham TW1
off Cassilis Rd . . . **144/145** E6
Norfolk Cres, W2 . . . . **15** H3
Sidcup DA15 . . . . **157** H7
Norfolk Gdns, Bexh. DA7 . **159** F1
Borehamwood WD6 . . . . **38** D4
Norfolk Ho, SE3 . . . . **135** E6
Norfolk Ho Rd, SW16 . . . . **168** D3
Norfolk Ms, W10
off Blagrove Rd **108** C5
Norfolk Pl, W2 . . . . **15** F3
Welling DA16 . . . . **158** A2
Norfolk Rd, E6 . . . . **116** C1
E17 . . . . **77** G2
NW8 . . . . **109** G1
NW10 . . . . **88** E7
SW19 . . . . **167** H7
Barking IG11 . . . . **99** H7
Barnet EN5 . . . . **40** D3
Dagenham RM10 . . . . . . **101** H5
Enfield EN3 . . . . **45** E6
Esher (Clay.) KT10 . . . . . **194** B5
Feltham TW13 . . . . **160** C1
Harrow HA1 . . . . **67** H5
Ilford IG3 . . . . **99** H1
Romford RM7 . . . . **83** J6
Thornton Heath CR7 . . . **187** J3
Norfolk Row, SE1 . . . . **34** C1
Norfolk Sq, W2 . . . . **15** F4
Norfolk Sq Ms, W2 . . . . **15** F4
Norfolk St, E7 . . . . **97** G4
Norfolk Ter, W6
off Field Rd **128** B5
Norgrove St, SW12 . . . . . **150** A7
Norhyrst Av, SE25 . . . . . . **188** C3
Norland Ho, W11 . . . . **128** A1
Norland Pl, W11 . . . . **128** B1
Norland Rd, W11 . . . . **128** A1
Norlands Cres, Chis. BR7 . **192** E1
Norlands Gate, Chis. BR7 . **193** E1
Norland Sq, W11 . . . . **128** B1
Norley Vale, SW15 . . . . . . **165** G1
Norlington Rd, E10 . . . . **96** C1
E11 . . . . **96** C1
Norman Av, N22 . . . . **75** H1
Feltham TW13 . . . . **161** E2
Southall UB1 . . . . **103** E7
Twickenham TW1 . . . . . **145** E7
Normanby Cl, SW15
off Manfred Rd **148** C5
Normanby Rd, NW10 . . . . . **89** F4
Norman Cl, Orp. BR6 . . . . **207** F3
Romford RM5 . . . . **83** H2
Norman Ct, Ilf. IG2 . . . . **81** G7
Woodford Green IG8
off Monkhams Av **63** H5
Norman Cres, Houns.TW5 . **142** D1
Pinner HA5 . . . . **66** C1
Normand Gdns, W14
off Greyhound Rd **128** B6
Normand Ms, W14
off Normand Rd **128** B6
Normand Rd, W14 . . . . . . **128** C6
Normandy Av, Barn. EN5 . . **40** C5
Normandy Cl, SE26 . . . . . **171** H3
Normandy Rd, SW9 . . . . . **151** G1
Normandy Ter, E16 . . . . . . **115** H6
Norman Gro, E3 . . . . **113** H2
Normanhurst Av, Bexh.
DA7 . . . . **158** D1
Normanhurst Dr, Twick.
TW1 *off St. Margarets*
Rd **144/145** E5
Normanhurst Rd, SW2 . . . **169** F2
Norman Rd, E6 . . . . **116** C4
E11 . . . . **96** D2
N15 . . . . **76** C5
SE10 . . . . **134** B7
SW19 . . . . **167** F7
Belvedere DA17 . . . . . . **139** H3
Ilford IG1 . . . . **99** E5
Sutton SM1 . . . . **198** D5
Norman Rd, Th. Hth. CR7 . **187** H5
Norman's Bldgs, EC1
off Ironmonger Row . . **111** J3
Normans Cl, NW10 . . . . . . **88** D6
Normansfield Av, Tedd.
TW11 . . . . **163** F7
Normanshire Av, E4 . . . . . . **62** C4
Normanshire Dr, E4 . . . . . . **62** A4
Normans Mead, NW10 . . . **88** D6
Norman St, EC1 . . . . **11** J4
Normanton Av, SW19 . . . **166** D2
Normanton Pk, E4 . . . . **62** E3
Normanton Rd, S.Croy.
CR2 . . . . **202** B6
Normanton St, SE23 . . . . **171** G2
Norman Way, N14 . . . . **58** E2
W3 . . . . **106** B5
Normington Cl, SW16 . . . **169** G5
Norrice Lea, N2 . . . . **73** G5
Norris St, SW1 . . . . **17** H6
Norroy Rd, SW15 . . . . **148** A4
Norrys Cl, Barn. EN4 . . . . . **41** J5
Norrys Rd, Barn. EN4 . . . . . **41** J4
Norseman Cl, Ilf. IG3 . . . . **100** B1
Norseman Way, Grnf. UB6
off Olympic Way **103** H1
Norstead Pl, SW15 . . . . . . **165** G2
North Access Rd, E17 . . . . **77** G6
North Acre, NW9 . . . . **71** E1
NORTH ACTON, W3 . . . . . **106** D4
North Acton Rd, NW10 . . . **106** D3
Northall Rd, Bexh. DA7 . . **159** J2
Northampton Gro, N1 . . . . **94** A5
Northampton Pk, N1 . . . . . **93** J6
Northampton Rd, EC1 . . . . **11** F5
Croydon CR0 . . . . **202** D2
Enfield EN3 . . . . **45** H4
Northampton Row, EC1 . . . **11** F4
Northampton Sq, EC1 . . . . **11** G4
Northampton St, N1 . . . . . **93** J7
Northanger Rd, SW16 . . . **168** E6
North Arc, Croy. CR0
off North End **201** J2
North Audley St, W1 . . . . . **16** B4
North Av, N18 . . . . **60** D4
W13 . . . . **104** E6
Carshalton SM5 . . . . . . **199** J7
Harrow HA2 . . . . **67** H6
Hayes UB3 . . . . **102** A7
Richmond TW9
off Sandycombe Rd . . **146** A1
Southall UB1 . . . . **103** F7
North Bk, NW8 . . . . **7** F4
Northbank Rd, E17 . . . . **78** C2
NORTH BECKTON, E6 . . . **116** B4
North Birkbeck Rd, E11 . . . **96** D3
Northborough Rd, SW16 . **186** D3
Northbourne, Brom. BR2 . **191** G7
Northbourne Rd, SW4 . . . **150** D4
North Branch Av, W10
off Harrow Rd **107** J3
Northbrook Rd, N22 . . . . . **59** E7
SE13 . . . . **154** D5
Barnet EN5 . . . . **40** B6
Croydon CR0 . . . . **188** A5
Ilford IG1 . . . . **98** D2
Northburgh St, EC1 . . . . . . **11** H5
North Carriage Dr, W2 . . . . **15** G5
NORTH CHEAM, Sutt.
SM3 . . . . **197** J3
Northchurch, SE17 . . . . **36** C3
Northchurch Rd, N1 . . . . . . **94** A7
Wembley HA9 . . . . **87** J6
Northchurch Ter, N1 . . . . . . **94** B7
North Circular Rd, E4
(A406) **61** J7
E6 (A406) **117** E2
E11 (A406) **79** J2
E12 (A406) **98** D5
E17 (A406) **61** J7
E18 (A406) **79** J2
N3 (A406) **72** E3
N11 (A406) **73** G1
N12 (A406) **73** G1
N13 (A406) **59** G5
N18 (A406) **60** B5
NW2 (A406) **88** E3
NW10 (A406) **88** B7
NW11 (A406) **72** B4
W3 (A406) **125** J2
W4 (A406) **125** J2
W5 (A406) **125** J2
Barking (A406) IG11 . . . . **117** E2
Ilford (A406) IG1, IG4 . . . **98** B1
Northcliffe Cl, Wor.Pk.
KT4 . . . . **197** E3
Northcliffe Dr, N20 . . . . **56** C1
North Cl, Barn. EN5 . . . . . . **39** J5
Bexleyheath DA6 . . . . . **158** D4
North Cl, Dag. RM10 . . . . **119** G1
Feltham TW14
off North Rd **141** G6
Morden SM4 . . . . **184** B4
North Colonnade, E14 . . . **134** A1
North Common Rd, W5 . . **105** H7
Northcote, Pnr. HA5 . . . . . . **66** C2
Northcote Av, W5 . . . . **105** H7
Isleworth TW7 . . . . **144** D5
Southall UB1 . . . . **103** E7
Surbiton KT5 . . . . **182** A7
Northcote Ms, SW11
off Northcote Rd **149** H4
Northcote Rd, E17 . . . . **77** H4
NW10 . . . . **89** E7
SW11 . . . . **149** H4
Croydon CR0 . . . . **188** A6
New Malden KT3 . . . . . **182** C3
Sidcup DA14 . . . . **175** H4
Twickenham TW1 . . . . . **144** D5
Northcott Av, N22 . . . . **75** E1
North Countess Rd, E17 . . . **77** J2
NORTH CRAY, Sid. DA14 . **177** G3
North Cray Rd, Bex. DA5 . . **177** F3
Sidcup DA14 . . . . **176** E6
North Cres, E16 . . . . **114** D4
N3 . . . . **72** C2
WC1 . . . . **17** H1
Northcroft Rd, W13 . . . . . **124** E2
Epsom KT19 . . . . **196** D7
Northcroft Ter, W13
off Northcroft Rd . **124/125** E2
North Cross Rd, SE22 . . . **152** C5
Ilford IG6 . . . . **81** F4
North Dene, NW7 . . . . **54** D3
Northdene, Chig. IG7 . . . . . **65** G5
North Dene, Houns. TW3 . **143** H1
Northdene Gdns, N15 . . . . **76** C6
Northdown Gdns, Ilf. IG2 . . **81** H5
Northdown Rd, Well.
DA16 . . . . **158** B2
Northdown St, N1 . . . . **10** B1
North Dr, SW16 . . . . **168** C4
Hounslow TW3 . . . . **143** J2
Orpington BR6 . . . . **207** H4
North End, NW3 . . . . **91** F2
Buckhurst Hill IG9 . . . . . . **47** J7
Croydon CR0 . . . . **201** J2
North End Av, NW3 . . . . . . **91** F2
North End Cres, W14 . . . . **128** C4
North End Ho, W14 . . . . . **128** B4
North End Par, W14
off North End Rd **128** B4
North End Rd, NW11 . . . . . **90** D1
SW6 . . . . **128** C6
W14 . . . . **128** B4
Wembley HA9 . . . . **88** A3
North End Way, NW3 . . . . . **91** F2
Northern Av, N9 . . . . **60** C2
Northernhay Wk, Mord.
SM4 . . . . **184** B4
Northern Perimeter Rd,
Houns. (Hthrw Air.)
TW6 . . . . **141** F1
Northern Perimeter Rd W,
Houns. (Hthrw Air.)
TW6 . . . . **140** A1
Northern Relief Rd, Bark.
IG11 . . . . **99** E7
Northern Rd, E13 . . . . **115** H1
Northern Service Rd, Barn.
EN5 . . . . **40** B3
North Eyot Gdns, W6 . . . . **127** G5
Northey St, E14 . . . . **113** H7
Northfield, Loug. IG10 . . . . **48** A4
Northfield Av, W5 . . . . **125** E2
W13 . . . . **125** E2
Pinner HA5 . . . . **66** D4
Northfield Cl, Brom. BR1 . **192** B1
Hayes UB3 . . . . **121** J3
Northfield Cres, Sutt.
SM3 . . . . **198** B4
Northfield Gdns, Dag. RM9
off Northfield Rd **101** F4
Northfield Ind Est, NW10 . **106** A3
Northfield Pk, Hayes UB3 . **121** J3
Northfield Path, Dag.
RM9 . . . . **101** F3
Northfield Rd, E6 . . . . **98** C7
N16 . . . . **76** B7
W13 . . . . **124** E2
Barnet EN4 . . . . **41** H3
Borehamwood WD6 . . . . **38** B1
Dagenham RM9 . . . . . . **101** F4
Enfield EN3 . . . . **44** E5
Hounslow TW5 . . . . **122** D6
Northfields, SW18 . . . . . . **148** D4
Northfields Ind Est, Wem.
HA0 . . . . **106** A1

Northfields Rd, W3 . . . . . . **106** B5
NORTH FINCHLEY, N12 . . . **57** G5
North Flockton St, SE16 . . **29** H3
North Gdn, E14
off Westferry Circ **133** J1
North Gdns, SW19 . . . . . . **167** G7
Northgate Dr, NW9 . . . . . . **70** E6
Northgate Ind Pk, Rom.
RM5 . . . . **83** F2
North Glade, The, Bex.
DA5 . . . . **159** F7
North Gower St, NW1 . . . . . **9** G4
North Grn, NW9
off Clayton Fld **54/55** E7
North Gro, N6 . . . . **74** A7
N15 . . . . **76** A5
NORTH HARROW, Har.
HA2 . . . . **67** G6
North Hatton Rd, Houns.
(Hthrw Air.) TW6 . . . . . **141** G1
North Hill, N6 . . . . **73** J6
North Hill Av, N6 . . . . **74** A6
NORTH HYDE, Sthl. UB2 . **123** E4
North Hyde Gdns, Hayes
UB3 . . . . **122** A4
North Hyde La, Houns.
TW5 . . . . **123** E5
Southall UB2 . . . . **123** E5
North Hyde Rd, Hayes
UB3 . . . . **121** J3
Northiam, N12 . . . . **56** D3
Northiam St, E9 . . . . **113** E1
Northington St, WC1 . . . . . **10** C6
NORTH KENSINGTON,
W10 . . . . **107** J6
Northlands Av, Orp. BR6 . **207** H4
Northlands St, SE5 . . . . . **151** J2
North La, Tedd. TW11 . . . . **162** C6
North Lo Cl, SW15
off Westleigh Av **148** A5
North Mall, N9
off St. Martins Rd . . **60/61** E2
North Ms, WC1 . . . . **10** D6
Northolm, Edg. HA8 . . . . . **54** D4
Northolme Gdns, Edg.
HA8 . . . . **70** A1
Northolme Ri, Orp. BR6 . . **207** H2
Northolme Rd, N5 . . . . **93** J4
NORTHOLT, UB5 . . . . **85** F7
Northolt Av, Ruis. HA4 . . . . **84** B5
Northolt Gdns, Grnf.
UB6 . . . . **86** C5
Northolt Rd, Har. HA2 . . . . **85** H4
Hounslow (Hthrw Air.)
TW6 . . . . **140** A1
Northover, Brom. BR1 . . . **173** F3
North Par, Chess. KT9 . . . **195** H5
North Pk, SE9 . . . . **166** C6
North Pas, SW18 . . . . **148** D4
North Peckham Est, SE15 . **37** E7
North Pl, Mitch. CR4 . . . . **167** J7
Teddington TW11 . . . . . . **162** C6
Northpoint, Brom. BR1
off Sherman Rd **191** G1
North Pole La, Kes. BR2 . . **205** F6
North Pole Rd, W10 . . . . . **107** J5
Northport St, N1 . . . . **112** A1
North Ride, W2 . . . . **15** G6
North Rd, N6 . . . . **74** A7
N7 . . . . **92** E6
N9 . . . . **60** E1
SE18 . . . . **137** H4
SW19 . . . . **167** F6
W5 . . . . **125** G3
Belvedere DA17 . . . . . . **139** H3
Brentford TW8 . . . . **125** H6
Bromley BR1 . . . . **191** H1
Edgware HA8 . . . . **70** B1
Feltham TW14 . . . . **141** G6
Ilford IG3 . . . . **99** H2
Richmond TW9 . . . . **146** A3
Romford (Chad.Hth)
RM6 . . . . **82** E5
Southall UB1 . . . . **103** G7
Surbiton KT6 . . . . **181** G6
West Drayton UB7 . . . . **120** C3
West Wickham BR4 . . . . **204** B1
Northrop Rd, Houns.
(Hthrw Air.) TW6 . . . . . **141** H1
North Row, W1 . . . . **16** A5
North Several, SE3
off Orchard Rd **154** D2
NORTH SHEEN, Rich.
TW9 . . . . **146** A2
Northside Rd, Brom. BR1
off Mitchell Way **191** G1
North Side Wandsworth
Common, SW18 . . . . **149** F5
Northspur Rd, Sutt. SM1 . **198** D3
North Sq, N9
off St. Martins Rd . . **60/61** E2
NW11 . . . . **72** D5
Northstead Rd, SW2 . . . . **169** G2
North St, E13 . . . . **115** G2
NW4 . . . . **71** J5
SW4 . . . . **150** C3
Barking IG11 . . . . **99** E6
Bexleyheath DA7 . . . . . **159** G4
Bromley BR1 . . . . **191** G1
Carshalton SM5 . . . . . . **199** J3
Isleworth TW7 . . . . **144** D3
North St Pas, E13 . . . . . . **115** H2
North Tenter St, E1 . . . . **21** G4
North Ter, SW3 . . . . **23** G6
Northumberland All, EC3 . . **21** E4
Northumberland Av, E12 . . **97** J1
WC2 . . . . **26** A1
Enfield EN1 . . . . **45** E1
Isleworth TW7 . . . . **144** C1
Welling DA16 . . . . **157** G4
Northumberland Cl, Erith
DA8 . . . . **139** J7
Staines (Stanw.) TW19 . **140** B6
Northumberland Cres, Felt.
TW14 . . . . **141** H6
Northumberland Gdns,
N9 . . . . **60** C3
Bromley BR1 . . . . **192** D4
Isleworth TW7 . . . . **124** D7
Mitcham CR4 . . . . **186** D5
Northumberland Gro, N17 . **60** E7
NORTHUMBERLAND HEATH,
Erith DA8 . . . . **139** J7
Northumberland Pk, N17 . . **60** C7
Erith DA8 . . . . **139** J7
Northumberland Pl, W2 . . **108** D6
Richmond TW10 . . . . . . **145** G5
Northumberland Rd, E6 . . **116** B6
E17 . . . . **78** A7
Barnet EN5 . . . . **41** F6
Harrow HA2 . . . . **67** F5
Northumberland Row, Twick.
TW2 *off Colne Rd* **162** B1
Northumberland St, WC2 . **26** A1
Northumberland Way, Erith
DA8 . . . . **159** J1
Northumbria St, E14 . . . . **114** A6
North Verbena Gdns, W6
off St. Peter's Sq **127** G5
Northview, N7 . . . . **93** E3
North Vw, SW19 . . . . **165** H5
W5 . . . . **105** F4
Pinner HA5 . . . . **66** C7
Northview Cres, NW10 . . . **89** F4
North Vw Dr, Wdf.Grn. IG8 . [illegible] A2
North Vw Rd, N8 . . . . **74** D3
North Vil, NW1 . . . . **92** D6
North Wk, W2 . . . . **14** C6
Croydon (New Adgtn)
CR0 . . . . **204** B5
North Way, N9 . . . . **61** F2
N11 . . . . **58** C6
NW9 . . . . **70** B7
Northway, NW11 . . . . **72** E5
Morden SM4 . . . . **184** B3
North Way, Pnr. HA5 . . . . . **66** C3
Northway, Wall. SM6 . . . . **200** C4
Northway Circ, NW7 . . . . . **54** D4
Northway Cres, NW7 . . . . . **54** D4
Northway Ho, N20 . . . . **57** F1
Northway Rd, SE5 . . . . . . **151** J3
Croydon CR0 . . . . **188** C6
Northways Par, NW3
off Finchley Rd **91** G7
Northweald La, Kings.T.
KT2 . . . . **163** G5
NORTH WEMBLEY, Wem.
HA0 . . . . **87** E2
Northwest Pl, N1 . . . . **11** F1
North Wf Rd, W2 . . . . **14** E2
Northwick Av, Har. HA3 . . . **68** D6
Northwick Circle, Har. HA3 . **69** F6
Northwick Cl, NW8 . . . . **6** E5
Harrow HA1
off Nightingale Av . . **68/69** E7
Northwick Pk Rd, Har.
HA1 . . . . **68** C6
Northwick Rd, Wat. WD19 . **50** C4
Wembley HA0 . . . . **105** G1
Northwick Ter, NW8 . . . . **6** E5
Northwick Wk, Har. HA1 . . **68** C7
Northwold Dr, Pnr. HA5
off Cuckoo Hill **66** C3
Northwold Est, E5 . . . . **94** D2
Northwold Rd, E5 . . . . **94** C2
N16 . . . . **94** C2
North Wd Ct, SE25
off Regina Rd **188** D3
Northwood Gdns, N12 . . . . **57** G5
Greenford UB6 . . . . **86** C5
Ilford IG5 . . . . **80** D4
Northwood Hall, N6 . . . . . . **74** C7
Northwood Ho, SE27 . . . . **170** A4
Northwood Pl, Erith DA18 **139** F3
Northwood Rd, N6 . . . . **74** B7
SE23 . . . . **171** J1
Carshalton SM5 . . . . . . **200** A6
Hounslow (Hthrw Air.)
TW6 . . . . **140** A1
Thornton Heath CR7 . . . **187** H2
Northwood Twr, E17 . . . . . **78** C4
Northwood Way, SE19
off Roman Ri **170** A6
Northwood HA6 . . . . **50** A7
NORTH WOOLWICH, E16 . **136** B2
North Woolwich Rd, E16 . **135** G1
North Woolwich Roundabout,
E16 *off North*
Woolwich Rd **136** A1
★**North Woolwich Sta Mus**,
E16 . . . . **136** D2
North Worple Way, SW14 . **146** D3
Norton Av, Surb. KT5 . . . . **182** B7
Norton Cl, E4 . . . . **62** A5
Borehamwood WD6 . . . . **38** A1
Enfield EN1
off Brick La **44/45** E2
Norton Folgate, E1 . . . . **21** E1
Norton Gdns, SW16 . . . . . **186** E2
Norton Rd, E10 . . . . **95** J1
Wembley HA0 . . . . **87** G6
Norval Rd, Wem. HA0 . . . . **86** E2
Norway Gate, SE16 . . . . . **133** H3
Norway Pl, E14
off Commercial Rd . . . **113** J6
Norway St, SE10 . . . . **134** B6
Norwich Ho, E14
off Cordelia St **114** B6
Norwich Ms, Ilf. IG3
off Ashgrove Rd **100** A1
Norwich Pl, Bexh. DA6 . . **159** G4
Norwich Rd, E7 . . . . **97** G5
Dagenham RM9 . . . . . . **119** G2
Greenford UB6 . . . . **103** H1
Thornton Heath CR7 . . . **187** J3
Norwich St, EC4 . . . . **19** E3
Norwich Wk, Edg. HA8 . . . **54** C7
NORWOOD, SE19 . . . . **170** B6
Norwood Av, Wem. HA0 . **105** J1
Norwood Cl, NW2 . . . . **90** B3
Southall UB2 . . . . **123** G4
Twickenham TW2
off Fourth Cross Rd . . . **162** A2
Norwood Cres, Houns.
(Hthrw Air.) TW6 . . . . . **141** F1
Norwood Dr, Har. HA2 . . . . **67** F6
Norwood Gdns, Hayes
UB4 . . . . **102** C4
Southall UB2 . . . . **123** F4
NORWOOD GREEN, Sthl.
UB2 . . . . **123** G4
Norwood Grn Rd, Sthl.
UB2 . . . . **123** G4
Norwood High St, SE27 . **169** H3
NORWOOD NEW TOWN,
SE19 . . . . **169** J6
Norwood Pk Rd, SE27 . . . **169** J5
Norwood Rd, SE24 . . . . . **169** H1
SE27 . . . . **169** H2
Southall UB2 . . . . **123** F4
Norwood Ter, Sthl. UB2
off Tentelow La **123** H4
Notley St, SE5 . . . . **36** B7
Notre Dame Est, SW4 . . . **150** C4
Notson Rd, SE25 . . . . **188** E4
Notting Barn Rd, W10 . . . **108** A4
Nottingdale Sq, W11
off Wilsham St **128** B1
Nottingham Av, E16 . . . . . **115** J5
Nottingham Ct, WC2 . . . . . **18** A4
Nottingham Pl, W1 . . . . **8** B6
Nottingham Rd, E10 . . . . . **78** C6
SW17 . . . . **167** J1
Isleworth TW7 . . . . **144** C2
South Croydon CR2 . . . **201** J4
Nottingham St, W1 . . . . . . **16** B1
Nottingham Ter, NW1 . . . . . **8** B6
NOTTING HILL, W11 . . . . **108** B7
Notting Hill Gate, W11 . . . **128** D1
Nova, E14 *off Newton Pl* . **134** A4
Nova Ms, Sutt. SM3 . . . . . **198** B1
Novar Cl, Orp. BR6 . . . . . **193** J7
Nova Rd, Croy. CR0 . . . . . **187** H7
Novar Rd, SE9 . . . . **175** F1
Novello St, SW6 . . . . **148** D1
Novello Way, Borwd. WD6 . **38** D1
Nowell Rd, SW13 . . . . **127** G6
Nower Hill, Pnr. HA5 . . . . . **67** F4
Noyna Rd, SW17 . . . . **167** J3
Nuding Cl, SE13 . . . . **154** A3
Nugent Rd, N19 . . . . **93** E1
SE25 . . . . **188** C3
Nugents Ct, Pnr. HA5
off St. Thomas' Dr . . **66/67** E1
Nugents Pk, Pnr. HA5 . . . . **67** E1
Nugent Ter, NW8 . . . . **6** D2
Numa Ct, Brent. TW8
off Justin Cl **125** G7
★**No. 2 Willow Rd**, NW3 . . **91** H4
Nun Ct, EC2 . . . . **20** B3
Nuneaton Rd, Dag. RM9 . **100** D7
NUNHEAD, SE15 . . . . **153** F3
Nunhead Cres, SE15 . . . . **152** E3
Nunhead Est, SE15 . . . . . **152** E4
Nunhead Grn, SE15 . . . . . **153** E3
Nunhead Gro, SE15 . . . . . **153** E3
Nunhead La, SE15 . . . . . . **152** E3
Nunhead Pas, SE15
off Peckham Rye **152** D3
Nunnington Cl, SE9 . . . . . **174** B3
Nunns Rd, Enf. EN2 . . . . . . **43** J2
Nupton Dr, Barn. EN5 . . . . **39** J6
Nursery Av, N3 . . . . **73** F2
Bexleyheath DA7 . . . . . **159** F3
Croydon CR0 . . . . **203** G2
Nursery Cl, SE4 . . . . **153** J2
SW15 . . . . **148** A4
Croydon CR0 . . . . **203** G2
Enfield EN3 . . . . **45** G1
Feltham TW14 . . . . **142** B7
Romford RM6 . . . . **82** D6
Woodford Green IG8 . . . **63** H5
Nursery Ct, N17
off Nursery St **60** C7
Nursery Gdns, Chis. BR7 . **174** E6
Enfield EN3 . . . . **45** G1
Hounslow TW4 . . . . **143** F5
Nursery La, E2 . . . . **112** C1
E7 . . . . **97** G6
W10 . . . . **107** J5
Nurserymans Rd, N11 . . . . **58** A2
Nursery Rd, E9
off Morning La **95** F6
N2 . . . . **73** G1
N14 . . . . **42** C7
SW9 . . . . **151** F4
Loughton IG10 . . . . **47** J5
Loughton (High Beach)
IG10 . . . . **47** H1
Pinner HA5 . . . . **66** C3
Sutton SM1 . . . . **199** F4
Thornton Heath CR7 . . . **188** A4
Nursery Rd Merton,
SW19 . . . . **185** E2
Nursery Rd Mitcham,
Mitch. CR4 . . . . **185** H3
Nursery Rd Wimbledon,
SW19 *off Worple Rd* . . **166** B7
Nursery Row, SE17 . . . . . . **36** B2
Barnet EN5
off St. Albans Rd **40** B3
Nursery St, N17 . . . . **60** C7
Nursery Wk, NW4 . . . . **71** H3
Nurstead Rd, Erith DA8 . . **139** G7
Nutbourne St, W10 . . . . . . **108** B3
Nutbrook St, SE15 . . . . . . **152** D3
Nutbrowne Rd, Dag. RM9 . **119** F1
Nutcroft Rd, SE15 . . . . . . **132** E7
Nutfield Cl, N18 . . . . **60** D6
Carshalton SM5 . . . . . . **199** H3
Nutfield Gdns, Ilf. IG3 . . . . **99** J2
Northolt UB5 . . . . **102** C2
Nutfield Rd, E15 . . . . **96** C4
NW2 . . . . **89** G2
SE22 . . . . **152** C5
Thornton Heath CR7 . . . **187** H4
Nutfield Way, Orp. BR6 . . **206** D2
Nutford Pl, W1 . . . . **15** H3
Nuthatch Gdns, SE28 . . . **137** G2
Nuthurst Av, SW2 . . . . . . **169** F2
Nutley Ter, NW3 . . . . **91** F6
Nutmead Cl, Bex. DA5 . . . **177** J1
Nutmeg Cl, E16
off Cranberry La . . **114/115** E4
Nutmeg La, E14 . . . . **114** D6
Nuttall St, N1 . . . . **12** E1
Nutter La, E11 . . . . **79** J6
Nutt Gro, Edg. HA8 . . . . . . **53** G2
Nutt St, SE15 . . . . **37** G7
Nutwell St, SW17 . . . . **167** H5
Nuxley Rd, Belv. DA17 . . . **139** F6
Nyanza St, SE18 . . . . **137** G6
Nye Bevan Est, E5 . . . . **95** G3
Nylands Av, Rich. TW9 . . . **146** A1
Nymans Gdns, SW20
off Hidcote Gdns **183** H3

Nynehead St, SE14 . . . . . **133** H7
Nyon Gro, SE6 . . . . **171** J2
Nyssa Cl, Wdf.Grn. IG8
off Gwynne Pk Av **64** C6
Nyton Cl, N19
off Courtauld Rd . . . **92/93** E1

O

O2 Shop Cen, NW3
off Finchley Rd **91** F6
Oak Apple Ct, SE12 . . . . . **173** G2
Oak Av, N8 . . . . **74** E4
N10 . . . . **58** B7
N17 . . . . **60** A7
Croydon CR0 . . . . **204** A2
Hampton TW12 . . . . **161** E5
Hounslow TW5 . . . . **122** D7
West Drayton UB7 . . . . **120** D3
Oak Bk, Croy. (New Adgtn) CR0 . . . . **204** C6
Oakbank Av, Walt. KT12 . . **179** F7
Oakbank Gro, SE24 . . . . . **151** J4
Oakbrook Cl, Brom. BR1 . **173** H4
Oakbury Rd, SW6 . . . . . . **149** E2
Oak Cl, N14 . . . . **42** B7
Sutton SM1 . . . . **199** F2
Oakcombe Cl, N.Mal. KT3 *off Traps La* . . **182/183** E1
Oak Cottage Cl, SE6 . . . . . **173** F1
Oak Cres, E16 . . . . **115** E5
Oakcroft Cl, Pnr. HA5 . . . . . **66** B2
Oakcroft Rd, SE13 . . . . . . **154** D2
Chessington KT9 . . . . . . **195** J4
Oakcroft Vil, Chess. KT9 . . **195** J4
Oakdale, N14 . . . . **58** B1
Oakdale Av, Har. HA3 . . . . . **69** H5
Northwood HA6 . . . . **66** A2
Oakdale Cl, Wat. WD19 . . . . **50** C4
Oakdale Gdns, E4 . . . . **62** C5
Oakdale Rd, E7 . . . . **97** H7
E11 . . . . **96** D2
E18 . . . . **79** H2
N4 . . . . **75** J6
SE15 . . . . **153** F3
SW16 . . . . **169** E5
Watford WD19 . . . . **50** C3
Oakdale Way, Mitch. CR4
off Wolseley Rd **186** A7
Oakdene, SE15
off Carlton Gro . . . **152/153** E1
Oak Dene, W13
off The Dene **104/105** E5
Oakdene Av, Chis. BR7 . . . **174** D5
Erith DA8 . . . . **139** J6
Thames Ditton KT7 . . . . **194** D1
Oakdene Cl, Pnr. HA5 . . . . **51** F7
Oakdene Dr, Surb. KT5 . . **182** C7
Oakdene Ms, Sutt. SM3 . . **198** C1
Oakdene Pk, N3 . . . . **56** C7
Oakdene Rd, Orp. BR5 . . . . **193** J5
Oakden St, SE11 . . . . **35** F1
Oake Ct, SW15 . . . . **148** B5
Oaken Dr, Esher (Clay.) KT10 . . . . **194** C6
Oakenholt Ho, SE2
off Hartslock Dr **138** D2
Oaken La, Esher (Clay.) KT10 . . . . **194** B5
Oakenshaw Cl, Surb. KT6 . **181** H7
Oakes Cl, E6
off Savage Gdns **116** C6
Oakeshott Av, N6 . . . . **92** A2
Oakey La, SE1 . . . . **27** E5
Oak Fm, Borwd. WD6 . . . . . **38** C5
Oakfield, E4 . . . . **62** B5
Oakfield Av, Har. HA3 . . . . **69** E3
Oakfield Cl, N.Mal. KT3
off Blakes La **183** F5
Oakfield Ct, N8 . . . . **74** E7
NW2 *off Hendon Way* . . . **72** A7
Borehamwood WD6 . . . . **38** B3
Oakfield Gdns, N18 . . . . . . **60** B4
SE19 . . . . **170** B5
Beckenham BR3 . . . . . . **190** A5
Carshalton SM5 . . . . . . **199** H1
Greenford UB6 . . . . **104** A4
Oakfield La, Kes. BR2 . . . . **205** J4
Oakfield Rd, E6 . . . . **116** B1
E17 . . . . **77** H2
N3 . . . . **72** E1
N4 . . . . **75** G6
N14 . . . . **58** E3
SE20 . . . . **171** E7
SW19 . . . . **166** A3
Croydon CR0 . . . . **201** J1
Ilford IG1 . . . . **99** E2
Oakfields Rd, NW11 . . . . . . **72** B6
Oakfield St, SW10 . . . . **30** C5
Oakford Rd, NW5 . . . . **92** C4
Oak Gdns, Croy. CR0 . . . . **204** A2
Edgware HA8 . . . . **70** C2
Oak Gro, NW2 . . . . **90** B4
Ruislip HA4 . . . . **66** B7
Sunbury-on-Thames TW16 . . . . **160** B7
West Wickham BR4 . . . . **204** C2
Oak Gro Rd, SE20 . . . . . . **189** F1
Oakhall Ct, E11 . . . . **79** H6
Oak Hall Rd, E11 . . . . **79** H6
Oakham Cl, SE6
off Rutland Wk **171** J2
Barnet EN4 . . . . **41** J3
Oakham Dr, Brom. BR2 . . **191** F4
Oakhampton Rd, NW7 . . . . **56** A7
Oakhill, Esher (Clay.) KT10 . . . . **194** D6
Oak Hill, Surb. KT6 . . . . . . **181** H7
Woodford Green IG8 . . . **62** D7
Oakhill Av, NW3 . . . . **90** E4
Pinner HA5 . . . . **66** E2
Oak Hill Cl, Wdf.Grn. IG8 . . **62** D7
Oakhill Ct, SW19 . . . . **166** A7
Oak Hill Cres, Surb. KT6 . **181** H7
Woodford Green IG8 . . . **62** D7
Oakhill Dr, Surb. KT6 . . . . **181** H7
Oak Hill Gdns, Wdf.Grn. IG8 . . . . **79** E1
Oak Hill Gro, Surb. KT6 . . **181** H6
Oak Hill Pk, NW3 . . . . **91** E4
Oak Hill Pk Ms, NW3 . . . . . **91** F4
Oakhill Path, Surb. KT6 . . **181** H6
Oakhill Pl, SW15
off Oakhill Rd **148** D5
Oakhill Rd, SW15 . . . . **148** C5
SW16 . . . . **187** E1
Beckenham BR3 . . . . . . **190** C2
Orpington BR6 . . . . **207** J1
Oak Hill Rd, Surb. KT6 . . . **181** H6
Oakhill Rd, Sutt. SM1 . . . . **199** E3
Oak Hill Way, NW3 . . . . **91** F4
Oakhouse Rd, Bexh. DA6 . **159** G5
Oakhurst Av, Barn. EN4 . . . **41** H7
Bexleyheath DA7 . . . . . **138** E7
Oakhurst Cl, E17 . . . . **78** E4
Chislehurst BR7 . . . . . . **192** C1
Ilford IG6 . . . . **81** F1
Teddington TW11 . . . . . . **162** B5
Oakhurst Gdns, E4 . . . . **63** F1
E17 . . . . **78** E4
Bexleyheath DA7 . . . . . **139** E7
Oakhurst Gro, SE22 . . . . . **152** D4
Oakhurst Rd, Epsom KT19 . . . . **196** C6
Oakington Av, Har. HA2 . . . **67** G7
Hayes UB3 . . . . **121** G4
Wembley HA9 . . . . **87** J3
Oakington Cl, Sun. TW16
off Oakington Dr **178** C2
Oakington Dr, Sun. TW16 . **178** C2
Oakington Manor Dr, Wem. HA9 . . . . **88** A5
Oakington Rd, W9 . . . . . . **108** D4
Oakington Way, N8 . . . . . . **75** E6
Oakland Pl, Buck.H. IG9 . . . **63** G2
Oakland Rd, E15 . . . . **96** D4
Oaklands, N21 . . . . **59** F2
Twickenham TW2 . . . . . **143** J7
Oaklands Av, N9 . . . . **44** E6
Esher KT10 . . . . **194** A1
Isleworth TW7 . . . . **124** C6
Sidcup DA15 . . . . **157** J7
Thornton Heath CR7 . . . **187** G4
Watford WD19 . . . . **50** B1
West Wickham BR4 . . . . **204** B3
Oaklands Cl, Bexh. DA6 . . **159** F5
Chessington KT9 . . . . . . **195** F4
Orpington BR5 . . . . **193** H6
Oaklands Ct, Wem. HA0 . . . **87** G5
Oaklands Est, SW4 . . . . . **150** C6
Oaklands Gro, W12 . . . . . **127** G1
Oaklands La, Barn. EN5 . . . **39** H4
Oaklands Pk Av, Ilf. IG1
off High Rd **99** G2
Oaklands Pl, SW4
off St. Alphonsus Rd . . **150** C4
Oaklands Rd, N20 . . . . **40** C7
NW2 . . . . **90** A4
SW14 . . . . **146** D3
W7 . . . . **124** C2
Bexleyheath DA6 . . . . . **159** F4
Bromley BR1 . . . . **173** E7
Oaklands Way, Wall. SM6 . **200** D7
Oakland Way, Epsom KT19 . . . . **196** D6
Oak La, E14 . . . . **113** J7
N2 . . . . **73** G2
Oak La, N11 . . . . **58** D6
Isleworth TW7 . . . . **144** B4
Twickenham TW1 . . . . . **144** D7
Woodford Green IG8 . . . **63** F4
Oakleafe Gdns, Ilf. IG6 . . . . **80** E3
Oaklea Pas, Kings.T. KT1 . **181** G3
Oakleigh Av, N20 . . . . **57** G2
Edgware HA8 . . . . **70** B2
Surbiton KT6 . . . . **196** A1
Oakleigh Cl, N20 . . . . **57** J3
Oakleigh Ct, Barn. EN4
off Church Hill Rd **41** H6
Edgware HA8 . . . . **70** C2
Oakleigh Cres, N20 . . . . . . **57** H2
Oakleigh Gdns, N20 . . . . . . **57** F1
Edgware HA8 . . . . **53** J5
Orpington BR6 . . . . **207** H4
Oakleigh Ms, N20
off Oakleigh Rd N **57** F2
OAKLEIGH PARK, N20 . . . . **57** G1
Oakleigh Pk Av, Chis. BR7 . **192** D1
Oakleigh Pk N, N20 . . . . . . **57** G1
Oakleigh Pk S, N20 . . . . . . **57** H2
Oakleigh Rd, Pnr. HA5 . . . . **51** F6
Oakleigh Rd N, N20 . . . . . . **57** G2
Oakleigh Rd S, N11 . . . . . . **58** A3
Oakleigh Way, Mitch. CR4 . **186** B1
Surbiton KT6 . . . . **196** A1
Oakley Av, W5 . . . . **106** A7
Barking IG11 . . . . **99** J7
Croydon CR0 . . . . **201** E4
Oakley Cl, E4 . . . . **62** C3
E6
off Northumberland Rd . . **116** B6
W7 . . . . **104** B7
Isleworth TW7 . . . . **144** A1
Oakley Ct, Loug. IG10
off Hillyfields **48** D2
Mitcham CR4
off London Rd **200** A1
Oakley Cres, EC1 . . . . **11** H2
Oakley Dr, SE9 . . . . **175** G1
SE13 . . . . **154** D6
Bromley BR2 . . . . **206** B3
Oakley Gdns, N8 . . . . **75** F5
SW3 . . . . **31** H5
Oakley Pk, Bex. DA5 . . . . **158** C7
Oakley Pl, SE1 . . . . **37** F4
Oakley Rd, N1 . . . . **94** A7
SE25 . . . . **188** E5
Bromley BR2 . . . . **206** B3
Harrow HA1 . . . . **68** B6
Oakley Sq, NW1 . . . . **9** G2
Oakley St, SW3 . . . . **31** G5
Oakley Wk, W6 . . . . **128** A6
Oakley Yd, E2 . . . . **13** G5
Oak Lo Av, Chig. IG7 . . . . . **65** G5
Oak Lo Cl, Stan. HA7
off Dennis La **53** F5
Oak Lo Dr, W.Wick. BR4 . . **190** B7
Oak Manor Dr, Wem. HA9
off Oakington Manor Dr . **87** J5
Oakmead Av, Brom. BR2 . **191** G6
Oakmeade, Pnr. HA5 . . . . . **51** G6
Oakmead Gdns, Edg. HA8 . **54** D4
Oakmead Pl, Mitch. CR4 . **185** H1
Oakmead Rd, SW12 . . . . . **168** A1
Croydon CR0 . . . . **186** D6
Oakmere Rd, SE2 . . . . **138** A6
Oakmoor Way, Chig. IG7 . . **65** H5
Oakmount Pl, Orp. BR6 . . **207** G1
Oak Pk Gdns, SW19 . . . . . **148** A7
Oak Pk Ms, E5
off Brooke Rd **94** C3
Oak Pl, SW18
off East Hill **148/149** E5
Oakridge Dr, N2 . . . . **73** G3
Oakridge La, Brom. BR1
off Downham Way . . . **172** D5
Oakridge Rd, Brom. BR1 . **172** D4
Oak Ri, Buck.H. IG9 . . . . . . **64** A3
Oak Rd, W5
off The Broadway **105** G7
Erith (Northumb.Hth) DA8 . . . . **139** J7
New Malden KT3 . . . . . **182** D2
Oak Row, SW16 . . . . **186** C2
Oaks, The, N12 . . . . **57** E4
SE18 . . . . **137** F5
Watford WD19 . . . . **50** C1
Woodford Green IG8 . . . **63** E6
Oaks Av, SE19 . . . . **170** B5
Feltham TW13 . . . . **160** E2
Romford RM5 . . . . **83** J2
Worcester Park KT4 . . . . **197** H3
Oaksford Av, SE26 . . . . . . **170** E3
Oaks Gro, E4 . . . . **62** E2
Oakshade Rd, Brom. BR1 . **172** D4
Oakshaw Rd, SW18 . . . . . **149** E7
Oaks La, Croy. CR0 . . . . . **203** F3
Ilford IG2 . . . . **81** H5
Oaks Rd, Croy. CR0 . . . . . **202** E5
Staines (Stanw.) TW19 . **140** A6
Oak St, Rom. RM7 . . . . **83** J5
Oaks Way, Cars. SM5 . . . . **199** J7
Surbiton KT6 . . . . **195** G2
Oakthorpe Rd, N13 . . . . . . **59** G5
Oaktree Av, N13 . . . . **59** H3
Oak Tree Cl, W5
off Pinewood Gro **105** F6
Loughton IG10 . . . . **49** F1
Stanmore HA7 . . . . **53** F7
Oak Tree Dell, NW9 . . . . . . **70** C5
Oak Tree Dr, N20 . . . . **57** E1
Oak Tree Gdns, Brom. BR1 . . . . **173** H5
Oaktree Gro, Ilf. IG1 . . . . . . **99** G5
Oak Tree Rd, NW8 . . . . **7** F4
Oakview Gdns, N2 . . . . **73** G4
Oakview Gro, Croy. CR0 . **203** H1
Oakview Rd, SE6 . . . . **172** B5
Oak Village, NW5 . . . . **92** A4
Oak Wk, Wall. SM6
off Helios Rd **200** A1
Oak Way, N14 . . . . **42** B7
Oakway, SW20 . . . . **183** J4
Oak Way, W3 . . . . **126** E1
Oakway, Brom. BR2 . . . . . **190** D2
Oak Way, Croy. CR0 . . . . . **189** G6
Oakway Cl, Bex. DA5 . . . . **159** E6
Oakways, SE9 . . . . **156** E6
OAKWOOD, N14 . . . . **42** D6
Oakwood Av, N14 . . . . **42** D7
Beckenham BR3 . . . . . . **190** C2
Borehamwood WD6 . . . . **38** B4
Bromley BR2 . . . . **191** H3
Mitcham CR4 . . . . **185** G2
Southall UB1 . . . . **103** G7
Oakwood Cl, N14 . . . . **42** C6
Chislehurst BR7 . . . . . . **174** C6
Woodford Green IG8
off Green Wk **64** B6
Oakwood Ct, W14 . . . . . . **128** C3
Oakwood Cres, N21 . . . . . . **43** E6
Greenford UB6 . . . . **86** D6
Oakwood Dr, SE19 . . . . . . **170** A6
Edgware HA8 . . . . **54** C6
Oakwood Gdns, Ilf. IG3 . . . **99** J2
Orpington BR6 . . . . **207** F2
Sutton SM1 . . . . **198** D2
Oakwood Hill, Loug. IG10 . **48** C6
Oakwood Hill Ind Est, Loug. IG10 . . . . **49** F5
Oakwood La, W14 . . . . . . **128** C3
Oakwood Pk Rd, N14 . . . . . **42** D7
Oakwood Pl, Croy. CR0 . . **187** G6
Oakwood Rd, NW11 . . . . . . **72** E5
SW20 . . . . **183** G1
Croydon CR0 . . . . **187** G6
Orpington BR6 . . . . **207** F2
Pinner HA5 . . . . **66** B2
Oakwood Vw, N14 . . . . **42** D6
Oakworth Rd, W10 . . . . . . **107** J5
Oarsman Pl, E.Mol. KT8 . . **180** B4
Oates Cl, Brom. BR2 . . . . **190** D3
Oatfield Ho, N15
off Bushey Rd **76** B6
Oatfield Rd, Orp. BR6 . . . **207** J1
Oatland Ri, E17 . . . . **77** H2
Oatlands Rd, Enf. EN3 . . . . **45** F1
Oat La, EC2 . . . . **19** J3
Oban Cl, E13 . . . . **115** J4
Oban Ho, Bark. IG11
off Wheelers Cross . . . **117** G2
Oban Rd, E13 . . . . **115** J3
SE25 . . . . **188** A4
Oban St, E14 . . . . **114** D6
Oberon Cl, Borwd. WD6 . . . **38** C1
Oberstein Rd, SW11 . . . . . **149** G4
Oborne Cl, SE24 . . . . **151** H5
Observatory Gdns, W8 . . . **128** D2
Observatory Ms, E14
off Storers Quay **134** D4
Observatory Rd, SW14 . . . **146** C4
Occupation La, SE18 . . . . **156** E1
W5 . . . . **125** G4
Occupation Rd, SE17 . . . . . **35** J3
W13 . . . . **124** E2
Ocean Est, E1 . . . . **113** G4
Ocean St, E1 . . . . **113** G5
Ocean Wf, E14 . . . . **134** A2
Ockendon Ms, N1
off Ockendon Rd **94** A6
Ockendon Rd, N1 . . . . **94** A6
Ockham Dr, Orp. BR5 . . . . **176** A7
Ockley Ct, Sutt. SM1
off Oakhill Rd **199** F4
Ockley Rd, SW16 . . . . **168** E3

Ockley Rd, Croy. CR0 . . . . 187 F7
Octagon Arc, EC2 . . . . 20 D2
Octavia Cl, Mitch. CR4 . . . 185 H5
Octavia Ms, W9 *off Bravington Rd* 108 C4
Octavia Rd, Islw. TW7 . . . 144 C2
Octavia St, SW11 . . . . 149 H1
Octavia Way, SE28 *off Booth Cl* 118 B7
Octavius St, SE8 . . . . 134 A7
Odard Rd, W.Mol. KT8 *off Down St* 179 G4
Oddesey Rd, Borwd. WD6 . . . . 38 B1
Odell Cl, Bark. IG11 . . . . . . 99 J7
Odeon, The, Bark. IG11 *off Longbridge Rd* 99 G7
Odessa Rd, E7 . . . . 97 F3
NW10 . . . . 107 G2
Odessa St, SE16 . . . . 133 J2
Odger St, SW11 . . . . 149 J2
Odhams Wk, WC2 . . . . 18 B4
Odyssey Business Pk, Ruis. HA4 . . . . 84 B5
Offa's Mead, E9 *off Lindisfarne Way* 95 H4
Offenbach Ho, E2 . . . . 113 G2
Offenham Rd, SE9 . . . . . . 174 C4
Offers Ct, Kings.T. KT1 *off Winery La* 181 J3
Offerton Rd, SW4 . . . . 150 C3
Offham Slope, N12 . . . . . . 56 C5
Offley Pl, Islw. TW7 . . . . . 144 A2
Offley Rd, SW9 . . . . 35 E7
Offord Cl, N17 . . . . 60 D7
Offord Rd, N1 . . . . 93 F7
Offord St, N1 . . . . 93 F7
Ogilby St, SE18 . . . . 136 C4
Oglander Rd, SE15 . . . . . . 152 C4
Ogle St, W1 . . . . 17 F1
Oglethorpe Rd, Dag. RM10 . . . . 101 F3
Ohio Rd, E13 . . . . 115 F4
Oil Mill La, W6 . . . . 127 G5
Okeburn Rd, SW17 . . . . . . 168 A5
Okehampton Cl, N12 . . . . . . 57 G5
Okehampton Cres, Well. DA16 . . . . 158 B1
Okehampton Rd, NW10 . . 107 J1
Olaf St, W11 . . . . 108 A7
Oldacre Ms, SW12 *off Balham Gro* 150 B7
★**Old Admiralty Bldgs (M.o.D.)**, SW1 . . . . 25 J2
Old Bailey, EC4 . . . . 19 H4
Old Barge Ho All, SE1 *off Upper Grd* 131 G1
Old Barn Cl, Sutt. SM2 . . . 198 B7
Old Barrack Yd, SW1 . . . . . 24 B3
Old Barrowfield, E15 *off New Plaistow Rd*. 114/115 E1
Old Bellgate Pl, E14 . . . . . 134 A3
Oldberry Rd, Edg. HA8 . . . . 54 D6
Old Bethnal Grn Rd, E2 . . . 13 H3
OLD BEXLEY, Bex. DA5 . . 159 H7
Old Billingsgate Wk, EC3 *off Lower Thames St* . . 112 B6
Old Bond St, W1 . . . . 17 F6
Oldborough Rd, Wem. HA0 87 F2
Old Brewers Yd, WC2 . . . . . 18 A4
Old Brewery Ms, NW3 *off Hampstead High St* . . 91 G4
Old Br Cl, Nthlt. UB5 . . . . 103 G2
Old Br St, Kings.T. (Hmptn W.) KT1 . . . . . . 181 G2
Old Broad St, EC2 . . . . 20 C4
Old Bromley Rd, Brom. BR1 . . . . 172 D5
Old Brompton Rd, SW5 . . 128 D5
SW7 . . . . 128 D5
Old Bldgs, WC2 . . . . 18 E3
Old Burlington St, W1 . . . . 17 F5
Oldbury Pl, W1 . . . . 16 C1
Oldbury Rd, Enf. EN1 . . . . . 44 D2
Old Canal Ms, SE15 . . . . . . 37 G4
Old Castle St, E1 . . . . 21 F2
Old Cavendish St, W1 . . . . 16 D3
Old Change Ct, EC4 *off Carter La* 111 J6
Old Chelsea Ms, SW3 . . . . 31 F6
Old Ch La, NW9 . . . . 88 C2
Greenford UB6 *off Perivale La* 104 D3
Stanmore HA7 . . . . 53 F7
Old Ch Rd, E1 . . . . 113 G6
E4 . . . . 62 A4
Old Ch St, SW3 . . . . 31 F4
Old Claygate La, Esher (Clay.) KT10 . . . . 194 D6
Old Clem Sq, SE18 *off Kempt St* 136 D6
Old Coal Yd, SE28 *off Pettman Cres* 137 G4
Old Compton St, W1 . . . . . 17 H5
Old Cote Dr, Houns. TW5 . 123 G6
Old Ct Pl, W8 . . . . 22 A3
★**Old Curiosity Shop**, WC2 . 18 C3
Old Dairy Ms, SW12 *off Chestnut Gro* 150 A7
Old Deer Pk Gdns, Rich. TW9 . . . . 145 H3
Old Devonshire Rd, SW12 . . . . 150 B7
Old Dock Cl, Rich. TW9 *off Watcombe Cotts*. . . 126 A6
Old Dover Rd, SE3 . . . . . . 135 G7
Old Fm Av, N14 . . . . 42 C7
Sidcup DA15 . . . . 175 G1
Old Fm Cl, Houns. TW4 . . 143 F4
Old Fm Pas, Hmptn. TW12 . . . . 179 J1
Old Fm Rd, N2 . . . . 73 G1
Hampton TW12 . . . . 161 F6
West Drayton UB7 . . . . 120 A2
Old Fm Rd E, Sid. DA15 . . 176 A2
Old Fm Rd W, Sid. DA15 . 175 J2
Oldfield Cl, Brom. BR1 . . . 192 C4
Greenford UB6 . . . . 86 B5
Stanmore HA7 . . . . 52 D5
Oldfield Fm Gdns, Grnf. UB6 . . . . 104 A1
Oldfield Gro, SE16 . . . . . . 133 G4
Oldfield La N, Grnf. UB6 . . 86 B6
Oldfield La S, Grnf. UB6 . . 103 J4
Oldfield Ms, N6 . . . . 74 C7
Oldfield Rd, N16 . . . . 94 B3
NW10 . . . . 89 F7
SW19 . . . . 166 B6
W3 *off Valetta Rd* 127 F2
Bexleyheath DA7 . . . . . 159 E2
Bromley BR1 . . . . 192 C4
Hampton TW12 . . . . 179 F1
Oldfields Circ, Nthlt. UB5 . . 85 J6
Oldfields Rd, Sutt. SM1 . . 198 C3
Oldfields Trd Est, Sutt. SM1 . . . . 198 D3
Old Fish St Hill, EC4 . . . . . . 19 J5
Old Fleet La, EC4 . . . . 19 G3
Old Fold Cl, Barn. EN5 *off Old Fold La* 40 C1
Old Fold La, Barn. EN5 . . . . 40 C1
Old Fold Vw, Barn. EN5 . . . 39 J3
OLD FORD, E3 . . . . 95 J7
Old Ford Rd, E2 . . . . 113 F2
E3 . . . . 113 H2
Old Forge Cl, Stan. HA7 . . . 52 D4
Old Forge Ms, W12 *off Goodwin Rd* 127 H2
Old Forge Rd, N19 *off Elthorne Rd* 92 D2
Old Forge Way, Sid. DA14 . 176 B4
Old Fox Footpath, S.Croy. CR2 *off Essenden Rd* . . 202 B7
Old Gloucester St, WC1 . . . 18 B1
Old Hall Cl, Pnr. HA5 . . . . . 67 E1
Old Hall Dr, Pnr. HA5 . . . . . 66 E1
Oldham Ter, W3 . . . . 126 C1
Old Hill, Chis. BR7 . . . . . . 192 D1
Orpington BR6 . . . . 207 G6
Oldhill St, N16 . . . . 94 D1
Old Homesdale Rd, Brom. BR2 . . . . 191 J4
Old Hosp Cl, SW12 . . . . . . 167 J1
Old Ho Cl, SW19 . . . . 166 B5
Old Ho Gdns, Twick. TW1 . 145 F5
Old Jamaica Rd, SE16 . . . . 29 H5
Old James St, SE15 . . . . . 152 E3
Old Jewry, EC2 . . . . 20 B4
Old Kenton La, NW9 . . . . . 70 B5
Old Kent Rd, SE1 . . . . 28 C6
SE15 . . . . 37 J5
Old Kingston Rd, Wor.Pk. KT4 . . . . 196 C3
Old Lo Pl, Twick. TW1 *off St. Margarets Rd* . 144/145 E6
Old Lo Way, Stan. HA7 . . . . 52 D5
Old London Rd, Kings.T. KT2 . . . . 181 H2
Old Maidstone Rd, Sid. DA14 . . . . 177 F7
OLD MALDEN, Wor.Pk. KT4 . . . . 196 D1
Old Malden La, Wor.Pk. KT4 . . . . 196 D2
Old Manor Dr, Islw. TW7 . 143 J6
Old Manor Rd, Sthl. UB2 . 122 D4
Old Manor Way, Chis. BR7 . . . . 174 C5
Old Manor Yd, SW5 *off Earls Ct Rd* . . . 128/129 E4
Old Mkt Sq, E2 . . . . 13 F3
Old Marylebone Rd, NW1 . 15 H2
Old Ms, Har. HA1 *off Hindes Rd* 68 B5
Old Mill Ct, E18 . . . . 79 J3
Old Mill Rd, SE18 . . . . 137 G6
Old Mitre Ct, EC4 *off Fleet St* 111 G6
Old Montague St, E1 . . . . . 21 H2
Old Nichol St, E2 . . . . 13 F5
Old N St, WC1 . . . . 18 C1
Old Oak Cl, Chess. KT9 . . 195 J4
OLD OAK COMMON, NW10 . . . . 107 F5
Old Oak Common La, NW10 . . . . 107 E5
W3 . . . . 107 E5
Old Oak La, NW10 . . . . . . 107 E3
Old Oak Rd, W3 . . . . 107 F7
★**Old Operating Thea Mus & Herb Garret**, SE1 . . . . . . 28 C2
Old Orchard, Sun. TW16 . . 178 C2
Old Orchard, The, NW3 *off Nassington Rd* 91 J4
Old Palace La, Rich. TW9 . 145 F5
Old Palace Rd, Croy. CR0 . 201 H3
Old Palace Ter, Rich. TW9 *off King St* 145 G5
Old Palace Yd, SW1 . . . . . . 26 A5
Richmond TW9 . . . . 145 F5
Old Paradise St, SE11 . . . . 34 C1
Old Pk Av, SW12 . . . . 150 A6
Enfield EN2 . . . . 43 J4
Old Pk Gro, Enf. EN2 . . . . . 43 J4
Old Pk La, W1 . . . . 24 C2
Old Pk Ms, Houns. TW5 . . 123 F7
Old Pk Ridings, N21 . . . . . . 43 H6
Old Pk Rd, N13 . . . . 59 F4
SE2 . . . . 138 A5
Enfield EN2 . . . . 43 H3
Old Pk Rd S, Enf. EN2 . . . . 43 H4
Old Pk Vw, Enf. EN2 . . . . . 43 G3
Old Perry St, Chis. BR7 . . 175 H7
Old PO La, SE3 *off Kidbrooke Pk Rd* . . 155 H3
Old Pound Cl, Islw. TW7 . . 144 D1
Old Pye St, SW1 . . . . 25 H5
Old Quebec St, W1 . . . . . . 16 A4
Old Queen St, SW1 . . . . . . 25 J4
Old Rectory Gdns, Edg. HA8 . . . . 54 A6
Old Redding, Har. HA3 . . . . 51 J4
Oldridge Rd, SW12 . . . . . . 150 A7
Old River Lea Towpath, E15 *off City Mill River Towpath* 96 B7
Old Rd, SE13 . . . . 155 E4
Enfield EN3 . . . . 45 F1
Old Rope Wk, Sun. TW16 *off The Avenue* 178 B3
Old Royal Free Pl, N1 *off Liverpool Rd* 111 G1
Old Royal Free Sq, N1 . . . 111 G1
Old Ruislip Rd, Nthlt. UB5 . 102 D2
Old Savill's Cotts, Chig. IG7 *off The Chase* 65 F4
Old Sch Cl, SE10 . . . . 135 E3
SW19 . . . . 184 D2
Beckenham BR3 . . . . . . 189 G2
Old Sch Cres, E7 . . . . 97 F6
Old Sch Pl, Croy. CR0 . . . . 201 G4
Old Sch Sq, E14 *off Pelling St* 114 A6
Thames Ditton KT7 . . . . 180 C6
Old Seacoal La, EC4 . . . . . . 19 G3
Old S Cl, Pnr. HA5 . . . . 66 D1
Old S Lambeth Rd, SW8 . . 34 B7
★**Old Spitalfields Mkt**, E1 . 21 F1
Old Sq, WC2 . . . . 18 D3
Old Sta Rd, Hayes UB3 . . 121 J3
Loughton IG10 . . . . 48 B5
Old Sta Yd, Brom. BR2 *off Bourne Way* 205 F1
Oldstead Rd, Brom. BR1 . 172 D4
Old Stockley Rd, West Dr. UB7 . . . . 120 E2
Old St, E13 . . . . 115 H2
EC1 . . . . 11 J5
Old Swan Yd, Cars. SM5 . 199 J4
Old Town, SW4 . . . . 150 C3
Croydon CR0 . . . . 201 H3
Old Tram Yd, SE18 *off Lakedale Rd* 137 H4
Old Woolwich Rd, SE10 . . 134 D6
Old York Rd, SW18 . . . . . . 149 E5
Oleander Cl, Orp. BR6 . . . 207 G5
O'Leary Sq, E1 . . . . 113 F5
Olga St, E3 . . . . 113 H2
Olinda Rd, N16 . . . . 76 C6
Oliphant St, W10 . . . . 108 A3
Oliver Av, SE25 . . . . 188 C3
Oliver Cl, W4 . . . . 126 B6
Oliver Gdns, E6 . . . . 116 B6
Oliver-Goldsmith Est, SE15 . . . . 152 D1
Oliver Gro, SE25 . . . . 188 C4
Oliver Ms, SE15 . . . . 152 D2
Olive Rd, E13 . . . . 115 J3
NW2 . . . . 89 J4
SW19 *off Norman Rd* . . 167 F7
W5 . . . . 125 G3
Oliver Rd, E10 . . . . 96 B2
E17 . . . . 78 C5
NW10 . . . . 106 C2
New Malden KT3 . . . . . 182 C2
Sutton SM1 . . . . 199 G4
Olivers Yd, EC1 . . . . 12 C5
Olivette St, SW15 . . . . . . 148 A3
Ollards Gro, Loug. IG10 . . . 48 A4
Ollerton Grn, E3 . . . . 113 J1
Ollerton Rd, N11 . . . . 58 D5
Olley Cl, Wall. SM6 . . . . . . 200 E7
Ollgar Cl, W12 . . . . 127 F1
Olliffe St, E14 . . . . 134 C3
Olmar St, SE1 . . . . 37 H5
Olney Rd, SE17 . . . . 35 J5
Olron Cres, Bexh. DA6 . . . 158 D5
Olven Rd, SE18 . . . . 137 F7
Olveston Wk, Cars. SM5 . 185 G6
Olwen Ms, Pnr. HA5 . . . . . 66 D2
Olyffe Av, Well. DA16 . . . . 158 A2
Olyffe Dr, Beck. BR3 . . . . . 190 C1
★**Olympia**, W14 . . . . 128 B3
Olympia Ms, W2 . . . . 14 B6
Olympia Way, W14 . . . . . . 128 B3
Olympic Way, Grnf. UB6 . 103 H1
Wembley HA9 . . . . 88 A4
Olympus Sq, E5 *off Nolan Way* 94 D4
Oman Av, NW2 . . . . 89 J4
O'Meara St, SE1 . . . . 28 A2
Omega Cl, E14 *off Tiller Rd* 134 B3
Omega Pl, N1 . . . . 10 B2
Omega St, SE14 . . . . 154 A1
Ommaney Rd, SE14 . . . . . 153 G1
Omnibus Way, E17 . . . . 78 A2
Ondine Rd, SE15 . . . . 152 C4
Onega Gate, SE16 . . . . . . 133 H3
O'Neill Path, SE18 *off Kempt St* 136 D6
One Tree Cl, SE23 . . . . 153 F6
Ongar Cl, Rom. RM6 . . . . . 82 C5
Ongar Rd, SW6 . . . . 128 D6
Onra Rd, E17 . . . . 78 A7
Onslow Av, Rich. TW10 . . 145 H5
Onslow Cl, E4 . . . . 62 C2
Thames Ditton KT7 . . . . 194 B1
Onslow Cres, Chis. BR7 . . 192 E1
Onslow Dr, Sid. DA14 . . . 176 D2
Onslow Gdns, E18 . . . . 79 H3
N10 . . . . 74 D5
N21 . . . . 43 G5
SW7 . . . . 30 E2
Thames Ditton KT7 . . . . 194 B1
Wallington SM6 . . . . . . 200 C6
Onslow Ms E, SW7 . . . . . . 31 E2
Onslow Ms W, SW7 . . . . . . 30 E2
Onslow Rd, Croy. CR0 . . . 187 F7
New Malden KT3 . . . . . 183 G4
Richmond TW10 . . . . . . 145 H5
Onslow Sq, SW7 . . . . 31 F1
Onslow St, EC1 . . . . 11 F6
Onslow Way, T.Ditt. KT7 . . 194 B1
Ontario St, SE1 . . . . 27 H6
Ontario Way, E14 . . . . 114 A7
On The Hill, Wat. WD19 . . . 50 E2
Onyx Ms, E15 *off Vicarage La* 96 E6
Opal Cl, E16 . . . . 116 A6
Opal Ms, NW6 *off Priory Pk Rd* 108 C1
Ilford IG1 *off Ley St* 98/99 E2
Opal St, SE11 . . . . 35 G2
Openshaw Rd, SE2 . . . . . 138 B4
Openview, SW18 . . . . 167 F1
Ophelia Gdns, NW2 *off Hamlet Sq* 90 B3
Ophir Ter, SE15 . . . . 152 D1
Opossum Way, Houns. TW4 . . . . 142 C2
Oppenheim Rd, SE13 . . . . 154 C2
Oppidans Ms, NW3 *off Meadowbank* 91 J7
Oppidans Rd, NW3 . . . . . . 91 J7

Orange Ct, E1 29 J2
Orange Gro, E11 96 E3
Chigwell IG7 65 F6
Orange Hill Rd, Edg. HA8 54 C7
Orange Pl, SE16
off Lower Rd 133 F3
Orangery, The, Rich. TW10 163 F2
Orangery La, SE9 156 C5
Orange Sq, SW1 32 C2
Orange St, WC2 17 H6
Orange Yd, W1 17 J4
Oransay Rd, N1 93 J6
Oransay Wk, N1
off Clephane Rd 93 J6
Oratory La, SW3 31 F3
Orbain Rd, SW6 128 B7
Orbel St, SW11 149 H1
Orb St, SE17 36 B2
Orchard, The, N14 42 B5
N21 44 A6
NW11 72 D5
SE3 154 D2
W4 126 D4
W5 105 G5
Epsom KT17 197 F7
Hounslow TW3 143 J2
Orchard Av, N3 72 D3
N14 42 C6
N20 57 G2
Belvedere DA17 139 E6
Croydon CR0 189 H7
Feltham TW14 141 G5
Hounslow TW5 123 E7
Mitcham CR4 200 A1
New Malden KT3 183 E2
Southall UB1 123 E1
Thames Ditton KT7 194 D1
Orchard Cl, E4
off Chingford Mt Rd 62 A4
E11 79 H4
N1 *off Morton Rd* 93 J7
NW2 89 G3
SE23
off Brenchley Gdns 153 F6
SW20 *off Grand Dr* 183 J4
W10 108 B5
Bexleyheath DA7 158 E1
Bushey (Bushey Hth)
WD23 52 A1
Edgware HA8 53 H6
Epsom (W.Ewell) KT19 196 B6
Northolt UB5 85 J5
Surbiton KT6 181 E7
Walton-on-Thames
KT12 178 B7
Wembley HA0 105 H1
Orchard Ct, Islw. TW7
off Thornbury Av 144 A1
Twickenham TW2 162 A2
Wallington SM6
off Parkgate Rd 200 B5
Worcester Park KT4 197 G1
Orchard Cres, Edg. HA8 54 C5
Enfield EN1 44 C1
Orchard Dr, SE3
off Orchard Rd 154/155 E2
Edgware HA8 53 J5
Orchard Est, Wdf.Grn. IG8 63 J7
Orchard Gdns, Chess.
KT9 195 H4
Sutton SM1 198 D5
Orchard Gate, NW9 70 E4
Esher KT10 194 A1
Greenford UB6 86 E6
Orchard Grn, Orp. BR6 207 H2
Orchard Gro, SE20 170 D7
Croydon CR0 189 H7
Edgware HA8 70 A1
Harrow HA3 69 J5
Orpington BR6 207 J2
Orchard Hill, SE13
off Coldbath St 154 B2
Carshalton SM5 199 J5
Orchard La, SW20 183 H1
East Molesey KT8 180 A6
Woodford Green IG8 63 J4
Orchardleigh Av, Enf. EN3 45 F2
Orchardmede, N21 44 A6
Orchard Ms, N1
off Southgate Gro 94 A7
Orchard Pl, E5 95 E5
E14 114 E7
N17 60 C7
Orchard Ri, Croy. CR0 203 H1
Kingston upon Thames
KT2 182 C1
Richmond TW10 146 B4
Orchard Ri E, Sid. DA15 157 J5
Orchard Ri W, Sid. DA15 157 H5
Orchard Rd, N6 74 B7
SE3 154 E2
SE18 137 G4
Barnet EN5 40 C4
Belvedere DA17 139 G4
Brentford TW8 125 F6
Bromley BR1 191 J1
Chessington KT9 195 H4
Dagenham RM10 119 G1
Enfield EN3 45 F5
Hampton TW12 161 F7
Hounslow TW4 143 F5
Kingston upon Thames
KT1 181 H2
Mitcham CR4 200 A1
Orpington (Farnboro.)
BR6 207 E5
Richmond TW9 146 A3
Romford RM7 83 H1
Sidcup DA14 175 H4
Sunbury-on-Thames TW16
off Hanworth Rd 160 B7
Sutton SM1 198 D5
Twickenham TW1 144 D5
Welling DA16 158 B3
Orchardson St, NW8 7 E6
Orchard Sq, W14
off Sun Rd 128 C5
Orchard St, E17 77 H4
W1 16 B4
Orchard Ter, Enf. EN1
off Great Cambridge Rd 44 D6
Orchard Vil, Sid. DA14 176 C6
Orchard Way, Beck. BR3 189 H5
Croydon CR0 203 H1
Enfield EN1 44 B3
Sutton SM1 199 G4
Orchid Cl, E6 116 B5
Chessington KT9 195 F7
Southall UB1 103 E6
Orchid Rd, N14 42 C7
Orchid St, W12 107 G7
Orde Hall St, WC1 10 C6
Ordell Rd, E3 113 J2
Ordnance Cl, Felt. TW13 160 A3
Ordnance Cres, SE10 134 D2
Ordnance Hill, NW8 109 G1
Ordnance Ms, NW8 7 F1
Ordnance Rd, E16 115 F5
SE18 136 D6
Oregano Dr, E14 114 D6
Oregon Av, E12 98 C4
Oregon Cl, N.Mal. KT3
off Georgia Rd 182 C4
Oregon Sq, Orp. BR6 207 G1
Orestes Ms, NW6
off Aldred Rd 90 D5
Orford Ct, SE27 169 H2
Orford Gdns, Twick. TW1 162 C2
Orford Rd, E17 78 A5
E18 79 H3
SE6 172 B3
Organ La, E4 62 C2
Oriel Cl, Mitch. CR4 186 D4
Oriel Ct, NW3
off Heath St 91 F4
Oriel Dr, SW13 127 H6
Oriel Gdns, Ilf. IG5 80 C3
Oriel Pl, NW3
off Heath St 91 F4
Oriel Rd, E9 95 G6
Oriel Way, Nthlt. UB5 85 H7
Oriental Rd, E16 136 A1
Oriental St, E14
off Morant St 114 A7
Orient Ind Pk, E10 96 A2
Orient St, SE11 35 G1
Orient Way, E5 95 G3
E10 95 H2
Oriole Way, SE28 118 B7
Orion Pt, E14
off Crews St 134 A4
Orion Rd, N11 58 B6
Orissa Rd, SE18 137 H5
Orkney St, SW11 150 A2
Orlando Rd, SW4 150 C3
Orleans Cl, Esher KT10 194 A2
★**Orleans Ho Gall**, Twick.
TW1 163 E1
Orleans Rd, SE19 170 A6
Twickenham TW1 145 E7
Orleston Ms, N7 93 G6
Orleston Rd, N7 93 G6
Orley Fm Rd, Har. HA1 86 B3
Orlop St, SE10 134 E5
Ormanton Rd, SE26 170 D4
Orme Ct, W2 14 A6
Orme Ct Ms, W2 14 B6
Orme La, W2 14 A6
Ormeley Rd, SW12 168 B1
Orme Rd, Kings.T. KT1 182 B2
Sutton SM1
off Grove Rd 198/199 E6
Ormerod Gdns, Mitch.
CR4 186 A2
Ormesby Cl, SE28
off Wroxham Rd 118 D7
Ormesby Way, Har. HA3 69 J6
Orme Sq, W2 14 A6
Ormiston Gro, W12 127 H1
Ormiston Rd, SE10 135 G5
Ormond Av, Hmptn.
TW12 179 H1
Richmond TW10
off Ormond Rd 145 G5
Ormond Cl, WC1 18 B1
Ormond Cres, Hmptn.
TW12 179 H1
Ormond Dr, Hmptn.
TW12 161 H7
Ormonde Av, Orp. BR6 207 F2
Ormonde Gate, SW3 32 A4
Ormonde Pl, SW1 32 B2
Ormonde Ri, Buck.H. IG9 63 J1
Ormonde Rd, SW14 146 B3
Ormonde Ter, NW8 109 J1
Ormond Ms, WC1 10 B6
Ormond Rd, N19 93 E1
Richmond TW10 145 G5
Ormond Yd, SW1 25 G1
Ormsby, Sutt. SM2
off Grange Rd 198/199 E7
Ormsby Gdns, Grnf. UB6 103 J2
Ormsby Pl, N16
off Victorian Gro 94 C3
Ormsby Pt, SE18
off Troy Ct 136/137 E4
Ormsby St, E2 13 F1
Ormside St, SE15 133 F6
Ormskirk Rd, Wat. WD19 50 D4
Ornan Rd, NW3 91 H5
Orpen Wk, N16 94 B3
Orpheus St, SE5 152 A1
ORPINGTON, BR5 &
BR6 207 H1
Orpington Gdns, N18 60 B3
Orpington Rd, N21 59 H1
Chislehurst BR7 193 H3
Orpwood Cl, Hmptn.
TW12 161 F5
Orsett St, SE11 34 D3
Orsett Ter, W2 14 B3
Woodford Green IG8 79 J1
Orsman Rd, N1 112 B1
Orton St, E1 29 H2
Orville Rd, SW11 149 G2
Orwell Ct, N5 93 J4
Orwell Rd, E13 115 J2
Osbaldeston Rd, N16 94 D2
Osberton Rd, SE12 155 G5
Osbert St, SW1 33 H2
Osborn Cl, E8 112 D1
Osborne Cl, Barn. EN4 41 J3
Beckenham BR3 189 H4
Feltham TW13 160 D5
Osborne Gdns, Th.Hth.
CR7 187 J2
Osborne Gro, E17 77 J4
N4 93 G1
Osborne Ms, E17
off Osborne Gro 77 J4
Osborne Pl, Sutt. SM1 199 G5
Osborne Rd, E7 97 H5
E9 95 J6
E10 96 B3
N4 93 F1
N13 59 G3
NW2 89 H6
W3 126 B3
Belvedere DA17 139 F5
Buckhurst Hill IG9 63 H1
Dagenham RM9 101 F5
Enfield EN3 45 H2
Hounslow TW3 143 F3
Kingston upon Thames
KT2 163 H7
Southall UB1 103 J6
Thornton Heath CR7 187 J2
Osborne Sq, Dag. RM9 101 F4
Osborne Ter, SW17
off Church La 168 A5
Osborne Way, Chess. KT9
off Bridge Rd 195 J5
Osborn Gdns, NW7 56 A7
Osborn La, SE23 153 H7
Osborn St, E1 21 G2
Osborn Ter, SE3
off Lee Rd 155 F4
Osbourne Av, NW7 56 A7
Oscar Faber Pl, N1
off St. Peter's Way 94 B7
Oscar St, SE8 154 A1
Oseney Cres, NW5 92 C6
Osgood Av, Orp. BR6 207 J5
Osgood Gdns, Orp. BR6 207 J5
OSIDGE, N14 58 B1
Osidge La, N14 58 A1
Osier Cres, N10 73 J1
Osier La, SE10 135 F3
Osier Ms, W4 127 F6
Osiers Rd, SW18 148 D4
Osier St, E1 113 F4
Osier Way, E10 96 B3
Mitcham CR4 185 H5
Oslac Rd, SE6 172 B5
Oslo Ct, NW8 7 G2
Oslo Sq, SE16 133 H3
Osman Cl, N15
off Tewkesbury Rd 76 A6
Osman Rd, N9 60 D3
W6 *off Batoum Gdns* 127 J3
Osmond Cl, Har. HA2 85 J2
Osmond Gdns, Wall.
SM6 200 C5
Osmund St, W12
off Braybrook St 107 F6
Osnaburgh St, NW1 9 E6
NW1 (north section) 9 E4
Osnaburgh Ter, NW1 8 E5
Osney Ho, SE2
off Hartslock Dr 138 D2
Osney Wk, Cars. SM5 185 G6
Osprey Cl, E6
off Dove App 116 B5
E11 79 G4
E17 61 H7
Sutton SM1
off Sandpiper Rd 198 C5
West Drayton UB7 120 A2
Osprey Hts, SW11
off Bramlands Cl 149 H3
Osprey Ms, Enf. EN3 45 E5
Ospringe Cl, SE20 171 F7
Ospringe Ct, SE9
off Alderwood Rd 157 G6
Ospringe Rd, NW5 92 C4
Osram Ct, W6
off Lena Gdns 127 J3
Osram Rd, Wem. HA9 87 G3
Osric Path, N1 12 D2
Ossian Ms, N4 75 F7
Ossian Rd, N4 75 F7
Ossington Bldgs, W1 16 B1
Ossington Cl, W2
off Ossington St 108/109 E7
Ossington St, W2 108 D7
Ossory Rd, SE1 37 H4
Ossulston St, NW1 9 H2
Ossulton Pl, N2
off East End Rd 73 F3
Ossulton Way, N2 73 F4
Ostade Rd, SW2 151 F7
Osten Ms, SW7 22 B6
OSTERLEY, Islw. TW7 123 J7
Osterley Av, Islw. TW7 124 A7
Osterley Ct, Islw. TW7 144 A1
Osterley Cres, Islw. TW7 144 B1
Osterley Gdns, Th.Hth.
CR7 187 J2
Osterley Ho, E14
off Giraud St 114 B6
Osterley La, Islw. TW7 124 B5
Southall UB2 123 G5
Osterley Pk, Islw. TW7 124 A5
★**Osterley Park Ho**, Islw.
TW7 123 J5
Osterley Pk Rd, Sthl. UB2 123 F3
Osterley Pk Vw Rd, W7 124 B2
Osterley Rd, N16 94 B4
Isleworth TW7 124 B7
Osterley Views, Sthl. UB2
off West Pk Rd 123 J1
Oster Ter, E17
off Southcote Rd 77 G5
Ostliffe Rd, N13 59 J5
Oswald Rd, Sthl. UB1 123 E1
Oswald's Mead, E9
off Lindisfarne Way 95 H4
Oswald St, E5 95 G3
Oswald Ter, NW2
off Temple Rd 89 J3
Osward Pl, N9 60 E2
Osward Rd, SW17 167 J2
Oswell Ho, E1 133 E1
Oswin St, SE11 35 H1
Oswyth Rd, SE5 152 B2
Otford Cl, SE20 189 F1

Otford Cl, Bex. DA5
off Southwold Rd **159** H6
Bromley BR1 .... **192** D3
Otford Cres, SE4 ...... **153** J6
Othello Cl, SE11 .... **35** G3
Otho Ct, Brent. TW8 .... **125** G7
Otis St, E3 .... **114** C3
Otley App, Ilf. IG2 .... **81** E6
Otley Dr, Ilf. IG2 .... **80** E5
Otley Rd, E10 .... **115** J6
Otley Ter, E5 .... **95** G2
Otley Way, Wat. WD19 .... **50** C3
Ottaway St, E5
off Stellman Cl **94** D3
Ottenden Cl, Orp. BR6
off Southfleet Rd **207** H4
Otterbourne Rd, E4 ..... **62** D3
Croydon CR0 .... **201** J2
Otterburn Gdns, Islw.
TW7 .... **124** D7
Otterburn Ho, SE5 ...... **35** J7
Otterburn St, SW17 .... **167** J6
Otter Cl, E15 .... **114** C1
Otterden St, SE6 ...... **172** A4
Otter Rd, Grnf. UB6 .... **103** J4
Otto Cl, SE26 .... **170** E3
Otto St, SE17 .... **35** G6
Oulton Cl, E5
off Mundford Rd **95** F2
SE28
off Rollesby Way **118** C6
Oulton Cres, Bark. IG11 ... **99** J6
Oulton Rd, N15 .... **76** A5
Oulton Way, Wat. WD19 ... **51** E4
Ouseley Rd, SW12 ...... **167** J1
Outer Circle, NW1 .... **8** B6
Outgate Rd, NW10 ...... **89** F7
Outram Pl, N1 .... **111** E1
Outram Rd, E6 .... **116** B1
N22 .... **74** D1
Croydon CR0 .... **202** C1
Outwich St, EC3 .... **20** E3
★**Oval, The, Surrey County** ..
Cricket Club, SE11 .... **34** D5
Oval, The, E2 .... **112** E2
Sidcup DA15 .... **158** A7
Oval Pl, SW8 .... **34** C7
Oval Rd, NW1 .... **110** B1
Croydon CR0 .... **202** B1
Oval Rd N, Dag. RM10 ... **119** H1
Oval Rd S, Dag. RM10 ... **119** H2
Oval Way, SE11 .... **34** D4
Overbrae, Beck. BR3 .... **172** A6
Overbrook Wk, Edg. HA8 .. **54** A7
Overbury Av, Beck. BR3 .. **190** B3
Overbury Rd, N15 .... **76** A6
Overbury St, E5 .... **95** G4
Overcliff Rd, SE13 ...... **154** A3
Overcourt Cl, Sid. DA15 .. **158** B6
Overdale Av, N.Mal. KT3 . **182** C2
Overdale Rd, W5 .... **125** F3
Overdown Rd, SE6 ...... **172** A4
Overhill Rd, SE22 ...... **152** D7
Overhill Way, Beck. BR3 .. **190** D5
Overlea Rd, E5 .... **76** D7
Overmead, Sid. DA15 .... **157** G7
Oversley Ho, W2 .... **108** D5
Overstand Cl, Beck. BR3 . **190** A5
Overstone Gdns, Croy.
CR0 .... **189** J7
Overstone Rd, W6 ...... **127** J3
Overton Cl, NW10 .... **88** C6
Isleworth TW7
off Avenue Rd **144** C1
Overton Ct, E11 .... **79** G7
Overton Dr, E11 .... **79** H7
Romford RM6 .... **82** C7
Overton Ho, SW15
off Tangley Gro **147** F7
Overton Rd, E10 .... **95** H1
N14 .... **42** E5
SE2 .... **138** C3
SW9 .... **151** G2
Sutton SM2 .... **198** D6
Overton Rd E, SE2 ...... **138** D3
Overtons Yd, Croy. CR0 .. **201** J3
Ovesdon Av, Har. HA2 .... **85** F1
Ovett Cl, SE19 .... **170** B6
Ovex Cl, E14 .... **134** C2
Ovington Gdns, SW3 ..... **23** H6
Ovington Ms, SW3 ...... **23** H6
Ovington Sq, SW3 ...... **23** H6
Ovington St, SW3 ...... **23** H6
Owen Cl, SE28 .... **138** C1
Croydon CR0 .... **188** A6
Hayes UB4 .... **102** B3
Owen Gdns, Wdf.Grn. IG8 .. **64** B6
Owenite St, SE2 .... **138** B4
Owen Rd, N13 .... **59** J5
Owen Rd, Hayes UB4 .... **102** B3
Owen's Ct, EC1 .... **11** G3
Owen's Row, EC1 .... **11** G3
Owen St, EC1 .... **11** G2
Owens Way, SE23 ...... **153** H7
Owen Wk, SE20
off Sycamore Gro **170** D7
Owen Waters Ho, Ilf.
IG5 .... **80** C1
Owen Way, NW10 .... **88** C6
Owgan Cl, SE5
off Benhill Rd **132** A7
Owl Pk, Loug. (High Beach)
IG10 .... **47** F2
Oxberry Av, SW6 .... **148** B2
Oxendon St, SW1 .... **17** H6
Oxenford St, SE15 ...... **152** C3
Oxenholme, NW1 .... **9** G2
Oxenpark Av, Wem. HA9 .. **69** H7
Oxestalls Rd, SE8 .... **133** H5
Oxford Av, SW20 .... **184** B2
Hayes UB3 .... **121** J7
Hounslow TW5 .... **123** G5
★**Oxford Circ**, W1 .... **17** F3
Oxford Circ Av, W1 ...... **17** F4
Oxford Cl, N9 .... **60** E2
Mitcham CR4 .... **186** C3
Oxford Ct, EC4 .... **20** B5
W3 .... **106** A6
Feltham TW13
off Oxford Way **160** D4
Oxford Cres, N.Mal. KT3 . **182** D6
Oxford Dr, SE1 .... **28** D2
Ruislip HA4 .... **84** C2
Oxford Gdns, N20 .... **57** G1
N21 .... **43** J7
W4 .... **126** A5
W10 .... **108** B6
Oxford Gate, W6 .... **128** A4
Oxford Ms, Bex. DA5 .... **159** G7
Oxford Pl, NW10
off Neasden La N **88** D3
Oxford Rd, E15 .... **96** D6
N4 .... **93** G1
N9 .... **61** E2
NW6 .... **108** D2
SE19 .... **170** A6
SW15 .... **148** B4
W5 .... **105** G7
Carshalton SM5 ...... **199** H6
Enfield EN3 .... **45** E5
Harrow HA1 .... **67** J6
Harrow (Wldste) HA3 ... **68** C3
Ilford IG1 .... **99** F4
Sidcup DA14 .... **176** B5
Teddington TW11 ...... **162** A5
Wallington SM6 .... **200** C5
Woodford Green IG8 ... **63** J5
Oxford Rd N, W4 .... **126** B6
Oxford Rd S, W4 .... **126** A5
Oxford Sq, W2 .... **15** H4
Oxford St, W1 .... **17** G3
Oxford Wk, Sthl. UB1 .... **123** F1
Oxford Way, Felt. TW13 .. **160** D4
Oxgate Gdns, NW2 ...... **89** H3
Oxgate La, NW2 .... **89** H2
Oxhawth Cres, Brom.
BR2 .... **192** D5
Oxhey Dr, Nthwd. HA6 ... **50** B5
Watford WD19 .... **50** C3
Oxhey Dr S, Nthwd. HA6 .. **50** B5
Oxhey La, Har. HA3 ...... **51** G5
Pinner HA5 .... **51** G5
Watford WD19 .... **51** F2
Oxhey Ridge Cl, Nthwd.
HA6 .... **50** A5
Oxleas, E6 .... **116** E6
Oxleas Cl, Well. DA16 .... **157** G2
Oxleay Ct, Har. HA2 ...... **85** G1
Oxleay Rd, Har. HA2 ..... **85** G1
Oxleigh Cl, N.Mal. KT3 ... **183** E5
Oxley Cl, SE1 .... **37** G3
Oxleys Rd, NW2 .... **89** H3
Oxlip Cl, Croy. CR0
off Marigold Way **203** G1
Oxlow La, Dag. RM9,
RM10 .... **101** G4
Oxonian St, SE22 .... **152** C4
Oxo Twr Wf, SE1 .... **19** F6
Oxted Cl, Mitch. CR4 .... **185** G3
Oxtoby Way, SW16 ...... **186** D2
Oyster Catchers Cl, E16
off Freemasons Rd ... **115** H6
Oyster Catcher Ter, Ilf. IG5
off Tiptree Cres **80** D3
Oystergate Wk, EC4
off Upper Thames St .. **112** A7
Oyster Row, E1
off Lukin St **113** F6
Oyster Wf, SW11
off Lombard Rd **149** G2
Ozolins Way, E16 .... **115** G6

P

Pablo Neruda Cl, SE24
off Shakespeare Rd ... **151** H4
Pace Pl, E1
off Bigland St **112/113** E6
Pacific Rd, E16 .... **115** G6
Pacific Wf, SE16
off Rotherhithe St **133** G1
Packham Ct, Wor.Pk. KT4
off Lavender Av **197** J3
Packington Rd, W3 ...... **126** C3
Packington Sq, N1 ...... **111** J1
Packington St, N1 .... **111** H1
Packmores Rd, SE9 ..... **157** G5
Padbury, SE17 .... **36** D4
Padbury Ct, E2 .... **13** G4
Padcroft Rd, West Dr.
UB7 .... **120** A1
Padden Ct, NW7
off Bittacy Hill **56** B7
Paddenswick Rd, W6 .... **127** G3
PADDINGTON, W2 .... **14** C2
Paddington Cl, Hayes
UB4 .... **102** D4
Paddington Grn, W2 ...... **15** F1
Paddington St, W1 .... **16** B1
Paddock Cl, SE3 .... **155** G2
SE26 .... **171** G4
Northolt UB5 .... **103** G2
Orpington BR6
off State Fm Av .. **206/207** E4
Worcester Park KT4 .... **196** E1
Paddock Gdns, SE19
off Westow St **170** B6
Paddock Rd, NW2 .... **89** G3
Bexleyheath DA6 ..... **159** E4
Ruislip HA4 .... **84** D3
Paddocks, The, NW7 ..... **56** B6
Barnet EN4 .... **41** J3
Wembley HA9 .... **88** B2
Paddocks Cl, Har. HA2 .... **86** H1
Paddock Way, SW15 ..... **147** J7
Chislehurst BR7 ...... **175** G7
Padfield Ct, Wem. HA9
off Forty Av **87** J3
Padfield Rd, SE5 .... **151** J3
Padley Cl, Chess. KT9 ... **195** J5
Padnall Ct, Rom. RM6
off Padnall Rd **82** D3
Padnall Rd, Rom. RM6 .... **82** D4
Padstow Cl, Orp. BR6 ... **207** J4
Padstow Rd, Enf. EN2 .... **43** H2
Padua Rd, SE20 .... **189** F1
Pagden St, SW8 .... **150** B1
Pageant Av, NW9 .... **70** D1
Pageant Cres, SE16
off Rotherhithe St **133** H1
Pageantmaster Ct, EC4 ... **19** G4
Pageant Wk, Croy. CR0 .. **202** B3
Page Av, Wem. HA9 ...... **88** C3
Page Cl, Dag. RM9 ...... **101** E5
Hampton TW12 .... **161** E6
Harrow HA3 .... **69** J6
Page Cres, Croy. CR0 .... **201** G5
Page Grn Rd, N15 .... **76** D5
Page Grn Ter, N15 .... **76** C5
Page Heath La, Brom.
BR1 .... **192** A3
Page Heath Vil, Brom.
BR1 .... **192** A3
Pagehurst Rd, Croy. CR0 . **188** E7
Page Meadow, NW7 ..... **55** G7
Page Rd, Felt. TW14 ..... **141** G6
Pages Hill, N10 .... **74** A2
Pages La, N10 .... **74** A2
Page St, NW7 .... **71** G1
SW1 .... **33** J1
Pages Wk, SE1 .... **36** D1
Pages Yd, W4
off Church St **126/127** E6
Paget Av, Sutt. SM1 ..... **199** G3
Paget Cl, Hmptn. TW12 .. **162** A4
Paget Gdns, Chis. BR7 ... **192** E1
Paget La, Islw. TW7 ..... **144** A3
Paget Pl, Kings.T. KT2 .. **164** C6
Thames Ditton KT7
off Brooklands Rd **194** D1
Paget Ri, SE18 .... **136** D7
Paget Rd, N16 .... **94** A1
Ilford IG1 .... **98** E4
Paget St, EC1 .... **11** G3
Paget Ter, SE18 .... **136** D6
Pagitts Gro, Barn. EN4 .... **40** E1
Pagnell St, SE14 .... **133** J7
Pagoda Av, Rich. TW9 .... **145** J3
Pagoda Gdns, SE3 ...... **154** D2
Pagoda Vista, Rich. TW9 .. **145** J2
Paignton Rd, N15 .... **76** B6
Ruislip HA4 .... **84** A3
Paines Cl, Pnr. HA5 ...... **67** E3
Paines La, Pnr. HA5 ...... **66** E1
Pains Cl, Mitch. CR4 ..... **186** B2
Painsthorpe Rd, N16
off Oldfield Rd **94** B3
Painters Ms, SE16
off Macks Rd **132** D4
Painters Rd, Ilf. IG2 ...... **81** J3
Paisley Rd, N22 .... **75** H1
Carshalton SM5 ...... **199** G1
Pakeman St, N7 .... **93** F3
Pakenham Cl, SW12
off Balham Pk Rd **168** A1
Pakenham St, WC1 .... **10** D4
Palace Av, W8 .... **22** B2
Palace Ct, NW3 .... **91** E5
W2 .... **14** A5
Bromley BR1
off Palace Gro **191** H1
Harrow HA3 .... **69** H6
Palace Ct Gdns, N10 ..... **74** C3
Palace Gdns, Buck.H. IG9 .. **64** A1
Palace Gdns Ms, W8 .... **128** D1
Palace Gdns Prec, Enf. EN2
off Sydney Rd **44** A3
Palace Gdns Ter, W8 ..... **128** D1
Palace Gate, W8 .... **22** C4
Palace Gates Rd, N22 ..... **74** D1
Palace Grn, W8 .... **22** B3
Croydon CR0 .... **203** J7
Palace Gro, SE19 .... **170** C7
Bromley BR1 .... **191** H1
Palace Ms, E17 .... **77** J4
SW1 .... **32** C2
SW6
off Hartismere Rd **128** C7
Palace of Industry, Wem.
HA9 .... **88** A4
Palace Par, E17 .... **78** A4
Palace Pl, SW1 .... **25** F5
Palace Rd, N8 .... **74** D5
N11 .... **58** E7
SE19 .... **170** C7
SW2 .... **169** F1
Bromley BR1 .... **191** H1
East Molesey KT8 ..... **180** A3
Kingston upon Thames
KT1 .... **181** G4
Ruislip HA4 .... **84** E4
Palace Rd Est, SW2 ..... **169** F1
Palace Sq, SE19 .... **170** C7
Palace St, SW1 .... **25** F5
Palace Vw, SE12 .... **173** G2
Bromley BR1 .... **191** G3
Croydon CR0 .... **203** J4
Palace Vw Rd, E4 .... **62** B5
Palamos Rd, E10 .... **96** A1
Palatine Av, N16
off Stoke Newington Rd . **94** C4
Palatine Rd, N16 .... **94** B4
Palermo Rd, NW10 ...... **107** G2
Palestine Gro, SW19 .... **185** G1
Palewell Common Dr,
SW14 .... **146** D5
Palewell Pk, SW14 ...... **146** D5
Paley Gdns, Loug. IG10 ... **49** E3
Palfrey Pl, SW8 .... **34** D7
Palgrave Av, Sthl. UB1 ... **103** G7
Palgrave Gdns, NW1 ...... **7** H5
Palgrave Rd, W12 .... **127** F3
Palissy St, E2 .... **13** F4
Palladino Ho, SW17
off Laurel Cl **167** H5
Pallant Way, Orp. BR6 ... **206** D3
Pallet Way, SE18 .... **156** B1
Palliser Rd, W14 .... **128** B5
Pallister Ter, SW15
off Roehampton Vale . **165** F3
Pall Mall, SW1 .... **25** G2
Pall Mall E, SW1 .... **25** J1
Palmar Cres, Bexh. DA7 .. **159** G3
Palmar Rd, Bexh. DA7 ... **159** G2
Palm Av, Sid. DA14 ...... **176** D6
Palm Cl, E10 .... **96** B3
Palmeira Rd, Bexh. DA7 .. **158** D3
Palmer Av, Sutt. SM3 .... **197** J4
Palmer Cl, Houns. TW5 ... **143** G1
West Wickham BR4 .... **204** D3
Palmer Cres, Kings.T. KT1 . **181** H3
Palmer Gdns, Barn. EN5 .. **40** A5
Palmer Pl, N7 .... **93** G5
Palmer Rd, E13 .... **115** H4
Dagenham RM8 ...... **100** D1

PALMERS GREEN, N13 . . . 59 G3
Palmers Gro, W.Mol. KT8. 179 G4
Palmers La, Enf. EN1, EN3. 45 E1
Palmers Pas, SW14
off Palmers Rd 146 C3
Palmers Rd, E2 . . . . 113 G2
N11 . . . . 58 C5
SW14. . . . . 146 C3
SW16. . . . . 187 F2
Borehamwood WD6 . . . . 38 B1
Palmerston Cres, N13 . . . . 59 F5
SE18 . . . . 137 F6
Palmerston Gro, SW19. . . 166 D7
Palmerston Rd, E7 . . . . 97 H5
E17 . . . . 77 J4
N22 . . . . 59 F7
NW6 . . . . 90 D7
SW14. . . . . 146 C4
SW19. . . . . 166 D7
W3. . . . . 126 C3
Buckhurst Hill IG9 . . . . . . 63 H2
Carshalton SM5 . . . . . . 199 J4
Croydon CR0. . . . . 188 A5
Harrow HA3 . . . . 68 C3
Hounslow TW3 . . . . 143 J1
Orpington BR6 . . . . 207 F4
Sutton SM1
off Vernon Rd 199 F5
Twickenham TW2 . . . . . 144 C6
Palmerston Way, SW8
off Bradmead 130 B7
Palmer St, SW1 . . . . 25 H4
Palm Gro, W5 . . . . 125 H3
Palm Rd, Rom. RM7. . . . . . 83 J5
Pamela Gdns, Pnr. HA5 . . . 66 B5
Pamela Wk, E8
off Marlborough Av. . . 112 D1
Pampisford Rd, S.Croy.
CR2 . . . . 201 H7
Pams Way, Epsom KT19. . 196 D5
Pancras La, EC4 . . . . 20 A4
Pancras Rd, NW1 . . . . 9 H1
Pandora Rd, NW6. . . . . 90 D6
Panfield Ms, Ilf. IG2
off Cranbrook Rd 80 D6
Panfield Rd, SE2. . . . . 138 A3
Pangbourne Av, W10 . . . . 107 J5
Pangbourne Dr, Stan. HA7. 53 G5
Pangbourne Ho, N7 . . . . . . 92 E5
Panhard Pl, Sthl. UB1. . . . 103 H7
Pank Av, Barn. EN5 . . . . . . 41 F5
Pankhurst Av, E16
off Wesley Av 135 H1
Pankhurst Cl, SE14
off Briant St. 133 G7
Isleworth TW7 . . . . 144 C3
Pankhurst Rd, Walt. KT12. 178 C7
Panmuir Rd, SW20. . . . . . 183 H1
Panmure Cl, N5 . . . . 93 H4
Panmure Rd, SE26 . . . . . . 170 E3
Pansy Gdns, W12 . . . . 107 G7
Panther Dr, NW10 . . . . 88 D5
Pantiles, The, NW11
off Willifield Way. 72 C5
Bexleyheath DA7 . . . . . 139 F7
Bromley BR1 . . . . 192 B3
Pantiles Cl, N13 . . . . 59 H5
Panton St, SW1 . . . . 17 H6
Panyer All, EC4. . . . . 19 J4
Papermill Cl, Cars. SM5 . . 200 A4
Papillons Wk, SE3 . . . . . . 155 G2
Papworth Gdns, N7
off Liverpool Rd 93 F5
Papworth Way, SW2 . . . . 151 G7
Parade, The, SW11 . . . . 32 A7
Esher (Clay.) KT10. . . . . 194 B6
Hampton TW12
off Hampton Rd 162 A5
Watford (Carp.Pk) WD19 . 50 E3
Watford (S.Oxhey) WD19
off Prestwick Rd 50 D3
Parade Ms, SE27
off Norwood Rd 169 H2
Paradise Pas, N7 . . . . 93 G5
Paradise Path, SE28
off Birchdene Dr 138 A1
Paradise Pl, SE18
off Woodhill. 136 B4
Paradise Rd, SW4. . . . . . . 150 E2
Richmond TW9 . . . . 145 G5
Paradise Row, E2
off Bethnal Grn Rd. 112/113 E3
Paradise St, SE16. . . . . . . 132 E2
Paradise Wk, SW3 . . . . 31 J6
Paragon, The, SE3 . . . . . . 155 F2
Paragon Cl, E16 . . . . 115 G6
Paragon Gro, Surb. KT5. . 181 J6
Paragon Ms, SE1 . . . . 36 C1
Paragon Pl, SE3 . . . . 155 F2
Paragon Pl, Surb. KT5
off Berrylands Rd 181 J6
Paragon Rd, E9. . . . . 95 F6
Parbury Ri, Chess. KT9. . . 195 H6
Parbury Rd, SE23. . . . . . . 153 H6
Parchmore Rd, Th.Hth.
CR7 . . . . 187 H2
Parchmore Way, Th.Hth.
CR7 . . . . 187 H2
Pardoner St, SE1 . . . . 28 C5
Pardon St, EC1 . . . . 11 H5
Parfett St, E1 . . . . 21 J2
Parfitt Cl, NW3
off North End 91 F2
Parfrey St, W6 . . . . 127 J6
Parham Dr, Ilf. IG2 . . . . 80 E6
Parham Way, N10 . . . . 74 C2
Paris Gdn, SE1 . . . . 27 G1
Parish Gate Dr, Sid. DA15. 157 H6
Parish La, SE20. . . . . 171 G6
Parish Ms, SE20 . . . . 171 G7
Parish Wf, SE18
off Woodhill. 136 B4
Park, The, N6 . . . . 74 A6
NW11. . . . . 90 E1
SE19 . . . . 170 B7
SE23 *off Park Hill* . . 170/171 E1
W5. . . . . 125 G1
Carshalton SM5 . . . . . . 199 J5
Sidcup DA14 . . . . 175 J5
Park App, Well. DA16 . . . . 158 B4
Park Av, E6 . . . . 116 D1
E15 . . . . 96 E6
N3 . . . . 73 E1
N13 . . . . 59 G3
N18 . . . . 60 D4
N22 . . . . 75 E2
NW2 . . . . 89 H6
NW10. . . . . 105 J3
NW11. . . . . 90 E1
SW14. . . . . 146 D4
Barking IG11 . . . . 99 F6
Bromley BR1 . . . . 173 F6
Carshalton SM5 . . . . . . 200 A6
Enfield EN1 . . . . 44 B6
Hounslow TW3 . . . . 143 H6
Ilford IG1. . . . . 98 D2
Mitcham CR4. . . . . 168 B7
Orpington (Farnboro.)
BR6 . . . . 206 C3
Southall UB1. . . . . 123 G1
West Wickham BR4 . . . . 204 C2
Woodford Green IG8 . . . 63 H5
Park Av E, Epsom KT17 . . 197 G6
Park Av Ms, Mitch. CR4
off Park Av. 168 B7
Park Av N, N8. . . . . 74 D3
NW10 . . . . 89 H5
Park Av Rd, N17 . . . . 61 E7
Park Av S, N8 . . . . 74 D4
Park Av W, Epsom KT17. . 197 G6
Park Chase, Wem. HA9 . . . 87 J4
Park Cl, E9 . . . . 113 F1
NW2 . . . . 89 H3
NW10. . . . . 105 J3
SW1. . . . . 23 J4
W4. . . . . 126 D5
W14. . . . . 128 C3
Carshalton SM5 . . . . . . 199 J6
Hampton TW12 . . . . 179 J1
Harrow HA3 . . . . 68 B1
Hounslow TW3 . . . . 143 J5
Kingston upon Thames
KT2 . . . . 182 A1
Park Ct, SE26 . . . . 171 E6
Kingston upon Thames
(Hmptn W.) KT1. . . . . . 181 F1
New Malden KT3 . . . . . 182 D4
Wembley HA9. . . . . 87 H5
Park Cres, N3 . . . . 57 E7
W1. . . . . 8 D6
Enfield EN2. . . . . 44 A4
Erith DA8. . . . . 139 J6
Harrow HA3 . . . . 68 B1
Twickenham TW2 . . . . . 162 A1
Park Cres Ms E, W1 . . . . 8 E6
Park Cres Ms W, W1 . . . . . . 16 D1
Park Cft, Edg. HA8 . . . . 70 C1
Parkcroft Rd, SE12 . . . . . . 155 F7
Park Dale, N11 . . . . 58 D6
Parkdale Cres, Wor.Pk.
KT4 . . . . 196 D3
Parkdale Rd, SE18 . . . . . . 137 H5
Park Dr, N21. . . . . 43 J6
NW11. . . . . 90 E1
SE7 . . . . 136 B6
SW14. . . . . 146 D4
W3. . . . . 126 A3
Dagenham RM10. . . . . . 101 J3
Park Dr, Har. (Har.Wld) HA3. 52 B6
Harrow (N.Har.) HA2 . . . . 67 G7
Park Dr Cl, SE7. . . . . 136 B5
Park End, NW3
off South Hill Pk 91 H4
Bromley BR1 . . . . 191 F1
Parker Cl, E16 . . . . 136 B1
Carshalton SM5 . . . . . . 199 J6
Parker Ms, WC2 . . . . 18 B3
Parke Rd, SW13 . . . . 147 G1
Sunbury-on-Thames
TW16. . . . . 178 A4
Parker Rd, Croy. CR0 . . . . 201 J4
Parkers Row, SE1. . . . . 29 G4
Parker St, E16. . . . . 136 B1
WC2. . . . . 18 B3
Parkes Rd, Chig. IG7 . . . . . 65 H5
Park Fm Cl, N2 . . . . 73 F3
Pinner HA5
off Field End Rd 66 B5
Park Fm Rd, Brom. BR1 . . 192 A1
Kingston upon Thames
KT2 . . . . 163 H7
Parkfield Av, SW14. . . . . . 146 E4
Feltham TW13 . . . . 160 A3
Harrow HA2 . . . . 67 J2
Northolt UB5. . . . . 102 D2
Parkfield Cl, Edg. HA8 . . . . 54 B6
Northolt UB5. . . . . 102 E2
Parkfield Cres, Felt. TW13. 160 A3
Harrow HA2 . . . . 67 J2
Ruislip HA4. . . . . 84 E3
Parkfield Dr, Nthlt. UB5 . . 102 D2
Parkfield Gdns, Har. HA2 . . 67 H3
Parkfield Rd, NW10 . . . . . . 89 G7
SE14 . . . . 153 J1
Feltham TW13 . . . . 160 A3
Harrow HA2 . . . . 85 J3
Northolt UB5. . . . . 102 E2
Parkfields, SW15 . . . . 147 J4
Croydon CR0. . . . . 203 J1
Parkfields Av, NW9. . . . . . . 88 D1
SW20. . . . . 183 H1
Parkfields Cl, Cars. SM5
off Devonshire Rd. . . . 200 A4
Parkfields Rd, Kings.T.
KT2 . . . . 163 J5
Parkfield St, N1 . . . . 11 F1
Parkfield Way, Brom. BR2 . 192 C6
Park Gdns, NW9. . . . . 70 B3
Kingston upon Thames
KT2 . . . . 163 J5
Park Gate, N2. . . . . 73 G3
N21 . . . . 43 F7
Parkgate, SE3. . . . . 155 F3
Park Gate, W5. . . . . 105 G5
Parkgate Av, Barn. EN4 . . . 41 F1
Parkgate Cl, Kings.T. KT2
off Warboys App 164 B6
Parkgate Cres, Barn. EN4. . 41 F2
Parkgate Gdns, SW14 . . . 146 D5
Parkgate Ms, N6
off Stanhope Rd 74 C7
Parkgate Rd, SW11. . . . . . 129 H7
Wallington SM6 . . . . . . 200 A5
Park Gates, Har. HA2 . . . . . 85 G4
Park Gro, E15 . . . . 115 G1
N11 . . . . 58 D7
Bexleyheath DA7 . . . . . 159 J4
Bromley BR1 . . . . 191 H1
Edgware HA8 . . . . 53 J5
Park Gro Rd, E11 . . . . 96 E2
Park Hall Rd, N2. . . . . 73 H4
SE21 . . . . 169 J3
Parkham Ct, Brom. BR2 . . 191 E2
Parkham St, SW11 . . . . . . 149 H1
Park Hill, SE23 . . . . 171 E2
SW4. . . . . 150 D5
W5. . . . . 105 G5
Bromley BR1 . . . . 192 B4
Carshalton SM5 . . . . . . 199 H6
Loughton IG10 . . . . 48 A5
Richmond TW10 . . . . . . 145 J6
Park Hill Cl, Cars. SM5. . . 199 H5
Park Hill Ct, SW17
off Beeches Rd 167 J3
Park Hill Ri, Croy. CR0 . . . 202 B2
Parkhill Rd, E4 . . . . 62 C1
NW3 . . . . 91 J5
Bexley DA5 . . . . 159 F7
Park Hill Rd, Brom. BR2 . . 190 E2
Croydon CR0. . . . . 202 B2
Parkhill Rd, Sid. DA15 . . . 175 G3
Park Hill Rd, Wall. SM6 . . 200 B7
Parkhill Wk, NW3 . . . . 91 J5
Parkholme Rd, E8. . . . . 94 C6
Park Ho, N21 . . . . 43 F7
Park Ho Gdns, Twick. TW1 . 145 F6
Parkhouse St, SE5 . . . . 36 C7
Parkhurst Gdns, Bex.
DA5 . . . . 159 G7
Parkhurst Rd, E12 . . . . 98 D4
E17 . . . . 77 H4
N7 . . . . 92 E4
N11 . . . . 58 A4
N17 . . . . 76 D2
N22 . . . . 59 F7
Bexley DA5 . . . . 159 G7
Sutton SM1. . . . . 199 G4
Parkland Cl, Chig. IG7 . . . . 65 F3
Parkland Gdns, SW19 . . . 166 A1
Parkland Rd, N22. . . . . 75 F2
Woodford Green IG8 . . . 63 G7
Parklands, N6. . . . . 74 B7
Chigwell IG7 . . . . 65 F3
Surbiton KT5. . . . . 181 J5
Parklands Cl, SW14 . . . . . 146 C5
Ilford IG2. . . . . 81 F7
Parklands Ct, Houns. TW5. 142 D2
Parklands Dr, N3 . . . . 72 B3
Parklands Rd, SW16. . . . . 168 B5
Parklands Way, Wor.Pk.
KT4 . . . . 197 E3
Parkland Wk, N4. . . . . 75 F7
N6 . . . . 74 D7
N10 . . . . 74 B4
Park La, E15 *off High St* . . 114 D1
N9 . . . . 60 C3
N17 . . . . 60 D7
W1. . . . . 24 C2
Carshalton SM5 . . . . . . 200 A4
Croydon CR0. . . . . 202 A3
Harrow HA2 . . . . 85 H3
Hounslow TW5 . . . . 122 A7
Richmond TW9 . . . . 145 G4
Romford (Chad.Hth)
RM6. . . . . 82 D6
Stanmore HA7 . . . . 52 D3
Sutton SM3. . . . . 198 B6
Teddington TW11. . . . . . 162 C6
Wallington SM6 . . . . . . 200 A4
Wembley HA9. . . . . 87 H5
Park La Cl, N17. . . . . 60 D7
PARK LANGLEY, Beck.
BR3 . . . . 190 C5
Park Lawns, Wem. HA9 . . . 87 J4
Parklea Cl, NW9 . . . . 71 E1
Parkleigh Rd, SW19 . . . . . 184 E2
Parkleys, Rich. TW10. . . . . 163 G4
Parkmead, SW15 . . . . 147 H6
Park Mead, Har. HA2 . . . . . 85 H3
Parkmead, Loug. IG10 . . . . 48 D5
Park Mead, Sid. DA15 . . . 158 B5
Parkmead Gdns, NW7 . . . . 55 F6
Park Ms, SE24
off Croxted Rd. 151 J6
Chislehurst BR7 . . . . . . 175 E6
East Molesey KT8 . . . . . 179 J4
Hampton (Hmptn H.)
TW12 *off Park Rd* 161 J5
Parkmore Cl, Wdf.Grn. IG8 . 63 G4
Park Par, NW10. . . . . 107 F2
Park Pl, E14. . . . . 134 A1
SW1. . . . . 25 F2
W3. . . . . 126 A4
W5. . . . . 125 G1
Hampton (Hmptn H.)
TW12. . . . . 161 J6
Wembley HA9. . . . . 87 J4
Park Pl Vil, W2 . . . . 14 D1
Park Ridings, N8 . . . . 75 G3
Park Ri, SE23 . . . . 171 H1
Harrow HA3 . . . . 68 B1
Park Ri Rd, SE23. . . . . 171 H1
Park Rd, E6. . . . . 115 J1
E10 . . . . 96 A1
E12 . . . . 97 H1
E15. . . . . 115 G1
E17 . . . . 77 J5
N2. . . . . 73 G3
N8 . . . . 74 C4
N11 . . . . 58 D7
N14 . . . . 42 D7
N15 . . . . 75 H4
N18 . . . . 60 C4
NW1 . . . . 7 G3
NW4 . . . . 71 G7
NW8 . . . . 7 G3
NW9 . . . . 70 D7
NW10. . . . . 106 E1
SE25 . . . . 188 B4
SW19. . . . . 167 G6
W4. . . . . 126 C7
W7. . . . . 104 C7
Barnet EN5 . . . . 40 C4
Barnet (New Barn.) EN4 . 41 H4
Beckenham BR3 . . . . . . 171 J7
Bromley BR1 . . . . 191 H1

Park Rd, Chis. BR7 175 E6
East Molesey KT8 179 J4
Feltham TW13 160 D4
Hampton (Hmptn H.) TW12 161 H4
Hounslow TW3 143 J4
Ilford IG1 99 G3
Isleworth TW7 144 E1
Kingston upon Thames KT2 163 J5
Kingston upon Thames (Hmptn W.) KT1 181 F1
New Malden KT3 182 D4
Richmond TW10 145 J6
Sunbury-on-Thames TW16 160 B7
Surbiton KT5 181 J5
Sutton SM3 198 B6
Teddington TW11 162 C6
Twickenham TW1 145 F6
Wallington SM6 200 B5
Wallington (Hackbr.) SM6 200 B2
Wembley HA0 87 H6
Park Rd E, W3 126 B2
Park Rd N, W3 126 B2
W4 126 D5
Park Row, SE10 134 D6
PARK ROYAL, NW10 106 A3
Park Royal Rd, NW10 106 C3
W3 106 C3
Parkshot, Rich. TW9 145 H4
Parkside, N3 72 E1
NW2 89 G3
NW7 55 G6
SE3 135 F7
SW19 166 A4
Buckhurst Hill IG9 63 H2
Hampton (Hmptn H.) TW12 162 A5
Sidcup DA14 176 B2
Sutton SM3 198 B6
Parkside Av, SW19 166 A5
Bromley BR1 192 B4
Parkside Business Est, SE8 *off Rolt St* 133 H6
Parkside Cl, SE20 171 F7
Parkside Cres, N7 93 G3
Surbiton KT5 182 C6
Parkside Dr, Edg. HA8 54 A3
Parkside Est, E9 *off Rutland Rd* 113 F1
Parkside Gdns, SW19 166 A4
Barnet EN4 57 J1
Parkside Ho, Dag. RM10 101 J3
Parkside Rd, SW11 150 A1
Belvedere DA17 139 J4
Hounslow TW3 143 H5
Parkside Ter, N10 *off Great Cambridge Rd* 60 A4
Orpington BR6 *off Willow Wk* 206/207 E3
Parkside Wk, SE10 134 E5
Parkside Way, Har. HA2 67 H4
Park S, SW11 *off Austin Rd* 150 A1
Park Sq E, NW1 8 D5
Park Sq Ms, NW1 8 D6
Park Sq W, NW1 8 D5
Parkstead Rd, SW15 147 G5
Parkstone Av, N18 60 C5
Parkstone Rd, E17 78 C3
SE15 *off Rye La* 152 D2
Park St, SE1 27 J1
W1 16 B5
Croydon CR0 201 J2
Teddington TW11 162 B6
Park Ter, Wor.Pk. KT4 197 G1
Parkthorne Cl, Har. HA2 67 H6
Parkthorne Dr, Har. HA2 67 G6
Parkthorne Rd, SW12 150 D7
Park Vw, N21 43 F7
W3 106 C5
New Malden KT3 183 F3
Pinner HA5 67 F1
Wembley HA9 88 B5
Parkview Ct, SW18 *off Broomhill Rd* 148 D6
Park Vw Ct, Ilf. IG2 *off Brancaster Rd* 81 H6
Park Vw Cres, N11 58 B4
Parkview Dr, Mitch. CR4 185 G2
Park Vw Est, E2 113 G2
N5 93 J4
Park Vw Gdns, NW4 71 J5
Ilford IG4 80 C4
Park Vw Ho, SE24 *off Hurst St* 151 H6
Park Vw Ms, SW9 151 F2
Park Vw Rd, N3 73 E1
N17 76 D3
NW10 89 F4
Parkview Rd, SE9 174 E2
Park Vw Rd, W5 105 H5
Parkview Rd, Croy. CR0 202 D1
Park Vw Rd, Pnr. HA5 50 B7
Southall UB1 123 G1
Welling DA16 158 C3
Park Vw Rd Est, N17 76 E2
Park Village E, NW1 110 B2
Park Village W, NW1 8 D1
Park Vil, Rom. RM6 82 D6
Parkville Rd, SW6 128 C7
Park Vista, SE10 134 D6
Park Wk, N6 *off North Rd* 74 A7
SE10 *off Crooms Hill* 134 D7
SW10 30 D5
Parkway, N14 58 E2
Park Way, N20 57 J4
Parkway, NW1 110 B1
Park Way, NW11 72 B5
Parkway, SW20 184 A4
Park Way, Edg. HA8 70 B1
Enfield EN2 43 G2
Parkway, Erith DA18 139 E3
Park Way, Felt. TW14 142 B7
Parkway, Ilf. IG3 99 J3
Park Way, Ruis. HA4 84 A1
West Molesey KT8 179 H3
Parkway, Wdf.Grn. IG8 63 J5
Parkway, The, Hayes UB3, UB4 102 C6
Hounslow (Cran.) TW4, TW5 142 B2
Northolt UB5 102 D3
Southall UB2 122 A5
Parkway Trd Est, Houns. TW5 122 C6
Park W, W2 15 H4
Park W Pl, W2 15 H3
Parkwood, N20 57 J3
Beckenham BR3 190 A1
Parkwood Gro, Sun. TW16 178 A3
Parkwood Ms, N6 74 B6
Parkwood Rd, SW19 166 C5
Bexley DA5 159 F7
Isleworth TW7 144 C1
Parliament Ct, E1 *off Sandy's Row* 112 B5
Parliament Hill, NW3 91 H4
Parliament Ms, SW14 *off Thames Bk* 146 C2
Parliament Sq, SW1 26 A4
Parliament St, SW1 26 A4
Parliament Vw Apartments, SE1 34 C1
Parma Cres, SW11 149 J4
Parmiter St, E2 113 E2
Parmoor Ct, EC1 11 J5
Parnell Cl, W12 127 H3
Edgware HA8 54 B4
Parnell Rd, E3 113 J1
Parnham St, E14 *off Blount St* 113 H6
Parolles Rd, N19 92 C1
Paroma Rd, Belv. DA17 139 G3
Parr Cl, N9 60 E4
N18 60 E4
Parr Ct, N1 12 B1
Feltham TW13 160 C4
Parr Pl, W4 *off Chiswick High Rd* 127 F4
Parr Rd, E6 116 A1
Stanmore HA7 69 G1
Parrs Pl, Hmptn. TW12 161 G7
Parr St, N1 12 B1
Parry Av, E6 116 C6
Parry Cl, Epsom KT17 197 G7
Parry Pl, SE18 137 E4
Parry Rd, SE25 188 B3
W10 108 B3
Parry St, SW8 34 A5
Parsifal Rd, NW6 90 D5
Parsley Gdns, Croy. CR0 *off Primrose La* 203 G1
Parsloes Av, Dag. RM9 100 D4
Parsonage Gdns, Enf. EN2 43 J2
Parsonage La, Enf. EN1, EN2 44 A2
Sidcup DA14 177 F4
Parsonage Manorway, Belv. DA17 139 G6
Parsonage St, E14 134 C4
Parsons Cl, Sutt. SM1 198 E3
Parsons Cres, Edg. HA8 54 A3
PARSONS GREEN, SW6 148 D1
Parsons Grn, SW6 148 D1
Parsons Grn La, SW6 148 D1
Parsons Gro, Edg. HA8 54 A3
Parsons Ho, SW2 *off New Pk Rd* 150/151 E7
Parson's Ho, W2 7 E6
Parson's Mead, Croy. CR0 201 H1
Parsons Mead, E.Mol. KT8 179 J3
Parsons Rd, E13 *off Old St* 115 J2
Parson St, NW4 71 J4
Parthenia Rd, SW6 148 D1
Partingdale La, NW7 56 A5
Partington Cl, N19 92 D1
Partridge Cl, E16 *off Fulmer Rd* 116 A5
Barnet EN5 39 J6
Bushey WD23 51 H1
Stanmore HA7 53 H4
Partridge Ct, EC1 *off Percival St* 111 H4
Partridge Dr, Orp. BR6 207 F3
Partridge Grn, SE9 174 D3
Partridge Rd, Hmptn. TW12 161 F6
Sidcup DA14 175 H3
Partridge Sq, E6 *off Nightingale Way* 116 B5
Partridge Way, N22 75 E1
Parvin St, SW8 150 D1
Pasadena Cl, Hayes UB3 122 B2
Pasadena Cl Trd Est, Hayes UB3 *off Pasadena Cl* 122 B2
Pascal St, SW8 33 J7
Pascoe Rd, SE13 154 D5
Pasley Cl, SE17 35 J4
Pasquier Rd, E17 77 H3
Passey Pl, SE9 156 C6
Passfield Dr, E14 *off Uamvar St* 114 B5
Passfield Path, SE28 *off Booth Cl* 118 B7
Passing All, EC1 11 H6
Passmore Gdns, N11 58 D6
Passmore St, SW1 32 B2
★**Passport Office**, SW1 32 E1
Pasteur Cl, NW9 71 F2
Pasteur Gdns, N18 59 H5
Paston Cl, E5 *off Caldecott Way* 95 G3
Wallington SM6 200 C3
Paston Cres, SE12 155 H7
Pastor St, SE11 35 H1
Pasture Cl, Wem. HA0 86 E3
Pasture Rd, SE6 173 F1
Dagenham RM9 101 F4
Wembley HA0 86 E2
Pastures, The, N20 56 C1
Patcham Ter, SW8 150 B1
Patching Way, Hayes UB4 102 E5
Paternoster Row, EC4 19 J4
Paternoster Sq, EC4 19 H4
Pater St, W8 128 D3
Pates Manor Dr, Felt. TW14 141 G7
Path, The, SW19 184 E1
Pathfield Rd, SW16 168 D6
Pathway, The, Wat. WD19 *off Anthony Cl* 50 D1
Patience Rd, SW11 149 H2
Patio Cl, SW4 150 D6
Patmore Est, SW8 150 C1
Patmore St, SW8 150 C1
Patmos Rd, SW9 131 H7
Paton Cl, E3 114 A3
Paton St, EC1 11 J4
Patricia Ct, Chis. BR7 *off Manor Pk Rd* 193 G1
Welling DA16 138 B7
Patrick Connolly Gdns, E3 *off Talwin St* 114 B3
Patrick Rd, E13 115 J3
Patriot Sq, E2 113 E2
Patrol Pl, SE6 154 B6
Patshull Pl, NW5 *off Patshull Rd* 92 C6
Patshull Rd, NW5 92 C6
Patten All, Rich. TW10 *off The Hermitage* 145 G5
Pattenden Rd, SE6 171 J1
Patten Rd, SW18 149 H7
Patterdale Cl, Brom. BR1 173 F6
Patterdale Rd, SE15 133 F7
Patterson Ct, SE19 170 C7
Patterson Rd, SE19 170 C6
Pattina Wk, SE16 133 J1
Pattison Pt, E16 *off Fife Rd* 115 G5
Pattison Rd, NW2 90 D3
Pattison Wk, SE18 137 F5
Paul Cl, E15 96 E7
Paulet Rd, SE5 151 H2
Paul Gdns, Croy. CR0 202 C2
Paulhan Rd, Har. HA3 69 G4
Paulin Dr, N21 43 G7
Pauline Cres, Twick. TW2 161 J1
Paul Julius Cl, E14 114 D7
Paul Robeson Cl, E6 *off Eastbourne Rd* 116 D3
Paul St, E15 114 D1
EC2 12 C6
Paul's Wk, EC4 19 H5
Paultons Sq, SW3 31 F5
Paultons St, SW3 31 F6
Pauntley St, N19 92 C1
Paved Ct, Rich. TW9 145 G5
Paveley Dr, SW11 129 H7
Paveley St, NW8 7 H5
Pavement, The, SW4 150 C4
W5 *off Popes La* 125 H3
Pavement Ms, Rom. RM6 *off Clarissa Rd* 82 D7
Pavement Sq, Croy. CR0 202 D1
Pavet Cl, Dag. RM10 101 H6
Pavilion La, Beck. BR3 171 J6
Pavilion Ms, N3 *off Windermere Av* 72 D2
Pavilion Rd, SW1 24 A6
Ilford IG1 80 C7
Pavilion Sq, SW17 167 J3
Pavilion St, SW1 24 A6
Pavilion Ter, E.Mol. KT8 180 C4
Ilford IG2 *off Southdown Cres* 81 H5
Pavilion Way, Edg. HA8 54 B7
Ruislip HA4 84 C2
Pawleyne Cl, SE20 171 F7
Pawsey Cl, E13 *off Plashet Rd* 115 G1
Pawson's Rd, Croy. CR0 187 J6
Paxford Rd, Wem. HA0 86 E2
Paxton Cl, Rich. TW9 145 J2
Walton-on-Thames KT12 178 C7
Paxton Pl, SE27 170 B4
Paxton Rd, N17 60 C7
SE23 171 H3
W4 126 E6
Bromley BR1 173 G7
Paxton Ter, SW1 33 E5
Payne Cl, Bark. IG11 99 H7
Paynell Ct, SE3 *off Lawn Ter* 154/155 E3
Payne Rd, E3 114 B2
Paynesfield Av, SW14 146 D3
Payne St, SE8 133 J6
Paynes Wk, W6 128 B6
Peabody Av, SW1 32 D3
Peabody Cl, SE10 *off Devonshire Dr* 154 B1
SW1 32 E4
Croydon CR0 *off Shirley Rd* 203 F1
Peabody Dws, WC1 10 A5
Peabody Est, EC1 12 A6
N1 (Islington) *off Greenman St* 93 J7
N17 76 B1
SE1 27 F2
SE24 151 J7
SW3 31 H5
W6 *off The Square* 127 J5
W10 107 J5
Peabody Hill, SE21 169 H1
Peabody Hill Est, SE21 151 H7
Peabody Sq, SE1 27 G4
Peabody Twr, EC1 *off Golden La* 111 J4
Peabody Trust, SE1 27 J2
Peabody Yd, N1 *off Greenman St* 111 J1
Peace Cl, N14 42 B5
SE25 188 B4
Peace Gro, Wem. HA9 88 B3
Peace St, SE18 *off Nightingale Vale* 136/137 E6
Peaches Cl, Sutt. SM2 198 B7
Peach Rd, W10 108 A3
Peachum Rd, SE3 135 F6
Peachwalk Ms, E3 *off Grove Rd* 113 G2
Peacock St, SE17 35 H2
Peacock Wk, E16 115 H6
Peacock Yd, SE17 35 H2
Peak, The, SE26 171 F3
Peaketon Av, Ilf. IG4 80 A4
Peak Hill, SE26 171 F4
Peak Hill Av, SE26 171 F4
Peak Hill Gdns, SE26 171 F4

Peal Gdns, W13
off Ruislip Rd E . . . **104** D4
Peall Rd, Croy. CR0 . . . **187** F6
Pearce Cl, Mitch. CR4 . . . **186** A2
Pearcefield Av, SE23 . . . **171** F1
Pearce Rd, W.Mol. KT8 . . . **179** H3
Pear Cl, NW9 . . . **70** D4
SE14
off Southerngate Way . **133** H7
Pearcroft Rd, E11 . . . **96** D2
Peardon St, SW8 . . . **150** B2
Peareswood Gdns, Stan.
HA7 . . . **69** G1
Pearfield Rd, SE23 . . . **171** H3
Pearl Cl, E6 . . . **116** D6
NW2 *off Marble Dr* . . . **72** A7
Pearl Rd, E17 . . . **78** A3
Pearl St, E1
off Penang St . . . **132/133** E1
Pearman St, SE1 . . . **27** F5
Pear Pl, SE1 . . . **27** E3
Pear Rd, E11 . . . **96** D3
Pearscroft Ct, SW6 . . . **149** E1
Pearscroft Rd, SW6 . . . **148** E1
Pearse St, SE15 . . . **36** E6
Pearson Cl, SE5
off Medlar St . . . **151** J1
Pearson Ms, SW4
off Edgeley Rd . . . **150** D3
Pearsons Av, SE14
off Tanners Hill . . . **154** A1
Pearson St, E2 . . . **13** E1
Pears Rd, Houns. TW3 . . . **143** J3
Peartree Av, SW17 . . . **167** F3
Pear Tree Cl, E2 . . . **112** C1
Chessington KT9 . . . **196** A5
Mitcham CR4 . . . **185** H2
Peartree Ct, E18
off Churchfields . . . **79** H1
Pear Tree Ct, EC1 . . . **11** F6
Peartree Gdns, Dag. RM8 . **100** B4
Romford RM7 . . . **83** H2
Peartree La, E1
off Glamis Rd . . . **113** F7
Peartree Rd, Enf. EN1 . . . **44** B3
Pear Tree St, EC1 . . . **11** H5
Peartree Way, SE10 . . . **135** G4
Peary Pl, E2
off Kirkwall Pl . . . **113** F3
Peatfield Cl, Sid. DA15
off Woodside Rd . . . **175** H3
Pebble Way, W3 . . . **126** B1
Pebworth Rd, Har. HA1 . . . **86** D2
Peckarmans Wd, SE26 . . . **170** D3
Peckett Sq, N5
off Highbury Gra . . . **93** J4
Peckford Pl, SW9 . . . **151** G2
PECKHAM, SE15 . . . **152** D1
Peckham Gro, SE15 . . . **36** E7
Peckham High St, SE15 . . **152** D1
Peckham Hill St, SE15 . . . **37** H7
Peckham Pk Rd, SE15 . . . **37** H7
Peckham Rd, SE5 . . . **152** B1
SE15 . . . **152** B1
Peckham Rye, SE15 . . . **152** D3
SE22 . . . **152** D4
Pecks Yd, E1 . . . **21** F1
Peckwater St, NW5 . . . **92** C5
Pedlars Wk, N7 . . . **93** E6
Pedley Rd, Dag. RM8 . . . **100** C1
Pedley St, E1 . . . **13** G6
Pedro St, E5 . . . **95** G3
Pedworth Gdns, SE16
off Rotherhithe New Rd . **133** F4
Peek Cres, SW19 . . . **166** A5
Peel Cl, E4 . . . **62** B2
N9 *off Plevna Rd* . . . **60** D3
Peel Dr, NW9 . . . **71** F3
Ilford IG5 . . . **80** B3
Peel Gro, E2 . . . **113** F2
Peel Pas, W8 *off Peel St* . . **128** D1
Peel Pl, Ilf. IG5 . . . **80** B2
Peel Prec, NW6 . . . **108** D2
Peel Rd, E18 . . . **79** F1
NW6 . . . **108** C3
Harrow (Wldste) HA3 . . . **68** C3
Orpington BR6 . . . **207** F5
Wembley HA9 . . . **87** G3
Peel St, W8 . . . **128** D1
Peerless St, EC1 . . . **12** B4
Pegamoid Rd, N18 . . . **61** F3
Pegasus Cl, N16
off Green Las . . . **94** A4
Pegasus Pl, SE11 . . . **35** E5
SW6 *off Ackmar Rd* . . . **148** D1
Pegasus Rd, Croy. CR0 . . . **201** G6
Pegasus Way, N11 . . . **58** B6
Pegg Rd, Houns. TW5 . . . **122** D7
Pegley Gdns, SE12 . . . **173** G2
Pegwell St, SE18 . . . **137** H7
Pekin Cl, E14
off Pekin St . . . **114** A6
Pekin St, E14 . . . **114** A6
Peldon Ct, Rich. TW9 . . . **145** J4
Peldon Pas, Rich. TW10
off Worple Way . . . **145** J4
Peldon Wk, N1
off Britannia Row . . . **111** H1
Pelham Av, Bark. IG11 . . . **117** J1
Pelham Cl, SE5 . . . **152** B2
Pelham Cres, SW7 . . . **31** G2
Pelham Pl, SW7 . . . **31** G2
W13 *off Ruislip Rd E* . . . **104** C4
Pelham Rd, E18 . . . **79** H3
N15 . . . **76** C4
N22 . . . **75** G2
SW19 . . . **166** D7
Beckenham BR3 . . . **189** F2
Bexleyheath DA7 . . . **159** G3
Ilford IG1 . . . **99** G2
Pelham St, SW7 . . . **31** F1
Pelican Est, SE15 . . . **152** C1
Pelican Pas, E1
off Cambridge
Heath Rd . . . **113** F4
Pelier St, SE17 . . . **36** A5
Pelinore Rd, SE6 . . . **172** E2
Pellant Rd, SW6 . . . **128** B7
Pellatt Gro, N22 . . . **75** G1
Pellatt Rd, SE22 . . . **152** C5
Wembley HA9 . . . **87** G2
Pellerin Rd, N16 . . . **94** B5
Pelling St, E14 . . . **114** A6
Pellipar Cl, N13 . . . **59** G3
Pellipar Gdns, SE18 . . . **136** C5
Pelly Rd, E13 . . . **115** G2
Pelter St, E2 . . . **13** F3
Pelton Rd, SE10 . . . **134** E5
Pembar Av, E17 . . . **77** H3
Pemberley Chase, Epsom
(W.Ewell) KT19 . . . **196** B5
Pemberley Cl, Epsom
(W.Ewell) KT19 . . . **196** B5
Pember Rd, NW10 . . . **108** A3
Pemberton Gdns, N19 . . . **92** C3
Romford RM6 . . . **82** E5
Pemberton Ho, SE26
off High Level Dr . . . **170** D4
Pemberton Pl, E8
off Mare St . . . **94/95** E7
Pemberton Rd, N4 . . . **75** G5
East Molesey KT8 . . . **179** J4
Pemberton Row, EC4 . . . **19** F3
Pemberton Ter, N19 . . . **92** C3
Pembridge Av, Twick. TW2 . **161** F1
Pembridge Cres, W11 . . . **108** D7
Pembridge Gdns, W2 . . . **108** D7
Pembridge Ms, W11 . . . **108** D7
Pembridge Pl, SW15 . . . **148** D5
W2 . . . **108** D7
Pembridge Rd, W11 . . . **108** D7
Pembridge Sq, W2 . . . **108** D7
Pembridge Vil, W2 . . . **108** D7
W11 . . . **108** D7
Pembroke Av, N1 . . . **111** E1
Harrow HA3 . . . **68** D3
Pinner HA5 . . . **84** D1
Surbiton KT5 . . . **182** B5
Pembroke Cl, SW1 . . . **24** C4
Pembroke Cotts, W8
off Pembroke Sq . . . **128** D3
Pembroke Gdns, W8 . . . **128** C4
Dagenham RM10 . . . **101** H3
Pembroke Gdns Cl, W8 . . **128** D3
Pembroke Ms, E3
off Morgan St . . . **113** H3
N10 *off Pembroke Rd* . . . **74** A1
W8 *off Earls Wk* . . . **128** D3
Pembroke Pl, W8 . . . **128** D3
Edgware HA8 . . . **54** A7
Isleworth TW7
off Thornbury Rd . . . **144** B2
Pembroke Rd, E6 . . . **116** C5
E17 . . . **78** B5
N8 . . . **74** E4
N10 . . . **74** A1
N13 . . . **59** J3
N15 . . . **76** C5
SE25 . . . **188** B4
W8 . . . **128** D4
Bromley BR1 . . . **191** J2
Erith DA8 . . . **139** J5
Greenford UB6 . . . **103** H4
Ilford IG3 . . . **99** J1
Mitcham CR4 . . . **186** A2
Wembley HA9 . . . **87** G3
Pembroke Sq, W8 . . . **128** D3
Pembroke St, N1 . . . **93** E7
Pembroke Studios, W8 . . . **128** C3
Pembroke Vil, W8 . . . **128** D4
Richmond TW9 . . . **145** G4
Pembroke Wk, W8 . . . **128** D4
Pembroke Way, Hayes
UB3 . . . **121** F3
Pembry Cl, SW9 . . . **151** G1
Pembury Av, Wor.Pk. KT4 . **183** G7
Pembury Cl, Brom. BR2 . . **191** F7
Pembury Ct, Hayes UB3 . . **121** G6
Pembury Cres, Sid. DA14 . **176** E2
Pembury Pl, E5 . . . **94** E5
Pembury Rd, E5 . . . **94** E5
N17 . . . **76** C2
SE25 . . . **188** D4
Bexleyheath DA7 . . . **139** E7
Pemdevon Rd, Croy. CR0 . **187** G7
Pemell Cl, E1
off Colebert Av . . . **113** F4
Pemerich Cl, Hayes UB3 . **121** J5
Pempath Pl, Wem. HA9 . . . **87** G2
Penally Pl, N1
off Shepperton Rd . . . **112** A1
Penang St, E1 . . . **133** E1
Penard Rd, Sthl. UB2 . . . **123** G3
Penarth St, SE15 . . . **133** F6
Penates, Esher KT10 . . . **194** A4
Penberth Rd, SE6 . . . **172** C2
Penbury Rd, Sthl. UB2 . . . **123** F4
Pencombe Ms, W11
off Denbigh Rd . . . **108** C7
Pencraig Way, SE15 . . . **132** E6
Pendall Cl, Barn. EN4 . . . **41** H4
Penda Rd, Erith DA8 . . . **139** H7
Pendarves Rd, SW20 . . . **183** J1
Penda's Mead, E9
off Lindisfarne Way . . . **95** H4
Pendell Av, Hayes UB3 . . . **121** J7
Pendennis Rd, N17 . . . **76** A3
SW16 . . . **168** E4
Penderel Rd, Houns. TW3 . **143** G5
Penderry Ri, SE6 . . . **172** D2
Penderyn Way, N7 . . . **92** D4
Pendle Rd, SW16 . . . **168** B6
Pendlestone Rd, E17 . . . **78** A5
Pendragon Rd, Brom.
BR1 . . . **173** F3
Pendragon Wk, NW9 . . . **70** E6
Pendrell Rd, SE4 . . . **153** H2
Pendrell St, SE18 . . . **137** G7
Pendula Dr, Hayes UB4 . . **102** D4
Pendulum Ms, E8
off Birkbeck Rd . . . **94** C5
Penerley Rd, SE6 . . . **172** B1
Penfold Cl, Croy. CR0
off Epsom Rd . . . **201** G3
Penfold La, Bex. DA5 . . . **176** D2
Penfold Pl, NW1 . . . **15** F1
Penfold Rd, N9 . . . **61** G1
Penfold St, NW1 . . . **7** F6
NW8 . . . **7** F6
Penford Gdns, SE9 . . . **156** A3
Penford St, SE5 . . . **151** H2
Pengarth Rd, Bex. DA5 . . **158** D5
PENGE, SE20 . . . **171** F7
Penge Ho, SW11
off Wye St . . . **149** G3
Penge La, SE20 . . . **171** F7
Penge Rd, E13 . . . **97** J7
SE20 . . . **188** D3
SE25 . . . **188** D3
Penhall Rd, SE7 . . . **136** A4
Penhill Rd, Bex. DA5 . . . **158** C7
Penhurst Pl, SE1 . . . **26** D6
Penhurst Rd, Ilf. IG6 . . . **65** E7
Penifather La, Grnf. UB6 . **104** A3
Peninsula Apartments, W2
off Praed St . . . **109** G5
Peninsula Hts, SE1
off Albert Embk . . . **130** E5
Peninsular Cl, Felt. TW14 . **141** G6
Peninsular Pk Rd, SE7 . . . **135** G4
Penistone Rd, SW16 . . . **168** E7
Penketh Dr, Har. HA1 . . . **86** A3
Penmon Rd, SE2 . . . **138** A3
Pennack Rd, SE15 . . . **37** G6
Pennant Ms, W8 . . . **30** A1
Pennant Ter, E17 . . . **77** J2
Pennard Rd, W12 . . . **127** J2
Pennards, The, Sun. TW16 . **178** C2
Penn Cl, Grnf. UB6 . . . **103** H2
Harrow HA3 . . . **69** F4
Penner Cl, SW19 . . . **166** B2
Penners Gdns, Surb. KT6 . **181** H7
Pennethorne Cl, E9
off Victoria Pk Rd . . . **113** F1
Pennethorne Ho, SW11
off Wye St . . . **149** G3
Pennethorne Rd, SE15 . . . **132** E7
Penn Gdns, Chis. BR7 . . . **192** E2
Pennine Dr, NW2 . . . **90** B2
Pennine Ho, N9
off Plevna Rd . . . **60** D3
Pennine La, NW2
off Pennine Dr . . . **90** B2
Pennine Way, Hayes UB3 . **121** G7
Pennington Cl, SE27
off Hamilton Rd . . . **170** A4
Pennington Dr, N21 . . . **43** E5
Pennington St, E1 . . . **21** J6
Pennington Way, SE12 . . . **173** H2
Penniston Cl, N17 . . . **75** J2
Penn La, Bex. DA5 . . . **158** D5
Penn Rd, N7 . . . **93** E5
Penn St, N1 . . . **112** A1
Pennyfather La, Enf. EN2 . . **43** J2
Pennyfields, E14 . . . **114** A7
Penny Ms, SW12
off Caistor Rd . . . **150** B7
Pennymoor Wk, W9
off Ashmore Rd . . . **108** C3
Penny Rd, NW10 . . . **106** B3
Pennyroyal Av, E6 . . . **116** D6
Penpoll Rd, E8 . . . **94** E6
Penpool La, Well. DA16 . . **158** B3
Penrhyn Av, E17 . . . **77** J1
Penrhyn Cres, E17 . . . **78** A1
SW14 . . . **146** C4
Penrhyn Gdns, Kings.T. KT1
off Surbiton Rd . . . **181** G4
Penrhyn Gro, E17 . . . **78** A1
Penrhyn Rd, Kings.T. KT1 . **181** H3
Penrith Cl, SW15 . . . **148** B5
Beckenham BR3
off Albemarle Rd . . . **190** B1
Penrith Pl, SE27
off Harpenden Rd . . . **169** H2
Penrith Rd, N15 . . . **76** A5
Ilford IG6 . . . **65** J6
New Malden KT3 . . . **182** D4
Thornton Heath CR7 . . . **187** J2
Penrith St, SW16 . . . **168** C6
Penrose Av, Wat. WD19 . . . **50** D2
Penrose Gro, SE17 . . . **35** J4
Penrose Ho, SE17 . . . **35** J4
Penrose St, SE17 . . . **35** J4
Penryn St, NW1 . . . **9** H1
Penry St, SE1 . . . **37** E2
Pensbury Pl, SW8 . . . **150** C2
Pensbury St, SW8 . . . **150** C2
Penscroft Gdns, Borwd.
WD6 . . . **38** D4
Pensford Av, Rich. TW9 . . . **146** A2
Penshurst Av, Sid. DA15 . **158** A6
Penshurst Gdns, . . . **54** B5
Penshurst Grn, Brom.
BR2 . . . **191** F5
Penshurst Rd, E9 . . . **95** G7
N17 . . . **60** C7
Bexleyheath DA7 . . . **159** F1
Thornton Heath CR7 . . . **187** H5
Penshurst Wk, Brom. BR2
off Hayesford Pk Dr . . . **191** F5
Penshurst Way, Sutt.
SM2 . . . **198** D7
Pensilver Cl, Barn. EN4 . . . **41** H4
Penstemon Cl, N3 . . . **56** D7
Penstock Footpath, N22 . . **75** E3
Pentavia Retail Pk, NW7
off Bunns La . . . **55** F7
Pentelow Gdns, Felt.
TW14 . . . **142** A6
Pentire Rd, E17 . . . **78** D1
Pentland Av, Edg. HA8 . . . **54** B2
Pentland Cl, N9 . . . **61** F2
NW11 . . . **90** B2
Pentland Gdns, SW18
off St. Ann's Hill . . . **149** F6
Pentland Pl, Nthlt. UB5 . . **102** E1
Pentlands Cl, Mitch. CR4 . **186** B3
Pentland St, SW18 . . . **149** F6
Pentlow St, SW15 . . . **147** J3
Pentlow Way, Buck.H. IG9 . **48** B7
Pentney Rd, E4 . . . **62** D1
SW12 . . . **168** C1
SW19 *off Midmoor Rd* . **184** B1
Penton Gro, N1 . . . **11** E2
Penton Ho, SE2
off Hartslock Dr . . . **138** D2
Penton Pl, SE17 . . . **35** H3
Penton Ri, WC1 . . . **10** D3
Penton St, N1 . . . **10** E1
PENTONVILLE, N1 . . . **10** E2
Pentonville Rd, N1 . . . **10** C2
Pentridge St, SE15 . . . **132** C7
Pentyre Av, N18 . . . **60** A5
Penwerris Av, Islw. TW7 . . **123** J7
Penwith Rd, SW18 . . . **166** E2

Penwood Ho, SW15
off Tunworth Cres **147** F6
Penwortham Rd, SW16 **168** B6
Penylan Pl, Edg. HA8 **54** A7
Penywern Rd, SW5 **128** D5
Penzance Pl, W11 **128** B1
Penzance St, W11 **128** B1
Peony Ct, Wdf.Grn. IG8
off The Bridle Path **62/63** E7
Peony Gdns, W12 **107** G7
Pepler Ms, SE5 **37** F5
Peploe Rd, NW6 **108** A2
Peplow Cl, West Dr. UB7
off Tavistock Rd **120** A1
Pepper All, Loug.
(High Beach) IG10 **47** G1
Pepper Cl, E6 **116** C5
Peppercorn Cl, Th.Hth.
CR7 **188** A2
Peppermead Sq, SE13 **154** A5
Peppermint Cl, Croy. CR0 **186** E7
Peppermint Pl, E11
off Birch Gro **96/97** E3
Pepper St, E14 **134** B3
SE1 **27** J3
Peppie Cl, N16
off Bouverie Rd **94** B2
Pepys Cres, E16
off Britannia Gate **135** G1
Barnet EN5 **39** J5
Pepys Ri, Orp. BR6 **207** J1
Pepys Rd, SE14 **153** G1
SW20 **183** J1
Pepys St, EC3 **21** E5
Perceval Av, NW3 **91** H5
Percheron Cl, Islw. TW7 **144** D3
Percheron Rd, Borwd. WD6 **38** D6
Perch St, E8 **94** C4
Percival Ct, N17
off High Rd **60** C7
Northolt UB5 **85** G5
★**Percival David Foundation**
of Chinese Art, WC1
off Gordon Sq **9** J6
Percival Gdns, Rom. RM6 **82** C6
Percival Rd, SW14 **146** C4
Enfield EN1 **44** C4
Orpington BR6 **207** E2
Percival St, EC1 **11** G5
Percival Way, Epsom
KT19 **196** C4
Percy Bush Rd, West Dr.
UB7 **120** C3
Percy Circ, WC1 **10** D3
Percy Gdns, Enf. EN3 **45** G5
Isleworth TW7 **144** D2
Worcester Park KT4 **196** D1
Percy Ms, W1 **17** H2
Percy Pas, W1 **17** G2
Percy Rd, E11 **78** E7
E16 **115** E5
N12 **57** F5
N21 **43** J7
SE20 **189** G1
SE25 **188** D5
W12 **127** G2
Bexleyheath DA7 **159** E2
Hampton TW12 **161** G7
Ilford IG3 **82** A7
Isleworth TW7 **144** D4
Mitcham CR4 **186** A7
Romford RM7 **83** H3
Twickenham TW2 **161** H1
Percy St, W1 **17** H2
Percy Way, Twick. TW2 **161** J1
Percy Yd, WC1 **10** D3
Peregrine Cl, NW10 **88** D5
Peregrine Ct, SW16
off Leithcote Gdns **169** F4
Welling DA16 **157** J1
Peregrine Gdns, Croy.
CR0 **203** H2
Peregrine Ho, EC1 **11** H3
Peregrine Way, SW19 **165** J7
Perham Rd, W14 **128** B5
Peridot St, E6 **116** B5
Perifield, SE21 **169** J1
Perimeade Rd, Grnf. UB6 **105** F2
Periton Rd, SE9 **156** A4
PERIVALE, Grnf. UB6 **105** F1
Perivale Gdns, W13
off Bellevue Rd **104/105** E4
Perivale Gra, Grnf. UB6 **104** D3
Perivale Ind Pk, Grnf. UB6 **104** E2
Perivale La, Grnf. UB6 **104** D3
Perivale New Business Cen,
Grnf. UB6 **105** E2
Perkin Cl, Houns. TW3 **143** H4
Wembley HA0 **86** E5
Perkin's Rents, SW1 **25** H5
Perkins Rd, Ilf. IG2 **81** G5
Perkins Sq, SE1 **28** A1
Perks Cl, SE3
off Hurren Cl **154/155** E3
Perpins Rd, SE9 **157** H6
Perran Rd, SW2
off Christchurch Rd **169** H2
Perran Wk, Brent. TW8 **125** H5
Perren St, NW5
off Ryland Rd **92** B6
Perrers Rd, W6 **127** H4
Perrin Rd, Wem. HA0 **86** D4
Perrins Ct, NW3
off Hampstead High St **91** F4
Perrins La, NW3 **91** F4
Perrin's Wk, NW3 **91** F4
Perrott St, SE18 **137** F4
Perry Av, W3 **106** D6
Perry Ct, E14
off Napier Av **134** A5
N15 *off Albert Rd* **76** B6
Perryfield Way, NW9 **71** F6
Richmond TW10 **163** E2
Perry Gdns, N9
off Deansway **60** B3
Perry Garth, Nthlt. UB5 **102** C1
Perry Hall Rd, Orp. BR6 **193** J6
Perry Hill, SE6 **171** J3
Perry Ho, SW2
off Tierney Rd **150/151** E7
Perry How, Wor.Pk. KT4 **197** F1
Perryman Ho, Bark. IG11 **117** F1
Perrymans Fm Rd, Ilf. IG2 **81** G6
Perry Mead, Enf. EN2 **43** H2
Perrymead St, SW6 **148** D1
Perryn Rd, SE16
off Drummond Rd **132/133** E3
W3 **106** D7
Perry Ri, SE23 **171** H3
Perry Rd, Dag. RM9 **119** F4
Perrys Pl, W1 **17** H3
Perry St, Chis. BR7 **175** G6
Perry St Gdns, Chis. BR7
off Old Perry St **175** H6
Perry Vale, SE23 **171** F2
Persant Rd, SE6 **172** E2
Perseverance Pl, SW9 **131** G7
Richmond TW9
off Shaftesbury Rd **145** H3
Pershore Cl, Ilf. IG2 **81** E5
Pershore Gro, Cars. SM5 **185** G6
Pert Cl, N10 **58** B7
Perth Av, NW9 **70** D7
Hayes UB4 **102** C4
Perth Cl, SW20
off Huntley Way **183** G2
Perth Rd, E10 **95** H1
E13 **115** H2
N4 **93** G1
N22 **75** H1
Barking IG11 **117** G2
Beckenham BR3 **190** C2
Ilford IG2 **80** D6
Perth Ter, Ilf. IG2 **81** F7
Perwell Av, Har. HA2 **85** F1
Perwell Ct, Har. HA2 **85** F1
Peter Av, NW10 **89** H7
Peterboat Cl, SE10
off Tunnel Av **134/135** E4
Peterborough Gdns, Ilf.
IG1 **80** B7
Peterborough Ms, SW6 **148** D2
Peterborough Rd, E10 **78** C5
SW6 **148** D2
Carshalton SM5 **185** H6
Harrow HA1 **86** B1
Peterborough Vil, SW6 **148** E1
Peterchurch Ho, SE15 *off*
Commercial Way **132/133** E6
Petergate, SW11 **149** F4
Peter Heathfield Ho, E15
off High St **114** D1
Peterhouse Gdns, SW6
off Bagley's La **148/149** E1
Peter James Business Cen,
Hayes UB3 **122** A2
Peterley Business Cen, E2
off Hackney Rd **112/113** E2
★**Peter Pan Statue**, W2 **23** E1
Peters Cl, Dag. RM8 **100** D1
Stanmore HA7 **53** G6
Welling DA16 **157** H2
Petersfield Cl, N18 **59** J5
Petersfield Ri, SW15 **165** H1
Petersfield Rd, W3 **126** C2
PETERSHAM, Rich. TW10 **163** H1
Petersham Cl, Rich. TW10 **163** G2
Sutton SM1 **198** D5
Petersham Dr, Orp. BR5 **193** J2
Petersham Gdns, Orp.
BR5 **193** J2
Petersham La, SW7 **22** C5
Petersham Ms, SW7 **22** C6
Petersham Pl, SW7 **22** C5
Petersham Rd, Rich. TW10 **145** H6
Petersham Ter, Croy. CR0
off Richmond Grn **200/201** E3
Peters Hill, EC4 **19** J5
Peter's La, EC1 **10** H1
Peters Path, SE26 **170** E4
Peterstone Rd, SE2 **138** B3
Peterstow Cl, SW19 **166** B2
Peter St, W1 **17** G5
Peterwood Way, Croy.
CR0 **201** F2
Petherton Rd, N5 **93** J5
Petley Rd, W6 **127** J6
Peto Pl, NW1 **8** E5
Peto St N, E16
off Victoria Dock Rd **115** F7
Petrie Cl, NW2 **90** B6
★**Petrie Mus of Egyptian**
Archaeology, WC1
off Malet Pl **9** H6
★**Petticoat La (Market)**, E1 **21** E2
Petticoat Sq, E1 **21** F3
Petticoat Twr, E1
off Petticoat Sq **112** C6
Pettits Pl, Dag. RM10 **101** G5
Pettits Rd, Dag. RM10 **101** G5
Pettiward Cl, SW15 **147** J4
Pettman Cres, SE28 **137** G3
Pettsgrove Av, Wem. HA0 **87** F5
Petts Hill, Nthlt. UB5 **85** H5
Pett St, SE18 **136** B4
PETTS WOOD, Orp. BR5 **193** G5
Petts Wd Rd, Orp. BR5 **193** F5
Petty France, SW1 **25** G5
Petty Wales, EC3
off Lower Thames St **112** B7
Petworth Cl, Nthlt. UB5 **85** F7
Petworth Gdns, SW20
off Hidcote Gdns **183** H3
Petworth Rd, N12 **57** H5
Bexleyheath DA6 **159** G5
Petworth St, SW11 **149** H1
Petyt Pl, SW3 **31** G6
Petyward, SW3 **31** H2
Pevensey Av, N11 **58** D5
Enfield EN1 **44** A2
Pevensey Cl, Islw. TW7 **123** J7
Pevensey Rd, E7 **97** F4
SW17 **167** G4
Feltham TW13 **160** E1
Peverel, E6 *off Downings* **116** D6
Peverel Ho, Dag. RM10 **101** G2
Peveret Cl, N11
off Woodland Rd **58** B5
Peveril Dr, Tedd. TW11 **162** A5
Pewsey Cl, E4 **62** A5
Peyton Pl, SE10 **134** C7
Pharaoh Cl, Mitch. CR4 **185** J7
Pheasant Cl, E16
off Maplin Rd **115** G6
Phelp St, SE17 **36** B5
Phelps Way, Hayes UB3 **121** J4
Phene St, SW3 **31** H5
Philbeach Gdns, SW5 **128** D5
Phil Brown Pl, SW8
off Daley Thompson
Way **150** B2
Philchurch Pl, E1 **21** J4
Philimore Cl, SE18 **137** H5
Philip Gdns, Croy. CR0 **203** J2
Philip La, N15 **76** A4
Philipot Path, SE9 **156** C6
Philippa Gdns, SE9 **156** A5
Philips Cl, Cars. SM5 **200** A1
Philip St, E13 **115** G4
Philip Wk, SE15 **152** D3
Phillimore Gdns, NW10 **107** J1
W8 **128** D2
Phillimore Gdns Cl, W8
off Phillimore Gdns **128** D3
Phillimore Pl, W8 **128** D2
Phillimore Wk, W8 **128** D3
Phillipp St, N1 **112** B1
Philpot La, EC3 **20** D5
Philpot Path, Ilf. IG1
off Sunnyside Rd **99** F3
Philpot Sq, SW6
off Peterborough
Rd **148/149** E3
Philpot St, E1 **113** E6
Phineas Pett Rd, SE9 **156** B3
Phipps Br Rd, SW19 **185** F2
Mitcham CR4 **185** F2
Phipp's Ms, SW1 **24** E6
Phipp St, EC2 **12** D5
Phoebeth Rd, SE4 **154** A5
Phoenix Cl, E8
off Stean St **112** C1
E17 **77** J2
West Wickham BR4 **204** E2
Phoenix Dr, Kes. BR2 **206** A3
Phoenix Pk, Brent. TW8 **125** G5
Phoenix Pl, WC1 **10** D5
Phoenix Rd, NW1 **9** H3
SE20 **171** F6
Phoenix St, WC2 **17** J4
Phoenix Way, Houns. TW5 **122** C6
Phoenix Wf, SE10 **135** F2
Phoenix Wf Rd, SE1 **29** G4
Phoenix Yd, WC1 **10** D4
★**Photographers' Gall**,
WC2 **17** J5
Phyllis Av, N.Mal. KT3 **183** H5
★**Physical Energy Statue**,
W2 **22** D2
Physic Pl, SW3 **31** J5
Piazza, The, WC2
off Covent Gdn **110/111** E7
Picardy Manorway, Belv.
DA17 **139** H3
Picardy Rd, Belv. DA17 **139** G4
Picardy St, Belv. DA17 **139** G3
Piccadilly, W1 **24** E2
Piccadilly Arc, SW1 **25** F1
Piccadilly Circ, W1 **17** H6
Piccadilly Pl, W1 **17** G6
Pickard St, EC1 **11** H3
Pickering Av, E6 **116** D2
Pickering Cl, E9
off Cassland Rd **95** G7
Pickering Gdns, N11 **58** A6
Croydon CR0 **188** C6
Pickering Ms, W2 **14** B3
Pickering Pl, SW1 **25** G2
Pickering St, N1
off Essex Rd **111** H1
Pickets Cl, Bushey
(Bushey Hth) WD23 **52** A1
Pickets St, SW12 **150** B7
Pickett Cft, Stan. HA7 **69** G1
Picketts Lock La, N9 **61** F2
Pickford Cl, Bexh. DA7 **158** E2
Pickford La, Bexh. DA7 **159** E2
Pickford Rd, Bexh. DA7 **158** E3
Pickfords Wf, N1 **11** J2
Pickhurst Grn, Brom. BR2 **191** F7
Pickhurst La, Brom. BR2 **205** F1
West Wickham BR4 **191** E6
Pickhurst Mead, Brom.
BR2 **191** F7
Pickhurst Pk, Brom. BR2 **191** E5
Pickhurst Ri, W.Wick. BR4 **190** C7
Pickle Herring St, SE1
off Tooley St **132** B1
Pickwick Cl, Houns. TW4
off Dorney Way **142/143** E5
Pickwick Ct, SE9
off West Pk **174** D1
Pickwick Ms, N18 **60** B5
Pickwick Pl, Har. HA1 **68** B7
Pickwick Rd, SE21 **152** A7
Pickwick St, SE1 **27** J4
Pickwick Way, Chis. BR7 **175** F6
Pickworth Cl, SW8
off Kenchester Cl **130/131** E7
Picton Pl, W1 **16** C4
Surbiton KT6 **196** A1
Picton St, SE5 **132** A7
Piedmont Rd, SE18 **137** G5
Pier Head, E1 *off*
Wapping High St **132/133** E1
Piermont Grn, SE22 **152** E5
Piermont Pl, Brom. BR1 **192** B2
Piermont Rd, SE22 **152** E5
Pier Par, E16
off Pier Rd **136** D1
Pierrepoint Arc, N1
off Islington High St **111** H2
Pierrepoint Rd, W3 **106** B7
Pierrepoint Row, N1 **11** G1
Pier Rd, E16 **136** C2
Feltham TW14 **142** B5
Pier St, E14 **134** C4
Pier Ter, SW18
off Jew's Row **149** F4
Pier Way, SE28 **137** G3
Pigeon La, Hmptn. TW12 **161** G4
Pigott St, E14 **114** A6
Pike Cl, Brom. BR1 **173** H5
Pike Rd, NW7
off Ellesmere Av **54** D4
Pikes End, Pnr. HA5 **66** B4

Pikestone Cl, Hayes UB4
off *Berrydale Rd* 102/103 E4
Pilgrimage St, SE1 28 B4
Pilgrim Cl, Mord. SM4 185 E7
Pilgrim Hill, SE27 169 J4
Pilgrims Cl, N13 59 F4
Northolt UB5 85 J5
Pilgrims Ct, SE3 155 G1
Pilgrim's La, NW3 91 G4
Pilgrims Ms, E14
off *Blackwall Way* 114 C7
Pilgrims Pl, NW3
off *Hampstead High St* 91 G4
Pilgrims Ri, Barn. EN4 41 H5
Pilgrim St, EC4 19 G4
Pilgrims Way, E6
off *High St N* 116 B1
N19 92 D1
South Croydon CR2 202 C5
Pilgrim's Way, Wem. HA9 88 B1
Pilkington Rd, SE15 152 E2
Orpington BR6 207 F2
Pilot Cl, SE8 133 J6
Pilsdon Cl, SW19
off *Inner Pk Rd* 166 A1
Piltdown Rd, Wat. WD19 50 D4
Pilton Est, The, Croy.
(Pitlake) CR0
off *Pitlake* 201 H2
Pilton Pl, SE17 36 A3
Pimento Ct, W5
off *Olive Rd* 125 G3
PIMLICO, SW1 33 F3
Pimlico Rd, SW1 32 B3
Pimlico Wk, N1 12 D3
Pinchbeck Rd, Orp. BR6 207 J6
Pinchin St, E1 21 J5
Pincott Pl, SE4 153 G4
Pincott Rd, SW19 167 F7
Bexleyheath DA6 159 G5
Pindar St, EC2 20 D1
Pindock Ms, W9 6 B6
Pineapple Ct, SW1 25 F5
Pine Av, E15 96 D5
West Wickham BR4 204 B1
Pine Cl, E10
off *Walnut Rd* 96 B2
N14 42 C7
N19 off *Hargrave Pk* 92 C2
SE20 189 F1
Stanmore HA7 52 E4
Pine Coombe, Croy. CR0 203 G4
Pinecrest Gdns, Orp. BR6 207 E4
Pinecroft Cres, Barn. EN5
off *Hillside Gdns* 40 B4
Pinedene, SE15
off *Meeting Ho La* 152/153 E1
Pinefield Cl, E14 114 A7
Pine Gdns, Ruis. HA4 84 B1
Surbiton KT5 182 A6
Pine Glade, Orp. BR6 206 C4
Pine Gro, N4 93 E2
N20 56 C1
SW19 166 C5
Pinehurst Wk, Orp. BR6 207 H1
Pinelands Cl, SE3
off *St. John's Pk* 135 F7
Pinemartin Cl, NW2 89 J3
Pine Ms, NW10
off *Clifford Gdns* 108 A2
Pine Rd, N11 58 A2
NW2 89 J4
Pines, The, N14 42 C5
Sunbury-on-Thames
TW16 178 A3
Woodford Green IG8 63 G3
Pines Rd, Brom. BR1 192 B2
Pine St, EC1 11 E5
Pine Tree Cl, Houns. TW5 142 B1
Pine Wk, Brom. BR1 191 J1
Surbiton KT5 182 A6
Pine Wd, Sun. TW16 178 A1
Pinewood Av, Pnr. HA5 51 H6
Sidcup DA15 175 H1
Pinewood Cl, Borwd. WD6 38 D1
Croydon CR0 203 H3
Northwood HA6 50 B5
Orpington BR6 207 G1
Pinner HA5 51 H6
Pinewood Dr, Orp. BR6 207 H5
Pinewood Gro, W5 105 F6
Pinewood Ms, Stai. (Stanw.)
TW19 140 A6
Pinewood Rd, SE2 138 D6
Bromley BR2 191 G4
Feltham TW13 160 B3
Pinfold Rd, SW16 168 E4
Pinglestone Cl, West Dr.
UB7 120 B7
Pinkcoat Cl, Felt. TW13
off *Tanglewood Way* 160 B3
Pinkerton Pl, SW16
off *Riggindale Rd* 168 D4
Pinkham Way, N11 58 A7
Pinkwell Av, Hayes UB3 121 G4
Pinkwell La, Hayes UB3 121 F4
Pinley Gdns, Dag. RM9
off *Stamford Rd* 118 B1
Pinnacle Hill, Bexh. DA7 159 H4
Pinnacle Hill N, Bexh.
DA7 159 H3
Pinnell Rd, SE9 156 A4
PINNER, HA5 67 E4
Pinner Ct, Pnr. HA5 67 G4
PINNER GREEN, Pnr. HA5 66 C1
Pinner Grn, Pnr. HA5 66 C2
Pinner Gro, Pnr. HA5 67 E4
Pinner Hill, Pnr. HA5 66 C1
Pinner Hill Rd, Pnr. HA5 66 C2
Pinner Pk, Pnr. HA5 67 G1
Pinner Pk Av, Har. HA2 67 H3
Pinner Pk Gdns, Har. HA2 67 J2
Pinner Rd, Har. HA1, HA2 67 H5
Pinner HA5 67 F4
Pinner Vw, Har. HA1, HA2 67 J6
PINNERWOOD PARK, Pnr.
HA5 50 C7
Pintail Cl, E6
off *Swan App* 116 B5
Pintail Rd, Wdf.Grn. IG8 63 H7
Pintail Way, Hayes UB4 102 D5
Pinter Ho, SW9
off *Grantham Rd* 150/151 E2
Pinto Cl, Borwd. WD6
off *Percheron Rd* 38 D6
Pinto Way, SE3 155 H4
Pioneers Ind Pk, Croy.
CR0 200 E1
Pioneer St, SE15 152 D1
Pioneer Way, W12
off *Du Cane Rd* 107 H6
Piper Cl, N7 93 F6
Piper Rd, Kings.T. KT1 182 A3
Piper's Gdns, Croy. CR0 189 H7
Pipers Grn, NW9 70 C5
Pipers Grn La, Edg. HA8 53 H3
Pipewell Rd, Cars. SM5 185 H6
Pippin Cl, NW2 89 H3
Croydon CR0 203 J1
Pippins Cl, West Dr. UB7 120 A3
Piquet Rd, SE20 189 F2
Pirbright Cres, Croy.
(New Adgtn) CR0 204 C6
Pirbright Rd, SW18 166 C1
Pirie Cl, SE5
off *Denmark Hill* 152 A3
Pirie St, E16 135 H1
Pitcairn Cl, Rom. RM7 83 G4
Pitcairn Rd, Mitch. CR4 167 J7
Pitcairn's Path, Har. HA2
off *Eastcote Rd* 85 J3
Pitchford St, E15 96 D7
Pitfield Cres, SE28 138 A1
Pitfield Est, N1 12 C3
Pitfield St, N1 12 D4
Pitfield Way, NW10 88 C6
Enfield EN3 45 F1
Pitfold Cl, SE12 155 G6
Pitfold Rd, SE12 155 G6
Pitlake, Croy. CR0 201 H2
Pitman Ho, SE8
off *Tanners Hill* 154 A1
Pitman St, SE5 35 J7
Pitmaston Ho, SE13
off *Lewisham Rd* 154 C2
Pitmaston Rd, SE13
off *Morden Hill* 154 C2
Pitsea Pl, E1
off *Pitsea St* 113 G6
Pitsea St, E1 113 G6
Pitshanger La, W5 105 E4
★**Pitshanger Manor & Gall**,
W5 125 F1
Pitshanger Pk, W13 105 F3
Pitt Cres, SW19 166 E4
Pittman Gdns, Ilf. IG1 99 F5
Pitt Rd, Croy. CR0 187 J5
Orpington BR6 207 F4
Thornton Heath CR7 187 J5
Pitt's Head Ms, W1 24 C2
Pittsmead Av, Brom. BR2 191 G7
Pitt St, W8 128 D2
Pittville Gdns, SE25 188 D3
Pixfield Ct, Brom. BR2
off *Beckenham La* 191 F2
Pixley St, E14 113 J6
Place Fm Av, Orp. BR6 207 G1
PLAISTOW, E13 115 F3
PLAISTOW, Brom. BR1 173 F6
Plaistow Gro, E15 115 F1
Bromley BR1 173 H7
Plaistow La, Brom. BR1 173 H7
Plaistow Pk Rd, E13 115 H2
Plaistow Rd, E13 115 F1
E15 115 F1
Plane St, SE26 170 E3
★**Planetarium**, NW1 8 A6
Plane Tree Cres, Felt.
TW13 160 B3
Plane Tree Wk, N2 73 G3
SE19
off *Central Hill* 170 B6
Plantagenet Cl, Wor.Pk.
KT4 196 D4
Plantagenet Gdns, Rom.
RM6 82 D7
Plantagenet Pl, Rom. RM6
off *Broomfield Rd* 82 D7
Plantagenet Rd, Barn. EN5 41 F4
Plantain Gdns, E11
off *Hollydown Way* 96 D3
Plantain Pl, SE1 28 B3
Plantation, The, SE3 155 G2
Plantation Wf, SW11 149 F3
Plasel Ct, E13
off *Plashet Rd* 115 G1
Plashet Gro, E6 115 J1
Plashet Rd, E13 115 G1
Plassy Rd, SE6 154 B7
Platina St, EC2 12 C5
Plato Rd, SW2 151 E4
Platt, The, SW15 148 A3
Platt's Eyot, Hmptn. TW12 179 G2
Platt's La, NW3 90 D4
Platts Rd, Enf. EN3 45 F1
Platt St, NW1 9 H1
Plawsfield Rd, Beck. BR3 189 G1
Plaxtol Cl, Brom. BR1 191 J1
Plaxtol Rd, Erith DA8 139 G7
Plaxton Ct, E11
off *Woodhouse Rd* 97 F3
Playfair St, W6
off *Winslow Rd* 127 J5
Playfield Av, Rom. RM5 83 J1
Playfield Cres, SE22 152 C5
Playfield Rd, Edg. HA8 70 C2
Playford Rd, N4 93 F2
Playgreen Way, SE6 172 A4
Playground Cl, Beck. BR3
off *Churchfields Rd* 189 G2
Playhouse Ct, SE1
off *Southwark Br Rd* 131 J2
Playhouse Yd, EC4 19 G4
Plaza Par, NW6
off *Kilburn High Rd* 108/109 E2
Plaza Shop Cen, The, W1 17 G3
Plaza W, Houns. TW3 143 H1
Pleasance, The, SW15 147 H4
Pleasance Rd, SW15 147 H5
Pleasant Gro, Croy. CR0 203 J3
Pleasant Pl, N1 93 H7
Pleasant Row, NW1 110 B1
Pleasant Vw Pl, Orp. BR6
off *High St* 206/207 E5
Pleasant Way, Wem. HA0 105 F2
Plender St, NW1 110 C1
Pleshey Rd, N7 92 D4
Plevna Cres, N15 76 B6
Plevna Rd, N9 60 D3
Hampton TW12 179 H1
Plevna St, E14 134 C3
Pleydell Av, SE19 170 C7
W6 127 F4
Pleydell Ct, EC4 19 F4
Pleydell Est, EC1
off *Radnor St* 111 J3
Pleydell St, EC4 19 F4
Plimsoll Cl, E14
off *Grundy St* 114 B6
Plimsoll Rd, N4 93 G3
Plough Ct, EC3 20 C5
Plough La, SE22 152 C6
SW17 167 E5
SW19 167 E5
Teddington TW11 162 D5
Wallington SM6 200 E4
Plough La Cl, Wall. SM6 200 E5
Ploughmans Cl, NW1
off *Crofters Way* 110 D1
Ploughmans End, Islw.
TW7 144 A5
Ploughmans Wk, N2
off *Long La* 73 F2
Plough Ms, SW11
off *Plough Ter* 149 G4
Plough Pl, EC4 19 F3
Plough Rd, SW11 149 G3
Plough St, E1 21 H3
Plough Ter, SW11 149 G4
Plough Way, SE16 133 G4
Plough Yd, EC2 12 E6
Plover Way, SE16 133 H3
Hayes UB4 102 D6
Plowden Bldgs, EC4
off *Middle Temple La* 111 G6
Plowman Cl, N18 60 A5
Plowman Way, Dag. RM8 100 C1
Plumbers Row, E1 21 H2
Plumbridge St, SE10
off *Blackheath Hill* 154 C1
Plum Cl, Felt. TW13
off *Highfield Rd* 160 A1
Plum Garth, Brent. TW8 125 G4
Plum La, SE18 137 E7
Plummer La, Mitch. CR4 185 J2
Plummer Rd, SW4 150 D7
Plumpton Cl, Nthlt. UB5 85 G6
Plumpton Way, Cars.
SM5 199 H3
PLUMSTEAD, SE18 137 H5
Plumstead Common Rd,
SE18 136 E6
Plumstead High St, SE18 137 H4
Plumstead Rd, SE18 137 E4
Plumtree Cl, Dag. RM10 101 H6
Wallington SM6 200 D7
Plumtree Ct, EC4 19 F3
Plumtree Mead, Loug.
IG10 48 D3
Plymouth Rd, E16 115 G5
Bromley BR1 191 H1
Plymouth Wf, E14 134 D4
Plympton Av, NW6 90 C7
Plympton Cl, Belv. DA17
off *Halifield Dr* 138/139 E3
Plympton Pl, NW8 7 G6
Plympton Rd, NW6 90 C7
Plympton St, NW8 7 G6
Plymstock Rd, Well. DA16 138 C7
Pocklington Cl, NW9 70 E2
Pocock Av, West Dr. UB7 120 C3
Pocock St, SE1 27 G3
Podmore Rd, SW18 149 F4
Poets Rd, N5 94 A5
Poets Way, Har. HA1
off *Blawith Rd* 68 B4
Pointalls Cl, N3 73 F2
Point Cl, SE10
off *Point Hill* 154 C1
Pointer Cl, SE28 118 D6
Pointers Cl, E14 134 B5
Point Hill, SE10 134 C7
Point of Thomas Path, E1
off *Glamis Rd* 113 F7
Point Pl, Wem. HA9 88 B7
Point Pleasant, SW18 148 D4
Point W, SW7
off *Cromwell Rd* 128 E4
Point Wf La, Brent. TW8
off *High St* 125 H6
Poland Ho, E15 114 D1
Poland Ct, W1 17 G4
Polebrook Rd, SE3 155 J3
Pole Cat All, Brom. BR2 205 F2
Polecroft La, SE6 171 J2
Polehamptons, The, Hmptn.
TW12
off *High St* 161 J7
Pole Hill Rd, E4 46 C7
Polesden Gdns, SW20 183 H2
Polesworth Ho, W2 108 D5
Polesworth Rd, Dag. RM9 100 D7
★**Polish Inst & Sikorski Mus**,
SW7 off *Princes Gate* 23 F4
Pollard Cl, E16 115 G7
N7 93 F5
Pollard Rd, N20 57 H2
Morden SM4 185 G5
Pollard Row, E2 13 J3
Pollards Cl, Loug. IG10 47 J5
Pollards Cres, SW16 187 E3
Pollards Hill E, SW16 187 F3
Pollards Hill N, SW16 187 E3
Pollards Hill S, SW16 187 E3
Pollards Hill W, SW16 187 E3
Pollard St, E2 13 J3
Pollards Wd Rd, SW16 187 E2
Pollard Wk, Sid. DA14 176 C6
Pollen St, W1 17 E4
Pollitt Dr, NW8 7 E5
★**Pollock's Toy Mus**, W1 17 G1
Polperro Cl, Orp. BR6
off *Cotswold Ri* 193 J6
Polperro Ms, SE11 35 F1
Polsted Rd, SE6 153 J7
Polthorne Est, SE18 137 G4

Polthorne Gro, SE18 . . . . 137 F4
Polworth Rd, SW16 . . . . . 168 E5
Polygon, The, SW4
off Old Town 150 C4
Polygon Rd, NW1 . . . . 9 H2
Polytechnic St, SE18 . . . . 136 D4
Pomell Way, E1 . . . . 21 G3
Pomeroy St, SE14 . . . . . . 153 F1
Pomfret Rd, SE5
off Flaxman Rd 151 H3
Pomoja La, N19 . . . . 92 D2
Pond Cl, N12
off Summerfields Av. . . 57 H6
SE3 . . . . 155 F2
Pond Cottage La, W.Wick.
BR4 . . . . 204 A1
Pond Cotts, SE21 . . . . 170 B1
PONDERS END, Enf. EN3. . 45 F5
Ponders End Ind Est, Enf.
EN3 . . . . 45 J4
Pond Fld End, Loug. IG10 . 47 J7
Pondfield Rd, Brom. BR2 . 205 E1
Dagenham RM10 . . . . . . 101 H5
Orpington BR6 . . . . 207 E3
Pond Hill Gdns, Sutt.
SM3 . . . . 198 B6
Pond Mead, SE21 . . . . 152 A6
Pond Path, Chis. BR7
off Heathfield La. . 174/175 E6
Pond Pl, SW3 . . . . 31 G2
Pond Rd, E15 . . . . 114 E2
SE3 . . . . 155 F2
Pondside Cl, Hayes UB3
off Providence La 121 G7
Pond Sq, N6
off South Gro 92 A1
Pond St, NW3 . . . . 91 H5
Pond Way, Tedd. TW11
off Holmesdale Rd . . . 163 F6
Pondwood Ri, Orp. BR6. . 193 H7
Ponler St, E1 . . . . 112 E6
Ponsard Rd, NW10 . . . . . 107 H3
Ponsford St, E9 . . . . 95 F6
Ponsonby Pl, SW1 . . . . 33 J3
Ponsonby Rd, SW15 . . . . 147 H7
Ponsonby Ter, SW1 . . . . . . 33 J3
Pontefract Rd, Brom. BR1. 173 F5
Ponton Rd, SW8 . . . . 33 J6
Pont St, SW1 . . . . 23 J6
Pont St Ms, SW1 . . . . 23 J6
Pontypool Pl, SE1 . . . . 27 G3
Pool Cl, Beck. BR3 . . . . . . 172 A5
West Molesey KT8 . . . . 179 F5
Pool Ct, SE6 . . . . 172 A2
Poole Ct Rd, Houns. TW4
off Vicarage Fm Rd. 142/143 E2
Poole Rd, E9 . . . . 95 G6
Epsom KT19 . . . . 196 D6
Pooles Bldgs, EC1 . . . . 10 E6
Pooles La, SW10
off Lots Rd 129 F7
Dagenham RM9 . . . . . . 119 E2
Pooles Pk, N4
off Seven Sisters Rd . . . 93 G2
Poole St, N1 . . . . 112 A1
Poolmans St, SE16 . . . . . . 133 G2
Pool Rd, Har. HA1 . . . . 68 A7
West Molesey KT8 . . . . 179 F6
Poolsford Rd, NW9 . . . . 71 E4
Poonah St, E1
off Hardinge St 113 F6
Pope Cl, SW19 . . . . 167 G6
Pope Rd, Brom. BR2 . . . . . 192 A5
Popes Av, Twick. TW2 . . . . 162 B2
Popes Dr, N3 . . . . 72 D1
Popes Gro, Croy. CR0 . . . . 203 J3
Twickenham TW1, TW2 . 162 C2
Pope's Head All, EC3
off Cornhill 112 A6
Popes La, W5 . . . . 125 G3
Popes Rd, SW9 . . . . 151 G3
Pope St, SE1 . . . . 29 E4
Popham Cl, Felt. TW13 . . . 161 F3
Popham Gdns, Rich. TW9
off Lower
Richmond Rd 146 A3
Popham Rd, N1 . . . . 111 J1
Popham St, N1 . . . . 111 H1
POPLAR, E14 . . . . 114 B7
Poplar Av, Mitch. CR4 . . . . 185 J1
Orpington BR6 . . . . 207 E2
Southall UB2 . . . . 123 H3
Poplar Bath St, E14
off Lawless St 114 B7
Poplar Business Pk, E14. . 114 C7
Poplar Cl, E9 off
Lee Conservancy Rd. . . 95 J5
Pinner HA5 . . . . 66 D1
Poplar Ct, SW19 . . . . 166 D5
Poplar Cres, Epsom KT19. 196 C6
Poplar Fm Cl, Epsom
KT19 . . . . 196 C6
Poplar Gdns, N.Mal. KT3 . 182 D2
Poplar Gro, N11 . . . . 58 A6
W6 . . . . 127 J2
New Malden KT3 . . . . . 182 D3
Wembley HA9 . . . . 88 C3
Poplar High St, E14 . . . . . 114 A7
Poplar Mt, Belv. DA17 . . . 139 H4
Poplar Pl, SE28 . . . . 118 C7
W2 . . . . 14 A5
Hayes UB3
off Central Av 102 A7
Poplar Rd, SE24 . . . . 151 J4
SW19 . . . . 184 D2
Sutton SM3 . . . . 198 C1
Poplar Rd S, SW19 . . . . . . 184 D3
Poplars, The, N14 . . . . 42 B5
Poplars Av, NW10 . . . . 89 J6
Poplars Rd, E17 . . . . 78 B6
Poplar St, Rom. RM7 . . . . . 83 J4
Poplar Vw, Wem. HA9
off Magnet Rd 87 G2
Poplar Wk, SE24 . . . . 151 J4
Croydon CR0 . . . . 201 J2
Poplar Way, Felt. TW13 . . . 160 A3
Ilford IG6 . . . . 81 F4
Poppins Ct, EC4 . . . . 19 G4
Poppleton Rd, E11 . . . . 79 E6
Poppy Cl, Belv. DA17 . . . . 139 H3
Northolt UB5 . . . . 85 F6
Wallington SM6 . . . . . . 200 A1
★Poppy Factory Mus, The,
Rich. TW10 . . . . 145 G6
Poppy La, Croy. CR0 . . . . . 189 F7
Porchester Cl, SE5 . . . . . . 151 J4
Porchester Gdns, W2 . . . . . 14 A5
Porchester Gdns Ms, W2 . . 14 B4
Porchester Mead, Beck.
BR3 . . . . 172 B6
Porchester Ms, W2 . . . . 14 B3
Porchester Pl, W2 . . . . 15 H4
Porchester Rd, W2 . . . . 14 A3
Kingston upon Thames
KT1 . . . . 182 B2
Porchester Sq, W2 . . . . 14 B3
Porchester Ter, W2 . . . . 14 C4
Porchester Ter N, W2 . . . . . 14 B3
Porch Way, N20 . . . . 57 J3
Porcupine Cl, SE9 . . . . 174 B2
Porden Rd, SW2 . . . . 151 F4
Porlock Av, Har. HA2 . . . . . 85 J1
Porlock Rd, W10
off Ladbroke Gro 108 A4
Enfield EN1 . . . . 44 C7
Porlock St, SE1 . . . . 28 B3
Porrington Cl, Chis. BR7. . 192 C1
Portal Cl, SE27 . . . . 160 C3
Ruislip HA4 . . . . 84 A4
Portal Way, W3
off Victoria Rd 106 D5
Portbury Cl, SE15
off Clayton Rd 152 D1
Port Cres, E13
off Jenkins Rd 115 H4
★Portcullis Ho, SW1 . . . . . 26 A3
Portcullis Lo Rd, Enf. EN2 . 44 A3
Portelet Ct, N1
off De Beauvoir Est . . . 112 B1
Portelet Rd, E1 . . . . 113 G3
Porten Rd, W14 . . . . 128 B3
Porter Rd, E6 . . . . 116 C6
Porters Av, Dag. RM8,
RM9 . . . . 100 B6
Portersfield Rd, Enf. EN1 . . 44 B4
Porter Sq, N19
off Hornsey Rd 92/93 E1
Porter St, SE1 . . . . 28 A1
W1 . . . . 16 A1
Porters Wk, E1
off Pennington St. 112/113 E7
Porters Way, West Dr. UB7. 120 C3
Porteus Rd, W2 . . . . 14 D2
Portgate Cl, W9 . . . . 108 C4
Porthallow Cl, Orp. BR6
off Sevenoaks Rd 207 J4
Porthcawe Rd, SE26 . . . . . 171 H4
Porthkerry Av, Well. DA16 158 A4
Portia Way, E3 . . . . 113 J4
Portinscale Rd, SW15 . . . . 148 B5
Portland Av, N16 . . . . 76 C7
New Malden KT3 . . . . . 183 F7
Sidcup DA15 . . . . 158 A6
Portland Cl, Rom. RM6 . . . 82 E5
Worcester Park KT4 . . . . 183 H7
Portland Cres, SE9 . . . . . . 174 B2
Greenford UB6 . . . . 103 H4
Stanmore HA7 . . . . 69 G2
Portland Gdns, N4 . . . . 75 H6
Romford RM6 . . . . 82 D5
Portland Gro, SW8 . . . . . . 151 F1
Portland Ms, W1 . . . . 17 G4
Portland Pl, W1 . . . . 16 E2
Portland Ri, N4 . . . . 93 H1
Portland Ri Est, N4 . . . . 93 J1
Portland Rd, N15 . . . . 76 C4
SE9 . . . . 174 B2
SE25 . . . . 188 D4
W11 . . . . 108 B7
Bromley BR1 . . . . 173 J4
Kingston upon Thames
KT1 . . . . 181 H3
Mitcham CR4 . . . . 185 H2
Southall UB2 . . . . 123 F3
Portland Sq, E1
off Watts St 132/133 E1
Portland St, SE17 . . . . 36 B3
Portland Ter, Rich. TW9 . . . 145 G4
Portland Wk, SE17 . . . . 36 C5
Portman Av, SW14 . . . . . . 146 D3
Portman Cl, W1 . . . . 16 A3
Bexleyheath DA7
off Queen Anne's Gate . 158 D3
Portman Dr, Wdf.Grn. IG8 . 80 A2
Portman Gdns, NW9 . . . . . . 70 D2
Portman Gate, NW1 . . . . 7 H6
Portman Hall, Har. HA3 . . . 52 A4
Portman Ms S, W1 . . . . 16 B4
Portman Pl, E2 . . . . 113 F3
Portman Rd, Kings.T. KT1 . 181 J2
Portman Sq, W1 . . . . 16 A3
Portman St, W1 . . . . 16 B4
Portmeadow Wk, SE2 . . . . 138 D2
Portmeers Cl, E17
off Lennox Rd 77 J6
Portnall Rd, W9 . . . . 108 C2
Portobello Ct, W11
off Westbourne Gro . . . 108 C7
Portobello Ms, W11
off Portobello Rd 108 D7
Portobello Rd, W10 . . . . . 108 C6
W11 . . . . 108 C6
Porton Ct, Surb. KT6 . . . . 181 F6
Portpool La, EC1 . . . . 18 E1
Portree Cl, N22
off Nightingale Rd 59 F7
Portree St, E14 . . . . 114 D6
Portsdown, Edg. HA8
off Rectory La 54 A5
Portsdown Av, NW11 . . . . . 72 C6
Portsdown Ms, NW11 . . . . 72 C6
Portsea Ms, W2 . . . . 15 H4
Portsea Pl, W2 . . . . 15 H4
Portslade Rd, SW8 . . . . . . 150 C2
Portsmouth Av, T.Ditt. KT7 . 180 D7
Portsmouth Ms, E16
off Wesley Av 135 H1
Portsmouth Rd, SW15 . . . . 147 H7
Kingston upon Thames
KT1 . . . . 181 F5
Surbiton KT6 . . . . 181 F5
Thames Ditton KT7 . . . . 194 B2
Portsmouth St, WC2 . . . . . . 18 C4
Portsoken St, E1 . . . . 21 F5
Portugal Gdns, Twick. TW2
off Fulwell Pk Av 161 J2
Portugal St, WC2 . . . . 18 C4
Portway, E15 . . . . 115 F1
Portway Gdns, SE18
off Shooter's Hill Rd . . 136 A7
Postern Grn, Enf. EN2 . . . . 43 G2
Post La, Twick. TW2 . . . . . 162 A1
Postmill Cl, Croy. CR0 . . . . 203 G3
Post Office App, E7 . . . . . . 97 H5
Post Office Ct, EC3 . . . . . . 20 C4
Post Office Way, SW8 . . . . 33 H7
Post Rd, Sthl. UB2 . . . . . . 123 H3
Postway Ms, Ilf. IG1
off Clements Rd 98/99 E3
Potier St, SE1 . . . . 28 C6
Potter Cl, Mitch. CR4 . . . . 186 B2
Potterne Cl, SW19 . . . . . . 148 A7
Potters Cl, SE15
off Chandler Way 132 B7
Croydon CR0 . . . . 203 H1
Loughton IG10 . . . . 48 B2
Potters Flds, SE1 . . . . 29 E2
Potters Gro, N.Mal. KT3 . . 182 C4
Potters Hts Cl, Pnr. HA5 . . . 50 B7
Potters La, SW16 . . . . 168 D6
Barnet EN5 . . . . 40 D4
Borehamwood WD6 . . . . 38 C1
Potters Rd, SW6 . . . . 149 F2
Barnet EN5 . . . . 40 E4
Potter St, Nthwd. HA6 . . . . 66 A1
Pinner HA5 . . . . 66 B1
Potter St Hill, Pnr. HA5 . . . 50 B6
Pottery La, W11
off Portland Rd 108 B7
Pottery Rd, Bex. DA5 . . . . 177 J2
Brentford TW8 . . . . 125 H6
Pottery St, SE16 . . . . 132 E2
Pott St, E2 . . . . 113 E3
Poulett Gdns, Twick. TW1 . 162 D1
Poulett Rd, E6 . . . . 116 C2
Poulner Way, SE15
off Daniel Gdns 132 C7
Poulters Wd, Kes. BR2 . . . 206 A5
Poulton Av, Sutt. SM1 . . . 199 G3
Poulton Cl, E8
off Spurstowe Ter . . 94/95 E5
Poultry, EC2 . . . . 20 B4
Pound Cl, Orp. BR6 . . . . . 207 G2
Surbiton KT6 . . . . 195 F1
Pound Ct Dr, Orp. BR6 . . . 207 G2
Pound Fm Cl, Esher KT10 . 194 A1
Poundfield Rd, Loug. IG10 . 48 D5
Pound La, NW10 . . . . 89 G6
Pound Pk Rd, SE7 . . . . 136 A4
Pound Pl, SE9 . . . . 156 D6
Pound St, Cars. SM5 . . . . . 199 J5
Pound Way, Chis. BR7
off Royal Par 175 F7
Pountney Rd, SW11 . . . . . 150 A3
POVEREST, Orp. BR5 . . . . 193 J5
Poverest Rd, Orp. BR5 . . . 193 J5
Powder Mill La, Twick.
TW2 . . . . 161 F1
Powell Cl, Chess. KT9
off Coppard Gdns 195 G5
Edgware HA8 . . . . 53 J6
Wallington SM6 . . . . . . 200 D7
Powell Gdns, Dag. RM10 . 101 G4
Powell Rd, E5 . . . . 95 E3
Buckhurst Hill IG9 . . . . . 47 J7
Powell's Wk, W4 . . . . 127 E6
Powergate Business Pk,
NW10 . . . . 106 D3
Power Rd, W4 . . . . 126 A4
Powers Ct, Twick. TW1 . . . 145 G7
Powerscroft Rd, E5 . . . . . . 95 F4
Sidcup DA14 . . . . 176 C6
Powis Gdns, NW11 . . . . 72 C7
W11 . . . . 108 C6
Powis Ms, W11
off Westbourne Pk Rd . 108 C6
Powis Pl, WC1 . . . . 10 B6
Powis Rd, E3 . . . . 114 B3
Powis Sq, W11 . . . . 108 C6
Powis St, SE18 . . . . 136 D3
Powis Ter, W11 . . . . 108 C6
Powle Ter, Ilf. IG1
off Oaktree Gro 99 F5
Powlett Pl, NW1
off Harmood St 92 B6
Pownall Gdns, Houns.
TW3 . . . . 143 H4
Pownall Rd, E8 . . . . 112 C1
Hounslow TW3 . . . . 143 H4
Pownsett Ter, Ilf. IG1
off Buttsbury Rd 99 F5
Powster Rd, Brom. BR1 . . 173 H5
Powys Cl, Bexh. DA7 . . . . 138 D6
Powys Ct, Borwd. WD6
off Kensington Way 38 D3
Powys La, N13 . . . . 58 E5
N14 . . . . 58 E4
Poynders Ct, SW4
off Poynders Rd 150 C6
Poynders Gdns, SW4 . . . . 150 C7
Poynders Rd, SW4 . . . . . . 150 C6
Poynings Rd, N19 . . . . 92 C3
Poynings Way, N12 . . . . 56 D5
Poyntell Cres, Chis. BR7. . 193 G1
Poynter Ho, W11 . . . . 128 A1
Poynter Rd, Enf. EN1 . . . . . 44 D5
Poynton Rd, N17 . . . . 76 D2
Poyntz Rd, SW11 . . . . 149 J2
Poyser St, E2 . . . . 113 E2
Praed Ms, W2 . . . . 15 F3
Praed St, W2 . . . . 15 G2
Pragel St, E13 . . . . 115 H2
Pragnell Rd, SE12 . . . . . . 173 H2
Prague Pl, SW2 . . . . 150 E5
Prah Rd, N4 . . . . 93 G2
Prairie St, SW8 . . . . 150 A2
Pratt Ms, NW1
off Pratt St 110 C1
Pratts Pas, Kings.T. KT1
off Eden St 181 H2
Pratt St, NW1 . . . . 110 C1
Pratt Wk, SE11 . . . . 34 D1
Prayle Gro, NW2 . . . . 90 A1
Prebend Gdns, W4 . . . . . . 127 F3
W6 . . . . 127 F3
Prebend St, N1 . . . . 111 J1

Precinct, The, W.Mol. KT8
off Victoria Av 179 H3
Precinct Rd, Hayes UB3 . . 102 A7
Precincts, The, Mord. SM4
off Green La 184 D6
Premier Cor, W9
off Kilburn La 108 C2
Premiere Pl, E14
off Garford St 114 A7
Premier Pk, NW10 . . . . . . 106 B1
Premier Pk Rd, NW10. . . . 106 B2
Premier Pl, SW15
off Putney High St. . . . 148 B4
Prendergast Rd, SE3 . . . . 155 E3
Prentis Rd, SW16 . . . . 168 D4
Prentiss Ct, SE7 . . . . 136 A4
Presburg Rd, N.Mal. KT3 . 183 E5
Presburg St, E5
off Glyn Rd 95 G3
Prescelly Pl, Edg. HA8 . . . . 69 J1
Prescot St, E1. . . . . 21 G5
Prescott Av, Orp. BR5. . . . 192 E6
Prescott Cl, SW16 . . . . . . 168 E7
Prescott Grn, Loug. IG10 . . 49 F3
Prescott Ho, SE17 . . . . 35 H6
Prescott Pl, SW4 . . . . 150 D3
Presentation Ms, SW2
off Palace Rd. 169 F1
President Dr, E1
off Waterman Way. 132/133 E1
President St, EC1 . . . . 11 J3
Prespa Cl, N9
off Hudson Way 61 F2
Press Rd, NW10 . . . . 88 D3
Prestage Way, E14 . . . . . . 114 C7
Prestbury Rd, E7 . . . . 97 J7
Prestbury Sq, SE9 . . . . . . 174 C4
Prested Rd, SW11
off St. John's Hill. 149 H4
Prestige Way, NW4
off Heriot Rd 71 J5
PRESTON, Wem. HA9 . . . . 69 G7
Preston Av, E4 . . . . 62 D6
Preston Cl, SE1 . . . . 36 D1
Twickenham TW2 . . . . . 162 B3
Preston Dr, E11. . . . . 79 J5
Bexleyheath DA7 . . . . . 158 D1
Epsom KT19 . . . . 197 E6
Preston Gdns, NW10
off Church Rd. 88/89 E6
Ilford IG1. . . . . 80 B6
Preston Hill, Har. HA3 . . . . 69 J6
Preston Pl, NW2. . . . . 89 G6
Richmond TW10 . . . . 145 H5
Preston Rd, E11 . . . . 79 E6
SE19 . . . . 169 H6
SW20. . . . . 165 F7
Harrow HA3 . . . . 69 H7
Wembley HA9. . . . . 87 H2
Prestons Rd, E14 . . . . 134 C2
Bromley BR2. . . . . 205 G3
Preston Waye, Har. HA3. . . 87 H1
Prestwick Cl, Sthl. UB2
off Ringway 122/123 E5
Prestwick Rd, Wat. WD19. . . 50 D5
Prestwood Av, Har. HA3 . . 69 E4
Prestwood Cl, SE18 . . . . . 138 A7
Harrow HA3 . . . . 69 F4
Prestwood Gdns, Croy.
CR0 . . . . 187 J7
Prestwood St, N1 . . . . 12 A2
Pretoria Av, E17 . . . . 77 H4
Pretoria Cl, N17
off Pretoria Rd. 60 C7
Pretoria Cres, E4 . . . . 62 C1
Pretoria Rd, E4. . . . . 62 C1
E11. . . . . 96 D1
E16. . . . . 115 F3
N17 . . . . 60 C7
SW16. . . . . 168 B6
Ilford IG1. . . . . 98 E5
Romford RM7 . . . . 83 J4
Pretoria Rd N, N18. . . . . . . 60 C6
Prevost Rd, N11 . . . . 58 A2
Price Cl, NW7. . . . . 56 B6
SW17. . . . . 167 J3
Price Rd, Croy. CR0 . . . . . 201 H5
Price's Ct, SW11 . . . . 149 G3
Price's St, SE1 . . . . 27 H2
Price's Yd, N1 . . . . 111 F1
Price Way, Hmptn. TW12
off Victors Dr 160/161 E6
Pricklers Hill, Barn. EN5. . . 41 E6
Prickley Wd, Brom. BR2 . . 205 F1
Priddy's Yd, Croy. CR0
off Church St. 201 J2
Prideaux Pl, W3
off Friars Pl La. 106 D7
WC1. . . . . 10 D3
Prideaux Rd, SW9 . . . . . . 151 E3
Pridham Rd, Th.Hth. CR7 . 188 A4
Priest Ct, EC2. . . . . 19 J3
Priestfield Rd, SE23 . . . . . 171 H3
Priestlands Pk Rd, Sid.
DA15 . . . . 175 J3
Priestley Cl, N16
off Ravensdale Rd. 76 C7
Priestley Gdns, Rom. RM6. 82 B6
Priestley Rd, Mitch. CR4. . 186 A2
Priestley Way, E17 . . . . 77 G3
NW2 . . . . 89 G1
Priestman Pt, E3
off Rainhill Way 114 B3
Priest Pk Av, Har. HA2 . . . . 85 G2
Priests Br, SW14 . . . . 147 E4
SW15. . . . . 147 E4
Prima Rd, SW9. . . . . 35 E7
Primrose Av, Enf. EN2 . . . . 44 A1
Romford RM6 . . . . 82 B7
Primrose Cl, N3
off Rosemary Av 72 E2
SE6 . . . . 172 C5
Harrow HA2 . . . . 85 F4
Wallington SM6 . . . . . . 200 B1
Primrose Dr, West Dr.
UB7 . . . . 120 A4
Primrose Gdns, NW3 . . . . . 91 H6
Ruislip HA4 . . . . 84 C5
PRIMROSE HILL, NW8 . . . 109 J1
Primrose Hill, EC4 . . . . 19 F4
Primrose Hill Ct, NW3 . . . . 91 J7
Primrose Hill Rd, NW3 . . . . 91 H7
Primrose Hill Studios, NW1
off Fitzroy Rd. 110 A1
Primrose La, Croy. CR0 . . 203 G1
Primrose Ms, NW1
off Sharpleshall St 91 J7
SE3 . . . . 135 H7
W5 *off St. Mary's Rd*. . . 125 G2
Primrose Rd, E10 . . . . 96 B1
E18 . . . . 79 H2
Primrose Sq, E9 . . . . 95 F7
Primrose St, EC2 . . . . 20 D1
Primrose Wk, SE14
off Alexandra St 133 H7
Epsom KT17 . . . . 197 F7
Primrose Way, Wem. HA0. 105 G2
Primula St, W12 . . . . 107 G6
Prince Albert Rd, NW1 . . . . . 7 H2
NW8 . . . . 7 H2
Prince Arthur Ms, NW3
off Perrins La. 91 F4
Prince Arthur Rd, NW3. . . . 91 F5
Prince Charles Dr, NW4 . . . 71 J7
Prince Charles Rd, SE3. . . 155 F1
Prince Charles Way, Wall.
SM6. . . . . 200 B3
Prince Consort Dr, Chis.
BR7 . . . . 193 G1
Prince Consort Rd, SW7 . . 22 D5
Princedale Rd, W11. . . . . . 128 B1
Prince Edwards Rd, E9. . . . 95 J6
Prince George Av, N14. . . . 42 C4
Prince George Duke of Kent Ct, Chis. BR7
off Holbrook La 175 G7
Prince George Rd, N16. . . . 94 B4
Prince George's Av, SW20 . 183 J2
Prince George's Rd, SW19. 185 G1
Prince Henry Rd, SE7. . . . 136 A7
★**Prince Henry's Room**,
EC4 . . . . 19 E4
Prince Imperial Rd, SE18 . 156 C1
Chislehurst BR7 . . . . . . 175 E7
Prince John Rd, SE9. . . . . 156 B5
Princelet St, E1 . . . . 21 G1
Prince of Orange La, SE10
off Greenwich High Rd . 134 C7
Prince of Wales Cl, NW4
off Church Ter 71 H4
Prince of Wales Dr, SW8 . 130 B7
SW11 . . . . 149 J1
Prince of Wales Gate, SW7 . 23 G3
Prince of Wales Pas, NW1 . . 9 F4
Prince of Wales Rd, NW5 . . 92 A6
SE3 . . . . 155 F1
Sutton SM1. . . . . 199 G2
Prince of Wales Ter, W4 . . 126 E5
W8. . . . . 22 B4
Prince Regent La, E13 . . . 115 H3
E16. . . . . 115 J5
Prince Regent Ms, NW1. . . . 9 F4
Prince Regent Rd, Houns.
TW3. . . . . 143 J3
Prince Rd, SE25 . . . . 188 B5
Prince Rupert Rd, SE9 . . . 156 C4
Prince's Arc, SW1 . . . . 25 G1
Princes Av, N3 . . . . 72 D1
Princes Av, N10. . . . . 74 A3
N13 . . . . 59 G5
N22 . . . . 74 D1
NW9 . . . . 70 B4
W3. . . . . 126 A3
Carshalton SM5 . . . . . . 199 J7
Greenford UB6 . . . . 103 H6
Orpington BR5 . . . . 193 H5
Surbiton KT6. . . . . 196 A1
Woodford Green IG8 . . . 63 H4
Princes Cl, N4. . . . . 93 H1
NW9 . . . . 70 A4
SW4 *off Old Town* 150 C3
Edgware HA8 . . . . 54 A5
Sidcup DA14 . . . . 176 D3
Teddington TW11. . . . . . 162 A4
Princes Ct, E1 . . . . 113 E7
SE16 . . . . 133 J3
Wembley HA9. . . . . 87 H5
Princes Dr, Har. HA1 . . . . . 68 B3
Princes Gdns, SW7 . . . . . . 23 F5
W3. . . . . 106 A5
W5. . . . . 105 F4
Princes Gate, SW7 . . . . 23 G4
Princes Gate Ct, SW7. . . . . 23 F4
Princes Gate Ms, SW7 . . . . 23 F5
Princes La, N10. . . . . 74 B3
Princes Ms, W2. . . . . 14 A5
Princes Pk Av, NW11 . . . . . 72 B6
Princes Pl, SW1 . . . . 25 G1
W11 . . . . 128 B1
Princes Plain, Brom. BR2 . 192 B7
Princes Ri, SE13 . . . . 154 C2
Princes Riverside Rd,
SE16 . . . . 133 G1
Princes Rd, N18 . . . . 61 F4
SE20 . . . . 171 G6
SW14. . . . . 146 D3
SW19. . . . . 166 D6
W13
off Broomfield Rd . 124/125 E1
Buckhurst Hill IG9. . . . . . 63 J2
Ilford IG6. . . . . 81 G4
Kingston upon Thames
KT2 . . . . 164 A7
Richmond TW10 . . . . . . 145 J5
Richmond (Kew) TW9 . . 125 J7
Teddington TW11. . . . . . 162 A4
Princess Alice Way, SE28 . 137 G2
Princess Av, Wem. HA9 . . . 87 H2
Princess Cl, SE28
off Redbourne Dr. 118 D6
Princess Cres, N4. . . . . 93 H2
Princesses Wk, Rich. TW9
off Kew Rd 125 H7
Princess Louise Cl, W2. . . . 15 F1
Princess May Rd, N16 . . . . 94 B4
Princess Ms, NW3
off Belsize Cres 91 G6
Kingston upon Thames
KT1 . . . . 181 J3
Princess Par, Orp. BR6
off Crofton Rd 206 D3
Princess Pk Manor, N11 . . . 58 A5
Princess Sq, W2. . . . . 14 A5
Princess Rd, NW1 . . . . 110 A1
NW6 . . . . 108 D2
Croydon CR0. . . . . 187 J6
Princess St, SE1 . . . . 27 H6
Princes St, EC2. . . . . 20 B3
N17 *off Queen St* 60 B6
W1. . . . . 17 E4
Bexleyheath DA7 . . . . . 159 F4
Richmond TW9
off Sheen Rd. 145 H5
Sutton SM1. . . . . 199 G4
Princes Ter, E13. . . . . 115 H1
Prince St, SE8 . . . . 133 J6
Princes Way, SW19. . . . . . 148 A7
Buckhurst Hill IG9. . . . . . 63 J2
Croydon CR0. . . . . 201 F5
Ruislip HA4 . . . . 84 E4
West Wickham BR4 . . . . 205 F4
Princes Yd, W11
off Princedale Rd. 128 B1
Princethorpe Ho, W2 . . . . . 14 A1
Princethorpe Rd, SE26 . . . 171 G4
Princeton Ct, SW15
off Felsham Rd 148 A3
Princeton St, WC1 . . . . 18 C1
Principal Sq, E9
off Chelmer Rd 95 G5
Pringle Gdns, SW16. . . . . 168 C4
Printers Inn Ct, EC4 . . . . . . 19 E3
Printers Ms, E3. . . . . 113 H1
Printer St, EC4 . . . . 19 F3
Printing Ho La, Hayes
UB3. . . . . 121 H2
Printing Ho Yd, E2 . . . . 13 E3
Print Village, SE15
off Chadwick Rd 152 C2
Priolo Rd, SE7 . . . . 135 J5
Prior Av, Sutt. SM2. . . . . . 199 H7
Prior Bolton St, N1. . . . . . . 93 H6
Prioress Rd, SE27. . . . . . . 169 H3
Prioress St, SE1 . . . . 28 C6
Prior Rd, Ilf. IG1 . . . . 98 D3
Priors Cft, E17 . . . . 77 H2
Priors Fm La, Nthlt. UB5 . . 85 F6
Priors Fld, Nthlt. UB5
off Arnold Rd. 84/85 E6
Priors Gdns, Ruis. HA4 . . . 84 C5
Priors Mead, Enf. EN1 . . . . 44 B1
Priors Shop Cen, The, N12
off High Rd 57 F5
Prior St, SE10. . . . . 134 C7
Priory, The, SE3 . . . . 155 F4
Priory Av, E4. . . . . 61 J3
E17 . . . . 78 A5
N8 . . . . 74 D4
W4. . . . . 127 E4
Orpington BR5 . . . . 193 G6
Sutton SM3. . . . . 198 A4
Wembley HA0. . . . . 86 C4
Priory Cl, E4 . . . . 61 J3
E18 . . . . 79 G1
N3 *off Church Cres* 72 C1
N14 . . . . 42 B5
N20 . . . . 40 C7
SW19
off High Path 184/185 E1
Beckenham BR3 . . . . . . 189 H3
Chislehurst BR7 . . . . . . 192 C1
Hampton TW12
off Priory Gdns 179 F1
Hayes UB3. . . . . 102 B7
Stanmore HA7 . . . . 52 C3
Sunbury-on-Thames
TW16
off Staines Rd E 160 A7
Wembley (Sudbury)
HA0 . . . . 86 C4
Priory Ct, E17 . . . . 77 J3
EC4 *off Carter La* 111 H6
SW8. . . . . 150 D1
Priory Ct Est, E17
off Priory Ct. 77 J2
Priory Cres, SE19 . . . . 169 J7
Sutton SM3. . . . . 198 A4
Wembley HA0. . . . . 86 D3
Priory Dr, SE2. . . . . 138 D5
Stanmore HA7 . . . . 52 C3
Priory Fld Dr, Edg. HA8 . . . 54 B4
Priory Gdns, N6 . . . . 74 B6
SE25 . . . . 188 C4
SW13. . . . . 147 F3
W4. . . . . 127 E4
W5 *off Hanger La* 105 H3
Hampton TW12 . . . . 161 F7
Wembley HA0. . . . . 86 D4
Priory Grn Est, N1 . . . . 10 D1
Priory Gro, SW8. . . . . 150 E1
Barnet EN5 . . . . 40 D5
Priory Hill, Wem. HA0 . . . . 86 D4
Priory La, SW15 . . . . 147 E6
Richmond TW9
off Forest Rd 126 A7
West Molesey KT8 . . . . 179 G4
Priory Ms, SW8 . . . . 150 D1
Priory Pk, SE3 . . . . 155 F3
Priory Pk Rd, NW6 . . . . . . 108 C1
Wembley HA0. . . . . 86 D4
Priory Rd, E6. . . . . 116 A1
N8 . . . . 74 D4
NW6 . . . . 108 E1
SW19. . . . . 167 G7
W4. . . . . 126 D3
Barking IG11 . . . . 99 G7
Chessington KT9. . . . . . 195 H3
Croydon CR0. . . . . 187 G7
Hampton TW12 . . . . 161 F7
Hounslow TW3 . . . . 143 J5
Loughton IG10 . . . . 48 B4
Richmond TW9 . . . . 126 A6
Sutton SM3. . . . . 198 A4
Priory St, E3
off St. Leonards St . . . 114 B3
Priory Ter, NW6. . . . . 108 E1
Sunbury-on-Thames TW16
off Staines Rd E 160 A7
Priory Wk, SW10 . . . . 30 D4
Priory Way, Har. HA2 . . . . . 67 H4
Southall UB2. . . . . 122 D3
West Drayton UB7 . . . . 120 B6
Priscilla Cl, N15
off Conway Rd 75 J5
Pritchard's Rd, E2. . . . . . . 112 D1
Priter Rd, SE16. . . . . 29 J6

Priter Way, SE16
off Dockley Rd **132** D3
Private Rd, Enf. EN1 . . . . . **44** B5
Probert Rd, SW2 . . . . **151** G5
Probyn Rd, SW2 . . . . **169** H2
Procter St, WC1 . . . . **18** C2
Proctor Cl, Mitch. CR4 . . . **186** A1
Proctors Cl, Felt. TW14 . . . **160** A1
Progress Business Pk,
Croy. CR0 . . . . **201** F2
Progress Way, N22 . . . . **75** G1
Croydon CR0 . . . . **201** F2
Enfield EN1 . . . . **44** D5
Promenade, The, W4 . . . . **147** E1
Promenade App Rd, W4 . . **126** E7
Promenade Mans, Edg.
HA8 *off Hale La* **54** B5
Prospect Business Pk,
Loug. IG10 . . . . **49** F4
Prospect Cl, SE26 . . . . **170** E4
Belvedere DA17 . . . . . . **139** G4
Hounslow TW3 . . . . **143** F1
Ruislip HA4 . . . . **66** D7
Prospect Cotts, SW18
off Point Pleasant **148** D4
Prospect Cres, Twick.
TW2 . . . . **143** J6
Prospect Hill, E17 . . . . **78** B4
Prospect Pl, E1 . . . . **133** F1
N2 . . . . **73** G4
N7 *off Parkhurst Rd* . . **92/93** E4
N17 . . . . **76** B1
NW2 *off Ridge Rd* **90** C3
NW3 *off Holly Wk* **91** F4
W4
off Chiswick High Rd . . **126** D5
Bromley BR2 . . . . **191** H3
Romford RM5 . . . . **83** J2
Prospect Quay, SW18 . . . **148** D4
Prospect Ring, N2 . . . . **73** G3
Prospect Rd, NW2 . . . . **90** C3
Barnet EN5 . . . . **40** D5
Surbiton KT6 . . . . **181** F6
Woodford Green IG8 . . . **63** J5
Prospect St, SE16
off Jamaica Rd . . . **132/133** E2
Prospect Vale, SE18 . . . . . **136** B4
Prospero Rd, N19 . . . . **92** C1
Protea Cl, E16
off Hermit Rd **115** F4
Prothero Gdns, NW4 . . . . . **71** H5
Prothero Ho, NW10 . . . . . . **88** D7
Prothero Rd, SW6 . . . . . . **128** B7
Prout Gro, NW10 . . . . **89** E4
Prout Rd, E5 . . . . **95** E3
Provence St, N1
off St. Peters St **111** J2
Providence Cl, E9
off Wetherell Rd **113** C1
Providence Ct, W1 . . . . **16** C5
Providence La, Hayes
UB3 . . . . **121** G7
Providence Pl, N1
off Upper St **111** H1
Romford RM5 . . . . **83** F2
Providence Rd, West Dr.
UB7 . . . . **120** B1
Providence Row, N1
off Pentonville Rd **111** F2
Providence Row Cl, E2
off Ainsley St **112/113** E3
Providence Sq, SE1
off Jacob St **132** C2
Providence St, N1
off St. Peters St **111** J2
Providence Yd, E2 . . . . **13** H3
Provident Ind Est, Hayes
UB3 . . . . **122** A2
Provost Est, N1 . . . . **12** B3
Provost Rd, NW3 . . . . **91** J7
Provost St, N1 . . . . **12** B4
Prowse Av, Bushey
(Bushey Hth) WD23 . . . . **51** J2
Prowse Pl, NW1
off Bonny St **92** B7
Pruden Cl, N14 . . . . **58** C2
Prudent Pas, EC2 . . . . **20** A3
Prusom St, E1 . . . . **133** E1
Pryors, The, NW3 . . . . **91** G3
★**P.S. Tattershall Castle**,
SW1 . . . . **26** B2
★**Public Record Office**,
Rich. TW9 . . . . **126** B7
Pudding La, EC3 . . . . **20** C6
Chigwell IG7 . . . . **65** J1
Pudding Mill La, E15 . . . . **114** B1
Puddle Dock, EC4 . . . . **19** H5
Puffin Cl, Bark. IG11 . . . . . **118** B3
Beckenham BR3 . . . . . . **189** G5
Puffin Ter, Ilf. IG5
off Tiptree Cres **80** D3
Pulborough Rd, SW18 . . . **148** C7
Pulborough Way, Houns.
TW4 . . . . **142** C4
Pulford Rd, N15 . . . . **76** A6
Pulham Av, N2 . . . . **73** F4
Puller Rd, Barn. EN5 . . . . . **40** B2
Pulleyns Av, E6 . . . . **116** B3
Pullman Ct, SW2 . . . . **169** E1
Pullman Gdns, SW15 . . . . **147** J6
Pullman Pl, SE9 . . . . **156** B5
Pulross Rd, SW9 . . . . **151** F3
Pulteney Cl, E3 . . . . **113** J1
Isleworth TW7
off Gumley Gdns **144** D3
Pulteney Gdns, E18
off Pulteney Rd **79** H3
Pulteney Rd, E18 . . . . **79** H3
Pulteney Ter, N1 . . . . **111** F1
Pulton Pl, SW6 . . . . **128** D7
Puma Ct, E1 . . . . **21** F1
Pump All, Brent. TW8 . . . . **125** G7
Pump Cl, Nthlt. UB5
off Union Rd **103** G2
Pump Ct, EC4 . . . . **19** E4
Pumphandle Path, N2
off Tarling Rd **73** F2
Pump Hill, Loug. IG10 . . . . **48** C2
Pump Ho Cl, SE16
off Renforth St **133** F2
Bromley BR2 . . . . **191** F2
Pump Ho Ms, E1 . . . . **21** H5
Pumping Sta Rd, W4 . . . . **127** E7
Pump La, SE14 . . . . **133** F7
Hayes UB3 . . . . **122** B2
Pump Pail N, Croy. CR0
off Old Town **201** J3
Pump Pail S, Croy. CR0
off Southbridge Rd . . . **201** J3
Pundersons Gdns, E2 . . . . **113** E3
Punjab La, Sthl. UB1
off Herbert Rd **123** F1
Purbeck Av, N.Mal. KT3 . . **183** F6
Purbeck Dr, NW2 . . . . **90** B2
Purbrook Est, SE1 . . . . **29** E4
Purbrook St, SE1 . . . . **29** E5
Purcell Cres, SW6 . . . . **128** B7
Purcell Ms, NW10
off Suffolk Rd **88/89** E7
Purcell Rd, Grnf. UB6 . . . . **103** H5
Purcells Av, Edg. HA8 . . . . **54** A5
Purcell St, N1 . . . . **12** D1
Purchese St, NW1 . . . . **9** J1
Purdy St, E3 . . . . **114** B4
Purelake Ms, SE13 . . . . . . **154** D3
Purland Cl, Dag. RM8 . . . . **101** F1
Purland Rd, SE28 . . . . **137** J2
Purleigh Av, Wdf.Grn. IG8 . **64** B6
Purley Av, NW2 . . . . **90** B3
Purley Cl, Ilf. IG5 . . . . **80** D2
Purley Pl, N1
off Islington Pk St **93** H7
Purley Rd, N9 . . . . **60** A3
South Croydon CR2 . . . **202** A7
Purley Way, Croy. CR0 . . . **187** F7
Purley CR8 . . . . **201** G7
Purley Way Cres, Croy. CR0
off Purley Way **187** F7
Purneys Rd, SE9 . . . . **156** A4
Purrett Rd, SE18 . . . . **137** J5
Purser's Cross Rd, SW6 . . **148** C1
Pursewardens Cl, W13 . . . **125** F1
Pursley Rd, NW7 . . . . **55** H7
Purves Rd, NW10 . . . . **107** J2
Puteaux Ho, E2 . . . . **113** G2
PUTNEY, SW15 . . . . **148** B4
Putney Br, SW6 . . . . **148** B3
SW15 . . . . **148** B3
Putney Br App, SW6 . . . . **148** B3
Putney Br Rd, SW15 . . . . **148** B4
SW18 . . . . **148** B4
Putney Common, SW15 . **147** J3
Putney Ex Shop Cen,
SW15 . . . . **148** A4
Putney Gdns, Rom.
(Chad.Hth) RM6
off Heathfield Pk Dr . . . **82** B6
PUTNEY HEATH, SW15 . . **147** J6
Putney Heath, SW15 . . . . **147** J6
Putney Heath La, SW15 . . **148** A6
Putney High St, SW15 . . . **148** A4
Putney Hill, SW15 . . . . . . **148** A6
Putney Pk Av, SW15 . . . . . **147** G4
Putney Pk La, SW15 . . . . . **147** H4
PUTNEY VALE, SW15 . . . . **165** F3
Putney Wf Twr, SW15 . . . . **148** B3
Puttenham Cl, Wat. WD19 . **50** C3
Pycroft Way, N9 . . . . **60** D4
Pyecombe Cor, N12 . . . . . . **56** C4
Pylbrook Rd, Sutt. SM1 . . **198** D3
Pylon Way, Croy. CR0 . . . . **201** E1
Pym Cl, Barn. EN4 . . . . **41** G5
Pymers Mead, SE21 . . . . . **169** J1
Pymmes Cl, N13 . . . . **59** F5
N17 . . . . **76** E1
Pymmes Gdns N, N9 . . . . . **60** C3
Pymmes Gdns S, N9 . . . . . **60** C3
Pymmes Grn Rd, N11 . . . . . **58** B4
Pymmes Rd, N13 . . . . **59** E6
Pymms Brook Dr, Barn.
EN4 . . . . **41** H4
Pyne Rd, Surb. KT6 . . . . . **196** A1
Pyne Ter, SW19
off Windlesham Gro . . **166** A1
Pynfolds, SE16
off Paradise St . . . **132/133** E2
Pynham Cl, SE2 . . . . **138** A3
Pynnacles Cl, Stan. HA7 . . **52** E5
Pyrland Rd, N5 . . . . **94** A5
Richmond TW10 . . . . . . **145** J6
Pyrles Grn, Loug. IG10 . . . . **48** E1
Pyrles La, Loug. IG10 . . . . . **48** E2
Pyrmont Gro, SE27 . . . . . **169** H3
Pyrmont Rd, W4 . . . . **126** A6
Ilford IG1
off High Rd **99** F2
Pytchley Cres, SE19 . . . . . **169** J6
Pytchley Rd, SE22 . . . . . . **152** B3

Q

Quadrangle, The, W2 . . . . . **15** G3
Quadrangle Cl, SE1 . . . . . . **36** D1
Quadrangle Ho, E15
off Romford Rd **96** E6
Quadrangle Ms, Stan. HA7 . **53** F7
Quadrant, The, SE24
off Herne Hill **151** J5
SW20 . . . . **184** B1
Bexleyheath DA7 . . . . . **138** D7
Richmond TW9 . . . . **145** H4
Sutton SM2 . . . . **199** F6
Quadrant Arc, W1 . . . . **17** G6
Quadrant Cl, NW4
off The Burroughs **71** H5
Quadrant Gro, NW5 . . . . . . **91** J5
Quadrant Ho, Sutt. SM2 . **199** F6
Quadrant Rd, Rich. TW9 . . **145** G4
Thornton Heath CR7 . . . **187** H4
Quad Rd, Wem. HA9
off Courtenay Rd **87** G3
Quaggy Wk, SE3 . . . . **155** G4
Quainton St, NW10 . . . . . . **88** D3
Quaker Ct, E1 . . . . **13** F6
Quaker La, Sthl. UB2 . . . . **123** G3
Quakers Course, NW9 . . . . **71** F1
Quakers La, Islw. TW7 . . . **144** D1
Quaker's Pl, E7 . . . . **98** A5
Quaker St, E1 . . . . **13** F6
Quakers Wk, N21 . . . . **44** A6
Quality Ct, WC2 . . . . **18** E3
Quantock Cl, Hayes UB3 . **121** G7
Quantock Dr, Wor.Pk. KT4 . **197** J2
Quantock Gdns, NW2 . . . . **90** A2
Quantock Ms, SE15
off Choumert Gro **152** D2
Quarley Way, SE15 . . . . **37** F7
Quarrendon St, SW6 . . . . **148** D2
Quarr Rd, Cars. SM5 . . . . **185** G6
Quarry Pk Rd, Sutt. SM1 . . **198** C6
Quarry Ri, Sutt. SM1 . . . . **198** C6
Quarry Rd, SW18 . . . . **149** F6
Quarterdeck, The, E14 . . . **134** A2
Quarter Mile La, E10 . . . . . **96** B4
Quayside Wk, Kings.T. KT1
off Bishop's Hall **181** G2
Quay W, Tedd. TW11 . . . . . **162** E5
Quebec Ms, W1 . . . . **16** A4
Quebec Rd, Hayes UB4 . . . **102** C7
Ilford IG1, IG2 . . . . **81** E7
Quebec Way, SE16 . . . . . . **133** G2
Queen Adelaide Rd, SE20 . **171** F6
Queen Alexandra's Ct,
SW19 . . . . **166** C5
Queen Anne Av, N15
off Suffield Rd **76** C5
Bromley BR2 . . . . **191** F3
Queen Anne Dr, Esher
(Clay.) KT10 . . . . **194** B7
Queen Anne Ms, W1 . . . . . **16** E2
Queen Anne Rd, E9 . . . . . . **95** G6
Queen Anne's Cl, Twick.
TW2 . . . . **162** A3
Queen Anne's Gdns, W4 . **127** E3
Queen Annes Gdns, W5 . . **125** H2
Enfield EN1 . . . . **44** B6
Queen Anne's Gdns, Mitch.
CR4 . . . . **185** J3
Queen Anne's Gate, SW1 . . **25** H4
Bexleyheath DA7 . . . . . **158** D3
Queen Anne's Gro, W4 . . . **126** E3
Queen Annes Gro, W5 . . . **125** H2
Enfield EN1 . . . . **44** A7
Queen Annes Pl, Enf. EN1 . **44** B6
Queen Anne St, W1 . . . . . . **16** D3
Queen Anne's Wk, WC1
off Guilford St **110/111** E4
Queen Anne Ter, E1
off Sovereign Cl . . **112/113** E7
Queenborough Gdns, Chis.
BR7 . . . . **175** G6
Ilford IG2 . . . . **80** D4
Queen Caroline Est, W6 . . **127** J5
Queen Caroline St, W6 . . . **127** J4
Queen Elizabeth Gdns,
Mord. SM4 . . . . **184** D4
★**Queen Elizabeth Hall &**
Purcell Room, SE1 . . . . **26** C1
Queen Elizabeth Rd, E17 . . **77** H3
Kingston upon Thames
KT2 . . . . **181** J1
Queen Elizabeths Cl, N16 . **94** A2
Queen Elizabeths Dr, N14 . **58** E1
★**Queen Elizabeth II Conf**
Cen, SW1 . . . . **25** J4
★**Queen Elizabeth's**
Hunting Lo, Epping
Forest, E4 . . . . **47** F7
Queen Elizabeth St, SE1 . . **29** E3
Queen Elizabeths Wk, N16 . **94** A2
Queen Elizabeth's Wk, Wall.
SM6 . . . . **200** D4
Queen Elizabeth Wk,
SW13 . . . . **147** H1
Queenhithe, EC4 . . . . **20** A5
Queen Margaret's Gro, N1 . **94** B5
Queen Mary Av, Mord.
SM4 . . . . **184** A5
Queen Mary Cl, Surb.
KT6 . . . . **196** A3
Queen Mary Rd, SE19 . . . **169** H6
Queen Mary's Av, Cars.
SM5 . . . . **199** J7
★**Queen Mary's Gdns**,
NW1 . . . . **8** B4
Queen of Denmark Ct,
SE16 . . . . **133** J3
Queens Acre, Sutt. SM3 . . **198** A7
Queens Av, N3 . . . . **57** F7
N10 . . . . **74** A3
N20 . . . . **57** G2
Queen's Av, N21 . . . . **59** H1
Queens Av, Felt. TW13 . . . **160** C4
Greenford UB6 . . . . **103** H6
Stanmore HA7 . . . . **69** F3
Woodford Green IG8 . . . **63** H5
Queensberry Ms W, SW7 . . **30** E1
Queensberry Pl, E12 . . . . . . **98** A5
SW7 . . . . **30** E1
Richmond TW9
off Friars La **145** G5
Queensberry Way, SW7 . . . **31** E1
Queensborough Ms, W2 . . **14** C5
Queensborough Pas, W2 . . **14** C5
Queensborough S Bldgs,
W2 *off Porchester Ter* . **109** F7
Queensborough Studios,
W2 . . . . **14** C5
Queensborough Ter, W2 . . . **14** B5
Queensbridge Pk, Islw.
TW7 . . . . **144** B5
Queensbridge Rd, E2 . . . . **112** C1
E8 . . . . **94** C7
QUEENSBURY, Har. HA3 . . **69** G3
Queensbury Circle Par, Har.
HA3 *off Streatfield Rd* . . **69** H3
Stanmore HA7
off Streatfield Rd **69** H3
Queensbury Rd, NW9 . . . . **70** D7
Wembley HA0 . . . . **105** J2
Queensbury Sta Par, Edg.
HA8 . . . . **69** J3
Queensbury St, N1 . . . . . . **93** J7
Queen's Circ, SW8
off Queenstown Rd . . . **130** B7
SW11
off Queenstown Rd . . . **130** B7
Queens Cl, Edg. HA8 . . . . . **54** A5
Wallington SM6
off Queens Rd **200** B5
★**Queens Club (Tennis Cen)**,
W14 . . . . **128** B5
Queens Club Gdns, W14 . **128** B6
Queens Ct, SE23 . . . . **171** F1
Richmond TW10 . . . . . . **145** J6

Queenscourt, Wem. HA9 . . **87** H4
Queen's Cres, NW5 . . . . . . **92** A6
Queens Cres, Rich. TW10 . **145** J5
Queenscroft Rd, SE9 . . . . **156** A5
Queensdale Cres, W11 . . . **128** A1
Queensdale Pl, W11 . . . . . **128** B1
Queensdale Rd, W11 . . . . **128** A1
Queensdale Wk, W11 . . . . **128** B1
Queensdown Rd, E5 . . . . . **94** E4
Queens Dr, E10 . . . . **78** A7
N4 . . . . **93** H2
W3 . . . . **105** J6
W5 . . . . **105** J6
Surbiton KT5 . . . . **182** A7
Thames Ditton KT7 . . . . **180** D7
Queens Elm Par, SW3
off Old Ch St **129** G5
Queen's Elm Sq, SW3 . . . . **31** F4
Queensferry Wk, N17
off Jarrow Rd **76/77** E4
★**Queen's Gall, The**, SW1 . **24** E4
Queens Gdns, NW4 . . . . . . **71** J5
W2 . . . . **14** C5
W5 . . . . **105** F4
Queen's Gdns, Houns. TW5 . . . . **142** E1
Queen's Gate, SW7 . . . . . . **22** D4
Queen's Gate Gdns, SW7 . **22** D6
Queens Gate Gdns, SW15
off Upper Richmond Rd . . **147** H4
Queensgate Gdns, Chis. BR7 . . . . **193** G1
Queen's Gate Ms, SW7 . . . **22** D4
Queensgate Pl, NW6 . . . . . **90** D7
Queen's Gate Pl, SW7 . . . . **22** D6
Queen's Gate Pl Ms, SW7 . **22** D6
Queen's Gate Ter, SW7 . . . **22** C5
Queen's Gro, NW8 . . . . . . **109** G1
Queen's Gro Ms, NW8 . . . **109** G1
Queens Gro Rd, E4 . . . . . . **62** D1
Queen's Head Pas, EC4 . . . **19** J3
Queen's Head St, N1 . . . . **111** H1
Queens Head Yd, SE1 . . . . **28** B2
Queens Ho, Tedd. TW11 . . **162** C6
★**Queen's Ice Rink**, W2
off Queensway **14** B6
Queensland Av, N18 . . . . . **59** J6
SW19 . . . . **184** E1
Queensland Cl, E17 . . . . . . **77** J2
Queensland Ho, E16
off Rymill St **136** D1
Queens La, N10 . . . . **74** B3
Queens Mkt, E13
off Green St **115** J1
Queensmead, NW8 . . . . . **109** G1
Queensmead Rd, Brom. BR2 . . . . **191** F2
Queensmere Cl, SW19 . . . **166** A2
Queensmere Rd, SW19 . . **166** A2
Queens Ms, W2 . . . . **14** B5
Queensmill Rd, SW6 . . . . **128** A7
Queens Par, N11
off Colney Hatch La . . . **57** J5
W5 . . . . **105** J6
Queens Par Cl, N11
off Colney Hatch La . . . **57** J5
Queens Pk Ct, W10 . . . . . . **108** A3
★**Queens Park Rangers FC**, W12 . . . . **127** H1
Queens Pas, Chis. BR7
off High St **174/175** E6
Queens Pl, Mord. SM4 . . . **184** D4
Queen's Prom, Kings.T. KT1
off Portsmouth Rd **181** G3
Queen Sq, WC1 . . . . **10** B6
Queen Sq Pl, WC1 . . . . **10** B6
Queens Reach, E.Mol. KT8 . . . . **180** B4
Queens Ride, SW13 . . . . . **147** G3
SW15 . . . . **147** G3
Queen's Ride, Rich. TW10 . **164** B1
Queens Ri, Rich. TW10 . . . **145** J6
Queens Rd, E11 . . . . **78** D7
E13 . . . . **115** H1
Queen's Rd, E17 . . . . **77** J6
Queens Rd, N3 . . . . **73** F1
N9 . . . . **60** E3
Queen's Rd, N11 . . . . **58** E7
Queens Rd, NW4 . . . . **71** J5
SE14 . . . . **152** E1
SE15 . . . . **152** E1
SW14 . . . . **146** D3
SW19 . . . . **166** C6
W5 . . . . **105** H6
Barking IG11 . . . . **99** F7
Barnet EN5 . . . . **40** A3
Beckenham BR3 . . . . . . **189** H2
Bromley BR1 . . . . **191** G2
Buckhurst Hill IG9 . . . . . . **63** H2
Queens Rd, Chis. BR7 . . . **175** E6
Queen's Rd, Croy. CR0 . . . **187** H6
Queens Rd, Enf. EN1 . . . . . **44** B4
Feltham TW13 . . . . **160** B1
Hampton (Hmptn H.) TW12 . . . . **161** H4
Queen's Rd, Houns. TW3 . **143** H3
Queens Rd, Kings.T. KT2 . **164** A7
Loughton IG10 . . . . **48** B3
Mitcham CR4 . . . . **185** G3
Morden SM4 . . . . **184** D4
New Malden KT3 . . . . . **183** F4
Richmond TW10 . . . . . . **145** J5
Southall UB2 . . . . **122** D2
Queen's Rd, Tedd. TW11 . . **162** B6
Thames Ditton KT7 . . . . **180** C5
Queens Rd, Twick. TW1 . . . **162** C1
Wallington SM6 . . . . . . **200** B5
Queen's Rd, Well. DA16 . . **158** B2
Queens Rd, West Dr. UB7 . **120** C2
Queens Rd W, E13 . . . . . . **115** G2
Queen's Row, SE17 . . . . . . **36** B5
Queens Ter, E13 . . . . **115** H1
Queen's Ter, NW8 . . . . **7** E1
Queens Ter, Islw. TW7 . . . **144** D4
Queens Ter Cotts, W7
off Boston Rd **124** B2
Queensthorpe Rd, SE26 . . **171** G4
★**Queen's Twr**, SW7 . . . . . . **23** E5
Queenstown Ms, SW8
off Queenstown Rd . . . **150** B2
Queenstown Rd, SW8 . . . . **32** D6
Queen St, EC4 . . . . **20** A5
N17 . . . . **60** B6
W1 . . . . **24** D1
Bexleyheath DA7 . . . . . **159** F3
Croydon CR0 . . . . **201** J4
Queen St Pl, EC4 . . . . **20** A6
Queensville Rd, SW12 . . . **150** D7
Queens Wk, E4
off The Green Wk **62** D1
NW9 . . . . **88** C2
Queen's Wk, SE1 . . . . **26** C2
SW1 . . . . **25** F2
Queens Wk, W5 . . . . **105** F4
Queen's Wk, Har. HA1 . . . . **68** B4
Queens Wk, Ruis. HA4 . . . . **84** D3
Queens Way, NW4 . . . . **71** J5
Queensway, W2 . . . . **14** B4
Queens Way, Croy. CR0 . . **201** F6
Queensway, Enf. EN3 . . . . **45** E4
Queens Way, Felt. TW13 . . **160** C4
Queensway, Orp. BR5 . . . **193** F5
Sunbury-on-Thames TW16 . . . . **178** B2
West Wickham BR4 . . . . **205** E3
Queenswell Av, N20 . . . . . . **57** H3
Queenswood Av, E17 . . . . . **78** C1
Hampton TW12 . . . . **161** H6
Hounslow TW3 . . . . **143** F2
Thornton Heath CR7 . . . **187** G5
Wallington SM6 . . . . . . **200** D4
Queenswood Gdns, E11 . . . **97** G1
Queenswood Pk, N3 . . . . . **72** B2
Queen's Wd Rd, N10 . . . . . **74** B6
Queenswood Rd, SE23 . . **171** G3
Sidcup DA15 . . . . **157** J5
Queens Yd, WC1 . . . . **9** G6
Queen Victoria Av, Wem. HA0 . . . . **87** G7
★**Queen Victoria Mem**, SW1 . . . . **25** F3
Queen Victoria St, EC4 . . . . **19** H5
Queen Victoria Ter, E1
off Sovereign Cl . . **112/113** E7
Quemerford Rd, N7 . . . . . . **93** F5
Quentin Pl, SE13 . . . . **155** E3
Quentin Rd, SE13 . . . . **155** E3
Quernmore Cl, Brom. BR1 **173** G6
Quernmore Rd, N4 . . . . **75** G6
Bromley BR1 . . . . **173** G6
Querrin St, SW6 . . . . **149** F2
Quex Ms, NW6
off Quex Rd **108** D1
Quex Rd, NW6 . . . . **108** D1
Quick Rd, W4 . . . . **126** E5
Quicks Rd, SW19 . . . . **167** E7
Quick St, N1 . . . . **11** H2
Quick St Ms, N1 . . . . **11** G2
Quickswood, NW3
off King Henry's Rd **91** H7
Quiet Nook, Brom. BR2
off Croydon Rd **206** A3
Quill La, SW15 . . . . **148** A4
Quill St, N4 . . . . **93** G3
W5 . . . . **105** H3
Quilp St, SE1 . . . . **27** J3
Quilter St, E2 . . . . **13** H3
SE18 . . . . **137** J5
Quilting Ct, SE16
off Poolmans St **133** G2
Quince Rd, SE13 . . . . **154** B2
Quinta Dr, Barn. EN5 . . . . . **39** H5
Quintin Av, SW20 . . . . **184** C1
Quintin Cl, Pnr. HA5
off High Rd **66** B5
Quinton Cl, Beck. BR3 . . . **190** C3
Hounslow TW5 . . . . **122** B7
Wallington SM6 . . . . . . **200** B4
Quinton Rd, T.Ditt. KT7 . . . **194** D1
Quinton St, SW18 . . . . . . **167** F2
Quixley St, E14 . . . . **114** D7
Quorn Rd, SE22 . . . . **152** B4

R

Rabbit Row, W8
off Kensington Mall . . **128** D1
Rabbits Rd, E12 . . . . **98** B4
Rabournmead Dr, Nthlt. UB5 . . . . **84** E5
Raby Rd, N.Mal. KT3 . . . . **182** D4
Raby St, E14
off Salmon La **113** H6
Raccoon Way, Houns. TW4 . . . . **142** C2
Rachel Cl, Ilf. IG6 . . . . **81** G3
Rachel Pt, E5
off Muir Rd **94** D4
Rackham Cl, Well. DA16 . . **158** B2
Rackham Ms, SW16
off Westcote Rd **168** C6
Racton Rd, SW6 . . . . **128** D6
Radbourne Av, W5 . . . . . . **125** F4
Radbourne Cl, E5
off Overbury St **95** G4
Radbourne Cres, E17 . . . . . **78** D2
Radbourne Rd, SW12 . . . . **150** C7
Radcliffe Av, NW10 . . . . . . **107** G2
Enfield EN2 . . . . **43** J1
Radcliffe Gdns, Cars. SM5 . **199** H7
Radcliffe Ms, Hmptn. (Hmptn H.) TW12
off Taylor Cl **161** J5
Radcliffe Path, SW8
off Robertson St **150** B2
Radcliffe Rd, N21 . . . . **59** H1
SE1 . . . . **29** E5
Croydon CR0 . . . . **202** C2
Harrow HA3 . . . . **68** D2
Radcliffe Sq, SW15 . . . . . . **148** A6
Radcliffe Way, Nthlt. UB5 . **102** D3
Radcot Pt, SE23 . . . . **171** G3
Radcot St, SE11 . . . . **35** F4
Raddington Rd, W10 . . . . . **108** B5
Radfield Way, Sid. DA15 . **157** G7
Radford Rd, SE13 . . . . **154** C6
Radford Way, Bark. IG11 . . **117** J3
Radipole Rd, SW6 . . . . **148** C1
Radius Pk, Felt. TW14 . . . . **141** J4
Radland Rd, E16 . . . . **115** F6
Radlet Av, SE26 . . . . **171** E3
Radlett Cl, E7 . . . . **97** F6
Radlett Pl, NW8 . . . . **109** H1
Radley Av, Ilf. IG3 . . . . **99** J4
Radley Ct, SE16
off Thame Rd **133** G2
Radley Gdns, Har. HA3 . . . **69** H4
Radley Ho, SE2
off Wolvercote Rd **138** D2
Radley Ms, W8 . . . . **128** D3
Radley Rd, N17 . . . . **76** B2
Radley's La, E18 . . . . **79** G2
Radleys Mead, Dag. RM10 . **101** H6
Radley Sq, E5
off Dudlington Rd **95** F2
Radlix Rd, E10 . . . . **96** A1
Radnor Av, Har. HA1 . . . . . **68** B5
Welling DA16 . . . . **158** B5
Radnor Cl, Chis. BR7
off Homewood Cres . . **175** H6
Mitcham CR4 . . . . **187** E4
Radnor Cres, SE18 . . . . . . **138** A6
Ilford IG4 . . . . **80** C5
Radnor Gdns, Enf. EN1 . . . **44** B1
Twickenham TW1 . . . . . **162** C2
Radnor Ms, W2 . . . . **15** F4
Radnor Pl, W2 . . . . **15** G4
Radnor Rd, NW6 . . . . **108** B1
SE15 . . . . **37** H7
Harrow HA1 . . . . **68** A5
Twickenham TW1 . . . . . **162** C2
Radnor St, EC1 . . . . **12** A4
Radnor Ter, W14 . . . . **128** C4
Radnor Wk, E14
off Copeland Dr **134** A4
SW3 . . . . **31** H4
Radnor Wk, Croy. CR0 . . . **189** J6
Radnor Way, NW10 . . . . . **106** B4
Radstock Av, Har. HA3 . . . . **68** D3
Radstock Cl, N11
off Martock Gdns **58** A6
Radstock St, SW11 . . . . . . **129** H7
Raeburn Gdns, Barn. EN5 . **39** H5
Raeburn Av, Surb. KT5 . . . **182** B6
Raeburn Cl, NW11 . . . . **73** F6
Kingston upon Thames KT1 . . . . **163** G7
Raeburn Rd, Edg. HA8 . . . . **70** A2
Sidcup DA15 . . . . **157** H6
Raeburn St, SW2 . . . . **151** E4
Rafford Way, Brom. BR1 . . **191** H2
Raft Rd, SW18
off North Pas **148** D4
★**Ragged Sch Mus**, E3
off Copperfield Rd **113** H5
Raggleswood, Chis. BR7 . **192** D1
Raglan Cl, Houns. TW4
off Vickers Way . . . **142/143** E5
Raglan Ct, SE12 . . . . **155** G5
South Croydon CR2 . . . **201** H5
Wembley HA9 . . . . **87** J4
Raglan Gdns, Wat. WD19 . . **50** B1
Raglan Rd, E17 . . . . **78** C5
SE18 . . . . **137** F5
Belvedere DA17 . . . . . . **139** F4
Bromley BR2 . . . . **191** J4
Enfield EN1 . . . . **44** B7
Raglan St, NW5 . . . . **92** B6
Raglan Ter, Har. HA2 . . . . . **85** H4
Raglan Way, Nthlt. UB5 . . . **85** J6
Ragley Cl, W3
off Church Rd **126** C2
Ragwort Ct, SE26 . . . . **170** E5
Rahere Ho, EC1
off Central St **111** J3
Raider Cl, Rom. RM7 . . . . . **83** G1
Railey Ms, NW5 . . . . **92** C5
Railshead Rd, Islw. TW7 . . **144** E4
Railton Rd, SE24 . . . . **151** G4
Railway App, N4
off Wightman Rd **75** G6
SE1 . . . . **28** C1
Harrow HA3 . . . . **68** C4
Twickenham TW1 . . . . . **144** D7
Wallington SM6 . . . . . . **200** B6
Railway Av, SE16 . . . . **133** F2
Railway Children Wk, SE12
off Baring Rd **173** G2
Bromley BR1
off Reigate Rd **173** G2
Railway Ms, E3
off Wellington Way . . . **114** A3
W10 *off Ladbroke Gro* . . **108** B6
Railway Pas, Tedd. TW11
off Victoria Rd **162** D6
Railway Pl, SW19
off Hartfield Rd **166** C6
Belvedere DA17 . . . . . . **139** G3
Railway Ri, SE22
off Grove Vale **152** B4
Railway Rd, Tedd. TW11 . . **162** C4
Railway Side, SW13 . . . . . **147** E3
Railway St, N1 . . . . **10** B2
Romford RM6 . . . . **100** C1
Railway Ter, SE13
off Ladywell Rd **154** B5
Feltham TW13 . . . . **160** A1
Rainborough Cl, NW10 . . . **88** C6
Rainbow Av, E14 . . . . **134** B5
Rainbow Quay, SE16 . . . . **133** H3
Rainbow St, SE5 . . . . **132** B7
Raines Ct, N16
off Northwold Rd **94** C2
Raine St, E1 . . . . **133** E1
Rainham Cl, SE9 . . . . **157** G6
SW11 . . . . **149** H6
Rainham Rd, NW10 . . . . . **107** J3
Rainham Rd N, Dag. RM10 . . . . **101** H2
Rainham Rd S, Dag. RM10 . . . . **101** H4
Rainhill Way, E3 . . . . **114** A3
Rainsborough Av, SE8 . . . **133** H4
Rainsford Cl, Stan. HA7
off Coverdale Cl **53** F5
Rainsford Rd, NW10 . . . . . **106** B3
Rainsford St, W2 . . . . **15** G3
Rainton Rd, SE7 . . . . **135** G5
Rainville Rd, W6 . . . . **127** J6
Raisins Hill, Pnr. HA5 . . . . . **66** C3
Raith Av, N14 . . . . **58** D3
Raleana Rd, E14 . . . . **134** C1
Raleigh Av, Hayes UB4 . . . **102** B5
Wallington SM6 . . . . . . **200** D4
Raleigh Cl, NW4 . . . . **71** J5

Raleigh Cl, Pnr. HA5. . . . . . **66** D7
Raleigh Ct, SE16
off Rotherhithe St **133** G1
SE19 *off Lymer Av*. **170** C5
Beckenham BR3 . . . . . . **190** B1
Wallington SM6 . . . . . . **200** B6
Raleigh Dr, N20 . . . . **57** H3
Esher (Clay.) KT10. . . . . **194** A5
Surbiton KT5. . . . . **196** C1
Raleigh Gdns, SW2
off Brixton Hill. **151** F6
Mitcham CR4. . . . . **185** J2
Raleigh Ms, N1
off Queen's Head St. . . **111** H1
Orpington BR6
off Osgood Av. **207** J5
Raleigh Rd, N8. . . . . **75** G4
SE20 . . . . **171** G7
Enfield EN2. . . . . **44** A4
Richmond TW9 . . . . **145** J3
Southall UB2. . . . . **122** E5
Raleigh St, N1. . . . . **111** H1
Raleigh Way, N14. . . . . **58** D1
Feltham TW13 . . . . **160** C5
Ralph Ct, W2 . . . . **14** B3
Ralph Perring Ct, Beck.
BR3 . . . . **190** A4
Ralston St, SW3. . . . . **31** J4
Ralston Way, Wat. WD19 . . **50** D2
Rama Cl, SW16 . . . . **168** D7
Rama Ct, Har. HA1. . . . . . . **86** B2
Ramac Way, SE7 . . . . **135** H4
Rama La, SE19. . . . . **170** C7
Rambler Cl, SW16 . . . . . . **168** C4
Rame Cl, SW17 . . . . **168** A5
Ramilles Cl, SW2 . . . . . . **151** E6
Ramillies Pl, W1 . . . . **17** F4
Ramillies Rd, NW7. . . . . . . **54** E2
W4. . . . . **126** D4
Sidcup DA15 . . . . **158** B6
Ramillies St, W1. . . . . **17** F4
Rampart St, E1
off Commercial Rd . **112/113** E6
Ram Pas, Kings.T. KT1
off High St. **181** G2
Rampayne St, SW1 . . . . . . **33** H3
Ram Pl, E9
off Chatham Pl **95** F6
Rampton Cl, E4 . . . . **62** A3
Ramsay Ms, SW3. . . . . **31** G5
Ramsay Pl, Har. HA1 . . . . . **86** B1
Ramsay Rd, E7. . . . . **97** E4
W3. . . . . **126** C3
Ramscroft Cl, N9 . . . . **44** B7
Ramsdale Rd, SW17 . . . . **168** A5
Ramsden Rd, N11. . . . . **57** J5
SW12. . . . . **150** A6
Ramsey Cl, NW9 . . . . **71** F6
Greenford UB6 . . . . **85** J5
Ramsey Ho, Wem. HA9 . . . **87** H6
Ramsey Ms, N4
off Monsell Rd **93** H3
Ramsey Rd, Th.Hth. CR7 . **187** F6
Ramsey Ct, E2 . . . . **13** J6
Ramsey Wk, N1 . . . . **94** A6
Ramsey Way, N14 . . . . **42** C7
Ramsgate Cl, E16
off Hanameel St **135** H1
Ramsgate St, E8
off Dalston La **94** C6
Ramsgill App, Ilf. IG2 . . . . . **81** J4
Ramsgill Dr, Ilf. IG2 . . . . . . **81** J5
Rams Gro, Rom. RM6 . . . . **83** E4
Ram St, SW18 . . . . **148** E5
Ramulis Dr, Hayes UB4 . . . **102** D4
Ramus Wd Av, Orp. BR6 . **207** H5
Rancliffe Gdns, SE9 . . . . . **156** B4
Rancliffe Rd, E6 . . . . **116** B2
Randall Av, NW2 . . . . **89** F3
Randall Cl, SW11 . . . . **149** H1
Erith DA8. . . . . **139** J6
Randall Ct, NW7
off Page St **55** G7
Randall Pl, SE10. . . . . **134** C7
Randall Rd, SE11 . . . . **34** C3
Randall Row, SE11. . . . . . . **34** C2
Randell's Rd, N1 . . . . **111** E1
Randle Rd, Rich. TW10 . . . **163** F4
Randlesdown Rd, SE6 . . . **172** A4
Randolph App, E16. . . . . . **116** A6
Randolph Av, W9 . . . . **6** D5
Randolph Cl, Bexh. DA7 . **159** J3
Kingston upon Thames
KT2 . . . . **164** C5
Randolph Cres, W9 . . . . **6** C6
Randolph Gdns, NW6 . . . . . **6** A2
Randolph Gro, Rom. RM6
off Donald Dr **82** C5
Randolph Ho, Croy. CR0 . **201** J1
Randolph Ms, W9. . . . . **6** D6
Randolph Rd, E17 . . . . **78** B5
W9. . . . . **6** C6
Bromley BR2. . . . . **206** C1
Southall UB1. . . . . **123** F2
Randolph St, NW1 . . . . **92** C7
Randon Cl, Har. HA2 . . . . . **67** H2
Ranelagh Av, SW6 . . . . . . **148** C3
SW13. . . . . **147** G2
Ranelagh Br, W2
off Gloucester Ter. **108/109** E5
Ranelagh Cl, Edg. HA8. . . . **54** A4
Ranelagh Dr, Edg. HA8 . . . **54** A4
Twickenham TW1 . . . . . **145** E5
★**Ranelagh Gdns**, SW3 . . . **32** B4
Ranelagh Gdns, E11. . . . . . **79** J5
SW6. . . . . **148** C3
W4 *off Grove Pk Gdns* . **126** C7
W6. . . . . **127** F3
Ilford IG1. . . . . **98** D1
Ranelagh Gdns Mans, SW6
off Ranelagh Gdns . . . **148** B3
Ranelagh Gro, SW1 . . . . . . **32** C3
Ranelagh Ms, W5
off Ranelagh Rd **125** G2
Ranelagh Pl, N.Mal. KT3 . **182** E5
Ranelagh Rd, E6. . . . . **116** D1
E11. . . . . **96** E4
E15. . . . . **115** E1
N17 . . . . **76** B3
N22 . . . . **75** F1
NW10. . . . . **107** F2
SW1. . . . . **33** G4
W5. . . . . **125** G2
Southall UB1. . . . . **122** D1
Wembley HA0. . . . . **87** G5
Ranfurly Rd, Sutt. SM1 . . **198** D2
Rangefield Rd, Brom. BR1. **172** E5
Rangemoor Rd, N15. . . . . . **76** C5
Rangers Rd, E4. . . . . **47** E7
Loughton IG10 . . . . **47** E7
Rangers Sq, SE10. . . . . . . **154** D1
Rangeworth Pl, Sid. DA15
off Priestlands Pk Rd. . **175** J3
Rangoon St, EC3 . . . . **21** F4
Rankin Cl, NW9 . . . . **71** E3
Ranleigh Gdns, Bexh.
DA7 . . . . **139** F7
Ranmere St, SW12
off Ormeley Rd **168** B1
Ranmoor Cl, Har. HA1 . . . . **68** A4
Ranmoor Gdns, Har. HA1 . **68** A4
Ranmore Av, Croy. CR0 . . **202** C3
Rannoch Cl, Edg. HA8 . . . . **54** B2
Rannoch Rd, W6. . . . . **127** J6
Rannock Av, NW9 . . . . **70** E7
Ranskill Rd, Borwd. WD6. . **38** A1
**Ransome's Dock Business
Cen**, SW11
off Parkgate Rd **129** H7
Ransom Rd, SE7
off Floyd Rd **135** J5
Ransom Wk, SE7
off Woolwich Rd **135** J5
Ranston St, NW1 . . . . **15** G1
Ranulf Rd, NW2 . . . . **90** C4
Ranwell Cl, E3
off Beale Rd. **113** J1
Ranwell St, E3 . . . . **113** J1
Ranworth Rd, N9 . . . . **61** F2
Ranyard Cl, Chess. KT9 . . **195** J3
Raphael Dr, T.Ditt. KT7 . . . **180** C7
Raphael St, SW7 . . . . **23** J4
Rashleigh St, SW8
off Peardon St. **150** B2
Rasper Rd, N20 . . . . **57** F2
Rastell Av, SW2 . . . . **168** D2
Ratcliffe Cl, SE12 . . . . **155** G7
Ratcliffe Cross St, E1 . . . . **113** G6
Ratcliffe La, E14 . . . . **113** H6
Ratcliffe Orchard, E1. . . . . **113** G7
Ratcliff Rd, E7. . . . . **97** J5
Rathbone Mkt, E16
off Barking Rd **115** F5
Rathbone Pl, W1 . . . . **17** H3
Rathbone Pt, E5
off Nolan Way. **94** D4
Rathbone St, E16 . . . . **115** F5
W1. . . . . **17** G2
Rathcoole Av, N8 . . . . **75** F4
Rathcoole Gdns, N8. . . . . . **75** F5
Rathfern Rd, SE6 . . . . **171** J1
Rathgar Av, W13. . . . . **125** E1
Rathgar Cl, N3 . . . . **72** C2
Rathgar Rd, SW9
off Coldharbour La . . . **151** H3
Rathmell Dr, SW4 . . . . . . **150** D6
Rathmore Rd, SE7 . . . . . . **135** H5
Rattray Rd, SW2. . . . . **151** G4
Raul Rd, SE15. . . . . **152** D1
Raveley St, NW5 . . . . **92** C4
Raven Cl, NW9
off Eagle Dr **70/71** E2
Raven Ct, E5
off Stellman Cl **94** D3
Ravenet St, SW11
off Strasburg Rd **150** B1
Ravenfield Rd, SW17 . . . . **167** J3
Ravenhill Rd, E13 . . . . **115** J2
Ravenna Rd, SW15. . . . . . **148** A5
Ravenoak Way, Chig. IG7 . . **65** H5
Ravenor Pk Rd, Grnf. UB6. **103** H3
Raven Rd, E18 . . . . **79** J2
Raven Row, E1 . . . . **113** E5
Ravensbourne Av, Beck.
BR3 . . . . **172** D7
Bromley BR2. . . . . **172** D7
Ravensbourne Gdns, W13. **104** E5
Ilford IG5. . . . . **80** D1
Ravensbourne Pk, SE6. . . **154** A7
Ravensbourne Pk Cres,
SE6 . . . . **153** J7
Ravensbourne Pl, SE13 . . **154** B2
Ravensbourne Rd, SE6 . . **153** J7
Bromley BR1. . . . . **191** G3
Twickenham TW1 . . . . . **145** F6
Ravensbury Av, Mord.
SM4. . . . . **185** F5
Ravensbury Ct, Mitch. CR4
off Ravensbury Gro. . . **185** G4
Ravensbury Gro, Mitch.
CR4 . . . . **185** G4
Ravensbury La, Mitch.
CR4 . . . . **185** G4
Ravensbury Path, Mitch.
CR4. . . . . **185** G4
Ravensbury Rd, SW18 . . . **166** D2
Orpington BR5 . . . . **193** J4
Ravensbury Ter, SW18 . . . **166** E2
Ravenscar Rd, Brom BR1 . **172** E4
Surbiton KT6. . . . . **195** J2
Ravens Cl, Brom. BR2 . . . **191** F2
Chessington KT9. . . . . . **181** G6
Enfield EN1 . . . . **44** B2
Ravenscourt Av, W6 . . . . . **127** G4
Ravenscourt Gdns, W6. . . **127** G4
Ravenscourt Pk, W6. . . . . **127** G3
Ravenscourt Pl, W6 . . . . . **127** H4
Ravenscourt Rd, W6. . . . . **127** H4
Ravenscourt Sq, W6. . . . . **127** G3
Ravenscraig Rd, N11 . . . . . **58** B4
Ravenscroft Av, NW11 . . . . **72** C7
Wembley HA9. . . . . **87** J1
Ravenscroft Cl, E16 . . . . . **115** G5
Ravenscroft Cres, SE9 . . . **174** C3
Ravenscroft Pk, Barn.
EN5 . . . . **40** A4
Ravenscroft Pt, E9
off Kenton Rd **95** G6
Ravenscroft Rd, E16. . . . . **115** G5
W4. . . . . **126** C4
Beckenham BR3 . . . . . . **189** F2
Ravenscroft St, E2 . . . . **13** G2
Ravensdale Av, N12 . . . . . . **57** F4
Ravensdale Gdns, SE19 . . **170** A7
Hounslow TW4 . . . . **142** E3
Ravensdale Rd, N16. . . . . . **76** C7
Hounslow TW4 . . . . **142** E3
Ravensdon St, SE11. . . . . . **35** F4
Ravensfield Cl, Dag. RM9. **100** D4
Ravensfield Gdns, Epsom
KT19 . . . . **197** E5
Ravenshaw St, NW6 . . . . . **90** C5
Ravenshill, Chis. BR7 . . . . **192** E1
Ravenshurst Av, NW4 . . . . **71** J4
Ravenside Cl, N18 . . . . **61** G6
Ravenside Retail Pk, N18. . **61** G5
Ravenslea Rd, SW12 . . . . **149** J7
Ravensmead Rd, Brom.
BR2 . . . . **172** D7
Ravensmede Way, W4 . . . **127** F4
Ravens Ms, SE12
off Ravens Way **155** G5
Ravenstone, SE17 . . . . **36** E4
Ravenstone Rd, N8 . . . . . . **75** G3
NW9
off West Hendon Bdy . . **71** F6
Ravenstone St, SW12 . . . **168** A1
Ravens Way, SE12 . . . . . . **155** G5
Ravenswood, Bex. DA5 . . **177** E1
Ravenswood Av, Surb.
KT6 . . . . **195** J2
West Wickham BR4. . . . **204** C1
Ravenswood Ct, Kings.T.
KT2 . . . . **164** B6
Ravenswood Cres, Har.
HA2. . . . . **85** F2
West Wickham BR4. . . . **204** C1
Ravenswood Gdns, Islw.
TW7. . . . . **144** B1
Ravenswood Pk, Nthwd.
HA6. . . . . **50** A6
Ravenswood Rd, E17. . . . . **78** B4
SW12. . . . . **150** B7
Croydon CR0 . . . . **201** H3
Ravensworth Rd, NW10. . **107** H3
SE9 . . . . **174** C4
Ravey St, EC2. . . . . **12** D5
Ravine Gro, SE18 . . . . **137** H6
Rav Pinter Cl, N16 . . . . **76** B7
Rawlings Cl, Beck. BR3
off Creswell Dr **190** B5
Orpington BR6 . . . . **207** J5
Rawlings Cres, Wem. HA9 . **88** B3
Rawlings St, SW3 . . . . **31** J1
Rawlins Cl, N3 . . . . **72** B3
South Croydon CR2 . . . **203** H7
Rawnsley Av, Mitch. CR4 . **185** G5
Rawreth Wk, N1
off Basire St. **111** J1
Rawson St, SW11
off Strasburg Rd **150** A1
Rawsthorne Cl, E16
off Kennard St. **136** C1
Rawstone Wk, E13 . . . . . . **115** G2
Rawstorne Pl, EC1 . . . . **11** G3
Rawstorne St, EC1 . . . . **11** G3
Ray Cl, Chess. KT9
off Merritt Gdns **195** F6
Raydean Rd, Barn. EN5 . . . **40** E5
Raydons Gdns, Dag. RM9. **101** E5
Raydons Rd, Dag. RM9 . . **100** E5
Raydon St, N19 . . . . **92** B2
Rayfield Cl, Brom. BR2. . . **192** B6
Rayford Av, SE12 . . . . **155** F7
Ray Gdns, Bark. IG11 . . . . **118** A2
Stanmore HA7 . . . . **53** E5
Rayleas Cl, SE18 . . . . **156** E1
Rayleigh Av, Tedd. TW11 . . **162** B6
Rayleigh Cl, N13
off Rayleigh Rd. **60** A3
Rayleigh Ct, Kings.T. KT1. **181** J2
Rayleigh Ri, S.Croy. CR2 . **202** B6
Rayleigh Rd, E16 . . . . **135** H1
N13 . . . . **59** J3
SW19. . . . . **184** C1
Woodford Green IG8 . . . **63** J6
Ray Lo Rd, Wdf.Grn. IG8 . . **63** J6
Ray Massey Way, E6
off Ron Leighton Way . **116** B1
Raymead, NW4
off Tenterden Gro **71** J4
Raymead Av, Th.Hth. CR7. **187** G5
Raymead Pas, Th.Hth. CR7
off Raymead Av. **187** G5
Raymere Gdns, SE18. . . . **137** G7
Raymond Av, E18. . . . . **79** F3
W13. . . . . **124** D3
Raymond Bldgs, WC1 . . . . **18** D1
Raymond Cl, SE26 . . . . . . **171** F5
Raymond Ct, N10
off Pembroke Rd **58** A7
Sutton SM2
off Mulgrave Rd. . **198/199** E6
Raymond Rd, E13 . . . . **97** J7
SW19. . . . . **166** B6
Beckenham BR3 . . . . . . **189** H4
Ilford IG2. . . . . **81** G7
Raymond Way, Esher (Clay.)
KT10. . . . . **194** D6
Raymouth Rd, SE16. . . . . **133** E4
Rayne Ct, E18. . . . . **79** F4
Rayners Cl, Wem. HA0. . . . **87** G5
Rayners Ct, Har. HA2. . . . . **85** G1
Rayners Cres, Nthlt. UB5 . **102** B3
Rayners Gdns, Nthlt. UB5 . **102** B2
RAYNERS LANE, Har. HA2. **85** F1
Rayners La, Har. HA2. . . . . **85** H2
Pinner HA5 . . . . **67** F6
Rayners Rd, SW15 . . . . . . **148** B5
Rayner Twr, E10 . . . . **78** A7
Raynes Av, E11 . . . . **79** J7
RAYNES PARK, SW20 . . . **183** H3
Raynham Av, N18. . . . . **60** D6
Raynham Rd, N18 . . . . **60** D5
W6. . . . . **127** H4
Raynham Ter, N18 . . . . **60** D5
Raynor Cl, Sthl. UB1 . . . . **123** F1
Raynor Pl, N1
off Elizabeth Av **111** J1
Raynton Cl, Har. HA2. . . . . **85** E1
Ray Rd, W.Mol. KT8 . . . . . **179** H5
Rays Av, N18 . . . . **61** F4
Rays Rd, N18 . . . . **61** F4
West Wickham BR4. . . . **190** C7
Ray St, EC1. . . . . **11** F6
Ray St Br, EC1 . . . . **11** F6

Ray Wk, N7
off Andover Rd 93 F2
Raywood Cl, Hayes UB3 121 F7
Reachview Cl, NW1
off Baynes St 92 C7
Read Cl, T.Ditt. KT7 180 D7
Reade Wk, NW10
off Denbigh Cl 88/89 E7
Reading La, E8 94 E6
Reading Rd, Nthlt. UB5 85 H5
Sutton SM1 199 F5
Reading Way, NW7 56 A5
Reads Cl, Ilf. IG1
off Chapel Rd 98/99 E3
Reapers Cl, NW1
off Crofters Way 110 D1
Reapers Way, Islw. TW7
off Hall Rd 144 A5
Reardon Ct, N21
off Cosgrove Cl 59 J2
Reardon Path, E1 133 E1
Reardon St, E1 132 E1
Reaston St, SE14 133 F7
Reckitt Rd, W4 126 E5
Record St, SE15 133 F6
Recovery St, SW17 167 H5
Recreation Av, Rom. RM7 83 J5
Recreation Rd, SE26 171 G4
Bromley BR2 191 F2
Sidcup DA15
off Woodside Rd 175 H3
Southall UB2 122 E4
Recreation Way, Mitch.
CR4 186 D3
Rector St, N1 111 J1
Rectory Cl, E4 62 A3
N3 72 C1
SW20 183 J3
Sidcup DA14 176 B4
Stanmore HA7 53 E6
Surbiton KT6 195 F1
Rectory Cres, E11 79 J6
Rectory Fld Cres, SE7 135 J7
Rectory Gdns, N8 74 E4
SW4 *off Fitzwilliam Rd* 150 C3
Northolt UB5 103 F1
Rectory Grn, Beck. BR3 189 J1
Rectory Gro, SW4 150 C3
Croydon CR0 201 H2
Hampton TW12 161 F4
Rectory La, SW17 168 A6
Edgware HA8 54 A6
Loughton IG10 48 D2
Sidcup DA14 176 B4
Stanmore HA7 52 E5
Surbiton KT6 195 E1
Wallington SM6 200 C4
Rectory Orchard, SW19 166 B4
Rectory Pk Av, Nthlt. UB5 103 F3
Rectory Pl, SE18 136 D4
Rectory Rd, E12 98 C5
E17 78 B3
N16 94 C3
SW13 147 G2
W3 120 D1
Beckenham BR3 190 A1
Dagenham RM10 101 G7
Hayes UB3 102 A6
Hounslow TW4 142 B1
Keston BR2 206 A7
Southall UB2 123 F3
Sutton SM1 198 D3
Rectory Sq, E1 113 G5
Reculver Ms, N18
off Lyndhurst Rd 60 D4
Reculver Rd, SE16 133 G5
Red Anchor Cl, SW3 31 G6
Redan Pl, W2 14 A4
Redan St, W14 128 A3
Redan Ter, SE5
off Flaxman Rd 151 J2
Red Barracks Rd, SE18 136 C4
Redberry Gro, SE26 171 F3
Redbourne Av, N3 72 D1
Redbourne Dr, SE28 118 D6
REDBRIDGE, Ilf. IG 80 C6
Redbridge Enterprise Cen,
Ilf. IG1 99 F2
Redbridge Gdns, SE5 132 B7
Redbridge La E, Ilf. IG4 80 A6
Redbridge La W, E11 79 H6
Redburn St, SW3 31 J5
Redcar Cl, Nthlt. UB5 85 H5
Redcar St, SE5 131 J7
Redcastle Cl, E1 113 F7
Red Cedars Rd, Orp. BR6 193 H7
Redchurch St, E2 13 F5
Redcliffe Cl, SW5
off Warwick Rd 128/129 E5
Redcliffe Gdns, SW5 30 B4
SW10 30 B4
W4 126 B7
Ilford IG1 98 D1
Redcliffe Ms, SW10 30 B4
Redcliffe Pl, SW10 30 C6
Redcliffe Rd, SW10 30 C4
Redcliffe Sq, SW10 30 B4
Redcliffe St, SW10 30 B5
Redclose Av, Mord. SM4 184 D5
Redclyffe Rd, E6 115 J1
Redcroft Rd, Sthl. UB1 103 J7
Redcross Way, SE1 28 A3
Reddings, The, NW7 55 F3
Reddings Cl, NW7 55 F4
Reddins Rd, SE15 37 H6
Reddons Rd, Beck. BR3 171 H7
Redenham Ho, SW15
off Tangley Gro 147 F7
Rede Pl, W2
off Chepstow Pl 108 D6
Redesdale Gdns, Islw.
TW7 124 D7
Redesdale St, SW3 31 H5
Redfern Av, Houns. TW4 143 G7
Redfern Rd, NW10 89 E7
SE6 154 C7
Redfield La, SW5 128 D4
Redfield Ms, SW5
off Redfield La 128 D4
Redford Av, Th.Hth. CR7 187 F4
Wallington SM6 200 E6
Redford Wk, N1
off Britannia Row 111 H1
Redgate Dr, Brom. BR2 205 H2
Redgate Ter, SW15
off Lytton Gro 148 A6
Redgrave Cl, Croy. CR0 188 C6
Redgrave Rd, SW15 148 A3
Red Hill, Chis. BR7 174 D5
Redhill Dr, Edg. HA8 70 C2
Redhill St, NW1 8 E3
Red Ho La, Bexh. DA6 158 D4
Redhouse Rd, Croy. CR0 186 D6
Red Ho Sq, N1
off Ashby Gro 93 J6
★Red Ho (William Morris Ho),
The, Bexh. DA6 158 E4
Redington Gdns, NW3 90 E4
Redington Rd, NW3 90 E4
Redland Gdns, W.Mol. KT8
off Dunstable Rd 179 F4
Redlands Ct, Brom. BR1 173 F7
Redlands Rd, Enf. EN3 45 H1
Redlands Way, SW2 151 F7
Red La, Esher (Clay.)
KT10 194 D6
Redleaf Cl, Belv. DA17 139 G6
Redlees Cl, Islw. TW7 144 D4
Red Lion Cl, SE17 36 A5
Red Lion Ct, EC4 19 F3
Red Lion Hill, N2 73 G2
Red Lion La, SE18 136 D7
Red Lion Pl, SE18
off Shooter's Hill Rd 156 D1
Red Lion Rd, Surb. KT6 195 J2
Red Lion Row, SE17 36 A5
Red Lion Sq, SW18
off Wandsworth
High St 140 D5
WC1 18 C2
Red Lion St, WC1 18 C1
Richmond TW9 145 G5
Red Lion Yd, W1 24 C1
Red Lo Rd, Beck. BR3 190 D6
West Wickham BR4 204 C1
Redman Cl, Nthlt. UB5 102 C2
Redman's Rd, E1 113 F5
Redmead La, E1 29 H2
Redmead Rd, Hayes
UB3 121 H4
Redmore Rd, W6 127 H4
Red Oak Cl, Orp. BR6 207 E3
Red Path, E9 95 J6
Red Pl, W1 16 B5
Redpoll Way, Erith DA18 138 D3
Red Post Hill, SE21 152 A5
SE24 152 A4
Redriffe Rd, E13 115 F1
Redriff Est, SE16 133 J3
Redriff Rd, SE16 133 G4
Romford RM7 83 H2
Redroofs Cl, Beck. BR3 190 B1
Redruth Cl, N22
off Palmerston Rd 59 F7
Redruth Rd, E9 113 G1
Red Sq, N16 94 A3
Redstart Cl, E6
off Columbine Av 116 B5
Redstart Cl, SE14
off Southerngate Way 133 H7
Redston Rd, N8 74 D4
Redvers Rd, N22 75 G2
Redvers St, N1 13 E3
Redwald Rd, E5 95 G4
Redway Dr, Twick. TW2 143 J7
Redwing Path, SE28 137 G2
Redwing Rd, Wall. SM6 201 E7
Redwood Cl, E3 114 A2
N14 *off The Vale* 42 D7
SE16 133 H1
Buckhurst Hill IG9
off Beech La 63 H2
Sidcup DA15 158 A7
Watford WD19 50 C4
Redwood Ct, NW6
off The Avenue 90 B7
Redwood Est, Houns.
TW5 122 B6
Redwood Gdns, E4 46 B6
Redwood Ms, SW4
off Hannington Rd 150 B3
Redwoods, SW15 165 G1
Redwood Wk, Surb. KT6 195 G1
Redwood Way, Barn. EN5 40 A5
Reece Ms, SW7 30 E1
Reed Av, Orp. BR6 207 H3
Reed Cl, E16 115 G5
SE12 155 G5
Reede Gdns, Dag. RM10 101 H5
Reede Rd, Dag. RM10 101 G6
Reede Way, Dag. RM10 101 H6
Reedham Cl, N17 76 E4
Reedham St, SE15 152 D2
Reedholm Vil, N16
off Winston Rd 94 A4
Reed Rd, N17 76 C2
Reeds Pl, NW1
off Royal Coll St 92 C7
Reedworth St, SE11 35 F2
Ree La Cotts, Loug. IG10
off Englands La 48 D2
Reenglass Rd, Stan. HA7 53 G4
Rees Dr, Stan. HA7 53 H4
Rees Gdns, Croy. CR0 188 C6
Reesland Cl, E12 98 D6
Rees St, N1 111 J1
Reets Fm Cl, NW9 71 E6
Reeves Av, NW9 70 D7
Reeves Cor, Croy. CR0
off Roman Way 201 H2
Reeves Ms, W1 16 B6
Reeves Rd, E3 114 B4
SE18 136 E6
Reflection, The, E16
off Woolwich
Manor Way 136/137 E2
Reform Row, N17 76 C2
Reform St, SW11 149 J2
Regal Cl, E1 21 J1
W5 105 G5
Regal Ct, N18
off College Cl 60 C5
Regal Cres, Wall. SM6 200 B3
Regal Dr, N11 58 B5
Regal La, NW1
off Regents Pk Rd 110 A1
Regal Pl, E3 *off Coborn St* 113 J3
SW6
off Maxwell Rd 128/129 E7
Regal Row, SE15
off Astbury Rd 153 F1
Regal Way, Har. HA3 69 H6
Regan Way, N1 12 D2
Regatta Ho, Tedd. TW11
off Twickenham Rd 162 D4
Regency Cl, W5 105 H6
Chigwell IG7 65 F5
Hampton TW12 161 F5
Regency Ct, Sutt. SM1
off Brunswick Rd 198/199 E4
Regency Cres, NW4 72 A2
Regency Ho, SW6
off The Boulevard 149 F1
Regency Lo, Buck.H. IG9 64 A2
Regency Ms, NW10
off High Rd 89 G6
SW9 *off Lothian Rd* 131 H7
Beckenham BR3 190 C1
Isleworth TW7
off Queensbridge Pk 144 B5
Regency Pl, SW1 33 J1
Regency St, SW1 33 H1
Regency Ter, SW7
off Fulham Rd 129 G5
Regency Wk, Croy. CR0 189 H6
Richmond TW10
off Grosvenor Rd 145 H5
Regency Way, Bexh.
DA6 158 D3
Regent Cl, N12
off Nether St 57 F5
Harrow HA3 69 H6
Hounslow TW4 142 B1
Regent Gdns, Ilf. IG3 82 A6
Regent Pl, SW19
off Haydons Rd 166/167 E5
W1 17 G5
Croydon CR0
off Grant Rd 202 C1
Regent Rd, SE24 151 H6
Surbiton KT5 181 J5
Regents Av, N13 59 F5
Regents Br Gdns, SW8 34 B7
Regents Cl, S.Croy. CR2 202 B6
Regents Dr, Kes. BR2 206 A5
Woodford Green IG8 64 D7
Regents Ms, NW8 6 D1
REGENT'S PARK, NW1 8 C2
★Regent's Park, NW1 7 J3
Regent's Pk Est, NW1 9 F4
Regents Pk Rd, N3 72 C3
NW1 109 J1
Regents Pk Ter, NW1
off Oval Rd 110 B1
Regent's Pl, SE3 155 G2
Regents Pl, Loug. IG10 48 A7
Regent Sq, E3 114 B3
WC1 10 B4
Belvedere DA17 139 H4
Regents Row, E8 112 D1
Regent St, NW10
off Wellington Rd 108 A3
SW1 17 H6
W1 17 E3
W4 126 A5
Regents Wf, N1 10 C1
Regina Cl, Barn. EN5 40 A3
Reginald Rd, E7 97 G7
SE8 134 A7
Reginald Sq, SE8 134 A7
Regina Pt, SE16
off Renforth St 133 F3
Regina Rd, N4 93 F1
SE25 188 D3
W13 124 D1
Southall UB2 122 E4
Regina Ter, W13 124 D1
Regis Pl, SW2 151 F4
Regis Rd, NW5 92 B5
Regnart Bldgs, NW1 9 G5
Reid Cl, Pnr. HA5 66 A4
Reidhaven Rd, SE18 137 H4
Reigate Av, Sutt. SM1 198 D1
Reigate Rd, Brom. BR1 173 F3
Ilford IG3 99 J2
Reigate Way, Wall. SM6 201 E5
Reighton Rd, E5 94 D3
Reinickendorf Av, SE9 157 F5
Reizel Cl, N16 94 C1
Relay Rd, W12 107 J7
Relf Rd, SE15 152 D3
Reliance Sq, EC2 13 E5
Relko Gdns, Sutt. SM1 199 G5
Relton Ms, SW7 23 H5
Rembrandt Cl, E14 134 D3
SW1 32 B2
Rembrandt Ct, Epsom
KT19 197 F6
Rembrandt Rd, SE13 154 E4
Edgware HA8 70 A2
Remington Rd, E6 116 B6
N15 76 A6
Remington St, N1 11 H2
Remnant St, WC2 18 C3
Remus Rd, E3
off Monier Rd 96 A7
Renaissance Wk, SE10
off Teal St 135 F3
Rendle Cl, Croy. CR0 188 C5
Rendlesham Rd, E5 94 D4
Enfield EN2 43 H1
Renforth St, SE16 133 F2
Renfrew Cl, E6 116 D7
Renfrew Rd, SE11 35 G1
Hounslow TW4 142 D2
Kingston upon Thames
KT2 164 B7
Renmuir St, SW17 167 J6
Rennell St, SE13 154 C3
Rennels Way, Islw. TW7
off St. John's Rd 144 B2
Renness Rd, E17 77 H3
Rennets Cl, SE9 157 H5
Rennets Wd Rd, SE9 157 G5
Rennie Est, SE16 133 E4
Rennie St, SE1 27 G1

Renovation, The, E16 *off Woolwich Manor Way* **136/137** E2
Renown Cl, Croy. CR0 **201** H1
Romford RM7 **83** G1
Rensburg Rd, E17 **77** G5
Renshaw Cl, Belv. DA17 *off Grove Rd* **139** F6
Renters Av, NW4 **71** J6
Renwick Ind Est, Bark. IG11 **118** B1
Renwick Rd, Bark. IG11 **118** B4
Repens Way, Hayes UB4 *off Stipularis Dr.* **102** D4
Rephidim St, SE1 **28** D6
Replingham Rd, SW18 **166** C1
Reporton Rd, SW6 **148** B1
Repository Rd, SE18 **136** C6
Repton Av, Hayes UB3 **121** G4
Wembley HA0 **87** F4
Repton Cl, Cars. SM5 **199** H5
Repton Ct, Beck. BR3 **190** B1
Ilford IG5 *off Repton Gro* **80** C1
Repton Gro, Ilf. IG5 **80** C1
Repton Rd, Har. HA3 **69** J4
Repton St, E14 **113** H6
Repulse Cl, Rom. RM5 **83** H1
Reservoir Cl, Th.Hth. CR7 **188** A4
Reservoir Rd, N14 **42** C5
SE4 **153** H2
Resham Cl, Sthl. UB2 **122** C3
Resolution Wk, SE18 **136** C3
Resolution Way, SE8 *off Deptford High St* **134** A7
Restell Cl, SE3 **135** E6
Restmor Way, Wall. SM6 **200** A2
Reston Pl, SW7 **22** C4
Restons Cres, SE9 **157** G6
Restormel Cl, Houns. TW3 **143** G5
Retcar Cl, N19 *off Dartmouth Pk Hill* **92** B2
Retcar Pl, N19 **92** B2
Retford St, N1 **13** E2
Retingham Way, E4 **62** B2
Retreat, The, NW9 **70** D5
SW14 *off South Worple Way* **146/147** E3
Harrow HA2 **67** G7
Surbiton KT5 **181** J6
Thornton Heath CR7 **188** A4
Worcester Park KT4 **197** H2
Retreat Cl, Har. HA3 **69** F5
Retreat Pl, E9 **95** F6
Retreat Rd, Rich. TW9 **145** G5
Reunion Row, E1 *off Pennington St* **112/113** E7
Reveley Sq, SE16 *off Howland Way* **133** H2
Revell Ri, SE18 **137** J6
Revell Rd, Kings.T. KT1 **182** B1
Sutton SM1 **198** C6
Revelon Rd, SE4 **153** H4
Revelstoke Rd, SW18 **166** C2
Reventlow Rd, SE9 **175** F1
Reverdy Rd, SE1 **37** H2
Reverend Cl, Har. HA2 **85** H3
Revesby Rd, Cars. SM5 **185** G6
Review Rd, NW2 **89** F2
Dagenham RM10 **119** H1
Rewell St, SW6 **129** F7
Rewley Rd, Cars. SM5 **185** G6
Rex Pl, W1 **16** C6
Reydon Av, E11 **79** J6
Reynard Cl, SE4 *off Foxwell St* **153** H3
Bromley BR1 **192** C3
Reynard Dr, SE19 **170** C7
Reynard Pl, SE14 *off Milton Ct Rd* **133** H6
Reynardson Rd, N17 **59** J7
Reynolah Gdns, SE7 *off Rathmore Rd* **135** H5
Reynolds Av, E12 **98** D5
Chessington KT9 **195** H7
Romford RM6 **82** C7
Reynolds Cl, NW11 **72** E7
SW19 **185** G1
Carshalton SM5 **199** J1
Reynolds Ct, E11 *off Cobbold Rd* **97** F3
Romford RM6 **82** D3
Reynolds Dr, Edg. HA8 **69** J3
Reynolds Pl, SE3 **135** H7
Richmond TW10 *off Cambrian Rd* **145** J6
Reynolds Rd, SE15 **153** F5
Reynolds Rd, W4 **126** C3
Hayes UB4 **102** C4
New Malden KT3 **182** D7
Reynolds Way, Croy. CR0 **202** B4
Rheidol Ms, N1 **11** J1
Rheidol Ter, N1 **11** H1
Rheola Cl, N17 **76** C1
Rhoda St, E2 **13** G5
Rhodes Av, N22 **74** C1
Rhodesia Rd, E11 **96** D2
SW9 **151** E2
Rhodes Moorhouse Ct, Mord. SM4 **184** D6
Rhodes St, N7 *off Mackenzie Rd* **93** F5
Rhodeswell Rd, E14 **113** H5
Rhodrons Av, Chess. KT9 **195** H5
Rhondda Gro, E3 **113** H3
Rhyl Rd, Grnf. UB6 **104** C2
Rhyl St, NW5 **92** A6
Rhys Av, N11 **58** D7
Rialto Rd, Mitch. CR4 **186** A2
Ribble Cl, Wdf.Grn. IG8 *off Prospect Rd* **63** J6
Ribblesdale Av, N11 **58** A6
Northolt UB5 **85** H6
Ribblesdale Rd, N8 **75** F4
SW16 **168** B6
Ribbon Dance Ms, SE5 *off Camberwell Gro* **152** A1
Ribchester Av, Grnf. UB6 **104** C3
Ribston Cl, Brom. BR2 **206** C1
Ricardo Path, SE28 *off Byron Cl* **138** C1
Ricardo St, E14 **114** B6
Ricards Rd, SW19 **166** C5
Richard Cl, SE18 **136** B4
Richard Fell Ho, E12 *off Walton Rd* **98** D4
Richard Foster Cl, E17 **77** J7
Richard Ho Dr, E16 **116** A6
Richards Av, Rom. RM7 **83** J5
Richards Cl, Har. HA1 **68** D5
Hayes UB3 **121** G6
Richardson Cl, E8 *off Clarissa St* **112** C1
Richardson Rd, E15 **114** E2
Richardson's Ms, W1 **9** F6
Richards Pl, E17 **78** A3
SW3 **31** H1
Richard St, E1 *off Commercial Rd* **112/113** E6
Richbell Pl, WC1 **18** C1
Richborne Ter, SW8 **34** D7
Richborough Rd, NW2 **90** A4
Richens Cl, Houns. TW3 **144** A2
Riches Rd, Ilf. IG1 **99** F2
Richford Rd, E15 **115** F1
Richford St, W6 **127** J2
Richlands Av, Epsom KT17 **197** G4
Rich La, SW5 **30** A4
RICHMOND, TW9 & TW10 **145** H6
Richmond Av, E4 **62** D5
N1 **111** F1
NW10 **89** J6
SW20 **184** B1
Feltham TW14 **141** H6
Richmond Br, Rich. TW9 **145** G6
Twickenham TW1 **145** G6
Richmond Bldgs, W1 **17** H4
Richmond Cl, E17 **77** J6
Borehamwood WD6 **38** D5
Richmond Cres, E4 **62** D5
N1 **111** F1
N9 **60** D1
Richmond Dr, Wdf.Grn. IG8 **64** D7
Richmond Gdns, NW4 **71** G5
Harrow HA3 **52** C6
Richmond Grn, Croy. CR0 **201** E3
Richmond Gro, N1 **93** H7
Surbiton KT5 **181** J6
Richmond Hill, Rich. TW10 **145** H6
Richmond Hill Ct, Rich. TW10 **145** H6
Richmond Ms, W1 **17** H4
Teddington TW11 *off Broad St* **162** C6
★**Richmond Palace (remains)**, Rich. TW9 **145** F5
★**Richmond Park**, Rich. TW10 **164** A1
Richmond Pk, Kings.T. KT2 **164** A1
Loughton IG10 *off Fallow Flds* **47** J7
Richmond TW10 **164** A1
Richmond Pk Rd, SW14 **146** C5
Kingston upon Thames KT2 **163** H7
Richmond Pl, SE18 **137** F4
Richmond Rd, E4 **62** D1
E7 **97** H5
E8 **94** C7
E11 **96** D2
N2 **73** F2
N11 **58** E6
N15 **76** B6
SW20 **183** H1
W5 **125** H2
Barnet EN5 **41** E5
Croydon CR0 **200** E3
Ilford IG1 **99** F3
Isleworth TW7 **144** D3
Kingston upon Thames KT2 **163** G5
Thornton Heath CR7 **187** H3
Twickenham TW1 **145** F6
Richmond St, E13 **115** G2
Richmond Ter, SW1 **26** A3
Richmond Ter Ms, SW1 *off Parliament St* **130/131** E2
Richmond Way, E11 **97** G2
W12 **128** A2
W14 **128** A3
Richmount Gdns, SE3 **155** G3
Rich St, E14 **113** J7
Rickard Cl, NW4 **71** H4
SW2 **169** F1
West Drayton UB7 **120** A3
Rickards Cl, Surb. KT6 **195** H1
Rickett St, SW6 **128** D6
Rickman St, E1 *off Mantus Rd* **113** F3
Rickmansworth Rd, Pnr. HA5 **66** B2
Rick Roberts Way, E15 **114** C1
Rickthorne Rd, N19 *off Landseer Rd* **92/93** E2
Rickyard Path, SE9 **156** B4
Ridding La, Grnf. UB6 **86** C5
Riddons Rd, SE12 **173** J3
Ride, The, Brent. TW8 **125** E5
Enfield EN3 **45** F3
Rideout St, SE18 **136** C4
Rider Cl, Sid. DA15 **157** H6
Ridgdale St, E3 **114** B2
Ridge, The, Bex. DA5 **159** F7
Orpington BR6 **207** G2
Surbiton KT5 **182** A5
Twickenham TW2 **144** A7
Ridge Av, N21 **43** J7
Ridgebrook Rd, SE3 **155** J4
Ridge Cl, NW4 **72** A2
NW9 **70** D4
SE20 **107** G2
Ridge Crest, Enf. EN2 **43** F1
Ridgecroft Cl, Bex. DA5 **177** J1
Ridge Hill, NW11 **90** B1
Ridgemont Gdns, Edg. HA8 **54** C4
Ridgemount Av, Croy. CR0 **203** G1
Ridgemount Cl, SE20 **170** E7
Ridgemount Gdns, Enf. EN2 **43** H2
Ridge Rd, N8 **75** F6
N21 **59** J1
NW2 **90** C3
Mitcham CR4 **168** B7
Sutton SM3 **198** B1
Ridgeview Cl, Barn. EN5 **40** A6
Ridgeview Rd, N20 **57** E3
Ridge Way, SE19 *off Central Hill* **170** B6
Ridgeway, SE28 *off Pettman Cres* **137** G4
Bromley BR2 **205** G2
Ridge Way, Felt. TW13 **160** E3
Ridgeway, Wdf.Grn. IG8 **63** J4
Ridgeway, The, E4 **62** B2
N3 **56** E7
N11 **57** J4
N14 **59** E2
NW7 **55** G4
NW9 **70** E4
NW11 **90** C1
W3 **126** A3
Croydon CR0 **201** F3
Enfield EN2 **43** G1
Harrow (Kenton) HA3 **69** F6
Harrow (N.Har.) HA2 **67** G6
Ruislip HA4 **66** A7
Stanmore HA7 **53** F6
Ridgeway Av, Barn. EN4 **41** J6
Ridgeway Cres, Orp. BR6 **207** H3
Ridgeway Cres Gdns, Orp. BR6 **207** H2
Ridgeway Dr, Brom. BR1 **173** H4
Ridgeway E, Sid. DA15 **157** J5
Ridgeway Gdns, N6 **74** C7
Ilford IG4 **80** B5
Ridgeway Rd, SW9 **151** H3
Isleworth TW7 **124** B7
Ridgeway Rd N, Islw TW7 **124** B6
Ridgeway Wk, Nthlt. UB5 *off Fortunes Mead* **84/85** E6
Ridgeway W, Sid. DA15 **157** H5
Ridgewell Cl, N1 *off Basire St* **111** J1
SE26 **171** J4
Dagenham RM10 **119** H1
Ridgmount Gdns, WC1 **9** H6
Ridgmount Pl, WC1 **17** H1
Ridgmount Rd, SW18 **149** E5
Ridgmount St, WC1 **17** H1
Ridgway, SW19 **166** A6
Ridgway, The, Sutt. SM2 **199** G7
Ridgway Gdns, SW19 **166** A7
Ridgway Pl, SW19 **166** B6
Ridgwell Rd, E16 **115** J5
Riding, The, NW11 *off Golders Grn Rd* **72** C7
Riding Ho St, W1 **17** F2
Ridings, The, E11 *off Malcolm Way* **79** G5
W5 **105** J4
Sunbury-on-Thames TW16 **178** A1
Surbiton KT5 **182** A5
Ridings Av, N21 **43** H4
Ridings Cl, N6 *off Hornsey La Gdns* **74** C7
Ridley Av, W13 **124** E3
Ridley Cl, Bark. IG11 **99** J7
Ridley Rd, E7 **97** J4
E8 **94** C5
NW10 **107** G2
SW19 **166** E7
Bromley BR2 **191** F3
Welling DA16 **158** B1
Ridsdale Rd, SE20 **188** E1
Riefield Rd, SE9 **157** F4
Riesco Dr, Croy. CR0 **203** F6
Riffel Rd, NW2 **89** J5
Rifle Pl, SE11 **35** F5
Rifle St, E14 **114** B5
Rigault Rd, SW6 **148** B2
Rigby Cl, Croy. CR0 **201** G3
Rigby La, Hayes UB3 **121** G2
Rigby Ms, Ilf. IG1 *off Cranbrook Rd* **98/99** E2
Rigden St, E14 **114** B6
Rigeley Rd, NW10 **107** G3
Rigg App, E10 **06** C1
Rigge Pl, SW4 **150** D4
Riggindale Rd, SW16 **168** D5
Riley Rd, SE1 **29** E5
Riley St, SW10 **31** E7
Rinaldo Rd, SW12 **150** B7
Ring, The, W2 **15** G5
Ring Cl, Brom. BR1 *off Garden Rd* **173** H7
Ringcroft St, N7 **93** G5
Ringers Rd, Brom. BR1 **191** G3
Ringford Rd, SW18 **148** C5
Ringlet Cl, E16 **115** H5
Ringlewell Cl, Enf. EN1 *off Central Av* **44/45** E2
Ringmer Av, SW6 **148** B1
Ringmer Gdns, N19 *off Sussex Way* **92/93** E2
Ringmer Pl, N21 **44** A5
Ringmer Way, Brom. BR1 **192** C5
Ringmore Ri, SE23 **153** E7
Ring Rd, W12 **107** J7
Ringslade Rd, N22 **75** F2
Ringstead Rd, SE6 **154** B7
Sutton SM1 **199** G4
Ringway, N11 **58** C6
Southall UB2 **123** E5
Ringwold Cl, Beck. BR3 **171** H7
Ringwood Av, N2 **73** J2
Croydon CR0 **187** E7
Ringwood Cl, Pnr. HA5 **66** C3
Ringwood Gdns, E14 *off Inglewood Cl* **134** A4
SW15 **165** G2
Ringwood Rd, E17 **77** J6
Ringwood Way, N21 **59** H1
Hampton (Hmptn H.) TW12 **161** G4
Ripley Cl, Brom. BR1 *off Ringmer Way* **192** C5

Ripley Cl, Croy. (New Adgtn) CR0 **204** C6
Ripley Gdns, SW14 **146** D3
Sutton SM1 **199** F4
Ripley Ms, E11
off Wadley Rd **78/79** E7
Ripley Rd, E16 **115** J6
Belvedere DA17 **139** G4
Enfield EN2 **43** J1
Hampton TW12 **161** G7
Ilford IG3 **99** J2
Ripley Vil, W5
off Castlebar Rd **105** F6
Riplington Ct, SW15
off Longwood Dr. **147** G7
Ripon Cl, Nthlt. UB5 **85** G5
Ripon Gdns, Chess. KT9 **195** G5
Ilford IG1 **80** B6
Ripon Rd, N9 **44** E7
N17 **76** A3
SE18 **136** E6
Ripon Way, Borwd. WD6 **38** C5
Rippersley Rd, Well. DA16 **158** A1
Ripple Rd, Bark. IG11 **99** F7
Dagenham RM9 **118** B1
Rippleside Commercial Est, Bark. IG11 **118** C2
Ripplevale Gro, N1 **93** F7
Rippolson Rd, SE18 **137** J5
Risborough Dr, Wor.Pk. KT4 **183** G7
Risborough St, SE1 **27** H3
Risdon St, SE16 **133** F2
Rise, The, E11 **79** G5
N13 **59** G4
NW7 **55** F6
NW10 **88** D4
Bexley DA5 **158** C7
Buckhurst Hill IG9 **48** A7
Edgware HA8 **54** B5
Greenford UB6 **86** D5
Risedale Rd, Bexh. DA7 **159** H3
Riseldine Rd, SE23 **153** H6
Risinghill St, N1 **10** E1
Risingholme Cl, Har. HA3 **68** B1
Risingholme Rd, Har. HA3 **68** B2
Risings, The, E17 **78** D4
Rising Sun Ct, EC1 **19** H2
Risley Av, N17 **75** J1
Rita Rd, SW8 **34** B6
Ritches Rd, N15 **75** J5
Ritchie Rd, Croy. CR0 **189** E6
Ritchie St, N1 **11** F1
Ritchings Av, E17 **77** H4
Ritherdon Rd, SW17 **168** A2
Ritson Rd, E8 **94** D6
Ritter St, SE18 **136** D6
Ritz Par, W5
off Connell Cres **105** J4
Rivaz Pl, E9 **95** F6
Rivenhall Gdns, E18 **79** F4
River Av, N13 **59** H3
Thames Ditton KT7 **180** D7
River Bk, N21 **43** J7
East Molesey KT8 **180** B6
Thames Ditton KT7 **180** C5
West Molesey KT8 **179** F3
Riverbank Way, Brent. TW8 **125** F6
River Barge Cl, E14
off Stewart St **134** C2
River Brent Business Pk, W7 **124** B3
River Cl, E11 **79** J6
Southall UB2 **123** J2
Surbiton KT6
off Catherine Rd **181** G5
Rivercourt Rd, W6 **127** H4
River Crane Wk, Felt. TW13 **160** D1
Hounslow TW4 **160** D1
River Crane Way, Felt. TW13
off Watermill Way **161** F2
Riverdale, SE13
off Lewisham High St. **154** C3
Riverdale Cl, Bark. IG11 **118** B4
Riverdale Dr, SW18
off Strathville Rd **166/167** E1
Riverdale Gdns, Twick. TW1 **145** F6
Riverdale Rd, SE18 **137** J5
Bexley DA5 **159** F7
Erith DA8 **139** H5
Feltham TW13 **161** E4
Twickenham TW1 **145** F6
Riverdene, Edg. HA8 **54** C3
Riverdene Rd, Ilf. IG1 **98** D3
River Front, Enf. EN1 **44** A3
River Gdns, Cars. SM5 **200** A2
River Gdns, Felt. TW14 **142** B5
River Gro Pk, Beck. BR3 **189** J1
Riverhead Cl, E17 **77** G2
River La, Rich. TW10 **163** G1
Rivermead, E.Mol. KT8 **179** J3
Rivermead Cl, Tedd. TW11 **163** E5
Rivermead Ct, SW6 **148** C3
Rivermead Ho, E9
off Kingsmead Way **95** H5
Rivermead Rd, N18 **61** G6
Rivermeads Av, Twick. TW2 **161** G3
Rivermill, SW1
off Grosvenor Rd **130** D5
Rivernook Cl, Walt. KT12 **178** C5
River Pk Gdns, Brom. BR2 **172** D7
River Pk Rd, N22 **75** F2
River Pl, N1 **93** J7
River Reach, Tedd. TW11 **163** F5
River Rd, Bark. IG11 **117** H2
Buckhurst Hill IG9 **64** B1
River Rd Business Pk, Bark. IG11 **117** J3
Riversdale Rd, N5 **93** H3
Thames Ditton KT7 **180** D5
Riversfield Rd, Enf. EN1 **44** B3
Riverside, NW4 **71** H7
SE7 **135** H3
Twickenham TW1 **162** E1
Riverside, The, E.Mol. KT8 **180** A3
Riverside Av, E.Mol. KT8 **180** A5
Riverside Business Cen, SW18 **167** E1
Riverside Cl, E5 **95** F1
W7 **104** B4
Kingston upon Thames KT1 **181** G4
Wallington SM6 **200** B3
Riverside Ct, E4
off Chelwood Cl **46** B6
SW8 **33** J5
Riverside Dr, NW11 **72** B6
W4 **126** D7
Mitcham CR4 **185** H5
Richmond TW10 **162** E2
Riverside Gdns, N3 **72** B3
W6 **127** H5
Enfield EN2 **43** J2
Wembley HA0 **105** H2
Riverside Ind Est, Bark. IG11 **118** A3
Enfield EN3 **45** H6
Riverside Mans, E1
off Milk Yd **113** F7
Riverside Ms, Croy. CR0
off Wandle Rd **200/201** E3
Riverside Pl, Stai. (Stanw.) TW19 **140** A6
Riverside Rd, E15 **114** C2
N15 **76** D6
SW17 **167** E4
Sidcup DA14 **177** E3
Staines (Stanw.) TW19 **140** A5
Riverside Twr, SW6 **149** F2
Riverside Wk, E14
off Ferry St **134** C5
Bexley DA5 **158** C7
Isleworth TW7 **144** B3
Kingston upon Thames KT1
off High St. **181** G2
Loughton IG10 **48** E6
West Wickham BR4
off The Alders **204** B1
Riverside W, SW18
off Smugglers Way **148/149** E4
Riverside Yd, SW17
off Riverside Rd **167** F4
River St, EC1 **11** E3
River Ter, W6
off Crisp Rd. **127** J5
Riverton Cl, W9 **108** C3
River Vw, Enf. EN2
off Chase Side **43** J3
Riverview Gdns, SW13 **127** H6
Twickenham TW1 **162** C2
Riverview Gro, W4 **126** B6
River Vw Hts, SE16 **29** H3
Riverview Pk, SE6 **172** A2
Riverview Rd, W4 **126** B6
Epsom KT19 **196** C4
River Wk, Walt. KT12 **178** A6
Riverway, N13 **59** G5
River Way, Epsom KT19 **196** D5
Loughton IG10 **48** D6
Twickenham TW2 **161** H2
Riverwood La, Chis. BR7 **193** G1
Rivington Av, Wdf.Grn. IG8 **80** A2
Rivington Ct, NW10 **107** G1
Rivington Cres, NW7 **55** F7
Rivington Pl, EC2 **12** E4
Rivington St, EC2 **12** D4
Rivington Wk, E8
off Wilde Cl **112** D1
Rivulet Rd, N17 **59** J7
Rixon Ho, SE18
off Barnfield Rd **136/137** E6
Rixon St, N7 **93** G3
Rixsen Rd, E12 **98** B5
Roach Rd, E3 **96** A7
Roads Pl, N19
off Hornsey Rd **92/93** E2
Roan St, SE10 **134** C6
Robarts Cl, Pnr. HA5
off Field End Rd **66** B5
Robb Rd, Stan. HA7 **52** D6
Robert Adam St, W1 **16** B3
Roberta St, E2 **13** H3
Robert Burns Ms, SE24
off Mayall Rd. **151** H5
Robert Cl, W9 **6** D6
Chigwell IG7 **65** J5
Robert Dashwood Way, SE17 **35** J2
Robert Keen Cl, SE15
off Cicely Rd **152** D1
Robert Lowe Cl, SE14 **133** G7
Roberton Dr, Brom. BR1 **191** J1
Robert Owen Ho, SW6 **148** A1
Robertsbridge Rd, Cars. SM5 **199** F1
Roberts Cl, SE9 **175** G1
SE16 **133** G2
Sutton SM3 **198** A7
Thornton Heath CR7
off Kitchener Rd **188** A3
West Drayton UB7 **120** B1
Roberts Ms, SW1 **24** B6
Robertson Rd, E15 **114** C1
Robertson St, SW8 **150** B3
Robert's Pl, EC1 **11** F5
Robert Sq, SE13
off Bonfield Rd **154** C4
Roberts Rd, E17 **78** B1
NW7 **56** B6
Belvedere DA17 **139** G5
Robert St, E16 **136** E1
NW1 **8** E4
SE18 **137** G4
WC2 **18** B6
Croydon CR0
off High St. **201** J3
Robeson St, E3
off Ackroyd Dr. **113** J5
Robeson Way, Borwd. WD6 **38** C1
Robina Cl, Bexh. DA6 **158** D4
Robin Cl, NW7 **54** E3
Hampton TW12 **161** E5
Robin Ct, SE16 **37** H1
Wallington SM6
off Carew Rd **200** C6
Robin Cres, E6 **116** A5
Robin Gro, N6 **92** A2
Brentford TW8 **125** F6
Harrow HA3 **69** J6
Robin Hill Dr, Chis. BR7 **174** B6
Robinhood Cl, Mitch. CR4 **186** C3
Robin Hood Dr, Har. HA3 **52** C7
Robin Hood Gdns, E14
off Woolmore St **114** C7
Robin Hood La, E14 **114** C7
SW15 **164** E4
Bexleyheath DA6 **159** E5
Robinhood La, Mitch. CR4 **186** C3
Robin Hood La, Sutt. SM1 **198** D5
Robin Hood Rd, SW19 **165** H5
Robin Hood Way, SW15 **165** E4
SW20 **165** E4
Greenford UB6 **86** C6
Robin Ho, NW8
off Newcourt St. **109** H2
Robinia Cl, SE20
off Sycamore Gro **188** D1
Ilford IG6 **65** H6
Robinia Cres, E10 **96** B2
Robins Ct, SE12 **173** J3
Robinscroft Ms, SE10
off Sparta St **154** B1
Robins Gro, W.Wick. BR4 **205** G3
Robinson Cl, E11 **97** E3
Robinson Cres, Bushey (Bushey Hth) WD23 **51** J1
Robinson Rd, E2 **113** F2
SW17 **167** H6
Robinson Rd, Dag. RM10 **101** G4
Robinsons Cl, W13 **104** D5
Robinson St, SW3 **31** J5
Robinwood Pl, SW15 **164** D4
Robsart St, SW9 **151** F2
Robson Av, NW10 **107** G1
Robson Cl, E6
off Linton Gdns **116** B6
Enfield EN2 **43** H2
Robson Rd, SE27 **169** H3
Rocastle Rd, SE4
off Turnham Rd **153** H5
Roch Av, Edg. HA8 **69** J2
Rochdale Rd, E17 **78** A7
SE2 **138** B5
Rochdale Way, SE8
off Octavius St **134** A7
Rochelle Cl, SW11 **149** G4
Rochelle St, E2 **13** F4
Rochemont Wk, E8
off Pownall Rd. **112** C1
Roche Rd, SW16 **187** F1
Rochester Av, E13 **115** J1
Bromley BR1 **191** H2
Rochester Cl, SW16 **169** E7
Enfield EN1 **44** B1
Sidcup DA15 **158** B6
Rochester Dr, Bex. DA5 **159** F6
Pinner HA5 **66** D5
Rochester Gdns, Croy. CR0 **202** B3
Ilford IG1 **80** C7
Rochester Ms, NW1 **92** C7
Rochester Pl, NW1 **92** C6
Rochester Rd, NW1 **92** C6
Carshalton SM5 **199** J4
Rochester Row, SW1 **33** G1
Rochester Sq, NW1 **92** C7
Rochester St, SW1 **25** H6
Rochester Ter, NW1 **92** C6
Rochester Wk, SE1 **28** B1
Rochester Way, SE3 **155** H1
SE9 **156** C3
Rochester Way Relief Rd, SE3 **155** H1
SE9 **156** B4
Roche Wk, Cars. SM5 **185** G6
Rochford Av, Loug. IG10 **49** F3
Romford RM6 **82** C5
Rochford Cl, E6
off Boleyn Rd. **116** A2
Rochford Grn, Loug. IG10 **49** F3
Rochford St, NW5 **91** J5
Rochford Wk, E8
off Wilman Gro **94** D7
Rochford Way, Croy. CR0 **186** E6
Rock Av, SW14
off South Worple Way **146** D3
Rockbourne Rd, SE23 **171** G1
★**Rock Circ**, W1 **17** H6
Rockells Pl, SE22 **153** E6
Rockford Av, Grnf. UB6 **104** D2
Rock Gdns, Dag. RM10 **101** H5
Rock Gro Way, SE16 **37** J1
Rockhall Rd, NW2 **90** A4
Rockhall Way, NW2
off Midland Ter **90** A3
Rockhampton Cl, SE27
off Rockhampton Rd **169** G4
Rockhampton Rd, SE27 **169** G4
South Croydon CR2 **202** B6
Rock Hill, SE26 **170** C4
Rockingham Cl, SW15 **147** F4
Rockingham Est, SE1 **27** J6
Rockingham St, SE1 **27** J6
Rockland Rd, SW15 **148** B4
Rocklands Dr, Stan. HA7 **69** E2
Rockley Rd, W14 **128** A2
Rockmount Rd, SE18 **137** J5
SE19 **170** A6
Rocks La, SW13 **147** G1
Rock St, N4 **93** G2
Rockware Av, Grnf. UB6 **104** A1
Rockways, Barn. EN5 **39** F6
Rockwell Gdns, SE19 **170** B5
Rockwell Rd, Dag. RM10 **101** H5
Rockwood Pl, W12 **127** J2
Rocliffe St, N1 **11** H2
Rocombe Cres, SE23 **153** F7
Rocque La, SE3 **155** F3
Rodborough Rd, NW11 **90** D1
Roden Ct, N6
off Hornsey La. **74** D7
Roden Gdns, Croy. CR0 **188** B6
Rodenhurst Rd, SW4 **150** C6
Roden St, N7 **93** F3
Ilford IG1 **98** D3
Roderick Rd, NW3 **91** J4
Roding Av, Wdf.Grn. IG8 **64** B6

Roding Gdns, Loug. IG10 . . 48 B6
Roding La, Buck.H. IG9 . . . 64 B1
Chigwell IG7 . . . . 64 D1
Roding La N, Wdf.Grn. IG8 . 80 A2
Roding La S, Ilf. IG4 . . . . . . 80 A4
Woodford Green IG8 . . . 80 A4
Roding Ms, E1 . . . . 29 J1
Roding Rd, E5 . . . . 95 G4
E6 . . . . 116 E5
Loughton IG10 . . . . 48 B5
Rodings, The, Wdf.Grn.
IG8 . . . . 63 J6
Rodings Row, Barn. EN5
off Leecroft Rd 40 B5
Roding Trd Est, Bark. IG11 . 98 E7
Roding Vw, Buck.H. IG9 . . . 64 A1
Rodmarton St, W1 . . . . 16 A2
Rodmell Cl, Hayes UB4 . . 102 E4
Rodmell Slope, N12 . . . . . . 56 C5
Rodmere St, SE10
off Trafalgar Rd . . . 134/135 E5
Rodmill La, SW2 . . . . 151 E7
Rodney Cl, Croy. CR0 . . . . 201 H1
New Malden KT3 . . . . . 182 E5
Pinner HA5 . . . . 66 E7
Rodney Ct, W9 . . . . 6 D5
Rodney Gdns, Pnr. HA5 . . . 66 B5
West Wickham BR4 . . . . 205 G4
Rodney Pl, E17 . . . . 77 H2
SE17 . . . . 36 A1
SW19 . . . . 185 F1
Rodney Rd, E11 . . . . 79 H4
SE17 . . . . 36 A1
Mitcham CR4 . . . . 185 H2
New Malden KT3 . . . . . 182 E5
Twickenham TW2 . . . . . 143 G6
Rodney St, N1 . . . . 10 D1
Rodney Way, Rom. RM7 . . 83 G1
Rodway Rd, SW15 . . . . . . 147 G7
Bromley BR1 . . . . 191 H1
Rodwell Cl, Ruis. HA4 . . . . 84 C1
Rodwell Pl, Edg. HA8
off Whitchurch La 54 A6
Rodwell Rd, SE22 . . . . . . 152 C6
Roebourne Way, E16 . . . . 136 D2
Roebuck Cl, Felt. TW13 . . . 160 D4
Roebuck La, N17
off High Rd 60 C6
Buckhurst Hill IG9 . . . . . . 47 J7
Roebuck Rd, Chess. KT9 . 196 A5
Roedean Av, Enf. EN3 . . . . 45 F1
Roedean Cl, Enf. EN3 . . . . . 45 F1
Roedean Cres, SW15 . . . . 146 E6
Roe End, NW9 . . . . 70 C4
Roe Grn, NW9 . . . . 70 C5
ROEHAMPTON, SW15 . . . 147 G5
Roehampton Cl, SW15 . . . 147 G4
Roehampton Dr, Chis.
BR7 . . . . 175 F6
Roehampton Gate, SW15 . 146 E6
Roehampton High St,
SW15 . . . . 147 H7
Roehampton La, SW15 . . 147 G4
Roehampton Vale, SW15 . 166 E3
Roe La, NW9 . . . . 70 B4
Roe Way, Wall. SM6 . . . . . 201 E6
Roffey St, E14 . . . . 134 C2
Rogate Ho, E5
off Muir Rd 94 D3
Roger Dowley Ct, E2 . . . . 113 F2
Rogers Gdns, Dag. RM10 . 101 G5
Rogers Rd, E16 . . . . 115 F6
SW17 . . . . 167 G4
Dagenham RM10 . . . . . . 101 G5
Roger St, WC1 . . . . 10 D6
Rogers Wk, N12
off Brook Meadow . . 56/57 E3
Rojack Rd, SE23 . . . . 171 G1
Rokeby Gdns, Wdf.Grn.
IG8 . . . . 79 G1
Rokeby Pl, SW20 . . . . 165 H7
Rokeby Rd, SE4 . . . . 153 J2
Rokeby St, E15 . . . . 114 E1
Rokesby Cl, Well. DA16 . . 157 G2
Rokesby Pl, Wem. HA0 . . . . 87 G5
Rokesly Av, N8 . . . . 74 E5
Roland Gdns, SW7 . . . . 30 D3
Feltham TW13 . . . . 161 E3
Roland Ms, E1
off Stepney Grn 113 G5
Roland Rd, E17 . . . . 78 D4
Roland Way, SE17 . . . . 36 C4
SW7 . . . . 30 D3
Worcester Park KT4 . . . . 197 F2
Roles Gro, Rom. RM6 . . . . 82 D4
Rolfe Cl, Barn. EN4 . . . . . . 41 H4
Rolinsden Way, Kes. BR2 . 206 A4
Rollesby Rd, Chess. KT9 . 196 A6
Rollesby Way, SE28 . . . . . 118 C7
Rolleston Av, Orp. BR5 . . . 192 E6
Rolleston Cl, Orp. BR5 . . . 193 E7
Rolleston Rd, S.Croy. CR2 . 202 A7
Roll Gdns, Ilf. IG2 . . . . 80 D5
Rollins St, SE15 . . . . 133 F6
Rollit Cres, Houns. TW3 . . 143 G5
Rollit St, N7
off Hornsey Rd 93 F5
Rolls Bldgs, EC4 . . . . 19 E3
Rollscourt Av, SE24 . . . . . 151 J5
Rolls Pk Av, E4 . . . . 62 A6
Rolls Pk Rd, E4 . . . . 62 B5
Rolls Pas, EC4 . . . . 18 E3
Rolls Rd, SE1 . . . . 37 G3
Rolt St, SE8 . . . . 133 H6
Rolvenden Gdns, Brom.
BR1 . . . . 174 A7
Rolvenden Pl, N17
off Manor Rd 76 D1
★**Roman Bath**, WC2
off Strand La 18 D5
Roman Cl, W3
off Avenue Gdns 126 B2
Feltham TW14 . . . . 142 C5
Romanfield Rd, SW2 . . . . 151 F7
Romanhurst Av, Brom.
BR2 . . . . 191 E4
Romanhurst Gdns, Brom.
BR2 . . . . 190 E4
Roman Ind Est, Croy. CR0 . 188 B7
Roman Ri, SE19 . . . . 170 A6
Roman Rd, E2 . . . . 113 F3
E3 . . . . 113 H2
E6 . . . . 116 B4
N10 . . . . 58 B7
NW2 . . . . 89 J3
W4 . . . . 127 E4
Ilford IG1 . . . . 99 E6
Roman Sq, SE28 . . . . 138 A1
Roman Way, N7 . . . . 93 F6
SE15 *off Clifton Way* . . . 133 F7
Croydon CR0 . . . . 201 H2
Enfield EN1 . . . . 44 C5
Roman Way Ind Est, N1
off Offord St 93 F7
Romany Gdns, E17
off McEntee Av 77 H1
Sutton SM3 . . . . 184 D7
Romany Ri, Orp. BR5 . . . . 207 F1
Roma Read Cl, SW15
off Bessborough Rd . . 147 H7
Roma Rd, E17 . . . . 77 H3
Romberg Rd, SW17 . . . . . 168 A3
Romborough Gdns, SE13 . 154 C5
Romborough Way, SE13 . 154 C5
Romero Cl, SW9
off Stockwell Rd 151 F3
Romero Sq, SE3 . . . . 155 J4
Romeyn Rd, SW16 . . . . . . 169 F3
Romford Rd, E7 . . . . 97 H5
E12 . . . . 98 B4
E15 . . . . 96 E7
Romford St, E1 . . . . 21 J2
Romilly Dr, Wat. WD19 . . . 51 F4
Romilly Rd, N4 . . . . 93 H2
Romilly St, W1 . . . . 17 H5
Rommany Rd, SE27 . . . . . 170 A4
Romney Cl, N17 . . . . 76 E1
NW11 . . . . 91 F1
SE14 *off Kender St* 133 F7
Chessington KT9 . . . . . . 195 H4
Harrow HA2 . . . . 67 G7
Romney Dr, Brom. BR1 . . 174 A7
Harrow HA2 . . . . 67 G7
Romney Gdns, Bexh. DA7 . 159 F1
Romney Ms, W1 . . . . 16 B1
Romney Rd, SE10 . . . . . . 134 C6
New Malden KT3 . . . . . 182 D6
Romney Row, NW2
off Brent Ter 90 A2
Romney St, SW1 . . . . 25 J6
Romola Rd, SE24 . . . . 169 H1
Romsey Cl, Orp. BR6 . . . . 207 E4
Romsey Gdns, Dag. RM9 . 118 D1
Romsey Rd, W13 . . . . 104 D7
Dagenham RM9 . . . . . . 118 D1
Romulus Ct, Brent. TW8
off Justin Cl 125 G7
Ronald Av, E15 . . . . 115 E3
Ronald Cl, Beck. BR3 . . . . 189 J4
Ronald Ho, SE3
off Cambert Way 155 J4
Ronalds Rd, N5 . . . . 93 G5
Bromley BR1 . . . . 191 G1
Ronaldstone Rd, Sid.
DA15 . . . . 157 H6
Ronald St, E1
off Devonport St 113 F6
Rona Rd, NW3 . . . . 92 A4
Ronart St, Har. (Wldste)
HA3 *off Stuart Rd* 68 C3
Rona Wk, N1
off Ramsey Wk 94 A6
Rondu Rd, NW2 . . . . 90 B5
Ronelean Rd, Surb. KT6 . . 195 J3
Ron Leighton Way, E6 . . . 116 B1
Ronnie La, E12
off Walton Rd 98 D4
Ronver Rd, SE12 . . . . 166 F7
Rood La, EC3 . . . . 20 D5
Rookby Ct, N21
off Carpenter Gdns 59 H2
Rook Cl, Wem. HA9 . . . . . . 88 B3
Rookeries Cl, Felt. TW13 . . 160 B3
Rookery Cl, NW9 . . . . 71 F5
Rookery Cres, Dag. RM10 . 101 H7
Rookery Dr, Chis. BR7 . . . 192 D1
Rookery La, Brom. BR2 . . 192 A6
Rookery Rd, SW4 . . . . 150 C4
Rookery Way, NW9 . . . . . . 71 F5
Rooke Way, SE10 . . . . 135 F5
Rookfield Av, N10 . . . . 74 C4
Rookfield Cl, N10
off Cranmore Way 74 C4
Rookstone Rd, SW17 . . . . 167 J5
Rook Wk, E6
off Allhallows Rd 116 B6
Rookwood Av, Loug. IG10 . 49 F3
New Malden KT3 . . . . . 183 G4
Wallington SM6 . . . . . . 200 D4
Rookwood Gdns, E4
off Whitehall Rd 63 F1
Loughton IG10 . . . . 49 F3
Rookwood Ho, Bark. IG11
off St. Marys 117 G2
Rookwood Rd, N16 . . . . . . 76 C7
★**Roosevelt Mem**, W1 . . . . 16 C5
Rootes Dr, W10 . . . . 108 A4
Ropemaker Rd, SE16 . . . . 133 H3
Ropemakers Flds, E14
off Narrow St 113 J7
Ropemaker St, EC2 . . . . . . 20 B1
Roper La, SE1 . . . . 29 E4
Ropers Av, E4 . . . . 62 C5
Ropers Orchard, SW3 . . . . 31 F6
Roper St, SE9 . . . . 156 C6
Ropers Wk, SW2
off Brockwell Pk Gdns . 151 G7
Roper Way, Mitch. CR4 . . . 186 A2
Ropery St, E3 . . . . 113 J4
Rope St, SE16 . . . . 133 H4
Rope Wk, Sun. TW16 . . . . 178 C3
Rope Wk Gdns, E1 . . . . 21 J4
Ropewalk Ms, E8
off Middleton Rd 94 C7
Rope Yd Rails, SE18 . . . . . 136 E3
Ropley St, E2 . . . . 13 H2
Rosa Alba Ms, N5
off Kelross Rd 93 J4
Rosaline Rd, SW6 . . . . . . 128 B7
Rosamond St, SE26 . . . . . 170 E3
Rosamund Cl, S.Croy.
CR2 . . . . 202 A4
Rosamun St, Sthl. UB2 . . 123 E4
Rosary Cl, Houns. TW3 . . . 142 E2
Rosary Gdns, SW7 . . . . 30 D2
Rosaville Rd, SW6 . . . . . . 128 C7
Roscoe St, EC1 . . . . 12 A6
Roscoff Cl, Edg. HA8 . . . . . 70 C1
Roseacre Cl, W13
off Middlefielde . . 104/105 E5
Roseacre Rd, Well. DA16 . 158 B3
Rose All, EC2
off Bishopsgate 112 B5
SE1 . . . . 28 A1
Rose & Crown Ct, EC2 . . . . 19 J3
Rose & Crown Yd, SW1 . . . 25 G1
Roseary Cl, West Dr. UB7 . 120 A4
Rose Av, E18 . . . . 79 H2
Mitcham CR4 . . . . 185 J1
Morden SM4 . . . . 185 F5
Rosebank, SE20 . . . . 170 E7
Rosebank Av, Wem. HA0 . . 86 C4
Rosebank Cl, N12 . . . . 57 H5
Teddington TW11 . . . . . . 162 D6
Rosebank Gdns, E3 . . . . . 113 J2
Rosebank Gro, E17 . . . . . . 77 J3
Rosebank Rd, E17 . . . . 78 B6
W7 . . . . 124 B2
Rosebank Vil, E17 . . . . 78 A4
Rosebank Wk, NW1
off Maiden La 92 D7
SE18 *off Woodhill* 136 B4
Rosebank Way, W3 . . . . . 106 D6
Rose Bates Dr, NW9 . . . . . 70 A4
Roseberry Gdns, N4 . . . . . . 75 H6
Orpington BR6 . . . . 207 H3
Roseberry Pl, E8 . . . . 94 C6
Roseberry St, SE16 . . . . . 132 E4
Rosebery Av, E12 . . . . 98 B6
EC1 . . . . 10 E6
N17 . . . . 76 D2
Harrow HA2 . . . . 85 F4
New Malden KT3 . . . . . 183 F2
Sidcup DA15 . . . . 157 H7
Thornton Heath CR7 . . . 187 J2
Rosebery Cl, Mord. SM4 . 184 A6
Rosebery Ct, EC1
off Rosebery Av 111 G4
Rosebery Gdns, N8 . . . . . . 74 E5
W13 . . . . 104 D6
Sutton SM1 . . . . 199 E4
Rosebery Ms, N10 . . . . 74 C2
SW2
off Rosebery Rd . . 150/151 E6
Rosebery Rd, N9 . . . . 60 D3
N10 . . . . 74 C2
SW2 . . . . 150 E6
Hounslow TW3 . . . . 143 J5
Kingston upon Thames
KT1 . . . . 182 B2
Sutton SM1 . . . . 198 C6
Rosebery Sq, EC1 . . . . 10 E6
Kingston upon Thames
KT1 . . . . 182 A2
Rosebine Av, Twick. TW2 . 144 A7
Rosebury Rd, SW6 . . . . . . 149 E2
Rosebury Sq, Wdf.Grn.
IG8 . . . . 64 D7
Rose Ct, E1 . . . . 21 F2
Pinner HA5
off Nursery Rd 66 C3
Rosecourt Rd, Croy. CR0 . 187 F6
Rosecroft Av, NW3 . . . . 90 D3
Rosecroft Gdns, NW2 . . . . 89 G3
Twickenham TW2 . . . . . 162 A1
Rosecroft Rd, Sthl. UB1 . . 103 G4
Rosecroft Wk, Pnr. HA5 . . . 66 D5
Wembley HA0 . . . . 87 G5
Rose Dale, Orp. BR6 . . . . . 207 E2
Rosedale Cl, SE2
off Finchale Rd 138 B3
W7 *off Boston Rd* 124 C2
Stanmore HA7 . . . . 53 E6
Rosedale Ct, N5 . . . . 93 H4
Rosedale Gdns, Dag.
RM9 . . . . 100 B7
Rosedale Pl, Croy. CR0 . . . 189 G7
Rosedale Rd, E7 . . . . 97 J5
Dagenham RM9 . . . . . . 100 B7
Epsom KT17 . . . . 197 G5
Richmond TW9 . . . . 145 H4
Romford RM1 . . . . 83 J2
Rosedale Ter, W6
off Dalling Rd 127 H3
Rosedene, NW6 . . . . 108 A1
Rosedene Av, SW16 . . . . . 169 F3
Croydon CR0 . . . . 187 F7
Greenford UB6 . . . . 103 G3
Morden SM4 . . . . 184 D5
Rosedene Gdns, Ilf. IG2 . . . 80 D4
Rosedene Ter, E10 . . . . 96 D2
Rosedew Rd, W6 . . . . 128 A6
Rose End, Wor.Pk. KT4 . . . 198 A1
Rosefield Cl, Cars. SM5 . . 199 H5
Rosefield Gdns, E14 . . . . . 114 A7
Roseford Ct, W12 . . . . 128 A2
Rose Gdn Cl, Edg. HA8 . . . 53 H6
Rose Gdns, W5 . . . . 125 G3
Feltham TW13 . . . . 160 A2
Southall UB1 . . . . 103 G4
Staines (Stanw.) TW19
off Diamedes Av 140 A7
Rose Glen, NW9 . . . . 70 D4
Rosehart Ms, W11
off Westbourne Gro . . . 108 D6
Rosehatch Av, Rom. RM6 . 82 D3
Roseheath Rd, Houns.
TW4 . . . . 143 F5
ROSEHILL, Sutt. SM1 . . . . 198 E1
Rosehill, Esher (Clay.)
KT10 . . . . 194 D6
Hampton TW12 . . . . 179 G1
Rose Hill, Sutt. SM1 . . . . . 199 E3
Rosehill Av, Sutt. SM1 . . . 199 F1
Rosehill Gdns, Grnf. UB6 . . 86 C5
Sutton SM1 . . . . 199 E2
Rosehill Pk W, Sutt. SM1 . 199 F1
Rosehill Rd, SW18 . . . . . . 149 F6
Roseland Cl, N17
off Cavell Rd 60 A7
Rose La, Rom. RM6 . . . . . . 82 D3
Rose Lawn, Bushey
(Bushey Hth) WD23 . . . . 51 J1
Roseleigh Av, N5 . . . . 93 H4
Roseleigh Cl, Twick. TW1 . 145 G6
Rosemary Av, N3 . . . . 73 E2

Rosemary Av, N9 . . . . **60** E1
Enfield EN2 . . . . **44** A1
Hounslow TW4 . . . . **142** D2
West Molesey KT8 . . . . **179** G3
Rosemary Cl, Croy. CR0 . . **186** E6
Rosemary Dr, E14 . . . . **114** D6
Ilford IG4 . . . . **80** A5
Rosemary Gdns, SW14
off Rosemary La **146** C3
Chessington KT9 . . . . . . **195** H4
Dagenham RM8 . . . . . . **101** F1
Rosemary La, SW14 . . . . . **146** C3
Rosemary Rd, SE15 . . . . . . **37** G7
SW17 . . . . **167** F3
Welling DA16 . . . . **157** J1
Rosemary St, N1
off Shepperton Rd **112** A1
Rosemead, NW9 . . . . **71** F7
Rosemead Av, Mitch.
CR4 . . . . **186** C2
Wembley HA9 . . . . **87** H5
Rosemont Av, N12 . . . . **57** F6
Rosemont Rd, NW3 . . . . . . **91** F6
W3 . . . . **106** B7
New Malden KT3 . . . . . **182** C3
Richmond TW10 . . . . . . **145** H6
Wembley HA0 . . . . **105** H1
Rosemoor St, SW3 . . . . . . **31** J2
Rosemount Cl, Wdf.Grn. IG8
off Chapelmount Rd . . . **64** C6
Rosemount Dr, Brom.
BR1 . . . . **192** C4
Rosemount Pt, SE23
off Dacres Rd **171** G3
Rosemount Rd, W13 . . . . **104** D6
Rosenau Cres, SW11 . . . . **149** H1
Rosenau Rd, SW11 . . . . . . **149** H1
Rosendale Rd, SE21 . . . . . **151** J7
SE24 . . . . **151** J7
Roseneath Av, N21 . . . . . . **59** H1
Roseneath Rd, SW11 . . . . **150** A6
Roseneath Wk, Enf. EN1 . . **44** B4
Rosens Wk, Edg. HA8 . . . . **54** B3
Rosenthal Rd, SE6 . . . . . . **154** B6
Rosenthorpe Rd, SE15 . . . **153** G5
Rose Pk Cl, Hayes UB4 . . **102** C4
Rosepark Ct, Ilf. IG5 . . . . . . **80** C2
Roserton St, E14 . . . . **134** C2
Rosery, The, Croy. CR0 . . . **189** G6
Roses, The, Wdf.Grn. IG8 . . **63** F7
Rose Sq, SW3 . . . . **31** F3
Rose St, EC4 . . . . **19** H3
WC2 . . . . **18** A5
Rosethorn Cl, SW12 . . . . . **150** C7
Rosetta Cl, SW8 . . . . **131** E7
Rosetti Ter, Dag. RM8
off Marlborough Rd . . **100** B4
Roseveare Rd, SE12 . . . . . **173** J4
Roseville Av, Houns.TW3 . **143** G5
Roseville Rd, Hayes UB3 . **122** A5
Rosevine Rd, SW20 . . . . . **183** J1
Rose Wk, Surb. KT5 . . . . . **182** B5
West Wickham BR4 . . . . **204** D2
Rose Way, SE12 . . . . **155** G5
Roseway, SE21 . . . . **152** A6
Rose Way, Edg. HA8 . . . . . . **54** C4
Rosewell Cl, SE20 . . . . . . **170** E7
Rosewood, Esher KT10 . . **194** D2
Rosewood Av, Grnf. UB6 . . **86** D5
Rosewood Cl, Sid. DA14 . **176** C3
Rosewood Ct, Brom. BR1 . **191** J1
Romford RM6 . . . . **82** C5
Rosewood Gdns, SE13
off Morden Hill **154** C2
Rosewood Gro, Sutt.
SM1 . . . . **199** F2
Rosewood Sq, W12
off Primula St **107** G6
Rosewood Ter, SE20
off Laurel Gro **171** F7
Rosher Cl, E15 . . . . **96** D7
Rosina St, E9 . . . . **95** G5
Roskell Rd, SW15 . . . . **148** A3
Roslin Rd, W3 . . . . **126** B3
Roslin Sq, W3 . . . . **126** B3
Roslin Way, Brom. BR1 . . **173** G5
Roslyn Cl, Mitch. CR4 . . . . **185** G2
Roslyn Rd, N15 . . . . **76** A5
Rosmead Rd, W11 . . . . . . **108** B7
Rosoman Pl, EC1 . . . . **11** F5
Rosoman St, EC1 . . . . **11** F4
Rossall Cres, NW10 . . . . . **105** J3
Ross Av, NW7 . . . . **56** B5
Dagenham RM8 . . . . . . **101** F2
Ross Cl, Har. HA3 . . . . **51** J7
Hayes UB3 . . . . **121** G4
Northolt UB5 . . . . **86** A4
Ross Ct, SW15 . . . . **148** A7
Rossdale, Sutt. SM1 . . . . . **199** H5
Rossdale Dr, N9 . . . . **45** F6
NW9 . . . . **88** C1
Rossdale Rd, SW15 . . . . . **147** J4
Rosse Ms, SE3 . . . . **155** H1
Rossendale St, E5 . . . . **94** E2
Rossendale Way, NW1 . . . . **92** C7
Rossetti Rd, SE16 . . . . **132** E5
Rossignol Gdns, Cars.
SM5 . . . . **200** A2
Rossindel Rd, Houns.
TW3 . . . . **143** G5
Rossington St, E5 . . . . **94** D2
Rossiter Flds, Barn. EN5 . . **40** B6
Rossiter Rd, SW12 . . . . . . **168** B1
Rossland Cl, Bexh. DA6 . . **159** H5
Rosslyn Av, E4 . . . . **63** F2
SW13 . . . . **147** E3
Barnet EN4 . . . . **41** H6
Dagenham RM8 . . . . **83** F7
Feltham TW14 . . . . **142** A6
Rosslyn Cl, W.Wick. BR4 . **205** F3
Rosslyn Cres, Har. HA1 . . . **68** C5
Wembley HA9 . . . . **87** H4
Rosslyn Gdns, Wem. HA9
off Rosslyn Cres **87** H3
Rosslyn Hill, NW3 . . . . **91** G4
Rosslyn Ms, NW3
off Rosslyn Hill **91** G4
Rosslyn Pk Ms, NW3
off Lyndhurst Rd **91** G5
Rosslyn Rd, E17 . . . . **78** C4
Barking IG11 . . . . **99** G7
Twickenham TW1 . . . . . **145** F6
Rossmore Ct, NW1 . . . . **7** J5
Rossmore Rd, NW1 . . . . **7** H6
Ross Par, Wall. SM6 . . . . . **200** B6
Ross Rd, SE25 . . . . **188** A3
Twickenham TW2 . . . . . **161** H1
Wallington SM6 . . . . . . **200** C5
Ross Way, SE9 . . . . **156** B3
Rosswood Gdns, Wall.
SM6 . . . . **200** C6
Rostella Rd, SW17 . . . . . . **167** G4
Rostrevor Av, N15 . . . . **76** C6
Rostrevor Gdns, Hayes
UB3 . . . . **121** H1
Southall UB2 . . . . **122** E5
Rostrevor Ms, SW6 . . . . . **148** C1
Rostrevor Rd, SW6 . . . . . **148** C1
SW19 . . . . **166** D5
Rotary St, SE1 . . . . **27** G5
Rothbury Gdns, Islw.
TW7 . . . . **124** D7
Rothbury Rd, E9 . . . . **95** J7
Rothbury Wk, N17 . . . . **60** D7
Rotherfield Rd, Cars.
SM5 . . . . **200** A4
Rotherfield St, N1 . . . . **93** J7
Rotherham Wk, SE1 . . . . . . **27** G2
Rotherhill Av, SW16 . . . . . **168** D6
ROTHERHITHE, SE16 . . . . **133** G3
★Rotherhithe Heritage Mus, SE16 . . . . **133** H1
Rotherhithe New Rd,
SE16 . . . . **37** J4
Rotherhithe Old Rd,
SE16 . . . . **133** G4
Rotherhithe St, SE16 . . . . **133** F2
Rotherhithe Tunnel, E1 . . . **133** F1
Rotherhithe Tunnel App,
E14 . . . . **113** H7
SE16 . . . . **133** F2
Rothermere Rd, Croy.
CR0 . . . . **201** F5
Rotherwick Hill, W5 . . . . . **105** J4
Rotherwick Rd, NW11 . . . . **72** D7
Rotherwood Cl, SW20 . . . **184** B1
Rotherwood Rd, SW15 . . **148** A3
Rothery St, N1
off Gaskin St **111** H1
Rothery Ter, SW9 . . . . **131** H7
Rothesay Av, SW20 . . . . . **184** B2
Greenford UB6 . . . . **86** A6
Richmond TW10 . . . . . . **146** B4
Rothesay Rd, SE25 . . . . . . **188** B4
Rothsay Rd, E7 . . . . **97** J6
Rothsay St, SE1 . . . . **28** D5
Rothsay Wk, E14
off Charnwood Gdns . **134** A4
Rothschild Rd, W4 . . . . . . **126** C4
Rothschild St, SE27 . . . . . **169** H4
Roth Wk, N7
off Durham Rd **93** F3
Rothwell Gdns, Dag.
RM9 . . . . **100** C7
Rothwell Rd, Dag. RM9 . . **118** C1
Rothwell St, NW1 . . . . . . **109** J1
Rotten Row, SW1 . . . . **24** B3
SW7 . . . . **23** G3
Rotterdam Dr, E14 . . . . . . **134** C3
Rouel Rd, SE16 . . . . **29** H6
Rougemont Av, Mord.
SM4 . . . . **184** D6
Roundacre, SW19
off Inner Pk Rd **166** A2
Roundaway Rd, Ilf. IG5 . . . **80** C2
Roundel Cl, SE4
off Adelaide Av **153** J4
Round Gro, Croy. CR0 . . . **189** G7
Roundhay Cl, SE23 . . . . . **171** G2
Round Hill, SE26 . . . . **171** F2
Roundhill Dr, Enf. EN2 . . . . **43** F4
Roundmead Av, Loug.
IG10 . . . . **48** D3
Roundmead Cl, Loug.
IG10 . . . . **48** D3
Roundshaw Cen, Wall. SM6
off Meteor Way . . **200/201** E7
Roundtable Rd, Brom.
BR1 . . . . **173** F3
Roundtree Rd, Wem. HA0 . **86** E5
Roundway, The, N17 . . . . . **75** J1
Esher (Clay.) KT10 . . . . . **194** C5
Roundwood, Chis. BR7 . . **192** E2
Roundwood Av, Uxb.
UB11 . . . . **121** F1
Roundwood Rd, NW10 . . . **89** F6
Rounton Rd, E3 . . . . **114** A4
Roupell Rd, SW2 . . . . **169** F1
Roupell St, SE1 . . . . **27** F2
Rousden St, NW1 . . . . **92** C7
Rouse Gdns, SE21 . . . . . . **170** B4
Rous Rd, Buck.H. IG9 . . . . . **64** B1
Routemaster Cl, E13 . . . . **115** H3
Routh Rd, SW18 . . . . **149** H7
Routh St, E6 . . . . **116** C5
Routledge Cl, N19 . . . . **92** D1
Rover Av, Ilf. IG6 . . . . **65** J6
Rowallan Rd, SW6 . . . . . . **128** B7
Rowan Av, E4 . . . . **61** J6
Rowan Cl, SW16 . . . . **186** C1
W5 . . . . **125** H2
Ilford IG1 . . . . **99** G5
New Malden KT3 . . . . . **182** E2
Stanmore HA7
off Woodlands Dr **52** C6
Wembley HA0 . . . . **86** D3
Rowan Cres, SW16 . . . . . **186** C1
Rowan Dr, NW9 . . . . **71** G4
Rowan Gdns, Croy. CR0
off Radcliffe Rd **202** C3
Rowan Rd, SW16 . . . . **186** C2
W6 . . . . **128** A4
Bexleyheath DA7 . . . . . **159** E3
Brentford TW8 . . . . **125** E7
West Drayton UB7 . . . . **120** A4
Rowans, The, N13 . . . . **59** H3
Rowans Way, Loug. IG10 . . **48** C4
Rowan Ter, SE20
off Sycamore Gro **188** D1
W6 *off Bute Gdns* **128** A4
Rowantree Cl, N21 . . . . **60** A1
Rowantree Rd, N21 . . . . . . **60** A1
Enfield EN2 . . . . **43** H2
Rowan Wk, N2 . . . . **73** F6
N19 *off Bredgar Rd* **92** C2
W10 *off Droop St* **108** B4
Barnet EN5
off Station Rd **40/41** E5
Bromley BR2 . . . . **206** C3
Rowan Way, Rom. RM6 . . . **82** C3
Rowanwood Av, Sid.
DA15 . . . . **176** A1
Rowanwood Ms, Enf.
EN2 . . . . **43** H2
Rowben Cl, N20 . . . . **56** E1
Rowberry Cl, SW6 . . . . . . **127** J7
Rowcross St, SE1 . . . . **37** F3
Rowdell Rd, Nthlt. UB5 . . **103** G1
Rowden Pk Gdns, E4
off Rowden Rd **62** A6
Rowden Rd, E4 . . . . **62** A6
Beckenham BR3 . . . . . . **189** H1
Epsom KT19 . . . . **196** B4
Rowditch La, SW11 . . . . . **150** A2
Rowdon Av, NW10 . . . . **89** H7
Rowdowns Rd, Dag.
RM9 . . . . **119** F1
Rowe Gdns, Bark. IG11 . . . **117** J2
Rowe La, E9 . . . . **95** F5
Rowena Cres, SW11 . . . . . **149** H2
Rowe Wk, Har. HA2 . . . . . . **85** G3
Rowfant Rd, SW17 . . . . . . **168** A1
Rowhill Rd, E5 . . . . **95** E4
Rowington Cl, W2 . . . . **14** A1
Rowland Av, Har. HA3 . . . . **69** F4
Rowland Ct, E16 . . . . **115** F4
Rowland Cres, Chig. IG7 . . **65** H4
Rowland Gro, SE26
off Dallas Rd **170/171** E3
Rowland Hill Av, N17 . . . . . **59** J7
Rowland Hill St, NW3 . . . . **91** H5
Rowlands Av, Pnr. HA5 . . . **51** G6
Rowlands Cl, N6
off North Hill **74** A6
NW7 . . . . **55** G7
Rowlands Rd, Dag. RM8 . **101** F2
Rowland Way, SW19
off Hayward Cl . . . **184/185** E1
Rowley Av, Sid. DA15 . . . **158** B7
Rowley Cl, Wem. HA0 . . . . **87** J7
Rowley Gdns, N4 . . . . **75** J7
ROWLEY GREEN, Barn.
EN5 . . . . **39** F4
Rowley Grn Rd, Barn. EN5 . **39** F5
Rowley Ind Pk, W3 . . . . . . **126** B3
Rowley La, Barn. EN5 . . . . **39** F5
Borehamwood WD6 . . . . **38** D1
Rowley Rd, N15 . . . . **75** J5
Rowley Way, NW8 . . . . . . **109** E1
Rowlheys Pl, West Dr.
UB7 . . . . **120** B3
Rowlls Rd, Kings.T. KT1 . . **181** J3
Rowney Gdns, Dag. RM9 . **100** C6
Rowney Rd, Dag. RM9 . . . **100** B6
Rowntree Clifford Cl, E13
off Liddon Rd **115** H3
Rowntree Path, SE28
off Booth Cl **118** B7
Rowntree Rd, Twick. TW2 . **162** B1
Rowse Cl, E15 . . . . **96** C7
Rowsley Av, NW4 . . . . **71** J3
Rowstock Gdns, N7 . . . . . . **92** D5
Rowton Rd, SE18 . . . . **137** F7
Roxborough Av, Har. HA1 . **68** A7
Isleworth TW7 . . . . **124** C7
Roxborough Pk, Har. HA1 . **68** B7
Roxborough Rd, Har. HA1 . **68** A5
Roxbourne Cl, Nthlt. UB5 . **84** D6
Roxburgh Rd, SE27 . . . . . **169** H5
Roxby Pl, SW6 . . . . **128** D6
ROXETH, Har. HA2 . . . . **86** A2
Roxeth Grn Av, Har. HA2 . . **85** H3
Roxeth Gro, Har. HA2 . . . . **85** H4
Roxeth Hill, Har. HA2 . . . . . **86** A2
Roxley Rd, SE13 . . . . **154** B6
Roxton Gdns, Croy. CR0 . **204** A5
Roxwell Rd, W12 . . . . **127** G2
Barking IG11 . . . . **118** A2
Roxwell Trd Pk, E10 . . . . . . **77** H7
Roxwell Way, Wdf.Grn.
IG8 . . . . **63** J7
Roxy Av, Rom. RM6 . . . . . . **82** C7
★Royal Acad of Arts, W1 . . **17** F6
★Royal Acad of Dramatic Art (R.A.D.A.), WC1 . . . **17** H1
★Royal Acad of Music,
NW1 . . . . **8** C6
★Royal Air Force Museums,
NW9 . . . . **71** G2
Royal Albert Dock, E16 . . . **116** C7
★Royal Albert Hall, SW7 . . **22** F4
Royal Albert Roundabout, E16
off Royal Albert Way . . **116** B7
Royal Albert Way, E16 . . . **116** A7
Royal Arc, W1 . . . . **17** F6
Royal Artillery Barracks, SE18
off Repository Rd **136** D5
Royal Av, SW3 . . . . **31** J3
Worcester Park KT4 . . . . **197** E2
★Royal Botanic Gdns, Kew, Rich. TW9 . . . . . . **125** H7
Royal Circ, SE27 . . . . **169** G3
Royal Cl, N16
off Manor Rd **94** B1
SE8 . . . . **133** J6
SW19 . . . . **166** A2
Ilford IG3 . . . . **82** A7
Orpington BR6 . . . . **206** E4
Worcester Park KT4 . . . . **196** E2
★Royal Coll of Art, SW7 . . **22** D4
★Royal Coll of Music,
SW7 . . . . **22** E5
★Royal Coll of Surgeons,
WC2 . . . . **18** D3
Royal Coll St, NW1 . . . . . . **92** C7
Royal Ct, EC3
off Cornhill **112** A6
SE16 . . . . **133** J3
★Royal Courts of Justice,
WC2 . . . . **18** D4
Royal Cres, W11 . . . . **128** A1
Ruislip HA4 . . . . **84** E4
Royal Cres Ms, W11
off Queensdale Rd . . . **128** A1
Royal Docks Rd, E6 . . . . . **117** E6
Royal Dr, N11 . . . . **58** A5

Royal Duchess Ms, SW12
off Dinsmore Rd **150** B7
Royale Leisure Pk, W3 ... **106** A4
★**Royal Exchange**, EC3 ... **20** C4
Royal Ex Av, EC3 .... **20** C4
Royal Ex Bldgs, EC3...... **20** C4
Royal Ex Steps, EC3
off Cornhill **112** A6
★**Royal Festival Hall**, SE1 .. **26** C1
Royal Gdns, W7 .... **124** D3
★**Royal Geographical Society**, SW7 .... **23** E4
Royal Herbert Pavilions, SE18 .... **156** C1
Royal Hill, SE10 .... **134** C7
★**Royal Horticultural Society (Lawrence Hall)**, SW1 .. **25** H6
★**Royal Horticultural Society (Lindley Hall)**, SW1.... **33** H1
★**Royal Hosp Chelsea & Mus**, SW3........... **32** B4
Royal Hosp Rd, SW3 ..... **31** J5
Royal London Est, The, N17 .... **60** E6
★**Royal Mews, The**, SW1 .. **24** E5
★**Royal Military Acad**, SE18 .... **136** C7
Royal Mint Ct, EC3....... **21** G6
Royal Mint Pl, E1 .... **21** G5
Royal Mint St, E1........ **21** G5
Royal Mt Ct, Twick. TW2 .. **162** B3
★**Royal Nat Thea**, SE1 .... **26** D1
Royal Naval Pl, SE14 .... **133** J7
Royal Oak Ct, N1
off Pitfield St **112** B3
Royal Oak Pl, SE22...... **153** E6
Royal Oak Rd, E8 .... **94** E6
Bexleyheath DA6 ..... **159** F5
Royal Oak Yd, SE1 .... **28** E4
Royal Opera Arc, SW1 .... **25** H1
★**Royal Opera Ho**, WC2 ... **18** B4
Royal Orchard Cl, SW18.. **148** B7
Royal Par, SE3 .... **155** E2
SW6 *off Dawes Rd* **128** B7
W5 *off Western Av*..... **105** H3
Chislehurst BR7 ...... **175** F7
Richmond TW9
off Station App **146** A1
Royal Par Ms, SE3
off Royal Par **155** F2
Chislehurst BR7 ...... **175** F7
Royal Pl, SE10 .... **134** C7
Royal Quarter, Kings.T. KT2
off Seven Kings Way.. **181** H1
Royal Rd, E16.......... **116** A6
SE17 .... **35** G5
Sidcup DA14 .... **176** D3
Teddington TW11...... **162** A5
Royal Route, Wem. HA9... **87** J4
Royal St, SE1........... **26** D5
Royalty Ms, W1 .... **17** H4
Royal Victoria Dock, E16.. **115** H7
Royal Victoria Patriotic Bldg, SW18 *off Fitzhugh Gro* . **149** G6
Royal Victoria Pl, E16
off Wesley Av **135** H1
Royal Victoria Sq, E16
off Western Gateway.. **115** H7
Royal Victor Pl, E3 ...... **113** G2
Royal Wk, Wall. SM6
off Prince Charles Way . **200** B3
Roycraft Av, Bark. IG11 ... **117** J2
Roycraft Cl, Bark. IG11 ... **117** J2
Roycroft Cl, E18 .... **79** H1
SW2................ **169** G1
Roydene Rd, SE18 ...... **137** H6
Roydon Cl, SW11
off Reform St **149** J2
Loughton IG10 .... **48** B7
Roydon St, SW11
off Southolm St **150** B1
Roy Gdns, Ilf. IG2........ **81** H4
Roy Gro, Hmptn. TW12 .. **161** H6
Royle Cres, W13 .... **104** D4
Roy Sq, E14
off Narrow St........ **113** H7
Royston Av, E4.......... **62** A5
Sutton SM1.......... **199** G3
Wallington SM6 ...... **200** D4
Royston Cl, Houns. TW5 . **142** B1
Royston Ct, SE24
off Burbage Rd **151** J6
Richmond TW9
off Lichfield Rd **145** J1
Surbiton KT6
off Hook Ri N........ **196** A3
Royston Gdns, Ilf. IG1 .... **80** A6
Royston Gro, Pnr. HA5.... **51** F6
Royston Par, Ilf. IG1 ...... **80** A6
Royston Pk Rd, Pnr. HA5.. **51** F6
Royston Rd, SE20 ...... **189** G1
Richmond TW10 ...... **145** H5
Roystons, The, Surb. KT5. **182** B5
Royston St, E2 .... **113** F2
Rozel Ct, N1 .... **112** B1
Rozel Rd, SW4 .... **150** C2
Rubastic Rd, Sthl. UB2... **122** B3
Rubens Pl, SW4
off Dolman St **151** F4
Rubens Rd, Nthlt. UB5... **102** C2
Rubens St, SE6 .... **171** J2
Ruby Ms, E17 *off Ruby Rd*. **78** A3
Ruby Rd, E17 .... **78** A3
Ruby St, NW10
off Diamond St....... **88** D7
SE15 .... **132** E6
Ruby Triangle, SE15
off Sandgate St .. **132/133** E6
Ruckholt Cl, E10......... **96** B3
Ruckholt Rd, E10 .... **96** A4
Rucklidge Av, NW10..... **107** F2
Rudall Cres, NW3
off Willoughby Rd..... **91** G4
Ruddington Cl, E5 .... **95** H4
Ruddock Cl, Edg. HA8 .... **54** C7
Ruddstreet Cl, SE18..... **137** E4
Rudgwick Ter, NW8
off Avenue Rd **109** H1
Rudland Rd, Bexh. DA7 .. **159** H3
Rudloe Rd, SW12....... **150** C7
Rudolf Pl, SW8.......... **34** B6
Rudolph Ct, SE22....... **152** D7
Rudolph Rd, E13........ **115** F2
NW6 .... **108** D2
Rudyard Gro, NW7....... **54** C6
Ruffetts, The, S.Croy. CR2 . **203** E7
Ruffetts Cl, S.Croy. CR2 .. **202** E7
Ruffle Cl, West Dr. UB7 .. **120** B2
Rufford Cl, Har. HA3...... **68** D6
Rufford St, N1.......... **111** E1
Rufford Twr, W3 .... **126** B1
Rufus Cl, Ruis. HA4 ...... **84** E3
Rufus St, N1........... **12** D4
Rugby Av, N9 .... **60** C1
Greenford UB6 .... **86** A6
Wembley HA0......... **87** E5
Rugby Cl, Har. HA1 ...... **68** B5
★**Rugby Football Union Twickenham**, Twick. TW2 .... **144** B6
Rugby Gdns, Dag. RM9 .. **100** C6
Rugby Rd, NW9 .... **70** B4
W4................. **126** E2
Dagenham RM9 ...... **100** B7
Twickenham TW1 ..... **144** B6
Rugby St, WC1 .... **10** C6
Rugg St, E14........... **114** A7
Ruislip Cl, Grnf. UB6 .... **103** H4
RUISLIP MANOR, Ruis. HA4 .... **84** A2
Ruislip Rd, Grnf. UB6 ... **103** G3
Northolt UB5......... **102** D2
Southall UB1 .... **103** G3
Ruislip Rd E, W7........ **104** A4
W13................ **104** A4
Greenford UB6 .... **104** A4
Ruislip St, SW17 .... **167** J4
Rumbold Rd, SW6 ...... **129** E7
Rum Cl, E1 .... **113** F7
Rumsey Cl, Hmptn. TW12 . **161** F6
Rumsey Ms, N4
off Monsell Rd **93** H3
Rumsey Rd, SW9....... **151** F3
Runbury Circle, NW9..... **88** D2
Runcorn Cl, N17......... **76** E4
Runcorn Pl, W11 .... **108** B7
Rundell Cres, NW4....... **71** H5
Runes Cl, Mitch. CR4 .... **185** G4
Runnel Fld, Har. HA1 ..... **86** B3
Running Horse Yd, Brent. TW8 *off Pottery Rd*... **125** H6
Runnymede, SW19...... **185** G1
Runnymede Cl, Twick. TW2 .... **143** H6
Runnymede Ct, Croy. CR0 .... **202** C2
Runnymede Cres, SW16 . **186** D1
Runnymede Gdns, Grnf. UB6 .... **104** A2
Twickenham TW2 ..... **143** H6
Runnymede Ho, E9
off Kingsmead Way.... **95** H4
Runnymede Rd, Twick. TW2 .... **143** H6
Runway, The, Ruis. HA4... **84** B5
Rupack St, SE16
off St. Marychurch St . **133** F2
Rupert Av, Wem. HA9 .... **87** H5
Rupert Ct, W1........... **17** H5
West Molesey KT8
off St. Peter's Rd..... **179** G4
Rupert Gdns, SW9...... **151** H2
Rupert Rd, N19
off Holloway Rd **92** D3
NW6 .... **108** C2
W4................. **127** E3
Rupert St, W1........... **17** H5
Rural Way, SW16 .... **168** B7
Rusbridge Cl, E8
off Amhurst Rd....... **94** D5
Ruscoe Rd, E16......... **115** F6
Ruscombe Way, Felt. TW14............. **141** J7
Rush, The, SW19
off Kingston Rd...... **184** C1
Rusham Rd, SW12...... **149** J6
Rushbrook Cres, E17 ..... **77** J1
Rushbrook Rd, SE9 ..... **175** F2
Rush Common Ms, SW2 . **151** F7
Rushcroft Rd, E4 .... **62** A7
SW2................ **151** G4
Rushden Cl, SE19....... **170** A7
Rushdene, SE2......... **138** D3
Rushdene Av, Barn. EN4 .. **41** H7
Rushdene Cl, Nthlt. UB5 . **102** C3
Rushdene Cres, Nthlt. UB5 .... **102** C2
Rushdene Rd, Pnr. HA5 ... **66** D6
Rushden Gdns, NW7 ..... **55** J6
Ilford IG5............. **80** D3
Rushen Wk, Cars. SM5
off Paisley Rd **199** G1
Rushett Cl, T.Ditt. KT7.... **194** E1
Rushett Rd, T.Ditt. KT7 ... **180** E7
Rushey Cl, N.Mal. KT3... **182** D4
Rushey Grn, SE6 .... **154** B7
Rushey Hill, Enf. EN2..... **43** F4
Rushey Mead, SE4...... **154** A5
Rushford Rd, SE4....... **153** J6
RUSH GREEN, Rom. RM7 . **83** J7
Rush Grn Gdns, Rom. RM7............... **101** J1
Rush Grn Rd, Rom. RM7 . **101** J1
Rushgrove Av, NW9...... **71** F5
Rush Gro St, SE18 ...... **136** C4
Rush Hill Ms, SW11
off Rush Hill Rd...... **150** A3
Rush Hill Rd, SW11 ..... **150** A3
Rushley Cl, Kes. BR2 .... **206** A4
Rushmead, E2
off Florida St..... **112/113** E3
Richmond TW10 ...... **163** E3
Rushmead Cl, Croy. CR0 . **202** C4
Rushmere Ct, Wor.Pk. KT4
off The Avenue **197** G2
Rushmere Ho, SW15
off Fontley Way...... **165** G1
Rushmere Pl, SW19 ..... **166** A5
Rushmoor Cl, Pnr. HA5 ... **66** B4
Rushmore Cl, Brom. BR1 . **192** B3
Rushmore Cres, E5
off Rushmore Rd...... **95** G4
Rushmore Rd, E5........ **95** F4
Rusholme Av, Dag. RM10. **101** G3
Rusholme Gro, SE19 .... **170** B5
Rusholme Rd, SW15 .... **148** A6
Rushout Av, Har. HA3 .... **68** E6
Rushton St, N1 .... **12** C1
Rushworth Av, NW4
off Rushworth Gdns ... **71** G3
Rushworth Gdns, NW4 ... **71** G4
Rushworth St, SE1 ...... **27** H3
Rushy Meadow La, Cars. SM5............... **199** H2
Ruskin Av, E12.......... **98** B6
Feltham TW14 .... **141** J6
Richmond TW9 .... **126** A7
Welling DA16 .... **158** A3
Ruskin Cl, NW11 .... **72** E6
Ruskin Dr, Orp. BR6..... **207** H3
Welling DA16 .... **158** A3
Worcester Park KT4.... **197** H2
Ruskin Gdns, W5 .... **105** G4
Harrow HA3 .... **69** J4
Ruskin Gro, Well. DA16 .. **158** A2
Ruskin Pk Ho, SE5 ...... **152** A3
Ruskin Rd, N17 .... **76** C1
Belvedere DA17 ...... **139** G4
Carshalton SM5 ...... **199** J5
Croydon CR0......... **201** H2
Isleworth TW7 .... **144** C3
Southall UB1......... **102** E7
Ruskin Wk, N9
off Durham Rd **60** D2
SE24 .... **151** J5
Bromley BR2......... **192** C6
Ruskin Way, SW19 ...... **185** G1
Rusland Av, Orp. BR6.... **207** G3
Rusland Hts, Har. HA1
off Rusland Pk Rd..... **68** B4
Rusland Pk Rd, Har. HA1 .. **68** B4
Rusper Cl, NW2 .... **89** J3
Stanmore HA7 .... **53** F4
Rusper Rd, N22 .... **75** J2
Dagenham RM9 ...... **100** C6
Russell Av, N22 .... **75** H2
Russell Cl, NW10 .... **88** C7
SE7 .... **135** J7
W4................. **127** F6
Beckenham BR3 ...... **190** B3
Bexleyheath DA7 ..... **159** G4
Ruislip HA4........... **84** C2
Russell Ct, SW1 .... **25** G2
Russell Dr, Stai. (Stanw.) TW19............. **140** A6
Russell Gdns, N20 .... **57** H2
NW11................ **72** B6
W14................ **128** B3
Richmond TW10 ...... **163** F2
West Drayton UB7 .... **120** D5
Russell Gdns Ms, W14 .... **128** B3
Russell Gro, NW7........ **54** E5
SW9................ **131** G7
Russell Kerr Cl, W4
off Burlington La..... **126** C7
Russell La, N20 .... **57** H2
Russell Mead, Har. (Har.Wld) HA3 .... **68** C1
Russell Par, NW11
off Golders Grn Rd.... **72** B6
Russell Pl, NW3
off Aspern Gro **91** H5
SE16 *off Onega Gate* .. **133** H3
Russell Rd, E4 .... **61** J4
E10 .... **78** B6
E16................. **115** G6
E17 .... **77** J3
N8 .... **74** D6
N13 .... **59** F6
N15 .... **76** B5
N20 .... **57** H2
NW9 .... **71** F6
SW19............... **166** D7
W14................ **128** B3
Buckhurst Hill IG9...... **63** H1
Mitcham CR4......... **185** H3
Northolt UB5.......... **85** J5
Twickenham TW2 ..... **144** C6
Walton-on-Thames KT12 .... **178** A6
Russell's Footpath, SW16 . **169** E5
Russell Sq, WC1 .... **10** A6
Russell St, WC2 .... **18** B5
Russell Wk, Rich. TW10
off Park Hill **145** J6
Russell Way, Sutt. SM1 .. **198** D5
Russet Cres, N7
off Stock Orchard Cres . **93** F5
Russet Dr, Croy. CR0 .... **203** H1
Russets Cl, E4
off Larkshall Rd....... **62** D4
Russett Way, SE13 ...... **154** B2
Russia Ct, EC2 .... **20** A3
Russia Dock Rd, SE16 ... **133** H1
Russia La, E2 .... **113** F2
Russia Row, EC2 .... **20** A4
Russia Wk, SE16........ **133** H2
Rusthall Av, W4 .... **126** D4
Rusthall Cl, Croy. CR0 ... **189** F6
Rustic Av, SW16........ **168** B7
Rustic Pl, Wem. HA0 ..... **87** G4
Rustic Wk, E16
off Lambert Rd **115** H6
Rustington Wk, Mord. SM4............... **184** C7
Ruston Av, Surb. KT5.... **182** B7
Ruston Gdns, N14
off Farm La **42** A6
Ruston Ms, W11
off St. Marks Rd **108** B6
Ruston Rd, SE18 .... **136** B3
Ruston St, E3 .... **113** J1
Rust Sq, SE5 .... **36** B7
Rutford Rd, SW16 ...... **168** E5
Ruth Cl, Stan. HA7....... **69** J4
Rutherford Cl, Borwd. WD6 .... **38** C2
Sutton SM2.......... **199** G6
Rutherford St, SW1 ...... **33** H1
Rutherford Twr, Sthl. UB1 . **103** H6
Rutherford Way, Bushey (Bushey Hth) WD23.... **52** A1
Wembley HA9......... **88** A4
Rutherglen Rd, SE2 ..... **138** A6
Rutherwyke Cl, Epsom KT17 .... **197** G6

Ruthin Cl, NW9 . . . . 70 E6
Ruthin Rd, SE3. . . . . 135 G6
Ruthven St, E9
off Lauriston Rd 113 G1
Rutland Av, Sid. DA15 . . . 158 A7
Rutland Cl, SW14. . . . . . . 146 C3
SW19 *off Rutland Rd*. . . 167 H7
Bexley DA5 . . . . 176 D1
Chessington KT9. . . . . . 195 J6
Rutland Ct, Enf. EN3 . . . . . 45 F5
Rutland Dr, Mord. SM4 . . 184 C6
Richmond TW10 . . . . . . 163 G1
Rutland Gdns, N4 . . . . 75 H6
SW7. . . . . 23 H4
W13 . . . . 104 D5
Croydon CR0. . . . . 202 B4
Dagenham RM8 . . . . 100 C5
Rutland Gdns Ms, SW7 . . . 23 H4
Rutland Gate, SW7 . . . . . . 23 H4
Belvedere DA17 . . . . . . 139 H5
Bromley BR2. . . . . 191 F4
Rutland Gate Ms, SW7 . . . 23 G4
Rutland Gro, W6. . . . . 127 H5
Rutland Ms, NW8
off Boundary Rd. . 108/109 E1
Rutland Ms E, SW7 . . . . . . 23 G5
Rutland Ms S, SW7 . . . . . . 23 G5
Rutland Ms W, SW7
off Ennismore St. 129 H3
Rutland Pk, NW2 . . . . 89 J6
SE6 . . . . 171 J2
Rutland Pk Gdns, NW2
off Rutland Pk. 89 J6
Rutland Pk Mans, NW2
off Walm La. 89 J6
Rutland Pl, EC1 . . . . 11 J6
Bushey (Bushey Hth)
WD23 *off The Rutts*. . . . 52 A1
Rutland Rd, E7. . . . . 98 A7
E9. . . . . 113 F1
E11. . . . . 79 H5
E17 . . . . 78 A6
SW19. . . . . 167 H7
Harrow HA1 . . . . 67 J6
Hayes UB3 . . . . 121 G4
Ilford IG1. . . . . 99 E4
Southall UB1. . . . . 103 G5
Twickenham TW2 . . . . . 162 A2
Rutland St, SW7 . . . . 23 H5
Rutland Wk, SE6 . . . . 171 J2
Rutley Cl, SE17 . . . . 35 G5
Rutlish Rd, SW19. . . . . . . 184 D1
Rutter Gdns, Mitch. CR4 . 185 F4
Rutters Cl, West Dr. UB7 . 120 D2
Rutts, The, Bushey
(Bushey Hth) WD23. . . . 52 A1
Rutts Ter, SE14. . . . . 153 G1
Ruvigny Gdns, SW15. . . . 148 A3
Ruxley Cl, Epsom KT19 . . 196 B5
Sidcup DA14 . . . . 176 D6
Ruxley Cor Ind Est, Sid.
DA14 . . . . 176 D6
Ruxley Cres, Esher (Clay.)
KT10 . . . . 194 E6
Ruxley La, Epsom KT19 . . 196 D5
Ruxley Ms, Epsom KT19 . 196 B5
Ruxley Ridge, Esher (Clay.)
KT10 . . . . 194 D7
Ryalls Ct, N20 . . . . 57 J3
Ryan Cl, SE3. . . . . 155 J4
Ruislip HA4. . . . . 84 B1
Ryan Dr, Brent. TW8. . . . . 124 D6
Ryarsh Cres, Orp. BR6 . . . 207 H4
Rycott Path, SE22
off Lordship La 152 D7
Rycroft Way, N17 . . . . 76 C3
Ryculff Sq, SE3. . . . . 155 F2
Rydal Cl, NW4 . . . . 72 B1
Rydal Cres, Grnf. UB6 . . . 105 E3
Rydal Dr, Bexh. DA7 . . . . 159 G1
West Wickham BR4. . . . 205 E2
Rydal Gdns, NW9. . . . . 71 E5
SW15. . . . . 164 E5
Hounslow TW3 . . . . 143 H6
Wembley HA9. . . . . 87 F1
Rydal Rd, SW16 . . . . 168 D4
Rydal Way, Enf. EN3. . . . . . 45 F6
Ruislip HA4. . . . . 84 C4
Ryde Pl, Twick. TW1 . . . . . 145 F6
Ryder Cl, Brom. BR1 . . . . 173 H5
Ryder Ct, SW1 . . . . 25 G1
Ryder Dr, SE16. . . . . 132 E5
Ryder Ms, E9
off Homerton High St. . 95 F5
Ryders Ter, NW8. . . . . 6 C1
Ryder St, SW1 . . . . 25 G1
Ryder Yd, SW1 . . . . 25 G1
Ryde Vale Rd, SW12. . . . . 168 B2
Rydons Cl, SE9. . . . . 156 B3
Rydon St, N1
off St. Paul St. 111 J1
Rydston Cl, N7
off Sutterton St. 93 F7
Rye, The, N14. . . . . 42 C7
Rye Cl, Bex. DA5 . . . . 159 H6
Ryecotes Mead, SE21 . . . 170 B1
Ryecroft Av, Ilf. IG5 . . . . . . 80 E2
Twickenham TW2 . . . . . 143 H7
Ryecroft Cres, Barn. EN5 . . 39 H5
Ryecroft Rd, SE13 . . . . . . 154 C5
SW16. . . . . 169 G6
Orpington BR5 . . . . 193 G6
Ryecroft St, SW6 . . . . 148 E1
Ryedale, SE22 . . . . 152 E6
Ryefield Ct, Nthwd. HA6
off Ryefield Cres 66 A2
Ryefield Cres, Nthwd.
HA6 . . . . 66 A2
Ryefield Par, Nthwd. HA6
off Ryefield Cres 66 A2
Ryefield Path, SW15 . . . . 165 G1
Ryefield Rd, SE19. . . . . . . 169 J6
Ryegates, SE15
off Caulfield Rd . . 152/153 E2
Rye Hill Pk, SE15 . . . . 153 F4
Ryelands Cres, SE12 . . . . 155 J6
Rye La, SE15 . . . . 152 D1
Rye Pas, SE15. . . . . 152 D3
Rye Rd, SE15 . . . . 153 G4
Rye Wk, SW15
off Chartfield Av 148 A5
Rye Way, Edg. HA8
off Canons Dr 53 J6
Ryfold Rd, SW19 . . . . 166 D3
Ryhope Rd, N11 . . . . 58 B4
Rylandes Rd, NW2. . . . . . . 89 G3
Ryland Ho, Croy. CR0. . . . 201 J3
Ryland Rd, NW5. . . . . 92 B6
Rylett Cres, W12. . . . . 127 F3
Rylett Rd, W12 . . . . 127 F2
Rylston Rd, N13. . . . . 60 A3
SW6. . . . . 128 C6
Rymer Rd, Croy. CR0 . . . . 188 B7
Rymer St, SE24 . . . . 151 H6
Rymill St, E16. . . . . 136 D1
Rysbrack St, SW3 . . . . 23 J5
Rythe Cl, Chess. KT9
off Nigel Fisher Way . . 195 F7
Rythe Ct, T.Ditt. KT7 . . . . . 180 D7
Rythe Rd, Esher (Clay.)
KT10 . . . . 194 A5

S

★**Saatchi Gall**, SE1 . . . . . . 26 C4
Sabbarton St, E16
off Victoria Dock Rd. . . 115 F6
Sabella Ct, E3. . . . . 113 J2
Sabine Rd, SW11 . . . . 149 J3
Sable Cl, Houns. TW4. . . . 142 C3
Sable St, N1. . . . . 93 H7
Sach Rd, E5 . . . . 95 E2
Sackville Av, Brom. BR2. . 205 G1
Sackville Cl, Har. HA2 . . . . 86 A3
Sackville Est, SW16 . . . . . 169 E3
Sackville Gdns, Ilf. IG1. . . . 98 C1
Sackville Rd, Sutt. SM2 . . 198 D7
Sackville St, W1 . . . . 17 G6
Sackville Way, SE22
off Dulwich Common . 170 D1
Saddlers Cl, Barn. (Arkley)
EN5 . . . . 39 H5
Borehamwood WD6
off Farriers Way. 38 D6
Pinner HA5 . . . . 51 G6
Saddlers Ms, SW8
off Portland Gro 151 F1
Kingston upon Thames
(Hmptn W.) KT1. . . . . . 181 F1
Wembley HA0
off The Boltons 86 C4
Saddlers Path, Borwd.
WD6 . . . . 38 D5
Saddlescombe Way, N12 . . 56 D5
Saddle Yd, W1 . . . . 24 D1
Sadler Cl, Mitch. CR4 . . . . 185 J2
Sadlers Ride, W.Mol. KT8. 179 J2
★**Sadler's Wells Thea**, EC1 . 11 G3
Saffron Av, E14. . . . . 114 D7
Saffron Cl, NW11 . . . . 72 C5
Croydon CR0. . . . . 186 E6
Saffron Ct, Felt. TW14
off Staines Rd. 141 F7
Saffron Hill, EC1. . . . . 11 F6
Saffron Rd, Rom. RM5. . . . 83 J2
Saffron St, EC1. . . . . 19 F1
Saffron Way, Surb. KT6 . . 195 G1
Sage Cl, E6
off Bradley Stone Rd. . 116 C5
Sage Ms, SE22
off Lordship La 152 C5
Sage St, E1 *off Cable St*. . 113 F7
Sage Way, WC1 . . . . 10 C4
Saigasso Cl, E16
off Royal Rd. 116 A6
Sail Ct, E14
off Newport Av 114 D7
Sailmakers Ct, SW6
off William Morris Way . 149 F3
Sail St, SE11. . . . . 34 D1
Sainfoin Rd, SW17. . . . . . 168 A2
Saini Ms, N8
off Harringay Gdns 75 H3
Sainsbury Rd, SE19 . . . . . 170 B5
St. Agatha's Dr, Kings.T.
KT2 . . . . 163 J6
St. Agathas Gro, Cars.
SM5. . . . . 199 J1
St. Agnes Cl, E9
off Gore Rd 113 F1
St. Agnes Pl, SE11 . . . . 35 G6
St. Agnes Well, EC1
off Old St. 112 A4
St. Aidans Ct, W13
off St. Aidans Rd . 124/125 E2
Barking IG11
off Choats Rd. 118 B3
St. Aidan's Rd, SE22. . . . . 152 E6
St. Aidans Rd, W13. . . . . . 125 E2
St. Albans Av, E6 . . . . 116 C3
St. Alban's Av, W4 . . . . . . 126 D4
St. Albans Av, Felt. TW13 . 160 D5
St. Albans Cl, NW11 . . . . . . 90 D1
St. Albans Ct, EC2 . . . . 20 A3
St. Albans Cres, N22 . . . . . 75 G1
St. Alban's Cres, Wdf.Grn.
IG8 . . . . 63 G7
St. Alban's Gdns, Tedd.
TW11. . . . . 162 D5
St. Albans Gro, W8. . . . . . . 22 B5
St. Alban's Gro, Cars.
SM5. . . . . 185 H7
St. Albans La, NW11
off West Heath Dr 90 D1
St. Alban's Pl, N1 . . . . 111 H1
St. Albans Rd, NW5 . . . . . . 92 A3
NW10. . . . . 106 E1
Barnet EN5 . . . . 40 A1
Ilford IG3. . . . . 99 J1
St. Alban's Rd, Kings.T.
KT2 . . . . 163 H6
Sutton SM1 . . . . 198 C4
Woodford Green IG8 . . . 63 G7
St. Albans St, SW1. . . . . . . 17 H6
St. Albans Ter, W6
off Margravine Rd. . . . 128 B6
St. Alban's Vil, NW5
off Highgate Rd. 92 A3
St. Alfege Pas, SE10 . . . . . 134 C6
St. Alfege Rd, SE7 . . . . . . 136 A6
St. Alphage Gdns, EC2. . . . 20 A2
St. Alphage Highwalk, EC2 . 20 B2
St. Alphage Wk, Edg. HA8 . 70 C2
St. Alphege Rd, N9. . . . . . . 45 F7
St. Alphonsus Rd, SW4 . . 150 C4
St. Amunds Cl, SE6 . . . . . 172 A4
St. Andrews Av, Wem.
HA0. . . . . 86 D4
St. Andrew's Cl, N12
off Woodside Av 57 F4
St. Andrews Cl, NW2 . . . . . 89 H3
SE16 *off Ryder Dr* . 132/133 E5
SE28 . . . . 118 D6
St. Andrew's Cl, Islw. TW7 . 144 A1
St. Andrews Cl, Ruis. HA4 . 84 D2
Stanmore HA7 . . . . 69 F2
Thames Ditton KT7 . . . . 194 E1
St. Andrew's Ct, SW18
off Waynflete St. 167 F2
St. Andrews Dr, Stan. HA7 . 69 F1
St. Andrew's Gro, N16 . . . . 94 A1
St. Andrew's Hill, EC4 . . . . 19 H5
St. Andrew's Ms, N16 . . . . 94 B1
St. Andrews Ms, SE3
off Mycenae Rd. 135 G7
St. Andrews Pl, NW1 . . . . . . 8 E5
St. Andrews Rd, E11. . . . . . 78 E6
E13. . . . . 115 H3
E17 . . . . 77 G2
N9. . . . . 45 F7
NW9 . . . . 88 D1
NW10 . . . . 89 H6
NW11. . . . . 72 C6
W3. . . . . 107 E7
W7
off Churchfield Rd. . . . 124 B2
St. Andrews Rd, W14 . . . . 128 B6
Carshalton SM5 . . . . . . 199 H3
Croydon CR0
off Lower Coombe St . 201 J4
Enfield EN1 . . . . 44 A3
Ilford IG1. . . . . 80 C7
Sidcup DA14 . . . . 176 D3
St. Andrew's Rd, Surb.
KT6 . . . . 181 G6
St. Andrews Rd, Wat.
WD19. . . . . 50 D3
St. Andrews Sq, W11
off St. Marks Rd 108 B6
St. Andrew's Sq, Surb.
KT6 . . . . 181 G6
St. Andrews Twr, Sthl.
UB1 . . . . 103 J7
St. Andrew St, EC4 . . . . . . 19 F2
St. Andrews Way, E3 . . . . 114 B4
St. Anna Rd, Barn. EN5
off Sampson Av 40 A5
St. Annes Av, Stai. (Stanw.)
TW19. . . . . 140 A7
St. Anne's Cl, N6
off Highgate W Hill 92 A3
Watford WD19. . . . . 50 C4
St. Anne's Ct, W1 . . . . 17 H4
St. Annes Gdns, NW10. . . 105 J3
St. Annes Pas, E14
off Newell St 113 J6
St. Annes Rd, E11. . . . . 96 D2
St. Anne's Rd, Wem. HA0. . 87 G5
St. Anne's Row, E14
off Commercial Rd . . . 113 J6
St. Anne St, E14
off Commercial Rd . . . 113 J6
St. Ann's, Bark. IG11 . . . . . 117 F1
St. Ann's Cres, SW18 . . . . 149 F6
St. Ann's Gdns, NW5
off Queen's Cres 92 A6
St. Ann's Hill, SW18 . . . . . 149 E5
St. Ann's La, SW1 . . . . 25 J5
St. Ann's Pk Rd, SW18. . . . 149 F6
St. Ann's Pas, SW13. . . . . 147 E3
St. Anns Rd, N9 . . . . 60 C2
St. Ann's Rd, N15. . . . . 75 H5
SW13. . . . . 147 F2
St. Anns Rd, W11 . . . . 108 A7
St. Ann's Rd, Bark. IG11
off Axe St. 117 F1
Harrow HA1 . . . . 68 B6
St. Ann's Shop Cen, Har.
HA1. . . . . 68 B6
St. Ann's St, SW1. . . . . 25 J5
St. Ann's Ter, NW8 . . . . 7 F1
St. Anns Vil, W11 . . . . 128 A1
St. Anns Way, S.Croy.
CR2 . . . . 201 H6
St. Anselm's Pl, W1 . . . . . . 16 D4
St. Anselms Rd, Hayes
UB3. . . . . 121 J2
St. Anthonys Av, Wdf.Grn.
IG8 . . . . 63 J6
St. Anthonys Cl, E1 . . . . . . 29 H1
SW17
off College Gdns. 167 H2
St. Anthony's Way, Felt.
TW14. . . . . 141 J4
St. Antony's Rd, E7 . . . . . . 97 H7
St. Arvans Cl, Croy. CR0. . 202 B3
St. Asaph Rd, SE4 . . . . . . 153 G3
St. Aubins Ct, N1
off De Beauvoir Est. . . 112 A1
St. Aubyn's Av, SW19. . . . 166 C5
St. Aubyns Av, Houns.
TW3 . . . . 143 G5
St. Aubyns Cl, Orp. BR6. . 207 J3
St. Aubyns Gdns, Orp.
BR6 . . . . 207 J2
St. Aubyn's Rd, SE19 . . . . 170 C6
St. Audrey Av, Bexh.
DA7 . . . . 159 G2
St. Augustine's Av, W5 . . . 105 H2
St. Augustines Av, Brom.
BR2 . . . . 192 B5
St. Augustine's Av, S.Croy.
CR2 . . . . 201 J6
St. Augustines Av, Wem.
HA9. . . . . 87 H3
St. Augustine's Path, N5
off Highbury New Pk . . 93 J4
St. Augustines Rd, NW1 . . 92 D7
St. Augustine's Rd, Belv.
DA17 . . . . 139 F4
St. Austell Cl, Edg. HA8 . . . 69 J2
St. Austell Rd, SE13 . . . . . 154 C2
St. Awdry's Rd, Bark. IG11 . 99 G7
St. Awdry's Wk, Bark. IG11
off Station Par. 99 F7

St. Barnabas Cl, SE22 *off East Dulwich Gro* . . 152 B5
Beckenham BR3 . . . . . . 190 C2
St. Barnabas Ct, Har. HA3 . 67 J1
St. Barnabas Gdns, W.Mol. KT8 . . . . 179 G5
St. Barnabas Rd, E17 . . . . . 78 A6
Mitcham CR4 . . . . 168 A7
Sutton SM1 . . . . 199 G5
Woodford Green IG8 . . . 79 H1
St. Barnabas St, SW1 . . . . 32 C3
St. Barnabas Ter, E9 . . . . . . 95 G5
St. Barnabas Vil, SW8 . . . 151 E1
St. Bartholomews Cl, SE26 . . . . 171 F4
St. Bartholomew's Rd, E6 . 116 B1
★**St. Bartholomew-the-Great Ch**, EC1 . . . . 19 H2
St. Benedict's Cl, SW17 *off Church La* 168 A5
St. Benet's Cl, SW17 *off College Gdns* 167 H2
St. Benet's Gro, Cars. SM5 . . . . 185 F7
St. Benet's Pl, EC3 . . . . 20 C5
St. Bernards, Croy. CR0 . . 202 B3
St. Bernard's Cl, SE27 *off St. Gothard Rd* 170 A4
St. Bernard's Rd, E6 . . . . . 116 A1
St. Blaise Av, Brom. BR1 . 191 H2
St. Botolph Row, EC3 . . . . 21 F4
St. Botolph St, EC3 . . . . . . 21 F4
St. Brides Av, EC4 . . . . 19 G4
Edgware HA8 . . . . 69 J1
★**St. Bride's Ch & Crypt Mus**, EC4 . . . . 19 G4
St. Brides Cl, Erith DA18 *off St. Katherines Rd* . . 138 D2
St. Bride's Pas, EC4 . . . . . . 19 G4
St. Bride St, EC4 . . . . 19 G3
St. Catherines Cl, SW17 *off College Gdns* 167 H2
St. Catherines Dr, SE14 *off Kitto Rd* 153 G2
St. Catherine's Ms, SW3 . . 31 J1
St. Catherines Rd, E4 . . . . . 62 A2
St. Catherines Twr, E10 *off Kings Cl* 78 B7
St. Cecilia's Cl, Sutt. SM3 . 198 B1
St. Chads Cl, Surb. KT6 . . 181 F7
St. Chad's Gdns, Rom. RM6 . . . . 82 E7
St. Chad's Pl, WC1 . . . . 10 B3
St. Chad's Rd, Rom. RM6 . . 82 E6
St. Chad's St, WC1 . . . . 10 B3
St. Charles Pl, W10 *off Chesterton Rd* 108 B5
St. Charles Sq, W10 . . . . . 108 D5
St. Christopher's Cl, Islw. TW7 . . . . 144 B1
St. Christopher's Dr, Hayes UB3 . . . . 102 B7
St. Christophers Gdns, Th.Hth. CR7 . . . . 187 G3
St. Christophers Ms, Wall. SM6 . . . . 200 C5
St. Christopher's Pl, W1 . . . 16 C3
St. Clair Dr, Wor.Pk. KT4 . 197 H3
St. Clair Rd, E13 . . . . 115 H2
St. Clair's Rd, Croy. CR0 . . 202 B2
St. Clare Business Pk, Hmptn. TW12 . . . . 161 J6
St. Clare Cl, Ilf. IG5 . . . . 80 C2
St. Clare St, EC3 . . . . 21 F4
★**St. Clement Danes Ch**, WC2 . . . . 18 D4
St. Clements Ct, EC4 *off Clements La* 112 A7
N7 *off Arundel Sq* 93 G6
St. Clements Hts, SE26 . . 170 D3
St. Clement's La, WC2 . . . . 18 D4
St. Clements St, N7 . . . . . . 93 G6
St. Clements Yd, SE22 *off Archdale Rd* 152 C5
St. Cloud Rd, SE27 . . . . . . 169 J4
St. Crispins Cl, NW3 . . . . . 91 H4
Southall UB1 . . . . 103 F6
St. Cross St, EC1 . . . . 19 F1
St. Cuthberts Gdns, Pnr. HA5 *off Westfield Pk* . . . 51 F7
St. Cuthberts Rd, N13 . . . . 59 G6
NW2 . . . . 90 C6
St. Cyprian's St, SW17 . . . 167 J4
St. Davids Cl, SE16 *off Masters Dr* . . . 132/133 E5
Wembley HA9 . . . . 88 C3
St. David's Cl, W.Wick. BR4 . . . . 190 B7
St. David's Ct, E17 . . . . 78 C3
St. Davids Dr, Edg. HA8 . . . 69 J1
St. Davids Ms, E3 *off Morgan St* 113 H3
St. Davids Pl, NW4 . . . . 71 H7
St. Davids Sq, E14 . . . . . . 134 B5
St. Denis Rd, SE27 . . . . . . 170 A4
St. Dionis Rd, SW6 . . . . . . 148 C2
St. Donatts Rd, SE14 . . . . . 153 J1
St. Dunstan's All, EC3 . . . . 20 D5
St. Dunstans Av, W3 . . . . . 106 D7
St. Dunstans Cl, Hayes UB3 . . . . 121 J4
St. Dunstan's Ct, EC4 *off Fleet St* 111 G6
St. Dunstans Gdns, W3 *off St. Dunstans Av* . . . 106 D7
St. Dunstan's Hill, EC3 . . . . 20 D6
Sutton SM1 . . . . 198 B5
St. Dunstan's La, EC3 . . . . 20 D6
Beckenham BR3 . . . . . . 190 C6
St. Dunstan's Rd, E7 . . . . . 97 J6
St. Dunstans Rd, SE25 . . . 188 C4
W6 . . . . 128 A5
W7 . . . . 124 B2
Hounslow TW4 . . . . 142 C2
St. Edmunds Cl, NW8 *off St. Edmunds Ter* . . . 109 J1
SW17 *off College Gdns* 167 H2
Erith DA18 *off St. Katherines Rd* . . 138 D2
St. Edmunds Dr, Stan. HA7 . . . . 68 D1
St. Edmund's La, Twick. TW2 . . . . 143 H7
St. Edmunds Rd, N9 . . . . . 44 D7
Ilford IG1 . . . . 80 C6
St. Edmunds Sq, SW13 . . 127 J6
St. Edmunds Ter, NW8 . . . . . 7 H1
St. Edwards Cl, NW11 . . . . 72 D6
St. Egberts Way, E4 . . . . . . 62 C1
St. Elmo Rd, W12 . . . . 127 F1
St. Elmos Rd, SE16 . . . . . 133 G2
St. Erkenwald Ms, Bark. IG11 *off St. Erkenwald Rd* . . 117 G1
St. Erkenwald Rd, Bark. IG11 . . . . 117 G1
St. Ermin's Hill, SW1 . . . . . 25 H5
St. Ervans Rd, W10 . . . . . . 108 B5
St. Faiths Cl, Enf. EN2 . . . . 43 J1
St. Faith's Rd, SE21 . . . . . 169 H1
St. Fillans Rd, SE6 . . . . . . 172 C1
St. Francis Cl, Orp. BR5 . . 193 H6
Watford WD19 . . . . 50 B1
St. Francis Rd, SE22 . . . . . 152 B4
St. Francis Way, Ilf. IG1 . . . 99 H4
St. Frideswides Ms, E14 *off Lodore St* 114 C6
St. Gabriel's Cl, E11 . . . . . . 97 H2
St. Gabriels Rd, NW2 . . . . . 90 A5
St. Georges Av, E7 . . . . 97 H7
N7 . . . . 92 D4
NW9 . . . . 70 C4
St. George's Av, W5 . . . . . 125 G2
St. Georges Av, Sthl. UB1 . 103 F7
St. Georges Cen, Har. HA1 *off St. Ann's Rd* 68 B6
St. Georges Circ, SE1 . . . . . 27 G5
St. Georges Cl, NW11 . . . . 72 C6
SE28 *off Redbourne Dr* 118 D6
St. George's Cl, SW8 *off Patmore St* 150 C1
St. Georges Cl, Wem. HA0 . 86 D3
St. Georges Ct, E6 . . . . . . 116 C4
EC4 . . . . 19 G3
SW7 . . . . 22 C5
St. George's Dr, SW1 . . . . . 33 F3
St. Georges Dr, Wat. WD19 . . . . 50 E3
St. Georges Flds, W2 . . . . . 15 H4
St. George's Gdns, Surb. KT6 *off Hamilton Av* . . 196 B2
St. Georges Gro, SW17 . . 167 G3
St. Georges Gro Est, SW17 . . . . 167 G3
St. Georges Ind Est, Kings.T. KT2 *off Richmond Rd* . 163 G5
St. Georges La, EC3 . . . . . . 20 D5
St. Georges Ms, NW1 *off Regents Pk Rd* 91 J7
SE1 . . . . 27 F5
St. Georges Pl, Twick. TW1 *off Church St* 162 D1
St. Georges Rd, E7 . . . . 97 H6
E10 . . . . 96 C3
N9 . . . . 60 D3
N13 . . . . 59 F3
NW11 . . . . 72 C6
St. Georges Rd, SE1 . . . . . 27 F5
St. George's Rd, SW19 . . . 166 C6
St. Georges Rd, W4 . . . . . 126 E2
W7 . . . . 124 C1
St. George's Rd, Beck. BR3 . . . . 190 B1
St. Georges Rd, Brom. BR1 . . . . 192 C2
Dagenham RM9 . . . . . . 100 E5
St. George's Rd, Felt. TW13 . . . . 160 D4
St. Georges Rd, Ilf. IG1 . . . 80 C7
St. George's Rd, Kings.T. KT2 . . . . 164 A7
Mitcham CR4 . . . . 186 B3
Orpington BR5 . . . . 193 G6
St. Georges Rd, Rich. TW9 . . . . 145 J3
St. George's Rd, Sid. DA14 . . . . 176 D6
St. Georges Rd, Twick. TW1 . . . . 145 E5
Wallington SM6 . . . . . . 200 B5
St. Georges Rd W, Brom. BR1 . . . . 192 B1
St. Georges Sq, E7 . . . . 97 H7
E14 *off Narrow St* 113 H7
SE8 . . . . 133 J4
St. George's Sq, SW1 . . . . . 33 H3
New Malden KT3 *off High St* 182/183 E3
St. George's Sq Ms, SW1 . . 33 H4
St. Georges Ter, NW1 *off Regents Pk Rd* 91 J7
St. George St, W1 . . . . 17 E4
St. Georges Wk, Croy. CR0 . . . . 201 J3
St. Georges Way, SE15 . . . 36 D6
St. George Wf, SW8 . . . . . . 34 A4
St. Gerards Cl, SW4 . . . . . 150 C5
St. German's Pl, SE3 . . . . 155 G1
St. Germans Rd, SE23 . . . 171 H1
St. Giles Av, Dag. RM10 . . 101 H7
St. Giles Cl, Dag. RM10 *off St. Giles Av* 101 H7
Hounslow TW5 *off Vicarage Fm Rd* . . . 123 F7
Orpington BR6 . . . . 207 G5
St. Giles Ct, WC2 *off St. Giles High St* . 110/111 E6
St. Giles High St, WC2 . . . . 17 J3
St. Giles Pas, WC2 . . . . 17 J4
St. Giles Rd, SE5 . . . . 132 B7
St. Gilles Ho, E2 . . . . 113 G2
St. Gothard Rd, SE27 . . . . 170 A4
St. Gregory Cl, Ruis. HA4 . . 84 C4
St. Helena Rd, SE16 . . . . . 133 G4
St. Helena St, WC1 . . . . 10 E4
St. Helens Cres, SW16 *off St. Helens Rd* 187 F1
St. Helens Gdns, W10 . . . . 108 A6
St. Helens Pl, EC3 . . . . 20 D3
St. Helens Rd, SW16 . . . . 187 F1
St. Helen's Rd, W13 *off Dane Rd* 124/125 E1
St. Helens Rd, Erith DA18 . 138 D2
Ilford IG1 . . . . 80 C6
ST. HELIER, Cars. SM5 . . . 185 G7
St. Helier Av, Mord. SM4 . 185 F7
St. Heliers Av, Houns. TW3 . . . . 143 G5
St. Heliers Rd, E10 . . . . 78 C6
St. Hildas Cl, NW6 . . . . 90 A7
SW17 . . . . 167 H2
St. Hilda's Rd, SW13 . . . . 127 H6
St. Hughe's Cl, SW17 *off College Gdns* 167 H2
St. Hughs Rd, SE20 *off Ridsdale Rd* . . 188/189 E1
St. James Av, N20 . . . . 57 H3
W13 . . . . 124 D1
Sutton SM1 . . . . 198 D5
St. James Cl, N20 . . . . 57 H3
SE18 *off Congleton Gro* 137 F5
Barnet EN4 . . . . 41 G4
New Malden KT3 . . . . . 183 F5
Ruislip HA4 . . . . 84 C2
St. James Gdns, Rom. (Lt.Hth) RM6 . . . . 82 B4
Wembley HA0 . . . . 87 G7
St. James Gate, NW1 *off St. Paul's Cres* 92 D7
St. James Gro, SW11 *off Reform St* 149 J2
St. James Ms, E14 . . . . . . 134 C3
E17 *off St. James's St* 77 H5
St. James Rd, E15 . . . . 97 F5
St. James Rd, N9 *off Queens Rd* 60/61 E2
Carshalton SM5 . . . . 199 H3
Kingston upon Thames KT1 . . . . 181 H2
Mitcham CR4 . . . . 168 A7
Surbiton KT6 . . . . 181 G6
Sutton SM1 . . . . 198 D5
ST. JAMES'S, SW1 . . . . 25 G2
St. James's, SE14 . . . . 153 H1
St. James's Av, E2 . . . . . . 113 F2
Beckenham BR3 . . . . . . 189 H3
Hampton (Hmptn H.) TW12 . . . . 161 J5
St. James's Cl, SW17 *off St. James's Dr* 167 J2
St. James's Cotts, Rich. TW9 *off Paradise Rd* . . 145 G5
St. James's Ct, SW1 . . . . . 25 G5
St. James's Cres, SW9 . . . 151 G3
St. James's Dr, SW12 . . . 167 J1
SW17 . . . . 167 J1
St. James's Gdns, W11 . . . 128 B1
St. James's La, N10 . . . . . . 74 B4
St. James's Mkt, SW1 . . . . 17 H6
★**St. James's Palace**, SW1 . 25 G3
★**St. James's Park**, SW1 . . 25 H3
St. James's Pk, Croy. CR0 . 187 J7
St. James's Pas, EC3 . . . . . 21 E4
St. James's Pl, SW1 . . . . . . 25 F2
St. James's Rd, SE1 . . . . . . 37 J3
SE16 . . . . 29 J5
Croydon CR0 . . . . 187 H7
Hampton (Hmptn H.) TW12 . . . . 161 H5
St. James's Sq, SW1 . . . . . 25 G1
St. James's St, E17 . . . . . . 77 H5
SW1 . . . . 25 F1
St. James's Ter, NW8 . . . . . . 7 J1
St. James's Ter Ms, NW8 . 109 J1
St. James St, W6 . . . . 127 J5
St. James's Wk, EC1 . . . . . . 11 G5
St. James Way, Sid. DA14 . . . . 177 E5
St. Joans Rd, N9 . . . . 60 C1
St. John Fisher Rd, Erith DA18 . . . . 138 D3
ST. JOHN'S, SE8 . . . . 154 A2
St. Johns Av, N11 . . . . 57 J5
St. John's Av, NW10 . . . . . 107 F1
SW15 . . . . 148 A5
St. John's Ch Rd, E9 . . . . . 95 F5
St. Johns Cl, N14 *off Chase Rd* 42 C6
St. John's Cl, SW6 *off Dawes Rd* 128 D7
Wembley HA9 . . . . 87 H5
St. John's Cotts, SE20 *off Maple Rd* 171 F7
St. Johns Cotts, Rich. TW9 *off Kew Foot Rd* 145 H4
St. Johns Ct, Buck.H. IG9 . . 63 H1
St. John's Ct, Islw. TW7 . . 144 C2
St. John's Cres, SW9 . . . . 151 G3
St. Johns Dr, SW18 . . . . . 166 E1
St. John's Est, N1 . . . . 12 C2
SE1 . . . . 29 F3
St. John's Gdns, W11 . . . . 108 C7
★**St. John's Gate & Mus of the Order of St. John**, EC1 . . . . 11 G6
St. Johns Gro, N19 . . . . 92 C2
SW13 *off Terrace Gdns* 147 F2
Richmond TW9 *off Kew Foot Rd* 145 H4
St. John's Hill, SW11 . . . . 149 G4
St. John's Hill Gro, SW11 . 149 G4
St. John's La, EC1 . . . . 11 G6
St. John's Ms, W11 *off Ledbury Rd* 108 D6
St. Johns Par, Sid. DA14 . 176 A4
St. John's Pk, SE3 . . . . . . 135 F7
St. John's Pas, SW19 *off Ridgway Pl* 166 B6
St. John's Path, EC1 . . . . . . 11 G6
St. Johns Pathway, SE23 *off Devonshire Rd* 171 F1
St. John's Pl, EC1 . . . . 11 G6
St. John's Rd, E4 . . . . 62 B3
E6 *off Ron Leighton Way* . 116 B1
St. Johns Rd, E16 . . . . 115 G6
St. John's Rd, E17 . . . . 78 B2
N15 . . . . 76 B6
St. Johns Rd, NW11 . . . . . . 72 C6
St. John's Rd, SE20 . . . . . 171 F7
SW11 . . . . 149 H4
SW19 . . . . 166 B7

St. John's Rd, Barking IG11 ... **117** H1
Carshalton SM5 ... **199** H3
St. Johns Rd, Croy. CR0 *off Sylverdale Rd.* ... **201** H3
East Molesey KT8 ... **180** A4
St. John's Rd, Felt. TW13 . **161** E4
Harrow HA1 ... **68** C6
St. Johns Rd, Ilf. IG2 ... **81** G7
St. John's Rd, Islw. TW7 . . **144** B2
Kingston upon Thames (Hmptn W.) KT1 ... **181** F2
St. Johns Rd, Loug. IG10 . . **48** C2
New Malden KT3 ... **182** C3
St. John's Rd, Orp. BR5 . . **193** G6
Richmond TW9 ... **145** H4
St. Johns Rd, Sid. DA14 . . **176** B4
Southall UB2 ... **122** E3
Sutton SM1 ... **198** D2
St. John's Rd, Well. DA16. **158** B3
Wembley HA9 ... **87** G4
St. John's Sq, EC1 ... **11** G6
St. Johns Ter, E7 ... **97** H6
SE18 ... **137** F6
SW15 *off Kingston Vale* ... **164** D4
W10 *off Harrow Rd* ... **108** A4
St. John St, EC1 ... **11** H6
St. Johns Vale, SE8 ... **154** A2
St. Johns Vil, N19 ... **92** D2
St. John's Vil, W8 ... **22** B6
St. Johns Way, N19 ... **92** D1
ST. JOHN'S WOOD, NW8 . . . **6** E3
St. John's Wd Ct, NW8 ... **7** F4
St. John's Wd High St, NW8 ... **7** F2
St. John's Wd Pk, NW8 . . **109** G1
St. John's Wd Rd, NW8 ... **6** E5
St. John's Wd Ter, NW8 ... **7** G1
St. Josephs Cl, W10 *off Bevington Rd* ... **108** B5
St. Joseph's Cl, Orp. BR6 . **207** J4
St. Joseph's Ct, SE7 ... **135** H6
St. Josephs Dr, Sthl. UB1 . **123** E1
St. Joseph's Gro, NW4 ... **71** H4
St. Josephs Rd, N9 ... **45** E7
St. Josephs St, SW8 *off Battersea Pk Rd* ... **150** B1
St. Joseph's Vale, SE3 ... **154** D2
St. Jude's Rd, E2 ... **113** E2
St. Jude St, N16 ... **94** B5
St. Julian's Cl, SW16 ... **169** G4
St. Julian's Fm Rd, SE27 . **169** G4
St. Julian's Rd, NW6 ... **90** C7
★**St. Katharine's Dock**, E1 . **21** G6
St. Katharines Prec, NW1 . . **8** D1
St. Katharine's Way, E1 ... **29** G1
St. Katherines Rd, Erith DA18 ... **138** D2
St. Katherine's Row, EC3 . . **21** E4
St. Katherine's Wk, W11 *off Freston Rd* ... **108** A7
St. Keverne Rd, SE9 ... **174** B4
St. Kilda Rd, W13 ... **124** D1
Orpington BR6 ... **207** J1
St. Kilda's Rd, N16 ... **94** A1
Harrow HA1 ... **68** B6
St. Kitts Ter, SE19 ... **170** B5
St. Laurence Cl, NW6 ... **108** A1
St. Lawrence Cl, Edg. HA8. **53** J7
St. Lawrence Dr, Pnr. HA5. **66** B6
★**St. Lawrence Jewry Ch**, EC2 ... **20** A3
St. Lawrence St, E14 ... **134** C1
St. Lawrence Ter, W10 ... **108** B5
St. Lawrence Way, SW9 . . **151** G1
St. Leonards Av, E4 ... **62** D6
Harrow HA3 ... **69** F4
St. Leonard's Cl, Well. DA16 *off Hook La* ... **158** A3
St. Leonards Ct, N1 ... **12** A3
St. Leonard's Gdns, Houns. TW5 ... **122** E7
St. Leonards Gdns, Ilf. IG1. **99** F5
St. Leonards Ri, Orp. BR6 ... **207** H4
St. Leonards Rd, E14 ... **114** B5
NW10 ... **106** D4
St. Leonard's Rd, SW14 . . **146** B3
St. Leonards Rd, W13 ... **105** F7
Croydon CR0 ... **201** H3
Esher (Clay.) KT10 ... **194** C6
St. Leonard's Rd, Surb. KT6 ... **181** G5
St. Leonards Rd, T.Ditt. KT7 ... **180** D6
St. Leonards Sq, NW5 ... **92** A6
St. Leonard's Sq, Surb. KT6 *off St. Leonard's Rd* . . **181** G5

St. Leonards St, E3 ... **114** B3
St. Leonard's Ter, SW3 ... **31** J4
St. Leonards Wk, SW16 . . **169** F7
St. Loo Av, SW3 ... **31** H5
St. Louis Rd, SE27 ... **169** J4
St. Loy's Rd, N17 ... **76** B2
St. Lucia Dr, E15 ... **115** F1
ST. LUKE'S, EC1 ... **12** A5
St. Luke's Av, SW4 ... **150** D4
Ilford IG1 ... **99** E5
St. Luke's Cl, EC1 ... **12** A5
SE25 ... **189** E6
St. Luke's Est, EC1 ... **12** B4
St. Lukes Ms, W11 *off Basing St* ... **108** C6
St. Lukes Rd, W11 ... **108** C5
St. Lukes Sq, E16 ... **115** F6
St. Luke's St, SW3 ... **31** G3
St. Luke's Yd, W9 ... **108** C2
St. Malo Av, N9 ... **61** F3
ST. MARGARETS, Twick. TW1 ... **144** D5
St. Margarets, Bark. IG11 . **117** G1
St. Margarets Av, N15 ... **75** H4
N20 ... **57** F2
Harrow HA2 ... **85** J3
Sidcup DA15 ... **175** G3
St. Margaret's Av, Sutt. SM3 ... **198** B3
St. Margarets Cl, EC2 *off Lothbury* ... **112** A6
St. Margaret's Ct, SE1 ... **28** A2
St. Margaret's Cres, SW15 ... **147** H5
St. Margaret's Dr, Twick. TW1 ... **144** E5
St. Margaret's Gro, E11 ... **97** F3
SE18 ... **137** F6
St. Margarets Gro, Twick. TW1 ... **144** D6
St. Margarets La, W8 ... **22** A6
St. Margarets Pas, SE13 *off Church Ter.* ... **154/155** E3
St. Margarets Path, SE18. **137** F5
St. Margarets Rd, E12 ... **97** J2
St. Margaret's Rd, N17 ... **76** B3
NW10 ... **107** J3
St. Margarets Rd, SE4 ... **153** J4
W7 ... **124** B2
Edgware HA8 ... **54** B5
Isleworth TW7 ... **144** E4
Twickenham TW1 ... **144** E4
St. Margarets Sq, SE4 *off Adelaide Av* ... **153** J4
St. Margaret's St, SW1 ... **26** A4
St. Margaret's Ter, SE18 . . **137** F5
St. Marks Cl, SE10 *off Ashburnham Gro.* . **134** C7
SW6 *off Ackmar Rd.* ... **148** D1
W11 *off Lancaster Rd* . . **108** B6
St. Mark's Cl, Barn. EN5 ... **40** E3
St. Marks Cl, Har. HA1 *off Nightingale Av* . . **68/69** E7
St. Marks Cres, NW1 ... **110** A1
St. Mark's Gate, E9 *off Cadogan Ter.* ... **95** J7
St. Mark's Gro, SW10 ... **30** B7
St. Mark's Hill, Surb. KT6. **181** H6
St. Mark's Pl, SW19 *off Wimbledon Hill Rd.* **166** C6
St. Marks Pl, W11 ... **108** B6
St. Marks Ri, E8 ... **94** C5
St. Marks Rd, SE25 *off Coventry Rd.* ... **188** D4
St. Mark's Rd, W5 *off The Common* ... **125** H1
St. Marks Rd, W7 ... **124** B2
W10 ... **108** A6
W11 ... **108** B6
Bromley BR2 ... **191** H3
Enfield EN1 ... **44** C6
Mitcham CR4 ... **185** J2
St. Mark's Rd, Tedd. TW11 ... **163** E7
St. Marks Sq, NW1 ... **110** A1
St. Mark St, E1 ... **21** G4
★**St. Martin-in-the-Fields Ch**, WC2 ... **18** A6
St. Martins Av, E6 ... **116** A2
St. Martins Cl, NW1 ... **110** C1
Enfield EN1 ... **44** E1
Erith DA18 *off St. Helens Rd.* ... **138** D2
St. Martin's Cl, Wat. WD19 *off Muirfield Rd.* ... **50** C4
West Drayton UB7 *off St. Martin's Rd* ... **120** A3
St. Martin's Ct, WC2 *off St. Martin's La* ... **110** D7

St. Martins Est, SW2 ... **169** G1
St. Martin's La, WC2 ... **18** A5
St. Martins La, Beck. BR3. **190** B5
St. Martin's-le-Grand, EC1 . **19** J3
St. Martin's Ms, WC2 ... **18** A6
St. Martin's Pl, WC2 ... **18** A6
St. Martins Rd, N9 ... **60** E2
St. Martin's Rd, SW9 ... **151** F2
West Drayton UB7 ... **120** A3
St. Martin's St, WC2 ... **17** J6
St. Martins Ter, N10 *off Pages La* ... **74** A2
St. Martins Way, SW17 . . **167** F3
St. Mary Abbots Pl, W8 . . **128** C3
St. Mary Abbots Ter, W14 *off Holland Pk Rd* ... **128** C3
St. Mary at Hill, EC3 ... **20** D6
★**St. Mary at Hill Ch**, EC3 . **20** D6
St. Mary Av, Wall. SM6 . . **200** A3
St. Mary Axe, EC3 ... **20** D4
St. Marychurch St, SE16 . **133** F2
★**St. Mary-le-Bow Ch**, EC2 . **20** A4
St. Mary Rd, E17 ... **78** A4
St. Marys, Bark. IG11 ... **117** G1
St. Marys App, E12 ... **98** C5
St. Marys Av, E11 ... **79** H6
St. Mary's Av, N3 ... **72** B2
Bromley BR2 ... **191** E3
Staines (Stanw.) TW19 . **140** A7
Teddington TW11 ... **162** C6
St. Mary's Av Cen, Sthl. UB2 ... **123** H4
St. Mary's Av N, Sthl. UB2 ... **123** H4
St. Mary's Av S, Sthl. UB2 ... **123** H4
St. Mary's Cl, N17 *off Kemble Rd.* ... **76** C1
St. Marys Cl, Chess. KT9 . **195** J7
Epsom KT17 ... **197** G7
St. Mary's Cl, Stai. (Stanw.) TW19 ... **140** A7
Sunbury-on-Thames TW16 *off Green Way* ... **178** A4
St. Mary's Copse, Wor.Pk. KT4 ... **196** E2
St. Marys Ct, E6 ... **116** C4
St. Mary's Ct, SE7 ... **136** A7
W5 *off St. Mary's Rd.* . **125** G2
St. Mary's Cres, NW4 ... **71** H3
St. Marys Cres, Islw. TW7 . **124** A7
St. Mary's Cres, Stai. (Stanw.) TW19 ... **140** A7
St. Marys Dr, Felt. TW14 . **141** F7
St. Mary's Gdns, SE11 ... **35** F1
St. Mary's Gate, W8 ... **22** A6
St. Marys Grn, N2 *off Thomas More Way* . . **73** F3
St. Mary's Gro, N1 ... **93** H6
SW13 ... **147** H3
W4 ... **126** B6
Richmond TW9 ... **145** J4
St. Marys Mans, W2 ... **14** E1
St. Mary's Ms, NW6 *off Priory Rd* ... **90/91** E7
Richmond TW10 ... **163** F2
St. Marys Path, N1 ... **111** H1
St. Mary's Pl, SE9 *off Eltham High St* ... **156** D6
W5 *off St. Mary's Rd.* . **125** G2
W8 ... **22** A6
St. Marys Rd, E10 ... **96** C3
E13 ... **115** H2
N8 *off High St* ... **74/75** E4
N9 ... **61** F1
St. Mary's Rd, NW10 ... **107** E1
St. Marys Rd, NW11 ... **72** B7
St. Mary's Rd, SE15 ... **153** F1
SE25 ... **188** B3
SW19 (Wimbledon) ... **166** B5
W5 ... **125** G2
Barnet EN4 ... **41** J7
Bexley DA5 ... **177** J1
St. Marys Rd, E.Mol. KT8. **180** A5
Ilford IG1 ... **99** F2
Surbiton KT6 ... **181** G6
Surbiton (Long Dit.) KT6 ... **181** F7
St. Mary's Rd, Wor.Pk. KT4 ... **197** E2
St. Marys Sq, W2 ... **14** E1
St. Mary's Sq, W5 *off St. Mary's Rd* ... **125** G2
St. Marys Ter, W2 ... **14** E1
St. Mary's Twr, EC1 *off Fortune St.* ... **111** J4
St. Mary St, SE18 ... **136** C4
St. Marys Vw, Har. HA3 ... **69** F5
St. Mary's Wk, SE11 ... **35** F1

St. Mary's Way, Chig. IG7 . **64** D5
St. Matthew's Av, Surb. KT6 ... **195** H1
St. Matthew's Dr, Brom. BR1 ... **192** C3
St. Matthew's Rd, SW2 . . **151** F4
St. Matthews Rd, W5 *off The Common* ... **125** H1
St. Matthew's Row, E2 ... **13** H4
St. Matthew St, SW1 ... **25** H6
St. Matthias Cl, NW9 ... **71** F5
St. Maur Rd, SW6 ... **148** C1
St. Mellion Cl, SE28 *off Redbourne Dr.* ... **118** D6
St. Merryn Cl, SE18 ... **137** G7
St. Michael's All, EC3 ... **20** C4
St. Michaels Av, N9 ... **45** F7
St. Michael's Av, Wem. HA9 ... **88** A6
St. Michaels Cl, E16 *off Fulmer Rd* ... **116** A5
St. Michael's Cl, N3 ... **72** C2
St. Michaels Cl, N12 ... **57** H5
Bromley BR1 ... **192** B3
Erith DA18 *off St. Helens Rd.* ... **138** D2
Worcester Park KT4 ... **197** F2
St. Michaels Cres, Pnr. HA5 ... **67** E6
St. Michaels Gdns, W10 *off St. Lawrence Ter.* . . **108** B5
St. Michaels Rd, NW2 ... **89** J4
St. Michael's Rd, SW9 ... **151** F2
St. Michaels Rd, Croy. CR0 ... **201** J1
Wallington SM6 ... **200** C6
Welling DA16 ... **158** B3
St. Michaels St, W2 ... **15** F3
St. Michaels Ter, N22 ... **75** E2
St. Mildred's Ct, EC2 *off Poultry* ... **112** A6
St. Mildreds Rd, SE12 ... **155** E7
St. Nicholas Cen, Sutt. SM1 *off St. Nicholas Way*. **198/199** E4
St. Nicholas Glebe, SW17 . **168** A6
St. Nicholas Pl, Loug. IG10 . **48** D4
St. Nicholas Rd, SE18 ... **137** J5
Sutton SM1 ... **199** E5
Thames Ditton KT7 ... **180** C6
St. Nicholas St, SE8 *off Lucas St.* ... **154** A1
St. Nicholas Way, Sutt. SM1 ... **198** E4
St. Nicolas La, Chis. BR7 . **192** B1
St. Ninian's Ct, N20 ... **57** J3
St. Norbert Grn, SE4 ... **153** H4
St. Norbert Rd, SE4 ... **153** H4
St. Olaf's Rd, SW6 ... **128** B7
St. Olaves Ct, EC2 ... **20** B4
St. Olave's Est, SE1 ... **29** E3
St. Olaves Gdns, SE11 ... **34** E1
St. Olaves Rd, E6 ... **116** D1
St. Olave's Wk, SW16 ... **186** C2
St. Olav's Sq, SE16 ... **133** F3
St. Oswald's Pl, SE11 ... **34** C4
St. Oswald's Rd, SW16 ... **187** H1
St. Oswulf St, SW1 ... **33** J2
ST. PANCRAS, WC1 ... **10** A4
St. Pancras Way, NW1 ... **92** C7
St. Patrick's Ct, Wdf.Grn. IG8 ... **63** E7
St. Paul's All, EC4 *off St. Paul's Chyd* ... **111** H6
St. Paul's Av, NW2 ... **89** H6
SE16 ... **133** G1
St. Pauls Av, Har. HA3 ... **69** J5
★**St. Paul's Cath**, EC4 ... **19** J4
St. Paul's Chyd, EC4 ... **19** H4
St. Paul's Cl, SE7 ... **136** A5
W5 ... **125** J2
Carshalton SM5 ... **199** H1
St. Pauls Cl, Chess. KT9 . . **195** G4
Hayes UB3 ... **121** G5
St. Paul's Cl, Houns. TW3 . **143** E2
St. Paul's Ct, W14 *off Colet Gdns.* ... **128** A4
St. Pauls Ctyd, SE8 *off Deptford High St* . . **134** A7
St. Pauls Cray Rd, Chis. BR7 ... **193** G1
St. Paul's Cres, NW1 ... **92** D7
St. Pauls Dr, E15 ... **96** D5
St. Paul's Ms, NW1 *off St. Paul's Cres* ... **92** D7
St. Paul's Pl, N1 ... **94** A6
St. Pauls Ri, N13 ... **59** H6
St. Paul's Rd, N1 ... **93** H6
N17 ... **60** D7
Barking IG11 ... **117** F1

St. Paul's Rd, Brent. TW8 . 125 G6
Erith DA8 . . . . 139 J7
Richmond TW9 . . . . 145 J3
Thornton Heath CR7 . . . 187 J3
St. Paul's Shrubbery, N1 . . 94 A6
St. Pauls Sq, Brom. BR2 . 191 G2
St. Paul's Ter, SE17 . . . . . . 35 H5
St. Pauls Twr, E10 . . . . 78 B7
St. Paul St, N1 . . . . 111 J1
St. Pauls Wk, Kings.T. KT2
off Alexandra Rd 164 A7
St. Pauls Way, E3 . . . . 113 J5
E14 . . . . 113 J5
St. Paul's Way, N3 . . . . 56 E7
St. Pauls Wd Hill, Orp.
BR5 . . . . 193 H2
St. Peter's All, EC3 . . . . 20 C4
St. Peter's Av, E2 . . . . 13 J2
E17 . . . . 78 E4
St. Peters Av, N18 . . . . 60 D4
St. Petersburgh Ms, W2 . . . 14 A5
St. Petersburgh Pl, W2 . . . . 14 A5
St. Peter's Cl, E2 . . . . 13 J2
St. Peters Cl, SW17
off College Gdns 167 H2
St. Peter's Cl, Barn. EN5 . . 39 H5
St. Peters Cl, Bushey
(Bushey Hth) WD23 . . . . 52 A1
Chislehurst BR7 . . . . . . 175 G7
Ilford IG2 . . . . 81 H4
St. Peter's Cl, Ruis. HA4 . . . 84 D2
St. Peter's Ct, NW4 . . . . . . 71 J5
St. Peters Ct, SE3
off Eltham Rd 155 F4
SE4 *off Wickham Rd* . . . 153 J2
West Molesey KT8 . . . . 179 G4
St. Peter's Gdns, SE27 . . . 169 G3
St. Peter's Gro, W6 . . . . . . 127 G4
St. Peters Ms, N4
off Warham Rd 75 H5
St. Peter's Pl, W9 . . . . 6 A6
St. Peters Rd, N9 . . . . 61 F1
St. Peter's Rd, W6 . . . . 127 G5
Croydon CR0 . . . . 202 A4
St. Peters Rd, Kings.T.
KT1 . . . . 182 A2
Southall UB1 . . . . 103 G5
Twickenham TW1 . . . . . 145 E5
St. Peter's Rd, W.Mol.
KT8 . . . . 179 G4
St. Peter's Sq, E2 . . . . 13 J2
W6 . . . . 127 G5
St. Peters St, N1 . . . . 111 H1
St. Peter's St, S.Croy.
CR2 . . . . 202 A5
St. Peters Ter, SW6 . . . . . . 128 B7
St. Peter's Vil, W6 . . . . 127 G4
St. Peter's Way, N1 . . . . 94 B7
St. Peters Way, W5 . . . . . . 105 G5
Hayes UB3 . . . . 121 G5
St. Philip's Av, Wor.Pk.
KT4 . . . . 197 H2
St. Philips Gate, Wor.Pk.
KT4 . . . . 197 H2
St. Philip Sq, SW8 . . . . . . 150 B2
St. Philip's Rd, E8 . . . . 94 D6
St. Philips Rd, Surb. KT6 . 181 G6
St. Philip St, SW8 . . . . . . 150 B2
St. Philip's Way, N1
off Linton St 111 J1
St. Quentin Ho, SW18
off Fitzhugh Gro 149 G6
St. Quentin Rd, Well.
DA16 . . . . 157 J3
St. Quintin Av, W10 . . . . . 107 J5
St. Quintin Gdns, W10 . . . 107 J5
St. Quintin Rd, E13 . . . . . . 115 H2
St. Raphael's Way, NW10 . . 88 C5
St. Regis Cl, N10 . . . . 74 B2
St. Ronans Cres, Wdf.Grn.
IG8 . . . . 63 G7
St. Rule St, SW8 . . . . 150 C2
St. Saviour's Est, SE1 . . . . 29 F5
St. Saviour's Rd, SW2 . . . 151 F5
St. Saviours Rd, Croy.
CR0 . . . . 187 J6
Saints Cl, SE27
off Wolfington Rd 169 H4
Saints Dr, E7 . . . . 98 A5
St. Silas Pl, NW5 . . . . 92 A6
St. Silas St Est, NW5 . . . . . 92 A6
St. Simon's Av, SW15 . . . 147 J5
St. Stephens Av, E17 . . . . . 78 C5
W12 . . . . 127 H2
W13 . . . . 104 E6
St. Stephens Cl, E17 . . . . . 78 B5
NW8 *off Avenue Cl* 109 H1
Southall UB1 . . . . 103 G5
St. Stephens Cres, W2 . . . 108 D6
St. Stephens Cres, Th. Hth.
CR7 . . . . 187 G3
St. Stephens Gdn Est, W2
off Shrewsbury Rd . . . 108 D6
St. Stephens Gdns, SW15
off Manfred Rd 148 C5
W2 . . . . 108 D6
Twickenham TW1 . . . . . 145 F6
St. Stephens Gro, SE13 . . 154 C3
St. Stephens Ms, W2
off Chepstow Rd 108 D5
St. Stephen's Par, E7
off Green St 97 J7
St. Stephen's Pas, Twick.
TW1 *off Richmond Rd* . 145 F6
St. Stephen's Rd, E3 . . . . . 113 J2
St. Stephens Rd, E6 . . . . . . 97 J7
St. Stephen's Rd, E17
off Grove Rd 78 B5
St. Stephens Rd, W13 . . . 105 E6
St. Stephen's Rd, Barn.
EN5 . . . . 40 A5
St. Stephens Rd, Houns.
TW3 . . . . 143 G6
St. Stephen's Rd, West Dr.
UB7 . . . . 120 A1
St. Stephens Row, EC4 . . . 20 B4
St. Stephens Ter, SW8 . . . 131 F7
St. Stephen's Wk, SW7 . . . 30 C1
St. Swithin's La, EC4 . . . . . 20 B5
St. Swithun's Rd, SE13 . . 154 D5
St. Theresa's Rd, Felt.
TW14 . . . . 141 J4
St. Thomas' Cl, Surb. KT6 . . 195 J1
St. Thomas Ct, Bex. DA5 . 159 G7
St. Thomas Dr, Orp. BR5 . 207 F1
St. Thomas' Dr, Pnr. HA5 . . 67 E1
St. Thomas Gdns, Ilf. IG1 . . 99 F6
St. Thomas Pl, NW1
off Maiden La 92 D7
St. Thomas Rd, E16 . . . . . 115 G6
N14 . . . . 42 D7
St. Thomas' Rd, W4 . . . . . 126 C6
St. Thomas Rd, Belv.
DA17 . . . . 139 J2
St. Thomas's Gdns, NW5
off Queen's Cres 92 A6
St. Thomas's Pl, E9 . . . . 95 F7
St. Thomas's Rd, N4 . . . . . . 93 G2
NW10 . . . . 107 E1
St. Thomas's Sq, E9 . . . . . . 95 E7
St. Thomas St, SE1 . . . . . . 28 B2
St. Thomas's Way, SW6 . . 128 C7
St. Timothy's Ms, Brom.
BR1 *off Wharton Rd* . . 191 H1
St. Ursula Gro, Pnr. HA5 . . 66 D5
St. Ursula Rd, Sthl. UB1 . . 103 G6
St. Vincent Cl, SE27 . . . . . 169 H5
St. Vincent Rd, Twick.
TW2 . . . . 143 J6
St. Vincent St, W1 . . . . 16 C2
St. Wilfrids Cl, Barn. EN4 . . 41 H5
St. Wilfrids Rd, Barn. EN4 . 41 G5
St. Winefride's Av, E12 . . . . 98 C5
St. Winifreds Cl, Chig. IG7 . 65 F5
St. Winifred's Rd, Tedd.
TW11 . . . . 163 E6
Sala Ho, SE3
off Pinto Way 155 H4
Salamanca Pl, SE1 . . . . 34 C2
Salamanca St, SE1 . . . . . . 34 B2
Salamander Cl, Kings.T.
KT2 . . . . 163 F5
Salcombe Dr, Mord. SM4 . 198 A1
Romford RM6 . . . . 83 F6
Salcombe Gdns, NW7 . . . . 55 J6
Salcombe Pk, Loug. IG10 . . 48 A5
Salcombe Rd, E17 . . . . 77 J7
N16 . . . . 94 B5
Salcombe Way, Ruis. HA4 . 84 A2
Salcott Rd, SW11 . . . . 149 H5
Croydon CR0 . . . . 201 E3
Salehurst Cl, Har. HA3 . . . . 69 H5
Salehurst Rd, SE4 . . . . . . 153 J6
Salem Pl, Croy. CR0 . . . . . 201 J3
Salem Rd, W2 . . . . 14 B5
Sale Pl, W2 . . . . 15 G2
Sale St, E2 . . . . 13 H5
Salford Rd, SW2 . . . . 168 D1
Salhouse Cl, SE28
off Rollesby Way 118 C6
Salisbury Av, N3 . . . . 72 C3
Barking IG11 . . . . 99 H7
Sutton SM1 . . . . 198 C6
Salisbury Cl, SE17 . . . . 36 B1
Worcester Park KT4 . . . . 197 F3
Salisbury Ct, EC4 . . . . 19 G4
Salisbury Gdns, SW19 . . . 166 B7
Buckhurst Hill IG9 . . . . . . 64 A2
Salisbury Hall Gdns, E4 . . . 62 A6
Salisbury Ho, E14
off Hobday St 114 B6
Salisbury Ms, SW6
off Dawes Rd 128 C7
Bromley BR2
off Salisbury Rd 192 B5
Salisbury Pl, SW9 . . . . . . 131 H7
W1 . . . . 15 J1
Salisbury Rd, E4 . . . . 62 A3
E7 . . . . 97 G6
E10 . . . . 96 C2
E12 . . . . 98 A5
E17 . . . . 78 C5
N4 . . . . 75 H5
N9 . . . . 60 D3
N22 . . . . 75 H1
SE25 . . . . 188 D6
SW19 . . . . 166 B7
W13 . . . . 124 D2
Barnet EN5 . . . . 40 B3
Bexley DA5 . . . . 177 G1
Bromley BR2 . . . . 192 B5
Carshalton SM5 . . . . 199 J6
Dagenham RM10 . . . . . . 101 H6
Feltham TW13 . . . . 160 C1
Harrow HA1 . . . . 68 A5
Hounslow TW4 . . . . 142 C3
Hounslow (Hthrw Air.)
TW6 . . . . 141 F5
Ilford IG3 . . . . 99 H2
New Malden KT3 . . . . . 182 D3
Pinner HA5 . . . . 66 A4
Richmond TW9 . . . . 145 H4
Southall UB2 . . . . 123 E4
Worcester Park KT4 . . . . 197 F3
Salisbury Sq, EC4 . . . . 19 F4
Salisbury St, NW8 . . . . 7 F6
W3 . . . . 126 C2
Salisbury Ter, SE15 . . . . . . 153 F3
Salisbury Wk, N19 . . . . 92 C2
Salix Cl, Sun. TW16
off Oak Gro 160 B7
Salliesfield, Twick. TW2 . . . 144 A6
Sally Murrey Cl, E12
off Grantham Rd 98 D4
Salmen Rd, E13 . . . . 115 F2
Salmond Cl, Stan. HA7
off Robb Rd 52 D6
Salmon La, E14 . . . . 113 H6
Salmon Rd, Belv. DA17 . . 139 G5
Salmons Rd, N9 . . . . 60 D1
Chessington KT9 . . . . . . 195 G6
Salmon St, E14
off Salmon La 113 J6
NW9 . . . . 88 B1
Salomons Rd, E13
off Chalk Rd 115 J5
Salop Rd, E17 . . . . 77 G6
Saltash Cl, Sutt. SM1 . . . . 198 C4
Saltash Rd, Ilf. IG6 . . . . 65 G7
Welling DA16 . . . . 158 C1
Saltcoats Rd, W4 . . . . 126 E2
Saltcroft Cl, Wem. HA9 . . . . 88 B1
Salter Cl, Har. HA2 . . . . 85 F3
Salterford Rd, SW17 . . . . . 168 A6
Salter Rd, SE16 . . . . 133 G1
Salters Hall Ct, EC4 . . . . . . 20 B5
Salters Hill, SE19 . . . . 170 A5
Salters Rd, E17 . . . . 78 D4
W10 . . . . 108 A4
Salter St, E14 . . . . 114 A7
NW10 . . . . 107 G3
Salterton Rd, N7 . . . . 93 E3
Saltley Cl, E6
off Dunnock Rd 116 B6
Saltoun Rd, SW2 . . . . 151 G4
Saltram Cl, N15 . . . . 76 C4
Saltram Cres, W9 . . . . 108 C3
Saltwell St, E14 . . . . 114 A7
Saltwood Gro, SE17 . . . . . 36 B4
Salusbury Rd, NW6 . . . . . 108 B1
Salutation Rd, SE10 . . . . . 135 E4
Salvia Gdns, Grnf. UB6
off Selborne Gdns 104 D2
Salvin Rd, SW15 . . . . 148 A3
Salway Cl, Wdf.Grn. IG8 . . 63 F7
Salway Pl, E15
off Broadway 96/97 E6
Salway Rd, E15
off Great Eastern Rd . . . 96 D6
Samantha Cl, E17 . . . . 77 J7
Sam Bartram Cl, SE7 . . . . 135 J5
Sambruck Ms, SE6 . . . . . . 172 B1
Samels Ct, W6
off South Black Lion La . 127 G5
Samford St, NW8 . . . . 7 F6
Samira Cl, E17
off Colchester Rd 78 A6
Samos Rd, SE20 . . . . 189 E2
Sampson Av, Barn. EN5 . . . 40 A5
Sampson Cl, Belv. DA17
off Carrill Way 138 D3
Sampson St, E1 . . . . 29 J2
Samson St, E13 . . . . 115 J2
Samuel Cl, E8
off Pownall Rd 112 C1
SE14 . . . . 133 G6
SE18 . . . . 136 B4
Samuel Gray Gdns, Kings.T.
KT2 . . . . 181 G1
Samuel Johnson Cl, SW16
off Curtis Fld Rd 169 G4
Samuel Lewis Trust Dws, E8
off Amhurst Rd 94 D4
N1 *off Liverpool Rd* 93 G7
SW3 . . . . 31 G2
SW6 . . . . 128 D7
Samuels Cl, W6
off South Black Lion La . 127 G5
Samuel St, SE15 . . . . 37 F7
SE18 . . . . 136 C4
Sancroft Cl, NW2 . . . . 89 H3
Sancroft Rd, Har. HA3 . . . . 68 C2
Sancroft St, SE11 . . . . 34 D3
Sanctuary, The, SW1 . . . . . 25 J4
Bexley DA5 . . . . 158 D6
Morden SM4 . . . . 184 D6
Sanctuary Rd, Houns.
(Hthrw Air.) TW6 . . . . . 140 D6
Sanctuary St, SE1 . . . . 28 A4
Sandale Cl, N16
off Stoke Newington
Ch St 94 A3
Sandall Cl, W5 . . . . 105 H4
Sandall Rd, NW5 . . . . 92 C6
W5 . . . . 105 H4
Sandal Rd, N18 . . . . 60 D5
New Malden KT3 . . . . . 182 D5
Sandal St, E15 . . . . 114 E1
Sandalwood Cl, E1
off Solebay St 113 H4
Sandalwood Rd, Felt.
TW13 . . . . 160 B3
Sandbach Pl, SE18 . . . . . . 137 F4
Sandbourne Av, SW19 . . . 184 E3
Sandbourne Rd, SE4 . . . . 153 H2
Sandbrook Cl, NW7 . . . . . . 54 D6
Sandbrook Rd, N16 . . . . . . 94 B3
Sandby Grn, SE9 . . . . 156 B3
Sandcroft Cl, N13 . . . . 59 H6
Sandell St, SE1 . . . . 27 E3
Sanders Cl, Hmptn.
(Hmptn H.) TW12 . . . . . 161 J5
Sanders La, NW7 . . . . 56 A7
Sanderson Cl, NW5 . . . . . . 92 B4
Sanderstead Av, NW2 . . . . 90 B2
Sanderstead Cl, SW12
off Atkins Rd 150 C7
Sanderstead Rd, E10 . . . . . 95 H1
South Croydon CR2 . . . 202 A7
Sanders Way, N19
off Sussex Way 92 D1
Sandfield Gdns, Th.Hth.
CR7 . . . . 187 H3
Sandfield Pas, Th.Hth.
CR7 . . . . 187 J3
Sandfield Rd, Th.Hth.
CR7 . . . . 187 H3
Sandford Av, N22 . . . . 59 J7
Loughton IG10 . . . . 49 F3
Sandford Cl, E6 . . . . 116 C4
Sandford Ct, N16 . . . . 94 B1
Sandford Rd, E6 . . . . 116 B4
Bexleyheath DA7 . . . . . 159 E4
Bromley BR2 . . . . 191 G4
Sandford St, SW6
off King's Rd 128/129 E7
Sandgate La, SW18 . . . . . 167 H1
Sandgate Rd, Well.
DA16 . . . . 138 C7
Sandgate St, SE15 . . . . . . 132 E6
Sandham Pt, SE18
off Troy Ct 136/137 E4
Sandhills, Wall. SM6 . . . . 200 D4
Sandhurst Av, Har. HA2 . . . 67 H6
Surbiton KT5 . . . . 182 B7
Sandhurst Cl, NW9 . . . . 70 A3
Sandhurst Dr, Ilf. IG3 . . . . . 99 J4
Sandhurst Rd, N9 . . . . 45 F6
NW9 . . . . 70 A3
SE6 . . . . 172 D1
Bexley DA5 . . . . 158 D5
Sidcup DA15 . . . . 175 J3
Sandhurst Way, S.Croy.
CR2 . . . . 202 B7
Sandifer Dr, NW2 . . . . 90 A3
Sandiford Rd, Sutt. SM3 . 198 C2

Sandiland Cres, Brom. BR2 **205** F2
Sandilands, Croy. CR0 **202** D2
Sandilands Rd, SW6 **148** E1
Sandison St, SE15 **152** C3
Sandland St, WC1 **18** D2
Sandling Ri, SE9 **174** D3
Sandlings, The, N22 **75** G2
Sandlings Cl, SE15
off Pilkington Rd **152/153** E2
Sandmartin Way, Wall. SM6 **200** A1
Sandmere Rd, SW4 **150** E4
Sandon Cl, Esher KT10 **180** A7
Sandow Cres, Hayes UB3 **121** J3
Sandown Av, Dag. RM10 **101** J6
Sandown Cl, Houns. TW5 **142** A1
Sandown Ct, Sutt. SM2
off Grange Rd **198/199** E7
Sandown Rd, SE25 **188** E5
Sandown Way, Nthlt. UB5 **85** E6
Sandpiper Cl, E17 **77** G1
SE16 **133** J2
Sandpiper Rd, Sutt. SM1 **198** C5
Sandpit Pl, SE7 **136** B5
Sandpit Rd, Brom. BR1 **172** E5
Sandpits Rd, Croy. CR0 **203** G4
Richmond TW10 **163** G2
Sandra Cl, N22
off New Rd **75** J1
Hounslow TW3 **143** H5
Sandridge Cl, Har. HA1 **68** B4
Sandridge St, N19 **92** C2
Sandringham Av, SW20 **184** B2
Sandringham Cl, SW19 **166** A1
Enfield EN1 **44** B2
Ilford IG6 **81** F3
Sandringham Ct, W9 **6** D4
Sandringham Cres, Har. HA2 **85** G2
Sandringham Dr, Well. DA16 **157** H2
Sandringham Gdns, N8 **75** E6
N12 **57** F6
Hounslow TW5 **142** A1
Ilford IG6 **81** F3
West Molesey KT8
off Rosemary Av **179** G4
Sandringham Ms, W5
off High St **105** G7
Hampton TW12
off Oldfield Rd **179** F1
Sandringham Rd, E7 **97** J5
E8 **94** C5
E10 **78** D6
N22 **75** J3
NW2 **89** H6
NW11 **72** B7
Barking IG11 **99** J6
Bromley BR1 **173** G5
Hounslow (Hthrw Air.) TW6 **140** B5
Northolt UB5 **85** G7
Thornton Heath CR7 **187** J5
Worcester Park KT4 **197** G3
Sandrock Pl, Croy. CR0 **203** G4
Sandrock Rd, SE13 **154** A3
SANDS END, SW6 **149** F1
Sand's End La, SW6 **149** E1
Sandstone La, E10 **115** H7
Sandstone Pl, N19 **92** B2
Sandstone Rd, SE12 **173** H2
Sands Way, Wdf.Grn. IG8 **64** B6
Sandtoft Rd, SE7 **135** H6
Sandwell Cres, NW6 **90** D6
Sandwich St, WC1 **10** A4
Sandwick Cl, NW7
off Sebergham Gro **55** G7
Sandy Bury, Orp. BR6 **207** G3
Sandycombe Rd, Felt. TW14 **160** A1
Richmond TW9 **146** A3
Sandycoombe Rd, Twick. TW1 **145** F6
Sandycroft, SE2 **138** A6
Sandy Hill Av, SE18 **136** E5
Sandy Hill Rd, SE18 **136** E5
Sandyhill Rd, Ilf. IG1 **98** E4
Sandy La, Har. HA3 **69** J6
Kingston upon Thames KT1 **162** D7
Mitcham CR4 **186** A1
Northwood HA6 **50** A5
Richmond TW10 **163** F2
Sidcup DA14 **176** D7
Sutton SM2 **198** B7
Teddington TW11 **162** D7
Walton-on-Thames KT12 **178** B6
Sandy La Est, Rich. TW10 **163** G2
Sandy La N, Wall. SM6 **200** D6
Sandy La S, Wall. SM6 **200** D6
Sandymount Av, Stan. HA7 **53** F5
Sandy Ridge, Chis. BR7 **174** D6
Sandy Rd, NW3 **90** E3
Sandy's Row, E1 **21** E2
Sandy Way, Croy. CR0 **203** J3
Sanford La, N16
off Lawrence Bldgs **94** C2
Sanford St, SE14 **133** H6
Sanford Ter, N16 **94** C3
Sanford Wk, N16
off Sanford Ter **94** C2
SE14
off Cold Blow La **133** H6
Sanger Av, Chess. KT9 **195** H5
Sangley Rd, SE6 **154** B7
SE25 **188** B4
Sangora Rd, SW11 **149** G4
Sansom Rd, E11 **97** E2
Sansom St, SE5 **132** A7
Sans Wk, EC1 **11** F5
Santley St, SW4 **151** F4
Santos Rd, SW18 **148** D5
Santway, The, Stan. HA7 **52** B5
Sapcote Trd Cen, NW10 **89** F5
Saperton Wk, SE11 **34** D1
Saphora Cl, Orp. BR6
off Oleander Cl **207** G5
Sapperton Ct, EC1 **11** J5
Sapphire Cl, E6 **116** D6
Dagenham RM8 **100** C1
Sapphire Rd, SE8 **133** H4
Saracen Cl, Croy. CR0 **188** A6
Saracen's Head Yd, EC3 **21** E4
Saracen St, E14 **114** A6
Sara Ct, Beck. BR3
off Albemarle Rd **190** B1
Sarah Ho, SW15 **147** F4
Saratoga Rd, E5 **95** F4
Sardinia St, WC2 **18** C4
Sarita Cl, Har. HA3 **68** A2
Sarjant Path, SW19
off Queensmere Rd **166** A2
Sark Cl, Houns. TW5 **123** G7
Sark Wk, E16 **115** H6
Sarnesfield Ho, SE15
off Pencraig Way **132/133** E6
Sarnesfield Rd, Enf. EN2
off Church St **44** A3
Sarre Rd, NW2 **90** C5
Sarsen Av, Houns. TW3 **143** F2
Sarsfeld Rd, SW12 **167** J1
Sarsfield Rd, Grnf. UB6 **105** E2
Sartor Rd, SE15 **153** G4
Sarum Ter, E3
off Bow Common La **113** H4
Satanita Cl, E16
off Fulmer Rd **116** A6
Satchell Mead, NW9 **71** F1
Satchwell Rd, E2 **13** H4
Sattar Ms, N16
off Clissold Rd **94** A3
Sauls Grn, E11
off Napier Rd **96/97** E3
Saunders Cl, E14
off Limehouse Causeway **113** J7
Saunders Ness Rd, E14 **134** C5
Saunders Rd, SE18 **137** J5
Saunders St, SE11 **34** E1
Saunders Way, SE28
off Oriole Way **118** B7
Saunderton Rd, Wem. HA0 **86** E5
Saunton Av, Hayes UB3 **121** J7
Savage Gdns, E6 **116** C6
EC3 **21** E5
Savannah Cl, SE15
off Chandler Way **132** C7
Savernake Rd, N9 **44** D6
NW3 **91** J4
Savery Dr, Surb. KT6 **181** F7
Savile Cl, N.Mal. KT3 **183** E5
Thames Ditton KT7 **194** C1
Savile Gdns, Croy. CR0 **202** C2
Savile Row, W1 **17** F5
Saville Rd, E16 **136** B1
W4 **126** D3
Romford RM6 **83** F6
Twickenham TW1 **162** C1
Saville Row, Brom. BR2 **205** F1
Enfield EN3 **45** G2
Savill Gdns, SW20
off Bodnant Gdns **183** G3
Savill Row, Wdf.Grn. IG8 **63** F6
Savona Cl, SW19 **166** B7
Savona Est, SW8 **130** C7
Savona St, SW8 **130** C7
Savoy Av, Hayes UB3 **121** H5
Savoy Bldgs, WC2 **18** C6
Savoy Cl, E15
off Arthingworth St **114/115** E1
Edgware HA8 **54** A5
Savoy Ct, WC2 **18** B6
Savoy Hill, WC2 **18** C6
Savoy Ms, SW9
off Clapham Rd **150** E3
Savoy Pl, WC2 **18** B6
Savoy Row, WC2 **18** C5
Savoy Steps, WC2
off Savoy St **111** F7
Savoy St, WC2 **18** C5
Savoy Way, WC2 **18** C6
Sawbill Cl, Hayes UB4 **102** D5
Sawkins Cl, SW19 **166** B2
Sawley Rd, W12 **127** F1
Sawmill Yd, E3 **113** H1
Sawtry Cl, Cars. SM5 **185** H7
Sawyer Cl, N9
off Lion Rd **60** D2
Sawyers Cl, Dag. RM10 **101** J6
Sawyer's Hill, Rich. TW10 **146** B7
Sawyers Lawn, W13 **104** C6
Sawyer St, SE1 **27** J3
Saxby Rd, SW2 **150** E7
Saxham Rd, Bark. IG11 **117** H2
Saxlingham Rd, E4 **62** D3
Saxon Av, Felt. TW13 **161** F2
Saxonbury Av, Sun. TW16 **178** B3
Saxonbury Cl, Mitch. CR4 **185** G3
Saxonbury Gdns, Surb. KT6 **195** F1
Saxon Cl, E17 **78** A7
Surbiton KT6 **181** G6
Saxon Dr, W3 **106** B6
Saxonfield Cl, SW2 **151** F7
Saxon Gdns, Sthl. UB1
off Saxon Rd **102/103** E7
Saxon Rd, E3 **113** J2
E6 **116** C4
N22 **75** H1
SE25 **188** A5
Bromley BR1 **173** F7
Ilford IG1 **99** E6
Kingston upon Thames KT2 **181** H1
Southall UB1 **123** E1
Wembley HA9 **88** C3
Saxon Wk, Sid. DA14 **176** C6
Saxon Way, N14 **42** D6
Saxton Cl, SE13 **154** D3
Sayers Wk, Rich. TW10
off Stafford Pl **145** J7
Sayesbury La, N18 **60** D5
Sayes Ct, SE8
off Sayes Ct St **133** J5
Sayes Ct St, SE8 **133** J6
Scadbury Pk, Chis. BR7 **175** J6
Scads Hill Cl, Orp. BR6 **193** J6
Scala St, W1 **17** G1
Scales Rd, N17 **76** C3
Scampston Ms, W10 **108** A6
Scampton Rd, Houns. (Hthrw Air.) TW6
off Southampton Rd **140** C6
Scandrett St, E1 **132** E1
Scarba Wk, N1
off Marquess Rd **94** A6
Scarborough Rd, E11 **96** D1
N4 **75** G7
N9 **45** F7
Hounslow (Hthrw Air.) TW6 *off Southern Perimeter Rd* **141** F6
Scarborough St, E1 **21** G4
Scarbrook Rd, Croy. CR0 **201** J3
Scarle Rd, Wem. HA0 **87** G6
Scarlet Rd, SE6 **172** E3
Scarlette Manor Way, SW2
off Papworth Way **151** G7
Scarsbrook Rd, SE3 **156** A3
Scarsdale Pl, W8 **22** A5
Scarsdale Rd, Har. HA2 **85** J3
Scarsdale Vil, W8 **128** D3
Scarth Rd, SW13 **147** F3
Scawen Cl, Cars. SM5 **200** A4
Scawen Rd, SE8 **133** H5
Scawfell St, E2 **13** G2
Scaynes Link, N12 **56** D5
Sceaux Est, SE5 **152** B1
Sceptre Rd, E2 **113** F3
Schofield Wk, SE3
off Dornberg Cl **135** H7
Scholars Pl, N16
off Oldfield Rd **94** B3
Scholars Rd, E4 **62** C1
SW12 **168** C1
Scholefield Rd, N19 **92** D1
Schonfeld Sq, N16 **94** A2
Schoolbank Rd, SE10 **135** F4
Schoolbell Ms, E3
off Arbery Rd **113** H2
Schoolhouse Gdns, Loug. IG10 **48** E4
Schoolhouse La, E1 **113** G7
School Ho La, Tedd. TW11 **163** E7
School La, Chig. IG7 **65** J4
Kingston upon Thames KT1
off School Rd **181** F1
Pinner HA5 **66** E4
Surbiton KT6 **196** A1
Welling DA16 **158** B3
School Pas, Kings.T. KT1 **181** J2
Southall UB1 **123** F1
School Rd, E12
off Sixth Av **98** C4
NW10 **106** D4
Chislehurst BR7 **193** F1
Dagenham RM10 **119** G1
East Molesey KT8 **180** A4
Hampton (Hmptn H.) TW12 **161** J6
Hounslow TW3 **143** J3
Kingston upon Thames KT1 **181** F1
West Drayton UB7 **120** A6
School Rd Av, Hmptn. (Hmptn H.) TW12 **161** J6
School Way, N12
off High Rd **57** F4
Schoolway, N12 (Woodhouse Rd) **57** G6
School Way, Dag. RM8 **100** C3
Schooner Cl, E14 **134** D3
SE16 *off Kinburn St* **133** G2
Barking IG11 **118** B3
Schubert Rd, SW15 **148** C5
★**Science Mus**, SW7 **23** F6
Sclater St, E1 **13** F5
Scoble Pl, N16
off Amhurst Rd **94** C4
Scoles Cres, SW2 **169** G1
Scope Way, Kings.T. KT1 **181** H4
Scoresby St, SE1 **27** G2
Scorton Av, Grnf. UB6 **104** D2
Scotch Common, W13 **104** D5
Scoter Cl, Wdf.Grn. IG8
off Mallards Rd **63** H7
Scot Gro, Pnr. HA5 **50** D7
Scotia Rd, SW2 **151** G7
Scotland Grn, N17 **76** C2
Scotland Grn Rd, Enf. EN3 **45** G5
Scotland Grn Rd N, Enf. EN3 **45** G4
Scotland Pl, SW1 **26** A1
Scotland Rd, Buck.H. IG9 **63** J1
Scotney Cl, Orp. BR6 **206** D4
Scotsdale Cl, Orp. BR5 **193** H4
Sutton SM3 **198** B7
Scotsdale Rd, SE12 **155** H5
Scotswood St, EC1 **11** F5
Scotswood Wk, N17 **60** D7
Scott Cl, SW16 **187** F1
Epsom KT19 **196** C5
West Drayton UB7 **120** C4
Scott Ct, W3
off Petersfield Rd **126** C2
Scott Cres, Har. HA2 **85** H1
Scott Ellis Gdns, NW8 **6** E4
Scottes La, Dag. RM8
off Valence Av **100** D1
Scott Fm Cl, T.Ditt. KT7 **194** E1
Scott Gdns, Houns. TW5 **122** D7
Scott Ho, E13
off Queens Rd W **115** G2
N18 **60** D5
Scott Lidgett Cres, SE16 **29** H4
Scott Russell Pl, E14
off Westferry Rd **134** B5
Scotts Av, Brom. BR2 **190** D2
Scotts Dr, Hmptn. TW12 **161** H7
Scotts Fm Rd, Epsom KT19 **196** C6
Scotts La, Brom. BR2 **190** D3
Scotts Pas, SE18
off Spray St **136** E4
Scotts Rd, E10 **96** C1
W12 **127** H2
Bromley BR1 **173** G7
Southall UB2 **122** C3
Scott St, E1 **112** E4
Scott Trimmer Way, Houns. TW3 **143** E2

Scottwell Dr, NW9 . . . . **71** F5
Scoulding Rd, E16 . . . . . . **115** F6
Scouler St, E14
off Quixley St **114** D7
Scout App, NW10 . . . . **88** E4
Scout La, SW4
off Old Town **150** C3
Scout Way, NW7 . . . . **54** D4
Scovell Cres, SE1 . . . . **27** J4
Scovell Rd, SE1 . . . . **27** J4
Scrattons Ter, Bark. IG11 . . **118** D2
Scriven St, E8 . . . . **112** C1
Scrooby St, SE6 . . . . **154** B6
Scrubs La, NW10 . . . . **107** G3
W10 . . . . **107** G3
Scrutton Cl, SW12 . . . . . . **150** D7
Scrutton St, EC2 . . . . **12** D6
Scudamore La, NW9 . . . . . **70** C3
Scutari Rd, SE22 . . . . **153** F5
Scylla Cres, Houns.
(Hthrw Air.) TW6 . . . . . **141** E7
Scylla Rd, SE15 . . . . **152** E3
Hounslow (Hthrw Air.)
TW6 . . . . **141** E6
Seabright St, E2 *off*
Bethnal Grn Rd . . . **112/113** E3
Seabrook Dr, W.Wick.
BR4 . . . . **204** E2
Seabrook Gdns, Rom.
RM7 . . . . **83** G7
Seabrook Rd, Dag. RM8 . . **100** D3
Seacole Cl, W3 . . . . **106** D5
Seacon Twr, E14
off Hutchings St **134** A2
Seacourt Rd, SE2 . . . . **138** D2
Seacroft Gdns, Wat. WD19 . **50** D3
Seafield Rd, N11 . . . . **58** D4
Seaford Rd, E17 . . . . **78** B3
N15 . . . . **76** A5
W13 . . . . **124** E1
Enfield EN1 . . . . **44** B4
Hounslow (Hthrw Air.)
TW6 . . . . **140** A5
Seaford St, WC1 . . . . **10** B4
Seaforth Av, N.Mal. KT3 . . **183** H5
Seaforth Cres, N5 . . . . **93** J5
Seaforth Gdns, N21 . . . . . . **43** F7
Epsom KT19 . . . . **197** F4
Woodford Green IG8 . . . **63** J5
Seaforth Pl, SW1
off Buckingham Gate . **130** C3
Seagrave Rd, SW6 . . . . . . **128** D6
Seagry Rd, E11 . . . . **79** G6
Seagull Cl, Bark. IG11 . . . . **118** A3
Seagull La, E16 . . . . **115** G7
Sealand Rd, Houns.
(Hthrw Air.) TW6 . . . . . **140** D6
Sealand Wk, Nthlt. UB5
off Wayfarer Rd . . **102/103** E3
Seal St, E8 . . . . **94** C4
Searle Pl, N4
off Evershot Rd **93** F1
Searles Cl, SW11 . . . . **129** H7
Searles Dr, E6 . . . . **116** F5
Searles Rd, SE1 . . . . **36** C1
Sears St, SE5 . . . . **36** B7
Seasprite Cl, Nthlt. UB5 . . **102** D3
Seaton Av, Ilf. IG3 . . . . **99** H5
Seaton Cl, E13
off New Barn St **115** H4
SE11 . . . . **35** F3
SW15 . . . . **165** H1
Twickenham TW2 . . . . . **144** A6
Seaton Gdns, Ruis. HA4 . . **84** A3
Seaton Pt, E5
off Nolan Way **94/95** E4
Seaton Rd, Hayes UB3 . . . **121** G4
Mitcham CR4 . . . . **185** H2
Twickenham TW2 . . . . . **143** J6
Welling DA16 . . . . **138** C7
Wembley HA0 . . . . **105** H2
Seaton Sq, NW7
off Tavistock Av **56** A7
Seaton St, N18 . . . . **60** D5
Sebastian Ct, Bark. IG11
off Meadow Rd **99** J7
Sebastian St, EC1 . . . . **11** H4
Sebastopol Rd, N9 . . . . **60** D4
Sebbon St, N1 . . . . **93** H7
Sebergham Gro, NW7 . . . . **55** G7
Sebert Rd, E7 . . . . **97** H5
Sebright Pas, E2 . . . . **13** J2
Sebright Rd, Barn. EN5 . . . **40** A2
Secker Cres, Har. HA3 . . . . **67** J1
Secker St, SE1 . . . . **27** E2
Second Av, E12 . . . . **98** B4
E13 . . . . **115** G3
E17 . . . . **78** A5
N18 . . . . **61** F4
Second Av, NW4 . . . . **72** A4
SW14 . . . . **146** E3
W3 . . . . **127** F1
W10 . . . . **108** B4
Dagenham RM10 . . . . . . **119** H1
Enfield EN1 . . . . **44** C5
Hayes UB3 . . . . **121** J1
Romford RM6 . . . . **82** C5
Walton-on-Thames
KT12 . . . . **178** B6
Wembley HA9 . . . . **87** G2
Second Cl, W.Mol. KT8 . . . **179** J4
Second Cross Rd, Twick.
TW2 . . . . **162** B2
Second Way, Wem. HA9 . . . **88** B4
Sedan Way, SE17 . . . . **36** D3
Sedcombe Cl, Sid. DA14
off Knoll Rd **176** B4
Sedcote Rd, Enf. EN3 . . . . . **45** F5
Sedding St, SW1 . . . . **32** B1
Seddon Highwalk, EC2
off Beech St **111** J5
Seddon Ho, EC2
off The Barbican **111** J5
Seddon Rd, Mord. SM4 . . **185** G5
Seddon St, WC1 . . . . **10** D4
Sedgebrook Rd, SE3 . . . . **156** A2
Sedgecombe Av, Har.
HA3 . . . . **69** F5
Sedgeford Rd, W12 . . . . . **127** F1
Sedgehill Rd, SE6 . . . . **172** A4
Sedgemere Av, N2 . . . . **73** F3
Sedgemere Rd, SE2 . . . . . **138** C3
Sedgemoor Dr, Dag.
RM10 . . . . **101** G4
Sedge Rd, N17 . . . . **61** F7
Sedgeway, SE6 . . . . **173** F1
Sedgewood Cl, Brom.
BR2 . . . . **191** F7
Sedgmoor Pl, SE5 . . . . . . **132** B7
Sedgwick Rd, E10 . . . . **96** C2
Sedgwick St, E9 . . . . **95** G5
Sedleigh Rd, SW18 . . . . . **148** C6
Sedlescombe Rd, SW6 . . **128** C6
Sedley Pl, W1 . . . . **16** D4
Sedley Ri, Loug. IG10 . . . . . **48** C2
Sedum Cl, NW9 . . . . **70** B5
Seeley Dr, SE21 . . . . **170** B4
Seelig Av, NW9 . . . . **71** G7
Seely Rd, SW17 . . . . **168** A6
Seething La, EC3 . . . . **21** E6
Seething Wells La, Surb.
KT6 . . . . **181** F6
Sefton Av, NW7 . . . . **54** D5
Harrow HA3 . . . . **68** A1
Sefton Cl, Orp. BR5 . . . . . **193** J4
Sefton Rd, Croy. CR0 . . . . **202** D1
Orpington BR5 . . . . **193** J4
Sefton St, SW15 . . . . **147** J2
Segal Cl, SE23 . . . . **153** H7
Sekforde St, EC1 . . . . **11** G6
Sekhon Ter, Felt. TW13 . . . **161** G3
Selan Gdns, Hayes UB4 . . **102** B5
Selbie Av, NW10 . . . . **89** F5
Selborne Av, E12
off Walton Rd **98** D4
Bexley DA5 . . . . **176** E1
Selborne Gdns, NW4 . . . . . **71** G4
Greenford UB6 . . . . **104** D1
Selborne Rd, E17 . . . . **77** J5
N14 . . . . **58** E3
N22 . . . . **75** F1
SE5 *off Denmark Hill* . . . **152** A2
Croydon CR0 . . . . **202** B3
Ilford IG1 . . . . **98** D2
New Malden KT3 . . . . . **182** E2
Sidcup DA14 . . . . **176** B4
Selbourne Av, E17 . . . . **77** J4
Surbiton KT6 . . . . **195** J2
Selbourne Wk, E17
off Selbourne Wk
Shop Cen **77** J4
Selbourne Wk Shop Cen,
E17 . . . . **77** J4
Selby Chase, Ruis. HA4 . . . **84** B2
Selby Cl, E6
off Linton Gdns **116** B5
Chessington KT9 . . . . . . **195** H7
Chislehurst BR7 . . . . **174** D6
Selby Gdns, Sthl. UB1 . . . **103** G4
Selby Grn, Cars. SM5 . . . . **185** H7
Selby Rd, E11 . . . . **96** E3
E13 . . . . **115** H5
N17 . . . . **60** B6
SE20 . . . . **188** D2
W5 . . . . **105** E4
Carshalton SM5 . . . . . . **185** H7
Selby St, E1 . . . . **13** J6
Selden Rd, SE15 . . . . **153** F2
Selden Wk, N7
off Durham Rd **93** F2
★**Selfridges**, W1 . . . . **16** C4
SELHURST, SE25 . . . . **188** B6
Selhurst Cl, SW19 . . . . . . **166** A1
Selhurst New Rd, SE25 . . **188** B6
Selhurst Pl, SE25 . . . . **188** B6
Selhurst Rd, N9 . . . . **60** A3
SE25 . . . . **188** B5
Selinas La, Dag. RM8 . . . . . **83** E7
Selkirk Rd, SW17 . . . . **167** H4
Twickenham TW2 . . . . . **161** J2
Sellers Cl, Borwd. WD6 . . . **38** C1
Sellers Hall Cl, N3 . . . . **56** D7
Sellincourt Rd, SW17 . . . . **167** H5
Sellindge Cl, Beck. BR3 . . **171** J7
Sellons Av, NW10 . . . . **107** F1
Sellwood Dr, Barn. EN5 . . . **40** A5
Sellwood St, SW2
off Tulse Hill **151** G7
Selsdon Av, S.Croy. CR2 . **202** A6
Selsdon Cl, Rom. RM5 . . . . **83** J1
Surbiton KT6 . . . . **181** H5
Selsdon Rd, E11 . . . . **79** G7
E13 . . . . **115** J1
NW2 . . . . **89** F2
SE27 . . . . **169** H3
South Croydon CR2 . . . **202** A5
Selsdon Rd Ind Est, S.Croy.
CR2 *off Selsdon Rd* . . . **202** A6
Selsdon Way, E14 . . . . **134** B3
Selsea Pl, N16
off Crossway **94** B5
Selsey Cres, Well. DA16 . . **158** D1
Selsey St, E14 . . . . **114** A5
Selvage La, NW7 . . . . **54** D5
Selway Cl, Pnr. HA5 . . . . . . **66** B4
Selwood Pl, SW7 . . . . **30** E3
Selwood Rd, Chess. KT9 . **195** G4
Croydon CR0 . . . . **202** E2
Sutton SM3 . . . . **198** C1
Selwood Ter, SW7 . . . . **31** E3
Selworthy Cl, E11 . . . . **79** G5
Selworthy Ho, SW11 . . . . **149** G1
Selworthy Rd, SE6 . . . . . . **171** J3
Selwyn Av, E4 . . . . **62** C6
Ilford IG3 . . . . **81** H6
Richmond TW9 . . . . **145** H3
Selwyn Cl, Houns. TW4 . . **143** E4
Selwyn Ct, SE3 . . . . **155** E3
Edgware HA8
off Camrose Av **54** B7
Selwyn Cres, Well. DA16 . **158** B4
Selwyn Rd, E3 . . . . **113** J2
E13 . . . . **115** H1
NW10 . . . . **88** D7
New Malden KT3 . . . . . **182** D5
Semley Pl, SW1 . . . . **32** C2
Semley Rd, SW16 . . . . **107** E2
Senate St, SE15 . . . . **153** F2
Senator Wk, SE28
off Broadwater Rd **137** G3
Sendall Ct, SW11 . . . . **149** G3
Seneca Rd, Th.Hth. CR7 . . **187** J4
Senga Rd, Wall. SM6 . . . . **200** A1
Senhouse Rd, Sutt. SM3 . **198** A3
Senior St, W2 . . . . **14** A1
Senlac Rd, SE12 . . . . **173** H1
Sennen Rd, Enf. EN1 . . . . . **44** C7
Sennen Wk, SE9 . . . . **174** B3
Senrab St, E1 . . . . **113** G6
Sentinel Cl, Nthlt. UB5 . . . **103** E4
Sentinel Sq, NW4 . . . . **71** J4
September Way, Stan.
HA7 . . . . **53** E6
Sequoia Cl, Bushey
(Bushey Hth) WD23
off Giant Tree Hill **52** A1
Sequoia Gdns, Orp.
BR6 . . . . **193** J7
Sequoia Pk, Pnr. HA5 . . . . . **51** H6
Serbin Cl, E10 . . . . **78** C7
Serenaders Rd, SW9 . . . . **151** G2
Serjeants Inn, EC4 . . . . **19** F4
Serle St, WC2 . . . . **18** D3
Sermon La, EC4 . . . . **19** J4
★**Serpentine, The**, W2 . . . . **23** G2
★**Serpentine Gall**, W2 . . . . **23** F2
Serpentine Rd, W2 . . . . **23** J2
Serviden Dr, Brom. BR1 . . **192** A1
Setchell Rd, SE1 . . . . **37** F1
Setchell Way, SE1 . . . . **37** F1
Seth St, SE16
off Swan Rd **133** F2
Seton Gdns, Dag. RM9 . . **100** C7
Settle Pt, E13
off London Rd **115** G2
Settle Rd, E13
off London Rd **115** G2
Settlers Ct, E14
off Newport Av **114** D7
Settles St, E1 . . . . **21** J2
Settrington Rd, SW6 . . . . **148** E2
Seven Acres, Cars. SM5 . . **199** H2
Northwood HA6 . . . . **50** A6
SEVEN KINGS, Ilf. IG3 . . . . **81** H7
Seven Kings Rd, Ilf. IG3 . . . **99** J2
Seven Kings Way, Kings.T.
KT2 . . . . **181** H1
Sevenoaks Cl, Bexh. DA7 . **159** J4
Sevenoaks Ho, SE25 . . . . **188** D3
Sevenoaks Rd, SE4 . . . . . **153** H6
Orpington BR6 . . . . **207** J5
Orpington (Grn St Grn)
BR6 . . . . **207** J7
Sevenoaks Way, Orp. BR5 . **176** C7
Sidcup DA14 . . . . **176** C7
Seven Sisters Rd, N4 . . . . . **93** F3
N7 . . . . **93** F3
N15 . . . . **75** J7
Seven Stars Cor, W12
off Goldhawk Rd **127** G3
Seven Stars Yd, E1 . . . . **21** G1
Seventh Av, E12 . . . . **98** C4
Hayes UB3 . . . . **122** A1
Severnake Cl, E14 . . . . . . **134** A4
Severn Dr, Esher KT10 . . . **194** D2
Severn Way, NW10 . . . . **89** F5
Severus Rd, SW11 . . . . . . **149** H4
Seville Ms, N1 . . . . **94** B7
Seville St, SW1 . . . . **24** A4
Sevington Rd, NW4 . . . . **71** H6
Sevington St, W9 . . . . **6** A6
Seward Rd, W7 . . . . **124** D2
Beckenham BR3 . . . . . . **189** G2
SEWARDSTONE, E4 . . . . . . **46** C1
SEWARDSTONEBURY, E4 . **47** E4
Sewardstone Gdns, E4 . . . **46** B5
Sewardstone Grn, E4 . . . . . **46** E4
Sewardstone Rd, E2 . . . . . **113** F2
E4 . . . . **46** B7
Seward St, EC1 . . . . **11** H5
Sewdley St, E5 . . . . **95** G3
Sewell Rd, SE2 . . . . **138** A3
Sewell St, E13 . . . . **115** G3
Sextant Av, E14 . . . . **134** D4
Sexton Ct, E14
off Newport Av **114** D7
Seymour Av, N17 . . . . **76** D2
Morden SM4 . . . . **184** A7
Seymour Cl, E.Mol. KT8 . . **179** J5
Loughton IG10 . . . . **48** B6
Pinner HA5 . . . . **67** F1
Seymour Ct, E4 . . . . **63** F2
Seymour Dr, Brom. BR2 . **206** C1
Seymour Gdns, SE4 . . . . . **153** H3
Feltham TW13 . . . . **160** C4
Ilford IG1 . . . . **98** C1
Ruislip HA4 . . . . **84** D1
Surbiton KT5 . . . . **181** J5
Twickenham TW1 . . . . . **144** E7
Seymour Ms, W1 . . . . **16** B3
Seymour Pl, SE25 . . . . **188** E4
W1 . . . . **15** J2
Seymour Rd, E4 . . . . **62** B1
E6 . . . . **116** A2
E10 . . . . **95** J1
N3 . . . . **57** E7
N8 . . . . **75** G5
N9 . . . . **61** E2
SW18 . . . . **148** C7
SW19 . . . . **166** A2
W4 . . . . **126** C4
Carshalton SM5 . . . . . . **200** A5
East Molesey KT8 . . . . . **179** J5
Hampton (Hmptn H.)
TW12 . . . . **161** J5
Kingston upon Thames
KT1 . . . . **181** G1
Mitcham CR4 . . . . **186** A7
Seymours, The, Loug.
IG10 . . . . **48** D1
Seymour St, SE18 . . . . **137** F3
W1 . . . . **15** J4
W2 . . . . **15** J4
Seymour Ter, SE20 . . . . . . **188** E1
Seymour Vil, SE20 . . . . . . **188** E1
Seymour Wk, SW10 . . . . . . **30** C5
Seyssel St, E14 . . . . **134** C4
Shaa Rd, W3 . . . . **106** D7
Shacklegate La, Tedd.
TW11 . . . . **162** B4
Shackleton Cl, SE23
off Featherstone Av . **170/171** E2
Shackleton Ct, E14
off Maritime Quay **134** A5
W12 . . . . **127** H2
Shackleton Rd, Sthl. UB1 . **103** F7

SHACKLEWELL, N16 . . . . . **94** C4
Shacklewell Grn, E8. . . . . . **94** C4
Shacklewell La, E8. . . . . . . **94** C5
Shacklewell Rd, N16 . . . . . **94** C4
Shacklewell Row, E8 . . . . . **94** C4
Shacklewell St, E2. . . . . . . **13** G5
Shadbolt Av, E4 . . . . **61** H5
Shadbolt Cl, Wor.Pk. KT4 . **197** F2
Shad Thames, SE1 . . . . **29** F2
SHADWELL, E1. . . . . **113** F7
Shadwell Ct, Nthlt. UB5 *off Shadwell Dr* **103** F2
Shadwell Dr, Nthlt. UB5. . **103** F3
Shadwell Gdns Est, E1 *off Martha St*. **113** F6
Shadwell Pierhead, E1 *off Glamis Rd* **113** F7
Shadwell Pl, E1 *off Sutton St* **113** F7
Shaef Way, Tedd. TW11 . . . **162** D7
Shafter Rd, Dag. RM10. . . . **101** J6
Shaftesbury, Loug. IG10 . . **48** A3
Shaftesbury Av, W1 . . . . . . **17** H5
WC2. . . . . **17** H5
Barnet EN5 . . . . **41** F4
Enfield EN3. . . . . **45** G2
Feltham TW14 . . . . **142** A6
Harrow HA2 . . . . **85** H1
Harrow (Kenton) HA3 . . . **69** G6
Southall UB2. . . . . **123** G4
Shaftesbury Circle, Har. HA2 *off Shaftesbury Av* **85** J1
Shaftesbury Ct, N1 *off Shaftesbury St*. . . . **112** A2
Shaftesbury Gdns, NW10. **107** E4
Shaftesbury Ms, SW4 *off Clapham Common S Side* **150** C5
W8 *off Stratford Rd*. . . . **128** D3
Shaftesbury Pl, W14 *off Warwick Rd* **128** C4
Shaftesbury Pt, E13 *off High St*. **115** H2
Shaftesbury Rd, E4 . . . . . . **62** D1
E7 . . . . **97** J7
E10 . . . . **96** A1
E17 . . . . **78** B6
N18 . . . . **60** B6
N19 . . . . **92** E1
Beckenham BR3 . . . . . . **189** J2
Carshalton SM5 . . . . . . **185** G7
Richmond TW9 . . . . **145** H3
Shaftesburys, The, Bark. IG11. . . . . **117** F1
Shaftesbury St, N1 . . . . . . **12** A2
Shaftesbury Way, Twick. TW2. . . . . **162** A3
Shaftesbury Waye, Hayes UB4 . . . . **102** B5
Shafto Ms, SW1. . . . . **23** J6
Shafton Rd, E9 . . . . **113** G1
Shakespeare Av, N11 . . . . . **58** C5
NW10. . . . . **106** D1
Feltham TW14 . . . . **142** A6
Hayes UB4. . . . . **102** D4
Shakespeare Cres, E12 . . . **98** C6
NW10. . . . . **106** D1
Shakespeare Dr, Har. HA3 . **69** J6
Shakespeare Gdns, N2 . . . **73** J4
Shakespeare Ho, N14 *off High St*. **58** D2
Shakespeare Rd, E17 . . . . . **77** G2
N3 *off Popes Dr*. **72** D1
NW7 . . . . **55** F4
SE24 . . . . **151** H5
W3. . . . . **126** C1
W7. . . . . **104** C7
Bexleyheath DA7 . . . . . **158** E1
★**Shakespeare's Globe Thea**, SE1 . . . . **19** J6
Shakespeare Sq, Ilf. IG6. . . **65** F6
Shakespeare Twr, EC2 . . . . **20** A1
Shakespeare Way, Felt. TW13. . . . . **160** C4
Shakspeare Ms, N16 *off Shakspeare Wk* **94** B4
Shakspeare Wk, N16 . . . . . **94** B4
Shalbourne Sq, E9. . . . . . . **95** J6
Shalcomb St, SW10. . . . . . **30** D6
Shalden Ho, SW15 *off Tunworth Cres* **147** F6
Shaldon Dr, Mord. SM4. . **184** B5
Ruislip HA4. . . . . **84** C3
Shaldon Rd, Edg. HA8 . . . . **69** J1
Shalfleet Dr, W10 . . . . **108** A7
Shalford Cl, Orp. BR6. . . . **207** F4
Shalimar Gdns, W3 . . . . . **106** C7
Shalimar Rd, W3 *off Hereford Rd*. **106** C7
Shallons Rd, SE9 . . . . **174** E4
Shalstone Rd, SW14 . . . . **146** B3
Shalston Vil, Surb. KT6 . . **181** J6
Shamrock Ho, SE26 *off Talisman Sq* **170** D4
Shamrock Rd, Croy. CR0 . **187** F6
Shamrock St, SW4. . . . . . **150** D3
Shamrock Way, N14. . . . . . **58** B1
Shandon Rd, SW4 . . . . . . **150** C6
Shand St, SE1 . . . . **28** D3
Shandy St, E1. . . . . **113** G5
Shanklin Gdns, Wat. WD19 . . . . **50** C4
Shanklin Rd, N8 . . . . **74** D5
N15 . . . . **76** D4
Shanklin Way, SE15 *off Pentridge St*. **132** C7
Shannon Cl, NW2 . . . . **90** A3
Southall UB2. . . . . **122** D5
Shannon Gro, SW9 . . . . . **151** F4
Shannon Pl, NW8 . . . . **7** H1
Shannon Way, Beck. BR3 . **172** B6
Shap Cres, Cars. SM5 . . . **199** J1
Shapland Way, N13 . . . . . . **59** F5
Shapwick Cl, N11 *off Friern Barnet Rd* . . . **57** J5
Shardcroft Av, SE24 . . . . . **151** H5
Shardeloes Rd, SE4 . . . . . **153** J3
SE14 . . . . **153** J3
Sharland Cl, Th.Hth. CR7 *off Dunheved Rd N*. . . **187** G6
Sharman Ct, Sid. DA14 . . **176** A4
Sharnbrooke Cl, Well. DA16 . . . . **158** C3
Sharon Cl, Surb. KT6 . . . . **195** G1
Sharon Gdns, E9 . . . . **113** F1
Sharon Rd, W4. . . . . **126** D5
Enfield EN3. . . . . **45** H2
Sharpe Cl, W7 *off Templeman Rd*. . . . **104** C5
Sharpleshall St, NW1. . . . . **91** J7
Sharpness Cl, Hayes UB4 . **102** E5
Sharratt St, SE15 . . . . **133** F6
Sharsted St, SE17 . . . . **35** G4
Sharvel La, Nthlt. UB5 . . . **102** A1
Shavers Pl, SW1. . . . . **17** H6
Shaw Av, Bark. IG11 . . . . . **118** E2
Shawbrooke Rd, SE9. . . . . **155** J5
Shawbury Rd, SE22. . . . . . **152** C5
Shaw Cl, SE28 . . . . **138** B1
Bushey (Bushey Hth) WD23 . . . . **52** B2
Shaw Ct, SW11 . . . . **149** G3
Shaw Dr, Walt. KT12 . . . . **178** C7
Shawfield Ct, West Dr. UB7 . . . . **120** B3
Shawfield Pk, Brom. BR1. **192** A2
Shawfield St, SW3. . . . . . . **31** H4
Shawford Ct, SW15 . . . . . **147** G7
Shawford Rd, Epsom KT19 . . . . **196** D6
Shaw Gdns, Bark. IG11. . . **118** E2
Shaw Rd, SE22 . . . . **152** B4
Bromley BR1. . . . . **173** F3
Enfield EN3. . . . . **45** G1
Shaws Cotts, SE23. . . . . . **171** H3
Shaw Sq, E17. . . . . **77** H1
Shaw Way, Wall. SM6 . . . **200** E7
Shearing Dr, Cars. SM5 *off Stavordale Rd* **185** F7
Shearling Way, N7 . . . . **93** E6
Shearman Rd, SE3. . . . . . . **155** F4
Shearsmith Ho, E1. . . . . . . **21** J5
Shearwater Cl, Bark. IG11. . . . . **118** A3
Shearwater Rd, Sutt. SM1. . . . . **198** C5
Shearwater Way, Hayes UB4 . . . . **102** D6
Sheaveshill Av, NW9 . . . . . **71** E4
Sheen Common Dr, Rich. TW10. . . . . **146** A4
Sheen Ct, Rich. TW10. . . . **146** A4
Sheen Ct Rd, Rich. TW10 . **146** A4
Sheendale Rd, Rich. TW9 . **145** J4
Sheenewood, SE26 . . . . . **171** E5
Sheen Gate Gdns, SW14 . **146** C4
Sheen Gro, N1 *off Richmond Av* **111** G1
Sheen La, SW14. . . . . **146** C3
Sheen Pk, Rich. TW9 . . . . **145** J4
Sheen Rd, Orp. BR5. . . . . **193** J4
Richmond TW9, TW10 . . **145** H5
Sheen Way, Wall. SM6 . . . **201** F5
Sheen Wd, SW14 . . . . **146** C5
Sheepcote Cl, Houns. TW5. . . . . **122** A7
Sheepcote La, SW11 . . . . **149** J2
Sheepcote Rd, Har. HA1 . . **68** C6
Sheepcotes Rd, Rom. RM6. . . . . **82** D4
Sheephouse Way, N.Mal. KT3 . . . . **182** E7
Sheep La, E8. . . . . **112** E1
Sheep Wk Ms, SW19 . . . . **166** A6
Sheerness Ms, E16. . . . . . **137** E2
Sheerwater Rd, E16 . . . . . **116** A5
Sheffield Rd, Houns. (Hthrw Air.) TW6 *off Southern Perimeter Rd*. **141** G5
Sheffield Sq, E3 *off Malmesbury Rd* . . . **113** J3
Sheffield St, WC2. . . . . **18** C4
Sheffield Ter, W8. . . . . . . **128** D1
Shefton Ri, Nthwd. HA6 . . **50** A7
Shelbourne Cl, Pnr. HA5 . . **67** F3
Shelbourne Pl, Beck. BR3. **171** J7
Shelbourne Rd, N17. . . . . . **76** E2
Shelburne Dr, Houns. TW4 *off Hanworth Rd* **143** G6
Shelburne Rd, N7. . . . . **93** F4
Shelbury Cl, Sid. DA14. . . **176** A3
Shelbury Rd, SE22 . . . . . . **153** E5
Sheldon Av, N6 . . . . **73** H7
Ilford IG5. . . . . **80** E2
Sheldon Cl, SE12 . . . . **155** H5
SE20 . . . . **189** E1
Sheldon Rd, N18 . . . . **60** B4
NW2 . . . . **90** A4
Bexleyheath DA7 . . . . . **159** F1
Dagenham RM9 . . . . . . **100** E7
Sheldon Sq, W2 . . . . **14** D2
Sheldon St, Croy. CR0 . . . **201** J3
Sheldrake Cl, E16. . . . . . . **136** C1
Sheldrake Pl, W8 . . . . **128** C2
Sheldrick Cl, SW19. . . . . . **185** G2
Shelduck Cl, E15 . . . . **97** F5
Sheldwich Ter, Brom. BR2. **192** B6
Shelford Pl, N16 *off Stoke Newington Ch St*. **94** A3
Shelford Ri, SE19 . . . . **170** C7
Shelford Rd, Barn. EN5 . . . **39** J6
Shelgate Rd, SW11. . . . . . **149** H5
★**Shell Cen**, SE1 . . . . **26** D2
Shell Cl, Brom. BR2 . . . . . **192** C6
Shellduck Cl, NW9 *off Swan Dr*. **70/71** E2
Shelley Av, E12. . . . . **98** B6
Greenford UB6 . . . . **104** A3
Shelley Cl, SE15. . . . . **153** E2
Edgware HA8 . . . . **54** A4
Greenford UB6 . . . . **104** A3
Hayes UB4. . . . . **102** A5
Orpington BR6 . . . . **207** H3
Shelley Cres, Houns. TW5 . **142** D2
Southall UB1. . . . . **103** F6
Shelley Dr, Well. DA16 . . . **157** H1
Shelley Gdns, Wem. HA0. . **87** F2
Shelley Gro, Loug. IG10. . . **48** C4
Shelley Rd, NW10 . . . . . . **106** D1
Shelley Way, SW19. . . . . . **167** G6
Shellgrove Est, N16 . . . . . . **94** B5
Shellness Rd, E5 . . . . **95** E5
Shell Rd, SE13 . . . . **154** B3
Shellwood Rd, SW11 . . . . **149** J2
Shelmerdine Cl, E3. . . . . . **114** A5
Shelton Rd, SW19 . . . . . . **184** D1
Shelton St, WC2. . . . . **18** A4
Shenfield Ho, SE18 *off Shooter's Hill Rd* . . **136** A7
Shenfield Rd, Wdf.Grn. IG8. . . . . **63** H7
Shenfield St, N1. . . . . **12** E2
Shenley Rd, SE5. . . . . **152** B1
Borehamwood WD6 . . . . **38** A4
Hounslow TW5 . . . . **142** E1
Shepcot Ho, N14 . . . . **42** C6
Shepherd Cl, W1 *off Lees Pl* **110** A7
Feltham (Han.) TW13. . . **160** E4
Shepherdess Pl, N1 . . . . . . **12** A3
Shepherdess Wk, N1 . . . . . **12** A1
Shepherd Mkt, W1. . . . . . . **24** D1
SHEPHERD'S BUSH, W12 . . . . **127** J1
Shepherds Bush Grn, W12. . . . . **127** J2
Shepherds Bush Mkt, W12. . . . . **127** J2
Shepherds Bush Pl, W12 . **128** A2
Shepherds Bush Rd, W6 . **127** J4
Shepherds Cl, N6. . . . . **74** B6
Orpington BR6 *off Stapleton Rd* **207** J3
Romford RM6. . . . . **82** D5
Stanmore HA7 . . . . **52** E5
Shepherds Ct, W12 *off Shepherds Bush Grn*. **128** A2
Shepherds Grn, Chis. BR7. **175** G7
Shepherds Hill, N6. . . . . . . **74** B6
Shepherds La, E9. . . . . **95** G5
SE28 *off Hill Vw Dr* **137** H1
Shepherds Path, Nthlt. UB5 *off Fortunes Mead*. . **84/85** E6
Shepherd's Pl, W1 . . . . **16** B5
Shepherd St, W1 . . . . **24** D2
Shepherds Wk, NW2 . . . . . **89** G2
NW3 . . . . **91** G5
Bushey (Bushey Hth) WD23 . . . . **52** A2
Shepherds Way, S.Croy. CR2 . . . . **203** G7
Shepiston La, Hayes UB3 . **121** G4
West Drayton UB7 . . . . **121** F4
Shepley Cl, Cars. SM5 . . . **200** A3
Sheppard Cl, Enf. EN1 . . . . **45** E1
Kingston upon Thames KT1 *off Beaufort Rd* . . **181** H4
Sheppard Dr, SE16. . . . . . **132** E5
Sheppard St, E16 . . . . **115** F4
Shepperton Cl, Borwd. WD6 . . . . **38** D1
Shepperton Rd, N1. . . . . . **111** J1
Orpington BR5 . . . . **193** F6
Sheppey Gdns, Dag. RM9 *off Sheppey Rd* **100** C7
Sheppey Rd, Dag. RM9 . . **100** B7
Sheppey Wk, N1 *off Ashby Gro* **93** J7
Sherard Ct, N7 *off Manor Gdns*. . . . **92/93** E3
Sherard Rd, SE9. . . . . **156** B5
Sheraton Business Cen, Grnf. UB6 . . . . **105** E2
Sheraton St, W1. . . . . **17** H4
Sherborne Av, Enf. EN3 . . . **45** F2
Southall UB2. . . . . **123** G4
Sherborne Cl, Hayes UB4 . **102** C6
Sherborne Cres, Cars. SM5. . . . . **185** H7
Sherborne Gdns, NW9. . . . **70** A3
W13. . . . . **105** E6
Sherborne La, EC4. . . . . . . **20** B5
Sherborne Rd, Chess. KT9 . . . . **195** H5
Feltham TW14 . . . . **141** G7
Orpington BR5 . . . . **193** J4
Sutton SM3. . . . . **198** D2
Sherborne St, N1 . . . . **112** A1
Sherboro Rd, N15 *off Ermine Rd* **76** C6
Sherbourne Pl, Stan. HA7 . **52** D6
Sherbrooke Cl, Bexh. DA6 . . . . **159** G4
Sherbrooke Rd, SW6 . . . . **128** C7
Sherbrooke Way, Wor.Pk. KT4 . . . . **183** H7
Sherbrook Gdns, N21 . . . . **43** H7
Shere Cl, Chess. KT9 . . . . **195** G5
Sheredan Rd, E4 . . . . **62** D5
Shere Rd, Ilf. IG2 . . . . **80** D5
Sherfield Cl, N.Mal. KT3 . **182** B4
Sherfield Gdns, SW15 . . . **147** F6
Sheridan Ct, Houns. TW4 *off Vickers Way* **143** F5
Northolt UB5. . . . . **85** H5
Sheridan Cres, Chis. BR7 . **192** E2
Sheridan Gdns, Har. HA3. . **69** G6
Sheridan Ms, E11 *off Woodbine Pl* **79** G6
Sheridan Pl, SW13 *off Brookwood Av*. . . . **147** F2
Hampton TW12 . . . . **179** H1
Sheridan Rd, E7 . . . . **97** F3
E12 . . . . **98** B5
SW19. . . . . **184** C1
Belvedere DA17 . . . . . . **139** G4
Bexleyheath DA7 . . . . . **158** E3
Richmond TW10 . . . . . . **163** F3
Sheridan St, E1 *off Watney St* **112/113** E6
Sheridan Ter, Nthlt. UB5 *off Whitton Av W*. **85** H5
Sheridan Wk, NW11 . . . . . . **72** D6
Carshalton SM5 *off Carshalton Pk Rd*. . **199** J5
Sheridan Way, Beck. BR3 *off Turners Meadow Way* **189** J1
Sheringham Av, E12. . . . . . **98** C4
N14 . . . . **42** D5
Feltham TW13 . . . . **160** A3
Romford RM7. . . . . **83** J6
Twickenham TW2 . . . . . **161** F1
Sheringham Dr, Bark. IG11 . **99** J5

Sheringham Rd, N7 93 F6
SE20 189 E3
Sheringham Twr, Sthl. UB1 103 H7
Sherington Av, Pnr. HA5 51 G7
Sherington Rd, SE7 135 H6
Sherland Rd, Twick. TW1 162 C1
Sherlies Av, Orp. BR6 207 H2
★**Sherlock Holmes Mus**, NW1 8 A6
Sherlock Ms, W1 16 B1
Sherman Rd, Brom. BR1 191 G1
Shernhall St, E17 78 C5
Sherrard Rd, E7 97 J6
E12 98 A6
Sherrards Way, Barn. EN5 40 D5
Sherrick Grn Rd, NW10 89 H5
Sherriff Rd, NW6 90 D6
Sherringham Av, N17 76 D2
Sherrin Rd, E10 96 A4
Sherrock Gdns, NW4 71 G4
Sherry Ms, Bark. IG11
off Cecil Av 99 G7
Sherwin Rd, SE14 153 G1
Sherwood Av, E18 79 H3
SW16 168 D7
Greenford UB6 86 B6
Hayes UB4 102 B4
Sherwood Cl, SW13
off Lower Common S 147 H3
W13 124 E1
Bexley DA5 158 C6
Sherwood Gdns, E14 134 A4
SE16 37 J4
Barking IG11 99 G7
Sherwood Pk Av, Sid. DA15 158 A7
Sherwood Pk Rd, Mitch. CR4 186 C4
Sutton SM1 198 D5
Sherwood Rd, NW4 71 J3
SW19 166 C7
Croydon CR0 188 E7
Hampton (Hmptn H.) TW12 161 J5
Harrow HA2 85 J2
Ilford IG6 81 G4
Welling DA16 157 H2
Sherwood St, N20 57 G3
W1 17 G5
Sherwood Ter, N20
off Green Rd 57 G3
Sherwood Way, W.Wick. BR4 204 B2
Shetland Cl, Borwd. WD6
off Percheron Rd 38 D6
Shetland Rd, E3 113 J2
Shield Dr, Brent. TW8 124 D6
Shieldhall St, SE2 138 C4
Shifford Path, SE23 171 G3
Shillibeer Pl, W1 15 H1
Shillibeer Wk, Chig. IG7 65 J3
Shillingford Cl, NW7 56 A7
Shillingford St, N1
off Cross St 93 H7
Shinfield St, W12 107 J6
Shinglewell Rd, Erith DA8 139 G7
Shinners Cl, SE25 188 D5
Ship All, W4
off Thames Rd 126 A6
Ship & Mermaid Row, SE1 28 C3
Shipka Rd, SW12 168 B1
Ship La, SW14 146 C2
Shipman Rd, E16 115 H6
SE23 171 G2
Ship St, SE8 154 A1
Ship Tavern Pas, EC3 20 D5
Shipton Cl, Dag. RM8 100 D3
Shipton St, E2 13 G3
Shipwright Rd, SE16 133 H2
Shipwright Yd, SE1 28 D2
Ship Yd, E14
off Napier Av 134 B5
Shirburn Cl, SE23
off Tyson Rd 153 F7
Shirbutt St, E14 114 B7
Shirebrook Rd, SE3 156 A3
Shire Ct, Epsom KT17 197 F7
Erith DA18
off St. John Fisher Rd 138 D3
Shirehall Cl, NW4 72 A6
Shirehall Gdns, NW4 72 A6
Shirehall La, NW4 72 A6
Shirehall Pk, NW4 72 A6
Shire Horse Way, Islw. TW7 144 C3
Shire La, Kes. BR2 206 C7
Shire La, Orp. BR6 207 G6
Shire Pl, SW18
off Swaffield Rd 148/149 E7
Shires, The, Rich. TW10 163 H4
Shirland Ms, W9 108 C3
Shirland Rd, W9 108 D3
SHIRLEY, Croy. CR0 203 G3
Shirley Av, Bex. DA5 158 D7
Croydon CR0 203 F1
Sutton SM1 199 H4
Shirley Ch Rd, Croy. CR0 203 G3
Shirley Cl, E17
off Addison Rd 78 B5
Hounslow TW3 143 J5
Shirley Ct, Croy. CR0 203 G3
Shirley Cres, Beck. BR3 189 H4
Shirley Dr, Houns. TW3 143 J5
Shirley Gdns, W7 124 C1
Barking IG11 99 H6
Shirley Gro, N9 45 F7
SW11 150 A3
Shirley Hills Rd, Croy. CR0 203 G5
Shirley Ho Dr, SE7 135 J7
Shirley Oaks Rd, Croy. CR0 203 G1
Shirley Pk Rd, Croy. CR0 203 E1
Shirley Rd, E15 97 E7
W4 126 D2
Croydon CR0 189 E7
Enfield EN2 43 J3
Sidcup DA15 175 H3
Shirley St, E16 115 F6
Shirley Way, Croy. CR0 203 H3
Shirlock Rd, NW3 91 J4
Shirwell Cl, NW7 56 A7
Shobden Rd, N17 76 A1
Shobroke Cl, NW2 89 J3
Shoebury Rd, E6 98 C7
Shoe La, EC4 19 F3
Sholto Rd, Houns. (Hthrw Air.) TW6 140 C5
Shooters Av, Har. HA3 69 F4
SHOOTER'S HILL, SE18 157 F1
Shooter's Hill, SE18 156 D1
Welling DA16 156 D1
Shooter's Hill Rd, SE3 155 F1
SE10 154 D1
SE18 135 H7
Shooters Rd, Enf. EN2 43 H1
Shoot Up Hill, NW2 90 B5
Shore Cl, Felt. TW14 142 A7
Hampton TW12
off Stewart Cl 160/161 E5
SHOREDITCH, E1 13 F6
Shoreditch High St, E1 13 F6
Shoreditch Ho, N1 12 C4
Shore Gro, Felt. TW13 161 G2
Shoreham Cl, SW18
off Ram St 148/149 E5
Bexley DA5 176 D1
Croydon CR0 189 F6
Shoreham Rd E, Houns. (Hthrw Air.) TW6 140 B5
Shoreham Rd W, Houns. (Hthrw Air.) TW6 140 B5
Shoreham Way, Brom. BR2 191 G6
Shore Pl, E9 95 F7
Shore Rd, E9 95 F7
Shorncliffe Rd, SE1 37 F3
Shorndean St, SE6 172 C1
Shorne Cl, Sid. DA15 158 B6
Shornefield Cl, Brom. BR1 192 D3
Shornells Way, SE2
off Willrose Cres 138 C5
Shorrolds Rd, SW6 128 C7
Shortcroft Rd, Epsom KT17 197 F7
Shortcrofts Rd, Dag. RM9 101 F6
Shorter St, E1 21 F5
Shortgate, N12 56 C4
Short Hedges, Houns. TW3, TW5 143 H1
Short Hill, Har. HA1
off High St 86 B1
SHORTLANDS, Brom. BR1 190 E3
Shortlands, W6 128 A4
Hayes UB3 121 G6
Shortlands Cl, N18 60 A3
Belvedere DA17 139 F3
Shortlands Gdns, Brom. BR2 191 E2
Shortlands Gro, Brom. BR2 190 D3
Shortlands Rd, E10 78 B7
Bromley BR2 190 D3
Shortlands Rd, Kings.T. KT2 163 J7
Short Path, SE18
off Westdale Rd 136/137 E6
Short Rd, E11 96 E2
E15 114 D1
W4 126 E6
Hounslow (Hthrw Air.) TW6 140 B6
Shorts Cft, NW9 70 B4
Shorts Gdns, WC2 18 A4
Shorts Rd, Cars. SM5 199 H4
Short St, NW4
off New Brent St 71 J4
SE1 27 F3
Short Wall, E15 114 C3
Shortway, N12 57 H6
Short Way, SE9 156 B3
Twickenham TW2 143 J7
Shotfield, Wall. SM6 200 B6
Shott Cl, Sutt. SM1
off Turnpike La 199 F5
Shottendane Rd, SW6 148 D1
Shottery Cl, SE9 174 B3
Shottfield Av, SW14 146 E4
Shoulder of Mutton All, E14 *off Narrow St* 113 H7
Shouldham St, W1 15 H2
Showers Way, Hayes UB3 122 A1
Shrapnel Cl, SE18 136 B7
Shrapnel Rd, SE9 156 C3
Shrewsbury Av, SW14 146 C4
Harrow HA3 69 H4
Shrewsbury Cl, Surb. KT6 195 H2
Shrewsbury Ct, EC1
off Whitecross St 111 J4
Shrewsbury Cres, NW10 106 D1
Shrewsbury La, SE18 156 E1
Shrewsbury Ms, W2
off Chepstow Rd 108 D5
Shrewsbury Rd, E7 98 A5
N11 58 C6
W2 108 D6
Beckenham BR3 189 H3
Carshalton SM5 185 H6
Hounslow (Hthrw Air.) TW6 141 F6
Shrewsbury St, W10 107 J4
Shrewsbury Wk, Islw. TW7
off South St 144 D3
Shrewton Rd, SW17 167 J7
Shroffold Rd, Brom. BR1 173 E4
Shropshire Cl, Mitch. CR4 187 E4
Shropshire Ho, N18
off Cavendish Rd 60/61 E5
Shropshire Pl, WC1 9 G6
Shropshire Rd, N22 59 F7
Shroton St, NW1 15 G1
Shrubberies, The, E18 79 G2
Chigwell IG7 65 F5
Shrubbery, The, E11 79 H5
Shrubbery Cl, N1
off St. Paul St 111 J1
Shrubbery Gdns, N21 43 H7
Shrubbery Rd, N9 60 D3
SW16 168 E4
Southall UB1 123 F1
Shrubland Gro, Wor.Pk. KT4 197 J3
Shrubland Rd, E8 112 D1
E10 78 A7
E17 78 A5
Shrublands Av, Croy. CR0 204 A4
Shrublands Cl, N20 57 G1
SE26 171 F3
Chigwell IG7 65 F6
Shrubsall Cl, SE9 174 B1
Shuna Wk, N1
off St. Paul's Rd 94 A6
Shurland Av, Barn. EN4 41 G6
Shurland Gdns, SE15 37 G7
Shurlock Dr, Orp. BR6 207 F4
Shuters Sq, W14
off Sun Rd 128 C5
Shuttle Cl, Sid. DA15 157 J7
Shuttlemead, Bex. DA5 159 F7
Shuttle St, E1 13 H6
Shuttleworth Rd, SW11 149 H2
Siamese Ms, N3
off Station Rd 72 D1
Sibella Rd, SW4 150 D2
Sibley Cl, Bexh. DA6 159 E5
Bromley BR1
off Southborough Rd 192 B5
Sibley Gro, E12 98 B7
Sibthorpe Rd, SE12 155 H6
Sibton Rd, Cars. SM5 185 H7
Sicilian Av, WC1 18 B2
Sidbury St, SW6 148 B1
SIDCUP, DA14 & DA15 175 J4
Sidcup Bypass, Chis. BR7 175 H4
Orpington BR5 176 D7
Sidcup DA14 175 H4
Sidcup High St, Sid. DA14 176 A4
Sidcup Hill, Sid. DA14 176 B4
Sidcup Hill Gdns, Sid. DA14
off Sidcup Hill 176 C5
Sidcup Pl, Sid. DA14 176 A5
Sidcup Rd, SE9 156 A7
SE12 155 H5
Sidcup Tech Cen, Sid. DA14 176 D5
Siddeley Dr, Houns. TW4 142 E3
Siddons La, NW1 8 A6
Siddons Rd, N17 76 D1
SE23 171 H2
Croydon CR0 201 G3
Side Rd, E17 77 J5
Sidewood Rd, SE9 175 G1
Sidford Pl, SE1 26 D6
Sidi Ct, N15
off Milton Rd 75 H3
Sidings, The, E11 96 C1
Loughton IG10 48 B6
Sidings Ms, N7 93 G3
Sidmouth Av, Islw. TW7 144 B2
Sidmouth Cl, Wat. WD19 50 B2
Sidmouth Dr, Ruis. HA4 84 A3
Sidmouth Par, NW2
off Sidmouth Rd 89 J7
Sidmouth Rd, E10 96 C3
NW2 89 J7
Welling DA16 138 C7
Sidmouth St, WC1 10 B4
Sidney Av, N13 59 F5
Sidney Elson Way, E6
off Edwin Av 116 D2
Sidney Gdns, Brent. TW8 125 F6
Sidney Gro, EC1 11 G2
Sidney Rd, E7 97 G3
N22 59 F7
SE25 188 D5
SW9 151 F2
Beckenham BR3 189 H2
Harrow HA2 67 J3
Twickenham TW1 144 D6
Walton-on-Thames KT12 178 A7
Sidney Sq, E1 113 F6
Sidney St, E1 113 E5
Sidworth St, E8 95 E7
Siebert Rd, SE3 135 G6
Siemens Rd, SE18 136 A3
Sigdon Rd, E8 94 D5
Sigers, The, Pnr. HA5 66 B6
Signmakers Yd, NW1
off Delancey St 110 B1
Sigrist Sq, Kings.T. KT2 181 H1
Silbury Av, Mitch. CR4 185 H1
Silbury Ho, SE26
off Sydenham Hill 170 D3
Silbury St, N1 12 B3
Silchester Rd, W10 108 A6
Silecroft Rd, Bexh. DA7 159 G1
Silesia Bldgs, E8
off London La 94/95 E7
Silex St, SE1 27 H4
Silk Cl, SE12 155 G5
Silkfield Rd, NW9 71 E5
Silkin Ho, Wat. WD19 50 C3
Silk Mills Pas, SE13
off Russett Way 154 B2
Silk Mills Path, SE13
off Lewisham Rd 154 C2
Silk Mills Sq, E9 95 J6
Silkstream Rd, Edg. HA8 70 C1
Silk St, EC2 20 A1
Silsoe Rd, N22 75 F2
Silver Birch Av, E4 61 J6
Silver Birch Cl, N11 58 A6
SE6 171 J3
SE28 138 A1
Silver Birch Gdns, E6 116 C4
Silver Birch Ms, Ilf. IG6
off Fencepiece Rd 65 F6
Silverbirch Wk, NW3
off Queen's Cres 92 A6
Silvercliffe Gdns, Barn. EN4 41 H4
Silver Cl, SE14
off Southerngate Way 133 H7
Harrow HA3 52 A7
Silver Cres, W4 126 B4
Silverdale, SE26 171 F4
Enfield EN2 43 E4
Silverdale Av, Ilf. IG3 81 H5

Silverdale Cl, W7 124 B1
Northolt UB5 85 F5
Sutton SM1 198 C4
Silverdale Dr, SE9 174 B2
Sunbury-on-Thames TW16 178 B2
Silverdale Gdns, Hayes UB3 122 A2
Silverdale Rd, E4 62 D6
Bexleyheath DA7 159 H2
Hayes UB3 122 A2
Orpington (Petts Wd) BR5 193 F4
Silvergate, Epsom KT19 196 C5
Silverhall St, Islw. TW7 144 D3
Silverholme Cl, Har. HA3 69 G7
Silver Jubilee Way, Houns. TW4 142 B2
Silverland St, E16 136 C1
Silver La, W.Wick. BR4 204 D2
Silverleigh Rd, Th.Hth. CR7 187 F4
Silvermead, E18 *off Churchfields* 63 G7
Silvermere Dr, N18 61 G6
Silvermere Rd, SE6 154 B6
Silver Pl, W1 17 G5
Silver Rd, SE13 154 B3
W12 108 A7
Silver Spring Cl, Erith DA8 139 H6
Silverston Way, Stan. HA7 53 F6
Silver St, N18 60 B4
Enfield EN1 44 A3
Silverthorne Rd, SW8 150 B2
Silverthorn Gdns, E4 62 A2
Silverton Rd, W6 128 A6
SILVERTOWN, E16 135 J2
Silvertown Way, E16 115 F6
Silvertree La, Grnf. UB6 *off Cowgate Rd* 104 A3
Silver Wk, SE16 133 J1
Silver Way, Rom. RM7 83 H3
Silverwood Cl, Beck. BR3 172 A7
Silvester Rd, SE22 152 C5
Silvester St, SE1 28 A4
Silvocea Way, E14 114 D6
Silwood Est, SE16 133 F4
Silwood St, SE16 133 F4
Simla Ho, SE1 28 C4
Simmil Rd, Esher (Clay.) KT10 194 B5
Simmons Cl, N20 57 H1
Chessington KT9 195 F7
Simmons La, E4 62 D2
Simmons Rd, SE18 136 E5
Simmons Way, N20 57 H2
Simms Cl, Cars. SM5 199 H2
Simms Gdns, N2 73 F2
Simms Rd, SE1 37 H2
Simnel Rd, SE12 155 H7
Simon Cl, W11 *off Portobello Rd* 108 C7
Simonds Rd, E10 96 A2
Simone Cl, Brom. BR1 102 A1
Simons Wk, E15 *off Waddington Rd* 96 D5
Simpson Cl, N21 *off Macleod Rd* 42/43 E5
Simpson Dr, W3 106 D6
Simpson Rd, Houns. TW4 143 F6
Richmond TW10 163 F4
Simpsons Rd, E14 114 B7
Bromley BR2 191 G3
Simpson St, SW11 149 H2
Simrose Ct, SW18 *off Wandsworth High St* 148 D5
Sims Wk, SE3 155 F4
Sinclair Ct, Beck. BR3 172 A7
Sinclair Gdns, W14 128 A2
Sinclair Gro, NW11 72 A6
Sinclair Pl, SE4 154 A6
Sinclair Rd, E4 61 J5
W14 128 A2
Sinclare Cl, Enf. EN1 44 C1
Singapore Rd, W13 124 D1
Singer St, EC2 12 C4
Singleton Cl, SW17 167 J7
Croydon CR0 *off St. Saviours Rd* 187 J7
Singleton Rd, Dag. RM9 101 F5
Singleton Scarp, N12 56 D5
Sinnott Rd, E17 77 G1
Sion Rd, Twick. TW1 162 E1
SIPSON, West Dr. UB7 120 D6
Sipson Cl, West Dr. UB7 120 D6
Sipson La, Hayes UB3 120 D6
West Drayton UB7 120 D6
Sipson Rd, West Dr. UB7 120 D5
Sipson Way, West Dr. UB7 120 D7
Sir Alexander Cl, W3 127 F1
Sir Alexander Rd, W3 127 F1
Sir Cyril Black Way, SW19 166 D7
Sirdar Rd, N22 75 H3
W11 108 A7
Mitcham CR4 *off Grenfell Rd* 168 A6
Sirinham Pt, SW8 34 D6
Sirius Rd, Nthwd. HA6 50 A5
Sir John Kirk Cl, SE5 35 J7
★**Sir John Soane's Mus**, WC2 *off Lincoln's Inn Flds* 18 C3
Sir Thomas More Est, SW3 31 F6
Sise La, EC4 20 B4
Siskin Cl, Borwd. WD6 38 A4
Sisley Rd, Bark. IG11 117 H1
Sispara Gdns, SW18 148 C6
Sissinghurst Rd, Croy. CR0 188 D7
Sissulu Ct, E6 115 J1
Sister Mabel's Way, SE15 37 H7
Sisters Av, SW11 149 J4
Sistova Rd, SW12 168 B1
Sisulu Pl, SW9 151 G3
Sittingbourne Av, Enf. EN1 44 A6
Sitwell Gro, Stan. HA7 52 C5
Siverst Cl, Nthlt. UB5 85 H6
Sivill Ho, E2 13 G3
Siviter Way, Dag. RM10 101 H7
Siward Rd, N17 76 A1
SW17 167 F3
Bromley BR2 191 H3
Six Acres Est, N4 93 G2
Six Bridges Trd Est, SE1 37 J4
Sixth Av, E12 98 C4
W10 108 B3
Hayes UB3 121 J1
Sixth Cross Rd, Twick. TW2 161 J3
Skardu Rd, NW2 90 B5
Skeena Hill, SW18 148 B7
Skeffington Rd, E6 116 B1
Skeffington St, SE18 137 F3
Skelbrook St, SW18 167 E2
Skelgill Rd, SW15 148 C4
Skelley Rd, E15 97 F7
Skelton Cl, E8 *off Buttermere Wk* 94 C6
Skelton Rd, E7 97 G6
Skeltons La, E10 78 B7
Skelwith Rd, W6 127 J6
Skenfrith Ho, SE15 *off Commercial Way* 132/133 E6
Skerne Rd, Kings.T. KT2 181 G1
Skerne Wk, Kings.T. KT2 181 G1
Sketchley Gdns, SE16 133 G5
Sketty Rd, Enf. EN1 44 B3
Skiers St, E15 114 E1
Skiffington Cl, SW2 169 G1
Skinner Ct, E2 *off Parmiter St* 112/113 E2
Skinner Pl, SW1 32 B2
★**Skinners' Hall**, EC4 *off Dowgate Hill* 20 B5
Skinners La, EC4 20 A5
Hounslow TW5 143 H1
Skinner St, EC1 11 F4
Skipsea Ho, SW18 *off Fitzhugh Gro* 149 G6
Skipsey Av, E6 116 C3
Skipton Cl, N11 *off Ribblesdale Av* 58 A6
Skipton Dr, Hayes UB3 121 F3
Skipworth Rd, E9 113 F1
Skomer Wk, N1 *off Ashby Gro* 93 J6
Skylines Village, E14 134 C2
Sky Peals Rd, Wdf.Grn. IG8 78 D1
Skyport Dr, West Dr. UB7 120 A7
Slade, The, SE18 137 H6
Sladebrook Rd, SE3 156 A3
Sladedale Rd, SE18 137 H5
Slade Ho, Houns. TW4 143 F6
Slades Cl, Enf. EN2 43 G3
Slades Dr, Chis. BR7 175 F3
Slades Gdns, Enf. EN2 43 G2
Slades Hill, Enf. EN2 43 G3
Slades Ri, Enf. EN2 43 G3
Slade Twr, E10 96 B2
Slade Wk, SE17 35 H6
Slagrove Pl, SE13 154 A5
Slaidburn St, SW10 30 D6
Slaithwaite Rd, SE13 154 C4
Slaney Pl, N7 *off Hornsey Rd* 93 G5
Slater Cl, SE18 *off Woolwich New Rd* 136 D5
Slattery Rd, Felt. TW13 160 C1
Sleaford Grn, Wat. WD19 50 D3
Sleaford Ho, E3 *off Chiltern Rd* 114 A4
Sleaford St, SW8 33 F7
Slievemore Cl, SW4 *off Voltaire Rd* 150 D3
Slingsby Pl, WC2 18 A5
Slippers Pl, SE16 133 E3
Sloane Av, SW3 31 G1
Sloane Ct E, SW3 32 B3
Sloane Ct W, SW3 32 B3
Sloane Gdns, SW1 32 B2
Orpington BR6 207 F3
Sloane Sq, SW1 32 B2
Sloane St, SW1 24 A5
Sloane Ter, SW1 32 A1
Sloane Wk, Croy. CR0 189 J6
Slocum Cl, SE28 118 C7
Slough La, NW9 70 C6
Sly St, E1 *off Cannon St Rd* 112/113 E6
Smaldon Cl, West Dr. UB7 *off Walnut Av* 120 D3
Smallberry Av, Islw. TW7 144 C2
Smallbrook Ms, W2 14 E4
Smalley Cl, N16 94 C3
Smalley Rd Est, N16 *off Smalley Cl* 94 C3
Smallwood Rd, SW17 167 G4
Smardale Rd, SW18 *off Alma Rd* 149 F5
Smarden Cl, Belv. DA17 *off Essenden Rd* 139 G5
Smarden Gro, SE9 174 C4
Smarts La, Loug. IG10 48 A4
Smarts Pl, N18 *off Fore St* 60 D5
Smart's Pl, WC2 18 B3
Smart St, E2 113 G3
Smeaton Cl, Chess. KT9 *off Merritt Gdns* 195 G6
Smeaton Rd, SW18 148 D7
Woodford Green IG8 64 C5
Smeaton St, E1 132 E1
Smedley St, SW4 150 D2
SW8 150 D2
Smeed Rd, E3 96 A7
Smiles Pl, SE13 154 C2
Smith Cl, SE16 133 G1
★**Smithfield Cen Mkt**, EC1 19 H2
Smithfield St, EC1 19 G2
Smithies Ct, E15 96 C5
Smithies Rd, SE2 138 B4
Smith's Ct, W1 17 G5
Smiths Fm Est, Nthlt. UB5 103 G2
Smithson Rd, N17 76 A1
Smiths Pt, E13 *off Brooks Rd* 115 G1
Smith Sq, SW1 26 A6
Smith St, SW3 31 J3
Surbiton KT5 181 J6
Smiths Yd, SW18 *off Summerley St* 167 F2
Smith's Yd, Croy. CR0 *off St. Georges Wk* 201 J3
Smith Ter, SW3 31 J4
Smithwood Cl, SW19 166 B1
Smithy St, E1 113 F5
Smock Wk, Croy. CR0 187 J6
Smokehouse Yd, EC1 19 H1
Smugglers Way, SW18 149 E4
Smyrks Rd, SE17 36 E4
Smyrna Rd, NW6 90 D7
Smythe St, E14 114 B7
Snakes La, Barn. EN4 42 B3
Snakes La E, Wdf.Grn. IG8 63 J6
Snakes La W, Wdf.Grn. IG8 63 G6
SNARESBROOK, E11 79 E5
Snaresbrook Dr, Stan. HA7 53 G4
Snaresbrook Rd, E11 78 E4
Snarsgate St, W10 107 J5
Sneath Av, NW11 72 C7
Snells Pk, N18 60 C6
Sneyd Rd, NW2 89 J4
Snowberry Cl, E15 96 D4
Snowbury Rd, SW6 149 E2
Snowden St, EC2 12 D6
Snowdon Cres, Hayes UB3 121 F3
Snowdon Dr, NW9 70 E6
Snowdon Rd, Houns. (Hthrw Air.) TW6 *off Southern Perimeter Rd* 141 F5
Snowdown Cl, SE20 189 G1
Snowdrop Cl, Hmptn. TW12 *off Gresham Rd* 161 G6
Snow Hill, EC1 19 G2
Snow Hill Ct, EC1 19 H3
Snowman Ho, NW6 109 E1
Snowsfields, SE1 28 C3
Snowshill Rd, E12 98 B5
Snowy Fielder Waye, Islw. TW7 144 E2
Soames St, SE15 152 C3
Soames Wk, N.Mal. KT3 182 E1
Soane Cl, W5 125 G2
Soap Ho La, Brent. TW8 125 H7
Socket La, Brom. BR2 191 H6
SOHO, W1 17 H5
Soho Sq, W1 17 H3
Soho St, W1 17 H3
Sojourner Truth Cl, E8 *off Richmond Rd* 94/95 E6
Solander Gdns, E1 *off Dellow St* 112/113 E7
Solebay St, E1 113 H4
Solent Ri, E13 115 G3
Solent Rd, NW6 90 D5
Hounslow (Hthrw Air.) TW6 140 C6
Soley Ms, WC1 10 E3
Solna Av, SW15 147 J5
Solna Rd, N21 60 A1
Solomon Av, N9 60 D4
Solomon's Pas, SE15 152 E4
Solon New Rd, SW4 150 E4
Solon New Rd Est, SW4 *off Solon New Rd* 150/151 E4
Solon Rd, SW2 151 E4
Solway Cl, E8 *off Buttermere Wk* 94 C6
Hounslow TW4 143 E3
Solway Rd, N22 75 H1
SE22 152 D4
Somaford Gro, Barn. EN4 41 G6
Somali Rd, NW2 90 C4
Somborne Ho, SW15 *off Fontley Way* 147 G7
Somerby Rd, Bark. IG11 99 G7
Somercoates Cl, Barn. EN4 41 H3
Somerfield Rd, N4 93 H2
SE16 *off Oldfield Gro* 133 G5
Somerford Cl, Pnr. HA5 66 A4
Somerford Gro, N16 94 C4
N17 60 D7
Somerford Gro Est, N16 *off Somerford Gro* 94 C4
Somerford St, E1 112 E4
Somerford Way, SE16 133 H2
Somerhill Av, Sid. DA15 158 B7
Somerhill Rd, Well. DA16 158 B2
Somerleyton Pas, SW9 151 H4
Somerleyton Rd, SW9 151 G4
Somersby Gdns, Ilf. IG4 80 C5
Somers Cl, NW1 9 H1
Somers Cres, W2 15 G4
Somerset Av, SW20 183 H2
Chessington KT9 195 G4
Welling DA16 157 J5
Somerset Cl, N17 76 A2
New Malden KT3 183 E6
Woodford Green IG8 79 G1
Somerset Est, SW11 149 G1
Somerset Gdns, N6 74 A7
N17 60 B7
SE13 154 B2
SW16 187 F3
Teddington TW11 162 B5
★**Somerset Ho**, WC2 18 C5
Somerset Ho, SW19 166 A3
Somerset Rd, E17 78 A5
N17 76 C3
N18 60 C5
NW4 71 J4
SW19 166 B4
W4 126 D3
W13 125 E1
Barnet EN5 41 E5
Brentford TW8 125 F6
Harrow HA1 67 J5
Kingston upon Thames KT1 181 J2
Southall UB1 103 F5
Teddington TW11 162 B5
Somerset Sq, W14 128 B2
Somerset Waye, Houns. TW5 122 E6

Somersham Rd, Bexh.
DA7 . . . . **159** E2
Somers Ms, W2 . . . . **15** G4
Somers Pl, SW2 . . . . **151** F7
Somers Rd, E17 . . . . **77** J4
SW2. . . . . **151** F6
SOMERS TOWN, NW1 . . . . . **9** J3
Somerton Av, Rich. TW9 . **146** B3
Somerton Rd, NW2 . . . . . . **90** B3
SE15 . . . . **153** E4
Somertrees Av, SE12 . . . . **173** H2
Somervell Rd, Har. HA2 . . . **85** F5
Somerville Av, SW13 . . . . **127** H6
Somerville Rd, SE20 . . . . **171** G7
Romford RM6 . . . . **82** C6
Sonderburg Rd, N7 . . . . . . **93** F2
Sondes St, SE17 . . . . **36** B5
Sonia Ct, Har. HA1 . . . . **68** C6
Sonia Gdns, N12
off Woodside Av **57** F4
NW10 . . . . **89** F4
Hounslow TW5 . . . . **123** G7
Sonning Gdns, Hmptn.
TW12 . . . . **161** E6
Sonning Rd, SE25 . . . . . . **188** D6
Soper Cl, E4 . . . . **61** J5
SE23 . . . . **171** G1
Sophia Cl, N7
off Mackenzie Rd **93** F6
Sophia Rd, E10. . . . . **96** B1
E16. . . . . **115** H6
Sophia Sq, SE16
off Rotherhithe St **113** H7
Sopwith Av, Chess. KT9. . **195** H5
Sopwith Cl, Kings.T. KT2 . **163** J5
Sopwith Rd, Houns. TW5. **122** C7
Sopwith Way, SW8 . . . . . . **32** D7
Kingston upon Thames
KT2 . . . . **181** H1
Sorrel Cl, SE28 . . . . **138** A1
Sorrel Gdns, E6 . . . . **116** B5
Sorrel La, E14 . . . . **114** D6
Sorrell Cl, SE14
off Southerngate Way. **133** H7
Sorrento Rd, Sutt. SM1 . . **198** E3
Sotheby Rd, N5 . . . . **93** H3
Sotheran Cl, E8 . . . . **112** D1
Sotheron Rd, SW6 . . . . . . **129** E7
Soudan Rd, SW11 . . . . . . **149** J1
Souldern Rd, W14 . . . . . . **128** A3
South Access Rd, E17 . . . . **77** H7
Southacre Way, Pnr. HA5. . **66** C1
SOUTH ACTON, W3 . . . . . **126** A3
South Acton Est, W3 . . . . **126** B2
South Africa Rd, W12. . . . **127** H1
SOUTHALL, UB1 & UB2 . **122** D1
Southall La, Houns. TW5 . **122** B6
Southall UB2 . . . . **122** B6
Southall Pl, SE1 . . . . **28** B4
Southampton Bldgs, WC2 . **18** E3
Southampton Gdns,
Mitch. CR4. . . . . **186** E5
Southampton Ms, E16
off Wesley Av **135** H1
Southampton Pl, WC1 . . . . **18** B2
Southampton Rd, NW5 . . . **91** J5
Hounslow (Hthrw Air.)
TW6 . . . . **140** D6
Southampton Row, WC1 . . **18** B1
Southampton St, WC2. . . . **18** B5
Southampton Way, SE5. . . **36** C7
Southam St, W10. . . . . . . **108** B4
South Audley St, W1 . . . . . **16** C6
South Av, E4 . . . . **46** B7
Carshalton SM5 . . . . . . **199** J7
Richmond TW9
off Sandycombe Rd . . **146** A2
Southall UB1 . . . . **103** F7
South Av Gdns, Sthl. UB1. **103** F7
South Bk, Chis. BR7. . . . . **175** F4
Surbiton KT6. . . . . **181** H6
Southbank, T.Ditt. KT7 . . . **180** E7
Southbank Business Cen,
SW8 . . . . **33** J6
South Bk Ter, Surb. KT6. . **181** H6
SOUTH BEDDINGTON,
Wall. SM6. . . . . **200** D6
South Birkbeck Rd, E11 . . . **96** D3
South Black Lion La, W6 . **127** G5
South Bolton Gdns, SW5 . **30** B3
SOUTHBOROUGH, Brom.
BR2 . . . . **192** C6
Southborough Cl, Surb.
KT6 . . . . **195** G1
Southborough La, Brom.
BR2 . . . . **192** B5
Southborough Rd, E9. . . . **113** F1
Bromley BR1 . . . . **192** B3
Surbiton KT6. . . . . **195** H1
Southbourne, Brom. BR2. **191** G7
Southbourne Av, NW9. . . . **70** C2
Southbourne Cl, Pnr. HA5 . **67** E7
Southbourne Cres, NW4 . . **72** B4
Southbourne Gdns, SE12 . **155** H5
Ilford IG1 . . . . **99** F5
Ruislip HA4 . . . . **84** B1
Southbridge Pl, Croy.
CR0 . . . . **201** J4
Southbridge Rd, Croy.
CR0 . . . . **201** J4
Southbridge Way, Sthl.
UB2 . . . . **123** E2
Southbrook Ms, SE12 . . . **155** F6
Southbrook Rd, SE12 . . . **155** F6
SW16. . . . . **187** E1
Southbury Av, Enf. EN1 . . . **44** D5
Southbury Rd, Enf. EN1,
EN3 . . . . **44** A3
South Carriage Dr, SW1 . . **23** J3
SW7. . . . . **23** F4
SOUTH CHINGFORD, E4 . . **61** J5
Southchurch Rd, E6 . . . . . **116** C2
South Circular Rd, SE6
(A205) **154** D7
SE9 (A205) **156** C3
SE12 (A205). **155** H6
SE18 (A205). **136** D6
SE21 (A205). **170** B1
SE22 (A205). **171** E1
SE23 (A205). **171** J1
SW2 (A205) **169** G1
SW4 (A205) **150** A5
SW11 (A3) **149** H5
SW12 (A205) **169** G1
SW14 (A205) **147** E4
SW15 (A205) **147** J4
SW18 (A3) **149** H5
W4 (A205) **126** A5
Brentford (A205) TW8 . . **126** A5
Richmond (A205) TW9 . **146** B2
South Cl, N6. . . . . **74** B6
Barnet EN5 . . . . **40** C3
Bexleyheath DA6 . . . . . **158** D4
Dagenham RM10. . . . . . **119** G1
Morden SM4 . . . . **184** D6
Pinner HA5 . . . . **67** F7
Twickenham TW2 . . . . . **161** G3
West Drayton UB7 . . . . **120** C3
South Colonnade, E14. . . **134** A1
Southcombe St, W14. . . . **128** B4
Southcote Av, Surb. KT5 . **182** B7
Southcote Rd, E17. . . . . . . **77** G5
N19 . . . . **92** C4
SE25 . . . . **189** E6
Southcott Ms, NW8 . . . . **7** G2
South Countess Rd, E17 . . **77** J3
South Cres, E16 . . . . **114** D4
WC1. . . . . **17** H2
Southcroft Av, Well.
DA16 . . . . **157** H3
West Wickham BR4 . . . . **204** C2
Southcroft Rd, SW16. . . . **168** A6
SW17 . . . . **168** A6
Orpington BR6 . . . . **207** H3
South Cross Rd, Ilf. IG6 . . . **81** F5
South Croxted Rd, SE21 . **170** A3
SOUTH CROYDON, CR2. . **201** J6
Southdale, Chig. IG7 . . . . . **65** G6
Southdean Gdns, SW19. . **166** C2
South Dene, NW7 . . . . **54** D3
Southdown Av, W7 . . . . . **124** D3
Southdown Cres, Har.
HA2 . . . . **85** H1
Ilford IG2. . . . . **81** H5
Southdown Dr, SW20
off Crescent Rd **166** A7
Southdown Rd, SW20 . . . **184** A1
South Dr, Orp. BR6 . . . . . **207** H5
South Ealing Rd, W5 . . . . **125** G2
South Eastern Av, N9. . . . . **60** C3
South Eaton Pl, SW1 . . . . . **32** C1
South Eden Pk Rd, Beck.
BR3. . . . . **190** B6
South Edwardes Sq, W8 . **128** C3
SOUTHEND, SE6 . . . . **172** B4
South End, W8. . . . . **22** B5
Croydon CR0. . . . . **201** J4
South End Cl, NW3 . . . . . . **91** H4
Southend Cl, SE9. . . . . . . **156** E6
Southend Cres, SE9. . . . . **156** D6
South End Grn, NW3
off South End Rd **91** H4
Southend La, SE6 . . . . . . **171** J4
SE26 . . . . **171** J4
Southend Rd, E4 . . . . **61** H5
E6 . . . . **98** C7
E17 . . . . **78** B1
E18 . . . . **79** G1
South End Rd, NW3. . . . . . **91** H4
Southend Rd, Beck. BR3 . **172** A7
Woodford Green IG8 . . . **79** J2
South End Row, W8. . . . . . **22** B5
Southern Av, SE25 . . . . . . **188** C3
Feltham TW14 . . . . **160** A1
Southern Dr, Loug. IG10 . . **48** C6
Southerngate Way, SE14 . **133** H7
Southern Gro, E3 . . . . **113** J3
Southernhay, Loug. IG10. . **48** A5
Southern Perimeter Rd, Houns.
(Hthrw Air.) TW6 . . . . . **141** G5
Southern Rd, E13 . . . . **115** H2
N2 . . . . **73** J4
Southern Row, W10 . . . . . **108** B4
Southern St, N1 . . . . **10** C1
Southern Way, SE10. . . . . **135** F4
Romford RM7 . . . . **83** G6
Southerton Rd, W6 . . . . . **127** J3
South Esk Rd, E7 . . . . **97** J6
Southey Ms, E16
off Wesley Av **135** G1
Southey Rd, N15 . . . . **76** B5
SW9. . . . . **151** G1
SW19. . . . . **166** D7
Southey St, SE20. . . . . . . **171** G7
Southfield, Barn. EN5 . . . . **40** A6
Southfield Cotts, W7
off Oaklands Rd **124** C2
Southfield Gdns, Twick.
TW1 . . . . **162** C4
Southfield Pk, Har. HA2. . . **67** H4
Southfield Rd, N17
off The Avenue **76** B2
W4. . . . . **126** E3
Chislehurst BR7 . . . . . . **193** J3
Enfield EN3. . . . . **45** E6
SOUTHFIELDS, SW18 . . . **166** D1
Southfields, NW4. . . . . **71** G3
East Molesey KT8 . . . . . . **180** B6
Southfields Ct, SW19. . . . **166** B1
Sutton SM1 *off*
Sutton Common Rd . . **198** D2
Southfields Ms, SW18
off Southfields Rd. . . . **148** D6
Southfields Pas, SW18. . . **148** D6
Southfields Rd, SW18 . . . **148** D6
Southfleet Rd, Orp. BR6 . **207** H3
South Gdns, SW19. . . . . . **167** G7
SOUTHGATE, N14 . . . . **58** C2
Southgate Circ, N14
off The Bourne **58** D1
Southgate Gro, N1. . . . . . . **94** A7
Southgate Rd, N1. . . . . . . **112** A1
South Gipsy Rd, Well.
DA16 . . . . **158** D3
South Glade, The, Bex.
DA5 . . . . **177** F1
South Grn, NW9
off Clayton Fld. **70/71** E1
South Gro, E17 . . . . **77** J5
N6 . . . . **92** A1
N15 . . . . **76** A5
South Gro Ho, N6
off Highgate W Hill **92** A1
SOUTH HACKNEY, E9 . . . . **95** F7
SOUTH HAMPSTEAD,
NW6 . . . . **91** E7
SOUTH HARROW, Har.
HA2 . . . . **85** H3
South Hill, Chis. BR7 . . . . **174** C6
South Hill Av, Har. HA1,
HA2 . . . . **85** J3
South Hill Gro, Har. HA1 . . **86** B4
South Hill Pk, NW3 . . . . . . **91** H4
South Hill Pk Gdns, NW3 . **91** H4
South Hill Rd, Brom.
BR2 . . . . **190** E3
Southholme Cl, SE19. . . . **188** B1
South Huxley, N18. . . . . . . **60** A5
Southill La, Pnr. HA5 . . . . . **66** A4
Southill Rd, Chis. BR7 . . . **174** B7
Southill St, E14
off Chrisp St **114** B6
South Island Pl, SW9. . . . **131** F7
SOUTH KENSINGTON,
SW7 . . . . **30** C2
South Kensington Sta Arc,
SW7 *off Pelham St* . . . **129** G4
SOUTH LAMBETH, SW8 . **151** E1
South Lambeth Pl, SW8 . . **34** B5
South Lambeth Rd, SW8. . **34** B6
Southland Rd, SE18. . . . . **137** J7
Southlands Av, Orp. BR6 . **207** G4
Southlands Dr, SW19. . . . **166** A2
Southlands Gro, Brom.
BR1 . . . . **192** B3
Southlands Rd, Brom. BR1,
BR2 . . . . **191** J5
Southland Way, Houns.
TW3. . . . . **144** A5
South La, Kings.T. KT1 . . . **181** G3
New Malden KT3 . . . . . **182** D4
South La W, N.Mal. KT3. . **182** D4
South Lo Av, Mitch. CR4 . **186** E4
South Lo Cres, Enf. EN2 . . **42** D4
South Lo Dr, N14. . . . . **42** E5
★**South London Art Gall**,
SE5 . . . . **152** B1
Southly Cl, Sutt. SM1 . . . **198** D3
South Mall, N9
off Edmonton Grn
Shop Cen **60** D3
South Mead, NW9 . . . . **71** F1
Epsom KT19 . . . . **197** E7
South Meadows, Wem.
HA9 . . . . **87** J5
Southmead Rd, SW19 . . . **166** B1
South Molton La, W1. . . . . **16** D4
South Molton Rd, E16 . . . **115** G6
South Molton St, W1. . . . . **16** D4
Southmont Rd, Esher
KT10 . . . . **194** B2
Southmoor Way, E9. . . . . . **95** J6
SOUTH NORWOOD, SE25. **188** C3
South Norwood Hill,
SE25 . . . . **188** B2
South Oak Rd, SW16. . . . **169** F4
Southold Ri, SE9 . . . . **174** C3
Southolm St, SW11 . . . . . **150** B1
Southover, N12 . . . . **56** D4
Bromley BR1 . . . . **173** G5
SOUTH OXHEY, Wat.
WD19 . . . . **50** C3
South Par, SW3 . . . . **31** F3
W4. . . . . **126** D4
South Pk, SW6. . . . . **148** D2
South Pk Cres, SE6 . . . . . **173** F1
Ilford IG1 . . . . **99** G3
South Pk Dr, Bark. IG11 . . . **99** H4
Ilford IG3. . . . . **99** H4
South Pk Gro, N.Mal. KT3. **182** C4
South Pk Hill Rd, S.Croy.
CR2 . . . . **202** A5
South Pk Ms, SW6. . . . . . **148** E3
South Pk Rd, SW19 . . . . . **166** D6
Ilford IG1 . . . . **99** G3
South Pk Ter, Ilf. IG1 . . . . . **99** G3
South Pk Way, Ruis. HA4. . **84** C6
South Penge Pk Est, SE20. **188** E2
South Pl, EC2. . . . . **20** C1
Enfield EN3. . . . . **45** F5
Surbiton KT5. . . . . **181** J7
South Pl Ms, EC2. . . . . **20** C2
South Pt, Sutt. SM1. . . . . **199** F6
Southport Rd, SE18 . . . . . **137** G4
South Quay Plaza, E14
off Marsh Wall **134** B2
Southridge Pl, SW20 . . . . **166** A7
South Ri Way, SE18 . . . . . **137** G5
South Rd, N9 . . . . **60** D1
SE23 . . . . **171** G2
SW19 . . . . **167** F6
W5. . . . . **125** G4
Edgware HA8 . . . . **70** B1
Feltham TW13 . . . . **160** D5
Hampton TW12 . . . . **161** E6
Romford (Chad.Hth) RM6 . **82** E6
Romford (Lt.Hth) RM6 . . **82** C5
Southall UB1. . . . . **123** F2
Twickenham TW2 . . . . . **162** A3
West Drayton UB7 . . . . . **120** C3
South Row, SE3. . . . . **155** F2
SOUTH RUISLIP, Ruis.
HA4. . . . . **84** C4
Southsea Rd, Kings.T.
KT1 . . . . **181** H4
South Sea St, SE16 . . . . . **133** J3
South Side, W6 . . . . **127** F3
Southside Common,
SW19. . . . . **165** J6
Southspring, Sid. DA15 . . **157** G7
South Sq, NW11 . . . . **72** E6
WC1. . . . . **18** E2
South St, W1 . . . . **24** C1
Bromley BR1 . . . . **191** G2
Enfield EN3. . . . . **45** G5
Isleworth TW7 . . . . **144** D3
Rainham RM13 . . . . **119** J2
South Tenter St, E1 . . . . . . **21** G5
South Ter, SW7 . . . . **31** G1
Surbiton KT6. . . . . **181** H6
SOUTH TOTTENHAM, N15. **76** B5
South Vale, SE19 . . . . **170** B6
Harrow HA1 . . . . **86** B4
Southvale Rd, SE3. . . . . . **155** E2
South Vw, Brom. BR1 . . . **191** H2
Southview Av, NW10. . . . . **89** F5

Southview Cl, SW17 168 A5
Bexley DA5 159 F6
Southview Cres, Ilf. IG2 80 E6
South Vw Dr, E18 79 H3
Southview Gdns, Wall. SM6 200 C7
South Vw Rd, N8 74 D3
Southview Rd, Brom. BR1 172 D4
South Vw Rd, Loug. IG10 48 C6
Pinner HA5 50 B6
South Vil, NW1 92 D6
Southville, SW8 150 D1
Southville Rd, T.Ditt. KT7 180 E7
South Wk, W.Wick. BR4 204 E3
SOUTHWARK, SE1 27 H2
Southwark Br, EC4 28 A1
SE1 28 A1
Southwark Br Rd, SE1 27 H5
★**Southwark Cath**, SE1 28 B1
Southwark Pk Est, SE16 133 E4
Southwark Pk Rd, SE16 37 G1
Southwark Pl, Brom. BR1 *off St. Georges Rd* 192 C3
Southwark St, SE1 27 H1
Southwater Cl, E14 113 J6
Beckenham BR3 172 B7
South Way, N9 61 F2
N11 *off Ringway* 58 C6
Southway, N20 56 D2
NW11 72 E6
SW20 183 J4
South Way, Brom. BR2 191 G7
Croydon CR0 203 H3
Harrow HA2 67 G4
Southway, Wall. SM6 200 C4
South Way, Wem. HA9 88 A5
Southwell Av, Nthlt. UB5 85 G6
Southwell Gdns, SW7 30 C1
Southwell Gro Rd, E11 96 E2
Southwell Rd, SE5 151 J3
Croydon CR0 187 G6
Harrow HA3 69 G6
South Western Rd, Twick. TW1 144 D6
Southwest Rd, E11 96 D1
South Wf Rd, W2 15 E3
Southwick Ms, W2 15 F3
Southwick Pl, W2 15 G4
Southwick St, W2 15 G3
SOUTH WIMBLEDON, SW19 166 E7
Southwold Dr, Bark. IG11 100 A5
Southwold Rd, E5 95 E2
Bexley DA5 159 H6
Southwood Av, N6 74 B7
Kingston upon Thames KT2 182 C1
Southwood Cl, Brom. BR1 192 C4
Worcester Park KT4 198 A1
Southwood Dr, Surb. KT5 182 C7
SOUTH WOODFORD, E18 79 F2
South Woodford to Barking Relief Rd, E11 79 J4
E12 98 D3
E18 79 J4
Barking IG11 98 D3
Ilford IG1, IG4 98 D3
Southwood Gdns, Esher KT10 194 D3
Ilford IG2 80 E4
Southwood La, N6 74 A7
Southwood Lawn Rd, N6 74 A7
Southwood Rd, SE9 174 E2
SE28 138 B1
Southwood Smith St, N1 *off Old Royal Free Sq* 111 G1
South Worple Av, SW14 146 E3
South Worple Way, SW14 146 D3
Sovereign Cl, E1 113 E7
W5 105 F5
Barnet EN4 41 J3
Sovereign Ct, W.Mol. KT8 179 F4
Sovereign Cres, SE16 *off Rotherhithe St* 133 H1
Sovereign Gro, Wem. HA0 87 G3
Sovereign Ms, E2 13 F1
Barnet EN4 *off Bournwell Cl* 41 J3
Sovereign Pk, NW10 106 B4
Sovereign Pl, Har. HA1 68 C5
Sovereign Rd, Bark. IG11 118 C3
Sowerby Cl, SE9 156 B5
Space Waye, Felt. TW14 142 A5
Spa Cl, SE25 188 B1
Spafield St, EC1 11 E5
Spa Grn Est, EC1 11 F3
Spa Hill, SE19 188 A1
Spalding Cl, Edg. HA8 *off Blundell Rd* 54/55 E7
Spalding Rd, NW4 71 J6
SW17 168 B5
Spanby Rd, E3 114 A4
Spaniards Cl, NW11 91 G1
Spaniards End, NW3 91 F1
Spaniards Rd, NW3 91 F2
Spanish Pl, W1 16 C3
Spanish Rd, SW18 149 F5
Spareleaze Hill, Loug. IG10 48 C5
Sparkbridge Rd, Har. HA1 68 B4
Sparkford Gdns, N11 *off Friern Barnet Rd* 58 A5
Sparkford Ho, SW11 149 G1
Sparks Cl, W3 *off Joseph Av* 106 D6
Dagenham RM8 100 D2
Hampton TW12 *off Victors Dr* 160/161 E6
Spa Rd, SE16 29 F6
Sparrow Cl, Hmptn. TW12 160 E6
Sparrow Dr, Orp. BR5 207 F1
Sparrow Fm Dr, Felt. TW14 142 D7
Sparrow Fm Rd, Epsom KT17 197 G4
Sparrow Grn, Dag. RM10 101 H3
Sparrows La, SE9 157 F7
Sparsholt Rd, N19 93 F1
Barking IG11 117 H1
Sparta St, SE10 154 B1
★**Speaker's Cor**, W2 16 A5
Speaker's Ct, Croy. CR0 *off St. James's Rd* 202 A1
Spearman St, SE18 136 D6
Spear Ms, SW5 128 D4
Spearpoint Gdns, Ilf. IG2 81 J4
Spears Rd, N19 92 E1
Speart La, Houns. TW5 122 E7
Spedan Cl, NW3 91 E3
Speechly Ms, E8 *off Alvington Cres* 94 C5
Speed Highwalk, EC2 *off Beech St* 111 J5
Speed Ho, EC2 20 B1
Speedwell St, SE8 *off Comet St* 134 A7
Speedy Pl, WC1 10 A4
Speer Rd, T.Ditt. KT7 180 C5
Speirs Cl, N.Mal. KT3 183 F6
Spekehill, SE9 174 C3
Speke Ho, SE5 131 J7
Speke Rd, Th.Hth. CR7 188 A2
Speldhurst Cl, Brom. BR2 191 F5
Speldhurst Rd, E9 95 G7
W4 126 D3
Spellbrook Wk, N1 *off Basire St* 111 J1
Spelman St, E1 21 H1
Spence Cl, SE16 *off Vaughan St* 133 J2
Spencer Av, N13 59 F6
Hayes UB4 102 A5
Spencer Cl, N3 72 C2
NW10 105 J3
Orpington BR6 207 H2
Woodford Green IG8 63 J5
Spencer Ct, NW8 *off Marlborough Pl* 109 F2
Spencer Dr, N2 73 F6
Spencer Gdns, SE9 156 C5
SW14 146 C5
Spencer Hill, SW19 166 B6
Spencer Hill Rd, SW19 166 B7
★**Spencer Ho**, SW1 25 F2
Spencer Ms, SW8 *off Lansdowne Way* 151 F1
W6 *off Greyhound Rd* 128 B6
Spencer Pk, SW18 149 G5
Spencer Pas, E2 *off Pritchard's Rd* 112/113 E2
Spencer Pl, N1 *off Canonbury La* 93 H7
Croydon CR0 *off Gloucester Rd* 188 A7
Spencer Ri, NW5 92 B4
Spencer Rd, E6 116 A1
E17 78 C1
N8 75 F5
N11 58 B4
N17 76 D1
SW18 149 G4
SW20 183 H1
W3 126 C1
W4 126 C7
Bromley BR1 173 E7
Spencer Rd, E. Mol. KT8 179 J5
Harrow HA3 68 B2
Ilford IG3 99 J1
Isleworth TW7 144 A1
Mitcham CR4 186 A3
Mitcham (Bedd.Cor.) CR4 186 A7
South Croydon CR2 202 B5
Twickenham TW2 162 B3
Wembley HA0 87 F2
Spencer St, EC1 11 G4
Southall UB2 122 D2
Spencer Wk, NW3 91 G4
SW15 148 A4
Spencer Yd, SE3 *off Blackheath Village* 155 F2
Spenser Gro, N16 94 B4
Spenser Ms, SE21 *off Croxted Rd* 170 A1
Spenser Rd, SE24 151 G5
Spenser St, SW1 25 G5
Spensley Wk, N16 *off Clissold Rd* 94 A3
Speranza St, SE18 137 J5
Sperling Rd, N17 76 B2
Spert St, E14 113 H7
Speyside, N14 42 C6
Spey St, E14 114 C5
Spezia Rd, NW10 107 G2
Spice Quay Hts, SE1 29 G2
Spicer Cl, SW9 151 H2
Walton-on-Thames KT12 178 C6
Spice's Yd, Croy. CR0 201 J4
Spigurnell Rd, N17 76 A1
Spikes Br Moorings, Hayes UB4 102 E6
Spikes Br Rd, Sthl. UB1 103 E6
Spilsby Cl, NW9 *off Kenley Av* 70/71 E2
Spindle Cl, SE18 136 B3
Spindlewood Gdns, Croy. CR0 202 B4
Spindrift Av, E14 134 B4
Spinel Cl, SE18 137 J5
Spinnaker Cl, Bark. IG11 118 B3
Spinnells Rd, Har. HA2 85 F1
Spinney, The, N21 43 G7
SW16 168 D3
Barnet EN5 41 E2
Sidcup DA14 176 E5
Stanmore HA7 53 H4
Sunbury-on-Thames TW16 178 A1
Sutton SM3 197 J4
Wembley HA0 86 D3
Spinney Cl, Beck. BR3 190 B4
New Malden KT3 182 E5
Worcester Park KT4 197 F3
Spinney Dr, Felt. TW14 141 F7
Spinney Gdns, SE19 170 C5
Dagenham RM9 101 E5
Spinney Oak, Brom. BR1 192 B2
Spinneys, The, Brom. BR1 192 C2
Spire Ho, W2 *off Lancaster Gate* 109 F7
Spires Shop Cen, The, Barn. EN5 40 B3
Spirit Quay, E1 29 J1
★**Spitalfields Comm Fm**, E1 13 H6
Spital Sq, E1 21 E1
Spital St, E1 21 H1
Spital Yd, E1 21 E1
Spitfire Est, Houns. TW5 122 C5
Spitfire Rd, Wall. SM6 200 E7
Spitfire Way, Houns. TW5 122 C5
Spode Wk, NW6 *off Lymington Rd* 90/91 E6
Spondon Rd, N15 76 D4
Spoonbill Way, Hayes UB4 *off Cygnet Way* 102 D5
Spooners Ms, W3 *off Churchfield Rd* 126 D1
Spooner Wk, Wall. SM6 200 D5
Sporle Ct, SW11 149 G3
Sportsbank St, SE6 154 C7
Spotted Dog Path, E7 *off Upton La* 97 G6
Spottons Gro, N17 *off Gospatrick Rd* 75 J1
Spout Hill, Croy. CR0 204 A5
Spratt Hall Rd, E11 79 G6
Spray La, Twick. TW2 144 B6
Spray St, SE18 137 E4
Spreighton Rd, W.Mol. KT8 179 H4
Sprimont Pl, SW3 31 J3
Springall St, SE15 133 E7
Springbank, N21 43 F6
Springbank Rd, SE13 154 D6
Springbank Wk, NW1 *off St. Paul's Cres* 92 D7
Springbourne Ct, Beck. BR3 190 C1
Spring Br Ms, W5 *off Spring Br Rd* 105 G7
Spring Br Rd, W5 105 G7
Spring Cl, Barn. EN5 40 A5
Borehamwood WD6 38 A1
Dagenham RM8 100 D1
Springclose La, Sutt. SM3 198 B6
Spring Cotts, Surb. KT6 *off St. Leonard's Rd* 181 G5
Spring Ct, Sid. DA15 *off Station Rd* 176 A3
Springcroft Av, N2 73 J4
Springdale Ms, N16 *off Springdale Rd* 94 A4
Springdale Rd, N16 94 A4
Spring Dr, Pnr. HA5 *off Eastcote Rd* 66 A6
Springfield, E5 94 E1
Bushey (Bushey Hth) WD23 52 A1
Springfield Av, N10 74 C3
SW20 184 C3
Hampton TW12 161 H6
Springfield Cl, N12 56 E5
Stanmore HA7 52 D3
Springfield Ct, Wall. SM6 *off Springfield Rd* 200 B5
Springfield Dr, Ilf. IG2 81 F6
Springfield Gdns, E5 95 E1
NW9 70 D5
Bromley BR1 192 C4
Ruislip HA4 84 B1
West Wickham BR4 204 B2
Woodford Green IG8 63 J7
Springfield Gro, SE7 135 J6
Springfield La, NW6 108 E1
Springfield Mt, NW9 70 E5
Springfield Pl, N.Mal. KT3 182 C4
Springfield Ri, SE26 170 E3
Springfield Rd, E4 62 E1
E6 98 C7
E15 115 E3
E17 77 J6
N11 58 B5
N15 76 D4
NW8 109 F1
SE26 171 E5
SW19 166 C5
W7 124 B1
Bexleyheath DA7 159 H3
Bromley BR1 192 C4
Harrow HA1 68 B6
Hayes UB4 122 C1
Kingston upon Thames KT1 181 H3
Teddington TW11 162 D5
Thornton Heath CR7 187 J1
Twickenham TW2 161 G1
Wallington SM6 200 B5
Welling DA16 158 B3
Springfield Wk, NW6 108 E1
Orpington BR6 *off Place Fm Av* 207 G1
Spring Gdns, N5 *off Grosvenor Av* 93 J5
SW1 25 J1
Romford RM7 83 J5
Wallington SM6 200 C5
West Molesey KT8 179 J5
Woodford Green IG8 63 J7
Spring Gdns Ind Est, Rom. RM7 83 J5
SPRING GROVE, Islw. TW7 144 C1
Spring Gro, SE19 *off Alma Pl* 170 C7
W4 126 A5
Hampton TW12 *off Plevna Rd* 179 H1
Loughton IG10 48 A6
Mitcham CR4 186 A1
Spring Gro Cres, Houns. TW3 143 J1
Spring Gro Rd, Houns. TW3 143 H1
Isleworth TW7 143 H1
Richmond TW10 145 J5
Spring Hill, E5 76 D7
SE26 171 F4
Springhill Cl, SE5 152 A3

Springhurst Cl, Croy. CR0 . **203** J4
Spring Lake, Stan. HA7 . . . **52** E4
Spring La, E5 . . . . **95** E1
N10 . . . . **74** A3
SE25 . . . . **188** E6
Spring Ms, W1 . . . . **16** A1
Richmond TW9
off Rosedale Rd **145** H4
Spring Pk Av, Croy. CR0 . **203** G2
Spring Pk Dr, N4 . . . . **93** J1
Springpark Dr, Beck. BR3. **190** C3
Spring Pk Rd, Croy. CR0 . **203** G2
Spring Pas, SW15
off Embankment **148** A3
Spring Path, NW3 . . . . **91** G5
Spring Pl, N3
off Windermere Av **72** D2
NW5 . . . . **92** B5
Springpond Rd, Dag.
RM9. . . . . **101** E5
Springrice Rd, SE13 . . . . . **154** C6
Spring St, W2. . . . . **15** E4
Spring Ter, Rich. TW9 . . . . **145** H5
Springtide Cl, SE15
off Staffordshire St . . . **152** D1
Spring Vale, Bexh. DA7 . . **159** H4
Springvale Av, Brent. TW8. **125** G5
Springvale Est, W14
off Blythe Rd. **128** B3
Springvale Ter, W14 . . . . . **128** A3
Spring Vil Rd, Edg. HA8 . . . **54** A7
Spring Wk, E1. . . . . **21** H1
Springwater Cl, SE18. . . . . **156** D1
Springway, Har. HA1 . . . . . **68** A7
Springwell Av, NW10 . . . . **107** F1
Springwell Cl, SW16
off Etherstone Rd **169** G4
Springwell Ct, Houns.
TW4. . . . . **142** D2
Springwell Rd, SW16. . . . **169** G4
Hounslow TW4, TW5 . . . **142** D1
Springwood Cres, Edg.
HA8. . . . . **54** B2
Sprowston Ms, E7 . . . . **97** G6
Sprowston Rd, E7 . . . . **97** G5
Spruce Ct, W5
off Elderberry Rd. **125** H3
Sprucedale Gdns, Croy.
CR0 . . . . **203** G4
Spruce Hills Rd, E17. . . . . . **78** C2
Spruce Pk, Brom. BR2
off Cumberland Rd . . . **191** F4
Sprules Rd, SE4 . . . . **153** H2
Spurfield, W.Mol. KT8 . . . **179** H3
Spurgeon Av, SE19. . . . . . **188** A1
Spurgeon Rd, SE19 . . . . . **188** A1
Spurgeon St, SE1 . . . . **28** B6
Spurling Rd, SE22 . . . . . . **152** C4
Dagenham RM9 . . . . . . **101** F6
Spur Rd, N15
off Philip La. **76** A4
SE1 . . . . **26** E3
SW1 . . . . **35** F4
Barking IG11 . . . . **117** F2
Edgware HA8 . . . . **53** H4
Feltham TW14 . . . . **142** B5
Isleworth TW7 . . . . **124** E7
Spur Rd Est, Edg. HA8. . . . **53** J4
Spurstowe Rd, E8
off Marcon Pl. **94/95** E6
Spurstowe Ter, E8 . . . . **94** E5
Square, The, W6 . . . . **127** J5
Carshalton SM5 . . . . . . **200** A5
Hayes UB3 . . . . **121** G1
Ilford IG1. . . . . **80** D7
Richmond TW9 . . . . **145** G5
Woodford Green IG8 . . . **63** G5
Square Rigger Row, SW11
off York Pl **149** F3
Squarey St, SW17 . . . . . . **167** F3
Squire Gdns, NW8. . . . . **7** E4
Squires, The, Rom. RM7. . . **83** J6
Squires Ct, SW19. . . . . . . **166** D4
Squires La, N3 . . . . **73** E2
Squires Mt, NW3
off East Heath Rd **91** G3
Squires Wd Dr, Chis. BR7. **174** B7
Squirrel Cl, Houns. TW4. . **142** C2
Squirrel Ms, W13 . . . . **104** D7
Squirrels, The, SE13
off Belmont Hill. **154** D3
Pinner HA5 . . . . **67** F3
Squirrels Cl, N12
off Woodside Av **57** F4
Squirrels Grn, Wor.Pk.
KT4 . . . . **197** F1
Squirrels La, Buck.H. IG9 . . **64** A3
Squirrels Trd Est, The,
Hayes UB3 . . . . **122** A3
Squirries St, E2 . . . . **13** J3
Stable Cl, Nthlt. UB5 . . . . **103** G2
Stable Ms, Twick. TW1 . . . **162** C1
Stables, The, Buck.H. IG9. . **47** J7
Stables End, Orp. BR6 . . . **207** F3
Stables Ms, SE27. . . . . . . **169** J5
Stables Way, SE11 . . . . **35** E3
Stable Wk, N1
off Wharfdale Rd **110** E2
N2 *off Old Fm Rd* **73** G1
Stable Way, W10
off Latimer Rd. **107** J6
Stable Yd, SW1 . . . . **25** F3
SW9
off Broomgrove Rd. . . **151** F2
SW15 *off Danemere St*. **147** J3
Stable Yd Rd, SW1. . . . . . . **25** F2
Stacey Av, N18. . . . . **61** F4
Stacey Cl, E10
off Halford Rd **78** D5
Stacey St, N7. . . . . **93** G3
WC2. . . . . **17** J4
Stackhouse St, SW3 . . . . . **23** J5
Stacy Path, SE5
off Harris St. **132** B7
Stadium Business Cen,
Wem. HA9. . . . . **88** B3
Stadium Retail Pk, Wem. HA9
off Wembley Pk Dr **88** A3
Stadium Rd, NW2 . . . . **71** H7
SE18 . . . . **136** B7
Stadium Rd E, NW2. . . . . . **71** J7
Stadium St, SW10 . . . . . . **129** F7
Stadium Way, Wem. HA9. . **87** J4
Staffa Rd, E10. . . . . **95** H1
Stafford Cl, E17 . . . . **77** J6
N14 . . . . **42** C5
NW6 . . . . **108** D3
Sutton SM3. . . . . **198** B6
Stafford Ct, W8. . . . . **128** D3
Stafford Cross, Croy. CR0 . **201** F5
Stafford Gdns, Croy. CR0. **201** F5
Stafford Pl, SW1 . . . . **25** F5
Richmond TW10 . . . . . . **145** J7
Stafford Rd, E3. . . . . **113** J2
E7 . . . . **97** J7
NW6 . . . . **108** D3
Croydon CR0. . . . . **201** G4
Harrow HA3 . . . . **51** J7
New Malden KT3 . . . . . **182** C3
Sidcup DA14 . . . . **175** H4
Wallington SM6 . . . . . . **200** C6
Staffordshire St, SE15 . . . **152** D1
Stafford St, W1. . . . . **25** F1
Stafford Ter, W8 . . . . **128** D3
Staff St, EC1. . . . . **12** C4
Stag Cl, Edg. HA8 . . . . **70** B2
Staggart Grn, Chig. IG7 . . . **65** J6
Stag La, NW9. . . . . **70** C3
SW15. . . . . **165** F2
Buckhurst Hill IG9. . . . . . . **63** H2
Edgware HA8 . . . . **70** B2
Stag Pl, SW1 . . . . **25** F5
Stag Ride, SW19 . . . . **165** H3
Stags Way, Islw. TW7. . . . **124** C6
Stainbank Rd, Mitch. CR4 . **186** B3
Stainby Cl, West Dr. UB7 . **120** B3
Stainby Rd, N15. . . . . **76** C4
Stainer Ho, SE3
off Ryan Cl **155** J4
Stainer St, SE1. . . . . **28** C2
Staines Av, Sutt. SM3 . . . **198** A2
Staines Rd, Felt. TW14 . . . **141** G7
Hounslow TW3, TW4 . . . **143** H3
Ilford IG1. . . . . **99** F4
Twickenham TW2 . . . . . **161** G3
Staines Rd E, Sun. TW16 . **160** A7
Staines Wk, Sid. DA14
off Evry Rd **176** C6
Stainforth Rd, E17 . . . . **78** A4
Ilford IG2. . . . . **81** G7
Staining La, EC2 . . . . **20** A3
Stainmore Cl, Chis. BR7. . **193** G1
Stainsbury St, E2
off Royston St. **113** F2
Stainsby Pl, E14
off Stainsby Rd **114** A6
Stainsby Rd, E14 . . . . **114** A6
Stainton Rd, SE6 . . . . **154** D6
Enfield EN3. . . . . **45** F1
Stalbridge St, NW1 . . . . . . **15** H1
Stalham St, SE16. . . . . . . **133** E3
Stalham Way, Ilf. IG6 . . . . . **80** E1
Stambourne Way, SE19 . . **170** B7
West Wickham BR4. . . . **204** C3
Stamford Brook Av, W6 . . **127** F3
Stamford Brook Gdns, W6
off Stamford Brook Rd . **127** F3
Stamford Brook Rd, W6. . **127** F3
Stamford Cl, N15. . . . . **76** D4
Harrow HA3 . . . . **52** B7
Southall UB1. . . . . **103** G7
Stamford Cotts, SW10. . . . **30** B7
Stamford Ct, W6
off Goldhawk Rd. **127** F4
Stamford Dr, Brom. BR2 . **191** F4
Stamford Gdns, Dag.
RM9. . . . . **100** C7
Stamford Gro E, N16
off Oldhill St **94** D1
Stamford Gro W, N16
off Oldhill St **94** D1
STAMFORD HILL, N16 . . . . **94** B1
Stamford Hill, N16. . . . . . . **94** C2
Stamford Hill Est, N16. . . . **94** C1
Stamford Rd, E6. . . . . **116** B1
N1 . . . . **94** B7
N15 . . . . **76** D5
Dagenham RM9 . . . . . . **118** B1
Stamford St, SE1. . . . . **27** E2
Stamp Pl, E2 . . . . **13** F3
Stanard Cl, N16 . . . . **76** B7
Stanborough Cl, Hmptn.
TW12 . . . . **161** F6
Stanborough Pas, E8
off Abbot St. **94** C6
Stanborough Rd, Houns.
TW3 . . . . **144** A3
Stanbridge Pl, N21. . . . . . . **59** H2
Stanbridge Rd, SW15. . . . **147** J3
Stanbrook Rd, SE2. . . . . . **138** B2
Stanbury Rd, SE15. . . . . . **153** E1
Stancroft, NW9 . . . . **70** E4
Standard Ind Est, E16 . . . **136** C2
Standard Pl, EC2 . . . . **12** E4
Standard Rd, NW10 . . . . . **106** C4
Belvedere DA17 . . . . . . **139** G5
Bexleyheath DA6 . . . . . **159** E4
Hounslow TW4 . . . . **143** E3
Standen Rd, SW18. . . . . . **148** C7
Standfield Gdns, Dag. RM10
off Standfield Rd. **101** G6
Standfield Rd, Dag. RM10. **101** G5
Standish Ho, SE3
off Elford Cl. **155** J4
Standish Rd, W6 . . . . **127** G4
Standlake Pt, SE23. . . . . . **171** G3
Stane Cl, SW19
off Hayward Cl. . . **184/185** E1
Stane Way, SE18 . . . . **136** A7
Stanfield Rd, E3 . . . . **113** H2
Stanford Cl, Hmptn.
TW12 . . . . **161** F6
Romford RM7 . . . . **83** H6
Woodford Green IG8 . . . **64** B5
Stanford Ct, SW6
off Bagley's La . . . **148/149** E1
Stanford Ho, Bark. IG11 . . **118** D2
Stanford Pl, SE17. . . . . **36** D2
Stanford Rd, N11 . . . . **57** J5
SW16. . . . . **186** D2
W8. . . . . **22** B5
Stanford St, SW1. . . . . **33** H2
Stanford Way, SW16 . . . . **186** D2
Stangate Cres, Borwd.
WD6 . . . . **38** E5
Stangate Gdns, Stan. HA7. **53** E4
Stanger Rd, SE25. . . . . . . **188** D4
Stanhope Av, N3 . . . . **72** C3
Bromley BR2. . . . . **205** F1
Harrow HA3 . . . . **68** A1
Stanhope Cl, SE16
off Middleton Dr. **133** G2
Stanhope Gdns, N4 . . . . . . **75** H6
N6 . . . . **74** B6
NW7 . . . . **55** F5
SW7. . . . . **30** D1
Dagenham RM8 . . . . . . **101** F3
Ilford IG1. . . . . **98** C1
Stanhope Gate, W1 . . . . . . **24** C1
Stanhope Gro, Beck. BR3. **189** J5
Stanhope Ms E, SW7. . . . . **30** D1
Stanhope Ms S, SW7. . . . . **30** D2
Stanhope Ms W, SW7 . . . . **30** D1
Stanhope Par, NW1. . . . . . . **9** F3
Stanhope Pk Rd, Grnf.
UB6 . . . . **103** J4
Stanhope Pl, W2 . . . . **15** J4
Stanhope Rd, E17 . . . . **78** B5
N6 . . . . **74** C6
N12 . . . . **57** F5
Barnet EN5 . . . . **39** J6
Bexleyheath DA7 . . . . . **159** E2
Carshalton SM5 . . . . . . **200** A7
Croydon CR0. . . . . **202** B3
Dagenham RM8 . . . . . . **101** F2
Greenford UB6 . . . . **103** J5
Sidcup DA15 . . . . **176** A4
Stanhope Row, W1 . . . . . . **24** D2
Stanhope St, NW1. . . . . **9** F4
Stanhope Ter, W2 . . . . **15** F5
Stanier Cl, W14
off Aisgill Av **128** C5
Stanlake Ms, W12 . . . . . . **127** J1
Stanlake Rd, W12. . . . . . . **127** H1
Stanlake Vil, W12 . . . . **127** H1
Stanley Av, Bark. IG11 . . . **117** J2
Beckenham BR3 . . . . . . **190** C2
Dagenham RM8 . . . . . . **101** F1
Greenford UB6 . . . . **103** J1
New Malden KT3 . . . . . **183** G5
Wembley HA0. . . . . **87** H7
Stanley Cl, SW8. . . . . **34** C6
Wembley HA0. . . . . **87** H7
Stanley Ct, Cars. SM5
off Stanley Pk Rd **200** A7
Stanley Cres, W11. . . . . . . **108** C7
Stanleycroft Cl, Islw. TW7 . **144** B1
Stanley Gdns, NW2 . . . . . . **89** J5
W3. . . . . **126** E1
W11 . . . . **108** C7
Mitcham CR4
off Ashbourne Rd **168** A6
Wallington SM6 . . . . . . **200** C6
Stanley Gdns Ms, W11
off Stanley Cres. **108** C7
Stanley Gdns Rd, Tedd.
TW11. . . . . **162** B5
Stanley Gro, SW8 . . . . . . **150** A2
Croydon CR0. . . . . **187** G6
Stanley Pk Dr, Wem. HA0. . **87** J7
Stanley Pk Rd, Cars.
SM5. . . . . **199** J7
Wallington SM6 . . . . . . **200** B6
Stanley Rd, E4 . . . . **62** D1
E10 . . . . **78** B6
E12 . . . . **98** B5
E15. . . . . **114** D1
E18 . . . . **79** F1
N2 . . . . **73** G3
N9 . . . . **60** C1
N10 . . . . **58** B7
N11 . . . . **58** D6
N15 . . . . **75** H4
NW9
off West Hendon Bdy . . **71** G7
SW14. . . . . **146** B4
SW19. . . . . **166** D7
W3. . . . . **126** C3
Bromley BR2. . . . . **191** H4
Carshalton SM5 . . . . . . **200** A7
Croydon CR0. . . . . **187** G7
Enfield EN1. . . . . **44** B3
Harrow HA2 . . . . **85** J2
Hounslow TW3 . . . . **143** J4
Ilford IG1. . . . . **99** G2
Mitcham CR4 . . . . **168** A7
Morden SM4. . . . . **184** D4
Northwood HA6 . . . . **66** A1
Sidcup DA14 . . . . **176** A3
Southall UB1. . . . . **102** E7
Sutton SM2. . . . . **198** E6
Teddington TW11. . . . . . **162** B4
Twickenham TW2 . . . . . **162** A3
Wembley HA9. . . . . **87** J6
Stanley St, SE8 . . . . **133** J7
Stanley Ter, N19 . . . . **92** E2
Stanmer St, SW11 . . . . . . **149** H1
STANMORE, HA7. . . . . **52** D5
Stanmore Gdns, Rich.
TW9. . . . . **145** J3
Sutton SM1. . . . . **199** F3
Stanmore Hall, Stan. HA7 . **52** E3
Stanmore Hill, Stan. HA7. . **52** D3
Stanmore Pl, NW1
off Arlington Rd. **110** B1
Stanmore Rd, E11 . . . . **97** F1
N15 . . . . **75** H4
Belvedere DA17 . . . . . . **139** J4
Richmond TW9 . . . . **145** J3
Stanmore St, N1
off Caledonian Rd **111** F1
Stanmore Ter, Beck. BR3 . **190** A2
Stanmore Way, Loug.
IG10. . . . . **48** D1
Stannard Ms, E8 . . . . **94** D6
Stannard Rd, E8. . . . . **94** D6
Stannary Pl, SE11. . . . . **35** F4
Stannary St, SE11 . . . . **35** F5
Stannet Way, Wall. SM6. . **200** C4
Stannington Path, Borwd.
WD6 . . . . **38** A1
Stansfeld Rd, E6. . . . . **116** A5
Stansfield Rd, SW9 . . . . . **151** F3
Hounslow TW4 . . . . **142** B2
Stansgate Rd, Dag. RM10 . **101** G2
Stanstead Cl, Brom. BR2 . **191** F5

Stanstead Gro, SE6
off Stanstead Rd **171** J1
Stanstead Manor, Sutt.
SM1 .... **198** D6
Stanstead Rd, E11 .... **79** H5
SE6 .... **171** G1
SE23 .... **171** G1
Hounslow (Hthrw Air.)
TW6 .... **140** C6
Stansted Cres, Bex. DA5 . **176** D1
Stanswood Gdns, SE5 ... **132** B7
Stanthorpe Cl, SW16 .... **168** E5
Stanthorpe Rd, SW16 ... **168** E5
Stanton Av, Tedd. TW11 .. **162** B5
Stanton Cl, Epsom KT19 . **196** B5
Worcester Park KT4.... **198** A1
Stanton Ho, SE16
off Rotherhithe St **133** J2
Stanton Rd, SE26
off Stanton Way **171** J4
SW13............... **147** F2
SW20............... **184** A2
Croydon CR0......... **187** J7
Stanton Sq, SE26
off Stanton Way **171** J4
Stanton Way, SE26...... **171** J4
Stanway Cl, Chig. IG7 .... **65** H5
Stanway Ct, N1 .... **13** E2
Stanway Gdns, W3 ..... **126** A1
Edgware HA8 .... **54** C5
Stanway St, N1 .... **12** E1
STANWELL, Stai. TW19 .. **140** B7
Stanwell Cl, Stai. (Stanw.)
TW19............. **140** A6
Stanwell Gdns, Stai.
(Stanw.) TW19 ...... **140** A6
Stanwell Rd, Felt. TW14.. **141** F7
Stanwick Rd, W14 ...... **128** C4
Stanworth St, SE1....... **29** F4
Stanwyck Dr, Chig. IG7 ... **65** F5
Stapenhill Rd, Wem. HA0 . **86** E3
Staplefield Cl, SW2 ..... **169** E1
Pinner HA5 .... **50** E7
Stapleford Av, Ilf. IG2..... **81** H5
Stapleford Cl, E4 .... **62** C3
SW19............... **148** B7
Kingston upon Thames
KT1 .... **182** A3
Stapleford Rd, Wem. HA0 . **87** G7
Stapleford Way, Bark.
IG11............... **118** B3
Staplehurst Rd, SE13.... **154** E5
Carshalton SM5 ...... **199** H7
Staple Inn, WC1 .... **19** E2
Staple Inn Bldgs, WC1 .... **18** E2
Staples Cl, SE16........ **133** H1
Staples Cor, NW2 .... **89** H1
Staples Cor Business Pk,
NW2 .... **89** H1
Staples Rd, Loug. IG10 ... **48** B3
Staple St, SE1 .... **28** C4
Stapleton Gdns, Croy.
CR0 .... **201** G5
Stapleton Hall Rd, N4 .... **75** F7
Stapleton Rd, SW17 ..... **168** A6
Bexleyheath DA7 ..... **139** F7
Orpington BR6 .... **207** J3
Stapley Rd, Belv. DA17 .. **139** G5
Stapylton Rd, Barn. EN5 .. **40** B3
Star All, EC3 .... **20** F5
Star & Garter Hill, Rich.
TW10............... **163** H1
Starboard Way, E14 ..... **134** A3
Starch Ho La, Ilf. IG6 ..... **81** G2
Starcross St, NW1 .... **9** G4
Starfield Rd, W12 .... **127** G2
Star La, E16 .... **115** E4
Starling Cl, Buck.H. IG9 ... **63** G1
Pinner HA5 .... **66** C3
Starling Wk, Hmptn. TW12
off Oak Av **160/161** E6
Starmans Cl, Dag. RM9 .. **119** E1
Star Path, Nthlt. UB5
off Brabazon Rd **103** G2
Star Pl, E1 .... **21** G6
Star Rd, W14 .... **128** C6
Isleworth TW7 .... **144** A2
Star St, E16 .... **115** F5
W2.................. **15** F3
Starts Cl, Orp. BR6...... **206** D3
Starts Hill Av, Orp. BR6 .. **207** E4
Starts Hill Rd, Orp. BR6 .. **206** D3
Starveall Cl, West Dr. UB7. **120** C3
Star Yd, WC2 .... **18** E3
State Fm Av, Orp. BR6 ... **207** E4
Staten Gdns, Twick. TW1 . **162** C1
Statham Gro, N16
off Green Las **93** J4
N18 .... **60** B5
Station App, E4 (Highams Pk)
off The Avenue **62** D6
E7 *off Woodford Rd* **97** H4
E11 (Snaresbrook)
off High St **79** G5
N11
off Friern Barnet Rd ... **58** B5
N12 (Woodside Pk) **56** E4
N16 (Stoke Newington)
off Stamford Hill **94** C2
NW10 *off Station Rd* ... **107** F3
SE1 .... **26** D2
SE3 *off Kidbrooke Pk Rd* . **155** H3
SE9 (Mottingham) **174** C1
SE26 (Lwr Sydenham)
off Worsley Br Rd **171** J5
SE26 (Sydenham)
off Sydenham Rd **171** F4
SW6................ **148** B3
SW16............... **168** D5
W7................. **124** B1
Barnet EN5 .... **41** F4
Bexley DA5
off Bexley High St **159** G7
Bexleyheath DA7
off Avenue Rd ... **158/159** E2
Bexleyheath (Barne.)
DA7 .... **159** J2
Bromley (Hayes) BR2 .. **205** G1
Buckhurst Hill IG9
off Cherry Tree Ri **64** A4
Chislehurst BR7 ...... **192** D1
Chislehurst (Elm.Wds)
BR7 .... **174** B6
Epsom (Stoneleigh)
KT19 .... **197** G5
Esher (Hinch.Wd) KT10. **194** C3
Greenford UB6 .... **86** A7
Hampton TW12
off Milton Rd **179** G1
Harrow HA1 .... **68** B7
Hayes UB3 .... **121** J2
Kingston upon Thames
KT1 .... **182** A1
Loughton IG10 .... **48** B5
Loughton (Debden) IG10.. **49** F4
Orpington BR6 .... **207** J2
Pinner HA5 .... **66** E3
Pinner (Hatch End) HA5
off Uxbridge Rd **51** G7
Richmond TW9 .... **146** A1
Ruislip (S.Ruis.) HA4.... **84** B5
Sunbury-on-Thames
TW16.............. **178** A1
Sutton (Cheam) SM2 .. **198** B7
Watford (Carp.Pk) WD19
off Prestwick Rd **50** D3
Welling DA16 .... **157** J2
Wembley HA0......... **87** E6
West Drayton UB7 .... **120** B1
Worcester Park KT4.... **197** G1
Station App N, Sid. DA15 . **176** A2
Station App Path, SE9
off Glenlea Rd **156** C5
Station App Rd, W4 ..... **126** C7
Station Av, SW9
off Coldharbour La ... **151** H3
New Malden KT3 ..... **183** E3
Richmond TW9 .... **146** A1
Station Cl, N3 .... **72** D1
N12 (Woodside Pk) **56** E4
Hampton TW12 .... **179** H1
Station Ct, SW6
off Townmead Rd **149** F1
Station Cres, N15........ **76** A4
SE3 .... **135** G5
Wembley HA0......... **87** E6
Stationers Hall Ct, EC4
off Ludgate Hill **111** H6
Station Est, Beck. BR3
off Elmers End Rd **189** G4
Station Est Rd, Felt.
TW14.............. **160** B1
Station Gar Ms, SW16
off Estreham Rd **168** D6
Station Gdns, W4....... **126** C7
Station Gro, Wem. HA0 ... **87** H6
Station Hill, Brom. BR2 .. **205** G2
Station Ho Ms, N9
off Fore St **60** D4
Station Par, E11 .... **79** G5
N14 *off High St* **58** D1
NW2 .... **89** J6
SW12
off Balham High Rd .. **168** A1
W3................. **106** A6
Barking IG11 .... **99** F7
Barnet EN4
off Cockfosters Rd **42** A4
Station Par, Felt. TW14... **142** B7
Richmond TW9 .... **146** A1
Station Pas, E18
off Maybank Rd **79** H2
SE15 .... **153** F1
Station Path, E8
off Amhurst Rd **94/95** E6
Station Pl, N4
off Seven Sisters Rd ... **93** G2
Station Ri, SE27
off Norwood Rd **169** H2
Station Rd, E4 (Chingford) . **62** D1
E7 .... **97** G4
E12 .... **98** A4
E17 .... **77** H6
N3 .... **72** D1
N11 .... **58** B5
N17 .... **76** D3
N19 .... **92** C3
N21 .... **59** H1
N22 .... **75** F2
NW4 .... **71** G6
NW7 .... **55** E5
NW10............... **107** F2
SE13 .... **154** C3
SE20 .... **171** F6
SE25 (Norwood Junct.). **188** C4
SW13............... **147** G3
SW19............... **185** F1
W5................. **105** J6
W7 (Hanwell)......... **124** B1
Barnet EN5 .... **40** E5
Belvedere DA17 ...... **139** G3
Bexleyheath DA7 ..... **159** E3
Borehamwood WD6 .... **38** A4
Brentford TW8........ **125** F6
Bromley BR1......... **191** G1
Bromley (Short.) BR2 .. **191** E2
Carshalton SM5 ...... **199** J4
Chessington KT9...... **195** H5
Chigwell IG7 .... **64** E3
Croydon (E.Croy.) CR0 . **202** A2
Croydon (W.Croy.) CR0 . **201** J1
Edgware HA8 .... **54** A6
Esher KT10 .... **194** A2
Esher (Clay.) KT10..... **194** A5
Hampton TW12 .... **179** G1
Harrow HA1 .... **68** C7
Harrow (N.Har.) HA2.... **67** H5
Hayes UB3 .... **121** J3
Hounslow TW3 .... **143** H4
Ilford IG1............ **98** E3
Ilford (Barkingside) IG6.. **81** G3
Kingston upon Thames
KT2 .... **182** A1
Kingston upon Thames
(Hmptn W.) KT1...... **181** F1
Loughton IG10 .... **48** B4
New Malden (Mots.Pk)
KT3 .... **183** H5
Orpington BR6 .... **207** J2
Romford (Chad.Hth)
RM6................ **82** D7
Sidcup DA15 .... **176** A4
Sunbury-on-Thames
TW16.............. **160** A7
Teddington TW11...... **162** C5
Thames Ditton KT7.... **180** C7
Twickenham TW1 ..... **162** C1
West Drayton UB7 .... **120** A1
West Wickham BR4.... **204** C1
Station Rd N, Belv. DA17. **139** H3
Station Sq, Orp. (Petts Wd)
BR5 .... **193** F5
Station St, E15.......... **96** D7
E16 .... **136** E1
Station Ter, NW10 ...... **108** A2
SE5 .... **151** J1
Station Vw, Grnf. UB6 ... **104** A1
Station Way, Buck.H.
(Rod.Val.) IG9 .... **63** J4
Esher (Clay.) KT10..... **194** B6
Sutton (Cheam) SM3 .. **198** B6
Station Yd, Twick. TW1 .. **144** D7
Staunton Rd, Kings.T.
KT2 .... **163** H6
Staunton St, SE8........ **133** J6
★**Stave Hill Ecological Pk**,
SE16 .... **133** H2
Staveley Cl, E9
off Churchill Wk **95** F5
N7 *off Penn Rd* **92/93** E4
SE15
off Asylum Rd ... **152/153** E1
Staveley Gdns, W4...... **146** D1
Staveley Rd, W4........ **126** D7
Staverton Rd, NW2 ...... **89** J7
Stave Yd Rd, SE16 ...... **133** H1
Stavordale Rd, N5 .... **93** H4
Stavordale Rd, Cars. SM5. **185** F7
Stayner's Rd, E1........ **113** G4
Stayton Rd, Sutt. SM1 ... **198** D3
Steadfast Rd, Kings.T.
KT1 .... **181** G1
Stead St, SE17.......... **36** B2
Steam Fm La, Felt. TW14 . **141** J4
Stean St, E8 .... **112** C1
Stebbing Ho, W11....... **128** A1
Stebbing Way, Bark. IG11 . **118** A2
Stebondale St, E14 ..... **134** C5
Stedham Pl, WC1 .... **18** A3
Steedman St, SE17 ...... **35** J2
Steeds Rd, N10 .... **73** J1
Steeds Way, Loug. IG10 ... **48** B3
Steele Rd, E11 .... **96** E4
N17 .... **76** B3
NW10............... **106** C2
W4................. **126** C3
Isleworth TW7 .... **144** D4
Steeles Ms N, NW3
off Steeles Rd **91** J6
Steeles Ms S, NW3
off Steeles Rd **91** J6
Steeles Rd, NW3 .... **91** J6
Steele Wk, Erith DA8 .... **139** H6
Steel's La, E1
off Devonport St **113** F6
Steelyard Pas, EC4
off Upper Thames St .. **112** A7
Steen Way, SE22
off East Dulwich Gro .. **152** B5
Steep Cl, Orp. BR6...... **207** J6
Steep Hill, SW16 .... **168** D3
Croydon CR0......... **202** B4
Steeple Cl, SW6........ **148** B2
SW19............... **166** B5
Steeple Ct, E1
off Coventry Rd .. **112/113** E4
Steeplestone Cl, N18..... **59** J5
Steeple Wk, N1
off Basire St **111** J1
Steerforth St, SW18..... **167** E2
Steers Mead, Mitch. CR4 . **185** J1
Steers Way, SE16....... **133** H2
Stellar Ho, N17.......... **60** C6
Stella Rd, SW17........ **167** J6
Stellman Cl, E5 .... **94** D3
Stembridge Rd, SE20.... **188** E2
Stephan Cl, E8 .... **112** D1
Stephen Cl, Orp. BR6.... **207** J3
Stephendale Rd, SW6 ... **149** E2
Stephen Ms, W1......... **17** H2
Stephen Pl, SW4
off Rectory Gro **150** C3
Stephen Rd, Bexh. DA7 .. **159** J3
Stephenson Rd, E17 ..... **77** H5
W7................. **104** C6
Twickenham TW2 ..... **143** G7
Stephenson St, E16 ..... **114** E4
NW10............... **107** E3
Stephenson Way, NW1 .... **9** G5
Stephen's Rd, E15 ...... **115** E1
Stephen St, W1 .... **17** H2
STEPNEY, E1 .... **113** F5
Stepney Causeway, E1... **113** G6
Stepney Grn, E1 .... **113** F5
Stepney High St, E1..... **113** G5
Stepney Way, E1........ **112** E5
Sterling Av, Edg. HA8 .... **53** J4
Sterling Cl, N9 .... **61** F1
NW10 .... **89** G6
Sterling Gdns, SE14..... **133** H6
Sterling Ho, SE3
off Cambert Way **155** H4
Sterling Ind Est, Dag.
RM10.............. **101** H4
Sterling Pl, W5 .... **125** H4
Sterling St, SW7 .... **23** H5
Sterling Way, N18 .... **60** A5
★**Sternberg Cen**, N3 ..... **72** E2
Stern Cl, Bark. IG11..... **118** C2
Sterndale Rd, W14...... **128** A3
Sterne St, W12......... **128** A2
Sternhall La, SE15 ...... **152** D3
Sternhold Av, SW2...... **168** D2
Sterry Cres, Dag. RM10
off Alibon Rd **101** G5
Sterry Dr, Epsom KT19 .. **196** E4
Thames Ditton KT7.... **180** B6
Sterry Gdns, Dag. RM10.. **101** G6
Sterry Rd, Bark. IG11 .... **117** J1
Dagenham RM10...... **101** G4
Sterry St, SE1 .... **28** B4
Steucers La, SE23 ...... **153** H7
Steve Biko La, SE6...... **172** A4
Steve Biko Rd, N7 .... **93** G3
Steve Biko Way, Houns.
TW3............... **143** G3

Stevedale Rd, Well. DA16. **158** C2
Stevedore St, E1
off Waterman Way. **132/133** E1
Stevenage Rd, E6. . . . . **98** D6
SW6. . . . . **128** A7
Stevens Av, E9 . . . . **95** F6
Stevens Cl, Beck. BR3 . . . **172** A6
Hampton TW12 . . . . **161** E6
Pinner HA5
off Bridle Rd **66** C5
Stevens Grn, Bushey
(Bushey Hth) WD23. . . . **51** J1
Stevens La, Esher (Clay.)
KT10 . . . . **194** D7
Stevenson Cl, Barn. EN5 . . **41** G6
Stevenson Cres, SE16 . . . . **37** J3
Stevens Rd, Dag. RM8 . . . **100** B3
Stevens St, SE1 . . . . **29** E5
Stevens Way, Chig. IG7 . . . **65** H4
Steventon Rd, W12. . . . . . **107** F7
Stewards Holte Wk, N11
off Coppies Gro **58** B4
Steward St, E1. . . . . **21** E2
Stewart Cl, NW9 . . . . **70** C6
Chislehurst BR7 . . . . . . **175** E5
Hampton TW12 . . . . **161** E5
Stewart Rainbird Ho, E12 . **98** D5
Stewart Rd, E15. . . . . **96** C4
Stewartsby Cl, N18 . . . . . . **59** J5
Stewart's Gro, SW3 . . . . . . **31** F3
Stewart's Rd, SW8. . . . . . **130** C7
Stewart St, E14 . . . . **134** C2
Stew La, EC4 . . . . **19** J5
Steyne Rd, W3 . . . . **126** C1
Steyning Gro, SE9 . . . . . . **174** C4
Steynings Way, N12. . . . . . **56** D5
Steyning Way, Houns.
TW4. . . . . **142** C4
Steynton Av, Bex. DA5. . . **176** D2
Stickland Rd, Belv. DA17
off Picardy Rd **139** G4
Stickleton Cl, Grnf. UB6. . **103** H3
Stilecroft Gdns, Wem.
HA0 . . . . **86** E3
Stile Hall Gdns, W4 . . . . . **126** A5
Stile Hall Par, W4
off Chiswick High Rd. . **126** A5
Stile Path, Sun. TW16. . . . **178** A4
Stiles Cl, Brom. BR2. . . . . **192** C6
Erith DA8
off Riverdale Rd **139** H5
Stillingfleet Rd, SW13 . . . **127** G6
Stillington St, SW1 . . . . . . **33** G1
Stillness Rd, SE23 . . . . . . **153** H6
Stipularis Dr, Hayes UB4 . **102** D4
Stirling Av, Pnr. HA5 . . . . . **66** F7
Wallington SM6 . . . . . . **200** E7
Stirling Cl, SW16 . . . . **186** C1
Stirling Cor, Barn. EN5 . . . **38** D6
Borehamwood WD6 . . . . **38** D6
Stirling Gro, Houns. TW3 . **143** J2
Stirling Rd, E13. . . . . **115** H2
E17 . . . . **77** H3
N17 . . . . **76** [illegible]
N22 . . . . **75** H1
SW9. . . . . **150** E2
W3. . . . . **126** B3
Harrow HA3 . . . . **68** C3
Hayes UB3. . . . . **102** B7
Hounslow (Hthrw Air.)
TW6 . . . . **140** C6
Twickenham TW2 . . . . . **143** G7
Stirling Rd Path, E17 . . . . . **77** H3
Stirling Wk, N.Mal. KT3 . . **182** C5
Surbiton KT5. . . . . **182** B6
Stirling Way, Borwd. WD6 . **38** D6
Croydon CR0. . . . . **186** E7
Stiven Cres, Har. HA2 . . . . **85** F3
Stockbury Rd, Croy. CR0 . **189** F6
Stockdale Rd, Dag. RM8 . **101** F2
Stockdove Way, Grnf.
UB6 . . . . **104** C3
Stocker Gdns, Dag. RM9 . **100** C7
★**Stock Exchange**, EC2 . . . **19** H3
Stockfield Rd, SW16 . . . . **169** F3
Esher (Clay.) KT10. . . . . **194** B5
Stockholm Ho, E1. . . . . . . **112** D7
Stockholm Rd, SE16 . . . . **133** F5
Stockholm Way, E1 . . . . . . **29** H1
Stockhurst Cl, SW15 . . . . **147** J2
Stockingswater La, Enf.
EN3 . . . . **45** H3
Stockley Cl, West Dr. UB7 . **120** E2
Stockley Fm Rd, West Dr.
UB7
off Stockley Rd. . . **120/121** E3
Stockley Pk, Uxb. UB11 . . **121** E1
Stockley Pk Roundabout,
Uxb. UB11. . . . . **120** E1
Stockley Rd, West Dr.
UB7 . . . . **120** E4
Stock Orchard Cres, N7 . . . **93** F5
Stock Orchard St, N7. . . . . **93** F5
Stockport Rd, SW16. . . . . **186** D1
Stocksfield Rd, E17 . . . . . . **78** C3
Stocks Pl, E14
off Grenade St. **113** J7
Stock St, E13 . . . . **115** G2
Stockton Cl, Barn. EN5 . . . **41** F4
Stockton Gdns, N17
off Stockton Rd. **59** J7
NW7 . . . . **54** E3
Stockton Rd, N17. . . . . **59** J7
N18 . . . . **60** D6
STOCKWELL, SW9. . . . . . **151** F1
Stockwell Av, SW9. . . . . . **151** F3
Stockwell Cl, Brom. BR1 . **191** H2
Edgware HA8
off Burnt Oak Bdy **70** C2
Stockwell Gdns, SW9 . . . **151** F2
Stockwell Gdns Est, SW9. **151** E2
Stockwell Grn, SW9. . . . . **151** F2
Stockwell La, SW9. . . . . . **151** F2
Stockwell Ms, SW9
off Stockwell Rd **151** F2
Stockwell Pk Cres, SW9. . **151** F2
Stockwell Pk Est, SW9. . . **151** F2
Stockwell Pk Rd, SW9 . . . **151** F1
Stockwell Pk Wk, SW9. . . **151** F3
Stockwell Rd, SW9 . . . . . **151** F2
Stockwell St, SE10. . . . . . **134** C6
Stockwell Ter, SW9 . . . . . **151** F1
Stodart Rd, SE20 . . . . **189** F1
Stofield Gdns, SE9
off Aldersgrove Av . . . **174** A3
Stoford Cl, SW19 . . . . **148** B7
Stokenchurch St, SW6. . . **148** E1
STOKE NEWINGTON,
N16 . . . . **94** B2
Stoke Newington Ch St,
N16 . . . . **94** A3
Stoke Newington Common,
N16 . . . . **94** C3
Stoke Newington High St,
N16 . . . . **94** C3
Stoke Newington Rd,
N16 . . . . **94** C5
Stoke Pl, NW10 . . . . **107** F3
Stoke Rd, Kings.T. KT2. . . **164** C7
Stokesby Rd, Chess. KT9. **195** J6
Stokesley St, W12 . . . . . . **107** F6
Stokes Rd, E6. . . . . **116** B4
Croydon CR0. . . . . **189** G6
Stoll Cl, NW2 . . . . **89** J3
Stonard Rd, N13 . . . . **59** G3
Dagenham RM8 . . . . . . **100** B5
Stonards Hill, Loug. IG10. . **48** C6
Stondon Pk, SE23 . . . . . . **153** H7
Stondon Wk, E6 . . . . **116** A2
Stonebanks, Walt. KT12 . . **178** A7
STONEBRIDGE, NW10 . . . **106** B1
Stonebridge Common, E8
off Mayfield Rd **94** C7
Stonebridge Pk, NW10. . . . **88** D7
Stonebridge Rd, N15 . . . . . **76** B5
Stonebridge Way, Wem.
HA9. . . . . **88** B6
Stone Bldgs, WC2 . . . . **18** D2
Stonechat Sq, E6
off Peridot St. **116** B5
Stone Cl, SW4
off Larkhall Ri **150** C2
Dagenham RM8 . . . . . . **101** F2
West Drayton UB7 . . . . **120** C1
Stonecot Cl, Sutt. SM3 . . **198** B1
Stonecot Hill, Sutt. SM3 . **198** B1
Stone Cres, Felt. TW14. . . **141** J7
Stonecroft Cl, Barn. EN5 . . **39** H4
Stonecroft Rd, Erith DA8 . **139** J7
Stonecroft Way, Croy.
CR0 . . . . **187** E7
Stonecrop Cl, NW9 . . . . . . **70** D3
Stonecutter Ct, EC4
off Stonecutter St **111** H6
Stonecutter St, EC4. . . . . . **19** G3
Stonefield Cl, Bexh. DA7 . **159** G3
Ruislip HA4 . . . . **84** E5
Stonefield St, N1 . . . . **111** G1
Stonefield Way, SE7
off Greenbay Rd **136** A7
Ruislip HA4. . . . . **84** E4
Stonegrove, Edg. HA8 . . . . **53** H4
Stonegrove Est, Edg. HA8 . **53** J4
Stonegrove Gdns, Edg.
HA8 . . . . **53** J5
Stonehall Av, Ilf. IG1 . . . . **80** B6
Stone Hall Gdns, W8 . . . . . **22** A6
Stone Hall Pl, W8. . . . . **22** A6
Stone Hall Rd, N21 . . . . . . **43** F7
Stoneham Rd, N11. . . . . . . **58** C6
Stonehill Cl, SW14. . . . . . **146** D5
Stonehill Grn, Dart. DA2 . **177** J7
Stonehill Rd, SW14 . . . . . **146** C5
W4 *off Wellesley Rd* . . . **126** A5
Stonehills Business Pk, N18
off Silvermere Dr **61** G6
Stonehills Ct, SE21 . . . . . **170** B3
Stonehill Wds Pk, Sid.
DA14 . . . . **177** H10
Stonehorse Rd, Enf. EN3 . . **45** F5
Stone Ho Ct, EC3. . . . . **20** D3
Stone Lake Retail Pk,
SE7 . . . . **135** H4
STONELEIGH, Epsom
KT17 . . . . **197** G5
Stoneleigh Av, Enf. EN1. . . **45** E1
Worcester Park KT4. . . . **197** G4
Stoneleigh Bdy, Epsom
KT17 . . . . **197** G5
Stoneleigh Cres, Epsom
KT19 . . . . **197** F5
Stoneleigh Ms, E3
off Stanfield Rd **113** H2
Stoneleigh Pk Av, Croy.
CR0 . . . . **189** G6
Stoneleigh Pk Rd, Epsom
KT19 . . . . **197** F6
Stoneleigh Pl, W11 . . . . . . **108** A7
Stoneleigh Rd, N17 . . . . . . **76** C3
Carshalton SM5 . . . . . . **185** H7
Ilford IG5. . . . . **80** B3
Stoneleigh St, W11. . . . . . **108** A7
Stoneleigh Ter, N19 . . . . . . **92** B2
Stonells Rd, SW11
off Chatham Rd. **149** J5
Stonemasons Cl, N15 . . . . **76** A4
Stonenest St, N4 . . . . **93** F1
Stone Pk Av, Beck. BR3 . . **190** A4
Stone Pl, Wor.Pk. KT4. . . . **197** G2
Stone Rd, Brom. BR2. . . . . **191** F5
Stones End St, SE1 . . . . . . **27** J4
Stone St, Croy. CR0 . . . . . **201** G5
Stonewall, E6 . . . . **116** D5
Stoney All, SE18. . . . . **156** D2
Stoneyard La, E14
off Poplar High St **114** B7
Stoneycroft Cl, SE12 . . . . **155** F7
Stoneycroft Rd, Wdf.Grn.
IG8. . . . . **64** B6
Stoneydeep, Tedd. TW11
off Twickenham Rd . . . **162** D4
Stoneydown, E17. . . . . **77** H4
Stoneydown Av, E17 . . . . . **77** H4
Stoneyfields Gdns, Edg.
HA8 . . . . [illegible]
Stoneyfields La, Edg. HA8 . **54** C5
Stoney La, E1 . . . . **21** E3
SE19 *off Church Rd*. . . . **170** C6
Stoney St, SE1. . . . . **28** B1
Stonhouse St, SW4 . . . . . **150** D3
Stonor Rd, W14 . . . . **128** C4
Stonycroft Cl, Enf. EN3
off Brimsdown Av. **45** H7
Stony Path, Loug. IG10 . . . **48** C2
Stopes St, SE15 . . . . **132** C7
Stopford Rd, E13 . . . . **115** G1
SE17 . . . . **35** H4
Store Rd, E16 . . . . **136** D2
Storers Quay, E14 . . . . . . **134** D4
Store St, E15 . . . . **96** D5
WC1. . . . . **17** H2
Storey Rd, E17 . . . . **77** J4
N6 . . . . **73** J6
Storey's Gate, SW1 . . . . . . **25** J4
Storey St, E16 . . . . **136** D1
Stories Ms, SE5 . . . . **152** B2
Stories Rd, SE5 . . . . **152** B3
Stork Rd, E7. . . . . **97** F6
Storksmead Rd, Edg. HA8. **54** E7
Storks Rd, SE16 . . . . **29** J6
Stormont Rd, N6 . . . . **73** J7
SW11. . . . . **150** A3
Stormont Way, Chess.
KT9 . . . . **195** F5
Stormount Dr, Hayes
UB3 . . . . **121** F2
Storrington Rd, Croy.
CR0 . . . . **202** C1
Story St, N1
off Carnoustie Dr **93** F7
Stothard Pl, EC2
off Bishopsgate **112** B5
Stothard St, E1
off Colebert Av **113** F4
Stott Cl, SW18. . . . . **149** G6
Stoughton Av, Sutt. SM3. **198** A5
Stoughton Cl, SE11 . . . . . . **34** D2
Stoughton Cl, SW15
off Bessborough Rd . . **165** G1
Stour Av, Sthl. UB2 . . . . . **123** G3
Stourcliffe St, W1. . . . . **15** J4
Stour Cl, Kes. BR2 . . . . . . **205** J4
Stourhead Cl, SW19
off Castlecombe Dr. . . **148** A7
Stourhead Gdns, SW20 . . **183** G3
Stour Rd, E3. . . . . **96** A7
Dagenham RM10. . . . . . **101** G2
Stourton Av, Felt. TW13 . . **161** F4
Stowage, SE8. . . . . **134** A6
Stow Cres, E17. . . . . **61** H7
Stowe Gdns, N9. . . . . **60** C1
Stowe Pl, N15 . . . . **76** B3
Stowe Rd, W12. . . . . **127** H2
Stowting Rd, Orp. BR6 . . **207** H4
Stox Mead, Har. HA3 . . . . . **68** A1
Stracey Rd, E7 . . . . **97** G4
NW10. . . . . **106** D1
Strachan Pl, SW19
off Woodhayes Rd. . . . **165** J6
Stradbroke Dr, Chig. IG7 . . **64** D6
Stradbroke Gro, Buck.H.
IG9 . . . . **64** A1
Ilford IG5. . . . . **80** B3
Stradbroke Pk, Chig. IG7 . . **64** E6
Stradbroke Rd, N5 . . . . **93** J4
Stradbrook Cl, Har. HA2
off Stiven Cres **85** F3
Stradella Rd, SE24. . . . . . **151** J6
Strafford Av, Ilf. IG5 . . . . . **80** D2
Strafford Rd, W3. . . . . **126** C2
Barnet EN5 . . . . **40** B3
Hounslow TW3 . . . . **143** F3
Twickenham TW1 . . . . . **144** D7
Strafford St, E14. . . . . **134** A2
Strahan Rd, E3 . . . . **113** H3
Straight, The, Sthl. UB1 . . **122** D2
Straightsmouth, SE10 . . . **134** C7
Strait Rd, E6 . . . . **116** B7
Straker's Rd, SE22 . . . . . . **152** E4
STRAND, WC2 . . . . **18** A5
Strand, WC2 . . . . **18** A6
Strand Ct, SE18
off Strandfield Cl. **137** H5
Strand Dr, Rich. TW9
off Bessant Dr. **126** B7
Strandfield Cl, SE18. . . . . **137** H5
Strand La, WC2 . . . . **18** D5
Strand on the Grn, W4. . . **126** A6
Strand Pl, N18 . . . . **60** A4
Strand Sch App, W4
off Thames Rd. **126** A6
Strangways Ter, W14
off Melbury Rd **128** C3
Stranraer Rd, Houns.
(Hthrw Air.) TW6 . . . . . **140** B6
Stranraer Way, N1 . . . . **93** E7
Strasburg Rd, SW11 . . . . . **150** D1
Stratfield Pk Cl, N21 . . . . . **43** H7
Stratfield Rd, Borwd. WD6. **38** A3
STRATFORD, E15. . . . . **96** C6
Stratford Av, W8
off Stratford Rd. **128** D3
Stratford Cen, The, E15 . . . **96** D7
Stratford Cl, Bark. IG11 . . **100** A7
Dagenham RM10. . . . . . **101** J7
Stratford Ct, N.Mal. KT3
off Kingston Rd. **182** D4
Stratford Gro, SW15 . . . . **148** A4
Stratford Ho Av, Brom.
BR1 . . . . **192** B3
Stratford Pl, W1 . . . . **16** D4
Stratford Rd, E13 . . . . **115** F1
NW4 . . . . **72** A4
W8. . . . . **128** D3
Hayes UB4. . . . . **102** B4
Hounslow (Hthrw Air.)
TW6 . . . . **141** E6
Southall UB2. . . . . **122** E4
Thornton Heath CR7. . . . **187** G4
Stratford Vil, NW1 . . . . **92** C7
Strathan Cl, SW18 . . . . . . **148** B6
Strathaven Rd, SE12 . . . . **155** H6
Strathblaine Rd, SW11. . . **149** G4
Strathbrook Rd, SW16. . . **169** F7
Strathcona Rd, Wem. HA9. **87** G2
Strathdale, SW16. . . . . . . **169** F5
Strathdon Dr, SW17. . . . . **167** G3
Strathearn Av, Hayes
UB3 . . . . **121** J7
Twickenham TW2 . . . . . **161** H1
Strathearn Pl, W2. . . . . **15** F5
Strathearn Rd, SW19 . . . . **166** D5
Sutton SM1. . . . . **198** D5
Stratheden Par, SE3
off Stratheden Rd **135** G7
Stratheden Rd, SE3 . . . . . **155** G1

Strathfield Gdns, Bark. IG11 **99** G6
Strathleven Rd, SW2 **151** E5
Strathmore Gdns, N3 **72** E1
W8 *off Palace Gdns Ter* **128** D1
Edgware HA8 **70** B2
Strathmore Rd, SW19 **166** D3
Croydon CR0 **187** J7
Teddington TW11 **162** B4
Strathnairn St, SE1 **37** J2
Strathray Gdns, NW3 **91** H6
Strath Ter, SW11 **149** H4
Strathville Rd, SW18 **166** E2
Strathyre Av, SW16 **187** G3
Stratton Cl, SW19 **184** D2
Bexleyheath DA7 **159** E3
Edgware HA8 **53** J6
Hounslow TW3 **143** F1
Strattondale St, E14 **134** C3
Stratton Dr, Bark. IG11 **99** J5
Stratton Gdns, Sthl. UB1 **103** F6
Stratton Rd, SW19 **184** D2
Bexleyheath DA7 **159** E3
Stratton St, W1 **25** E1
Strauss Rd, W4 **126** D2
STRAWBERRY HILL, Twick. TW1 **162** B3
Strawberry Hill, Twick. TW1 **162** C3
Strawberry Hill Cl, Twick. TW1 **162** C3
Strawberry Hill Rd, Twick. TW1 **162** C3
Strawberry La, Cars. SM5 **199** J3
Strawberry Vale, N2 **73** G1
Twickenham TW1 **162** D3
Streakes Fld Rd, NW2 **89** G2
Streamdale, SE2 **138** A6
Stream La, Edg. HA8 **54** B5
Streamline Ms, SE22 **170** D1
Streamside Cl, N9 **60** C1
Bromley BR2 **191** G4
Streamway, Belv. DA17 **139** G6
Streatfield Av, E6 **116** C1
Streatfield Rd, Har. HA3 **69** G3
STREATHAM, SW16 **169** E4
Streatham Cl, SW16 **169** E2
Streatham Common N, SW16 **168** E5
Streatham Common S, SW16 **169** E6
Streatham Ct, SW16 **168** E3
Streatham High Rd, SW16 **168** E5
STREATHAM HILL, SW2 **151** F7
Streatham Hill, SW2 **169** E2
STREATHAM PARK, SW16 **168** C4
Streatham Pl, SW2 **150** E7
Streatham Rd, SW16 **186** A1
Mitcham CR4 **186** A1
Streatham St, WC1 **17** J3
STREATHAM VALE, SW16 **168** D7
Streatham Vale, SW16 **168** C7
Streathbourne Rd, SW17 **168** A2
Streatley Pl, NW3 *off New End Sq* **91** F4
Streatley Rd, NW6 **90** C7
Streeters La, Wall. SM6 **200** D3
Streetfield Ms, SE3 **155** G3
Streimer Rd, E15 **114** C2
Strelley Way, W3 **106** E7
Stretton Mans, SE8 *off Glaisher St* **134** A6
Stretton Rd, Croy. CR0 **188** B7
Richmond TW10 **163** F2
Strickland Row, SW18 **149** G7
Strickland St, SE8 **154** A2
Strickland Way, Orp. BR6 **207** J4
Stride Rd, E13 **115** F2
Strimon Cl, N9 **61** F2
Strode Cl, N10 *off Pembroke Rd* **58** A7
Strode Rd, E7 **97** G4
N17 **76** B2
NW10 **89** G6
SW6 **128** A7
Strone Rd, E7 **97** J6
E12 **98** A6
Strone Way, Hayes UB4 **102** E4
Strongbow Cres, SE9 **156** C5
Strongbow Rd, SE9 **156** C5
Strongbridge Cl, Har. HA2 **85** G1
Stronsa Rd, W12 **127** F2
Stroud Cres, SW15 **165** G3
Stroudes Cl, Wor.Pk. KT4 **183** E7
Stroud Fld, Nthlt. UB5 **84** E6
Stroud Gate, Har. HA2 **85** H4
STROUD GREEN, N4 **75** F6
Stroud Grn Gdns, Croy. CR0 **189** F7
Stroud Grn Rd, N4 **93** F1
Stroud Grn Way, Croy. CR0 **189** E7
Stroudley Wk, E3 **114** B3
Stroud Rd, SE25 **188** D6
SW19 **166** D3
Strouds Cl, Rom. (Chad.Hth) RM6 **82** B5
Strouts Pl, E2 **13** F3
Strutton Grd, SW1 **25** H5
Strype St, E1 **21** F2
Stuart Av, NW9 **71** G7
W5 **125** J1
Bromley BR2 **205** G1
Harrow HA2 **85** F3
Stuart Cres, N22 **75** F1
Croydon CR0 **203** J3
Stuart Evans Cl, Well. DA16 **158** C3
Stuart Gro, Tedd. TW11 **162** B5
Stuart Pl, Mitch. CR4 **185** J1
Stuart Rd, NW6 **108** D3
SE15 **153** F4
SW19 **166** D3
W3 **126** C1
Barking IG11 **99** J7
Barnet EN4 **41** H7
Harrow HA3 **68** C2
Richmond TW10 **163** E2
Thornton Heath CR7 **187** J4
Welling DA16 **158** B1
Stuart Twr, W9 **6** C4
Stubbs Cl, NW9 **70** C5
Stubbs Dr, SE16 **132** E5
Stubbs Ms, Dag. RM8 *off Marlborough Rd* **100** B4
Stubbs Pt, E13 **115** H4
Stubbs Way, SW19 *off Brangwyn Cres* **185** G1
Stucley Pl, NW1 *off Hawley Cres* **92** B7
Stucley Rd, Houns. TW5 **123** J7
Studdridge St, SW6 **148** D2
Studd St, N1 **111** H1
Studholme Ct, NW3 **90** D4
Studholme St, SE15 **132** E7
Studio Pl, SW1 **24** A4
Studio Way, Borwd. WD6 **38** C2
Studland, SE17 **36** B3
Studland Cl, Sid. DA15 **175** J3
Studland Rd, SE26 **171** G5
W7 **104** A6
Kingston upon Thames KT2 **163** H6
Studland St, W6 **127** H4
Studley Av, E4 **62** D7
Studley Cl, E5 **95** H5
Studley Ct, E14 *off Newport Av* **114** D7
Sidcup DA14 **176** B5
Studley Dr, Ilf. IG4 **80** A6
Studley Est, SW4 **151** E1
Studley Gra Rd, W7 **124** B2
Studley Rd, E7 **97** H6
SW4 **150** E1
Dagenham RM9 **100** D7
Stukeley Rd, E7 **97** H7
Stukeley St, WC2 **18** B3
Stumps Hill La, Beck. BR3 **172** A6
Sturdy Rd, SE15 **153** E2
Sturge Av, E17 **78** B2
Sturgeon Rd, SE17 **35** J4
Sturges Fld, Chis. BR7 **175** G6
Sturgess Av, NW4 **71** H7
Sturge St, SE1 **27** J3
Sturmer Way, N7 **93** F5
Sturminster Cl, Hayes UB4 **102** C6
Sturrock Cl, N15 **76** A4
Sturry St, E14 **114** B6
Sturt St, N1 **12** A2
Stutfield St, E1 **21** J4
Styles Gdns, SW9 **151** H3
Styles Way, Beck. BR3 **190** C4
Sudbourne Rd, SW2 **151** E5
Sudbrooke Rd, SW12 **149** J6
Sudbrook Gdns, Rich. TW10 **163** G3
Sudbrook La, Rich. TW10 **163** H1
SUDBURY, Wem. HA0 **86** D5
Sudbury, E6 *off Newark Knok* **116** D6
Sudbury Av, Wem. HA0 **87** G3
Sudbury Ct Dr, Har. HA1 **86** C3
Sudbury Ct Rd, Har. HA1 **86** C3
Sudbury Cres, Brom. BR1 **173** G6
Wembley HA0 **87** E5
Sudbury Cft, Wem. HA0 **86** C4
Sudbury Gdns, Croy. CR0 **202** B4
Sudbury Hts Av, Grnf. UB6 **86** C5
Sudbury Hill, Har. HA1 **86** B2
Sudbury Hill Cl, Wem. HA0 **86** C4
Sudbury Ho, SW18 *off Wandsworth High St* **148** E5
Sudbury Rd, Bark. IG11 **99** J5
Sudeley St, N1 **11** H2
Sudlow Rd, SW18 **148** D4
Sudrey St, SE1 **27** J4
Suez Av, Grnf. UB6 **104** C2
Suez Rd, Enf. EN3 **45** H4
Suffield Rd, E4 **62** B3
N15 **76** C5
SE20 **189** F2
Suffolk Cl, Borwd. WD6 *off Clydesdale Cl* **38** D5
Suffolk Ct, E10 **78** A7
Ilford IG3 **81** H6
Suffolk La, EC4 **20** B5
Suffolk Pk Rd, E17 **77** H4
Suffolk Pl, SW1 **25** J1
Suffolk Rd, E13 **115** F3
N15 **76** A6
NW10 **89** E7
SE25 **188** C4
SW13 **127** F7
Barking IG11 **99** G7
Dagenham RM10 **101** J5
Enfield EN3 **45** E5
Harrow HA2 **67** F6
Ilford IG3 **81** H6
Sidcup DA14 **176** C6
Worcester Park KT4 **197** F2
Suffolk St, E7 **97** G5
SW1 **25** J1
Sugar Bakers Ct, EC3 *off Creechurch La* **112** B6
Sugar Ho La, E15 **114** C2
Sugar Loaf Wk, E2 *off Victoria Pk Sq* **113** F3
Sugar Quay Wk, EC3 **20** E6
Sugden Rd, SW11 **150** A3
Thames Ditton KT7 **194** E1
Sugden Way, Bark. IG11 **117** J2
Sulgrave Gdns, W6 *off Sulgrave Rd* **127** J2
Sulgrave Rd, W6 **127** J2
Sulina Rd, SW2 **150** E7
Sulivan Ct, SW6 **148** D3
Sulivan Rd, SW6 **148** D3
Sullivan Av, E16 **116** A5
Sullivan Cl, SW11 **149** H3
Hayes UB4 **102** C5
West Molesey KT8 *off Victoria Av* **179** G3
Sullivan Rd, SE11 **35** F1
Sultan Rd, E11 **79** H4
Sultan St, SE5 **35** J7
Beckenham BR3 **189** G2
Sultan Ter, N22 *off Vincent Rd* **75** G2
Sumatra Rd, NW6 **90** D5
Sumburgh Rd, SW12 **150** A6
Summer Av, E.Mol. KT8 **180** B5
Summercourt Rd, E1 **113** F6
Summerene Cl, SW16 **168** C7
Summerfield Av, NW6 **108** B2
Summerfield La, Surb. KT6 **195** G2
Summerfield Rd, W5 **105** E4
Loughton IG10 **48** A6
Summerfields Av, N12 **57** H6
Summerfield St, SE12 **155** F7
Summer Gdns, E.Mol. KT8 **180** B5
Summer Hill, Borwd. (Elstree) WD6 **38** A5
Chislehurst BR7 **192** D2
Summerhill Cl, Orp. BR6 **207** H3
Summerhill Gro, Enf. EN1 **44** B6
Summerhill Rd, N15 **76** A4
Summer Hill Vil, Chis. BR7 **192** D1
Summerhill Way, Mitch. CR4 **186** A1
Summerhouse Av, Houns. TW5 **142** E1
Summerhouse La, West Dr. UB7 **120** A6
Summerhouse Rd, N16 **94** B2
Summerland Gdns, N10 **74** B3
Summerlands Av, W3 **106** C7
Summerlee Av, N2 **73** J4
Summerlee Gdns, N2 **73** J4
Summerley St, SW18 **167** E2
Summer Rd, E.Mol. KT8 **180** B5
Thames Ditton KT7 **180** C5
Summersby Rd, N6 **74** B6
Summers Cl, Sutt. SM2 *off Overton Rd* **198** D7
Wembley HA9 **88** B1
Summerskille Cl, N9 *off Plevna Rd* **60/61** E2
Summers La, N12 **57** G7
Summers Row, N12 **57** H6
SUMMERSTOWN, SW17 **166** E3
Summerstown, SW17 **167** F3
Summer St, EC1 **11** E6
Summerton Way, SE28 **118** D6
Summer Trees, Sun. TW16 *off The Avenue* **178** B1
Summerville Gdns, Sutt. SM1 **198** C6
Summerwood Rd, Islw. TW7 **144** C5
Summit, The, Loug. IG10 **48** C1
Summit Av, NW9 **70** D5
Summit Cl, N14 **58** C2
NW9 **70** D4
Edgware HA8 **54** A7
Summit Ct, NW2 **90** B5
Summit Dr, Wdf.Grn. IG8 **80** A2
Summit Est, N16 **76** D7
Summit Rd, E17 **78** B4
Northolt UB5 **85** G7
Summit Way, N14 **58** B2
SE19 **170** B7
Sumner Av, SE15 *off Peckham Rd* **152** C1
Sumner Cl, Orp. BR6 **207** F4
Sumner Est, SE15 **132** C7
Sumner Gdns, Croy. CR0 **201** G1
Sumner Pl, SW7 **31** F2
Sumner Pl Ms, SW7 **31** F2
Sumner Rd, SE15 **37** G6
Croydon CR0 **201** G1
Harrow HA1 **67** J7
Sumner Rd S, Croy. CR0 **201** G1
Sumner St, SE1 **27** H1
Sumpter Cl, NW3 **91** F6
Sun All, Rich. TW9 *off Kew Rd* **145** H4
Sunbeam Cres, W10 **107** J4
Sunbeam Rd, NW10 **106** C4
Sunbury Av, NW7 **54** D5
SW14 **146** D4
Sunbury Cl, Walt. KT12 **178** A6
Sunbury Ct, Sun. TW16 **178** D2
Sunbury Ct Island, Sun. TW16 **178** D3
Sunbury Ct Ms, Sun. TW16 *off Lower Hampton Rd* **178** D2
Sunbury Ct Rd, Sun. TW16 **178** C2
Sunbury Gdns, NW7 **54** D5
Sunbury La, SW11 **149** G1
Walton-on-Thames KT12 **178** A6
Sunbury Lock Ait, Walt. KT12 **178** B4
Sunbury Rd, Sutt. SM3 **198** A3
Sunbury St, SE18 **136** C3
Sunbury Way, Felt. TW13 **160** C5
Sun Ct, EC3 **20** C4
Suncroft Pl, SE26 **171** F3
Sunderland Ct, SE22 **152** D7
Sunderland Mt, SE23 *off Sunderland Rd* **171** G2
Sunderland Rd, SE23 **171** G1
W5 **125** G3
Sunderland Ter, W2 **14** A3
Sunderland Way, E12 **98** A2
Sundew Av, W12 **107** G7
Sundial Av, SE25 **188** C3
Sundorne Rd, SE7 **135** H5
Sundra Wk, E1 *off Beaumont Gro* **113** G4
SUNDRIDGE, Brom. BR1 **173** J6
Sundridge Av, Brom. BR1 **192** A1
Chislehurst BR7 **174** A7
Welling DA16 **157** G2
Sundridge Ho, Brom. BR1 *off Burnt Ash La* **173** H5
Sundridge Pl, Croy. CR0 *off Inglis Rd* **202** D1
Sundridge Rd, Croy. CR0 **188** C7
Sunfields Pl, SE3 **135** H7
Sunken Rd, Croy. CR0 **203** F5
Sunland Av, Bexh. DA6 **159** E4
Sun La, SE3 **135** H7
Sunleigh Rd, Wem. HA0 **105** H1

Sunley Gdns, Grnf. UB6. . **104** D1
Sunlight Cl, SW19 . . . . . . **167** F6
Sunlight Sq, E2 . . . . **113** E3
Sunmead Rd, Sun. TW16 . **178** A3
Sunna Gdns, Sun. TW16 . **178** B2
Sunningdale, N14
off Wilmer Way **58** D5
Sunningdale Av, W3 . . . . . **107** E7
Barking IG11 . . . . **117** G1
Feltham TW13 . . . . **160** E2
Ruislip HA4 . . . . **84** C1
Sunningdale Cl, E6. . . . . . **116** C3
SE16 *off Ryder Dr* . **132/133** E5
SE28 . . . . **118** E6
Stanmore HA7 . . . . **52** D7
Surbiton KT6
off Culsac Rd. **195** H2
Sunningdale Gdns, NW9 . . **70** C5
W8 *off Lexham Ms* **128** D3
Sunningdale Rd, Brom.
BR1 . . . . **192** B4
Sutton SM1. . . . . **198** C4
Sunningfields Cres, NW4. . **71** H2
Sunningfields Rd, NW4 . . . **71** H2
Sunninghill Rd, SE13. . . . **154** B2
Sunny Bk, SE25 . . . . **188** D3
Sunny Cres, NW10. . . . . . . **88** C7
Sunnycroft Rd, SE25 . . . . **188** D3
Hounslow TW3 . . . . **143** H2
Southall UB1. . . . . **103** G5
Sunnydale, Orp. BR6 . . . . **206** D2
Sunnydale Gdns, NW7. . . . **54** D6
Sunnydale Rd, SE12. . . . . **155** H5
Sunnydene Av, E4 . . . . **62** D5
Ruislip HA4 . . . . **84** A2
Sunnydene Gdns, Wem.
HA0 . . . . **87** F6
Sunnydene St, SE26 . . . . **171** H4
Sunnyfield, NW7 . . . . **55** F4
Sunny Gdns Par, NW4
off Great N Way **71** J2
Sunny Gdns Rd, NW4 . . . . **71** H2
Sunny Hill, NW4. . . . . **71** H3
Sunnyhill Cl, E5 . . . . **95** H4
Sunnyhill Rd, SW16 . . . . . **168** E4
Sunnyhurst Cl, Sutt. SM1 . **198** D3
Sunnymead Av, Mitch.
CR4 . . . . **186** C3
Sunnymead Rd, NW9 . . . . **70** D7
SW15. . . . . **147** H5
Sunnymede Dr, Ilf. IG6 . . . **80** E4
Sunny Nook Gdns, S.Croy.
CR2 . . . . **202** A6
Sunny Rd, The, Enf. EN3 . . **45** G1
Sunnyside, NW2 . . . . **90** C3
SW19. . . . . **166** B6
Walton-on-Thames
KT12 . . . . **178** C5
Sunnyside Dr, E4 . . . . **46** C7
Sunnyside Pas, SW19 . . . **166** B6
Sunnyside Pl, SW19
off Sunnyside **166** B6
Sunnyside Rd, E10. . . . . . . **96** A1
N19 . . . . **74** D7
W5. . . . . **125** G1
Ilford IG1. . . . . **99** F3
Teddington TW11. . . . . . **162** A4
Sunnyside Rd E, N9. . . . . . **60** D3
Sunnyside Rd N, N9. . . . . . **60** C3
Sunnyside Rd S, N9. . . . . . **60** C3
Sunnyside Ter, NW9
off Edgware Rd. **70** D3
Sunny Vw, NW9. . . . . **70** D5
Sunny Way, N12. . . . . **57** H7
Sun Pas, SE16 . . . . **29** H5
Sunray Av, SE24. . . . . **152** A4
Bromley BR2. . . . . **192** B6
Surbiton KT5. . . . . **196** B2
West Drayton UB7 . . . . **120** A2
Sunrise Cl, Felt. TW13
off Exeter Rd. **161** F3
Sun Rd, W14. . . . . **128** C5
Sunset Av, E4. . . . . **62** B1
Woodford Green IG8 . . . **63** F4
Sunset Ct, Wdf.Grn. IG8
off Navestock Cres **63** J7
Sunset Gdns, SE25 . . . . . **188** C2
Sunset Rd, SE5 . . . . **151** J4
SE28 . . . . **138** A2
Sunset Vw, Barn. EN5 . . . . **40** B2
Sunshine Way, Mitch.
CR4 . . . . **185** J2
Sun St, EC2 . . . . **20** D2
Sun St Pas, EC2. . . . . **20** D2
Sun Wk, E1. . . . . **21** H6
Sunwell Cl, SE15
off Cossall Wk . . . **152/153** E1
Superior Dr, Orp. BR6 . . . **207** J6
SURBITON, KT6 . . . . **181** J7
Surbiton Ct, Surb. KT6 . . **181** F6
Surbiton Cres, Kings.T.
KT1 . . . . **181** H4
Surbiton Hall Cl, Kings.T.
KT1 . . . . **181** H4
Surbiton Hill Pk, Surb.
KT5 . . . . **182** A5
Surbiton Hill Rd, Surb.
KT6 . . . . **181** H4
Surbiton Par, Surb. KT6
off St. Mark's Hill. **181** H6
Surbiton Rd, Kings.T. KT1 . **181** H4
Surlingham Cl, SE28 . . . . **118** D7
Surma Cl, E1. . . . . **112** E4
Surmans Cl, Dag. RM9. . . **118** C1
Surrendale Pl, W9. . . . . . . **108** D4
Surrey Canal Rd, SE14 . . . **133** F6
SE15 . . . . **133** F6
Surrey Cres, W4 . . . . **126** A5
★**Surrey Docks City Fm**,
SE16 . . . . **133** J2
Surrey Gdns, N4
off Finsbury Pk Av. **75** J6
Surrey Gro, SE17 . . . . **36** D4
Sutton SM1. . . . . **199** G3
Surrey La, SW11. . . . . **149** H1
Surrey La Est, SW11. . . . . **149** H1
Surrey Lo, SE1 . . . . **26** E6
Surrey Ms, SE27
off Hamilton Rd. **170** B4
Surrey Mt, SE23. . . . . **171** E1
Surrey Quays Retail Cen,
SE16 . . . . **133** G3
Surrey Quays Rd, SE16 . . **133** F3
Surrey Rd, SE15. . . . . **153** G5
Barking IG11 . . . . **117** H1
Dagenham RM10. . . . . . **101** H5
Harrow HA1 . . . . **67** J5
West Wickham BR4. . . . **204** B1
Surrey Row, SE1 . . . . **27** G3
Surrey Sq, SE17. . . . . **36** D3
Surrey St, E13. . . . . **115** H3
WC2. . . . . **18** D5
Croydon CR0. . . . . **201** J3
Surrey Ter, SE17. . . . . **36** E3
Surrey Water Rd, SE16. . . **133** G1
Surridge Gdns, SE19
off Hancock Rd **170** A6
Surr St, N7. . . . . **92** E5
Sury Basin, Kings.T. KT2 . **181** H1
Susan Cl, Rom. RM7 . . . . . **83** J3
Susan Constant Ct, E14
off Newport Av **114** D7
Susan Lawrence Ho, E12
off Walton Rd **98** D4
Susannah St, E14. . . . . . . **114** B6
Susan Rd, SE3 . . . . **155** H2
Susan Wd, Chis. BR7 . . . . **192** D1
Sussex Av, Islw. TW7 . . . . **144** D3
Sussex Cl, N19
off Cornwallis Rd. . . **92/93** E2
Ilford IG4. . . . . **80** C6
New Malden KT3 . . . . . **183** E4
Twickenham TW1
off Westmorland Cl . **144/145** E6
Sussex Cres, Nthlt. UB5. . . **85** G6
Sussex Gdns, N4 . . . . **75** J5
N6 *off Great N Rd*. **73** J5
W2. . . . . **15** E5
Chessington KT9. . . . . . **195** G6
Sussex Ms, SE6
off Ravensbourne Pk. . **154** A7
Sussex Ms E, W2 . . . . **15** F4
Sussex Ms W, W2. . . . . **15** F5
Sussex Pl, NW1 . . . . **7** J4
W2. . . . . **15** F4
W6. . . . . **127** J5
Erith DA8. . . . . **139** H7
New Malden KT3 . . . . . **183** E4
Sussex Ring, N12. . . . . **56** D5
Sussex Rd, E6. . . . . **116** D1
Carshalton SM5 . . . . . . **199** J6
Erith DA8. . . . . **139** H7
Harrow HA1 . . . . **67** J5
Mitcham CR4
off Lincoln Rd. . . . **186/187** E5
New Malden KT3 . . . . . **183** E4
Sidcup DA14 . . . . **176** B5
South Croydon CR2 . . . **202** A6
Southall UB2. . . . . **122** D3
West Wickham BR4. . . . **204** B1
Sussex Sq, W2. . . . . **15** F5
Sussex St, E13 . . . . **115** H3
SW1. . . . . **32** E4
Sussex Way, N7 . . . . **93** E2
N19 . . . . **92** E1
Barnet EN4 . . . . **42** A5
Sutcliffe Cl, NW11 . . . . **73** E5
Sutcliffe Ho, Hayes UB3. . **102** A6
Sutcliffe Rd, SE18 . . . . . . **137** H6
Welling DA16 . . . . **158** C2
Sutherland Av, W9 . . . . **6** C4
W13. . . . . **104** E6
Hayes UB3 . . . . **122** A4
Orpington BR5 . . . . **193** J6
Welling DA16 . . . . **157** H4
Sutherland Cl, Barn. EN5. . **40** B4
Sutherland Ct, NW9. . . . . . **70** B5
Sutherland Dr, SW19 . . . . **185** G1
Sutherland Gdns, SW14 . **147** E3
Worcester Park KT4. . . . **197** H1
Sutherland Gro, SW18. . . **148** B6
Teddington TW11. . . . . . **162** B5
Sutherland Pl, W2. . . . . . . **108** D6
Sutherland Rd, E17 . . . . . . **77** G2
N9 . . . . **60** D1
N17 . . . . **60** D7
W4. . . . . **126** E6
W13. . . . . **104** D6
Belvedere DA17 . . . . . . **139** G3
Croydon CR0. . . . . **187** G7
Enfield EN3. . . . . **45** G5
Southall UB1. . . . . **103** F6
Sutherland Rd Path, E17 . . **77** G3
Sutherland Row, SW1 . . . . **32** E3
Sutherland Sq, SE17 . . . . . **35** J4
Sutherland St, SW1 . . . . . . **32** D3
Sutherland Wk, SE17 . . . . . **36** A4
Sutlej Rd, SE7 . . . . **135** J7
Sutterton St, N7. . . . . **93** F6
SUTTON, SM1 - SM3. . . . . **198** E6
Sutton Cl, Beck. BR3
off Albemarle Rd. **190** B1
Loughton IG10 . . . . **48** B7
Pinner HA5 . . . . **66** A5
Sutton Common Rd, Sutt.
SM1, SM3. . . . . **184** C7
Sutton Ct, W4. . . . . **126** C6
Sutton SM2. . . . . **199** F6
Sutton Ct Rd, E13. . . . . . . **115** J3
W4. . . . . **126** C7
Sutton SM1. . . . . **199** F6
Sutton Cres, Barn. EN5 . . . **40** A5
Sutton Dene, Houns. TW3. **143** H1
Sutton Est, SW3 . . . . **31** H3
W10 . . . . **107** J5
Sutton Est, The, N1 . . . . . . **93** H7
Sutton Gdns, Bark. IG11
off Sutton Rd. **117** H1
Croydon CR0. . . . . **188** C5
Sutton Grn, Bark. IG11
off Sutton Rd. **117** H1
Sutton Gro, Sutt. SM1 . . . **199** G4
Sutton Hall Rd, Houns.
TW5 . . . . **123** G7
★**Sutton Heritage Cen**,
Cars. SM5 . . . . **199** J4
★**Sutton Ho**, E9 . . . . **95** F5
Sutton La, EC1 . . . . **11** H6
Hounslow TW3 . . . . **143** F3
Sutton La N, W4. . . . . **126** C5
Sutton La S, W4. . . . . **126** C6
Sutton Par, NW4
off Church Rd **71** J4
Sutton Pk Rd, Sutt. SM1 . **198** E6
Sutton Path, Borwd. WD6
off Stratfield Rd **38** A2
Sutton Pl, E9 . . . . **95** F5
Sutton Rd, E13 . . . . **115** F4
E17 . . . . **77** G1
N10 . . . . **74** A2
Barking IG11 . . . . **117** H2
Hounslow TW5 . . . . **143** G1
Sutton Row, W1. . . . . **17** J3
Sutton Sq, E9
off Urswick Rd **95** F5
Hounslow TW5 . . . . **143** F1
Sutton St, E1 . . . . **113** F6
Sutton's Way, EC1 . . . . **12** A6
Sutton Wk, SE1 . . . . **26** D2
Sutton Way, W10 . . . . **107** J5
Hounslow TW5 . . . . **143** F1
Swaby Rd, SW18. . . . . **167** F1
Swaffham Way, N22
off White Hart La. **59** H7
Swaffield Rd, SW18. . . . . **149** E7
Swain Cl, SW16 . . . . **168** B6
Swain Rd, Th.Hth. CR7 . . . **187** J5
Swains Cl, West Dr. UB7 . **120** B2
Swains La, N6 . . . . **92** A3
Swainson Rd, W3. . . . . **127** F2
Swains Rd, SW17. . . . . . . **167** J7
Swain St, NW8 . . . . **7** G5
Swaledale Cl, N11
off Ribblesdale Av. **58** A6
Swallands Rd, SE6. . . . . . **172** A3
Swallow Cl, SE14. . . . . . . **153** F1
Bushey WD23 . . . . **51** J1
Swallow Dr, NW10
off Kingfisher Way **88** D6
Northolt UB5. . . . . **103** G2
Swallowfield Rd, SE7. . . . **135** H5
Swallowfield Way, Hayes
UB3 . . . . **121** G2
Swallow Gdns, SW16 . . . **168** D5
Swallow Ho, NW8
off Allitsen Rd **109** H2
Swallow Pas, W1 . . . . **17** E4
Swallow Pl, W1 . . . . **17** E4
Swallow St, E6. . . . . **116** B5
W1. . . . . **17** G6
Swanage Rd, E4. . . . . **62** C7
SW18. . . . . **149** F6
Swanage Waye, Hayes
UB4 . . . . **102** C6
Swan App, E6. . . . . **116** B5
Swanbridge Rd, Bexh.
DA7 . . . . **159** G1
Swan Cl, E17 . . . . **77** H1
Croydon CR0. . . . . **188** B7
Feltham TW13 . . . . **161** E4
Swan Ct, SW3 . . . . **31** H4
Swandon Way, SW18. . . . **149** E4
Swan Dr, NW9. . . . . **70** E2
Swanfield St, E2 . . . . **13** F4
Swan La, EC4. . . . . **20** B6
N20 . . . . **57** F3
Loughton IG10 . . . . **47** J7
Swanley Rd, Well. DA16. . **158** C1
Swan Mead, SE1 . . . . **28** D6
Swan Pas, E1
off Cartwright St **112** C7
Swan Path, E10
off Jesse Rd **96** C1
Swan Pl, SW13. . . . . **147** F2
Swan Rd, SE16. . . . . **133** F2
SE18 . . . . **136** A3
Feltham TW13 . . . . **160** E5
Southall UB1. . . . . **103** H6
West Drayton UB7 . . . . **120** A2
Swanscombe Ho, W11
off St. Anns Rd **128** A1
Swanscombe Rd, W4. . . . **127** E5
W11 . . . . **128** A1
Swansea Ct, E16
off Fishguard Way . **136/137** E1
Swansea Rd, Enf. EN3. . . . **45** F4
Hounslow (Hthrw Air.)
TW6 *off Southern*
Perimeter Rd. **141** F6
Swanshope, Loug. IG10. . . **49** E2
Swansland Gdns, E17
off McEntee Av **77** H1
Swanston Path, Wat.
WD19 . . . . **50** C3
Swan St, SE1. . . . . **28** A5
Isleworth TW7 . . . . **144** E3
Swanton Gdns, SW19 . . . **166** A1
Swanton Rd, Erith DA8 . . **139** H7
Swan Wk, SW3 . . . . **31** J5
Swan Way, Enf. EN3. . . . . . **45** G2
Swanwick Cl, SW15. . . . . . **147** F7
Swan Yd, N1
off Highbury Sta Rd . . . **93** H6
Swaton Rd, E3 . . . . **114** A4
Swaylands Rd, Belv.
DA17 . . . . **139** G6
Swaythling Cl, N18 . . . . . . **61** E4
Swaythling Ho, SW15
off Tunworth Cres **147** F6
Swedenborg Gdns, E1. . . . **21** J5
Sweden Gate, SE16 . . . . . **133** H3
Sweeney Cres, SE1 . . . . . . **29** G4
Sweet Briar Grn, N9. . . . . . **60** C3
Sweet Briar Gro, N9. . . . . . **60** C3
Sweet Briar Wk, N18 . . . . . **60** C4
Sweetmans Av, Pnr. HA5. . **66** D3
Sweets Way, N20. . . . . **57** G2
Swetenham Wk, SE18
off Sandbach Pl. **137** F5
Swete St, E13. . . . . **115** G2
Sweyn Pl, SE3 . . . . **155** G2
Swift Cl, E17. . . . . **61** H7
Harrow HA2 . . . . **85** H2
Swift Rd, Felt. TW13. . . . . **161** E3
Southall UB2. . . . . **123** F3
Swiftsden Way, Brom.
BR1 . . . . **173** E6
Swift St, SW6 . . . . **148** C1
Swinbrook Rd, W10 . . . . . **108** B5
Swinburne Ct, SE5
off Basingdon Way . . . **152** A4
Swinburne Cres, Croy.
CR0 . . . . **189** F6
Swinburne Rd, SW15. . . . **147** G4
Swinderby Rd, Wem.
HA0 . . . . **87** H6

Swindon Cl, Ilf. IG3
off Salisbury Rd 99 H2
Swindon Rd, Houns.
(Hthrw Air.) TW6 141 F5
Swindon St, W12 127 H1
Swinfield Cl, Felt. TW13 160 E4
Swinford Gdns, SW9 151 H3
Swingate La, SE18 137 H6
Swinnerton St, E9 95 H5
Swinton Cl, Wem. HA9 88 B1
Swinton Pl, WC1 10 C3
Swinton St, WC1 10 C3
Swires Shaw, Kes. BR2 206 A4
Swiss Ct, W1 17 J6
Swiss Ter, NW6 91 G7
Switch Ho, E14
off Blackwall Way 114 D7
Swithland Gdns, SE9 174 D4
Swyncombe Av, W5 125 E4
Swynford Gdns, NW4
off Handowe Cl 71 G4
Sybil Ms, N4
off Lothair Rd N 75 H6
Sybil Phoenix Cl, SE8 133 G5
Sybourn St, E17 77 J7
Sycamore Av, E3 113 J1
W5 125 G3
Sidcup DA15 157 J6
Sycamore Cl, E16
off Clarence Rd. 114/115 E4
N9 *off Pycroft Way* 60 D4
SE9 174 B2
W3
off Bromyard Av 126/127 E1
Barnet EN4 41 G6
Carshalton SM5 199 J4
Edgware HA8
off Ash Cl 54 C4
Feltham TW13 160 A3
Loughton IG10
off Cedar Dr. 48/49 E2
Northolt UB5 103 E1
South Croydon CR2 202 B5
Sycamore Ct, Surb. KT6
off Penners Gdns 181 H7
Sycamore Gdns, W6 127 H2
Mitcham CR4 185 G2
Sycamore Gro, NW9 70 C7
SE6 154 C6
SE20 170 D7
New Malden KT3 182 D3
Sycamore Hill, N11 58 A6
Sycamore Ms, SW4 150 C3
Sycamore Rd, SW19 165 J6
Sycamore St, EC1 11 J6
Sycamore Wk, W10
off Fifth Av. 108 B4
Ilford IG6
off Civic Way 81 F4
Sycamore Way, Tedd.
TW11 163 F6
Thornton Heath CR7 187 G5
SYDENHAM, SE26 171 F5
Sydenham Av, N21
off Fleming Dr. 43 F5
SE26 171 E5
Sydenham Cotts, SE12 173 J2
Sydenham Hill, SE23 170 E1
SE26 170 D3
Sydenham Hill Est, SE26 170 D3
Sydenham Pk, SE26 171 F3
Sydenham Pk Rd, SE26 171 F3
Sydenham Ri, SE23 170 E2
Sydenham Rd, SE26 171 F5
Croydon CR0 188 A7
Sydmons Ct, SE23 153 F7
Sydner Ms, N16
off Sydner Rd 94 C4
Sydner Rd, N16 94 C4
Sydney Cl, SW3 31 F2
Sydney Gro, NW4 71 J5
Sydney Ms, SW3 31 F2
Sydney Pl, SW7 31 F2
Sydney Rd, E11
off Mansfield Rd 79 H6
N8 75 G4
N10 74 A1
SE2 138 C3
SW20 184 A2
W13 124 D1
Bexleyheath DA6 158 D4
Enfield EN2 44 A4
Feltham TW14 160 A1
Ilford IG6 81 F2
Richmond TW9 145 H4
Sidcup DA14 175 H4
Sutton SM1 198 D4
Teddington TW11 162 C5
Woodford Green IG8 63 G4
Sydney St, SW3 31 G3
Sylvan Av, N3 72 D2
N22 59 F7
NW7 55 F6
Romford RM6 83 F6
Sylvan Ct, N12
off Holden Rd 56/57 E4
Sylvan Est, SE19 188 C1
Sylvan Gdns, Surb. KT6 181 G7
Sylvan Gro, NW2 90 A4
SE15 133 E7
Sylvan Hill, SE19 188 B1
Sylvan Rd, E7 97 G6
E11 79 G5
E17 78 A5
SE19 188 C1
Ilford IG1
off Hainault St. 99 F2
Sylvan Wk, Brom. BR1 192 C3
Sylvan Way, Dag. RM8 100 B3
West Wickham BR4 204 E4
Sylverdale Rd, Croy. CR0 201 H3
Sylvester Av, Chis. BR7 174 C6
Sylvester Path, E8
off Sylvester Rd. 94/95 E6
Sylvester Rd, E8 95 E6
E17 77 J7
N2 73 F2
Wembley HA0 87 F5
Sylvestrus Cl, Kings.T.
KT1 182 A1
Sylvia Av, Pnr. HA5 51 F6
Sylvia Ct, Wem. HA9
off Harrow Rd 88 B7
Sylvia Gdns, Wem. HA9 88 B7
Symes Ms, NW1 9 F1
Symington Ms, E9
off Coopersale Rd. 95 G5
Symister Ms, N1 12 D4
Symons St, SW3 32 A2
Symphony Ms, W10
off Third Av 108 B3
Syon Gate Way, Brent.
TW8 124 D7
★**Syon Ho & Pk**, Brent.
TW8 145 F1
Syon La, Islw. TW7 124 E7
Syon Pk Gdns, Islw. TW7 124 C7
Syon Vista, Rich. TW9 145 G1

T

Tabard Cen, SE1
off Prioress St 132 A3
Tabard Gdn Est, SE1 28 C4
Tabard St, SE1 28 B4
Tabernacle Av, E13
off Barking Rd 115 G4
Tabernacle St, EC2 12 C6
Tableer Av, SW4 150 D5
Tabley Rd, N7 92 E4
Tabor Gdns, Sutt. SM3 198 C6
Tabor Gro, SW19 166 B7
Tabor Rd, W6 127 H3
Tachbrook Est, SW1 33 J4
Tachbrook Ms, SW1 33 F1
Tachbrook Rd, Felt. TW14 141 J7
Southall UB2 122 D4
Tachbrook St, SW1 33 G2
Tack Ms, SE4 154 A3
Tadema Rd, SW10 30 D7
Tadmor St, W12 128 A1
Tadworth Av, N.Mal. KT3 183 F5
Tadworth Rd, NW2 89 G2
Taeping St, E14 134 B4
Taffy's How, Mitch. CR4 185 H3
Taft Way, E3
off St. Leonards St 114 B3
Tagg's Island, Hmptn.
TW12 180 A2
Tailworth St, E1 21 H2
Tait Rd, Croy. CR0 188 B7
Takhar Ms, SW11
off Cabul Rd 149 H2
Talacre Rd, NW5 92 A6
Talbot Av, N2 73 G3
Talbot Cl, N15 76 C4
Talbot Ct, EC3 20 C5
Talbot Cres, NW4 71 G5
Talbot Gdns, Ilf. IG3 100 A2
Talbot Ho, E14
off Giraud St 114 B6
N7 *off Harvist Est* 93 G3
Talbot Pl, SE3 154 E2
Talbot Rd, E6 116 D2
E7 97 G4
N6 74 A6
N15 76 C4
Talbot Rd, N22 74 C2
SE22 152 B4
W2 108 C6
W11 108 C6
W13 104 D7
Bromley BR2
off Masons Hill 191 H4
Carshalton SM5 200 A5
Dagenham RM9 101 F6
Harrow HA3 68 C2
Isleworth TW7 144 D4
Southall UB2 123 E4
Thornton Heath CR7 188 A4
Twickenham TW2 162 B1
Wembley HA0 87 G5
Talbot Sq, W2 15 F4
Talbot Wk, NW10
off Garnet Rd. 88/89 E6
W11 108 B6
Talbot Yd, SE1 28 B2
Talfourd Pl, SE15 152 C1
Talfourd Rd, SE15 152 C1
Talgarth Rd, W6 128 B5
W14 128 B5
Talgarth Wk, NW9 70 E5
Talisman Cl, Ilf. IG3 100 B1
Talisman Sq, SE26 170 D4
Talisman Way, Wem. HA9 87 J3
Tallack Cl, Har. HA3
off College Hill Rd. 52 B7
Tallack Rd, E10 95 J1
Tall Elms Cl, Brom. BR2 191 F5
Tallis Cl, E16 115 H6
Tallis Gro, SE7 135 H6
Tallis St, EC4 19 F5
Tallis Vw, NW10 88 D6
Tall Trees, SW16 187 F3
Tally Ho Cor, N12 57 F5
Talma Gdns, Twick. TW2 144 B6
Talmage Cl, SE23
off Tyson Rd 153 F7
Talman Gro, Stan. HA7 53 G6
Talma Rd, SW2 151 G4
Talwin St, E3 114 B3
Tamar Cl, E3
off Lefevre Wk 113 J1
Tamarind Yd, E1 29 J1
Tamarisk Sq, W12 107 F7
Tamar Sq, Wdf.Grn. IG8 63 H6
Tamar St, SE7
off Woolwich Rd 136 B3
Tamar Way, N17 76 D3
Tamesis Gdns, Wor.Pk.
KT4 196 E1
Tamian Way, Houns. TW4 142 C4
Tamworth Av, Wdf.Grn.
IG8 63 E6
Tamworth La, Mitch. CR4 186 B2
Tamworth Pk, Mitch. CR4 186 B4
Tamworth Pl, Croy. CR0 201 J2
Tamworth Rd, Croy. CR0 201 H2
Tamworth St, SW6 128 D6
Tancred Rd, N4 75 H6
Tandem Cen, SW19
off Prince George's Rd. 185 G1
Tandem Way, SW19 185 G1
Tandridge Dr, Orp. BR6 207 G1
Tandridge Pl, Orp. BR6
off Tandridge Dr. 193 G7
Tanfield Av, NW2 89 F4
Tanfield Rd, Croy. CR0 201 J4
Tangier Rd, Rich. TW10 146 B3
Tanglebury Cl, Brom. BR1 192 C4
Tangle Tree Cl, N3 73 E2
Tanglewood Cl, Croy.
CR0 203 F3
Stanmore HA7 52 B2
Tanglewood Way, Felt.
TW13 160 B3
Tangley Gro, SW15 147 F7
Tangley Pk Rd, Hmptn.
TW12 161 F6
Tangmere Gdns, Nthlt.
UB5 102 C2
Tangmere Gro, Kings.T.
KT2 163 G5
Tangmere Way, NW9 71 E2
Tanhurst Wk, SE2
off Alsike Rd 138 D3
Tankerton Rd, Surb. KT6 195 J2
Tankerton St, WC1 10 B4
Tankerville Rd, SW16 168 D6
Tankridge Rd, NW2 89 H2
Tanner Pt, E13
off Pelly Rd 115 G1
Tanners Cl, Walt. KT12 178 B6
Tanners End La, N18 60 B4
Tanners Hill, SE8 153 J1
Tanners La, Ilf. IG6 81 F3
Tanners Ms, SE8
off Tanners Hill 153 J1
Tanner St, SE1 28 E4
Barking IG11 99 F6
Tannery Cl, Beck. BR3 189 G5
Dagenham RM10 101 H3
Tannington Ter, N5 93 G3
Tannsfeld Rd, SE26 171 G5
Tansley Cl, N7
off Hilldrop Rd 92 D5
Tanswell Est, SE1 27 F4
Tanswell St, SE1 27 E4
Tansy Cl, E6 116 D6
Tantallon Rd, SW12 168 A1
Tant Av, E16 115 F6
Tantony Gro, Rom. RM6 82 D3
Tanworth Gdns, Pnr. HA5 66 B2
Tanyard La, Bex. DA5 159 G7
Tanza Rd, NW3 91 J4
Tapestry Cl, Sutt. SM2 198 E7
Taplow, NW3 91 G7
SE17 36 D4
Taplow Rd, N13 59 J4
Taplow St, N1 12 A2
Tappesfield Rd, SE15 153 F3
Tapp St, E1 113 E4
Tapster St, Barn. EN5 40 C4
Tara Ms, N8
off Edison Rd 74 D6
Taransay Wk, N1
off Essex Rd 94 A6
Tarbert Ms, N15
off Roslyn Rd 76 B5
Tarbert Rd, SE22 152 B5
Tarbert Wk, E1
off Juniper St 113 F7
Target Cl, Felt. TW14 141 H6
Tariff Cres, SE8 133 J4
Tariff Rd, N17 60 D6
Tarleton Gdns, SE23 171 E1
Tarling Cl, Sid. DA14 176 B3
Tarling Rd, E16 115 F6
N2 73 F2
Tarling St, E1 113 E6
Tarling St Est, E1 113 F6
Tarnbank, Enf. EN2 43 E5
Tarn St, SE1 27 J6
Tarnwood Pk, SE9 174 C1
Tarquin Ho, SE26 170 D4
Tarragon Cl, SE14 133 H7
Tarragon Gro, SE26 171 G6
Tarrant Pl, W1 15 J2
Tarrington Cl, SW16 168 D3
Tarver Rd, SE17 35 H4
Tarves Way, SE10 134 B7
Tash Pl, N11
off Woodland Rd 58 B5
Tasker Cl, Hayes UB3 121 F7
Tasker Ho, Bark. IG11
off Dovehouse Mead 117 G2
Tasker Rd, NW3 91 J5
Tasman Ct, E14
off Westferry Rd 134 B4
Tasmania Ter, N10 55 J6
Tasman Rd, SW9 151 E3
Tasman Wk, E16
off Royal Rd. 116 A6
Tasso Rd, W6 128 B6
Tatam Rd, NW10 88 C7
Tatchbury Ho, SW15
off Tunworth Cres 147 F6
Tate & Lyle Jetty, E16 136 B2
★**Tate Britain**, SW1 34 A2
★**Tate Modern**, SE1 27 H1
Tate Rd, E16
off Newland St 136 C1
Sutton SM1 198 D5
Tatham Pl, NW8
off Acacia Rd 109 G2
Tatnell Rd, SE23 153 H6
Tattersall Cl, SE9 156 B5
Tatton Cres, N16
off Clapton Common 76 C7
Tatum St, SE17 36 C2
Tauheed Cl, N4 93 J2
Taunton Av, SW20 183 H2
Hounslow TW3 143 J2
Taunton Cl, Ilf. IG6 65 J6
Sutton SM3 198 D1
Taunton Dr, N2 73 F2
Enfield EN2 43 G3
Taunton Ms, NW1 7 J6
Taunton Pl, NW1 7 J5
Taunton Rd, SE12 155 E5
Greenford UB6 103 H1
Taunton Way, Stan. HA7 69 H3
Tavern Cl, Cars. SM5 185 H7
Taverners Cl, W11
off Addison Av 128 B1

Taverner Sq, N5
off Highbury Gra. 93 J4
Taverners Way, E4
off Douglas Rd. 62/63 E1
Tavern La, SW9 151 G2
Tavistock Av, E17 77 H3
NW7 56 A7
Greenford UB6 104 D2
Tavistock Cl, N16
off Crossway 94 B5
Tavistock Ct, WC2
off Tavistock St 110/111 E7
Tavistock Cres, W11 108 C5
Mitcham CR4 186 E4
Tavistock Gdns, Ilf. IG3 99 H4
Tavistock Gate, Croy. CR0 202 A1
Tavistock Gro, Croy. CR0 188 A7
Tavistock Ms, E18
off Avon Way 79 G4
W11 *off Lancaster Rd* 108 C6
Tavistock Pl, E18
off Avon Way 79 G3
N14 *off Chase Side* 42 B7
WC1 9 J5
Tavistock Rd, E7 97 F4
E15 97 F6
E18 79 G3
N4 76 A6
NW10 107 F2
W11 108 C6
Bromley BR2 191 F4
Carshalton SM5 199 G1
Croydon CR0 202 A1
Edgware HA8 70 A1
Welling DA16 158 C1
West Drayton UB7 120 A1
Tavistock Sq, WC1 9 J5
Tavistock St, WC2 18 B5
Tavistock Ter, N19 92 D3
Tavistock Twr, SE16
off Finland St 133 H3
Tavistock Wk, Cars. SM5
off Tavistock Rd 199 G1
Taviton St, WC1 9 H5
Tavy Cl, SE11 35 F3
Tawney Rd, SE28 118 B7
Tawny Cl, W13 124 E1
Feltham TW13
off Chervil Cl 160 A3
Tawny Way, SE16 133 G4
Tayben Av, Twick. TW2 144 B6
Taybridge Rd, SW11 150 A3
Tayburn Cl, E14 114 C6
Taylor Av, Rich. TW9 146 B2
Taylor Cl, N17 60 D7
SE8 133 J6
Hampton (Hmptn H.)
TW12 161 J5
Hounslow TW3 143 J1
Orpington BR6 207 J4
Taylor Ct, E15
off Clays La 96 C5
Taylor Rd, Mitch. CR4 167 H7
Wallington SM6 200 D5
Taylors Bldgs, SE18
off Spray St 136/137 E4
Taylors Cl, Sid. DA14 175 J4
Taylors Grn, W3
off Long Dr. 106/107 E6
Taylors La, NW10 88 E7
SE26 170 E4
Barnet EN5 40 C1
Taymount Ri, SE23 171 F2
Tayport Cl, N1 93 E7
Tayside Dr, Edg. HA8 54 B3
Taywood Rd, Nthlt. UB5 103 F3
Teak Cl, SE16 133 H1
Teal Cl, E16 *off Fulmer Rd* 116 A5
Teal Ct, Wall. SM6
off Carew Rd 200 C6
Teale St, E2 13 J1
Tealing Dr, Epsom KT19 196 D4
Teal Pl, Sutt. SM1
off Sandpiper Rd 198 C5
Teal St, SE10 135 F3
Teasel Cl, Croy. CR0 203 G1
Teasel Cres, SE28 137 H1
Teasel Way, E15 114 E3
Tebworth Rd, N17 60 C7
Teck Cl, Islw. TW7 144 D2
Tedder Cl, Chess. KT9 195 F5
Ruislip HA4
off West End Rd 84 B5
Tedder Rd, S.Croy. CR2 203 F7
TEDDINGTON, TW11 162 D6
Teddington Lock, Tedd.
TW11 162 E4
Teddington Pk, Tedd.
TW11 162 C5
Teddington Pk Rd, Tedd.
TW11 162 C4
Tedworth Gdns, SW3 31 J4
Tedworth Sq, SW3 31 J4
Tee, The, W3 106 E6
Tees Av, Grnf. UB6 104 B2
Teesdale Av, Islw. TW7 144 D1
Teesdale Cl, E2 13 J2
Teesdale Gdns, SE25 188 B2
Isleworth TW7 144 D1
Teesdale Rd, E11 79 H6
Teesdale St, E2 112 E2
Teesdale Yd, E2 13 J1
Teeswater Ct, Erith DA18
off Middle Way 138 D3
Teevan Cl, Croy. CR0 188 D7
Teevan Rd, Croy. CR0 188 D7
Teignmouth Cl, SW4 150 D4
Edgware HA8 69 J2
Teignmouth Gdns, Grnf.
UB6 104 C2
Teignmouth Rd, NW2 90 A5
Welling DA16 158 C2
Telcote Way, Ruis. HA4
off Woodlands Av 66 C7
★**Telecom Twr**, W1 17 F1
Telegraph Hill, NW3 90 E3
Telegraph La, Esher (Clay.)
KT10 194 C6
Telegraph Ms, Ilf. IG3 100 A1
Telegraph Path, Chis. BR7 174 E5
Telegraph Pl, E14 134 B4
Telegraph Rd, SW15 147 H7
Telegraph St, EC2 20 B3
Telemann Sq, SE3 155 H3
Telephone Pl, SW6
off Lillie Rd 128 C6
Telfer Cl, W3
off Church Rd 126 C2
Telferscot Rd, SW12 168 D1
Telford Av, SW2 168 E1
Telford Cl, E17 77 H7
SE19
off St. Aubyn's Rd 170 C6
Telford Dr, Walt. KT12 178 C7
Telford Rd, N11 58 C6
NW9
off West Hendon Bdy 71 G6
SE9 175 G2
W10 108 B5
Southall UB1 103 H7
Twickenham TW2 143 G7
Telfords Yd, E1 21 J6
Telford Ter, SW1 33 F5
Telford Way, W3 106 E5
Hayes UB4 102 E5
Telham Rd, E6 116 D2
Tell Gro, SE22 152 C4
Tellson Av, SE18 156 B1
Telscombe Cl, Orp. BR6 207 H2
Temeraire Pl, Brent. TW8
off Green Dragon La 125 J5
Temeraire St, SE16
off Albion St 133 F2
Temperley Rd, SW12 150 A7
Templar Dr, SE28 118 D6
Templar Ho, NW2
off Shoot Up Hill 90 C6
Templar Pl, Hmptn. TW12 161 G7
Templars Av, NW11 72 C6
Templars Cres, N3 72 D2
Templars Dr, Har. HA3 52 A6
Templar St, SE5 151 H2
Temple, EC4 111 G7
★**Temple, The**, EC4 19 E5
Temple Av, EC4 19 F5
N20 41 G7
Croydon CR0 203 J2
Dagenham RM8 101 G1
★**Temple Bar**, EC4 18 E4
Temple Cl, E11
off Wadley Rd 78/79 E7
N3 *off Cyprus Rd* 72 C2
SE28 137 F3
Templecombe Rd, E9 113 F1
Templecombe Way, Mord.
SM4 184 B5
Temple Ct, E1
off Rectory Sq 113 G5
Temple Fortune Hill, NW11 72 D5
Temple Fortune La, NW11 72 D6
Temple Fortune Par, NW11
off Finchley Rd 72 C5
Temple Gdns, N21
off Barrowell Grn 59 H2
NW11 72 C6
Dagenham RM8 100 D3
Temple Gro, NW11 72 D6
Enfield EN2 43 H3
Templehof Av, NW2 71 J7
Temple La, EC4 19 F4
Templeman Rd, W7 104 C5
Templemead Cl, W3 106 E6
Temple Mead Cl, Stan.
HA7 52 E6
Templemead Ho, E9
off Kingsmead Way 95 H4
Temple Mill La, E15 96 B4
★**Temple of Mithras**, EC4
off Queen Victoria St 20 B4
Temple Pl, WC2 18 D5
Temple Rd, E6 116 B1
N8 75 F4
NW2 89 J4
W4 126 C3
W5 125 G3
Croydon CR0 202 A4
Hounslow TW3 143 H4
Richmond TW9 145 J3
Temple Sheen, SW14 146 C5
Temple Sheen Rd, SW14 146 B4
Temple St, E2 112 E2
Templeton Av, E4 62 A4
Templeton Cl, N16
off Boleyn Rd 94 B5
SE19 188 A1
Templeton Ct, NW7
off Kingsbridge Dr 56 A7
Templeton Pl, SW5 128 D4
Templeton Rd, N15 76 A6
Temple Way, Sutt. SM1 199 G3
Temple W Ms, SE11 27 G6
Templewood, W13 105 E5
Templewood Av, NW3 90 E3
Templewood Gdns, NW3 91 E3
Templewood Pt, NW2
off Granville Rd 90 C2
Temple Yd, E2
off Temple St 112 E3
Tempsford Av, Borwd.
WD6 38 D4
Tempsford Cl, Enf. EN2
off Gladbeck Way 43 J3
Temsford Cl, Har. HA2 67 J2
Tenbury Cl, E7
off Romford Rd 98 A5
Tenbury Ct, SW2 168 D1
Tenby Av, Har. HA3 68 E2
Tenby Cl, N15
off Hanover Rd 76 C4
Romford RM6 82 E6
Tenby Gdns, Nthlt. UB5 85 G6
Tenby Rd, E17 77 H5
Edgware HA8 69 J1
Enfield EN3 45 F3
Romford RM6 83 E6
Welling DA16 158 D1
Tench St, E1 132 E1
Tenda Rd, SE16
off Roseberry St. 132/133 E4
Tendring Way, Rom. RM6 82 C5
Tenham Av, SW2 168 D1
Tenison Ct, W1 17 F5
Tenison Way, SE1 20 E2
Tenniel Cl, W2 14 C4
Tennis Ct La, E.Mol. KT8
off Hampton Ct Way 180 C3
Tennison Av, Borwd. WD6 38 B5
Tennison Rd, SE25 188 C4
Tennis St, SE1 28 B3
Tenniswood Rd, Enf. EN1 44 C1
Tennyson Av, E11 79 G7
E12 98 B7
NW9 70 C3
New Malden KT3 183 H5
Twickenham TW1 162 C1
Tennyson Cl, Enf. EN3 45 G5
Feltham TW14 141 J6
Welling DA16 157 H1
Tennyson Rd, E10 96 B2
E15 96 E7
E17 77 J6
NW6 108 C1
NW7 55 G5
SE20 171 G7
SW19 167 F6
W7 104 C7
Hounslow TW3 143 J2
Tennyson St, SW8 150 B2
Tensing Rd, Sthl. UB2 123 G3
Tentelow La, Sthl. UB2 123 G5
Tenterden Cl, NW4 72 A3
SE9 174 C4
Tenterden Dr, NW4 72 A3
Tenterden Gdns, NW4 72 A3
Croydon CR0 188 D7
Tenterden Gro, NW4 72 A4
Tenterden Rd, N17 60 C7
Tenterden Rd, Croy. CR0 188 D7
Dagenham RM8 101 F2
Tenterden St, W1 16 E4
Tenter Grd, E1 21 F2
Tenter Pas, E1 21 G4
Tent Peg La, Orp. BR5 193 F5
Tent St, E1 112 E4
Terborch Way, SE22
off East Dulwich Gro. 152 B5
Teredo St, SE16 133 G3
Terence Ct, Belv. DA17
off Nuxley Rd 139 F6
Teresa Ms, E17 78 A4
Teresa Wk, N10
off Connaught Gdns 74 B5
Terling Cl, E11 97 F3
Terling Rd, Dag. RM8 101 G2
Terling Wk, N1
off Britannia Row 111 J1
Terminus Pl, SW1 25 E6
Terrace, The, E4
off Chingdale Rd 62/63 E3
N3 *off Hendon La* 72 C2
NW6 108 D1
SW13 147 E2
Woodford Green IG8
off Broadmead Rd 63 G6
Terrace Gdns, SW13 147 F2
Terrace La, Rich. TW10 145 H6
Terrace Rd, E9 95 F7
E13 115 G1
Walton-on-Thames
KT12 178 A7
Terrace Wk, Dag. RM9 101 E5
Terrapin Rd, SW17 168 B3
Terretts Pl, N1
off Upper St 93 H7
Terrick Rd, N22 75 E1
Terrick St, W12 107 H6
Terrilands, Pnr. HA5 67 F3
Terront Rd, N15 75 J5
Tersha St, Rich. TW9 145 J4
Tessa Sanderson Pl, SW8 150 B3
Tessa Sanderson Way,
Grnf. UB6
off Lilian Board Way 86 A5
Testerton Wk, W11 108 A7
Tetbury Pl, N1
off Upper St 111 H1
Tetcott Rd, SW10 30 C7
Tetherdown, N10 74 A3
Tetty Way, Brom. BR2 191 G2
Teversham La, SW8 151 E1
Teviot Cl, Well. DA16 158 B1
Teviot St, E14 114 C5
Tewkesbury Av, SE23 171 E1
Pinner HA5 67 E5
Tewkesbury Cl, N15
off Tewkesbury Rd 76 A6
Barnet EN4
off Approach Rd 41 G4
Loughton IG10 48 B6
Tewkesbury Gdns, NW9 70 B3
Tewkesbury Rd, N15 76 A6
W13 104 D7
Carshalton SM5 199 G1
Tewkesbury Ter, N11 58 C6
Tewson Rd, SE18 137 H5
Teynham Av, Enf. EN1 44 A6
Teynham Grn, Brom. BR2 191 G5
Teynton Ter, N17 75 J1
Thackeray Av, N17 76 D2
Thackeray Cl, SW19 166 A7
Harrow HA2 85 G1
Isleworth TW7 144 D2
Thackeray Dr, Rom. RM6 82 A7
Thackeray Rd, E6 116 A2
SW8 150 B2
Thackeray St, W8 22 B4
Thakeham Cl, SE26 170 E5
Thalia Cl, SE10 134 D6
Thame Rd, SE16 133 G2
Thames Av, SW10 149 F1
Dagenham RM9 119 H4
Greenford UB6 104 C2
Thames Bk, SW14 146 C2
Thamesbank Pl, SE28 118 C6
Thames Circle, E14
off Westferry Rd 134 A4
Thames Cl, Hmptn.
TW12 179 H2
Thames Ct, W.Mol. KT8 179 H2
Thames Cres, W4
off Corney Rd. 126/127 E7
THAMES DITTON, KT7 180 C6
Thames Ditton Island,
T.Ditt. KT7 180 D5
★**Thames Flood Barrier &
Visitors Cen**, SE18 136 A2

Thamesgate Cl, Rich. TW10 *off Locksmeade Rd* . **162/163** E4
Thames Gateway, Dag. RM9 . . . . **119** F2
Thameshill Av, Rom. RM5 . **83** J2
★**Thames Ho**, SW1 . . . . . . **34** A1
Thameside, Tedd. TW11 . . **163** G7
Thameside Ind Est, E16 . . **136** B2
Thameside Wk, SE28 . . . . **117** J6
THAMESMEAD, SE28 . . . **137** J1
Thamesmead, Walt. KT12 . **178** A7
THAMESMEAD NORTH, SE28 . . . . **118** C6
Thames Meadow, W.Mol. KT8 . . . . **179** G2
Thamesmead Spine Rd, Belv. DA17. . . . . **139** H2
THAMESMEAD WEST, SE18 . . . . **137** E3
Thamesmere Dr, SE28 . . . **118** A7
Thames Pl, SW15. . . . . . . **148** A3
Thames Pt, SW6 *off The Boulevard* **149** F1
Thames Quay, SW10 *off Harbour Av* **149** F1
Thames Rd, E16. . . . . **136** A1
W4. . . . . **126** A6
Barking IG11 . . . . **117** J3
Thames Side, Kings.T. KT1 . . . . **181** G1
Thames St, SE10 . . . . **134** B6
Hampton TW12 . . . . **179** H1
Kingston upon Thames KT1 . . . . **181** G2
Sunbury-on-Thames TW16. . . . . **178** B4
Thames Tunnel Mills, SE16 *off Rotherhithe St* **133** F2
Thamesvale Cl, Houns. TW3 . . . . **143** G3
Thames Village, W4 . . . . . **146** C1
Thames Wf, E16. . . . . **135** F1
Thanescroft Gdns, Croy. CR0 . . . . **202** B3
Thanet Dr, Kes. BR2 *off Phoenix Dr*. **206** A3
Thanet Pl, Croy. CR0 . . . . **201** J4
Thanet Rd, Bex. DA5 . . . . **159** G7
Thanet St, WC1 . . . . **10** A4
Thane Vil, N7 . . . . **93** F3
Thane Wks, N7. . . . . **93** F3
Thanington Ct, SE9 . . . . . **157** H6
Thant Cl, E10 . . . . **96** B3
Tharp Rd, Wall. SM6 . . . . **200** D5
Thatcham Gdns, N20. . . . . **41** F7
Thatcher Cl, West Dr. UB7 *off Classon Cl* **120** B2
Thatchers Cl, Loug. IG10 . . **49** F2
Thatchers Way, Islw. TW7 . **144** A5
Thatches Gro, Rom. RM6 . **82** E4
Thavies Inn, EC1 . . . . **19** F3
Thaxted Ct, N1. . . . . **12** B2
Thaxted Ho, Dag. RM10 . . **101** H7
Thaxted Pl, SW20 . . . . . . **166** A7
Thaxted Rd, SE9 . . . . **175** F2
Buckhurst Hill IG9 . . . . . . **48** B7
Thaxton Rd, W14 . . . . **128** C6
Thayers Fm Rd, Beck. BR3 . . . . **189** H1
Thayer St, W1. . . . . **16** C2
★**Theatre Mus**, WC2 *off Russell St*. **18** B5
★**Theatre Royal**, WC2 . . . . **18** B4
Theatre Sq, E15 *off Great Eastern Rd* . . . **96** D6
Theatre St, SW11 . . . . **149** J3
Theberton St, N1 . . . . **111** G1
Theed St, SE1 . . . . **27** E2
Thelma Gdns, SE3. . . . . . **156** A1
Feltham TW13 . . . . **161** E3
Thelma Gro, Tedd. TW11 . . **162** D6
Theobald Cres, Har. HA3 . . **67** H1
Theobald Rd, E17. . . . . **77** J7
Croydon CR0. . . . . **201** H2
Theobalds Av, N12. . . . . . . **57** F4
Theobalds Ct, N4 *off Queens Dr* **93** J2
Theobald's Rd, WC1 . . . . . . **18** C1
Theobald St, SE1. . . . . **28** B6
Theodore Rd, SE13 . . . . . . **154** C6
Therapia La, Croy. CR0 . . . **187** E6
Therapia Rd, SE22 . . . . . . **153** F6
Theresa Rd, W6 . . . . **127** G4
Therfield Ct, N4 *off Brownswood Rd* . . . **93** J2
Thermopylae Gate, E14 . . **134** B4
Theseus Wk, N1 . . . . **11** H2
Thesiger Rd, SE20 . . . . . . **171** G7
Thessaly Rd, SW8 . . . . . . **130** C7
Thetford Cl, N13. . . . . **59** H6
Thetford Gdns, Dag. RM9 . **100** D7
Thetford Rd, Dag. RM9 . . **118** D1
New Malden KT3 . . . . . **182** D6
Thetis Ter, Rich. TW9 *off Kew Grn*. **126** A6
Theydon Gro, Wdf.Grn. IG8. . . . . **63** J6
Theydon Pk Rd, Epp. (They.B.) CM16 . . . . **49** H1
Theydon Rd, E5 . . . . **95** F2
Theydon St, E17. . . . . **77** J7
Thicket Cres, Sutt. SM1 . . **199** F4
Thicket Gro, SE20 *off Anerley Rd*. **170** D7
Dagenham RM9 . . . . . . **100** C6
Thicket Rd, SE20 . . . . **170** D7
Sutton SM1. . . . . **199** F4
Third Av, E12 . . . . **98** B4
E13. . . . . **115** G3
E17 . . . . **78** A5
W3. . . . . **127** F1
W10 . . . . **108** B3
Dagenham RM10. . . . . . **119** H1
Enfield EN1 . . . . **44** C5
Hayes UB3 . . . . **121** J1
Romford RM6 . . . . **82** C6
Wembley HA9. . . . . **87** G2
Third Cl, W.Mol. KT8 . . . . **179** H4
Third Cross Rd, Twick. TW2 . . . . **162** A2
Third Way, Wem. HA9 . . . . **88** B4
Thirleby Rd, SW1. . . . . **25** G6
Edgware HA8 . . . . **70** D1
Thirlmere Av, Grnf. UB6 . . **105** F3
Thirlmere Gdns, Wem. HA9. . . . . **87** F1
Thirlmere Ho, Islw. TW7 *off Summerwood Rd* . **144** C5
Thirlmere Ri, Brom. BR1 . **173** F6
Thirlmere Rd, N10 . . . . **74** B1
SW16. . . . . **168** D4
Bexleyheath DA7 . . . . . **159** J2
Thirsk Cl, Nthlt. UB5 . . . . . **85** G6
Thirsk Rd, SE25 . . . . **188** A4
SW11. . . . . **150** A3
Mitcham CR4. . . . . **168** A7
Thirston Path, Borwd. WD6 . . . . **38** A2
Thistlebrook, SE2. . . . . . . **138** C3
Thistlebrook Ind Est, SE2. **138** C2
Thistlecroft Gdns, Stan. HA7. . . . . **69** G1
Thistledene, T.Ditt. KT7. . . **180** B6
Thistledene Av, Har. HA2 . . **85** E3
Thistlefield Cl, Bex. DA5 . **176** D1
Thistle Gro, SW10 . . . . **30** D3
Thistlemead, Chis. BR7 . . **192** E2
Thistle Mead, Loug. IG10. . **48** D3
Thistlewaite Rd, E5 . . . . . . **95** E3
Thistlewood Cl, N7 . . . . . . **93** F2
Thistleworth Cl, Islw. TW7. . . . . **124** A7
Thistley Cl, N12 *off Summerfields Av*. . . **57** H6
Thistley Ct, SE8 *off Glaisher St*. **134** B6
Thomas a'Beckett Cl, Wem. HA0. . . . . **86** C4
Thomas Baines Rd, SW11. **149** G3
Thomas Cribb Ms, E6. . . . **116** C6
Thomas Darby Ct, W11. . . **108** B6
Thomas Dean Rd, SE26 *off Kangley Br Rd* **171** J4
Thomas Dinwiddy Rd, SE12 . . . . **173** H2
Thomas Doyle St, SE1. . . . **27** G5
Thomas Hardy Ho, N22 . . . **59** F7
Thomas La, SE6. . . . . **154** A7
Thomas More Ho, EC2 *off The Barbican*. **111** J5
Thomas More St, E1 . . . . . **21** H6
Thomas More Way, N2 . . . **73** F3
Thomas Pl, W8. . . . . **22** A6
Thomas Rd, E14 . . . . **113** J6
Thomas St, SE18 . . . . **136** D4
Thomas Wall Cl, Sutt. SM1 *off Clarence Rd* . . **198/199** E5
Thompson Av, Rich. TW9 . **146** A3
Thompson Cl, Ilf. IG1 *off High Rd* **99** F2
Sutton SM3 *off Barrington Rd* **198** D1
Thompson Rd, SE22 . . . . **152** C6
Dagenham RM9 . . . . . . **101** F3
Hounslow TW3 . . . . **143** H4
Thompson's Av, SE5 . . . . . **35** J7
Thompson's La, Loug. (High Beach) IG10. . . . . **47** F1
Thomson Cres, Croy. CR0 . **201** G1
Thomson Rd, Har. HA3 . . . **68** B3
Thorburn Sq, SE1 . . . . **37** H2
Thorburn Way, SW19 . . . . **185** F1
Thoresby St, N1 . . . . **12** A3
Thorkhill Gdns, T.Ditt. KT7 . . . . **194** D1
Thorkhill Rd, T.Ditt. KT7 . . **180** E7
Thornaby Gdns, N18 . . . . . **60** D6
Thorn Av, Bushey (Bushey Hth) WD23. . . . **51** J1
Thornbury Av, Islw. TW7 . **124** A7
Thornbury Cl, N16 *off Boleyn Rd* **94** B5
NW7 *off Kingsbridge Dr* **56** A7
Thornbury Gdns, Borwd. WD6 . . . . **38** C4
Thornbury Rd, SW2 . . . . . **150** E6
Isleworth TW7 . . . . **144** A1
Thornbury Sq, N6 . . . . **92** C1
Thornby Rd, E5 . . . . **95** F3
Thorncliffe Rd, SW2 . . . . . **150** E6
Southall UB2. . . . . **123** F5
Thorn Cl, Brom. BR2 . . . . **192** D6
Northolt UB5. . . . . **103** F3
Thorncombe Rd, SE22 . . . **152** B5
Thorncroft Rd, Sutt. SM1 . **198** E4
Thorncroft St, SW8 . . . . . **130** E7
Thorndean St, SW18 . . . . **167** F2
Thorndene Av, N11. . . . . . . **58** A1
Thorndike Av, Nthlt. UB5 . **102** D1
Thorndike Cl, SW10 . . . . . . **30** C7
Thorndike Rd, N1. . . . . **93** J6
Thorndike St, SW1. . . . . . . **33** H3
Thorndon Cl, Orp. BR5. . . . **193** J2
Thorndon Gdns, Epsom KT19 . . . . **196** E4
Thorndon Rd, Orp. BR5 . . . **193** J2
Thorndyke Ct, Pnr. HA5 *off Westfield Pk*. **51** F7
Thorne Cl, E11 . . . . **96** E4
E16. . . . . **115** G6
Erith DA8. . . . . **139** J6
Thorneloe Gdns, Croy. CR0 . . . . **201** G5
Thorne Pas, SW13 . . . . . . **147** E2
Thorne Rd, SW8. . . . . **130** E7
Thornes Cl, Beck. BR3 . . . **190** C3
Thorne St, E16 . . . . **115** F6
SW13. . . . . **147** E3
Thornet Wd Rd, Brom. BR1 . . . . **192** D3
Thorney Cres, SW11. . . . . **129** G7
Thorneycroft Cl, Walt. KT12 . . . . **178** C6
Thorney Hedge Rd, W4 . . **126** B4
Thorney St, SW1 . . . . **34** A1
Thornfield Av, NW7 . . . . . . **72** B1
Thornfield Rd, W12 . . . . . **127** H2
Thornford Rd, SE13 . . . . . **154** C5
Thorngate Rd, W9 . . . . . . **108** D4
Thorngrove Rd, E13 . . . . . **115** H1
Thornham Gro, E15 . . . . . . **96** D5
Thornham Ct, SE10 . . . . . **134** B6
Thornhaugh Ms, WC1 . . . . . **9** J6
Thornhaugh St, WC1 . . . . . **17** J1
Thornhill Av, SE18 . . . . . . **137** H7
Surbiton KT6. . . . . **195** H2
Thornhill Br Wf, N1 *off Caledonian Rd* **111** F1
Thornhill Cres, N1 . . . . **93** F7
Thornhill Gdns, E10 . . . . . . **96** B2
Barking IG11 . . . . **99** H7
Thornhill Gro, N1 *off Lofting Rd* **93** F7
Thornhill Rd, E10 . . . . **96** B2
N1 . . . . **93** G7
Croydon CR0. . . . . **187** J7
Surbiton KT6. . . . . **195** H2
Thornhill Sq, N1. . . . . **93** F7
Thorn Ho, Beck. BR3 . . . . **189** H1
Thornlaw Rd, SE27 . . . . . **169** G4
Thornley Cl, N17 . . . . **60** D7
Thornley Dr, Har. HA2 . . . . **85** H2
Thornley Pl, SE10 *off Caradoc St* . . . **134/135** E5
Thornsbeach Rd, SE6. . . . **172** C1
Thornsett Pl, SE20 . . . . . . **188** E2
Thornsett Rd, SE20 . . . . . **188** E2
SW18. . . . . **167** E2
Thornside, Edg. HA8 *off High St*. **54** A6
Thorn Ter, SE15 *off Nunhead Gro*. **153** F3
Thornton Av, SW2 . . . . . . **168** D1
W4. . . . . **127** E4
Croydon CR0. . . . . **187** F6
West Drayton UB7 . . . . **120** C3
Thornton Cl, West Dr. UB7 . . . . **120** C3
Thornton Ct, SW20 . . . . . **184** A5
Thornton Dene, Beck. BR3 . . . . **190** A2
Thornton Gdns, SW12 . . . **168** D1
Thornton Gro, Pnr. HA5. . . **51** G6
THORNTON HEATH, CR7 . **187** H4
Thornton Hill, SW19. . . . . **166** B7
Thornton Pl, W1 . . . . **16** A1
Thornton Rd, E11 . . . . **96** D2
N18 . . . . **61** F3
SW12. . . . . **150** D7
SW14. . . . . **146** D3
SW19. . . . . **166** A6
Barnet EN5 . . . . **40** B3
Belvedere DA17 . . . . . . **139** H4
Bromley BR1. . . . . **173** G5
Carshalton SM5 . . . . . . **199** G1
Croydon CR0. . . . . **187** F7
Ilford IG1. . . . . **98** E4
Thornton Heath CR7 . . . **187** F7
Thornton Rd E, SW19 *off Thornton Rd*. **166** A6
Thornton Rd Retail Pk, Croy. CR0 . . . . **187** F6
Thornton Row, Th.Hth. CR7 *off London Rd*. **187** G5
Thornton St, SW9 . . . . . . **151** G2
Thornton Way, NW11 . . . . . **73** E5
Thorntree Rd, SE7 . . . . . . **136** A5
Thornville Gro, Mitch. CR4 . . . . **185** F2
Thornville St, SE8 . . . . . . **154** A1
Thornwood Cl, E18 . . . . . . **79** H2
Thornwood Rd, SE13. . . . . **154** E5
Thorogood Gdns, E15 . . . . **97** E5
Thorold Rd, N22. . . . . **59** E7
Ilford IG1. . . . . **98** E2
Thorparch Rd, SW8 . . . . . **150** D1
Thorpebank Rd, W12 . . . . **127** G1
Thorpe Cl, W10 *off Cambridge Gdns* . . **108** B6
Orpington BR6 . . . . **207** H2
Thorpe Cres, E17 . . . . **77** J2
Thorpedale Gdns, Ilf. IG2, IG6. . . . . **80** D4
Thorpedale Rd, N4. . . . . . . **93** E1
Thorpe Hall Rd, E17. . . . . . **78** C1
Thorpe Rd, E6. . . . . **116** C1
E7 . . . . **97** F4
E17 . . . . **78** C2
N15 . . . . **76** B6
Barking IG11 . . . . **99** G7
Kingston upon Thames KT2 . . . . **163** H7
Thorpe Wk, Grnf. UB6 . . . **104** B2
Thorpewood Av, SE26 . . . **171** E2
Thorsden Way, SE19 *off Oaks Av* **170** B4
Thorverton Rd, NW2 . . . . . **90** B3
Thoydon Rd, E3 . . . . **113** H2
Thrale Rd, SW16 . . . . **168** C5
Thrale St, SE1 . . . . **28** A2
Thrasher Cl, E8 *off Stean St*. **112** C1
Thrawl St, E1 . . . . **21** G2
Threadneedle St, EC2 . . . . **20** C4
Three Barrels Wk, EC4 . . . . **20** A5
Three Colts Cor, E2 . . . . . . **13** H5
Three Colts La, E2 . . . . . . **113** E4
Three Colt St, E14 . . . . . . **113** J7
Three Cors, Bexh. DA7. . . **159** H2
Three Cranes Wk, EC4 *off Upper Thames St* . . **111** J7
Three Cups Yd, WC1. . . . . . **18** D2
Three Kings Rd, Mitch. CR4 . . . . **186** A3
Three Kings Yd, W1 . . . . . . **16** D5
Three Mill La, E3 . . . . **114** C3
Three Oak La, SE1 . . . . **29** F3
Three Quays Wk, EC3. . . . . **20** E6
Threshers Pl, W11. . . . . . . **108** B7
Thriffwood, SE26 . . . . **171** F3
Thrift Fm La, Borwd. WD6 . **38** B2
Thrigby Rd, Chess. KT9 . . **195** J6
Throckmorten Rd, E16 . . . **115** H6
Throgmorton Av, EC2 . . . . **20** C3
Throgmorton St, EC2. . . . . **20** C3
Throwley Cl, SE2 . . . . **138** C3
Throwley Rd, Sutt. SM1. . **199** E5
Throwley Way, Sutt. SM1. **199** E4
Thrupp Cl, Mitch. CR4 . . . **186** B2
Thrush Grn, Har. HA2. . . . . **67** G4
Thrush St, SE17. . . . . **35** J3
Thruxton Way, SE15. . . . . . **37** G7
Thunderer Rd, Dag. RM9 . **118** E4
Thurbarn Rd, SE6. . . . . . . **172** B5
Thurland Rd, SE16. . . . . . . **29** H5

Thurlby Cl, Har. HA1
off Gayton Rd 68 D6
Woodford Green IG8 64 C5
Thurlby Rd, SE27 169 G4
Wembley HA0 87 G6
Thurleigh Av, SW12 150 A6
Thurleigh Rd, SW12 150 A6
Thurleston Av, Mord.
SM4 184 B5
Thurlestone Av, N12 57 J6
Ilford IG3 99 J4
Thurlestone Rd, SE27 169 G3
Thurloe Cl, SW7 31 G1
Thurloe Pl, SW7 31 F1
Thurloe Pl Ms, SW7 31 F1
Thurloe Sq, SW7 31 G1
Thurloe St, SW7 31 F1
Thurlow Cl, E4
off Higham Sta Av 62 B6
Thurlow Gdns, Ilf. IG6 65 G6
Wembley HA0 87 G5
Thurlow Hill, SE21 169 J1
Thurlow Pk Rd, SE21 169 H1
Thurlow Rd, NW3 91 G5
W7 124 D2
Thurlow St, SE17 36 C3
Thurlow Ter, NW5 92 A5
Thurlstone Rd, Ruis. HA4 84 A3
Thurnby Ct, Twick. TW2 162 B3
Thursland Rd, Sid. DA14 176 E5
Thursley Cres, Croy.
(New Adgtn) CR0 204 D7
Thursley Gdns, SW19 166 A2
Thursley Rd, SE9 174 C3
Thurso St, SW17 167 G4
Thurstan Rd, SW20 165 H7
Thurston Rd, SE13 154 B2
Southall UB1 103 F6
Thurston Rd Ind Est, SE13
off Jerrard St 154 B3
Thurtle Rd, E2 112 C1
Thwaite Cl, Erith DA8 139 J6
Thyer Cl, Orp. BR6
off Isabella Dr 207 F4
Thyme Cl, SE3
off Nelson Mandela Rd 155 J3
Thyra Gro, N12 57 E6
Tibbatts Rd, E3 114 B4
Tibbenham Pl, SE6 172 A2
Tibbenham Wk, E13 115 F2
Tibberton Sq, N1
off Popham Rd 93 J7
Tibbets Cl, SW19 166 A1
Tibbet's Cor, SW15 148 A7
Tibbet's Cor Underpass,
SW15 *off West Hill* 148 A7
Tibbet's Ride, SW15 148 A7
Tiber Gdns, N1
off Copenhagen St 111 F1
Ticehurst Cl, Orp. BR5
off Grovelands Rd 176 A7
Ticehurst Rd, SE23 171 H2
Tickford Cl, SE2
off Ampleforth Rd 138 C2
Tidal Basin Rd, E16 115 F7
Tidenham Gdns, Croy.
CR0 202 B3
Tideswell Rd, SW15 147 J5
Croydon CR0 204 A3
Tideway Cl, Rich. TW10
off Locksmeade Rd 162/163 E4
Tideway Ind Est, SW8 33 G6
Tideway Wk, SW8
off Cringle St 130 C7
Tidey St, E3 114 A5
Tidford Rd, Well. DA16 157 J2
Tidworth Rd, E3 114 A4
Tiepigs La, Brom. BR2 205 E2
West Wickham BR4 205 E2
Tierney Rd, SW2 168 E1
Tiger La, Brom. BR2 191 H4
Tiger Way, E5 94 E4
Tigris Cl, N9 61 F2
Tilbrook Rd, SE3 155 J3
Tilbury Cl, SE15 37 G7
Tilbury Rd, E6 116 C2
E10 78 C7
Tildesley Rd, SW15 147 J6
Tile Fm Rd, Orp. BR6 207 G3
Tilehurst Pt, SE2
off Yarnton Way 138 C2
Tilehurst Rd, SW18 167 G1
Sutton SM3 198 B5
Tile Kiln La, N6
off Winchester Rd 92 B1
N13 59 J5
Bexley DA5 177 J2
Tile Yd, E14
off Commercial Rd 113 J6
Tileyard Rd, N7 92 E7
Tilford Gdns, SW19 166 A2
Tilia Cl, Sutt. SM1 198 C5
Tilia Rd, E5
off Clarence Rd 94/95 E4
Tilia Wk, SW9
off Moorland Rd 151 H4
Tiller Rd, E14 134 A3
Tillett Cl, NW10 88 C6
Tillett Sq, SE16
off Howland Way 133 H2
Tillett Way, E2 13 H3
Tillingbourne Gdns, N3 72 C3
Tillingbourne Way, N3
off Tillingbourne Gdns 72 C3
Tillingham Way, N12 56 D4
Tilling Rd, NW2 89 J1
Tilling Way, Wem. HA9 87 G2
Tillman St, E1
off Bigland St 112/113 E6
Tilloch St, N1
off Carnoustie Dr 93 F7
Tillotson Rd, N9 60 C2
Harrow HA3 51 H7
Ilford IG1 80 D7
Tilney Ct, EC1 12 A5
Tilney Dr, Buck.H. IG9 63 G2
Tilney Gdns, N1 94 A6
Tilney Rd, Dag. RM9 101 F6
Southall UB2 122 C4
Tilney St, W1 24 C1
Tilson Cl, SE5
off Coleman Rd 132 B7
Tilson Gdns, SW2 150 E7
Tilson Ho, SW2
off Tilson Gdns 150/151 E7
Tilson Rd, N17 76 D1
Tilston Cl, E11
off Matcham Rd 97 F3
Tilton St, SW6 128 B6
Tiltwood, The, W3
off Acacia Rd 106 C7
Tilt Yd App, SE9 156 C6
Timber Cl, Chis. BR7 192 D2
Timbercroft, Epsom KT19 196 E4
Timbercroft La, SE18 137 H6
Timberdene, NW4 72 A2
Timberdene Av, Ilf. IG6 81 E1
Timberland Cl, SE15
off Peckham Hill St 132 D7
Timberland Rd, E1 113 E6
Timber Mill Way, SW4 150 D3
Timber Pond Rd, SE16 133 G2
Timber St, EC1 11 J5
Timberwharf Rd, N16 76 D6
Timbrell Pl, SE16
off Silver Wk 133 J1
Time Sq, E8 94 C5
Times Sq, Sutt. SM1 199 E5
Times Sq Shop Cen, Sutt.
SM1 *off High St* 198/199 E5
Timothy Cl, SW4
off Elms Rd 150 C5
Bexleyheath DA6 159 F5
Timothy Ho, Erith DA18
off Kale Rd 138/139 E2
Timothy Rd, E3 113 J5
Timsbury Wk, SW15 165 G1
Tindal St, SW9 151 H1
Tinderbox All, SW14 146 D3
Tine Rd, Chig. IG7 65 H5
Tinniswood Cl, N5
off Drayton Pk 93 G5
Tinsley Rd, E1 113 F5
Tintagel Cres, SE22 152 C4
Tintagel Dr, Stan. HA7 53 G4
Tintagel Gdns, SE22
off Oxonian St 152 C4
Tintern Av, NW9 70 B3
Tintern Cl, SW15 148 B5
SW19 167 F7
Tintern Ct, W13
off Green Man La 104 D7
Tintern Gdns, N14 43 E7
Tintern Path, NW9
off Ruthin Cl 70/71 E6
Tintern Rd, N22 75 J1
Carshalton SM5 199 G1
Tintern St, SW4 151 E4
Tintern Way, Har. HA2 85 H1
Tinto Rd, E16 115 G4
Tinwell Ms, Borwd. WD6
off Cranes Way 38 C5
Tinworth St, SE11 34 B3
Tippetts Cl, Enf. EN2 43 J1
Tipthorpe Rd, SW11 150 A3
Tipton Dr, Croy. CR0 202 B4
Tiptree Cl, E4
off Mapleton Rd 62 C3
Tiptree Cres, Ilf. IG5 80 D3
Tiptree Dr, Enf. EN2 44 A4
Tiptree Est, Ilf. IG5 80 D3
Tiptree Rd, Ruis. HA4 84 B4
Tirlemont Rd, S.Croy.
CR2 201 J7
Tirrell Rd, Croy. CR0 187 J6
Tisbury Ct, W1
off Rupert St 110 D7
Tisbury Rd, SW16 186 E2
Tisdall Pl, SE17 36 C2
Titchborne Row, W2 15 H4
Titchfield Rd, NW8 109 J1
Carshalton SM5 199 G1
Titchfield Wk, Cars. SM5
off Titchfield Rd 185 G7
Titchwell Rd, SW18 149 G7
Tite St, SW3 31 J4
Tithe Barn Cl, Kings.T.
KT2 181 J1
Tithe Barn Way, Nthlt.
UB5 102 B3
Tithe Cl, NW7 71 G1
Walton-on-Thames
KT12 178 B6
Tithe Fm Av, Har. HA2 85 G3
Tithe Fm Cl, Har. HA2 85 G3
Tithe Wk, NW7 71 G1
Titley Cl, E4 62 A5
Titmuss Av, SE28 118 B7
Titmuss St, W12
off Goldhawk Rd 127 J2
Tiverton Av, Ilf. IG5 80 D3
Tiverton Cl, Croy. CR0
off Exeter Rd 188 C7
Tiverton Dr, SE9 175 F1
Tiverton Ho, Enf. EN3 45 G3
Tiverton Rd, N15 76 A6
N18 60 B5
NW10 108 A1
Edgware HA8 69 J2
Hounslow TW3 143 J2
Ruislip HA4 84 A3
Thornton Heath CR7
off Willett Rd 187 G5
Wembley HA0 105 H2
Tiverton St, SE1 27 J6
Tiverton Way, NW7 56 A7
Chessington KT9 195 F5
Tivoli Ct, SE16 133 J2
Tivoli Gdns, SE18 136 B4
Tivoli Rd, N8 74 D5
SE27 169 J5
Hounslow TW4 142 E4
Toad La, Houns. TW4 143 F4
Tobacco Dock, E1 112 E7
Tobacco Quay, E1
off Wapping La 112/113 E7
Tobago St, E14
off Manilla St 134 A2
Tobin Cl, NW3 91 H7
Toby La, E1 113 H4
Toby Way, Surb. KT5 196 B2
Todds Wk, N7
off Andover Rd 93 F2
Tokenhouse Yd, EC2 20 B3
Token Yd, SW15
off Montserrat Rd 148 B4
TOKYNGTON, Wem. HA9 88 B6
Tokyngton Av, Wem. HA9 88 A6
Toland Sq, SW15 147 G5
Tolcarne Dr, Pnr. HA5 66 B3
Toley Av, Wem. HA9 69 H7
Tollbridge Cl, W10
off Kensal Rd 108 B4
Tollesbury Gdns, Ilf. IG6 81 G3
Tollet St, E1 113 G4
Tollgate Dr, SE21 170 B2
Hayes UB4 102 D7
Tollgate Gdns, NW6 6 A1
Tollgate Rd, E6 116 A5
E16 115 J5
Tollhouse Way, N19 92 C2
Tollington Pk, N4 93 F2
Tollington Pl, N4 93 F2
Tollington Rd, N7 93 F4
Tollington Way, N7 92 E3
Tolmers Sq, NW1 9 G5
Tolpuddle Av, E13
off Rochester Av 115 J1
Tolpuddle St, N1 10 E1
Tolsford Rd, E5 95 E5
Tolson Rd, Islw. TW7 144 D3
Tolverne Rd, SW20 183 J1
TOLWORTH, Surb. KT6 196 A2
Tolworth Bdy, Surb. KT6 196 B1
Tolworth Cl, Surb. KT6 196 B1
Tolworth Gdns, Rom.
RM6 82 D5
Tolworth Pk Rd, Surb.
KT6 195 J2
Tolworth Ri N, Surb. KT5
off Elmbridge Av 182 C7
Tolworth Ri S, Surb. KT5
off Warren Dr S 196 C1
Tolworth Rd, Surb. KT6 195 H2
Tolworth Twr, Surb. KT6 196 B2
Tomahawk Gdns, Nthlt. UB5
off Javelin Way 102 D3
Tom Coombs Cl, SE9
off Well Hall Rd 156 B4
Tom Cribb Business Cen,
SE28 *off Tom Cribb Rd* 137 G3
Tom Cribb Rd, SE28 137 F3
Tom Gros Cl, E15
off Maryland St 96 D5
Tom Hood Cl, E15
off Maryland St 96 D5
Tom Jenkinson Rd, E16 135 G1
Tomlins Gro, E3 114 A3
Tomlinson Cl, E2 13 G4
W4 126 B5
Tomlins Orchard, Bark.
IG11 117 F1
Tomlins Ter, E14
off Rhodeswell Rd 113 J5
Tomlins Wk, N7
off Briset Way 93 F2
Tom Mann Cl, Bark. IG11 117 H1
Tom Nolan Cl, E15 114 E2
Tompion St, EC1 11 G4
Tom Smith Cl, SE10
off Maze Hill 134/135 E6
Tomswood Ct, Ilf. IG6 81 F1
Tomswood Hill, Ilf. IG6 65 E7
Tomswood Rd, Chig. IG7 64 D6
Tom Thumbs Arch, E3
off Malmesbury Rd 114 A2
Tom Williams Ho, SW6
off Clem Attlee Ct 128 C6
Tonbridge Cres, Har. HA3 69 H4
Tonbridge Ho, SE25 188 D3
Tonbridge Rd, W.Mol. KT8 179 E4
Tonbridge St, WC1 10 A3
Tonbridge Wk, WC1
off Tonbridge St 110/111 E3
Tonfield Rd, Sutt. SM3 198 C1
Tonge Cl, Beck. BR3 190 A5
Tonsley Hill, SW18 149 E5
Tonsley Pl, SW18 149 E5
Tonsley Rd, SW18 149 E5
Tonsley St, SW18 149 E5
Tonstall Rd, Mitch. CR4 186 A2
Tony Cannell Ms, E3
off Maplin St 113 J3
Tooke Cl, Pnr. HA5 66 E1
Tookey Cl, Har. HA3 69 J7
Took's Ct, EC4 19 E3
Tooley St, SE1 28 C1
Toorack Rd, Har. HA3 68 A2
Tooting Bec Gdns, SW16 168 D4
Tooting Bec Rd, SW16 168 A3
SW17 168 A3
TOOTING GRAVENEY,
SW17 167 H6
Tooting Gro, SW17 167 H5
Tooting High St, SW17 167 H6
Tootswood Rd, Brom.
BR2 190 E5
Topaz Ho, E15
off Romford Rd 97 F6
Topaz Wk, NW2
off Marble Dr 72 A7
Topcliffe Dr, Orp. BR6 207 G4
Topham Sq, N17 75 J1
Topham St, EC1 11 E5
Top Ho Ri, E4
off Parkhill Rd 46 C7
Topiary Sq, Rich. TW9 145 J3
Topley St, SE9 156 A4
Topmast Pt, E14 134 A2
Top Pk, Beck. BR3 190 E5
Topp Wk, NW2 89 J2
Topsfield Cl, N8
off Wolseley Rd 74 D5
Topsfield Par, N8
off Tottenham La 74/75 E5
Topsfield Rd, N8 74 E5
Topsham Rd, SW17 167 J3
Torbay Rd, NW6 90 C7
Harrow HA2 84 E2
Torbay St, NW1
off Hawley Rd 92 B7
Torbitt Way, Ilf. IG2 81 J5
Torbridge Cl, Edg. HA8 53 H7
Torbrook Cl, Bex. DA5 159 E6
Torcross Dr, SE23 171 F2
Torcross Rd, Ruis. HA4 84 B3

Tor Gdns, W8 **128** D2
Tor Gro, SE28 **137** H1
Tormead Cl, Sutt. SM1 **198** D6
Tormount Rd, SE18 **137** H6
Toronto Av, E12 **98** C4
Toronto Rd, E11 **96** D4
Ilford IG1 **99** E1
Torquay Gdns, Ilf. IG4 **80** A4
Torquay St, W2 **14** A2
Torrance Cl, SE7 **136** A6
Torrens Rd, E15 **97** F6
SW2 **151** F5
Torrens Sq, E15 **97** E6
Torrens St, EC1 **11** F2
Torres Sq, E14
off Maritime Quay **134** A5
Torre Wk, Cars. SM5 **199** H1
Torrey Dr, SW9
off Overton Rd **151** G2
Torriano Av, NW5 **92** D5
Torriano Cotts, NW5
off Torriano Av **92** C5
Torriano Ms, NW5
off Torriano Av **92** D5
Torridge Gdns, SE15 **153** F4
Torridge Rd, Th.Hth. CR7 **187** H5
Torridon Rd, SE6 **172** D1
SE13 **154** D7
Torrington Av, N12 **57** G5
Torrington Cl, N12 **57** G4
Esher (Clay.) KT10 **194** B6
Torrington Dr, Har. HA2 **85** H4
Loughton IG10 **49** F4
Torrington Gdns, N11 **58** C6
Greenford UB6 **87** F7
Loughton IG10 **49** F4
Torrington Gro, N12 **57** H5
Torrington Pk, N12 **57** F5
Torrington Pl, E1 **29** J1
WC1 **17** G1
Torrington Rd, E18 **79** G3
Dagenham RM8 **101** F1
Esher (Clay.) KT10 **194** B6
Greenford UB6 **105** F1
Torrington Sq, WC1 **9** J6
Croydon CR0
off Tavistock Gro **188** A7
Torrington Way, Mord.
SM4 **184** D6
Tor Rd, Well. DA16 **158** C1
Torr Rd, SE20 **171** G7
Torver Rd, Har. HA1 **68** B4
Torver Way, Orp. BR6 **207** G3
Torwood Rd, SW15 **147** G5
Tothill St, SW1 **25** H4
Totnes Rd, Well. DA16 **138** B7
Totnes Wk, N2 **73** G4
Tottan Ter, E1 **113** G6
Tottenhall Rd, N13 **59** G6
TOTTENHAM, N17 **76** B1
Tottenham Ct Rd, W1 **9** G6
Tottenham Grn E, N15 **76** C4
TOTTENHAM HALE, N17 **76** E3
Tottenham Hale Retail Pk,
N15 **76** D4
★**Tottenham Hotspur FC**,
N17 **60** C7
Tottenham La, N8 **74** E5
Tottenham Ms, W1 **17** G1
Tottenham Rd, N1 **94** B6
Tottenham St, W1 **17** G2
Totterdown St, SW17 **167** J4
TOTTERIDGE, N20 **56** B1
Totteridge Common, N20 **55** G2
Totteridge Grn, N20 **56** D2
Totteridge Ho, SW11 **149** G2
Totteridge La, N20 **56** D2
Totteridge Village, N20 **56** B1
Totternhoe Cl, Har. HA3 **69** F5
Totton Rd, Th.Hth. CR7 **187** G3
Toulmin St, SE1 **27** J4
Toulon St, SE5 **35** J7
Tournay Rd, SW6 **128** C7
Tours Pas, SW11 **149** G4
Toussaint Wk, SE16 **29** J5
Tovil Cl, SE20 **188** D2
Towcester Rd, E3 **114** B4
Tower 42, EC2 **20** D3
Tower Br, E1 **29** F2
SE1 **29** F2
Tower Br App, E1 **29** F1
★**Tower Br Exhib**, SE1 **29** F2
Tower Br Piazza, SE1 **29** F2
Tower Br Rd, SE1 **28** D6
Tower Br Wf, E1 **29** H2
Tower Cl, NW3
off Lyndhurst Rd **91** G5
SE20 **170** E7
Ilford IG6 **65** E6
Tower Cl, Orp. BR6 **207** J2
Tower Ct, WC2 **18** A4
Tower Gdns, Esher (Clay.)
KT10 **194** D7
Tower Gdns Rd, N17 **75** J1
Tower Hamlets Rd, E7 **97** F4
E17 **78** A3
Tower Hill, EC3 **21** E6
Tower Hill Ter, EC3
off Tower Hill **112** B7
Tower La, Wem. HA9
off Main Dr **87** G3
Tower Ms, E17 **78** A4
★**Tower Millennium Pier**,
EC3 **29** E1
Tower Mill Rd, SE15 **36** D6
★**Tower of London**, EC3 **21** F6
Tower Pl, EC3 **20** E6
Tower Pt, Enf. EN2 **44** A4
Tower Ri, Rich. TW9
off Jocelyn Rd **145** H3
Tower Rd, NW10 **89** G7
Belvedere DA17 **139** J4
Bexleyheath DA7 **159** H4
Orpington BR6 **207** J2
Twickenham TW1 **162** C3
Tower Royal, EC4 **20** A5
Towers Pl, Rich. TW9
off Eton St **145** H5
Towers Rd, Pnr. HA5 **66** E1
Southall UB1 **103** G4
Tower St, WC2 **17** J4
Tower Ter, N22
off Mayes Rd **75** F2
SE4 *off Foxberry Rd* **153** H4
Tower Vw, Croy. CR0 **189** G7
Towfield Rd, Felt. TW13 **161** F2
Towing Path Wk, N1 **10** A1
Town, The, Enf. EN2 **44** A3
Towncourt Cres, Orp.
BR5 **193** F5
Towncourt La, Orp. BR5 **193** G6
Town Ct Path, N4 **93** J1
Towney Mead, Nthlt. UB5 **103** F2
Towney Mead Ct, Nthlt. UB5
off Towney Mead **103** F2
Town Fm Way, Stai. (Stanw.)
TW19 *off Town La* **140** A7
Townfield Rd, Hayes UB3 **121** J1
Townfield Sq, Hayes UB3 **121** J1
Town Fld Way, Islw. TW7 **144** D2
Town Hall App, N16
off Milton Gro **94** B4
Town Hall App Rd, N15 **76** C4
Town Hall Av, W4 **126** D5
Town Hall Rd, SW11 **149** J3
Townholm Cres, W7 **124** C3
Town La, Stai. (Stanw.)
TW19 **140** A6
Townley Ct, E15 **97** F6
Townley Rd, SE22 **152** B5
Bexleyheath DA6 **159** F5
Townley St, SE17 **36** B3
Townmead Business Cen,
SW6 *off William Morris Way* **149** F3
Town Meadow, Brent.
TW8 **125** G7
Townmead Rd, SW6 **149** F2
Richmond TW9 **146** B2
Town Quay, Bark. IG11 **117** E1
Town Rd, N9 **60** E2
Townsend Av, N14 **58** D4
Townsend Ind Est, NW10 **106** D2
Townsend La, NW9 **70** D7
Townsend Rd, N15 **76** C5
Southall UB1 **122** E1
Townsend St, SE17 **36** C2
Townsend Yd, N6 **92** B1
Townshend Cl, Sid. DA14 **176** B6
Townshend Est, NW8 **7** G1
Townshend Rd, NW8 **109** H1
Chislehurst BR7 **174** E5
Richmond TW9 **145** J4
Townshend Ter, Rich. TW9 **145** J4
Townson Av, Nthlt. UB5 **102** A3
Townson Way, Nthlt. UB5
off Townson Av **102** A2
Towpath Rd, N18 **61** G6
Towpath Wk, E9 **95** J5
Towpath Way, Croy. CR0 **188** C6
Towton Rd, SE27 **169** J2
Toynbec Cl, Chis. BR7
off Beechwood Ri **174/175** E4
★**Toynbee Hall**, E1 **21** G2
Toynbee Rd, SW20 **184** B1
Toynbee St, E1 **21** F2
Toyne Way, N6
off Gaskell Rd **73** J6
Tracey Av, NW2 **89** J5
Tracy Ct, Stan. HA7 **53** F7
Trade Cl, N13 **59** G4
Trader Rd, E6 **116** E6
Tradescant Rd, SW8 **131** E7
Trading Est Rd, NW10 **106** C4
Trafalgar Av, N17 **60** B6
SE15 **37** G4
Worcester Park KT4 **198** A1
Trafalgar Business Cen,
Bark. IG11 **117** J4
Trafalgar Cl, SE16
off Greenland Quay **133** H4
Trafalgar Ct, E1
off Glamis Rd **113** F7
Trafalgar Gdns, E1 **113** G5
W8 **22** B5
Trafalgar Gro, SE10 **134** D6
Trafalgar Ms, E9 **95** J6
Trafalgar Pl, E11 **79** G4
N18 **60** D5
Trafalgar Rd, SE10 **134** D6
SW19 **167** E7
Twickenham TW2 **162** A2
Trafalgar Sq, SW1 **25** J1
WC2 **25** J1
Trafalgar St, SE17 **36** B3
Trafalgar Ter, Har. HA1
off Nelson Rd **86** B1
Trafalgar Way, E14 **134** C1
Croydon CR0 **201** F2
Trafford Cl, E15 **96** B5
Ilford IG6 **65** J6
Trafford Rd, Th.Hth. CR7 **187** F5
Tralee Ct, SE16
off Masters Dr **132/133** E5
Tramsheds Ind Est, Croy.
CR0 **186** D7
Tramway Av, E15 **96** E7
N9 **45** E7
Tramway Cl, SE20 **189** F1
Tramway Path, Mitch.
CR4 **185** J5
Tranby Pl, E9
off Homerton High St **95** G5
Tranley Ms, NW3
off Fleet Rd **91** H5
Tranmere Rd, N9 **44** C7
SW18 **167** F2
Twickenham TW2 **143** H7
Tranquil Pas, SE3
off Tranquil Vale **155** F2
Tranquil Vale, SE3 **155** E2
Transept St, NW1 **15** G2
Transmere Cl, Orp. BR5 **193** F6
Transmere Rd, Orp. BR5 **193** F6
Transom Cl, SE16
off Plough Way **133** H4
Transom Sq, E14 **134** B4
Transport Av, Brent. TW8 **124** D5
Tranton Rd, SE16 **29** J5
Traps Hill, Loug. IG10 **48** C3
Traps La, N.Mal. KT3 **182** E1
Travellers Way, Houns.
TW4 **142** C2
Travers Cl, E17 **77** G1
Travers Rd, N7 **93** G3
Treacy Cl, Bushey
(Bushey Hth) WD23 **51** J2
Treadgold St, W11 **108** A7
Treadway St, E2 **112** E2
Treasury Cl, Wall. SM6 **200** D5
Treaty Cen, Houns. TW3 **143** H3
Treaty Rd, Houns. TW3
off Hanworth Rd **143** H3
Treaty St, N1 **111** F1
Trebeck St, W1 **24** D1
Trebovir Rd, SW5 **128** D5
Treby St, E3 **113** J4
Trecastle Way, N7
off Carleton Rd **92** D4
Tredegar Ms, E3
off Tredegar Ter **113** J3
Tredegar Rd, E3 **113** J2
N11 **58** D7
Tredegar Sq, E3 **113** J3
Tredegar Ter, E3 **113** J3
Trederwen Rd, E8 **112** D1
Tredown Rd, SE26 **171** F5
Tredwell Cl, SW2
off Hillside Rd **169** F2
Bromley BR2 **192** B4
Tredwell Rd, SE27 **169** H4
Tree Cl, Rich. TW10 **163** G1
Treen Av, SW13 **147** F3
Tree Rd, E16 **115** J6
Treeside Cl, West Dr. UB7 **120** A4
Treetops Cl, SE2 **139** E5
Treetops Vw, Loug. IG10 **48** A7
Treeview Cl, SE19 **188** B1
Treewall Gdns, Brom.
BR1 **173** H4
Trefgarne Rd, Dag. RM10 **101** G2
Trefil Wk, N7 **93** E4
Trefoil Ho, Erith DA18
off Kale Rd **138/139** E2
Trefoil Rd, SW18 **149** F5
Tregaron Av, N8 **74** E6
Tregaron Gdns, N.Mal. KT3
off Avenue Rd **182/183** E4
Tregarvon Rd, SW11 **150** A4
Tregenna Av, Har. HA2 **85** F4
Tregenna Cl, N14 **42** C5
Tregenna Ct, Har. HA2 **85** G4
Tregony Rd, Orp. BR6 **207** J4
Trego Rd, E9 **96** A7
Tregothnan Rd, SW9 **151** E3
Tregunter Rd, SW10 **30** C5
Trehearn Rd, Ilf. IG6 **65** G7
Treherne Ct, SW9
off Eythorne Rd **151** G1
SW17 **168** A4
Trehern Rd, SW14 **146** D3
Trehurst St, E5 **95** H5
Trelawney Cl, E17
off Orford Rd **78** B4
Trelawney Est, E9 **95** F6
Trelawney Rd, Ilf. IG6 **65** G7
Trelawn Rd, E10 **96** C3
SW2 **151** G5
Trellick Twr, W10 **108** C4
Trellis Sq, E3
off Malmesbury Rd **113** J3
Treloar Gdns, SE19
off Hancock Rd **170** A6
Tremadoc Rd, SW4 **150** D4
Tremaine Cl, SE4 **154** A2
Tremaine Rd, SE20 **189** E2
Trematon Pl, Tedd. TW11 **163** F7
Tremlett Gro, N19 **92** C3
Tremlett Ms, N19 **92** C3
Trenance Gdns, Ilf. IG3 **100** A3
Trenchard Av, Ruis. HA4 **84** B4
Trenchard Cl, NW9
off Fulbeck Dr **70/71** E1
Stanmore HA7 **52** D6
Trenchard Ct, Mord. SM4
off Green La **184** D6
Trenchard St, SE10 **134** D5
Trenchold St, SW8 **34** A6
Trenholme Cl, SE20 **171** E7
Trenholme Rd, SE20 **170** E7
Trenholme Ter, SE20 **170** E7
Trenmar Gdns, NW10 **107** H3
Trent Av, W5 **125** F3
Trentbridge Cl, Ilf. IG6 **65** J6
Trent Gdns, N14 **42** B6
Trentham St, SW18 **166** D1
★**Trent Park Country Pk**,
Barn. EN4 **42** B2
Trent Rd, SW2 **151** F5
Buckhurst Hill IG9 **63** H1
Trent Way, Wor.Pk. KT4 **197** J3
Trentwood Side, Enf. EN2 **43** F3
Treport St, SW18 **149** E7
Tresco Cl, Brom. BR1 **172** E6
Trescoe Gdns, Har. HA2 **67** E7
Tresco Gdns, Ilf. IG3 **100** A2
Tresco Rd, SE15 **153** E4
Tresham Cres, NW8 **7** G5
Tresham Rd, Bark. IG11 **99** J7
Tresham Wk, E9
off Churchill Wk **95** F5
Tresilian Av, N21 **43** F5
Tressell Cl, N1
off Sebbon St **93** H7
Tressillian Cres, SE4 **154** A3
Tressillian Rd, SE4 **153** J4
Trestis Cl, Hayes UB4
off Jollys La **102/103** E5
Treswell Rd, Dag. RM9 **119** E1
Tretawn Gdns, NW7 **55** E4
Tretawn Pk, NW7 **55** E4
Trevanion Rd, W14 **128** B5
Treve Av, Har. HA1 **67** J7
Trevelyan Av, E12 **98** C4
Trevelyan Cres, Har. HA3 **69** G7
Trevelyan Gdns, NW10 **107** J1
Trevelyan Rd, E15 **97** E4
SW17 **167** H5
Treveris St, SE1 **27** G2
Treverton St, W10 **108** A4
Treves Cl, N21 **43** F5
Treville St, SW15 **147** H7
Treviso Rd, SE23
off Farren Rd **171** G2
Trevithick St, SE8 **134** A5
Trevone Gdns, Pnr. HA5 **67** E6

Trevor Cl, Barn. EN4 . . . . . . **41** G5
Bromley BR2 . . . . **191** F7
Harrow HA3
off Kenton La **52** C7
Isleworth TW7 . . . . **144** C5
Northolt UB5 . . . . **102** C2
Trevor Gdns, Edg. HA8 . . . . **70** D1
Northolt UB5 . . . . **102** C2
Trevor Pl, SW7 . . . . **23** H4
Trevor Rd, SW19 . . . . **166** B7
Edgware HA8 . . . . **70** D1
Hayes UB3 . . . . **121** H2
Woodford Green IG8 . . . **63** G7
Trevor Sq, SW7 . . . . **23** J4
Trevor St, SW7 . . . . **23** H4
Trevor Wk, SW7
off Trevor Sq **129** J2
Trevose Rd, E17 . . . . **78** D1
Trevose Way, Wat. WD19 . . **50** C3
Trewenna Dr, Chess. KT9 . **195** G5
Trewince Rd, SW20 . . . . . **183** J1
Trewint St, SW18 . . . . **167** F2
Trewsbury Ho, SE2
off Hartslock Dr **138** D2
Trewsbury Rd, SE26 . . . . . . **171** G5
Triandra Way, Hayes UB4 . **102** D5
Triangle, The, EC1 . . . . **11** H5
N13 *off Lodge Dr* **59** G4
Barking IG11
off Tanner St **99** F6
Hampton TW12
off High St **179** J1
Kingston upon Thames
KT1 *off Kenley Rd* **182** C2
Triangle Business Cen, NW10
off Enterprise Way **107** G3
Triangle Ct, E16
off Tollgate Rd **116** A5
Triangle Est, SE11 . . . . **35** E4
Triangle Pas, Barn. EN4
off Station App **41** F4
Triangle Pl, SW4 . . . . **150** D4
Triangle Rd, E8 . . . . **112** E1
Trident Gdns, Nthlt. UB5
off Jetstar Way **102** D3
Trident St, SE16 . . . . **133** G4
Trident Way, Sthl. UB2 . . . **122** B3
Trig La, EC4 . . . . **19** J5
Trigon Rd, SW8 . . . . **34** D7
Trilby Rd, SE23 . . . . **171** G2
Trimmer Wk, Brent. TW8 . **125** H6
Trim St, SE14 . . . . **133** J6
Trinder Gdns, N19
off Trinder Rd **92/93** E1
Trinder Ms, Tedd. TW11 . . . **162** D5
Trinder Rd, N19 . . . . **93** E1
Barnet EN5 . . . . **39** J5
Tring Av, W5 . . . . **125** J1
Southall UB1 . . . . **103** F6
Wembley HA9 . . . . **88** A6
Tring Cl, Ilf. IG2 . . . . **81** F5
Trinidad St, E14 . . . . **113** J7
Trinity Av, N2 . . . . **73** G3
Enfield EN1 . . . . **44** C6
Trinity Buoy Wf, E14 . . . . . **115** F7
Trinity Ch Pas, SW13 . . . . **127** H6
Trinity Ch Rd, SW13 . . . . . **127** H6
Trinity Ch Sq, SE1 . . . . **28** A5
Trinity Cl, E8 . . . . **94** C6
E11 . . . . **97** E2
NW3
off Hampstead High St . **91** G4
SE13 *off Wisteria Rd* . . . **154** D4
SW4 *off The Pavement* . **150** C4
Bromley BR2 . . . . **206** B1
Hounslow TW4 . . . . **143** E4
Trinity Cotts, Rich. TW9
off Trinity Rd **145** J3
Trinity Ct, N1
off Downham Rd **94** B7
NW2 *off Anson Rd* **89** J5
SE7 *off Charlton La* **136** A4
Trinity Cres, SW17 . . . . . . **167** J2
Trinity Gdns, E16
off Cliff Wk **115** F4
SW9 . . . . **151** F4
Trinity Gro, SE10 . . . . **154** C1
★**Trinity Ho**, EC3 . . . . **21** E5
Trinity Ms, SE20 . . . . **189** E1
W10
off Cambridge Gdns . . **108** A6
Trinity Path, SE26 . . . . **171** F3
Trinity Pl, EC3 . . . . **21** F6
Bexleyheath DA6 . . . . . **159** F4
Trinity Ri, SW2 . . . . **169** G1
Trinity Rd, N2 . . . . **73** G3
N22 . . . . **75** E1
SW17 . . . . **167** J2
SW18 . . . . **149** G5
Trinity Rd, SW19 . . . . **166** D6
Ilford IG6 . . . . **81** F3
Richmond TW9 . . . . **145** J3
Southall UB1 . . . . **122** E1
Trinity Sq, EC3 . . . . **21** E6
Trinity St, E16
off Vincent St **115** G5
SE1 . . . . **28** A4
Enfield EN2 . . . . **43** J2
Trinity Wk, NW3 . . . . **91** F6
Trinity Way, E4 . . . . **61** J6
W3 . . . . **107** E7
Trio Pl, SE1 . . . . **28** A4
Tristan Sq, SE3 . . . . **155** E3
Tristram Cl, E17 . . . . **78** D3
Tristram Dr, N9
off Barbot Cl **60** D3
Tristram Rd, Brom. BR1 . . **173** F4
Triton Sq, NW1 . . . . **9** F5
Tritton Av, Croy. CR0 . . . . **201** E4
Tritton Rd, SE21 . . . . **170** A3
Triumph Cl, Hayes UB3 . . **121** F7
Triumph Ho, Bark. IG11 . . . **118** B3
Triumph Rd, E6 . . . . **116** C6
★**Trocadero Cen**, W1 . . . . . **17** H6
Trojan Ct, NW6
off Willesden La **90** B7
Trojan Way, Croy. CR0 . . . **201** F3
Troon Cl, SE16
off Masters Dr . . . **132/133** E5
SE28 *off Fairway Dr* **118** D6
Troon St, E1
off White Horse Rd . . . **113** H6
Trosley Rd, Belv. DA17 . . . **139** G6
Trossachs Rd, SE22 . . . . . **152** B5
Trothy Rd, SE1 . . . . **37** J1
Trott Rd, N10 . . . . **57** J7
Trott St, SW11 . . . . **149** H1
Trotwood, Chig. IG7 . . . . . . **65** G6
Troughton Rd, SE7 . . . . . . **135** H5
Troutbeck Rd, SE14 . . . . . **153** H1
Trout Rd, West Dr. UB7 . . **120** A1
Trouville Rd, SW4 . . . . **150** C6
Trowbridge Est, E9
off Osborne Rd **95** J6
Trowbridge Rd, E9 . . . . **95** J6
Trowlock Av, Tedd. TW11 . **163** F6
Trowlock Island, Tedd.
TW11 . . . . **163** G5
Trowlock Way, Tedd. TW11 . **163** G6
Troy Ct, SE18 . . . . **137** E4
Troy Rd, SE19 . . . . **170** A6
Troy Town, SE15 . . . . **152** D3
Trubshaw Rd, Sthl. UB2
off Havelock Rd **123** H3
Truesdale Rd, E6 . . . . **116** C6
Trulock Ct, N17 . . . . **60** D7
Trulock Rd, N17 . . . . **60** D7
Truman Cl, Edg. HA8
off Pavilion Way **54** B7
Truman's Rd, N16 . . . . **94** B5
Trumpers Way, W7 . . . . . . **124** B3
Trumpington Rd, E7 . . . . . . **97** F4
Trump St, EC2 . . . . **20** A4
Trundlers Way, Bushey
(Bushey Hth) WD23 . . . . **52** B1
Trundle St, SE1 . . . . **27** J3
Trundleys Rd, SE8 . . . . . . **133** G5
Trundleys Ter, SE8 . . . . . . **133** G4
Truro Gdns, Ilf. IG1 . . . . . . **80** B7
Truro Rd, E17 . . . . **77** J4
N22 . . . . **59** E7
Truro St, NW5 . . . . **92** A6
Truslove Rd, SE27 . . . . . . **169** G5
Trussley Rd, W6 . . . . **127** J3
Trust Wk, SE21
off Peabody Hill **169** H1
Tryfan Cl, Ilf. IG4 . . . . **80** A5
Tryon Cres, E9 . . . . **113** F1
Tryon St, SW3 . . . . **31** J3
Trystings Cl, Esher (Clay.)
KT10 . . . . **194** D6
Tuam Rd, SE18 . . . . **137** G6
Tubbenden Cl, Orp. BR6 . . **207** H2
Tubbenden Dr, Orp. BR6 . **207** G4
Tubbenden La, Orp. BR6 . **207** H3
Tubbenden La S, Orp.
BR6 . . . . **207** G5
Tubbs Rd, NW10 . . . . **107** F2
Tudor Av, Hmptn. TW12 . . **161** G6
Worcester Park KT4 . . . . **197** H3
Tudor Cl, N6 . . . . **74** C7
NW3 . . . . **91** H5
NW7 . . . . **55** G6
NW9 . . . . **88** C2
SW2 *off Elm Pk* **151** F6
Chessington KT9 . . . . . . **195** H5
Chigwell IG7 . . . . **64** D4
Chislehurst BR7 . . . . . . **192** C1
Tudor Cl, Pnr. HA5 . . . . **66** A5
Sutton SM3 . . . . **198** A5
Wallington SM6 . . . . . . **200** C7
Woodford Green IG8 . . . **63** H5
Tudor Ct, E17 . . . . **77** H7
Feltham TW13 . . . . **160** C4
Tudor Ct N, Wem. HA9 . . . . **88** A5
Tudor Ct S, Wem. HA9 . . . . **88** A5
Tudor Cres, Enf. EN2 . . . . . **43** H1
Ilford IG6 . . . . **65** E6
Tudor Dr, Kings.T. KT2 . . . **163** H5
Morden SM4 . . . . **184** A6
Tudor Est, NW10 . . . . **106** B2
Tudor Gdns, NW9 . . . . **88**
SW13 *off Treen Av* . **146/147** E3
W3 . . . . **106** A6
Harrow HA3
off Tudor Rd **68** A2
Twickenham TW1 . . . . . **162** C1
West Wickham BR4 . . . . **204** C3
Tudor Gro, E9 . . . . **95** F7
N20 *off Church Cres* **57** H3
Tudor Ho, Surb. KT6
off Lenelby Rd **196** A1
Tudor Pl, Mitch. CR4 . . . . . **167** H7
Tudor Rd, E4 . . . . **62** B6
E6 . . . . **115** J1
E9 . . . . **113** E1
N9 . . . . **45** E7
SE19 . . . . **170** C7
SE25 . . . . **189** E5
Barking IG11 . . . . **117** J1
Barnet EN5 . . . . **40** D3
Beckenham BR3 . . . . . . **190** B3
Hampton TW12 . . . . **161** G7
Harrow HA3 . . . . **68** A2
Hounslow TW3 . . . . **144** A4
Kingston upon Thames
KT2 . . . . **164** A7
Pinner HA5 . . . . **66** C2
Southall UB1 . . . . **102** E7
Tudor St, EC4 . . . . **19** F5
Tudor Wk, Bex. DA5 . . . . . **159** E6
Tudor Way, N14 . . . . **58** D1
W3 . . . . **126** A2
Orpington BR5 . . . . **193** G6
Tudor Well Cl, Stan. HA7 . . **53** E5
Tudway Rd, SE3 . . . . **155** H3
TUFNELL PARK, N7 . . . . . . **92** D4
Tufnell Pk Rd, N7 . . . . **92** C4
N19 . . . . **92** C4
Tufter Rd, Chig. IG7 . . . . . . **65** J5
Tufton Gdns, W.Mol. KT8 . **179** H2
Tufton Rd, E4 . . . . **62** A4
Tufton St, SW1 . . . . **25** J5
Tugboat St, SE28 . . . . **137** H2
Tugela Rd, Croy. CR0 . . . . **188** A6
Tugela St, SE6 . . . . **171** J2
Tugmutton Cl, Orp. BR6
off Acorn Way . . . **206/207** E4
Tuilerie St, E2 . . . . **13** H1
Tulip Cl, E6
off Bradley Stone Rd . . **116** C5
Croydon CR0 . . . . **203** G1
Hampton TW12
off Partridge Rd **161** F6
Southall UB2
off Chevy Rd **123** J2
Tulip Ct, Pnr. HA5 . . . . **66** C3
Tulip Gdns, Ilf. IG1 . . . . **98** E6
Tulip Way, West Dr. UB7 . . **120** A4
Tull St, Mitch. CR4 . . . . . . **185** J7
Tulse Cl, Beck. BR3 . . . . . . **190** C3
TULSE HILL, SE21 . . . . **169** J1
Tulse Hill, SW2 . . . . **151** G6
Tulse Hill Est, SW2 . . . . . . **151** G6
Tulsemere Rd, SE27 . . . . . **169** J2
Tumbling Bay, Walt.
KT12 . . . . **178** A6
Tummons Gdns, SE25 . . . **188** B2
Tuncombe Rd, N18 . . . . **60** B4
Tunis Rd, W12 . . . . **127** H1
Tunley Grn, E14
off Burdett Rd **113** J5
Tunley Rd, NW10 . . . . **106** E1
SW17 . . . . **168** A1
Tunmarsh La, E13 . . . . **115** J3
Tunnan Leys, E6 . . . . **116** D6
Tunnel Av, SE10 . . . . **134** D2
Tunnel Gdns, N11 . . . . **58** C7
Tunnel Rd, SE16
off St. Marychurch St . **133** F2
Tunstall Cl, Orp. BR5 . . . . **207** H4
Tunstall Rd, SW9 . . . . **151** F4
Croydon CR0 . . . . **202** B1
Tunstall Wk, Brent. TW8 . . **125** H6
Tunstock Way, Belv. DA17 . **139** E3
Tunworth Cl, NW9 . . . . **70** C6
Tunworth Cres, SW15 . . . **147** F6
Tun Yd, SW8
off Peardon St **150** B2
Tupelo Rd, E10 . . . . **96** B2
Tuppy St, SE28 . . . . **137** F3
Turenne Cl, SW18 . . . . **149** F4
Turin Rd, N9 . . . . **45** F7
Turin St, E2 . . . . **13** H4
Turkey Oak Cl, SE19 . . . . . **188** B1
Turk's Head Yd, EC1 . . . . . . **19** G1
Turks Row, SW3 . . . . **32** A3
Turle Rd, N4 . . . . **93** F1
SW16 . . . . **186** E2
Turlewray Cl, N4 . . . . **93** F1
Turley Cl, E15 . . . . **115** E1
Turnagain La, EC4 . . . . **19** G3
Turnage Rd, Dag. RM8 . . . **100** E1
Turnberry Cl, NW4 . . . . **72** A2
SE16 *off Ryder Dr* . **132/133** E5
Turnberry Ct, Wat. WD19 . . **50** C3
Turnberry Quay, E14
off Pepper St **134** B3
Turnberry Way, Orp. BR6 . **207** G1
Turnbury Cl, SE28 . . . . **118** D6
Turnchapel Ms, SW4
off Cedars Rd **150** B3
Turner Av, N15 . . . . **76** B4
Mitcham CR4 . . . . **185** J1
Twickenham TW2 . . . . . **161** J3
Turner Cl, NW11 . . . . **72** E6
SW9 . . . . **151** H1
Wembley HA0 . . . . **87** G5
Turner Dr, NW11 . . . . **72** E6
Turner Pl, SW11
off Cairns Rd **149** H5
Turner Rd, E17 . . . . **78** C3
Edgware HA8 . . . . **69** J3
New Malden KT3 . . . . . . **182** D7
Turners Meadow Way,
Beck. BR3 . . . . **189** J1
Turners Rd, E3 . . . . **113** J5
Turner St, E1 . . . . **112** E5
E16 . . . . **115** F6
Turners Way, Croy. CR0 . . **201** G2
Turners Wd, NW11 . . . . **73** F7
Turneville Rd, W14 . . . . . . **128** C6
Turney Grn, E14
off Wallwood St **113** J5
Turney Rd, SE21 . . . . **152** A7
Turnham Grn Ter, W4 . . . . **126** E4
Turnham Grn Ter Ms, W4
off Turnham Grn Ter . **126/127** E4
Turnham Rd, SE4 . . . . **153** H5
Turnmill St, EC1 . . . . **11** F6
Turnpike Cl, SE8
off Amersham Vale . . . **133** J7
Turnpike Ho, EC1 . . . . **11** H4
Turnpike La, N8 . . . . **75** F4
Sutton SM1 . . . . **199** F5
Turnpike Link, Croy. CR0 . **202** B2
Turnpike Ms, N8
off Turnpike La **75** G3
Turnpike Way, Islw. TW7 . . **144** D1
Turnpin La, SE10 . . . . **134** C6
Turnstone Cl, E13 . . . . **115** G3
NW9 *off Kestrel Cl* . . . **70/71** E2
Turpentine La, SW1 . . . . . . **32** E3
Turpington Cl, Brom. BR2 . **192** B6
Turpington La, Brom. BR2 . **192** B7
Turpin Rd, Felt. TW14
off Staines Rd **141** J6
Turpins La, Wdf.Grn. IG8 . . **64** C5
Turpin Way, N19
off Elthorne Rd **92** D2
Wallington SM6 . . . . . . **200** B7
Turquand St, SE17 . . . . **36** A2
Turret Gro, SW4 . . . . **150** C3
Turton Rd, Wem. HA0 . . . . . **87** H5
Turville St, E2 . . . . **13** F5
Tuscan Rd, SE18 . . . . **137** G5
Tuskar St, SE10 . . . . **134** E5
Tustin Est, SE15 . . . . **133** F6
Tuttlebee La, Buck.H. IG9 . . **63** G2
Tweedale Ct, E15 . . . . **96** C5
Tweeddale Rd, Cars.
SM5 . . . . **199** G1
Tweedmouth Rd, E13 . . . . **115** H2
Tweedy Cl, Enf. EN1 . . . . . . **44** C5
Tweedy Rd, Brom. BR1 . . **191** F1
Tweezer's All, WC2 . . . . **18** E5
Twelve Acre Ho, E12
off Grantham Rd **98** D3
Twelvetrees Cres, E3 . . . . **114** C4
Twentyman Cl, Wdf.Grn.
IG8 . . . . **63** G5
TWICKENHAM, TW1 &
TW2 . . . . **162** D2
Twickenham Br, Rich.
TW9 . . . . **145** F5
Twickenham TW1 . . . . . **145** F5

Twickenham Cl, Croy. CR0 . . . **201** F3
Twickenham Gdns, Grnf. UB6 . . . **86** D5
Harrow HA3 . . . **52** B7
Twickenham Rd, E11 . . . **96** D2
Feltham TW13 . . . **161** F3
Isleworth TW7 . . . **144** D3
Richmond TW9 . . . **145** F4
Teddington TW11 . . . **162** D5
Twickenham Trd Est, Twick. TW1 . . . **144** C6
Twig Folly Cl, E2
off Roman Rd . . . **113** G2
Twilley St, SW18 . . . **148** E7
Twine Cl, Bark. IG11
off Thames Rd . . . **118** B3
Twine Ct, E1 . . . **113** F7
Twineham Grn, N12
off Tillingham Way . . . **56** D4
Twine Ter, E3
off Ropery St . . . **113** J4
Twining Av, Twick. TW2 . . . **161** J3
Twinn Rd, NW7 . . . **56** B6
Twin Tumps Way, SE28 . . . **118** A7
Twisden Rd, NW5 . . . **92** B4
Twybridge Way, NW10 . . . **88** C7
Twycross Ms, SE10
off Blackwall La . . **134/135** E4
Twyford Abbey Rd, NW10 . **105** J3
Twyford Av, N2 . . . **73** J3
W3 . . . **106** A7
Twyford Cres, W3 . . . **126** A1
Twyford Ho, N15
off Chisley Rd . . . **76** B6
Twyford Pl, WC2 . . . **18** C3
Twyford Rd, Cars. SM5 . . **199** G1
Harrow HA2 . . . **85** H1
Ilford IG1 . . . **99** F5
Twyford St, N1 . . . **111** F1
Tyas Rd, E16 . . . **115** F4
Tybenham Rd, SW19 . . . **184** D3
Tyberry Rd, Enf. EN3 . . . **45** E3
Tyburn La, Har. HA1 . . . **68** B7
Tyburn Way, W1 . . . **16** A5
Tycehurst Hill, Loug. IG10 . **48** C4
Tye La, Orp. BR6 . . . **207** F5
Tyers Est, SE1 . . . **28** D3
Tyers Gate, SE1 . . . **28** D3
Tyers St, SE11 . . . **34** C3
Tyers Ter, SE11 . . . **34** C4
Tyeshurst Cl, SE2 . . . **139** E5
Tylecroft Rd, SW16 . . . **186** E2
Tylehurst Gdns, Ilf. IG1 . . . **99** F5
Tyler Cl, E2 . . . **13** F1
Erith DA8
off Brook St . . . **139** H7
Tyler Rd, Sthl. UB2
off McNair Rd . . . **123** H3
Tylers Cl, Loug. IG10 . . . **48** B7
Tyler's Ct, W1 . . . **17** H4
Tylers Gate, Har. HA3 . . . **69** H6
Tylers Path, Cars. SM5
off Rochester Rd . . . **199** J4
Tyler St, SE10 . . . **135** E5
Tylney Av, SE19 . . . **170** C5
Tylney Rd, E7 . . . **97** J4
Bromley BR1 . . . **192** A2
Tymperley Ct, SW19
off Windlesham Gro . . **166** B1
Tynan Cl, Felt. TW14
off Sandycombe Rd . . **160** A1
Tyndale Ct, E14 . . . **134** B5
Tyndale La, N1
off Upper St . . . **93** H7
Tyndale Ter, N1
off Canonbury La . . . **93** H7
Tyndall Rd, E10 . . . **96** C2
Welling DA16 . . . **157** J3
Tyneham Cl, SW11
off Shirley Gro . . . **150** A3
Tyneham Rd, SW11 . . . **150** A2
Tynemouth Cl, E6
off Covelees Wall . **116/117** E6
Tynemouth Rd, N15 . . . **76** C4
SE18 . . . **137** J5
Mitcham CR4 . . . **168** A7
Tynemouth St, SW6 . . . **149** F2
Tyne St, E1 . . . **21** G3
Tynsdale Rd, NW10
off Mayo Rd . . . **88/89** E6
Tynwald Ho, SE26
off Sydenham Hill . . . **170** D3
Type St, E2 . . . **113** G2
Tyrawley Rd, SW6 . . . **148** E1
Tyre La, NW9
off Sheaveshill Av . . **70/71** E4
Tyrell Cl, Har. HA1 . . . **86** B4
Tyrell Ct, Cars. SM5 . . . **199** J4
Tyrols Rd, SE23
off Wastdale Rd . . . **171** G1
Tyrone Rd, E6 . . . **116** C2
Tyron Way, Sid. DA14 . . . **175** H4
Tyrrell Av, Well. DA16 . . . **158** A5
Tyrrell Rd, SE22 . . . **152** D4
Tyrrell Sq, Mitch. CR4 . . . **185** H1
Tyrrel Way, NW9 . . . **71** F7
Tyrwhitt Rd, SE4 . . . **154** A3
Tysoe St, EC1 . . . **11** E4
Tyson Rd, SE23 . . . **153** F7
Tyssen Pas, E8 . . . **94** C6
Tyssen Rd, N16 . . . **94** C3
Tyssen St, E8 . . . **94** C6
N1 . . . **12** E1
Tytherton Rd, N19 . . . **92** D3

U

Uamvar St, E14 . . . **114** B5
Uckfield Gro, Mitch. CR4 . **186** A1
Udall St, SW1 . . . **33** G2
Udney Pk Rd, Tedd. TW11 . **162** D5
Uffington Rd, NW10 . . . **107** G1
SE27 . . . **169** G4
Ufford Cl, Har. HA3
off Ufford Rd . . . **51** H7
Ufford Rd, Har. HA3 . . . **51** H7
Ufford St, SE1 . . . **27** F3
Ufton Gro, N1 . . . **94** A7
Ufton Rd, N1 . . . **94** A7
Uhura Sq, N16 . . . **94** B3
Ujima Ct, SW16
off Sunnyhill Rd . . **168/169** E4
Ullathorne Rd, SW16 . . . **168** C4
Ulleswater Rd, N14 . . . **59** E4
Ullin St, E14
off St. Leonards Rd . . . **114** C5
Ullswater Cl, SW15 . . . **164** D4
Bromley BR1 . . . **173** E6
Ullswater Ct, Har. HA2
off Oakington Av . . . **67** G7
Ullswater Cres, SW15 . . . **164** D4
Ullswater Rd, SE27 . . . **169** H2
SW13 . . . **127** G7
Ulster Gdns, N13 . . . **59** J4
Ulster Pl, NW1 . . . **8** D6
Ulster Ter, NW1 . . . **8** D5
Ulundi Rd, SE3 . . . **135** E6
Ulva Rd, SW15
off Ravenna Rd . . . **148** A5
Ulverscroft Rd, SE22 . . . **152** C5
Ulverstone Rd, SE27 . . . **169** H2
Ulverston Rd, E17 . . . **78** D2
Ulysses Rd, NW6 . . . **90** C5
Umberston St, E1
off Hessel St . . . **112/113** E6
Umbria St, SW15 . . . **147** G6
Umfreville Rd, N4 . . . **75** H6
Undercliff Rd, SE13 . . . **154** A3
UNDERHILL, Barn. EN5 . . . **40** D5
Underhill, Barn. EN5 . . . **40** D5
Underhill Pas, NW1
off Camden High St . . . **110** B1
Underhill Rd, SE22 . . . **152** E6
Underhill St, NW1
off Camden High St . . . **110** B1
Underne Av, N14 . . . **58** B2
Undershaft, EC3 . . . **20** D4
Undershaw Rd, Brom. BR1 . . . **173** E3
Underwood, Croy. (New Adgtn) CR0 . . . **204** C5
Underwood, The, SE9 . . . **174** C2
Underwood Rd, E1 . . . **13** H6
E4 . . . **62** B5
Woodford Green IG8 . . . **64** A7
Underwood Row, N1 . . . **12** A3
Underwood St, N1 . . . **12** A3
Undine Rd, E14 . . . **134** B4
Undine St, SW17 . . . **167** J5
Uneeda Dr, Grnf. UB6 . . . **104** A1
Unicorn Ho, Brom. BR1
off Elmfield Rd . . . **191** G3
Union Cl, E11 . . . **96** D4
Union Cotts, E15
off Welfare Rd . . . **96/97** E7
Union Ct, EC2 . . . **20** D3
Richmond TW9
off Eton St . . . **145** H5
Union Dr, E1
off Canal Cl . . . **113** H4
Union Gro, SW8 . . . **150** D2
Union Jack Club, SE1
off Waterloo Rd . . . **131** G2
Union Rd, N11 . . . **58** D6
SW4 . . . **150** D2
SW8 . . . **150** D2
Union Rd, Brom. BR2 . . . **192** A5
Croydon CR0 . . . **187** J7
Northolt UB5 . . . **103** G2
Wembley HA0 . . . **87** H6
Union Sq, N1 . . . **111** J1
Union St, E15 . . . **114** C1
SE1 . . . **27** H2
Barnet EN5 . . . **40** B4
Kingston upon Thames KT1 . . . **181** G2
Union Wk, E2 . . . **13** E3
Union Wf, N1 . . . **11** J2
Unity Cl, NW10 . . . **89** G6
SE19 *off Crown Dale* . . . **169** J5
Unity Ter, Har. HA2
off Scott Cres . . . **85** H2
Unity Trd Est, Wdf.Grn. IG8 . . . **80** A3
Unity Way, SE18 . . . **136** A3
Unity Wf, SE1 . . . **29** G3
University Cl, NW7 . . . **55** F7
★**University Coll London**, WC1 . . . **9** H5
University Gdns, Bex. DA5 . . . **159** F7
★**University of London**, WC1 . . . **9** J6
University Pl, Erith DA8
off Belmont Rd . . . **139** H7
University Rd, SW19 . . . **167** G6
University St, WC1 . . . **9** G6
University Way, E16 . . . **116** D7
Unwin Av, Felt. TW14 . . . **141** H5
Unwin Cl, SE15 . . . **37** H6
Unwin Rd, SW7 . . . **23** F5
Isleworth TW7 . . . **144** B3
Upbrook Ms, W2 . . . **14** D4
Upcerne Rd, SW10 . . . **129** F7
Upchurch Cl, SE20 . . . **171** E7
Upcroft Av, Edg. HA8 . . . **54** C5
Updale Rd, Sid. DA14 . . . **175** J4
Upfield, Croy. CR0 . . . **203** E2
Upfield Rd, W7 . . . **104** C4
Upgrove Manor Way, SW2
off Trinity Ri . . . **151** G7
Uphall Rd, Ilf. IG1 . . . **99** E5
Upham Pk Rd, W4 . . . **127** E4
Uphill Dr, NW7 . . . **55** E5
NW9 . . . **70** C5
Uphill Gro, NW7 . . . **55** E4
Uphill Rd, NW7 . . . **54** E4
Upland Ms, SE22
off Upland Rd . . . **152** D5
Upland Rd, E13
off Sutton Rd . . . **115** F4
SE22 . . . **152** D5
Bexleyheath DA7 . . . **159** F3
South Croydon CR2 . . . **202** A5
Sutton SM2 . . . **199** G7
Uplands, Beck. BR3 . . . **190** A2
Uplands, The, Loug. IG10 . . **48** C3
Ruislip HA4 . . . **84** A1
Uplands Av, E17
off Blackhorse La . . . **77** G2
Uplands Business Pk, E17 . **77** G2
Uplands Cl, SW14
off Monroe Dr . . . **146** B5
Uplands End, Wdf.Grn. IG8 . . . **64** B7
Uplands Pk Rd, Enf. EN2 . . **43** G3
Uplands Rd, N8 . . . **75** F5
Barnet EN4 . . . **58** A1
Romford RM6 . . . **82** D3
Woodford Green IG8 . . . **64** B7
Uplands Way, N21 . . . **43** G5
Upney La, Bark. IG11 . . . **99** H6
Upnor Way, SE17 . . . **37** E3
Uppark Dr, Ilf. IG2 . . . **81** F6
Upper Abbey Rd, Belv. DA17 . . . **139** F4
Upper Addison Gdns, W14 . . . **128** B2
Upper Bk St, E14 . . . **134** B1
Upper Bardsey Wk, N1
off Clephane Rd . . . **93** J6
Upper Belgrave St, SW1 . . **24** C5
Upper Berkeley St, W1 . . . **15** J4
Upper Beulah Hill, SE19 . . **188** B1
Upper Brighton Rd, Surb. KT6 . . . **181** G6
Upper Brockley Rd, SE4 . . **153** J2
Upper Brook St, W1 . . . **16** B6
Upper Butts, Brent. TW8 . **125** F6
Upper Caldy Wk, N1
off Clephane Rd . . . **93** J6
Upper Camelford Wk, W11
off Lancaster Rd . . . **108** B6
Upper Cavendish Av, N3 . . **72** D3
Upper Cheyne Row, SW3 . **31** G6
UPPER CLAPTON, E5 . . . **94** E1
Upper Clapton Rd, E5 . . . **94** E1
Upper Clarendon Wk, W11
off Lancaster Rd . . . **108** B6
Upper Dengie Wk, N1
off Popham Rd . . . **111** J1
UPPER EDMONTON, N18 . **60** D6
UPPER ELMERS END, Beck. BR3 . . . **189** J6
Upper Elmers End Rd, Beck. BR3 . . . **189** H4
Upper Fm Rd, W.Mol. KT8 . . . **179** F4
Upper Fosters, NW4
off New Brent St . . . **71** J5
Upper Grn E, Mitch. CR4 . **185** J3
Upper Grn W, Mitch. CR4
off London Rd . . . **185** J3
Upper Grenfell Wk, W11
off Whitchurch Rd . . . **108** A7
Upper Grosvenor St, W1 . . **16** B6
Upper Grotto Rd, Twick. TW1 . . . **162** C2
Upper Grd, SE1 . . . **26** E1
Upper Gro, SE25 . . . **188** B4
Upper Gro Rd, Belv. DA17 . **139** F6
Upper Gulland Wk, N1
off Clephane Rd . . . **93** J6
Upper Ham Rd, Kings.T. KT2 . . . **163** G4
Richmond TW10 . . . **163** G4
Upper Handa Wk, N1
off Clephane Rd . . . **94** A6
Upper Hawkwell Wk, N1
off Popham Rd . . . **111** J1
Upper Hitch, Wat. WD19 . . . **51** E1
UPPER HOLLOWAY, N19 . . **92** C3
Upper Holly Hill Rd, Belv. DA17 . . . **139** H5
Upper James St, W1 . . . **17** G5
Upper John St, W1 . . . **17** G5
Upper Lismore Wk, N1
off Clephane Rd . . . **93** J6
Upper Mall, W6 . . . **127** G5
Upper Marsh, SE1 . . . **26** D5
Upper Montagu St, W1 . . . **15** J1
Upper Mulgrave Rd, Sutt. SM2 . . . **198** B7
Upper N St, E14 . . . **114** A5
UPPER NORWOOD, SE19 . **170** A7
Upper Palace Rd, E.Mol. KT8 . . . **179** J3
Upper Pk, Loug. IG10 . . . **48** A4
Upper Pk Rd, N11 . . . **58** B5
NW3 . . . **91** J5
Belvedere DA17 . . . **139** H4
Bromley BR1 . . . **191** H1
Kingston upon Thames KT2 . . . **164** A6
Upper Phillimore Gdns, W8 . . . **128** D2
Upper Ramsey Wk, N1
off Clephane Rd . . . **94** A6
Upper Rawreth Wk, N1
off Popham Rd . . . **111** J1
Upper Richmond Rd, SW15 . . . **148** B4
Upper Richmond Rd W, SW14 . . . **146** B4
Richmond TW10 . . . **146** A4
Upper Rd, E13 . . . **115** G3
Wallington SM6 . . . **200** D5
Upper St. Martin's La, WC2 . . . **18** A5
Upper Selsdon Rd, S.Croy. CR2 . . . **202** C7
Upper Sheppey Wk, N1
off Clephane Rd . . . **93** J7
Upper Sheridan Rd, Belv. DA17 *off Coleman Rd* . **139** G4
Upper Shirley Rd, Croy. CR0 . . . **203** F2
Upper Sq, Islw. TW7 . . . **144** D3
Upper St, N1 . . . **11** F1
Upper Sunbury Rd, Hmptn. TW12 . . . **179** E1
Upper Sutton La, Houns. TW5 . . . **123** G7
UPPER SYDENHAM, SE26 . . . **170** D4
Upper Tachbrook St, SW1 . **33** F1
Upper Tail, Wat. WD19 . . . **51** E3
Upper Talbot Wk, W11
off Lancaster Rd . . . **108** B6
Upper Teddington Rd, Kings.T. KT1 . . . **181** F1
Upper Ter, NW3 . . . **91** F3
Upper Thames St, EC4 . . . **19** H5
Upper Tollington Pk, N4 . . . **93** G1

Upperton Rd, Sid. DA14. . **175** J5
Upperton Rd E, E13
off Inniskilling Rd **115** J3
Upperton Rd W, E13. . . . . **115** J3
UPPER TOOTING, SW17. . **167** H3
Upper Tooting Pk, SW17 . **167** J2
Upper Tooting Rd, SW17 . **167** J4
Upper Town Rd, Grnf.
UB6 . . . . **103** H4
Upper Tulse Hill, SW2 . . . **151** F7
Upper Vernon Rd, Sutt.
SM1. . . . . **199** G5
UPPER WALTHAMSTOW,
E17 . . . . **78** B4
Upper Walthamstow Rd,
E17 . . . . **78** D4
Upper Wickham La, Well.
DA16. . . . . **138** B7
Upper Wimpole St, W1 . . . **16** D1
Upper Woburn Pl, WC1 . . . . **9** J4
Uppingham Av, Stan. HA7. **69** E1
Upsdell Av, N13 . . . . **59** G6
Upstall St, SE5. . . . . **151** H1
UPTON, E7 . . . . **97** H7
Upton Av, E7 . . . . **97** G7
Upton Cl, NW2
off Somerton Rd **90** B3
Bexley DA5 . . . . **159** F6
Upton Ct, SE20
off Blean Gro. **171** F7
Upton Dene, Sutt. SM2 . . **198** E7
Upton Gdns, Har. HA3. . . . **69** E5
Upton La, E7 . . . . **97** G7
UPTON PARK, E6 . . . . **115** J1
Upton Pk Rd, E7. . . . . **97** H7
Upton Rd, N18 . . . . **60** D5
SE18 . . . . **137** F6
Bexley DA5 . . . . **159** F6
Bexleyheath DA6 . . . . . **158** E4
Hounslow TW3 . . . . **143** G3
Thornton Heath CR7 . . . **188** A2
Upton Rd S, Bex. DA5 . . . **159** F6
Upway, N12 . . . . **57** H7
Upwood Rd, SE12 . . . . . . **155** F6
SW16. . . . . **187** E1
Urlwin St, SE5 . . . . **35** J6
Urlwin Wk, SW9. . . . . **151** G2
Urmston Dr, SW19. . . . . . **166** B1
Ursula Ms, N4
off Portland Ri. **93** J1
Ursula St, SW11 . . . . **149** H1
Urswick Gdns, Dag. RM9
off Urswick Rd . . . **100/101** E7
Urswick Rd, E9. . . . . **95** F5
Dagenham RM9 . . . . . . **100** D7
Usborne Ms, SW8 . . . . **34** C7
Usher Rd, E3. . . . . **113** J2
Usk Rd, SW11. . . . . **149** F4
Usk St, E2. . . . . **113** G3
Utopia Village, NW1
off Chalcot Rd **110** A1
Uvedale Rd, Dag. RM10 . . **101** G3
Enfield EN2 . . . . **44** A5
Uverdale Rd, SW10 . . . . . **129** F7
Uxbridge Gdns, Felt. TW13
off Marlborough Rd . . **160** D2
Uxbridge Rd, W3 . . . . **105** H7
W5. . . . . **105** F7
W5 (Ealing Com.) **105** H7
W7. . . . . **124** B1
W12. . . . . **127** G1
W13. . . . . **124** E1
Feltham TW13 . . . . **160** C2
Hampton (Hmptn H.)
TW12 . . . . **161** G4
Harrow HA3 . . . . **51** J7
Hayes UB4. . . . . **102** C7
Kingston upon Thames
KT1 . . . . **181** G4
Pinner HA5 . . . . **51** H7
Southall UB1. . . . . **123** G1
Stanmore HA7 . . . . **52** C6
Uxbridge St, W8. . . . . **128** D1
Uxendon Cres, Wem. HA9 . **87** H1
Uxendon Hill, Wem. HA9 . . **87** J1

V

Valance Av, E4 . . . . **63** F1
Valan Leas, Brom. BR2. . . **191** E3
Vale, The, N10. . . . . **74** A1
N14 . . . . **42** D7
NW11. . . . . **90** A3
SW3. . . . . **31** E5
W3. . . . . **126** D1
Croydon CR0. . . . . **203** G2
Feltham TW14 . . . . **142** B6
Hounslow TW5 . . . . **122** E6
Vale, The, Ruis. HA4. . . . . . **84** C4
Sunbury-on-Thames TW16
off Ashridge Way. **160** A6
Woodford Green IG8 . . . **63** G7
Vale Av, Borwd. WD6 . . . . . **38** B5
Vale Cl, N2
off Church Vale **73** J3
W9. . . . . **6** C4
Orpington BR6 . . . . **206** D4
Vale Cotts, SW15
off Kingston Vale. **164** D4
Vale Ct, W9. . . . . **6** C4
Vale Cres, SW15. . . . . **165** E3
Vale Cft, Esher (Clay.)
KT10 . . . . **194** B7
Pinner HA5 . . . . **66** E5
Vale Dr, Barn. EN5 . . . . **40** C4
Vale End, SE22
off Grove Vale **152** B4
Vale Gro, N4. . . . . **75** J7
W3 *off The Vale* **126** D1
Vale La, W3. . . . . **106** A5
Valence Av, Dag. RM8 . . . **100** D3
Valence Circ, Dag. RM8 . . **100** D3
★**Valence Ho Mus**, Dag.
RM8. . . . . **100** E2
Valence Wd Rd, Dag.
RM8. . . . . **100** D3
Valencia Rd, Stan. HA7 . . . **53** F4
Valentia Pl, SW9
off Brixton Sta Rd. . . . **151** G4
Valentine Av, Bex. DA5 . . **176** E2
Valentine Ct, SE23 . . . . . . **171** G2
Valentine Pl, SE1 . . . . **27** G3
Valentine Rd, E9. . . . . **95** G6
Harrow HA2 . . . . **85** J3
Valentine Row, SE1 . . . . . **27** G4
Valentines Rd, Ilf. IG1 . . . . **98** E1
Vale of Health, NW3
off East Heath Rd **91** G3
Vale Par, SW15
off Kingston Vale. **164** D4
Valerian Way, E15. . . . . . . **115** E3
Valerie Ct, Sutt. SM2
off Stanley Rd . . . **198/199** E7
Vale Ri, NW11. . . . . **90** C1
Vale Rd, E7. . . . . **97** H6
N4 . . . . **75** J7
Bromley BR1 . . . . **192** D2
Epsom KT19 . . . . **197** F4
Mitcham CR4. . . . . **186** D3
Sutton SM1. . . . . **198** E4
Worcester Park KT4. . . . **197** F4
Vale Rd N, Surb. KT6 . . . . **195** H2
Vale Rd S, Surb. KT6 . . . . **195** H2
Vale Row, N5
off Gillespie Rd. **93** H3
Vale Royal, N7 . . . . **92** E7
Valery Pl, Hmptn. TW12 . . **161** C7
Vale St, SE27 . . . . **170** A3
Valeswood Rd, Brom.
BR1 . . . . **173** F5
Vale Ter, N4 . . . . **75** J6
Valetta Gro, E13 . . . . **115** G2
Valetta Rd, W3 . . . . **126** E2
Valette St, E9 . . . . **95** E6
Valiant Cl, Nthlt. UB5
off Ruislip Rd. **102** D3
Romford RM7 . . . . **83** G2
Valiant Ho, SE7 . . . . **135** J5
Valiant Path, NW9
off Blundell Rd. **54/55** E7
Valiant Way, E6. . . . . **116** C5
Vallance Rd, E1 . . . . **13** J4
E2 . . . . **13** J4
N22 . . . . **74** C2
Vallentin Rd, E17 . . . . **78** C4
Valley Av, N12 . . . . **57** G4
Valley Cl, Loug. IG10 . . . . . **48** C6
Pinner HA5
off Alandale Dr **66** B2
Valley Dr, NW9. . . . . **70** A6
Valleyfield Rd, SW16 . . . . **169** F5
Valley Flds Cres, Enf. EN2 . **43** G2
Valley Gdns, SW19. . . . . . **167** G7
Wembley HA0. . . . . **87** J7
Valley Gro, SE7 . . . . **135** J5
Valley Hill, Loug. IG10 . . . . **48** B7
Valley Link Ind Est, Enf.
EN3 . . . . **45** H6
Valley Ms, Twick. TW1
off Cross Deep **162** D2
Valley Rd, SW16. . . . . **169** F4
Belvedere DA17 . . . . . . **139** H4
Bromley BR2. . . . . **191** E2
Valley Side, E4 . . . . **62** A2
Valley Side Par, E4
off Valley Side. **62** A2
Valley Vw, Barn. EN5 . . . . . **40** B6
Valley Wk, Croy. CR0 . . . . **203** F2
Valliere Rd, NW10 . . . . . . **107** H3
Valliers Wd Rd, Sid. DA15 . **175** G1
Vallis Way, W13 . . . . **104** D5
Chessington KT9. . . . . . **195** G4
Valmar Rd, SE5 . . . . **151** J1
Val McKenzie Av, N7
off Parkside Cres. **93** G3
Valnay St, SW17 . . . . **167** J5
Valognes Av, E17 . . . . **77** H1
Valonia Gdns, SW18 . . . . **148** C6
Vambery Rd, SE18 . . . . . . **137** F6
Vanbrough Cres, Nthlt.
UB5 . . . . **102** C1
Vanbrugh Cl, E16
off Fulmer Rd **116** A5
Vanbrugh Dr, Walt. KT12 . **178** C7
Vanbrugh Flds, SE3 . . . . . **135** F7
Vanbrugh Hill, SE3. . . . . . **135** F5
SE10 . . . . **135** F5
Vanbrugh Pk, SE3 . . . . . . **135** F7
Vanbrugh Pk Rd, SE3. . . . **135** F7
Vanbrugh Pk Rd W, SE3. . **135** F7
Vanbrugh Rd, W4. . . . . . . **126** D3
Vanbrugh Ter, SE3 . . . . . . **155** F1
Vanburgh Cl, Orp. BR6. . . **207** H1
Vancouver Cl, Orp. BR6 . . **207** J4
Vancouver Rd, SE23. . . . . **171** H2
Edgware HA8 . . . . **70** B1
Hayes UB4. . . . . **102** B4
Richmond TW10 . . . . . . **163** F4
Vanderbilt Rd, SW18 . . . . **167** F1
Vanderville Gdns, N2
off Tarling Rd. **73** F2
Vandome Cl, E16 . . . . **115** H6
Vandon Pas, SW1. . . . . **25** G5
Vandon St, SW1. . . . . **25** G5
Van Dyck Av, N.Mal. KT3 . **182** D7
Vandyke Cl, SW15 . . . . . . **148** A7
Vandyke Cross, SE9. . . . . **156** B5
Vandy St, EC2 . . . . **12** D6
Vane Cl, NW3. . . . . **91** G4
Harrow HA3 . . . . **69** J6
Vanessa Cl, Belv. DA17 . . **139** G5
Vane St, SW1. . . . . **33** G1
Van Gogh Cl, Islw. TW7
off Twickenham Rd . . . **144** D3
Vanguard Cl, E16 . . . . **115** G5
Croydon CR0. . . . . **201** H1
Romford RM7 . . . . **83** H2
Vanguard St, SE8. . . . . . . **154** A1
Vanguard Way, Wall.
SM6. . . . . **200** E7
Vanneck Sq, SW15. . . . . . **147** G5
Vanner Pt, E9
off Wick Rd **95** G6
Vanoc Gdns, Brom. BR1 . **173** G3
Vansittart Rd, E7 . . . . **97** F4
Vansittart St, SE14. . . . . . **133** H7
Vanston Pl, SW6 . . . . **128** D7
Vantage Ms, E14
off Prestons Rd **134** C1
Vantage Pl, W8
off Abingdon Rd **128** D3
Vant Rd, SW17. . . . . **167** J5
Varcoe Rd, SE16. . . . . **133** E5
Vardens Rd, SW11 . . . . . . **149** G4
Varden St, E1 . . . . **112** E6
Vardon Cl, W3. . . . . **106** D6
Varley Par, NW9. . . . . **70** E4
Varley Rd, E16 . . . . **115** H6
Varley Way, Mitch. CR4 . . **185** G2
Varna Rd, SW6. . . . . **128** B7
Hampton TW12 . . . . **179** H1
Varndell St, NW1. . . . . **9** F3
Varnishers Yd, N1
off Caledonian Rd **110** E2
Varsity Dr, Twick. TW1 . . . **144** B5
Varsity Row, SW14
off William's La **146** C2
Vartry Rd, N15 . . . . **76** A6
Vassall Rd, SW9. . . . . **131** G7
Vauban Est, SE16. . . . . **29** G6
Vauban St, SE16 . . . . **29** G6
Vaughan Av, NW4 . . . . **71** G5
W6. . . . . **127** F4
Vaughan Cl, Hmptn. TW12
off Oak Av **160/161** E6
Vaughan Gdns, Ilf. IG1. . . . **80** C7
Vaughan Rd, E15 . . . . **97** F6
SE5 . . . . **151** J3
Harrow HA1 . . . . **67** J7
Thames Ditton KT7 . . . . **180** E7
Welling DA16 . . . . **157** J2
Vaughan St, SE16 . . . . **133** J2
Vaughan Way, E1. . . . . **21** H6
Vaughan Williams Cl, SE8
off Watson's St **134** A7
VAUXHALL, SE11 . . . . **34** B4
Vauxhall Br, SE1 . . . . **34** A4
SW1. . . . . **34** A4
Vauxhall Br Rd, SW1 . . . . . **33** G1
Vauxhall Gdns, S.Croy.
CR2 . . . . **201** J6
Vauxhall Gdns Est, SE11 . . **34** D4
Vauxhall Gro, SW8. . . . . . . **34** C5
Vauxhall St, SE11. . . . . **34** D4
Vauxhall Wk, SE11 . . . . **34** C3
Vawdrey Cl, E1 . . . . **113** F4
Veals Mead, Mitch. CR4 . . **185** H1
Vectis Gdns, SW17
off Vectis Rd **168** B6
Vectis Rd, SW17. . . . . **168** B6
Veda Rd, SE13 . . . . **154** A4
Veldene Way, Har. HA2 . . . **85** F3
Velde Way, SE22
off East Dulwich Gro. . **152** B5
Velletri Ho, E2. . . . . **113** G2
Vellum Dr, Cars. SM5 . . . **200** A3
Venables Cl, Dag. RM10 . . **101** H4
Venables St, NW8 . . . . **15** F1
Vencourt Pl, W6 . . . . **127** G5
Venetian Rd, SE5 . . . . **151** J2
Venetia Rd, N4. . . . . **75** H6
W5. . . . . **125** G2
Venner Rd, SE26 . . . . **171** F6
Venn St, SW4. . . . . **150** C4
Ventnor Av, Stan. HA7. . . . **69** E1
Ventnor Dr, N20. . . . . **56** E3
Ventnor Gdns, Bark.
IG11 . . . . **99** H6
Ventnor Rd, SE14. . . . . . . **133** G7
Sutton SM2. . . . . **199** E7
Venture Cl, Bex. DA5 . . . . **158** E7
Venue St, E14. . . . . **114** C5
Venus Ho, E14
off Crews St **134** A4
Venus Rd, SE18 . . . . **136** C3
Vera Av, N21. . . . . **43** G5
Vera Lynn Cl, E7
off Dames Rd **97** G4
Vera Rd, SW6. . . . . **148** B1
Verbena Cl, E16
off Pretoria Rd. **115** F4
West Drayton UB7
off Magnolia St. **120** A5
Verbena Gdns, W6 . . . . . . **127** G5
Verdant La, SE6 . . . . **173** E1
Verdayne Av, Croy. CR0 . . **203** G1
Verdun Rd, SE18 . . . . **138** A6
SW13. . . . . **127** G6
Vereker Dr, Sun. TW16 . . . **178** A3
Vereker Rd, W14. . . . . **128** B5
Vere Rd, Loug. IG10 . . . . . . **49** F4
Vere St, W1 . . . . **16** D4
Verity Cl, W11 . . . . **108** B6
Vermeer Gdns, SE15
off Elland Rd. **153** F4
Vermont Cl, Enf. EN2. . . . . . **43** H4
Vermont Rd, SE19 . . . . . . **170** A6
SW18. . . . . **149** E6
Sutton SM1. . . . . **198** E3
Verney Gdns, Dag. RM9. . **100** E4
Verney Rd, SE16 . . . . **37** J5
Dagenham RM9 . . . . . . **100** E5
Verney St, NW10 . . . . **88** D3
Verney Way, SE16. . . . . . . **132** E5
Vernham Rd, SE18. . . . . . . **137** F6
Vernon Av, E12. . . . . **98** C4
SW20. . . . . **184** A2
Woodford Green IG8 . . . **63** H7
Vernon Cl, Epsom KT19 . . **196** C6
Vernon Ct, Stan. HA7
off Vernon Dr **68/69** E1
Vernon Cres, Barn. EN4 . . . **42** A6
Vernon Dr, Stan. HA7. . . . . **68** D1
Vernon Ms, E17
off Vernon Rd **77** J4
W14 *off Vernon St*. **128** B4
Vernon Pl, WC1 . . . . **18** B2
Vernon Ri, WC1 . . . . **10** D3
Greenford UB6 . . . . **86** A5
Vernon Rd, E3. . . . . **113** J2
E11. . . . . **97** E1
E15 . . . . **97** E7
E17 . . . . **77** J5
N8 . . . . **75** G3
SW14. . . . . **146** D3
Ilford IG3. . . . . **99** J1
Sutton SM1. . . . . **199** F5
Vernon Sq, WC1 . . . . **10** D3
Vernon St, W14 . . . . **128** B4
Vernon Yd, W11
off Portobello Rd. **108** C7
Veroan Rd, Bexh. DA7 . . . **158** E2
Verona Ct, W4
off Chiswick La. . . **126/127** E5
Verona Dr, Surb. KT6 . . . . **195** H2

Verona Rd, E7 *off Upton La* 97 G7
Veronica Gdns, SW16 186 C1
Veronica Rd, SW17 168 B3
Veronique Gdns, Ilf. IG6 81 E5
Verran Rd, SW12 *off Balham Gro* 150 B7
Versailles Rd, SE20 170 D7
Verulam Av, E17 77 J6
Verulam Bldgs, WC1 18 D1
Verulam Rd, Grnf. UB6 103 G4
Verulam St, WC1 18 E1
Verwood Dr, Barn. EN4 41 J3
Verwood Rd, Har. HA2 67 J2
Vesey Path, E14 *off East India Dock Rd* 114 B6
Vespan Rd, W12 127 G2
Vesta Rd, SE4 153 H2
Vestris Rd, SE23 171 G2
Vestry Ms, SE5 152 B1
Vestry Rd, E17 78 B4
SE5 152 B1
Vestry St, N1 12 B3
Vevey St, SE6 171 J2
Veysey Gdns, Dag. RM10 101 G3
Viaduct Pl, E2 *off Viaduct St* 112/113 E3
Viaduct St, E2 112 E3
Vian St, SE13 154 B3
Vibart Gdns, SW2 151 F7
Vibart Wk, N1 *off Outram Pl* 110/111 E1
Vicarage Av, SE3 155 G1
Vicarage Cl, Erith DA8 139 J6
Northolt UB5 85 F7
Worcester Park KT4 196 E1
Vicarage Ct, W8 22 A3
Feltham TW14 141 F7
Vicarage Cres, SW11 149 G1
Vicarage Dr, SW14 146 D5
Barking IG11 99 F7
Beckenham BR3 190 A1
Vicarage Fm Rd, Houns. TW3, TW5 142 E2
Vicarage Flds, Walt. KT12 178 C6
Vicarage Fld Shop Cen, Bark. IG11 99 F7
Vicarage Gdns, SW14 *off Vicarage Rd* 146 C5
W8 128 D1
Mitcham CR4 185 H3
Vicarage Gate, W8 22 A3
Vicarage Gro, SE5 152 A1
Vicarage La, E6 116 C3
E15 97 E7
Chigwell IG7 65 F2
Ilford IG1 99 G1
Vicarage Pk, SE18 137 F5
Vicarage Path, N8 74 E7
Vicarage Rd, E10 96 B1
E15 97 F7
N17 60 D7
NW4 71 G6
SE18 137 F5
SW14 146 C5
Bexley DA5 177 H1
Croydon CR0 201 G3
Dagenham RM10 101 H6
Kingston upon Thames KT1 181 G2
Kingston upon Thames (Hmptn W.) KT1 181 F1
Sutton SM1 198 E4
Teddington TW11 162 D5
Twickenham TW2 162 B2
Twickenham (Whitton) TW2 143 J6
Woodford Green IG8 64 B7
Vicarage Wk, SW11 *off Battersea Ch Rd* 149 G1
Vicarage Way, NW10 88 D3
Harrow HA2 67 G7
Vicars Br Cl, Wem. HA0 105 H2
Vicars Cl, E9 *off Northiam St* 113 F1
E15 115 G1
Enfield EN1 44 B2
Vicars Hill, SE13 154 B4
Vicars Moor La, N21 43 G7
Vicars Oak Rd, SE19 170 B6
Vicars Rd, NW5 92 A5
Vicars Wk, Dag. RM8 100 B3
Viceroy Cl, N2 *off Market Pl* 73 H4
Viceroy Ct, NW8 7 H1
Viceroy Par, N2 *off High Rd* 73 H3
Viceroy Rd, SW8 150 E1
Vickers Cl, Wall. SM6 201 F7
Vickers Way, Houns. TW4 143 E5
Victor Gro, Wem. HA0 87 H7
★**Victoria & Albert Mus**, SW7 23 F6
Victoria Arc, SW1 *off Terminus Pl* 130 B3
Victoria Av, E6 116 A1
EC2 20 E2
N3 72 C1
Barnet EN4 41 G4
Hounslow TW3 143 F5
Surbiton KT6 181 G7
Wallington SM6 200 A3
Wembley HA9 88 B6
West Molesey KT8 179 G3
Victoria Cl, Barn. EN4 41 G4
West Molesey KT8 *off Victoria Av* 179 G3
★**Victoria Coach Sta**, SW1 32 D2
Victoria Cotts, Rich. TW9 145 J1
Victoria Ct, Wem. HA9 88 A6
Victoria Cres, N15 76 B5
SE19 170 B6
SW19 166 C7
Victoria Dock Rd, E16 115 F6
Victoria Dr, SW19 148 A7
Victoria Embk, EC4 18 C6
SW1 26 B3
WC2 18 C6
★**Victoria Embankment Gdns**, WC2 18 B6
Victoria Gdns, W11 128 D1
Hounslow TW5 142 E1
Victoria Gro, N12 57 F5
W8 22 C5
Victoria Gro Ms, W2 *off Ossington St* 108/109 E7
Victoria Ind Est, NW10 106 E3
Victoria La, Barn. EN5 40 C4
Hayes UB3 121 F5
Victoria Ms, E8 *off Dalston La* 94 D5
NW6 108 D1
SW4 *off Victoria Ri* 150 B4
SW18 167 F1
Victorian Gro, N16 94 B3
Victorian Rd, N16 94 B3
★**Victoria Park**, E9 95 H7
Victoria Pk Rd, E9 113 F1
Victoria Pk Sq, E2 113 F3
Victoria Pas, NW8 7 E5
Victoria Pl, SE22 *off Underhill Rd* 152 D5
SW1 32 E1
Richmond TW9 145 G5
Victoria Pt, E13 *off Victoria Rd* 115 G2
Victoria Retail Pk, Ruis. HA4 84 E5
Victoria Ri, SW4 150 B3
Victoria Rd, E4 63 E1
E11 96 E4
E13 115 G2
E17 78 C2
E18 79 H2
N4 75 F7
N9 60 C4
N15 76 D4
N18 60 C4
N22 74 C1
NW4 71 J4
NW6 108 C1
NW7 55 F5
NW10 106 D5
SW14 146 D3
W3 106 D5
W5 105 E5
W8 22 C6
Barking IG11 99 E6
Barnet EN4 41 G4
Bexleyheath DA6 159 G4
Bromley BR2 192 A5
Buckhurst Hill IG9 64 A2
Bushey WD23 51 H1
Chislehurst BR7 174 D5
Dagenham RM10 101 H5
Feltham TW13 160 B1
Kingston upon Thames KT1 181 J2
Mitcham CR4 167 H7
Ruislip HA4 84 C5
Sidcup DA15 175 J3
Southall UB2 123 F3
Surbiton KT6 181 G6
Sutton SM1 199 G5
Teddington TW11 162 D6
Twickenham TW1 144 D7
Victoria Sq, SW1 24 E5
Victoria Sta, SW1 33 E1
Victoria Steps, Brent. TW8 *off Kew Br Rd* 125 J6
Victoria St, E15 96 E7
SW1 25 F6
Belvedere DA17 139 F5
Victoria Ter, N4 93 G1
NW10 *off Old Oak La* 106/107 E3
Harrow HA1 86 B1
★**Victoria Twr**, SW1 26 A5
Victoria Vil, Rich. TW9 145 J3
Victoria Way, SE7 135 H5
Victoria Wf, E14 113 H7
Victoria Yd, E1 *off Fairclough St* 112 D6
Victor Rd, NW10 107 H3
SE20 171 G7
Harrow HA2 67 J3
Teddington TW11 162 B4
Victors Dr, Hmptn. TW12 161 E6
Victors Way, Barn. EN5 40 C3
Victor Vil, N9 60 A3
Victor Wk, NW9 70 E1
Victory Av, Mord. SM4 185 F5
Victory Business Cen, Islw. TW7 144 C3
Victory Pl, E14 *off Northey St* 113 H7
SE17 36 A1
SE19 *off Westow St* 170 B6
Victory Rd, E11 79 H4
SW19 167 F7
Victory Rd Ms, SW19 *off Victory Rd* 167 F7
Victory Wk, SE8 *off Ship St* 154 A1
Victory Way, SE16 133 H2
Hounslow TW5 122 C5
Romford RM7 83 H2
Vidler Cl, Chess. KT9 *off Merritt Gdns* 195 F6
Vienna Cl, Ilf. IG5 80 A3
View, The, SE2 139 E5
View Cl, N6 73 J7
Chigwell IG7 65 G5
Harrow HA1 68 A4
Viewfield Cl, Har. HA3 69 H7
Viewfield Rd, SW18 148 C6
Bexley DA5 176 C1
Viewland Rd, SE18 137 J5
View Rd, N6 73 J7
Viga Rd, N21 43 G6
Vigilant Cl, SE26 170 D4
Vignoles Rd, Rom. RM7 83 G7
Vigo St, W1 17 F6
Viking Cl, E3 *off Selwyn Rd* 113 H2
Viking Ct, SW6 128 D6
Viking Gdns, E6 *off Jack Dash Way* 116 B4
Viking Pl, E10 95 J1
Viking Rd, Sthl. UB1 103 E7
Viking Way, Erith DA8 139 J3
Villacourt Rd, SE18 138 A7
Village, The, SE7 135 J6
Village Arc, E4 *off Station Rd* 62 D1
Village Cl, E4 62 C5
NW3 *off Belsize La* 91 G5
Village Ct, E17 *off Eden Rd* 78 B5
Village Hts, Wdf.Grn. IG8 63 F5
Village Ms, NW9 88 D2
Village Pk Cl, Enf. EN1 44 B6
Village Rd, N3 72 B1
Enfield EN1 44 B6
Village Row, Sutt. SM2 198 D7
Village Way, NW10 88 D4
SE21 152 A6
Beckenham BR3 190 A2
Pinner HA5 67 E7
Village Way E, Har. HA2 67 F7
Villa Rd, SW9 151 G3
Villas Rd, SE18 137 F4
Villa St, SE17 36 C4
Villiers Av, Surb. KT5 181 J5
Twickenham TW2 161 F1
Villiers Cl, E10 96 A2
Surbiton KT5 181 J4
Villiers Ct, N20 *off Buckingham Av* 41 F7
Villiers Path, Surb. KT5 181 H5
Villiers Rd, NW2 89 G6
Beckenham BR3 189 G2
Isleworth TW7 144 B2
Kingston upon Thames KT1 181 J3
Southall UB1 123 F1
Villiers St, WC2 18 A6
Vincam Cl, Twick. TW2 143 G7
Vincent Av, Surb. KT5 196 B1
Vincent Cl, SE16 133 H2
Barnet EN5 40 D3
Bromley BR2 191 H4
Ilford IG6 65 F6
Sidcup DA15 175 H1
West Drayton UB7 120 D6
Vincent Gdns, NW2 89 F3
Vincent Ms, E3 114 A2
Vincent Rd, E4 62 D6
N15 75 J4
N22 75 G2
SE18 137 E4
W3 126 C3
Croydon CR0 188 B7
Dagenham RM9 100 E7
Hounslow TW4 142 D2
Isleworth TW7 144 A1
Kingston upon Thames KT1 182 A3
Wembley HA0 87 J7
Vincent Row, Hmptn. (Hmptn H.) TW12 161 J6
Vincents La, NW7 55 J4
Vincents Path, Nthlt. UB5 *off Arnold Rd* 84/85 E6
Vincent Sq, SW1 33 G1
Vincent St, E16 115 F5
SW1 33 H1
Vincent Ter, N1 11 G1
Vince St, EC1 12 C4
Vine Cl, Surb. KT5 181 J6
Sutton SM1 199 F3
West Drayton UB7 120 D4
Vine Ct, E1 21 J2
Harrow HA3 69 H6
Vinegar All, E17 78 B4
Vine Gdns, Ilf. IG1 99 F5
Vinegar St, E1 *off Reardon St* 132/133 E1
Vinegar Yd, SE1 28 D3
Vine Hill, EC1 10 E6
Vine La, SE1 28 E2
Vine Pl, W5 *off The Common* 125 H1
Hounslow TW3 143 H4
Viner Cl, Walt. KT12 178 C6
Vineries, The, N14 42 C6
Enfield EN1 44 B3
Vineries Bk, NW7 55 H5
Vineries Cl, Dag. RM9 *off Heathway* 101 G6
West Drayton UB7 120 D6
Vine Rd, E15 97 F7
SW13 147 F3
East Molesey KT8 179 J4
Orpington BR6 207 J6
Vines Av, N3 72 E1
Vine Sq, W14 128 C5
Vine St, EC3 21 F5
W1 17 G6
Romford RM7 83 J5
Vine St Br, EC1 11 F6
Vine Yd, SE1 28 A3
Vineyard, The, Rich. TW10 145 H5
Vineyard Av, NW7 56 B7
Vineyard Cl, SE6 172 A1
Kingston upon Thames KT1 181 J3
Vineyard Gro, N3 73 E1
Vineyard Hill Rd, SW19 166 D4
Vineyard Pas, Rich. TW9 *off Paradise Rd* 145 H5
Vineyard Path, SW14 146 D3
Vineyard Rd, Felt. TW13 160 A3
Vineyard Row, Kings.T. (Hmptn W.) KT1 181 F1
Vineyard Wk, EC1 11 E5
Viney Rd, SE13 154 B3
Vining St, SW9 151 G4
★**Vinopolis**, SE1 28 A1
Vintners Ct, EC4 20 A5
Vintners Pl, EC4 *off Upper Thames St* 111 J7
Vintry Ms, E17 *off Cleveland Pk Cres* 78 A4
Viola Av, SE2 138 B4
Feltham TW14 142 C6
Viola Sq, W12 107 F7
Violet Cl, E16 115 E4
SE8 *off Dorking Cl* 133 J6
Sutton SM3 198 B1
Wallington SM6 200 B1
Violet Gdns, Croy. CR0 201 H5
Violet Hill, NW8 6 C2
Violet La, Croy. CR0 201 H5
Violet Rd, E3 114 B4
E17 78 A6

Violet Rd, E18 79 H2
Violet St, E2
off Three Colts La 112/113 E4
Virgil Pl, W1 15 J2
Virgil St, SE1 26 D5
Virginia Cl, N.Mal. KT3
off Willow Rd 182 C4
Virginia Gdns, Ilf. IG6 81 F2
Virginia Rd, E2 13 F4
Thornton Heath CR7 187 H1
Virginia St, E1 21 J6
Virginia Wk, SW2 151 F6
Viscount Cl, N11 58 B5
Viscount Dr, E6 116 C5
Viscount Gro, Nthlt. UB5 102 D3
Viscount St, EC1 11 J6
Viscount Way, Houns. (Hthrw Air.) TW6 141 H4
Vista, The, E4
off Forest Vw 46 D7
SE9 156 A6
Sidcup DA14
off Langdon Shaw 175 J5
Vista Av, Enf. EN3 45 G2
Vista Bldg, The, SE18
off Calderwood St 136 D3
Vista Dr, Ilf. IG4 80 A5
Vista Way, Har. HA3 69 H6
Viveash Cl, Hayes UB3 121 J3
Vivian Av, NW4 71 H5
Wembley HA9 88 A5
Vivian Cl, Wat. WD19 50 A1
Vivian Comma Cl, N4
off Blackstock Rd 93 H3
Vivian Gdns, Wat. WD19 50 A1
Wembley HA9 88 A5
Vivian Rd, E3 113 H2
Vivian Sq, SE15
off Scylla Rd 152/153 E3
Vivian Way, N2 73 G5
Vivien Cl, Chess. KT9 195 H7
Vivienne Cl, Twick. TW1 145 F6
Voce Rd, SE18 137 G7
Voewood Cl, N.Mal. KT3 183 F6
Volta Cl, N9
off Hudson Way 61 F3
Voltaire Rd, SW4 150 D3
Volt Av, NW10 106 D3
Volta Way, Croy. CR0 201 F1
Voluntary Pl, E11 79 G6
Vorley Rd, N19 92 C2
Voss Ct, SW16 169 E6
Voss St, E2 13 J4
Voyagers Cl, SE28 118 C6
Voysey Cl, N3 72 B3
Vulcan Cl, E6 116 D6
Vulcan Gate, Enf. EN2 43 G2
Vulcan Rd, SE4 153 J2
Vulcan Sq, E14
off Britannia Rd 134 A4
Vulcan Ter, SE4 153 J2
Vulcan Way, N7 93 F6
Vyne, The, Bexh. DA7 159 H3
Vyner Rd, W3 106 D7
Vyner St, E2 113 E1
Vyse Cl, Barn. EN5 39 J4

W

Wadbrook St, Kings.T. KT1 181 G2
Wadding St, SE17 36 B2
Waddington Cl, Enf. EN1 44 B4
Waddington Rd, E15 96 D5
Waddington St, E15 96 D6
Waddington Way, SE19 169 J7
WADDON, Croy. CR0 201 G2
Waddon Cl, Croy. CR0 201 G3
Waddon Ct Rd, Croy. CR0 201 G4
Waddon Marsh Way, Croy. CR0 201 F1
Waddon New Rd, Croy. CR0 201 H3
Waddon Pk Av, Croy. CR0 201 G4
Waddon Rd, Croy. CR0 201 G3
Waddon Way, Croy. CR0 201 H6
Wades Gro, N21 43 G7
Wades Hill, N21 43 G6
Wades La, Tedd. TW11
off High St 162 D5
Wades Ms, N21
off Wades Hill 43 G7
Wadeson St, E2 113 E2
Wades Pl, E14 114 B7
Wadeville Av, Rom. RM6 83 F7
Wadeville Cl, Belv. DA17 139 G6
Wadham Av, E17 62 B7
Wadham Gdns, NW3 109 H1
Wadham Gdns, Grnf. UB6 86 A6
Wadham Rd, E17 78 B1
SW15 148 B4
Wadhurst Cl, SE20 188 E2
Wadhurst Rd, SW8 150 C1
W4 126 D3
Wadley Rd, E11 78 E7
Wadsworth Business Cen, Grnf. UB6 105 F2
Wadsworth Cl, Enf. EN3 45 G5
Greenford UB6 105 F2
Wadsworth Rd, Grnf. UB6 105 E2
Wager St, E3 113 J4
Waggon Ms, N14
off Chase Side 58 C1
Waghorn Rd, E13 115 J1
Harrow HA3 69 G3
Waghorn St, SE15 152 D3
Wagner St, SE15 133 F7
Wagstaff Gdns, Dag. RM9 100 C7
Wagtail Cl, NW9
off Swan Dr 70/71 E2
Wagtail Wk, Beck. BR3 190 C5
Waights Ct, Kings.T. KT2 181 H1
Wainfleet Av, Rom. RM5 83 J2
Wainford Cl, SW19
off Windlesham Gro 166 A1
Wainwright Gro, Islw. TW7 144 A4
Waite Davies Rd, SE12 155 F7
Waite St, SE15 37 F5
Waithman St, EC4 19 G4
Wakefield Gdns, SE19 170 B7
Ilford IG1 80 B6
Wakefield Ms, WC1 10 B4
Wakefield Rd, N11 58 D5
N15 76 C5
Richmond TW10 145 G5
Wakefield St, E6 116 A1
N18 60 D5
WC1 10 B5
Wakeford Cl, SW4
off Clapham Common S Side 150 C5
Wakehams Hill, Pnr. HA5 67 F3
Wakeham St, N1 94 A6
Wakehurst Rd, SW11 149 H5
Wakeling Rd, W7 104 C5
Wakeling St, E14 113 H6
Wakelin Rd, E15 114 E2
Wakeman Rd, NW10 107 J3
Wakemans Hill Av, NW9 70 D5
Wakering Rd, Bark. IG11 99 F6
Wakerley Cl, E6
off Truesdale Rd 116 C6
Wakley St, EC1 11 G3
Walberswick St, SW8 131 E7
Walbrook, EC4 20 B5
Walbrook Ho, N9 61 F1
Walbrook Wf, EC4
off Upper Thames St 111 J7
Walburgh St, E1
off Bigland St 112/113 E6
Walcorde Av, SE17 36 A2
Walcot Rd, Enf. EN3 45 J2
Walcot Sq, SE11 35 F1
Walcott St, SW1 33 G1
Waldair Ct, E16
off Barge Ho Rd 136/137 E2
Waldair Wf, E16 136 E2
Waldeck Gro, SE27 169 H3
Waldeck Rd, N15 75 H4
SW14
off Lower Richmond Rd 146 C3
W4 126 A6
W13 104 E6
Waldeck Ter, SW14
off Lower Richmond Rd 146 C3
Waldegrave Av, Tedd. TW11
off Waldegrave Rd 162 C5
Waldegrave Gdns, Twick. TW1 162 C2
Waldegrave Pk, Twick. TW1 162 C4
Waldegrave Rd, N8 75 G3
SE19 170 C7
W5 105 J6
Bromley BR1 192 B4
Dagenham RM8 100 C2
Teddington TW11 162 C4
Twickenham TW1 162 C4
Waldegrove, Croy. CR0 202 C3
Waldemar Av, SW6 148 B1
W13 125 F1
Waldemar Rd, SW19 166 D5
Walden Av, N13 59 J4
Chislehurst BR7 174 C4
Walden Cl, Belv. DA17 139 F5
Walden Gdns, Th.Hth. CR7 187 F3
Walden Par, Chis. BR7
off Walden Rd 174 C6
Walden Rd, N17 76 A1
Chislehurst BR7 174 C6
Waldenshaw Rd, SE23 171 F1
Walden St, E1 112 E6
Walden Way, NW7 56 A6
Ilford IG6 65 H7
Waldo Cl, SW4 150 C5
Waldo Pl, Mitch. CR4 167 H7
Waldo Rd, NW10 107 G3
Bromley BR1 192 A3
Waldram Cres, SE23 171 F1
Waldram Pk Rd, SE23 171 G1
Waldram Pl, SE23
off Waldram Cres 171 F1
Waldrist Way, Erith DA18 139 F2
Waldron Gdns, Brom. BR2 190 D3
Waldronhyrst, S.Croy. CR2 201 H4
Waldron Ms, SW3 31 F5
Waldron Rd, SW18 167 F3
Harrow HA1, HA2 86 B1
Waldrons, The, Croy. CR0 201 H4
Waldrons Path, S.Croy. CR2 201 J4
Waldstock Rd, SE28 118 A7
Waleran Cl, Stan. HA7 52 C6
Walerand Rd, SE13 154 C2
Waleran Flats, SE1
off Old Kent Rd 132 B4
Wales Av, Cars. SM5 199 J5
Wales Cl, SE15 132 E7
Wales Fm Rd, W3 106 D5
Waleton Acres, Wall. SM6 200 C6
Waley St, E1 113 G5
Walfield Av, N20 41 E7
Walford Rd, N16 94 B4
Walfrey Gdns, Dag. RM9 101 E7
WALHAM GREEN, SW6 128 E7
Walham Grn Ct, SW6
off Waterford Rd 128/129 E7
Walham Gro, SW6 128 D7
Walham Ri, SW19 166 B6
Walham Yd, SW6
off Walham Gro 128 D7
Walkden Rd, Chis. BR7 174 D5
Walker Cl, N11 58 C4
SE18 137 F4
W7 124 B1
Hampton TW12
off Fearnley Cres 161 F6
Walker Ms, SW2
off Effra Rd 151 G5
Walkers Ct, E8
off Wilton Way 94 D6
W1 17 H5
Walkerscroft Mead, SE21 169 J1
Walkers Pl, SW15
off Felsham Rd 148 B3
Walkford Way, SE15
off Daniel Gdns 132 C7
Walks, The, N2 73 G3
Walkynscroft, SE15
off Firbank Rd 152/153 E2
Wallace Cl, SE28
off Haldane Rd 118 D7
★**Wallace Collection**, W1 16 B3
Wallace Cres, Cars. SM5 199 J5
Wallace Rd, N1 93 J6
Wallace Way, N19
off Giesbach Rd 92 D2
Wallbutton Rd, SE4 153 H2
Wallcote Av, NW2 90 A1
Wall End Rd, E6 98 C7
Waller Dr, Nthwd. HA6 66 A2
Waller Rd, SE14 153 G1
Wallers Cl, Dag. RM9 119 E1
Woodford Green IG8 64 C6
Wallers Hoppit, Loug. IG10 48 B2
Waller Way, SE10
off Greenwich High Rd 134 B7
Wallflower St, W12 107 F7
Wallgrave Rd, SW5 30 A1
Wallingford Av, W10 108 A5
WALLINGTON, SM6 200 C5
Wallington Cor, Wall. SM6
off Manor Rd N 200 B4
Wallington Rd, Ilf. IG3 81 J7
Wallington Sq, Wall. SM6
off Woodcote Rd 200 B6
Wallis All, SE1 28 A3
Wallis Cl, SW11 149 G3
Wallis Ms, N22
off Brampton Pk Rd 75 G3
Wallis Rd, E9 95 J6
Southall UB1 103 H6
Wallis's Cotts, SW2 150 E7
Wallman Pl, N22
off Bounds Grn Rd 75 F1
Wallorton Gdns, SW14 146 D4
Wallside, EC2 20 A2
Wall St, N1 94 A6
Wallwood Rd, E11 96 D1
Wallwood St, E14 113 J5
Walmar Cl, Barn. EN4 41 G1
Walmer Cl, E4 62 B2
Orpington BR6
off Tubbenden La S 207 G4
Romford RM7 83 H2
Walmer Gdns, W13 124 D2
Walmer Ho, N9 44 C7
Walmer Pl, W1 15 J1
Walmer Rd, W10
off Latimer Rd 107 J6
W11 108 B7
Walmer St, W1 15 J1
Walmer Ter, SE18 137 F4
Walmgate Rd, Grnf. UB6 104 E1
Walmington Fold, N12 56 D6
Walm La, NW2 90 A5
Walmsley Ho, SW16
off Colson Way 168 C4
Walney Wk, N1
off St. Paul's Rd 93 J6
Walnut Av, West Dr. UB7 120 D3
Walnut Cl, SE8
off Clyde St 133 J6
Carshalton SM5 199 J5
Ilford IG6
off Civic Way 81 F4
Walnut Ct, W5 125 H2
Walnut Gdns, E15
off Burgess Rd 96/97 E4
Walnut Gro, Enf. EN1 44 A5
Walnut Ms, Sutt. SM2 199 F7
Walnut Rd, E10 96 A2
Walnut Tree Av, Mitch. CR4
off De'Arn Gdns 185 H3
Walnut Tree Cl, SW13 147 F1
Chislehurst BR7 193 F1
Walnut Tree Cotts, SW19
off Church Rd 166 B4
Walnut Tree Rd, SE10 135 E5
Brentford TW8 125 H6
Dagenham RM8 100 D2
Hounslow TW5 123 F6
Walnut Tree Wk, SE11 34 E1
Walnut Way, Buck.H. IG9 64 A3
Ruislip HA4 84 C6
Walpole Av, Rich. TW9 145 J2
Walpole Cl, W13 125 F2
Pinner HA5 51 G6
Walpole Cres, Tedd. TW11 162 C5
Walpole Gdns, W4 126 C5
Twickenham TW2 162 B2
Walpole Ms, NW8
off Queen's Gro 109 G1
SW19 *off Walpole Rd* 167 G6
Walpole Pk, W5 125 F1
Walpole Pl, SE18
off Brookhill Rd 136/137 E4
Teddington TW11 162 C5
Walpole Rd, E6 97 J7
E17 77 H4
E18 79 F1
N17 (Downhills Way) 75 J3
N17 (Lordship La) 75 J2
SW19 167 G6
Bromley BR2 192 A5
Croydon CR0 202 A2
Surbiton KT6 181 H6
Teddington TW11 162 C5
Twickenham TW2 162 B2
Walpole St, SW3 31 J3
Walrond Av, Wem. HA9 87 H5
Walsham Cl, N16
off Braydon Rd 76 D7
SE28 118 D7
Walsham Rd, SE14 153 G2
Feltham TW14 142 B7
Walsingham Gdns, Epsom KT19 197 E4
Walsingham Pk, Chis. BR7 193 G2
Walsingham Pl, SW4
off Clapham Common W Side 149 J4
SW11 150 A6
Walsingham Rd, E5 94 D3
W13 124 D1
Enfield EN2 44 A4

Walsingham Rd, Mitch. CR4 . . . . . **185** J5
Walsingham Wk, Belv. DA17 . . . . . **139** G6
Walter Hurford Par, E12 *off Walton Rd* **98** D4
Walter Rodney Cl, E6 *off Stevenage Rd* **98** C6
Walters Cl, SE17 . . . . . **36** A2
Hayes UB3 *off St. Anselms Rd* . . . **121** J2
Walters Ho, SE17 . . . . . **35** G6
Walters Rd, SE25 . . . . . **188** B4
Enfield EN3 . . . . . **45** F5
Walter St, E2 . . . . . **113** G3
Kingston upon Thames KT2 *off Sopwith Way* . **181** H1
Walters Way, SE23 . . . . . **153** G6
Walters Yd, Brom. BR1 . . . **191** G2
Walter Ter, E1 . . . . . **113** G6
Walterton Rd, W9 . . . . . **108** C4
Walter Wk, Edg. HA8 . . . . . **54** C6
Waltham Av, NW9 . . . . . **70** A6
Hayes UB3 . . . . . **121** F3
Waltham Dr, Edg. HA8 . . . . **70** A2
Waltham Pk Way, E17 . . . . **78** A1
Waltham Rd, Cars. SM5 . . **185** G7
Southall UB2 . . . . . **122** E3
Woodford Green IG8 . . . **64** B6
WALTHAMSTOW, E17 . . . . **78** B2
Walthamstow Av, E4 . . . . . **62** A7
Walthamstow Business Cen, E17 . . . . . **78** C2
Waltham Way, E4 . . . . . **61** J4
Waltheof Av, N17 . . . . . **76** A1
Waltheof Gdns, N17 . . . . . **76** A1
Walton Av, Har. HA2 . . . . . **85** F5
New Malden KT3 . . . . . **183** F4
Sutton SM3 . . . . . **198** C3
Wembley HA9 . . . . . **88** B3
Walton Cl, E5 *off Orient Way* **95** G3
NW2 . . . . . **89** H2
SW8 . . . . . **34** B7
Harrow HA1 . . . . . **68** A4
Walton Cres, Har. HA2 . . . . **85** F4
Walton Dr, NW10 *off Mitchellbrook Way* . . **88** D6
Harrow HA1 . . . . . **68** A4
Walton Gdns, W3 . . . . . **106** B5
Wembley HA9 . . . . . **87** H2
Walton Grn, Croy. (New Adgtn) CR0 . . . . **204** C7
Walton Pl, SW3 . . . . . **23** J5
Walton Rd, E12 . . . . . **98** D4
E13 . . . . . **115** J2
N15 . . . . . **76** C5
East Molesey KT8 . . . . . **179** G4
Harrow HA1 . . . . . **68** A4
Sidcup DA14 . . . . . **176** C2
Walton-on-Thames KT12 . . . . . **178** C5
West Molesey KT8 . . . . **179** E5
Walton St, SW3 . . . . . **31** H1
Enfield EN2 . . . . . **44** A1
Walton Way, W3 . . . . . **106** B5
Mitcham CR4 . . . . . **186** C4
Walt Whitman Cl, SE24 *off Shakespeare Rd* . . . **151** H4
WALWORTH, SE17 . . . . . **35** J3
★Walworth Garden Farm - Horticultural Training Cen, SE17 . . . . . **35** H4
Walworth Pl, SE17 . . . . . **36** A4
Walworth Rd, SE1 . . . . . **35** J1
SE17 . . . . . **35** J1
Walwyn Av, Brom. BR1 . . **192** A3
Wanborough Dr, SW15 . . **165** H1
Wanderer Dr, Bark. IG11 . . **118** B3
Wandle Bk, SW19 . . . . . **167** G6
Croydon CR0 . . . . . **200** E3
Wandle Ct, Epsom KT19 . **196** C4
Wandle Ct Gdns, Croy. CR0 . . . . . **200** E4
Wandle Rd, SW17 . . . . . **167** H2
Croydon CR0 . . . . . **201** J3
Croydon (Waddon) CR0 . **201** E3
Morden SM4 . . . . . **185** F4
Wallington SM6 . . . . . **200** B2
Wandle Side, Croy. CR0 . . **201** F3
Wallington SM6 . . . . . **200** B3
Wandle Tech Pk, Mitch. CR4 *off Goat Rd* **185** J7
Wandle Trd Est, Mitch. CR4 *off Budge La* **185** J7
Wandle Way, SW18 . . . . . **166** E1
Mitcham CR4 . . . . . **185** J5
Wandon Rd, SW6 . . . . . **129** E7
WANDSWORTH, SW18 . . **148** C5
Wandsworth Br, SW6 . . . **149** E3
SW18 . . . . . **149** E3
Wandsworth Br Rd, SW6 . **148** E1
Wandsworth Common, SW12 . . . . . **149** H6
Wandsworth Common W Side, SW18 . . . . . **149** F5
Wandsworth High St, SW18 . . . . . **148** D5
★Wandsworth Mus, SW18 *off Garratt La* . . **148** E5
Wandsworth Plain, SW18 . **148** E5
Wandsworth Rd, SW8 . . . . **34** A5
Wandsworth Shop Cen, SW18 . . . . . **148** E6
Wangey Rd, Rom. RM6 . . . **82** D7
Wanless Rd, SE24 . . . . . **151** J3
Wanley Rd, SE5 . . . . . **152** A4
Wanlip Rd, E13 . . . . . **115** H4
Wannock Gdns, Ilf. IG6 . . . **65** E7
Wansbeck Rd, E3 . . . . . **95** J7
E9 . . . . . **95** J7
Wansdown Pl, SW6 . . . . . **30** A7
Wansey St, SE17 . . . . . **35** J2
Wansford Pk, Borwd. WD6 . **38** E4
Wansford Rd, Wdf.Grn. IG8 . **79** J1
WANSTEAD, E11 . . . . . **79** H7
Wanstead Cl, Brom. BR1 . **191** J2
Wanstead La, Ilf. IG1 . . . . . **80** A6
Wanstead Pk, E11 . . . . . **80** A7
Wanstead Pk Av, E12 . . . . **98** A2
Wanstead Pk Rd, Ilf. IG1 . . **98** C1
Wanstead Pl, E11 . . . . . **79** G6
Wanstead Rd, Brom. BR1 . **191** J2
Wansunt Rd, Bex. DA5 . . . **177** J1
Wantage Rd, SE12 . . . . . **155** F5
Wantz Rd, Dag. RM10 . . . **101** H4
WAPPING, E1 . . . . . **29** J1
Wapping Dock St, E1 *off Cinnamon St* . **132/133** E1
Wapping High St, E1 . . . . . **29** H2
Wapping La, E1 . . . . . **113** E7
Wapping Wall, E1 . . . . . **133** F1
Warbank La, Kings.T. KT2 . **165** F7
Warbeck Rd, W12 . . . . . **127** H1
Warberry Rd, N22 . . . . . **75** F2
Warboys App, Kings.T. KT2 . . . . . **164** B6
Warboys Cres, E4 . . . . . **62** C5
Warboys Rd, Kings.T. KT2 . **164** B6
Warburton Cl, N1 *off Culford Rd* **94** B6
Harrow HA3 . . . . . **52** A6
Warburton Rd, E8 . . . . . **95** E7
Twickenham TW2 . . . . . **161** H1
Warburton St, E8 *off Warburton Rd* . **112/113** E1
Warburton Ter, E17 . . . . . **78** B2
Wardalls Gro, SE14 . . . . . **133** F7
Ward Cl, S.Croy. CR2 . . . **202** B5
Wardell Cl, NW7 . . . . . **55** E7
Wardell Fld, NW9 . . . . . **71** E1
Warden Av, Har. HA2 . . . . . **85** F1
Warden Rd, NW5 . . . . . **92** A6
Wardens Fld Cl, Orp. BR6 . . . . . **207** H6
Wardens Gro, SE1 . . . . . **27** J2
Wardle St, E9 . . . . . **95** G5
Wardley St, SW18 *off Garratt La* **148/149** F7
Wardo Av, SW6 . . . . . **148** B1
Wardour Ms, W1 . . . . . **17** G4
Wardour St, W1 . . . . . **17** H5
Ward Rd, E15 . . . . . **114** D1
N19 . . . . . **92** C3
Wardrobe Pl, EC4 *off Carter La* **111** H6
Wardrobe Ter, EC4 . . . . . **19** H4
Wards Rd, Ilf. IG2 . . . . . **81** G7
Wards Wf App, E16 . . . . . **136** A2
Wareham Cl, Houns. TW3 . **143** H4
Waremead Rd, Ilf. IG2 . . . **80** E5
Warenford Way, Borwd. WD6 . . . . . **38** A1
Ware Pt Dr, SE28 . . . . . **137** G2
Warfield Rd, NW10 . . . . . **108** A3
Feltham TW14 . . . . . **141** H7
Hampton TW12 . . . . . **179** H1
Warfield Yd, NW10 *off Warfield Rd* **108** A3
Wargrave Av, N15 . . . . . **76** C6
Wargrave Rd, Har. HA2 . . . **85** J3
Warham Rd, N4 . . . . . **75** G5
Harrow HA3 . . . . . **68** C2
South Croydon CR2 . . . **201** J5
Warham St, SE5 . . . . . **35** H7
Waring Cl, Orp. BR6 . . . . **207** J6
Waring Dr, Orp. BR6 . . . . **207** J6
Waring Rd, Sid. DA14 . . . . **176** C6
Waring St, SE27 . . . . . **169** J4
Warkworth Gdns, Islw. TW7 . . . . . **124** D7
Warkworth Rd, N17 . . . . . **60** A7
Warland Rd, SE18 . . . . . **137** G7
Warley Av, Dag. RM8 . . . . . **83** F7
Hayes UB4 . . . . . **102** A5
Warley Cl, E10 *off Millicent Rd* **95** J1
Warley Rd, N9 . . . . . **61** F2
Hayes UB4 . . . . . **102** A6
Ilford IG5 . . . . . **80** D1
Woodford Green IG8 . . . **63** H7
Warley St, E2 . . . . . **113** G3
Warlingham Rd, Th.Hth. CR7 . . . . . **187** H4
Warlock Rd, W9 . . . . . **108** D4
Warlters Cl, N7 *off Warlters Rd* **92/93** E4
Warlters Rd, N7 . . . . . **93** E4
Warltersville Rd, N19 . . . . . **74** E7
Warmington Cl, E5 *off Orient Way* **95** G3
Warmington Rd, SE24 . . . **151** J6
Warmington St, E13 *off Barking Rd* **115** G4
Warminster Gdns, SE25 . . **188** D2
Warminster Rd, SE25 . . . . **188** C2
Warminster Sq, SE25 . . . . **188** D2
Warminster Way, Mitch. CR4 . . . . . **186** B1
Warndon St, SE16 . . . . . **133** G4
Warneford Rd, Har. HA3 . . . **69** G3
Warneford St, E9 . . . . . **113** E1
Warne Pl, Sid. DA15 *off Westerham Dr* **158** B6
Warner Av, Sutt. SM3 . . . . **198** B2
Warner Cl, E15 . . . . . **97** E5
NW9 . . . . . **71** F7
Hampton TW12 *off Tangley Pk Rd* **161** F5
Hayes UB3 . . . . . **121** G7
Warner Ho, SE13 *off Conington Rd* **154** B2
Warner Par, Hayes UB3 . . **121** G7
Warner Pl, E2 . . . . . **13** J2
Warner Rd, E17 . . . . . **77** H4
N8 . . . . . **74** D4
SE5 . . . . . **151** J1
Bromley BR1 . . . . . **173** F7
Warners Cl, Wdf.Grn. IG8 . . **63** G5
Warners La, Kings.T. KT2 . **163** G4
Warners Path, Wdf.Grn. IG8 . . . . . **63** G5
Warner St, EC1 . . . . . **11** E6
Warner Ter, E14 *off Broomfield St* **114** A5
Warner Yd, EC1 . . . . . **10** E6
Warnford Ho, SW15 *off Tunworth Cres* **147** F6
Warnford Ind Est, Hayes UB3 . . . . . **121** H2
Warnford Rd, Orp. BR6 . . **207** J5
Warnham Ct Rd, Cars. SM5 . . . . . **199** J7
Warnham Rd, N12 . . . . . **57** H5
Warple Ms, W3 *off Warple Way* . . . **126/127** E2
Warple Way, W3 . . . . . **126** E1
Warren, The, E12 . . . . . **98** B4
Hayes UB4 . . . . . **102** A6
Hounslow TW5 . . . . . **123** F7
Worcester Park KT4 . . . . **196** D4
Warren Av, E10 . . . . . **96** C3
Bromley BR1 . . . . . **172** E7
Orpington BR6 . . . . . **207** J5
Richmond TW10 . . . . . **146** B4
South Croydon CR2 . . . **203** G7
Warren Cl, N9 . . . . . **45** G7
SE21 *off Lairdale Cl* . . . **151** J7
Bexleyheath DA6 . . . . . **159** G5
Hayes UB4 . . . . . **102** C5
Wembley HA9 . . . . . **87** G2
Warren Ct, SE7 *off Charlton Ch La* **135** J5
Chigwell IG7 . . . . . **65** G4
Warren Cres, N9 . . . . . **44** C7
Warren Cutting, Kings.T. KT2 . . . . . **164** D7
Warrender Rd, N19 . . . . . **92** C3
Warrender Way, Ruis. HA4 . . . . . **66** A7
Warren Dr, Grnf. UB6 . . . . **103** H4
Ruislip HA4 . . . . . **66** D7
Warren Dr, The, E11 . . . . . **79** J7
Warren Dr N, Surb. KT5 . . **196** B1
Warren Dr S, Surb. KT5 . . **196** C1
Warren Flds, Stan. HA7 *off Valencia Rd* **53** F4
Warren Footpath, Twick. TW1 . . . . . **163** F1
Warren Gdns, E15 *off Ashton Rd* **96** D5
Warren Gro, Borwd. WD6 . . **38** D4
Warren Hts, Loug. IG10 . . . **47** J5
Warren Hill, Loug. IG10 . . . **47** J6
Warren Ho, E3 *off Bromley High St* . . **114** B3
Warren La, SE18 . . . . . **136** E3
Stanmore HA7 . . . . . **52** C3
Warren La Gate, SE18 . . . **136** E3
Warren Ms, W1 . . . . . **9** F6
Warren Pk, Kings.T. KT2 . . **164** C6
Warren Pk Rd, Sutt. SM1 . **199** G6
Warren Pond Rd, E4 . . . . . **63** F1
Warren Ri, N.Mal. KT3 . . . **182** D1
Warren Rd, E4 . . . . . **62** C2
E10 . . . . . **96** C3
E11 . . . . . **97** J1
NW2 . . . . . **89** F2
SW19 . . . . . **167** H6
Bexleyheath DA6 . . . . . **159** G5
Bromley BR2 . . . . . **205** G2
Bushey (Bushey Hth) WD23 . . . . . **51** J1
Croydon CR0 . . . . . **202** B1
Ilford IG6 . . . . . **81** G5
Kingston upon Thames KT2 . . . . . **164** C6
Orpington BR6 . . . . . **207** J5
Sidcup DA14 . . . . . **176** C3
Twickenham TW2 . . . . . **143** J6
Warrens Shawe La, Edg. HA8 . . . . . **54** B1
Warren St, W1 . . . . . **9** E6
Warren Ter, Rom. RM6 . . . **82** D4
Warren Wk, SE7 . . . . . **135** J6
Warren Way, NW7 . . . . . **56** B6
Warren Wd Cl, Brom. BR2 . **205** F2
Warriner Dr, N9 . . . . . **60** D3
Warriner Gdns, SW11 . . . . **149** J1
Warrington Cres, W9 . . . . . **6** C6
Warrington Gdns, W9 . . . . . **6** C6
Warrington Pl, E14 *off Yabsley St* **134** C1
Warrington Rd, Croy. CR0 . **201** H3
Dagenham RM8 . . . . . **100** D2
Harrow HA1 . . . . . **68** B5
Richmond TW10 . . . . . **145** G5
Warrington Sq, Dag. RM8 . **100** D2
Warrior Sq, E12 . . . . . **98** D4
Warsaw Cl, Ruis. HA4 *off Glebe Av* **84** B6
Warsdale Dr, NW9 *off Mardale Dr* **70** D5
Warspite Rd, SE18 . . . . . **136** B3
Warton Rd, E15 . . . . . **96** C7
Warwall, E6 . . . . . **116** E6
Warwick Av, W2 . . . . . **6** C6
W9 . . . . . **6** C6
Edgware HA8 . . . . . **54** B3
Harrow HA2 . . . . . **85** F4
Warwick Bldg, SW8 *off Queenstown Rd* . . . **130** B6
Warwick Cl, Barn. EN4 . . . . **41** G5
Bexley DA5 . . . . . **159** F7
Hampton TW12 . . . . . **161** J7
Warwick Ct, SE15 . . . . . **152** D2
WC1 . . . . . **18** D2
Surbiton KT6 *off Hook Rd* **195** H2
Warwick Cres, W2 . . . . . **14** C1
Warwick Dene, W5 . . . . . **125** H1
Warwick Dr, SW15 . . . . . **147** H3
Warwick Est, W2 . . . . . **14** B2
Warwick Gdns, N4 . . . . . **75** J5
W14 . . . . . **128** C3
Ilford IG1 . . . . . **99** E1
Thames Ditton KT7 . . . . **180** C5
Warwick Gro, E5 . . . . . **94** E1
Surbiton KT5 . . . . . **181** J7
Warwick Ho St, SW1 . . . . . **25** J1
Warwick La, EC4 . . . . . **19** H4
Warwick Pas, EC4 . . . . . **19** H3
Warwick Pl, W5 *off Warwick Rd* **125** G2
W9 . . . . . **14** C1
Warwick Pl N, SW1 . . . . . **33** F2
Warwick Rd, E4 . . . . . **62** A5
E11 . . . . . **79** H5
E12 . . . . . **98** B5
E15 . . . . . **97** F6
E17 . . . . . **77** J1
N11 . . . . . **58** D6
N18 . . . . . **60** B4
SE20 . . . . . **189** E3
SW5 . . . . . **128** C4
W5 . . . . . **125** G2

Warwick Rd, W14 **128** C4
Barnet EN5 **40** E4
Borehamwood WD6 **38** D3
Hounslow TW4 **142** B3
Kingston upon Thames KT1 **181** F1
New Malden KT3 **182** C3
Sidcup DA14 **176** B5
Southall UB2 **123** F3
Sutton SM1 **199** F4
Thames Ditton KT7 **180** C5
Thornton Heath CR7 **187** G3
Twickenham TW2 **162** B1
Welling DA16 **158** C3
West Drayton UB7 **120** B2
Warwick Row, SW1 **25** E5
Warwickshire Path, SE8 **133** J7
Warwick Sq, EC4 **19** H3
SW1 **33** F3
Warwick Sq Ms, SW1 **33** F2
Warwick St, W1 **17** G5
Warwick Ter, SE18 **137** G6
Warwick Way, SW1 **33** F2
Warwick Yd, EC1 **12** A6
Washington Av, E12 **98** B4
Washington Cl, E3 *off St. Leonards St* **114** B3
Washington Rd, E6 *off St. Stephens Rd.* **97** J7
E18 **79** F2
SW13 **127** G7
Kingston upon Thames KT1 **182** A2
Worcester Park KT4 **197** H2
Wastdale Rd, SE23 **171** G1
Watchfield Ct, W4 **126** C5
Watcombe Cotts, Rich. TW9 **126** A6
Watcombe Pl, SE25 *off Albert Rd.* **188/189** E5
Watcombe Rd, SE25 **188** E5
Waterbank Rd, SE6 **172** B3
Waterbeach Rd, Dag. RM9 **100** C6
Waterbrook La, NW4 **71** J5
Watercress Pl, N1 *off Hertford Rd* **94** B7
Waterdale Rd, SE2 **138** A6
Waterden Rd, E15 **96** A5
Waterer Ri, Wall. SM6 **200** D6
Waterfall Cl, N14 **58** C3
Waterfall Cotts, SW19 **167** G6
Waterfall Rd, N11 **58** B4
N14 **58** C3
SW19 **167** G6
Waterfall Ter, SW17 **167** H6
Waterfield Cl, SE28 **138** B1
Belvedere DA17 **139** G3
Waterfield Gdns, SE25 **188** B5
Waterford Rd, SW6 **149** E1
Waterfront Studios Business Cen, E16 *off Dock Rd* **135** F1
Water Gdns, Stan. HA7 **53** E6
Water Gdns, The, W2 **15** H3
Watergardens, The, Kings.T. KT2 **164** C6
Watergate, EC4 **19** G5
Watergate, The, Wat. WD19 **50** D2
Watergate St, SE8 **134** A6
Watergate Wk, WC2 **26** B1
Waterhall Av, E4 **62** E4
Waterhall Cl, E17 **77** G1
Waterhouse Cl, E16 **116** A5
NW3 *off Lyndhurst Rd* **91** G5
W6 *off Great Ch La* **128** A4
Waterhouse Sq, EC1 **19** E2
Wateridge Cl, E14 *off Westferry Rd* **134** A3
Water La, E15 **97** E6
EC3 **20** D6
N9 **60** E1
NW1 *off Kentish Town Rd* **92** B7
SE14 **133** F7
Ilford IG3 **99** H3
Kingston upon Thames KT1 **181** G1
Richmond TW9 **145** G5
Sidcup DA14 **177** F2
Twickenham TW1 *off The Embankment* **162** D1
Water Lily Cl, Sthl. UB2 *off Navigator Dr* **123** J2
Waterloo Br, SE1 **18** C6
WC2 **18** C6
Waterloo Cl, E9 *off Churchill Wk* **95** F5
Waterloo Est, E2 **113** F2
Waterloo Gdns, E2 **113** F2
N1 *off Barnsbury St* **93** H7
Waterloo Pas, NW6 **90** C7
Waterloo Pl, SW1 **25** H1
Richmond TW9 *off Sheen Rd* **145** H5
Richmond (Kew) TW9 **126** A6
Waterloo Rd, E6 **97** J7
E7 *off Wellington Rd* **97** F5
E10 **78** A7
NW2 **89** G1
SE1 **27** E3
Ilford IG6 **81** F2
Sutton SM1 **199** G5
Waterloo Ter, N1 **93** H7
Waterlow Ct, NW11 *off Heath Cl* **72/73** E7
Waterlow Rd, N19 **92** C1
★**Watermans Art Cen**, Brent. TW8 **125** H6
Waterman's Cl, Kings.T. KT2 *off Woodside Rd* **163** H7
Waterman St, SW15 **148** A3
Waterman's Wk, EC4 *off Upper Thames St* **112** A7
Watermans Wk, SE16 **133** H3
Waterman Way, E1 **132** E1
Watermead Ho, E9 *off Kingsmead Way* **95** H5
Watermead La, Cars. SM5 *off Middleton Rd* **185** J7
Watermeadow La, SW6 **149** F2
Watermead Rd, SE6 **172** C4
Watermead Way, N17 **76** E3
Watermen's Sq, SE20 **171** F7
Water Ms, SE15 **153** F4
Watermill Cl, Rich. TW10 **163** F3
Watermill La, N18 **60** B5
Watermill Way, SW19 **185** F1
Feltham TW13 **161** F2
Watermint Quay, N16 **76** D7
Water Rd, Wem. HA0 **105** J1
Watersedge, Epsom KT19 **196** C4
Watersfield Way, Edg. HA8 **53** G7
Waters Gdns, Dag. RM10 **101** G5
Waterside, Beck. BR3 **190** A1
Waterside Av, Beck. BR3 *off Creswell Dr* **190** B5
Waterside Cl, E3 **113** J1
SE16 **29** J4
SE28 *off Barnham Dr* **137** J1
Barking IG11 **100** A4
Northolt UB5 **103** F3
Surbiton KT6 *off Culsac Rd* **195** H2
Waterside Ct, SE13 *off Weardale Rd* **154** D4
Waterside Dr, Walt. KT12 **178** A5
Waterside Path, SW18 *off Smugglers Way* **148/149** E4
Waterside Pl, NW1 *off Princess Rd* **110** A1
Waterside Pt, SW11 **31** H7
Waterside Rd, Sthl. UB2 **123** G3
Waterside Twr, SW6 **149** F1
Waterside Trd Cen, W7 **124** B3
Waterside Way, SW17 **167** F4
Watersmeet Way, SE28 **118** C6
Waterson St, E2 **13** E3
Waters Pl, SW15 *off Danemere St* **147** J2
Watersplash Cl, Kings.T. KT1 **181** H3
Watersplash La, Hayes UB3 **122** A4
Hounslow TW5 **122** B5
Waters Rd, SE6 **172** E3
Kingston upon Thames KT1 **182** B2
Waters Sq, Kings.T. KT1 **182** B3
Water St, WC2 **18** D5
Water Twr Hill, Croy. CR0 **202** A4
Water Twr Pl, N1 *off Old Royal Free Sq* **111** G1
Waterview Ho, E14 **113** H5
Waterworks Cor, E18 **79** E2
Waterworks La, E5 **95** G2
Waterworks Rd, SW2 **151** F6
Waterworks Yd, Croy. CR0 *off Surrey St* **201** J3
Watery La, SW20 **184** C2
Northolt UB5 **102** C2
Sidcup DA14 **176** B6
Wates Way, Mitch. CR4 **185** J6
Wates Way Ind Est, Mitch. CR4 *off Wates Way* **185** J6
Wateville Rd, N17 **75** J1
Watford Cl, SW11 *off Petworth St* **149** H1
WATFORD HEATH, Wat. WD19 **50** E1
Watford Rd, E16 **115** G5
Harrow HA1 **86** D2
Wembley HA0 **86** D2
Watford Way, NW4 **71** G4
NW7 **71** G4
Watkin Rd, Wem. HA9 **88** B3
Watkinson Rd, N7 **93** F6
Watling Av, Edg. HA8 **54** D7
Watling Ct, EC4 **20** A4
Watling Fm Cl, Stan. HA7 **53** F1
Watling Gdns, NW2 **90** B6
Watlings Cl, Croy. CR0 **189** H6
Watling St, EC4 **19** J4
SE15 **36** E6
Bexleyheath DA6 **159** H4
Watlington Gro, SE26 **171** H5
Watney Mkt, E1 *off Commercial Rd* **112/113** E6
Watney Rd, SW14 **146** C3
Watneys Rd, Mitch. CR4 **186** D5
Watney St, E1 **113** E6
Watson Av, E6 **98** D7
Sutton SM3 **198** B2
Watson Cl, N16 *off Matthias Rd* **94** A5
SW19 **167** H6
Watson's Ms, W1 **15** H2
Watsons Rd, N22 **75** F1
Watson's St, SE8 **134** A7
Watson St, E13 **115** H2
Watsons Yd, NW2 *off North Circular Rd* **89** F2
Wattisfield Rd, E5 **95** F3
Watts Cl, N15 *off Seaford Rd* **76** B5
Watts Gro, E3 **114** B5
Watts La, Chis. BR7 **193** E1
Teddington TW11 **162** D5
Watts Rd, T.Ditt. KT7 **180** D7
Watts St, E1 **133** E1
SE15 **152** C1
Watts Way, SW7 **23** F5
Wat Tyler Rd, SE3 **154** C2
SE10 **154** C2
Wauthier Cl, N13 **59** H5
Wavell Dr, Sid. DA15 **157** H6
Wavel Ms, N8 **74** D4
NW6 *off Acol Rd* **90/91** E7
Wavel Pl, SE26 *off Sydenham Hill* **170** C4
Wavendon Av, W4 **126** D5
Waveney Av, SE15 **153** E4
Waveney Cl, E1 **29** J1
Waverley Av, E4 **61** J4
E17 **78** D3
Surbiton KT5 **182** B6
Sutton SM1 **199** E2
Twickenham TW2 **161** F1
Wembley HA9 **87** J5
Waverley Cl, E18 **79** J1
Bromley BR2 **192** A5
Hayes UB3 **121** G4
West Molesey KT8 **179** G5
Waverley Cres, SE18 **137** G5
Waverley Gdns, E6 *off Oliver Gdns* **116** B5
NW10 **105** J3
Barking IG11 **117** H2
Ilford IG6 **81** F2
Northwood HA6 **66** A1
Waverley Gro, N3 **72** B3
Waverley Ind Est, Har. HA1 **68** A3
Waverley Pl, N4 *off Adolphus Rd* **93** H2
NW8 **6** E1
Waverley Rd, E17 **78** C3
E18 **79** J1
N8 **74** D6
N17 **60** E7
SE18 **137** F5
SE25 **188** E4
Enfield EN2 **43** H4
Epsom KT17 **197** H5
Harrow HA2 **85** F1
Southall UB1 **103** G7
Waverley Vil, N17 **76** C2
Waverley Wk, W2 **108** D5
Waverley Way, Cars. SM5 **199** H6
Waverton Ho, E3 **113** J1
Waverton Rd, SW18 **149** F7
Waverton St, W1 **24** C1
Wavertree Ct, SW2 *off Streatham Hill* **169** F1
Wavertree Rd, E18 **79** G2
SW2 **169** E1
Waxlow Cres, Sthl. UB1 **103** G6
Waxlow Rd, NW10 **106** C2
Waxwell Cl, Pnr. HA5 **66** D2
Waxwell La, Pnr. HA5 **66** D2
Waye Av, Houns. TW5 **142** A1
Wayfarer Rd, Nthlt. UB5 **102** D4
Wayfield Link, SE9 **157** G6
Wayford St, SW11 **149** H2
Wayland Av, E8 **94** D5
Waylands Mead, Beck. BR3 **190** B1
Wayleave, The, SE28 **118** B7
Waylett Pl, SE27 **169** H3
Wembley HA0 **87** G4
Wayman Ct, E8 **94** E6
Wayne Cl, Orp. BR6 **207** J3
Waynflete Av, Croy. CR0 **201** H3
Waynflete Sq, W10 **108** A7
Waynflete St, SW18 **167** F2
Wayside, NW11 **90** B1
SW14 **146** C5
Croydon CR0 *off Field Way* **204** B6
Wayside Cl, N14 **42** C6
Wayside Commercial Est, Bark. IG11 **118** A1
Wayside Ct, Twick. TW1 **145** F6
Wembley HA9 *off Oakington Av* **88** A3
Wayside Gdns, SE9 *off Wayside Gro* **174** C4
Dagenham RM10 **101** G5
Wayside Gro, SE9 **174** C4
Wayside Ms, Ilf. IG2 *off Gaysham Av* **80** D5
Weald, The, Chis. BR7 **174** C6
Weald Cl, SE16 *off Stevenson Cres* **132/133** E5
Bromley BR2 **206** B2
Weald La, Har. HA3 **68** A2
Weald Ri, Har. HA3 **52** C7
Weald Sq, E5 *off Rossington St* **94/95** E2
WEALDSTONE, Har. HA3 **68** C3
Wealdstone Rd, Sutt. SM3 **198** C2
Weald Way, Rom. RM7 **83** H6
Wealdwood Gdns, Pnr. HA5 *off Highbanks Rd* **51** H6
Weale Rd, E4 **62** D3
Weardale Gdns, Enf. EN2 **44** A1
Weardale Rd, SE13 **154** D4
Wear Pl, E2 **112** E3
Wearside Rd, SE13 **154** B4
Weatherley Cl, E3 **113** J5
Weaver Cl, E6 *off Trader Rd* **116/117** C7
Croydon CR0 **202** C4
Weavers Cl, Islw. TW7 **144** B4
Weavers Ter, SW6 **128** D6
Weaver St, E1 **13** H6
Weavers Way, NW1 **110** D1
Weaver Wk, SE27 **169** H4
Webb Cl, W10 **107** J4
Webber Row, SE1 **27** F5
Webber St, SE1 **27** F3
Webb Est, E5 **76** D7
Webb Gdns, E13 *off Kelland Rd* **115** G4
Webb Pl, NW10 *off Old Oak La* **107** F3
Webb Rd, SE3 **135** F6
Webbscroft Rd, Dag. RM10 **101** H4
Webbs Rd, SW11 **149** J5
Hayes UB4 **102** B3
Webb St, SE1 **28** D6
Webheath Est, NW6 **90** C7
Webster Gdns, W5 **125** G1
Webster Rd, E11 **96** C3
SE16 **29** J6
Wedderburn Rd, NW3 **91** G5
Barking IG11 **117** G1
Wedgewood Wk, NW6 *off Lymington Rd* **90/91** E5
Wedgwood Ms, W1 **17** J4
Wedgwood Wk, NW6 *off Dresden Cl* **90** E5
Wedgwood Way, SE19 **169** J7
Wedlake St, W10 *off Kensal Rd* **108** B4
Wedmore Av, Ilf. IG5 **80** D1
Wedmore Gdns, N19 **92** D2
Wedmore Ms, N19 *off Wedmore St* **92** D3
Wedmore Rd, Grnf. UB6 **104** A3
Wedmore St, N19 **92** D3

Weech Rd, NW6 . . . . **90** D4
Weedington Rd, NW5 . . . . **92** A5
Weekley Sq, SW11
off Thomas Baines Rd. **149** G3
Weigall Rd, SE12 . . . . **155** G4
Weighhouse St, W1 . . . . . . **16** C4
Weighton Rd, SE20 . . . . . **188** E2
Harrow HA3 . . . . **68** A1
Weihurst Gdns, Sutt. SM1 . . . . **199** G5
Weimar St, SW15. . . . . . . **148** B3
Weirdale Av, N20 . . . . **57** J2
Weir Est, SW12 . . . . **150** C7
Weir Hall Av, N18 . . . . **60** A6
Weir Hall Gdns, N18 . . . . . **60** A5
Weir Hall Rd, N17. . . . . **60** A5
N18 . . . . **60** A5
Weir Rd, SW12. . . . . **150** C7
SW19. . . . . **167** E3
Bexley DA5 . . . . **159** H7
Walton-on-Thames KT12 . . . . **178** A6
Weirside Gdns, West Dr. UB7 . . . . **120** A1
Weir's Pas, NW1. . . . . **9** J3
Weiss Rd, SW15. . . . . **148** A3
Welbeck Av, Brom. BR1 . . **173** G4
Hayes UB4. . . . . **102** B4
Sidcup DA15 . . . . **176** A1
Welbeck Cl, N12
off Torrington Pk **57** G5
Borehamwood WD6 . . . . **38** A3
Epsom KT17 . . . . **197** G7
New Malden KT3 . . . . . **183** F5
Welbeck Rd, E6. . . . . **116** A3
Barnet EN4 . . . . **41** G6
Carshalton SM5 . . . . . . **199** H1
Harrow HA2 . . . . **85** H1
Sutton SM1. . . . . **199** G2
Welbeck St, W1 . . . . **16** D3
Welbeck Wk, Cars. SM5
off Welbeck Rd **199** H1
Welbeck Way, W1. . . . . **16** D3
Welby St, SE5 . . . . **151** H1
Welch Pl, Pnr. HA5. . . . . . . **66** C1
Weldon Cl, Ruis. HA4. . . . . **84** B6
Weldon Dr, W.Mol. KT8 . . **179** F4
Weld Pl, N11. . . . . **58** B5
Welfare Rd, E15 . . . . **97** E7
Welford Cl, E5
off Denton Way. **95** G3
Welford Pl, SW19. . . . . . . **166** B4
Welham Rd, SW16. . . . . . **168** A5
SW17. . . . . **168** A5
Welhouse Rd, Cars. SM5. **199** H1
Wellacre Rd, Har. HA3 . . . . **69** E6
Wellan Cl, Sid. DA15 . . . . **158** B5
Welland Gdns, Grnf. UB6. **104** C2
Welland Ms, E1 . . . . **29** J1
Wellands Cl, Brom. BR1. . **192** C2
Welland St, SE10 . . . . **134** C6
Well App, Barn. EN5 . . . . . **39** J5
Wellbrook Rd, Orp. BR6. . **206** D4
Well Cl, SW16. . . . . **169** F4
Ruislip HA4
off Parkfield Cres . . . **84/85** E3
Wellclose Sq, E1 . . . . **21** J5
Wellclose St, E1. . . . . **21** J6
★**Wellcome Trust**, NW1 . . . . **9** G5
Well Cottage Cl, E11. . . . . . . **70** J7
Well Ct, EC4. . . . . **20** A4
SW16. . . . . **169** F4
Welldon Cres, Har. HA1 . . . **68** B6
Weller St, SE1 . . . . **27** J3
Wellesley Av, W6 . . . . **127** H3
Wellesley Cl, SE7
off Wellington Gdns . . **135** J5
Wellesley Ct, W9 . . . . **6** C3
Wellesley Ct Rd, Croy. CR0 . . . . **202** A2
Wellesley Cres, Twick. TW2 . . . . **162** B2
Wellesley Gro, Croy. CR0. **202** A2
Wellesley Pk Ms, Enf. EN2. **43** H2
Wellesley Pas, Croy. CR0
off Wellesley Rd. **201** J2
Wellesley Pl, NW1 . . . . **9** H4
Wellesley Rd, E11 . . . . **79** G5
E17 . . . . **78** A6
N22 . . . . **75** G2
NW5 . . . . **92** A5
W4. . . . . **126** A5
Croydon CR0 . . . . **201** J1
Harrow HA1 . . . . **68** B5
Ilford IG1. . . . . **98** E2
Sutton SM2. . . . . **199** F6
Twickenham TW2 . . . . . **162** A3
Wellesley St, E1 . . . . **113** G5
Wellesley Ter, N1 . . . . **12** A3
Wellfield Av, N10 . . . . **74** B3
Wellfield Rd, SW16 . . . . . **169** E4
Wellfields, Loug. IG10 . . . . **48** D3
Wellfield Wk, SW16 . . . . . **169** F5
Wellfit St, SE24
off Hinton Rd. **151** H3
Wellgarth, Grnf. UB6 . . . . . **86** E6
Wellgarth Rd, NW11. . . . . . **91** E1
Well Gro, N20. . . . . **41** F7
Well Hall Par, SE9
off Well Hall Rd **156** C4
Well Hall Rd, SE9. . . . . . . **156** C3
Wellhouse La, Barn. EN5 . . **39** J4
Wellhouse Rd, Beck. BR3. **189** J4
WELLING, DA16. . . . . **158** A3
Welling High St, Well. DA16 . . . . **158** B3
Wellings Ho, Hayes UB3 . **122** B1
★**Wellington Arch**, W1 . . . . **24** C3
Wellington Av, E4. . . . . **62** A2
N9 . . . . **61** E3
N15 . . . . **76** C6
Hounslow TW3 . . . . **143** G5
Pinner HA5 . . . . **67** F1
Sidcup DA15 . . . . **158** A6
Worcester Park KT4. . . . **197** J4
Wellington Bldgs, SW1 . . . **32** C4
Wellington Cl, SE14
off Rutts Ter. **153** G1
W11 *off Ledbury Rd*. . . . **108** D6
Dagenham RM10. . . . . . **101** J7
Watford WD19
off Highfield **51** F3
Wellington Ct, NW8. . . . . . . **7** E2
Staines TW19
off Clare Rd. **140** B7
Wellington Cres, N.Mal. KT3 . . . . **182** C3
Wellington Dr, Dag. RM10. **101** J7
Wellington Gdns, SE7 . . . **135** J6
Twickenham TW2 . . . . . **162** A4
Wellington Gro, SE10
off Crooms Hill **134** D7
Wellington Ms, SE7 . . . . . **135** J6
SE22 *off Peckham Rye* . **152** D4
SW16
off Woodbourne Av. . . **168** D3
Wellington Pk Est, NW2 . . **89** G2
Wellington Pas, E11
off Wellington Rd **79** G5
Wellington Pl, N2
off Great N Rd. **73** H5
NW8 . . . . **7** F3
Wellington Rd, E6. . . . . . . **116** C2
E7 . . . . **97** F4
E10 . . . . **95** H1
E11. . . . . **79** G5
E17 . . . . **77** H3
NW8 . . . . **7** E1
NW10. . . . . **108** A3
SW19. . . . . **166** D2
W5. . . . . **125** F3
Belvedere DA17 . . . . . . **139** F5
Bexley DA5 . . . . **158** D5
Bromley BR2 . . . . **191** J4
Croydon CR0. . . . . **187** H7
Enfield EN1 . . . . **44** B4
Feltham TW14 . . . . **141** H5
Hampton TW12 . . . . **162** A5
Harrow HA3 . . . . **68** D6
Pinner HA5 . . . . **67** F1
Twickenham TW2 . . . . . **162** A5
Wellington Rd N, Houns. TW4 . . . . **143** F3
Wellington Rd S, Houns. TW4 . . . . **143** F4
Wellington Row, E2 . . . . . . **13** G3
Wellington Sq, SW3. . . . . . **31** J3
Wellington St, SE18. . . . . **136** D4
WC2. . . . . **18** B5
Barking IG11
off Axe St. **117** F1
Wellington Ter, E1 . . . . . . **132** E1
W2 *off*
Notting Hill Gate . **108/109** E7
Harrow HA1
off West St. **86** A1
Wellington Way, E3 . . . . . **114** A3
Welling Way, SE9. . . . . . . **157** G3
Welling DA16 . . . . **157** G3
Well La, SW14 . . . . **146** C5
Wellmeadow Rd, SE6 . . . **155** E7
SE13 . . . . **154** E6
W7. . . . . **124** D4
Wellow Wk, Cars. SM5. . . **199** G1
Well Pas, NW3 . . . . **91** G3
Well Rd, NW3. . . . . **91** G3
Barnet EN5 . . . . **39** J5
Wells, The, N14. . . . . **42** D7
Wells Cl, Nthlt. UB5
off Yeading La **102** C3
South Croydon CR2 . . . **202** B5
Wells Dr, NW9 . . . . **88** D1
Wells Gdns, Dag. RM10 . . **101** H5
Ilford IG1. . . . . **80** B7
Wells Ho Rd, NW10 . . . . . **106** E5
Wellside Cl, Barn. EN5. . . . **39** J4
Wellside Gdns, SW14
off Well La. **146** C5
Wells Ms, W1 . . . . **17** G2
Wellsmoor Gdns, Brom. BR1 . . . . **192** D3
Wells Pk Rd, SE26 . . . . . . **170** D3
Wells Pl, SW18. . . . . **149** F7
Wells Ri, NW8 . . . . **109** J1
Wells Rd, W12 . . . . **127** J2
Bromley BR1. . . . . **192** C2
Wells Sq, WC1 . . . . **10** C4
Wells St, W1. . . . . **17** F2
Wellstead Av, N9 . . . . **45** F7
Wellstead Rd, E6 . . . . **116** D2
Wells Ter, N4. . . . . **93** G2
Well St, E9 . . . . **95** E7
E15 . . . . **96** E6
Wells Way, SE5. . . . . **36** C5
SW7. . . . . **22** E5
Wells Yd S, N7
off George's Rd. **93** G5
Well Wk, NW3 . . . . **91** G4
Wellwood Rd, Ilf. IG3 . . . . **100** A1
Welmar Ms, SW4
off Clapham Pk Rd . . . **150** D4
Welsford St, SE1 . . . . **37** H3
Welsh Cl, E13 . . . . **115** G3
Welshpool Ho, E8
off Benjamin Cl **112** D1
Welshpool St, E8
off Broadway Mkt. **112/113** E1
Welshside Wk, NW9
off Fryent Gro **70/71** E6
Welstead Way, W4 . . . . . . **127** F4
Weltje Rd, W6. . . . . **127** G5
Welton Rd, SE18 . . . . **137** H7
Welwyn Av, Felt. TW14. . . **141** J6
Welwyn St, E2
off Globe Rd **113** F3
WEMBLEY, HA0 & HA9. . . **87** H5
Wembley Commercial Cen, Wem. HA9 . . . . **87** G2
★**Wembley Conf Cen**, Wem. HA9. . . . . **87** J4
Wembley Hill Rd, Wem. HA9. . . . . **87** J5
WEMBLEY PARK, Wem. HA9. . . . . **87** J2
Wembley Pk Business Cen, Wem. HA9 . . . . **88** B3
Wembley Pk Dr, Wem. HA9. . . . . **87** J3
Wembley Pt, Wem. HA9. . . **88** B7
Wembley Rd, Hmptn. TW12 . . . . **161** G7
★**Wembley Stadium (under redevelopment)**, Wem. HA9. . . . . **88** A4
Wembley Way, Wem. HA9 . **88** B6
Wemborough Rd, Stan. HA7. . . . . **53** F7
Wembury Ms, N6
off Wembury Rd **74** B7
Wembury Rd, N6 . . . . **74** B7
Wemyss Rd, SE3 . . . . **155** F2
Wendela Ct, Har. HA1 . . . . **86** B3
Wendell Rd, W12 . . . . **127** F2
Wendle Ct, SW8. . . . . **34** A6
Wendling Rd, Sutt. SM1. . **199** G1
Wendon St, E3 . . . . **113** J1
Wendover, SE17. . . . . **36** D4
Wendover Cl, Hayes UB4. **102** E4
Wendover Dr, N.Mal. KT3 . **183** F6
Wendover Rd, NW10 . . . . **107** F2
SE9 . . . . **156** A3
Bromley BR2. . . . . **191** H3
Wendover Way, Well. DA16 . . . . **158** A5
Wendy Cl, Enf. EN1 . . . . . . **44** C6
Wendy Way, Wem. HA0 . . **105** H1
Wenlock Ct, N1 . . . . **12** C2
Wenlock Gdns, NW4
off Rickard Cl. **71** G4
Wenlock Rd, N1 . . . . **11** J1
Edgware HA8 . . . . **54** B7
Wenlock St, N1 . . . . **12** A2
Wennington Rd, E3 . . . . . **113** G2
Wensley Av, Wdf.Grn. IG8 . **63** F7
Wensley Cl, N11
off Pickering Gdns **58** A6
SE9 . . . . **156** C6
Wensleydale Av, Ilf. IG5 . . . **80** B2
Wensleydale Gdns, Hmptn. TW12 . . . . **161** H7
Wensleydale Pas, Hmptn. TW12. . . . . **179** G1
Wensleydale Rd, Hmptn. TW12 . . . . **161** G6
Wensley Rd, N18 . . . . **60** E6
Wentland Cl, SE6. . . . . . . **172** D2
Wentland Rd, SE6 . . . . . . **172** D2
Wentworth Av, N3 . . . . **56** D7
Wentworth Cl, N3 . . . . **56** E7
SE28 . . . . **118** D6
Bromley BR2
off Hillside La **205** G2
Morden SM4. . . . . **184** D7
Orpington BR6 . . . . **207** H5
Surbiton KT6. . . . . **195** G2
Wentworth Ct, Surb. KT6
off Culsac Rd. **195** H2
Wentworth Cres, SE15. . . **132** D7
Hayes UB3 . . . . **121** G3
Wentworth Dr, Pnr. HA5 . . **66** A5
Wentworth Gdns, N13. . . . **59** H4
Wentworth Hill, Wem. HA9. . . . . **87** J1
Wentworth Ms, E3
off Eric St. **113** J4
Wentworth Pk, N3 . . . . **56** D7
Wentworth Pl, Stan. HA7
off Greenacres Dr . . **52/53** E6
Wentworth Rd, E12 . . . . . . **98** A4
NW11. . . . . **72** C6
Barnet EN5 . . . . **40** A3
Croydon CR0. . . . . **187** G7
Southall UB2. . . . . **122** C4
Wentworth St, E1 . . . . **21** F3
Wentworth Way, Pnr. HA5. **66** D4
Wenvoe Av, Bexh. DA7 . . **159** H2
Wepham Cl, Hayes UB4. . **102** D5
Wernbrook St, SE18. . . . . **137** F6
Werndee Rd, SE25 . . . . . . **188** D4
Werneth Hall Rd, Ilf. IG5 . . **80** C3
Werrington St, NW1 . . . . . . **9** G2
Werter Rd, SW15 . . . . **148** B4
Wesleyan Pl, NW5
off Gordon Ho Rd. **92** B4
Wesley Av, E16. . . . . **135** G1
NW10. . . . . **106** D3
Hounslow TW3 . . . . **143** E2
Wesley Cl, N7. . . . . **93** F2
SE17 . . . . **35** H2
Harrow HA2 . . . . **85** J2
Wesley Rd, E10. . . . . **78** C7
NW10. . . . . **106** C1
Hayes UB3. . . . . **102** A7
★**Wesley's Ho**, EC1 . . . . . . **12** C5
Wesley Sq, W11
off Bartle Rd **108** B6
Wesley St, W1 . . . . **16** C2
Wessex Av, SW19. . . . . . . **184** D2
Wessex Cl, Ilf. IG3 . . . . **81** H6
Kingston upon Thames KT1
off Gloucester Rd **182** B1
Thames Ditton KT7 . . . . **194** C2
Wessex Ct, Wem. HA9
off The Avenue **87** J2
Wessex Dr, Pnr. HA5 . . . . . **51** E7
Wessex Gdns, NW11 . . . . . **90** B1
Wessex La, Grnf. UB6 . . . **104** A2
Wessex St, E2. . . . . **113** F3
Wessex Way, NW11 . . . . . . **72** B7
West 12 Shop Cen, W12
off Shepherds Bush Grn. **128** A2
Westacott Cl, N19 . . . . **92** D1
WEST ACTON, W3 . . . . . . **106** A6
Westall Rd, Loug. IG10 . . . **49** E3
West App, Orp. BR5 . . . . . **193** F5
West Arbour St, E1. . . . . . **113** G6
West Av, E17 . . . . **78** B4
N3 . . . . **56** D6
NW4 . . . . **72** A5
Pinner HA5 . . . . **67** F6
Southall UB1 . . . . **103** F7
Wallington SM6 . . . . . . **201** E5
West Av Rd, E17. . . . . **78** A4
West Bk, N16 . . . . **76** B7
Barking IG11
off Highbridge Rd. **116/117** E1
Enfield EN2. . . . . **43** J2
Westbank Rd, Hmptn. (Hmptn H.) TW12. . . . . **161** J6
WEST BARNES, N.Mal. KT3 . . . . **183** G5
West Barnes La, SW20. . . **183** H3
New Malden KT3 . . . . . **183** H3
Westbeech Rd, N22 . . . . . . **75** G3
Westbere Dr, Stan. HA7. . . **53** G4

Westbere Rd, NW2 . . . . . . 90 B4
Westbourne Av, W3 . . . . . 106 D6
Sutton SM3 . . . . 198 B2
Westbourne Br, W2 . . . . . . 14 C2
Westbourne Cl, Hayes UB4 . . . . 102 B4
Westbourne Cres, W2 . . . . 14 E5
Westbourne Cres Ms, W2 . 14 E5
Westbourne Dr, SE23 . . . . 171 G2
Westbourne Gdns, W2 . . . . 14 A3
WESTBOURNE GREEN, W2 . . . . 108 D5
Westbourne Gro, W2 . . . . 108 D6
W11 . . . . 108 C7
Westbourne Gro Ms, W11 *off Westbourne Gro* . . . 108 D6
Westbourne Gro Ter, W2 . . 14 A3
Westbourne Pk Ms, W2 . . . 14 A3
Westbourne Pk Pas, W2 *off Westbourne Pk Vil* . 108 D5
Westbourne Pk Rd, W2 . . 108 D5
W11 . . . . 108 B6
Westbourne Pk Vil, W2 . . . 108 D5
Westbourne Pl, N9 *off Eastbournia Av* . . 60/61 E3
Westbourne Rd, N7 . . . . . . 93 G6
SE26 . . . . 171 G6
Bexleyheath DA7 . . . . . 138 E7
Croydon CR0 . . . . 188 C6
Westbourne St, W2 . . . . . . 15 E5
Westbourne Ter, SE23 *off Westbourne Dr* 171 G2
W2 . . . . 14 D3
Westbourne Ter Ms, W2 . . . 14 C3
Westbourne Ter Rd, W2 . . . 14 C2
Westbridge Rd, SW11 . . . 149 G1
WEST BROMPTON, SW10 . . . . 30 A5
Westbrook Av, Hmptn. TW12 . . . . 161 F7
Westbrook Cl, Barn. EN4 . . 41 G3
Westbrook Cres, Barn. EN4 . . . . 41 G3
Westbrooke Cres, Well. DA16 . . . . 158 C3
Westbrooke Rd, Sid. DA15 . . . . 175 G2
Welling DA16 . . . . 158 B3
Westbrook Rd, SE3 . . . . . 155 H1
Hounslow TW5 . . . . 123 F7
Thornton Heath CR7 . . . 188 A1
Westbrook Sq, Barn. EN4 *off Westbrook Cres* 41 G3
Westbury Av, N22 . . . . 75 H3
Esher (Clay.) KT10 . . . . . 194 C6
Southall UB1 . . . . 103 G4
Wembley HA0 . . . . 87 H7
Westbury Cl, Ruis. HA4 . . . 66 A7
Westbury Gro, N12 . . . . . . 56 D6
Westbury La, Buck.H. IG9 . 63 J2
Westbury Lo Cl, Pnr. HA5 . 66 D3
Westbury Par, SW12 *off Balham Hill* 150 B6
Westbury Pl, Brent. TW8 . 125 G6
Westbury Rd, E7 . . . . 97 H5
E17 . . . . 78 A4
N11 . . . . 58 E6
N12 . . . . 56 D6
SE20 . . . . 189 G1
W5 . . . . 105 H6
Barking IG11 . . . . 117 G1
Beckenham BR3 . . . . . . 189 H3
Bromley BR1 . . . . 192 A1
Buckhurst Hill IG9 . . . . . . 63 J2
Croydon CR0 . . . . 188 A6
Feltham TW13 . . . . 160 D1
Ilford IG1 . . . . 98 C2
New Malden KT3 . . . . . 182 D4
Wembley HA0 . . . . 87 H7
Westbury St, SW8 . . . . . . 150 C2
Westbury Ter, E7 . . . . 97 H6
West Carriage Dr, W2 . . . . . 23 F2
West Cen St, WC1 . . . . 18 A3
West Cen Av, W10 *off Harrow Rd* 107 H3
West Chantry, Har. HA3 *off Chantry Rd* 67 H1
Westchester Dr, NW4 . . . . 72 A3
Westcliffe Apartments, W2 *off Praed St* 109 G5
West Cl, N9 . . . . 60 C3
Barnet EN5 . . . . 39 H5
Barnet (Cockfos.) EN4 . . . 42 A4
Greenford UB6 . . . . 103 J2
Hampton TW12 *off Oak Av* 160/161 E6
Wembley HA9 . . . . 87 J1
Westcombe Av, Croy. CR0 . . . . 187 E6
Westcombe Ct, SE3 *off Westcombe Pk Rd* . 135 F7
Westcombe Dr, Barn. EN5 . 40 D5
Westcombe Hill, SE3 . . . . 135 G5
SE10 . . . . 135 G5
Westcombe Pk Rd, SE3 . . 135 E6
West Common Rd, Brom. BR2 . . . . 205 G2
Keston BR2 . . . . 205 H4
Westcoombe Av, SW20 . . 183 F1
Westcote Rd, SW16 . . . . . 168 C5
West Cotts, NW6 . . . . 90 D5
Westcott Cl, N15 *off Ermine Rd* 76 C6
Bromley BR1 *off Ringmer Way* 192 B5
Westcott Cres, W7 . . . . . . 104 B6
Westcott Rd, SE17 . . . . 35 G5
West Ct, SE18 *off Prince Imperial Rd* . 156 C1
Westcourt, Sun. TW16 . . . 178 B2
West Ct, Wem. HA0 . . . . . . 87 F2
Westcroft Cl, NW2 . . . . 90 B4
Westcroft Gdns, Mord. SM4 . . . . 184 C3
Westcroft Rd, Cars. SM5 . 200 A4
Wallington SM6 . . . . . . 200 A4
Westcroft Sq, W6 . . . . 127 G4
Westcroft Way, NW2 . . . . . 90 B4
West Cromwell Rd, SW5 . 128 C4
W14 . . . . 128 C4
West Cross Cen, Brent. TW8 . . . . 124 D6
West Cross Route, W10 . . 108 A7
W11 . . . . 108 A7
West Cross Way, Brent. TW8 . . . . 124 E6
Westdale Pas, SE18 . . . . . 136 E6
Westdale Rd, SE18 . . . . . . 137 E6
Westdean Av, SE12 . . . . . 173 H1
Westdean Cl, SW18 . . . . . 149 E6
West Dene, Sutt. SM3 *off Park La* 198 B6
Westdown Rd, E15 . . . . . . 96 C4
SE6 . . . . 154 A7
WEST DRAYTON, UB7 . . . 120 A3
West Drayton Pk Av, West Dr. UB7 . . . . 120 B3
West Dr, SW16 . . . . 168 C4
Harrow HA3 . . . . 52 A6
West Dr Gdns, Har. HA3 . . 52 A6
WEST DULWICH, SE21 . . . 170 A3
West Eaton Pl, SW1 . . . . . . 32 B1
West Eaton Pl Ms, SW1 . . . 32 B1
West Ella Rd, NW10 . . . . . . 88 E7
West End Av, E10 . . . . 78 C5
Pinner HA5 . . . . 66 D4
West End Cl, NW10 . . . . . . 88 C7
West End Ct, Pnr. HA5 . . . . 66 D4
West End Gdns, Nthlt. UB5 *off Edward Cl* 102 C2
West End La, NW6 . . . . 90 D7
Barnet EN5 . . . . 40 A4
Hayes UB3 . . . . 121 F7
Pinner HA5 . . . . 66 D3
West End Rd, Nthlt. UB5 . . 84 C7
Ruislip HA4 . . . . 84 B5
Southall UB1 . . . . 122 E1
Westerdale Rd, SE10 . . . . 135 G5
Westerfield Rd, N15 . . . . . . 76 C5
Westergate Rd, SE2 . . . . . 138 E5
Westerham Av, N9 . . . . 60 A3
Westerham Dr, Sid. DA15 . 158 B6
Westerham Rd, E10 . . . . . . 78 B7
Keston BR2 . . . . 206 A6
Westerley Cres, SE26 . . . . 171 J5
Westerley Ware, Rich. TW9 *off Kew Grn* 126 A6
Western Av, NW11 . . . . 72 A6
W3 . . . . 106 D5
W5 . . . . 105 J3
Dagenham RM10 . . . . . . 101 J6
Greenford UB6 . . . . 104 C3
Northolt UB5 . . . . 103 F1
Western Av Business Pk, W3 *off Mansfield Rd* 106 B4
Western Av Underpass, W5 *off Western Av* 105 J3
Western Beach Apartments, E16 *off Hanover Av* . . . 135 G1
Western Ct, N3 *off Huntley Dr* 56 D6
Western Gdns, W5 . . . . . . 106 A7
Western Gateway, E16 . . . 115 G7
Western La, SW12 . . . . . . 150 A7
Western Ms, W9 *off Great Western Rd* . . 108 C4
Western Par, Barn. EN5 *off Great N Rd* 40 D5
Western Pl, SE16 *off Canon Beck Rd* . . . 133 F2
Western Rd, E13 . . . . 115 J1
E17 . . . . 78 C5
N2 . . . . 73 J4
N22 . . . . 75 F2
NW10 . . . . 106 C4
SW9 . . . . 151 G3
SW19 . . . . 185 G1
W5 . . . . 105 G7
Mitcham CR4 . . . . 185 G1
Southall UB2 . . . . 122 D3
Sutton SM1 . . . . 198 D5
Western Ter, W6 *off Chiswick Mall* 127 G5
Western Trd Est, NW10 . . . 106 C4
Western Vw, Hayes UB3 . 121 J2
Westernville Gdns, Ilf. IG2 . 81 F7
Western Way, SE28 . . . . . 137 G3
Barnet EN5 . . . . 40 D6
WEST EWELL, Epsom KT19 . . . . 196 E7
Westferry Circ, E14 . . . . . . 133 J1
Westferry Rd, E14 . . . . 134 A1
Westfield, Loug. IG10 . . . . . 47 J5
Westfield Cl, NW9 . . . . 70 C3
SW10 . . . . 129 F7
Enfield EN3 . . . . 45 H3
Sutton SM1 . . . . 198 C4
Westfield Dr, Har. HA3 . . . . 69 G5
Westfield Gdns, Har. HA3 . 69 G4
Westfield La, Har. HA3 . . . . 69 G4
Westfield Pk, Pnr. HA5 . . . . 51 F7
Westfield Pk Dr, Wdf.Grn. IG8 . . . . 64 B6
Westfield Rd, NW7 . . . . 54 D3
W13 . . . . 124 D1
Beckenham BR3 . . . . . . 189 J2
Bexleyheath DA7 . . . . . 159 J2
Croydon CR0 . . . . 201 H2
Dagenham RM9 . . . . . . 101 E4
Mitcham CR4 . . . . 185 J2
Surbiton KT6 . . . . 181 G5
Sutton SM1 . . . . 198 C4
Walton-on-Thames KT12 . . . . 179 E7
Westfields, SW13 . . . . 147 F3
Westfields Av, SW13 . . . . 147 E3
Westfields Rd, W3 . . . . . . 106 B5
Westfield St, SE18 . . . . . . 136 A3
Westfield Way, E1 . . . . 113 H3
West Gdn Pl, W2 . . . . 15 H4
West Gdns, E1 . . . . 113 E7
SW17 . . . . 167 H6
West Gate, W5 . . . . 105 H3
Westgate Ho, Brent. TW8 . 125 G5
Westgate Rd, SE25 . . . . . 188 E4
Beckenham BR3 . . . . . . 190 B2
Westgate St, E8 . . . . 112 E1
Westgate Ter, SW10 . . . . . . 30 B4
Westglade Ct, Har. HA3 . . . 69 G5
WEST GREEN, N15 . . . . . . 75 J3
West Grn Pl, Grnf. UB6 *off Uneeda Dr* 101 A1
West Grn Rd, N15 . . . . 75 H4
West Gro, SE10 . . . . 154 C1
Woodford Green IG8 . . . 63 J6
Westgrove La, SE10 . . . . . 154 C1
West Halkin St, SW1 . . . . . 24 B5
West Hallowes, SE9 . . . . . 174 A1
West Hall Rd, Rich. TW9 . . 146 B1
WEST HAM, E15 . . . . 97 F7
West Ham La, E15 . . . . 96 E7
West Ham Pk, E7 . . . . 97 G7
WEST HAMPSTEAD, NW6 . 90 E5
West Hampstead Ms, NW6 . . . . 90 E6
★**West Ham United FC**, E13 . . . . 115 J2
West Harding St, EC4 . . . . 19 F3
WEST HARROW, Har. HA1 . 67 J7
Westhay Gdns, SW14 . . . 146 B5
WEST HEATH, SE2 . . . . . . 138 D6
West Heath Av, NW11 . . . . 90 D1
West Heath Cl, NW3 . . . . . 90 D3
West Heath Dr, NW11 . . . . 90 D1
West Heath Gdns, NW3 . . . 90 D3
West Heath Rd, NW3 . . . . . 90 D2
SE2 . . . . 138 D6
WEST HENDON, NW9 . . . . 71 E7
West Hendon Bdy, NW9 . . . 71 F6
West Hill, SW15 . . . . 148 A7
SW18 . . . . 148 D5
Harrow HA2 . . . . 86 B2
Wembley HA9 . . . . 87 J1
West Hill Ct, N6 . . . . 92 A3
West Hill Pk, N6 *off Merton La* 91 J2
West Hill Rd, SW18 . . . . . 148 D6
West Hill Way, N20 . . . . 56 E1
Westholm, NW11 . . . . 72 E4
West Holme, Erith DA8 . . 159 J1
Westholme, Orp. BR6 . . . 193 H7
Westholme Gdns, Ruis. HA4 . . . . 84 A1
Westhorne Av, SE9 . . . . . 155 J6
SE12 . . . . 155 G7
Westhorpe Gdns, NW4 . . . 71 J3
Westhorpe Rd, SW15 . . . . 147 J3
West Ho Cl, SW19 . . . . . . 166 B1
Westhurst Dr, Chis. BR7 . 175 E5
West India Av, E14 . . . . . . 134 A1
West India Dock Rd, E14 . 113 J6
WEST KILBURN, W9 . . . . . 108 C3
Westlake Cl, N13 . . . . 59 G3
Hayes UB4 *off Lochan Cl* 102/103 E4
Westlake Rd, Wem. HA9 . . 87 G2
Westland Cl, Stai. (Stanw.) TW19 . . . . 140 B6
Westland Dr, Brom. BR2 . 205 F2
Westland Ho, E16 *off Rymill St* 136 D1
Westland Pl, N1 . . . . 12 B3
Westlands Cl, Hayes UB3 *off Granville Rd* 122 A4
Westlands Ter, SW12 *off Gaskarth Rd* 150 C6
West La, SE16 . . . . 132 E2
Westlea Rd, W7 . . . . 124 D3
Westleigh Av, SW15 . . . . . 147 H5
Westleigh Dr, Brom. BR1 . 192 B1
Westleigh Gdns, Edg. HA8 . . . . 70 A1
Westlinks, Wem. HA0 *off Alperton La* 105 G3
Westlinton Cl, NW7 . . . . . . 56 B6
West Lo Av, W3 . . . . 126 A1
West Mall, W8 *off Palace Gdns Ter* . . . 128 D1
Westmark Pt, SW15 *off Norley Vale* 165 H1
Westmead, SW15 . . . . 147 H6
West Mead, Epsom KT19 . 197 E6
Ruislip HA4 . . . . 84 C4
Westmead Cor, Cars. SM5 *off Colston Av* 199 H4
Westmead Rd, Sutt. SM1 . 199 G4
Westmede, Chig. IG7 . . . . . 65 F6
Westmere Dr, NW7 . . . . . . 54 D3
West Mersea Cl, E16 *off Hanameel St* 135 H1
West Ms, N17 . . . . 60 E6
SW1 . . . . 33 E2
Westmill Ct, N4 *off Brownswood Rd* . . . 93 J2
WESTMINSTER, SW1 . . . . 25 F5
★**Westminster Abbey**, SW1 . . . . 26 A5
★**Westminster Abbey Mus**, SW1 . . . . 26 A5
Westminster Av, Th.Hth. CR7 . . . . 187 H2
Westminster Br, SE1 . . . . . 26 B4
SW1 . . . . 26 B4
Westminster Br Rd, SE1 . . 26 D4
★**Westminster Cath**, SW1 . 25 F6
★**Westminster City Hall**, SW1 . . . . 25 G5
Westminster Cl, Felt. TW14 . . . . 160 A1
Ilford IG6 . . . . 81 G2
Teddington TW11 . . . . . . 162 D5
Westminster Dr, N13 . . . . . 58 E5
Westminster Gdns, E4 . . . . 63 E1
SW1 . . . . 34 A1
Barking IG11 . . . . 117 H2
Ilford IG6 . . . . 81 F2
★**Westminster Millennium Pier**, SW1 . . . . 26 B3
Westminster Rd, N9 . . . . . . 61 E1
W7 . . . . 124 B1
Sutton SM1 . . . . 199 G2
Westmoat Cl, Beck. BR3 . 172 C7
WEST MOLESEY, KT8 . . . 179 F5
Westmont Rd, Esher KT10 . . . . 194 B2
Westmoor Gdns, Enf. EN3 . 45 G2
Westmoor Rd, Enf. EN3 . . . 45 G2
Westmoor St, SE7 . . . . . . 135 J3
Westmoreland Av, Well. DA16 . . . . 157 H3
Westmoreland Bldgs, EC1 *off Bartholomew Cl* . . . 111 J5
Westmoreland Pl, SW1 . . . 33 E4
W5 . . . . 105 G5
Bromley BR1 . . . . 191 G3
Westmoreland Rd, NW9 . . 70 A4

Westmoreland Rd, SE17 . . 36 A5
SW13. . . . . 147 F1
Bromley BR1, BR2. . . . . 191 E5
Westmoreland St, W1 . . . . 16 C2
Westmoreland Ter, SW1. . . 32 E4
Westmoreland Wk, SE17 . . 36 C5
Westmorland Cl, E12 . . . . . 98 A2
Twickenham TW1 . . . . . 144 E6
Westmorland Rd, E17 . . . . 78 A6
Harrow HA1 . . . . 67 H5
Westmorland Sq, Mitch. CR4 *off Westmorland Way* 186/187 E5
Westmorland Ter, SE20 . . 171 E7
Westmorland Way, Mitch. CR4. . . . . 186 D4
Westmount Rd, SE9. . . . . 156 C2
WEST NORWOOD, SE27 . . . . 169 J3
West Oak, Beck. BR3 . . . . 190 D1
Westoe Rd, N9. . . . . 61 E2
Weston Av, T.Ditt. KT7 . . . 180 B7
West Molesey KT8 . . . . 179 E3
Weston Ct, N4 *off Queens Dr* 93 J3
N20 *off Farnham Cl*. 41 F7
Weston Dr, Stan. HA7 . . . . 68 E1
West One Shop Cen, W1 . . 16 C4
Weston Gdns, Islw. TW7 . 144 A1
WESTON GREEN, T.Ditt. KT7 . . . . 194 C1
Weston Grn, Dag. RM9 . . 101 F4
Thames Ditton KT7. . . . 194 B1
Weston Grn Rd, Esher KT10 . . . . 194 A1
Thames Ditton KT7. . . . 194 B1
Weston Gro, Brom. BR1. . 191 F1
Weston Pk, N8. . . . . 75 E6
Kingston upon Thames KT1 *off Fairfield W* . . . 181 H2
Thames Ditton KT7. . . . 194 B1
Weston Pk Cl, T.Ditt. KT7 *off Weston Pk* 194 B1
Weston Ri, WC1 . . . . 10 D2
Weston Rd, W4. . . . . 126 C3
Bromley BR1. . . . . 173 F7
Dagenham RM9 . . . . . . 101 E4
Enfield EN2. . . . . 44 A1
Thames Ditton KT7. . . . 194 B1
Weston St, SE1 . . . . 28 C5
Weston Wk, E8 *off Mare St*. 94/95 E7
Westover Hill, NW3 . . . . . . 90 D2
Westover Rd, SW18. . . . . . 149 F6
Westow Hill, SE19 . . . . 170 B6
Westow St, SE19 . . . . 170 B6
West Pk, SE9 . . . . 174 B2
West Pk Av, Rich. TW9 . . . 146 A1
West Pk Cl, Houns. TW5 *off Heston Gra La* 123 F6
Romford RM6 . . . . 82 D5
West Pk Rd, Rich. TW9. . . 146 A1
Southall UB2. . . . . 123 J1
West Parkside, SE10 . . . . 135 E2
West Pier, E1 *off Wapping High St*. 132/133 E1
West Pl, SW19 . . . . 165 J5
Westpoint Trd Est, W3 . . . 106 B6
Westpole Av, Barn. EN4. . . 42 A4
Westport Rd, E13 . . . . 115 H4
Westport St, E1 . . . . 113 G6
West Poultry Av, EC1 . . . . . 19 G2
West Quarters, W12 . . . . . 107 G6
West Quay Dr, Hayes UB4 . . . . 102 E5
West Ramp, Houns. (Hthrw Air.) TW6 . . . . . 140 D1
West Ridge Gdns, Grnf. UB6 . . . . 103 J2
West Rd, E15 . . . . 115 F1
N17 . . . . 60 E6
SW3. . . . . 32 A4
SW4. . . . . 150 D5
W5. . . . . 105 H5
Barnet EN4 . . . . 58 A1
Feltham TW14 . . . . 141 G6
Kingston upon Thames KT2 . . . . 182 C1
Romford (Chad.Hth) RM6. . . . . 82 D6
West Drayton UB7 . . . . 120 C3
Westrow, SW15 . . . . 147 J5
West Row, W10 . . . . 108 B4
Westrow Dr, Bark. IG11 . . . 99 J6
Westrow Gdns, Ilf. IG3. . . . 99 J2
West Sheen Vale, Rich. TW9. . . . . 145 J4
Westside, NW4 . . . . 71 H2
West Side Common, SW19. . . . . 165 J5
West Smithfield, EC1. . . . . 19 G2
West Sq, SE11 . . . . 27 G6
West St, E2. . . . . 113 E2
E11. . . . . 96 E3
E17 *off Grove Rd*. 78 B5
WC2. . . . . 17 J4
Bexleyheath DA7 . . . . . 159 F4
Brentford TW8. . . . . 125 F6
Bromley BR1. . . . . 191 G1
Carshalton SM5 . . . . . . 199 J3
Croydon CR0. . . . . 201 J4
Harrow HA1 . . . . 86 A1
Sutton SM1. . . . . 198 E5
West St La, Cars. SM5. . . 199 J4
West Temple Sheen, SW14. . . . . 146 B4
West Tenter St, E1 . . . . 21 G4
West Thamesmead Business Pk, SE28 . . . 137 J3
West Twrs, Pnr. HA5. . . . . . 66 D6
Westvale Ms, W3 . . . . 127 E1
West Vw, NW4. . . . . 71 J4
Feltham TW14 . . . . 141 F7
Loughton IG10 . . . . 48 C3
Westview Cl, NW10. . . . . . 89 F5
W7. . . . . 104 B6
W10 . . . . 107 J6
Westview Cres, N9 . . . . . . 44 B7
Westview Dr, Wdf.Grn. IG8 . . . . 80 A2
Westville Rd, W12 . . . . . . 127 G2
Thames Ditton KT7. . . . 194 D1
West Wk, W5 . . . . 105 H5
Barnet EN4 . . . . 42 A7
Hayes UB3 . . . . 122 A1
West Walkway, The, Sutt. SM1 *off Cheam Rd*. . . . 198/199 E5
Westward Rd, E4 . . . . 61 J5
Westward Way, Har. HA3. . 69 H6
West Warwick Pl, SW1. . . . 33 F2
West Way, N18. . . . . 60 A4
NW10 . . . . 88 D3
Westway, SW20. . . . . 183 H3
W2. . . . . 108 D5
W9. . . . . 108 D5
W10 . . . . 108 B6
W12 . . . . 107 G7
West Way, Croy. CR0 . . . . 203 H2
Edgware HA8 . . . . 54 B6
Hounslow TW5 . . . . 143 F1
Westway, Orp. BR5 . . . . . 193 G5
West Way, Pnr. HA5. . . . . . 66 D4
West Wickham BR4. . . . 190 D6
Westway Cl, SW20. . . . . . 183 H3
Westway Cross Shop Pk, Grnf. UB6 . . . . 104 B1
West Way Gdns, Croy. CR0 . . . . 203 G2
Westways, Epsom KT19 . 197 F4
Westwell Rd, SW16 . . . . . 168 E6
Westwell Rd App, SW16 *off Westwell Rd* . . 168/169 E6
Westwick Gdns, W14. . . . 128 A2
Hounslow TW4 . . . . 142 B2
WEST WICKHAM, BR4 . . . 204 C2
Westwood Av, SE19. . . . . 107 J1
Harrow HA2 . . . . 85 H4
Westwood Cl, Brom. BR1 192 A3
Westwood Gdns, SW13. . 147 F3
Westwood Hill, SE26 . . . . 170 D5
Westwood La, Sid. DA15. 158 A5
Welling DA16 . . . . 157 J3
Westwood Pk, SE23. . . . . 153 E7
Westwood Pl, SE26 . . . . . 170 D4
Westwood Rd, E16. . . . . . 135 H1
SW13. . . . . 147 F3
Ilford IG3. . . . . 99 J1
West Woodside, Bex. DA5 . . . . 159 E7
West World, W5 . . . . 105 H3
Wetheral Dr, Stan. HA7 . . . 69 E1
Wetherby Cl, Nthlt. UB5 . . 85 H6
Wetherby Gdns, SW5 . . . . 30 C2
Wetherby Ms, SW5 . . . . . . 30 A3
Wetherby Pl, SW7 . . . . 30 C2
Wetherby Rd, Enf. EN2 . . . 43 J1
Wetherby Way, Chess. KT9 . . . . 195 H7
Wetherden St, E17. . . . . . . 77 J7
Wetherell Rd, E9. . . . . 113 G1
Wetherill Rd, N10. . . . . 74 A1
★**Wetland Cen, The**, SW13. . . . . 127 H7
Wexford Rd, SW12. . . . . . 149 J7
Weybourne St, SW18. . . . 167 F2
Weybridge Ct, SE16. . . . . . 37 J4
Weybridge Pt, SW11. . . . . 150 A2
Weybridge Rd, Th.Hth. CR7 . . . . 187 G4
Wey Ct, Epsom KT19 . . . . 196 C4
Weydown Cl, SW19 . . . . . 166 B1
Weyhill Rd, E1 . . . . 21 J3
Weylond Rd, Dag. RM8 . . 101 F3
Weyman Rd, SE3 . . . . 155 J1
Weymouth Av, NW7 . . . . . 54 E5
W5. . . . . 125 F3
Weymouth Cl, E6 *off Covelees Wall* . 116/117 E6
Weymouth Ct, Sutt. SM2. 198 D7
Weymouth Ms, W1 . . . . . . 16 D1
Weymouth St, W1 . . . . 16 C2
Weymouth Ter, E2 . . . . 13 G1
Weymouth Wk, Stan. HA7. 52 D6
Whadcote St, N4 *off Seven Sisters Rd*. . . 93 G2
Whalebone Av, Rom. RM6. 83 F6
Whalebone Ct, EC2 . . . . . . 20 C3
Whalebone Gro, Rom. RM6. . . . . 83 F6
Whalebone La, E15 *off West Ham La* . . . 96/97 E7
Whalebone La N, Rom. RM6. . . . . 83 E5
Whalebone La S, Dag. RM8. . . . . 83 F7
Romford RM6 . . . . 83 F7
Whales Yd, E15 *off West Ham La* 96 E7
Wharfdale Cl, N11 *off Ribblesdale Av*. 58 A6
Wharfdale Ct, E5 *off Rushmore Rd*. 95 G4
Wharfdale Rd, N1. . . . . 10 B1
Wharfedale Gdns, Th.Hth. CR7 . . . . 187 F4
Wharfedale St, SW10. . . . . 30 A4
Wharf La, Twick. TW1 . . . . 162 D1
Wharf Pl, E2 . . . . 112 D1
Wharf Rd, E15. . . . . 114 D1
N1 . . . . 11 J1
Enfield EN3. . . . . 45 H6
Wharfside Rd, E16 . . . . . . 114 E5
Wharf St, E16. . . . . 114 E5
Wharncliffe Dr, Sthl. UB1. 124 A1
Wharncliffe Gdns, SE25 . . 188 B2
Wharncliffe Rd, SE25 . . . . 188 B2
Wharton Cl, NW10. . . . . . . 89 E6
Wharton Cotts, WC1 *off Wharton St*. 111 F3
Wharton Rd, Brom. BR1 . 191 H1
Wharton St, WC1. . . . . 10 D4
Whateley Rd, SE20. . . . . . 171 G7
SE22 . . . . 152 C5
Whatley Av, SW20 . . . . . . 184 B3
Whatman Rd, SE23 . . . . . 153 G7
Wheatfields, E6 *off Oxleas* 116/117 E6
Enfield EN3. . . . . 45 H2
Wheatfield Way, Kings.T. KT1 . . . . 181 H2
Wheathill Rd, SE20 . . . . . 188 E3
Wheatlands, Houns. TW5. 123 G6
Wheatlands Rd, SW17 *off Stapleton Rd* 168 A3
Wheatley Cl, NW4 . . . . 71 G2
Wheatley Cres, Hayes UB3 . . . . 102 A7
Wheatley Gdns, N9 . . . . . . 60 B2
Wheatley Ho, SW15 *off Tangley Gro* 147 G7
Wheatley Rd, Islw. TW7 . . 144 C3
Wheatley's Ait, Sun. TW16. . . . . 178 A5
Wheatley St, W1 . . . . 16 C2
Wheat Sheaf Cl, E14 . . . . 134 B4
Wheatsheaf Cl, Nthlt. UB5. 84 E5
Wheatsheaf La, SW6 . . . . 127 J7
SW8. . . . . 34 B7
Wheatsheaf Ter, SW6. . . . 128 C7
Wheatstone Cl, Mitch. CR4 . . . . 185 H1
Wheatstone Rd, W10 . . . . 108 B5
Wheeler Cl, Wdf.Grn. IG8 *off Chigwell Rd*. 64 C5
Wheeler Gdns, N1 *off Outram Pl* 110/111 E1
Wheelers Cross, Bark. IG11. . . . . 117 G2
Wheel Fm Dr, Dag. RM10. 101 J3
Wheelock Cl, Erith DA8 . . 139 H7
Wheelwright St, N7. . . . . . 93 F7
Whelan Way, Wall. SM6 . . 200 D3
Wheler St, E1. . . . . 13 F6
Whellock Rd, W4 . . . . 126 E3
Whenman Av, Bex. DA5. . 177 J2
Whernside Cl, SE28 . . . . . 118 C7
WHETSTONE, N20. . . . . . . 57 E2
Whetstone Cl, N20 *off Oakleigh Rd N* 57 G2
Whetstone Pk, WC2. . . . . . 18 C3
Whetstone Rd, SE3 . . . . . 155 J2
Whewell Rd, N19. . . . . 93 E2
Whichcote St, SE1 . . . . 26 E2
Whidborne Cl, SE8 *off Cliff Ter*. 154 A2
Whidborne St, WC1 . . . . . . 10 B4
Whimbrel Cl, SE28 . . . . . . 118 C7
Whimbrel Way, Hayes UB4 . . . . 102 D6
Whinchat Rd, SE28 . . . . . 137 G3
Whinfell Cl, SW16 . . . . . . 168 D5
Whinyates Rd, SE9. . . . . . 156 B3
Whipps Cross Rd, E11 . . . . 78 D5
Whiskin St, EC1 . . . . 11 G4
Whisperwood Cl, Har. HA3. 52 B7
Whistler Gdns, Edg. HA8. . 69 J2
Whistler Ms, SE15 *off Kelly Av* 132 C7
Dagenham RM8 *off Fitzstephen Rd*. . . . 100 B5
Whistlers Av, SW11 . . . . . 129 G7
Whistler St, N5 . . . . 93 H4
Whistler Wk, SW10 . . . . . . 30 D7
Whiston Rd, E2 . . . . 13 F1
Whitacre Ms, SE11 *off Stannary St* 131 G5
Whitakers Way, Loug. IG10 . . . . 48 C1
Whitbread Cl, N17 . . . . 76 D1
Whitbread Rd, SE4. . . . . . 153 H4
Whitburn Rd, SE13. . . . . . 154 B4
Whitby Av, NW10. . . . . . . 106 B3
Whitby Gdns, NW9 . . . . . . 70 A3
Sutton SM1. . . . . 199 G2
Whitby Rd, SE18 . . . . 136 C4
Harrow HA2 . . . . 85 J3
Ruislip HA4 . . . . 84 B3
Sutton SM1. . . . . 199 G2
Whitby St, E1. . . . . 13 F5
Whitcher Cl, SE14 . . . . . . 133 H6
Whitcher Pl, NW1 *off Rochester Rd* 92 C7
Whitchurch Av, Edg. HA8. . 53 J7
Whitchurch Cl, Edg. HA8. . 53 J6
Whitchurch Gdns, Edg. HA8. . . . . 53 J6
Whitchurch La, Edg. HA8. . 53 G7
Whitchurch Rd, W11 . . . . 108 A7
Whitcomb Ct, WC2 *off Whitcomb St* 110 D7
Whitcombe Ms, Rich. TW9 . . . . 146 B1
Whitcomb St, WC2 . . . . . . 17 J6
Whiteadder Way, E14. . . . 134 B4
Whitear Wk, E15. . . . . 96 D6
Whitebarn La, Dag. RM10 . 119 G1
Whitebeam Av, Brom. BR2 . . . . 192 D6
Whitebeam Cl, SW9 *off Clapham Rd*. 131 F7
Whitebeams, Hat. AL10 . . 121 H3
White Bear Pl, NW3 *off New End Sq*. 91 G4
White Br Av, Mitch. CR4. . 185 G4
Whitebridge Cl, Felt. TW14. . . . . 141 J6
White Butts Rd, Ruis. HA4. 84 D3
WHITECHAPEL, E1. . . . . . . 21 H4
★**Whitechapel Art Gall**, E1. 21 G3
Whitechapel High St, E1 . . 21 G3
Whitechapel Rd, E1 . . . . . . 21 H3
White Ch La, E1 . . . . 21 H3
White Ch Pas, E1 . . . . 21 H3
White City Cl, W12 . . . . . . 107 J7
White City Est, W12 . . . . . 107 H7
White City Rd, W12 . . . . . 107 H7
White Conduit St, N1. . . . . 11 F1
Whitecote Rd, Sthl. UB1 . 103 H6
White Craig Cl, Pnr. HA5 . . 51 G5
Whitecroft Cl, Beck. BR3 . 190 D4
Whitecroft Way, Beck. BR3 . . . . 190 C5
Whitecross Pl, EC2. . . . . . . 20 C1
Whitecross St, EC1 . . . . . . 12 A5
Whitefield Av, NW2 . . . . . . 71 J7
Whitefield Cl, SW15. . . . . 148 B6
Whitefoot La, Brom. BR1 . 172 C4
Whitefoot Ter, Brom. BR1 173 E3
Whitefriars Av, Har. HA3 . . 68 B2
Whitefriars Dr, Har. HA3 . . 68 A2
Whitefriars St, EC4 . . . . . . 19 F4
White Gdns, Dag. RM10. . 101 G6
Whitegate Gdns, Har. HA3. 52 C7
Whitehall, SW1 . . . . 26 A1

Whitehall Ct, SW1 . . . **26** A2
Whitehall Cres, Chess. KT9 . . . **195** G5
Whitehall Gdns, E4 . . . **62** E1
SW1 . . . **26** A2
W3 . . . **126** A1
W4 . . . **126** B6
Whitehall La, Buck.H. IG9 . **63** G2
Whitehall Pk, N19 . . . **92** C1
Whitehall Pk Rd, W4 . . . **126** B6
Whitehall Pl, E7 *off Station Rd* . . . **97** G5
SW1 . . . **26** A2
Wallington SM6 *off Bernard Rd* . . . **200** B4
Whitehall Rd, E4 . . . **62** E2
W7 . . . **124** D2
Bromley BR2 . . . **192** A5
Harrow HA1 . . . **68** B7
Thornton Heath CR7 . . . **187** G5
Woodford Green IG8 . . . **62** E2
Whitehall St, N17 . . . **60** C7
White Hart Av, SE18 *off North Rd* . . . **137** J2
White Hart Ct, EC2 *off Bishopsgate* . . . **112** B6
White Hart La, N17 . . . **60** A7
N22 . . . **75** G1
NW10 *off Church Rd* . . . **89** F6
SW13 . . . **147** E3
Romford RM7 . . . **83** G1
White Hart Rd, SE18 . . . **137** H4
White Hart Slip, Brom. BR1 *off Market Sq.* . . . **191** G2
White Hart St, EC4 . . . **19** H3
SE11 . . . **35** F3
White Hart Yd, SE1 . . . **28** B2
Whitehaven Cl, Brom. BR2 . . . **191** G4
Whitehaven St, NW8 . . . **7** G6
Whitehead Cl, N18 . . . **60** A5
SW18 . . . **149** F7
Whitehead's Gro, SW3 . . . **31** H3
White Heron Ms, Tedd. TW11 . . . **162** C6
Whitehills Rd, Loug. IG10 . **48** D3
White Horse All, EC1 . . . **19** G1
Whitehorse Hill, Chis. BR7 . . . **174** D4
White Horse La, E1 . . . **113** G4
Whitehorse La, SE25 . . . **188** A4
White Horse Ms, SE1 . . . **27** F5
White Horse Rd, E1 . . . **113** H6
E6 . . . **116** C3
Whitehorse Rd, Croy. CR0 . . . **188** A6
Thornton Heath CR7 . . . **188** A6
White Horse St, W1 . . . **24** D2
White Horse Yd, EC2 . . . **20** B3
Whitehouse Av, Borwd. WD6 . . . **38** B3
White Ho Dr, Stan. HA7 . . . **53** F4
Whitehouse Way, N14 . . . **58** B2
Whitehurst Dr, N18 . . . **61** G5
White Kennett St, E1 . . . **21** E3
Whiteledges, W13 . . . **105** F6
Whitelegg Rd, E13 . . . **115** F2
Whiteley Rd, SE19 . . . **170** A5
Whiteleys Shop Cen, W2 . . **14** A4
Whiteleys Way, Felt. TW13 . . . **161** G3
White Lion Ct, EC3 . . . **20** D4
White Lion Hill, EC4 . . . **19** H5
White Lion St, N1 . . . **11** E2
White Lo, SE19 . . . **169** H7
White Lo Cl, N2 . . . **73** G6
Isleworth TW7 . . . **144** D2
Sutton SM2 . . . **199** F7
White Lyon Ct, EC2 *off Fann St.* . . . **111** J4
White Oak Dr, Beck. BR3 . **190** C2
White Oak Gdns, Sid. DA15 . . . **157** J7
Whiteoaks La, Grnf. UB6 . **104** A2
White Orchards, N20 . . . **40** C7
Stanmore HA7 . . . **52** D5
White Post La, E9 . . . **95** J7
SE13 . . . **154** A3
White Post St, SE15 . . . **133** F7
White Rd, E15 . . . **97** E7
Whites Av, Ilf. IG2 . . . **81** H6
Whites Grds, SE1 . . . **28** E4
Whites Grds Est, SE1 . . . **28** E3
White's Row, E1 . . . **21** F2
White's Sq, SW4 *off Nelson's Row* . . . **150** D4
Whitestile Rd, Brent. TW8 . **125** F5
Whitestone La, NW3 *off Heath St.* . . . **91** F3
Whitestone Wk, NW3 *off North End Way* . . . **91** F3
White St, Sthl. UB1 . . . **122** D2
White Swan Ms, W4 *off Bennett St.* . . . **126/127** E6
Whitethorn Gdns, Croy. CR0 . . . **203** E2
Enfield EN2 . . . **44** A5
Whitethorn St, E3 . . . **114** A4
Whitewebbs Way, Orp. BR5 . . . **193** J1
Whitfield Pl, W1 . . . **9** F6
Whitfield Rd, E6 . . . **97** J7
SE3 . . . **154** D1
Bexleyheath DA7 . . . **139** F7
Whitfield St, W1 . . . **17** H2
Whitford Gdns, Mitch. CR4 . . . **185** J3
Whitgift Av, S.Croy. CR2 . **201** J5
Whitgift Cen, Croy. CR0 . . **201** J2
Whitgift Ho, SW11 *off Westbridge Rd* . . . **149** H1
Whitgift St, SE11 . . . **34** C1
Croydon CR0 . . . **201** J3
Whiting Av, Bark. IG11 . . . **99** E7
Whitings, Ilf. IG2 . . . **81** G5
Whitings Rd, Barn. EN5 . . . **39** J5
Whitings Way, E6 . . . **116** D5
Whitland Rd, Cars. SM5 . **199** G1
Whitley Cl, Stai. (Stanw.) TW19 . . . **140** B6
Whitley Rd, N17 . . . **76** B2
Whitlock Dr, SW19 . . . **148** B7
Whitman Rd, E3 *off Mile End Rd* . . . **113** H4
Whitmead Cl, S.Croy. CR2 . . . **202** B6
Whitmore Cl, N11 . . . **58** B5
Whitmore Est, N1 . . . **112** B1
Whitmore Gdns, NW10 . . **107** J2
Whitmore Rd, N1 . . . **112** B1
Beckenham BR3 . . . **189** J3
Harrow HA1 . . . **67** J7
Whitnell Way, SW15 . . . **148** A5
Whitney Av, Ilf. IG4 . . . **80** A4
Whitney Rd, E10 . . . **78** B7
Whitney Wk, Sid. DA14 . . **176** E6
Whitstable Cl, Beck. BR3 . **189** J1
Whitstable Ho, W10 . . . **108** A6
Whitstable Pl, Croy. CR0 . **201** J4
Whitstone La, Beck. BR3 . **190** B5
Whittaker Av, Rich. TW9 *off Hill St.* . . . **145** G5
Whittaker Rd, E6 . . . **97** J7
Sutton SM3 . . . **198** C3
Whittaker St, SW1 . . . **32** B2
Whittaker Way, SE1 . . . **37** J2
Whitta Rd, E12 . . . **98** A4
Whittell Gdns, SE26 . . . **171** F3
Whittingstall Rd, SW6 . . . **148** C1
Whittington Av, EC3 . . . **20** D4
Whittington Ct, N2 . . . **73** J5
Whittington Ms, N12 *off Fredericks Pl* . . . **57** F4
Whittington Rd, N22 . . . **58** E7
Whittington Way, Pnr. HA5 . . . **67** E5
Whittlebury Cl, Cars. SM5 . . . **199** J7
Whittle Cl, E17 . . . **77** H6
Southall UB1 . . . **103** H6
Whittle Rd, Houns. TW5 . . **122** C7
Southall UB2 *off Post Rd* . . . **123** H2
Whittlesea Cl, Har. HA3 . . . **51** J7
Whittlesea Path, Har. HA3 . **67** J1
Whittlesea Rd, Har. HA3 . . **67** J1
Whittlesey St, SE1 . . . **27** E2
WHITTON, Twick. TW2 . . . **143** H7
Whitton Av E, Grnf. UB6 . . **86** B5
Whitton Av W, Grnf. UB6 . . **85** J5
Northolt UB5 . . . **85** J5
Whitton Cl, Grnf. UB6 . . . **87** E6
Whitton Dene, Houns. TW3 . . . **143** H5
Isleworth TW7 . . . **144** A5
Whitton Dr, Grnf. UB6 . . . **86** D6
Whitton Manor Rd, Islw. TW7 . . . **143** J5
Whitton Rd, Houns. TW3 . **143** H4
Twickenham TW1, TW2 . **144** C6
Whitton Wk, E3 . . . **114** A2
Whitton Waye, Houns. TW3 . . . **143** G6
Whitwell Rd, E13 . . . **115** G3
Whitworth Pl, SE18 . . . **137** E4
Whitworth Rd, SE18 . . . **136** D7
SE25 . . . **188** B3
Whitworth St, SE10 . . . **135** E5
Whorlton Rd, SE15 . . . **152** E3
Whychcote Pt, NW2 *off Claremont Rd* . . . **71** J7
Whymark Av, N22 . . . **75** G3
Whytecroft, Houns. TW5 . **122** D7
Whyteville Rd, E7 . . . **97** H6
Wickersley Rd, SW11 . . . **150** A2
Wickers Oake, SE19 . . . **170** C4
Wicker St, E1 *off Burslem St* . . . **112/113** E6
Wicket, The, Croy. CR0 . **204** A5
Wicket Rd, Grnf. UB6 . . . **104** D3
Wickets Way, Ilf. IG6 . . . **65** J6
Wickford St, E1 . . . **113** F4
Wickford Way, E17 . . . **77** G4
Wickham Av, Croy. CR0 . . **203** H2
Sutton SM3 . . . **197** J5
Wickham Chase, W.Wick. BR4 . . . **190** D7
Wickham Cl, E1 . . . **113** F5
Enfield EN3 . . . **45** E3
New Malden KT3 . . . **183** F5
Wickham Ct Rd, W.Wick. BR4 . . . **204** C2
Wickham Cres, W.Wick. BR4 . . . **204** C2
Wickham Gdns, SE4 . . . **153** J3
Wickham La, SE2 . . . **138** A5
Welling DA16 . . . **138** A5
Wickham Ms, SE4 . . . **153** J2
Wickham Rd, E4 . . . **62** C7
SE4 . . . **153** J4
Beckenham BR3 . . . **190** B2
Croydon CR0 . . . **203** G2
Harrow HA3 . . . **68** A2
Wickham St, SE11 . . . **34** C3
Welling DA16 . . . **157** H2
Wickham Way, Beck. BR3 . **190** C4
Wick La, E3 . . . **114** A2
Wickliffe Av, N3 . . . **72** B2
Wickliffe Gdns, Wem. HA9 . **88** B2
Wicklow St, WC1 . . . **10** C3
Wick Rd, E9 . . . **95** G6
Teddington TW11 . . . **163** E7
Wicks Cl, SE9 . . . **174** A4
Wicksteed Ho, Brent. TW8 *off Green Dragon La.* . **125** J5
Wickwood St, SE5 . . . **151** H2
Widdecombe Av, Har. HA2 . . . **84** E2
Widdenham Rd, N7 . . . **93** F4
Widdin St, E15 . . . **96** D7
Widecombe Gdns, Ilf. IG4 . **80** B4
Widecombe Rd, SE9 . . . **174** B3
Widecombe Way, N2 . . . **73** G5
Widegate St, E1 . . . **21** E2
Widenham Cl, Pnr. HA5 *off Bridle Rd* . . . **66** C5
Wide Way, Mitch. CR4 . . . **186** D3
Widewing Cl, Tedd. TW11 . **163** E7
Widgeon Cl, E16 *off Maplin Rd* . . . **115** H6
Widley Rd, W9 . . . **108** D3
WIDMORE, Brom. BR1 . . . **191** H3
WIDMORE GREEN, Brom. BR1 . . . **191** J1
Widmore Lo Rd, Brom. BR1 . . . **192** A2
Widmore Rd, Brom. BR1 . **191** G2
Wieland Rd, Nthwd. HA6 . . **50** A7
Wigan Ho, E5 *off Warwick Gro* . . . **94/95** E1
Wigeon Path, SE28 . . . **137** G3
Wigeon Way, Hayes UB4 . **102** D6
Wiggins La, Rich. TW10 . . **163** F2
Wiggins Mead, NW9 . . . **55** F7
Wigginton Av, Wem. HA9 . **88** B6
Wigham Ho, Bark. IG11 . . . **99** F7
Wightman Rd, N4 . . . **75** G5
N8 . . . **75** G4
Wigley Rd, Felt. TW13 . . . **160** D1
Wigmore Ct, W13 *off Singapore Rd* . . . **124** D1
Wigmore Pl, W1 . . . **16** D3
Wigmore Rd, Cars. SM5 . **199** G2
Wigmore St, W1 . . . **16** B4
Wigmore Wk, Cars. SM5 . **199** G2
Wigram Rd, E11 . . . **79** J6
Wigram Sq, E17 . . . **78** C2
Wigston Cl, N18 . . . **60** B5
Wigston Rd, E13 . . . **115** H4
Wigton Gdns, Stan. HA7 . . **69** H1
Wigton Pl, SE11 . . . **35** F4
Wigton Rd, E17 . . . **77** J1
Wilberforce Ms, SW4 *off Stonhouse St.* . . . **150** D4
Wilberforce Rd, N4 . . . **93** H2
NW9 . . . **71** G6
Wilberforce Way, SW19 . . **166** A6
Wilbraham Pl, SW1 . . . **32** A1
Wilbury Way, N18 . . . **60** A5
Wilby Ms, W11 . . . **128** C1
Wilcox Cl, SW8 . . . **34** B7
Borehamwood WD6 . . . **38** C1
Wilcox Pl, SW1 . . . **25** G6
Wilcox Rd, SW8 . . . **34** A7
Sutton SM1 . . . **198** E4
Teddington TW11 . . . **162** A4
Wild Ct, WC2 . . . **18** C3
Wildcroft Gdns, Edg. HA8 . **53** G6
Wildcroft Rd, SW15 . . . **147** J7
Wilde Cl, E8 . . . **112** D1
Wilde Pl, N13 *off Medesenge Way* . . . **59** H6
SW18 *off Heathfield Rd* . . . **149** G7
Wilder Cl, Ruis. HA4 . . . **84** B1
Wilderness, The, E.Mol. KT8 . . . **179** J5
Hampton (Hmptn H.) TW12 *off Park Rd* . . . **161** H4
Wilderness Ms, SW4 *off The Chase* . . . **150** B4
Wilderness Rd, Chis. BR7 . **175** E7
Wilde Rd, Erith DA8 . . . **139** H7
Wilderton Rd, N16 . . . **76** B7
Wildfell Rd, SE6 . . . **154** B7
Wild Goose Dr, SE14 . . . **153** F1
Wild Hatch, NW11 . . . **72** D6
Wild's Rents, SE1 . . . **28** D5
Wild St, WC2 . . . **18** B4
Wildwood Cl, SE12 . . . **155** F7
Wildwood Gro, NW3 *off North End Way* . . . **91** F1
Wildwood Ri, NW11 . . . **91** F1
Wildwood Rd, NW11 . . . **73** F7
Wildwood Ter, NW3 . . . **91** F1
Wilford Cl, Enf. EN2 . . . **44** A3
Wilfred Owen Cl, SW19 *off Tennyson Rd* . . . **167** F6
Wilfred St, SW1 . . . **25** F5
Wilfred Turney Est, W6 *off Hammersmith Gro.* . **127** J3
Wilfrid Gdns, W3 . . . **106** C5
Wilkes Rd, Brent. TW8 . . . **125** H6
Wilkes St, E1 . . . **21** G1
Wilkie Way, SE22 *off Lordship La* . . . **170** D1
Wilkins Cl, Hayes UB3 . . . **121** J5
Mitcham CR4 . . . **185** H1
Wilkinson Rd, E16 . . . **115** J6
Wilkinson St, SW8 . . . **131** F7
Wilkinson Way, W4 . . . **126** D2
Wilkin St, NW5 . . . **92** B6
Wilkin St Ms, NW5 *off Wilkin St.* . . . **92** B6
Wilks Gdns, Croy. CR0 . . . **203** H1
Wilks Pl, N1 . . . **12** E2
Willan Rd, N17 . . . **76** A2
Willan Wall, E16 *off Victoria Dock Rd* . . . **115** F7
Willard St, SW8 . . . **150** B3
Willcocks Cl, Chess. KT9 . **195** H3
Willcott Rd, W3 . . . **126** B1
Will Crooks Gdns, SE9 . . . **155** J4
Willen Fld Rd, NW10 . . . **106** C2
Willenhall Av, Barn. EN5 . . **41** F6
Willenhall Rd, SE18 . . . **136** E5
Willersley Av, Orp. BR6 . . **207** G3
Sidcup DA15 . . . **175** J1
Willersley Cl, Sid. DA15 . . **175** J1
WILLESDEN, NW10 . . . **89** F6
WILLESDEN GREEN, NW10 . . . **89** H7
Willesden La, NW2 . . . **90** A6
NW6 . . . **90** A6
Willes Rd, NW5 . . . **92** B6
Willett Cl, Nthlt. UB5 *off Broomcroft Av* . . . **102** C3
Orpington BR5 . . . **193** H6
Willett Ho, E13 *off Queens Rd W* . . . **115** G2
Willett Pl, Th.Hth. CR7 *off Willett Rd* . . . **187** G5
Willett Rd, Th.Hth. CR7 . . . **187** G5
Willett Way, Orp. BR5 . . . **193** G5
William Barefoot Dr, SE9 . **174** D4
William Bonney Est, SW4 . **150** D4
William Booth Rd, SE20 . **188** D1
William Carey Way, Har. HA1 . . . **68** B7
William Cl, N2 *off King St.* . . . **73** G3
SE13 . . . **154** C2
Romford RM5 . . . **83** J1
Southall UB2 *off Windmill Av* . . . **123** J2
William Dr, Stan. HA7 . . . **52** E5

William Dunbar Ho, NW6. **108** C2
William Dyce Ms, SW16 *off Babington Rd*. **168** D4
William Ellis Way, SE16 . . . **29** J6
William IV St, WC2. . . . . . . **18** A6
William Gdns, SW15 . . . . **147** H5
William Guy Gdns, E3 *off Talwin St*. **114** B3
William Harvey Ho, SW19 *off Whitlock Dr* **166** B1
William Henry Wk, SW8. . . **33** H6
William Margrie Cl, SE15 *off Moncrieff St*. **152** D2
William Ms, SW1 . . . . **24** A4
William Morley Cl, E6. . . . **116** A1
William Morris Cl, E17 . . . . **77** J3
★**William Morris Gall, Lloyd Pk**, E17 . . . . **78** A3
William Morris Way, SW6. **149** F3
William Perkin Ct, Grnf. UB6 *off Greenford Rd*. . **86** B6
William Pl, E3 *off Roman Rd* **113** J2
William Rd, NW1 . . . . **9** E4
SW19. . . . . **166** B7
Sutton SM1 . . . . **199** F5
Williams Av, E17 . . . . **77** J1
William Saville Ho, NW6 . **108** C2
Williams Bldgs, E2 . . . . . . **113** F4
Williams Cl, N8 *off Coolhurst Rd* **74** D6
SW6 *off Pellant Rd* **128** B7
Williams Dr, Houns. TW3 . **143** G4
Williams Gro, N22 . . . . **75** G1
Surbiton KT6. . . . . **181** F6
William's La, SW14 . . . . . **146** C3
Williams La, Mord. SM4 . . **185** F5
Williamson Cl, SE10 *off Lenthorp Rd*. **135** F4
Williamson Rd, N4. . . . . . . **75** H6
Williamson St, N7 . . . . **93** E4
Williamson Way, NW7 . . . . **56** B6
William Sq, SE16 *off Rotherhithe St* **113** H7
Williams Rd, W13 . . . . **104** D7
Southall UB2. . . . . **122** E4
Williams Ter, Croy. CR0 . . **201** G6
William St, E10. . . . . **78** B6
N17 . . . . **60** C7
SW1. . . . . **24** A4
Barking IG11 . . . . **99** F7
Carshalton SM5 . . . . . . **199** H3
Willifield Way, NW11 . . . . . **72** C4
Willingale Cl, Loug. IG10 *off Willingale Rd* **49** F2
Woodford Green IG8 . . . **64** A6
Willingale Rd, Loug. IG10 . **49** F3
Willingdon Rd, N22 . . . . . . **75** H2
Willingham Cl, NW5 *off Leighton Rd*. **92** C5
Willingham Ter, NW5 *off Leighton Rd*. **92** C5
Willingham Way, Kings.T. KT1. . . . . **182** A3
Willington Ct, E5 *off Mandeville St* **95** H3
Willington Rd, SW9 . . . . . **150** E3
Willis Av, Sutt. SM2 . . . . . **199** H6
Willis Ho, E12 *off Grantham Rd*. **98** D3
Willis Rd, E15 . . . . **115** F1
Croydon CR0. . . . . **187** J7
Erith DA8. . . . . **139** J4
Willis St, E14 . . . . **114** B6
Willmore End, SW19 . . . . **184** E1
Willoughby Av, Croy. CR0 . . . . **201** F4
Willoughby Gro, N17 . . . . . **60** E7
Willoughby Ho, EC2 *off The Barbican*. **111** J5
Willoughby La, N17 . . . . . . **61** E7
Willoughby Ms, SW4 *off Wixs La* **150** B4
Willoughby Pk Rd, N17 . . . **60** E7
Willoughby Pas, E14 . . . . **134** A1
Willoughby Rd, N8. . . . . . . **75** G3
NW3 . . . . **91** G4
Kingston upon Thames KT2 . . . . **181** J1
Twickenham TW1 . . . . . **145** G6
Willoughbys, The, SW14 *off Upper Richmond Rd W* **146/147** E4
Willoughby St, WC1. . . . . . **18** A2
Willoughby Way, SE7. . . . **135** H4
Willow Av, SW13 . . . . **147** F2
Sidcup DA15. . . . . **158** A6
Willow Bk, SW6. . . . . **148** B3
Richmond TW10 . . . . . . **163** E3
Willowbay Cl, Barn. EN5 *off Chesterfield Rd* **40** A6
Willow Br Rd, N1 . . . . **93** J6
Willowbrook Est, SE15 *off Sumner Rd* **132** C7
Willowbrook Rd, SE15. . . . **37** G6
Southall UB2. . . . . **123** G3
Willow Business Cen, Mitch. CR4 *off Willow La* **185** J5
Willow Cl, SE6 *off Verdant La* **172** E1
Bexley DA5 . . . . **159** F6
Brentford TW8. . . . . **125** F6
Bromley BR2. . . . . **192** C5
Buckhurst Hill IG9. . . . . . **64** A3
Thornton Heath CR7 . . . **187** H6
Willow Cotts, Mitch. CR4. **186** C3
Richmond TW9 *off Kew Grn*. **126** A6
Willow Ct, EC2. . . . . **12** D5
Edgware HA8 . . . . **53** H4
Willowcourt Av, Har. HA3 . **69** E5
Willowdene, N6 *off Denewood Rd* **73** J7
Willow Dene, Pnr. HA5 . . . **66** D2
Willowdene Cl, Twick. TW2 . . . . **143** J7
Willow Dr, Barn. EN5. . . . . **40** B4
Willow End, N20 . . . . **56** D2
Northwood HA6 . . . . **50** A6
Surbiton KT6. . . . . **195** H1
Willow Fm La, SW15 *off Queens Ride* **147** H3
Willowfield Cl, SE18. . . . . **137** H5
Willow Gdns, Houns. TW3 . . . . **143** G1
Willow Grn, NW9 *off Clayton Fld*. **70/71** E1
Borehamwood WD6 . . . . **38** D5
Willow Gro, E13 *off Libra Rd* **115** G2
Chislehurst BR7. . . . . . . **174** D6
Willowhayne Dr, Walt. KT12. . . . . **178** B7
Willowhayne Gdns, Wor.Pk. KT4. . . . . **197** J3
Willow La, SE18. . . . . **136** C4
Mitcham CR4. . . . . **185** J5
Willowmead Cl, W5 . . . . . **105** G5
Willow Mt, Croy. CR0 *off Langton Way* **202** B3
Willow Pl, SW1 . . . . **33** G1
Willow Rd, NW3 . . . . **91** G4
W5. . . . . **125** H2
Enfield EN1 . . . . **44** B3
New Malden KT3 . . . . . **182** C4
Romford RM6 . . . . **83** E6
Wallington SM6 . . . . . . **200** B7
Willows, The, Buck.H. IG9 . **64** A3
Esher (Clay.) KT10. . . . . **194** B6
Willows Av, Mord. SM4 . . **185** E5
Willows Cl, Pnr. HA5 . . . . . **66** C2
Willow St, E4. . . . . **46** D7
EC2 . . . . **12** D5
Romford RM7 . . . . **83** J4
Willow Tree Cl, E3 *off Birdsfield La*. **113** J1
SW18 *off Cargill Rd* **166/167** E1
Hayes UB4. . . . . **102** C4
Willow Tree La, Hayes UB4 . . . . **102** C4
Willowtree Marina, Hayes UB4 . . . . **103** E6
Willow Tree Wk, Brom. BR1 . . . . **191** H1
Willowtree Way, Th.Hth. CR7 *off Kensington Av* **187** G1
Willow Vale, W12 . . . . **127** G1
Chislehurst BR7. . . . . . . **174** E6
Willow Vw, SW19. . . . . . . **185** G1
Willow Wk, E17 . . . . **77** J5
N2 . . . . **73** G2
N15 . . . . **75** H4
N21 . . . . **43** F6
SE1 . . . . **37** E1
Orpington BR6 . . . . **206** E3
Sutton SM3. . . . . **198** C3
Willow Way, N3 . . . . **56** E7
SE26 . . . . **171** E3
W11 *off Freston Rd* **128** A1
Epsom KT19 . . . . **196** D6
Sunbury-on-Thames TW16. . . . . **178** A4
Twickenham TW2 . . . . . **161** H2
Wembley HA0. . . . . **86** D3
Willow Wd Cres, SE25 . . . **188** B6
Willrose Cres, SE2 . . . . . . **138** C5
Wills Cres, Houns. TW3 . . **143** H6
Wills Gro, NW7 . . . . **55** G5
Wilman Gro, E8 . . . . **94** D7
Wilmar Gdns, W.Wick. BR4 . . . . **204** B1
Wilmcote Ho, W2. . . . . **14** A1
Wilmer Cl, Kings.T. KT2 . . **163** J5
Wilmer Cres, Kings.T. KT2. **163** J5
Wilmer Gdns, N1 . . . . **112** B1
Wilmer Lea Cl, E15. . . . . . . **96** C7
Wilmer Pl, N16 *off Stoke Newington Ch St*. **94** C2
Wilmer Way, N14 . . . . **58** D5
Wilmington Av, W4 . . . . . **126** D7
Wilmington Gdns, Bark. IG11 . . . . **99** G6
Wilmington Sq, WC1 . . . . . **11** E4
Wilmington St, WC1 . . . . . **11** E4
Wilmot Cl, N2 . . . . **73** F2
SE15 . . . . **132** D7
Wilmot Pl, NW1. . . . . **92** C7
W7 *off Boston Rd* **124** B1
Wilmot Rd, E10 . . . . **96** B2
N17 . . . . **76** A3
Carshalton SM5 . . . . . . **199** J5
Wilmot St, E2. . . . . **112** E4
Wilmount St, SE18 . . . . . **136** E4
Wilna Rd, SW18. . . . . **149** F7
Wilsham St, W11 . . . . **128** A1
Wilshaw Cl, NW4. . . . . **71** G3
Wilshaw St, SE14. . . . . . . **154** A1
Wilsmere Dr, Har. HA3. . . . **52** C7
Northolt UB5. . . . . **85** E6
Wilson Av, Mitch. CR4 . . . **167** H7
Wilson Cl, S.Croy. CR2 *off Bartlett St*. **202** A5
Wembley HA9. . . . . **69** J7
Wilson Dr, Wem. HA9 . . . . **69** J7
Wilson Gdns, Har. HA1 . . . **67** J7
Wilson Gro, SE16. . . . . . . **132** E2
Wilson Rd, E6. . . . . **116** A3
SE5 . . . . **152** B1
Chessington KT9. . . . . . **195** J6
Ilford IG1. . . . . **80** C7
Wilsons Pl, E14 *off Salmon La* **113** J6
Wilsons Rd, W6 . . . . **128** A5
Wilson St, E17 . . . . **78** C5
EC2 . . . . **20** C1
N21 . . . . **43** G7
Wilstone Cl, Hayes UB4. . **102** E4
Wilthorne Gdns, Dag. RM10 *off Acre Rd* **101** H7
Wilton Av, W4. . . . . **127** E5
Wilton Cl, West Dr. UB7 . . **120** A6
Wilton Cres, SW1. . . . . **24** B4
SW19. . . . . **184** C1
Wilton Gdns, W.Mol. KT8. **179** G3
Wilton Gro, SW19 . . . . . . **184** C1
New Malden KT3 . . . . . **183** F6
Wilton Ms, SW1. . . . . **24** C5
Wilton Par, Felt. TW13 *off Highfield Rd*. **160** A2
Wilton Pk Ct, SE18 *off Prince Imperial Rd*. **156** D1
Wilton Pl, SW1. . . . . **24** B4
Wilton Rd, N10. . . . . **74** A2
SE2 . . . . **138** C3
SW1. . . . . **25** E6
SW19. . . . . **167** H7
Barnet (Cockfos.) EN4. . . **41** J4
Hounslow TW4 . . . . **142** D3
Ilford IG1 *off Ilford La* **98/99** E3
Wilton Row, SW1 . . . . **24** B4
Wilton Sq, N1. . . . . **112** A1
Wilton St, SW1 . . . . **24** D5
Wilton Ter, SW1 . . . . **24** B5
Wilton Vil, N1 . . . . **112** A1
Wilton Way, E8. . . . . **94** D6
Wiltshire Cl, NW7 . . . . **55** F5
SW3. . . . . **31** J1
Wiltshire Gdns, N4. . . . . . . **75** J6
Twickenham TW2 . . . . . **161** J1
Wiltshire Rd, SW9 . . . . . . **151** G3
Thornton Heath CR7 . . . **187** G3
Wiltshire Row, N1 . . . . . . **112** A1
Wilverley Cres, N.Mal. KT3 . . . . **183** E6
Wimbart Rd, SW2 . . . . . . **151** F7
WIMBLEDON, SW19 . . . . **166** B6
★**Wimbledon (All England Tenn & Croquet Club)**, SW19 . . . . **166** B4
Wimbledon Br, SW19. . . . **166** C6
★**Wimbledon Common**, SW19. . . . . **165** F4
Wimbledon Hill Rd, SW19. . . . . **166** B6
WIMBLEDON PARK, SW19. . . . . **166** C3
Wimbledon Pk, SW19 . . . **166** C2
Wimbledon Pk Est, SW19. . . . . **166** B1
Wimbledon Pk Rd, SW18. **148** C7
SW19. . . . . **166** C1
Wimbledon Pk Side, SW19. . . . . **166** A2
Wimbledon Rd, SW17 . . . **167** F4
Wimbledon Stadium Business Cen, SW17 *off Riverside Rd* **166** E3
Wimbledon Sta, SW19. . . **166** C6
★**Wimbledon Windmill Mus**, SW19 . . . . **165** H2
Wimbolt St, E2. . . . . **13** H3
Wimborne Av, Hayes UB4. **102** B6
Southall UB2. . . . . **123** G4
Wimborne Cl, SE12 . . . . . **155** F5
Buckhurst Hill IG9. . . . . . **63** H2
Worcester Park KT4. . . . **197** J1
Wimborne Dr, NW9 . . . . . . **70** A3
Pinner HA5 . . . . **66** D7
Wimborne Gdns, W13 . . . **105** E6
Wimborne Rd, N9 . . . . **60** D2
N17 . . . . **76** B2
Wimborne Way, Beck. BR3 . . . . **189** G3
Wimbourne Av, Chis. BR7. **193** J4
Orpington BR5 . . . . **193** J4
Wimbourne Ct, N1. . . . . . . **12** B1
Wimbourne St, N1. . . . . . . **12** B1
Wimpole Cl, Brom. BR2 . . **191** J4
Kingston upon Thames KT1 . . . . **181** J2
Wimpole Ms, W1 . . . . **16** D1
Wimpole Rd, West Dr. UB7 . . . . **120** A1
Wimpole St, W1. . . . . **16** D3
Wimshurst Cl, Croy. CR0 . **201** E1
Winans Wk, SW9 . . . . **151** G2
Wincanton Cres, Nthlt. UB5. . . . . **85** G5
Wincanton Gdns, Ilf. IG6 . . **80** E3
Wincanton Rd, SW18. . . . **148** C7
Winchcombe Rd, Cars. SM5. . . . . **185** G7
Winchcomb Gdns, SE9 . . **156** A3
Winchelsea Av, Bexh. DA7 . . . . **139** F7
Winchelsea Cl, SW15. . . . **148** A5
Winchelsea Rd, E7. . . . . . . **97** G3
N17 . . . . **76** B3
NW10. . . . . **106** D1
Winchelsey Ri, S.Croy. CR2 . . . . **202** C6
Winchendon Rd, SW6 . . . **128** C7
Teddington TW11. . . . . . **162** A4
Winchester Av, NW6 . . . . **108** B1
NW9 . . . . **70** A3
Hounslow TW5 . . . . **123** F6
Winchester Cl, E6 *off Boultwood Rd* **116** B6
SE17 . . . . **35** H2
Bromley BR2. . . . . **191** F3
Enfield EN1 . . . . **44** B5
Kingston upon Thames KT2. . . . . **164** D7
Winchester Ct, E17 *off Billet Rd*. **77** H1
Winchester Dr, Pnr. HA5 . . **66** D5
Winchester Ho, SE18 *off Shooter's Hill Rd* . . **136** A7
Winchester Ms, NW3 *off Winchester Rd* **91** G7
Winchester Pk, Brom. BR2 . . . . **191** F3
Winchester Pl, E8 *off Kingsland High St* . . **94** C5
N6 . . . . **92** B1
W3 *off Avenue Rd*. **126** C2
Winchester Rd, E4 . . . . **62** C7
N6 . . . . **92** B1
N9 . . . . **60** D1
NW3 . . . . **91** G7
Bexleyheath DA7 . . . . . **158** D2
Bromley BR2. . . . . **191** F3
Feltham TW13 . . . . **161** F3
Harrow HA3 . . . . **69** H4
Hayes UB3 . . . . **121** H7
Ilford IG1. . . . . **99** G3
Twickenham TW1 . . . . . **144** E6
Winchester Sq, SE1 . . . . . . **28** B1
Winchester St, SW1. . . . . . **32** E3
W3. . . . . **126** C1
Winchester Wk, SE1. . . . . . **28** B1
Winchet Wk, Croy. CR0 . . **189** F6
Winchfield Cl, Har. HA3 . . . **69** F6

Winchfield Ho, SW15
off Highcliffe Dr ... **147** F6
Winchfield Rd, SE26 ... **171** H5
Winchilsea Cres, W.Mol.
KT8 ... **179** J2
WINCHMORE HILL, N21 ... **43** F7
Winchmore Hill Rd, N14 ... **58** D1
N21 ... **58** D1
Winckley Cl, Har. HA3 ... **69** J5
Wincott St, SE11 ... **35** F1
Wincrofts Dr, SE9 ... **157** G4
Windall Cl, SE19 ... **188** D1
Windborough Rd, Cars.
SM5 ... **200** A7
Windermere Av, N3 ... **72** D3
NW6 ... **108** B1
SW19 ... **184** E3
Harrow HA3 ... **69** F7
Ruislip HA4 ... **66** C7
Wembley HA9 ... **69** F7
Windermere Cl, Orp. BR6 . **206** E3
Windermere Ct, SW13 ... **127** F6
Wembley HA9
off Windermere Av ... **69** F7
Windermere Gdns, Ilf. IG4 . **80** B5
Windermere Gro, Wem. HA9
off Windermere Av ... **87** F1
Windermere Ho, Islw. TW7
off Summerwood Rd . **144** C5
Windermere Pt, SE15
off Ilderton Rd ... **133** F7
Windermere Rd, N10 ... **74** B1
N19 *off Holloway Rd* ... **92** C2
SW15 ... **164** E4
SW16 ... **186** C1
W5 ... **125** F3
Bexleyheath DA7 ... **159** J2
Croydon CR0 ... **202** C1
Southall UB1 ... **103** F5
West Wickham BR4 ... **204** E2
Windermere Way, West Dr.
UB7 *off Providence Rd* . **120** C1
Winders Rd, SW11 ... **149** H2
Windfield Cl, SE26 ... **171** G4
Windham Rd, Rich. TW9 . **145** J3
Winding Way, Dag. RM8 . **100** C3
Harrow HA1 ... **86** B4
Windlass Pl, SE8 ... **133** H4
Windlesham Gro, SW19 .. **166** A1
Windley Cl, SE23 ... **171** F2
Windmill All, W4
off Windmill Rd .. **126/127** E4
Windmill Av, Sthl. UB2 .. **123** J2
Windmill Br Ho, Croy.
CR0 ... **202** B1
Windmill Cl, SE1 ... **37** J1
SE13 ... **154** C2
Surbiton KT6 ... **195** E1
Windmill Ct, NW2 ... **90** B6
Windmill Dr, NW2 ... **90** B3
SW4 ... **150** C5
Keston BR2 ... **205** J4
Windmill Gdns, Enf. EN2 .. **43** G3
Windmill Gro, Croy. CR0 . **187** J7
Windmill Hill, NW3 ... **91** F3
Enfield EN2 ... **43** H3
Windmill Ho, E14
off Westferry Rd ... **134** A4
Windmill La, E15 ... **96** D6
Barnet EN5 ... **39** F6
Bushey (Bushey Hth)
WD23 ... **52** B1
Greenford UB6 ... **103** J5
Isleworth TW7 ... **124** B4
Southall UB2 ... **123** J3
Surbiton KT6 ... **181** E6
Windmill Ms, W4
off Windmill Rd .. **126/127** E4
Windmill Pas, W4 ... **126** E4
Windmill Ri, Kings.T. KT2 . **164** B7
Windmill Rd, N18 ... **60** A4
SW18 ... **149** G6
SW19 ... **165** H1
W4 ... **126** E4
W5 ... **125** F4
Brentford TW8 ... **125** G5
Croydon CR0 ... **187** J7
Hampton (Hmptn H.)
TW12 ... **161** H5
Mitcham CR4 ... **186** C5
Windmill Row, SE11 ... **35** E4
Windmill St, W1 ... **17** H2
Bushey (Bushey Hth)
WD23 ... **52** B1
Windmill Wk, SE1 ... **27** F2
Windmore Cl, Wem. HA0 . **86** D5
Windover Av, NW9 ... **70** D4
Windrose Cl, SE16 ... **133** G2
Windrush, N.Mal. KT3 ... **182** B4
Windrush Cl, SW11
off Maysoule Rd ... **149** G4
W4 ... **146** C1
Windrush La, SE23 ... **171** G3
Windrush Rd, NW10 ... **106** D1
Windrush Sq, SW2
off Rushcroft Rd ... **151** G4
Windsock Cl, SE16 ... **133** J4
Windsor Av, E17 ... **77** H2
SW19 ... **185** F1
Edgware HA8 ... **54** B4
New Malden KT3 ... **182** C5
Sutton SM3 ... **198** B3
West Molesey KT8 ... **179** G3
Windsor Cen, The, SE27
off Advance Rd ... **169** J4
Windsor Cl, N3 ... **72** B2
SE27 ... **169** J4
Borehamwood WD6 ... **38** A1
Brentford TW8 ... **124** E6
Chislehurst BR7 ... **175** E5
Harrow HA2 ... **85** G3
Northwood HA6 ... **66** A2
Windsor Ct, N14 ... **42** C7
Sunbury-on-Thames
TW16 *off Windsor Rd* . **160** A6
Windsor Cres, Har. HA2 ... **85** G4
Wembley HA9 ... **88** B3
Windsor Dr, Barn. EN4 ... **41** J6
Windsor Gdns, W9 ... **108** D5
Croydon CR0
off Richmond Rd . **200/201** E3
Hayes UB3 ... **121** G3
Windsor Gro, SE27 ... **169** J4
Windsor Ms, SE6 ... **172** C1
SE23 ... **171** H1
Windsor Pk Rd, Hayes
UB3 ... **121** J7
Windsor Pl, SW1 ... **25** G6
Windsor Rd, E4
off Chivers Rd ... **62** B4
E7 ... **97** H5
E10 ... **96** B2
E11 ... **97** G1
N3 ... **72** B2
N7 ... **93** E3
N13 ... **59** G3
N17 ... **76** D2
NW2 ... **89** H6
W5 ... **105** H7
Barnet EN5 ... **40** B6
Bexleyheath DA6 ... **158** E4
Dagenham RM8 ... **101** E3
Harrow HA3 ... **68** A1
Hounslow TW4 ... **142** B2
Ilford IG1 ... **99** F4
Kingston upon Thames
KT2 ... **163** H7
Richmond TW9 ... **145** J2
Southall UB2 ... **123** F3
Sunbury-on-Thames
TW16 ... **160** A6
Teddington TW11 ... **162** A5
Thornton Heath CR7 ... **187** H2
Worcester Park KT4 ... **197** G2
Windsors, The, Buck.H.
IG9 ... **64** B2
Windsor St, N1 ... **111** H1
Windsor Ter, N1 ... **12** A3
Windsor Wk, SE5 ... **152** A2
Windsor Way, W14 ... **128** A4
Windsor Wf, E9 ... **95** J5
Windspoint Dr, SE15
off Ethnard Rd ... **132/133** E6
Windus Rd, N16 ... **94** C1
Windus Wk, N16 ... **94** C1
Windy Ridge, Brom. BR1 . **192** B1
Windyridge Cl, SW19 ... **166** A5
Wine Cl, E1 ... **113** F7
Wine Office Ct, EC4 ... **19** F3
Winery La, Kings.T. KT1 .. **181** J3
Winey Cl, Chess. KT9
off Nigel Fisher Way . **195** F7
Winford Ho, E3 ... **95** J7
Winford Par, Sthl. UB1
off Telford Rd ... **103** H6
Winforton St, SE10 ... **154** C1
Winfrith Rd, SW18 ... **149** F7
Wingate Cres, Croy. CR0 . **186** D6
Wingate Rd, W6 ... **127** H3
Ilford IG1 ... **99** E5
Sidcup DA14 ... **176** C5
Wingate Trd Est, N17 ... **60** D7
Wingfield Ct, E14
off Newport Av ... **114** D7
Wingfield Ms, SE15
off Wingfield St ... **152** D3
Wingfield Rd, E15 ... **96** E5
E17 ... **78** B5
Wingfield Rd, Kings.T
KT2 ... **164** A6
Wingfield St, SE15 ... **152** D3
Wingfield Way, Ruis.
HA4 ... **84** B6
Wingford Rd, SW2 ... **150** E6
Wingmore Rd, SE24 ... **151** J3
Wingrave Rd, W6 ... **127** J6
Wingrove Rd, SE6 ... **173** E2
Wings Cl, Sutt. SM1 ... **198** D4
Winifred Cl, Barn. EN5 ... **39** F6
Winifred Gro, SW11 ... **149** J4
Winifred Pl, N12
off High Rd ... **57** F5
Winifred Rd, SW19 ... **184** D1
Dagenham RM8 ... **101** E2
Hampton (Hmptn H.)
TW12 ... **161** G4
Winifred St, E16 ... **136** C1
Winifred Ter, E13
off Victoria Rd ... **115** G2
Enfield EN1
off Great Cambridge Rd . **44** C7
Winkfield Rd, E13 ... **115** H2
N22 ... **75** G1
Winkley St, E2 ... **112** E2
Winlaton Rd, Brom. BR1 . **172** D4
Winmill Rd, Dag. RM8 ... **101** F3
Winn Common Rd, SE18 . **137** H6
Winnett St, W1 ... **17** H5
Winningales Ct, Ilf. IG5
off Vienna Cl ... **80** B3
Winnings Wk, Nthlt. UB5
off Arnold Rd ... **84/85** E6
Winnington Cl, N2 ... **73** G6
Winnington Rd, N2 ... **73** G7
Winnipeg Dr, Orp. BR6 .. **207** J6
Winnock Rd, West Dr.
UB7 ... **120** A1
Winn Rd, SE12 ... **173** G1
Winns Av, E17 ... **77** H3
Winns Ms, N15
off Grove Pk Rd ... **76** B4
Winns Ter, E17 ... **78** A2
Winsbeach, E17 ... **78** D3
Winscombe Cres, W5 ... **105** G4
Winscombe St, N19 ... **92** B2
Winscombe Way, Stan.
HA7 ... **52** D5
Winsford Rd, SE6 ... **171** J3
Winsford Ter, N18 ... **60** A5
Winsham Gro, SW11 ... **150** A5
Winslade Rd, SW2 ... **151** E5
Winslade Way, SE6
off Rushey Grn ... **154** B7
Winsland Ms, W2 ... **15** E3
Winsland St, W2 ... **15** E3
Winsley St, W1 ... **17** F3
Winslow, SE17 ... **36** D4
Winslow Cl, NW10
off Neasden La N ... **88/89** E3
Pinner HA5 ... **66** B6
Winslow Gro, E4 ... **62** E2
Winslow Rd, W6 ... **127** J6
Winslow Way, Felt. TW13 . **160** D3
Winsor Ter, E6 ... **116** D5
Winstanley Est, SW11 ... **149** G3
Winstanley Rd, SW11 ... **149** G3
Winstead Gdns, Dag.
RM10 ... **101** J5
Winston Av, NW9 ... **70** E7
Winston Cl, Har. HA3 ... **52** C6
Romford RM7 ... **83** H4
Winston Ct, Har. HA3 ... **51** H7
Winston Rd, N16 ... **94** A4
Winston Wk, W4
off Beaconsfield Rd ... **126** D4
Winston Way, Ilf. IG1 ... **99** E3
Winstre Rd, Borwd. WD6 .. **38** A1
Winter Av, E6 ... **116** B1
Winterborne Av, Orp. BR6 . **207** G3
Winterbourne Rd, SE6 ... **171** J1
Dagenham RM8 ... **100** C2
Thornton Heath CR7 ... **187** G3
Winter Box Wk, Rich.
TW10 ... **145** J4
Winterbrook Rd, SE24 ... **151** J6
Winterburn Cl, N11 ... **58** A6
Winterfold Cl, SW19 ... **166** B2
Wintergreen Cl, E6
off Yarrow Cres ... **116** B5
Winters Rd, T.Ditt. KT7 ... **180** E7
Winterstoke Gdns, NW7 ... **55** G5
Winterstoke Rd, SE6 ... **171** J1
Winterton Ho, E1 ... **113** E6
Winterton Pl, SW10 ... **30** D5
Winterwell Rd, SW2 ... **151** E5
Winthorpe Rd, SW15 ... **148** B4
Winthrop St, E1 ... **112** E5
Winthrop Wk, Wem. HA9
off Everard Way ... **87** H3
Winton Av, N11 ... **58** C7
Winton Cl, N9 ... **45** G7
Winton Gdns, Edg. HA8 ... **53** J7
Winton Rd, Orp. BR6 ... **206** E4
Winton Way, SW16 ... **169** G5
Wirrall Ho, SE26
off Sydenham Hill ... **170** D3
Wisbeach Rd, Croy. CR0 . **188** A5
Wisdons Cl, Dag. RM10 .. **101** H1
Wise La, NW7 ... **55** H6
West Drayton UB7 ... **120** A4
Wiseman Ct, SE19 ... **170** B5
Wiseman Rd, E10 ... **96** A2
Wise Rd, E15 ... **114** D1
Wiseton Rd, SW17 ... **167** H1
Wishart Rd, SE3 ... **156** A1
Wisley Rd, SW11 ... **150** A5
Orpington BR5 ... **176** A7
Wisteria Cl, NW7 ... **55** F6
Ilford IG1 ... **98** E5
Orpington BR6 ... **207** E2
Wisteria Rd, SE13 ... **154** D4
Witan St, E2 ... **113** E3
Witham Cl, Loug. IG10 ... **48** B6
Witham Rd, SE20 ... **189** F3
W13 ... **124** D1
Dagenham RM10 ... **101** G5
Isleworth TW7 ... **144** A1
Witherby Cl, Croy. CR0 .. **202** B5
Witherington Rd, N5 ... **93** G5
Withers Cl, Chess. KT9
off Coppard Gdns ... **195** F6
Withers Mead, NW9 ... **71** F1
Witherston Way, SE9 ... **174** D2
Withycombe Rd, SW19 .. **148** A7
Withy Mead, E4 ... **62** D3
Witley Cres, Croy.
(New Adgtn) CR0 ... **204** C6
Witley Gdns, Sthl. UB2 .. **123** F4
Witley Pt, SW15
off Wanborough Dr ... **165** H1
Witley Rd, N19
off Holloway Rd ... **92** C2
Witney Cl, Pnr. HA5 ... **51** F6
Witney Path, SE23 ... **171** G3
Wittenham Way, E4 ... **62** D3
Wittering Cl, Kings.T. KT2 . **163** G5
Wittersham Rd, Brom.
BR1 ... **173** F5
Wivenhoe Cl, SE15 ... **152** E3
Wivenhoe Ct, Houns.
TW3 ... **143** F4
Wivenhoe Rd, Bark. IG11 . **118** A2
Wiverton Rd, SE26 ... **171** F6
Wixom Ho, SE3
off Romero Sq ... **155** J4
Wix Rd, Dag. RM9 ... **110** D1
Wixs La, SW4 ... **150** B4
Woburn Cl, SE28
off Summerton Way .. **118** D6
SW19 *off Tintern Cl* ... **167** F6
Woburn Ct, SE16
off Masters Dr ... **132/133** E5
Woburn Pl, WC1 ... **9** J5
Woburn Rd, Cars. SM5 .. **199** H1
Croydon CR0 ... **201** J1
Woburn Sq, WC1 ... **9** J6
Woburn Wk, WC1 ... **9** J4
Wodehouse Av, SE5 ... **152** C1
Woffington Cl, Kings.T.
KT1 ... **181** F1
Woking Cl, SW15 ... **147** F4
Woldham Pl, Brom. BR2 . **191** J4
Woldham Rd, Brom.
BR2 ... **191** J4
Wolds Dr, Orp. BR6 ... **206** D4
Wolfe Cl, Brom. BR2 ... **191** G6
Hayes UB4
off Ayles Rd ... **102** B3
Wolfe Cres, SE7 ... **136** A5
SE16 ... **133** G2
Wolferton Rd, E12 ... **98** C4
Wolffe Gdns, E15 ... **97** F6
Wolffram Cl, SE13 ... **154** E5
Wolfington Rd, SE27 ... **169** H4
Wolftencroft Cl, SW11 ... **149** G3
Wollaston Cl, SE1 ... **35** J1
Wolmer Cl, Edg. HA8 ... **54** B4
Wolmer Gdns, Edg. HA8 .. **54** A3
Wolseley Av, SW19 ... **166** D2
Wolseley Gdns, W4 ... **126** B6
Wolseley Rd, E7 ... **97** H7
N8 ... **74** D6
N22 ... **75** F1
W4 ... **126** C4
Harrow HA3 ... **68** B3
Mitcham CR4 ... **186** A7

Wolseley St, SE1 29 G4
Wolsey Av, E6 116 D3
E17 77 J3
Thames Ditton KT7 180 C5
Wolsey Cl, SW20 165 H7
Hounslow TW3 143 J4
Kingston upon Thames KT2 182 B1
Southall UB2 123 J3
Worcester Park KT4 197 G4
Wolsey Cres, Mord. SM4 184 B7
Wolsey Dr, Kings.T. KT2 163 H5
Wolsey Gdns, Ilf. IG6 65 F6
Wolsey Gro, Edg. HA8 54 D7
Wolsey Ms, NW5 92 C6
Orpington BR6 *off Osgood Av* 207 J5
Wolsey Rd, N1 94 A5
East Molesey KT8 180 A4
Enfield EN1 45 E2
Hampton (Hmptn H.) TW12 161 H6
Wolsey St, E1 *off Sidney St* 113 F5
Wolsey Way, Chess. KT9 196 A5
Wolstonbury, N12 56 D5
Wolvercote Rd, SE2 138 D2
Wolverley St, E2 *off Bethnal Grn Rd* 112/113 E3
Wolverton, SE17 36 C3
Wolverton Av, Kings.T. KT2 182 A1
Wolverton Gdns, W5 105 J7
W6 128 A4
Wolverton Rd, Stan. HA7 53 E6
Wolverton Way, N14 42 C5
Wolves La, N13 59 G7
N22 59 G7
Womersley Rd, N8 75 F6
Wonford Cl, Kings.T. KT2 183 E1
Wontner Cl, N1 *off Greenman St* 93 J7
Wontner Rd, SW17 167 J2
Woodall Cl, E14 *off Lawless St* 114 B7
Chessington KT9 195 G6
Woodall Rd, Enf. EN3 45 G6
Woodbank Rd, Brom. BR1 173 F3
Woodbastwick Rd, SE26 171 G5
Woodberry Av, N21 59 G2
Harrow HA2 67 H4
Woodberry Cl, NW7 56 A7
Sunbury-on-Thames TW16 *off Ashridge Way* 160 A6
Woodberry Cres, N10 74 B3
Woodberry Down, N4 75 J7
Woodberry Down Est, N4 75 J7
Woodberry Gdns, N12 57 F6
Woodberry Gro, N4 75 J7
N12 57 F6
Woodberry Way, E4 62 C1
N12 57 F6
Woodbine Cl, Twick. TW2 162 A2
Woodbine Gro, SE20 171 E7
Woodbine La, Wor.Pk. KT4 197 J3
Woodbine Pl, E11 79 G6
Woodbine Rd, Sid. DA15 175 H1
Woodbines Av, Kings.T. KT1 181 G3
Woodbine Ter, E9 *off Morning La* 95 F6
Woodborough Rd, SW15 147 H4
Woodbourne Av, SW16 168 D3
Woodbourne Cl, SW16 *off Woodbourne Av* 168/169 E3
Woodbourne Dr, Esher (Clay.) KT10 194 C6
Woodbourne Gdns, Wall. SM6 200 B7
Woodbridge Cl, N7 93 F2
NW2 89 G3
Woodbridge Ct, Wdf.Grn. IG8 64 B7
Woodbridge Rd, Bark. IG11 99 J5
Woodbridge St, EC1 11 G5
Woodbrook Rd, SE2 138 A6
Woodburn Cl, NW4 72 A5
Woodbury Cl, E11 79 H4
Croydon CR0 202 C2
Woodbury Hill, Loug. IG10 48 B3
Woodbury Hollow, Loug. IG10 48 B2
Woodbury Pk Rd, W13 104 E4
Woodbury Rd, E17 78 B4
Woodbury St, SW17 167 H5
Woodchester Sq, W2 14 A1
Woodchurch Cl, Sid. DA14 175 G3
Woodchurch Dr, Brom. BR1 174 A7
Woodchurch Rd, NW6 90 D7
Wood Cl, E2 13 H5
NW9 70 D7
Harrow HA1 68 A7
Woodclyffe Dr, Chis. BR7 192 D2
Woodcock Ct, Har. HA3 69 H7
Woodcock Dell Av, Har. HA3 69 G7
Woodcock Hill, Har. HA3 69 G7
Woodcocks, E16 115 J5
Woodcombe Cres, SE23 171 F1
Woodcote Av, NW7 55 J6
Thornton Heath CR7 187 H4
Wallington SM6 200 B7
Woodcote Cl, Enf. EN3 45 F6
Kingston upon Thames KT2 163 J5
Woodcote Dr, Orp. BR6 207 G1
Woodcote Ms, Loug. IG10 48 A7
Wallington SM6 200 B6
Woodcote Pl, SE27 169 H5
Woodcote Rd, E11 79 G7
Wallington SM6 200 B6
Woodcott Ho, SW15 *off Ellisfield Dr* 147 G7
Woodcroft, N21 59 F1
SE9 174 C3
Greenford UB6 86 D6
Woodcroft Av, NW7 55 E7
Stanmore HA7 68 C1
Woodcroft Ms, SE8 *off Croft St* 133 H4
Woodcroft Rd, Th.Hth. CR7 187 H5
Wood Dr, Chis. BR7 174 B6
Woodedge Cl, E4 63 F1
Woodend, SE19 169 J6
Sutton SM1 199 F2
Wood End Av, Har. HA2 85 H4
Wood End Cl, Nthlt. UB5 86 A5
Woodend Gdns, Enf. EN2 42 E4
Wood End Gdns, Nthlt. UB5 85 J5
Wood End La, Nthlt. UB5 85 H6
Woodend Rd, E17 78 C2
Wood End Rd, Har. HA1 86 A4
Wood End Way, Nthlt. UB5 85 J5
Wooder Gdns, E7 97 F4
Wooderson Cl, SE25 188 B4
Woodfall Av, Barn. EN5 40 C5
Woodfall Rd, N4 93 G1
Woodfall St, SW3 31 J4
Woodfarrs, SE5 152 A4
Woodfield Av, NW9 71 E4
SW16 168 D3
W5 105 F4
Carshalton SM5 200 A6
Wembley HA0 87 F3
Woodfield Cl, SE19 169 J7
Enfield EN1 44 B4
Woodfield Cres, W5 105 F4
Woodfield Dr, Barn. EN4 58 A1
Woodfield Gdns, W9 *off Woodfield Rd* 108 C5
New Malden KT3 183 F5
Woodfield Gro, SW16 168 D3
Woodfield La, SW16 168 D3
Woodfield Pl, W9 108 C4
Woodfield Rd, W5 105 F4
W9 108 C5
Hounslow TW4 142 B2
Thames Ditton KT7 194 C2
Woodfield Way, N11 58 D7
WOODFORD, Wdf.Grn. IG8 63 H6
Woodford Av, Ilf. IG2, IG4 80 C5
Woodford Green IG8 80 A3
WOODFORD BRIDGE, Wdf.Grn. IG8 64 C7
Woodford Br Rd, Ilf. IG4 80 A3
Woodford Ct, W12 *off Shepherds Bush Grn* 128 A2
Woodford Cres, Pnr. HA5 66 B2
WOODFORD GREEN, IG8 63 F4
Woodford New Rd, E17 78 E4
E18 79 E1
Woodford Green IG8 79 E1
Woodford Pl, Wem. HA9 87 H1
Woodford Rd, E7 97 H4
E18 79 G4
WOODFORD WELLS, Wdf.Grn. IG8 63 H4
Woodgate Av, Chess. KT9 195 G5
Woodgate Cres, Nthwd. HA6 50 A6
Woodgate Dr, SW16 168 D7
Woodger Rd, W12 *off Goldhawk Rd* 127 J2
Woodget Cl, E6 *off Remington Rd* 116 B6
Woodgrange Av, N12 57 G6
W5 126 A1
Enfield EN1 44 D6
Harrow HA3 69 F5
Woodgrange Cl, Har. HA3 69 G5
Woodgrange Gdns, Enf. EN1 44 D6
Woodgrange Rd, E7 97 H4
Woodgrange Ter, Enf. EN1 *off Great Cambridge Rd* 44 D6
WOOD GREEN, N22 74 E1
Wood Grn Shop City, N22 75 G2
Woodhall Av, SE21 170 C3
Pinner HA5 66 E2
Woodhall Dr, SE21 170 C3
Pinner HA5 66 D1
Woodhall Gate, Pnr. HA5 50 D7
Woodhall Ho, SW18 *off Fitzhugh Gro* 149 G6
Woodhall La, Wat. WD19 50 D4
Woodhall Rd, Pnr. HA5 50 D7
Woodham Ct, E18 79 F4
Woodham Rd, SE6 172 C3
Woodhatch Cl, E6 *off Remington Rd* 116 B6
Woodhaven Gdns, Ilf. IG6 *off Brandville Gdns* 81 F3
Woodhayes Rd, SW19 165 J7
Woodhead Dr, Orp. BR6 *off Sherlies Av* 207 H2
Woodheyes Rd, NW10 88 D5
Woodhill, SE18 136 B4
Woodhill Cres, Har. HA3 69 G6
Wood Ho, SW17 *off Laurel Cl* 167 H5
Woodhouse Av, Grnf. UB6 104 C2
Woodhouse Cl, Grnf. UB6 104 C2
Hayes UB3 121 H3
Woodhouse Eaves, Nthwd. HA6 50 A5
Woodhouse Gro, E12 98 B6
Woodhouse Rd, E11 97 F3
N12 57 G6
Woodhurst Av, Orp. BR5 193 F6
Woodhurst Rd, SE2 138 A5
W3 106 C7
Woodington Cl, SE9 156 D6
Woodknoll Dr, Chis. BR7 192 C1
Woodland App, Grnf. UB6 86 D6
Woodland Cl, NW9 70 C6
SE19 *off Woodland Hill* 170 B6
Epsom KT19 197 E6
Woodford Green IG8 63 H3
Woodland Cres, SE10 134 E6
SE16 133 G2
Woodland Gdns, N10 74 B5
Isleworth TW7 144 B2
Woodland Gro, SE10 134 E5
Woodland Hill, SE19 170 B6
Woodland Ms, SW16 168 E2
Woodland Ri, N10 74 B4
Greenford UB6 86 D6
Woodland Rd, E4 62 C1
N11 58 B5
SE19 170 B5
Loughton IG10 48 B3
Thornton Heath CR7 187 G4
WOODLANDS, Islw. TW7 144 B2
Woodlands, NW11 72 B6
SW20 183 J4
Harrow HA2 67 G4
Woodlands, The, N14 58 B1
SE13 154 D7
SE19 169 J7
Beckenham BR3 190 C1
Isleworth TW7 144 C2
Woodlands Av, E11 97 H1
N3 57 F7
W3 126 B1
New Malden KT3 182 C1
Romford RM6 82 E6
Ruislip HA4 84 C1
Sidcup DA15 175 H1
Worcester Park KT4 197 F2
Woodlands Cl, NW11 72 B5
Borehamwood WD6 38 B4
Bromley BR1 192 C2
Esher (Clay.) KT10 194 C7
Woodlands Dr, Stan. HA7 52 C6
Sunbury-on-Thames TW16 178 C2
Woodlands Gro, Islw. TW7 144 B2
Woodlands Pk, Bex. DA5 177 J4
Woodlands Pk Rd, N15 75 H5
SE10 134 E6
Woodlands Rd, E11 96 E2
E17 78 C3
N9 61 F1
SW13 147 F3
Bexleyheath DA7 159 E3
Bromley BR1 192 B2
Enfield EN2 44 A1
Harrow HA1 68 C5
Ilford IG1 99 F3
Isleworth TW7 144 B2
Southall UB1 122 D1
Surbiton KT6 181 G7
Woodlands St, SE13 154 D7
Woodland St, E8 *off Dalston La* 94 C6
Woodlands Way, SW15 *off Oakhill Rd* 148 C5
Woodland Ter, SE7 136 B4
Woodland Wk, NW3 91 H5
SE10 *off Woodland Gro* 134/135 E5
Bromley BR1 172 E4
Epsom KT19 196 A6
Woodland Way, N21 59 G2
NW7 55 E6
SE2 138 D4
Croydon CR0 203 H1
Mitcham CR4 168 A7
Morden SM4 184 C4
Orpington BR5 193 F4
Surbiton KT5 196 B2
West Wickham BR4 204 B4
Woodford Green IG8 63 H3
Wood La, N6 74 B6
NW9 70 E7
W12 107 J6
Dagenham RM8, RM9, RM10 100 C4
Isleworth TW7 124 C7
Stanmore HA7 52 D3
Woodford Green IG8 63 F5
Woodlawn Cl, SW15 148 C5
Woodlawn Cres, Twick. TW2 161 H2
Woodlawn Dr, Felt. TW13 160 D2
Woodlawn Rd, SW6 128 A7
Woodlea Dr, Brom. BR2 191 E5
Woodlea Rd, N16 94 B3
Woodleigh, E18 *off Churchfields* 79 G1
Woodleigh Av, N12 57 H6
Woodleigh Gdns, SW16 169 E3
Woodley Cl, SW17 *off Arnold Rd* 167 J7
Woodley La, Cars. SM5 199 G3
Wood Lo Gdns, Brom. BR1 174 B7
Wood Lo La, W.Wick. BR4 204 C3
Woodman La, E4 46 E5
Woodman Path, Ilf. IG6 65 H6
Woodmans Gro, NW10 89 F5
Woodmans Ms, W12 107 H5
Woodmansterne Rd, SW16 186 D1
Woodman St, E16 136 D1
Woodmere, SE9 174 C1
Woodmere Av, Croy. CR0 189 G7
Woodmere Cl, SW11 *off Lavender Hill* 150 A3
Croydon CR0 189 G7
Woodmere Gdns, Croy. CR0 189 G7
Woodmere Way, Beck. BR3 190 D5
Woodnook Rd, SW16 168 B5
Woodpecker Cl, N9 44 E6
Bushey WD23 51 J1
Harrow HA3 68 C1
Woodpecker Ms, SE13 *off Mercator Rd* 154 D4
Woodpecker Rd, SE14 133 H6
SE28 118 C7
Wood Pt, E16 *off Fife Rd* 115 G5
Woodquest Av, SE24 151 J5
Wood Retreat, SE18 137 G7
Wood Ride, Barn. EN4 41 G1
Orpington BR5 193 G4
Woodridge Cl, Enf. EN2 43 G1
Woodridings Av, Pnr. HA5 67 F1
Woodridings Cl, Pnr. HA5 51 E7
Woodriffe Rd, E11 78 D7

Wood Ri, Pnr. HA5 . . . . **66** A5
Wood Rd, NW10. . . . . **88** C7
Woodrow, SE18 . . . . **136** C4
Woodrow Cl, Grnf. UB6 . . . **87** E7
Woodrow Ct, N17
off Heybourne Rd . . **60/61** E7
Woodrush Cl, SE14
off Southerngate Way . **133** H7
Woodrush Way, Rom.
RM6. . . . . **82** D4
Woods, The, Nthwd. HA6. . **50** A5
Wood's Bldgs, E1
off Whitechapel Rd. **112/113** E5
Woodseer St, E1 . . . . **21** G1
Woodsford, SE17 . . . . **36** B4
Woodsford Sq, W14 . . . . . **128** B2
Woodshire Rd, Dag.
RM10. . . . . **101** H3
WOODSIDE, Croy. CR0. . . **188** D6
Woodside, NW11 . . . . **72** D5
SW19. . . . . **166** C6
Buckhurst Hill IG9. . . . . . **63** J2
Woodside Av, N6 . . . . **73** J5
N10 . . . . **73** J5
N12 . . . . **57** F4
SE25 . . . . **188** E6
Chislehurst BR7 . . . . . . **175** F5
Esher KT10 . . . . **180** B7
Wembley HA0 . . . . **105** H1
Woodside Cl, Stan. HA7 . . **52** E5
Surbiton KT5. . . . . **182** C7
Wembley HA0 . . . . **105** H1
Woodside Ct, N12
off Woodside Av **57** F4
Woodside Ct Rd, Croy.
CR0 . . . . **188** D7
Woodside Cres, Sid.
DA15 . . . . **175** H3
Woodside End, Wem.
HA0 . . . . **105** H1
Woodside Gdns, E4 . . . . . . **62** B5
N17 . . . . **76** B2
Woodside Gra Rd, N12 . . . **57** E4
Woodside Grn, SE25 . . . . **188** E6
Woodside Gro, N12 . . . . . . **57** F3
Woodside La, N12 . . . . **57** E3
Bexley DA5 . . . . **158** D6
Woodside Ms, SE22
off Heber Rd **152** C6
Woodside Pk, SE25 . . . . . **188** D5
Woodside Pk Av, E17 . . . . . **78** D4
Woodside Pk Rd, N12 . . . . **57** E4
Woodside Pl, Wem. HA0 . **105** H1
Woodside Rd, E13 . . . . . . **115** J4
N22 . . . . **59** F7
SE25 . . . . **188** E6
Bromley BR1 . . . . **192** B5
Kingston upon Thames
KT2 . . . . **163** H7
New Malden KT3 . . . . . **182** D2
Sidcup DA15 . . . . **175** H3
Sutton SM1 . . . . **199** F3
Woodford Green IG8 . . . **63** G4
Woodside Way, Croy. CR0. **189** E6
Mitcham CR4. . . . . **186** B1
Woods Ms, W1 . . . . **16** A5
Woodsome Rd, NW5 . . . . . **92** A3
Woods Pl, SE1 . . . . **28** E6
Woodspring Rd, SW19. . . **166** B2
Woods Rd, SE15. . . . . **152** E1
Woodstead Gro, Edg. HA8. **53** H6
Woodstock Av, NW11. . . . . **72** B7
W13. . . . . **124** D3
Isleworth TW7 . . . . **144** D5
Southall UB1 . . . . **103** F3
Sutton SM3. . . . . **184** C7
Woodstock Cl, Bex. DA5 . **177** F1
Stanmore HA7 . . . . **69** H2
Woodstock Ct, SE12 . . . . **155** G6
Woodstock Cres, N9 . . . . . **44** E6
Woodstock Gdns, Beck.
BR3 . . . . **190** B1
Ilford IG3 . . . . **100** A2
Woodstock Gro, W12 . . . . **128** A2
Woodstock La N, Surb.
KT6 . . . . **195** F2
Woodstock La S, Chess.
KT9 . . . . **195** F4
Esher (Clay.) KT10. . . . . **194** E5
Woodstock Ms, W1 . . . . . . **16** C2
Woodstock Ri, Sutt. SM3. **184** C7
Woodstock Rd, E7 . . . . **97** J7
E17 . . . . **78** D2
N4 . . . . **93** G1
NW11. . . . . **72** C7
W4. . . . . **127** E3
Carshalton SM5 . . . . . . **200** A5
Croydon CR0. . . . . **202** A3
Wembley HA0. . . . . **87** J7
Woodstock St, W1 . . . . **16** D4
Woodstock Ter, E14 . . . . . **114** B7
Woodstock Way, Mitch.
CR4 . . . . **186** B2
Woodstone Av, Epsom
KT17 . . . . **197** G5
Wood St, E17 . . . . **78** C3
EC2 . . . . **20** A4
W4. . . . . **126** E5
Barnet EN5 . . . . **39** J4
Kingston upon Thames
KT1 . . . . **181** G1
Mitcham CR4. . . . . **186** A7
Woodsyre, SE26. . . . . **170** C4
Woodthorpe Rd, SW15 . . **147** H4
Woodtree Cl, NW4
off Ashley La. **71** J2
Wood Vale, N10 . . . . **74** C5
SE23 . . . . **170** E1
Woodvale Av, SE25 . . . . . **188** C3
Wood Vale Est, SE23 . . . . **153** F6
Woodvale Wk, SE27
off Elder Rd. **169** J5
Woodvale Way, NW11
off The Vale **90** A3
Woodview Av, E4. . . . . **62** C4
Woodview Cl, N4. . . . . **75** H7
SW15. . . . . **164** D4
Orpington BR6
off Crofton Rd **207** F2
Woodville, SE3. . . . . **155** H1
Woodville Cl, SE12. . . . . . **155** G5
Teddington TW11. . . . . . **162** D4
Woodville Gdns, NW11 . . . **72** A7
W5. . . . . **105** H6
Ilford IG6. . . . . **80** E3
Woodville Gro, Well.
DA16 . . . . **158** A3
Woodville Rd, E11 . . . . **97** F1
E17 . . . . **77** H4
E18 . . . . **79** H2
N16 . . . . **94** B5
NW6 . . . . **108** C2
NW11. . . . . **72** A7
W5. . . . . **105** G6
Barnet EN5 . . . . **40** E3
Morden SM4. . . . . **184** D4
Richmond TW10 . . . . . . **163** E3
Thornton Heath CR7 . . . **187** J4
Woodville St, SE18
off Woodhill. **136** B4
Woodward Av, NW4 . . . . . **71** G5
Woodward Cl, Esher (Clay.)
KT10 . . . . **194** C6
Woodwarde Rd, SE22 . . . **152** B6
Woodward Gdns, Dag. RM9
off Woodward Rd **100** C7
Stanmore HA7 . . . . **52** C7
Woodward Rd, Dag. RM9 **100** B7
Wood Way, Orp. BR6 . . . . **206** D2
Woodway Cres, Har. HA1 . **68** D6
Woodwell St, SW18
off Huguenot Pl. **149** F5
Wood Wf, SE10. . . . . **134** B6
Woodyard Cl, NW5
off Gillies St **92** A5
Woodyard La, SE21 . . . . . **152** B7
Woodyates Rd, SE12 . . . . **155** G6
Woolacombe Rd, SE3 . . . **155** J1
Woolacombe Way, Hayes
UB3. . . . . **121** H4
Wooler St, SE17. . . . . **36** B4
Woolf Cl, SE28 . . . . **138** B1
Woolf Ms, WC1 . . . . **9** J5
Woollaston Rd, N4. . . . . . . **75** H6
Woolmead Av, NW9. . . . . . **71** G7
Woolmer Gdns, N18 . . . . . **60** D5
Woolmer Rd, N18. . . . . **60** D5
Woolmore St, E14 . . . . . . **114** C7
Woolneigh St, SW6 . . . . . **148** E3
Wool Rd, SW20 . . . . **165** H6
Woolstaplers Way, SE16 . . **29** H6
Woolston Cl, E17
off Riverhead Cl **77** G2
Woolstone Rd, SE23 . . . . **171** H2
WOOLWICH, SE18 . . . . . . **136** D5
Woolwich Ch St, SE18. . . **136** B3
★**Woolwich Common**,
SE18 . . . . **136** C7
Woolwich Common,
SE18 . . . . **136** D6
Woolwich Ferry Pier, E16. **136** D2
Woolwich Foot Tunnel,
E16 . . . . **136** D2
SE18 . . . . **136** D2
Woolwich Garrison, SE18 . **136** C6
Woolwich High St, SE18 . **136** D3
Woolwich Ind Est, SE28
off Hadden Rd. **137** H3
Woolwich Manor Way, E6. **116** C4
E16. . . . . **117** E7
Woolwich Mkt, SE18 . . . . **136** E4
Woolwich New Rd, SE18. **136** D5
Woolwich Rd, SE2 . . . . . . **138** D6
SE7 . . . . **135** G5
SE10 . . . . **135** F5
Belvedere DA17 . . . . . . **138** D6
Bexleyheath DA7 . . . . . **159** G4
Woolwich Trade Pk, SE28
off Pettman Cres **137** G3
Wooster Gdns, E14. . . . . . **114** D6
Wooster Ms, Har. HA2
off Fairfield Dr. **67** J3
Wooster Pl, SE1 . . . . **36** C1
Wootton Gro, N3 . . . . **72** D1
Wootton St, SE1 . . . . **27** F3
Worbeck Rd, SE20 . . . . . **189** E2
Worcester Av, N17 . . . . **60** D7
Worcester Cl, NW2
off Newfield Ri **89** H3
Croydon CR0. . . . . **203** J2
Mitcham CR4. . . . . **186** A2
Worcester Cres, NW7. . . . . **54** E3
Woodford Green IG8 . . . **63** H5
Worcester Dr, W4. . . . . . . **127** E2
Worcester Gdns, SW11
off Grandison Rd **149** J5
Greenford UB6 . . . . **85** J6
Ilford IG1 . . . . **80** B7
Worcester Park KT4. . . . **197** E3
Worcester Ms, NW6
off Lymington Rd. . . **90/91** E6
WORCESTER PARK, KT4 . **197** F2
Worcester Pk Rd, Wor.Pk.
KT4 . . . . **196** C3
Worcester Rd, E12 . . . . **98** C4
E17 . . . . **77** G2
SW19. . . . . **166** C5
Sutton SM2. . . . . **199** E6
Wordsworth Av, E12 . . . . . **98** B6
E18 . . . . **79** F3
Greenford UB6 . . . . **104** A2
Wordsworth Dr, Sutt.
SM3. . . . . **197** J4
Wordsworth Rd, N16 . . . . . **94** B4
SE1 . . . . **37** F2
SE20 . . . . **171** G7
Hampton TW12 . . . . **161** F4
Wallington SM6 . . . . . . **200** C6
Welling DA16 . . . . **157** H1
Wordsworth Wk, NW11 . . . **72** D4
Wordsworth Way, West Dr.
UB7. . . . . **120** B4
Worfield St, SW11 . . . . . . **129** H7
Worgan St, SE11 . . . . **34** C3
SE16 . . . . **133** G3
Worland Rd, E15 . . . . **97** E7
WORLD'S END, Enf. EN2 . . **43** G3
World's End Est, SW10 . . . **30** E7
Worlds End La, N21 . . . . . . **43** F5
Enfield EN2 . . . . **43** F5
Orpington BR6 . . . . **207** J6
World's End Pas, SW10 . . . **30** E7
World's End Pl, SW10
off King's Rd **129** F7
Worlidge St, W6 . . . . **127** J5
Worlingham Rd, SE22 . . . **152** C4
Wormholt Rd, W12. . . . . . **107** G7
Wormwood St, EC2 . . . . . . **20** D3
Wornington Rd, W10 . . . . **108** B5
Woronzow Rd, NW8. . . . . **109** G1
Worple Av, SW19 . . . . **166** A7
Isleworth TW7 . . . . **144** D5
Worple Cl, Har. HA2. . . . . . **85** F1
Worple Rd, SW19. . . . . . . **166** B7
SW20. . . . . **183** J2
Isleworth TW7 . . . . **144** D4
Worple Rd Ms, SW19. . . . **166** C6
Worple St, SW14 . . . . **146** D3
Worple Way, Har. HA2 . . . . **85** F1
Richmond TW10 . . . . . . **145** H5
Worship St, EC2. . . . . **12** C6
Worslade Rd, SW17. . . . . . **167** G4
Worsley Br Rd, SE26 . . . . **171** J4
Beckenham BR3 . . . . . . **171** J5
Worsley Gra, Chis. BR7
off Kemnal Rd. **175** F6
Worsley Gro, E5. . . . . **94** D4
Worsley Rd, E11 . . . . **96** E4
Worsopp Dr, SW4 . . . . . . **150** C5
Worth Cl, Orp. BR6 . . . . . **207** H4
Worthfield Cl, Epsom
KT19 . . . . **196** D7
Worth Gro, SE17 . . . . **36** B4
Worthing Cl, E15
off Mitre Rd **114/115** E2
Worthing Rd, Houns.
TW5 . . . . **123** F6
Worthington Cl, Mitch.
CR4 . . . . **186** B3
Worthington Rd, Surb.
KT6 . . . . **195** J1
Worthy Down Ct, SE18
off Prince Imperial Rd. **156** D1
Wortley Rd, E6. . . . . **98** A7
Croydon CR0. . . . . **187** G7
Worton Gdns, Islw. TW7 . **144** A2
Worton Hall Ind Est, Islw
TW7 . . . . **144** B4
Worton Rd, Islw. TW7. . . . **144** B3
Worton Way, Houns. TW3 . **144** A2
Isleworth TW7 . . . . **143** J1
Wotton Rd, NW2 . . . . **89** J4
SE8 . . . . **133** J6
Wouldham Rd, E16. . . . . . **115** F6
Wragby Rd, E11 . . . . **97** E3
Wrampling Pl, N9. . . . . **60** D1
Wrangthorn Wk, Croy. CR0
off Epsom Rd **201** G4
Wray Av, Ilf. IG5 . . . . **80** D3
Wray Cres, N4 . . . . **93** E2
Wrayfield Rd, Sutt. SM3. . **198** A3
Wraysbury Cl, Houns.
TW4 . . . . **142** E5
Wrekin Rd, SE18 . . . . **137** F7
Wren Av, NW2 . . . . **89** J5
Southall UB2. . . . . **123** F4
Wren Cl, E16
off Ibbotson Av **115** F6
N9 *off Chaffinch Cl* **61** G1
Wren Cres, Bushey WD23 . **51** J1
Wren Dr, West Dr. UB7. . . **120** A3
Wren Gdns, Dag. RM9 . . . **100** D5
Wren Landing, E14
off Cabot Sq **134** A1
Wren Ms, SE13
off Lee High Rd . . **154/155** E4
Wren Path, SE28 . . . . **137** G3
Wren Rd, SE5. . . . . **152** A1
Dagenham RM9 . . . . . . **100** D5
Sidcup DA14 . . . . **176** C4
Wren St, WC1. . . . . **10** D5
Wren Ter, Ilf. IG5
off Tiptree Cres **80** D3
Wrentham Av, NW10 . . . . **108** A2
Wrenthorpe Rd, Brom.
BR1. . . . . **172** E4
Wrenwood Way, Pnr. HA5 . **66** B4
Wrestlers Ct, EC3
off Camomile St **112** B6
Wrexham Rd, E3. . . . . **114** A2
Wricklemarsh Rd, SE3 . . . **155** H1
Wrigglesworth St, SE14. . **133** G7
Wright Rd, N1
off Burder Cl **94** B6
Hounslow TW5 . . . . **122** C7
Wrights All, SW19 . . . . . . **165** J6
Wrights Cl, SE13
off Wisteria Rd **154** D4
Dagenham RM10. . . . . . **101** H3
Wrights Grn, SW4
off Nelson's Row. **150** D4
Wrights La, W8. . . . . **22** A5
Wrights Pl, NW10
off Mitchell Way **88** C6
Wrights Rd, E3 . . . . **113** J2
SE25 . . . . **188** B3
Wrights Row, Wall. SM6 . **200** B4
Wrights Wk, SW14 . . . . . . **146** D3
Wrigley Cl, E4. . . . . **62** D5
Wrotham Rd, NW1
off Agar Pl. **92** C7
W13
off Mattock La . . . **124/125** E1
Barnet EN5 . . . . **40** B2
Welling DA16 . . . . **158** C1
Wroths Path, Loug. IG10 . . **48** C1
Wrottesley Rd, NW10. . . . **107** G2
SE18 . . . . **137** F6
Wroughton Rd, SW11 . . . **149** J6
Wroughton Ter, NW4 . . . . . **71** J4
Wroxall Rd, Dag. RM9 . . . **100** C6
Wroxham Gdns, N11 . . . . . **58** C7
Wroxham Rd, SE28 . . . . . **118** D7
Wroxham Way, Ilf. IG6 . . . . **80** E1
Wroxton Rd, SE15 . . . . . . **153** E2
WRYTHE, THE, Cars. SM5 . **199** H2
Wrythe Grn, Cars. SM5
off Wrythe Grn Rd. . . . **199** J3
Wrythe Grn Rd, Cars.
SM5. . . . . **199** J3
Wrythe La, Cars. SM5 . . . **199** F1
Wulfstan St, W12 . . . . **107** F6
Wyatt Cl, SE16 . . . . **133** J2
Feltham TW13 . . . . **160** C1
Hayes UB4. . . . . **102** A5
Wyatt Dr, SW13 . . . . **127** J7

Wyatt Pk Rd, SW2 ... **169** E2
Wyatt Rd, E7 ... **97** G6
N5 ... **93** J3
Wyatts La, E17 ... **78** C3
Wybert St, NW1 ... **9** E5
Wyborne Way, NW10 ... **88** C7
Wyburn Av, Barn. EN5 ... **40** C3
Wyche Gro, S.Croy. CR2 . **201** J7
Wych Elm Dr, Brom. BR1
off London La ... **173** F7
Wych Elm Pas, Kings.T.
KT2 ... **163** J7
Wycherley Cl, SE3 ... **135** F7
Wycherley Cres, Barn. EN5 . **40** E6
Wychwood Av, Edg. HA8 .. **53** G6
Thornton Heath CR7 ... **187** J3
Wychwood Cl, Edg. HA8 .. **53** G6
Sunbury-on-Thames
TW16 ... **160** A6
Wychwood End, N6 ... **74** C7
Wychwood Gdns, Ilf. IG5 .. **80** C4
Wychwood Way, SE19
off Roman Ri ... **170** A6
Wycliffe Cl, Well. DA16 ... **157** J1
Wycliffe Rd, SW11 ... **150** A2
SW19 ... **167** E6
Wyclif St, EC1 ... **11** G4
Wycombe Gdns, NW11 ... **90** D2
Wycombe Pl, SW18 ... **149** F6
Wycombe Rd, N17 ... **76** D1
Ilford IG2 ... **80** C5
Wembley HA0 ... **106** A1
Wycombe Sq, W8
off Aubrey Wk ... **128** D1
Wydehurst Rd, Croy. CR0 . **188** D7
Wydell Cl, Mord. SM4 ... **183** J6
Wydeville Manor Rd,
SE12 ... **173** H4
Wye Cl, Orp. BR6 ... **193** J7
Wyemead Cres, E4 ... **62** E2
Wye St, SW11 ... **149** G2
Wyevale Cl, Pnr. HA5 ... **66** A3
Wyfields, Ilf. IG5
off Ravensbourne
Gdns ... **80/81** E1
Wyfold Ho, SE2
off Wolvercote Rd ... **138** D2
Wyfold Rd, SW6 ... **128** B7
Wyhill Wk, Dag. RM10 ... **101** J6
Wyke Cl, Islw. TW7 ... **124** C6
Wyke Gdns, W7 ... **124** D3
Wykeham Av, Dag. RM9 . **100** C6
Wykeham Cl, West Dr.
UB7 ... **120** D5
Wykeham Grn, Dag. RM9 . **100** C6
Wykeham Hill, Wem. HA9 . **87** J1
Wykeham Ri, N20 ... **56** B1
Wykeham Rd, NW4 ... **71** J5
Harrow HA3 ... **68** E4
Wyke Rd, E3 ... **96** A7
SW20 ... **183** J2
Wyldes Cl, NW11
off Wildwood Rd ... **91** F1
Wyldfield Gdns, N9 ... **60** C2
Wyld Way, Wem. HA9 ... **88** B6
Wyleu St, SE23 ... **153** H7
Wylie Rd, Sthl. UB2 ... **123** G3
Wyllen Cl, E1 ... **113** F4
Wylo Dr, Barn. EN5 ... **39** G6
Wymering Rd, W9 ... **108** D3
Wymond St, SW15 ... **147** J3
Wynan Rd, E14 ... **134** B5
Wynash Gdns, Cars. SM5 . **199** H5
Wynaud Ct, N22
off Palmerston Rd ... **59** F6
Wyncham Av, Sid. DA15 . **175** H1
Wynchgate, N14 ... **58** D1
N21 ... **58** E1
Harrow HA3 ... **52** B7
Wyncroft Cl, Brom. BR1 .. **192** C3
Wyndale Av, NW9 ... **70** A6
Wyndcliff Rd, SE7 ... **135** H6
Wyndcroft Cl, Enf. EN2 ... **43** H3
Wyndham Cl, Orp. BR6 .. **207** F1
Sutton SM2 ... **198** D7
Wyndham Cres, N19 ... **92** C3
Hounslow TW4 ... **143** G6
Wyndham Est, SE5 ... **36** A7
Wyndham Ms, W1 ... **15** J2
Wyndham Pl, W1 ... **15** J2
Wyndham Rd, E6 ... **98** A7
SE5 ... **131** H7
W13 ... **124** E3
Barnet EN4 ... **57** J1
Kingston upon Thames
KT2 ... **163** J7
Wyndham St, W1 ... **15** J1
Wyndham Yd, W1 ... **15** J2
Wyneham Rd, SE24 ... **152** A5
Wynell Rd, SE23 ... **171** G3
Wynford Pl, Belv. DA17 .. **139** G6
Wynford Rd, N1 ... **10** C1
Wynford Way, SE9 ... **174** C3
Wynlie Gdns, Pnr. HA5 ... **66** B2
Wynn Br Cl, Wdf.Grn. IG8
off Chigwell Rd ... **79** J1
Wynndale Rd, E18 ... **79** H1
Wynne Rd, SW9 ... **151** G2
Wynns Av, Sid. DA15 ... **158** A5
Wynnstay Gdns, W8 ... **128** D3
Wynter St, SW11 ... **149** F4
Wynton Gdns, SE25 ... **188** C5
Wynton Pl, W3 ... **106** B6
Wynyard Ter, SE11 ... **34** D3
Wynyatt St, EC1 ... **11** G4
Wyre Gro, Edg. HA8 ... **54** B3
Hayes UB3 ... **122** A4
Wyresdale Cres, Grnf.
UB6 ... **104** C3
Wythburn Pl, W1 ... **15** J4
Wythenshawe Rd, Dag.
RM10 ... **101** G3
Wythens Wk, SE9 ... **156** E6
Wythes Cl, Brom. BR1 ... **192** C2
Wythes Rd, E16 ... **136** B1
Wythfield Rd, SE9 ... **156** C6
Wyvenhoe Rd, Har. HA2 .. **85** J3
Wyvern Est, N.Mal. KT3 .. **183** G4
Wyvern Gro, Hayes UB3 . **121** E7
Wyvil Est, SW8 ... **34** A7
Wyvil Rd, SW8 ... **34** A6
Wyvis St, E14 ... **114** B5

Y

Yabsley St, E14 ... **134** C1
Yalding Rd, SE16 ... **29** H6
Yale Cl, Houns. TW4 ... **143** F5
Yaohan Plaza, NW9 ... **70** D3
Yarborough Rd, SW19 ... **185** G1
Yardley Cl, E4 ... **46** B5
Yardley Ct, Sutt. SM3
off Hemingford Rd ... **197** J4
Yardley La, E4 ... **46** B5
Yardley St, WC1 ... **10** E4
Yarmouth Cres, N17 ... **76** E5
Yarmouth Pl, W1 ... **24** D2
Yarnfield Sq, SE15
off Clayton Rd ... **152** D1
Yarnton Way, SE2 ... **138** D2
Erith DA18 ... **139** F3
Yarrow Cres, E6 ... **116** B5
Yateley St, SE18 ... **136** A3
Yates Ct, NW2 ... **90** A6
YEADING, Hayes UB4 ... **102** B3
Yeading Av, Har. HA2 ... **84** E2
Yeading Fork, Hayes UB4 . **102** C5
Yeading Gdns, Hayes UB4 . **102** B5
Yeading La, Hayes UB4 .. **102** B6
Northolt UB5 ... **102** C3
Yeames Cl, W13 ... **104** D6
Yeate St, N1 ... **94** A7
Yeatman Rd, N6 ... **73** J6
Yeats Cl, NW10 ... **88** E6
Yeats Ct, N15
off Tynemouth Rd ... **76** C4
Yeend Cl, W.Mol. KT8 ... **179** G4
Yeldham Rd, W6 ... **128** A5
Yellow Hammer Ct, NW9
off Eagle Dr ... **70/71** E2
Yelverton Rd, SW11 ... **149** G2
Yenston Cl, Mord. SM4 .. **184** D6
Yeoman Cl, E6
off Ferndale St ... **116/117** E7
SE27 ... **169** H3
Yeoman Rd, Nthlt. UB5 ... **85** E7
Yeomans Acre, Ruis. HA4 .. **66** A6
Yeoman's Ms, Islw. TW7
off Queensbridge Pk .. **144** B5
Yeoman's Row, SW3 ... **23** H6
Yeoman St, SE8 ... **133** H4
Yeomans Way, Enf. EN3 ... **45** F2
Yeomans Yd, E1 ... **21** G5
Yeomen Way, Ilf. IG6 ... **65** F6
Yeo St, E3 ... **114** B5
Yeovil Cl, Orp. BR6 ... **207** H2
Yeovilton Pl, Kings.T. KT2 . **163** F5
Yerbury Rd, N19 ... **92** D3
Yester Dr, Chis. BR7 ... **174** B7
Yester Pk, Chis. BR7 ... **174** C7
Yester Rd, Chis. BR7 ... **174** C7
Yew Cl, Buck.H. IG9 ... **64** A2
Yewdale Cl, Brom. BR1 .. **173** E6
Yewfield Rd, NW10 ... **89** F7
Yew Gro, NW2 ... **90** A4
Yew Tree Cl, N21 ... **43** G7
Yewtree Cl, N22 ... **74** C1
Harrow HA2 ... **67** H4
Yew Tree Cl, Well. DA16 .. **158** A1
Worcester Park KT4 ... **197** E1
Yew Tree Gdns, Rom.
(Chad.Hth) RM6 ... **83** E5
Yew Tree Rd, W12 ... **107** F7
Yewtree Rd, Beck. BR3 ... **189** J3
Yew Tree Wk, Houns. TW4 . **143** F5
Yew Wk, Har. HA1 ... **86** B1
YIEWSLEY, West Dr. UB7 . **120** B1
Yoakley Rd, N16 ... **94** B2
Yoke Cl, N7 *off Ewe Cl* . **92/93** E6
Yolande Gdns, SE9 ... **156** B5
Yonge Pk, N4 ... **93** G3
York Av, SW14 ... **146** C5
W7 ... **124** B1
Sidcup DA15 ... **175** H2
Stanmore HA7 ... **68** E1
York Br, NW1 ... **8** B5
York Bldgs, WC2 ... **18** B6
York Cl, E6
off Boultwood Rd ... **116** C6
W7 *off York Av* ... **124** B1
Morden SM4 ... **184** E4
York Cres, Borwd. WD6 ... **38** D2
Loughton IG10 ... **48** B3
York Gate, N14 ... **42** E7
NW1 ... **8** B6
York Gro, SE15 ... **153** F1
York Hill, SE27 ... **169** H3
Loughton IG10 ... **48** B3
York Hill Est, SE27 ... **169** H3
York Ho, Wem. HA9 ... **87** J4
York Ho Pl, W8 ... **22** A3
Yorkland Av, Well. DA16 .. **157** J3
York Ms, NW5
off Kentish Town Rd ... **92** B5
Ilford IG1
off York Rd ... **98** D3
York Par, Brent. TW8 ... **125** G5
York Pl, SW11 ... **149** G3
WC2 ... **18** B6
Dagenham RM10 ... **101** J6
Ilford IG1
off York Rd ... **98** D2
York Ri, NW5 ... **92** B3
Orpington BR6 ... **207** H1
York Rd, E4 ... **62** A5
York Rd, E7 ... **97** G6
E10 ... **96** C3
E17 ... **77** G5
N11 ... **58** D6
N18 ... **60** E6
N21 ... **44** A7
SE1 ... **26** D3
SW11 ... **149** F4
SW18 ... **149** F4
SW19 ... **167** F6
W3 ... **106** C6
W5 ... **125** F3
Barnet EN5 ... **41** G5
Brentford TW8 ... **125** G5
Croydon CR0 ... **187** G7
Hounslow TW3 ... **143** H3
Ilford IG1 ... **98** D3
Kingston upon Thames
KT2 ... **163** J7
Northwood HA6 ... **66** A2
Richmond TW10
off Albert Rd ... **145** J5
Sutton SM2 ... **198** D6
Teddington TW11 ... **162** B4
Yorkshire Cl, N16 ... **94** B3
Yorkshire Gdns, N18 ... **60** E5
Yorkshire Grey Pl, NW3
off Heath St ... **91** F4
Yorkshire Grey Yd, WC1 ... **18** C2
Yorkshire Rd, E14 ... **113** H6
Mitcham CR4 ... **186** E5
York Sq, E14 ... **113** H6
York St, W1 ... **16** A1
Barking IG11
off Abbey Rd ... **117** F1
Mitcham CR4 ... **186** A7
Twickenham TW1 ... **162** D1
York Ter, Erith DA8 ... **159** J1
York Ter E, NW1 ... **8** C6
York Ter W, NW1 ... **8** B6
Yorkton St, E2 ... **13** H2
York Way, N1 ... **111** E1
N7 ... **92** D6
N20 ... **57** J3
Borehamwood WD6 ... **38** D2
Chessington KT9 ... **195** H7
Feltham TW13 ... **161** F3
York Way Ct, N1 ... **111** E1
York Way Est, N7
off York Way ... **92/93** E6
Youngmans Cl, Enf. EN2 .. **43** J1
Young Rd, E16 ... **115** J6
Young's Bldgs, EC1 ... **12** A5
★**Young's Ram Brewery**,
SW18 ... **148** E5
Youngs Rd, Ilf. IG2 ... **81** G5
Young St, W8 ... **22** A4
Yoxley App, Ilf. IG2 ... **81** F6
Yoxley Dr, Ilf. IG2 ... **81** F6
Yukon Rd, SW12 ... **150** B7
Yuletide Cl, NW10 ... **88** E7
Yunus Khan Cl, E17 ... **78** A5

Z

Zambezie Dr, N9 ... **61** F3
Zampa Rd, SE16 ... **133** F5
Zander Ct, E2 ... **13** J2
Zangwill Rd, SE3 ... **156** A1
Zealand Av, West Dr. UB7 . **120** A7
Zealand Rd, E3 ... **113** H2
Zeland Cl, NW2 ... **89** J1
Zennor Rd, SW12 ... **168** C1
Zenoria St, SE22 ... **152** C4
Zermatt Rd, Th.Hth. CR7 . **187** J4
Zetland St, E14 ... **114** B5
Zion Pl, Th.Hth. CR7 ... **188** A4
Zion Rd, Th.Hth. CR7 ... **188** A4
Zoar St, SE1 ... **27** J1
Zoffany St, N19 ... **92** D2